CPSIA information can be obtained
at www.ICGtesting.com
Printed in the USA
LVHW011738280520
656344LV00014B/1034

Rabbinic

Reference Bible

The Connection between Tanach and Tradition™

Volume VIb:
Isaiah, Jeremiah,
Ezekiel, The Twelve

cover photo: JeremyWhat/Shutterstock.com
Printed in the United States of America

First printing, 2019

ISBN: 978-1-970063-21-9

Library of Congress Control Number: 2019909513

Set in New Times Roman, Papyrus, and Cambria

Ordering information: Special discounts are available on quantity purchases by bookstores, corporations, associations, and others. For details, contact the publisher at:
   sales@braughlerbooks.com
   or at 937-58-BOOKS

For questions or comments about this book, please write to:
   info@braughlerbooks.com

Braughler™
Books
braughlerbooks.com

Introduction

Traversing the sea of Rabbinic commentaries is nearly impossible unless one has a key. For nearly two decades, my search for this Mafteach proved fruitless. While small indexes and reference guides were found but they proved to be of limited help. What was desired was one source that would tell the reader where in Talmuds, Midrashim, or wherever, a certain verse was referenced. Since nothing like this existed [at least to the knowledge of this writer], the search for this tome of Rabbinic knowledge ended in April 2012. Throughout 2018, the first five volumes, featuring the Chumash, were released with the help of *Ohalecha Ya'akov* and *Braughler Books*. What you, our esteemed reader, now hold, is a continuation of that dream: the rabbinic key to the Neviim, and this volume completes the prophets. We hope this work will serve our community as *The Connection between Tanach and Tradition*™.

A work such as this cannot be accomplished without its author utilizing previously published works. I would like to acknowledge those brilliant minds and give credit to them. The authors of most of the books listed in the Bibliography have painstakingly documented Biblical passages in their intellectual work and in their translations. These I have culled from their pages and I have attempted to properly enter them into my spreadsheet.[1] Thus, I have sorted them, removed duplicate entries, and entered them as footnotes in my word-processing program.[2] Every attempt way made to show the textual differences between the Masoretic Text and the DSS Biblical books[3] and the Septuagint[4], because these differences can illumine and provide insight into the different Biblical autographs. I have also included variants found in the Mesorah[5]. Please refer to *Rabbinic Reference Bible Volume One: Genesis* for the complete bibliography of sources from which non-Biblical sources references came.

Further Comments:

The author and editors would never purport to be perfect, and if only one percent of all the references contained in these volumes are mistakes, that would mean there are more than 60,000 errors. Therefore, our staff would like to ask a favor, our esteemed reader. If you find a missing reference, a spelling error, a grammatical error, or an incorrect reference, please send a correction to the email address below. We will verify the error, correct the mistake, and your name will appear in subsequent printings under a *Special Thanks*. While we cannot make any claims beyond what is stated here, we greatly appreciate anything you do to assist in making this a treasured reference work, B"H.

RabRef@mail.com

---

[1] *Microsoft® Excel* for Mac
[2] *Microsoft Word* for Mac
[3] Abegg Jr, Martin & Peter Flint & Eugene Ulrich — *The Dead Sea Scrolls Bible; The Oldest Known Bible Translated for the First Time into English.* New York, NY, Harper Collins Publishers, Inc., ©1999.
[4] Brenton, Sir Lancelot C. L. — *The Septuagint with Apocrypha: Greek and English.* Chicago, IL, Hendrickson Publishers, Inc., ©1851, 1986, 1987, 1990, 1992, 1995, 1997.
[5] Ginsburg L.L.D., Christian D — *Introduction to the Massoretico-Critical Edition of the Hebrew Bible with a Prolegomenon by Harry M Orlinsky; The Masoretic Text: A Critical Evaluation.* New York, NY; Ktav Publishing House Inc., ©1897, 1966.

Table of Contents

Yeshayashu b'Amotz

Isaiah[1] – Chapter 1[2]

חֲזוֹן יְשַׁעְיָהוּ בֶן־אָמוֹץ אֲשֶׁר חָזָה עַל־יְהוּדָה
וִירוּשָׁלָ͏ִם בִּימֵי עֻזִּיָּהוּ יוֹתָם אָחָז יְחִזְקִיָּהוּ מַלְכֵי
יְהוּדָה

1[3]   The Vision of Isaiah[4] the son of Amoz, which he saw concerning Judah and Jerusalem, in the days of Uzziah, Jotham, Ahaz, and *Hezekiah*[5], kings of Judah.

שִׁמְעוּ שָׁמַיִם וְהַאֲזִינִי אֶרֶץ כִּי יְהוָה דִּבֵּר בָּנִים
גִּדַּלְתִּי וְרוֹמַמְתִּי וְהֵם פָּשְׁעוּ בִי

2[6]   Hear, O heavens, and give ear, O earth, for the LORD has spoken: Children I have reared, and brought up, And they have rebelled against Me.

יָדַע שׁוֹר קֹנֵהוּ וַחֲמוֹר אֵבוּס בְּעָלָיו יִשְׂרָאֵל לֹא
יָדַע עַמִּי לֹא הִתְבּוֹנָן

3[7]   The ox knows his owner, And the donkey his master's crib; *But*[8] Israel does not know, [9]My people do not consider.

הוֹי גּוֹי חֹטֵא עַם כֶּבֶד עָוֺן זֶרַע מְרֵעִים בָּנִים
מַשְׁחִיתִים עָזְבוּ אֶת־יְהוָה נִאֲצוּ אֶת־קְדוֹשׁ יִשְׂרָאֵל
נָזֹרוּ אָחוֹר

4[10]   Ah sinful nation, A people laden with iniquity, A seed of evil doers, Children who deal corruptly; They have forsaken the LORD, They have provoked the Holy One of Israel, *They have turned away, backward*[11].

---

[1] Isaiah - Ein Yaakov Berachot:57b

[2] Isaiah 1 - 1QIsaa, Midrash Psalms 27:7

[3] Isaiah 1:1 - 2 Chronicles 26:1-33, 2 Corinthians 12:1, 2 Kings 15:1 15:7 15:32-16:20 18:1-20:21, 2 Peter 1:21, 3Q4 frag 1 Il.1-4, Acts 10:17 2:19, Amos 1:1, b.Bava Batra 15b, b.Megillah 10b, b.Pesachim 87a, b.Sotah 10b, Ein Yaakov Bava Batra 15b, Ein Yaakov Megillah 9b, Ein Yaakov Pesachim 87b, Ein Yaakov Sotah 10b, Genesis.R 13:12, Guide for the Perplexed 1:4, Habakkuk 2:2, Hosea 1:1, Isaiah 2:1 6:1 7:1 13:1 21:2 16:9, Isaiah has 26 Sedrim, Jeremiah 23:16, Leviticus.R 36:3, Matthew 17:9, Micah 1:1, Midrash Psalms 135:2, Nahum 1:1, Numbers 12:6 24:4 24:16, Psalms 89:20, Seder Olam 20:Flee, Siman 79:9, y.Sanhedrin 10:1
Isaiah 1:1-3 - 11QIsaa, 4QIsaa
Isaiah 1:1-6 - 4QIsab, 4QIsai
Isaiah 1:1-13 - mt.Hilchot Teshuvah 1:1
Isaiah 1:1-20 - Haftarah Massei [Teimon]
Isaiah 1:1-27 - Haftarah Devarim [Isaiah 1:1-1:27], mt.Hilchot Tefilah 13:19, Siman 122:6
Isaiah 1:1-28 - Haftarah Devorim [Ashkenaz and Sephard]

[4] LXX *Esaias*

[5] MT: *Yehezkiyahu*; 1QIsaa *Yehezkiyah*

[6] Isaiah 1:2 - Acts 4:20, Amos 3:1, Apocalypse of Elijah 5:25 2, Deuteronomy 1:31 4:7-4:8 4:26 9:22-9:24 6:19 8:1, Deuteronomy.R 10:4, Ecclesiastes.R 1:9, Ezekiel 16:6-16:14 20:5-20:32 12:4, Isaiah 5:1-5:2 6:1 6:9 46:3-46:4 63:9-63:10 17:2, Jeremiah 2:5-2:13 6:19 13:15 22:29 7:10, Malachi 1:6, Mekilta de R'Ishmael Pisha 12:22, Micah 1:2 3:8 6:1-6:2, Midrash Tanchuma Haazinu 2, Midrash Tanchuma Pekudei 2, Numbers.R 2:15 2:15, Psalms 50:4, Romans 3:1-3:2 9:4-9:5, Saadia Opinions 2:10, Sifre Devarim {Ha'azinu Hashamayim} 306, Sifre Devarim Nitzavim 306, z.Vaetchanan 263a

[7] Isaiah 1:3 - 2 Peter 3:5, b.Makkot 23a, Deuteronomy 32:28-32:29, Ein Yaakov Makkot:23a, Gates of Repentance 3.061, Isaiah 5:12 3:11 20:18, Jeremiah 4:22 8:7 9:4-9:7 10:8 10:14, Leviticus.R 27:8, Matthew 13:13-13:15 13:19, Mesillat Yesharim 2:Traits of Zehirus, Midrash Shmuel 1:1, Midrash Tanchuma Emor 11, Midrash Tanchuma Ki Tissa 30, mt.Hilchot Sanhedrin v'Hainshin Hameurim Lahem 16:8, mt.Hilchot Teshuvah 4:2 4:2, Pesikta de R'Kahana 9.8, Pirkei de R'Eliezer 45, Proverbs 6:6, Psalms 94:8, Romans 1:28, Sifre Devarim {Ha'azinu Hashamayim} 306 309, Sifre Devarim Nitzavim 306 309

[8] Missing in 1QIsaj

[9] 1QIsa adds *and*

[10] Isaiah 1:4 - 1 Corinthians 10:22, Acts 7:51-7:52, b.Kiddushin 36a, Colossians 1:24, Deuteronomy 5:24 7:16 8:19, Exodus.R 15:29, Ezekiel 16:33, Gates of Repentance 3.125, Genesis 13:13, Guide for the Perplexed 3:8, Isaiah 1:23 3:8 5:19 5:24 10:6 12:6 14:20 5:19 6:9 30:11-12 6:15 13:23 17:14 17:16 17:20 57:3-4 17:3, Jastrow 1060b, Jeremiah 2:5 2:13 2:17 2:19 2:31 2:33 7:19 7:26 16:11-12 2:29 3:5, Judges 10:10, Mas.Kallah Rabbati 6:1, Matthew 3:7 11:28 23:33, Midrash Tanchuma Bechukkotai 2, mt.Hilchot Teshuvah 4:2 4:2, Numbers 8:14, Pesikta de R'Kahana S6.1, Pesikta Rabbati 31:3, Psalms 58:4 78:8 78:40 89:19, Revelation 18:5, Romans 8:7, Sifre Devarim {Ha'azinu Hashamayim} 308, Sifre Devarim Nitzavim 308
Isaiah 1:4-8 - MurIsa

[11] Missing in LXX

עַל מֶה תֻכּוּ עוֹד תּוֹסִיפוּ סָרָה כָּל־רֹאשׁ לָחֳלִי וְכָל־לֵבָב דַּוָּי

5[1] On what part will you yet be stricken, Seeing you stray away more and more? The whole head is sick, And the whole heart faints;

מִכַּף־רֶגֶל וְעַד־רֹאשׁ אֵין־בּוֹ מְתֹם פֶּצַע וְחַבּוּרָה וּמַכָּה טְרִיָּה לֹא־זֹרוּ וְלֹא חֻבָּשׁוּ וְלֹא רֻכְּכָה בַּשָּׁמֶן

6[2] From the sole of the foot to the head , there is no soundness in it; But wounds, and bruises, and festering sores: *They have not been pressed, nor bound, nor mollified with oil*[3].

אַרְצְכֶם שְׁמָמָה עָרֵיכֶם שְׂרֻפוֹת אֵשׁ אַדְמַתְכֶם לְנֶגְדְּכֶם זָרִים אֹכְלִים אֹתָהּ וּשְׁמָמָה כְּמַהְפֵּכַת זָרִים

7[4] Your country is desolate; Your cities are burned with fire; Your land, strangers devour it in your presence, *And it is desolate*[5], as overthrown by *floods*[6].

וְנוֹתְרָה בַת־צִיּוֹן כְּסֻכָּה בְכָרֶם כִּמְלוּנָה בְמִקְשָׁה כְּעִיר נְצוּרָה

8[7] And the daughter of Zion is left as a booth in a vineyard, [8]as a *lodge*[9] in a garden of cucumbers, [10]as a besieged city.

לוּלֵי יְהוָה צְבָאוֹת הוֹתִיר לָנוּ שָׂרִיד כִּמְעָט כִּסְדֹם הָיִינוּ לַעֲמֹרָה דָּמִינוּ

9[11] Except the LORD of *hosts*[12] has left to us a tiny remnant, We should have been like Sodom, We should have been like Gomorrah.

שִׁמְעוּ דְבַר־יְהוָה קְצִינֵי סְדֹם הַאֲזִינוּ תּוֹרַת אֱלֹהֵינוּ עַם עֲמֹרָה

10[13] Hear the word of the LORD, You rulers of Sodom; Give ear to the law of *our*[14] God, You people of Gomorrah.

לָמָּה־לִּי רֹב־זִבְחֵיכֶם יֹאמַר יְהוָה שָׂבַעְתִּי עֹלוֹת אֵילִים וְחֵלֶב מְרִיאִים וְדַם פָּרִים וּכְבָשִׂים וְעַתּוּדִים לֹא חָפָצְתִּי

11[15] To what purpose is the abundance of your sacrifices to Me? Says the LORD; I am full of the [16]burnt offerings of rams, And the fat of fed beasts; And I do not delight in the *blood of bullocks, or of lambs, or of male goats*[17].

---

[1] Isaiah 1:5 - 2 Chronicles 4:22, Daniel 9:8-9:11, Ezekiel 24:13, Hebrews 12:5-8, Isaiah 1:23 9:14 9:22 7:6 9:24, Jeremiah 2:30 5:3 5:5 5:31 6:28-30 9:4, Lamentations.R 1:57, Nehemiah 9:34, Pesikta de R'Kahana 16.11, Pesikta Rabbati 33:13, Revelation 16:8-11, Zephaniah 3:1-4

[2] Isaiah 1:6 - 2 Chronicles 6:28-29, Ein Yaakov Yevamot:49b, Gates of Repentance 2.12, Hosea 5:12-13, Jeremiah 6:14 8:21-22 6:12 9:6, Job 2:7-8 5:18, Leviticus.R 3:1, Luke 10:34 16:20-21, Malachi 3:20, Matthew 9:12, Nahum 3:19, Pesikta Rabbati 33:13, Psalms 38:4-6 77:3

[3] LXX *It is not possible to apply a plaister, nor oil, nor bandages*

[4] Isaiah 1:7 - 2 Chronicles 4:5 28:16-21, Deuteronomy 4:33 4:43 28:48-52, Ezekiel 6:12, Hosea 7:9 8:7, Isaiah 5:5-6 5:9 5:17 6:11 9:6 24:10-12 10:9, Jeremiah 2:15 6:8, Lamentations 5:2, Lamentations.R Petichata D'Chakimei:21, Leviticus 2:34, Pesikta Rabbati 33:13, Psalms 11:34 11:39

[5] 1QIsa *they brought desolation upon it*

[6] LXX *strange nations*

[7] Isaiah 1:8 - b.Eruvin [Tosefot] 25b, Isaiah 4:4 8:8 10:32 13:22 14:11, Jeremiah 4:17, Job 3:18, John 12:15, Lamentations 2:1 2:6, Luke 19:43-44, Midrash Tanchuma Ekev 6, Psalms 9:15, Sifre Devarim Vaetchanan 27, Testament of Joseph 19:12, Zechariah 2:10 9:9

[8] 1QIsa LXX adds *and*

[9] LXX *storehouse of fruits*

[10] 1QIsa adds *and*

[11] Isaiah 1:9 - 1 Kings 19:18, 2 Peter 2:6, Amos 4:11, b.Berachot 19a 60a, b.Ketubot 8b, Deuteronomy 5:22, Ein Yaakov Ketubot:8b, Ezekiel 6:8 14:22, Genesis 18:26 18:32 19:24, Habakkuk 3:2, Isaiah 6:13 10:20-22 17:6 24:13 13:4 37:31-32, Joel 3:5, Lamentations 3:22 4:6, Luke 17:29-30, Matthew 7:14, Philo Quaestiones et Solutiones in Genesin II 43, Romans 9:27 9:29 11:4-6, Sifre Devarim Ha'azinu Hashamayim 322, Sifre Devarim Nitzavim 322, Song of Songs.R 8:13, Zechariah 13:8-9, Zephaniah 2:9

[12] LXX *Sabaoth*

[13] Isaiah 1:10 - 1 Kings 22:19-22:23, Amos 3:1 3:8 9:7, b.Moed Katan [Tosefot] 18a, Deuteronomy 8:32, Ein Yaakov Ketubot:8b, Ezekiel 16:46 16:49, Genesis 13:13, Isaiah 3:9 8:20 4:14, Jeremiah 9:27 23:14, Martyrdom and Ascension of Isaiah 3:10, Micah 3:8-3:12, Pesikta de R'Kahana 14.3, Revelation 11:8, Romans 9:29
Isaiah 1:10-16 - 4QIsaf

[14] Missing in LXX

[15] Isaiah 1:11 - 1 Samuel 15:22, 2 Enoch 45:3, Amos 5:21, b.Berachot 32b, b.Chagigah 4b, Ein Yaakov Berachot:32b, Ein Yaakov Chagigah:4b, Guide for the Perplexed 3:32, Isaiah 18:3, Jeremiah 6:20 7:21, Malachi 1:10, Matthew 9:13, Micah 6:7, mt.Hilchot Tefilah 1:9, Pesikta Rabbati 29/30A:10, Proverbs 15:8 21:27, Psalms 50:8 51:17, Sibylline Oracles 8.390
Isaiah 1:11-13 - mt.Hilchot Teshuvah 1:1
Isaiah 1:11-14 - MurIsa
Isaiah 1:11-15 - Midrash Tanchuma Vayera 1

[16] LXX adds *burnt*

[17] LXX *fat of lambs, and the blood of bulls and goats*

כִּי תָבֹאוּ לֵרָאוֹת פָּנָי מִי־בִקֵּשׁ זֹאת מִיֶּדְכֶם רְמֹס חֲצֵרָי

12[1] *When you come to appear before Me, Who has required this from your hand, To trample My courts[2]?*

לֹא תוֹסִיפוּ הָבִיא מִנְחַת־שָׁוְא קְטֹרֶת תּוֹעֵבָה הִיא לִי חֹדֶשׁ וְשַׁבָּת קְרֹא מִקְרָא לֹא־אוּכַל אָוֶן וַעֲצָרָה

13[3] Do not bring more vain oblations; It is an offering of abomination to Me; New moon and sabbath, the holding of convocations. I cannot endure iniquity along with *the[4]* solemn assembly.

חָדְשֵׁיכֶם וּמוֹעֲדֵיכֶם שָׂנְאָה נַפְשִׁי הָיוּ עָלַי לָטֹרַח נִלְאֵיתִי נְשֹׂא

14[5] Your new moons and your appointed seasons My soul hates; They are a burden to Me; I am weary to bear them.

וּבְפָרִשְׂכֶם כַּפֵּיכֶם אַעְלִים עֵינַי מִכֶּם גַּם כִּי־תַרְבּוּ תְפִלָּה אֵינֶנִּי שֹׁמֵעַ יְדֵיכֶם דָּמִים מָלֵאוּ

15[6] And when you spread forth your hands, I will hide My eyes from you; *Yes, when you make many[7]* prayers, I will not hear; Your hands are full of blood[8].

רַחֲצוּ הִזַּכּוּ הָסִירוּ רֹעַ מַעַלְלֵיכֶם מִנֶּגֶד עֵינָי חִדְלוּ הָרֵעַ

16[9] Wash, [10]make yourself clean, [11]put away your evil deeds from before My eyes, stop doing evil;

לִמְדוּ הֵיטֵב דִּרְשׁוּ מִשְׁפָּט אַשְּׁרוּ חָמוֹץ שִׁפְטוּ יָתוֹם רִיבוּ אַלְמָנָה

17[12] Learn to do well; Seek justice, relieve the oppressed, Judge the fatherless, plead for the widow.

---

[1] Isaiah 1:12 - b.Chagigah 4b, b.Yevamot [Rashi] 102b, Deuteronomy 16:16, Ecclesiastes 5:2, Ein Yaakov Chagigah:4b, Exodus 23:17 10:23, Isaiah 58:1-2, Matthew 23:5, Mekhilta de R'Shimon bar Yochai Kaspa 79:2, Micah 6:8, mt.Hilchot Teshuvah 7:7, Psalms 40:7

Isaiah 1:12-15 - z.Bamidbar 120b

[2] LXX *nor shall you come with these to appear before me; for who has required these things at your hands? You shall no longer tread my court*

[3] Isaiah 1:13 - 1 Chronicles 23:31, 1 Corinthians 11:17, Deuteronomy 16:1-22, Ephesians 4:30, Exodus 12:16, Ezekiel 20:39, Isaiah 18:3, Jeremiah 7:9-10, Joel 1:14 2:15, Lamentations 2:6, Leviticus 23:1-44, Luke 11:42, Malachi 1:10, Matthew 15:9, Midrash Psalms 45:1, Numbers 28:1-29, Philippians 1:15, Proverbs 21:27, Psalms 78:40

Isaiah 1:13 [LXX] - Joseph and Aseneth 14:1

[4] 1QIsa *her*

[5] Isaiah 1:14 - Amos 2:13 5:21, b.Megillah 31b, b.Shabbat 145b, Ein Yaakov Shabbat:145b, Isaiah 7:13 5:1 19:24 13:8, Jastrow 686a, Malachi 2:17, Midrash Tanchuma Pinchas 17, Numbers.R 21:25, z.Yitro 88b, Zechariah 11:8

Isaiah 1:14-15 - Exodus.R 15:29 22:3

Isaiah 1:14-31 - mt.Hilchot Tefilah 13:4

[6] Isaiah 1:15 - 1 Kings 8:22 8:54, 1 Timothy 2:8, 4 Ezra 1:26, b.Berachot 32b, b.Niddah 13b, b.Sanhedrin [Tosefot] 35b, Ein Yaakov Berachot:32b, Ezekiel 8:17-18, Ezra 9:5, Guide for the Perplexed 1:45, Isaiah 8:17 10:7 59:2-3, Jeremiah 7:8-10 14:12, Job 27:8-9 3:20, Jubilees 1:12, Lamentations.R 1:57, Luke 13:25-28, Matthew 6:7 23:13, Micah 3:4 3:9-11, mt.Hilchot Nesiat Kapayim 15:1, mt.Hilchot Tefilah 1:7, mt.Hilchot Teshuvah 7:7, Pesikta de R'Kahana 16.11, Pesikta Rabbati 33:13, Proverbs 1:28, Psalms 55:2 66:18 14:2, Saadia Opinions 5:6, Siman 151:1, y.Berachot 4:1, y.Taanit 4:1, z.Vayechi 244a, z.Vayeshev 188a, Zechariah 7:13

[7] 1QIsa adds *multiply*

[8] 1QIsa adds *your fingers with iniquity*

[9] Isaiah 1:16 - 1 Peter 2:1 3:11, 2 Corinthians 7:1, Acts 22:16, Amos 5:15, Ecclesiastes.R 11:1, Ephesians 4:22-29, Ezekiel 18:30-31, Genesis.R 48:10, Isaiah 4:11 55:6-7, James 4:8, Jeremiah 4:14 1:5, Job 11:13-14, Matthew 3:8, Numbers.R 14:2, Pesikta Rabbati 40:5, Psalms 26:6 34:15 37:27, Revelation 7:14, Romans 12:9, Sibylline Oracles 4.165, Titus 2:11-14, y.Rosh Hashanah 4:7, Zechariah 1:3-4

Isaiah 1:16-17 - Midrash Tanchuma Vayishlach 2

[10] 1QIsa adds *and*

[11] 1QIsa adds *and*

[12] Isaiah 1:17 - 2 Enoch 42:9 9:1, b.Ketubot [Rashi] 10b, b.Kiddushin 53a, b.Sanhedrin 35a, b.Yoma 39b, Daniel 4:24, Ein Yaakov Kiddushin:53a, Ein Yaakov Yoma:39b, Isaiah 1:23, Jastrow 478b 479a, Jeremiah 22:3 22:15-22:16, Micah 6:8, Midrash Tanchuma Mishpatim 6, mt.Hilchot Sanhedrin v'Hainshin Hameurim Lahem 21:3, Numbers.R 14:10, Pesikta Rabbati 40:5, Proverbs 7:9, Psalms 82:3-4, y.Rosh Hashanah 4:7, Zechariah 7:9-10 8:16, Zephaniah 2:3

Hebrew		English
לְכוּ־נָא וְנִוָּכְחָה יֹאמַר יְהוָה אִם־יִהְיוּ חֲטָאֵיכֶם כַּשָּׁנִים כַּשֶּׁלֶג יַלְבִּינוּ אִם־יַאְדִּימוּ כַתּוֹלָע כַּצֶּמֶר יִהְיוּ	18[1]	Come now, and let us reason together, says the LORD; Though your sins are as *scarlet*[2], They shall be as white as snow; Though they are *red*[3] like crimson, They shall be as [4]wool.
לְכוּ־נָא וְנִוָּכְחָה יֹאמַר יְהוָה אִם־יִהְיוּ חֲטָאֵיכֶם כַּשָּׁנִים כַּשֶּׁלֶג יַלְבִּינוּ אִם־יַאְדִּימוּ כַתּוֹלָע כַּצֶּמֶר יִהְיוּ	19[5]	If you are willing and *obedient*[6], You shall eat the good of the land;
אִם־תֹּאבוּ וּשְׁמַעְתֶּם טוּב הָאָרֶץ תֹּאכֵלוּ	20[7]	*But*[8] if you *refuse and rebel*[9], You shall be devoured *by*[10] the sword; For the mouth of the LORD has spoken.
אֵיכָה הָיְתָה לְזוֹנָה קִרְיָה נֶאֱמָנָה מְלֵאֲתִי מִשְׁפָּט צֶדֶק יָלִין בָּהּ וְעַתָּה מְרַצְּחִים	21[11]	How has the faithful city[12] become a harlot? She who was full of justice, Righteousness lodged in her, but now murderers.
אֵיכָה הָיְתָה לְזוֹנָה קִרְיָה נֶאֱמָנָה מְלֵאֲתִי מִשְׁפָּט צֶדֶק יָלִין בָּהּ וְעַתָּה מְרַצְּחִים	22[13]	Your silver has become *dross*[14], Your *wine mixed*[15] with water.
שָׂרַיִךְ סוֹרְרִים וְחַבְרֵי גַּנָּבִים כֻּלּוֹ אֹהֵב שֹׁחַד וְרֹדֵף שַׁלְמֹנִים יָתוֹם לֹא יִשְׁפֹּטוּ וְרִיב אַלְמָנָה לֹא־יָבוֹא אֲלֵיהֶם	23[16]	Your princes are rebellious and companions of thieves; everyone loves *bribes*[17], and *follows*[18] after rewards; they do not judge the fatherless, nor does the cause of the widow come before them.
לָכֵן נְאֻם הָאָדוֹן יְהוָה צְבָאוֹת אֲבִיר יִשְׂרָאֵל הוֹי אֶנָּחֵם מִצָּרַי וְאִנָּקְמָה מֵאוֹיְבָי	24[19]	Therefore, says the Lord, the LORD of hosts, The Mighty One of Israel: *Ah, I will get relief*

---

[1] Isaiah 1:18 - 1 Samuel 12:7, Acts 17:2 18:4 24:25, Apocryphon of Ezekiel Fragment 2, b.Berachot [Rashi] 57a, b.Menachot [Tosefot] 3a, b.Shabbat [Rashi] 129b, b.Shabbat 86a 89b, b.Yoma [Rashi] 39a, b.Yoma [Tosefot] 41b, b.Yoma 67a 68b, Ein Yaakov Shabbat:89b, Ein Yaakov Yoma:66b, Ephesians 1:6-8, Genesis.R 99 [Excl]:8, Isaiah 17:1 17:21 43:24-26 20:22, Jastrow 690a 1604b 1605a 1652b, Jeremiah 2:5, Leviticus.R 1:2 27:6, m.Shabbat 9:3, m.Yoma 6:8, Micah 6:2 7:18-19, Midrash Tanchuma Emor 10, Midrash Tanchuma Vayechi 10, Midrash Tanchuma Vayishlach 2, mt.Hilchot Teshuvah 1:2, Numbers.R 2:15 8:1 10:1, Pesikta de R'Kahana 6.4 9.5, Pesikta Rabbati 16:7 40:5 29/30A:10, Psalms 51:8, Revelation 7:14, Romans 5:20, Selichot, Sifre Devarim Devarim 6, Sifre Devarim Vaetchanan 28, Siman 131:1, Song of Songs.R 1:37 6:2 7:11, Tanya Igeret Hakodesh §22a, y.Rosh Hashanah 4:7, y.Shabbat 9:3, y.Yoma 6:5 6:7, z.Shemot 20a, z.Terumah 135a
Isaiah 1:18-31 - 4QIsaf

[2] 1QIsaa singular; MT plural; LXX *purple*

[3] 1QIsaa unclear: *be red* or *be like*; missing in LXX

[4] LCC adds *white as*

[5] Isaiah 1:19 - b.Gittin [Rashi] 76a, b.Kiddushin 61b, b.Sheviit [Tosefot] 36b, Deuteronomy 30:15-30:16, Deuteronomy.R 4:2, Guide for the Perplexed 3:33, Hebrews 5:9, Hosea 14:3-14:6, Isaiah 3:10 55:1-3 55:6-7, Jeremiah 3:12-14 31:19-21, Joel 2:26, Joseph and Aseneth 2:5, Lamentations.R Petichata D'Chakimei:30, Leviticus.R 35:6, Matthew 21:28-32, Sifre Devarim Ekev 40
Isaiah 1:19-20 - Midrash Proverbs 8, Pesikta de R'Kahana 14.3

[6] LXX *listen to me*

[7] Isaiah 1:20 - 1 Samuel 12:25 15:29, 2 Chronicles 36:14-16, Guide for the Perplexed 1:46, Hebrews 2:1-3, Isaiah 3:11 3:25 16:5 10:14 17:12, Jastrow 497a, Leviticus 2:33, Leviticus.R 13:4, Mekilta de R'Ishmael Pisha 12:26, Micah 4:4, Numbers 23:19, Titus 1:2
Isaiah 1:21 - 2 Chronicles 19:9, 2 Samuel 8:15, Acts 7:52, b.Megillah 31b, b.Sanhedrin 35a, b.Yoma [Tosefot] 56a, Bahir 75 120, Ecclesiastes.R 3:19, Ezekiel 16:1-63 22:1-23, Genesis.R 43:6, Hebrews 12:22, Hosea 12:1, Isaiah 5:7 24:2 57:3-57:9, Jastrow 1152a, Jeremiah 2:20-21 3:1, Lamentations 1:8-9, Lamentations.R 1:1 2:4 Petichata D'Chakimei:12, Leviticus.R 4:1, Luke 13:34, Micah 3:2-3, Midrash Shmuel 1:1, Midrash Tanchuma Pinchas 13, Midrash Tanchuma Shoftim 1 8, mt.Hilchot Matnot Aniyim 9:4, mt.Hilchot Tefilah 13:19, Nehemiah 11:1, Numbers.R 21:21, Pesikta de R'Kahana 5.17 6.4 15.6-7, Pesikta Rabbati 15:24 16:7, Psalms 46:5 48:2 48:9, Revelation 11:2 11:8, Song of Songs.R 1:51 5:17, z.Metzorah 53a, Zechariah 8:3, Zephaniah 3:1-3

[8] Missing in 1QIsaf

[9] LXX *are not willing, nor Listen to me*

[10] Explicite *by* in 1QIsaa; Implicite *with* in MT

[11] Isaiah 1:21-31 - Haftarah Devorim [Teimon]

[12] LXX adds *Sion*

[13] Isaiah 1:22 - 2 Corinthians 2:17, b.Avodah Zara [Rashi] 70b, b.Bava Batra 15b, b.Eruvin [Tosefot] 37a, Ein Yaakov Bava Batra:15b, Exodus.R 31:4, Ezekiel 22:18-22, Genesis.R 28:7, Hosea 4:18 6:4, Jeremiah 6:28-30, Lamentations 4:1-2, Midrash Tanchuma Mishpatim 9, Pesikta de R'Kahana 15.8

[14] LXX *worthless*

[15] LXX *wine merchants mix the wine*

[16] Isaiah 1:23 - 2 Chronicles 24:17-21 12:14, Acts 4:5-11, Daniel 9:5-6, Deuteronomy 16:19, Exodus 23:8, Exodus.R 30:19, Ezekiel 22:6-12, Hosea 4:18 7:3-5 9:15, Isaiah 3:14 10:1-2 9:15, Jastrow 43a, Jeremiah 5:5 5:28-29 22:17, Luke 18:2-5 19:46, Malachi 3:5, Mark 11:17, Matthew 21:13, Micah 3:1-3 3:11 7:3, Pesikta de R'Kahana 15.9, Proverbs 17:23 5:24, Zechariah 7:10

[17] Plural in 1QIsaa, singular in MT

[18] Plural in 1QIsaa, singular in MT

[19] Isaiah 1:24 - Deuteronomy 28:63 8:43, Ezekiel 5:13 16:42 21:22, Hebrews 10:13, Isaiah 6:29 11:4 1:26 12:16 13:2 15:4, Jeremiah 2:34, Midrash Tanchuma Shoftim 1, Pesikta de R'Kahana 15.10 15.11, Proverbs 1:25-26, Psalms 12:2, Revelation 18:8

from[1] My[2] adversaries, And *avenge Myself*[3] on My[4] enemies;

וְאָשִׁיבָה יָדִי עָלַיִךְ וְאֶצְרֹף כַּבֹּר סִיגָיִךְ וְאָסִירָה כָּל־בְּדִילָיִךְ	25[5]	And I[6] will turn My hand upon you, and *purge your dross as with lye, And will take away all your alloy*[7];
וְאָשִׁיבָה שֹׁפְטַיִךְ כְּבָרִאשֹׁנָה וְיֹעֲצַיִךְ כְּבַתְּחִלָּה אַחֲרֵי־כֵן יִקָּרֵא לָךְ עִיר הַצֶּדֶק קִרְיָה נֶאֱמָנָה	26[8]	And I will restore your judges as before, And your counsellors as at the beginning; Afterward *you shall be called*[9] The city of righteousness, The faithful *city*[10].
צִיֹּון בְּמִשְׁפָּט תִּפָּדֶה וְשָׁבֶיהָ בִּצְדָקָה	27[11]	*Zion shall be redeemed with justice, And they who return to her [will do so in]with righteousness*[12].
וְשֶׁבֶר פֹּשְׁעִים וְחַטָּאִים יַחְדָּו וְעֹזְבֵי יְהוָה יִכְלוּ	28[13]	But the destruction of the transgressors and the sinners shall be together, And they who forsake the LORD shall be consumed.
כִּי יֵבֹשׁוּ מֵאֵילִים אֲשֶׁר חֲמַדְתֶּם וְתַחְפְּרוּ מֵהַגַּנֹּות אֲשֶׁר בְּחַרְתֶּם	29[14]	For they shall be ashamed of the *terebinths you have desired*[15], And you shall be confounded for the gardens you chose.
כִּי תִהְיוּ כְּאֵלָה נֹבֶלֶת עָלֶהָ וּכְגַנָּה אֲשֶׁר־מַיִם אֵין לָהּ	30[16]	For you shall be as a *terebinth*[17] *whose leaf fades*[18], And as a garden that has no water.
וְהָיָה הֶחָסֹן לִנְעֹרֶת וּפֹעֲלֹו לְנִיצֹוץ וּבָעֲרוּ שְׁנֵיהֶם יַחְדָּו וְאֵין מְכַבֶּה	31[19]	*And the strong*[20] shall be as tow, And *his*[21] work as a spark; And *they*[22] shall both burn together, And no one shall quench them.

---

[1] LXX *for my wrath shall not cease against*

[2] 1QIsaa *his*

[3] LXX *I will execute judgment*

[4] 1QIsaa *his*

[5] Isaiah 1:25 - b.Megillah 14b, b.Sanhedrin 98a, b.Shabbat 139a, Ein Yaakov Megillah:17b, Ein Yaakov Sanhedrin:97b, Ein Yaakov Shabbat:139a, Ezekiel 20:38 22:20 22:22, Isaiah 1:22 4:4 6:11-13, Jeremiah 6:29 9:8, Malachi 3:3, Matthew 3:12, Revelation 3:19, Zechariah 13:7-9, Zephaniah 3:11

[6] 1QIsaa *He*

[7] LXX *thee completely, and I will destroy the rebellious, and will take away from thee all transgressors*

[8] Isaiah 1:26 - 1 Samuel 12:2-12:5, b.Megillah 14b, b.Sanhedrin 98a, Ein Yaakov Megillah:17b, Ein Yaakov Sanhedrin:97b, Ein Yaakov Shabbat:139a, Ezekiel 34:23-24 37:24-25 21:8, Isaiah 1:21 32:1-2 9:5 12:14 60:17-18 12:21 62:1-2, Jastrow 595b, Jeremiah 7:24 9:7 9:11 33:15-17, Midrash Tanchuma Mishpatim 3, Midrash Tanchuma Shoftim 1, mt.Hilchot Sanhedrin v'Hainshin Hameurim Lahem 4:11, Numbers 12:3 16:15, Pesikta de R'Kahana 15.11, Revelation 21:27, Zechariah 8:3 8:8, Zephaniah 3:9 3:13

[9] 1QIsaa *they will call*

[10] LXX *mother-city of Sion*

[11] Isaiah 1:27 - 1 Corinthians 1:30, 1 Peter 1:18-1:19, 2 Corinthians 5:21, b.Sanhedrin 98a, b.Shabbat 139a, Deuteronomy.R 3:7, Ein Yaakov Sanhedrin:97b, Ein Yaakov Shabbat:139a, Ephesians 1:7-1:8, Exodus.R 30:14 30:15, Isaiah 5:16 45:21-45:25 14:12 15:4, Midrash Proverbs 11, Midrash Psalms 119:53, Midrash Tanchuma Mishpatim 3, mt.Hilchot Matnot Aniyim 10:1, Pesikta de R'Kahana 15.11, Pesikta Rabbati 41:1, Romans 3:24-3:26 11:26-11:27, Siman 34:1, Tanya Igeret Hakodesh §04, Titus 2:14, Verse for names ה-צ [Pisukim Lesheimot Anoshim]

[12] LXX *For her captives shall be saved with judgment, and with mercy*

[13] Isaiah 1:28 - 1 Chronicles 4:9, 1 Kings 9:6-9:9, 1 Samuel 12:25, 1 Thessalonians 5:3, 2 Peter 3:7, 2 Thessalonians 1:8-1:9, b.Berachot 8a, b.Megillah [Tosefot] 23b, b.Megillah 14b, Ein Yaakov Megillah:17b, Gates of Repentance 3.170, Isaiah 6:13 2:11 17:11 18:24, Job 7:3, Luke 12:45-12:46, Midrash Psalms 119:53, mt.Hilchot Tefilah 8:7 12:9, Proverbs 5:1, Psalms 1:6 5:7 9:6 37:38 73:27 92:10 93:5 5:5, Revelation 21:8, Siman 15:10, Tanya Igeret Hakodesh §23, Zephaniah 1:4-1:6

[14] Isaiah 1:29 - Ezekiel 6:13 16:63 36:31, Hosea 4:13 14:5 14:10, Isaiah 6:22 7:7 21:16 9:5 17:3 18:17, Jeremiah 2:20 3:6, Romans 6:21, y.Megillah 4:4, z.Beshallach 59a

[15] LXX *idols, in which they delighted*

[16] Isaiah 1:30 - Ezekiel 17:9-17:10 17:24 31:4-31:18, Isaiah 5:6 10:11, Jeremiah 17:5-17:6 7:13, Matthew 21:19, Mekilta de R'Ishmael Amalek 4:31

[17] LXX *turpentine tree*

[18] LXX *that has cast its leaves*

[19] Isaiah 1:31 - b.Shabbat 20b, Ezekiel 21:3-20:4 8:21, Isaiah 5:24 9:20 2:11 3:4 9:14 34:9-34:10 19:17 2:11 18:24, Judges 15:14, Lamentations.R 1:50, Malachi 3:19, Mark 9:43-9:49, Matthew 3:10, Perek Shirah [the Bat], Revelation 6:14-6:17 14:10-14:11 19:20 20:10, Saadia Opinions 9:5, y.Shabbat 2:1

[20] 1QIsaa *The your strong one*; Alternate reading in MT *Your treasure*

[21] 1QIsaa *your*

[22] LXX *transgressors and the sinners*

Isaiah – Chapter 2[1]

הַדָּבָר֙ אֲשֶׁ֣ר חָזָ֔ה יְשַֽׁעְיָ֖הוּ בֶּן־אָמ֑וֹץ עַל־יְהוּדָ֖ה
וִירֽוּשָׁלָֽ͏ִם

1[2] The word that *Isaiah*[3] the son of Amoz saw concerning Judah and [4]Jerusalem.

הַדָּבָר֙ אֲשֶׁ֣ר חָזָ֔ה יְשַֽׁעְיָ֖הוּ בֶּן־אָמ֑וֹץ עַל־יְהוּדָ֖ה
וִירֽוּשָׁלָֽ͏ִם

2[5] *And it shall come to pass*[6] in the end of days, that the mountain of the LORD's house shall be established as the top of *the*[7] mountains, and *it shall*[8] be exalted above the hills; and all nations shall flow *to*[9] it.

וְהָלְכ֞וּ עַמִּ֣ים רַבִּ֗ים וְאָמְרוּ֙ לְכ֣וּ וְנַעֲלֶ֣ה אֶל־הַר־
יְהֹוָ֗ה אֶל־בֵּית֙ אֱלֹהֵ֣י יַעֲקֹ֔ב וְיֹרֵ֙נוּ֙ מִדְּרָכָ֔יו וְנֵלְכָ֖ה
בְּאֹרְחֹתָ֑יו כִּ֤י מִצִּיּוֹן֙ תֵּצֵ֣א תוֹרָ֔ה וּדְבַר־יְהֹוָ֖ה
מִירֽוּשָׁלָֽ͏ִם

3[10] And many peoples shall go and say: 'Come, and let us go up to the mountain of the LORD, to the house of the God of Jacob; And *He*[11] will teach us of His ways, and we will walk in His paths.' For from Zion shall go forth the law, and the word of the LORD from Jerusalem.

וְשָׁפַט֙ בֵּ֣ין הַגּוֹיִ֔ם וְהוֹכִ֖יחַ לְעַמִּ֣ים רַבִּ֑ים וְכִתְּת֨וּ
חַרְבוֹתָ֜ם לְאִתִּ֗ים וַחֲנִיתֽוֹתֵיהֶם֙ לְמַזְמֵר֔וֹת לֹא־יִשָּׂ֨א
ג֤וֹי אֶל־גּוֹי֙ חֶ֔רֶב וְלֹא־יִלְמְד֥וּ ע֖וֹד מִלְחָמָֽה

4[12] And He shall judge between the nations, And *shall decide*[13] for[14] many peoples; And they shall beat their swords into plowshares, And their spears into *pruning hooks*[15]; [16]Nation shall not lift up sword against nation, nor shall they learn war any longer.

בֵּ֖ית יַעֲקֹ֑ב לְכ֥וּ וְנֵלְכָ֖ה בְּא֥וֹר יְהֹוָֽה

5[17] O house of Jacob, come, and let us walk In the light of the LORD.

---

[1] Isaiah 2 - 1QIsaa

[2] Isaiah 2:1 - Amos 1:1, Guide for the Perplexed 1:16, Habakkuk 1:1, Isaiah 1:1 13:1, Micah 1:1 6:9
Isaiah 2:1-3 - 4QIsaf
Isaiah 2:1-4 - 4QIsae

[3] 1QIsaa *Yeshayah*; MT *Yeshayahu*

[4] LXX adds *concerning*

[5] Isaiah 2:2 - 2 Peter 3:3, 2 Timothy 3:1, Acts 2:17, b.Bava Batra 4a, Daniel 2:28 2:35 2:45 10:14, Ein Yaakov Bava Batra:4a, Ezekiel 14:16, Genesis 1:1, Genesis.R 98 [Excl]:2, Hebrews 1:2, Isaiah 11:10 3:13 6:29 1:6 8:7 60:11-12 18:20, Jeremiah 3:17 23:20 6:24 24:47 1:39, Job 19:25, Malachi 3:12, Micah 4:1-3, Midrash Psalms 36:6 50:1 68:9 87:3, Midrash Tanchuma Ekev 3, mt.Hilchot Melachim u'Michamoteihem 11:4, mt.Hilchot Teshuvah 9:2 9:2, Numbers 24:14, Pesikta de R'Kahana 21.4, Psalms 2:8 22:28 68:16-17 72:8 72:17-19 86:9, Revelation 11:15 20:4 21:10-27, Sifre Devarim Vaetchanan 28, z.Ki Tissa 189b, z.Pekudei 232a, z.Vaetchanan 270a, Zechariah 8:3
Isaiah 2:2-3 - Sifre Devarim Devarim 1, t.Menachot 13:23
Isaiah 2:2-4 - Psalms of Solomon 17:31

[6] LXX *For*

[7] Missing in 1QIsaa

[8] Missing in 1QIsaa

[9] 1QIsaa *over*

[10] Isaiah 2:3 - Acts 1:8 10:33 13:46-48, Attah Haraisah [Simchat Torah], b.Bava Batra 21a, b.Berachot 63b, b.Pesachim 88a, b.Rosh Hashanah [Tosefot] 25a, b.Sanhedrin [Rashi] 11b, b.Taanit [Rashi] 16a, Deuteronomy 6:1, Ein Yaakov Bava Batra:21a, Ein Yaakov Berachot:63b, Guide for the Perplexed 1:23 2:29, Isaiah 51:4-5, James 1:23, Jeremiah 7:17 50:4-5, John 7:17, Kuzari 2.20 3.39, Leviticus.R 24:4, Luke 11:28 24:47, Matthew 7:24, Midrash Psalms 2:5 14:6 81:2, mt.Hilchot Beit Habechirah 6:10 6:10, mt.Hilchot Kiddush HaChodesh 1:8 5:13, mt.Hilchot Sanhedrin v'Hainshin Hameurim Lahem 4:6, mt.Hilchot Talmud Torah 6:14, mt.Hilchot Talmud Torah 6:14, Opening the ark to take the Sefer Torah [Vayhi Binsoa], Pesikta Rabbati 39:2 40:6 41:1 41:2, Psalms 25:8-9 14:2, Romans 10:18, Sibylline Oracles 3.718 3.772, Sifre Devarim Ekev 37, Sifre Devarim Nitzavim 317, Sifre Devarim Vaetchanan 28, Sifre Devarim Vezot Habracha 352, Tanya Igeret Hakodesh §27, y.Nedarim 6:8, y.Sanhedrin 1:2, z.Naso 148a, z.Pekudei 221b 232b, z.Vayakhel 218a, z.Yitro 69b, Zechariah 8:20-23
Isaiah 2:3-16 - 4QIsab

[11] 1QIsaa *they*

[12] Isaiah 2:4 - 1 Samuel 2:10, Acts 17:31, Apocalypse of Daniel 5:11, b.Shabbat 63a, Hosea 2:18, Isaiah 9:6 9:8 11:3-11:4 11:6-11:9 8:18 60:17-60:18, Jastrow 42a, Joel 4:10, John 16:8-16:11, Micah 4:3, Midrash Tanchuma Shoftim 19, mt.Hilchot Chametz u'Matzah 19:1, Pesikta de R'Kahana S2.2 S5.1, Psalms 46:10 72:3-72:7 82:8 96:13 14:6, Revelation 19:11, Saadia Opinions 8:8, Sibylline Oracles 5.381, y.Shabbat 6:4, Zechariah 9:10

[13] 1QIsaa *give judgment*

[14] The scribe of 1QIsaa wrote *between*, crossed it out, and wrote *for*

[15] LXX *sickles*

[16] 1QIsaa LXX adds *and*

[17] Isaiah 2:5 - 1 John 1:5 1:7, 1 Thessalonians 5:5-6, Ephesians 5:8, Exodus.R 28:2, Guide for the Perplexed 1:24, Isaiah 2:3 50:10-11 10:1 60:1-2 60:19-20, John 12:35-36, Luke 1:79, Motzei Shabbat [Viyiten Lecha], Pesikta de R'Kahana 51.2, Pesikta Rabbati 39:2, Psalms 89:16, Revelation 21:23-24, Romans 13:12-14, Siman 221:8, Tanya Likutei Aramim §36, Tefillat Haderech

כִּי נָטַשְׁתָּה עַמְּךָ בֵּית יַעֲקֹב כִּי מָלְאוּ מִקֶּדֶם
וְעֹנְנִים כַּפְּלִשְׁתִּים וּבְיַלְדֵי נָכְרִים יַשְׂפִּיקוּ

6[1] For you have forsaken Your people, the house of *Jacob; For they are replenished from the east, And with soothsayers like the Philistines, they please themselves in the brood of aliens*[2].

וַתִּמָּלֵא אַרְצוֹ כֶּסֶף וְזָהָב וְאֵין קֵצֶה לְאֹצְרֹתָיו
וַתִּמָּלֵא אַרְצוֹ סוּסִים וְאֵין קֵצֶה לְמַרְכְּבֹתָיו

7[3] Their land is full of silver and gold, nor is there an end to their treasures; Their land is full of horses, nor is there an end of their chariots.

וַתִּמָּלֵא אַרְצוֹ אֱלִילִים לְמַעֲשֵׂה יָדָיו יִשְׁתַּחֲווּ
לַאֲשֶׁר עָשׂוּ אֶצְבְּעֹתָיו

8[4] Their land also is full of idols; everyone worships the work of his own hands, What his own fingers have made.

וַיִּשַּׁח אָדָם וַיִּשְׁפַּל־אִישׁ וְאַל־תִּשָּׂא לָהֶם

9[5] And [6]man bows down, And [7]man lowers himself, *And you cannot bear with them*[8].

בּוֹא בַצּוּר וְהִטָּמֵן בֶּעָפָר מִפְּנֵי פַּחַד יְהֹוָה וּמֵהֲדַר
גְּאֹנוֹ

10[9] *Enter into the rock, And hide in the dust, From before the terror of the LORD, And from the glory of His majesty*[10].

עֵינֵי גַּבְהוּת אָדָם שָׁפֵל וְשַׁח רוּם אֲנָשִׁים וְנִשְׂגַּב
יְהֹוָה לְבַדּוֹ בַּיּוֹם הַהוּא

11[11] [12]*The lofty looks of man shall be brought low*[13], And the haughtiness of men shall be bowed down, And the LORD alone shall be exalted in that day.

כִּי [יוֹם] לַיהֹוָה צְבָאוֹת עַל כָּל־גֵּאֶה וָרָם וְעַל כָּל־
נִשָּׂא וְשָׁפֵל

12[14] For the LORD of hosts has a day for all who are proud and lofty, *and on all who are lifted up*[15], and it shall be brought low;

וְעַל כָּל־אַרְזֵי הַלְּבָנוֹן הָרָמִים וְהַנִּשָּׂאִים וְעַל כָּל־
אַלּוֹנֵי הַבָּשָׁן

13[16] And on all the cedars of Lebanon That are high and lifted up, And on all the oaks of Bashan;

---

[1] Isaiah 2:6 - 1 Chronicles 10:13, 1 Kings 11:1-2, 2 Chronicles 15:2 24:20, 2 Kings 1:2 16:7-16:8, Deuteronomy 18:10-18:14 21:11-21:13 31:16-31:17, Exodus 22:18 10:16, Guide for the Perplexed 2:11 [T.Jonathan] 1:7 2:11, Isaiah 8:19 47:12-47:13, Jeremiah 10:2, Lamentations 5:20, Leviticus 19:31 20:6, Nehemiah 13:23, Numbers 23:7 25:1-25:2, Proverbs 6:1, Psalms 10:35, Romans 11:1-11:2 11:20, Sifre Devarim {Ha'azinu Hashamayim} 318, Sifre Devarim Nitzavim 318

[2] LXX *Israel, because their land is filled as at the beginning with divinations, as the land of the Philistines, and many strange children were born to them*

[3] Isaiah 2:7 - 1 Kings 4:26 10:21-27, 2 Chronicles 9:20-25, Deuteronomy 17:16-17, Hosea 14:5, Isaiah 6:16 7:1, James 5:1-3, Jeremiah 5:27-28, Micah 5:11, Psalms 20:8, Revelation 18:3 18:11-17
Isaiah 2:7-8 - Sifre Devarim {Ha'azinu Hashamayim} 318, Sifre Devarim Nitzavim 318
Isaiah 2:7-10 - 4QIsaa

[4] Isaiah 2:8 - 2 Chronicles 3:2 28:2-28:4 28:23-28:25 33:3-33:7, Acts 17:16, Deuteronomy 4:28, Ezekiel 16:23-16:25, Hosea 8:6 12:13 13:2 14:5, Isaiah 10:10-10:11 17:8 13:19 44:15-44:20 9:5, Jeremiah 2:28 11:13, Psalms 115:4-115:8, Revelation 9:20

[5] Isaiah 2:9 - Colossians 2:18 2:23, Isaiah 5:15 3:11 9:9, Jastrow 1547a 1617a, Jeremiah 5:4-5:5 18:23, Joshua 24:19, Mark 3:29, Midrash Tanchuma Ki Tissa 4, Nehemiah 4:5, Numbers.R 10:2, Pesikta de R'Kahana 2.3, Pesikta Rabbati 10:6, Psalms 49:3 62:10, Revelation 6:15-6:17, Romans 3:23

[6] LXX adds *the mean*

[7] LXX adds *the great*

[8] Missing in 1QIsaa because this appears to be a later addition, though it's included in the later texts of 4QIsaa, 4QIsaab, MT, and LXX.

[9] Isaiah 2:10 - 2 Thessalonians 1:9, Hosea 10:8, Isaiah 2:19-21 6:3-5 10:3 18:22, Jeremiah 10:7 10:10, Job 30:5-6 7:23 37:22-24, Judges 6:1-2, Luke 12:5 23:30, Psalms 90:11, Revelation 6:15-16 15:3-4

[10] Missing in 1QIsaa because this appears to be a later addition, though it's included in the later texts of 4QIsaa, 4QIsaab, MT, and LXX; LXX *Now Therefore, enter into the rocks, and hide yourselves in the earth, for fear of the LORD, and because the glory of his might, when he shall arise to strike terribly the earth*

[11] Isaiah 2:11 - 1 Corinthians 1:29-31, 1 Peter 5:5, 2 Corinthians 10:5 10:17, Amos 9:11, b.Rosh Hashanah 31a, b.Sanhedrin 92b 97a, Ein Yaakov Rosh Hashanah:31a, Ein Yaakov Sanhedrin:92b 97a, Ezekiel 14:14 14:19 15:11 15:22, Genesis.R 77:1, Hosea 2:16 2:18 2:21, Isaiah 2:17 4:1 5:15-16 11:10-11 12:1 12:4 13:11 24:21 1:9 2:17:1-2 27:12-13 4:5 5:18 6:23 13:23 4:6, Jeremiah 9:25 30:7-8 50:31-32, Job 40:10-12, Joel 4:18, Lamentations.R 2:17, Luke 18:14, Malachi 3:19, Micah 4:6 5:11 7:11-12, Midrash Psalms 8:8 114:3, Midrash Tanchuma Pekudei 3, Obadiah 1:8, Pesikta de R'Kahana S5.1, Psalms 18:28, z.Pekudei 232b, z.Shemot 19b, z.Vayishlach 177b, z.Yitro 67b, Zechariah 9:16, Zephaniah 3:11 3:16

[12] 1QIsaa adds *And*

[13] LXX *For the eyes of the LORD are high, but man is low*

[14] Isaiah 2:12 - 1 Corinthians 5:5, 1 Thessalonians 5:2, Amos 5:18, Daniel 4:34 5:20-24, Exodus.R 5:15, Ezekiel 13:5, Guide for the Perplexed 2:29, Isaiah 13:6 13:9 23:9 24:4 24:21, James 4:6, Jeremiah 22:10, Job 40:11-12, Luke 14:11, Malachi 3:19 3:23, Matthew 23:12, Mekhilta de R'Shimon bar Yochai Shirata 28:1, Proverbs 6:16-17 16:5, Sibylline Oracles 3.741, z.Metzorah 54a
Isaiah 2:12-17 - Mekhilta de R'Ishmael Shirata 2:8-12
Isaiah 2:12-18 - Midrash Tanchuma Beshallach 12

[15] 1QIsaa *and lifted up*

[16] Isaiah 2:13 - Amos 2:5, Ezekiel 31:3-12, Isaiah 10:33-34 14:8 13:24, Zechariah 11:1-2

וְעַל כָּל־הֶהָרִים הָרָמִים וְעַל כָּל־הַגְּבָעוֹת הַנִּשָּׂאוֹת	14[1]	And on all the high mountains, And on all the hills *that are lifted up*[2];
וְעַל כָּל־מִגְדָּל גָּבֹהַ וְעַל כָּל־חוֹמָה בְצוּרָה	15[3]	And on every lofty tower, And on every fortified wall;
וְעַל כָּל־אֳנִיּוֹת תַּרְשִׁישׁ וְעַל כָּל־שְׂכִיּוֹת הַחֶמְדָּה	16[4]	And on all the ships of *Tarshish, And on all delightful imagery*[5].
וְשַׁח גַּבְהוּת הָאָדָם וְשָׁפֵל רוּם אֲנָשִׁים וְנִשְׂגַּב יְהוָה לְבַדּוֹ בַּיּוֹם הַהוּא	17[6]	And the loftiness of man shall be bowed down, And the haughtiness of men shall be brought low; And the LORD alone shall be exalted in that day.
וְהָאֱלִילִים כָּלִיל יַחֲלֹף	18[7]	*And the idols shall utterly perish*[8].
וּבָאוּ בִּמְעָרוֹת צֻרִים וּבִמְחִלּוֹת עָפָר מִפְּנֵי פַּחַד יְהוָה וּמֵהֲדַר גְּאוֹנוֹ בְּקוּמוֹ לַעֲרֹץ הָאָרֶץ	19[9]	*And men shall go into the caves of the rocks, And into the holes of the earth*[10], From before the terror of the LORD, And from the glory of His majesty, When He arises to shake mightily the earth.
בַּיּוֹם הַהוּא יַשְׁלִיךְ הָאָדָם אֵת אֱלִילֵי כַסְפּוֹ וְאֵת אֱלִילֵי זְהָבוֹ אֲשֶׁר עָשׂוּ־לוֹ לְהִשְׁתַּחֲוֹת לַחְפֹּר פֵּרוֹת וְלָעֲטַלֵּפִים	20[11]	In that day a man shall cast away his idols of silver, and his idols of gold, which *they made for themselves*[12] to worship, To the moles and to the bats[13];
לָבוֹא בְּנִקְרוֹת הַצֻּרִים וּבִסְעִפֵי הַסְּלָעִים מִפְּנֵי פַּחַד יְהוָה וּמֵהֲדַר גְּאוֹנוֹ בְּקוּמוֹ לַעֲרֹץ הָאָרֶץ	21[14]	To go into the clefts of the rocks, And into the crevices of the crags, From before the terror of the LORD, And from the glory of His majesty, When he arises to shake mightily the earth.
חִדְלוּ לָכֶם מִן־הָאָדָם אֲשֶׁר נְשָׁמָה בְּאַפּוֹ כִּי־בַמֶּה נֶחְשָׁב הוּא	22[15]	*Cease from man, in whose nostrils is a breath; For how little is he to be accounted!*[16]

Isaiah – Chapter 3[17]

כִּי הִנֵּה הָאָדוֹן יְהוָה צְבָאוֹת מֵסִיר מִירוּשָׁלַ͏ִם וּמִיהוּדָה מַשְׁעֵן וּמַשְׁעֵנָה כֹּל מִשְׁעַן־לֶחֶם וְכֹל מִשְׁעַן־מָיִם	1[18]	For, behold, the Lord, the LORD of hosts, Does take away from Jerusalem and from Judah *drop*

---

[1] Isaiah 2:14 - 2 Corinthians 10:5, b.Sanhedrin 6b, b.Sotah 5b, Ein Yaakov Sotah:5b, Isaiah 6:25 16:4, mt.Pirkei Avot 4:4, Psalms 68:17 110:5-6

[2] Missing in LXX

[3] Isaiah 2:15 - Isaiah 1:12

[4] Isaiah 2:16 - 1 Kings 10:22 22:48-22:49, Isaiah 23:1 12:9, Numbers 9:52, Psalms 47:8, Revelation 18:11 18:17-18:19

[5] LXX *the sea, and upon every display of fine ships*

[6] Isaiah 2:17 - Ezekiel 28:2-7, Genesis.R 12:10, Isaiah 2:11 13:11, Jeremiah 48:29-30, Midrash Tanchuma Tetzaveh 10, Numbers.R 10:2, z.Vayetze 164a

[7] Isaiah 2:18 - Ezekiel 12:25 13:23, Genesis.R 12:10, Hosea 14:10, Isaiah 21:9 3:9, Mekhilta de R'Shimon bar Yochai Pisha 9:3, Mekhilta de R'Shimon bar Yochai Shirata 34:1, Mekilta de R'Ishmael Shirata 8:15, Midrash Tanchuma Shoftim 9, Midrash Tanchuma Tetzaveh 10, Numbers.R 10:2, Pesikta de R'Kahana S5.1, Sibylline Oracles 8.224, z.Vayetze 164a, Zechariah 13:2, Zephaniah 1:3 Isaiah 2:18-20 - Exodus.R 5:15, Sibylline Oracles 3.608

[8] LXX *And they shall hide all idols made with hands*

[9] Isaiah 2:19 - 1 Samuel 13:6 14:11, 2 Peter 3:10-3:13, 2 Thessalonians 1:9, Habakkuk 3:3-3:14, Haggai 2:6 2:21-2:22, Hebrews 11:38 12:26, Hosea 10:8, Isaiah 2:10 2:21 6:32, Jeremiah 16:16, Luke 23:30, Micah 1:3-1:4 7:17, Nahum 1:3-1:6, Psalms 7:7 18:7-18:16 76:8-76:10 114:5-114:7, Revelation 6:12-6:15 9:6 11:13 11:19 16:18 20:11, z.Lech Lecha 84a, z.Shemot 7b

[10] LXX *having carried them into the caves, and into the clefts of the rocks, and into the caverns of the earth*

[11] Isaiah 2:20 - Hosea 14:10, Isaiah 6:22 7:7 22:1 22:6, Joseph and Aseneth 10:12, Leviticus 11:19, Midrash Psalms 97:2, Perek Shirah, Pesikta de R'Kahana S5.1, Philippians 3:7-3:8, z.Shemot 5b
Isaiah 2:20-21 - Mekhilta de R'Shimon bar Yochai Shirata 34:1, Mekilta de R'Ishmael Shirata 8:13-14

[12] 1QIsaa *their finger have made*

[13] LXX *in order to worship vanities and bats*

[14] Isaiah 2:21 - Exodus 9:22, Isaiah 2:10 2:19, Job 6:6, Song of Songs 2:14, Tanya Likutei Aramim §36
Isaiah 2:21 [Targum] - mt.Hilchot Tumat Meit 13:3

[15] Isaiah 2:22 - 1QS 5.17-17, b.Berachot 14a, b.Sotah 4b, Ein Yaakov Berachot:14a, Ein Yaakov Sotah:4b, Esther.R 7:8, Genesis 2:7 7:22, Genesis.R 8:10, Isaiah 16:15, James 4:14, Jastrow 508a, Jeremiah 17:5, Job 7:15-21 3:3, mt.Hilchot Tefilah 6:4, mt.Pirkei Avot 4:4, Psalms 8:5 62:10 144:3-4 2:3, Siman 8:5, z.Tetzaveh 182a

[16] Missing in LXX

[17] Isaiah 3 - 1QIsaa

[18] Isaiah 3:1 - b.Chagigah 14a, Ezekiel 4:16-17 14:13, Isaiah 1:24 2:22 5:13 12:12 3:22, Jeremiah 13:21 14:9, Leviticus 2:26, Midrash

and crumb[1], Every *crump*[2] of bread, and every drop of water;

גִּבּוֹר וְאִישׁ מִלְחָמָה שׁוֹפֵט וְנָבִיא וְקֹסֵם וְזָקֵן 2[3]

The [4]mighty man, and the man of war; The judge, and the prophet, And the *diviner*[5], and the elder;

שַׂר־חֲמִשִּׁים וּנְשׂוּא פָנִים וְיוֹעֵץ וַחֲכַם חֲרָשִׁים וּנְבוֹן לָחַשׁ 3[6]

The captain of fifty, *and the man of rank, And the counsellor, and the cunning charmer, and the skillful enchanter*[7].

וְנָתַתִּי נְעָרִים שָׂרֵיהֶם וְתַעֲלוּלִים יִמְשְׁלוּ־בָם 4[8]

And I will give children to be their princes, And *babes*[9] shall rule over them.

וְנִגַּשׂ הָעָם אִישׁ בְּאִישׁ וְאִישׁ בְּרֵעֵהוּ יִרְהֲבוּ הַנַּעַר בַּזָּקֵן וְהַנִּקְלֶה בַּנִּכְבָּד 5[10]

And the people shall *oppress one another*[11], Every man his friend, and every man his neighbor; The child shall behave insolently against the aged, And the base against the honorable,

כִּי־יִתְפֹּשׂ אִישׁ בְּאָחִיו בֵּית אָבִיו שִׂמְלָה לְכָה קָצִין תִּהְיֶה־לָּנוּ וְהַמַּכְשֵׁלָה הַזֹּאת תַּחַת יָדֶךָ 6[12]

For a man shall take hold of his brother of the house of his father: 'You have a mantle, you be our ruler, And let *this ruin be under your hand*[13].'

יִשָּׂא בַיּוֹם הַהוּא לֵאמֹר לֹא־אֶהְיֶה חֹבֵשׁ וּבְבֵיתִי אֵין לֶחֶם וְאֵין שִׂמְלָה לֹא תְשִׂימֻנִי קְצִין עָם 7[14]

[15]In that day shall he swear, saying: 'I will not be a *healer*[16]; For in my house is neither bread nor mantle; *You shall not make me ruler of a*[17] people.'

כִּי כָשְׁלָה יְרוּשָׁלַ͏ִם וִיהוּדָה נָפָל כִּי־לְשׁוֹנָם וּמַעַלְלֵיהֶם אֶל־יְהֹוָה לַמְרוֹת עֵנֵי כְבוֹדוֹ 8[18]

For Jerusalem is ruined, And Judah is *fallen*[19]; *Because their tongue and deeds are against the LORD, To provoke the eyes of His glory*[20].

Psalms 23:5, Psalms 9:16

Isaiah 3:1-4 - Ein Yaakov Chagigah:13b

[1] LXX *the mighty man and mighty woman*

[2] LXX *strength*

[3] Isaiah 3:2 - 2 Kings 24:14-24:16, Amos 2:3, b.Chagigah 14a, Ezekiel 8:12 9:5 17:13, Isaiah 2:13-2:15 9:15-9:16, Jastrow 409a 1396b 1539a 1593a, Lamentations 5:12-5:14, Psalms 74:9

[4] LXX adds *great and*

[5] LXX *counsellor*

[6] Isaiah 3:3 - 1 Samuel 8:12, b.Chagigah 13a 14a, b.Chagigah 14a, b.Pesachim 112b, b.Taanit 25a, b.Yoma 53b, Deuteronomy 1:15, Ein Yaakov Chagigah:12b, Exodus 4:10 4:14-16 18:21, Guide for the Perplexed 1:37, Jastrow 704b 937b, Judges 8:18, Lamentations.R 1:1, mt.Hilchot Sanhedrin v'Hainshin Hameurim Lahem 2:6, Numbers.R 18:21, Ralbag SOS 6, Tanya Igeret Hakodesh §22a

[7] LXX *also, and the honorable counsellor, and the wise artificer, and the intelligent hearer*

[8] Isaiah 3:4 - 1 Kings 3:7-3:9, 2 Chronicles 9:1 10:1 12:2 12:5 12:9 12:11, b.Chagigah 14a, Ecclesiastes 10:16, Jastrow 921b 1683b, z.Shemot 10a, z.Terumah 175a 176a

[9] LXX *mockers*

[10] Isaiah 3:5 - 2 Kings 2:23, 2 Samuel 16:5-16:9, Amos 4:1, b.Chagigah 14a, Ecclesiastes 10:5-10:7, Ein Yaakov Chagigah:13b, Ein Yaakov Eruvin, Ezekiel 22:6-22:7 22:12, Isaiah 1:4 9:20-9:22 11:13, James 2:6 5:4, Jeremiah 9:4-9:9 22:17, Job 30:1-30:12, Leviticus 19:32, Luke 22:64, Malachi 3:5, Mark 14:65, Matthew 26:67 27:28-30, Micah 3:1-3 3:11 7:3-6, Zechariah 7:9-7:11

[11] LXX *fall, man upon man*

[12] Isaiah 3:6 - b.Chagigah 14a, b.Gittin 43a, b.Shabbat 119b, Bahir 150, Ein Yaakov Chagigah:13b, Ein Yaakov Chagigah:14b, Ein Yaakov Gittin:43a, Ein Yaakov Shabbat:119b, Genesis.R 80:5, Isaiah 4:1, Jastrow 1596b, John 6:15, Judges 11:6-11:8, Lamentations.R 1:57, Midrash Tanchuma Acharei Mot 8, Numbers.R 7:10 9:11 9:47

[13] LXX *my meat be under you*

[14] Isaiah 3:7 - b.Chagigah 14a, b.Shabbat 120a, Deuteronomy 8:40, Ein Yaakov Chagigah:13b, Ezekiel 10:4, Genesis 14:22, Hosea 5:13 6:1, Isaiah 10:12, Jeremiah 14:19, Lamentations 2:13, Revelation 10:5-6

[15] 1QIsaa adds *but*

[16] LXX *ruler*

[17] LXX *I will not be the ruler of this*

[18] Isaiah 3:8 - 1 Corinthians 10:22, 2 Chronicles 28:5-7 4:18 33:6-7 9:11 36:17-19, Ezekiel 8:4-6 8:12 8:17-18 9:9, Habakkuk 1:13, Hosea 7:16, Isaiah 1:7 5:18-19 9:18 9:4 65:3-5, Jeremiah 2:6 2:18, Jude 1:15, Lamentations 5:16-17, Malachi 3:13-15, Matthew 12:36-37, Mesillat Yesharim 24:Trait of Yiras Cheit, Micah 3:12, Midrash Psalms 39:1, Psalms 73:8-11

[19] 1QIsaa feminine; MT masculine

[20] LXX *and their tongues have spoken with iniquity, disobedient as they are toward the LORD*

הֻכָּרַת פְּנֵיהֶם עָנְתָה בָּם וְחַטָּאתָם כִּסְדֹם הִגִּידוּ לֹא כִחֵדוּ אוֹי לְנַפְשָׁם כִּי־גָמְלוּ לָהֶם רָעָה   9[1]

2The *shame*[3] of their countenance witnesses against them; And they declare their sin as Sodom, **4**they do not hide it. Woe to their soul! For they have worked evil to themselves.

אִמְרוּ צַדִּיק כִּי־טוֹב כִּי־פְרִי מַעַלְלֵיהֶם יֹאכֵלוּ   10[5]

Say of the righteous so it shall be well with him[6]; For they shall eat the fruit of their deeds.

אוֹי לְרָשָׁע רָע כִּי־גְמוּל יָדָיו יֵעָשֶׂה לּוֹ   11[7]

Woe to the wicked! It shall be ill with him; For the work of his *hands shall be done*[8] to him.

עַמִּי נֹגְשָׂיו מְעוֹלֵל וְנָשִׁים מָשְׁלוּ בוֹ עַמִּי מְאַשְּׁרֶיךָ מַתְעִים וְדֶרֶךְ אֹרְחֹתֶיךָ בִּלֵּעוּ   12[9]

As for My people, a babe is their master, And women rule over them. O My people, *they who lead you cause you to err, And destroy the way of your paths*[10].

נִצָּב לָרִיב יְהוָה וְעֹמֵד לָדִין עַמִּים   13[11]

The LORD stands up to plead, And stands to judge the peoples.

יְהוָה בְּמִשְׁפָּט יָבוֹא עִם־זִקְנֵי עַמּוֹ וְשָׂרָיו וְאַתֶּם בִּעַרְתֶּם הַכֶּרֶם גְּזֵלַת הֶעָנִי בְּבָתֵּיכֶם   14[12]

The LORD will enter into judgment With the elders of *His*[13] people, and its princes: 'It is you who have eaten up the vineyard; The spoil of the poor is in your houses;

'מַלָּכֶם' "מַה־לָּכֶם" תְּדַכְּאוּ עַמִּי וּפְנֵי עֲנִיִּים תִּטְחָנוּ נְאֻם־אֲדֹנָי יְהוִה צְבָאוֹת   15[14]

Why have you crushed My people, And ground the face of the poor?' *says the Lord, the GOD of hosts*[15].

וַיֹּאמֶר יְהוָה יַעַן כִּי גָבְהוּ בְּנוֹת צִיּוֹן וַתֵּלַכְנָה 'נְטֻוֹת' "נְטוּיוֹת" גָּרוֹן וּמְשַׂקְּרוֹת עֵינָיִם הָלוֹךְ וְטָפֹף תֵּלַכְנָה וּבְרַגְלֵיהֶם תְּעַכַּסְנָה   16[16]

Moreover the LORD said: Because the daughters of Zion are haughty, And walk with stretched-forth necks And wanton eyes,

---

[1] Isaiah 3:9 - 1 Samuel 15:32, 2 Kings 9:30, b.Bechorot 46b, b.Yevamot 120a, Daniel 7:20, Ezekiel 23:16, Genesis 13:13 18:20-18:21 19:5-19:9, Genesis.R 65:20 73:5, Hosea 13:9, Isaiah 3:16, Jeremiah 3:3 6:15 44:16-44:17, Lamentations 5:16, Leviticus.R 33:5, Mas.Derek Eretz Rabbah 1:13, Mas.Derek Eretz Zutta 8:8, Midrash Psalms 119:8, Proverbs 8:36 6:13, Psalms 10:5 73:6-73:7, Romans 6:23, Ruth.R 7:12, Sifre Devarim {Ha'azinu Hashamayim} 308, y.Sotah 9:3, y.Yevamot 16:3, z.Yitro 75a

[2] LXX adds *Now their glory has been brought low*

[3] 1QIsaa plural; MT singular

[4] 1QIsaa adds *and*

[5] Isaiah 3:10 - Avot de R'Natan 40, b.Bava Batra [Rashi] 80b, b.Bava Batra 11a, b.Chagigah 12a, b.Kiddushin 40a, b.Succah 56b, b.Yoma 38b, Deuteronomy 28:1-28:14, Ecclesiastes 8:12, Ein Yaakov Bava Batra:11a, Ein Yaakov Chagigah:12a, Ein Yaakov Kiddushin:40a, Ein Yaakov Sukkah:56b, Ein Yaakov Yoma:38b, Ezekiel 9:4 18:9-19, Galatians 6:7-8, Hebrews 6:10, Isaiah 26:20-21, Jeremiah 15:11, Leviticus.R 27:1, Malachi 3:18, Mas.Derek Eretz Rabbah 2:21, Mesillat Yesharim 19:For-the-Benefit-of-One's-Fellow, Midrash Psalms 62:4 72:1-2 114:2 118:1-2, Midrash Tanchuma Emor 5, Numbers.R 3:1, Pesikta de R'Kahana 9.1, Psalms 18:24-25 128:1-2, Ralbag Wars 4:6, Romans 2:5-2:11, Sifre Devarim Nitzavim 324, t.Peah 1:2 4:18, y.Peah 1:1, z.Bereshit 33a, z.Lech Lecha 82b, z.Noach 60a, z.Shemot 11b, z.Terumah 128b, Zephaniah 2:3

[6] LXX *saying against themselves, Let us bind the just, for he is burdensome to us*

[7] Isaiah 3:11 - 2 Corinthians 5:10, Avot de R'Natan 40, b.Kiddushin 40a, Deuteronomy 28:15-28:68, Ecclesiastes 8:13, Ein Yaakov Kiddushin:40a, Gates of Repentance 3.125, Isaiah 24:22 57:20-57:21 65:13-65:15 17:20, James 2:13, Jastrow 1485a, Leviticus.R 27:1, Midrash Psalms 115:1 118:2, Midrash Tanchuma Emor 5, Pesikta de R'Kahana 9.1, Proverbs 1:31, Psalms 1:3-1:5 11:6-11:7 28:4 62:13 120:3-120:4, Ralbag Wars 4:6, Sifre Devarim {Ha'azinu Hashamayim} 324, Sifre Devarim Nitzavim 324, t.Peah 1:3, y.Peah 1:1, z.Bereshit 54b, z.Vayechi 219b

[8] 1QIsaa *hand will be repaid*

[9] Isaiah 3:12 - 2 Kings 11:1, Esther.R 3:3, Guide for the Perplexed 3:8, Isaiah 3:4 9:16-9:17 28:14-28:15, Jastrow 1052a 1321a, Jeremiah 5:31, Matthew 15:14 23:13, Nahum 3:13, Numbers 6:23-6:27, z.Vayikra 20b

[10] LXX *your exactors strip you, and extortioners rule over you: O my people, they that pronounce you blessed lead you astray, and pervert the path of your feet*

[11] Isaiah 3:13 - Genesis.R 82:8, Hosea 4:1-2, Micah 6:2, Midrash Tanchuma Kedoshim 1, Pesikta Rabbati 12:5, Proverbs 22:22-23 23:10-11, Psalms 12:6

[12] Isaiah 3:14 - Amos 4:1, b.Bava Kamma [Tosefot] 73b, b.Berachot 6b, b.Shabbat 54b, Deuteronomy.R 1:10, Ein Yaakov Berachot:6b, Ein Yaakov Shabbat:54b, Exodus.R 5:12, Isaiah 3:2-3:3 5:7, James 2:6, Jeremiah 5:27, Job 22:4 24:2-24:7 24:9 10:23, Matthew 21:33, Micah 2:2 6:10, Midrash Tanchuma Kedoshim 1, Midrash Tanchuma Mishpatim 7, Midrash Tanchuma Shemot 29, Psalms 14:4 23:2, Ruth.R Petichata:6

Isaiah 3:14-22 - 4QIsab

[13] Not in 4QIsab

[14] Isaiah 3:15 - Amos 2:6-2:7 8:4-8:6, Exodus 5:14, Ezekiel 18:2, Gates of Repentance 3.024, Isaiah 10:4, Jonah 1:6, Lamentations.R 2:11, Mas.Soferim 7:3, Micah 3:2-3:3, Pesikta de R'Kahana 17.6, Psalms 94:5

[15] 1QIsaa *says my Lord, the LORD of Hosts*; missing in LXX

[16] Isaiah 3:16 - b.Bava Batra [Tosefot] 75b, b.Sanhedrin [Rashi] 21a, b.Shabbat 62b, b.Sotah 47b, b.Yoma 9b, Ein Yaakov Sotah 47b, Ein Yaakov Yoma 9a, Ezekiel 16:49-50, Genesis.R 18:2, Isaiah 1:8 3:18 4:4 24:4 32:9-11, Jastrow 124a 218b 225a 656a 1021a 1079a 1360b 1482a 1538b, Lamentations.R 4:18, Leviticus.R 16:1 17:3, Luke 23:28, Matthew 21:5, Midrash Tanchuma Naso 1, Midrash Tanchuma Tazria 11, Midrash Tanchuma Vayeshev 6, mt.Hilchot Deot 5:8, Pesikta de R'Kahana 16.11, Pesikta Rabbati 27/28:1 31:7

Walking and mincing as they go, And making a tinkling with *their*[1] feet;

וְשִׂפַּח אֲדֹנָי קָדְקֹד בְּנוֹת צִיּוֹן וַיהוָה פָּתְהֵן יְעָרֶה   17[2]

Therefore, *the Lord*[3] will strike with a scab The crown of the head of the daughters of Zion, And *the LORD*[4] will lay bare their secret parts.

בַּיּוֹם הַהוּא יָסִיר אֲדֹנָי אֵת תִּפְאֶרֶת הָעֲכָסִים וְהַשְּׁבִיסִים וְהַשַּׂהֲרֹנִים   18[5]

In that day *the*[6] Lord will take the *bravery of their anklets, and the fillets*[7], and the crescents;

הַנְּטִיפוֹת וְהַשֵּׁירוֹת וְהָרְעָלוֹת   19[8]

[9]The pendants, and the bracelets, and the veils[10];

הַפְּאֵרִים וְהַצְּעָדוֹת וְהַקִּשֻּׁרִים וּבָתֵּי הַנֶּפֶשׁ וְהַלְּחָשִׁים: 20[11]

[12]The headdresses, and the armlets, and *the*[13] sashes, and the corselets, and the amulets[14];

הַטַּבָּעוֹת וְנִזְמֵי הָאָף   21[15]

[16]The rings, and the nose jewels[17];

הַמַּחֲלָצוֹת וְהַמַּעֲטָפוֹת וְהַמִּטְפָּחוֹת וְהָחֲרִיטִים   22[18]

[19]The aprons, and *the*[20] mantles, and the cloaks, and the girdles[21];

וְהַגִּלְיֹנִים וְהַסְּדִינִים וְהַצְּנִיפוֹת וְהָרְדִידִים   23[22]

And the gauze robes, and the fine linen, and the turbans, and the mantles[23].

וְהָיָה תַחַת בֹּשֶׂם מַק יִהְיֶה וְתַחַת חֲגוֹרָה נִקְפָּה וְתַחַת מַעֲשֶׂה מִקְשֶׁה קָרְחָה וְתַחַת פְּתִיגִיל מַחֲגֹרֶת שָׂק כִּי־תַחַת יֹפִי   24[24]

And it shall come to pass, that Instead of *sweet spices, there shall be rottenness*[25]; And instead of a girdle, *rags*[26]; And instead of *curled hair*,

---

33:13, Proverbs 16:18 6:13, Siman 3:7, Song of Songs 3:11, t.Sotah 14:9, y.Shabbat 6:4, Zephaniah 3:11

Isaiah 3:16-17 - Lamentations.R 1:57 4:18

[1] 1QIsaa feminine; MT masculine [incorrect]

[2] Isaiah 3:17 - b.Shabbat 62b, Deuteronomy 4:27, Ezekiel 16:36-16:37 23:25-23:29, Isaiah 20:4 47:2-47:3, Jastrow 614a 1012b 1618b, Jeremiah 13:22, Leviticus 13:29-13:30 13:43-13:44, Leviticus.R 17:3, Mas.Soferim 7:4, Micah 1:11, Midrash Tanchuma Metzora 4, Midrash Tanchuma Tazria 11, Nahum 3:5, Numbers.R 7:5, Per Massorah: Soferim altered "Hashem" to "Adonai", Pesikta de R'Kahana 17.6, Pesikta Rabbati 31:7, Revelation 16:2

[3] 1QIsaa *My Lord to the LORD*; LXX *God*

[4] 1QIsaa *my Lord*

[5] Isaiah 3:18 - Ecclesiastes.R 7:7, Jastrow 993b 1341b 1514a, Judges 8:21 8:26, mt.Hilchot Keilim 22:14, Numbers.R 9:11, Per Massorah: Soferim altered "Hashem" to "Adonai", y.Shabbat 6:4

Isaiah 3:18-24 - Genesis.R 18:1, Song of Songs.R 4:23

[6] 1QIsaa *my*

[7] LXX *glory of their raiment, the curls, and the fringes*

[8] Isaiah 3:19 - Exodus 11:22, Ezekiel 16:11, Genesis 24:22 24:30 24:53 14:18 14:25, Jastrow 645a 1487b, Numbers 7:50, Numbers.R 9:11, y.Shabbat 6:4

[9] LXX adds *and*

[10] LXX *and the chains, and the ornaments of their faces*

[11] Isaiah 3:20 - b.Bava Batra [Tosefot] 156b, Exodus 8:2 15:28, Ezekiel 16:12, Genesis 11:4, Hosea 2:13, Jastrow 90a 703a 1139b 1321a, y.Shabbat 6:4

[12] LXX dds *and*

[13] Missing in 1QIsaa

[14] LXX *and the array of glorious ornaments, and the armlets, and the bracelets, and the wreathed work, and the finger-rings, and the ornaments for the right hand*

[15] Isaiah 3:21 - 1 Peter 3:3-4, 1 Timothy 2:9-10, Esther 8:12, Ezekiel 16:12, Genesis 24:47 17:42, Genesis.R 36:1, James 2:2, Jastrow 453a, Luke 15:22, Song of Songs 5:14, y.Shabbat 6:4

[16] LXX adds *and*

[17] Missing in LXX

[18] Isaiah 3:22 - Jastrow 818b 951a 1226b 1328a, y.Shabbat 6:4

[19] LXX adds *and*

[20] Missing in 1QIsaa

[21] Missing in LXX

[22] Isaiah 3:23 - 1 Chronicles 15:27, b.Bava Batra [Tosefot] 156b, Exodus 14:8, Ezekiel 16:10, Genesis 24:65 17:42, Jastrow 249a 713a 957a, Luke 16:19, Revelation 19:8 19:14, Ruth 3:15, Song of Songs 5:7, y.Shabbat 3:4

[23] LXX *and the earrings, and the garments with scarlet borders, and the garments with purple grounds, and the shawls to be worn in the house, and the Spartan transparent dresses, and those made of fine linen, and the purple ones, and the scarlet ones, and the fine linen, interwoven with gold and purple, and the light coverings for couches*

[24] Isaiah 3:24 - 1 Peter 3:3, Amos 8:10, b.Shabbat 62b, Deuteronomy 4:22 8:24, Esther 2:12, Ezekiel 7:18 3:31, Isaiah 4:4 15:3 22:12 32:9-11 9:9, Jastrow 935a 1285b, Jeremiah 4:8 6:26 24:37 1:3, Job 16:15, Joel 1:8, Lamentations 2:10, Leviticus 2:16, m.Negaim 1:1, Micah 1:16, Proverbs 7:17 7:24, Psalms of Solomon 2:20, Revelation 11:3 16:9 18:9

[25] 1QIsaa LXX *perfume there will be stench*

[26] LXX *you shall gird yourself with a rope*

מְתַיִךְ בַּחֶרֶב יִפֹּלוּ וּגְבוּרָתֵךְ בַּמִּלְחָמָה   25[4]

וְאָנוּ וְאָבְלוּ פְּתָחֶיהָ וְנִקָּתָה לָאָרֶץ תֵּשֵׁב   26[8]

baldness[1]; And instead of a *bodice, a girding of*[2] sackcloth; *Branding instead of beauty*[3]. *Your men*[5] shall fall by the sword, And your *mighty*[6] *in the war*[7].

And *her gates shall lament and*[9] mourn; And utterly bereft she shall sit upon the ground.

Isaiah – Chapter 4[10]

וְהֶחֱזִיקוּ שֶׁבַע נָשִׁים בְּאִישׁ אֶחָד בַּיּוֹם הַהוּא לֵאמֹר לַחְמֵנוּ נֹאכֵל וְשִׂמְלָתֵנוּ נִלְבָּשׁ רַק יִקָּרֵא שִׁמְךָ עָלֵינוּ אֱסֹף חֶרְפָּתֵנוּ   1[11]

בַּיּוֹם הַהוּא יִהְיֶה צֶמַח יְהוָה לִצְבִי וּלְכָבוֹד וּפְרִי הָאָרֶץ לְגָאוֹן וּלְתִפְאֶרֶת לִפְלֵיטַת יִשְׂרָאֵל   2[12]

וְהָיָה הַנִּשְׁאָר בְּצִיּוֹן וְהַנּוֹתָר בִּירוּשָׁלַם קָדוֹשׁ יֵאָמֶר לוֹ כָּל־הַכָּתוּב לַחַיִּים בִּירוּשָׁלָם   3[15]

אִם רָחַץ אֲדֹנָי אֵת צֹאַת בְּנוֹת־צִיּוֹן וְאֶת־דְּמֵי יְרוּשָׁלַם יָדִיחַ מִקִּרְבָּהּ בְּרוּחַ מִשְׁפָּט וּבְרוּחַ בָּעֵר   4[16]

וּבָרָא יְהוָה עַל כָּל־מְכוֹן הַר־צִיּוֹן וְעַל־מִקְרָאֶהָ עָנָן יוֹמָם וְעָשָׁן וְנֹגַהּ אֵשׁ לֶהָבָה לָיְלָה כִּי עַל־כָּל־כָּבוֹד חֻפָּה   5[19]

And seven women shall take hold of one man in that day, saying: 'We will eat our own bread, and wear our own apparel; only let us be called by your name; take away our reproach.'

In that day *the growth of the LORD shall be beautiful and glorious, And the fruit of the land excellent and beautiful for those who escaped from* [13]Israel[14].

And it shall come to pass, that he who remains in Zion, and he who remains in Jerusalem, shall be called holy, everyone who is written for life in Jerusalem;

when the Lord shall wash away the filth of the [17]daughters of Zion, and shall purge the blood of Jerusalem from its midst, by the spirit of judgment, and by the spirit of *destruction*[18].

And the LORD will create over the whole habitation of mount Zion, and over her assemblies, a cloud and smoke by day, *and the*

---

[1] LXX *a golden ornament for the head, you shall have baldness on account of your works*

[2] LXX *tunic with a scarlet ground, you shall gird thyself with*

[3] 1QIsaa *instead of beauty, shame*

[4] Isaiah 3:25 - 2 Chronicles 5:9, Amos 9:10, Isaiah 1:20, Jeremiah 11:22 14:18 18:21 19:7 21:9, Lamentations 2:21, Sifre Devarim Vezot Habracha 347

[5] LXX *your most beautiful son whom you love*

[6] 1QIsaa *forces*

[7] LXX *men shall fall by the sword, and shall be brought low*

[8] Isaiah 3:26 - b.Niddah 60b, Ezekiel 2:16, Guide for the Perplexed 1:54, Isaiah 23:1, Jeremiah 14:2, Job 2:8 2:13, Lamentations 1:4 2:10, Lamentations.R Petichata D'Chakimei:7, Luke 19:44, y.Horayot 3:3, y.Pesachim 8:8, y.Sanhedrin 2:1

[9] LXX *the stores of your ornaments shall*

[10] Isaiah 4 - 1QIsaa

[11] Isaiah 4:1 - 1 Samuel 1:6, 2 Thessalonians 3:12, Genesis 6:23, Guide for the Perplexed 1:30, Isaiah 2:11 2:17 3:25-3:26 10:20 13:12 17:7, Lamentations.R 5:11, Luke 1:25 21:22

[12] Isaiah 4:2 - 2 Corinthians 4:6, 2 Peter 1:16, Exodus 4:2, Ezekiel 7:16 17:22-23, Hosea 2:22-25, Isaiah 10:20-10:22 11:1-2 11:4 3:6 27:12-13 6:23 37:31-32 31:8 5:2 12:21, Jeremiah 23:5 9:15 20:14 20:28, Joel 3:5 4:18, John 1:14, Luke 21:36, Matthew 24:22, Obadiah 1:17, Psalms 67:7 72:16 85:12-13, Revelation 7:9-14, Romans 11:4-5, Zechariah 3:8 6:12 9:17

[13] LXX *God shall shine gloriously in counsel on the earth, to exalt and glorify the remnant of*

[14] 1QIsaa adds *and Judah*

[15] Isaiah 4:3 - 1 Peter 2:9, Acts 13:48, Avot de R'Natan 31, b.Bava Batra 75b, b.Sanhedrin 92a, Colossians 3:12, Ein Yaakov Bava Batra:75b, Ein Yaakov Sanhedrin:92a, Ephesians 1:4, Exodus 32:32-33, Ezekiel 13:9 36:24-28 19:12, Hebrews 12:14, Isaiah 1:27 4:1 12:21, Leviticus.R 35:6, Luke 10:20, Mas.Kallah Rabbati 10:1, Midrash Tanchuma Kedoshim 5, Numbers.R 13:5, Pesikta de R'Kahana 5.9, Pesikta Rabbati 15:14/15, Philippians 4:3, Psalms 69:29, Revelation 3:5 13:8 17:8 20:15 21:27, Romans 11:5, Ruth.R Petichata:7, Song of Songs.R 2:33, z.Beshallach 57b, z.Lech Lecha 94b, z.Mishpatim 121a, z.Vayechi 219a, z.Vayera 119a, z.Vayetze 164a, Zechariah 14:20-14:21

[16] Isaiah 4:4 - b.Sotah 12b, Ecclesiastes.R 11:1, Ein Yaakov Sotah:12a, Ezekiel 16:6-9 22:15 22:18-22 24:7-14 12:25 12:29, Genesis.R 48:10, Isaiah 1:15 1:31 3:16-26 9:6 26:20-21 4:6, Joel 4:21, John 16:8-11, Lamentations 1:9, Lamentations.R 1:23, Malachi 3:2-3 3:19, Matthew 3:11-12 23:37, Midrash Tanchuma Emor 22, Midrash Tanchuma Ki Tetze 3, Midrash Tanchuma Vayera 4, Midrash Tanchuma Vayigash 10, Numbers.R 14:2, Per Massorah: Soferim altered "Hashem" to "Adonai", Pesikta Rabbati 29/30B:4, Tanya Igeret Hakodesh §22a, Zechariah 3:3-4 13:1 13:9, Zephaniah 3:1
Isaiah 4:4-6 - Mekilta de R'Ishmael Pisha 14:16-18

[17] LXX adds *sons and*

[18] 1QIsaa *storm*; LXX *burning*

[19] Isaiah 4:5 - b.Bava Batra [Tosefot] 75ab, Ein Yaakov Bava Batra:75ab, Exodus 13:21-22 14:19-20 14:24 2:1 2:7 40:34-38, Exodus.R 50:5, Genesis.R 44:22, Isaiah 31:4-5 8:18 9:20 13:35 22:13 12:1, Matthew 18:20 4:20, Mekhilta de R'Shimon bar Yochai

וְסֻכָּה תִּהְיֶה לְצֵל־יוֹמָם מֵחֹרֶב וּלְמַחְסֶה וּלְמִסְתּוֹר מִזֶּרֶם וּמִמָּטָר

6[2]

shining of a flaming fire by night; for over all the glory shall be a canopy[1].
And there shall be a pavilion for shade in the daytime[3] from the heat, and for a refuge and for concealment from storm and from rain.

Isaiah – Chapter 5

אָשִׁירָה נָּא לִידִידִי שִׁירַת דּוֹדִי לְכַרְמוֹ כֶּרֶם הָיָה לִידִידִי בְּקֶרֶן בֶּן־שָׁמֶן

1[4]

Let me[5] sing of my well-beloved, a song of my beloved touching his vineyard. My well-beloved had a vineyard In a very fruitful hill;

וַיְעַזְּקֵהוּ וַיְסַקְּלֵהוּ וַיִּטָּעֵהוּ שֹׂרֵק וַיִּבֶן מִגְדָּל בְּתוֹכוֹ וְגַם־יֶקֶב חָצֵב בּוֹ וַיְקַו לַעֲשׂוֹת עֲנָבִים וַיַּעַשׂ בְּאֻשִׁים

2[6]

And he dug it, and cleared it of stones[7], And planted it with the choicest vine, And built a tower in its midst, And also hewed out a vat there; And he looked so it should bring forth grapes, And it brought forth *wild grapes*[8].

וְעַתָּה יוֹשֵׁב יְרוּשָׁלַ͏ִם וְאִישׁ יְהוּדָה שִׁפְטוּ־נָא בֵּינִי וּבֵין כַּרְמִי

3[9]

And now, O *inhabitants*[10] of Jerusalem and men of Judah, judge[11], please, between me and my vineyard.

מַה־לַּעֲשׂוֹת עוֹד לְכַרְמִי וְלֹא עָשִׂיתִי בּוֹ מַדּוּעַ קִוֵּיתִי לַעֲשׂוֹת עֲנָבִים וַיַּעַשׂ בְּאֻשִׁים

4[12]

What could have been done more *for*[13] my vineyard, that I have not done in it? Why, when I looked that it should bring forth grapes, brought it forth *wild grapes*[14]?

Beshallach 20:4, Mekilta de R'Ishmael Beshallah 1:174, Mesillat Yesharim 4:To Acquire Zehirus, Midrash Psalms 16:10, Midrash Tanchuma Bo 9, Midrash Tanchuma Pinchas 14, Midrash Tanchuma Tzav 12, Midrash Tanchuma Vayakhel 10, Nehemiah 9:12, Numbers 9:15-22, Numbers.R 21:22, Pesikta Rabbati 31:6, Psalms 78:14 85:10 87:2-3 89:8 15:1, z.Vayechi 219a, Zechariah 2:5-10 Isaiah 4:5-6 - 4Q162 1:1-6, 4QIsaa, Midrash Tanchuma Terumah 5

[1] Missing in 1QIsaa; apparently the scribe skipped from *by day* in 4:5 and continued after the *by day* in 4:6

[2] Isaiah 4:6 - b.Succah 2a 6b, Ecclesiastes.R 11:1, Ezekiel 11:16, Genesis.R 1:6 48:10, Guide for the Perplexed 3:20, Hebrews 6:18 11:7, Isaiah 8:14 1:4 8:2 32:18-19, Matthew 7:24-27, Mekhilta de R'Shimon bar Yochai Beshallach 20:4, Mekilta de R'Ishmael Beshallah 1:175, Mekilta de R'Ishmael Pisha 14:19, Midrash Psalms 13:4, Midrash Tanchuma Bo 9, mt.Hilcnot Shofar Sukkah v'Lulav 4:2 5:9, Numbers.R 14:2, Pesikta de R'Kahana S2.1 S2.3-5, Proverbs 18:10, Psalms 27:5 91:1 121:5-6, Revelation 7:16, Song of Songs.R 1:45, y.Sukkah 1:1

Isaiah 4:26 - b.Chullin [Tosefot] 60a

[3]

[4] Isaiah 5:1 - 3 Baruch 1:2, 4QIsaa, b.Menachot 53b, b.Succah 49a, Deuteronomy 31:19-31:22, Ein Yaakov Sukkah:49a, Genesis.R 21:9, Isaiah 27:2-27:3, Jeremiah 2:21, John 15:1, Judges 5:1-5:31, Lamentations.R 2:6, Luke 20:9, Mark 12:1, Matthew 21:33, Midrash Psalms 75:5, Midrash Tanchuma Terumah 5, Midrash Tanchuma Vayeilech 2, Pesikta de R'Kahana S2.5, Psalms 45:2 80:9 5:1, Sifre Devarim Ekev 37, Sifre Devarim Vezot Habracha 352, Song of Songs 2:16 5:2 5:16 6:3 8:11-8:12, y.Chagigah 3:1, z.Lech Lecha 95b

Isaiah 5:1-2 - t.Sukkah 3:15

Isaiah 5:1-7 - z.Shemot 4a

Isaiah 5:1-30 - 1QIsaa

[5] 1QIsaa *I will*

[6] Isaiah 5:2 - 1 Corinthians 9:7, b.Chullin [Rashi] 94a, b.Menachot [Tosefot] 84a 85b, b.Rosh Hashanah [Tosefot] 12b, b.Rosh Hashanah 23b, b.Succah 39b 49a, Deuteronomy 32:6 32:8-9 32:32-33, Ein Yaakov Sukkah:49a, Exodus 33:16, Exodus.R 20:5, Genesis.R 19:12, Hosea 10:1, Isaiah 1:2-1:4 1:8 1:21-23 5:7 63:2-3, Jastrow 1570a, Jeremiah 2:21, Judges 16:4, Luke 13:6-7 20:10-18, Mark 11:13 12:2, Matthew 21:19 21:34, Micah 4:8, Midrash Tanchuma Mishpatim 5, Midrash Tanchuma Vayeilech 2, Nehemiah 13:15, Numbers 23:9, Psalms 44:2-4, Revelation 14:18-20, Romans 9:4, t.Meilah 1:16, Testament of Joseph 19:12, y.Rosh Hashanah 2:1, y.Sukkah 4:6

[7] LXX *I made a hedge round it, and dug a trench*

[8] LXX *thorns*

[9] Isaiah 5:3 - Jeremiah 2:4-2:5, Luke 20:15-20:16, Mark 12:9-12:12, Matthew 21:40-21:41, Micah 6:2-6:3, Psalms 50:4-50:6 51:5, Romans 2:5 3:4

Isaiah 5:3-4 - Sifre Devarim {Ha'azinu Hashamayim} 306, Sifre Devarim Nitzavim 306

[10] MT collective singular; 1QIsaa plural

[11] Misspelling in 1QIsaa

[12] Isaiah 5:4 - 2 Chronicles 36:14-36:16, Acts 7:51-7:60, Ezekiel 24:13, Isaiah 1:5, Jeremiah 2:5 2:30-2:31 6:29-6:30, Matthew 23:37, Micah 6:3-6:4, Midrash Tanchuma Mishpatim 17, Numbers.R 16:24

[13] 1QIsaa *in*

[14] LXX *thorns*

וְעַתָּה אוֹדִיעָה־נָּא אֶתְכֶם אֵת אֲשֶׁר־אֲנִי עֹשֶׂה לְכַרְמִי הָסֵר מְשׂוּכָּתוֹ וְהָיָה לְבָעֵר פָּרֹץ גְּדֵרוֹ וְהָיָה לְמִרְמָס	5⁵ And *now*[2] come, I will tell you What I will do to my vineyard: I will take away the hedge, and it *shall be consumed*[3]; I will break down its fence, And it shall be trodden down;
וַאֲשִׁיתֵהוּ בָתָה לֹא יִזָּמֵר וְלֹא יֵעָדֵר וְעָלָה שָׁמִיר וָשָׁיִת וְעַל הֶעָבִים אֲצַוֶּה מֵהַמְטִיר עָלָיו מָטָר	6⁴ And I will lay it waste: It shall not be pruned nor hoed, But there shall come up briers and thorns; I will command the clouds that they do not rain on it.
כִּי כֶרֶם יְהוָה צְבָאוֹת בֵּית יִשְׂרָאֵל וְאִישׁ יְהוּדָה נְטַע שַׁעֲשׁוּעָיו וַיְקַו לְמִשְׁפָּט וְהִנֵּה מִשְׂפָּח לִצְדָקָה וְהִנֵּה צְעָקָה	7⁵ For the vineyard of the LORD of hosts is the house of Israel, and the men of Judah the plant of His *delight*[6]; and He looked for justice, but saw *violence*[7]; for righteousness, but saw a cry.
הוֹי מַגִּיעֵי בַיִת בְּבַיִת שָׂדֶה בְשָׂדֶה יַקְרִיבוּ עַד אֶפֶס מָקוֹם וְהוּשַׁבְתֶּם לְבַדְּכֶם בְּקֶרֶב הָאָרֶץ	8⁸ Woe to those who join house *to*[9] house, who lay field to field, until there is no room, and *you are made to live alone*[10] in the midst of the land!
בְּאָזְנָי יְהוָה צְבָאוֹת אִם־לֹא בָּתִּים רַבִּים לְשַׁמָּה יִהְיוּ גְּדֹלִים וְטוֹבִים מֵאֵין יוֹשֵׁב	9¹¹ In my ears said the LORD of hosts: Of a truth many houses shall be desolate, great and fair, without inhabitant.
כִּי עֲשֶׂרֶת צִמְדֵּי־כֶרֶם יַעֲשׂוּ בַּת אֶחָת וְזֶרַע חֹמֶר יַעֲשֶׂה אֵיפָה	10¹² *For ten acres of vineyard shall yield*[13] one[14] bath, And *the seed of a homer shall yield an ephah*[15].
הוֹי מַשְׁכִּימֵי בַבֹּקֶר שֵׁכָר יִרְדֹּפוּ מְאַחֲרֵי בַנֶּשֶׁף יַיִן יַדְלִיקֵם	11¹⁶ Woe to those who rise up early in the morning, so they may follow strong drink; *who tarry late into the night*[17] until wine inflames them!

---

[1] Isaiah 5:5 - 2 Chronicles 36:4-36:10, 4Q162 1.1, 4Q162 1.3-4, Daniel 8:13, Deuteronomy 28:49-28:52, Genesis 11:4 11:7, Isaiah 10:6 25:10 27:10-27:11 28:3 28:18, Lamentations 1:2-1:9 1:15 4:12, Leviticus 26:31-26:35, Luke 21:24, Mekhilta de R'Shimon bar Yochai Nezikin 71:1, Nehemiah 2:3, Psalms 74:1-74:10 80:13-80:17, Revelation 11:2, y.Bava Kamma 1:1

[2] Misspelling in 1QIsaa

[3] 1QIsaa *will be for eating*

[4] Isaiah 5:6 - 1 Kings 17:1, 2 Chronicles 36:19-36:21, Amos 4:7, Deuteronomy 28:23-28:24 29:22, Ecclesiastes.R 11:3, Ein Yaakov Yevamot:105a, Exodus.R 32:2, Genesis.R 21:8, Guide for the Perplexed 2:47, Hebrews 6:6-6:8, Hosea 3:4, Isaiah 5:9-5:10 6:11-6:12 7:23-7:25 24:1-24:3 24:12 30:23 32:13-32:14, Jeremiah 14:1 14:22 25:11 45:4, Leviticus 26:33-26:35, Luke 21:24, Midrash Psalms 73:2, Midrash Tanchuma Mishpatim 17, Revelation 14:16-14:17

[5] Isaiah 5:7 - 1 Corinthians 6:8-6:11, 1 John 3:7-3:8, Deuteronomy 15:9, Exodus 2:23-2:24 3:7 22:21-22:27, Exodus.R 5:12 34:3, Gates of Repentance 3.161, Genesis 4:10, Isaiah 1:6 3:14 3:17 5:2 58:6-58:8 62:5, James 5:4, Jeremiah 12:10, Job 31:38-31:39 34:28, John 15:2, Leviticus.R 32:1, Luke 18:7, Matthew 3:8-3:10 23:23, Micah 6:8, Midrash Proverbs 19, Midrash Psalms 10:1 12:5, Midrash Tanchuma Chayyei Sarah 4, Midrash Tanchuma Re'eh 9, Midrash Tanchuma Shemini 9, Midrash Tanchuma Shemot 29, mt.Hilchot Talmud Torah 5:4, Nehemiah 5:1-5:5, Pesikta de R'Kahana 16.9, Pesikta Rabbati 29/30B:3, Philo De Somniis II 175, Proverbs 21:13, Psalms 80:9-80:12 80:16 147:11 149:4, Song of Songs 7:7, Song of Songs.R 2:44 7:18 8:14, Zechariah 7:9-7:14, Zephaniah 3:17

[6] LXX *beloved plant*

[7] 1QIsaa places a prefix in front of *bloodshed* that is not present in the MT

[8] Isaiah 5:8 - 1 Kings 21:16-21:20, Ezekiel 11:15 9:24, Genesis.R 68:13, Habakkuk 2:9-2:12, Jeremiah 22:13-22:17, Lamentations.R Petichata D'Chakimei:22, Luke 12:16-12:24, Matthew 23:13, Micah 2:2

[9] Missing in 1QIsaa

[10] 1QIsaa *you place yourself alone*

[11] Isaiah 5:9 - 2 Chronicles 12:21, 4Q162 2.1, Amos 3:7 5:11 6:11, b.Berachot 58b, Ein Yaakov Berachot:58b, Isaiah 5:6 6:11-6:12 22:14 3:10, Lamentations.R Petichata D'Chakimei:22, Matthew 22:7 23:38, Midrash Psalms 125:1

[12] Isaiah 5:10 - 1 Enoch 10:19, 4Q1621:7-2:2, b.Taanit [Tosefot] 9a, Ezekiel 45:10-45:11, Haggai 1:6 1:9-1:11 2:16, Joel 1:17, Leviticus 2:26 3:16

[13] LXX *For where ten yoke of oxen plough the land*

[14] MT familine; 1QIsaa masculine

[15] LXX *he who sows six homers shall produce three measures*

[16] Isaiah 5:11 - 1 Corinthians 6:10, 1 Thessalonians 5:6-7, b.Shabbat 119b, b.Sotah 48a, Ecclesiastes 10:16-17, Ein Yaakov Sotah:47b, Esther.R 5:1, Galatians 5:21, Gates of Repentance 1.031, Genesis.R 36:4, Habakkuk 2:15, Hosea 7:5-6, Isaiah 5:22 4:1 28:7-8, Luke 21:34, Midrash Tanchuma Shemini 5, Proverbs 20:1 23:29-30 23:32, Ralbag SOS 1, Romans 13:13, z.Beshallach 62b
Isaiah 5:11-13 - Ein Yaakov Shabbat:119b
Isaiah 5:11-14 - 4Q162 2:2-6

[17] 1QIsaa *holding on in the night*

וְהָיָה כִנּוֹר וָנֶבֶל תֹּף וְחָלִיל וָיַיִן מִשְׁתֵּיהֶם וְאֵת פֹּעַל יְהֹוָה לֹא יַבִּיטוּ וּמַעֲשֵׂה יָדָיו לֹא רָאוּ

12[1] *And the*[2] harp and the psaltery, the tambourine and the pipe, And wine, are in their festivals; But they do not regard the work of the LORD, nor do they consider the action of His hands.

לָכֵן גָּלָה עַמִּי מִבְּלִי־דָעַת וּכְבוֹדוֹ מְתֵי רָעָב וַהֲמוֹנוֹ צִחֵה צָמָא

13[3] Therefore, My people go into captivity, For want of knowledge; And *its*[4] honorable men are famished, And *the*[5] multitudes are parched with thirst.

לָכֵן הִרְחִיבָה שְּׁאוֹל נַפְשָׁהּ וּפָעֲרָה פִיהָ לִבְלִי־חֹק וְיָרַד הֲדָרָהּ וַהֲמוֹנָהּ וּשְׁאוֹנָהּ וְעָלֵז בָּהּ

14[6] Therefore, the netherworld enlarges her desire, And opens her mouth without measure; And down goes their glory, and their tumult, and their uproar, And he who rejoices among them.

וַיִּשַּׁח אָדָם וַיִּשְׁפַּל־אִישׁ וְעֵינֵי גְבֹהִים תִּשְׁפַּלְנָה

15[7] *And man is*[8] bowed down, And *man is humbled*[9], And the eyes of the lofty are humbled;

וַיִּגְבַּה יְהֹוָה צְבָאוֹת בַּמִּשְׁפָּט וְהָאֵל הַקָּדוֹשׁ נִקְדָּשׁ בִּצְדָקָה

16[10] But the LORD of hosts is exalted through justice, And God the Holy One is *sanctified*[11] through righteousness.

וְרָעוּ כְבָשִׂים כְּדָבְרָם וְחָרְבוֹת מֵחִים גָּרִים יֹאכֵלוּ

17[12] *Then the lambs shall feed as in their pasture, And the wanderers shall eat the waste places of the fat ones*[13].

הוֹי מֹשְׁכֵי הֶעָוֹן בְּחַבְלֵי הַשָּׁוְא וְכַעֲבוֹת הָעֲגָלָה חַטָּאָה

18[14] Woe to those who draw iniquity with cords of vanity, And sin as it were with a *cart rope*[15],

הָאֹמְרִים יְמַהֵר יָחִישָׁה מַעֲשֵׂהוּ לְמַעַן נִרְאֶה וְתִקְרַב וְתָבוֹאָה עֲצַת קְדוֹשׁ יִשְׂרָאֵל וְנֵדָעָה

19[16] Who says: 'Let Him make speed, let Him hasten His work, so we may see it; And let the counsel of the Holy One of Israel draw near and come, so we may know it.'

---

[1] Isaiah 5:12 - Amos 6:4-6:6, b.Shabbat 75a 119b, b.Sotah 48a, Daniel 5:1-5:4 5:23, Ein Yaakov Shabbat:69b, Ein Yaakov Sotah:47b, Gates of Repentance 1.031, Genesis 7:27, Hosea 4:10-4:11, Isaiah 5:19 22:13, Job 21:11-21:14 10:27, Jude 1:12, Luke 16:19, Midrash Tanchuma Bamidbar 2, Psalms 28:5 92:6-92:7, Saadia Opinions 1:1 1:3

[2] LXX *For they drink wine with*

[3] Isaiah 5:13 - 2 Chronicles 28:5-28:8, 2 Kings 17:6, 2 Peter 3:5, Amos 8:13, b.Sanhedrin 92a, b.Shabbat 119b, b.Sotah 48a, Ein Yaakov Sanhedrin:92a, Ein Yaakov Sotah:47b, Esther.R 5:1, Hosea 4:6, Isaiah 1:3 1:7 3:11 42:22-42:25, Jeremiah 8:7 14:3 14:18, John 3:19-3:20, Lamentations 4:4-4:5 4:9, Luke 19:44, Matthew 23:16-23:27, Numbers.R 3:6, Romans 1:28
Isaiah 5:13-14 - 4QIsaf

[4] 1QIsaa *My*

[5] Missing in LXX

[6] Isaiah 5:14 - 1 Samuel 25:36-25:38, 2 Baruch 56:6, 2 Samuel 13:28-13:29, Acts 12:21-12:23, b.Sanhedrin 111a, b.Sotah 48a, Daniel 5:3-5:6 5:30, Ecclesiastes.R 10:1, Ein Yaakov Sanhedrin:111a, Ein Yaakov Sotah:48b, Exodus.R 19:4, Ezekiel 32:18-32:30, Habakkuk 2:5, Isaiah 14:9 21:4 6:33, Luke 12:19-12:20 16:20-16:23 17:27 21:34, Matthew 7:13, Midrash Psalms 6:1 104:23 17A:9, Midrash Tanchuma Lech Lecha 20, Midrash Tanchuma Tazria 5, Nahum 1:10, Numbers 16:30-16:34, Proverbs 1:12 3:20 6:16, Psalms 49:15 55:16, Psalms of Solomon 4:13, Revelation 20:13-15, y.Kiddushin 1:9

[7] Isaiah 5:15 - 1 Peter 5:5, b.Sotah 48a, Daniel 4:34, Ein Yaakov Sotah:47b, Exodus 9:17, Isaiah 2:9 2:11 2:17 9:15-18 10:12 10:33 13:11 24:2-4 13:23 13:29, James 1:9-11, Jastrow 1618a, Jeremiah 5:4-5 5:9, Job 40:11-12, Psalms 62:10, Revelation 6:15-16
Isaiah 5:15-28 - 4QIsab

[8] 1QIsaa *And people are*

[9] LXX *the great man shall be disgraced*

[10] Isaiah 5:16 - 1 Chronicles 5:11, 1 Peter 1:16 2:15, 3 Enoch 24:21, b.Berachot 12b, Deuteronomy.R 5:7, Ezekiel 4:22 12:23 14:23, Isaiah 2:11 2:17 6:3 8:13 12:4 4:17 5:23 6:18 9:5 9:15 13:8, Leviticus 10:3, Leviticus.R 24:1, Midrash Proverbs 14, Midrash Psalms 3:1 8:8 101:1, Midrash Tanchuma Kedoshim 1, Midrash Tanchuma Shoftim 15, Pirkei de R'Eliezer 35, Psalms 9:17 21:14 46:11, Revelation 3:7 4:8 15:3-15:4 19:1-19:5, Romans 2:5, Tefillat Rosh Hashanah-Tefillat Yom Kippur

[11] LXX *glorified*

[12] Isaiah 5:17 - Amos 4:1-4:3, b.Pesachim 68a, Deuteronomy 4:33 8:15, Ein Yaakov Pesachim:68a, Hosea 8:7, Isaiah 1:7 7:21-7:22 7:25 10:16 17:2 8:14 16:11 17:10, Jeremiah 5:28, Lamentations 5:2, Lamentations.R 1:33, Luke 21:24, Micah 2:12, Nehemiah 9:37, Pesikta de R'Kahana 17.6, Psalms 17:10 17:14 73:7 119:70, Saadia Opinions 8:6, Zephaniah 2:6 2:14

[13] LXX *And they who were spoiled shall be fed as bulls, and lambs shall feed on the waste places of those who are taken away*

[14] Isaiah 5:18 - 2 Samuel 16:20-16:23, Acts 2:9, b.Berachot 24b, b.Sanhedrin 99b, b.Sheviit [Rashi] 3b 20b, b.Succah 52a, Chibbur Yafeh 27 {120b} 30 {136a}, Ein Yaakov Berachot:24b, Ein Yaakov Sanhedrin:99b, Ein Yaakov Sukkah:52a, Ezekiel 13:10-13:11 13:22, Genesis.R 22:6, Isaiah 4:15 59:4-8, Jastrow 1037a 1380b, Jeremiah 5:31 8:5-9 23:10 23:14 23:24 28:15-16 44:15-19, John 16:2, Judges 17:5 17:13, Psalms 10:12 14:1 36:3 94:5-11, z.Bereshit 57a 5a, z.Mikketz 199a, Zephaniah 1:12

[15] LXX *thong of the heifer's yoke*

[16] Isaiah 5:19 - 2 Peter 3:3-3:4, Amos 5:18-5:19, Ezekiel 12:22 12:27, Isaiah 6:11 18:5, Jastrow 1080a 1331a, Jeremiah 5:12-5:13 17:15 23:18 23:36, Lamentations.R 4:18, Leviticus.R 16:1, Mesillat Yesharim 7:Elements of Zerizus, Pesikta de R'Kahana 17.6, Pesikta Rabbati 31:7, Sifre Devarim {Ha'azinu Hashamayim} 325, Sifre Devarim Nitzavim 325

20[1]	Woe to those who call evil good, And good evil; Who change darkness into light, And light into darkness; Who change bitter into sweet, And sweet into bitter.

הוֹי הָאֹמְרִים לָרַע טוֹב וְלַטּוֹב רָע שָׂמִים חֹשֶׁךְ לְאוֹר וְאוֹר לְחֹשֶׁךְ שָׂמִים מַר לְמָתוֹק וּמָתוֹק לְמָר

21[2]	Woe to those who are wise in their own eyes, And prudent in their own sight!

הוֹי חֲכָמִים בְּעֵינֵיהֶם וְנֶגֶד פְּנֵיהֶם נְבֹנִים

22[3]	Woe to those who are mighty to drink wine, And men of strength to mingle strong drink;

הוֹי גִּבּוֹרִים לִשְׁתּוֹת יָיִן וְאַנְשֵׁי־חַיִל לִמְסֹךְ שֵׁכָר

23[4]	who justify the wicked for a reward, And take away the righteousness of the righteous from him!

מַצְדִּיקֵי רָשָׁע עֵקֶב שֹׁחַד וְצִדְקַת צַדִּיקִים יָסִירוּ מִמֶּנּוּ

24[5]	Therefore, as the *tongue*[6] of fire devours the stubble, And as *the chaff is consumed in the flame*[7], So their root shall be as rottenness, And their blossom shall go up as dust; Because they rejected the law of the LORD of hosts, And disdained the word of the Holy One of Israel.

לָכֵן כֶּאֱכֹל קַשׁ לְשׁוֹן אֵשׁ וַחֲשַׁשׁ לֶהָבָה יִרְפֶּה שָׁרְשָׁם כַּמָּק יִהְיֶה וּפִרְחָם כָּאָבָק יַעֲלֶה כִּי מָאֲסוּ אֵת תּוֹרַת יְהוָה צְבָאוֹת וְאֵת אִמְרַת קְדוֹשׁ־יִשְׂרָאֵל נִאֵצוּ

25[8]	*Therefore*[9], the anger of the *LORD*[10] is kindled against His people, And He has stretched forth His *hand*[11] against them, and has struck them, And the hills trembled, And their carcasses were as refuse in the midst of the streets. For all this His anger is not turned away, But His *hand is*[12] stretched out still.

עַל־כֵּן חָרָה אַף־יְהוָה בְּעַמּוֹ וַיֵּט יָדוֹ עָלָיו וַיַּכֵּהוּ וַיִּרְגְּזוּ הֶהָרִים וַתְּהִי נִבְלָתָם כַּסּוּחָה בְּקֶרֶב חוּצוֹת בְּכָל־זֹאת לֹא־שָׁב אַפּוֹ וְעוֹד יָדוֹ נְטוּיָה

26[13]	And He will lift up a signal to the nations from far, And will hiss to them from the end of the earth; And, behold, they shall come swiftly with speed;

וְנָשָׂא־נֵס לַגּוֹיִם מֵרָחוֹק וְשָׁרַק לוֹ מִקְצֵה הָאָרֶץ וְהִנֵּה מְהֵרָה קַל יָבוֹא

27[14]	No one *among them shall be weary or stumble*[15] among them; No one shall slumber or sleep; [16]nor shall the girdle of their loins *be loosened*[17], Nor shall the latchet of their shoes break;

אֵין־עָיֵף וְאֵין־כּוֹשֵׁל בּוֹ לֹא יָנוּם וְלֹא יִישָׁן וְלֹא נִפְתַּח אֵזוֹר חֲלָצָיו וְלֹא נִתַּק שְׂרוֹךְ נְעָלָיו

---

[1] Isaiah 5:20 - 2 Peter 2:1 2:18-2:19, 2 Timothy 3:1-3:5, 3 Baruch 4:15 [Gk], 4Q471 2 8, 4Q471a frag 1 1.8, Amos 5:7, b.Sotah 41b 47b, Ein Yaakov Sotah:41b 47b, Job 17:12, Luke 11:34-11:35 16:15, Malachi 2:17 3:15, Matthew 6:22-6:23 15:3-15:6 23:16-23:23, mt.Hilchot Deot 2:1 2:1, mt.Pirkei Avot 4:22, Proverbs 17:15, t.Sotah 14:8

[2] Isaiah 5:21 - 1 Corinthians 3:18-20, Job 11:12, John 9:41, Proverbs 3:7 2:12 2:16, Romans 1:22 11:25 12:16

[3] Isaiah 5:22 - Habakkuk 2:15, Isaiah 5:11 28:1-28:3 4:7 8:12, Leviticus.R 5:5, Numbers.R 10:8, Proverbs 23:19-23:20

[4] Isaiah 5:23 - 1 Kings 21:13, 2 Chronicles 19:7, Deuteronomy 16:19, Exodus 23:6-23:9, Genesis.R 65:5, Isaiah 1:23 10:2, James 5:6, Matthew 23:35 27:24-25, Micah 3:11 7:3, Proverbs 17:15 17:23 24:24 31:4-5, Psalms 94:21, Testament of Moses 5:5

[5] Isaiah 5:24 - 1 Corinthians 3:12-3:13, 1 Samuel 15:23 15:26, 1 Thessalonians 4:8, 2 Kings 17:14-17:15, 2 Samuel 12:9-12:10, Acts 13:41, Amos 2:9, Apocalypse of Elijah 1:4, b.Sotah 41b, Ein Yaakov Sotah:41b, Exodus 15:7, Hebrews 10:28-10:29, Hosea 5:12 9:16, Isaiah 8:6 9:15-9:18 6:9 6:12 23:14, Jeremiah 6:19 8:9, Job 18:16, Joel 2:5, John 12:48, Lamentations.R Petichata D'Chakimei:2, Luke 3:17 7:30 10:16, Malachi 3:19, Matthew 3:12, Midrash Tanchuma Metzora 4, Nahum 1:10, Nehemiah 9:26, Numbers.R 7:5, Pesikta de R'Kahana 15.5, Psalms 50:17, Sifre Devarim Ekev 41
Isaiah 5:24-25 - 4Q162 2:7-10, 4Q162 2.7-10

[6] LXX *coal*

[7] 1QIsaa *fire sinks down in the flames*

[8] Isaiah 5:25 - 1 Kings 14:11 16:4 21:24, 1 Thessalonians 2:16, 2 Chronicles 12:16, 2 Kings 9:37 13:3 22:13-22:17, 4QIsaf, Daniel 9:16, Deuteronomy 7:17 32:19-32:22, Habakkuk 3:10, Hosea 14:6, Isaiah 9:13-9:14 9:18 9:22 10:4 14:26-14:27, Jeremiah 4:8 4:24 8:2 9:23 15:3 16:4, Lamentations 2:1-2:3 5:22, Leviticus 26:14-26:46, Micah 1:4, Nahum 1:5, Pesikta Rabbati 33:13, Psalms 18:8 68:9 77:19 78:38 83:11 10:40 18:7, Revelation 20:11, Zephaniah 1:17

[9] 1QIsab *Upon*

[10] 1QIsab adds *of Hosts*

[11] 1QIsaa *hands*

[12] 1QIsaa *hands are*

[13] Isaiah 5:26 - Deuteronomy 4:49, Habakkuk 1:8, Isaiah 7:18 11:12 13:2 13:5 18:3 6:16 15:3, Jeremiah 4:13 5:15 3:27, Joel 2:7, Lamentations 4:19, Malachi 1:11, Psalms 72:8, Zechariah 10:8

[14] Isaiah 5:27 - 1 Kings 2:5, Daniel 5:6, Deuteronomy 8:25, Ephesians 6:13-14, Isaiah 11:5 21:1 5, Job 12:18 12:21, Joel 2:7-2, Psalms 18:33 93:1

[15] 1QIsaa *No one is weary or stumbles*

[16] 1QIsaa adds *and*

[17] 1QIsaa *come undone*

Hebrew		English
אֲשֶׁר חִצָּיו שְׁנוּנִים וְכָל־קַשְּׁתֹתָיו דְּרֻכוֹת פַּרְסוֹת סוּסָיו כַּצַּר נֶחְשָׁבוּ וְגַלְגִּלָּיו כַּסּוּפָה	28[1]	Whose arrows are sharp, And all their bows bent; Their horses' hoofs shall be counted like *flint*[2], And their *wheels like a whirlwind*[3];
שְׁאָגָה לוֹ כַּלָּבִיא ׳וְשָׁאַג׳ ״יִשְׁאַג״ כַּכְּפִירִים וְיִנְהֹם וְיֹאחֵז טֶרֶף וְיַפְלִיט וְאֵין מַצִּיל	29[4]	*Their roaring shall be like a lion, They shall roar like young lions, yes, they shall roar*[5], And take hold of the prey, and safely carry it away, And there shall be no one to deliver.
וְיִנְהֹם עָלָיו בַּיּוֹם הַהוּא כְּנַהֲמַת־יָם וְנִבַּט לָאָרֶץ וְהִנֵּה־חֹשֶׁךְ צַר וָאוֹר חָשַׁךְ בַּעֲרִיפֶיהָ	30[6]	*And*[7] they shall roar against them in that day Like the roaring of the sea; And if one looks to the land, Behold darkness and distress, And the light is darkened in the skies.

Isaiah – Chapter 6

Hebrew		English
בִּשְׁנַת־מוֹת הַמֶּלֶךְ עֻזִּיָּהוּ וָאֶרְאֶה אֶת־אֲדֹנָי יֹשֵׁב עַל־כִּסֵּא רָם וְנִשָּׂא וְשׁוּלָיו מְלֵאִים אֶת־הַהֵיכָל	1[8]	In the year king *Uzziah*[9] died I saw the Lord sitting upon *a*[10] throne high and lifted up, and *His train filled the temple*[11].
שְׂרָפִים עֹמְדִים מִמַּעַל לוֹ שֵׁשׁ כְּנָפַיִם שֵׁשׁ כְּנָפַיִם לְאֶחָד בִּשְׁתַּיִם יְכַסֶּה פָנָיו וּבִשְׁתַּיִם יְכַסֶּה רַגְלָיו וּבִשְׁתַּיִם יְעוֹפֵף	2[12]	*Above Him stood the seraphim*[13]; each one had six wings: with two *he covered his*[14] face and with two *he covered his*[15] feet, and with two *he*[16] flew.

[1] Isaiah 5:28 - Ezekiel 21:14-16, Isaiah 21:1, Jeremiah 5:16 23:3, Judges 5:22, Micah 4:13, Nahum 2:4-5 3:2, Psalms 7:13-14 45:6 24:4
Isaiah 5:28-30 - pap4QIsaP
[2] LXX *solid rock*
[3] LXX *chariot-wheels are as a storm*
[4] Isaiah 5:29 - Amos 3:8, Genesis 1:9, Hosea 11:10, Isaiah 10:6 7:4 18:22 49:24-49:25, Jeremiah 4:7 1:19 2:17 3:38, Micah 5:9, Numbers 24:9, Psalms 50:22, Zechariah 11:3, Zephaniah 3:3
Isaiah 5:29-30 - 4Q162 3.1-3
[5] 1QIsaa *With a roar like a lion they roar; and like young lions, they growl*; LXX *They rage as lions, and draw near as a lion's whelps*
[6] Isaiah 5:30 - Amos 8:9, Exodus 10:21-10:23, Ezekiel 32:7-32:8, Guide for the Perplexed 1:4, Isaiah 8:22 13:10, Jastrow 882a, Jeremiah 4:23-4:28 6:23 2:42, Joel 2:10, Lamentations 3:2, Luke 21:25-21:26, Matthew 24:29, Midrash Psalms 106:4, Psalms 93:3-93:4, Revelation 6:12 16:10-16:11
[7] Missing in 1QIsaa
[8] Isaiah 6:1 - 1 Enoch 14:18 2 Enoch 20:1 20:3 3 Enoch 24:23, 1 Kings 8:10-8:11 22:19, 1 Timothy 6:16, 2 Chronicles 26:22-26:23, 2 Kings 15:7, b.Chagigah [Rashi] 13b, b.Yevamot 49b, Daniel 7:9, Ecclesiastes.R 1:31, Ein Yaakov Yevamot:49b, Ephesians 1:20-1:21, Exodus 24:10-24:11, Exodus.R 1:34, Ezekiel 1:1 1:25-1:28 10:1, Guide for the Perplexed 3:6, Isaiah 11:12:4 9:15 18:1, John 1:18 12:41, Kuzari 4.003, Martyrdom and Ascension of Isaiah 3:10, Matthew 1:31, Mekhilta de R'Shimon bar Yochai Shirata 33:1, Mekilta de R'Ishmael Shirata 7:5, Midrash Tanchuma Kedoshim 1, Midrash Tanchuma Naso 11, Midrash Tanchuma Tzav 13, Numbers 12:8, Per Massorah: Soferim altered "Hashem" to "Adonai", Pesikta Rabbati 21:6, Psalms 46:11 12:6 17:5, Psalms of Solomon 2:5, Revelation 3:21 4:2 4:10 5:1 5:7 6:16 7:15-7:17 15:8, Seder Olam 20:Flee, Song of Songs.R 1:46, Testament of Levi 2:5 3:4, z.Bereshit 18a, z.Yitro 82a
Isaiah 6:1-2 - 2 Baruch 21:7, Exodus.R 33:4 35:6 43:4, Sefer Yetzirah 1:12
Isaiah 6:1-3 - Derech Hashem Part IV 6§14, Questions of Ezra 29
Isaiah 6:1-5 - Testament of Levi 5:1
Isaiah 6:1-8 - Apocalypse of Zephaniah A
Isaiah 6:1-13 - 1QIsaa, Haftarah Yitro [continues with Isaiah 9:5 [Teimon]], Haftarah Yitro [Sephard]
Isaiah 6:1-7:6 - Haftarah Yitro [continues with Isaiah 9:5 [Ashkenaz]], Haftarah Yitro Part One [Isaiah 6:1-7:6]
[9] MT *Uzziyahu*; 1QIsaa *Uzziyah*
[10] 1QIsaa *His*
[11] LXX *the house was full of his glory*
[12] Isaiah 6:2 - 8 16, 1 Kings 6:24 6:27 8:7 19:13 22:19, 3 Enoch 22:13 26:8, Apocalypse of Elijah 5:2, b.Chagigah 13b, b.Chullin [Tosefot] 92a, b.Sanhedrin [Tosefot] 37b, b.Shabbat [Rashi] 30a, b.Sotah [Rashi] 40b, Bahir 21, Daniel 7:10 9:21, Deuteronomy.R 6:10, Exodus 3:6 1:20 13:9, Ezekiel 1:4 1:6 1:9 1:11 1:24 10:16 10:21, Genesis 17:3, Genesis.R 1:3 3:8 56:5 65:21, Guide for the Perplexed 1:43, Hebrews 1:7, Hellenistic Synagogal Prayers 12:82, Isaiah 6:6, Job 1:6 4:18 15:15, Kuzari 4.003, Ladder of Jacob 2:15, Leviticus.R 27:3, Luke 1:10, Midrash Psalms 1:2 24:4, Midrash Tanchuma Bereshit 5, Midrash Tanchuma Emor 16, Midrash Tanchuma Kedoshim 6, Midrash Tanchuma Tzav 13, mt.Hilchot Yesodei haTorah 2:7, Numbers.R 12:8, Pesikta de R'Kahana 1.3 9.3 16.1, Pesikta Rabbati 29/30A:1 33:11, Psalms 18:11 89:8 7:20 8:4, Revelation 4:8 7:11 8:13 14:6, Ruth.R 5:4 Petichata:1, Saadia Opinions 9:8, Sefer Yetzirah 1:7, Sifre Devarim {Ha'azinu Hashamayim} 306, Sifre Devarim Nitzavim 306, Tanya Likutei Aramim §40, Testament of Adam 1:4 18:34, y.Berachot 7:4, y.Rosh Hashanah 1:2, z.Pekudei 233b, z.Terumah 147b 139a, Zechariah 3:4
Isaiah 6:2-3 - 2 Enoch 21:1, Exodus.R 15:6 23:7 25:2, Tanna Devei Eliyahu 2
[13] LXX *And seraphs stood round about him*
[14] LXX *they covered their*
[15] LXX *they covered their*
[16] LXX *they*

וַיִּקְרָא זֶה אֶל־זֶה וְאָמַר קָדוֹשׁ קָדוֹשׁ קָדוֹשׁ יְהוָה
צְבָאוֹת מְלֹא כָל־הָאָרֶץ כְּבוֹדוֹ

3[1]

And one called to another and said[2]: **Holy, holy, *holy*[3], is the LORD of hosts; The whole earth is full of His glory**.

וַיָּנֻעוּ אַמּוֹת הַסִּפִּים מִקּוֹל הַקּוֹרֵא וְהַבַּיִת יִמָּלֵא
עָשָׁן

4[4]

And the posts of the door moved at the voice of those who called, and the house was *filled with*[5] smoke.

וָאֹמַר אוֹי־לִי כִי־נִדְמֵיתִי כִּי אִישׁ טְמֵא־שְׂפָתַיִם
אָנֹכִי וּבְתוֹךְ עַם־טְמֵא שְׂפָתַיִם אָנֹכִי יוֹשֵׁב כִּי אֶת־
הַמֶּלֶךְ יְהוָה צְבָאוֹת רָאוּ עֵינָי

5[6]

Then I said: Woe is me! For I am *undone*[7]; Because I am a man of *unclean*[8] lips, And I live in the midst of a people of unclean lips; For My eyes have seen the King, the LORD of hosts.

וַיָּעָף אֵלַי אֶחָד מִן־הַשְּׂרָפִים וּבְיָדוֹ רִצְפָּה
בְּמֶלְקָחַיִם לָקַח מֵעַל הַמִּזְבֵּחַ

6[9]

Then one of the seraphim flew to me, with a glowing stone in his hand, which he took with the tongs from the altar;

וַיַּגַּע עַל־פִּי וַיֹּאמֶר הִנֵּה נָגַע זֶה עַל־שְׂפָתֶיךָ וְסָר
עֲוֺנֶךָ וְחַטָּאתְךָ תְּכֻפָּר

7[10]

And he touched my mouth with it, and said: Lo, this has touched *your*[11] lips; And your iniquity is taken away, your *sin*[12] is forgiven.

וָאֶשְׁמַע אֶת־קוֹל אֲדֹנָי אֹמֵר אֶת־מִי אֶשְׁלַח וּמִי
יֵלֶךְ־לָנוּ וָאֹמַר הִנְנִי שְׁלָחֵנִי

8[13]

And I heard the voice of the Lord, saying: Whom shall I send, And who will go for us? Then I said: 'Here am I; send me.'

---

[1] Isaiah 6:3 - 3 Enoch 1:3 19:7 20:2 22B:7 35:6 38:1 40:2 48B:2 4 Baruch 9:3, Avot de R'Natan 12, b.Berachot 43b, b.Chullin [Rashi] 92a, b.Chullin 91b, b.Kiddushin 31a, Bahir 128 171, Blessings for Kriat Shema [Shacharit], Deuteronomy.R 2:33, Ein Yaakov Berachot 43b, Ein Yaakov Chullin 91b, Ein Yaakov Kiddushin 31a, Ephesians 1:18, Exodus 15:11 15:20-21, Exodus.R 30:9, Ezra 3:11, Genesis.R 52:5 74:7, Guide for the Perplexed 1:64 3:52, Habakkuk 2:14, Hammeir Lah'aretz, Hellenistic Synagogal Prayers 12:84 4:10, Isaiah 11:9-10 24:16 16:5, Jastrow 682b 1314a, Kedusha [all Services] U'vah Letzion [Shacharit, Kuzari 4.003, Leviticus.R 1:13 2:8 24:9, Maariv Motzoei Shabbat], Mekhilta de R'Shimon bar Yochai Shirata 30:1, Mekilta de R'Ishmael Beshallah 1:211, Mekilta de R'Ishmael Shirata 4:69, Mesillat Yesharim 25:To Acquire Yirah Cheit, Midrash Tanchuma Beshallach 5, Midrash Tanchuma Kedoshim 5, Midrash Tanchuma Naso 4, Midrash Tanchuma Tzav 13, Midrash Tanchuma Vayikra 8, mt.Hilchot Deot 5:6 5:8, mt.Hilchot Tefilah 7:17 8:4 9:5, Numbers 14:21, Pesikta Rabbati 20:4, Pirkei de R'Eliezer 4, Pirkei de R'Eliezer 10, Psalms 19:2-4 24:7-10 57:12 72:19, Revelation 4:8-9 15:3-4, Sefer Yetzirah 6:4 Sefer Yetzirah [Long] 6:1, Shabbat, Sifre Devarim {Ha'azinu Hashamayim} 306, Siman 1:1 15:9, t.Berachot 1:9, Tanna Devei Eliyahu 6, Tanya Igeret Hakodesh §15, Tanya Igeret Hateshuvah §4-5, Tanya Kuntress Acharon §4, Tanya Likutei Aramim §41 §48-49, Testament of Abraham 20:12, Yom Tov Minchah, z.Bo 42b, z.Noach 71b, z.Terumah 171a, Zechariah 14:9
Isaiah 6:3 [LXX] - Hellenistic Synagogal Prayers 4:10
Isaiah 6:3-8 - 4QIsaf
[2] 1QIsaa *They called to each other*
[3] Missing in 1QIsaa
[4] Isaiah 6:4 - 1 Kings 8:10-8:12, 2 Chronicles 5:13-6:1, Amos 9:1, b.Pesachim [Rashi] 87a, b.Yoma 53a, Exodus 16:34, Exodus.R 9:13, Ezekiel 1:24 10:5, Guide for the Perplexed 1:19, Mekilta de R'Ishmael Pisha 6:4, Mekilta de R'Ishmael Pisha 11:37, Midrash Psalms 18:11, Midrash Tanchuma Chayyei Sarah 3, Midrash Tanchuma Tzav 13, Midrash Tanchuma Vaera 13, Psalms 18:9, Revelation 11:19 15:8, Testament of Levi 3:10, z.Yitro 81b
Isaiah 6:4-8 - 4QIsaa
[5] 1QIsaa *full of*
[6] Isaiah 6:5 - b.Yevamot 49b, Daniel 10:6-10:8, Ein Yaakov Yevamot:49b, Exodus 4:10 6:12 6:30 9:20, Ezekiel 2:6-2:8 9:31, Habakkuk 3:16, Isaiah 5:13 9:17, James 3:1-3:2 3:6-3:10, Jastrow 314a, Jeremiah 1:6 9:4-9:9 3:57, Job 42:5-42:6, Judges 6:22 13:22, Life of Adam and Eve [Vita] 6:2, Luke 5:8-5:9, Matthew 12:34-12:37, Midrash Tanchuma Vayishlach 2, Pesikta Rabbati 11:2 33:3, Revelation 1:5-1:7 1:16-1:17, Zechariah 3:1-3:7
[7] LXX *pricked to the heart*
[8] Misspelled in 1QIsaa
[9] Isaiah 6:6 - 3 Enoch 36:2, Acts 2:3, b.Nedarim [Ran] 57b, Daniel 9:21-9:23, Deuteronomy.R 8:2, Ein Yaakov Berachot:4b, Exodus.R 33:4, Ezekiel 10:2, Hebrews 1:7 1:14 9:22-9:26 13:10, Isaiah 6:2, Jastrow 328a 793b 1495a, Leviticus 16:12, Leviticus.R 6:3, Matthew 3:11, Midrash Tanchuma Vayakhel 7, Midrash Tanchuma Vayishlach 2, Pesikta Rabbati 11:2 33:3, Revelation 8:3-8:5, y.Rosh Hashanah 1:2, z.Bereshit 46b
[10] Isaiah 6:7 - 1 John 1:7 2:1-2:2, b.Berachot 57a, b.Shabbat 119b, Daniel 10:16, Ein Yaakov Shabbat:119b, Guide for the Perplexed 1:18, Hebrews 9:13-9:14, Isaiah 19:25 5:5 5:10, Jeremiah 1:9, Mas.Kallah Rabbati 6:1, Matthew 9:2, Mesillat Yesharim 4:To Acquire Zehirus, Midrash Tanchuma Vayishlach 2, Pesikta Rabbati 33:3, z.Acharei Mot 57b 75b
[11] 1QIsaf *the*
[12] Misspelled in 1QIsaa
[13] Isaiah 6:8 - 1 Kings 22:20, Acts 9:4 20:24 22:21 26:16-26:17 28:25-28:28, Avot de R'Natan 34, Deuteronomy 4:33-4:36, Ephesians 3:8, Exodus 4:10-4:13, Ezekiel 1:24 10:5, Genesis 1:26 3:8-3:10 3:22 11:7, Guide for the Perplexed 2:44 2:45, Isaiah 17:1, Leviticus.R 10:2, Matthew 4:20-4:22, Per Massorah: Soferim altered "Hashem" to "Adonai", Pesikta de R'Kahana 164, Pesikta Rabbati 29/30A:5 33:3

וַיֹּ֙אמֶר֙ לֵ֔ךְ וְאָמַרְתָּ֖ לָעָ֣ם הַזֶּ֑ה שִׁמְע֤וּ שָׁמ֙וֹעַ֙ וְאַל־תָּבִ֔ינוּ וּרְא֥וּ רָא֖וֹ וְאַל־תֵּדָֽעוּ׃ 9[1]

And He said: 'Go, and tell this people: Hear indeed, but understand *not*[2]; And[3] see indeed, but perceive not.

הַשְׁמֵן֙ לֵב־הָעָ֣ם הַזֶּ֔ה וְאָזְנָ֥יו הַכְבֵּ֖ד וְעֵינָ֣יו הָשַׁ֑ע פֶּן־יִרְאֶ֨ה בְעֵינָ֜יו וּבְאָזְנָ֣יו יִשְׁמָ֗ע וּלְבָב֛וֹ יָבִ֥ין וָשָׁ֖ב וְרָ֥פָא לֽוֹ׃ 10[4]

Make the heart of this people fat, And make their ears heavy, And shut their eyes; Lest they, seeing with their eyes, And hearing with their ears, And understanding with their heart, Return, and be healed.'

וָאֹמַ֕ר עַד־מָתַ֖י אֲדֹנָ֑י וַיֹּ֡אמֶר עַ֣ד אֲשֶׁר֩ אִם־שָׁא֨וּ עָרִ֜ים מֵאֵ֣ין יוֹשֵׁ֗ב וּבָתִּים֙ מֵאֵ֣ין אָדָ֔ם וְהָאֲדָמָ֖ה תִּשָּׁאֶ֥ה שְׁמָמָֽה׃ 11[5]

Then said I: '*Lord*[6], how long?' And He answered: 'Until cities are waste without inhabitant, And houses without man, And the land becomes utterly waste,

וְרִחַ֥ק יְהוָ֖ה אֶת־הָאָדָ֑ם וְרַבָּ֥ה הָעֲזוּבָ֖ה בְּקֶ֥רֶב הָאָֽרֶץ׃ 12[7]

And the LORD has removed men far away, And *the*[8] forsaken places are many in the midst of the land[9].

וְע֥וֹד בָּהּ֙ עֲשִׂ֣רִיָּ֔ה וְשָׁ֖בָה וְהָיְתָ֣ה לְבָעֵ֑ר כָּאֵלָ֣ה וְכָאַלּ֗וֹן אֲשֶׁ֤ר בְּשַׁלֶּ֙כֶת֙ מַצֶּ֣בֶת בָּ֔ם זֶ֥רַע קֹ֖דֶשׁ מַצַּבְתָּֽהּ׃ 13[10]

And if there is yet a tenth in it, it shall again be eaten up; as a terebinth, and as an oak, *whose stock remains, when they cast their leaves*[11], so the holy seed shall be its stock.[12]'

Isaiah – Chapter 7

וַיְהִ֡י בִּימֵ֣י אָ֠חָז בֶּן־יוֹתָ֨ם בֶּן־עֻזִיָּ֜הוּ מֶ֣לֶךְ יְהוּדָ֗ה עָלָ֣ה רְצִ֣ין מֶֽלֶךְ־אֲ֠רָם וּפֶ֨קַח בֶּן־רְמַלְיָ֤הוּ מֶֽלֶךְ־יִשְׂרָאֵל֙ יְר֣וּשָׁלִַ֔ם לַמִּלְחָמָ֖ה עָלֶ֑יהָ וְלֹ֥א יָכֹ֖ל לְהִלָּחֵ֥ם עָלֶֽיהָ׃ 1[13]

And it came to pass in the days of Ahaz the son of Jotham, the son of Uzziah, king of Judah, that Rezin the king of Aram, and Pekah the son of Remaliah, king of Israel, went up to Jerusalem to war against it; but *could not prevail against it*[14].

וַיֻּגַּ֗ד לְבֵ֤ית דָּוִד֙ לֵאמֹ֔ר נָ֥חָה אֲרָ֖ם עַל־אֶפְרָ֑יִם וַיָּ֤נַע לְבָבוֹ֙ וּלְבַ֣ב עַמּ֔וֹ כְּנ֥וֹעַ עֲצֵי־יַ֖עַר מִפְּנֵי־רֽוּחַ׃ 2[15]

And it was told to the house of David, saying: 'Aram is confederate with Ephraim.' And *his*

---

[1] Isaiah 6:9 - 4Q162 3.7-8, Acts 28:26-28:27, Avot de R'Natan 34, Exodus 32:7-32:10, Hosea 1:9, Isaiah 5:13 30:8-30:11 19:8 44:18-44:20, Jeremiah 15:1-2, John 12:40, Luke 8:10, Mark 4:12, Matthew 13:14-15, Romans 11:8, Sibylline Oracles 1.360

[2] Misspelled in 1QIsaa

[3] Missing in 1QIsaa

[4] Isaiah 6:10 - 2 Corinthians 2:16, Acts 3:19 4:27, b.Berachot [Rashi] 61a, b.Megillah 14b, b.Rosh Hashanah 14b, b.Shabbat [Rashi] 152a, b.Shabbat 33b, Deuteronomy 2:30 8:15, Ein Yaakov Megillah:17b, Ein Yaakov Rosh Hashanah:17b, Exodus 7:3 10:27 11:10 14:17, Ezekiel 3:6-3:11, Gates of Repentance 1.023 4.001, Isaiah 19:22 5:10 15:17, Jastrow 1489a, Jeremiah 5:21 John 3:19-3:20, Matthew 13:15, Mekilta de R'Ishmael Bahodesh 1:78, Mesillat Yesharim 3:Elements of Zehirus, mt.Hilchot Teshuvah 6:3 6:3, mt.Shemonah Perakim 8:6, Psalms 17:10 119:70, Saadia Opinions 4:6, Shemonah Perachim VIII, Tanya Igeret Hakodesh §10 §24, y.Berachot 2:4, Zechariah 7:11
Isaiah 6:10-13 - 4QIsaf

[5] Isaiah 6:11 - Isaiah 1:7 3:26 24:1-24:12, Leviticus 2:31, Per Massorah: Soferim altered "Hashem" to "Adonai", Psalms 74:10 79:5 90:13 94:3, Psalms of Solomon 2:14, Tanya Igeret Hakodesh §19

[6] 1QIsaa *LORD*

[7] Isaiah 6:12 - 2 Kings 1:11 1:21, Deuteronomy 28:64, Ecclesiastes.R 3:10, Guide for the Perplexed 2:29, Isaiah 2:15, Jeremiah 4:29 12:7 15:4 52:28-52:30, Lamentations 5:20, Romans 11:1-11:2 11:15

[8] Missing in 1QIsaa

[9] LXX *ones who are left upon the land shall be multiplied*

[10] Isaiah 6:13 - b.Ketubot 112b, b.Menachot [Rashi] 63a, Ein Yaakov Ketubot:112b, Ezra 9:2, Galatians 3:16-3:19 3:28-3:29, Genesis 22:18, Isaiah 1:9 4:3 10:20-10:22 65:8-65:9, Jastrow 1281a, Job 14:7-14:9, John 15:1-15:3, Malachi 2:15, Mark 13:20, Matthew 24:22, Pesikta Rabbati 33:13 40:5, Romans 9:5 11:5-11:6 11:16-11:29, z.Bereshit 15a

[11] 1QIsaa *the stump of which felled, remained*

[12] LXX *And yet there shall be a tenth upon it, and again it shall be for a spoil, as a turpentine tree, and as an acorn when it falls out of its husk.*

[13] Isaiah 7:1 - 2 Chronicles 28:1-28:6, 2 Kings 15:25 15:37 16:1, b.Megillah 10b, Ein Yaakov Megillah:9b, Esther.R Petichata:11, Genesis.R 42:3 63:1, Isaiah 1:1 7:4-7:9 8:6 8:9-8:10, Leviticus.R 11:7, Psalms 83:4-83:6, Ruth.R Petichata:7
Isaiah 7:1-6 - Seder Olam 22:Shallum
Isaiah 7:1-25 - 1QIsaa

[14] 1QIsaa *they were unsuccessful*

[15] Isaiah 7:2 - 1 Kings 11:32 12:16 13:2, 2 Chronicles 1:10 4:12, 2 Kings 7:6-7, 2 Samuel 7:16, b.Sanhedrin 95b 96a, Deuteronomy 28:65-66, Ezekiel 37:16-19, Genesis.R 16:3, Hosea 12:3, Isaiah 6:13 7:13 7:17 8:12 9:10 11:13 22:22 13:27 13:35, Jeremiah 21:12 27:1-2 112:7-8
Leviticus 26:36-37, Matthew 2:3, Mekhilta de R'Shimon bar Yochai Bachodesh 56:1, Numbers 14:1-3, Proverbs 4:1, Psalms 11:2 27:1-2 112:7-8

heart was moved, and the heart of his people[1], as the trees of the forest are moved with the wind.

וַיֹּ֤אמֶר יְהוָה֙ אֶל־יְשַׁעְיָ֔הוּ צֵא־נָא֙ לִקְרַ֣את אָחָ֔ז אַתָּ֕ה וּשְׁאָ֖ר יָשׁ֣וּב בְּנֶ֑ךָ אֶל־קְצֵ֗ה תְּעָלַת֙ הַבְּרֵכָ֣ה הָעֶלְיוֹנָ֔ה אֶל־מְסִלַּ֖ת שְׂדֵ֥ה כוֹבֵֽס

3 [2]

Then said the LORD to Isaiah: 'Go forth now to meet Ahaz, you, and Shear-jashub your son, at the end of the conduit of the upper pool, in the highway of the fullers' field;

וְאָמַרְתָּ֣ אֵלָ֗יו הִשָּׁמֵ֤ר וְהַשְׁקֵט֙ אַל־תִּירָ֔א וּלְבָבְךָ֖ אַל־יֵרַ֑ךְ מִשְּׁנֵ֨י זַנְב֜וֹת הָאוּדִ֤ים הָעֲשֵׁנִים֙ הָאֵ֔לֶּה בָּחֳרִי־אַ֛ף רְצִ֥ין וַאֲרָ֖ם וּבֶן־רְמַלְיָֽהוּ

4 [3]

And say to him: Keep calm, and be quiet; do not fear, nor let your heart be faint, because of these two tails of smoking firebrands, *for the fierce anger of Rezin and Aram, and of the son of Remaliah*[4].

יַ֗עַן כִּֽי־יָעַ֥ץ עָלֶ֛יךָ אֲרָ֖ם רָעָ֑ה אֶפְרַ֥יִם וּבֶן־רְמַלְיָ֖הוּ לֵאמֹֽר

5 [5]

Because Aram has counseled evil against you, Ephraim also, and the son of Remaliah, saying:

נַעֲלֶ֤ה בִֽיהוּדָה֙ וּנְקִיצֶ֔נָּה וְנַבְקִעֶ֖נָּה אֵלֵ֑ינוּ וְנַמְלִ֥יךְ מֶ֙לֶךְ֙ בְּתוֹכָ֔הּ אֵ֖ת בֶּן־טָֽבְאַֽל

6 [6]

Let us go up against Judah, and vex it, and let us make a breach therein for us, and set up a king in the midst of it, the son of Tabeel;

כֹּ֥ה אָמַ֖ר אֲדֹנָ֣י יְהוִ֑ה לֹ֥א תָק֖וּם וְלֹ֥א תִֽהְיֶֽה

7 [7]

thus says the Lord GOD: It shall not stand, neither shall it come to pass.

כִּ֣י רֹ֤אשׁ אֲרָם֙ דַּמֶּ֔שֶׂק וְרֹ֥אשׁ דַּמֶּ֖שֶׂק רְצִ֑ין וּבְע֗וֹד שִׁשִּׁ֤ים וְחָמֵשׁ֙ שָׁנָ֔ה יֵחַ֥ת אֶפְרַ֖יִם מֵעָֽם

8 [8]

For the head of Aram is Damascus, And the head of Damascus is Rezin; And within 65 years shall Ephraim be broken, that it be not a people;

וְרֹ֤אשׁ אֶפְרַ֙יִם֙ שֹׁמְר֔וֹן וְרֹ֥אשׁ שֹׁמְר֖וֹן בֶּן־רְמַלְיָ֑הוּ אִ֚ם לֹ֣א תַאֲמִ֔ינוּ כִּ֖י לֹ֥א תֵאָמֵֽנוּ

9 [9]

And the head of Ephraim is Samaria, And the head of Samaria is Remaliah's son. If you will not have faith, surely you shall not *be established*[10].'

וַיּ֣וֹסֶף יְהוָ֔ה דַּבֵּ֥ר אֶל־אָחָ֖ז לֵאמֹֽר

10 [11]

And the LORD spoke again to Ahaz, saying:

שְׁאַל־לְךָ֣ א֗וֹת מֵעִם֙ יְהוָ֣ה אֱלֹהֶ֔יךָ הַעְמֵ֣ק שְׁאָ֔לָה א֖וֹ הַגְבֵּ֥הַּ לְמָֽעְלָה

11 [12]

'Ask a sign of the LORD your God: ask it either in the depth, or in the height above.'

וַיֹּ֖אמֶר אָחָ֑ז לֹא־אֶשְׁאַ֖ל וְלֹֽא־אֲנַסֶּ֥ה אֶת־יְהוָֽה

12 [13]

But Ahaz said: 'I will not ask, nor will I try the LORD.'

וַיֹּ֕אמֶר שִׁמְעוּ־נָ֖א בֵּ֣ית דָּוִ֑ד הַמְעַ֤ט מִכֶּם֙ הַלְא֣וֹת אֲנָשִׁ֔ים כִּ֥י תַלְא֖וּ גַּ֥ם אֶת־אֱלֹהָֽי

13 [14]

And he said: 'Hear now, O house of David: Is it a small thing for you to weary men, that you will weary my God also?

---

[1] 1QIsaa *the heart of his people trembled*

[2] Isaiah 7:3 - 2 Kings 18:17 20:20, b.Sanhedrin 41a, Ein Yaakov Sanhedrin:104a, Exodus 7:15, Isaiah 6:13 10:21 12:2 7:7, Jastrow 610a, Jeremiah 19:2-19:3 22:1, Leviticus.R 36:3, Romans 9:27, y.Sanhedrin 10:1

[3] Isaiah 7:4 - 1 Samuel 17:32, 2 Chronicles 20:17, 2 Kings 15:29-30, Amos 4:11, Deuteronomy 20:3, Exodus 14:13-14, Isaiah 7:1 7:8 8:4 8:11-14 10:24 6:7 6:15 11:4 17:14 51:12-13, Lamentations 3:26, Matthew 10:28 24:6, Numbers.R 18:22, z.Tetzaveh 185a, Zechariah 3:2

[4] LXX *for when my fierce anger is over, I will heal again*

[5] Isaiah 7:5 - Nahum 1:11, Psalms 2:2 83:4-83:5, Zechariah 1:15

[6] Isaiah 7:6 - Jastrow 516a, Midrash Tanchuma Korach 12, Numbers.R 18:21, y.Avodah Zarah 1:1, z.Tetzaveh 185a

[7] Isaiah 7:7 - Acts 4:25-4:28, Daniel 4:32, Genesis.R 76:4, Isaiah 8:10 10:6-10:12 13:29 46:10-46:11, Lamentations 3:37, Proverbs 21:30, Psalms 2:4-2:6 33:11 76:11, z.Vaetchanan 269b

[8] Isaiah 7:8 - 2 Kings 17:5-17:23, 2 Samuel 8:6, b.Moed Katan [Tosefot] 7b, Ezra 4:2, Genesis 14:15, Hosea 1:6-1:10, Isaiah 8:4 17:1-17:3, Seder Olam 28:Darius

[9] Isaiah 7:9 - 1 John 5:10, 1 Kings 16:24-29, 2 Chronicles 20:20, 2 Kings 15:27, Acts 3:11 3:25, Hebrews 11:6, Isaiah 8:6-8:8 30:12-30:14, Josephus Antiquities 13.9.1, m.Maaser Sheni 5:2, m.Shekalim 1:5, Romans 11:20

[10] LXX *understand*

[11] Isaiah 7:10 - Hosea 13:2, Isaiah 1:5 1:13 8:5 10:20

[12] Isaiah 7:11 - 2 Kings 19:29 20:8-20:11, Genesis.R 44:8, Isaiah 13:30 38:7-38:8 14:22, Jastrow 916a, Jeremiah 19:1 19:10 51:63-51:64, Judges 6:36-6:40, Matthew 12:38-12:40 16:1-16:4, Midrash Psalms 2:10, z.Vayikra 2a

[13] Isaiah 7:12 - 1 Corinthians 10:9, 2 Chronicles 4:22, 2 Kings 16:15, Acts 5:9, Deuteronomy 6:16, Ezekiel 9:31, Malachi 3:15 Isaiah 7:12-14 - Sibylline Oracles 5.157

[14] Isaiah 7:13 - 2 Chronicles 21:7 36:15-36:16, Acts 7:51, Amos 3:13, Ezekiel 16:20 16:47 10:18, Genesis 6:15, Hebrews 3:10, Isaiah 1:24 7:2 1:1 19:24 15:10 65:3-65:5, Jeremiah 6:11 21:12, Luke 1:69, Malachi 2:17, Numbers 16:9 16:13

לָכֵן יִתֵּן אֲדֹנָי הוּא לָכֶם אוֹת הִנֵּה הָעַלְמָה הָרָה 14[1]
וְיֹלֶדֶת בֵּן וְקָרָאת שְׁמוֹ עִמָּנוּ אֵל

14[1] Therefore, *the Lord*[2] Himself shall give you a sign: behold, *the young woman*[3] shall conceive, and bear a son, and *shall call his name*[4] Immanuel.

חֶמְאָה וּדְבַשׁ יֹאכֵל לְדַעְתּוֹ מָאוֹס בָּרָע וּבָחוֹר 15[5]
בַּטּוֹב

15[5] Curd and honey shall he eat, when he knows to refuse the evil, and choose the good.

כִּי בְּטֶרֶם יֵדַע הַנַּעַר מָאֹס בָּרָע וּבָחֹר בַּטּוֹב תֵּעָזֵב 16[6]
הָאֲדָמָה אֲשֶׁר אַתָּה קָץ מִפְּנֵי שְׁנֵי מְלָכֶיהָ

16[6] Yes, before the child shall know *to refuse the evil, and choose the good*[7], the land whose two kings you have a horror of shall be forsaken.

יָבִיא יְהוָה עָלֶיךָ וְעַל־עַמְּךָ וְעַל־בֵּית אָבִיךָ יָמִים 17[8]
אֲשֶׁר לֹא־בָאוּ לְמִיּוֹם סוּר־אֶפְרַיִם מֵעַל יְהוּדָה אֵת
מֶלֶךְ אַשּׁוּר

17[8] [9]The LORD shall bring on you, and on your people, and on your father's house, days that have not come, from the day that Ephraim departed from Judah; the king of Assyria.'

וְהָיָה בַּיּוֹם הַהוּא יִשְׁרֹק יְהוָה לַזְּבוּב אֲשֶׁר בִּקְצֵה 18[10]
יְאֹרֵי מִצְרָיִם וְלַדְּבוֹרָה אֲשֶׁר בְּאֶרֶץ אַשּׁוּר

18[10] And it shall come to pass in that day, That the LORD shall hiss for the fly that is in the uttermost part of the rivers of Egypt, And for the bee that is in the land of Assyria.

וּבָאוּ וְנָחוּ כֻלָּם בְּנַחֲלֵי הַבַּתּוֹת וּבִנְקִיקֵי הַסְּלָעִים 19[11]
וּבְכֹל הַנַּעֲצוּצִים וּבְכֹל הַנַּהֲלֹלִים

19[11] And they shall come, and shall rest all of them In the rugged valleys, and in the holes of the rocks, *And on all thorns, and on all brambles*[12].

בַּיּוֹם הַהוּא יְגַלַּח אֲדֹנָי בְּתַעַר הַשְּׂכִירָה בְּעֶבְרֵי 20[13]
נָהָר בְּמֶלֶךְ אַשּׁוּר אֶת־הָרֹאשׁ וְשַׂעַר הָרַגְלָיִם וְגַם
אֶת־הַזָּקָן תִּסְפֶּה

20[13] In that day the Lord shall shave with a razor that is hired in the parts beyond the River, with the king of Assyria, the head and the hair of the feet; and it shall also sweep away the beard.

וְהָיָה בַּיּוֹם הַהוּא יְחַיֶּה־אִישׁ עֶגְלַת בָּקָר וּשְׁתֵּי־ 21[14]
צֹאן

21[14] And it shall come to pass in that day, that a man shall rear a young cow, and two sheep;

וְהָיָה מֵרֹב עֲשׂוֹת חָלָב יֹאכַל חֶמְאָה כִּי־חֶמְאָה 22[15]
וּדְבַשׁ יֹאכַל כָּל־הַנּוֹתָר בְּקֶרֶב הָאָרֶץ

22[15] And it shall come to pass, for the abundance of milk that they shall give, he shall eat curd; for

---

[1] Isaiah 7:14 - 1 Samuel 1:20 4:21, 1 Timothy 3:16, Apocryphon of Ezekiel Fragment 3, Exodus.R 18:5, Genesis 3:15 4:1-4:2 4:25 16:11 5:32 6:6 6:8, Isaiah 8:8 8:10 9:7, Jeremiah 7:23, John 1:1-1:2 1:14, Liber Antiquitatum Biblicarum 43:1, Luke 1:31 1:35, Mas.Soferim 4:8, Matthew 1:23, Per Massorah: Soferim altered "Hashem" to "Adonai", Ralbag SOS 1, Romans 9:5, Testament of Solomon 11:6 15:12 6:8, virgin [LXX] vs. "young woman" [MT]
Isaiah 7:14 [LXX] - Lives of the Prophets 2:8
Isaiah 7:14-15 - 4QIsaI

[2] 1QIsaa *the LORD*

[3] LXX *a virgin*; Heb. *almah* is generally *young [unmarried] woman/damsel* of good report; Heb. *Betulah* is not *virgin* but *righteous woman*; Heb. *zanah* is a woman of ill repute.

[4] 1QIsaa *his name will be*

[5] Isaiah 7:15 - Amos 5:15, Isaiah 7:22, Luke 1:35 2:40 2:52, Matthew 3:4, Numbers.R 14:2, Philippians 1:9-10, Psalms 51:6, Romans 12:9, Testament of Job 13:2

[6] Isaiah 7:16 - 2 Kings 15:29-15:30 16:9, Amos 1:3-1:5, Deuteronomy 1:39, Hosea 5:9, Isaiah 8:4 9:12 17:1-3, Jonah 4:11
Isaiah 7:16-18 - 4QIsaf

[7] LXX *good or evil, he refuses evil, to choose the good*

[8] Isaiah 7:17 - 1 Kings 12:16-12:19, 2 Chronicles 10:16-10:19 28:19-28:21 32:1-32:33 9:11 36:6-36:20, 2 Kings 18:1-18:19, 4Q266 frag 9 3.17-18, 4Q267 frag 9 5.2-4, Cairo Damascus 13.23-14.1, Cairo Damascus 7:10-12 13.23-14.1, Cairo Damascus 7.11-12, Isaiah 8:7-8:8 10:5-10:6 36:1-36:22, Nehemiah 9:32
Isaiah 7:17-20 - 4QIsae

[9] 1QIsaa *And*

[10] Isaiah 7:18 - 2 Kings 23:33-34, Deuteronomy 1:44 7:20, Exodus 8:17 8:20, Exodus.R 30:5, Isaiah 5:26 7:17 13:5 30:1-2 7:1, Joshua 24:12, Midrash Tanchuma Chukkat 1, Midrash Tanchuma Vayeshev 3, Numbers.R 18:22, Psalms 22:12, Seder Olam 20:Gad

[11] Isaiah 7:19 - 2 Chronicles 9:11, b.Megillah 10b, Ein Yaakov Megillah:9b, Isaiah 2:19 2:21, Jastrow 200b, Jeremiah 16:16, Micah 7:17, Midrash Tanchuma Chukkat 1

[12] LXX *and into the caves, and into every ravine*

[13] Isaiah 7:20 - 2 Chronicles 28:20-21, 2 Kings 16:7-8 18:13-16, Ein Yaakov Sanhedrin:95b, Ezekiel 5:1-4 5:18 5:20, Isaiah 1:5 8:7 9:15-18 10:5-6 10:15 11:15 24:1-2, Jeremiah 27:6-7, m.Kilayim 28:10, Per Massorah: Soferim altered "Hashem" to "Adonai", Song of Songs.R 8:8

[14] Isaiah 7:21 - b.Chullin 135a, b.Sanhedrin 94b, Ein Yaakov Sanhedrin:94b, Genesis.R 42:3 48:10 70:6, Isaiah 5:17 7:25 17:2 13:30, Jeremiah 15:10, Leviticus.R 11:7, Midrash Tanchuma Shemini 9, Numbers.R 13:5, Ruth.R Petichata:7, Sifre Devarim Shoftim 166, Sifre Devarim {Shoftim} 166
Isaiah 7:21-22 - t.Arachin 4:27

[15] Isaiah 7:22 - 2 Samuel 17:29, Isaiah 7:15, Matthew 3:4
Isaiah 7:22-25 - QIsab

curd and honey shall *everyone*[1] eat that is left in the midst of the land.

וְהָיָה בַיּוֹם הַהוּא יִהְיֶה כָל־מָקוֹם אֲשֶׁר יִהְיֶה־שָּׁם אֶלֶף גֶּפֶן בְּאֶלֶף כָּסֶף לַשָּׁמִיר וְלַשַּׁיִת יִהְיֶה	23[2]	And it shall come to pass in that day that every place, where there were a thousand vines at a thousand silverlings, shall *be for briers*[3] and thorns.
בַּחִצִּים וּבַקֶּשֶׁת יָבוֹא שָׁמָּה כִּי־שָׁמִיר וָשַׁיִת תִּהְיֶה כָל־הָאָרֶץ	24[4]	With arrows and with bow[5] shall one come there; because all the land shall become briers and thorns.
וְכֹל הֶהָרִים אֲשֶׁר בַּמַּעְדֵּר יֵעָדֵרוּן לֹא־תָבוֹא שָׁמָּה יִרְאַת שָׁמִיר וָשָׁיִת וְהָיָה לְמִשְׁלַח שׁוֹר וּלְמִרְמַס שֶׂה	25[6]	And all the hills that were dug with the pickaxe, you shall not go there for fear of [7]briers and thorns, but it shall be for the sending forth of oxen, and for the treading of sheep.

Isaiah – Chapter 8

וַיֹּאמֶר יְהֹוָה אֵלַי קַח־לְךָ גִּלָּיוֹן גָּדוֹל וּכְתֹב עָלָיו בְּחֶרֶט אֱנוֹשׁ לְמַהֵר שָׁלָל חָשׁ בַּז	1[8]	And the LORD said to me: 'Take you a *great tablet, and write upon it in common script: The spoil speeds, the prey hurries*[9];
וְאָעִידָה לִּי עֵדִים נֶאֱמָנִים אֵת אוּרִיָּה הַכֹּהֵן וְאֶת־זְכַרְיָהוּ בֶּן יְבֶרֶכְיָהוּ	2[10]	And *I will take to Me*[11] faithful witnesses to record, Uriah the priest, and Zechariah the son of *Jeberechiah*[12].'
וָאֶקְרַב אֶל־הַנְּבִיאָה וַתַּהַר וַתֵּלֶד בֵּן וַיֹּאמֶר יְהֹוָה אֵלַי קְרָא שְׁמוֹ מַהֵר שָׁלָל חָשׁ בַּז	3[13]	And I went to the prophetess[14]; and she conceived, and bore a son. Then the LORD said to me: 'Call his name *Maher-shalal-hashbaz*[15].
כִּי בְּטֶרֶם יֵדַע הַנַּעַר קְרֹא אָבִי וְאִמִּי יִשָּׂא אֶת־חֵיל דַּמֶּשֶׂק וְאֵת שְׁלַל שֹׁמְרוֹן לִפְנֵי מֶלֶךְ אַשּׁוּר	4[16]	For before the child *shall have knowledge to cry*[17]: my father and my mother, the riches of Damascus and the spoil of Samaria shall be carried away before the king of Assyria.'
וַיֹּסֶף יְהֹוָה דַּבֵּר אֵלַי עוֹד לֵאמֹר	5[18]	And the LORD spoke to me yet again, saying:

---

[1] 1QIsaa *the one*

[2] Isaiah 7:23 - b.Sanhedrin 94b, Ein Yaakov Sanhedrin:94b, Hebrews 6:8, Isaiah 5:6 32:12-14, Jeremiah 4:26, Matthew 21:33, Song of Songs 8:11-12
Isaiah 7:23-25 - 4QIsaf

[3] LXX *become barren land*

[4] Isaiah 7:24 - Genesis 27:3

[5] 1QIsaa plural; MT singular

[6] Isaiah 7:25 - Isaiah 5:17 7:21-22 13:20-22 17:2, y.Nazir 9:6, Zephaniah 2:6

[7] 1QIsaa adds *iron*

[8] Isaiah 8:1 - 1QIsab, 4QIsaf, Habakkuk 2:2-2:3, Isaiah 8:3 30:8, Jeremiah 36:2 36:28 36:32, Job 19:23-19:24, Midrash Psalms 15:4, Revelation 13:18 21:17, z.Ki Tissa 192b
Isaiah 8:1-23 - 1QIsaa, Philo Quaestiones et Solutiones in Genesin I 100

[9] LXX *volume of a great new book, and write in it with a man's pen concerning a rapid plunder of spoils; for it is near at hand*

[10] Isaiah 8:2 - 2 Corinthians 13:1, 2 Kings 16:10-11 16:15-16 18:2, b.Makkot 24b, Ein Yaakov Makkot:24b, Lamentations.R 5:18, Midrash Tanchuma Massei 13, Pesikta de R'Kahana 13.12, Ruth 4:2 4:10-4:11, Sifre Devarim Ekev 43
Isaiah 8:2-14 - 4QIsae

[11] 1QIsaa *call*

[12] LXX *Barachias*

[13] Isaiah 8:3 - 2 Kings 22:14, Exodus.R 18:5, Hosea 1:3-1:9, Isaiah 7:13-7:14, Jastrow 1585a, Judges 4:4, Saadia Opinions 10:6

[14] 1QIsaa masculine; MT feminine

[15] LXX *Spoil quickly, plunder speedily*

[16] Isaiah 8:4 - 2 Kings 15:29 16:9 17:3 17:5-6, Deuteronomy 1:39, Isaiah 7:8-9 7:15-16 10:6-14 17:3, Jonah 4:11, Romans 9:11
Isaiah 8:4-11 - 4QIsaf

[17] 1QIsaa *can call*

[18] Isaiah 8:5 - Genesis.R 61:4, Isaiah 7:10

וַיַּעַן כִּי מָאַס הָעָם הַזֶּה אֵת מֵי הַשִּׁלֹחַ הַהֹלְכִים
לְאַט וּמְשׂוֹשׂ אֶת־רְצִין וּבֶן־רְמַלְיָהוּ

6[1] Because as this people has refused The waters of Shiloah that go softly, *And rejoices with Rezin and Remaliah's son*[2];

וְלָכֵן הִנֵּה אֲדֹנָי מַעֲלֶה עֲלֵיהֶם אֶת־מֵי הַנָּהָר
הָעֲצוּמִים וְהָרַבִּים אֶת־מֶלֶךְ אַשּׁוּר וְאֶת־כָּל־כְּבוֹדוֹ
וְעָלָה עַל־כָּל־אֲפִיקָיו וְהָלַךְ עַל־כָּל־גְּדוֹתָיו

7[3] Now therefore, behold, *the Lord*[4] brings upon them the waters of the River, mighty and many, the king of Assyria and all his glory; and he shall come over *all his channels, and go over all his banks*[5];

וְחָלַף בִּיהוּדָה שָׁטַף וְעָבַר עַד־צַוָּאר יַגִּיעַ וְהָיָה
מֻטּוֹת כְּנָפָיו מְלֹא רֹחַב־אַרְצְךָ עִמָּנוּ אֵל

8[6] And he shall sweep through Judah Overflowing as he passes through He shall reach to the neck; and the stretching out of his wings shall fill the breadth of your land, O *Immanuel*[7].

רֹעוּ עַמִּים וָחֹתּוּ וְהַאֲזִינוּ כֹּל מֶרְחַקֵּי־אָרֶץ הִתְאַזְּרוּ
וָחֹתּוּ הִתְאַזְּרוּ וָחֹתּוּ

9[8] *Make an uproar, O peoples, and you shall be broken in pieces; And give ear, all you of far countries; Gird yourselves, and you shall be broken in pieces*[9]; *Gird yourselves, and you shall be broken in pieces*[10].

עֻצוּ עֵצָה וְתֻפָר דַּבְּרוּ דָבָר וְלֹא יָקוּם כִּי עִמָּנוּ אֵל

10[11] Take counsel together, and it shall be brought to nothing; Speak the word, and it shall not stand; *For God is with us*[12].

כִּי כֹה אָמַר יְהוָה אֵלַי כְּחֶזְקַת הַיָּד וְיִסְּרֵנִי מִלֶּכֶת
בְּדֶרֶךְ הָעָם־הַזֶּה לֵאמֹר

11[13] For the LORD spoke thus to me with a strong hand, admonishing me that I should not walk in the way of this people, saying:

לֹא־תֹאמְרוּן קֶשֶׁר לְכֹל אֲשֶׁר־יֹאמַר הָעָם הַזֶּה
קָשֶׁר וְאֶת־מוֹרָאוֹ לֹא־תִירְאוּ וְלֹא תַעֲרִיצוּ

12[14] 'Do not say: A conspiracy, concerning all this people who say: A conspiracy; nor fear their fear, nor account it dreadful.

[1] Isaiah 8:6 - 16:6, 1 Kings 7:16, 2 Chronicles 13:8-13:18, b.Sanhedrin 94b, Ein Yaakov Sanhedrin:94b, Genesis.R 78:14, Isaiah 5:24 7:1-7:2 7:6, Jeremiah 2:13 2:18 18:14, John 9:7, Judges 9:16-9:20, Lamentations.R Petichata D'Chakimei:19, Lives of the Prophets 1:1, Midrash Tanchuma Korach 12, Nehemiah 3:15, Numbers.R 18:21, Pesikta de R'Kahana 6.2, Pesikta Rabbati 16:6
[2] LXX *but wants to have Rassin, and the son of Romelias to be king over you*
[3] Isaiah 8:7 - 2 Kings 17:3-17:6 18:9-18:12, Amos 8:8 9:5, b.Sanhedrin 94b, Daniel 9:26 11:10 11:22, Deuteronomy 28:49-28:52, Ein Yaakov Sanhedrin:94b, Exodus.R 49:1, Ezekiel 31:3-31:18, Ezra 4:10, Genesis 6:17, Isaiah 7:1-7:6 7:17 7:20 10:8-10:14 17:12-17:13 28:17 59:19, Jeremiah 46:7-46:8, Luke 6:48, Nahum 1:8, Numbers.R 2:16, Per Massorah: Soferim altered "Hashem" to "Adonai", Pesikta de R'Kahana 6.2, Pesikta Rabbati 16:6 31:9, Psalms 72:8, Revelation 12:15-12:16 17:15, Saadia Opinions 7:4 7Variant:5, Song of Songs.R 8:8
Isaiah 8:7-8 - 4Q163 frag 2 ll.1-3
[4] 1QIsaa *the LORD God*
[5] LXX *every valley of yours, and shall walk over every wall of yours*
[6] Isaiah 8:8 - b.Sanhedrin 94b 95b, Ein Yaakov Sanhedrin:95b, Ezekiel 17:3, Isaiah 7:14 10:28-10:32 22:1-22:7 28:14-28:22 29:1-29:9 30:28 36:1-36:22, Jastrow 741a 1280a, Mas.Soferim 4:8, Matthew 1:23, Midrash Psalms 79:1, Midrash Tanchuma Tazria 8, Midrash Tanchuma Tazria 8 states Immanuel refers to the tribe of Judah, Testament of Solomon 11:6 15:12 6:8
[7] 1QIsaa 4QIsae 4QIsaf one word, MT two words
[8] Isaiah 8:9 - 1 Kings 20:11, Daniel 2:34-2:35, Ezekiel 38:9-38:23, Isaiah 7:1-7:2 14:5-14:6 17:12-17:13 28:13 37:36 54:15, Jeremiah 46:9-46:11, Joel 4:9-4:14, Leviticus.R 6:5, Micah 4:11-4:13, Proverbs 11:21, Psalms 37:14-37:15, Revelation 17:12-17:14 20:8-20:9, Zechariah 14:1-14:3
[9] LXX *Know, you Gentiles, and be conquered; listen to the extremity of the earth: be conquered, after you have strengthened yourselves*
[10] 1QIsaa *gird yourselves but be shattered*
[11] Isaiah 8:10 - 1 John 4:4, 2 Chronicles 13:12 33:7-33:8, 2 Samuel 15:31 17:4 17:23, Acts 5:38-5:39, After Aleinu [Shacharit, Deuteronomy 20:1, Esther.R 7:13, Guide for the Perplexed 3:52, Isaiah 7:5-7:7 7:14 8:8 9:7 41:10, Job 5:12, Joshua 1:5, Lamentations 3:37, Maariv, Matthew 1:23 28:20, Minchah, Motzoei Shabbat [Ribbon Ha'olamim], Mussaf Al Tirah Mipachad], Nahum 1:9-1:12, Proverbs 21:30, Psalms 2:1-2:2 33:10-33:11 46:2 46:8 46:12 83:4-83:19, Romans 8:13 8:31
[12] 1QIsaa 4QIsae one words; MT two words
[13] Isaiah 8:11 - 1QIs 1.14-16 4Q174 4QFlor 1.14-16, 4Q174 3.15-16, 4Q174 3.15-16, Acts 4:20, Ezekiel 2:6-2:8 3:14, Jeremiah 15:19 20:7 20:9, Proverbs 1:15, Psalms 32:8, Ralbag SOS 2
Isaiah 8:11-14 - 4QIsal
[14] Isaiah 8:12 - 1 Peter 3:14-15, 2 Kings 16:5-7, b.Sanhedrin 26a, Gates of Repentance 3.050, Isaiah 7:2-6 30:1 51:12-13 57:9-11, Jastrow 1433a, Luke 12:4-5 21:9, Matthew 28:2-5, Psalms 53:6

אֶת־יְהוָה צְבָאוֹת אֹתוֹ תַקְדִּישׁוּ וְהוּא מוֹרַאֲכֶם
וְהוּא מַעֲרִצְכֶם

13[1] The LORD *of hosts*[2], you shall sanctify Him; and let Him be your fear, and let Him be your dread[3].

וְהָיָה לְמִקְדָּשׁ וּלְאֶבֶן נֶגֶף וּלְצוּר מִכְשׁוֹל לִשְׁנֵי בָתֵּי
יִשְׂרָאֵל לְפַח וּלְמוֹקֵשׁ לְיוֹשֵׁב יְרוּשָׁלָ͏ִם

14[4] And [5]He shall be a sanctuary; but for a stone of stumbling and for a rock of offense to both the houses of Israel, for a trap and for a snare to the inhabitants of Jerusalem.

וְכָשְׁלוּ בָם רַבִּים וְנָפְלוּ וְנִשְׁבָּרוּ וְנוֹקְשׁוּ וְנִלְכָּדוּ

15[6] And many among them shall stumble and fall, and be broken, *and be snared, and be taken*[7].'

צוֹר תְּעוּדָה חֲתוֹם תּוֹרָה בְּלִמֻּדָי

16[8] 'Bind up the testimony, seal the instruction among My disciples.'

וְחִכִּיתִי לַיהוָה הַמַּסְתִּיר פָּנָיו מִבֵּית יַעֲקֹב וְקִוֵּיתִי־
לוֹ

17[9] [10]And I will wait for the LORD, who hides His face from the house of Jacob, and I will look for Him.

הִנֵּה אָנֹכִי וְהַיְלָדִים אֲשֶׁר נָתַן־לִי יְהוָה לְאֹתוֹת
וּלְמוֹפְתִים בְּיִשְׂרָאֵל מֵעִם יְהוָה צְבָאוֹת הַשֹּׁכֵן
בְּהַר צִיּוֹן

18[11] Behold, I and the children whom the LORD has given me *shall be for signs and for wonders*[12] in Israel from the LORD of hosts, who dwells in mount Zion.

וְכִי־יֹאמְרוּ אֲלֵיכֶם דִּרְשׁוּ אֶל־הָאֹבוֹת וְאֶל־
הַיִּדְּעֹנִים הַמְצַפְצְפִים וְהַמַּהְגִּים הֲלוֹא־עַם אֶל־
אֱלֹהָיו יִדְרֹשׁ בְּעַד הַחַיִּים אֶל־הַמֵּתִים

19[13] And when they shall say to you: 'Seek to the ghosts and the familiar spirits, who chirp and who mutter; should not a people seek their God[14]? On behalf of the living to the dead

לְתוֹרָה וְלִתְעוּדָה אִם־לֹא יֹאמְרוּ כַּדָּבָר הַזֶּה אֲשֶׁר
אֵין־לוֹ שָׁחַר

20[15] *For instruction and for testimony?'* Surely they will speak according to this word, in which there is no light[16].

---

[1] Isaiah 8:13 - Genesis 31:53, Isaiah 26:3-26:4 29:23, Leviticus 10:3, Luke 12:5, Malachi 2:5, Matthew 10:28, Numbers 20:12-20:13 27:14, Psalms 76:8, Revelation 15:4, Romans 4:20, the abbreviation מ stands for מוראכם

[2] Missing in LXX

[3] Missing in LXX

[4] Isaiah 8:14 - 1 Peter 2:8, b.Sanhedrin 38a, Ein Yaakov Sanhedrin:38a, Ezekiel 11:16, Isaiah 4:6 24:17-24:18 26:20 28:16, Luke 2:34 21:35, Matthew 13:57, Proverbs 18:10, Psalms 11:7 46:2-46:3 69:23, Romans 9:32-9:33 11:9-11:11 11:35, Sibylline Oracles 1.346

[5] LXX adds *if you shall trust in him*

[6] Isaiah 8:15 - 1 Corinthians 1:23, Isaiah 28:13 59:10, John 6:66, Luke 20:17-18, Matthew 11:6 15:14 21:44, Romans 9:32

[7] LXX *and they shall draw near, and men shall be taken securely*

[8] Isaiah 8:16 - 1 Corinthians 2:14, 1 John 5:9-5:12, 2 Kings 11:12, b.Sanhedrin 103b, Daniel 9:24 12:4 12:9-12:10, Deuteronomy 4:45, Esther.R Petichata:11, Genesis.R 42:3, Hebrews 3:5, Isaiah 8:1-8:2 8:20 29:11-29:12 54:13, John 3:32-3:33, Leviticus.R 11:7, Mark 4:10-4:11 4:34 10:10, Matthew 13:11, Midrash Tanchuma Tetzaveh 15, Proverbs 8:8-8:9, Psalms 25:14, Revelation 2:17 5:1 5:5 10:4 19:10, Ruth.R Petichata:7, z.Emor 90b, z.Tzav 35a

[9] Isaiah 8:17 - 1 Thessalonians 1:10, 2 Thessalonians 3:5, b.Megillah 24a, Deuteronomy 31:17-18 32:20, Esther.R Petichata:11, Ezekiel 39:23-24, Genesis 49:18, Genesis.R 42:3, Habakkuk 2:3, Hebrews 9:28 10:36-39, Hosea 12:8, Isaiah 1:15 25:9 26:8 33:2 50:10 54:8 59:2 64:5 64:8, Lamentations 3:25-26, Leviticus.R 11:7, Luke 2:38, Micah 3:4 7:7, Psalms 27:14 33:20 37:34 39:8 40:2 130:5, Ralbag Wars 4:3, Ruth.R Petichata:7, Song of Songs.R 5:11, y.Sanhedrin 10:2, z.Mikketz 204a

[10] LXX adds *And one shall say*

[11] Isaiah 8:18 - 1 Chronicles 23:25, 1 Corinthians 4:9-13, b.Kiddushin [Rashi] 30b, Esther.R Petichata:11, Ezekiel 14:8, Genesis.R 42:3, Hebrews 2:13-14 10:33 12:22, Isaiah 7:3 7:16 8:3 12:6 14:32 24:23 53:10, Leviticus.R 11:7, Luke 2:34, Midrash Psalms 90:4, Psalms 9:12 22:31 71:7, Ruth.R Petichata:7, y.Sanhedrin 10:2, z.Vayeilech 284b, Zechariah 3:8 8:3

[12] 1QIsaa *as a sign and a wonder*

[13] Isaiah 8:19 - 1 Chronicles 10:13, 1 Samuel 28:8 28:11 28:16, 1 Thessalonians 1:9, 2 Baruch 14:5, 2 Chronicles 33:6, 2 Kings 1:3 21:6 23:24, 2 Peter 2:1, b.Sotah 12b, Deuteronomy 18:11, Ein Yaakov Sotah:12a, Exodus.R 1:24, Isaiah 19:3 29:4, Jastrow 331a 1269a 1296b, Jeremiah 10:10, Leviticus 19:31 20:6, Leviticus.R 6:6, Midrash Tanchuma Emor 2, Midrash Tanchuma Ki Tissa 24, Midrash Tanchuma Shoftim 10, Psalms 106:28, Sibylline Oracles 3.227

[14] 1QIsaa singular; MT plural

[15] Isaiah 8:20 - 2 Peter 1:9 1:19, 2 Timothy 3:15-3:17, Acts 17:11, Galatians 3:8-3:29 4:21-4:22, Hosea 6:3, Isaiah 1:10 8:16 30:8-30:11, Jeremiah 8:9, John 5:39 5:46-5:47, Leviticus.R 6:6, Luke 10:26 16:29-16:31, Malachi 3:20, Mark 7:7-7:9, Matthew 6:23 22:29, Micah 3:6, Midrash Tanchuma Emor 2, Proverbs 4:18, Psalms 19:8-19:9 119:130, Romans 1:22, z.Emor 90b
Isaiah 8:20 [LXX] - Hellenistic Synagogal Prayers 12:69

[16] LXX *For he has given the law for a help, that they should not speak according to this word, concerning which there are no gifts to give for it*

וַיַּעֲבַר בָּהּ נִקְשֶׁה וְרָעֵב וְהָיָה כִי־יִרְעַב וְהִתְקַצַּף 21[1]
וְקִלֵּל בְּמַלְכּוֹ וּבֵאלֹהָיו וּפָנָה לְמָעְלָה

[2]And they who are wretched and hungry shall pass this way; and it shall come to pass that, when they shall be hungry, they shall fret themselves, and curse by their king and *by their Gods*[3], and, whether they turn their faces upward,

וְאֶל־אֶרֶץ יַבִּיט וְהִנֵּה צָרָה וַחֲשֵׁכָה מְעוּף צוּקָה 22[4]
וַאֲפֵלָה מְנֻדָּח

Or look to the earth, behold distress and darkness, the gloom of anguish, and outspread thick darkness[5].

כִּי לֹא מוּעָף לַאֲשֶׁר מוּצָק לָהּ כָּעֵת הָרִאשׁוֹן הֵקַל 23[6]
אַרְצָה זְבֻלוּן וְאַרְצָה נַפְתָּלִי וְהָאַחֲרוֹן הִכְבִּיד דֶּרֶךְ
הַיָּם עֵבֶר הַיַּרְדֵּן גְּלִיל הַגּוֹיִם

Is there no gloom to she who was steadfast? Now the former has lightly afflicted the [7]land of Zebulun and the land of Naphtali, but the latter has dealt a more grievous blow by the way of the sea, beyond the Jordan, in the *district of the nations*[8].

Isaiah – Chapter 9

הָעָם הַהֹלְכִים בַּחֹשֶׁךְ רָאוּ אוֹר גָּדוֹל יֹשְׁבֵי בְּאֶרֶץ 1[9]
צַלְמָוֶת אוֹר נָגַהּ עֲלֵיהֶם

The people who walked in darkness have seen a great light; they who lived in the land of the shadow of death, on them the light has shined.

הִרְבִּיתָ הַגּוֹי 'לֹא' "לוֹ" הִגְדַּלְתָּ הַשִּׂמְחָה שָׂמְחוּ 2[10]
לְפָנֶיךָ כְּשִׂמְחַת בַּקָּצִיר כַּאֲשֶׁר יָגִילוּ בְּחַלְּקָם שָׁלָל

You have multiplied the nation, you have increased their joy; They joy before You according to the joy in harvest, As men rejoice when they divide the spoil.

כִּי אֶת־עֹל סֻבֳּלוֹ וְאֵת מַטֵּה שִׁכְמוֹ שֵׁבֶט הַנֹּגֵשׂ בּוֹ 3[11]
הַחִתֹּתָ כְּיוֹם מִדְיָן

For the yoke of his burden, And the staff of his shoulder, The rod of his oppressor, *You have broken*[12] as in the day of Midian[13].

כִּי כָל־סְאוֹן סֹאֵן בְּרַעַשׁ וְשִׂמְלָה מְגוֹלָלָה בְדָמִים 4[14]
וְהָיְתָה לִשְׂרֵפָה מַאֲכֹלֶת אֵשׁ

For every boot stamped with fierceness, And every cloak rolled in blood, Shall be for burning, for fuel of fire.

---

[1] Isaiah 8:21 - 2 Kings 6:33 25:3, b.Avodah Zara [Rashi] 44b, b.Avodah Zara 54a, Deuteronomy 28:33-28:34 28:53-28:57, Esther.R Petichata:11, Exodus 22:28, Isaiah 8:7-8:8 9:21, Jeremiah 14:18 52:6, Job 1:11 2:5 2:9, Lamentations 4:4-4:5 4:9-4:10, Mekilta de R'Ishmael Bahodesh 10:11, Midrash Tanchuma Yitro 16, mt.Hilchot Avodat Kochavim v'Chukkoteihem 8:10, Proverbs 19:3, Revelation 9:20-9:21 16:9-16:11, y.Avodah Zarah 4:5
Isaiah 8:21-22 - mt.Hilchot Avodat Kochavim v'Chukkoteihem 8:10
[2] LXX adds *And severe famine shall come upon you*
[3] 1QIsaa singular; MT plural; LXX *your fathers' ordinances*
[4] Isaiah 8:22 - 2 Chronicles 15:5-6, Amos 5:18-20, b.Avodah Zara 54a, Isaiah 5:30 8:20 9:2, Jeremiah 13:16 23:12 30:6-7, Job 18:18, Jude 1:13, Luke 21:25-26, Matthew 8:12 22:13 24:29, mt.Hilchot Avodat Kochavim v'Chukkoteihem 8:10, Proverbs 14:32, Zephaniah 1:14-15
[5] LXX *and they shall look on the earth below, and behold severe distress, and darkness, affliction, and anguish, and darkness so that one cannot see; and he who is in anguish shall not be distressed only for a time*
[6] Isaiah 8:23 - b.Sanhedrin 94b 104b, Ein Yaakov Sanhedrin:104b 94b, Jastrow 249a 355b 781a 1073b 1270a, Lamentations.R Petichata D'Chakimei:5, Numbers.R 23:14, Seder Olam 23:Sennacherib, Sifre Devarim Ekev 43, z.Beshallach 56b
[7] LXX *Drink this first. Act quickly, O*
[8] LXX *Galilee of the Gentiles*
[9] Isaiah 9:1 - Derech Hashem Part I 4§04, Midrash Psalms 22:15, Midrash Tanchuma Noach 3, mt.Hilchot Deot 5:5
Isaiah 9:1-20 - 1QIsaa
[10] Isaiah 9:2 - 1 Chronicles 5:26, 1 Kings 15:19-15:20, 2 Chronicles 16:4, 2 Enoch 46:3, 2 Kings 15:29 17:5-17:6, Isaiah 8:22, Leviticus 26:24 26:28, Mas.Soferim 6:6, Matthew 4:15-4:16, z.Vayechi 236b, z.Vayera 116a
[11] Isaiah 9:3 - 1 John 1:5-1:7, 1 Peter 2:9, Amos 5:8, Ecclesiastes.R 8:12, Ephesians 5:8 5:13-5:14, Genesis.R 26:6, Isaiah 9:2 50:10 60:1-60:3 60:19, Job 10:21, John 8:12 12:35 12:46, Luke 1:78-1:79 2:32, Matthew 4:16, Micah 7:8-7:9, Psalms 23:4 107:10 107:14
Isaiah 9:3-12 - 4QIsac
[12] 4QIsac *I have broken*
[13] 1QIsaa *Midiam*
[14] Isaiah 9:4 - 1 Peter 1:8, 1 Samuel 30:16, 2 Chronicles 20:25-20:28, 4Q257 3.4, Acts 8:8, b.Sotah 8b 9a, Hosea 4:7, Isaiah 12:1 16:9-16:10 25:9 26:15 35:2 35:10 49:20-49:22 54:1 55:12 61:7 61:10 65:18 66:10, Jastrow 947b, Jeremiah 31:8 31:13-31:15, Judges 5:3, Luke 11:22, Midrash Psalms 81:2, Nehemiah 9:23, Numbers.R 9:24, Philippians 4:4, Psalms 4:8 107:38 119:162 126:5-126:6, t.Sotah 3:1, y.Sotah 1:7, Zechariah 2:11 8:23 10:8

כִּי־יֶלֶד יֻלַּד־לָנוּ בֵּן נִתַּן־לָנוּ וַתְּהִי הַמִּשְׂרָה עַל־ שִׁכְמוֹ וַיִּקְרָא שְׁמוֹ פֶּלֶא יוֹעֵץ אֵל גִּבּוֹר אֲבִיעַד שַׂר־שָׁלוֹם

5[1] For a child is born to us, a son is given to us; and the government is on his shoulder; And *his* name[2] is called *Pele-joez-el-gibbor-Abi-ad-sar-shalom*[3] [Wonderful, Counsellor, God Almighty, Everlasting Father, Prince of Peace];

לְמַרְבֵּה ״לְמַרְבֵּה״ הַמִּשְׂרָה וּלְשָׁלוֹם אֵין־קֵץ עַל־ כִּסֵּא דָוִד וְעַל־מַמְלַכְתּוֹ לְהָכִין אֹתָהּ וּלְסַעֲדָהּ בְּמִשְׁפָּט וּבִצְדָקָה מֵעַתָּה וְעַד־עוֹלָם קִנְאַת יְהוָה צְבָאוֹת תַּעֲשֶׂה־זֹּאת

6[4] So the government may be increased, And of peace there is no end, Upon the throne of David, and on his kingdom, To establish *it*[5], and to uphold *it*[6] through justice and through righteousness From henceforth forever. The zeal of the LORD of hosts performs this.

דָּבָר שָׁלַח אֲדֹנָי בְּיַעֲקֹב וְנָפַל בְּיִשְׂרָאֵל

7[7] The Lord[8] sent a word into Jacob, And it rests on Israel.

וְיָדְעוּ הָעָם כֻּלּוֹ אֶפְרַיִם וְיוֹשֵׁב שֹׁמְרוֹן בְּגַאֲוָה וּבְגֹדֶל לֵבָב לֵאמֹר

8[9] And all the people *shall know*[10], Ephraim and the inhabitant of Samaria, Who say in pride and in the arrogance of heart:

לְבֵנִים נָפָלוּ וְגָזִית נִבְנֶה שִׁקְמִים גֻּדָּעוּ וַאֲרָזִים נַחֲלִיף

9[11] 'The bricks have fallen, but we will build with hewn stones; The sycamores are cut down, but cedars *we will put in their place*[12].'

וַיְשַׂגֵּב יְהוָה אֶת־צָרֵי רְצִין עָלָיו וְאֶת־אֹיְבָיו יְסַכְסֵךְ

10[13] Therefore, the LORD sets on high the enemies of Rezin against him, And *spur*[14] his enemies;

אֲרָם מִקֶּדֶם וּפְלִשְׁתִּים מֵאָחוֹר וַיֹּאכְלוּ אֶת־יִשְׂרָאֵל בְּכָל־פֶּה בְּכָל־זֹאת לֹא־שָׁב אַפּוֹ וְעוֹד יָדוֹ נְטוּיָה

11[15] The Arameans on the east, and the *Philistines*[16] on the west; And they devour Israel with open mouth. For all this His anger is not turned away, But His hand[17] is *stretched out still*[18].

---

[1] Isaiah 9:5 - 1QH 9.09-10, 3 Enoch 26:8, b.Sanhedrin 94a, Deuteronomy.R 1:20, Ein Yaakov Sanhedrin:94a, Genesis 27:40, Genesis.R 97:1, Isaiah 10:5 10:26-10:27 14:3-14:5 14:25 30:31-30:32 47:6 49:26 51:13 54:14, Jeremiah 30:8, Joseph and Aseneth 3:4, Judges 6:1-6:6 7:22-7:25 8:10-8:12, Leviticus 26:13, Mas.Perek Hashalom 1:11, Nahum 1:13, Numbers.R 2:10, Pesikta Rabbati 46:3, Psalms 83:10-83:12 125:3, Ruth.R 7:2
Isaiah 9:5 [LXX] - Hellenistic Synagogal Prayers 12:1
Isaiah 9:5-6 - Haftarah Yitro Part Two [continued from Isaiah 7:6 Ashkenaz; Isaiah 6:13 Teimon]
[2] 1QIsaa *he*
[3] LXX *the Messenger of great counsel: for I will bring peace upon the princes, and health to him*
[4] Isaiah 9:6 - 1 Samuel 14:19, 2 Thessalonians 1:8, Acts 2:3 2:19, Apocalypse of Elijah 2:6, b.Sanhedrin 94a, b.Shabbat 55a, Ein Yaakov Sanhedrin:94a, Ezekiel 39:8-39:10, Genesis.R 97:1, Isaiah 4:4 10:16-10:17 13:4 30:33 37:36 66:15-66:16, Jeremiah 47:3, Joel 2:5, Leviticus 3:11 3:16, Leviticus.R 36:6, Malachi 3:2-3:3, Mas.Soferim 7:3, Matthew 3:11, Nahum 3:2, Numbers.R 11:7, Psalms 46:10, Ruth.R 7:2, Testament of Solomon 12:3, There is a final mem in the middle of the word לְמַרְבֵּה; this is a case of ketiv and qere, where a word space was written but should not be read, y.Sanhedrin 10:1, z.Tzav 30b
[5] 1QIsaa masculine refers to *the throne*; MT feminine refers to *the kingdom*
[6] 1QIsaa masculine refers to *the throne*; MT feminine refers to *the kingdom*
[7] Isaiah 9:7 - 1 Corinthians 1:30 15:25, 1 John 4:10-4:14 5:20, 1 Timothy 3:16, 2 Corinthians 5:19, Acts 10:36 20:28, b.Chullin 91a, Colossians 1:20-1:21 2:3, Daniel 9:24-9:25, Deuteronomy 10:17, Ephesians 1:21-1:22 2:14-2:18, Hebrews 1:8 2:13-2:14 7:2-7:3 13:20, Isaiah 7:14 8:18 10:21 11:1-11:2 11:6-11:9 22:21-22:22 26:3 26:12 28:29 45:24-45:25 53:2 53:5 53:10 63:16 66:12, Jeremiah 23:5-23:6 31:23, John 1:1-1:2 1:14 1:16 3:16-3:17 14:27, Judges 13:18, Luke 1:35 2:11 2:14 21:15, Matthew 1:23 11:27 28:18, Micah 5:5-5:6, Nehemiah 9:32, Proverbs 8:23, Psalms 2:6-2:12 45:4 45:7 50:1 72:3 72:7 72:17 85:11 110:1-110:4, Revelation 19:16, Romans 5:1-5:10 8:32 9:5, Titus 2:13, Zechariah 6:12-6:13 9:9-9:10
[8] 1QIsaa *The LORD*
[9] Isaiah 9:8 - 1 Corinthians 15:24-15:28, 2 Kings 19:31, 2 Samuel 7:16, Daniel 2:35 2:44 7:14 7:27, Ezekiel 36:21-36:23, Hebrews 1:8, Isaiah 11:3-11:5 16:5 32:1-32:2 37:32 42:3-42:4 59:16-59:17 63:4-63:6, Jeremiah 23:5 33:15-33:21, Luke 1:32-33, Per Massorah: Soferim altered "Hashem" to "Adonai", Psalms 2:8 45:5-45:7 72:1-72:3 72:7-72:11 89:36-89:38, Revelation 19:11, the abbreviation וכ stands for וכגדל
[10] 1QIsaa *were evil*
[11] Isaiah 9:9 - Isaiah 7:7-7:8 8:4-8:8, Matthew 24:35, Micah 1:1-1:9, Zechariah 1:6 5:1-5:4
[12] LXX *and let us build for ourselves a tower*
[13] Isaiah 9:10 - 1 Kings 22:25, 1 Peter 5:5, Ezekiel 7:9 7:27 30:19 33:33, Isaiah 7:8-7:9 10:9-10:11 26:11 46:12 48:4, Jeremiah 32:24 44:28-44:29, Job 21:19-21:20, Malachi 3:13 3:19, mt.Pirkei Avot 4:22, Proverbs 16:18
Isaiah 9:10-11 - 4QIsab
[14] LXX *scatter*
[15] Isaiah 9:11 - 1 Kings 7:9-7:12 10:27, b.Bava Batra [Tosefot] 25a, Esther.R Petichata:11, Genesis.R 42:3 43:3, Jastrow 1059a, Lamentations.R 1:57, Leviticus.R 11:7 14:1, Malachi 1:4, Pesikta de R'Kahana 16:11, Pesikta Rabbati 33:13
Isaiah 9:11-12 - 4Q163 frags 4-7 ll.4-5
[16] LXX *Greeks*
[17] 1QIsaa plural; MT singular
[18] LXX *yet exalted*

וְהָעָם לֹא־שָׁב עַד־הַמַּכֵּהוּ וְאֶת־יְהוָה צְבָאוֹת לֹא דָרָשׁוּ

12[1] Yet the people do not turn to He who strikes them, nor do they seek the LORD of hosts.

וַיַּכְרֵת יְהוָה מִיִּשְׂרָאֵל רֹאשׁ וְזָנָב כִּפָּה וְאַגְמוֹן יוֹם אֶחָד

13[2] Therefore, the LORD cuts off from Israel head and tail, Palm-branch and rush, in one day.

זָקֵן וּנְשׂוּא־פָנִים הוּא הָרֹאשׁ וְנָבִיא מוֹרֶה־שֶּׁקֶר הוּא הַזָּנָב

14[3] The elder and the man of rank, he is the head; And the prophet who teaches lies, he is the tail.

וַיִּהְיוּ מְאַשְּׁרֵי הָעָם־הַזֶּה מַתְעִים וּמְאֻשָּׁרָיו מְבֻלָּעִים

15[4] For they who lead this people cause them to err; And they who are led are destroyed.

עַל־כֵּן עַל־בַּחוּרָיו לֹא־יִשְׂמַח אֲדֹנָי וְאֶת־יְתֹמָיו וְאֶת־אַלְמְנֹתָיו לֹא יְרַחֵם כִּי כֻלּוֹ חָנֵף וּמֵרַע וְכָל־פֶּה דֹּבֵר נְבָלָה בְּכָל־זֹאת לֹא־שָׁב אַפּוֹ וְעוֹד יָדוֹ נְטוּיָה

16[5] Therefore, the Lord shall *have no joy in*[6] their young men, nior shall He have compassion on their fatherless and widows; for everyone is ungodly and an evil-doer, And every mouth speaks wantonness. For all this His anger is not turned away, and His hand is *stretched out still*[7].

כִּי־בָעֲרָה כָאֵשׁ רִשְׁעָה שָׁמִיר וָשַׁיִת תֹּאכֵל וַתִּצַּת בְּסִבְכֵי הַיַּעַר וַיִּתְאַבְּכוּ גֵּאוּת עָשָׁן

17[8] For wickedness burns as the fire; It devours the briers and thorns; Yes, it kindles in the thickets of the forest, And they roll upward in thick clouds of smoke.

בְּעֶבְרַת יְהוָה צְבָאוֹת נֶעְתַּם אָרֶץ וַיְהִי הָעָם כְּמַאֲכֹלֶת אֵשׁ אִישׁ אֶל־אָחִיו לֹא יַחְמֹלוּ

18[9] Through the wrath of the LORD of hosts is the land burnt up; The people also are like the fuel of fire; No man spares his brother.

וַיִּגְזֹר עַל־יָמִין וְרָעֵב וַיֹּאכַל עַל־שְׂמֹאול וְלֹא שָׂבֵעוּ אִישׁ בְּשַׂר־זְרֹעוֹ יֹאכֵלוּ

19[10] And one snatches on the right hand, and is hungry; And he eats on the left hand, and is not satisfied; every man eats the flesh of his own arm:

מְנַשֶּׁה אֶת־אֶפְרַיִם וְאֶפְרַיִם אֶת־מְנַשֶּׁה יַחְדָּו הֵמָּה עַל־יְהוּדָה בְּכָל־זֹאת לֹא־שָׁב אַפּוֹ וְעוֹד יָדוֹ נְטוּיָה

20[11] *Manasseh, Ephraim; and Ephraim, Manasseh*[12]; And they together are against Judah. For all this His anger is not turned away, But His hand is *stretched out still*[13].

---

[1] Isaiah 9:12 - 2 Kings 15:29 16:9, Isaiah 7:8 8:4-7 10:9-11 17:1-5

[2] Isaiah 9:13 - 2 Chronicles 28:18, 2 Kings 16:6, Deuteronomy 31:17, Isaiah 5:25 9:18 9:22 10:4, Jeremiah 4:8 10:25 35:11, Psalms 79:7 129:3-6
Isaiah 9:13-16 - 4Q163 frags 4-7 ll.6-9

[3] Isaiah 9:14 - 2 Chronicles 28:22, Deuteronomy 4:29, Ecclesiastes.R 1:3, Ezekiel 24:13, Hosea 3:4-3:5 5:15 7:10 7:16, Isaiah 1:5 26:11 31:1 57:17, Jeremiah 5:3 29:11 31:19-31:21 50:4-50:5, Job 36:13, Midrash Tanchuma Shoftim 10

[4] Isaiah 9:15 - 2 Kings 17:6-17:20, Amos 2:14-2:16 3:12 5:2-5:3 6:11 7:8-7:9 7:17 9:1-9:9, Hosea 1:4 1:6 1:9 4:5 5:12-5:14 8:8 9:11-9:17 10:15 13:3, Isaiah 3:2-3:3 10:17 19:15 30:13, Micah 1:6-1:8, Revelation 18:8 18:10 18:17

[5] Isaiah 9:16 - 1 John 4:1, 1 Kings 13:18 22:22-22:24, 1 Samuel 9:6, 2 Corinthians 11:13-11:15, 2 Peter 2:1-2:3, 2 Thessalonians 2:9-2:12, 2 Timothy 4:2-4:3, b.Ketubot 8b, b.Shabbat 33a, Ein Yaakov Ketubot:8b, Ein Yaakov Shabbat:33a, Ezekiel 13:1-13:16 13:19 13:22, Galatians 1:8-1:9, Gates of Repentance 3.211 3.229, Hosea 9:8, Isaiah 3:2-3:3 3:5 5:13 28:17 29:10, Jeremiah 5:31 14:14-14:15 23:9 23:14-23:15 23:25-23:27 27:9-27:10 27:14-27:15 28:15-28:16 29:21-29:22, Lamentations.R 1:57, Malachi 2:9, Mas.Kallah Rabbati 3:15, Matthew 7:15 24:24, Mesillat Yesharim 11:Traits-of-Nekuyut, Pesikta de R'Kahana 16.11, Revelation 19:20

[6] 1QIsaa *spare*

[7] LXX *yet exalted*

[8] Isaiah 9:17 - 1 Kings 8:55-8:56, 2 Chronicles 30:27, Hebrews 7:7, Isaiah 3:12, Matthew 15:14 23:16-23:36, Numbers 6:23-6:26, Per Massorah: Soferim altered "Hashem" to "Adonai", Pesikta Rabbati 29/30:1
Isaiah 9:17-20 - 4Q163 frags 4-7 ll.14-19, 4QIsae

[9] Isaiah 9:18 - Ezekiel 20:33, Isaiah 1:4 5:25 9:13 9:22 10:2 10:4 10:6 13:18 27:11 32:6-32:7 62:5 65:19, Jeremiah 5:1 18:21, Job 15:34, Matthew 12:34 16:3, Micah 7:2, Psalms 147:10, Saadia Opinions 10:5, Zechariah 9:17

[10] Isaiah 9:19 - Amos 7:4, b.Bava Batra 25b, b.Shabbat 33a, b.Taanit 5a, Deuteronomy 32:22, Ein Yaakov Bava Batra:25b, Ein Yaakov Shabbat:33a, Ein Yaakov Taanit:5a, Ezekiel 21:3-20:4, Hebrews 6:8, Hosea 13:3, Isaiah 1:31 5:24 10:16-10:18 27:4 30:30 30:33 33:12 34:8-34:10 66:16-66:17, Job 31:11-31:12, Joel 2:20, Malachi 3:19, Mark 9:43-9:50, Matthew 13:49-13:50 25:41, Nahum 1:6 1:10, Numbers 11:1-11:3, Psalms 37:20 83:15, Revelation 14:11

[11] Isaiah 9:20 - 2 Peter 2:4, Acts 2:20, Amos 5:18, Ezekiel 9:5, Isaiah 1:31 5:30 8:22 13:9 13:13 13:18 24:6 24:11-24:12 60:2, Jeremiah 13:16, Joel 2:2, Matthew 27:45, Micah 7:2 7:6

[12] LXX *For Manasses shall eat the flesh of Ephraim, and Ephraim the flesh of Manasses*

[13] LXX *yet exalted*

Isaiah – Chapter 10

הוֹי הַחֹקְקִים חִקְקֵי־אָוֶן וּמְכַתְּבִים עָמָל כִּתֵּבוּ	1[1] Woe unto those who *decree*[2] unrighteous decrees, And to the writers who pen iniquity;
לְהַטּוֹת מִדִּין דַּלִּים וְלִגְזֹל מִשְׁפַּט עֲנִיֵּי עַמִּי לִהְיוֹת אַלְמָנוֹת שְׁלָלָם וְאֶת־יְתוֹמִים יָבֹזּוּ	2[3] To turn aside the needy from judgment, And to take away the right of the poor of My people, so widows may be their spoil, And so they may make the fatherless their prey!
וּמַה־תַּעֲשׂוּ לְיוֹם פְּקֻדָּה וּלְשׁוֹאָה מִמֶּרְחָק תָּבוֹא עַל־מִי תָּנוּסוּ לְעֶזְרָה וְאָנָה תַעַזְבוּ כְּבוֹדְכֶם	3[4] And what will you do in the day of visitation, And in the ruin which shall come from far? To whom will you flee for help? And where will you leave your glory?
בִּלְתִּי כָרַע תַּחַת אַסִּיר וְתַחַת הֲרוּגִים יִפֹּלוּ בְּכָל־זֹאת לֹא־שָׁב אַפּוֹ וְעוֹד יָדוֹ נְטוּיָה	4[5] They can do nothing except crouch under *the captives*[6], And fall under the slain.
הוֹי אַשּׁוּר שֵׁבֶט אַפִּי וּמַטֶּה־הוּא בְיָדָם זַעְמִי	5[7] O Asshur, the rod of My anger, In whose hand as a staff is My indignation!
בְּגוֹי חָנֵף אֲשַׁלְּחֶנּוּ וְעַל־עַם עֶבְרָתִי אֲצַוֶּנּוּ לִשְׁלֹל שָׁלָל וְלָבֹז בַּז וּלְשׂימוֹ וּלְשׂוּמוֹ מִרְמָס כְּחֹמֶר חוּצוֹת	6[8] I send him against an ungodly nation, And against the people of My wrath I give him a charge, To take the spoil, and to *take the prey, And to walk on them like mire in the streets*[9].
וְהוּא לֹא־כֵן יְדַמֶּה וּלְבָבוֹ לֹא־כֵן יַחְשֹׁב כִּי לְהַשְׁמִיד בִּלְבָבוֹ וּלְהַכְרִית גּוֹיִם לֹא מְעָט	7[10] Yet he does not intend this, nor does his heart think so; But it is in his heart to destroy, And to cut off nations not a few.
כִּי יֹאמַר הֲלֹא שָׂרַי יַחְדָּו מְלָכִים	8[11] *For he says: 'Are not all my princes kings*[12]?
הֲלֹא כְּכַרְכְּמִישׁ כַּלְנוֹ אִם־לֹא כְאַרְפַּד חֲמָת אִם־לֹא כְדַמֶּשֶׂק שֹׁמְרוֹן	9[13] *Is not Calno as Carchemish? Is not Hamath as Arpad? Is not Samaria as Damascus*[14]?
כַּאֲשֶׁר מָצְאָה יָדִי לְמַמְלְכֹת הָאֱלִיל וּפְסִילֵיהֶם מִירוּשָׁלִַם וּמִשֹּׁמְרוֹן	10[15] As my hand has reached the kingdoms of the idols, Whose graven images exceeded them of Jerusalem and of Samaria;
הֲלֹא כַּאֲשֶׁר עָשִׂיתִי לְשֹׁמְרוֹן וְלֶאֱלִילֶיהָ כֵּן אֶעֱשֶׂה לִירוּשָׁלִַם וְלַעֲצַבֶּיהָ	11[16] Shall I not, as I have done to Samaria and her idols, do so to Jerusalem and her idols?'

---

[1] Isaiah 10:1 - 1 Kings 21:13, Daniel 6:9-6:10, Esther 3:10-3:13, Habakkuk 2:6 2:9 2:12 2:15 2:19, Isaiah 3:11 5:8 5:11 5:18 5:20-5:22, Jeremiah 22:13, John 9:22 19:6, Jude 1:11, Leviticus.R 35:5, Luke 11:42-11:44 11:46-11:47 11:52, Matthew 11:21 23:13-23:16 23:23 23:27 23:29 26:24, Micah 3:1-3:4 3:9-3:11 6:16, Psalms 58:3 94:20-94:21
Isaiah 10:1-10 - 4QIsae
Isaiah 10:1-34 - 1QIsaa
[2] 1QIsaa *ones enacting*
[3] Isaiah 10:2 - 4Q266 frag 3 2.22, Amos 2:7 5:11-5:12, Cairo Damascus 6:16-17, Cairo Damascus 6.16-17, Ezekiel 22:7, Isaiah 1:23 3:14 5:7 5:23 29:21, Jeremiah 7:6, Lamentations 3:35, Malachi 3:5, Matthew 23:13
[4] Isaiah 10:3 - 1 Peter 2:12, 2 Kings 7:6-7:8 7:15, Deuteronomy 28:49, Ezekiel 24:13-24:14, Genesis 31:1, Hosea 5:13 9:7, Isaiah 2:20-2:21 5:14 5:26 20:6 26:21 30:1-30:3 30:16 30:27-30:28 31:1-31:3 33:14 39:3 39:6-39:7, Jeremiah 5:31, Job 31:14, Luke 19:44, Proverbs 11:4, Psalms 49:17-49:18, Revelation 6:15-6:16, Zephaniah 1:18
[5] Isaiah 10:4 - Deuteronomy 31:15-18 32:30, Hosea 9:12, Isaiah 5:25 9:13 9:18 9:22 22:2 24:22 34:3 66:16, Jeremiah 37:10, Leviticus 26:17 26:36-37
[6] 1QIsaa *those in fetters*
[7] Isaiah 10:5 - Genesis 10:11, Isaiah 8:4 10:15 13:5 14:5-14:6 14:25 30:30 66:14, Jeremiah 51:20-51:24, Midrash Psalms 17:10, Pesikta Rabbati 29/30A:8, Psalms 17:14 125:3, Saadia Opinions 4:5, Zephaniah 2:13
Isaiah 10:5-11 - Psalms of Solomon 2:24
[8] Isaiah 10:6 - 2 Samuel 22:43, Guide for the Perplexed 2:47, Isaiah 5:29 9:18 9:20 10:13-10:14 19:17 22:5 29:13 30:9-30:11 33:14 37:26-37:27 41:25 45:1-45:5 63:3 63:6, Jeremiah 3:10 4:14 25:9 34:22 47:6-47:7, Leviticus.R 12:5, Matthew 15:7, Micah 7:10, Saadia Opinions 5:3, Zechariah 10:5
[9] LXX *make them dust*
[10] Isaiah 10:7 - Acts 2:23 13:27-13:30, Genesis 50:20, Isaiah 36:18-36:20 37:11-13, Micah 4:11-12
[11] Isaiah 10:8 - 2 Kings 18:24 19:10, Daniel 2:37, Ezekiel 26:7, Isaiah 36:8
[12] LXX *And if they should say to him, you alone are ruler*
[13] Isaiah 10:9 - 2 Chronicles 35:20, 2 Kings 16:9 17:5-17:6 17:24 18:9-18:10, 2 Samuel 8:9, Amos 6:1-6:2, Genesis 10:10, Isaiah 7:8 17:3 36:19 37:13, Jeremiah 46:2 49:23
[14] LXX *then shall he say, Have I not taken the country above Babylon and Chalanes, where the tower was built? and have I not taken Arabia, and Damascus, and Samaria*
[15] Isaiah 10:10 - 2 Chronicles 32:12-16 32:19, 2 Kings 18:33-35 19:12-13 19:17-19, Isaiah 10:14, Leviticus.R 33:6, Midrash Psalms 18:18, Numbers.R 15:14, Sifre Devarim Ha'azinu Hashamayim 318, Sifre Devarim Nitzavim 318, Song of Songs.R 6:14
[16] Isaiah 10:11 - Isaiah 2:8 36:19-36:20 37:10-37:13

וְהָיָ֗ה כִּֽי־יְבַצַּ֤ע אֲדֹנָי֙ אֶת־כָּל־מַֽעֲשֵׂ֔הוּ בְּהַ֥ר צִיּ֖וֹן וּבִירֽוּשָׁלִָ֑ם אֶפְקֹ֗ד עַל־פְּרִי־גֹ֙דֶל֙ לְבַ֣ב מֶֽלֶךְ־אַשּׁ֔וּר וְעַל־תִּפְאֶ֖רֶת ר֥וּם עֵינָֽיו	12[1]	When it shall come to pass, when the Lord has performed His whole work on mount Zion and on Jerusalem, I will punish the fruit of the arrogant heart of the king of Assyria, and the glory of his haughty looks.
כִּ֣י אָמַ֗ר בְּכֹ֤חַ יָדִי֙ עָשִׂ֔יתִי וּבְחָכְמָתִ֖י כִּ֣י נְבֻנ֑וֹתִי וְאָסִ֣יר ׀ גְּבוּלֹ֣ת עַמִּ֗ים 'וַעֲתִידֹֽתֵיהֶם' "וַעֲתוּדֹֽתֵיהֶם" שׁוֹשֵׂ֔תִי וְאוֹרִ֥יד כַּאבִּ֖יר יוֹשְׁבִֽים	13[2]	For he has said: By the strength of my hand I have done it, And by my wisdom, for I am prudent; In that I have removed the bounds of the peoples, And have robbed their treasures, And have brought down as one mighty the inhabitants;
וַתִּמְצָ֨א כַקֵּ֤ן ׀ יָדִי֙ לְחֵ֣יל הָֽעַמִּ֔ים וְכֶאֱסֹף֙ בֵּיצִ֣ים עֲזֻב֔וֹת כָּל־הָאָ֖רֶץ אֲנִ֣י אָסָ֑פְתִּי וְלֹ֤א הָיָה֙ נֹדֵ֣ד כָּנָ֔ף וּפֹצֶ֥ה פֶ֖ה וּמְצַפְצֵֽף	14[3]	And my hand has found as a nest the riches of the peoples; And as one gathers eggs that are forsaken, I have gathered all the earth; And there was no one *who moved the wing, Or that opened mouth, or chirped*[4].
הֲיִתְפָּאֵר֙ הַגַּרְזֶ֔ן עַ֖ל הַחֹצֵ֣ב בּ֑וֹ אִם־יִתְגַּדֵּ֤ל הַמַּשּׂוֹר֙ עַל־מְנִיפ֔וֹ כְּהָנִ֥יף שֵׁ֙בֶט֙ וְאֶת־מְרִימָ֔יו כְּהָרִ֥ים מַטֶּ֖ה לֹא־עֵֽץ	15[5]	Should the axe boast itself against he who hews with it? Should the saw magnify itself against he who moves it? *As if a rod should move those who lift it up, Or as if a staff should lift up he who is not wood*[6].
לָ֠כֵן יְשַׁלַּ֨ח הָאָד֜וֹן יְהוָ֧ה צְבָא֛וֹת בְּמִשְׁמַנָּ֖יו רָז֑וֹן וְתַ֧חַת כְּבֹד֛וֹ יֵקַ֥ד יְקֹ֖ד כִּיק֥וֹד אֵֽשׁ	16[7]	Therefore, will the Lord, the LORD of hosts, Send *among his fat ones leanness; And under his glory a burning like the burning of fire shall be kindled*[8].
וְהָיָ֤ה אֽוֹר־יִשְׂרָאֵל֙ לְאֵ֔שׁ וּקְדוֹשׁ֖וֹ לְלֶהָבָ֑ה וּבָעֲרָ֗ה וְאָֽכְלָ֛ה שִׁית֥וֹ וּשְׁמִיר֖וֹ בְּי֥וֹם אֶחָֽד	17[9]	And the light of Israel shall be for a fire, And his Holy One for a flame; *And it shall burn and devour his thorns And his briers in one day*[10].
וּכְב֤וֹד יַעְרוֹ֙ וְכַרְמִלּ֔וֹ מִנֶּ֥פֶשׁ וְעַד־בָּשָׂ֖ר יְכַלֶּ֑ה וְהָיָ֖ה כִּמְסֹ֥ס נֹסֵֽס	18[11]	*And the glory of his forest and of his fruitful field, He will consume both soul and body; And it shall be as when a sick man wastes away*[12].

---

[1] Isaiah 10:12 - 1 Peter 4:17, 2 Kings 19:31, Daniel 4:34, Ezekiel 31:10 31:14, Isaiah 2:11 5:15 9:10 10:5-10:6 10:16-10:19 10:25-10:34 14:24-14:27 17:12-17:14 27:9 28:21-28:22 29:7-29:8 30:30-30:33 31:5-31:9 37:36-37:38 46:10-46:11 50:11 65:7, Jeremiah 50:18, Job 40:11-40:12, Matthew 12:33 15:19, Midrash Tanchuma Beshallach 10, Per Massorah: Soferim altered "Hashem" to "Adonai", Proverbs 30:13, Psalms 18:28 21:11 76:11, Saadia Opinions 4:5 10:12

[2] Isaiah 10:13 - 1 Chronicles 5:26, 2 Kings 15:29 16:8 17:6 17:24 18:11 18:15 18:32 19:22-19:24, Amos 5:27-6:2 6:13, b.Berachot 28a, b.Yevamot [Tosefot] 76b, b.Yoma 54a, Bahir 45, Daniel 4:27, Deuteronomy 8:17, Ein Yaakov Berachot:28a, Ezekiel 25:3 26:2 28:2-28:9 29:3, Gates of Repentance 3.175, Genesis.R 89:6, Habakkuk 1:16, Hosea 13:15-13:16, Isaiah 10:8 37:23-37:25, m.Yadayim 4:4, Midrash Tanchuma Massei 13, Midrash Tanchuma Metzora 4, Pirkei de R'Eliezer 44, Saadia Opinions 10:12, t.Yadayim 2:17

[3] Isaiah 10:14 - Habakkuk 2:5-2:11, Hosea 12:9-12:10, Isaiah 5:8, Jastrow 1296a, Jeremiah 49:16, Job 31:25, Mekilta de R'Ishmael Beshallah 2:131, Midrash Tanchuma Metzora 4, Nahum 2:10-3:2, Numbers.R 13:14, Obadiah 1:4, Proverbs 18:12 21:6-21:7, Tanna Devei Eliyahu 7, y.Avodah Zarah 3:1

[4] LXX *who shall escape me, or contradict me*

[5] Isaiah 10:15 - Ahiqar 104, Ezekiel 28:9, Isaiah 10:5 29:16 45:9, Jeremiah 51:20-51:23, Psalms 17:13-17:14, Romans 9:20-9:21, Saadia Opinions 1:3, z.Bereshit 31b

[6] LXX *as if one should lift a rod or staff? but it shall not be so*

[7] Isaiah 10:16 - 2 Chronicles 32:21, Acts 12:23, b.Sanhedrin 94a 95b, b.Shabbat 113b, Ein Yaakov Sanhedrin:94a, Ein Yaakov Sanhedrin:95b, Ein Yaakov Shabbat:113b, Exodus.R 18:5, Isaiah 5:17 8:7 9:6 10:18 14:24-14:27 17:4 29:5-29:8 30:30-30:33 33:10-33:14 37:6-37:7 37:29 37:36, Leviticus.R 7:6, Midrash Psalms 11:5, Midrash Tanchuma Tzav 2, Psalms 106:15 Isaiah 10:16-19 - 1QIsab

[8] LXX *dishonor upon your honor, and burning fire shall be kindled upon your glory*

[9] Isaiah 10:17 - 2 Thessalonians 1:7-1:9, Deuteronomy.R 1:12, Exodus.R 15:26, Hebrews 12:29, Isaiah 9:19 27:4 30:27-30:28 31:9 33:14 37:23 37:36 60:19 64:2-64:3 66:15-66:16 66:24, Jeremiah 4:4 7:20, Malachi 3:19-4:21, Matthew 3:12, Midrash Psalms 22:2 22:11 27:1, Nahum 1:5-1:6 1:10, Numbers 11:1-11:3 16:35, Pesikta Rabbati 11:7, Psalms 18:9 21:10 27:1 50:3 83:15-83:16 84:12 97:3, Revelation 21:23 22:5, z.Terumah 149b Isaiah 10:17-19 - 4Q163 6-7 ii 2-9, 4Q163 frags 6-7 2.2-3

[10] LXX *and it shall devour the wood as grass*

[11] Isaiah 10:18 - 2 Kings 19:23 19:28, b.Sanhedrin [Rashi] 98a, Ezekiel 21:3-20:4, Isaiah 9:19 10:33-10:34, Jeremiah 21:14, Midrash Psalms 79:5, Tanya Igeret Hakodesh §09

[12] LXX *In that day the mountains shall be consumed, and the hills, and the forests, and fire shall devour both soul and body: and he who flees shall be as one fleeing from burning flame*

19[1] וּשְׁאָר עֵץ יַעְרוֹ מִסְפָּר יִהְיוּ וְנַעַר יִכְתְּבֵם

And the remnant of the trees of his forest shall be few[2], *so a child may write them down.*

20[3] וְהָיָה בַּיּוֹם הַהוּא לֹא־יוֹסִיף עוֹד שְׁאָר יִשְׂרָאֵל וּפְלֵיטַת בֵּית־יַעֲקֹב לְהִשָּׁעֵן עַל־מַכֵּהוּ וְנִשְׁעַן עַל־יְהוָה קְדוֹשׁ יִשְׂרָאֵל בֶּאֱמֶת

And it shall come to pass in that day, That the remnant of Israel, And they who escaped from the house of Jacob, Shall not again lean on he who struck them; But shall lean upon the LORD, the Holy One of Israel, in truth.

21[4] שְׁאָר יָשׁוּב שְׁאָר יַעֲקֹב אֶל־אֵל גִּבּוֹר

A remnant shall return, the remnant of Jacob, to God the Mighty.

22[5] כִּי אִם־יִהְיֶה עַמְּךָ יִשְׂרָאֵל כְּחוֹל הַיָּם שְׁאָר יָשׁוּב בּוֹ כִּלָּיוֹן חָרוּץ שׁוֹטֵף צְדָקָה

For though your people, O Israel, are as the sand of the sea, Only a remnant shall return; *An extermination is determined, overflowing with righteousness*[6].

23[7] כִּי כָלָה וְנֶחֱרָצָה אֲדֹנָי יְהוִה צְבָאוֹת עֹשֶׂה בְּקֶרֶב כָּל־הָאָרֶץ

For an extermination wholly determined Shall the Lord, the GOD of hosts, make in the midst of all the earth[8].

24[9] לָכֵן כֹּה־אָמַר אֲדֹנָי יְהוִה צְבָאוֹת אַל־תִּירָא עַמִּי יֹשֵׁב צִיּוֹן מֵאַשּׁוּר בַּשֵּׁבֶט יַכֶּכָּה וּמַטֵּהוּ יִשָּׂא־עָלֶיךָ בְּדֶרֶךְ מִצְרָיִם

Therefore, thus says the Lord, the GOD of hosts: O My people who live in Zion, do not fear *Asshur, though he strikes you with the rod, and*[10] lifts up his staff against you, after the manner of Egypt.

25[11] כִּי־עוֹד מְעַט מִזְעָר וְכָלָה זַעַם וְאַפִּי עַל־תַּבְלִיתָם

For yet a very little while, and the indignation shall be accomplished, and My anger shall be to their destruction.

26[12] וְעוֹרֵר עָלָיו יְהוָה צְבָאוֹת שׁוֹט כְּמַכַּת מִדְיָן בְּצוּר עוֹרֵב וּמַטֵּהוּ עַל־הַיָּם וּנְשָׂאוֹ בְּדֶרֶךְ מִצְרָיִם

And the LORD of hosts *shall stir up against him a scourge*[13], as in the slaughter of Midian at the Rock of Oreb; and as His rod was over the sea, so shall He lift it up after the manner of Egypt.

27[14] וְהָיָה בַּיּוֹם הַהוּא יָסוּר סֻבֳּלוֹ מֵעַל שִׁכְמֶךָ וְעֻלּוֹ מֵעַל צַוָּארֶךָ וְחֻבַּל עֹל מִפְּנֵי־שָׁמֶן

And it shall come to pass in that day, His burden shall depart from off your shoulder, And his yoke from off your neck, And the yoke shall be destroyed *because of fatness*[15].

---

[1] Isaiah 10:19 - 4Q163 frags 6-7 2.1, 4Q163 frags 6-7 2.5, b.Sanhedrin 95b, Ein Yaakov Sanhedrin:95b, Isaiah 21:17 37:36, Jastrow 1025a, Lamentations.R 4:15 4:15, Midrash Psalms 79:1
Isaiah 10:19-23 - Odes of Solomon 11:22

[2] LXX *And they who are left of them shall be a small number*

[3] Isaiah 10:20 - 2 Chronicles 28:20, 2 Kings 16:7, Ezra 9:14, Hosea 5:13 14:5, Isaiah 1:9 4:2-4:3 6:13 11:11 17:7-17:8 26:3-26:4 37:4 37:31-37:32 48:1-48:2 50:10, Romans 9:27-9:29
Isaiah 10:20-22 - 4Q163 6-7 ii 10-17, 4Q163 frags 6-7 2.10-13

[4] Isaiah 10:21 - 2 Corinthians 3:14-16, Acts 26:20, Hosea 6:1 7:10 7:16 14:3, Isaiah 7:3 9:7 9:14 19:22 55:7 65:8-65:9, z.Toledot 146b

[5] Isaiah 10:22 - 1 Kings 4:20, Acts 17:31, Daniel 9:27, Genesis 18:25, Hosea 2:1, Isaiah 6:11 6:13 8:8 27:10-27:11 28:15-28:22, Revelation 20:8, Romans 2:5 3:5-3:6 9:27-9:28 11:5-11:6
Isaiah 10:22-23 - 4Q161 2.5, 4Q161 2+3+4 1-9, 4Q163 frags 6-7 2.14-17

[6] Missing in LXX

[7] Isaiah 10:23 - Daniel 4:32, Isaiah 14:26-14:27 24:1-24:23 28:22, Romans 9:28, y.Berachot 2:8
Isaiah 10:23-33 - 4QIsac

[8] LXX *He will finish the work, and cut it short in righteousness: because the Lord will make a short work in all the world*

[9] Isaiah 10:24 - 4Q163 frags 6-7 2.19, Exodus 1:10-1:16 5:14 14:9 14:21-14:31 15:6-15:10, Hebrews 12:22-12:24, Isaiah 4:3 8:12-8:13 9:5 10:5 12:6 14:29 27:7 30:19 33:14-33:16 35:4 37:6 37:22 37:33-37:35 46:13 61:3, Psalms 87:5-87:6, z.Vaetchanan 269b
Isaiah 10:24-27 - 4Q161 2.10-15, 4Q161 2+3+4 9-14

[10] 1QIsaa *the Assyrian, of the rod that strikes you*

[11] Isaiah 10:25 - 2 Kings 19:35, Daniel 11:36, Hebrews 10:37, Isaiah 10:5 10:33-10:34 12:1-12:2 14:24-14:25 17:12-17:14 30:30-30:33 31:4-31:9 37:36-37:38 54:7, Psalms 37:10

[12] Isaiah 10:26 - 2 Kings 19:35, Exodus 14:16 14:25-27, Habakkuk 3:7-15, Isaiah 9:5 10:16-19 10:24 11:16 37:36-38 51:9-10, Judges 7:25, Nehemiah 9:10-11, Psalms 35:23 83:12 106:10-11, Revelation 11:18 19:15

[13] 1QIsaa *will brandish a whip against it*

[14] Isaiah 10:27 - 1 John 2:20 2:27, 2 Kings 18:13-18:14, 2 Samuel 1:21, Acts 4:27, b.Sanhedrin [Rashi] 20a, b.Sanhedrin 94b, Daniel 9:24-9:26, Ein Yaakov Sanhedrin:94b, Isaiah 9:5 14:25 37:35, John 1:41, Luke 4:18, Nahum 1:9-1:13, Psalms 2:1-2:3 2:6 20:7 45:8 84:10 89:21-89:53 105:15 132:10 132:17-132:18, Song of Songs.R 1:21

[15] LXX *from off your shoulders*

בָּא עַל־עַיַּת עָבַר בְּמִגְרוֹן לְמִכְמָשׂ יַפְקִיד כֵּלָיו	28[1]	He shall come *to*[2] *Aiath*[3], He shall pass through *Migron*[4]; At Michmas he lays up his baggage;
עָבְרוּ מַעְבָּרָה גֶּבַע מָלוֹן לָנוּ חָרְדָה הָרָמָה גִּבְעַת שָׁאוּל נָסָה	29[5]	They have gone over the pass; *They have taken up their lodging at Geba; Ramah trembles; Gibeath-shaul is fled*[6].
צַהֲלִי קוֹלֵךְ בַּת־גַּלִּים הַקְשִׁיבִי לַיְשָׁה עֲנִיָּה עֲנָתוֹת	30[7]	Cry with a shrill voice, O daughter of Gallim! Listen, O Laish! O you poor Anathoth!
נָדְדָה מַדְמֵנָה יֹשְׁבֵי הַגֵּבִים הֵעִיזוּ	31[8]	*Madmenah*[9] is in insane flight; The inhabitants of Gebim flee for cover.
עוֹד הַיּוֹם בְּנֹב לַעֲמֹד יְנֹפֵף יָדוֹ הַר 'בֵּית־בַּת־צִיּוֹן' גִּבְעַת יְרוּשָׁלִָם	32[10]	This very day shall he halt at Nob, Shaking his hand at the mount of the daughter of Zion, The hill of Jerusalem.
הִנֵּה הָאָדוֹן יְהוָה צְבָאוֹת מְסָעֵף פֻּארָה בְּמַעֲרָצָה וְרָמֵי הַקּוֹמָה גְּדֻעִים וְהַגְּבֹהִים יִשְׁפָּלוּ	33[11]	Behold, the Lord, the LORD of hosts, Shall lop the boughs with terror; And the high ones of stature shall be hewn down, And the lofty shall be laid low.
וְנִקַּף סִבְכֵי הַיַּעַר בַּבַּרְזֶל וְהַלְּבָנוֹן בְּאַדִּיר יִפּוֹל	34[12]	And *He shall cut down the thickets of the forest with iron*[13], And Lebanon shall fall by a mighty one.

Isaiah – Chapter 11

וְיָצָא חֹטֶר מִגֵּזַע יִשָׁי וְנֵצֶר מִשָּׁרָשָׁיו יִפְרֶה	1[14]	And there shall come forth a shoot from the stock of Jesse, And a *twig*[15] shall grow forth from his roots.
וְנָחָה עָלָיו רוּחַ יְהוָה רוּחַ חָכְמָה וּבִינָה רוּחַ עֵצָה וּגְבוּרָה רוּחַ דַּעַת וְיִרְאַת יְהוָה	2[16]	And the spirit of the LORD shall rest upon him, The spirit of wisdom and understanding, The

---

[1] Isaiah 10:28 - 1 Samuel 13:2 13:5 14:2 14:5 14:31 17:22, b.Bava Kamma [Tosefot] 60b, b.Sanhedrin 94b, Joshua 7:2, Judges 18:21, Nehemiah 11:31
Isaiah 10:28-32 - 4Q161 2.21-25, 4Q161 5+6 19-23, Ein Yaakov Sanhedrin:94b, Seder Olam 23:Sennacherib
[2] 1QIsaa *on*
[3] LXX *Angai*
[4] LXX *Maggedo*
[5] Isaiah 10:29 - 1 Kings 15:23, 1 Samuel 7:17 11:4 13:2 13:16 13:23 14:4 15:34, b.Avodah Zara [Tosefot] 65a, b.Sanhedrin 94b, b.Taanit 5a, Hosea 5:8 9:9 10:9, Jeremiah 31:16, Joshua 18:24-18:25 21:17, Judges 19:12-19:15
[6] LXX *and shall arrive at Angai: fear shall seize upon Rama, the city of Saul*
[7] Isaiah 10:30 - 1 Kings 2:26, 1 Samuel 25:44, b.Sanhedrin 94b 95a, Jastrow 689b 710a 1097b 1269b, Jeremiah 1:1 32:8, Joshua 21:18, Judges 18:7 18:29, Lamentations.R Petichata D'Chakimei:1, Pesikta de R'Kahana 13.1, z.Noach 63a, z.Vayechi 249a
[8] Isaiah 10:31 - b.Sanhedrin 94b, Joshua 15:31
[9] 1QIsaa *Marmenah*; LXX *Madebena*
[10] Isaiah 10:32 - 1 Samuel 21:1 22:19, b.Megillah 31a, b.Sanhedrin 94b 95a, b.Sanhedrin 94b 95a, Ein Yaakov Sanhedrin:95a, Isaiah 1:8 2:2 10:24 11:15 13:2 19:16 37:22, Jastrow 561a, Jeremiah 6:23, Mekhilta de R'Shimon bar Yochai Shirata 32:1, Mekhilta de R'Ishmael Shirata 2:83, Nehemiah 11:32, Sifre Devarim Devarim 6, z.Beshallach 49b, z.Pekudei 224a, Zechariah 2:9
Isaiah 10:32 [Targum] - Midrash Tanchuma Vayikra 8
Isaiah 10:32-12:6 - Haftarah 8th day Pesach [Chutz L'Aretz], mt.Hilchot Tefilah 13:8
[11] Isaiah 10:33 - 2 Chronicles 32:21, 2 Kings 19:21-19:37, Amos 2:9, b.Sotah 5a, Daniel 4:34, Ein Yaakov Sotah:4b, Isaiah 2:11-2:17 10:16-10:19 37:24-37:36 37:38, Job 40:11-40:12, Luke 14:11, Mesillat Yesharim 22:Trait of Anavah, mt.Pirkei Avot 4:4
Isaiah 10:33-34 - 4Q161 3.5-7, 4Q161 8+9+10 5-14
[12] Isaiah 10:34 - 2 Peter 2:11, 2 Thessalonians 1:7, Avot de R'Natan 4, b.Bava Kamma [Tosefot] 119b, b.Gittin [Rashi] 59b, b.Gittin 56b, b.Shabbat [Rashi] 62b, b.Sotah [Rashi] 48a, Daniel 4:10-4:11 4:20, Ein Yaakov Gittin:56b, Isaiah 10:18 31:8 37:24 37:36, Jeremiah 22:7 46:22-23 48:2, Lamentations.R 1:31 1:51, Mekhilta de R'Shimon bar Yochai Amalek 45:1, Mekhilta de R'Ishmael Amalek 2:45, Midrash Proverbs 15, Midrash Psalms 29:2, Nahum 1:4, Psalms 103:20, Revelation 10:1 18:21, Sifre Devarim Devarim 6, Sifre Devarim Vaetchanan 28, y.Berachot 2:4, Zechariah 11:1-2
Isaiah 10:34-11:1 - 11Q14 frag 1 1.11, 4Q285 5 1-3, 4Q285 frag 7 ll.1-3
[13] LXX *the lofty ones shall fall by the sword*
[14] Isaiah 11:1 - 1 Samuel 17:58, Acts 13:22-13:23, Isaiah 4:2 9:8 11:10 53:2, Jeremiah 23:5 33:15, Lamentations.R 1:51, Luke 2:23-2:32, Matthew 1:6-1:16, Midrash Psalms 72:3, Pesikta Rabbati 33:6, Revelation 5:5 22:16, Romans 15:12, Ruth 4:17, Sibylline Oracles 6.16 6.8 7.38 8.254, Testament of Judah 24:4, y.Berachot 2:4, Zechariah 3:8 6:12
Isaiah 11:1-3 - Testament of Levi 2:3
Isaiah 11:1-5 - 4Q161 3.15-20, 4Q161 8+9+10 15-29
Isaiah 11:1-10 - mt.Hilchot Melachim u'Michamoteihem 11:2
Isaiah 11:1-16 - 1QIsaa
[15] LXX *blossom*
[16] Isaiah 11:2 - 1 Corinthians 1:30, 1QSb 5:25, 1QSb 5.24-26, 2 Timothy 1:7, 3 Enoch 23:9, Acts 10:38, b.Sanhedrin 93b, Colossians

spirit of counsel and might, The spirit of knowledge and *of the fear of the LORD*[1].

3[2] וַהֲרִיחוֹ בְּיִרְאַת יְהוָה וְלֹא־לְמַרְאֵה עֵינָיו יִשְׁפּוֹט וְלֹא־לְמִשְׁמַע אָזְנָיו יוֹכִיחַ

And his delight shall be in the fear of the LORD[3]; And he will not judge from the sight of his eyes, nor decide from the hearing of his ears;

4[4] וְשָׁפַט בְּצֶדֶק דַּלִּים וְהוֹכִיחַ בְּמִישׁוֹר לְעַנְוֵי־אָרֶץ וְהִכָּה־אֶרֶץ בְּשֵׁבֶט פִּיו וּבְרוּחַ שְׂפָתָיו יָמִית רָשָׁע

But he shall judge the poor with righteousness, and decide with equity for the meek of the land; And he shall strike the land with the rod of his mouth, And with the breath of his lips he shall slay the wicked[5].

5[6] וְהָיָה צֶדֶק אֵזוֹר מָתְנָיו וְהָאֱמוּנָה אֵזוֹר חֲלָצָיו

And righteousness shall be the girdle of his loins, And *faithfulness the girdle of his reins*[7].

6[8] וְגָר זְאֵב עִם־כֶּבֶשׂ וְנָמֵר עִם־גְּדִי יִרְבָּץ וְעֵגֶל וּכְפִיר וּמְרִיא יַחְדָּו וְנַעַר קָטֹן נֹהֵג בָּם

And the wolf shall live with the lamb, And the leopard shall lie down with the kid; And the calf and the young lion *and the fatling*[9] together; And a little child shall lead them.

7[10] וּפָרָה וָדֹב תִּרְעֶינָה יַחְדָּו יִרְבְּצוּ יַלְדֵיהֶן וְאַרְיֵה כַּבָּקָר יֹאכַל־תֶּבֶן

And the cow and the bear feed; Their young ones shall lie down together[11]; And the lion shall eat straw like the ox.

8[12] וְשִׁעֲשַׁע יוֹנֵק עַל־חֻר פָּתֶן וְעַל מְאוּרַת צִפְעוֹנִי גָּמוּל יָדוֹ הָדָה

And the sucking child shall *play*[13] on the hole of the asp, *and the weaned child shall put his hand on the basilisk's den*[14].

9[15] לֹא־יָרֵעוּ וְלֹא־יַשְׁחִיתוּ בְּכָל־הַר קָדְשִׁי כִּי־מָלְאָה הָאָרֶץ דֵּעָה אֶת־יְהוָה כַּמַּיִם לַיָּם מְכַסִּים

They shall not hurt nor destroy in all my holy mountain; for the earth *shall be full of the*

1:8-1:9 2:2-2:3, Deuteronomy 34:9, Ein Yaakov Sanhedrin:93b, Ephesians 1:17-1:18, Genesis.R 2:4 8:1 97:1, Isaiah 42:1 48:16 59:21 61:1, James 3:17-3:18, Jastrow 798b 852a, John 1:32-1:33 3:34 14:17 15:26 16:13, Matthew 3:16, Mekilta de R'Ishmael Pisha 1:156, Numbers 11:25-11:26, Numbers.R 10:5 13:11 14:10, Pesikta Rabbati 33:6, Pirkei de R'Eliezer 3, Psalms of Solomon 17:37, Ruth.R 7:2, Testament of Judah 24:2, Testament of Levi 18:7, Upon taking the Sefer Torah from the ark on Holidays [Ribbon Shel Olam], z.Tetzaveh 179b, z.Vayera 103b

[1] LXX *godliness shall fill him*

[2] Isaiah 11:3 - 1 Corinthians 2:13-2:15 4:3-4:5, 1 Kings 3:9 3:28, 1 Samuel 16:7, 2 Samuel 14:17, b.Sanhedrin 93b, Bahir 187, Ein Yaakov Sanhedrin:93b, Hebrews 5:14, Isaiah 33:6, Jastrow 1473b, Job 12:11 34:3, John 2:25 7:24 8:15-8:16, Luke 2:52, Midrash Psalms 72:3, Perek Shirah, Philippians 1:9-1:10, Proverbs 2:5 2:9, z.Vayakhel 213b

[3] LXX *the spirit of the fear of God*; These seven attributes: with the first and the seven, the second and the sixth, and he third and the fifth tying together like the branches of the menorah. The fourth attribute is the foundation of the menorah.

[4] Isaiah 11:4 - 1 Kings 10:8-10:9, 1QSb 5:21-22 1QSb 5:24-25, 1QSb 5:21-22, 1QSb 5:24-26, 2 Baruch 40:2 4 Ezra 13:10, 2 Corinthians 10:1, 2 Samuel 8:15 23:2-23:4, 2 Thessalonians 2:8, Acts 9:1, b.Sanhedrin 93b, Galatians 5:23, Isaiah 1:17 3:14 9:8 16:5 29:19 30:33 32:1 61:1, James 3:13, Job 4:9, Malachi 3:24, Martyrdom and Ascension of Isaiah 4:18, Matthew 5:5 11:5, Mekhilta de R'Shimon bar Yochai Amalek 47:1, Midrash Psalms 2:3 21:3 72:3 72:4, Midrash Tanchuma Shoftim 19, Midrash Tanchuma Terumah 7, Midrash Tanchuma Toledot 14, Pesikta Rabbati 37:1, Proverbs 31:8-31:9, Psalms 2:9 18:9 45:7-45:8 72:1-72:4 72:12-72:14 82:2-82:4 110:2, Psalms of Solomon 17:36, Revelation 1:16 2:16 19:11 19:15, Ruth.R 5:6, Song of Songs.R 6:25, Titus 3:2, z.Vayera 103b, Zephaniah 2:3
Isaiah 11:4-11 - 4QIsac

[5] 1QIsaa *the wicked will be killed*

[6] Isaiah 11:5 - 1 John 1:9, 1 Peter 4:1, 1QSb 5:25-26, 1QSb 5.24-26, 2 Corinthians 6:7, Ephesians 6:14, Hebrews 2:17, Hosea 2:20, Isaiah 25:1 59:17, Mekhilta de R'Shimon bar Yochai Amalek 47:1, Psalms 93:1, Revelation 1:13 3:14, z.Balak 198b

[7] LXX *his sides clothed with truth*

[8] Isaiah 11:6 - 1 Corinthians 6:9-6:11, 2 Corinthians 5:14-5:21, Acts 9:13-9:20, Colossians 3:3-3:8, Ephesians 4:22-4:32, Ezekiel 34:25, Galatians 3:26-3:27, Guide for the Perplexed 3:11, Hosea 2:18, Isaiah 65:25, Jastrow 53a 1031b, Mekhilta de R'Shimon bar Yochai Amalek 47:1, mt.Hilchot Melachim u'Michamoteihem 12:1, mt.Hilchot Teshuvah 8:7 9:2 10:1, Philemon 1:9-1:16, Revelation 5:9-5:10, Romans 14:17, Saadia Opinions 8:8, Sibylline Oracles 13.28, Titus 3:3-3:5
Isaiah 11:6-8 - Sibylline Oracles 3.788
Isaiah 11:6-9 - 2 Baruch 73:7

[9] 1QIsaa *will graze*; LXX uses *young calf and bull and lion shall feed together*

[10] Isaiah 11:7 - Exodus.R 15:21, Midrash Tanchuma Vayishlach 1, mt.Hilchot Melachim u'Michamoteihem 12:1, Pesikta Rabbati 33:13, Saadia Opinions 8:8
Isaiah 11:7-9 - 4QIsab

[11] 1QIsaa *The cow and the bear will graze together, and their young will lie down*; LXX *And the ox and bear shall feed together; and their young shall be together*

[12] Isaiah 11:8 - Isaiah 59:5, Pesikta Rabbati 33:13, Psalms 140:4, Saadia Opinions 8:8

[13] LXX *put his hand*

[14] LXX *and on the nest of young asps*

[15] Isaiah 11:9 - 1 Thessalonians 5:15, Acts 2:41-2:47 4:29-4:35, b.Bava Batra 74b, b.Shekalim [Taklin Chadatin] 16b, Derech Hashem

knowledge of the LORD[1], as the waters cover the sea.

וְהָיָה בַּיּוֹם הַהוּא שֹׁרֶשׁ יִשַׁי אֲשֶׁר עֹמֵד לְנֵס עַמִּים אֵלָיו גּוֹיִם יִדְרֹשׁוּ וְהָיְתָה מְנֻחָתוֹ כָּבוֹד

10[2] And it shall come to pass in that day, that the root of Jesse, *who stands for a banner of the peoples, to him shall the nations seek*[3]; And his resting place shall be glorious.

וְהָיָה בַּיּוֹם הַהוּא יוֹסִיף אֲדֹנָי שֵׁנִית יָדוֹ לִקְנוֹת אֶת־שְׁאָר עַמּוֹ אֲשֶׁר יִשָּׁאֵר מֵאַשּׁוּר וּמִמִּצְרַיִם וּמִפַּתְרוֹס וּמִכּוּשׁ וּמֵעֵילָם וּמִשִּׁנְעָר וּמֵחֲמָת וּמֵאִיֵּי הַיָּם

11[4] And it shall come to pass in that day, the Lord will set His hand again the second time To recover the remnant of His people, who shall remain in Assyria, and in Egypt, *and in Pathros, and in Cush, and in Elam, and in Shinar, and in Hamath, and in the islands of the sea*[5].

וְנָשָׂא נֵס לַגּוֹיִם וְאָסַף נִדְחֵי יִשְׂרָאֵל וּנְפֻצוֹת יְהוּדָה יְקַבֵּץ מֵאַרְבַּע כַּנְפוֹת הָאָרֶץ

12[6] And He will set up an ensign for the nations, and will assemble the dispersed of Israel, and gather together the scattered of Judah from the *four*[7] compass points of the earth.

וְסָרָה קִנְאַת אֶפְרַיִם וְצֹרְרֵי יְהוּדָה יִכָּרֵתוּ אֶפְרַיִם לֹא־יְקַנֵּא אֶת־יְהוּדָה וִיהוּדָה לֹא־יָצֹר אֶת־אֶפְרָיִם

13[8] The envy of Ephraim will depart, and they who harass Judah shall be cut off; Ephraim will not envy Judah, and Judah will not vex Ephraim.

וְעָפוּ בְכָתֵף פְּלִשְׁתִּים יָמָּה יַחְדָּו יָבֹזּוּ אֶת־בְּנֵי־קֶדֶם אֱדוֹם וּמוֹאָב מִשְׁלוֹח יָדָם וּבְנֵי עַמּוֹן מִשְׁמַעְתָּם

14[9] And they shall fly *down on the shoulder*[10] of the Philistines *on the west; together*[11] they shall *spoil the children of*[12] the east[13]; They shall put forth their hand upon Edom and Moab; And the children of Ammon shall obey them.

Part II 8§04, Ein Yaakov Bava Batra:74a, Galatians 5:22-5:24, Habakkuk 2:14, Isaiah 2:4 11:13 30:26 35:9 45:6 49:6 52:10 59:19 60:1-60:22, Job 5:23, Matthew 5:44-5:45, Mekhilta de R'Shimon bar Yochai Amalek 47:1, Mekhilta de R'Shimon bar Yochai Shirata 36:3, Mekhilta de R'Ishmael Shirata 10:70, Micah 4:2-4:4, Midrash Psalms 1:18, mt.Hilchot Chametz u'Matzah 19:1, mt.Hilchot Megillah v'Chanukah 2:18, mt.Hilchot Melachim u'Michamoteihem 12:5, mt.Hilchot Teshuvah 9:2 9:2, mt.Perek Chelek Intro:11, Odes of Solomon 6:8, Philippians 2:14-2:15, Psalms 22:28-22:32 72:19 98:2-98:3, Revelation 20:2-20:6 21:27, Romans 11:25-11:26 12:17-12:21, Rosh Hashanah, Saadia Opinions 8:8 Intro:2, Seder Tashlich, Song of Songs.R 1:19, Tanya Igeret Hakodesh §12, Testament of Levi 18:5, y.Sotah 1:9, z.Vayikra 23a, Zechariah 14:9

[1] 1QIsaa *will be full of the knowledge of the LORD*

[2] Isaiah 11:10 - 1 Peter 1:7-1:9 5:10, 2 Thessalonians 1:7-1:12, Acts 11:18 26:17-26:18 28:28, Genesis 49:10, Genesis.R 97:1 98 [Excl]:9 99 [Excl]:8, Haggai 2:9, Hebrews 4:1 4:9-4:16, Isaiah 2:11 11:1 14:3 28:12 32:17-32:18 49:22 59:19 60:3 60:5 66:10-66:12 66:19, Jeremiah 6:16, John 3:14-3:15 12:20-12:21 12:32, Luke 2:32, Matthew 2:1-2:2 8:11 11:28-11:30 12:21, Midrash Psalms 21:1, Midrash Tanchuma Vayechi 10, Psalms 91:1 91:4 116:7 149:5, Revelation 22:16, Romans 15:9-15:12, z.Lech Lecha 88b, z.Pekudei 221b, z.Terumah 172b

[3] LXX *and he who shall arise to rule over the Gentiles; in him shall the Gentiles trust*

[4] Isaiah 11:11 - 2 Corinthians 3:16, Amos 9:14-9:15, Daniel 8:2 11:18, Deuteronomy 4:27-4:31 30:3-30:6, Exodus.R 1:5, Ezekiel 11:16-11:20 27:6 30:14 34:23-34:28 36:24-36:28 37:1-37:28, Genesis 10:5-10:7 10:10 10:22 11:2 14:1, Genesis.R 70:6, Hosea 2:2 3:4-3:5 12:1, Isaiah 10:9 10:20 11:16 19:23-19:24 24:15 27:12-27:13 42:4 42:10 42:12 45:14 60:1-60:22 66:19, Jeremiah 23:7-23:8 25:25 30:8-30:11 31:11 31:37-31:41 33:24-33:26 44:1 49:23, Joel 4:1-4:21, Lamentations.R 1:23 1:57, Leviticus 26:40-26:42, Micah 7:12 7:14-7:15, Midrash Psalms 6:2 60:3 107:4, Midrash Tanchuma Shemot 3, Numbers.R 13:5, Per Massorah: Soferim altered "Hashem" to "Adonai", Pesikta de R'Kahana 16.11, Pesikta Rabbati 33:13, Psalms 68:23, Romans 11:15 11:26, Ruth.R Petichata:7, Saadia Opinions 8:8, Tanya Igeret Hakodesh §02, z.Beshallach 54a, Zechariah 5:11 9:2 10:8-10:12 12:1-12:14, Zephaniah 2:11
Isaiah 11:11-12 - 4Q165 frag 11 ll.3-5
Isaiah 11:11-15 - 4QIsaa

[5] LXX *country of Babylon, and from Ethiopia, and from the Elamites, and from the rising of the sun, and out of Arabia*

[6] Isaiah 11:12 - Deuteronomy 32:26, Genesis.R 98 [Excl]:2, Isaiah 11:10 18:3 27:13 43:6 49:11-49:12 56:8 59:19 62:10, James 1:1, John 7:35, Lamentations.R 1:23, Midrash Psalms 107:4, Midrash Tanchuma Massei 13, Midrash Tanchuma Vayechi 8, Numbers.R 23:14, Pesikta de R'Kahana 4.1, Pesikta Rabbati 14:15 29/30B:4, Psalms 68:23 147:2, Revelation 5:9, Zechariah 10:6, Zephaniah 3:10

[7] Missing in 1QIsaa

[8] Isaiah 11:13 - Ezekiel 37:16-37:24, Genesis.R 95:2 95:2, Hosea 2:2, Isaiah 7:1-7:6 9:22, Jastrow 2a 129b, Jeremiah 3:18, Mekhilta de R'Shimon bar Yochai Beshallach 25:3, Mekilta de R'Ishmael Beshallah 6:154, Mesillat Yesharim 11:Nekiyut-from-Envy, Midrash Tanchuma Vayigash 4 9

[9] Isaiah 11:14 - Amos 9:12, Daniel 11:41, Ecclesiastes.R 1:3, Ezekiel 38:1-38:23, Isaiah 16:14 25:10 33:1 34:5-34:6 59:19 60:14 66:19-66:20, Jeremiah 49:28, Joel 4:19, Matthew 8:11, Midrash Psalms 60:3, mt.Perek Chelek Intro:11, Numbers 24:17, Numbers.R 14:1, Obadiah 1:18-1:19, Zechariah 9:5-9:7, Zephaniah 2:5
Isaiah 11:14-15 - 4QIsae
Isaiah 11:14-16 - 4QIsac

[10] LXX *in the ships*

[11] 1QIsaa *in the west together, and*

[12] LXX *at the same time spoil the sea, and those who come from*

[13] LXX adds *and Idumea*

וְהֶחֱרִים יְהֹוָה אֵת לְשׁוֹן יָם־מִצְרַיִם וְהֵנִיף יָדוֹ עַל־הַנָּהָר בַּעְיָם רוּחוֹ וְהִכָּהוּ לְשִׁבְעָה נְחָלִים וְהִדְרִיךְ בַּנְּעָלִים	15[1]	And the LORD will utterly destroy the tongue of the Egyptian sea; And *with His[2] scorching wind He will shake His hand over the River, And will strike it into seven streams[3]*, And cause men to march over dry shod.
וְהָיְתָה מְסִלָּה לִשְׁאָר עַמּוֹ אֲשֶׁר יִשָּׁאֵר מֵאַשּׁוּר כַּאֲשֶׁר הָיְתָה לְיִשְׂרָאֵל בְּיוֹם עֲלֹתוֹ מֵאֶרֶץ מִצְרָיִם	16[4]	And there shall be a highway for the remnant of His people who shall remain in Assyria, like as there was for Israel in the day he came up out of the land of Egypt.

Isaiah – Chapter 12

וְאָמַרְתָּ בַּיּוֹם הַהוּא אוֹדְךָ יְהֹוָה כִּי אָנַפְתָּ בִּי יָשֹׁב אַפְּךָ וּתְנַחֲמֵנִי	1[5]	And in that day you shall say: 'I will give thanks to You, for though you were angry with me, your anger turned away, and you comfort me.
הִנֵּה אֵל יְשׁוּעָתִי אֶבְטַח וְלֹא אֶפְחָד כִּי־עָזִּי וְזִמְרָת יָהּ יְהֹוָה וַיְהִי־לִי לִישׁוּעָה	2[6]	Behold, God is my salvation; I will trust[7], and will not be afraid; For GOD the LORD is my *strength and song[8]*; And He has become my salvation.'
וּשְׁאַבְתֶּם־מַיִם בְּשָׂשׂוֹן מִמַּעַיְנֵי הַיְשׁוּעָה	3[9]	Therefore, with joy you shall draw water out of the wells of salvation.
וַאֲמַרְתֶּם בַּיּוֹם הַהוּא הוֹדוּ לַיהֹוָה קִרְאוּ בִשְׁמוֹ הוֹדִיעוּ בָעַמִּים עֲלִילֹתָיו הַזְכִּירוּ כִּי נִשְׂגָּב שְׁמוֹ	4[10]	And in that day you shall say: '[11]*Give thanks[12]* to the LORD, proclaim His name, Declare His deeds among the peoples, Make mention that His name is exalted.
זַמְּרוּ יְהֹוָה כִּי גֵאוּת עָשָׂה 'מְיֻדַּעַת' "מוּדַעַת" זֹאת בְּכָל־הָאָרֶץ	5[13]	Sing [14]to the LORD; for He has done gloriously; *This is known[15]* in all the land.

[1] Isaiah 11:15 - 4 Ezra 13:47, b.Eruvin [Tosefot] 47b, Exodus 7:19-7:21 14:21, Ezekiel 29:10 30:12, Isaiah 7:20 19:5-19:10 19:16 50:2 51:9-51:10, Leviticus.R 27:4, Midrash Psalms 92:2, Midrash Tanchuma Emor 9, Pesikta Rabbati 48:2, Psalms 74:13-74:15, Revelation 16:12, Saadia Opinions 8:8, z.Bo 42b, Zechariah 10:11

[2] 1QIsaa *a*

[3] LXX *he shall lay his hand on the river with a strong wind, and he shall smite the seven channels*

[4] Isaiah 11:16 - Exodus 14:26-14:29, Isaiah 11:11 19:23 27:13 35:8-35:10 40:3-40:4 42:15-42:16 48:20-48:21 49:12 51:10 57:14 62:10 63:12-63:13, Mekhilta de R'Shimon bar Yochai Beshallach 20:5, Pesikta Rabbati 48:2, Saadia Opinions 8:8

Isaiah 12:1-6 - 1QIsaa, 4QIsae

[5] Isaiah 12:1 - 4QIsac, b.Niddah 31a, Derech Hashem Part II 3§12, Deuteronomy 30:1-3, Ein Yaakov Niddah:31a, Ezekiel 39:24-29, Gates of Repentance 4.012, Hosea 6:1 11:8 14:6-11, Isaiah 2:11 10:4 10:25 11:10-11 11:16 19:23 25:1 25:9 26:1 27:1-3 27:12-13 35:10 40:1-40:2 49:13 51:3 54:8 57:15-18 60:18-19 66:13, Jeremiah 31:19-21, Leviticus.R 32:1, Midrash Psalms 12:5 60:2 118:3 118:19 136:3, Midrash Tanchuma Shemot 3, Psalms 30:6 34:2-23 67:2-5 69:35-37 72:15-19 85:2-4 149:6-9, Ralbag Wars 4:2 4:5, Revelation 15:3-4 19:1-7, Romans 11:15, Zechariah 14:9 14:20

[6] Isaiah 12:2 - 1 Timothy 3:16, 4QIsab, Exodus 15:2, Exodus.R 23:6, Hosea 1:7, Isaiah 7:14 9:7-9:8 26:3-26:4 32:2 45:17 45:22-45:25 62:11, Jeremiah 3:23 23:6, Jonah 2:9, Luke 2:30-2:32, Matthew 1:21-1:23, Prayer for one who will engage in commerce that day, Psalms 27:1 83:19 118:14, Revelation 7:10, Romans 1:16, z.Beshallach 55a

Isaiah 12:2-3 - Havdala, Motzoei Shabbat

Isaiah 12:2-6 - Motzoei Shabbat [Viyiten Lecha]

[7] LXX adds *in HIm*

[8] LXX *glory and my praise*

[9] Isaiah 12:3 - b.Shabbat [Tosefot] 21a, b.Succah [Rashi] 48a, b.Succah 48b 50b, Guide for the Perplexed 1:30 [T.Jonathan] 1:30, Isaiah 49:10 55:1-55:3, Jeremiah 2:13, John 1:16 4:10-4:14 7:37-7:39, Psalms 36:10, Revelation 7:17 22:1 22:17, Ruth.R 4:8, Song of Songs 2:3, y.Sukkah 5:1

Isaiah 12:3-6 - 1QIsab

[10] Isaiah 12:4 - 1 Chronicles 16:8 5:11, b.Avodah Zara 24b, Ein Yaakov Avodah Zarah:24b, Exodus 15:2 9:19 34:5-34:7, Isaiah 2:11 2:17 12:1 24:15 1:1 9:5 18:19, Jeremiah 2:2 51:9-10, John 17:26, Midrash Psalms 18:35, Nehemiah 9:5, Philippians 2:9-2:11, Psalms 9:12 18:47 21:14 22:32 34:4 40:6 46:11 57:6 71:16-18 73:28 96:3 97:9 9:1 106:47-48 11:22 113:1-3 17:5 117:1-2 145:4-6, z.Vayeilech 286a, z.Yitro 90b

Isaiah 12:4-6 - 4QIsaa

[11] 1QIsaa adds *I*

[12] LXX *sing*

[13] Isaiah 12:5 - Exodus 15:1 15:21, Habakkuk 2:14, Isaiah 16:9, Midrash Psalms 118:22, Psalms 68:33-68:36 72:19 98:1 9:2, Revelation 11:15-11:17 15:3 19:1-19:3, Song of Songs.R 4:20, Tanya Igeret Hakodesh §15 §25

[14] LXX adds *praise*

[15] LXX *declare this*

Hebrew	Verse	English
צַהֲלִי וָרֹנִּי יוֹשֶׁבֶת צִיּוֹן כִּי־גָדוֹל בְּקִרְבֵּךְ קְדוֹשׁ יִשְׂרָאֵל	6[1]	*Cry aloud and shout[2], inhabitant of Zion, for great is the Holy One of Israel in your midst[3].'*

Isaiah – Chapter 13

Hebrew	Verse	English
מַשָּׂא בָּבֶל אֲשֶׁר חָזָה יְשַׁעְיָהוּ בֶּן־אָמוֹץ	1[4]	The burden of Babylon, that Isaiah the son of Amoz saw.
עַל הַר־נִשְׁפֶּה שְׂאוּ־נֵס הָרִימוּ קוֹל לָהֶם הָנִיפוּ יָד וְיָבֹאוּ פִּתְחֵי נְדִיבִים	2[5]	Set up an ensign upon the *high mountain[6]*, lift up the voice to them, wave the hand so *they[7]* may go into the gates of the nobles[8].
אֲנִי צִוֵּיתִי לִמְקֻדָּשָׁי גַּם קָרָאתִי גִבּוֹרַי לְאַפִּי עַלִּיזֵי גַּאֲוָתִי	3[9]	I have commanded My consecrated ones, *yes, I have called My mighty ones for My anger, My proudly exulting ones[10]*.
קוֹל הָמוֹן בֶּהָרִים דְּמוּת עַם־רָב קוֹל שְׁאוֹן מַמְלְכוֹת גּוֹיִם נֶאֱסָפִים יְהוָה צְבָאוֹת מְפַקֵּד צְבָא מִלְחָמָה	4[11]	Hear, a *tumult[12]* in the mountains, as from a great people. Hear, the uproar of the kingdoms Of the nations gathered together. The LORD of hosts musters the host of the battle.
בָּאִים מֵאֶרֶץ מֶרְחָק מִקְצֵה הַשָּׁמָיִם יְהוָה וּכְלֵי זַעְמוֹ לְחַבֵּל כָּל־הָאָרֶץ	5[13]	They come from a far country, from the *end[14]* of heaven, the LORD, and the weapons of His indignation, to destroy the whole earth.
הֵילִילוּ כִּי קָרוֹב יוֹם יְהוָה כְּשֹׁד מִשַּׁדַּי יָבוֹא	6[15]	Howl for the day of the LORD is at hand; As destruction from the Almighty shall it come.
עַל־כֵּן כָּל־יָדַיִם תִּרְפֶּינָה וְכָל־לְבַב אֱנוֹשׁ יִמָּס	7[16]	Therefore, all hands shall be slack, And every *heart of man shall melt[17]*.
וְנִבְהָלוּ צִירִים וַחֲבָלִים יֹאחֵזוּן כַּיּוֹלֵדָה יְחִילוּן אִישׁ אֶל־רֵעֵהוּ יִתְמָהוּ פְּנֵי לְהָבִים פְּנֵיהֶם	8[18]	And they shall be frightened; Pangs and throes shall take hold of them; They shall be in pain as a woman in travail; They shall look aghast one to another; Their faces shall be faces of flame.

[1] Isaiah 12:6 - Ezekiel 19:7 24:35, Isaiah 8:18 10:24 24:23 6:19 9:24 16:9 17:14 17:16 1:26 52:7-52:10 6:1, Kuzari 4.003, Luke 19:37-19:40, Midrash Psalms 118:22, Psalms 9:12 68:17 71:22 89:19 12:14, Sibylline Oracles 3.785, Song of Songs.R 1:29, y.Berachot 1:5, y.Taanit 2:3, Zechariah 2:5 2:10-2:11 8:3-8:8, Zephaniah 2:5 3:14-3:17

[2] LXX *Exalt and rejoice*

[3] LXX *for the Holy One of Israel is exalted in the midst of her*

[4] Isaiah 13:1 - Daniel 5:6 5:28, Ezekiel 12:10, Habakkuk 1:1, Isaiah 1:1 13:19 14:4-14:23 14:28 15:1 17:1 19:1 21:1-21:11 21:13 22:1 22:25-23:1 19:14 44:1-44:2 47:1-47:15, Jeremiah 23:33-23:38 25:12-25:26 50:1-51:64, Leviticus.R 14:2, Malachi 1:1, Nahum 1:1, Revelation 17:1-17:18, Sibylline Oracles 5.434, Zechariah 9:1 12:1

Isaiah 13:1-4 - 4QIsae

Isaiah 13:1-8 - 1QIsab

Isaiah 13:1-16 - 4QIsaa

Isaiah 13:1-22 - 1QIsaa

[5] Isaiah 13:2 - b.Bava Metzia [Rashi] 15a 70a, b.Menachot [Rashi] 27b, b.Zevachim [Rashi] 12b, Isaiah 5:26 10:32 11:12 11:15 18:3 45:1-45:3, Jeremiah 2:2 3:25 51:27-51:28 3:58

[6] LXX *mountain of the plain*

[7] 1QIsaa *he*

[8] LXX *beckon with the hand, open the gates, you rulers*

[9] Isaiah 13:3 - b.Berachot 8b, Ein Yaakov Berachot:8b, Ezra 1:1-11 6:1-22 7:12-26, Guide for the Perplexed 2:47, Isaiah 23:11 44:27-28 45:4-5, Jeremiah 50:21-46 51:20-24, Joel 4:11, Psalms 5:2 149:5-9, Revelation 17:12-18 18:4-8 18:20-19:7

Isaiah 13:3-18 - 4QIsab

[10] LXX *and I bring them: giants are coming to fulfil my wrath, rejoicing at the same time and insulting*

[11] Isaiah 13:4 - Ezekiel 38:3-23, Isaiah 10:5-6 22:1-22:9 45:1-2, Jeremiah 50:2-3 50:14-15 50:21-46 51:6-25 51:27-28, Joel 2:1-11 2:25 4:14, Revelation 9:7-9:19 18:8 19:11-19:21, Zechariah 14:1-3 14:13-14

[12] LXX *voice*

[13] Isaiah 13:5 - Guide for the Perplexed 2:47, Isaiah 5:26 13:17 24:1, Jeremiah 2:3 2:9 3:11 51:20-51:46, Matthew 24:31, Midrash Psalms 5:7 86:7, Midrash Tanchuma Tazria 9, Pesikta de R'Kahana 24.11, Saadia Opinions 2:3, y.Taanit 2:1

[14] LXX *utmost foundation*

[15] Isaiah 13:6 - 1 Thessalonians 5:2-3, Amos 5:18, Ezekiel 21:17 30:2-3, Isaiah 2:12 13:9 14:31 23:1 10:8 4:5 17:14, James 5:1, Jeremiah 1:34 1:3 3:8, Job 7:23, Joel 1:5 1:11 1:13 1:15 2:11 3:4, Malachi 3:23, Pesikta Rabbati 41:3, Revelation 18:10, Zephaniah 1:7 1:14 2:2-3

[16] Isaiah 13:7 - Exodus 15:15, Ezekiel 7:17 21:12, Isaiah 10:3-10:4 19:1 13:27 3:20, Jeremiah 2:43, Nahum 1:6 2:11

[17] LXX *utmost foundation*

[18] Isaiah 13:8 - 1 Thessalonians 5:3, Daniel 5:5-5:6, Isaiah 21:3-21:4 2:17, Jeremiah 4:31 6:6 2:43, Joel 2:6, John 16:21, Nahum 2:11, Psalms 48:6-48:7, Saadia Opinions 9:8

Hebrew	Verse	English
הִנֵּה יוֹם־יְהוָה בָּא אַכְזָרִי וְעֶבְרָה וַחֲרוֹן אַף לָשׂוּם הָאָרֶץ לְשַׁמָּה וְחַטָּאֶיהָ יַשְׁמִיד מִמֶּנָּה	9[1]	Behold, the day of the LORD comes, *cruel*[2], and full of wrath, and fierce anger; To make the earth a desolation, And to destroy the sinners from it,
כִּי־כוֹכְבֵי הַשָּׁמַיִם וּכְסִילֵיהֶם לֹא יָהֵלּוּ אוֹרָם חָשַׁךְ הַשֶּׁמֶשׁ בְּצֵאתוֹ וְיָרֵחַ לֹא־יַגִּיהַ אוֹרוֹ	10[3]	For the stars of heaven and *its constellations*[4] shall not *beam*[5] their light; The sun shall be darkened in his track, And the moon shall not cause her light to shine.
וּפָקַדְתִּי עַל־תֵּבֵל רָעָה וְעַל־רְשָׁעִים עֲוֺנָם וְהִשְׁבַּתִּי גְּאוֹן זֵדִים וְגַאֲוַת עָרִיצִים אַשְׁפִּיל	11[6]	And I will visit upon the world their evil, And upon the wicked their iniquity; And I will cause the arrogance of the proud to cease, And will lay low the haughtiness of the tyrants.
אוֹקִיר אֱנוֹשׁ מִפָּז וְאָדָם מִכֶּתֶם אוֹפִיר	12[7]	I will make man more rare than fine gold, man than the pure gold of Ophir.
עַל־כֵּן שָׁמַיִם אַרְגִּיז וְתִרְעַשׁ הָאָרֶץ מִמְּקוֹמָהּ בְּעֶבְרַת יְהוָה צְבָאוֹת וּבְיוֹם חֲרוֹן אַפּוֹ	13[8]	Therefore, I will make the heavens tremble, and the earth shall be shaken from her place, For the wrath of the LORD of hosts, And for the day of His fierce anger.
וְהָיָה כִּצְבִי מֻדָּח וּכְצֹאן וְאֵין מְקַבֵּץ אִישׁ אֶל־עַמּוֹ יִפְנוּ וְאִישׁ אֶל־אַרְצוֹ יָנוּסוּ	14[9]	And it shall come to pass, that as the chased gazelle, And as sheep that no man gathers, every man shall turn to his own people, And every man shall flee to his own land.
כָּל־הַנִּמְצָא יִדָּקֵר וְכָל־הַנִּסְפֶּה יִפּוֹל בֶּחָרֶב	15[10]	Everyone who is found shall be thrust through; And everyone who is caught shall fall by the sword.
וְעֹלְלֵיהֶם יְרֻטְּשׁוּ לְעֵינֵיהֶם יִשַּׁסּוּ בָּתֵּיהֶם וּנְשֵׁיהֶם 'תִּשָּׁגַלְנָה' "תִּשָּׁכַבְנָה"	16[11]	Their babes also shall be dashed in pieces before their eyes; Their houses shall be spoiled, And their wives ravished[12].
הִנְנִי מֵעִיר עֲלֵיהֶם אֶת־מָדָי אֲשֶׁר־כֶּסֶף לֹא יַחְשֹׁבוּ וְזָהָב לֹא יַחְפְּצוּ־בוֹ	17[13]	Behold, I will stir up the Medes against them, Who shall not regard silver, And as for gold, they shall not delight in it.
וּקְשָׁתוֹת נְעָרִים תְּרַטַּשְׁנָה וּפְרִי־בֶטֶן לֹא יְרַחֵמוּ עַל־בָּנִים לֹא־תָחוּס עֵינָם	18[14]	And their bows shall dash the young men in pieces; And *they shall have no pity on the fruit of the womb*[15]; Their eye shall not spare children.

---

[1] Isaiah 13:9 - Isaiah 13:6 13:15-13:18 47:10-47:15, Jeremiah 6:22-6:23 50:40-50:42 51:35-51:58, Malachi 3:19, Mekilta de R'Ishmael Pisha 7:26, Mekilta de R'Ishmael Pisha 11:82, Midrash Psalms 2:7, Nahum 1:2 1:6, Proverbs 2:22, Psalms 8:35, Revelation 17:16-17:17 18:8 19:17-19:21, Saadia Opinions 10:4, z.Vayera 107a 107b
Isaiah 13:9-13 - Testament of Levi 3:9
[2] LXX *that cannot be escaped*
[3] Isaiah 13:10 - Amos 8:9-8:10, Apocalypse of Adam 5:10, Ezekiel 32:7-32:8, Guide for the Perplexed 2:29, Isaiah 5:30 24:21 24:23, Joel 2:10 3:4 4:15, Luke 21:25, Mark 13:24, Matthew 24:29, Mekhilta de R'Shimon bar Yochai Shirata 30:1, Mekilta de R'Ishmael Shirata 5:11, Midrash Tanchuma Bereshit 6, Pesikta de R'Kahana S6.2, Ralbag Wars 6part02:5, Revelation 6:12-6:14 8:12, Song of Songs.R 5:5, z.Mikketz 196b, z.Vayeshev 182a, z.Vayigash 210a, Zephaniah 1:15-1:16
[4] LXX *Orion, and all the host of heaven*
[5] 1QIsaa *shine*
[6] Isaiah 13:11 - Daniel 5:22-5:23, Isaiah 2:11 2:17 3:11 5:15 11:4 14:12-14:16 14:21 24:4-24:6 2:21, Jeremiah 50:29-50:32 51:34-51:38, Mekhilta de R'Shimon bar Yochai Shirata 30:1, Mekilta de R'Ishmael Shirata 5:14, Revelation 12:9-10 18:2-3
[7] Isaiah 13:12 - Isaiah 4:1 13:15-18 24:6, Job 4:16, Midrash Psalms 116:5, Psalms 17:9, z.Vayera 107b
[8] Isaiah 13:13 - 2 Peter 3:10, Guide for the Perplexed 2:29, Haggai 2:6-2:7 2:21-2:22, Hebrews 12:26-12:27, Isaiah 10:4 3:6, Jeremiah 4:23-24, Joel 4:16, Matthew 24:29 24:35, Nahum 1:4-1:6, Psalms 110:5-6, Revelation 6:13-14 20:11
[9] Isaiah 13:14 - 1 Kings 22:17 22:36, Isaiah 17:13 23:15, Jeremiah 2:16 3:9, Revelation 18:9-18:10
[10] Isaiah 13:15 - Isaiah 14:19-22 47:9-14, Jeremiah 2:25 2:27 50:35-42 51:3-4
[11] Isaiah 13:16 – Deuteronomy 28:30, Hosea 10:14, Isaiah 13:18, Lamentations 5:11, Nahum 3:10, Psalms 137:8-9, the word ישגלנה [ravish], is substituted by ישכבנה [lie with] to remove indelicate expressions, Zechariah 14:2
Isaiah 13:16-19 - 1QIsab
[12] 4QIsaa *taken*
[13] Isaiah 13:17 - Daniel 5:28-5:31, Esther.R 5:3, Isaiah 13:3-13:5 21:2 17:25, Jeremiah 2:9 3:11 51:27-51:28, Proverbs 6:34-35, Saadia Opinions 10:13
[14] Isaiah 13:18 - 2 Chronicles 12:17, 2 Kings 8:12, Esther.R 5:3, Ezekiel 9:5-9:6 9:10, Hosea 14:1, Isaiah 13:16, Nahum 2:2 3:10
[15] 1QIsaa *on infants they shall have no pity, and*

וְהָיְתָה בָבֶל צְבִי מַמְלָכוֹת תִּפְאֶרֶת גְּאוֹן כַּשְׂדִּים כְּמַהְפֵּכַת אֱלֹהִים אֶת־סְדֹם וְאֶת־עֲמֹרָה

19[1] And Babylon, the glory of kingdoms, The beauty of the Chaldeans' pride, Shall be as when God overthrew Sodom and Gomorrah.

לֹא־תֵשֵׁב לָנֶצַח וְלֹא תִשְׁכֹּן עַד־דּוֹר וָדוֹר וְלֹא־יַהֵל שָׁם עֲרָבִי וְרֹעִים לֹא־יַרְבִּצוּ שָׁם

20[2] It shall never be inhabited, nor shall it be lived in from generation to generation; nor shall the Arabian pitch a tent there; nor shall the shepherds make their fold there.

וְרָבְצוּ־שָׁם צִיִּים וּמָלְאוּ בָתֵּיהֶם אֹחִים וְשָׁכְנוּ שָׁם בְּנוֹת יַעֲנָה וּשְׂעִירִים יְרַקְּדוּ־שָׁם

21[3] But wild *cats*[4] shall lie there; And their houses shall be full of *ferrets*; And ostriches shall live there, And satyrs shall dance there[5].

וְעָנָה אִיִּים בְּאַלְמְנוֹתָיו וְתַנִּים בְּהֵיכְלֵי עֹנֶג וְקָרוֹב לָבוֹא עִתָּהּ וְיָמֶיהָ לֹא יִמָּשֵׁכוּ

22[6] And *jackals* shall howl in their castles, And *wild dogs* in the pleasant palaces; And her time is near to come, And her days shall not be prolonged[7].

Isaiah – Chapter 14

כִּי יְרַחֵם יְהוָה אֶת־יַעֲקֹב וּבָחַר עוֹד בְּיִשְׂרָאֵל וְהִנִּיחָם עַל־אַדְמָתָם וְנִלְוָה הַגֵּר עֲלֵיהֶם וְנִסְפְּחוּ עַל־בֵּית יַעֲקֹב

1[8] For the LORD will have compassion on Jacob, and will yet choose Israel, and set them in their own land; and the stranger shall join himself with them, and they shall cleave to the house of Jacob.

וּלְקָחוּם עַמִּים וֶהֱבִיאוּם אֶל־מְקוֹמָם וְהִתְנַחֲלוּם בֵּית־יִשְׂרָאֵל עַל אַדְמַת יְהוָה לַעֲבָדִים וְלִשְׁפָחוֹת וְהָיוּ שֹׁבִים לְשֹׁבֵיהֶם וְרָדוּ בְּנֹגְשֵׂיהֶם

2[9] And *the*[10] peoples shall take them, and bring them to their[11] place; and the house of Israel shall possess them in the land of the LORD for servants and for handmaids; and they shall take them captive, whose captives they were; and they shall rule over their oppressors.

וְהָיָה בְּיוֹם הָנִיחַ יְהוָה לְךָ מֵעָצְבְּךָ וּמֵרָגְזֶךָ וּמִן־הָעֲבֹדָה הַקָּשָׁה אֲשֶׁר עֻבַּד־בָּךְ

3[12] And it shall come to pass in the day the LORD shall give you rest from your *travail*[13], and from your trouble, and from the hard service in which you were made to serve,

---

[1] Isaiah 13:19 - Amos 4:11, Daniel 2:37-2:38 4:27, Deuteronomy 5:22, Genesis 19:24, Isaiah 14:4-14:6 14:12-14:15, Jeremiah 1:18 2:40 3:41, Zephaniah 2:9

[2] Isaiah 13:20 - 2 Chronicles 17:11, Isaiah 14:23 34:10-34:15, Jeremiah 2:3 2:13 2:21 2:39 2:45 3:25 3:29 3:37 3:43 51:62-51:64, Revelation 18:21-18:23

[3] Isaiah 13:21 - 2 Baruch 10:8, b.Berachot [Rashi] 62a, b.Chullin 64b, b.Shabbat [Rashi] 149b, Genesis.R 65:15, Isaiah 34:11-34:15, Leviticus.R 5:1 22:8, Revelation 18:2, Sifre Devarim {Ha'azinu Hashamayim} 306

[4] LXX *beasts*

[5] LXX *howling; and monsters shall rest there, and devils shall dance there*

[6] Isaiah 13:22 - 2 Peter 2:3 3:9-3:10, Deuteronomy 8:35, Ezekiel 7:7-7:10, Habakkuk 2:3, Isaiah 1:2 10:13 11:7, *Jeremiah 3:33*

[7] LXX *satyrs shall live there; and hedgehogs shall make their nests in their houses. It will come soon, and will not tarry*

[8] Isaiah 14:1 - 2 Enoch 29:3, Acts 15:14-15:17, b.Kiddushin 70b, b.Niddah [Rashi] 13b, b.Yevamot [Rashi] 19b, b.Yevamot 47b, Derech Hashem Part II 4§07, Deuteronomy 4:29-4:31 30:3-30:5, Ein Yaakov Yevamot:47b, Ephesians 2:12-2:19, Esther 8:17, Exodus.R 19:4, Ezekiel 36:24-36:28 39:25-39:29, Isaiah 19:24-19:25 3:6 40:1-40:2 17:8 20:1 44:21-44:22 1:7 1:13 49:16-49:23 54:7-54:8 56:6-56:8 60:3-60:5 18:20, Jastrow 1012b, Jeremiah 12:15-12:16 24:6-24:7 5:14 30:18-30:22 31:9-31:13 32:37-32:41 50:4-50:6 50:17-50:20 2:33 51:4-51:6 51:34-51:37, Leviticus 26:40-26:45, Luke 1:54 1:72-1:74 2:32, Malachi 1:11, Mas.Kallah Rabbati 2:4, mt.Hilchot Tumat Tzaraat 1:2, Nehemiah 1:8-1:9, Psalms 98:3 6:14 136:10-24 23:12, Ruth 1:14-1:18, Zechariah 1:17 2:11-12 8:22-23
Isaiah 14:1-5 - 4QIsac
Isaiah 14:1-13 - 4QIsae
Isaiah 14:1-32 - 1QIsaa

[9] Isaiah 14:2 - 2 Corinthians 8:4-8:5 10:5, Daniel 7:18 7:25-7:27, Ephesians 4:8, Ezra 2:65, Galatians 5:13, Genesis.R 16:5 40:5, Isaiah 18:7 1:23 60:9-60:12 12:14 13:5, Jeremiah 6:16, Numbers.R 14:2, Pesikta de R'Kahana 12.17, Psalms 68:19, Revelation 3:9 11:11-11:18 18:20-18:24, Romans 15:27, Saadia Opinions 8:6 8:6, Sifre Devarim {Ha'azinu Hashamayim} 332, Sifre Devarim Nitzavim 332, the abbreviation וה stands for והתנחלתם, Zechariah 14:2-14:3

[10] 1QIsaa *many*

[11] 1QIsaa adds *land and to their*

[12] Isaiah 14:3 - Deuteronomy 4:48 28:65-28:68, Ezekiel 4:24, Ezra 9:8-9:9, Isaiah 11:10 12:1 8:18, Jeremiah 6:10 46:27-46:28 2:34, Revelation 18:20 19:1-19:3, Sibylline Oracles 5.173, Song of Songs.R 3:6, z.Bereshit 48b, z.Yitro 89a, Zechariah 8:2 8:8

[13] LXX *sorrow and vexation*

וְנָשָׂאתָ הַמָּשָׁל הַזֶּה עַל־מֶלֶךְ בָּבֶל וְאָמָרְתָּ אֵיךְ שָׁבַת נֹגֵשׂ שָׁבְתָה מַדְהֵבָה	4[1] that you shall take up this parable against the king of Babylon, and say: How the oppressor ceased. The *exactress of gold*[2] ceased.
שָׁבַר יְהוָה מַטֵּה רְשָׁעִים שֵׁבֶט מֹשְׁלִים	5[3] The LORD has broken the *staff*[4] of the wicked, the *scepter*[5] of the rulers,
מַכֶּה עַמִּים בְּעֶבְרָה מַכַּת בִּלְתִּי סָרָה רֹדֶה בָאַף גּוֹיִם מֻרְדָּף בְּלִי חָשָׂךְ	6[6] Who struck the peoples in wrath With an *incessant stroke, who ruled the nations in anger, with a persecution that no one restrained*[7].
נָחָה שָׁקְטָה כָּל־הָאָרֶץ פָּצְחוּ רִנָּה	7[8] *The whole earth is at rest and is quiet; they break forth into singing*[9].
גַּם־בְּרוֹשִׁים שָׂמְחוּ לְךָ אַרְזֵי לְבָנוֹן מֵאָז שָׁכַבְתָּ לֹא־יַעֲלֶה הַכֹּרֵת עָלֵינוּ	8[10] Yes, the *cypresses*[11] rejoice at you, And the cedars of Lebanon: 'Since you are laid down, no one has come up to cut us down.'
שְׁאוֹל מִתַּחַת רָגְזָה לְךָ לִקְרַאת בּוֹאֶךָ עוֹרֵר לְךָ רְפָאִים כָּל־עַתּוּדֵי אָרֶץ הֵקִים מִכִּסְאוֹתָם כֹּל מַלְכֵי גוֹיִם	9[12] The netherworld from beneath is moved for you to meet you at your coming; *The shades are stirred for you, all the chief ones of the earth*[13]; All the kings of the nations raise from their thrones.
כֻּלָּם יַעֲנוּ וְיֹאמְרוּ אֵלֶיךָ גַּם־אַתָּה חֻלֵּיתָ כָמוֹנוּ אֵלֵינוּ נִמְשָׁלְתָּ	10[14] They all answer And say to you: 'Have you become weak as us? Are you becoming like us?
הוּרַד שְׁאוֹל גְּאוֹנֶךָ הֶמְיַת נְבָלֶיךָ תַּחְתֶּיךָ יֻצַּע רִמָּה וּמְכַסֶּיךָ תּוֹלֵעָה	11[15] Your pomp is brought down to the netherworld, And the noise of your psalteries; The maggot is spread under you, And *the worms cover you.*[16]'
אֵיךְ נָפַלְתָּ מִשָּׁמַיִם הֵילֵל בֶּן־שָׁחַר נִגְדַּעְתָּ לָאָרֶץ חוֹלֵשׁ עַל־גּוֹיִם	12[17] How you have fallen from[18] *heaven, O Daystar, son of the morning! How you are cut down to the ground, you who cast lots over the nations*[19].

---

[1] Isaiah 14:4 - 2 Chronicles 12:18, b.Shabbat 149b, Daniel 2:38 7:19-7:25, Ezekiel 5:15, Habakkuk 1:2-1:10 2:6-2:12 2:17, Isaiah 9:5 13:19 14:6 14:17 45:2-45:3 23:5 1:26 3:23, Jastrow 281a 731b 732a, Jeremiah 24:9 25:9-25:14 27:6-27:7 50:22-50:23 51:20-51:24 51:34-51:35, Lamentations 4:1, Leviticus.R 15:9, Midrash Tanchuma Tazria 11, Numbers.R 9:24, Pesikta Rabbati 5:9, Revelation 13:15-13:17 16:5-16:6 17:6 18:5-18:8 18:16 18:20

[2] LXX *taskmaster*

[3] Isaiah 14:5 - b.Shabbat 139a, Ein Yaakov Shabbat:139a, Isaiah 9:5 10:5 14:29, Jastrow 831a, Jeremiah 48:15-17, Midrash Psalms 47:1 95:1, Numbers.R 12:7, Pesikta de R'Kahana 5.9, Pesikta Rabbati 5:9 15:13 15:14/15, Psalms 5:3, Song of Songs.R 2:32, y.Megillah 1:11

[4] LXX *yoke*

[5] LXX *yoke*

[6] Isaiah 14:6 - 2 Chronicles 12:17, Daniel 4:32 7:19-7:21, Isaiah 10:14 13:14-13:18 21:1-21:10 9:1 46:10-46:11 47:1-47:15, James 2:13, Jeremiah 1:9 1:26 2:31, Job 9:13, Midrash Psalms 47:1 95:1, Proverbs 21:30, Revelation 17:16-17:17 18:8-18:10

[7] LXX *incurable plague smiting a nation with a wrathful plague, which spared them not, he rested in quiet*

[8] Isaiah 14:7 - b.Shabbat 149b, Isaiah 1:13, Jeremiah 3:48, Midrash Psalms 47:1 95:1, Proverbs 11:10, Psalms 96:11-96:13 98:1 98:7-98:9 126:1-126:3, Revelation 18:20 19:1-19:6

[9] LXX *All the earth cries aloud with joy*

[10] Isaiah 14:8 - 4Q163 frags 8-10 ll.1-3, Ezekiel 7:16, Guide for the Perplexed 2:30 [T.Jonathan] 2:47 4Q163 8-10 1-3, Isaiah 55:12-55:13, Lamentations.R 1:30, Zechariah 11:2

[11] LXX *trees also of Libanus*

[12] Isaiah 14:9 - Ezekiel 32:21-32:32, Jeremiah 2:8, Proverbs 15:24, Psalms of Solomon 4:13, Saadia Opinions 8:7

[13] LXX *all the great ones who have ruled over the earth have risen up together against you*

[14] Isaiah 14:10 - b.Shabbat 149b, Ecclesiastes 2:16, Ezekiel 8:21, Luke 16:20-23, Psalms 49:7-15 49:21 82:6-7

[15] Isaiah 14:11 - Amos 6:3-6:7, Daniel 5:1-5:4 5:25-5:30, Ezekiel 2:13 32:19-32:20, Isaiah 21:4-21:5 22:2 18:24, Job 17:13-17:14 21:11-21:15 24:19-24:20, Mark 9:43-9:48, Revelation 18:11-18:19, Ruth.R 3:3

[16] 1QIsaa *your covering is a worm*

[17] Isaiah 14:12 - 2 Baruch 4:7 [Slav], 2 Peter 1:19 2:4, Apocalypse of Elijah 4:11, b.Arachin [Rashi] 31b, b.Gittin [Rashi] 74b, b.Shabbat 149b, Exodus.R 15:6, Ezekiel 28:13-28:17, Isaiah 13:10 14:4-14:6 10:4, Jastrow 474b 1146a, Jeremiah 2:23 51:20-51:24, Luke 10:18, Mekhilta de R'Shimon bar Yochai Shirata 28:2, Mekhilta de R'Ishmael Shirata 2:117, Midrash Tanchuma Beshallach 13, Revelation 2:28 8:10 9:1 12:7-12:10 22:16, Sibylline Oracles 5.212 5.72, Song of Songs.R 8:19
Isaiah 14:12 [LXX] - Greek Apocalypse of Ezra 4:28
Isaiah 14:12-15 - Life of Adam and Eve [Vita] 12:1

[18] 1QIsaa adds *the*

[19] LXX *Lucifer, that rose in the morning, fallen from heaven! He who sent orders to all the nations is crushed to the earth*

וְאַתָּה אָמַרְתָּ בִלְבָבְךָ הַשָּׁמַיִם אֶעֱלֶה מִמַּעַל לְכוֹכְבֵי־אֵל אָרִים כִּסְאִי וְאֵשֵׁב בְּהַר־מוֹעֵד בְּיַרְכְּתֵי צָפוֹן	13[1]	And you said in your heart: 'I will ascend into heaven, Above the stars of God I will exalt my throne, And I will sit on the mount of meeting, In the uttermost parts of the north;
אֶעֱלֶה עַל־בָּמֳתֵי עָב אֶדַּמֶּה לְעֶלְיוֹן	14[2]	I will ascend above the heights of the clouds; I will be like the Most High.'
אַךְ אֶל־שְׁאוֹל תּוּרָד אֶל־יַרְכְּתֵי־בוֹר	15[3]	Yet you shall be brought down to the netherworld, To the uttermost parts of the pit.
רֹאֶיךָ אֵלֶיךָ יַשְׁגִּיחוּ אֵלֶיךָ יִתְבּוֹנָנוּ הֲזֶה הָאִישׁ מַרְגִּיז הָאָרֶץ מַרְעִישׁ מַמְלָכוֹת	16[4]	They who saw you look narrowly upon you, They gaze earnestly at you: 'Is this the man who made the earth tremble, *who*[5] shook kingdoms;
שָׂם תֵּבֵל כַּמִּדְבָּר וְעָרָיו הָרָס אֲסִירָיו לֹא־פָתַח בָּיְתָה	17[6]	Who made the world a wilderness, And destroyed its cities; who did not open the house of his prisoners?'
כָּל־מַלְכֵי גוֹיִם כֻּלָּם שָׁכְבוּ בְכָבוֹד אִישׁ בְּבֵיתוֹ	18[7]	All the kings of the nations, *All of them*[8], sleep in glory, Everyone in his own house.
וְאַתָּה הָשְׁלַכְתָּ מִקִּבְרְךָ כְּנֵצֶר נִתְעָב לְבוּשׁ הֲרֻגִים מְטֹעֲנֵי חָרֶב יוֹרְדֵי אֶל־אַבְנֵי־בוֹר כְּפֶגֶר מוּבָס	19[9]	But you are cast forth *away from your grave*[10] like an *abhorred offshoot*[11], In the raiment of the slain, that are thrust through with the sword, That go down to the *pavement of the*[12] pit, as a carcass trodden under foot.
לֹא־תֵחַד אִתָּם בִּקְבוּרָה כִּי־אַרְצְךָ שִׁחַתָּ עַמְּךָ הָרָגְתָּ לֹא־יִקָּרֵא לְעוֹלָם זֶרַע מְרֵעִים	20[13]	You shall not be *joined*[14] with them in burial, because you have destroyed your land, You have slain your people; *The seed of evildoers shall not be named*[15] forever.
הָכִינוּ לְבָנָיו מַטְבֵּחַ בַּעֲוֹן אֲבוֹתָם בַּל־יָקֻמוּ וְיָרְשׁוּ אָרֶץ וּמָלְאוּ פְנֵי־תֵבֵל עָרִים	21[16]	Prepare slaughter for his children For the iniquity of their fathers; so they may not rise and possess the earth, *And fill the face of the world with cities*[17].

---

[1] Isaiah 14:13 - 2 Thessalonians 2:4, 4QIsac, Daniel 4:27-4:28 5:22-5:23 8:10-8:12, Exodus.R 21:3, Ezekiel 3:3 4:2 4:9 28:12-28:16 5:3, Isaiah 2:2 47:7-47:10, Jastrow 1418a 1703a, Leviticus.R 18:2, Life of Adam and Eve [Vita] 15:3, Matthew 11:23, Mekhilta de R'Shimon bar Yochai Shirata 28:1 34:1, Mekhilta de R'Ishmael Shirata 6:49, Midrash Psalms 14:2, Midrash Tanchuma Tazria 8, Midrash Tanchuma Tzav 2, Numbers.R 9:24, Psalms 48:3, Psalms of Solomon 1:5, Revelation 18:7-18:8, Sibylline Oracles 1.314, t.Sotah 3:19, Zephaniah 2:15

Isaiah 14:13-15 - Greek Apocalypse of Ezra 4:32, Mekhilta de R'Ishmael Shirata 2:85-87, Midrash Tanchuma Beshallach 12

Isaiah 14:13-16 - Sibylline Oracles 3.360

[2] Isaiah 14:14 - 2 Enoch 29:4, 2 Thessalonians 2:4, b.Chagigah 13a, b.Chullin 89a, b.Pesachim 94a, Genesis 3:5, Isaiah 37:23-37:24 23:8, Mekhilta de R'Shimon bar Yochai Shirata 32:1, Mekhilta de R'Ishmael Shirata 6:51, Mekhilta de R'Ishmael Shirata 8:31, Midrash Tanchuma Balak 1, Midrash Tanchuma Beshallach 16, Midrash Tanchuma Tzav 2, Midrash Tanchuma Vaera 9, Numbers.R 9:24 20:1, Pirkei de R'Eliezer 35, t.Sotah 3:19

Isaiah 14:14-15 - Exodus.R 8:2

[3] Isaiah 14:15 - Acts 12:22-12:23, b.Chagigah 13a, b.Pesachim 94a, Ezekiel 28:8-28:9 8:23, Isaiah 14:3-14:11, Luke 10:15, Matthew 11:23, Mekhilta de R'Shimon bar Yochai Shirata 28:1 34:1, Midrash Tanchuma Vaera 9, Midrash Tanchuma Vezot Habracha 6, Numbers.R 9:24, Pirkei de R'Eliezer 35, Revelation 19:20, Sibylline Oracles 5.177 8.100, t.Sotah 3:19

[4] Isaiah 14:16 - Isaiah 14:4-14:5, Jeremiah 2:23 51:20-51:23, Psalms 52:8 58:11-58:12 64:10

[5] 1QIsaa *he one who*

[6] Isaiah 14:17 - 2 Chronicles 28:8-15, Ezekiel 6:14, Ezra 1:2-4, Genesis.R 83:2, Isaiah 13:19-22 21:13 10:6 16:11, Joel 2:3, Leviticus.R 18:2 19:6, Midrash Tanchuma Tazria 8, Zephaniah 2:13-14

[7] Isaiah 14:18 - 2 Chronicles 24:16 24:25, b.Shabbat 149b, Ecclesiastes 6:3 12:5, Ezekiel 32:18-32:32, Isaiah 22:16, Job 6:23

[8] Missing in 1QIsaa

[9] Isaiah 14:19 - 1 Kings 21:19 21:24, 2 Kings 9:25 9:34-9:36, 4Q165 frag 3 1.1, Ezekiel 8:23, Isaiah 22:16-22:18, Jeremiah 8:1-8:2 16:6 22:19 17:7 17:9, Leviticus.R 18:2, Midrash Tanchuma Tazria 8, Seder Olam 28:Daniel, Tanna Devei Eliyahu 5

[10] LXX *on the mountains*

[11] LXX *loathed carcass*

[12] Missing in 1QIsaa

[13] Isaiah 14:20 - Isaiah 1:4 13:15-13:19, Job 18:16 18:19, Psalms 21:11 37:28 13:13 137:8-137:9

Isaiah 14:20-24 - 4QIsae

[14] 1QIsaa *under*

[15] 1QIsaa plural verb with singular noun; LXX *May you not remember forever the evil seed*

[16] Isaiah 14:21 - b.Taanit [Tosefot] 5a, Esther.R 4:2, Exodus 20:5, Habakkuk 2:8-2:12, Isaiah 3:6, Leviticus 2:39, Matthew 23:35

[17] LXX *nor fill the earth with wars*

וַהֲקִמֹתִי עֲלֵיהֶם נְאֻם יְהוָה צְבָאוֹת וְהִכְרַתִּי לְבָבֶל
שֵׁם וּשְׁאָר וְנִין וָנֶכֶד נְאֻם־יְהוָה

22[1] And I will rise against them, says the LORD of hosts, and cut off from Babylon name and *remnant, and offshoot and offspring*[2], says the LORD.

וְשַׂמְתִּיהָ לְמוֹרַשׁ קִפֹּד וְאַגְמֵי־מָיִם וְטֵאטֵאתִיהָ
בְּמַטְאֲטֵא הַשְׁמֵד נְאֻם יְהוָה צְבָאוֹת

23[3] I will also make *it*[4] a possession for the *bittern*[5], and pools of water; and I will sweep it with the besom of destruction, says the LORD of hosts.

נִשְׁבַּע יְהוָה צְבָאוֹת לֵאמֹר אִם־לֹא כַּאֲשֶׁר דִּמִּיתִי
כֵּן הָיָתָה וְכַאֲשֶׁר יָעַצְתִּי הִיא תָקוּם

24[6] *The LORD of hosts has sworn*[7], saying: Surely as I have thought, so it shall come to pass; And as I have planned, so shall it stand,

לִשְׁבֹּר אַשּׁוּר בְּאַרְצִי וְעַל־הָרַי אֲבוּסֶנּוּ וְסָר
מֵעֲלֵיהֶם עֻלּוֹ וְסֻבֳּלוֹ מֵעַל שִׁכְמוֹ יָסוּר

25[8] That I will break Asshur in My land, And on My mountains tread him under foot; Then his yoke shall depart *from off them*[9], And his burden depart *from off their shoulder*[10].

זֹאת הָעֵצָה הַיְּעוּצָה עַל־כָּל־הָאָרֶץ וְזֹאת הַיָּד
הַנְּטוּיָה עַל־כָּל־הַגּוֹיִם

26[11] This is the purpose that is planned on the whole earth; And this is the hand that is stretched out on all the nations.

כִּי־יְהוָה צְבָאוֹת יָעָץ וּמִי יָפֵר וְיָדוֹ הַנְּטוּיָה וּמִי
יְשִׁיבֶנָּה

27[12] For the LORD of hosts has purposed, And who shall reverse it? And His hand is stretched out, And who shall turn it back?

בִּשְׁנַת־מוֹת הַמֶּלֶךְ אָחָז הָיָה הַמַּשָּׂא הַזֶּה

28[13] In the year that king Ahaz died was this burden.

אַל־תִּשְׂמְחִי פְלֶשֶׁת כֻּלֵּךְ כִּי נִשְׁבַּר שֵׁבֶט מַכֵּךְ כִּי־
מִשֹּׁרֶשׁ נָחָשׁ יֵצֵא צֶפַע וּפִרְיוֹ שָׂרָף מְעוֹפֵף

29[14] Do not rejoice, O Philistia, all of you, Because the rod who smote you is broken: For out of the serpent's root shall come forth *a basilisk*[15], And his fruit shall be a flying serpent.

וְרָעוּ בְּכוֹרֵי דַלִּים וְאֶבְיוֹנִים לָבֶטַח יִרְבָּצוּ וְהֵמַתִּי
בָרָעָב שָׁרְשֵׁךְ וּשְׁאֵרִיתֵךְ יַהֲרֹג

30[16] And *the firstborn of*[17] the poor shall feed, And the needy shall lie down in safety; And I will kill your root with famine, *And your remnant shall be slain*[18].

---

[1] Isaiah 14:22 - 1 Kings 14:10, b.Avodah Zara [Tosefot] 10a, b.Megillah 10b, Ein Yaakov Megillah:9b, Esther.R Petichata:12, Isaiah 13:5 21:9 19:14 47:9-14, Jeremiah 50:26-27 50:29-35 51:3-4 51:56-57 51:62-64, Job 18:16-19, Midrash Tanchuma Nitzavim 1, Proverbs 10:7

[2] 1QIsaa *remnant, and offspring, and posterity*; LXX *and posterity*

[3] Isaiah 14:23 - 1 Kings 14:10, 2 Kings 21:13, b.Bava Batra [Rashbam] 119b, b.Bava Kamma 55a, b.Berachot 57b 58a, b.Eruvin 18b, b.Megillah 18a, b.Rosh Hashanah 26b, b.Yoma [Rashi] 9b, Ein Yaakov Bava Kamma:55a, Genesis.R 79:7, Isaiah 13:21-22 34:11-15, Jeremiah 50:39-40 51:25-26 51:42-43, Revelation 14:8 18:2 18:21-23, y.Berachot 9:1, Zephaniah 2:14

[4] LXX *the region of Babylon desert*

[5] 1QIsaa *hedgehog* [misspelled in 1QIsaa]

[6] Isaiah 14:24 - Acts 4:28, Amos 8:7, b.Sanhedrin 94b, Ein Yaakov Sanhedrin:94b, Ephesians 1:9, Exodus 17:16, Hebrews 4:3 6:16-6:18, Isaiah 46:10-46:11, Jeremiah 23:20 5:11 20:26, Job 23:13, Lamentations 3:37, Matthew 11:25, Midrash Tanchuma Shoftim 16, Proverbs 19:21 21:30, Psalms 33:10 92:6 14:4

[7] LXX *I have sworn*

[8] Isaiah 14:25 - b.Sanhedrin 94b, Ein Yaakov Sanhedrin:94b, Ezekiel 15:4, Isaiah 9:5 10:12 10:16-19 10:24-27 10:32-34 14:5 17:12-14 30:30-33 31:8-9 37:36-38, Mekhilta de R'Shimon bar Yochai Beshallach 25:3, Mekilta de R'Ishmael Beshallah 6:153, Nahum 1:13

[9] 1QIsaa *from you*

[10] 1QIsaa *from your shoulder*

[11] Isaiah 14:26 - Exodus 15:12, Isaiah 5:25 23:9, Mekhilta de R'Shimon bar Yochai Beshallach 25:3, Zephaniah 3:6-8
Isaiah 14:26-27 - 4Q163 8-10 4-7, 4Q163 frags 8-10 ll.4-7, Mekilta de R'Ishmael Beshallah 6:156

[12] Isaiah 14:27 - 2 Chronicles 20:6, Daniel 4:28-4:32, Isaiah 9:13 23:9 19:13 22:11, Jeremiah 4:28 3:59, Job 9:12 23:13 16:8, Mekhilta de R'Shimon bar Yochai Beshallach 25:3, Proverbs 19:21 21:30, Psalms 33:11, Romans 8:28 8:31

[13] Isaiah 14:28 - 2 Chronicles 4:27, 2 Kings 16:20, Isaiah 6:1 13:1
Isaiah 14:28-30 - 4Q163 frags 8-10 ll.11-14
Isaiah 14:28-32 - 4QIsao, Josephus Antiquities 9.8.3

[14] Isaiah 14:29 - 1 Samuel 6:17-6:18, 2 Chronicles 2:6 4:18, 2 Kings 18:8, Ezekiel 2:2 11:15, Hosea 9:1, Isaiah 11:8 6:6, Joshua 13:3, Micah 7:8, Obadiah 1:12, Proverbs 24:17, Zephaniah 3:11

[15] LXX *the young asps*

[16] Isaiah 14:30 - Amos 1:6-1:8, Ezekiel 25:15-25:17, Isaiah 3:15 5:17 7:21-7:22 8:21 9:21 30:23-30:24 9:16 13:30 3:19 65:13-65:14, Jeremiah 47:1-47:7, Job 18:13, Joel 4:4-4:8, Zechariah 9:5-9:7, Zephaniah 2:4-2:7

[17] Missing in LXX

[18] 1QIsaa *and I will slay your remnant*

הֵילִ֨ילִי שַׁ֜עַר זַֽעֲקִי־עִ֗יר נָמ֛וֹג פְּלֶ֥שֶׁת כֻּלֵּ֖ךְ כִּ֥י מִצָּפ֣וֹן עָשָׁ֣ן בָּ֑א וְאֵ֥ין בּוֹדֵ֖ד בְּמוֹעָדָֽיו

31[1] Howl, *O gate; cry, O city*[2]; Melt away, O Philistia, all of you; For a smoke comes out of the north, And there is *no straggler in his ranks*[3].

וּמַֽה־יַּעֲנֶ֖ה מַלְאֲכֵי־ג֑וֹי כִּ֤י יְהֹוָה֙ יִסַּ֣ד צִיּ֔וֹן וּבָ֥הּ יֶחֱס֖וּ עֲנִיֵּ֥י עַמּֽוֹ

32[4] What then shall *one*[5] answer the *messengers*[6] of the nation? That the LORD has founded Zion, And in *her*[7] shall the *afflicted*[8] of His people take refuge.

Isaiah – Chapter 15

מַשָּׂ֖א מוֹאָ֑ב כִּ֠י בְּלֵ֞יל שֻׁדַּ֨ד עָ֤ר מוֹאָב֙ נִדְמָ֔ה כִּ֗י בְּלֵ֛יל שֻׁדַּ֥ד קִיר־מוֹאָ֖ב נִדְמָֽה

1[9] *The oracle of Moab*[10]. For in the night that *Ar*[11] of Moab is laid waste, He is brought to ruin; For in the night that *Kir*[12] of Moab is laid waste, He is brought to ruin.

עָלָ֨ה הַבַּ֧יִת וְדִיבֹ֛ן הַבָּמ֖וֹת לְבֶ֑כִי עַל־נְב֞וֹ וְעַ֤ל מֵֽידְבָא֙ מוֹאָ֣ב יְיֵלִ֔יל בְּכׇל־רֹאשָׁ֣יו קׇרְחָ֔ה כׇּל־זָקָ֖ן גְּרוּעָֽה

2[13] *He is gone up to Baith, and to Dibon, to the high places, to weep; Upon Nebo, and upon Medeba, Moab howls; On all their*[14] *heads is baldness, Every beard is shaven*[15].

בְּחֽוּצֹתָ֖יו חָ֣גְרוּ שָׂ֑ק עַ֣ל גַּגּוֹתֶ֧יהָ וּבִרְחֹבֹתֶ֛יהָ כֻּלֹּ֥ה יְיֵלִ֖יל יֹרֵ֥ד בַּבֶּֽכִי

3[16] In their streets they clothe themselves with sackcloth; On their housetops, and in their broad places, Every one howls, weeping profusely.

וַתִּזְעַ֤ק חֶשְׁבּוֹן֙ וְאֶלְעָלֵ֔ה עַד־יַ֖הַץ נִשְׁמַ֣ע קוֹלָ֑ם עַל־כֵּ֗ן חֲלֻצֵ֤י מוֹאָב֙ יָרִ֔יעוּ נַפְשׁ֖וֹ יָ֥רְעָה לּֽוֹ

4[17] And Heshbon cries out, and Elealeh; Their voice is heard in Jahaz; Therefore, *the armed men*[18] of Moab cry aloud; *His soul is faint within him*[19].

---

[1] Isaiah 14:31 - Isaiah 3:26 13:6 14:29 16:7 20:1 24:12, Jeremiah 1:14 25:16-25:20

[2] LXX *you gates of cities; let the cities be troubled and cry*

[3] 1QIsaa *none who metes out payment* [error?] *among its kinsmen*; LXX *no possibility of living*

[4] Isaiah 14:32 - 2 Kings 20:12-20:19, 2 Samuel 8:10, Exodus.R 5:12 31:5 31:13, Hebrews 12:22, Isaiah 4:6 11:4 12:6 1:4 4:16 13:9 13:32 15:1 20:28 6:11, James 2:5, Matthew 16:18 24:15-24:16, Midrash Tanchuma Kedoshim 1, Midrash Tanchuma Mishpatim 9, Midrash Tanchuma Shemot 29, Proverbs 18:10, Psalms 87:1 87:5 6:17 6:29 132:13-132:14, Zechariah 11:7 11:11, Zephaniah 3:12

[5] 1QIsaa *they*

[6] 1QIsaa *kings*

[7] 1QIsaa *it*

[8] LXX *poor*

[9] Isaiah 15:1 - 1 Thessalonians 5:1-3, 2 Kings 3:25, Amos 2:1-3, Deuteronomy 2:9 2:18, Exodus 12:29-30, Ezekiel 25:8-11, Genesis.R 41:3, Isaiah 11:14 13:1 14:28 16:7 16:11 1:10, Jeremiah 9:27 48:1-47, Lamentations.R 1:38, Leviticus.R 14:2, Numbers 21:28, Pesikta Rabbati 33:3, Zephaniah 2:8-11
Isaiah 15:1-2 - 4QIsao
Isaiah 15:1-9 - 1QIsaa

[10] LXX *The word against the land of Moab*

[11] LXX *the land*

[12] 1QIsaa *the city*; LXX *the wall of the land*

[13] Isaiah 15:2 - Deuteronomy 14:1 10:1, Ezekiel 7:18, Isaiah 3:24 14:31 15:3 16:7 16:12 22:12, Jastrow 271b, Jeremiah 7:29 23:5 24:1 24:18 48:22-23 24:31 48:37-39, Job 1:20, Joshua 13:16-17, Leviticus 19:27-28 21:5, m.Kilayim 22:3, Numbers 21:30 8:3 8:38

[14] 1QIsaa *its*

[15] LXX *Grieve for yourselves; for Debon, where your altar is, shall be destroyed: there you shall go up to weep, over Nabau of the land of Moab: howl: baldness shall be on every head, and all arms shall be wounded*

[16] Isaiah 15:3 - 2 Kings 6:30, 2 Samuel 3:31, Deuteronomy 22:8, Isaiah 15:2 22:1 22:4, Jeremiah 19:13 48:38-39, Jonah 3:6-8, Matthew 11:21
Isaiah 15:3-9 - 1QIsab

[17] Isaiah 15:4 - 1 Kings 19:4, Deuteronomy 2:32, Genesis 3:46, Isaiah 16:8-9, Jeremiah 8:3 20:18 24:34, Job 3:21-23 7:15-16, Jonah 4:3 4:8, Joshua 13:18, Judges 11:20, Numbers 11:15 21:23 32:3-4, Revelation 9:6
Isaiah 15:4-5 - 4Q165 frag 4.1-2

[18] LXX *the loins of the region*

[19] LXX *her soul shall know*

לְבִּי לְמוֹאָב יִזְעָק בְּרִיחֶהָ עַד־צֹעַר עֶגְלַת שְׁלִשִׁיָּה
כִּי מַעֲלֵה הַלּוּחִית בִּבְכִי יַעֲלֶה־בּוֹ כִּי דֶּרֶךְ חוֹרֹנַיִם
זַעֲקַת־שֶׁבֶר יְעֹעֵרוּ

5[1] My heart cries out for Moab; Her fugitives reach *Zoar*[2], A heifer of three years old; For by the ascent of Luhith with weeping they go up; For in the way of Horonaim they raise up a cry of destruction[3].

כִּי־מֵי נִמְרִים מְשַׁמּוֹת יִהְיוּ כִּי־יָבֵשׁ חָצִיר כָּלָה
דֶּשֶׁא יֶרֶק לֹא הָיָה

6[4] For the Waters of Nimrim shall be desolate; for the grass has withered, the herbage fails, there is no green thing.

עַל־כֵּן יִתְרָה עָשָׂה וּפְקֻדָּתָם עַל גַּחַל הָעֲרָבִים
יִשָּׂאוּם

7[5] Therefore, the abundance they received, and what they stored away, they shall carry away to the brook of the *willows*[6].

כִּי־הִקִּיפָה הַזְּעָקָה אֶת־גְּבוּל מוֹאָב עַד־אֶגְלַיִם
יְלָלָתָהּ וּבְאֵר אֵילִים יְלָלָתָהּ

8[7] For the cry has gone around The borders of Moab; its howling to Eglaim, And its howling to Beer-elim.

כִּי מֵי דִימוֹן מָלְאוּ דָם כִּי־אָשִׁית עַל־דִּימוֹן
נוֹסָפוֹת לִפְלֵיטַת מוֹאָב אַרְיֵה וְלִשְׁאֵרִית אֲדָמָה

9[8] For the waters of *Dimon*[9] are full of blood; For I will bring *yet more*[10] upon *Dimon*[11], *A lion upon him who escapes of Moab, And upon the remnant of the land*[12].

Isaiah – Chapter 16

שִׁלְחוּ־כַר מֹשֵׁל־אֶרֶץ מִסֶּלַע מִדְבָּרָה אֶל־הַר בַּת־
צִיּוֹן

1[13] Send the *lambs*[14] for the ruler of the land from *the crags*[15] that are toward the wilderness, to the mount of the daughter of Zion.

וְהָיָה כְעוֹף־נוֹדֵד קֵן מְשֻׁלָּח תִּהְיֶינָה בְּנוֹת מוֹאָב
מַעְבָּרֹת לְאַרְנוֹן

2[16] *For it shall be that, as wandering birds, As a scattered nest*[17], So shall the daughters of Moab be At the fords of Arnon.

הָבִיאוּ "הָבִיאִי" עֵצָה עֲשׂוּ פְלִילָה שִׁיתִי כַלַּיִל
צִלֵּךְ בְּתוֹךְ צָהֳרַיִם סַתְּרִי נִדָּחִים נֹדֵד אַל־תְּגַלִּי

3[18] 'Give counsel, execute justice; Make your shadow as the night in the midst of noonday; *Hide the outcasts; do not betray the fugitive*[19].

יָגוּרוּ בָךְ נִדָּחַי מוֹאָב הֱוִי־סֵתֶר לָמוֹ מִפְּנֵי שׁוֹדֵד
כִּי־אָפֵס הַמֵּץ כָּלָה שֹׁד תַּמּוּ רֹמֵס מִן־הָאָרֶץ

4[20] *Let my outcasts live with you; As for Moab, be a covert to him from the face of the spoiler.'*
For the extortion is at an end, spoiling ceases,

---

[1] Isaiah 15:5 - 2 Samuel 15:23 15:30, b.Sotah [Rashi] 18b, Genesis 13:10 14:2 19:22, Isaiah 16:9-11 16:14 22:5, Jeremiah 4:20 8:18-19 9:11 9:19-20 13:17 17:16 24:5 48:31-36, Luke 19:41-44, Romans 9:1-3

[2] LXX *Segor*

[3] LXX *and trembling*

[4] Isaiah 15:6 - Habakkuk 3:17-18, Isaiah 16:9-10 19:5-7, Jeremiah 24:34, Joel 1:10-12, Joshua 13:27, Numbers 8:3 8:36, Revelation 8:7, z.Beshallach 52b

[5] Isaiah 15:7 - Isaiah 5:29 10:6 10:14 6:6, Jeremiah 24:36, Nahum 2:13-2:14, Psalms 137:1-137:2

[6] 1QIsaa *Arabs*; LXX replaced verse with *Shall Moab thus be delivered? For I will bring the Arabians upon the valley, and they shall take it*

[7] Isaiah 15:8 - Ezekiel 23:10, Isaiah 15:2-15:5, Jeremiah 48:20-48:24 48:31-48:34, z.Vayikra 25b

[8] Isaiah 15:9 - 2 Kings 17:25, Amos 5:19, Jeremiah 15:3 48:43-45 2:17, Leviticus 2:18 26:21-22 2:24 28

[9] 1QIsaa *Dimon*

[10] LXX *Arabians*

[11] 1QIsaa *Dimon*

[12] LXX *and I will take away the seed of Moab, and Ariel, and the remnant of Adama*

[13] Isaiah 16:1 - 2 Kings 3:4 14:7, 2 Samuel 8:2, b.Niddah 31b, b.Sanhedrin 96b, Ein Yaakov Sanhedrin:96b, Ezra 7:17, Isaiah 10:32 18:11, Jastrow 128b, Micah 4:8

Isaiah 16:1-2 - 1QIsab

Isaiah 16:1-14 - 1QIsaa

[14] LXX *reptiles*

[15] *Dimon*[15] selah

[16] Isaiah 16:2 - Deuteronomy 2:36 3:8 3:12, Isaiah 13:14, Jeremiah 24:20, Joshua 13:16, Judges 11:18, Midrash Tanchuma Ki Tetze 2, Numbers 21:13-21:15, Proverbs 3:8, z.Yitro 89a

[17] LXX replaces verse with *For you shall be as a young bird taken away from a bird that has flown*

[18] Isaiah 16:3 - 1 Kings 18:4, Daniel 4:24, Ezekiel 45:9-45:12, Hebrews 13:2, Isaiah 1:17 9:7 1:4 8:2 8:8, Jeremiah 21:12 22:3, Jonah 4:5-8, Judges 9:15, Matthew 1:35, Obadiah 1:12-14, Psalms 82:3-82:4, Zechariah 7:9

[19] LXX *they are amazed; do not be led captive*

[20] Isaiah 16:4 - Deuteronomy 23:17-23:17 24:14, Isaiah 9:5 14:4 15:6 1:10 9:1 3:13, Jeremiah 21:12 24:8 24:18, Luke 21:24, Malachi 3:21, Revelation 11:2, Romans 16:20, z.Yitro 89a, Zechariah 9:8 10:5

They who trampled down are consumed from the land[1];

And a throne is established through mercy, And sits there in truth, in the tent of David, One who judges, and seeks justice, and is ready in righteousness.

5[2]

וְהוּכַן בַּחֶסֶד כִּסֵּא וְיָשַׁב עָלָיו בֶּאֱמֶת בְּאֹהֶל דָּוִד שֹׁפֵט וְדֹרֵשׁ מִשְׁפָּט וּמְהִר צֶדֶק

We have heard of the pride of Moab; *He is very proud[4]*; of his haughtiness, and his pride, and his arrogance, His ill-founded boastings[5].

6[3]

שָׁמַעְנוּ גְאוֹן־מוֹאָב גֵּא מְאֹד גַּאֲוָתוֹ וּגְאוֹנוֹ וְעֶבְרָתוֹ לֹא־כֵן בַּדָּיו

Therefore, Moab shall wail for Moab, Everyone shall wail[7]; you shall mourn for the sweet cakes of Kir-hareseth, Sorely stricken.

7[6]

לָכֵן יְיֵלִיל מוֹאָב לְמוֹאָב כֻּלֹּה יְיֵלִיל לַאֲשִׁישֵׁי קִיר־חֲרֶשֶׂת תֶּהְגּוּ אַךְ־נְכָאִים

For the fields of Heshbon languish, And the vine of Sibmah, *whose choice plants overcame the lords of nations; they reached through to Jazer, they wandered into the wilderness; her branches were spread abroad, they passed over the sea[9].*

8[8]

כִּי שַׁדְמוֹת חֶשְׁבּוֹן אֻמְלָל גֶּפֶן שִׂבְמָה בַּעֲלֵי גוֹיִם הָלְמוּ שְׂרוּקֶּיהָ עַד־יַעְזֵר נָגָעוּ תָּעוּ מִדְבָּר שְׁלֻחוֹתֶיהָ נִטְּשׁוּ עָבְרוּ יָם

Therefore, I will weep with the weeping of Jazer For the vine of Sibmah[11]; I will water you with my tears, O Heshbon, and Elealeh; For upon your summer fruits and upon your harvest, the battle shout is fallen[12].

9[10]

עַל־כֵּן אֶבְכֶּה בִּבְכִי יַעְזֵר גֶּפֶן שִׂבְמָה אֲרַיָּוֶךְ דִּמְעָתִי חֶשְׁבּוֹן וְאֶלְעָלֵה כִּי עַל־קֵיצֵךְ וְעַל־קְצִירֵךְ הֵידָד נָפָל

And gladness and joy are taken away from the *fruitful field[14]*; And in the vineyards there shall be no singing[15], nor shall there be shouting[16]; No treader shall tread out wine in the presses; I have made the vintage shout to cease.

10[13]

וְנֶאֱסַף שִׂמְחָה וָגִיל מִן־הַכַּרְמֶל וּבַכְּרָמִים לֹא־יְרֻנָּן לֹא יְרֹעָע יַיִן בַּיְקָבִים לֹא־יִדְרֹךְ הַדֹּרֵךְ הֵידָד הִשְׁבַּתִּי

When my heart moans like a harp for Moab, and *my inward parts for Kir-heres[18]*.

11[17]

עַל־כֵּן מֵעַי לְמוֹאָב כַּכִּנּוֹר יֶהֱמוּ וְקִרְבִּי לְקִיר חָרֶשׂ

---

[1] LXX *The fugitives of Moab shall sojourn with you; they shall be to you a shelter from the face of the pursuer: for your alliance has been taken away, and the oppressing ruler has perished from off the earth*

[2] Isaiah 16:5 - 1 Kings 10:9, 2 Chronicles 7:20, 2 Peter 3:11-12, 2 Samuel 5:9 7:16 23:3, 3 Enoch 31:2, Acts 15:16-17, Amos 9:11, Daniel 7:14 7:27, Genesis.R 97:1, Hebrews 1:8-9, Isaiah 9:7-8 11:1-5 32:1-2 7:4, Jeremiah 23:5-6, Luke 1:31-33 1:69-75, Mesillat Yesharim 11:Nekiyut-from-Falsehood, Micah 4:7, Midrash Psalms 89:2 110:4, Proverbs 20:28 5:14, Psalms 61:7-8 72:2-4 85:11 89:2-3 89:15 96:13 98:9 99:4, z.Mishpatim 122a, z.Pekudei 220b, z.Yitro 89a, Zechariah 9:9

[3] Isaiah 16:6 - 1 Peter 5:5, Amos 2:1, Isaiah 2:11 4:15 4:18 20:25, Jeremiah 24:26 48:29-30 24:42 2:36, Obadiah 1:3-4, Zephaniah 2:8-10

[4] 1QIsaa *how he became very proud*

[5] 1QIsaa *of his haughtiness, and his pride, and his arrogance, indeed, of his boasting*; LXX *but you shall care for those who live in Seth, and you shall not be ashamed*

[6] Isaiah 16:7 - 1 Chronicles 16:3, 2 Kings 3:25, Isaiah 8:19 15:1-15:5 16:11, Jeremiah 24:20
Isaiah 16:7-12 - 1QIsab

[7] 1QIsaa *Therefore, let not Moab wait, [but] let everyone wail for Moab.*

[8] Isaiah 16:8 - 2 Samuel 1:21, Isaiah 10:7 15:4 16:9 24:7, Jeremiah 27:6-7 24:32, Joshua 13:19 13:25, Numbers 8:3 8:38

[9] Missing in 1QIsaa; LXX *swallowing up the nations, trample her vines, to Jazer: you shall not come together; wander in the desert: they who were sent are deserted, for they have gone over to the sea*

[10] Isaiah 16:9 - Isaiah 9:4 15:4-5, Jeremiah 16:10 16:12 48:32-34, Judges 9:27

[11] Missing test in 1QIsaa

[12] LXX *Esebon and Eleale cast down your trees; for I will trample on your harvest and on your vintages, and all your plants shall fall*

[13] Isaiah 16:10 - Amos 5:11 5:17, Habakkuk 3:17-18, Isaiah 24:7-9 8:10, Jeremiah 24:33, Job 24:11, Judges 9:27, t.Kippurim 4:10, Zephaniah 1:13

[14] LXX *vineyards*

[15] 1QIsaa *and in the vineyards people will sing no songs*; Missing in LXX

[16] Missing in LXX

[17] Isaiah 16:11 - Hosea 11:8, Isaiah 15:5 15:15, Jeremiah 4:19 7:21 24:36, Midrash Tanchuma Balak 1, Philippians 2:1

[18] LXX *you hast repaired my inward parts as a wall*

וְהָיָה כִי־נִרְאָה כִּי־נִלְאָה מוֹאָב עַל־הַבָּמָה וּבָא אֶל־מִקְדָּשׁוֹ לְהִתְפַּלֵּל וְלֹא יוּכָל

12[1] *And it shall come to pass*[2], when it is seen that Moab has *wearied himself*[3] on the high place, that he shall come to his sanctuary to pray; but *he shall not prevail*[4].

זֶה הַדָּבָר אֲשֶׁר דִּבֶּר יְהוָה אֶל־מוֹאָב מֵאָז

13[5] This is the word that the LORD spoke concerning Moab in times past.

וְעַתָּה דִּבֶּר יְהוָה לֵאמֹר בְּשָׁלֹשׁ שָׁנִים כִּשְׁנֵי שָׂכִיר וְנִקְלָה כְּבוֹד מוֹאָב בְּכֹל הֶהָמוֹן הָרָב וּשְׁאָר מְעַט מִזְעָר לוֹא כַבִּיר

14[6] *But now the LORD has spoken, saying*[7]: 'Within three years, as the years of a hireling, and the glory of Moab shall grow contemptible for all his great multitude; and the remnant shall be very small and without strength.'

Isaiah – Chapter 17

מַשָּׂא דַּמֶּשֶׂק הִנֵּה דַמֶּשֶׂק מוּסָר מֵעִיר וְהָיְתָה מְעִי מַפָּלָה

1[8] The oracle of *Damascus*[9]. Behold, *Damascus*[10] is taken away from being a city, And it shall be a ruinous waste.

עֲזֻבוֹת עָרֵי עֲרֹעֵר לַעֲדָרִים תִּהְיֶינָה וְרָבְצוּ וְאֵין מַחֲרִיד

2[11] The cities of *Aroer*[12] are forsaken; They shall be for flocks, Which shall lie down, and no one shall make them afraid.

וְנִשְׁבַּת מִבְצָר מֵאֶפְרַיִם וּמַמְלָכָה מִדַּמֶּשֶׂק וּשְׁאָר אֲרָם כִּכְבוֹד בְּנֵי־יִשְׂרָאֵל יִהְיוּ נְאֻם יְהוָה צְבָאוֹת

3[13] *The fortress shall cease from Ephraim, And the kingdom from Damascus*[14]*; And the remnant of Aram shall be as the glory of the children of Israel*[15], Says the LORD of hosts.

וְהָיָה בַּיּוֹם הַהוּא יִדַּל כְּבוֹד יַעֲקֹב וּמִשְׁמַן בְּשָׂרוֹ יֵרָזֶה

4[16] And it shall come to pass in that day, That the glory of Jacob shall be made thin, And the *fatness of his flesh shall grow lean*[17].

וְהָיָה כֶּאֱסֹף קָצִיר קָמָה וּזְרֹעוֹ שִׁבֳּלִים יִקְצוֹר וְהָיָה כִּמְלַקֵּט שִׁבֳּלִים בְּעֵמֶק רְפָאִים

5[18] And it shall be as when the harvester gathers the standing corn, and reaps the ears with his arm; yes, it shall be as when one gleans ears in *the valley of Rephaim*[19].

---

[1] Isaiah 16:12 - 1 Kings 11:7 18:29, 2 Kings 3:27 19:12 19:16-19, Isaiah 15:2 2:16 13:38 23:13, Jastrow 686a, Jeremiah 10:5 24:7 24:13 24:35 24:46, Numbers 22:39 22:41-3 23:14 23:28 24:17, Proverbs 1:28, Psalms 115:3-7, Psalms of Solomon 4:13

[2] LXX *And it shall be to your shame*

[3] 1QIsaa *comes*

[4] LXX *they shall not be at all able to deliver him*

[5] Isaiah 16:13 - Isaiah 20:8

[6] Isaiah 16:14 - b.Kiddushin [Tosefot] 14a, b.Sotah [Tosefot] 9a, Deuteronomy 15:8, Esther 5:11, Genesis 7:1, Isaiah 7:16 15:5 17:4 21:16 23:9 1:10, Jeremiah 9:24 24:42 48:46-48:47, mt.Hilchot Avadim 2:5, Nahum 2:10-2:11, Seder Olam 23:Sennacherib

[7] LXX *And now I say*

[8] Isaiah 17:1 - 1 Chronicles 18:5, 1 Kings 11:24, 2 Chronicles 4:5 4:23, 2 Kings 16:9, Acts 9:2, Amos 1:3-1:5, Esther.R 3:4, Genesis 14:15 15:2, Isaiah 7:8 8:4 10:9 13:1 15:1 19:1 1:2 13:26, Jeremiah 1:2 49:23-27, Micah 1:6 3:12, Song of Songs.R 1:38, Zechariah 9:1 Isaiah 17:1-2 - Lamentations.R Petichata D'Chakimei:10 Isaiah 17:1-14 - 1QIsaa

[9] 1QIsaa *Dramascus*

[10] 1QIsaa *Dramascus*

[11] Isaiah 17:2 - Deuteronomy 2:36 3:12, Ezekiel 1:5, Isaiah 5:17 7:21 7:23-7:25, Jeremiah 7:33 24:19, Joshua 13:16, Micah 4:4, Numbers 8:34, Song of Songs.R 1:38, Zephaniah 2:6

[12] 1QIsaa *Oraru*; LXX *forever*

[13] Isaiah 17:3 - 2 Kings 16:9 17:6, Amos 2:6-9 3:9-15 5:25-27 6:7-11 8:14-10, Hosea 1:4 1:6 3:4 5:13-14 8:8 9:11 9:16-17 10:14 13:7-8 13:15-16, Isaiah 7:8 7:16 8:4 10:9 16:14 17:4 28:1-4, Micah 1:4-9

[14] 1QIsaa *Dramascus*

[15] LXX *And she shall no longer be a strong place to which Ephraim can flee, and there shall no longer be a kingdom in Damascus, or a remnant of Syrians; for you are no better than the children of Israel, than their glory*

[16] Isaiah 17:4 - Deuteronomy 32:15-27, Ezekiel 10:20, Isaiah 9:9 9:22 10:4 10:16 24:13 24:16, z.Vayechi 228a, Zephaniah 2:11

[17] LXX *riches of his glory shall be shaken*

[18] Isaiah 17:5 - 2 Samuel 5:18 5:22, Hosea 6:11, Isaiah 17:11, Jeremiah 9:23 3:33, Joel 4:13, Joshua 15:8 18:16, Matthew 13:30 13:39-42, Revelation 14:15-20

[19] LXX *a rich valley*

וְנִשְׁאַר־בּוֹ עוֹלֵלֹת כְּנֹקֶף זַיִת שְׁנַיִם שְׁלֹשָׁה
גַּרְגְּרִים בְּרֹאשׁ אָמִיר אַרְבָּעָה חֲמִשָּׁה בִּסְעִפֶיהָ
פֹּרִיָּה נְאֻם־יְהוָה אֱלֹהֵי יִשְׂרָאֵל

6[1] Yet gleanings shall remain, As at the beating of an olive tree, two or three berries in the top of the uppermost bough, Four or five in the branches of the fruitful tree, says the LORD, the God of Israel.

בַּיּוֹם הַהוּא יִשְׁעֶה הָאָדָם עַל־עֹשֵׂהוּ וְעֵינָיו אֶל־
קְדוֹשׁ יִשְׂרָאֵל תִּרְאֶינָה

7[2] In that day a man shall *regard*[3] his Maker, And his eyes shall look to the Holy One of Israel.

וְלֹא יִשְׁעֶה אֶל־הַמִּזְבְּחוֹת מַעֲשֵׂה יָדָיו וַאֲשֶׁר עָשׂוּ
אֶצְבְּעֹתָיו לֹא יִרְאֶה וְהָאֲשֵׁרִים וְהָחַמָּנִים

8[4] And he shall not *regard*[5] the altars, The work of his hands, nor shall he look to what his fingers have made, Either the Asherim, or the sun images.

בַּיּוֹם הַהוּא יִהְיוּ עָרֵי מָעֻזּוֹ כַּעֲזוּבַת הַחֹרֶשׁ
וְהָאָמִיר אֲשֶׁר עָזְבוּ מִפְּנֵי בְּנֵי יִשְׂרָאֵל וְהָיְתָה
שְׁמָמָה

9[6] In that day his strong cities shall be *the forsaken places, which were forsaken from before the children of Israel, after the manner of woods and lofty forests*[7]; and it shall be a desolation.

כִּי שָׁכַחַתְּ אֱלֹהֵי יִשְׁעֵךְ וְצוּר מָעֻזֵּךְ לֹא זָכָרְתְּ עַל־
כֵּן תִּטְּעִי נִטְעֵי נַעֲמָנִים וּזְמֹרַת זָר תִּזְרָעֶנּוּ

10[8] For you have forgotten the God of your salvation, And you have not been mindful of *the Rock of your stronghold*[9]; Therefore, you planted *plants of pleasantness, And set it with slips of a stranger*[10];

בְּיוֹם נִטְעֵךְ תְּשַׂגְשֵׂגִי וּבַבֹּקֶר זַרְעֵךְ תַּפְרִיחִי נֵד
קָצִיר בְּיוֹם נַחֲלָה וּכְאֵב אָנוּשׁ

11[11] In the day of your planting *you made it to grow, And in the morning you made your seed to blossom*— A heap of boughs in the day of grief And of desperate pain[12].

הוֹי הֲמוֹן עַמִּים רַבִּים כַּהֲמוֹת יַמִּים יֶהֱמָיוּן וּשְׁאוֹן
לְאֻמִּים כִּשְׁאוֹן מַיִם כַּבִּירִים יִשָּׁאוּן

12[13] *Ah, the uproar of many peoples, who roar like the roaring of the seas; And the rushing of nations, who rush like the rushing of mighty waters!*[14]

---

[1] Isaiah 17:6 - 1 Kings 19:18, 4 Ezra 16:29, b.Gittin [Rashi] 59b, b.Sanhedrin 95b, Deuteronomy 4:27, Ein Yaakov Sanhedrin:95b, Ezekiel 36:8-15 37:19-25 15:29, Isaiah 1:9 10:22 24:13 3:12, Jastrow 908b, Judges 8:2, Lamentations.R 4:15 4:15 Petichata D'Chakimei:30, Micah 7:1, Midrash Psalms 79:1, mt.Hilcnot Shofar Sukkah v'Lulav 4:5, Obadiah 1:5, Romans 9:27 11:4-6 11:26

[2] Isaiah 17:7 - 2 Chronicles 30:10-11 30:18-20 7:1 35:17-18, Hosea 3:5 6:1 14:3-14:5, Isaiah 10:20-21 19:22 22:11 24:14-15 29:18-19 5:24, Jeremiah 3:12-14 3:18-23 31:5-11, Judges 10:15-16, Micah 7:7, Midrash Tanchuma Bechukkotai 4, y.Peah 7:3

[3] LXX *trust in*

[4] Isaiah 17:8 - 2 Chronicles 14:4 10:4 34:6-34:7, Exodus 10:13, Ezekiel 12:25, Hosea 8:4-8:6 10:1-10:2 13:1-13:2 14:10, Isaiah 1:29 2:8 2:18-2:21 3:9 6:22 31:6-31:7 20:15 44:19-44:20, Micah 5:14-5:15, Zechariah 13:2, Zephaniah 1:3
Isaiah 17:8-14 - 4QIsab

[5] 1QIsaa *look upon*; LXX *trust in*

[6] Isaiah 17:9 - Amos 3:11-3:15 7:9, Hosea 10:14 13:15-13:16, Isaiah 6:11-6:13 7:16-7:20 9:10-9:13 17:4-17:5 24:1-24:12 3:10 28:1-28:4, Lamentations.R 2:1, Micah 5:12 6:16 7:13
Isaiah 17:9-14 - 4QIsaa

[7] 1QIsaa *like the deserted places of the Hivites and Amorites, which were deserted before the Israelites*

[8] Isaiah 17:10 - 1 Chronicles 16:35, Amos 5:11, Deuteronomy 6:12 8:11 8:14 8:19 4:30 28:38-28:42 8:4 8:15 8:18 8:31, Habakkuk 3:18, Hosea 2:13-16 4:6 8:14 13:6-7, Isaiah 12:2 2:4 3:13 65:21-22, Jeremiah 2:32 12:13 17:13, Leviticus 2:16 2:20, Psalms 9:18 18:3 31:3 65:6 68:20-21 79:9 85:5 10:13 10:21, Zephaniah 1:13

[9] LXX *the LORD your helper*

[10] LXX *a false plant and a false seed*

[11] Isaiah 17:11 - Galatians 6:7-6:8, Hosea 8:7 9:1-9:4 9:16 10:12-10:15, Isaiah 18:5-18:6 65:13-65:14, Jastrow 82b 208b 209a 879a 975a 1213b 1406a, Jeremiah 5:31, Job 4:8, Joel 1:5-1:12, Leviticus.R 18:3, Matthew 8:11-8:12, Midrash Tanchuma Shelach 12, Numbers.R 7:4 16:20, Pirkei de R'Eliezer 23, Psalms 90:6, Romans 2:5 2:8-2:9

[12] LXX *you shall be deceived; but if you sow in the morning, the seed shall spring up for a crop in the day in which you shall obtain an inheritance, and as a man's father, you shall obtain an inheritance for your sons*

[13] Isaiah 17:12 - Exodus.R 49:1, Ezekiel 19:2, Isaiah 5:26-5:30 8:7-8:8 9:6 4:17, Jeremiah 6:23, Lamentations.R 3:?, Luke 21:25, Midrash Psalms 3:5/6 15:4 17:9 83:2 93:7, Midrash Tanchuma Ki Tissa 4, Midrash Tanchuma Shoftim 16, Numbers.R 2:16, Pesikta de R'Kahana 2.1, Pesikta Rabbati 31:9, Pirkei de R'Eliezer 9, Psalms 18:5 29:3 46:2-46:4 65:7-65:8 93:3-93:4, Revelation 17:1 17:15, Sibylline Oracles 1.314, Song of Songs.R 8:8

[14] LXX *Woe to the multitude of many nations, as the swelling sea, so shall you be confounded; and the force of many nations shall sound like water*

לְאֻמִּים כִּשְׁאוֹן מַיִם רַבִּים יִשָּׁאוּן וְגָעַר בּוֹ וְנָס
מִמֶּרְחָק וְרֻדַּף כְּמֹץ הָרִים לִפְנֵי־רוּחַ וּכְגַלְגַּל לִפְנֵי
סוּפָה

13[1]

The nations shall rush like the rushing of many waters; but He shall rebuke them, and they shall flee far off, and shall be chased as the chaff of the mountains before the wind, and like the whirling dust before the storm[2].

לְעֵת עֶרֶב וְהִנֵּה בַלָּהָה בְּטֶרֶם בֹּקֶר אֵינֶנּוּ זֶה חֵלֶק
שׁוֹסֵינוּ וְגוֹרָל לְבֹזְזֵינוּ

14[3]

At evening, behold terror; and before morning they are no more. This is the portion of those who spoil us, and the lot of those who rob us.

Isaiah – Chapter 18

הוֹי אֶרֶץ צִלְצַל כְּנָפָיִם אֲשֶׁר מֵעֵבֶר לְנַהֲרֵי־כוּשׁ

1[4]

Ah, land of the buzzing of wings[5] that is beyond the rivers of Ethiopia;

הַשֹּׁלֵחַ בַּיָּם צִירִים וּבִכְלֵי־גֹמֶא עַל־פְּנֵי־מַיִם לְכוּ
מַלְאָכִים קַלִּים אֶל־גּוֹי מְמֻשָּׁךְ וּמוֹרָט וְאֶל־עַם
נוֹרָא מִן־הוּא וָהָלְאָה גּוֹי קַו־קָו וּמְבוּסָה אֲשֶׁר־
בָּזְאוּ נְהָרִים אַרְצוֹ

2[6]

Who sends ambassadors by the sea, in vessels of papyrus on the waters! Go, you swift messengers, To a nation tall and of glossy skin, To a people terrible from their beginning onward; A nation *that is sturdy and treads down, Whose land the rivers divide*[7]!

כָּל־יֹשְׁבֵי תֵבֵל וְשֹׁכְנֵי אָרֶץ כִּנְשֹׂא־נֵס הָרִים תִּרְאוּ
וְכִתְקֹעַ שׁוֹפָר תִּשְׁמָעוּ

3[8]

All you inhabitants of the world, and You dwellers on the earth[9], when an ensign is lifted up on the mountains, look; And when the horn is blown, hear.

כִּי כֹה אָמַר יְהוָה אֵלַי 'אֶשְׁקוֹטָה' 'אֶשְׁקֳטָה'
וְאַבִּיטָה בִמְכוֹנִי כְּחֹם צַח עֲלֵי־אוֹר כְּעָב טַל בְּחֹם
קָצִיר

4[10]

For thus has the LORD said to me: I will hold Me still, and I will look on in My dwelling place, Like clear heat in sunshine, Like a cloud of dew in the heat of harvest.

כִּי־לִפְנֵי קָצִיר כְּתָם־פֶּרַח וּבֹסֶר גֹּמֵל יִהְיֶה נִצָּה
וְכָרַת הַזַּלְזַלִּים בַּמַּזְמֵרוֹת וְאֶת־הַנְּטִישׁוֹת הֵסִיר
הֵתַז

5[11]

For before the harvest, when the blossom is over and the bud becomes a ripening grape, He will cut off the sprigs with pruning hooks, and the shoots will He take away and lop off.

יֵעָזְבוּ יַחְדָּו לְעֵיט הָרִים וּלְבֶהֱמַת הָאָרֶץ וְקָץ עָלָיו
הָעַיִט וְכָל־בֶּהֱמַת הָאָרֶץ עָלָיו תֶּחֱרָף

6[12]

They shall be left together for the ravenous birds of the mountains, And to the beasts of the earth; And the ravenous birds shall summer upon them, And all the beasts of the earth shall winter upon them.

בָּעֵת הַהִיא יוּבַל־שַׁי לַיהוָה צְבָאוֹת עַם מְמֻשָּׁךְ
וּמוֹרָט וּמֵעַם נוֹרָא מִן־הוּא וָהָלְאָה גּוֹי קַו־קָו

7[13]

In that time a present shall be brought to the LORD of hosts of a people tall and *of glossy*

---

[1] Isaiah 17:13 - Daniel 2:35, Hosea 13:3, Isaiah 10:15-10:16 10:33-10:34 14:25 25:4-25:5 3:1 5:5 30:30-30:33 31:8-31:9 33:1-33:3 33:9-33:12 37:29-37:38 41:15-41:16, Job 21:18 14:11, Mark 4:39-4:41, Midrash Psalms 15:4, Psalms 1:4 9:6 35:5 46:6-46:12 83:14-83:16, Song of Songs.R 2:3

[2] LXX *many nations like much water, as when much water rushes violently: and they shall drive him away, and pursue him afar, as the dust of chaff when men winnow before the wind, and as a storm whirling the dust of the wheel*

[3] Isaiah 17:14 - 2 Kings 19:3 19:35, Ezekiel 15:10, Habakkuk 2:16-2:17, Isaiah 10:28-10:32 9:1, Jeremiah 2:3 13:25, Job 20:29, Judges 5:31, Proverbs 22:23, Psalms 37:36, Zephaniah 2:9-2:10

[4] Isaiah 18:1 - 1QIsab, 2 Kings 19:9, b.Bava Kamma [Tosefot] 116b, Ezekiel 30:4-30:5 6:9, Isaiah 20:3-20:6 30:2-30:3 7:1, Matthew 23:37, Psalms 17:8 36:8 57:2 61:5 63:8 91:4, Ruth 2:12, Saadia Opinions 8:6, z.Kedoshim 80b, Zephaniah 2:12 3:10
Isaiah 18:1-7 - 1QIsaa

[5] LXX *Woe to you, you wings of the land of ships*

[6] Isaiah 18:2 - 2 Chronicles 12:2-12:4 14:8 16:8, Exodus 2:3, Ezekiel 6:9, Genesis 10:8-10:9, Isaiah 18:7 19:5-19:7 30:2-30:4, Saadia Opinions 8:6, Variant of קוקו is קו־קו

[7] LXX *not looked for, and trodden down*

[8] Isaiah 18:3 - Amos 3:6-3:8, Avot de R'Natan 37, Isaiah 1:2 5:26 7:18 13:2 2:11, Jeremiah 22:29, Matthew 13:9 13:16, Micah 6:2 6:9, mt.Hilcnot Shofar Sukkah v'Lulav 3:9, Mussaf Rosh Hashanah, Psalms 49:2-49:3 50:1, Zechariah 9:14

[9] LXX *Now all the rivers of the land shall be inhabited as an inhabited country; their land shall be as*

[10] Isaiah 18:4 - 2 Samuel 23:4, Hosea 5:15 14:7, Isaiah 12:6 14:32 18:7 2:19 2:21 7:9 22:13, Joel 4:17, Psalms 72:6 132:13-14

[11] Isaiah 18:5 - b.Sanhedrin 98a, Ein Yaakov Sanhedrin:97b, Ezekiel 17:6-10, Isaiah 17:10-11, Song of Songs 2:13 2:15
Isaiah 18:5-7 - 4QIsab

[12] Isaiah 18:6 - Ezekiel 32:4-32:6 39:17-39:20, Genesis.R 34:11, Isaiah 14:19 34:1-34:7 8:9, Jastrow 1339b, Jeremiah 7:33 15:3, Lamentations.R 1:40, Midrash Psalms 150:1, Revelation 19:17-19:18, Seder Olam 3:Plagues

[13] Isaiah 18:7 - 2 Chronicles 8:23, Acts 8:27-8:28, b.Sanhedrin 98a, Ein Yaakov Sanhedrin:97b, Genesis.R 97:1, Isaiah 16:1 18:4

וּמְבוּסָ֔ה אֲשֶׁ֨ר בָּזְא֤וּ נְהָרִים֙ אַרְצ֔וֹ אֶל־מְק֛וֹם שֵׁם־
יְהוָ֥ה צְבָא֖וֹת הַר־צִיּֽוֹן׃

skin[1], and from a people terrible from their beginning onward; a nation that is sturdy and treads down, whose land the rivers divide, to the place of the name of the LORD *of hosts*[2], the mount Zion.

Isaiah – Chapter 19

מַשָּׂ֖א מִצְרָ֑יִם הִנֵּ֨ה יְהוָ֜ה רֹכֵ֤ב עַל־עָב֙ קַל֙ וּבָ֣א
מִצְרַ֔יִם וְנָע֞וּ אֱלִילֵ֤י מִצְרַ֙יִם֙ מִפָּנָ֔יו וּלְבַ֥ב מִצְרַ֖יִם
יִמַּ֥ס בְּקִרְבּֽוֹ׃

1[3] The oracle of Egypt. Behold, the LORD rides on a swift cloud and comes to Egypt; And the idols of Egypt shall be moved at His presence, And the heart of Egypt shall melt within it.

וְסִכְסַכְתִּ֤י מִצְרַ֙יִם֙ בְּמִצְרַ֔יִם וְנִלְחֲמ֥וּ אִישׁ־בְּאָחִ֖יו
וְאִ֣ישׁ בְּרֵעֵ֑הוּ עִ֣יר בְּעִ֔יר מַמְלָכָ֖ה בְּמַמְלָכָֽה׃

2[4] And I will spur Egypt against Egypt; And everyone shall fight against his brother, and everyone against his neighbor; city against city, and *kingdom against kingdom*[5].

וְנָבְקָ֤ה רֽוּחַ־מִצְרַ֙יִם֙ בְּקִרְבּ֔וֹ וַעֲצָת֖וֹ אֲבַלֵּ֑עַ וְדָרְשׁ֤וּ
אֶל־הָֽאֱלִילִים֙ וְאֶל־הָ֣אִטִּ֔ים וְאֶל־הָאֹב֖וֹת וְאֶל־
הַיִּדְּעֹנִֽים׃

3[6] And the spirit of Egypt shall be made empty within it; And I will make void its counsel; And they shall seek the idols, and to the whisperers, And to the ghosts, and to the familiar spirits.

וְסִכַּרְתִּי֙ אֶת־מִצְרַ֔יִם בְּיַ֖ד אֲדֹנִ֣ים קָשֶׁ֑ה וּמֶ֤לֶךְ עַז֙
יִמְשָׁל־בָּ֔ם נְאֻ֥ם הָאָד֖וֹן יְהוָ֥ה צְבָאֽוֹת׃

4[7] And I will give the Egyptians into the hand of a cruel lord; And a fierce king shall rule over them, says the Lord, the LORD of hosts.

וְנִשְּׁתוּ־מַ֖יִם מֵהַיָּ֑ם וְנָהָ֖ר יֶחֱרַ֥ב וְיָבֵֽשׁ׃

5[8] And the *waters shall fail from*[9] the *sea*[10], and the *river*[11] shall be drained dry,

וְהֶאֶזְנִ֣יחוּ נְהָר֔וֹת דָּלֲל֥וּ וְחָרְב֖וּ יְאֹרֵ֣י מָצ֑וֹר קָנֶ֥ה
וָס֖וּף קָמֵֽלוּ׃

6[12] And the rivers shall become foul; The streams of Egypt shall be fouled and dried up; The reeds and flags shall wither[13].

עָר֥וֹת עַל־יְא֖וֹר עַל־פִּ֣י יְא֑וֹר וְכֹל֙ מִזְרַ֣ע יְא֔וֹר יִיבַ֖שׁ
נִדַּ֥ף וְאֵינֶֽנּוּ׃

7[14] The mosses *by the Nile*[15], by the brink of the Nile, And all that is sown by the Nile, Shall *become dry, be driven away*[16], *and be no more*[17].

23:17-23:18 21:14 60:6-60:9, Malachi 1:11, Matthew 2:11, Micah 4:13, Midrash Psalms 87:6 120:5, Psalms 68:30-68:32 72:9-72:15, Saadia Opinions 8:6, Variant of קוקו is קז־קו, Zechariah 14:16-14:17, Zephaniah 3:10

[1] 1QIsaa *handsome*

[2] Missing in 1QIsaa

[3] Isaiah 19:1 - 1 Samuel 5:2-4, 3 Enoch 24:3 24:17, Deuteronomy 9:26, Exodus 12:12 15:14-16, Exodus.R 15:19, Ezekiel 29:1-21 6:13, Greek Apocalypse of Ezra 5:7, Guide for the Perplexed 1:49, Isaiah 13:1 13:7 19:16 21:9 46:1-2, Jeremiah 1:19 43:8-13 44:29-30 46:1-28 2:2 3:44, Joel 4:19, Joshua 2:9 2:11 2:24, Lamentations.R 2:1, Matthew 26:64-26:65, Midrash Psalms 104:6, Psalms 18:11-13 68:5 68:34-35 8:3 8:34, Revelation 1:7, Sibylline Oracles 3.313, Tanna Devei Eliyahu 7, z.Bo 43a, z.Shemot 6b 7a, Zechariah 10:11 14:18

Isaiah 19:1 [LXX] - Lives of the Prophets 2:8

Isaiah 19:1-25 - 1QIsaa, 4QIsab, Haftarah Bo [Teimon]

[4] Isaiah 19:2 - 1 Samuel 14:16 14:20, 2 Chronicles 20:22-20:23, 4 Ezra 13:31, b.Chullin [Rashi] 14b, Ezekiel 14:21, Isaiah 9:22 19:13-19:14, Jastrow 654b, Judges 7:22 9:23, Lamentations.R 1:53, Matthew 10:21 10:36 12:25, Revelation 17:12-17:17

[5] LXX *law against law*

[6] Isaiah 19:3 - 1 Chronicles 10:13, 1 Corinthians 3:19-3:20, 1 Samuel 1:37, 2 Chronicles 25:16-25:20, 2 Samuel 15:31 17:14 17:23, Daniel 2:2 4:3-4:4 5:7, Ezekiel 21:12 22:14, Guide for the Perplexed 1:40, Isaiah 8:19 14:27 15:2 19:1 19:11-19:13 20:25 23:12 9:16, Jeremiah 22:15, Job 5:12-5:13, Proverbs 21:30, Psalms 76:13 11:27

[7] Isaiah 19:4 - 1 Samuel 23:7, Ezekiel 5:19, Isaiah 19:2 20:4, Jastrow 992b, Jeremiah 22:26, Lamentations.R 1:53, Midrash Tanchuma Bamidbar 3, Numbers.R 1:3, Psalms 31:9

[8] Isaiah 19:5 - Ezekiel 6:12, Jeremiah 3:36, Zechariah 10:11 14:18

Isaiah 19:5-8 - Sibylline Oracles 5.92

[9] LXX *Egyptians shall drink the water that is by*

[10] 1QIsaa *Nile*

[11] 1QIsaa *riverbed*

[12] Isaiah 19:6 - 2 Kings 19:24, b.Sotah 12b, Ein Yaakov Sotah:12a, Exodus 2:3 7:18, Exodus.R 1:21, Isaiah 15:6 18:2 13:25, Job 8:11

[13] 1QIsaa *and they shall wither away*

[14] Isaiah 19:7 - Ezekiel 19:13, Isaiah 23:3 8:20, Jeremiah 14:4, Joel 1:17-1:18

Isaiah 19:7-17 - 1QIsab

[15] Missing in 1QIsaa

[16] LXX *be blasted with the wind and dried up*

[17] 1QIsaa *and there will be nothing in it*

Hebrew		English
וְאָנוּ הַדַּיָּגִים וְאָבְלוּ כָּל־מַשְׁלִיכֵי בַיְאוֹר חַכָּה וּפֹרְשֵׂי מִכְמֹרֶת עַל־פְּנֵי־מַיִם אֻמְלָלוּ	8[1]	The fishermen also lament, And all those who cast angle into the Nile shall mourn, And those who spread nets on the waters[2] shall languish.
וּבֹשׁוּ עֹבְדֵי פִשְׁתִּים שְׂרִיקוֹת וְאֹרְגִים חוֹרָי	9[3]	Moreover, they who work in combed flax, And they who weave cotton, shall be ashamed.
וְהָיוּ שָׁתֹתֶיהָ מְדֻכָּאִים כָּל־עֹשֵׂי שֶׂכֶר אַגְמֵי־נָפֶשׁ	10[4]	*And her foundations shall be crushed; all they who make dams shall be grieved in soul*[5].
אַךְ־אֱוִלִים שָׂרֵי צֹעַן חַכְמֵי יֹעֲצֵי פַרְעֹה עֵצָה נִבְעָרָה אֵיךְ תֹּאמְרוּ אֶל־פַּרְעֹה בֶּן־חֲכָמִים אָנִי בֶּן־מַלְכֵי־קֶדֶם	11[6]	The princes of *Zoan*[7] are utter fools; The wisest counsellors of Pharaoh are a senseless counsel; How can you say to Pharaoh: 'I am the son of the wise, The son of ancient kings?'
אַיָּם אֵפוֹא חֲכָמֶיךָ וְיַגִּידוּ נָא לָךְ וְיֵדְעוּ מַה־יָּעַץ יְהוָה צְבָאוֹת עַל־מִצְרָיִם	12[8]	Where are they, then, your wise men? And let them tell you now; And let them know what the LORD *of hosts*[9] has designed concerning Egypt.
נוֹאֲלוּ שָׂרֵי צֹעַן נִשְּׁאוּ שָׂרֵי נֹף הִתְעוּ אֶת־מִצְרַיִם פִּנַּת שְׁבָטֶיהָ	13[10]	The princes of *Zoan*[11] have become fools, the princes of *Noph*[12] are deceived; They have caused Egypt to go astray, *who are the cornerstone of her tribes*[13].
יְהוָה מָסַךְ בְּקִרְבָּהּ רוּחַ עִוְעִים וְהִתְעוּ אֶת־מִצְרַיִם בְּכָל־מַעֲשֵׂהוּ כְּהִתָּעוֹת שִׁכּוֹר בְּקִיאוֹ	14[14]	The LORD has *mingled*[15] within her a spirit of dizziness; And they caused Egypt to stagger in its every work, as a drunken man staggers in his vomit.
וְלֹא־יִהְיֶה לְמִצְרַיִם מַעֲשֶׂה אֲשֶׁר יַעֲשֶׂה רֹאשׁ וְזָנָב כִּפָּה וְאַגְמוֹן	15[16]	Nor shall there be for Egypt any work, *which head or tail, palm branch or rush, may do*[17].[18]
בַּיּוֹם הַהוּא יִהְיֶה מִצְרַיִם כַּנָּשִׁים וְחָרַד וּפָחַד מִפְּנֵי תְּנוּפַת יַד־יְהוָה צְבָאוֹת אֲשֶׁר־הוּא מֵנִיף עָלָיו	16[19]	In that day *Egypt shall*[20] be like women; and *it*[21] shall tremble and fear *because of the shaking of the hand of the LORD of hosts, which He shakes over it*[22].

---

[1] Isaiah 19:8 - Exodus 7:21, Ezekiel 23:10, Habakkuk 1:15, Numbers 11:5, y.Horayot 3:3, y.Pesachim 8:8, y.Sanhedrin 2:1

[2] LXX adds *and the anglers*

[3] Isaiah 19:9 - 1 Kings 10:28, Ezekiel 3:7, Jastrow 1029b, Midrash Tanchuma Balak 18, Midrash Tanchuma Vayeilech 2, Proverbs 7:16, Seder Olam 23:Sennacherib
Isaiah 19:9-12 - 4Q163 frag 11 2.1-5

[4] Isaiah 19:10 - b.Bava Metzia [Rashi] 24b, b.Menachot [Tosefot] 64b, Deuteronomy 11:10, Exodus 7:19 8:1

[5] 1QIsaa *Its weavers will be broken in piceses, and all who work for wages will be sick at heart*; LXX *And they who work at them shall be in pain, and all who make beer shall be grieved and pained in their souls*

[6] Isaiah 19:11 - 1 Corinthians 1:19-1:20, 1 Kings 4:30, Acts 7:22, Exodus.R 1:14 5:14, Ezekiel 7:26 6:14, Genesis 41:38-41:39, Isaiah 19:3 19:13 5:14 6:4 20:25, Jeremiah 10:14 10:21 1:7, Job 5:12-5:13 12:17, Midrash Proverbs 27, Midrash Tanchuma Vaera 5, Numbers 13:22, Proverbs 6:2, Psalms 33:10 73:22 78:12 78:43 92:7, Tanna Devei Eliyahu 7

[7] LXX *Tanis*

[8] Isaiah 19:12 - 1 Corinthians 1:20, Isaiah 5:21 14:24 40:13-40:14 41:22-41:23 20:7 47:10-47:13, Jeremiah 2:28, Job 11:6-11:7, Judges 9:38, Midrash Tanchuma Mikketz 3, Romans 9:17 11:33-11:34

[9] Missing in 1QIsaa

[10] Isaiah 19:13 - 1 Peter 2:7, 1 Samuel 14:38, b.Berachot 63b, b.Makkot 10a, b.Taanit 7a, Ein Yaakov Berachot:63b, Ein Yaakov Taanit:6b, Ezekiel 6:13 6:16, Isaiah 19:11, Jeremiah 2:16 22:14 22:19, Numbers 24:17, Romans 1:22, Zechariah 10:4

[11] LXX *Tanis*

[12] LXX *Memphis*

[13] LXX *by tribes*

[14] Isaiah 19:14 - 1 Kings 22:20-23, 2 Thessalonians 2:11, 4Q471 2 6, 4Q471a frag 1 1.6, b.Taanit 7a, Ezekiel 14:7-9, Isaiah 19:2 28:7-8 29:9-10 5:14 47:10-11, Jeremiah 25:15-16 1:27 24:26, Job 12:16 12:25, Matthew 17:17, Psalms of Solomon 8:14, z.Vayeshev 192b

[15] 4QIsab *poured*

[16] Isaiah 19:15 - 1 Thessalonians 4:11-4:12, Habakkuk 3:17, Haggai 1:11, Isaiah 9:15-9:16, Proverbs 14:23, Psalms 8:2

[17] LXX *shall make head or tail, or beginning or end*

[18] 4QIsab adds *on that day*

[19] Isaiah 19:16 - Exodus.R 8:2, Hebrews 10:31, Isaiah 10:32 11:15 6:17 30:30-30:32, Jeremiah 30:5-30:7 2:37 3:30, Joseph and Aseneth 9:1, Midrash Tanchuma Vaera 9, Nahum 3:13, Psalms 48:7, Zechariah 2:9

[20] 1QIsaa *the Egyptians shall*

[21] 1QIsaa *they*

[22] 1QIsaa *at the uplifted hand of the LORD of Hosts whe he bradishes His hand against her*

וְהָיְתָ֩ה אַדְמַ֨ת יְהוּדָ֤ה לְמִצְרַ֙יִם֙ לְחָגָּ֔א כֹּל֩ אֲשֶׁ֨ר יַזְכִּ֥יר אֹתָ֛הּ אֵלָ֖יו יִפְחָ֑ד מִפְּנֵ֗י עֲצַ֛ת יְהוָ֥ה צְבָא֖וֹת אֲשֶׁר־ה֥וּא יוֹעֵ֖ץ עָלָֽיו	17¹	And the land of Judah shall become a terror to Egypt, whenever one makes mention of it; it shall be afraid, because of the purpose of the ²LORD of hosts, which He designs against it.
בַּיּ֣וֹם הַה֗וּא יִֽהְי֞וּ חָמֵ֤שׁ עָרִים֙ בְּאֶ֣רֶץ מִצְרַ֔יִם מְדַבְּרוֹת֙ שְׂפַ֣ת כְּנַ֔עַן וְנִשְׁבָּע֖וֹת לַיהוָ֣ה צְבָא֑וֹת עִ֣יר הַהֶ֔רֶס יֵאָמֵ֖ר לְאֶחָֽת	18³	In that day there shall be five cities in the land of Egypt that speak the language of Canaan, and swear to the LORD of hosts; one shall be called The *city of destruction*⁴.
בַּיּ֣וֹם הַה֗וּא יִֽהְיֶ֞ה מִזְבֵּ֤חַ לַֽיהוָה֙ בְּת֖וֹךְ אֶ֣רֶץ מִצְרָ֑יִם וּמַצֵּבָ֥ה אֵֽצֶל־גְּבוּלָ֖הּ לַיהוָֽה	19⁵	In that day shall there be an altar to the LORD⁶ in the midst of the land of Egypt, and a pillar at its border to the LORD.
וְהָיָ֨ה לְא֥וֹת וּלְעֵ֛ד לַֽיהוָ֥ה צְבָא֖וֹת בְּאֶ֣רֶץ מִצְרָ֑יִם כִּֽי־יִצְעֲק֤וּ אֶל־יְהוָה֙ מִפְּנֵ֣י לֹֽחֲצִ֔ים וְיִשְׁלַ֥ח לָהֶ֛ם מוֹשִׁ֥יעַ וָרָ֖ב וְהִצִּילָֽם	20⁷	And it shall be for a sign and for a witness ⁸to the LORD of hosts in the land of Egypt; for they shall cry to the LORD because of their oppressors, and He will send them a savior, *and a defender, who will deliver them*⁹.
וְנוֹדַ֤ע יְהוָה֙ לְמִצְרַ֔יִם וְיָדְע֥וּ מִצְרַ֛יִם אֶת־יְהוָ֖ה בַּיּ֣וֹם הַה֑וּא וְעָֽבְדוּ֙ זֶ֣בַח וּמִנְחָ֔ה וְנָדְרוּ־נֵ֥דֶר לַֽיהוָ֖ה וְשִׁלֵּֽמוּ	21¹⁰	And the LORD shall make Himself known to Egypt, and the Egyptians shall know the LORD in that day; yes, they shall worship with sacrifice and offering, and shall vow a vow to the LORD, and shall perform it.
וְנָגַ֧ף יְהוָ֛ה אֶת־מִצְרַ֖יִם נָגֹ֣ף וְרָפ֑וֹא וְשָׁ֙בוּ֙ עַד־יְהוָ֔ה וְנֶעְתַּ֥ר לָהֶ֖ם וּרְפָאָֽם	22¹¹	And the LORD will strike Egypt, striking and healing; and they shall return to the LORD, and He will be entreated by them, and will heal them.
בַּיּ֣וֹם הַה֗וּא תִּהְיֶ֨ה מְסִלָּ֜ה מִמִּצְרַ֣יִם אַשּׁ֗וּרָה וּבָֽא־אַשּׁ֤וּר בְּמִצְרַ֙יִם֙ וּמִצְרַ֣יִם בְּאַשּׁ֔וּר וְעָבְד֥וּ מִצְרַ֖יִם אֶת־אַשּֽׁוּר	23¹²	In that day there shall be a highway out of Egypt to Assyria, and the Assyrian shall come into Egypt, and the Egyptian into Assyria; and *the Egyptian*¹³ shall worship with the Assyrian.
בַּיּ֣וֹם הַה֗וּא יִהְיֶ֤ה יִשְׂרָאֵל֙ שְׁלִֽישִׁיָּ֔ה לְמִצְרַ֖יִם וּלְאַשּׁ֑וּר בְּרָכָ֖ה בְּקֶ֥רֶב הָאָֽרֶץ	24¹⁴	In that day Israel shall be the third with Egypt and with Assyria, a blessing in the midst of the earth;
אֲשֶׁ֧ר בֵּרֲכ֛וֹ יְהוָ֥ה צְבָא֖וֹת לֵאמֹ֑ר בָּר֨וּךְ עַמִּ֜י מִצְרַ֗יִם וּמַעֲשֵׂ֤ה יָדַי֙ אַשּׁ֔וּר וְנַחֲלָתִ֖י יִשְׂרָאֵֽל	25¹⁵	For the LORD of hosts has blessed him, saying: 'Blessed be Egypt, My people, and

---

¹ Isaiah 19:17 - Daniel 4:32, Ezekiel 29:6-7, Isaiah 14:24 14:26-27 20:2-5 12:1 46:10-11, Jeremiah 1:19 25:27-31 43:8-13 44:28-30
² 1QIsaa adds *hand of the*
³ Isaiah 19:18 - b.Menachot 19b 11a, city of righteousness vs. "city of the sun" or "the city of destruction", Deuteronomy 10:20, Genesis 11:1, Isaiah 2:11 11:11 19:19 19:21 3:13 45:23-45:24, Jastrow 368b 369a 504b, Jeremiah 12:16, Nehemiah 10:30, Pesikta de R'Kahana 7.5, Pesikta Rabbati 17:4, Psalms 68:32, Seder Olam 23:Sennacherib, Zechariah 2:11, Zephaniah 3:9
Isaiah 19:18-23 - Josephus Wars 7.11.3
⁴ 1QIsaa 4QIsab Vulgate *City of the Sun* [cf. Jeremiah 43:13]; LXX *Asedec*
⁵ Isaiah 19:19 - b.Menachot 19b 11a, Exodus 24:4, Genesis 12:7 4:18, Hebrews 13:10, Isaiah 18:23, Joshua 22:10 22:26, Mekhilta de R'Shimon bar Yochai Pisha 15:4, Mekilta de R'Ishmael Beshallah 1:7, Seder Olam 23:Sennacherib, Sibylline Oracles 5.501, y.Yoma 6:3, Zechariah 6:15
⁶ 4QIsab adds *of hosts*
⁷ Isaiah 19:20 - 2 Kings 13:4-5, Exodus 2:23 3:7, Isaiah 19:4 20:4 13:36 45:21-22 49:25-26 4:5 7:13, James 5:4, Joshua 4:20-4:21 22:27-28 22:34 24:26-27, Luke 2:11, Midrash Psalms 71:2, Psalms 50:15, Titus 2:13
Isaiah 19:20-25 - 1QIsab
⁸ LXX adds *forever*
⁹ 1QIsaa *and he will go down and will rescue them*
¹⁰ Isaiah 19:21 - 1 Kings 8:43, 1 Peter 2:5 2:9, 1 Samuel 17:46, Ecclesiastes 5:5, Galatians 4:8-9, Habakkuk 2:14, Isaiah 7:5 8:7 11:9 13:20 20:5, John 4:21-24 17:3, Jonah 1:16, Malachi 1:11, Psalms 67:3 98:2-3, Romans 15:27-28, Zechariah 14:16-18, Zephaniah 3:10
¹¹ Isaiah 19:22 - Acts 26:17-20 28:26-27, Amos 4:6-12, b.Megillah 13b, Deuteronomy 8:39, Ein Yaakov Megillah:13b, Hebrews 12:11, Hosea 5:15 6:2 14:3, Isaiah 6:10 19:1-15 21:14 7:7, Job 5:18, Song of Songs.R 4:13, Tanna Devei Eliyahu 7, z.Bo 36a
¹² Isaiah 19:23 - Ephesians 2:18-2:22 3:6-8, Isaiah 11:16 3:13 35:8-10 40:3-5
¹³ 1QIsaa *they*
¹⁴ Isaiah 19:24 - Deuteronomy 8:43, Ezekiel 10:26, Galatians 3:14, Genesis 12:2, Isaiah 6:13 1:6 1:22 17:8 17:22 18:12 66:19-21, Luke 2:32, Midrash Tanchuma Beha'alotcha 9, Midrash Tanchuma Tzav 2, Numbers.R 15:14, Psalms 117:1-2, Romans 10:11-13 15:9-12 15:27, Zechariah 2:10-11 8:13 8:20-23
Isaiah 19:24-25 - 4QIsaa
¹⁵ Isaiah 19:25 - 1 Peter 2:10, Colossians 3:10-11, Deuteronomy 8:9, Ephesians 1:3 2:10, Galatians 6:15, Hosea 2:23, Isaiah 5:23 21:11 12:21 13:9 16:9 17:23, Midrash Psalms 5:1, Numbers 6:24 6:27 24:1, Philippians 1:6, Psalms 67:7-8 4:3 19:15 18:8, Romans

Assyria, the work of My hands, and Israel My inheritance.'

Isaiah – Chapter 20

בִּשְׁנַת בֹּא תַרְתָּן אַשְׁדּוֹדָה בִּשְׁלֹחַ אֹתוֹ סַרְגוֹן מֶלֶךְ אַשּׁוּר וַיִּלָּחֶם בְּאַשְׁדּוֹד וַיִּלְכְּדָהּ	1[1] In the year that *Tartan came into Ashdod[2]*, when Sargon the king of Assyria sent him, and he fought against Ashdod and took it;
בָּעֵת הַהִיא דִּבֶּר יְהוָה בְּיַד יְשַׁעְיָהוּ בֶן־אָמוֹץ לֵאמֹר לֵךְ וּפִתַּחְתָּ הַשַּׂק מֵעַל מָתְנֶיךָ וְנַעַלְךָ תַחֲלֹץ מֵעַל רַגְלֶיךָ וַיַּעַשׂ כֵּן הָלֹךְ עָרוֹם וְיָחֵף	2[3] at that time the LORD spoke by Isaiah the son of Amoz, saying: 'Go, and remove the sackcloth from your loins, and take your shoe from your foot.' And he did so, walking naked and barefoot.
וַיֹּאמֶר יְהוָה כַּאֲשֶׁר הָלַךְ עַבְדִּי יְשַׁעְיָהוּ עָרוֹם וְיָחֵף שָׁלֹשׁ שָׁנִים אוֹת וּמוֹפֵת עַל־מִצְרַיִם וְעַל־כּוּשׁ	3[4] And the LORD said: 'Like as My servant Isaiah has walked naked and barefoot to be for three years a sign and a wonder upon Egypt and upon Ethiopia,
כֵּן יִנְהַג מֶלֶךְ־אַשּׁוּר אֶת־שְׁבִי מִצְרַיִם וְאֶת־גָּלוּת כּוּשׁ נְעָרִים וּזְקֵנִים עָרוֹם וְיָחֵף וַחֲשׂוּפַי שֵׁת עֶרְוַת מִצְרָיִם	4[5] so shall the king of Assyria lead away the captives of Egypt, and the exiles of Ethiopia, young and old, naked and barefoot, *and with buttocks uncovered[6]*, to the shame of Egypt.
וְחַתּוּ וָבֹשׁוּ מִכּוּשׁ מַבָּטָם וּמִן־מִצְרַיִם תִּפְאַרְתָּם	5[7] And they shall be dismayed and ashamed, because of Ethiopia their expectation, and of Egypt their glory.
וְאָמַר יֹשֵׁב הָאִי הַזֶּה בַּיּוֹם הַהוּא הִנֵּה־כֹה מַבָּטֵנוּ אֲשֶׁר־נַסְנוּ שָׁם לְעֶזְרָה לְהִנָּצֵל מִפְּנֵי מֶלֶךְ אַשּׁוּר וְאֵיךְ נִמָּלֵט אֲנָחְנוּ	6[8] And the inhabitant of this coastland shall say in that day: Behold, such is our expectation, *where we fled[9]* for help to be delivered from the king of Assyria; and how shall we escape?'

Isaiah – Chapter 21

מַשָּׂא מִדְבַּר־יָם כְּסוּפוֹת בַּנֶּגֶב לַחֲלֹף מִמִּדְבָּר בָּא מֵאֶרֶץ נוֹרָאָה	1[10] The burden of the wilderness *of the sea[11]*. As whirlwinds in the South sweeping on, It comes from the wilderness, from a dreadful land.
חָזוּת קָשָׁה הֻגַּד־לִי הַבּוֹגֵד בּוֹגֵד וְהַשּׁוֹדֵד שׁוֹדֵד עֲלִי עֵילָם צוּרִי מָדַי כָּל־אַנְחָתָה הִשְׁבַּתִּי	2[12] A grievous vision is declared to me: 'The treacherous dealer deals treacherously, *and the*

3:29 9:24-25

[1] Isaiah 20:1 - 1 Samuel 5:1 6:17, 1QIsab, 2 Kings 18:17, Amos 1:8, b.Sanhedrin 94a, Jeremiah 1:20 25:29-25:30, Seder Olam 23:Sennacherib
Isaiah 20:1-4 - 4QIsab
Isaiah 20:1-6 - 1QIsaa, 4QIsaa

[2] LXX *Tanathan came to Azotus*

[3] Isaiah 20:2 - 1 Samuel 19:24, 2 Kings 1:8, 2 Samuel 6:20, Acts 19:16, b.Yoma 77a, Ein Yaakov Shabbat:113a, Exodus 3:5, Ezekiel 4:5 24:17 24:23, Isaiah 13:1, Jeremiah 13:1-13:11 19:1-19:15, Job 1:20-21, John 21:7, Joshua 5:15, Matthew 3:4 16:24, Micah 1:8 1:11, Revelation 11:3, Zechariah 13:4

[4] Isaiah 20:3 - b.Megillah [Rashi] 24a, b.Shabbat 114a, Ein Yaakov Shabbat:114a, Ezekiel 4:5-4:6, Guide for the Perplexed 2:46, Isaiah 8:18 18:1-18:7 13:9 19:3, Jastrow 575b, Numbers 14:34, Revelation 11:2-11:3, Sifre Devarim {Vaetchanan} 27, Sifre Devarim Vaetchanan 27

[5] Isaiah 20:4 - 2 Samuel 10:4, b.Megillah [Rashi] 25b, Ezekiel 6:18, Genesis.R 36:6, Isaiah 3:17 19:4 23:3, Jeremiah 13:22 13:26 22:26, Micah 1:11, Midrash Tanchuma Noach 15, Revelation 3:18
Isaiah 20:4-6 - 4QIsaf

[6] Missing in LXX

[7] Isaiah 20:5 - 1 Corinthians 3:21, 2 Kings 18:21, Ezekiel 29:6-29:7, Isaiah 2:22 6:3 6:5 6:7 12:6, Jeremiah 9:24-9:25 17:5

[8] Isaiah 20:6 - 1 Thessalonians 5:3, Hebrews 2:3, Isaiah 10:3 4:17 30:1-30:7 30:15-30:16 31:1-31:3, Jeremiah 30:15-30:17 23:4, Job 6:20 22:30, Matthew 23:33

[9] 1QIsaa *on whom we rely*

[10] Isaiah 21:1 - Daniel 11:40, Ezekiel 6:11 7:12, Isaiah 13:1 13:4-13:5 13:17-13:18 13:20-13:22 14:23 17:1, Jastrow 1085a 1597a, Jeremiah 3:42, Job 13:9, Mekilta de R'Ishmael Vayassa 1:50, Midrash Psalms 80:6, Song of Songs.R 3:6, Zechariah 9:14
Isaiah 21:1-16 - 4QIsaa
Isaiah 21:1-17 - 1QIsaa

[11] Missing in LXX

[12] Isaiah 21:2 - 1 Samuel 24:13, Daniel 5:28 8:20, Exodus.R 15:16, Genesis.R 44:6, Isaiah 13:2-4 13:17-18 14:1-3 22:6 24:16 9:1

עַל־כֵּן מָלְאוּ מָתְנַי חַלְחָלָה צִירִים אֲחָזוּנִי כְּצִירֵי יוֹלֵדָה נַעֲוֵיתִי מִשְּׁמֹעַ נִבְהַלְתִּי מֵרְאוֹת 3[2]

תָּעָה לְבָבִי פַּלָּצוּת בִּעֲתָתְנִי אֵת נֶשֶׁף חִשְׁקִי שָׂם לִי לַחֲרָדָה 4[3]

עָרֹךְ הַשֻּׁלְחָן צָפֹה הַצָּפִית אָכוֹל שָׁתֹה קוּמוּ הַשָּׂרִים מִשְׁחוּ מָגֵן 5[4]

כִּי כֹה אָמַר אֵלַי אֲדֹנָי לֵךְ הַעֲמֵד הַמְצַפֶּה אֲשֶׁר יִרְאֶה יַגִּיד 6[5]

וְרָאָה רֶכֶב צֶמֶד פָּרָשִׁים רֶכֶב חֲמוֹר רֶכֶב גָּמָל וְהִקְשִׁיב קֶשֶׁב רַב־קָשֶׁב 7[6]

וַיִּקְרָא אַרְיֵה עַל־מִצְפֶּה אֲדֹנָי אָנֹכִי עֹמֵד תָּמִיד יוֹמָם וְעַל־מִשְׁמַרְתִּי אָנֹכִי נִצָּב כָּל־הַלֵּילוֹת 8[8]

וְהִנֵּה־זֶה בָא רֶכֶב אִישׁ צֶמֶד פָּרָשִׁים וַיַּעַן וַיֹּאמֶר נָפְלָה נָפְלָה בָּבֶל וְכָל־פְּסִילֵי אֱלֹהֶיהָ שִׁבַּר לָאָרֶץ 9[10]

מְדֻשָׁתִי וּבֶן־גָּרְנִי אֲשֶׁר שָׁמַעְתִּי מֵאֵת יְהוָה צְבָאוֹת אֱלֹהֵי יִשְׂרָאֵל הִגַּדְתִּי לָכֶם 10[12]

spoiler spoils. Go up, O Elam! Besiege, O Media! All its sighing I have made it cease[1].' Therefore, my loins are filled with convulsion; pangs have taken hold of me, as the pangs of a woman in travail; I am bent so I cannot hear; I am afraid, so I cannot see.

My heart is bewildered, terror overwhelms me; The twilight I longed for has been turned to trembling for me.

They prepare the table, they light the lamps, they eat, they drink. 'Rise up, princes, anoint the shield.'

For thus has the Lord said to me: Go, set a watchman; let him declare what he sees!

And when he sees a troop, horsemen by pairs, A troop of donkeys, a troop of camels[7], He shall listen diligently with much heed.

And he cried as a lion: 'Upon the watchtower, O Lord[9], I stand continually in the daytime, And I am set in my ward all the nights.'

And, behold, *there came a troop of men, horsemen by pairs*[11]. And he spoke and said: 'Fallen, fallen is Babylon; And all the graven images of her gods are broken to the ground.'

O my threshing, and the winnowing of my floor[13], what I have heard from the LORD of hosts, The God of Israel, I declared to you.

11:10 23:6, Jastrow 1300b, Jeremiah 31:12-13 7:21 7:26 21:3 1:34 2:14 2:34 51:3-4 3:11 51:27-28 3:44 51:48-49 3:53, Lamentations 1:22, Micah 7:8-10, Proverbs 13:15, Psalms 12:6 60:4 79:11 137:1-3, Revelation 13:10, Song of Songs.R 3:6, Zechariah 1:15-16

[1] LXX *the transgressor transgresses. The Elamites are upon me, and the ambassadors of the Persians come against me: now I will groan and comfort myself*

[2] Isaiah 21:3 - 1 Thessalonians 5:3, b.Bechorot 45a, Daniel 5:5-5:6, Deuteronomy 28:67, Habakkuk 3:16, Isaiah 13:8 15:5 16:9 16:11 2:17, Jastrow 1280b, Jeremiah 24:41 1:22 2:43, Lamentations.R 5:9, Micah 4:9-4:10, Pesikta Rabbati 33:11, Psalms 48:7, Psalms of Solomon 8:5, Sifre Devarim Nitzavim 319, Song of Songs.R 3:6

[3] Isaiah 21:4 - 1 Samuel 25:36-38, 2 Samuel 13:28-13:29, Daniel 5:1 5:5 5:30, Deuteronomy 28:67, Ecclesiastes.R 1:36, Esther 5:12 7:6-10, Isaiah 5:11-14, Jastrow 716b, Jeremiah 3:39 3:57, Job 21:11-13, Luke 21:34-36, Nahum 1:10

[4] Isaiah 21:5 - 1 Corinthians 15:32, Daniel 5:1-5, Gates of Repentance 3.168, Genesis.R 63:14, Isaiah 13:2 13:17-18 22:13-14 45:1-3, Jastrow 802b, Jeremiah 3:11 51:27-28 3:39 3:57, Mesillat Yesharim 5:Factors Detracting from Zehirus

[5] Isaiah 21:6 - 2 Kings 9:17-20, Ezekiel 3:17 33:2-7, Habakkuk 2:1-2, Isaiah 14:6, Jeremiah 51:12-13, Per Massorah: Soferim altered "Hashem" to "Adonai"

[6] Isaiah 21:7 - Hebrews 2:1, Isaiah 21:9 13:24

[7] LXX *And I saw two mounted horsemen, and a rider on an ass, and a rider on a camel*

[8] Isaiah 21:8 - 1 Peter 5:8, Bahir 88, Habakkuk 2:1-2:2, Isaiah 5:29 8:10 14:6, Jeremiah 4:7 1:38 1:19 2:44, Mekhilta de R'Shimon bar Yochai Pisha 16:5, Per Massorah: Soferim altered "Hashem" to "Adonai", Psalms 63:7 7:1
Isaiah 21:8-11 - Mekhilta de R'Shimon bar Yochai Pisha 16:5
Isaiah 21:8-12 - Seder Olam 28:Belshazzar

[9] LXX *and call thou Urias to the watch-tower: the Lord has spoken*

[10] Isaiah 21:9 - 2 Baruch 70:10, Genesis.R 44:17, Isaiah 13:19 14:4 46:1-46:2, Jeremiah 50:2-50:3 2:9 2:29 2:38 2:42 3:8 3:27 3:44 3:47 3:52 51:64, Lamentations.R 2:11, Leviticus.R 13:5, Mekhilta de R'Shimon bar Yochai Pisha 9:3, Mekilta de R'Ishmael Bahodesh 9:37, Pirkei de R'Eliezer 28, Revelation 14:8 18:2 18:21
Isaiah 21:9-10 - 4Q165 frag 5 ll.1-2

[11] LXX *he comes riding in a chariot and pair*

[12] Isaiah 21:10 - 1 Kings 22:14, 2 Kings 13:7, Acts 20:26-20:27, Ezekiel 3:17-3:19, Habakkuk 3:12, Isaiah 41:15-41:16, Jeremiah 3:33, Matthew 3:12, Mesillat Yesharim Afterword, Micah 4:13, Midrash Tanchuma Bamidbar 19, Numbers.R 4:1

[13] LXX *Hear, you who are left, and you who are in pain*

מַשָּׂא דּוּמָה אֵלַי קֹרֵא מִשֵּׂעִיר שֹׁמֵר מַה־מִלַּיְלָה שֹׁמֵר מַה־מִלֵּיל

11[1] The burden of *Dumah*[2]. One calls to me out of Seir: '*Watchman, what of the night? Watchman, what of the night?*[3]'

אָמַר שֹׁמֵר אָתָה בֹקֶר וְגַם־לָיְלָה אִם־תִּבְעָיוּן בְּעָיוּ שֻׁבוּ אֵתָיוּ

12[4] *The watchman said*[5]: 'The morning comes, and also the night. If you will inquire, inquire; *return, come*[6].'

מַשָּׂא בַּעְרָב בַּיַּעַר בַּעְרָב תָּלִינוּ אֹרְחוֹת דְּדָנִים

13[7] *The burden on Arabia. In the thickets in Arabia you shall lodge, O caravans*[8] *of Dedanites.*

לִקְרַאת צָמֵא הֵתָיוּ מָיִם יֹשְׁבֵי אֶרֶץ תֵּימָא בְּלַחְמוֹ קִדְּמוּ נֹדֵד

14[9] To him who is thirsty, bring water! The inhabitants of the land of Tema met the fugitive with his bread[10].

כִּי־מִפְּנֵי חֲרָבוֹת נָדָדוּ מִפְּנֵי חֶרֶב נְטוּשָׁה וּמִפְּנֵי קֶשֶׁת דְּרוּכָה וּמִפְּנֵי כֹּבֶד מִלְחָמָה

15[11] *For they fled from the swords, from the drawn sword, And from the bent bow, and from the grievousness of war.*[12]

כִּי־כֹה אָמַר אֲדֹנָי אֵלָי בְּעוֹד שָׁנָה כִּשְׁנֵי שָׂכִיר וְכָלָה כָּל־כְּבוֹד קֵדָר

16[13] For thus has the Lord said to me: 'Within a year, according to the years of a hireling, and all the glory of Kedar shall fail;

וּשְׁאָר מִסְפַּר־קֶשֶׁת גִּבּוֹרֵי בְנֵי־קֵדָר יִמְעָטוּ כִּי יְהוָה אֱלֹהֵי־יִשְׂרָאֵל דִּבֵּר

17[14] and the remnant of the number of the archers, the mighty men of the children of Kedar, shall be diminished; for the LORD, the God of Israel, has spoken it.'

Isaiah – Chapter 22

מַשָּׂא גֵּיא חִזָּיוֹן מַה־לָּךְ אֵפוֹא כִּי־עָלִית כֻּלָּךְ לַגַּגּוֹת

1[15] The burden concerning the Valley of *Vision*[16]. What ails you now, that you have wholly gone up to the housetops,

---

[1] Isaiah 21:11 - 1 Chronicles 1:30, Amos 1:6 1:11-1:12, Apocalypse of Zephaniah 3:2, Avot de R'Natan 1, b.Sanhedrin 94a, Deuteronomy 2:5, Ein Yaakov Sanhedrin:94a, Ezekiel 35:1-35:15, Genesis 1:14 8:4, Isaiah 21:6 34:1-34:17 63:1-63:6, Jastrow 383a 1461a 1536b 1611a, Jeremiah 13:17 49:7-49:22, Joel 4:19, Malachi 1:2-1:4, Numbers 24:18, Numbers.R 11:5, Obadiah 1:1-1:16, Pesikta Rabbati 33:3 33:4, Psalms 17:7, y.Taanit 1:1, z.Terumah 130b, z.Toledot 144a, z.Vayikra 22a
Isaiah 21:11-12 - Sifre.z Numbers Naso 6:24
Isaiah 21:11-14 - 4QIsab
Isaiah 21:11-15 - 4Q165 frag 5 ll.3-5
[2] LXX *Idumea*
[3] LXX *you guard the bulwarks*
[4] Isaiah 21:12 - Acts 2:37-2:38 17:19-17:20 17:30-17:32, b.Bava Kamma 3b, b.Middot [Rashi] 34a, b.Sanhedrin 94a, Exodus.R 18:12 23:6, Ezekiel 7:5-7:7 7:10 7:12 14:1-6 18:30-32, Isaiah 17:14 7:7, Jastrow 181a, Jeremiah 42:19-42:22 2:27, Midrash Tanchuma Shelach 13, Numbers.R 16:23, Pesikta Rabbati 33:4, y.Taanit 1:1
[5] Missing in LXX
[6] LXX *and live by me*
[7] Isaiah 21:13 - 1 Chronicles 1:9 1:32, 1 Kings 10:15, b.Rosh Hashanah [Rashi] 16b, Ezekiel 3:15 27:20-27:21, Galatians 4:25, Genesis 1:3, Genesis.R 53:14, Isaiah 13:1 13:20, Jeremiah 25:23-24 49:28-33, Midrash Psalms 5:8, Midrash Tanchuma Yitro 5, Pesikta de R'Kahana 19.2, Pesikta Rabbati 33:3, Sifre Devarim {Ha'azinu Hashamayim} 322, y.Taanit 4:5
Isaiah 21:13-15 - Lamentations.R 1:56 2:4
[8] LXX *You mayest lodge in the forest in the evening, or in the way*
[9] Isaiah 21:14 - 1 Chronicles 1:30, 1 Peter 4:9, b.Taanit 7a, Ein Yaakov Taanit:6b, Genesis 1:15, Isaiah 16:3-16:4, Job 6:19, Judges 8:4-8:8, Midrash Psalms 5:8, Midrash Tanchuma Yitro 5, Proverbs 1:21, Romans 12:20, y.Taanit 4:5
[10] LXX *You who live in the country of Thaeman, bring water to meet him who is thirsty*
[11] Isaiah 21:15 - b.Sanhedrin 95b, Ein Yaakov Sanhedrin:95b, Exodus.R 27:1, Isaiah 13:14, Job 6:19-6:20, Midrash Tanchuma Yitro 5, Pirkei de R'Eliezer 30, y.Taanit 4:5
[12] LXX *meet the fugitives with bread, because of the multitude of the slain, and because of the multitude of those who lose their way, and because of the multitude of swords, and because of the multitude of bent bows, and because of the multitude of they who have fallen in war*
[13] Isaiah 21:16 - 1 Chronicles 1:29, Ezekiel 3:21, Genesis 1:13, Isaiah 16:14 18:11 12:7, Jeremiah 1:28, Job 7:1, Mas.Kallah Rabbati 4:12, Per Massorah: Soferim altered "Hashem" to "Adonai", Psalms 24:5, Song of Songs 1:5
[14] Isaiah 21:17 - Isaiah 1:20 10:18-19 17:4-5, Jeremiah 20:29, Matthew 24:35, Numbers 23:19, Psalms 11:39, Zechariah 1:6
[15] Isaiah 22:1 - 1 Samuel 3:1 11:5, 2 Kings 6:28, 2 Samuel 14:5, Avot de R'Natan 34, b.Shekalim 14b, b.Taanit 29a, Deuteronomy 22:8, Ein Yaakov Taanit:28b, Genesis 21:17, Isaiah 13:1 15:3, Jeremiah 21:13 24:38, Joel 4:12 4:14, Judges 18:23, Lamentations.R Petichata D'Chakimei:21 Petichata D'Chakimei:24, Leviticus.R 19:6, Micah 3:6, Proverbs 5:18, Psalms 18:5 5:2 147:19-147:20, Romans 9:4-9:5, y.Shekalim 6:2, z.Mikketz 202b
Isaiah 22:1-25 - 1QIsaa
[16] LXX *Sion*

תְּשֻׁאוֹת מְלֵאָה עִיר הוֹמִיָּה קִרְיָה עַלִּיזָה חֲלָלַיִךְ לֹא חַלְלֵי־חֶרֶב וְלֹא מֵתֵי מִלְחָמָה	2[1]	You, who are full of uproar, a tumultuous city, a joyous town? Your slain are not slain with the sword, nor dead in battle.
כָּל־קְצִינַיִךְ גָּדְדוּ־יַחַד מִקֶּשֶׁת אֻסָּרוּ כָּל־נִמְצָאַיִךְ אֻסְּרוּ יַחְדָּו מֵרָחוֹק בָּרָחוּ	3[2]	All your rulers fled together, Without the bow *they are bound*[3]; All who are found in you are bound together, they fled far off.
עַל־כֵּן אָמַרְתִּי שְׁעוּ מִנִּי אֲמָרֵר בַּבֶּכִי אַל־תָּאִיצוּ לְנַחֲמֵנִי עַל־שֹׁד בַּת־עַמִּי	4[4]	Therefore, I said: 'Look away from me, I will weep bitterly; Strain not to comfort me, for the destruction of *the daughter of my people*[5].'
כִּי יוֹם מְהוּמָה וּמְבוּסָה וּמְבוּכָה לַאדֹנָי יְהֹוָה צְבָאוֹת בְּגֵיא חִזָּיוֹן מְקַרְקַר קִר וְשׁוֹעַ אֶל־הָהָר	5[6]	For it is a day of trouble, and of trampling, and of perplexity, From the Lord, the GOD of hosts, in the Valley of Vision; *Kir shouting, and Shoa at the mount*[7].
וְעֵילָם נָשָׂא אַשְׁפָּה בְּרֶכֶב אָדָם פָּרָשִׁים וְקִיר עֵרָה מָגֵן	6[8]	And Elam bore the quiver, with troops of men, horsemen; And *Kir uncovered the shield*[9].
וַיְהִי מִבְחַר־עֲמָקַיִךְ מָלְאוּ רָכֶב וְהַפָּרָשִׁים שֹׁת שָׁתוּ הַשָּׁעְרָה	7[10]	And it came to pass, when your choicest valleys were full of chariots, And the horsemen set themselves in array at the gate,
וַיְגַל אֵת מָסַךְ יְהוּדָה וַתַּבֵּט בַּיּוֹם הַהוּא אֶל־נֶשֶׁק בֵּית הַיָּעַר	8[11]	And *the covering of Judah was laid bare*[12], so you looked in that day *to the armor in the house of the forest*[13].
וְאֵת בְּקִיעֵי עִיר־דָּוִד רְאִיתֶם כִּי־רָבּוּ וַתְּקַבְּצוּ אֶת־מֵי הַבְּרֵכָה הַתַּחְתּוֹנָה	9[14]	*And you saw the breaches of the city*[15] of David, that they were many; and you gathered together the waters of the lower pool.
וְאֶת־בָּתֵּי יְרוּשָׁלַ͏ִם סְפַרְתֶּם וַתִּתְצוּ הַבָּתִּים לְבַצֵּר הַחוֹמָה	10[16]	And you numbered the houses of Jerusalem, and you broke down the houses to fortify the wall;
וּמִקְוָה עֲשִׂיתֶם בֵּין הַחֹמֹתַיִם לְמֵי הַבְּרֵכָה הַיְשָׁנָה וְלֹא הִבַּטְתֶּם אֶל־עֹשֶׂיהָ וְיֹצְרָהּ מֵרָחוֹק לֹא רְאִיתֶם	11[17]	You made a basin between the *two*[18] walls for the water of the old pool; But you do not *look*

---

[1] Isaiah 22:2 - Amos 6:3-6:6, b.Shekalim 14b, b.Taanit 29a, Ein Yaakov Taanit:28b, Isaiah 22:12-22:13 23:7 8:13 13:33 13:36, Jastrow 292a 426a 836a, Jeremiah 14:18 14:2 4:6, Lamentations 2:20 4:9-4:10, Lamentations.R Petichata D'Chakimei:21 Petichata D'Chakimei:24, y.Shekalim 6:2

[2] Isaiah 22:3 - 2 Kings 25:4-25:7 25:18-25:21, Isaiah 3:1-3:8, Jastrow 1431a 1433b, Jeremiah 39:4-39:7 52:24-52:27, Lamentations.R Petichata D'Chakimei:21 Petichata D'Chakimei:24

[3] 1QIsaa *she is captured*

[4] Isaiah 22:4 - Isaiah 15:3 9:7, Jeremiah 4:19 6:26 8:18 9:2 13:17 7:16, Lamentations.R Petichata D'Chakimei:21 Petichata D'Chakimei:24, Luke 1:2 19:41, Matthew 2:18 26:75, Micah 1:8, Midrash Psalms 137:3, Midrash Tanchuma Vayigash 10, Pesikta Rabbati 28:2 29:1, Psalms 77:3, Ruth 1:20-1:21, z.Mikketz 203a

[5] 1QIsaa *my beloved people*

[6] Isaiah 22:5 - 2 Kings 19:3 1:10, Amos 5:18-5:20, b.Taanit 29a, Ein Yaakov Taanit:28b, Esther 3:15, Hosea 10:8, Isaiah 5:5 10:6 22:1 1:10 13:3, Jastrow 729b 1427a 1538a, Jeremiah 6:7, Lamentations 1:5 2:2, Lamentations.R Petichata D'Chakimei:21 Petichata D'Chakimei:24, Luke 23:30, Matthew 24:16, Micah 7:4, Pesikta de R'Kahana S6.2, Revelation 6:16-6:17, z.Chayyei Sarah 132a 132b, z.Vaetchanan 270a

[7] 1QIsaa *a battering down of his holiness on the mountain*

[8] Isaiah 22:6 - 2 Kings 16:9, Amos 1:5 9:7, Genesis 10:22, Isaiah 15:1 21:2, Jeremiah 49:35-49:39, Lamentations.R Petichata D'Chakimei:21 Petichata D'Chakimei:24

[9] LXX *there was a gathering for battle*

[10] Isaiah 22:7 - Isaiah 8:7-8:8 10:28-10:32 13:34, Jastrow 859a, Jeremiah 39:1-39:3, Lamentations.R Petichata D'Chakimei:21 Petichata D'Chakimei:24

[11] Isaiah 22:8 - 1 Kings 7:2 10:17 14:27-14:28, Ecclesiastes.R 10:18, Isaiah 36:1-36:3, Lamentations.R Petichata D'Chakimei:21 Petichata D'Chakimei:24 Petichata D'Chakimei:24, Leviticus.R 19:4, Midrash Psalms 137:10, Pesikta de R'Kahana 15.7, Song of Songs 4:4, y.Yoma 1:1

[12] LXX *they shall uncover the gates of Juda*

[13] LXX *on the choice houses of the city*

[14] Isaiah 22:9 - 2 Chronicles 32:1-6 8:30, 2 Kings 20:20, Lamentations.R Petichata D'Chakimei:21 Petichata D'Chakimei:24, Nehemiah 3:16

[15] LXX *And they shall uncover the secret places of the houses of the citadel*

[16] Isaiah 22:10 - Lamentations.R Petichata D'Chakimei:21 Petichata D'Chakimei:24
Isaiah 22:10-14 - 4QIsac

[17] Isaiah 22:11 - 2 Chronicles 6:6 16:7-9 32:3-4, 2 Kings 20:20 1:4, Isaiah 8:17 17:7 7:1 13:26, Jeremiah 33:2-3 15:4, Micah 7:7, Nehemiah 3:16
Isaiah 22:11-18 - 1QIsab

[18] Missing in 1QIsaa

וַיִּקְרָ֞א אֲדֹנָ֧י יְהוִ֛ה צְבָא֖וֹת בַּיּ֣וֹם הַה֑וּא לִבְכִי֙ וּלְמִסְפֵּ֔ד וּלְקׇרְחָ֖ה וְלַחֲגֹ֥ר שָֽׂק׃   12[2]

וְהִנֵּ֣ה ׀ שָׂשׂ֣וֹן וְשִׂמְחָ֗ה הָרֹ֤ג ׀ בָּקָר֙ וְשָׁחֹ֣ט צֹ֔אן אָכֹ֥ל בָּשָׂ֖ר וְשָׁת֣וֹת יָ֑יִן אָכ֣וֹל וְשָׁת֔וֹ כִּ֥י מָחָ֖ר נָמֽוּת׃   13[3]

וְנִגְלָ֥ה בְאׇזְנָ֖י יְהוָ֣ה צְבָא֑וֹת אִם־יְכֻפַּ֞ר הֶעָוֺ֤ן הַזֶּה֙ לָכֶם֙ עַד־תְּמֻת֔וּן אָמַ֛ר אֲדֹנָ֥י יְהוִ֖ה צְבָאֽוֹת׃   14[4]

כֹּ֥ה אָמַ֛ר אֲדֹנָ֥י יְהוִ֖ה צְבָא֑וֹת לֶךְ־בֹּא֙ אֶל־הַסֹּכֵ֣ן הַזֶּ֔ה עַל־שֶׁבְנָ֖א אֲשֶׁ֥ר עַל־הַבָּֽיִת׃   15[5]
מַה־לְּךָ֥ פֹה֙ וּמִ֣י לְךָ֣ פֹ֔ה כִּי־חָצַ֧בְתָּ לְּךָ֛ פֹּ֖ה קָ֑בֶר חֹצְבִ֤י מָרוֹם֙ קִבְר֔וֹ חֹקְקִ֥י בַסֶּ֖לַע מִשְׁכָּ֥ן לֽוֹ׃   16[8]

הִנֵּ֤ה יְהוָה֙ מְטַלְטֶלְךָ֔ טַלְטֵלָ֖ה גָּ֑בֶר וְעֹטְךָ֖ עָטֹֽה׃   17[9]

צָנ֤וֹף יִצְנׇפְךָ֙ צְנֵפָ֔ה כַּדּ֕וּר אֶל־אֶ֖רֶץ רַחֲבַ֣ת יָדָ֑יִם שָׁ֣מָּה תָמ֗וּת וְשָׁ֙מָּה֙ מַרְכְּב֣וֹת כְּבוֹדֶ֔ךָ קְל֖וֹן בֵּ֥ית אֲדֹנֶֽיךָ׃   18[11]

וַהֲדַפְתִּ֖יךָ מִמַּצָּבֶ֑ךָ וּמִמַּעֲמָדְךָ֖ יֶהֶרְסֶֽךָ׃   19[13]

וְהָיָ֖ה בַּיּ֣וֹם הַה֑וּא וְקָרָ֥אתִי לְעַבְדִּ֖י לְאֶלְיָקִ֥ים בֶּן־חִלְקִיָּֽהוּ׃   20[14]

---

to[1] Him who has done this, nor have you respected Him who fashioned it long ago.

12[2] And in that day the Lord, the GOD of hosts, called to weeping, and to lamentation, and to baldness, and to wearing sackcloth;

13[3] And behold joy and gladness, slaying oxen and killing sheep, eating flesh and drinking wine; 'Let us eat and drink, for tomorrow we shall die!'

14[4] And the LORD of hosts revealed Himself in My ears: Surely this iniquity shall not be forgiven until you die, says the LORD of hosts.

15[5] Thus says *the LORD of hosts*[6]: Go, get to this steward, to *Shebna, who is over the house*[7]:

16[8] What have you here, and whom have you here, That you have hewed out here a sepulcher, You who hews out a sepulcher on high, And graves as a dwelling for yourself in the rock?

17[9] Behold, the LORD *will hurl you up and down with a man's throw; Yes, He will wind you round and around*[10];

18[11] He will violently roll and toss you like a ball into a large country; There you shall die, *and there shall be the chariots of your glory, You shame of the lord's house*[12].

19[13] And I will thrust you from your post, And from your station you shall be pulled down.

20[14] And it shall come to pass in that day, That I will call my servant Eliakim the son of *Hilkiah*[15];

---

[1] 1QIsaa *look upon*

[2] Isaiah 22:12 - 2 Chronicles 11:25, Amos 8:10, b.Avodah Zara 3b, b.Chagigah 5b, Ecclesiastes 3:4 3:11, Ecclesiastes.R 3:10, Ein Yaakov Avodah Zarah:3b, Ezra 9:3, Isaiah 15:2, James 4:8-4:10 5:1, Job 1:20, Joel 1:13 2:17, Jonah 3:6, Lamentations.R 1:1 1:23, Micah 1:16, Midrash Psalms 20:1, Midrash Tanchuma Vayigash 10, Nehemiah 8:9-8:12 9:9, Pesikta de R'Kahana 15.3, Pesikta Rabbati 29:1, Sifre Devarim {Nitzavim} 305, Sifre Devarim Haazinu 305, z.Vayigash 210a

[3] Isaiah 22:13 - 1 Corinthians 15:32, 4Q177 1.15, 4Q177 5+6 15, Amos 6:3-6:7, b.Taanit 11a, Ein Yaakov Taanit:11a, Gates of Repentance 4.004, Isaiah 5:12 5:22 21:4-21:5 28:7-28:8 8:12, James 5:5, Luke 17:26-17:29, mt.Hilchot Deot 5:1 5:1 Isaiah 22:13-25 - 4QIsaa

[4] Isaiah 22:14 - 1 Samuel 3:14 9:15, Amos 3:7, Avot de R'Natan 29, b.Taanit 11a, b.Yoma 86a, Ein Yaakov Yoma:86a, Ezekiel 24:13, Gates of Repentance 1.47 4.4 4.6, Hebrews 10:26-27, Isaiah 5:9 13:11 2:21 6:13, John 8:21-24, Mekilta de R'Ishmael Bahodesh 7:24, Midrash Proverbs 10, Midrash Tanchuma Vayeshev 2, mt.Hilchot Teshuvah 1:4, Numbers 15:25-31, Pirkei de R'Eliezer 38, Revelation 22:11-12, t.Kippurim 4:8, y.Sanhedrin 10:1, y.Sheviit 1:6, y.Yoma 8:7, z.Bamidbar 121a Isaiah 22:14-22 - 4QIsaf

[5] Isaiah 22:15 - 1 Chronicles 3:25, 1 Kings 4:6, 2 Kings 10:5 18:18 18:26 18:37 19:2, Acts 8:27, b.Sanhedrin 26b, b.Shabbat [Tosefot] 12b, Exodus.R 1:10, HaMadrikh 35:9, Isaiah 12:3 12:11 12:22 13:2, Jastrow 992a, Leviticus.R 5:5, z.Vaetchanan 269b

[6] 1QIsaa *the LORD God of hosts*

[7] LXX *Somnas the treasurer, and say to him, Why art you here?*

[8] Isaiah 22:16 - 2 Chronicles 16:14, 2 Samuel 18:18, b.Sanhedrin 26a, Ein Yaakov Sanhedrin:26a, HaMadrikh 35:9, Isaiah 14:18 4:5, Jastrow 494a 1311a, Job 3:15, Leviticus.R 5:5, Matthew 27:60, Micah 2:10

[9] Isaiah 22:17 - b.Sanhedrin 26a, Esther 7:8, Jastrow 411a 536a 1700a, Jeremiah 14:3, Job 9:24, Leviticus.R 5:5 17:3, Ralbag SOS 1, z.Bereshit 14b

[10] LXX *of hosts casts forth and will utterly destroy such a man, and will take away your robe and your glorious crown*

[11] Isaiah 22:18 - Amos 7:17, b.Chullin [Tosefot] 64a, b.Ketubot 22a, b.Sanhedrin 26a, Ein Yaakov Sanhedrin:26a, Isaiah 17:13, Jastrow 655b, Leviticus.R 5:5

[12] LXX *and he will bring your fair chariot to shame, and the house of your prince to be trodden down*

[13] Isaiah 22:19 - Ezekiel 17:24, Job 40:11-40:12, Luke 1:52, Psalms 75:7-75:8

[14] Isaiah 22:20 - 2 Kings 18:18 18:37, b.Shabbat [Tosefot] 12b, Isaiah 12:3 12:11 12:22 13:2, Mas.Kallah Rabbati 8:9, Sifre Devarim {Vaetchanan} 27, Sifre Devarim Vaetchanan 27

[15] 1QIsaa 4QIsaf *Hilkiyah*, MT 4QIsaa *Hilkiyahu*

וְהִלְבַּשְׁתִּיו כֻּתָּנְתֶּךָ וְאַבְנֵטְךָ אֲחַזְּקֶנּוּ וּמֶמְשַׁלְתְּךָ אֶתֵּן בְּיָדוֹ וְהָיָה לְאָב לְיוֹשֵׁב יְרוּשָׁלַ͏ִם וּלְבֵית יְהוּדָה

21[1] And I will clothe him with your *robe*[2], *And bind him with your girdle, And I will commit your government into his hand*[3]; And he shall be a father to the inhabitants of Jerusalem, and to the house of Judah.

וְנָתַתִּי מַפְתֵּחַ בֵּית־דָּוִד עַל־שִׁכְמוֹ וּפָתַח וְאֵין סֹגֵר וְסָגַר וְאֵין פֹּתֵחַ

22[4] And I will lay the key of the house of David upon his shoulder; *And he shall open, and no ne shall shut; And he shall shut, and no one shall open*[5].

וּתְקַעְתִּיו יָתֵד בְּמָקוֹם נֶאֱמָן וְהָיָה לְכִסֵּא כָבוֹד לְבֵית אָבִיו

23[6] *And I will fasten him as a peg*[7] in a sure place; And he shall be a throne of honor to his father's house.

וְתָלוּ עָלָיו כֹּל כְּבוֹד בֵּית־אָבִיו הַצֶּאֱצָאִים וְהַצְּפִעוֹת כֹּל כְּלֵי הַקָּטָן מִכְּלֵי הָאַגָּנוֹת וְעַד כָּל־כְּלֵי הַנְּבָלִים

24[8] *And they shall hang on him all the glory of his father's house, the offspring and the issue, all vessels of small quantity, from the vessels of cups to all the vessels of flagons*[9].

בַּיּוֹם הַהוּא נְאֻם יְהוָה צְבָאוֹת תָּמוּשׁ הַיָּתֵד הַתְּקוּעָה בְּמָקוֹם נֶאֱמָן וְנִגְדְּעָה וְנָפְלָה וְנִכְרַת הַמַּשָּׂא אֲשֶׁר־עָלֶיהָ כִּי יְהוָה דִּבֵּר

25[10] In that day, says *the LORD*[11] of hosts, *the peg that was fastened in a sure place shall give way; and it shall be hewn down, and fall, and the burden that was upon it shall be cut off*[12]; for the LORD has spoken.

Isaiah – Chapter 23

מַשָּׂא צֹר הֵילִילוּ אֳנִיּוֹת תַּרְשִׁישׁ כִּי־שֻׁדַּד מִבַּיִת מִבּוֹא מֵאֶרֶץ כִּתִּים נִגְלָה־לָמוֹ

1[13] The burden of Tyre. Howl, you ships of *Tarshish*[14], For it is laid waste, so that there is no house, no entering in; From the land of *Kittim*[15] it is revealed to them[16].

דֹּמּוּ יֹשְׁבֵי אִי סֹחֵר צִידוֹן עֹבֵר יָם מִלְאוּךְ

2[17] Be still, you inhabitants of the coastland; *You whom the merchants of Zidon, who pass over*[18] the sea, have replenished.

---

[1] Isaiah 22:21 - 1 Samuel 18:4, b.Shabbat [Tosefot] 12b, Esther 8:2 8:15, Genesis 41:42-43 21:8, Isaiah 9:7-8, Leviticus.R 5:5
[2] 1QIsaa plural, MT singular
[3] LXX *and I will grant him your crown with power, and I will give your stewardship into his hands*
[4] Isaiah 22:22 - b.Shabbat [Tosefot] 137b, Isaiah 7:2, Job 12:14, Matthew 16:18-16:19 18:18-18:19, Revelation 1:18 3:7, Midrash Tanchuma Noach 3, Seder Olam 25:Nebuchadnezzar, Sifre Devarim {Ha'azinu Hashamayim} 321
[5] LXX *And I will give him the glory of David; and he shall rule, and there shall be none to speak against him*
[6] Isaiah 22:23 - 1 Samuel 2:8, 4QIsac, Ecclesiastes 12:11, Esther 4:14 10:3, Exodus.R 37:1, Ezra 9:8, Genesis 45:9-45:13, Jastrow 603a, Job 12:7, Luke 22:29-22:30, Psalms of Solomon 2:19, Revelation 3:21, Zechariah 10:4
[7] LXX *And I will make him a ruler*
[8] Isaiah 22:24 - 2 Timothy 2:20-2:21, b.Menachot [Tosefot] 53b, Daniel 6:2-6:4, Ezekiel 15:3, Genesis 41:44-41:45 47:11-47:25, John 5:22-5:27 20:21-20:23, Matthew 4:18, Romans 9:22-9:23
Isaiah 22:24-25 - 1QIsab, 4QIsab
[9] LXX *And every one who is glorious in the house of his father shall trust in him, from the least to the greatest; and they shall depend upon him in that day*
[10] Isaiah 22:25 - 4QIsaf, Esther 9:5-9:14 9:24-9:25, Ezekiel 5:13 5:15 5:17, Isaiah 22:15-22:16 22:23 22:11 24:15, Jeremiah 4:28 17:5-17:6, Micah 4:4, Psalms 52:6 2:3
[11] 4QIsaf *the LORD God*
[12] LXX *The man who is fastened in the sure place shall be removed and be taken away, and shall fall; and the glory that is upon him shall be utterly destroyed*
[13] Isaiah 23:1 - 1 Kings 5:1 10:22 22:48, 2 Chronicles 9:21, Amos 1:9-1:10, Daniel 11:30, Ezekiel 26:1-28:24, Genesis 10:4, Isaiah 2:16 15:1-15:2 15:8 23:12 24:10 12:9, Jeremiah 2:10 25:10-25:11 1:15 1:22 23:4, Joel 4:4-4:8, Joshua 19:29, Numbers 24:24, Psalms 48:8, Revelation 18:17-18:19 18:22-18:23, Zechariah 9:2-9:4
Isaiah 23:1-4 - 1QIsab
Isaiah 23:1-12 - 4QIsaa
Isaiah 23:1-18 - 1QIsaa
[14] LXX *Carthage*
[15] *Cyprus*; LXX *the Citians*
[16] LXX *she is led captive*
[17] Isaiah 23:2 - Ezekiel 27:3-27:4 27:8-27:36 4:2, Habakkuk 2:20, Isaiah 17:1 23:5, Psalms 46:11
[18] 1QIsaa 4QIsaa LXX *you merchants of Sidon, whose messengers crossed over*

Hebrew		English
וּבְמַיִם רַבִּים זֶרַע שִׁחֹר קְצִיר יְאוֹר תְּבוּאָתָהּ וַתְּהִי סְחַר גּוֹיִם	3[1]	And on great waters *the seed of Shihor, The harvest of the Nile, was her revenue; And she was the market of*[2] nations.
בּוֹשִׁי צִידוֹן כִּי־אָמַר יָם מָעוֹז הַיָּם לֵאמֹר לֹא־חַלְתִּי וְלֹא־יָלַדְתִּי וְלֹא גִדַּלְתִּי בַּחוּרִים רוֹמַמְתִּי בְתוּלוֹת	4[3]	Be ashamed, O Zidon; for the sea has spoken, The stronghold of the sea, saying: 'I have not travailed, nor brought forth, nor have I reared young men, nor brought up virgins.'
כַּאֲשֶׁר־שֵׁמַע לְמִצְרָיִם יָחִילוּ כְּשֵׁמַע צֹר	5[4]	When the report comes to Egypt, They shall be sorely pained at the report of Tyre.
עִבְרוּ תַּרְשִׁישָׁה הֵילִילוּ יֹשְׁבֵי אִי	6[5]	Pass over to Tarshish; howl, you inhabitants of the *coastland*[6].
הֲזֹאת לָכֶם עַלִּיזָה מִימֵי־קֶדֶם קַדְמָתָהּ יֹבִלוּהָ רַגְלֶיהָ מֵרָחוֹק לָגוּר	7[7]	*Is this your joyous city, whose feet in antiquity, in ancient days, Carried her afar to sojourn*[8]?
מִי יָעַץ זֹאת עַל־צֹר הַמַּעֲטִירָה אֲשֶׁר סֹחֲרֶיהָ שָׂרִים כִּנְעָנֶיהָ נִכְבַּדֵּי־אָרֶץ	8[9]	Who has devised this against Tyre, *the crowning city, Whose merchants are princes, Whose merchants are the honorable of the earth?*[10]
יְהוָה צְבָאוֹת יְעָצָהּ לְחַלֵּל גְּאוֹן כָּל־צְבִי לְהָקֵל כָּל־נִכְבַּדֵּי־אָרֶץ	9[11]	The LORD of hosts has devised it, to pollute the pride of *all*[12] glory, to bring into contempt all the honorable of the earth.
עִבְרִי אַרְצֵךְ כַּיְאֹר בַּת־תַּרְשִׁישׁ אֵין מֵזַח עוֹד	10[13]	*Overflow your land as the Nile, O daughter of Tarshish! there is no girdle any longer*[14].
יָדוֹ נָטָה עַל־הַיָּם הִרְגִּיז מַמְלָכוֹת יְהוָה צִוָּה אֶל־כְּנַעַן לַשְׁמִד מָעֻזְנֶיהָ	11[15]	He has stretched out His hand over the sea, He has shaken the kingdoms; The LORD[16] has given commandment concerning Canaan, To destroy its strongholds;
וַיֹּאמֶר לֹא־תוֹסִיפִי עוֹד לַעְלוֹז הַמְעֻשָּׁקָה בְּתוּלַת בַּת־צִידוֹן כתיים "כִּתִּים" קומי עֲבֹרִי גַּם־שָׁם לֹא־יָנוּחַ לָךְ	12[17]	And He said: 'You shall *rejoice no longer*[18].' O oppressed virgin daughter of Zidon, Arise, pass over to Kittim; there you shall have no rest.

---

[1] Isaiah 23:3 - 1 Chronicles 13:5, Deuteronomy 11:10, Ezekiel 27:3-27:23 3:33 4:4, Isaiah 19:7 23:8 8:20, Jeremiah 2:18, Joel 4:5, Revelation 18:11-13

[2] LXX *a generation of merchants? As when the harvest is gathered in, so are these traders with the*

[3] Isaiah 23:4 - Ezekiel 26:3-26:6, Genesis 10:15 10:19, Hosea 9:11-9:14, Jeremiah 47:3-47:4, Midrash Psalms 114:9, Pesikta Rabbati 22:1, Revelation 18:23, Saadia Opinions 2:10

[4] Isaiah 23:5 - Exodus 15:14-16, Exodus.R 9:13, Ezekiel 26:15-21 27:29-36 4:19, Isaiah 19:16, Joshua 2:9-2:11, Midrash Tanchuma Bo 4, Midrash Tanchuma Vaera 13, Pesikta de R'Kahana 7.11, Pesikta Rabbati 17:8 49:9, Revelation 18:1719

[5] Isaiah 23:6 - Isaiah 16:7 21:15 23:1-2 23:10 23:12

[6] LXX *island*

[7] Isaiah 23:7 - Ecclesiastes 10:7, Genesis.R 61:7, Isaiah 22:2 8:13 47:1-2, Joshua 19:29

[8] LXX *Was not this your pride from the beginning, before she was given up*

[9] Isaiah 23:8 - b.Bava Batra 75a, b.Pesachim 50a, Deuteronomy 29:23-29:27, Ein Yaakov Bava Batra:75a, Ezekiel 28:2-28:6 28:12-28:18, Isaiah 10:8 12:9, Jeremiah 50:44-50:45, Leviticus.R 17:5, Midrash Tanchuma Massei 9, Numbers.R 23:10, Pesikta de R'Kahana S2.4, Pesikta Rabbati 13:2, Revelation 18:8
Isaiah 23:8-18 - 4QIsac

[10] LXX *Is she inferior or has she no strength? Her merchants were the glorious princes of the earth*

[11] Isaiah 23:9 - 1 Corinthians 1:26-29, Acts 4:28, Daniel 4:34, Ephesians 1:11 3:11, Isaiah 2:11 2:17 5:13 5:15-16 9:16 10:33 13:11 14:24 14:27 46:10-11, James 4:6, Jeremiah 47:6-7 51:62, Job 12:21 40:11-12, Malachi 3:19, Pesikta Rabbati 13:2, Psalms 11:40, Saadia Opinions 10:4

[12] Missing in 1QIsaa

[13] Isaiah 23:10 - 1 Samuel 4:20, Haggai 2:22, Isaiah 23:14, Job 12:21, Lamentations 1:6, Psalms 18:33, Romans 5:6

[14] LXX *Till your land; for ships no longer come out of Carthage*

[15] Isaiah 23:11 - Exodus 14:21 15:8-15:10, Ezekiel 2:10 26:15-26:19 27:34-27:35 7:16, Genesis 9:25 10:15-10:19, Haggai 2:7, Hosea 12:9-12:10, Isaiah 2:19 10:6 14:16-14:17 23:3 1:2, Jeremiah 23:7, John 2:16, Mark 11:17, Nahum 1:14, Psalms 46:7 71:3, Zechariah 9:3-9:4 14:21

[16] LXX adds *of hosts*

[17] Isaiah 23:12 - Deuteronomy 28:64-67, Ezekiel 26:13-14 3:6, Genesis 10:15-19 1:13, Isaiah 23:1-2 23:7 13:22 23:1 23:5, Jeremiah 14:17 22:11, Joshua 11:8, Lamentations 1:3 1:15 4:15, Numbers 24:24, Revelation 18:22, Variant of קומו is קומי;

[18] 1QIsaa *not take refuge to rejoice*

הֵן ׀ אֶרֶץ כַּשְׂדִּים זֶה הָעָם לֹא הָיָה אַשּׁוּר יְסָדָהּ
לְצִיִּים הֵקִימוּ ׳בְחִינָיו׳ ״בַחוּנָיו״ עֹרְרוּ אַרְמְנוֹתֶיהָ
שָׂמָהּ לְמַפֵּלָה

13[1] *Behold[2]*, the land of the Chaldeans, this is the people who were not *when Asshur founded it for shipmen[3]*, they set up their [4]towers, they overthrew its palaces; it is made a ruin.

הֵילִילוּ אֳנִיּוֹת תַּרְשִׁישׁ כִּי שֻׁדַּד מָעֻזְּכֶן

14[5] Howl, you ships of Tarshish, For your stronghold is laid waste.

וְהָיָה בַּיּוֹם הַהוּא וְנִשְׁכַּחַת צֹר שִׁבְעִים שָׁנָה כִּימֵי
מֶלֶךְ אֶחָד מִקֵּץ שִׁבְעִים שָׁנָה יִהְיֶה לְצֹר כְּשִׁירַת
הַזּוֹנָה

15[6] And it shall come to pass in that day, that Tyre *shall be forgotten seventy years, according to the days of one king; after the end of seventy years it shall fare with Tyre[7]* as in the song of the harlot:

קְחִי כִנּוֹר סֹבִּי עִיר זוֹנָה נִשְׁכָּחָה הֵיטִיבִי נַגֵּן
הַרְבִּי־שִׁיר לְמַעַן תִּזָּכֵרִי

16[8] Take a harp, Go about the city, You harlot long forgotten; Make sweet melody, Sing many songs, So you may be remembered.

וְהָיָה מִקֵּץ שִׁבְעִים שָׁנָה יִפְקֹד יְהוָה אֶת־צֹר
וְשָׁבָה לְאֶתְנַנָּה וְזָנְתָה אֶת־כָּל־מַמְלְכוֹת הָאָרֶץ
עַל־פְּנֵי הָאֲדָמָה

17[9] And it shall come to pass after the end of seventy years, that the LORD will remember Tyre, and she shall return to her *hire[10]*, and shall have commerce with all the kingdoms of the world on the face of the earth.

וְהָיָה סַחְרָהּ וְאֶתְנַנָּהּ קֹדֶשׁ לַיהוָה לֹא יֵאָצֵר וְלֹא
יֵחָסֵן כִּי לַיֹּשְׁבִים לִפְנֵי יְהוָה יִהְיֶה סַחְרָהּ לֶאֱכֹל
לְשָׂבְעָה וְלִמְכַסֶּה עָתִיק

18[11] And her gain and her hire shall be holiness to the LORD; it shall not be treasured nor laid up; *for her gain shall be for those who live before the LORD, to eat their fill, and for stately clothing[12]*.

Isaiah – Chapter 24

הִנֵּה יְהוָה בּוֹקֵק הָאָרֶץ וּבוֹלְקָהּ וְעִוָּה פָנֶיהָ וְהֵפִיץ
יֹשְׁבֶיהָ

1[13] Behold, the *LORD[14]* makes the earth empty and makes it waste, And turns it upside down, and scatters its inhabitants abroad.

וְהָיָה כָעָם כַּכֹּהֵן כַּעֶבֶד כַּאדֹנָיו כַּשִּׁפְחָה כַּגְבִרְתָּהּ
כַּקּוֹנֶה כַּמּוֹכֵר כַּמַּלְוֶה כַּלֹּוֶה כַּנֹּשֶׁה כַּאֲשֶׁר נֹשֶׁא בוֹ

2[15] And it shall be, as with the people, so with the priest; As with the servant, so with his master;

---

[1] Isaiah 23:13 - 2 Chronicles 9:11, 2 Kings 17:24 20:12, Acts 7:4, b.Succah 52b, Daniel 4:27, Ezekiel 26:7-26:21 5:18, Ezra 4:9-4:10, Genesis 2:14 10:10-10:11 11:9 11:28 11:31, Habakkuk 1:6, Isaiah 10:5 10:7 13:19, Job 1:17, Leviticus.R 17:4, Pesikta de R'Kahana 7.10 14.3, Pesikta Rabbati 17:6 35:1, Psalms 72:9, Ruth.R 2:10, y.Taanit 3:4, z.Yitro 82b

[2] LXX *And if you depart to*

[3] 1QIsaa *Assyria. They mde Tyre for desert creatures*

[4] 1QIsaa adds *siege*

[5] Isaiah 23:14 - Ezekiel 27:25-27:30, Isaiah 2:16 23:1 23:6, Midrash Tanchuma Bamidbar 2, Revelation 18:11-18:19

[6] Isaiah 23:15 - b.Sanhedrin 99a, Daniel 7:14 8:21, Ein Yaakov Sanhedrin:99a, Ezekiel 3:25 5:11, Hosea 2:15, Jeremiah 25:9-25:11 1:22 27:3-7 5:10, Leviticus.R 5:5, Revelation 17:10

[7] 1QIsaa is missing all the test between the two *Tyre*s.

[8] Isaiah 23:16 - Jeremiah 6:14, Proverbs 7:10-7:12

[9] Isaiah 23:17 - 1 Peter 5:2, 1 Timothy 3:3 3:8, Acts 15:14, Deuteronomy 23:20, Ezekiel 16:26 16:31 22:13 27:6-36, Hosea 12:9-10, Jeremiah 5:10, Micah 1:7 3:11, Nahum 3:4, Revelation 17:1-5 18:9-14 19:2, Saadia Opinions 8:3, Zephaniah 2:7

[10] LXX *primitive state*

[11] Isaiah 23:18 - 2 Chronicles 2:6-8 2:10-15, Acts 9:39 21:3-5, b.Pesachim 118b, b.Succah [Rashi] 45b, Deuteronomy 12:18-12:19 26:12-14, Ecclesiastes 2:26, Ecclesiastes.R 1:21, Ein Yaakov Pesachim:118b, Exodus 4:36, Exodus.R 31:17, Galatians 6:6, Guide for the Perplexed 3:Introduction, Isaiah 60:5-60:9, Jastrow 653a 1129b, Luke 8:3 12:18-20 12:33 16:9-13, Malachi 3:10, Mark 3:8, Matthew 6:19-21 25:35-40, Micah 4:13, Midrash Tanchuma Balak 14, Numbers.R 20:20, Philippians 4:17-18, Proverbs 3:9-10 13:22 4:8, Psalms 45:13 72:10, Romans 15:25-27, z.Emor 105b, Zechariah 14:20-21

[12] 1QIsaa *but her merchandise will become abundant food and choice attire for those who live in the presence of the LORD*; LXX adds *and for a covenant and a memorial before the LORD*

[13] Isaiah 24:1 - 2 Kings 21:13, Acts 17:6, Deuteronomy 4:27 28:64 8:26, Ezekiel 5:2 5:14 6:6 12:20 24:11 11:14, Isaiah 1:7-1:9 2:19 5:6 6:11-6:12 7:17-7:25 24:20 3:10 5:16 32:13-32:14 9:9 18:15, James 1:1, Jeremiah 4:7 9:17 16:15 2:17, Luke 21:24, Nahum 2:11, Nehemiah 1:8, Psalms 2:9, Zechariah 13:7-13:9
Isaiah 24:1-3 - 4QIsaf
Isaiah 24:1-15 - 4QIsac
Isaiah 24:1-23 - 1QIsaa
Isaiah 24:1-27:13 - Cairo Damascus 1:13-14

[14] 4QIsac *Lord*

[15] Isaiah 24:2 - 2 Chronicles 36:14-36:17 12:20, 4QIsab, b.Pesachim 25b, b.Shabbat 119b, Daniel 9:5-9:8, Deuteronomy 23:21-23:21, Ein Yaakov Shabbat:119b, Ephesians 6:8-6:9, Ezekiel 7:12-7:13 14:8-14:10, Genesis 17:50, Hosea 4:9, Isaiah 2:9 3:2-3:8 5:15 9:15-

As with the maid, so with her mistress; As with the buyer, so with the seller; As with the lender, so with the borrower; As with the creditor, so with the debtor.

הִבּוֹק תִּבּוֹק הָאָרֶץ וְהִבּוֹז‎ תִּבּוֹז כִּי יְהוָה דִּבֶּר אֶת־הַדָּבָר הַזֶּה

3[1] The earth shall be utterly emptied, and clean despoiled; For the LORD has spoken this word.

אָבְלָה נָבְלָה הָאָרֶץ אֻמְלְלָה נָבְלָה תֵּבֵל אֻמְלָלוּ מְרוֹם עַם־הָאָרֶץ

4[2] The earth faints and fades away, The world fails and fades away, The lofty people of the earth fail.

וְהָאָרֶץ חָנְפָה תַּחַת יֹשְׁבֶיהָ כִּי־עָבְרוּ תוֹרֹת חָלְפוּ חֹק הֵפֵרוּ בְּרִית עוֹלָם

5[3] The earth also is defiled under her inhabitants, because they have transgressed the laws, violated the statute, broken the everlasting covenant.

עַל־כֵּן אָלָה אָכְלָה אֶרֶץ וַיֶּאְשְׁמוּ יֹשְׁבֵי בָהּ עַל־כֵּן חָרוּ יֹשְׁבֵי אֶרֶץ וְנִשְׁאַר אֱנוֹשׁ מִזְעָר

6[4] Therefore, a curse devoured *the earth*[5], And they who live there are found guilty; Therefore, the inhabitants of the earth waste away, And few men remain.

אָבַל תִּירוֹשׁ אֻמְלְלָה־גָפֶן נֶאֶנְחוּ כָּל־שִׂמְחֵי־לֵב

7[6] The new wine fails, the vine[7] fades; All the merry-hearted shall sigh.

שָׁבַת מְשׂוֹשׂ תֻּפִּים חָדַל שְׁאוֹן עַלִּיזִים שָׁבַת מְשׂוֹשׂ כִּנּוֹר

8[8] The mirth of *drums*[9] ceases, *the noise of those who rejoice ends*[10], The joy of the harp ceases.

בַּשִּׁיר לֹא יִשְׁתּוּ־יָיִן יֵמַר שֵׁכָר לְשֹׁתָיו

9[11] They do not drink wine with a song; Strong drink is bitter to those who drink it.

נִשְׁבְּרָה קִרְיַת־תֹּהוּ סֻגַּר כָּל־בַּיִת מִבּוֹא

10[12] *Broken down is the wasted city*[13]; Every house is shut up, so no one may come in.

צְוָחָה עַל־הַיַּיִן בַּחוּצוֹת עָרְבָה כָּל־שִׂמְחָה גָּלָה מְשׂוֹשׂ הָאָרֶץ

11[14] There is a crying in the streets *amid*[15] the wine; all joy is darkened; the land's mirth is gone.

נִשְׁאַר בָּעִיר שַׁמָּה וּשְׁאִיָּה יֻכַּת־שָׁעַר

12[16] In the city is left desolation, And the *gate*[17] is struck and ruined.

9:18, Jastrow 1081b, Jeremiah 5:3-5:6 23:11-23:13 17:2 18:18 44:11-44:13 52:24-52:30, Lamentations 4:13 5:12-5:14, Leviticus 25:36-25:37, Ralbag SOS 1
[1] Isaiah 24:3 - 2 Chronicles 12:21, Deuteronomy 5:22 5:27, Ein Yaakov Shabbat:119b, Ezekiel 12:4, Isaiah 6:11 21:17 22:25 24:1, Jeremiah 13:15, Leviticus 26:30-26:35, Micah 4:4
[2] Isaiah 24:4 - 4QIsab, Hosea 4:3, Isaiah 2:11-2:12 3:26 4:1 9:9 16:7, Jeremiah 4:28 12:4
[3] Isaiah 24:5 - 2 Chronicles 9:9, 2 Kings 17:7-17:23 22:13-22:17 23:26-23:27, 2 Samuel 23:5, Daniel 7:25 9:5 9:10, Deuteronomy 8:15 8:20, Ezekiel 7:20-7:24 20:13 20:24 22:24-22:31 13:26, Ezra 9:6-9:7, Genesis 3:17-3:18 6:11-6:13 17:13-17:14, Hebrews 9:1 13:20, Isaiah 1:2-1:5 10:6 2:1 59:1-59:3 59:12-59:15, Jastrow 484b 485a, Jeremiah 3:1-3:2 2:5, Joshua 24:25, Leviticus 18:24-18:28 20:22, Luke 1:6, Mark 7:7-7:9, Micah 2:10, Midrash Tanchuma Re'eh 14, Numbers 35:33-35:34, Pesikta de R'Kahana 10.5, Pesikta Rabbati 25:3, Pirkei de R'Eliezer 34, Psalms 55:6 9:10 106:36-106:39, Romans 8:20-8:21, z.Noach 61a
[4] Isaiah 24:6 - 2 Peter 3:10, Deuteronomy 4:27 28:15-28:20 28:62 29:21-29:27 30:18-30:19, Ezekiel 5:3, Isaiah 1:31 42:24-42:25, Joshua 23:15-23:16, Leviticus 2:22, Malachi 2:2 3:9 3:19 3:24, Matthew 7:14 3:25, Midrash Tanchuma Vayeshev 2, Romans 9:27, Zechariah 5:3-5:4
[5] Missing in 1QIsaa
[6] Isaiah 24:7 - Hosea 9:1-9:2, Isaiah 16:8 16:10 32:9-32:13, Joel 1:10-1:12
[7] 4QIsac adds *the oil*
[8] Isaiah 24:8 - Ezekiel 2:13, Hosea 2:11, Isaiah 5:12 23:15-23:16, Jeremiah 7:34 16:9 1:10, Revelation 18:22
[9] LXX *timbrels*
[10] Missing in LXX
[11] Isaiah 24:9 - Amos 6:5-6:7 8:3 8:10, b.Chagigah [Rashi] 15b, b.Gittin 7a, b.Sotah 48a, Ecclesiastes 9:7, Ein Yaakov Gittin:6b, Ein Yaakov Sotah:47b 48a, Ephesians 5:18-5:19, Isaiah 5:11-5:12 5:20 5:22, Lamentations.R 5:15 Petichata D'Chakimei:23, m.Sotah 9:11, mt.Hilchot Taaniot 5:14, Psalms 69:13, y.Sotah 9:12, Zechariah 9:15
[12] Isaiah 24:10 - 2 Kings 1:4 25:9-25:10, Genesis 11:9, Isaiah 23:1 24:12 1:2 3:10 8:14 10:11 34:13-34:15, Jeremiah 9:26-9:27 15:4 15:8 4:7 52:13-52:14, Luke 19:43 21:24, Matthew 23:34-23:35, Micah 2:13 3:12, Revelation 11:7-11:8 17:5-17:6 18:2
[13] LXX *All the city has become desolate*
[14] Isaiah 24:11 - Amos 5:16-5:20, Hosea 7:14, Isaiah 8:22 9:20 16:10 24:7-24:9 8:13, Jeremiah 24:33, Joel 1:15, Lamentations 5:14-5:15, Luke 16:25, Matthew 22:11-22:13, Midrash Tanchuma Shemini 5, Proverbs 7:6
[15] LXX *for*
[16] Isaiah 24:12 - b.Bava Kamma 21a 97a, Ein Yaakov Sotah:47b, Isaiah 8:14, Jeremiah 9:12, Lamentations 1:1 1:4 2:9 5:18, Matthew 22:7, Micah 1:9 1:12
[17] LXX *houses*

כִּי כֹה יִהְיֶה בְּקֶרֶב הָאָרֶץ בְּתוֹךְ הָעַמִּים כְּנֹקֶף זַיִת כְּעוֹלֵלֹת אִם־כָּלָה בָצִיר	13[1]	For thus shall it be *in the midst of the earth, among the peoples*[2], as at the beating of an olive tree, as at the gleanings when the vintage is done.
הֵמָּה יִשְׂאוּ קוֹלָם יָרֹנּוּ בִּגְאוֹן יְהוָה צָהֲלוּ מִיָּם	14[3]	Those yonder lift up their voice, they sing for joy; for the majesty of the LORD they shout from *the sea*[4]:
עַל־כֵּן בָּאֻרִים כַּבְּדוּ יְהוָה בְּאִיֵּי הַיָּם שֵׁם יְהוָה אֱלֹהֵי יִשְׂרָאֵל	15[5]	'Therefore, [6]glorify the LORD in the regions of light, the name of the LORD, the God of Israel, in the isles of the sea.'
מִכְּנַף הָאָרֶץ זְמִרֹת שָׁמַעְנוּ צְבִי לַצַּדִּיק וָאֹמַר רָזִי־לִי רָזִי־לִי אוֹי לִי בֹּגְדִים בָּגָדוּ וּבֶגֶד בּוֹגְדִים בָּגָדוּ	16[7]	From the uttermost part of the earth we have heard *songs*[8]: '*Glory to the righteous.*' But I say: I waste away, I waste away, woe is me! *The treacherous deal treacherously; Yes, the treacherous deal very treacherously*[9].
פַּחַד וָפַחַת וָפָח עָלֶיךָ יוֹשֵׁב הָאָרֶץ	17[10]	Terror, and the pit, and the trap, are upon you, O inhabitant of the earth.
וְהָיָה הַנָּס מִקּוֹל הַפַּחַד יִפֹּל אֶל־הַפַּחַת וְהָעוֹלֶה מִתּוֹךְ הַפַּחַת יִלָּכֵד בַּפָּח כִּי־אֲרֻבּוֹת מִמָּרוֹם נִפְתָּחוּ וַיִּרְעֲשׁוּ מוֹסְדֵי אָרֶץ	18[11]	And it shall come to pass, that he who flees from the noise of the terror shall fall into the pit; And he who comes up from the midst of the pit shall be taken in the trap; For the windows on high are opened, And the foundations of the earth shake;
רֹעָה הִתְרֹעֲעָה הָאָרֶץ פּוֹר הִתְפּוֹרְרָה אָרֶץ מוֹט הִתְמוֹטְטָה אָרֶץ	19[12]	The earth is broken, broken down, The earth is crumbled in pieces, The earth trembles and totters;
נוֹעַ תָּנוּעַ אֶרֶץ כַּשִּׁכּוֹר וְהִתְנוֹדְדָה כַּמְּלוּנָה וְכָבַד עָלֶיהָ פִּשְׁעָהּ וְנָפְלָה וְלֹא־תֹסִיף קוּם	20[13]	The earth reels to and fro like a drunken man, And sways to and fro as a *lodge*[14]; And its transgression is heavy upon it, And it shall *fall*[15], and not rise again.

---

[1] Isaiah 24:13 - Ezekiel 6:8-11 7:16 9:4-6 11:16-20 14:22-23, Isaiah 1:9 6:13 10:20-22 17:5-6, Jeremiah 20:28, Matthew 24:22, Micah 2:12, Revelation 3:4 11:2-3, Romans 11:2-6

[2] LXX *in the land in the midst of the nations*

[3] Isaiah 24:14 - b.Arachin 11a, Isaiah 12:1-12:6 1:1 2:1 3:2 11:2 11:10 16:9 42:10-42:12 20:23 3:11 52:7-52:9 6:1, Jeremiah 6:19 7:13 9:11, Numbers.R 6:10, Zechariah 2:10, Zephaniah 3:14-3:20

[4] 4QIsac *the day*

[5] Isaiah 24:15 - 1 Peter 1:7 3:15 4:12-4:14, Acts 16:25, Genesis 10:4-10:5, Habakkuk 3:17-3:18, Isaiah 11:11-11:12 1:3 17:5 18:4 18:10 1:1 3:5 12:9 18:19, Job 35:9-35:10, Malachi 1:11, Pesikta de R'Kahana 21.1, Revelation 15:2-15:4, Shepherd Vision II 1:2, Siman 131:14, Zechariah 10:9-10:12 13:8-13:9, Zephaniah 2:11

[6] 1QIsaa adds *in the east*; 4QIsac adds *in the east, in Aram*

[7] Isaiah 24:16 - Acts 13:47, b.Sanhedrin 37b 94a, Ecclesiastes.R 1:19, Ein Yaakov Sanhedrin:37b 94a, Exodus 15:11, Guide for the Perplexed 1:43, Habakkuk 1:3, Hosea 5:7 6:7, Isaiah 10:16 17:4 21:2 2:15 4:5 9:1 45:22-25 24:8 4:10 12:21 66:19-20, Jastrow 152b 1464b, Jeremiah 3:20 5:11 12:1 12:6, Lamentations 1:2, Mark 13:27, Micah 5:5, Midrash Psalms 1:20, Numbers.R 10:2, Perek Shirah [the Earth], Pesikta de R'Kahana 16.1, Pesikta Rabbati 29/30A:1 33:13, Pirkei de R'Eliezer 37, Psalms 2:8 22:28-32 58:11 67:8 72:8-11 98:3 10:15 107:1-43, Revelation 15:3 16:5-7 19:1-6, Ruth.R 5:4, Saadia Opinions 2:10 8:5, Song of Songs.R 2:2, z.Vayeilech 284a

[8] LXX *wonderful things*

[9] LXX *and there is hope to the godly: but they shall say, Woe to the despisers, that despise the law*

[10] Isaiah 24:17 - 1 Kings 19:17, Amos 5:19, Cairo Damascus 4:12-18 4:14, Ezekiel 14:21, Guide for the Perplexed 2:29, Jeremiah 8:3 48:43-44, Leviticus 26:21-22
Isaiah 24:17-20 - Testament of Levi 3:9

[11] Isaiah 24:18 - 1 Kings 20:29-20:30, 2 Kings 7:2, Amos 5:19, Deuteronomy 32:22-32:26, Genesis 7:11 19:24, Job 18:8-18:16 20:24, Joshua 10:10-10:11, Psalms 18:8 18:16 46:3-46:4
Isaiah 24:18-23 - 1QIsab, Testament of Levi 3:10

[12] Isaiah 24:19 - 3 Enoch 48A:4, Deuteronomy 11:6, Habakkuk 3:6, Isaiah 24:1-24:5 34:4-34:10, Jeremiah 4:23-4:28, Matthew 24:3, Midrash Psalms 60:3, Midrash Tanchuma Kedoshim 4, Nahum 1:5, Revelation 20:11
Isaiah 24:19-23 - 4QIsac

[13] Isaiah 24:20 - Amos 8:14, Daniel 11:19, Hosea 4:1-4:5, Isaiah 1:8 1:28 5:7-5:30 19:14 5:9 14:12 19:27, Jeremiah 8:4 1:27, Lamentations 1:14, Matthew 23:35-23:36, Mekhilta de R'Shimon bar Yochai Bachodesh 56:1, Mekhilta de R'Ishmael Bahodesh 9:43, Psalms 38:5 11:27, Revelation 18:21, Zechariah 5:5-5:8

[14] LXX *storehouse of fruits*

[15] 1QIsaa masculine, referring to *the earth*

וְהָיָה בַּיּוֹם הַהוּא יִפְקֹד יְהוָה עַל־צְבָא הַמָּרוֹם בַּמָּרוֹם וְעַל־מַלְכֵי הָאֲדָמָה עַל־הָאֲדָמָה	21[1]	And *it shall come to pass in that day, That the LORD*[2] will punish the host of the high heaven *on high*[3], And the kings of the earth upon the earth.
וְאֻסְּפוּ אֲסֵפָה אַסִּיר עַל־בּוֹר וְסֻגְּרוּ עַל־מַסְגֵּר וּמֵרֹב יָמִים יִפָּקֵדוּ	22[4]	And they shall be gathered together, as prisoners are gathered in the dungeon, And shall be shut up in the prison, And after many days shall they be punished.
וְחָפְרָה הַלְּבָנָה וּבוֹשָׁה הַחַמָּה כִּי־מָלַךְ יְהוָה צְבָאוֹת בְּהַר צִיּוֹן וּבִירוּשָׁלִַם וְנֶגֶד זְקֵנָיו כָּבוֹד	23[5]	*Then the moon shall be perplexed, and the sun ashamed*[6]; For the LORD of hosts will reign in mount Zion, And in Jerusalem, and before His elders shall be Glory.

Isaiah – Chapter 25

יְהוָה אֱלֹהַי אַתָּה אֲרוֹמִמְךָ אוֹדֶה שִׁמְךָ כִּי עָשִׂיתָ פֶּלֶא עֵצוֹת מֵרָחוֹק אֱמוּנָה אֹמֶן	1[7]	O LORD, you are my God, I will exalt You, I will praise Your name, for you have done wonderful things; counsels of old, in faithfulness and truth[8].
כִּי שַׂמְתָּ מֵעִיר לַגָּל קִרְיָה בְצוּרָה לְמַפֵּלָה אַרְמוֹן זָרִים מֵעִיר לְעוֹלָם לֹא יִבָּנֶה	2[9]	For you have made of a city a heap, Of a fortified city a ruin; A *castle of strangers*[10] to be no city, It shall never be built.
עַל־כֵּן יְכַבְּדוּךָ עַם־עָז קִרְיַת גּוֹיִם עָרִיצִים יִירָאוּךָ	3[11]	*Therefore, the strong people shall glorify You, The city of the terrible nations shall fear You*[12].
כִּי־הָיִיתָ מָעוֹז לַדָּל מָעוֹז לָאֶבְיוֹן בַּצַּר־לוֹ מַחְסֶה מִזֶּרֶם צֵל מֵחֹרֶב כִּי רוּחַ עָרִיצִים כְּזֶרֶם קִיר	4[13]	For you have been a stronghold to the poor, A stronghold to the needy in his distress, *A refuge*

---

[1] Isaiah 24:21 - b.Makkot [Rashi] 12a, Bahir 200, Exodus.R 9:9, Ezekiel 38:1-38:23, Haggai 2:21-2:22, Isaiah 10:12 10:25-10:27 14:1-14:2 25:10-25:12 34:2-34:17, Joel 4:9-4:17 4:19, Jubilees 15:32, Lamentations.R Petichata D'Chakimei:2, Mekhilta de R'Shimon bar Yochai Shirata 28:2, Mekhilta de R'Ishmael Shirata 2:115, Midrash Psalms 82:3 104:1 145:1, Midrash Tanchuma Beshallach 13, Midrash Tanchuma Bo 4, Midrash Tanchuma Mishpatim 18, Pesikta Rabbati 42:9, Psalms 76:13 149:6-149:9, Revelation 6:14-6:17 17:14 18:9 19:18-19:21, Song of Songs.R 8:19, Tanna Devei Eliyahu 4, z.Beshallach 46b 54b, z.Naso 147a, z.Noach 69a, z.Pekudei 232b, z.Shemot 6b 18a, z.Terumah 175a, Zechariah 14:12-14:19

[2] LXX *God*

[3] i.e., *in Heaven*

[4] Isaiah 24:22 - Ezekiel 14:8, Isaiah 2:19 10:4 24:17 18:22, Jeremiah 38:6-38:13, Joshua 10:16-10:17 10:22-10:26, Midrash Psalms 145:1, Saadia Opinions 9:8, Sifre Devarim {Ha'azinu Hashamayim} 325, Sifre Devarim Nitzavim 325, Zechariah 9:11
Isaiah 24:22-23 - Testament of Levi 18:12

[5] Isaiah 24:23 - 29, b.Avodah Zara 14a, b.Bava Batra 10b, b.Nedarim 90a, b.Pesachim 68a, b.Sanhedrin 91b, b.Sotah 34b, Daniel 7:9-10 7:18 7:27, Deuteronomy.R 1:14, Ecclesiastes.R 1:3 1:30, Ein Yaakov Avodah Zarah:17a, Ein Yaakov Bava Batra:10b, Midrash Shmuel 6:9, Ein Yaakov Pesachim:68a, Ein Yaakov Sanhedrin:91b, Ein Yaakov Sotah:34b, Exodus 15:21, Exodus.R 5:12 45:5, Ezekiel 32:7-8, Guide for the Perplexed 2:29, Guide for the Perplexed 2:29 3:13, Hebrews 12:22, Isaiah 12:6 13:10 6:26 4:7 12:19, Job 38:4-7, Joel 3:4 4:15, Jubilees 1:28, Leviticus.R 11:8, Mark 13:24-13:26, Martyrdom and Ascension of Isaiah 4:15, Mas.Kallah Rabbati 8:8 8:9, Mas.Soferim 21:9, Matthew 6:10 6:13, Mesillat Yesharim 22:Trait of Anavah, Micah 4:7, Midrash Psalms 31:5 72:4 145:1, Midrash Tanchuma Shemini 11, Midrash Tanchuma Shemot 24 29, Midrash Tanchuma Vayigash 7, mt.Pirkei Avot 6:8, Numbers.R 2:13 13:11, Pirkei Avot 6:8 [Shabbat afternoon], Psalms 97:1, Revelation 6:12-14 11:15 14:1 19:4 19:6 21:23 22:5, Sifre.z Numbers Beha'alotcha 11:16, t.Sanhedrin 11:8, y.Avodah Zara 4:7, y.Sanhedrin 11:3, Zechariah 9:9

[6] LXX *And the brick shall decay, and the wall shall fall*

[7] Isaiah 25:1 - 1 Chronicles 29:10-29:20, Daniel 3:32-3:33, Ephesians 1:11, Exodus 15:2, Ezekiel 38:17-38:23, Hebrews 6:17-6:18, Isaiah 2:13 4:29 22:10 13:10, Jeremiah 32:17-32:24, Mekhilta de R'Shimon bar Yochai Beshallach 21:7 22:2, Mekhilta de R'Ishmael Beshallah 2:230, Mekhilta de R'Ishmael Beshallah 3:147, Midrash Psalms 115:3 145:1, mt.Hilchot Temurah 4:13, mt.Shemonah Perakim 4:6, Numbers 23:19, Perek Shirah [the Locust], Psalms 33:10-33:11 40:6 46:11 78:4 98:1 99:5 107:8-107:43 15:4 22:28 1:1 2:2, Revelation 5:9-5:14 7:12 15:3 19:11, Romans 11:25-11:29, z.Balak 193b, z.Noach 73a
Isaiah 25:1-2 - 4QIsac
Isaiah 25:1-8 - 1QIsab
Isaiah 25:1-12 - 1QIsaa

[8] LXX adds *so be it*

[9] Isaiah 25:2 - Deuteronomy 13:17, Isaiah 13:22 14:23 17:1 17:3 21:9 23:13 1:12, Jeremiah 3:26, Nahum 3:12-15, Revelation 18:2-3 18:19

[10] 4QIsac *foreigners' palace*

[11] Isaiah 25:3 - Ezekiel 14:23 39:21-39:22, Isaiah 13:11 49:23-49:26 60:10-60:14 66:18-66:20, Psalms 46:11-46:12 66:3 72:8-72:11, Revelation 11:13 11:15-11:17, Zechariah 14:9 14:16

[12] LXX *Therefore, the poor people shall bless you, and cities of injured men shall bless you*

[13] Isaiah 25:4 - Ezekiel 13:11-13:13, Isaiah 4:5-4:6 11:4 14:32 17:10 3:5 5:5 5:19 8:2 32:18-32:19 9:2 9:16 37:3-37:4 13:36 1:25 18:2, James 2:5, Job 5:15-5:16, Matthew 7:25-7:27, Psalms 12:6 35:10 72:4 72:13 11:41 23:31, Zephaniah 3:12

from the storm, a shadow from the heat; For the blast of the terrible ones was as a storm against the wall[1].

כְּחֹרֶב בְּצָיוֹן שְׁאוֹן זָרִים תַּכְנִיעַ חֹרֶב בְּצֵל עָב זְמִיר עָרִיצִים יַעֲנֶה 5[2]

As the heat in a dry place, you subdued the noise of strangers; As the heat by the shadow of a cloud, the song of the terrible ones was brought low[3].

וְעָשָׂה יְהוָה צְבָאוֹת לְכָל־הָעַמִּים בָּהָר הַזֶּה מִשְׁתֵּה שְׁמָנִים מִשְׁתֵּה שְׁמָרִים שְׁמָנִים מְמֻחָיִם מְזֻקָּקִים שְׁמָרִים 6[4]

And in this mountain the LORD of hosts will make to all peoples a festival of fat things, a festival of wines on the lees, Of fat things full of marrow, of well refined wines on the lees.

וּבִלַּע בָּהָר הַזֶּה פְּנֵי־הַלּוֹט הַלּוֹט עַל־כָּל־הָעַמִּים וְהַמַּסֵּכָה הַנְּסוּכָה עַל־כָּל־הַגּוֹיִם 7[5]

And He will destroy in this mountain The face of the covering that is cast over all peoples, And the veil that is spread over all nations[6].

בִּלַּע הַמָּוֶת לָנֶצַח וּמָחָה אֲדֹנָי יְהוִה דִּמְעָה מֵעַל כָּל־פָּנִים וְחֶרְפַּת עַמּוֹ יָסִיר מֵעַל כָּל־הָאָרֶץ כִּי יְהוָה דִּבֵּר 8[7]

He will swallow up death forever; And[8] the Lord GOD will wipe away tears from all faces; And He will take away the reproach of His people from off all the earth; For the LORD has spoken it.

וְאָמַר בַּיּוֹם הַהוּא הִנֵּה אֱלֹהֵינוּ זֶה קִוִּינוּ לוֹ וְיוֹשִׁיעֵנוּ זֶה יְהוָה קִוִּינוּ לוֹ נָגִילָה וְנִשְׂמְחָה בִּישׁוּעָתוֹ 9[9]

And it shall be said[10] in that day: 'Lo[11], this is our God, For whom we waited, so He might save us; This is the LORD, for whom we waited, We will be glad and rejoice in His salvation.'

כִּי־תָנוּחַ יַד־יְהוָה בָּהָר הַזֶּה וְנָדוֹשׁ מוֹאָב תַּחְתָּיו כְּהִדּוּשׁ מַתְבֵּן בְּמֵי "בְּמוֹ" מַדְמֵנָה 10[12]

For the hand of the LORD will rest in this mountain, And Moab shall be trodden down in his place, *as straw is trodden in the dunghill[13].*

---

[1] LXX you shalt deliver them from wicked men: you have been a shelter of those who thirst, and a refreshing air to injured men

[2] Isaiah 25:5 - Daniel 7:23-7:27 11:36-11:45, Ezekiel 32:18-32:32 38:9-39:10, Isaiah 10:8-10:15 10:32-10:34 13:11 14:10-14:16 14:19 17:12-17:14 18:4 30:30-30:33 1:10 49:25-49:26 54:15-54:17 64:2-64:3, Jeremiah 50:11-50:15 51:38-51:43 51:53-51:57, Job 8:16-8:19, Jonah 4:5-4:6, Liber Antiquitatum Biblicarum 16:2, Psalms 74:3-74:23 79:10-79:12 9:39, Revelation 16:1-16:19 20:8-20:9, z.Bereshit 1a, z.Vayakhel 220a

[3] LXX *We were as faint-hearted men thirsting in Sion, because ungodly men to whom you delivered us*

[4] Isaiah 25:6 - b.Chullin [Rashi] 64a, Daniel 7:14, Hebrews 12:22, Isaiah 1:19 2:2-2:3 1:10 49:6-49:10 55:1-55:2, Jastrow 1208b, Jeremiah 31:13-31:14, Luke 5:39 14:16-14:23 22:30, Mark 16:15, Matthew 8:11 22:1-22:10 2:29, Micah 4:1-4:2, Proverbs 9:1-9:5, Psalms 63:6 72:14-72:16 78:68, Revelation 19:9, Sifre Devarim {Ha'azinu Hashamayim} 324, Sifre Devarim Nitzavim 324, Song of Songs 1:2 1:4 2:3-5 5:1, t.Shabbat 8:25, Zechariah 8:3 9:16-17

[5] Isaiah 25:7 - 2 Corinthians 3:13-18, Acts 17:30, Ephesians 3:5-6 4:18 5:8, Exodus.R 28:4, Hebrews 9:8 9:24 10:19-21, Isaiah 60:1-3, Luke 2:32, Matthew 3:51, Saadia Opinions 3:5

[6] LXX *they shall anoint themselves with ointment in this mountain. Impart all these things to the nations; for this is God's counsel upon all the nations*

[7] Isaiah 25:8 - 1 Corinthians 15:26 15:54, 1 Peter 4:14, 2 Timothy 1:10, After leaving a cemetery, Apocalypse of Elijah 5:38, b.Bava Batra [Rashi] 88a, b.Moed Katan 28b, b.Pesachim 68a, b.Sanhedrin 90a, b.Sanhedrin 91b, Deuteronomy.R 2:30, Ecclesiastes.R 1:7, Ein Yaakov Pesachim:68a, Ein Yaakov Pesachim:68a, Ein Yaakov Pesachim:68a, Ein Yaakov Pesachim:68a, Ein Yaakov Sanhedrin:91b, Exodus.R 15:21 30:3, Genesis.R 26:2, Hebrews 2:14-15, Hosea 13:14, Isaiah 6:19 6:26 11:10 13:3 3:11 6:4 12:15 13:7 17:19 18:5, Lamentations.R 1:41, m.Moed Katan 3:9, Malachi 3:17-3:18, Matthew 5:11-12, Mekilta de R'Ishmael Pisha 12:29, Midrash Psalms 119:17, Midrash Tanchuma Emor 3, Midrash Tanchuma Vayechi 3, Midrash Tanchuma Yitro 17, Pesikta de R'Kahana S2.8 S6.1, Pesikta Rabbati 36:1, Psalms 69:10 89:51-52, Revelation 7:17 20:14 21:4, Saadia Opinions 7Variant:8, Siman 221:8, Tanna Devei Eliyahu 5, y.Moed Katan 3:9, z.Bereshit 29a 34a 38a 54a, z.Chayyei Sarah 124a 127a 131a, z.Emor 107b, z.Noach 70b, z.Pekudei 236a 240b 269a, z.Tetzaveh 185a, z.Vayakhel 199b, z.Vayechi 219b, z.Vayera 114a, z.Vayetze 160b 164a Isaiah 25:8-12 - 4QIsac

[8] LXX *Death has prevailed and swallowed men up; but again*

[9] Isaiah 25:9 - 1 Peter 1:6 1:8, 2 Peter 3:12, Attah Haraisah [Simchat Torah], b.Taanit 31a, Derech Hashem Part IV 7§06, Ein Yaakov Aggadot, Ein Yaakov Taanit:31a, Exodus.R 23:14, Genesis 1:18, Isaiah 8:17 12:1-12:6 26:8-26:9 30:18-30:19 9:22 11:2 11:4 11:10 16:9 49:25-49:26 12:16 66:10-66:14, Lamentations.R 2:3, Luke 2:25 2:28-2:30, Mekhilta de R'Shimon bar Yochai Bachodesh 49:5, Micah 7:7, Midrash Psalms 17:13 40:1 48:5 119:17, Midrash Tanchuma Bamidbar 17, Midrash Tanchuma Devarim 1, Midrash Tanchuma Ekev 3, Midrash Tanchuma Tzav 12, Motzoei Shabbat [Viyiten Lecha], Pesikta de R'Kahana 16.11, Philippians 3:1 3:3, Psalms 9:15 20:6 21:2 27:14 37:5-37:7 62:2-62:3 62:6-62:8 95:1 4:1, Revelation 1:7 19:1-19:7 22:20, Romans 5:2-5:3 8:23-8:25, Saadia Opinions 7Variant:9, Titus 2:13, z.Beshallach 55b, Zechariah 9:9, Zephaniah 3:14-3:20

[10] 1QIsaa *And you will say*; LXX *And they will say*

[11] 1QIsaa adds *the LORD*

[12] Isaiah 25:10 - Amos 2:1-2:3, Ezekiel 24:35, Isaiah 5:25 10:6 10:31 11:10 11:14 12:6 14:19 15:1-15:9 18:4 1:6 2:6 41:15-41:16, Jeremiah 24:2, Lamentations 1:15, Micah 4:13, Numbers 24:17, Psalms 83:11 132:13-14, Zechariah 9:9-11, Zephaniah 2:9 3:15-17

[13] LXX *as they tread the floor with wagons*

וּפֵרַשׂ יָדָיו בְּקִרְבּוֹ כַּאֲשֶׁר יְפָרֵשׂ הַשֹּׂחֶה לִשְׂחֽוֹת וְהִשְׁפִּיל גַּאֲוָתוֹ עִם אָרְבּוֹת יָדָֽיו	11[1]	And when he shall spread forth his hands in the midst, *as he who swims spreads forth his hands to swim*[2], His pride shall be brought down together with the cunning of his hands.
וּמִבְצַר מִשְׂגַּב חוֹמֹתֶיךָ הֵשַׁח הִשְׁפִּיל הִגִּיעַ לָאָרֶץ עַד־עָפָֽר	12[3]	And the high fortress of your walls He will bring down, lay low, And bring to the ground, to the dust.

Isaiah – Chapter 26

בַּיּוֹם הַהוּא יוּשַׁר הַשִּׁיר־הַזֶּה בְּאֶרֶץ יְהוּדָה עִיר עָז־לָנוּ יְשׁוּעָה יָשִׁית חוֹמוֹת וָחֵֽל	1[4]	In that day *this song shall be sung*[5] in the land of Judah: We have a strong city; Walls and bulwarks does He appoint for salvation.
פִּתְחוּ שְׁעָרִים וְיָבֹא גוֹי־צַדִּיק שֹׁמֵר אֱמֻנִֽים	2[6]	Open *the*[7] gates, so the righteous nation who keeps faithfulness may enter.
יֵצֶר סָמוּךְ תִּצֹּר שָׁלוֹם שָׁלוֹם כִּי בְךָ בָּטֽוּחַ	3[8]	The mind stayed on You. You keep in perfect peace; because *he trusts in you*[9].[10]
בִּטְחוּ בַיהוָה עֲדֵי־עַד כִּי בְּיָהּ יְהוָה צוּר עוֹלָמִֽים	4[11]	Trust in the LORD forever, For the LORD is GOD, an everlasting Rock.
כִּי הֵשַׁח יֹשְׁבֵי מָרוֹם קִרְיָה נִשְׂגָּבָה יַשְׁפִּילֶנָּה יַשְׁפִּילָהּ עַד־אֶרֶץ יַגִּיעֶנָּה עַד־עָפָֽר	5[12]	For *He has brought down*[13] those who live on high, The lofty city, laying it low, *laying it low*[14] to the ground, Bringing it to the dust.
תִּרְמְסֶנָּה רָגֶל רַגְלֵי עָנִי פַּעֲמֵי דַלִּֽים	6[15]	*The foot shall tread it down, the feet of the poor, and*[16] the steps of the needy.

---

[1] Isaiah 25:11 - b.Shekalim 14a, Colossians 2:15, Daniel 4:34, Isaiah 2:11 5:25 10:33 13:11 14:26 16:6 16:14 1:5 5:12 17:2, James 4:6, Jeremiah 24:29 24:42 50:31-32 3:44, Psalms 2:5 2:8-12 110:1-7, Revelation 18:6-8 19:18-20, y.Shekalim 6:2

[2] LXX *as he also brings down man to destroy him*

[3] Isaiah 25:12 - 2 Corinthians 10:4-5, Exodus.R 40:4, Hebrews 11:30, Isaiah 13:19-22 14:23 15:1 2:5, Jeremiah 3:58 51:64, Revelation 18:21

[4] Isaiah 26:1 - 2 Samuel 22:1-22:51, Ephesians 5:19-5:20, Exodus 15:2-15:21, Ezra 3:11, Isaiah 2:11 2:20 5:1 12:1 24:21-23 1:9 27:1-27:2 12:18 14:11, Jeremiah 9:11, Judges 5:1-5:31, Matthew 16:18, Numbers 21:17, Psalms 31:22 48:13 137:3-4, Revelation 19:1-19:7 21:12-21:22, Song of Songs.R 1:36, Zechariah 2:5
Isaiah 26:1-2 - 1QIsaa
Isaiah 26:1-5 - 1QIsab, 4QIsab
Isaiah 26:1-9 - 4QIsac

[5] 1QIsaa *one will sing that song*

[6] Isaiah 26:2 - 1 Peter 2:9, 2 Peter 3:13, Acts 2:47, b.Bava Kamma [Tosefot] 38a, b.Sanhedrin 11b, b.Shabbat 119b, Deuteronomy 4:6-8, Ein Yaakov Sanhedrin:110b, Ein Yaakov Shabbat:119b, Exodus 19:6, Exodus.R 15:29, Ezekiel 48:31-34, Guide for the Perplexed 2:29, Isaiah 6:14 10:8 12:11 12:21 14:2 14:10, Jude 1:3, Mekilta de R'Ishmael Beshallah 7:145, Mesillat Yesharim 11:Traits-of-Nekuyut, Midrash Tanchuma Beshallach 10, Pesikta de R'Kahana S6.1, Pirkei de R'Eliezer 15, Psalms 10:5 22:20, Revelation 5:9 21:24, y.Sheviit 4:8, z.Vayakhel 202a, z.Vayeilech 285b, z.Yitro 75b, Zechariah 8:20

[7] 1QIsaa *your*

[8] Isaiah 26:3 - 1 Chronicles 5:20, 2 Chronicles 13:18 16:8, Ephesians 2:14-16, Genesis.R 22:6, Isaiah 9:7-8 7:1 24:2 2:1 57:19-21, Jeremiah 17:7-8, John 14:27 16:33, Mas.Perek Hashalom 1:15, Micah 5:6, Philippians 4:7, Psalms 9:11 85:8-9, Romans 4:18-21 5:1

[9] 1QIsaa *he is in you*

[10] v.3-4 in LXX *read supporting truth, and keeping peace: for on you, O LORD, they have trusted with confidence forever, the great, the eternal God*

[11] Isaiah 26:4 - 1 Samuel 2:2, 2 Chronicles 20:20 8:8, 3 Enoch 42:5, b.Menachot [Tosefot] 29b, b.Menachot 29b, Deuteronomy 8:4 8:15, Exodus.R 15:22, Genesis.R 12:10, Guide for the Perplexed 1:16, Isaiah 12:2 17:10 8:2 21:17 21:24 2:10 15:1, Job 9:19, Maariv Motzoei Shabbat], Matthew 6:13 4:18, Midrash Psalms 62:1 70:4 114:3 118:14, Midrash Tanchuma Chayyei Sarah 3, Midrash Tanchuma Vayikra 7, Perek Shirah [the Ducks], Pesikta Rabbati 21:21, Philippians 4:13, Proverbs 3:5-3:6, Psalms 18:3 46:2 55:23 62:9 62:12 66:7 93:1 5:1, Shabbat and Yom Tov Minchah, Tanya Igeret Hakodesh §05, Tefillat Haderech, U'voh Letzion [Shacharit], y.Chagigah 2:1, z.Vaera 22a

[12] Isaiah 26:5 - b.Rosh Hashanah 31b, Ein Yaakov Rosh Hashanah:31b, Genesis.R 97:1, Isaiah 2:12 13:11 14:13 25:11-25:12 8:19 23:1, Jeremiah 50:31-50:32 51:25-51:26 3:37 51:64, Job 40:11-40:13, Midrash Psalms 62:1, Revelation 18:2

[13] 1QIsaa *he has made drunk*

[14] Missing in 1QIsaa

[15] Isaiah 26:6 - 1 Corinthians 1:26, b.Chagigah 3a, Daniel 7:27, Genesis.R 97:1, Isaiah 3:15 1:10 13:25 12:14, James 2:5, Jeremiah 2:45, Joshua 10:24, Luke 1:51-53 10:19, Malachi 3:21, Midrash Psalms 60:3 62:1, Revelation 2:26 3:9, Romans 16:20, Sifre Devarim Ha'azinu Hashamayim 325, Sifre Devarim Re'eh 143, Song of Songs.R 2:3, Zephaniah 3:11

[16] 1QIsaa *The feet of the oppressed trample*

אֹרַח לַצַּדִּיק מֵישָׁרִים יָשָׁר מַעְגַּל צַדִּיק תְּפַלֵּס 7[1]

The way of the just is straight; You, Most Upright, make plain the path of the just[2].

אַף אֹרַח מִשְׁפָּטֶיךָ יְהוָה קִוִּינוּךָ לְשִׁמְךָ וּלְזִכְרְךָ תַּאֲוַת־נָפֶשׁ 8[3]

Yes, in the way of Your judgments, O LORD, have we waited for You; To Your name and to Your memorial is the desire of our soul.

נַפְשִׁי אִוִּיתִיךָ בַּלַּיְלָה אַף־רוּחִי בְקִרְבִּי אֲשַׁחֲרֶךָּ כִּי כַּאֲשֶׁר מִשְׁפָּטֶיךָ לָאָרֶץ צֶדֶק לָמְדוּ יֹשְׁבֵי תֵבֵל 9[4]

With my soul have I desired You in the night[5]; Yes, with my spirit within me have I sought You earnestly; For when Your judgments are in the earth[6], The inhabitants of the world learn righteousness.

יֻחַן רָשָׁע בַּל־לָמַד צֶדֶק בְּאֶרֶץ נְכֹחוֹת יַעֲוֵל וּבַל־יִרְאֶה גֵּאוּת יְהוָה 10[7]

Let favor be shown to the wicked, yet he will not learn righteousness; he will deal wrongfully in the land of uprightness[8], And will not witness the majesty of the LORD.

יְהוָה רָמָה יָדְךָ בַּל־יֶחֱזָיוּן יֶחֱזוּ וְיֵבֹשׁוּ קִנְאַת־עָם אַף־אֵשׁ צָרֶיךָ תֹאכְלֵם 11[9]

LORD, Your hand was lifted up, yet they do not see; They shall see with shame Your zeal for the people; Yes[10], fire shall devour your adversaries.

יְהוָה תִּשְׁפֹּת שָׁלוֹם לָנוּ כִּי גַּם כָּל־מַעֲשֵׂינוּ פָּעַלְתָּ לָּנוּ 12[11]

LORD, you will establish peace for us; For you have indeed worked all our works for us.

יְהוָה אֱלֹהֵינוּ בְּעָלוּנוּ אֲדֹנִים זוּלָתֶךָ לְבַד־בְּךָ נַזְכִּיר שְׁמֶךָ 13[12]

O LORD our God, other lords beside You have had dominion over us; But by You only do we make mention of Your name[13].

מֵתִים בַּל־יִחְיוּ רְפָאִים בַּל־יָקֻמוּ לָכֵן פָּקַדְתָּ וַתַּשְׁמִידֵם וַתְּאַבֵּד כָּל־זֵכֶר לָמוֹ 14[14]

The dead do not live, the shades do not rise[15]; To that end you have punished and destroyed them, And made all their memory perish[16].

---

[1] Isaiah 26:7 - 1 Chronicles 5:17, 1 Corinthians 4:5, 1 John 3:7 3:10, 1 Samuel 2:2-2:4, 2 Corinthians 1:12, Ephesians 2:10, Isaiah 11:8 18:16, Job 27:5-27:6 7:6, Proverbs 20:7, Psalms 1:6 11:5 11:8 18:24-18:27, Zephaniah 3:5 Isaiah 26:7-19 - 4QIsab

[2] 1QIsaa The way of the righteous is level, O Upright One, you bring the path of justice

[3] Isaiah 26:8 - 2 Samuel 23:5, 2 Thessalonians 3:5, Acts 1:4, Exodus 3:15, Genesis.R 98 [Excl]:14, Isaiah 12:4 1:9 6:18 9:2 8:1 64:5-64:6, James 5:7-5:11, Job 23:10-23:12, Luke 1:6, Malachi 3:22, Mesillat Yesharim 19:Love-of-Hashem, Micah 7:7, Numbers 12:13, Psalms 13:2-13:3 18:24 37:3-37:7 44:18-44:19 63:2-63:4 65:7 73:25 77:11-77:13 84:3 10:3 143:5-143:6, Romans 8:25, Selichot, Song of Songs 1:2-1:4 2:3-2:5 5:8, the abbreviation ול stands for ולזכר

[4] Isaiah 26:9 - b.Sanhedrin 90a, b.Yoma [Rashi] 29a, Exodus.R 13:4 15:10, Hosea 5:15, Isaiah 3:9 7:6, Luke 6:12, Mark 1:35, Matthew 6:33, Mesillat Yesharim 19:Love-of-Hashem, Midrash Tanchuma Metzora 4, Numbers 14:21-23, Numbers.R 3:1, Proverbs 8:17, Psalms 58:12 63:2 63:7-63:8 64:10 77:3-4 78:34 83:19 119:62 10:6, Revelation 11:13, Saadia Opinions 2:13, Song of Songs 3:1-4 5:2-8, Tanya Likutei Aramim §44, Tanya Shaar Hayichud §09, z.Acharei Mot 67a, z.Lech Lecha 83a 83a

[5] LXX very early in the morning

[6] LXX O God, for your commandments are a light on the earth

[7] Isaiah 26:10 - 1 Samuel 15:17, b.Megillah 6a, Deuteronomy 32:15, Deuteronomy.R 7:4, Ecclesiastes 3:16, Ein Yaakov Megillah:6a, Exodus 8:11 8:27-32 9:34, Ezekiel 22:2-16, Gates of Repentance 3.75, Genesis.R 67:5, Guide for the Perplexed 3:13, Hosea 9:3 11:7 13:6, Isaiah 2:10 5:12 22:12-13 24:5 27:13 32:6 63:9-10, Jastrow 484a, Jeremiah 2:7 31:24, John 5:37-38, Matthew 4:5, Micah 2:10 3:10-12, Pirkei de R'Eliezer 39, Proverbs 1:32, Psalms 28:4-5 78:54-58 106:43 143:10, Revelation 2:21, Romans 2:4-5, z.Terumah 132a

[8] LXX For the ungodly one is put down: no one who will not learn righteousness on the earth, shall be able to do the truth: let the ungodly be taken away

[9] Isaiah 26:11 - 1 Peter 3:16, 1 Samuel 5:6-5:11 6:9, 2 Thessalonians 1:8, Acts 28:27, Exodus 9:14, Hebrews 10:27, Isaiah 5:24 11:13 18:3 44:9 44:18 60:14, Jeremiah 5:3 44:28, Job 34:27, Luke 16:23, Malachi 3:19, Matthew 25:41, Micah 5:10, Midrash Psalms 23:7 145:1, Pesikta de R'Kahana 24.11, Psalms 10:13 21:9 86:17, Revelation 3:9 19:20, Saadia Opinions 9:5, z.Mishpatim 112b

[10] LXX jealousy shall seize upon an untaught nation

[11] Isaiah 26:12 - b.Berachot 56b, Deuteronomy 30:6, Ein Yaakov Berachot:56b, Ephesians 2:10, Ezekiel 20:9 20:14 20:22 36:25, Hebrews 13:20, Isaiah 57:10, Jeremiah 33:6, John 14:27, Pesikta de R'Kahana S2.8, Psalms 29:11 57:3

[12] Isaiah 26:13 - 1 Corinthians 4:7, 2 Chronicles 12:8, Amos 6:10, Hebrews 13:15, Isaiah 2:8 10:11 12:4 51:22 63:7, John 8:32, Joshua 23:7, Midrash Psalms 28:2, Romans 6:22, Selichot, z.Shemot 9a

[13] LXX take possession of us: O LORD, we know no other beside you: we name your name

[14] Isaiah 26:14 - b.Ketubot 111b, b.Sanhedrin 11b, Deuteronomy 4:28, Ein Yaakov Ketubot:111b, Ein Yaakov Sanhedrin:110b, Exodus 14:30, Habakkuk 2:18-2:20, Isaiah 8:19 10:3 14:19-14:22 26:19 51:12-51:13, Matthew 2:20, Pirkei de R'Eliezer 34, Proverbs 10:7, Psalms 9:7 106:28 109:13, Revelation 18:2-18:3 19:19-19:21 20:5, z.Bereshit 25b

[15] LXX neither shall physicians by any means raise them up

[16] 1QIsaa And made all their memory to be imprisoned; LXX and hast taken away all their males. Bring more evils on them, O LORD

יָסַפְתָּ לַגּוֹי יְהֹוָה יָסַפְתָּ לַגּוֹי נִכְבָּדְתָּ רִחַקְתָּ כָּל־קַצְוֵי־אָרֶץ	15[1]	*You have gotten honor with the nations, O LORD, Yes, exceeding great honor with the nations; You are honored to the farthest ends of the earth*[2]
יְהֹוָה בַּצַּר פְּקָדוּךָ צָקוּן לַחַשׁ מוּסָרְךָ לָמוֹ	16[3]	LORD, in trouble they have sought You, they pour out a silent prayer when Your chastening was upon them.
כְּמוֹ הָרָה תַּקְרִיב לָלֶדֶת תָּחִיל תִּזְעַק בַּחֲבָלֶיהָ כֵּן הָיִינוּ מִפָּנֶיךָ יְהֹוָה	17[4]	Like as a woman with child, who draws near the time of her delivery, Is in pain and cries out in her pangs; So have we been at Your presence, O LORD.
הָרִינוּ חַלְנוּ כְּמוֹ יָלַדְנוּ רוּחַ יְשׁוּעֹת בַּל־נַעֲשֶׂה אֶרֶץ וּבַל־יִפְּלוּ יֹשְׁבֵי תֵבֵל	18[5]	[6]We have been with child, we have been in pain, We have, as it were, brought forth wind; We have not worked a deliverance in the land; nor are the inhabitants of the world come to life.
יִחְיוּ מֵתֶיךָ נְבֵלָתִי יְקוּמוּן הָקִיצוּ וְרַנְּנוּ שֹׁכְנֵי עָפָר כִּי טַל אוֹרֹת טַלֶּךָ וָאָרֶץ רְפָאִים תַּפִּיל	19[7]	Your dead shall live; my dead bodies shall arise. Awake and sing, you who live in the dust. For Your dew is as the dew *of light, And the earth shall bring to life the shades*[8].
לֵךְ עַמִּי בֹּא בַחֲדָרֶיךָ וּסְגֹר "דְּלָתִיךָ" "דְּלָתְךָ" בַּעֲדֶךָ חֲבִי כִמְעַט־רֶגַע 'עַד־יַעֲבוֹר־יַעֲבָר־זָעַם'	20[9]	Come, my people, enter into your chambers, And shut your doors after you; Hide yourself for a little moment, until the indignation passes.
"עַד־כִּי־יַעֲבָר־הַגָּה" יְהֹוָה יֹצֵא מִמְּקוֹמוֹ לִפְקֹד עֲוֹן יֹשֵׁב־הָאָרֶץ עָלָיו וְגִלְּתָה הָאָרֶץ אֶת־דָּמֶיהָ וְלֹא־תְכַסֶּה עוֹד עַל־הֲרוּגֶיהָ	21[10]	For, behold, the LORD *comes forth from*[11] His place to visit the iniquity on the inhabitants of the earth; the earth also shall disclose her blood, And shall cover her slain no longer.

---

[1] Isaiah 26:15 - 1 Kings 8:46, 2 Kings 17:6 17:23 23:27, Deuteronomy 4:27-4:28 10:22 28:25 28:64 32:26-32:27, Ezekiel 5:12 36:24, Genesis 12:2 13:16, HaMadrikh 35:3, Isaiah 6:12 9:4 10:22 33:17 44:23 54:2-54:3 60:21, Jeremiah 30:19 32:37, John 12:23-12:28 13:31-13:32 15:8 17:1, Luke 21:24, Midrash Tanchuma Pinchas 16, Nehemiah 9:23, Numbers 23:10, Numbers.R 21:23, Pesikta de R'Kahana 28.b 28.c 28.1, Pesikta Rabbati 52:1, Psalms 86:9-86:10, Revelation 11:15-11:18

[2] LXX *bring more evils on the glorious ones of the earth*

[3] Isaiah 26:16 - 1 Samuel 1:15, 2 Chronicles 6:37-38 33:12-13, Deuteronomy 4:29-30, Exodus.R 46:4, Hosea 5:15 7:14, Isaiah 37:3, Jeremiah 22:23, Judges 10:9-10, Lamentations 2:19, Midrash Psalms 1:20 63:1, Psalms 42:5 50:15 77:2-3 91:15 142:3, Revelation 3:19, z.Beshallach 47a

[4] Isaiah 26:17 - 1 Thessalonians 5:3, Isaiah 13:8 21:3, Jeremiah 4:31 6:24 30:6, John 16:21, Psalms 48:7, z.Ki Tissa 189a

[5] Isaiah 26:18 - 1 John 5:19, 1 Samuel 11:13 14:45, 2 Kings 19:3, b.Niddah 8b, Exodus 5:22-5:23, Hosea 13:13, Isaiah 33:11 37:3 59:4, John 7:7, Joshua 7:7-7:9, Psalms 17:14, t.Niddah 1:7, y.Niddah 1:3, y.Yevamot 4:11

[6] LXX adds *because of your fear*

[7] Isaiah 26:19 - 1 Corinthians 15:20 15:22-15:23, 1 Thessalonians 4:14-4:15, 2 Baruch 29:8, Acts 24:15, b.Ketubot 111ab, b.Sanhedrin [Rashi] 11b, b.Sanhedrin 90b, b.Sotah 5a, Daniel 12:2, Deuteronomy 32:2 33:13 33:28, Ecclesiastes.R 1:19, Ein Yaakov Ketubot:111a, Ein Yaakov Sanhedrin:90b, Ein Yaakov Sotah:4b, Ephesians 5:14, Ezekiel 37:1-37:14, Genesis 2:5-2:6, Hosea 6:2 13:14 14:7, Isaiah 25:8 51:17 52:1-52:2 60:1-60:2, Jastrow 1179a, Job 29:19, John 5:28-5:29 11:25-11:26, Matthew 27:52 27:58, Midrash Psalms 1:20 17:13 18:11, Midrash Tanchuma Naso 24, mt.Pirkei Avot 4:4, Pesikta Rabbati 5:3, Philippians 3:10 3:21, Pirkei de R'Eliezer 34, Psalms 22:16 71:20 110:3, Pseudo-Phocylides 104, Revelation 11:8-11:11 20:5-20:6 20:12-20:13, Saadia Opinions 7:3 7Variant:4 7Variant:4, Song of Songs.R 2:2, Tanna Devei Eliyahu 5 5, y.Berachot 5:2, y.Taanit 1:1, z.Chayyei Sarah 130b 130b 131a, z.Mishpatim 105b, z.Terumah 151b, z.Vaera 28b, z.Vayakhel 199b 220a, z.Vayeshev 182a, Zechariah 8:12
Isaiah 26:19 [LXX] - Apocryphon of Ezekiel Fragment 1

[8] LXX *healing to them: but the land of the ungodly shall perish*

[9] Isaiah 26:20 - 1 Enoch 72:5, 2 Corinthians 4:17, b.Avodah Zara 4b, b.Bava Kamma 60b, b.Berachot 7a, b.Sanhedrin 25b 105b, Ecclesiastes.R 7:19, Ein Yaakov Bava Kamma:60b, Ein Yaakov Berachot:7a, Exodus 12:22-12:23, Ezekiel 11:16, Genesis 7:1 7:16, Genesis.R 91:3, Isaiah 10:25 32:18-32:19 51:4 51:16 54:7-54:8, Jeremiah 7:23 31:15, Matthew 6:6 23:37, Mekilta de R'Ishmael Pisha 11:63, Midrash Tanchuma Massei 1, Midrash Tanchuma Vayechi 6, Numbers.R 23:1, Pesikta Rabbati 31:2, Proverbs 18:10, Psalms 17:8 27:5 30:6 31:21 32:7 57:2 91:1 91:4 143:9, Song of Songs.R 7:14, y.Berachot 7:2, y.Nazir 5:3, z.Mikketz 200b, z.Vayeshev 182b

[10] Isaiah 26:21 - 1 Enoch 1:4, 2 Thessalonians 1:7-1:10, Ezekiel 8:6 9:3-9:6 10:3-10:5 10:18-10:19 24:7-24:8, Genesis 4:10-4:11, Guide for the Perplexed 1:23, Hosea 5:14-5:15, Isaiah 13:11 18:4 30:12-30:14, Job 16:18, Jude 1:14-1:15, Luke 11:40 11:50, Micah 1:3-1:8, Numbers 35:32-35:33, Pesikta Rabbati 21:4, Psalms 50:2-50:3, Revelation 6:9-6:11 16:6 18:24, y.Taanit 2:1

[11] LXX *is bringing wrath from*

Isaiah – Chapter 27

בַּיּ֣וֹם הַה֡וּא יִפְקֹ֣ד יְהוָה֩ בְּחַרְבּ֨וֹ הַקָּשָׁ֜ה וְהַגְּדוֹלָ֣ה וְהַחֲזָקָ֗ה עַ֤ל לִוְיָתָן֙ נָחָ֣שׁ בָּרִ֔חַ וְעַל֙ לִוְיָתָ֔ן נָחָ֖שׁ עֲקַלָּת֑וֹן וְהָרַ֥ג אֶת־הַתַּנִּ֖ין אֲשֶׁ֥ר בַּיָּֽם׃ 1[1]

בַּיּ֖וֹם הַה֑וּא כֶּ֥רֶם חֶ֖מֶד עַנּוּ־לָֽהּ׃ 2[6]

אֲנִ֤י יְהוָה֙ נֹֽצְרָ֔הּ לִרְגָעִ֖ים אַשְׁקֶ֑נָּה פֶּ֚ן יִפְקֹ֣ד עָלֶ֔יהָ לַ֥יְלָה וָי֖וֹם אֶצֳּרֶֽנָּה׃ 3[8]

חֵמָ֖ה אֵ֣ין לִ֑י מִֽי־יִתְּנֵ֜נִי שָׁמִ֥יר שַׁ֙יִת֙ בַּמִּלְחָמָ֔ה אֶפְשְׂעָ֣ה בָ֔הּ אֲצִיתֶ֖נָּה יָּֽחַד׃ 4[10]

א֚וֹ יַחֲזֵ֣ק בְּמָעוּזִּ֔י יַעֲשֶׂ֥ה שָׁל֖וֹם לִ֑י שָׁל֖וֹם יַֽעֲשֶׂה־לִֽי׃ 5[12]

הַבָּאִים֙ יַשְׁרֵ֣שׁ יַֽעֲקֹ֔ב יָצִ֥יץ וּפָרַ֖ח יִשְׂרָאֵ֑ל וּמָלְא֥וּ פְנֵי־תֵבֵ֖ל תְּנוּבָֽה׃ 6[14]

הַכְּמַכַּ֥ת מַכֵּ֖הוּ הִכָּ֑הוּ אִם־כְּהֶ֥רֶג הֲרֻגָ֖יו הֹרָֽג׃ 7[16]

1[1] In that day the LORD with His *terrible*[2] and great and strong sword *will punish leviathan*[3] the slant serpent, and leviathan the *tortuous*[4] serpent; and He will slay the dragon *in the sea*[5].

2[6] In that day sing of her: 'A *vineyard of foaming wine*[7]!'

3[8] *I the LORD guards it, I water it every moment; in case My anger visit it, I guard it night and day*[9].

4[10] *Fury is not in Me; Would that I was as the briers and thorns in flame! I would with one step burn it altogether*[11].

5[12] *Or else let him take hold of My strength, so he may make peace with Me; yes, let him make peace with Me*[13].

6[14] *In days to come Jacob shall take root, Israel shall blossom and bud*[15]; And the face of the world shall be filled with fruit.

7[16] Has He struck him as He struck those who struck him? Or has he killed according to the slaughter of those who were killed by Him?

---

[1] Isaiah 27:1 - 2 Baruch 29:4 3 Enoch 32:1, 4QIsaf, b.Bava Batra 74b, Deuteronomy 32:41-32:42, Ein Yaakov Bava Batra:74a, Exodus.R 3:12, Ezekiel 29:3 32:2-32:5, Isaiah 26:21 34:5-34:6 51:9 65:25 66:16, Jeremiah 47:6 51:13 51:34, Job 3:9 12:1-12:25 26:13 40:19, Midrash Tanchuma Vaera 3, Pesikta Rabbati 42:9, Psalms 45:4 74:13-74:14 104:26, Revelation 2:16 12:3-13:2 13:4 13:11 16:13 17:1 17:15 19:21 20:2, Sefer Yetzirah 6:1, Sibylline Oracles 8.88, Testament of Asher 7:3
Isaiah 27:1-13 - 1QIsaa
[2] LXX *holy*
[3] LXX *upon the dragon*
[4] 1QIsaa *gliding*
[5] Missing in LXX
[6] Isaiah 27:2 - Isaiah 5:1-5:7, Jeremiah 2:21, Luke 20:9-20:18, Matthew 21:33-21:46, Midrash Psalms 8:1, Midrash Tanchuma Mishpatim 5, Midrash Tanchuma Vayeilech 2, Numbers 21:17, Numbers.R 10:2, Psalms 80:9-80:20, Song of Songs.R 8:19
Isaiah 27:2-5 - Exodus.R 30:1
[7] 1QIsaa *diminishing vineyard*
[8] Isaiah 27:3 - 1 Samuel 2:9, Deuteronomy 33:26-29, Ezekiel 34:11 34:24 37:14 37:28, Genesis 6:17 9:9, Genesis.R 13:17, Isaiah 5:6 35:6-7 41:13-19 46:4 46:9 55:10-11 58:11 60:16, John 10:27-30 15:1-2, Psalms 46:6 46:12 121:3-5, y.Avodah Zarah 3:5, y.Berachot 9:2, y.Taanit 1:3
[9] LXX *I am a strong city, a city in a siege: in vain shall I water it; for it shall be taken by night, and by day the wall shall fall*
[10] Isaiah 27:4 - 2 Peter 2:9, 2 Samuel 23:6, b.Avodah Zara 4a, b.Nedarim 32a, Ein Yaakov Nedarim:32a, Ezekiel 16:63, Hebrews 6:8, Isaiah 9:19 10:17 12:1 26:20-26:21 54:6-54:10, Malachi 3:21, Matthew 3:12, Mekhilta de R'Shimon bar Yochai Shirata 31:2, Mekilta de R'Ishmael Shirata 5:62, Midrash Psalms 6:3 7:6 65:1, Midrash Tanchuma Beshallach 15, Midrash Tanchuma Mishpatim 5, Nahum 1:3-1:7, Psalms 85:4 103:9
[11] LXX *There is no woman who has not taken hold of it; who will set me to watch stubble in the field? Because of this enemy I have set her aside; Therefore, on this account the LORD has done all that he appointed*
[12] Isaiah 27:5 - 2 Corinthians 5:19-21, b.Sanhedrin 99b, Colossians 1:20-21, Ein Yaakov Sanhedrin 99b, Ephesians 2:16-17, Ezekiel 34:25-26, Hebrews 6:18, Hosea 2:18-22, Isaiah 25:4 26:3-4 45:24 56:2 57:19 64:8, Job 22:21, Joshua 9:24-9:25 10:6, Leviticus.R 34:16, Luke 13:34 14:32 19:42, Midrash Tanchuma Mishpatim 5, Numbers.R 13:15-16, Romans 5:1-5:10, z.Bamidbar 118a
Isaiah 27:5-6 - 4QIsaf
[13] LXX *I am burnt up; they who live in her shall cry, Let us make peace with him, let us make peace*
[14] Isaiah 27:6 - b.Shabbat 145b, Ein Yaakov Shabbat:145b, Galatians 3:29, Hosea 2:23 14:7-8, Isaiah 6:13 37:31 49:20-23 54:1-3 60:22, Jeremiah 30:19, Philippians 3:3, Psalms 92:14-16, Revelation 11:15, Romans 11:16-26, Song of Songs.R 7:8, Zechariah 2:11 10:8-9
Isaiah 27:6-28:13 - Haftarah Shemot Part One [continues at Isaiah 29:22 Ashkenaz]
[15] LXX *They that are coming are the children of Jacob. Israel shall bud and blossom*
[16] Isaiah 27:7 - Daniel 2:31-2:35, Isaiah 10:20-10:25 14:22-14:23 17:3 17:14 37:36-37:38, Jeremiah 30:11-30:16 50:33-50:34 50:40 51:24, Nahum 1:14 3:19, Pesikta de R'Kahana 11.4

בְּסַאסְּאָה בְּשַׁלְחָהּ תְּרִיבֶנָּה הָגָה בְּרוּחוֹ הַקָּשָׁה בְּיוֹם קָדִים	8[1]	*In full measure, when you send her away, you contend with her; He has removed her with His rough blast in the day of the east wind*[2].
לָכֵן בְּזֹאת יְכֻפַּר עֲוֹן־יַעֲקֹב וְזֶה כָּל־פְּרִי הָסִר חַטָּאתוֹ בְּשׂוּמוֹ כָּל־אַבְנֵי מִזְבֵּחַ כְּאַבְנֵי־גִר מְנֻפָּצוֹת לֹא־יָקֻמוּ אֲשֵׁרִים וְחַמָּנִים	9[3]	Therefore, by this the iniquity of Jacob shall be atoned, And this is *all the fruit of taking*[4] away his sin: When he makes all the stones of the altar as chalkstones that are beaten in pieces, *So the Asherim and the sun images shall rise any more*[5].
כִּי עִיר בְּצוּרָה בָּדָד נָוֶה מְשֻׁלָּח וְנֶעֱזָב כַּמִּדְבָּר שָׁם יִרְעֶה עֵגֶל וְשָׁם יִרְבָּץ וְכִלָּה סְעִפֶיהָ	10[6]	*For the fortified city is solitary, A habitation abandoned and forsaken, like the wilderness*[7]; There the calf shall feed, and there he shall lie down, *And consume its branches.*[8]
בִּיבֹשׁ קְצִירָהּ תִּשָּׁבַרְנָה נָשִׁים בָּאוֹת מְאִירוֹת אוֹתָהּ כִּי לֹא עַם־בִּינוֹת הוּא עַל־כֵּן לֹא־יְרַחֲמֶנּוּ עֹשֵׂהוּ וְיֹצְרוֹ לֹא יְחֻנֶּנּוּ	11[9]	*When the boughs there are withered, they shall be broken off; The women shall come, and*[10] set them *on fire*[11]; For this is a people of no understanding; Therefore, He who made them will not have compassion on them, And He who formed them will not be gracious to them.
וְהָיָה בַּיּוֹם הַהוּא יַחְבֹּט יְהוָה מִשִּׁבֹּלֶת הַנָּהָר עַד־נַחַל מִצְרָיִם וְאַתֶּם תְּלֻקְּטוּ לְאַחַד אֶחָד בְּנֵי יִשְׂרָאֵל	12[12]	And it shall come to pass in that day, That the LORD will *beat off [His fruit] from the flood of the River to the Brook of Egypt*[13], And you shall be gathered one by one, O children of Israel.
וְהָיָה בַּיּוֹם הַהוּא יִתָּקַע בְּשׁוֹפָר גָּדוֹל וּבָאוּ הָאֹבְדִים בְּאֶרֶץ אַשּׁוּר וְהַנִּדָּחִים בְּאֶרֶץ מִצְרָיִם וְהִשְׁתַּחֲווּ לַיהוָה בְּהַר הַקֹּדֶשׁ בִּירוּשָׁלָ͏ִם	13[14]	And it shall come to pass in that day, That a great horn shall be blown; And they shall come who were lost in the land of Assyria, And they

---

[1] Isaiah 27:8 - 1 Corinthians 10:13, 1 Peter 1:6, b.Sanhedrin 1a, b.Shabbat 105b, b.Sotah 8b 9a, Ein Yaakov Sanhedrin:100a, Ein Yaakov Shabbat:105b, Ein Yaakov Sotah:8b, Ezekiel 19:12, Hosea 4:1 6:1-6:2 11:7-11:9 13:15, Isaiah 1:5 1:18-1:20 5:3-5:4 10:5-10:6 10:12 50:1 54:7 57:16, Jastrow 947b 1563a, Jeremiah 2:17-2:37 4:11 4:27 10:24 30:11 46:28, Job 23:6, Judges 10:10-10:16, Mekhilta de R'Shimon bar Yochai Beshallach 24:4, Mekilta de R'Ishmael Beshallah 5:102, Micah 6:2-6:5, Midrash Psalms 17:4 81:2, Numbers.R 9:24, Pesikta de R'Kahana 11.4, Psalms 6:2 38:2 76:11 78:38 103:14, Sifre.z Numbers Beha'alotcha 12:15, t.Sotah 3:1, the abbreviation בסא stands for בסאכאה, y.Sotah 1:7, z.Vayera 113b
Isaiah 27:8-12 - 4QIsaf
[2] LXX *Fighting and reproaching he will dismiss them; didn't you meditate with a harsh spirit, to slay them with a wrathful spirit?*
[3] Isaiah 27:9 - 1 Corinthians 11:32, 2 Chronicles 14:4 34:4 36:19, 2 Kings 25:9 25:13-17, Avot de R'Natan 34, b.Avodah Zara 54a, Daniel 11:35, Exodus 34:13, Ezekiel 11:18 20:38 24:11-24:14, Ezra 3:2-3, Hebrews 12:6 12:9-12:11, Hosea 14:10, Isaiah 1:24-25 1:29 2:12-21 4:4 17:8 48:10, Lamentations.R 2:3, Malachi 3:2-3, Micah 5:14-15, mt.Hilchot Avodat Kochavim v'Chukkoteihem 8:12, Proverbs 20:30, Psalms 119:67 119:71, Romans 11:27, Sifre Devarim Nitzavim 315, y.Avodah Zarah 4:4, Zechariah 13:2
[4] LXX *his blessing, when I shall have*
[5] LXX *and their trees shall not remain, and their idols shall be cut off, as a thicket afar off*
[6] Isaiah 27:10 - b.Sanhedrin [Rashi] 11a, Exodus.R 1:26, Ezekiel 36:4, Isaiah 5:9-5:10 6:11-6:12 7:25 17:2 17:9 25:2 32:13-32:14 64:11, Jeremiah 26:6 26:18, Lamentations 1:4 2:5-2:9 5:18, Luke 19:43-19:44 21:20-21:24, Micah 3:12, Midrash Tanchuma Shemot 8, Midrash Tanchuma Tazria 8
[7] LXX *The flock that dwelt there shall be left, as a deserted flock; and the ground shall be for a long time for pasture*
[8] "*come, and*" missing in LXX
[9] Isaiah 27:11 - 1 Thessalonians 2:16, 2 Chronicles 36:16-36:17, 2 Thessalonians 1:8-1:9, 4Q266 frag 3 2.4, b.Bava Batra [Tosefot] 8a, b.Bava Batra 10b, b.Berachot 33a, Cairo Damascus 5:16, Cairo Damascus 5.16, Deuteronomy 4:6 32:18-32:25 32:28-32:29, Ein Yaakov Berachot:33a, Ein Yaakov Berachot:33b, Ein Yaakov Sanhedrin:92a, Ezekiel 9:10 15:2-15:8 21:3, Genesis 6:6-6:7, Hosea 4:6, Isaiah 1:3 9:18 43:1 43:7 44:2 44:18-44:21 44:24, James 2:13, Jastrow 1467a, Jeremiah 4:22 5:4-5:5 5:21-5:22 8:7, John 15:6, Matthew 3:10 13:15 13:19, Psalms 80:16-80:17 106:40, Romans 1:28 1:31
[10] Missing in 1QIsaa
[11] LXX *And after a time no green thing shall be in it because of the grass being parched. Come here, you women who come from a sight*
[12] Isaiah 27:12 - Amos 9:9, Deuteronomy 30:3-4, Genesis 15:18, Isaiah 11:11-16 17:6 24:13-16 56:8, Jeremiah 3:14, John 6:37 10:16, Luke 15:4, Matthew 18:12-14, Nehemiah 1:9, Psalms 68:23 72:8
[13] LXX *fence men off from the channel of the river as far as Rhinocorura*
[14] Isaiah 27:13 - 1 Chronicles 15:24, 1 Thessalonians 4:16, 2 Kings 17:6, b.Berachot 56b, b.Makkot 24a, b.Rosh Hashanah 11b, b.Sanhedrin [Rashi] 92a 97a, b.Sanhedrin 11b, Derech Hashem Part IV 8§04, Ecclesiastes.R 1:20, Ein Yaakov Makkot:24a, Ein Yaakov Rosh Hashanah:11b, Ein Yaakov Sanhedrin:110b, Esther.R Petichata:11, Gates of Repentance 3.159, Genesis.R 42:3 56:2 70:6, Greek Apocalypse of Ezra 4:36, Hebrews 12:22, Hosea 8:13 9:3 12:1, Isaiah 2:3 2:11 11:12 11:16 16:3-16:4 18:3 19:21 19:23-19:25 25:6 56:8 66:18, Jastrow 878a, Jeremiah 43:7 44:28, John 4:21-4:24, Leviticus 25:9, Luke 4:18, Malachi 1:11, Mas.Derek Eretz Zutta 10:1, Matthew 24:31, Mekilta de R'Ishmael Bahodesh 4:29, Midrash Psalms 147:3, mt.Hilcnot Shofar Sukkah v'Lulav 3:9,

who were dispersed in the land of Egypt; And they shall *worship*[1] the LORD in the holy mountain at Jerusalem.

Isaiah – Chapter 28

הוֹי עֲטֶרֶת גֵּאוּת שִׁכֹּרֵי אֶפְרַיִם וְצִיץ נֹבֵל צְבִי תִפְאַרְתּוֹ אֲשֶׁר עַל־רֹאשׁ גֵּיא־שְׁמָנִים הֲלוּמֵי יָיִן

1[2] Woe to the crown of pride *of the drunkards*[3] of Ephraim, and to the fading flower of his glorious beauty, which is on the *head of the fat valley of those who are struck down with wine*[4]!

הִנֵּה חָזָק וְאַמִּץ לַאדֹנָי כְּזֶרֶם בָּרָד שַׂעַר קָטֶב כְּזֶרֶם מַיִם כַּבִּירִים שֹׁטְפִים הִנִּיחַ לָאָרֶץ בְּיָד

2[5] Behold, *the Lord*[6] has a mighty and strong one[7], as a storm of hail, a tempest of destruction, as a storm of mighty waters overflowing, that casts down to the earth with violence.

בְּרַגְלַיִם תֵּרָמַסְנָה עֲטֶרֶת גֵּאוּת שִׁכֹּרֵי אֶפְרָיִם

3[8] The crown of pride *of the drunkards*[9] of Ephraim shall be *trodden under foot*[10];

וְהָיְתָה צִיצַת נֹבֵל צְבִי תִפְאַרְתּוֹ אֲשֶׁר עַל־רֹאשׁ גֵּיא שְׁמָנִים כְּבִכּוּרָהּ בְּטֶרֶם קַיִץ אֲשֶׁר יִרְאֶה הָרֹאֶה אוֹתָהּ בְּעוֹדָהּ בְּכַפּוֹ יִבְלָעֶנָּה

4[11] And the fading flower of his glorious beauty, Which is on the head of the fat valley, Shall be as the first-ripe fig *before the summer*[12], Which when one looks on it, While it is yet in his hand he eats it.

בַּיּוֹם הַהוּא יִהְיֶה יְהוָה צְבָאוֹת לַעֲטֶרֶת צְבִי וְלִצְפִירַת תִּפְאָרָה לִשְׁאָר עַמּוֹ

5[13] In that day the LORD of hosts shall *be For a crown of glory, and for a diadem of beauty, to the remnant*[14] of His people;

וּלְרוּחַ מִשְׁפָּט לַיּוֹשֵׁב עַל־הַמִּשְׁפָּט וְלִגְבוּרָה מְשִׁיבֵי מִלְחָמָה שָׁעְרָה

6[15] And for a spirit of judgment to him who sits in judgment, And for strength to those who turn back the battle at the gate.

וְגַם־אֵלֶּה בַּיַּיִן שָׁגוּ וּבַשֵּׁכָר תָּעוּ כֹּהֵן וְנָבִיא שָׁגוּ בַשֵּׁכָר נִבְלְעוּ מִן־הַיַּיִן תָּעוּ מִן־הַשֵּׁכָר שָׁגוּ בָּרֹאֶה פָּקוּ פְּלִילִיָּה

7[16] But these also reel through wine, And stagger through strong drink; The priest and the prophet reel through strong drink, They are

Mussaf Rosh Hashanah, Numbers 10:2-10:4, Numbers.R 13:5, Psalms 47:6 81:4 89:16, Revelation 8:2 8:6-9:1 9:14 10:7 11:15-11:18, Romans 10:18, Ruth.R Petichata:7, t.Sanhedrin 13:12, y.Sanhedrin 10:4, z.Beshallach 46b, z.Vaetchanan 266b, z.Vayigash 210a, Zechariah 9:13-9:16 10:8-10:12 14:16

[1] 1QIsaa *bow down to*

[2] Isaiah 28:1 - 2 Chronicles 28:6 30:6-30:7, 2 Kings 14:25-14:27 15:29 18:10-18:12, Amos 2:8 2:12 6:1 6:6, Hosea 4:11 5:5 6:10 7:5, Isaiah 5:11 5:22 7:8-7:9 8:4 9:10 28:3-28:4 28:7, Midrash Tanchuma Shemini 11, Proverbs 23:29
Isaiah 28:1-29 - 1QIsaa

[3] LXX *the hirelings*

[4] LXX *top of the fertile mountain, they who are drunk without wine*

[5] Isaiah 28:2 - b.Sheviit 35a, Ezekiel 13:11 30:10-30:11, Isaiah 8:7-8:8 9:10-9:13 25:4 27:1 28:15-28:19 29:6 30:30 40:10, Matthew 7:25-7:27, Midrash Psalms 47:1, Nahum 1:8, Per Massorah: Soferim altered "Hashem" to "Adonai", Revelation 18:8

[6] 1QIsaa *the LORD*; LXX *the anger of the LORD*

[7] LXX *is strong and severe*

[8] Isaiah 28:3 - 2 Kings 9:33, Daniel 8:13, Genesis.R 99 [Excl]:8, Hebrews 10:29, Isaiah 25:10 26:6 28:1, Lamentations 1:15, Midrash Tanchuma Vayechi 10, Revelation 11:2

[9] LXX *the hirelings*

[10] LXX *beaten down with the hands and with the feet*

[11] Isaiah 28:4 - Genesis.R 22:5, Hosea 6:4 9:10-9:11 9:16 13:1 13:15, Isaiah 28:1, James 1:10-1:11, Micah 7:1, Nahum 3:12, Psalms 73:19-73:20, Revelation 6:13

[12] Missing in LXX

[13] Isaiah 28:5 - 1 Corinthians 1:30-1:31, 1 Peter 5:4, 2 Corinthians 4:17, b.Megillah 15b, b.Rosh Hashanah [Tosefot] 11a, b.Sanhedrin 111b, Ein Yaakov Megillah:15b, Greek Apocalypse of Ezra 6:17, Isaiah 10:20-10:21 11:16 37:31-37:32 41:16 45:25 60:1-60:3 60:19 62:3, Jastrow 1065a 1561b, Jeremiah 9:24-25, Job 29:14, Luke 2:32, Psalms 90:16-90:17, Romans 11:5-6, Zechariah 6:13-15
Isaiah 28:5-6 - Midrash Tanchuma Vayechi 10

[14] LXX *shall be the crown of hope, the woven crown of glory, to the remnant*

[15] Isaiah 28:6 - 1 Corinthians 12:8, 1 Kings 3:28, 2 Chronicles 32:8, b.Sanhedrin 111b, Deuteronomy 20:4, Genesis 41:38-39, Isaiah 11:2-4 32:15-16, John 3:34 5:30, Joshua 1:9, Numbers 11:16-17 27:16-18, Proverbs 20:8, Psalms 18:33-35 46:2 46:12 72:1-4
Isaiah 28:6-9 - 4QIsaf
Isaiah 28:6-14 - 4QIsac

[16] Isaiah 28:7 - b.Megillah 15b, Ecclesiastes 10:17, Ein Yaakov Megillah:15b, Ephesians 5:28, Esther.R 5:1, Ezekiel 13:7 44:21, Genesis.R 36:4, Guide for the Perplexed 3:8 3:48, Hosea 4:11-4:12, Isaiah 3:12 5:11 5:22 9:16-9:17 19:14 22:13 24:2 29:11 56:10-56:12, Jastrow 1169a 1182a, Jeremiah 14:14 23:13 23:16, Lamentations 2:4, Leviticus 10:9-10:10, Luke 21:34, Matthew 24:29, Micah

confused because of wine, They stagger because of strong drink; *They reel in vision, they totter in judgment*[1].

8[2] כִּי כָּל־שֻׁלְחָנוֹת מָלְאוּ קִיא צֹאָה בְּלִי מָקוֹם

For all tables are full of filthy vomit, and no place is clean[3].

9[4] אֶת־מִי יוֹרֶה דֵעָה וְאֶת־מִי יָבִין שְׁמוּעָה גְּמוּלֵי מֵחָלָב עַתִּיקֵי מִשָּׁדָיִם

To whom shall one teach knowledge? And to whom shall one make understand the message[5]? They who are weaned from the milk, They who are drawn from the breasts?

10[6] כִּי צַו לָצָו צַו לָצָו קַו לָקָו קַו לָקָו זְעֵיר שָׁם זְעֵיר שָׁם

For it is precept by precept, precept by precept, line by line, line by line; here a little, there a little[7].

11[8] כִּי בְּלַעֲגֵי שָׂפָה וּבְלָשׁוֹן אַחֶרֶת יְדַבֵּר אֶל־הָעָם הַזֶּה

For with stammering lips and with a strange tongue[9] it shall be spoken to this people;

12[10] אֲשֶׁר אָמַר אֲלֵיהֶם זֹאת הַמְּנוּחָה הָנִיחוּ לֶעָיֵף וְזֹאת הַמַּרְגֵּעָה וְלֹא אָבוּא שְׁמוֹעַ

To whom it was said: 'This is the rest, Give rest to the weary; And this is the refreshing'[11]; Yet they would not hear.

13[12] וְהָיָה לָהֶם דְּבַר־יְהוָה צַו לָצָו צַו לָצָו קַו לָקָו קַו לָקָו זְעֵיר שָׁם זְעֵיר שָׁם לְמַעַן יֵלְכוּ וְכָשְׁלוּ אָחוֹר וְנִשְׁבָּרוּ וְנוֹקְשׁוּ וְנִלְכָּדוּ

And so the word of the LORD is to them precept by precept, precept by precept, line by line, line by line; here a little, there a little; so they may go, and fall backward, and be broken, and snared, and[13] taken.

14[14] לָכֵן שִׁמְעוּ דְבַר־יְהוָה אַנְשֵׁי לָצוֹן מֹשְׁלֵי הָעָם הַזֶּה אֲשֶׁר בִּירוּשָׁלָ͏ִם

Therefore, hear the word of the LORD, *you scoffers, The ballad-mongers*[15] of this people who are in Jerusalem:

15[16] כִּי אֲמַרְתֶּם כָּרַתְנוּ בְרִית אֶת־מָוֶת וְעִם־שְׁאוֹל עָשִׂינוּ חֹזֶה *"שִׁיט" "שׁוֹט"* שׁוֹטֵף *"כִּי־עָבַר" "כִּי־ יַעֲבֹר"* לֹא יְבוֹאֵנוּ כִּי שַׂמְנוּ כָזָב מַחְסֵנוּ וּבַשֶּׁקֶר נִסְתָּרְנוּ

Because you have said: 'We have made a covenant with death, And with the nether-world are we at agreement; When the scouring scourge shall pass through, It shall not come to us; For we have made lies our refuge, And in falsehood we have hid ourselves;'

2:11, Midrash Tanchuma Shemini 5, Proverbs 20:1 31:4-31:5, Psalms 107:27

[1] LXX *they have erred: this is their vision*

[2] Isaiah 28:8 - Ein Yaakov Sotah:12a, Guide for the Perplexed 3:8, Habakkuk 2:15-2:16, Jeremiah 48:26, mt.Hilchot Deot 5:1 5:1 5:2 5:2, mt.Pirkei Avot 3:3, Pirkei Avot 3:4 [Shabbat afternoon], Proverbs 26:11, Saadia Opinions 10:5, Tanna Devei Eliyahu 4, Tanya Likutei Aramim §24, z.Emor 104a, z.Terumah 153b

[3] LXX *curse shall devour this counsel, for this is their counsel for the sake of covetousness*

[4] Isaiah 28:9 - 1 Peter 2:2, 3 Enoch 48C:12, b.Sotah 12b, b.Zara Avodah 3b, Ein Yaakov Avodah Zarah:3b, Ein Yaakov Sotah:12a, Exodus.R 1:25, Isaiah 28:26 30:10-30:12 30:20 48:17 50:4 53:1 54:13, Jeremiah 5:31 6:10, John 3:19 12:38 12:47-12:48, Mark 10:15, Mas.Kallah Rabbati 2:9, Matthew 11:25 21:15-16, Proverbs 1:29, Psalms 50:17 131:2, Tanna Devei Eliyahu 5, y.Yevamot 1:6

[5] LXX *To whom have we reported evils? And to whom have we reported a message?*

[6] Isaiah 28:10 - 2 Chronicles 36:15-36:16, 2 Timothy 3:7, Deuteronomy 6:1-6:6, Hebrews 5:12, Isaiah 5:4 28:13, Jeremiah 11:7 25:3-25:7, Matthew 21:34-21:41, Nehemiah 9:29-9:30, Philippians 3:1, Tanna Devei Eliyahu 4

[7] LXX *Expect you affliction on affliction, hope upon hope: yet a little, and yet a little*

[8] Isaiah 28:11 - 1 Corinthians 14:21, b.Sanhedrin 11b, Deuteronomy 28:49, Isaiah 33:19, Jeremiah 5:15

[9] LXX *because the contemptuous words of the lips, by means of another language*

[10] Isaiah 28:12 - 2 Chronicles 16:8-16:9, Hebrews 12:25, Isaiah 11:10 30:15, Jeremiah 6:16 44:16, Matthew 11:28-11:29, Psalms 81:12-81:14, Zechariah 7:11 7:14

[11] LXX *This is the rest to him who is hungry, and this is the calamity*

[12] Isaiah 28:13 - 1 Peter 2:7-2:8, 2 Corinthians 2:16, 2 Peter 3:16, Hosea 6:5 8:12, Isaiah 6:9-6:10 8:14-8:15 28:10, Jeremiah 23:36-23:38, Matthew 13:14 21:44, Psalms 69:23, Romans 11:9

[13] LXX *Therefore, the oracle of God shall be to them affliction on affliction, hope on hope, yet a little, and yet a little, that they may go and fall backward; and they shall be crushed and shall be in danger, and shall be*

[14] Isaiah 28:14 - Acts 13:41, Hosea 7:5, Isaiah 1:10 5:9 28:22 29:20, Mesillat Yesharim 5:Factors Detracting from Zehirus, Proverbs 1:22 3:34 29:8

[15] LXX *you afflicted men, and you princes*

[16] Isaiah 28:15 - 2 Thessalonians 2:9-11, Amos 2:4, Daniel 11:22, Ecclesiastes 8:8, Ezekiel 8:12 13:16 13:22, Hosea 2:18, Isaiah 5:18-19 8:7-8 9:16 28:2 28:18 29:15 30:10 30:28, Jeremiah 5:31 14:13 16:19 28:15-17 44:17, Job 5:23 15:25-27, Jonah 2:8, Zephaniah 1:12 Isaiah 28:15-20 - 1QIsab

לָכֵן כֹּה אָמַר אֲדֹנָי יְהוִה הִנְנִי יִסַּד בְּצִיּוֹן אָבֶן אֶבֶן בֹּחַן פִּנַּת יִקְרַת מוּסָד מוּסָּד הַמַּאֲמִין לֹא יָחִישׁ	16[1]	Therefore, thus says the Lord GOD: Behold, I lay in Zion as a foundation a stone, A tried stone, a costly corner-stone of sure foundation; He who believes *shall not make haste*[2].
וְשַׂמְתִּי מִשְׁפָּט לְקָו וּצְדָקָה לְמִשְׁקָלֶת וְיָעָה בָרָד מַחְסֵה כָזָב וְסֵתֶר מַיִם יִשְׁטֹפוּ	17[3]	*And I will make justice the line, And righteousness the plummet; And the hail shall sweep away the refuge of lies, And the waters shall overflow the hiding place*[4].
וְכֻפַּר בְּרִיתְכֶם אֶת־מָוֶת וְחָזוּתְכֶם אֶת־שְׁאוֹל לֹא תָקוּם שׁוֹט שׁוֹטֵף כִּי יַעֲבֹר וִהְיִיתֶם לוֹ לְמִרְמָס	18[5]	And your covenant with death shall be voided and your agreement with the nether-world shall not stand; When the scouring scourge passes through, Then you shall be trodden down by it,
מִדֵּי עָבְרוֹ יִקַּח אֶתְכֶם כִּי־בַבֹּקֶר בַּבֹּקֶר יַעֲבֹר בַּיּוֹם וּבַלָּיְלָה וְהָיָה רַק־זְוָעָה הָבִין שְׁמוּעָה	19[6]	As often as it passes through, it shall take you; For morning by morning it shall pass *through, By day and by night; And it shall be sheer terror to understand the message*[7].
כִּי־קָצַר הַמַּצָּע מֵהִשְׂתָּרֵעַ וְהַמַּסֵּכָה צָרָה כְּהִתְכַּנֵּס	20[8]	*For the bed is too short for a man to stretch himself; And the sheet too narrow when he gathers himself up*[9].
כִּי כְהַר־פְּרָצִים יָקוּם יְהוָה כְּעֵמֶק בְּגִבְעוֹן יִרְגָּז לַעֲשׂוֹת מַעֲשֵׂהוּ זָר מַעֲשֵׂהוּ וְלַעֲבֹד עֲבֹדָתוֹ נָכְרִיָּה עֲבֹדָתוֹ	21[10]	For the LORD will rise as in mount *Perazim*[11], He will be angry as in the valley of Gibeon; so He may do His work, strange is His work, *and bring to pass His act, strange is His act.*[12]
וְעַתָּה אַל־תִּתְלוֹצָצוּ פֶּן־יֶחְזְקוּ מוֹסְרֵיכֶם כִּי־כָלָה וְנֶחֱרָצָה שָׁמַעְתִּי מֵאֵת אֲדֹנָי יְהוִה צְבָאוֹת עַל־כָּל־הָאָרֶץ	22[13]	*Now, therefore*[14] do not be *scoffers*[15], Lest your bands be made strong; For I have heard a wholly determined extermination from *the Lord, the GOD*[16] of hosts, on the whole land.
הַאֲזִינוּ וְשִׁמְעוּ קוֹלִי הַקְשִׁיבוּ וְשִׁמְעוּ אִמְרָתִי	23[17]	Give ear, and hear my voice; pay attention, and hear my speech.

---

[1] Isaiah 28:16 - 1 Corinthians 3:11, 1 Peter 2:6-2:8, 1QS 8:7, 1QS 8.7, 4Q259 2.14, Acts 4:11-4:12, Deuteronomy.R 3:13, Ephesians 2:20, Genesis 49:10 49:24, Habakkuk 2:3-2:4, Isaiah 8:14-8:15 30:18, James 5:7-5:8, Leviticus.R 17:7, Luke 20:17-20:18, Mark 12:10, Matthew 21:42, Midrash Tanchuma Ekev 10, Psalms 112:7-112:8 118:22, Romans 9:33 10:11, Testament of Solomon 22:7, y.Yoma 5:3, z.Toledot 140b, z.Vaetchanan 269b, z.Vayechi 231a, Zechariah 3:9
Isaiah 28:16-18? - 4QIsaf
[2] LXX *on him shall by no means be ashamed*
[3] Isaiah 28:17 - 2 Kings 21:13, 2 Peter 3:6-3:7, Amos 7:7-7:9, Daniel 11:22, Exodus 9:18-9:19, Ezekiel 13:10-13:16 38:22, Isaiah 5:16 10:22 25:4 28:2 28:15 30:28 32:2 32:18-32:19, Jeremiah 7:4-7:8 7:14 7:20 23:19 30:23-30:24, Job 22:16, Joshua 10:11, Matthew 7:27, Psalms 94:15, Revelation 8:7 11:19 16:21 19:2, Romans 2:2 2:5 9:28
[4] LXX *And I will cause judgment to be for hope, and my compassion shall be for just measures, and you who trust vainly in falsehood shall fall: for the storm shall by no means pass by you*
[5] Isaiah 28:18 - Daniel 8:9-8:13 9:26-9:27 11:40, Ezekiel 17:15, Isaiah 2:15 7:7 8:8 8:10 28:3 28:15, Jeremiah 44:28 47:2, Malachi 3:19-4:21, Revelation 12:15 17:15, Zechariah 1:6
[6] Isaiah 28:19 - 1 Samuel 3:11, 2 Kings 17:6 18:13 21:12 24:2, b.Sanhedrin 95b, Daniel 7:28 8:27, Ein Yaakov Sanhedrin:95b, Ezekiel 21:24-21:28, Habakkuk 3:16, Isaiah 10:5-10:6 33:7 36:22 37:3 50:4, Jeremiah 19:3, Job 18:11, Luke 21:25-21:26, Midrash Tanchuma Bechukkotai 1
[7] LXX *in the day, and in the night there shall be an evil hope. Learn to hear...*
[8] Isaiah 28:20 - 1 Corinthians 1:18-31, b.Sanhedrin 103b, b.Yoma 9b, Ein Yaakov Yoma 9a, Isaiah 57:12-13 59:5-6 64:7 66:3-6, Jastrow 1632a 1634b, Jeremiah 7:8-10, Lamentations.R Petichata D'Chakimei 22, Leviticus.R 17:7, Mekilta de R'Ishmael Beshallah 4:74, Midrash Tanchuma Re'eh 16, Midrash Tanchuma Bechukkotai 3, Numbers.R 7:10, Pesikta de R'Kahana 10.8, Romans 9:30-32
[9] LXX *you who are distressed; we cannot fight, but we are ourselves too weak for you to be gathered*
[10] Isaiah 28:21 - 1 Chronicles 14:11 14:16, 2 Samuel 5:20 5:25, Deuteronomy 29:20-23, Ezekiel 33:21, Isaiah 10:12 28:19 29:14, Jeremiah 30:14, Joshua 10:10 10:12, Lamentations 2:15 3:33, Luke 19:41-44
[11] LXX *ungodly men*
[12] Missing in LXX
[13] Isaiah 28:22 - 2 Chronicles 30:10 33:11 36:16, 4QIsaf, Acts 13:40-13:41 17:32, b.Avodah Zara 18b, Daniel 9:26-9:27, Ein Yaakov Avodah Zarah:18b, Gates of Repentance 3.177, Isaiah 10:22-10:23 24:1-24:23 28:14-28:15 32:12-32:14, Jeremiah 15:17 20:7 25:11 39:7, Lamentations 1:14, Luke 21:24, Matthew 27:39 27:44, Mesillat Yesharim 5:Factors Detracting from Zehirus, Pesikta de R'Kahana 13.2, Psalms 107:16, Revelation 22:18-22:19, y.Berachot 2:8
[14] 1QIsaa *But as for you*
[15] LXX *rejoice*
[16] 1QIsaa *the LORD*
[17] Isaiah 28:23 - Deuteronomy 32:1, Isaiah 1:2, Jeremiah 22:29, Revelation 2:7 2:11 2:14 2:29

Hebrew	Verse	English
הֲכֹל הַיּוֹם יַחֲרֹשׁ הַחֹרֵשׁ לִזְרֹעַ יְפַתַּח וִישַׂדֵּד אַדְמָתוֹ	24[1]	Is the plowman never done with plowing to sow, *With the opening and harrowing of his ground*[2]?
הֲלוֹא אִם־שִׁוָּה פָנֶיהָ וְהֵפִיץ קֶצַח וְכַמֹּן יִזְרֹק וְשָׂם חִטָּה שׂוֹרָה וּשְׂעֹרָה נִסְמָן וְכֻסֶּמֶת גְּבֻלָתוֹ	25[3]	When he has made the face plain, does he not cast abroad the *black cumin, and scatter the cumin, And plant the wheat in rows and the barley in the appointed place and the spelt in its border*[4]?
וְיִסְּרוֹ לַמִּשְׁפָּט אֱלֹהָיו יוֹרֶנּוּ	26[5]	*For He does instruct him correctly; His God teaches him*[6].
כִּי לֹא בֶחָרוּץ יוּדַשׁ קֶצַח וְאוֹפַן עֲגָלָה עַל־כַּמֹּן יוּסָּב כִּי בַמַּטֶּה יֵחָבֶט קֶצַח וְכַמֹּן בַּשָּׁבֶט	27[7]	For the *black cumin*[8] is not threshed with a threshing-sledge, nor is a cart-wheel turned about on the cumin; But the *black cumin is beaten with a staff, And the cumin with a rod*[9].
לֶחֶם יוּדָק כִּי לֹא לָנֶצַח אָדוֹשׁ יְדוּשֶׁנּוּ וְהָמַם גִּלְגַּל עֶגְלָתוֹ וּפָרָשָׁיו לֹא־יְדֻקֶּנּוּ	28[10]	Is *bread corn crushed*[11]? No, he will not ever be threshing it[12]; And though the roller of his wagon and its sharp edges move noisily, He does not crush it[13].
גַּם־זֹאת מֵעִם יְהוָה צְבָאוֹת יָצָאָה הִפְלִיא עֵצָה הִגְדִּיל תּוּשִׁיָּה	29[14]	*This also comes forth from the LORD of hosts: Wonderful is His counsel, and great His wisdom*[15].

Isaiah – Chapter 29

Hebrew	Verse	English
הוֹי אֲרִיאֵל אֲרִיאֵל קִרְיַת חָנָה דָוִד סְפוּ שָׁנָה עַל־שָׁנָה חַגִּים יִנְקֹפוּ	1[16]	Ah, *Ariel, Ariel*[17], the city *where David encamped! Add year to year, Let the holidays come around*[18]!
וַהֲצִיקוֹתִי לַאֲרִיאֵל וְהָיְתָה תַאֲנִיָּה וַאֲנִיָּה וְהָיְתָה לִּי כַּאֲרִיאֵל	2[19]	Then will I distress *Ariel*[20], And there shall be mourning and moaning; and she shall be to Me as a hearth of God[21].

---

[1] Isaiah 28:24 - 4QIsaf, Hosea 10:11-10:12, Jeremiah 4:3

[2] LXX *or will he prepare the seed beforehand, before he tills the ground*

[3] Isaiah 28:25 - Exodus 9:31-32, Ezekiel 4:9, Gates of Repentance 4.19, Jastrow 204b 623b 1310a 1566b, Matthew 23:23, y.Challah 1:1

[4] LXX *small black poppy, or cumin, and afterward sow wheat, and barley, and millet, and bread-corn in thy borders*

[5] Isaiah 28:26 - b.Sanhedrin 105a, Daniel 1:17, Ein Yaakov Sanhedrin:105a, Exodus 28:3 31:3-31:6 36:2, James 1:17, Job 35:11 39:17, Psalms 144:1, y.Challah 1:1
Isaiah 28:26-29 - 4QIsak

[6] LXX *So you shall be chastened by the judgment of your God, and shall rejoice*

[7] Isaiah 28:27 - 2 Kings 13:7, Amos 1:3, Isaiah 27:7-27:8 41:15, Jeremiah 10:24 46:28

[8] 1QIsaa *caraway*; LXX *black poppy*

[9] LXX *black poppy is threshed with a rod, and the cumin shall be eaten with bread*

[10] Isaiah 28:28 - 1 Corinthians 3:9 9:9-10, Amos 9:9, Isaiah 21:10, John 12:24, Luke 22:31-32, Matthew 3:12 13:37-43

[11] 1QIsaa *is ground for bread*; missing in LXX

[12] Missing in LXX

[13] 1QIsaa *although his horses may scatter it, he does not grind it*; LXX *for I will not be wroth with you for ever, neither shall the voice of my anger crush you*

[14] Isaiah 28:29 - b.Avodah Zara 14b, b.Nazir 23b, b.Sanhedrin 26b, Daniel 3:32-33, Ein Yaakov Sanhedrin:26b, Isaiah 9:7 28:21-22, Jastrow 1641a 1705a, Jeremiah 32:19, Job 5:9 37:23, Psalms 40:6 92:6, Romans 11:33

[15] LXX *And these signs came forth from the LORD of hosts. Take counsel, exalt vain comfort*

[16] Isaiah 29:1 - 2 Samuel 5:9, Amos 4:4-5, Avot de R'Natan 1, b.Berachot [Rashi] 18a, b.Chagigah [Tosefot] 5b, b.Middot 37a, b.Sanhedrin [Rashi] 76b, Exodus.R 29:9, Ezekiel 43:15-43:16, Hebrews 10:1, Hosea 5:6 8:13 9:4, Isaiah 1:11-15 22:12-13 31:9 66:3, Jastrow 119a 343b 482b 1397a 1419b, Jeremiah 7:21, Lamentations.R Petichata D'Chakimei:26, m.Middot 4:7, Micah 6:6-7, mt.Hilchot Beit Habechirah 4:5 4:5, Pesikta de R'Kahana 13.15, Pesikta Rabbati 27/28:1
Isaiah 29:1-8 - 1QIsab
Isaiah 29:1-9 - 4QIsak
Isaiah 29:1-24 - 1QIsaa

[17] 1QIsaa *Aruel Aruel*I; LXX has one "*Ariel*"

[18] LXX *which David besieged. Gather fruits year by year; eat, for you shall eat with Moab*

[19] Isaiah 29:2 - Ezekiel 22:31 24:3-13 39:17, Isaiah 3:26 5:25-30 10:5-6 10:32 17:14 24:1-12 33:7-9 34:6 36:22 37:3, Jastrow 979b, Jeremiah 32:28-32 39:4-5, Lamentations 2:5, Lamentations.R Petichata D'Chakimei:26, m.Middot 4:7, Revelation 19:17-18, z.Vaera 30b, Zephaniah 1:7-8

[20] 1QIsaa *Aruel*

[21] LXX *and her strength and her wealth shall be mine*

וְחָנִיתִי כַדּוּר עָלָיִךְ וְצַרְתִּי עָלָיִךְ מֻצָּב וַהֲקִימֹתִי עָלַיִךְ מְצֻרֹת

3[1] And I will encamp around and against you[2], And will lay siege against you with a mound, And I will raise siege works against you.

וְשָׁפַלְתְּ מֵאֶרֶץ תְּדַבֵּרִי וּמֵעָפָר תִּשַּׁח אִמְרָתֵךְ וְהָיָה כְּאוֹב מֵאֶרֶץ קוֹלֵךְ וּמֵעָפָר אִמְרָתֵךְ תְּצַפְצֵף

4[3] And brought down, you shall speak out of the ground, And your speech shall be low out of the dust; And your voice shall be as *of a ghost out of the ground*[4], And your speech shall chirp out of the dust.

וְהָיָה כְּאָבָק דַּק הֲמוֹן זָרָיִךְ וּכְמֹץ עֹבֵר הֲמוֹן עָרִיצִים וְהָיָה לְפֶתַע פִּתְאֹם

5[5] But the *multitude of your foes shall be like small dust*[6], And the multitude of the terrible ones as chaff that passes away; Yes, it shall be at an instant suddenly.

מֵעִם יְהֹוָה צְבָאוֹת תִּפָּקֵד בְּרַעַם וּבְרַעַשׁ וְקוֹל גָּדוֹל סוּפָה וּסְעָרָה וְלַהַב אֵשׁ אוֹכֵלָה

6[7] There shall be a visitation from the LORD of hosts With thunder, and with earthquake, and great noise, With whirlwind and tempest, and the flame of a devouring fire.

וְהָיָה כַּחֲלוֹם חֲזוֹן לַיְלָה הֲמוֹן כָּל־הַגּוֹיִם הַצֹּבְאִים עַל־אֲרִיאֵל וְכָל־צֹבֶיהָ וּמְצֹדָתָהּ וְהַמְּצִיקִים לָהּ

7[8] *And the multitude of all the nations who war against Ariel, all who war against her*[9], and *the bulwarks*[10] about her, and they who distress her, Shall be as a dream, a vision of the night.

וְהָיָה כַּאֲשֶׁר יַחֲלֹם הָרָעֵב וְהִנֵּה אוֹכֵל וְהֵקִיץ וְרֵיקָה נַפְשׁוֹ וְכַאֲשֶׁר יַחֲלֹם הַצָּמֵא וְהִנֵּה שֹׁתֶה וְהֵקִיץ וְהִנֵּה עָיֵף וְנַפְשׁוֹ שׁוֹקֵקָה כֵּן יִהְיֶה הֲמוֹן כָּל־הַגּוֹיִם הַצֹּבְאִים עַל־הַר צִיּוֹן

8[11] And it shall be as when a hungry man dreams, and, behold, he eats, But he awakens, and his soul is empty; Or as when a thirsty man dreams, and, behold, he drinks, But he awakens, and, behold, he is faint, and his soul has appetite, So shall the *multitude*[12] of all the nations be, who fight against mount Zion.

הִתְמַהְמְהוּ וּתְמָהוּ הִשְׁתַּעַשְׁעוּ וָשֹׁעוּ שָׁכְרוּ וְלֹא־יַיִן נָעוּ וְלֹא שֵׁכָר

9[13] Stupefy yourselves, and be stupid! Blind yourselves, and be blind! You who are drunk, but not with wine, who stagger, but not with strong drink.

כִּי־נָסַךְ עֲלֵיכֶם יְהֹוָה רוּחַ תַּרְדֵּמָה וַיְעַצֵּם אֶת־עֵינֵיכֶם אֶת־הַנְּבִיאִים וְאֶת־רָאשֵׁיכֶם הַחֹזִים כִּסָּה

10[14] For the LORD has poured on you the spirit of deep sleep, And has closed your eyes; The prophets, and your heads, the seers, He has covered.

וַתְּהִי לָכֶם חָזוּת הַכֹּל כְּדִבְרֵי הַסֵּפֶר הֶחָתוּם אֲשֶׁר־יִתְּנוּ אֹתוֹ אֶל־יוֹדֵעַ הַסֵּפֶר לֵאמֹר קְרָא נָא־זֶה וְאָמַר לֹא אוּכַל כִּי חָתוּם הוּא

11[15] And the vision of all this has become to you as the words of a writing that is sealed, which men deliver to one who is learned, saying: 'Read

---

[1] Isaiah 29:3 - 2 Kings 18:17 19:32 24:11-12 25:1-4, Ezekiel 21:27, Luke 19:43-44, Matthew 22:7

[2] LXX adds *like David*

[3] Isaiah 29:4 - b.Rosh Hashanah 31b, b.Sanhedrin 65b, Ein Yaakov Rosh Hashanah:31b, Gates of Repentance 1.029, Isaiah 2:11-21 3:8 8:19 51:23, Jastrow 1559b, Lamentations 1:9, Midrash Tanchuma Shoftim 10, Psalms 44:26, Ralbag Wars 6part2:14, Song of Songs.R 1:21, y.Sanhedrin 7:10

[4] LXX *they who speak out of the earth*

[5] Isaiah 29:5 - 1 Thessalonians 5:3, Isaiah 10:16-19 17:13-14 25:5 30:13 31:3 31:8 37:36, Job 21:18, Psalms 1:4 35:5 46:6-7 76:6-7

[6] LXX *wealth of the ungodly shall be as dust from a wheel*

[7] Isaiah 29:6 - 1 Samuel 2:10 12:17-12:18, 2 Samuel 22:14, Isaiah 5:26-5:30 28:2 30:30 33:11-33:14, Luke 21:11, Mark 13:8, Matthew 24:7, Revelation 11:13 11:19 16:18, Sibylline Oracles 3.690

[8] Isaiah 29:7 - Isaiah 17:14 37:36 41:11-12, Jeremiah 25:31-33 51:42-44, Job 20:8, Micah 4:11-12, Nahum 1:3-12, Psalms 73:20, Revelation 20:8-9, Zechariah 12:3-5 12:9 14:1-3 14:12-15

[9] LXX *wealth of all the nations together, as many as have fought against Ariel, and all they who war against Jerusalem*

[10] 1QIsaa *the mountain stronghold*; LXX *all who gather*

[11] Isaiah 29:8 - 2 Chronicles 32:21, 4QIsaf, Isaiah 10:7-16 44:12, Psalms 73:20, Saadia Opinions Intro:4

[12] LXX *wealth*

[13] Isaiah 29:9 - Acts 13:40-41, Genesis.R 17:5 44:17, Habakkuk 1:5, Isaiah 1:2 19:14 22:12-13 28:7-8 29:10 33:13-14 49:26 51:17 51:21-22, Jeremiah 2:12 23:9 25:27 51:7, Lamentations 4:21, Mark 14:41, Matthew 26:45, Midrash Psalms 75:4, Revelation 17:6

[14] Isaiah 29:10 - 1 Samuel 9:9 26:12, 2 Corinthians 4:4, 2 Thessalonians 2:9-12, Acts 28:26-27, Amos 7:12-13, Exodus.R 38:4, Ezekiel 14:9, Isaiah 3:2-3 6:9-10 29:14 30:10 44:18, Jeremiah 26:8-11, Micah 3:1 3:6, Numbers.R 14:4, Pesikta Rabbati 8:3 33:13, Psalms 69:24, Romans 11:8, Sifre Devarim Ekev 41
Isaiah 29:10-12 - 4Q163 frags 15-16 ll.1-4

[15] Isaiah 29:11 - Daniel 12:4 12:9, Guide for the Perplexed 2:29 2:46, Isaiah 8:16, Matthew 11:25 13:11 16:17, Revelation 5:1-9 6:1

this, Please'; and he says: 'I cannot, for it is sealed';

12[1]
וְנִתַּן הַסֵּפֶר עַל אֲשֶׁר לֹא־יָדַע סֵפֶר לֵאמֹר קְרָא נָא־זֶה וְאָמַר לֹא יָדַעְתִּי סֵפֶר

and the writing is delivered to one who is not learned, saying: 'Read this, Please'; and he says: 'I am not learned.'

13[2]
וַיֹּאמֶר אֲדֹנָי יַעַן כִּי נִגַּשׁ הָעָם הַזֶּה בְּפִיו וּבִשְׂפָתָיו כִּבְּדוּנִי וְלִבּוֹ רִחַק מִמֶּנִּי וַתְּהִי יִרְאָתָם אֹתִי מִצְוַת אֲנָשִׁים מְלֻמָּדָה

And the Lord said: Because as this people draw near, And with their mouth and with their lips honor Me, But have removed their heart far from Me, And their fear of Me is a commandment of men learned by rote;

14[3]
לָכֵן הִנְנִי יוֹסִף לְהַפְלִיא אֶת־הָעָם־הַזֶּה הַפְלֵא וָפֶלֶא וְאָבְדָה חָכְמַת חֲכָמָיו וּבִינַת נְבֹנָיו תִּסְתַּתָּר

Therefore, behold, I will again do a marvelous work among this people, a marvelous work and a wonder; And the wisdom of their wise men shall perish, And the prudence of their prudent men shall be hidden.

15[4]
הוֹי הַמַּעֲמִיקִים מֵיהוָה לַסְתִּר עֵצָה וְהָיָה בְמַחְשָׁךְ מַעֲשֵׂיהֶם וַיֹּאמְרוּ מִי רֹאֵנוּ וּמִי יוֹדְעֵנוּ

Woe to those who seek deep to hide their counsel from the LORD, And their works are in the dark, And they say: 'Who sees us? and who knows us?'

16[5]
הַפְכְּכֶם אִם־כְּחֹמֶר הַיֹּצֵר יֵחָשֵׁב כִּי־יֹאמַר מַעֲשֶׂה לְעֹשֵׂהוּ לֹא עָשָׂנִי וְיֵצֶר אָמַר לְיוֹצְרוֹ לֹא הֵבִין

O your perversity[6]! Shall the potter be esteemed as clay; so the thing made should say of he who made it: 'He did not make me'; Or the thing framed say of he who framed it: 'He has no understanding?'

17[7]
הֲלוֹא־עוֹד מְעַט מִזְעָר וְשָׁב לְבָנוֹן לַכַּרְמֶל וְהַכַּרְמֶל לַיַּעַר יֵחָשֵׁב

Is it not yet a very little while, And Lebanon shall be turned into a fruitful field, And the fruitful field shall be esteemed as a forest?

18[8]
וְשָׁמְעוּ בַיּוֹם־הַהוּא הַחֵרְשִׁים דִּבְרֵי־סֵפֶר וּמֵאֹפֶל וּמֵחֹשֶׁךְ עֵינֵי עִוְרִים תִּרְאֶינָה

And in that day the deaf shall hear the words of a book, And the eyes of the blind shall see out of obscurity and out of darkness.

19[9]
וְיָסְפוּ עֲנָוִים בַּיהוָה שִׂמְחָה וְאֶבְיוֹנֵי אָדָם בִּקְדוֹשׁ יִשְׂרָאֵל יָגִילוּ

The humble shall increase their joy in the LORD, And the neediest among men shall exult in the Holy One of Israel.

---

[1] Isaiah 29:12 - Hosea 4:6, Isaiah 28:12-13 29:18, Jeremiah 5:4, John 7:15-16, Midrash Psalms 119:56

[2] Isaiah 29:13 - 2 Chronicles 29:1-31, Colossians 2:22, Ezekiel 33:31-33, Gates of Repentance 3.15, Guide for the Perplexed 1:18, Isaiah 10:6 48:1-2 58:2-3, Jeremiah 3:10 5:2 12:2 42:2-4 42:20, Mark 7:2-13, Matthew 15:2-9, Per Massorah: Soferim altered "Hashem" to "Adonai", Proverbs 30:6, Psalms 17:1, Siman 6:1, Tanya Likutei Aramim §39

[3] Isaiah 29:14 - 1 Corinthians 1:19-24 3:19, Acts 28:26-27, b.Shabbat 138b, Ein Yaakov Shabbat:138b, Exodus.R 5:14, Gates of Repentance 3.15, Guide for the Perplexed 2:11, Habakkuk 1:5, Isaiah 6:9-10 19:3 19:11-14 28:21 29:9-10, Jastrow 1181a, Jeremiah 8:7-9 49:7, Job 5:13, John 9:29-34 9:39-41, Lamentations.R 1:37, Luke 10:24, Midrash Proverbs 27, Midrash Tanchuma Vaera 5, Obadiah 1:8, Romans 1:21-22 1:28, Siman 6:1, z.Vaera 30b

[4] Isaiah 29:15 - 1 Corinthians 4:5, 2 Corinthians 4:2, b.Bava Kamma 79b, Ein Yaakov Bava Kamma:79a, Exodus.R 14:2, Ezekiel 8:12 9:9, Gates of Repentance 3.193, Genesis.R 1:6 2:3 24:1, Isaiah 5:18-19 28:15 28:17 30:1 47:10 57:12, Jeremiah 23:24, Job 22:13-14 24:13-17 34:22, John 3:19, Leviticus.R 27:1, Luke 12:1-3, Malachi 2:17, Mekilta de R'Ishmael Nezikin 15:25, Midrash Psalms 14:1, Midrash Tanchuma Bo 2, Midrash Tanchuma Emor 5, Midrash Tanchuma Naso 4, Midrash Tanchuma Noach 4, Numbers.R 1:1 2:10 9:1 9:45, Pesikta de R'Kahana 9.1, Psalms 10:12-14 59:8 64:6-7 73:11 94:7-9 139:1-8, Revelation 2:23, Song of Songs.R 1:3, t.Bava Kamma 7:3, z.Noach 68a, Zephaniah 1:12
Isaiah 29:15-16 - 4Q163 frags 17 ll.1

[5] Isaiah 29:16 - Acts 17:6, Genesis.R 24:1, Isaiah 24:1 45:9-11 64:9, Jastrow 1271b, Jeremiah 18:1-10, Liber Antiquitatum Biblicarum 53:13, Midrash Psalms 14:1, Psalms 94:8-9, Romans 9:19-21

[6] 1QIsaa *He has overturned things from you*

[7] Isaiah 29:17 - 4Q163 21, 4Q163 frag 21 ll.1-2, b.Yoma [Rashi] 9b, Ezekiel 21:2-3, Genesis.R 24:1, Habakkuk 2:3, Haggai 2:6, Hebrews 10:37, Hosea 1:9-1:10 3:4, Isaiah 5:6 32:15 35:1-2 41:19 49:5-6 55:13 63:18 65:12-16, Jastrow 441a, Matthew 19:30 21:18-21:19 21:43, Micah 3:12, Psalms 84:7 107:33 107:35, Romans 11:11-17 11:19-27, Zechariah 11:1-2

[8] Isaiah 29:18 - 1 Peter 2:9, 2 Corinthians 3:14-18 4:2-6, Acts 26:18, Deuteronomy 29:3, Ephesians 1:17-1:19 5:14, Genesis.R 24:1, Isaiah 29:10-29:12 29:24 32:3 35:5 42:16-18, Jeremiah 31:34-35, John 6:45, Luke 4:18 7:22, Mark 7:37, Matthew 11:5 13:14-13:16 16:17, Proverbs 20:12, Psalms 119:18, Revelation 3:18
Isaiah 29:18-23 - 4Q163 frags 18-19 ll.1-6

[9] Isaiah 29:19 - 1 Corinthians 1:26-29, 1 Peter 2:1-3, Ecclesiastes.R 7:5, Ephesians 4:2, Galatians 5:22-23, Habakkuk 3:18, Isaiah 11:4 14:30 14:32 41:16-18 57:15 61:1 61:10 66:2, James 1:9 1:21 2:5 3:13-18, Matthew 5:3 5:5 11:5 11:29, Midrash Psalms 9:12, Midrash Tanchuma Tazria 5, Numbers.R 11:1, Philippians 2:1-3 3:1-3 4:4, Psalms 9:19 12:6 25:9 37:11 149:4, Zephaniah 2:3 3:12-18

כִּי־אָפֵס עָרִיץ וְכָלָה לֵץ וְנִכְרְתוּ כָּל־שֹׁקְדֵי אָוֶן	20[1]	For the terrible one is brought to nothing, And the scorner ceases, And all those who watch for iniquity are cut off;
מַחֲטִיאֵי אָדָם בְּדָבָר וְלַמּוֹכִיחַ בַּשַּׁעַר יְקֹשׁוּן וַיַּטּוּ בַּתֹּהוּ צַדִּיק	21[2]	That make a man an offender by words, And lay a snare for he who reproves in the gate, And turn aside the just with a thing of nothing.
לָכֵן כֹּה־אָמַר יְהֹוָה אֶל־בֵּית יַעֲקֹב אֲשֶׁר פָּדָה אֶת־אַבְרָהָם לֹא־עַתָּה יֵבוֹשׁ יַעֲקֹב וְלֹא עַתָּה פָּנָיו יֶחֱוָרוּ	22[3]	Therefore, thus says the LORD, who redeemed Abraham, concerning the house of Jacob: Jacob shall not now be ashamed, nor shall his face now grow pale;
כִּי בִרְאֹתוֹ יְלָדָיו מַעֲשֵׂה יָדַי בְּקִרְבּוֹ יַקְדִּישׁוּ שְׁמִי וְהִקְדִּישׁוּ אֶת־קְדוֹשׁ יַעֲקֹב וְאֶת־אֱלֹהֵי יִשְׂרָאֵל יַעֲרִיצוּ	23[4]	When he sees his children, the work of My hands, in his midst, so they sanctify My name; Yes, they shall sanctify the Holy One of Jacob, And shall stand in awe of the God of Israel.
וְיָדְעוּ תֹעֵי־רוּחַ בִּינָה וְרוֹגְנִים יִלְמְדוּ־לֶקַח	24[5]	They also who err in spirit shall come to understanding, And they who murmur shall learn instruction.

Isaiah – Chapter 30

הוֹי בָּנִים סוֹרְרִים נְאֻם־יְהֹוָה לַעֲשׂוֹת עֵצָה וְלֹא מִנִּי וְלִנְסֹךְ מַסֵּכָה וְלֹא רוּחִי לְמַעַן סְפוֹת חַטָּאת עַל־חַטָּאת	1[6]	Woe to the rebellious children, says the LORD, who take counsel, but not of Me; And who form projects, but not of My spirit, That they may add sin to sin;
הַהֹלְכִים לָרֶדֶת מִצְרַיִם וּפִי לֹא שָׁאָלוּ לָעוֹז בְּמָעוֹז פַּרְעֹה וְלַחְסוֹת בְּצֵל מִצְרָיִם	2[7]	Who walk to go down into Egypt, And have not asked at My mouth; To take refuge in the stronghold of Pharaoh, And to take shelter in the shadow of Egypt!
וְהָיָה לָכֶם מָעוֹז פַּרְעֹה לְבֹשֶׁת וְהֶחָסוּת בְּצֵל־מִצְרַיִם לִכְלִמָּה	3[8]	Therefore, the stronghold of Pharaoh shall turn to your shame, And the shelter in the shadow of Egypt to your *confusion*[9].
כִּי־הָיוּ בְצֹעַן שָׂרָיו וּמַלְאָכָיו חָנֵס יַגִּיעוּ	4[10]	For his princes are at Zoan, and his emissaries have come to Hanes.

[1] Isaiah 29:20 - Daniel 7:7 7:19-25, Habakkuk 1:6-7, Isaiah 13:3 25:4-5 28:14-22 29:5 49:25 51:13 59:4, Luke 6:7 13:14-17 16:14 20:20-23 23:11 23:35, Mark 2:6-7 3:2-6, Micah 2:1, Revelation 12:10

[2] Isaiah 29:21 - Acts 3:14, Amos 5:10-5:12 7:10-7:17, Ezekiel 13:19, Isaiah 32:7, James 5:6, Jeremiah 18:18 20:7-20:10 26:2-26:8, Judges 12:6, Luke 11:53-11:54, Malachi 3:5, Matthew 22:15 26:15, Micah 2:6-2:7, Proverbs 28:21

[3] Isaiah 29:22 - 1 Peter 1:18-1:19, b.Sanhedrin 19b, Ein Yaakov Sanhedrin:19b, Ezekiel 37:24 37:28 39:25-40:48, Genesis 48:16, Genesis.R 63:2, Isaiah 41:8-41:9 41:14 44:21-44:26 45:17 45:25 46:3-46:4 49:7-49:26 51:2 51:11 54:4 60:1-60:9 61:7-61:11 63:16, Jeremiah 30:5-30:7 30:10 31:11-31:13 33:24-33:26, Joel 2:27, Joshua 24:2-24:5, Leviticus.R 36:4, Luke 1:68, Midrash Psalms 14:1, Midrash Tanchuma Shemot 4, Midrash Tanchuma Toledot 4, mt.Hilchot Yesodei haTorah 5:4, Nehemiah 9:7-9:8, Numbers.R 2:13, Pesikta Rabbati 11:5, Revelation 5:9, Tanya Kuntress Acharon §07, Tanya Likutei Aramim §32 §45, z.Acharei Mot 57a, z.Vaetchanan 269b, z.Vayetze 154b

Isaiah 29:22-23 - Haftarah Shemot Part Two [continued from Isaiah 28:13 Ashkenaz]

[4] Isaiah 29:23 - b.Megillah 16b, Ein Yaakov Megillah:17b, Ephesians 2:10, Hosea 3:5, Isaiah 5:16 8:13 19:25 43:21 45:11 49:20-49:26 60:21, Leviticus 10:3, Matthew 6:9, Midrash Psalms 114:5, Midrash Tanchuma Kedoshim 1, mt.Hilchot Yesodei haTorah 5:4, Numbers.R 2:13, Pesikta Rabbati 11:5, Revelation 11:15-11:17 15:4 19:5, Song of Songs.R 1:22 1:64 4:2, Tanya Igeret Hakodesh §27, y.Berachot 2:4

[5] Isaiah 29:24 - 1 Corinthians 6:11, 1 Timothy 1:13-1:15, Acts 2:37 6:7 9:19-9:20, Ein Yaakov Megillah:17b, Hebrews 5:2, Isaiah 28:7 29:10-29:11 30:21 41:20 60:16, Luke 7:47 15:17-15:19, Matthew 21:28-21:32, Revelation 20:2-20:3, Song of Songs.R 4:2, y.Berachot 2:4, Zechariah 12:10

[6] Isaiah 30:1 - 1 Chronicles 10:13-10:14, 2 Timothy 3:13, Acts 7:51-7:52, Apocalypse of Elijah 1:2, Deuteronomy 9:7 9:24 29:18, Ezekiel 2:3 3:9 3:26-3:27 12:2-12:3, Hosea 4:10-4:12 7:13 13:2, Isaiah 1:2 1:5 4:5 5:18 8:12 8:19 28:15 28:20 29:15 30:9 32:2 63:10 65:2, Jeremiah 4:17 5:23, Numbers 32:14, Psalms 61:5 91:1-91:4, Psalms of Solomon 3:10, Romans 2:5

Isaiah 30:1-5 - 4Q163 frag 21 ll.9-15

Isaiah 30:1-33 - 1QIsaa

[7] Isaiah 30:2 - 1 Kings 22:7, 2 Kings 17:4, b.Eruvin [Rashi] 54b, b.Eruvin 13b, b.Horayot 12a, b.Kereitot 6a, b.Sanhedrin 81b, b.Sotah 49a, b.Succah [Rashi] 45b, Deuteronomy 28:68, Ezekiel 29:6-29:7, Isaiah 16:3 18:1 20:5-20:6 31:1-31:3 36:6 36:9, Jeremiah 21:2 37:5 42:2 42:20 43:7, Joshua 9:14, Judges 9:15, Lamentations 4:20, Numbers 27:21

[8] Isaiah 30:3 - Isaiah 20:5 30:5-30:7 36:6 45:16-45:17, Jeremiah 17:5-17:6 37:5-37:10, Midrash Proverbs 8, Romans 5:5 10:11

[9] 1QIsaa *longing*; LXX *humiliation*

[10] Isaiah 30:4 - 2 Kings 17:4, b.Ketubot 112a, b.Sotah 34b, Ein Yaakov Ketubot:112a, Ezekiel 30:14 30:18, Hosea 7:11-7:12 7:16, Isaiah 19:11 57:9, Jeremiah 43:7, Numbers 13:22, Sifre Devarim {Ekev} 37, Sifre Devarim Ekev 37

כָּל ׳הִבְאִישׁ׳ ׳הֹבִישׁ׳ עַל־עַם לֹא־יוֹעִילוּ לָמוֹ לֹא
לְעֵזֶר וְלֹא לְהוֹעִיל כִּי לְבֹשֶׁת וְגַם־לְחֶרְפָּה

5[1] *They shall all be ashamed*[2] of a people who cannot profit them, who are neither helpful nor profitable, but a shame, and a reproach.

מַשָּׂא בַּהֲמוֹת נֶגֶב בְּאֶרֶץ צָרָה וְצוּקָה לָבִיא וָלַיִשׁ
מֵהֶם אֶפְעֶה וְשָׂרָף מְעוֹפֵף יִשְׂאוּ עַל־כֶּתֶף עֲיָרִים
חֵילֵהֶם וְעַל־דַּבֶּשֶׁת גְּמַלִּים אוֹצְרֹתָם עַל־עַם לֹא
יוֹעִילוּ

6[3] The burden of the beasts of the South. Through the land of trouble[4] and anguish, *From where come*[5] the lioness and the lion, the viper and flying serpent; they carry their riches upon the shoulders of young donkeys and their treasures on the humps of camels, to a people who shall not profit them.

וּמִצְרַיִם הֶבֶל וָרִיק יַעְזֹרוּ לָכֵן קָרָאתִי לָזֹאת רַהַב
הֵם שָׁבֶת

7[6] For Egypt helps in vain, and to no purpose; Therefore, have I called her arrogance who sits still.

עַתָּה בּוֹא כָתְבָהּ עַל־לוּחַ אִתָּם וְעַל־סֵפֶר חֻקָּהּ
וּתְהִי לְיוֹם אַחֲרוֹן לָעַד עַד־עוֹלָם

8[7] Now go, write it before them on a tablet, and inscribe it in a book so it may be for the time to come forever and ever.

כִּי עַם מְרִי הוּא בָּנִים כֶּחָשִׁים בָּנִים לֹא־אָבוּ
שְׁמוֹעַ תּוֹרַת יְהוָה

9[8] For it is a rebellious people, lying children, Children who refuse to hear the teaching of the LORD;

אֲשֶׁר אָמְרוּ לָרֹאִים לֹא תִרְאוּ וְלַחֹזִים לֹא תֶחֱזוּ־
לָנוּ נְכֹחוֹת דַּבְּרוּ־לָנוּ חֲלָקוֹת חֲזוּ מַהֲתַלּוֹת

10[9] Who say to the seers: 'Do not see,' And to the prophets: 'Do not prophesy right things to us, Speak smooth things, prophetic delusions to us;

סוּרוּ מִנֵּי־דֶרֶךְ הַטּוּ מִנִּי־אֹרַח הַשְׁבִּיתוּ מִפָּנֵינוּ
אֶת־קְדוֹשׁ יִשְׂרָאֵל

11[10] Get out of the way, Turn aside from the path, Cause the Holy One of Israel to cease from before us.'

לָכֵן כֹּה אָמַר קְדוֹשׁ יִשְׂרָאֵל יַעַן מָאָסְכֶם בַּדָּבָר
הַזֶּה וַתִּבְטְחוּ בְּעֹשֶׁק וְנָלוֹז וַתִּשָּׁעֲנוּ עָלָיו

12[11] When thus says the Holy One of Israel: Because you despise this word, And trust in oppression and *perverseness*[12], And stay there;

לָכֵן יִהְיֶה לָכֶם הֶעָוֹן הַזֶּה כְּפֶרֶץ נֹפֵל נִבְעֶה בְּחוֹמָה
נִשְׂגָּבָה אֲשֶׁר־פִּתְאֹם לְפֶתַע יָבוֹא שִׁבְרָהּ

13[13] Therefore, this iniquity shall be to you as a breach ready to fall, swelling out in a high wall, *Whose breaking comes suddenly, instantly*[14].

---

[1] Isaiah 30:5 - Isaiah 20:5-20:6 30:7 30:16 31:1-31:3, Jeremiah 2:36, Saadia Opinions 5:5

[2] 1QIsaa *Destruction is odius*

[3] Isaiah 30:6 - 1 Kings 10:2, 2 Chronicles 9:1 16:2 28:20-28:23, Avot de R'Natan 39, b.Sanhedrin [Tosefot] 15b, b.Sanhedrin 90a, Deuteronomy 4:20 8:15 17:16, Exodus 1:14 5:10-5:21, Hosea 8:9-8:10 12:3, Isaiah 8:22 15:7 19:4 46:1-46:2 57:9, Jastrow 1079b, Jeremiah 2:6 11:4, Matthew 12:42, Mekhilta de R'Shimon bar Yochai Vayassa 37:1, Mekilta de R'Ishmael Vayassa 1:51, Midrash Proverbs 20, Midrash Tanchuma Beshallach 18, Numbers 21:6-21:7

[4] 1QIsaa adds *and dryness*

[5] 1QIsaa *where there is no water*

[6] Isaiah 30:7 - 4 Ezra 6:50, Birchat HaChammah.Alenu, Exodus 14:13, Hosea 5:13, Isaiah 2:22 7:4 28:12 30:15 31:1-31:5 51:9, Jeremiah 37:7, Lamentations 3:26, Midrash Psalms 90:15, Psalms 76:9-76:10 118:8-118:9

[7] Isaiah 30:8 - 1 Timothy 4:1, 2 Peter 3:3, Deuteronomy 4:30 31:19 31:22 31:29, Ezekiel 38:16, Habakkuk 2:2, Hosea 3:5, Isaiah 2:2 8:1, Jeremiah 23:20 36:2 36:28-36:32 48:47 51:60, Job 19:23-19:25, Jude 1:18, Numbers 24:14
Isaiah 30:8-17 - 4QIsac

[8] Isaiah 30:9 - 2 Chronicles 33:10 36:15-36:16, Acts 7:51, Deuteronomy 31:27-31:29 32:20, Hosea 4:2, Isaiah 1:4 1:10 28:15 30:1 59:3-59:4 63:8, Jeremiah 7:13 9:4 44:2-44:17, Matthew 23:31-23:33, Midrash Tanchuma Yitro 4, Nehemiah 9:29-9:30, Proverbs 28:9, Revelation 21:8 22:15, Romans 2:21-2:23, Zechariah 1:4-6 7:11-7:12, Zephaniah 3:2

[9] Isaiah 30:10 - 1 Kings 21:20 22:8-13 22:27, 1 Thessalonians 2:15-16, 2 Chronicles 16:10 18:7-27 24:19-21 25:16, Acts 4:17 5:28, Amos 2:12 7:13, Ezekiel 13:7-10 13:18-22, Galatians 4:16, Jeremiah 5:31 6:13-14 8:10-11 11:21 23:17 23:26-29 26:11 26:20-23 29:27 38:4, John 7:7 8:45, Micah 2:6 2:11, mt.Hilchot Deot 2:6, Pesikta de R'Kahana S5.3, Revelation 11:7, Romans 16:18
Isaiah 30:10-14 - 1QIsab

[10] Isaiah 30:11 - Amos 7:13, Ephesians 4:18, Isaiah 29:21, Job 21:14, John 15:23-15:24, Romans 1:28 1:30 8:7

[11] Isaiah 30:12 - 1 Thessalonians 4:8, 2 Samuel 12:9-12:10, Amos 2:4, Isaiah 5:7 5:24 28:15 30:1 30:7 30:15-30:17 31:1-31:3 47:10, Jeremiah 13:25, Luke 10:16, Psalms 52:8 62:11

[12] 1QIsaa *you rejoice*

[13] Isaiah 30:13 - 1 Kings 20:30, 1 Thessalonians 5:1-5:3, Ezekiel 13:10-13:15, Isaiah 29:5, Job 36:18, Luke 6:49, Matthew 7:27, Proverbs 29:1, Psalms 62:4 73:19-73:20

[14] 1QIsab *whose crash comes suddenly, in an instant*

וְשִׁבְרָהּ כְּשֵׁבֶר נֵבֶל יוֹצְרִים כָּתוּת לֹא יַחְמֹל וְלֹא־יִמָּצֵא בִמְכִתָּתוֹ חֶרֶשׂ לַחְתּוֹת אֵשׁ מִיָּקוּד וְלַחְשֹׂף מַיִם מִגֶּבֶא	14[1]	And He shall break it as a potter's vessel is broken, Breaking it in pieces *without sparing*[2]; So there shall not be found among its pieces a sherd To take fire from the hearth, Or to take water out of the cistern.
כִּי כֹה־אָמַר אֲדֹנָי יְהוִה קְדוֹשׁ יִשְׂרָאֵל בְּשׁוּבָה וָנַחַת תִּוָּשֵׁעוּן בְּהַשְׁקֵט וּבְבִטְחָה תִּהְיֶה גְּבוּרַתְכֶם וְלֹא אֲבִיתֶם	15[3]	For thus said *the Lord GOD*[4], the Holy One of Israel: In sitting still and rest you shall be saved, In quietness and in confidence shall be your strength; And you would not.
וַתֹּאמְרוּ לֹא־כִי עַל־סוּס נָנוּס עַל־כֵּן תְּנוּסוּן וְעַל־קַל נִרְכָּב עַל־כֵּן יִקַּלּוּ רֹדְפֵיכֶם	16[5]	But you said: 'No, for we will flee on horses'; Therefore, you shall flee; And: 'We will ride on the swift'; Therefore, they who pursue you shall be swift.
אֶלֶף אֶחָד מִפְּנֵי גַּעֲרַת אֶחָד מִפְּנֵי גַּעֲרַת חֲמִשָּׁה תָּנֻסוּ עַד אִם־נוֹתַרְתֶּם כַּתֹּרֶן עַל־רֹאשׁ הָהָר וְכַנֵּס עַל־הַגִּבְעָה	17[6]	One thousand shall flee *at the rebuke of*[7] one, At the rebuke of five you shall flee; until you are left as a beacon on the top of a mountain, And as an ensign on a hill.
וְלָכֵן יְחַכֶּה יְהוָה לַחֲנַנְכֶם וְלָכֵן יָרוּם לְרַחֶמְכֶם כִּי־אֱלֹהֵי מִשְׁפָּט יְהוָה אַשְׁרֵי כָּל־חוֹכֵי לוֹ	18[8]	And, therefore, the LORD will wait, so He may be gracious to you, And, therefore, He will be exalted, so He may have compassion on you for the LORD is a God of justice, Happy are all those who wait for Him.
כִּי־עַם בְּצִיּוֹן יֵשֵׁב בִּירוּשָׁלִָם בָּכוֹ לֹא־תִבְכֶּה חָנוֹן יָחְנְךָ לְקוֹל זַעֲקֶךָ כְּשָׁמְעָתוֹ עָנָךְ	19[9]	O people who live in Zion *at Jerusalem*[10], You shall weep no more; He will surely be gracious to you at the voice of your cry, When He shall hear, He will answer you.

---

[1] Isaiah 30:14 - 2 Peter 2:4-2:5, Deuteronomy 29:19, Esther.R 7:10, Ezekiel 5:11 7:4 7:9 8:18 9:10 15:3-15:8 24:14, Isaiah 27:11 47:14, Jeremiah 13:14 19:10-19:11 48:38, Job 27:22, Luke 4:2, m.Shabbat 8:7, Midrash Tanchuma Terumah 7, Psalms 2:9 31:13, Revelation 2:27, Romans 8:32 11:21, y.Shabbat 8:7

[2] 1QIsaa *he does not take pity*

[3] Isaiah 30:15 - 1 Chronicles 5:20, 2 Chronicles 16:8 32:8, b.Sanhedrin 97b, Ecclesiastes.R 4:5, Ein Yaakov Sanhedrin:97b, Exodus.R 16:2, Hebrews 12:25, Hosea 14:3-14:5, Isaiah 7:4 26:3-26:4 30:7 30:11 32:17, Jastrow 904a, Jeremiah 3:22-3:23 23:36 44:16-44:17, John 5:40, Leviticus.R 3:1, Luke 13:34, Matthew 22:3 23:37, Midrash Tanchuma Bechukkotai 3, mt.Hilchot Deot 2:5 2:5, Numbers.R 7:10, Psalms 80:12-80:14 125:1-125:2, y.Taanit 1:1, z.Vaetchanan 269b
Isaiah 30:15-18 - 4Q163 23 ii, 4Q163 frag 232.3-9

[4] 1QIsaa *the LORD*

[5] Isaiah 30:16 - 2 Kings 25:5, Amos 2:14-16 9:1, Deuteronomy 28:25 28:49, Habakkuk 1:8, Isaiah 5:26-30 10:28-32 31:1 31:3, Jeremiah 4:13 52:7, Lamentations 4:19, Micah 1:13, Psalms 33:17 147:10

[6] Isaiah 30:17 - Deuteronomy 28:25 32:30, Isaiah 1:7-1:8 6:13 27:11 37:3-37:4, Jastrow 1658a, Jeremiah 37:10, John 15:2-15:6, Joshua 23:10, Leviticus 26:8 26:36, Matthew 24:21-24:22, Nehemiah 1:2-1:3, Proverbs 28:1, Romans 11:17, Sibylline Oracles 3.533, Sifre Devarim Ekev 47, Zechariah 13:8-13:9, Zephaniah 3:12

[7] 1QIsaa *before*

[8] Isaiah 30:18 - 1 Samuel 2:3, 2 Peter 3:9 3:15, Acts 2:33-2:39 5:31, b.Succah 45b, Deuteronomy 32:4, Ein Yaakov Sanhedrin:97b, Ein Yaakov Sukkah:45b, Ephesians 1:6 1:8 1:20-1:23, Exodus 34:6, Hosea 2:14 5:15-6:2 11:8-11:9, Isaiah 5:16 8:17 18:4 25:9 26:7-26:8 33:5 33:10-33:12 40:31 42:1-42:4 42:14 55:8 57:17-57:18, James 5:11, Jastrow 461b[~, Jeremiah 10:24-10:25 17:7 31:19-31:21, Job 35:14, Jonah 3:4-3:10, Lamentations 3:25-3:26, Luke 2:25 15:20 24:26-24:27, Malachi 2:17, Matthew 15:22-15:28, Mekhilta de R'Shimon bar Yochai Shirata 27:1, Micah 7:7-7:9 7:18-7:20, Midrash Psalms 17:10 72:3, Numbers.R 11:1, Pesikta de R'Kahana S1.3, Pesikta Rabbati 31:9 34:2, Proverbs 16:20, Psalms 2:12 27:14 28:6-28:7 34:9 40:2-40:4 46:11-46:12 62:2-62:3 62:6-62:9 76:6-76:11 84:13 99:4, Romans 2:2-2:10 5:20 8:25-8:28 9:15-9:18 9:22
Isaiah 30:18-19 - Midrash Proverbs 23

[9] Isaiah 30:19 - 1 John 5:14-15, Ein Yaakov Sotah:49a, Ephesians 3:20, Ezekiel 20:40 36:37 37:25-28, Guide for the Perplexed 2:29, Isaiah 10:24 12:3-6 25:8 35:10 40:1-2 46:13 54:6-14 58:9 60:20 61:1-3 65:9 65:18 65:24, Jeremiah 29:11-13 30:12 31:7 31:10 31:13 33:3 50:4-5 50:28 51:10, Lamentations.R 1:23, Luke 6:21, Matthew 7:7-11, Micah 4:9, Midrash Psalms 116:1, Midrash Tanchuma Mishpatim 16, Midrash Tanchuma Vaetchanan 4, Numbers.R 11:1 11:6, Pesikta de R'Kahana S6.1, Pesikta Rabbati 29/30B:4 34:2, Psalms 50:15, Revelation 5:4 7:17, Romans 11:26, Zechariah 1:16-17 2:4-7 8:3-8, Zephaniah 3:14-20
Isaiah 30:19-21 - 4Q163 frag 232.15-19

[10] 1QIsaa *and in Jerusalem*

וְנָתַן לָכֶם אֲדֹנָי לֶחֶם צָר וּמַיִם לָחַץ וְלֹא־יִכָּנֵף
עוֹד מוֹרֶיךָ וְהָיוּ עֵינֶיךָ רֹאוֹת אֶת־מוֹרֶיךָ

20[1] And though the Lord gave you sparing bread and *scant water*[2], Yet your Teacher shall not hide Himself any longer, But your eyes shall see your Teacher;

וְאָזְנֶיךָ תִּשְׁמַעְנָה דָבָר מֵאַחֲרֶיךָ לֵאמֹר זֶה הַדֶּרֶךְ
לְכוּ בוֹ כִּי תַאֲמִינוּ וְכִי תַשְׂמְאִילוּ

21[3] And your ears shall hear a word behind you, saying: 'This is the way, walk in it, when you turn to the right hand, and when you turn to the left.'

וְטִמֵּאתֶם אֶת־צִפּוּי פְּסִילֵי כַסְפֶּךָ וְאֶת־אֲפֻדַּת
מַסֵּכַת זְהָבֶךָ תִּזְרֵם כְּמוֹ דָוָה צֵא תֹּאמַר לוֹ

22[4] And you shall defile your graven images overlaid with silver, And your molten images covered with gold; You shall put them far away as one unclean; You shall say to it: 'Get away.'

וְנָתַן מְטַר זַרְעֲךָ אֲשֶׁר־תִּזְרַע אֶת־הָאֲדָמָה וְלֶחֶם
תְּבוּאַת הָאֲדָמָה וְהָיָה דָשֵׁן וְשָׁמֵן יִרְעֶה מִקְנֶיךָ
בַּיּוֹם הַהוּא כַּר נִרְחָב

23[5] And He will give the rain for your seed, with which you sow the ground, And bread from the increase of the ground, and it shall be fat and plentiful; In that day your cattle shall feed in large pastures.

וְהָאֲלָפִים וְהָעֲיָרִים עֹבְדֵי הָאֲדָמָה בְּלִיל חָמִיץ
יֹאכֵלוּ אֲשֶׁר־זֹרֶה בָרַחַת וּבַמִּזְרֶה

24[6] The oxen and the young donkeys that till the ground shall eat *savory food*[7], which has been winnowed with the shovel and with the fan.

וְהָיָה עַל־כָּל־הַר גָּבֹהַּ וְעַל כָּל־גִּבְעָה נִשָּׂאָה
פְּלָגִים יִבְלֵי־מָיִם בְּיוֹם הֶרֶג רָב בִּנְפֹל מִגְדָּלִים

25[8] And there shall be streams and *watercourses*[9] on every lofty mountain, and on every high hill, in the day of the great slaughter, when the towers fall.

וְהָיָה אוֹר־הַלְּבָנָה כְּאוֹר הַחַמָּה וְאוֹר הַחַמָּה יִהְיֶה
שִׁבְעָתַיִם כְּאוֹר שִׁבְעַת הַיָּמִים בְּיוֹם חֲבֹשׁ יְהוָה
אֶת־שֶׁבֶר עַמּוֹ וּמַחַץ מַכָּתוֹ יִרְפָּא

26[10] Moreover the light of the moon shall be as the light of the sun, And the light of the sun shall be sevenfold, *as the light of the seven days*[11], In

---

[1] Isaiah 30:20 - 1 Kings 22:27, 2 Chronicles 18:26, Acts 14:22, Amos 8:11-8:12, Deuteronomy 16:3, Ein Yaakov Eruvin:13b, Ein Yaakov Keritot:6a, Ephesians 4:11, Exodus.R 21:3 38:3, Ezekiel 4:13-4:17 24:22-24:23, Guide for the Perplexed 1:43, Jastrow 651a, Joseph and Aseneth 8:5, m.Sanhedrin 9:5, Matthew 9:38, Midrash Tanchuma Balak 14, Midrash Tanchuma Ki Tetze 11, mt.Hilchot Talmud Torah 4:2, mt.Hilchot Talmud Torah 4:2, Numbers.R 20:20, Per Massorah: Soferim altered "Hashem" to "Adonai", Pesikta de R'Kahana 3.16, Pesikta Rabbati 12:9, Psalms 30:6 74:9 80:6 102:10 127:2, Sifre Devarim {Ha'azinu Hashamayim} 310, Sifre Devarim Nitzavim 310, t.Sanhedrin 12:7, Tanya Likutei Aramim §36, y.Sanhedrin 9:6
Isaiah 30:20-21 - 4Q163 22 1-3, 4QI63 frag 22 l.1
[2] 1QIsaa *the water of affliction*
[3] Isaiah 30:21 - 1 John 2:20 2:27, 2 Kings 22:2, b.Megillah 32a, b.Shabbat 153a, Deuteronomy 5:32, Ein Yaakov Megillah:32a, Ein Yaakov Shabbat:153a, Isaiah 29:24 35:8-35:9 42:16 48:17 58:11, Jeremiah 6:16, Joshua 1:7 23:6, Lamentations.R 1:57, Mas.Derek Eretz Zutta 4:8, Pesikta de R'Kahana 16.11, Proverbs 3:5-3:6 4:27, Psalms 25:8-25:9 32:8 143:8-143:10, Sifre Devarim {Ha'azinu Hashamayim} 310, Sifre Devarim Nitzavim 310, y.Shabbat 6:9
Isaiah 30:21-26 - 1QIsab
[4] Isaiah 30:22 - 2 Chronicles 31:1 34:3-34:7, 2 Kings 23:4-23:20, b.Avodah Zara 47b, b.Chullin 128a, b.Shabbat 82b, Ein Yaakov Shabbat:82a, Exodus 32:2-32:4, Ezekiel 18:6 36:31, Hosea 14:10, Isaiah 2:20-2:21 17:7-17:8 27:9 31:7 46:6, Jastrow 912a, Joseph and Aseneth 10:12, Judges 17:3-17:4, Lamentations 1:17, m.Avodah Zarah 3:6, m.Shabbat 9:1, Micah 5:11-5:15, Midrash Tanchuma Ki Tetze 3, mt.Hilchot Issurei Mizbeiach 4:4, mt.Hilchot Shaar Avot Hatuman 6:3, Pesikta de R'Kahana 132, Revelation 19:20, t.Avodah Zarah 5:6, y.Avodah Zarah 3:6, y.Shabbat 9:1, Zechariah 13:2
[5] Isaiah 30:23 - 1 Timothy 4:8, 4Q163 frag 22 l.4, 4QIsar, Amos 4:7-8, b.Menachot 87a, Ezekiel 36:25-26, Genesis 41:18 41:26 41:47, Genesis.R 75:8 89:4, Hosea 2:21-25 4:16, Isaiah 4:2 5:6 32:20 44:2-4 55:10-11 58:11, Jastrow 16a 636b, Jeremiah 14:22, Joel 2:21-26, Malachi 3:10 3:20, Matthew 6:33, Psalms 36:9 65:10-14 104:13-14 107:35-38 144:12-14, Zechariah 8:11-12 10:1
[6] Isaiah 30:24 - 1 Corinthians 9:9-10, 1 Samuel 8:12, b.Avodah Zara [Tosefot] 15b, b.Niddah [Rashi] 31a, b.Succah [Tosefot] 14a, Deuteronomy 21:4 25:4, Exodus 34:21, Genesis 45:6, Luke 3:17, Matthew 3:12, Midrash Tanchuma Mishpatim 17, y.Maasrot 1:4
[7] 1QIsaa *leavened*
[8] Isaiah 30:25 - 2 Corinthians 10:4, b.Bechorot [Tosefot] 56a, Ezekiel 17:22 34:13 34:26 39:17-39:20, Isaiah 2:14-2:15 32:14 34:2-34:10 35:6-35:7 37:36 41:18-41:19 43:19-43:20 44:3-44:4 63:1-63:6, John 7:38, Midrash Psalms 111:1, Nahum 3:12, Numbers.R 14:2, Revelation 16:1-16:19 22:1, Sibylline Oracles 3.682
[9] 1QIsaa *canals of water*
[10] Isaiah 30:26 - 2 Enoch 11:1 66:8 3 Enoch 26:5, Amos 9:11, b.Bava Batra 8b, b.Pesachim 68a, b.Sanhedrin 91b, Bahir 55 57, Birchat HaChammah.Vihi Ratzon, Deuteronomy 32:39, Ecclesiastes.R 11:6, Ein Yaakov Pesachim:68a, Ein Yaakov Pesachim 68a, Ein Yaakov Sanhedrin:91b, Exodus.R 15:21 18:11, Genesis.R 3:6 10:4 12:6, Guide for the Perplexed 2:29, Hebrews 6:1-2, Hosea 6:1, Isaiah 1:5-6 11:9 24:23 60:19-20, Jeremiah 33:5-6, Job 5:18, Lamentations 2:13, Midrash Psalms 111:1 147:3, Midrash Tanchuma Bereshit 6, Midrash Tanchuma Pinchas 14, Midrash Tanchuma Vayakhel 10, Numbers.R 13:12 21:22, Pesikta de R'Kahana S6.2, Pesikta Rabbati 2:6 42:4, Pirkei de R'Eliezer 51, Revelation 21:23 22:5, Saadia Opinions 7Variant:5, z.Bereshit 34a, z.Chayyei Sarah 131a, z.Noach 70b, z.Pekudei 232a, z.Terumah 172b, z.Vayeshev 181b, Zechariah 12:8 14:7
[11] Missing in LXX

the day the LORD binds up the bruise of His people, And heals the stroke of their wound.

27[1] הִנֵּה שֵׁם־יְהוָה בָּא מִמֶּרְחָק בֹּעֵר אַפּוֹ וְכֹבֶד מַשָּׂאָה שְׂפָתָיו מָלְאוּ זַעַם וּלְשׁוֹנוֹ כְּאֵשׁ אֹכָלֶת

Behold, the name of the LORD comes from far, With His anger burning, and in thick uplifting of smoke; His lips are full of indignation, And His tongue is like a devouring fire;

28[2] וְרוּחוֹ כְּנַחַל שׁוֹטֵף עַד־צַוָּאר יֶחֱצֶה לַהֲנָפָה גוֹיִם בְּנָפַת שָׁוְא וְרֶסֶן מַתְעֶה עַל לְחָיֵי עַמִּים

And His breath is like an overflowing stream, that divides to the neck, To *sift*[3] the nations with the sieve of destruction; And a bridle that causes err shall be in the jaws of the peoples.

29[4] הַשִּׁיר יִהְיֶה לָכֶם כְּלֵיל הִתְקַדֶּשׁ־חָג וְשִׂמְחַת לֵבָב כַּהוֹלֵךְ בֶּחָלִיל לָבוֹא בְהַר־יְהוָה אֶל־צוּר יִשְׂרָאֵל

You shall have a song As in the night when a holiday is hallowed; And gladness of heart, as when one goes with the pipe To come into the mountain of the LORD, to the Rock of Israel.

30[5] וְהִשְׁמִיעַ יְהוָה אֶת־הוֹד קוֹלוֹ וְנַחַת זְרוֹעוֹ יַרְאֶה בְּזַעַף אַף וְלַהַב אֵשׁ אוֹכֵלָה נֶפֶץ וָזֶרֶם וְאֶבֶן בָּרָד

And the LORD will cause His glorious voice to *be heard*[6], And will show the lighting down of His arm, With furious anger, and the flame of a devouring fire, With a bursting of clouds, and a storm of rain, and hailstones.

31[7] כִּי־מִקּוֹל יְהוָה יֵחַת אַשּׁוּר בַּשֵּׁבֶט יַכֶּה

For through the voice of the LORD shall Asshur be dismayed, The rod with which He struck.

32[8] וְהָיָה כֹּל מַעֲבַר מַטֵּה מוּסָדָה אֲשֶׁר יָנִיחַ יְהוָה עָלָיו בְּתֻפִּים וּבְכִנֹּרוֹת וּבְמִלְחֲמוֹת תְּנוּפָה 'נִלְחַם־בָּה' "נִלְחַם־בָּם"

And in every place where the appointed staff shall pass, which the LORD shall lay on him, it shall be with tabrets and harps; And in battles of wielding will He fight with *them*[9].

33[10] כִּי־עָרוּךְ מֵאֶתְמוּל תָּפְתֶּה 'גַּם־הֵוא' "גַּם־הִיא" לַמֶּלֶךְ הוּכָן הֶעֱמִיק הִרְחִב מְדֻרָתָהּ אֵשׁ וְעֵצִים הַרְבֵּה נִשְׁמַת יְהוָה כְּנַחַל גָּפְרִית בֹּעֲרָה בָּהּ

For *a hearth*[11] is ordered of old; Yes, for the king it is prepared, Deep and large; its pile is fire and much wood; The breath of the LORD, like a stream of brimstone, kindles it.

---

[1] Isaiah 30:27 - 2 Thessalonians 2:8, Daniel 7:9, Deuteronomy 32:22 33:2, Guide for the Perplexed 1:46, Hebrews 12:29, Isaiah 9:6 10:5 10:16-10:17 33:12 34:9 59:19 66:14, Lamentations 1:12-1:13, Nahum 1:5-1:6, Psalms 18:8-18:10 79:5, Zephaniah 3:8

[2] Isaiah 30:28 - 1 Kings 22:20-22:22, 2 Kings 19:28, 2 Samuel 17:14, 2 Thessalonians 2:8 2:11, Amos 9:9, Ezekiel 14:7-14:9, Habakkuk 3:12-3:15, Hebrews 4:12, Hosea 13:3, Isaiah 8:8 11:4 19:3 19:12-14 28:17-18 29:6 33:10-12 37:29, Jastrow 889a, Job 39:17, Luke 22:31, Matthew 3:12, Pesikta Rabbati 41:2, Proverbs 26:3, Psalms 18:16 32:9, Revelation 1:16 2:16

[3] 1QIsaa *winnow*

[4] Isaiah 30:29 - 12, 1 Chronicles 13:7-13:8, 2 Chronicles 20:27-20:28, b.Arachin 10b, b.Pesachim 95b, Deuteronomy 16:6 16:14 32:4 32:31, Ein Yaakov Arachin:10b, Exodus 15:1-15:21, Genesis.R 6:2, Isaiah 2:3 12:1 26:1 26:4, Jeremiah 19:1-19:7 33:11, Leviticus 23:32, Matthew 26:30, Mekhilta de R'Shimon bar Yochai Shirata 27:1 28:1, Mekhilta de R'Ishmael Shirata 1:17, Mekhilta de R'Ishmael Shirata 2:3, Midrash Psalms 1:20 18:1 113:1 113:2, Midrash Tanchuma Beshallach 10 12, mt.Hilchot Korban Pesach 10:15, mt.Hilchot Megillah v'Chanukah 3:6, Psalms 18:32 32:7 42:5 81:2-81:5 95:1-95:2 150:3-150:5, Revelation 15:3, Song of Songs.R 2:1, y.Pesachim 9:3, y.Sukkah 5:1, z.Emor 96a

[5] Isaiah 30:30 - 1 Enoch 14:11, 1 Samuel 7:10, 2 Thessalonians 1:8, Exodus 15:16, Ezekiel 10:5 38:19-22, Isaiah 28:2 29:6 32:19 51:9 62:8, Job 37:2-5 40:9, Joshua 10:11, Luke 1:51, Matthew 24:7, Micah 1:4, Nahum 1:2-6, Psalms 2:5 18:14-15 29:3-9 46:7 50:1-3 76:6-9 97:3-5 98:1, Revelation 1:15 6:12-17 11:19 14:16-20 16:18-21, Sibylline Oracles 3.690

Isaiah 30:30-32 - 4Q163 frag 25 l.1

[6] 1QIsaa *make heard make heard*

[7] Isaiah 30:31 - Isaiah 9:5 10:5 10:12 10:15 10:24 11:4 30:30 37:32-38, Micah 5:6-5:7, Psalms 17:13-14 125:5

[8] Isaiah 30:32 - 1 Samuel 10:5, Ezekiel 32:10, Genesis 31:27, Hebrews 12:26, Isaiah 2:19 11:15 19:16 24:8 30:29, Jastrow 1256b 1265a 1680b, Job 16:12 21:11-12, Leviticus.R 28:6, Pesikta de R'Kahana 8.4, Pesikta Rabbati 18:4/5, Psalms 81:2-3

[9] 1QIsaa *her*

[10] Isaiah 30:33 - 1 Peter 1:8, 2 Kings 23:10, b.Eruvin 19a, b.Menachot [Rashi] 99b, b.Menachot 1a, b.Nedarim 39b, b.Pesachim 54a, Chibbur Yafeh 27 {119b}, Ein Yaakov Eruvin, Ein Yaakov Nedarim:39b, Ezekiel 32:22-23, Genesis 19:24, Genesis.R 4:6, Hebrews 13:8, Isaiah 14:9-20 30:27-28 37:38, Jastrow 1090a 1115a 1117a 1252b, Jeremiah 7:31-32 19:6 19:11-14, Jude 1:4, Leviticus.R 31:10, Matthew 4:22 18:8-9 25:41, Mekhilta de R'Shimon bar Yochai Beshallach 24:4, Mekhilta de R'Ishmael Beshallah 5:101, Midrash Tanchuma Bechukkotai 6, Midrash Tanchuma Chayyei Sarah 3, Midrash Tanchuma Naso 11, mt.Hilchot Teshuvah 8:5, Pesikta Rabbati 41:3, Psalms 40:6-7, Revelation 14:10-11 19:18-20, Saadia Opinions 9:5 9:8

[11] 1QIsaa *an opening place*; MT *its burning place*

Isaiah – Chapter 31[1]

הוֹי הַיֹּרְדִים מִצְרַיִם לְעֶזְרָה עַל־סוּסִים יִשָּׁעֵנוּ וַיִּבְטְחוּ עַל־רֶכֶב כִּי רָב וְעַל פָּרָשִׁים כִּי־עָצְמוּ מְאֹד וְלֹא שָׁעוּ עַל־קְדוֹשׁ יִשְׂרָאֵל וְאֶת־יְהוָה לֹא דָרָשׁוּ	1[2]	Woe to those who go down to Egypt for help, and rely on horses, and trust in chariots, because they are many, And in horsemen, because they are exceeding mighty; But they do not look to the Holy One of Israel, nor seek the LORD!
וְגַם־הוּא חָכָם וַיָּבֵא רָע וְאֶת־דְּבָרָיו לֹא הֵסִיר וְקָם עַל־בֵּית מְרֵעִים וְעַל־עֶזְרַת פֹּעֲלֵי אָוֶן	2[3]	Yet He also is wise, And brings evil, And does not call back His words; But will arise against the house of the evil doers, And against the help of those who work iniquity.
וּמִצְרַיִם אָדָם וְלֹא־אֵל וְסוּסֵיהֶם בָּשָׂר וְלֹא־רוּחַ וַיהֹוָה יַטֶּה יָדוֹ וְכָשַׁל עוֹזֵר וְנָפַל עָזֻר וְיַחְדָּו כֻּלָּם יִכְלָיוּן	3[4]	Now the Egyptians are men, and not God, And their horses flesh, and not spirit; So when the LORD shall stretch out His hand, Both he who helps shall stumble, and he who is helped shall fall, And they all shall perish together.
כִּי כֹה אָמַר־יְהוָה אֵלַי כַּאֲשֶׁר יֶהְגֶּה הָאַרְיֵה וְהַכְּפִיר עַל־טַרְפּוֹ אֲשֶׁר יִקָּרֵא עָלָיו מְלֹא רֹעִים מִקּוֹלָם לֹא יֵחָת וּמֵהֲמוֹנָם לֹא יַעֲנֶה כֵּן יֵרֵד יְהוָה צְבָאוֹת לִצְבֹּא עַל־הַר־צִיּוֹן וְעַל־גִּבְעָתָהּ	4[5]	For the LORD says to me: Like as the lion, or the young lion, growling over his *prey*[6], *Though a multitude of shepherds are called forth against him, he will not be dismayed at their voice, nor abase himself for their noise*[7]; So the LORD of hosts will come down To fight on mount Zion, and on its hill.
כְּצִפֳּרִים עָפוֹת כֵּן יָגֵן יְהוָה צְבָאוֹת עַל־יְרוּשָׁלָ͏ִם גָּנוֹן וְהִצִּיל פָּסֹחַ וְהִמְלִיט	5[8]	As birds hovering, So will the LORD of hosts protect Jerusalem; He will deliver it as He protects it, *He will rescue it as He passes over*[9].
שׁוּבוּ לַאֲשֶׁר הֶעְמִיקוּ סָרָה בְּנֵי יִשְׂרָאֵל	6[10]	Turn to Him *against whom*[11] you have deeply rebelled, O children of Israel.
כִּי בַּיּוֹם הַהוּא יִמְאָסוּן אִישׁ אֱלִילֵי כַסְפּוֹ וֶאֱלִילֵי זְהָבוֹ אֲשֶׁר עָשׂוּ לָכֶם יְדֵיכֶם חֵטְא	7[12]	For in that day every man shall cast away his idols of silver, and his idols of gold, which your own hands have made *for you for a sin*[13].
וְנָפַל אַשּׁוּר בְּחֶרֶב לֹא־אִישׁ וְחֶרֶב לֹא־אָדָם תֹּאכְלֶנּוּ וְנָס לוֹ מִפְּנֵי־חֶרֶב וּבַחוּרָיו לָמַס יִהְיוּ	8[14]	Then Asshur shall fall *with the sword, not of man, And the sword, not of men, shall devour*

[1] Isaiah 31 - Ein Yaakov Pesachim:54a, Testament of Solomon 7:7

[2] Isaiah 31:1 - 2 Chronicles 16:7, 4Q163 frag 25 ll.5-7, Amos 5:4-5:8, Daniel 9:13, Deuteronomy 17:16, Esther.R Petichata:3, Ezekiel 17:15, Hosea 7:7 7:13-7:16 11:5 14:5, Isaiah 2:7 5:12 9:14 17:7-17:8 22:11 30:1-30:7 30:16 36:6 36:9 57:9 64:8, Jeremiah 2:13 17:5, Mekilta de R'Ishmael Beshallah 3:125, Psalms 20:8 33:16-33:17, y.Sukkah 5:1
Isaiah 31:1-9 - 1QIsaa

[3] Isaiah 31:2 - 1 Corinthians 1:21-1:29, 1 Samuel 2:3, Amos 3:6, Ezekiel 29:6, Guide for the Perplexed 1:12, Isaiah 20:4-20:6 22:14 28:21 30:3 30:13-30:14 31:3 32:6 45:7 63:4-63:5, Jeremiah 10:7 10:12 36:32 44:29-44:30, Job 5:13, Joshua 23:15, Jude 1:25, Leviticus.R 32:5, Matthew 24:35, Numbers 10:35 23:19, Numbers.R 9:8, Psalms 12:6-12:7 68:2-68:3 78:65-78:66, Romans 16:27, Tanya Shaar Hayichud §08 §09, y.Kiddushin 4:1, y.Yevamot 8:3, Zechariah 1:6, Zephaniah 3:8

[4] Isaiah 31:3 - 2 Thessalonians 2:4-8, Acts 12:22-23, Deuteronomy 32:30-31, Esther.R Petichata:3, Ezekiel 20:33-34 28:9, Isaiah 9:18 30:5 30:7 36:6 36:9, Jeremiah 15:6 37:7-10, Mekhilta de R'Shimon bar Yochai Beshallach 22:2, Mekhilta de R'Shimon bar Yochai Shirata 35:1, Mekhilta de R'Ishmael Shirata 9:22, Midrash Psalms 114:6, Pesikta Rabbati 49:1, Psalms 9:21 33:17 146:3-5, y.Sukkah 5:1

[5] Isaiah 31:4 - 2 Chronicles 20:15, Amos 3:8, Genesis.R 74:11, Hosea 11:10, Isaiah 10:16 12:6 37:35-37:36 42:13, Jeremiah 50:44, Numbers 24:8-24:9, Psalms 125:1-125:2, Revelation 5:5, Zechariah 2:5 9:8 9:15 12:8 14:3

[6] 1QIsaa plural; LXX singular

[7] LXX *which he has taken, and cry over it, until the mountains are filled with his voice, and the animals are awe-struck and tremble at the fierceness of his wrath*

[8] Isaiah 31:5 - b.Berachot 56b, b.Chullin [Tosefot] 139b, Deuteronomy 32:11, Ein Yaakov Berachot:56b, Exodus 12:27 19:4, Isaiah 10:14 37:35 38:6, Mekhilta de R'Shimon bar Yochai Pisha 14:1, Mekhilta de R'Ishmael Pisha 7:75, Mekhilta de R'Ishmael Pisha 11:91, Psalms 37:40 46:6 91:4

[9] 1QIsaa *he will pass over and bring it to safety*; LXX *and he shall rescue, and save and deliver*

[10] Isaiah 31:6 - 2 Chronicles 33:9-33:16 36:14, Acts 3:19 26:20, Gates of Repentance 1.001, Hosea 9:9 14:3-14:5, Isaiah 1:4-1:5 29:15 48:8 55:7, Jeremiah 3:10 3:14 3:22 5:23 31:19-31:21, Joel 2:12-2:13, Saadia Opinions 5:6

[11] 1QIsaa *against whom against whom*

[12] Isaiah 31:7 - 1 Kings 12:28-30, Deuteronomy 7:25, Ezekiel 36:25, Hosea 8:11 14:10, Isaiah 2:20 30:22, Joseph and Aseneth 10:12, Sibylline Oracles 3.605

[13] Missing in LXX

[14] Isaiah 31:8 - 1QM 1.002 1QM 11.41225, 1QM 11:11-12, 1QM 11.11-12, 2 Chronicles 32:21, 2 Kings 19:34-19:37, Genesis 49:15,

him; *And he shall flee from* [1]*the sword, and his young men shall become tributary*[2].
And his rock shall pass away because of terror, And his princes shall be dismayed at the ensign, says the LORD, whose fire is in Zion, And His furnace in Jerusalem[4].

9[3] וְסַלְעוֹ מִמָּגוֹר יַעֲבוֹר וְחַתּוּ מִנֵּס שָׂרָיו נְאֻם־יְהֹוָה אֲשֶׁר־אוּר לוֹ בְּצִיּוֹן וְתַנּוּר לוֹ בִּירוּשָׁלָֽם

Isaiah – Chapter 32

1[5] הֵן לְצֶדֶק יִמְלָךְ־מֶלֶךְ וּלְשָׂרִים לְמִשְׁפָּט יָשֹׂרוּ

Behold, a king shall reign in righteousness, And as for princes, they shall rule in justice.

2[6] וְהָיָה־אִישׁ כְּמַחֲבֵא־רוּחַ וְסֵתֶר זָרֶם כְּפַלְגֵי־מַיִם בְּצָיוֹן כְּצֵל סֶלַע־כָּבֵד בְּאֶרֶץ עֲיֵפָֽה

And a man shall be as in a hiding place from the wind, And concealed from the tempest; As by the watercourses in a dry place, *As in the shadow of a great rock in a weary land*[7].

3[8] וְלֹא תִשְׁעֶינָה עֵינֵי רֹאִים וְאָזְנֵי שֹׁמְעִים תִּקְשַׁבְנָה

And the eyes of those who see shall not be closed, And the ears of those who hear shall focus[9].

4[10] וּלְבַב נִמְהָרִים יָבִין לָדָעַת וּלְשׁוֹן עִלְּגִים תְּמַהֵר לְדַבֵּר צָחֽוֹת

The heart *also of the rash shall understand knowledge*[11], And the tongue of the stammerers shall be ready to speak plainly.

5[12] לֹא־יִקָּרֵא עוֹד לְנָבָל נָדִיב וּלְכִילַי לֹא יֵאָמֵר שֽׁוֹעַ

The vile person shall no longer be called liberal, Nor the miser said to be noble[13].

6[14] כִּי נָבָל נְבָלָה יְדַבֵּר וְלִבּוֹ יַעֲשֶׂה־אָוֶן לַעֲשׂוֹת חֹנֶף וּלְדַבֵּר אֶל־יְהֹוָה תּוֹעָה לְהָרִיק נֶפֶשׁ רָעֵב וּמַשְׁקֵה צָמֵא יַחְסִֽיר

For the vile person will speak villainy, And his heart *will work*[15] iniquity, to practice ungodliness, and to utter wickedness against the LORD, to *make empty*[16] the souls of the hungry, And to cause the drink of the thirsty to fail.

Hosea 1:7, Isaiah 10:12 10:16-10:19 10:33-10:34 14:25 29:5 30:27-30:33 37:7 37:35-37:38

[1] 1QIsaa adds *before*

[2] LXX *not the sword of a great man, nor the sword of a mean man shall devour him; neither shall he flee from the face of the sword: but the young men shall be overthrown*

[3] Isaiah 31:9 - b.Eruvin 19a, Deuteronomy 32:31 32:37, Ein Yaakov Eruvin, Ezekiel 22:18-22:22, Genesis.R 6:6 26:6, Isaiah 4:4 10:17 11:10 18:3 29:6 30:33, Jastrow 60a, Leviticus 6:13, Malachi 3:19, Mekilta de R'Ishmael Bahodesh 9:26, Midrash Psalms 15:1 19:13 52:8, Midrash Tanchuma Bamidbar 2, Midrash Tanchuma Pekudei 8, Numbers.R 1:2, Pesikta de R'Kahana S2.2, Pirkei de R'Eliezer 28, Zechariah 2:5

[4] LXX *for they shall be compassed with rocks as with a trench, and shall be worse; and he who flees shall be taken. The Lord says, Blessed is he who has a seed in Sion, and household friends in Jerusalem*

[5] Isaiah 32:1 - 2 Chronicles 31:20-21, 2 Samuel 23:3, Ezekiel 37:24, Hebrews 1:8-9, Hosea 3:5, Isaiah 9:7-8 11:4 28:6 40:1-5, Jastrow 205a, Jeremiah 23:5-6 33:15, Psalms 45:2 45:7-8 72:1-4 99:4, Revelation 17:14 19:11, Romans 5:21, Song of Songs.R 2:20, Zechariah 9:9
Isaiah 32:1-20 - 1QIsaa

[6] Isaiah 32:2 - 1 Timothy 3:16, b.Avodah Zara 5b, b.Bava Kamma 2b 3a 14a 55b, b.Chullin 141b, Isaiah 4:5-4:6 7:14 8:10-8:14 9:7 25:4 26:20-26:21 28:17 32:18-32:19 35:6-7 41:18 43:20 44:3, John 7:37, Liber Antiquitatum Biblicarum 16:2, Matthew 7:24-7:27, Micah 5:5-6, Psalms 31:3-4 32:7 63:2 143:9 146:3-5, Revelation 22:1, Zechariah 13:7

[7] Missing in LXX

[8] Isaiah 32:3 - 1 John 2:20-2:21, 2 Corinthians 4:6, Acts 26:18, Isaiah 29:18 29:24 30:26 35:5-35:6 54:13 60:1-60:2, Jeremiah 31:35, Mark 7:37 8:22-8:25, Matthew 13:11

[9] LXX *And they shall no longer trust in men, but they shall incline their ears to hear.*

[10] Isaiah 32:4 - Acts 2:4-2:12 4:13 6:7 26:9-26:11, Exodus 4:11, Galatians 1:23, Isaiah 29:24, Luke 21:14-21:15, Matthew 11:25 16:17, Nehemiah 8:8-8:12, Song of Songs 7:10

[11] LXX *of the weak ones shall attend to hear*

[12] Isaiah 32:5 - 1 Samuel 25:3-8 1:25, b.Sotah 41b, Ein Yaakov Sotah 41b, Isaiah 5:20, Malachi 3:18, Proverbs 23:6-8, Psalms 15:4 Isaiah 32:5-7 - 4Q165 frag 6 ll.2-6

[13] LXX *And they shall no more at all tell a fool to rule, and thy servants shall no more at all say, Be silent*

[14] Isaiah 32:6 - 1 Samuel 24:13 25:10-25:11, Acts 5:3-5:4 8:21-8:22, Amos 2:6-2:7 8:6, Guide for the Perplexed 1:59, Hosea 7:6-7:7, Isaiah 3:15 9:18, James 1:14-1:15 1:27 3:5-3:6, Jeremiah 13:23, Job 22:5-22:9 24:2-24:16, Matthew 12:34-12:36 15:19 23:13, Micah 2:1-2:2 3:1-3:3, Proverbs 11:24-11:26 19:3, Psalms 58:2-58:3

[15] 1QIsaa Iplans

[16] LXX *scatter*

וְכֵלַ֤י כֵּלָ֣יו רָעִ֔ים ה֖וּא זִמּ֣וֹת יָעָ֑ץ לְחַבֵּ֤ל עֲנָוִים֙ 'עֲנָוִים' "עֲנִיִּים" בְּאִמְרֵי־שֶׁ֔קֶר וּבְדַבֵּ֥ר אֶבְי֖וֹן מִשְׁפָּֽט	7[1]	The instruments also of the boor are evil; He devises wicked devices to destroy the poor with lying words, And the needy when he speaks right.
וְנָדִ֖יב נְדִיב֣וֹת יָעָ֑ץ וְה֖וּא עַל־נְדִיב֥וֹת יָקֽוּם	8[2]	*But the liberal devises liberal things; And by liberal things shall he stand[3].*
נָשִׁים֙ שַֽׁאֲנַנּ֔וֹת קֹ֖מְנָה שְׁמַ֣עְנָה קוֹלִ֑י בָּנוֹת֙ בֹּ֣טְח֔וֹת הַאְזֵ֖נָּה אִמְרָתִֽי	9[4]	Rise up, you women who are *at ease[5]*, and hear my voice; You confident daughters, give ear to my speech.
יָמִים֙ עַל־שָׁנָ֔ה תִּרְגַּ֖זְנָה בֹּטְח֑וֹת כִּ֚י כָּלָ֣ה בָצִ֔יר אֹ֖סֶף בְּלִ֥י יָבֽוֹא	10[6]	*After a year and days you shall be troubled, you confident women[7]; For the vintage shall fail, the harvest shall not come.*
חִרְדוּ֙ שַֽׁאֲנַנּ֔וֹת רְגָ֖זָה בֹּֽטְח֑וֹת פְּשֹׁ֣טָֽה וְעֹ֔רָה וַחֲג֖וֹרָה עַל־חֲלָצָֽיִם	11[8]	*Tremble, you women who are at ease; Be troubled[9], you confident ones; Strip, and make yourself bare, And wrap sackcloth [10]upon your loins,*
עַל־שָׁדַ֖יִם סֹֽפְדִ֑ים עַל־שְׂדֵי־חֶ֕מֶד עַל־גֶּ֖פֶן פֹּרִיָּֽה	12[11]	Strike upon the breasts for the pleasant fields, for the fruitful vine;
עַ֚ל אַדְמַ֣ת עַמִּ֔י ק֥וֹץ שָׁמִ֖יר תַּֽעֲלֶ֑ה כִּ֚י עַל־כָּל־בָּתֵּ֣י מָשׂ֔וֹשׂ קִרְיָ֖ה עַלִּיזָֽה	13[12]	For the land of my people, where thorns and briers come up; Yes, for all the houses of joy And the joyous city[13].
כִּֽי־אַרְמ֣וֹן נֻטָּ֔שׁ הֲמ֥וֹן עִ֖יר עֻזָּ֑ב עֹ֣פֶל וָבַ֜חַן הָיָ֨ה בְעַ֤ד מְעָרוֹת֙ עַד־עוֹלָ֔ם מְשׂ֥וֹשׂ פְּרָאִ֖ים מִרְעֵ֥ה עֲדָרִֽים	14[14]	*For the palace shall be forsaken; The city with its noise shall be deserted; The mound and the tower shall be for dens[15] forever, A joy of wild donkeys, a pasture of flocks;*
עַד־יֵ֠עָרֶה עָלֵ֨ינוּ ר֜וּחַ מִמָּר֗וֹם וְהָיָ֤ה מִדְבָּר֙ לַכַּרְמֶ֔ל 'וְכַרְמֶ֖ל' "וְהַכַּרְמֶ֖ל" לַיַּ֥עַר יֵחָשֵֽׁב	15[16]	Until the spirit is poured on us from on high, and *the wilderness becomes a fruitful field, And the fruitful field is counted as a forest[17].*
וְשָׁכַ֥ן בַּמִּדְבָּ֖ר מִשְׁפָּ֑ט וּצְדָקָ֖ה בַּכַּרְמֶ֥ל תֵּשֵֽׁב	16[18]	Then justice shall live in the wilderness, And righteousness shall live in *the fruitful field[19].*

---

[1] Isaiah 32:7 - 1 Kings 21:10-21:14, 4Q177 1.6, 4Q177 5+6 6, Acts 6:11-6:13, Isaiah 1:23 5:23 59:3-59:4 13:1, Jeremiah 5:26-5:28 18:18, Matthew 2:4 26:14-16 26:59-26:60, Micah 2:11 7:2-7:3, Psalms 10:8-10:11 64:5-64:7 82:2-82:5, y.Sanhedrin 10:2

[2] Isaiah 32:8 - 2 Corinthians 8:2 9:6-9:11, 2 Samuel 9:1-9:13, Acts 9:39 11:29-11:30, Job 31:16-31:21, Luke 6:33-6:35, Proverbs 11:24-11:25, Psalms 16:9, Tanya Igeret Hakodesh §19 §32

[3] LXX *But the godly have devised wise measures, and this counsel shall stand*

[4] Isaiah 32:9 - Amos 6:1-6, b.Berachot 14a, Deuteronomy 4:56, Ein Yaakov Berachot:17a, Isaiah 3:16 4:23 47:7-8, Jeremiah 6:2-6 48:11-12, Judges 9:7, Lamentations 4:5, Matthew 13:9, Psalms 49:2-3, Tanna Devei Eliyahu 4, z.Vayikra 18b, Zephaniah 2:15

[5] LXX *rich*

[6] Isaiah 32:10 - Habakkuk 3:17, Hosea 2:12 3:4, Isaiah 3:17-26 5:5-6 7:23 16:10 24:7-12, Jeremiah 8:13 25:10-11, Joel 1:7 1:12, Zephaniah 1:13

[7] LXX *Remember for a full year in pain, yet with hope*

[8] Isaiah 32:11 - b.Moed Katan 27b, Deuteronomy 4:48, Hosea 2:3, Isaiah 2:19 2:21 3:24 15:3 20:4 22:4-5 9:14 47:1-3, James 5:5, Jeremiah 4:8 6:26 1:3, Lamentations.R Petichata D'Chakimei:24, Luke 23:27-30, Micah 1:8-11

[9] LXX *Be amazed, be pained*

[10] 1QIsaa adds *and beat your breasts*

[11] Isaiah 32:12 - b.Menachot [Tosefot] 37a, b.Moed Katan 27b, Deuteronomy 8:7-8 11:11-12, Ezekiel 20:6 20:15, Lamentations 2:11 4:3-4, Lamentations.R Petichata D'Chakimei:24, Nahum 2:8, t.Moed Katan 2:17, y.Sotah 7:5

[12] Isaiah 32:13 - Avot de R'Natan 34, Hosea 9:6 10:8, Isaiah 5:6 6:11 7:23 22:2 22:12-22:13 10:13, Jeremiah 15:8, Psalms 11:34, Revelation 18:7-8

[13] LXX *and joy shall be removed from every house*

[14] Isaiah 32:14 - 2 Kings 1:9, Isaiah 5:9 6:11 13:19-13:22 24:1-24:3 24:10 24:12 1:2 3:10 34:11-34:17, Lamentations.R 1:23 3:?, Luke 21:20 21:24, Psalms 8:11, Revelation 18:2-18:3

[15] LXX *As for the rich city, the houses are deserted; they shall abandon the wealth of the city, and the pleasant houses: and the villages shall be caves*

[16] Isaiah 32:15 - 2 Corinthians 3:8, Acts 2:17-2:18 2:33, Ezekiel 15:29, Hosea 2:1-2:2, Isaiah 11:2-11:3 5:17 35:1-35:2 11:7 20:3 21:8 54:1-54:3 55:11-55:13 59:19-60:22 61:3-61:5 15:11, Joel 3:1-3:2, John 7:39, Lamentations.R 1:23 3:?, Luke 24:49, Pesikta Rabbati 29/30B:4, Proverbs 1:23, Psalms 8:30 11:33 11:35, Romans 11:18-26, Titus 3:5-6, z.Lech Lecha 83a, Zechariah 12:10

[17] LXX *and Chermel shall be desert, and Chermel shall be counted for a forest*

[18] Isaiah 32:16 - 1 Corinthians 6:9-6:11, 1 Peter 2:9-2:12 4:1-4:4, Hosea 3:5, Isaiah 11:8 18:4 56:6-56:8 12:21, Mas.Semachot 8:9, Psalms 94:14-94:15, Titus 2:11-2:12

[19] LXX *Carmel*

וְהָיָה מַעֲשֵׂה הַצְּדָקָה שָׁלוֹם וַעֲבֹדַת הַצְּדָקָה
הַשְׁקֵט וָבֶטַח עַד־עוֹלָם

17[1] And the work of righteousness shall be peace; And the effect of righteousness: quietness and confidence forever.

וְיָשַׁב עַמִּי בִּנְוֵה שָׁלוֹם וּבְמִשְׁכְּנוֹת מִבְטַחִים
וּבִמְנוּחֹת שַׁאֲנַנּוֹת

18[2] And my people will live in a peaceful lodging, And in secure dwellings, and in quiet resting places.

וּבָרַד בְּרֶדֶת הַיָּעַר וּבַשִּׁפְלָה תִּשְׁפַּל הָעִיר

19[3] And it shall hail, in the downfall of the forest; But *the city shall descend into the valley*[4].[5]

אַשְׁרֵיכֶם זֹרְעֵי עַל־כָּל־מָיִם מְשַׁלְּחֵי רֶגֶל־הַשּׁוֹר
וְהַחֲמוֹר

20[6] Happy are you who sow beside all waters, who send forth freely the feet of the ox and the donkey.

Isaiah – Chapter 33

הוֹי שׁוֹדֵד וְאַתָּה לֹא שָׁדוּד וּבוֹגֵד וְלֹא־בָגְדוּ בוֹ
כַּהֲתִמְךָ שׁוֹדֵד תּוּשַּׁד כַּנְּלֹתְךָ לִבְגֹּד יִבְגְּדוּ־בָךְ

1[7] Woe to you who spoils, and you were not spoiled; And deals treacherously, and they did not deal treacherously with you. When you *cease*[8] spoiling, you will be spoiled; And when you are weary with dealing treacherously, they shall deal treacherously with you.

יְהֹוָה חָנֵּנוּ לְךָ קִוִּינוּ הֱיֵה זְרֹעָם לַבְּקָרִים אַף־
יְשׁוּעָתֵנוּ בְּעֵת צָרָה

2[9] O LORD, *be gracious*[10] to us; We have waited for You; *Be their arm every morning*[11], Our salvation in the time of trouble.

מִקּוֹל הָמוֹן נָדְדוּ עַמִּים מֵרוֹמְמֻתֶךָ נָפְצוּ גּוֹיִם

3[12] At the noise of turmoil the peoples flee; At the lifting up of Yourself the nations are scattered.

וְאֻסַּף שְׁלַלְכֶם אֹסֶף הֶחָסִיל כְּמַשַּׁק גֵּבִים שׁוֹקֵק
בּוֹ

4[13] *And your spoil is gathered as the caterpillar gathers; As locusts leap do they leap on it*[14].

---

[1] Isaiah 32:17 - 1 Enoch 11:2, 1 John 3:18-3:24 4:17, 2 Corinthians 1:12, 2 Peter 1:10-1:11, b.Bava Batra 9a, Ein Yaakov Bava Batra:9a, Ezekiel 37:21-37:22 13:25 15:29, Hebrews 6:11, Isaiah 2:3-2:4 9:8 11:6-11:9 11:13 2:3 6:15 24:18 54:13-54:14 7:12 9:19 18:12, James 3:17-3:18, Mas.Kallah Rabbati 2:13, Micah 4:3-4:4, mt.Hilchot Matnot Aniyim 10:2 10:6, Numbers.R 11:7 14:10, Philippians 4:6-4:9, Proverbs 14:26, Psalms 72:2-72:3 85:9 112:6-112:9 119:165, Romans 14:17, Saadia Opinions 10:16, Siman 34:1 34:11 z.Beshallach 59a, Tanya Igeret Hakodesh §05 §12

[2] Isaiah 32:18 - 1 John 4:16, Ezekiel 34:25-34:26, Hebrews 4:9, Hosea 2:18-2:25, Isaiah 33:20-33:22 35:9-35:10 60:17-60:18, Jeremiah 23:5-23:6 9:16, Midrash Psalms 92:5, Numbers.R 11:7, Saadia Opinions 10:16, Song of Songs.R 7:1, Zechariah 2:5 2:8

[3] Isaiah 32:19 - Exodus 9:18-9:26, Ezekiel 13:11-13, Isaiah 10:19 14:22-14:23 24:10 1:4 2:5 3:10 4:2 4:17 6:30 13:24, Matthew 7:25, Nahum 1:1 1:8 2:11-14, Revelation 8:7 18:21, Zechariah 11:2

[4] 1QIsaa *the wood will be completely laid low*; due to the term, *forest*, it appears 1QIsaa holds the superior reading.

[5] LXX reads, *And if the hail should come down, it shall not come upon you; and they that live in the forests shall be in confidence, as those in the plain country*

[6] Isaiah 32:20 - 1 Corinthians 3:6 9:9-9:11, Acts 2:41 4:4 5:14, Ecclesiastes 11:1, Ein Yaakov Avodah Zarah:5b, Ein Yaakov Bava Kamma:17a, Isaiah 19:5-19:7 30:23-30:24 55:10-55:11, James 3:18, Midrash Tanchuma Bereshit 1, Tanna Devei Eliyahu 2, y.Bava Kamma 1:1, z.Beshallach 64b

[7] Isaiah 33:1 - 2 Chronicles 28:16-28:21, 2 Kings 18:13-18:17, Exodus.R 31:15, Habakkuk 2:5-2:8, Isaiah 10:5-10:6 10:12 17:14 21:2 24:16 37:36-37:38, Jastrow 137a, Jeremiah 25:12-25:14, Judges 1:7, Matthew 7:2, Midrash Tanchuma Mishpatim 12, Obadiah 1:10-1:16, Revelation 13:10 16:6 17:12-17:14 17:17, Zechariah 14:1-14:3
Isaiah 33:1-24 - 1QIsaa

[8] 1QIsaa *sunk down in*

[9] Isaiah 33:2 - 2 Corinthians 1:3-1:4, Companion verse for third "Hashem" recited in Birchat Kohanim, Deuteronomy.R 2:4, Exodus 14:27, Genesis.R 98 [Excl]:14, Hosea 14:4, Isaiah 1:4 1:9 2:8 2:16 30:18-30:19 16:10 11:16, Jeremiah 2:27-2:28 14:8, Lamentations 3:23 3:25-3:26, Mnemonic at the end of the book of Genesis, Numbers.R 11:6 12:4, Pesikta Rabbati 34:1, Psalms 25:3 27:13-27:14 37:39 46:2 46:6 50:15 60:12 62:2 62:6 62:9 90:15 91:15 3:2 130:4-130:8 23:8
Isaiah 33:2-8 - 4QIsac

[10] LXX *have mercy*

[11] LXX *the seed of the rebellious is gone to destruction*

[12] Isaiah 33:3 - 3 Enoch 18:7, b.Sanhedrin 95b, Ein Yaakov Sanhedrin:95b, Isaiah 10:13-14 10:32-34 17:12-14 37:11-18 37:29-36 59:16-18, Psalms 46:7, the abbreviation ובמ stands for ובמים, This is the middle verse of the book of Isaiah per the Massorah

[13] Isaiah 33:4 - 2 Chronicles 14:12 20:25, 2 Kings 7:15-7:16, b.Sanhedrin 94b, Ein Yaakov Sanhedrin:94b, Isaiah 9:23, Joel 2:9 2:25, mt.Hilchot Shechitah 1:3, Song of Songs.R 1:16

[14] LXX *And now shall the spoils of your small and great be gathered: as if one should gather locusts, so shall they mock you*

Hebrew	#	English
נִשְׂגָּב יְהוָה כִּי שֹׁכֵן מָרֹום מִלֵּא צִיֹּון מִשְׁפָּט וּצְדָקָה	5[1]	*The LORD is exalted, for He dwells on high*[2]; He fills Zion with justice and righteousness.
וְהָיָה אֱמוּנַת עִתֶּיךָ חֹסֶן יְשׁוּעֹת חָכְמַת וָדָעַת יִרְאַת יְהוָה הִיא אֹוצָרֹו	6[3]	*And the stability of your times shall be a hoard of salvation: wisdom and knowledge, And the fear of the LORD which is His treasure*[4].
הֵן אֶרְאֶלָּם צָעֲקוּ חֻצָה מַלְאֲכֵי שָׁלֹום מַר יִבְכָּיוּן	7[5]	Behold, *their valiant ones cry outside; The ambassadors of peace weep bitterly*[6].
נָשַׁמּוּ מְסִלֹּות שָׁבַת עֹבֵר אֹרַח הֵפֵר בְּרִית מָאַס עָרִים לֹא חָשַׁב אֱנֹושׁ	8[7]	The highways lie waste, The wayfaring man ceases; He has broken the covenant, He has despised *the cities*[8], He does not regard man.
אָבַל אֻמְלְלָה אָרֶץ הֶחְפִּיר לְבָנֹון קָמֵל הָיָה הַשָּׁרֹון כָּעֲרָבָה וְנֹעֵר בָּשָׁן וְכַרְמֶל	9[9]	The land mourns and languishes; Lebanon is ashamed, it withers; Sharon is as a wilderness; And *Bashan and Carmel are clean bare*[10].
עַתָּה אָקוּם יֹאמַר יְהוָה עַתָּה אֵרֹומָם עַתָּה אֶנָּשֵׂא	10[11]	Now I will arise, *says the LORD*[12]; Now I will be exalted; Now I will lift Myself.
תַּהֲרוּ חֲשַׁשׁ תֵּלְדוּ קַשׁ רוּחֲכֶם אֵשׁ תֹּאכַלְכֶם	11[13]	*You conceive chaff, you shall bring forth stubble; Your breath is a fire that shall devour you*[14].
וְהָיוּ עַמִּים מִשְׂרְפֹות שִׂיד קֹוצִים כְּסוּחִים בָּאֵשׁ יִצַּתּוּ	12[15]	And the people shall be as the burnings of lime; As thorns cut down, that are burned in the fire.
שִׁמְעוּ רְחֹוקִים אֲשֶׁר עָשִׂיתִי וּדְעוּ קְרֹובִים גְּבֻרָתִי	13[16]	*Hear, you who are far off,*[17] what I have done; *and, you who are near, acknowledge*[18] My might.

[1] Isaiah 33:5 - 2 Chronicles 31:20-31:21, Daniel 4:34, Ephesians 1:20-1:21, Exodus 9:16-17 15:1 15:6 18:11, Isaiah 1:26-27 2:11 2:17 4:2-4 12:4 4:6 8:1 32:15-18 9:10 13:20 4:1 54:11-14 9:15 12:21 13:3 61:11-1 18:1, Job 40:9-14, Kuzari 2.50, Psalms 21:12-14 46:10-11 97:8-9 113:5-6 115:1-2 22:16 3:1, Psalms of Solomon 18:10, Revelation 19:2-6, Romans 3:26 11:26

[2] LXX *The God who dwells on high is holy*

[3] Isaiah 33:6 - 1 Timothy 4:8 6:6, 2 Chronicles 32:20-32:21 32:27-32:29, 2 Corinthians 6:10, b.Berachot 33b, b.Shabbat 31a, Bahir 186, Ecclesiastes 7:12 7:19 9:14-9:18, Ein Yaakov Berachot:33b, Midrash Shmuel 1:1, Ein Yaakov Shabbat:31a, Exodus.R 30:14 40:1, Isaiah 11:2-11:5 38:5-38:6 3:6, Jastrow 162b 1338b, Jeremiah 22:15-22:17, Matthew 6:33, Midrash Tanchuma Korach 12, Motzoei Shabbat [Viyiten Lecha], Numbers.R 18:21, Pesikta de R'Kahana S1.2, Proverbs 14:27 15:16 19:23 24:3-24:7 4:2 28:15-28:16 5:4, Psalms 27:1-27:2 28:8 45:5 112:1-3 20:8, z.Pekudei 223a

[4] LXX *They shall be delivered up to the law: our salvation is our treasure: there are wisdom and knowledge and piety toward the Lord; these are the treasures of righteousness*

[5] Isaiah 33:7 - 2 Kings 18:18 18:37-19:3, 3 Enoch 33:1, b.Chagigah 5b, Esther.R 7:13, Genesis.R 56:5 59:5 65:10, Isaiah 12:3 12:22, Jastrow 113b 559b 848a, Lamentations.R 1:23, Midrash Tanchuma Shoftim 11, mt.Hilchot Yesodei haTorah 2:7, Pesikta de R'Kahana S5.3 S6.2, Pesikta Rabbati 40:6, Pirkei de R'Eliezer 31, Tanna Devei Eliyahu 5, z.Shemot 2b 18a, z.Vayakhel 196a, z.Vayera 120a, z.Vayeshev 182a, z.Vayigash 210a

[6] LXX *these shall be terrified with fear of you: those whom you feared shall cry out because of you: messengers shall be sent, bitterly weeping, entreating for peace*

[7] Isaiah 33:8 - 1 Samuel 17:10 17:26, 2 Kings 18:13-17 18:20-21, b.Shabbat 77a, Genesis.R 56:5 56:8, Isaiah 10:9-11 10:13-14 10:29-31 11:8 12:1, Judges 5:6, Lamentations 1:4, Lamentations.R Petichata D'Chakimei:24, Luke 18:2-4, m.Sotah 8:7, Pesikta Rabbati 40:6, Psalms 10:6

[8] 1QIsaa *witnesses*

[9] Isaiah 33:9 - 4Q522 1 i 9, b.Shabbat 31a, Deuteronomy 3:4, Isaiah 1:7-1:8 2:13 3:26 14:8 24:1 24:4-24:6 24:19-24:20 11:2 13:24 17:10, Jeremiah 4:20-4:26 2:19, Micah 7:14, Nahum 1:4, Ralbag SOS Pesichta, Song of Songs 2:1, Zechariah 11:1-11:3

[10] LXX *Galilee shall be laid bare, and Chermel*

[11] Isaiah 33:10 - Amos 6:1, Deuteronomy 32:36-32:43, Exodus 14:18 15:9-15:12, Isaiah 2:21 10:16 10:33 30:17-30:18 42:13-42:14 59:16-59:17, Midrash Psalms 2:14, Pesikta Rabbati 29/30A:10, Psalms 7:7 12:6 46:11 78:65 102:14-102:19, Song of Songs.R 4:18, Verse for names א-ע [Pisukim Lesheimot Anoshim], Zephaniah 3:8

[12] 1QIsaa *the LORD has said*

[13] Isaiah 33:11 - Acts 5:4, b.Sanhedrin 18a, Ein Yaakov Sanhedrin:108a, Genesis.R 6:6 26:6, Isaiah 1:31 5:24 8:9-8:10 10:7-10:14 17:13 2:18 29:5-29:8 30:30-30:33 31:8-31:9 37:23-37:29 11:4, James 1:15, Job 15:35, mt.Perek Chelek Intro:11, Nahum 1:5-1:10, Numbers.R 19:18, Psalms 2:1 7:15 83:6-83:19, Saadia Opinions 9:5, t.Sanhedrin 13:6, y.Niddah 1:3, y.Yevamot 4:11

[14] LXX *Now you shall see, now you shall perceive; the strength of your breath, shall be vain; fire shall devour you*

[15] Isaiah 33:12 - 2 Samuel 23:6-7, Amos 2:1, b.Sotah 35b, Ein Yaakov Sotah:35b, Genesis.R 44:4, Isaiah 9:19 10:17 3:4 13:36, Leviticus.R 23:5, Midrash Psalms 2:13 2:14 37:2 45:1, Midrash Tanchuma Bamidbar 19, Midrash Tanchuma Chukkat 25, Midrash Tanchuma Re'eh 9, Numbers.R 2:17 19:32, Pesikta Rabbati 10:4 10:5 11:5, Pirkei de R'Eliezer 40, Song of Songs.R 2:8, z.Shemot 21b

[16] Isaiah 33:13 - 1 Samuel 17:46, Acts 2:5-2:11, Daniel 3:27-3 6:26-28, Ephesians 2:11-18, Exodus 15:14, Isaiah 18:3 13:20 1:1 9:19, Joshua 2:9-11 9:9-10, Psalms 67:46-12 48:11 97:8 98:1-2 99:2-3 147:12-14 4:14

[17] 1QIsaa *Those who are far off heard*

[18] 1QIsaa *Those who are far off acknowledged*

פָּחֲדוּ בְצִיּוֹן חַטָּאִים אָחֲזָה רְעָדָה חֲנֵפִים מִי יָגוּר לָנוּ אֵשׁ אוֹכֵלָה מִי־יָגוּר לָנוּ מוֹקְדֵי עוֹלָם

14[1] The sinners in Zion are afraid; Trembling has seized the ungodly: '*Who among us shall live with the devouring fire? Who among us shall live with everlasting burnings[2]?*'

הֹלֵךְ צְדָקוֹת וְדֹבֵר מֵישָׁרִים מֹאֵס בְּבֶצַע מַעֲשַׁקּוֹת נֹעֵר כַּפָּיו מִתְּמֹךְ בַּשֹּׁחַד אֹטֵם אָזְנוֹ מִשְּׁמֹעַ דָּמִים וְעֹצֵם עֵינָיו מֵרְאוֹת בְּרָע

15[3] He who walks righteously, and speaks uprightly; He who despises the gain of oppression, who shakes his *hands[4]* from holding of bribes, who stops his *ears[5]* from hearing of blood, And shuts his eyes from looking upon evil;

הוּא מְרוֹמִים יִשְׁכֹּן מְצָדוֹת סְלָעִים מִשְׂגַּבּוֹ לַחְמוֹ נִתָּן מֵימָיו נֶאֱמָנִים

16[6] He shall live on high; His place of defense shall be the munitions of rocks; His bread shall be given; his waters shall be sure.

מֶלֶךְ בְּיָפְיוֹ תֶּחֱזֶינָה עֵינֶיךָ תִּרְאֶינָה אֶרֶץ מַרְחַקִּים

17[7] Your eyes shall see the king in his beauty; They shall behold a land stretching afar.

לִבְּךָ יֶהְגֶּה אֵימָה אַיֵּה סֹפֵר אַיֵּה שֹׁקֵל אַיֵּה סֹפֵר אֶת־הַמִּגְדָּלִים

18[8] *Your heart shall muse on the terror: 'Where is he who counted, where is he who weighed? Where is he who counted the towers[9]?'*

אֶת־עַם נוֹעָז לֹא תִרְאֶה עַם עִמְקֵי שָׂפָה מִשְּׁמוֹעַ נִלְעַג לָשׁוֹן אֵין בִּינָה

19[10] *You shall not see the fierce people; A people of a deep speech you cannot see, Of a stammering tongue you cannot understand[11].*

חֲזֵה צִיּוֹן קִרְיַת מוֹעֲדֵנוּ עֵינֶיךָ תִרְאֶינָה יְרוּשָׁלַ͏ִם נָוֶה שַׁאֲנָן אֹהֶל בַּל־יִצְעָן בַּל־יִסַּע יְתֵדֹתָיו לָנֶצַח וְכָל־חֲבָלָיו בַּל־יִנָּתֵקוּ

20[12] Look upon Zion, the city of our solemn gatherings; your eyes shall see Jerusalem a peaceful habitation, A tent that shall not be removed, The stakes of which shall never be pulled up, nor shall any of its cords be broken.

---

[1] Isaiah 33:14 - 2 Thessalonians 1:8, b.Berachot 60a, b.Shabbat 82a, Deuteronomy 5:24-5:25 32:21-32:24, Ein Yaakov Berachot:60a, Genesis.R 48:6, Hebrews 12:29, Isaiah 5:24 7:2 9:18 10:6 28:14-28:15 28:17-28:22 5:6 5:13 8-30:11 30:27-30:33 8:11 10:9 18:24, Job 15:21-15:22 18:11, Luke 16:23-16:26, Mark 9:43-9:49, Matthew 18:8 22:12 24:51 1:41 1:46, Mesillat Yesharim 9:Factors Detracting from Zerizut, Midrash Psalms 14:5 119:52 17A:21, Nahum 1:6, Numbers 17:27-17:13, Pesikta Rabbati 52:3, Proverbs 4:1, Psalms 11:7 21:10 50:3 53:6, Revelation 6:15-6:17 14:10 20:10, Saadia Opinions 9:9

[2] LXX *Who will tell you that a fire is kindled? Who will tell you of the eternal place?*

[3] Isaiah 33:15 - 1 John 3:7, 1 Samuel 12:3 24:4-7 26:8-11, 2 Enoch 9:1, 2 Peter 2:14-16, Acts 8:18-23, b.Avodah Zara [Rashi] 19b, b.Bava Batra 57b, b.Makkot 24a, b.Shabbat 77b, b.Sotah [Rashi] 22a, Deuteronomy 16:19, Ein Yaakov Bava Batra:57b, Ein Yaakov Makkot:24a, Ephesians 5:11-13, Exodus 23:6-9, Ezekiel 18:15-17, Genesis.R 43:2 48:6 53:12, Isaiah 56:1-2 10:8, James 5:4, Jastrow 78b, Jeremiah 5:26-28 40:15-16, Job 31:13-25 31:29-31, Leviticus.R 23:13, Luke 1:6 3:12-14 19:8, Malachi 2:6, Mas.Derek Eretz Rabbah 1:13, Mas.Kallah Rabbati 8:9, Matthew 2:15, Mekhilta de R'Shimon bar Yochai Bachodesh 51:1, Micah 7:3-4, Midrash Psalms 17A:21, Midrash Tanchuma Shoftim 9, mt.Hilchot Teshuvah 7:1, Nehemiah 5:7-13, Numbers 16:15, Pesikta Rabbati 1:3 24:2, Psalms 1:1-3 15:1-2 24:4-5 26:1-2 26:4-6 26:9-11 10:3 23:37, Romans 2:7, Titus 2:11-12

[4] 1QIsaa *hand*

[5] 1QIsaa *ear*

[6] Isaiah 33:16 - b.Bava Batra 10b, b.Makkot 24a, Ein Yaakov Bava Batra:10b, Ein Yaakov Makkot:24a, Genesis.R 48:6, Habakkuk 3:19, Isaiah 1:4 26:1-5 8:18 1:10, Luke 12:29-31, Mas.Derek Eretz Rabbah 1:13, Midrash Psalms 40:2 17A:21, Pesikta Rabbati 24:2, Proverbs 1:33 18:10, Psalms 15:1 18:34 33:18 34:11 37:3 90:1 91:1-10 91:14 11:41 15:5, Tanya Igeret Hakodesh §23
Isaiah 33:16-17 - 4QIsaa, Exodus.R 25:8
Isaiah 33:16-23 - 4QIsac

[7] Isaiah 33:17 - 1 John 3:2, 2 Chronicles 8:23, 2 Corinthians 4:18, b.Sanhedrin 22b, b.Taanit 14a, b.Yoma [Rashi] 73b, b.Yoma 78b, Genesis.R 48:6, Hebrews 11:13-15, Isaiah 6:5 2:15 32:1-2 13:1, John 1:14 14:21 17:24, Leviticus.R 23:13, Mas.Derek Eretz Rabbah 1:13, Matthew 17:2, mt.Hilchot Melachim u'Michamoteihem 2:5, mt.Hilchot Shevitat Asor 3:1, mt.Hilchot Shevitat Esor 3:1, Pesikta Rabbati 1:3 24:2, Psalms 31:9 45:3, Song of Songs 5:10, y.Sanhedrin 8:1, y.Yoma 9:17

[8] Isaiah 33:18 - 1 Corinthians 1:20, 1 Samuel 25:33-25:36 6:6, 2 Corinthians 1:8-1:10, 2 Kings 15:19 18:14 18:31, 2 Timothy 3:11, b.Chagigah 15b, Deuteronomy.R 6:7, Ein Yaakov Chagigah:15a, Ein Yaakov Sanhedrin:106b, Genesis 23:16, Isaiah 10:16-10:19 17:14 38:9-38:22, Midrash Proverbs 16, Psalms 31:8-31:9 31:23 71:20

[9] LXX *Your soul shall meditate terror. Where are the scribes? where are the counsellors, where is he who numbers those who are growing up*

[10] Isaiah 33:19 - 1 Corinthians 14:21, 2 Kings 19:32, Deuteronomy 28:49-50, Exodus 14:13, Ezekiel 3:5-6, Isaiah 4:11, Jeremiah 5:15
Isaiah 33:19-20 - Exodus.R 25:8

[11] LXX *the small and great people? with whom he took not counsel, neither did he understand a people of deep speech, so that a despised people should not hear, and there is no understanding to he who hears*

[12] Isaiah 33:20 - Deuteronomy 12:5, Ezekiel 24:35, Isaiah 8:18 13:33 6:2, Matthew 16:18, Mekhilta de R'Shimon bar Yochai Shirata 29:1 35:2, Mekilta de R'Ishmael Shirata 3:48, Mekilta de R'Ishmael Shirata 9:51, Psalms 46:6 48:13-14 78:68-69 125:1-2 8:5, Revelation 3:12, Song of Songs.R 1:37, z.Bereshit 52b, z.Ki Tissa 194a

כִּי אִם־שָׁם אַדִּיר יְהוָה לָנוּ מְקוֹם־נְהָרִים יְאֹרִים
רַחֲבֵי יָדָיִם בַּל־תֵּלֶךְ בּוֹ אֳנִי־שַׁיִט וְצִי אַדִּיר לֹא
יַעַבְרֶנּוּ

21[1] In which no galley with oars shall go, nor shall gallant ship pass by. But there the LORD will be with us in majesty, In a place of broad rivers and streams;

כִּי יְהוָה שֹׁפְטֵנוּ יְהוָה מְחֹקְקֵנוּ יְהוָה מַלְכֵּנוּ הוּא
יוֹשִׁיעֵנוּ

22[2] *For the LORD is our Judge, [3]the LORD is our Lawgiver, [4]the LORD is our King; [5]He will save us[6].*

נִטְּשׁוּ חֲבָלָיִךְ בַּל־יְחַזְּקוּ כֵן־תָּרְנָם בַּל־פָּרְשׂוּ נֵס
אָז חֻלַּק עַד־שָׁלָל מַרְבֶּה פִּסְחִים בָּזְזוּ בַז

23[7] Your tacklings are loosened; They do not *firmly*[8] hold the stand of their mast, They do not spread the sail; Then the prey of a great spoil is divided; The lame take the prey.

וּבַל־יֹאמַר שָׁכֵן חָלִיתִי הָעָם הַיֹּשֵׁב בָּהּ נְשֻׂא עָוֹן

24[9] And the inhabitant shall not say: 'I am sick'; The people who live there shall have their iniquity forgiven.

Isaiah – Chapter 34

קִרְבוּ גוֹיִם לִשְׁמֹעַ וּלְאֻמִּים הַקְשִׁיבוּ תִּשְׁמַע
הָאָרֶץ וּמְלֹאָהּ תֵּבֵל וְכָל־צֶאֱצָאֶיהָ

1[10] Come near, you nations, to hear, And attend, you people; Let the earth hear, and its fulness, The world, and all things that come forth of it.

כִּי קֶצֶף לַיהוָה עַל־כָּל־הַגּוֹיִם וְחֵמָה עַל־כָּל־
צְבָאָם הֶחֱרִימָם נְתָנָם לַטָּבַח

2[11] For the LORD has indignation against all the nations, And fury against all their host; He has utterly destroyed them, He has delivered them to the slaughter.

וְחַלְלֵיהֶם יֻשְׁלָכוּ וּפִגְרֵיהֶם יַעֲלֶה בָאְשָׁם וְנָמַסּוּ
הָרִים מִדָּמָם

3[12] Their slain shall be cast out, And the stench of their carcasses shall come up, And the mountains shall be melted with their blood.

וְנָמַקּוּ כָּל־צְבָא הַשָּׁמַיִם וְנָגֹלּוּ כַסֵּפֶר הַשָּׁמָיִם
וְכָל־צְבָאָם יִבּוֹל כִּנְבֹל עָלֶה מִגֶּפֶן וּכְנֹבֶלֶת
מִתְּאֵנָה

4[13] *And all the host of heaven shall rot away*[14], And the heavens shall be rolled together as a scroll; And all their host shall fall down, As the leaf falls off from the vine, And as a falling fig from the fig tree.

---

[1] Isaiah 33:21 - 2 Corinthians 4:4-4:6, Acts 7:2, b.Rosh Hashanah 23a, b.Sanhedrin [Rashi] 16a, b.Shekalim 14a, b.Yoma 77b, Isaiah 17:18 24:18 18:12, Midrash Psalms 5:1, Midrash Tanchuma Chukkat 21, Numbers.R 19:26, Psalms 29:3 46:5-46:6, t.Sukkah 3:7[8], y.Shekalim 6:2, z.Bereshit 33b

[2] Isaiah 33:22 - 2 Corinthians 5:10, Acts 5:31, b.Shabbat 82a, Deuteronomy 9:2, Deuteronomy.R 5:12, Genesis 18:25, Hebrews 5:9, Isaiah 11:4 12:2 16:5 1:9 11:4, James 4:12, Jeremiah 23:5-6, Luke 2:11, Matthew 1:21-23 21:5 1:34, Nehemiah 10:15, Psalms 44:5 50:6 74:12 75:8 89:19 98:9 147:19-20, Revelation 19:16, Selichot, Titus 3:4-6, Zechariah 9:9, Zephaniah 3:15-17

[3] 1QIsaa adds *and*

[4] 1QIsaa adds *and*

[5] 1QIsaa adds *and*

[6] LXX *For my God is great: the LORD our judge shall not pass me by: the LORD is our prince, the LORD is our king; the LORD, he shall save us*

[7] Isaiah 33:23 - 1 Corinthians 1:27, 1 Samuel 6:10 30:22-24, 2 Chronicles 20:25, 2 Kings 7:8 7:16, Acts 3:19 27:30-32 27:40-41, b.Bechorot 39a, Ezekiel 27:26-34, Isaiah 9:1 9:4 9:21, Psalms 68:13

[8] 1QIsaa *indeed*

[9] Isaiah 33:24 - 1 John 1:7-1:9, 2 Chronicles 6:20, b.Ketubot 111a, b.Shekalim [Rashi] 9b, Deuteronomy 7:15 4:27, Ein Yaakov Ketubot:111a, Exodus 15:26, Gates of Repentance 2.003, Isaiah 6:26 20:22 10:8, James 5:14, Jeremiah 33:6-33:8 2:20, Mas.Gerim 4:3, Micah 7:18-7:19, Midrash Psalms 85:2, mt.Hilchot Melachim u'Michamoteihem 5:11, Pesikta Rabbati 1:6, Revelation 21:4 22:2, Sifre Devarim {Ha'azinu Hashamayim} 333, Sifre Devarim Nitzavim 333

[10] Isaiah 34:1 - 1 Corinthians 10:26, Apocalypse of Zephaniah 3:8, Deuteronomy 4:26 8:1, Isaiah 1:2 18:3 9:13 17:1 19:9 1:1, Jeremiah 22:29, Judges 5:3 5:31, Mark 16:15-16:16, Micah 6:1-6:2, Psalms 24:1 49:2-49:3 50:1 96:10, Revelation 2:7
Isaiah 34:1-17 - 1QIsaa, Midrash Tanchuma Vaera 13

[11] Isaiah 34:2 - Amos 1:1-2, Isaiah 13:5 24:1-23 6:25 30:27-30, Jeremiah 25:15-29, Joel 4:9-14, Lamentations.R 2:3, Nahum 1:2-6, Revelation 6:12-17 14:15-20 19:15-21 20:9 20:15, Romans 1:18, Zechariah 14:3 14:12-16, Zephaniah 3:8

[12] Isaiah 34:3 - 2 Kings 9:35-37, Amos 4:10, Ezekiel 14:19 32:5-6 11:6 14:22 15:4 15:11, Guide for the Perplexed 2:29, Isaiah 14:19-20 10:7, Jeremiah 8:1-2 22:19, Joel 2:20, Revelation 14:20 16:3-4

[13] Isaiah 34:4 - 2 Peter 3:7-3:12, Acts 2:19-2:20, Ecclesiastes.R 1:3, Ein Yaakov Avodah Zarah:17a, Ezekiel 32:7-32:8, Isaiah 13:10 13:13 14:12, Jeremiah 4:23-4:24, Joel 3:3-3:4 4:15, Mark 13:24-13:25, Matthew 24:29 24:35, Mekhilta de R'Shimon bar Yochai Amalek 47:1, Mekilta de R'Ishmael Amalek 4:31, Midrash Psalms 92:2 150:1, Midrash Tanchuma Vaetchanan 6, Pesikta de R'Kahana S2.1, Pirkei de R'Eliezer 51, Psalms 102:26-27, Revelation 6:13-14 8:12 20:11, Sibylline Oracles 3.82 8.233 8.413

[14] 1QIsaa *The valley will be split and all the host of heaven will fall*

כִּי־רִוְּתָה בַשָּׁמַיִם חַרְבִּי הִנֵּה עַל־אֱדוֹם תֵּרֵד
וְעַל־עַם חֶרְמִי לְמִשְׁפָּט

5[1] For My sword *drank its fill[2]* in heaven; Behold, it shall come down on Edom, And on the people of My ban, to judgment.

חֶרֶב לַיהֹוָה מָלְאָה דָם הֻדַּשְׁנָה מֵחֵלֶב מִדַּם כָּרִים
וְעַתּוּדִים מֵחֵלֶב כִּלְיוֹת אֵילִים כִּי זֶבַח לַיהֹוָה
בְּבָצְרָה וְטֶבַח גָּדוֹל בְּאֶרֶץ אֱדוֹם

6[3] The sword of the LORD is filled with blood, It is made fat with fatness, With the blood of lambs and goats, With the fat of the kidneys of rams; For the LORD has a sacrifice in Bozrah, And a great slaughter in the land of Edom.

וְיָרְדוּ רְאֵמִים עִמָּם וּפָרִים עִם־אַבִּירִים וְרִוְּתָה
אַרְצָם מִדָּם וַעֲפָרָם מֵחֵלֶב יְדֻשָּׁן

7[4] And the *wild oxen[5]* shall come down with them, And the bullocks with the bulls; And their land shall be drunk with blood, And their dust made fat with fatness.

כִּי יוֹם נָקָם לַיהֹוָה שְׁנַת שִׁלּוּמִים לְרִיב צִיּוֹן

8[6] For the LORD has a day of vengeance, A year of recompense for the controversy of Zion.

וְנֶהֶפְכוּ נְחָלֶיהָ לְזֶפֶת וַעֲפָרָהּ לְגָפְרִית וְהָיְתָה
אַרְצָהּ לְזֶפֶת בֹּעֵרָה

9[7] And its *streams[8]* shall be turned to pitch, and its dust into brimstone, and its land shall become burning pitch.

לַיְלָה וְיוֹמָם לֹא תִכְבֶּה לְעוֹלָם יַעֲלֶה עֲשָׁנָהּ מִדּוֹר
לָדוֹר תֶּחֱרָב לְנֵצַח נְצָחִים אֵין עֹבֵר בָּהּ

10[9] *It shall not be quenched, neither night nor day, its smoke shall go up forever; From generation to generation it shall lie waste: no one shall pass through it forever and ever[10].*

וִירֵשׁוּהָ קָאַת וְקִפּוֹד וְיַנְשׁוֹף וְעֹרֵב יִשְׁכְּנוּ־בָהּ
וְנָטָה עָלֶיהָ קַו־תֹהוּ וְאַבְנֵי־בֹהוּ

11[11] But *the pelican and the bittern shall possess it, And the owl[12]* and the raven shall live there; And He shall stretch over it *the line of confusion[13]*, and *the cliff of emptiness[14]*.

חֹרֶיהָ וְאֵין־שָׁם מְלוּכָה יִקְרָאוּ וְכָל־שָׂרֶיהָ יִהְיוּ
אָפֶס

12[15] As for her nobles, no one shall be there to be called to the kingdom; And all her princes shall be nothing.

---

[1] Isaiah 34:5 - 1 Corinthians 16:22, 2 Peter 2:14, 3 Enoch 32:1, Amos 1:11-1:12, Deuteronomy 27:15-27:26 29:17-29:20 8:14 32:41-32:42, Exodus.R 21:1, Ezekiel 21:8-21:10 21:14-21:16 25:12-25:14, Galatians 3:10, Genesis.R 75:1 98 [Excl]:2, Isaiah 24:6 15:1, Jastrow 1459a, Jeremiah 22:10 23:6 49:7-49:22, Malachi 1:4, Matthew 1:41, Mekhilta de R'Shimon bar Yochai Shirata 28:2, Mekilta de R'Ishmael Shirata 2:118, Midrash Psalms 17:10 150:1, Midrash Tanchuma Beshallach 13, Obadiah 1:1-1:14, Psalms 17:13 17:7, Revelation 1:16, Song of Songs.R 8:19, z.Shemot 19b, Zephaniah 2:12
[2] 1QIsaa *will be seen*
[3] Isaiah 34:6 - b.Shabbat [Rashi] 29b, Deuteronomy 8:14, Ezekiel 21:9-21:10 21:15 39:17-39:20, Genesis.R 65:11 83:5, Isaiah 10:5 15:1 15:3, Jastrow 516b, Jeremiah 1:13 2:27 3:40, Midrash Psalms 150:1, Pesikta de R'Kahana 4.9 5.18 17:8, Revelation 19:17-19:18, Sifre Devarim {Ha'azinu Hashamayim} 332, Sifre Devarim Nitzavim 332, Song of Songs.R 2:44, z.Bereshit 53b, z.Metzorah 54a, z.Vaera 28b 29a 32a, Zephaniah 1:7
Isaiah 34:6-7 - Pesikta de R'Kahana 7.11
[4] Isaiah 34:7 - b.Avodah Zara 14a, b.Sheviit [Rashi] 47b, Deuteronomy 9:17, Jastrow 1461b, Jeremiah 22:21 2:11 2:27, Job 39:9-39:10, Midrash Psalms 150:1, Midrash Tanchuma Bo 4, Numbers 23:22 24:8, Pesikta Rabbati 17:8, Psalms 68:31 92:11
[5] LXX *mighty ones*
[6] Isaiah 34:8 - 2 Thessalonians 1:6-10, Deuteronomy 8:35 32:41-43, Isaiah 2:21 11:4 1:26 59:17-18 13:2 15:4, Jeremiah 22:10, Luke 18:7, Micah 6:1, Midrash Psalms 150:1, Psalms 94:1, Revelation 6:10-11 18:20 19:2, Romans 2:5 2:8-9
[7] Isaiah 34:9 - Deuteronomy 5:22, Genesis 19:28, Genesis.R 51:2, Job 18:15, Jude 1:7, Luke 17:29, Midrash Psalms 18:11, Midrash Tanchuma Bo 4, Pesikta de R'Kahana 7.11, Pesikta Rabbati 17:8, Psalms 11:7, Revelation 19:20 21:8, z.Vaera 30b
Isaiah 34:9-10 - Exodus.R 9:13, Midrash Tanchuma Vaera 13
[8] LXX *valleys*
[9] Isaiah 34:10 - Bahir 169, Ezekiel 21:3-20:4 5:11, Isaiah 1:31 13:20 24:1 18:24, Jeremiah 7:20, Malachi 1:3-1:4, Mark 9:43-9:48, Midrash Psalms 18:11, Midrash Tanchuma Terumah 11, Revelation 14:10-14:11 18:18 19:3
[10] 1QIsaa *It will burn night and day and will never be extinguished. Its smoke will go up from generation to generation, and it will lie waste forever and ever*; LXX *and it shall never be quenched, and her smoke shall go up: it shall be made desolate throughout her generations*
[11] Isaiah 34:11 - 2 Kings 21:13, 2 Samuel 8:2, b.Bava Batra [Rashbam] 129a, b.Bava Kamma [Tosefot] 116b, b.Bechorot [Tosefot] 8a, b.Chagigah 12a, b.Moed Katan [Rashi] 25b, Ein Yaakov Chagigah:12a, Isaiah 13:20-13:22 14:23 24:10, Jastrow 1183a, Lamentations 2:8, Leviticus.R 6:6, Malachi 1:3-1:4, Midrash Tanchuma Bo 4, Pesikta de R'Kahana 7.11, Pesikta Rabbati 17:8, Revelation 18:2 18:21-23, Sefer Yetzirah [Saadia] 4:6, Testament of Solomon 7:7, z.Bereshit 11b, Zephaniah 2:14
Isaiah 34:11-15 - Sibylline Oracles 8.
[12] LXX *for a long time birds and hedgehogs, and ibises*
[13] 1QIsaa *a line, and chaos*
[14] LXX *satyrs shall live in it*
[15] Isaiah 34:12 - 1 Corinthians 8:4 13:2, 2 Corinthians 12:11, Ecclesiastes 10:16-17, Isaiah 3:6-8 41:11-12 17:24, Jeremiah 3:20 15:6

וְעָלְתָה אַרְמְנֹתֶיהָ סִירִים קִמּוֹשׂ וָחוֹחַ בְּמִבְצָרֶיהָ
וְהָיְתָה נְוֵה תַנִּים חָצִיר לִבְנוֹת יַעֲנָה

13[1] And thorns shall come up in her palaces, nettles and thistles in its fortresses; and it shall be a habitation of *wild-dogs*[2], an enclosure for ostriches.

וּפָגְשׁוּ צִיִּים אֶת־אִיִּים וְשָׂעִיר עַל־רֵעֵהוּ יִקְרָא
אַךְ־שָׁם הִרְגִּיעָה לִּילִית וּמָצְאָה לָהּ מָנוֹחַ

14[3] And *the wild cats shall meet with the jackals, And the satyr shall cry to his fellow; Yes, the night monster shall*[4] *rest there, And shall find her a place of rest.*

שָׁמָּה קִנְּנָה קִפּוֹז וַתְּמַלֵּט וּבָקְעָה וְדָגְרָה בְצִלָּהּ
אַךְ־שָׁם נִקְבְּצוּ דַיּוֹת אִשָּׁה רְעוּתָהּ

15[5] *There the great owl shall make her nest, and lay, And hatch, and brood under her shadow; indeed*[6], *the vultures shall gather, each one with her mate*[7].

דִּרְשׁוּ מֵעַל־סֵפֶר יְהוָה וּקְרָאוּ אַחַת מֵהֵנָּה לֹא
נֶעְדָּרָה אִשָּׁה רְעוּתָהּ לֹא פָקָדוּ כִּי־פִי הוּא צִוָּה
וְרוּחוֹ הוּא קִבְּצָן

16[8] Search the book of the LORD, and read; Not one *of these*[9] shall be missing, No one shall want her mate; *For My mouth has commanded, and of its breath has gathered them*[10].[11]

וְהוּא־הִפִּיל לָהֶן גּוֹרָל וְיָדוֹ חִלְּקַתָּה לָהֶם בַּקָּו
עַד־עוֹלָם יִירָשׁוּהָ לְדוֹר וָדוֹר יִשְׁכְּנוּ־בָהּ

17[12] And He cast the lot for them, and His hand divided it to them by line; They shall possess it forever, *From generation to generation they shall live there*[13].

Isaiah – Chapter 35

יְשֻׂשׂוּם מִדְבָּר וְצִיָּה וְתָגֵל עֲרָבָה וְתִפְרַח
כַּחֲבַצָּלֶת

1[14] *The wilderness and the parched land shall be glad; And the desert shall rejoice, and blossom as the rose*[15].

פָּרֹחַ תִּפְרַח וְתָגֵל אַף גִּילַת וְרַנֵּן כְּבוֹד הַלְּבָנוֹן
נִתַּן־לָהּ הֲדַר הַכַּרְמֶל וְהַשָּׁרוֹן הֵמָּה יִרְאוּ כְבוֹד־
יְהוָה הֲדַר אֱלֹהֵינוּ

2[16] *It shall blossom abundantly, and rejoice, with joy and singing; The glory of Lebanon shall be given to it, The excellency of Carmel and Sharon; They shall see the glory of the LORD, The excellency of our God*[17].

---

[1] Isaiah 34:13 - 2 Baruch 10:8, Hosea 9:6, Isaiah 13:21-22 32:13-32:14 11:7, Jeremiah 9:12 10:22 1:33 50:39-50:40 3:37, Malachi 1:3, Psalms 44:20, Revelation 18:2 18:20-18:24, Zephaniah 2:9

[2] LXX *monsters*

[3] Isaiah 34:14 - Isaiah 13:21-22, Sifre Devarim {Ha'azinu Hashamayim} 306, z.Bereshit 33b, z.Vayikra 19a

[4] LXX *devils shall meet with satyrs, and they shall cry one to the other: there shall satyrs*

[5] Isaiah 34:15 - b.Chullin 140b, Deuteronomy 14:13, Jastrow 279b

[6] 1QIsaa *indeed indeed*

[7] LXX *There has the hedgehog made its nest, and the earth has safely preserved its young: there have the deer met, and seen one another's faces*

[8] Isaiah 34:16 - 2 Peter 1:19, Amos 3:7, b.Bava Kamma [Tosefot] 11a, Daniel 10:21, Deuteronomy 7:21, Genesis 6:17, Genesis.R 32:8, Isaiah 1:20 6:8 10:14, John 5:39 10:35, Joshua 1:8, Luke 21:33, Malachi 3:16, Matthew 5:18, mt.Hilchot Kiddush HaChodesh 19:16, Proverbs 23:12, Psalms 33:6 33:9, Tanya Igeret Hakodesh §29, z.Beshallach 56a, z.Terumah 130b

[9] Missing in 1QIsaa

[10] 1QIsaa *For it his mouth that has commanded, and it is his spirit that has gathered them.*

[11] LXX *They passed by in full number, and not one of them perished: they sought not one another; for the Lord commanded them, and his Spirit gathered them*

[12] Isaiah 34:17 - Acts 13:19 17:26, Guide for the Perplexed 2:47, Isaiah 13:20-13:22 17:14 10:10, Jastrow 474a, Jeremiah 13:25, Joshua 18:8, Psalms 78:55

[13] Missing in 1QIsaa but a different author inserted the text to match the MT and LXX

[14] Isaiah 35:1 - Ezekiel 12:35, Hosea 14:7-8, Isaiah 4:2 3:6 3:10 5:17 32:15-16 16:3 41:18-19 3:3 52:9-10 55:12-13 61:10-11 66:10-14, Midrash Psalms 1:20, Midrash Tanchuma Bamidbar 2, Midrash Tanchuma Devarim 1, Numbers.R 1:2 15:10 23:4, Perek Shirah [the Wilderness], Psalms 48:12 97:8, Revelation 19:1-7, Song of Songs.R 2:2, Testament of Simeon 6:2
Isaiah 35:1-2 - Midrash Tanchuma Beha'alotcha 6, Midrash Tanchuma Massei 3
Isaiah 35:1-10 - 1QIsaa

[15] Missing in 1QIsaa

[16] Isaiah 35:2 - 1 Chronicles 16:33, 2 Corinthians 3:18 4:6, Acts 4:32-33, Amos 9:13-15, b.Shabbat 77a, b.Yoma 21b 39b, Ein Yaakov Yoma 21b 39b, Exodus 33:18-19, Ezekiel 34:25-26, Habakkuk 2:14, Hosea 14:8-9, Isaiah 6:3 1:9 8:15 9:9 16:5 17:19 42:10-12 1:13 55:12-13 60:1-3 12:13 12:21 13:13 65:8-10 66:18-19, John 12:41 17:24, m.Sotah 8:7, Micah 7:14-15, Midrash Tanchuma Devarim 1, Psalms 50:2 65:13-14 72:16 72:19 89:13 96:11-13 97:6 98:7-9 102:16-17 148:9-13, Revelation 21:23, Romans 10:15 15:10, Song of Songs 7:6, Song of Songs.R 3:22, Tanya Igeret Hakodesh §23, y.Yoma 4:4, Zechariah 10:7 14:20-21, Zephaniah 3:19-20

[17] Missing in 1QIsaa

חִזְּק֖וּ יָדַ֣יִם רָפ֑וֹת וּבִרְכַּ֥יִם כֹּשְׁל֖וֹת אַמֵּֽצוּ	3[1]	Strengthen the weak hands, And make firm the tottering knees.
אִמְרוּ֙ לְנִמְהֲרֵי־לֵ֔ב חִזְק֖וּ אַל־תִּירָ֑אוּ הִנֵּ֤ה אֱלֹֽהֵיכֶם֙ נָקָ֣ם יָב֔וֹא גְּמ֖וּל אֱלֹהִ֑ים ה֥וּא יָב֖וֹא וְיֹשַׁעֲכֶֽם	4[2]	Say to those who are of a fearful heart: 'Be strong, fear not'; Behold, your God will *come with*[3] vengeance, With the recompense of God He will come and save you.
אָ֥ז תִּפָּקַ֖חְנָה עֵינֵ֣י עִוְרִ֑ים וְאָזְנֵ֥י חֵרְשִׁ֖ים תִּפָּתַֽחְנָה	5[4]	Then the eyes of the blind shall be opened, And the ears of the deaf shall be unstopped.
אָ֣ז יְדַלֵּ֤ג כָּֽאַיָּל֙ פִּסֵּ֔חַ וְתָרֹ֖ן לְשׁ֣וֹן אִלֵּ֑ם כִּֽי־נִבְקְע֤וּ בַמִּדְבָּר֙ מַ֔יִם וּנְחָלִ֖ים בָּעֲרָבָֽה	6[5]	Then shall the lame man leap as a hart, And the tongue of the dumb shall sing; For in the wilderness waters shall break out, And streams[6] in the desert.
וְהָיָ֤ה הַשָּׁרָב֙ לַאֲגַ֔ם וְצִמָּא֖וֹן לְמַבּ֣וּעֵי מָ֑יִם בִּנְוֵ֤ה תַנִּים֙ רִבְצָ֔הּ חָצִ֖יר לְקָנֶ֥ה וָגֹֽמֶא	7[7]	And the parched land shall become a pool, And the thirsty ground springs of water; In the habitation of jackals, *herds shall lie down, It shall be an enclosure for*[8] reeds and rushes.
וְהָיָה־שָׁ֞ם מַסְל֣וּל וָדֶ֗רֶךְ וְדֶ֤רֶךְ הַקֹּ֙דֶשׁ֙ יִקָּ֣רֵא לָ֔הּ לֹֽא־יַעַבְרֶ֥נּוּ טָמֵ֖א וְהוּא־לָ֑מוֹ הֹלֵ֥ךְ דֶּ֛רֶךְ וֶאֱוִילִ֖ים לֹ֥א יִתְעֽוּ	8[9]	And a highway shall be *there*[10], and a way, And it shall be called The *way*[11] of holiness; The unclean shall not pass over it; but it shall be for those; The wayfaring men, yes fools, shall not err there.
לֹא־יִהְיֶ֨ה שָׁ֜ם אַרְיֵ֗ה וּפְרִ֤יץ חַיּוֹת֙ בַּל־יַעֲלֶ֔נָּה לֹ֥א תִמָּצֵ֖א שָׁ֑ם וְהָלְכ֖וּ גְּאוּלִֽים	9[12]	No lion shall be there, Nor shall any ravenous beast go there, They shall not be found there; But the redeemed shall walk there;
וּפְדוּיֵ֨י יְהֹוָ֜ה יְשֻׁב֗וּן וּבָ֤אוּ צִיּוֹן֙ בְּרִנָּ֔ה וְשִׂמְחַ֥ת עוֹלָ֖ם עַל־רֹאשָׁ֑ם שָׂשׂ֤וֹן וְשִׂמְחָה֙ יַשִּׂ֔יגוּ וְנָ֖סוּ יָג֥וֹן וַאֲנָחָֽה	10[13]	And the ransomed of the LORD shall return, And come to Zion with singing, And everlasting joy shall be upon their heads; They

---

[1] Isaiah 35:3 - Acts 18:23, Hebrews 12:12, Isaiah 40:1-2 52:1-2 57:14-16, Jastrow 676a 1489a 1490a, Job 4:3-4 16:5, Judges 7:11, Leviticus.R 19:5, Luke 22:32 22:43, Saadia Opinions 7Variant:1

[2] Isaiah 35:4 - 1 Chronicles 4:20, 2 Timothy 2:1, Daniel 10:19, Deuteronomy 32:35-43, Ephesians 6:10, Habakkuk 2:3, Haggai 2:4, Hebrews 9:28 10:37-38, Hosea 1:7, Isaiah 1:24 1:9 26:20-21 4:16 8:4 9:22 10:8 40:9-11 41:10-14 43:1-6 20:2 52:7-10 54:4-5 13:2 18:15, James 5:7-9, Joshua 1:6-1:7, Leviticus.R 19:5, Luke 21:28, Malachi 3:1, Matthew 1:21-23, Midrash Tanchuma Vaera 13, Psalms 50:3 20:11, Revelation 1:7 2:10 22:20, Zechariah 2:8-10, Zephaniah 3:16-17
Isaiah 35:4-6 - 1QIsab

[3] 1QIsaa *bring*

[4] Isaiah 35:5 - Acts 9:17-18 2:18, Ephesians 1:17-18 5:14, Exodus 4:11, Genesis.R 95:1, Guide for the Perplexed 3:54, Isaiah 5:18 32:3-4 42:6-7 18:16 19:8 24:8 2:4, Jeremiah 6:10, Job 9:16, John 9:1-7 9:39 11:37, Luke 4:18 7:20-23, Mark 7:32-37 8:22-25 9:25-26, Matthew 9:27-9:30 11:3-5 12:22 20:30-34 21:14, Mekhilta de R'Shimon bar Yochai Shirata 27:1, Mekilta de R'Ishmael Shirata 1:6, Midrash Psalms 146:5, Midrash Tanchuma Beshallach 10, Midrash Tanchuma Metzora 2, Midrash Tanchuma Vayigash 8, Pesikta de R'Kahana 5.16 12.19, Pesikta Rabbati 15:2, Proverbs 20:12, Psalms 2:8, Saadia Opinions 7:9
Isaiah 35:5-6 - z.Yitro 82b

[5] Isaiah 35:6 - 4 Maccabees 10:21, Acts 3:2 3:6-8 8:7 14:8-10, b.Pesachim [Rashi] 68a, b.Sanhedrin 91b, Colossians 3:16, Ein Yaakov Sanhedrin:91b, Exodus 17:6, Ezekiel 47:1-11, Genesis.R 95:1, Isaiah 8:4 11:6 41:17-18 43:19-20 24:21 49:10-11, John 5:8-9 7:37-39, Luke 1:64 11:14, Mark 7:32-37 9:17-25, Matthew 9:32-33 11:5 12:22 15:30-31 21:14, Mekhilta de R'Shimon bar Yochai Shirata 27:1, Mekilta de R'Ishmael Shirata 1:6, Midrash Tanchuma Beshallach 10, Midrash Tanchuma Devarim 2, Midrash Tanchuma Metzora 2, Nehemiah 9:15, Numbers 20:11, Pesikta de R'Kahana 5.16 12.19, Pesikta Rabbati 15:2, Psalms 46:5 51:16 78:15-16, Revelation 22:1 22:17, Saadia Opinions 7:9 7Variant:8, Zechariah 14:8

[6] 1QIsaa adds *will run*

[7] Isaiah 35:7 - 1 Corinthians 6:9-6:11, 1 John 5:19-5:20, Acts 2:18, Chibbur Yafeh 27 {123b}, Hosea 2:1-2:2, Isaiah 13:22 19:6 5:17 10:13 44:3-44:4 1:10, John 4:14 7:38, Luke 13:29, Matthew 21:43, Revelation 12:9-12:12 18:2 20:2-20:3, Saadia Opinions 8:6 7Variant:8

[8] 1QIsaa *a grassy resting place with*

[9] Isaiah 35:8 - 1 John 2:20 2:27, 1 Peter 1:14-1:15 2:9-2:10, 1 Thessalonians 4:7, 2 Peter 3:13, 2 Timothy 1:9, Ephesians 2:10, Ezekiel 19:12 20:9, Hebrews 10:20-10:23 12:14, Isaiah 4:3 11:16 19:23 6:21 9:8 40:3-40:4 18:16 49:10-49:12 4:1 4:11 9:14 12:21 14:10, Jeremiah 7:22 32:39-32:40 50:4-50:5, Joel 4:17, John 7:17 14:6, Matthew 1:23 7:13-7:14, Midrash Tanchuma Massei 3, mt.Hilchot Teshuvah 8:3 8:4 8:4, Numbers.R 23:4, Proverbs 4:18 8:20, Psalms 19:8 23:4 25:8-25:9 119:130, Revelation 7:15-7:17 21:27, Tanya Igeret Hakodesh §27, Titus 2:11-2:14, Zechariah 14:20-14:21

[10] 1QIsaa *there there*

[11] MT repeats *way*

[12] Isaiah 35:9 - 1 Peter 1:18, Exodus 15:13, Ezekiel 10:25, Galatians 3:13, Hosea 2:18, Isaiah 11:6-11:9 6:6 14:12 15:4 17:25, Leviticus 2:6, Psalms 11:2, Revelation 5:9 20:1-20:3, Titus 2:14
Isaiah 35:9-10 - 4QIsa

[13] Isaiah 35:10 - 1 Timothy 2:6, Avot de R'Natan 34 34, b.Berachot 55b, b.Sanhedrin 11b, b.Shabbat 88a, b.Succah 48b, Ein Yaakov

shall obtain gladness and joy[1], And sorrow and sighing shall flee.

Isaiah – Chapter 36

1[2] Now it came to pass in the fourteenth year of king *Hezekiah*[3], that Sennacherib king of Assyria came against all the fortified cities of Judah, and took them.

וַיְהִ֡י בְּאַרְבַּע֩ עֶשְׂרֵ֨ה שָׁנָ֜ה לַמֶּ֣לֶךְ חִזְקִיָּ֗הוּ עָלָ֞ה סַנְחֵרִ֤יב מֶֽלֶךְ־אַשּׁוּר֙ עַ֣ל כָּל־עָרֵ֧י יְהוּדָ֛ה הַבְּצֻר֖וֹת וַֽיִּתְפְּשֵֽׂם

2[4] And the king of Assyria sent Rabshakeh from Lachish to Jerusalem to king *Hezekiah*[5] with a great army. And he stood by the conduit of the upper pool in the highway of the fullers' field.

וַיִּשְׁלַ֣ח מֶֽלֶךְ־אַשּׁ֣וּר ׀ אֶת־רַב־שָׁקֵ֨ה מִלָּכִ֜ישׁ יְרוּשָׁלַ֗͏ְמָה אֶל־הַמֶּ֤לֶךְ חִזְקִיָּ֙הוּ֙ בְּחֵ֣יל כָּבֵ֔ד וַֽיַּעֲמֹ֗ד בִּתְעָלַת֙ הַבְּרֵכָ֣ה הָעֶלְיוֹנָ֔ה בִּמְסִלַּ֖ת שְׂדֵ֥ה כוֹבֵֽס

3[6] Then Eliakim the son of Hilkiah, who was over the household, and Shebna the scribe, and Joah the son of Asaph the recorder came forth to him.

וַיֵּצֵ֥א אֵלָ֛יו אֶלְיָקִ֥ים בֶּן־חִלְקִיָּ֖הוּ אֲשֶׁ֣ר עַל־הַבָּ֑יִת וְשֶׁבְנָא֙ הַסֹּפֵ֔ר וְיוֹאָ֥ח בֶּן־אָסָ֖ף הַמַּזְכִּֽיר

4[7] And Rabshakeh said to them: 'Say now to *Hezekiah*[8]: Thus says the great king, the king of Assyria: *What confidence is this in which you trust*[9]?

וַיֹּ֤אמֶר אֲלֵיהֶם֙ רַב־שָׁקֵ֔ה אִמְרוּ־נָ֖א אֶל־חִזְקִיָּ֑הוּ כֹּֽה־אָמַ֞ר הַמֶּ֣לֶךְ הַגָּד֗וֹל מֶ֚לֶךְ אַשּׁ֔וּר מָ֧ה הַבִּטָּח֛וֹן הַזֶּ֖ה אֲשֶׁ֥ר בָּטָֽחְתָּ

5[10] I said: It is but vain words; for counsel and strength are for the war. Now on whom do you trust, that you have rebelled against me?

אָמַ֙רְתִּי֙ אַךְ־דְּבַר־שְׂפָתַ֔יִם עֵצָ֥ה וּגְבוּרָ֖ה לַמִּלְחָמָ֑ה עַתָּה֙ עַל־מִ֣י בָטַ֔חְתָּ כִּ֥י מָרַ֖דְתָּ בִּֽי

6[11] Behold, you trust on the staff of this bruised reed, on Egypt; on which if a man lean, it will go into his hand, and pierce it; so is Pharaoh king of Egypt to all who trust on him.

הִנֵּ֣ה בָטַ֡חְתָּ עַל־מִשְׁעֶנֶת֩ הַקָּנֶ֨ה הָרָצ֤וּץ הַזֶּה֙ עַל־מִצְרַ֔יִם אֲשֶׁ֨ר יִסָּמֵ֥ךְ אִישׁ֙ עָלָ֔יו וּבָ֥א בְכַפּ֖וֹ וּנְקָבָ֑הּ כֵּ֚ן פַּרְעֹ֣ה מֶֽלֶךְ־מִצְרַ֔יִם לְכָֽל־הַבֹּטְחִ֖ים עָלָֽיו

7[12] But if you say to me: We trust in the LORD our God; *is not He, whose high places and whose altars Hezekiah has taken away, and has said to Judah and to Jerusalem: You shall worship before this altar*[13]?[14]

וְכִֽי־תֹאמַ֣ר אֵלַ֔י אֶל־יְהֹוָ֥ה אֱלֹהֵ֖ינוּ בָּטָ֑חְנוּ הֲלוֹא־ה֗וּא אֲשֶׁ֨ר הֵסִ֤יר חִזְקִיָּ֙הוּ֙ אֶת־בָּמֹתָ֣יו וְאֶת־מִזְבְּחֹתָ֔יו וַיֹּ֤אמֶר לִֽיהוּדָה֙ וְלִיר֣וּשָׁלַ֔͏ִם לִפְנֵ֛י הַמִּזְבֵּ֥חַ הַזֶּ֖ה תִּֽשְׁתַּחֲוֽוּ

Sanhedrin:110b, Ein Yaakov Shabbat:88a, Exodus.R 15:21 23:11, Hellenistic Synagogal Prayers 16:14 16:4, Isaiah 1:8 6:19 51:10-51:11 12:20 17:19, Jeremiah 31:12-31:15 9:11, John 16:22, Jude 1:21, Matthew 20:28, Mekilta de R'Ishmael Beshallah 1:176, Mekilta de R'Ishmael Pisha 14:20, Midrash Psalms 107:1 147:3, Midrash Tanchuma Vayigash 5, Motzoei Shabbat [Viyiten Lecha], Numbers.R 23:14, Pesikta Rabbati 28:3 29/30B:4 37:3 41:2, Psalms 84:8, Revelation 7:9-7:17 14:1-14:4 15:2-15:4 18:20 19:1-19:7 21:4, Seder Hatavat Chalom [Order of making good a bad dream], t.Sanhedrin 13:11, y.Sanhedrin 10:4, z.Yitro 90b

[1] 1QIsaa adds *in it*, referring to Zion but marks it for deletion.

[2] Isaiah 36:1 - 2 Chronicles 8:1, 2 Kings 18:13 18:17, Isaiah 1:7-1:8 7:17 8:7-8:8 10:28-10:32 33:7-33:8, Josephus Antiquities 10.1.1, Leviticus.R 10:5, Mekhilta de R'Shimon bar Yochai Bachodesh 48:1

Isaiah 36:1-2 - 4QIsab

Isaiah 36:1-22 - 1QIsaa, Mas.Soferim 8:2

[3] MT *Hizkiyahu*; 1QIsaa *Hizkiyah*

[4] Isaiah 36:2 - 2 Chronicles 32:9-32:23, 2 Kings 18:17-18:37, Ein Yaakov Megillah:11b, Isaiah 7:3 22:9-22:11, Leviticus.R 17:6, western wrote ירושלמה and Eastern wrote ירולם [j.Megillah 1:9]

Isaiah 36:2-22 - Josephus Antiquities 10.1.2

[5] MT *Hizkiyahu*; 1QIsaa *Hizkiyah*

[6] Isaiah 36:3 - 2 Samuel 8:16-8:17 20:24-20:25, Isaiah 22:15-22:21, Leviticus.R 5:5

[7] Isaiah 36:4 - 2 Chronicles 32:7-32:10 32:14-32:16, 2 Kings 18:5 18:19-18:37 19:10, Acts 12:22-12:23, Daniel 4:27, Ezekiel 31:3-31:18, Isaiah 10:8-10:14 37:11-37:15, Jude 1:16, Proverbs 16:18, Psalms 42:4 42:11 71:10-71:11

[8] MT *Hizkiyahu*; 1QIsaa *Hizkiyah*

[9] LXX *Why are you secure*

[10] Isaiah 36:5 - 2 Kings 18:7 24:1, Ezekiel 17:15, Jeremiah 4:3, Nehemiah 2:19-20, Proverbs 21:30-31 24:5-6

[11] Isaiah 36:6 - 2 Kings 17:4 18:21, Ezekiel 29:6-7, Isaiah 20:5-6 30:1-7 7:3, Jeremiah 37:5-37:8

[12] Isaiah 36:7 - 1 Chronicles 5:20, 1 Corinthians 2:15, 2 Chronicles 16:7-16:9 6:14 7:1 32:7-32:8 8:12, 2 Kings 18:4-18:5 18:22, Deuteronomy 12:2-12:6 12:13-14, Psalms 22:5-22:6 42:6 42:11-12

[13] Missing in LXX

[14] 1QIsaa adds *in Jerusalem*

וְעַתָּה הִתְעָרֶב נָא אֶת־אֲדֹנִי הַמֶּלֶךְ אַשּׁוּר וְאֶתְּנָה לְךָ אַלְפַּיִם סוּסִים אִם־תּוּכַל לָתֶת לְךָ רֹכְבִים עֲלֵיהֶם	8[1]	Now therefore, please, make a wager with my master, the king of Assyria, and I will give you two thousand horses, if you be able, on your part, to set riders upon them.
וְאֵיךְ תָּשִׁיב אֵת פְּנֵי פַחַת אַחַד עַבְדֵי אֲדֹנִי הַקְּטַנִּים וַתִּבְטַח לְךָ עַל־מִצְרַיִם לְרֶכֶב וּלְפָרָשִׁים	9[2]	How then can you turn away the face of one captain, of the least of my master's servants? Yet you put your trust on Egypt for chariots and for horsemen!
וְעַתָּה הֲמִבַּלְעֲדֵי יְהוָה עָלִיתִי עַל־הָאָרֶץ הַזֹּאת לְהַשְׁחִיתָהּ יְהוָה אָמַר אֵלַי עֲלֵה אֶל־הָאָרֶץ הַזֹּאת וְהַשְׁחִיתָהּ	10[3]	And have I come up without the LORD against this land to destroy it? The LORD said to me: Go up against this land, and destroy it.'
וַיֹּאמֶר אֶלְיָקִים וְשֶׁבְנָא וְיוֹאָח אֶל־רַב־שָׁקֵה דַּבֶּר־נָא אֶל־עֲבָדֶיךָ אֲרָמִית כִּי שֹׁמְעִים אֲנָחְנוּ וְאַל־תְּדַבֵּר אֵלֵינוּ יְהוּדִית בְּאָזְנֵי הָעָם אֲשֶׁר עַל־הַחוֹמָה	11[4]	Then said Eliakim and Shebna and Joah to Rabshakeh: 'Speak, please, to your servants in the Aramean language, for we understand it; and do not speak *to us in the Jews' language, in the ears of the people who are on the wall*[5].'
וַיֹּאמֶר רַב־שָׁקֵה הַאֶל אֲדֹנֶיךָ וְאֵלֶיךָ שְׁלָחַנִי אֲדֹנִי לְדַבֵּר אֶת־הַדְּבָרִים הָאֵלֶּה הֲלֹא עַל־הָאֲנָשִׁים הַיֹּשְׁבִים עַל־הַחוֹמָה לֶאֱכֹל "אֶת־חַרְאֵיהֶם" "אֶת־צוֹאָתָם" וְלִשְׁתּוֹת "אֶת־שֵׁינֵיהֶם" "אֶת־מֵימֵי" "רַגְלֵיהֶם" עִמָּכֶם	12[6]	But Rabshakeh said: 'Has my master sent me to your master, and to you, to speak these words? Has he not sent me to the men who sit on the wall, to eat their own *dung*[7], and to drink their own *urine*[8] with you?'
וַיַּעֲמֹד רַב־שָׁקֵה וַיִּקְרָא בְקוֹל־גָּדוֹל יְהוּדִית וַיֹּאמֶר שִׁמְעוּ אֶת־דִּבְרֵי הַמֶּלֶךְ הַגָּדוֹל מֶלֶךְ אַשּׁוּר	13[9]	Then Rabshakeh stood, and cried with a loud voice in the Jews' language, and said: 'Hear the words of the great king, the king of Assyria.
כֹּה אָמַר הַמֶּלֶךְ אַל־יַשִּׁא לָכֶם חִזְקִיָּהוּ כִּי לֹא־יוּכַל לְהַצִּיל אֶתְכֶם	14[10]	Thus says the king[11]: Let not *Hezekiah*[12] beguile you, for he will not be able to deliver you;
וְאַל־יַבְטַח אֶתְכֶם חִזְקִיָּהוּ אֶל־יְהוָה לֵאמֹר הַצֵּל יַצִּילֵנוּ יְהוָה לֹא תִנָּתֵן הָעִיר הַזֹּאת בְּיַד מֶלֶךְ אַשּׁוּר	15[13]	Nor let *Hezekiah*[14] make you trust in the LORD, saying: The LORD will surely deliver us; this city shall not be given into the hand of the king of Assyria.
אַל־תִּשְׁמְעוּ אֶל־חִזְקִיָּהוּ ס כִּי כֹה אָמַר הַמֶּלֶךְ אַשּׁוּר עֲשׂוּ־אִתִּי בְרָכָה וּצְאוּ אֵלַי וְאִכְלוּ אִישׁ־גַּפְנוֹ וְאִישׁ תְּאֵנָתוֹ וּשְׁתוּ אִישׁ מֵי־בוֹרוֹ	16[15]	Do not listen to *Hezekiah*[16]; for thus says the king of Assyria: Make your peace with me, and come out to me; and every one of you will eat of his vine, and of his fig-tree, and drink the waters of his own cistern;

---

[1] Isaiah 36:8 - 1 Kings 20:10 20:18, 1 Samuel 17:40-17:43, 2 Kings 14:14 18:23, Isaiah 10:13-10:14, Nehemiah 4:2-4:5, Psalms 20:8-20:9 123:3-123:4

[2] Isaiah 36:9 - 2 Kings 18:24, Deuteronomy 17:16, Isaiah 10:8 20:5 30:2-30:5 6:7 30:16-17 7:3 12:6, Jeremiah 2:36, Proverbs 21:31

[3] Isaiah 36:10 - 1 Kings 13:18, 2 Chronicles 11:21, 2 Kings 18:25, Amos 3:6, Isaiah 10:5-10:7 13:28

[4] Isaiah 36:11 - 2 Kings 18:26-18:27, Daniel 2:4, Ezra 4:7

[5] 1QIsaa *this message so that the men sitting onm the wall can hear*

[6] Isaiah 36:12 - 2 Kings 6:25-29 18:27, Deuteronomy 28:53-57, Ezekiel 4:16, Isaiah 9:21, Jastrow 1564a, Jeremiah 19:9, Lamentations 4:9-10, Leviticus 2:29

[7] To remove indelicate expressions the word חריהם *excrement* is substituted by צואה *deposit*

[8] To remove indelicate expressions the word שיניהם *urine* is substituted by ממי רגליהם *water of the feet*

[9] Isaiah 36:13 - 1 Samuel 17:8-17:11, 2 Chronicles 8:18, 2 Kings 18:28, 2 Kings 18:28-18:32, compare דברי *the words of* here with דבר *the word of* at, Daniel 4:34, Ezekiel 31:3-31:10, Isaiah 8:7 10:8-13 12:4, Psalms 17:10-13 73:8-9 82:6-7

[10] Isaiah 36:14 - 2 Chronicles 8:11 32:13-19, 2 Kings 19:10-13 19:22, 2 Thessalonians 2:4, Daniel 3:15-17 6:21 7:25, Isaiah 37:10-37:13, Revelation 13:5-13:6

[11] 1QIsaa adds *of Assyria*

[12] MT *Hizkiyahu*; 1QIsaa *Hizkiyah*

[13] Isaiah 36:15 - Isaiah 12:7 13:10 37:23-24, Matthew 3:43, Psalms 4:3 22:8-9 71:9-11

[14] MT *Hizkiyahu*; 1QIsaa *Hizkiyah*

[15] Isaiah 36:16 - 1 Kings 4:20 4:25, 1 Samuel 11:3 1:27, 2 Corinthians 9:5, 2 Kings 5:15 18:31 24:12-24:16, 2 Samuel 8:6, Genesis 8:21 9:11, Micah 4:4, Proverbs 5:15, Zechariah 3:10

[16] MT *Hizkiyahu*; 1QIsaa *Hizkiyah*

17[1] until I come and take you away to a land like your own land, a land of corn and wine, a land of bread and vineyards.

עַד־בֹּאִי וְלָקַחְתִּי אֶתְכֶם אֶל־אֶרֶץ כְּאַרְצְכֶם אֶרֶץ דָּגָן וְתִירוֹשׁ אֶרֶץ לֶחֶם וּכְרָמִים

18[2] Beware lest *Hezekiah*[3] persuade you, saying: The LORD will deliver us. has any of the gods of the nations delivered his land out of the hand of the king of Assyria?

פֶּן־יַסִּית אֶתְכֶם חִזְקִיָּהוּ לֵאמֹר יְהוָה יַצִּילֵנוּ הַהִצִּילוּ אֱלֹהֵי הַגּוֹיִם אִישׁ אֶת־אַרְצוֹ מִיַּד מֶלֶךְ אַשּׁוּר

19[4] Where are the gods of Hamath and Arpad? where are the gods of Sepharvaim? and have they delivered Samaria out of my hand?

אַיֵּה אֱלֹהֵי חֲמָת וְאַרְפָּד אַיֵּה אֱלֹהֵי סְפַרְוָיִם וְכִי־הִצִּילוּ אֶת־שֹׁמְרוֹן מִיָּדִי

20[5] Who are they among all the gods of these countries, that have delivered their country out of my hand, that the LORD should deliver Jerusalem out of my hand?'

מִי בְּכָל־אֱלֹהֵי הָאֲרָצוֹת הָאֵלֶּה אֲשֶׁר־הִצִּילוּ אֶת־אַרְצָם מִיָּדִי כִּי־יַצִּיל יְהוָה אֶת־יְרוּשָׁלַ͏ִם מִיָּדִי

21[6] But they held their peace, and answered him not a word; for the king's commandment was, saying: 'Do not answer him.'

וַיַּחֲרִישׁוּ וְלֹא־עָנוּ אֹתוֹ דָּבָר כִּי־מִצְוַת הַמֶּלֶךְ הִיא לֵאמֹר לֹא תַעֲנֻהוּ

22[7] Then Eliakim the son of Hilkiah came, who was over the household, and Shebna the scribe, and Joah the son of Asaph the recorder, to *Hezekiah*[8] with their clothes rent, and told him the words of Rabshakeh.

וַיָּבֹא אֶלְיָקִים בֶּן־חִלְקִיָּהוּ אֲשֶׁר־עַל־הַבַּיִת וְשֶׁבְנָא הַסֹּפֵר וְיוֹאָח בֶּן־אָסָף הַמַּזְכִּיר אֶל־חִזְקִיָּהוּ קְרוּעֵי בְגָדִים וַיַּגִּידוּ לוֹ אֵת דִּבְרֵי רַב־שָׁקֵה

Isaiah – Chapter 37

1[9] And it came to pass, when king Hezekiah heard it, he rent his clothes, and covered himself with sackcloth, and went into the house of the LORD.

וַיְהִי כִּשְׁמֹעַ הַמֶּלֶךְ חִזְקִיָּהוּ וַיִּקְרַע אֶת־בְּגָדָיו וַיִּתְכַּס בַּשָּׂק וַיָּבֹא בֵּית יְהוָה

2[10] And he sent Eliakim, who was over the household, and Shebna the scribe, and the elders of the priests, covered with sackcloth, to Isaiah the prophet the son of Amoz.

וַיִּשְׁלַח אֶת־אֶלְיָקִים אֲשֶׁר־עַל־הַבַּיִת וְאֵת שֶׁבְנָא הַסֹּפֵר וְאֵת זִקְנֵי הַכֹּהֲנִים מִתְכַּסִּים בַּשַּׂקִּים אֶל־יְשַׁעְיָהוּ בֶן־אָמוֹץ הַנָּבִיא

3[11] And they said to him: 'Thus says Hezekiah: This day is a day of trouble, and of rebuke, and of insult; for the children come to the birth, and there is no strength to bring forth.

וַיֹּאמְרוּ אֵלָיו כֹּה אָמַר חִזְקִיָּהוּ יוֹם־צָרָה וְתוֹכֵחָה וּנְאָצָה הַיּוֹם הַזֶּה כִּי בָאוּ בָנִים עַד־מַשְׁבֵּר וְכֹחַ אַיִן לְלֵדָה

---

[1] Isaiah 36:17 - 2 Kings 17:6-23 18:9-12 18:32 24:11, Deuteronomy 8:7-9 11:12, Exodus 3:8, Job 20:17, Leviticus.R 17:6, Proverbs 12:10

[2] Isaiah 36:18 - 2 Chronicles 32:13-17, 2 Kings 18:33-35 19:12-13 19:17-18, Daniel 3:15, Habakkuk 2:19-20, Isaiah 12:7 12:10 12:15 13:10 37:12-13 37:17-18, Jeremiah 10:3-5 10:10-12, Psalms 12:5 92:6-8 115:2-8 135:5-6 135:15-18
Isaiah 36:18-20 - Ein Yaakov Sanhedrin 94a

[3] MT *Hizkiyahu*; 1QIsaa *Hizkiyah*

[4] Isaiah 36:19 - 2 Kings 17:5-7 17:24 18:10-12, 2 Samuel 8:9, Isaiah 10:9-11 37:11-13, Jeremiah 1:23, Numbers 10:8

[5] Isaiah 36:20 - 1 Kings 20:23, 2 Chronicles 8:15 8:19, 2 Kings 19:22-19:37, b.Megillah 11b, b.Sotah [Tosefot] 9a, b.Succah 14a, Daniel 3:15, Ecclesiastes.R 5:1, Ein Yaakov Megillah:11b, Exodus 5:2, Isaiah 37:18-37:19 37:23-37:29 45:16-45:17, Job 15:25-15:26 40:9-40:12, Leviticus.R 18:2, Mekilta de R'Ishmael Shirata 8:30, Psalms 50:21 73:9

[6] Isaiah 36:21 - 2 Kings 18:26 18:37, Amos 5:13, Matthew 7:6, Proverbs 9:7-8 2:4, Psalms 38:14-16 39:2

[7] Isaiah 36:22 - 2 Kings 5:7, b.Shabbat 12b, Ezra 9:3, Isaiah 9:7 12:3 12:11 37:1-2, Matthew 26:65, mt.Hilchot Avodat Kochavim v'Chukkoteihem 2:10 2:10

[8] MT *Hizkiyahu*; 1QIsaa *Hizkiyah*

[9] Isaiah 37:1 - 2 Kings 19:1-19:37 22:11, Ezra 9:5, Isaiah 36:22-37:38, Jeremiah 12:24, Job 1:20-1:21, Jonah 3:5-3:6, Matthew 11:21, mt.Hilchot Avodat Kochavim v'Chukkoteihem 2:10 2:10, Tanya Igeret Hakodesh §19
Isaiah 37:1-8 - Josephus Antiquities 10.1.3
Isaiah 37:1-38 - 1QIsaa

[10] Isaiah 37:2 - 2 Chronicles 20:20, 2 Kings 18:18 19:2 22:12-22:14, Isaiah 1:1 12:3 13:14, Joel 1:13, Leviticus.R 5:5
Isaiah 37:2-36 - Mas.Soferim 8:2

[11] Isaiah 37:3 - 2 Chronicles 15:4, 2 Kings 19:3, Esther.R 7:13, Hosea 5:15-6:1 13:13, Isaiah 22:5 1:8 26:17-18 9:2 18:9, Jeremiah 6:7, Numbers.R 13:4, Psalms 50:15 91:15 95:8 116:3-4, Revelation 3:19, Ruth.R 5:6, Song of Songs.R 6:25, y.Shabbat 2:6

אוּלַי יִשְׁמַע יְהֹוָה אֱלֹהֶיךָ אֵת ׀ דִּבְרֵי רַב־שָׁקֵה אֲשֶׁר שְׁלָחוֹ מֶלֶךְ־אַשּׁוּר ׀ אֲדֹנָיו לְחָרֵף אֱלֹהִים חַי וְהוֹכִיחַ בַּדְּבָרִים אֲשֶׁר שָׁמַע יְהֹוָה אֱלֹהֶיךָ וְנָשָׂאתָ תְפִלָּה בְּעַד הַשְּׁאֵרִית הַנִּמְצָאָה	4[1]	It may be the LORD your God will hear the words of Rabshakeh, whom the king of Assyria his master has sent to taunt the living God, and will rebuke the words which the LORD your God has heard; therefore, pray for the remnant who are left[2].'
וַיָּבֹאוּ עַבְדֵי הַמֶּלֶךְ חִזְקִיָּהוּ אֶל־יְשַׁעְיָהוּ	5	So the servants of king Hezekiah came to Isaiah.
וַיֹּאמֶר אֲלֵיהֶם יְשַׁעְיָהוּ כֹּה תֹאמְרוּן אֶל־אֲדֹנֵיכֶם כֹּה ׀ אָמַר יְהֹוָה אַל־תִּירָא מִפְּנֵי הַדְּבָרִים אֲשֶׁר שָׁמַעְתָּ אֲשֶׁר גִּדְּפוּ נַעֲרֵי מֶלֶךְ־אַשּׁוּר אוֹתִי	6[3]	And Isaiah said to them: 'Thus shall you say to your master: Thus says the LORD: Do not be afraid of the words you have heard, with which the servants of the king of Assyria have blasphemed Me.
הִנְנִי נוֹתֵן בּוֹ רוּחַ וְשָׁמַע שְׁמוּעָה וְשָׁב אֶל־אַרְצוֹ וְהִפַּלְתִּיו בַּחֶרֶב בְּאַרְצוֹ	7[4]	Behold, I will put a spirit in him, and he shall hear a rumor, and shall return to his own land; and I will cause him to fall by the sword in his own land.'
וַיָּשָׁב רַב־שָׁקֵה וַיִּמְצָא אֶת־מֶלֶךְ אַשּׁוּר נִלְחָם עַל־לִבְנָה כִּי שָׁמַע כִּי נָסַע מִלָּכִישׁ	8[5]	So Rabshakeh returned, and found the king of Assyria warring against Libnah; for he had heard that he departed from Lachish.
וַיִּשְׁמַע עַל־תִּרְהָקָה מֶלֶךְ־כּוּשׁ לֵאמֹר יָצָא לְהִלָּחֵם אִתָּךְ וַיִּשְׁמַע וַיִּשְׁלַח מַלְאָכִים אֶל־חִזְקִיָּהוּ לֵאמֹר	9[6]	And he heard say *about*[7] Tirhakah king of Ethiopia: 'He has come out to fight against you.' And when he heard it, he sent messengers to Hezekiah, saying:
כֹּה תֹאמְרוּן אֶל־חִזְקִיָּהוּ מֶלֶךְ־יְהוּדָה לֵאמֹר אַל־יַשִּׁאֲךָ אֱלֹהֶיךָ אֲשֶׁר אַתָּה בּוֹטֵחַ בּוֹ לֵאמֹר לֹא תִנָּתֵן יְרוּשָׁלַ͏ִם בְּיַד מֶלֶךְ אַשּׁוּר	10[8]	'Thus shall you speak to Hezekiah king of Judah, saying: Let not your God in whom you trust beguile you, saying: Jerusalem shall not be given into the hand of the king of Assyria.
הִנֵּה ׀ אַתָּה שָׁמַעְתָּ אֲשֶׁר עָשׂוּ מַלְכֵי אַשּׁוּר לְכָל־הָאֲרָצוֹת לְהַחֲרִימָם וְאַתָּה תִּנָּצֵל	11[9]	Behold, you have heard what the kings of Assyria have done to all lands, by destroying them utterly; and shall you be delivered?
הַהִצִּילוּ אוֹתָם אֱלֹהֵי הַגּוֹיִם אֲשֶׁר הִשְׁחִיתוּ אֲבוֹתַי אֶת־גּוֹזָן וְאֶת־חָרָן וְרֶצֶף וּבְנֵי־עֶדֶן אֲשֶׁר בִּתְלַשָּׂר	12[10]	Have the gods of the nations delivered them, which my fathers destroyed, Gozan, and Haran, and Rezeph, and the children of Eden who were in *Telassar*[11]?
אַיֵּה מֶלֶךְ־חֲמָת וּמֶלֶךְ אַרְפָּד וּמֶלֶךְ לָעִיר סְפַרְוָיִם הֵנַע וְעִוָּה	13[12]	Where is the king of Hamath, and the king of Arpad, and the king of the city of *Sepharvaim, of Hena, and Ivvah*[13]?'

---

[1] Isaiah 37:4 - 1 Samuel 7:8 12:19 12:23 14:6 17:26 17:36, 2 Chronicles 4:19 32:15-32:20, 2 Kings 17:18 18:9-18:16 19:4 19:22-19:23, 2 Samuel 16:12, Amos 5:15, Isaiah 1:9 8:7-8:8 10:5-10:6 10:22 12:13 12:18 12:20 37:23-37:24 51:7-51:8, James 5:16, Joel 2:17, Joshua 14:12, Mas.Soferim 8:2, Psalms 50:21 10:23, Romans 9:27

[2] 1QIsaa adds *in the city*

[3] Isaiah 37:6 - 2 Chronicles 20:15-20:20, 2 Kings 19:5-19:7 22:15-22:20, Exodus 14:13, Isaiah 7:4 10:24-10:25 11:4 41:10-41:14 43:1-43:2 51:12-51:13, Jastrow 1279b, Joshua 11:6, Leviticus 2:8, Mark 4:40 5:36, z.Vaetchanan 269b

[4] Isaiah 37:7 - 2 Chronicles 8:21, 2 Kings 7:6, Isaiah 10:16-18 10:33-34 17:13-14 29:5-8 30:28-33 31:8-9 33:10-12 13:9 37:36-38, Job 4:9 15:21, Psalms 58:10

[5] Isaiah 37:8 - 2 Chronicles 21:10, 2 Kings 8:22 19:8-9, Joshua 10:29 10:31-34 12:11 15:39 21:13, Numbers 33:20-21
Isaiah 37:8-12 - 1QIsab

[6] Isaiah 37:9 - 1 Samuel 23:27-28, Isaiah 18:1 20:5 13:7
Isaiah 37:9-35 - Josephus Antiquities 10.1.4

[7] 1QIsaa misspells this word

[8] Isaiah 37:10 - 2 Chronicles 32:7-8 32:15-19, 2 Kings 18:5 19:10-13, Isaiah 12:4 12:15 12:20, Matthew 3:43, Psalms 22:9, the abbreviation ירש stands for ירושלם

[9] Isaiah 37:11 - 2 Kings 17:4-6 18:33-35, Isaiah 10:7-10:14 14:17 36:18-20 37:18-19

[10] Isaiah 37:12 - 2 Kings 17:6 18:11 19:12, Acts 7:2, Amos 1:5, Ezekiel 3:23 4:13, Genesis 2:8 11:31 12:1-4 12:14 4:10 5:4, Genesis.R 37:4, Isaiah 12:20 46:5-7

[11] LXX *Theemath*

[12] Isaiah 37:13 - 2 Kings 17:24 17:30-31 18:34 19:13, Isaiah 10:9 12:19, Jeremiah 1:23, Pirkei de R'Eliezer 31

[13] LXX *Eppharuaim, and of Anagugana*

וַיִּקַּ֨ח חִזְקִיָּ֧הוּ אֶת־הַסְּפָרִ֛ים מִיַּ֥ד הַמַּלְאָכִ֖ים וַיִּקְרָאֵ֑הוּ וַיַּ֙עַל֙ בֵּ֣ית יְהֹוָ֔ה וַיִּפְרְשֵׂ֥הוּ חִזְקִיָּ֖הוּ לִפְנֵ֥י יְהֹוָֽה	14[1] And Hezekiah received the letter from the hand of the messengers, and read it; and Hezekiah went up to the house of the LORD, and spread it before the LORD.
וַיִּתְפַּלֵּל֙ חִזְקִיָּ֔הוּ אֶל־יְהֹוָ֖ה לֵאמֹֽר	15[2] And Hezekiah prayed to the LORD, saying:
יְהֹוָ֨ה צְבָא֜וֹת אֱלֹהֵ֤י יִשְׂרָאֵל֙ יֹשֵׁ֣ב הַכְּרֻבִ֔ים אַתָּה־ה֤וּא הָֽאֱלֹהִים֙ לְבַדְּךָ֔ לְכֹ֖ל מַמְלְכ֣וֹת הָאָ֑רֶץ אַתָּ֣ה עָשִׂ֔יתָ אֶת־הַשָּׁמַ֖יִם וְאֶת־הָאָֽרֶץ	16[3] 'O LORD of hosts, the God of Israel, who sits upon the cherubim, you are the God, you alone, of all the kingdoms of the earth; you have made heaven and earth.
הַטֵּ֨ה יְהֹוָ֤ה ׀ אׇזְנְךָ֙ וּֽשְׁמָ֔ע פְּקַ֧ח יְהֹוָ֛ה עֵינֶ֖ךָ וּרְאֵ֑ה וּשְׁמַ֗ע אֵ֚ת כׇּל־דִּבְרֵ֣י סַנְחֵרִ֔יב אֲשֶׁ֣ר שָׁלַ֔ח לְחָרֵ֖ף אֱלֹהִ֥ים חָֽי	17[4] Incline your ear, O LORD, and hear; open your eyes, O LORD, and see; and hear all the words of Sennacherib, who has sent to taunt the living God.
אׇמְנָ֖ם יְהֹוָ֑ה הֶחֱרִ֜יבוּ מַלְכֵ֥י אַשּׁ֛וּר אֶת־כׇּל־הָאֲרָצ֖וֹת וְאֶת־אַרְצָֽם	18[5] Truly, LORD, the kings of Assyria has laid to waste all the countries, and their land,
וְנָתֹ֥ן אֶת־אֱלֹהֵיהֶ֖ם בָּאֵ֑שׁ כִּי֩ לֹ֨א אֱלֹהִ֜ים הֵ֗מָּה כִּ֣י אִם־מַעֲשֵׂ֧ה יְדֵֽי־אָדָ֛ם עֵ֥ץ וָאֶ֖בֶן וַֽיְאַבְּדֽוּם	19[6] and have cast their gods into the fire; for they were no gods, but the work of men's hands, wood and stone; Therefore, they destroyed them.
וְעַתָּה֙ יְהֹוָ֣ה אֱלֹהֵ֔ינוּ הוֹשִׁיעֵ֖נוּ מִיָד֑וֹ וְיֵֽדְעוּ֙ כׇּל־מַמְלְכ֣וֹת הָאָ֔רֶץ כִּֽי־אַתָּ֥ה יְהֹוָ֖ה לְבַדֶּֽךָ	20[7] Now therefore, O LORD our God, [8]save us from his hand, so all the kingdoms of the earth may know that you alone *are the LORD*[9].'
וַיִּשְׁלַח֙ יְשַֽׁעְיָ֣הוּ בֶן־אָמ֔וֹץ אֶל־חִזְקִיָּ֖הוּ לֵאמֹ֑ר כֹּֽה־אָמַ֤ר יְהֹוָה֙ אֱלֹהֵ֣י יִשְׂרָאֵ֔ל אֲשֶׁ֧ר הִתְפַּלַּ֛לְתָּ אֵלַ֖י אֶל־סַנְחֵרִ֥יב מֶ֥לֶךְ אַשּֽׁוּר	21[10] Then Isaiah the son of Amoz sent to Hezekiah, saying: 'Thus says the LORD, the God of Israel: *Since you have prayed to Me*[11] about Sennacherib king of Assyria,
זֶ֣ה הַדָּבָ֔ר אֲשֶׁר־דִּבֶּ֥ר יְהֹוָ֖ה עָלָ֑יו בָּזָ֨ה לְךָ֜ לָעֲגָ֣ה לְךָ֗ בְּתוּלַת֙ בַּת־צִיּ֔וֹן אַחֲרֶ֙יךָ֙ רֹ֣אשׁ הֵנִ֔יעָה בַּ֖ת יְרוּשָׁלָֽ͏ִם	22[12] this is the word the LORD has spoken concerning him: The virgin daughter of Zion has despised you and laughed you to scorn; The daughter of Jerusalem has shaken her head at you.
אֶת־מִ֤י חֵרַ֙פְתָּ֙ וְגִדַּ֔פְתָּ וְעַל־מִ֖י הֲרִימ֣וֹתָה קּ֑וֹל וַתִּשָּׂ֥א מָר֛וֹם עֵינֶ֖יךָ אֶל־קְד֥וֹשׁ יִשְׂרָאֵֽל	23[13] Whom have you taunted and blasphemed? And against whom have you exalted your voice? Yes, you have lifted your eyes on high, against the Holy One of Israel!

---

[1] Isaiah 37:14 - 1 Kings 8:28-30 8:38 9:3, 2 Chronicles 6:20-22, 2 Kings 19:14, Isaiah 13:1, Joel 2:17-20, Psalms 27:5 62:2-4 74:10 76:2-4 123:1-4 23:6

[2] Isaiah 37:15 - 1 Samuel 7:8-9, 2 Chronicles 14:10 20:6-12, 2 Kings 19:15-19, 2 Samuel 7:1829, Daniel 9:3-4, Ecclesiastes.R 9:29, James 5:13, Philippians 4:6-7

[3] Isaiah 37:16 - 1 Kings 18:32, 1 Samuel 4:4, 2 Kings 5:15, 2 Samuel 7:26, Colossians 1:16, Deuteronomy 10:17, Exodus 1:22, Exodus.R 33:4, Genesis 1:1, Hebrews 4:16, Isaiah 6:3 8:13 13:20 16:28 43:10-43:11 20:6 20:24 21:22 6:5, Jeremiah 10:10-10:12, John 1:3, Joseph and Aseneth 8:9, Kuzari 2.050, Numbers.R 13:3, Pesikta Rabbati 7:2, Psalms 46:8 46:12 80:2 86:10 99:1 136:2-136:3 2:6, Revelation 11:15-11:17, Selichot

[4] Isaiah 37:17 - 1 Peter 3:12, 2 Chronicles 6:40, 2 Samuel 16:12, Daniel 9:17-19, Isaiah 13:4, Job 12:7, Midrash Psalms 71:2, Psalms 10:15-16 17:6 71:2 74:10 74:22 79:12 89:51-52 130:1-2

[5] Isaiah 37:18 - 1 Chronicles 5:26, 2 Kings 15:29 16:9 17:6 17:24, Nahum 2:12-2:13

[6] Isaiah 37:19 - 2 Samuel 5:21, Exodus 8:20, Hosea 8:6, Isaiah 10:9-10:11 2:14 36:18-36:20 40:19-40:21 17:7 17:24 17:29 44:9-10 20:17 46:1-2, Jeremiah 10:3-6 10:11, Mekilta de R'Ishmael Bahodesh 6:23, Psalms 115:4-8, Sifre Devarim Ekev 43

[7] Isaiah 37:20 - 1 Kings 8:43 18:36-37, 1 Samuel 17:45-47, Exodus 9:15-16, Ezekiel 12:23, Isaiah 18:8, Joshua 7:8-9, Lamentations.R 1:23, Leviticus.R 7:6, Malachi 1:11, Psalms 46:11 59:14 67:2-3 83:18-19

[8] 1QIsaa adds *I will*

[9] 1QIsaa *LORD, are God*

[10] Isaiah 37:21 - 2 Kings 19:20-19:21, 2 Samuel 15:31 17:23, Acts 4:31, Daniel 9:20-9:23, Isaiah 13:2 38:3-38:6 10:9 17:24, Job 22:27, Psalms 91:15, z.Vaetchanan 269b

[11] 1QIsaa *to whom you prayed*

[12] Isaiah 37:22 - 1 Samuel 17:36 17:44-47, Amos 5:2, Isaiah 1:8 8:9-10 10:32 23:12 14:11, Jeremiah 14:17, Job 16:4, Joel 4:9-12, Lamentations 1:15 2:13, Matthew 21:5 3:39, Psalms 2:2-4 9:15 22:8-9 27:1-3 31:19 46:2-8, Zechariah 2:10 9:9, Zephaniah 3:14

[13] Isaiah 37:23 - 2 Chronicles 8:17, 2 Kings 19:4 19:22, 2 Thessalonians 2:4, Daniel 5:20-23 7:25, Exodus 5:2 9:17 15:11, Ezekiel 4:2 4:9 15:7, Habakkuk 1:12-13, Isaiah 2:11 10:13-15 10:20 12:6 14:13-14 17:7 30:11-13 13:4 37:10-13 17:14 17:16 19:3 19:14, Proverbs 6:13, Psalms 44:17 73:9 74:18 74:23, Revelation 13:1-13:6, Tanna Devei Eliyahu 7

בְּיַד עֲבָדֶיךָ חֵרַפְתָּ ׀ אֲדֹנָי וַתֹּאמֶר בְּרֹב רִכְבִּי אֲנִי עָלִיתִי מְרוֹם הָרִים יַרְכְּתֵי לְבָנוֹן וְאֶכְרֹת קוֹמַת אֲרָזָיו מִבְחַר בְּרֹשָׁיו וְאָבוֹא מְרוֹם קִצּוֹ יַעַר כַּרְמִלּוֹ

24[1] By your servants you have taunted the Lord, And have said: With the multitude of my chariots I have come up to the height of the mountains, To the innermost parts of Lebanon; And I have cut down its tall cedars, And its choice cypress trees; And I have entered into his farthest height, The forest of his fruitful field.

אֲנִי קַרְתִּי וְשָׁתִיתִי מָיִם וְאַחְרִב בְּכַף־פְּעָמַי כֹּל יְאֹרֵי מָצוֹר

25[2] I have *dug*[3] and drunk [4]water, And with the sole of my feet have I dried up all the rivers of Egypt[5].

הֲלוֹא־שָׁמַעְתָּ לְמֵרָחוֹק אוֹתָהּ עָשִׂיתִי מִימֵי קֶדֶם וִיצַרְתִּיהָ עַתָּה הֲבֵאתִיהָ וּתְהִי לְהַשְׁאוֹת גַּלִּים נִצִּים עָרִים בְּצֻרוֹת

26[6] Have you not heard? Long ago I made it, In ancient times I fashioned it; Now I have brought it to pass, Yes, it is done; that fortified cities Should be laid waste into *ruined*[7] piles.

וְיֹשְׁבֵיהֶן קִצְרֵי־יָד חַתּוּ וָבֹשׁוּ הָיוּ עֵשֶׂב שָׂדֶה וִירַק דֶּשֶׁא חֲצִיר גַּגּוֹת וּשְׁדֵמָה לִפְנֵי קָמָה

27[8] Therefore, their inhabitants were of small power, They were dismayed and confused; They were as the grass of the field, And as the green herb, As the grass on the housetops, And as a field of corn before it is grown up.

וְשִׁבְתְּךָ וְצֵאתְךָ וּבוֹאֲךָ יָדָעְתִּי וְאֵת הִתְרַגֶּזְךָ אֵלָי

28[9] But I know your [10]sitting down, and your going out, and your coming in, And your raging against Me.

יַעַן הִתְרַגֶּזְךָ אֵלַי וְשַׁאֲנַנְךָ עָלָה בְאָזְנָי וְשַׂמְתִּי חַחִי בְּאַפֶּךָ וּמִתְגִּי בִּשְׂפָתֶיךָ וַהֲשִׁיבֹתִיךָ בַּדֶּרֶךְ אֲשֶׁר־בָּאתָ בָּהּ

29[11] *Because of your raging against Me*[12], And for that, your uproar has come up into My ears, Therefore, will I put My hook in your nose, And My bridle in your lips, And I will turn you back the way *by which you came*[13].

וְזֶה־לְּךָ הָאוֹת אָכוֹל הַשָּׁנָה סָפִיחַ וּבַשָּׁנָה הַשֵּׁנִית שָׁחִיס וּבַשָּׁנָה הַשְּׁלִישִׁית זִרְעוּ וְקִצְרוּ וְנִטְעוּ כְרָמִים "וְאָכוֹל" "וְאִכְלוּ" פִרְיָם

30[14] And this shall be the sign to you: you shall eat this year what grows of itself, and in the second year what springs of the same; and in the third year sow, and reap, and plant vineyards, and eat its fruit.

וְיָסְפָה פְּלֵיטַת בֵּית־יְהוּדָה הַנִּשְׁאָרָה שֹׁרֶשׁ לְמָטָּה וְעָשָׂה פְרִי לְמָעְלָה

31[15] And the remnant of the house of Judah who escaped shall [16]again take root downward, and bear fruit upward.

---

[1] Isaiah 37:24 - 2 Kings 19:22-23, Avot de R'Natan 27, b.Sanhedrin 94b, Daniel 4:5-11 4:17-19 4:27, Ein Yaakov Sanhedrin:94b, Exodus 15:9, Exodus.R 23:5, Ezekiel 31:3-31:18, Isaiah 10:13-14 10:18 14:8 5:17 12:9 36:15-20 13:4, Josephus Wars 1.13.2, Mekilta de R'Ishmael Shirata 6:47, Numbers.R 9:24, Per Massorah: Soferim altered "Hashem" to "Adonai", Psalms 20:8, Zechariah 11:1-2

[2] Isaiah 37:25 - 1 Kings 20:10, 2 Kings 19:23-19:24, b.Sanhedrin 95b, Deuteronomy 11:10, Ein Yaakov Sanhedrin:95b, Isaiah 12:12, Midrash Tanchuma Bereshit 7

[3] 1QIsaa *cried out*

[4] 1QIsaa adds *foreign*

[5] LXX reads, *and I have made a bridge, and dried up the waters, and every pool of water*

[6] Isaiah 37:26 - 1 Peter 2:8, Acts 2:23 4:27-28, Amos 3:6, Genesis 2:20, Isaiah 10:5-6 10:15 25:1-2 21:7 46:10-11, Jude 1:4, Psalms 17:13 76:11

[7] 1QIsaa *besieged*

[8] Isaiah 37:27 - 1 Peter 1:24, 2 Kings 19:26, Isaiah 19:16 40:6-8, James 1:10-11, Jeremiah 5:10 13:10, Numbers 14:9, Psalms 37:2 90:5-6 92:8 7:15 127:1-2 9:6

[9] Isaiah 37:28 - Jeremiah 23:23-23:24, Proverbs 5:21 15:3, Psalms 139:1-139:11, Revelation 2:13

[10] 1QIsaa adds *rising up and your*

[11] Isaiah 37:29 - 2 Kings 19:27-28, Acts 9:4 22:22, Amos 4:2, Ezekiel 5:4 14:4, Isaiah 10:12 6:28 12:4 12:10 13:10 13:34, Job 15:25-26 16:26, John 15:22-23, Matthew 3:24, Nahum 1:9-11, Psalms 2:1-3 32:9 46:7 74:4 74:23 83:3 93:3-4 Isaiah 37:29-32 - 4QIsab

[12] 1QIsaa *I have heard of your arrogance*

[13] 1QIsaa *on which is destruction*

[14] Isaiah 37:30 - 1 Kings 13:3-13:5, 2 Kings 19:29 20:9, 4Q177 1.2, 4Q177 5+6 2, Exodus 3:12, Isaiah 7:14 7:21-25 14:7, Leviticus 25:4-5 25:20-22, Mas.Soferim 7:1, Seder Olam 23 Sennacherib

[15] Isaiah 37:31 - 2 Kings 19:30-19:31, Galatians 3:29, Isaiah 1:9 6:13 10:20-10:22 3:6 17:9, Jeremiah 6:19 20:28, Psalms 80:10, Romans 9:27 11:5

[16] 1QIsaa adds *gather and those who are found shall*

כִּי מִירוּשָׁלִַ֙ם תֵּצֵ֣א שְׁאֵרִ֔ית וּפְלֵיטָ֖ה מֵהַ֣ר צִיּ֑וֹן קִנְאַ֛ת יְהוָ֥ה צְבָא֖וֹת תַּעֲשֶׂה־זֹּֽאת	32[1]	For out of *Jerusalem*[2] shall go forth a remnant, and out of mount Zion they who shall escape; the zeal of the LORD of hosts shall perform this.
לָכֵ֗ן כֹּֽה־אָמַ֤ר יְהוָה֙ אֶל־מֶ֣לֶךְ אַשּׁ֔וּר לֹ֤א יָבוֹא֙ אֶל־הָעִ֣יר הַזֹּ֔את וְלֹֽא־יוֹרֶ֥ה שָׁ֖ם חֵ֑ץ וְלֹֽא־יְקַדְּמֶ֣נָּה מָגֵ֔ן וְלֹֽא־יִשְׁפֹּ֥ךְ עָלֶ֖יהָ סֹלְלָֽה	33[3]	Therefore, thus says the LORD concerning the king of Assyria: He shall not come to this city, *nor shoot an arrow there, nor shall he come before it with shield, nor cast a mound against it*[4].
בַּדֶּ֥רֶךְ אֲשֶׁר־בָּ֖א בָּ֣הּ יָשׁ֑וּב וְאֶל־הָעִ֥יר הַזֹּ֛את לֹ֥א יָב֖וֹא נְאֻם־יְהוָֽה	34[5]	By the way he came, by the same shall he return, and he shall not come to this city, says the LORD.
וְגַנּוֹתִ֛י עַל־הָעִ֥יר הַזֹּ֖את לְהֽוֹשִׁיעָ֑הּ לְמַֽעֲנִ֖י וּלְמַ֥עַן דָּוִ֥ד עַבְדִּֽי	35[6]	For I will defend this city to save it, for My own sake, and for My servant David's sake.'
וַיֵּצֵ֣א מַלְאַ֣ךְ יְהוָ֗ה וַיַּכֶּה֙ בְּמַחֲנֵ֣ה אַשּׁ֔וּר מֵאָ֛ה וּשְׁמֹנִ֥ים וַחֲמִשָּׁ֖ה אָ֑לֶף וַיַּשְׁכִּ֣ימוּ בַבֹּ֔קֶר וְהִנֵּ֥ה כֻלָּ֖ם פְּגָרִ֥ים מֵתִֽים	36[7]	And the angel of the LORD went forth, and struck 185,000 in the camp of the Assyrians; and when men arose early in the morning, behold, they were all dead corpses.
וַיִּסַּ֣ע וַיֵּ֔לֶךְ וַיָּ֖שׇׁב סַנְחֵרִ֣יב מֶֽלֶךְ־אַשּׁ֑וּר וַיֵּ֖שֶׁב בְּנִֽינְוֵֽה	37[8]	So Sennacherib king of Assyria departed, and went, and returned, and lived at Nineveh.
וַיְהִ֙י ה֧וּא מִֽשְׁתַּחֲוֶ֣ה בֵּ֣ית ׀ נִסְרֹ֣ךְ אֱלֹהָ֗יו וְֽאַדְרַמֶּ֣לֶךְ וְשַׂרְאֶ֣צֶר בָּנָ֗יו הִכֻּ֣הוּ בַחֶ֔רֶב וְהֵ֥מָּה נִמְלְט֖וּ אֶ֣רֶץ אֲרָרָ֑ט וַיִּמְלֹ֛ךְ אֵֽסַר־חַדֹּ֥ן בְּנ֖וֹ תַּחְתָּֽיו	38[9]	And it came to pass, as he was worshipping in the house of Nisroch his god, Adrammelech and Sarezer his sons struck him with the sword; and they escaped into the land of Ararat. And Esarhaddon his son reigned in his place.

Isaiah – Chapter 38[10]

בַּיָּמִ֣ים הָהֵ֔ם חָלָ֥ה חִזְקִיָּ֖הוּ לָמ֑וּת וַיָּב֣וֹא אֵלָ֡יו יְשַׁעְיָ֣הוּ בֶן־אָמוֹץ֩ הַנָּבִ֨יא וַיֹּ֤אמֶר אֵלָיו֙ כֹּה־אָמַ֣ר יְהוָ֔ה צַ֣ו לְבֵיתֶ֔ךָ כִּ֛י מֵ֥ת אַתָּ֖ה וְלֹ֥א תִחְיֶֽה	1[11]	In those days Hezekiah was deathly sick, and Isaiah the prophet the son of Amoz came to him, and said to him: 'Thus says the LORD: Set your house in order; for you shall die, and not live.'
וַיַּסֵּ֧ב חִזְקִיָּ֛הוּ פָּנָ֖יו אֶל־הַקִּ֑יר וַיִּתְפַּלֵּ֖ל אֶל־יְהוָֽה	2[12]	Then Hezekiah turned his face to the wall, and prayed to the LORD,

---

[1] Isaiah 37:32 - 2 Kings 19:31, Isaiah 9:8 13:20 11:17, Joel 2:18, Zechariah 1:14

[2] 1QIsaa *Zion*

[3] Isaiah 37:33 - 2 Kings 19:32-35, Ezekiel 21:27, Isaiah 8:7-10 10:32-34 17:12 17:14 9:20, Luke 19:43-44, z.Vaetchanan 269b

[4] 1QIsaa *nor build up a siege-mound against it, nor shoot an arrow there, nor oppose it with a shield*

[5] Isaiah 37:34 - Isaiah 13:29, Proverbs 21:30

[6] Isaiah 37:35 - 1 Kings 11:12-13 11:36 15:4, 2 Kings 20:6, Deuteronomy 8:27, Ephesians 1:6 1:14, Ezekiel 20:9 12:22 37:24-25, Isaiah 7:5 14:6 19:25 48:9-11, Jeremiah 23:5-6 6:9 33:15-16, Mesillat Yesharim 22:Trait of Anavah, z.Acharei Mot 71b, z.Pekudei 232b

[7] Isaiah 37:36 - 1 Chronicles 21:12 21:16, 1 Thessalonians 5:2-5:3, 2 Chronicles 32:21-32:22, 2 Kings 19:35, 2 Samuel 24:16, Acts 12:23, Avot de R'Natan 27, b.Sanhedrin 95b, Ein Yaakov Sanhedrin:94a, Ein Yaakov Sanhedrin:95b, Exodus 12:23 12:30, Isaiah 10:12 10:16-10:19 10:33-10:34 30:30-30:33 7:8 33:10-33:12, Job 20:5-20:7 24:24, Numbers.R 9:24 20:13, Psalms 35:5-35:6 46:7-46:12 76:6-76:8, Sifre.z Numbers Naso 6:26, Song of Songs.R 4:20, Testament of Adam 4:7
Isaiah 37:36-37 - Josephus Antiquities 10.1.5

[8] Isaiah 37:37 - Birchat HaChammah.Vihi Noam, Genesis 10:11-10:12, Isaiah 7:9 13:7 13:29, Jonah 1:2 3:3 4:11, Matthew 12:41, Nahum 1:1

[9] Isaiah 37:38 - 2 Chronicles 8:14 8:19 8:21, 2 Kings 19:36-19:37, Ezra 4:2, Genesis 8:4, Isaiah 14:9 14:12 12:15 12:18 13:10, Jeremiah 3:27

[10] Isaiah 38 - mt.Hilchot Yesodei haTorah 10:4

[11] Isaiah 38:1 - 2 Chronicles 8:24, 2 Kings 20:1-11, 2 Samuel 17:23, Acts 9:37, Avot de R'Natan 2, b.Berachot 10a, Deuteronomy.R 8:1, Ecclesiastes 9:10, Ecclesiastes.R 5:4, Isaiah 1:1 13:2 13:21 38:1-38:8 39:3-4, Jeremiah 18:7-10, John 11:1-5, Jonah 3:4 3:10, Leviticus.R 10:5, Philippians 2:27-30, Ruth.R 5:6, Saadia Opinions 3:9, y.Sanhedrin 10:2, z.Terumah 174b, z.Vaetchanan 269b
Isaiah 38:1-22 - 1QIsaa, Josephus Antiquities 10.2.1

[12] Isaiah 38:2 - 1 Kings 8:30, b.Berachot 5b 10b, Deuteronomy.R 8:1, Ecclesiastes.R 5:4, Ein Yaakov Berachot:10b, Ein Yaakov Berachot:5b, Jastrow 1368a, Matthew 6:6, Midrash Psalms 26:2, mt.Hilchot Tefilah 5:6, Psalms 50:15 91:15, Sifre Devarim {Vaetchanan} 29, Sifre Devarim Vaetchanan 29, Siman 12:10 18:8, y.Sanhedrin 10:2, z.Bereshit 11a, z.Chayyei Sarah 132a,

Hebrew	v.	English
וַיֹּאמַר אָנָּה יְהוָה זְכָר־נָא אֵת אֲשֶׁר הִתְהַלַּכְתִּי לְפָנֶיךָ בֶּאֱמֶת וּבְלֵב שָׁלֵם וְהַטּוֹב בְּעֵינֶיךָ עָשִׂיתִי וַיֵּבְךְּ חִזְקִיָּהוּ בְּכִי גָדוֹל	3[1]	and said: 'Remember now, O LORD, I beg You, how I have walked before You in truth and with a whole heart, and have done what is good in Your sight.' And Hezekiah wept bitterly.
וַיְהִי דְּבַר־יְהוָה אֶל־יְשַׁעְיָהוּ לֵאמֹר	4[2]	Then the word of the LORD came to Isaiah, saying:
הָלוֹךְ וְאָמַרְתָּ אֶל־חִזְקִיָּהוּ כֹּה־אָמַר יְהוָה אֱלֹהֵי דָּוִד אָבִיךָ שָׁמַעְתִּי אֶת־תְּפִלָּתֶךָ רָאִיתִי אֶת־דִּמְעָתֶךָ הִנְנִי יוֹסִף עַל־יָמֶיךָ חֲמֵשׁ עֶשְׂרֵה שָׁנָה	5[3]	'Go, and say to Hezekiah: Thus says the LORD, the God of David your father: I have heard your prayer, I have seen your tears; behold, I will add fifteen years to your days.
וּמִכַּף מֶלֶךְ־אַשּׁוּר אַצִּילְךָ וְאֵת הָעִיר הַזֹּאת וְגַנּוֹתִי עַל־הָעִיר הַזֹּאת	6[4]	And I will deliver you and this city out of the hand of the king of Assyria; and I will defend this city[5].
וְזֶה־לְּךָ הָאוֹת מֵאֵת יְהוָה אֲשֶׁר יַעֲשֶׂה יְהוָה אֶת־הַדָּבָר הַזֶּה אֲשֶׁר דִּבֵּר	7[6]	And this shall be the sign to you from the LORD, that the LORD will do this thing that He has spoken:
הִנְנִי מֵשִׁיב אֶת־צֵל הַמַּעֲלוֹת אֲשֶׁר יָרְדָה בְמַעֲלוֹת אָחָז בַּשֶּׁמֶשׁ אֲחֹרַנִּית עֶשֶׂר מַעֲלוֹת וַתָּשָׁב הַשֶּׁמֶשׁ עֶשֶׂר מַעֲלוֹת בַּמַּעֲלוֹת אֲשֶׁר יָרָדָה	8[7]	behold, I will cause the shadow of the dial, which is gone down on the [8]sundial of Ahaz, to return backward ten degrees.' So the sun returned ten degrees, by which degrees it was gone down.
מִכְתָּב לְחִזְקִיָּהוּ מֶלֶךְ־יְהוּדָה בַּחֲלֹתוֹ וַיְחִי מֵחָלְיוֹ	9[9]	The writing of Hezekiah king of Judah, when he was sick, and recovered of his sickness.
אֲנִי אָמַרְתִּי בִּדְמִי יָמַי אֵלֵכָה בְּשַׁעֲרֵי שְׁאוֹל פֻּקַּדְתִּי יֶתֶר שְׁנוֹתָי	10[10]	I said: In the noon of my days I shall go, to the gates of the netherworld; I am deprived of the *remnant*[11] of my years.
אָמַרְתִּי לֹא־אֶרְאֶה יָּהּ יָהּ בְּאֶרֶץ הַחַיִּים לֹא־אַבִּיט אָדָם עוֹד עִם־יוֹשְׁבֵי חָדֶל	11[12]	I said: I shall not see the LORD, the LORD in the land of the living; I shall see man no more with the inhabitants of the world.
דּוֹרִי נִסַּע וְנִגְלָה מִנִּי כְּאֹהֶל רֹעִי קִפַּדְתִּי כָאֹרֵג חַיַּי מִדַּלָּה יְבַצְּעֵנִי מִיּוֹם עַד־לַיְלָה תַּשְׁלִימֵנִי	12[13]	My habitation *is plucked up and carried away*[14] from me as a shepherd's tent; I have

---

z.Terumah 133a 174b, z.Vaetchanan 260a, z.Vayechi 228a

Isaiah 38:2-4 - t.Maaser Sheni 5:24

Isaiah 38:2-8 - Mas.Soferim 8:2

[1] Isaiah 38:3 - 1 Chronicles 5:9 5:19, 1 John 3:21-3:22, 1 Kings 2:4 15:14, 2 Chronicles 16:9 1:2 31:20-31:21, 2 Corinthians 1:12, 2 Kings 18:5-18:6, 2 Samuel 12:21-12:22, b.Berachot 10b, Deuteronomy 6:18, Ein Yaakov Berachot:10b, Ein Yaakov Berachot:10b, Ezra 10:1, Genesis 5:22-5:23 6:9 17:1, Hebrews 5:7 6:10, Hosea 12:6, Job 23:11-23:12, John 1:47, Mesillat Yesharim 22:Trait of Anavah, Nehemiah 1:4 5:19 13:14 13:22 13:31, Psalms 6:9 16:8 18:21-18:28 20:2-20:4 26:3 32:2 5:2 6:10 119:80, z.Terumah 128b

[2] Isaiah 38:4 - Ecclesiastes.R 5:4, y.Sanhedrin 10:2

[3] Isaiah 38:5 - 1 Chronicles 17:2-4, 1 John 5:14-15, 1 Kings 8:25 9:4-5 11:12-13 15:4, 2 Chronicles 10:3, 2 Corinthians 7:6, 2 Kings 18:2 18:13 19:20, 2 Samuel 7:3-5, Acts 3:24, Deuteronomy.R 1:13 8:1, Ecclesiastes.R 3:4, Ein Yaakov Yevamot:49b, Genesis.R 61:4, Isaiah 7:13-14, Job 14:5, Leviticus.R 10:5, Luke 1:13, Matthew 22:32, Pirkei de R'Eliezer 52, Psalms 34:6-7 39:13 56:9 89:4-5 20:15 3:3, Revelation 7:17, Saadia Opinions 3:9, Sifre.z Numbers Pinchas 27:1, y.Sanhedrin 10:2, z.Vaetchanan 269b

[4] Isaiah 38:6 - 2 Chronicles 8:22, 2 Timothy 4:17, Isaiah 12:6 31:4-31:5 13:35

[5] 1QIsaa adds *for My sake and my servant David's sake*

[6] Isaiah 38:7 - 2 Kings 20:8-20:21, Genesis 9:13, Isaiah 7:11-14 13:30 14:22, Judges 6:17-6:22 6:37-6:39

Isaiah 38:7-8 - Midrash Tanchuma Vaera 3

[7] Isaiah 38:8 - 2 Chronicles 8:24 8:31, 2 Kings 20:9-20:11, b.Sanhedrin 96a, Josephus Against Apion 2.2, Joshua 10:12-10:14, Matthew 16:1, Pirkei de R'Eliezer 52, Psalms of Solomon 18:12, Seder Olam 23:Sennacherib

[8] 1QIsaa adds *upper*

[9] Isaiah 38:9 - 1 Samuel 2:1-10, 2 Chronicles 5:30, Deuteronomy 8:39, Exodus 15:1-21, Genesis.R 65:9 97 [Excl], Guide for the Perplexed 1:42, Hosea 6:1-2, Isaiah 12:1-6, Job 5:18, Jonah 2:1-9, Judges 5:1-31, Pirkei de R'Eliezer 52, Psalms 18:2 30:12-13 107:17-22 116:1-4 118:18-19, z.Terumah 174b

[10] Isaiah 38:10 - 2 Corinthians 1:9, Isaiah 14:1, Job 6:11 7:7 17:11-16, Pesikta Rabbati 24:1, Psalms 6:25 11:18

[11] 1QIsaa *bitterness*

[12] Isaiah 38:11 - Ecclesiastes 9:5-6, Job 35:14-15, Midrash Tanchuma Chukkat 16, Pirkei de R'Eliezer 19, Psalms 6:5-6 27:13 31:23 116:8-9, z.Noach 65b 66a

[13] Isaiah 38:12 - 2 Corinthians 5:1 5:4, 2 Peter 1:13-14, b.Nedarim 40a, Ein Yaakov Nedarim:40a, Hebrews 1:12, Isaiah 1:8 13:20, James 4:14, Job 4:20 6:9 7:3-7 9:25-26 14:2 17:1, Psalms 31:23 73:14 89:46-48 6:12 102:24-25 23:23

Isaiah 38:12-22 - 1QIsab

[14] 1QIsaa *vanishes*

		rolled up[1] like a weaver my life; He will cut me off from the thrum; From day to night You will make an end of me.
שִׁוִּיתִי עַד־בֹּקֶר כָּאֲרִי כֵּן יְשַׁבֵּר כָּל־עַצְמוֹתָי מִיּוֹם עַד־לַיְלָה תַּשְׁלִימֵנִי	13[2]	*The more I make myself like a lion until morning, The more it breaks all my bones*[3]; From day to night you will make an end of me.
שִׁוִּיתִי עַד־בֹּקֶר כָּאֲרִי כֵּן יְשַׁבֵּר כָּל־עַצְמוֹתָי מִיּוֹם עַד־לַיְלָה תַּשְׁלִימֵנִי	14[4]	Like a swallow or a crane, so I chatter, I do moan as a dove; My eyes fail with looking upward. O LORD, *I am oppressed*[5], be my surety.
מַה־אֲדַבֵּר וְאָמַר־לִי וְהוּא עָשָׂה אֲדַדֶּה כָל־שְׁנוֹתַי עַל־מַר נַפְשִׁי	15[6]	*What shall I say? He has both spoken to me, And Himself has done it; I shall go softly all my years for the bitterness of my soul*[7].
אֲדֹנָי עֲלֵיהֶם יִחְיוּ וּלְכָל־בָּהֶן חַיֵּי רוּחִי וְתַחֲלִימֵנִי וְהַחֲיֵנִי	16[8]	O Lord, by these things men live, And altogether within is the life of my spirit; therefore recover me, and make me live.
הִנֵּה לְשָׁלוֹם מַר־לִי מָר וְאַתָּה חָשַׁקְתָּ נַפְשִׁי מִשַּׁחַת בְּלִי כִּי הִשְׁלַכְתָּ אַחֲרֵי גֵוְךָ כָּל־חֲטָאָי	17[9]	Behold, for my peace I had *great bitterness*[10]; But you have in love to my soul delivered it From the pit of *corruption*[11]; For you have cast all my sins behind Your back.
כִּי לֹא שְׁאוֹל תּוֹדֶךָּ מָוֶת יְהַלְלֶךָּ לֹא־יְשַׂבְּרוּ יוֹרְדֵי־בוֹר אֶל־אֲמִתֶּךָ	18[12]	For the netherworld cannot praise You, death cannot celebrate You; those who go down into the pit cannot hope for Your truth.
חַי חַי הוּא יוֹדֶךָ כָּמוֹנִי הַיּוֹם אָב לְבָנִים יוֹדִיעַ אֶל־אֲמִתֶּךָ	19[13]	The living, *the living*[14], he shall praise You, as I do this day; the father to the children shall make known Your truth.
יְהוָה לְהוֹשִׁיעֵנִי וּנְגִנוֹתַי נְנַגֵּן כָּל־יְמֵי חַיֵּינוּ עַל־בֵּית יְהוָה	20[15]	The LORD is ready to save me[16]; Therefore, we will sing songs to the stringed instruments All the days of our life in the house of the LORD.

---

[1] 1QIsaa *made an accounting*

[2] Isaiah 38:13 - 1 Corinthians 11:30-32, 1 Kings 13:24-26 20:36, Daniel 6:25, Hosea 5:14, Job 10:16-17 16:12-14, Psalms 39:11 50:22 51:9

[3] 1QIsaa *I am laid bare until morning. Jut like a lion, he breaks all my bones*

[4] Isaiah 38:14 - b.Berachot [Rashi] 56b, Ezekiel 7:16, Isaiah 11:11, Job 17:3 6:29, Lamentations 4:17, Mas.Derek Eretz Rabbah 2:8, Midrash Psalms 119:54, Nahum 2:8, Per Massorah: Soferim altered "Hashem" to "Adonai", Perek Shirah [the Dove], Psalms 69:4 102:5-102:8 119:122-119:123 119:82 123:1-123:4 23:7, z.Vayechi 218b

[5] 1QIsab *I have desire*

[6] Isaiah 38:15 - 1 Kings 21:27, 1 Samuel 1:10, 2 Kings 4:27, Ezra 9:10, Job 7:11 10:1 21:25, John 12:27, Joshua 7:8, Psalms 39:10-11

[7] Missing in LXX

[8] Isaiah 38:16 - 1 Corinthians 11:32, 2 Corinthians 4:17, b.Berachot55a 57b, b.Menachot 44b, Deuteronomy 8:3, Ein Yaakov Menachot:44b, Genesis.R 20:10, Hebrews 12:10-12:11, Isaiah 16:6, Job 33:19-33:28, Matthew 4:4, mt.Hilchot Tefillin u'Mezuzah v'Sefer Torah 4:26, Per Massorah: Soferim altered "Hashem" to "Adonai", Pesikta de R'Kahana 19.5, Psalms 71:20 23:25, Siman 10:1, Tanya Igeret Hakodesh §09 §27a, y.Gittin 7:1, y.Terumot 1:1, z.Pekudei 239b

[9] Isaiah 38:17 - b.Berachot 10b, Ein Yaakov Berachot:10b, Isaiah 19:25, Jeremiah 7:35, Job 3:26-27 5:18, Jonah 2:6, Leviticus.R 36:3, Mesillat Yesharim 22:Trait of Anavah, Micah 7:18-19, Psalms 10:3 30:4 30:7-8 40:3 85:3 86:13 88:5-7

[10] 1QIsaa *exceedingly bitter*; 1QIsab MT *bitter bitter*;

[11] 1QIsaa *confinement*

[12] Isaiah 38:18 - 50:1, b.Sanhedrin 97b, Ecclesiastes 9:10, Genesis.R 96 [New Version]:1, Luke 16:26-16:31, Matthew 8:12 1:46, Numbers 16:33, Pesikta Rabbati 50:1, Proverbs 14:32, Psalms 6:6 30:10 88:11-88:12 115:17-115:18

[13] Isaiah 38:19 - 11Q5 19.2, 11Q6 frags 4-5 1.4, Deuteronomy 4:9 6:7 11:19, Ecclesiastes 9:10, Exodus 12:26-27 13:14-15, Genesis 18:19, Joel 1:3, John 9:4, Joshua 4:21-22, Midrash Psalms 146:1, Psalms 78:3-6 22:17 119:175 1:4 2:2, Saadia Opinions 10:9, z.Vayigash 207b
Isaiah 38:19 - 11Q5 19:2

[14] Missing in LXX

[15] Isaiah 38:20 - Habakkuk 3:19, Pesikta de R'Kahana 17.1, Psalms 9:14-15 27:5-6 30:12-13 33:2 51:16 66:13-15 68:26 20:2 116:17-19 1:2 6:4

[16] This is where the original scribe of 1QIsaa ended verse 20. A second scribe continues and writes: *The living, the living will praise you as I do this day. Parents will make your loyalty known to their children. O LORD, save me!* A second scribe added the following to the verse: *And we will make music with stringed instruments all the days of our lives in the house of the LORD.*

וַיֹּאמֶר יְשַׁעְיָהוּ יִשְׂאוּ דְּבֶלֶת תְּאֵנִים וְיִמְרְחוּ עַל־הַשְּׁחִין וְיֶחִי | 21[1] | And Isaiah said: 'Let them take a cake of figs, and lay it for a plaster on the boil, and he shall recover.'

וַיֹּאמֶר חִזְקִיָּהוּ מָה אוֹת כִּי אֶעֱלֶה בֵּית יְהוָה | 22[2] | *And Hezekiah said.' What is the sign that I shall go up to the house of the LORD?[3]*

Isaiah – Chapter 39

בָּעֵת הַהִוא שָׁלַח מְרֹדַךְ בַּלְאֲדָן בֶּן־בַּלְאֲדָן מֶלֶךְ־בָּבֶל סְפָרִים וּמִנְחָה אֶל־חִזְקִיָּהוּ וַיִּשְׁמַע כִּי חָלָה וַיֶּחֱזָק | 1[4] | At that time Merodach-baladan the son of Baladan, king of Babylon, sent a letter and a present to Hezekiah; *for*[5] he heard that he was sick, and recovered.

וַיִּשְׂמַח עֲלֵיהֶם חִזְקִיָּהוּ וַיַּרְאֵם אֶת־בֵּית 'נְכֹתֹה' "נְכֹתוֹ" אֶת־הַכֶּסֶף וְאֶת־הַזָּהָב וְאֶת־הַבְּשָׂמִים וְאֵת הַשֶּׁמֶן הַטּוֹב וְאֵת כָּל־בֵּית כֵּלָיו וְאֵת כָּל־אֲשֶׁר נִמְצָא בְּאֹצְרֹתָיו לֹא־הָיָה דָבָר אֲשֶׁר לֹא־הֶרְאָם חִזְקִיָּהוּ בְּבֵיתוֹ וּבְכָל־מֶמְשַׁלְתּוֹ | 2[6] | And Hezekiah was glad of them, and showed them his treasure house, the silver, and the gold, and the spices, and the precious oil, and all the house of his armor, and all that was found in his treasures; there was nothing in his house, nor in all his dominion, that Hezekiah did not show them.

וַיָּבֹא יְשַׁעְיָהוּ הַנָּבִיא אֶל־הַמֶּלֶךְ חִזְקִיָּהוּ וַיֹּאמֶר אֵלָיו מָה אָמְרוּ הָאֲנָשִׁים הָאֵלֶּה וּמֵאַיִן יָבֹאוּ אֵלֶיךָ וַיֹּאמֶר חִזְקִיָּהוּ מֵאֶרֶץ רְחוֹקָה בָּאוּ אֵלַי מִבָּבֶל | 3[7] | Then Isaiah the prophet came to king Hezekiah, and said to him: 'What did these men say? And from where did they come to you?' And Hezekiah said: 'They are come from a far country to me, from Babylon.'

וַיֹּאמֶר מָה רָאוּ בְּבֵיתֶךָ וַיֹּאמֶר חִזְקִיָּהוּ אֵת כָּל־אֲשֶׁר בְּבֵיתִי רָאוּ לֹא־הָיָה דָבָר אֲשֶׁר לֹא־הִרְאִיתִים בְּאוֹצְרֹתָי | 4[8] | Then said he: 'What have they seen in your house?' And Hezekiah answered: 'All that is in my house have they seen; there is nothing among my treasures that I did not shown them.'

וַיֹּאמֶר יְשַׁעְיָהוּ אֶל־חִזְקִיָּהוּ שְׁמַע דְּבַר־יְהוָה צְבָאוֹת | 5[9] | Then said Isaiah to Hezekiah: 'Hear the word of the LORD of hosts:

הִנֵּה יָמִים בָּאִים וְנִשָּׂא כָּל־אֲשֶׁר בְּבֵיתֶךָ וַאֲשֶׁר אָצְרוּ אֲבֹתֶיךָ עַד־הַיּוֹם הַזֶּה בָּבֶל לֹא־יִוָּתֵר דָּבָר אָמַר יְהוָה | 6[10] | Behold, the days come, that all that is in your house, and what your fathers have laid up in store until this day, [11]shall be carried to Babylon; nothing shall be left, says the LORD.

וּמִבָּנֶיךָ אֲשֶׁר יֵצְאוּ מִמְּךָ אֲשֶׁר תּוֹלִיד יִקָּחוּ וְהָיוּ סָרִיסִים בְּהֵיכַל מֶלֶךְ בָּבֶל | 7[12] | And of your sons who shall issue from *you*[13], whom you shall father, they shall take away;

---

[1] Isaiah 38:21 - 2 Kings 20:7-8, John 9:6, m.Negaim 1:1, Mark 7:33, Mekhilta de R'Shimon b' Yochai Vayassa 37:2, Mekilta de R'Ishmael Vayassa 1:121, Midrash Tanchuma Beshallach 24, Ruth.R 5:6

[2] Isaiah 38:22 - 2 Kings 20:8, John 5:14, Mekhilta de R'Shimon bar Yochai Beshallach 21:3, Psalms 42:2-3 84:2-3 84:11-13 118:18-19 2:1

[3] Missing in the original version of 1QIsaa, but was added by a third scribe; LXX *And Ezekias said, This is a sign to Ezekias, that I shall go up to the house of God*

[4] Isaiah 39:1 - 2 Chronicles 8:23 8:31, 2 Kings 20:12-19, 2 Samuel 8:10 10:2, b.Sanhedrin 96a, Ein Yaakov Sanhedrin:96a, Esther.R 3:1, Isaiah 13:1 13:19 14:4 23:1 39:1-8, Numbers.R 20:6, Pesikta de R'Kahana 2.5, Song of Songs.R 3:6, z.Mikketz 202a
Isaiah 39:1-2 - Mas.Soferim 8:2
Isaiah 39:1-8 - 1QIsaa, 1QIsab, 4QIsab, Josephus Antiquities 10.2.2

[5] 1QIsaa *when*

[6] Isaiah 39:2 - 1 John 1:8, 1 Kings 10:2 10:10 10:15 10:25, 2 Chronicles 9:1 9:9 8:25 8:27 8:31, 2 Corinthians 12:7, 2 Kings 18:15-18:16 20:13, b.Sanhedrin 41a, Ecclesiastes 7:20, Ein Yaakov Sanhedrin:104a, Jeremiah 17:9, Job 7:25, Mesillat Yesharim 4:To Acquire Zehirus, Pirkei de R'Eliezer 52, Proverbs 4:23, Psalms 146:3-146:4, Song of Songs.R 3:6

[7] Isaiah 39:3 - 2 Chronicles 16:7 19:2 1:15, 2 Kings 20:14-20:15, 2 Samuel 12:1, 5QIsa, 5QIsaI, Deuteronomy 4:49, Genesis.R 52:5, Isaiah 14:1 14:5, Jeremiah 5:15 22:1-22:2, Joshua 9:6 9:9, Leviticus.R 1:13 29:2, Numbers.R 2:12 20:6
Isaiah 39:3-8 - Mas.Soferim 8:2

[8] Isaiah 39:4 - 1 John 1:9, Job 7:33, Joshua 7:19, Proverbs 23:5 4:13

[9] Isaiah 39:5 - 1 Samuel 13:13-13:14 15:16

[10] Isaiah 39:6 - 2 Chronicles 12:10 12:18, 2 Kings 20:17-19 24:13 25:13-15, Avot de R'Natan 39, b.Yoma 53b, Daniel 1:2, Ein Yaakov Yoma:53b, Jeremiah 20:5 27:21-22 52:17-19, Numbers.R 20:6, Pirkei de R'Eliezer 52, y.Shekalim 6:1, z.Mikketz 202a

[11] 1QIsaa adds *They will come in and*

[12] Isaiah 39:7 - 2 Chronicles 9:11 12:10 12:20, 2 Kings 24:12 24:15 25:6-7, b.Sanhedrin 93b, Daniel 1:1-1:7, Ezekiel 17:12-20, Jeremiah 15:7, Lives of the Prophets 4:1, Mesillat Yesharim 4:To Acquire Zehirus, Pirkei de R'Eliezer 52

[13] 1QIsaa *your lions*

and they shall be officers in the palace of the king of Babylon.'

וַיֹּ֤אמֶר חִזְקִיָּ֙הוּ֙ אֶֽל־יְשַׁעְיָ֔הוּ ט֥וֹב דְּבַר־יְהֹוָ֖ה אֲשֶׁ֣ר דִּבַּ֑רְתָּ וַיֹּ֕אמֶר כִּ֥י יִהְיֶ֛ה שָׁל֥וֹם וֶאֱמֶ֖ת בְּיָמָֽי

8[1] Then said Hezekiah to Isaiah: 'Good is the word of the LORD which you have spoken.' He said moreover: '*If there shall*[2] be peace and truth in my days.'

Isaiah – Chapter 40

נַחֲמ֥וּ נַחֲמ֖וּ עַמִּ֑י יֹאמַ֖ר אֱלֹהֵיכֶֽם

1[3] Comfort, comfort My people, says your God.

דַּבְּר֞וּ עַל־לֵ֤ב יְרֽוּשָׁלַ֙͏ִם֙ וְקִרְא֣וּ אֵלֶ֔יהָ כִּ֤י מָֽלְאָה֙ צְבָאָ֔הּ כִּ֥י נִרְצָ֖ה עֲוֺנָ֑הּ כִּ֤י לָקְחָה֙ מִיַּ֣ד יְהֹוָ֔ה כִּפְלַ֖יִם בְּכׇל־חַטֹּאתֶֽיהָ

2[4] *Bid Jerusalem to take heart, and proclaim to her, that her time of service*[5] is accomplished, that her guilt is paid off; that she has received of the LORD's hand double for all her sins.

ק֣וֹל קוֹרֵ֔א בַּמִּדְבָּ֕ר פַּנּ֖וּ דֶּ֣רֶךְ יְהֹוָ֑ה יַשְּׁרוּ֙ בָּעֲרָבָ֔ה מְסִלָּ֖ה לֵאלֹהֵֽינוּ

3[6] *Listen! One calls: 'Clear in the wilderness the way of the LORD, Make plain in the desert a highway for our God*[7].

כׇּל־גֶּיא֙ יִנָּשֵׂ֔א וְכׇל־הַ֥ר וְגִבְעָ֖ה יִשְׁפָּ֑לוּ וְהָיָ֤ה הֶֽעָקֹב֙ לְמִישׁ֔וֹר וְהָרְכָסִ֖ים לְבִקְעָֽה

4[8] Every valley shall be lifted up, And every mountain and hill shall be made low; *And the rugged shall be made level*[9], And the rough places a plain;

[1] Isaiah 39:8 - 1 Peter 5:6, 1 Samuel 3:18, 2 Chronicles 8:26 10:28, 2 Samuel 15:26, Bahir 75, Job 1:21, Lamentations 3:22 3:39, Leviticus 10:3, Psalms 39:10, Zechariah 8:16 8:19

[2] LXX *Let there, I pray*

[3] Isaiah 40:1 - 29/30A:1-10 29/30B:1-4 30:1-4 33:3, 29/30A:10, 1 Thessalonians 4:18, 2 Corinthians 1:4, Genesis.R 100 [Excl]:9, Hebrews 6:17-18, Isaiah 3:10 12:1 35:3-4 41:10-14 17:27 49:13-16 2:10 3:3 3:12 4:9 57:15-19 60:1-3 62:11-62:12 65:13-14 66:10-14, Jastrow 867b, Jeremiah 31:11-15, Leviticus.R 10:2, Midrash Psalms 4:8 23:7, Midrash Tanchuma Devarim 1, Nehemiah 8:10, Pesikta de R'Kahana 16.1-2 16.4-11, Pesikta Rabbati 29/30A:6, Psalms 85:9, Siman 128:4, Verse for names נ-ם [Pisukim Lesheimot Anoshim], Zechariah 1:13 9:9, Zephaniah 3:14-17
Isaiah 40:1-3 - 11QIsaa, Lamentations.R 1:23 1:57
Isaiah 40:1-4 - 4QIsab
Isaiah 40:1-5 - 4Q176 1+2 i 4-9, 4Q176 frags 1-2 1.4-9
Isaiah 40:1-11 - mt.Hilchot Melachim u'Michamoteihem 11:2
Isaiah 40:1-26 - Haftarah Vaetchanan [Ashkenaz, mt.Hilchot Tefilah 13:19, Sephard]
Isaiah 40:1-27 - continues at Isaiah 41:17], Haftarah Vaetchanan [Teimon
Isaiah 40:1-31 - Shabbat after Tisha b'Av [Pesikta Rabbati 29/30B]
Isaiah 40:1-40:26 - Haftarah Vaetchanan [Isaiah 40:1-40:26]
Isaiah 40:1-66:24 - Psalms of Solomon ch. 11

[4] Isaiah 40:2 - 1 Corinthians 6:9-11, 2 Chronicles 30:22, Acts 1:7, Daniel 9:2 9:12 9:24-27 11:35 12:4 12:9, Ecclesiastes.R 1:36 3:10, Galatians 4:4, Genesis 10:3, Genesis.R 80:7, Habakkuk 2:3, Hosea 2:14, Isaiah 12:1 9:24 11:4 41:11-13 19:25 20:22 1:25 13:7, Jeremiah 16:18 17:18 5:11 31:34-35 33:8-9, Job 42:10-12, Leviticus.R 21:7, Midrash Psalms 4:8 22:22, Midrash Tanchuma Devarim 1, Perek Shirah [the Stork], Pesikta de R'Kahana 16.2 16.6 16.11, Pesikta Rabbati 29/30A:2-3 29/30A:7 29/30B:1 33:13, Psalms 32:1 102:14-29, Revelation 6:10-11 11:15-18 18:6, Saadia Opinions 8:1, Song of Songs 2:11-13, y.Berachot 5:1, Zechariah 1:15 9:12
Isaiah 40:2-3 - 1QIsab
Isaiah 40:2-6 - Genesis.R 78:4

[5] LXX *Speak, you priests, to the heart of Jerusalem; comfort her, for her humiliation*

[6] Isaiah 40:3 - 8:12-14, 1QS 8:14 1QS 9:19-20, 1QS 8.13-16 1QS 8.13-16, 1QS 8.14, 4Q259 3.19-20, 4Q259 3.5, Cairo Damascus 9:20, Isaiah 11:15-11:16 35:8 43:19 49:11 57:14 62:10-62:11, Jastrow 1396b, John 1:23, 1QS 9.20, Luke 1:16-1:17 1:76-1:77 3:2-3:6, Malachi 3:1 3:23-4:24, Mark 1:2-1:5, Mas.Kallah Rabbati 8:9, Matthew 3:1-3:3, Perek Shirah [the Wild Goose], Pesikta Rabbati 29/30B:4, Psalms 68:5, Psalms of Solomon 8:17,

[7] LXX *The voice of one crying in the wilderness, "Prepare the way of the LORD, make straight the paths of our God,"* or *The voice of one crying, "In the wilderness, prepare the way of the LORD, make straight the paths of our God,"*

[8] Isaiah 40:4 - 1 Samuel 2:8, b.Eruvin 54a, b.Nedarim 55b, Deuteronomy.R 4:11, Ein Yaakov Eruvin, Ein Yaakov Nedarim:55a, Ezekiel 17:24 21:31, Isaiah 2:12-15 42:11 42:15-16 45:2, Jastrow 1480b, Job 40:11-13, Luke 1:52-53 3:5 18:14, Mekhilta de R'Shimon bar Yochai Beshallach 20:5, Mekhilta de R'Ishmael Beshallah 1:185, Numbers.R 1:2, Proverbs 2:15, Psalms 113:7-8, Psalms of Solomon 11:4, Sibylline Oracles 3.680 8.234, Sifre Devarim Nitzavim 306, y.Eruvin 8:8

[9] LXX *and all the crooked ways shall become straight*

וְנִגְלָה כְּבוֹד יְהוָה וְרָאוּ כָל־בָּשָׂר יַחְדָּו כִּי פִּי יְהוָה דִּבֵּר	5[1]	And the glory of the LORD shall be revealed, And all flesh shall *see it together*[2]; For the mouth of the LORD has spoken it.'
קוֹל אֹמֵר קְרָא וְאָמַר מָה אֶקְרָא כָּל־הַבָּשָׂר חָצִיר וְכָל־חַסְדּוֹ כְּצִיץ הַשָּׂדֶה	6[3]	'Listen!' one says: 'Proclaim!' And he says: 'What shall I proclaim?' 'All flesh is grass, And all its goodliness is as the flower of the field;
יָבֵשׁ חָצִיר נָבֵל צִיץ כִּי רוּחַ יְהוָה נָשְׁבָה בּוֹ אָכֵן חָצִיר הָעָם	7[4]	*The grass withers, the flower fades; Because the breath of the LORD blows upon it; Surely the people are grass*[5].
יָבֵשׁ חָצִיר נָבֵל צִיץ וּדְבַר־אֱלֹהֵינוּ יָקוּם לְעוֹלָם	8[6]	The grass withers, the flower fades; But the word of our God shall stand forever.'
עַל הַר־גָּבֹהַ עֲלִי־לָךְ מְבַשֶּׂרֶת צִיּוֹן הָרִימִי בַכֹּחַ קוֹלֵךְ מְבַשֶּׂרֶת יְרוּשָׁלִָם הָרִימִי אַל־תִּירָאִי אִמְרִי לְעָרֵי יְהוּדָה הִנֵּה אֱלֹהֵיכֶם	9[7]	O you who tell good tidings to Zion, Get up into the high mountain; O you who tell good tidings to Jerusalem, Lift up your voice with strength; Lift it up, be not afraid; Say to the cities of Judah: 'Behold your God!'
הִנֵּה אֲדֹנָי יְהוִה בְּחָזָק יָבוֹא וּזְרֹעוֹ מֹשְׁלָה לוֹ הִנֵּה שְׂכָרוֹ אִתּוֹ וּפְעֻלָּתוֹ לְפָנָיו	10[8]	Behold, the Lord GOD will come as a Mighty One, And His arm will rule for Him; Behold, His reward is with Him, And His reward before Him.
כְּרֹעֶה עֶדְרוֹ יִרְעֶה בִּזְרֹעוֹ יְקַבֵּץ טְלָאִים וּבְחֵיקוֹ יִשָּׂא עָלוֹת יְנַהֵל	11[9]	Even as a shepherd who feeds his flock, who gathers the lambs in his arm, And carries them in his bosom, And gently leads those that nurse.
מִי־מָדַד בְּשָׁעֳלוֹ מַיִם וְשָׁמַיִם בַּזֶּרֶת תִּכֵּן וְכָל בַּשָּׁלִשׁ עֲפַר הָאָרֶץ וְשָׁקַל בַּפֶּלֶס הָרִים וּגְבָעוֹת בְּמֹאזְנָיִם	12[10]	Who has measured the waters[11] in the hollow of his hand, And meted out heaven with the span, and comprehended the dust of the earth in a measure, And weighed the mountains in scales, and the hills in a balance?

[1] Isaiah 40:5 - 29/30A:10, 2 Corinthians 3:18 4:6, Acts 2:17, Habakkuk 2:14, Hebrews 1:3, Isaiah 1:20 6:3 11:9 35:2 49:6 52:10 58:14 60:1 66:16 66:23, Jeremiah 9:13 32:27, Joel 3:1, John 1:14 12:41 17:2, Kuzari 4.003, Leviticus.R 1:14, Luke 2:10-2:14 2:32 3:6, Mekilta de R'Ishmael Pisha 12:24, Micah 4:4, Midrash Psalms 17:14, Pesikta Rabbati 33:13, Psalms 72:19 96:6 102:17, Revelation 21:23, Tanya Igeret Hakodesh §12, Tanya Likutei Aramim §33 §36 §49, Tanya Shaar Hayichud 03, When carrying the Sefer Torah to the Bima [Shabbat and Yom Tov Shacharit], z.Mishpatim 126a, z.Vayigash 205b, Zechariah 2:13
[2] LXX *he salvation of God*
[3] Isaiah 40:6 - 1 Peter 1:24-25, Guide for the Perplexed 1:21, Hosea 5:8, Isaiah 12:6 37:27 40:3 58:1 61:1-2, James 1:10-11, Jastrow 1652a, Jeremiah 2:2 31:7, Job 14:2, Life of Adam and Eve [Vita] 10:2, Mesillat Yesharim 19:Longing-for-the-Redemption, Midrash Psalms 35:2 146:3, Perek Shirah [the fly], Psalms 90:5-6 92:8 102:12 103:15-16
Isaiah 40:6-7 - 2 Baruch 82:7
Isaiah 40:6-8 - 4Q185 1-2 i 4-13
[4] Isaiah 40:7 - Jastrow 869b, Job 41:13, Midrash Psalms 1:20 35:2 119:12 119:20 119:35 138:1
[5] Missing in LXX and original scribe's work on 1QIsaa; a second scribe added the text and substituted four dots for Hashem.
[6] Isaiah 40:8 - 1 Peter 1:25, Genesis.R 53:3, Isaiah 46:10-11 55:10-11 59:21, John 10:35 12:34, Mark 13:31, Matthew 5:18 24:35, Midrash Psalms 1:20 119:12 119:20 119:35, Midrash Tanchuma Shelach 3, Numbers.R 16:3, Perek Shirah [the fly], Psalms 119:89-91, Romans 3:1-3:3, Saadia Opinions 8:1, Tanya Likutei Aramim §25, Tanya Shaar Hayichud §1, Zechariah 1:6
[7] Isaiah 40:9 - 1 John 5:20-5:21, 1 Peter 3:14, 1 Samuel 26:13-26:14, 1 Timothy 3:16, 2 Chronicles 13:4, Acts 2:14 4:13 4:29 5:41-5:42, Ephesians 6:19, Ezra 1:1-1:2, Isaiah 12:2 25:9 35:3-35:4 41:27 51:7 51:12 52:7-52:8 58:4 61:1, Jeremiah 22:20, Judges 9:7, Leviticus.R 27:2, Luke 24:47, Midrash Psalms 138:1, Philippians 1:28-1:29, Romans 10:18
[8] Isaiah 40:10 - 1 John 3:8, Ephesians 1:20-1:22, Hebrews 2:14, Isaiah 9:7-9:8 49:4 49:24-49:25 53:12 59:15-60:22 62:11, John 12:13 12:15, Malachi 3:1, Midrash Tanchuma Ki Tissa 37, Numbers.R 2:8, Philippians 2:10-2:11, Psalms 2:8-2:9 66:3 110:1-110:2 110:6, Revelation 2:26-27 17:14 19:11-16 20:11 22:12, Saadia Opinions 3:Exordium, Zechariah 2:8-11
[9] Isaiah 40:11 - 1 Corinthians 3:1-3:2, 1 Peter 2:25 5:4, 4Q165 1-2, 4Q165 frags 1-2 l.2, Ezekiel 34:12-34:14 34:16 34:23 34:31 37:24, Genesis 33:13 49:24, Hebrews 13:20, Isaiah 42:3 49:9-49:10 63:11, John 10:11-10:16 21:15-21:17, Micah 5:5, Midrash Proverbs 27, mt.Hilchot Melachim u'Michamoteihem 2:6, Psalms 23:1-23:6 78:71-78:72 80:2, Revelation 7:17, Zechariah 11:7
Isaiah 40:11 [LXX] - Greek Apocalypse of Ezra 7:6
[10] Isaiah 40:12 - 2 Enoch 47:6, 4Q165 frags 1-2 ll.3-4, 4Q511 30 4-5, b.Eruvin 21a, b.Menachot [Tosefot] 35b, b.Sanhedrin 39a 1a, Deuteronomy.R 6:2, Ein Yaakov Sanhedrin:100a, Ein Yaakov Sanhedrin:39a, Exodus.R 25:3, Genesis.R 10:1, Hebrews 1:10-12, Isaiah 48:13, Jastrow 1548b 1611a, Job 11:7-9 28:25 38:4-11, Mekhilta de R'Shimon bar Yochai Shirata 34:2, Midrash Psalms 95:2 149:1, Midrash Tanchuma Bereshit 5, Midrash Tanchuma Chayyei Sarah 3, Midrash Tanchuma Emor 15, Midrash Tanchuma Pinchas 12, Midrash Tanchuma Shemini 6, Numbers.R 2:17 21:17, Pesikta Rabbati 48:3, Proverbs 8:26-28 30:4, Psalms 102:26-27 104:2-3, Revelation 20:11, Saadia Opinions 8:2, z.Bereshit 30b, z.Terumah 175b
Isaiah 40:12 [LXX] - Greek Apocalypse of Ezra 7:5
[11] 1QIsaa adds *of the sea*

Hebrew		English
מִי־תִכֵּן אֶת־רוּחַ יְהוָה וְאִישׁ עֲצָתוֹ יוֹדִיעֶנּוּ	13[1]	Who has meted out the spirit of the LORD? Or who was His counsellor that he might instruct Him?
אֶת־מִי נוֹעָץ וַיְבִינֵהוּ וַיְלַמְּדֵהוּ בְּאֹרַח מִשְׁפָּט וַיְלַמְּדֵהוּ דַעַת וְדֶרֶךְ תְּבוּנוֹת יוֹדִיעֶנּוּ	14[2]	With whom does He take counsel, and who instructed Him, and taught Him in the right path, and taught Him knowledge, and made Him to know the way of discernment?
הֵן גּוֹיִם כְּמַר מִדְּלִי וּכְשַׁחַק מֹאזְנַיִם נֶחְשָׁבוּ הֵן אִיִּים כַּדַּק יִטּוֹל	15[3]	Behold, the nations are as a drop of a bucket, And are counted as the small dust of the balance; Behold the isles are as a mote in weight.
וּלְבָנוֹן אֵין דֵּי בָּעֵר וְחַיָּתוֹ אֵין דֵּי עוֹלָה	16[4]	And Lebanon is not sufficient fuel, nor its beasts sufficient for burnt offerings.
כָּל־הַגּוֹיִם כְּאַיִן נֶגְדּוֹ מֵאֶפֶס וָתֹהוּ נֶחְשְׁבוּ־לוֹ	17[5]	All the nations are as nothing before Him; They are accounted by Him as nothing, and vanity.
וְאֶל־מִי תְּדַמְּיוּן אֵל וּמַה־דְּמוּת תַּעַרְכוּ לוֹ	18[6]	To whom, then, will you compare God? Or what likeness will you compare to Him?
הַפֶּסֶל נָסַךְ חָרָשׁ וְצֹרֵף בַּזָּהָב יְרַקְּעֶנּוּ וּרְתֻקוֹת כֶּסֶף צוֹרֵף	19[7]	The image perchance, which the craftsman has melted, and the goldsmith spread over with gold, *the silversmith casting silver chains*[8]?
הַמְסֻכָּן תְּרוּמָה עֵץ לֹא־יִרְקַב יִבְחָר חָרָשׁ חָכָם יְבַקֶּשׁ־לוֹ לְהָכִין פֶּסֶל לֹא יִמּוֹט	20[9]	*A holm-oak is set apart, he chooses a*[10] tree that will not rot; he seeks a cunning craftsman to set up an image, that shall not be moved.
הֲלוֹא תֵדְעוּ הֲלוֹא תִשְׁמָעוּ הֲלוֹא הֻגַּד מֵרֹאשׁ לָכֶם הֲלוֹא הֲבִינֹתֶם מוֹסְדוֹת הָאָרֶץ	21[11]	Do you not know? Do you not hear? Has it not been told you from the beginning? Have you not understood the foundations of the earth?
הַיֹּשֵׁב עַל־חוּג הָאָרֶץ וְיֹשְׁבֶיהָ כַּחֲגָבִים הַנּוֹטֶה כַדֹּק שָׁמַיִם וַיִּמְתָּחֵם כָּאֹהֶל לָשָׁבֶת	22[12]	It is He who sits above the sphere of the earth, And its inhabitants are as grasshoppers; who

---

[1] Isaiah 40:13 - 1 Corinthians 2:16, 2 Baruch 75:2, 2 Enoch 33:4, Ein Yaakov Sanhedrin 92b, Ephesians 1:11, Guide for the Perplexed 1:40, Job 21:22 36:22-23, John 1:13, Luke 10:22, Romans 11:34

[2] Isaiah 40:14 - 1 Corinthians 12:4-12:6, Colossians 2:3, James 1:17, Job 21:22, Lamentations.R 1:23

[3] Isaiah 40:15 - 2 Baruch 82:5 4 Ezra 6:57, Apocalypse of Zephaniah 2:5, b.Bava Batra [Rashbam] 58b, Daniel 11:18, Genesis 10:5, Genesis.R 99 [Excl]:7, Guide for the Perplexed 3:11, Isaiah 11:11 29:5 40:22 41:5 59:18 66:19, Jeremiah 10:10, Job 34:14-34:15, Liber Antiquitatum Biblicarum 12:4 7:3, Midrash Psalms 18:33, Saadia Opinions 8:2, Zephaniah 2:11
Isaiah 40:15 [LXX] - 2 Baruch 82:6, Liber Antiquitatum Biblicarum 7:3

[4] Isaiah 40:16 - 5QIsa, Hebrews 10:5-10:10, Mekilta de R'Ishmael Pisha 16:40 16:43, Micah 6:6-7, Midrash Psalms 91:1, Midrash Tanchuma Bo 11, Midrash Tanchuma Ki Tissa 10, Midrash Tanchuma Naso 11, Numbers.R 12:3, Pesikta de R'Kahana 2.10 6.4, Pesikta Rabbati 16:7, Psalms 40:7 50:9-12

[5] Isaiah 40:17 - 2 Corinthians 12:11, b.Moed Katan [Tosefot] 28a, b.Sanhedrin 39a, Daniel 4:31-32, Ein Yaakov Sanhedrin:39a, Isaiah 29:7, Job 25:6, Leviticus.R 27:7, Midrash Psalms 119:21, Midrash Tanchuma Bamidbar 4 20, Midrash Tanchuma Emor 11, Midrash Tanchuma Re'eh 9, Midrash Tanchuma Vayeshev 3, Numbers.R 1:4 4:2, Pesikta de R'Kahana 9.6 16.1, Psalms 62:10, Song of Songs.R 7:8, t.Berachot 6:18, Tanya Likutei Aramim §19, y.Berachot 9:1, z.Bereshit 10a, z.Bo 37a, z.Mishpatim 96a

[6] Isaiah 40:18 - 1 Samuel 2:2, Acts 17:29, Colossians 1:15, Deuteronomy 33:26, Exodus 8:6 9:14 15:11 20:4, Guide for the Perplexed 1:56, Hebrews 1:3, Isaiah 40:25 46:5 46:9, Jeremiah 10:6 10:16, Job 40:9, Micah 7:18, mt.Perek Chelek Intro:11, Psalms 86:8-10 89:7 89:9 113:5, Saadia Opinions 2:9, z.Bo 42b
Isaiah 40:18-19 - 5QIsa
Isaiah 40:18-26 - Sibylline Oracles 3.12

[7] Isaiah 40:19 - b.Sheviit [Rashi] 32b, Exodus 32:2-32:4, Habakkuk 2:18-2:19, Hosea 8:6, Isaiah 2:20 37:18-37:19 41:6-41:7 44:10-44:12 46:6-46:7, Jeremiah 10:3-10:5 10:9, Judges 17:4, Psalms 115:4-115:8 135:15 135:18, Saadia Opinions 2:9, Sibylline Oracles 5.80

[8] LXX *and made it a likeness*

[9] Isaiah 40:20 - 1 Samuel 5:3-5:4, Daniel 5:23, Isaiah 2:8-2:9 41:7 44:13-44:19 46:7, Jeremiah 10:3-10:4, Saadia Opinions 2:9

[10] 1QIsaa *the poor person an offering*

[11] Isaiah 40:21 - Acts 14:17, Isaiah 27:11 44:20 46:8 48:13 51:13, Jeremiah 10:8-12, Psalms 19:2-6 50:6 115:8, Romans 1:19-21 1:28 3:1-2, Saadia Opinions Intro:6, z.Noach 59b, z.Terumah 176a
Isaiah 40:21-26 - Apocalypse of Elijah 1:3

[12] Isaiah 40:22 - 2 Enoch 47:4 3 Enoch 17:6, b.Bechorot [Rashi] 16a, b.Bechorot 28a, b.Chagigah 12b, b.Gittin [Rashi] 56a, b.Menachot [Rashi] 79a, b.Pesachim [Rashi] 73a, b.Zevachim [Rashi] 35b 85b, Ein Yaakov Chagigah:12b, Exodus.R 29:6 33:4, Genesis.R 1:6 4:5 48:8, Guide for the Perplexed 1:11 3:13, Hebrews 1:10-1:12, Hellenistic Synagogal Prayers 12:16 3:5, Isaiah 19:1 40:15 40:17 42:5 44:24 51:13 66:1, Jeremiah 10:12, Job 9:8 22:14 36:29 37:18 38:4-38:9, Mekilta de R'Shimon bar Yochai Bachodesh 50:2, Mekilta de R'Shimon bar Yochai Vayassa 40:3, Mekilta de R'Ishmael Vayassa 4:66, Midrash Psalms 2:2 4:3 19:6, Midrash Tanchuma Tzav 12, Numbers 13:33, Numbers.R 12:11, Numbers.R 12:11, Pesikta Rabbati 5:3, Pirkei de R'Eliezer 3, Proverbs 8:27, Psalms 2:4 29:10 68:34 102:26-102:27 104:2, y.Berachot 1:1, Zechariah 12:1

stretches out the heavens as a curtain, And spreads them out as a tent in which to live; Who brings princes to nothing; He makes the judges of the earth as a thing of nothing.

הַנּוֹתֵן רוֹזְנִים לְאָיִן שֹׁפְטֵי אֶרֶץ כַּתֹּהוּ עָשָׂה   23[1]

Scarce are they planted, Scarce are they sown, Scarce has their stock taken root in the earth[3]; When He blows on them, they wither, And the whirlwind takes them away as stubble.

אַף בַּל־נִטָּעוּ אַף בַּל־זֹרָעוּ אַף בַּל־שֹׁרֵשׁ בָּאָרֶץ גִּזְעָם וְגַם־נָשַׁף בָּהֶם וַיִּבָשׁוּ וּסְעָרָה כַּקַּשׁ תִּשָּׂאֵם   24[2]

To whom then will you liken Me, that I should be equal? says the Holy One.

וְאֶל־מִי תְדַמְּיוּנִי וְאֶשְׁוֶה יֹאמַר קָדוֹשׁ   25[4]

Lift up your eyes on high, And see: who has created these? He who brings out their host by number, He calls them all by name; By the greatness of His might, and for that He is strong in power, Not one fails.

שְׂאוּ־מָרוֹם עֵינֵיכֶם וּרְאוּ מִי־בָרָא אֵלֶּה הַמּוֹצִיא בְמִסְפָּר צְבָאָם לְכֻלָּם בְּשֵׁם יִקְרָא מֵרֹב אוֹנִים וְאַמִּיץ כֹּחַ אִישׁ לֹא נֶעְדָּר   26[5]

Why do you say, O Jacob, And speak, O Israel: 'My way is hidden from the LORD, And my right is passed over from my God?'

לָמָּה תֹאמַר יַעֲקֹב וּתְדַבֵּר יִשְׂרָאֵל נִסְתְּרָה דַרְכִּי מֵיהוָה וּמֵאֱלֹהַי מִשְׁפָּטִי יַעֲבוֹר   27[6]

Have you not known? Have you not heard that the everlasting God, the LORD, the Creator of the ends of the earth, neither faints nor is weary? His discernment is past searching out.

הֲלוֹא יָדַעְתָּ אִם־לֹא שָׁמַעְתָּ אֱלֹהֵי עוֹלָם יְהוָה בּוֹרֵא קְצוֹת הָאָרֶץ לֹא יִיעַף וְלֹא יִיגָע אֵין חֵקֶר לִתְבוּנָתוֹ   28[7]

He gives power to the weary; And to him who has no might He increases strength.

נֹתֵן לַיָּעֵף כֹּחַ וּלְאֵין אוֹנִים עָצְמָה יַרְבֶּה   29[8]

Even the youths shall faint and be weary, and the young men shall utterly fall;

וְיִעֲפוּ נְעָרִים וְיִגָעוּ וּבַחוּרִים כָּשׁוֹל יִכָּשֵׁלוּ   30[9]

Isaiah 40:22-26 - 4QIsab

[1] Isaiah 40:23 - Ecclesiastes.R 8:18, Isaiah 19:13-14 23:9 24:21-22 34:12, Jeremiah 25:18-27, Job 12:21 34:19-20, Luke 1:51-52, Midrash Psalms 2:2, Psalms 76:13 107:40, Revelation 19:18-20

[2] Isaiah 40:24 - 1 Kings 21:21-22, 2 Kings 10:11, 2 Samuel 22:16, b.Sanhedrin 95a, Haggai 1:9, Hosea 13:3 13:15, Isaiah 11:4 14:21-22 17:11 17:13 30:33 37:7 40:7 41:16, Jeremiah 22:30 23:19, Job 4:9 15:30-33 18:16-19 21:18, Midrash Tanchuma Balak 8, Midrash Tanchuma Noach 18, Nahum 1:14, Numbers.R 20:13, Proverbs 1:27, Psalms 58:10, Song of Songs.R 7:8, Zechariah 7:14 9:14

[3] LXX *For they shall not plant, neither shall they sow, neither shall their root be fixed in the ground*

[4] Isaiah 40:25 - Deuteronomy 4:15-18 4:33 5:8, Guide for the Perplexed 1:55, Isaiah 40:18, Midrash Tanchuma Bechukkotai 4, Midrash Tanchuma Vayakhel 4, mt.Hilchot Yesodei haTorah 1:8, mt.Perek Chelek Intro:11, Saadia Opinions 2:9, z.Bereshit 22b, z.Bo 42a

Isaiah 40:25-26 - Exodus.R 48:2

Isaiah 40:25-41:17 - Haftarah Lech Lecha [Teimon]

[5] Isaiah 40:26 - 3 Enoch 46:2, Ahiqar 116, Colossians 1:16-1:17, Deuteronomy 4:19, Genesis 2:1-2:2, Guide for the Perplexed 2:19, Isaiah 34:16 42:5 44:24 45:7 48:13 51:6, Jeremiah 10:11-10:12 32:17-32:19, Job 31:26-31:28, Midrash Psalms 19:11, Midrash Tanchuma Bechukkotai 4, Midrash Tanchuma Vayakhel 4, Numbers.R 11:7, Psalms 8:4-8:5 19:2 89:12-89:14 102:26 147:4-147:5 148:3-148:6, Saadia Opinions 2:9, Sefer Yetzirah 4:6, z.Bereshit 1b 2a 30a, z.Chayyei Sarah 131a 131a, z.Mishpatim 105a, z.Pekudei 220a 231b, z.Terumah 168b 171b

[6] Isaiah 40:27 - Ecclesiastes.R 4:3, Genesis.R 91:10 94:3, Isaiah 49:4 49:14, Job 27:2, Lamentations.R 3:?, Luke 18:7-18:8, Midrash Psalms 7:6, Pesikta de R'Kahana 17.3, Saadia Opinions 8:2, Song of Songs.R 1:23

Isaiah 40:27-41:16 - Haftarah Lech Lecha [Ashkenaz and Sephard]

[7] Isaiah 40:28 - 1 Corinthians 2:16 6:3-6:5 6:9 6:16 6:19, 1 Samuel 2:10, 1 Timothy 1:17, Acts 13:47, b.Taanit 2a 9b, Deuteronomy 33:27, Ein Yaakov Taanit:2a, Ein Yaakov Taanit:2a, Ein Yaakov Taanit:9b, Exodus.R 13:1, Genesis 21:33, Hebrews 9:14, Isaiah 40:21 45:22 55:8-55:9 57:15 59:1 66:9, Jeremiah 4:22 10:10, John 5:17 14:9, Luke 24:25, Mark 8:17-8:18 9:19 16:14, Midrash Tanchuma Mikketz 1, Midrash Tanchuma Vayigash 2, Pesikta Rabbati 23:5, Philippians 1:6, Psalms 90:2 138:8 139:6 147:5, Romans 11:33-11:34 16:26, Saadia Opinions 2:1, Tanya Likutei Aramim §04

Isaiah 40:28-29 - Mekilta de R'Ishmael Bahodesh 7:104-105

Isaiah 40:28-31 - Testament of Joseph 2:5, Testament of Judah 25:5

[8] Isaiah 40:29 - 2 Corinthians 12:9-12:10, Colossians 1:11, Deuteronomy 33:25, Genesis 49:24, Genesis.R 25:3 40:3 64:2, Hebrews 11:34, Isaiah 41:10 50:4, Jastrow 1418b, Jeremiah 31:26, Philippians 4:13, Psalms 29:11, Ruth.R 1:4, Zechariah 10:12

[9] Isaiah 40:30 - Amos 2:14, Ecclesiastes 9:11, Isaiah 9:18 13:18, Jeremiah 6:11 9:22, Psalms 33:16 34:11 39:6

וְקוֹיֵ יְהֹוָה יַחֲלִיפוּ כֹחַ יַעֲלוּ אֵבֶר כַּנְּשָׁרִים יָרוּצוּ
וְלֹא יִיגָעוּ יֵלְכוּ וְלֹא יִיעָפוּ

31[1] But they who wait for the LORD shall renew their strength; [2]they shall mount up with wings as eagles; they shall run, and not be weary; they shall walk, and not faint.

Isaiah – Chapter 41

הַחֲרִישׁוּ אֵלַי אִיִּים וּלְאֻמִּים יַחֲלִיפוּ כֹחַ יִגְּשׁוּ אָז
יְדַבֵּרוּ יַחְדָּו לַמִּשְׁפָּט נִקְרָבָה

1[3] *Keep silence before Me*[4], O islands, And let the peoples renew their strength; Let them draw near, then let them speak; Let us come near together to judgment.

מִי הֵעִיר מִמִּזְרָח צֶדֶק יִקְרָאֵהוּ לְרַגְלוֹ יִתֵּן לְפָנָיו
גּוֹיִם וּמְלָכִים יַרְדְּ יִתֵּן כֶּעָפָר חַרְבּוֹ כְּקַשׁ נִדָּף
קַשְׁתּוֹ

2[5] Who has raised up one from the east, At whose steps victory attends? He gives nations before him, And makes him rule over kings; His sword makes them as the dust, His bow as the driven stubble.

יִרְדְּפֵם יַעֲבוֹר שָׁלוֹם אֹרַח בְּרַגְלָיו לֹא יָבוֹא

3[6] He pursues them, and passes on safely; The way with his feet *he does not tread*[7].

מִי־פָעַל וְעָשָׂה קֹרֵא הַדֹּרוֹת מֵרֹאשׁ אֲנִי יְהֹוָה
רִאשׁוֹן וְאֶת־אַחֲרֹנִים אֲנִי־הוּא

4[8] Who has worked and done it? He who called the generations from the beginning. I, the LORD, who is the first, and with the last I am the same.

רָאוּ אִיִּים וְיִירָאוּ קְצוֹת הָאָרֶץ יֶחֱרָדוּ קָרְבוּ
וַיֶּאֱתָיוּן

5[9] The isles saw, and feared; The ends of the earth *trembled*[10]; They drew near, and came.

אִישׁ אֶת־רֵעֵהוּ יַעְזֹרוּ וּלְאָחִיו יֹאמַר חֲזָק

6[11] Everyone helped his neighbor; And everyone said to his brother: 'Be of good courage.'

וַיְחַזֵּק חָרָשׁ אֶת־צֹרֵף מַחֲלִיק פַּטִּישׁ אֶת־הוֹלֶם
פָּעַם אֹמֵר לַדֶּבֶק טוֹב הוּא וַיְחַזְּקֵהוּ בְמַסְמְרִים
לֹא יִמּוֹט

7[12] So the carpenter encouraged the goldsmith, And he who smooths with the hammer, he who smites the anvil, Saying of the soldering: 'It is

---

[1] Isaiah 40:31 - 1 Thessalonians 1:10, 2 Corinthians 1:8-10 4:1 4:8-10 4:16 12:9-10, b.Kiddushin 82ab, b.Sanhedrin 92b, Ein Yaakov Kiddushin:82a 82b, Exodus 19:4, Galatians 6:9, HaMadrikh 14, Hebrews 12:1 12:3, Isaiah 8:17 25:9 30:18, Job 17:9 33:24-26, Judges 16:28, Lamentations 3:25-3:26, Luke 18:1, m.Kiddushin 4:14, Mas.Soferim 16:1, Midrash Psalms 40:1 149:1, Pesikta Rabbati 29/30B:4, Psalms 25:3 25:5 25:21 27:13-14 37:34 40:2 84:8 92:2 92:14 103:5 123:2 138:3, Revelation 2:3 4:7, Romans 8:25, Saadia Opinions 4:3, Sifre.z Numbers Naso 6:24, Song of Songs 8:5, t.Kiddushin 5:16, Testament of Moses 10:8, y.Kiddushin 4:12, Zechariah 10:12

[2] 1QIsaa adds *then*

[3] Isaiah 41:1 - Habakkuk 2:20, Isaiah 1:18 8:9-8:10 11:11 10:1 41:6-41:7 41:21-41:22 24:16 1:1 2:8, Job 23:3-23:7 31:35-31:36 14:3 40:7-40:10, Joel 4:10-4:11, Micah 6:1-6:3, Midrash Tanchuma Noach 3, Psalms 46:11, Saadia Opinions 4:3, Zechariah 2:13
Isaiah 41:1-29 - 1QIsaa

[4] LXX *Hold a festival to me*

[5] Isaiah 41:2 - 2 Chronicles 12:23, 2 Kings 13:7, 2 Samuel 22:43, b.Bava Batra 15a, b.Sanhedrin 18b, b.Shabbat 156b, b.Taanit 21a, Ein Yaakov Bava Batra:14b, Ein Yaakov Sanhedrin:108b, Ein Yaakov Shabbat:156b, Ein Yaakov Taanit:21a, Exodus.R 15:26, Ezra 1:2, Genesis 11:31 12:1-12:3 14:14-14:15 17:1, Genesis.R 2:3 43:3, Hebrews 7:1 11:8-11:10, Isaiah 16:24 41:15-41:16 17:25 21:1 21:13 22:11, Jastrow 601a 1263b, Leviticus.R 9:1, Mekhilta de R'Shimon bar Yochai Beshallach 25:2, Midrash Proverbs 1, Midrash Psalms 1:4 77:3 110:1 110:2, Midrash Tanchuma Beshallach 16, Midrash Tanchuma Lech Lecha 9, Numbers.R 2:13, Pesikta de R'Kahana S4.3, Pesikta Rabbati 6:5, z.Bereshit 45b, z.Lech Lecha 85b, z.Naso 125a, z.Terumah 139b
Isaiah 41:2-3 - Mekilta de R'Ishmael Shirata 6:36-38, Midrash Tanchuma Lech Lecha 15, Mekhilta de R'Shimon bar Yochai Shirata 32:1

[6] Isaiah 41:3 - Genesis.R 43:3, Isaiah 9:2, Job 5:24, Midrash Psalms 110:3, Midrash Tanchuma Beshallach 16, Pesikta Rabbati 49:5, z.Lech Lecha 86a
Isaiah 41:3-23 - 1QIsab

[7] 1QIsaa *he does not come*; LXX *shall proceed in peace*

[8] Isaiah 41:4 - Acts 15:18 17:26, b.Shabbat [Rashi] 32a, Deuteronomy 32:7-32:8, Ein Yaakov Eduyot:4a, Esther.R Petichata:10, Isaiah 16:12 16:26 17:26 18:24 19:10 44:6-44:7 46:3-46:4 22:10 48:3-48:7 24:12, m.Eduyot 2:9, Matthew 1:23 4:20, Mekhilta de R'Shimon bar Yochai Shirata 30:1, Mekhilta de R'Ishmael Bahodesh 5:32, Mekhilta de R'Ishmael Shirata 4:29, Midrash Psalms 139:6, Midrash Tanchuma Beshallach 16, Midrash Tanchuma Ki Tissa 12, Numbers.R 1:2, Pesikta de R'Kahana 5.18 27.10, Pesikta Rabbati 15:25 51:3, Ralbag Wars 2:4, Revelation 1:8 1:11 1:17 2:8 22:13, t.Eduyot 1:14, y.Sanhedrin 1:1, z.Lech Lecha 86a, z.Vayechi 227b

[9] Isaiah 41:5 - Exodus 15:14, Ezekiel 26:15-16, Genesis 10:5, Genesis.R 44:7, Jastrow 1403b, Joshua 2:10 5:1, Psalms 65:9 66:3 67:8

[10] 1QIsaa *together*

[11] Isaiah 41:6 - 1 Samuel 4:7-4:9 5:3-5:5, Acts 19:24-19:28, Daniel 3:1-3:7, Genesis.R 44:7, Isaiah 11:4 16:19 20:12, Joel 4:9-4:11

[12] Isaiah 41:7 - b.Menachot [Rashi] 27b, b.Succah [Rashi] 52b, Daniel 3:1-3:7, Genesis.R 44:7, Isaiah 40:19-20 44:12-15 46:6-7, Jastrow 354a 1304a, Jeremiah 10:3-5 10:9, Judges 18:17-18 18:24

good'; And he fastened it with nails, so it should not move.

וְאַתָּה יִשְׂרָאֵל עַבְדִּי יַעֲקֹב אֲשֶׁר בְּחַרְתִּיךָ זֶרַע אַבְרָהָם אֹהֲבִי

8[1] But you, Israel, My servant, Jacob whom I have chosen, the seed of Abraham *My friend*[2];

אֲשֶׁר הֶחֱזַקְתִּיךָ מִקְצוֹת הָאָרֶץ וּמֵאֲצִילֶיהָ קְרָאתִיךָ וָאֹמַר לְךָ עַבְדִּי־אַתָּה בְּחַרְתִּיךָ וְלֹא מְאַסְתִּיךָ

9[3] You whom I have taken hold of from the ends of the earth, And called you from its uttermost parts, And said to you: 'You are My servant, I have chosen you and not cast you away';

אַל־תִּירָא כִּי עִמְּךָ־אָנִי אַל־תִּשְׁתָּע כִּי־אֲנִי אֱלֹהֶיךָ אִמַּצְתִּיךָ אַף־עֲזַרְתִּיךָ אַף־תְּמַכְתִּיךָ בִּימִין צִדְקִי

10[4] Do not fear, for I am with you, Do not be dismayed, for I am your God; I strengthen you, yes, I help you; Yes, I uphold you with My victorious right hand.

הֵן יֵבֹשׁוּ וְיִכָּלְמוּ כֹּל הַנֶּחֱרִים בָּךְ יִהְיוּ כְאַיִן וְיֹאבְדוּ אַנְשֵׁי רִיבֶךָ

11[5] Behold, all those who were incensed against you shall be ashamed and perplexed; They who strove with you *shall be as nothing, and shall perish*[6].

תְּבַקְשֵׁם וְלֹא תִמְצָאֵם אַנְשֵׁי מַצֻּתֶךָ יִהְיוּ כְאַיִן וּכְאֶפֶס אַנְשֵׁי מִלְחַמְתֶּךָ

12[7] You shall seek them, and shall not find them, those who contended with you; those who warred against you Shall be as nothing, and as a thing of nothing.

כִּי אֲנִי יְהוָה אֱלֹהֶיךָ מַחֲזִיק יְמִינֶךָ הָאֹמֵר לְךָ אַל־תִּירָא אֲנִי עֲזַרְתִּיךָ

13[8] For I, the LORD your God, hold your right hand, Who says to you: 'Fear not, I will help you.'

אַל־תִּירְאִי תּוֹלַעַת יַעֲקֹב מְתֵי יִשְׂרָאֵל אֲנִי עֲזַרְתִּיךְ נְאֻם־יְהוָה וְגֹאֲלֵךְ קְדוֹשׁ יִשְׂרָאֵל

14[9] Fear not, *you worm*[10] Jacob[11], And you men of Israel; I help you, says the LORD, And your Redeemer, the Holy One of Israel.

הִנֵּה שַׂמְתִּיךְ לְמוֹרַג חָרוּץ חָדָשׁ בַּעַל פִּיפִיּוֹת תָּדוּשׁ הָרִים וְתָדֹק וּגְבָעוֹת כַּמֹּץ תָּשִׂים

15[12] Behold, I make you a new threshing-sledge Having sharp teeth; You shall thresh the

---

[1] Isaiah 41:8 - 2 Chronicles 20:7, Apocalypse of Abraham 9:7, b.Sotah [Tosefot] 22b, Bahir 77 78, Chibbur Yafeh 5 {19a}, Deuteronomy 7:6-7:8 10:15 14:2, Ein Yaakov Sotah:31a, Esther.R 4:2, Exodus 19:5-19:6, Exodus.R 27:1 44:9, Galatians 3:19 4:22-4:31, Genesis.R 44:3, Isaiah 5:22 19:1 44:1-44:2 20:21 24:12 1:3 3:2 15:16, James 2:23, Jastrow 564b, Jeremiah 9:24, John 8:33-8:44 15:14-15:15, Jubilees 19:9 2:20, Leviticus 1:42, m.Avot 5:19, m.Avot 5:2, Mas.Gerim 4:2, Mas.Kallah Rabbati 8:1, Matthew 3:9, Mekilta de R'Ishmael Nezikin 18:23, Mesillat Yesharim 4:To Acquire Zehirus, Midrash Psalms 112:2, Midrash Tanchuma Ki Tetze 9, Midrash Tanchuma Lech Lecha 1, Midrash Tanchuma Shelach 3, Midrash Tanchuma Shemini 9, Midrash Tanchuma Tzav 8, Midrash Tanchuma Yitro 5, mt.Hilchot Teshuvah 10:2, mt.Pirkei Avot 5:17, Numbers.R 3:2 8:2 16:3, Pesikta de R'Kahana S1.20, Psalms 33:12 9:6 105:42-105:45 15:4, Romans 4:12-4:13 9:4-9:8, Sefer Yetzirah 6:7 Sefer Yetzirah [Long] 6:8, Sifre Devarim Vaetchanan 27 32, Tanya Igeret Hakodesh §13, z.Beshallach 48b, z.Lech Lecha 76b 85a, z.Vayera 100b 105a
Isaiah 41:8 [LXX] - Testament of Abraham 1:6
Isaiah 41:8-9 - 4Q176 frags 1-2 1.9-11
Isaiah 41:8-11 - 4QIsab
[2] LXX *whom I have loved*
[3] Isaiah 41:9 - 1 Corinthians 1:26-29, 1 Samuel 12:22, Deuteronomy 7:6-7, Isaiah 17:2 17:8 43:5-6, James 2:5, Jastrow 1185a, Jeremiah 33:25-26, Joshua 24:2-4, Luke 13:29, Nehemiah 9:7-38, Psalms 94:14 107:2-3, Revelation 5:9, Romans 11:1-2
[4] Isaiah 41:10 - 1 Chronicles 12:17, 2 Chronicles 20:17 8:8, 2 Corinthians 12:9, Deuteronomy 20:1 31:6-31:8 33:27-33:29, Ephesians 3:16, Genesis 15:1, Genesis.R 65:19, Guide for the Perplexed 3:51, Hosea 1:9, Isaiah 12:2 40:29-40:31 41:13-41:14 43:1-43:2 19:5 20:2 1:8 51:12-51:13 4:7 12:19, Jastrow 1537b, John 8:54-8:55, Joshua 1:9, Luke 1:13 1:30 2:10-2:11, Philippians 4:13, Pirkei de R'Eliezer 28, Psalms 27:1 29:11 37:17 37:24 41:13 46:2-46:3 46:8 46:12 63:9 65:6 89:14-89:15 99:4 24:8 24:11 1:14 3:12, Romans 8:31, Sibylline Oracles 3.709, Zechariah 10:12 13:9
[5] Isaiah 41:11 - Acts 13:8-11 16:39, Daniel 4:32, Exodus 11:8 23:22, Isaiah 5:8 16:17 17:24 17:29 21:24 1:26 6:17 60:12-14, Revelation 3:9, Saadia Opinions 10:13, z.Ki Tissa 188b, Zechariah 12:3
[6] 1QIsaa *will all die*; 1QIsab *will become nothing and be ashamed*
[7] Isaiah 41:12 - Isaiah 17:14, Job 20:7-20:9, Psalms 37:35-37:36, Saadia Opinions 10:13
[8] Isaiah 41:13 - 2 Timothy 4:17, Deuteronomy 33:26-33:29, Isaiah 17:10 18:6 19:6 21:1 3:18, Numbers.R 2:13, Pesikta Rabbati 11:5, Pirkei de R'Eliezer 28, Psalms 63:9 73:23 13:31
[9] Isaiah 41:14 - Deuteronomy 7:7, Exodus.R 49:2, Galatians 3:13, Genesis.R 100 [Excl]:3, HaMadrikh 35:6, Isaiah 19:14 20:6 20:24 23:4 24:17 1:7 1:26 6:5 6:8 11:20 12:16 15:16, Jeremiah 2:34, Job 19:25 1:6, Kuzari 3.011, Luke 12:32, Matthew 7:14, Mekilta de R'Shimon bar Yochai Beshallach 22:1, Mekilta de R'Ishmael Beshallah 3:38, Midrash Psalms 22:20 118:13, Midrash Tanchuma Beshallach 9, Midrash Tanchuma Terumah 5, Psalms 19:15 22:7, Revelation 5:9, Romans 9:27, Titus 2:14, z.Vayishlach 177b
[10] Missing in LXX
[11] LXX *few in number*
[12] Isaiah 41:15 - 2 Corinthians 10:4-10:5, b.Avodah Zara 24b, b.Menachot 22a, b.Zevachim 116b, Habakkuk 3:12, Isaiah 21:10 4:27, Micah 4:13, Midrash Psalms 22:20, Psalms 18:43, Zechariah 4:7

mountains, and beat them small, And shall make the hills as chaff.

16[1] תְּזְרֵם֙ וְר֣וּחַ תִּשָּׂאֵ֔ם וּסְעָרָ֖ה תָּפִ֣יץ אוֹתָ֑ם וְאַתָּה֙ תָּגִ֣יל בַּֽיהֹוָ֔ה בִּקְד֥וֹשׁ יִשְׂרָאֵ֖ל תִּתְהַלָּֽל

You shall fan them, and the wind shall carry them away, And the whirlwind shall scatter them; And you shall rejoice in the LORD, you shall glory in the Holy One of Israel.

17[2] הָעֲנִיִּ֨ים וְהָאֶבְיוֹנִ֜ים מְבַקְשִׁ֥ים מַ֨יִם֙ וָאַ֔יִן לְשׁוֹנָ֖ם בַּצָּמָ֣א נָשָׁ֑תָּה אֲנִ֤י יְהֹוָה֙ אֶעֱנֵ֔ם אֱלֹהֵ֥י יִשְׂרָאֵ֖ל לֹ֥א אֶעֶזְבֵֽם

The poor *and needy seek[3]* water and there is none, And their tongue fails for thirst; I the LORD will answer them, I the God of Israel will not forsake them.

18[4] אֶפְתַּ֤ח עַל־שְׁפָיִים֙ נְהָר֔וֹת וּבְת֥וֹךְ בְּקָע֖וֹת מַעְיָנ֑וֹת אָשִׂ֤ים מִדְבָּר֙ לַאֲגַם־מַ֔יִם וְאֶ֥רֶץ צִיָּ֖ה לְמוֹצָ֥אֵי מָֽיִם

I will open rivers on the high hills, And fountains in the midst of the valleys; I will make the wilderness a pool of water, And the dry land springs of water.

19[5] אֶתֵּ֤ן בַּמִּדְבָּר֙ אֶ֣רֶז שִׁטָּ֔ה וַהֲדַ֖ס וְעֵ֣ץ שָׁ֑מֶן אָשִׂ֣ים בָּעֲרָבָ֗ה בְּר֛וֹשׁ תִּדְהָ֥ר וּתְאַשּׁ֖וּר יַחְדָּֽו

I will plant in the wilderness the cedar, the *acacia tree, And the myrtle, and the oil tree; I will set in the desert the cypress, the plane tree, and the larch together[6]*;

20[7] לְמַ֧עַן יִרְא֣וּ וְיֵדְע֗וּ וְיָשִׂ֤ימוּ וְיַשְׂכִּ֙ילוּ֙ יַחְדָּ֔ו כִּ֛י יַד־יְהֹוָ֖ה עָ֣שְׂתָה זֹּ֑את וּקְד֥וֹשׁ יִשְׂרָאֵ֖ל בְּרָאָֽהּ

So they may see, and know, And consider, and understand together, That the hand of the LORD has done this, And the Holy One of Israel has created it.

21[8] קָרְב֥וּ רִֽיבְכֶ֖ם יֹאמַ֣ר יְהֹוָ֑ה הַגִּ֙ישׁוּ֙ עֲצֻמ֣וֹתֵיכֶ֔ם יֹאמַ֖ר מֶ֥לֶךְ יַעֲקֹֽב

Produce your cause[9], says the LORD; Bring forth your reasons, says the King of Jacob.

22[10] יַגִּ֙ישׁוּ֙ וְיַגִּ֣ידוּ לָ֔נוּ אֵ֖ת אֲשֶׁ֣ר תִּקְרֶ֑ינָה הָרִאשֹׁנ֣וֹת ׀ מָ֣ה הֵ֗נָּה הַגִּ֜ידוּ וְנָשִׂ֤ימָה לִבֵּ֙נוּ֙ וְנֵֽדְעָ֣ה אַחֲרִיתָ֔ן א֥וֹ הַבָּא֖וֹת הַשְׁמִיעֻֽנוּ

Let them bring them forth, and declare to us the things that shall happen; the former things, what are they? Declare so we may consider, and know the end of them; Or announce to us things to come.

23[11] הַגִּ֙ידוּ֙ הָאֹתִיּ֣וֹת לְאָח֔וֹר וְנֵ֣דְעָ֔ה כִּ֥י אֱלֹהִ֖ים אַתֶּ֑ם אַף־תֵּיטִ֤יבוּ וְתָרֵ֙עוּ֙ וְנִשְׁתָּ֣עָה "וְנִרְא' "וְנֵרֶ֔א" יַחְדָּֽו

Declare the things that are to come hereafter, so we may know you are gods; Yes, do good, or do evil, so we may be dismayed, and see it together.

---

[1] Isaiah 41:16 - 1 Corinthians 1:30-1:31, 1 Samuel 2:1-2:2, b.Avodah Zara 44a, Genesis.R 83:5, Habakkuk 3:18, Isaiah 12:6 17:13 25:1-25:3 45:24-45:25 61:10-61:11, Jastrow 322b, Jeremiah 9:24-9:25 15:7 3:2, Luke 1:46-1:47, Matthew 3:12, Midrash Psalms 18:33, Philippians 3:3, Psalms 1:4, Romans 5:11, Song of Songs.R 7:8

[2] Isaiah 41:17 - 2 Corinthians 12:9, Amos 8:11-8:13, continued from Isaiah 40:27], Exodus 17:3 17:6, Genesis 4:15, Haftarah Vaetchanan [Teimon, Hebrews 13:5-13:6, Isaiah 6:19 18:16 19:20 20:3 7:1 13:1 18:2, John 4:10-4:15 7:37-7:39, Judges 15:18-15:19, Lamentations 4:4, Luke 16:24, Matthew 5:3 5:6, Midrash Psalms 5:6 63:1, Psalms 22:16 34:7 42:3 50:15 63:2-63:3 68:10-68:11 72:12-72:13 94:14 102:17-18 107:5-6, Revelation 21:6 22:17
Isaiah 41:17-20 - Apocalypse of Elijah 1:3

[3] 1QIsaa *the needy, those seeking*

[4] Isaiah 41:18 - Ezekiel 47:1-47:8, Isaiah 12:3 6:25 8:2 35:6-35:7 43:19-43:20 20:3 24:21 49:9-49:10 10:11, Joel 4:18, Midrash Tanchuma Massei 3, Numbers.R 14:2 23:4, Psalms 46:5 78:15-16 9:41 11:35, Revelation 7:17 22:1, Zechariah 14:8

[5] Isaiah 41:19 - b.Bava Batra 80b, b.Ketubot [Tosefot] 14a, b.Rosh Hashanah 23a, b.Succah 37a, b.Taanit 25b, Ein Yaakov Bava Batra:80b, Ein Yaakov Rosh Hashanah:23a, Exodus.R 35:1, Ezekiel 17:22-24 23:12, Genesis.R 15:1, Isaiah 3:6 8:15 11:1 37:31-32 3:3 7:13 12:13 12:21 13:3 13:11, Jastrow 88b 1170a 1505b 1542a 1658a, Midrash Psalms 1:20, Midrash Tanchuma Massei 3, Midrash Tanchuma Pinchas 14, Midrash Tanchuma Terumah 9, Numbers.R 21:22 23:4, Psalms 92:14-15, Song of Songs.R 2:2, y.Ketubot 7:9

[6] LXX *box, the myrtle and cypress, and white poplar*

[7] Isaiah 41:20 - 2 Thessalonians 1:10, Ephesians 2:6-10, Exodus 9:16, Isaiah 43:7-13 19:21 20:23 45:6-8 18:18, Job 12:9, Numbers 23:23, Psalms 13:27

[8] Isaiah 41:21 - Jastrow 1332b, Job 23:3-4 7:37 14:3 40:7-9, Micah 6:1-2, Midrash Psalms 20:3, Midrash Tanchuma Vayechi 2, Pesikta Rabbati 29/30A:10

[9] LXX *Your judgment draws near*

[10] Isaiah 41:22 - Isaiah 18:9 43:9-12 20:7 21:21 22:10 24:14, John 13:19 16:14, Saadia Opinions Intro:6

[11] Isaiah 41:23 - Acts 15:18, Isaiah 18:9 44:7-8 21:3 45:7-8 22:7 46:9-10, Jeremiah 10:5, John 13:19, Mas.Soferim 7:2

הֶן־אַתֶּם מֵאַיִן וּפָעָלְכֶם מֵאָפַע תּוֹעֵבָה יִבְחַר בָּכֶם	24[1]	Behold, *you are nothing, And your work a thing of nothing*[2]; An abomination is he who chooses you.
הַעִירוֹתִי מִצָּפוֹן וַיַּאת מִמִּזְרַח־שֶׁמֶשׁ יִקְרָא בִשְׁמִי וְיָבֹא סְגָנִים כְּמוֹ־חֹמֶר וּכְמוֹ יוֹצֵר יִרְמָס־טִיט	25[3]	*I have*[4] awakened one from the north, and he has come, From the rising of the sun one who calls on My name; *And he shall come on rulers as on mortar*[5], And as the potter treads clay.
מִי־הִגִּיד מֵרֹאשׁ וְנֵדָעָה וּמִלְּפָנִים וְנֹאמַר צַדִּיק אַף אֵין־מַגִּיד אַף אֵין מַשְׁמִיעַ אַף אֵין־שֹׁמֵעַ אִמְרֵיכֶם	26[6]	Who has declared from the beginning, that we may know? And in their past, so we may say he is right? Yes, there is no one who declares, Yes, there is no one who announces, Yes, there is no one who hears your utterances.
רִאשׁוֹן לְצִיּוֹן הִנֵּה הִנָּם וְלִירוּשָׁלַ͏ִם מְבַשֵּׂר אֶתֵּן	27[7]	*A harbinger*[8] to Zion will I give: 'Behold, behold them[9],' and to Jerusalem a messenger of good tidings.
וְאֵרֶא וְאֵין אִישׁ וּמֵאֵלֶּה וְאֵין יוֹעֵץ וְאֶשְׁאָלֵם וְיָשִׁיבוּ דָבָר	28[10]	And I look, but there is no man; among them, but there is no counsellor, That, when I ask of them, can give an answer.
הֵן כֻּלָּם אָוֶן אֶפֶס מַעֲשֵׂיהֶם רוּחַ וָתֹהוּ נִסְכֵּיהֶם	29[11]	*Behold, all of them, Their works are vanity and nothing; Their molten images are wind and confusion*[12].

Isaiah – Chapter 42

הֵן עַבְדִּי אֶתְמָךְ־בּוֹ בְּחִירִי רָצְתָה נַפְשִׁי נָתַתִּי רוּחִי עָלָיו מִשְׁפָּט לַגּוֹיִם יוֹצִיא	1[13]	Behold My servant, whom I uphold; My elect, in whom My soul delights; I have put My spirit on him, He shall make the right to go forth to the nations.
לֹא יִצְעַק וְלֹא יִשָּׂא וְלֹא־יַשְׁמִיעַ בַּחוּץ קוֹלוֹ	2[14]	He shall not cry, nor lift up, nor cause his voice to be heard in the street.
קָנֶה רָצוּץ לֹא יִשְׁבּוֹר וּפִשְׁתָּה כֵהָה לֹא יְכַבֶּנָּה לֶאֱמֶת יוֹצִיא מִשְׁפָּט	3[15]	He shall not break a bruised reed, And he shall not quench the dimly burning wick; He shall make the right go forth according to the truth.

[1] Isaiah 41:24 - 1 Corinthians 8:4, Deuteronomy 7:26 3:15, Isaiah 13:19 17:29 44:9-10 18:24, Jastrow 1202b 1655a, Jeremiah 10:8 10:14 51:17-18, Leviticus.R 27:7, Midrash Tanchuma Emor 11, Midrash Tanchuma Tazria 4, Pesikta de R'Kahana 9.6, Psalms 19:8, Revelation 17:5

[2] 1QIsaa *you and your work are nothing*

[3] Isaiah 41:25 - 2 Samuel 22:43, 5QIsa, 5QIsaI, Ezra 1:2-1:3, Isaiah 10:6 21:2 17:2 44:28-45:6 21:13 46:10-46:11, Jeremiah 2:3 51:27-51:29, Leviticus.R 9:6, Micah 7:10, Numbers.R 13:2, Song of Songs.R 4:32, z.Vayeshev 186b, Zechariah 10:5

[4] 1QIsaa *You are*

[5] 1QIsaa *Rulers will come like mire*

[6] Isaiah 41:26 - Habakkuk 2:18-2:20, Isaiah 17:22 19:9 20:7 21:21

[7] Isaiah 41:27 - b.Pesachim 5a, Exodus.R 15:1, Ezra 1:1-1:2, Genesis.R 63:8, Isaiah 16:9 17:4 19:10 20:6 20:28 24:3 24:12 4:7, Leviticus.R 30:16, Luke 2:10-2:11, Motzoei Shabbat [Ribbon HaOlamim], Nahum 2:1, Pesikta de R'Kahana 27.1, Pesikta Rabbati 51:3, Revelation 2:8, Romans 10:15

[8] LXX *dominion*

[9] 1QIsaa *there is slumber*

[10] Isaiah 41:28 - Daniel 2:10-2:11 4:4-5 5:8, Isaiah 40:13-14 2:2 11:16 15:5

[11] Isaiah 41:29 - Habakkuk 2:18, Isaiah 17:24 44:9-20, Jeremiah 5:13 10:2-16, Psalms 115:4-8 135:15-18

[12] LXX *For these are your makers, as you think, and they who cause you to err in vain*

[13] Isaiah 42:1 - 1 Peter 2:4 2:6, 2 Baruch 70:10, Acts 9:15 10:38 11:18 26:17-18 4:28, Apocalypse of Adam 6:9, Colossians 1:13, Ephesians 1:4 1:6 3:8, Isaiah 2:4 11:2-5 8:16 17:8 19:10 49:3-8 50:4-9 4:13 5:11 11:21 13:1, John 1:32-1:34 3:34 6:27 16:32, Luke 3:22 9:35, Malachi 1:11, Mark 1:10-11, Martyrdom and Ascension of Isaiah 8:8, Matthew 3:16-17 12:18-21 17:5, Midrash Psalms 2:9 42/43:5, Pesikta Rabbati 36:1, Philippians 2:7, Psalms 89:20-21, Romans 15:8-16, Testament of Benjamin 11:2, Zechariah 3:8
Isaiah 42:1-4 - Psalms of Solomon 12:6 17:21
Isaiah 42:1-16 - Haftarah Bereshit [Teimon]
Isaiah 42:1-25 - 1QIsaa

[14] Isaiah 42:2 - 1 Peter 2:23, 2 Baruch 72:3, 2 Timothy 2:24, Luke 17:20, Matthew 11:29 12:16-20, Zechariah 9:9
Isaiah 42:2-7 - 4QIsab

[15] Isaiah 42:3 - b.Berachot 56b, b.Yevamot 93b, Ezekiel 10:16, Hebrews 2:17-2:18, Isaiah 11:3-11:4 35:3-35:4 16:11 40:29-40:31 2:4 2:10 57:15-57:18 61:1-61:3 18:2, Jeremiah 30:12-30:17 31:19-31:21 7:26, John 5:30 20:19-20:21 20:27, Luke 22:31-22:32, Matthew 11:28 18:10-18:14, Micah 7:9, Psalms 72:2-72:4 96:13 98:9 103:13-103:14 3:3, Revelation 19:11

לֹא יִכְהֶה֙ וְלֹ֣א יָר֔וּץ עַד־יָשִׂ֥ים בָּאָ֖רֶץ מִשְׁפָּ֑ט וּלְתוֹרָת֖וֹ אִיִּ֥ים יְיַחֵֽילוּ	4[1]	He shall not fail nor be crushed, until he has set the right in the earth; And the isles shall wait for his teaching.
כֹּֽה־אָמַ֞ר הָאֵ֣ל׀ יְהוָ֗ה בּוֹרֵ֤א הַשָּׁמַ֙יִם֙ וְנ֣וֹטֵיהֶ֔ם רֹקַ֥ע הָאָ֖רֶץ וְצֶאֱצָאֶ֑יהָ נֹתֵ֤ן נְשָׁמָה֙ לָעָ֣ם עָלֶ֔יהָ וְר֖וּחַ לַהֹלְכִ֥ים בָּֽהּ	5[2]	Thus says *God the LORD*[3], He who created the heavens, and stretched them forth, He who spread forth the earth and what comes from it, He who gives breath to the people upon it, and spirit to those who walk in it:
אֲנִ֧י יְהוָ֛ה קְרָאתִ֥יךָֽ בְצֶ֖דֶק וְאַחְזֵ֣ק בְּיָדֶ֑ךָ וְאֶצָּרְךָ֗ וְאֶתֶּנְךָ֛ לִבְרִ֥ית עָ֖ם לְא֥וֹר גּוֹיִֽם	6[4]	I *the LORD*[5] have called you in righteousness, And have taken hold of your hand, And kept you, and set you for *a covenant of the people*[6], For a light of the nations;
לִפְקֹ֖חַ עֵינַ֣יִם עִוְר֑וֹת לְהוֹצִ֤יא מִמַּסְגֵּר֙ אַסִּ֔יר מִבֵּ֥ית כֶּ֖לֶא יֹ֥שְׁבֵי חֹֽשֶׁךְ	7[7]	To open the blind eyes, to release *the prisoners*[8] from the dungeon, And those who sit in darkness out of the prison house.
אֲנִ֥י יְהוָ֖ה ה֣וּא שְׁמִ֑י וּכְבוֹדִי֙ לְאַחֵ֣ר לֹֽא־אֶתֵּ֔ן וּתְהִלָּתִ֖י לַפְּסִילִֽים	8[9]	I am the LORD, that is My name; And I will not give My glory to another, nor My praise to graven images.
הָרִֽאשֹׁנ֖וֹת הִנֵּה־בָ֑אוּ וַֽחֲדָשׁוֹת֙ אֲנִ֣י מַגִּ֔יד בְּטֶ֥רֶם תִּצְמַ֖חְנָה אַשְׁמִ֥יעַ אֶתְכֶֽם	9[10]	Behold, the former things have come to pass, And new things I declare; Before they spring forth I tell you of them.
שִׁ֤ירוּ לַֽיהוָה֙ שִׁ֣יר חָדָ֔שׁ תְּהִלָּת֖וֹ מִקְצֵ֣ה הָאָ֑רֶץ יוֹרְדֵ֤י הַיָּם֙ וּמְלֹא֔וֹ אִיִּ֖ים וְיֹשְׁבֵיהֶֽם	10[11]	Sing to the LORD a new song, And His praise from the end of the earth; You who go down to the sea, and all who are in it, the isles, and its inhabitants.
יִשְׂא֤וּ מִדְבָּר֙ וְעָרָ֔יו חֲצֵרִ֖ים תֵּשֵׁ֣ב קֵדָ֑ר יָרֹ֙נּוּ֙ יֹ֣שְׁבֵי סֶ֔לַע מֵרֹ֥אשׁ הָרִ֖ים יִצְוָֽחוּ	11[12]	Let the wilderness and its cities lift up their voice, the villages that Kedar inhabits; Let the

[1] Isaiah 42:4 - 1 Corinthians 9:21, 1 Peter 2:22-2:24, Genesis 1:10, Hebrews 12:2-12:4, Isaiah 2:2-4 9:8 11:9-12 24:15-16 17:5 18:12 1:1 49:5-10 52:13-15 53:2-12 7:5 12:9 18:19, John 17:4-17:5, LXX Footnote: "*and in his mane shall the Gentiles trust.*", Matthew 12:21, Micah 4:1-3, mt.Perek Chelek Intro:11, Psalms 22:28 72:8-11 98:2-3, Romans 16:26, Zechariah 2:11
Isaiah 42:4-11 - 4QIsah

[2] Isaiah 42:5 - 2 Enoch 47:4 3 Enoch 44:7, Abnormal Dagesh in מ on נשמה, Abnormal Dagesh in נ on נשמה נתן, Acts 17:25, Amos 9:6, b.Berachot 52b, b.Ketubot 111a, Daniel 5:23, Deuteronomy.R 5:15, Ein Yaakov Ketubot:111a, Genesis 1:10-1:12 1:24-1:25 2:7, Genesis.R 12:12 74:1 96:5, Hebrews 1:2 1:10-1:12, Isaiah 16:12 16:22 16:28 20:24 21:12 21:18 24:13, Jeremiah 10:12 8:17, Job 12:10 3:3 9:4 10:14, Midrash Tanchuma Bereshit 7, Midrash Tanchuma Vayechi 3, Pesikta de R'Kahana 22.5a, Pesikta Rabbati 1:6 1:7, Psalms 24:1-24:2 33:6 102:26-102:27 104:2-104:35 16:6, y.Ketubot 12:3, y.Ketubot 12:3, y.Kilayim 9:3, z.Vaetchanan 269b, Zechariah 12:1
Isaiah 42:5-9 - Maamad [Sunday]
Isaiah 42:5-21 - Haftarah Bereshit [Sephard]
Isaiah 42:5-43:11 - Haftarah Bereshit [Ashkenaz]
[3] 1QIsaa *the God, and God*
[4] Isaiah 42:6 - 1 Peter 2:9, 2 Corinthians 1:20, Acts 13:47 2:23, Apocalypse of Adam 6:1, Galatians 3:15-17, Hebrews 1:8-9 7:2 7:26 8:6 9:15 12:24 13:20, Isaiah 2:3 8:1 17:13 18:1 19:1 21:13 49:1-3 1:6 1:8 51:4-5 60:1-3, Jeremiah 23:5-6 33:15-16, John 8:12, Luke 1:69-72 2:32, Two Letters Part II, Matthew 2:28, mt.Hilchot Melachim u'Michamoteihem 8:10, Psalms 45:7-8, Romans 3:25-26 15:8-9
[5] Missing in 1QIsaa
[6] 4QIsah *an everlasting covenant*
[7] Isaiah 42:7 - 1 Peter 2:9, 2 Corinthians 4:6, 2 Timothy 2:26, Acts 2:18, Ephesians 1:17-18, Hebrews 2:14-15, Isaiah 9:3 5:18 11:5 18:16 18:22 1:9 13:1, John 9:39, Joseph and Aseneth 15:12 2 4:10, Luke 4:18-21 24:45, Matthew 11:5, Psalms 107:10-116 146:7-18, Revelation 3:18, Selichot, Zechariah 9:11-12
[8] 1QIsaa *those bound*
[9] Isaiah 42:8 - b.Chullin [Tosefot] 66b, Ecclesiastes.R 7:33, Exodus 3:13-15 4:5 20:3-5 10:14, Genesis.R 17:4, Isaiah 19:11 24:11, John 5:23 8:58, Midrash Psalms 8:2, Midrash Tanchuma Chukkat 6, Midrash Tanchuma Naso 24, Midrash Tanchuma Shemini 8, Numbers.R 19:3, Pesikta de R'Kahana 4.3 7.2 21.2, Pesikta Rabbati 5:3 14:9 17:1 21:8, Psalms 83:19, z.Mishpatim 94b, z.Vayishlach 174a, z.Yitro 86a
[10] Isaiah 42:9 - 1 Kings 8:15-20 11:36, 1 Peter 1:10-12, 2 Baruch 70:10, 2 Peter 1:19-21, Acts 15:18, Ein Yaakov Avodah Zarah:3b, Exodus.R 15:17 15:21, Genesis 15:12-16, Isaiah 41:22-23 19:19 44:7-8 46:9-10, John 13:19, Joshua 21:45 23:14-15
Isaiah 42:9-12 - 4QIsab
[11] Isaiah 42:10 - 1 Chronicles 16:32, Ecclesiastes.R 1:28, Isaiah 24:14-16 18:4 20:23 1:6 1:13 3:5 12:9 17:14, Jastrow 1568b, Mekhilta de R'Shimon bar Yochai Shirata 27:1, Mekilta de R'Ishmael Shirata 1:73, Midrash Psalms 98:1 104:23, Psalms 33:3 40:4 96:1-3 96:11 97:1 98:1-4 107:23-32 117:1-2 148:1-14 6:6, Revelation 5:9 14:3, Romans 15:9-11, Zephaniah 2:11
Isaiah 42:10-16 - Maamad [Monday]
Isaiah 42:10-21 - HaMadrikh 32
[12] Isaiah 42:11 - Deuteronomy.R 7:6, Genesis 1:23, Genesis.R 13:6, Isaiah 16:1 21:16 8:16 11:1 11:6 16:3 41:18-41:19 19:19 4:7 12:7,

inhabitants of Sela exult, Let them shout from the top of the mountains.

יָשִׂימוּ לַיהוָה כָּבוֹד וּתְהִלָּתוֹ בָּאִיִּים יַגִּידוּ 12[1]

Let them give glory to the LORD, And declare His praise in the islands.

יְהוָה כַּגִּבּוֹר יֵצֵא כְּאִישׁ מִלְחָמוֹת יָעִיר קִנְאָה יָרִיעַ אַף־יַצְרִיחַ עַל־אֹיְבָיו יִתְגַּבָּר 13[2]

The LORD will go forth as a mighty man, He will stir up jealousy like a man of war; *He will cry, yes, He will shout aloud*[3], *He will prove Himself*[4] mighty against His enemies.

הֶחֱשֵׁיתִי מֵעוֹלָם אַחֲרִישׁ אֶתְאַפָּק כַּיּוֹלֵדָה אֶפְעֶה אֶשֹּׁם וְאֶשְׁאַף יָחַד 14[5]

[6]I have held My peace for a long time, I have been still, and refrained Myself; Now I will cry like a travailing woman, Gasping and panting at once.

אַחֲרִיב הָרִים וּגְבָעוֹת וְכָל־עֶשְׂבָּם אוֹבִישׁ וְשַׂמְתִּי נְהָרוֹת לָאִיִּים וַאֲגַמִּים אוֹבִישׁ 15[7]

I will make the mountains and hills waste, and dry up all their herbs; and I will make the rivers islands, And will dry up the pools.

וְהוֹלַכְתִּי עִוְרִים בְּדֶרֶךְ לֹא יָדָעוּ בִּנְתִיבוֹת לֹא־יָדְעוּ אַדְרִיכֵם אָשִׂים מַחְשָׁךְ לִפְנֵיהֶם לָאוֹר וּמַעֲקַשִּׁים לְמִישׁוֹר אֵלֶּה הַדְּבָרִים עֲשִׂיתִם וְלֹא עֲזַבְתִּים 16[8]

And I will bring the blind by a way they never knew, I will lead them in paths they never knew; I will make darkness light before them, and rugged places plain. These things I will do, And I will not leave them undone.

נָסֹגוּ אָחוֹר יֵבֹשׁוּ בֹשֶׁת הַבֹּטְחִים בַּפָּסֶל הָאֹמְרִים לְמַסֵּכָה אַתֶּם אֱלֹהֵינוּ 17[9]

They shall be turned back, greatly ashamed, That trust in graven images, who say to molten images: 'You are our gods.'

הַחֵרְשִׁים שְׁמָעוּ וְהַעִוְרִים הַבִּיטוּ לִרְאוֹת 18[10]

Hear, you deaf, And look, you blind, so you may see.

מִי עִוֵּר כִּי אִם־עַבְדִּי וְחֵרֵשׁ כְּמַלְאָכִי אֶשְׁלָח מִי עִוֵּר כִּמְשֻׁלָּם וְעִוֵּר כְּעֶבֶד יְהוָה 19[11]

Who is blind, but My servant? Or deaf, as My messenger whom I send? Who is blind as he who is wholehearted, And blind as the LORD's servant?

רָאִיתָ "רָאוֹת" רַבּוֹת וְלֹא תִשְׁמֹר פָּקוֹחַ אָזְנַיִם וְלֹא יִשְׁמָע 20[12]

Seeing many things, you do not observe; Opening the ears, he does not hear.

Jeremiah 21:13 24:28 1:16, Midrash Psalms 104:23, Midrash Tanchuma Bamidbar 2, Nahum 2:1, Numbers.R 1:2, Obadiah 1:3, Psalms 72:8-72:10 24:5, Sifre Devarim Nitzavim 333

Isaiah 42:11-12 - Perek Shirah [the Bear]

[1] Isaiah 42:12 - Isaiah 24:15-24:16 18:4 66:18-66:19, Midrash Psalms 104:23, Psalms 22:28 96:3-96:10 117:1-117:2, Revelation 5:9-5:10 7:9-7:12, Romans 15:9-15:11, Tanna Devei Eliyahu 2, z.Vayishlach 173b

[2] Isaiah 42:13 - Amos 1:2, Avot de R'Natan 2, b.Bechorot 15b, Esther.R 7:18, Exodus 15:1-15:3, Exodus.R 18:8 30:18, Hosea 11:10, Isaiah 9:8 2:11 7:4 59:16-59:19 63:1-63:4 18:14, Jastrow 1352b, Jeremiah 1:30, Joel 4:16, Leviticus.R 27:11, Mekhilta de R'Shimon bar Yochai Shirata 27:1 34:2, Mekilta de R'Ishmael Shirata 1:112, Midrash Psalms 2:4 80:3, Midrash Tanchuma Beshallach 11, Midrash Tanchuma Emor 13, Midrash Tanchuma Metzora 2, Midrash Tanchuma Shoftim 14, Nahum 1:2, Perek Shirah [the Lion], Pesikta de R'Kahana 9.11, Pesikta Rabbati 9:3, Psalms 78:65 110:5-110:6 22:16, Song of Songs.R 1:49, z.Beshallach 47b, z.Vayishlach 174a, Zephaniah 1:18 3:8

[3] 1QIsaa *showing his anger, he shouts aloud*

[4] Missing in LXX

[5] Isaiah 42:14 - 2 Peter 3:9-3:10 3:15, b.Avodah Zara 3b, b.Sotah 11b, Ecclesiastes 8:11-8:12, Ecclesiastes.R 3:10, Ein Yaakov Avodah Zarah:3b, Guide for the Perplexed 3:7, Jeremiah 15:6 20:22, Job 8:18 8:20, Luke 18:7, Mekhilta de R'Shimon bar Yochai Shirata 34:1, Midrash Psalms 65:1 109:1, Midrash Tanchuma Tazria 4, Psalms 50:2 83:2-83:3, Saadia Opinions 2:12

Isaiah 42:14-15 - Mekhilta de R'Ishmael Shirata 8:20-23

Isaiah 42:14-17 - Mekhilta de R'Shimon bar Yochai Shirata 34:1

Isaiah 42:14-25 - 4QIsag

[6] 1QIsaa adds *Certainly*

[7] Isaiah 42:15 - Ezekiel 14:20, Habakkuk 3:6-10, Haggai 2:6, Isaiah 2:12-16 11:15-16 20:27 1:11 2:2, Jeremiah 4:24, Nahum 1:4-6, Psalms 18:8 107:33-34 114:3-7, Revelation 6:12-17 8:7-12 11:13 16:12 16:18 20:11, Zechariah 10:11

[8] Isaiah 42:16 - 1 Peter 1:3-5, 2 Thessalonians 2:13-14, 4Q434 frag 1 1.9, 4Q435 frag 1 1.8, Ecclesiastes 1:15 7:13, Ephesians 5:8, Ezekiel 14:23, Hebrews 13:5, Hosea 2:6 2:14, Isaiah 5:18 5:24 6:21 8:3 11:5 11:8 16:4 17:3 21:2 24:17 6:13 60:1-2 60:19-20, Jeremiah 31:9-10 32:39-41, Joshua 3:4, Luke 1:78-79 3:5, Midrash Tanchuma Chukkat 8, Midrash Tanchuma Devarim 1, Numbers.R 19:6, Pesikta de R'Kahana 4.7, Pesikta Rabbati 14:1, Psalms 94:18, Romans 5:8-10 8:29-31, z.Vaetchanan 261b

[9] Isaiah 42:17 - Exodus 8:4 8:8, Habakkuk 2:18-2:20, Isaiah 1:29 20:11 20:17 45:16-45:17, Jeremiah 2:26-2:27, Psalms 97:7

[10] Isaiah 42:18 - Exodus 4:11, Isaiah 5:18 11:5 19:8, Luke 7:22, Mark 7:34-7:37, Pesikta Rabbati 33:13, Proverbs 20:12, Revelation 3:17-3:18, Tanya Igeret Hakodesh §09

[11] Isaiah 42:19 - 2 Corinthians 3:14-15 4:4, Ezekiel 12:2, Isaiah 6:9 2:3 29:9-14 17:8 20:26 8:10, Jeremiah 4:22 5:21, John 7:47-49 9:39 9:41 12:40, Mark 8:17-8:18, Matthew 13:14-15 15:14-16 23:16-24, Romans 2:17-23 11:7-10 11:25

[12] Isaiah 42:20 - Acts 28:22-28:27, Deuteronomy 4:9 29:1-29:3, Ezekiel 9:31, Guide for the Perplexed 1:2, Isaiah 1:3 48:6-48:8 10:2,

יְהוָה חָפֵץ לְמַעַן צִדְקוֹ יַגְדִּיל תּוֹרָה וְיַאְדִּיר	21[1]	The LORD was pleased, for His righteousness' sake, To make the teaching great and glorious.
וְהוּא עַם־בָּזוּז וְשָׁסוּי הָפֵחַ בַּחוּרִים כֻּלָּם וּבְבָתֵּי כְלָאִים הָחְבָּאוּ הָיוּ לָבַז וְאֵין מַצִּיל מְשִׁסָּה וְאֵין־אֹמֵר הָשֵׁב	22[2]	But this is a people robbed and spoiled, all of them are snared in holes, and they are hid in prison houses; they are for a prey, and no one delivers, for a spoil, and no one says: 'Restore.'
מִי בָכֶם יַאֲזִין זֹאת יַקְשֵׁב וְיִשְׁמַע לְאָחוֹר	23[3]	Who among you will give ear to this? Who will pay attention and hear for the time to come?
מִי־נָתַן לִמְשׁוֹסָה "לִמְשִׁסָּה" יַעֲקֹב וְיִשְׂרָאֵל לְבֹזְזִים הֲלוֹא יְהוָה זוּ חָטָאנוּ לוֹ וְלֹא־אָבוּ בִדְרָכָיו הָלוֹךְ וְלֹא שָׁמְעוּ בְּתוֹרָתוֹ	24[4]	Who gave Jacob as a spoil, and Israel to the robbers? Did not the LORD? He, against whom we have sinned, and in whose ways they would not walk, nor were they obedient to His law.
וַיִּשְׁפֹּךְ עָלָיו חֵמָה אַפּוֹ וֶעֱזוּז מִלְחָמָה וַתְּלַהֲטֵהוּ מִסָּבִיב וְלֹא יָדָע וַתִּבְעַר־בּוֹ וְלֹא־יָשִׂים עַל־לֵב	25[5]	Therefore, He poured on him the fury of His anger, And the strength of battle; And it set him on fire all around, yet he never knew, and it burned him, yet he never laid it to heart.

Isaiah – Chapter 43

וְעַתָּה כֹּה־אָמַר יְהוָה בֹּרַאֲךָ יַעֲקֹב וְיֹצֶרְךָ יִשְׂרָאֵל אַל־תִּירָא כִּי גְאַלְתִּיךָ קָרָאתִי בְשִׁמְךָ לִי־אָתָּה	1[6]	But now thus says the LORD who created you, O Jacob, And He who formed you, O Israel: Fear not, for I have redeemed you, I have called you by your name, you are Mine.
כִּי־תַעֲבֹר בַּמַּיִם אִתְּךָ־אָנִי וּבַנְּהָרוֹת לֹא יִשְׁטְפוּךָ כִּי־תֵלֵךְ בְּמוֹ־אֵשׁ לֹא תִכָּוֶה וְלֶהָבָה לֹא תִבְעַר־בָּךְ	2[7]	When you pass through the waters, I will be with you, and through the rivers, they shall not overflow you; when you walk through the fire, you shall not be burned, nor shall the flame kindle on you.

Jeremiah 6:10 42:2-42:5, John 9:37-9:40 11:37-11:50, Mark 6:19-6:20, Nehemiah 9:10-9:17, Numbers 14:22, Psalms 106:7-106:13 11:43, Romans 2:21

[1] Isaiah 42:21 - 1 John 3:4-5, 2 Corinthians 5:19-21, At the end of each Perek of Pirkei Avot [Shabbat afternoon], Avot de R'Natan 41, b.Chullin 66b, b.Makkot 23b, b.Megillah 16a, b.Niddah 51b, Birchat HaChammah.R'Chananya, Daniel 9:24-27, Ein Yaakov Makkot 23b, Ein Yaakov Megillah:27a, Midrash Shmuel 6:11, Exodus.R 9:1, Galatians 3:13 3:21 5:22-23, Hagbaha, Hebrews 8:10, Isaiah 1:24-127 18:4 46:12-13, John 8:29 13:31-32 15:10 17:4-17:5, Leviticus.R 31:8, m.Avot 6:11, m.Makkot 3:16, Maariv Motzoei Shabbat], Mas.Gerim 4:3, Mas.Soferim 14:8 16:9, Matthew 3:15 3:17 5:17-20 17:5, Mekilta de R'Ishmael Nezikin 18:43, Mekilta de R'Ishmael Pisha 16:58, Midrash Psalms 17A:12, Midrash Tanchuma Beha'alotcha 2, Midrash Tanchuma Shelach 15, Midrash Tanchuma Tazria 9, Midrash Tanchuma Vaera 11, Midrash Tanchuma Vayera 8, Motzoei Shabbat [Viyiten Lecha], mt.Emor R'Chaninah b'Akashya 1:11, mt.Hilchot Talmud Torah 2:7, mt.Hilchot Talmud Torah 2:7, Numbers.R 14:10 15:2 17:5, Pesikta Rabbati 40:1 40:3/4, Philippians 3:9, Psalms 40:9 71:16 71:19 85:10-85:13, Romans 3:25-26 3:31 7:12 8:3-4 10:4, Saadia Opinions 3:1, Shabbat, U'voh Letzion Shacharit, y.Makkot 3:13, Yom Tov Minchah, z.Vayetze 154a

[2] Isaiah 42:22 - Deuteronomy 28:29-28:33, Isaiah 1:7 14:17 18:2 24:18 24:22 12:1 18:7 21:13 3:23 52:4-52:5 8:9, Jastrow 418a, Jeremiah 2:17 51:34-51:35 52:4-52:11 4:31, Luke 19:41-19:44 21:20-21:24, Psalms 50:22 6:21, y.Kilayim 5:3

[3] Isaiah 42:23 - 1 Peter 4:2-3, Acts 3:19 3:22-23, Deuteronomy 4:29-31 8:29, Isaiah 1:18-20 24:18, Jeremiah 3:4-7 3:13, Leviticus 26:40-42, Matthew 21:28-31, Micah 6:9, Proverbs 1:22-23

[4] Isaiah 42:24 - 2 Chronicles 15:6 12:17, Amos 3:6, b.Avodah Zara [Tosefot] 65a, b.Gittin 58a, Deuteronomy 4:49 8:30, Ein Yaakov Gittin:58a, Isaiah 10:5-10:6 6:15 21:7 23:6 50:1-50:2 59:1-59:2 15:10, Jeremiah 5:15 25:8-25:9, Judges 2:14 3:8 10:7, Lamentations 1:14 1:18, Lamentations.R 4:4, Mas.Soferim 7:4, Matthew 22:7, Nehemiah 9:26-9:27, Psalms 106:40-106:42, t.Bava Kamma 2:4, t.Horayot 2:5 2:6, y.Horayot 3:4, z.Chayyei Sarah 134a

[5] Isaiah 42:25 - 2 Kings 1:9, Deuteronomy 8:22, Ezekiel 7:8-9 20:34 22:21-22, Gates of Repentance 2.2, Hosea 7:9, Isaiah 9:14 5:13 23:7 9:1 9:11, Jeremiah 5:3, Lamentations.R 2:8 4:14, Leviticus 26:15-46, Malachi 2:2, Midrash Tanchuma Behar 3, Nahum 1:6, Psalms 79:5-6, Revelation 9:18-9:21 16:1-21

[6] Isaiah 43:1 - 2 Timothy 2:19, Acts 3:20 3:25, Deuteronomy 8:9, Ephesians 2:10, Exodus 15:13 19:5-6 9:17, Exodus.R 40:4, Ezekiel 16:8, Genesis 8:29, Hebrews 8:8-10, Isaiah 35:9-10 17:14 18:6 19:7 43:14-15 19:21 20:2 44:5-6 44:21-24 45:3-4 24:17 1:1 54:4-5 14:12 15:16, Jeremiah 7:4 9:24 9:26 2:34, Leviticus.R 36:4, Malachi 3:17, Midrash Psalms 31:2, Pesikta Rabbati 26:1/2, Psalms 4:3 6:19, Revelation 5:9, Titus 2:14, z.Vaetchanan 269b, z.Vayetze 154b, z.Vayishlach 177b, Zechariah 13:9

Isaiah 43:1-2 - 4Q176 frag 3 ll.1-3

Isaiah 43:1-4 - 4QIsag

Isaiah 43:1-13 - 1QIsab

Isaiah 43:1-28 - 1QIsaa

[7] Isaiah 43:2 - 1 Corinthians 3:13-15, 1 Peter 4:12-13, 2 Corinthians 12:9-10, 2 Timothy 4:17 4:22, 4 Maccabees 18:14, Amos 9:8-9, b.Chullin 64b, Daniel 3:25-27, Deuteronomy 31:6-31:8, Exodus 14:29, Genesis.R 76:5, Guide for the Perplexed 3:51, Hebrews 11:29 11:33-38, Isaiah 8:7-8:10 11:15-16 5:6 6:27 17:10 17:14, Joshua 1:5 1:9 3:15-17, Luke 21:12-21:18, Malachi 3:2-3:3 3:19, Matthew 1:23 7:25-27, Midrash Psalms 17:9 40:4 119:55, Midrash Tanchuma Bereshit 7, Midrash Tanchuma Pekudei 8, Pesikta Rabbati 11:5, Psalms 23:4 46:5-46:8 66:10 66:12 91:3-91:5 91:15, Zechariah 13:9

Hebrew	Verse	English
כִּ֗י אֲנִי֙ יְהוָ֣ה אֱלֹהֶ֔יךָ קְד֥וֹשׁ יִשְׂרָאֵ֖ל מוֹשִׁיעֶ֑ךָ נָתַ֤תִּי כָפְרְךָ֙ מִצְרַ֔יִם כּ֥וּשׁ וּסְבָ֖א תַּחְתֶּֽיךָ	3[1]	For I am the LORD your God, the Holy One of Israel, your *Savior*[2]; I have given Egypt as your ransom, *Ethiopia and Seba for you*[3].
מֵאֲשֶׁ֨ר יָקַ֧רְתָּ בְעֵינַ֛י נִכְבַּ֖דְתָּ וַאֲנִ֣י אֲהַבְתִּ֑יךָ וְאֶתֵּ֤ן אָדָם֙ תַּחְתֶּ֔יךָ וּלְאֻמִּ֖ים תַּ֥חַת נַפְשֶֽׁךָ	4[4]	Since you are precious in My sight, and honorable, And I have loved you; I will give men for you, And peoples for your life.
אַל־תִּירָ֖א כִּ֣י אִתְּךָ־אָ֑נִי מִמִּזְרָח֙ אָבִ֣יא זַרְעֶ֔ךָ וּמִֽמַּעֲרָ֖ב אֲקַבְּצֶֽךָ	5[5]	Fear not, for I am with you; I will bring your seed from the east, And gather you from the west;
אֹמַ֤ר לַצָּפוֹן֙ תֵּ֔נִי וּלְתֵימָ֖ן אַל־תִּכְלָ֑אִי הָבִ֤יאִי בָנַי֙ מֵרָח֔וֹק וּבְנוֹתַ֖י מִקְצֵ֥ה הָאָֽרֶץ	6[6]	I will say to the north: 'Give up,' and to the south: 'Do not keep back, bring My sons from far, and My daughters from the end of the earth;
כֹּ֚ל הַנִּקְרָ֣א בִשְׁמִ֔י וְלִכְבוֹדִ֖י בְּרָאתִ֑יו יְצַרְתִּ֖יו אַף־עֲשִׂיתִֽיו	7[7]	Everyone who is called by My name, and whom I have created for My glory, I have formed him, yes, I have made him.'
הוֹצִ֥יא עַם־עִוֵּ֖ר וְעֵינַ֣יִם יֵ֑שׁ וְחֵרְשִׁ֖ים וְאָזְנַ֥יִם לָֽמוֹ	8[8]	The blind people who have eyes shall be brought forth, And the deaf who have ears.
כָּֽל־הַגּוֹיִ֞ם נִקְבְּצ֣וּ יַחְדָּ֗ו וְיֵאָֽסְפוּ֙ לְאֻמִּ֔ים מִ֤י בָהֶם֙ יַגִּ֣יד זֹ֔את וְרִאשֹׁנ֖וֹת יַשְׁמִיעֻ֑נוּ יִתְּנ֤וּ עֵֽדֵיהֶם֙ וְיִצְדָּ֔קוּ וְיִשְׁמְע֖וּ וְיֹאמְר֥וּ אֱמֶֽת	9[9]	All the nations are gathered together, And the peoples are assembled; who among them can declare this, And announce *to us*[10] former things? Let them bring their witnesses, so they may be justified; And let them *hear*[11], and say: 'It is truth.'
אַתֶּ֤ם עֵדַי֙ נְאֻם־יְהוָ֔ה וְעַבְדִּ֖י אֲשֶׁ֣ר בָּחָ֑רְתִּי לְמַ֣עַן תֵּדְע֡וּ וְתַאֲמִ֣ינוּ לִי֩ וְתָבִ֨ינוּ כִּֽי־אֲנִ֣י ה֗וּא לְפָנַי֙ לֹא־נ֣וֹצַר אֵ֔ל וְאַחֲרַ֖י לֹ֥א יִהְיֶֽה	10[12]	You are My witnesses, says the LORD, And My servant whom I have chosen; so you may know and believe Me, and understand That I

[1] Isaiah 43:3 - 2 Chronicles 14:8-14:13, Exodus 10:7 20:2, Exodus.R 11:2, Hosea 13:4, Isaiah 20:3 6:11 17:14 21:15 21:21 1:26 12:16, Jude 1:25, Mekhilta de R'Shimon bar Yochai Pisha 9:3, Midrash Psalms 119:55, Proverbs 11:8 21:18, Sifre Devarim {Ha'azinu Hashamayim} 333, Titus 2:10-14 3:4-6
Isaiah 43:3-4 - Mekhilta de R'Ishmael Nezikin 10:179, Sifre Devarim Nitzavim 333
[2] 1QIsaa *redeemer*
[3] 1QIsaa *Cush and the people of Seba in exchange for you*
[4] Isaiah 43:4 - 1 Peter 1:7 2:9, b.Bava Kamma [Tosefot] 38a, b.Berachot 62b, b.Yevamot [Tosefot] 61a, Deuteronomy 7:6-7:8 14:2 2:18 32:9-32:14, Ecclesiastes.R 5:10, Exodus 19:5-19:6, Exodus.R 15:11, Genesis 12:2, Genesis.R 10:7, Hosea 11:1, Isaiah 15:9, Jeremiah 7:4, John 5:44 16:27 17:23 17:26, Leviticus.R 22:4, Malachi 1:2 3:17, Midrash Tanchuma Bamidbar 19, Midrash Tanchuma Vayishlach 4, Numbers.R 4:1, Psalms 16:9 15:4, Revelation 3:9, Titus 2:14, y.Shabbat 6:9
Isaiah 43:4-6 - 4Q176 4+5 1-4
[5] Isaiah 43:5 - 1 Kings 8:46-51, Acts 18:9-10, Bahir 73 155 156 159, Deuteronomy 6:3, Ezekiel 36:24-27 37:21-28 39:25-29, Genesis.R 96 [Excl]:1, Isaiah 11:11-12 27:12-13 17:8 17:10 17:14 19:2 20:2 1:12 60:1-11 66:19-20, Jeremiah 30:10-11 30:18-19 31:9-10 46:27-28, John 10:16, Luke 13:29, Micah 2:12, Psalms 22:28-32 10:47 11:3, Zechariah 8:7
[6] Isaiah 43:6 - 2 Corinthians 6:17-18, b.Menachot 11a, Esther.R 2:14, Galatians 3:26-3:29, Hosea 2:1-2, Isaiah 18:7, Jeremiah 3:14 3:18-3:19, Leviticus.R 9:6, Midrash Psalms 20:3, Numbers.R 13:2, Perek Shirah [the Wind], Psalms 9:25-9:26, Saadia Opinions 8:6, Sifre Devarim {Ha'azinu Hashamayim} 314, Sifre Devarim Nitzavim 314, Song of Songs.R 4:32
[7] Isaiah 43:7 - 1 Peter 2:9 4:11 4:14, 2 Corinthians 5:17, Acts 11:26, Avot de R'Natan 41, b.Bava Batra 75b, b.Shekalim 14a, b.Yoma 38a, Bahir 78, Derech Hashem Part IV 6§13, Ein Yaakov Bava Batra:75b, Ephesians 1:6 1:12 2:4-7 2:10, Exodus.R 46:5, Galatians 6:15, Gates of Repentance 3.17 3.143, Guide for the Perplexed 3:13, Isaiah 5:23 19:1 19:21 24:11 8:5 62:2-5 15:19, James 2:7, Jeremiah 9:16, John 3:3-7 15:8, m.Avot 6:11, m.Makkot 3:16, Mas.Kallah Rabbati 8:9, Mesillat Yesharim 11:Nekiyut-from-Chillul-Hashem, Midrash Psalms 20:3 148:5, Midrash Shmuel 6:11, mt.Pirkei Avot 6:11, Pesikta Rabbati 50:1, Pirkei Avot 6:11 [Shabbat afternoon], Psalms 50:23 95:6-7 4:3, Revelation 3:12, Romans 9:23, Saadia Opinions 3:Exordium, Sefer Yetzirah 1:4, Shepherd Similitudes 9:14:3, Sifre Devarim Ekev 49, Song of Songs.R 3:10, t.Kippurim 2:5, Titus 3:5-7, y.Shekalim 5:1, y.Yoma 3:9, z.Bo 42a, z.Lech Lecha 96b
[8] Isaiah 43:8 - 2 Corinthians 4:4-4:6, Deuteronomy 29:1-29:3, Ezekiel 12:2, Genesis.R 95:1, Isaiah 6:9 42:18-42:20 44:18-44:20, Jeremiah 5:21, Midrash Tanchuma Vayigash 8
[9] Isaiah 43:9 - 1 Kings 18:21-18:24 18:36-18:39, b.Avodah Zara 2ab 4b, Ein Yaakov Avodah Zarah:2a, Ein Yaakov Avodah Zarah:2b, Ein Yaakov Avodah Zarah:3a, Isaiah 17:1 41:21-41:26 19:26 44:7-44:9 45:20-45:21 22:10 48:5-48:6 24:14, Joel 4:11, Joshua 24:15-24:24, Midrash Tanchuma Shoftim 9, Pesikta de R'Kahana S2.1, Psalms 49:2-49:3 50:1, t.Berachot 1:11
[10] Missing in 1QIsaa
[11] 1QIsaa *proclaim*
[12] Isaiah 43:10 - 1 Corinthians 15:15, 2 Baruch 70:10, Acts 1:8, b.Taanit 11a, Colossians 1:7, Derech Hashem Part IV 4§1, Ein Yaakov Taanit:11a, Genesis.R 95:1, Isaiah 40:21-22 17:4 17:8 17:20 18:1 19:12 44:6-8 21:6 46:8-9 7:4, John 1:7-8 15:27 20:31, Midrash Psalms 51:3, Midrash Tanchuma Vayigash 8, Philippians 2:7, Revelation 1:2 1:5 3:14, Saadia Opinions 2:11, Tanna Devei Eliyahu 6, z.Kedoshim 86a

am He; Before Me no God was formed, nor shall any be after Me.

אָנֹכִ֥י אָנֹכִ֖י יְהוָ֑ה וְאֵ֥ין מִבַּלְעָדַ֖י מוֹשִֽׁיעַ

11[1] I, I, am the LORD; And beside Me there is no savior.

אָנֹכִ֞י הִגַּ֤דְתִּי וְהוֹשַׁ֙עְתִּי֙ וְהִשְׁמַ֔עְתִּי וְאֵ֥ין בָּכֶ֖ם זָ֑ר וְאַתֶּ֥ם עֵדַ֛י נְאֻם־יְהוָ֖ה וַֽאֲנִי־אֵֽל

12[2] I have declared, and I have saved, And I have announced, And there was no strange god among you; Therefore, you are My witnesses, says the LORD, and I am God.

גַּם־מִיּוֹם֙ אֲנִ֣י ה֔וּא וְאֵ֥ין מִיָּדִ֖י מַצִּ֑יל אֶפְעַ֖ל וּמִ֥י יְשִׁיבֶֽנָּה

13[3] Yes, since the day was, I am He, And there is no one who can deliver out of My hand; I will work, and who can reverse it?

כֹּֽה־אָמַ֤ר יְהוָה֙ גֹּאַלְכֶ֣ם קְד֣וֹשׁ יִשְׂרָאֵ֔ל לְמַעַנְכֶ֗ם שִׁלַּ֣חְתִּי בָבֶ֔לָה וְהוֹרַדְתִּ֥י בָֽרִיחִ֖ים כֻּלָּ֑ם וְכַשְׂדִּ֖ים בָּאֳנִיּ֥וֹת רִנָּתָֽם

14[4] Thus says the LORD, your Redeemer, The Holy One of Israel: For your sake I have sent to Babylon, And I will bring down all of them as fugitives, the Chaldeans, in the ships of their shouting.

אֲנִ֥י יְהוָ֖ה קְדֽוֹשְׁכֶ֑ם בּוֹרֵ֥א יִשְׂרָאֵ֖ל מַלְכְּכֶֽם

15[5] I am the LORD, your Holy One, The Creator of Israel, your King.

כֹּ֣ה אָמַ֣ר יְהוָ֔ה הַנּוֹתֵ֥ן בַּיָּ֖ם דָּ֑רֶךְ וּבְמַ֥יִם עַזִּ֖ים נְתִיבָֽה

16[6] Thus says the LORD, who makes a way in the sea, And a path in the mighty waters;

הַמּוֹצִ֥יא רֶֽכֶב־וָס֖וּס חַ֣יִל וְעִזּ֑וּז יַחְדָּ֤ו יִשְׁכְּבוּ֙ בַּל־יָק֔וּמוּ דָּעֲכ֖וּ כַּפִּשְׁתָּ֥ה כָבֽוּ

17[7] Who brings forth the chariot and horse, The army and the power: they lie down together, they shall not rise, They are extinct, they are quenched as a wick.

אַֽל־תִּזְכְּר֖וּ רִֽאשֹׁנ֑וֹת וְקַדְמֹנִיּ֖וֹת אַל־תִּתְבֹּנָֽנוּ

18[8] Do not remember the former things, nor consider the things of old.

הִנְנִ֨י עֹשֶׂ֤ה חֲדָשָׁה֙ עַתָּ֣ה תִצְמָ֔ח הֲל֖וֹא תֵדָע֑וּהָ אַ֣ף אָשִׂ֤ים בַּמִּדְבָּר֙ דֶּ֔רֶךְ בִּֽישִׁמ֖וֹן נְהָרֽוֹת

19[9] Behold, I will do a new thing; Now it shall spring forth; shall you not know it? I will make a way in the wilderness, And *rivers*[10] in the desert.

[1] Isaiah 43:11 - 1 John 4:14 5:20-21, 2 Peter 3:18, Acts 4:12, Deuteronomy 6:4, Hosea 1:7 13:4, Isaiah 12:2 19:3 20:6 20:8 45:21-22, John 10:28-30, Jude 1:25, Luke 1:47 2:11, Revelation 1:11 1:17-18 7:10-12, Sibylline Oracles 3.628 5.173, Titus 2:10 2:13 3:4-6

[2] Isaiah 43:12 - b.Chagigah 16a, Derech Hashem Part IV 4§01, Deuteronomy 8:12, Ein Yaakov Chagigah:16a, Exodus.R 29:5, Isaiah 13:7 13:20 37:35-37:36 19:10 20:8 46:9-46:10 48:4-48:7, Leviticus.R 6:1 6:5 21:5, Mekilta de R'Ishmael Bahodesh 8:93, Mekilta de R'Ishmael Shabbata 1:50, Midrash Psalms 123:2, Pesikta de R'Kahana 12.6, Psalms 81:10-81:11, Sifre Devarim {Vezot Habracha} 346, Sifre Devarim Vezot Habracha 346
Isaiah 43:12-15 - 4QIsab

[3] Isaiah 43:13 - 1 Timothy 1:17, Daniel 4:32, Deuteronomy 4:31 8:39, Ephesians 1:11, Habakkuk 1:12, Hebrews 13:8, Hosea 2:10 5:14, Isaiah 14:27 17:4 22:10 9:15, Job 9:12 34:14-34:15 10:29, John 1:1-1:2 8:58, Micah 5:3, Proverbs 8:23 21:30, Psalms 50:22 90:2 93:2, Revelation 1:8, Romans 9:18-9:19, Saadia Opinions 2:11 2:11

[4] Isaiah 43:14 - b.Megillah 29a, Ein Yaakov Megillah:29a, Exodus.R 15:16 23:5, Ezekiel 27:29-27:36, Isaiah 23:13 19:1 43:3-43:4 20:6 44:24-45:5 54:5-54:8, Jastrow 392b, Jeremiah 51:50-51:58 50:27-50:34 51:1-51:11 3:24 51:34-51:37, Lamentations.R 1:53 5:13, Leviticus.R 32:8, Mekilta de R'Ishmael Pisha 14:103, Midrash Psalms 137:3, Midrash Tanchuma Behar 1, Numbers.R 7:10, Pesikta Rabbati 8:4 28:2 29/30:1 30:2, Psalms 19:15, Revelation 5:9 18:11-18:21, Song of Songs.R 4:18, y.Taanit 1:1, z.Vaetchanan 269b

[5] Isaiah 43:15 - Habakkuk 1:12, Isaiah 6:11 9:22 16:25 17:14 17:16 19:1 19:3 19:7 19:21 21:11 24:17, Jeremiah 3:5, Matthew 1:34, Pesikta Rabbati 49:5, Psalms 74:12, Revelation 3:7

[6] Isaiah 43:16 - b.Chullin 139b, Exodus 14:16 14:21-22 14:29, Genesis.R 6:5, Isaiah 11:15-16 19:2 3:10 3:15 63:11-13, Jeremiah 7:36, Joshua 3:13-16, Leviticus.R 35:8, Midrash Psalms 104:23, Nehemiah 9:11, Psalms 74:13-14 77:20 78:13 10:9 114:3-5 136:13-15, Revelation 16:12, Song of Songs.R 2:43, y.Shabbat 2:6, z.Bereshit 48b, z.Mikketz 197b, z.Vaetchanan 269b, z.Vayakhel 215a
Isaiah 43:16-17 - Exodus.R 15:15
Isaiah 43:16-24 - 4QIsag

[7] Isaiah 43:17 - Exodus 14:4-14:9 14:23-14:28 15:4, Ezekiel 38:8-38:18, Isaiah 1:31 14:20-14:22, Mekhilta de R'Shimon bar Yochai Shirata 32:2, Mekilta de R'Ishmael Shirata 6:85, Pesikta Rabbati 35:1, Psalms 46:9-46:10 76:6-76:7 22:12, Revelation 19:17-19:21 20:8-20:9, Song of Songs.R 2:42

[8] Isaiah 43:18 - 1 Chronicles 16:12, 2 Corinthians 3:10, b.Berachot 13a, Deuteronomy 7:18 8:2, Ein Yaakov Berachot:13a, Isaiah 22:9 17:17, Jeremiah 16:14-15 23:7-8, Midrash Psalms 149:1 149:3, t.Berachot 1:11, Tanna Devei Eliyahu 1, y.Berachot 1:6

[9] Isaiah 43:19 - 2 Corinthians 5:17, b.Berachot 13a, Deuteronomy 8:15, Exodus 17:6, Isaiah 35:6-35:10 40:3-40:4 17:18 18:9 24:6 48:21-48:22, Jeremiah 7:23, Luke 3:4-3:5, Midrash Psalms 149:1 149:3, Midrash Tanchuma Massei 3, Numbers 20:11, Numbers.R 23:4, Pirkei de R'Eliezer 51, Psalms 78:16-78:20 9:41, Revelation 21:5, y.Berachot 1:6

[10] 1QIsaa *paths*

Hebrew	Verse	English

תְּכַבְּדֵ֙נִי֙ חַיַּ֣ת הַשָּׂדֶ֔ה תַּנִּ֖ים וּבְנ֣וֹת יַֽעֲנָ֑ה כִּֽי־נָתַ֨תִּי בַמִּדְבָּ֜ר מַ֗יִם נְהָרוֹת֙ בִּֽישִׁימֹ֔ן לְהַשְׁק֖וֹת עַמִּ֥י בְחִירִֽי

20[1] The beasts of the field shall *honor*[2] Me, the jackals and the ostriches; because I give waters in the wilderness, And rivers in the desert, To give drink to My people, My elect;

עַם־זוּ֙ יָצַ֣רְתִּי לִ֔י תְּהִלָּתִ֖י יְסַפֵּֽרוּ

21[3] The people whom I formed for Myself, so they might *tell*[4] of My praise.

וְלֹא־אֹתִ֥י קָרָ֖אתָ יַֽעֲקֹ֑ב כִּֽי־יָגַ֥עְתָּ בִּ֖י יִשְׂרָאֵֽל

22[5] Yet you have not called on Me, O Jacob, nor have you wearied yourself about Me, O Israel.

לֹֽא־הֵבֵ֤יאתָ לִּי֙ שֵׂ֣ה עֹֽלֹתֶ֔יךָ וּזְבָחֶ֖יךָ לֹ֣א כִבַּדְתָּ֑נִי לֹ֤א הֶֽעֱבַדְתִּ֙יךָ֙ בְּמִנְחָ֔ה וְלֹ֥א הֽוֹגַעְתִּ֖יךָ בִּלְבוֹנָֽה

23[6] You have not brought Me the *small cattle*[7] of your burnt offerings; nor have you honored Me with your sacrifices. *I have not burdened you with a meal offering*[8], Nor wearied you with frankincense.

לֹֽא־קָנִ֨יתָ לִּ֤י בַכֶּ֙סֶף֙ קָנֶ֔ה וְחֵ֥לֶב זְבָחֶ֖יךָ לֹ֣א הִרְוִיתָ֑נִי אַ֗ךְ הֶעֱבַדְתַּ֙נִי֙ בְּחַטֹּאותֶ֔יךָ הֽוֹגַעְתַּ֖נִי בַּֽעֲוֹנֹתֶֽיךָ

24[9] You have not bought me sweet cane with money, *nor have you satisfied Me with the fat of your sacrifices*[10]; but you have burdened Me with your sins, you have wearied Me with your iniquities.

אָֽנֹכִ֧י אָֽנֹכִ֛י ה֖וּא מֹחֶ֣ה פְשָׁעֶ֑יךָ לְמַֽעֲנִ֔י וְחַטֹּאתֶ֖יךָ לֹ֥א אֶזְכֹּֽר

25[11] I, I, am He who blots out your transgressions for My own sake; And your sins I will not remember.

הַזְכִּירֵ֕נִי נִשָּׁפְטָ֖ה יָ֑חַד סַפֵּ֥ר אַתָּ֖ה לְמַ֥עַן תִּצְדָּֽק

26[12] Put Me in remembrance, let us plead together; Declare, that you may be justified.

אָבִ֥יךָ הָֽרִאשׁ֖וֹן חָטָ֑א וּמְלִֽיצֶ֖יךָ פָּ֥שְׁעוּ בִֽי

27[13] Your first father sinned, And your intercessors have transgressed against Me.

וַֽאֲחַלֵּ֖ל שָׂ֣רֵי קֹ֑דֶשׁ וְאֶתְּנָ֤ה לַחֵ֙רֶם֙ יַֽעֲקֹ֔ב וְיִשְׂרָאֵ֖ל לְגִדּוּפִֽים

28[14] *Therefore, I have profaned the princes of the sanctuary*[15], And I have given Jacob to condemnation, And Israel to reviling.

---

[1] Isaiah 43:20 - 1 Chronicles 16:13, 1 Peter 2:9, 2 Baruch 10:8, Isaiah 11:6-10 13:22 17:17 19:19 24:21 1:10 55:1-2 17:15, Jeremiah 7:10, Joel 4:18, John 4:10 4:14 7:37-39, Mark 13:20, Midrash Psalms 149:1 149:3, Psalms 33:12 8:21 4:10, Revelation 17:14 21:6 22:17

[2] LXX *bless*

[3] Isaiah 43:21 - 1 Corinthians 6:19-6:20 10:31, 1 Peter 2:9, Colossians 1:16, Ephesians 1:5-1:12 3:21, Hebrews 13:15, Isaiah 2:7 12:21 13:3, Luke 1:74-1:75, Mekhilta de R'Shimon bar Yochai Shirata 29:1 35:2 35:5, Mekhilta de R'Ishmael Shirata 9:119, Mekhilta de R'Ishmael Shirata 9:29, Midrash Proverbs 14, Midrash Psalms 5:10 104:1 109:1 149:1 149:3, Numbers.R 5:6, Proverbs 16:4, Psalms 4:4 6:19, Sifre Devarim Vezot Habracha 355, Titus 2:14, z.Ki Tissa 188a

Isaiah 43:21-44:6 - Haftarah Vayikra [Teimon]

Isaiah 43:21-44:23 - Haftarah Vayikroh [Ashkenaz and Sephard]

[4] 1QIsaa *speak*; 4QIsa6 *recount*

[5] Isaiah 43:22 - b.Yoma 19b, Daniel 9:13, Esther.R 3:4, Genesis.R 96 [New Version]:1, Hosea 7:10-14 14:3-4, Isaiah 16:8, James 4:2-3, Jastrow 1425a, Jeremiah 2:5 2:11-13 2:31-32 10:25, Job 21:14-15 27:9-10, John 6:66-69, Lamentations.R Petichata D'Chakimei 10, Malachi 1:13 3:14, Micah 6:3, Midrash Tanchuma Vayechi 8, mt.Hilchot Kriat Shema 2:8, Pesikta Rabbati 29/30:1, Psalms 14:4 79:6

[6] Isaiah 43:23 - Amos 5:21-22 5:25, Esther.R 3:4, Isaiah 1:11-15 18:3, Jeremiah 7:22, Lamentations.R Petichata D'Chakimei:10, Leviticus 2:1, Malachi 1:6-8 1:13-14 3:8, Matthew 11:30, Pesikta Rabbati 29/30:1, Proverbs 15:8 21:27, Zechariah 7:5-6

Isaiah 43:23-27 - 1QIsab

[7] LXX *sheep*

[8] 1QIsaa *You have not made meal offerings for me*

[9] Isaiah 43:24 - Amos 2:13, Esther.R 3:4, Exodus 6:7 30:23-24 6:34, Ezekiel 6:9 16:43, Isaiah 1:14 1:24 7:13 15:10, Jeremiah 6:20, Lamentations.R Petichata D'Chakimei:10, Leviticus 3:16 4:31, Malachi 1:14 2:13-17, Pesikta Rabbati 29/30:1, Psalms 50:9-13 95:10

[10] LXX *neither have I desired the fat of thy sacrifices*

[11] Isaiah 43:25 - 4 10, Acts 3:19, Ephesians 1:6 1:8, Ezekiel 20:9 20:14 20:22 12:22 12:32, Hebrews 8:12 10:17, Isaiah 1:18 13:35 14:17 19:11 20:22 48:8-48:10, Jeremiah 7:35 2:20, Mark 2:7, Micah 7:18-7:19, Midrash Tanchuma Shemini 10, Psalms 25:7 25:11 51:10 79:8-79:9, Romans 5:20, Selichot, Tefillat Yom Kippur, z.Lech Lecha 87b

[12] Isaiah 43:26 - Ezekiel 12:37, Genesis 8:13, Isaiah 1:18 17:1 19:9 2:8, Jeremiah 2:21-2:35, Job 16:21 23:3-23:6 40:4-40:5 40:7-40:8, Luke 10:29 16:15 18:9-18:14, Pesikta Rabbati 40:3/04, Psalms 21:2, Romans 8:33 10:3 11:35

[13] Isaiah 43:27 - Acts 5:17-5:18 7:51, Ezekiel 16:3 22:25-22:28, Hosea 4:6, Isaiah 3:12 9:16 4:7 56:10-56:12, Jeremiah 3:25 5:31 23:11-23:15, John 11:49-11:53, Lamentations 4:13-4:14, Malachi 2:4-2:8 3:7, Matthew 15:14 3:1 3:41, Micah 3:11, Numbers 8:14, Psalms 78:8 106:6-106:7, Romans 5:12, Zechariah 1:4-1:6

[14] Isaiah 43:28 - 1 Thessalonians 2:16, 2 Samuel 1:21, Daniel 9:14, Deuteronomy 28:15-20 29:20-27, Ezekiel 5:15, Isaiah 42:24-25 23:6 17:15, Jeremiah 24:9, Lamentations 2:2 2:6-7 4:20, Lamentations.R 2:5, Luke 21:21-24, Psalms 79:4 82:6-7 89:40, Zechariah 8:13

[15] LXX *And the princes have defiled my sanctuaries*

Isaiah – Chapter 44

וְעַתָּה שְׁמַע יַעֲקֹב עַבְדִּי וְיִשְׂרָאֵל בָּחַרְתִּי בוֹ:	1[1] Yet now hear, O Jacob My servant, And Israel, whom I have chosen;
כֹּה־אָמַר יְהוָה עֹשֶׂךָ וְיֹצֶרְךָ מִבֶּטֶן יַעְזְרֶךָּ אַל־תִּירָא עַבְדִּי יַעֲקֹב וִישֻׁרוּן בָּחַרְתִּי בוֹ	2[2] Thus says the LORD who made you, And formed you from the womb, who will help you: Fear not, O Jacob My servant, And you, *Jeshurun*[3], whom I have chosen.
כִּי אֶצָּק־מַיִם עַל־צָמֵא וְנֹזְלִים עַל־יַבָּשָׁה אֶצֹּק רוּחִי עַל־זַרְעֶךָ וּבִרְכָתִי עַל־צֶאֱצָאֶיךָ	3[4] For I will pour water on the thirsty land, and streams on the dry ground; I will pour My spirit on your seed, and My blessing on your offspring;
וְצָמְחוּ בְּבֵין חָצִיר כַּעֲרָבִים עַל־יִבְלֵי־מָיִם	4[5] And they shall spring up *among*[6] the grass, As willows by the watercourses.
זֶה יֹאמַר לַיהוָה אָנִי וְזֶה יִקְרָא בְשֵׁם־יַעֲקֹב וְזֶה יִכְתֹּב יָדוֹ לַיהוָה וּבְשֵׁם יִשְׂרָאֵל יְכַנֶּה	5[7] One shall say: 'I am the LORD's'; And another shall call himself by the name of Jacob; And another shall subscribe with his hand unto the LORD, And surname himself by the name of Israel.
כֹּה־אָמַר יְהוָה מֶלֶךְ־יִשְׂרָאֵל וְגֹאֲלוֹ יְהוָה צְבָאוֹת אֲנִי רִאשׁוֹן וַאֲנִי אַחֲרוֹן וּמִבַּלְעָדַי אֵין אֱלֹהִים	6[8] Thus says the LORD, the King of Israel, And his Redeemer the LORD of hosts[9]: I am the first, and I am the *last*[10], And beside Me there is no God.
וּמִי־כָמוֹנִי יִקְרָא וְיַגִּידֶהָ וְיַעְרְכֶהָ לִי מִשּׂוּמִי עַם־עוֹלָם וְאֹתִיּוֹת וַאֲשֶׁר תָּבֹאנָה יַגִּידוּ לָמוֹ	7[11] And who, as I, can proclaim, let him declare it, and set it in order for Me, *since I appointed the*[12] ancient people? And the things that are coming, and that shall come to pass, let them declare.
אַל־תִּפְחֲדוּ וְאַל־תִּרְהוּ הֲלֹא מֵאָז הִשְׁמַעְתִּיךָ וְהִגַּדְתִּי וְאַתֶּם עֵדָי הֲיֵשׁ אֱלוֹהַּ מִבַּלְעָדַי וְאֵין צוּר בַּל־יָדָעְתִּי	8[13] Fear not, nor be afraid; Have I not announced to you of old, and declared it? And you are My

---

[1] Isaiah 44:1 - Deuteronomy 7:6-8, Genesis 17:7, Hebrews 3:7-8, Isaiah 17:8 18:23 19:1 48:16-18 7:3, Jeremiah 4:7 6:10 46:27-28, Jubilees 2:20, Luke 13:34, Midrash Tanchuma Beshallach 15, Psalms 81:12-14 9:6 105:42-43, Romans 11:5-6
Isaiah 44:1-2 - z.Vayishlach 177b
Isaiah 44:1-28 - 1QIsaa
[2] Isaiah 44:2 - 1 Thessalonians 1:4, Deuteronomy 8:15 9:5, Ephesians 1:4, Ezekiel 16:4-8 20:5-12, Hebrews 4:16, Isaiah 17:10 17:14 19:1 19:5 19:7 19:21 20:21 20:24 46:3-4 1:1, Jeremiah 1:5, Luke 12:32, Midrash Psalms 18:4 111:1, Pesikta Rabbati 29/30:1, Psalms 46:6 71:6, Romans 8:30, Saadia Opinions 2:3, z.Vaetchanan 269b
[3] LXX *beloved Israel*
[4] Isaiah 44:3 - Acts 2:17 2:33 2:39 10:45, Ezekiel 10:26 15:29, Isaiah 8:2 8:15 35:6-7 17:17 43:19-20 24:21 1:10 11:21 13:9 17:23, Joel 3:1 4:18, John 7:37-39, Matthew 12:43, Midrash Psalms 111:1, Proverbs 1:23, Psalms 63:2 78:15-16 11:35, Revelation 21:6 22:17, Titus 3:5-6, z.Bereshit 11a, Zechariah 12:10
Isaiah 44:3-7 - 4QIsac
[5] Isaiah 44:4 - Acts 2:41-47 4:4 5:14, Esther.R 9:2, Ezekiel 17:5, Isaiah 10:11 13:11, Job 16:22, Leviticus 23:40, Midrash Psalms 111:1, Psalms 1:3 92:14-16 137:1-2
[6] 1QIsaa *like*
[7] Isaiah 44:5 - 1 Peter 2:9, 2 Corinthians 8:5, Avot de R'Natan 36, Avot de R'Natan 36, Deuteronomy 26:17-19, Exodus 13:9, Galatians 6:16, Jeremiah 2:5, Mas.Gerim 4:2-3, Mekilta de R'Ishmael Nezikin 18:45, Micah 4:2, Midrash Psalms 111:1 17A:13, Nehemiah 10:1-30, Numbers.R 8:2, Psalms 20:16, z.Lech Lecha 95b, Zechariah 8:20-23 13:9
[8] Isaiah 44:6 - 1 Timothy 3:16, 2 Enoch 33:8 36:1 47:3 4 Ezra 8:7, Avot de R'Natan 34, Deuteronomy 4:35 4:39 6:4 8:39, Deuteronomy.R 1:10, Exodus.R 15:1 29:5 29:9, Genesis.R 63:8 81:2, Isaiah 9:22 13:16 13:20 17:4 17:14 17:21 18:8 19:1 43:10-11 43:14-15 20:8 20:24 45:5-6 45:21-22 24:17 6:5 11:20, Jeremiah 2:34, Leviticus 1:14, Malachi 1:14, Matthew 1:34 3:37, Mekhilta de R'Shimon bar Yochai Shirata 30:1, Mekilta de R'Ishmael Bahodesh 5:30, mt.Hilcnot Shofar Sukkah v'Lulav 3:9, Mussaf Rosh Hashanah, Pirkei de R'Eliezer 11, Revelation 1:8 1:11 1:17-1:18 2:8 22:13, Saadia Opinions Intro:6, Sibylline Oracles 5.173 8.377, Sifre Devarim Ha'azinu Hashamayim 329, Sifre Devarim Nitzavim 329, Song of Songs.R 1:46, Testament of Isaac 6:34, y.Sanhedrin 1:1, z.Bereshit 10a, z.Metzorah 56a, z.Vaetchanan 269b
[9] 1QIsaa add *is his name*
[10] LXX *hereafter*
[11] Isaiah 44:7 - Acts 17:26, Deuteronomy 8:8, Genesis 17:7-17:8, Isaiah 17:4 17:22 17:26 19:9 19:12 21:21 46:9-46:10 48:3-48:8, Midrash Psalms 3:2, Saadia Opinions Intro:6, z.Vaera 25a
[12] 1QIsaa *making them an*
[13] Isaiah 44:8 - 1 John 1:2, 1 Samuel 2:2, 2 Samuel 22:32, Acts 1:8 14:15 17:23-31, Daniel 2:28 2:47 3:16-3:28 4:22 5:23-5:30 6:23, Deuteronomy 4:25-4:31 4:35 4:39 28:1-28:68 8:4 8:31 8:39, Ezra 1:2 8:22, Genesis 15:13-15:21 28:13-28:15 22:3 24:19 49:1-49:28,

witnesses. Is there a God beside Me? *Yes, there is no Rock; I know not any*[1].

9[2] *Those who fashion a*[3] *graven image are all vanity, And their delectable things shall not profit; And their own witnesses do not see, nor know; so they may be ashamed.*

יֹצְרֵי־פֶסֶל כֻּלָּם תֹּהוּ וַחֲמוּדֵיהֶם בַּל־יוֹעִילוּ
וְעֵדֵיהֶם הֵמָּה בַּל־יִרְאוּ וּבַל־יֵדְעוּ לְמַעַן יֵבֹשׁוּ

10[4] Who has fashioned a god, or molten an image that is profitable for nothing?

מִי־יָצַר אֵל וּפֶסֶל נָסָךְ לְבִלְתִּי הוֹעִיל

11[5] Behold, all its fellows shall be ashamed; And the craftsmen skilled above men; Let them all be gathered together, let them stand up; [6]They shall fear, they shall be ashamed together.

הֵן כָּל־חֲבֵרָיו יֵבֹשׁוּ וְחָרָשִׁים הֵמָּה מֵאָדָם
יִתְקַבְּצוּ כֻלָּם יַעֲמֹדוּ יִפְחֲדוּ יֵבֹשׁוּ יָחַד

12[7] *The smith makes an axe, and works in the coals, and fashions it with hammers, and works it with his strong arm*[8]; *yes, he is hungry, and his strength fails; he drinks no water, and is faint.*

חָרַשׁ בַּרְזֶל מַעֲצָד וּפָעַל בַּפֶּחָם וּבַמַּקָּבוֹת יִצְּרֵהוּ
וַיִּפְעָלֵהוּ בִּזְרוֹעַ כֹּחוֹ גַּם־רָעֵב וְאֵין כֹּחַ לֹא־שָׁתָה
מַיִם וַיִּיעָף

13[9] *The carpenter stretches out a line; He marks it out with a pencil; He fits it with planes, And he marks it out with the compasses, And makes it after the figure of a man, According to the beauty of a man, to live*[10] *in the house.*

חָרַשׁ עֵצִים נָטָה קָו יְתָאֲרֵהוּ בַשֶּׂרֶד יַעֲשֵׂהוּ
בַּמַּקְצֻעוֹת וּבַמְּחוּגָה יְתָאֲרֵהוּ וַיַּעֲשֵׂהוּ כְּתַבְנִית
אִישׁ כְּתִפְאֶרֶת אָדָם לָשֶׁבֶת בָּיִת

14[11] *He hews down cedars, And takes the cypress and the oak, And strengthens for himself one among the trees of the forest; He plants a fir tree, and the rain nourishes it*[12].

לִכְרָת־לוֹ אֲרָזִים וַיִּקַּח תִּרְזָה וְאַלּוֹן וַיְאַמֶּץ־לוֹ
בַּעֲצֵי־יָעַר נָטַע אֹרֶן וְגֶשֶׁם יְגַדֵּל

15[13] Then a man uses it for fuel; And he takes from it, and warms himself; Yes, he kindles it, and bakes bread; *Yea*[14], he makes a god, and worships it; He makes it a graven image, and falls down to it.

וְהָיָה לְאָדָם לְבָעֵר וַיִּקַּח מֵהֶם וַיָּחָם אַף־יַשִּׂיק
וְאָפָה לָחֶם אַף־יִפְעַל־אֵל וַיִּשְׁתָּחוּ עָשָׂהוּ פֶסֶל
וַיִּסְגָּד־לָמוֹ

Hebrews 12:1, Isaiah 6:29 41:10-41:14 18:9 19:10 19:12 20:2 20:6 45:5-45:6 22:9 24:5, Jeremiah 10:7 30:10-11, Joel 2:27, John 1:1 6:10 10:30, Leviticus 26:1-46, Proverbs 3:25-26, Psalms 18:32, Saadia Opinions Intro:6, Selichot
Isaiah 44:8-20 - Sibylline Oracles 3.586
[1] Missing in LXX
[2] Isaiah 44:9 - 1 Corinthians 8:4, 1 Kings 18:26-40, 2 Corinthians 4:4, b.Avodah Zara 2a, Daniel 5:23 11:38, Deuteronomy 3:15, Ephesians 4:18 5:8, Extraordinary points of the Soferim: הֵמָּה is pointed and is cancelled since it's a dittography of הם from the previous word , וְעֵדֵיהֶם this pointed word is missing from the Syriac. Therefore "*As for their witnesses, they* [i.e., the idols] *neither see them nor know them*", Habakkuk 2:18-20, Hosea 8:4-6, Isaiah 2:20-2:21 37:18-37:20 17:24 17:29 18:18 19:8 20:18 20:20 21:20 46:1-46:2 46:6-46:7, Jeremiah 2:11 2:27-28 10:3-8 10:14-15 14:22 16:19-20, Judges 10:14, Psalms 97:7 19:8 15:18, Romans 1:22, the text should read, y.Avodah Zarah 1:2, y.Berachot 8:6, y.Eruvin 5:1, z.Bereshit 10a
Isaiah 44:9-20 - Sibylline Oracles 5.80 8.378
[3] 1QIsaa *Now, all forming of*
[4] Isaiah 44:10 - 1 Corinthians 8:4, 1 Kings 12:28, Acts 19:26, Daniel 3:1 3:14, Habakkuk 2:18, Isaiah 17:29, Jeremiah 10:5
[5] Isaiah 44:11 - 1 Kings 18:19-29 18:40, 1 Samuel 5:3-7 6:4-5, Acts 19:24-34, Daniel 3:1-7 5:1-6, Genesis.R 24:7, Isaiah 1:29 41:5-7 18:17 21:16, Jeremiah 2:26-27 10:14 3:17, Judges 6:29-32 16:23-30, Psalms 97:7, Revelation 19:19-21
[6] 1QIsaa adds *Then*
[7] Isaiah 44:12 - Exodus 8:4 8:8, Habakkuk 2:13, Isaiah 16:19 41:6-7 46:6-7, Jeremiah 10:3-11, Tanya Igeret Hateshuvah §7
[8] LXX *For the artificer sharpens the iron; he fashions the idol with an axe, and fixes it with an awl, and fashions it with the strength of his arm*
[9] Isaiah 44:13 - Acts 17:29, b.Eruvin [Tosefot] 58b, b.Nedarim [Ran] 61b, b.Shabbat [Rashi] 123b, Deuteronomy 4:16-18 4:28 3:15, Exodus 20:4-5, Ezekiel 8:12, Genesis 7:19 7:30 7:32 11:2, Genesis.R 21:2, Guide for the Perplexed 1:1, Isaiah 17:7, Judges 17:4-5 18:24, mt.Hilchot Keilim 5:1, Psalms 115:5-7, Romans 1:23
[10] LXX *The artificer having chosen a piece of wood, marks it out with a rule, and fits it with glue, and makes it as the form of a man, and as the beauty of a man, to set it up*
[11] Isaiah 44:14 - Habakkuk 2:19, Hosea 4:12, Isaiah 16:20, Jeremiah 10:3-8, Traditional MT Small ן in אֹרֶן
[12] LXX *He cuts wood out of the forest, which the Lord planted, a pine tree, and the rain made it grow*
[13] Isaiah 44:15 - 2 Chronicles 1:14, Isaiah 20:10 21:20, Judges 2:19, Revelation 9:20
[14] 1QIsaa *Or perhaps*

חֶצְיוֹ שָׂרַף בְּמוֹ־אֵשׁ עַל־חֶצְיוֹ בָּשָׂר יֹאכֵל יִצְלֶה צָלִי וְיִשְׂבָּע אַף־יָחֹם וְיֹאמַר הֶאָח חַמּוֹתִי רָאִיתִי אוּר

16[1] He burns its half in the fire; With its half he eats meat; *He roasts roast, and is satisfied; Yes, he warms himself, and says*[2]: 'Aha, I am warm, I *have seen*[3] the fire';

וּשְׁאֵרִיתוֹ לְאֵל עָשָׂה לְפִסְלוֹ יִסְגּוֹד־יִסְגָּד־לוֹ וְיִשְׁתַּחוּ וְיִתְפַּלֵּל אֵלָיו וְיֹאמַר הַצִּילֵנִי כִּי אֵלִי אָתָּה

17[4] And the rest of it he makes a god, his graven image; He falls down to it and worships, and prays to it, And says: 'Deliver me, for you are my god.'

לֹא יָדְעוּ וְלֹא יָבִינוּ כִּי טַח מֵרְאוֹת עֵינֵיהֶם מֵהַשְׂכִּיל לִבֹּתָם

18[5] They do not know, nor do they understand; For their eyes are bedaubed, that they cannot see, And their hearts, so they cannot understand.

וְלֹא־יָשִׁיב אֶל־לִבּוֹ וְלֹא דַעַת וְלֹא־תְבוּנָה לֵאמֹר חֶצְיוֹ שָׂרַפְתִּי בְמוֹ־אֵשׁ וְאַף אָפִיתִי עַל־גֶּחָלָיו לֶחֶם אֶצְלֶה בָשָׂר וְאֹכֵל וְיִתְרוֹ לְתוֹעֵבָה אֶעֱשֶׂה לְבוּל עֵץ אֶסְגּוֹד

19[6] And no one considers in his heart, nor is there knowledge nor understanding *to say*[7]: 'I have burned half of it in the fire; Yes, also I have baked bread on its coals; I have roasted meat and eaten it; And shall I make its remnant an abomination? Shall I fall down to the stock of a tree?'

רֹעֶה אֵפֶר לֵב הוּתַל הִטָּהוּ וְלֹא־יַצִּיל אֶת־נַפְשׁוֹ וְלֹא יֹאמַר הֲלוֹא שֶׁקֶר בִּימִינִי

20[8] He strives after ashes, A deceived heart has turned him aside, so he cannot deliver his soul, nor say: *Is there not a lie in my right hand?*[9]

זְכָר־אֵלֶּה יַעֲקֹב וְיִשְׂרָאֵל כִּי עַבְדִּי־אָתָּה יְצַרְתִּיךָ עֶבֶד־לִי אַתָּה יִשְׂרָאֵל לֹא תִנָּשֵׁנִי

21[10] Remember these things, O Jacob, And Israel, for you are My servant; I have formed you, you are My own servant; O Israel, *you should not forget Me*[11].

מָחִיתִי כָעָב פְּשָׁעֶיךָ וְכֶעָנָן חַטֹּאותֶיךָ שׁוּבָה אֵלַי כִּי גְאַלְתִּיךָ

22[12] I have blotted out, as a thick cloud, your transgressions, And, as a cloud, your sins; Return to Me, for I have redeemed you.

רָנּוּ שָׁמַיִם כִּי־עָשָׂה יְהוָה הָרִיעוּ תַּחְתִּיּוֹת אָרֶץ פִּצְחוּ הָרִים רִנָּה יַעַר וְכָל־עֵץ בּוֹ כִּי־גָאַל יְהוָה יַעֲקֹב וּבְיִשְׂרָאֵל יִתְפָּאָר

23[13] *Sing, O heavens, for the LORD has done it; Shout, you lowest parts of the earth; Break forth into singing, you mountains, O forest, and every tree in it; For the LORD has redeemed Jacob, And glorifies Himself in Israel*[14].

---

[1] Isaiah 44:16 - b.Chullin [Rashi] 8a, b.Taanit [Rashi] 24b

[2] 1QIsaa *He sits by its coals, warms himself*

[3] 1QIsaa *in front of*

[4] Isaiah 44:17 - 1 Kings 18:26, Daniel 3:17 3:29 6:17 6:21-23 6:28, Isaiah 36:19-20 13:38 21:20

[5] Isaiah 44:18 - 2 Corinthians 4:3-4, 2 Peter 2:14, 2 Thessalonians 2:9-12, Acts 14:16, Daniel 12:10, Genesis.R 38:4, Hosea 14:11, Isaiah 1:3 6:9-10 5:10 20:9 20:20 21:20 46:7-8 8:11, Jeremiah 5:21 10:8 10:14, John 5:44 8:43 12:39-40, Matthew 12:34 13:14-15, Midrash Tanchuma Shelach 5, Numbers.R 16:6, Proverb 2:5-9 4:5, Psalms 81:13 92:7, Romans 1:21-23 1:28 11:8-10

[6] Isaiah 44:19 - 1 Kings 11:5 11:7, 2 Kings 23:13, Deuteronomy 3:15 8:46, Exodus 7:23, Ezekiel 16:4, Haggai 1:5, Hosea 7:2, Isaiah 5:13 21:20 22:8

Isaiah 44:19-28 - 4QIsab

[7] 1QIsaa *to think to think*

[8] Isaiah 44:20 - 1 Kings 22:20-23, 1 Timothy 4:2, 2 Thessalonians 2:9-11, 2 Timothy 2:13 3:13, Habakkuk 2:18, Hosea 4:12 12:3, Isaiah 28:15-17 59:3-4 11:13, Jeremiah 16:19, Job 15:2 15:31, Luke 15:16, Proverbs 15:14, Psalms 6:10, Revelation 12:9 13:14 18:23 20:3, Romans 1:20-22 1:25 1:28

[9] 1QIsaa LXX *There is a lie in my right hand*

[10] Isaiah 44:21 - 2 Baruch 70:10, Deuteronomy 4:9 4:23 31:19-21 8:18, Isaiah 41:8-9 18:23 19:1 19:7 19:15 44:1-2 46:8-9 49:15-16, Romans 11:28-29, Tanna Devei Eliyahu 1, Zechariah 10:9

Isaiah 44:21-28 - 1QIsab

[11] 1QIsaa *you will not be forgotten by me*

[12] Isaiah 44:22 - 1 Corinthians 6:20, 1 Peter 1:18-1:19, Acts 3:18-3:19, Hosea 14:3-14:6, Isaiah 1:18 1:27 19:1 19:25 24:20 3:11 7:7 59:20-59:21, Jeremiah 3:1 3:12-3:14 18:23 9:8, Job 13:11, Lamentations 3:42-3:44, Lamentations.R 1:23, Luke 1:73-1:74, Nehemiah 4:5, Pesikta Rabbati 29/30B:4, Psalms 51:2 51:10 7:12 13:14, Selichot, Tanna Devei Eliyahu 1, Tanya Igeret Hateshuvah §10, Tefillat Yom Kippur, Titus 2:12-2:14

Isaiah 44:22-23 - Motzoei Shabbat [Viyiten Lecha]

[13] Isaiah 44:23 - 1 Peter 4:11, 2 Thessalonians 1:10-12, 4QIsac, Bahir 4, Deuteronomy.R 10:4, Ephesians 1:6-7 3:21, Ezekiel 12:1 12:8 15:13, Isaiah 2:15 42:10-12 1:3 1:13 55:12-13 12:21 13:3, Jeremiah 3:48, Luke 2:10-14, Mekhilta de R'Shimon bar Yochai Shirata 32:3, Mekhilta de R'Ishmael Shirata 6:144, Midrash Psalms 19:3, Pesikta de R'Kahana S6.2, Psalms 69:35 96:11-12 98:7-8 4:7, Revelation 5:8-14 12:12 18:20 19:1-6, Sifre Devarim Ha'azinu Hashamayim 333, Testament of Levi 18:5

[14] LXX *Rejoice, you heavens; for God has had mercy upon Israel: sound the trumpet, you foundations of the earth: you mountains, shout with joy, you hills, and all the trees therein: for God has redeemed Jacob, and Israel shall be glorified*

כֹּה־אָמַ֤ר יְהוָה֙ גֹּֽאֲלֶ֔ךָ וְיֹצֶרְךָ֖ מִבָּ֑טֶן אָנֹכִ֤י יְהוָה֙ עֹ֣שֶׂה כֹּ֔ל נֹטֶ֤ה שָׁמַ֙יִם֙ לְבַדִּ֔י רֹקַ֥ע הָאָ֖רֶץ 'מִי' 'אִתִּ֖י' "מֵאִתִּֽי" 24[1]

Thus says the LORD, your Redeemer, And He who formed you from the womb: I am the LORD, who makes all things; who stretched forth the heavens alone; who spread abroad the earth by Myself;

מֵפֵ֖ר אֹת֣וֹת בַּדִּ֑ים וְקֹסְמִ֖ים יְהוֹלֵ֑ל מֵשִׁ֤יב חֲכָמִים֙ אָח֔וֹר וְדַעְתָּ֖ם יְשַׂכֵּֽל 25[2]

Who frustrates the tokens of *the imposters, And makes diviners mad; who turns wise men backward*[3], And makes their knowledge *foolish*[4];

מֵקִ֙ים֙ דְּבַ֣ר עַבְדּ֔וֹ וַעֲצַ֥ת מַלְאָכָ֖יו יַשְׁלִ֑ים הָאֹמֵ֤ר לִירוּשָׁלִַ֙ם֙ תּוּשָׁ֔ב וּלְעָרֵ֤י יְהוּדָה֙ תִּבָּנֶ֔ינָה וְחָרְבוֹתֶ֖יהָ אֲקוֹמֵֽם 26[5]

Who confirms the word of His servant, and performs the counsel of His messengers; who says of Jerusalem: 'She shall be inhabited'; And of the cities of Judah: 'They shall be built, And I will raise up the waste places there';

הָאֹמֵ֥ר לַצּוּלָ֖ה חֳרָ֑בִי וְנַהֲרֹתַ֖יִךְ אוֹבִֽישׁ 27[6]

Who says to the deep: 'Be dry, and I will dry up your rivers';

הָאֹמֵ֤ר לְכ֙וֹרֶשׁ֙ רֹעִ֔י וְכָל־חֶפְצִ֖י יַשְׁלִ֑ם וְלֵאמֹ֤ר לִירוּשָׁלִַ֙ם֙ תִּבָּנֶ֔ה וְהֵיכָ֖ל תִּוָּסֵֽד 28[7]

Who says of Cyrus: 'He is My shepherd, And shall perform all My pleasure[8]; saying of Jerusalem: 'She shall be built'; And to the temple: 'My foundation shall be laid.'

Isaiah – Chapter 45

כֹּה־אָמַ֣ר יְהוָה֮ לִמְשִׁיחוֹ֮ לְכ֣וֹרֶשׁ אֲשֶׁר־הֶחֱזַ֣קְתִּי בִֽימִינ֗וֹ לְרַד־לְפָנָיו֙ גּוֹיִ֔ם וּמָתְנֵ֥י מְלָכִ֖ים אֲפַתֵּ֑חַ לִפְתֹּ֤חַ לְפָנָיו֙ דְּלָתַ֔יִם וּשְׁעָרִ֖ים לֹ֥א יִסָּגֵֽרוּ 1[9]

Thus says the LORD to His anointed, to Cyrus, whose right hand I have grasped, to subdue nations before him, and to loosen the loins of kings; to open the doors before him, And so the gates may not be shut:

אֲנִי֙ לְפָנֶ֣יךָ אֵלֵ֔ךְ וַהֲדוּרִ֖ים 'אוֹשִׁ֑ר' "אֲיַשֵּׁ֑ר" דַּלְת֤וֹת נְחוּשָׁה֙ אֲשַׁבֵּ֔ר וּבְרִיחֵ֥י בַרְזֶ֖ל אֲגַדֵּֽעַ 2[10]

I will go before you, *And make the crooked places straight*[11]; I will break in pieces the doors of brass, And *cut apart the*[12] bars of iron;

---

[1] Isaiah 44:24 - 2 Enoch 47:4, Apocalypse of Elijah 1:3, Bahir 22, Colossians 1:16-1:17, Ephesians 3:9, Galatians 1:15, Genesis.R 1:3 3:8 82:2, Hebrews 1:2 1:10-1:12, Isaiah 16:22 18:5 19:1 19:7 19:14 20:2 20:6 21:12 21:18 46:3-4 24:13 24:17 1:1 1:7 1:26 3:13 6:5 6:8 11:20 12:16 15:16, Jeremiah 2:34 3:15, Job 9:8 2:7 7:15, John 1:3, Mas.Soferim 7:3, Midrash Psalms 24:4 149:1, Pesikta Rabbati 33:8, Psalms 71:6 78:35 8:2 139:13-16, Revelation 5:9, Saadia Opinions 1:1, z.Vaetchanan 269b

[2] Isaiah 44:25 - 1 Corinthians 1:20-27 3:19-20, 1 Kings 22:11-12 22:22-25 22:37, 2 Chronicles 18:11 18:34, 2 Samuel 15:31 16:23 17:23, b.Gittin 56b, Daniel 1:20 2:10-12 4:4 5:6-8, Ein Yaakov Gittin:56b, Exodus 9:11, Isaiah 19:11-14 5:14 47:12-14, Jastrow 139b, Jeremiah 27:9-10 28:9-17 1:7 2:36 3:57, Job 5:12-14, Midrash Tanchuma Balak 14, mt.Hilchot Avodat Kochavim v'Chukkoteihem 11:6, mt.Hilchot Yesodei haTorah 10:3, Numbers.R 20:20, Psalms 33:10, Sibylline Oracles 3.227, Sifre Devarim Nitzavim 333

[3] LXX *those who have divining spirits, and prophecies from the heart of man? turning the wise back*

[4] 1QIsaa 1QIsab 4QIsab LXX *wise*

[5] Isaiah 44:26 - 1 Kings 13:3-5 18:36-38, 2 Peter 1:19-21, Acts 2:25-28, Amos 9:14, Daniel 9:25, Exodus 11:4-6 12:29-30, Exodus.R 18:1, Ezekiel 12:10 36:33-36 14:17, Ezra 2:70, Genesis.R 78:3, Isaiah 18:9 6:3 54:11-12 10:12 12:10 13:4, Jeremiah 6:18 7:5 31:39-41 8:15 8:44 9:7, Luke 24:44, Matthew 5:18 2:56, Midrash Psalms 83:1, Midrash Tanchuma Vayechi 6, Midrash Tanchuma Vayera 16, Nehemiah 1:3 2:3 3:1-32, Pesikta de R'Kahana 7.3, Pesikta Rabbati 17:2 49:11, Psalms 102:14-17 3:2, Saadia Opinions 8:1, Zechariah 1:6 2:4 12:6 14:10-11

[6] Isaiah 44:27 - b.Megillah [Tosefot] 9a, b.Menachot [Rashi] 52a, b.Sanhedrin 93ab, b.Zevachim [Rashi] 113b, Ecclesiastes.R 12:7, Ein Yaakov Sanhedrin:93a, Isaiah 11:15-11:16 18:15 19:16 3:15, Jastrow 385b 1284a, Jeremiah 2:38 3:32 3:36, Lamentations.R Petichata D'Chakimei:23, Midrash Psalms 69:2, Psalms 74:15, Revelation 16:12, y.Berachot 4:1
Isaiah 44:27-45:1 - Sibylline Oracles 3.28

[7] Isaiah 44:28 - 2 Chronicles 36:22-1:3, Daniel 10:1, Ezra 6:3-18, Isaiah 14:32 18:15 21:1 21:3 21:13 22:11 48:14-15 15:11, Josephus Antiquities 11.1.2, Psalms 78:71-72

[8] LXX *Who bids Cyrus be wise, and he shall perform all my will*

[9] Isaiah 45:1 - 1 Kings 19:15, b.Megillah 12a, Daniel 5:6 5:28-30 7:5 8:3, Ein Yaakov Megillah:12a, Esther.R 2:1, Ezekiel 30:21-24, Ezra 1:1, Isaiah 13:3 17:2 17:13 17:25 18:6 20:28 21:5, Jeremiah 3:6 2:3 2:35 3:11 51:20-24, Job 12:21, Josephus Antiquities 11.1.2, Nahum 2:7, Psalms 73:23, z.Vaetchanan 269b
Isaiah 45:1-4 - 4QIsac
Isaiah 45:1-13 - 1QIsab
Isaiah 45:1-25 - 1QIsaa

[10] Isaiah 45:2 - Acts 1:15, Apocalypse of Zephaniah 5:5, Isaiah 13:4-17 16:4 18:16, Jastrow 332b 772b, Jeremiah 3:30, Luke 3:5, Mas.Kallah Rabbati 2:15, Mas.Soferim 7:4, Odes of Solomon 17:10, Psalms 11:16

[11] 1QIsaa LXX *and he will make the mountains level*

[12] LXX *burst*

וְנָתַתִּי לְךָ אוֹצְרוֹת חֹשֶׁךְ וּמַטְמֻנֵי מִסְתָּרִים לְמַעַן
תֵּדַע כִּי־אֲנִי יְהוָה הַקּוֹרֵא בְשִׁמְךָ אֱלֹהֵי יִשְׂרָאֵל

3[1] And I will give you the treasures of darkness, And hidden riches of secret places, so you may know that I am the LORD, who called you by your name, the God of Israel.

לְמַעַן עַבְדִּי יַעֲקֹב וְיִשְׂרָאֵל בְּחִירִי וָאֶקְרָא לְךָ
בִּשְׁמֶךָ אֲכַנְּךָ וְלֹא יְדַעְתָּנִי

4[2] For the sake of Jacob My servant, And Israel My elect, *I have called you by your name, I have surnamed you*[3], though you have not known Me.

אֲנִי יְהוָה וְאֵין עוֹד זוּלָתִי אֵין אֱלֹהִים אֲאַזֶּרְךָ
וְלֹא יְדַעְתָּנִי

5[4] I am the LORD, and there is no one else, beside Me there is no God; I have clothed you, though you have not known Me;

לְמַעַן יֵדְעוּ מִמִּזְרַח־שֶׁמֶשׁ וּמִמַּעֲרָבָה כִּי־אֶפֶס
בִּלְעָדָי אֲנִי יְהוָה וְאֵין עוֹד

6[5] So they may know from the rising of the sun, and from the west, there is no one beside Me; *I am the LORD; and there is no one else*[6];

יוֹצֵר אוֹר וּבוֹרֵא חֹשֶׁךְ עֹשֶׂה שָׁלוֹם וּבוֹרֵא רָע
אֲנִי יְהוָה עֹשֶׂה כָל־אֵלֶּה

7[7] I form the light, and create darkness; I make *peace*[8], and create evil; I am the LORD who does all these things.

הַרְעִיפוּ שָׁמַיִם מִמַּעַל וּשְׁחָקִים יִזְּלוּ־צֶדֶק תִּפְתַּח־
אֶרֶץ וְיִפְרוּ־יֶשַׁע וּצְדָקָה תַצְמִיחַ יַחַד אֲנִי יְהוָה
בְּרָאתִיו

8[9] *Drop down, you heavens, from above, And let the skies pour down righteousness; Let the earth open, so they may bring forth salvation, And let her cause righteousness to spring up together; I the LORD have created it*[10].

הוֹי רָב אֶת־יֹצְרוֹ חֶרֶשׂ אֶת־חַרְשֵׂי אֲדָמָה הֲיֹאמַר
חֹמֶר לְיֹצְרוֹ מַה־תַּעֲשֶׂה וּפָעָלְךָ אֵין־יָדַיִם לוֹ

9[11] *Woe to him who strives with his Maker*[12], As a potsherd with the potsherds of the earth! *Shall the clay say*[13] to him who fashioned it: 'What made you?' Or: 'Your work, it has no [14]hands?'

הוֹי אֹמֵר לְאָב מַה־תּוֹלִיד וּלְאִשָּׁה מַה־תְּחִילִין

10[15] Woe to him who says to his father. What fathered you?' Or to *a woman*[16]: 'What travails you?'

---

[1] Isaiah 45:3 - Esther.R 2:1, Exodus 9:12 9:17, Ezekiel 29:19-20, Ezra 1:2, Isaiah 17:23 19:1 24:15 1:1, Jeremiah 27:5-7 17:8 2:37 3:53

[2] Isaiah 45:4 - 1 Thessalonians 4:5, Acts 17:23, Ephesians 2:12, Exodus 19:5-19:6, Galatians 4:8-4:9, Isaiah 41:8-41:9 43:3-43:4 19:14 20:1 44:28-45:1, Jeremiah 50:17-50:20, Mark 13:20, Matthew 24:22, Romans 9:6 11:7

[3] 1QIsaa *I have called you and he has established you with a name*; LXX *and accept you*

[4] Isaiah 45:5 - 1 Kings 8:60, 2 Enoch 36:1 47:3, Apocalypse of Adam 2:5, Aristobulus Fragment 4:5, b.Shabbat 103b, Deuteronomy 4:35 4:39 8:39, Ezra 1:2, Hebrews 1:8-9, Hellenistic Synagogal Prayers 4:27, Isaiah 22:21 20:6 20:8 45:14-18 45:21-22 22:9, Jastrow 73a, Job 12:18 12:21, Joel 2:27, John 1:1, Psalms 18:33 18:40, Pseudo-Orpheus 16, Sibylline Oracles 3.628 8.377, Tanna Devei Eliyahu 6

Isaiah 45:5-6 - 2 Enoch 33:8

[5] Isaiah 45:6 - 1 Samuel 17:46-17:47, Ezekiel 14:23 15:21, Isaiah 13:20 21:5, Malachi 1:11, Psalms 46:11 83:19 102:16-102:17, Saadia Opinions 2:2, Tanya Likutei Aramim §35

Isaiah 45:6-8 - 4QIsac

[6] Missing in LXX

[7] Isaiah 45:7 - 2 Corinthians 4:6, Acts 4:28, Amos 3:6 4:13 5:6, b.Berachot 11b 52b, Bahir 12 13, Birchat Yotzer Or [Altered], Ecclesiastes 7:13-7:14, Ein Yaakov Berachot:11b, Exodus 10:21-10:23 14:20, Exodus.R 28:7, Ezekiel 14:15-14:21 8:8, Genesis 1:3-1:5 1:17-1:18, Genesis.R 1:9 3:6, Guide for the Perplexed 3:10, Isaiah 10:5-10:6 7:2, James 1:17, Jastrow 1418a, Jeremiah 13:16 18:7-18:10 7:36 3:20, Job 2:10 10:29, Joel 2:2, Jude 1:6 1:13, Kuzari 2.002, Midrash Tanchuma Yitro 12, Nahum 1:8, Numbers.R 12:4, Psalms 8:4 29:11 75:8 104:20-104:23, Saadia Opinions 1:3 1:3, Shacharit, Sibylline Oracles 5.173, y.Berachot 8:6, z.Terumah 155a

[8] 1QIsaa *goodness*

[9] Isaiah 45:8 - 1 Corinthians 3:6-9, Acts 2:33, Avot de R'Natan 16, b.Taanit 7b, Bahir 74 120, Ein Yaakov Taanit:7b, Ephesians 2:10 4:24, Ezekiel 10:26, Genesis.R 13:13, Hosea 10:12 14:7-10, Isaiah 4:2 11:1 8:15 20:3 5:2 12:21 13:3 13:11 65:17-65:18 18:22, Jastrow 1251a, Jeremiah 7:23, Joel 3:1-2 4:18, Midrash Psalms 42/43:5, Psalms 72:3 72:6 85:10-13, Sifre Devarim Vezot Habracha 356, Titus 3:3-6, y.Berachot 9:2, y.Taanit 1:3

[10] 1QIsaa *Shout out, skies above and clouds, and let righteousness stream down. The one who says to the Earh, "Let salvation bloom, and let righteousness sprout forth.";* LXX *Let the heaven rejoice from above, and let the clouds rain righteousness: let the earth bring forth, and blossom with mercy, and bring forth righteousness likewise: I am the LORD who created you*

[11] Isaiah 45:9 - 1 Corinthians 10:22, Exodus 9:16-9:17, Isaiah 10:15 5:16 16:9, Jeremiah 18:6 2:24, Job 15:24-15:26 40:8-40:9, Midrash Psalms 7:17, Proverbs 21:30, Psalms 2:2-2:9, Romans 9:20-9:21, Saadia Opinions 6:4, y.Megillah 4:5

[12] LXX *What excellent thing have I prepared as clay of the potter?*

[13] 1QIsaa *Woe to the one who says*

[14] 1QIsaa adds *human*

[15] Isaiah 45:10 - Deuteronomy 3:16, Hebrews 12:9, Malachi 1:6

[16] LXX *his mother*

כֹּה־אָמַר יְהוָה קְדוֹשׁ יִשְׂרָאֵל וְיֹצְרוֹ הָאֹתִיּוֹת
שְׁאָלוּנִי עַל־בָּנַי וְעַל־פֹּעַל יָדַי תְּצַוֻּנִי

11[1] Thus says the LORD, *The Holy One of Israel, and his Maker: Ask Me of the things that are to come; Concerning My sons, and concerning the work*[2] *of My hands, command Me.*

אָנֹכִי עָשִׂיתִי אֶרֶץ וְאָדָם עָלֶיהָ בָרָאתִי אֲנִי יָדַי
נָטוּ שָׁמַיִם וְכָל־צְבָאָם צִוֵּיתִי

12[3] I, I, have made the earth, And created man on it; I, My hands, have stretched out the heavens and I have commanded all their host.

אָנֹכִי הַעִירֹתִהוּ בְצֶדֶק וְכָל־דְּרָכָיו אֲיַשֵּׁר הוּא־
יִבְנֶה עִירִי וְגָלוּתִי יְשַׁלֵּחַ לֹא בִמְחִיר וְלֹא בְשֹׁחַד
אָמַר יְהוָה צְבָאוֹת

13[4] *I have roused him up in victory, And I make level all his ways*[5]; He shall build My city, And he shall let My exiles go free, not for price nor reward, says the LORD of hosts.

כֹּה אָמַר יְהוָה יְגִיעַ מִצְרַיִם וּסְחַר־כּוּשׁ וּסְבָאִים
אַנְשֵׁי מִדָּה עָלַיִךְ יַעֲבֹרוּ וְלָךְ יִהְיוּ אַחֲרַיִךְ יֵלֵכוּ
בַּזִּקִּים יַעֲבֹרוּ וְאֵלַיִךְ יִשְׁתַּחֲווּ אֵלַיִךְ יִתְפַּלָּלוּ אַךְ
בָּךְ אֵל וְאֵין עוֹד אֶפֶס אֱלֹהִים

14[6] Thus says the LORD: The labor of Egypt, and the merchandise of Ethiopia, And of the Sabeans, men of stature, shall come over to you, and they shall be yours; They shall go after you, in chains they shall come over; and they shall fall down to you, They shall make petitions to you: surely God is in you, and there is no one else; there is no other God.

אָכֵן אַתָּה אֵל מִסְתַּתֵּר אֱלֹהֵי יִשְׂרָאֵל מוֹשִׁיעַ

15[7] Truly you are a God who hides Yourself, O God of Israel, the Savior.

בּוֹשׁוּ וְגַם־נִכְלְמוּ כֻּלָּם יַחְדָּו הָלְכוּ בַכְּלִמָּה חָרָשֵׁי
צִירִים

16[8] They shall be ashamed, yes, confounded, all of them; They shall go in confusion together who are makers of idols.

יִשְׂרָאֵל נוֹשַׁע בַּיהוָה תְּשׁוּעַת עוֹלָמִים לֹא־תֵבֹשׁוּ
וְלֹא־תִכָּלְמוּ עַד־עוֹלְמֵי עַד

17[9] O Israel, who are saved by the LORD with an everlasting salvation; You shall not be ashamed nor confounded, world without end.

כִּי כֹה אָמַר־יְהוָה בּוֹרֵא הַשָּׁמַיִם הוּא הָאֱלֹהִים
יֹצֵר הָאָרֶץ וְעֹשָׂהּ הוּא כוֹנְנָהּ לֹא־תֹהוּ בְרָאָהּ
לָשֶׁבֶת יְצָרָהּ אֲנִי יְהוָה וְאֵין עוֹד

18[10] For thus says the Lord who created the heavens, He is God; who formed the earth and made it, He established it, He created it not a

---

[1] Isaiah 45:11 - 2 Corinthians 6:18, 4 Ezra 8:7, Daniel 2:18 9:2-9:3 9:24-9:27, Ephesians 2:10, Ezekiel 12:37 15:7, Galatians 3:26-3:29, Genesis 8:27, Hosea 2:1 12:6, Isaiah 19:25 5:23 19:3 19:7 19:15 19:21 24:17 12:21 16:9, Jeremiah 3:19 7:2 7:10 9:3, Joshua 10:12, Judges 16:23, Mark 11:24, Mekhilta de R'Shimon bar Yochai Beshallach 23:1, Mekhilta de R'Ishmael Beshallah 4:78, Midrash Tanchuma Pinchas 11, Numbers.R 21:2, Romans 9:4-9:8, z.Vaetchanan 269b

[2] 1QIsaa *the creator of the signs: Question me concerning my children and concerning the work*

[3] Isaiah 45:12 - Genesis 1:26-1:27 2:1, Genesis.R 5:5 9:13 12:5, Guide for the Perplexed 2:29, Hebrews 11:3, Isaiah 16:12 16:22 16:28 18:5 20:24 21:18, Jeremiah 3:5 8:17, Mekhilta de R'Shimon bar Yochai Shirata 34:2, Mekhilta de R'Ishmael Shirata 4:66, Midrash Psalms 8:2, Nehemiah 9:6, Pesikta Rabbati 33:8, Psalms 6:26, Saadia Opinions 4:Exordium, Tanna Devei Eliyahu 5, Tanya Likutei Aramim §40, z.Lech Lecha 87b, z.Toledot 134b, z.Vayigash 205b, Zechariah 12:1

[4] Isaiah 45:13 - 1 Peter 1:18-19, 2 Chronicles 36:22-23, b.Arachin [Tosefot] 6a, Ezra 1:3, Isaiah 13:17 17:2 17:25 18:6 44:28-45:6 22:11 48:14-15 1:25 52:2-3 4:5, Midrash Psalms 118:10, Pirkei de R'Eliezer 45, Psalms 65:6, Romans 3:24-26

[5] LXX *I have raised him up to be a king with righteousness, and all his ways are right*

[6] Isaiah 45:14 - 1 Corinthians 8:4-8:6 14:25, 1 Thessalonians 1:9, 2 Samuel 21:20, Acts 10:25-10:26, Esther 8:17, Exodus 11:8, Ezekiel 23:42 7:3, Isaiah 10:33 14:1-14:2 18:7 19:23-19:25 23:18 19:3 20:8 45:5-45:6 21:24 1:23 60:5-60:16 61:5-61:6 13:9 66:19-66:20, Jastrow 302a 646b, Jeremiah 16:19, Job 1:15, Joel 4:8, Mekhilta de R'Shimon bar Yochai Beshallach 21:3, Mekhilta de R'Ishmael Beshallah 2:78, Midrash Psalms 94:1, Midrash Tanchuma Beshallach 7, Numbers 13:32, Psalms 68:31-68:32 72:10-72:15 5:6 5:8, Revelation 3:9, Seder Olam 23:Sennacherib 23:Sennacherib, Sibylline Oracles 3.628, Song of Songs.R 4:20, z.Vaetchanan 269b, Zechariah 8:20-8:23
Isaiah 45:14-17 - Maamad [Friday

[7] Isaiah 45:15 - 2 Peter 3:18, Acts 5:31 13:23, Isaiah 8:17 12:2 19:3 19:11 21:17 22:13 9:17 12:16, John 4:22 4:42 13:7, Matthew 1:22-1:23, Mekhilta de R'Ishmael Beshallah 2:82, Midrash Psalms 94:1, Midrash Tanchuma Beshallach 7, Psalms 44:25 68:27 77:20, Romans 11:33-34, Song of Songs.R 4:20

[8] Isaiah 45:16 - Isaiah 17:19 18:17 20:9 20:11 21:20, Jeremiah 2:26-2:27 10:14-10:15, Psalms 97:7

[9] Isaiah 45:17 - 1 Corinthians 1:30-1:31, 1 John 4:15 5:11-5:13, 1 Peter 2:6, 2 Corinthians 5:17-5:21, 2 Thessalonians 2:13-2:14 2:16, b.Makkot 23b, Ein Yaakov Makkot:23b, Hebrews 5:9, Hosea 1:7, Isaiah 2:4 5:22 21:25 1:23 3:6 3:8 6:4 6:8 12:19, Jeremiah 7:4, Joel 2:26-2:27, John 5:24 6:40 10:28, Mekhilta de R'Shimon bar Yochai Shirata 27:1 29:1, Mekhilta de R'Ishmael Shirata 1:81, Midrash Psalms 22:5 31:2 50:3 71:1 88:1 107:2, Midrash Tanchuma Acharei Mot 12, Motzoei Shabbat [Viyiten Lecha], Pesikta de R'Kahana 12.25, Philippians 3:8-3:9, Psalms 25:3 7:17, Romans 2:28-2:29 8:1 9:33 10:11 11:26, Selichot, Sifre Devarim Vezot Habracha 356, Zephaniah 3:11

[10] Isaiah 45:18 - b.Arachin 2b, b.Avodah Zara [Tosefot] 13a, b.Bava Batra 13a, b.Bechorot [Tosefot] 29a, b.Bechorot 47a, b.Chagigah 2b, b.Gittin 41b, b.Megillah 16a, b.Moed Katan 8b, b.Pesachim 88b, b.Yevamot 62a, Ein Yaakov Megillah:27a, Ezekiel 36:10-12, Genesis 1:2 1:26 1:28 9:1, Genesis.R 19:5 20:8, Guide for the Perplexed 3:13, Isaiah 18:5 45:5-6 21:12, Jeremiah 10:12 3:15, m.Eduyot 1:13, m.Gittin 4:5, Numbers.R 12:4, Psalms 19:16, Saadia Opinions 1:1 2:3 2:13, y.Gittin 4:5, z.Vaetchanan 269b

waste, He formed it to be inhabited: I am the LORD, and there is no one else.

לֹא בַסֵּתֶר דִּבַּרְתִּי בִּמְקוֹם אֶרֶץ חֹשֶׁךְ לֹא אָמַרְתִּי לְזֶרַע יַעֲקֹב תֹּהוּ בַקְּשׁוּנִי אֲנִי יְהוָה דֹּבֵר צֶדֶק מַגִּיד מֵישָׁרִים

19[1] I have not spoken in secret, In a place of the land of darkness; I did not say to the seed of Jacob: *'Seek Me in vain'; I the LORD speak righteousness, I declare things that are right[2]*.

הִקָּבְצוּ וָבֹאוּ הִתְנַגְּשׁוּ יַחְדָּו פְּלִיטֵי הַגּוֹיִם לֹא יָדְעוּ הַנֹּשְׂאִים אֶת־עֵץ פִּסְלָם וּמִתְפַּלְלִים אֶל־אֵל לֹא יוֹשִׁיעַ

20[3] Assemble yourselves and come, draw near together, You who escaped out of the nations; They who carry the wood of their graven image have no knowledge, And pray to a god that cannot save.

הַגִּידוּ וְהַגִּישׁוּ אַף יִוָּעֲצוּ יַחְדָּו מִי הִשְׁמִיעַ זֹאת מִקֶּדֶם מֵאָז הִגִּידָהּ הֲלוֹא אֲנִי יְהוָה וְאֵין־עוֹד אֱלֹהִים מִבַּלְעָדַי אֵל־צַדִּיק וּמוֹשִׁיעַ אַיִן זוּלָתִי

21[4] Declare, and bring them near. Yes, let them take counsel together: Who has announced this from ancient time, And declared it of old? Have not I the LORD? And there is no God else beside Me, A just God and a Savior; There is no one beside Me.

פְּנוּ־אֵלַי וְהִוָּשְׁעוּ כָּל־אַפְסֵי־אָרֶץ כִּי אֲנִי־אֵל וְאֵין עוֹד

22[5] Look to Me, and be saved, All the ends of the earth; For I am God, and there is no one else.

בִּי נִשְׁבַּעְתִּי יָצָא מִפִּי צְדָקָה דָּבָר וְלֹא יָשׁוּב כִּי־לִי תִּכְרַע כָּל־בֶּרֶךְ תִּשָּׁבַע כָּל־לָשׁוֹן

23[6] By Myself have I sworn, The word is gone forth from My mouth in righteousness, And shall not come back, so to Me every knee shall bow, Every tongue shall swear[7].

אַךְ בַּיהוָה לִי אָמַר צְדָקוֹת וָעֹז עָדָיו יָבוֹא וְיֵבֹשׁוּ כֹּל הַנֶּחֱרִים בּוֹ

24[8] *Only in the LORD, shall one say of Me, is victory and strength; to Him shall men come in confusion, All they who were incensed against Him[9].*

בַּיהוָה יִצְדְּקוּ וְיִתְהַלְלוּ כָּל־זֶרַע יִשְׂרָאֵל

25[10] In the LORD shall all the seed of Israel be justified, and shall glory.

[1] Isaiah 45:19 - 1 Chronicles 4:8, 2 Chronicles 15:2, Acts 2:4-2:8, Amos 5:4, Deuteronomy 5:28 30:11-30:14 8:4, Ezra 8:22, Genesis.R 47:9, Guide for the Perplexed 3:49, Isaiah 1:15 8:19 43:9-43:10 21:23 24:16 55:6-55:7 58:1-58:3 15:1, James 4:3, Jastrow 1186a, Jeremiah 29:13-29:14, John 7:26 7:28 7:37-7:39 18:20, Malachi 3:13-3:14, Matthew 15:8-15:9, Mekhilta de R'Shimon bar Yochai Bachodesh 48:1 52:1, Mekilta de R'Ishmael Bahodesh 1:91, Numbers 23:19-23:20, Proverbs 1:21 8:1-8:4 8:6 15:8 6:5, Psalms 9:11 12:7 19:8-11 24:6 69:14 69:33 111:7-8 119:137-138, Tanna Devei Eliyahu 2, z.Lech Lecha 86a

[2] LXX *Seek vanity: I, I, am the LORD, speaking righteousness, and proclaiming truth*

[3] Isaiah 45:20 - 1 Kings 18:26-29, 4QIsad, Aleinu [Shacharit, Birchat HaChammah.Alenu, Ephesians 2:12 2:16, Habakkuk 2:18-20, Isaiah 4:2 41:5-6 17:21 42:17-18 19:9 44:17-20 22:1 46:6-7 48:5-7, Jeremiah 2:27-28 10:5 10:8 10:14 25:15-29 2:28 51:6-9 51:17-18, Kiddush Levonoh, Maariv, Minchah, Mussaf, Mussaf Rosh Hashanah, Psalms 19:8, Revelation 18:3-18, Romans 1:21-23, Seder Brit Milah]
Isaiah 45:20-25 - 4QIsa

[4] Isaiah 45:21 - Isaiah 41:1-41:4 41:22-41:23 17:26 19:3 19:9 19:11 44:7-44:8 21:5 21:14 21:18 21:25 46:9-46:10 24:3 24:14 15:1, Jeremiah 23:5-23:6 2:2, Joel 4:9-4:12, Psalms 26:7 71:17-71:18 96:10, Romans 3:25-3:26, Saadia Opinions 2:2, Tanna Devei Eliyahu 6, Titus 2:13-2:14, Zechariah 9:9, Zephaniah 3:5 3:17

[5] Isaiah 45:22 - 2 Chronicles 20:12, 2 Peter 1:1, Hebrews 12:2, Isaiah 21:21 1:6 1:12, John 3:13-16 6:40 10:28-30, Micah 7:7, Midrash Psalms 9:11 100:1, Numbers 21:8-9, Psalms 22:18 65:6, Ruth.R 4:1, Saadia Opinions 2:2 Intro 2, Titus 2:13, y.Yevamot 8:3, Zechariah 12:10

[6] Isaiah 45:23 - 2 Chronicles 15:14-15:15, Amos 6:8, b.Niddah 30b, Deuteronomy 6:13, Ein Yaakov Niddah:30b, Genesis 22:15-22:18 7:53, Hebrews 6:13-6:18, Isaiah 19:18-19:21 44:3-44:5 21:19 7:11 17:16, Jeremiah 22:5 1:13, Mas.Kallah Rabbati 3:1, Mekhilta de R'Shimon bar Yochai Shirata 31:1, Mekhilta de R'Ishmael Shirata 5:35, Midrash Psalms 100:1, Nehemiah 10:30, Numbers 23:19, Philippians 2:10, Psalms 63:12 12:2, Romans 11:4 14:10-14:12

[7] LXX adds *by God*

[8] Isaiah 45:24 - 1 Corinthians 1:30, 2 Corinthians 5:21 12:9-12:10, 2 Peter 1:1, 2 Timothy 4:17-18, Colossians 1:11, Ephesians 3:16 6:10, Genesis 1:10, Isaiah 2:4 17:11 20:8 21:25 6:17 7:5 12:9 13:10, Jeremiah 23:5-6 9:16, John 7:37 12:32, Luke 13:17 19:27, Matthew 11:27-28, Philippians 4:13, Psalms 2:1-12 21:9-10 72:9 14:2, Revelation 11:18 22:17, Zechariah 10:6 10:12

[9] LXX *saying, Righteousness and glory shall come to him: and all who remove them from their borders shall be ashamed*

[10] Isaiah 45:25 - 1 Chronicles 16:13, 1 Corinthians 1:31 6:11, 2 Corinthians 5:21 10:17, Acts 13:39, Galatians 3:27-29 6:14, Gates of Repentance 2.1 3.27, Isaiah 17:16 21:17 21:19 21:24 13:9 17:9 17:23, Jeremiah 9:24-25, Philippians 3:3, Psalms 22:24 64:11, Romans 3:24-25 4:16 5:1 5:18-19 8:1 8:30 8:33-34 9:6-9:8

Isaiah – Chapter 46

Hebrew	Verse	English
כָּרַע בֵּל קֹרֵס נְבֹו הָיוּ עֲצַבֵּיהֶם לַחַיָּה וְלַבְּהֵמָה נְשֻׂאֹתֵיכֶם עֲמוּסֹות מַשָּׂא לַעֲיֵפָה	1[1]	*Bel bows down, Nebo stoops[2]*; their idols are on the beasts, and on the cattle; *The things you carried about are made a load, A burden to the weary beast[3].*
קָרְסוּ כָרְעוּ יַחְדָּו לֹא יָכְלוּ מַלֵּט מַשָּׂא וְנַפְשָׁם בַּשְּׁבִי הָלָכָה	2[4]	*They stoop, they bow down together, They could not deliver the burden; And themselves go into captivity[5].*
שִׁמְעוּ אֵלַי בֵּית יַעֲקֹב וְכָל־שְׁאֵרִית בֵּית יִשְׂרָאֵל הַעֲמֻסִים מִנִּי־בֶטֶן הַנְּשֻׂאִים מִנִּי־רָחַם	3[6]	Listen to Me, O house of Jacob, and all the remnant of the house of Israel who are borne from birth, who are carried from the womb:
וְעַד־זִקְנָה אֲנִי הוּא וְעַד־שֵׂיבָה אֲנִי אֶסְבֹּל אֲנִי עָשִׂיתִי וַאֲנִי אֶשָּׂא וַאֲנִי אֶסְבֹּל וַאֲמַלֵּט	4[7]	Even to [your] old age I am the same, And to gray hairs I will carry you; I have made, and I will bear; Yes, I will carry, and I will deliver.
לְמִי תְדַמְיוּנִי וְתַשְׁווּ וְתַמְשִׁלוּנִי וְנִדְמֶה	5[8]	*To whom will you compare Me, and make Me equal, and compare Me so we may be alike?[9]*
הַזָּלִים זָהָב מִכִּיס וְכֶסֶף בַּקָּנֶה יִשְׁקֹלוּ יִשְׂכְּרוּ צֹורֵף וְיַעֲשֵׂהוּ אֵל יִסְגְּדוּ אַף־יִשְׁתַּחֲווּ	6[10]	You who lavish gold out of the bag, And weigh silver in the balance; You who hire a goldsmith, so he makes it a god, To fall down before, yes, to worship.
יִשָּׂאֻהוּ עַל־כָּתֵף יִסְבְּלֻהוּ וְיַנִּיחֻהוּ תַחְתָּיו וְיַעֲמֹד מִמְּקֹומֹו לֹא יָמִישׁ אַף־יִצְעַק אֵלָיו וְלֹא יַעֲנֶה מִצָּרָתֹו לֹא יֹושִׁיעֶנּוּ	7[11]	He is borne on the shoulder, he is carried, and set in his place, and he stands, *From his place he does not remove[12]*; Yes, though one cries to him, he cannot answer, Nor save him from his trouble.
זִכְרוּ־זֹאת וְהִתְאֹשָׁשׁוּ הָשִׁיבוּ פֹושְׁעִים עַל־לֵב	8[13]	Remember this, *and stand fast; Bring it to mind, you transgressors[14].*

---

[1] Isaiah 46:1 - 1 Samuel 5:3, According to the Massorah, b.Megillah 25b, b.Sanhedrin 63b, b.Zevachim [Rashi] 96a, Exodus 12:12, Isaiah 2:20 21:9 41:6-7, Jastrow 1427b, Jeremiah 10:5 48:1-25 2:2 3:44 3:47 3:52, Song of Songs.R 7:15, בל "Bel" was not altered to become באל "Baal"
Isaiah 46:1-3 - 4QIsab
Isaiah 46:1-13 - 1QIsa

[2] LXX *Bel has fallen, Nabo is broken to pieces*

[3] 1QIsaa *Your loads are more burdensome than their report;* LXX *you take them packed up as a burden to the weary, exhausted, hungry, and at the same time helpless man*

[4] Isaiah 46:2 - 2 Samuel 5:21, Apocalypse of Elijah 5:11, b.Megillah 25b, b.Sanhedrin 63b, Hosea 10:5-6, Isaiah 36:18-19 13:12 13:19 20:17 21:20, Jeremiah 43:12-13 24:7, Judges 18:17-18 18:24

[5] LXX *who will not be able to save themselves from war, but they themselves are led away captive.*

[6] Isaiah 46:3 - Deuteronomy 1:31 32:11-12, Deuteronomy.R 1:10, Exodus 19:4, Exodus.R 25:9, Ezekiel 16:6-16, Isaiah 1:9 10:22 11:11 13:4 44:1-2 20:21 22:12 24:1 48:17-18 49:1-49:2 3:1 3:7 15:9, Mas.Soferim 20:1, Midrash Tanchuma Bamidbar 20, Midrash Tanchuma Haazinu 2, mt.Hilchot Berachot 10:16, Numbers.R 4:2 9:33, Psalms 22:10-11 71:6 81:9-14
Isaiah 46:3-13 - 1QIsab

[7] Isaiah 46:4 - 3 Enoch 4:6, After Aleinu [Shacharit, b.Sanhedrin 38b, Deuteronomy.R 7:11, Ecclesiastes.R 7:15, Ein Yaakov Sanhedrin:38b, Esther.R 7:13, Exodus.R 29:6 36:4, Genesis.R 90:2, Hebrews 1:12 13:8, Isaiah 17:4 19:13 19:25, James 1:17, Leviticus.R 4:8 24:9, Maariv, Malachi 2:16 3:6, Mekilta de R'Ishmael Bahodesh 5:30, Midrash Psalms 32:4 137:3 149:1, Midrash Tanchuma Bereshit 9, Midrash Tanchuma Tetzaveh 2, Minchah, Mussaf-Al Tirah Mipachad], Pesikta Rabbati 28:2, Psalms 48:15 71:18 92:15 102:27-102:28, Romans 11:29

[8] Isaiah 46:5 - Colossians 1:15, Exodus 15:11, Hebrews 1:3, Isaiah 16:18 16:25, Jeremiah 10:6-10:7 10:16, Philippians 2:6, Psalms 86:8 89:7 89:9 17:5, Saadia Opinions 2:9, y.Kiddushin 3:5

[9] LXX *To whom have you compared me? see, consider, you who go astray*

[10] Isaiah 46:6 - 1 Kings 12:28, Acts 17:29, b.Bava Batra 25ab, Daniel 3:5-3:15, Ein Yaakov Bava Batra:25a 25b, Exodus 32:2-32:4, Habakkuk 2:18-2:20, Hosea 8:4-8:6, Isaiah 2:8 40:19-40:20 41:6-41:7 44:12-44:19 21:20, Jeremiah 10:3-10:4 10:9 10:14, Judges 17:3-17:4, Saadia Opinions 2:9, y.Bava Batra 9:6, y.Kiddushin 3:5, y.Kilayim 8:1, y.Sotah 2:5, y.Yevamot 1:1
Isaiah 46:6-7 - Fragments of Pseudo-Greek Poets 5

[11] Isaiah 46:7 - 1 Kings 18:26 18:40, 1 Samuel 5:3, Daniel 3:1, Deuteronomy.R 2:10 2:20, Isaiah 13:38 21:20 22:1, Jeremiah 2:28 10:5, Jonah 1:5 1:14-1:16, Jubilees 12:5, Judges 10:12-10:14, Mekilta de R'Shimon bar Yochai Bachodesh 53:1, Mekilta de R'Ishmael Bahodesh 6:29, Midrash Psalms 4:3 31:3, Sifre Devarim {Ekev} 43, y.Berachot 9:1

[12] 1QIsaa *and does not move from its place*

[13] Isaiah 46:8 - 1 Corinthians 14:20, Deuteronomy 8:29, Ephesians 5:14, Ezekiel 18:28, Haggai 1:5 1:7, Isaiah 44:18-44:21 23:7, Jeremiah 10:8, Luke 15:17, Psalms 19:8 15:18
Isaiah 46:8-13 - 4QIsac

[14] LXX *and groan: repent, you who have gone astray, return in your heart*

זִכְר֥וּ רִאשֹׁנ֖וֹת מֵעוֹלָ֑ם כִּ֣י אָנֹכִ֥י אֵל֙ וְאֵ֣ין ע֔וֹד אֱלֹהִ֖ים וְאֶ֥פֶס כָּמֽוֹנִי	9[1]	Remember the former things of old: *That I am God, and there is no one else*[2]; I am God, and there is no one like Me;

מַגִּ֤יד מֵֽרֵאשִׁית֙ אַחֲרִ֔ית וּמִקֶּ֖דֶם אֲשֶׁ֣ר לֹא־נַעֲשֹׂ֑וּ אֹמֵר֙ עֲצָתִ֣י תָק֔וּם וְכָל־חֶפְצִ֖י אֶעֱשֶֽׂה

10[3] Declaring the end from the beginning, And from ancient times things that are not yet done[4]; Saying: 'My counsel shall stand, And I will do all My pleasure.'

קֹרֵ֤א מִמִּזְרָח֙ עַ֔יִט מֵאֶ֥רֶץ מֶרְחָ֖ק אִ֣ישׁ *עֲצָתֹ֑ו* *עֲצָתִ֔י* אַף־דִּבַּ֙רְתִּי֙ אַף־אֲבִיאֶ֔נָּה יָצַ֖רְתִּי אַף־אֶעֱשֶֽׂנָּה

11[5] Calling a bird of prey from the east, *The man of My counsel from a far country*; Yes, I have spoken, and I will bring it to pass, I have designed, and I will do it[6].

שִׁמְע֥וּ אֵלַ֖י אַבִּ֣ירֵי לֵ֑ב הָרְחוֹקִ֖ים מִצְּדָקָֽה

12[7] Listen to Me, you stout-hearted, who are far from righteousness:

קֵרַ֤בְתִּי צִדְקָתִי֙ לֹ֣א תִרְחָ֔ק וּתְשׁוּעָתִ֖י לֹ֣א תְאַחֵ֑ר וְנָתַתִּ֤י בְצִיּוֹן֙ תְּשׁוּעָ֔ה לְיִשְׂרָאֵ֖ל תִּפְאַרְתִּֽי

13[8] I bring My righteousness near, it shall not be far off, And My salvation shall not tarry; And I will place salvation in Zion for Israel My glory.

Isaiah – Chapter 47

רְדִ֣י ׀ וּשְׁבִ֣י עַל־עָפָ֗ר בְּתוּלַת֙ בַּת־בָּבֶ֔ל שְׁבִי־לָאָ֥רֶץ אֵין־כִּסֵּ֖א בַּת־כַּשְׂדִּ֑ים כִּ֣י לֹ֣א תוֹסִ֔יפִי יִקְרְאוּ־לָ֖ךְ רַכָּ֥ה וַעֲנֻגָּֽה

1[9] Come down, and sit in the dust, virgin daughter of Babylon, Sit on the ground *without a throne*[10], daughter of the Chaldeans; For you shall not be called tender and delicate any longer.

קְחִ֤י רֵחַ֙יִם֙ וְטַ֣חֲנִי קָ֔מַח גַּלִּ֥י צַמָּתֵ֖ךְ חֶשְׂפִּי־שֹׁ֑בֶל גַּלִּי־שׁ֖וֹק עִבְרִ֥י נְהָרֽוֹת

2[11] Take the millstones, and grind meal; remove your veil, *strip off the train*[12], uncover the leg, pass through the rivers.

---

[1] Isaiah 46:9 - 2 Enoch 33:8 36:1 47:3, Daniel 9:6-9:15, Deuteronomy 8:7 9:26, Isaiah 18:9 45:5-6 21:14 21:18 45:21-22 22:5 17:17, Jeremiah 23:7-23:8, mt.Hilchot Teshuvah 5:5, Nehemiah 9:7-9:37, Psalms 78:1-72 105:1-45 15:4

[2] Missing in LXX

[3] Isaiah 46:10 - 2 Enoch 29:4, Acts 3:23 4:27-28 5:39 15:18, Daniel 4:32, Deuteronomy 4:24-31 28:15-68, Deuteronomy.R 2:22, Ephesians 1:9-11, Exodus.R 9:1 15:27 38:7, Genesis 3:15 12:2-3 1:10 49:22-26, Genesis.R 4:6 16:2 42:7, Hebrews 6:17, Isaiah 41:22-23 19:13 20:7 21:21 22:11, Jastrow 1164a, Midrash Tanchuma Lech Lecha 8, Midrash Tanchuma Shelach 9, Midrash Tanchuma Tazria 8, Midrash Tanchuma Vaera 4 11, mt.Hilchot Teshuvah 5:5, Numbers 24:17-24, Numbers.R 5:5 16:16, Proverbs 19:21 21:30, Psalms 33:11 15:6, Romans 11:33-34, Saadia Opinions 2:13, z.Bereshit 28a, z.Lech Lecha 82a
Isaiah 46:10-13 - 4QIsad

[4] LXX adds *and they are accomplished together*

[5] Isaiah 46:11 - Acts 4:28 5:39, b.Menachot [Rashbam] 88b, Ephesians 1:11 3:11, Ezekiel 15:4, Ezra 1:2, Genesis.R 15:4 49:2 54:2, Isaiah 13:2-4 14:24-27 21:7-21:9 14:15 17:2 17:25 44:28-36 21:13 48:14-15, Jeremiah 2:29 2:45 51:20-29, Job 23:13, Numbers 23:19, Psalms 76:11 23:24

[6] LXX *and from a land afar off, for the things that I have planned: I have spoken, and brought him; I have created and made him; I have brought him, and prospered his way*

[7] Isaiah 46:12 - Acts 7:51, Ein Yaakov Berachot 17b, Ephesians 2:13 5:14, Isaiah 4:23 21:20 22:3 24:1 24:4, Jastrow 549a, Jeremiah 2:5, Malachi 3:13-15, Proverbs 1:22-23 8:1-5, Psalms 49:2 76:6 119:150 119:155, Revelation 3:17-18, y.Maaser Sheni 5:5, z.Lech Lecha 76b, Zechariah 7:11-12

[8] Isaiah 46:13 - 1 Peter 2:6, 2 Thessalonians 1:10 1:12, Ephesians 1:6, Habakkuk 2:3, Haggai 1:8, Hebrews 10:37, Isaiah 12:2 4:16 19:7 20:23 3:5 12:21 13:3 13:11 14:11, Jeremiah 9:9, Joel 4:17, John 17:10, Leviticus.R 5:7, Psalms 14:7 46:2 46:6, Romans 1:17 3:21-26 10:3-15

[9] Isaiah 47:1 - Deuteronomy 28:56-28:57, Ezekiel 2:16 4:17, Haggai 2:22, Isaiah 3:26 14:13-14 23:12 2:5 32:9-11 13:22 47:7-47:9 4:2, Jeremiah 13:18 22:11 24:18 2:42 3:33, Job 2:8 2:13, Jonah 3:6, Lamentations 2:10 2:21 4:5, Midrash Tanchuma Tazria 11, Obadiah 1:3-1:4, Psalms 18:28 89:45 17:8, Revelation 18:7, Sibylline Oracles 3.356, Song of Songs.R 3:6, Zechariah 2:7
Isaiah 47:1-6 - 4QIsad
Isaiah 47:1-14 - 1QIsab
Isaiah 47:1-15 - 1QIsaa

[10] Missing in LXX

[11] Isaiah 47:2 - b.Berachot 24a, b.Sanhedrin 96b, b.Shabbat [Rashi] 82a, Ein Yaakov Chagigah:16a, Ein Yaakov Sanhedrin:96b, Exodus 11:5, Ezekiel 16:37-16:39, Genesis 24:65, Hosea 2:3, Isaiah 3:17 20:4 8:11, Jastrow 1292a 1381a, Jeremiah 13:22 13:26 3:7, Job 7:10, Judges 16:21, Lamentations 5:13, Lamentations.R 1:41, Luke 17:35, Matthew 24:41, Micah 1:11, Nahum 3:5-3:6, Numbers.R 9:45, Song of Songs.R 3:6

[12] LXX *uncover your white hairs*

תִּגָּל עֶרְוָתֵךְ גַּם תֵּרָאֶה חֶרְפָּתֵךְ נָקָם אֶקָּח וְלֹא אֶפְגַּע אָדָם — 3[1]

Your nakedness shall be uncovered; Yes, your *shame shall be seen*[2]; I will take vengeance, and will let no man intercede.

גֹּאֲלֵנוּ יְהוָה צְבָאוֹת שְׁמוֹ קְדוֹשׁ יִשְׂרָאֵל — 4[3]

Our Redeemer, the LORD of hosts is His name, The Holy One of Israel.

שְׁבִי דוּמָם וּבֹאִי בַחֹשֶׁךְ בַּת־כַּשְׂדִּים כִּי לֹא תוֹסִיפִי יִקְרְאוּ־לָךְ גְּבֶרֶת מַמְלָכוֹת — 5[4]

Sit silent[5], and get into darkness, O daughter of the Chaldeans; For you shall no longer be called the *mistress*[6] of kingdoms.

קָצַפְתִּי עַל־עַמִּי חִלַּלְתִּי נַחֲלָתִי וָאֶתְּנֵם בְּיָדֵךְ לֹא־שַׂמְתְּ לָהֶם רַחֲמִים עַל־זָקֵן הִכְבַּדְתְּ עֻלֵּךְ מְאֹד — 6[7]

I was angry with My people, I profaned My inheritance, and gave them into your hand; you showed them no mercy; you have laid your heavy yoke upon the aged.

וַתֹּאמְרִי לְעוֹלָם אֶהְיֶה גְּבָרֶת עַד לֹא־שַׂמְתְּ אֵלֶּה עַל־לִבֵּךְ לֹא זָכַרְתְּ אַחֲרִיתָהּ — 7[8]

And you said: 'forever shall I be mistress'; so that you did not lay these things to your heart, nor remembered the end.

וְעַתָּה שִׁמְעִי־זֹאת עֲדִינָה הַיּוֹשֶׁבֶת לָבֶטַח הָאֹמְרָה בִּלְבָבָהּ אֲנִי וְאַפְסִי עוֹד לֹא אֵשֵׁב אַלְמָנָה וְלֹא אֵדַע שְׁכוֹל — 8[9]

Now, therefore, hear this, you who are given to pleasures, who sit securely, who says in your heart: 'I am, and there is no one else beside me; I shall not sit as a widow, nor shall I know the loss of children';

וְתָבֹאנָה לָּךְ שְׁתֵּי־אֵלֶּה רֶגַע בְּיוֹם אֶחָד שְׁכוֹל וְאַלְמֹן כְּתֻמָּם בָּאוּ עָלַיִךְ בְּרֹב כְּשָׁפַיִךְ בְּעָצְמַת חֲבָרַיִךְ מְאֹד — 9[10]

But these two things shall come to you in a moment. In one day, the loss of children, and widowhood; *in their full measure they shall come on you, For the multitude of your sorceries, And the great abundance*[11] of your enchantments.

וַתִּבְטְחִי בְרָעָתֵךְ אָמַרְתְּ אֵין רֹאָנִי חָכְמָתֵךְ וְדַעְתֵּךְ הִיא שׁוֹבְבָתֶךְ וַתֹּאמְרִי בְלִבֵּךְ אֲנִי וְאַפְסִי עוֹד — 10[12]

And you have been secure in your wickedness; you have said: 'No one sees me'; your wisdom and your knowledge has perverted you; And you have said in your heart. 'I am, and there is no one else besides me.'

וּבָא עָלַיִךְ רָעָה לֹא תֵדְעִי שַׁחְרָהּ וְתִפֹּל עָלַיִךְ הֹוָה לֹא תוּכְלִי כַּפְּרָהּ וְתָבֹא עָלַיִךְ פִּתְאֹם שׁוֹאָה לֹא תֵדָעִי — 11[13]

Yet evil shall come upon you; you will not know how to charm it away; And calamity shall fall on you; you shall not be able to put it

---

[1] Isaiah 47:3 - b.Berachot 24a, Deuteronomy 8:35 32:41-32:43, Ezekiel 16:37, Hebrews 10:30-10:31, Isaiah 34:1-34:8 59:17-59:18 63:4-63:6, Jeremiah 13:22 13:26 50:27-50:28 3:4 3:11 51:20-51:24 51:34-51:36 3:56, Nahum 3:5, Psalms 94:1-94:2 137:8-137:9, Revelation 6:9-6:10 16:19 18:5-18:8 18:20, Romans 12:19
[2] LXX *reproaches shall be brought to light*
[3] Isaiah 47:4 - Blessings for Kriat Shema [Shacharit, Ecclesiastes.R 4:1, Isaiah 17:14 19:3 19:14 20:6 1:26 6:5, Jastrow 216b, Jeremiah 7:12 50:33-50:34, Leviticus.R 32:8, Motzoei Shabbat [Viyiten Lecha], Song of Songs.R 3:6 4:17, Tzur Israel]
[4] Isaiah 47:5 - 1 Samuel 2:9, Daniel 2:37-38, Habakkuk 2:20, Isaiah 13:10 13:19-20 14:4 14:23 23:1 23:7, Jastrow 884b, Jeremiah 8:14 1:10, Jude 1:13, Lamentations 1:1, Leviticus.R 13:5, Matthew 22:12-13, Psalms 31:18 46:11, Revelation 17:3-5 17:18 18:7 18:16-19 18:21-24, Sibylline Oracles 5.436, Zechariah 2:13
[5] LXX *Sit down pierced with woe*
[6] LXX *strength*
[7] Isaiah 47:6 - 2 Chronicles 4:9, 2 Samuel 24:14, Deuteronomy 4:50, Ezekiel 24:21 4:16, Isaiah 10:6 13:16 14:17 42:24-42:25 19:28, James 2:13, Lamentations 2:13, Leviticus.R 13:5, Matthew 7:2, Midrash Tanchuma Tazria 11, Obadiah 1:10 1:16, Pesikta Rabbati 13:3, Psalms 69:27, Sifre.z Numbers Beha'alotcha 11:16, Zechariah 1:15
[8] Isaiah 47:7 - Daniel 4:26 5:18-23, Deuteronomy 8:29, Ezekiel 7:3-9 4:2 28:12-14 5:3, Isaiah 18:25 46:8-9 23:5, Jeremiah 5:31
[9] Isaiah 47:8 - 2 Thessalonians 2:4, Daniel 4:19 4:27 5:1-5:4 5:23 5:30 11:36, Exodus.R 15:16, Habakkuk 2:5-2:8, Isaiah 21:4-21:5 22:12-22:13 8:9 21:6 21:18 23:10, Jeremiah 2:11 50:31-50:32 3:53, Judges 18:7 18:27, Luke 12:18-12:20 17:27-17:29, Nahum 1:10, Psalms 10:6-10:7, Revelation 18:3-18:8, Sibylline Oracles 11.290 3.77 5.173, Tanya Likutei Aramim §22 §36, Zephaniah 2:15 Isaiah 47:8 [LXX] - Joseph and Aseneth 11:13 2 Isaiah 47:8-9 - 4QIsa
[10] Isaiah 47:9 - 1 Thessalonians 5:3, 2 Thessalonians 2:9-10, Daniel 2:2 4:4 5:7, Isaiah 13:18-22 14:22-23 47:12-13 51:18-19, Jeremiah 3:29 51:62-51:64, Luke 7:12-13, Nahum 3:4, Psalms 73:19, Revelation 9:20-21 18:8-10 18:21-23 21:8 22:15, Ruth 1:5 1:20, Sibylline Oracles 5.169
[11] LXX *shall come suddenly upon you, for your sorcery, for the strength*
[12] Isaiah 47:10 - 1 Corinthians 1:19-21 3:19, Ecclesiastes 8:8, Ezekiel 8:12 9:9 28:2-6, Isaiah 5:21 4:15 5:15 20:20 11:4, Jeremiah 23:24, Job 22:13-14, Psalms 10:12 52:8 62:10-11 64:6 94:7-9, Romans 1:22, St. Petersburg Codex has אמרת but revisers state אמרתי with ילק "the Yod is to be cancelled", Tanya Likutei Aramim §36
[13] Isaiah 47:11 - 1 Thessalonians 5:3, Daniel 5:25-5:30, Exodus 12:29-12:30, Isaiah 13:36, Jeremiah 51:39-51:42, Luke 12:59,

away; and ruin shall come on you suddenly, before you know.

עִמְדִי־נָא בַחֲבָרַ֫יִךְ וּבְרֹב כְּשָׁפַ֫יִךְ בַּאֲשֶׁר יָגַ֫עַתְּ מִנְּעוּרָ֑יִךְ אוּלַי תּוּכְלִי הוֹעִיל אוּלַי תַּעֲרֽוֹצִי

12[1] Stand now with your enchantments, And with the multitude of your sorceries, I which you labored from your youth; *perhaps you can profit, perhaps you can prevail*[2].

נִלְאֵית בְּרֹב עֲצָתָ֑יִךְ יַעַמְדוּ־נָא וְיוֹשִׁיעֻ֫ךְ 'הָבְרוּ' "הֹבְרֵי" שָׁמַ֫יִם הַחֹזִים֙ בַּכּֽוֹכָבִים מֽוֹדִיעִם֙ לֶחֳדָשִׁ֔ים מֵאֲשֶׁ֥ר יָבֹ֖אוּ עָלָֽיִךְ

13[3] You are wearied in the multitude of your counsels; let the *astrologers, the stargazers, the monthly prognosticators*[4], Stand up, and save you from the things that shall come on *you*[5].

הִנֵּה הָיוּ כְקַשׁ אֵשׁ שְׂרָפָ֫תַם לֹֽא־יַצִּ֫ילוּ אֶת־נַפְשָׁם מִיַּד לֶהָבָ֑ה אֵין־גַּחֶ֫לֶת לַחְמָם אוּר לָשֶׁ֫בֶת נֶגְדּֽוֹ

14[6] Behold, they *shall be as stubble; the fire shall burn them; they shall not deliver themselves from the power of the flame; it shall not be a coal to warm at, nor a fire to sit before*[7].

כֵּן הָיוּ־לָךְ אֲשֶׁר יָגָ֑עַתְּ סֹחֲרַ֫יִךְ מִנְּעוּרַ֫יִךְ אִישׁ לְעֶבְרוֹ תָּעוּ אֵין מוֹשִׁיעֵֽךְ

15[8] Thus shall they be to you with whom you have labored; everyone who has traded with you from your youth shall wander to his quarter; there shall be no one to save you.

Isaiah – Chapter 48

שִׁמְעוּ־זֹאת בֵּית־יַעֲקֹב֙ הַנִּקְרָאִים֙ בְּשֵׁם יִשְׂרָאֵל וּמִמֵּי יְהוּדָה יָצָ֑אוּ הַנִּשְׁבָּעִים֙ בְּשֵׁם יְהֹוָה וּבֵאלֹהֵי יִשְׂרָאֵל֙ יַזְכִּ֫ירוּ לֹא בֶאֱמֶת וְלֹא בִצְדָקָֽה

1[9] Hear this, O house of Jacob, who are called by the name of Israel, and come forth from the fountain of Judah; who swear by the name of the LORD, and make mention of the God of Israel, but not in truth, nor in righteousness.

כִּֽי־מֵעִיר הַקֹּ֫דֶשׁ נִקְרָ֫אוּ וְעַל־אֱלֹהֵי יִשְׂרָאֵל נִסְמָ֑כוּ יְהֹוָה צְבָאוֹת שְׁמֽוֹ

2[10] For they call themselves of the holy city, And stay themselves upon the God of Israel, The LORD of hosts is His name.

הָרִֽאשֹׁנוֹת מֵאָז הִגַּ֫דְתִּי וּמִפִּי יָצְאוּ וְאַשְׁמִיעֵ֑ם פִּתְאֹם עָשִׂ֫יתִי וַתָּבֹֽאנָה

3[11] I have declared the former things from of old; Yes, they went forth from My mouth, and I announced them; Suddenly I did them, and they came to pass.

מִדַּעְתִּ֫י כִּי קָשֶׁה אָ֑תָּה וְגִיד בַּרְזֶל עָרְפֶּ֫ךָ וּמִצְחֲךָ נְחוּשָֽׁה

4[12] *Because I knew*[13] you are obstinate, And your neck is an iron sinew, and your brow brass;

Matthew 18:34, Nehemiah 4:11, Psalms 50:22, Revelation 3:3 18:9-18:10

[1] Isaiah 47:12 - 2 Thessalonians 2:9-2:12, Acts 13:8-13:12, Daniel 5:7-5:9, Exodus 7:11 8:3 8:14-8:19 9:11, Isaiah 8:19 19:3 20:25 47:9-47:10, Jeremiah 2:28, Nahum 3:4, Revelation 17:4-17:6, Sibylline Oracles 3.225

[2] *Missing in 1QIsaa; LXX if you can be profited*

[3] Isaiah 47:13 - Daniel 2:2-10 5:7-8 5:15-16 5:30, Derech Hashem Part II 7§4, Ezekiel 24:12, Genesis.R 85:2, Guide for the Perplexed 1:22, Habakkuk 2:13, Isaiah 20:25 23:15 9:10, Jeremiah 3:58, mt.Hilchot Yesodei haTorah 10:3, Numbers.R 20:7, z.Pekudei 232a
Isaiah 47:13-14 - Midrash Tanchuma Balak 4

[4] LXX *astrologers of the heavens*

[5] 1QIsaa *them*

[6] Isaiah 47:14 - Ezekiel 15:7, Isaiah 5:24 10:17 6:14 16:24 17:2, Jeremiah 51:25-51:26 3:30 3:32 3:58, Joel 2:5, Malachi 3:19, Matthew 10:28 16:26, Nahum 1:10, Obadiah 1:18, Pesikta Rabbati 12:6, Psalms 83:14-83:16, Revelation 18:21

[7] LXX *all shall be burned up as sticks in the fire; neither shall they at all deliver their life from the flame. Because you have coals of fire, sit you upon them*

[8] Isaiah 47:15 - Ezekiel 27:12-27:25, Isaiah 8:11, Jeremiah 51:6-51:9, Revelation 18:11-18:19

[9] Isaiah 48:1 - 1 Timothy 4:2, 2 Kings 17:34, 2 Timothy 3:2-5, Deuteronomy 5:28 6:13 10:20 9:28, Exodus 23:13, Genesis 8:29 11:10, Isaiah 1:10-14 2:13 20:5 10:2 14:8 17:16, Jeremiah 4:2 5:2 7:9-10, John 1:47 4:24, Leviticus 19:12, Malachi 3:5, Matthew 15:8-9 23:13, Numbers 24:7, Proverbs 5:16, Psalms 50:16-20 63:12 66:3 68:27, Revelation 2:9 3:9, Romans 2:17 2:28-29 9:6 9:8, Zephaniah 1:5
Isaiah 48:1-22 - 1QIsaa

[10] Isaiah 48:2 - 1 Samuel 4:3-5, b.Chagigah 16a, Daniel 9:24, Isaiah 10:20 23:4 3:13 4:1 64:11-12, Jeremiah 7:4-11 10:16 21:2, John 8:40-41, Judges 17:13, Matthew 4:5 3:53, Micah 3:11, Nehemiah 11:1 11:18, Psalms 48:2 87:3, Revelation 11:2 21:2 22:19, Romans 2:17

[11] Isaiah 48:3 - Isaiah 10:12-19 10:33-34 13:7 13:29 37:36-38 17:22 18:9 19:9 44:7-8 21:21 46:9-10, Joshua 21:45 23:14-15

[12] Isaiah 48:4 - 2 Chronicles 6:8 12:13, 2 Kings 17:14, Acts 7:51, Daniel 5:20, Deuteronomy 10:16 7:27, Exodus 8:9 9:3 9:5, Ezekiel 3:4-9, Guide for the Perplexed 3:8, Hebrews 3:13, Isaiah 22:12, Jeremiah 3:3 5:3 7:26 19:15, Midrash Tanchuma Terumah 11, mt.Hilchot Teshuvah 4:2, Nehemiah 9:16-17 9:28, Proverbs 5:1, Psalms 75:6 78:8, Romans 2:5, Zechariah 7:11-12

[13] 1QIsaa *Because of my knowledge*

וָאַגִּיד לְךָ מֵאָז בְּטֶרֶם תָּבוֹא הִשְׁמַעְתִּיךָ פֶּן־תֹּאמַר
עָצְבִּי עָשָׂם וּפִסְלִי וְנִסְכִּי צִוָּם

5[1] Therefore, I have declared it to you from old; Before it came to pass I announced it to you; Lest you should say: 'My idol have done this, And my graven image, and my molten image, commanded them.'

שָׁמַעְתָּ חֲזֵה כֻּלָּהּ וְאַתֶּם הֲלוֹא תַגִּידוּ הִשְׁמַעְתִּיךָ
חֲדָשׁוֹת מֵעַתָּה וּנְצֻרוֹת וְלֹא יְדַעְתָּם

6[2] You have heard, see, all this; And you, will you not declare it? I have announced to you new things from this time, hidden things, which you have not known.

עַתָּה נִבְרְאוּ וְלֹא מֵאָז וְלִפְנֵי־יוֹם וְלֹא שְׁמַעְתָּם
פֶּן־תֹּאמַר הִנֵּה יְדַעְתִּין

7 They are created now, and not from of old, And before this day you have not heard them; lest you should say: 'Behold, I knew them.'

גַּם לֹא־שָׁמַעְתָּ גַּם לֹא יָדַעְתָּ גַּם מֵאָז לֹא־פִתְּחָה
אָזְנֶךָ כִּי יָדַעְתִּי בָּגוֹד תִּבְגּוֹד וּפֹשֵׁעַ מִבֶּטֶן קֹרָא
לָךְ

8[3] Yes, you never heard; Yes, you never knew; Yes, from of old your ear was not opened; For I knew you would deal very treacherously, And were called a transgressor from the womb.

לְמַעַן שְׁמִי אַאֲרִיךְ אַפִּי וּתְהִלָּתִי אֶחֱטָם־לָךְ
לְבִלְתִּי הַכְרִיתֶךָ

9[4] *For My name's sake I will defer my anger, and for My praise I will refrain for you, so I do not cut you off[5].*

הִנֵּה צְרַפְתִּיךָ וְלֹא בְכָסֶף בְּחַרְתִּיךָ בְּכוּר עֹנִי

10[6] Behold, I have *refined*[7] you, but not as silver; I have *tried*[8] you in the furnace of affliction.

לְמַעֲנִי לְמַעֲנִי אֶעֱשֶׂה כִּי אֵיךְ יֵחָל וּכְבוֹדִי לְאַחֵר
לֹא־אֶתֵּן

11[9] For my own sake, *for my own sake*[10], I do it; For how should it be profaned? And My glory I will not give to another.

שְׁמַע אֵלַי יַעֲקֹב וְיִשְׂרָאֵל מְקֹרָאִי אֲנִי־הוּא אֲנִי
רִאשׁוֹן אַף אֲנִי אַחֲרוֹן

12[11] Listen to Me, O Jacob, And Israel My called: I am He; I am the first, and I am the last.

אַף־יָדִי יָסְדָה אֶרֶץ וִימִינִי טִפְּחָה שָׁמָיִם קֹרֵא אֲנִי
אֲלֵיהֶם יַעַמְדוּ יַחְדָּו

13[12] Yes, My hand laid the foundation of the earth, And My right hand spread out the heavens; When I call to them, They stand up together.

---

[1] Isaiah 48:5 - Acts 15:18, Deuteronomy.R 2:18, Gates of Repentance 3.231, Isaiah 42:8-9 20:7 22:10 46:10, Jeremiah 44:15-18, Luke 1:70

[2] Isaiah 48:6 - 1 Corinthians 2:9, 1 Peter 1:10-12, Acts 1:8, Amos 3:6, Daniel 12:8-13, Isaiah 21:10 18:9 43:8-10 19:19, Jeremiah 2:31 2:2, John 15:15, Matthew 10:27, Micah 6:9, Psalms 40:10-11 71:15-18 78:3-6 11:43 23:13 145:4-5, Revelation 1:19 4:1 5:1-2 6:1-17, Romans 16:25-26
Isaiah 48:6-8 - 4QIsab

[3] Isaiah 48:8 - Deuteronomy 9:7-24, Ephesians 2:3, Ezekiel 16:3-5, Gates of Repentance 3.2, Hosea 5:7 6:7, Isaiah 6:9-10 21:2 2:11 29:10-11 42:19-20 22:8 24:4 2:5, Jeremiah 3:7-11 3:20 5:11 5:21 6:10, John 12:39-40, Malachi 2:11, Matthew 13:13-15, Pesikta Rabbati 12:1, Psalms 40:7 51:6 58:4 139:1-4
Isaiah 48:8-22 - 4QIsad

[4] Isaiah 48:9 - 1 Samuel 12:22, Bahir 5, Daniel 9:17-19, Ezekiel 20:9 20:14 20:22 20:44, Isaiah 6:18 13:35 19:25 24:11, Jeremiah 14:7, Joshua 7:9, Midrash Tanchuma Bamidbar 24, Nehemiah 9:30-31, Numbers.R 5:6, Proverbs 19:11, Psalms 25:11 78:38 79:9 103:8-10 10:8 23:11

[5] LXX *For my own sake will I show you my wrath, and will bring before you my glorious acts, that I may not utterly destroy you*

[6] Isaiah 48:10 - 1 Kings 8:51, 1 Peter 1:7 4:12, b.Chagigah 9b, Deuteronomy 4:20, Ezekiel 20:38 22:18-22, Hebrews 12:10-11, Isaiah 1:25-26, Jeremiah 9:8, Job 23:10, Malachi 3:2-3, Proverbs 17:3, Psalms 66:10, Revelation 3:19, Zechariah 13:8-9
Isaiah 48:10-15 - 4QIsac

[7] LXX *sold*

[8] LXX *rescued*

[9] Isaiah 48:11 - 1 Samuel 12:22, 3 Enoch 48A:9, b.Pesachim 114a, b.Sanhedrin 98a, Deuteronomy 32:26-32:27, Ein Yaakov Pesachim:117a, Ein Yaakov Sanhedrin:97b, Ezekiel 20:9 20:14 20:22 20:39 20:44, Isaiah 13:35 18:8 19:25 24:5 4:5, Jeremiah 14:7, John 5:23, Mekhilta de R'Shimon bar Yochai Beshallach 23:1, Mekhilta de R'Ishmael Beshallah 4:48, Midrash Psalms 107:1, Numbers 14:15-14:16, Romans 2:24, Ruth.R 2:11

[10] Missing in LXX

[11] Isaiah 48:12 - 1 Corinthians 1:24, 1 Peter 2:9, Deuteronomy 8:39, Ein Yaakov Shabbat:54b, Exodus.R 1:6, Isaiah 10:1 17:4 19:11 20:6 22:3 1:1 3:1 3:4 3:7 7:3, Jastrow 404a, Leviticus.R 29:7, Matthew 20:16, Mekhilta de R'Shimon bar Yochai Shirata 30:1, Midrash Psalms 14:7, Midrash Tanchuma Shemot 3, Pesikta de R'Kahana 23.7, Pesikta Rabbati 40:5 41:5, Proverbs 7:24 8:32, Revelation 1:8 1:11 1:17-1:18 2:8 17:14 22:13, Romans 1:6 8:28, y.Sotah 7:4

[12] Isaiah 48:13 - 6:59, 7:11, 3 Enoch 44:7, 4 Esdras 6:5, Assumption of Moses 1:12, b.Chagigah 12a, b.Ketubot 5a, b.Menachot 36b, Bahir 45, Chibbur Yafeh 6 {23a}, Ein Yaakov Chagigah:12a, Ein Yaakov Ketubot:5a, Exodus 20:11, Genesis.R 1:15 36:2, Hebrews 1:10-1:12, Isaiah 16:12 16:22 16:26 18:5 21:18, Job 13:18, Joseph and Aseneth 12:2, Lamentations.R 1:50 1:51, Leviticus.R 36:1, m.Tehorot 2:13-14, Mas.Kallah Rabbati 8:9, Mekhilta de R'Shimon bar Yochai Shirata 34:2 36:1, Mekhilta de R'Ishmael Pisha 17:132, Mekhilta de R'Ishmael Shirata 10:40, Midrash Psalms 50:1 137:3, Midrash Tanchuma Bereshit 5, Midrash Tanchuma Bo 14, Pesikta Rabbati 28:2, Pirkei de R'Eliezer 19, Psalms 6:26 119:89-91 3:4 148:5-8, Saadia Opinions 2:5, Sefer Yetzirah 1:3, Sifre Devarim

הִקָּבְצ֤וּ כֻלְּכֶם֙ וּֽשֲׁמָ֔עוּ מִ֥י בָהֶ֖ם הִגִּ֣יד אֶת־אֵ֑לֶּה יְהֹוָ֣ה אֲהֵב֗וֹ יַעֲשֶׂ֤ה חֶפְצוֹ֙ בְּבָבֶ֔ל וּזְרֹע֖וֹ כַּשְׂדִּֽים	14[1]	Assemble yourselves, all you, and hear; which among them has declared these things? He whom the LORD loves shall perform His pleasure on Babylon, And show His arm on the Chaldeans.
אֲנִ֥י אֲנִ֛י דִּבַּ֖רְתִּי אַף־קְרָאתִ֑יו הֲבִיאֹתִ֖יו וְהִצְלִ֥יחַ דַּרְכּֽוֹ	15[2]	I, I, have spoken, yes, I have called him; I have brought him, and he shall make his way prosperous.
קִרְב֧וּ אֵלַ֣י שִׁמְעוּ־זֹ֗את לֹ֤א מֵרֹאשׁ֙ בַּסֵּ֣תֶר דִּבַּ֔רְתִּי מֵעֵ֥ת הֱיוֹתָ֖הּ שָׁ֣ם אָ֑נִי וְעַתָּ֗ה אֲדֹנָ֧י יֱהֹוִ֛ה שְׁלָחַ֖נִי וְרוּחֽוֹ	16[3]	Come near to Me, hear this: From the beginning I have not spoken in secret; From the time that was, there am I; And now the Lord GOD has sent me, and His spirit.
כֹּֽה־אָמַ֧ר יְהֹוָ֛ה גֹּאַלְךָ֖ קְד֣וֹשׁ יִשְׂרָאֵ֑ל אֲנִ֨י יְהֹוָ֤ה אֱלֹהֶ֙יךָ֙ מְלַמֶּדְךָ֣ לְהוֹעִ֔יל מַדְרִֽיכֲךָ֖ בְּדֶ֥רֶךְ תֵּלֵֽךְ	17[4]	Thus says the LORD, your Redeemer, The Holy One of Israel: I am the LORD your God, *who teaches you for your profit, Who leads you by the way you should go*[5].
ל֥וּא הִקְשַׁ֖בְתָּ לְמִצְוֺתָ֑י וַיְהִ֤י כַנָּהָר֙ שְׁלוֹמֶ֔ךָ וְצִדְקָתְךָ֖ כְּגַלֵּ֥י הַיָּֽם	18[6]	Oh that you would listen to my commandments! Then your peace would be like a river, And your righteousness as the waves of the sea;
וַיְהִ֤י כַחוֹל֙ זַרְעֶ֔ךָ וְצֶאֱצָאֵ֥י מֵעֶ֖יךָ כִּמְעֹתָ֑יו לֹֽא־יִכָּרֵ֧ת וְֽלֹא־יִשָּׁמֵ֛ד שְׁמ֖וֹ מִלְּפָנָֽי	19[7]	Your seed would be as the sand, And the offspring *of your body*[8] like its grains; His name would not be cut off nor destroyed from before Me.
צְא֣וּ מִבָּבֶל֮ בִּרְח֣וּ מִכַּשְׂדִּים֒ בְּק֣וֹל רִנָּ֗ה הַגִּ֤ידוּ הַשְׁמִ֙יעוּ֙ זֹ֔את הוֹצִיא֖וּהָ עַד־קְצֵ֣ה הָאָ֑רֶץ אִמְר֕וּ גָּאַ֥ל יְהֹוָ֖ה עַבְדּ֥וֹ יַעֲקֹֽב	20[9]	Go forth from Babylon, flee from the Chaldeans; With a voice of singing declare, tell this, utter it to the end of the earth; say: 'The LORD has redeemed His servant Jacob.
וְלֹ֣א צָמְא֗וּ בׇּחֳרָבוֹת֙ הֽוֹלִיכָ֔ם מַ֥יִם מִצּ֖וּר הִזִּ֣יל לָ֑מוֹ וַיִּ֨בְקַע־צ֔וּר וַיָּזֻ֖בוּ מָֽיִם	21[10]	And they did not thirst when He led them through the deserts; He caused the waters to flow out of the rock for them; He cleaved the rock also, and the waters gushed out[11].'

Vaetchanan 35, y.Chagigah 2:1, z.Bereshit 30a, z.Bo 37a

[1] Isaiah 48:14 - Isaiah 13:4-13:5 13:17-13:18 17:22 19:9 20:7 44:28-45:3 45:20-45:21 46:10-46:11, Jeremiah 50:21-50:29 51:20-51:24, Mark 10:21, mt.Hilchot Teshuvah 4:2

[2] Isaiah 48:15 - Ezekiel 1:2, Isaiah 45:1-45:2, Joshua 1:8, Leviticus.R 1:9, Psalms 45:5

[3] Isaiah 48:16 - b.Moed Katan 16b, b.Shabbat 86b, Ecclesiastes.R 1:29, Ein Yaakov Moed Katan:9b, Exodus.R 28:6, Isaiah 11:1-11:5 17:1 21:19 48:3-48:6 61:1-61:3, John 3:34 18:20 20:21-20:22, Luke 4:18, Midrash Tanchuma Yitro 11, Saadia Opinions 2:3, Tanna Devei Eliyahu 2, Zechariah 2:8-2:11

[4] Isaiah 48:17 - 1 Kings 8:36, Deuteronomy 8:17-8:18, Ein Yaakov Makkot:9b, Ephesians 4:21, Isaiah 2:3 6:20 19:14 19:16 44:6-44:24 24:20 1:7 49:9-49:10 6:5 6:13, Jastrow 1019a, Jeremiah 6:16 31:34-31:35, Job 22:21-22:22 12:22, John 6:45, Leviticus.R 29:7, Micah 4:2, Midrash Tanchuma Shelach 14, Numbers.R 17:1, Pesikta de R'Kahana 23.7, Psalms 25:8-25:9 25:12 32:8 71:17 73:24, Saadia Opinions 1:4 Intro:2, Sefer Yetzirah 6:4, z.Vaetchanan 269b

Isaiah 48:17-19 - 4QIsac

Isaiah 48:17-22 - 1QIsab

[5] LXX *I have shown you how you should find the way you should walk*

[6] Isaiah 48:18 - Amos 5:24, b.Avodah Zara 5a, b.Berachot 6a, Deuteronomy 5:29 8:29, Isaiah 32:15-32:18 21:8 18:12, Luke 19:41-19:42, Matthew 23:37, Numbers.R 5:9, Psalms 36:9 81:14-81:17 119:165, Romans 14:17

Isaiah 48:18-19 - Ein Yaakov Berachot:6a

[7] Isaiah 48:19 - 1 Kings 9:7, b.Avodah Zara 5a, b.Berachot 6a, Genesis 13:16 22:17, Hosea 2:1, Isaiah 9:15 10:22 14:22 24:9 8:5 18:22, Jeremiah 9:22, Joshua 7:9, Mekilta de R'Ishmael Nezikin 18:110, Psalms 9:6 13:13, Romans 9:27, Ruth 4:10, Zephaniah 1:4

[8] Missing in 1QIsaa

[9] Isaiah 48:20 - 2 Samuel 7:23, Exodus 15:1-15:21 19:4-19:6, Isaiah 12:1 2:1 45:22-45:23 24:6 1:13 4:9 4:11 15:9, Jeremiah 7:11 31:13-31:14 2:2 3:6 3:45 3:48, Psalms 6:1, Revelation 18:4 18:20 19:1-19:6, Zechariah 2:6-2:7

[10] Isaiah 48:21 - Exodus 17:6, Isaiah 6:25 35:6-35:7 41:17-41:18 43:19-43:20 1:10, Jeremiah 7:10, Nehemiah 9:15, Numbers 20:11, Psalms 78:15 78:20 9:41

[11] LXX adds *and my people shall drink*

אֵין שָׁלוֹם אָמַר יְהוָה לָרְשָׁעִים 22[1]

There is no *peace*[2], says the LORD concerning the wicked.

Isaiah – Chapter 49

שִׁמְעוּ אִיִּים אֵלַי וְהַקְשִׁיבוּ לְאֻמִּים מֵרָחוֹק יְהוָה 1[3]
מִבֶּטֶן קְרָאָנִי מִמְּעֵי אִמִּי הִזְכִּיר שְׁמִי

Listen to me, O isles, *and Listen, you peoples, in afar nations: The LORD has called me from the womb, From the womb of my mother He mentioned my name*[4];

וַיָּשֶׂם פִּי כְּחֶרֶב חַדָּה בְּצֵל יָדוֹ הֶחְבִּיאָנִי וַיְשִׂימֵנִי 2[5]
לְחֵץ בָּרוּר בְּאַשְׁפָּתוֹ הִסְתִּירָנִי

And He has made my mouth like a sharp sword, In the shadow of His hand has He hid me; And He has made me a polished shaft, In His quiver has He concealed me;

וַיֹּאמֶר לִי עַבְדִּי-אָתָּה יִשְׂרָאֵל אֲשֶׁר-בְּךָ אֶתְפָּאָר 3[6]

And He said to me: 'You are My servant, Israel, in whom I will be glorified.'

וַאֲנִי אָמַרְתִּי לְרִיק יָגַעְתִּי לְתֹהוּ וְהֶבֶל כֹּחִי כִלֵּיתִי 4[7]
אָכֵן מִשְׁפָּטִי אֶת-יְהוָה וּפְעֻלָּתִי אֶת-אֱלֹהָי

But I said: 'I have labored in vain, I have spent my strength for nothing and vanity; Yet surely my cause is with the LORD, And my recompense with my God.'

וְעַתָּה אָמַר יְהוָה יֹצְרִי מִבֶּטֶן לְעֶבֶד לוֹ לְשׁוֹבֵב 5[8]
יַעֲקֹב אֵלָיו וְיִשְׂרָאֵל "לֹא" "לוֹ" יֵאָסֵף וְאֶכָּבֵד
בְּעֵינֵי יְהוָה וֵאלֹהַי הָיָה עֻזִּי

And now says [9]the Lord who formed me from the womb to be His servant, To bring Jacob back to Him, so Israel may be gathered to Him, for I am honorable in the eyes of the LORD, And my God is become my strength.

וַיֹּאמֶר נָקֵל מִהְיוֹתְךָ לִי עֶבֶד לְהָקִים אֶת-שִׁבְטֵי 6[10]
יַעֲקֹב "וּנְצִירֵי" "וּנְצוּרֵי" יִשְׂרָאֵל לְהָשִׁיב וּנְתַתִּיךָ
לְאוֹר גּוֹיִם לִהְיוֹת יְשׁוּעָתִי עַד-קְצֵה הָאָרֶץ

Yes, He says: '*It is too light a thing that you should be*[11] My servant to raise up the tribes of Jacob, and to *restore the offspring*[12] of Israel; I will also give you as a light of the nations, so My salvation may be to the end of the earth.'

---

[1] Isaiah 48:22 - b.Chagigah 15a, b.Ketubot 41a, b.Shabbat 152b, Deuteronomy.R 5:15, Ein Yaakov Chagigah:15a, Ein Yaakov Ketubot:104a, Ein Yaakov Shabbat:152b, Isaiah 9:21, Job 15:20-15:24, Luke 19:42, Midrash Psalms 116:7, Numbers.R 11:7, Romans 3:17, z.Lech Lecha 76b, z.Mikketz 205a

[2] LXX *joy*

[3] Isaiah 49:1 - 1 Peter 1:20, Ephesians 2:17, Galatians 1:15, Genesis.R 98 [Excl]:2, Hebrews 12:25, Isaiah 7:14 9:7 17:1 42:1-4 18:12 20:2 20:24 21:22 22:3 1:5 3:5 7:3 9:19 12:9 18:19, Jeremiah 1:5, John 10:36, Luke 1:15 1:31 2:10-2:11, Matthew 1:20-21, Midrash Psalms 9:7 58:2 139:6, Psalms 71:5-6, Sibylline Oracles 3.710, Zephaniah 2:11
Isaiah 49:1-6 - Psalms of Solomon 12:6 17:21
Isaiah 49:1-15 - 1QIsab, 4QIsad
Isaiah 49:1-26 - 1QIsaa

[4] LXX *and attend, you Gentiles; after a long time it shall come to pass, says the LORD: from my mother's womb he called my name*

[5] Isaiah 49:2 - 4Q437 frag 2 1.8-9, Hebrews 4:12, Hosea 6:5, Isaiah 11:4 18:1 2:4 3:16 61:1-61:3, Jeremiah 1:18 15:19-15:20, Luke 23:46, Midrash Psalms 58:2, Psalms 45:3-45:6 91:1, Revelation 1:16 2:12 19:15, z.Acharei Mot 62a, z.Vayikra 4b

[6] Isaiah 49:3 - 1 Peter 2:9, 2 Baruch 70:10 3 Enoch 10:3, b.Yoma 86a, Birchat HaChammah.Ribono Shel Olam, Chibbur Yafeh 23 {102b}, Ein Yaakov Yoma:86a, Ephesians 1:6, Esther.R 7:10, Exodus.R 21:4, Gates of Repentance 3.113, Genesis.R 68:12, Isaiah 18:1 19:21 20:23 4:13 5:10, John 12:28 13:31-32 15:8 17:1 17:4, Kuzari 2.50, Leviticus.R 2:5, Luke 2:10-14, Mas.Kallah Rabbati 8:9, Matthew 17:5, Mekhilta de R'Shimon bar Yochai Shirata 29:1, Mekilta de R'Ishmael Shirata 3:22, Midrash Psalms 58:2, Midrash Tanchuma Balak 12, Midrash Tanchuma Kedoshim 1 2, Midrash Tanchuma Ki Tissa 8, Midrash Tanchuma Shemini 2, mt.Hilchot Yesodei haTorah 5:11, Numbers.R 20:19, Pesikta de R'Kahana 2.7, Philippians 2:6-11, Sifre Devarim Vezot Habracha 355, z.Bamidbar 120b, z.Beha'alotcha 155a, z.Lech Lecha 96a, z.Noach 73a, z.Shemini 41b, z.Terumah 152b 160b 176a, z.Vaetchanan 265a, z.Vayakhel 201a 203a 209a, z.Vayikra 8b 22a, z.Vayishlach 169a, z.Yitro 79a 84a 87b, Zechariah 3:8

[7] Isaiah 49:4 - 2 Corinthians 2:15 12:15, Exodus.R 52:3, Ezekiel 3:19, Galatians 4:11, Genesis.R 62:2, Hebrews 12:2, Isaiah 11:4 16:10 53:10-12 14:11 17:2 17:23, John 1:11 17:4-5, Leviticus 2:20, Luke 24:26, Matthew 17:17 23:37, Midrash Tanchuma Bereshit 1, Midrash Tanchuma Vayechi 4, Philippians 2:9-10, Psalms 22:23-32, Romans 10:21, y.Avodah Zarah 3:1, z.Yitro 90b

[8] Isaiah 49:5 - 1 Peter 3:22, 1 Thessalonians 2:15-16, Acts 10:36, Avot de R'Natan 34, Ephesians 1:20-22, Isaiah 11:12 12:2 19:4 1:1 2:4 4:13 8:8, John 3:35 5:20-27, Luke 19:42, Mas.Soferim 6:6, Matthew 3:17 11:27 15:24 17:5 21:37-41 23:37 4:18, Midrash Tanchuma Haazinu 2, Pesikta Rabbati 26:1/2, Psalms 110:1-3, Romans 15:8, Sifre Devarim Vaetchanan 27

[9] 1QIsaa adds *my LORD*

[10] Isaiah 49:6 - 2 Kings 3:18 20:10, Acts 13:47 2:18, Isaiah 11:10 24:14-24:16 18:6 22:13 4:10 12:3, Jastrow 929a, John 1:4-1:9, Luke 2:32 24:46-24:47, mt.Hilchot Deot 5:13 5:13, Psalms 98:2-98:3, Psalms of Solomon 17:28, Sibylline Oracles 14.214, Testament of Levi 14:3, y.Sheviit 4:8

[11] LXX *It is a great thing for you to be called*

[12] LXX *recover the dispersion*

כֹּה אָמַר־יְהֹוָה גֹּאֵל יִשְׂרָאֵל קְדוֹשׁוֹ לִבְזֹה־נֶפֶשׁ לִמְתָעֵב גּוֹי לְעֶבֶד מֹשְׁלִים מְלָכִים יִרְאוּ וָקָמוּ שָׂרִים וְיִשְׁתַּחֲוּוּ לְמַעַן יְהֹוָה אֲשֶׁר נֶאֱמָן קְדֹשׁ יִשְׂרָאֵל וַיִּבְחָרֶךָ	7[1]	Thus says the LORD, The Redeemer of Israel, his Holy One, To he who is despised of men, to he who is abhorred of nations, to a servant of rulers: kings shall see and rise, princes shall prostrate themselves; because of the Lord who is faithful, the Holy One of Israel, who has chosen you.
כֹּה אָמַר יְהֹוָה בְּעֵת רָצוֹן עֲנִיתִיךָ וּבְיוֹם יְשׁוּעָה עֲזַרְתִּיךָ וְאֶצָּרְךָ וְאֶתֶּנְךָ לִבְרִית עָם לְהָקֵים אֶרֶץ לְהַנְחִיל נְחָלוֹת שֹׁמֵמוֹת	8[2]	Thus says the LORD: In an acceptable time I have answered you, and in a day of salvation I have helped you; and I *will preserve*[3] you, and give you as a covenant to the people, to raise up the land, to inherit the desolate heritages;
לֵאמֹר לַאֲסוּרִים צֵאוּ לַאֲשֶׁר בַּחֹשֶׁךְ הִגָּלוּ עַל־דְּרָכִים יִרְעוּ וּבְכָל־שְׁפָיִים מַרְעִיתָם	9[4]	Saying to the prisoners: 'Go forth'; To those who are in darkness: 'Show yourselves'; They shall feed *in the ways*[5], And their pasture shall be in all high hills.
לֹא יִרְעָבוּ וְלֹא יִצְמָאוּ וְלֹא־יַכֵּם שָׁרָב וָשָׁמֶשׁ כִּי־מְרַחֲמָם יְנַהֲגֵם וְעַל־מַבּוּעֵי מַיִם יְנַהֲלֵם	10[6]	They shall not hunger nor thirst, nor shall the heat or sun strike them; for He who has compassion on them will lead them, He will guide them by the springs of water.
וְשַׂמְתִּי כָל־הָרַי לַדָּרֶךְ וּמְסִלֹּתַי יְרֻמוּן	11[7]	And I will make all My mountains a way, And My highways shall be raised on high.
הִנֵּה־אֵלֶּה מֵרָחוֹק יָבֹאוּ וְהִנֵּה־אֵלֶּה מִצָּפוֹן וּמִיָּם וְאֵלֶּה מֵאֶרֶץ סִינִים	12[8]	Behold, these shall come from far; And these from the north and from the west, And these from the land of *Sinim*[9].
רָנּוּ שָׁמַיִם וְגִילִי אָרֶץ "יִפְצְחוּ" "וּפִצְחוּ" הָרִים רִנָּה כִּי־נִחַם יְהֹוָה עַמּוֹ וַעֲנִיָּו יְרַחֵם	13[10]	Sing, O heavens, and be joyful, O earth, And break forth into singing, O mountains; For the LORD has comforted His people, And has compassion on His afflicted.

[1] Isaiah 49:7 - 1 Peter 2:4, 4Q176 frag 1-2 2.1-6, b.Sanhedrin 97b, b.Taanit 14a, Ein Yaakov Sanhedrin 97b, Ein Yaakov Taanit 15a, Exodus.R 15:17, Isaiah 18:1 24:7 24:17 1:1 1:23 2:6 4:15 5:3 12:3 12:10 12:16, John 18:40 19:6 19:15, Joseph and Aseneth 27:10, Luke 22:27 23:18 23:23 23:35, Mas.Derek Eretz Rabbah 2:14, Matthew 20:28 26:67 27:38-44, Midrash Tanchuma Mishpatim 5, Psalms 2:10-12 22:7-9 68:32 69:8-10 69:20 72:10-11, Revelation 3:7 11:15, z.Vaetchanan 269b, Zechariah 11:8

[2] Isaiah 49:8 - 2 Corinthians 6:2, Acts 2:24-32, b.Berachot 8a, b.Gittin [Tosefot] 50a, b.Sanhedrin 102a, Ein Yaakov Berachot 8a, Ein Yaakov Sanhedrin:102a, Ephesians 1:6 2:12-19, Gates of Repentance 2.14, Hebrews 5:7 8:6 12:24, Isaiah 2:3 18:1 18:6 20:26 1:19 50:7-9 3:3 3:16 6:3 10:12 13:4, Jastrow 962b, John 11:41-42, Matthew 2:28, Midrash Psalms 69:2, Pesikta Rabbati 31:1, Psalms 2:8 69:14 75:4, Siman 12:7, z.Vaetchanan 269b
Isaiah 49:8-9 - Midrash Tanchuma Noach 1
[3] LXX *have formed*
[4] Isaiah 49:9 - 1 Peter 2:9, 1 Thessalonians 5:5-5:6, 2 Corinthians 4:4-4:6, Acts 2:18, Colossians 1:13, Deuteronomy 8:13, Ephesians 5:8 5:14, Ezekiel 34:13-34:15 10:23 10:29, Isaiah 5:17 9:3 17:18 18:7 18:16 55:1-55:2 60:1-60:2 13:1 17:13, Joel 4:18, John 6:53-6:58 8:12 10:9, Joseph and Aseneth 4:10, Lamentations.R 2:9, Luke 1:79 4:18, Numbers.R 16:25, Pesikta Rabbati 31:1, Psalms 22:27 23:1-23:2 69:34 6:21 107:10-107:16 2:7, y.Sanhedrin 10:5, Zechariah 9:11-9:12
[5] 1QIsaa *upon all the mountains*
[6] Isaiah 49:10 - Apocalypse of Elijah 1:10 5:6, b.Bava Kamma 92b, b.Bava Metzia 107b, b.Sanhedrin 92a, Ein Yaakov Bava Kamma:92b, Ein Yaakov Bava Metzia:107b, Ezekiel 10:23, Isaiah 4:6 14:1 1:4 8:2 9:16 11:7 16:11 6:10, Jeremiah 7:10, John 6:35 10:3-10:4, Lamentations R 1:23, Matthew 5:6, Mekhilta de R'Shimon bar Yochai Beshallach 20:5, Pesikta Rabbati 31:1, Psalms 23:2-23:4 121:5-121:6, Revelation 7:16-7:17
[7] Isaiah 49:11 - Isaiah 11:16 35:8-10 40:3-4 19:19 9:14 14:10, John 14:6, Luke 3:4-5, Pesikta de R'Kahana S6.1, Pesikta Rabbati 31:1, Psalms 11:4 11:7
[8] Isaiah 49:12 - Exodus.R 51:8, Isaiah 2:2-3 11:10-11 43:5-6 60:9-14 66:19-20, Luke 13:29, Matthew 8:11, Micah 4:2, Numbers.R 16:25, Pesikta de R'Kahana 12.22, Pesikta Rabbati 31:1, Psalms 22:28 72:10-11 72:17, Revelation 7:9 11:15, Zechariah 2:11 8:20-23
[9] 1QIsaa *Syene*; LXX *the Persians*
[10] Isaiah 49:13 - 2 Corinthians 7:6, 2 Thessalonians 2:16-17, Exodus.R 31:5 31:13, Isaiah 12:1 40:1-2 42:10-11 20:23 3:3 4:9 7:12 61:2-3 66:13-14, Jeremiah 7:14, Luke 2:13-14 15:10, Mekhilta de R'Shimon bar Yochai Shirata 32:3, Mekilta de R'Ishmael Shirata 6:147, Midrash Proverbs 19, Midrash Tanchuma Mishpatim 9, Pesikta Rabbati 31:8 31:10, Psalms 96:11-13 98:4-9, Revelation 5:8-13 7:9-12, z.Shemot 20a
Isaiah 49:13-17 - 4Q176 frag 1-2 2.1-6

וַתֹּאמֶר צִיּוֹן עֲזָבַנִי יְהֹוָה וַאדֹנָי שְׁכֵחָנִי	14[1]	But Zion said: 'The LORD has forsaken me, And *the Lord*[2] has forgotten me.'
הֲתִשְׁכַּח אִשָּׁה עוּלָהּ מֵרַחֵם בֶּן־בִּטְנָהּ גַּם־אֵלֶּה תִשְׁכַּחְנָה וְאָנֹכִי לֹא אֶשְׁכָּחֵךְ	15[3]	Can a woman forget her sucking child, so she should not have compassion on the son of her womb? Yes, these may forget, Yet I will not forget you[4].
הֵן עַל־כַּפַּיִם חַקֹּתִיךְ חוֹמֹתַיִךְ נֶגְדִּי תָּמִיד	16[5]	Behold, I have en*graved you on the palms of My hands; your walls are always before Me*[6].
מִהֲרוּ בָּנָיִךְ מְהָרְסַיִךְ וּמַחֲרִבַיִךְ מִמֵּךְ יֵצֵאוּ	17[7]	*Your children*[8] hurry; *Your destroyers*[9] and those who made you desolate shall go forth from you.
שְׂאִי־סָבִיב עֵינַיִךְ וּרְאִי כֻּלָּם נִקְבְּצוּ בָאוּ־לָךְ חַי־אָנִי נְאֻם־יְהֹוָה כִּי כֻלָּם כָּעֲדִי תִלְבָּשִׁי וּתְקַשְּׁרִים כַּכַּלָּה	18[10]	Lift up your eyes all around, and see: All these gather themselves together, and come to you. As I live, says the LORD, You shall surely clothe yourself with them as an ornament, And clothe yourself with them, like a bride.
כִּי חָרְבֹתַיִךְ וְשֹׁמְמֹתַיִךְ וְאֶרֶץ הֲרִסֻתֵיךְ כִּי עַתָּה תֵּצְרִי מִיּוֹשֵׁב וְרָחֲקוּ מְבַלְּעָיִךְ	19[11]	For your wasted and desolate places And your land that has been destroyed; Surely you shall be too strict for the inhabitants, And they who swallowed you shall be far away.
עוֹד יֹאמְרוּ בְאָזְנַיִךְ בְּנֵי שִׁכֻּלָיִךְ צַר־לִי הַמָּקוֹם גְּשָׁה־לִּי וְאֵשֵׁבָה	20[12]	The children of your bereavement shall yet say in your ears: 'The place is too strict for me; Give me a place so I may live.'
וְאָמַרְתְּ בִּלְבָבֵךְ מִי יָלַד־לִי אֶת־אֵלֶּה וַאֲנִי שְׁכוּלָה וְגַלְמוּדָה גֹּלָה וְסוּרָה וְאֵלֶּה מִי גִדֵּל הֵן אֲנִי נִשְׁאַרְתִּי לְבַדִּי אֵלֶּה אֵיפֹה הֵם	21[13]	Then you shall say in your heart: 'Who has birthed these to me, Seeing I *have been bereft of my children, and am solitary, an exile, and wandering to and fro*[14]? And who has brought these? Behold, I was left alone; These, where were they?'

---

[1] Isaiah 49:14 - b.Berachot 32b, Ein Yaakov Berachot:32b, Isaiah 16:27, Jastrow 1061a 1572a, Jeremiah 23:39, Lamentations 5:20, Lamentations.R 1:23 3:?, Midrash Psalms 10:6, Per Massorah: Soferim altered "Hashem" to "Adonai", Pesikta de R'Kahana 17.1-6, Pesikta Rabbati 27/28:2 31:1-10, Psalms 13:2 22:2 31:23 77:7-10 89:39-47, Romans 11:1-5, z.Haazinu 298a
Isaiah 49:14-51:3 - Haftarah Ekev [Isaiah 49:14-51:3], Second Shabbat after Tisha b'Av [Pesikta Rabbati 31]
[2] 1QIsaa *my God*
[3] Isaiah 49:15 - 33:13, 1 Kings 3:26-27, 2 Kings 6:28-29 11:1-2, b.Berachot 32b, Deuteronomy 28:56-57, Hosea 11:1, Isaiah 20:21, Jeremiah 7:21, Lamentations 4:3 4:10, Lamentations.R 5:20, Leviticus 2:29, Malachi 3:17, Matthew 7:11, Midrash Psalms 10:6 32:2 121:3, Pesikta de R'Kahana 17.7-8, Pesikta Rabbati 31:8, Psalms 7:13, Romans 1:31 11:28-29, Song of Songs.R 8:6, z.Haazinu 298a 298b, z.Vayechi 228a
[4] LXX adds *says the LORD*
[5] Isaiah 49:16 - 2 Baruch 4:2, b.Taanit 4a, Ein Yaakov Taanit:4a, Exodus 13:9, Haggai 2:23, Isaiah 2:1 6:12 12:18 14:6, Jeremiah 22:24, Midrash Tanchuma Pekudei 1, Pesikta de R'Kahana 17.8, Pesikta Rabbati 27/28:2, Psalms 48:13-48:14, Revelation 21:10-21:21, Song of Songs 8:6, Song of Songs.R 8:6, z.Vayechi 228a
[6] LXX *painted your walls on my hands, and you are continually before me*
[7] Isaiah 49:17 - Ezekiel 4:24, Ezra 1:5, Isaiah 10:6 1:19 3:13 51:18-20 51:22-23 14:5, Midrash Tanchuma Pekudei 1, Nehemiah 2:4-9 2:17
[8] 1QIsaa *builders*
[9] LXX *And you shall soon be built by those who destroyed you,*
[10] Isaiah 49:18 - Deuteronomy.R 2:37, Exodus.R 21:4, Galatians 3:28-29, Genesis 13:14 22:16, Hebrews 6:13-6:18, Isaiah 43:5-6 21:23 1:12 1:22 4:1 54:1-3 6:7 6:9 60:4-11 13:10 66:12-13 18:20, Jastrow 639b, Jeremiah 2:32 7:9, Matthew 13:41-42, Midrash Tanchuma Tazria 8, Numbers.R 11:2 13:2, Pesikta de R'Kahana 22.5 S5.3, Pesikta Rabbati 31:1, Proverbs 17:6, Revelation 21:2 22:15, Sifre Devarim Vezot Habracha 356, Song of Songs.R 4:22
[11] Isaiah 49:19 - Ezekiel 12:3 36:9-15, Hosea 2:1-2:2, Isaiah 5:6 1:8 1:17 49:25-26 3:3 54:1-2, Jeremiah 6:16 30:18-19 33:10-11 3:33 3:44, Proverbs 1:12, Psalms 56:2-3 4:3, Zechariah 2:4 2:11 10:10
[12] Isaiah 49:20 - 2 Kings 6:1, Avot de R'Natan 35, Galatians 4:26-4:28, Hosea 2:1, Isaiah 3:3 54:1-54:3 12:4, Joshua 17:14-17:16, m.Avot 5:5, Matthew 3:9, Midrash Tanchuma Tzav 12, Pesikta de R'Kahana 20.7, Pesikta Rabbati 33:13, Song of Songs.R 7:11
[13] Isaiah 49:21 - b.Sotah 42a, Ein Yaakov Sotah:42a, Galatians 3:29 4:26-4:29, Genesis.R 79:7, Isaiah 1:8 3:26 5:13 51:17-51:20 4:2 54:3-54:8 12:15 14:4 16:11, Jastrow 250b, Jeremiah 31:16-31:18, Lamentations 1:1-1:3, Lamentations.R 1:23, Luke 21:24, Matthew 24:29-30, Pesikta de R'Kahana 20.1, Pesikta Rabbati 31:10 32:2, Romans 11:11-17 11:24 11:26-31, y.Berachot 9:1
Isaiah 49:21-23 - 4QIsab
[14] LXX *I was childless, and a widow*

כֹּה־אָמַר אֲדֹנָי יְהוִה הִנֵּה אֶשָּׂא אֶל־גּוֹיִם יָדִי וְאֶל־עַמִּים אָרִים נִסִּי וְהֵבִיאוּ בָנַיִךְ בְּחֹצֶן וּבְנֹתַיִךְ עַל־כָּתֵף תִּנָּשֶׂאנָה

22[1]   Thus says *the Lord GOD*[2]: Behold, I will lift up my hand to the nations, And set up my banner to the peoples, And they shall bring your sons in their bosom, And your daughters shall be carried on their shoulders.

וְהָיוּ מְלָכִים אֹמְנַיִךְ וְשָׂרוֹתֵיהֶם מֵינִיקֹתַיִךְ אַפַּיִם אֶרֶץ יִשְׁתַּחֲווּ לָךְ וַעֲפַר רַגְלַיִךְ יְלַחֵכוּ וְיָדַעַתְּ כִּי־אֲנִי יְהוָה אֲשֶׁר לֹא־יֵבֹשׁוּ קֹוָי

23[3]   And kings shall be your foster-fathers, and their queens your nursing mothers; they shall bow to you with their face to the earth, and lick the dust of your feet; and you shall know I am the LORD, For those who wait for Me shall not be ashamed.

הֲיֻקַּח מִגִּבּוֹר מַלְקוֹחַ וְאִם־שְׁבִי צַדִּיק יִמָּלֵט

24[4]   *Shall prey be taken from the mighty*[5], *or the captives of the victorious*[6] *be delivered?*

כִּי־כֹה אָמַר יְהוָה גַּם־שְׁבִי גִבּוֹר יֻקָּח וּמַלְקוֹחַ עָרִיץ יִמָּלֵט וְאֶת־יְרִיבֵךְ אָנֹכִי אָרִיב וְאֶת־בָּנַיִךְ אָנֹכִי אוֹשִׁיעַ

25[7]   But thus says the LORD: the captives of the mighty shall be taken away, and the prey of the terrible shall be delivered; and I will contend with he who contends with you, and I will save your children.

וְהַאֲכַלְתִּי אֶת־מוֹנַיִךְ אֶת־בְּשָׂרָם וְכֶעָסִיס דָּמָם יִשְׁכָּרוּן וְיָדְעוּ כָל־בָּשָׂר כִּי אֲנִי יְהוָה מוֹשִׁיעֵךְ וְגֹאֲלֵךְ אֲבִיר יַעֲקֹב

26[8]   And I will feed those who oppress you with their own flesh; and they shall be drunk with their own blood, as sweet wine; and all flesh shall know I, the LORD, am your Savior, *And your Redeemer, the Mighty One of Jacob*[9].

Isaiah – Chapter 50

כֹּה אָמַר יְהוָה אֵי זֶה סֵפֶר כְּרִיתוּת אִמְּכֶם אֲשֶׁר שִׁלַּחְתִּיהָ אוֹ מִי מִנּוֹשַׁי אֲשֶׁר־מָכַרְתִּי אֶתְכֶם לוֹ הֵן בַּעֲוֹנֹתֵיכֶם נִמְכַּרְתֶּם וּבְפִשְׁעֵיכֶם שֻׁלְּחָה אִמְּכֶם

1[10]   Thus says the LORD: Where is the bill of your mother's divorce, by which I put her away? Or to which of My creditors have I sold you? Behold, you were sold for your iniquities, and your mother was put away for your transgressions.

מַדּוּעַ בָּאתִי וְאֵין אִישׁ קָרָאתִי וְאֵין עוֹנֶה הֲקָצוֹר קָצְרָה יָדִי מִפְּדוּת וְאִם־אֵין־בִּי כֹחַ לְהַצִּיל הֵן

2[11]   Why, when I came, was there no man? When I called, was there no one to answer? *Is My hand*

---

[1] Isaiah 49:22 - 4QIsac, Isaiah 2:2-2:3 11:10-11:12 14:2 42:1-42:4 1:12 60:3-60:11 18:20, Jastrow 1286b, Luke 13:29, Malachi 1:11, Midrash Psalms 4:10, Numbers.R 12:17, Psalms 22:28 67:5-67:8 72:8 72:17 86:9, Saadia Opinions 8:6, Sifre Devarim {Ha'azinu Hashamayim} 314, Sifre Devarim Nitzavim 314, Sifre.z Numbers Naso 7:3, z.Vaetchanan 269b

[2] 1QIsaa *the LORD*; MT *My Lord the LORD*

[3] Isaiah 49:23 - 1 Peter 2:6, b.Avodah Zara [Tosefot] 26a, b.Megillah [Tosefot] 22b, b.Sheviit [Tosefot] 16b, b.Zevachim 19a, Chibbur Yafeh Pesichta 4a, Derech Hashem Part IV 8§2, Esther 8:1-10, Ezra 1:2-4 6:7-12 7:11-28, Genesis 19:26, Genesis.R 75:8, Isaiah 1:9 21:14 1:7 4:15 12:3 60:10- 11 12:14 12:16 14:2 16:5, Joel 2:27, Leviticus.R 27:4 33:6 36:2, Micah 7:17, Midrash Psalms 2:3 4:10 40:1, Midrash Tanchuma Emor 9 24, Midrash Tanchuma Vayigash 10, mt.Hilchot Avodat Kochavim v'Chukkoteihem 9:16, Nehemiah 2:6-10, Numbers 11:12, Pesikta de R'Kahana 9.4, Pesikta Rabbati 11:2, Psalms 2:10-12 25:3 34:23 68:32 69:7 72:9-11 18:4, Revelation 3:9 21:24-26, Romans 5:5 9:33 10:11, Saadia Opinions 8:6, Song of Songs.R 6:24 6:26, t.Sotah 4:2, y.Avodah Zarah 2:1

[4] Isaiah 49:24 - Ezekiel 13:3 13:11, Ezra 9:9 9:13, Isaiah 18:22 5:12, Jeremiah 25:6-9 25:11-14, Luke 11:21-22, Matthew 12:29, Nehemiah 9:33 9:37, Psalms 124:6-7 126:1-3, Psalms of Solomon 5:3

[5] LXX *Will any one take spoils from a giant*

[6] LXX *and if one should take a man captive unjustly, shall he*

[7] Isaiah 49:25 - 1 John 3:8, Galatians 4:26, Genesis 12:3, Hebrews 2:14-15, Isaiah 10:27 14:2 1:9 11:4 41:11-12 52:2-5 6:13 54:15-17, Jeremiah 5:10 50:17-19 50:33-34 51:35-36, Numbers 23:8-9, Revelation 18:20, Romans 8:31-39, z.Vaetchanan 269b, Zechariah 9:11 9:13-16 12:3-6 14:3 14:12

[8] Isaiah 49:26 - Ezekiel 15:7, Gates of Repentance 3.024, Isaiah 9:5 9:21 41:14-41:20 19:3 21:6 12:16, Joseph and Aseneth 27:10 8:9, Judges 7:22, Leviticus.R 33:6, Psalms 9:17 58:11-58:12 83:19, Revelation 14:20 15:3-15:4 16:6 17:6

[9] LXX *and who upholds the strength of Jacob*

[10] Isaiah 50:1 - 1 Kings 21:25, 2 Baruch 3:2, 2 Kings 4:1 17:17, b.Sanhedrin 105a, Deuteronomy 24:1-24:4 8:30, Ein Yaakov Sanhedrin:105a, Esther 7:4, Exodus 21:7, Exodus.R 31:11, Hosea 2:2-2:6, Isaiah 4:3 59:1-59:2, Jeremiah 3:1 3:8 4:18, Lamentations.R 1:3, Leviticus 1:39, Mark 10:4-10:12, Matthew 18:25, Midrash Tanchuma Mishpatim 11, Nehemiah 5:5, Psalms 44:13, Sifre Devarim {Ha'azinu Hashamayim} 306, Sifre Devarim Nitzavim 306, Tanya Igeret Hateshuvah §06, z.Bereshit 22b, z.Ki Tissa 189b, z.Vaetchanan 269b, z.Vayechi 237a, z.Vayeshev 182a, z.Vayikra 8a
Isaiah 50:1-11 - 1QIsaa

[11] Isaiah 50:2 - 2 Baruch 21:6 4 Ezra 8:23, 2 Chronicles 8:15, b.Berachot 6b, Daniel 3:15 3:29 6:21 6:28, Ein Yaakov Berachot:6b,

בְּגַעֲרָתִי אַחֲרִיב יָם אָשִׂים נְהָרוֹת מִדְבָּר תִּבְאַשׁ
דְּגָתָם מֵאֵין מַיִם וְתָמֹת בַּצָּמָא

shortened at all, that it cannot redeem[1]? Or have I no power to deliver? Behold, at My rebuke I dry up the sea, I make the rivers a wilderness; Their fish *become foul*[2], because there is no water, And die for thirst.

אַלְבִּישׁ שָׁמַיִם קַדְרוּת וְשַׂק אָשִׂים כְּסוּתָם 3[3]

I clothe the heavens with blackness, And I make sackcloth their covering.

אֲדֹנָי יְהֹוִה נָתַן לִי לְשׁוֹן לִמּוּדִים לָדַעַת לָעוּת 4[4]
אֶת־יָעֵף דָּבָר יָעִיר בַּבֹּקֶר בַּבֹּקֶר יָעִיר לִי אֹזֶן
לִשְׁמֹעַ כַּלִּמּוּדִים

The Lord GOD gave me the tongue of *those who are taught*[5], *so I should know how to sustain with words he who is weary; He wakens morning by morning, He wakens my ear to hear as those who are taught*[6].

אֲדֹנָי יְהֹוִה פָּתַח־לִי אֹזֶן וְאָנֹכִי לֹא מָרִיתִי אָחוֹר 5[7]
לֹא נְסוּגֹתִי

The Lord GOD opened my ear, and I was not rebellious, nor turned backward[8].

גֵּוִי נָתַתִּי לְמַכִּים וּלְחָיַי לְמֹרְטִים פָּנַי לֹא הִסְתַּרְתִּי 6[9]
מִכְּלִמּוֹת וָרֹק

I gave my back to assailants, and my cheeks to those who plucked off the hair; I have not hid my face from shame *and*[10] spitting.

וַאדֹנָי יְהֹוִה יַעֲזָר־לִי עַל־כֵּן לֹא נִכְלָמְתִּי עַל־כֵּן 7[11]
שַׂמְתִּי פָנַי כַּחַלָּמִישׁ וָאֵדַע כִּי־לֹא אֵבוֹשׁ

For the Lord GOD will help me; therefore, have I not been confused; but have I set my face like flint, And I know that I shall not be ashamed.

קָרוֹב מַצְדִּיקִי מִי־יָרִיב אִתִּי נַעַמְדָה יָּחַד מִי־בַעַל 8[12]
מִשְׁפָּטִי יִגַּשׁ אֵלָי

He who justifies me is near; *who will contend with me? Let us stand up together; who is my adversary? Let him come near to me*[13].

הֵן אֲדֹנָי יְהֹוִה יַעֲזָר־לִי מִי־הוּא יַרְשִׁיעֵנִי הֵן כֻּלָּם 9[14]
כַּבֶּגֶד יִבְלוּ עָשׁ יֹאכְלֵם

Behold, the Lord GOD will help me; Who is he who shall condemn me? Behold, they all shall grow old as a garment, the moth shall eat them.

מִי בָכֶם יְרֵא יְהֹוָה שֹׁמֵעַ בְּקוֹל עַבְדּוֹ אֲשֶׁר הָלַךְ 10[15]
חֲשֵׁכִים וְאֵין נֹגַהּ לוֹ יִבְטַח בְּשֵׁם יְהֹוָה וְיִשָּׁעֵן
בֵּאלֹהָיו

Who is among you who fears the LORD, who obeys the voice of His servant? Though he walks in darkness, and has no light, let him

---

Exodus 7:18 7:21 14:21 14:29, Genesis 18:14, Hosea 11:2 11:7, Isaiah 19:5 12:20 17:28 18:15 19:16 3:10 11:1 11:16 15:13 17:12 18:4, Jeremiah 5:1 7:13 8:6 11:15, John 1:11 3:19, Joshua 3:16, Mark 4:39, Nahum 1:4, Numbers 11:23, Proverbs 1:24, Psalms 10:9 11:33 114:3-114:7, Song of Songs.R 1:57, z.Naso 126a, z.Terumah 131b, z.Vayikra 4b

[1] LXX *Is not my hand strong to redeem*

[2] LXX *shall be dried up*

[3] Isaiah 50:3 - b.Berachot 59a, Esther.R 7:13, Exodus 10:21, Lamentations.R 3:10 3:?, Matthew 3:45, Pesikta de R'Kahana 15.3 S6.2, Pesikta Rabbati 31:1, Psalms 18:12-18:13, Revelation 6:12, z.Shemot 18a, z.Vayigash 210a

[4] Isaiah 50:4 - Exodus 4:11-12, Isaiah 57:15-19, Jeremiah 1:9, John 7:15-17 7:46, Luke 4:22 21:15, Matthew 11:28 13:54 22:46, Pesikta Rabbati 33:3, Proverbs 15:23 1:11, Psalms 5:4 45:3 119:147 23:8, Saadia Opinions Intro:2, y.Avodah Zarah 1:2, y.Berachot 8:6, y.Eruvin 5:1
Isaiah 50:4-9 - Psalms of Solomon 12:6 17:21

[5] LXX *instruction*

[6] LXX *to know when it is fit to speak a word: he has appointed for me early, he has given me an ear to hear*

[7] Isaiah 50:5 - Acts 2:19, Hebrews 5:8 10:5-10:9, Isaiah 11:5 24:8, Jastrow 1125a, John 8:29 14:31 15:10, Matthew 2:39, Pesikta Rabbati 33:3, Philippians 2:8, Psalms 40:7-40:9

[8] LXX *and the instruction of the Lord, the Lord, opens my ears, and I do not disobey, nor dispute*

[9] Isaiah 50:6 - Hebrews 12:2, Isaiah 5:5, Jastrow 527b, John 18:22, Lamentations 3:30, Leviticus.R 10:2, Luke 22:63-22:64, Mark 14:65 15:19, Matthew 5:39 26:67 3:26 3:30, Micah 5:2, Midrash Tanchuma Tazria 9, Nehemiah 13:25, Pesikta de R'Kahana 16.4, Pesikta Rabbati 29/30A:5, Psalms of Solomon 10:2, Sibylline Oracles 8.290, t.Bava Kamma 9:31

[10] LXX *or*

[11] Isaiah 50:7 - 1 Peter 4:1 4:16, Ezekiel 3:8-3:9, Hebrews 13:6, Isaiah 18:1 1:8 2:9, Jeremiah 1:18, John 16:33, Luke 9:51 11:39-11:54, Matthew 23:13-23:36, Mesillat Yesharim 5:Factors Detracting from Zehirus 20:Weighing Implementation of Chassidus, Psalms 89:22-89:28 14:1, Romans 1:16
Isaiah 50:7-11 - 11QIsab

[12] Isaiah 50:8 - 1 Timothy 3:16, Deuteronomy 19:17, Exodus 22:9, Isaiah 17:1 17:21 19:26, Job 23:3-23:7, Matthew 5:25, Midrash Psalms 60:1, Midrash Tanchuma Devarim 3, Revelation 12:10, Romans 8:32-8:34, Zechariah 3:1-3:10

[13] LXX *who is he who pleads with me? Let him stand up against me at the same time: yes, who is he who pleads with me*

[14] Isaiah 50:9 - Hebrews 1:11-1:12, Isaiah 17:10 51:6-51:8, Job 13:28, Psalms 39:12 6:27

[15] Isaiah 50:10 - 1 Chronicles 5:20, 1 Peter 5:7, 1 Samuel 6:6, 2 Chronicles 20:12 20:20, 2 Corinthians 1:8-10, b.Berachot 6b, Ecclesiastes 12:13, Ein Yaakov Berachot:6b, Genesis.R 60:1, Hebrews 5:9, Isaiah 9:3 26:3-4 18:1 49:2-3 2:4 5:11 11:9, Job 13:15 23:8-10 5:3, John 8:12 12:46, Lamentations 3:2 3:25-3:26, Malachi 3:16, Micah 7:7-9, Midrash Psalms 31:1 70:4, Psalms 23:4 25:12

trust in the name of the LORD, and stay upon his God.

הֵן כֻּלְּכֶם קֹדְחֵי אֵשׁ מְאַזְּרֵי זִיקוֹת לְכוּ בְּאוּר אֶשְׁכֶם וּבְזִיקוֹת בִּעַרְתֶּם מִיָּדִי הָיְתָה־זֹּאת לָכֶם לְמַעֲצֵבָה תִּשְׁכָּבוּן

11[1] Behold, all you who kindle a fire, who gird yourselves with firebrands, *begone in the flame of your fire, and among the brands you have kindled[2]*. This shall you have of My hand; You shall lie down in sorrow.

Isaiah – Chapter 51

שִׁמְעוּ אֵלַי רֹדְפֵי צֶדֶק מְבַקְשֵׁי יְהוָה הַבִּיטוּ אֶל־צוּר חֻצַּבְתֶּם וְאֶל־מַקֶּבֶת בּוֹר נֻקַּרְתֶּם

1[3] Listen to Me, you who follow after righteousness, you who seek the LORD; look to the rock from where you were hewn, and to the hole of the pit from where you were dug.

הַבִּיטוּ אֶל־אַבְרָהָם אֲבִיכֶם וְאֶל־שָׂרָה תְּחוֹלֶלְכֶם כִּי־אֶחָד קְרָאתִיו וַאֲבָרְכֵהוּ וְאַרְבֵּהוּ

2[4] Look to Abraham your father, and to Sarah who bore you; for when he was but one I called him, I *blessed him[5], and made him many[6]*.

כִּי־נִחַם יְהוָה צִיּוֹן נִחַם כָּל־חָרְבֹתֶיהָ וַיָּשֶׂם מִדְבָּרָהּ כְּעֵדֶן וְעַרְבָתָהּ כְּגַן־יְהוָה שָׂשׂוֹן וְשִׂמְחָה יִמָּצֵא בָהּ תּוֹדָה וְקוֹל זִמְרָה

3[7] For the LORD has comforted Zion; He has comforted all her ruined places, And has made her wilderness like Eden, And her desert like the garden of the LORD; Joy and gladness shall be found there, Thanksgiving, and the voice of melody. *Sorrow and mourning will flee away[8]*.

הַקְשִׁיבוּ אֵלַי עַמִּי וּלְאוּמִּי אֵלַי הַאֲזִינוּ כִּי תוֹרָה מֵאִתִּי תֵצֵא וּמִשְׁפָּטִי לְאוֹר עַמִּים אַרְגִּיעַ

4[9] *Listen to Me[10]*, My people, *My nation[11]*, and give ear to Me; For a law shall go forth from Me, And *My judgment as a light to the peoples[12]*; I will provide rest.

25:14 27:13-14 28:7 40:2-5 42:12 62:9 111:10-112:1 8:1 1:21, Tanya Igeret Hakodesh §30, z.Balak 196a, z.Terumah 131b

[1] Isaiah 50:11 - 2 Thessalonians 1:8-1:9, 4Q266 frag 3 2.1, 6Q15 frag 2 1.1, Amos 4:4-5, b.Bava Batra [Rashbam] 75a, b.Ketubot 41a, Cairo Damascus 5.13, Ecclesiastes.R 3:11, Ein Yaakov Ketubot:104a, Exodus 11:9-11:10, Ezekiel 20:39, Isaiah 8:22 28:15-20 30:15-16 7:2 65:13-16, James 3:6, Jeremiah 17:5-7, John 8:24 9:39, Jonah 2:8, Matthew 8:12 15:6-8 22:13, Midrash Psalms 116:7, Numbers.R 6:2 11:7, Pesikta Rabbati 36:1, Proverbs 2:18, Psalms 16:4 20:8-9 32:10, Revelation 19:20 20:15, Romans 1:21-22 10:3

[2] LXX *walk in the light of your fire, and in the flame you have kindled*

[3] Isaiah 51:1 - 1 Timothy 6:11, 2 Timothy 2:22, Amos 5:6, b.Horayot [Rashi] 10b, b.Nazir [Rashi] 23a, b.Yevamot 64a, Ein Yaakov Yevamot:64b, Ephesians 2:11-12, Esther.R 7:10, Exodus.R 51:7, Genesis 17:15-17, Hebrews 12:14, Isaiah 21:19 46:3-4 24:12 3:4 3:7 55:2-3 7:6, Liber Antiquitatum Biblicarum 23:4, Matthew 5:6 6:33, Midrash Psalms 52:5 53:2, Midrash Tanchuma Pekudei 8, Philippians 3:13, Proverbs 15:9 21:21, Psalms 24:6 94:15 105:3-4, Romans 9:30-32 14:19, Saadia Opinions Intro:6, Sefer Yetzirah 1:10, Sifre Devarim Ha'azinu Hashamayim 319, z.Chayyei Sarah 122b, Zephaniah 2:3
Isaiah 51:1-2 - 4QIsab, Sifre Devarim Nitzavim 319
Isaiah 51:1-10 - 1QIsab
Isaiah 51:1-23 - 1QIsaa

[4] Isaiah 51:2 - b.Yevamot 64b, Exodus.R 46:5, Ezekiel 9:24, Galatians 3:9-3:14, Genesis 12:1-12:3 13:14-13:17 15:1-15:2 15:4-15:5 18:11-18:13 22:17 24:1 24:35, Hebrews 11:8-11:12, Isaiah 5:22, Joshua 24:3, Midrash Psalms 52:8 53:2, Midrash Tanchuma Chayyei Sarah 4, Midrash Tanchuma Vayera 16, Nehemiah 9:7-9:8, Pesikta de R'Kahana 5.2, Pesikta Rabbati 15:2, Romans 4:1-4:5 4:16-4:24, Saadia Opinions Intro:6, z.Bereshit 22b

[5] 1QIsaa *made him fruitful*

[6] LXX *and loved him, and multiplied him*

[7] Isaiah 51:3 - 1 Peter 1:8, 2 Corinthians 1:3-1:4, Ezekiel 31:8-31:10, Genesis 2:8-2:9 13:10, Genesis.R 15:2 97:1 100 [Excl]:12, Isaiah 12:1 1:9 35:1-35:2 35:7-35:10 40:1-40:2 41:18-41:19 20:26 1:8 1:13 3:12 4:9 54:6-54:8 61:1-61:4 66:10-66:14, Jeremiah 31:13-31:15 7:26 33:11-33:13, Joel 2:3, Midrash Tanchuma Vayechi 17, Midrash Tanchuma Vayera 23, Motzoei Shabbat [Viyiten Lecha], Pesikta de R'Kahana S5.3, Psalms 85:9 102:14-102:15, Revelation 19:1-19:7, Zephaniah 3:14-3:20

[8] 1QIsaa; Missing in LXX

[9] Isaiah 51:4 - 1 Corinthians 9:21, 1 Peter 2:9, Exodus 19:6 9:13, Exodus.R 52:5, Isaiah 2:3 2:2 42:1-4 18:6 1:6, John 16:8-11, Leviticus.R 13:3, Liber Antiquitatum Biblicarum 51:4 51:6, Luke 2:32, Matthew 12:18-20, Micah 4:2, Midrash Psalms 23:1, Numbers.R 12:8, Pesikta de R'Kahana 1.3, Proverbs 6:23, Psalms 33:12 50:7 78:1 10:5 3:20, Romans 8:2-4, Song of Songs.R 2:45 3:25 6:24

[10] LXX *Hear me, hear me*

[11] Missing in LXX

[12] LXX *judgment shall be for a light of the nations*

קָרוֹב צִדְקִי יָצָא יִשְׁעִי וּזְרֹעַי עַמִּים יִשְׁפֹּטוּ אֵלַי אִיִּים יְקַוּוּ וְאֶל־זְרֹעִי יְיַחֵלוּן	5[1]

My favor is near, My salvation has gone forth[2], and My arms shall judge the peoples; the isles shall wait for Me, And they shall trust in My arm.

שְׂאוּ לַשָּׁמַיִם עֵינֵיכֶם וְהַבִּיטוּ אֶל־הָאָרֶץ מִתַּחַת כִּי־שָׁמַיִם כֶּעָשָׁן נִמְלָחוּ וְהָאָרֶץ כַּבֶּגֶד תִּבְלֶה וְיֹשְׁבֶיהָ כְּמוֹ־כֵן יְמוּתוּן וִישׁוּעָתִי לְעוֹלָם תִּהְיֶה וְצִדְקָתִי לֹא תֵחָת	6[3]

Lift up your eyes to the heavens, And look on the earth beneath; *For the heavens shall vanish away like smoke, And the earth shall grow old like a garment[4],* And they who live there shall die in like manner; But My *salvation shall be forever, And My favor shall not be abolished[5].*

שִׁמְעוּ אֵלַי יֹדְעֵי צֶדֶק עַם תּוֹרָתִי בְלִבָּם אַל־תִּירְאוּ חֶרְפַּת אֱנוֹשׁ וּמִגִּדֻּפֹתָם אַל־תֵּחָתּוּ	7[6]

Listen to Me, you who know righteousness, the people in whose heart is My law; Do not fear the taunt of men, nor be dismayed at their insults.

כִּי כַבֶּגֶד יֹאכְלֵם עָשׁ וְכַצֶּמֶר יֹאכְלֵם סָס וְצִדְקָתִי לְעוֹלָם תִּהְיֶה וִישׁוּעָתִי לְדוֹר דּוֹרִים	8[7]

For the moth shall eat them like a garment, And the worm shall eat them like wool[8]; But My favor shall be forever, And My salvation to all generations.

עוּרִי עוּרִי לִבְשִׁי־עֹז זְרוֹעַ יְהוָה עוּרִי כִּימֵי קֶדֶם דֹּרוֹת עוֹלָמִים הֲלוֹא אַתְּ־הִיא הַמַּחְצֶבֶת רַהַב מְחוֹלֶלֶת תַּנִּין	9[9]

Awake, awake, put on strength, O arm of the LORD; Awake, as in the days of old, The generations of ancient times. Are you not he who *hewed[10] Rahab[11]* in pieces, who pierced the dragon?[12]

הֲלוֹא אַתְּ־הִיא הַמַּחֲרֶבֶת יָם מֵי תְּהוֹם רַבָּה הַשָּׂמָה מַעֲמַקֵּי־יָם דֶּרֶךְ לַעֲבֹר גְּאוּלִים	10[13]

Are you not he who dried up the sea, the waters of the great deep; Who made the depths of the sea a way for the *redeemed to pass over[14]?*

וּפְדוּיֵי יְהוָה יְשׁוּבוּן וּבָאוּ צִיּוֹן בְּרִנָּה וְשִׂמְחַת עוֹלָם עַל־רֹאשָׁם שָׂשׂוֹן וְשִׂמְחָה יַשִּׂיגוּן נָסוּ יָגוֹן וַאֲנָחָה	11[15]

And the *ransomed[16]* of the LORD shall return, and come with singing unto Zion, and eternal joy shall be on their heads; they shall obtain gladness and joy, And sorrow and sighing shall flee.

---

[1] Isaiah 51:5 - 1 Samuel 2:10, 2 Corinthians 5:10, Acts 17:31, Deuteronomy 6:14, Ezekiel 47:1-47:5, Isaiah 2:2-2:3 16:10 18:4 22:13 1:1 8:1 12:9 15:5, Joel 4:12, John 5:22-5:23, Luke 24:47, Mark 16:15, Matthew 3:2 4:18, Psalms 50:4-50:6 67:5 85:10 96:13 98:9 14:6, Romans 1:16-1:17 2:16 10:6-10:10 10:17-10:18 15:9-15:12, Sibylline Oracles 3.710, Zephaniah 2:11

[2] LXX My righteousness speedily draws nigh, and my salvation shall go forth as light

[3] Isaiah 51:6 - 2 Peter 3:10-12, 2 Thessalonians 2:16, b.Avodah Zara 14a, Daniel 9:24, Deuteronomy 4:19, Deuteronomy.R 3:15, Ecclesiastes.R 1:3, Ein Yaakov Avodah Zarah:17a, Esther.R Petichata:11, Genesis.R 34:11 42:3, Hebrews 1:10-12 5:9 9:12 9:15, Isaiah 13:13 10:4 16:26 21:17 2:9 3:8, John 3:15-16 5:24 10:27-29, Leviticus.R 11:7, Matthew 24:35, Midrash Proverbs 6, Midrash Psalms 92:2 150:1, Midrash Tanchuma Shemini 9, Midrash Tanchuma Vaetchanan 6, Numbers.R 13:5, Pirkei de R'Eliezer 51, Psalms 8:4-5 102:26-27 7:17, Revelation 6:12-14 20:11, Ruth.R Petichata:7, Saadia Opinions 7:7, z.Bereshit 24b

[4] 1QIsaa *and see who created these.*

[5] LXX *righteousness shall not fail*

[6] Isaiah 51:7 - 1 Peter 4:4 4:14, 2 Corinthians 3:3, Acts 5:41, Ezekiel 2:6, Gates of Repentance 3.167, Hebrews 10:16, Isaiah 3:1, Jeremiah 1:17 31:34-31:35, Luke 6:22 12:4-12:5, Matthew 5:11 10:28, Philippians 3:8 3:10, Psalms 37:31 40:9, Titus 2:11-2:12

[7] Isaiah 51:8 - b.Sanhedrin [Rashi] 98a, Hosea 5:12, Isaiah 21:17 22:13 2:9 3:6 18:24, Job 4:19 13:28, Luke 1:50
Isaiah 51:8-16 - 4QIsac

[8] LXX *For as a garment will be devoured by time, and as wool will be devoured by a moth, so shall they be consumed*

[9] Isaiah 51:9 - 3 Enoch 48A:3 4 Ezra 6:50, Deuteronomy 4:34, Ezekiel 5:3, Habakkuk 2:19 3:13, Isaiah 3:1 6:7 3:5 3:17 4:1 5:1 59:16-59:17 14:8, Job 2:12, John 12:38, Judges 6:13, Leviticus.R 10:2, Luke 1:51, Midrash Psalms 50:3, Midrash Tanchuma Devarim 1, Nehemiah 9:7-15, Pesikta de R'Kahana 16.4, Pesikta Rabbati 33:3, Psalms 7:7 21:14 44:2 44:24 59:5 74:13-14 78:65 87:4 89:11 93:1, Revelation 11:17 12:9, z.Vayakhel 217b
Isaiah 51:9-10 - Mekhilta de R'Shimon bar Yochai Beshallach 23:1, Mekilta de R'Ishmael Beshallah 4:16-20

[10] 1QIsaa *broke*

[11] 1QIsaa *Rehob*

[12] LXX says *Awake, awake, O Jerusalem, and put on the strength of your arm; awake as in the early time, as the ancient generation*

[13] Isaiah 51:10 - 4 Ezra 8:23, Exodus 14:21-22 15:13, Isaiah 18:15 19:16 2:2 63:11-12, Psalms 74:13

[14] LXX *delivered and redeemed*

[15] Isaiah 51:11 - 2 Corinthians 4:17-18, 2 Thessalonians 2:16, Acts 2:41-47, Isaiah 1:8 11:10 20:23 24:20 1:13 60:19-20 13:7 17:19, Jeremiah 30:18-19 31:12-13 9:11, Jude 1:24, Midrash Tanchuma Massei 13, mt.Hilchot Teshuvah 8:2, Numbers.R 16:25, Pesikta Rabbati 37:3, Revelation 5:9-13 7:9-10 7:17 14:1-4 19:1-19:7 21:1 21:4 22:3

[16] 1QIsaa *dispersed*

אָנֹכִי אָנֹכִי הוּא מְנַחֶמְכֶם מִי־אַתְּ וַתִּירְאִי מֵאֱנוֹשׁ יָמוּת וּמִבֶּן־אָדָם חָצִיר יִנָּתֵן

12[1] I, I, am He who comforts you: Who are you, who you are afraid of man who shall die, And of the son of man who shall be made as grass;

וַתִּשְׁכַּח יְהוָה עֹשֶׂךָ נוֹטֶה שָׁמַיִם וְיֹסֵד אָרֶץ וַתְּפַחֵד תָּמִיד כָּל־הַיּוֹם מִפְּנֵי חֲמַת הַמֵּצִיק כַּאֲשֶׁר כּוֹנֵן לְהַשְׁחִית וְאַיֵּה חֲמַת הַמֵּצִיק

13[2] And have forgotten the LORD your Maker, who stretched forth the heavens, and laid the foundations of the earth and fears continually all the day because of the fury of the oppressor, as he prepares to destroy? And where is the fury of the oppressor?

מִהַר צֹעֶה לְהִפָּתֵחַ וְלֹא־יָמוּת לַשַּׁחַת וְלֹא יֶחְסַר לַחְמוֹ

14[3] *He who is bent down*[4] shall speedily be loosed; And he shall not descend dying into the pit, nor shall his bread fail[5].

וְאָנֹכִי יְהוָה אֱלֹהֶיךָ רֹגַע הַיָּם וַיֶּהֱמוּ גַּלָּיו יְהוָה צְבָאוֹת שְׁמוֹ

15[6] For I am the LORD your God, who stirs up the sea, so its waves roar; the LORD of hosts is His name.

וָאָשִׂים דְּבָרַי בְּפִיךָ וּבְצֵל יָדִי כִּסִּיתִיךָ לִנְטֹעַ שָׁמַיִם וְלִיסֹד אָרֶץ וְלֵאמֹר לְצִיּוֹן עַמִּי־אָתָּה

16[7] And I have put My words in your mouth, And have covered you in the shadow of My hand, so I may plant the heavens, and lay the foundations of the earth, and say unto Zion: 'You are My people.'

הִתְעוֹרְרִי הִתְעוֹרְרִי קוּמִי יְרוּשָׁלַ͏ִם אֲשֶׁר שָׁתִית מִיַּד יְהוָה אֶת־כּוֹס חֲמָתוֹ אֶת־קֻבַּעַת כּוֹס הַתַּרְעֵלָה שָׁתִית מָצִית

17[8] Awake, awake, stand up, Jerusalem, who has drunk at the hand of the LORD the cup of His fury; *you drank the beaker, the cup of staggering, And emptied it*[9].

אֵין־מְנַהֵל לָהּ מִכָּל־בָּנִים יָלָדָה וְאֵין מַחֲזִיק בְּיָדָהּ מִכָּל־בָּנִים גִּדֵּלָה

18[10] There is no one to guide *her*[11] among all the sons whom she has brought forth; nor is there any who takes her by the hand of all the sons whom she has brought up.

שְׁתַּיִם הֵנָּה קֹרְאֹתַיִךְ מִי יָנוּד לָךְ הַשֹּׁד וְהַשֶּׁבֶר וְהָרָעָב וְהַחֶרֶב מִי אֲנַחֲמֵךְ

19[12] These two things have befallen you; Who shall bemoan you? Desolation and destruction, And

---

[1] Isaiah 51:12 - 1 Peter 1:24, 2 Corinthians 1:3-5 7:5-6, Acts 9:31, Daniel 3:16-18, Gates of Repentance 3.32 3.167, Isaiah 2:22 40:6-7 19:25 3:3 51:7-8 57:15-18 18:13, James 1:10-11, Jastrow 881b, John 14:18 14:26-27, Lamentations.R 1:57, Leviticus.R 10:2, Life of Adam and Eve [Vita] 10:2, Luke 12:4-5, Matthew 10:28, Midrash Tanchuma Devarim 1, Pesikta de R'Kahana 16.4 16.11 19.1 19.5 S6.1, Pesikta Rabbati 21:15 29/30A:5 33:1-13, Proverbs 5:26, Psalms 90:5-6 92:8 103:15-16 22:6 2:4
Isaiah 51:12-52:12 - Fourth Shabbat after Tisha b'Av [Pesikta Rabbati 33], Haftarah Ki Tetze, Haftarah Shoftim
[2] Isaiah 51:13 - 1 Corinthians 1:20 15:55, Acts 12:23, Daniel 3:15 3:19 4:29-30, Deuteronomy 8:18, Esther 5:14 7:10, Exodus 14:10-13 15:9-10, Genesis.R 76:1, Hebrews 1:9-12 11:15, Isaiah 7:4 8:12-13 10:29-34 14:16-17 16:4 17:10 33:18-19 37:36-38 16:22 18:5 20:24 21:12 24:13 9:11, Jeremiah 2:32 10:11-12 3:15, Job 9:8 20:5-9 13:18, Lamentations.R 1:26, Matthew 2:16-20, Pesikta de R'Kahana 19.5, Pesikta Rabbati 33:5, Psalms 9:7-8 37:35-36 76:11 102:26-27 8:2, Revelation 19:20 20:9, Saadia Opinions Intro:6, Tanna Devei Eliyahu 5
[3] Isaiah 51:14 - Acts 12:7-8, b.Berachot 57ab, b.Menachot [Tosefot] 94a, b.Pesachim 118a, Ein Yaakov Pesachim:118a, Ezra 1:5, Genesis.R 20:10, Isaiah 24:20 1:10 4:2, Jastrow 1195b, Jeremiah 13:16 38:6-13, Lamentations 3:53-54, Pesikta de R'Kahana 19.5, Pesikta Rabbati 33:5, Zechariah 9:11
Isaiah 51:14-16 - 4QIsab
[4] 1QIsaa *Distress*
[5] LXX reads *For in your deliverance he shall not halt nor tarry*
[6] Isaiah 51:15 - Amos 9:5-9:6, b.Pesachim 118a, Ein Yaakov Pesachim:118a, Isaiah 23:4 24:2 3:10 6:5, Jeremiah 10:16 7:36, Job 2:12, Nehemiah 9:11, Pesikta de R'Kahana 19.6, Pesikta Rabbati 33:5, Psalms 74:13 114:3-114:5 16:13
[7] Isaiah 51:16 - 2 Peter 3:13, 4 Ezra 15:2, b.Chagigah 5b, b.Sanhedrin 99b, Deuteronomy 18:18 9:27, Ein Yaakov Chagigah:5b, Ein Yaakov Sanhedrin:99b, Exodus 9:22, Genesis.R 2:5, Hebrews 8:10, Isaiah 21:18 24:13 1:2 1:8 2:4 11:21 60:14-15 12:21 13:3 17:17 18:22, Jeremiah 7:34 8:38, John 3:34 8:38-8:40 17:8, Midrash Tanchuma Pekudei 3, Midrash Tanchuma Re'eh 1, Midrash Tanchuma Yitro 14, Pesikta de R'Kahana 19.6, Psalms 75:4 92:14, Revelation 1:1, Saadia Opinions 7:8, Tanya Igeret Hateshuvah §09 §10, y.Megillah 3:6, y.Taanit 4:2, z.Bereshit 4b 5a, z.Tzav 35a, Zechariah 8:8 13:9
[8] Isaiah 51:17 - 1 Corinthians 15:34, Deuteronomy 4:28 4:34, Ephesians 5:14, Ezekiel 23:31-34, Isaiah 3:9 4:1 60:1-2, Jeremiah 25:15-17 1:27, Job 21:20, Judges 5:12, Leviticus.R 10:2, Midrash Tanchuma Devarim 1, Pesikta de R'Kahana 16.4, Pesikta Rabbati 29/30A:5 33:3, Psalms 11:7 60:4 75:9 75:11, Revelation 14:10 16:19 18:6, Sibylline Oracles Fragment 3.39, Zechariah 12:2
Isaiah 51:17-23 - Psalms of Solomon 8:14
[9] *LXX for you have drunk out and drained the cup of calamity, the cup of wrath*
[10] Isaiah 51:18 - Acts 9:8 13:11, Hebrews 8:9, Isaiah 3:4-8 17:13 21:1 1:21, Jeremiah 7:33, Job 8:20, Mark 8:23, Matthew 9:36 15:14, Mesillat Yesharim 19:Longing-for-the-Redemption, Psalms 88:19 22:5
[11] 1QIsaa LXX *you*
[12] Isaiah 51:19 - 2 Corinthians 7:6-7 7:13, 2 Thessalonians 2:16-17, Amos 7:2, Ecclesiastes 4:1, Ezekiel 14:21, Isaiah 14:30 22:4 23:9 13:2, Jeremiah 9:18-22, Job 2:11 18:11, Lamentations 1:9 1:12 1:16-17, Psalms 69:21, z.Shemot 19b

the famine and the sword; How shall I comfort you?

בָּנַיִךְ עֻלְּפוּ שָׁכְבוּ בְּרֹאשׁ כָּל־חוּצוֹת כְּתוֹא מִכְמָר הַמְלֵאִים חֲמַת־יְהוָה גַּעֲרַת אֱלֹהָיִךְ **20**[1]

Your sons have fainted, they *lie at the head of all the streets as an antelope in a net*[2]; they are full of the fury of the LORD, *the rebuke of your God*[3].

לָכֵן שִׁמְעִי־נָא זֹאת עֲנִיָּה וּשְׁכֻרַת וְלֹא מִיָּיִן **21**[4]

Therefore, hear this, you afflicted, and drunkard, but not with wine;

כֹּה־אָמַר אֲדֹנַיִךְ יְהוָה וֵאלֹהַיִךְ יָרִיב עַמּוֹ הִנֵּה לָקַחְתִּי מִיָּדֵךְ אֶת־כּוֹס הַתַּרְעֵלָה אֶת־קֻבַּעַת כּוֹס חֲמָתִי לֹא־תוֹסִיפִי לִשְׁתּוֹתָהּ עוֹד **22**[5]

Thus says *your Lord the LORD, And your God who pleads the case for His people: Behold, I have taken the cup of staggering out of your hand; The beaker, the cup of My fury*[6], You shall not drink it again;

וְשַׂמְתִּיהָ בְּיַד־מוֹגַיִךְ אֲשֶׁר־אָמְרוּ לְנַפְשֵׁךְ שְׁחִי וְנַעֲבֹרָה וַתָּשִׂימִי כָאָרֶץ גֵּוֵךְ וְכַחוּץ לַעֹבְרִים **23**[7]

And I will put it into the hand of those who afflict[8] you; who have said to your soul: 'Bow down, so we may pass over'; And you have laid your back as the ground, And as the street, to those who pass over.

Isaiah – Chapter 52

עוּרִי עוּרִי לִבְשִׁי עֻזֵּךְ צִיּוֹן לִבְשִׁי בִּגְדֵי תִפְאַרְתֵּךְ יְרוּשָׁלִַם עִיר הַקֹּדֶשׁ כִּי לֹא יוֹסִיף יָבֹא־בָךְ עוֹד עָרֵל וְטָמֵא **1**[9]

Awake, awake, put on your strength, O Zion; put on your beautiful garments, O Jerusalem, the holy city; from now on, he uncircumcised and the unclean shall no longer come in to you.

הִתְנַעֲרִי מֵעָפָר קוּמִי שְּׁבִי יְרוּשָׁלִָם 'הִתְפַּתְּחוּ' "הִתְפַּתְּחִי" מוֹסְרֵי צַוָּארֵךְ שְׁבִיָּה בַּת־צִיּוֹן **2**[10]

Shake yourself from the dust; arise, and sit down, O Jerusalem; loose the bands from your neck, O captive daughter of Zion.

כִּי־כֹה אָמַר יְהוָה חִנָּם נִמְכַּרְתֶּם וְלֹא בְכֶסֶף תִּגָּאֵלוּ **3**[11]

For thus says the LORD: You were sold for nothing; And you shall be redeemed without payment.

---

[1] Isaiah 51:20 - Deuteronomy 14:5, Ein Yaakov Bava Kamma:117a, Ezekiel 12:13 17:20 15:19, Isaiah 5:25 8:21 9:20-22 5:9 16:30 1:26 3:17 3:21, Jeremiah 14:16 14:18, Lamentations 1:15 1:19 2:11-12 3:15-16 4:2 5:13, Psalms 88:16-17, Revelation 14:10 16:9-11
[2] LXX *sleep at the top of every street as a half-boiled beet*
[3] LXX *caused to faint by the LORD God*
[4] Isaiah 51:21 - b.Eruvin 65a, Ein Yaakov Eruvin:65a, Isaiah 5:9 3:17 6:11, Jastrow 1157a 1576b, Midrash Psalms 35:1, Midrash Tanchuma Pinchas 12, y.Berachot 5:1
[5] Isaiah 51:22 - 1 Samuel 1:39, Ezekiel 15:29, Isaiah 1:25 3:17 54:7-54:9 14:8, Jeremiah 2:34 3:36, Joel 4:2, Micah 7:9, Midrash Psalms 146:6, Proverbs 22:23, Psalms 35:1, z.Vaetchanan 269b
Isaiah 51:22-23 - 4Q176 frags 6-7 ll.1-3
[6] LXX *the LORD God who judges his people, Behold, I have taken out of your hand the cup of calamity, the cup of my wrath*
[7] Isaiah 51:23 - Exodus.R 12:1, Genesis.R 41:9 69:5, Isaiah 49:25-26, Jastrow 703b 738a 1179b, Jeremiah 25:15-29, Joshua 10:24, Midrash Psalms 146:6, Proverbs 11:8 21:18, Psalms 65:12-13, Revelation 11:2 13:16-17 17:6-8 17:18, Zechariah 12:2
[8] 1QIsaa adds *and oppressed*
[9] Isaiah 52:1 - Daniel 10:9 10:16-19, Ephesians 4:24 6:10, Exodus 4:2 4:40, Ezekiel 20:9, Haggai 2:4, Isaiah 1:21 1:26 2:2 11:8 24:2 3:9 3:17 12:21 13:3 13:10, Jeremiah 7:24, Luke 15:22, Matthew 4:5, Mekilta de R'Ishmael Beshallah 4:14, Midrash Tanchuma Lech Lecha 20, Midrash Tanchuma Vayigash 10, Nahum 2:1, Nehemiah 11:1, Pesikta Rabbati 29/30B:4, Pirkei de R'Eliezer 29, Psalms 14:3, Psalms of Solomon 11:7, Revelation 19:8 19:14 21:2 21:27, Romans 3:22 13:14, z.Vayishlach 172b, Zechariah 3:4 14:20-21
Isaiah 52:1-3 - 4Q176 frags 8-11 ll.2-4
Isaiah 52:1-15 - 1QIsaa
[10] Isaiah 52:2 - 4QIsab, Ein Yaakov Rosh Hashanah:31b, Genesis.R 75:1, Isaiah 3:26 5:4 1:21 3:14 3:23 13:1, Jastrow 921a, Jeremiah 3:6 3:45 3:50, Lamentations.R 1:23, Luke 4:18 21:24, Midrash Psalms 119:12, mt.Hilchot Sanhedrin v'Hainshin Hameurim Lahem 14:12, Pesikta Rabbati 26:7, Revelation 18:4, Song of Songs.R 4:18, Tanya Igeret Hakodesh §23, z.Bamidbar 118a, z.Chayyei Sarah 134a, z.Shemot 7a, z.Vayikra 6b, Zechariah 2:6
[11] Isaiah 52:3 - 1 Peter 1:18, b.Megillah 24a, b.Sanhedrin 97b, Ein Yaakov Sanhedrin:97b, Isaiah 21:13 2:1, Jeremiah 15:13, Mas.Soferim 11:1, Midrash Tanchuma Behar 1, Midrash Tanchuma Nitzavim 3, Pirkei de R'Eliezer 50, Psalms 44:13, Romans 7:14-7:25, y.Taanit 1:1, z.Vaetchanan 269b
Isaiah 52:3-5 - mt.Hilchot Tefilah 12:14

כִּי כֹה אָמַר אֲדֹנָי יְהֹוִה מִצְרַיִם יֲרַד־עַמִּי בָרִאשֹׁנָה לָגוּר שָׁם וְאַשּׁוּר בְּאֶפֶס עֲשָׁקוֹ

4[1] For thus says *the Lord GOD*[2]: In the past, My people went down into Egypt to sojourn there; and the Assyrian oppressed them without cause.

וְעַתָּה מִי־לִי־מַה־לִי־פֹה נְאֻם־יְהֹוָה כִּי־לֻקַּח עַמִּי חִנָּם מֹשְׁלוֹ יְהֵילִילוּ נְאֻם־יְהֹוָה וְתָמִיד כָּל־הַיּוֹם שְׁמִי מִנֹּאָץ

5[3] *Now, therefore, what[4] shall I do, says the LORD, Seeing that My people are taken away for nothing? They who rule over them howl[5], says the LORD, And My name is blasphemed, continually all the day[6].*

לָכֵן יֵדַע עַמִּי שְׁמִי לָכֵן בַּיּוֹם הַהוּא כִּי־אֲנִי־הוּא הַמְדַבֵּר הִנֵּנִי

6[7] Therefore, My people shall know My name; *Therefore*[8] they shall know in that day that I, He who spoke, behold, here I am.

מַה־נָּאווּ עַל־הֶהָרִים רַגְלֵי מְבַשֵּׂר מַשְׁמִיעַ שָׁלוֹם מְבַשֵּׂר טוֹב מַשְׁמִיעַ יְשׁוּעָה אֹמֵר לְצִיּוֹן מָלַךְ אֱלֹהָיִךְ

7[9] The feet of the messenger of *good tidings*[10] are beautiful on the mountains, he who announces peace, the harbinger of *good tidings*[11], who announces salvation; who says to Zion: 'Your God reigns!'

קוֹל צֹפַיִךְ נָשְׂאוּ קוֹל יַחְדָּו יְרַנֵּנוּ כִּי עַיִן בְּעַיִן יִרְאוּ בְּשׁוּב יְהֹוָה צִיּוֹן

8[12] Listen to your watchmen! They lift up the voice, together they sing; for they shall see, eye to eye, the LORD returning to Zion[13].[14]

פִּצְחוּ רַנְּנוּ יַחְדָּו חָרְבוֹת יְרוּשָׁלָ͏ִם כִּי־נִחַם יְהֹוָה עַמּוֹ גָּאַל יְרוּשָׁלָ͏ִם

9[15] Break forth *into joy, sing together*[16], you ruined places of Jerusalem; for the LORD has comforted His people, He has redeemed Jerusalem.

---

[1] Isaiah 52:4 - Acts 7:14-7:15, b.Megillah 24a, Genesis 22:6, Isaiah 14:25 36:1-36:22, Jeremiah 2:17, Job 2:3, John 15:25, Mas.Soferim 11:1, Psalms 25:3 69:5, z.Shemot 7a, z.Vaetchanan 269b
Isaiah 52:4-7 - 4QIsad

[2] 1QIsaa *the LORD*

[3] Isaiah 52:5 - 1AQM 11.5-7, b.Megillah 24a, b.Succah 52b, Exodus 1:13-1:16 2:23-24 3:7, Ezekiel 20:9 20:14 36:20-23, Isaiah 22:16 13:6 13:28 23:6 3:20 3:23 4:3, Jeremiah 2:17, Judges 18:3, Lamentations 1:21 2:3 5:13-5:15, Mas.Soferim 11:1, Midrash Psalms 20:1, Midrash Tanchuma Pekudei 1, Psalms 44:13 44:17 74:10 74:18 74:22-23 137:1-2, Romans 2:24, z.Vaetchanan 267a, Zephaniah 1:10

[4] MT *who*; 1QIsaa *what*

[5] 1QIsaa *are deluded*

[6] LXX reads *And now why are you here? Thus says the LORD, because my people were taken for nothing, wonder and howl. Thus says the LORD, On account of you my name is continually blasphemed among the Gentiles.*

[7] Isaiah 52:6 - Exodus 9:19 34:5-34:7, Ezekiel 20:44 37:13-37:14 39:27-39:29, Hebrews 6:14-6:18 8:10-8:11, Isaiah 18:9 1:23, Midrash Psalms 91:8, Numbers 23:19, Pesikta Rabbati 22:7, Psalms 48:11, Zechariah 10:9-10:12

[8] Mssing in 1QIsaa

[9] Isaiah 52:7 - 11Q13 2.15-16 2.23, 4QIsab, Acts 10:36-38, b.Berachot 56b, Deuteronomy.R 5:15, Ephesians 6:15, Isaiah 24:23 9:22 16:9 61:1-3, Kuzari 4.3, Lamentations.R 1:57, Leviticus.R 9:9, Luke 2:10 24:47, Mark 13:10 16:15, Mas.Perek Hashalom 1:13, Matthew 1:34 4:18, Micah 4:7, Midrash Psalms 29:2 74:3 147:1-2, Midrash Tanchuma Toledot 14, Midrash Tanchuma Vayigash 10, Motzoei Shabbat [Ribbon HaOlamim], Nahum 2:1, Pesikta de R'Kahana 5.9 16.11 S5.1-2 S5.4, Pesikta Rabbati 15:14/15 33:13 35:4, Psalms 59:14 68:12 93:1 96:10 97:1 99:1, Psalms of Solomon 11:1, Revelation 11:15 14:6, Romans 10:12-15, Song of Songs 2:8, Song of Songs.R 4:18, Zechariah 9:9
Isaiah 52:7-15 - 1QIsab

[10] 1QIsaa *peace*

[11] 1QIsaa *news of good things*

[12] Isaiah 52:8 - 1 Corinthians 1:10 13:12, Acts 2:1 2:46-47 4:32, b.Megillah [Tosefot] 2b, b.Sanhedrin 91b, Ein Yaakov Sanhedrin 91b, Ephesians 1:17-18, Ezekiel 3:17 9:7, Hebrews 13:17, Isaiah 12:4-6 24:14 2:1 3:2 6:26 11:10 16:9 24:20 8:10 10:1 14:6, Jeremiah 6:17 31:7-8 8:39 9:11, Lamentations.R 1:23 1:57, Leviticus.R 14:2, Mekhilta de R'Shimon bar Yochai Bachodesh 49:5, Midrash Psalms 13:2 17:13 147:1 147:2, Midrash Tanchuma Bamidbar 17, Midrash Tanchuma Devarim 1, Midrash Tanchuma Ekev 7, Motzoei Shabbat [Ribbon HaOlamim], Pesikta de R'Kahana 16.11 S5.3, Pesikta Rabbati 29/30B:4 33:13, Revelation 5:8-10 18:20 19:4, Shacharit], Song of Songs 3:3 5:7, Tanya Igeret Hakodesh §9, Tanya Likutei Aramim §36, Tanya Shaar Hayichud §3, When carrying the Sefer Torah to the Bimah [Shabbat, Yom Tov], z.Beshallach 55b, z.Mishpatim 126a, z.Pekudei 240b, z.Yitro 81a, Zechariah 12:8, Zephaniah 3:9

[13] 1QIsaa adds *with compassion*

[14] LXX reads *For the voice of those who guard you is exalted, and with the voice together they shall rejoice: for eyes shall look to eyes, when the LORD shall have mercy upon Sion.*

[15] Isaiah 52:9 - Galatians 4:27, Isaiah 14:7 42:10-42:11 20:23 20:26 24:20 1:13 3:3 54:1-54:3 7:12 13:4 65:18-19 66:10-13, Midrash Psalms 147:1 147:2, Psalms 96:11-96:12 98:4, Zephaniah 3:14-15

[16] 1QIsaa *together, sing for joy*

חָשַׂף יְהֹוָה אֶת־זְרוֹעַ קָדְשׁוֹ לְעֵינֵי כָּל־הַגּוֹיִם וְרָאוּ כָּל־אַפְסֵי־אָרֶץ אֵת יְשׁוּעַת אֱלֹהֵינוּ

10[1] The LORD has made His holy arm the feet of the messenger of *good tidings*[2] in the eyes of all the nations; and all the ends of the earth shall see the salvation of our God.

סוּרוּ סוּרוּ צְאוּ מִשָּׁם טָמֵא אַל־תִּגָּעוּ צְאוּ מִתּוֹכָהּ הִבָּרוּ נֹשְׂאֵי כְּלֵי יְהֹוָה

11[3] Depart you, depart, *do not go out from there*[4], touch no unclean thing; go out of the midst of her; *be clean*[5], you who bear the vessels of the LORD.

כִּי לֹא בְחִפָּזוֹן תֵּצֵאוּ וּבִמְנוּסָה לֹא תֵלֵכוּן כִּי־הֹלֵךְ לִפְנֵיכֶם יְהֹוָה וּמְאַסִּפְכֶם אֱלֹהֵי יִשְׂרָאֵל

12[6] For you shall not go out in haste, nor shall you go by flight; for the LORD will go before you, and the God of Israel will be your rear guard[7].

הִנֵּה יַשְׂכִּיל עַבְדִּי יָרוּם וְנִשָּׂא וְגָבַהּ מְאֹד

13[8] Behold, My servant shall *prosper*[9], He shall be exalted and lifted up, and shall be very high.

כַּאֲשֶׁר שָׁמְמוּ עָלֶיךָ רַבִּים כֵּן־מִשְׁחַת מֵאִישׁ מַרְאֵהוּ וְתֹאֲרוֹ מִבְּנֵי אָדָם

14[10] *According as many were appalled at you. So marred was his visage unlike that of a man, And his form unlike that of the sons of men*[11].

כֵּן יַזֶּה גּוֹיִם רַבִּים עָלָיו יִקְפְּצוּ מְלָכִים פִּיהֶם כִּי אֲשֶׁר לֹא־סֻפַּר לָהֶם רָאוּ וַאֲשֶׁר לֹא־שָׁמְעוּ הִתְבּוֹנָנוּ

15[12] So he shall startle[13] many nations, Kings shall be silent because of him; for what had not been told to them they shall see, and what they had not heard they shall perceive.

---

[1] Isaiah 52:10 - 3 Enoch 48A:10, Acts 2:5-11 13:47, Isaiah 1:6 3:9 66:18-19, Jastrow 510b, Luke 3:6, Midrash Psalms 2:6 98:1 137:7, Midrash Tanchuma Ekev 7, Midrash Tanchuma Kedoshim 4, Motzoei Shabbat [Ribbon HaOlamim], Psalms 22:28 98:1-3, Revelation 11:15-17 14:6 15:4, y.Berachot 9:1
Isaiah 52:10-15 - 4QIsac
[2] 1QIsaa *peace*
[3] Isaiah 52:11 - 1 Peter 1:14-16 2:5 2:11, 2 Corinthians 6:17, Acts 10:14 10:28, Ephesians 5:11, Ezekiel 20:23, Ezra 1:7-11 8:25-30, Haggai 2:13-14, Isaiah 1:16 24:20, Jeremiah 2:8 3:6 3:45, Jubilees 22:16, Leviticus 5:2-3 10:3 11:26-27 11:45 11:47 15:5-33 22:2-33, Revelation 18:4, Romans 14:14, Sifre Devarim {Ha'azinu Hashamayim} 333, z.Vayakhel 218a, Zechariah 2:6-7
[4] LXX *go out from there*
[5] LXX *separate yourselves*
[6] Isaiah 52:12 - 1 Chronicles 14:15, Deuteronomy 20:4, Exodus 12:11 12:33 12:39 13:21-22 14:8 14:19-20, Exodus.R 15:17 19:6, Isaiah 4:16 21:2 3:14 10:8, Judges 4:14, Mekilta de R'Ishmael Pisha 7:18, Micah 2:13, Midrash Tanchuma Devarim 1, Numbers 10:25, Pesikta de R'Kahana 5.19, Pesikta Rabbati 15:3, Saadia Opinions 7:7, Tanya Likutei Aramim §31, z.Bamidbar 118a, z.Mishpatim 94b
[7] 1QIsaa adds *He is called the God of all the earth.*
[8] Isaiah 52:13 - Ephesians 1:20-1:23, Ezekiel 10:23, Hebrews 1:3, Isaiah 9:7-9:8 11:2-11:3 18:1 1:1 1:3 49:5-49:7 53:10-53:11 9:15, Jeremiah 23:5, John 3:31 5:22-5:23, Joshua 1:7-1:8, Kuzari 4.022, Matthew 4:18, Midrash Psalms 2:9, Midrash Tanchuma Toledot 14, mt.Hilchot Melachim u'Michamoteihem 11:4, Philippians 2:7-2:11, Psalms 2:6-2:9 110:1-110:2, Revelation 5:6-5:13, Tanya Kuntress Acharon §06, z.Shemini 38a, z.Vayeshev 181a, Zechariah 3:8
Isaiah 52:13 [LXX] - Martyrdom and Ascension of Isaiah 4:21
Isaiah 52:13-53:12 - Psalms of Solomon 12:6 17:21, Kuzari 2.034
[9] LXX *understand*
[10] Isaiah 52:14 - Isaiah 2:6 53:2-53:5, Luke 2:47 4:36 5:26 22:64, Mark 5:42 6:51 7:37 10:26 10:32, Matthew 7:28 22:22-22:23 26:67 3:14 27:29-27:30, Psalms 22:7-22:8 22:16 22:18 71:7 102:4-102:6
[11] LXX *As many shall be amazed at you, so shall your face be without glory from men, and your glory shall not be honored by the sons of men*
[12] Isaiah 52:15 - 1 Peter 1:2, Acts 2:33, Ephesians 3:5-9, Ezekiel 12:25, Hebrews 9:1314 10:22 11:28 12:24, Isaiah 1:7 1:23 3:5 7:5, Job 29:9-10 16:4, Matthew 4:19, Micah 7:16-17, Numbers 8:7, Psalms 72:9-11, Romans 15:20-21 16:25-26, Titus 3:5-6, Zechariah 2:13
[13] 1QIsaa or *sprinkle*

Isaiah – Chapter 53[1]

מִי הֶאֱמִין לִשְׁמֻעָתֵנוּ וּזְרוֹעַ יְהוָה עַל־מִי נִגְלָתָה

1[2]   'Who would have believed our report? And to whom has the arm of the LORD been revealed?

וַיַּעַל כַּיּוֹנֵק לְפָנָיו וְכַשֹּׁרֶשׁ מֵאֶרֶץ צִיָּה לֹא־תֹאַר לוֹ וְלֹא הָדָר וְנִרְאֵהוּ וְלֹא־מַרְאֶה וְנֶחְמְדֵהוּ

2[3]   *For he shot forth as a sapling*[4], And as a root out of a dry ground; He had no form *nor allure*[5], that we should *look on him*[6], nor beauty that we should delight in him.

נִבְזֶה וַחֲדַל אִישִׁים אִישׁ מַכְאֹבוֹת וִידוּעַ חֹלִי וּכְמַסְתֵּר פָּנִים מִמֶּנּוּ נִבְזֶה וְלֹא חֲשַׁבְנֻהוּ

3[7]   *He was despised, and forsaken of men*[8], A man of pains, and acquainted with disease, And as one from whom men hide their face: *He was despised, and we did not esteemed him*[9].

אָכֵן חֳלָיֵנוּ הוּא נָשָׂא וּמַכְאֹבֵינוּ סְבָלָם וַאֲנַחְנוּ חֲשַׁבְנֻהוּ נָגוּעַ מֻכֵּה אֱלֹהִים וּמְעֻנֶּה

4[10]   *Surely our diseases he bore, and our pains he carried; while we considered him stricken, struck of God, and afflicted*[11].

וְהוּא מְחֹלָל מִפְּשָׁעֵנוּ מְדֻכָּא מֵעֲוֹנֹתֵינוּ מוּסַר שְׁלוֹמֵנוּ עָלָיו וּבַחֲבֻרָתוֹ נִרְפָּא־לָנוּ

5[12]   But he was impaled because of our transgressions, he was crushed because of our iniquities: the chastisement of our *peace was on him, and with his wounds*[13] we were healed ourselves.

כֻּלָּנוּ כַּצֹּאן תָּעִינוּ אִישׁ לְדַרְכּוֹ פָּנִינוּ וַיהוָה הִפְגִּיעַ בּוֹ אֵת עֲוֹן כֻּלָּנוּ

6[14]   All we, like sheep, go astray, *everyone turned to his way*; And the LORD made to him the *iniquity of us all*[15].

נִגַּשׂ וְהוּא נַעֲנֶה וְלֹא יִפְתַּח־פִּיו כַּשֶּׂה לַטֶּבַח יוּבָל וּכְרָחֵל לִפְנֵי גֹזְזֶיהָ נֶאֱלָמָה וְלֹא יִפְתַּח פִּיו

7[16]   *He was oppressed, though humbled himself*[17] and did not open his mouth; as a lamb that is led to the slaughter, And as a sheep before her shearer is dumb; Yes, he did not opened his mouth.

---

[1] Isaiah 53 - and 3 missing letters for light in verse 11, contains 10 spelling differences 4 stylistic changes, for a total of 17 differences [MT]

[2] Isaiah 53:1 - 1 Corinthians 1:18 1:24, Ephesians 1:18-19, Guide for the Perplexed 1:46, Isaiah 16:5 3:9 4:10 14:8, John 1:7 1:12 12:38, Matthew 11:25 16:17, Romans 1:16-18 10:16-17
Isaiah 53:1-3 - 4QIsac
Isaiah 53:1-12 - 1QIsaa, 1QIsab

[3] Isaiah 53:2 - 1 Peter 2:14, Ezekiel 17:22-24, Isaiah 11:1 4:14, Jeremiah 23:5, John 1:10-14 9:28-29 18:40 19:5 19:14-15, Luke 2:7 2:39-40 2:51-52 9:58, Mark 6:3 9:12, Philippians 2:6-7, Romans 8:3, Zechariah 6:12
Isaiah 53:2-3 - Sibylline Oracles 8.257

[4] LXX *We brought a report as of a child before him*

[5] 1QIsaa *and he had no majesty*

[6] 1QIsaa possible reading of *look at ourselves*

[7] Isaiah 53:3 - 4Q471b frag 1a-d ll.1-2, Acts 3:13-15, Deuteronomy 8:15, Hebrews 2:15-18 4:15 5:7 12:2-3, Isaiah 1:7 2:6 5:4 5:10, John 1:10-11 8:48 11:35, Luke 8:53 9:22 16:14 18:31-33 19:41 23:18-25, Mark 9:12 14:34 15:19, Matthew 26:37-38 26:67 27:9-10 27:39-44 27:63, Micah 5:2, Psalms 22:7-9 69:11-13 69:20-21 69:30, Zechariah 11:8 11:12-13

[8] LXX *But his form was ignoble, and inferior to that of the children of men*

[9] 1QIsaa *and we despised him and we did not value him*

[10] Isaiah 53:4 - 1 John 2:2, 1 Peter 2:24 3:18, b.Sanhedrin 98ab, Galatians 3:13, Hebrews 9:28, Isaiah 53:5-53:6 53:11-53:12, John 19:7, Kuzari 2.035 2.044, Matthew 8:17 2:37, Psalms 69:27, z.Vayakhel 212a

[11] LXX *He bears our sins, and is pained for us: yet we accounted him to be in trouble, and in suffering, and in affliction*

[12] Isaiah 53:5 - 1 Corinthians 15:3, 1 Peter 2:24-25 3:18, 2 Corinthians 5:21, b.Sanhedrin 98a, Daniel 9:24, Ephesians 5:2, Genesis 3:15, Hebrews 9:12-15 9:28 10:10 10:14, Isaiah 53:6-8 53:10-12, Matthew 20:28, Romans 3:24-26 4:25 5:6-10 5:15-21, Ruth.R 5:6, z.Pinchas 218a, z.Vayakhel 212a, Zechariah 13:7

[13] LXX *peace was upon him; and by his bruises*

[14] Isaiah 53:6 - 1 Peter 2:25 3:18, Ezekiel 3:18, Isaiah 5:10 7:7 8:11, James 5:20, Luke 15:3-7, Matthew 18:12-14, Psalms 69:5 119:176, Romans 3:10-19 4:25, Sibylline Oracles 3.721
Isaiah 53:6-8 - 4QIsac

[15] LXX *everyone has gone astray in his way; and the Lord gave him up for our sins*

[16] Isaiah 53:7 - 1 Peter 2:23, 4 Ezra 15:10, Acts 8:32-8:33, John 19:9, Liber Antiquitatum Biblicarum 30:5, Luke 23:9, Mark 14:61 15:5, Matthew 26:63 27:12-27:14, Midrash Tanchuma Noach 13, z.Vaera 29b
Isaiah 53:7-12 - 4 Maccabees 10:18

[17] LXX *And he, because of his affliction*

מֵעֹצֶר וּמִמִּשְׁפָּט לֻקָּח וְאֶת־דּוֹרוֹ מִי יְשׂוֹחֵחַ כִּי
נִגְזַר מֵאֶרֶץ חַיִּים מִפֶּשַׁע עַמִּי נֶגַע לָמוֹ

8[1] By oppression and judgment *he was taken away*[2], And with his generation who reasoned? For he was cut off from the land of the living, *an affliction*[3] for the transgression of my people.

וַיִּתֵּן אֶת־רְשָׁעִים קִבְרוֹ וְאֶת־עָשִׁיר בְּמֹתָיו עַל
לֹא־חָמָס עָשָׂה וְלֹא מִרְמָה בְּפִיו

9[4] And they made his grave with the wicked, and with the rich his tomb; although he did no violence, nor was any deceit in his mouth.'

וַיהוָה חָפֵץ דַּכְּאוֹ הֶחֱלִי אִם־תָּשִׂים אָשָׁם נַפְשׁוֹ
יִרְאֶה זֶרַע יַאֲרִיךְ יָמִים וְחֵפֶץ יְהוָה בְּיָדוֹ יִצְלָח

10[5] Yet it pleased the LORD to crush him *by disease*[6]; *to see if his soul would offer itself as a guilt offering, so he might see his seed, prolong his days, And the purpose of the LORD might prosper in his hand*[7]:

מֵעֲמַל נַפְשׁוֹ יִרְאֶה יִשְׂבָּע בְּדַעְתּוֹ יַצְדִּיק צַדִּיק
עַבְדִּי לָרַבִּים וַעֲוֹנֹתָם הוּא יִסְבֹּל

11[8] *Of the travail of his soul he shall see to the full*[9], My servant, who by his knowledge justified the Righteous One to the many, and their iniquities he bore.

לָכֵן אֲחַלֶּק־לוֹ בָרַבִּים וְאֶת־עֲצוּמִים יְחַלֵּק שָׁלָל
תַּחַת אֲשֶׁר הֶעֱרָה לַמָּוֶת נַפְשׁוֹ וְאֶת־פֹּשְׁעִים נִמְנָה
וְהוּא חֵטְא־רַבִּים נָשָׂא וְלַפֹּשְׁעִים יַפְגִּיעַ

12[10] Therefore, I will divide to him a portion among the great, and he shall divide the spoil with the mighty; because he bore his soul to death, and was numbered with the transgressors; yet he bore the sin of many, And made intercession for *the transgressors*[11].

---

[1] Isaiah 53:8 - 1 Peter 3:18, Acts 8:33, Daniel 9:26, Isaiah 5:5 5:12, John 11:49-52 19:7, Matthew 1:1 26:65-66, Psalms 22:13-22 69:13, Romans 1:4
Isaiah 53:8-12 - 4QIsad

[2] 1QIsab *he was taken away*

[3] 1QIsaa *he was stricken*

[4] Isaiah 53:9 - 1 Corinthians 15:4, 1 John 3:5, 1 Peter 2:22, 2 Corinthians 5:21, Hebrews 4:15 7:26, Isaiah 42:1-42:3, John 19:38-19:42, Luke 23:50-23:53, Mark 15:43-15:46, Matthew 27:57-27:60

[5] Isaiah 53:10 - 1 John 4:9-10, 1 Peter 2:24, 2 Corinthians 5:21, 2 Thessalonians 1:11, Acts 2:24-28, b.Berachot 57b, b.Yoma [Rashi] 88a, Daniel 7:13-14 9:24, Ein Yaakov Berachot:5a, Ephesians 1:5 1:9 5:2, Ezekiel 9:11 13:25, Galatians 3:13, Genesis.R 20:10, Hebrews 2:13 7:27 9:14 9:25-26 10:6-12 13:10-12, Isaiah 9:8 18:1 22:10 53:3-6 5:12 55:11-13 62:3-5, Jeremiah 8:41, John 6:37-40 12:24, Luke 1:33 15:5-7 15:23-24, Matthew 3:17 17:5, Mesillat Yesharim Afterword, Micah 7:18, Pesikta de R'Kahana 19.5, Psalms 16:9-11 21:5 22:31 45:17-18 69:27 72:7 72:17 85:11-13 89:30 89:37 14:3 3:11 5:4, Revelation 1:18, Romans 6:9 8:8 8:32, Tanna Devei Eliyahu 6, z.Toledot 140a, z.Vayeshev 186b, Zechariah 13:7, Zephaniah 3:17

[6] LXX *with a blow*; MT *he made him suffer*

[7] LXX *If you can give an offering for sin, your soul shall see a long-lived seed*

[8] Isaiah 53:11 - 1 Corinthians 6:11, 1 John 2:1, 1 Peter 2:24 3:18, 2 Corinthians 4:6, 2 John 1:1 1:3, 2 Peter 1:2-3 3:18, Galatians 4:19, Hebrews 9:28 12:2, Isaiah 18:1 21:25 1:3 53:4-6 5:8 5:12, John 10:14-18 12:24 12:27-32 16:21 17:3, light omitted [MT], Luke 22:44, Matthew 20:28, Philippians 3:8-10, Revelation 5:9-10 7:9-17, Romans 3:22-24 4:24-5:1 5:9 5:18-19, Titus 3:6-7
Isaiah 53:11-12 - 4QIsab

[9] MT *He will see some of the suffering of his soul*; 1QIsaa 1QIsab 1QIsad *Out of he suffering of his soul he will see light*

[10] Isaiah 53:12 - 1 John 2:1 2:12, 1 Timothy 2:5-2:6, Acts 2:18, b.Shekalim 13b, b.Sotah 14a, Colossians 1:13-14 2:15, Daniel 2:45, Ein Yaakov Sotah:14a, Genesis 3:15, Hebrews 2:14-2:15 7:25 9:24 9:26 9:28 12:2, Isaiah 49:24-49:25 4:13 4:15 5:6 5:8 53:10-11, Luke 22:37 23:25 23:32-34, Mark 15:27, Matthew 12:28-29 26:38-39 2:42, Numbers.R 13:2, Philippians 2:8-11 2:17, Psalms 2:8 22:15, Psalms of Solomon 16:2, Romans 8:34, Sifre Devarim Vezot Habracha 355, Titus 2:14, y.Shekalim 5:1

[11] 1QIsaa *their transgressions*

Isaiah – Chapter 54

רָנִּי עֲקָרָה לֹא יָלָדָה פִּצְחִי רִנָּה וְצַהֲלִי לֹא־חָלָה
כִּי־רַבִּים בְּנֵי־שׁוֹמֵמָה מִבְּנֵי בְעוּלָה אָמַר יְהוָה

1[1] Sing, O barren, you who did not bear, break forth into singing, and cry aloud, you who did not travail; For more are the children of the desolate than the children of the married wife, says the LORD.

הַרְחִיבִי מְקוֹם אָהֳלֵךְ וִירִיעוֹת מִשְׁכְּנוֹתַיִךְ יַטּוּ
אַל־תַּחְשֹׂכִי הַאֲרִיכִי מֵיתָרַיִךְ וִיתֵדֹתַיִךְ חַזֵּקִי

2[2] Enlarge the place of your tent, and let them stretch forth the curtains of your habitations, do not spare; lengthen your ropes, and strengthen your stakes.

כִּי־יָמִין וּשְׂמֹאול תִּפְרֹצִי וְזַרְעֵךְ גּוֹיִם יִירָשׁ
וְעָרִים נְשַׁמּוֹת יוֹשִׁיבוּ

3[3] For you shall spread abroad on the right hand and on the left; And your seed shall possess the nations, And make the desolate cities inhabited.

אַל־תִּירְאִי כִּי־לֹא תֵבוֹשִׁי וְאַל־תִּכָּלְמִי כִּי לֹא
תַחְפִּירִי כִּי בֹשֶׁת עֲלוּמַיִךְ תִּשְׁכָּחִי וְחֶרְפַּת
אַלְמְנוּתַיִךְ לֹא תִזְכְּרִי־עוֹד

4[4] Fear not, for you shall not be ashamed. Nor will you be puzzled, for you shall not be put to shame; For you shall forget the shame of your youth, And the reproach of your widowhood you shall remember no more.

כִּי בֹעֲלַיִךְ עֹשַׂיִךְ יְהוָה צְבָאוֹת שְׁמוֹ וְגֹאֲלֵךְ קְדוֹשׁ
יִשְׂרָאֵל אֱלֹהֵי כָל־הָאָרֶץ יִקָּרֵא

5[5] For your Maker is your *husband*[6], The LORD of hosts is His name; And the Holy One of Israel is your Redeemer, The God of the whole earth shall He be called.

כִּי־כְאִשָּׁה עֲזוּבָה וַעֲצוּבַת רוּחַ קְרָאֵךְ יְהוָה
וְאֵשֶׁת נְעוּרִים כִּי תִמָּאֵס אָמַר אֱלֹהָיִךְ

6[7] *For the LORD has called you as a wife, forsaken and grieved in spirit; and a wife of youth, can she be rejected*[8]? says *your God*[9].

בְּרֶגַע קָטֹן עֲזַבְתִּיךְ וּבְרַחֲמִים גְּדֹלִים אֲקַבְּצֵךְ

7[10] For a small moment I have forsaken you; but with great *compassion I will gather you*[11].

---

[1] Isaiah 54:1 - 1 Samuel 2:5, 2 Baruch 10:14 4 Ezra 2:2, Apocalypse of Elijah 2:38, b.Berachot 10a, Ein Yaakov Berachot:10a, Galatians 4:27, Hebrews 11:11-12, Isaiah 42:10-11 20:23 1:13 1:20 55:12-13 14:4, Pesikta de R'Kahana 20.1-5, Pesikta Rabbati 32:2, Philo De Praemiis et Poenis 158, Psalms 67:4-6 98:3-9 17:9, Psalms of Solomon 1:3, Revelation 7:9-10, Song of Songs 8:8, Song of Songs.R 1:29 1:36 4:12, z.Mishpatim 103b, Zechariah 9:9, Zephaniah 3:14
Isaiah 54:1-2 - 4Q265 frag 1 ll.4-5
Isaiah 54:1-6 - 1QIsab
Isaiah 54:1-10 - Haftarah Noach [Sephard], Haftarah Noach Sephard [Isaiah 54:1-10], Siman 128:4, Third Shabbat after Tisha b'Av [Pesikta Rabbati 32]
Isaiah 54:1-11 - 4QIsad
Isaiah 54:1-17 - 1QIsaa
Isaiah 54:1-54:10 - Haftarah Ki Tetze [Isaiah 54:1-54:10]
Isaiah 54:1-55:3 - Haftarah Noach [Teimon]
Isaiah 54:1-55:5 - Haftarah Noach [Ashkenaz]
[2] Isaiah 54:2 - Exodus 11:18 15:40, Genesis.R 5:7, Isaiah 9:20 49:19-49:20, Jeremiah 10:20, Leviticus.R 10:9, Midrash Tanchuma Tzav 12, Pesikta de R'Kahana 12.22 20.7
[3] Isaiah 54:3 - Colossians 1:23, Ezekiel 36:35-36, Genesis 4:14 1:10, Genesis.R 69:5, Isaiah 2:2-4 11:9-12 35:1-2 42:1-12 43:5-6 1:8 1:12 49:18-49:19 4:9 7:5 60:3-13 61:5-9, Leviticus.R 10:9, Pesikta de R'Kahana 20.7, Psalms 72:8-11, Romans 9:25-26 10:18 11:12, Song of Songs.R 7:11, z.Bereshit 50b
Isaiah 54:3-5 - 4QIsac
[4] Isaiah 54:4 - 1 Peter 2:6, Ezekiel 16:22 16:43 16:60-63, Hosea 3:1-3:5, Isaiah 17:10 17:14 45:16-17 3:7 13:7, Jeremiah 7:20, Midrash Psalms 31:2
Isaiah 54:4-5 - z.Vayeshev 187b
Isaiah 54:4-10 - 4Q176 frags 8-11 ll.5-12
[5] Isaiah 54:5 - 2 Corinthians 11:2-11:3, b.Sanhedrin 22b, Ein Yaakov Sanhedrin:22b, Ephesians 5:25-5:27 5:32, Exodus.R 15:31, Ezekiel 16:8, Hosea 2:19-2:22, Isaiah 6:3 19:14 24:2 24:17 3:15, Jeremiah 3:14 10:16 3:19, John 3:29, Joseph and Aseneth 27:10, Luke 1:32, Psalms 45:11-45:18, Revelation 11:15, Romans 3:29-3:30, Zechariah 14:9
[6] LXX *maker*
[7] Isaiah 54:6 - 2 Corinthians 7:6 7:9-7:10, b.Sanhedrin 22a, Ecclesiastes 9:9, Hosea 2:1-4 2:14-17, Isaiah 49:14-49:21 50:1-50:2 14:4, Malachi 2:14, Matthew 11:28, Proverbs 5:18
[8] LXX *The LORD has not called you as a deserted and faint-hearted woman, nor as a woman hated from her youth*
[9] 1QIsaa *the LORD you God*
[10] Isaiah 54:7 - 2 Corinthians 4:17, 2 Peter 3:8, Deuteronomy 6:3, Ephesians 1:10, Ezekiel 12:24, Isaiah 11:11 2:20 3:12 16:11 43:5-43:6 1:18 8:8 12:4 12:10 18:18, Matthew 23:37, Micah 4:6, Psalms 30:6 10:47, Saadia Opinions 8:1
Isaiah 54:7-17 - 4QIsac
[11] LXX *mercy I will have compassion upon you*

בְּשֶׁצֶף קֶצֶף הִסְתַּרְתִּי פָנַי רֶגַע מִמֵּךְ וּבְחֶסֶד עוֹלָם רִחַמְתִּיךְ אָמַר גֹּאֲלֵךְ יְהוָה. 8[1]

In a little wrath I hid My face from you for a moment; but with everlasting kindness I will have compassion on you, says the LORD your Redeemer.

כִּי־מֵי נֹחַ זֹאת לִי אֲשֶׁר נִשְׁבַּעְתִּי מֵעֲבֹר מֵי־נֹחַ עוֹד עַל־הָאָרֶץ כֵּן נִשְׁבַּעְתִּי מִקְּצֹף עָלַיִךְ וּמִגְּעָר־בָּךְ. 9[2]

For this is like the waters of Noah to Me; For as I swore that the waters of Noah should never cover the earth, So I have sworn I will not be angry with you, nor rebuke you.

כִּי הֶהָרִים יָמוּשׁוּ וְהַגְּבָעוֹת תְּמוּטֶנָה וְחַסְדִּי מֵאִתֵּךְ לֹא־יָמוּשׁ וּבְרִית שְׁלוֹמִי לֹא תָמוּט אָמַר מְרַחֲמֵךְ יְהוָה. 10[3]

For the mountains may depart and the hills removed; but My kindness shall not depart from you, nor shall My covenant of peace be removed, says the Lord who has compassion on you.

עֲנִיָּה סֹעֲרָה לֹא נֻחָמָה הִנֵּה אָנֹכִי מַרְבִּיץ בַּפּוּךְ אֲבָנַיִךְ וִיסַדְתִּיךְ בַּסַּפִּירִים. 11[4]

O you afflicted, *tossed with tempest*[5], And not comforted, Behold, I will set your stones in fair colors, and lay your foundations with sapphires.

וְשַׂמְתִּי כַּדְכֹד שִׁמְשֹׁתַיִךְ וּשְׁעָרַיִךְ לְאַבְנֵי אֶקְדָּח וְכָל־גְּבוּלֵךְ לְאַבְנֵי־חֵפֶץ. 12[6]

And I will make your *pinnacles of rubies*[7], And your gates *of carbuncles*[8], And all your border of precious stones.

וְכָל־בָּנַיִךְ לִמּוּדֵי יְהוָה וְרַב שְׁלוֹם בָּנָיִךְ. 13[9]

And all your children shall be taught of the LORD; And great shall be the peace of your children.

בִּצְדָקָה תִּכּוֹנָנִי רַחֲקִי מֵעֹשֶׁק כִּי־לֹא תִירָאִי וּמִמְּחִתָּה כִּי לֹא־תִקְרַב אֵלָיִךְ. 14[10]

In righteousness you shall be established; be far from oppression, for you shall not fear, and from ruin, for it shall not come near you.

---

[1] Isaiah 54:8 - 1 Timothy 1:16, 2 Thessalonians 2:16, Ezekiel 39:23-39:24, Isaiah 8:17 21:15 23:6 24:17 1:26 6:5 6:10 7:3 57:16-57:17 12:10, Jeremiah 7:4, Psalms 13:2 27:9 7:17, Zechariah 1:15

[2] Isaiah 54:9 - According to Madinchai כי־מי is one word, b.Bava Batra [Rashbam] 74a, b.Sanhedrin 99a, b.Sheviit 36a, b.Sotah 10a, Ein Yaakov Sanhedrin:99a, Ein Yaakov Sotah:11a, Exodus.R 1:9, Ezekiel 15:20, Genesis 8:21 9:11-16, Genesis.R 34:6, Hebrews 6:16-18, Isaiah 12:1 7:11, Jeremiah 31:36-37 33:20-26, Lamentations.R 5:21, Leviticus.R 10:1, Mekhilta de R'Shimon bar Yochai Amalek 46:1, Mekhilta de R'Shimon bar Yochai Bachodesh 50:2, Mekhilta de R'Ishmael Amalek 3:11, Mekhilta de R'Ishmael Bahodesh 5:57, Midrash Proverbs 21, Midrash Tanchuma Noach 11, Pesikta de R'Kahana 16.4 19.3, Pesikta Rabbati 29/30A:4, Pirkei de R'Eliezer 23, Psalms 8:9, Sibylline Oracles 1.318, Song of Songs.R 2:42, t.Taniyot 2:13, y.Taanit 3:9, z.Noach 67b 72b, z.Vayikra 14b

[3] Isaiah 54:10 - 2 Peter 3:10-3:13, 2 Samuel 23:5, b.Avodah Zara 14a, Deuteronomy.R 3:7, Ein Yaakov Avodah Zarah:17a, Ephesians 2:4-2:5, Genesis.R 76:1, Guide for the Perplexed 2:29, Hebrews 8:6-8:13 13:20-13:21, Isaiah 1:10 51:6-51:7 6:8 7:3, Jastrow 740b, Leviticus.R 36:6, Malachi 2:5, Matthew 5:18 16:18 24:35, Midrash Psalms 46:3, Midrash Tanchuma Vaetchanan 6, Pirkei de R'Eliezer 19, Psalms 46:3 89:34-89:35, Romans 11:29, Titus 3:5, y.Sanhedrin 10:1, z.Bereshit 33a
Isaiah 54:10-13 - 4QIsaq

[4] Isaiah 54:11 - 1 Chronicles 5:2, 1 Kings 5:17, 1 Peter 2:4-6, 4Q164 frag 1 l.1, Acts 14:22 27:18-20, b.Bava Batra [Tosefot] 75a, Deuteronomy 7:17, Ephesians 2:20, Exodus 2:23 3:2 3:7 24:10 28:17-20 39:10-14, Ezekiel 1:26 10:1 40:1-42, Isaiah 14:32 4:16 1:14 51:17-19 3:21 51:23-52:5 6:6 12:15, Jastrow 967b 1121b, Jeremiah 6:17, John 16:20-22 16:33, Lamentations 1:1-2 1:16-17 1:21, Matthew 8:24, Midrash Psalms 53:2 87:1, Pesikta de R'Kahana 18.1 18.3-4, Pesikta Rabbati 30:3 32:1-3/4 33:8, Psalms 34:20 129:1-3, Revelation 11:3-10 12:13-17 21:18-21, Song of Songs 5:14, z.Mishpatim 126a
Isaiah 54:11-12 - Exodus.R 15:21
Isaiah 54:11-55:5 - Haftarah Re'eh [Isaiah 54:11-55:5], Siman 128:4

[5] 1QIsaa *passed back and forth*

[6] Isaiah 54:12 - 4Q164 frag 1 l.6, 4Q164 frag 1 ll.3-4, b.Bava Batra 75a, b.Sanhedrin 1a, b.Sotah [Rashi] 10a, Ein Yaakov Bava Batra:75a, Ein Yaakov Sanhedrin:100a, Jastrow 315a, Midrash Psalms 87:2 87:3, Pesikta de R'Kahana 18.5-6, Pesikta Rabbati 32:3/4, Saadia Opinions 8:6

[7] LXX *buttresses jasper*

[8] LXX *crystal*

[9] Isaiah 54:13 - 1 Corinthians 2:10, 1 John 2:20 2:27, 1 Thessalonians 4:9, b.Berachot 94a, b.Kereitot 28b, b.Nazir 66b, b.Tamid 32b, b.Yevamot 122b, Deuteronomy.R 6:14, Ein Yaakov Farewell:64a, Ein Yaakov Nazir:66b, Ephesians 4:21, Exodus.R 15:29 21:3 38:3, Ezekiel 10:25 10:28 13:26, Galatians 5:22, Genesis.R 95:3, Hebrews 8:10, Hosea 2:18, Isaiah 2:3 11:9 2:3 32:15-32:18 24:18 7:12, Jastrow 176b, Jeremiah 7:35 9:6, John 6:45 14:26-14:27 16:33, Luke 10:21-10:22 24:45, Matthew 11:25-11:29 16:17, Midrash Psalms 45:2 122:7, Midrash Tanchuma Vayigash 11, mt.Hilchot Tefilah 7:11, Mussaf Shabbat], Numbers.R 11:7, Omar Rebbe Elazar [Kabbalat Shabbat, Pesikta de R'Kahana 12.21 18.6, Pesikta Rabbati 32:3/4, Philippians 4:7, Psalms 25:8-25:12 71:17 119:165, Romans 5:1 14:17 15:13, Sifre Devarim {Ha'azinu Hashamayim} 336, Sifre Devarim Haazinu 336, y.Berachot 9:5, z.Lech Lecha 96b, z.Noach 64b, z.Terumah 169b

[10] Isaiah 54:14 - 2 Peter 3:13, Ezekiel 36:27-36:28 37:23-37:26, Isaiah 1:26 2:4 9:5 21:24 3:13 4:1 12:21 61:10-62:1, Jeremiah 23:3-23:4 6:10 7:24, Joel 4:17-4:21, Micah 4:3-4:4, mt.Hilchot Matnot Aniyim 10:1, Proverbs 3:25-3:26, Siman 34:1, Tanya Igeret Hakodesh §06, z.Beshallach 59a, Zechariah 2:4-2:5 8:3 9:8, Zephaniah 3:13-3:16

הֵן גּוֹר יָגוּר אֶפֶס מֵאוֹתִי מִי־גָר אִתָּךְ עָלַיִךְ יִפּוֹל

15[1] Behold, they may gather together, but not by Me; Whoever *gathers together against*[2] *you shall fall*[3] because of you.

"הֵן" "הִנֵּה" אָנֹכִי בָּרָאתִי חָרָשׁ נֹפֵחַ בְּאֵשׁ פֶּחָם וּמוֹצִיא כְלִי לְמַעֲשֵׂהוּ וְאָנֹכִי בָּרָאתִי מַשְׁחִית לְחַבֵּל

16[4] Behold, I have created *the smith*[5] who blows the fire of coals, and brings forth a weapon for his work; *And I have created the waster to destroy*[6].

כָּל־כְּלִי יוּצַר עָלַיִךְ לֹא יִצְלָח וְכָל־לָשׁוֹן תָּקוּם־אִתָּךְ לַמִּשְׁפָּט תַּרְשִׁיעִי זֹאת נַחֲלַת עַבְדֵי יְהוָה וְצִדְקָתָם מֵאִתִּי נְאֻם־יְהוָה

17[7] No weapon that is formed against you *shall prosper*[8]; and you shall condemn every tongue *that shall rise against you in judgment*[9]. This is the heritage of the servants of the LORD, And their due reward from Me, says the LORD.[10]

Isaiah – Chapter 55

הוֹי כָּל־צָמֵא לְכוּ לַמַּיִם וַאֲשֶׁר אֵין־לוֹ כָּסֶף לְכוּ שִׁבְרוּ וֶאֱכֹלוּ וּלְכוּ שִׁבְרוּ בְּלוֹא־כֶסֶף וּבְלוֹא מְחִיר יַיִן וְחָלָב

1[11] Everyone who thirsts, come for water, And he who has no money; come, *buy, and eat; Yes, come*[12], *buy wine and milk without money and without price*[13].

לָמָּה תִשְׁקְלוּ־כֶסֶף בְּלוֹא־לֶחֶם וִיגִיעֲכֶם בְּלוֹא לְשָׂבְעָה שִׁמְעוּ שָׁמוֹעַ אֵלַי וְאִכְלוּ־טוֹב וְתִתְעַנַּג בַּדֶּשֶׁן נַפְשְׁכֶם

2[14] Why do you spend money for what is not bread? And your gain for what does not satisfy? Listen diligently to Me, and eat what is good, And let your soul delight itself in fatness.

---

[1] Isaiah 54:15 - b.Avodah Zara [Rashi] 3b, b.Yevamot 24b, Ecclesiastes.R 1:18, Ein Yaakov Yevamot 24b, Ezekiel 38:8-23, Isaiah 41:11-16 43:3-4 19:14, Joel 4:9-14, Joseph and Aseneth 15:7, Psalms 37:12-13, Revelation 16:14 19:19-21 20:8-9, Zechariah 2:8 12:3 12:9 14:2-3

[2] 1QIsaa *will attack*

[3] 1QIsaa *they will fall*

[4] Isaiah 54:16 - Cairo Damascus 6:3-11, Cairo Damascus 6.8, Daniel 4:31-4:32, Exodus 9:16, Exodus.R 48:5, Isaiah 10:5-10:6 10:15 13:26 22:11, John 19:11, Mas.Soferim 7:2, Proverbs 16:4, There is a dagesh with vowel but without consonant in הֵן [or הֵן] to be read הִנֵּה.

[5] LXX *you, not as the coppersmith*

[6] LXX *but I have created you, not for ruin, that I should destroy you*

[7] Isaiah 54:17 - 1 Corinthians 1:30, 2 Corinthians 5:21, 2 Peter 1:1, Abnormal Dagesh in ל on וכל־לישון, Daniel 3:26 6:21, Deuteronomy.R 3:6, Esther.R 10:13, Ezekiel 38:9-10, Genesis.R 32:10, Isaiah 5:8 45:24-25 2:8 6:15 10:14 13:10, Jeremiah 23:6, Job 1:11 2:5 22:5-30 18:7, John 10:28-30, Matthew 16:18, Midrash Tanchuma Toledot 5, Philippians 3:9, Psalms 2:1-6 32:6 61:6 71:16 71:19, Revelation 12:10, Romans 3:22 6:22-23 8:1 8:28-39 10:4, Song of Songs.R 4:8, z.Emor 104a, Zechariah 3:1-4

[8] 1QIsaa *will be effective*

[9] Missing in 1QIsaa

[10] LXX reads *I will not allow any weapon formed against you to prosper; and every voice that shall rise up against you for judgment, you shall vanquish them all; and your adversaries shall be condemned. There is an inheritance to those who serve the LORD, and you shall be righteous before me, says the LORD.*

[11] Isaiah 55:1 - 1 Corinthians 3:2, 1 Peter 2:2, Avot de R'Natan 41, b.Avodah Zara 5b, b.Bava Kamma 14a 82a, b.Bechorot 6b, b.Kiddushin [Rashi] 40b, b.Kiddushin 30b, b.Sanhedrin [Rashi] 7a, b.Succah [Rashi] 52a, b.Succah 52b, b.Taanit 7a, Bahir 51 136, Chibbur Yafeh 27 {118a}, Deuteronomy.R 7:3, Ecclesiastes.R 11:1, Ein Yaakov Bava Kamma:17a, Ein Yaakov Kiddushin:30b, Ein Yaakov Sukkah:52b, Ein Yaakov Taanit:6b, Ephesians 2:4-8, Exodus.R 2:5 9:1 15:27 25:8, Genesis.R 41:9 54:1 66:2 84:16, Hosea 14:6, Isaiah 41:17-18 20:3 4:3, Joel 4:18, John 2:3-10 4:10-14 7:37-38, Lamentations 5:4, Mas.Derek Eretz Zutta 8:1, Matthew 10:8 13:44 2:29, Mekhilta de R'Shimon bar Yochai Vayassa 37:2, Mekilta de R'Ishmael Vayassa 1:75, Midrash Psalms 1:18 15:4 34:2 87:5, Midrash Tanchuma Bamidbar 6, Midrash Tanchuma Bereshit 1, Midrash Tanchuma Beshallach 19, Midrash Tanchuma Ki Tavo 3, Midrash Tanchuma Vayakhel 8, mt.Hilchot Talmud Torah 3:9, mt.Hilchot Tefilah 12:1, Numbers.R 1:7 1:8, Proverbs 1:21-23 8:4, Psalms 42:2-3 63:2 23:6, Ralbag SOS 1, Revelation 3:18 21:6 22:1 22:17, Romans 3:24, Ruth 4:1, Sifre Devarim Ekev 48, Song of Songs 1:2 1:4 5:1, Song of Songs.R 1:19, Tanna Devei Eliyahu 2, Tanya Likutei Aramim §10 §40, z.Beshallach 60a, z.Terumah 128a, Zechariah 2:6 9:15 10:7

Isaiah 55:1-7 - 4QIsac

Isaiah 55:1-13 - 1QIsaa

[12] Missing in 1QIsaa; LXX *go and buy*

[13] LXX *and eat and drink wine and fat without money or price.*

[14] Isaiah 55:2 - Deuteronomy 11:13, Ecclesiastes 6:2, Exodus 15:26, Habakkuk 2:13, Hebrews 13:9, Hosea 8:7 12:3, Isaiah 1:19 1:6 20:20 22:6 3:1 3:4 3:7, Jeremiah 2:13 7:15, John 6:48-6:58, Leviticus.R 30:1, Luke 15:15-15:16 15:23, Mark 7:14, Matthew 15:9 22:4, Midrash Psalms 98:2, Pesikta de R'Kahana 27.1, Pesikta Rabbati 51:1, Philippians 3:4-3:7, Proverbs 1:33 7:23 8:32 9:5, Psalms 22:27 34:12 36:9 63:6, Romans 9:31 10:2-3 10:17

Isaiah 55:2-13 - 1QIsab

Hebrew	Verse	English

הַטּוּ אָזְנְכֶם וּלְכוּ אֵלַי שִׁמְעוּ וּתְחִי נַפְשְׁכֶם
וְאֶכְרְתָה לָכֶם בְּרִית עוֹלָם חַסְדֵי דָוִד הַנֶּאֱמָנִים

3[1] Incline your ear, *and come to Me*[2]; Hear, and your soul shall live[3]; And I will make an eternal covenant with you, the sure mercies of David.

הֵן עֵד לְאוּמִּים נְתַתִּיו נָגִיד וּמְצַוֵּה לְאֻמִּים

4[4] Behold, I have given him as a witness to the peoples, A prince and commander to the peoples.

הֵן גּוֹי לֹא־תֵדַע תִּקְרָא וְגוֹי לֹא־יְדָעוּךָ אֵלֶיךָ
יָרוּצוּ לְמַעַן יְהוָה אֱלֹהֶיךָ וְלִקְדוֹשׁ יִשְׂרָאֵל כִּי
פֵאֲרָךְ

5[5] Behold, you shall call a nation whom you do not know, And a nation that never knew you shall run to you[6]; Because of the LORD your God, And for the Holy One of Israel, for He has glorified you.

הֵן גּוֹי לֹא־תֵדַע תִּקְרָא וְגוֹי לֹא־יְדָעוּךָ אֵלֶיךָ
יָרוּצוּ לְמַעַן יְהוָה אֱלֹהֶיךָ וְלִקְדוֹשׁ יִשְׂרָאֵל כִּי
פֵאֲרָךְ

6[7] Seek the LORD while He may be found, call upon Him while He is near;

יַעֲזֹב רָשָׁע דַּרְכּוֹ וְאִישׁ אָוֶן מַחְשְׁבֹתָיו וְיָשֹׁב אֶל־
יְהוָה וִירַחֲמֵהוּ וְאֶל־אֱלֹהֵינוּ כִּי־יַרְבֶּה לִסְלוֹחַ

7[8] Let the wicked forsake his way, And the man of iniquity his thoughts; And let him return to the LORD, and He will have compassion on him, And to our God, for He will abundantly pardon[9]

כִּי לֹא מַחְשְׁבוֹתַי מַחְשְׁבוֹתֵיכֶם וְלֹא דַרְכֵיכֶם
דְּרָכָי נְאֻם יְהוָה

8[10] For My thoughts are not your thoughts, nor are your ways My ways, says the LORD.

כִּי־גָבְהוּ שָׁמַיִם מֵאָרֶץ כֵּן גָּבְהוּ דְרָכַי מִדַּרְכֵיכֶם
וּמַחְשְׁבֹתַי מִמַּחְשְׁבֹתֵיכֶם

9[11] For as the heavens are higher than the earth, so are My ways higher than your ways, and My thoughts than your thoughts.

---

[1] Isaiah 55:3 - 2 Samuel 7:8-17 23:5, Acts 13:34, Deuteronomy.R 10:1, Exodus.R 27:9, Ezekiel 37:24-37:25, Gates of Repentance 2.012, Genesis 17:7, Hebrews 13:20, Isaiah 6:8 13:8, Jastrow 1394a, Jeremiah 6:9 8:40 33:20-21 9:26 2:5, John 5:24-25 6:37 6:44-45 7:37 8:47 10:27, Leviticus 18:5, Matthew 11:28 13:16 17:5, Pesikta de R'Kahana 14.2, Proverbs 4:20, Psalms 78:1 89:29 89:36-38 119:112, Romans 10:5, Tanya Igeret Hakodesh §01, z.Bereshit 8a, z.Terumah 169a, z.Vayechi 219a

[2] LXX and *follow my ways*

[3] LXX adds *in prosperity*

[4] Isaiah 55:4 - 1 Timothy 6:13, 2 Thessalonians 1:8, Daniel 9:25, Ephesians 5:24, Ezekiel 34:23-24, Hebrews 2:10 5:9, Hosea 3:5, Isaiah 9:7-9:8 49:8-49:10, Jeremiah 6:9, John 3:16 10:3 10:27 12:26 13:13 18:37, Matthew 2:6 28:18-20, Micah 5:3-5:5, Midrash Psalms 40:2 51:3, Psalms 2:6 18:44, Revelation 1:5 3:14

[5] Isaiah 55:5 - 1 Peter 1:11, Acts 3:13 5:31, Ephesians 2:11 3:5, Genesis 1:10, Hebrews 5:5, Hosea 2:1, Isaiah 11:10-11 21:23 1:6 4:15 7:4 8:8 12:5 12:9, John 13:31-32 17:1, Luke 24:26, Psalms 18:44 110:1-3, Pesikta de R'Kahana S6.1, Psalms of Solomon 17:31, Romans 15:20, Zechariah 2:11 8:20-23

Isaiah 55:5-6 - Midrash Tanchuma Haazinu 4

[6] LXX adds *for refuge*

[7] Isaiah 55:6 - 1 Chronicles 4:9, 2 Chronicles 19:3, 2 Corinthians 6:1-2, Amos 5:6, b.Rosh Hashanah 18a, b.Yevamot 49b 105a, Deuteronomy 4:7, Ein Yaakov Rosh Hashanah:18a, Ein Yaakov Yevamot:49b, Ephesians 3:13, Ezekiel 8:6, Gates of Repentance 2.014, Hebrews 2:3 3:13, Isaiah 12:6 21:19 22:12 1:8 17:24, Jeremiah 29:12-29:14, Job 8:5, John 7:33-34 8:21 12:35-36, Luke 13:25, Matthew 5:25 7:7-8 25:11-12, Midrash Proverbs 1, Midrash Psalms 10:2, Midrash Tanchuma Haazinu 4, mt.Hilchot Teshuvah 2:6 2:6, Numbers.R 11:7, Pesikta de R'Kahana S7.1-3, Pesikta Rabbati 31:3 44:5, Psalms 14:2 27:8 32:6 75:2 95:7 1:18 4:14, Siman 130:1, Verse for names ד-ב [Pisukim Lesheimot Anoshim], y.Berachot 5:1, z.Vayera 105b

Isaiah 55:6-7 - Pesikta de R'Kahana S7.3, Selichot [Neilah Yom Kippur]

Isaiah 55:6-56:8 - Haftarah Minchah [Fast Days and Tisha B'Av [Ashkenaz]], Mas.Soferim 17:7, mt.Hilchot Tefilah 13:18

Isaiah 55:6-56:8 - Fast of Esther, Haftarah Vayeilech, Minor Fasts [Fast of Gedaliah, Seventeenth of Tammuz, Siman 121:1, Tenth of Tevet, Tisha B'Av] Morning Haftarah

[8] Isaiah 55:7 - 1 Corinthians 6:9-6:11, 1 Timothy 1:15-1:16, 2 Chronicles 7:14, Acts 3:19 8:21-8:22 2:20, b.Megillah 14b, Ein Yaakov Megillah:17b, Ephesians 1:6-1:8, Exodus 34:6-34:7, Ezekiel 3:18-3:19 18:21-18:23 18:27-18:32 9:11 33:14-33:16, Gates of Repentance 1.011 1.011, Genesis 6:5, Hosea 14:3-14:4, Isaiah 1:16-1:18 8:7 16:2 19:25 20:22 6:10 11:7, James 1:15 4:8-4:10, Jastrow 703b, Jeremiah 3:3 3:12-3:13 4:14 8:4-8:6, Jonah 3:10, Leviticus.R 3:3, Luke 7:47 11:39-11:40 15:10 15:24, Mark 7:21 7:23, Matthew 9:13 15:18-15:19 23:25-23:26, Midrash Proverbs 28, Midrash Psalms 25:3 38:2 103:9, mt.Hilchot Teshuvah 2:2 2:2 7:3 7:3, Numbers 14:18-14:19, Pesikta Rabbati 44:1, Proverbs 4:13, Psalms 51:2 66:18 10:7, Romans 5:16-5:21, Saadia Opinions 5:7 5:8, Siman 127:1, Tanya Igeret Hateshuvah §01 §07 §11, y.Berachot 2:4, Zechariah 8:17

[9] LXX adds *your sins*

[10] Isaiah 55:8 - 2 Samuel 7:19, 4 Ezra 4:13, Daniel 4:34, Ezekiel 18:29, Hosea 14:11, Isaiah 5:6, Jeremiah 3:1, Midrash Proverbs 1 11, mt.Hilchot Melachim u'Michamoteihem 11:4, mt.Hilchot Teshuvah 5:5 5:5, Pesikta de R'Kahana 24.1, Pesikta Rabbati 44:2, Proverbs 21:8 1:3, Psalms 25:10 40:6 92:6, Tanya Likutei Aramim §02 §21 §48, Tanya Likutei Aramim §04, Tanya Shaar Hayichud §07, z.Bereshit 58a, z.Vayikra 5b

[11] Isaiah 55:9 - Matthew 11:25, Perek Shirah, Psalms 36:6 77:20 89:3 7:11, Romans 11:31-36, Saadia Opinions 3:2, Tanya Shaar Hayichud §7 §10

Hebrew		English
כִּי כַּאֲשֶׁר יֵרֵד הַגֶּשֶׁם וְהַשֶּׁלֶג מִן־הַשָּׁמַיִם וְשָׁמָּה לֹא יָשׁוּב כִּי אִם־הִרְוָה אֶת־הָאָרֶץ וְהוֹלִידָהּ וְהִצְמִיחָהּ וְנָתַן זֶרַע לַזֹּרֵעַ וְלֶחֶם לָאֹכֵל	10¹	For as the rain comes down and the snow from heaven, And does not return, except it water the earth, and make it bring forth and bud, And give seed to the sower and bread to the eater;
כֵּן יִהְיֶה דְבָרִי אֲשֶׁר יֵצֵא מִפִּי לֹא־יָשׁוּב אֵלַי רֵיקָם כִּי אִם־עָשָׂה אֶת־אֲשֶׁר חָפַצְתִּי וְהִצְלִיחַ אֲשֶׁר שְׁלַחְתִּיו	11²	So shall My word be that goes forth from My mouth: It shall not return to *Me void, except it accomplish what I please, And make the thing for which I sent it prosper*³.
כִּי־בְשִׂמְחָה תֵצֵאוּ וּבְשָׁלוֹם תּוּבָלוּן הֶהָרִים וְהַגְּבָעוֹת יִפְצְחוּ לִפְנֵיכֶם רִנָּה וְכָל־עֲצֵי הַשָּׂדֶה יִמְחֲאוּ־כָף	12⁴	For you shall go out with joy, And *be led forth*⁵ with peace; The mountains and the hills shall break forth before you in singing, And all the trees of the field shall clap their hands.
תַּחַת הַנַּעֲצוּץ יַעֲלֶה בְרוֹשׁ "תַּחַת' וְתַחַת" הַסִּרְפַּד יַעֲלֶה הֲדַס וְהָיָה לַיהוָה לְשֵׁם לְאוֹת עוֹלָם לֹא יִכָּרֵת	13⁶	Instead of the thorn shall come up the cypress, And instead of the brier shall come up the myrtle; And it shall be to the LORD for *a memorial, For an everlasting sign*⁷ that shall not be cut off.

Isaiah – Chapter 56

Hebrew		English
כֹּה אָמַר יְהוָה שִׁמְרוּ מִשְׁפָּט וַעֲשׂוּ צְדָקָה כִּי־קְרוֹבָה יְשׁוּעָתִי לָבוֹא וְצִדְקָתִי לְהִגָּלוֹת	1⁸	Thus says the LORD: Keep justice, and do righteousness; For My salvation is near to come, And My favor to be revealed.
אַשְׁרֵי אֱנוֹשׁ יַעֲשֶׂה־זֹּאת וּבֶן־אָדָם יַחֲזִיק בָּהּ שֹׁמֵר שַׁבָּת מֵחַלְּלוֹ וְשֹׁמֵר יָדוֹ מֵעֲשׂוֹת כָּל־רָע	2⁹	Happy is the man who does this, and the son of man who holds fast by it: who keeps from profaning the sabbath, And keeps his hand from doing any evil.
וְאַל־יֹאמַר בֶּן־הַנֵּכָר הַנִּלְוָה אֶל־יְהוָה לֵאמֹר הַבְדֵּל יַבְדִּילַנִי יְהוָה מֵעַל עַמּוֹ וְאַל־יֹאמַר הַסָּרִיס הֵן אֲנִי עֵץ יָבֵשׁ	3¹⁰	Nor let the alien who has joined himself to the LORD, speak, saying: 'The LORD will surely

---

Isaiah 55:9-11 - Sefer Yetzirah 1:11

¹ Isaiah 55:10 - 1 Samuel 23:4, 2 Corinthians 9:9-9:11, 2 Enoch 5:2, b.Chagigah [Tosefot] 12b, b.Taanit 6b 8b, Deuteronomy 8:2, Ecclesiastes.R 3:22, Ezekiel 10:26, Genesis.R 12:11, Guide for the Perplexed 1:7, Hosea 10:12, Isaiah 5:6 6:23 13:11, Jastrow 182a, Psalms 65:10-65:14 72:6-72:7, Revelation 11:6, Sifre Devarim {Ekev} 39, Sifre Devarim Ekev 39

² Isaiah 55:11 - 1 Corinthians 1:18 3:6-9, 1 Peter 1:23, 1 Thessalonians 2:13, 3 Enoch 48C:10-11, Deuteronomy 8:2, Ephesians1:9-11, Exodus.R 38:1, Hebrews 6:7, Isaiah 44:26-28 21:23 22:10 6:9, James 1:18, John 6:63, Luke 8:11-16, Matthew 24:35, Midrash Tanchuma Bechukkotai 3, Romans 10:17, z.Pekudei 240a

³ LXX *until all the things that I willed shall have been accomplished; and I will make you ways prosperous, and will affect my commands*

⁴ Isaiah 55:12 - 1 Chronicles 16:32-33, b.Succah 48b, Colossians 1:11, Galatians 5:22, Guide for the Perplexed 2:47, Isaiah 14:8 35:1-2 11:10 42:10-11 20:23 24:20 49:9-10 1:13 3:11 6:10 6:13 65:13-14, Jeremiah 6:19 31:13-15 9:6 9:11, Luke 15:10, Midrash Psalms 13:4, Motzoei Shabbat [Viyiten Lecha], Pesikta de R'Kahana S2.6 S6.2, Pesikta Rabbati 41:5, Psalms 47:2 65:14 96:11-13 98:7-9 9:43 148:4-13, Revelation 19:1-6, Romans 5:1 5:11 15:13, Saadia Opinions 2:10, Sifre Devarim Ha'azinu Hashamayim 333, Sifre Devarim Nitzavim 333, z.Balak 212b, z.Bamidbar 118a, z.Vayikra 8b, Zechariah 2:7-10

⁵ 1QIsaa *come back*

⁶ Isaiah 55:13 - 1 Corinthians 6:9-6:11, 1 Peter 2:9-10 4:11, 2 Corinthians 5:17, 2 Enoch 47:4, b.Megillah 10b, Ein Yaakov Megillah:9b, Ephesians 3:20-3:21, Esther.R 10:10, Isaiah 5:6 11:6-9 17:19 19:21 6:10 12:13 12:21 13:3 15:12, Jastrow 198a 921a 1476a, Jeremiah 13:11 9:9 2:5, John 15:8, Luke 2:14, Micah 7:4, Midrash Tanchuma Pinchas 14, Numbers.R 21:22, Romans 6:19, Song of Songs.R 1:6

⁷ 1QIsaa *sign for an everlasting renown*

⁸ Isaiah 56:1 - b.Bava Batra 10a, b.Makkot 24a, b.Megillah [Tosefot] 21a, Deuteronomy.R 5:7, Ein Yaakov Bava Batra:10a, Exodus.R 30:24, Isaiah 1:16-1:19 26:7-26:8 22:13 3:5 7:7, Jeremiah 7:3-7:11, John 7:17, Luke 3:3-3:9, Malachi 3:22, Mark 1:15, Matthew 3:2 4:17, Mekilta de R'Ishmael Nezikin 18:101, Midrash Psalms 119:53 17A:23, Midrash Tanchuma Mishpatim 3 4, Midrash Tanchuma Shoftim 8 9, Psalms 24:4-24:6 50:23 85:10, Romans 1:17 10:6-10:10 13:11-13:14, Sifre Devarim {Vezot Habracha} 355, Sifre Devarim Vezot Habracha 355, z.Vaetchanan 269b

Isaiah 56:1-8 - Maamad [Shabbat]

Isaiah 56:1-12 - 1QIsaa, 1QIsab

⁹ Isaiah 56:2 - b.Ketubot [Tosefot] 5a, b.Shabbat 118b, Ecclesiastes 7:18, Ein Yaakov Shabbat:118b, Exodus 20:8 20:10 31:13-31:16, Exodus.R 25:12, Ezekiel 20:12 20:20, Isaiah 8:4 8:6 10:13, Jeremiah 17:21-17:22, John 13:17, Leviticus 19:30, Leviticus.R 21:6 25:2, Luke 11:28 12:43, Mekhilta de R'Shimon bar Yochai Vayassa 42:1, Mekilta de R'Ishmael Vayassa 6:10, Midrash Psalms 92:2, mt.Hilchot Chametz u'Matzah 16:15, Nehemiah 13:17, Pirkei de R'Eliezer 19, Proverbs 4:13 4:27 14:16 16:6 16:17, Psalms 1:1-1:3 15:1-15:5 34:15 37:27 10:3 16:1 119:1-119:5 119:101 8:1, Revelation 22:14, Romans 12:9, Siman 72:3, z.Vayakhel 204b

¹⁰ Isaiah 56:3 - 1 Corinthians 6:17, 1 Peter 1:1, Acts 8:26-8:40 10:1-10:2 10:34 13:47-13:48 17:4 18:7, Daniel 1:3-1:21, Deuteronomy

separate me from His people'; nor let the eunuch say: 'Behold, I am a dry tree.'

4[1] For thus says the LORD concerning the eunuchs who keep My sabbaths, and choose the things that please Me, And hold fast by My covenant:

5[2] Even to them I will give in My house and within My walls a monument and a memorial better than sons and daughters; I will give them an everlasting memorial, so shall not be cut off.

6[3] Also the aliens who join themselves to the LORD, *to minister to Him, and to love the name of the LORD*[4], To be His servants, Everyone who keeps the sabbath from profaning it, And holds fast by My covenant:

7[5] I will bring them to My holy mountain, And make them joyful in My house of prayer; Their burnt offerings and their sacrifices Shall be accepted on My altar; for My house shall be called A house of prayer for all peoples.

8[6] Says the Lord GOD who gathers the dispersed of Israel: I will yet gather others to him, beside those of him who are gathered.

9[7] *All you beasts*[8] of the field, come to devour, Yes, *all you beasts*[9] in the forest.

10[10] His watchmen are all blind, without knowledge; they are all dumb dogs, they cannot bark; *raving, lying down*[11], loving to slumber.

11[12] Yes, the dogs are greedy, they do not know when they have enough; *and these are*

כִּי־כֹה ׀ אָמַר יְהֹוָה לַסָּרִיסִים אֲשֶׁר יִשְׁמְרוּ אֶת־שַׁבְּתוֹתַי וּבָחֲרוּ בַּאֲשֶׁר חָפָצְתִּי וּמַחֲזִיקִים בִּבְרִיתִֽי

וְנָתַתִּי לָהֶם בְּבֵיתִי וּבְחוֹמֹתַי יָד וָשֵׁם טוֹב מִבָּנִים וּמִבָּנוֹת שֵׁם עוֹלָם אֶתֶּן־לוֹ אֲשֶׁר לֹא יִכָּרֵֽת

וּבְנֵי הַנֵּכָר הַנִּלְוִים עַל־יְהֹוָה לְשָׁרְתוֹ וּֽלְאַהֲבָה אֶת־שֵׁם יְהֹוָה לִהְיוֹת לוֹ לַעֲבָדִים כָּל־שֹׁמֵר שַׁבָּת מֵֽחַלְּלוֹ וּמַחֲזִיקִים בִּבְרִיתִֽי

וַהֲבִיאוֹתִים אֶל־הַר קָדְשִׁי וְשִׂמַּחְתִּים בְּבֵית תְּפִלָּתִי עוֹלֹתֵיהֶם וְזִבְחֵיהֶם לְרָצוֹן עַל־מִזְבְּחִי כִּי בֵיתִי בֵּית־תְּפִלָּה יִקָּרֵא לְכָל־הָעַמִּֽים

נְאֻם אֲדֹנָי יְהֹוִה מְקַבֵּץ נִדְחֵי יִשְׂרָאֵל עוֹד אֲקַבֵּץ עָלָיו לְנִקְבָּצָֽיו

כֹּל חַיְתוֹ שָׂדָי אֵתָיוּ לֶאֱכֹל כָּל־חַיְתוֹ בַּיָּֽעַר

צֹפָו "צֹפָיו" עִוְרִים כֻּלָּם לֹא יָדָעוּ כֻּלָּם כְּלָבִים אִלְּמִים לֹא יוּכְלוּ לִנְבֹּחַ הֹזִים שֹׁכְבִים אֹהֲבֵי לָנֽוּם

וְהַכְּלָבִים עַזֵּי־נֶפֶשׁ לֹא יָדְעוּ שָׂבְעָה וְהֵמָּה רֹעִים לֹא יָדְעוּ הָבִין כֻּלָּם לְדַרְכָּם פָּנוּ אִישׁ לְבִצְעוֹ מִקָּצֵֽהוּ

23:3-23:4, Ephesians 2:12 2:22, Exodus.R 19:4, Isaiah 14:1 15:7 8:5, Jeremiah 38:7-38:13 39:16-39:17 2:5, Liber Antiquitatum Biblicarum 50:1, Luke 7:6-7:8, Matthew 8:10-8:11 15:26-15:27 19:12-19:30, Midrash Tanchuma Bamidbar 25, Numbers 18:4 18:7, Numbers.R 5:3, Romans 2:10-2:11 15:9-15:12 15:16, Zechariah 8:20-8:23, Zephaniah 2:11

[1] Isaiah 56:4 - 2 Samuel 23:5, b.Sanhedrin 93b, b.Shabbat 118b, Ein Yaakov Shabbat:118b, Hebrews 6:17, Isaiah 3:5 7:3 8:2 8:6, Jeremiah 2:5, Joshua 24:15, Luke 10:42, Pirkei de R'Eliezer 52, Psalms 119:111, z.Kedoshim 82a, z.Vaetchanan 269b

[2] Isaiah 56:5 - 1 John 3:1, 1 Samuel 1:8, 1 Timothy 3:15, b.Sanhedrin 93b, Ein Yaakov Sanhedrin:93b, Ephesians 2:22, Hebrews 3:6, Isaiah 2:1 24:19 7:13 12:18 14:12, John 1:12, Matthew 16:18, Midrash Tanchuma Vayakhel 1, Pirkei de R'Eliezer 52, Revelation 3:5 3:12, z.Yitro 82b

[3] Isaiah 56:6 - 1 Corinthians 16:22, 1 Thessalonians 1:9-1:10, 2 Corinthians 8:5, Acts 2:41 11:23, b.Ketubot 5a, Ephesians 6:24, Galatians 5:6, Isaiah 20:5 56:2-56:4 10:13 12:10 13:5, James 1:12 2:5, Jeremiah 2:5, Joseph and Aseneth 15:7, Mark 12:30-12:34, Mas.Gerim 4:3, Mekilta de R'Ishmael Nezikin 18:19, Mekilta de R'Ishmael Nezikin 18:22, Mekilta de R'Ishmael Nezikin 18:27, Numbers.R 8:2, Revelation 1:10, Romans 8:28

[4] Missing in 1QIsaa due to homoioteleuton

[5] Isaiah 56:7 - 1 Peter 1:1-1:2 2:5, 1 Timothy 2:8, b.Berachot 7a, b.Megillah 18a, b.Shabbat 118b, Ein Yaakov Berachot:7a, Ein Yaakov Megillah:18a, Ein Yaakov Shabbat:118b, Ephesians 2:11-2:13, Hebrews 12:22 13:15, Isaiah 2:2-2:3 66:19-66:20, John 4:21-23 12:20-26, Lamentations.R 1:23, Luke 19:46, Malachi 1:11, Mark 11:17, Mas.Gerim 4:3, Matthew 21:13, Mekilta de R'Ishmael Nezikin 18:29, Micah 4:1-4:2, Midrash Tanchuma Re'eh 18, Numbers.R 8:2, Pesikta de R'Kahana 10.1, Psalms 2:6, Romans 12:1, Selichot, Shepherd Similitudes 5:5:3, y.Berachot 2:4 4:5, z.Mikketz 203a, Zechariah 8:3 Isaiah 56:7-8 - 4QIsai

[6] Isaiah 56:8 - Ephesians 1:10 2:14-16, Genesis 1:10, Genesis.R 98 [Excl]:2, Hosea 2:2, Isaiah 11:11-12 27:12-13 19:6 1:12 1:22 6:7 60:3-11 66:18-21, Jeremiah 6:17 7:11, John 10:16 11:52, Micah 4:6, Psalms 10:47 107:2-3 3:2, Zechariah 10:8-10, Zephaniah 3:18-20

[7] Isaiah 56:9 - Deuteronomy 4:26, Ezekiel 5:5 15:17, Isaiah 18:6, Jeremiah 12:9, Revelation 19:17-18

[8] 1QIsaa *Every wild animal*

[9] 1QIsaa *Every wild animal*

[10] Isaiah 56:10 - Ezekiel 3:15-3:18 3:26-3:27 13:16 9:6, Hosea 4:6 9:7-9:8, Isaiah 5:10 4:8 10:1, Jeremiah 6:13-6:14 14:13-14:14 23:13-23:14, Jonah 1:2-1:6, Luke 6:39-6:40, Mark 13:34-13:37, Matthew 15:14 23:16-23:26, Nahum 3:18, Philippians 3:2, Proverbs 6:4-6:10 24:30-24:34, Traditional Enlarged צ in צֹפָו

[11] LXX *dreaming of rest*

[12] Isaiah 56:11 - 1 Peter 5:2, 1 Samuel 2:12-2:17 2:29, 1 Timothy 3:3 3:8, 2 Corinthians 4:4, 2 Peter 2:3 2:14-2:16, Acts 20:29 20:33, b.Berachot 56b, Ecclesiastes 5:11, Exodus 23:3, Ezekiel 13:19 34:2-34:3, Isaiah 1:3 9:17, Jeremiah 22:17, John 8:43, Jude 1:11 1:16, Malachi 1:10, Matthew 13:14-13:15, Mesillat Yesharim 11:Traits-of-Nekuyut, Micah 3:5-3:6 3:11, Midrash Psalms 4:11, Philippians

shepherds[1] who cannot understand; they all turn to their own way, *each one to his gain, one and all*[2].

אָתָיוּ אֶקְחָה־יַיִן וְנִסְבְּאָה שֵׁכָר וְהָיָה כָזֶה יוֹם מָחָר גָּדוֹל יֶתֶר מְאֹד

12[3] 'Come, I will fetch wine, And we will fill ourselves with strong drink; And tomorrow shall be like day, And much more abundant.'

Isaiah – Chapter 57

הַצַּדִּיק אָבָד וְאֵין אִישׁ שָׂם עַל־לֵב וְאַנְשֵׁי־חֶסֶד נֶאֱסָפִים בְּאֵין מֵבִין כִּי־מִפְּנֵי הָרָעָה נֶאֱסַף הַצַּדִּיק

1[4] The righteous perish, and no man lays it to heart, and *godly men*[5] are taken away, no one considers the righteous are taken away from the evil to come.

יָבוֹא שָׁלוֹם יָנוּחוּ עַל־מִשְׁכְּבוֹתָם הֹלֵךְ נְכֹחוֹ

2[6] He enters into peace, they rest in their beds, each one who walks in *his*[7] uprightness[8].

וְאַתֶּם קִרְבוּ־הֵנָּה בְּנֵי עֹנְנָה זֶרַע מְנָאֵף וַתִּזְנֶה

3[9] But draw near here, *You sons of the sorceress*[10], the seed of the adulterer and *the harlot*[11].

עַל־מִי תִּתְעַנָּגוּ עַל־מִי תַּרְחִיבוּ פֶה תַּאֲרִיכוּ לָשׁוֹן הֲלוֹא־אַתֶּם יִלְדֵי־פֶשַׁע זֶרַע שָׁקֶר

4[12] Against whom do you *sport yourselves*[13]? Against whom do you make a wide mouth, And draw out the tongue? Are you not children of transgression, A seed of *falsehood*[14],

הַנֶּחָמִים בָּאֵלִים תַּחַת כָּל־עֵץ רַעֲנָן שֹׁחֲטֵי הַיְלָדִים בַּנְּחָלִים תַּחַת סְעִפֵי הַסְּלָעִים

5[15] You who *inflame yourselves among the terebinths*[16], under every leafy tree; who slay the children in the valleys, under the clefts of the rocks?

3:2 3:19, Revelation 22:15, Saadia Opinions 10:5, Titus 1:7 1:11, z.Kedoshim 80a, Zechariah 11:15-17

[1] LXX *and they are wicked*

[2] LXX *each according to his will*

[3] Isaiah 56:12 - 1 Corinthians 15:32, Amos 6:3-6:6, b.Taanit 11a, Ein Yaakov Taanit:11a, Hosea 4:11, Isaiah 5:11 5:22 22:13-22:14 28:7-28:8, Jeremiah 18:18, Luke 12:19-12:20 12:45-12:46 21:34, Matthew 24:49-24:51, Midrash Tanchuma Ki Tissa 14, Midrash Tanchuma Re'eh 16, Proverbs 23:35 3:1 31:4-31:5, Psalms 10:7, Titus 1:7

[4] Isaiah 57:1 - 1 Enoch 81:9, 1 Kings 14:13, 2 Chronicles 8:33 10:28 11:24, 2 Kings 22:20, b.Bava Kamma 60a, b.Sanhedrin 113b, b.Taanit 11a, Ein Yaakov Bava Kamma:60a, Ein Yaakov Sanhedrin:113b, Ein Yaakov Taanit:11a, Isaiah 18:25 23:7 9:11, Malachi 2:2, Mas.Kallah Rabbati 3:26 6:1 6:1 6:1, Mas.Semachot 8:8, Micah 7:2, Midrash Psalms 149:5, Pirkei de R'Eliezer 17, Psalms 12:2, t.Sotah 10:2, z.Beshallach 57b, z.Vaetchanan 266b, z.Vayeshev 180a

Isaiah 57:1-2 - 11QIsaa

Isaiah 57:1-3 - Mekilta de R'Ishmael Nezikin 18:69-73

Isaiah 57:1-4 - 11QIsab

[5] 1QIsaa *people of the mercy*

[6] Isaiah 57:2 - 2 Chronicles 16:14, 2 Corinthians 5:1 5:8, After learning Mishnayot for the deceased, b.Ketubot 14a, b.Shabbat 152b, b.Sotah 5a, Derech Hashem Part I 3§11, Deuteronomy.R 11:10, Ecclesiastes 12:7, Ein Yaakov Shabbat:152b, Ezekiel 8:25, Genesis 17:1, Genesis.R 25:2, HaMadrikh 35:8, Isaiah 14:18 2:7, Job 3:18, Luke 1:6 2:29 7:50 16:22, Luke 16:22, Mas.Kallah Rabbati 6:1, Mas.Semachot 8:8, Matthew 1:21, Midrash Psalms 30:3 116:7, Numbers.R 11:7, Pesikta Rabbati 2:3 44:8, Philippians 1:23, Pirkei de R'Eliezer 20, Revelation 14:13, Sifre.z Numbers Naso 6:26, t.Sotah 10:2, Tanna Devei Eliyahu 2 5, y.Sotah 1:10, Yalkut Isaiah 487, Yalkut Psalms 889, z.Noach 63a, z.Vayakhel 199a, z.Vayakhel 200b

[7] 1QIsaa *her*

[8] LXX reads *His burial shall be in peace: he has been removed out of the way*

[9] Isaiah 57:3 - 1 John 3:10, Genesis 3:15, Hosea 1:2, Isaiah 1:21 21:20, James 4:4, Joel 4:9-4:11, John 8:40-8:44, Luke 3:7, Mas.Kallah Rabbati 6:1, Matthew 3:7 12:34 16:4 23:33, Revelation 17:1-17:5, t.Sotah 10:2

[10] LXX *you lawless children*

[11] MT *she has practices prostitution* [problematic]; LXX *harlots*

[12] Isaiah 57:4 - 2 Peter 2:13, Acts 9:4, Colossians 3:6, Ephesians 2:2-2:3 5:6, Exodus 9:17 16:7-16:8, Ezekiel 2:4, Hosea 10:9, Isaiah 1:4 10:15 6:1 6:9 13:23 13:29, Job 16:9-16:10, Joshua 10:21, Judges 16:25-16:27, Lamentations 2:15-2:16, Luke 10:16, Matthew 13:38 3:29 27:39-44, Numbers 16:11, Psalms 22:8 22:14 22:18 35:21 69:13, Tanya Igeret Hakodesh §27

[13] LXX *riot*

[14] LXX *lawlessness*

[15] Isaiah 57:5 - 1 Kings 14:23, 2 Chronicles 4:3, 2 Kings 16:3-4 17:10 23:10, Amos 2:7-8, b.Niddah 13a, Deuteronomy 12:2, Exodus 8:6, Ezekiel 6:13 16:20 20:26 20:31, Gates of Repentance 3.112, Hosea 4:11-13 7:4-7, Isaiah 1:29, Jeremiah 2:20 3:6 3:13 7:31 17:2 8:35 2:38 3:7, Leviticus 18:21 20:2-5, Mas.Kallah 1:17, Numbers 25:1-2 1:6, Pesikta Rabbati 33:13, Psalms 106:37-38, Revelation 17:1-5 18:3

Isaiah 57:5 [Targum] - mt.Hilchot Tumat Meit 13:3

Isaiah 57:5-8 - 4QIsai

[16] LXX *call upon idols under the leafy trees*

בְּחַלְקֵי־נַחַל חֶלְקֵךְ הֵם הֵם גּוֹרָלֵךְ גַּם־לָהֶם
שָׁפַכְתְּ נֶסֶךְ הֶעֱלִית מִנְחָה הַעַל אֵלֶּה אֶנָּחֵם

6[1] *Among the smooth stones of the valley[2] is your portion; They, yes, they are[3]* your lot; you have poured a drink offering to them, You have offered a meal offering. Should I pacify Myself for these things?

עַל הַר־גָּבֹהַּ וְנִשָּׂא שַׂמְתְּ מִשְׁכָּבֵךְ גַּם־שָׁם עָלִית
לִזְבֹּחַ זָבַח

7[4] Upon a high and lofty mountain you set your bed; You also went up there to offer sacrifice.

וְאַחַר הַדֶּלֶת וְהַמְּזוּזָה שַׂמְתְּ זִכְרוֹנֵךְ כִּי מֵאִתִּי
גִלִּית וַתַּעֲלִי הִרְחַבְתְּ מִשְׁכָּבֵךְ וַתִּכְרָת־לָךְ מֵהֶם
אָהַבְתְּ מִשְׁכָּבָם יָד חָזִית

8[5] *And behind the doors and the posts you set up your symbol; For you have uncovered, and have gone up from Me, you have enlarged your bed, And chosen those whose bed you love, Whose hand you saw[6].*

וַתָּשֻׁרִי לַמֶּלֶךְ בַּשֶּׁמֶן וַתַּרְבִּי רִקֻּחָיִךְ וַתְּשַׁלְּחִי
צִרַיִךְ עַד־מֵרָחֹק וַתַּשְׁפִּילִי עַד־שְׁאוֹל

9[7] *And you went to the king with ointment, and increased your perfumes, and sent your ambassadors far off, down to the netherworld[8].*

בְּרֹב דַּרְכֵּךְ יָגַעַתְּ לֹא אָמַרְתְּ נוֹאָשׁ חַיַּת יָדֵךְ
מָצָאת עַל־כֵּן לֹא חָלִית

10[9] You were wearied with the length of your way; yet you did not say: 'There is no hope'; you found a renewal of your strength; Therefore, you were not affected[10].

וְאֶת־מִי דָּאַגְתְּ וַתִּירְאִי כִּי תְכַזֵּבִי וְאוֹתִי לֹא זָכַרְתְּ
לֹא־שַׂמְתְּ עַל־לִבֵּךְ הֲלֹא אֲנִי מַחְשֶׁה וּמֵעֹלָם
וְאוֹתִי לֹא תִירָאִי

11[11] And of whom have you been afraid and in fear, so you would fail? And as for Me, you have not remembered Me, nor laid it to your heart[12]. Have not I held My peace a long time? Therefore, you did not fear Me.

אֲנִי אַגִּיד צִדְקָתֵךְ וְאֶת־מַעֲשַׂיִךְ וְלֹא יוֹעִילוּךְ

12[13] I will declare *your righteousness[14]*; your *works[15]* also[16]; they shall not profit you.

בְּזַעֲקֵךְ יַצִּילֻךְ קִבּוּצַיִךְ וְאֶת־כֻּלָּם יִשָּׂא־רוּחַ יִקַּח־
הָבֶל וְהַחוֹסֶה בִי יִנְחַל־אֶרֶץ וְיִירַשׁ הַר־קָדְשִׁי

13[17] When you cry, let those whom you gathered deliver you; but the wind shall carry them all away, a breath shall bear them off; but he who takes refuge in Me shall possess the land, and shall inherit My holy mountain.

[1] Isaiah 57:6 - Deuteronomy 32:37-38, Ein Yaakov Megillah:31a, Ezekiel 20:39, Habakkuk 2:19, Isaiah 17:11 18:3, Jeremiah 3:9 5:9 5:29 7:18 9:10 19:13 8:29 44:17-25, m.Demai 1:3, y.Avodah Zarah 3:5
[2] LXX *this*
[3] 1QIsaa *There they go as*
[4] Isaiah 57:7 - Ezekiel 16:16 16:25 20:28-20:29 23:17 23:41, Jeremiah 2:20 3:2 3:6
[5] Isaiah 57:8 - b.Shabbat 116a, Ezekiel 8:8-12 16:25-28 16:32 23:2-20 23:41, Lamentations.R Petichata D'Chakimei:22, t.Shabbat 13:5
[6] LXX *and behind the posts of your door you didst place your memorials. Did you think that if you should depart from me, you would gain? You have loved those who lay with you.*
[7] Isaiah 57:9 - 2 Kings 16:7-11, Colossians 2:18, Ezekiel 16:33 23:16 23:40, Hosea 7:11 12:3, Isaiah 2:9 30:1-6 31:1-3, Proverbs 7:17 Isaiah 57:9-21 - 4QIsad
[8] LXX *and you have multiplied your whoredom with them, and you have increased the number of those who are far from you, and have sent ambassadors beyond your borders, and have been debased to hell*
[9] Isaiah 57:10 - 2 Chronicles 28:22-23, Ezekiel 24:12, Habakkuk 2:13, Isaiah 23:13, Jeremiah 2:25 2:36 3:3 5:3 9:6 18:12 44:17-18, Romans 7:9
[10] LXX *I will cease to strengthen myself: for you have done these things; therefore you have not supplicated me*
[11] Isaiah 57:11 - 1 Timothy 4:2, 2 Thessalonians 2:9, Acts 5:3, Ecclesiastes 8:11, Ezekiel 13:22, Galatians 2:12-13, Hosea 12:1, Isaiah 2:10 6:9 51:12-13 59:3-4, Jeremiah 2:32 3:21 9:4-6 18:20, Matthew 26:69-75, Proverbs 5:25, Psalms 50:21, Revelation 21:8 22:15
[12] 1QIsaa *these things*; LXX *me*
[13] Isaiah 57:12 - Gates of Repentance 3.189, Isaiah 1:11-15 5:15 58:2-6 59:6-8 16:6 66:3-4, Jeremiah 7:4-11, Matthew 23:5 23:13, Micah 3:2-4, Pesikta Rabbati 30:4, Romans 3:10-20 10:2-3
[14] 1QIsaa *your justice*
[15] LXX *sins*
[16] 1QIsaa adds *your contingent [of idols]*
[17] Isaiah 57:13 - 2 Kings 3:13, b.Bava Batra 91b, Ein Yaakov Bava Batra:91b, Ezekiel 20:40, Genesis.R 84:1, Hosea 13:3, Isaiah 11:9 26:3-26:4 16:24 17:16 8:7 57:9-57:10 17:9 17:11 17:25 18:20, Jastrow 633b, Jeremiah 17:7-17:8 22:20 22:22, Job 21:18, Joel 4:17, Judges 10:14, Proverbs 4:25, Psalms 1:4 37:3 37:9 58:10 84:13 5:1, Zechariah 7:13

וְאָמַר סֹלּוּ־סֹלּוּ פַּנּוּ־דָרֶךְ הָרִימוּ מִכְשׁוֹל מִדֶּרֶךְ עַמִּי	14[1]	And He will say: *Cast up, cast up, clear the way*[2], Take the stumbling block out of the way of My people.
כִּי כֹה אָמַר רָם וְנִשָּׂא שֹׁכֵן עַד וְקָדוֹשׁ שְׁמוֹ מָרוֹם וְקָדוֹשׁ אֶשְׁכּוֹן וְאֶת־דַּכָּא וּשְׁפַל־רוּחַ לְהַחֲיוֹת רוּחַ שְׁפָלִים וּלְהַחֲיוֹת לֵב נִדְכָּאִים	15[3]	For thus says *the High and Lofty One who inhabits eternity, whose name is Holy: I live in the high and holy place, with he who is of a contrite and humble spirit, to revive the spirit of the humble, and to revive the heart of the contrite ones*[4].
כִּי לֹא לְעוֹלָם אָרִיב וְלֹא לָנֶצַח אֶקְצוֹף כִּי־רוּחַ מִלְּפָנַי יַעֲטוֹף וּנְשָׁמוֹת אֲנִי עָשִׂיתִי	16[5]	For I will not contend forever, nor will I always be angry; for the spirit that enwraps itself is from Me, And the souls that I have made.
בַּעֲוֹן בִּצְעוֹ קָצַפְתִּי וְאַכֵּהוּ הַסְתֵּר וְאֶקְצֹף וַיֵּלֶךְ שׁוֹבָב בְּדֶרֶךְ לִבּוֹ	17[6]	For the iniquity of *his covetousness*[7] I was angry and struck him, I hid Me and was angry; And he went forward in the way of his heart.
דְּרָכָיו רָאִיתִי וְאֶרְפָּאֵהוּ וְאַנְחֵהוּ וַאֲשַׁלֵּם נִחֻמִים לוֹ וְלַאֲבֵלָיו	18[8]	I have seen his ways, and will heal him; *I will lead him*[9], *and requite with comfort to him and his mourners*[10].
בּוֹרֵא "נוב" "נִיב" שְׂפָתָיִם שָׁלוֹם שָׁלוֹם לָרָחוֹק וְלַקָּרוֹב אָמַר יְהוָה וּרְפָאתִיו	19[11]	Peace, *peace*[12], to he who is far off and to he who is near, says the LORD who creates the fruit of the lips; And I will heal him.

---

[1] Isaiah 57:14 - 1 Corinthians 1:23 8:9 8:13 10:32-10:33, 2 Corinthians 6:3, b.Moed Katan 5a, b.Shabbat [Tosefot] 41b, b.Succah 52a, Chibbur Yafeh 27 {117a}, Ein Yaakov Sukkah:52a, Hebrews 12:13, Isaiah 11:8 16:3 14:10, Jastrow 784b, Jeremiah 18:15, Luke 3:5-3:6, Midrash Tanchuma Beha'alotcha 10, Numbers.R 15:16, Pesikta de R'Kahana S6.1, Romans 14:13
Isaiah 57:14-15 - Gates of Repentance 1.023
Isaiah 57:14-58:14 - Haftarah Shacharit Yom Kippur [Ashkenaz, mt.Hilchot Tefilah 13:11, Sephard; Teimon continue at Isaiah 59:20]
[2] LXX *Clear the ways before him*
[3] Isaiah 57:15 - 1 Kings 8:27, 1 Peter 5:5, 1 Samuel 2:2, 1 Timothy 1:17 6:16, 2 Chronicles 33:12-13 10:27, 2 Corinthians 1:4 2:7 7:6, 3 Enoch 1:5 35:6, Acts 3:14, Apocalypse of Zephaniah 2:9, b.Megillah 31a, b.Shekalim 9b, b.Sotah [Rashi] 5a, b.Sotah 5a, Daniel 4:14 4:21-22 4:31, Deuteronomy 9:27, Ein Yaakov Megillah:31a, Ein Yaakov Sotah:4b, Exodus 15:11, Ezekiel 9:4 16:63, Gates of Repentance 1.23 1.33, Genesis 21:33, Guide for the Perplexed 1:20 1:34, Hebrews 9:14, Isaiah 6:1 6:3 16:28 4:13 61:1-3 66:1-2, James 4:6, Jeremiah 10:10, Job 6:10, Lamentations.R 1:23, Leviticus.R 7:2, Luke 1:49 4:18 15:20-24, Mas.Kallah Rabbati 10:24, Matthew 5:3-4 6:9, Mekilta de R'Ishmael Bahodesh 9:101, Micah 5:3, Midrash Psalms 4:3 68:9, Midrash Tanchuma Vayera 2, Motzoei Shabbat [Viyiten Lecha], mt.Hilchot Matnot Aniyim 10:5, mt.Hilchot Megillah v'Chanukah 2:17, mt.Hilchot Shevitat Yom Tov 6:18, mt.Pirkei Avot 4:4, Pesikta Rabbati 34:2 50:1, Proverbs 8:23, Psalms 34:19 51:18 68:5-6 83:19 90:2 93:2 97:9 99:3 15:9 113:4-6 19:3 3:1 18:6 3:3, Psalms of Solomon 18:10, Revelation 3:7 4:8 15:4, Romans 1:20, Sefer Yetzirah 1:1, Siman 142:1, Song of Songs.R 1:9 5:1, Tanya Igeret Hakodesh §5 §6 §12 §30, Tanya Igeret Hateshuvah §9, y.Shabbat 1:3, y.Shekalim 3:3, z.Pekudei 233a, z.Vayeshev 181a, z.Vayikra 9a, Zechariah 2:13
[4] LXX *Most High, who dwells on high forever, Holy in the holies, is his name, the Most High resting in the holies, and giving patience to the faint-hearted, and giving life to the broken-hearted*
[5] Isaiah 57:16 - 3 Enoch 43:3, b.Avodah Zara 5a, b.Eruvin 54a, b.Niddah 13b, b.Yevamot 62a 63b, Bahir 51, Ecclesiastes 12:7, Ecclesiastes.R 1:12, Ein Yaakov Chagigah:12b, Ein Yaakov Eruvin, Ein Yaakov Yevamot:63b, Gates of Repentance 1.013 1.015 1.023 1.023, Genesis 6:3, Genesis.R 24:4, Hebrews 12:9, Isaiah 18:5, Jastrow 1064a 1406b 1578b, Jeremiah 10:24 14:16, Job 34:14-34:15, Lamentations.R 5:20, Leviticus.R 15:1, Mas.Kallah Rabbati 2:4, Micah 7:18, Numbers 16:22, Pesikta Rabbati 9:3, Psalms 78:38-78:39 85:6 103:9-103:16, Tanya Likutei Aramim §01, y.Berachot 9:2, z.Mishpatim 99b, Zechariah 12:1
Isaiah 57:16-18 - Gates of Repentance 1.023
[6] Isaiah 57:17 - 1 Timothy 6:9, 2 Peter 2:3 2:14, b.Avodah Zara [Rashi] 7b, b.Shabbat [Rashi] 87a, b.Sotah [Rashi] 5a, Colossians 3:5, Ecclesiastes 6:9, Ephesians 5:3-5:5, Ezekiel 9:31, Isaiah 1:4 5:8-5:9 8:17 9:14 21:15 8:11, Jastrow 1650a, Jeremiah 2:30 5:3 6:13 8:10 22:17, Leviticus.R 16:9, Luke 12:15 15:14-15:16, Micah 2:2-2:3, z.Mishpatim 106b
Isaiah 57:17-21 - 11QIsab
[7] LXX *sin*
[8] Isaiah 57:18 - b.Sotah [Rashi] 5a, Ecclesiastes 9:4, Ezekiel 16:60-63 36:22-38, Gates of Repentance 1.23 3.82, Hosea 14:6-10, Isaiah 1:18 12:1 6:26 43:24-25 48:8-11 1:10 9:15 61:1-3 66:10-13, Jeremiah 3:22 13:17 7:4 31:19-21 9:6, Leviticus.R 16:9, Luke 15:20, Psalms 23:2 51:13, Psalms of Solomon 15:3, Revelation 7:17, Romans 5:20, z.Mishpatim 106b
[9] Missing in 1QIsaa LXX
[10] LXX *and comforted him, and given him true comfort*
[11] Isaiah 57:19 - 2 Corinthians 5:20-5:21, Acts 2:39 10:36, b.Bava Kamma 60a, b.Berachot 34b 55b, b.Sanhedrin 99a, b.Sotah [Rashi] 5a, Colossians 4:3-4:4, Companion verse for the word "Shalom" in Birchat Kohanim, Deuteronomy.R 5:15, Ein Yaakov Berachot:34b, Ein Yaakov Berachot:34b, Ein Yaakov Sanhedrin:99a, Ephesians 2:14-2:17 6:19, Exodus 4:11-4:12, Hebrews 13:15, Hosea 14:4, Isaiah 6:7, Jastrow 48b 249b 688b 883a 902a 1469b 1680b 1703a, Leviticus.R 16:9, Luke 2:14 10:5-10:6 21:15, Mark 16:15, Mas.Soferim 7:4, Matthew 10:13, Midrash Psalms 10:7 104:24 120:7, Motzoei Shabbat [Viyiten Lecha], mt.Hilchot Teshuvah 3:14 3:14 7:6 7:6, Numbers.R 8:4 11:7, Perek Shirah [the fly], Pesikta Rabbati 33:8 44:8, Seder Hatavat Chalom [Order of making good a bad dream], y.Berachot 5:5, z.Bereshit 5b, z.Vayikra 21a
[12] Missing in 1QIsaa

וְהָרְשָׁעִים כַּיָּם נִגְרָשׁ כִּי הַשְׁקֵט לֹא יוּכָל וַיִּגְרְשׁוּ מֵימָיו רֶפֶשׁ וָטִיט	20[1]	But the wicked are like the troubled sea; For it cannot rest, *and its waters cast up mire and dirt*[2].
אֵין שָׁלוֹם אָמַר אֱלֹהַי לָרְשָׁעִים	21[3]	There is no peace, says my God concerning the wicked.

Isaiah – Chapter 58

קְרָא בְגָרוֹן אַל־תַּחְשֹׂךְ כַּשּׁוֹפָר הָרֵם קוֹלֶךָ וְהַגֵּד לְעַמִּי פִּשְׁעָם וּלְבֵית יַעֲקֹב חַטֹּאתָם	1[4]	[5]Cry aloud, spare not, lift up your voice like a horn, and declare to My people their transgression, and to the house of Jacob their sins.
וְאוֹתִי יוֹם יוֹם יִדְרֹשׁוּן וְדַעַת דְּרָכַי יֶחְפָּצוּן כְּגוֹי אֲשֶׁר־צְדָקָה עָשָׂה וּמִשְׁפַּט אֱלֹהָיו לֹא עָזָב יִשְׁאָלוּנִי מִשְׁפְּטֵי־צֶדֶק קִרְבַת אֱלֹהִים יֶחְפָּצוּן	2[6]	Yet they seek Me daily, and delight to know My ways; as a nation who did righteousness, and did not forsake the ordinance of their God, they ask of Me righteous ordinances, they delight to draw near to God.
לָמָּה צַּמְנוּ וְלֹא רָאִיתָ עִנִּינוּ נַפְשֵׁנוּ וְלֹא תֵדָע הֵן בְּיוֹם צֹמְכֶם תִּמְצְאוּ־חֵפֶץ וְכָל־עַצְּבֵיכֶם תִּנְגֹּשׂוּ	3[7]	[8]'Why have we fasted, and you do not see? Why have we afflicted our soul, and you have no knowledge?' Behold, in the day of your fast you pursue your business, *and exact all your labors*[9].
הֵן לְרִיב וּמַצָּה תָּצוּמוּ וּלְהַכּוֹת בְּאֶגְרֹף רֶשַׁע לֹא־תָצוּמוּ כַיּוֹם לְהַשְׁמִיעַ בַּמָּרוֹם קוֹלְכֶם	4[10]	Behold, you fast for strife and [11]contention, and to strike with the fist of wickedness; You do not fast this day to make your voice heard on high.
הֲכָזֶה יִהְיֶה צוֹם אֶבְחָרֵהוּ יוֹם עַנּוֹת אָדָם נַפְשׁוֹ הֲלָכֹף כְּאַגְמֹן רֹאשׁוֹ וְשַׂק וָאֵפֶר יַצִּיעַ הֲלָזֶה תִּקְרָא־צוֹם וְיוֹם רָצוֹן לַיהוָה	5[12]	Have I chosen such a fast? The day for a man to afflict his soul? Is it to bow down his head as a bulrush, And to spread sackcloth and ashes

---

[1] Isaiah 57:20 - Ein Yaakov Sotah:4b, Isaiah 3:11, Job 15:20-15:24 18:5-18:14 20:11-20:29, Jude 1:12, Midrash Psalms 2:1 2:2 11:4 120:7 149:5, Midrash Tanchuma Vayikra 7, Proverbs 4:16-4:17, Psalms 73:18-73:20, Sefer Yetzirah 1:11, Song of Songs.R 2:46, z.Noach 74b, z.Terumah 149b, z.Vayishlach 171b
[2] Missing in LXX
[3] Isaiah 57:21 - 2 Kings 9:22, Deuteronomy.R 11:10, Isaiah 3:11 24:22 11:8, Leviticus.R 17:1, Midrash Psalms 30:3, Pesikta Rabbati 2:3, Romans 3:16-3:17
[4] Isaiah 58:1 - 4 Ezra 1:5, Acts 7:51-7:52 20:26-20:27, b.Bava Metzia 33b, Ein Yaakov Bava Metzia:33b, Ezekiel 2:3-2:8 3:5-3:9 3:17-3:21 20:4 22:2, Hosea 8:1, Isaiah 3:13 16:6 40:9-40:10 8:10, Jastrow 447b, Jeremiah 1:7-1:10 1:17-1:19 7:8-7:11 15:19-15:20, Life of Adam and Eve [Apocalypse] 22:1, Matthew 3:7-3:9, Micah 3:8-3:12, Pesikta Rabbati 33:13, Psalms 40:10-40:11, Psalms of Solomon 3:3, Revelation 1:10 4:1 14:9-14:10, Saadia Opinions 6:5, Titus 2:15, variant of תחשך is תחשוך is found
Isaiah 58:1-3 - 4QIsad
Isaiah 58:1-11 - Apocalypse of Elijah 1:16 3
Isaiah 58:1-14 - 1QIsaa, 1QIsab
[5] 1QIsaa adds *But*
[6] Isaiah 58:2 - 1 Peter 2:1-2:2, 1 Samuel 15:21-15:25, b.Chagigah 5b, Deuteronomy 5:28-5:29, Ein Yaakov Chagigah:5b, Exodus.R 25:9 42:7, Ezekiel 33:30-33:33, Guide for the Perplexed 1:18, Hebrews 6:4-6:6, Isaiah 1:11-1:15 5:13 48:1-48:2, James 1:21-1:22 4:8, Jeremiah 18:2 18:20, John 5:35, Mark 4:16-4:17 6:20 12:14, Matthew 15:7-15:9, Proverbs 15:8, Tanya Igeret Hakodesh §18, Titus 1:16, y.Rosh Hashanah 4:8
[7] Isaiah 58:3 - Daniel 10:2-10:3, Exodus 2:23-2:24, Isaiah 22:13 23:6, Jeremiah 34:9-34:17, Jonah 3:6-3:8, Leviticus 16:29 16:31 23:27, Luke 15:29 18:9-18:12, Malachi 3:14, Matthew 18:28-18:35 20:11-20:12, Micah 3:9-3:11, Nehemiah 5:7, Numbers 23:4, Proverbs 4:9, Psalms 69:11, Saadia Opinions 5:7, t.Taniyot 1:8, Zechariah 7:5-7:7
[8] LXX adds *saying*
[9] LXX *and all those who are under your power you wound*
[10] Isaiah 58:4 - 1 Kings 21:9-21:13, Acts 23:1-23:2, Isaiah 11:2 11:6, Joel 2:13-2:14, John 18:28, Jonah 3:7, Leviticus.R 32:4, Luke 20:47, Matthew 6:16-18 23:13, Philippians 1:14-15, Proverbs 21:27
Isaiah 58:4-5 - t.Taniyot 1:8
[11] 1QIsaa adds *for*
[12] Isaiah 58:5 - 1 Kings 21:27-29, 1 Peter 2:5, 2 Chronicles 20:3, 2 Kings 6:30, b.Kiddushin 62b, b.Menachot [Rashi] 71a, b.Shabbat 54b, b.Succah [Rashi] 36b, Daniel 9:3-19, Esther 4:3 4:16, Ezra 10:6, Isaiah 1:8 10:3 13:2, Jastrow 12b, Job 2:8, Jonah 3:5-8, Leviticus 16:29, Luke 4:19, Nehemiah 9:1-2, Pesikta Rabbati 23:1, Psalms 69:14, Romans 12:2, y.Shabbat 5:3, y.Taanit 2:1, Zechariah 7:5
Isaiah 58:5-7 - 4QIsad

under him? Will you call this a fast, And an acceptable day *to the LORD*[1]?

Is this not the fast I chose? To loosen the fetters of wickedness, to undo the bands of the yoke, and to let the oppressed go free, and so you break every yoke[3]?

הֲלוֹא זֶה צוֹם אֶבְחָרֵהוּ פַּתֵּחַ חַרְצֻבּוֹת רֶשַׁע הַתֵּר אֲגֻדּוֹת מוֹטָה וְשַׁלַּח רְצוּצִים חָפְשִׁים וְכָל־מוֹטָה תְּנַתֵּקוּ   6[2]

Is it not to give your bread to the hungry, and that you bring the poor who are cast out to your house? When you see the naked, that you cover him[5], and not to *hide yourself*[6] from your own flesh?

הֲלוֹא פָרֹס לָרָעֵב לַחְמֶךָ וַעֲנִיִּים מְרוּדִים תָּבִיא בָיִת כִּי־תִרְאֶה עָרֹם וְכִסִּיתוֹ וּמִבְּשָׂרְךָ לֹא תִתְעַלָּם   7[4]

Then your light shall break forth like the morning, and your healing shall speedily spring forth; And your righteousness shall go before you, The glory of the LORD shall be your rearguard.

אָז יִבָּקַע כַּשַּׁחַר אוֹרֶךָ וַאֲרֻכָתְךָ מְהֵרָה תִצְמָח וְהָלַךְ לְפָנֶיךָ צִדְקֶךָ כְּבוֹד יְהוָה יַאַסְפֶךָ   8[7]

Then you shall call, and the LORD will answer; You shall cry, and He will say: 'Here I am.' If you take away the yoke from your midst, the putting forth of the finger, and speaking wickedness;

אָז תִּקְרָא וַיהוָה יַעֲנֶה תְּשַׁוַּע וְיֹאמַר הִנֵּנִי אִם־תָּסִיר מִתּוֹכְךָ מוֹטָה שְׁלַח אֶצְבַּע וְדַבֶּר־אָוֶן   9[8]

And if you draw out your soul to the hungry, And satisfy the afflicted soul; Then your light shall rise in darkness, And your gloom will be as the noonday;

וְתָפֵק לָרָעֵב נַפְשֶׁךָ וְנֶפֶשׁ נַעֲנָה תַּשְׂבִּיעַ וְזָרַח בַּחֹשֶׁךְ אוֹרֶךָ וַאֲפֵלָתְךָ כַּצָּהֳרָיִם   10[9]

And the LORD will guide you continually, And satisfy your soul in drought, And make your bones strong; And you shall be like a watered

וְנָחֲךָ יְהוָה תָּמִיד וְהִשְׂבִּיעַ בְּצַחְצָחוֹת נַפְשֶׁךָ וְעַצְמֹתֶיךָ יַחֲלִיץ וְהָיִיתָ כְּגַן רָוֶה וּכְמוֹצָא מַיִם אֲשֶׁר לֹא־יְכַזְּבוּ מֵימָיו   11[10]

---

[1] Missing in LXX

[2] Isaiah 58:6 - 1 Timothy 6:1, b.Megillah [Rashi] 31a, Isaiah 10:9, Jeremiah 34:8-11, Micah 3:2-4, Nehemiah 5:10-12, t.Taniyot 1:8, y.Taanit 2:1

[3] LXX *I have not chosen such a fast, says the LORD; but do you loosen every burden of iniquity, do thou untie the knots of hard bargains, set the bruised free, and cancel every unjust account*

[4] Isaiah 58:7 - 1 John 3:17-3:18, 1 Timothy 5:10, 2 Chronicles 4:15, 2 Corinthians 9:6-9:10, 2 Enoch 63:1 9:1, Acts 16:15 16:34, b.Bava Batra [Rashbam] 141a, b.Bava Batra 9ab 10a, b.Ketubot 52b 86a, b.Sheviit 39a, Daniel 4:24, Ecclesiastes 11:1-11:2, Ein Yaakov Bava Batra:10a 9a 9b, Ein Yaakov Shevuot:39a, Exodus.R 31:3, Ezekiel 18:7 18:16, Gates of Repentance 3.071, Genesis 18:2-18:5 19:2 19:14, Genesis.R 17:3, Hebrews 13:2-13:3, Isaiah 16:3-16:4 10:10, James 2:15-2:16, Jastrow 1232a, Job 22:7 31:18-31:21, Judges 9:2 19:20-19:21, Lamentations.R 4:7, Leviticus.R 34:11, Leviticus.R 34:13 34:14, Luke 3:11 10:26-10:36 11:41 19:8, Matthew 25:35-25:45, mt.Hilchot Issurei Biah 2:14, Nehemiah 5:5, Philemon 1:7, Proverbs 22:9 1:21 4:27, Psalms 16:9, Pseudo-Phocylides 24-25, Romans 12:13 12:20-12:21, Sibylline Oracles 2.82, Siman 152:16, t.Sotah 7:2, y.Ketubot 11:3, y.Peah 5:5, y.Taanit 2:1, z.Vayakhel 198a

[5] 1QIsaa adds *with clothing*

[6] 1QIsaa *raise yourself up*

[7] Isaiah 58:8 - Acts 10:4 10:31 10:35, b.Avodah Zara 5a, b.Bava Batra 9b 11a, b.Bava Kamma [Tosefot] 16b, b.Sotah 3b 9b, Ein Yaakov Bava Batra:11a 9b, Ein Yaakov Sotah:11a 3b, Exodus 14:19, Guide for the Perplexed 3:51, HaMadrikh 16 35:8, Hosea 6:2-3 14:6, Isaiah 8:26 4:12 9:18 58:10-11, Jeremiah 6:17 9:6, Job 11:17, Leviticus.R 34:15, m.Sotah 1:9, Malachi 3:20, Mas.Derek Eretz Rabbah 2:18, Matthew 13:15, Mekilta de R'Ishmael Shirata 1:5, Midrash Proverbs 14, Midrash Psalms 18:36 22:5, Midrash Tanchuma Beshallach 10, Midrash Tanchuma Mishpatim 8, Numbers.R 11:7, Odes of Solomon 20:9 8:19, Pesikta Rabbati 2:3, Pirkei de R'Eliezer 34, Proverbs 4:18, Psalms 37:6 85:14 97:11 16:4, Saadia Opinions 2:5 9:3, Sifre.z Numbers Pinchas 27:12, Siman 34:1, t.Peah 4:18, y.Sotah 1:10, Yalkut Psalms 889, z.Beshallach 59a, z.Emor 104a, z.Lech Lecha 96b, z.Mikketz 203b

[8] Isaiah 58:9 - 1 John 3:21-3:22, 1 Samuel 3:4-3:8, b.Bava Batra 9b, b.Chagigah [Tosefot] 5a, b.Sanhedrin 76b, b.Yevamot 63a, Bahir 139, Ein Yaakov Yevamot:63a, Ezekiel 13:8, Genesis 3:18, Isaiah 1:15 6:19 9:4 10:6 59:3-59:4 11:13 17:24, Jeremiah 29:12-29:13, Leviticus.R 31:3 34:15, Mas.Derek Eretz Rabbah 2:17, Mas.Derek Eretz Zutta 9:10, Matthew 7:7-7:8, Midrash Psalms 116:1, Midrash Tanchuma Shemot 15, mt.Hilchot Matnot Aniyim 10:16, Proverbs 6:13, Psalms 12:3 34:16-34:18 37:4 50:15 66:18-66:19 91:15 22:5, Siman 179:1, y.Taanit 2:1, Zechariah 10:2

Isaiah 58:9-14 - Maamad [Shabbat]

[9] Isaiah 58:10 - b.Bava Batra 9b, Deuteronomy 15:7-15:10, Gates of Repentance 4.011, Isaiah 5:18 18:16 58:7-58:8, Jastrow 1485b, Job 11:17, Leviticus.R 34:13 34:15 34:15, Luke 18:22, Mas.Derek Eretz Zutta 4:8, Mas.Kallah Rabbati 5:1, Midrash Psalms 41:4, Proverbs 11:24-11:25 14:31 4:27, Psalms 37:6 41:2 112:5-112:9

Isaiah 58:10-12 - Ein Yaakov Bava Batra:9b

Isaiah 58:10-14 - z.Terumah 155b

[10] Isaiah 58:11 - 1 Thessalonians 3:11, b.Avodah Zara 65a, b.Bava Batra 9b, b.Yevamot 102b, Ezekiel 12:35, Genesis.R 85:5, Hosea 13:5, Isaiah 9:16 1:10 13:11, Jastrow 150a 387b 412b 465b 472b, Jeremiah 17:8 7:13, Job 5:20 6:15-6:20, John 4:14 16:13, Joseph

garden, And like a spring of water, whose waters do not fail.

12[1] *And those of you shall build the old ruined places, the restorer of paths in which to live*[2].

וּבָנוּ מִמְּךָ חָרְבוֹת עוֹלָם מוֹסְדֵי דוֹר־וָדוֹר תְּקוֹמֵם וְקֹרָא לְךָ גֹּדֵר פֶּרֶץ מְשֹׁבֵב נְתִיבוֹת לָשָׁבֶת

13[3] If you turn away your foot because of the sabbath, from pursuing your business on My holy day; and call the sabbath a delight, *And the holy of the LORD honorable; And shall honor it, not doing your wonton ways, nor pursuing your business, nor speaking of it*[4];

אִם־תָּשִׁיב מִשַּׁבָּת רַגְלֶךָ עֲשׂוֹת חֲפָצֶיךָ בְּיוֹם קָדְשִׁי וְקָרָאתָ לַשַּׁבָּת עֹנֶג לִקְדוֹשׁ יְהוָה מְכֻבָּד וְכִבַּדְתּוֹ מֵעֲשׂוֹת דְּרָכֶיךָ מִמְּצוֹא חֶפְצְךָ וְדַבֵּר דָּבָר

14[5] Then you shall *delight yourself in*[6] the LORD, *and I*[7] will make you ride upon the high places of the earth, *and I*[8] will feed you with the heritage of Jacob your father; For the mouth of the LORD has spoken it.

אָז תִּתְעַנַּג עַל־יְהוָה וְהִרְכַּבְתִּיךָ עַל־בָּמֳתֵי אָרֶץ וְהַאֲכַלְתִּיךָ נַחֲלַת יַעֲקֹב אָבִיךָ כִּי פִּי יְהוָה דִּבֵּר

Isaiah – Chapter 59

1[9] Behold, the LORD's hand is not short, so it cannot save, nor His ear heavy, so it cannot hear;

הֵן לֹא־קָצְרָה יַד־יְהוָה מֵהוֹשִׁיעַ וְלֹא־כָבְדָה אָזְנוֹ מִשְּׁמוֹעַ

---

and Aseneth 16:16, Pesikta de R'Kahana 17.5, Proverbs 3:8 11:25 13:4 4:25, Psalms 25:9 32:8 33:19 34:10-34:11 37:19 48:15 73:24 92:15 11:9, Ralbag SOS 5, Ruth.R 2:4, Siman 128:13, Song of Songs 4:15, Song of Songs.R 1:22, z.Beshallach 55a, z.Emor 104a, z.Mishpatim 97a, z.Terumah 142b, z.Terumah 171a, z.Toledot 141a 141a 141b, z.Vaetchanan 266a, z.Vayakhel 210b, z.Vayechi 224b 224b

Isaiah 58:11 [LXX] - Joseph and Aseneth 24:19

[1] Isaiah 58:12 - Amos 9:11 9:14, b.Bava Batra 9b, Daniel 9:25, Ezekiel 12:4 36:8-11 12:33, Isaiah 20:28 1:8 3:3 4:9 13:4, Jastrow 1238a, Jeremiah 7:39, Leviticus.R 34:16, Nehemiah 2:5 2:17 4:1-7 6:1

[2] 1QIsaa *And your people will rebuild the ancient ruin; you wil raise up the fundations of many generations, and people will call you, "Repairer of the Breach, Restorer of Streets Upon Which to Live;"* LXX *And your old waste desert places shall be built up, and your foundations shall last through all generations; and you shall be called a repairer of breaches, and you shall cause your paths between to be in peace*

[3] Isaiah 58:13 - b.Avodah Zara [Rashi] 7a 15a, b.Bava Metzia 54a, b.Beitzah [Rashi] 37a, b.Beitzah 34b, b.Chullin 111a, b.Eruvin [Rashi] 39a, b.Eruvin 52b, b.Ketubot [Rashi] 5a, b.Pesachim [Rashbam] 101a, b.Pesachim 68b, b.Sanhedrin [Rashi] 101a, b.Shabbat 113a 118b 119a 150a, Deuteronomy 5:12-15, Deuteronomy.R 3:1, Ein Yaakov Pesachim 68b, Ein Yaakov Pesachim 68b, Ein Yaakov Shabbat 113a 118b 119a 150a, Exodus 20:8-11 31:13-17 36:2-3, Isaiah 56:2-6, Jastrow 366a 492b 1054a 1092a 1271b, Jeremiah 17:21-27, Jubilees 2:29, Leviticus.R 34:16, Mesillat Yesharim 11:Nekiyut-from-Chillul-Hashem 19:Honoring-Hashem-Beautify-Mitzvot, Midrash Psalms 92:1 92:3, Midrash Tanchuma Bereshit 2, Midrash Tanchuma Metzora 9, Midrash Tanchuma Noach 1, Midrash Tanchuma Re'eh 11, Midrash Tanchuma Vayera 1, mt.Hilchot Chametz u'Matzah 21:29 23:12 23:19 24:1-2 24:4-5 29:8 30:1 30:5 30:15 58:14-15, mt.Hilchot Shevitat Yom Tov 6:16, Nehemiah 13:15-22, Pesikta de R'Kahana 10.2, Pesikta Rabbati 27:4, Psalms 27:4 42:5 84:3 84:11 92:2-3 2:1, Revelation 1:10, Siman 103:1 131:14 72:16 77:14 77:22 90:1, z.Bereshit 5b, z.Beshallach 47a 47b, z.Emor 105a, z.Yitro 89a

Isaiah 58:13-14 - 4QIsan, Derech Hashem Part IV 7§04, Exodus.R 25:12, Kiddusha Rabba [Shabbat morning], Mekilta de R'Ishmael Bahodesh 7:78 8:27-28, Siman 72:3

[4] LXX *holy to God; if you shall not lift up your foot to work, nor speak a word in anger out of your mouth*

[5] Isaiah 58:14 - 1 Peter 1:8, b.Shabbat 118a, Bahir 190, Deuteronomy 8:13 9:29, Deuteronomy.R 3:1, Ein Yaakov Shabbat:118b, Guide for the Perplexed 1:70, Habakkuk 3:18-3:19, Isaiah 1:19-1:20 9:16 16:5, Jeremiah 3:19, Job 22:26 3:10 10:9, Leviticus.R 34:16, Matthew 24:35, Mekilta de R'Ishmael Pisha 12:31, Micah 4:4, Midrash Tanchuma Bereshit 2, Midrash Tanchuma Re'eh 11, Midrash Tanchuma Vezot Habracha 5, Pesikta de R'Kahana 10.2 S1.19, Philippians 4:4, Psalms 36:9 37:4 37:11 105:9-105:11 15:12 16:21, Tanya Igeret Hakodesh §29, z.Emor 104a, z.Vayakhel 209a, z.Vayechi 216a, z.Yitro 83a 88a

[6] LXX *trust on*

[7] 1QIsaa *and he*

[8] 1QIsaa *and he*

[9] Isaiah 59:1 - Genesis 18:14, Hebrews 7:25, Isaiah 6:10 2:2 10:9 15:1 17:24, Jeremiah 8:17, Lamentations.R 1:23, Matthew 13:15, Midrash Psalms 42/43:5, Numbers 11:23, Pesikta de R'Kahana 17.2, Saadia Opinions 8:2

Isaiah 59:1-2 - 11QIsaa

Isaiah 59:1-8 - 11QIsab

כִּי אִם־עֲוֺנֹתֵיכֶם הָיוּ מַבְדִּלִים בֵּינֵכֶם לְבֵין 2[1]
אֱלֹהֵיכֶם וְחַטֹּאותֵיכֶם הִסְתִּירוּ פָנִים מִכֶּם מִשְּׁמוֹעַ

But your iniquities have separated between you and your God, And your sins have hid His face from you, *so He will not hear*[2].

כִּי כַפֵּיכֶם נְגֹאֲלוּ בַדָּם וְאֶצְבְּעוֹתֵיכֶם בֶּעָוֺן 3[3]
שִׂפְתוֹתֵיכֶם דִּבְּרוּ־שֶׁקֶר לְשׁוֹנְכֶם עַוְלָה תֶהְגֶּה

For your hands are defiled with blood, You shall raise up the foundations of many generations; and you shall be called the repairer of the breach, and your fingers with iniquity; your lips *have spoken lies, Your tongue*[4] mutters wickedness.

אֵין־קֹרֵא בְצֶדֶק וְאֵין נִשְׁפָּט בֶּאֱמוּנָה בָּטוֹחַ עַל־ 4[5]
תֹּהוּ וְדַבֶּר־שָׁוְא הָרוֹ עָמָל וְהוֹלֵיד אָוֶן

No one sue in righteousness, And no one pleads in truth; They trust in vanity, and speak lies, They conceive mischief, and birth iniquity.

בֵּיצֵי צִפְעוֹנִי בִּקֵּעוּ וְקוּרֵי עַכָּבִישׁ יֶאֱרֹגוּ הָאֹכֵל 5[6]
מִבֵּיצֵיהֶם יָמוּת וְהַזּוּרֶה תִּבָּקַע אֶפְעֶה

They hatch *basilisks'*[7] eggs, and weave the spider's web; *he who eats of their eggs dies, and what is crushed breaks out into a viper*[8].

קוּרֵיהֶם לֹא־יִהְיוּ לְבֶגֶד וְלֹא יִתְכַּסּוּ בְּמַעֲשֵׂיהֶם 6[9]
מַעֲשֵׂיהֶם מַעֲשֵׂי־אָוֶן וּפֹעַל חָמָס בְּכַפֵּיהֶם

Their webs shall not become garments, nor shall men cover themselves with their works; Their works are works of iniquity, And the act of violence is in their hands.

רַגְלֵיהֶם לָרַע יָרֻצוּ וִימַהֲרוּ לִשְׁפֹּךְ דָּם נָקִי 7[10]
מַחְשְׁבוֹתֵיהֶם מַחְשְׁבוֹת אָוֶן שֹׁד וָשֶׁבֶר בִּמְסִלּוֹתָם

Their feet run to evil, And they rush to shed innocent blood; Their thoughts are thoughts of iniquity, Desolation and destruction[11] are in their paths.

דֶּרֶךְ שָׁלוֹם לֹא יָדָעוּ וְאֵין מִשְׁפָּט בְּמַעְגְּלוֹתָם 8[12]
נְתִיבוֹתֵיהֶם עִקְּשׁוּ לָהֶם כֹּל דֹּרֵךְ בָּהּ לֹא יָדַע שָׁלוֹם

They do not know the way of peace, And there is no right in their goings; They have made themselves crooked paths, Whoever goes there does not know peace.

עַל־כֵּן רָחַק מִשְׁפָּט מִמֶּנּוּ וְלֹא תַשִּׂיגֵנוּ צְדָקָה 9[13]
נְקַוֶּה לָאוֹר וְהִנֵּה־חֹשֶׁךְ לִנְגֹהוֹת בָּאֲפֵלוֹת נְהַלֵּךְ

Therefore, justice is far from us, nor does righteousness overtake us; We look for light, but see darkness, For brightness, but we walk in *deep darkness*[14].

נְגַשְׁשָׁה כַעִוְרִים קִיר וּכְאֵין עֵינַיִם נְגַשֵּׁשָׁה 10[15]
כָּשַׁלְנוּ בַצָּהֳרַיִם כַּנֶּשֶׁף בָּאַשְׁמַנִּים כַּמֵּתִים

We grope for the wall like the blind, Yes, we grope as those who have no eyes; we stumble

---

[1] Isaiah 59:2 - b.Sanhedrin 65b, b.Sanhedrin 98a, b.Yoma 86b, Deuteronomy 31:17-31:18 32:19-32:20, Ein Yaakov Sanhedrin:65b, Ezekiel 39:23-39:24 15:29, Guide for the Perplexed 3:51, Isaiah 1:15 2:1 9:17 10:4, Jeremiah 5:25, Joshua 7:11, Mekilta de R'Ishmael Pisha 11:103, Micah 3:4, mt.Hilchot Teshuvah 7:7 7:7, mt.Shemonah Perakim 7:6, Pesikta de R'Kahana 17.2, Proverbs 15:29, Ralbag Wars 4:6, Shemonah Perachim VII, Sifre Devarim {Shoftim} 173, Sifre Devarim Shoftim 173, Tanya Igeret Hateshuvah §08, Tanya Likutei Aramim §14

[2] LXX *so as not to have mercy upon you*

[3] Isaiah 59:3 - 1 Timothy 4:2, b.Shabbat 139a, Ein Yaakov Shabbat:139a, Ezekiel 7:23 9:9 13:8 22:2 11:6, Hosea 4:2 7:3 7:13, Isaiah 1:15 1:21, Jeremiah 2:30 2:34 7:8 9:4-9:7 22:17, Matthew 3:4, Mesillat Yesharim 11:Nekiyut-from-Falsehood, Micah 3:10-3:12 6:12 7:2, Pesikta Rabbati 33:13

[4] Missing in 1QIsaa

[5] Isaiah 59:4 - Ezekiel 22:29-31, Isaiah 6:12 11:3 59:13-14 11:16, James 1:15, Jeremiah 5:1 5:4-5 7:4 7:8, Job 15:31 15:35, Micah 2:1 7:2-5, Proverbs 4:16, Psalms 7:14-15 62:5 62:11

[6] Isaiah 59:5 - 4Q266 frag 3 2.1-2, 6Q15 frag 2 ll.2.1-2, Cairo Damascus 5.13-14, Isaiah 14:29, Job 8:14, Matthew 3:7 12:34, Proverbs 23:32

[7] LXX *asps'*

[8] LXX *and he who is going to eat of their eggs, having crushed an addled egg, has found also in it a basilisk*

[9] Isaiah 59:6 - Amos 3:10 6:3, Ezekiel 7:11 7:23, Genesis 6:11, Habakkuk 1:2-4, Isaiah 5:7 28:18-20 6:1 30:12-14 9:12 10:4 16:7, Jeremiah 6:7, Job 8:14-15, Micah 2:1-3 2:8 3:1-11 6:12, Psalms 58:3, Revelation 3:17-18, Romans 3:20-22 4:6-8, Zephaniah 1:9 3:3-4

[10] Isaiah 59:7 - Acts 8:20-22, Ezekiel 9:9 22:6, Isaiah 11:3 12:18, Jeremiah 22:17, Lamentations 4:13, Mark 7:21-22, Matthew 23:31-37, Proverbs 1:16 6:17 15:26 24:9, Revelation 17:6, Romans 3:15-17

[11] 1QIsaa adds *and violence*

[12] Isaiah 59:8 - Amos 6:1-6:6, Gates of Repentance 3.231, Hosea 4:1-4:2, Isaiah 5:7 24:22 57:20-57:21 59:14-59:15, Jeremiah 5:1, Luke 1:79, Mas.Kallah Rabbati 3:4, Matthew 23:23, Proverbs 2:15 3:17 4:18, Psalms 58:2-58:3 5:5, Romans 3:17

[13] Isaiah 59:9 - 1 Thessalonians 5:3, Amos 5:18-5:20, Habakkuk 1:13, Isaiah 5:30, Jeremiah 8:15 14:19, Job 6:26, Lamentations 5:16-5:17, Micah 1:12, Midrash Psalms 146:5

[14] MT *deep darkness* or *gloom*; 1QIsaa *darkness*

[15] Isaiah 59:10 - 1 John 2:11, Amos 8:9, Deuteronomy 4:29, Exodus.R 36:2, Isaiah 8:15, Jeremiah 13:16, Job 5:14, John 11:9-10 12:35 12:40, Lamentations 3:6 4:14, Midrash Psalms 146:5, Midrash Tanchuma Tetzaveh 4, Numbers.R 15:5, Proverbs 4:19

at noonday as in the twilight; we are in dark places like the dead.

נֶהֱמֶה כַדֻּבִּים כֻּלָּנוּ וְכַיּוֹנִים הָגֹה נֶהְגֶּה נְקַוֶּה לַמִּשְׁפָּט וָאַיִן לִישׁוּעָה רָחֲקָה מִמֶּנּוּ

11[1] We all growl like bears, And mourn sore like doves; We look for right, but there is none; For salvation, but it is far off from us.

כִּי־רַבּוּ פְשָׁעֵינוּ נֶגְדֶּךָ וְחַטֹּאותֵינוּ עָנְתָה בָּנוּ כִּי־פְשָׁעֵינוּ אִתָּנוּ וַעֲוֹנֹתֵינוּ יְדַעֲנוּם

12[2] For our transgressions are multiplied before You, And our sins testify against us; For our transgressions are present to us, And as for our iniquities, we know them:

פָּשֹׁעַ וְכַחֵשׁ בַּיהוָה וְנָסוֹג מֵאַחַר אֱלֹהֵינוּ דַּבֶּר־עֹשֶׁק וְסָרָה הֹרוֹ וְהֹגוֹ מִלֵּב דִּבְרֵי־שָׁקֶר

13[3] Transgressing and denying the LORD, And turning away from following our God, Speaking oppression and perverseness, *conceiving and[4] uttering from the heart words of falsehood.*

וְהֻסַּג אָחוֹר מִשְׁפָּט וּצְדָקָה מֵרָחוֹק תַּעֲמֹד כִּי־כָשְׁלָה בָרְחוֹב אֱמֶת וּנְכֹחָה לֹא־תוּכַל לָבוֹא

14[5] *And justice turns backward[6],* and righteousness stands afar off; *For truth has stumbled in the broad place, and uprightness cannot enter[7].*

וַתְּהִי הָאֱמֶת נֶעְדֶּרֶת וְסָר מֵרָע מִשְׁתּוֹלֵל וַיַּרְא יְהוָה וַיֵּרַע בְּעֵינָיו כִּי־אֵין מִשְׁפָּט

15[8] *And truth is lacking, And he who departs from evil makes himself a victim[9].* And the LORD saw, and it displeased Him; there is no justice;

וַיַּרְא כִּי־אֵין אִישׁ וַיִּשְׁתּוֹמֵם כִּי אֵין מַפְגִּיעַ וַתּוֹשַׁע לוֹ זְרֹעוֹ וְצִדְקָתוֹ הִיא סְמָכָתְהוּ

16[10] And He saw that there was no man, And was astonished that there was no intercessor; Therefore, His own arm brought salvation to Him; And His *righteousness[11],* it sustained Him;

וַיִּלְבַּשׁ צְדָקָה כַּשִּׁרְיָן וְכוֹבַע יְשׁוּעָה בְּרֹאשׁוֹ וַיִּלְבַּשׁ בִּגְדֵי נָקָם תִּלְבֹּשֶׁת וַיַּעַט כַּמְעִיל קִנְאָה

17[12] And He put on righteousness as a coat of mail, And a helmet of salvation on His *head[13],* And He put on garments of vengeance for clothing, And was clad with zeal as a cloak.

כְּעַל גְּמֻלוֹת כְּעַל יְשַׁלֵּם חֵמָה לְצָרָיו גְּמוּל לְאֹיְבָיו לָאִיִּים גְּמוּל יְשַׁלֵּם

18[14] *According to their deeds, accordingly He will repay, Fury to His adversaries, recompense to*

---

[1] Isaiah 59:11 - Ezekiel 7:16, Hosea 7:14, Isaiah 14:14 3:20 11:9, Jeremiah 8:15 9:2, Job 30:28-30:29, Mas.Derek Eretz Rabbah 2:8, Psalms 32:3-32:4 38:9 85:10 119:155

[2] Isaiah 59:12 - 1 Thessalonians 2:15-16, Daniel 9:5-8, Ezekiel 5:6 7:23 8:8-16 16:51-52 22:2-12 22:24-30 23:2-49 24:6-24:14, Ezra 9:6 9:13, Hosea 4:2 5:5 7:10, Isaiah 1:4 3:9, Jeremiah 3:2 5:3-9 5:25-29 7:8-10 14:7, Matthew 23:32-33, Nehemiah 9:33, Romans 3:19-3:20, Tanya Igeret Hateshuvah §9

[3] Isaiah 59:13 - Acts 5:3-4, Ezekiel 6:9 18:25, Hebrews 3:12, Hosea 1:2 6:7 7:13 12:1, Isaiah 5:7 7:6 8:6 24:8 9:11 59:3-4, James 1:15 3:6, Jastrow 366b, Jeremiah 2:13 2:19-21 3:10 3:20 5:23 9:3-6 17:13 8:40 18:20, Mark 7:21-22, Matthew 10:33 12:34-36, Midrash Psalms 21:1, Pesikta Rabbati 24:3, Proverbs 6:9, Psalms 18:22 78:36, Romans 3:10-3:18, Titus 1:16

[4] Missing in 1QIsaa

[5] Isaiah 59:14 - 4 Ezra 5:10, Amos 5:7 5:11, Ecclesiastes 3:16, Habakkuk 1:4, Isaiah 1:21 5:23 10:1-2 11:4, Jeremiah 5:27-28 5:31, Micah 3:9-11 7:3-7:5, Psalms 82:2-5, Zephaniah 3:1-3

[6] 1QIsaa *I will drive back justice*

[7] LXX *for truth is consumed in their ways, and they could not pass by a straight path*

[8] Isaiah 59:15 - 1 John 3:11-12, 2 Chronicles 21:7, 2 Corinthians 5:13, 2 Kings 9:11, 2 Samuel 11:27, Acts 9:1 9:23 2:24, b.Sanhedrin 97a, Ein Yaakov Sanhedrin:97a, Genesis 14:10, Habakkuk 1:13-14, Hebrews 11:36-38, Hosea 4:1-2 9:7, Isaiah 24:1, Jastrow 1045b 1046a 1585a, Jeremiah 5:1-2 7:28 5:26, John 8:52 10:20, Mark 3:21, Micah 7:2, Pesikta de R'Kahana 5.9, Pesikta Rabbati 15:14/15, Psalms 5:10 12:2-3, Romans 8:36, Song of Songs.R 2:33, Tanna Devei Eliyahu 10, z.Pekudei 236b Isaiah 59:15-16 - 4QIsae

[9] LXX *And truth has been taken away, and they have turned aside their mind from understanding*

[10] Isaiah 59:16 - 3 Enoch 48A:6, b.Chagigah 12b, b.Sanhedrin 98a, Ein Yaakov Sanhedrin 97b, Exodus.R 30:24, Ezekiel 22:30, Genesis 18:23-32, Isaiah 17:28 2:2 4:10 63:3-5 16:8, Jeremiah 5:1, Mark 6:6, Mesillat Yesharim 19:Longing-for-the-Redemption, Midrash Psalms 71:2, Psalms 98:1 10:23

[11] 1QIsaa *his righteous acts*

[12] Isaiah 59:17 - 1 Thessalonians 5:8, 2 Corinthians 6:7, 2 Thessalonians 1:8, 3 Enoch 28:8, ApE14:30, b.Bava Batra 9b, b.Chagigah 12b, Bahir 75, Deuteronomy 32:35-32:43, Deuteronomy.R 2:37, Ein Yaakov Chagigah:12b, Ephesians 6:14 6:17, Exodus.R 38:8, Hebrews 10:30, Isaiah 9:8 11:5 3:9 15:3 15:15, Job 5:14, John 2:17, Mekhilta de R'Shimon bar Yochai Shirata 30:1, Mekilta de R'Ishmael Shirata 4:6, Mesillat Yesharim 16:Trait of Taharah, Midrash Psalms 71:2 93:1, Pesikta de R'Kahana 22.5 S6.5, Pesikta Rabbati 37:2, Psalms 69:10 94:1, Revelation 19:11, Romans 13:12-13:14, Saadia Opinions 2:10, Song of Songs.R 1:49 4:22, Tanya Igeret Hakodesh §03, Zechariah 1:14

[13] MT singular, 1QIsaa plural

[14] Isaiah 59:18 - Ezekiel 5:13 6:12 14:18, Isaiah 1:24 49:25-49:26 15:3 15:6 18:15, Jeremiah 17:10 2:29, Job 10:11, Lamentations 4:11, Luke 19:27 21:22, Matthew 16:27, Mekhilta de R'Shimon bar Yochai Beshallach 25:3 26:1, Mekilta de R'Ishmael Beshallah

His enemies; To the islands He will repay recompense[1].

וְיִירְא֤וּ מִֽמַּעֲרָב֙ אֶת־שֵׁ֣ם יְהוָ֔ה וּמִמִּזְרַח־שֶׁ֖מֶשׁ אֶת־כְּבוֹד֑וֹ כִּֽי־יָב֤וֹא כַנָּהָר֙ צָ֔ר ר֥וּחַ יְהוָ֖ה נֹ֥סְסָה בֽוֹ   19[2]

So shall they fear the name of the LORD from the west, And His glory from the rising of the sun; For distress will come in like a flood, Which the breath of the LORD drives.

וּבָ֤א לְצִיּוֹן֙ גּוֹאֵ֔ל וּלְשָׁבֵ֥י פֶ֖שַׁע בְּיַעֲקֹ֑ב נְאֻ֖ם יְהוָֽה   20[3]

And a redeemer will come to Zion, And to those who turn from transgression in Jacob, *says the LORD*[4].

וַאֲנִ֗י זֹ֣את בְּרִיתִ֤י אוֹתָם֙ אָמַ֣ר יְהוָ֔ה רוּחִי֙ אֲשֶׁ֣ר עָלֶ֔יךָ וּדְבָרַ֖י אֲשֶׁר־שַׂ֣מְתִּי בְּפִ֑יךָ לֹֽא־יָמ֡וּשׁוּ מִפִּ֡יךָ וּמִפִּי֩ זַרְעֲךָ֨ וּמִפִּ֜י זֶ֣רַע זַרְעֲךָ֗ אָמַ֤ר יְהוָה֙ מֵעַתָּ֖ה וְעַד־עוֹלָֽם   21[5]

And as for Me[6], this is My covenant with them, says the LORD; My spirit that is on you, and My words I have put in your mouth, shall not depart from your mouth, nor from the mouth of your seed, *nor from the mouth of your seed's seed*[7], *says the LORD*[8], from now and forever.

Isaiah – Chapter 60

ק֥וּמִי א֖וֹרִי כִּ֣י בָ֣א אוֹרֵ֑ךְ וּכְב֥וֹד יְהוָ֖ה עָלַ֥יִךְ זָרָֽח   1[9]

Arise, shine, for your light has come, and the glory of the LORD is risen on you.

כִּֽי־הִנֵּ֤ה הַחֹ֙שֶׁךְ֙ יְכַסֶּה־אֶ֔רֶץ וַעֲרָפֶ֖ל לְאֻמִּ֑ים וְעָלַ֙יִךְ֙ יִזְרַ֣ח יְהוָ֔ה וּכְבוֹד֖וֹ עָלַ֥יִךְ יֵרָאֶֽה   2[10]

For, behold, darkness shall cover the earth, And gross darkness the peoples; But on you the LORD will arise, And His glory shall be seen on you.

7:14, Midrash Psalms 119:8 121:3, Midrash Tanchuma Ki Tetze 2, Nahum 1:2, Psalms 18:25-18:27 21:9-21:10 62:13, Revelation 16:19 19:15 20:12-20:13, Romans 2:6

[1] LXX *as one about to render a recompence, reproach to his adversaries*

[2] Isaiah 59:19 - 2 Thessalonians 2:8, b.Berachot 56b, b.Sanhedrin 98a, Daniel 7:27, Ein Yaakov Sanhedrin:97b, Isaiah 11:9-16 24:14-16 6:28 1:12 66:18-20, Malachi 1:11, Midrash Tanchuma Bechukkotai 3, Psalms 22:28 102:16-17 17:3, Revelation 11:15 12:10 12:15-17 17:14-15 20:1-3, Zechariah 4:6, Zephaniah 3:8-9

[3] Isaiah 59:20 - Acts 2:36-2:39 3:19 3:26 2:20, Daniel 9:13, Deuteronomy 30:1-30:10, Ein Yaakov Sanhedrin:97b, Ezekiel 18:30-18:31, Genesis.R 38:14, Hebrews 12:14, Isaiah 16:9, Jastrow 216b, Joel 3:5, Lamentations.R 1:23 1:26 1:33 1:52, Midrash Tanchuma Bechukkotai 3, mt.Hilchot Teshuvah 7:5, Obadiah 1:17-1:21, Pesikta de R'Kahana 18.3 25.1 S5.4, Pesikta Rabbati 32:2, Romans 11:26-11:27, Titus 2:11-2:14

Isaiah 59:20-21 - 11QIsab, continued from Isaiah 58:14 Teimon], Haftarah Shacharit Yom Kippur, Maariv Motzoei Shabbat], Mekilta de R'Ishmael Nezikin 18:113-116, mt.Hilchot Tefilah 9:5, Shabbat and Yom Tov Minchah, U'voh Letzion [Shacharit]

[4] Missing in LXX

[5] Isaiah 59:21 - 1 Corinthians 15:3-58, 2 Corinthians 3:8 3:17-18, b.Bava Batra [Rashbam] 59a, b.Bava Metzia [Rashi] 21b, b.Bava Metzia 85a, Ein Yaakov Bava Metzia:85a, Exodus.R 31:2, Ezekiel 36:25-27 37:25-27 39:25-29, Hebrews 8:6-13 10:16, Isaiah 11:1-3 20:3 1:8 3:16 7:3 61:1-3, Jeremiah 31:32-35 32:38-41, John 1:33 3:34 4:14 7:16-17 7:39 8:38 17:8, Midrash Psalms 59:1 119:34 119:75, Midrash Tanchuma Noach 3, Romans 8:9, Tanna Devei Eliyahu 3, z.Emor 98a, z.Pekudei 236b, z.Vayechi 240b

[6] Missing in LXX

[7] Missing in LXX

[8] Missing in 1QIsaa

[9] Isaiah 60:1 - 1 Peter 4:14, Ephesians 5:8 5:14, Exodus.R 15:23 15:27, Genesis.R 2:5 6:3, Isaiah 9:3 52:1-52:2 10:8 60:19-60:20, John 1:9 3:19 8:12 12:46, Kuzari 4.003, Luke 1:78-1:79 2:32, Malachi 3:20, Matthew 4:16 5:16, Midrash Psalms 22:5 22:11 27:1 97:2 119:34, Midrash Tanchuma Beha'alotcha 2, Midrash Tanchuma Pinchas 14, Midrash Tanchuma Vayakhel 10, Numbers.R 2:10 11:5 15:2 21:22, Perek Shirah [the Sun], Pesikta de R'Kahana 21.1 21.2 21.3 21.4 S5.3, Pesikta Rabbati 8:4 15:20 36:1-2, Philippians 2:15, Revelation 21:23 22:5, Saadia Opinions 8:6, Sibylline Oracles 14.214 3.787, Sifre.z Numbers Naso 6:25, z.Bamidbar 118a

Isaiah 60:1-2 - Mekilta de R'Shimon bar Yochai Beshallach 24:3, Mekilta de R'Ishmael Beshallah 5:42-43, Pesikta de R'Kahana 5.14

Isaiah 60:1-3 - Apocalypse of Elijah 3:3, Testament of Levi 4:2

Isaiah 60:1-22 - 1QIsaa, 1QIsab, Haftarah Ki Tavo, 7th Shabbat after Tisha b'Av [Pesikta Rabbati 36]

[10] Isaiah 60:2 - 1 Kings 8:11, 1 Peter 2:9, 2 Corinthians 3:18 4:4-4:6, Acts 14:16 17:23 17:30-17:31 2:18, b.Bava Batra 99a, Colossians 1:13, Ein Yaakov Sanhedrin:99a, Ephesians 4:17-4:20, Exodus.R 14:3, Ezekiel 10:4, Habakkuk 3:3-3:4, Haggai 2:7-2:9, HaMadrikh 35:7, Hebrews 1:2-1:3, Jeremiah 13:16, John 1:1 1:14 1:18 8:55, Leviticus 9:23, Leviticus.R 6:6, Malachi 3:20, Matthew 15:14 23:19 23:24, Midrash Psalms 22:3 27:1, Midrash Tanchuma Bo 4, Midrash Tanchuma Tetzaveh 7, Numbers 16:19, Numbers.R 21:22, Pesikta de R'Kahana 7.12 21.6 S6.5, Pesikta Rabbati 15:20 17:8 36:1-2 53:2, Psalms 80:2, Romans 1:21-1:32, Saadia Opinions 2:3 8:6, Sifre.z Numbers Naso 6:25, z.Bamidbar 119a, z.Shemot 7b

וְהָלְכוּ גוֹיִם לְאוֹרֵךְ וּמְלָכִים לְנֹגַהּ זַרְחֵךְ

3[1] And nations[2] shall walk at your light, And kings[3] *at the brightness*[4] of your rising.

שְׂאִי־סָבִיב עֵינַיִךְ וּרְאִי כֻּלָּם נִקְבְּצוּ בָאוּ־לָךְ בָּנַיִךְ מֵרָחוֹק יָבֹאוּ וּבְנֹתַיִךְ עַל־צַד תֵּאָמַנָה

4[5] Lift up your eyes all around, and see: *They all*[6] gather together, and come to you; Your sons come from far, And your daughters are borne on the side.

אָז תִּרְאִי וְנָהַרְתְּ וּפָחַד וְרָחַב לְבָבֵךְ כִּי־יֵהָפֵךְ עָלַיִךְ הֲמוֹן יָם חֵיל גוֹיִם יָבֹאוּ לָךְ

5[7] Then you shall see and be radiant, And your heart shall *throb and*[8] swell with joy; Because the abundance of the sea shall be turned to you, The wealth of the nations shall come to you.

שִׁפְעַת גְּמַלִּים תְּכַסֵּךְ בִּכְרֵי מִדְיָן וְעֵיפָה כֻּלָּם מִשְּׁבָא יָבֹאוּ זָהָב וּלְבוֹנָה יִשָּׂאוּ וּתְהִלֹּת יְהוָה יְבַשֵּׂרוּ

6[9] The caravan of camels shall cover you, And of the young camels of Midian and *Ephah*[10], All coming from *Sheba*[11]; They shall bring gold and *incense, And shall proclaim the praises*[12] of the LORD.

כָּל־צֹאן קֵדָר יִקָּבְצוּ לָךְ אֵילֵי נְבָיוֹת יְשָׁרְתוּנֶךְ יַעֲלוּ עַל־רָצוֹן מִזְבְּחִי וּבֵית תִּפְאַרְתִּי אֲפָאֵר

7[13] All the flocks of Kedar shall be gathered together to you, the rams of Nebaioth shall minister to you; they shall come up with acceptance on My altar, And I will glorify My glorious house.

מִי־אֵלֶּה כָּעָב תְּעוּפֶינָה וְכַיּוֹנִים אֶל־אֲרֻבֹּתֵיהֶם

8[14] Who are these who fly as a cloud, And as the doves *to their windows*[15]?

כִּי־לִי אִיִּים יְקַוּוּ וָאֳנִיּוֹת תַּרְשִׁישׁ בָּרִאשֹׁנָה לְהָבִיא בָנַיִךְ מֵרָחוֹק כַּסְפָּם וּזְהָבָם אִתָּם לְשֵׁם יְהוָה אֱלֹהַיִךְ וְלִקְדוֹשׁ יִשְׂרָאֵל כִּי פֵאֲרָךְ

9[16] Surely the isles shall wait for Me, and the ships of Tarshish first, to bring your sons from far, their silver and their gold with them, for the name of the LORD your God, and for the Holy One of Israel, because He has glorified you.

---

[1] Isaiah 60:3 - Acts 13:47 15:17, Amos 9:12, b.Bava Batra 75a, Ein Yaakov Bava Batra:75a, Esther.R 7:11, Exodus.R 15:21 36:1, Genesis 1:10, Genesis.R 59:5, Isaiah 2:2-5 11:10 19:23-25 21:14 49:6-7 1:12 1:23 54:1-3 12:10 12:16 18:12 66:19-20, John 12:20-21 12:32, Luke 24:47, Matthew 2:1-11 4:19, Micah 4:1-2, Midrash Psalms 36:6 72:5, Midrash Tanchuma Beha'alotcha 2, Midrash Tanchuma Tetzaveh 8, Numbers.R 21:22, Pesikta de R'Kahana 21.4 S6.5, Pesikta Rabbati 36:2, Psalms 2:10 22:28 67:2-5 68:30 72:11 72:17-19 98:2-3 117:1-2 18:4, Revelation 11:15 21:24, Romans 11:11-15 15:9-12, Saadia Opinions 8:6, Song of Songs.R 1:21 1:66 4:2, Tanya Likutei Aramim §36, Zechariah 2:11 8:20-23

[2] LXX *kings*

[3] LXX *netions*

[4] 1QIsaa *before the dawn*

[5] Isaiah 60:4 - Acts 13:44, Galatians 3:28-3:29, Isaiah 11:12 18:6 19:6 1:18 49:20-49:22 66:11-66:12, John 4:35, Matthew 8:11, Pesikta de R'Kahana 22.3 S6.5, Song of Songs.R 1:30

[6] LXX *your children*

[7] Isaiah 60:5 - 1 Samuel 2:1, 2 Corinthians 6:1-6:13 10:15, Acts 10:45 11:17 24:17, Hosea 2:1-2:2 3:5, Isaiah 23:18 24:14-24:15 6:2 12:11 13:6, Jeremiah 9:9, Mekhilta de R'Shimon bar Yochai Shirata 27:1, Mekhilta de R'Ishmael Shirata 1:5, Midrash Tanchuma Beshallach 10, Psalms 34:6 96:7-96:9 98:7-98:9, Revelation 21:26, Romans 11:25 15:26

[8] Missing in 1QIsaa

[9] Isaiah 60:6 - 1 Kings 10:2, 1 Peter 2:5 2:9, 2 Chronicles 9:1, 2 Kings 8:9, b.Sanhedrin [Rashi] 52a, Genesis 10:7 25:3-25:4 1:13, Isaiah 6:6 18:10 21:14 13:6, Judges 6:5 7:12, Malachi 1:11, Matthew 2:11, Philippians 2:17, Psalms 72:10 72:15, Revelation 5:9-5:10 7:9-7:12, Romans 15:9

[10] 1QIsaa *Ephu*; LXX *Gaepha*

[11] 1QIsaa *Shebu*

[12] LXX *shall bring frankincense, and they shall publish the salvation*

[13] Isaiah 60:7 - b.Avodah Zara 23b 24a, Genesis 1:13, Haggai 2:7-2:9, Hebrews 13:10 13:15-13:16, Isaiah 18:11 8:7 12:13, Job 18:8, Mesillat Yesharim 16:Trait of Taharah, Midrash Psalms 68:15, Psalms of Solomon 2:5, Romans 12:1 15:16, y.Avodah Zarah 2:1, z.Yitro 84a

[14] Isaiah 60:8 - b.Bava Batra 75b, Ein Yaakov Bava Batra:75b, Exodus.R 51:8, Genesis 8:8-8:11, Hebrews 12:1, Isaiah 21:22 1:21 12:4, Luke 13:29, Mekhilta de R'Shimon bar Yochai Beshallach 25:2, Mekhilta de R'Ishmael Beshallah 6:109, Mekhilta de R'Ishmael Beshallah 6:113, Midrash Psalms 48:4, Midrash Tanchuma Balak 14, Midrash Tanchuma Beshallach 23, Midrash Tanchuma Tzav 12, Numbers.R 20:20, Pesikta Rabbati 1:3, Revelation 7:9, Saadia Opinions 8:6, z.Mishpatim 105a

[15] LXX *with young ones to me*

[16] Isaiah 60:9 - 1 Kings 8:41 10:1 10:22 22:48, 2 Corinthians 8:4-8:5, Acts 9:15, Exodus 9:19 34:5-34:7, Galatians 3:26 4:26, Genesis 9:27 10:2-5, Isaiah 2:16 11:11 14:1-2 18:4 18:10 19:4 19:6 1:1 3:5 52:1-6 7:5 9:17 12:4 66:19-20, Jeremiah 3:17 6:19, John 17:26, Joshua 9:9, Luke 2:32, m.Oholot 13:1 8:3, Proverbs 18:20, Psalms 68:31-32 72:10, Saadia Opinions 8:6, Zechariah 14:14, Zephaniah 2:11

וּבָנוּ בְנֵי־נֵכָר֙ חֹמֹתַ֔יִךְ וּמַלְכֵיהֶ֖ם יְשָׁרְת֑וּנֶךְ כִּ֤י בְקִצְפִּי֙ הִכִּיתִ֔יךְ וּבִרְצוֹנִ֖י רִחַמְתִּֽיךְ	10[1]	And aliens shall build up your walls, And their kings shall minister to you; For in My wrath I struck you, But in My favor I have compassion on you.
וּפִתְּח֨וּ שְׁעָרַ֜יִךְ תָּמִ֗יד יוֹמָ֧ם וָלַ֛יְלָה לֹ֥א יִסָּגֵ֖רוּ לְהָבִ֤יא אֵלַ֙יִךְ֙ חֵ֣יל גּוֹיִ֔ם וּמַלְכֵיהֶ֖ם נְהוּגִֽים	11[2]	Your gates shall be open continually, Day and night, they shall not be shut; so men may bring unto you the *wealth of the nations, And their kings in procession*[3].
כִּֽי־הַגּ֧וֹי וְהַמַּמְלָכָ֛ה אֲשֶׁ֥ר לֹא־יַעַבְד֖וּךְ יֹאבֵ֑דוּ וְהַגּוֹיִ֖ם חָרֹ֥ב יֶחֱרָֽבוּ	12[4]	For that nation and kingdom that will not serve you shall perish; Yes, those nations shall be utterly wasted.
כְּב֤וֹד הַלְּבָנוֹן֙ אֵלַ֣יִךְ יָב֔וֹא בְּר֛וֹשׁ תִּדְהָ֥ר וּתְאַשּׁ֖וּר יַחְדָּ֑ו לְפָאֵר֙ מְק֣וֹם מִקְדָּשִׁ֔י וּמְק֥וֹם רַגְלַ֖י אֲכַבֵּֽד	13[5]	[6]The glory of Lebanon [7]shall come to you, The cypress, *the plane tree and the larch together*[8]; To beautify the place of My sanctuary, And I will make the place of My feet glorious.
וְהָלְכ֨וּ אֵלַ֤יִךְ שְׁח֙וֹחַ֙ בְּנֵ֣י מְעַנַּ֔יִךְ וְהִֽשְׁתַּחֲו֛וּ עַל־כַּפּ֥וֹת רַגְלַ֖יִךְ כָּל־מְנַֽאֲצָ֑יִךְ וְקָ֤רְאוּ לָךְ֙ עִ֣יר יְהֹוָ֔ה צִיּ֖וֹן קְד֥וֹשׁ יִשְׂרָאֵֽל	14[9]	And the sons of those who afflicted you shall come bending to you, and all they who despised you shall bow at the soles of your feet; and they shall call you The city of the LORD, The Zion of the Holy One of Israel.
תַּ֧חַת הֱיוֹתֵ֛ךְ עֲזוּבָ֥ה וּשְׂנוּאָ֖ה וְאֵ֣ין עוֹבֵ֑ר וְשַׂמְתִּיךְ֙ לִגְא֣וֹן עוֹלָ֔ם מְשׂ֖וֹשׂ דּ֥וֹר וָדֽוֹר	15[10]	Although you have been forsaken and hated, So no man passed through you, I will make you an eternal excellency, a joy from generation to generation.
וְיָנַקְתְּ֙ חֲלֵ֣ב גּוֹיִ֔ם וְשֹׁ֥ד מְלָכִ֖ים תִּינָ֑קִי וְיָדַ֗עַתְּ כִּ֣י אֲנִ֤י יְהֹוָה֙ מֽוֹשִׁיעֵ֔ךְ וְגֹאֲלֵ֖ךְ אֲבִ֥יר יַעֲקֹֽב	16[11]	You shall suck the milk of the nations, And shall *suck the breast*[12] of kings; And you shall know I, the LORD, am your Savior, And I, the *Mighty One of Jacob*[13], your Redeemer.
תַּ֣חַת הַנְּחֹ֜שֶׁת אָבִ֣יא זָהָ֗ב וְתַ֤חַת הַבַּרְזֶל֙ אָבִ֣יא כֶ֔סֶף וְתַ֤חַת הָעֵצִים֙ נְחֹ֔שֶׁת וְתַ֥חַת הָאֲבָנִ֖ים בַּרְזֶ֑ל וְשַׂמְתִּ֤י פְקֻדָּתֵךְ֙ שָׁל֔וֹם וְנֹגְשַׂ֖יִךְ צְדָקָֽה	17[14]	For brass I will bring gold, And for iron I will bring silver, And for wood, brass, And for stone, iron; I will also make your officers peace, And righteousness your magistrates.
לֹא־יִשָּׁמַ֨ע ע֤וֹד חָמָס֙ בְּאַרְצֵ֔ךְ שֹׁ֥ד וָשֶׁ֖בֶר בִּגְבוּלָ֑יִךְ וְקָרָ֤את יְשׁוּעָה֙ חוֹמֹתַ֔יִךְ וּשְׁעָרַ֖יִךְ תְּהִלָּֽה	18[15]	*Violence*[16] shall no longer be heard in your land, Desolation nor destruction within your borders; But you shall call your walls Salvation, And your gates *Praise*[17].

---

[1] Isaiah 60:10 - Ezra 6:3-6:12 7:12-7:28, Isaiah 12:1 14:1-14:2 1:23 54:7-8 57:17-18 12:3 13:5 18:21, Nehemiah 2:7-2:9, Psalms 30:6, Revelation 21:24 21:26, Saadia Opinions 8:8, Zechariah 6:15

[2] Isaiah 60:11 - Isaiah 12:5 12:18 14:10, m.Oholot 13:1, Nehemiah 13:19, Psalms 5:8, Revelation 21:25-26, Saadia Opinions 8:8

[3] LXX *power of the Gentiles, and their kings as captives*

[4] Isaiah 60:12 - Daniel 2:35 2:44-2:45, Exodus.R 2:4 18:12, Gates of Repentance 3.167, Isaiah 14:2 17:11 6:15, Luke 19:27, Matthew 21:44, Midrash Tanchuma Bamidbar 7, Midrash Tanchuma Tetzaveh 11, Numbers.R 1:8, Psalms 2:12, Revelation 2:26-2:27, Saadia Opinions 8:8, Song of Songs.R 4:5, y.Sotah 7:5, Zechariah 12:2-12:4 14:12-14:19

[5] Isaiah 60:13 - 1 Chronicles 4:2, Ezra 7:27, Hosea 14:8-14:9, Isaiah 11:2 41:19-41:20 7:13 18:1, Jastrow 56b, Psalms 96:6 12:7

[6] 1QIsaa adds *He has given you*

[7] 1QIsaa adds *and it*

[8] LXX *and pine, and cedar together*

[9] Isaiah 60:14 - Derech Hashem Part IV 8§02, Hebrews 12:22, Isaiah 1:26 14:1-14:2 21:14 1:23 14:12, Jeremiah 16:19, Lamentations.R 1:23, Pesikta Rabbati 29/30B:4, Psalms 87:3, Revelation 3:9 3:12 14:1

[10] Isaiah 60:15 - Isaiah 1:7-1:9 4:2 6:12 11:10 49:14-49:23 54:6-54:14 13:7 17:18, Jeremiah 6:17 9:11, Lamentations 1:1-1:2, Psalms 78:60-78:61, Revelation 11:2 11:15-11:17

[11] Isaiah 60:16 - Ezekiel 10:30, Isaiah 43:3-43:4 1:23 11:20 13:6 66:11-66:12 18:14, Joseph and Aseneth 8:9

[12] LXX *eat the wealth*

[13] LXX *Holy One of Israel*

[14] Isaiah 60:17 - 1 Kings 10:21-10:27, 2 Peter 3:13, 3 Enoch 45:2, b.Avodah Zara [Rashi] 4a, b.Bava Batra 9a, b.Rosh Hashanah 23a, b.Temurah 16a, Ein Yaakov Bava Batra:9a, Ein Yaakov Rosh Hashanah:23a, Hebrews 11:40, Isaiah 1:26 6:26 32:1-32:2, Midrash Psalms 79:4 129:2, Midrash Tanchuma Bamidbar 21, Numbers.R 4:4, Pesikta de R'Kahana S2.2, Zechariah 12:8

[15] Isaiah 60:18 - Isaiah 2:4 11:9 2:1, Lamentations.R 1:23, Micah 4:3, Psalms 72:3-72:7, Revelation 19:1-19:6, Zechariah 9:8

[16] LXX *Injustice*

[17] LXX *Sculptured Work*

לֹא־יִהְיֶה־לָּ֣ךְ ע֤וֹד הַשֶּׁ֨מֶשׁ֙ לְא֣וֹר יוֹמָ֔ם וּלְנֹ֕גַהּ
הַיָּרֵ֖חַ לֹא־יָאִ֣יר לָ֑ךְ וְהָֽיָה־לָ֤ךְ יְהֹוָה֙ לְא֣וֹר עוֹלָ֔ם
וֵאלֹהַ֖יִךְ לְתִפְאַרְתֵּֽךְ

19[1]

The sun shall no longer be your light by day, nor for brightness shall the moon give light to you[2]; But the LORD shall be to you an everlasting light, *And your God your glory*[3].

לֹא־יָב֥וֹא עוֹד֙ שִׁמְשֵׁ֔ךְ וִירֵחֵ֖ךְ לֹ֣א יֵֽאָסֵ֑ף כִּ֣י יְהֹוָ֗ה
יִֽהְיֶה־לָּךְ֙ לְא֣וֹר עוֹלָ֔ם וְשָׁלְמ֖וּ יְמֵ֥י אֶבְלֵֽךְ

20[4]

Your sun shall no longer go down, nor shall your moon withdraw itself; For the LORD shall be your everlasting light[5], And the days of your mourning shall be ended.

וְעַמֵּךְ֙ כֻּלָּ֣ם צַדִּיקִ֔ים לְעוֹלָ֖ם יִ֣ירְשׁוּ אָ֑רֶץ נֵ֧צֶר
מַטָּעַוֹ "*מַטָּעַי*" מַעֲשֵׂ֥ה יָדַ֖י לְהִתְפָּאֵֽר

21[6]

Your people also shall be all righteous, They shall inherit the land forever; *The branch*[7] of My planting[8], the work of My hands, in which I glory.

הַקָּטֹן֙ יִהְיֶ֣ה לָאֶ֔לֶף וְהַצָּעִ֖יר לְג֣וֹי עָצ֑וּם אֲנִ֥י יְהֹוָ֖ה
בְּעִתָּ֥הּ אֲחִישֶֽׁנָּה

22[9]

The smallest shall become a thousand, And the least a mighty nation; I the LORD will hasten it in its time.

Isaiah – Chapter 61

ר֛וּחַ אֲדֹנָ֥י יֱהֹוִ֖ה עָלָ֑י יַ֡עַן מָשַׁח֩ יְהֹוָ֨ה אֹתִ֜י לְבַשֵּׂ֣ר
עֲנָוִ֗ים שְׁלָחַ֙נִי֙ לַחֲבֹ֣שׁ לְנִשְׁבְּרֵי־לֵ֔ב לִקְרֹ֤א
לִשְׁבוּיִם֙ דְּר֔וֹר וְלַאֲסוּרִ֖ים פְּקַח־קֽוֹחַ

1[10]

The spirit of *the Lord God*[11] on me; Because the LORD has anointed me To bring good tidings to the humble; He has sent me to bind up the broken-hearted, To proclaim liberty to the captives, And the *opening of the eyes*[12] to them who are bound;

---

[1] Isaiah 60:19 - Exodus.R 15:21, Genesis.R 59:5, Jastrow 1095b, Luke 2:32, Midrash Psalms 17:8 36:6 72:4, Midrash Tanchuma Nitzavim 1, Midrash Tanchuma Tetzaveh 4, Pesikta de R'Kahana 21.5, Pesikta Rabbati 8:4 21:19, Psalms 3:4 4:3 36:10 62:8, Revelation 21:23 22:5, Song of Songs.R 2:19, Tanya Likutei Aramim §36, Zechariah 2:5

[2] 1QIsaa adds *at night*

[3] Missing in 1QIsaa due to a homoioteleuton between *the LORD shall be unto you an everlasting light* in verse 19 and the similar phrase in verse 20.

[4] Isaiah 60:20 - 4 Ezra 2:35, Amos 8:9, Guide for the Perplexed 2:29, Isaiah 1:8 6:19 6:26 11:10 17:19, Malachi 3:20, Psalms 27:1 84:12, Revelation 7:15-17 21:4, Saadia Opinions 7:4, Song of Songs.R 2:19
Isaiah 60:20-22 - 4QIsa

[5] Missing in 1QIsaa due to a homoioteleuton between *the LORD shall be unto you an everlasting light* in verse 19 and the similar phrase in verse 20.

[6] Isaiah 60:21 - 2 Baruch 84:3 4 Ezra 8:7, 2 Peter 3:13, 2 Thessalonians 1:10, b.Pesachim 53b, b.Sanhedrin 98a, Before reciting Pirkei Avot [Shabbat afternoon], Chibbur Yafeh 11 {43a} 12 {43b}, Ein Yaakov Sanhedrin 89b 97b, Ephesians 1:6 1:12 2:7 2:10, Gates of Repentance 3.154, Isaiah 4:3-4 19:25 5:23 19:7 19:21 20:23 21:11 1:3 3:2 4:1 9:13 13:3 13:7 14:4, John 15:2, Lamentations.R 1:23, Leviticus.R 5:7, m.Sanhedrin 10:1, Matthew 5:5 15:13, Midrash Tanchuma Bamidbar 19, Midrash Tanchuma Chayyei Sarah 8, mt.Hilchot Shevitat Asor 3:10, mt.Hilchot Teshuvah 3:5 3:5, mt.Perek Chelek Intro:11, Numbers.R 11:1, Psalms 37:11 37:22 92:14, Revelation 5:10 21:7 21:27, Tanya Igeret Hakodesh §17, z.Bamidbar 121a, z.Bereshit 33a 35b, z.Beshallach 59b, z.Lech Lecha 84a 92a 93a 95b, z.Mishpatim 114a, z.Noach 69a, z.Pekudei 238a, z.Vaera 23a, z.Vayechi 216a 219b 251a, z.Vayetze 164b, z.Vayishlach 177b 179a, Zechariah 14:20-14:21 The smallest shall become a thousand, And the least a mighty nation; I the LORD will hasten it in its time.

[7] Missing in 4QIsam; LXX *guarding*

[8] 1QIsaa adds *of the LORD*

[9] Isaiah 60:22 - 2 Peter 3:8, Acts 2:41 5:14, Avot de R'Natan 21, b.Bava Batra 133b, b.Sanhedrin 98a, Daniel 2:35 2:44, Ecclesiastes.R 11:4, Ein Yaakov Sanhedrin:97b, Exodus.R 18:12, Genesis.R 65:12, Habakkuk 2:3, Hebrews 10:36, Isaiah 5:19 18:8, Lamentations.R 3:?, Luke 18:7, Matthew 13:31-13:32, Midrash Tanchuma Bechukkotai 3, Midrash Tanchuma Chayyei Sarah 8, Revelation 7:9, Song of Songs.R 8:19, y.Taanit 1:1, z.Vayera 116b 117b

[10] Isaiah 61:1 - 11Q13 2.4, 2 Col 2+4 1.12, 2 Corinthians 7:6, 2 Timothy 2:25-26, 4Q521 frags, 4QIsam, Acts 4:27 10:38 2:18, b.Arachin [Rashi] 16b, b.Avodah Zara 20b, Daniel 9:24, Hebrews 1:9, Hosea 6:1, Isaiah 11:2-5 18:1 18:7 24:16 1:9 49:24-25 4:9 9:15 11:21 18:2, Jastrow 1251b, Jeremiah 10:8, John 1:32-33 1:41 3:34 8:32-36, Lamentations.R 3:?, Leviticus.R 10:2, Luke 4:18-19 7:22, LXX footnote: *preach liberty to the captives and recovery of sight to the blind*, Mas.Kallah Rabbati 2:6, Matthew 3:16 5:3-5 11:5, Mekilta de R'Ishmael Bahodesh 9:103, Pesikta de R'Kahana 16.4 S5.4, Pesikta Rabbati 29/30A:5 33:3, Psalms 2:6 22:27 25:9 34:19 45:8 51:18 69:33 6:21 3:3 5:4, recovery of sight to the blind omitted, Romans 6:16-22 7:23-25, Saadia Opinions 8:6, z.Terumah 136b, Zechariah 9:11-12
Isaiah 61:1-1 - 11QIsaa
Isaiah 61:1-2 - 1QIsaa 1QIsab "The Spirit of Hashem is upon me" vs. "The Spirit of Hashem, 1QIsab, Hashem, is upon me"
Isaiah 61:1-3 - 4QIsab

[11] 1QIsaa *the LORD*

[12] or *release from darkness*

לִקְרֹא שְׁנַת־רָצוֹן לַיהֹוָה וְיוֹם נָקָם לֵאלֹהֵינוּ לְנַחֵם כָּל־אֲבֵלִים	2[1]	To proclaim the year of the LORD's good pleasure, And the day of *vengeance of our God*[2]; To comfort all who mourn;
לָשׂוּם ׀ לַאֲבֵלֵי צִיּוֹן לָתֵת לָהֶם פְּאֵר תַּחַת אֵפֶר שֶׁמֶן שָׂשׂוֹן תַּחַת אֵבֶל מַעֲטֵה תְהִלָּה תַּחַת רוּחַ כֵּהָה וְקֹרָא לָהֶם אֵילֵי הַצֶּדֶק מַטַּע יְהֹוָה לְהִתְפָּאֵר	3[3]	To appoint to those who mourn in Zion, To give to them a garland for ashes, The oil of joy for mourning, The mantle of praise for the spirit of heaviness; so *they might be called*[4] terebinths of righteousness, The planting of the LORD, in which He might glory.
וּבָנוּ חָרְבוֹת עוֹלָם שֹׁמְמוֹת רִאשֹׁנִים יְקוֹמֵמוּ וְחִדְּשׁוּ עָרֵי חֹרֶב שֹׁמְמוֹת דּוֹר וָדוֹר	4[5]	And they shall build the old ruins, They shall raise up the former desolations, And they shall renew the ruined cities[6], The desolations of many generations.
וְעָמְדוּ זָרִים וְרָעוּ צֹאנְכֶם וּבְנֵי נֵכָר אִכָּרֵיכֶם וְכֹרְמֵיכֶם	5[7]	And strangers shall stand and feed your flocks, And aliens shall be your plowmen and your vinedressers.
וְאַתֶּם כֹּהֲנֵי יְהֹוָה תִּקָּרֵאוּ מְשָׁרְתֵי אֱלֹהֵינוּ יֵאָמֵר לָכֶם חֵיל גּוֹיִם תֹּאכֵלוּ וּבִכְבוֹדָם תִּתְיַמָּרוּ	6[8]	But you shall be named the priests of the LORD, Men shall call you the ministers of our God; You shall eat the *wealth of the nations, And you shall revel in their splendor*[9].
תַּחַת בָּשְׁתְּכֶם מִשְׁנֶה וּכְלִמָּה יָרֹנּוּ חֶלְקָם לָכֵן בְּאַרְצָם מִשְׁנֶה יִירָשׁוּ שִׂמְחַת עוֹלָם תִּהְיֶה לָהֶם	7[10]	*For your shame that was double, And for that they rejoiced: 'Confusion is their portion'; Therefore, in their land they shall possess double, Everlasting joy shall be to them*[11].
כִּי אֲנִי יְהֹוָה אֹהֵב מִשְׁפָּט שֹׂנֵא גָזֵל בְּעוֹלָה וְנָתַתִּי פְעֻלָּתָם בֶּאֱמֶת וּבְרִית עוֹלָם אֶכְרוֹת לָהֶם	8[12]	For I the LORD loves justice, I hate robbery with iniquity; And I will give them their recompense in truth, And I will make an everlasting covenant with them.
וְנוֹדַע בַּגּוֹיִם זַרְעָם וְצֶאֱצָאֵיהֶם בְּתוֹךְ הָעַמִּים כָּל־רֹאֵיהֶם יַכִּירוּם כִּי הֵם זֶרַע בֵּרַךְ יְהֹוָה	9[13]	And their seed shall be known among the nations, And their offspring among the peoples;

---

[1] Isaiah 61:2 - 1 Thessalonians 2:16, 11Q13 2:19-20, 11Q13 2.9, 2 Corinthians 1:4-5 6:2, 2 Thessalonians 1:7-9 2:16-17, Isaiah 1:8 10:8 11:4 1:8 9:18 59:17-18 63:1-6 66:10-12 18:14, Jeremiah 7:14 22:10, John 16:20-22, Leviticus 25:9-13, Luke 4:19 6:21 7:44-50 21:22-24, Malachi 3:19-4:21, Matthew 5:4, Psalms 110:5-6, Saadia Opinions 8:6

[2] LXX *recompence*

[3] Isaiah 61:3 - 1 Corinthians 6:20, 1 Peter 2:9 4:9-11 4:14, 11Q13 2.14, 2 Thessalonians 1:10, b.Bava Batra 60b, b.Taanit 16a, Ecclesiastes 9:8, Ein Yaakov Bava Batra:60b, Esther 4:1-3 8:15 9:22, Ezekiel 16:8-13, Isaiah 12:1 60:20-21 13:10, Jeremiah 17:7-8, John 15:8 16:20, Luke 15:22, Mas.Derek Eretz Rabbah 2:20, Matthew 5:16 7:17-19, Midrash Psalms 5:1 137:6, Midrash Tanchuma Noach 13, mt.Hilchot Taaniot 4:1, Pesikta de R'Kahana S6.2, Pesikta Rabbati 34:1, Philippians 1:11, Psalms 23:5 30:12 45:8 92:13-16 8:15, Psalms of Solomon 14:3, Revelation 7:9-14, Saadia Opinions 8:6, Zechariah 3:5
Isaiah 61:3-6 - 4QIsam

[4] 1QIsaa *the people will call them*

[5] Isaiah 61:4 - Amos 9:14-15, Ezekiel 36:23-26 36:33-36, Isaiah 49:6-8 10:12, Saadia Opinions 8:6

[6] 1QIsaa adds *they will erect again*

[7] Isaiah 61:5 - b.Berachot 35b, b.Pesachim 68a, b.Sanhedrin 91b 105a, Ecclesiastes.R 2:11, Ein Yaakov Pesachim:68a, Ein Yaakov Pesachim:68a, Ein Yaakov Sanhedrin:91b, Ephesians 2:12-20, Isaiah 14:1-2 60:10-14, Mekilta de R'Ishmael Shabbata 1:84 2:20, mt.Perek Chelek Intro:11, Saadia Opinions 8:6, Sifre Devarim Ekev 42, z.Toledot 143b

[8] Isaiah 61:6 - 1 Corinthians 3:5 4:1, 1 Peter 2:5 2:9, 2 Corinthians 6:4 11:23, Acts 11:28-11:30, Ephesians 4:11-4:12, Exodus 19:6, Ezekiel 14:11, Isaiah 23:18 60:5-7 60:10-11 60:16-17 18:12 18:21, Mas.Gerim 4:3, Mekilta de R'Ishmael Nezikin 18:20, Numbers.R 8:2, Pesikta Rabbati 29/30B:4 33:13, Revelation 1:6 5:10 20:6, Romans 12:1 15:26-15:27, Song of Songs.R 7:8

[9] LXX *strength of nations, and shall be admired because of their wealth*

[10] Isaiah 61:7 - 2 Corinthians 4:17, 2 Kings 2:9, 2 Thessalonians 2:16, b.Chagigah 15a 16a, Deuteronomy 21:17, Genesis.R 9:5, Isaiah 11:10 16:2 3:11 60:19-20, Job 18:10, Matthew 1:46, Mesillat Yesharim Afterword, Midrash Psalms 31:6, Psalms 16:11, Saadia Opinions 8:1, Zechariah 9:12

[11] LXX *Thus shall they inherit the land a second time, and everlasting joy shall be upon their head*

[12] Isaiah 61:8 - 1 Samuel 15:21-15:24, 2 Samuel 23:5, 2 Thessalonians 3:5, Amos 5:21-5:24, b.Bava Batra [Tosefot] 26b, b.Succah 30a, Deuteronomy.R 5:7, Ein Yaakov Sukkah:30a, Genesis 17:7, Hebrews 13:20-13:21, Isaiah 1:11-1:13 5:16 7:3, Jastrow 1344b, Jeremiah 7:8-7:11 9:25 8:40, Matthew 23:13, Mesillat Yesharim 11:Traits-of-Nekuyut, Midrash Psalms 99:2, Midrash Tanchuma Chukkat 24, Midrash Tanchuma Tzav 1 14, Proverbs 3:6 8:20, Psalms 11:8 25:8-25:12 32:8 33:5 37:28 45:8 50:5 99:4, Saadia Opinions 2:11, Zechariah 8:16-8:17

[13] Isaiah 61:9 - Acts 3:26, Exodus.R 15:29 46:4, Genesis 22:18, Isaiah 20:3 17:23, Leviticus.R 23:6 25:8, Midrash Tanchuma Bereshit 6, Midrash Tanchuma Re'eh 4, Numbers.R 16:24, Perek Shirah [the Starling], Pesikta de R'Kahana S6.1, Pesikta Rabbati 34:1, Psalms 19:14, Romans 9:3-4 11:16-24, Saadia Opinions 8:6, Song of Songs.R 2:9 5:23 6:26, z.Shemini 41b, Zechariah 8:13
Isaiah 61:9-63:9 - Haftarah Netzavim [Teimon]

All who see them shall acknowledge them, they are the seed that the LORD has blessed.

שׂוֹשׂ אָשִׂישׂ בַּיהֹוָה תָּגֵל נַפְשִׁי בֵּאלֹהַי כִּי הִלְבִּישַׁנִי בִּגְדֵי־יֶשַׁע מְעִיל צְדָקָה יְעָטָנִי כֶּחָתָן יְכַהֵן פְּאֵר וְכַכַּלָּה תַּעְדֶּה כֵלֶיהָ

10[1] I will greatly rejoice in the LORD, My soul shall be joyful in my God; For He clothes me with the garments of salvation, He covers me with the robe of victory, As a bridegroom *puts on a priestly*[2] diadem, And as a bride adorns herself with her jewels.

כִּי כָאָרֶץ תּוֹצִיא צִמְחָהּ וּכְגַנָּה זֵרוּעֶיהָ תַצְמִיחַ כֵּן אֲדֹנָי יְהֹוִה יַצְמִיחַ צְדָקָה וּתְהִלָּה נֶגֶד כָּל־הַגּוֹיִם

11[3] For as the earth brings forth her growth, And as the garden causes the things that are sown in it to spring forth; so the Lord GOD causes victory and glory to spring forth before all the nations.

Isaiah – Chapter 62

לְמַעַן צִיּוֹן לֹא אֶחֱשֶׁה וּלְמַעַן יְרוּשָׁלַ͏ִם לֹא אֶשְׁקוֹט עַד־יֵצֵא כַנֹּגַהּ צִדְקָהּ וִישׁוּעָתָהּ כְּלַפִּיד יִבְעָר

1[4] For Zion's sake will I not *hold My peace*[5], And for Jerusalem's sake I will not rest, Until her triumph goes forth like brightness, And her salvation as a burning torch.

וְרָאוּ גוֹיִם צִדְקֵךְ וְכָל־מְלָכִים כְּבוֹדֵךְ וְקֹרָא לָךְ שֵׁם חָדָשׁ אֲשֶׁר פִּי יְהֹוָה יִקֳּבֶנּוּ

2[6] And the nations shall see your *triumph*[7], And all kings your glory; And you shall be called by a new name, which the mouth of the LORD shall mark out.

וְהָיִית עֲטֶרֶת תִּפְאֶרֶת בְּיַד־יְהֹוָה וּצְנוֹף׳ ״וּצְנִיף״ מְלוּכָה בְּכַף־אֱלֹהָיִךְ

3[8] You shall be a crown of beauty in the hand of the LORD, And a royal diadem in the open hand of your God.

לֹא־יֵאָמֵר לָךְ עוֹד עֲזוּבָה וּלְאַרְצֵךְ לֹא־יֵאָמֵר עוֹד שְׁמָמָה כִּי לָךְ יִקָּרֵא חֶפְצִי־בָהּ וּלְאַרְצֵךְ בְּעוּלָה כִּי־חָפֵץ יְהֹוָה בָּךְ וְאַרְצֵךְ תִּבָּעֵל

4[9] You shall not be called Forsaken, nor shall your land be called Desolate any longer; but you shall be called, My delight is in her, and your land, *Espoused*[10]; for the LORD delights in you, And your land shall be *Espoused*[11].

---

[1] Isaiah 61:10 - 1 Peter 1:8, 1 Samuel 2:1, 2 Chronicles 6:41, b.Moed Katan 28b, Deuteronomy.R 2:37, Exodus 28:2-28:43, Ezekiel 16:8-16:16, Galatians 3:27, Genesis 24:53, Habakkuk 3:18, Isaiah 1:9 11:10 1:18 3:11 4:1 13:3, Jeremiah 2:32, Leviticus.R 10:2, Life of Adam and Eve [Apocalypse] 20:2, Luke 1:46-1:47 15:22, Mas.Kallah Rabbati 8:1, Mesillat Yesharim 16:Trait of Taharah, Midrash Tanchuma Devarim 1, Nehemiah 8:10, Numbers.R 13:2, Pesikta de R'Kahana 16.4 22.1-5 S6.1-5, Pesikta Rabbati 29/30A:5 33:3 37:1-3, Philippians 3:1-3 3:9 4:4, Psalms 28:7 45:9-10 45:14-15 12:9 12:16, Revelation 4:4 7:9-14 19:7-8 21:2 21:9, Romans 3:22 5:11 13:14 14:17, Song of Songs.R 1:29 1:30 4:22, z.Yitro 90b, Zechariah 10:7
Isaiah 61:10-63:9 - Haftarah Nitzavim [Isaiah 61:10-63:9], Shabbat Vayelech with Rosh Hashanah on Monday and Tuesday [Pesikta Rabbati 37]

[2] 1QIsaa

[3] Isaiah 61:11 - 1 Peter 2:9, b.Shabbat 84b, Isaiah 21:8 55:10-11 10:11 12:18 14:1 14:7, m.Shabbat 9:2, Mark 4:26-32, Matthew 13:3 13:8 13:23, Midrash Psalms 67:1, Pesikta de R'Kahana 22.5a, Psalms 72:3 72:16 85:12, Song of Songs 4:16-5:1, Testament of Judah 24:2, y.Kilayim 3:1, y.Shabbat 9:2

[4] Isaiah 62:1 - 1 Peter 2:9, 2 Thessalonians 3:1, Hebrews 7:25, Isaiah 1:26-1:27 32:15-32:17 51:5-51:6 51:9 61:10-61:11 62:6-62:7, Luke 2:30-2:32 10:2, Matthew 5:16, Micah 4:2, Philippians 2:15-2:16, Proverbs 4:18, Psalms 51:19 98:1-98:3 102:14-102:17 122:6-122:9 137:6, Zechariah 2:12
Isaiah 62:1-12 - 1QIsaa

[5] 1QIsaa *keep silent*

[6] Isaiah 62:2 - Acts 9:15 11:26 26:23, Colossians 1:23, Genesis 17:5 17:15 32:29, Isaiah 49:6 49:23 52:10 60:1-3 60:11 60:16 61:9 62:4 62:12 65:15 66:12 66:19, Jeremiah 33:16, Micah 5:9, Midrash Psalms 67:1, Pesikta de R'Kahana 22.5a, Pesikta Rabbati 34:1, Psalms 72:10-11 138:4-5, Revelation 2:17, Sifre Devarim Ha'azinu Hashamayim 306, Sifre Devarim Nitzavim 306
Isaiah 62:2-12 - 1QIsab

[7] LXX *righteousness*

[8] Isaiah 62:3 - 1 Thessalonians 2:19, 3 Enoch 22:9, Greek Apocalypse of Ezra 6:17, Isaiah 28:5, Luke 2:14, Mas.Soferim 7:4, Song of Songs.R 4:26 8:6, y.Shabbat 6:4, Zechariah 9:16

[9] Isaiah 62:4 - 1 Peter 2:10, 2 Corinthians 11:2, Ephesians 5:25-5:27, Hebrews 13:5, Hosea 1:9-1:10 2:19-2:22, Isaiah 32:14-32:15 49:14 54:1 54:5-54:7 60:15 61:10 62:5 62:12, Jeremiah 3:14 32:41, John 3:29, Joseph and Aseneth 15:7, Midrash Psalms 22:22, Pesikta Rabbati 33:13, Psalms 149:4, Revelation 21:2 21:9-21:10, Romans 9:25-9:27, Zephaniah 3:17

[10] LXX *inhabited*

[11] LXX *inhabited*

5[1] כִּי־יִבְעַל בָּחוּר בְּתוּלָה יִבְעָלוּךְ בָּנָיִךְ וּמְשׂוֹשׂ חָתָן עַל־כַּלָּה יָשִׂישׂ עָלַיִךְ אֱלֹהָיִךְ

For[2] as a young man *espouses*[3] a virgin, So shall your sons espouse you; And as the bridegroom rejoices over the bride, So shall your God rejoice over you.

6[4] עַל־חוֹמֹתַיִךְ יְרוּשָׁלַ͏ִם הִפְקַדְתִּי שֹׁמְרִים כָּל־הַיּוֹם וְכָל־הַלַּיְלָה תָּמִיד לֹא יֶחֱשׁוּ הַמַּזְכִּרִים אֶת־יְהוָה אַל־דֳּמִי לָכֶם

I have set watchmen upon your walls, O Jerusalem, they shall *never*[5] hold their peace day or night; '*You who remember the LORD, do not take a rest,*[6]

7[7] וְאַל־תִּתְּנוּ דֳמִי לוֹ עַד־יְכוֹנֵן וְעַד־יָשִׂים אֶת־יְרוּשָׁלַ͏ִם תְּהִלָּה בָּאָרֶץ

And do not give Him rest, until He establishes[8], and until He *makes*[9] Jerusalem a praise in the earth.'

8[10] נִשְׁבַּע יְהוָה בִּימִינוֹ וּבִזְרוֹעַ עֻזּוֹ אִם־אֶתֵּן אֶת־דְּגָנֵךְ עוֹד מַאֲכָל לְאֹיְבַיִךְ וְאִם־יִשְׁתּוּ בְנֵי־נֵכָר תִּירוֹשֵׁךְ אֲשֶׁר יָגַעַתְּ בּוֹ

The LORD has sworn by His right hand, And by the arm of His strength: Surely I will not give your corn to be food for your enemies any longer; and strangers shall not drink your wine, for which you have labored;

9[11] כִּי מְאַסְפָיו יֹאכְלֻהוּ וְהִלְלוּ אֶת־יְהוָה וּמְקַבְּצָיו יִשְׁתֻּהוּ בְּחַצְרוֹת קָדְשִׁי

But those who gather it shall eat it, And praise the[12] LORD, And those who gather it shall drink it in the courts of My sanctuary[13].

10[14] עִבְרוּ עִבְרוּ בַּשְּׁעָרִים פַּנּוּ דֶּרֶךְ הָעָם סֹלּוּ סֹלּוּ הַמְסִלָּה סַקְּלוּ מֵאֶבֶן הָרִימוּ נֵס עַל־הָעַמִּים

Go through, *go through*[15], go through the gates, Clear the way of the people; Cast up, cast up the highway, remove the stones; *Lift up an ensign over the peoples*[16].

11[17] הִנֵּה יְהוָה הִשְׁמִיעַ אֶל־קְצֵה הָאָרֶץ אִמְרוּ לְבַת־צִיּוֹן הִנֵּה יִשְׁעֵךְ בָּא הִנֵּה שְׂכָרוֹ אִתּוֹ וּפְעֻלָּתוֹ לְפָנָיו

Behold, the LORD has proclaimed to the end[18] of the earth: say to the daughter of Zion: 'Behold, your salvation comes; Behold, His reward is with Him, His reward is before Him.'

12[19] וְקָרְאוּ לָהֶם עַם־הַקֹּדֶשׁ גְּאוּלֵי יְהוָה וְלָךְ יִקָּרֵא דְרוּשָׁה עִיר לֹא נֶעֱזָבָה

And they shall call them the holy people, the redeemed of the LORD; And you shall be called Sought out, A city not forsaken.

---

[1] Isaiah 62:5 - b.Moed Katan 2a, b.Sanhedrin 99a, b.Succah [Rashi] 33b, Deuteronomy.R 2:37, Ein Yaakov Sanhedrin 99a, Hebrews 12:2, Isaiah 49:18-22 62:4 65:19, Jeremiah 32:41, Midrash Psalms 90:17, Midrash Tanchuma Beshallach 28, Midrash Tanchuma Ekev 7, Midrash Tanchuma Tzav 14, Midrash Tanchuma Vayishlach 10, mt.Hilchot Shevuot 2:6, Pesikta de R'Kahana 22.5 S6.1 S6.2, Pesikta Rabbati 1:7 29/30B:4 33:13, Psalms 45:12-17, Song of Songs 3:11, Song of Songs.R 4:22

[2] 1QIsaa adds *just*

[3] LXX *lives with*

[4] Isaiah 62:6 - 1 Corinthians 12:28, 1 Thessalonians 5:17, 2 Chronicles 8:14, Acts 10:4 10:31, b.Menachot 87a, Ein Yaakov Menachot:87a, Ephesians 4:11-12, Exodus.R 18:5, Ezekiel 3:17-21 33:2-9, Genesis 8:13 8:27, Hebrews 13:17, Isaiah 19:26 4:8 8:10 14:1, Jeremiah 6:17, Luke 11:5-13 18:1-8 18:39, Matthew 15:22-27, Midrash Psalms 83:1, Numbers 14:17-19, Pesikta de R'Kahana S6.2, Pesikta Rabbati 35:2, Psalms 74:2 74:18 134:1-2, Psalms of Solomon 3:3, Revelation 4:6-8 6:10, Song of Songs 3:3 5:7, Tanya Igeret Hakodesh §22b, z.Bereshit 34a, z.Lech Lecha 77b, z.Vayakhel 212a, z.Yitro 89b

[5] 1QIsaa *not*

[6] LXX *making mention of the LORD*

[7] Isaiah 62:7 - Isaiah 12:18 61:11-62:3, Jeremiah 9:9, Luke 18:1-18:8, Matthew 6:9-6:10 6:13, Midrash Psalms 83:1, Revelation 11:15, Selichot, Zephaniah 3:19-3:20

[8] LXX *For there is none like you, when he shall have established*

[9] 1QIsaa *prepares and establishes*

[10] Isaiah 62:8 - b.Berachot 10a, b.Nazir 3b, Deuteronomy 4:31 4:33 8:40, Ein Yaakov Berachot:6a, Ezekiel 20:5, Isaiah 1:7 65:21-65:23, Jastrow 1687b, Jeremiah 5:17, Judges 6:3-6:6, Lamentations.R 1:37, Leviticus 2:16, Mekhilta de R'Shimon bar Yochai Shirata 35:1, Mekilta de R'Ishmael Shirata 9:14, Midrash Psalms 22:17, Midrash Tanchuma Noach 11, Midrash Tanchuma Shemot 3, Pirkei de R'Eliezer 41, Saadia Opinions 8:8, z.Vayikra 24a, Sifre Devarim Ekev 42

[11] Isaiah 62:9 - Deuteronomy 12:7 12:12 14:23-14:29 16:11 16:14, Sifre Devarim Ekev 42

[12] 1QIsaa adds *the name of*

[13] 1QIsaa adds *says your God*

[14] Isaiah 62:10 - Birchat HaChammah.Ana Bekoach, Exodus 17:15, Hebrews 12:13, Isaiah 11:10 11:12 11:16 18:3 16:3 24:20 1:22 4:11 9:14 12:11, Lamentations.R 1:23, Matthew 22:9, Midrash Psalms 114:2, Midrash Tanchuma Beha'alotcha 10, Numbers.R 15:16, Pesikta de R'Kahana S6.1, z.Toledot 140a

[15] Missing in 1QIsaa

[16] 1QIsaa *speak among the peoples*

[17] Isaiah 62:11 - Deuteronomy.R 1:23, Isaiah 40:9-40:10 1:4 1:6, John 12:15, Mark 16:15, Matthew 21:5, Midrash Tanchuma Acharei Mot 12, Psalms 98:1-98:3, Revelation 22:12, Romans 10:11-10:18, Zechariah 9:9

[18] 1QIsaa *Behold the LORD! Proclaim to the ends*

[19] Isaiah 62:12 - 1 Peter 1:18-1:19 2:9, Deuteronomy 7:6 2:19 4:9, Ezekiel 34:11-34:16, Hebrews 13:5, Isaiah 11:9 18:16 12:21 14:4

Isaiah – Chapter 63

מִי־זֶה בָּא מֵאֱדוֹם חֲמוּץ בְּגָדִים מִבָּצְרָה זֶה הָדוּר בִּלְבוּשׁוֹ צֹעֶה בְּרֹב כֹּחוֹ אֲנִי מְדַבֵּר בִּצְדָקָה רַב לְהוֹשִׁיעַ	1[1] 'Who is this who comes from Edom, with crimson garments from *Bozrah*[2]? This who is glorious in his apparel, stately in the greatness of his strength?' 'I, who speak in victory, mighty to save.'
מַדּוּעַ אָדֹם לִלְבוּשֶׁךָ וּבְגָדֶיךָ כְּדֹרֵךְ בְּגַת	2[3] 'Why is your apparel red, And Your garments like his who treads in the *winepress*[4]?'
פּוּרָה דָּרַכְתִּי לְבַדִּי וּמֵעַמִּים אֵין־אִישׁ אִתִּי וְאֶדְרְכֵם בְּאַפִּי וְאֶרְמְסֵם בַּחֲמָתִי וְיֵז נִצְחָם עַל־בְּגָדַי וְכָל־מַלְבּוּשַׁי אֶגְאָלְתִּי	3[5] 'I have tread the winepress alone, And of the peoples there was no man with Me; Yes, I stepped on them in My anger, And trampled them in My fury; And their lifeblood is dashed against My garments, And I have stained all My raiment.
כִּי יוֹם נָקָם בְּלִבִּי וּשְׁנַת גְּאוּלַי בָּאָה	4[6] For the day of vengeance was in My heart, And My year of redemption has come.
וְאַבִּיט וְאֵין עֹזֵר וְאֶשְׁתּוֹמֵם וְאֵין סוֹמֵךְ וַתּוֹשַׁע לִי זְרֹעִי וַחֲמָתִי הִיא סְמָכָתְנִי	5[7] And I looked, and there was no one *to help*[8], And I saw in astonishment, and there was no one to uphold; therefore, My own arm brought salvation to Me, and My fury, upheld Me.
וְאָבוּס עַמִּים בְּאַפִּי וַאֲשַׁכְּרֵם בַּחֲמָתִי וְאוֹרִיד לָאָרֶץ נִצְחָם	6[9] And I walked on the peoples in My anger, And made them drunk from My fury, And I poured their lifeblood on the earth.'
חַסְדֵי יְהוָה אַזְכִּיר תְּהִלֹּת יְהוָה כְּעַל כֹּל אֲשֶׁר־גְּמָלָנוּ יְהוָה וְרַב־טוּב לְבֵית יִשְׂרָאֵל אֲשֶׁר־גְּמָלָם כְּרַחֲמָיו וּכְרֹב חֲסָדָיו	7[10] *I will mention the mercies of the LORD, And the praises of the LORD, According to all the LORD has bestowed on us; And the great goodness toward the house of Israel, which He bestowed on them according to His*

17:1, John 4:23 10:16, Luke 15:4-15:5 19:10, Matthew 16:18 18:10-18:13 4:20, Midrash Tanchuma Ki Tetze 3, Midrash Tanchuma Tazria 11, Psalms 11:2, Revelation 5:9

[1] Isaiah 63:1 - 1 Peter 1:5, Amos 1:11-12, b.Makkot 12a, b.Pesachim [Rashbam] 118a, Ein Yaakov Makkot:12a, Ein Yaakov Megillah 29a, Exodus.R 15:16, Genesis.R 16:5, Hebrews 7:25, Isaiah 9:6 34:5-6 21:19 21:23 63:2-3, Jastrow 457b 928b 1104a, John 10:28-30, Jude 1:24-25, Matthew 21:10, Mekilta de R'Ishmael Pisha 14:105, Midrash Proverbs 14, Midrash Psalms 20:3 29:2 68:13 93:1, Midrash Tanchuma Kedoshim 1, Midrash Tanchuma Ki Tissa 32, Numbers 23:19, Numbers.R 7:10 14:1 14:10, Pesikta de R'Kahana 22.5, Pesikta Rabbati 29/30B:4 40:3/4, Pirkei de R'Eliezer 30, Psalms 24:7-10 45:4-5 17:7, Revelation 11:17-18 19:13, Song of Songs 3:6 6:10 8:5, Song of Songs.R 4:22, z.Beshallach 51b 56b, z.Bo 36a, z.Emor 89a, z.Vayechi 238a, z.Vayigash 211b, z.Vayishlach 174a, Zephaniah 3:17
Isaiah 63:1-19 - 1QIsaa, 1QIsab

[2] LXX *Bosor*

[3] Isaiah 63:2 - Deuteronomy.R 2:37, Exodus.R 30:18, Genesis.R 63:12 75:4, Mekhilta de R'Shimon bar Yochai Bachodesh 53:3, Midrash Psalms 8:8 68:13 84:1, Pesikta de R'Kahana 22.5 S6.5, Pesikta Rabbati 37:2, Revelation 19:13 19:15, Song of Songs.R 4:22

[4] 1QIsaa *coriander* or *clothing*; MT has a misspelling of *winepress*

[5] Isaiah 63:3 - 2 Kings 9:33, b.Berachot 58a, b.Chullin 92a, Ein Yaakov Berachot:58a, Esther.R 1:6, Exodus.R 15:16 15:17, Ezekiel 38:18-38:22, Genesis.R 16:4 99 [Excl]:11, Isaiah 22:5 1:10 34:2-34:5 15:6, Lamentations 1:15, Leviticus.R 13:5, Malachi 3:21, Micah 7:10, Midrash Psalms 8:1 60:3 84:1, Midrash Tanchuma Mishpatim 5, Midrash Tanchuma Vayechi 12, Numbers.R 11:7 14:1, Revelation 14:19-20 19:13-15, Sifre.z Numbers Naso 6:26, z.Vayechi 238a, z.Vayigash 208b, Zechariah 10:5

[6] Isaiah 63:4 - 1:7, b.Sanhedrin 99a, Ecclesiastes.R 11:4 12:9, Ein Yaakov Sanhedrin:99a, Genesis.R 65:12, Isaiah 10:8 11:4 13:2, Jeremiah 3:6, Luke 21:22, Mekhilta de R'Shimon bar Yochai Pisha 16:5, Midrash Psalms 7:11 9:2 14:6 84:1 90:17, Midrash Tanchuma Behar 1, Midrash Tanchuma Ekev 7, Pesikta Rabbati 1:7, Revelation 6:9-6:17 11:13 18:20, Zechariah 3:8

[7] Isaiah 63:5 - 1 Corinthians 1:24, 3 Enoch 48A:8, Hebrews 2:14-2:15, Hosea 1:7, Isaiah 16:10 17:28 2:2 3:9 4:10 59:16-59:18 15:3, John 16:32, Mesillat Yesharim 19:Longing-for-the-Redemption, Psalms 44:4 98:1, Tanna Devei Eliyahu 11

[8] 1QIsaa *to take hold of me*

[9] Isaiah 63:6 - Isaiah 25:10-12 26:5-6 5:9 1:26 51:21-23 63:2-3, Jeremiah 25:16-17 25:26-27, Job 21:20, Lamentations 3:15, Midrash Psalms 84:1, Psalms 60:4 75:9, Revelation 14:10 16:6 16:19 18:3-6 18:21, variant ואשברם of ואשכרם is found

[10] Isaiah 63:7 - 1 Kings 8:66, 1 Timothy 1:14, 2 Chronicles 7:10, Ephesians 1:6-7 2:4, Exodus 34:6-7, Ezekiel 16:6-14, Guide for the Perplexed 2:29 3:53, Hosea 2:19, Isaiah 41:8-9 3:2 6:8 7:7, Lamentations 3:32, Mekhilta de R'Shimon bar Yochai Shirata 35:2, Mekilta de R'Ishmael Shirata 9:25, Midrash Psalms 84:1 89:1 119:8, Nehemiah 9:7-15 9:19-21 9:25 9:27 9:31 9:35, Numbers 14:18-19, Psalms 51:2 63:4 78:11-72 86:5 86:15 105:5-45 11:8 11:15 11:21 11:31 136:1-26 147:19-20, Romans 2:4 5:20, Titus 3:4-7, z.Bereshit 7a, z.Emor 104a, z.Terumah 127a, Zechariah 9:17

compassions, And according to the multitude of His mercies[1].

וַיֹּ֨אמֶר֙ אַךְ־עַמִּ֣י הֵ֔מָּה בָּנִ֖ים לֹ֣א יְשַׁקֵּ֑רוּ וַיְהִ֥י לָהֶ֖ם לְמוֹשִֽׁיעַ	8[2]

For He said: 'Surely, they are My people, Children who will not deal falsely'; So He was their Savior.

בְּכָל־צָרָתָ֣ם ׀ לֹ֣א ״לוֹ״ ׳לֹא׳ צָ֗ר וּמַלְאַ֤ךְ פָּנָיו֙ הוֹשִׁיעָ֔ם בְּאַהֲבָת֥וֹ וּבְחֶמְלָת֖וֹ ה֣וּא גְאָלָ֑ם וַֽיְנַטְּלֵ֥ם וַֽיְנַשְּׂאֵ֖ם כָּל־יְמֵ֥י עוֹלָֽם	9[3]

In all their affliction He was afflicted, And the angel of His presence saved them; In His love and in His pity He redeemed them; And He *bore them, and carried them*[4] all the days of old.

וְהֵ֛מָּה מָר֥וּ וְעִצְּב֖וּ אֶת־ר֣וּחַ קָדְשׁ֑וֹ וַיֵּהָפֵ֧ךְ לָהֶ֛ם לְאוֹיֵ֖ב ה֥וּא נִלְחַם־בָּֽם	10[5]

But they rebelled, and grieved His holy spirit; Therefore, He was turned to be their enemy; He, Himself, fought against them.

וַיִּזְכֹּ֥ר יְמֵֽי־עוֹלָ֖ם מֹשֶׁ֣ה עַמּ֑וֹ אַיֵּ֣ה ׀ הַֽמַּעֲלֵ֣ם מִיָּ֗ם אֵ֚ת רֹעֵ֣י צֹאנ֔וֹ אַיֵּ֛ה הַשָּׂ֥ם בְּקִרְבּ֖וֹ אֶת־ר֥וּחַ קָדְשֽׁוֹ	11[6]

Then His people remembered the days of old, *the days of Moses*[7]: 'Where is He who brought them up out of the sea with the shepherds of His flock? Where is He who put His holy spirit In their midst?

מוֹלִיךְ֙ לִימִ֣ין מֹשֶׁ֔ה זְר֖וֹעַ תִּפְאַרְתּ֑וֹ בּ֤וֹקֵֽעַ מַ֙יִם֙ מִפְּנֵיהֶ֔ם לַעֲשׂ֥וֹת ל֖וֹ שֵׁ֥ם עוֹלָֽם	12[8]

Who caused His glorious arm to go at the right hand of Moses? Who divided the water before them, to make Himself an everlasting name?

מוֹלִיכָ֖ם בַּתְּהֹמ֑וֹת כַּסּ֥וּס בַּמִּדְבָּ֖ר לֹ֥א יִכָּשֵֽׁלוּ	13[9]

Who led them through the deep, as a horse in the wilderness, without stumbling?

כַּבְּהֵמָה֙ בַּבִּקְעָ֣ה תֵרֵ֔ד ר֥וּחַ יְהוָ֖ה תְּנִיחֶ֑נּוּ כֵּ֤ן נִהַ֙גְתָּ֙ עַמְּךָ֔ לַעֲשׂ֥וֹת לְךָ֖ שֵׁ֥ם תִּפְאָֽרֶת	14[10]

As the cattle that go down into the valley, the spirit of the LORD caused them to rest; so you lead Your people, to glorify Your name.'

---

[1] LXX *I remembered the mercy of the LORD, the praises of the LORD in all things wherein he recompenses us. The LORD is a good judge to the house of Israel; he deals with us according to his mercy, and according to the abundance of his righteousness*

[2] Isaiah 63:8 - 1 John 4:14, Colossians 3:9, Deuteronomy 9:23, Ephesians 4:25, Exodus 3:7 4:22-23 6:7 19:5-6 24:7, Genesis 17:7, Hosea 13:4, Isaiah 12:2 17:8 19:3 19:11 3:4 9:11, Jeremiah 14:8, John 1:47, Jude 1:25, Mekilta de R'Ishmael Bahodesh 1:70, Mesillat Yesharim 11:Nekiyut-from-Falsehood, Pesikta de R'Kahana S6.1, Psalms 78:36-37 10:21, Romans 11:1-2 11:28, Zephaniah 3:7 Isaiah 63:8-9 [LXX] - Apocalypse of Elijah 1:5

[3] Isaiah 63:9 - 1 Corinthians 10:9, 1 John 4:9-4:10, Acts 7:30-7:32 7:34-7:35 7:38 9:4 12:11, b.Bava Batra [Rashbam] 74a, b.Chullin [Tosefot] 65a, b.Sotah 31a, b.Taanit 16a, Chibbur Yafeh 11 {43a}, Derech Hashem Part IV 8§02, Deuteronomy 1:31 7:7-7:8 32:10-32:12, Ein Yaakov Sotah:31a, Ein Yaakov Taanit:16a, Exodus 3:7-3:9 14:19 19:4 23:20-23:21 9:14, Exodus.R 2:5, Genesis 22:11-22:17 24:16, Guide for the Perplexed 1:20 2:29, Hebrews 2:18 4:15, Hosea 1:7 12:5-12:7, Isaiah 46:3-46:4, Jubilees 1:29, Judges 10:16, Luke 15:5, m.Taanit 2:1, Malachi 3:1, Mas.Soferim 6:6, Matthew 1:40 1:45, Mekhilta de R'Shimon bar Yochai Pisha 16:4, Mekhilta de R'Shimon bar Yochai Sanya 1:2, Mekhilta de R'Ishmael Amalek 2:169, Mekhilta de R'Ishmael Bahodesh 1:70, Mekhilta de R'Ishmael Pisha 14:90, Midrash Psalms 27:2, Midrash Tanchuma Beshallach 28, Midrash Tanchuma Vayishlach 10, mt.Hilchot Taaniot 4:1, Pirkei de R'Eliezer 40, Psalms 78:38 106:7-106:10, Revelation 1:5 5:9, Titus 2:14, z.Balak 203b, z.Terumah 165a, z.Vayera 120b, z.Vayigash 208b, Zechariah 2:8

[4] 1QIsaa *carried them and lifted them up*

[5] Isaiah 63:10 - Acts 7:51, Deuteronomy 9:7 9:22-24 28:15-68 32:19-25, Ecclesiastes.R 3:10, Ephesians 4:30, Exodus 15:24 16:8 23:21 8:8, Ezekiel 2:3 2:7 6:9 20:8 20:13 20:21, Guide for the Perplexed 1:29 2:29, Isaiah 1:2 17:2, Jeremiah 21:5 6:14, Lamentations 1:18 1:20 2:4-5, Lamentations.R 1:57, Leviticus 26:17-46, Matthew 22:7, Mekhilta de R'Shimon bar Yochai Shirata 31:2, Mekilta de R'Ishmael Shirata 5:66, Midrash Tanchuma Bechukkotai 2, Midrash Tanchuma Beshallach 15, Midrash Tanchuma Vayera 10, Nehemiah 9:16-17 9:26 9:29, Numbers 14:9-11 16:1-35, Pesikta de R'Kahana 16.11, Pesikta Rabbati 33:13, Psalms 51:12 78:8 78:40 78:49 78:56 95:9-11

[6] Isaiah 63:11 - Daniel 4:5, Deuteronomy 4:30-4:31, Deuteronomy.R 9:9, Ecclesiastes.R 2:19 9:20, Exodus 14:22 14:30 32:11-32:12, Exodus.R 30:4, Haggai 2:5, Isaiah 51:9-51:10 15:15, Jeremiah 2:6, Lamentations.R 5:21, Leviticus 26:40-26:45, Luke 1:54-1:55, Midrash Tanchuma Beshallach 10, Midrash Tanchuma Chukkat 8, Nehemiah 9:20, Numbers 11:17 11:25 11:29 14:13-14:25, Numbers.R 14:4, Pesikta Rabbati 12:1, Psalms 25:6 77:6-77:12 77:21 89:48-89:51 23:5, Sifre Devarim {Ekev} 41, Sifre Devarim Ekev 41, Tanna Devei Eliyahu 4, y.Sanhedrin 10:1, y.Sotah 5:4, z.Beshallach 47a, z.Noach 67b, Zechariah 4:6 Isaiah 63:11-12 - Exodus.R 21:6

[7] LXX *saying*

[8] Isaiah 63:12 - 3 Enoch 48A:3, Exodus 14:16-17 14:21-22 15:6 15:13 15:16, Isaiah 11:15 7:13, Joshua 3:16, Kuzari 2.55, Mekhilta de R'Shimon bar Yochai Beshallach 23:1, Mekhilta de R'Ishmael Beshallah 4:49, Midrash Psalms 44:1, Midrash Tanchuma Vaetchanan 6, Nehemiah 9:11, Psalms 78:13 80:2 114:5-7 136:13-16, Romans 9:17, z.Noach 67b, z.Vayeilech 283a

[9] Isaiah 63:13 - Habakkuk 3:15, Jeremiah 7:10, Psalms 10:9

[10] Isaiah 63:14 - 1 Chronicles 5:13, 2 Samuel 7:23, Avot de R'Natan 33, Ephesians 1:6 1:12, Hebrews 4:8-4:11, Isaiah 15:12, Joshua 22:4 23:1, Luke 2:14, Midrash Psalms 44:1 114:7, Nehemiah 9:5, Numbers 14:21

הַבֵּט מִשָּׁמַיִם וּרְאֵה מִזְּבֻל קָדְשְׁךָ וְתִפְאַרְתֶּךָ אַיֵּה קִנְאָתְךָ וּגְבוּרֹתֶךָ הֲמוֹן מֵעֶיךָ וְרַחֲמֶיךָ אֵלַי הִתְאַפָּקוּ | 15[1]
Look down from heaven, and see, from Your holy and glorious habitation; Where is Your zeal and Your mighty acts, the yearning of Your heart and Your compassions, now restrained toward me?

כִּי־אַתָּה אָבִינוּ כִּי אַבְרָהָם לֹא יְדָעָנוּ וְיִשְׂרָאֵל לֹא יַכִּירָנוּ אַתָּה יְהוָה אָבִינוּ גֹּאֲלֵנוּ מֵעוֹלָם שְׁמֶךָ | 16[2]
For you are our Father; for Abraham does not know us, And Israel does not acknowledge us; You[3], O LORD, are our Father, Our Redeemer; *from everlasting is Your name*[4].

לָמָּה תַתְעֵנוּ יְהוָה מִדְּרָכֶיךָ תַּקְשִׁיחַ לִבֵּנוּ מִיִּרְאָתֶךָ שׁוּב לְמַעַן עֲבָדֶיךָ שִׁבְטֵי נַחֲלָתֶךָ | 17[5]
O LORD, why do you make us err from Your ways, And harden our heart from Your fear? Return for Your servants' sake, The tribes of your inheritance.

לַמִּצְעָר יָרְשׁוּ עַם־קָדְשֶׁךָ צָרֵינוּ בּוֹסְסוּ מִקְדָּשֶׁךָ | 18[6]
Your holy people, they have been nearly driven out, Our adversaries have trodden down Your sanctuary[7].

הָיִינוּ מֵעוֹלָם לֹא־מָשַׁלְתָּ בָּם לֹא־נִקְרָא שִׁמְךָ עֲלֵיהֶם לוּא־קָרַעְתָּ שָׁמַיִם יָרַדְתָּ מִפָּנֶיךָ הָרִים נָזֹלּוּ | 19[8]
We became as those over whom You never ruled, As those not called by Your name.

Isaiah – Chapter 64

כִּקְדֹחַ אֵשׁ הֲמָסִים מַיִם תִּבְעֶה־אֵשׁ לְהוֹדִיעַ שִׁמְךָ לְצָרֶיךָ מִפָּנֶיךָ גּוֹיִם יִרְגָּזוּ | 1[9]
Oh, that you would rend the heavens, *that you would come down, That the mountains might quake at Your presence, as when fire kindles the brush-wood, and the fire causes the waters to boil*[10]; *To make Your name known to your adversaries*[11], so the nations might tremble at Your presence,

בַּעֲשׂוֹתְךָ נוֹרָאוֹת לֹא נְקַוֶּה יָרַדְתָּ מִפָּנֶיךָ הָרִים נָזֹלּוּ | 2[12]
When you did tremendous things for which we *did not look*[13]. Oh that you would come down, so the mountains might quake at Your presence!

---

[1] Isaiah 63:15 - 1 John 3:17, 1 Kings 8:27, 2 Chronicles 6:27, Avot de R'Natan 37, b.Chagigah 12b, Deuteronomy 2:15, Ein Yaakov Chagigah:12b, Exodus.R 33:4, Gates of Repentance 2.017, Guide for the Perplexed 1:46, Hosea 11:8, Isaiah 9:8 2:11 1:15 51:9-51:10 9:15 11:17 15:9 18:1, Jeremiah 7:21, Lamentations 3:50, Luke 1:78, Philippians 2:1, Psalms 25:6 33:14 77:8-77:10 80:15 89:50 102:20-102:21 113:5-113:6 3:1, Selichot, Testament of Moses 10:3

[2] Isaiah 63:16 - 1 Chronicles 5:10, 1 Peter 1:18-1:21, 3 Maccabees 2:21, b.Shabbat 89b, Deuteronomy 8:6, Ecclesiastes 9:5, Ein Yaakov Shabbat:89b, Exodus 4:22, Exodus.R 46:5, Genesis.R 60:12 67:7, Isaiah 17:14 19:14 20:6 6:5 15:12 16:9, Jastrow 1669a, Jeremiah 3:19 7:10, Job 14:21, Malachi 1:6 2:10, Mas.Kallah Rabbati 7:1, Matthew 6:9, Midrash Psalms 121:1, Pesikta Rabbati 30:2, Song of Songs.R 2:45, Testament of Job 33:3, z.Bereshit 29b, z.Vayigash 205a, z.Yitro 90a

[3] 1QIsaa *you are he*

[4] LXX *Your name has been upon us from the beginning*

[5] Isaiah 63:17 - 2 Thessalonians 2:11-12, Deuteronomy 2:30, Exodus.R 44:9, Ezekiel 14:7-9, Genesis.R 84:18, Isaiah 6:10 5:13, John 12:40, Joshua 11:20, mt.Shemonah Perakim 8:6, Numbers 10:36, Psalms 74:1-2 80:15 90:13 23:10 23:36 21:4, Romans 9:18-20, Saadia Opinions 4:6, Selichot, Shemonah Perachim VIII, Zechariah 1:12

[6] Isaiah 63:18 - 1 Peter 2:9, Daniel 8:24, Deuteronomy 7:6 2:19, Exodus 19:4-6, Guide for the Perplexed 2:29, Isaiah 14:12 64:12-13, Lamentations 1:10 4:1, Matthew 24:2, Midrash Psalms 42/43:5, Psalms 74:3-7, Psalms of Solomon 2:2, Revelation 11:2

[7] LXX *that we may inherit a small part of your holy mountain*

[8] Isaiah 63:19 - Mesillat Yesharim 24:Trait of Yiras Cheit
Isaiah 63:19-64:1 - Acts 14:16 15:17, Amos 9:12, Ephesians 2:12, Isaiah 17:1, Jeremiah 10:25, Psalms 79:6 15:4, Romans 9:4

[9] Isaiah 64:1 - 1QIsab, Avot de R'Natan 33, b.Avodah Zara [Rashi] 28b, b.Bava Kamma 4b, b.Bava Metzia [Rashi] 63b, Genesis.R 4:2, Liber Antiquitatum Biblicarum 15:6, Mekhilta de R'Shimon bar Yochai Bachodesh 51:1 51:2, Sefer Yetzirah 1:12
Isaiah 64:1-2 - Mekilta de R'Ishmael Bahodesh 4:52-53
Isaiah 64:1-11 - 1QIsaa

[10] LXX *trembling will take hold upon the mountains from thee, and they shall melt, as wax melts before the fire; and fire shall burn up the enemies*

[11] 1QIsaa *to your adversaries to make known your name to your adversaries before you*

[12] Isaiah 64:2 - 2 Peter 3:10-3:12, Amos 9:5 9:13, Exodus 3:8 19:11 19:18-19:19, Habakkuk 3:1-3:13, Isaiah 15:15, Judges 5:4-5:5, Mark 1:10, Micah 1:3-1:4, Nahum 1:5-1:6, Psalms 18:8-18:16 46:7 68:9 114:4-7 144:5-6, Revelation 20:11

[13] 1QIsaa *looked*

וּמֵעוֹלָם לֹא־שָׁמְעוּ לֹא הֶאֱזִינוּ עַיִן לֹא־רָאָתָה אֱלֹהִים זוּלָתְךָ יַעֲשֶׂה לִמְחַכֵּה־לוֹ	3[1]	*And from forever men have not heard, nor perceived by the ear, nor has the eye seen a God beside You, Who works for him who waits for Him[2].*
פָּגַעְתָּ אֶת־שָׂשׂ וְעֹשֵׂה צֶדֶק בִּדְרָכֶיךָ יִזְכְּרוּךָ הֵן אַתָּה קָצַפְתָּ וַנֶּחֱטָא בָּהֶם עוֹלָם וְנִוָּשֵׁעַ	4[3]	You took him away who joyfully worked righteousness, Those who remembered You in Your ways. Behold, you were angry, and we sinned; Upon them we stayed of old, so we might be saved.
וַנְּהִי כַטָּמֵא כֻּלָּנוּ וּכְבֶגֶד עִדִּים כָּל־צִדְקֹתֵינוּ וַנָּבֶל כֶּעָלֶה כֻּלָּנוּ וַעֲוֹנֵנוּ כָּרוּחַ יִשָּׂאֻנוּ	5[4]	And we are all become as one who is unclean, And all our righteousness are as a polluted garment; And we all fade as a leaf, And our iniquities, like the wind, take us away.
וְאֵין־קוֹרֵא בְשִׁמְךָ מִתְעוֹרֵר לְהַחֲזִיק בָּךְ כִּי־הִסְתַּרְתָּ פָנֶיךָ מִמֶּנּוּ וַתְּמוּגֵנוּ בְּיַד־עֲוֹנֵנוּ	6[5]	And there is no one who calls on Your name, who stirs himself to take hold of You; For you have hidden Your face from us, and has *consumed us by means of our iniquities[6].*
וְעַתָּה יְהוָה אָבִינוּ אָתָּה אֲנַחְנוּ הַחֹמֶר וְאַתָּה יֹצְרֵנוּ וּמַעֲשֵׂה יָדְךָ כֻּלָּנוּ	7[7]	*But now[8],* O LORD, you are our Father; We are the clay, and you our potter, And we all are the work of Your hand.
אַל־תִּקְצֹף יְהוָה עַד־מְאֹד וְאַל־לָעַד תִּזְכֹּר עָוֹן הֵן הַבֶּט־נָא עַמְּךָ כֻלָּנוּ	8[9]	Do not be terribly angry, O LORD, nor remember iniquity *forever[10]*; Behold, look, we implore You, we are all Your people.
עָרֵי קָדְשְׁךָ הָיוּ מִדְבָּר צִיּוֹן מִדְבָּר הָיָתָה יְרוּשָׁלִַם שְׁמָמָה	9[11]	Your holy cities became a wilderness, Zion became[12] a wilderness, Jerusalem a *desolation[13].*

---

[1] Isaiah 64:3 - 1 Kings 8:41-43, 1 Samuel 17:46-47, b.Avodah Zara 65a, b.Berachot 34b, b.Sanhedrin 99a, b.Shabbat 63a, Chibbur Yafeh 12 {55a}, Daniel 3:31-33 4:29-34 6:26-28, Derech Hashem Part I 3§4, Deuteronomy 2:25, Ecclesiastes.R 1:27 12:9, Ein Yaakov Berachot:34b, Ein Yaakov Sanhedrin:99a, Esther.R 2:1 2:5, Exodus 14:4 15:14-16, Exodus.R 30:24 45:6, Ezekiel 38:22-23 39:27-28, Isaiah 13:20 15:12, Jastrow 1045a, Jeremiah 5:22 9:9, Joel 4:16-17, Micah 7:15-17, Midrash Proverbs 13, Midrash Psalms 9:2, Midrash Tanchuma Bereshit 1, Midrash Tanchuma Devarim 1, Midrash Tanchuma Ki Tissa 27, Midrash Tanchuma Vayikra 8, mt.Hilchot Teshuvah 8:7, mt.Perek Chelek Intro:11, Pesikta Rabbati 37:1, Psalms 9:21 46:11 48:5-7 67:2-3 79:10 83:14 98:1-2 99:1 102:16-17 10:8, Ralbag SOS 5, Revelation 11:11-13, Saadia Opinions 9:5, Tanya Igeret Hakodesh §5, z.Bereshit 47a 4b 59a 6b, z.Chayyei Sarah 130b, z.Mishpatim 97a 100b, z.Noach 66a, z.Terumah 163a 166b, z.Vayakhel 210b 211a, z.Vayechi 217b

[2] LXX *From of old we have not heard, neither have our eyes seen a God beside you, and your works that you will perform to them who wait for mercy*

[3] Isaiah 64:4 - 2 Samuel 7:23, b.Taanit 8a, Deuteronomy 4:34 10:21, Ein Yaakov Taanit:8a, Exodus 10:10, Habakkuk 3:3 3:6, Isaiah 16:2, Judges 5:4-5:5, Liber Antiquitatum Biblicarum 26:13, Martyrdom of Polycarp 2:3, Midrash Psalms 38:1, Psalms 65:6-7 66:3 66:5 68:9 76:13 105:27-36 10:22, Sifre Numbers 135:1, z.Beshallach 63a, z.Terumah 156b, z.Vaetchanan 267b

[4] Isaiah 64:5 - 1 Corinthians 1:7 2:9-2:10, 1 John 3:1-3:2 4:10, 1 Thessalonians 1:10, 1 Timothy 3:16, b.Bava Batra 9b, b.Chullin [Rashi] 133a, Colossians 1:26-1:27, Ephesians 3:5-3:10 3:17-3:21, Genesis 1:18, Hebrews 11:16, Isaiah 1:9 6:18, James 5:7, Jastrow 1419b, John 14:3, Lamentations 3:25-3:26, Luke 2:25, Matthew 1:34, Mesillat Yesharim 16:Trait of Taharah, Psalms 31:20 62:2 10:5, Revelation 21:1-21:4 21:22-21:24 22:1-22:5, Romans 8:19 8:23-8:25

Isaiah 64:5-11 - 4QIsab

[5] Isaiah 64:6 - Acts 10:2-10:4 10:35, Exodus 20:21 1:22 29:42-29:43 6:6, Hebrews 4:16, Hosea 6:3 11:8, Isaiah 26:8-26:9 56:1-56:7 15:10, Jeremiah 31:19-31:21, Malachi 3:6, Philippians 3:13-3:15, Psalms 25:10 37:4 90:7-90:9 7:17 16:1, Selichot

Isaiah 64:6-7 - Exodus.R 46:4 46:5

Isaiah 64:6-8 - 1QIsab

[6] 1QIsaa *has gien us into the hands of our iniquity.*

[7] Isaiah 64:7 - 1 Peter 1:24-1:25, Ephesians 2:1-2:2, Hosea 4:19, Isaiah 6:5 40:6-40:8 22:12 24:1 5:6 57:12-57:13, James 1:10-1:11, Jeremiah 4:11-4:12, Job 14:3 15:14-15:16 1:4 16:4 42:5-42:6, Philippians 3:9, Psalms 1:4 51:6 90:5-6, Revelation 3:17-3:18 7:13, Romans 7:18 7:24, Tachanun [Monday and Thursday mornings], Titus 3:3, Zechariah 3:3 5:8-5:11

[8] 1QIsaa *But as for you*

[9] Isaiah 64:8 - Deuteronomy 31:17-18 32:19-25, Ezekiel 22:18-22 22:30 24:11, Hosea 5:15 7:7 7:14, Isaiah 1:15 3:5 2:2 6:8 8:4 9:17 11:2 11:4 11:16, Jeremiah 9:8, Job 8:4, Psalms 14:4, Selichot, Testament of Job 29:3, z.Mishpatim 97b

[10] 1QIsaa *for a long time*

[11] Isaiah 64:9 - b.Moed Katan 26a, b.Rosh Hashanah 23a, Deuteronomy 8:6, Ein Yaakov Rosh Hashanah:23a, Ephesians 2:10, Exodus 4:22, Galatians 3:26 3:29, Guide for the Perplexed 2:29, Isaiah 5:16 19:7 20:21 20:24 21:9 15:16, Jeremiah 18:2-6, Job 10:8-9, Midrash Psalms 9:8, Psalms 4:3 119:73 18:8, Romans 9:20-24, Upon seeing Judean cities or Jerusalem in their destruction

Isaiah 64:9-10 - mt.Hilchot Taaniot 5:16

[12] 1QIsaa adds *like*

[13] LXX *curse*

בֵּית קָדְשֵׁנוּ וְתִפְאַרְתֵּנוּ אֲשֶׁר הִלְלוּךָ אֲבֹתֵינוּ הָיָה לִשְׂרֵפַת אֵשׁ וְכָל־מַחֲמַדֵּינוּ הָיָה לְחָרְבָּה	10[1]	*Our holy and our beautiful house[2]*, where our fathers praised You is burned with fire; And all our *pleasant things[3]* are laid waste.
הַעַל־אֵלֶּה תִתְאַפַּק יְהֹוָה תֶּחֱשֶׁה וּתְעַנֵּנוּ עַד־מְאֹד	11[4]	*Will you refrain Yourself for these things, O LORD? Will you hold Your peace, and afflict us terribly?[5]*

Isaiah – Chapter 65

נִדְרַשְׁתִּי לְלוֹא שָׁאָלוּ נִמְצֵאתִי לְלֹא בִקְשֻׁנִי אָמַרְתִּי הִנֵּנִי הִנֵּנִי אֶל־גּוֹי לֹא־קֹרָא בִשְׁמִי	1[6]	I gave access to those who did not ask for Me, I was at hand for those who did not search for Me; I said: 'Behold Me, behold Me,' to a nation who was not called by My name.
פֵּרַשְׂתִּי יָדַי כָּל־הַיּוֹם אֶל־עַם סוֹרֵר הַהֹלְכִים הַדֶּרֶךְ לֹא־טוֹב אַחַר מַחְשְׁבֹתֵיהֶם	2[7]	I have spread out My hands all the day to a *rebellious[8]* people, who walk in a way that is not good, after their own thoughts;
הָעָם הַמַּכְעִיסִים אוֹתִי עַל־פָּנַי תָּמִיד זֹבְחִים בַּגַּנּוֹת וּמְקַטְּרִים עַל־הַלְּבֵנִים	3[9]	A people who provoke Me to My face continually, who sacrifice in gardens, And *burn incense[10]* on *bricks[11]*;
הַיֹּשְׁבִים בַּקְּבָרִים וּבַנְּצוּרִים יָלִינוּ הָאֹכְלִים בְּשַׂר הַחֲזִיר 'וּפְרַק' 'וּמְרַק' פִּגֻּלִים כְּלֵיהֶם	4[12]	*Who sit among the graves, And lodge in the vaults; who eat swine's flesh, And broth of abominable things is in their vessels[13];*
הָאֹמְרִים קְרַב אֵלֶיךָ אַל־תִּגַּשׁ־בִּי כִּי קְדַשְׁתִּיךָ אֵלֶּה עָשָׁן בְּאַפִּי אֵשׁ יֹקֶדֶת כָּל־הַיּוֹם	5[14]	Who say: 'Stand by yourself, do not *come near[15]* me, for I am *holier than you[16]*'; these are a smoke in My nose, a fire that burns all the day[17].
הִנֵּה כְתוּבָה לְפָנָי לֹא אֶחֱשֶׂה כִּי אִם־שִׁלַּמְתִּי וְשִׁלַּמְתִּי עַל־חֵיקָם	6[18]	Behold, it is written before Me; I will not keep silence, except when I have avenged, Yes, I will retaliate into their bosom,

---

[1] Isaiah 64:10 - 2 Peter 2:17, b.Moed Katan 26a, Habakkuk 3:2, Isaiah 19:25 9:17 12:10 15:19, Jeremiah 3:12 10:24, Lamentations 5:20, Lamentations.R 5:2, Malachi 1:4, Micah 7:18-7:20, Midrash Psalms 65:1 109:1, Psalms 6:2 38:2 74:1-74:2 79:5-79:9 79:13 119:94, Revelation 20:10, Selichot, Upon seeing the Temple in its destruction

[2] 1QIsaa *Our Holy Temple and our splendor*; LXX *The house, our sanctuary, and the glory*

[3] or *dearest places*

[4] Isaiah 64:11 - 2 Chronicles 36:19-36:21, 2 Kings 1:9, Daniel 9:26-9:27 12:7, Isaiah 1:7, Lamentations 1:1-1:4 2:4-2:8 5:18, Luke 21:21 21:24, Micah 3:12, Midrash Psalms 65:1 109:1 121:3, Psalms 79:1-79:7, Revelation 11:1-11:2, Selichot

[5] LXX *And for all these things you, O Lord, have withheld yourself and kept silent, and have brought us very low.*

[6] Isaiah 65:1 - 1 Peter 2:10, 1QIsaa "I became manifest to those who asked not for me" vs. "I am inquired of by those who asked not for me", 4QIsab, Ephesians 2:12-2:13, Exodus.R 25:4, Hosea 2:1, Isaiah 2:2-2:3 11:10 16:9 17:27 19:1 21:22 7:5 15:19, John 1:29, Midrash Psalms 10:2 61:1, Psalms 22:28, Romans 9:24-9:26 9:30 10:20, Zechariah 2:11 8:22-8:23
Isaiah 65:1-8 - Guide for the Perplexed 2:29
Isaiah 65:1-25 - 1QIsaa

[7] Isaiah 65:2 - 1 Thessalonians 2:15-2:16, Acts 7:51-7:52, Deuteronomy 9:7 5:18 7:27, Ezekiel 2:3-2:7, Genesis 6:5, Isaiah 1:2 1:23 7:7 59:7-59:8 15:10 18:18, James 1:14-1:15, Jeremiah 3:17 4:14 5:23 7:24, Luke 13:34 19:41-19:42, Matthew 12:33-12:34 15:19 23:37, Numbers 15:39, Proverbs 1:24 16:29, Psalms 36:5 81:12-81:13, Romans 2:5 10:21

[8] 1QIsaa *disobedient*; MT *obstinate*

[9] Isaiah 65:3 - 2 Kings 17:14-17 22:17, b.Bava Metzia 59a, Deuteronomy 32:16-19 8:21, Ein Yaakov Bava Metzia:59a, Exodus 20:21-25 30:1-10, Ezekiel 8:17-18 20:28, Isaiah 1:29 3:8 18:17, Jeremiah 3:6 32:30-35, Job 1:11 2:5, Lamentations.R Petichata D'Chakimei:2, Leviticus 17:5, Matthew 23:32-36, Midrash Psalms 68:2, Midrash Tanchuma Noach 4, Psalms 78:40 78:58

[10] 1QIsaa *waving their hands*

[11] 1QIsaa *stone altars*; LXX adds *to demons that do not exist*

[12] Isaiah 65:4 - Deuteronomy 14:3 14:8 14:21 18:11, Exodus 23:19 10:26, Ezekiel 4:14, Isaiah 18:3 18:17, Leviticus 11:7, Luke 8:27, Mark 5:2-5:5, Matthew 8:28, Midrash Psalms 68:2, Numbers 19:11 19:16-19:20

[13] LXX *They lie down to sleep in the tombs and in the caves for the sake of dreams, they who eat swine's flesh, and the broth of their sacrifices: all their vessels are defiled*

[14] Isaiah 65:5 - 1 Peter 5:5, Acts 22:21-22:22, b.Sheviit 18b, Deuteronomy 5:19 32:20-32:22, James 4:6, Jude 1:19, Luke 5:30 7:39 15:2 15:28-15:30 18:9-18:12, Matthew 9:11, Midrash Psalms 68:2, Proverbs 6:16-6:17 10:26 16:5, Romans 2:17-2:29

[15] 1QIsaa *touch*

[16] 1QIsaa *too holy for you*

[17] LXX reads *who say, Depart from me, do not draw near to me, for I am pure. This is the smoke of my wrath, a fire burns with it continually*

[18] Isaiah 65:6 - Deuteronomy 8:34, Exodus 17:14, Ezekiel 11:21 22:31, Isaiah 18:14 16:13, Jeremiah 16:18, Joel 4:4, Malachi 3:16, Psalms 50:3 50:21 56:9 79:12, Revelation 20:12, Saadia Opinions 5:1 9:3, Sifre Devarim {Ha'azinu Hashamayim} 325, Sifre Devarim Nitzavim 325

עֲוֺנֹתֵיכֶם וַעֲוֺנֹת אֲבוֹתֵיכֶם יַחְדָּו אָמַר יְהֹוָה אֲשֶׁר קִטְּרוּ עַל־הֶהָרִים וְעַל־הַגְּבָעוֹת חֵרְפוּנִי וּמַדֹּתִי פְעֻלָּתָם רִאשֹׁנָה 'עַל־אֵל־חֵיקָם'

7[1]
Your iniquities, and the iniquities of your fathers together, says the LORD, who have offered on the mountains, And blasphemed Me on the hills; Therefore, will I first measure their wage into their bosom.

כֹּה אָמַר יְהֹוָה כַּאֲשֶׁר יִמָּצֵא הַתִּירוֹשׁ בָּאֶשְׁכּוֹל וְאָמַר אַל־תַּשְׁחִיתֵהוּ כִּי בְרָכָה בּוֹ כֵּן אֶעֱשֶׂה לְמַעַן עֲבָדַי לְבִלְתִּי הַשְׁחִית הַכֹּל

8[2]
Thus says the LORD: *As, when wine is found in the cluster*[3], One says: 'Do not destroy it, for a blessing is in it'; so will I do for My servants' sakes, so I may not destroy all.

וְהוֹצֵאתִי מִיַּעֲקֹב זֶרַע וּמִיהוּדָה יוֹרֵשׁ הָרָי וִירֵשׁוּהָ בְחִירַי וַעֲבָדַי יִשְׁכְּנוּ־שָׁמָּה

9[4]
And I will bring forth a seed out of Jacob, And out of Judah an inheritor of My mountains; And My elect shall inherit it, And My servants shall live there.

וְהָיָה הַשָּׁרוֹן לִנְוֵה־צֹאן וְעֵמֶק עָכוֹר לְרֵבֶץ בָּקָר לְעַמִּי אֲשֶׁר דְּרָשׁוּנִי

10[5]
And *Sharon shall be a*[6] fold of flocks, And the valley of Achor a place *for herds to lie down*[7], for those of My people who searched for Me;

וְאַתֶּם עֹזְבֵי יְהֹוָה הַשְּׁכֵחִים אֶת־הַר קָדְשִׁי הַעֹרְכִים לַגַּד שֻׁלְחָן וְהַמְמַלְאִים לַמְנִי מִמְסָךְ

11[8]
But you who forsake the LORD, who forget My holy mountain, who prepare a table for Fortune, and who offer *mingled wine in full measure*[9] to Destiny,[10]

וּמָנִיתִי אֶתְכֶם לַחֶרֶב וְכֻלְּכֶם לַטֶּבַח תִּכְרָעוּ יַעַן קָרָאתִי וְלֹא עֲנִיתֶם דִּבַּרְתִּי וְלֹא שְׁמַעְתֶּם וַתַּעֲשׂוּ הָרַע בְּעֵינַי וּבַאֲשֶׁר לֹא־חָפַצְתִּי בְּחַרְתֶּם

12[11]
I will *destine*[12] you to the sword, And you shall all bow to the slaughter; because when I called, you did not answer, when I spoke, you did not hear; But you did what was evil in My eyes, And chose what I do not delight.

לָכֵן כֹּה־אָמַר אֲדֹנָי יְהֹוָה הִנֵּה עֲבָדַי יֹאכֵלוּ וְאַתֶּם תִּרְעָבוּ הִנֵּה עֲבָדַי יִשְׁתּוּ וְאַתֶּם תִּצְמָאוּ הִנֵּה עֲבָדַי יִשְׂמָחוּ וְאַתֶּם תֵּבֹשׁוּ

13[13]
Therefore, thus says *the Lord GOD*[14]: Behold, My servants shall eat, but you shall be hungry; Behold, My servants shall drink, But you shall be thirsty; Behold, My servants shall rejoice, But you shall be ashamed;

הִנֵּה עֲבָדַי יָרֹנּוּ מִטּוּב לֵב וְאַתֶּם תִּצְעֲקוּ מִכְּאֵב לֵב וּמִשֵּׁבֶר רוּחַ תְּיֵלִילוּ

14[15]
Behold, My servants shall sing For joy of heart, But you shall cry from the sorrow of heart and shall wail for vexation of spirit.

---

[1] Isaiah 65:7 - 1 Kings 22:43, 1 Thessalonians 2:16, 2 Kings 12:4 14:4 15:35 16:4, Daniel 9:8, Exodus 20:5, Ezekiel 18:6 20:27-20:28, Isaiah 22:14 9:7 17:6, Jeremiah 5:9 5:29 7:19-7:20 13:25, Leviticus 2:39, Matthew 23:31-23:36, Mekilta de R'Ishmael Beshallah 7:14, Numbers 8:14, Psalms 106:6-106:7

[2] Isaiah 65:8 - Amos 9:8-9:9, Genesis.R 29:2, Isaiah 6:13, Jastrow 128a, Jeremiah 6:11, Joel 2:14, Mark 13:20, Matthew 24:22, Perek Shirah [the Vine], Romans 9:27-9:29 11:5-11:6 11:24-11:26, Sifre Devarim Ekev 42, y.Nazir 2:1, z.Vaetchanan 269b

[3] LXX *As a grape-stone shall be found in the cluster*

[4] Isaiah 65:9 - Amos 9:11-15, Ezekiel 36:8-15 12:24 37:21-28 39:25-29, Isaiah 10:20-22 11:11-16 3:6 8:18 21:19 17:15 17:22, Jeremiah 31:37-41 33:17-26, Matthew 24:22, Obadiah 1:17-21, Romans 11:5-7 11:28, Zechariah 10:6-12, Zephaniah 3:20

[5] Isaiah 65:10 - b.Shabbat 77a, Ezekiel 34:13-34:14, Hosea 2:15, Isaiah 9:9 11:2 3:1, Joshua 7:24-7:26, Leviticus.R 22:10, m.Sotah 8:7, Midrash Tanchuma Pinchas 12, Numbers.R 21:18, Pesikta de R'Kahana 6.1, Pesikta Rabbati 16:4

[6] LXX *there shall be in the forest*

[7] 1QIsaa *for the resting of herds*

[8] Isaiah 65:11 - 1 Chronicles 4:9, 1 Corinthians 10:20-10:21, b.Sanhedrin 63b 92a, b.Shabbat [Rashi] 88b, b.Shabbat 67b, Deuteronomy 29:23-29:24 8:17, Ein Yaakov Sanhedrin:92a, Ezekiel 23:41-23:42, Hebrews 12:22, Isaiah 1:28 2:2 11:9 8:7 57:5-57:10 9:13 17:25, Jeremiah 2:28 17:13, Psalms 12:13, Revelation 21:2-21:3

[9] 1QIsaa *drink offerings*

[10] LXX reads *But you are they who have left me, and forgot my holy mountain, and prepared a table for the devil, and filled up the drink-offering to Fortune*

[11] Isaiah 65:12 - 2 Chronicles 36:15-36:16, Deuteronomy 8:25, Ezekiel 14:17-14:21, Isaiah 1:16 3:25 10:4 3:1 17:28 2:2 17:3 66:3-66:4, Jeremiah 7:13 16:17 18:21 10:17, John 1:11, Leviticus 2:25, Matthew 21:34-21:43 22:3 22:7, Proverbs 1:24-1:33, Zechariah 7:7 7:11-7:13, Zephaniah 1:4-1:6

[12] LXX *deliver*

[13] Isaiah 65:13 - b.Shabbat 153a, Daniel 12:2, Ecclesiastes.R 9:7, Ein Yaakov Shabbat:153a, Exodus.R 25:7, Guide for the Perplexed 2:29, Isaiah 1:19 17:17 20:9 13:7 18:5 18:14, Luke 14:23-14:24 16:24-16:25, Malachi 3:18, Midrash Psalms 119:6, Midrash Tanchuma Pinchas 13, Numbers.R 21:21, Psalms 34:11 37:19-20, Saadia Opinions 9:9, z.Vaetchanan 269b
Isaiah 65:13-14 - Midrash Proverbs 16

[14] 1QIsaa *the LORD*

[15] Isaiah 65:14 - b.Arachin [Rashi] 11a, Ein Yaakov Shabbat:153a, Isaiah 24:14 52:8-9, James 5:1 5:13, Jeremiah 7:8, Job 5:13, Luke 13:28, Matthew 8:12 13:42 22:13, Midrash Psalms 119:6, Psalms 66:4, Psalms of Solomon 3:2, Saadia Opinions 9:9

וְהִנַּחְתֶּם שִׁמְכֶם לִשְׁבוּעָה לִבְחִירַי וֶהֱמִיתְךָ אֲדֹנָי יֱהוִה וְלַעֲבָדָיו יִקְרָא שֵׁם אַחֵר	15[1]	And you shall leave your name for a curse to My elect: 'So may the Lord GOD kill you;' *But He shall call His servants by another name*[2];
אֲשֶׁר הַמִּתְבָּרֵךְ בָּאָרֶץ יִתְבָּרֵךְ בֵּאלֹהֵי אָמֵן וְהַנִּשְׁבָּע בָּאָרֶץ יִשָּׁבַע בֵּאלֹהֵי אָמֵן כִּי נִשְׁכְּחוּ הַצָּרוֹת הָרִאשֹׁנוֹת וְכִי נִסְתְּרוּ מֵעֵינָי	16[3]	*So he who blesses himself in the earth shall bless himself*[4] by the God of truth; And he who swears in the earth shall swear by the God of truth; because the former troubles are forgotten, *and because they are hid from My eyes*[5].
כִּי־הִנְנִי בוֹרֵא שָׁמַיִם חֲדָשִׁים וָאָרֶץ חֲדָשָׁה וְלֹא תִזָּכַרְנָה הָרִאשֹׁנוֹת וְלֹא תַעֲלֶינָה עַל־לֵב	17[6]	For, behold, I create new heavens and a new earth; And the former things shall not be remembered, nor come to mind.
כִּי־אִם־שִׂישׂוּ וְגִילוּ עֲדֵי־עַד אֲשֶׁר אֲנִי בוֹרֵא כִּי הִנְנִי בוֹרֵא אֶת־יְרוּשָׁלַם גִּילָה וְעַמָּהּ מָשׂוֹשׂ	18[7]	But be glad and rejoice forever in what I create; For, behold, I create Jerusalem as a rejoicing, and her people as a joy.
וְגַלְתִּי בִירוּשָׁלַם וְשַׂשְׂתִּי בְעַמִּי וְלֹא־יִשָּׁמַע בָּהּ עוֹד קוֹל בְּכִי וְקוֹל זְעָקָה	19[8]	And I will rejoice in Jerusalem, and joy in My people; and the voice of weeping shall no longer be heard in her, nor the voice of crying.
לֹא־יִהְיֶה מִשָּׁם עוֹד עוּל יָמִים וְזָקֵן אֲשֶׁר לֹא־יְמַלֵּא אֶת־יָמָיו כִּי הַנַּעַר בֶּן־מֵאָה שָׁנָה יָמוּת וְהַחוֹטֶא בֶּן־מֵאָה שָׁנָה יְקֻלָּל	20[9]	No longer shall there be *an infant*[10] of days, nor an old man, who has not filled his days; for the youngest shall die a hundred years old, And the sinner being a hundred years old shall be accursed.
וּבָנוּ בָתִּים וְיָשָׁבוּ וְנָטְעוּ כְרָמִים וְאָכְלוּ פִּרְיָם	21[11]	And they shall build houses, and live in them; and they will plant vineyards, and eat the fruit.
לֹא יִבְנוּ וְאַחֵר יֵשֵׁב לֹא יִטְּעוּ וְאַחֵר יֹאכֵל כִּי־כִימֵי הָעֵץ יְמֵי עַמִּי וּמַעֲשֵׂה יְדֵיהֶם יְבַלּוּ בְחִירָי	22[12]	They shall not build, and another inhabit, they shall not plant, and another eat; for as the days of a tree shall be the days of My people, and My elect shall long enjoy the work of their hands.
לֹא יִיגְעוּ לָרִיק וְלֹא יֵלְדוּ לַבֶּהָלָה כִּי זֶרַע בְּרוּכֵי יְהוָה הֵמָּה וְצֶאֱצָאֵיהֶם אִתָּם	23[13]	They shall not labor in vain, nor bring forth for terror; for they are the seed blessed of the LORD, And their offspring with them.

---

[1] Isaiah 65:15 - 1 Peter 2:9-10, 1 Thessalonians 2:16, Acts 11:26, Guide for the Perplexed 2:29, Isaiah 14:2 17:9 17:12 17:22 18:15, Jeremiah 5:22, Jubilees 20:6, Matthew 21:41 22:7, Numbers.R 9:40 11:1, Proverbs 10:7, Romans 9:26, Zechariah 8:13

[2] 1QIsaa *permanently*

[3] Isaiah 65:16 - Daniel 12:1 12:11, Deuteronomy 6:13 10:20 8:4, Exodus.R 23:11, Ezekiel 36:25-36:27, Genesis.R 75:8, Hebrews 6:17-6:18, Isaiah 11:16-12:1 19:18 11:10 45:23-45:25 24:1 6:4 17:19, Jeremiah 4:2 10:10 12:16 7:13, John 1:14 1:17 14:6, Martyrdom of Polycarp 2:3, mt.Hilchot Megillah v'Chanukah 2:18, mt.Hilchot Taaniot 5:19, Philippians 2:11, Psalms 31:6 63:12 72:17 86:15, Revelation 20:4, Romans 14:11, Zephaniah 1:5 3:14-3:20

[4] 1QIsaa *Then whoever takes an oath*

[5] LXX *it shall not come into their mind*

[6] Isaiah 65:17 - 1 Enoch 72:2 2 Baruch 32:7, 2 Peter 3:13, Apocalypse of Elijah 5:38, Genesis.R 1:13, Isaiah 19:18 3:16 18:22, Jeremiah 3:16, Jubilees 1:29, Lamentations.R 1:23, Midrash Psalms 46:2, Pesikta de R'Kahana 22.5a, Pesikta Rabbati 29/30B:4 44:7, Pirkei de R'Eliezer 51, Revelation 21:1-21:5, Saadia Opinions 8:6 9:6 7Variant:5, Sifre Devarim {Ha'azinu Hashamayim} 306, Sifre Devarim Nitzavim 306, Tanna Devei Eliyahu 1
Isaiah 65:17-25 - 1QIsab

[7] Isaiah 65:18 - 1 Thessalonians 5:16, Avot de R'Natan 34, Isaiah 12:4-6 1:9 42:10-12 20:23 1:13 3:11 52:7-10 66:10-14, Psalms 67:4-6 96:10-13 98:1-9, Revelation 11:15-18 19:1-6, Saadia Opinions 8:6 9:6, Zechariah 9:9, Zephaniah 3:14

[8] Isaiah 65:19 - Exodus.R 15:21, Isaiah 1:8 11:10 3:3 3:11 12:20 62:4-62:5, Jeremiah 7:13 8:41, Luke 15:3 15:5, Midrash Psalms 149:3, Midrash Tanchuma Beshallach 28, Midrash Tanchuma Devarim 1, Midrash Tanchuma Vayechi 3, Midrash Tanchuma Vayishlach 10, Pesikta Rabbati 30:1, Revelation 7:17 21:4, Saadia Opinions 8:6, Song of Songs 3:11, Zephaniah 3:17

[9] Isaiah 65:20 - b.Pesachim 68a, b.Sanhedrin 91b, Deuteronomy 4:40, Ecclesiastes 8:12-8:13, Ein Yaakov Pesachim:68a, Ein Yaakov Pesachim:68a, Ein Yaakov Sanhedrin:91b, Genesis.R 26:2, Isaiah 3:11, Job 5:26, Jubilees 23:28, Mekhilta de R'Shimon bar Yochai Kaspa 81:1, Midrash Psalms 1:12, Psalms 34:13, Romans 2:5-2:9, Saadia Opinions 7:9 7Variant:8, Tanya Igeret Hakodesh §26 §27a

[10] 1QIsaa *a young boy*

[11] Isaiah 65:21 - Amos 9:14, Deuteronomy 28:30-33, Isaiah 8:18 13:30 62:8-9, Jeremiah 31:5-6, Judges 6:1-6, Leviticus 2:16

[12] Isaiah 65:22 - Ecclesiastes.R 1:9 2:1, Genesis 5:5 5:27, Genesis.R 12:6, Genesis.R 12:6, Isaiah 17:9 17:15, Jastrow 957b 1623b, Leviticus 2:16, Leviticus.R 25:8, m.Kilayim 1:8, Midrash Psalms 45:7 90:17, Midrash Tanchuma Bereshit 6, Midrash Tanchuma Ekev 7, Midrash Tanchuma Kedoshim 11, Numbers.R 13:12, Pesikta Rabbati 1:7 33:13, Psalms 21:5 91:16 92:13-15, Revelation 20:3-5, Saadia Opinions 7:9 7Variant:8, Sifre Devarim Ekev 47, Song of Songs.R 5:23, z.Bereshit 38a, z.Emor 107b
Isaiah 65:22-23 - 4Q174 6:1-3, 4Q174 6.1-3, Mekilta de R'Ishmael Nezikin 18:107-109

[13] Isaiah 65:23 - 1 Corinthians 15:58, Acts 2:39 3:25-26, Deuteronomy 28:3-12 28:38-42, Galatians 3:29, Genesis 12:2 17:7, Haggai 1:6 2:19, Hosea 9:11-14, Isaiah 1:4 7:2 13:9, Jeremiah 32:38-39, Leviticus 26:3-10 2:20 2:22 2:29, Malachi 3:10, Midrash Psalms 2:2,

וְהָיָה טֶרֶם־יִקְרָאוּ וַאֲנִי אֶעֱנֶה עוֹד הֵם מְדַבְּרִים וַאֲנִי אֶשְׁמָע

24[1] And it shall come to pass that, before they call, I will answer, And while they are yet speaking, I will hear.

זְאֵב וְטָלֶה יִרְעוּ כְאֶחָד וְאַרְיֵה כַּבָּקָר יֹאכַל־תֶּבֶן וְנָחָשׁ עָפָר לַחְמוֹ לֹא־יָרֵעוּ וְלֹא־יַשְׁחִיתוּ בְּכָל־הַר קָדְשִׁי אָמַר יְהוָה

25[2] The wolf and the lamb shall feed together, and the lion shall eat straw like the ox; *and dust the serpent's food*[3]. they shall not hurt or destroy in all My holy mountain, says the LORD.

Isaiah – Chapter 66[4]

כֹּה אָמַר יְהוָה הַשָּׁמַיִם כִּסְאִי וְהָאָרֶץ הֲדֹם רַגְלָי אֵי־זֶה בַיִת אֲשֶׁר תִּבְנוּ־לִי וְאֵי־זֶה מָקוֹם מְנוּחָתִי

1[5] Thus says the LORD: the heaven is My throne, And the earth is My footstool; Where is the house that you may build to Me? And where is the place that may be My resting place?

וְאֶת־כָּל־אֵלֶּה יָדִי עָשָׂתָה וַיִּהְיוּ כָל־אֵלֶּה נְאֻם־יְהוָה וְאֶל־זֶה אַבִּיט אֶל־עָנִי וּנְכֵה־רוּחַ וְחָרֵד עַל־דְּבָרִי

2[6] For all these things My hand has made, And so all these things came to be, says the LORD; But on this man I will look, on he who is poor with a contrite spirit, And trembles at My word.

שׁוֹחֵט הַשּׁוֹר מַכֵּה־אִישׁ זוֹבֵחַ הַשֶּׂה עֹרֵף כֶּלֶב מַעֲלֵה מִנְחָה דַּם־חֲזִיר מַזְכִּיר לְבֹנָה מְבָרֵךְ אָוֶן גַּם־הֵמָּה בָּחֲרוּ בְּדַרְכֵיהֶם וּבְשִׁקּוּצֵיהֶם נַפְשָׁם חָפֵצָה

3[7] *He who kills an ox is as if he killed a man*[8]; He who sacrifices a lamb, as if he broke a dog's neck; He who offers a minchah, as if he offered swine's blood; He who makes a memorial offering of frankincense, as if he blessed an idol; According as they chose their own ways, And their soul delights in their abominations;

Midrash Tanchuma Naso 7, Psalms 115:14-15, Romans 4:16 9:7-8, Tanya Igeret Hakodesh §27a, Zechariah 10:8-9

[1] Isaiah 65:24 - 1 John 5:14-5:15, Acts 4:31 10:30-10:32 12:5-12:16, Aneinu in Amidah [public fast day], Daniel 9:20-9:23 10:12, Deuteronomy.R 2:10 2:12 2:17, Exodus.R 15:29 21:3, Isaiah 7:6 10:9, Lamentations.R 3:?, Luke 15:18-15:20, Mark 11:24, Mekhilta de R'Shimon bar Yochai Shirata 34:2, Midrash Psalms 4:5 22:19, Midrash Tanchuma Emor 16, Midrash Tanchuma Mishpatim 16, mt.Hilchot Tefilah 2:3, mt.Hilchot Teshuvah 7:7 7:7, Numbers.R 11:2, Psalms 32:5 50:15 91:15, Song of Songs.R 2:24, y.Taanit 2:2 3:11

[2] Isaiah 65:25 - 1 Corinthians 6:9-11, 3 Baruch 4:3 [Slav], Acts 9:1 9:19-9:21, b.Yoma 75a, Ein Yaakov Yoma:74b, Ezekiel 19:11, Genesis 3:14-15 95:1, Genesis.R 20:5 95:1, Isaiah 2:4 11:6-11:9 11:9 17:11, Mas.Kallah Rabbati 3:22, Mekhilta de R'Ishmael Pisha 12:49, Micah 4:3 7:17, Midrash Tanchuma Chukkat 19, Midrash Tanchuma Kedoshim 14, Midrash Tanchuma Metzora 2, Midrash Tanchuma Vayigash 8, Numbers.R 19:22, Pesikta Rabbati 33:13, Revelation 12:7-12:9 14:1 20:2-20:3, Romans 16:20, Sibylline Oracles 3.788, Titus 3:3-3:7, Zechariah 8:3 14:20-14:21

[3] LXX *and the serpent earth as bread*

[4] Isaiah 66 - Mas.Soferim 17:9

[5] Isaiah 66:1 - 1 Chronicles 4:2, 1 Enoch 84:2, 1 Kings 8:27, 2 Chronicles 6:18, 2 Samuel 7:5-7:7, Acts 7:48-7:50 17:24, Aristobulus Fragment 4:5, b.Berachot 59a, b.Chagigah 12a 14a, b.Kiddushin 31a, b.Sanhedrin 7a, b.Taanit [Rashi] 26b, Bahir 169, Ein Yaakov Chagigah:12a, Ein Yaakov Kiddushin:16a, Ein Yaakov Kiddushin:31a, Midrash Shmuel 6:11, Ein Yaakov Sanhedrin:7a, Exodus.R 17:1, Fragments of Pseudo-Greek Poets 8, Genesis.R 1:14, Guide for the Perplexed 1:9 1:46, Jeremiah 7:4-7:11, John 4:20-4:21, Leviticus.R 36:1, m.Avot 6:10, Malachi 1:11, Mas.Kallah Rabbati 8:9, Matthew 5:34-5:35 23:21-23:22 24:2, Mekhilta de R'Shimon bar Yochai Shirata 36:1, Mekhilta de R'Ishmael Pisha 16:47, Mesillat Yesharim 22:Trait of Anavah, Midrash Tanchuma Naso 5 11, Midrash Tanchuma Vayera 2, mt.Pirkei Avot 6:10, Numbers.R 12:3, Pesikta Rabbati 4:3, Pirkei Avot 6:10 [Shabbat afternoon], Pirkei de R'Eliezer 19, Psalms 11:5 99:9 12:7, Psalms of Solomon 2:19, Pseudo-Orpheus 33, Sibylline Oracles 1.139, y.Chagigah 2:1, z.Pekudei 241a, z.Vaetchanan 269b, z.Yitro 85b

Isaiah 66:1 [LXX] - Joseph and Aseneth 22:13

Isaiah 66:1-2 - Exodus.R 31:13, Sibylline Oracles 4.8

Isaiah 66:1-24 - 1QIsaa, 1QIsab, Haftarah Shabbat Rosh Chodesh, mt.Hilchot Tefilah 13:4, Pesikta Rabbati 1:1, Rosh Chodesh [Shabbat] Haftarah, Shabbat on Rosh Chodesh [Pesikta Rabbati 1], Siman 122:6 128:4 140:1 79:7

[6] Isaiah 66:2 - 2 Chronicles 34:27-34:28, 2 Kings 22:19-22:20, Acts 9:6 16:29-16:30, Colossians 1:17, Ezekiel 9:4-9:6, Ezra 9:4 10:3, Gates of Repentance 1.023 2.013, Genesis 1:1-1:31, Genesis.R 12:2, Habakkuk 3:16, Hebrews 1:2-1:3, Isaiah 16:26 9:15 13:1 18:5, Jeremiah 31:20-31:21, Luke 18:13-18:14, Matthew 5:3-4, Mekhilta de R'Ishmael Bahodesh 9:104, Mesillat Yesharim 24:Trait of Yiras Cheit, Midrash Psalms 146:1, Midrash Tanchuma Vayera 2, Pesikta Rabbati 4:1 4:3, Philippians 2:12, Proverbs 4:14, Psalms 34:19 51:18 119:120 119:161 18:6, Tanna Devei Eliyahu 1, z.Yitro 86b

[7] Isaiah 66:3 - Amos 5:21-5:22, Deuteronomy 14:8 23:20, Isaiah 1:11-1:15 9:17 65:3-65:4 17:12 18:17, Jastrow 1029a, Judges 5:8 10:14, Leviticus 2:2, Leviticus.R 22:6, Midrash Tanchuma Acharei Mot 12, mt.Hilchot Teshuvah 5:4 5:4, mt.Shemonah Perakim 8:6, Proverbs 15:8 21:27, Ralbag SOS 1, Shemonah Perakim VIII

[8] LXX *But the transgressor who sacrifices a calf to me, is as he who kills a dog*

גַּם־אֲנִי אֶבְחַר בְּתַעֲלֻלֵיהֶם וּמְגוּרֹתָם אָבִיא לָהֶם יַעַן קָרָאתִי וְאֵין עוֹנֶה דִּבַּרְתִּי וְלֹא שָׁמֵעוּ וַיַּעֲשׂוּ הָרַע בְּעֵינַי וּבַאֲשֶׁר לֹא־חָפַצְתִּי בָּחָרוּ

4[1] Even so I will choose their mocking, And will bring their fears on them; Because when I called, no one answered; When I spoke, they did not hear, But they did what was evil in My eyes, And chose what I do not delight.

שִׁמְעוּ דְּבַר־יְהֹוָה הַחֲרֵדִים אֶל־דְּבָרוֹ אָמְרוּ אֲחֵיכֶם שֹׂנְאֵיכֶם מְנַדֵּיכֶם לְמַעַן שְׁמִי יִכְבַּד יְהֹוָה וְנִרְאֶה בְשִׂמְחַתְכֶם וְהֵם יֵבֹשׁוּ

5[2] Hear the word of the LORD, You who tremble at His word: Your brothers who hate you, who cast you out for My name's sake, have said: 'Let the LORD be glorified, so we may gaze on your joy,' but they shall be ashamed.

קוֹל שָׁאוֹן מֵעִיר קוֹל מֵהֵיכָל קוֹל יְהֹוָה מְשַׁלֵּם גְּמוּל לְאֹיְבָיו

6[3] *Listen! An uproar from the city, Listen! It comes from the temple, Listen! the LORD renders recompense to His enemies[4].*

בְּטֶרֶם תָּחִיל יָלָדָה בְּטֶרֶם יָבוֹא חֵבֶל לָהּ וְהִמְלִיטָה זָכָר

7[5] Before she travailed, she gave birth; Before her pain came, She was delivered a son.

מִי־שָׁמַע כָּזֹאת מִי רָאָה כָּאֵלֶּה הֲיוּחַל אֶרֶץ בְּיוֹם אֶחָד אִם־יִוָּלֵד גּוֹי פַּעַם אֶחָת כִּי־חָלָה גַם־יָלְדָה צִיּוֹן אֶת־בָּנֶיהָ

8[6] Who has heard such a thing? Who has seen such things? Is a land born in one day? Is a nation brought forth at once? For as soon as Zion travailed, She brought forth her children.

הַאֲנִי אַשְׁבִּיר וְלֹא אוֹלִיד יֹאמַר יְהֹוָה אִם־אֲנִי הַמּוֹלִיד וְעָצַרְתִּי אָמַר אֱלֹהָיִךְ

9[7] *Shall I bring to the birth, and not cause to bring forth? Says the LORD; Shall I, who causes births, shut the womb[8]? Says your God.*

שִׂמְחוּ אֶת־יְרוּשָׁלַ͏ִם וְגִילוּ בָהּ כָּל־אֹהֲבֶיהָ שִׂישׂוּ אִתָּהּ מָשׂוֹשׂ כָּל־הַמִּתְאַבְּלִים עָלֶיהָ

10[9] Rejoice with Jerusalem, And be glad with her, all you who love her; Rejoice for joy with her, All you who mourn for her;

לְמַעַן תִּינְקוּ וּשְׂבַעְתֶּם מִשֹּׁד תַּנְחֻמֶיהָ לְמַעַן תָּמֹצּוּ וְהִתְעַנַּגְתֶּם מִזִּיז כְּבוֹדָהּ

11[10] So you may suckle, and be satisfied with her breast of consolations; so you may drink deeply with delight from the abundance of her glory.

כִּי־כֹה אָמַר יְהֹוָה הִנְנִי נֹטֶה־אֵלֶיהָ כְּנָהָר שָׁלוֹם וּכְנַחַל שׁוֹטֵף כְּבוֹד גּוֹיִם וִינַקְתֶּם עַל־צַד תִּנָּשֵׂאוּ וְעַל־בִּרְכַּיִם תְּשָׁעֳשָׁעוּ

12[11] For thus says the LORD: Behold, I will extend peace to her like a river, And the wealth of the nations like an overflowing stream, And you shall nurse from it: You shall be borne on the side, And shall be bounced on the knees.

---

[1] Isaiah 66:4 - 1 Kings 22:19-22:23, 2 Kings 21:2 21:6, 2 Thessalonians 2:10-2:12, Isaiah 2:2 17:3 17:12, Jeremiah 7:13, Matthew 22:2-22:7 24:24, mt.Shemonah Perakim 8:6, Proverbs 1:24 1:31-1:32 10:24, Psalms 81:13, Shemonah Perachim VIII
[2] Isaiah 66:5 - 1 John 3:13, 1 Peter 4:12-4:14, 1 Thessalonians 2:15-2:16, 1QS 6:24-7:25, 2 Thessalonians 1:6-1:10, Acts 2:33-2:47 26:9-26:10, b.Bava Metzia 33b, Ein Yaakov Bava Metzia:33b, Hebrews 9:28, Isaiah 5:19 12:15 18:2, Jeremiah 12:16 36:23-36:25, John 9:34 15:18-15:20 16:2, Luke 6:22-6:23 13:17, Matthew 5:10-5:12 10:22, Proverbs 13:13, Psalms 38:21, Shepherd Vision II 1:2, Song of Songs 1:6, Titus 2:13, z.Ki Tissa 188b
[3] Isaiah 66:6 - Amos 1:2, Exodus.R 9:13, Isaiah 10:8 11:18 65:5-65:7, Jastrow 1353a 1379b, Joel 4:7-4:16, Lamentations.R 2:11, Midrash Psalms 18:11 74:2 84:1, Midrash Tanchuma Bo 4, Midrash Tanchuma Vaera 13, Numbers.R 10:2, Pesikta de R'Kahana 7.11, Pesikta Rabbati 17:8
[4] LXX *A voice of a cry from the city, a voice from the temple, a voice of the Lord rendering recompence to his adversaries*
[5] Isaiah 66:7 - b.Bava Kamma [Tosefot] 80a, Galatians 4:26, Genesis.R 85:1, Isaiah 6:1, Jastrow 1608b, Leviticus.R 14:9, Revelation 12:1-12:5, Saadia Opinions 8:1, z.Vayakhel 220a
[6] Isaiah 66:8 - 1 Corinthians 2:9, Acts 2:41 4:4 21:20, Isaiah 49:20-22 16:5, Psalms of Solomon 2:8, Romans 15:18-21, Saadia Opinions 7Variant:3
[7] Isaiah 66:9 - Genesis 18:14, Isaiah 13:3, Pesikta Rabbati 29/30A:10
[8] LXX *But I have raised this expectation, yet you have not remembered me, says the LORD: behold, have not I made the bearing and barren woman*
[9] Isaiah 66:10 - b.Bava Batra 60b, b.Gittin 57a, b.Taanit 30b, Deuteronomy 8:43, Ein Yaakov Bava Batra:60b, Ezekiel 9:4, Isaiah 20:23 61:2-3 17:18, John 16:20-22, Pesikta de R'Kahana S5.3 S6.2, Pesikta Rabbati 28:3, Psalms 26:8 84:2-5 2:6 17:6, Revelation 11:3-15, Romans 15:9-12, Song of Songs.R 1:29, t.Bava Batra 2:17, t.Sotah 15:15, z.Bamidbar 118a, z.Vayigash 210a 210b Isaiah 66:10-11 - t.Taniyot 3:14
[10] Isaiah 66:11 - 1 Peter 2:2, Isaiah 12:5 12:16, Joel 4:18, Psalms 36:9
[11] Isaiah 66:12 - 2 Baruch 72:3, b.Berachot 56b, b.Niddah [Rashi] 48b, Deuteronomy.R 5:15, Ecclesiastes.R 3:10, Ein Yaakov Berachot:56b, Genesis.R 66:2, Isaiah 9:8 21:14 24:18 49:19-23 6:3 60:4-14 12:16 13:6 18:11 66:19-20, Leviticus.R 9:9, Midrash Tanchuma Tzav 7, Pesikta Rabbati 33:13 50:, Psalms 72:3-7, Song of Songs.R 7:1, z.Mikketz 193b, z.Vaetchanan 269b

כְּאִישׁ אֲשֶׁר אִמּוֹ תְּנַחֲמֶנּוּ כֵּן אָנֹכִי אֲנַחֶמְכֶם וּבִירוּשָׁלַ͏ִם תְּנֻחָמוּ	13[1]	As one whom his mother comforts, So will I comfort you; And you shall be comforted in Jerusalem.
וּרְאִיתֶם וְשָׂשׂ לִבְּכֶם וְעַצְמוֹתֵיכֶם כַּדֶּשֶׁא תִפְרַחְנָה וְנוֹדְעָה יַד־יְהוָה אֶת־עֲבָדָיו וְזָעַם אֶת־אֹיְבָיו	14[2]	And when you see this, your heart shall rejoice, And your bones shall flourish like young grass; And the hand of the LORD shall be known toward His servants, And *He will have indignation against His enemies*[3].
כִּי־הִנֵּה יְהוָה בָּאֵשׁ יָבוֹא וְכַסּוּפָה מַרְכְּבֹתָיו לְהָשִׁיב בְּחֵמָה אַפּוֹ וְגַעֲרָתוֹ בְּלַהֲבֵי־אֵשׁ	15[4]	For, behold, the LORD will come in fire, and His chariots shall be like the whirlwind; to render His anger with fury, and His rebuke with flames of fire.
כִּי בָאֵשׁ יְהוָה נִשְׁפָּט וּבְחַרְבּוֹ אֶת־כָּל־בָּשָׂר וְרַבּוּ חַלְלֵי יְהוָה	16[5]	For by fire the LORD will *contend*[6], and by His sword with all flesh; and the slain of the LORD shall be many.
הַמִּתְקַדְּשִׁים וְהַמִּטַּהֲרִים אֶל־הַגַּנּוֹת אַחַר 'אֶחָד' "אַחַת" בַּתָּוֶךְ אֹכְלֵי בְּשַׂר הַחֲזִיר וְהַשֶּׁקֶץ וְהָעַכְבָּר יַחְדָּו יָסֻפוּ נְאֻם־יְהוָה	17[7]	Those who sanctify themselves and purify themselves to go to the gardens, behind one in the midst, Eating swine's flesh, and the *detestable thing*[8], and the mouse, *shall be consumed*[9] together, says the LORD.
וְאָנֹכִי מַעֲשֵׂיהֶם וּמַחְשְׁבֹתֵיהֶם בָּאָה לְקַבֵּץ אֶת־כָּל־הַגּוֹיִם וְהַלְּשֹׁנוֹת וּבָאוּ וְרָאוּ אֶת־כְּבוֹדִי	18[10]	For I [know] their works and their thoughts; [the time] comes, that I will gather all nations and tongues; and they shall come, and shall see My glory.
וְשַׂמְתִּי בָהֶם אוֹת וְשִׁלַּחְתִּי מֵהֶם פְּלֵיטִים אֶל־הַגּוֹיִם תַּרְשִׁישׁ פּוּל וְלוּד מֹשְׁכֵי קֶשֶׁת תֻּבַל וְיָוָן הָאִיִּים הָרְחֹקִים אֲשֶׁר לֹא־שָׁמְעוּ אֶת־שִׁמְעִי וְלֹא־רָאוּ אֶת־כְּבוֹדִי וְהִגִּידוּ אֶת־כְּבוֹדִי בַּגּוֹיִם	19[11]	And I will work a sign among them, and I will send an escape for them from the nations, to Tarshish, Put[12] and Lud[13], who draw the bow, to Tubal[14] and Javan[15], to *the isles far off*[16], who have not heard My fame nor saw My glory; and they will declare My glory among the nations.

---

[1] Isaiah 66:13 - 1 Thessalonians 2:7, 2 Corinthians 1:4, Birchat Hamazon [for mourners], Isaiah 16:1 3:3 65:18-65:19 18:10, Pesikta de R'Kahana 19.3, Psalms 17:6

[2] Isaiah 66:14 - Ezekiel 37:1-37:14, Ezra 7:9 8:18 8:22 8:31, Hebrews 10:27, Hosea 14:6-10, Isaiah 10:5 2:19 10:11 65:12-16 18:5, John 16:22, Joseph and Aseneth 16:16, Lamentations.R 1:23, Malachi 3:18, Midrash Psalms 1:22, Proverbs 3:8 17:22, Saadia Opinions 7Variant:5, Zechariah 10:7

[3] LXX *he shall threaten the disobedient*

[4] Isaiah 66:15 - 2 Peter 3:10-3:12, 2 Thessalonians 1:6-9, Amos 7:4, b.Sanhedrin 39a, b.Sotah 11a, Daniel 11:40, Ein Yaakov Sanhedrin:39a, Ein Yaakov Sotah:11a, HaMadrikh 35:11, Isaiah 30:27-28 6:33, Jeremiah 4:3, Life of Adam and Eve [Vita] 25:2, Matthew 22:7, Midrash Tanchuma Bereshit 5, Psalms 11:7 21:10 50:3 68:18 97:3, Sefer Yetzirah 1:6

[5] Isaiah 66:16 - 3 Enoch 32:1, b.Sotah 11a, b.Zevachim 116a, Ein Yaakov Zevachim:116a, Exodus.R 1:9, Ezekiel 38:21-22 39:2-10, Isaiah 3:1 6:30 34:5-34:10, Midrash Psalms 1:20 11:5 29:2, Midrash Tanchuma Shoftim 9, Revelation 19:11-21, Sibylline Oracles 3.287 3.761 4.173, Song of Songs.R 2:3 2:42

[6] 1QIsaa *proceed to judgment*

[7] Isaiah 66:17 - b.Sanhedrin 20b, Deuteronomy 14:3-14:8, Guide for the Perplexed 3:33, Isaiah 1:28-1:29 65:3-65:4, Leviticus 11:2-11:8, Midrash Psalms 146:4, Numbers.R 12:44

[8] or *vermin*; LXX *abominations*

[9] Missing in 1QIsaa

[10] Isaiah 66:18 - 1 Corinthians 3:20, 2 Corinthians 4:4-4:6, Amos 5:12, Deuteronomy 7:21, Ezekiel 14:10 15:21, Hebrews 4:12, Isaiah 2:2 13:28 18:10, Job 18:2, Joel 4:2, John 5:42 17:24, Luke 5:22, Matthew 9:4 12:25, Psalms 67:3 72:11 72:17 82:8 86:9, Revelation 2:2 2:9 2:13 11:15, Romans 15:8-15:12 16:26, z.Bamidbar 121a

[11] Isaiah 66:19 - 1 Chronicles 1:7 1:11 16:24, Ephesians 3:8, Ezekiel 3:10 3:13 6:5 38:2-3 15:1, Genesis 10:2 10:4 10:13, Isaiah 2:16 11:10-11 18:3 18:7 24:15-16 5:24 18:4 19:6 1:1 1:12 1:22 3:5 4:15 7:5 12:9 14:10 17:1, Luke 2:34, Malachi 1:11, Mark 16:15, Matthew 7:11-12 4:19, Mekhilta de R'Shimon bar Yochai Beshallach 21:3, Mekilta de R'Ishmael Beshallah 2:77, Midrash Tanchuma Beshallach 7, Psalms 72:10, Romans 11:1-6 15:21, Saadia Opinions 8:6, Zephaniah 2:11

Isaiah 66:19-21 - 2 Baruch 72:3

[12] i.e., Lybia; LXX *Phud*

[13] i.e., Lydia

[14] LXX *Mosoch*

[15] i.e., Greece; LXX *Thobel*

[16] LXX *Greece, and to the isles afar off*

וְהֵבִיאוּ אֶת־כָּל־אֲחֵיכֶם מִכָּל־הַגּוֹיִם ׀ מִנְחָה
לַיהוָה בַּסּוּסִים וּבָרֶכֶב וּבַצַּבִּים וּבַפְּרָדִים
וּבַכִּרְכָּרוֹת עַל הַר קָדְשִׁי יְרוּשָׁלַ͏ִם אָמַר יְהוָה
כַּאֲשֶׁר יָבִיאוּ בְנֵי יִשְׂרָאֵל אֶת־הַמִּנְחָה בִּכְלִי
טָהוֹר בֵּית יְהוָה

20[1]

And they shall bring all your brothers from all[2] the nations for an offering to the LORD, on horses, and in chariots, and in wagons, and on mules[3], *and on swift beasts*[4], to My holy *mountain*[5] Jerusalem, says the LORD, as the children of Israel bring their offering *in a clean vessel*[6] into the house of the LORD.

וְגַם־מֵהֶם אֶקַּח לַכֹּהֲנִים לַלְוִיִּם אָמַר יְהוָה

21[7]

I will take[8] them for the priests and for the Levites, says the LORD.

כִּי כַאֲשֶׁר הַשָּׁמַיִם הַחֳדָשִׁים וְהָאָרֶץ הַחֲדָשָׁה
אֲשֶׁר אֲנִי עֹשֶׂה עֹמְדִים לְפָנַי נְאֻם־יְהוָה כֵּן יַעֲמֹד
זַרְעֲכֶם וְשִׁמְכֶם

22[9]

For as the new heavens and the new earth, which I will make, shall remain before Me, says the LORD, so shall your seed and your name remain.

וְהָיָה מִדֵּי־חֹדֶשׁ בְּחָדְשׁוֹ וּמִדֵּי שַׁבָּת בְּשַׁבַּתּוֹ יָבוֹא
כָל־בָּשָׂר לְהִשְׁתַּחֲוֺת לְפָנַי אָמַר יְהוָה

23[10]

And it shall come to pass, that from one new moon to another, and from one sabbath to sabbath, all flesh shall come to worship before Me[11], says the LORD.

וְיָצְאוּ וְרָאוּ בְּפִגְרֵי הָאֲנָשִׁים הַפֹּשְׁעִים בִּי כִּי
תוֹלַעְתָּם לֹא תָמוּת וְאִשָּׁם לֹא תִכְבֶּה וְהָיוּ דֵרָאוֹן
לְכָל־בָּשָׂר

24[12]

And they shall go forth, and look at the corpses of the men who rebelled against Me; for their worm shall not die, their fire shall not be sated; And they shall be abhorrent to all flesh.

וְהָיָה מִדֵּי־חֹדֶשׁ בְּחָדְשׁוֹ וּמִדֵּי שַׁבָּת בְּשַׁבַּתּוֹ יָבוֹא
כָל־בָּשָׂר לְהִשְׁתַּחֲוֺת לְפָנַי אָמַר יְהוָה

25

And it shall come to pass, that from one new moon to another, and from one sabbath to sabbath, all flesh shall come to worship before Me, says the LORD.

---

[1] Isaiah 66:20 - 1 Peter 2:5, 3 Enoch 48A:10, Isaiah 11:9 19:6 49:12-26 4:11 6:3 8:7 60:3-14 17:11 17:25, Jastrow 1703b, Midrash Psalms 87:6 149:6, Numbers.R 12:17, Philippians 2:17, Romans 12:1-12:2 15:16, Saadia Opinions 8:6, Sifre.z Numbers Naso 7:3, Song of Songs.R 4:19, y.Berachot 5:1, z.Tazria 52a, z.Vayera 119a
Isaiah 66:20-24 - 4QIsac
[2] 1QIsaa adds all; LXX adds *with awnings*
[3] 1QIsaa adds *yes and on mules*
[4] Missing in LXX
[5] LXX *city*
[6] LXX *with psalms*
[7] Isaiah 66:21 - 1 Peter 2:5 2:9, Exodus 19:6, Isaiah 13:6, Jeremiah 13:18-13:22, Mekilta de R'Ishmael Pisha 12:60, Midrash Psalms 87:6, Revelation 1:6 5:10 20:6
[8] 1QIsaa adds *for myself*
[9] Isaiah 66:22 - 1 Enoch 72:2, 1 Peter 1:4-5, 2 Peter 3:13, Deuteronomy.R 10:4, Guide for the Perplexed 2:29, Hebrews 12:26-28, Isaiah 17:17, John 10:27-29, Jubilees 1:29, Leviticus.R 29:12, Mas.Kallah Rabbati 8:9, Mas.Soferim 19:9, Matthew 4:20, Mekilta de R'Ishmael Nezikin 18:112, Midrash Tanchuma Nitzavim 4, Pesikta de R'Kahana 23.12, Pesikta Rabbati 27:4, Revelation 21:1, Saadia Opinions 9:6 9:6, Sifre Devarim Ekev 47, Two Letters Part II, z.Bereshit 25b 5a
[10] Isaiah 66:23 - 2 Kings 4:23, b.Megillah 31a, b.Sotah 5a, Colossians 2:16-2:17, Ein Yaakov Eduyot:4b, Ein Yaakov Sotah:4b, Exodus.R 15:29, Ezekiel 22:1 22:6, Isaiah 1:13-1:14 19:21, John 4:23, Lamentations.R 1:40, m.Eduyot 2:10, Malachi 1:11, Midrash Psalms 66:1 96:2, Pesikta Rabbati 1:1-7, Psalms 65:3 81:4-81:5 86:9, Revelation 15:4, Saadia Opinions 6:5 9:10, Seder Olam 3:Plagues, Selichot, z.Acharei Mot 79b, z.Terumah 156b, z.Vayeshev 181a, Zechariah 8:20-8:23 14:14 14:16
[11] LXX adds *in Jerusalem*
[12] Isaiah 66:24 - 1 Thessalonians 2:15-16, 4QIsab, b.Eruvin 19a, b.Pesachim 54a, b.Rosh Hashanah 14a, b.Sanhedrin 1b, b.Shabbat [Rashi] 33b, b.Taanit [Rashi] 7a, Daniel 12:2, Ecclesiastes.R 7:23, Ein Yaakov Pesachim:54a, Ein Yaakov Rosh Hashanah 17a, Ein Yaakov Sanhedrin:100b, Ezekiel 39:9-16, Gates of Repentance 3.162, Genesis.R 97:1, Greek Apocalypse of Ezra 1:24 4:19, Isaiah 1:31 14:11 10:10 17:15 18:16, Lamentations.R 1:40, Leviticus.R 32:1, Mark 9:43-49, Matthew 3:12, Midrash Psalms 1:22 4:12 12:5 149:6, Midrash Tanchuma Massei 4, Midrash Tanchuma Tzav 14, Midrash Tanchuma Vayikra 7, Numbers.R 23:5, Pesikta de R'Kahana 13.14 28.3, Pesikta Rabbati 52:3, Psalms 58:11-12, Revelation 14:10-11 19:17-21 21:8, Saadia Opinions 9:5 9:9-10, Seder Olam 3:Plagues, t.Berachot 5:31, t.Sanhedrin 13:5, Testament of Job 20:8, Vision of Ezra 35, y.Berachot 5:1, z.Bereshit 13a 59a, z.Mishpatim 106a, z.Terumah 151a, z.Vayakhel 212 214b, z.Yitro 85b, Zechariah 14:12 14:18-19

Yirmeyahu b'Hilkiyahu

Jeremiah[1] – Chapter 01

דִּבְרֵי יִרְמְיָהוּ בֶּן־חִלְקִיָּהוּ מִן־הַכֹּהֲנִים אֲשֶׁר בַּעֲנָתוֹת בְּאֶרֶץ בִּנְיָמִן

1[2]   *The words of*[3] Jeremiah the son of Hilkiah, of the priests who were in Anathoth in the land of Benjamin,

אֲשֶׁר הָיָה דְבַר־יְהוָה אֵלָיו בִּימֵי יֹאשִׁיָּהוּ בֶן־אָמוֹן מֶלֶךְ יְהוּדָה בִּשְׁלֹשׁ־עֶשְׂרֵה שָׁנָה לְמָלְכוֹ

2[4]   to whom the word of the LORD came in the days of Josiah the son of Amon, king of Judah, in the thirteenth year of his reign.

וַיְהִי בִּימֵי יְהוֹיָקִים בֶּן־יֹאשִׁיָּהוּ מֶלֶךְ יְהוּדָה עַד־תֹּם עַשְׁתֵּי עֶשְׂרֵה שָׁנָה לְצִדְקִיָּהוּ בֶן־יֹאשִׁיָּהוּ מֶלֶךְ יְהוּדָה עַד־גְּלוֹת יְרוּשָׁלַ͏ִם בַּחֹדֶשׁ הַחֲמִישִׁי

3[5]   It also came in the days of Jehoiakim the son of Josiah, king of Judah, to *the end of*[6] the eleventh year of Zedekiah the son of Josiah, king of Judah, when Jerusalem was carried captive in the fifth month.

וַיְהִי דְבַר־יְהוָה אֵלַי לֵאמֹר

4[7]   And the word of the LORD came to *me*[8], saying:

בְּטֶרֶם אֶצּוֹרְךָ בַבֶּטֶן יְדַעְתִּיךָ וּבְטֶרֶם תֵּצֵא מֵרֶחֶם הִקְדַּשְׁתִּיךָ נָבִיא לַגּוֹיִם נְתַתִּיךָ

5[9]   Before I formed you in the belly, I knew you. And before you came forth from the womb I sanctified you; I have appointed you a prophet to the nations.

וָאֹמַר אֲהָהּ אֲדֹנָי יְהוִֹה הִנֵּה לֹא־יָדַעְתִּי דַּבֵּר כִּי־נַעַר אָנֹכִי

6[10]   Then said I: 'Ah, Lord GOD! Behold, I cannot speak; for I am a child.'

וַיֹּאמֶר יְהוָה אֵלַי אַל־תֹּאמַר נַעַר אָנֹכִי כִּי עַל־כָּל־אֲשֶׁר אֶשְׁלָחֲךָ תֵּלֵךְ וְאֵת כָּל־אֲשֶׁר אֲצַוְּךָ תְּדַבֵּר

7[11]   But the LORD said to me: Say not: I am a child; For to whomever I shall send you, you shall go, and whatever I shall command you, you shall speak.

---

[1] Jeremiah - Ein Yaakov Berachot:57b

[2] Jeremiah 1:1 - 1 Chronicles 6:45, 2 Chronicles 12:21, Amos 1:1 7:10, b.Sanhedrin 95a, Ecclesiastes.R 1:2, Ein Yaakov Sanhedrin 95a, Ezekiel 1:3, Isaiah 1:1 2:1, Jeremiah 11:21 32:7-9, Jeremiah has 31 Sedarim, Joshua 21:17-18, Lamentations.R Petichata D'Chakimei:1, Leviticus.R 17:7, Lives of the Prophets 2:1, Pesikta de R'Kahana 4.10 13.1-3 13.5-9 13.12-14, Pesikta Rabbati 14:2, Ruth.R 1:5, Seder Olam 20:Zephaniah, z.Noach 63b
Jeremiah 1:1-3 - 2 Baruch 1:1, Pesikta de R'Kahana 13.15
Jeremiah 1:1-19 - First of the three Shabbats preceding Tisha bAv [Pesikta Rabbati 26]
Jeremiah 1:1-2:3 - Haftarah Mattot, Haftarah Shemos [Sephard], mt.Hilchot Tefilah 13:19, Siman 122:6

[3] LXX *The word of God that came to*

[4] Jeremiah 1:2 - 1 Kings 13:20, 2 Chronicles 3 4:1-34:33, 2 Kings 21:24-22:20, b.Megillah [Rashi] 14b, Hosea 1:1, Jeremiah 1:4 1:11 1:3 12:2, Jonah 1:1, Josephus Antiquities 10.5.1, Micah 1:1, Pesikta Rabbati 26:1/2, Tanna Devei Eliyahu 6

[5] Jeremiah 1:3 - 1 Chronicles 3:15, 2 Chronicles 36:5-36:8 36:11-36:21, 2 Kings 23:34 24:1-24:9 24:17-25:30, b.Megillah 10b, Ein Yaakov Megillah:9b, Esther.R Petichata:11, Genesis.R 42:3, Jastrow 247b, Jeremiah 21:1-21:14 25:1-25:3 26:1-26:24 28:1-28:17 34:1-35:19 37:1-37:21 15:2 52:1-52:34, Leviticus.R 11:7, Ruth.R Petichata:7, Zechariah 7:5 8:19

[6] Missing in LXX

[7] Jeremiah 1:4 - Ezekiel 1:3 3:16, Jeremiah 1:2, z.Shemini 41a

[8] LXX *him*

[9] Jeremiah 1:5 - 2 Timothy 2:19-2:21, Avot de R'Natan 2, Avot de R'Natan 34, b.Menachot [Tosefot] 53b, b.Yoma 82b, Ecclesiastes.R 6:9, Ephesians 1:22 4:11-4:12, Exodus 9:12 9:17, Exodus.R 29:9, Galatians 1:15-1:16, Genesis.R 63:6, Guide for the Perplexed 2:32, Isaiah 20:2 1:1 1:5, Jeremiah 1:10 25:15-25:26 2:34, Luke 1:15 1:41 1:76, Mekilta de R'Ishmael Pisha 16:89, Midrash Psalms 9:7 58:2 93:1 139:4, Midrash Tanchuma Balak 1, mt.Hilchot Deot 5:5, mt.Hilchot Teshuvah 5:2, Numbers.R 10:5, Pesikta Rabbati 26:1/2 27/28:1, Psalms 71:5-71:6 19:16, Romans 1:1 8:29, Seder Olam 30:Yehoiariv, Sefer Yetzirah [Long] 6:8 Sefer Yetzirah [Saadia] 8:5, Sifre Devarim Shoftim 175, z.Beshallach 53b
Jeremiah 1:5-6 - Midrash Tanchuma Toledot 12

[10] Jeremiah 1:6 - 1 Kings 3:7-3:9, Exodus 4:1 4:10-4:16 6:12 6:30, Guide for the Perplexed 2:32, Isaiah 6:5, Jeremiah 4:10 14:13 8:17, Kuzari 4.003, Liber Antiquitatum Biblicarum 56:6, Midrash Tanchuma Shemot 18, Pesikta Rabbati 26:1/2
Jeremiah 1:6-9 - Ahiqar 114

[11] Jeremiah 1:7 - 1 Kings 22:14, 2 Chronicles 18:13, Acts 20:27, Exodus 7:1-7:2, Exodus.R 4:3, Ezekiel 2:3-2:5 3:17-3:21 3:27, Jeremiah 1:17-1:18, Mark 16:15-16:16, Matthew 4:20, Midrash Tanchuma Shemot 18, Midrash Tanchuma Toledot 12, Numbers 22:20 22:38, Pesikta Rabbati 26:1/2 27/28:1

אַל־תִּירָא מִפְּנֵיהֶם כִּי־אִתְּךָ אֲנִי לְהַצִּלֶךָ נְאֻם־יְהוָה

8[1] Do not be afraid of them; For I am with you to deliver you, says the LORD.

וַיִּשְׁלַח יְהוָה אֶת־יָדוֹ וַיַּגַּע עַל־פִּי וַיֹּאמֶר יְהוָה אֵלַי הִנֵּה נָתַתִּי דְבָרַי בְּפִיךָ׃

9[2] Then the LORD put forth His hand, and touched my mouth; and the LORD said to me: Behold, I have put My words in your mouth;

רְאֵה הִפְקַדְתִּיךָ הַיּוֹם הַזֶּה עַל־הַגּוֹיִם וְעַל־הַמַּמְלָכוֹת לִנְתוֹשׁ וְלִנְתוֹץ וּלְהַאֲבִיד וְלַהֲרוֹס לִבְנוֹת וְלִנְטוֹעַ

10[3] See, I have this day set you over the nations and over the kingdoms, to root out and to pull down, and to destroy and to overthrow; to build, and to plant.

וַיְהִי דְבַר־יְהוָה אֵלַי לֵאמֹר מָה־אַתָּה רֹאֶה יִרְמְיָהוּ וָאֹמַר מַקֵּל שָׁקֵד אֲנִי רֹאֶה

11[4] Moreover, the word of the LORD came to me, saying: 'Jeremiah, what do you see?' And I said: 'I see a rod of an almond tree.'

וַיֹּאמֶר יְהוָה אֵלַי הֵיטַבְתָּ לִרְאוֹת כִּי־שֹׁקֵד אֲנִי עַל־דְּבָרִי לַעֲשֹׂתוֹ

12[5] Then said the LORD to me: 'You have seen well; for I watch over My word to perform it.'

וַיְהִי דְבַר־יְהוָה אֵלַי שֵׁנִית לֵאמֹר מָה אַתָּה רֹאֶה וָאֹמַר סִיר נָפוּחַ אֲנִי רֹאֶה וּפָנָיו מִפְּנֵי צָפוֹנָה

13[6] And the word of the LORD came to me the second time, saying: 'What do you see?' And I said: 'I see a seething pot; and its face is *from*[7] the north.'

וַיֹּאמֶר יְהוָה אֵלַי מִצָּפוֹן תִּפָּתַח הָרָעָה עַל כָּל־יֹשְׁבֵי הָאָרֶץ

14[8] Then the LORD said to me: 'From the north the evil shall break forth on all the inhabitants of the land.

כִּי הִנְנִי קֹרֵא לְכָל־מִשְׁפְּחוֹת מַמְלְכוֹת צָפוֹנָה נְאֻם־יְהוָה וּבָאוּ וְנָתְנוּ אִישׁ כִּסְאוֹ פֶּתַח שַׁעֲרֵי יְרוּשָׁלַ͏ִם וְעַל כָּל־חוֹמֹתֶיהָ סָבִיב וְעַל כָּל־עָרֵי יְהוּדָה

15[9] For, behold, I will call all the families of the kingdoms of the north, says the LORD; and they shall come, and they shall set their throne at the entrance of the gates of Jerusalem, and against all its walls, and against all the cities of Judah.

וְדִבַּרְתִּי מִשְׁפָּטַי אוֹתָם עַל כָּל־רָעָתָם אֲשֶׁר עֲזָבוּנִי וַיְקַטְּרוּ לֵאלֹהִים אֲחֵרִים וַיִּשְׁתַּחֲווּ לְמַעֲשֵׂי יְדֵיהֶם

16[10] And I will utter My judgments against them touching all their wickedness; in that they have forsaken me, and have offered to other gods, and worshipped the work of their own hands.

וְאַתָּה תֶּאְזֹר מָתְנֶיךָ וְקַמְתָּ וְדִבַּרְתָּ אֲלֵיהֶם אֵת כָּל־אֲשֶׁר אָנֹכִי אֲצַוֶּךָּ אַל־תֵּחַת מִפְּנֵיהֶם פֶּן־אֲחִתְּךָ לִפְנֵיהֶם

17[11] Therefore, gird up your loins, and rise, and speak to those all who I command; do not be dismayed at them, or I will dismay you before them.

---

[1] Jeremiah 1:8 - 2 Corinthians 1:8-1:10, 2 Timothy 4:17-4:18, Acts 4:13 4:29 7:9-7:10 18:10 2:17, Deuteronomy 7:6 7:8, Ephesians 6:20, Exodus 3:12, Ezekiel 2:6-2:7 3:8-3:9, Guide for the Perplexed 2:38, Hebrews 13:5-13:6, Isaiah 19:2 3:7 3:12, Jeremiah 1:17 15:20-15:21 20:11, Joshua 1:5 1:9, Luke 12:4-12:5, Matthew 10:26 4:20, Sifre Devarim {Haazinu Hashamayim} 325

[2] Jeremiah 1:9 - 4 Ezra 15:2 4 Ezra 15:2, Exodus 4:11-4:12 4:15-4:16, Ezekiel 3:10, Isaiah 6:6-6:7 1:2 2:4 3:16, Jeremiah 5:14, Luke 12:12 21:15, Matthew 10:19

[3] Jeremiah 1:10 - 1 Kings 17:1 19:17, 2 Corinthians 10:4-10:5, Amos 3:7 9:11, Ezekiel 8:18 12:36 19:3, Isaiah 44:26-44:28, Jeremiah 18:7-18:10 24:6 25:15-25:27 27:2-27:7 31:5-31:6 7:29 46:1-46:28, Revelation 11:3-11:6 19:19-19:21, Zechariah 1:6

[4] Jeremiah 1:11 - Amos 7:8 8:2, b.Bechorot [Tosefot] 8a, Ecclesiastes.R 12:7, Ezekiel 7:10, Guide for the Perplexed 2:29 2:43, Jastrow 696a 1621a, Jeremiah 24:3, Lamentations.R Petichata D'Chakimei:23, mt.Hilchot Yesodei haTorah 7:3, Numbers 17:23, Numbers.R 2:15, y.Taanit 4:5, Zechariah 4:2 5:2
Jeremiah 1:11-12 - z.Shemot 15b

[5] Jeremiah 1:12 - Amos 8:2, b.Gittin [Rashi] 88a, b.Sanhedrin [Rashi] 14a 38a, Deuteronomy 5:28 18:17 8:35, Ezekiel 12:22-12:23 12:25 12:28, Guide for the Perplexed 2:43, Jeremiah 39:1-39:18 52:1-52:34, Luke 10:28 20:39, mt.Hilchot Yesodei haTorah 7:3

[6] Jeremiah 1:13 - 2 Corinthians 13:1-13:2, Ezekiel 11:3 11:7 24:3-24:14, Genesis 17:32, Guide for the Perplexed 2:43, mt.Hilchot Yesodei haTorah 7:3, Numbers.R 2:15, Zechariah 4:2

[7] LXX *toward*

[8] Jeremiah 1:14 - b.Bava Batra 25b, b.Chagigah [Rashi] 13b, b.Gittin 6a, b.Kiddushin [Rashi] 71b, Bahir 162 164, Ein Yaakov Bava Batra:25b, Ezekiel 1:4, Isaiah 17:25, Jeremiah 4:6 6:1 6:22 10:22 7:9 22:20 2:9 2:41, Numbers.R 2:15, z.Vayakhel 203a, z.Vayetze 151a

[9] Jeremiah 1:15 - Bahir 164, Deuteronomy 28:49-28:53, Isaiah 22:7, Jeremiah 4:16 5:15 6:22 9:12 10:22 10:25 1:9 1:28 25:31-25:32 9:10 10:22 15:3 19:10 20:6, Lamentations 5:11, Midrash Psalms 79:4, Sibylline Oracles 3.667, Tanna Devei Eliyahu 6

[10] Jeremiah 1:16 - 2 Chronicles 7:19 15:2 10:25, 2 Kings 22:17, Acts 7:41, Deuteronomy 4:20 7:16, Ezekiel 8:9-8:11 24:14, Hosea 8:6 11:2, Isaiah 2:8 13:19 20:15 17:3, Jeremiah 2:13 2:17 4:12 4:28 5:9 5:29 7:9 10:8-10:9 10:15 11:12 11:17 15:6 16:11 17:13 19:4 20:17 3:17, Joel 2:11, Joshua 24:20, Matthew 23:35-23:36

[11] Jeremiah 1:17 - 1 Corinthians 9:16, 1 Kings 18:46, 1 Peter 1:13, 1 Thessalonians 2:2, 2 Kings 4:29 9:1, Acts 20:20 20:27, Exodus 3:12 7:2, Ezekiel 2:6-2:7 3:10-3:11 3:14-3:18 33:6-33:8, Jeremiah 1:7-1:8 17:18 23:28, Job 14:3, Jonah 3:2, Liber Antiquitatum Biblicarum 51:6, Luke 12:35

וַאֲנִי הִנֵּה נְתַתִּיךָ הַיּוֹם לְעִיר מִבְצָר וּלְעַמּוּד בַּרְזֶל וּלְחֹמוֹת נְחֹשֶׁת עַל־כָּל־הָאָרֶץ לְמַלְכֵי יְהוּדָה לְשָׂרֶיהָ לְכֹהֲנֶיהָ וּלְעַם הָאָרֶץ

18[1] For, behold, I have made you this day a fortified city, and an iron pillar, and brazen walls, against the whole land, against the kings of Judah, against its princes, against its priests, and against the people of the land.

וְנִלְחֲמוּ אֵלֶיךָ וְלֹא־יוּכְלוּ לָךְ כִּי־אִתְּךָ אֲנִי נְאֻם־יְהוָה לְהַצִּילֶךָ

19[2] And they shall fight against you; but they shall not prevail against you; For I am with you, says the LORD, to deliver you.'

Jeremiah – Chapter 02

וַיְהִי דְבַר־יְהוָה אֵלַי לֵאמֹר

1[3] *And the word of the LORD came to me, saying*[4]:

הָלֹךְ וְקָרָאתָ בְאָזְנֵי יְרוּשָׁלַ͏ִם לֵאמֹר כֹּה אָמַר יְהוָה זָכַרְתִּי לָךְ חֶסֶד נְעוּרַיִךְ אַהֲבַת כְּלוּלֹתָיִךְ לֶכְתֵּךְ אַחֲרַי בַּמִּדְבָּר בְּאֶרֶץ לֹא זְרוּעָה

2[5] *Go, and cry in the ears of Jerusalem, saying: Thus says the LORD: I remember for you the affection of your youth, the love of your advocates; how you went after Me in the wilderness, in a land that was not sown*[6].

קֹדֶשׁ יִשְׂרָאֵל לַיהוָה רֵאשִׁית תְּבוּאָתֹה כָּל־אֹכְלָיו יֶאְשָׁמוּ רָעָה תָּבֹא אֲלֵיהֶם נְאֻם־יְהוָה

3[7] *Israel is the LORD's holy portion*[8], *His first fruits of the increase; all who devour him shall be held guilty, evil shall come on them, says the LORD.*

שִׁמְעוּ דְבַר־יְהוָה בֵּית יַעֲקֹב וְכָל־מִשְׁפְּחוֹת בֵּית יִשְׂרָאֵל

4[9] *Hear the word of the LORD, O house of Jacob, and all the families of the house of Israel;*

כֹּה אָמַר יְהוָה מַה־מָּצְאוּ אֲבוֹתֵיכֶם בִּי עָוֶל כִּי רָחֲקוּ מֵעָלָי וַיֵּלְכוּ אַחֲרֵי הַהֶבֶל וַיֶּהְבָּלוּ

5[10] *Thus says the LORD: what unrighteousness have your fathers found in Me, that they have gone far from Me, and walked after things of nothing, and became nothing?*

[1] Jeremiah 1:18 - 2 Baruch 2:1 4 Baruch 1:1, Ezekiel 3:8-9, Isaiah 2:7, Jeremiah 6:27 15:20 21:4-30 26:12-15 10:3 34:20-22 36:27-32 13:7 14:2 14:18 18:22, John 1:42, Micah 3:8-9

[2] Jeremiah 1:19 - Jeremiah 1:8 11:19 15:10-21 20:1-6 20:11 26:11-24 29:25-32 37:11-21 38:6-13, Joshua 1:9, Psalms 9:2

[3] Jeremiah 2:1 - 2 Peter 1:21, Ezekiel 7:1, Hebrews 1:1, Jeremiah 1:11 7:1 23:28, Midrash Psalms 119:5

[4] LXX *And he said, Thus says the LORD*

[5] Jeremiah 2:2 - Avot de R'Natan 36, b.Sanhedrin 11b, Deuteronomy 2:7 8:2 8:15-8:16, Ecclesiastes.R 1:31, Ein Yaakov Sanhedrin:110b, Exodus 14:31-15:20 16:8 24:3-24:8, Ezekiel 7:1 16:8 16:22 23:3 23:8 23:19, Hosea 2:15 8:1, Isaiah 10:1 63:7-63:14, Jeremiah 2:6 7:2 11:6 19:2, Jonah 1:2, Luke 12:13, Matthew 11:15, Mekhilta de R'Shimon bar Yochai Beshallach 23:1, Mekhilta de R'Shimon bar Yochai Shirata 33:1, Mekhilta de R'Shimon bar Yochai Vayassa 37:1, Mekilta de R'Ishmael Beshallah 4:86, Mekilta de R'Ishmael Pisha 14:51, Mekilta de R'Ishmael Shirata 7:10, Mekilta de R'Ishmael Vayassa 1:13, Midrash Psalms 36:7 118:6 119:5, Midrash Tanchuma Bo 9, Midrash Tanchuma Vayigash 10, mt.Hilcnot Shofar Sukkah vLulav 3:9, Mussaf Rosh Hoshanna, Nehemiah 9:12-9:21, Numbers.R 2:15 2:15, Pesikta Rabbati 26:1/2, Proverbs 1:20 8:1-8:4, Song of Songs 3:11, z.Emor 103b, z.Vaetchanan 269b, z.Vayishlach 176b

[6] LXX *I remember the kindness of your youth, and the love of your espousals*

[7] Jeremiah 2:3 - 1 Peter 2:9, 4Q396 frags 1-2 4.5, 4Q397 frags 6-13 ll.11, Acts 9:4-9:5, Amos 6:1, b.Avodah Zara [Tosefot] 39a, b.Kiddushin 53a, b.Sanhedrin [Rashi] 91b, b.Shabbat [Rashi] 32a, Deuteronomy 7:6 14:2 2:19, Ein Yaakov Shabbat:32a, Ephesians 1:4, Exodus 4:22-4:23 19:5-19:6 22:29 23:16, Exodus.R 15:5 24:3 31:9 49:2, Genesis.R 81:1, Isaiah 17:11 23:6, James 1:18, Jastrow 1117b, Jeremiah 12:14 6:16 2:7, Joel 1:3 1:7-1:8, Leviticus.R 36:4, Mekhilta de R'Shimon bar Yochai Beshallach 23:1, Mekilta de R'Ishmael Beshallah 4:87, Mekilta de R'Ishmael Pisha 14:52, Midrash Psalms 14:4 53:2 80:5 104:1 150:1, Midrash Tanchuma Bamidbar 19, Midrash Tanchuma Bo 9, Midrash Tanchuma Mikketz 5, Numbers 18:12, Numbers.R 2:13 4:1 10:2, Psalms 81:15-81:16 105:14-105:15 105:25-105:36, Ralbag Wars 6part02:2, Revelation 14:4, Romans 11:16 16:5, Song of Songs.R 6:26, z.Bo 42a, z.Haazinu 297a, z.Mishpatim 101b 108b 121b 122a, z.Pekudei 225b 229b, z.Shemini 42a, z.Vaetchanan 266a, Zechariah 1:15 2:8 12:2-12:4 14:20-14:21

[8] LXX *in following the Holy One of Israel, says the Lord, Israel was the holy people to the LORD*

[9] Jeremiah 2:4 - Ecclesiastes.R 4:3, Exodus.R 27:9, Hosea 4:1, Isaiah 51:1-51:4, Jeremiah 5:21 7:2 13:15 19:3 7:2 9:24 10:4 44:24-44:26, Micah 6:1, Midrash Tanchuma Yitro 4, Pesikta de R'Kahana 14.3 14.4, Pesikta Rabbati 27:1-4
Jeremiah 2:4-28 - Haftarah Massai [continues at 3:4 Ashkenaz; continues at 4:1-2 Sephard], Haftarah Massai Part One, Haftarah Massai Part One Sephard [Jeremiah 2:4-28], mt.Hilchot Tefilah 13:4 13:19, Second of the three Shabbats preceding Tisha bAv [Pesikta Rabbati 27], Siman 122:6

[10] Jeremiah 2:5 - 1 Samuel 12:21, 2 Baruch 14:5, 2 Kings 17:15, Acts 14:15, Avot de R'Natan 36, b.Chagigah 9b, Deuteronomy 8:21, Deuteronomy.R 3:3, Ezekiel 11:15, Guide for the Perplexed 3:47, Isaiah 5:3-5:4 5:13 43:22-43:23 20:9, Jeremiah 2:31 10:8 10:14-10:15 12:2 14:22 51:17-51:18, Jonah 2:8, Mas.Derek Eretz Rabbah 11:14, Matthew 15:8, Micah 6:2-6:3, Pesikta de R'Kahana 14.3 14.5 14.6 14.7, Psalms 19:8, Romans 1:21, t.Chagigah 1:8, z.Vaetchanan 269b

וְלֹא אָמְרוּ אַיֵּה יְהֹוָה הַמַּעֲלֶה אֹתָנוּ מֵאֶרֶץ מִצְרָיִם הַמּוֹלִיךְ אֹתָנוּ בַּמִּדְבָּר בְּאֶרֶץ עֲרָבָה וְשׁוּחָה בְּאֶרֶץ צִיָּה וְצַלְמָוֶת בְּאֶרֶץ לֹא־עָבַר בָּהּ אִישׁ וְלֹא־יָשַׁב אָדָם שָׁם

6[1] Nor did they said: 'Where is the LORD who brought us up from the land of Egypt; who led us through the wilderness, through a land of deserts and of pits, through a land of drought and of the shadow of death, through a land that no man passed through, and where no man lived?'

וָאָבִיא אֶתְכֶם אֶל־אֶרֶץ הַכַּרְמֶל לֶאֱכֹל פִּרְיָהּ וְטוּבָהּ וַתָּבֹאוּ וַתְּטַמְּאוּ אֶת־אַרְצִי וְנַחֲלָתִי שַׂמְתֶּם לְתוֹעֵבָה

7[2] And I brought you to *a land of fruitful fields*[3], to eat its fruit and its good; but when you entered, you defiled My land, and made My heritage an abomination.

הַכֹּהֲנִים לֹא אָמְרוּ אַיֵּה יְהֹוָה וְתֹפְשֵׂי הַתּוֹרָה לֹא יְדָעוּנִי וְהָרֹעִים פָּשְׁעוּ בִי וְהַנְּבִיאִים נִבְּאוּ בַבַּעַל וְאַחֲרֵי לֹא־יוֹעִלוּ הָלָכוּ

8[4] The priests did not say: 'Where is the LORD?' and they who handle the law did not know Me, and the rulers transgressed against Me; the prophets prophesied by Baal, and walked after things that do not profit.

לָכֵן עֹד אָרִיב אִתְּכֶם נְאֻם־יְהֹוָה וְאֶת־בְּנֵי בְנֵיכֶם אָרִיב

9[5] Why I will yet plead with you, says the LORD, and with your children's children will I plead.

כִּי עִבְרוּ אִיֵּי כִתִּיִּים וּרְאוּ וְקֵדָר שִׁלְחוּ וְהִתְבּוֹנְנוּ מְאֹד וּרְאוּ הֵן הָיְתָה כָּזֹאת

10[6] For pass over to the isles of the Kittites, and see, and send to Kedar, and consider diligently, and see if there has been such a thing.

הַהֵימִיר גּוֹי אֱלֹהִים וְהֵמָּה לֹא אֱלֹהִים וְעַמִּי הֵמִיר כְּבוֹדוֹ בְּלוֹא יוֹעִיל

11[7] Has a nation changed its gods, which yet are no gods? But My people have changed its glory for what does not profit.

שֹׁמּוּ שָׁמַיִם עַל־זֹאת וְשַׂעֲרוּ חָרְבוּ מְאֹד נְאֻם־יְהֹוָה

12[8] Be astonished at this, O heavens, and be very afraid, be exceeding amazed, says the LORD.

כִּי־שְׁתַּיִם רָעוֹת עָשָׂה עַמִּי אֹתִי עָזְבוּ מְקוֹר מַיִם חַיִּים לַחְצֹב לָהֶם בֹּארוֹת בֹּארֹת נִשְׁבָּרִים אֲשֶׁר לֹא־יָכִלוּ הַמָּיִם

13[9] For My people have committed two evils: they have forsaken Me, the fountain of living waters, and hewed out cisterns, broken cisterns, that can hold no water.

---

[1] Jeremiah 2:6 - 2 Kings 2:14, b.Berachot 31a, b.Sotah 46b, Deuteronomy 8:14-8:16 8:10, Ein Yaakov Berachot:31a, Ein Yaakov Sotah:46b, Exodus 14:1-14:15, Exodus.R 32:5, Genesis.R 19:3, Guide for the Perplexed 3:50, Hosea 12:15 13:4, Isaiah 15:9 63:11-13 16:8, Jastrow 1285a 1531a, Jeremiah 2:2 2:8 5:2, Job 3:6 10:21-10:22 11:10, Judges 6:13, Matthew 4:16, Mekhilta de R'Shimon bar Yochai Vayassa 37:1, Mekhilta de R'Ishmael Vayassa 1:55, Midrash Tanchuma Beshallach 18, Psalms 23:4 77:6

[2] Jeremiah 2:7 - Deuteronomy 6:10-6:11 6:18 8:7-8:9 11:10-11:12 21:23, Ezekiel 20:6 12:17, Genesis.R 19:9 96:5 96 [Excl]:1, Jeremiah 3:1 3:9 16:18, Kuzari 2.022, Lamentations.R Petichata D'Chakimei:4, Leviticus 18:24-18:28, Micah 2:10, Midrash Tanchuma Kedoshim 7 11, Midrash Tanchuma Vayechi 3, Nehemiah 9:25, Numbers 13:27 14:7-14:8 35:33-35:34, Pesikta de R'Kahana 15.1, Psalms 78:58-78:59 106:38-106:39, Song of Songs.R 8:14, y.Ketubot 12:3, y.Kilayim 9:3, z.Acharei Mot 72a, z.Terumah 141b, z.Vayechi 226a

[3] LXX *Carmel*

[4] Jeremiah 2:8 - 1 Kings 18:22 18:29 18:40, 1 Samuel 2:12 12:21, 2 Corinthians 4:2, Derech Hashem Part III 4§10, Deuteronomy 9:10, Habakkuk 2:18, Hosea 4:6, Isaiah 4:7 5:10 6:5 56:9-56:12, Jeremiah 2:6 2:11 4:22 5:31 7:8 8:8-8:11 10:21 12:10 16:19 23:1-23:2 23:9-23:15, John 8:55 16:3, Liber Antiquitatum Biblicarum 30:4, Luke 11:52, Malachi 2:6-2:9, Matthew 16:26, Midrash Tanchuma Vayigash 2, Pesikta de R'Kahana 14.1, Pesikta Rabbati 27/28:2, Romans 2:17-2:24, Song of Songs.R 1:23, z.Tzav 32a

[5] Jeremiah 2:9 - Exodus 20:5, Ezekiel 20:35-20:36, Hosea 2:2, Isaiah 3:13 19:26, Jeremiah 2:29 2:35, Leviticus 20:5, Micah 6:2, Pesikta Rabbati 27:2

[6] Jeremiah 2:10 - 1 Chronicles 1:7 23:1 23:12, 1 Corinthians 5:1, b.Taanit 5b, Daniel 11:30, Ein Yaakov Taanit:5b, Ezekiel 3:6, Genesis 10:4-10:5 1:13, Isaiah 21:16, Jeremiah 18:13-18:14, Judges 19:30, Numbers 24:24, Psalms 24:5, Saadia Opinions 3:5

[7] Jeremiah 2:11 - 1 Corinthians 8:4, 1 Peter 1:18, But My people have changed My Glory by replacing כבודם [kevodam, Deuteronomy 9:29, Ein Yaakov Taanit:5b, Isaiah 13:19, Jeremiah 2:5 2:8 16:20, Mekhilta de R'Ishmael Shirata 6:19, Micah 4:5, Midrash Tanchuma Beshallach 16, my glory]., Psalms 3:4 10:20 19:4, Romans 1:23, Sifre.z Numbers Behaalotcha 12:12, their glory] back to כבודי [kevodi, This is the ninth of the Eighteen Emendations of the Sopherim. The text can be reconstructed to read

[8] Jeremiah 2:12 - Deuteronomy 8:1, Isaiah 1:2, Jeremiah 6:19 22:29, Matthew 3:45 27:50-27:53, Micah 6:2, Psalms of Solomon 2:9

[9] Jeremiah 2:13 - 1 Samuel 12:10, 2 Peter 2:17, b.Taanit 5ab, Ecclesiastes 1:2 1:14 2:11 2:21 2:26 4:4 12:8, Ein Yaakov Taanit:5a, Ein Yaakov Taanit:5b, Exodus.R 42:8, Genesis.R 70:8, Guide for the Perplexed 2:12, Isaiah 1:3 5:13 44:9-44:20 46:6-46:7 7:2 15:8, Jastrow 376b 1485a, Jeremiah 1:16 2:11 2:17 2:26 2:31-2:32 4:22 5:26 5:31 15:6 17:13 18:14, John 4:14 7:37, Joseph and Aseneth 2:12, Judges 10:13, m.Sukkah 5:1, Mekhilta de R'Shimon bar Yochai Bachodesh 53:3, Micah 2:8 6:3, Pesikta Rabbati 21:19, Philo De Fuga et Inventione 197, Psalms 36:10 81:12-81:14 115:4-115:8 146:3-146:4, Revelation 21:6 22:1 22:17, Sifre Devarim {Haazinu Hashamayim} 318, Sifre Devarim Nitzavim 318, Song of Songs.R 1:39, Tanya Igeret Hakodesh §09, y.Sukkah 5:5, z.Vaetchanan 266a, z.Vayeilech 286a

הַעֶבֶד יִשְׂרָאֵל אִם־יְלִיד בַּיִת הוּא מַדּוּעַ הָיָה לָבַז	14[1]	Is Israel a servant? Is he a home-born slave? Why has he become a prey?
עָלָיו יִשְׁאֲגוּ כְפִרִים נָתְנוּ קוֹלָם וַיָּשִׁיתוּ אַרְצוֹ לְשַׁמָּה עָרָיו 'נִצְּתָה' "נִצְּתוּ" מִבְּלִי יֹשֵׁב	15[2]	The young lions have roared on him, and let their voice echo; and they made his land desolate, his cities are laid waste, without inhabitant.
גַּם־בְּנֵי־נֹף 'וְתַחְפְּנֵס' "וְתַחְפַּנְחֵס" יִרְעוּךְ קָדְקֹד	16[3]	The children also of *Noph*[4] and Tahpanhes feed on the crown of your head.
הֲלוֹא־זֹאת תַּעֲשֶׂה־לָּךְ עָזְבֵךְ אֶת־יְהוָה אֱלֹהַיִךְ בְּעֵת מוֹלִיכֵךְ בַּדָּרֶךְ	17[5]	Has not forsaking the LORD your God causes this to happen to you, *that, when He led you by the way*[6]?
וְעַתָּה מַה־לָּךְ לְדֶרֶךְ מִצְרַיִם לִשְׁתּוֹת מֵי שִׁחוֹר וּמַה־לָּךְ לְדֶרֶךְ אַשּׁוּר לִשְׁתּוֹת מֵי נָהָר	18[7]	And now what have you to do in the way to Egypt, to drink the waters of *Shihor*[8]? Or what have you to do in the way to Assyria, to drink the waters of the River?
תְּיַסְּרֵךְ רָעָתֵךְ וּמְשֻׁבוֹתַיִךְ תּוֹכִחֻךְ וּדְעִי וּרְאִי כִּי־רַע וָמָר עָזְבֵךְ אֶת־יְהוָה אֱלֹהָיִךְ וְלֹא פַחְדָּתִי אֵלַיִךְ נְאֻם־אֲדֹנָי יְהוִה צְבָאוֹת	19[9]	Your own wickedness shall correct you, and your backslidings shall reprove you: know, therefore, and see it is an evil and a bitter thing, to forsake the LORD your God, nor is My fear in you, says the Lord GOD of hosts.
כִּי מֵעוֹלָם שָׁבַרְתִּי עֻלֵּךְ נִתַּקְתִּי מוֹסְרֹתַיִךְ וַתֹּאמְרִי לֹא 'אֶעֱבוֹד' "אֶעֱבוֹר" כִּי עַל־כָּל־גִּבְעָה גְּבֹהָה וְתַחַת כָּל־עֵץ רַעֲנָן אַתְּ צֹעָה זֹנָה	20[10]	For of old time I have broken your yoke, and burst your bands, and you said: '*I will not transgress.*' *Upon every high hill and under every leafy tree you laid, playing the harlot*[11].
וְאָנֹכִי נְטַעְתִּיךְ שֹׂרֵק כֻּלֹּה זֶרַע אֱמֶת וְאֵיךְ נֶהְפַּכְתְּ לִי סוּרֵי הַגֶּפֶן נָכְרִיָּה	21[12]	Yet I planted a noble vine, wholly a right seed. How then do you turn into the degenerate plant of a strange vine to Me?
כִּי אִם־תְּכַבְּסִי בַּנֶּתֶר וְתַרְבִּי־לָךְ בֹּרִית נִכְתָּם עֲוֹנֵךְ לְפָנַי נְאֻם אֲדֹנָי יְהוִה	22[13]	For though you wash with lye, and use a lot of soap, your iniquity is marked before Me, says the Lord GOD.

---

[1] Jeremiah 2:14 - Ecclesiastes 2:7, Exodus 4:22, Genesis 15:3, Isaiah 2:1, Pesikta Rabbati 27:3

[2] Jeremiah 2:15 - Amos 3:4 3:8 3:12, Ezekiel 5:14, Hosea 5:14 11:10 13:7-13:8, Isaiah 1:7 5:9 5:29 6:11 24:1, Jeremiah 4:7 5:6 9:12 1:30 2:9 9:10 10:22 20:22 2:17, Job 4:10, Judges 14:5, Nahum 2:12, Psalms 57:5, Zephaniah 1:18 2:5 3:6

[3] Jeremiah 2:16 - 2 Kings 18:21 23:33, Deuteronomy 9:20, Ezekiel 6:13 6:16, Isaiah 1:6-1:7 8:8 19:13 30:1-6 31:1-3, Jeremiah 43:7-9 20:1 22:14 22:19

[4] LXX *Memphis*

[5] Jeremiah 2:17 – 1 Chronicles 4:9, 2 Chronicles 7:19-7:20, Deuteronomy 28:15-28:68 8:10 8:19, Hosea 13:9, Isaiah 1:4 63:11-63:14, Jeremiah 2:13 2:19 4:18, Job 4:8, Leviticus 26:15-26:46, Numbers 8:23, Psalms 77:21 78:53-78:54 11:7 16:16

[6] Missing in LXX

[7] Jeremiah 2:18 - 2 Chronicles 28:20-28:21, 2 Kings 16:7-16:9, Ezekiel 17:15, Hosea 5:13 7:11, Isaiah 30:1-30:7 7:1, Jeremiah 2:36 37:5-37:10, Joshua 13:3, Lamentations 4:17, Lamentations.R Petichata D'Chakimei:19, Pesikta Rabbati 33:13

[8] LXX *Geon*

[9] Jeremiah 2:19 - Amos 8:10, Hosea 4:16 5:5 11:7 14:3, Isaiah 3:9 5:5 2:1, Jeremiah 2:17 3:6-3:8 3:11-3:14 3:22 4:18 5:6 5:22 8:5 36:23-36:24, Job 20:11-20:16, Midrash Psalms 14:5 36:2, Proverbs 1:31 5:22, Psalms 36:2, Romans 3:18, Zechariah 7:11

[10] Jeremiah 2:20 - 1 Kings 12:32, 1 Samuel 12:10, Deuteronomy 4:34 5:27 12:2 15:12 2:17, Exodus 3:8 19:8 24:3 34:14-34:16, Ezekiel 16:15-16:16 16:24-16:25 16:28 16:31 16:41 20:28 23:5, Hosea 2:5 3:3, Isaiah 1:21 9:5 10:27 14:25 57:5-57:7, Jeremiah 3:1-3:2 3:6-3:8 17:2 6:8, Joshua 1:16 24:24 24:26, Leviticus 2:13, Midrash Tanchuma Ekev 8, Nahum 1:13, Psalms 78:58

[11] LXX *I will not serve you, but will go upon every high hill, and under every shady tree, there will I indulge in my fornication*

[12] Jeremiah 2:21 - Deuteronomy 4:37 8:32, Exodus 15:17, Genesis 18:19 26:3-5 8:29, Isaiah 1:21 5:1-2 5:4 17:8 12:21 13:3, John 15:1, Joshua 24:31, Lamentations 4:1, Luke 20:9, Mark 12:1, Matthew 21:33, Mesillat Yesharim 11:Nekiyut-in-Character-Traits Sifre Devarim Nitzavim 323, Midrash Tanchuma Naso 7, Midrash Tanchuma Vayechi 10, Midrash Tanchuma Vayeilech 2, Midrash Tanchuma Vayeshev 1, Pirkei de R'Eliezer 39, Psalms 44:3 80:9 9:6, Sifre Devarim Haazinu Hashamayim 323, z.Lech Lecha 96b, z.Vayikra 14b

[13] Jeremiah 2:22 - Amos 8:7, b.Berachot [Rashi] 57a, b.Chagigah 15a, b.Rosh Hashanah 18a, b.Yevamot 105a, Deuteronomy 8:34, Ein Yaakov Chagigah:15a, Ein Yaakov Rosh Hashanah:18a, Ein Yaakov Yevamot:105a, Gates of Repentance 1.001, Hosea 13:12, Jeremiah 16:17 17:1, Job 9:30-9:31 14:17, Lamentations.R Petichata D'Chakimei:14, Midrash Tanchuma Haazinu 4, Numbers.R 11:7, Pesikta de R'Kahana S7.1, Pesikta Rabbati 48:3, Psalms 90:8 10:3, z.Noach 62a 63a 73b

אֵיךְ תֹּאמְרִי לֹא נִטְמֵאתִי אַחֲרֵי הַבְּעָלִים לֹא הָלַכְתִּי רְאִי דַרְכֵּךְ בַּגַּיְא דְּעִי מֶה עָשִׂית בִּכְרָה קַלָּה מְשָׂרֶכֶת דְּרָכֶיהָ 23[1]

פֶּרֶה׀ לִמֻּד מִדְבָּר בְּאַוַּת נַפְשׁוֹ "נַפְשָׁהּ" שָׁאֲפָה רוּחַ תַּאֲנָתָהּ מִי יְשִׁיבֶנָּה כָּל־מְבַקְשֶׁיהָ לֹא יִיעָפוּ בְּחָדְשָׁהּ יִמְצָאוּנְהָ 24[3]

מִנְעִי רַגְלֵךְ מִיָּחֵף "וּגְרוֹנֵךְ" "וּגְרֹנֵךְ" מִצִּמְאָה וַתֹּאמְרִי נוֹאָשׁ לוֹא כִּי־אָהַבְתִּי זָרִים וְאַחֲרֵיהֶם אֵלֵךְ 25[5]

כְּבֹשֶׁת גַּנָּב כִּי יִמָּצֵא כֵּן הֹבִישׁוּ בֵּית יִשְׂרָאֵל הֵמָּה מַלְכֵיהֶם שָׂרֵיהֶם וְכֹהֲנֵיהֶם וּנְבִיאֵיהֶם 26[7]

כְּבֹשֶׁת גַּנָּב כִּי יִמָּצֵא כֵּן הֹבִישׁוּ בֵּית יִשְׂרָאֵל הֵמָּה מַלְכֵיהֶם שָׂרֵיהֶם וְכֹהֲנֵיהֶם וּנְבִיאֵיהֶם 27[8]

וְאַיֵּה אֱלֹהֶיךָ אֲשֶׁר עָשִׂיתָ לָּךְ יָקוּמוּ אִם־יוֹשִׁיעוּךָ בְּעֵת רָעָתֶךָ כִּי מִסְפַּר עָרֶיךָ הָיוּ אֱלֹהֶיךָ יְהוּדָה 28[9]

לָמָּה תָרִיבוּ אֵלָי כֻּלְּכֶם פְּשַׁעְתֶּם בִּי נְאֻם־יְהוָה 29[10]

לַשָּׁוְא הִכֵּיתִי אֶת־בְּנֵיכֶם מוּסָר לֹא לָקָחוּ אָכְלָה חַרְבְּכֶם נְבִיאֵיכֶם כְּאַרְיֵה מַשְׁחִית 30[11]

הַדּוֹר אַתֶּם רְאוּ דְבַר־יְהוָה הֲמִדְבָּר הָיִיתִי לְיִשְׂרָאֵל אִם אֶרֶץ מַאְפֵּלְיָה מַדּוּעַ אָמְרוּ עַמִּי רַדְנוּ לוֹא־נָבוֹא עוֹד אֵלֶיךָ 31[12]

23[1] How can you say: 'I am not defiled, I have not gone after the Baalim?' *See your way in the Valley, know what you have done; you are a swift young camel traversing her ways*[2];

24[3] *A wild ass used to the wilderness, that sniffs up the wind in her desire; her lust, who can hinder it? All they who seek her will not weary themselves; in her month* [4]*they shall find her.*

25[5] Withhold your foot from being unshod, and your throat from thirst; but you said: '*There is no hope*[6]'; no, for I have loved strangers, and I will go after them.'

26[7] As the thief is ashamed when he is found, so is the house of Israel ashamed; they, their kings, their princes, and their priests, and their prophets;

27[8] Who says to a stock: 'You are my father,' and to a stone: 'You have brought us forth,' For they have turned their back to Me, and not their face; but in the time of their trouble they will say: 'Arise, and save us.'

28[9] But where are your gods you have made? Let them arise, if they can save you in the time of your trouble; for your gods number like your cities, O Judah.

29[10] Why will you contend with Me? You all have transgressed against Me, says the LORD.

30[11] I have struck your children in vain. They received no correction; your sword has devoured your prophets, like a destroying lion.

31[12] O generation, see the word of the LORD: have I been a wilderness to Israel, or a land of thick

[1] Jeremiah 2:23 - 1 John 1:8-10, 1 Samuel 15:13-14, b.Sanhedrin [Rashi] 52a, b.Shabbat 33a, Esther 8:16, Ezekiel 16:1-163 23:1-49, Gates of Repentance 1.037, Genesis 3:12-13, Isaiah 57:5-6, Jeremiah 2:33-35 3:2 7:31 9:15 7:23, Luke 10:29, Midrash Psalms 5:1, Proverbs 4:13 6:12 6:20, Psalms 36:3 50:21, Revelation 3:17-18, Romans 3:19, Sifre Devarim Haazinu Hashamayim 306

[2] LXX behold thy ways in the burial-ground, and know what thou have done: her voice has howled in the evening

[3] Jeremiah 2:24 - b.Nazir [Rashi] 7a, Deuteronomy.R 5:8, Hosea 5:15, Jastrow 1213a, Jeremiah 2:27 14:6, Job 11:12 39:5-8

[4] LXX *she has extended her ways over the waters of the desert; she was hurried along by the lusts of her soul; she is given up to them, who will turn her back? none that seek her shall be weary; at the time of her humiliation*

[5] Jeremiah 2:25 - 2 Chronicles 4:22, b.Yoma 77a, Deuteronomy 4:48 29:18-19 8:16, Guide for the Perplexed 3:4, Hosea 2:3, Isaiah 2:6 20:2-4 9:10, Jastrow 573b 1286b, Jeremiah 3:13 13:22 14:10 18:12 20:17, Lamentations 4:4, Luke 15:22 16:24, Romans 2:4-5 8:24

[6] LXX *I will strengthen myself*

[7] Jeremiah 2:26 - Daniel 9:6-8, Ezra 9:7, Isaiah 1:29, Jeremiah 2:36 3:24-25 8:32 24:27, Nehemiah 9:32-34, Proverbs 6:30-31, Romans 6:21

[8] Jeremiah 2:27 - b.Chullin 19b, b.Yevamot 48b, Ein Yaakov Yevamot 48b, Exodus.R 9:11 46:4, Ezekiel 8:16 23:35, Habakkuk 2:18-19, Hosea 5:15 7:14, Isaiah 2:16 44:9-20 46:6-8, Jastrow 1059a, Jeremiah 2:24 10:8 18:17 22:23 8:33, Judges 10:8-16, Lamentations.R Petichata D'Chakimei:13, Mas.Semachot 7:13, Midrash Psalms 13:2, Midrash Tanchuma Lech Lecha 3, mt.Hilchot Melachim uMichamoteihem 8:5, Pesikta de R'Kahana 13.4 13.8 16.1, Pesikta Rabbati 29/30A:1 33:13, Psalms 78:34-37 115:4-8, Ruth.R 5:3, Sifre Devarim Ki Tetze 213, Tanya Igeret Hakodesh §22

[9] Jeremiah 2:28 - 2 Kings 3:13 17:30-31, Apocalypse of Elijah 5:11, Deuteronomy 8:37, Hosea 10:1, Isaiah 21:20 22:2 22:7, Jeremiah 11:13, Judges 10:14, mt.Hilchot Yesodei haTorah 10:3, Pesikta Rabbati 27:4

[10] Jeremiah 2:29 - b.Bava Kamma 92a, Daniel 9:11, Ein Yaakov Bava Kamma 92a, Jeremiah 2:23 2:35 3:2 5:1 6:13 9:3-7, Romans 3:19

[11] Jeremiah 2:30 - 1 Kings 19:10 19:14, 1 Thessalonians 2:15, 2 Chronicles 24:21 4:22 12:16, Acts 7:52, b.Ketubot 72a, b.Shabbat 32b, b.Sheviit [Rashi] 20b, Ezekiel 24:13, Isaiah 1:5 9:14, Jeremiah 5:3 6:29-30 7:28 26:20-24 7:19, Luke 11:47-51 13:33-34, Mark 12:2-8, Mas.Kallah 1:21, Mas.Kallah Rabbati 1:12 2:10, Matthew 21:35-36 23:29 23:34-37, Nehemiah 9:26, Ralbag Wars 4:6, Revelation 9:20-21 16:9, Song of Songs.R 1:23, y.Gittin 4:3, y.Ketubot 7:6, y.Nedarim 3:2, y.Shabbat 2:5, y.Sheviit 3:8, Zephaniah 3:2

[12] Jeremiah 2:31 - 1 Corinthians 4:8, 2 Chronicles 7:10, 2 Samuel 12:7-12:9, Amos 1:1, Deuteronomy 8:12-8:14 7:20 8:15, Guide for the Perplexed 1:46 2:39 3:47, Hosea 2:7-2:10 13:6, Isaiah 21:19, Jastrow 354b 724a, Jeremiah 2:5-2:6, Malachi 3:9-3:11, Mekilta de

darkness? Why do My people say: 'We roam at large; we will no longer come to You?'

32[1] Can a maid forget her ornaments, or a bride her attire? Yet My people have forgotten Me days without number.

33[2] *How trim your ways[3]* to seek love! Therefore, you taught the wicked women your ways;

34[4] *Also in your skirts are found the blood of the souls of the innocent poor; you did not find them breaking in; yet for all these things[5]*

35[6] You said: 'I am innocent; surely His anger is turned from me' Behold, I will enter into judgment with you, because you say: 'I have not sinned.'

36[7] How greatly you cheapened yourself to change your way? You shall be ashamed of Egypt also, as you were ashamed of Asshur.

37[8] You go forth from him, with your hands on your head; for the LORD has rejected those in whom you did trust, and you shall not prosper in them, saying:

Jeremiah – Chapter 03

1[9] As follows: If a man put away his wife, and she goes from him, and become another man's, may he return to her again? Will not the land be greatly polluted? But you have played the harlot with many *lovers[10]*; and would yet return to Me? says the LORD.

2[11] Lift up your eyes to the high hills, and see: Where have you not been lain? By the ways you have sat for them, As an Arabian in the wilderness; and you have polluted the land with your harlotries and with your wickedness.

R'Ishmael Vayassa 6:78, Micah 6:9, Midrash Tanchuma Bamidbar 2, Midrash Tanchuma Beshallach 21, Midrash Tanchuma Massei 9, Nehemiah 9:21-9:25, Numbers.R 1:2 1:2 23:10, Proverbs 6:9, Psalms 10:5 12:5, Revelation 3:15-3:17

[1] Jeremiah 2:32 - 1 Peter 3:3-3:5, 2 Samuel 1:24, Exodus.R 42:7, Ezekiel 16:10-16:13 22:12, Genesis 24:22 24:30 24:53, Hosea 8:14, Isaiah 17:10 13:10, Jeremiah 2:11 3:21 13:10 13:25 18:15, Pesikta Rabbati 33:13, Psalms 9:18 45:14-45:15 10:21, Revelation 21:2

[2] Jeremiah 2:33 - 2 Chronicles 9:9, Ezekiel 16:27 16:47 16:51-16:52, Hosea 2:5-2:9 2:13, Isaiah 57:7-57:10, Jeremiah 2:23 2:36 3:1-2, Saadia Opinions 5:8

[3] LXX *What fair device will you yet employ in your ways*

[4] Jeremiah 2:34 - 2 Kings 21:16 24:4, b.Shabbat 32b, Ein Yaakov Shabbat:32b, Exodus 22:2, Ezekiel 16:20-16:21 20:31 24:7, Isaiah 9:5 11:7, Jeremiah 6:15 7:31 8:12 19:4, Leviticus.R 10:3, Mas.Kallah 1:20, Midrash Tanchuma Behaalotcha 14, Numbers.R 15:21, Pesikta Rabbati 33:13, Psalms 106:37-106:38, Tanya Igeret Hakodesh §16

[5] LXX *and in thine hands has been found the blood of innocent souls; I have not found them in holes, but on every oak*

[6] Jeremiah 2:35 - 1 John 1:8-1:10, Gates of Repentance 1.018 2.002, Isaiah 10:3, Jeremiah 2:9 2:23 2:29 1:31, Job 9:9, Midrash Psalms 80:1, Proverbs 4:13, Romans 7:9, y.Taanit 2:7

[7] Jeremiah 2:36 - 2 Chronicles 4:16 28:20-28:21, Ezekiel 5:7, Hosea 5:13 7:11 10:6 12:3 14:5, Isaiah 20:5 30:1-30:7 31:1-31:3, Jeremiah 2:18 2:23 2:33 7:23 13:7, Lamentations 4:17 5:6

[8] Jeremiah 2:37 - 2 Chronicles 13:12, 2 Samuel 13:19, Ezekiel 17:15-20, Isaiah 10:4, Jeremiah 2:36 17:5 8:5 37:7-10, Numbers 14:41

[9] Jeremiah 3:1 - b.Sanhedrin 56b, b.Yoma 86b, Deuteronomy 4:29-4:31 22:21 24:1-24:4, Deuteronomy.R 2:25, Ein Yaakov Sanhedrin:56b, Ein Yaakov Yoma:86b, Ezekiel 16:26 16:28-16:29 23:4-23:49 9:11, Genesis.R 16:6, Hosea 1:2 2:5-2:9 14:3-14:6, Isaiah 24:5 55:6-55:9, Jeremiah 2:7 2:20 2:23 3:9 3:12-3:14 3:22 4:1 4:14 8:4-8:6, Judges 19:2, Leviticus 18:24-18:28, Luke 15:16-15:24, Micah 2:10, Pesikta de R'Kahana 12.1, Pesikta Rabbati 44:6, Seder Olam 5:Marah, Sifre Devarim {Haazinu Hashamayim} 306, Sifre Devarim Ki Tetze 270 Sifre Devarim Nitzavim 306, Song of Songs.R 1:16, Tanna Devei Eliyahu 9, Zechariah 1:3

[10] LXX *shepherds*

[11] Jeremiah 3:2 - 1 Kings 11:3, 2 Kings 23:13, Deuteronomy 12:2, Ezekiel 8:4-8:6 16:16 16:24-16:25 20:28, Genesis 14:14, Jeremiah 2:7 2:20 2:23 3:1 3:9 3:21 7:29, Luke 16:23, Midrash Psalms 17A:10, Numbers.R 8:4, outrage] is substituted by שגלה [lie with]., Pirkei de R'Eliezer 17, Proverbs 7:11 23:28, Saadia Opinions 10:7, t.Kiddushin 1:4, the word ישגלנה [ravish, To remove indelicate expressions, violate, y.Kiddushin 4:1, y.Taanit 3:3

וַיִּמָּנְעוּ רְבִבִים וּמַלְקוֹשׁ לוֹא הָיָה וּמֵצַח אִשָּׁה זוֹנָה הָיָה לָךְ מֵאַנְתְּ הִכָּלֵם	3[1]	*Therefore, the showers have been withheld, and there has been no latter rain; yet you have a harlot's forehead, you refuse to be ashamed[2].*
הֲלוֹא מֵעַתָּה "קָרָאתי" "קָרָאת" לִי אָבִי אַלּוּף נְעֻרַי אָתָּה	4[3]	*Did you not just now cry to Me: 'My father, You are the friend of my youth[4].*
הֲיִנְטֹר לְעוֹלָם אִם־יִשְׁמֹר לָנֶצַח הִנֵּה "דברתי" "דִּבַּרְתְּ" וַתַּעֲשִׂי הָרָעוֹת וַתּוּכָל	5[5]	Will He bear a grudge forever? Will He keep it to the end?' Behold, you have spoken, but have done evil things, and have had your way.
וַיֹּאמֶר יְהֹוָה אֵלַי בִּימֵי יֹאשִׁיָּהוּ הַמֶּלֶךְ הֲרָאִיתָ אֲשֶׁר עָשְׂתָה מְשֻׁבָה יִשְׂרָאֵל הֹלְכָה הִיא עַל־כָּל־הַר גָּבֹהַּ וְאֶל־תַּחַת כָּל־עֵץ רַעֲנָן וַתִּזְנִי־שָׁם	6[6]	And the LORD said to me in the days of Josiah the king: 'You saw what backsliding Israel did? She went up on every high mountain and under every leafy tree, and played the harlot there.
וָאֹמַר אַחֲרֵי עֲשׂוֹתָהּ אֶת־כָּל־אֵלֶּה אֵלַי תָּשׁוּב וְלֹא־שָׁבָה "וַתִּרְאֶה" "וַתֵּרֶא" בָּגוֹדָה אֲחוֹתָהּ יְהוּדָה	7[7]	And I said: After she has done all these things, she will return to me; but she does not return. *And her treacherous sister Judah saw it[8].*
וָאֵרֶא כִּי עַל־כָּל־אֹדוֹת אֲשֶׁר נִאֲפָה מְשֻׁבָה יִשְׂרָאֵל שִׁלַּחְתִּיהָ וָאֶתֵּן אֶת־סֵפֶר כְּרִיתֻתֶיהָ אֵלֶיהָ וְלֹא יָרְאָה בֹּגֵדָה יְהוּדָה אֲחוֹתָהּ וַתֵּלֶךְ וַתִּזֶן גַּם־הִיא	8[9]	And I saw, when, because backsliding Israel had committed adultery, I had put her away and gave her a bill of divorce, yet treacherous Judah her sister feared not; but she also went and played the harlot;
וְהָיָה מִקֹּל זְנוּתָהּ וַתֶּחֱנַף אֶת־הָאָרֶץ וַתִּנְאַף אֶת־הָאֶבֶן וְאֶת־הָעֵץ	9[10]	*And it came to pass through the lightness of her harlotry, the land was fouled, and she committed adultery with stones and with stocks[11];*
וְגַם־בְּכָל־זֹאת לֹא־שָׁבָה אֵלַי בָּגוֹדָה אֲחוֹתָהּ יְהוּדָה בְּכָל־לִבָּהּ כִּי אִם־בְּשֶׁקֶר נְאֻם־יְהֹוָה	10[12]	and yet for all this her treacherous sister Judah has not returned to Me with her whole heart, but haphazardly, says the LORD
וַיֹּאמֶר יְהֹוָה אֵלַי צִדְּקָה נַפְשָׁהּ מְשֻׁבָה יִשְׂרָאֵל מִבֹּגֵדָה יְהוּדָה	11[13]	The LORD said to me, backsliding Israel has proven herself more righteous than treacherous Judah.
הָלֹךְ וְקָרָאתָ אֶת־הַדְּבָרִים הָאֵלֶּה צָפוֹנָה וְאָמַרְתָּ שׁוּבָה מְשֻׁבָה יִשְׂרָאֵל נְאֻם־יְהֹוָה לוֹא־אַפִּיל פָּנַי בָּכֶם כִּי־חָסִיד אֲנִי נְאֻם־יְהֹוָה לֹא אֶטּוֹר לְעוֹלָם	12[14]	Go, and proclaim these words toward the north, and say: Return, backsliding Israel, says the LORD; I will not frown on you; For I am

---

[1] Jeremiah 3:3 - Amos 4:7, b.Arachin 16a, b.Taanit 7b, b.Yevamot 78b, b.Zevachim 88b, Deuteronomy 4:23, Ein Yaakov Taanit:7b, Ein Yaakov Yevamot:78b, Ein Yaakov Zevachim:88b, Ezekiel 3:7 16:30-16:34, Gates of Repentance 3.094, Haggai 1:11, Hebrews 12:25, Isaiah 5:6, Jeremiah 5:3 5:24 6:15 8:12 9:13 14:4 14:22 44:16-44:17, Joel 1:16-1:20, Leviticus 2:19, Leviticus.R 10:6, Midrash Psalms 17A:10, Nehemiah 9:17, Numbers.R 8:4, Pesikta Rabbati 26:1/2, Philo De Cherubim 49, Pirkei de R'Eliezer 17, Song of Songs.R 4:8, y.Kiddushin 4:1, y.Sanhedrin 6:7, y.Taanit 3:3, y.Yoma 7:3, Zechariah 7:11-7:12, Zephaniah 3:5

[2] LXX *And you retained many shepherds for a stumbling-block to yourself: you had a whore's face, you became shameless toward all*

[3] Jeremiah 3:4 - b.Chagigah 16a, Ein Yaakov Chagigah:16a, Haftarah Massai [continued from 2:4-28 Ashkenaz], Haftarah Massei Part Two [Jeremiah 3:4], HaMadrikh 35:5, Hosea 2:15 14:3-14:5, Jeremiah 2:2 2:27 3:19 7:10 31:19-31:21, Malachi 2:14, Proverbs 1:4 2:17, Psalms 48:15 71:5 71:17 23:9, Second of the three Shabbats preceding Tisha bAv [Pesikta Rabbati 27], Siman 122:6

[4] LXX *Have you not called me as it were a home, and the father and guide of your virgin-time?*

[5] Jeremiah 3:5 - Ezekiel 22:6, Gates of Repentance 1.005, Isaiah 9:16 16:10, Jeremiah 3:12, Micah 2:1 7:3, Psalms 77:8-77:10 85:6 103:8-103:9, Zephaniah 3:1-3:5

[6] Jeremiah 3:6 - 1 Kings 14:23, 2 Kings 17:7-17:17, Ezekiel 16:24-16:25 16:31 20:28 23:11, Isaiah 9:7, Jeremiah 2:19-2:20 3:8 3:11-3:14 7:24 17:2

[7] Jeremiah 3:7 - 2 Chronicles 30:6-30:12, 2 Kings 17:13-17:14, Ezekiel 16:46 23:2-23:4, Hosea 6:1-6:4 14:3, Jeremiah 3:8-3:11, Mas.Soferim 7:2

[8] LXX *And faithless Juda saw her faithlessness*

[9] Jeremiah 3:8 - 2 Kings 17:6-17:19 18:9-18:11, Deuteronomy 24:1 24:3, Ezekiel 16:47 23:9 23:11-23:21, Hosea 2:2-2:5 3:4 4:15-4:17 9:15-9:17, Isaiah 2:1, Jeremiah 3:1, Lamentations.R 1:3

[10] Jeremiah 3:9 - Ezekiel 16:17 23:10, Habakkuk 2:19, Hosea 4:12, Isaiah 9:6, Jeremiah 2:7 2:27 3:2 10:8, Pesikta Rabbati 21:17, y.Challah 2:1

[11] LX *And her fornication was nothing accounted of; and she committed adultery with wood and stone*

[12] Jeremiah 3:10 - 2 Chronicles 34:33-35:18, Hosea 7:14, Isaiah 10:6, Jeremiah 12:2, Psalms 18:45 66:3 78:36-78:37

[13] Jeremiah 3:11 - Ezekiel 16:47 16:51-16:52 23:11, Hosea 4:16 11:7, Jeremiah 3:8 3:22

[14] Jeremiah 3:12 - 2 Chronicles 6:9, 2 Kings 15:29 17:6 17:23 18:1, b.Sanhedrin 11b, Deuteronomy 4:29-4:31 6:2, Deuteronomy.R 2:24, Ezekiel 9:11 15:25, Hosea 6:1 11:8-11:9 14:3-14:5, Isaiah 20:22, Jeremiah 3:1 3:5 3:7 3:14 3:18 3:22 4:1 23:8 6:11 7:9 7:21 9:26, Lamentations.R Petichata D'Chakimei:25, Micah 7:18-7:20, Midrash Proverbs 6, Midrash Psalms 16:11 86:1, Midrash

merciful, says the LORD, I will not bear a grudge forever.

13[1] Just acknowledge the iniquity you transgressed against the LORD your God, and scattered your ways to the strangers under every leafy tree, and you have not listened to My voice, says the LORD.

אַךְ דְּעִי עֲוֹנֵךְ כִּי בַּיהוָה אֱלֹהַיִךְ פָּשָׁעַתְּ וַתְּפַזְּרִי אֶת־דְּרָכַיִךְ לַזָּרִים תַּחַת כָּל־עֵץ רַעֲנָן וּבְקוֹלִי לֹא־שְׁמַעְתֶּם נְאֻם־יְהוָה

14[2] Return, O backsliding children, says the LORD; for I am a lord to you, and I will take one of a city, and two of a family, and I will bring you to Zion;

שׁוּבוּ בָנִים שׁוֹבָבִים נְאֻם־יְהוָה כִּי אָנֹכִי בָּעַלְתִּי בָכֶם וְלָקַחְתִּי אֶתְכֶם אֶחָד מֵעִיר וּשְׁנַיִם מִמִּשְׁפָּחָה וְהֵבֵאתִי אֶתְכֶם צִיּוֹן

15[3] and I will give you shepherds matching My heart, who shall feed you with knowledge and understanding.

וְנָתַתִּי לָכֶם רֹעִים כְּלִבִּי וְרָעוּ אֶתְכֶם דֵּעָה וְהַשְׂכֵּיל

16[4] And it shall come to pass, when you multiply and increase in the land, in those days, says the LORD, they shall no longer say: The ark of the covenant of the LORD; nor shall it come to mind; nor shall they mention it; nor shall they miss it; nor shall it be made any more.

וְהָיָה כִּי תִרְבּוּ וּפְרִיתֶם בָּאָרֶץ בַּיָּמִים הָהֵמָּה נְאֻם־יְהוָה לֹא־יֹאמְרוּ עוֹד אֲרוֹן בְּרִית־יְהוָה וְלֹא יַעֲלֶה עַל־לֵב וְלֹא יִזְכְּרוּ־בוֹ וְלֹא יִפְקֹדוּ וְלֹא יֵעָשֶׂה עוֹד

17[5] At that time they will call Jerusalem The Throne of the LORD; and all the nations shall be gathered to it, to the name of the LORD, to Jerusalem; nor shall they walk after the stubbornness of their evil heart.

בָּעֵת הַהִיא יִקְרְאוּ לִירוּשָׁלַם כִּסֵּא יְהוָה וְנִקְווּ אֵלֶיהָ כָל־הַגּוֹיִם לְשֵׁם יְהוָה לִירוּשָׁלָם וְלֹא־יֵלְכוּ עוֹד אַחֲרֵי שְׁרִרוּת לִבָּם הָרָע

18[6] In those days the house of Judah shall walk with the house of Israel, and they shall come together from the land of the north to the land I gave as an inheritance to your fathers.'

בַּיָּמִים הָהֵמָּה יֵלְכוּ בֵית־יְהוּדָה עַל־בֵּית יִשְׂרָאֵל וְיָבֹאוּ יַחְדָּו מֵאֶרֶץ צָפוֹן עַל־הָאָרֶץ אֲשֶׁר הִנְחַלְתִּי אֶת־אֲבוֹתֵיכֶם

19[7] But I said: 'How would I put you among the sons, and give you a pleasant land, The finest heritage of the nations.' And I said: 'You shall

וְאָנֹכִי אָמַרְתִּי אֵיךְ אֲשִׁיתֵךְ בַּבָּנִים וְאֶתֶּן־לָךְ אֶרֶץ חֶמְדָּה נַחֲלַת צְבִי צִבְאוֹת גּוֹיִם וָאֹמַר אָבִי תִּקְרְאוּ־תִקְרְאִי־לִי וּמֵאַחֲרַי לֹא תָשׁוּבוּ "תָשׁוּבִי"

Tanchuma Kedoshim 5, Pesikta de R'Kahana 24.16, Proverbs 4:13, Psalms 79:5 86:5 86:15 7:8 7:17 1:8, Romans 5:20-5:21, Sifre Devarim Ekev 49

[1] Jeremiah 3:13 - 1 John 1:8-1:10, Deuteronomy 12:2 30:1-30:3, Ezekiel 16:15 16:24-16:25, Jeremiah 2:20 2:25 3:2 3:6 3:25 14:20 31:19-31:21, Job 33:27-33:28, Leviticus 26:40-26:42, Luke 15:18-15:21, Proverbs 4:13

[2] Jeremiah 3:14 - b.Bechorot 31a, b.Sanhedrin 97b 111a, b.Yoma 86a, Chibbur Yafeh 3 {12a}, Chibbur Yafeh 3 {12a}, Ein Yaakov Sanhedrin:111a, Ein Yaakov Sanhedrin:97b, Ein Yaakov Yoma:86a, Ezekiel 34:11-34:14, Guide for the Perplexed 1:34, Hosea 2:19-2:22, Isaiah 1:9 6:13 10:22 11:11-11:12 17:6 24:13-24:15 6:5, Jeremiah 2:2 2:19 3:1 3:8 23:3 31:9-31:11 7:33, Lamentations.R Petichata D'Chakimei:21, Mekilta de R'Ishmael Bahodesh 7:21, Midrash Psalms 10:2 85:3, Midrash Tanchuma Behar 1, Pesikta Rabbati 30:4, Romans 9:27 11:4-11:6, Ruth.R 6:2, Saadia Opinions 8:5, t.Demai 2:9, y.Yoma 8:7, Zechariah 13:7-13:9

[3] Jeremiah 3:15 - 1 Corinthians 2:6 2:12-2:13 3:1-3:2, 1 Peter 2:2 5:1-5:4, 1 Samuel 13:14, Acts 20:28, Ephesians 4:11-4:12, Ezekiel 10:23 13:24, Guide for the Perplexed 1:39, Hebrews 5:12-5:14, Isaiah 30:20-30:21, Jeremiah 23:4, John 10:1-10:5 21:15-21:17, Luke 12:42, Micah 5:5-5:6, Proverbs 10:21, z.Vayikra 20b

[4] Jeremiah 3:16 - Amos 9:9 9:14-9:15, b.Rosh Hashanah [Tosefot] 3a, Ezekiel 36:8-36:12 13:26, Hebrews 9:9-9:12 10:8-10:9 10:19-10:21, Hosea 2:1-2:2, Isaiah 12:22 13:4 17:17 66:1-66:2, Jeremiah 7:4 6:19 7:9 7:28, John 4:20-4:24, Matthew 1:11 3:9, Zechariah 8:4-8:5 10:7-10:9, Zephaniah 3:11

[5] Jeremiah 3:17 - 2 Corinthians 10:4-5, Avot de R'Natan 35, Deuteronomy 5:28, Ephesians 4:17-19, Ezekiel 1:26 19:7, Galatians 4:26, Genesis 8:21, Genesis.R 5:7 49:2 64:4, Isaiah 2:2-2:4 6:1 2:8 49:18-49:23 8:6 11:19 60:3-60:9 18:1 18:20, Jeremiah 9:15 11:8 14:21 16:12 17:12 18:12 7:24, Judges 2:19, Lamentations.R 1:26, Leviticus.R 10:9, Micah 4:1-4:5, Midrash Psalms 9:8, Midrash Tanchuma Ki Tetze 11, Midrash Tanchuma Vayigash 10, Numbers 15:39, Pesikta de R'Kahana 3.15 20.7, Pesikta Rabbati 12:9 21:8, Psalms 78:8 87:3, Romans 1:21 6:14, z.Metzorah 56a, Zechariah 2:11 8:20-23

[6] Jeremiah 3:18 - Amos 9:15, Ezekiel 37:16-37:22 39:25-39:28, Hosea 2:2 12:1, Isaiah 11:11-11:13, Jeremiah 3:12 16:15 23:8 6:3 7:9 2:4 2:20, Midrash Psalms 5:1, Zechariah 10:6

[7] Jeremiah 3:19 - 1 John 3:1-3, 1 Peter 1:3-4, 2 Corinthians 6:17-18, Apocryphon of Ezekiel Fragment 2, b.Gittin 57a, b.Ketubot 112a, Daniel 8:9 11:16 11:41 11:45, Deuteronomy.R 2:2, Ein Yaakov Gittin:57a, Ein Yaakov Ketubot:112a, Ephesians 1:5, Ezekiel 20:6, Galatians 3:26 4:5-7, Hebrews 10:39, Hosea 11:8, Isaiah 15:16 16:9, Jastrow 1258a 1371b 1687b, Jeremiah 3:4 5:7 12:10 7:10 7:21 32:39-40, John 1:11-13, Matthew 6:8-9, Midrash Psalms 5:1, Midrash Tanchuma Kedoshim 12, Midrash Tanchuma Mishpatim 17, Midrash Tanchuma Reeh 8, Midrash Tanchuma Shelach 14, mt.Hilchot Berachot 2:3, mt.Hilchot Tefilah 11:5, Numbers.R 17:1 23:7, Proverbs 3:35, Psalms 10:24, Romans 8:15-17, Sifre Devarim Ekev 37
Jeremiah 3:19-20 - Exodus.R 32:2 32:5, Midrash Tanchuma Mishpatim 17

אָכֵן בָּגְדָה אִשָּׁה מֵרֵעָהּ כֵּן בְּגַדְתֶּם בִּי בֵּית יִשְׂרָאֵל נְאֻם־יְהוָה

20[1] Surely, as a wife treacherously departs from her husband, so have you dealt treacherously with Me, O house of Israel, says the LORD.

קוֹל עַל־שְׁפָיִים נִשְׁמָע בְּכִי תַחֲנוּנֵי בְּנֵי יִשְׂרָאֵל כִּי הֶעֱווּ אֶת־דַּרְכָּם שָׁכְחוּ אֶת־יְהוָֹה אֱלֹהֵיהֶם

21[2] *Listen! On the high hills is heard*[3] the pleading weeping of the children of Israel; for they have perverted their way, they have forgotten the LORD their God.

שׁוּבוּ בָּנִים שׁוֹבָבִים אֶרְפָּה מְשׁוּבֹתֵיכֶם הִנְנוּ אָתָנוּ לָךְ כִּי אַתָּה יְהוָֹה אֱלֹהֵינוּ

22[4] Return, you backsliding children, I will heal your backslidings. 'Here we are, we are coming to you; for you are the LORD our God.

אָכֵן לַשֶּׁקֶר מִגְּבָעוֹת הָמוֹן הָרִים אָכֵן בַּיהוָֹה אֱלֹהֵינוּ תְּשׁוּעַת יִשְׂרָאֵל

23[5] Truly vain have proved the hills, the uproar on the mountains. Truly the salvation of Israel is in the LORD our God.

וְהַבֹּשֶׁת אָכְלָה אֶת־יְגִיעַ אֲבוֹתֵינוּ מִנְּעוּרֵינוּ אֶת־צֹאנָם וְאֶת־בְּקָרָם אֶת־בְּנֵיהֶם וְאֶת־בְּנוֹתֵיהֶם

24[6] But the shameful thing has devoured the labor of our fathers from our youth; their flocks and their herds, their sons and their daughters.

נִשְׁכְּבָה בְּבָשְׁתֵּנוּ וּתְכַסֵּנוּ כְּלִמָּתֵנוּ כִּי לַיהוָֹה אֱלֹהֵינוּ חָטָאנוּ אֲנַחְנוּ וַאֲבוֹתֵינוּ מִנְּעוּרֵינוּ וְעַד־הַיּוֹם הַזֶּה וְלֹא שָׁמַעְנוּ בְּקוֹל יְהוָֹה אֱלֹהֵינוּ

25[7] Let us lie down in our shame, and let our confusion cover us; for we have sinned against the LORD our God, we and our fathers, from our youth to this day; and we have not listened to the voice of the LORD our God.'

Jeremiah – Chapter 04

אִם־תָּשׁוּב יִשְׂרָאֵל נְאֻם־יְהוָה אֵלַי תָּשׁוּב וְאִם־תָּסִיר שִׁקּוּצֶיךָ מִפָּנַי וְלֹא תָנוּד

1[8] If you will return, O Israel, says the LORD, yes, return to Me; and if you will put away your detestable things from My sight, and will not waver;

וְנִשְׁבַּעְתָּ חַי־יְהוָֹה בֶּאֱמֶת בְּמִשְׁפָּט וּבִצְדָקָה וְהִתְבָּרְכוּ בוֹ גּוֹיִם וּבוֹ יִתְהַלָּלוּ

2[9] And will swear: 'As the LORD lives' in truth, in justice, and in righteousness; then shall the nations bless themselves by Him, and in Him shall they glory.

---

[1] Jeremiah 3:20 - b.Sanhedrin 82a, Ezekiel 16:15-16:52, Hosea 3:1 5:7 6:7, Isaiah 24:8, Jastrow 1475b, Jeremiah 3:1-3:2 3:8-3:10 5:11, Malachi 2:11, Mas.Kallah Rabbati 2:2

[2] Jeremiah 3:21 - 2 Corinthians 7:10, Ezekiel 7:16 23:35, Hosea 8:14 13:6, Isaiah 15:2 17:10, Jeremiah 2:32 3:2 30:15-17 7:10 31:19-31:21 50:4-50:5, Job 9:27, Micah 3:9, Numbers 22:32, Proverbs 10:9 19:3, Zechariah 12:10-14

[3] LXX *A voice from the lips was heard*

[4] Jeremiah 3:22 - 3 Enoch 16:5, Avot de R'Natan 29, b.Avodah Zara 7b, b.Bava Batra [Rashbam] 88b, b.Chagigah 15a, b.Sanhedrin 97b, b.Yoma 86a, Bahir 67, Chibbur Yafeh 27 {127b-128a}, Ecclesiastes.R 7:16, Ein Yaakov Chagigah:15a, Ein Yaakov Sanhedrin:97b, Ein Yaakov Yoma:86a, Ein Yaakov Yoma:86a, Gates of Repentance 3.171 4.006, Hosea 3:5 6:1-6:2 13:4 14:3 14:6 14:10, Isaiah 3:8, Jeremiah 6:17 7:19 9:6, Leviticus.R 19:6, Mekilta de R'Ishmael Beshallah 6:98, Midrash Proverbs 10, Midrash Psalms 10:2, mt.Hilchot Avodat Kochavim vChukkoteihem 2:5, mt.Hilchot Teshuvah 1:4 1:4 3:14 6:3 6:3, Numbers.R 11:7, Pesikta de R'Kahana 13.11, Pesikta Rabbati 44:1 44:8, Shemonah Perachim III, Shepherd Vision I 1:9, Song of Songs 1:4, t.Demai 2:9, t.Kippurim 4:6, y.Sanhedrin 10:1, y.Sheviit 1:6, z.Naso 126a, z.Vayikra 4b, Zechariah 13:9

[5] Jeremiah 3:23 - Ezekiel 20:28, Hosea 1:7, Isaiah 12:2 19:11 20:9 21:15 21:17 21:20 46:7-46:8 15:1 15:16, Jeremiah 3:6 10:14-10:16 14:8 17:14, John 4:22, Jonah 2:8-2:9, Psalms 3:9 37:39-40 121:1-2

[6] Jeremiah 3:24 - Ezekiel 16:61 16:23, Hosea 2:8 9:10 10:6, Jeremiah 11:13

[7] Jeremiah 3:25 - Daniel 9:6-9:10 12:2, Deuteronomy 31:17-31:18, Deuteronomy.R 2:24, Ezekiel 7:18 12:32, Ezra 9:6-9:15, Genesis.R 68:13, Isaiah 24:8 2:11, Jeremiah 2:2 2:17 2:19 2:26 6:26 22:21, Judges 2:2, Lamentations 5:7 5:16, Nehemiah 9:32-9:34, Pesikta de R'Kahana 24.16, Proverbs 5:13, Psalms 10:7 13:29, Romans 6:21

[8] Jeremiah 4:1 - 1 Samuel 7:3, 2 Chronicles 15:8 9:8, 2 Kings 23:13 23:24, b.Pesachim [Tosefot] 107b, b.Sanhedrin 98a, Deuteronomy 3:15, Ein Yaakov Sanhedrin:97b, Ephesians 4:22-4:31, Ezekiel 11:18 18:13 20:7-20:8 19:9, Genesis 11:2, Hosea 2:2 7:16 14:3, Isaiah 7:6, Jeremiah 3:1 3:12 3:14 3:22 4:4 15:4 22:3-22:5 24:9 1:5 11:15 12:3, Joel 2:12, Joshua 24:14, Judges 10:16, Midrash Proverbs 6, Midrash Tanchuma Vayikra 7, mt.Hilchot Teshuvah 7:6 7:6, Pesikta Rabbati 44:5

Jeremiah 4:1-2 - Haftarah Massai [continued from 2:4-28 Sephard], Haftarah Massei Part Two Sephard [Jeremiah 4:1-2], Siman 122:6

[9] Jeremiah 4:2 - 1 Corinthians 1:31, 1 Kings 3:6, 2 Corinthians 10:17, Deuteronomy 10:20, Galatians 3:8, Genesis 22:18, Hosea 2:19, Isaiah 21:23 21:25 48:1-48:2 17:16, Jeremiah 5:2 9:25 12:16, Midrash Tanchuma Mattot 1, Midrash Tanchuma Vayikra 7, Numbers.R 9:40 22:1, Philippians 3:3, Psalms 72:17 99:4, Zechariah 8:8

כִּי־כֹה‏ אָמַ֣ר יְהֹוָ֗ה לְאִ֤ישׁ יְהוּדָה֙ וְלִיר֣וּשָׁלַ֔͏ִם גִּ֥ירוּ לָכֶ֖ם גִּ֑יר וְאַֽל־תִּזְרְע֖וּ אֶל־קוֹצִֽים׃ 3[1]

For thus says the LORD to the men of Judah and to Jerusalem: break up for yourself a fallow ground, and do not sow among thorns.

הִמֹּ֣לוּ לַֽיהֹוָ֗ה וְהָסִ֙רוּ֙ עׇרְל֣וֹת לְבַבְכֶ֔ם אִ֥ישׁ יְהוּדָ֖ה וְיֹשְׁבֵ֣י יְרֽוּשָׁלָ֑͏ִם פֶּן־תֵּצֵ֨א כָאֵ֜שׁ חֲמָתִ֗י וּבָעֲרָה֙ וְאֵ֣ין מְכַבֶּ֔ה מִפְּנֵ֖י רֹ֥עַ מַעַלְלֵיכֶֽם׃ 4[2]

Circumcise yourselves to the LORD, and take away the foreskins of your heart, you men of Judah and inhabitants of Jerusalem; lest My fury go forth like fire, and burn so no one can sate it, because of the evil of your deeds.

הַגִּ֣ידוּ בִיהוּדָ֗ה וּבִירוּשָׁלַ֙͏ִם֙ הַשְׁמִ֔יעוּ וְאִמְר֕וּ ׳וְתִקְע֥וּ׳ ׳תִּקְעוּ׳ שׁוֹפָ֖ר בָּאָ֑רֶץ קִרְא֤וּ מַלְאוּ֙ וְאִמְר֣וּ הֵאָסְפ֔וּ וְנָב֖וֹאָה אֶל־עָרֵ֥י הַמִּבְצָֽר׃ 5[3]

Declare in Judah, and publish in Jerusalem, and say: 'Blow the horn in the land;' Cry aloud and say: 'Assemble yourselves, and let us go into the fortified cities.'

שְׂאוּ־נֵ֣ס צִיּ֔וֹנָה הָעִ֖יזוּ אַֽל־תַּעֲמֹ֑דוּ כִּ֣י רָעָ֗ה אָנֹכִ֛י מֵבִ֥יא מִצָּפ֖וֹן וְשֶׁ֥בֶר גָּדֽוֹל׃ 6[4]

Set up a standard toward Zion; put yourselves under covert, do not stay[5]; For I will bring evil from the north, and a great destruction.

עָלָ֤ה אַרְיֵה֙ מִֽסֻּבְּכ֔וֹ וּמַשְׁחִ֣ית גּוֹיִ֔ם נָסַ֖ע יָצָ֣א מִמְּקֹמ֑וֹ לָשׂ֤וּם אַרְצֵךְ֙ לְשַׁמָּ֔ה עָרַ֥יִךְ תִּצֶּ֖ינָה מֵאֵ֥ין יוֹשֵֽׁב׃ 7[6]

A lion has gone up from his thicket, and a destroyer of nations has set out, gone forth from his place; to make your land desolate, so your cities are laid waste, without inhabitant.

עַל־זֹ֛את חִגְר֥וּ שַׂקִּ֖ים סִפְד֣וּ וְהֵילִ֑ילוּ כִּ֛י לֹא־שָׁ֥ב חֲרֽוֹן אַף־יְהֹוָ֖ה מִמֶּֽנּוּ׃ 8[7]

For this gird, yourself with sackcloth, lament and wail; for the fierce anger of the LORD has not turned back from us.

וְהָיָ֤ה בַיּוֹם־הַהוּא֙ נְאֻם־יְהֹוָ֔ה יֹאבַ֥ד לֵב־הַמֶּ֖לֶךְ וְלֵ֣ב הַשָּׂרִ֑ים וְנָשַׁ֙מּוּ֙ הַכֹּ֣הֲנִ֔ים וְהַנְּבִיאִ֖ים יִתְמָֽהוּ׃ 9[8]

And it shall come to pass on that day, says the LORD, that the heart of the king shall fail, and the heart of the princes; and the priests shall be astonished, and the prophets shall wonder.

וָאֹמַ֞ר אֲהָ֣הּ׀ אֲדֹנָ֣י יֱהֹוִ֗ה אָכֵן֩ הַשֵּׁ֨א הִשֵּׁ֜אתָ לָעָ֤ם הַזֶּה֙ וְלִירוּשָׁלַ֣͏ִם לֵאמֹ֔ר שָׁל֖וֹם יִֽהְיֶ֣ה לָכֶ֑ם וְנָגְעָ֥ה חֶ֖רֶב עַד־הַנָּֽפֶשׁ׃ 10[9]

Then said I: 'Ah, Lord GOD. Surely you have greatly deceived this people and Jerusalem, saying: You shall have peace; while the sword reaches to the soul.'

בָּעֵ֣ת הַהִ֗יא יֵאָמֵ֤ר לָֽעָם־הַזֶּה֙ וְלִיר֣וּשָׁלַ֔͏ִם ר֣וּחַ צַ֤ח שְׁפָיִים֙ בַּמִּדְבָּ֔ר דֶּ֖רֶךְ בַּת־עַמִּ֑י ל֥וֹא לִזְר֖וֹת וְל֥וֹא לְהָבַֽר׃ 11[10]

At that time shall it be said of this people and of Jerusalem: *A hot wind of the high hills in the wilderness toward the daughter of My people, neither to fan, nor to cleanse*[11];

ר֧וּחַ מָלֵ֛א מֵאֵ֖לֶּה יָ֣בוֹא לִ֑י עַתָּ֕ה גַּם־אֲנִ֛י אֲדַבֵּ֥ר מִשְׁפָּטִ֖ים אוֹתָֽם׃ 12[12]

A wind too strong for this shall come for Me; now I will also utter judgments against them.

---

[1] Jeremiah 4:3 - b.Bava Batra [Rashi] 24b, b.Menachot [Rashi] 85a, b.Pesachim 107b, Galatians 6:7-6:8, Genesis 3:18, Hosea 10:12, Luke 8:7 8:14, Mark 4:7 4:18-4:19, Matthew 13:7 13:22, t.Pisha 10:5, z.Vaetchanan 269b

[2] Jeremiah 4:4 - Amos 5:6, Colossians 2:11, Deuteronomy 10:16 6:6 8:22, Ezekiel 5:13-15 6:12 8:18 16:38 18:31 20:33 21:3-4 21:22 24:8 24:13, Isaiah 30:27-28 3:17, Jeremiah 9:27 21:5 21:12 23:19 12:7, Lamentations 4:11, Leviticus 2:28, Mark 9:43-50, Romans 2:28-29, Zephaniah 2:2

[3] Jeremiah 4:5 - 4QJerc, Amos 3:6 3:8, Ezekiel 33:2-33:6, Hosea 8:1, Jeremiah 5:20 6:1 8:14 9:13 11:2 11:11, Joshua 10:20

[4] Jeremiah 4:6 - Isaiah 14:10, Jeremiah 1:13-1:15 4:21 6:1 6:22 21:7 1:9 2:2 2:22 3:12 3:27 3:54, Zephaniah 1:10

[5] LXX Gather up your wares and flee to Sion: quickly, do not stay

[6] Jeremiah 4:7 - 2 Kings 24:1 1:1, b.Avodah Zara [Tosefot] 2b, b.Berachot 56b, b.Megillah 11a, b.Sanhedrin 94b, Daniel 5:19 7:4, Ein Yaakov Megillah:11a, Ein Yaakov Sanhedrin:94b, Exodus.R 29:9, Ezekiel 21:24-21:26 26:7-26:10 30:10-30:11, Isaiah 1:7 5:9 6:11, Jastrow 710a, Jeremiah 2:15 5:6 9:12 1:9 1:38 2:9 3:8 9:10 10:22 1:19 2:17 2:44, Lamentations.R Petichata D'Chakimei:1, Leviticus.R 13:5, Pesikta de R'Kahana 13.1 13.15, Pesikta Rabbati 27/28:1 33:13

[7] Jeremiah 4:8 - Amos 8:10, Ezekiel 21:17 6:2, History of the Rechabites 8:6, Isaiah 5:25 9:13 9:18 9:22 10:4 13:6 15:2-3 22:12 8:11, Jeremiah 6:26 6:24 24:20, Joel 2:12-13, Numbers 1:4, Psalms 78:49

[8] Jeremiah 4:9 - 1 Samuel 25:37-25:38, 2 Kings 1:4, Acts 13:41, Ezekiel 13:9-16, Isaiah 19:3 19:11-12 19:16 21:3-4 22:3-5 29:9-10, Jeremiah 5:31 6:13-14 13:19 39:4-5 4:7, Lamentations.R 1:51, Psalms 6:5

[9] Jeremiah 4:10 - 1 Kings 22:20-22:23, 2 Thessalonians 2:9-2:12, Exodus 9:14, Ezekiel 11:13 14:9-14:10, Isaiah 6:10 13:35 15:17, Jeremiah 1:6 4:18 5:12 6:14 8:11 14:13-14:14 23:17 8:17, Lamentations 2:21, Romans 1:24 1:26 1:28, Saadia Opinions 4:6

[10] Jeremiah 4:11 - Ezekiel 17:10 19:12, Hosea 13:3 13:15, Isaiah 22:4 3:8 17:16 16:7, Jeremiah 8:19 9:2 9:8 14:17 23:19 30:23-24 51:1-2, Lamentations 2:11 3:48 4:3 4:6 4:10, Luke 3:17, Matthew 3:12 Jeremiah 4:11-13 - Psalms of Solomon 8:2

[11] LXX *here is a spirit of error in the wilderness: the way of the daughter of my people is not purity, nor holiness*

[12] Jeremiah 4:12 - Ezekiel 5:8 6:11-6:13 7:8-7:9, Jeremiah 1:16

Hebrew	#	English
הִנֵּה כַּעֲנָנִים יַעֲלֶה וְכַסּוּפָה מַרְכְּבוֹתָיו קַלּוּ מִנְּשָׁרִים סוּסָיו אוֹי לָנוּ כִּי שֻׁדָּדְנוּ	13[1]	Behold, he comes up as clouds, and his chariots are like the whirlwind; his horses are swifter than eagles. Woe to us, for we are undone.'
כַּבְּסִי מֵרָעָה לִבֵּךְ יְרוּשָׁלַם לְמַעַן תִּוָּשֵׁעִי עַד־מָתַי תָּלִין בְּקִרְבֵּךְ מַחְשְׁבוֹת אוֹנֵךְ	14[2]	O Jerusalem, wash your heart from wickedness so you may be saved. How long shall your sinister thoughts lodge within you?
כִּי קוֹל מַגִּיד מִדָּן וּמַשְׁמִיעַ אָוֶן מֵהַר אֶפְרָיִם	15[3]	Listen. One declares from Dan, and announces calamity from the hills of Ephraim:
הַזְכִּירוּ לַגּוֹיִם הִנֵּה הַשְׁמִיעוּ עַל־יְרוּשָׁלַם נֹצְרִים בָּאִים מֵאֶרֶץ הַמֶּרְחָק וַיִּתְּנוּ עַל־עָרֵי יְהוּדָה קוֹלָם	16[4]	Make mention to the nations: Behold, publish concerning Jerusalem, watchers come from a far country, and give their voice against the cities of Judah.
כְּשֹׁמְרֵי שָׂדַי הָיוּ עָלֶיהָ מִסָּבִיב כִּי־אֹתִי מָרָתָה נְאֻם־יְהוָה	17[5]	As keepers of a field who are against her; because she has been rebellious against Me, says the LORD.
דַּרְכֵּךְ וּמַעֲלָלַיִךְ עָשׂוֹ אֵלֶּה לָךְ זֹאת רָעָתֵךְ כִּי מָר כִּי נָגַע עַד־לִבֵּךְ	18[6]	Your way and your deeds have procured these things to you; this is your wickedness; yes, it is bitter. Yes, it reaches to your heart.
מֵעַי מֵעַי 'אָחוּלָה' "אוֹחִילָה" קִירוֹת לִבִּי הֹמֶה־לִּי לִבִּי לֹא אַחֲרִישׁ כִּי קוֹל שׁוֹפָר 'שָׁמַעְתִּי' "שָׁמַעַתְּ" נַפְשִׁי תְּרוּעַת מִלְחָמָה	19[7]	My bowels, my bowels! I writhe in pain. *The chambers of my heart. My heart moans within me*[8]. I cannot hold my peace because you have heard, O my soul, the sound of the horn, the alarm of war.
שֶׁבֶר עַל־שֶׁבֶר נִקְרָא כִּי שֻׁדְּדָה כָּל־הָאָרֶץ פִּתְאֹם שֻׁדְּדוּ אֹהָלַי רֶגַע יְרִיעֹתָי	20[9]	Destruction follows destruction, for the whole land is spoiled; suddenly my tents are spoiled, my curtains *in a moment*[10].
עַד־מָתַי אֶרְאֶה־נֵּס אֶשְׁמְעָה קוֹל שׁוֹפָר	21[11]	How long shall I see *the standard*[12], shall I hear the sound of the horn?
כִּי אֱוִיל עַמִּי אוֹתִי לֹא יָדָעוּ בָּנִים סְכָלִים הֵמָּה וְלֹא נְבוֹנִים הֵמָּה חֲכָמִים הֵמָּה לְהָרַע וּלְהֵיטִיב לֹא יָדָעוּ	22[13]	For My people are foolish, they do not know Me. They are stupid children, and they have no understanding; they are wise to do evil, but to do good they have no knowledge.

---

[1] Jeremiah 4:13 - Daniel 7:4, Deuteronomy 4:49, Habakkuk 1:8, Hosea 8:1, Isaiah 5:28 13:5 19:1 18:15, Jeremiah 4:31 10:19, Lamentations 4:19, Life of Adam and Eve [Vita] 25:2, Matthew 24:30, Nahum 1:3 2:4-2:5, Revelation 1:7 Jeremiah 4:13-16 - 4QJerc

[2] Jeremiah 4:14 - 1 Corinthians 3:20, Acts 8:22, b.Rosh Hashanah 18a, Ein Yaakov Rosh Hashanah 18a, Ezekiel 18:31, Gates of Repentance 1.009, Isaiah 1:16-19 7:7, James 4:8, Jeremiah 13:27, Luke 11:39, Matthew 12:33 15:19-20 23:26-27, Midrash Tanchuma Haazinu 4, Numbers.R 11:7, Pesikta de R'Kahana S7.1, Pesikta Rabbati 48:3, Proverbs 1:22, Psalms 66:18 119:113, Romans 1:21

[3] Jeremiah 4:15 - Jeremiah 6:1 8:16, Joshua 17:15 20:7, Judges 18:29 20:1

[4] Jeremiah 4:16 - b.Shekalim [Taklin Chadatin] 2a, Deuteronomy 28:49-52, Ezekiel 21:27, Isaiah 10:1 15:3, Jeremiah 2:15 4:17 5:6 5:15 6:18 16:6 7:11 15:1 2:2

[5] Jeremiah 4:17 - 2 Kings 25:1-25:4, Daniel 9:7-9:19, Ezekiel 2:3-2:7, Isaiah 1:8 1:20-1:23 6:9, Jeremiah 5:23 6:2-6:3, Lamentations 1:8 1:18, Luke 19:43-19:44 21:20-21:24, Nehemiah 9:26 9:30

[6] Jeremiah 4:18 - Isaiah 2:1, Jeremiah 2:17 2:19 5:19 6:19 2:19, Job 20:5-20:16, Lamentations.R Petichata D'Chakimei:16, Pesikta Rabbati 31:2, Proverbs 1:31 5:22, Psalms 11:17

[7] Jeremiah 4:19 - Amos 3:6, b.Berachot 10b, Daniel 7:15 7:28 8:27, Ecclesiastes.R 5:4, Ein Yaakov Berachot:10b, Galatians 4:19, Genesis 1:6, Guide for the Perplexed 1:46, Habakkuk 3:16, Isaiah 15:5 16:11 21:3 22:4, Jeremiah 4:5 4:21 9:2 9:11 13:17 14:17-14:18 20:9 23:9 48:31-48:32, Judges 5:21, Lamentations 1:16 2:11 3:48-3:51, Luke 19:41-19:42, Numbers 10:9, Numbers.R 9:7, Pesikta Rabbati 26:1/2 27/28:1 33:13, Psalms 16:2 42:6-42:7 7:1 20:7 119:136 23:53 2:1, Psalms of Solomon 2:14, Romans 9:2-9:3 10:1, Song of Songs.R 5:4, Testament of Zebulun 2:5, y.Berachot 4:4, y.Rosh Hashanah 4:7, y.Sanhedrin 10:2, Zephaniah 1:15-1:16

[8] LXX *and the sensitive powers of my heart; my soul is in great commotion, my heart is torn*

[9] Jeremiah 4:20 - 2 Thessalonians 1:9, Exodus 9:5, Ezekiel 7:25-26 14:21, Habakkuk 3:7, Isaiah 13:6 9:20 23:9 6:2, Jeremiah 4:6 10:19-20 17:18, Joel 1:15, Lamentations 2:6-9 3:47, Leviticus 2:18 2:21 2:24 2:28, Matthew 10:28, Numbers 16:21 17:10, Psalms 42:8 72:19

[10] LXX *have been rent asunder*

[11] Jeremiah 4:21 - 2 Chronicles 11:25 12:3 36:6-36:7 12:10 12:17, Jeremiah 4:5-4:6 4:19 6:1

[12] LXX *fugitives*

[13] Jeremiah 4:22 - 1 Corinthians 1:20-1:21 14:20, 2 Samuel 13:3 16:21-16:23, b.Eruvin 26a, b.Kiddushin 36a, Deuteronomy 8:6 8:28, Exodus.R 25:8, Genesis.R 50:8, Guide for the Perplexed 3:54, Hosea 4:1 4:6 5:4, Isaiah 1:3 6:9-6:10 3:11 29:10-29:12 42:19-42:20, Jastrow 1553b, Jeremiah 5:4 5:21 8:7-8:9 10:8 13:23, John 16:3, Lamentations.R Petichata D'Chakimei:14, Leviticus.R 27:8, Luke 16:8, Matthew 23:16-23:26, Micah 2:1, mt.Pirkei Avot 5:13, Numbers.R 9:7, Pesikta de R'Kahana 9.8, Psalms 14:1-14:4, Romans 1:22 1:28 3:11 16:19, Sifre Devarim {Haazinu Hashamayim} 308, Sifre Devarim Nitzavim 308, y.Yevamot 12:6

רָאִיתִי אֶת־הָאָרֶץ וְהִנֵּה־תֹהוּ וָבֹהוּ וְאֶל־הַשָּׁמַיִם וְאֵין אוֹרָם

23[1]   I viewed the earth, and, lo, it was waste and void; and the heavens, and they had no light.

רָאִיתִי הֶהָרִים וְהִנֵּה רֹעֲשִׁים וְכָל־הַגְּבָעוֹת הִתְקַלְקָלוּ

24[2]   I viewed the mountains, and, lo, they trembled, and all the hills moved to and fro.

רָאִיתִי וְהִנֵּה אֵין הָאָדָם וְכָל־עוֹף הַשָּׁמַיִם נָדָדוּ

25[3]   I looked, and, lo, there was no man, and all the birds of the heavens fled.

רָאִיתִי וְהִנֵּה הַכַּרְמֶל הַמִּדְבָּר וְכָל־עָרָיו נִתְּצוּ מִפְּנֵי יְהוָה מִפְּנֵי חֲרוֹן אַפּוֹ

26[4]   I looked, and, lo, *the fruitful field*[5] was a wilderness, and all its cities *were broken down*[6] at the presence of the LORD, and before His fierce anger.

כִּי־כֹה אָמַר יְהוָה שְׁמָמָה תִהְיֶה כָּל־הָאָרֶץ וְכָלָה לֹא אֶעֱשֶׂה

27[7]   For thus says the LORD: The whole land shall be desolate; yet will I not make a full end.

עַל־זֹאת תֶּאֱבַל הָאָרֶץ וְקָדְרוּ הַשָּׁמַיִם מִמָּעַל עַל כִּי־דִבַּרְתִּי זַמֹּתִי וְלֹא נִחַמְתִּי וְלֹא־אָשׁוּב מִמֶּנָּה

28[8]   For this shall the earth mourn, and the heavens above will be black; because I have spoken it, I have intended it, and I have not repented, nor will I turn back from it.

מִקּוֹל פָּרָשׁ וְרֹמֵה קֶשֶׁת בֹּרַחַת כָּל־הָעִיר בָּאוּ בֶּעָבִים וּבַכֵּפִים עָלוּ כָּל־הָעִיר עֲזוּבָה וְאֵין־יוֹשֵׁב בָּהֵן אִישׁ

29[9]   The whole city flees for the noise of the horsemen and bowmen; they go into the thickets and climb up upon the rocks; every city is forsaken, and no one dwells in it.

וְאַתִּי שָׁדוּד מַה־תַּעֲשִׂי כִּי־תִלְבְּשִׁי שָׁנִי כִּי־תַעְדִּי עֲדִי־זָהָב כִּי־תִקְרְעִי בַפּוּךְ עֵינַיִךְ לַשָּׁוְא תִּתְיַפִּי מָאֲסוּ־בָךְ עֹגְבִים נַפְשֵׁךְ יְבַקֵּשׁוּ

30[10]   And you, who are spoiled, what will you do, you who clothe yourself with scarlet, you deck yourself with ornaments of gold, you enlarge your eyes with *paint*[11]? In vain you make yourself fair; your lovers despise you, they seek your life.

כִּי קוֹל כְּחוֹלָה שָׁמַעְתִּי צָרָה כְּמַבְכִּירָה קוֹל בַּת־צִיּוֹן תִּתְיַפֵּחַ תְּפָרֵשׂ כַּפֶּיהָ אוֹי־נָא לִי כִּי־עָיְפָה נַפְשִׁי לְהֹרְגִים

31[12]   For I have heard a voice as of a woman in travail, the anguish as of her who brings forth her first child, the voice of the daughter of Zion, who gasps for breath, who spreads her hands: 'Woe is me, now! for my soul faints *before the murderers*[13].'

---

[1] Jeremiah 4:23 - Acts 2:19-20, Amos 8:9, Deuteronomy.R 10:4, Esther.R Petichata:11, Ezekiel 32:7-8, Genesis 1:2, Genesis.R 2:2 2:4-5 42:3, Guide for the Perplexed 2:29, Isaiah 5:30 13:10 24:19-23, Jeremiah 9:11, Joel 2:10 3:3-4 4:15-16, Luke 21:25-26, Mark 13:24-25, Matthew 24:29 24:35, Pesikta de R'Kahana S6.2, Pesikta Rabbati 33:6, Revelation 20:11, Ruth.R Petichata:7

[2] Jeremiah 4:24 - 1 Kings 19:11, Ezekiel 14:20, Habakkuk 3:6 3:10, Isaiah 5:25, Jeremiah 8:16 10:10, Judges 5:4-5:5, Lamentations.R 1:3, Micah 1:4, Nahum 1:5-1:6, Pesikta de R'Kahana S5.2 S6.2, Psalms 18:8 77:19 97:4 114:4-114:7

[3] Jeremiah 4:25 - Hosea 4:3, Jeremiah 9:11 12:4, Zephaniah 1:2-1:3

[4] Jeremiah 4:26 - Deuteronomy 29:22-27, Isaiah 5:9-10 7:20-25, Jeremiah 12:4 14:2-6, Micah 3:12, Psalms 76:8 11:34, Ralbag SOS 5

[5] LXX *carmel*

[6] *LXX burnt with fire*

[7] Jeremiah 4:27 - 2 Chronicles 12:21, Amos 9:8-9:9, Ezekiel 6:14 11:13 9:28, Isaiah 6:11-6:12 24:1 24:3-24:13, Jeremiah 4:7 5:10 5:18 7:34 12:11-12:12 18:16 6:11 22:28, Leviticus 2:44, Midrash Psalms 50:1, Romans 9:27-9:29 11:1-11:7

[8] Jeremiah 4:28 - 1 Samuel 15:29, Ephesians 1:9 1:11, Ezekiel 24:14, Hebrews 7:21, Hosea 4:3 13:14, Isaiah 5:30 14:24-14:27 24:4 33:8-33:9 10:4 46:10-46:11 2:3, Jeremiah 4:23-4:26 7:16 12:4 12:11 14:2 14:11-14:12 15:1-15:9 23:10 23:20 6:24, Joel 1:10 3:3-3:4, Luke 23:44, Mark 15:33, Matthew 3:45, Numbers 23:19, Revelation 6:12

[9] Jeremiah 4:29 - 1 Samuel 13:6, 2 Chronicles 9:11, 2 Kings 25:4-25:7, Amos 9:1, Isaiah 2:19-2:21 6:17, Jeremiah 4:7 39:4-39:6 4:7, Lamentations.R 2:1 2:1, Luke 23:30, Mekilta de R'Ishmael Shirata 4:5, Revelation 6:15-6:17

[10] Jeremiah 4:30 - 2 Kings 9:30, b.Bava Batra 16b, b.Chagigah 15b, b.Pesachim [Tosefot] 114a, Ein Yaakov Bava Batra:16b, Ein Yaakov Chagigah:15a, Ezekiel 16:36-41 23:9-10 23:22-24 23:28-29 23:40-41 4:9 4:13, Hebrews 2:3, Isaiah 10:3 20:6 9:14, Jastrow 1502a, Jeremiah 5:31 13:21 22:20-22, Lamentations 1:2 1:19 4:17, Pesikta Rabbati 26:1/2, Revelation 17:2 17:4 17:13 17:16-18

[11] LXX *stibium*

[12] Jeremiah 4:31 - 1 Corinthians 9:16, 1 Thessalonians 5:3, b.Bava Batra 16b, Ezekiel 9:5-9:6 23:46-23:47, Genesis 3:46, Genesis.R 63:12, Hosea 13:13, Isaiah 1:15 6:5 13:8 21:3 18:14, Jeremiah 6:2 6:23-6:24 10:19 13:21 14:18 15:18 18:21 22:23 6:6 21:2 24:41 1:22 1:24 2:43, Job 10:1, Lamentations 1:17 1:20 2:21, Liber Antiquitatum Biblicarum 12:5, Matthew 21:5, Micah 7:1, Midrash Tanchuma Ki Tetze 4, Pesikta de R'Kahana 3.1, Pesikta Rabbati 12:4, Psalms 24:5, Sifre Devarim {Haazinu Hashamayim} 319, Sifre Devarim Nitzavim 319, z.Toledot 142b

[13] LXX *because of the slain*

Jeremiah – Chapter 05

שׁוֹטְט֞וּ בְּחוּצ֣וֹת יְרוּשָׁלִַ֗ם וּרְאוּ־נָ֤א וּדְעוּ֙ וּבַקְשׁ֣וּ בִרְחוֹבוֹתֶ֔יהָ אִם־תִּמְצְא֣וּ אִ֔ישׁ אִם־יֵ֛שׁ עֹשֶׂ֥ה מִשְׁפָּ֖ט מְבַקֵּ֣שׁ אֱמוּנָ֑ה וְאֶסְלַ֖ח לָֽהּ	1[1] Run to and fro through the streets of Jerusalem, and see now, and know, and look in its broad places, if you can find a man, if there are any who does justly, who seeks truth; and I will pardon her.
וְאִ֥ם חַי־יְהֹוָ֖ה יֹאמֵ֑רוּ לָכֵ֥ן לַשֶּׁ֖קֶר יִשָּׁבֵֽעוּ	2[2] And though they say: 'As the LORD lives,' surely they swear falsely.
יְהֹוָ֗ה עֵינֶיךָ֮ הֲל֣וֹא לֶאֱמוּנָה֒ הִכִּ֤יתָה אֹתָם֙ וְלֹֽא־חָ֔לוּ כִּלִּיתָ֕ם מֵאֲנ֖וּ קַ֣חַת מוּסָ֑ר חִזְּק֤וּ פְנֵיהֶם֙ מִסֶּ֔לַע מֵאֲנ֖וּ לָשֽׁוּב	3[3] O LORD, are your eyes not on truth? You have struck them, but they were not affected; you consumed them, but they refused to receive correction; they made their faces harder than a rock; they refused to return.
וַאֲנִ֣י אָמַ֔רְתִּי אַךְ־דַּלִּ֖ים הֵ֑ם נוֹאֲל֗וּ כִּ֣י לֹ֤א יָֽדְעוּ֙ דֶּ֣רֶךְ יְהֹוָ֔ה מִשְׁפַּ֖ט אֱלֹהֵיהֶֽם	4[4] And I said: 'Surely these are poor. They are foolish, for they do not know the way of the LORD, nor the ordinance of their God;
אֵֽלְכָה־לִּ֤י אֶל־הַגְּדֹלִים֙ וַאֲדַבְּרָ֣ה אוֹתָ֔ם כִּ֣י הֵ֗מָּה יָדְעוּ֙ דֶּ֣רֶךְ יְהֹוָ֔ה מִשְׁפַּ֖ט אֱלֹהֵיהֶ֑ם אַ֣ךְ הֵ֤מָּה יַחְדָּו֙ שָׁ֣בְרוּ עֹ֔ל נִתְּק֖וּ מוֹסֵרֽוֹת	5[5] I will get to the great men, and will speak to them; for they know the way of the LORD, and the ordinance of their God.' But these altogether broke the yoke, and burst the bands.
עַל־כֵּן֩ הִכָּ֨ם אַרְיֵ֜ה מִיַּ֗עַר זְאֵ֤ב עֲרָבוֹת֙ יְשָׁדְדֵ֔ם נָמֵ֣ר שֹׁקֵ֣ד עַל־עָרֵיהֶ֗ם כׇּל־הַיּוֹצֵ֤א מֵהֵ֙נָּה֙ יִטָּרֵ֔ף כִּ֤י רַבּוּ֙ פִּשְׁעֵיהֶ֔ם עָצְמ֖וּ 'מְשֻׁבוֹתֵיהֶם' "מְשׁוּבוֹתֵיהֶֽם":	6[6] Why a lion from the forest doesn't slay them, a wolf of the deserts does spoil them, a leopard watches over their cities, everyone who goes out there is torn in pieces; because their transgressions are many, their backslidings have increased.
אֵ֤י לָזֹאת֙ 'אֶסְלוֹחַ־אֶסְלַח־לָ֔ךְ' בָּנַ֣יִךְ עֲזָב֔וּנִי וַיִּשָּׁבְע֖וּ בְּלֹ֣א אֱלֹהִ֑ים וָאַשְׂבִּ֤עַ אוֹתָם֙ וַיִּנְאָ֔פוּ וּבֵ֥ית זוֹנָ֖ה יִתְגֹּדָֽדוּ	7[7] Why should I pardon you? The children have forsaken Me, and have sworn by no gods; and when I fed them to the full, they committed adultery, and assembled themselves in troops at the harlots' houses.
סוּסִ֥ים מְיֻזָּנִ֖ים מַשְׁכִּ֣ים הָי֑וּ אִ֛ישׁ אֶל־אֵ֥שֶׁת רֵעֵ֖הוּ יִצְהָֽלוּ	8[8] They became as well-fed horses, lusty stallions; everyone neighs after his neighbor's wife.

---

[1] Jeremiah 5:1 - 1 Kings 19:10, 2 Chronicles 16:9, 2 Thessalonians 2:10, Amos 8:12, b.Chagigah 14a, b.Shabbat 119b, Daniel 12:4, Ein Yaakov Chagigah:13b, Ein Yaakov Chagigah:14b, Ein Yaakov Shabbat 119b, Ezekiel 22:30, Genesis 18:23-18:32, Genesis.R 49:13, Isaiah 11:4 59:14-59:15, Joel 2:9, Luke 14:21, Micah 7:1-7:2, Midrash Tanchuma Vayera 8, Proverbs 2:4-2:6 8:3 20:6 23:23, Psalms 12:2 14:3 53:3-53:5, Song of Songs 3:2, Zechariah 2:4

[2] Jeremiah 5:2 - 1 Timothy 1:10, 2 Timothy 3:5, Hosea 4:1-4:2 4:15 10:4, Isaiah 24:1, Jeremiah 4:2 7:9, Leviticus 19:12, Malachi 3:5, Pesikta de R'Kahana 134 13.8, Pesikta Rabbati 27:4, Titus 1:16, Zechariah 5:3-5:4

[3] Jeremiah 5:3 - 2 Chronicles 16:9 4:22, Exodus.R 31:16, Ezekiel 3:7-3:9 24:13, Guide for the Perplexed 3:36, Hebrews 12:9, Isaiah 1:5-1:6 9:14 18:25 24:4, Jeremiah 2:30 7:26 7:28 19:15 8:19, Mekhilta de R'Shimon bar Yochai Beshallach 26:6, Mekilta de R'Ishmael Beshallah 7:154, Mesillat Yesharim 11:Traits-of-Nekuyut, Midrash Psalms 119:18, Midrash Tanchuma Mishpatim 12, mt.Hilchot Evel 13:12, Proverbs 21:29 22:12 23:35 3:22, Psalms 11:5-11:8 51:7, Romans 2:2 2:4-2:5, Siman 215:3, y.Taanit 3:6, Zechariah 7:11-7:12, Zephaniah 3:1-3:2 3:7

[4] Jeremiah 5:4 - Hosea 4:6, Isaiah 3:11 28:9-13, Jeremiah 4:22 7:8 8:7, John 7:48-49, Matthew 11:5

[5] Jeremiah 5:5 - Acts 4:26-4:27, Amos 4:1, Ezekiel 22:6-22:8 22:25-22:29, James 2:5-2:7, Jeremiah 2:20 6:13, Luke 18:24 19:14, Malachi 2:7, Matthew 19:23-19:26, Micah 3:1-3:4 3:11 7:3-7:4, Psalms 2:2-3, Zephaniah 3:3-5

[6] Jeremiah 5:6 - Amos 5:18-5:19, Daniel 7:4 7:6, Esther.R Petichata:5, Ezekiel 14:16-14:21 16:25 22:27 23:19, Ezra 9:6 10:10, Genesis.R 99 [Excl]:2, Habakkuk 1:8, Hosea 5:14 13:7-13:8, Isaiah 11:12, Jeremiah 2:15 2:17 2:19 4:7 9:13-9:15 14:7 16:10-16:12 1:38 6:14 6:24 1:19, Lamentations 1:5, Leviticus.R 13:5, mt.Hilchot Melachim uMichamoteihem 12:1, Nahum 2:12-2:13, Numbers 8:14, Pesikta Rabbati 33:13, Psalms 8:20, Revelation 13:2, Zephaniah 3:3

[7] Jeremiah 5:7 - 1 Corinthians 6:9 8:4, 4Q182 frag 1, Amos 8:14, Deuteronomy 8:15 8:21, Ezekiel 16:49-16:50 22:11, Galatians 4:8, Gates of Repentance 3.045, Guide for the Perplexed 3:49, Hebrews 13:4, Hosea 4:2 4:13-4:15 7:4 11:8 13:6, James 4:4 5:1-5:5, Jeremiah 2:11 2:31 3:19 9:3 12:16 13:27 23:10 29:22-29:23, Joshua 23:7, Leviticus 20:10, ll.4-5, Malachi 3:5, Matthew 23:37-23:38, Numbers 25:1-25:3, Psalms 50:18, Saadia Opinions 10:6, Zephaniah 1:5

[8] Jeremiah 5:8 - 2 Samuel 11:2-11:4, Deuteronomy 5:18 5:21, Exodus 20:13 20:14, Ezekiel 22:11, Gates of Repentance 4.020, Genesis 15:9, Guide for the Perplexed 3:8, Jeremiah 13:27 5:23, Job 7:9, Matthew 5:27-5:28, Midrash Psalms 79:4, Numbers.R 9:7 9:12, Pesikta Rabbati 27/28:1

Hebrew	Verse	English
הַעַל־אֵלֶּה לוֹא־אֶפְקֹד נְאֻם־יְהוָה וְאִם בְּגוֹי אֲשֶׁר־כָּזֶה לֹא תִתְנַקֵּם נַפְשִׁי	9[1]	Shall I not punish for these things, asks the LORD? And shall My soul not be avenged on such a nation as this?
הַעַל־אֵלֶּה לוֹא־אֶפְקֹד נְאֻם־יְהוָה וְאִם בְּגוֹי אֲשֶׁר־כָּזֶה לֹא תִתְנַקֵּם נַפְשִׁי	10[2]	Go up into her rows, and destroy, but do not make a full end. *Take away her shoots; for they are not the LORD's*[3].
כִּי בָגוֹד בָּגְדוּ בִּי בֵּית יִשְׂרָאֵל וּבֵית יְהוּדָה נְאֻם־יְהוָה	11[4]	For the house of Israel and the house of Judah dealt very treacherously against Me, says the LORD.
כִּחֲשׁוּ בַּיהוָה וַיֹּאמְרוּ לֹא־הוּא וְלֹא־תָבוֹא עָלֵינוּ רָעָה וְחֶרֶב וְרָעָב לוֹא נִרְאֶה	12[5]	They have denied the LORD and said: 'It is not He, nor shall evil come on us; nor shall we see sword nor famine;
וְהַנְּבִיאִים יִהְיוּ לְרוּחַ וְהַדִּבֵּר אֵין בָּהֶם כֹּה יֵעָשֶׂה לָהֶם	13[6]	And the prophets shall become wind, and the word is not in them; thus it will be done to them.'
לָכֵן כֹּה־אָמַר יְהוָה אֱלֹהֵי צְבָאוֹת יַעַן דַּבֶּרְכֶם אֶת־הַדָּבָר הַזֶּה הִנְנִי נֹתֵן דְּבָרַי בְּפִיךָ לְאֵשׁ וְהָעָם הַזֶּה עֵצִים וַאֲכָלָתַם	14[7]	Therefore, the LORD, the God of hosts says: Because you speak this word, behold, I will make My words fire in your mouth, and the people wood, and it shall devour them.
הִנְנִי מֵבִיא עֲלֵיכֶם גּוֹי מִמֶּרְחָק בֵּית יִשְׂרָאֵל נְאֻם־יְהוָה גּוֹי אֵיתָן הוּא גּוֹי מֵעוֹלָם הוּא גּוֹי לֹא־תֵדַע לְשֹׁנוֹ וְלֹא תִשְׁמַע מַה־יְדַבֵּר	15[8]	Lo, I will bring a nation on you from afar, O house of Israel, says the LORD; it is an enduring nation, it is an ancient nation, a nation whose language you do not know, nor understand what they say.
הִנְנִי מֵבִיא עֲלֵיכֶם גּוֹי מִמֶּרְחָק בֵּית יִשְׂרָאֵל נְאֻם־יְהוָה גּוֹי אֵיתָן הוּא גּוֹי מֵעוֹלָם הוּא גּוֹי לֹא־תֵדַע לְשֹׁנוֹ וְלֹא תִשְׁמַע מַה־יְדַבֵּר	16[9]	*Their quiver is an open sepulcher*[10], they are all mighty men.
וְאָכַל קְצִירְךָ וְלַחְמֶךָ יֹאכְלוּ בָּנֶיךָ וּבְנוֹתֶיךָ יֹאכַל צֹאנְךָ וּבְקָרֶךָ יֹאכַל גַּפְנְךָ וּתְאֵנָתֶךָ יְרֹשֵׁשׁ עָרֵי מִבְצָרֶיךָ אֲשֶׁר אַתָּה בּוֹטֵחַ בָּהֵנָּה בֶּחָרֶב	17[11]	And they shall eat your harvest and your bread, they shall eat your sons and your daughters, they shall eat your flocks and your herds, they shall eat your vines and your fig trees[12]; they shall batter your fortified cities in which you trust, with the sword.
וְגַם בַּיָּמִים הָהֵמָּה נְאֻם־יְהוָה לֹא־אֶעֱשֶׂה אִתְּכֶם כָּלָה	18[13]	But in those days, says the LORD, I will not make a full end of you.

---

[1] Jeremiah 5:9 - Deuteronomy 8:35 8:43, Ezekiel 5:13-5:15 7:9, Hosea 2:13 8:13, Isaiah 1:24, Jeremiah 5:29 9:10 23:2 20:22, Lamentations 4:22, Leviticus 2:25, Nahum 1:2, Numbers.R 9:7

[2] Jeremiah 5:10 - 2 Chronicles 12:17, 2 Kings 24:2-4, Amos 9:8, Ezekiel 9:5-7 12:16 14:17, Guide for the Perplexed 3:8, Hosea 1:9, Isaiah 10:5-7 13:1-5, Jeremiah 4:27 5:18 6:4-6 7:4-12 1:9 6:11 15:8 22:28 51:20-23, Matthew 22:7, Numbers.R 9:7, Psalms 78:61-62

[3] LXX *leave her buttresses: for they are the LORD's*

[4] Jeremiah 5:11 - Hosea 5:7 6:7, Isaiah 24:8, Jeremiah 3:6-11 3:20, Mekilta de R'Ishmael Nezikin 3:91

[5] Jeremiah 5:12 - 1 John 5:10, 1 Samuel 6:9, 1 Thessalonians 5:2-5:3, 2 Chronicles 12:16, Deuteronomy 5:18, Ecclesiastes.R 5:1, Exodus.R 30:5, Ezekiel 12:22-12:28 13:6, Guide for the Perplexed 3:17 3:32, Habakkuk 1:5-1:6, Isaiah 28:14-28:15, Jeremiah 4:10 5:31 14:13-14:14 23:14-23:17 4:4 28:15-28:17 43:2-43:3, Lamentations.R 1:57, Leviticus.R 19:2, Micah 2:11 3:11, Midrash Tanchuma Bereshit 1, Midrash Tanchuma Naso 2, Numbers.R 9:7, Pesikta de R'Kahana 16.11, Pesikta Rabbati 27:4 33:13, Psalms 10:7, Song of Songs.R 5:11

[6] Jeremiah 5:13 - Avot de R'Natan 34, Hosea 9:7, Jeremiah 14:13 14:15 18:18 20:8-11 4:3, Job 6:26 8:2

[7] Jeremiah 5:14 - 2 Kings 1:10-14, Hosea 6:5, Jeremiah 1:9 23:29 28:15-17, Revelation 11:5-6, z.Vaetchanan 269b, Zechariah 1:6

[8] Jeremiah 5:15 - 1 Corinthians 14:21, b.Sotah 46b, Daniel 2:37-38 7:7, Deuteronomy 4:49, Ezekiel 18:31, Habakkuk 1:5-10, Isaiah 5:7 5:26 4:11 5:3 5:6 9:19, Jeremiah 1:15 2:26 4:16 5:11 6:22 9:27 1:9, Matthew 3:9-10, Mekhilta de R'Shimon bar Yochai Beshallach 26:2, Mekhilta de R'Ishmael Beshallah 7:26

[9] Jeremiah 5:16 - b.Sotah 42b, Ein Yaakov Sotah:42b, Isaiah 5:28, Psalms 5:10, Romans 3:13

[10] Missing in LXX

[11] Jeremiah 5:17 - b.Bava Kamma 119a, Deuteronomy 28:30-28:31 4:33, Ein Yaakov Bava Kamma:119a, Ezekiel 12:4, Habakkuk 3:17-3:18, Hosea 8:14, Isaiah 14:9 17:22, Jeremiah 1:15 4:7 4:26 8:16 2:7 2:17, Judges 6:3-6:4, Lamentations 2:2, Leviticus 2:16, variant בטח of בוטח is found, Zephaniah 3:6

[12] LXX adds *and your olive yards*

[13] Jeremiah 5:18 - Ezekiel 9:8 11:13, Jeremiah 4:27 5:10, Romans 11:1-11:5

וְהָיָה֙ כִּ֣י תֹאמְר֔וּ תַּ֣חַת מֶ֗ה עָשָׂ֨ה יְהֹוָ֧ה אֱלֹהֵ֛ינוּ לָ֖נוּ אֶת־כׇּל־אֵ֑לֶּה וְאָמַרְתָּ֣ אֲלֵיהֶ֗ם כַּאֲשֶׁ֨ר עֲזַבְתֶּ֤ם אוֹתִי֙ וַתַּעַבְד֞וּ אֱלֹהֵ֤י נֵכָר֙ בְּאַרְצְכֶ֔ם כֵּ֚ן תַּעַבְד֣וּ זָרִ֔ים בְּאֶ֖רֶץ לֹ֥א לָכֶֽם

19[1] And it shall come to pass, when you say: 'Why has the LORD our God done all these things to us?' Then you shall say to them: 'Like you have forsaken Me, and served strange gods in your land, so shall you serve strangers in a land that is not yours.'

הַגִּ֥ידוּ זֹ֖את בְּבֵ֣ית יַעֲקֹ֑ב וְהַשְׁמִיע֥וּהָ בִיהוּדָ֖ה לֵאמֹֽר

20 Declare this in the house of Jacob and announce it in Judah, saying:

שִׁמְעוּ־נָ֣א זֹ֔את עַ֥ם סָכָ֖ל וְאֵ֣ין לֵ֑ב עֵינַ֤יִם לָהֶם֙ וְלֹ֣א יִרְא֔וּ אׇזְנַ֥יִם לָהֶ֖ם וְלֹ֥א יִשְׁמָֽעוּ

21[2] Hear this, O foolish people, and without understanding, who have eyes, and do not see, who have ears, and do not hear:

הַאוֹתִ֨י לֹא־תִירָ֜אוּ נְאֻם־יְהֹוָ֗ה אִ֤ם מִפָּנַי֙ לֹ֣א תָחִ֔ילוּ אֲשֶׁר־שַׂ֤מְתִּי חוֹל֙ גְּב֣וּל לַיָּ֔ם חׇק־עוֹלָ֖ם וְלֹ֣א יַעַבְרֶ֑נְהוּ וַיִּֽתְגָּעֲשׁוּ֙ וְלֹ֣א יוּכָ֔לוּ וְהָמ֥וּ גַלָּ֖יו וְלֹ֥א יַעַבְרֻֽנְהוּ

22[3] Do you not fear Me? says the LORD; will you not tremble at My presence? Who placed the sand as the boundary of the sea, an everlasting ordinance, which it cannot pass; and though its waves toss themselves, yet they cannot prevail; though they roar, yet they cannot pass over it.

וְלָעָ֤ם הַזֶּה֙ הָיָ֔ה לֵ֖ב סוֹרֵ֣ר וּמוֹרֶ֑ה סָ֖רוּ וַיֵּלֵֽכוּ

23[4] But this people have a revolting and a rebellious heart; they revolted, and are gone.

וְלֹֽא־אָמְר֣וּ בִלְבָבָ֗ם נִ֤ירָא נָא֙ אֶת־יְהֹוָ֣ה אֱלֹהֵ֔ינוּ הַנֹּתֵ֗ן גֶּ֛שֶׁם וְיֹרֶ֥ה וּמַלְק֖וֹשׁ בְּעִתּ֑וֹ שְׁבֻע֛וֹת חֻקּ֥וֹת קָצִ֖יר יִשְׁמׇר־לָֽנוּ

24[5] They do not say in their heart: 'Let us now fear the LORD our God who gives the former rain, and the latter in due season; who keeps for us the appointed weeks of the harvest.'

עֲוֺנֽוֹתֵיכֶ֖ם הִטּוּ־אֵ֑לֶּה וְחַטֹּ֣אותֵיכֶ֔ם מָנְע֥וּ הַטּ֖וֹב מִכֶּֽם

25[6] Your iniquities have turned away these things, and your sins have withheld good from you.

כִּי־נִמְצְא֥וּ בְעַמִּ֖י רְשָׁעִ֑ים יָשׁ֙וּר֙ כְּשַׁ֣ךְ יְקוּשִׁ֔ים הִצִּ֙יבוּ֙ מַשְׁחִ֔ית אֲנָשִׁ֖ים יִלְכֹּֽדוּ

26[7] For wicked men are found among My people. They pry, as fowlers lie in wait; they set a trap, they catch men.

כִּכְלוּב֙ מָ֣לֵא ע֔וֹף כֵּ֥ן בָּתֵּיהֶ֖ם מְלֵאִ֣ים מִרְמָ֑ה עַל־כֵּ֥ן גָּדְל֖וּ וַֽיַּעֲשִֽׁירוּ

27[8] As a cage is full of birds, so are the houses full of deceit; therefore, they became great, and grew rich;

שָׁמְנ֣וּ עָשְׁת֗וּ גַּ֤ם עָֽבְרוּ֙ דִבְרֵי־רָ֔ע דִּ֣ין לֹא־דָ֔נוּ דִּ֤ין יָתוֹם֙ וְיַצְלִ֔יחוּ וּמִשְׁפַּ֥ט אֶבְיוֹנִ֖ים לֹ֥א שָׁפָֽטוּ

28[9] *They grew fat, they became sleek. Yes, they overpass in deeds of wickedness; they do not plead the cause, the cause of the fatherless, so they might make it to prosper; and they do not judge the right of the needy[10].*

---

[1] Jeremiah 5:19 - 1 Kings 9:8-9, 2 Chronicles 7:21-22, Deuteronomy 4:25-28 28:47-48 29:23-27, Jeremiah 2:13 2:35 13:22 16:10-11 16:13 22:8-9, Lamentations 5:8, Lamentations.R Petichata D'Chakimei:21, Saadia Opinions 5:3, Sibylline Oracles 3.275

[2] Jeremiah 5:21 - Acts 4:26, Deuteronomy 5:3 8:6, Ezekiel 12:2, Hosea 7:11, Isaiah 6:9-6:10 3:11 20:18, Jeremiah 4:22 5:4 8:7 10:8, John 12:40, Mark 8:18, Matthew 13:13-13:15, Proverbs 17:16, Psalms 94:8, Romans 11:8

[3] Jeremiah 5:22 - 2 Enoch 28:4, Amos 9:6, b.Bava Batra [Rashi] 7b, b.Bava Batra 73a, Daniel 6:27, Deuteronomy 4:58, Exodus.R 15:22 21:6, Genesis.R 8:7, Hellenistic Synagogal Prayers 12:27, Isaiah 2:2 18:5, Jeremiah 10:7, Job 2:10 38:10-38:11, Luke 12:5, Mark 4:39, Matthew 10:28, Midrash Psalms 93:5, Midrash Tanchuma Bereshit 1, Midrash Tanchuma Chukkat 1, Nahum 1:4, Numbers.R 18:22, Pesikta Rabbati 22:1, Pirkei de R'Eliezer 5, Proverbs 8:29, Psalms 33:7 93:3-93:4 99:1 8:9 119:120, Revelation 15:4, Ruth.R 2:3, Sifre Devarim {Haazinu Hashamayim} 306, Sifre Devarim Nitzavim 306

[4] Jeremiah 5:23 - Deuteronomy 21:18, Ecclesiastes.R 1:36, Hebrews 3:12, Hosea 4:8 11:7, Isaiah 1:5 7:6, Jastrow 1021b, Jeremiah 5:5 6:28 17:9, Psalms 95:10

[5] Jeremiah 5:24 - 1 Kings 17:1, Acts 14:17, Amos 4:7, Deuteronomy 11:13-11:14 4:12, Ecclesiastes.R 1:4, Gates of Repentance 3.164, Genesis 8:22, Hosea 3:5 6:1, Isaiah 16:8, James 5:7 5:17-5:18, Jeremiah 5:22 14:22 2:5, Job 5:10 36:27-36:28 14:37, Joel 2:23, Leviticus.R 28:3, Matthew 5:45, Pesikta de R'Kahana 8.1, Pesikta Rabbati 18:2, Psalms 3:8, Revelation 11:6, Zechariah 10:1

[6] Jeremiah 5:25 - b.Kiddushin 82b, b.Taanit 23a, Deuteronomy 28:23-28:24, Ein Yaakov Kiddushin:82b, Ein Yaakov Taanit:23a, Isaiah 11:2, Jeremiah 2:17-2:19 3:3, Lamentations 3:39 4:22, Leviticus.R 5:3 35:10, Mekilta de R'Ishmael Pisha 11:103, mt.Hilchot Taaniot 1:2, Psalms 11:17 11:34

[7] Jeremiah 5:26 - 1 Samuel 19:10-19:11, Ezekiel 22:2-22:12, Habakkuk 1:14-1:15, Isaiah 10:1, Jeremiah 4:22 18:22, Luke 5:10, Midrash Psalms 18:6, Proverbs 1:11 1:17-18, Psalms 10:10-11 64:6

[8] Jeremiah 5:27 - Amos 8:4-8:6, b.Beitzah [Rashi] 24a, b.Moed Katan [Tosefot] 27b, b.Sanhedrin 1b, Ein Yaakov Yevamot:63b, Habakkuk 2:9-2:11, Hosea 12:9-12:10, Jeremiah 9:7, Micah 1:12 6:10-6:11, Proverbs 1:11-1:13, Revelation 18:2

[9] Jeremiah 5:28 - 1 Corinthians 5:1, Amos 4:1, Deuteronomy 8:15, Ezekiel 5:6-7 16:47-52, Isaiah 1:23, James 5:4-5, Jeremiah 2:33 7:6 12:1 22:15-19, Job 12:6 15:27-28 21:23-24 29:12-14, Psalms 72:4 73:6-7 73:12 82:2-4 119:70, Zechariah 7:10

[10] LXX *and they have transgressed the rule of judgment; they have not judged the cause of the orphan, nor have they judged the cause of the widow*

הַעַל־אֵ֣לֶּה לֹֽא־אֶפְקֹ֖ד נְאֻם־יְהֹוָ֑ה אִ֚ם בְּג֣וֹי אֲשֶׁר־כָּזֶ֔ה לֹ֥א תִתְנַקֵּ֖ם נַפְשִֽׁי	29[1]	Shall I not punish for these things? Says the LORD; Shall My soul not be avenged on such a nation as this?
שַׁמָּה֙ וְשַׁ֣עֲרוּרָ֔ה נִהְיְתָ֖ה בָּאָֽרֶץ	30[2]	An appalling and horrible thing came to pass in the land:
הַנְּבִיאִ֞ים נִבְּא֣וּ־בַשֶּׁ֗קֶר וְהַכֹּֽהֲנִים֙ יִרְדּ֣וּ עַל־יְדֵיהֶ֔ם וְעַמִּ֖י אָ֣הֲבוּ כֵ֑ן וּמַֽה־תַּעֲשׂ֖וּ לְאַחֲרִיתָֽהּ	31[3]	The prophets prophesy in the service of falsehood, and the priests *rule at their summons*[4]; and My people love to have it so. What then will you do in its end?

Jeremiah – Chapter 06

הָעִ֣זוּ ׀ בְּנֵ֣י בִנְיָמִ֗ן מִקֶּ֙רֶב֙ יְר֣וּשָׁלַ֔͏ִם וּבִתְק֙וֹעַ֙ תִּקְע֣וּ שׁוֹפָ֔ר וְעַל־בֵּ֥ית הַכֶּ֖רֶם שְׂא֣וּ מַשְׂאֵ֑ת כִּ֚י רָעָה֙ נִשְׁקְפָ֣ה מִצָּפ֔וֹן וְשֶׁ֖בֶר גָּדֽוֹל	1[5]	Put yourselves in refuge, children of Benjamin, away from the midst of Jerusalem, and blow the horn in Tekoa, and set up a signal on Beth-hacherem; for evil looks forth from the north, and a great destruction.
הַנָּוָה֙ וְהַמְעֻנָּגָ֔ה דָּמִ֖יתִי בַּת־צִיּֽוֹן	2[6]	I will cut off *the comely and delicate one*[7], the daughter of Zion.
אֵלֶ֛יהָ יָבֹ֥אוּ רֹעִ֖ים וְעֶדְרֵיהֶ֑ם תָּקְע֨וּ עָלֶ֤יהָ אֹֽהָלִים֙ סָבִ֔יב רָע֖וּ אִ֥ישׁ אֶת־יָדֽוֹ	3[8]	Shepherds with their flocks come to her; they pitch their tents against her; they will feed each man from his hand.
קַדְּשׁ֧וּ עָלֶ֣יהָ מִלְחָמָ֗ה ק֚וּמוּ וְנַעֲלֶ֣ה בַֽצׇּהֳרָ֔יִם א֥וֹי לָ֖נוּ כִּי־פָנָ֣ה הַיּ֑וֹם כִּ֥י יִנָּט֖וּ צִלְלֵי־עָֽרֶב	4[9]	'Prepare war against her. Arise, and let us go up at noon' 'Woe to us, for the day declines, for the shadows of evening are stretching out.'
ק֚וּמוּ וְנַעֲלֶ֣ה בַלָּ֔יְלָה וְנַשְׁחִ֖יתָה אַרְמְנוֹתֶֽיהָ	5[10]	'Arise, and let us go up by night, and let us destroy her *palaces*[11].'
כִּ֣י כֹ֤ה אָמַר֙ יְהֹוָ֣ה צְבָא֔וֹת כִּרְת֣וּ עֵצָ֔ה וְשִׁפְכ֥וּ עַל־יְרוּשָׁלַ֖͏ִם סֹלְלָ֑ה הִ֚יא הָעִ֣יר הׇפְקַ֔ד כֻּלָּ֖הּ עֹ֥שֶׁק בְּקִרְבָּֽהּ	6[12]	For thus has the LORD of hosts said: Hew down her trees, and cast up a mound against Jerusalem; this is the city to be punished; oppression is everywhere in her midst.
כְּהָקִ֥יר בְּו֙רִ֙ "בַּ֣יִר" מֵימֶ֔יהָ כֵּ֖ן הֵקֵ֣רָה רָעָתָ֑הּ חָמָ֣ס וָ֠שֹׁ֠ד יִשָּׁ֨מַע בָּ֧הּ עַל־פָּנַ֛י תָּמִ֖יד חֳלִ֥י וּמַכָּֽה	7[13]	As a cistern wells with her waters, So she wells with her wickedness; violence and spoil is heard in her; before Me continually is sickness and wounds.
הִוָּֽסְרִי֙ יְר֣וּשָׁלַ֔͏ִם פֶּן־תֵּקַ֥ע נַפְשִׁ֖י מִמֵּ֑ךְ פֶּן־אֲשִׂימֵ֣ךְ שְׁמָמָ֔ה אֶ֖רֶץ ל֥וֹא נוֹשָֽׁבָה	8[14]	Be corrected, O Jerusalem[15], lest My soul alienate from you, lest I make you desolate, an uninhabited land.

[1] Jeremiah 5:29 - James 5:4, Jeremiah 5:9 9:10, Malachi 3:5

[2] Jeremiah 5:30 - Hosea 6:10, Isaiah 1:2, Jeremiah 2:12 23:14

[3] Jeremiah 5:31 - 2 Corinthians 11:13-11:15, 2 Peter 2:1-2:2, 2 Thessalonians 2:9-2:11, 2 Timothy 4:3-4:4, Deuteronomy 8:29, Ezekiel 13:6 22:14, Isaiah 10:3 20:6 30:10-30:11 9:14, Jeremiah 4:30-4:31 14:14 22:22-22:23 23:25-23:26, John 3:19-3:21, Lamentations 1:9 2:14, Matthew 7:15-7:17, Micah 2:6 2:11 3:11, Zephaniah 2:2-2:3

[4] LXX *have clapped their hands*

[5] Jeremiah 6:1 - 2 Chronicles 11:6, 2 Samuel 14:2, Amos 1:1, Ezekiel 26:7-26:21, Jeremiah 1:14-1:15 4:5-4:6 4:19-4:20 4:29 6:22 10:17-10:18 10:22 1:9, Joshua 15:63 18:21-18:28, Judges 1:21, Leviticus.R 25:6, Nehemiah 3:14

[6] Jeremiah 6:2 - Isaiah 1:8 3:16-3:17, Jeremiah 4:31, Lamentations 2:1 2:13, z.Terumah 135a

[7] LXX *And your pride*

[8] Jeremiah 6:3 - 2 Kings 24:2 24:10-12 25:1-4, Jeremiah 4:16-17 12:10 39:1-3, Luke 19:43, Nahum 3:18

[9] Jeremiah 6:4 - b.Nazir [Rashi] 66a, b.Taanit 29a, Isaiah 5:26-30 13:2-5, Jeremiah 5:10 8:20 15:8 51:27-28, Joel 4:9, Mekhilta de R'Shimon bar Yochai Pisha 8:1 15:1, Mekhilta de R'Ishmael Pisha 5:123, Seder Olam 27:Siege, Song of Songs 2:17, t.Taniyot 3:10, y.Pesachim 5:1, z.Acharei Mot 64b, z.Chayyei Sarah 132b, z.Shemot 21b, z.Vaetchanan 270a, z.Vayeshev 182a, Zephaniah 2:4

[10] Jeremiah 6:5 - 2 Chronicles 12:19, Amos 2:5 3:10-11, Hosea 8:14, Isaiah 8:14, Jeremiah 9:22 17:27 4:13, Psalms 48:4, Zechariah 11:1

[11] LXX *foundations*

[12] Jeremiah 6:6 - Deuteronomy 20:19-20:20, Jeremiah 8:24

[13] Jeremiah 6:7 - b.Bava Metzia 59a, b.Berachot 56b, b.Eruvin 42a, Ein Yaakov Bava Metzia:59a, Ezekiel 7:11 7:23 22:3-12 24:7, Isaiah 9:20, James 3:10-12, Jeremiah 20:8, Mas.Soferim 7:4, Micah 2:1-2 2:8-10 3:1-3 3:9-12 7:2-3, Midrash Tanchuma Noach 4, Proverbs 4:23, Psalms 55:10-12

[14] Jeremiah 6:8 - Deuteronomy 8:29, Ezekiel 23:18, Hosea 9:12, Jeremiah 2:15 4:14 7:3-7:7 7:20 7:34 9:12 17:23 7:20 8:33 35:13-35:15, Leviticus 2:34, Proverbs 4:13, Psalms 2:10 50:17 94:12, Zechariah 11:8-11:9, Zephaniah 3:7

[15] LXX *adds with pain and the scourge*

כֹּה אָמַר יְהוָה צְבָאוֹת עוֹלֵל יְעוֹלְלוּ כַגֶּפֶן שְׁאֵרִית יִשְׂרָאֵל הָשֵׁב יָדְךָ כְּבוֹצֵר עַל־סַלְסִלּוֹת	9[1]	Thus says the LORD of hosts: They shall thoroughly glean as a vine the remnant of Israel; turn again your hand as a grape gatherer on the shoots.
עַל־מִי אֲדַבְּרָה וְאָעִידָה וְיִשְׁמָעוּ הִנֵּה עֲרֵלָה אָזְנָם וְלֹא יוּכְלוּ לְהַקְשִׁיב הִנֵּה דְבַר־יְהוָה הָיָה לָהֶם לְחֶרְפָּה לֹא יַחְפְּצוּ־בוֹ	10[2]	To whom shall I speak and give warning, so they may hear? Behold, their ear is dull, and they cannot attend. Behold, the word of the LORD has become a rebuke to them, they have no delight in it.
וְאֵת חֲמַת יְהוָה מָלֵאתִי נִלְאֵיתִי הָכִיל שְׁפֹךְ עַל־עוֹלָל בַּחוּץ וְעַל סוֹד בַּחוּרִים יַחְדָּו כִּי־גַם־אִישׁ עִם־אִשָּׁה יִלָּכֵדוּ זָקֵן עִם־מְלֵא יָמִים	11[3]	Therefore, I am full of the fury of the LORD, I am weary with holding in: Pour it out on the babes in the street, and on the assembly of young men together; for the husband with the wife shall be taken, the aged with he who is full of days.
וְאֵת חֲמַת יְהוָה מָלֵאתִי נִלְאֵיתִי הָכִיל שְׁפֹךְ עַל־עוֹלָל בַּחוּץ וְעַל סוֹד בַּחוּרִים יַחְדָּו כִּי־גַם־אִישׁ עִם־אִשָּׁה יִלָּכֵדוּ זָקֵן עִם־מְלֵא יָמִים	12[4]	And their houses shall be turned to others, Their fields and their wives together; for I will stretch out My hand on the inhabitants of the land, says the LORD.
כִּי מִקְּטַנָּם וְעַד־גְּדוֹלָם כֻּלּוֹ בּוֹצֵעַ בָּצַע וּמִנָּבִיא וְעַד־כֹּהֵן כֻּלּוֹ עֹשֶׂה שָּׁקֶר	13[5]	For from the least of them to the great of them, everyone is greedy for gain; and from the prophet to the priest, everyone deals falsely.
וַיְרַפְּאוּ אֶת־שֶׁבֶר עַמִּי עַל־נְקַלָּה לֵאמֹר שָׁלוֹם שָׁלוֹם וְאֵין שָׁלוֹם	14[6]	They have healed the hurt of My people lightly, saying: 'Peace, peace,' when there is no peace.
הֹבִישׁוּ כִּי תוֹעֵבָה עָשׂוּ גַּם־בּוֹשׁ לֹא־יֵבוֹשׁוּ גַּם־הַכְלִים לֹא יָדָעוּ לָכֵן יִפְּלוּ בַנֹּפְלִים בְּעֵת־פְּקַדְתִּים יִכָּשְׁלוּ אָמַר יְהוָה	15[7]	They shall be put to shame because they have committed abomination; yes, they are not at all ashamed, nor do they know how to blush; therefore, they shall fall among those who fall. When I punish them they shall stumble, says the LORD.
כֹּה אָמַר יְהוָה עִמְדוּ עַל־דְּרָכִים וּרְאוּ וְשַׁאֲלוּ לִנְתִבוֹת עוֹלָם אֵי־זֶה דֶרֶךְ הַטּוֹב וּלְכוּ־בָהּ וּמִצְאוּ מַרְגּוֹעַ לְנַפְשְׁכֶם וַיֹּאמְרוּ לֹא נֵלֵךְ	16[8]	Thus says the LORD: Stand in the ways and see, and ask for the old paths. Where is the good way, and walk in it, and you shall find rest for your souls. But they said: 'We will not walk in it.'

---

[1] Jeremiah 6:9 - Jeremiah 16:16 1:9 52:28-52:30, Midrash Tanchuma Noach 18, Obadiah 1:5-1:6, Revelation 14:18, Tanya Igeret Hakodesh §02, z.Vaetchanan 269b

[2] Jeremiah 6:10 - 2 Chronicles 36:15-36:16, 2 Timothy 4:3, Acts 7:51 7:60, Amos 7:10, b.Shabbat 18a, Colossians 1:28, Deuteronomy 5:3, Exodus 6:12, Ezekiel 3:18-3:21 9:3 9:9, Genesis.R 46:5, Hebrews 11:7, Isaiah 6:9-6:10 28:9-28:13 42:23-42:25 5:1, Jeremiah 4:4 5:4-5:5 7:26 20:8-20:9, John 7:7 9:40, Luke 11:45 20:19, Matthew 3:7, Midrash Tanchuma Lech Lecha 16, Pirkei de R'Eliezer 29, Psalms 1:2 40:9 23:16 119:174 23:24 23:35 119:70 119:77, Romans 7:22

[3] Jeremiah 6:11 - Acts 4:20 17:16 18:5, b.Shabbat 119b, compare use of א in the word מלתי with Job 32:18, Ein Yaakov Shabbat:119b, Ezekiel 3:14 9:6, Jeremiah 7:20 9:22 18:21 20:9, Job 32:18-32:19, Lamentations.R 2:24, Luke 17:34, Micah 3:8, Revelation 16:1, Sifre Devarim {Haazinu Hashamayim} 321, Sifre Devarim Nitzavim 321

[4] Jeremiah 6:12 - 1 Chronicles 21:16, Deuteronomy 28:30-28:33 28:39-28:43, Isaiah 5:25 9:13 9:18 9:22 10:4 65:21-65:22, Jeremiah 8:10 14:22, Lamentations 2:4-2:5 2:8 3:3 5:3 5:11, Zephaniah 1:13

[5] Jeremiah 6:13 - 1 Timothy 3:3, 2 Baruch 77:2, 2 Peter 2:3 2:14-15, Ezekiel 22:12 22:25-28 9:31, Isaiah 4:7 56:9-12 9:17, Jeremiah 2:8 2:26 5:31 8:10 14:18 22:17 23:11 23:14-15 26:7-8 8:32, Lamentations 4:13, Luke 16:14, Micah 2:1-2 3:2-3 3:5 3:11, Zephaniah 3:3-4

[6] Jeremiah 6:14 - 2 Baruch 48:32, 2 Peter 2:1 2:18-2:19, compare use of א in the word וירפאו [cf. Jeremiah 8:11], Ezekiel 13:10 13:22, Isaiah 1:6 6:26, Jeremiah 4:10 5:12 8:11-8:12 14:13 14:17 23:17 4:3, Lamentations 2:14, Micah 2:11

[7] Jeremiah 6:15 - b.Shabbat 119b, compare הכלים לא ידעו here with והכלם לא ידעו nor could they blush at Jeremiah 8:12 but both reading apparently originally read הכלם, Ein Yaakov Shabbat:119b, Exodus 8:34, Ezekiel 2:4 7:6-9 14:9-14:10 16:24-25 24:7, Hosea 9:7, Isaiah 3:9 10:4, Jeremiah 3:3 5:9 5:29 8:12 23:12, Matthew 15:14, Mekilta de R'Ishmael Bahodesh 9:91, Micah 3:6 7:4, Philippians 3:19, Proverbs 5:1, the word בגפלם among those who fall may be intended to read בנפלם they shall utterly fall when they do fall, Zephaniah 3:5

[8] Jeremiah 6:16 - Acts 17:11, Colossians 2:6, Deuteronomy 8:7, Gates of Repentance 1.005, Hebrews 6:12 11:2-12:1, Isaiah 2:5 8:20 4:12 6:21, Jeremiah 2:25 7:23 18:12 18:15 22:21 20:16, John 5:39 5:46-5:47 12:35 13:17, Luke 16:29, Malachi 3:22, Matthew 11:28-11:29 21:28-21:32, Midrash Psalms 119:5, Romans 4:1-4:6 4:12, Saadia Opinions 10:16, Sifre Devarim {Haazinu Hashamayim} 306, Sifre Devarim Nitzavim 306, Song of Songs 1:7-1:8, z.Vaetchanan 269b

Jeremiah 6:16-17 - Haftarah Tisha BAv Shacharit [continues at 8:13 [Teimon]

Hebrew	Verse	English
וַהֲקִמֹתִי עֲלֵיכֶם צֹפִים הַקְשִׁיבוּ לְקוֹל שׁוֹפָר וַיֹּאמְרוּ לֹא נַקְשִׁיב	17[1]	And I set watchmen over you: 'Focus on the sound of the horn,' But they said: 'We will not listen.'
לָכֵן שִׁמְעוּ הַגּוֹיִם וּדְעִי עֵדָה אֶת־אֲשֶׁר־בָּם	18[2]	Therefore, hear, you nations, and know, O congregation, what is against them.
שִׁמְעִי הָאָרֶץ הִנֵּה אָנֹכִי מֵבִיא רָעָה אֶל־הָעָם הַזֶּה פְּרִי מַחְשְׁבוֹתָם כִּי עַל־דְּבָרַי לֹא הִקְשִׁיבוּ וְתוֹרָתִי וַיִּמְאֲסוּ־בָהּ	19[3]	Hear, O earth: Behold, I will bring evil on this people, the fruit of their thoughts, because they have not focused on My words, and as for My teaching, they have rejected it.
לָמָּה־זֶּה לִי לְבוֹנָה מִשְּׁבָא תָבוֹא וְקָנֶה הַטּוֹב מֵאֶרֶץ מֶרְחָק עֹלוֹתֵיכֶם לֹא לְרָצוֹן וְזִבְחֵיכֶם לֹא־עָרְבוּ לִי	20[4]	To what purpose is the frankincense that comes from Sheba, and the sweet cane, from a far country? The burnt offerings are unacceptable, your sacrifices are unpleasing to Me.
לָכֵן כֹּה אָמַר יְהוָה הִנְנִי נֹתֵן אֶל־הָעָם הַזֶּה מִכְשֹׁלִים וְכָשְׁלוּ בָם אָבוֹת וּבָנִים יַחְדָּו שָׁכֵן וְרֵעוֹ "יֹאבֵדוּ" "וְאָבָדוּ"	21[5]	Therefore, thus says the LORD: Behold, I will lay stumbling blocks before this people, and the fathers and the sons together shall stumble against them, the neighbor and his friend, and they shall perish.
כֹּה אָמַר יְהוָה הִנֵּה עַם בָּא מֵאֶרֶץ צָפוֹן וְגוֹי גָּדוֹל יֵעוֹר מִיַּרְכְּתֵי־אָרֶץ	22[6]	Thus says the LORD: Behold, a people shall come from the north country, and a great nation shall be roused from the uttermost parts of the earth.
קֶשֶׁת וְכִידוֹן יַחֲזִיקוּ אַכְזָרִי הוּא וְלֹא יְרַחֵמוּ קוֹלָם כַּיָּם יֶהֱמֶה וְעַל־סוּסִים יִרְכָּבוּ עָרוּךְ כְּאִישׁ לַמִּלְחָמָה עָלַיִךְ בַּת־צִיּוֹן	23[7]	They lay hold on bow and spear; they are cruel and have no compassion; their voice is like the roaring sea, and they ride upon horses. Set in array, as a man for war, Against you, O daughter of Zion.
שָׁמַעְנוּ אֶת־שָׁמְעוֹ רָפוּ יָדֵינוּ צָרָה הֶחֱזִיקַתְנוּ חִיל כַּיּוֹלֵדָה	24[8]	'We heard of its fame, our hands grows feeble. Anguish has taken hold of us, and pain, as of a woman in travail.'
אַל־תֵּצְאִי "אַל־תֵּצְאוּ" הַשָּׂדֶה וּבַדֶּרֶךְ אַל־תֵּלֵכִי "אַל־תֵּלֵכוּ" כִּי חֶרֶב לְאֹיֵב מָגוֹר מִסָּבִיב	25[9]	Do not go forth into the field, nor walk by the way; for the sword of the enemy and terror is on every side.
בַּת־עַמִּי חִגְרִי־שָׂק וְהִתְפַּלְּשִׁי בָאֵפֶר אֵבֶל יָחִיד עֲשִׂי לָךְ מִסְפַּד תַּמְרוּרִים כִּי פִתְאֹם יָבֹא הַשֹּׁדֵד עָלֵינוּ	26[10]	O daughter of my people, bind yourself with sackcloth, and wallow yourself in ashes; make a mourning, as for an only son, a most bitter lamentation; for the spoiler shall suddenly come upon us.
בָּחוֹן נְתַתִּיךָ בְעַמִּי מִבְצָר וְתֵדַע וּבָחַנְתָּ אֶת־דַּרְכָּם	27[11]	I made you a tower and a fortress among My people; so you may know and try their way.

[1] Jeremiah 6:17 - Acts 20:27-20:31, Amos 3:6-3:8, Ezekiel 3:17-21 33:2-9, Habakkuk 2:1, Hebrews 13:17, Hosea 8:1, Isaiah 21:11 56:10 58:1, Jeremiah 25:4, Zechariah 7:11

[2] Jeremiah 6:18 - Deuteronomy 29:23-29:27, Isaiah 5:3, Jeremiah 4:10 31:11, Micah 6:5, Psalms 50:4-6, Sifre Devarim {Haazinu Hashamayim} 306, Sifre Devarim Nitzavim 306

[3] Jeremiah 6:19 - 1 Samuel 15:23 15:26, 2 Baruch 1:1, Acts 8:22, b.Kiddushin 40a, Deuteronomy 4:26 30:19 32:1, Ein Yaakov Kiddushin:40a, Hosea 4:6 10:13, Isaiah 1:2 59:7 66:18, Jeremiah 4:4 6:10 8:9 17:10 19:15 22:29, John 3:19-3:21 12:48, Micah 6:2, Pesikta Rabbati 29/30:2, Proverbs 1:24-1:31 15:26 28:9, Sifre Devarim Nitzavim 306, t.Peah 1:4

[4] Jeremiah 6:20 - 1 Kings 10:1-2 10:10, Amos 5:21-22, Exodus 30:23, Ezekiel 20:39 27:22, Isaiah 1:11 43:23-24 60:6 66:3, Jeremiah 7:21-23, Micah 6:6-6:8, Psalms 40:7 50:7-13 50:16-17 66:3

[5] Jeremiah 6:21 - 1 Peter 2:8, 2 Chronicles 36:17, Ezekiel 3:20 5:10 9:5-9:7, Isaiah 8:14 9:15-9:18 24:2-24:3, Jeremiah 9:22-9:23 13:16 15:2-15:9 16:3-16:9 18:21 19:7-19:9 21:7, Lamentations 2:20-2:22, Romans 9:33 11:9, z.Vaetchanan 269b

[6] Jeremiah 6:22 - Jeremiah 1:14-1:15 5:15 6:1 10:22 25:9 50:41-50:43, z.Vaetchanan 269b

[7] Jeremiah 6:23 - Ezekiel 23:22-25, Habakkuk 1:6-10, Isaiah 5:26-30 13:18 19:4, Jeremiah 4:13 4:29 5:16 30:14 50:42, Luke 21:25-26

[8] Jeremiah 6:24 - 1 Thessalonians 5:3, Ezekiel 21:11-12, Habakkuk 3:16, Jeremiah 4:6-9 4:19-21 4:31 13:21 22:23 30:6 49:24 50:43, Isaiah 21:3 28:19, Micah 4:9-10, Proverbs 1:27-28, Psalms 48:7

[9] Jeremiah 6:25 - 2 Chronicles 15:5, Isaiah 1:20, Jeremiah 4:5 4:10 8:14 14:18 20:3-20:4 20:10 49:29, Job 18:11, Jubilees 22:8, Judges 5:6-5:7, Lamentations.R Petichata D'Chakimei:31, Luke 19:43, Psalms 31:14, z.Vayeshev 180a

[10] Jeremiah 6:26 - Amos 8:10, b.Gittin 58a, b.Menachot [Tosefot] 32b, b.Moed Katan [Rashi] 14b, Ein Yaakov Gittin:58a, Ezekiel 7:16-7:18 27:30-27:31, Isaiah 22:4 22:12 30:13 32:11, James 4:9 5:1, Jeremiah 4:8 4:11 4:20 6:14 8:19 8:21-9:1 9:11 9:18-9:23 12:12 13:17 14:17 15:8 25:33-25:34, Lamentations 1:2 1:16 2:11 3:48 4:3 4:6 4:10, Luke 7:12, Micah 1:8-1:10, Zechariah 12:10

[11] Jeremiah 6:27 - Ezekiel 3:8-3:10 20:4 22:2, Jeremiah 1:18 9:8 15:20

Hebrew	Verse	English
כֻּלָּם סָרֵי סוֹרְרִים הֹלְכֵי רָכִיל נְחֹשֶׁת וּבַרְזֶל כֻּלָּם מַשְׁחִיתִים הֵמָּה	28[1]	They are all grievous rebels, going about with slanders; they are brass and iron; all of them deal corruptly.
נָחַר מַפֻּחַ 'מֵאִשְׁתַּם' 'מֵאֵשׁ' 'תַּם' עֹפָרֶת לַשָּׁוְא צָרַף צָרוֹף וְרָעִים לֹא נִתָּקוּ	29[2]	The bellows blow fiercely, the lead is consumed in the fire; in vain does the founder refines, for the wicked are not separated.
כֶּסֶף נִמְאָס קָרְאוּ לָהֶם כִּי־מָאַס יְהֹוָה בָּהֶם	30[3]	Junk silver shall men call them, because the LORD has rejected them.

Jeremiah – Chapter 07

Hebrew	Verse	English
הַדָּבָר אֲשֶׁר הָיָה אֶל־יִרְמְיָהוּ מֵאֵת יְהֹוָה לֵאמֹר	1[4]	The word *came to Jeremiah*[5] from the LORD, saying:
עֲמֹד בְּשַׁעַר בֵּית יְהֹוָה וְקָרָאתָ שָּׁם אֶת־הַדָּבָר הַזֶּה וְאָמַרְתָּ שִׁמְעוּ דְבַר־יְהֹוָה כָּל־יְהוּדָה הַבָּאִים בַּשְּׁעָרִים הָאֵלֶּה לְהִשְׁתַּחֲוֹת לַיהֹוָה	2[6]	*Stand in the gate of the LORD's house, and proclaim there this word, and say: Hear the word of the LORD, all you of Judah, who enter in these gates to worship the LORD*[7].
כֹּה־אָמַר יְהֹוָה צְבָאוֹת אֱלֹהֵי יִשְׂרָאֵל הֵיטִיבוּ דַרְכֵיכֶם וּמַעַלְלֵיכֶם וַאֲשַׁכְּנָה אֶתְכֶם בַּמָּקוֹם הַזֶּה	3[8]	Thus says the LORD of hosts, the God of Israel: Amend your ways and your deeds, and I will cause you to live in this place.
אַל־תִּבְטְחוּ לָכֶם אֶל־דִּבְרֵי הַשֶּׁקֶר לֵאמֹר הֵיכַל יְהֹוָה הֵיכַל יְהֹוָה הֵיכַל יְהֹוָה הֵמָּה	4[9]	Do not trust in lying words[10], saying: '*The temple of the LORD, the temple of the LORD*[11], the temple of the LORD, are these.'
כִּי אִם־הֵיטֵיב תֵּיטִיבוּ אֶת־דַּרְכֵיכֶם וְאֶת־מַעַלְלֵיכֶם אִם־עָשׂוֹ תַעֲשׂוּ מִשְׁפָּט בֵּין אִישׁ וּבֵין רֵעֵהוּ	5[12]	No, but if you thoroughly amend your ways and your deeds; if you thoroughly execute justice between a man and his neighbor;
גֵּר יָתוֹם וְאַלְמָנָה לֹא תַעֲשֹׁקוּ וְדָם נָקִי אַל־תִּשְׁפְּכוּ בַּמָּקוֹם הַזֶּה וְאַחֲרֵי אֱלֹהִים אֲחֵרִים לֹא תֵלְכוּ לְרַע לָכֶם	6[13]	If you do not oppress the stranger, the fatherless, and the widow, and do not shed innocent blood in this place, no walk after other gods to your harm;
וְשִׁכַּנְתִּי אֶתְכֶם בַּמָּקוֹם הַזֶּה בָּאָרֶץ אֲשֶׁר נָתַתִּי לַאֲבוֹתֵיכֶם לְמִן־עוֹלָם וְעַד־עוֹלָם	7[14]	then will I cause you to live in this place, in the land that I gave to your fathers, *forever and ever*[15].

[1] Jeremiah 6:28 - Ezekiel 22:18-22:22, Gates of Repentance 3.222, Isaiah 1:4-1:5 31:6, Jeremiah 5:23 6:30 9:5 18:18 20:10, Psalms 50:20, Revelation 11:18 19:2

[2] Jeremiah 6:29 - 1 Peter 1:7 4:12, b.Menachot 32b, Ezekiel 24:13, Hosea 11:7, Isaiah 49:4, Jastrow 864b, Jeremiah 9:8, Malachi 3:2-3, Mas.Soferim 7:3, Proverbs 17:3, Saadia Opinions 6:4, Testament of Abraham 12:14, the original spelling probably was ורעם while one school reads ורעים, y.Megillah 3:2, Zechariah 13:9

[3] Jeremiah 6:30 - 11, Exodus.R 31:4 31:10, Ezekiel 22:18-19, Gates of Repentance 1.023, Hosea 9:17, Isaiah 1:22 1:25, Jeremiah 7:29 14:19, Lamentations 5:22, Matthew 5:13, Midrash Tanchuma Mishpatim 9 11, Numbers.R 13:8, Pesikta Rabbati 7:7, Proverbs 25:4, Psalms 119:119, Romans 11:1, Saadia Opinions 6:4

[4] Jeremiah 7:1-2 - 4QJera

[5] Missing in LXX

[6] Jeremiah 7:2 - 1 Kings 22:19, Acts 5:20 5:42, Amos 7:16, Ezekiel 2:4-2:5, Hosea 5:1, Isaiah 1:10, Jeremiah 2:4 10:1 17:19-20 19:2-3 19:14 22:1-2 2 34:4 36:6 36:10 44:24, John 18:20, Matthew 13:9, Micah 1:2 3:1 3:9, Proverbs 1:20-21 8:2-3, Revelation 2:7 2:11 2:17 2:29 3:6 3:13 3:22

[7] LXX *all Judea*

[8] Jeremiah 7:3 - Ezekiel 18:30-31 33:4-11, Isaiah 1:16-19 55:7, James 4:8, Jeremiah 7:5-7 18:11 26:13 35:15, Matthew 3:8-10, Proverbs 28:13, z.Vaetchanan 269b

[9] Jeremiah 7:4 - 1 Samuel 4:3-4:4, b.Nazir 32b, Ezekiel 13:19, Jeremiah 6:14 7:8-7:12 28:15 29:23 29:31, Luke 3:8, Matthew 3:9-3:10, Micah 3:11, mt.Hilchot Beit Habechirah 1:5 1:5, Zephaniah 3:11

[10] LXX adds *for they shall not profit you at all*

[11] Missing in LXX

[12] Jeremiah 7:5 - 1 Kings 6:12-6:13, Ezekiel 18:8 18:17, Isaiah 1:19 16:3, Jeremiah 4:1-4:2 7:3 22:3, Judges 5:1 21:12

[13] Jeremiah 7:6 - 2 Kings 21:6 24:4, Deuteronomy 6:14-6:15 8:19 11:28 24:17 27:19, Exodus 22:21-22:24, Ezekiel 18:6 22:3-22:6, Isaiah 59:7, James 1:27, Jeremiah 2:30 2:34 7:5 13:10 19:4 22:3-22:4 22:15-22:17 26:15 26:23, Job 31:13-31:22, Lamentations 4:13, Malachi 3:5, Matthew 23:35-23:37 27:4 27:25, Psalms 82:3-82:4 106:38, Zechariah 7:9-7:12

[14] Jeremiah 7:7 - 2 Chronicles 33:8, Deuteronomy 4:40, Jeremiah 3:18 17:20-17:27 18:7-18:8 25:5

[15] LXX *of old and forever*

הִנֵּה אַתֶּם בֹּטְחִים לָכֶם עַל־דִּבְרֵי הַשֶּׁקֶר לְבִלְתִּי הוֹעִיל	8[1]	Behold, you trust in lying words, that cannot profit.

הֲגָנֹב רָצֹחַ וְנָאֹף וְהִשָּׁבֵעַ לַשֶּׁקֶר וְקַטֵּר לַבָּעַל וְהָלֹךְ אַחֲרֵי אֱלֹהִים אֲחֵרִים אֲשֶׁר לֹא־יְדַעְתֶּם

9[2] · will you steal, murder, and commit adultery, and swear falsely, and offer to Baal, and walk after other gods whom you have not known,

הֲגָנֹב רָצֹחַ וְנָאֹף וְהִשָּׁבֵעַ לַשֶּׁקֶר וְקַטֵּר לַבָּעַל וְהָלֹךְ אַחֲרֵי אֱלֹהִים אֲחֵרִים אֲשֶׁר לֹא־יְדַעְתֶּם

10[3] · *and come*[4] and stand before Me in this house, upon which My name is called, and say: 'We are delivered,' so you may do all these abominations?

הַמְעָרַת פָּרִצִים הָיָה הַבַּיִת הַזֶּה אֲשֶׁר־נִקְרָא־שְׁמִי עָלָיו בְּעֵינֵיכֶם גַּם אָנֹכִי הִנֵּה רָאִיתִי נְאֻם־יְהוָה

11[5] · Is this house, where My name is called, become a den of robbers in your eyes? Behold, I, I, have seen it, says the LORD.

כִּי לְכוּ־נָא אֶל־מְקוֹמִי אֲשֶׁר בְּשִׁילוֹ אֲשֶׁר שִׁכַּנְתִּי שְׁמִי שָׁם בָּרִאשׁוֹנָה וּרְאוּ אֵת אֲשֶׁר־עָשִׂיתִי לוֹ מִפְּנֵי רָעַת עַמִּי יִשְׂרָאֵל

12[6] · For you now go to My place which was in Shiloh, where I caused My name to live before, and see what I did to it for the wickedness of My people Israel.

וְעַתָּה יַעַן עֲשׂוֹתְכֶם אֶת־כָּל־הַמַּעֲשִׂים הָאֵלֶּה נְאֻם־יְהוָה וָאֲדַבֵּר אֲלֵיכֶם הַשְׁכֵּם וְדַבֵּר וְלֹא שְׁמַעְתֶּם וָאֶקְרָא אֶתְכֶם וְלֹא עֲנִיתֶם

13[7] · And now, because you have done these works, *says the LORD*[8], and I spoke to you, *speaking in good time and often*[9], but you did not hear, and I called you, but you did not answer;

וְעָשִׂיתִי לַבַּיִת אֲשֶׁר נִקְרָא־שְׁמִי עָלָיו אֲשֶׁר אַתֶּם בֹּטְחִים בּוֹ וְלַמָּקוֹם אֲשֶׁר־נָתַתִּי לָכֶם וְלַאֲבוֹתֵיכֶם כַּאֲשֶׁר עָשִׂיתִי לְשִׁלוֹ

14[10] · Therefore, will I do to the house, where My name is called, where you trust, and to the place I gave to you and to your fathers, as I did to Shiloh.

וְהִשְׁלַכְתִּי אֶתְכֶם מֵעַל פָּנָי כַּאֲשֶׁר הִשְׁלַכְתִּי אֶת־כָּל־אֲחֵיכֶם אֵת כָּל־זֶרַע אֶפְרָיִם

15[11] · And I will cast you from My sight, as I cast out all your brethren, the whole seed of Ephraim.

וְאַתָּה אַל־תִּתְפַּלֵּל בְּעַד־הָעָם הַזֶּה וְאַל־תִּשָּׂא בַעֲדָם רִנָּה וּתְפִלָּה וְאַל־תִּפְגַּע־בִּי כִּי־אֵינֶנִּי שֹׁמֵעַ אֹתָךְ

16[12] · Therefore, do not pray for this people, nor lift up cry nor prayer for them, nor make intercession to Me; for I will not hear you.

הַאֵינְךָ רֹאֶה מָה הֵמָּה עֹשִׂים בְּעָרֵי יְהוּדָה וּבְחֻצוֹת יְרוּשָׁלָ͏ִם

17[13] · Do you not see what they do in the cities of Judah and in the streets of Jerusalem?

---

[1] Jeremiah 7:8 - Ezekiel 13:6-13:16, Isaiah 28:15 30:10, Jeremiah 4:10 5:31 7:4 8:10 14:13-14:14 23:14-23:16 23:26 23:32

[2] Jeremiah 7:9 - 1 Corinthians 6:9-6:10, 1 Kings 18:21, 2 Timothy 3:2-3:5, b.Sanhedrin [Tosefot] 60b, Deuteronomy 32:17, Ephesians 5:5-5:7, Exodus 20:3, Ezekiel 18:10-18:13 33:25-33:26, Galatians 5:19-5:21, Guide for the Perplexed 3:32, Hosea 4:1-4:3, Isaiah 59:1-59:8, James 4:1-4:4, Jeremiah 7:6 9:3-9:10 11:13 11:17 13:10 32:29 44:3, Judges 5:8, Liber Antiquitatum Biblicarum 44:6, Malachi 3:5, Mekilta de R'Ishmael Bahodesh 8:85, Micah 3:8-3:12, Midrash Tanchuma Vayikra 7, Pesikta de R'Kahana 13.8, Pesikta Rabbati 27:4, Psalms 50:16-50:21, Revelation 21:8 22:15, Romans 2:2 2:17-2:29, Zechariah 5:3-5:4, Zephaniah 1:5

[3] Jeremiah 7:10 - 2 Chronicles 33:4 33:7, 2 Kings 21:4, Ezekiel 20:39 23:29 23:37 23:39 33:31, Isaiah 1:10-1:15 48:2 58:2-58:4, Jeremiah 7:11 7:14 7:30 32:34 34:15, John 13:18 13:26-13:27 18:28, Matthew 23:13, Proverbs 7:14-7:15 15:8

[4] LXX *so that it is evil with you; yet you have come*

[5] Jeremiah 7:11 - 2 Chronicles 6:33, Hebrews 4:13, Isaiah 56:7, Jeremiah 2:34 16:16-16:17 23:24 29:23, John 2:16, Luke 19:45-19:46, Mark 11:17, Matthew 21:13, Revelation 2:18-2:19

[6] Jeremiah 7:12 - 1 Samuel 1:3 4:3-4:4 4:10-4:11 4:22, Deuteronomy 12:5 12:11, Jeremiah 26:6, Joshua 18:1, Judges 18:31, Psalms 78:60-78:64

[7] Jeremiah 7:13 - 2 Chronicles 36:15-36:16, Hosea 11:2 11:7, Isaiah 50:2 65:12 66:4, Jeremiah 7:25 11:7 25:3 35:15 35:17 44:4, Matthew 23:37, Nehemiah 9:29-9:30, Pesikta Rabbati 33:9, Proverbs 1:24, Zechariah 7:13

[8] Missing in LXX

[9] Missing in LXX

[10] Jeremiah 7:14 - 1 Kings 9:7-8, 1 Samuel 4:10-11, 2 Chronicles 7:21 36:18-19, 2 Kings 25:9, Acts 6:13-14, Deuteronomy 12:5 28:52, Ezekiel 7:20-22 9:5-7 24:21, Isaiah 64:12, Jeremiah 7:4 7:10 7:12 26:6-9 26:18 52:13-23, Lamentations 2:7 4:1, Matthew 24:1-2, Micah 3:11-12, Psalms 74:6-8 78:60

[11] Jeremiah 7:15 - 2 Chronicles 15:9, 2 Kings 17:18-20 17:23 24:20, Hosea 1:4 9:3 9:9 9:16-17 12:3 14:1, Jeremiah 3:8 15:1 23:39 52:3, Lamentations.R 2:17, Psalms 78:67-68, Psalms of Solomon 2:4, Sifre Devarim {Vaetchanan} 26
Jeremiah 7:15-19 - 4QJera

[12] Jeremiah 7:16 - 1 John 5:16, 2 Samuel 8:18, b.Berachot 26b, b.Menachot [Tosefot] 53b, b.Sanhedrin 95b, b.Sotah 14a, b.Taanit 7b 8a, Deuteronomy 9:14, Deuteronomy.R 2:1, Ein Yaakov Berachot:26b, Ein Yaakov Sotah:14a, Ein Yaakov Taanit:7b, Ein Yaakov Taanit:8a, Exodus 32:10, Ezekiel 14:14-14:20, Genesis.R 68:9, Guide for the Perplexed 1:45, Isaiah 1:15, Jastrow 1133a, Jeremiah 11:14 14:11-14:12 15:1 18:20, Mekhilta de R'Shimon bar Yochai Beshallach 22:1, Mekilta de R'Ishmael Beshallah 3:35, Micah 3:4, Midrash Psalms 55:2, Midrash Tanchuma Beshallach 9, Midrash Tanchuma Mikketz 9, Numbers.R 2:1, Sifre Devarim Vaetchanan 26, y.Berachot 4:1, z.Shemot 15a

[13] Jeremiah 7:17 - Ezekiel 8:6-8:18 14:23, Jeremiah 6:27, Sifre Devarim {Haazinu Hashamayim} 306

הַבָּנִים מְלַקְטִים עֵצִים וְהָאָבוֹת מְבַעֲרִים אֶת־הָאֵשׁ וְהַנָּשִׁים לָשׁוֹת בָּצֵק לַעֲשׂוֹת כַּוָּנִים לִמְלֶכֶת הַשָּׁמַיִם וְהַסֵּךְ נְסָכִים לֵאלֹהִים אֲחֵרִים לְמַעַן הַכְעִסֵנִי	18[1] The children gather wood, and the fathers kindle the fire, and the women knead the dough, *to make cakes to the queen of heaven*[2], and to pour out drink offerings to other gods, so they may provoke Me.
הַאֹתִי הֵם מַכְעִסִים נְאֻם־יְהוָה הֲלוֹא אֹתָם לְמַעַן בֹּשֶׁת פְּנֵיהֶם	19[3] Do they provoke Me? says the LORD. Do they not provoke themselves, to the confusion of their own faces?
הַאֹתִי הֵם מַכְעִסִים נְאֻם־יְהוָה הֲלוֹא אֹתָם לְמַעַן בֹּשֶׁת פְּנֵיהֶם	20[4] Therefore, thus says the Lord GOD: Behold, my anger and My fury shall be poured out on this place, on man, and on beast, and on the trees of the field, and on the fruit of the land; and it shall burn, and shall not be quenched.
כֹּה אָמַר יְהוָה צְבָאוֹת אֱלֹהֵי יִשְׂרָאֵל עֹלוֹתֵיכֶם סְפוּ עַל־זִבְחֵיכֶם וְאִכְלוּ בָשָׂר	21[5] Thus says the LORD of hosts, the God of Israel: Add your burnt offerings to your sacrifices, and eat flesh.
כִּי לֹא־דִבַּרְתִּי אֶת־אֲבוֹתֵיכֶם וְלֹא צִוִּיתִים בְּיוֹם 'הוֹצִיא' "הוֹצִיאִי" אוֹתָם מֵאֶרֶץ מִצְרָיִם עַל־דִּבְרֵי עוֹלָה וָזָבַח	22[6] For I did not speak to your fathers, nor commanded them in the day I brought them from the land of Egypt, concerning burnt offerings or sacrifices;
כִּי אִם־אֶת־הַדָּבָר הַזֶּה צִוִּיתִי אוֹתָם לֵאמֹר שִׁמְעוּ בְקוֹלִי וְהָיִיתִי לָכֶם לֵאלֹהִים וְאַתֶּם תִּהְיוּ־לִי לְעָם וַהֲלַכְתֶּם בְּכָל־הַדֶּרֶךְ אֲשֶׁר אֲצַוֶּה אֶתְכֶם לְמַעַן יִיטַב לָכֶם	23[7] but this thing I commanded them, saying: 'Listen to My voice, and I will be your God, and you shall be My people; and walk in all the way I command you, so it may be well with you.'
וְלֹא שָׁמְעוּ וְלֹא־הִטּוּ אֶת־אָזְנָם וַיֵּלְכוּ בְּמֹעֵצוֹת בִּשְׁרִרוּת לִבָּם הָרָע וַיִּהְיוּ לְאָחוֹר וְלֹא לְפָנִים	24[8] But they did not listen, nor inclined their ear, but walked in their own counsels, in the stubbornness of their evil heart, and went backward and not forward,
לְמִן־הַיּוֹם אֲשֶׁר יָצְאוּ אֲבוֹתֵיכֶם מֵאֶרֶץ מִצְרַיִם עַד הַיּוֹם הַזֶּה וָאֶשְׁלַח אֲלֵיכֶם אֶת־כָּל־עֲבָדַי הַנְּבִיאִים יוֹם הַשְׁכֵּם וְשָׁלֹחַ	25[9] even since the day your fathers came up from the land of Egypt to this day; and though I have sent to you all My servants the prophets, sending them daily often and often,

---

Jeremiah 7:17-18 - Sifre Devarim Nitzavim 306

[1] Jeremiah 7:18 - 1 Corinthians 10:22, 1 Kings 14:9 16:2, b.Sanhedrin [Tosefot] 60b, Deuteronomy 4:19 32:16 32:21 32:37-32:38, Deuteronomy.R 10:4, Ezekiel 20:28, Isaiah 3:8 57:6 65:3 65:11, Jastrow 617a 619a, Jeremiah 11:17 19:13 25:7 32:29 44:17-44:19 44:25, Job 31:26-31:28, Lamentations.R 1:57, Pesikta de R'Kahana 16.11, Pesikta Rabbati 27/28:2 31:2, Psalms 16:4, Sifre Devarim Haazinu Hashamayim 306

[2] 4QJera spacing indicates a shorter text; LXX *to make cakes to the host of heaven*

[3] Jeremiah 7:19 - 1 Corinthians 10:22, Daniel 9:7-9:8, Deuteronomy 32:16 32:21-32:22, Ezekiel 8:17-8:18, Ezra 9:7, Isaiah 1:20 1:24 45:16, Jeremiah 2:17 2:19 9:20 20:11, Job 35:6, mt.Hilchot Yesodei haTorah 1:12, Saadia Opinions 4:4

[4] Jeremiah 7:20 - 2 Kings 22:17, Daniel 9:11, Ezekiel 21:3-20:4 22:22, Isaiah 42:25 66:24, Jeremiah 4:23-4:26 9:11-9:12 12:4 14:16 17:27 42:18 44:6, Lamentations 2:3-5 4:11, Malachi 3:19, Mark 9:43-48, Nahum 1:6, Revelation 14:10 16:1-21, z.Vaetchanan 269b

[5] Jeremiah 7:21 - Amos 5:21-5:23, b.Megillah 23b, Hosea 8:13, Isaiah 1:11-1:15, Jeremiah 6:20, Kuzari 2.048, Tanna Devei Eliyahu 6, z.Vaetchanan 269b

Jeremiah 7:21-28 - Haftarah Tzav [continues at 9:22 Teimon]

Jeremiah 7:21-8:3 - Haftarah Tzav [continues at 9:22 Ashkenaz and Sephard]

[6] Jeremiah 7:22 - 1 Samuel 15:22, Guide for the Perplexed 3:32, Hosea 6:6, Mark 12:33, Matthew 9:13, mt.Hilchot Teshuvah 1:1, Psalms 40:7 50:8-50:17 51:17-51:18

Jeremiah 7:22-23 - mt.Hilchot Teshuvah 1:1

[7] Jeremiah 7:23 - 2 Corinthians 10:5, Deuteronomy 4:10 5:16 5:29 5:33 6:3 11:27 13:5 30:2 30:8 30:20, Exodus 15:26 19:5-19:6, Hebrews 5:9, Jeremiah 11:4 11:7 31:34 42:6, Leviticus 26:3-26:12, mt.Hilchot Teshuvah 1:1, Romans 16:26

[8] Jeremiah 7:24 - Deuteronomy 29:18, Exodus 32:7-32:8, Ezekiel 20:8 20:13 20:16 20:21, Hosea 4:16, Jeremiah 2:27 3:17 7:26 8:5 11:7-11:8 15:6 23:17 32:33, Nehemiah 9:16-9:20 9:29, Numbers.R 2:10, Pesikta Rabbati 26:1/2, Psalms 81:12-81:13 106:7-106:48, t.Sotah 14:5

[9] Jeremiah 7:25 - 1 Samuel 8:7-8:8, 2 Chronicles 36:15, Avot de R'Natan 1, Avot de R'Natan 1, Deuteronomy 9:7 9:21-9:24, Ezekiel 2:3 20:5-20:32 23:2-23:3, Ezra 9:7, Jeremiah 7:13 25:4 32:30-32:31, Lamentations.R 2:17 Petichata D'Chakimei:31, Luke 20:10-20:12, m.Avot 1:1, Matthew 21:34-21:36, Nehemiah 9:16-9:18 9:26 9:30, Pesikta de R'Kahana 16.3, Pesikta Rabbati 29/30A:3 33:9, Psalms 106:13-106:22

וְלֹוא שָׁמְעוּ אֵלַי וְלֹא הִטּוּ אֶת־אָזְנָם וַיַּקְשׁוּ אֶת־עָרְפָּם הֵרֵעוּ מֵאֲבוֹתָם

26[1] yet they did not listen to Me, nor inclined their ear, but made their neck stiff; they did worse than their fathers.

וְדִבַּרְתָּ אֲלֵיהֶם אֶת־כָּל־הַדְּבָרִים הָאֵלֶּה וְלֹא יִשְׁמְעוּ אֵלֶיךָ וְקָרָאתָ אֲלֵיהֶם וְלֹא יַעֲנוּכָה

27[2] And you shall speak all these words to them, but they will not listen to you; you shall also call to them, but they will not answer you.

וְאָמַרְתָּ אֲלֵיהֶם זֶה הַגּוֹי אֲשֶׁר לוֹא־שָׁמְעוּ בְּקוֹל יְהוָה אֱלֹהָיו וְלֹא לָקְחוּ מוּסָר אָבְדָה הָאֱמוּנָה וְנִכְרְתָה מִפִּיהֶם

28[3] Therefore, you shall say to them: This is the nation who has not listened to the voice of the LORD their God, nor received correction; faithfulness has perished, and is cut off from their mouth.

גָּזִּי נִזְרֵךְ וְהַשְׁלִיכִי וּשְׂאִי עַל־שְׁפָיִם קִינָה כִּי מָאַס יְהוָה וַיִּטֹּשׁ אֶת־דּוֹר עֶבְרָתוֹ

29[4] Cut off your hair, and cast it away, and lament on the high hills; for the LORD has rejected and forsaken the generation of His wrath.

כִּי־עָשׂוּ בְנֵי־יְהוּדָה הָרַע בְּעֵינַי נְאֻום־יְהוָה שָׂמוּ שִׁקּוּצֵיהֶם בַּבַּיִת אֲשֶׁר־נִקְרָא־שְׁמִי עָלָיו לְטַמְּאוֹ

30[5] For the children of Judah have done what is evil in My sight, says the LORD; they set their detestable things in the house where My name is called, to defile it.

וּבָנוּ בָּמוֹת הַתֹּפֶת אֲשֶׁר בְּגֵיא בֶן־הִנֹּם לִשְׂרֹף אֶת־בְּנֵיהֶם וְאֶת־בְּנֹתֵיהֶם בָּאֵשׁ אֲשֶׁר לֹא צִוִּיתִי וְלֹא עָלְתָה עַל־לִבִּי

31[6] And they have built the high places of Topheth, which is in the valley of the son of Hinnom, to burn their sons and their daughters in the fire; which I never commanded, nor did it ever come into My *mind*[7].

לָכֵן הִנֵּה־יָמִים בָּאִים נְאֻם־יְהוָה וְלֹא־יֵאָמֵר עוֹד הַתֹּפֶת וְגֵיא בֶן־הִנֹּם כִּי אִם־גֵּיא הַהֲרֵגָה וְקָבְרוּ בְתֹפֶת מֵאֵין מָקוֹם

32[8] Therefore, behold, the days come, says the LORD, that it shall not called Topheth any longer, nor the valley of the son of Hinnom, but the valley of slaughter; for they shall bury in Topheth, for lack of room.

וְהָיְתָה נִבְלַת הָעָם הַזֶּה לְמַאֲכָל לְעוֹף הַשָּׁמַיִם וּלְבֶהֱמַת הָאָרֶץ וְאֵין מַחֲרִיד

33[9] And the carcasses of this people shall be food for the fowls of the heavens, and for the beasts of the earth; and no one shall frighten them away.

וְהִשְׁבַּתִּי מֵעָרֵי יְהוּדָה וּמֵחֻצוֹת יְרוּשָׁלִַם קוֹל שָׂשׂוֹן וְקוֹל שִׂמְחָה קוֹל חָתָן וְקוֹל כַּלָּה כִּי לְחָרְבָּה תִּהְיֶה הָאָרֶץ

34[10] Then I will cause the voice of mirth and the voice of gladness the voice of the bridegroom and the voice of the bride to cease from the cities of Judah, and from the streets of Jerusalem, for the land shall be desolate.

---

[1] Jeremiah 7:26 - 2 Chronicles 30:8 33:10, 2 Kings 17:14, Acts 7:51, Daniel 9:6, Isaiah 48:4, Jeremiah 6:17 7:24 11:8 16:12 17:23 19:15 25:3 25:7 26:5 29:19 34:14 44:16, Matthew 21:38 23:32, Nehemiah 9:16-9:17 9:29, Pesikta de R'Kahana 14.2, Proverbs 29:1, Romans 2:5

[2] Jeremiah 7:27 - Acts 20:27, Ezekiel 2:4-2:7 3:4-3:11 3:17-3:18, Isaiah 6:9-6:10 50:2 65:12, Jeremiah 1:7 1:19 26:2, Zechariah 7:13

[3] Jeremiah 7:28 - Hosea 4:1, Isaiah 1:4-1:5 59:14-59:15, Jeremiah 2:30 5:1 5:3 6:8 6:29-6:30 9:4-9:9 32:33, Micah 7:2-7:5, Proverbs 1:7, Psalms 50:17, Saadia Opinions 10:8, Zephaniah 3:2 3:7 Jeremiah 7:28-34 - 4QJera

[4] Jeremiah 7:29 - 2 Kings 17:20, Acts 2:40, b.Arachin [Rashi] 11b, b.Niddah 31a, b.Sotah 45b, b.Yoma 85a, Deuteronomy 32:5, Ein Yaakov Sotah:45b, Ezekiel 19:1 28:12, Isaiah 15:2-3, Jeremiah 6:30 9:18-22 16:6 47:5 48:37, Job 1:20, Matthew 3:7 12:39 16:4 23:36, Micah 1:16, Zechariah 11:8-9

[5] Jeremiah 7:30 - 2 Chronicles 33:4-33:5 33:7 33:15, 2 Kings 21:4 21:7 23:4-23:6 23:12, Daniel 9:27, Ezekiel 7:20 8:5-8:17 43:7-43:8, Jeremiah 23:11 32:34

[6] Jeremiah 7:31 - 2 Chronicles 28:3 33:6, 2 Kings 17:17 23:10 23:20, b.Nedarim 8b, b.Shabbat 33a, b.Taanit [Rashi] 4a, b.Eruvin 19a, Deuteronomy 12:31 17:3, Ezekiel 16:20, Jeremiah 19:2 19:5-19:6 32:35, Joshua 15:8, Lamentations.R 1:36, Leviticus 18:21 20:1-20:5, Psalms 106:37-106:38, Sibylline Oracles 2.292

[7] LXX *heart*

[8] Jeremiah 7:32 - 2 Kings 23:10, b.Nedarim 8b, b.Shabbat 33a, b.Eruvin 19a, Ezekiel 6:5-6:7, Jeremiah 7:31 19:6 19:11 19:13, Leviticus 26:30, Saadia Opinions 9:5

[9] Jeremiah 7:33 - Deuteronomy 28:26, Ezekiel 39:4 39:18-39:20, Jeremiah 8:1-8:2 9:23 12:9 16:4 19:7 22:19 25:33 34:20, Psalms 79:2-79:3, Psalms of Solomon 4:19, Revelation 19:17-19:18

[10] Jeremiah 7:34 - Deuteronomy.R 2:37, Ezekiel 26:13, Hosea 2:11, Isaiah 1:7 3:26 6:11 24:7-24:8, Jeremiah 4:27 16:9 25:10 33:10, Leviticus 26:33, Micah 7:13, Midrash Tanchuma Ki Tavo 4, Pesikta Rabbati 27:4 33:13, Revelation 18:23, Sifre Devarim Vezot Habracha 342, Song of Songs.R 4:22

Jeremiah – Chapter 08

בָּעֵת הַהִיא נְאֻם־יְהֹוָה ״וְיֹצִיאוּ״ ״יוֹצִיאוּ״ אֶת־ עַצְמוֹת מַלְכֵי־יְהוּדָה וְאֶת־עַצְמוֹת־שָׂרָיו וְאֶת־ עַצְמוֹת הַכֹּהֲנִים וְאֵת| עַצְמוֹת הַנְּבִיאִים וְאֵת עַצְמוֹת יוֹשְׁבֵי־יְרוּשָׁלָ͏ִם מִקִּבְרֵיהֶם	1[1] At that time, says the LORD, they shall bring out the bones of the kings of Judah, and the bones of his princes, and the bones of the priests, and the bones of the prophets, and the bones of the inhabitants of Jerusalem, from their graves;
וּשְׁטָחוּם לַשֶּׁמֶשׁ וְלַיָּרֵחַ וּלְכֹל| צְבָא הַשָּׁמַיִם אֲשֶׁר אֲהֵבוּם וַאֲשֶׁר עֲבָדוּם וַאֲשֶׁר הָלְכוּ אַחֲרֵיהֶם וַאֲשֶׁר דְּרָשׁוּם וַאֲשֶׁר הִשְׁתַּחֲווּ לָהֶם לֹא יֵאָסְפוּ וְלֹא יִקָּבֵרוּ לְדֹמֶן עַל־פְּנֵי הָאֲדָמָה יִהְיוּ	2[2] And they shall spread them before the sun, and *the moon, and all the host of heaven*[3], whom they have loved, and whom they have served, and after whom they have walked, and whom they have pursued, and whom they have worshipped; they shall not be gathered, nor be buried, they shall be dung upon the face of the earth.
וְנִבְחַר מָוֶת מֵחַיִּים לְכֹל הַשְּׁאֵרִית הַנִּשְׁאָרִים מִן־ הַמִּשְׁפָּחָה הָרָעָה הַזֹּאת בְּכָל־הַמְּקֹמוֹת הַנִּשְׁאָרִים אֲשֶׁר הִדַּחְתִּים שָׁם נְאֻם יְהֹוָה צְבָאוֹת	3[4] And death shall be chosen rather than life by all the remnant who remain of this evil family, who remain in all the places I have *driven them*[5], says the LORD of hosts.
וְאָמַרְתָּ אֲלֵיהֶם כֹּה אָמַר יְהֹוָה הֲיִפְּלוּ וְלֹא יָקוּמוּ אִם־יָשׁוּב וְלֹא יָשׁוּב	4[6] *Moreover, you shall say to them*[7]: Thus says the LORD: Do men fall, and not rise up again? Doesn't one turn away, and *not return*[8]?
מַדּוּעַ שׁוֹבְבָה הָעָם הַזֶּה יְרוּשָׁלַ͏ִם מְשֻׁבָה נִצַּחַת הֶחֱזִיקוּ בַּתַּרְמִית מֵאֲנוּ לָשׁוּב	5[9] Why then are the *people of Jerusalem*[10] slid back by a perpetual backsliding? They hold fast to deceit, they refuse to return.
הִקְשַׁבְתִּי וָאֶשְׁמָע לוֹא־כֵן יְדַבֵּרוּ אֵין אִישׁ נִחָם עַל־רָעָתוֹ לֵאמֹר מֶה עָשִׂיתִי כֻּלֹּה שָׁב ׳בִּמְרֻצֹתָם׳ ״בִּמְרוּצָתָם״ כְּסוּס שׁוֹטֵף בַּמִּלְחָמָה	6[11] I attended and listened, but they did not speak correctly; no man repented of his wickedness, Saying: 'What have I done?' Everyone turns away in his course, as a horse that rushes headlong in the battle.
גַּם־חֲסִידָה בַשָּׁמַיִם יָדְעָה מוֹעֲדֶיהָ וְתֹר ׳וְסוּס׳ ״וְסִיס״ וְעָגוּר שָׁמְרוּ אֶת־עֵת בֹּאָנָה וְעַמִּי לֹא יָדְעוּ אֵת מִשְׁפַּט יְהֹוָה	7[12] Yes, the stork in the heavens knows her appointed times; and the turtle and the swallow and the crane observe the time of their coming; but My people do not know the ordinance of the LORD.

---

[1] Jeremiah 8:1 - 1 Kings 13:2, 2 Chronicles 34:4-5, 2 Kings 23:16 23:20, Amos 2:1, Apocalypse of Daniel 8:2, b.Sanhedrin 96b, Ein Yaakov Sanhedrin 96b, Ezekiel 6:5 37:1, Jeremiah 7:32-34, m.Middot 3:4, m.Niddah 2:7, Midrash Psalms 79:5, Psalms of Solomon 4:19

Jeremiah 8:1-3 - 4QJerc

Jeremiah 8:1-12 - 4QJera

[2] Jeremiah 8:2 - 2 Chronicles 33:3-33:5, 2 Kings 9:36-9:37 17:16 21:3 21:5 23:5, Acts 7:42, b.Sanhedrin 96b, b.Yevamot 63b, Deuteronomy 4:19 17:3, Ecclesiastes 6:3, Ein Yaakov Sanhedrin:96b, Ein Yaakov Yevamot:63b, Ezekiel 8:16, Jeremiah 9:23 16:4 19:13 22:19 36:30 44:17-44:19, Jubilees 23:23, Psalms 83:11, Sibylline Oracles 3.227, Zephaniah 1:5 1:17

[3] 4QJerc *and all stars*

[4] Jeremiah 8:3 - 1 Kings 19:4, b.Yevamot 63b, Daniel 9:7, Deuteronomy 30:1 30:4, Ein Yaakov Yevamot:63b, Jeremiah 20:14-20:18 23:3 23:8 29:14 29:28 32:36-32:37 40:12, Job 3:21-3:23 7:15-7:16, Jonah 4:3, Revelation 6:16 9:6

[5] 4QJerc *scattered them*

[6] Jeremiah 8:4 - 1 Kings 8:38, Amos 5:2, b.Megillah 23b, Ezekiel 18:23, Hosea 6:1 7:10 14:3, Isaiah 44:22 55:7, Jeremiah 3:1 3:22 4:1 23:14 36:3, Micah 7:8, Numbers.R 11:7, Proverbs 24:16, z.Vaetchanan 269b

[7] Missing in LXX

[8] Missing in 4QJera

[9] Jeremiah 8:5 - 1 Thessalonians 5:21, 2 Thessalonians 2:9-2:12, b.Sanhedrin 105a, Ein Yaakov Sanhedrin:105a, Hebrews 12:25, Hosea 4:16 11:7, Isaiah 1:20 30:10 44:20, Jastrow 928a, Jeremiah 2:32 3:11-3:14 5:3 5:27 7:24-7:26 9:7, John 5:40, Proverbs 4:13, Revelation 2:25, Zechariah 7:11

[10] LXX *my people*

[11] Jeremiah 8:6 - 2 Peter 3:9, b.Shabbat [Rashi] 152a, Ezekiel 18:28 22:30, Gates of Repentance 1.010, Haggai 1:5 1:7, Isaiah 30:18 59:16, Jeremiah 2:24-2:25 5:1, Job 10:2 33:27-33:28 39:19-39:25, Joseph and Aseneth 9:2, Luke 15:17-15:19, Malachi 3:16, Mesillat Yesharim 2:Traits of Zehirus, Micah 7:2, Psalms 14:2, Revelation 9:20

[12] Jeremiah 8:7 - Exodus.R 25:8, Isaiah 1:3 5:12, Jeremiah 5:4-5:5, Mas.Soferim 7:4, Proverbs 6:6-6:8, Sifre Devarim {Haazinu Hashamayim} 306, Sifre Devarim Nitzavim 306, Song of Songs 2:12

Hebrew		English
אֵיכָה תֹאמְרוּ חֲכָמִים אֲנַחְנוּ וְתוֹרַת יְהוָה אִתָּנוּ אָכֵן הִנֵּה לַשֶּׁקֶר עָשָׂה עֵט שֶׁקֶר סֹפְרִים	8[1]	How do you say: 'We are wise, and the law of the LORD is with us?' Lo, certainly the scribes with in vain the vain pen.
הֹבִישׁוּ חֲכָמִים חַתּוּ וַיִּלָּכֵדוּ הִנֵּה בִדְבַר־יְהוָה מָאָסוּ וְחָכְמַת־מֶה לָהֶם	9[2]	The wise men are ashamed, they are dismayed and taken; lo, they have rejected the word of the LORD; so, what wisdom is in them?
לָכֵן אֶתֵּן אֶת־נְשֵׁיהֶם לַאֲחֵרִים שְׂדוֹתֵיהֶם לְיוֹרְשִׁים כִּי מִקָּטֹן וְעַד־גָּדוֹל כֻּלֹּה בֹּצֵעַ בָּצַע מִנָּבִיא וְעַד־כֹּהֵן כֻּלֹּה עֹשֶׂה שָּׁקֶר	10[3]	Therefore, will I give their wives to others, and their fields to those who shall possess them; *for from the least to the great, everyone is greedy for gain; from the prophet to the priest, everyone deals falsely*[4].
וַיְרַפּוּ אֶת־שֶׁבֶר בַּת־עַמִּי עַל־נְקַלָּה לֵאמֹר שָׁלוֹם שָׁלוֹם וְאֵין שָׁלוֹם	11[5]	*And they have healed the pain of the daughter of My people lightly, Saying: 'Peace, peace,' when there is no peace*[6].
הֹבִשׁוּ כִּי תוֹעֵבָה עָשׂוּ גַּם־בּוֹשׁ לֹא־יֵבֹשׁוּ וְהִכָּלֵם לֹא יָדָעוּ לָכֵן יִפְּלוּ בַנֹּפְלִים בְּעֵת פְּקֻדָּתָם יִכָּשְׁלוּ אָמַר יְהוָה	12[7]	*They shall be put to shame because they have committed abomination; Yes, they are not at all ashamed, nor do they know how to blush; therefore, they shall fall among those who fall, in the time of their visitation they shall stumble, says the LORD*[8].
אָסֹף אֲסִיפֵם נְאֻם־יְהוָה אֵין עֲנָבִים בַּגֶּפֶן וְאֵין תְּאֵנִים בַּתְּאֵנָה וְהֶעָלֶה נָבֵל וָאֶתֵּן לָהֶם יַעַבְרוּם	13[9]	*I will utterly consume them, says the LORD*[10]; There are no grapes on the vine, or figs on the fig tree, and the leaf is faded; and I gave them what they transgress.
עַל־מָה אֲנַחְנוּ יֹשְׁבִים הֵאָסְפוּ וְנָבוֹא אֶל־עָרֵי הַמִּבְצָר וְנִדְּמָה־שָּׁם כִּי יְהוָה אֱלֹהֵינוּ הֲדִמָּנוּ וַיַּשְׁקֵנוּ מֵי־רֹאשׁ כִּי חָטָאנוּ לַיהוָה	14[11]	'Why do we sit still? Assemble yourselves, and let us enter into the fortified cities, and let us be cut off there; for the LORD our God has cut us off, and gave us water of gall to drink, because we have sinned against the LORD.
קַוֵּה לְשָׁלוֹם וְאֵין טוֹב לְעֵת מַרְפֵּה וְהִנֵּה בְעָתָה	15[12]	We looked for peace, but no good came; and for a time of healing, and behold terror!'
מִדָּן נִשְׁמַע נַחְרַת סוּסָיו מִקּוֹל מִצְהֲלוֹת אַבִּירָיו רָעֲשָׁה כָּל־הָאָרֶץ וַיָּבוֹאוּ וַיֹּאכְלוּ אֶרֶץ וּמְלוֹאָהּ עִיר וְיֹשְׁבֵי בָהּ	16[13]	The snorting of his horses is heard from Dan; at the sound of the neighing of his strong ones the whole land trembles; for they came, and devoured the land and all that is in it, the city and those who live in it.

---

[1] Jeremiah 8:8 - 1 Corinthians 3:18-3:20, Gates of Repentance 2.013, Hosea 8:12, Isaiah 10:1-10:2, Job 5:12-5:13 11:12 12:20, John 9:41, Lamentations.R 1:1, Matthew 15:6, Pesikta de R'Kahana 15.6, Proverbs 17:6, Psalms 3:19, Romans 1:22 2:17-2:29

[2] Jeremiah 8:9 - 1 Corinthians 1:18-1:29, 2 Timothy 3:15, Deuteronomy 4:6, Ezekiel 7:26, Isaiah 8:20 19:11, Jeremiah 6:15 6:19 1:7, Job 5:12, Psalms 19:8 119:98-119:100

[3] Jeremiah 8:10 - 2 Baruch 77:2, 2 Peter 2:1-2:3, Amos 5:11, Deuteronomy 28:30-28:32, Ezekiel 22:27-22:28 9:31, Isaiah 4:7 56:10-56:12, Jeremiah 5:31 6:12-6:13 23:11-23:17 23:25-23:26 8:32, Lamentations 4:13, Micah 3:5 3:11, Titus 1:7 1:11, Zephaniah 1:13

[4] Missing in LXX

[5] Jeremiah 8:11 - 1 Kings 22:6 22:13, 2 Baruch 48:32, compare the lack of א in the word וירפו [cf. Jeremiah 6:14], Ezekiel 13:10-13:16 13:22, Jeremiah 6:14 14:14-14:15 27:9-27:10 28:3-28:9, Lamentations 2:14, Micah 2:11, Midrash Tanchuma Vayera 13, the word וירפו does not have an inserted א [cf. Jeremiah 6:14]

[6] Missing in LXX

[7] Jeremiah 8:12 - compare והכלם לא ידעו here with הכלים לא ילעו "neither could they blush" at Jeremiah 8:12 but both reading apparently originally read הכלם, Deuteronomy 8:35, Ezekiel 22:25-22:31, Hosea 4:5-4:6 5:9, Isaiah 3:9 9:14-9:18 24:2, Jeremiah 3:3 6:15, Philippians 3:19, Psalms 52:2 52:8, Zephaniah 3:5

[8] Missing in LXX

[9] Jeremiah 8:13 - b.Arachin [Rashi] 54a, b.Megillah 31b, Deuteronomy 28:39-42, Ezekiel 22:19-21 24:3-11, Habakkuk 3:17, Haggai 1:11 2:17, Hosea 2:8-11, Isaiah 5:4-6 5:10 24:21-22, James 1:11, Jeremiah 5:17 17:8, Joel 1:7 1:10-12, Lamentations.R 1:42, Leviticus 2:20, Luke 13:6-9, Matthew 21:19, Midrash Tanchuma Tazria 9, Pesikta Rabbati 33:13, Psalms 1:3-4 Jeremiah 8:13-9:23 - Haftarah Tisha BAv Shacharit [continued from 6:16-17], mt.Hilchot Tefilah 13:18, Siman 124:3

[10] Missing in LXX

[11] Jeremiah 8:14 - 2 Kings 7:3-7:4, 2 Samuel 20:6, Amos 6:10, Deuteronomy 5:17 8:32, Habakkuk 2:20, Jeremiah 4:5-4:6 9:16 14:20 23:15 11:11, Lamentations 3:19 3:27-3:28, Leviticus 10:3, Matthew 3:34, Numbers 5:18-5:24, Psalms 39:3 69:22, Zechariah 2:13

[12] Jeremiah 8:15 - 1 Thessalonians 5:3, Jeremiah 4:10 8:11 14:19, Micah 1:12

[13] Jeremiah 8:16 - 1 Corinthians 10:26 10:28, b.Gittin [Rashi] 68a, b.Sanhedrin 96a, Ein Yaakov Sanhedrin:96a, Genesis.R 43:2, Habakkuk 3:10, Jeremiah 4:15-4:16 4:24 6:23 10:25 23:3, Judges 5:22 18:29 20:1, Nahum 1:4-1:5 3:2, Psalms 24:1 Jeremiah 8:16-17 - Testament of Dan 5:6

כִּי הִנְנִי מְשַׁלֵּחַ בָּכֶם נְחָשִׁים צִפְעֹנִים אֲשֶׁר אֵין־לָהֶם לָחַשׁ וְנִשְּׁכוּ אֶתְכֶם נְאֻם־יְהוָה	17[1]	For, behold, I will send serpents, *basilisks, among you*[2], which will not be charmed; and they shall bite you, says the LORD.
מַבְלִיגִיתִי עֲלֵי יָגוֹן עָלַי לִבִּי דַוָּי	18[3]	*Though I would take comfort against sorrow, My heart is faint within me*[4].
הִנֵּה־קוֹל שַׁוְעַת בַּת־עַמִּי מֵאֶרֶץ מַרְחַקִּים הַיהוָה אֵין בְּצִיּוֹן אִם־מַלְכָּהּ אֵין בָּהּ מַדּוּעַ הִכְעִסוּנִי בִּפְסִלֵיהֶם בְּהַבְלֵי נֵכָר	19[5]	Behold the voice of the cry of the daughter of my people from a land far off: 'Is not the LORD in Zion? Is not her King in her?' 'Why have they provoked Me with their graven images, and with strange vanities?'
עָבַר קָצִיר כָּלָה קָיִץ וַאֲנַחְנוּ לוֹא נוֹשָׁעְנוּ	20[6]	'The harvest is past, the summer is ended, and we are not saved.'
עַל־שֶׁבֶר בַּת־עַמִּי הָשְׁבָּרְתִּי קָדַרְתִּי שַׁמָּה הֶחֱזִקָתְנִי	21[7]	For the *harm*[8] of the daughter of my people I *am seized with anguish; I am black, appalment has taken hold on me*[9].
הַצֳרִי אֵין בְּגִלְעָד אִם־רֹפֵא אֵין שָׁם כִּי מַדּוּעַ לֹא עָלְתָה אֲרֻכַת בַּת־עַמִּי	22[10]	Is there no balm in Gilead? Is there no physician there? Why then is not the health of the daughter of my people recovered?
מִי־יִתֵּן רֹאשִׁי מַיִם וְעֵינִי מְקוֹר דִּמְעָה וְאֶבְכֶּה יוֹמָם וָלַיְלָה אֵת חַלְלֵי בַת־עַמִּי	23[11]	*Oh, that my head were waters*[12], and my eyes a fountain of tears, so I might weep day and night for the slain of the daughter of my people!

Jeremiah – Chapter 09

מִי־יִתְּנֵנִי בַמִּדְבָּר מְלוֹן אֹרְחִים וְאֶעֶזְבָה אֶת־עַמִּי וְאֵלְכָה מֵאִתָּם כִּי כֻלָּם מְנָאֲפִים עֲצֶרֶת בֹּגְדִים	1[13]	Oh, that I was in the wilderness, in a lodging place of wayfaring men, so I might leave my people, and go from them! For they are all adulterers, an assembly of treacherous men.
וַיַּדְרְכוּ אֶת־לְשׁוֹנָם קַשְׁתָּם שֶׁקֶר וְלֹא לֶאֱמוּנָה גָּבְרוּ בָאָרֶץ כִּי מֵרָעָה אֶל־רָעָה יָצָאוּ וְאֹתִי לֹא־יָדָעוּ נְאֻם־יְהוָה	2[14]	And they bend their tongue, their bow of falsehood; and they are grown mighty in the land, but not for truth; for they proceed from

[1] Jeremiah 8:17 - Amos 5:19 9:3, Avot de R'Natan 39, Deuteronomy 8:24, Ecclesiastes 10:11, Isaiah 14:29, Numbers 21:6, Pesikta Rabbati 33:13, Psalms 58:5-58:6, Revelation 9:19

[2] Missing in LXX

[3] Jeremiah 8:18 - Daniel 10:16-10:17, Habakkuk 3:16, Isaiah 22:4, Jastrow 275a, Jeremiah 6:24 10:19-10:22, Job 7:13-7:14, Lamentations 1:16-1:17 5:17, Lamentations.R Petichata D'Chakimei:32
Jeremiah 8:18-19 - 4QJera

[4] LXX *mortally with the pain of your distressed heart*

[5] Jeremiah 8:19 - b.Taanit [Rashi] 29a, Deuteronomy 32:16-32:21, Guide for the Perplexed 1:36, Isaiah 1:4 12:6 13:5 9:22 15:3 4:1, Jastrow 1538a, Jeremiah 4:16-4:17 4:30-4:31 8:5-8:6 9:17 14:19 7:7, Joel 3:5 4:21, Lamentations.R Petichata D'Chakimei:32, Obadiah 1:17, Psalms 15:21 2:10 5:2, Revelation 2:1, Ruth.R Petichata:6

[6] Jeremiah 8:20 - Hebrews 3:7-3:15, Luke 13:25 19:44, Matthew 25:1-25:12, Midrash Psalms 40:1 119:30, Proverbs 10:5

[7] Jeremiah 8:21 - Jeremiah 4:19 9:2 14:17 17:16, Joel 2:6, Luke 19:41, Nahum 2:11, Nehemiah 2:3, Psalms 137:3-137:6, Romans 9:1-9:3, Song of Songs 1:5-1:6
Jeremiah 8:21-23 - 4QJerc

[8] LXX *breach*

[9] LXX *have been saddened: in my perplexity pangs have seized upon me as of a woman in travail*

[10] Jeremiah 8:22 - b.Taanit 4a, Ein Yaakov Taanit:4a, Genesis 37:25 43:11, Isaiah 1:5-1:6, Jeremiah 30:12-30:17 46:11 51:8, Luke 5:31-5:32 8:43, Matthew 9:11-9:12

[11] Jeremiah 8:23 - 4QJera, Lamentations.R 1:52, Pesikta Rabbati 29:2, Sifre Devarim {Haazinu Hashamayim} 332, Sifre Devarim Nitzavim 332

[12] LXX *Who will give water to my head*

[13] Jeremiah 9:1 - 2 Baruch 35:2, Ezekiel 21:11-21:12, Isaiah 16:9 22:4, Jeremiah 4:19 6:26 8:21-8:22 13:17 14:17, Lamentations 2:11 2:18-2:19 3:48-3:49, Lamentations.R 3:?, Midrash Tanchuma Bamidbar 2, mt.Hilchot Deot 6:1, mt.Hilchot Sanhedrin vHainshin Hameurim Lahem 2:14, mt.Shemonah Perakim 4:6, Numbers.R 1:2, Psalms 42:4 119:136, Shemonah Perachim IV, z.Acharei Mot 71b, z.Vayechi 225a
Jeremiah 9:1-2 - 4QJera
Jeremiah 9:1-5 - 4QJerc

[14] Jeremiah 9:2 - 1 Samuel 2:12, Ezekiel 22:10-22:11, Genesis.R 70:4, Guide for the Perplexed 3:8, Hosea 4:2 5:7 6:7 7:4, James 4:4, Jeremiah 5:7-5:8 12:1 12:6 23:10, Lamentations.R 1:57, Malachi 2:11, Micah 7:1-7:7, Midrash Tanchuma Shelach 4, Numbers.R 16:4, Pesikta de R'Kahana 13.8 16.11, Psalms 55:7-55:9 120:5-120:7, Zephaniah 3:4

evil to evil, and do not know Me, says the LORD[1].

3[2] Take heed everyone of his neighbor, and do not trust in a brother; for every brother acts slyly, and every neighbor goes about with slanders.

אִישׁ מֵרֵעֵהוּ הִשָּׁמֵרוּ וְעַל־כָּל־אָח אַל־תִּבְטָחוּ כִּי כָל־אָח עָקוֹב יַעְקֹב וְכָל־רֵעַ רָכִיל יַהֲלֹךְ

4[3] And everyone deceives his neighbor, and they do not speak truth; they have taught their tongue to speak lies, they weary themselves to commit iniquity.

וְאִישׁ בְּרֵעֵהוּ יְהָתֵלּוּ וֶאֱמֶת לֹא יְדַבֵּרוּ לִמְּדוּ לְשׁוֹנָם דַּבֶּר־שֶׁקֶר הַעֲוֵה נִלְאוּ

5[4] *Your habitation is in the midst of deceit[5];* through deceit they refuse to know Me, says the LORD.

שִׁבְתְּךָ בְּתוֹךְ מִרְמָה בְּמִרְמָה מֵאֲנוּ דַעַת־אוֹתִי נְאֻם־יְהוָה

6[6] Therefore, thus says the LORD of hosts: behold, I will smelt them and try them; for how else should I do, because of the daughter of My people?

לָכֵן כֹּה אָמַר יְהוָה צְבָאוֹת הִנְנִי צוֹרְפָם וּבְחַנְתִּים כִּי־אֵיךְ אֶעֱשֶׂה מִפְּנֵי בַּת־עַמִּי

7[7] Their tongue is a sharpened arrow, it speaks deceit; one speaks peaceably to his neighbor with his mouth, but in his heart he lays in wait for him.

חֵץ שׁוֹחֵט "שָׁחוּט" לְשׁוֹנָם מִרְמָה דִבֵּר בְּפִיו שָׁלוֹם אֶת־רֵעֵהוּ יְדַבֵּר וּבְקִרְבּוֹ יָשִׂים אָרְבּוֹ

8[8] Shall I not punish them for these things? Says the LORD. Shall not My soul be avenged on such a nation as this?

הַעַל־אֵלֶּה לֹא־אֶפְקָד־בָּם נְאֻם־יְהוָה אִם בְּגוֹי אֲשֶׁר־כָּזֶה לֹא תִתְנַקֵּם נַפְשִׁי

9[9] *For the mountains I will take up a weeping and wailing, and for the pastures of the wilderness a lamentation, because they are burned up, so that no one passes through. And they do not hear the voice of the cattle; both the fowl of the heavens and the beast fled and are gone[10].*

עַל־הֶהָרִים אֶשָּׂא בְכִי וָנֶהִי וְעַל־נְאוֹת מִדְבָּר קִינָה כִּי נִצְּתוּ מִבְּלִי־אִישׁ עֹבֵר וְלֹא שָׁמְעוּ קוֹל מִקְנֶה מֵעוֹף הַשָּׁמַיִם וְעַד־בְּהֵמָה נָדְדוּ הָלָכוּ

10[11] And I will make Jerusalem a ruin, a lair of *jackals[12]*; and I will make the cities of Judah desolate without an inhabitant.

וְנָתַתִּי אֶת־יְרוּשָׁלַ͏ִם לְגַלִּים מְעוֹן תַּנִּים וְאֶת־עָרֵי יְהוּדָה אֶתֵּן שְׁמָמָה מִבְּלִי יוֹשֵׁב

---

[1] 4QJerc adds *of HOsts*

[2] Jeremiah 9:3 - 2 Corinthians 4:4-4:6, 2 Timothy 3:13, Hosea 4:1-4:3, Isaiah 59:3-59:5 59:13-59:15, Jeremiah 4:22 7:26 9:6 9:9 22:16 31:35, John 8:54-8:55 17:3, Jude 1:3, Judges 2:10, Mark 8:38, Matthew 10:31-10:33, Micah 7:3-7:5, Philippians 1:28, Psalms 52:3-52:5 64:4-64:5 120:2-120:4, Revelation 12:11, Romans 1:16 1:28 3:13
Jeremiah 9:3-6 - Ahiqar 139

[3] Jeremiah 9:4 - 1 Peter 2:1-2:2, 1 Thessalonians 4:6, b.Succah 46b, b.Yevamot 63a, Chibbur Yafeh 12 {51b}, Ein Yaakov Yevamot:63a, Ezekiel 22:9, Gates of Repentance 3.186, Genesis 27:35-27:36 32:29, Jeremiah 6:28 12:6, Leviticus 19:16, Luke 21:16, Matthew 10:17 10:21 10:34-10:35, Mesillat Yesharim 11:Nekiyut-from-Falsehood, Micah 7:5-7:6, Pesikta de R'Kahana 13.4, Proverbs 6:16 6:19 10:18 25:18 26:24-26:25, Psalms 12:3-12:4 15:3 55:12-55:13

[4] Jeremiah 9:5 - 1 Timothy 4:2, Ephesians 4:25, Ezekiel 24:12, Gates of Repentance 3.147 3.211 4.005, Genesis 19:11, Habakkuk 2:13, Isaiah 5:18 41:6-41:7 44:12-44:14 57:10 59:13-59:15, Jeremiah 9:4 9:9, Job 11:3 15:5, Micah 6:3 6:12, mt.Hilchot Teshuvah 1:1, Proverbs 4:16, Psalms 7:15 50:19 64:4 140:4

[5] LXX *There is usury upon usury*

[6] Jeremiah 9:6 - 1 Corinthians 15:34, Hosea 4:6, Jeremiah 5:27 8:5 11:19 13:10 18:18 20:10, Job 21:14-21:15, John 3:19-3:20, Proverbs 1:24 1:29, Psalms 120:2-120:6, Romans 1:28

[7] Jeremiah 9:7 - 1 Peter 1:7 4:12, 2 Chronicles 36:15, b.Arachin 15b, b.Chullin 30ab, Ein Yaakov Arachin:15b, Ezekiel 22:18-22:22 26:11-26:12, Gates of Repentance 3.179, Hosea 6:4-6:5 11:8-11:9, Isaiah 1:25 48:10, Jastrow 493b 1546b, Jeremiah 6:27 6:29-6:30 31:21, Malachi 3:3, Mesillat Yesharim 11:Nekiyut-in-Giving-Advice, Midrash Proverbs 26, Midrash Psalms 12:2 58:2, Midrash Tanchuma Chukkat 9, Midrash Tanchuma Metzora 2, z.Vaetchanan 269b, Zechariah 1:14-1:16 13:9
Jeremiah 9:7-15 - 4QJera

[8] Jeremiah 9:8 - 2 Samuel 3:27 20:9-20:10, Gates of Repentance 3.179, Jeremiah 5:26 9:4 9:6, Matthew 26:48-26:49, Proverbs 26:24-26:26, Psalms 12:3 28:3 55:22 57:5 64:4-64:5 64:9 120:3

[9] Jeremiah 9:9 - b.Berachot 56b, b.Shabbat 145b, b.Yoma 54a, Ein Yaakov Shabbat:145b, Isaiah 1:24, Jastrow 1362b, Jeremiah 5:9 5:29, Lamentations.R Petichata D'Chakimei:34, Pesikta de R'Kahana 13.10 S5.2, Pesikta Rabbati 1:5, Seder Olam 27:Siege, y.Taanit 4:5

[10] LXX *Take up a lamentation for the mountains, and a mournful dirge for the paths of the wilderness, for they are desolate for want of men; they did not heard the sound of life from the birds of the sky, nor the cattle: they were amazed, they are gone*

[11] Jeremiah 9:10 - Ezekiel 14:15 29:11 33:28, Hosea 4:3, Isaiah 49:19, Jeremiah 2:6 4:19-4:26 7:29 8:18 12:4 12:10 13:16-13:17 14:6 23:10, Joel 1:10-12, Lamentations 1:16 2:11, Midrash Psalms 50:1

[12] LXX *dragons*

Hebrew		English
מִי־הָאִישׁ הֶחָכָם וְיָבֵן אֶת־זֹאת וַאֲשֶׁר דִּבֶּר פִּי־יְהוָה אֵלָיו וְיַגִּדָהּ עַל־מָה אָבְדָה הָאָרֶץ נִצְּתָה כַמִּדְבָּר מִבְּלִי עֹבֵר	11[1]	Who is the wise man, so he may understand this? And who is he to whom the mouth of the LORD has spoken, so he may declare it? Why is the land perished and laid waste like a wilderness, so that no one passes through?
וַיֹּאמֶר יְהוָה עַל־עָזְבָם אֶת־תּוֹרָתִי אֲשֶׁר נָתַתִּי לִפְנֵיהֶם וְלֹא־שָׁמְעוּ בְקוֹלִי וְלֹא־הָלְכוּ בָהּ	12[2]	And the LORD says: Because they have forsaken My law I set before them, and have not listened to My voice, *nor walked in it*[3];
וַיֵּלְכוּ אַחֲרֵי שְׁרִרוּת לִבָּם וְאַחֲרֵי הַבְּעָלִים אֲשֶׁר לִמְּדוּם אֲבוֹתָם	13[4]	But have walked after the stubbornness of their own heart, and after the Baalim, which their fathers taught them.
לָכֵן כֹּה־אָמַר יְהוָה צְבָאוֹת אֱלֹהֵי יִשְׂרָאֵל הִנְנִי מַאֲכִילָם אֶת־הָעָם הַזֶּה לַעֲנָה וְהִשְׁקִיתִים מֵי־רֹאשׁ	14[5]	Therefore, thus says the LORD of hosts, the God of Israel: Behold, I will feed them, this people, with *wormwood*[6], and give them water of gall to drink.
וַהֲפִצוֹתִים בַּגּוֹיִם אֲשֶׁר לֹא יָדְעוּ הֵמָּה וַאֲבוֹתָם וְשִׁלַּחְתִּי אַחֲרֵיהֶם אֶת־הַחֶרֶב עַד כַּלּוֹתִי אוֹתָם	15[7]	I will scatter them also among the nations, whom neither they nor their fathers have known; and I will send the sword after them, until I have consumed them.
כֹּה אָמַר יְהוָה צְבָאוֹת הִתְבּוֹנְנוּ וְקִרְאוּ לַמְקוֹנְנוֹת וּתְבוֹאֶינָה וְאֶל־הַחֲכָמוֹת שִׁלְחוּ וְתָבוֹאנָה	16[8]	Thus says the LORD of hosts: Consider and call for the mourning women, so they may come; and send for the wise women, *so they may come*[9];
וּתְמַהֵרְנָה וְתִשֶּׂנָה עָלֵינוּ נֶהִי וְתֵרַדְנָה עֵינֵינוּ דִּמְעָה וְעַפְעַפֵּינוּ יִזְּלוּ־מָיִם	17[10]	let them make haste, and take up a wailing for us, so our eyes may run down with tears, and our eyelids gush out with waters.
כִּי קוֹל נְהִי נִשְׁמַע מִצִּיּוֹן אֵיךְ שֻׁדָּדְנוּ בֹּשְׁנוּ מְאֹד כִּי־עָזַבְנוּ אָרֶץ כִּי הִשְׁלִיכוּ מִשְׁכְּנוֹתֵינוּ	18[11]	For a voice of wailing is heard from Zion: 'How are we undone! We are greatly confounded, because we have forsaken the land, because our houses have cast us out.'
כִּי־שְׁמַעְנָה נָשִׁים דְּבַר־יְהוָה וְתִקַּח אָזְנְכֶם דְּבַר־פִּיו וְלַמֵּדְנָה בְנוֹתֵיכֶם נֶהִי וְאִשָּׁה רְעוּתָהּ קִינָה	19[12]	Yes, hear the word of the LORD, O You women, and let your ear receive the word of His mouth, and teach your daughters wailing, and her neighbor lamentation:

---

[1] Jeremiah 9:11 - b.Bava Metzia 85a, b.Nedarim 81a, Ein Yaakov Bava Metzia:85a, Ein Yaakov Nedarim:81a, Isaiah 13:22 25:2 34:13 44:26, Jastrow 1242b, Jeremiah 10:22 25:11 25:18 26:9 26:18 34:22 51:37, Lamentations 2:2 2:7-2:8 3:47, Lamentations.R Petichata D'Chakimei:2, Micah 1:6 3:12 6:16, Nehemiah 4:2, Pesikta de R'Kahana 15.5, Pesikta Rabbati 29/30:2, Psalms 79:1, Revelation 18:2, y.Chagigah 1:6, z.Vayeshev 185a
Jeremiah 9:11-12 - Sifre Devarim Ekev 41, z.Beshallach 58b

[2] Jeremiah 9:12 - 1 Kings 9:8-9:9, b.Bava Metzia 85b, b.Nedarim 81a, Deuteronomy 29:21-29:27 32:29, Ein Yaakov Bava Metzia:85a, Ein Yaakov Nedarim:81a, Ezekiel 14:23 22:25-22:31, Hosea 14:11, Jastrow 1242b, Jeremiah 5:19-5:20 16:10-16:13 22:8-22:9, Lamentations.R Petichata D'Chakimei:2, Mas.Kallah Rabbati 8:9, Matthew 24:15, Pesikta de R'Kahana 15.5, Pesikta Rabbati 29/30:2, Psalms 107:34 107:43, Revelation 1:3, Tanya Igeret Hateshuvah §01, y.Chagigah 1:6, z.Vaetchanan 266b

[3] Missing in LXX

[4] Jeremiah 9:13 - 2 Chronicles 7:19, Ezra 9:10, Jeremiah 22:9, Proverbs 28:4, Psalms 89:31-89:33 119:53, Zephaniah 3:1-3:6

[5] Jeremiah 9:14 - 1 Peter 1:18, b.Avodah Zara [Rashi] 29a, Deuteronomy 31:16-31:17, Ephesians 2:3 4:17-4:19, Galatians 1:14, Genesis 6:5, Jeremiah 2:8 2:23 3:17 7:24 44:17, Romans 1:21-1:24, Zechariah 1:4-1:5

[6] LXX *trouble*

[7] Jeremiah 9:15 - Deuteronomy 29:17, Isaiah 2:17 2:22, Jeremiah 8:14 23:15 25:15, Lamentations 3:15 3:19, Psalms 60:4 69:22 75:9 80:6, Revelation 8:11, z.Vaetchanan 269b

[8] Jeremiah 9:16 - Deuteronomy 4:27 28:25 28:36 28:64 32:26, Ezekiel 5:2 5:12 11:17 12:15 14:17 20:23, James 1:1, Jeremiah 13:24 15:2-15:4 24:10 25:27 29:17 44:27 49:36-49:37, Lamentations.R Petichata D'Chakimei:2, Leviticus 26:33, Mas.Semachot 14:7, Nehemiah 1:8, Pesikta de R'Kahana 15.4, Psalms 106:27, Testament of Levi 10:4, Zechariah 7:14

[9] LXX *and let them utter their voice*

[10] Jeremiah 9:17 - 2 Chronicles 35:25, 3 Enoch 15:1, Amos 5:16-5:17, Ecclesiastes 12:5, Job 3:9, Lamentations.R Petichata D'Chakimei:2, Mark 5:38, Matthew 9:23, Pirkei de R'Eliezer 17, t.Shabbat 8:28, z.Vaetchanan 269b

[11] Jeremiah 9:18 - Isaiah 22:4, Jeremiah 6:26 9:2 9:11 9:21 13:17 14:17, Lamentations 1:2 2:11 2:18, Lamentations.R Petichata D'Chakimei:8, Luke 19:41, Pirkei de R'Eliezer 17

[12] Jeremiah 9:19 - b.Moed Katan 28b, Deuteronomy 28:29, Ezekiel 7:16-7:18, Jeremiah 2:14 4:13 4:20 4:30-4:31, Lamentations 4:15 5:2, Leviticus 18:25 18:28 20:22, m.Moed Katan 3:9, Micah 1:8-1:9 2:4 2:10, mt.Hilchot Evel 11:5, y.Moed Katan 3:9

כִּי־עָלָה מָוֶת בְּחַלּוֹנֵינוּ בָּא בְּאַרְמְנוֹתֵינוּ לְהַכְרִית עוֹלָל מִחוּץ בַּחוּרִים מֵרְחֹבוֹת	20[1]	'For death came up into our windows, it has entered into our palaces, to cut off the children from the street, and the young men from the broad places.
דַּבֵּר כֹּה נְאֻם־יְהֹוָה וְנָפְלָה נִבְלַת הָאָדָם כְּדֹמֶן עַל־פְּנֵי הַשָּׂדֶה וּכְעָמִיר מֵאַחֲרֵי הַקֹּצֵר וְאֵין מְאַסֵּף	21[2]	*Speak: Thus says the LORD*[3], and the carcasses of men fall as dung on the open field, and as the handful after the harvester, which no one gathers.'
כֹּה אָמַר יְהֹוָה אַל־יִתְהַלֵּל חָכָם בְּחָכְמָתוֹ וְאַל־יִתְהַלֵּל הַגִּבּוֹר בִּגְבוּרָתוֹ אַל־יִתְהַלֵּל עָשִׁיר בְּעָשְׁרוֹ	22[4]	Thus says the LORD: Do not let the wise man glory in his wisdom, nor let the mighty man glory in his might, do not let the rich man glory in his riches;
כִּי אִם־בְּזֹאת יִתְהַלֵּל הַמִּתְהַלֵּל הַשְׂכֵּל וְיָדֹעַ אוֹתִי כִּי אֲנִי יְהֹוָה עֹשֶׂה חֶסֶד מִשְׁפָּט וּצְדָקָה בָּאָרֶץ כִּי־בְאֵלֶּה חָפַצְתִּי נְאֻם־יְהֹוָה	23[5]	But let he who glories glory in this, that he understands, and knows Me, that I am the LORD who exercise mercy, justice, and righteousness, in the earth; for in these things I delight, says the LORD.
הִנֵּה יָמִים בָּאִים נְאֻם־יְהֹוָה וּפָקַדְתִּי עַל־כָּל־מוּל בְּעָרְלָה	24[6]	Behold, the days come, says the LORD, that I will punish all those who are circumcised in their uncircumcision:
עַל־מִצְרַיִם וְעַל־יְהוּדָה וְעַל־אֱדוֹם וְעַל־בְּנֵי עַמּוֹן וְעַל־מוֹאָב וְעַל כָּל־קְצוּצֵי פֵאָה הַיֹּשְׁבִים בַּמִּדְבָּר כִּי כָל־הַגּוֹיִם עֲרֵלִים וְכָל־בֵּית יִשְׂרָאֵל עַרְלֵי־לֵב	25[7]	Egypt, and *Judah*[8], and Edom, and the children of Ammon, and Moab, and *all who have the corners of their hair polled*[9], who live in the wilderness; for all the nations are uncircumcised, but all the house of Israel are uncircumcised in the heart.

Jeremiah – Chapter 10

שִׁמְעוּ אֶת־הַדָּבָר אֲשֶׁר דִּבֶּר יְהֹוָה עֲלֵיכֶם בֵּית יִשְׂרָאֵל	1[10]	Hear the word the LORD speaks to you, O house of Israel;

---

[1] Jeremiah 9:20 - b.Bava Kamma 60b, Ein Yaakov Bava Kamma:60b, Isaiah 3:4 3:16 32:9-32:13, Jastrow 1051b, Jeremiah 9:18-9:19, Job 22:22, Lamentations.R 1:37, Luke 23:27-23:30, Mekhilta de R'Shimon bar Yochai Shirata 27:1, Mekilta de R'Ishmael Shirata 1:145, Midrash Psalms 8:5 22:17, Midrash Tanchuma Beshallach 11, Testament of Job 25:1

[2] Jeremiah 9:21 - 2 Chronicles 36:17, Amos 6:10-6:11, Ezekiel 9:5-9:6 21:19-21:20, Jeremiah 6:11 15:7, Mas.Semachot 8:9

[3] Missing in LXX

[4] Jeremiah 9:22 - 2 Kings 9:37, 4Q460 frag 8 1.2, Ahiqar 207, b.Arachin 10b, Ein Yaakov Arachin:10b, Gates of Repentance 1.025 3.034, Guide for the Perplexed 3:54, Isaiah 5:25, Jeremiah 7:33 8:2 16:4 25:33, Midrash Psalms 52:7 112:1, Numbers.R 22:7, Psalms 83:11, Tanya Igeret Hakodesh §05, z.Vaetchanan 269b, Zephaniah 1:17
Jeremiah 9:22-23 - Haftarah Tzav [continued from 7:21-8:3 Ashkenaz and Sephard] [continued from 7:21-28 Teimon], Midrash Tanchuma Mattot 5
Jeremiah 9:22-25 - 4QJerb

[5] Jeremiah 9:23 - 1 Corinthians 1:19-1:21 1:27-1:29 3:18-3:20, 1 Kings 20:10-20:11, 1 Samuel 17:4-17:10 17:42, 1 Timothy 6:10, Acts 12:22-12:23, Amos 2:14-2:16, b.Megillah [Tosefot] 25a, Daniel 3:15 4:27-4:28 4:34 5:18-5:23, Derech Hashem Part I 4§08, Deuteronomy 8:17, Ecclesiastes 2:13-16 2:19 9:11, Ecclesiastes.R 12:9, Exodus.R 30:16, Ezekiel 7:19 28:2-28:9 29:9, Gates of Repentance 3.034, Genesis.R 35:3, Isaiah 5:21 10:8 10:12-10:13 36:8-9, James 3:14-16, Job 5:12-14 31:24-31:25, Luke 12:19-12:20, Mark 10:24, Midrash Psalms 52:7 89:1 112:1, Midrash Shmuel 1:1, Numbers.R 10:1, Proverbs 11:4, Psalms 33:16-17 49:7-14 49:17-19 52:7-8 62:11, Pseudo-Phocylides 53, Romans 1:22, Saadia Opinions 2:11, y.Peah 1:1, z.Vaetchanan 269b, Zephaniah 1:18

[6] Jeremiah 9:24 - 1 Corinthians 1:31, 1 John 5:20, 1 Maccabees 1:15, 1 Samuel 15:22, 2 Corinthians 4:6 10:17, Exodus 34:5-34:7, Galatians 6:14, Isaiah 41:16 45:25 61:8, Jeremiah 4:2 31:34-31:35, John 17:3, Leviticus.R 25:6, Luke 10:22, Matthew 11:27, Micah 6:8 7:18, Pesikta Rabbati 42:9, Philippians 3:3, Psalms 36:6-36:8 44:9 51:2 91:14 99:4 145:7-145:8 146:7-146:9, Romans 3:25-3:26 5:11

[7] Jeremiah 9:25 - Acts 7:51, Amos 1:1-1:2, Amos 3:2, b.Avodah Zara 16a, b.Nedarim 31b, Deuteronomy 30:6, Ein Yaakov Nedarim:31b, Ezekiel 24:1-24:27 44:7 44:9, Ezekiel 28:10 32:19-32:32, Galatians 5:2-5:6, Genesis.R 46:5, Isaiah 13:1-13:22 19:24-19:25, Jastrow 1119b, Jeremiah 4:4 25:9-25:26 27:3-27:7 46:1-46:28 49:32, Leviticus 26:41, m.Nedarim 3:11, Mekilta de R'Ishmael Amalek 3:107, mt.Hilchot Milah 3:8, mt.Hilchot Nedarim 9:22, Pirkei de R'Eliezer 16, Romans 2:28-2:29, Romans 2:8-2:9 2:25-2:26, y.Nedarim 3:9, z.Mishpatim 122a, Zephaniah 1:1-1:2

[8] LXX *Idumea*

[9] LXX *on everyone who completely shaves his face*

[10] Jeremiah 10:1 - 1 Kings 22:19, 1 Thessalonians 2:13, Amos 7:16, Hosea 4:1, Isaiah 1:10 28:14, Jeremiah 2:4 13:15-13:17 22:2 42:15, Psalms 50:7, Revelation 2:29
Jeremiah 10:1-5 - 4QJerb

2[1] Thus says the LORD: Do not learn the way of the nations, do not be dismayed at the signs of heaven; for the nations are dismayed at them.

כֹּה ׀ אָמַר יְהֹוָה אֶל־דֶּרֶךְ הַגּוֹיִם אַל־תִּלְמָדוּ וּמֵאֹתוֹת הַשָּׁמַיִם אַל־תֵּחָתּוּ כִּי־יֵחַתּוּ הַגּוֹיִם מֵהֵמָּה

3[2] For the customs of the peoples are vanity; for it is but a tree that one cuts from the forest, the work of the hands of the workman with the axe.

כִּי־חֻקּוֹת הָעַמִּים הֶבֶל הוּא כִּי־עֵץ מִיַּעַר כְּרָתוֹ מַעֲשֵׂה יְדֵי־חָרָשׁ בַּמַּעֲצָד

4[3] They deck it with silver and with gold, they fasten it with nails and with hammers, so it will not move.

בְּכֶסֶף וּבְזָהָב יְיַפֵּהוּ בְּמַסְמְרוֹת וּבְמַקָּבוֹת יְחַזְּקוּם וְלוֹא יָפִיק

5[4] *They are like a pillar in a garden of cucumbers, and do not speak; they must be carried, because they cannot move[5]*. Do not be afraid of them, for they cannot do evil, nor is it in them to do good.

כְּתֹמֶר מִקְשָׁה הֵמָּה וְלֹא יְדַבֵּרוּ נָשׂוֹא יִנָּשׂוּא כִּי לֹא יִצְעָדוּ אַל־תִּירְאוּ מֵהֶם כִּי־לֹא יָרֵעוּ וְגַם־הֵיטֵיב אֵין אוֹתָם

6[6] There is no one like to You, O LORD; you are great, and Your name is great in might.

מֵאֵין כָּמוֹךָ יְהֹוָה גָּדוֹל אַתָּה וְגָדוֹל שִׁמְךָ בִּגְבוּרָה

7[7] Who would not fear You, O king of the nations? For it befits You; because among all the wise men of the nations, and in all their royalty, there is none like to You.

מִי לֹא יִרָאֲךָ מֶלֶךְ הַגּוֹיִם כִּי לְךָ יָאָתָה כִּי בְכָל־חַכְמֵי הַגּוֹיִם וּבְכָל־מַלְכוּתָם מֵאֵין כָּמוֹךָ

8[8] But they are altogether brutish and foolish: the vanities by which they are instructed are but a stock;

וּבְאַחַת יִבְעֲרוּ וְיִכְסָלוּ מוּסַר הֲבָלִים עֵץ הוּא

9[9] Silver beaten into plates which is brought from Tarshish, and gold from Uphaz, *the work of the craftsman and of the hands of the goldsmith; blue and purple is their clothing; they are all the work of skillful men[10]*.

כֶּסֶף מְרֻקָּע מִתַּרְשִׁישׁ יוּבָא וְזָהָב מֵאוּפָז מַעֲשֵׂה חָרָשׁ וִידֵי צוֹרֵף תְּכֵלֶת וְאַרְגָּמָן לְבוּשָׁם מַעֲשֵׂה חֲכָמִים כֻּלָּם

---

[1] Jeremiah 10:2 - 1 Enoch 48:3 72:12, b.Shabbat 156a, b.Succah 29a, Birchat HaChammah. Vihi Noam, Deuteronomy 12:30-12:31, Ein Yaakov Shabbat:156a, Ezekiel 20:32, Genesis.R 44:12, Isaiah 47:12-47:14, Lamentations.R 1:1, Leviticus 18:3 20:23, Luke 21:25-21:28, Mekilta de R'Ishmael Pisha 2:49, Pirkei de R'Eliezer 7, Ralbag Wars 5 part 2:1, t.Sukkah 2:6, z.Bereshit 9a, z.Vaetchanan 269b
Jeremiah 10:2-16 - Exodus.R 16:2
[2] Jeremiah 10:3 - 1 Kings 18:26-18:28, 1 Peter 1:18, Ein Yaakov Sukkah:29a, Habakkuk 2:18-2:19, Hosea 8:4-8:6, Isaiah 40:19-40:31 44:9-44:20 45:20, Jeremiah 2:5 10:8, Jubilees 12:5, Leviticus 18:30, Matthew 6:7, Midrash Tanchuma Mishpatim 3, Romans 1:21
[3] Jeremiah 10:4 - Isaiah 40:19-40:20 41:6-41:7 44:12 46:7, Psalms 115:4 135:15
[4] Jeremiah 10:5 - 1 Corinthians 8:4 12:2, 4QJerb, Habakkuk 2:19, Isaiah 41:23-41:24 44:9-44:10 45:20 46:1 46:7, Midrash Psalms 1:21 22:1, Psalms 115:5-115:8 135:16-18, Revelation 13:14-13:15
[5] LXX *they will set them up so they may not move; it is wrought silver, they will not walk, it is forged silver They must certainly be borne, for they cannot ride of themselves*
[6] Jeremiah 10:6 - 2 Samuel 7:22, Daniel 3:33 4:31, Deuteronomy 32:31 33:26, Exodus 8:6 9:14 15:11, Guide for the Perplexed 1:55, Isaiah 12:6 40:18 40:25 46:5 46:9, Jeremiah 32:18, Malachi 1:11, Mekhilta de R'Shimon bar Yochai Shirata 27:1, Mekilta de R'Ishmael Shirata 1:113, Midrash Psalms 93:1, Midrash Tanchuma Bereshit 5, Midrash Tanchuma Beshallach 11, Nehemiah 4:14 9:32, Psalms 35:10 48:2 86:8-86:10 89:7-89:9 96:4 145:3 147:5
Jeremiah 10:6-7 - omitted [LXX] vs. included [MT], Selichot, z.Shemot 4b
Jeremiah 10:6-8 - 4QJerb [Not in LXX or 4QJerb] "There is none like to you, O Hashem; you are great, and your name is great in might; Who should not fear you, O King of the nations? For to you does it appertain; for as much as among all the wise men of the nations, and in all their royal estate, there is none like to you. But they are together brutish and foolish: the instruction of idols! It is but a stock" vs. "But Hashem is the true God; he is the living God, and an everlasting King; at his wrath the earth trembles, and the nations are not able to abide his indignation"
[7] Jeremiah 10:7 - 1 Corinthians 1:19-1:20, Exodus.R 29:9, Guide for the Perplexed 1:36, Isaiah 2:4, Jeremiah 5:22 10:6, Job 37:23-37:24, Luke 12:5, Mekhilta de R'Shimon bar Yochai Shirata 27:1, Mekilta de R'Ishmael Shirata 1:120, Midrash Psalms 93:1, Midrash Tanchuma Bereshit 5, Midrash Tanchuma Beshallach 11, mt.Hilchot Avodat Kochavim vChukkoteihem 1:1, Psalms 22:29 72:11 76:8 86:9 89:7, Revelation 11:15 15:4, z.Bereshit 9b, z.Bo 38a, z.Mishpatim 95b, z.Vayechi 218b, z.Yitro 90b, Zechariah 2:11
Jeremiah 10:7-8 - mt.Hilchot Avodat Kochavim vChukkoteihem 1:1
[8] Jeremiah 10:8 - b.Taanit 5a, Ein Yaakov Taanit:5a, Habakkuk 2:18, Hosea 4:12, Isaiah 41:29 44:19, Jeremiah 2:27 4:22 10:14 51:17-51:18, mt.Hilchot Avodat Kochavim vChukkoteihem 1:1, Numbers.R 3:12, Pesikta Rabbati 23:1 35:3, Psalms 115:8 135:18, Romans 1:21-1:22, Zechariah 10:2
[9] Jeremiah 10:9 - 1 Kings 10:22, 4QJerb, Daniel 10:5, Ezekiel 27:12, Isaiah 40:19, Mekhilta de R'Shimon bar Yochai Pisha 9:3, Psalms 115:4
Jeremiah 10:9-14 - 4QJera
[10] 4QJerb LXX *they are the products of skilled workers and the hands of the goldsmith, with blue and purple for their clothing.*

וַיהוָ֨ה אֱלֹהִ֣ים אֱמֶת֒ הֽוּא־אֱלֹהִ֥ים חַיִּ֖ים וּמֶ֣לֶךְ עוֹלָ֑ם מִקִּצְפּ֗וֹ תִּרְעַ֤שׁ הָאָ֨רֶץ֙ וְלֹֽא־יָכִ֣לוּ גוֹיִ֔ם זַעְמֽוֹ 10[1]

But the LORD God is the true God, He is the living God, and the everlasting King; at His wrath the earth trembles, and the nations are not able to survive His indignation[2].

כִּדְנָ֣ה תֵּאמְר֣וּן לְה֗וֹם אֱלָ֣הַיָּ֔א דִּֽי־שְׁמַיָּ֥א וְאַרְקָ֖א לָ֣א עֲבַ֑דוּ יֵאבַ֧דוּ מֵֽאַרְעָ֛א וּמִן־תְּח֥וֹת שְׁמַיָּ֖א אֵֽלֶּה 11[3]

Thus shall you say to them: 'The gods who have not made the heavens and the earth, these shall perish from the earth, and from under the heavens.'

עֹשֵׂ֥ה אֶ֨רֶץ֙ בְּכֹח֔וֹ מֵכִ֥ין תֵּבֵ֖ל בְּחָכְמָת֑וֹ וּבִתְבוּנָת֖וֹ נָטָ֥ה שָׁמָֽיִם 12[4]

He who made the earth by His power, Who established the world by His wisdom, and stretched out the heavens by His understanding;

לְק֨וֹל תִּתּ֜וֹ הֲמ֥וֹן מַ֨יִם֙ בַּשָּׁמַ֔יִם וַיַּעֲלֶ֥ה נְשִׂאִ֖ים מִקְצֵ֣ה *אָ֑רֶץ* "הָאָ֑רֶץ" בְּרָקִ֤ים לַמָּטָר֙ עָשָׂ֔ה וַיּ֥וֹצֵא ר֖וּחַ מֵאֹצְרֹתָֽיו 13[5]

At the sound of His giving a multitude of waters in the heavens, when He causes the vapors to ascend from the ends of the earth; when He makes lightnings with the rain, and brings forth the wind from His treasuries;

נִבְעַ֤ר כָּל־אָדָם֙ מִדַּ֔עַת הֹבִ֥ישׁ כָּל־צוֹרֵ֖ף מִפָּ֑סֶל כִּ֛י שֶׁ֥קֶר נִסְכּ֖וֹ וְלֹא־ר֥וּחַ בָּֽם 14[6]

Every man is proven to be brutish, without knowledge, every goldsmith is put to shame by the graven image, his molten image is a lie, and there is no breath in them.

הֶ֣בֶל הֵ֔מָּה מַעֲשֵׂ֖ה תַּעְתֻּעִ֑ים בְּעֵ֥ת פְּקֻדָּתָ֖ם יֹאבֵֽדוּ 15[7]

They are vanity, a work of delusion; in the time of their visitation they shall perish.

לֹֽא־כְאֵ֜לֶּה חֵ֣לֶק יַעֲקֹ֗ב כִּֽי־יוֹצֵ֤ר הַכֹּל֙ ה֔וּא וְיִ֨שְׂרָאֵ֔ל שֵׁ֖בֶט נַחֲלָת֑וֹ יְהוָ֥ה צְבָא֖וֹת שְׁמֽוֹ 16[8]

The portion of Jacob is not like these; for He is the former of all things, and Israel is the tribe of His inheritance; the LORD of hosts is His name.

---

[1] Jeremiah 10:10 - 1 John 5:20, 1 Kings 18:39, 1 Samuel 17:26 17:36, 1 Thessalonians 1:9, 1 Timothy 1:17 6:17, 2 Chronicles 15:3, 4QJerb [Not in LXX or 4QJerb] "There is none like to you, O Hashem; you are great, and your name is great in might; Who should not fear you, O King of the nations? For to you does it appertain; for as much as among all the wise men of the nations, and in all their royal estate, there is none like to you. But they are together brutish and foolish; the instruction of idols! It is but a stock" vs. "But Hashem is the true God; he is the living God, and an everlasting King; at his wrath the earth trembles, and the nations are not able to abide his indignation", Acts 14:15, Avot de R'Natan 34, b.Berachot 14b, b.Sotah [Rashi] 20a, Daniel 3:33 4:31 6:27 7:14, Deuteronomy 5:26 32:4, Exodus.R 15:10 38:1, Genesis.R 1:7 96 [Excl]:1, Habakkuk 3:6 3:10, Hebrews 10:31, Isaiah 37:4 37:17 57:15, Jeremiah 23:36, Job 9:6, Joel 2:11, John 17:3, Judges 5:4, Leviticus.R 6:6 26:1, Malachi 3:2, Matthew 16:16 26:63 27:51-27:52, Mekhilta de R'Shimon bar Yochai Pisha 9:3, Micah 1:4, Midrash Psalms 15:4, mt.Hilchot Kriat Shema 2:17, mt.Hilchot Yesodei haTorah 1:4, Nahum 1:6, O Hashem; you are great, Pesikta de R'Kahana 4.2, Pesikta Rabbati 14:4, Psalms 10:17 18:8 31:6 42:3 68:12 76:8 77:19 84:3 90:11 93:2 97:4 100:5 104:32 114:7 145:13 146:5, Revelation 20:11, Saadia Opinions 2:1 2:12, Siman 16:5, Song of Songs.R 1:46, Tanna Devei Eliyahu 7, Tanya Igeret Hakodesh §06, Tanya Likutei Aramim §35, y.Berachot 1:5 2:2
[2] 4QJerb *But the LORD is the true God. He is the living God and the everlasting King. At his anger the earth quakes and the nations cannot endure his wrath.*
[3] Jeremiah 10:11 - 2 Enoch 2:2, Avot de R'Natan 37, b.Bava Batra [Tosefot] 90b, b.Bava Kamma [Tosefot] 83a, b.Shabbat [Rashi] 115b, Genesis.R 74:14, Isaiah 2:18, Jastrow 63a 597b, Jeremiah 10:15 51:18, Lamentations 3:66, Lamentations.R 1:1, m.Yadayim 4:5, Mekhilta de R'Shimon bar Yochai Pisha 9:3, Midrash Psalms 68:1, Midrash Tanchuma Bereshit 7, Midrash Tanchuma Shoftim 12, Psalms 96:5, Revelation 20:2, y.Sotah 7:2, z.Bereshit 54b, Zechariah 13:2, Zephaniah 2:11
Jeremiah 10:11-12 - Midrash Tanchuma Tetzaveh 10
Jeremiah 10:11-21 - 4QJerb
[4] Jeremiah 10:12 - 2 Baruch 21:4, 3 Enoch 44:7, Birchat HaChammah.Vihi Noam, Colossians 1:16, Genesis 1:1 1:6-1:9, Genesis.R 5:4 13:4, Guide for the Perplexed 1:47, Isaiah 40:22 42:5 44:24 45:12 45:18 48:13 49:8, Jeremiah 10:13 32:17 51:15-51:19, Job 9:8 26:7 38:4-38:7, John 1:3, Perek Shirah [the Wind], Proverbs 3:19 30:4, Psalms 24:2 33:6 78:69 93:1 104:2 104:24 119:90 136:5-136:6 146:5-146:6 148:4-148:5, Tanya Shaar Hayichud §09, z.Bereshit 33b, Zechariah 12:1
Jeremiah 10:12-13 - 11Q5 26:14-15, 4QJerc
[5] Jeremiah 10:13 - 1 Kings 18:41 18:45-46, 1 Samuel 12:17-18, 3 Enoch 23:11 37:2, b.Berachot 59a, b.Megillah 15a, Ein Yaakov Megillah:15a, Exodus 9:23, Genesis.R 13:4, Job 36:27-33 37:2-5 38:22 38:25-27 38:34-35, Midrash Psalms 1:18, Perek Shirah [the Clouds], Psalms 18:14 29:3-10 68:34 135:7 135:17 147:8, Song of Songs.R 1:19, z.Beshallach 56b, Zechariah 10:1
[6] Jeremiah 10:14 - Habakkuk 2:18-2:19, Isaiah 42:17 44:11 44:18-44:20 45:16 46:7-8, Jeremiah 10:8 51:17-18, Midrash Psalms 9:16, Midrash Tanchuma Lech Lecha 12, Proverbs 30:2, Psalms 14:2 92:7 94:8 97:7 115:4-115:8 135:16-135:18, Romans 1:22-23
[7] Jeremiah 10:15 - 1 Samuel 12:21, Acts 14:15, b.Sanhedrin 92a, b.Shabbat [Tosefot] 137b, b.Taanit 5a, Deuteronomy 32:21, Ein Yaakov Sanhedrin:102a, Ein Yaakov Sanhedrin:92a, Ein Yaakov Taanit:5a, Gates of Repentance 3.180, Isaiah 2:18-21 41:24 41:29, Jeremiah 8:12 8:19 10:8 10:11 14:22 51:18, Jonah 2:8, Pesikta de R'Kahana 14.7, Pirkei de R'Eliezer 30, z.Vayera 118b, z.Vayishlach 177b, Zechariah 13:2, Zephaniah 1:3-1:4
[8] Jeremiah 10:16 - Deuteronomy 32:9, Exodus 19:5, Isaiah 45:7 47:4 47:6 51:15 54:5, Jeremiah 10:12 31:36 32:18 50:34 51:19, Lamentations 3:24, Lamentations.R 1:1, Leviticus.R 36:4, Mekhilta de R'Ishmael Shirata 8:83, Midrash Psalms 15:26 50:1, Pesikta de R'Kahana 14.7, Proverbs 16:4, Psalms 16:5-16:6 73:26 74:2 119:57 135:4 142:6, Saadia Opinions 2:13, Sifre Devarim {Haazinu Hashamayim} 312, Sifre Devarim Nitzavim 312, Siman 3:2, Tanya Likutei Aramim §02

אִסְפִּי מֵאֶרֶץ כִּנְעָתֵךְ "יֹשַׁבְתִּי" "יֹשֶׁבֶת" בַּמָּצוֹר	17[1]	*Gather up your wares from the ground, O you who live in the siege[2].*
כִּי־כֹה אָמַר יְהֹוָה הִנְנִי קוֹלֵעַ אֶת־יוֹשְׁבֵי הָאָרֶץ בַּפַּעַם הַזֹּאת וַהֲצֵרוֹתִי לָהֶם לְמַעַן יִמְצָאוּ	18[3]	For thus says the LORD: Behold, I will sling out the inhabitants of the land at this time, and will distress them, so they may feel it.
אוֹי לִי עַל־שִׁבְרִי נַחְלָה מַכָּתִי וַאֲנִי אָמַרְתִּי אַךְ זֶה חֳלִי וְאֶשָּׂאֶנּוּ	19[4]	Woe is me for my hurt! My wound is grievous; but I said: 'This is but a sickness, and I must bear it.'
אָהֳלִי שֻׁדָּד וְכָל־מֵיתָרַי נִתָּקוּ בָּנַי יְצָאֻנִי וְאֵינָם אֵין־נֹטֶה עוֹד אָהֳלִי וּמֵקִים יְרִיעוֹתָי	20[5]	My tent is spoiled, and all my cords are broken; My children went away from me, and they are no more; there is no one to stretch forth my tent anymore, and to set up my curtains.
כִּי נִבְעֲרוּ הָרֹעִים וְאֶת־יְהֹוָה לֹא דָרָשׁוּ עַל־כֵּן לֹא הִשְׂכִּילוּ וְכָל־מַרְעִיתָם נָפוֹצָה	21[6]	For the shepherds became brutish, and have not inquired of the LORD; therefore, they have not prospered, and all their flocks have scattered.
קוֹל שְׁמוּעָה הִנֵּה בָאָה וְרַעַשׁ גָּדוֹל מֵאֶרֶץ צָפוֹן לָשׂוּם אֶת־עָרֵי יְהוּדָה שְׁמָמָה מְעוֹן תַּנִּים	22[7]	Listen! A report, behold, it comes, and a great commotion from the north country, to make the cities of Judah desolate, a dwelling place of jackals.
יָדַעְתִּי יְהֹוָה כִּי לֹא לָאָדָם דַּרְכּוֹ לֹא־לְאִישׁ הֹלֵךְ וְהָכִין אֶת־צַעֲדוֹ	23[8]	O LORD, I know man's way is not his own; it is not in man to direct his steps as he walks.
יַסְּרֵנִי יְהֹוָה אַךְ־בְּמִשְׁפָּט אַל־בְּאַפְּךָ פֶּן־תַּמְעִטֵנִי	24[9]	O LORD, correct me, but in measure; not in your anger, lest you diminish me.
שְׁפֹךְ חֲמָתְךָ עַל־הַגּוֹיִם אֲשֶׁר לֹא־יְדָעוּךָ וְעַל מִשְׁפָּחוֹת אֲשֶׁר בְּשִׁמְךָ לֹא קָרָאוּ כִּי־אָכְלוּ אֶת־יַעֲקֹב וַאֲכָלֻהוּ וַיְכַלֻּהוּ וְאֶת־נָוֵהוּ הֵשַׁמּוּ	25[10]	Pour out Your wrath on the nations who do not know You, and on the families who do not call on Your name; For they devoured Jacob, Yes, they devoured him and consumed him, and laid waste to his dwelling.

Jeremiah – Chapter 11

הַדָּבָר אֲשֶׁר הָיָה אֶל־יִרְמְיָהוּ מֵאֵת יְהֹוָה לֵאמֹר	1	The word that came to Jeremiah from the LORD, saying:
שִׁמְעוּ אֶת־דִּבְרֵי הַבְּרִית הַזֹּאת וְדִבַּרְתָּם אֶל־אִישׁ יְהוּדָה וְעַל־יֹשְׁבֵי יְרוּשָׁלָ͏ִם	2[11]	'Hear the words of this covenant, and speak to the men of Judah, and to the inhabitants of Jerusalem;
וְאָמַרְתָּ אֲלֵיהֶם כֹּה־אָמַר יְהֹוָה אֱלֹהֵי יִשְׂרָאֵל אָרוּר הָאִישׁ אֲשֶׁר לֹא יִשְׁמַע אֶת־דִּבְרֵי הַבְּרִית הַזֹּאת	3[12]	And say to them: Thus says the LORD, the God of Israel: Cursed be the man who does not hear the words of this covenant

---

[1] Jeremiah 10:17 - Ezekiel 12:3-12:12, Jeremiah 6:1 21:13, Matthew 24:15, Micah 2:10

[2] LXX *He has gathered your substance from without the lodged in choice vessels*

[3] Jeremiah 10:18 - 1 Samuel 25:29, Deuteronomy 28:63-28:64, Ezekiel 6:10, Jeremiah 15:1-15:2 16:13 23:20, variant והצרתי of הצרותי is found, z.Vaetchanan 269b, Zechariah 1:6

[4] Jeremiah 10:19 - Isaiah 8:17, Jeremiah 4:19 4:31 8:21 9:2 14:17 17:13, Lamentations 1:2 1:12-22 2:11-22 3:18-21 3:39-40 3:48, Lamentations.R Petichata D'Chakimei:2, Micah 7:9, Midrash Psalms 5:1, Pesikta de R'Kahana 15.4, Psalms 39:10 77:11

[5] Jeremiah 10:20 - Isaiah 49:20-49:22 51:16 54:2, Jeremiah 4:20 31:16, Job 7:8, Lamentations 1:5 2:4-2:6, Pesikta Rabbati 28:1, Proverbs 12:7

[6] Jeremiah 10:21 - Ezekiel 22:25-22:30 34:2-34:10 34:12, Isaiah 56:10-12, Jeremiah 2:8 5:31 8:9 10:8 10:14 12:10 23:1-2 23:9-23:32 49:32 50:17, John 10:12-10:13, Zechariah 10:3 13:7

[7] Jeremiah 10:22 - Habakkuk 1:6-1:9, Jeremiah 1:15 4:6 5:15 6:1 6:22 9:12, Malachi 1:3

[8] Jeremiah 10:23 - 4QJera, Ahiqar 122, Proverbs 16:1 20:24, Psalms 17:5 37:23 119:116-117

[9] Jeremiah 10:24 - Gates of Repentance 4.13, Habakkuk 3:2, Isaiah 40:23 41:11-12, Jeremiah 30:11, Job 6:18, Midrash Psalms 6:7 38:1 78:8, Psalms 6:2 38:2

[10] Jeremiah 10:25 - 1 Corinthians 15:34, 1 Thessalonians 4:5, 2 Thessalonians 1:8, Acts 17:23, Ezekiel 25:6-25:8 35:5-35:10, Isaiah 43:22 64:8, Jeremiah 8:16 50:7 50:17 51:34-51:35, Job 18:21, John 17:25, Lamentations 2:22, Mekhilta de R'Shimon bar Yochai Shirata 29:1, Mekhilta de R'Ishmael Shirata 6:71 9:51, Obadiah 1:10-1:16, Psalms 14:2 27:2 79:6-7, Zechariah 1:15, Zephaniah 1:6 3:8

[11] Jeremiah 11:2 - 2 Chronicles 23:16 29:10 34:31, 2 Kings 11:17 23:2-23:3, Exodus 19:5, Jeremiah 11:6 34:13-34:16

[12] Jeremiah 11:3 - Deuteronomy 27:26 28:15-68 29:18-19, Galatians 3:10-13, Midrash Tanchuma Tazria 9, z.Vaetchanan 269b Jeremiah 11:3-6 - 4QJera

אֲשֶׁר צִוִּיתִי אֶת־אֲבוֹתֵיכֶם בְּיוֹם הוֹצִיאִי־אוֹתָם מֵאֶֽרֶץ־מִצְרַיִם מִכּוּר הַבַּרְזֶל לֵאמֹר שִׁמְעוּ בְקוֹלִי וַעֲשִׂיתֶם אוֹתָם כְּכֹל אֲשֶׁר־אֲצַוֶּה אֶתְכֶם וִהְיִיתֶם לִי לְעָם וְאָנֹכִי אֶהְיֶה לָכֶם לֵאלֹהִים

4[1] That I commanded your fathers in the day I brought them forth from the land of Egypt, from the iron furnace, saying: listen to My voice, and do them, according to all that I command you; so shall you be My people, and I will be your God;

לְמַעַן הָקִים אֶת־הַשְּׁבוּעָה אֲשֶׁר־נִשְׁבַּעְתִּי לַאֲבוֹתֵיכֶם לָתֵת לָהֶם אֶרֶץ זָבַת חָלָב וּדְבַשׁ כַּיּוֹם הַזֶּה וָאַעַן וָאֹמַר אָמֵן ׀ יְהוָה

5[2] So I may establish the oath which I swore to your fathers, to give them a land flowing with milk and honey, as this day.' Then I answered, and said: 'Amen, O LORD.'

וַיֹּאמֶר יְהוָה אֵלַי קְרָא אֶת־כָּל־הַדְּבָרִים הָאֵלֶּה בְּעָרֵי יְהוּדָה וּבְחֻצוֹת יְרוּשָׁלַ͏ִם לֵאמֹר שִׁמְעוּ אֶת־דִּבְרֵי הַבְּרִית הַזֹּאת וַעֲשִׂיתֶם אוֹתָם

6[3] And the LORD said to me: 'Proclaim all these words in the cities of Judah, and in the streets of Jerusalem, saying: Hear the words of this covenant, and do them.

כִּי הָעֵד הַעִדֹתִי בַּאֲבוֹתֵיכֶם בְּיוֹם הַעֲלוֹתִי אוֹתָם מֵאֶרֶץ מִצְרַיִם וְעַד־הַיּוֹם הַזֶּה הַשְׁכֵּם וְהָעֵד לֵאמֹר שִׁמְעוּ בְּקוֹלִי

7[4] *For I earnestly forewarned your fathers in the day I brought them up from the land of Egypt, to this day, forewarning often and often, saying: listen to My voice[5].*

וְלֹא שָׁמְעוּ וְלֹא־הִטּוּ אֶת־אָזְנָם וַיֵּלְכוּ אִישׁ בִּשְׁרִירוּת לִבָּם הָרָע וָאָבִיא עֲלֵיהֶם אֶת־כָּל־דִּבְרֵי הַבְּרִית־הַזֹּאת אֲשֶׁר־צִוִּיתִי לַעֲשׂוֹת וְלֹא עָשׂוּ

8[6] Yet they did not listen, *nor inclined their ear, but everyone walked in the stubbornness of his evil heart; therefore, I brought on them all the words of this covenant, which I commanded them to do, but they did not do them[7].*'

וַיֹּאמֶר יְהוָה אֵלָי נִמְצָא־קֶשֶׁר בְּאִישׁ יְהוּדָה וּבְיֹשְׁבֵי יְרוּשָׁלָ͏ִם

9[8] And the LORD said to me: 'A conspiracy is found among the men of Judah, and among the inhabitants of Jerusalem.

שָׁבוּ עַל־עֲוֺנֹת אֲבוֹתָם הָרִאשֹׁנִים אֲשֶׁר מֵאֲנוּ לִשְׁמוֹעַ אֶת־דְּבָרַי וְהֵמָּה הָלְכוּ אַחֲרֵי אֱלֹהִים אֲחֵרִים לְעָבְדָם הֵפֵרוּ בֵית־יִשְׂרָאֵל וּבֵית יְהוּדָה אֶת־בְּרִיתִי אֲשֶׁר כָּרַתִּי אֶת־אֲבוֹתָם

10[9] They turned back to the iniquities of their forefathers, who refused to hear My words; and they went after other gods to serve them; the house of Israel and the house of Judah have broken My covenant which I made with their fathers.

לָכֵן כֹּה אָמַר יְהוָה הִנְנִי מֵבִיא אֲלֵיהֶם רָעָה אֲשֶׁר לֹא־יוּכְלוּ לָצֵאת מִמֶּנָּה וְזָעֲקוּ אֵלַי וְלֹא אֶשְׁמַע אֲלֵיהֶם

11[10] Therefore, thus says the LORD: Behold, I will bring evil on them, which they shall not be able to escape; and though they shall cry to Me, I will not listen to them.

---

[1] Jeremiah 11:4 - 1 Kings 8:51, 1 Samuel 15:22, 2 Corinthians 6:16, Deuteronomy 4:20 5:2-5:3 11:27 28:1-28:14 29:9-29:14, Exodus 20:6 23:21-23:22 24:3-24:8, Ezekiel 11:20 14:11 20:6-20:12 36:28 37:23 37:27, Genesis 17:8, Hebrews 5:9 8:8-8:10, Isaiah 48:10, Jeremiah 7:22-7:23 24:7 26:13 30:22 31:32-31:34 32:28, Leviticus 26:3 26:12, Matthew 28:20, Tanya Shaar Hayichud §09, Zechariah 6:15 8:8 13:9

[2] Jeremiah 11:5 - 1 Corinthians 14:16, b.Ketubot 112a, Deuteronomy 6:3 7:12-7:13 27:15-27:26, Exodus 3:8-3:17 13:5, Genesis 22:16-22:18 26:3-26:5, Jeremiah 28:6, Leviticus 20:24, Matthew 6:13, Numbers.R 9:35, Psalms 105:9-105:11, Ruth.R Petichata:4, Sifre Devarim {Haazinu Hashamayim} 320, Sifre Devarim Nitzavim 320 320, y.Sotah 2:5

[3] Jeremiah 11:6 - Isaiah 58:1, James 1:22, Jeremiah 3:12 7:2 11:2-11:4 19:2, John 13:17, Psalms 15:5, Romans 2:13, Zechariah 7:7

[4] Jeremiah 11:7 - 1 Samuel 8:9, 2 Chronicles 36:15, 2 Thessalonians 3:12, Deuteronomy 4:6 5:29 6:2 8:6 10:12-10:13 11:26-11:28 13:1 28:1-28:14 30:20, Ephesians 4:17, Exodus 15:26 23:21-23:22, Jeremiah 7:13 7:23-7:25 11:4 25:4 35:15

[5] Missing in LXX

[6] Jeremiah 11:8 - Deuteronomy 28:15-28:68 29:20-29:23 30:17-30:19 31:17-31:18 32:20-32:26, Ezekiel 20:8 20:18-20:21 20:37-20:38, Jeremiah 3:17 6:16-6:17 7:24 7:26 9:14-9:15 35:15 44:17, Joshua 23:13-23:16, Leviticus 26:14-26:46, Nehemiah 9:16-9:17 9:26 9:29, Zechariah 7:11

[7] Missing in LXX

[8] Jeremiah 11:9 - Acts 23:12-23:15, Ezekiel 22:25-22:31, Hosea 6:9, Jeremiah 5:31 6:13 8:10, John 11:53, Matthew 21:38-21:39 26:3-26:4 26:15, Micah 3:11 7:2-7:3, Zephaniah 3:1-3:4

[9] Jeremiah 11:10 - 1 Samuel 15:11, 2 Chronicles 34:30-34:33, 2 Kings 17:7-17:20, Acts 7:51-7:52, Deuteronomy 9:7 31:16, Ezekiel 16:59 20:18-20:21 44:7, Hebrews 8:9, Hosea 6:4 6:7 7:16-8:1, Jeremiah 3:6-3:11 31:33, Judges 2:12-2:13 2:17 2:19, Leviticus 26:15, Psalms 78:8-78:10 78:57, Zechariah 1:4, Zephaniah 1:6

[10] Jeremiah 11:11 - 1 Thessalonians 5:3, 2 Chronicles 34:24, 2 Kings 22:16, Amos 2:14-2:15 5:19 9:1-9:4, b.Yevamot 63b, Ein Yaakov Yevamot:63b, Ezekiel 7:5 8:18, Hebrews 1:3, Isaiah 1:15 24:17, Jeremiah 6:19 11:14 11:17 14:12 15:2 19:3 19:15 23:12 35:17 36:31, Luke 13:24-13:28, Micah 3:4, Proverbs 1:28 29:1, Psalms 18:42 66:18, Revelation 6:16-6:17, variant ואל of ולא is found, z.Vaetchanan 269b, Zechariah 7:13

וְהָלְכֿוּ עָרֵי יְהוּדָה וְיֹשְׁבֵי֙ יְרוּשָׁלִַ֔ם וְזָעֲקוּ֙ אֶל־הָאֱלֹהִ֔ים אֲשֶׁ֕ר הֵ֥ם מְקַטְּרִ֖ים לָהֶ֑ם וְהוֹשֵׁ֤עַ לֹא־יוֹשִׁ֨יעוּ֙ לָהֶ֔ם בְּעֵ֖ת רָעָתָֽם	12¹	Then the cities of Judah and the inhabitants of Jerusalem shall go and cry to the gods to whom they offer; but they shall not save them at all in the time of their trouble.
כִּ֚י מִסְפַּ֣ר עָרֶ֔יךָ הָי֥וּ אֱלֹהֶ֖יךָ יְהוּדָ֑ה וּמִסְפַּ֞ר חֻצ֣וֹת יְרוּשָׁלִַ֗ם שַׂמְתֶּ֤ם מִזְבְּחוֹת֙ לַבֹּ֔שֶׁת מִזְבְּח֖וֹת לְקַטֵּ֥ר לַבָּֽעַל	13²	For according to the number of your cities are your gods, O Judah; and according to the number of the streets of Jerusalem have you set up altars to the shameful thing, altars to offer to Baal.
וְאַתָּ֗ה אַל־תִּתְפַּלֵּל֙ בְּעַד־הָעָ֣ם הַזֶּ֔ה וְאַל־תִּשָּׂ֥א בַעֲדָ֖ם רִנָּ֣ה וּתְפִלָּ֑ה כִּ֣י אֵינֶ֣נִּי שֹׁמֵ֗עַ בְּעֵ֛ת קָרְאָ֥ם אֵלַ֖י בְּעַ֥ד רָעָתָֽם	14³	Therefore, do not pray for this people, nor lift up a cry nor prayer for them; for I will not hear them when they cry to Me in their trouble.'
מֶ֣ה לִֽידִידִ֞י בְּבֵיתִ֗י עֲשׂוֹתָ֤הּ הַֽמְזִמָּ֙תָה֙ הָֽרַבִּ֔ים וּבְשַׂר־קֹ֖דֶשׁ יַעַבְר֣וּ מֵֽעָלָ֑יִךְ כִּ֥י רָעָתֵ֖כִי אָ֥ז תַּעֲלֹֽזִי	15⁴	What has My beloved to do in My house, seeing she has worked lewdness with many, and the hallowed flesh is passed from you? When you do evil, then you rejoice.
זַ֤יִת רַֽעֲנָן֙ יְפֵ֣ה פְרִי־תֹ֔אַר קָרָ֥א יְהוָ֖ה שְׁמֵ֑ךְ לְק֣וֹל ׀ הֲמוּלָּ֣ה גְדֹלָ֗ה הִצִּ֥ית אֵשׁ֙ עָלֶ֔יהָ וְרָע֖וּ דָּלִיּוֹתָֽיו	16⁵	The LORD called your name 'a leafy olive tree, fair with goodly fruit;' with the noise of a great tumult He kindled fire on it, and its branches are broken.
וַיהוָ֤ה צְבָאוֹת֙ הַנּוֹטֵ֣עַ אוֹתָ֔ךְ דִּבֶּ֥ר עָלַ֖יִךְ רָעָ֑ה בִּ֠גְלַל רָעַ֨ת בֵּֽית־יִשְׂרָאֵ֜ל וּבֵ֣ית יְהוּדָ֗ה אֲשֶׁ֨ר עָשׂ֤וּ לָהֶם֙ לְהַכְעִסֵ֔נִי לְקַטֵּ֖ר לַבָּֽעַל	17⁶	For the LORD of hosts, who planted you, has pronounced evil against you, because of the evil of the house of Israel and of the house of Judah, which they worked for themselves in provoking Me by offering to Baal.
וַֽיהוָ֥ה הֽוֹדִיעַ֖נִי וָאֵדָ֑עָה אָ֖ז הִרְאִיתַ֥נִי מַֽעַלְלֵיהֶֽם	18⁷	And the LORD gave me knowledge of it, and I knew it; then you showed me their deeds.
וַאֲנִ֕י כְּכֶ֥בֶשׂ אַלּ֖וּף יוּבַ֣ל לִטְב֑וֹחַ וְלֹֽא־יָדַ֜עְתִּי כִּֽי־עָלַ֣י ׀ חָשְׁב֣וּ מַחֲשָׁב֗וֹת נַשְׁחִ֨יתָה עֵ֤ץ בְּלַחְמוֹ֙ וְנִכְרְתֶ֙נּוּ֙ מֵאֶ֣רֶץ חַיִּ֔ים וּשְׁמ֖וֹ לֹֽא־יִזָּכֵ֥ר עֽוֹד	19⁸	But I was like a docile lamb who is led to the slaughter; and I did not know they devised devices against me: 'Let us destroy the tree with its fruit, and let us cut him off from the land of the living, so his name may be remembered no more.'
וַֽיהוָ֣ה צְבָא֗וֹת שֹׁפֵ֥ט צֶ֙דֶק֙ בֹּחֵ֣ן כְּלָי֣וֹת וָלֵ֔ב אֶרְאֶ֥ה נִקְמָֽתְךָ֖ מֵהֶ֑ם כִּ֥י אֵלֶ֖יךָ גִּלִּ֥יתִי אֶת־רִיבִֽי	20⁹	But, O LORD of hosts, who judges righteously, who tries the reins and the heart, let me see Your vengeance on them; for I have revealed my cause to You.

---

¹ Jeremiah 11:12 - 2 Chronicles 28:22, Deuteronomy 32:37, Isaiah 45:20, Jeremiah 2:28 44:17-27, Judges 10:14

² Jeremiah 11:13 - 2 Kings 21:4-21:5 23:4-23:5 23:13, Deuteronomy 32:16-32:17, Hosea 12:13, Isaiah 2:8, Jeremiah 2:28 3:1-3:2 3:24 7:9 19:5 32:35, Lamentations.R Petichata D'Chakimei:22, Sifre Devarim {Haazinu Hashamayim} 321, Sifre Devarim Nitzavim 321

³ Jeremiah 11:14 - 1 John 5:16, Exodus 32:10, Hosea 5:6, Jeremiah 7:16 11:11 14:11 15:1, Pirkei de R'Eliezer 3, Proverbs 26:24-26:25, Psalms 66:18

⁴ Jeremiah 11:15 - 1 Corinthians 13:6, b.Menachot 53b, Ein Yaakov Menachot:44b, Ein Yaakov Menachot:53b, Ezekiel 16:25-16:34 23:2-23:21, Gates of Repentance 3.231, Haggai 2:12-2:14, Hosea 3:1, Isaiah 1:11-1:15 50:1, James 4:16, Jeremiah 2:2 3:1-3:2 3:8 3:14 7:8-7:11 12:7 15:1, Lamentations.R 1:20 Petichata D'Chakimei:24, Luke 8:28, Matthew 22:11, Pesikta de R'Kahana S5.2, Pesikta Rabbati 14:15, Proverbs 2:14 10:23 15:8 21:27 26:18 28:9, Psalms 50:16, Romans 11:28, Sifre Devarim Vezot Habracha 352, Titus 1:15

⁵ Jeremiah 11:16 - b.Berachot 57a, b.Menachot 53b, Ein Yaakov Menachot:44b, Ein Yaakov Menachot:53b, Esther.R 9:2, Exodus.R 36:1 36:3, Ezekiel 15:4-15:7 21:3-20:4, Isaiah 1:30-1:31 27:11, Jastrow 477b 1488a, Jeremiah 21:14, John 15:6, Matthew 3:10, Midrash Psalms 128:4, Midrash Tanchuma Shelach 7, Numbers.R 16:11, Pesikta de R'Kahana 21.4, Psalms 52:9 80:17 83:3, Romans 11:17-11:24, y.Taanit 4:5

⁶ Jeremiah 11:17 - 2 Samuel 7:10, Ezekiel 17:5, Genesis.R 34:10, Isaiah 5:2 61:3, Jeremiah 2:21 7:9 11:11 12:2 16:10-16:11 18:8 19:15 24:6 26:13 26:19 35:17 36:7 40:2 42:10 45:4, Jubilees 7:34, Numbers.R 3:4, Psalms 44:3 80:9 80:16

⁷ Jeremiah 11:18 - 1 Samuel 23:11-23:12, 2 Kings 6:9-6:10 6:14-6:20, Ezekiel 8:6-8:18, Jeremiah 11:19, Matthew 21:3, Romans 3:7

⁸ Jeremiah 11:19 - Daniel 9:26, Isaiah 32:7 38:11 53:7-8, Jeremiah 18:18 20:10, Job 28:13, Luke 20:10-15, Matthew 26:3-4, Numbers 1:14, Proverbs 7:22 10:7, Psalms 27:13 31:14 35:15 37:32-33 52:6 83:5 109:13 112:6 116:9 142:6, Tanya Igeret Hakodesh §\8 Jeremiah 11:19-20 - 4QJera

⁹ Jeremiah 11:20 - 1 Chronicles 28:9 29:17, 1 Peter 2:23, 1 Samuel 16:7 24:15, 2 Baruch 48:39, 2 Timothy 4:14, Acts 17:31, Genesis 18:25, Jeremiah 12:1 15:15 17:10 17:18 18:20-18:23 20:12, Job 5:8, Midrash Proverbs 20, Philippians 4:6, Psalms 7:10 10:15-10:16 35:2 43:1 57:2 98:9, Revelation 2:23 6:9-6:10 18:20, Tanya Likutei Aramim §41

לָכֵן כֹּה־אָמַר יְהֹוָה עַל־אַנְשֵׁי עֲנָתוֹת הַמְבַקְשִׁים אֶת־נַפְשְׁךָ לֵאמֹר לֹא תִנָּבֵא בְּשֵׁם יְהֹוָה וְלֹא תָמוּת בְּיָדֵנוּ

21[1] Therefore, thus says the LORD concerning the men of Anathoth, who seek your life, saying: 'You shall not prophesy in the name of the LORD, so you will not die by our hand;'

לָכֵן כֹּה אָמַר יְהֹוָה צְבָאוֹת הִנְנִי פֹקֵד עֲלֵיהֶם הַבַּחוּרִים יָמֻתוּ בַחֶרֶב בְּנֵיהֶם וּבְנוֹתֵיהֶם יָמֻתוּ בָּרָעָב

22[2] Therefore, thus says the LORD of hosts: Behold, I will punish them; the young men shall die by the sword, their sons and their daughters shall die by famine;

וּשְׁאֵרִית לֹא תִהְיֶה לָהֶם כִּי־אָבִיא רָעָה אֶל־אַנְשֵׁי עֲנָתוֹת שְׁנַת פְּקֻדָּתָם

23 And there shall be no remnant to them; for I will bring evil upon the men of Anathoth, the year of their visitation.

Jeremiah – Chapter 12

צַדִּיק אַתָּה יְהֹוָה כִּי אָרִיב אֵלֶיךָ אַךְ מִשְׁפָּטִים אֲדַבֵּר אוֹתָךְ מַדּוּעַ דֶּרֶךְ רְשָׁעִים צָלֵחָה שָׁלוּ כָּל־בֹּגְדֵי בָגֶד

1[3] Right you would be, O LORD, if I to contend with You; yet I will reason with You: Why does the way of the wicked prosper? Why are all they secure who deal very treacherously?

נְטַעְתָּם גַּם־שֹׁרָשׁוּ יֵלְכוּ גַּם־עָשׂוּ פֶרִי קָרוֹב אַתָּה בְּפִיהֶם וְרָחוֹק מִכִּלְיוֹתֵיהֶם

2[4] You have planted them, yes, they have taken root; they grow, yes, they bring forth fruit; You are near in their mouth, and far from their reins.

וְאַתָּה יְהֹוָה יְדַעְתָּנִי תִּרְאֵנִי וּבָחַנְתָּ לִבִּי אִתָּךְ הַתִּקֵם כְּצֹאן לְטִבְחָה וְהַקְדִּשֵׁם לְיוֹם הֲרֵגָה

3[5] But You, O LORD, know me, You see me, and try my heart toward You; pull them out like sheep for the slaughter, and prepared them for the day of slaughter.

עַד־מָתַי תֶּאֱבַל הָאָרֶץ וְעֵשֶׂב כָּל־הַשָּׂדֶה יִיבָשׁ מֵרָעַת יֹשְׁבֵי־בָהּ סָפְתָה בְהֵמוֹת וָעוֹף כִּי אָמְרוּ לֹא יִרְאֶה אֶת־אַחֲרִיתֵנוּ

4[6] How long shall the land mourn, and the herbs of the whole field wither for the wickedness of those who live in it, the beasts and the birds are consumed because they said: 'He[7] does not see our end.'

כִּי אֶת־רַגְלִים רַצְתָּה וַיַּלְאוּךָ וְאֵיךְ תְּתַחֲרֶה אֶת־הַסּוּסִים וּבְאֶרֶץ שָׁלוֹם אַתָּה בוֹטֵחַ וְאֵיךְ תַּעֲשֶׂה בִּגְאוֹן הַיַּרְדֵּן

5[8] *'If you ran with the footmen, and they wearied you, how can you contend with horses? And though in a land of peace you are secure, how will you do in the thickets of the Jordan[9]?*

כִּי גַם־אַחֶיךָ וּבֵית־אָבִיךָ גַּם־הֵמָּה בָּגְדוּ בָךְ גַּם־הֵמָּה קָרְאוּ אַחֲרֶיךָ מָלֵא אַל־תַּאֲמֵן בָּם כִּי־יְדַבְּרוּ אֵלֶיךָ טוֹבוֹת

6[10] For your brothers and the house of your father have dealt treacherously with you, they have cried aloud after you; do not believe them, though they speak fair words to you.'

---

[1] Jeremiah 11:21 - Acts 7:51-52, Amos 2:12 7:13-16, Isaiah 30:10, Jeremiah 12:5-6 20:1-2 20:10 26:8 38:1-6, Luke 4:24 13:33-34, Matthew 10:21 10:34-36 21:35 22:6 23:34-37, Micah 2:6-11 7:6, Pesikta de R'Kahana 24.11, Pesikta Rabbati 27/28:1, z.Vaetchanan 269b

[2] Jeremiah 11:22 - 1 Thessalonians 2:15-2:16, 2 Chronicles 36:17, Jeremiah 9:22 18:21, Lamentations 2:21, Leviticus.R 10:5, z.Vaetchanan 269b

[3] Jeremiah 12:1 - b.Sanhedrin 96a, Daniel 9:7, Deuteronomy 32:4, Deuteronomy.R 1:17, Ein Yaakov Sanhedrin:96a, Ezra 9:15, Gates of Repentance 3.015, Genesis 18:25, Habakkuk 1:4 1:13-1:17, Hosea 6:7, Isaiah 41:21 48:8, Jeremiah 5:11 5:27-5:28 11:20 12:6, Job 12:6 13:3 21:7-21:15, Malachi 3:15, Midrash Psalms 90:2, Proverbs 1:32, Psalms 37:1 37:35 51:5 73:3-73:28 92:8 94:3-94:4 119:137 119:75 145:17, Romans 3:5-3:6, Saadia Opinions 5:3, Zephaniah 3:5 Jeremiah 12:1-6 - Tanna Devei Eliyahu 11

[4] Jeremiah 12:2 - b.Sanhedrin 96a, Ein Yaakov Sanhedrin:96a, Ezekiel 17:5-17:10 19:10-19:13 33:31, Gates of Repentance 3.015, Guide for the Perplexed 1:50 3:51, Isaiah 29:13, Jeremiah 3:10 11:17 45:4, Mark 7:6, Matthew 15:8, Titus 1:16 Jeremiah 12:3 - 1 Chronicles 29:17, 1 John 3:20-3:21, 2 Kings 20:3, James 5:5, Jeremiah 11:19-11:20 17:18 18:21-18:23 20:12 48:15 50:27 51:4, Job 23:10, John 21:17, Psalms 7:10 11:6 17:3 26:1 44:22-44:23 139:1-139:4 139:23, Sifre.z Numbers Behaalotcha 11:18

[5] Jeremiah 12:3-7 - 4QJera

[6] Jeremiah 12:4 - Ezekiel 7:2-7:13, Habakkuk 3:17, Hosea 4:3, Jeremiah 4:25 4:28 5:13 5:31 7:20 9:11 14:2 23:10, Joel 1:10-1:17, Psalms 50:21 107:34, Romans 8:22, Saadia Opinions 5:3

[7] 4QJera *The LORD*; LXX *God*

[8] Jeremiah 12:5 - 1 Chronicles 12:14, 1 Peter 4:12, b.Megillah [Rashi] 6b, b.Sanhedrin 96a, Ein Yaakov Sanhedrin:96a, Genesis.R 92:7, Hebrews 12:3-12:4, Jeremiah 26:8 36:26 38:4-38:6 49:19 50:44, Joshua 3:15, Proverbs 3:11 24:10, Psalms 42:8 69:2-69:3

[9] LXX *Your feet run and they cause you to faint; how will you prepare to ride upon horses? And you hast been confident in the land of your peace, how will you do in the roaring of Jordan?*

[10] Jeremiah 12:6 - Acts 16:22 18:12 19:24-29 21:28-30, Ahiqar 139, Ezekiel 33:30-31, Genesis 37:4-11, Isaiah 31:4, Jeremiah 9:5 11:19 11:21 20:10, Job 6:15, John 7:5, Mark 12:12, Matthew 10:21 22:16-18, Micah 7:5-7:6, Proverbs 26:25, Psalms 12:3 69:9

עָזַבְתִּי אֶת־בֵּיתִי נָטַשְׁתִּי אֶת־נַחֲלָתִי נָתַתִּי אֶת־
יְדִדוּת נַפְשִׁי בְּכַף אֹיְבֶיהָ

7[1] I have forsaken My house, I have cast off My heritage; I have given the dearly beloved of My soul into the hand of her enemies.

הָיְתָה־לִּי נַחֲלָתִי כְּאַרְיֵה בַיָּעַר נָתְנָה עָלַי בְּקוֹלָהּ
עַל־כֵּן שְׂנֵאתִיהָ

8[2] My heritage has become to Me as a lion in the forest; she has uttered her voice against Me; therefore, I have opposed her.

הַעַיִט צָבוּעַ נַחֲלָתִי לִי הַעַיִט סָבִיב עָלֶיהָ לְכוּ
אִסְפוּ כָּל־חַיַּת הַשָּׂדֶה הֵתָיוּ לְאָכְלָה

9[3] *Is My heritage to Me as a speckled bird of prey? Are the birds of prey against her[4]?* Come, assemble all the beasts of the field, bring them to devour.

רֹעִים רַבִּים שִׁחֲתוּ כַרְמִי בֹּסְסוּ אֶת־חֶלְקָתִי נָתְנוּ
אֶת־חֶלְקַת חֶמְדָּתִי לְמִדְבַּר שְׁמָמָה

10[5] Many shepherds have destroyed My vineyard, they trod My portion under foot, they made My pleasant portion a desolate wilderness.

שָׂמָהּ לִשְׁמָמָה אָבְלָה עָלַי שְׁמֵמָה נָשַׁמָּה כָּל־הָאָרֶץ
כִּי אֵין אִישׁ שָׂם עַל־לֵב

11[6] They made it desolate, it mourns to Me, being desolate; the whole land is desolate, because no man lays it to heart.

עַל־כָּל־שְׁפָיִם בַּמִּדְבָּר בָּאוּ שֹׁדְדִים כִּי חֶרֶב לַיהוָה
אֹכְלָה מִקְצֵה־אֶרֶץ וְעַד־קְצֵה הָאָרֶץ אֵין שָׁלוֹם
לְכָל־בָּשָׂר

12[7] Upon all the high hills in the wilderness spoilers have come; for the sword of the LORD devours from the one end of the land to the other end of the land, no flesh has peace.

זָרְעוּ חִטִּים וְקֹצִים קָצָרוּ נֶחְלוּ לֹא יוֹעִלוּ וּבֹשׁוּ
מִתְּבוּאֹתֵיכֶם מֵחֲרוֹן אַף־יְהוָה

13[8] They have sown wheat, and reaped thorns; they *put themselves to pain, they do not profit; be ashamed of your increase, because of the fierce anger of the LORD[9].*

כֹּה אָמַר יְהוָה עַל־כָּל־שְׁכֵנַי הָרָעִים הַנֹּגְעִים
בַּנַּחֲלָה אֲשֶׁר־הִנְחַלְתִּי אֶת־עַמִּי אֶת־יִשְׂרָאֵל הִנְנִי
נֹתְשָׁם מֵעַל אַדְמָתָם וְאֶת־בֵּית יְהוּדָה אֶתּוֹשׁ
מִתּוֹכָם

14[10] Thus says the LORD: As for My evil neighbors who touch the inheritance that I caused My people Israel to inherit, behold, I will pluck them up from off their land, and will pluck up the house of Judah from among them.

וְהָיָה אַחֲרֵי נָתְשִׁי אוֹתָם אָשׁוּב וְרִחַמְתִּים
וַהֲשִׁבֹתִים אִישׁ לְנַחֲלָתוֹ וְאִישׁ לְאַרְצוֹ

15[11] And it shall come to pass, after I have plucked them up, I will again have compassion on them; and I will bring them back, every man to his heritage, and every man to his land.

[1] Jeremiah 12:7 - b.Menachot 53b, Ezekiel 7:20-7:21 24:21, Hosea 9:15, Isaiah 2:6, Jeremiah 7:14 7:29 11:15 51:5, Joel 2:15 4:2, Lamentations 2:1-2:22, Luke 21:24, Pesikta de R'Kahana S5.3, Psalms 78:59-78:60, Sifre Devarim {Haazinu Hashamayim} 318, Sifre Devarim Nitzavim 318 Sifre Devarim Vezot Habracha 352

[2] Jeremiah 12:8 - Amos 6:8 R'Eliezer, b.Taanit 16b, b.Zevachim 119a, Ecclesiastes.R 3:10, Ein Yaakov Zevachim:119a, Gates of Repentance 3.210, Hosea 9:15, Jeremiah 2:15 51:38, Midrash Psalms 39:1 95:2 132:2, Midrash Tanchuma Vayigash 10, mt.Hilchot Tefilah 8:11, Numbers.R 16:20, Siman 15:11, Tanna Devei Eliyahu 11, y.Megillah 1:12, y.Taanit 2:1, Zechariah 11:8

[3] Jeremiah 12:9 - 2 Kings 24:2, b.Zevachim 119a, Ein Yaakov Zevachim:119a, Ezekiel 16:36-16:37 23:22-23:25 39:17-39:20, Isaiah 56:9, Jeremiah 2:15 7:33 15:3, Midrash Psalms 68:13 132:2, Pirkei de R'Eliezer 28, Revelation 17:16 19:17-19:18, y.Megillah 1:12

[4] LXX *Is not my inheritance to me a hyaena's cave, or a cave around her*

[5] Jeremiah 12:10 - b.Succah 14a, Isaiah 5:1-5:7 43:28 63:18, Jeremiah 3:19 6:3 23:1 25:9 39:3, Lamentations 1:10-1:11, Luke 20:9-20:16 21:14, Psalms 80:9-80:17, Revelation 11:2

[6] Jeremiah 12:11 - Ecclesiastes 7:2, Isaiah 42:25 57:1, Jeremiah 6:8 9:12 10:22 10:25 12:4-8 14:2 19:8 23:10, Lamentations 1:1-5, Malachi 2:2, Mas.Kallah Rabbati 6:1, mt.Hilchot Tefilah 7:6, Zechariah 7:5

[7] Jeremiah 12:12 - Amos 9:4, Ezekiel 5:2 14:17, Isaiah 34:6 57:21 66:15-66:16, Jeremiah 3:2 4:11-4:15 9:20-9:22 15:2 34:17 47:6 48:2, Leviticus 26:33, Matthew 24:21-24:22, Revelation 6:4 19:16-19:21, Zephaniah 2:12

[8] Jeremiah 12:13 - Deuteronomy 28:38, Habakkuk 2:13, Haggai 1:6 2:16-2:17, Isaiah 30:1-30:6 31:1-31:3 55:2, Jeremiah 3:23-3:25 4:26 25:37-25:38, Leviticus 26:16, Micah 6:15, Romans 6:21
Jeremiah 12:13-17 - 4QJera

[9] LXX *their portions shall not profit them: be ashamed of your boasting, because of reproach before the LORD*

[10] Jeremiah 12:14 - Amos 1:2-1:15 9:14-9:15, b.Berachot 8a, Deuteronomy 30:3, Ein Yaakov Berachot:8a, Ezekiel 25:1-25:17 28:25 34:12-34:13 35:1-35:15 36:24 37:21 39:27-39:28, Hosea 2:2, Isaiah 11:11-11:16, Jeremiah 2:3 3:18 32:37 48:1-49:1 49:7 50:9-50:17 51:33-51:35, mt.Hilchot Tefilah 8:1, Numbers.R 9:18, Obadiah 1:10-1:16, Psalms 105:15 106:47, t.Sotah 4:14, z.Vaetchanan 269b, Zechariah 1:15 2:8 10:6-10:12 12:2-12:4, Zephaniah 2:8-2:10 3:19-3:20

[11] Jeremiah 12:15 - Amos 9:14, Deuteronomy 3:20 30:3, Isaiah 23:17-23:18, Jeremiah 48:47 49:6 49:39, Numbers 32:18

וְהָיָה אִם־לָמֹד יִלְמְדוּ אֶת־דַּרְכֵי עַמִּי לְהִשָּׁבֵעַ בִּשְׁמִי חַי־יְהֹוָה כַּאֲשֶׁר לִמְּדוּ אֶת־עַמִּי לְהִשָּׁבֵעַ בַּבָּעַל וְנִבְנוּ בְּתוֹךְ עַמִּי

16[1] And it shall come to pass, if they will diligently learn the ways of My people to swear by My name: 'As the LORD lives, 'even as they taught My people to swear by Baal; then they shall be built up in the midst of My people.

וְאִם לֹא יִשְׁמָעוּ וְנָתַשְׁתִּי אֶת־הַגּוֹי הַהוּא נָתוֹשׁ וְאַבֵּד נְאֻם־יְהֹוָה

17[2] But if they will not listen, then will I pluck up that nation, plucking up and destroying it, says the LORD.

Jeremiah – Chapter 13

כֹּה־אָמַר יְהֹוָה אֵלַי הָלוֹךְ וְקָנִיתָ לְּךָ אֵזוֹר פִּשְׁתִּים וְשַׂמְתּוֹ עַל־מָתְנֶיךָ וּבַמַּיִם לֹא תְבִאֵהוּ

1[3] Thus said the LORD to me: 'Go, and get a linen girdle, and put it on your loins, and do not put it in water.'

וָאֶקְנֶה אֶת־הָאֵזוֹר כִּדְבַר יְהֹוָה וָאָשִׂם עַל־מָתְנָי

2[4] So I got a girdle according to the word of the LORD, and put it on my loins.

וַיְהִי דְבַר־יְהֹוָה אֵלַי שֵׁנִית לֵאמֹר

3[5] And the word of the LORD came to me *the second time*[6], saying:

קַח אֶת־הָאֵזוֹר אֲשֶׁר קָנִיתָ אֲשֶׁר עַל־מָתְנֶיךָ וְקוּם לֵךְ פְּרָתָה וְטָמְנֵהוּ שָׁם בִּנְקִיק הַסָּלַע

4[7] 'Take the girdle you have, which is on your loins, and arise, go to Perath, and hide it there in a cleft of the rock.'

וָאֵלֵךְ וָאֶטְמְנֵהוּ בִּפְרָת כַּאֲשֶׁר צִוָּה יְהֹוָה אוֹתִי

5[8] So I went, and hid it *in Perath*[9], as the LORD commanded *me*[10].

וַיְהִי מִקֵּץ יָמִים רַבִּים וַיֹּאמֶר יְהֹוָה אֵלַי קוּם לֵךְ פְּרָתָה וְקַח מִשָּׁם אֶת־הָאֵזוֹר אֲשֶׁר צִוִּיתִיךָ לְטָמְנוֹ־שָׁם

6 And it came to pass after many days, the LORD said to me: 'Arise, go to Perath, and take the girdle from there, which I commanded you to hide there.'

וָאֵלֵךְ פְּרָתָה וָאֶחְפֹּר וָאֶקַּח אֶת־הָאֵזוֹר מִן־הַמָּקוֹם אֲשֶׁר־טְמַנְתִּיו שָׁמָּה וְהִנֵּה נִשְׁחַת הָאֵזוֹר לֹא יִצְלַח לַכֹּל

7[11] Then I went to Perath, and dug, and took the girdle from the place where I hid it; and, behold, the girdle was marred and it was profitable for nothing.

וַיְהִי דְבַר־יְהֹוָה אֵלַי לֵאמֹר

8 Then the word of the LORD came to me, saying:

כֹּה אָמַר יְהֹוָה כָּכָה אַשְׁחִית אֶת־גְּאוֹן יְהוּדָה וְאֶת־גְּאוֹן יְרוּשָׁלַ͏ִם הָרָב

9[12] Thus says the LORD: In this manner I will mar the pride of Judah, and the great pride of Jerusalem,

הָעָם הַזֶּה הָרָע הַמֵּאֲנִים לִשְׁמוֹעַ אֶת־דְּבָרַי הַהֹלְכִים בִּשְׁרִרוּת לִבָּם וַיֵּלְכוּ אַחֲרֵי אֱלֹהִים

10[13] Even this evil people, who refuse to hear My words, who walk in the stubbornness of their heart, and went after other gods to serve them,

---

[1] Jeremiah 12:16 - 1 Corinthians 3:9, 1 Peter 2:4-2:6, Deuteronomy 10:20-10:21, Ephesians 2:19-2:22, Isaiah 9:19-9:22 19:23-19:25 45:23 49:6 56:5-56:6 65:16, Jeremiah 3:17 4:2 5:2, Joshua 23:7, Psalms 106:35-106:36, Romans 11:17 14:11, Song of Songs 1:8, Zechariah 2:11, Zephaniah 1:5

[2] Jeremiah 12:17 - 1 Peter 2:6-2:8, 2 Thessalonians 1:8, Daniel 7:4-7:8 11:4, Ezekiel 19:12, Isaiah 12:12, Jeremiah 12:14-12:17 18:7 7:29, Luke 19:27, Psalms 2:8-2:12, Zechariah 14:16-14:19

[3] Jeremiah 13:1 - Ezekiel 4:1-4:5, Hebrews 1:1, Jeremiah 13:11 19:1 3:2, z.Vaetchanan 269b
Jeremiah 13:1-7 - 4QJera
Jeremiah 13:1-27 - Derech Hashem Part III 4§08

[4] Jeremiah 13:2 - Ezekiel 2:8, Hosea 1:2-1:3, Isaiah 20:2, John 13:6-13:7 15:14, Proverbs 3:5

[5] Jeremiah 13:3 - Jeremiah 13:8

[6] Missing in LXX

[7] Jeremiah 13:4 - Guide for the Perplexed 2:46, Jeremiah 51:63-51:64, Micah 4:10, Psalms 17:1

[8] Jeremiah 13:5 - 2 Timothy 2:3, Acts 26:19-20, Exodus 39:42-43 16:16, Hebrews 11:8 11:17-19, John 2:5-8, Matthew 22:2-6

[9] LXX *by the Euphrates*

[10] Missing in 4QJera

[11] Jeremiah 13:7 - Ezekiel 15:3-5, Isaiah 16:7, Jeremiah 13:10 24:1-8, Luke 14:34-35, Philemon 1:11, Romans 3:12, Zechariah 3:3-4

[12] Jeremiah 13:9 - 1 Peter 5:5, Ezekiel 16:50 16:56, Isaiah 2:10-2:17 16:6 23:9, James 4:6, Jeremiah 13:15-13:17 18:4-18:6 24:29, Job 40:10-40:12, Lamentations 5:5-5:8, Leviticus 2:19, Luke 18:14, Nahum 2:3, Proverbs 16:18, z.Vaetchanan 269b, Zephaniah 3:11

[13] Jeremiah 13:10 - 2 Chronicles 36:15-36:16, Acts 7:51, Ecclesiastes 11:9, Ephesians 4:17-4:19, Hebrews 12:25, Isaiah 3:24, Jeremiah 3:17 5:23 7:24-7:28 8:5 9:15 11:7-11:8 11:18 13:7 15:1-15:4 16:4 16:12 25:3-25:7 34:14-34:17, Lamentations.R Petichata D'Chakimei:31, Numbers 14:11, Psalms 78:8, Sifre Numbers 85:2, Sifre.z Numbers Behaalotcha 11:1

אֲחֵרִים לְעָבְדָם וּלְהִשְׁתַּחֲוֺת לָהֶם וִיהִי כָּאֵזוֹר הַזֶּה אֲשֶׁר לֹא־יִצְלַח לַכֹּל

11¹ כִּי כַּאֲשֶׁר יִדְבַּק הָאֵזוֹר אֶל־מָתְנֵי־אִישׁ כֵּן הִדְבַּקְתִּי אֵלַי אֶת־כָּל־בֵּית יִשְׂרָאֵל וְאֶת־כָּל־בֵּית יְהוּדָה נְאֻם־יְהֹוָה לִהְיוֹת לִי לְעָם וּלְשֵׁם וְלִתְהִלָּה וּלְתִפְאָרֶת וְלֹא שָׁמֵעוּ

12² וְאָמַרְתָּ אֲלֵיהֶם אֶת־הַדָּבָר הַזֶּה ס כֹּה־אָמַר יְהֹוָה אֱלֹהֵי יִשְׂרָאֵל כָּל־נֵבֶל יִמָּלֵא יָיִן וְאָמְרוּ אֵלֶיךָ הֲיָדֹעַ לֹא נֵדַע כִּי כָל־נֵבֶל יִמָּלֵא יָיִן

13⁴ וְאָמַרְתָּ אֲלֵיהֶם כֹּה־אָמַר יְהֹוָה הִנְנִי מְמַלֵּא אֶת־כָּל־יֹשְׁבֵי הָאָרֶץ הַזֹּאת וְאֶת־הַמְּלָכִים הַיֹּשְׁבִים לְדָוִד עַל־כִּסְאוֹ וְאֶת־הַכֹּהֲנִים וְאֶת־הַנְּבִיאִים וְאֵת כָּל־יֹשְׁבֵי יְרוּשָׁלָ͏ִם שִׁכָּרוֹן

14⁵ וְנִפַּצְתִּים אִישׁ אֶל־אָחִיו וְהָאָבוֹת וְהַבָּנִים יַחְדָּו נְאֻם־יְהֹוָה לֹא־אֶחְמוֹל וְלֹא־אָחוּס וְלֹא אֲרַחֵם מֵהַשְׁחִיתָם

15⁶ שִׁמְעוּ וְהַאֲזִינוּ אַל־תִּגְבָּהוּ כִּי יְהֹוָה דִּבֵּר

16⁷ תְּנוּ לַיהֹוָה אֱלֹהֵיכֶם כָּבוֹד בְּטֶרֶם יַחְשִׁךְ וּבְטֶרֶם יִתְנַגְּפוּ רַגְלֵיכֶם עַל־הָרֵי נָשֶׁף וְקִוִּיתֶם לְאוֹר וְשָׂמָהּ לְצַלְמָוֶת "יָשִׁית׳ "וְשִׁית״ לַעֲרָפֶל

17⁹ וְאִם לֹא תִשְׁמָעוּהָ בְּמִסְתָּרִים תִּבְכֶּה־נַפְשִׁי מִפְּנֵי גֵוָה וְדָמֹעַ תִּדְמַע וְתֵרַד עֵינִי דִּמְעָה כִּי נִשְׁבָּה עֵדֶר יְהֹוָה

18¹⁰ אֱמֹר לַמֶּלֶךְ וְלַגְּבִירָה הַשְׁפִּילוּ שֵׁבוּ כִּי יָרַד מַרְאֲשׁוֹתֵיכֶם עֲטֶרֶת תִּפְאַרְתְּכֶם

and to worship them, so it be as this girdle, which is profitable for nothing.

11¹ For as the girdle cleaves to the loins of a man, so have I caused the whole house of Israel and the whole house of Judah to cleave to Me, says the LORD, so they might be to Me for a people, and for a name, and for a praise, and for a glory; but they would not listen.

12² *Moreover, you shall speak to them this word: Thus says the LORD, the God of Israel*[3]: 'Every bottle is filled with wine;' and when they shall say to you: 'Do we not know that every bottle is filled with wine?'

13⁴ Then shall you say to them: Thus says the LORD: Behold, I will fill all the inhabitants of this land, the kings who sit upon David's throne, and the priests, and the prophets, and all the inhabitants of Jerusalem, with drunkenness.

14⁵ And I will dash them one against another, the fathers and the sons together, says the LORD; I will not pity, nor spare, nor have compassion, so I should not destroy them.

15⁶ Hear, and give ear, do not be proud; for the LORD has spoken.

16⁷ Give glory to the LORD your God, before it grows dark, and before your feet stumble upon the mountains of twilight, and, while you look for light, he turns it into the shadow of death, and *makes it gross darkness*[8].

17⁹ But if you will not hear it, My soul shall weep in secret for your pride; and my eyes shall weep bitterly, and run down with tears, because the LORD's flock is carried away captive.

18¹⁰ Say to the king and to the queen mother: 'Sit down low; for your headdress shall come down, your beautiful crown.'

---

[1] Jeremiah 13:11 - 1 Peter 2:9, Apocryphon of Ezekiel Fragment 5, Deuteronomy 4:7 2:18 32:10-32:15, Ein Yaakov Sotah:4b, Exodus 19:5-19:6, Isaiah 19:21 14:12, Jeremiah 6:17 7:26 13:10 8:20 9:9, John 5:37-5:40, Leviticus.R 2:4, Midrash Tanchuma Kedoshim 5, Midrash Tanchuma Ki Tissa 8, Pesikta de R'Kahana 2.7, Psalms 81:12 15:4 3:20, Tanya Igeret Hakodesh §01

[2] Jeremiah 13:12 - Ezekiel 24:19, Midrash Psalms 136:4, z.Vaetchanan 269b

[3] LXX *And you shall say to this people*

[4] Jeremiah 13:13 - Habakkuk 2:16, Isaiah 5:9 1:26 3:17 3:21 15:6, Jeremiah 25:15-25:18 1:27 3:7 3:57, Psalms 60:4 75:9, z.Vaetchanan 269b

[5] Jeremiah 13:14 - 1 Samuel 14:16, 2 Chronicles 20:23, Deuteronomy 5:19, Ezekiel 5:10-5:11 7:4 7:9 8:18 9:5 9:10 24:14, Isaiah 9:21 3:11, Jeremiah 6:21 16:5 19:9-19:11 21:7 23:3 24:12, Judges 7:20-7:22, Mark 13:12, Matthew 10:21, Psalms 2:9

[6] Jeremiah 13:15 - Acts 4:19-4:20, Amos 7:15, b.Sotah 5a, Deuteronomy.R 4:2, Ein Yaakov Sotah:4b, Isaiah 28:14-28:22 18:23, James 4:10, Jeremiah 4:2, Joel 1:2, Revelation 2:29

[7] Jeremiah 13:16 - 1 John 2:10-2:11, 1 Peter 2:8, 1 Samuel 6:5, Amos 8:9-8:10, Ecclesiastes 11:8 12:1-12:2, Exodus 10:21, Guide for the Perplexed 1:64, Isaiah 5:30 8:22 11:9 12:2, Jastrow 875b, Jeremiah 4:23 8:15 14:19 23:12, John 12:35, Joshua 7:19, Lamentations 4:17, Lamentations.R 1:57 1:57 Petichata D'Chakimei:25, Numbers.R 8:3, Pesikta de R'Kahana 13.9 16.11, Pesikta Rabbati 33:11 33:13, Proverbs 4:19, Psalms 44:20 96:7-96:8, Tanna Devei Eliyahu 2, Tanya Igeret Hakodesh §23

[8] LXX *they shall be brought into darkness*

[9] Jeremiah 13:17 - 1 Samuel 15:11 15:35, b.Chagigah 5b, Ein Yaakov Chagigah:5b, Ezekiel 10:31 12:38, Isaiah 15:11, Jastrow 201b 812b, Jeremiah 9:2 13:19-13:20 14:17 17:16 22:5 23:1, Lamentations 1:2 1:16 2:18, Lamentations.R 1:57 Petichata D'Chakimei:25, Luke 19:41-42, Malachi 2:2, Pesikta Rabbati 33:11, Psalms 80:2 119:136, Romans 9:2-4, Tanya Igeret Hakodesh §13, z.Shemot 17b

[10] Jeremiah 13:18 - 1 Peter 5:6, 2 Chronicles 9:12 9:19 9:23, 2 Kings 24:12 24:15, Exodus 10:3, Ezekiel 19:2-19:14, Genesis.R 68:13, Isaiah 3:26 23:1, James 4:10, Jeremiah 22:26, Jonah 3:6, Lamentations 2:10, Matthew 18:4

עָרֵי הַנֶּגֶב סֻגְּרוּ וְאֵין פֹּתֵחַ הָגְלָת יְהוּדָה כֻּלָּהּ הָגְלָת שְׁלוֹמִים

19[1] The cities of the South are shut up, and there is no one to open them; Judah is carried away captive; it is wholly carried away captive.

שְׂאִי "שְׂאוּ" עֵינֵיכֶם "וּרְאִי" "וּרְאוּ" הַבָּאִים מִצָּפוֹן אַיֵּה הָעֵדֶר נִתַּן־לָךְ צֹאן תִּפְאַרְתֵּךְ

20[2] Lift up your eyes, and behold those who come from the north; where is the flock that was given you, your beautiful flock?

מַה־תֹּאמְרִי כִּי־יִפְקֹד עָלַיִךְ וְאַתְּ לִמַּדְתְּ אֹתָם עָלַיִךְ אַלֻּפִים לְרֹאשׁ הֲלוֹא חֲבָלִים יֹאחֱזוּךְ כְּמוֹ אֵשֶׁת לֵדָה

21[3] What will you say, when He shall set the friends over you as head, whom you yourself have trained against you? Shall not pangs take hold of you, as of a woman in travail?

וְכִי תֹאמְרִי בִּלְבָבֵךְ מַדּוּעַ קְרָאֻנִי אֵלֶּה בְּרֹב עֲוֹנֵךְ נִגְלוּ שׁוּלַיִךְ נֶחְמְסוּ עֲקֵבָיִךְ

22[4] And if you say in your heart: 'Why are these things befallen me?' For the greatness of your iniquity your skirts are uncovered, and your *heels*[5] *suffer violence*[6].

הֲיַהֲפֹךְ כּוּשִׁי עוֹרוֹ וְנָמֵר חֲבַרְבֻּרֹתָיו גַּם־אַתֶּם תּוּכְלוּ לְהֵיטִיב לִמֻּדֵי הָרֵעַ

23[7] Can the Ethiopian change his skin, or the leopard his spots? Then may you also do good, who are accustomed to do evil.

וַאֲפִיצֵם כְּקַשׁ־עוֹבֵר לְרוּחַ מִדְבָּר

24[8] Therefore, I will scatter them, as the stubble that blows away by the wind of the wilderness.

זֶה גוֹרָלֵךְ מְנָת־מִדַּיִךְ מֵאִתִּי נְאֻם־יְהוָה אֲשֶׁר שָׁכַחַתְּ אוֹתִי וַתִּבְטְחִי בַּשָּׁקֶר

25[9] This is your lot, the portion measured to you from Me, says the LORD; because you have forgotten Me, and trusted in falsehood.

וְגַם־אֲנִי חָשַׂפְתִּי שׁוּלַיִךְ עַל־פָּנָיִךְ וְנִרְאָה קְלוֹנֵךְ

26[10] Therefore, will I also uncover your skirts on your face, and your shame shall appear.

נִאֻפַיִךְ וּמִצְהֲלוֹתַיִךְ זִמַּת זְנוּתֵךְ עַל־גְּבָעוֹת בַּשָּׂדֶה רָאִיתִי שִׁקּוּצָיִךְ אוֹי לָךְ יְרוּשָׁלַ͏ִם לֹא תִטְהֲרִי אַחֲרֵי מָתַי עֹד

27[11] your adulteries, and your neighing, the lewdness of your harlotry, on the hills in the field I have seen your detestable acts. Woe to you, O Jerusalem! You will not be made clean! When shall it ever be?

Jeremiah – Chapter 14

אֲשֶׁר הָיָה דְבַר־יְהוָה אֶל־יִרְמְיָהוּ עַל־דִּבְרֵי הַבַּצָּרוֹת

1[12] The word of the LORD that came to Jeremiah concerning the droughts.

אָבְלָה יְהוּדָה וּשְׁעָרֶיהָ אֻמְלְלוּ קָדְרוּ לָאָרֶץ וְצִוְחַת יְרוּשָׁלַ͏ִם עָלָתָה

2[13] Judah mourns, and its gates languish, they bow down in black to the ground; and the cry of Jerusalem has gone up.

---

[1] Jeremiah 13:19 - 2 Kings 1:21, b.Bava Metzia [Rashi] 39a, Deuteronomy 4:15 4:52 28:64-28:68, Ezekiel 21:2-3, Jeremiah 17:26 20:4 9:13 15:9 4:27 4:30, Job 12:14, Joshua 18:5, Leviticus 26:31-33
[2] Jeremiah 13:20 - Acts 20:26-20:29, Ezekiel 34:7-34:10, Habakkuk 1:6, Isaiah 56:9-56:12, Jeremiah 1:14 6:22 10:22 13:17 23:2, John 10:12-10:13, Zechariah 11:16-11:17
[3] Jeremiah 13:21 - 1 Thessalonians 5:3, 2 Kings 16:7, Ezekiel 4:9, Genesis.R 75:3, Isaiah 10:3 13:8 21:3 39:2-39:4, Jeremiah 4:31 5:31 6:24 22:23 6:6 14:22 24:41
[4] Jeremiah 13:22 - 2QJer, 4QJera, Deuteronomy 7:17 8:17 18:21, Ezekiel 16:37-39 23:27-29, Hosea 2:3 2:10 12:10, Isaiah 3:17 20:4 47:2-3 23:8, Jeremiah 2:17-19 5:19 9:3-10 13:26 16:10-11, Lamentations 1:8, Luke 5:21-22, Nahum 3:5, Zephaniah 1:12
[5] i.e., *body*
[6] LXX *might be exposed*
[7] Jeremiah 13:23 - b.Shabbat 107b, b.Yoma [Rashi] 34b, Isaiah 1:5, Jastrow 914a 1497b, Jeremiah 2:22 2:30 5:3 6:29-30 9:6 17:9, Matthew 19:24-28, Proverbs 3:22
[8] Jeremiah 13:24 - Deuteronomy 4:27 28:64 8:26, Ezekiel 5:2 5:12 6:8 17:21, Hosea 13:3, Isaiah 17:13 17:16, Jeremiah 4:11-4:12, Leviticus 2:33, Luke 21:24, Psalms 1:4 83:14-16, Zephaniah 2:2
[9] Jeremiah 13:25 - Deuteronomy 32:16-18 32:37-38, Habakkuk 2:18-19, Isaiah 17:4 4:15, Jeremiah 2:13 2:32 7:4-8 10:14, Job 20:29, Matthew 24:51, Micah 3:11, Psalms 9:18 11:7 106:21-22
[10] Jeremiah 13:26 - Ezekiel 16:37 23:29, Hosea 2:10, Jeremiah 13:22, Lamentations 1:8
[11] Jeremiah 13:27 - 2 Corinthians 7:1 12:21, 4QJera, Ezekiel 2:10 6:13 16:15-16:22 20:28 23:2-23:21 24:6 24:13 12:25 12:37, Hosea 1:2 4:2 8:5, Isaiah 9:7 17:7, James 4:4, Jeremiah 2:20-2:24 3:1-3:2 3:6 4:13-4:14 5:7-5:8, Luke 11:9-11:13, Matthew 11:21, Proverbs 1:22, Psalms 94:7 94:8, Revelation 8:13, Saadia Opinions 10:6, Zephaniah 3:1
[12] Jeremiah 14:1 - b.Taanit 15a, Jeremiah 17:8, m.Taanit 2:3, y.Taanit 2:3
[13] Jeremiah 14:2 - 1 Samuel 5:12 9:16, b.Taanit 15a, Exodus 2:24, Hosea 4:3, Isaiah 3:26 5:7 15:5 24:4 24:7 9:9, Jeremiah 4:28 8:21 11:11 12:4 18:22, Job 10:28, Joel 1:10 2:6, Lamentations 2:9 4:8-4:9 5:10, Traditional Small צ in וְצִוְחַת, Zechariah 7:13

וְאַדִּרֵיהֶם שָׁלְחוּ 'צְעוֹרֵיהֶם' "צְעִירֵיהֶם" לַמָּיִם בָּאוּ עַל־גֵּבִים לֹא־מָצְאוּ מַיִם שָׁבוּ כְלֵיהֶם רֵיקָם בֹּשׁוּ וְהָכְלְמוּ וְחָפוּ רֹאשָׁם	**3[1]** And their nobles send their lads for water. They come to the pits, and find no water; their vessels return empty; they are ashamed and confounded, and cover their heads.
בַּעֲבוּר הָאֲדָמָה חַתָּה כִּי לֹא־הָיָה גֶשֶׁם בָּאָרֶץ בֹּשׁוּ אִכָּרִים חָפוּ רֹאשָׁם	**4[2]** Because of the ground that is cracked, for there has been no rain in the land, the plowmen are ashamed, they cover their heads.
כִּי גַם־אַיֶּלֶת בַּשָּׂדֶה יָלְדָה וְעָזוֹב כִּי לֹא־הָיָה דֶּשֶׁא	**5[3]** Yes, the hind also in the field calves, and forsakes her young, because there is no grass,
וּפְרָאִים עָמְדוּ עַל־שְׁפָיִם שָׁאֲפוּ רוּחַ כַּתַּנִּים כָּלוּ עֵינֵיהֶם כִּי־אֵין עֵשֶׂב	**6[4]** And the wild asses *stand on the high hills, they gasp for air like jackals*[5]; their eyes fail, because there is no herbage.
אִם־עֲוֹנֵינוּ עָנוּ בָנוּ יְהֹוָה עֲשֵׂה לְמַעַן שְׁמֶךָ כִּי־רַבּוּ מְשׁוּבֹתֵינוּ לְךָ חָטָאנוּ	**7[6]** Though our iniquities testify against us, O LORD, work you for Your name's sake; for our backslidings are many, we have sinned against You.
מִקְוֵה יִשְׂרָאֵל מוֹשִׁיעוֹ בְּעֵת צָרָה לָמָּה תִהְיֶה כְּגֵר בָּאָרֶץ וּכְאֹרֵחַ נָטָה לָלוּן	**8[7]** O, you hope of Israel, its savior in time of trouble, why should you be as a stranger in the land, and as a wayfaring man who turns aside to tarry for a night?
לָמָּה תִהְיֶה כְּאִישׁ נִדְהָם כְּגִבּוֹר לֹא־יוּכַל לְהוֹשִׁיעַ וְאַתָּה בְקִרְבֵּנוּ יְהֹוָה וְשִׁמְךָ עָלֵינוּ נִקְרָא אַל־תַּנִּחֵנוּ	**9[8]** Why should you be as a man *overcome*[9], as a mighty man who cannot save? Yet You, O LORD, are in our midst, and Your name is called on us; do not leave us.
כֹּה־אָמַר יְהֹוָה לָעָם הַזֶּה כֵּן אָהֲבוּ לָנוּעַ רַגְלֵיהֶם לֹא חָשָׂכוּ וַיהֹוָה לֹא רָצָם עַתָּה יִזְכֹּר עֲוֹנָם וְיִפְקֹד חַטֹּאתָם	**10[10]** Thus says the LORD to this people: so they have loved to wander, they have not refrained their feet; therefore, the LORD does not accept them, now He will remember their iniquity, and punish their sins.
וַיֹּאמֶר יְהֹוָה אֵלָי אַל־תִּתְפַּלֵּל בְּעַד־הָעָם הַזֶּה לְטוֹבָה	**11[11]** And the LORD said to me: 'Do not pray for this people for their good.
כִּי יָצֻמוּ אֵינֶנִּי שֹׁמֵעַ אֶל־רִנָּתָם וְכִי יַעֲלוּ עֹלָה וּמִנְחָה אֵינֶנִּי רֹצָם כִּי בַּחֶרֶב וּבָרָעָב וּבַדֶּבֶר אָנֹכִי מְכַלֶּה אוֹתָם	**12[12]** When they fast, I will not hear their cry; and when they offer burnt offering and meal offering, I will not accept them; but I will consume them by the sword, and by the famine, and by the pestilence.'

---

[1] Jeremiah 14:3 - 1 Kings 17:7 18:5-18:6, 2 Kings 18:31, 2 Samuel 15:30 19:4, Amos 4:8, b.Taanit 15a, Esther 6:12, Isaiah 45:16-45:17, Jeremiah 2:13 2:26-2:27 14:4 20:11, Job 6:20, Joel 1:20, Mas.Semachot 6:1, Mas.Soferim 7:4, Mekhilta de R'Shimon bar Yochai Vayassa 37:2, Mekilta de R'Ishmael Vayassa 1:72, Midrash Tanchuma Beshallach 19, Psalms 40:15 13:29

[2] Jeremiah 14:4 - b.Taanit 15a, Deuteronomy 28:23-28:24 5:22, Jeremiah 3:3, Joel 1:11 1:17 1:19-1:20, Leviticus 26:19-26:20 Jeremiah 14:4-7 - 4QJera

[3] Jeremiah 14:5 - b.Taanit 15a, Isaiah 15:6, Job 39:1-39:4, Psalms 29:9

[4] Jeremiah 14:6 - 1 Samuel 14:29, b.Taanit 15a, Jeremiah 2:24, Job 39:5-39:6, Joel 1:18, Lamentations 4:17 5:17

[5] LXX *stood by the forests, and snuffed up the wind*

[6] Jeremiah 14:7 - b.Taanit 15a, Daniel 9:5-9:16 9:18-9:19, Deuteronomy 8:27, Ephesians 1:6 1:12, Ezekiel 20:9 20:14 20:22, Ezra 9:6-9:7 9:15, Hosea 5:5 7:10, Isaiah 11:12, Jeremiah 2:19 3:6 5:6 8:14 14:20-14:21, Joshua 7:9, Nehemiah 9:33-9:34, Numbers.R 11:4, Psalms 25:11 19:1
Jeremiah 14:7-9 - Selichot, Tachanun [Monday and Thursday mornings]

[7] Jeremiah 14:8 - 1 Timothy 1:1, 2 Corinthians 1:4-1:5, Acts 4:20, b.Taanit 15a, Isaiah 19:3 19:11 21:15 21:21, Jeremiah 17:13 2:7, Joel 4:16, Judges 19:17, Midrash Tanchuma Behar 1, Midrash Tanchuma Lech Lecha 6, Psalms 9:10 10:2 37:39-40 46:2 50:15 91:15 18:7

[8] Jeremiah 14:9 - 1 Samuel 12:22, 2 Baruch 21:22, 2 Corinthians 6:16, b.Taanit 15a, Daniel 9:18-9:19, Deuteronomy 23:16, Exodus 29:45-29:46, Hebrews 13:5, Isaiah 12:6 50:1-50:2 3:9 11:1 15:19, Jeremiah 8:19 15:16, Leviticus 26:11-26:12, Midrash Tanchuma Mishpatim 11, Numbers 11:23 14:15-14:16, Psalms 27:9 44:24-44:27 46:6, Revelation 21:3, Zechariah 2:5

[9] LXX *asleep*

[10] Jeremiah 14:10 - 1 Kings 17:18, 1 Samuel 15:2, Amos 5:22, b.Taanit 15a, Hebrews 8:12, Hosea 8:13 9:9 11:7 11:9, Jeremiah 2:23-25 2:36 3:1-2 6:20 8:5 7:35 44:21-23, Malachi 1:8-13, Psalms 109:14-15 119:101, Sifre Numbers 85:2, Sifre.z Numbers Behaalotcha 11:1, z.Vaetchanan 269b

[11] Jeremiah 14:11 - Exodus 8:10 32:32-32:34, Jeremiah 7:16 11:14 15:1

[12] Jeremiah 14:12 - Ezekiel 5:12-5:17 8:18 14:21, Isaiah 1:11-1:15 10:3, Jeremiah 6:20 7:21-7:22 9:17 11:11 15:2-15:3 16:4 21:7-21:9 24:10 29:17-29:18, Micah 3:4, Proverbs 1:28 15:8 21:27 4:9, Zechariah 7:13

וָאֹמַ֞ר אֲהָהּ֣ אֲדֹנָ֣י יְהֹוִ֗ה הִנֵּ֤ה הַנְּבִאִים֙ אֹמְרִ֣ים לָהֶ֔ם לֹא־תִרְאוּ֙ חֶ֔רֶב וְרָעָ֖ב לֹא־יִהְיֶ֣ה לָכֶ֑ם כִּֽי־שְׁל֤וֹם אֱמֶת֙ אֶתֵּ֣ן לָכֶ֔ם בַּמָּק֖וֹם הַזֶּֽה

13[1] Then said I: 'Ah, Lord GOD! Behold, the prophets say to them: You shall not see the sword, nor shall you have famine; but I will give you assured peace [2]in this place.'

וַיֹּ֤אמֶר יְהֹוָה֙ אֵלַ֔י שֶׁ֚קֶר הַנְּבִאִ֣ים נִבְּאִ֣ים בִּשְׁמִ֔י לֹ֤א שְׁלַחְתִּים֙ וְלֹ֣א צִוִּיתִ֔ים וְלֹ֥א דִבַּ֖רְתִּי אֲלֵיהֶ֑ם חֲז֨וֹן שֶׁ֜קֶר וְקֶ֣סֶם (וֶאֱלוּל) [וֶאֱלִיל] (וְתַרְמוּת) [וְתַרְמִ֣ית] לִבָּ֔ם הֵ֖מָּה מִֽתְנַבְּאִ֥ים לָכֶֽם

14[3] Then the LORD said to me: 'The prophets prophesy lies in My name; I did not send, nor have I commanded them, nor have I spoke to them; they prophesy to you a lying vision, and divination, and a thing of nothing, and the deceit of their own heart.

לָכֵ֞ן כֹּֽה־אָמַ֣ר יְהֹוָ֗ה עַֽל־הַנְּבִאִ֡ים הַנִּבְּאִים֩ בִּשְׁמִ֨י וַאֲנִ֜י לֹֽא־שְׁלַחְתִּ֗ים וְהֵ֙מָּה֙ אֹ֣מְרִ֔ים חֶ֣רֶב וְרָעָ֔ב לֹ֥א יִהְיֶ֖ה בָּאָ֣רֶץ הַזֹּ֑את בַּחֶ֤רֶב וּבָֽרָעָב֙ יִתַּ֔מּוּ הַנְּבִאִ֖ים הָהֵֽמָּה

15[4] Therefore, thus says the LORD: As for the prophets who prophesy in My name, and I did not sent them, yet they say: Sword and famine shall not be in this land, by sword and famine shall those prophets be consumed;

וְהָעָ֣ם אֲשֶׁר־הֵ֣מָּה נִבְּאִ֣ים לָהֶ֗ם יִֽהְי֤וּ מֻשְׁלָכִים֙ בְּחֻצ֤וֹת יְרוּשָׁלַ֙͏ִם֙ מִפְּנֵ֣י הָרָעָ֣ב וְהַחֶ֔רֶב וְאֵ֥ין מְקַבֵּ֖ר לָהֵ֑מָּה הֵ֤מָּה נְשֵׁיהֶם֙ וּבְנֵיהֶ֣ם וּבְנֹֽתֵיהֶ֔ם וְשָׁפַכְתִּ֥י עֲלֵיהֶ֖ם אֶת־רָעָתָֽם

16[5] And the people to whom they prophesy shall be cast out in the streets of Jerusalem because of the famine and the sword; and they shall have no one to bury them, them, their wives, nor their sons, nor their daughters; for I will pour their evil on them.'

וְאָמַרְתָּ֤ אֲלֵיהֶם֙ אֶת־הַדָּבָ֣ר הַזֶּ֔ה תֵּרַ֨דְנָה עֵינַ֥י דִּמְעָ֛ה לַ֥יְלָה וְיוֹמָ֖ם וְאַל־תִּדְמֶ֑ינָה כִּי֩ שֶׁ֨בֶר גָּד֜וֹל נִשְׁבְּרָ֗ה בְּתוּלַת֙ בַּת־עַמִּ֔י מַכָּ֖ה נַחְלָ֥ה מְאֹֽד

17[6] And you shall say this word to them: Let my eyes run down with tears night and day, and let them not cease; for the virgin daughter of my people is broken with a great breach, with a very grievous blow.

אִם־יָצָ֣אתִי הַשָּׂדֶ֗ה וְהִנֵּה֙ חַֽלְלֵי־חֶ֔רֶב וְאִם֙ בָּ֣אתִי הָעִ֔יר וְהִנֵּ֖ה תַּחֲלוּאֵ֣י רָעָ֑ב כִּֽי־גַם־נָבִ֧יא גַם־כֹּהֵ֛ן סָחֲר֥וּ אֶל־אֶ֖רֶץ וְלֹ֥א יָדָֽעוּ

18[7] If I go forth into the field, then behold the dead with the sword. And if I enter into the city, then behold those who are sick with famine. For both the prophet and the priest are gone to a land, and did not know it.

הֲמָאֹ֨ס מָאַ֜סְתָּ אֶת־יְהוּדָ֗ה אִם־בְּצִיּוֹן֙ גָּעֲלָ֣ה נַפְשֶׁ֔ךָ מַדּ֙וּעַ֙ הִכִּיתָ֔נוּ וְאֵ֥ין לָ֖נוּ מַרְפֵּ֑א קַוֵּ֤ה לְשָׁלוֹם֙ וְאֵ֣ין ט֔וֹב וּלְעֵ֥ת מַרְפֵּ֖א וְהִנֵּ֥ה בְעָתָֽה

19[8] You utterly rejected Judah? Has Your soul loathed Zion? Why have you struck us, and there is no healing for us? We looked for peace, but no good came; and for a time of healing, and behold terror.

יָדַ֧עְנוּ יְהֹוָ֛ה רִשְׁעֵ֖נוּ עֲוֺ֣ן אֲבוֹתֵ֑ינוּ כִּ֥י חָטָ֖אנוּ לָֽךְ

20[9] We acknowledge, O LORD, our wickedness, the iniquity of our fathers; for we have sinned against You.

[1] Jeremiah 14:13 - 2 Peter 2:1, Ezekiel 13:10-13:16 13:22, Jeremiah 1:6 4:10 5:12 5:31 6:14 8:11 23:17 28:2-28:5, Micah 3:11
[2] LXX adds *on the land, and*
[3] Jeremiah 14:14 - 1 Timothy 4:2, 2 Thessalonians 2:9-2:11, Ezekiel 12:24 13:6-13:7 13:23 21:34, Isaiah 9:16 30:10-30:11, Jeremiah 5:31 23:14-23:16 23:21-23:32 27:9-27:10 27:14-27:15 4:13 4:15 29:8-29:9 5:21 5:31 13:19, Lamentations 2:14, Mas.Soferim 7:4, Micah 3:11, Zechariah 10:2 13:3
[4] Jeremiah 14:15 - 1 Kings 22:25, 2 Peter 2:1-2:3 2:14-2:17, Amos 7:17, Ezekiel 14:10, Jeremiah 5:12-5:13 6:15 8:12 20:6 23:14-23:15 28:15-28:17 29:20-29:21 29:31-29:32, Mas.Semachot 8:14, Revelation 19:20, z.Vaetchanan 269b
[5] Jeremiah 14:16 - Isaiah 9:17, Jeremiah 2:17-2:19 4:18 5:31 7:33 9:23 13:22-13:25 15:2-15:3 16:4 18:21 19:6-19:7, Matthew 15:14, Proverbs 1:31, Psalms 79:2-79:3, Revelation 16:1, Sifre Devarim {Haazinu Hashamayim} 321, Sifre Devarim Nitzavim 321
[6] Jeremiah 14:17 - Amos 5:2, Isaiah 13:22, Lamentations 1:15-16 2:13 2:18 3:48-49, Jeremiah 8:18 8:21 9:2 10:19 13:17 30:14-15, Micah 6:13, Pesikta Rabbati 29:2, Psalms 39:11 80:5-6 119:136
[7] Jeremiah 14:18 - 2 Peter 2:3, compare use of א in the word יצתי with Job 1:21 and Job 3:11, Deuteronomy 4:36 28:64, Ezekiel 7:15, Isaiah 4:7, Jeremiah 2:8 5:31 6:13 8:10 23:21 52:6-52:7, Lamentations 1:20 4:9 4:13-4:16, Micah 3:11, Sifre Devarim {Haazinu Hashamayim} 321, Sifre Devarim Nitzavim 321
[8] Jeremiah 14:19 - 1 Thessalonians 5:3, 2 Chronicles 12:16, 2 Kings 17:19-17:20, Exodus.R 31:10, Jeremiah 6:30 7:29 8:15 8:22 12:8 15:1 15:18 6:13, Job 6:26, Lamentations 2:13 4:17 5:22, Lamentations.R 5:20 Petichata D'Chakimei:24, Pesikta Rabbati 31:3, Psalms 78:59 80:13-80:14 89:39, Romans 11:1-11:6, Zechariah 11:8-11:9
Jeremiah 14:19-22 - Mas.Soferim 18:3
[9] Jeremiah 14:20 - 1 John 1:7-1:9, 2 Samuel 12:13 24:10, Daniel 9:5-9:8, Ezra 9:6-9:7, Jeremiah 3:13 3:25, Job 9:27, Leviticus 26:40-26:42, Luke 15:18-15:21, Nehemiah 9:2, Psalms 32:5 51:4-5 106:6-48

אַל־תִּנְאַץ לְמַעַן שִׁמְךָ אַל־תְּנַבֵּל אֶת־כִּסֵּא כְבוֹדֶךָ זְכֹר
אַל־תָּפֵר בְּרִיתְךָ אִתָּנוּ

21[1] Do not contemn us, for Your name's sake, do not *dishonor*[2] the throne of your glory; remember, do not break your covenant with us.

הֲיֵשׁ בְּהַבְלֵי הַגּוֹיִם מַגְשִׁמִים וְאִם־הַשָּׁמַיִם יִתְּנוּ
רְבִבִים הֲלֹא אַתָּה־הוּא יְהוָה אֱלֹהֵינוּ וּנְקַוֶּה־לָּךְ
כִּי־אַתָּה עָשִׂיתָ אֶת־כָּל־אֵלֶּה

22[3] Are there any among the vanities of the nations who can cause rain? *Or can the heavens give showers*[4]? Are you not He, O LORD our God, and do we not wait for You? For you have made all these things.

Jeremiah – Chapter 15

וַיֹּאמֶר יְהוָה אֵלַי אִם־יַעֲמֹד מֹשֶׁה וּשְׁמוּאֵל לְפָנַי
אֵין נַפְשִׁי אֶל־הָעָם הַזֶּה שַׁלַּח מֵעַל־פָּנַי וְיֵצֵאוּ

1[5] Then said the LORD to me: 'Though Moses and Samuel stood before Me, yet My mind could not be toward this people; cast them from My sight, and let them go forth.

וְהָיָה כִּי־יֹאמְרוּ אֵלֶיךָ אָנָה נֵצֵא וְאָמַרְתָּ אֲלֵיהֶם
כֹּה־אָמַר יְהוָה אֲשֶׁר לַמָּוֶת לַמָּוֶת וַאֲשֶׁר לַחֶרֶב
לַחֶרֶב וַאֲשֶׁר לָרָעָב לָרָעָב וַאֲשֶׁר לַשְּׁבִי לַשֶּׁבִי

2[6] And it shall come to pass, when they say to you: When shall we go forth? Then you shall tell them: Thus says the LORD: Such as are for death, to death; and such as are for the sword, to the sword; and such as are for the famine, to the famine; and such as are for captivity, to captivity.

וּפָקַדְתִּי עֲלֵיהֶם אַרְבַּע מִשְׁפָּחוֹת נְאֻם־יְהוָה אֶת־
הַחֶרֶב לַהֲרֹג וְאֶת־הַכְּלָבִים לִסְחֹב וְאֶת־עוֹף
הַשָּׁמַיִם וְאֶת־בֶּהֱמַת הָאָרֶץ לֶאֱכֹל וּלְהַשְׁחִית

3[7] And I will appoint over them four kinds, says the LORD: the sword to slay, and the dogs to drag, and the fowls of the heaven, and the beasts of the earth, to devour and to destroy.

וּנְתַתִּים "לְזַנְעָה" "לְזַעֲוָה" לְכֹל מַמְלְכוֹת הָאָרֶץ
בִּגְלַל מְנַשֶּׁה בֶן־יְחִזְקִיָּהוּ מֶלֶךְ יְהוּדָה עַל אֲשֶׁר־
עָשָׂה בִּירוּשָׁלָ͏ם

4[8] And I will cause them to be a horror among all the kingdoms of the earth, because of Manasseh the son of Hezekiah king of Judah, for what he did in Jerusalem.

כִּי מִי־יַחְמֹל עָלַיִךְ יְרוּשָׁלַ͏ם וּמִי יָנוּד לָךְ וּמִי יָסוּר
לִשְׁאֹל לְשָׁלֹם לָךְ

5[9] For who shall have pity on you, O Jerusalem? Or who shall bemoan you? Or who shall turn aside to ask of your welfare?

אַתְּ נָטַשְׁתְּ אֹתִי נְאֻם־יְהוָה אָחוֹר תֵּלֵכִי וָאַט אֶת־
יָדִי עָלַיִךְ וָאַשְׁחִיתֵךְ נִלְאֵיתִי הִנָּחֵם

6[10] You have cast Me off, says the LORD, you have gone backward; therefore, I stretch out

---

[1] Jeremiah 14:21 - 2 Baruch 46:4, Amos 6:8, Daniel 8:11-8:13 9:7 9:15-9:19, Deuteronomy 8:19, Ephesians 2:7, Exodus 8:13, Ezekiel 7:20-7:22 24:21 36:22-36:23 15:25 19:7, Hebrews 8:6-8:13, Isaiah 64:10-64:13, Jeremiah 3:17 14:7 14:19 17:12, Lamentations 1:10 2:6-2:7 2:20, Leviticus 2:11 26:42-26:45, Luke 1:72 21:24, Psalms 51:12 74:2-74:7 74:18-74:20 79:9-79:10 89:40-89:41 10:40 10:45, Revelation 11:2, Selichot Sifre Devarim Nitzavim 318, Zechariah 11:10-11:11

[2] LXX *destroy*

[3] Jeremiah 14:22 - 1 Kings 8:36 17:1 17:14 18:1 18:39-45, 4Q504 frags 1-2R 4.3-4, Acts 14:15-17, Amos 4:7, Deuteronomy 4:12 8:21, Habakkuk 3:17-19, Isaiah 6:18 6:23 17:29 44:12-20, Jeremiah 5:24 10:13 10:15 16:19 3:16, Job 5:10 38:26-28, Joel 2:23, Lamentations 3:25-26, Matthew 5:45, Micah 7:7, Psalms 25:3 25:21 27:14 74:1-2 10:5 15:7 3:8, Saadia Opinions 1:3, Zechariah 10:1-2

[4] LXX *and will the sky yield his fulness at their bidding*

[5] Jeremiah 15:1 - 1 Samuel 7:9 12:23, 2 Kings 17:20, 3 Enoch 48A:8, Ecclesiastes.R 8:11, Exodus 32:11-32:14, Exodus.R 46:4, Ezekiel 14:14 14:20-14:21, Genesis 19:27, Genesis.R 19:9 68:13, Guide for the Perplexed 1:13 1:41 3:8, Hebrews 9:24, Jastrow 109b, Jeremiah 7:15-7:16 11:14 14:11 15:19 18:20 23:39 11:19 4:3, Judges 5:9, Lamentations.R Petichata D'Chakimei:4, Midrash Psalms 1:3, Midrash Tanchuma Naso 7, Midrash Tanchuma Tzav 13, Numbers 14:13-14:20, Numbers.R 7:10, Pesikta de R'Kahana 15.1, Pesikta Rabbati 27:1, Proverbs 14:35, Psalms 99:6 10:23, Ruth.R Petichata:6, Zechariah 3:3 Jeremiah 15:1-2 - 4QJera

[6] Jeremiah 15:2 - Amos 5:19, b.Bava Batra 8b, Daniel 9:12, Ecclesiastes.R 8, Ezekiel 5:2 5:12 14:21, Isaiah 24:18, Jeremiah 14:12 24:9-24:10 19:11, Lamentations.R Petichata D'Chakimei:23, Numbers.R 9:49, Pesikta de R'Kahana 13.13 14.2, Revelation 6:3-6:8 13:10, Sifre Devarim Ekev 43, z.Vaetchanan 269b, Zechariah 11:9

[7] Jeremiah 15:3 - 1 Kings 21:23-21:24, 2 Kings 9:35-37, Deuteronomy 4:26, Ezekiel 14:21, Isaiah 18:6 56:9-10, Jeremiah 7:33, Josephus Antiquities 10.5.1, Leviticus 2:16 2:22 2:25, Revelation 6:8 19:17-18

[8] Jeremiah 15:4 - 2 Kings 21:2 21:11-21:13 21:16-21:17 23:26-23:27 24:3-24:4, b.Sanhedrin 102b, Deuteronomy 4:25 28:64, Ein Yaakov Sanhedrin:102b, Ezekiel 23:46, Jeremiah 9:17 24:9 5:18 10:17, Lamentations 1:8, Leviticus 2:33

[9] Jeremiah 15:5 - 1 Samuel 10:4 17:22 1:5, Exodus 18:7, Isaiah 3:19, Jeremiah 13:14 16:5 21:7, Job 19:21, Judges 18:15, Lamentations 1:12-1:16 2:15-2:16, Nahum 3:7, Psalms 69:21

[10] Jeremiah 15:6 - Amos 7:3-7:8, Ezekiel 12:26-12:28 14:9 1:7, Hosea 4:16 11:7 13:14, Isaiah 1:4 4:13, Jeremiah 1:16 2:13 2:17 2:19 6:11 6:19 7:24 8:5 20:9, Psalms 78:38-78:40, Zechariah 7:11, Zephaniah 1:4

My hand against you, and destroy you; I am weary with [false] repentance.

7[1] וָאֶזְרֵם בְּמִזְרֶה בְּשַׁעֲרֵי הָאָרֶץ שִׁכַּלְתִּי אִבַּדְתִּי אֶת־עַמִּי מִדַּרְכֵיהֶם לוֹא־שָׁבוּ

And I fan them with a fan in the gates of the land; I bereave them of children, I destroy My people, since they do not turn from their ways.

8[2] עָצְמוּ־לִי אַלְמְנֹתָו מֵחוֹל יַמִּים הֵבֵאתִי לָהֶם עַל־אֵם בָּחוּר שֹׁדֵד בַּצָּהֳרָיִם הִפַּלְתִּי עָלֶיהָ פִּתְאֹם עִיר וּבֶהָלוֹת

Their widows increase to Me above the sand of the seas; I bring on them, against the mother, a chosen one, a spoiler at noonday; I cause anguish and terrors to fall on her suddenly.

9[3] אֻמְלְלָה יֹלֶדֶת הַשִּׁבְעָה נָפְחָה נַפְשָׁהּ 'בָּאָה' "בָּא" שִׁמְשָׁהּ בְּעֹד יוֹמָם בּוֹשָׁה וְחָפֵרָה וּשְׁאֵרִיתָם לַחֶרֶב אֶתֵּן לִפְנֵי אֹיְבֵיהֶם נְאֻם־יְהוָה

She who has borne seven languishes; Her spirit droops; Her sun goes down while it was yet day, she is ashamed and confounded; and the remnant of those I will deliver to the sword before their enemies, says the LORD.'

10[4] אוֹי־לִי אִמִּי כִּי יְלִדְתִּנִי אִישׁ רִיב וְאִישׁ מָדוֹן לְכָל־הָאָרֶץ לֹא־נָשִׁיתִי וְלֹא־נָשׁוּ־בִי כֻּלֹּה מְקַלְלַוְנִי

Woe is me, my mother, that you bore me, a man of strife and a man of contention to the whole earth! I have not lent, nor have men lent to me; Yet every one of them curses me.

11[5] אָמַר יְהוָה אִם־לֹא 'שֵׁרוֹתִךָ' "שֵׁרִיתִךָ" לְטוֹב אִם־לוֹא הִפְגַּעְתִּי בְךָ בְּעֵת־רָעָה וּבְעֵת צָרָה אֶת־הָאֹיֵב

The LORD said: 'Verily I will release you for good; verily I will cause the enemy to make supplication to you in the time of evil and in the time of affliction.

12[6] הֲיָרֹעַ בַּרְזֶל בַּרְזֶל מִצָּפוֹן וּנְחֹשֶׁת

Can iron break iron from the north and brass?

13[7] חֵילְךָ וְאוֹצְרוֹתֶיךָ לָבַז אֶתֵּן לֹא בִמְחִיר וּבְכָל־חַטֹּאותֶיךָ וּבְכָל־גְּבוּלֶיךָ

Your substance and your treasures I will give as spoil without price, and that for all your sins, in all your borders.

14[8] וְהַעֲבַרְתִּי אֶת־אֹיְבֶיךָ בְּאֶרֶץ לֹא יָדָעְתָּ כִּי־אֵשׁ קָדְחָה בְאַפִּי עֲלֵיכֶם תּוּקָד

And I will *make you pass with*[9] your enemies into a land you do not know; for a fire kindles in My nostril, which shall burn on you.'

15[10] אַתָּה יָדַעְתָּ יְהוָה זָכְרֵנִי וּפָקְדֵנִי וְהִנָּקֶם לִי מֵרֹדְפַי אַל־לְאֶרֶךְ אַפְּךָ תִּקָּחֵנִי דַּע שְׂאֵתִי עָלֶיךָ חֶרְפָּה

You, O LORD, know; Remember me, and think of me, and avenge me of my persecutors; do not take me away because of Your long suffering; know that for Your sake I have suffered taunts.

16[11] נִמְצְאוּ דְבָרֶיךָ וָאֹכְלֵם וַיְהִי 'דְבָרֶיךָ' "דְבָרְךָ" לִי לְשָׂשׂוֹן וּלְשִׂמְחַת לְבָבִי כִּי־נִקְרָא שִׁמְךָ עָלַי יְהוָה אֱלֹהֵי צְבָאוֹת

Your words were found, and I ate them; and Your words were to me a joy and the rejoicing

[1] Jeremiah 15:7 - Amos 4:10-12, Deuteronomy 4:18 4:32 4:41 28:53-56, Ezekiel 24:21 24:25, Hosea 9:12-17, Isaiah 9:14 17:16, Jeremiah 4:11-12 5:3 8:4-5 9:22 18:21 3:2, Matthew 3:12, Midrash Tanchuma Massei 13, Numbers.R 23:14, Psalms 1:4, Zechariah 1:4

[2] Jeremiah 15:8 - Genesis.R 65:20, Isaiah 3:25-4:1, Jeremiah 4:16 5:6 6:4-5, Luke 21:35, y.Yevamot 16:3

[3] Jeremiah 15:9 - 1 Samuel 2:5, Amos 8:9-8:10, b.Gittin 88a, Ein Yaakov Gittin:88a, Ezekiel 5:12, Genesis.R 68:11 68:13, Isaiah 23:9, Jeremiah 15:2-3 21:7 20:27, Pesikta Rabbati 26:7, Lamentations 1:1 4:10, Lamentations.R 1:50, Mas.Soferim 7:2, Saadia Opinions 7Variant:5, z.Pekudei 235a

[4] Jeremiah 15:10 - 1 Corinthians 4:9-13, 1 Kings 18:17-18 21:20 22:8, Acts 16:20-22 17:6-8 19:8-9 19:25-28 4:22, Deuteronomy 23:21-21, Exodus 22:25, Ezekiel 2:6-7 3:7-9, Jeremiah 1:18-19 15:20 20:7-8 20:14-18, Job 3:2-27, Lamentations.R Petichata D'Chakimei:15, Leviticus 1:36, Luke 22:34 6:22, Matthew 5:44 10:21-23 24:9, Nehemiah 5:1-6, Philo De Cofusione Linguarum 44, Proverbs 2:2, Psalms 15:5 13:28 120:5-6

[5] Jeremiah 15:11 - Ecclesiastes 8:12, Jeremiah 21:2 29:11-29:14 13:3 39:11-39:12 40:2-40:6 18:2, Proverbs 16:7 21:1, Psalms 37:3-37:11 10:46

[6] Jeremiah 15:12 - Habakkuk 1:5-1:10, Isaiah 21:9, Jeremiah 1:18-1:19 21:4-21:5 4:14, Job 16:9

[7] Jeremiah 15:13 - Isaiah 4:3 4:5, Jeremiah 15:8 17:3 20:5, Psalms 44:13

[8] Jeremiah 15:14 - Amos 5:27, Deuteronomy 4:25 4:36 28:64 5:22 8:22, Hebrews 12:29, Isaiah 18:25 66:15-66:16, Jeremiah 4:4 14:18 15:4 16:13 17:4 4:27, Leviticus 26:38-26:39, Nahum 1:5-1:6, Psalms 21:10, variant תִּיקָד of תּוּקָד is found

[9] LXX *enslave you to*

[10] Jeremiah 15:15 - 1 Peter 4:14-4:16, 2 Corinthians 5:11, 2 Timothy 4:14, Isaiah 14:3, Jeremiah 11:18-11:21 12:3 15:10 17:16 20:8 20:12, Job 10:7, John 21:15-21:17, Luke 6:22-6:23 18:7-18:8 21:17, Matthew 5:10-5:12 10:22 19:29, Midrash Psalms 74:1 119:30, Nehemiah 5:19 6:14 13:22 13:31, Psalms 7:4-7:6 17:3 39:14 69:8-69:10 6:25 10:4 109:26-109:29 119:132-119:134 119:84, Revelation 6:10 18:20, Romans 8:35 12:19
Jeremiah 15:15-21 - Midrash Proverbs 1

[11] Jeremiah 15:16 - 2 Baruch 21:22, Ezekiel 3:1-3:3, Jeremiah 14:9, Job 23:12, Leviticus.R 12:2, Pesikta Rabbati 29/30A:3, Psalms

of my heart; because Your name was called on me, O LORD God of hosts.

לֹא־יָשַׁבְתִּי בְסוֹד־מְשַׂחֲקִים וָאֶעְלֹז מִפְּנֵי יָדְךָ בָּדָד יָשַׁבְתִּי כִּי־זַעַם מִלֵּאתָנִי

17[1] I did not sit in the assembly of those who make merry, nor rejoiced; I sat alone because of Your hand; for you have filled me with indignation.

לָמָּה הָיָה כְאֵבִי נֶצַח וּמַכָּתִי אֲנוּשָׁה מֵאֲנָה הֵרָפֵא הָיוֹ תִהְיֶה לִי כְּמוֹ אַכְזָב מַיִם לֹא נֶאֱמָנוּ

18[2] Why is my pain perpetual, and my wound incurable, so it refuses to be healed? Will you indeed be to me as a deceitful *brook, as waters that fail*[3]?

לָכֵן כֹּה־אָמַר יְהֹוָה אִם־תָּשׁוּב וַאֲשִׁיבְךָ לְפָנַי תַּעֲמֹד וְאִם־תּוֹצִיא יָקָר מִזּוֹלֵל כְּפִי תִהְיֶה יָשֻׁבוּ הֵמָּה אֵלֶיךָ וְאַתָּה לֹא־תָשׁוּב אֲלֵיהֶם

19[4] Therefore, thus says the LORD: If you return, and I bring you back, you shall stand before Me; and if you bring forth the precious from the vile, you shall be as My mouth; let them return to you, but you shall not return to them.

וּנְתַתִּיךָ לָעָם הַזֶּה לְחוֹמַת נְחֹשֶׁת בְּצוּרָה וְנִלְחֲמוּ אֵלֶיךָ וְלֹא־יוּכְלוּ לָךְ כִּי־אִתְּךָ אֲנִי לְהוֹשִׁיעֲךָ וּלְהַצִּילֶךָ נְאֻם־יְהֹוָה

20[5] And I will make you a fortified brazen wall to this people; and they shall fight against you, but they shall not prevail against you; for I am with you to save you and to deliver you, says the LORD.

וְהִצַּלְתִּיךָ מִיַּד רָעִים וּפְדִתִיךָ מִכַּף עָרִצִים

21[6] And I will deliver you from the hand of the wicked, and I will redeem you from the hand of *the terrible*[7].

Jeremiah – Chapter 16

וַיְהִי דְבַר־יְהֹוָה אֵלַי לֵאמֹר

1[8] The word of the LORD came also to me, saying:

לֹא־תִקַּח לְךָ אִשָּׁה וְלֹא־יִהְיוּ לְךָ בָּנִים וּבָנוֹת בַּמָּקוֹם הַזֶּה

2[9] You shall not take a wife, nor shall you have sons or daughters in this place.

כִּי־כֹה אָמַר יְהֹוָה עַל־הַבָּנִים וְעַל־הַבָּנוֹת הַיִּלּוֹדִים בַּמָּקוֹם הַזֶּה וְעַל־אִמֹּתָם הַיֹּלְדוֹת אוֹתָם וְעַל־אֲבוֹתָם הַמּוֹלִדִים אוֹתָם בָּאָרֶץ הַזֹּאת

3[10] For thus says the LORD concerning the sons and concerning the daughters who are born in this place, and concerning their mothers who bore them, and concerning their fathers who sired them in this land:

מְמוֹתֵי תַחֲלֻאִים יָמֻתוּ לֹא יִסָּפְדוּ וְלֹא יִקָּבֵרוּ לְדֹמֶן עַל־פְּנֵי הָאֲדָמָה יִהְיוּ וּבַחֶרֶב וּבָרָעָב יִכְלוּ וְהָיְתָה נִבְלָתָם לְמַאֲכָל לְעוֹף הַשָּׁמַיִם וּלְבֶהֱמַת הָאָרֶץ

4[11] They shall die of grievous deaths; they shall not be lamented, nor shall they be buried, *they shall be as dung*[12] on the face of the ground; and they shall be consumed by the sword, and by

---

19:11 119:101-119:103 119:111 119:72 119:97, Revelation 10:9-10:10, Saadia Opinions Intro:2

[1] Jeremiah 15:17 - 2 Corinthians 6:17, Daniel 7:28, Ezekiel 3:24-3:25, Jeremiah 1:10 6:11 13:17 16:8 20:8-20:9, Lamentations 3:28, Lamentations.R Petichata D'Chakimei:3, Pesikta de R'Kahana 15.2, Psalms 1:1 26:4-26:5 6:8, Sifre Devarim Vezot Habracha 356

[2] Jeremiah 15:18 - Jeremiah 1:18-1:19 14:3 14:19 20:7 6:12 6:15, Job 6:15-6:20 10:6, Lamentations 3:1-3:18, Mesillat Yesharim 15:To Acquire Pe - R'Ishus, Micah 1:9, Psalms 6:4 13:2-13:4

[3] LXX *water that has no faithfulness*

[4] Jeremiah 15:19 - 1 Kings 17:1, 2 Corinthians 5:16, Acts 20:27, b.Bava Metzia 85a, Ein Yaakov Bava Metzia:85a, Exodus 4:12 4:15-4:16 6:29-6:30, Ezekiel 2:7 3:10-3:11 22:26 20:23, Galatians 1:10 2:5, Hebrews 5:14, Isaiah 32:5-32:6, Jastrow 386b, Jeremiah 15:1 15:10-15:18 20:9 38:20-38:21, Jonah 3:2, Jude 1:24, Leviticus 10:10, Luke 1:19 10:16 12:12 21:15 21:36, Midrash Proverbs 2, Midrash Psalms 116:8, Proverbs 22:29, t.Horayot 2:7 2:7, z.Vaetchanan 269b, Zechariah 3:7

[5] Jeremiah 15:20 - 2 Baruch 2:1, 2 Timothy 4:16-4:17 4:22, Acts 4:8-4:13 4:29-4:31 5:29-5:32 18:9-18:10, Ein Yaakov Bava Batra:8b, Ezekiel 3:9, Isaiah 7:14 8:9-8:10 17:10, Jeremiah 1:8 1:18-1:19 6:27 20:11-20:12, Psalms 46:8 46:12 124:1-124:3 129:1-129:2, Romans 8:31-8:39

[6] Jeremiah 15:21 - 2 Corinthians 1:10, Genesis 24:16, Isaiah 25:3-5 5:5 5:20 49:24-25 6:17, Jeremiah 2:34, Matthew 6:13, Psalms 27:2 37:40, Romans 16:20

[7] LXX *pestilent men*

[8] Jeremiah 16:1 - Jeremiah 1:2 1:4 2:1

[9] Jeremiah 16:2 - 1 Corinthians 7:26-7:27, Genesis 19:14, Luke 21:23 23:29, Matthew 24:19

[10] Jeremiah 16:3 - Jeremiah 6:21 16:5 16:9, z.Vaetchanan 269b

[11] Jeremiah 16:4 - 1 Kings 14:10-11 21:23-24, 2 Kings 9:10 9:36-37, Amos 6:9-10, b.Sanhedrin 46b, Ein Yaakov Sanhedrin:46b, Ezekiel 5:12 39:17-20, Isaiah 5:25 18:6, Jeremiah 7:33 8:1-3 9:23 14:15-16 15:2-3 16:5-7 22:18-19 1:33 10:17 10:20 12:30 20:12 20:27, Numbers.R 9:49, Psalms 78:64 79:2-3 83:11, Pseudo-Phocylides 99, Revelation 19:17-18, Zephaniah 1:17

[12] LXX *they shall be for an example*

famine; and their carcasses shall be meat for the fowls of heaven, and for the beasts of the earth.

כִּי־כֹה ׀ אָמַר יְהֹוָה אַל־תָּבוֹא בֵּית מַרְזֵחַ וְאַל־תֵּלֵךְ לִסְפּוֹד וְאַל־תָּנֹד לָהֶם כִּי־אָסַפְתִּי אֶת־שְׁלוֹמִי מֵאֵת הָעָם־הַזֶּה נְאֻם־יְהֹוָה אֶת־הַחֶסֶד וְאֶת־הָרַחֲמִים 5[1]

For thus says the LORD: Do not enter into the house of mourning, nor go to lament, nor bemoan them; for I have taken away My peace from this people, *says the LORD, mercy and compassion*[2].

וּמֵתוּ גְדֹלִים וּקְטַנִּים בָּאָרֶץ הַזֹּאת לֹא יִקָּבֵרוּ וְלֹא־יִסְפְּדוּ לָהֶם וְלֹא יִתְגֹּדַד וְלֹא יִקָּרֵחַ לָהֶם 6[3]

Both the great and the small shall die in this land; they shall not be buried[4]; nor shall men lament for them, nor cut themselves, nor make themselves bald for them;

וְלֹא־יִפְרְסוּ לָהֶם עַל־אֵבֶל לְנַחֲמוֹ עַל־מֵת וְלֹא־יַשְׁקוּ אוֹתָם כּוֹס תַּנְחוּמִים עַל־אָבִיו וְעַל־אִמּוֹ 7[5]

Nor shall men break bread for them in mourning, to comfort them for the dead; nor shall men give them the cup of consolation to drink for their father or for their mother.

וּבֵית־מִשְׁתֶּה לֹא־תָבוֹא לָשֶׁבֶת אוֹתָם לֶאֱכֹל וְלִשְׁתּוֹת 8[6]

And you shall not go into the house of feasting to sit with them, to eat and to drink.

כִּי כֹה אָמַר יְהֹוָה צְבָאוֹת אֱלֹהֵי יִשְׂרָאֵל הִנְנִי מַשְׁבִּית מִן־הַמָּקוֹם הַזֶּה לְעֵינֵיכֶם וּבִימֵיכֶם קוֹל שָׂשׂוֹן וְקוֹל שִׂמְחָה קוֹל חָתָן וְקוֹל כַּלָּה 9[7]

For thus says the LORD of hosts, the God of Israel: Behold, I will cause the voice of mirth and the voice of gladness, the voice of the bridegroom and the voice of the bride to cease from this place before your eyes and in your days.

וְהָיָה כִּי תַגִּיד לָעָם הַזֶּה אֵת כָּל־הַדְּבָרִים הָאֵלֶּה וְאָמְרוּ אֵלֶיךָ עַל־מֶה דִבֶּר יְהֹוָה עָלֵינוּ אֵת כָּל־הָרָעָה הַגְּדוֹלָה הַזֹּאת וּמֶה עֲוֺנֵנוּ וּמֶה חַטָּאתֵנוּ אֲשֶׁר חָטָאנוּ לַיהֹוָה אֱלֹהֵינוּ 10[8]

And it shall come to pass, when you tell this people all these words, and they shall say to you: 'Why has the LORD pronounced all this great evil against us? Or what is our iniquity? Or what is the sin we have committed against the LORD our God?'

וְאָמַרְתָּ אֲלֵיהֶם עַל אֲשֶׁר־עָזְבוּ אֲבוֹתֵיכֶם אוֹתִי נְאֻם־יְהֹוָה וַיֵּלְכוּ אַחֲרֵי אֱלֹהִים אֲחֵרִים וַיַּעַבְדוּם וַיִּשְׁתַּחֲווּ לָהֶם וְאֹתִי עָזָבוּ וְאֶת־תּוֹרָתִי לֹא שָׁמָרוּ 11[9]

Then shall you say to them: 'Because your fathers forsook Me, says the LORD, and walked after other gods, and served them, and worshipped them, and forsaken Me, and did not keep My law;

וְאַתֶּם הֲרֵעֹתֶם לַעֲשׂוֹת מֵאֲבוֹתֵיכֶם וְהִנְּכֶם הֹלְכִים אִישׁ אַחֲרֵי שְׁרִרוּת לִבּוֹ־הָרָע לְבִלְתִּי שְׁמֹעַ אֵלָי 12[10]

and you have done worse than your fathers; for, behold, you all walk after the stubbornness of his evil heart, so that you do not listen to Me;

---

[1] Jeremiah 16:5 - 2 Chronicles 15:5-15:6, b.Bava Batra 10a, b.Ketubot 69b, Deuteronomy 7:17, Deuteronomy.R 3:7, Ein Yaakov Ketubot 69b, Ezekiel 24:16-23, Isaiah 3:11, Jastrow 840b, Jeremiah 15:1-4 16:6-7, Lamentations.R 1:23, Midrash Psalms 77:3, Pesikta de R'Kahana 13.13 17.1, Revelation 6:4, t.Peah 4:21, y.Moed Katan 3:5, z.Vaetchanan 269b, Zechariah 8:10
[2] Missing in LXX
[3] Jeremiah 16:6 - Amos 6:11, b.Megillah 9b, Deuteronomy 14:1, Ezekiel 9:5-6, Isaiah 9:15-18 22:12 24:2, Jeremiah 7:29 13:13 16:4 22:18-19 17:5 23:5 24:37, Leviticus 19:28, Revelation 6:15 20:12
[4] Missing in LXX
[5] Jeremiah 16:7 - Deuteronomy 2:14, Ezekiel 24:17, Hosea 9:4, Job 18:11, Josephus Wars 2.1.1, Lamentations.R 4:7, Proverbs 31:6-7
[6] Jeremiah 16:8 - 1 Corinthians 5:11, Amos 6:4-6, Ecclesiastes 7:2-4, Ephesians 5:11, Isaiah 22:12-14, Jeremiah 15:17, Luke 17:27-29, Matthew 24:38, Psalms 26:4
[7] Jeremiah 16:9 - b.Megillah 9b, Deuteronomy.R 7:1, Ezekiel 2:13, Hosea 2:11, Isaiah 24:7-24:12, Jeremiah 7:34 1:10, Revelation 18:22-18:23, z.Vaetchanan 269b
[8] Jeremiah 16:10 - 1 Kings 9:8-9, Deuteronomy 29:23-24, Hosea 12:10, Jeremiah 2:35 5:19 13:22 22:8-9
[9] Jeremiah 16:11 - 1 Kings 9:9, 1 Peter 4:3, Daniel 9:10-9:12, Deuteronomy 29:24-29:25, Ezekiel 11:21, Jeremiah 2:8 5:7-5:9 8:2 9:15 22:9, Judges 2:12-2:13 10:13-10:14, Lamentations.R Petichata D'Chakimei:2, Mas.Kallah Rabbati 8:9, Nehemiah 9:26-9:29, Pesikta de R'Kahana 15.5, Psalms 106:35-106:41, Sibylline Oracles 3.275
[10] Jeremiah 16:12 - 1 Samuel 15:23, 2 Timothy 3:13, Deuteronomy 9:27 5:18, Ecclesiastes 8:12 9:3, Genesis 6:5 8:21, Hebrews 3:12, Jeremiah 7:24 7:26 9:15 13:10 17:9, Judges 2:19, Mark 7:21

וְהֵטַלְתִּי אֶתְכֶם מֵעַל הָאָרֶץ הַזֹּאת עַל־הָאָרֶץ אֲשֶׁר לֹא יְדַעְתֶּם אַתֶּם וַאֲבוֹתֵיכֶם וַעֲבַדְתֶּם־שָׁם אֶת־אֱלֹהִים אֲחֵרִים יוֹמָם וָלַיְלָה אֲשֶׁר לֹא־אֶתֵּן לָכֶם חֲנִינָה	13[1]	Therefore, I will cast you from this land into a land you have not known, nor you nor your fathers; and there shall you serve *other gods day and night; because I will show you no favor*[2].'
לָכֵן הִנֵּה־יָמִים בָּאִים נְאֻם־יְהוָה וְלֹא־יֵאָמֵר עוֹד חַי־יְהוָה אֲשֶׁר הֶעֱלָה אֶת־בְּנֵי יִשְׂרָאֵל מֵאֶרֶץ מִצְרָיִם	14[3]	Therefore, behold, the days come, says the LORD, that it shall no longer be said: 'As the LORD lives, who brought up the children of Israel from the land of Egypt, '
כִּי אִם־חַי־יְהוָה אֲשֶׁר הֶעֱלָה אֶת־בְּנֵי יִשְׂרָאֵל מֵאֶרֶץ צָפוֹן וּמִכֹּל הָאֲרָצוֹת אֲשֶׁר הִדִּיחָם שָׁמָּה וַהֲשִׁבֹתִים עַל־אַדְמָתָם אֲשֶׁר נָתַתִּי לַאֲבוֹתָם	15[4]	But: 'As the LORD lives, who brought up the children of Israel from the land of the north, and from all the countries where He drove them;' and I will bring them back to their land that I gave to their fathers.
הִנְנִי שֹׁלֵחַ לְדַוָּגִים' "לְדַיָּגִים" רַבִּים נְאֻם־יְהוָה וְדִיגוּם וְאַחֲרֵי־כֵן אֶשְׁלַח לְרַבִּים צַיָּדִים וְצָדוּם מֵעַל כָּל־הַר וּמֵעַל כָּל־גִּבְעָה וּמִנְּקִיקֵי הַסְּלָעִים	16[5]	Behold, I will send for many fishers, says the LORD, and they shall fish them; and afterward I will send for many hunters, and they shall hunt them from every mountain, and from every hill, and from the clefts of the rocks.
כִּי עֵינַי עַל־כָּל־דַּרְכֵיהֶם לֹא נִסְתְּרוּ מִלְּפָנָי וְלֹא־נִצְפַּן עֲו‍ֹנָם מִנֶּגֶד עֵינָי	17[6]	For my eyes are on all their ways, they are not hidden from My face; nor is their iniquity concealed from my eyes.
וְשִׁלַּמְתִּי רִאשׁוֹנָה מִשְׁנֵה עֲו‍ֹנָם וְחַטָּאתָם עַל חַלְּלָם אֶת־אַרְצִי בְּנִבְלַת שִׁקּוּצֵיהֶם וְתוֹעֲבוֹתֵיהֶם מָלְאוּ אֶת־נַחֲלָתִי	18[7]	And first I will recompense their iniquity and their sin double; because they profaned My land; they filled my inheritance with the carcasses of their detestable things and their abominations.
יְהוָה עֻזִּי וּמָעֻזִּי וּמְנוּסִי בְּיוֹם צָרָה אֵלֶיךָ גּוֹיִם יָבֹאוּ מֵאַפְסֵי־אָרֶץ וְיֹאמְרוּ אַךְ־שֶׁקֶר נָחֲלוּ אֲבוֹתֵינוּ הֶבֶל וְאֵין־בָּם מוֹעִיל	19[8]	O LORD, my strength, and my stronghold, and my refuge, in the day of affliction, to You shall the nations come from the ends of the earth, and shall say: 'Our fathers have inherited nothing but lies, vanity, and things in which there is no profit.'
הֲיַעֲשֶׂה־לּוֹ אָדָם אֱלֹהִים וְהֵמָּה לֹא אֱלֹהִים	20[9]	Shall a man make to himself gods, and they are no gods?

---

[1] Jeremiah 16:13 - 2 Chronicles 7:20, b.Sanhedrin 98b, Deuteronomy 4:26-4:28 4:36 28:63-28:65 5:27 30:17-30:18, Ein Yaakov Sanhedrin:98b, Jeremiah 5:19 6:15 14:8 15:4 15:14 17:4 22:28, Joshua 23:15-23:16, Lamentations.R 1:51, Leviticus 18:27-18:28, Pesikta de R'Kahana 13.13 16.6, Pesikta Rabbati 29/30A:7, Psalms 81:13, Psalms of Solomon 9:1

[2] LXX *their other gods, who shall have no mercy upon you*

[3] Jeremiah 16:14 - b.Zevachim 54b, Derech Hashem Part II 2§04, Deuteronomy 15:15, Exodus 20:2, Hosea 3:4-3:5, Isaiah 43:18-43:19, Jeremiah 23:7-23:8, Mekhilta de R'Shimon bar Yochai Shirata 34:3, Micah 6:4
Jeremiah 16:14-15 - Mekilta de R'Ishmael Pisha 16:62-64 16:99-102, Mekilta de R'Ishmael Shirata 8:91-94

[4] Jeremiah 16:15 - Amos 9:14, b.Zevachim 54b, Deuteronomy 30:3-30:5, Ezekiel 34:12-34:14 12:24 37:21-37:22 15:28, Isaiah 11:11-16 13:5-13:6 14:1 27:12-13, Jeremiah 3:18 23:8 24:6 6:3 6:10 7:9 8:37 2:19, Midrash Proverbs 18, Psalms 10:47

[5] Jeremiah 16:16 - 1 Samuel 24:11 2:20, Amos 4:2 5:19 9:1-9:3, Genesis 10:9, Habakkuk 1:14-1:15, Isaiah 24:17-24:18, Jeremiah 1:9, Luke 17:34-37, Mas.Soferim 7:4, Micah 7:2, Revelation 6:15-6:17

[6] Jeremiah 16:17 - 1 Corinthians 4:5, 2 Chronicles 16:9, 2 Enoch 66:5, Ezekiel 8:12 9:9, Hebrews 4:13, Isaiah 5:15, Jeremiah 23:24 8:19, Job 34:21-34:22, Luke 12:1-12:2, Proverbs 5:21 15:3, Psalms 90:8 19:3
Jeremiah 16:17-17:14 - Haftarah Behar Sinai [Teimon]

[7] Jeremiah 16:18 - Ezekiel 11:18 11:21 43:7-43:9, Isaiah 24:5 16:2 13:7, Jeremiah 2:7 3:1-3:2 3:9 17:18, Leviticus 18:27-18:28 2:30, Micah 2:10, Numbers 35:33-35:34, Psalms 10:38, Revelation 18:6, Sifre Devarim {Haazinu Hashamayim} 325, Sifre Devarim Nitzavim 325, Zephaniah 3:1-3:5

[8] Jeremiah 16:19 - 1 Peter 1:18, Exodus.R 27:4, Ezekiel 11:16, Guide for the Perplexed 3:49, Habakkuk 2:18-19 3:19, Isaiah 2:2-3 11:9-10 1:4 8:2 20:10 1:6 60:1-3 14:2, Jeremiah 2:11 3:16-17 3:23 10:5 10:14-15 17:17, Malachi 1:11, Mekhilta de R'Shimon bar Yochai Beshallach 21:3, Mekhilta de R'Shimon bar Yochai Shirata 29:1 35:2, Mekilta de R'Ishmael Shirata 3:5, Micah 4:1-2, Midrash Psalms 42/43:5, mt.Hilchot Melachim uMichamoteihem 11:4, Nahum 1:7, Proverbs 18:10, Psalms 18:2-3 19:15 22:28-31 27:5 46:2 46:8 46:12 62:3 62:8 67:3-8 68:32 72:8-12 86:9 91:1-2 144:1-2, Revelation 7:9-11 11:15, Tanya Likutei Aramim §31, Zechariah 2:11 8:20-23
Jeremiah 16:19-17:14 - Haftarah Bechukosai [Ashkenaz and Sephard]
Jeremiah 16:19-20 - Mekilta de R'Ishmael Shirata 8

[9] Jeremiah 16:20 - Acts 19:26, Galatians 1:8 4:8, Hosea 8:4-6, Isaiah 12:19 13:19, Jeremiah 2:11, Psalms 115:4-8 135:14-18

Jeremiah – Chapter 17

לָכֵ֣ן הִנְנִ֤י מֽוֹדִיעָם֙ בַּפַּ֣עַם הַזֹּ֔את אוֹדִיעֵ֖ם אֶת־יָדִ֣י
וְאֶת־גְּבֽוּרָתִ֑י וְיָדְע֖וּ כִּֽי־שְׁמִ֥י יְהוָֽה

21¹ Therefore, behold, I will cause them to know, this once I will cause them to know My hand and My might; and they shall know that My name is the LORD.

חַטַּ֣את יְהוּדָ֗ה כְּתוּבָ֛ה בְּעֵ֥ט בַּרְזֶ֖ל בְּצִפֹּ֣רֶן שָׁמִ֑יר
חֲרוּשָׁה֙ עַל־ל֣וּחַ לִבָּ֔ם וּלְקַרְנ֖וֹת מִזְבְּחוֹתֵיכֶֽם

1² *The sin of Judah is written with a pen of iron, and with the point of a diamond; it is engraved on the tablet of their heart, and on the horns of your altars³.*

כִּזְכֹּ֤ר בְּנֵיהֶם֙ מִזְבְּחוֹתָ֔ם וַאֲשֵׁרֵיהֶ֖ם עַל־עֵ֣ץ רַעֲנָ֑ן
עַ֖ל גְּבָע֥וֹת הַגְּבֹהֽוֹת

2⁴ *Like the symbols of their sons are their altars, and their Asherim are by the leafy trees, upon the high hills⁵.*

הֲרָרִי֙ בַּשָּׂדֶ֔ה חֵילְךָ֥ כָל־אוֹצְרוֹתֶ֖יךָ לָבַ֣ז אֶתֵּ֑ן
בָּמֹתֶ֕יךָ בְּחַטָּ֖את בְּכָל־גְּבוּלֶֽיךָ

3⁶ *O, you who sit on the mountain in the field, I will give your substance and all your treasures as spoil, and your high places, because of sin, throughout all your borders⁷.*

וְשָׁמַטְתָּ֗ה וּבְךָ֙ מִנַּחֲלָֽתְךָ֙ אֲשֶׁ֣ר נָתַ֣תִּי לָ֔ךְ וְהַעֲבַדְתִּ֙יךָ֙
אֶת־אֹ֣יְבֶ֔יךָ בָּאָ֖רֶץ אֲשֶׁ֣ר לֹֽא־יָדָ֑עְתָּ כִּי־אֵ֛שׁ קְדַחְתֶּ֥ם
בְּאַפִּ֖י עַד־עוֹלָ֥ם תּוּקָֽד

4⁸ *And you, of yourself, shall discontinue from your heritage I gave you; and I will cause you to serve your enemies in the land you do not know; for you have kindled a fire in My nostril, which shall burn forever⁹.*

כֹּ֣ה ׀ אָמַ֣ר יְהוָ֗ה אָר֤וּר הַגֶּ֙בֶר֙ אֲשֶׁ֣ר יִבְטַ֣ח בָּֽאָדָ֔ם
וְשָׂ֥ם בָּשָׂ֖ר זְרֹע֑וֹ וּמִן־יְהוָ֖ה יָס֥וּר לִבּֽוֹ

5¹⁰ Thus says the LORD: Cursed is the man who trusts in man, and makes flesh his arm, and whose heart departs from the LORD.

וְהָיָה֙ כְּעַרְעָ֣ר בָּֽעֲרָבָ֔ה וְלֹ֥א יִרְאֶ֖ה כִּי־יָב֣וֹא ט֑וֹב
וְשָׁכַ֤ן חֲרֵרִים֙ בַּמִּדְבָּ֔ר אֶ֥רֶץ מְלֵחָ֖ה וְלֹ֥א תֵשֵֽׁב

6¹¹ For he shall be like a tamarisk in the desert, and shall not see when good comes; but shall inhabit the parched places in the wilderness, a salt land and not inhabited.

בָּר֣וּךְ הַגֶּ֔בֶר אֲשֶׁ֥ר יִבְטַ֖ח בַּֽיהוָ֑ה וְהָיָ֥ה יְהוָ֖ה מִבְטַחֽוֹ

7¹² Blessed is the man who trusts in the LORD, and whose trust is the LORD.

וְהָיָ֞ה כְּעֵ֣ץ ׀ שָׁת֣וּל עַל־מַ֗יִם וְעַל־יוּבַל֙ יְשַׁלַּ֣ח
שָֽׁרָשָׁ֔יו וְלֹ֤א *יִרָא* "יִרְאֶה" כִּֽי־יָבֹ֣א חֹ֔ם וְהָיָ֥ה עָלֵ֖הוּ

8¹³ For he shall be as a tree planted by the waters, and that spreads out its roots by the river, and

¹ Jeremiah 16:21 - Amos 5:8, Exodus 9:14-9:18 14:4 15:3, Ezekiel 6:7 24:24 24:27 1:14, Isaiah 19:3, Jeremiah 9:2, Leviticus.R 24:1, Psalms 9:17 83:19

² Jeremiah 17:1 - 2 Corinthians 3:3, Gates of Repentance 1.27, Hosea 12:13, Job 19:23-24, Leviticus 4:17-18 4:25, mt.Hilchot Gerusin 4:6, Proverbs 3:3 7:3

³ Missing in LXX

⁴ Jeremiah 17:2 - 2 Chronicles 24:18 9:3 9:19, b.Sanhedrin 63b, Ezekiel 20:28, Guide for the Perplexed 1:9, Hosea 4:13-4:14, Isaiah 1:29 17:8, Jeremiah 2:20 7:18, Judges 3:7, Psalms 78:58

⁵ Missing in LXX

⁶ Jeremiah 17:3 - 2 Kings 24:13 25:13-16, Ein Yaakov Yoma:87a, Ezekiel 6:3 7:20-22 16:39, Isaiah 2:2-3 3:9 39:4-6, Jeremiah 12:12 15:13 2:18 52:15-20, Lamentations 1:10 5:17-18, Leviticus 2:30, Micah 1:5-7 3:12-4:2

⁷ Missing in LXX

⁸ Jeremiah 17:4 - 1 Kings 9:7, 2 Kings 1:21, Deuteronomy 4:26-27 4:25 28:47-48 29:25-27 32:22-25, Ezekiel 21:3-4 21:36, Guide for the Perplexed 1:46, Isaiah 5:25 14:3 6:33 18:24, Jeremiah 5:29 7:20 12:7 15:14 16:13 25:9-11 27:12-13, Joshua 23:15-16, Lamentations 1:12 5:2, Leviticus 26:31-34, Mark 9:43-49, Nahum 1:5-6, Nehemiah 9:28

⁹ Missing in LXX

¹⁰ Jeremiah 17:5 - 2 Chronicles 8:8, Ezekiel 6:9 29:6-7, Hosea 1:2, Isaiah 2:22 30:1-7 31:1-9 12:6 11:15, Mekhilta de R'Shimon bar Yochai Beshallach 22:1, Mekhilta de R'Ishmael Beshallah 3:46, Midrash Tanchuma Tazria 9, Perek Shirah [the Wild Goose], Psalms 18:22 62:10 118:8-9 146:3-4, z.Vaetchanan 269b

¹¹ Jeremiah 17:6 - 2 Kings 7:2 7:19-7:20, Avot de R'Natan 22, Deuteronomy 5:22, Ezekiel 23:11, Isaiah 1:30, Jeremiah 24:6, Job 8:11-13 15:30-34 20:17 15:6, Judges 9:45, m.Avot 3:17, mt.Pirkei Avot 3:21 3:22 [Shabbat afternoon], Psalms 1:4 92:8 129:6-8, z.Chayyei Sarah 131a, z.Vayechi 224b, Zephaniah 2:9

¹² Jeremiah 17:7 - Birchat Hamazon, Deuteronomy.R 1:12 5:9, Ephesians 1:12, Isaiah 26:3-4 6:18, m.Peah 8:9, Maariv Motzoei Shabbat], Mekhilta de R'Shimon bar Yochai Beshallach 22:1, Mekhilta de R'Ishmael Beshallah 111:47, Midrash Proverbs 21, Midrash Tanchuma Vayeshev 8, Perek Shirah [the Wild Goose], mt.Hilchot Zechiyah Umatanah 12:17, Proverbs 16:20, Psalms 2:12 34:9 40:5 84:13 5:1 2:5, Shabbat and Yom Tov Minchah, Siman 34:16, Uvoh Letzion [daily Shacharit], y.Peah 8:8

¹³ Jeremiah 17:8 - Apocalypse of Adam 6:2, b.Bechorot 55b, Ezekiel 31:4-31:10 23:12, Isaiah 10:11, Jeremiah 14:1-14:6, Job 8:16, Joseph and Aseneth 16:16, Leviticus.R 22:10, m.Avot 3:17, Mas.Soferim 7:2, Midrash Shmuel 3:24, Midrash Tanchuma Pinchas 12, mt.Pirkei Avot 3:21, Numbers.R 21:18, Pesikta de R'Kahana 6.1, Pesikta Rabbati 16:4, Pirkei Avot 3:22 [Shabbat afternoon], Psalms

רַעֲנָן וּבִשְׁנַת בַּצֹּרֶת לֹא יִדְאָג וְלֹא יָמִישׁ מֵעֲשׂוֹת פֶּרִי

shall not see when heat comes, but its foliage shall be luxuriant; and shall not be anxious in the year of drought, nor shall cease from yielding fruit.

עָקֹב הַלֵּב מִכֹּל וְאָנֻשׁ הוּא מִי יֵדָעֶנּוּ

9[1] The heart is deceitful above all things, and *it is exceeding weak[2]*; who can know it?

אֲנִי יְהוָה חֹקֵר לֵב בֹּחֵן כְּלָיוֹת וְלָתֵת לְאִישׁ "כִּדְרָכוֹ" "כִּדְרָכָיו" כִּפְרִי מַעֲלָלָיו

10[3] I the LORD search the heart, I try the reins, to give every man according to his ways, according to the fruit of his deeds.

קֹרֵא דָגַר וְלֹא יָלָד עֹשֶׂה עֹשֶׁר וְלֹא בְמִשְׁפָּט בַּחֲצִי "יָמָו" "יָמָיו" יַעַזְבֶנּוּ וּבְאַחֲרִיתוֹ יִהְיֶה נָבָל

11[4] *As the partridge that broods over young she has not brought forth[5]*, so is he who gets riches, and not by right; in the midst of his days he shall leave them, and at his end he shall be a fool.

כִּסֵּא כָבוֹד מָרוֹם מֵרִאשׁוֹן מְקוֹם מִקְדָּשֵׁנוּ

12[6] *Your throne of glory, on high from the beginning, You, the place of our sanctuary[7]*, You hope of Israel, the LORD. All who forsake You shall be ashamed; they *who depart from You[9]* shall be written in the earth, because they have forsaken the LORD, the fountain of *living waters[10]*.

מִקְוֵה יִשְׂרָאֵל יְהוָה כָּל־עֹזְבֶיךָ יֵבֹשׁוּ "יִסּוֹרַי" "וְסוּרַי" בָּאָרֶץ יִכָּתֵבוּ כִּי עָזְבוּ מְקוֹר מַיִם־חַיִּים אֶת־יְהוָה

13[8]

רְפָאֵנִי יְהוָה וְאֵרָפֵא הוֹשִׁיעֵנִי וְאִוָּשֵׁעָה כִּי תְהִלָּתִי אָתָּה

14[11] Heal me, O LORD, and I shall be healed; save me, and I shall be saved; for you are my praise.

הִנֵּה־הֵמָּה אֹמְרִים אֵלָי אַיֵּה דְבַר־יְהוָה יָבוֹא נָא

15[12] Behold, they say to me: 'Where is the word of the LORD? let it come now.'

וַאֲנִי לֹא־אַצְתִּי מֵרֹעֶה אַחֲרֶיךָ וְיוֹם אָנוּשׁ לֹא הִתְאַוֵּיתִי אַתָּה יָדָעְתָּ מוֹצָא שְׂפָתַי נֹכַח פָּנֶיךָ הָיָה

16[13] *As for me, I have not hastened from being a shepherd[14]* after You; nor have I desired the

---

1:3 92:11-92:16, Ruth.R 7:2, z.Chayyei Sarah 131a, z.Mishpatim 98b
Jeremiah 17:8-26 - 4QJera
[1] Jeremiah 17:9 - 2 Baruch 83:3, Ecclesiastes 9:3, Genesis 6:5 8:21, Hebrews 3:12, James 1:14-15, Jeremiah 16:12, Job 15:14-16, Mark 7:21-22, Matthew 13:15 15:19, Midrash Psalms 14:1, Proverbs 4:26, Psalms 51:6 53:2-4
[2] LXX *and it is the man*
[3] Jeremiah 17:10 - 1 Chronicles 4:9 5:17, 1 Samuel 16:7, 2 Baruch 48:39, 2 Chronicles 6:30, Derech Hashem Part II 1§3, Ecclesiastes.R 1:36 11:4, Galatians 6:7-8, Genesis.R 65:12 67:8, Hebrews 4:12-4:13, Isaiah 3:10-3:11, Jeremiah 11:20 20:12 21:14 8:19, John 2:25, Mas.Derek Eretz Rabbah 2:12, Matthew 16:27, Mesillat Yesharim 4:To Acquire Zehirus, Micah 7:13, Midrash Psalms 14:1, Midrash Tanchuma Naso 5, Numbers.R 9:1, Pesikta Rabbati 42:3, Pirkei de R'Eliezer 43, Proverbs 17:3, Psalms 7:10 62:13 139:1-139:2 139:23-139:24, Revelation 2:23 20:12 22:12, Romans 2:6-2:8 6:21 8:27, Saadia Opinions 5:1 9:3, z.Bo 38b
Jeremiah 17:10-12 - Mekilta de R'Ishmael Kaspa 2:35-39
[4] Jeremiah 17:11 - 1 Timothy 6:9, 2 Peter 2:3 2:14, Amos 3:10 8:4-8:6, b.Chullin 140b, Ecclesiastes 5:14-5:17, Ezekiel 22:12-22:13, Habakkuk 2:6-2:12, Hosea 12:9-12:10, Isaiah 1:23-1:24, James 5:3-5:5, Jastrow 279b 878b, Jeremiah 5:27-5:28 22:13 22:17, Luke 12:20, Malachi 3:5, Matthew 23:13, Micah 2:1-2:2 2:9 6:10-6:12 7:3, Midrash Tanchuma Ki Tetze 2, Midrash Tanchuma Pekudei 5, Proverbs 1:18-1:19 13:11 15:27 21:6 23:5 4:8 4:16 4:20 4:22, Psalms 55:24, Titus 1:11, Zechariah 5:4 7:9-7:13, Zephaniah 1:9
[5] LXX *The partridge utters her voice, she gathers eggs she did not lay*
[6] Jeremiah 17:12 - 2 Baruch 46:4, 2 Chronicles 2:4-2:5, 3 Enoch 24:22, Avot de R'Natan 26, b.Nedarim 39b, b.Pesachim 5a 54a, b.Sanhedrin [Rashi] 94b, Ein Yaakov Nedarim:39b, Ein Yaakov Pesachim:54a, Exodus.R 15:1 25:8 33:4, Ezekiel 1:26 19:7, Genesis.R 1:4 3:4 63:8, Hebrews 4:16 12:2, Isaiah 6:1 18:1, Jeremiah 3:17 14:21, Leviticus.R 30:16 31:7, Matthew 1:31, Midrash Proverbs 8, Midrash Psalms 93:3, Midrash Tanchuma Ki Tetze 2, Midrash Tanchuma Naso 11, Midrash Tanchuma Pekudei 1, Midrash Tanchuma Vayakhel 7, Pesikta de R'Kahana 21.5 27.10, Pesikta Rabbati 32:1 51:3, Pirkei de R'Eliezer 3, Psalms 96:6 7:19, Revelation 3:21, Sifre Devarim Ekev 39
[7] LXX *An exalted throne of glory is our sanctuary*
[8] Jeremiah 17:13 - 1 Timothy 1:1, Acts 4:20, b.Yoma 85b, Daniel 12:2, Ezekiel 12:32 16:63 36:32, Isaiah 1:28 45:16-45:17 65:11-65:14 18:5, Jastrow 520a 829b, Jeremiah 2:13 2:17 2:26-2:27 14:8 17:5 17:17, Joel 4:16, John 4:10 4:14 7:37-7:38 8:6-8:8, Luke 10:20, m.Yoma 8:9, Midrash Psalms 4:9, Pesikta de R'Kahana 24.4 24.2, Pesikta Rabbati 44:8, Proverbs 10:7 14:14, Psalms 22:5 36:9-36:10 73:27 97:7, Revelation 7:17 20:15 21:6 22:1 22:17, Selichot, Tanya Igeret Hakodesh §09, y.Yoma 8:7
[9] 4QJera *and my faithless ones*
[10] LXX *life, the LORD*
[11] Jeremiah 17:14 - Deuteronomy 10:21 8:39, Isaiah 6:10 57:18-57:19, Jeremiah 15:20 7:19, Leviticus.R 16:9, Luke 4:18, Matthew 8:25 14:30, Mekilta de R'Ishmael Beshallah 6:97, Psalms 6:3 6:5 12:5 60:6 10:47 13:1 4:14
[12] Jeremiah 17:15 - 2 Peter 3:3-4, Amos 5:18, Ezekiel 12:22 12:27-28, Isaiah 5:19, Jeremiah 20:7-8
[13] Jeremiah 17:16 - 2 Corinthians 1:12 2:17, Acts 20:20 20:27, Amos 7:14-7:15, Ezekiel 3:14-3:19 33:7-33:9, James 1:19 3:1, Jeremiah 1:4-1:10 4:19-4:20 9:2 13:17 14:17-21 18:20 20:9, Romans 9:1-3
[14] LXX *But I have not wearied of following*

woeful day; you know it; what came from my lips was *manifest before You*[1].

Do not be a ruin to me; You are my refuge in the day of evil[3].

אַל־תִּהְיֵה־לִי לִמְחִתָּה מַחֲסִי־אַתָּה בְּיוֹם רָעָה

17 [2]

Let those who persecute me be ashamed, but let me not be ashamed; let them be dismayed, but let me not be dismayed; bring on them the day of evil, and destroy them with double calamity.

יֵבֹשׁוּ רֹדְפַי וְאַל־אֵבֹשָׁה אָנִי יֵחַתּוּ הֵמָּה וְאַל־אֵחַתָּה אָנִי הָבִיא עֲלֵיהֶם יוֹם רָעָה וּמִשְׁנֶה שִׁבָּרוֹן שָׁבְרֵם

18 [4]

Thus the LORD said to me: Go, and stand in the gate of the children of the people, in which the kings of Judah come, and by which they go out, and in all the gates of Jerusalem;

כֹּה־אָמַר יְהֹוָה אֵלַי הָלֹךְ וְעָמַדְתָּ בְּשַׁעַר 'בְּנֵי־עָם' "בְּנֵי־הָעָם" אֲשֶׁר יָבֹאוּ בוֹ מַלְכֵי יְהוּדָה וַאֲשֶׁר יֵצְאוּ בוֹ וּבְכֹל שַׁעֲרֵי יְרוּשָׁלָם

19 [5]

And say to them: Hear the word of the LORD, you kings of Judah, and all Judah, and all the inhabitants of Jerusalem, who enter in by these gates;

וְאָמַרְתָּ אֲלֵיהֶם שִׁמְעוּ דְבַר־יְהֹוָה מַלְכֵי יְהוּדָה וְכָל־יְהוּדָה וְכֹל יֹשְׁבֵי יְרוּשָׁלָם הַבָּאִים בַּשְּׁעָרִים הָאֵלֶּה

20 [6]

thus says the LORD: Take heed for the sake of your souls, and do not bear a burden on the Sabbath day, nor bring it in through the gates of Jerusalem;

כֹּה אָמַר יְהֹוָה הִשָּׁמְרוּ בְּנַפְשׁוֹתֵיכֶם וְאַל־תִּשְׂאוּ מַשָּׂא בְּיוֹם הַשַּׁבָּת וַהֲבֵאתֶם בְּשַׁעֲרֵי יְרוּשָׁלָם

21 [7]

Nor carry forth a burden from your houses on the Sabbath day, nor do any work; but hallow the Sabbath day, as I commanded your fathers;

וְלֹא־תוֹצִיאוּ מַשָּׂא מִבָּתֵּיכֶם בְּיוֹם הַשַּׁבָּת וְכָל־מְלָאכָה לֹא תַעֲשׂוּ וְקִדַּשְׁתֶּם אֶת־יוֹם הַשַּׁבָּת כַּאֲשֶׁר צִוִּיתִי אֶת־אֲבוֹתֵיכֶם

22 [8]

but they did not listen, nor inclined their ear, but made their neck stiff, so they might not hear, nor receive instruction.

וְלֹא שָׁמְעוּ וְלֹא הִטּוּ אֶת־אָזְנָם וַיַּקְשׁוּ אֶת־עָרְפָּם לְבִלְתִּי 'שׁוֹמֵעַ' "שְׁמוֹעַ" וּלְבִלְתִּי קַחַת מוּסָר

23 [9]

And it shall come to pass, if you diligently listen to Me, says the LORD, to bring in no burden through the gates of this city on the Sabbath day, but to hallow the Sabbath day, to do no work in it;

וְהָיָה אִם־שָׁמֹעַ תִּשְׁמְעוּן אֵלַי נְאֻם־יְהֹוָה לְבִלְתִּי הָבִיא מַשָּׂא בְּשַׁעֲרֵי הָעִיר הַזֹּאת בְּיוֹם הַשַּׁבָּת וּלְקַדֵּשׁ אֶת־יוֹם הַשַּׁבָּת לְבִלְתִּי 'עֲשׂוֹת־בֹּה' "עֲשׂוֹת־בָּוֹ" כָּל־מְלָאכָה

24 [10]

then kings and princes sitting on the throne of David shall enter in by the gates of this city, riding in chariots and on horses, they, and their princes, the men of Judah, and the inhabitants of Jerusalem; and this city shall be inhabited forever.

וּבָאוּ בְשַׁעֲרֵי הָעִיר הַזֹּאת מְלָכִים וְשָׂרִים יֹשְׁבִים עַל־כִּסֵּא דָוִד רֹכְבִים בָּרֶכֶב וּבַסּוּסִים הֵמָּה וְשָׂרֵיהֶם אִישׁ יְהוּדָה וְיֹשְׁבֵי יְרוּשָׁלָם וְיָשְׁבָה הָעִיר־הַזֹּאת לְעוֹלָם

25 [11]

---

[1] 4QJera *your mouth*

[2] Jeremiah 17:17 - Ephesians 6:13, Jeremiah 16:19 17:7 17:13, Job 7:23, Nahum 1:7, Psalms 41:2 59:17 77:3-77:10 88:16-88:17

[3] LXX *Do not be to me a stranger, but spare me in the evil day*

[4] Jeremiah 17:18 - b.Chagigah 15a, Ein Yaakov Chagigah:15a, Genesis.R 9:5, Jeremiah 11:20 14:17 16:18 17:16 18:19-18:23 20:11, Job 16:14, Psalms 25:2-25:3 35:4 35:8 35:26-35:27 40:15 70:3 71:1 83:18-83:19, Revelation 18:6

[5] Jeremiah 17:19 - Acts 5:20, Jeremiah 7:2 19:2 2:2 12:6 12:10, Proverbs 1:20-1:23 8:1 9:3

[6] Jeremiah 17:20 - Amos 4:1, Ezekiel 2:7 3:17, Hosea 5:1, Jeremiah 13:18 19:3 22:2, Micah 3:1, Psalms 49:2-49:3, Revelation 2:29

[7] Jeremiah 17:21 - Acts 20:28, Deuteronomy 4:9 4:15 4:23 11:16, Hebrews 2:1-2:3 12:15-12:16, Jeremiah 17:22-17:27, John 5:9-5:12, Joshua 23:11, Jubilees 2:29, Luke 8:18, Mark 4:24, Nehemiah 13:15-13:21, Numbers 15:32-15:36, Proverbs 4:23, Siman 84:1, z.Vaetchanan 269b
Jeremiah 17:21-26 - Maamad [Shabbat]

[8] Jeremiah 17:22 - Ahiqar 175, b.Beitzah 12a, b.Horayot 4a, Deuteronomy 5:12-5:15, Exodus 16:23-16:29 20:8-20:10 23:12 31:13-31:17, Ezekiel 20:12 20:20-20:21 22:8, Genesis 2:2-2:3, Isaiah 56:2-56:6 10:13, Leviticus 19:3 23:3, Luke 6:5 23:56, Pesikta Rabbati 27:4, Revelation 1:10, Saadia Opinions 3:9, y.Shabbat 1:1, y.Sheviit 1:1

[9] Jeremiah 17:23 - Acts 7:51, Ezekiel 20:13 20:16 20:21, Isaiah 24:4, Jeremiah 6:8 7:24-7:26 7:28 11:10 16:11-16:12 19:15 8:33 11:15, John 3:19-3:21, Proverbs 1:3 1:5 5:12 8:10 5:1, Psalms 50:17, Zechariah 7:11-7:12, Zephaniah 3:7

[10] Jeremiah 17:24 - 2 Peter 1:5-1:10, Deuteronomy 11:13 11:22, Exodus 15:26, Isaiah 21:7 7:2 58:13-58:14, Jeremiah 17:21-17:22, Pesikta Rabbati 27:4, Zechariah 6:15

[11] Jeremiah 17:25 - 1 Kings 9:4-9:5, 1 Samuel 8:11, 2 Samuel 7:16 8:4, Deuteronomy 17:16, Exodus 12:14, Hebrews 12:22, Isaiah 9:8, Jeremiah 13:13 22:4 22:30 9:15 9:17 9:21, Luke 1:32-1:33, Pesikta Rabbati 27:4, Psalms 89:30-89:38 132:11-132:14, the original ובסוסם was voweled as either ובסוסם "and on horses" or ובסוסם "and on their horses"

וּבָאוּ מֵעָרֵי־יְהוּדָה וּמִסְּבִיבוֹת יְרוּשָׁלַ͏ִם וּמֵאֶרֶץ בִּנְיָמִן וּמִן־הַשְּׁפֵלָה וּמִן־הָהָר וּמִן־הַנֶּגֶב מְבִאִים עוֹלָה וְזֶבַח וּמִנְחָה וּלְבוֹנָה וּמְבִאֵי תוֹדָה בֵּית יְהוָה

26[1] And they shall come from the cities of Judah, and from the places around Jerusalem, and from the land of Benjamin, and from the Lowland, and from the mountains, and from the South, bringing burnt offerings, and sacrifices, and *meal offerings, and frankincense, and bringing sacrifices of thanksgiving*[2], to the house of the LORD.

וְאִם־לֹא תִשְׁמְעוּ אֵלַי לְקַדֵּשׁ אֶת־יוֹם הַשַּׁבָּת וּלְבִלְתִּי שְׂאֵת מַשָּׂא וּבֹא בְּשַׁעֲרֵי יְרוּשָׁלַ͏ִם בְּיוֹם הַשַּׁבָּת וְהִצַּתִּי אֵשׁ בִּשְׁעָרֶיהָ וְאָכְלָה אַרְמְנוֹת יְרוּשָׁלַ͏ִם וְלֹא תִכְבֶּה

27[3] *But*[4] if you will not listen to Me to hallow the Sabbath day, and not to bear a burden and enter in at the gates of Jerusalem on the Sabbath day; then will I kindle a fire in its gates, and it shall devour the palaces of Jerusalem, and it shall not be quenched.

Jeremiah – Chapter 18

הַדָּבָר אֲשֶׁר הָיָה אֶל־יִרְמְיָהוּ מֵאֵת יְהוָה לֵאמֹר

1[5] The word which came to Jeremiah from the LORD, saying:

קוּם וְיָרַדְתָּ בֵּית הַיּוֹצֵר וְשָׁמָּה אַשְׁמִיעֲךָ אֶת־דְּבָרָי

2[6] 'Arise, and go down to the potter's house, and there I will cause you to hear My words.'

וָאֵרֵד בֵּית הַיּוֹצֵר 'וְהִנֵּהוּ' "וְהִנֵּה־הוּא" עֹשֶׂה מְלָאכָה עַל־הָאָבְנָיִם

3[7] Then I went down to the potter's house, and, behold, he was *at his work on the wheels*[8].

וְנִשְׁחַת הַכְּלִי אֲשֶׁר הוּא עֹשֶׂה בַּחֹמֶר בְּיַד הַיּוֹצֵר וְשָׁב וַיַּעֲשֵׂהוּ כְּלִי אַחֵר כַּאֲשֶׁר יָשַׁר בְּעֵינֵי הַיּוֹצֵר לַעֲשׂוֹת

4[9] And whenever the vessel he *made of clay was marred in the hand of the potter*[10], he made it again another vessel, as seemed good to the potter to make it.

וַיְהִי דְבַר־יְהוָה אֵלַי לֵאמוֹר

5 Then the word of the LORD came to me, saying:

הֲכַיּוֹצֵר הַזֶּה לֹא־אוּכַל לַעֲשׂוֹת לָכֶם בֵּית יִשְׂרָאֵל נְאֻם־יְהוָה הִנֵּה כַחֹמֶר בְּיַד הַיּוֹצֵר כֵּן־אַתֶּם בְּיָדִי בֵּית יִשְׂרָאֵל

6[11] '[12]O house of Israel, *I cannot*[13] do with you as this potter? says the LORD. Behold, as the clay is in the potter's hand, so are you in My hand, *O house of Israel*[14].

רֶגַע אֲדַבֵּר עַל־גּוֹי וְעַל־מַמְלָכָה לִנְתוֹשׁ וְלִנְתוֹץ וּלְהַאֲבִיד

7[15] At one instant I may speak concerning a nation, and concerning a kingdom, to pluck up and to break down and to destroy it;

---

[1] Jeremiah 17:26 - 1 Peter 2:5 2:9-2:10, Ezra 3:3-3:6 3:11, Hebrews 13:15, Jeremiah 8:44 9:11 9:13, Joshua 15:21-15:63, Leviticus 1:1-1:7, Psalms 11:22 20:17, Revelation 1:5, Zechariah 7:7

[2] LXX *incense, and manna, and frankincense, bringing praise*

[3] Jeremiah 17:27 - 2 Chronicles 12:19, 2 Kings 22:17 1:9, Amos 1:4 1:7 1:10 1:12 1:14 2:2 2:4-2:5, b.Shabbat 119b, Deuteronomy 8:22, Ein Yaakov Shabbat:119b, Ezekiel 16:41 21:3-20:4 22:8, Hebrews 12:25, Isaiah 1:20 1:31 9:19-9:20, Jeremiah 6:17 7:20 17:4 17:21-17:22 17:24 21:12 21:14 22:5 26:4-26:6 8:29 38:21-38:23 15:8 20:16 1:27 4:13, Jubilees 2:29, Lamentations 4:11, Mark 9:43-9:48, Pesikta Rabbati 27:4, Zechariah 7:11-7:14

[4] LXX *But it shall come to pass*

[5] Jeremiah 18:1-4 - Midrash Tanchuma Vayetze 8

[6] Jeremiah 18:2 - Acts 9:6, Amos 7:7, Ezekiel 4:1-4:5, Hebrews 1:1, Isaiah 20:2, Jeremiah 13:1 19:1-2 23:22

[7] Jeremiah 18:3 - According to the Massorah, Acts 2:19, b.Sotah 11b, Ein Yaakov Sotah:11b, Exodus.R 1:14, John 15:14, Jonah 1:3, Mas.Soferim 7:3, הנהו was altered to become והנ הו "and behold he"

[8] LXX *making a vessel on the stones*

[9] Jeremiah 18:4 - Isaiah 21:9, Jeremiah 18:6, Romans 9:20-9:23

[10] LXX *was making with his hands fell*

[11] Jeremiah 18:6 - b.Berachot 32a, b.Megillah [Rashi] 25a, b.Succah 52b, Daniel 4:20, Exodus.R 46:4, Genesis.R 72:6, Isaiah 21:9 16:9, Jeremiah 18:4, Matthew 20:15, Midrash Tanchuma Vayetze 8, Romans 9:20-9:21 11:34, z.Vayishlach 178a

[12] LXX adds *Shall I not be able*

[13] Missing in LXX

[14] Missing in LXX

[15] Jeremiah 18:7 - Amos 9:8, Exodus.R 45:1, Jeremiah 1:10 12:14-12:17 25:9-25:14 21:4, Jonah 3:4

וְשָׁב הַגּוֹי הַהוּא מֵרָעָתוֹ אֲשֶׁר דִּבַּרְתִּי עָלָיו וְנִחַמְתִּי עַל־הָרָעָה אֲשֶׁר חָשַׁבְתִּי לַעֲשׂוֹת לוֹ **8[1]**

רֶגַע אֲדַבֵּר עַל־גּוֹי וְעַל־מַמְלָכָה לִבְנֹת וְלִנְטֹעַ **9[2]**

וְעָשָׂה 'הָרָעָה' "הָרַע" בְּעֵינַי לְבִלְתִּי שְׁמֹעַ בְּקוֹלִי וְנִחַמְתִּי עַל־הַטּוֹבָה אֲשֶׁר אָמַרְתִּי לְהֵיטִיב אוֹתוֹ **10[3]**

וְעַתָּה אֱמָר־נָא אֶל־אִישׁ־יְהוּדָה וְעַל־יוֹשְׁבֵי יְרוּשָׁלַ͏ִם לֵאמֹר כֹּה אָמַר יְהוָה הִנֵּה אָנֹכִי יוֹצֵר עֲלֵיכֶם רָעָה וְחֹשֵׁב עֲלֵיכֶם מַחֲשָׁבָה שׁוּבוּ נָא אִישׁ מִדַּרְכּוֹ הָרָעָה וְהֵיטִיבוּ דַרְכֵיכֶם וּמַעַלְלֵיכֶם **11[4]**

וְאָמְרוּ נוֹאָשׁ כִּי־אַחֲרֵי מַחְשְׁבוֹתֵינוּ נֵלֵךְ וְאִישׁ שְׁרִרוּת לִבּוֹ־הָרָע נַעֲשֶׂה **12[5]**

לָכֵן כֹּה אָמַר יְהוָה שַׁאֲלוּ־נָא בַּגּוֹיִם מִי שָׁמַע כָּאֵלֶּה שַׁעֲרֻרִת עָשְׂתָה מְאֹד בְּתוּלַת יִשְׂרָאֵל **13[7]**

הֲיַעֲזֹב מִצּוּר שָׂדַי שֶׁלֶג לְבָנוֹן אִם־יִנָּתְשׁוּ מַיִם זָרִים קָרִים נוֹזְלִים **14[9]**

כִּי־שְׁכֵחֻנִי עַמִּי לַשָּׁוְא יְקַטֵּרוּ וַיַּכְשִׁלוּם בְּדַרְכֵיהֶם שְׁבִילֵי עוֹלָם לָלֶכֶת נְתִיבוֹת דֶּרֶךְ לֹא סְלוּלָה **15[11]**

לָשׂוּם אַרְצָם לְשַׁמָּה 'שְׁרוּקַת' "שְׁרִיקוֹת" עוֹלָם כֹּל עוֹבֵר עָלֶיהָ יִשֹּׁם וְיָנִיד בְּרֹאשׁוֹ **16[13]**

8[1] But if that nation turn from their evil, because of what I have spoken against it, I repent of the evil I thought to do to it.

9[2] And at one instant I may speak concerning a nation, and concerning a kingdom, to build and to plant it;

10[3] but if it does evil in My sight, that it does not listen to My voice, then I repent of the good, which I said I would benefit it.

11[4] Now, therefore, speak to the men of Judah, and to the inhabitants of Jerusalem, saying: Thus says the LORD: Behold, I frame evil against you, and devise a device against you; return now everyone from his evil way, and amend your ways and your deeds.

12[5] But they say: *There is no hope*[6]; but we will walk after our own devices, and everyone will do after the stubbornness of his evil heart.'

13[7] Therefore, thus says the LORD: Ask now among the nations, who has heard such things; the virgin of Israel has done *a very grievous thing*[8].

14[9] *Doesn't the snow of Lebanon fail from the rock of the field? Or are the strange cold flowing waters plucked up*[10]?

15[11] For My people have forgotten Me, they offer to vanity; and they have been made to stumble in their ways, in the ancient paths, *to walk in bypaths, in a way not built up*[12];

16[13] To make their land an astonishment, and a perpetual hissing; everyone who passes by shall be astonished, and shake his head.

---

[1] Jeremiah 18:8 - 1 Kings 8:33-8:34, 2 Chronicles 12:6, Amos 7:3-7:6, Deuteronomy 8:36, Exodus 8:12, Ezekiel 18:21 9:11 9:13, Hosea 11:8, Isaiah 1:16-1:19, Jeremiah 7:3-7:7 15:6 2:3 2:13 2:19 12:3 18:10, Joel 2:13-2:14, Jonah 2:5-2:10 3:9-3:10 4:2, Jubilees 5:17, Judges 2:18 10:15-10:16, Luke 13:3-13:5, Psalms 90:13 10:45 15:14
[2] Jeremiah 18:9 - Amos 9:11-9:15, Ecclesiastes 3:2, Jeremiah 1:10 11:17 6:18 7:5 7:29 7:39 8:41
[3] Jeremiah 18:10 - 1 Samuel 2:30 13:13 15:11 15:35, Ezekiel 18:24 9:18 21:20, Jeremiah 7:23-7:28, Mas.Soferim 7:2, Numbers 14:22 14:34, Psalms 5:5, Zephaniah 1:6
[4] Jeremiah 18:11 - 2 Kings 5:5 17:13 22:13, Acts 2:20, Ezekiel 13:22 18:23 18:30-18:32, Genesis 11:3-11:4 11:7, Isaiah 1:16-1:19 5:5 55:6-55:7, James 4:13 5:1, Jeremiah 3:1 3:22 4:6 4:23 7:3 11:19 18:18 1:5 2:3 2:13 11:15 12:3 12:7 3:11, Lamentations 3:39-3:41, Micah 2:3, z.Vaetchanan 269b, Zechariah 1:3
[5] Jeremiah 18:12 - 2 Kings 6:33, Deuteronomy 5:18, Ezekiel 13:11, Genesis 6:5 8:21, Isaiah 9:10, Jeremiah 2:25 3:17 7:24 11:8 16:12 23:17 20:17, Luke 1:51, Mark 7:21-7:22
[6] LXX *We will quit ourselves like men*
[7] Jeremiah 18:13 - 1 Corinthians 5:1, 1 Samuel 4:7, Hosea 6:10, Isaiah 12:22 18:8, Jeremiah 2:10-2:13 5:30 14:17 23:14 7:5, Lamentations 1:15, Lamentations.R 2:18, z.Vaetchanan 269b
[8] Missing in LXX
[9] Jeremiah 18:14 - John 6:68, Pesikta Rabbati 21:21
[10] LXX *Will fertilising streams fail to flow from a rock, or snow fail from Libanus? will water violently impelled by the wind turn aside*
[11] Jeremiah 18:15 - Hosea 2:13 11:2, Isaiah 3:12 9:17 17:29 9:14 14:10 17:7, Jeremiah 2:13 2:19 2:32 3:21 6:16 10:15 13:25 16:19 17:13 19:5 44:15-44:19 20:25, Malachi 2:8, Matthew 15:6, Pesikta Rabbati 27/28:2, Romans 14:21
Jeremiah 18:15-23 - 4QJera Jeremiah 18:14 - John 6:68, Pesikta Rabbati 21:21
[12] LXX *to enter upon impassable paths*
[13] Jeremiah 18:16 - 1 Kings 9:8, 2 Chronicles 7:20-7:21, Deuteronomy 4:59 5:22, Ezekiel 6:14 12:19 33:28-29, Isaiah 6:11 13:22, Jeremiah 9:12 19:8 1:9 1:13 2:13, Lamentations 2:15-2:16, Leviticus 26:33-34 2:43, Mark 15:29, Matthew 3:39, Micah 6:16, Psalms 22:8 44:15

כְּרוּחַ־קָדִים אֲפִיצֵם לִפְנֵי אוֹיֵב עֹרֶף וְלֹא־פָנִים אֶרְאֵם בְּיוֹם אֵידָם	17[1]	I will scatter them as with an east wind before the enemy; I will look on their back, and not their face, in the day of their calamity.
וַיֹּאמְרוּ לְכוּ וְנַחְשְׁבָה עַל־יִרְמְיָהוּ מַחֲשָׁבוֹת כִּי לֹא־תֹאבַד תּוֹרָה מִכֹּהֵן וְעֵצָה מֵחָכָם וְדָבָר מִנָּבִיא לְכוּ וְנַכֵּהוּ בַלָּשׁוֹן וְאַל־נַקְשִׁיבָה אֶל־כָּל־דְּבָרָיו	18[2]	Then said they: 'Come, and let us devise devices against Jeremiah; for instruction shall not perish from the priest, nor counsel from the wise, nor the word from the prophet. Come, and let us strike him with the tongue, and let us not give heed to any of his words.'
הַקְשִׁיבָה יְהוָה אֵלָי וּשְׁמַע לְקוֹל יְרִיבָי	19[3]	Give heed to me, O LORD, and listen to the voice of those who contend with me.
הַיְשֻׁלַּם תַּחַת־טוֹבָה רָעָה כִּי־כָרוּ שׁוּחָה לְנַפְשִׁי זְכֹר עָמְדִי לְפָנֶיךָ לְדַבֵּר עֲלֵיהֶם טוֹבָה לְהָשִׁיב אֶת־חֲמָתְךָ מֵהֶם	20[4]	Shall evil be recompensed for good? For they have dug a pit for my soul[5]. Remember how I stood before You to speak good for them, to turn Your wrath away from them.
לָכֵן תֵּן אֶת־בְּנֵיהֶם לָרָעָב וְהַגִּרֵם עַל־יְדֵי־חֶרֶב וְתִהְיֶנָה נְשֵׁיהֶם שַׁכֻּלוֹת וְאַלְמָנוֹת וְאַנְשֵׁיהֶם יִהְיוּ הֲרֻגֵי מָוֶת בַּחוּרֵיהֶם מֻכֵּי־חֶרֶב בַּמִּלְחָמָה	21[6]	Therefore, deliver their children to the famine, and hurl them to the power of the sword; and let their wives be bereaved of their children, and widows; and let their men be slain of death, and their young men struck of the sword in battle.
תִּשָּׁמַע זְעָקָה מִבָּתֵּיהֶם כִּי־תָבִיא עֲלֵיהֶם גְּדוּד פִּתְאֹם כִּי־כָרוּ שִׁיחָה שׁוּחָה לְלָכְדֵנִי וּפַחִים טָמְנוּ לְרַגְלָי	22[7]	Let a cry be heard from their houses, when you shall bring a troop suddenly on them; For they have dug a pit to take me, and hid snares for my feet.
וְאַתָּה יְהוָה יָדַעְתָּ אֶת־כָּל־עֲצָתָם עָלַי לַמָּוֶת אַל־תְּכַפֵּר עַל־עֲו‍ֹנָם וְחַטָּאתָם מִלְּפָנֶיךָ אַל־תֶּמְחִי וְהָיוּ וְיִהְיוּ מֻכְשָׁלִים לְפָנֶיךָ בְּעֵת אַפְּךָ עֲשֵׂה בָהֶם	23[8]	Yet, LORD, you know all their counsel against me to slay me; do not forgive their iniquity, nor blot out their sin from Your sight; but let them be made to stumble before You; deal with them in the time of your anger.

Jeremiah – Chapter 19

כֹּה אָמַר יְהוָה הָלוֹךְ וְקָנִיתָ בַקְבֻּק יוֹצֵר חָרֶשׂ וּמִזִּקְנֵי הָעָם וּמִזִּקְנֵי הַכֹּהֲנִים	19[9]	Thus said the LORD: Go, and get a potter's earthen bottle, and take of the elders of the people, and of the elders of the priests;

---

[1] Jeremiah 18:17 - Deuteronomy 4:25 28:64 7:17 8:35, Hosea 13:15, Jeremiah 2:27 13:24 8:33 22:21, Job 3:21, Judges 10:13-14, Mekhilta de R'Shimon bar Yochai Beshallach 24:4, Mekhilta de R'Ishmael Beshallah 5:88, Mekhilta de R'Ishmael Beshallah 5:95, Midrash Psalms 11:5, Proverbs 7:25-26, Psalms 48:8

[2] Jeremiah 18:18 - 1 Kings 22:24, 2 Samuel 15:31 17:14, 4Q177 12+13 i 6, 4Q177 4.6, Isaiah 8:7, Jeremiah 2:8 5:12-13 11:19 13:13-14 14:14-16 18:11 2:11 29:25-29 19:2 20:17, Job 5:13, John 7:47-49 9:40, Leviticus 10:11, Luke 11:45, Malachi 2:7, Micah 2:1-3, Proverbs 18:21, Psalms 21:12 52:3 57:5 64:4

[3] Jeremiah 18:19 - 2 Kings 19:16, Jeremiah 20:12, Luke 6:11-12, Micah 7:8, Nehemiah 4:4-5 6:9, Psalms 55:17-18 56:2:4 64:2-5 13:4 13:28

[4] Jeremiah 18:20 - 1 Samuel 24:17-19, Ecclesiastes 10:8, Ezekiel 22:30-31, Genesis 18:22-32, Jeremiah 7:16 11:14 14:7-11 14:20-15:1 18:22, Job 6:27, John 10:32 15:25, Midrash Psalms 109:4, Proverbs 17:13 2:27, Psalms 7:16 35:7 35:12 38:21 57:7 10:23 109:4-5 119:95, Zechariah 3:1-2

[5] LXX adds *and they hid their punishment for me*

[6] Jeremiah 18:21 - 2 Chronicles 12:17, 2 Timothy 4:14, Amos 4:10, Deuteronomy 8:25, Exodus 22:24, Jeremiah 9:22 11:20-11:23 12:3 15:2-15:3 15:8 16:3-16:4 20:1-20:6 20:11-20:12, Lamentations 5:3, Psalms 109:9-109:20

[7] Jeremiah 18:22 - b.Bava Kamma 16b, b.Temurah [Rashi] 28b, Ein Yaakov Bava Kamma:16b, Isaiah 10:30 22:1-4, Jeremiah 4:19-20 4:31 6:26 9:21-22 18:20 20:10 25:34-36 47:2-3 48:3-5, Matthew 22:15, Psalms 38:13 56:6-8 64:5-6 20:6, Zephaniah 1:10-11 1:16

[8] Jeremiah 18:23 - b.Bava Batra 9b, b.Bava Kamma 16b, Ein Yaakov Bava Batra:9b, Ein Yaakov Bava Kamma:16b, Isaiah 2:9 10:3, Jastrow 676b, Jeremiah 8:12 11:18-11:20 11:23 15:15 18:18, Luke 21:22, Nehemiah 4:4-4:5, Psalms 35:4 37:32-37:33 59:6 69:23-69:29 109:14-109:15, Romans 2:5

[9] Jeremiah 19:1 - 1 Chronicles 24:4-24:6, 2 Corinthians 4:7, 2 Kings 19:2, 4QJera, Acts 4:5-4:6, Ezekiel 8:11-8:12 9:6, Isaiah 6:14, Jeremiah 18:2-18:4 19:10-19:11 2:17 8:14, Lamentations 4:2, Matthew 2:3 3:1 27:41-27:42, Numbers 11:16, z.Vaetchanan 269b

וְיָצָ֙אתָ֙ אֶל־גֵּ֣יא בֶן־הִנֹּ֔ם אֲשֶׁ֕ר פֶּ֖תַח שַׁ֣עַר הַֽחַרְסוּת֒ "הַֽחַרְסִית" וְקָרָ֣אתָ שָּׁ֔ם אֶת־הַדְּבָרִ֖ים אֲשֶׁר־אֲדַבֵּ֥ר אֵלֶֽיךָ	2[1]	and go forth to the *valley of the son of Hinnom, which is by the entry of the gate Harsith*[2], and proclaim there the words I shall tell you;
וְאָ֣מַרְתָּ֔ שִׁמְע֥וּ דְבַר־יְהוָ֖ה מַלְכֵ֣י יְהוּדָ֑ה וְיֹשְׁבֵ֣י יְרוּשָׁלִָ֔ם כֹּֽה־אָמַ֞ר יְהוָ֣ה צְבָא֗וֹת אֱלֹהֵ֣י יִשְׂרָאֵ֔ל הִנְנִ֨י מֵבִ֤יא רָעָה֙ עַל־הַמָּק֣וֹם הַזֶּ֔ה אֲשֶׁ֥ר כָּל־שֹׁמְעָ֖הּ תִּצַּ֥לְנָה אָזְנָֽיו	3[3]	and say: Hear the word of the LORD, O kings of Judah, and inhabitants of Jerusalem; thus says the LORD of hosts, the God of Israel: Behold, I will bring evil on this place, which whoever hears, his ears shall tingle;
יַ֣עַן׀ אֲשֶׁ֣ר עֲזָבֻ֗נִי וַֽיְנַכְּר֞וּ אֶת־הַמָּק֣וֹם הַזֶּ֗ה וַיְקַטְּרוּ־בוֹ֙ לֵאלֹהִ֣ים אֲחֵרִ֔ים אֲשֶׁ֧ר לֹֽא־יְדָע֛וּם הֵ֥מָּה וַאֲבֽוֹתֵיהֶ֖ם וּמַלְכֵ֣י יְהוּדָ֑ה וּמָֽלְא֛וּ אֶת־הַמָּק֥וֹם הַזֶּ֖ה דַּ֥ם נְקִיִּֽם	4[4]	Because they have forsaken Me, and have estranged this place, and have offered in it to other gods, whom neither they nor their fathers have known, nor the kings of Judah; and have filled this place with the blood of innocents;
וּבָנ֞וּ אֶת־בָּמ֣וֹת הַבַּ֗עַל לִשְׂרֹ֧ף אֶת־בְּנֵיהֶ֛ם בָּאֵ֖שׁ עֹל֣וֹת לַבָּ֑עַל אֲשֶׁ֤ר לֹֽא־צִוִּ֙יתִי֙ וְלֹ֣א דִבַּ֔רְתִּי וְלֹ֥א עָלְתָ֖ה עַל־לִבִּֽי	5[5]	and have built the high places of Baal, to burn their sons in the fire for burnt offerings to Baal; which I never commanded, nor spoke, nor did it come into My mind.
לָכֵ֞ן הִנֵּֽה־יָמִ֤ים בָּאִים֙ נְאֻם־יְהוָ֔ה וְלֹא־יִקָּרֵא֩ לַמָּק֨וֹם הַזֶּ֥ה ע֛וֹד הַתֹּ֖פֶת וְגֵ֣יא בֶן־הִנֹּ֑ם כִּ֖י אִם־גֵּ֥יא הַהֲרֵגָֽה	6[6]	Therefore, behold, the days come, says the LORD, that this place shall no longer be called Topheth, or the valley of the son of Hinnom, but the valley of slaughter;
וּבַקֹּתִ֗י אֶת־עֲצַ֤ת יְהוּדָה֙ וִיר֣וּשָׁלִַ֔ם בַּמָּק֖וֹם הַזֶּ֑ה וְהִפַּלְתִּ֤ים בַּחֶ֙רֶב֙ לִפְנֵ֣י אֹֽיְבֵיהֶ֔ם וּבְיַ֖ד מְבַקְשֵׁ֣י נַפְשָׁ֑ם וְנָתַתִּ֤י אֶת־נִבְלָתָם֙ לְמַֽאֲכָ֔ל לְע֥וֹף הַשָּׁמַ֖יִם וּלְבֶהֱמַ֥ת הָאָֽרֶץ	7[7]	and I will make void the counsel of Judah and Jerusalem in this place; and I will cause them to fall by the sword before their enemies, and by the hand of those who seek their life; and I will give their carcasses as food for the fowls of the heaven, and for the beasts of the earth;
וְשַׂמְתִּי֙ אֶת־הָעִ֣יר הַזֹּ֔את לְשַׁמָּ֖ה וְלִשְׁרֵקָ֑ה כֹּ֚ל עֹבֵ֣ר עָלֶ֔יהָ יִשֹּׁ֥ם וְיִשְׁרֹ֖ק עַל־כָּל־מַכֹּתֶֽהָ	8[8]	and I will make this city an astonishment, and a hissing; everyone who passes by shall *be astonished*[9] and hiss because of all its plagues;
וְהַאֲכַלְתִּ֞ים אֶת־בְּשַׂ֣ר בְּנֵיהֶ֗ם וְאֵת֙ בְּשַׂ֣ר בְּנֹתֵיהֶ֔ם וְאִ֥ישׁ בְּשַׂר־רֵעֵ֖הוּ יֹאכֵ֑לוּ בְּמָצוֹר֙ וּבְמָצ֔וֹק אֲשֶׁ֨ר יָצִ֧יקוּ לָהֶ֛ם אֹיְבֵיהֶ֖ם וּמְבַקְשֵׁ֥י נַפְשָֽׁם	9[10]	and I will cause them to eat the flesh of their sons and the flesh of their daughters, and they shall eat the flesh of his friend, in the *siege and in the distress, with which their enemies, and they who seek their life, shall distress them*[11].
וְשָׁבַרְתָּ֖ הַבַּקְבֻּ֑ק לְעֵינֵי֙ הָֽאֲנָשִׁ֔ים הַהֹלְכִ֖ים אוֹתָֽךְ	10[12]	Then you shall break the bottle in the sight of the men who go with you,

[1] Jeremiah 19:2 - 2 Chronicles 4:3 9:6, 2 Kings 23:10, Acts 5:20 20:27, b.Eruvin 19a, Ezekiel 3:10-3:11, Jastrow 882a, Jeremiah 1:7 3:12 7:2 7:31-7:32 11:6 2:2 8:35, Jonah 3:2, Joshua 15:8, Mas.Soferim 7:4, Matthew 10:27, Nehemiah 3:29, Proverbs 1:20-1:22

[2] LXX *burial place of the sons of their children, which is at the entrance of the gate of Charsith*

[3] Jeremiah 19:3 - 1 Samuel 3:11 4:16-4:18, 2 Baruch 1:1, 2 Kings 21:12-21:13, Isaiah 4:19, Jeremiah 6:19 13:18 17:20, Matthew 10:18, Psalms 2:10 6:16 14:5, Revelation 2:29, z.Vaetchanan 269b

[4] Jeremiah 19:4 - 2 Chronicles 33:4-33:7, 2 Kings 21:4-7 21:16 22:16-17 23:11-12 24:4, Daniel 9:5-9:15, Deuteronomy 13:7 13:14 4:20 4:36 28:64 31:16-18 32:15-23, Isaiah 11:7 17:11, Jeremiah 2:13 2:17 2:19 2:30 2:34 5:6 7:9 7:31-32 11:13 15:6 16:11 17:13 18:15 22:17 2:15 2:23 32:29-35, Lamentations 4:13, Luke 11:50, Matthew 23:34-23:35, Revelation 16:6

[5] Jeremiah 19:5 - 2 Chronicles 4:3, 2 Kings 17:17, b.Taanit [Tosefot] 4a, Daniel 2:29, Deuteronomy 12:31, Ein Yaakov Taanit:4a, Ezekiel 16:20-21 20:26 14:10, Jeremiah 7:31-32 8:35, Leviticus 18:21, Midrash Tanchuma Bechukkotai 5, Numbers 22:41, Psalms 106:37-38, Sifre Devarim Shoftim 148

[6] Jeremiah 19:6 - b.Nedarim 8b, b.Eruvin 19a, Isaiah 6:33, Jeremiah 7:32-33 19:2 19:11, Joshua 15:8

[7] Jeremiah 19:7 - Deuteronomy 28:25-26, Isaiah 8:10 28:17-18 30:1-3, Jeremiah 7:33 8:2 9:22-23 15:2 15:9 16:4 18:21 22:19 22:25 10:20 22:26, Job 5:12-13, Lamentations 3:37, Leviticus 2:17, Proverbs 21:30, Psalms 33:10-11 79:2-3, Revelation 19:18-121, Romans 3:31 4:14

[8] Jeremiah 19:8 - 1 Kings 9:8, 2 Chronicles 7:20-7:21, Jeremiah 9:10-9:12 18:16 1:18 1:13 2:13, Lamentations 2:15-2:16, Leviticus 2:32, Zephaniah 2:15
Jeremiah 19:8-9 - 4QJerc

[9] LXX *scowl*

[10] Jeremiah 19:9 - 2 Kings 6:26-6:29, Deuteronomy 28:53-28:57, Ezekiel 5:10, Isaiah 9:21, Lamentations 2:20 4:10, Leviticus 2:29

[11] LXX *blockade, and in the siege with which their enemies shall besiege them*

[12] Jeremiah 19:10 - Jeremiah 19:1 24:12 51:63-51:64

11[1] and shall say to them: Thus says the LORD of hosts: so will I break this people and this city, as one breaks a potter's vessel, that cannot be made whole again; and *they shall bury in Topheth, for want of room to bury*[2].

וְאָמַרְתָּ אֲלֵיהֶם כֹּה־אָמַר יְהוָה צְבָאוֹת כָּכָה אֶשְׁבֹּר אֶת־הָעָם הַזֶּה וְאֶת־הָעִיר הַזֹּאת כַּאֲשֶׁר יִשְׁבֹּר אֶת־כְּלִי הַיּוֹצֵר אֲשֶׁר לֹא־יוּכַל לְהֵרָפֵה עוֹד וּבְתֹפֶת יִקְבְּרוּ מֵאֵין מָקוֹם לִקְבּוֹר

12[3] Thus I will do to this place, says the LORD, and to its inhabitants, *making this city as Topheth*[4];

כֵּן־אֶעֱשֶׂה לַמָּקוֹם הַזֶּה נְאֻם־יְהוָה וּלְיוֹשְׁבָיו וְלָתֵת אֶת־הָעִיר הַזֹּאת כְּתֹפֶת

13[5] and the houses of Jerusalem, and the houses of the kings of Judah that are defiled, shall be as the place of Topheth, all the houses on whose roofs they have offered to all the host of heaven, and have poured out drink offerings to other gods.

וְהָיוּ בָּתֵּי יְרוּשָׁלִַם וּבָתֵּי מַלְכֵי יְהוּדָה כִּמְקוֹם הַתֹּפֶת הַטְּמֵאִים לְכֹל הַבָּתִּים אֲשֶׁר קִטְּרוּ עַל־גַּגֹּתֵיהֶם לְכֹל צְבָא הַשָּׁמַיִם וְהַסֵּךְ נְסָכִים לֵאלֹהִים אֲחֵרִים

14[6] Then Jeremiah came from *Topheth*[7], where the LORD had sent him to prophesy; and he stood in the court of the LORD's house, and said to all the people:

וַיָּבֹא יִרְמְיָהוּ מֵהַתֹּפֶת אֲשֶׁר שְׁלָחוֹ יְהוָה שָׁם לְהִנָּבֵא וַיַּעֲמֹד בַּחֲצַר בֵּית־יְהוָה וַיֹּאמֶר אֶל־כָּל־הָעָם

15[8] 'Thus says the LORD *of hosts, the God of Israel*[9]: Behold, I will bring upon this city and upon all her towns all the evil I pronounced against it; because they have made their neck stiff, so they might not hear My words.'

כֹּה־אָמַר יְהוָה צְבָאוֹת אֱלֹהֵי יִשְׂרָאֵל הִנְנִי מֵבִי "מֵבִיא" אֶל־הָעִיר הַזֹּאת וְעַל־כָּל־עָרֶיהָ אֵת כָּל־הָרָעָה אֲשֶׁר דִּבַּרְתִּי עָלֶיהָ כִּי הִקְשׁוּ אֶת־עָרְפָּם לְבִלְתִּי שְׁמוֹעַ אֶת־דְּבָרָי

Jeremiah – Chapter 20

1[10] Now Pashhur the son of Immer the priest, who was chief officer in the house of the LORD, heard Jeremiah prophesying these things.

וַיִּשְׁמַע פַּשְׁחוּר בֶּן־אִמֵּר הַכֹּהֵן וְהוּא־פָקִיד נָגִיד בְּבֵית יְהוָה אֶת־יִרְמְיָהוּ נִבָּא אֶת־הַדְּבָרִים הָאֵלֶּה

2[11] Then Pashhur struck Jeremiah the prophet, and put him in the *stocks that were in the upper gate of Benjamin, which was in*[12] the house of the LORD.

וַיַּכֶּה פַשְׁחוּר אֵת יִרְמְיָהוּ הַנָּבִיא וַיִּתֵּן אֹתוֹ עַל־הַמַּהְפֶּכֶת אֲשֶׁר בְּשַׁעַר בִּנְיָמִן הָעֶלְיוֹן אֲשֶׁר בְּבֵית יְהוָה

3[13] And *it came to pass in the morning, that*[14] Pashhur brought forth Jeremiah from the stocks. Then said Jeremiah to him: 'The LORD has not called your name Pashhur, but *Magormissabib*[15].

וַיְהִי מִמָּחֳרָת וַיֹּצֵא פַשְׁחוּר אֶת־יִרְמְיָהוּ מִן־הַמַּהְפָּכֶת וַיֹּאמֶר אֵלָיו יִרְמְיָהוּ לֹא פַשְׁחוּר קָרָא יְהוָה שְׁמֶךָ כִּי אִם־מָגוֹר מִסָּבִיב

---

[1] Jeremiah 19:11 - Isaiah 6:14, Jeremiah 7:31-7:32 13:14 19:6, Lamentations 4:2, Psalms 2:9, Revelation 2:27, z.Vaetchanan 269b

[2] Missing in LXX

[3] Jeremiah 19:12 - Jeremiah 10:13 11:5, z.Vaetchanan 269b

[4] LXX *that this city may be given up, as one that is falling to ruin*

[5] Jeremiah 19:13 - 2 Kings 23:10 23:12 23:14, Acts 7:42, b.Nedarim 8b, Deuteronomy 4:19, Ezekiel 7:21-22 20:28, Jeremiah 7:18 8:29 20:18 4:13, Psalms 74:7 79:1, Saadia Opinions 9:5, Zephaniah 1:5

[6] Jeremiah 19:14 - 2 Chronicles 20:5 24:20-24:21, Acts 5:20, b.Nedarim 8b, Jeremiah 17:19 19:2-19:3 2:2, Luke 21:37-21:38

[7] LXX *the place of the Fall*

[8] Jeremiah 19:15 - 2 Chronicles 36:16-17, Acts 7:51-52, Jeremiah 7:26 17:23 35:15-17, Nehemiah 9:17 9:29, Psalms 58:3-6, z.Vaetchanan 269b, Zechariah 7:11-14

[9] Missing in LXX

[10] Jeremiah 20:1 - 1 Chronicles 24:14, 2 Chronicles 11:8, 2 Kings 1:18, Acts 4:1 5:24, Ezra 2:37-2:38, Nehemiah 7:40-7:41

[11] Jeremiah 20:2 - 1 Kings 22:27, 2 Chronicles 16:10 24:21, Acts 4:3 5:18 5:40 7:52 16:22-16:24, Amos 7:10-7:13, Hebrews 11:36-11:37, Jeremiah 1:19 19:14-19:15 2:8 5:26 12:26 13:13 37:15-37:16 38:6-38:7, Job 13:27, Matthew 5:10-5:12 21:35 23:34-23:37, Revelation 2:10 17:6, Zechariah 14:10
Jeremiah 20:2-6 - 4QJerc

[12] LXX *dungeon which was by the gate of the upper house that was set apart, which was by*

[13] Jeremiah 20:3 - Acts 4:5-4:7 16:30 16:35-16:39, Genesis 17:5 17:15 8:29, Hosea 1:4-1:9, Isaiah 8:3, Jeremiah 6:25 7:32 19:2 19:6 20:10 5:29 22:5, Lamentations 2:22, Psalms 31:14

[14] Missing in LXX

[15] Heb. *Terror-all-around*; LXX *Exile*

4[1] For thus says the LORD: Behold, I will *make you a terror to yourself, and to*[2] all your friends; and they shall fall by the sword of their enemies, and your eyes shall see it; and I will give all Judah into the hand of the king of Babylon, and he shall carry them captive to Babylon, and shall kill them with the sword.

כִּי כֹה אָמַר יְהוָה הִנְנִי נֹתֶנְךָ לְמָגוֹר לְךָ וּלְכָל־אֹהֲבֶיךָ וְנָפְלוּ בְּחֶרֶב אֹיְבֵיהֶם וְעֵינֶיךָ רֹאוֹת וְאֶת־כָּל־יְהוּדָה אֶתֵּן בְּיַד מֶלֶךְ־בָּבֶל וְהִגְלָם בָּבֶלָה וְהִכָּם בֶּחָרֶב

5[3] Moreover, I will give all the stores of this city, and all its gains, and all its wealth, yes, all the treasures of the kings of Judah will I give into the hand of their enemies, who shall spoil them, and take them, and carry them to Babylon.

וְנָתַתִּי אֶת־כָּל־חֹסֶן הָעִיר הַזֹּאת וְאֶת־כָּל־יְגִיעָהּ וְאֶת־כָּל־יְקָרָהּ וְאֵת כָּל־אוֹצְרוֹת מַלְכֵי יְהוּדָה אֶתֵּן בְּיַד אֹיְבֵיהֶם וּבְזָזוּם וּלְקָחוּם וֶהֱבִיאוּם בָּבֶלָה

6[4] And you, *Pashhur*[5], and all who live in your house shall go into captivity; and you shall come to Babylon, and there you shall die, and there shall you be buried, you, and all your friends, to whom you have prophesied falsely.'

וְאַתָּה פַשְׁחוּר וְכֹל יֹשְׁבֵי בֵיתֶךָ תֵּלְכוּ בַּשֶּׁבִי וּבָבֶל תָּבוֹא וְשָׁם תָּמוּת וְשָׁם תִּקָּבֵר אַתָּה וְכָל־אֹהֲבֶיךָ אֲשֶׁר־נִבֵּאתָ לָהֶם בַּשָּׁקֶר

7[6] O LORD, you have enticed me, and I was enticed, You have overcome me, and have prevailed; I became a laughing stock all the day, everyone mocks me.

פִּתִּיתַנִי יְהוָה וָאֶפָּת חֲזַקְתַּנִי וַתּוּכָל הָיִיתִי לִשְׂחוֹק כָּל־הַיּוֹם כֻּלֹּה לֹעֵג לִי

8[7] For as often as I speak, I cry out, I cry: 'Violence and spoil;' because the word of the LORD is made a reproach to me, and a derision, all the day.

כִּי־מִדֵּי אֲדַבֵּר אֶזְעָק חָמָס וָשֹׁד אֶקְרָא כִּי־הָיָה דְבַר־יְהוָה לִי לְחֶרְפָּה וּלְקֶלֶס כָּל־הַיּוֹם

9[8] *And if I say: 'I will not make mention of Him*[9], nor speak any more in His name,' then there is in my heart as it were a burning fire shut up in my bones, and I weary myself to hold it in, but cannot.

וְאָמַרְתִּי לֹא־אֶזְכְּרֶנּוּ וְלֹא־אֲדַבֵּר עוֹד בִּשְׁמוֹ וְהָיָה בְלִבִּי כְּאֵשׁ בֹּעֶרֶת עָצֻר בְּעַצְמֹתָי וְנִלְאֵיתִי כַּלְכֵל וְלֹא אוּכָל

10[10] For I have heard the whispering of many, terror on every side: 'Denounce, and we will denounce him;' of all my familiar friends, those who watch for my halting: 'Perhaps he will be enticed, and we shall prevail against him, and we shall take our revenge on him.'

כִּי שָׁמַעְתִּי דִּבַּת רַבִּים מָגוֹר מִסָּבִיב הַגִּידוּ וְנַגִּידֶנּוּ כֹּל אֱנוֹשׁ שְׁלוֹמִי שֹׁמְרֵי צַלְעִי אוּלַי יְפֻתֶּה וְנוּכְלָה לוֹ וְנִקְחָה נִקְמָתֵנוּ מִמֶּנּוּ

---

[1] Jeremiah 20:4 - 1 Samuel 2:33, 2 Kings 1:7, Deuteronomy 28:32-28:34 28:65-28:67, Ezekiel 26:17-26:21, Jeremiah 6:25 19:15 21:4-21:10 1:9 5:21 32:27-32:31 39:6-39:7 4:27, Job 18:11-18:21 20:23-20:26, Matthew 27:4-27:5, Psalms 73:19, z.Vaetchanan 269b
[2] LXX *give you up to captivity with*
[3] Jeremiah 20:5 - 2 Chronicles 12:10 36:17-36:19, 2 Kings 20:17-20:18 24:12-24:16 25:13-25:17, Daniel 1:2, Ezekiel 22:25, Jeremiah 3:24 4:20 12:12 15:13 17:3 24:8-24:10 27:19-27:22 32:3-32:5 15:2 15:8 52:7-52:23, Lamentations 1:7 1:10 4:12
[4] Jeremiah 20:6 - 9:3, 2 Peter 2:1-3, Acts 13:8-11, Deuteronomy 4:25, Ezekiel 13:4-16 13:22-23 22:28, Genesis.R 96:5, Isaiah 9:16, Jeremiah 5:31 6:13-15 8:10-11 14:14-15 20:4 23:14-17 23:25-26 23:32 28:15-17 29:21-22 5:32, Lamentations 2:14, Leviticus 2:17, Micah 2:11, Midrash Tanchuma Vayechi 3, Pesikta Rabbati 1:6, y.Ketubot 12:3, y.Kilayim 9:3, y.Kilayim 9:3, Zechariah 13:3
[5] Missing in LXX
[6] Jeremiah 20:7 - 1 Corinthians 4:9-13 9:6, 2 Kings 2:23, Acts 17:18 17:32, Exodus 5:22-23, Ezekiel 3:14, Gates of Repentance 3.175, Hebrews 11:36, Hosea 9:7, Jeremiah 1:6-8 1:18-19 15:10 15:18 17:16 20:9 5:26, Lamentations 3:14, Luke 16:14 22:63-64 23:11 23:35-36, Micah 3:8, Numbers 11:11-15, Pesikta de R'Kahana 13.14, Pesikta Rabbati 21:16 26:6, Psalms 22:7-8 35:15-16 69:10-13 Jeremiah 20:7-9 - 4QJerc, Two Letters Part II
[7] Jeremiah 20:8 - 1 Peter 4:14, 2 Chronicles 12:16, Guide for the Perplexed 2:37, Hebrews 11:26 13:13, Jeremiah 4:19-4:22 5:1 5:6 5:15-5:17 6:6-6:7 6:10 7:9 13:13-13:14 15:1-15:4 15:13-15:14 17:27 18:16-18:17 19:7-19:11 20:7 4:8, Lamentations 3:61-3:63, Luke 11:45
[8] Jeremiah 20:9 - 1 Corinthians 9:16-9:17, 1 Kings 19:3-19:4, 2 Corinthians 5:13-5:15, Acts 4:20 15:37-15:38 17:16 18:5, Ecclesiastes.R 1:36 8:11, Ezekiel 3:14, Jastrow 688b, Jeremiah 6:11, Job 32:18-32:20, John 1:2-1:3 4:2-3, Luke 9:62, Pesikta Rabbati 27/28:1, Psalms 39:4, y.Bava Kamma 6:4
[9] LXX *Then I said, I will by no means name the name of the LORD*
[10] Jeremiah 20:10 - 1 Kings 19:2 21:20 22:8 22:27, Acts 5:33 6:11-15 7:54 23:12-15 24:1-9 24:13, Ezekiel 22:9, Isaiah 5:21, Jeremiah 6:25 18:18, Job 19:19, Luke 11:53-54 12:52-53 20:20, Mark 6:19-28, Matthew 26:59-60, Nehemiah 6:6-13, Proverbs 10:18, Psalms 31:14 41:10 55:14-15 57:5 64:3-5

וַיהֹוָה אוֹתִי כְּגִבּוֹר עָרִיץ עַל־כֵּן רֹדְפַי יִכָּשְׁלוּ וְלֹא יֻכָלוּ בֹּשׁוּ מְאֹד כִּי־לֹא הִשְׂכִּילוּ כְּלִמַּת עוֹלָם לֹא תִשָּׁכֵחַ

11[1] But the LORD is with me as a mighty warrior; therefore, my persecutors shall stumble, and they shall not prevail; they shall be greatly ashamed, because they have not prospered, with an everlasting confusion that shall never be forgotten.

וַיהֹוָה צְבָאוֹת בֹּחֵן צַדִּיק רֹאֶה כְלָיוֹת וָלֵב אֶרְאֶה נִקְמָתְךָ מֵהֶם כִּי אֵלֶיךָ גִּלִּיתִי אֶת־רִיבִי

12[2] But, O LORD of hosts, who tries the righteous, who sees the reins and the heart, let me see Your vengeance on them; for I have revealed my cause to You.

שִׁירוּ לַיהֹוָה הַלְלוּ אֶת־יְהֹוָה כִּי הִצִּיל אֶת־נֶפֶשׁ אֶבְיוֹן מִיַּד מְרֵעִים

13[3] Sing to the LORD, praise the LORD; for He has delivered the soul of the needy from the hand of evildoers.

אָרוּר הַיּוֹם אֲשֶׁר יֻלַּדְתִּי בּוֹ יוֹם אֲשֶׁר־יְלָדַתְנִי אִמִּי אַל־יְהִי בָרוּךְ

14[4] Cursed be the day I was born; the day in which my mother bore me, let it not be blessed.

אָרוּר הָאִישׁ אֲשֶׁר בִּשַּׂר אֶת־אָבִי לֵאמֹר יֻלַּד־לְךָ בֵּן זָכָר שַׂמֵּחַ שִׂמְּחָהוּ

15[5] Cursed be the man who brought tidings to my father, saying: 'A baby boy is born to you;' making him very glad.

וְהָיָה הָאִישׁ הַהוּא כֶּעָרִים אֲשֶׁר־הָפַךְ יְהֹוָה וְלֹא נִחָם וְשָׁמַע זְעָקָה בַּבֹּקֶר וּתְרוּעָה בְּעֵת צָהֳרָיִם

16[6] And let that man be as the cities that the LORD overthrew, and did not repent; and let him hear a cry in the morning, and an alarm at noon;

אֲשֶׁר לֹא־מוֹתְתַנִי מֵרָחֶם וַתְּהִי־לִי אִמִּי קִבְרִי וְרַחְמָה הֲרַת עוֹלָם

17[7] Because He did not kill me from the womb; and so my mother would have been my grave, and her womb always great.

לָמָּה זֶּה מֵרֶחֶם יָצָאתִי לִרְאוֹת עָמָל וְיָגוֹן וַיִּכְלוּ בְּבֹשֶׁת יָמָי

18[8] Why have I come forth from the womb? To see labor and sorrow, so my days should be consumed in shame?

Jeremiah – Chapter 21

הַדָּבָר אֲשֶׁר־הָיָה אֶל־יִרְמְיָהוּ מֵאֵת יְהֹוָה בִּשְׁלֹחַ אֵלָיו הַמֶּלֶךְ צִדְקִיָּהוּ אֶת־פַּשְׁחוּר בֶּן־מַלְכִּיָּה וְאֶת־צְפַנְיָה בֶן־מַעֲשֵׂיָה הַכֹּהֵן לֵאמֹר

1[9] The word that came to Jeremiah from the LORD, when king Zedekiah sent to him Pashhur the son of Malchiah, and Zephaniah the son of Maaseiah the priest, saying:

דְּרָשׁ־נָא בַעֲדֵנוּ אֶת־יְהֹוָה כִּי נְבוּכַדְרֶאצַּר מֶלֶךְ־בָּבֶל נִלְחָם עָלֵינוּ אוּלַי יַעֲשֶׂה יְהֹוָה אוֹתָנוּ כְּכָל־נִפְלְאֹתָיו וְיַעֲלֶה מֵעָלֵינוּ

2[10] 'Inquire, please, of the LORD for us; for *Nebuchadrezzar*[11] king of Babylon makes war against us; perhaps the LORD will deal with us

---

[1] Jeremiah 20:11 - 2 Timothy 4:17, Daniel 12:2, Deuteronomy 32:35-32:36, Isaiah 17:10 17:14 21:16, Jeremiah 1:8 1:19 15:20 17:18 23:40, John 18:4-18:6, Odes of Solomon 5:4, Psalms 6:11 27:1-27:2 35:26 40:15 47:3 65:6 66:5, Romans 8:31

[2] Jeremiah 20:12 - 1 Peter 2:23 4:19, 1 Samuel 1:15, 2 Chronicles 24:22, Isaiah 13:14 14:14, Jeremiah 11:20 12:8 17:10 17:18 18:19-18:23, Psalms 7:10 11:6 17:3 26:2-26:3 54:8 59:11 62:9 86:4 109:6-109:20 19:23, Revelation 2:23 6:10 18:20 19:2-19:3

[3] Jeremiah 20:13 - 4Q434 1 ii 1, 4Q434 frag 1 1.1, Isaiah 1:4, James 2:5-2:6, Midrash Psalms 120:1 146:1, Psalms 34:7 35:9-35:11 69:34 72:4 109:30-109:31
Jeremiah 20:13-15 - 4QJerc

[4] Jeremiah 20:14 - 2 Baruch 10:6, Genesis.R 64:5, Jeremiah 15:10, Job 3:4-3:17, Pesikta Rabbati 26:1/2
Jeremiah 20:14-18 - 4QJera

[5] Jeremiah 20:15 - Genesis 21:5-21:6, Jeremiah 1:5, Luke 1:14

[6] Jeremiah 20:16 - 2 Peter 2:6, Amos 1:14 2:2 4:11, Deuteronomy 5:22, Ezekiel 21:27, Genesis 19:24-19:25, Hosea 10:14 11:8, Jeremiah 4:19 18:8 18:22 2:13 48:3-48:4, Jonah 3:4 3:9-3:10 4:2, Jude 1:7, Luke 17:29, Zephaniah 1:16 2:9

[7] Jeremiah 20:17 - Ecclesiastes 6:3, Jastrow 369a, Job 3:11-3:12 3:17 10:18-10:19

[8] Jeremiah 20:18 - 1 Corinthians 4:9-13, 1 Peter 4:14-16, 2 Timothy 1:12, Acts 5:41, compare use of א in the word יצתי with Job 1:21 and Job 3:11, Genesis 3:16-19, Hebrews 10:36 11:36 12:2 13:13, Isaiah 1:6 3:7, Jeremiah 8:18, Job 3:21 14:1 14:13, John 16:20, Lamentations 1:12 3:1, Psalms 69:20 90:9-10

[9] Jeremiah 21:1 - 1 Chronicles 3:15 9:12, 2 Chronicles 36:10-36:13, 2 Kings 24:17-24:18 25:18-25:21, 4QJera, Jeremiah 5:25 32:1-32:3 13:1 13:3 14:1 52:1-52:3 4:24, Nehemiah 11:12

[10] Jeremiah 21:2 - 1 Kings 14:2-14:3 22:3-22:8, 1 Samuel 7:10-7:12 10:22 14:6-14:14 17:45-17:50 4:6 4:15, 2 Chronicles 14:8-14:12 20:1-20:30 8:21, 2 Kings 1:3 3:11-3:14 22:13-22:14 25:1-25:2, b.Arachin [Rashi] 33a, Exodus 14:1-14:15, Ezekiel 14:3-14:7 20:1-20:3, Isaiah 59:1-59:2, Jeremiah 8:17 8:24 13:3 13:7 38:14-38:27 39:1-39:2 42:4-42:6 52:3-52:6, Joshua 10:1-10:11, Judges 4:1-4:5 20:27, Psalms 44:2-44:5 46:9-46:12 48:5-48:9 105:5-105:45 136:1-136:26

[11] LXX *the*

according to all His wondrous works, *that he may go up*[1] from us.'

3 Then Jeremiah said to them: Thus shall you say to Zedekiah:

4[2] Thus says the LORD, the God of Israel: Behold, I will turn back the weapons of war that are in your hands, with which you fight against *the king of Babylon, and against*[3] the Chaldeans, who besiege you outside the walls, and I will gather them to the midst of this city.

5[4] And I myself will fight against you with an outstretched hand and with a strong arm, in anger, and in fury, and in great wrath.

6[5] And I will strike the inhabitants of this city, both man and beast; they shall die of a great pestilence.

7[6] And afterward, says the LORD, I will deliver Zedekiah king of Judah, and his servants, and the people, and such as are left in this city from the *pestilence, from the sword, and from the famine*[7], into the hand of *Nebuchadrezzar king of Babylon, and into the hand of*[8] their enemies, and into the hand of those who seek their life; and he shall strike them with the edge of the sword; he shall not spare them, *nor have pity*[9], nor have compassion.

8[10] And to this people you shall say: Thus says the LORD: Behold, I[11] set before you the way of life and the way of death.

9[12] He who lives in this city shall die by the sword, and by the famine, and by the pestilence; but he who goes out, and falls to the Chaldeans who besiege you, he shall live, and his life shall be to him as prey.

10[13] For I have set My face against this city for evil, and not for good, says the LORD; it shall be given into the hand of the king of Babylon, and he shall burn it with fire.

וַיֹּ֙אמֶר֙ יִרְמְיָ֔הוּ אֲלֵיהֶ֑ם כֹּ֥ה תֹאמְרֻ֖ן אֶל־צִדְקִיָּֽהוּ

כֹּֽה־אָמַ֞ר יְהֹוָ֣ה אֱלֹהֵ֣י יִשְׂרָאֵ֗ל הִנְנִ֤י מֵסֵב֙ אֶת־כְּלֵ֣י הַמִּלְחָמָ֗ה אֲשֶׁ֤ר בְּיֶדְכֶם֙ אֲשֶׁ֨ר אַתֶּ֜ם נִלְחָמִ֣ים בָּ֗ם אֶת־מֶ֤לֶךְ בָּבֶל֙ וְאֶת־הַכַּשְׂדִּ֔ים הַצָּרִ֥ים עֲלֵיכֶ֖ם מִח֣וּץ לַחוֹמָ֑ה וְאָסַפְתִּ֣י אוֹתָ֔ם אֶל־תּ֖וֹךְ הָעִ֥יר הַזֹּֽאת

וְנִלְחַמְתִּ֤י אֲנִי֙ אִתְּכֶ֔ם בְּיָ֥ד נְטוּיָ֖ה וּבִזְר֣וֹעַ חֲזָקָ֑ה וּבְאַ֥ף וּבְחֵמָ֖ה וּבְקֶ֥צֶף גָּדֽוֹל

וְהִכֵּיתִ֗י אֶת־י֣וֹשְׁבֵי֙ הָעִ֣יר הַזֹּ֔את וְאֶת־הָאָדָ֖ם וְאֶת־הַבְּהֵמָ֑ה בְּדֶ֥בֶר גָּד֖וֹל יָמֻֽתוּ

וְאַחֲרֵי־כֵ֣ן נְאֻם־יְהֹוָ֡ה אֶתֵּ֣ן אֶת־צִדְקִיָּ֣הוּ מֶֽלֶךְ־יְהוּדָ֣ה וְאֶת־עֲבָדָ֣יו ׀ וְאֶת־הָעָ֡ם וְאֶת־הַנִּשְׁאָרִים֩ בָּעִ֨יר הַזֹּ֜את מִן־הַדֶּ֣בֶר ׀ מִן־הַחֶ֣רֶב וּמִן־הָרָעָ֗ב בְּיַד֙ נְבוּכַדְרֶאצַּ֣ר מֶֽלֶךְ־בָּבֶ֔ל וּבְיַד֙ אֹֽיְבֵיהֶ֔ם וּבְיַ֖ד מְבַקְשֵׁ֣י נַפְשָׁ֑ם וְהִכָּ֣ם לְפִי־חֶ֔רֶב לֹא־יָח֣וּס עֲלֵיהֶ֔ם וְלֹ֥א יַחְמֹ֖ל וְלֹ֥א יְרַחֵֽם

וְאֶל־הָעָ֤ם הַזֶּה֙ תֹּאמַ֔ר כֹּ֖ה אָמַ֣ר יְהֹוָ֑ה הִנְנִ֤י נֹתֵן֙ לִפְנֵיכֶ֔ם אֶת־דֶּ֥רֶךְ הַחַיִּ֖ים וְאֶת־דֶּ֥רֶךְ הַמָּֽוֶת

הַיֹּשֵׁב֙ בָּעִ֣יר הַזֹּ֔את יָמ֕וּת בַּחֶ֖רֶב וּבָרָעָ֣ב וּבַדָּ֑בֶר וְהַיּוֹצֵ֨א וְנָפַ֜ל עַל־הַכַּשְׂדִּ֗ים הַצָּרִ֤ים עֲלֵיכֶם֙ יִחְיֶ֔ה וְהָיְתָה־לּ֥וֹ נַפְשׁ֖וֹ לְשָׁלָֽל

כִּ֣י שַׂ֣מְתִּי פָנַ֞י בָּעִ֤יר הַזֹּאת֙ לְרָעָ֣ה וְלֹ֣א לְטוֹבָ֔ה נְאֻם־יְהֹוָ֑ה בְּיַד־מֶ֤לֶךְ בָּבֶל֙ תִּנָּתֵ֔ן וּשְׂרָפָ֖הּ בָּאֵֽשׁ

---

[1] LXX *and the king shall depart*

[2] Jeremiah 21:4 - Ezekiel 16:37-16:41, Hosea 9:12, Isaiah 5:5 10:4 13:4, Jeremiah 8:5 9:5 37:8-37:10 38:2-38:3 38:17-38:18 15:3 4:18, Lamentations 2:5 2:7, Matthew 22:7, Midrash Psalms 36:8, z.Vaetchanan 269b, Zechariah 14:2

[3] Missing in LXX

[4] Jeremiah 21:5 - Deuteronomy 4:23 4:34, Exodus 6:6 9:15, Ezekiel 20:33-34, Isaiah 5:25 9:13 9:18 9:22 10:4 15:10, Jeremiah 6:12 8:17 8:37, Lamentations 2:4-5, Midrash Psalms 36:8, Nahum 1:5-6

[5] Jeremiah 21:6 - Ezekiel 5:12-13 7:15 12:16 14:13 14:17 14:19 14:21 9:27 9:29, Genesis 6:7, Hosea 4:3, Isaiah 6:11 24:1-6, Jeremiah 7:20 12:3-12:4 14:12 8:24 9:12 10:17 12:29 18:22, Luke 1:24, Micah 3:12, Zephaniah 1:3

[6] Jeremiah 21:7 - 2 Chronicles 36:17-20, 2 Kings 25:5-7 25:18-21, Deuteronomy 4:50, Ezekiel 7:9 8:18 9:5-6 9:10 12:12-16 17:20-21 21:30-31, Habakkuk 1:6-10, Isaiah 13:17-18 3:11 23:6, Jeremiah 13:14 24:8-10 34:19-22 13:17 38:21-23 39:4-7 52:8-11 52:24-27 Jeremiah 21:7-10 - 4QJerc

[7] 4QJerc *the pestilence and the sword*; LXX *death, and famine, and the sword*

[8] Missing in LXX

[9] Missing in LXX

[10] Jeremiah 21:8 - b.Sanhedrin 37b, Deuteronomy 11:26 6:15 6:19, Isaiah 1:19-20, Joseph and Aseneth 24:7 2, Midrash Tanchuma Reeh 1, z.Vaetchanan 269b Jeremiah 21:8-9 - Ein Yaakov Sanhedrin:37b Jeremiah 21:8-14 - Testament of Asher 1:3

[11] 4QJerc adds *Myself*

[12] Jeremiah 21:9 - b.Sanhedrin 37b, Jeremiah 14:12 21:7 3:13 14:2 38:17-38:23 15:18 21:5

[13] Jeremiah 21:10 - 2 Chronicles 12:19, Amos 9:4, Ezekiel 15:7, Jeremiah 17:27 2:6 32:28-32:31 10:2 10:22 37:8-37:10 14:3 14:18 14:23 15:8 20:11 20:27 4:13, Leviticus 17:10 20:3-20:5 2:17, Psalms 34:17, Zechariah 1:6

וּלְבֵית מֶלֶךְ יְהוּדָה שִׁמְעוּ דְּבַר־יְהוָה ‎ 11[1]

And to the house of the king of Judah: Hear the word of the LORD;

בֵּית דָּוִד כֹּה אָמַר יְהוָה דִּינוּ לַבֹּקֶר מִשְׁפָּט וְהַצִּילוּ גָזוּל מִיַּד עוֹשֵׁק פֶּן־תֵּצֵא כָאֵשׁ חֲמָתִי וּבָעֲרָה וְאֵין מְכַבֶּה מִפְּנֵי רֹעַ 'מַעַלְלֵיהֶם' "מַעַלְלֵיכֶם" ‎ 12[2]

O house of David, thus says the LORD: Execute justice in the morning[3], and deliver the spoiled from the hand of the oppressor, lest My fury go forth like fire, and burn so no one can quench it, because *of the evil of your deeds*[4].

הִנְנִי אֵלַיִךְ יֹשֶׁבֶת הָעֵמֶק צוּר הַמִּישֹׁר נְאֻם־יְהוָה הָאֹמְרִים מִי־יֵחַת עָלֵינוּ וּמִי יָבוֹא בִּמְעוֹנוֹתֵינוּ ‎ 13[5]

Behold, I am against you, O inhabitant of the valley, and *rock of the plain, says the LORD; you who say: 'Who shall come down against us*[6]? Or who shall enter into our habitations?'

וּפָקַדְתִּי עֲלֵיכֶם כִּפְרִי מַעַלְלֵיכֶם נְאֻם־יְהוָה וְהִצַּתִּי אֵשׁ בְּיַעְרָהּ וְאָכְלָה כָּל־סְבִיבֶיהָ ‎ 14[7]

And I will punish you according to the fruit of your deeds, says the LORD[8]; and I will kindle a fire in her forest, and it shall devour all that is around her.

Jeremiah – Chapter 22

כֹּה אָמַר יְהוָה רֵד בֵּית־מֶלֶךְ יְהוּדָה וְדִבַּרְתָּ שָׁם אֶת־הַדָּבָר הַזֶּה ‎ 1[9]

Thus said the LORD: Go down to the house of the king of Judah, and speak this word,

וְאָמַרְתָּ שְׁמַע דְּבַר־יְהוָה מֶלֶךְ יְהוּדָה הַיֹּשֵׁב עַל־כִּסֵּא דָוִד אַתָּה וַעֲבָדֶיךָ וְעַמְּךָ הַבָּאִים בַּשְּׁעָרִים הָאֵלֶּה ‎ 2[10]

and say: Hear the word of the LORD, O king of Judah, who sits upon the throne of David, you, and your servants, and your people who enter in by these gates.

כֹּה אָמַר יְהוָה עֲשׂוּ מִשְׁפָּט וּצְדָקָה וְהַצִּילוּ גָזוּל מִיַּד עָשׁוֹק וְגֵר יָתוֹם וְאַלְמָנָה אַל־תֹּנוּ אַל־תַּחְמֹסוּ וְדָם נָקִי אַל־תִּשְׁפְּכוּ בַּמָּקוֹם הַזֶּה ‎ 3[11]

Thus says the LORD: Execute justice and righteousness, and deliver the spoiled from the hand of the oppressor; and do no wrong, do no violence, to the stranger, the fatherless, nor the widow, nor shed innocent blood in this place.

כִּי אִם־עָשׂוֹ תַּעֲשׂוּ אֶת־הַדָּבָר הַזֶּה וּבָאוּ בְשַׁעֲרֵי הַבַּיִת הַזֶּה מְלָכִים יֹשְׁבִים לְדָוִד עַל־כִּסְאוֹ רֹכְבִים בָּרֶכֶב וּבַסּוּסִים הוּא 'וְעַבְדּוֹ' "וַעֲבָדָיו" וְעַמּוֹ ‎ 4[12]

For if you do this thing, indeed, then kings sitting on the throne of David, riding in chariots and on horses, he, and his servants, and his people shall enter in by the gates of this house.

---

[1] Jeremiah 21:11 - Jeremiah 13:18 17:20, Micah 3:1

[2] Jeremiah 21:12 - 2 Samuel 8:15, b.Bava Batra [Rashbam] 113b, b.Megillah [Rashi] 14a, b.Sanhedrin 7b 19a, b.Shabbat 55a, Deuteronomy 8:22, Ecclesiastes 10:16-10:17, Ein Yaakov Sanhedrin:19a, Ein Yaakov Sanhedrin:7b, Ein Yaakov Shabbat:55a, Exodus 18:13, Ezekiel 21:3-20:4 22:18-22:22 22:31 24:8-24:14, Isaiah 1:17 1:31 7:2 7:13 16:3-16:5 31:1-31:2, Jeremiah 4:4 5:14 5:28 7:20 17:4 21:5 22:2-22:3 22:15-22:17 23:5 23:19 12:7, Job 5:17, Lamentations 2:3-2:4 4:11, Leviticus 2:28, Luke 1:69 18:3-18:5, m.Sanhedrin 2:2, Mark 9:43-9:48, Midrash Tanchuma Mishpatim 6, mt.Hilchot Melachim uMichamoteihem 3:7, Nahum 1:6, Numbers.R 3:6 10:4, Proverbs 24:11-24:12 31:8-31:9, Psalms 72:1-72:4 72:12-72:14 82:2-82:4 5:8, Romans 13:4, Tanna Devei Eliyahu 10, z.Mishpatim 122a, z.Vaetchanan 269b, Zechariah 7:9-7:11, Zephaniah 1:18 3:5

[3] LXX adds *and act rightly*

[4] Missing in LXX

[5] Jeremiah 21:13 - 2 Samuel 5:6-5:7, Exodus 13:8 13:20, Ezekiel 13:8, Isaiah 22:1, Jeremiah 7:4 21:5 23:30-32 49:4-49:5 1:16 2:31 3:25, Lamentations 4:12, Micah 3:11, Obadiah 1:3-4, Psalms 5:2

[6] LXX *of Sor; in the plain country, against those who say, Who shall alarm us*

[7] Jeremiah 21:14 - 2 Chronicles 12:19, Ezekiel 21:2-20:4, Galatians 6:7-6:8, Isaiah 3:10-3:11 10:12 10:18-10:19 24:21 27:10-27:11 13:24, Jeremiah 6:29 9:26 11:22 17:10 22:7 8:19 4:13, Proverbs 1:31, Zechariah 11:1

[8] Missing in LXX

[9] Jeremiah 22:1 - 1 Kings 21:18-21:20, 1 Samuel 15:16-15:23, 2 Chronicles 19:2-19:3 25:15-25:16 9:10, 2 Samuel 12:1 24:11-24:12, Amos 7:13, Hosea 5:1, Jeremiah 21:11 10:2, Luke 3:19-3:20, Mark 6:18, z.Vaetchanan 269b

[10] Jeremiah 22:2 - 1 Kings 22:19, Amos 7:16, Ezekiel 10:7, Isaiah 1:10 9:8 4:14, Jeremiah 7:2 13:18 17:20-17:27 19:3 22:4 22:29-22:30 29:16-29:17 5:20 12:30, Luke 1:32

[11] Jeremiah 22:3 - 2 Enoch 42:9 9:1, 2 Kings 24:4, 2 Samuel 23:3, 4QJera, Deuteronomy 10:18 16:18-20 19:10-13 24:7 1:1 3:19, Exodus 22:22 23:6-9, Ezekiel 22:7, Isaiah 1:15-20 1:23, James 1:27, Jeremiah 5:28 7:5-6 9:25 21:12 22:17 2:16, Job 22:9 24:9 29:7-17, Joel 4:19, Leviticus 19:15, Malachi 3:5, Micah 3:11 6:8, Proverbs 6:17 23:10, Psalms 68:6 72:2-4 94:6 94:21, z.Vaetchanan 269b, Zechariah 7:9-11
Jeremiah 22:3-16 - 4QJera

[12] Jeremiah 22:4 - Jeremiah 17:25
Jeremiah 22:4-6 - 4QJerc

וְאִם לֹא תִשְׁמְעוּ אֶת־הַדְּבָרִים הָאֵלֶּה בִּי נִשְׁבַּעְתִּי נְאֻם־יְהֹוָה כִּי־לְחָרְבָּה יִהְיֶה הַבַּיִת הַזֶּה	5[1]	But if you will not hear these words, I swear by Myself, says the LORD, that this house shall become desolate.
כִּי־כֹה ׀ אָמַר יְהֹוָה עַל־בֵּית מֶלֶךְ יְהוּדָה גִּלְעָד אַתָּה לִי רֹאשׁ הַלְּבָנוֹן אִם־לֹא אֲשִׁיתְךָ מִדְבָּר עָרִים לֹא 'נוֹשָׁבָה' "נוֹשָׁבוּ"	6[2]	For thus says the LORD concerning the house of the king of Judah: You are Gilead to Me, the head of Lebanon; yet I will surely make you a wilderness, cities that are not inhabited.
וְקִדַּשְׁתִּי עָלֶיךָ מַשְׁחִתִים אִישׁ וְכֵלָיו וְכָרְתוּ מִבְחַר אֲרָזֶיךָ וְהִפִּילוּ עַל־הָאֵשׁ	7[3]	And I will prepare destroyers against you, everyone with his weapons; and they shall cut down your choice cedars, and cast them into the fire.
וְעָבְרוּ גּוֹיִם רַבִּים עַל הָעִיר הַזֹּאת וְאָמְרוּ אִישׁ אֶל־רֵעֵהוּ עַל־מֶה עָשָׂה יְהֹוָה כָּכָה לָעִיר הַגְּדוֹלָה הַזֹּאת	8[4]	And many nations shall pass by this city, and they shall say to his neighbor: 'Why has the LORD done this to this great city?'
וְאָמְרוּ עַל אֲשֶׁר עָזְבוּ אֶת־בְּרִית יְהֹוָה אֱלֹהֵיהֶם וַיִּשְׁתַּחֲווּ לֵאלֹהִים אֲחֵרִים וַיַּעַבְדוּם	9[5]	Then they shall answer: 'Because they forsook the covenant of the LORD their God, and worshipped other gods, and served them.'
אַל־תִּבְכּוּ לְמֵת וְאַל־תָּנֻדוּ לוֹ בְּכוּ בָכוֹ לַהֹלֵךְ כִּי לֹא יָשׁוּב עוֹד וְרָאָה אֶת־אֶרֶץ מוֹלַדְתּוֹ	10[6]	Do not weep for the dead, nor bemoan him; but weep sorely for he who goes away, for he shall never return, nor see his native country.
כִּי כֹה אָמַר־יְהֹוָה אֶל־שַׁלֻּם בֶּן־יֹאשִׁיָּהוּ מֶלֶךְ יְהוּדָה הַמֹּלֵךְ תַּחַת יֹאשִׁיָּהוּ אָבִיו אֲשֶׁר יָצָא מִן־הַמָּקוֹם הַזֶּה לֹא־יָשׁוּב שָׁם עוֹד	11[7]	For thus says the LORD touching Shallum the son of Josiah, king of Judah, who reigned in place of Josiah his father, and who went forth from this place: he shall not return again;
כִּי בִּמְקוֹם אֲשֶׁר־הִגְלוּ אֹתוֹ שָׁם יָמוּת וְאֶת־הָאָרֶץ הַזֹּאת לֹא־יִרְאֶה עוֹד	12[8]	But in the place where they led him captive, there shall he die, and he shall not see this land again.
הוֹי בֹּנֶה בֵיתוֹ בְּלֹא־צֶדֶק וַעֲלִיּוֹתָיו בְּלֹא מִשְׁפָּט בְּרֵעֵהוּ יַעֲבֹד חִנָּם וּפֹעֲלוֹ לֹא יִתֶּן־לוֹ	13[9]	Woe to he who builds his house by unrighteousness, and his chambers by injustice; that uses his neighbor's service without wages, and does not give him his hire;
הָאֹמֵר אֶבְנֶה־לִּי בֵּית מִדּוֹת וַעֲלִיּוֹת מְרֻוָּחִים וְקָרַע לוֹ חַלּוֹנָי וְסָפוּן בָּאָרֶז וּמָשׁוֹחַ בַּשָּׁשַׁר	14[10]	Who says: 'I will build me a wide house and spacious chambers,' and cuts out windows, and a *ceiling*[11] of cedar, and paints with vermilion.
הֲתִמְלֹךְ כִּי אַתָּה מְתַחֲרֶה בָאָרֶז אָבִיךָ הֲלוֹא אָכַל וְשָׁתָה וְעָשָׂה מִשְׁפָּט וּצְדָקָה אָז טוֹב לוֹ	15[12]	Shall you reign, because you *strive to excel in cedar? Did your father not eat and drink, and*

[1] Jeremiah 22:5 - 2 Chronicles 7:19 7:22, Amos 6:8 8:7-8:8, Deuteronomy 32:40-32:42, Genesis 22:16, Hebrews 3:18 6:13 6:17, Isaiah 1:20, Jeremiah 7:13-7:14 17:27 26:6-26:9 15:8, Micah 3:12, Numbers 14:28-14:30, Psalms 95:11

[2] Jeremiah 22:6 - Deuteronomy 3:25, Ezekiel 33:27-33:28, Genesis 13:25, Isaiah 6:11 24:1-24:6 3:10, Jeremiah 4:20 7:34 9:12 19:7-19:8 21:11 21:14 22:24 25:9-25:10 26:6-26:9 2:18, Mekhilta de R'Shimon bar Yochai Amalek 45:1, Mekilta de R'Ishmael Amalek 2:87, Micah 3:12, Psalms 11:34, Sifre Devarim Devarim 6, Sifre Devarim Vaetchanan 28, Sifre Devarim Vezot Habracha 357, Song of Songs 5:15, z.Vaetchanan 269b

[3] Jeremiah 22:7 - Ezekiel 9:1-7, Isaiah 10:3-7 10:33-34 13:3-5 27:10-11 13:24 54:16-17, Jeremiah 4:6-7 5:15 21:14 50:20-23, Matthew 22:7, Sifre Devarim {Vezot Habracha} 357, Zechariah 11:1

[4] Jeremiah 22:8 - 1 Kings 9:8-9:9, 2 Chronicles 7:20-7:22, Apocalypse of Elijah 4:13, Daniel 9:7, Deuteronomy 29:22-29:25, Jeremiah 16:10, Lamentations 2:15-2:17 4:12, Midrash Psalms 48:3

[5] Jeremiah 22:9 - 2 Chronicles 10:25, 2 Kings 22:17, Apocalypse of Elijah 1:13, b.Sanhedrin 38b, Deuteronomy 29:24-29:27, Jeremiah 2:17-2:19 40:2-40:3 2:7

[6] Jeremiah 22:10 - 2 Chronicles 35:23-35:25, 2 Kings 22:20 23:30-23:34, b.Bava Batra 116a, b.Moed Katan 27b, Ecclesiastes 4:2, Ein Yaakov Bava Batra:116a, Ein Yaakov Moed Katan:27b, Ezekiel 19:3-19:4, Genesis.R 63:11, HaMadrikh 35:8, Isaiah 9:1, Jeremiah 22:11 22:18, Lamentations 4:9, Luke 23:28, mt.Hilchot Evel 13:11, Sifre Devarim Ekev 43, Siman 215:1, Tanna Devei Eliyahu 4 Jeremiah 22:10-28 - 4QJerc

[7] Jeremiah 22:11 - 1 Chronicles 3:15, 2 Chronicles 4:12 10:22 36:1-36:4, 2 Kings 23:31 23:34, z.Vaetchanan 269b

[8] Jeremiah 22:12 - 2 Kings 23:34, Jeremiah 22:18

[9] Jeremiah 22:13 - 2 Chronicles 12:4, 2 Kings 23:35-23:37, Deuteronomy 24:14-24:15, Habakkuk 2:9-2:11, James 5:4, Jeremiah 22:18, Job 24:10-24:11, Leviticus 19:13, Malachi 3:5, Micah 3:10, Perek Shirah [the Fox], Saadia Opinions 10:10, z.Tazria 51b

[10] Jeremiah 22:14 - 2 Chronicles 3:5, 2 Samuel 7:2, Daniel 4:27, Haggai 1:4, Isaiah 5:8-5:9 9:10, Luke 14:28-14:29, Malachi 1:4, Proverbs 17:19 24:27, Song of Songs 1:17

[11] LXX *wainscoted*

[12] Jeremiah 22:15 - 1 Chronicles 3:15, 1 Corinthians 10:31, 1 Kings 4:20-4:23 10:9, 2 Chronicles 10:2 35:7-35:8 35:12-35:18, 2 Kings 22:2 23:25, 2 Samuel 8:15, Acts 2:46, Deuteronomy 4:40, Ecclesiastes 2:24 9:7-9:10 10:17, Isaiah 3:10 9:8 9:16, Jeremiah 21:12 22:3

do justice and righteousness? Then it was well with him[1].

16[2]   He judged the cause of the poor and needy; then it was well. Is this not how one knows Me? says the LORD.

הֲנֶן דִּין־עָנִי וְאֶבְיֹון אָז טֹוב הֲלֹוא־הִיא הַדַּעַת אֹתִי נְאֻם־יְהוָה

17[3]   *But your eyes and your heart are not but for your covetousness*[4], and for shedding innocent blood, and for oppression, and for violence, to do it.

כִּי אֵין עֵינֶיךָ וְלִבְּךָ כִּי אִם־עַל־בִּצְעֶךָ וְעַל דַּם־הַנָּקִי לִשְׁפֹּוךְ וְעַל־הָעֹשֶׁק וְעַל־הַמְּרוּצָה לַעֲשֹׂות

18[5]   Therefore, thus says the LORD concerning Jehoiakim the son of Josiah, king of Judah: They shall not lament for him: 'Ah my brother!' or: 'Ah sister!' They shall not lament for him: 'Ah lord!' or: 'Ah his glory!'

לָכֵן כֹּה־אָמַר יְהוָה אֶל־יְהֹויָקִים בֶּן־יֹאשִׁיָּהוּ מֶלֶךְ יְהוּדָה לֹא־יִסְפְּדוּ לֹו הֹוי אָחִי וְהֹוי אָחֹות לֹא־יִסְפְּדוּ לֹו הֹוי אָדֹון וְהֹוי הֹדֹה

19[6]   He shall be buried with the burial of an ass, *drawn*[7] and cast forth beyond the gates of Jerusalem.

קְבוּרַת חֲמֹור יִקָּבֵר סָחֹוב וְהַשְׁלֵךְ מֵהָלְאָה לְשַׁעֲרֵי יְרוּשָׁלָ͏ִם

20[8]   Go to Lebanon, and cry, and lift up your voice in Bashan; and cry *from Abarim*[9], for all your lovers[10] are *destroyed*[11].

עֲלִי הַלְּבָנֹון וּצְעָקִי וּבַבָּשָׁן תְּנִי קֹולֵךְ וְצַעֲקִי מֵעֲבָרִים כִּי נִשְׁבְּרוּ כָּל־מְאַהֲבָיִךְ

21[12]   I spoke to you in your prosperity, but you said: 'I will not hear.' This has been your manner from your youth, you do not listen to My voice.

דִּבַּרְתִּי אֵלַיִךְ בְּשַׁלְוֹתַיִךְ אָמַרְתְּ לֹא אֶשְׁמָע זֶה דַרְכֵּךְ מִנְּעוּרַיִךְ כִּי לֹא־שָׁמַעַתְּ בְּקֹולִי

22[13]   The wind shall feed on all your shepherds, and your lovers shall go into captivity; surely then you shall be ashamed and confounded for all your wickedness.

כָּל־רֹעַיִךְ תִּרְעֶה־רוּחַ וּמְאַהֲבַיִךְ בַּשְּׁבִי יֵלֵכוּ כִּי אָז תֵּבֹשִׁי וְנִכְלַמְתְּ מִכֹּל רָעָתֵךְ

23[14]   O inhabitant of Lebanon, who are nestled in the cedars, How gracious shall you be when pangs come upon you, The pain as of a woman in travail!

"יֹשַׁבְתִּי" "יֹשַׁבְתְּ" בַּלְּבָנֹון "מְקֻנַּנְתִּי" "מְקֻנַּנְתְּ" בָּאֲרָזִים מַה־נֵּחַנְתְּ בְּבֹא־לָךְ חֲבָלִים חִיל כַּיֹּלֵדָה

22:18 23:5 18:6, Luke 11:41, Proverbs 20:28 21:3 1:5 5:4 7:9, Psalms 128:1-128:2

Jeremiah 22:15-16 - Mekhilta de R'Shimon bar Yochai Amalek 47:1

[1] LXX *are provoked with thy father Achaz? They shall not eat, and they shall not drink: it is better for you to execute judgment and justice*

[2] Jeremiah 22:16 - 1 Chronicles 4:9, 1 John 2:3-4, 1 Samuel 2:2, Gates of Repentance 4.005, Isaiah 1:17, Jeremiah 5:28 9:4 9:17 9:25 31:34-35, Job 29:12-17, John 8:19 8:54-55 16:3 17:3 17:6, Midrash Shmuel 1:1, Proverbs 24:11-12, Psalms 9:11 72:1-4 72:12-13 82:3-4 13:31, Titus 1:16

[3] Jeremiah 22:17 - 1 Corinthians 6:10, 1 John 2:15-2:16, 1 Kings 21:19, 1 Timothy 6:9-6:10, 2 Chronicles 12:8, 2 Kings 24:4, 2 Peter 2:3 2:14, Colossians 3:5, Ecclesiastes.R 1:36, Ephesians 5:3-5:5, Exodus 18:21, Ezekiel 19:6 9:31, James 1:14-1:15, Jeremiah 22:3 26:22-26:24, Job 7:7, Joshua 7:21, Luke 12:15-12:21 16:13-14, Mark 7:21-22, Psalms 10:4 119:36-37, Romans 1:29, Zephaniah 3:3

[4] LXX *Behold, your eyes are not good, nor your heart, but they go after your covetousness*

[5] Jeremiah 22:18 - 1 Kings 13:30, 2 Chronicles 21:19-21:20 11:25, 2 Samuel 1:26 3:33-3:38, Jeremiah 16:4 16:6 22:10 10:5, Sifre Devarim Ekev 43, z.Vaetchanan 269b

[6] Jeremiah 22:19 - 1 Kings 14:10 21:23-21:24, 2 Chronicles 12:6, 2 Kings 9:35, b.Avodah Zara [Rashi] 53a, b.Megillah [Rashi] 11b, b.Sanhedrin 82a 1 4a, Ein Yaakov Sanhedrin:104a, Jeremiah 15:3 12:6 12:30, Leviticus.R 19:6, Psalms of Solomon 2:27 2, Pseudo-Phocylides 99, Seder Olam 25:Nebuchadnezzar, Sifre Devarim Ekev 43

[7] LXX *he shall be dragged roughly along*

[8] Jeremiah 22:20 - 2 Kings 24:7, Deuteronomy 8:49, Ezekiel 23:9 23:22, Isaiah 20:5-6 30:1-7 31:1-3, Jeremiah 2:36-3:1 4:30 22:22 1:9 25:17-27 30:13-15, Lamentations 1:2 1:19, Numbers 3:12

[9] LXX *to the extremity of the sea*

[10] 4QJerc *supporters*

[11] 4QJerc *poured out*

[12] Jeremiah 22:21 - 2 Chronicles 9:10 36:16-36:17, Deuteronomy 9:7 9:24 7:27 32:15-32:20, Ezekiel 20:8 20:13 20:21 20:28 23:3-23:39, Isaiah 24:8, Jeremiah 2:31 3:25 6:16 7:22-7:28 8:30 11:15 36:21-36:26, Judges 2:11-2:19, Nehemiah 9:16-9:37, Proverbs 6:9, Psalms 106:6-106:48

[13] Jeremiah 22:22 - Acts 7:51-7:52, Ezekiel 34:2-34:10, Hosea 4:19 13:15, Isaiah 16:7, Jeremiah 2:8 2:26-2:27 2:37 4:11-4:13 5:30-5:31 10:21 12:10 20:11 23:1-23:2 30:23-30:24, Zechariah 11:8 11:17

[14] Jeremiah 22:23 - Amos 9:2, Habakkuk 2:9, Hosea 5:15-6:1 7:14, Jeremiah 3:21 4:30-4:31 6:24 21:13 22:6 30:5-30:6 24:28 1:16 50:4-50:5, Numbers 24:21, Obadiah 1:4, Zechariah 11:1-11:2

חַי־אָ֙נִי֙ נְאֻם־יְהוָ֔ה כִּ֣י אִם־יִהְיֶ֞ה כָּנְיָ֤הוּ בֶן־יְהֽוֹיָקִים֙ מֶ֣לֶךְ יְהוּדָ֔ה חוֹתָ֖ם עַל־יַ֣ד יְמִינִ֑י כִּ֥י מִשָּׁ֖ם אֶתְּקֶֽנְךָּ **24¹**	As I live, says the LORD, though Coniah the son of Jehoiakim king of Judah were the signet on My right hand, yet would I pluck you there; and I will give you into the hand of those who seek your life, and into the hand of those of whom you fear, in the hand of *Nebuchadrezzar king of Babylon, and in the hand of*[3] the Chaldeans.
וּנְתַתִּ֗יךָ בְּיַד֙ מְבַקְשֵׁ֣י נַפְשֶׁ֔ךָ וּבְיַ֖ד אֲשֶׁר־אַתָּ֣ה יָג֣וֹר מִפְּנֵיהֶ֑ם וּבְיַ֛ד נְבוּכַדְרֶאצַּ֥ר מֶֽלֶךְ־בָּבֶ֖ל וּבְיַ֥ד הַכַּשְׂדִּֽים **25²**	
וְהֵֽטַלְתִּ֣י אֹתְךָ֗ וְאֶֽת־אִמְּךָ֙ אֲשֶׁ֣ר יְלָדַ֔תְךָ עַ֚ל הָאָ֣רֶץ אַחֶ֔רֶת אֲשֶׁ֥ר לֹֽא־יֻלַּדְתֶּ֖ם שָׁ֑ם וְשָׁ֖ם תָּמֽוּתוּ **26⁴**	And I will cast you out, and your mother who bore you, into another country, where you were not born; and there shall you die.
וְעַל־הָאָ֗רֶץ אֲשֶׁר־הֵ֛ם מְנַשְּׂאִ֥ים אֶת־נַפְשָׁ֖ם לָשׁ֣וּב שָׁ֑ם שָׁ֖מָּה לֹ֥א יָשֽׁוּבוּ **27⁵**	But to the land into which they long to return, there they shall not return.
הַעֶ֣צֶב נִבְזֶ֗ה נָפ֙וּץ֙ הָאִ֣ישׁ הַזֶּ֔ה כָּנְיָ֕הוּ אִם־כְּלִ֖י אֵ֣ין חֵ֣פֶץ בּ֑וֹ מַדּ֤וּעַ הֽוּטֲלוּ֙ ה֣וּא וְזַרְע֔וֹ וְהֻ֨שְׁלְכ֔וּ עַל־הָאָ֖רֶץ אֲשֶׁ֥ר לֹא־יָדָֽעוּ **28⁶**	Is this man Coniah a despised, broken image? Is he a vessel in which is no pleasure? Why are they cast out, he and his seed, and are cast into the land that they do not know?
אֶ֥רֶץ אֶ֖רֶץ אָ֑רֶץ שִׁמְעִ֖י דְּבַר־יְהוָֽה **29⁷**	O land, land, land, Hear the word of the LORD.
כֹּ֣ה ׀ אָמַ֣ר יְהוָ֗ה כִּתְב֞וּ אֶת־הָאִ֤ישׁ הַזֶּה֙ עֲרִירִ֔י גֶּ֖בֶר לֹא־יִצְלַ֣ח בְּיָמָ֑יו כִּ֣י לֹ֣א יִצְלַ֣ח מִזַּרְע֗וֹ אִ֚ישׁ יֹשֵׁב֙ עַל־כִּסֵּ֣א דָוִ֔ד וּמֹשֵׁ֥ל ע֖וֹד בִּיהוּדָֽה **30⁸**	*Thus says the LORD: Write this man childless, a man who shall not prosper in his days; for no man of his seed shall prosper, sitting upon the throne of David, and ruling any longer in Judah*[9].

Jeremiah – Chapter 23

ה֣וֹי רֹעִ֗ים מְאַבְּדִ֧ים וּמְפִצִ֛ים אֶת־צֹ֥אן מַרְעִיתִ֖י נְאֻם־יְהוָֽה **1¹⁰**	*Woe to the shepherds who destroy and scatter the sheep of My pasture! says the LORD*[11].
לָ֠כֵן כֹּֽה־אָמַ֨ר יְהוָ֜ה אֱלֹהֵ֣י יִשְׂרָאֵ֗ל עַֽל־הָרֹעִים֮ הָרֹעִ֣ים אֶת־עַמִּי֒ אַתֶּ֞ם הֲפִצֹתֶ֤ם אֶת־צֹאנִי֙ וַתַּדִּח֔וּם וְלֹ֥א פְקַדְתֶּ֖ם אֹתָ֑ם הִנְנִ֨י פֹקֵ֧ד עֲלֵיכֶ֛ם אֶת־רֹ֥עַ מַעַלְלֵיכֶ֖ם נְאֻם־יְהוָֽה **2¹²**	*Therefore, thus says the LORD, the God of Israel, against the shepherds that feed My people: you have scattered My flock, and drove them away, and have not taken care of them; behold, I will visit on you the evil of your deeds, says the LORD*[13].

[1] Jeremiah 22:24 - 1 Chronicles 3:16, 2 Kings 24:6-24:8, Genesis.R 85:9, Haggai 2:23, Jastrow 944a 945a, Jeremiah 22:6 22:28 13:1, Matthew 1:11-1:12, Midrash Tanchuma Balak 13, mt.Hilchot Teshuvah 7:6 7:6, Numbers.R 20:20, Pesikta de R'Kahana 24.11, Pesikta Rabbati 47:1, Song of Songs 8:6, Song of Songs.R 8:5
Jeremiah 22:24-30 - z.Mishpatim 106a

[2] Jeremiah 22:25 - 2 Kings 24:15-24:16, Jeremiah 21:7 22:28 34:20-21 14:16, Leviticus.R 19:6 19:6, Proverbs 10:24

[3] Missing in LXX

[4] Jeremiah 22:26 - 2 Chronicles 36:9-36:10, 2 Kings 24:8 24:15, Ezekiel 19:9-19:14, Isaiah 22:17, Jastrow 592a 767b, Jeremiah 15:2-15:4, Psalms of Solomon 9:1

[5] Jeremiah 22:27 - 2 Kings 25:27-25:30, Jeremiah 22:11 20:14 52:31-52:34, Psalms 86:4

[6] Jeremiah 22:28 - 1 Chronicles 3:17-3:24, 1 Samuel 5:3-5:5, 2 Samuel 5:21, 2 Timothy 2:20-2:21, Hosea 8:8 13:15, Jeremiah 14:18 15:1 17:4 22:30 24:38, Leviticus.R 10:5, Matthew 1:12-1:16, Pesikta de R'Kahana 24.11, Psalms 31:13, Romans 9:21-9:23
Jeremiah 22:28-30 - 4QJerc

[7] Jeremiah 22:29 - 2 Baruch 6:8, b.Chullin 116a, Deuteronomy 4:26 7:19 8:1, Isaiah 1:1-1:2 10:1, Jeremiah 6:19, Micah 1:2 6:1-6:2, Midrash Psalms 19:1, Pesikta Rabbati 21:4

[8] Jeremiah 22:30 - 1 Chronicles 3:16-3:17, b.Sanhedrin [Rashi] 38a, b.Sanhedrin 37b, Ein Yaakov Sanhedrin:37b, Jeremiah 10:21 12:30, Luke 1:32-1:33, Matthew 1:11-1:16, Midrash Tanchuma Balak 13, mt.Hilchot Teshuvah 7:6 7:6, Numbers.R 20:20, Pesikta de R'Kahana 24.11, Pesikta Rabbati 47:1, Psalms 94:20, Song of Songs.R 8:5, z.Vaetchanan 269b

[9] LXX *Write this man an outcast: for there shall none of his seed at all grow up to sit on the throne of David, or as a prince in Juda*

[10] Jeremiah 23:1 - Ezekiel 13:3 22:25-22:29 34:2-34:10 10:21 10:31, Isaiah 56:9-56:12, Jeremiah 2:8 2:26 10:21 12:10 22:22 23:2 23:11-23:15 25:34-25:36 2:6, John 10:10 10:12, Luke 11:42-11:52, Matthew 9:36 15:14 23:13-23:29, Micah 3:11-3:12, Sifre Devarim {Devarim} 1, Zechariah 11:5-11:7 11:15-11:17, Zephaniah 3:3-3:4

[11] LXX *Woe to the shepherds who destroy and scatter the sheep of their pasture*

[12] Jeremiah 23:2 - Exodus 8:34, Hosea 2:13, James 1:27, Jeremiah 5:9 5:29 8:12 11:22 13:21 21:12 23:34, Matthew 1:36 1:43, Micah 7:4, Sifre Devarim {Devarim} 1, z.Vaetchanan 269b

[13] LXX *Therefore, thus says the LORD against them who tend my people; You have scattered my sheep, and driven them out, and you have not visited them: behold, I will take vengeance upon you according to your evil practices*

לָכֵן כֹּה־אָמַר יְהוָה אֱלֹהֵי יִשְׂרָאֵל עַל־הָרֹעִים
הָרֹעִים אֶת־עַמִּי אַתֶּם הֲפִצֹתֶם אֶת־צֹאנִי וַתַּדִּחוּם
וְלֹא פְקַדְתֶּם אֹתָם הִנְנִי פֹקֵד עֲלֵיכֶם אֶת־רֹעַ
מַעַלְלֵיכֶם נְאֻם־יְהוָה

3[1] *And I will gather the remnant of My flock from all the countries where I have driven them, and will bring them back to their folds; and they shall be fruitful and multiply[2].*

וַהֲקִמֹתִי עֲלֵיהֶם רֹעִים וְרָעוּם וְלֹא־יִירְאוּ עוֹד
וְלֹא־יֵחַתּוּ וְלֹא יִפָּקֵדוּ נְאֻם־יְהוָה

4[3] *And I will set up shepherds over them, who shall feed them; and they shall fear no more, nor be dismayed, nor shall any be lacking, says the LORD[4].*

הִנֵּה יָמִים בָּאִים נְאֻם־יְהוָה וַהֲקִמֹתִי לְדָוִד צֶמַח
צַדִּיק וּמָלַךְ מֶלֶךְ וְהִשְׂכִּיל וְעָשָׂה מִשְׁפָּט וּצְדָקָה
בָּאָרֶץ

5[5] *Behold, the days come, says the LORD, that I will raise to David a righteous shoot, and he shall reign as king and prosper, and shall execute justice and righteousness in the land[6].*

בְּיָמָיו תִּוָּשַׁע יְהוּדָה וְיִשְׂרָאֵל יִשְׁכֹּן לָבֶטַח וְזֶה־
שְּׁמוֹ אֲשֶׁר־יִקְרְאוֹ יְהוָה צִדְקֵנוּ

6[7] *In His day, Judah will be saved and Israel shall dwell safely, and the name by which he will be called shall be the LORD our righteousness[8].*

לָכֵן הִנֵּה־יָמִים בָּאִים נְאֻם־יְהוָה וְלֹא־יֹאמְרוּ עוֹד
חַי־יְהוָה אֲשֶׁר הֶעֱלָה אֶת־בְּנֵי יִשְׂרָאֵל מֵאֶרֶץ
מִצְרָיִם

7[9] *Therefore, behold, the days come, declares the LORD, they shall no longer say, 'As the LORD lives who brought the sons of Isael from the land of Egypt[10],*

כִּי אִם־חַי־יְהוָה אֲשֶׁר הֶעֱלָה וַאֲשֶׁר הֵבִיא אֶת־זֶרַע
בֵּית יִשְׂרָאֵל מֵאֶרֶץ צָפוֹנָה וּמִכֹּל הָאֲרָצוֹת אֲשֶׁר
הִדַּחְתִּים שָׁם וְיָשְׁבוּ עַל־אַדְמָתָם

8[11] *But as the LORD lives, who brought and led the seed of the house of Israel from the land of the north and from all the lands where I drove them, and they will live on their own land[12].*

לַנְּבִאִים נִשְׁבַּר לִבִּי בְקִרְבִּי רָחֲפוּ כָּל־עַצְמוֹתַי
הָיִיתִי כְּאִישׁ שִׁכּוֹר וּכְגֶבֶר עֲבָרוֹ יָיִן מִפְּנֵי יְהוָה
וּמִפְּנֵי דִּבְרֵי קָדְשׁוֹ

9[13] *Concerning the prohets who broke my heart and caused my bones to tremble: I am like a*

---

[1] Jeremiah 23:3 - 2 Baruch 78:7, Amos 9:14-9:15, Deuteronomy 30:3-30:5, Ezekiel 11:17 34:11-34:31 12:24 12:37 37:21-37:27 39:27-39:28, Isaiah 11:11-11:16 27:12-27:13 43:5-43:6, Jeremiah 5:14 6:3 7:9 8:37, Micah 7:12, Psalms 10:47, Zechariah 10:8-10:12, Zephaniah 3:19-3:20

[2] LXX *And I will gather in the remnant of my people in every land, where I have driven them out, and will set them in their pasture; and they shall increase and be multiplied*

[3] Jeremiah 23:4 - 1 Peter 1:5 5:1-5:4, Acts 20:28-20:29, Ezekiel 34:23-34:31, Hosea 3:3-3:5, Isaiah 11:11, Jeremiah 3:14-3:15 6:10 7:11 9:26 46:27-46:28, John 6:39-6:40 10:27-10:30 17:12 18:9 21:15-21:17, Micah 5:3 5:5-5:6 7:14, Numbers 7:49, Psalms 78:70-78:72

[4] LXX *And I will raise up shepherds to them, who shall feed them: and they shall fear no more, nor be alarmed, says the LORD*

[5] Jeremiah 23:5 - Amos 9:11, compare צמח צדיק "a righteous branch" here with צמח צדקה "the branch of righteousness" at Jeremiah 33:15, Daniel 9:24, Ezekiel 17:2-17:10 17:22-17:24 10:29, Hosea 3:5, Isaiah 4:2 9:8 11:1-11:5 32:1-32:2 40:9-40:11 4:13 5:2 5:10, Jeremiah 22:3 22:15 22:30 23:6 6:3 6:9 7:28 31:32-31:39 33:14-33:16, John 1:45 1:49, Luke 1:32-1:33, Matthew 2:2, Midrash Tanchuma Korach 12, Psalms 45:5 72:1-72:2 80:16, Psalms of Solomon 17:32, Revelation 19:11, Testament of Judah 24:4, Two Letters Part II, Zechariah 3:8 6:12-6:13 9:9

[6] LXX *Behold, the days come, says the LORD, when I will raise up to David a righteous branch, and a king shall reign and understand, and shall execute judgment and righteousness on the earth*

[7] Jeremiah 23:6 - 1 Corinthians 1:30, 1 Kings 4:25, 2 Corinthians 5:21, b.Bava Batra 75b, Daniel 9:24, Deuteronomy 33:28-33:29, Ein Yaakov Bava Batra:75b, Ezekiel 34:25-34:28 37:24-37:28, Hosea 7:2:18, Isaiah 2:4 7:14 9:7 12:1-12:2 9:22 11:9 21:17 45:24-45:25 6:17, Jastrow 1263b, Jeremiah 6:10 8:37 9:16, Lamentations.R 1:51, Luke 1:71-1:74 19:9-19:10, Mas.Soferim 13:13, Matthew 1:21-1:23, Midrash Proverbs 19, Midrash Psalms 21:2, Obadiah 1:17 1:21, Pesikta de R'Kahana 22.5a, Philippians 3:9, Psalms 130:7-130:8, Romans 3:22 11:26-11:27, Sifre Devarim {Devarim} 1, Tanya Igeret Hakodesh §23, Two Letters Part II, Zechariah 2:4-2:5 3:10 10:6 14:9-14:11, Zephaniah 3:13

[8] LXX *In his days both Juda shall be saved, and Israel shall live securely: and this is his name, which the Lord shall call him, Josedec among the prophets*

[9] Jeremiah 23:7 - b.Berachot 12b, b.Sanhedrin 69b, b.Sanhedrin 87a, b.Zevachim [Rashi] 54b, Ecclesiastes.R 1:30, Ein Yaakov Berachot:12b, Ein Yaakov Kiddushin:69b, Isaiah 43:18-43:19, Jastrow 1014b, Jeremiah 16:14-16:15 23:3 31:32-31:35, y.Berachot 1:6 Jeremiah 23:7-8 - t.Berachot 1:9

[10] LXX *Therefore, behold, the days come, says the LORD, when they shall no longer say, The LORD lives, who brought up the house of Israel from the land of Egypt*

[11] Jeremiah 23:8 - Amos 9:14-9:15, b.Berachot 12b, b.Kiddushin 69b, b.Sanhedrin 87a, b.Zevachim [Rashi] 54b, Ein Yaakov Berachot:12b, Ein Yaakov Kiddushin:69b, Ezekiel 10:13 12:24 13:25 15:28, Isaiah 14:1 27:12-27:13 43:5-43:6 65:8-65:10, Jeremiah 23:3, Zephaniah 3:20

[12] LXX *but The LORD lives, who has gathered the whole seed of Israel from the north land, and from all the countries where he had driven them out, and has restored them into their own land*

[13] Jeremiah 23:9 - 2 Kings 22:19-22:20, b.Sanhedrin 96a, Daniel 8:27, Ein Yaakov Sanhedrin:96a, Ezekiel 9:4 9:6, Guide for the Perplexed 1:21, Habakkuk 3:16, Isaiah 6:5 4:1 5:9 3:21, Jeremiah 5:31 9:2 14:17-14:18 25:15-25:18, Lamentations 3:15, Psalms 60:4, Psalms of Solomon 8:5, Romans 7:9

drunken man unconscious from wine before the LORD, from the words of His Holiness[1].

10[2] For adulterers fill the land; because of this curse, the land mourns and the pastures of the wilderness are drought ridden. Their couse is evil and their strength is not gracious[3].

11[4] *For both prophet and priest are ungodly; yes, in My house I have found their wickedness, says the LORD*[5].

12[6] So, their way shall be to them as slippery places in the darkness, they shall be thrust, and fall in it; for I will bring evil on them, the year of their visitation, *says the LORD*[7].

13[8] And I have seen unseemliness in the prophets of Samaria: they prophesied by Baal, and caused My people Israel to err.

14[9] But in the prophets of Jerusalem I have seen a horrible thing: they commit adultery, and walk in lies, and they strengthen the hands of evil doers, so no one turns from his wickedness; they are all became to Me as Sodom, and its inhabitants as Gomorrah.

15[10] Therefore, thus says the LORD *of hosts concerning the prophets*[11]: Behold, I will feed them with *wormwood*[12], and make them drink the water of gall; for ungodliness has gone forth into all the land from the prophets of Jerusalem.

16[13] Thus says the LORD of hosts: do not listen to the words of the prophets who prophesy to you, they lead you to vanity; they speak a vision of their own heart, and not from the mouth of the LORD.

כִּי מְנָאֲפִים מָלְאָה הָאָרֶץ כִּי־מִפְּנֵי אָלָה אָבְלָה הָאָרֶץ יָבְשׁוּ נְאוֹת מִדְבָּר וַתְּהִי מְרוּצָתָם רָעָה וּגְבוּרָתָם לֹא־כֵן

כִּי־גַם־נָבִיא גַם־כֹּהֵן חָנֵפוּ גַּם־בְּבֵיתִי מָצָאתִי רָעָתָם נְאֻם־יְהוָה

לָכֵן יִהְיֶה דַרְכָּם לָהֶם כַּחֲלַקְלַקּוֹת בָּאֲפֵלָה יִדַּחוּ וְנָפְלוּ בָהּ כִּי־אָבִיא עֲלֵיהֶם רָעָה שְׁנַת פְּקֻדָּתָם נְאֻם־יְהוָה

וּבִנְבִיאֵי שֹׁמְרוֹן רָאִיתִי תִפְלָה הִנַּבְּאוּ בַבַּעַל וַיַּתְעוּ אֶת־עַמִּי אֶת־יִשְׂרָאֵל

וּבִנְבִאֵי יְרוּשָׁלִַם רָאִיתִי שַׁעֲרוּרָה נָאוֹף וְהָלֹךְ בַּשֶּׁקֶר וְחִזְּקוּ יְדֵי מְרֵעִים לְבִלְתִּי־שָׁבוּ אִישׁ מֵרָעָתוֹ הָיוּ־לִי כֻלָּם כִּסְדֹם וְיֹשְׁבֶיהָ כַּעֲמֹרָה

לָכֵן כֹּה־אָמַר יְהוָה צְבָאוֹת עַל־הַנְּבִאִים הִנְנִי מַאֲכִיל אוֹתָם לַעֲנָה וְהִשְׁקִתִים מֵי־רֹאשׁ כִּי מֵאֵת נְבִיאֵי יְרוּשָׁלִַם יָצְאָה חֲנֻפָּה לְכָל־הָאָרֶץ

כֹּה־אָמַר יְהוָה צְבָאוֹת אַל־תִּשְׁמְעוּ עַל־דִּבְרֵי הַנְּבִאִים הַנִּבְּאִים לָכֶם מַהְבִּלִים הֵמָּה אֶתְכֶם חֲזוֹן לִבָּם יְדַבֵּרוּ לֹא מִפִּי יְהוָה

---

[1] LXX *My heart is broken within me; all my bones are shaken: I have become as a broken-down man, and as a man overcome with wine, because of the LORD, and because of the excellence of his glory*

[2] Jeremiah 23:10 - 1 Corinthians 6:9-6:10, 1 Timothy 1:10, b.Kiddushin 13a, b.Sheviit 39ab, Ein Yaakov Kiddushin:13a, Ein Yaakov Shevuot:39a, Ezekiel 22:9-22:11, Galatians 5:19-5:21, Hebrews 13:4, Hosea 4:2-4:3, Isaiah 24:6, James 4:4, Jeremiah 5:7-5:8 7:9 9:3 9:11 12:3-12:4 14:2, Joel 1:10, Lamentations 1:2-1:4, Malachi 3:5, Psalms 11:34, Zechariah 5:3-5:4

[3] LXX *For because of these things the land mourns; the pastures of the wilderness are dried up; and their course is become evil, and so also their strength*

[4] Jeremiah 23:11 - 2 Chronicles 9:5 9:7 12:14, Ezekiel 7:20 8:5-8:6 8:11 8:16 22:25-22:26 23:39, Jeremiah 5:31 6:13 7:10-7:11 7:30 8:10 11:15 23:15 8:34, Matthew 21:12-21:13, Saadia Opinions 5:7, Zephaniah 3:4

[5] LXX *For priest and prophet are defiled; and I have seen their iniquities in my house*

[6] Jeremiah 23:12 - 1 John 2:11, Exodus 8:34, Isaiah 8:22, Jeremiah 11:23 13:16 24:44 2:27, Job 18:18, John 12:35, Jude 1:13, Micah 7:4, Pesikta Rabbati 44:5, Proverbs 4:19, Psalms 35:6 73:18

[7] Missing in LXX

[8] Jeremiah 23:13 - 1 Kings 18:18-21 18:25-28 18:40, 2 Chronicles 9:9, Derech Hashem Part III 4§10, Hosea 9:7-8, Isaiah 9:17, Jastrow 1686b, Jeremiah 2:8, Josephus Antiquities 13.9.1 m.Maaser Sheni 5:2 m.Shekalim 1:5, Lamentations.R 2:18

[9] Jeremiah 23:14 - 1 Timothy 4:2, 2 Peter 2:1-2 2:6 2:14-19, 2 Thessalonians 2:9-11, Deuteronomy 8:32, Ezekiel 13:2-4 13:16 13:22-23 16:46-52 22:25, Gates of Repentance 3.187, Genesis 13:13 18:20, Isaiah 1:9-10 41:6-7, Jeremiah 5:30-31 14:14 18:13 20:16 23:17 23:25-26 23:32 5:23, Jude 1:7, Lamentations.R 2:18, Malachi 1:1, Matthew 11:24, Micah 3:11, Revelation 11:8 19:20 21:8 22:15, Zephaniah 3:4

[10] Jeremiah 23:15 - Esther.R 1:17, Jeremiah 8:14 9:16, Lamentations 3:5 3:15 3:19, Mas.Kallah Rabbati 4:16, Matthew 3:34, Numbers.R 9:18, Psalms 69:22, Revelation 8:11, t.Sotah 4:15, z.Vaetchanan 269b

[11] Missing in LXX

[12] LXX *pain*

[13] Jeremiah 23:16 - 1 John 4:1, 2 Corinthians 11:13-15, 2 Kings 17:15, Ezekiel 13:3 13:6 13:16 13:23 22:28, Galatians 1:8-9, Jeremiah 2:5 9:21 14:14 23:21 23:26 27:9-10 27:14-15 5:8, Matthew 7:15, Micah 2:11, Proverbs 19:27, Romans 1:21, Saadia Opinions 10:3, z.Vaetchanan 269b

Hebrew	v.	English
אֹמְרִים אָמוֹר לִמְנַאֲצַי דִּבֶּר יְהוָה שָׁלוֹם יִהְיֶה לָכֶם וְכֹל הֹלֵךְ בִּשְׁרִרוּת לִבּוֹ אָמְרוּ לֹא־תָבוֹא עֲלֵיכֶם רָעָה	17[1]	They say continually to those who despise Me: 'The LORD has said: You shall have peace;' and to everyone who walks in the stubbornness of his own heart they say: 'No evil shall come upon you;'
כִּי מִי עָמַד בְּסוֹד יְהוָה וְיֵרֶא וְיִשְׁמַע אֶת־דְּבָרוֹ מִי־הִקְשִׁיב ׳דְּבָרִי׳ ״דְּבָרוֹ״ וַיִּשְׁמָע	18[2]	For who has stood in the council of the LORD, that he should perceive and hear His word? Who has listened to His word, and heard it?
הִנֵּה סַעֲרַת יְהוָה חֵמָה יָצְאָה וְסַעַר מִתְחוֹלֵל עַל רֹאשׁ רְשָׁעִים יָחוּל	19[3]	Behold, a *storm*[4] of the LORD has gone forth in fury, yes, a whirling storm; it shall *whirl*[5] upon the head of the wicked.
לֹא יָשׁוּב אַף־יְהוָה עַד־עֲשֹׂתוֹ וְעַד־הֲקִימוֹ מְזִמּוֹת לִבּוֹ בְּאַחֲרִית הַיָּמִים תִּתְבּוֹנְנוּ בָהּ בִּינָה	20[6]	The anger of the LORD shall not return, until He have executed, and until He have performed the purposes of His heart; in the end of days you shall consider it perfectly.
לֹא־שָׁלַחְתִּי אֶת־הַנְּבִאִים וְהֵם רָצוּ לֹא־דִבַּרְתִּי אֲלֵיהֶם וְהֵם נִבָּאוּ	21[7]	I have not sent these prophets, yet they ran; I have not spoken to them, yet they prophesied.
וְאִם־עָמְדוּ בְּסוֹדִי וְיַשְׁמִעוּ דְבָרַי אֶת־עַמִּי וִישִׁבוּם מִדַּרְכָּם הָרָע וּמֵרֹעַ מַעַלְלֵיהֶם	22[8]	But if they have stood in My council, then let them cause My people to hear My words, and turn them from their evil way, and from the evil of their deeds.
הַאֱלֹהֵי מִקָּרֹב אָנִי נְאֻם־יְהוָה וְלֹא אֱלֹהֵי מֵרָחֹק	23[9]	Am I a God near at hand, says the LORD, and not a God afar off?
אִם־יִסָּתֵר אִישׁ בַּמִּסְתָּרִים וַאֲנִי לֹא־אֶרְאֶנּוּ נְאֻם־יְהוָה הֲלוֹא אֶת־הַשָּׁמַיִם וְאֶת־הָאָרֶץ אֲנִי מָלֵא נְאֻם־יְהוָה	24[10]	Can any hide himself in secret places that I cannot see him? says the LORD. Do I not fill the heavens and earth? says the LORD.
שָׁמַעְתִּי אֵת אֲשֶׁר־אָמְרוּ הַנְּבִאִים הַנִּבְּאִים בִּשְׁמִי שֶׁקֶר לֵאמֹר חָלַמְתִּי חָלָמְתִּי	25[11]	I heard what the prophets said, who prophesy lies in My name, saying: 'I have dreamed, I have dreamed.'
עַד־מָתַי הֲיֵשׁ בְּלֵב הַנְּבִאִים נִבְּאֵי הַשָּׁקֶר וּנְבִיאֵי תַּרְמִת לִבָּם	26[12]	How long shall this be? Is it in the heart of the prophets who prophesy lies, and the prophets of the deceit of their own heart?

---

[1] Jeremiah 23:17 - 1 Samuel 2:30, 1 Thessalonians 4:8, 2 Samuel 12:10, Amos 9:10, Deuteronomy 5:18, Ezekiel 13:10 13:15-16 13:22, Isaiah 3:10-3:11 9:21, Jeremiah 3:17 4:10 5:12 6:14 7:24 8:11 9:15 13:10 14:13-14 18:18 28:3-9, Lamentations 2:14, Luke 10:16, Malachi 1:6, Micah 3:5 3:11, Numbers 11:20, Zechariah 10:2, Zephaniah 1:12

[2] Jeremiah 23:18 - 1 Corinthians 2:16, 1 Kings 22:24, 2 Chronicles 18:23, Amos 3:7, Isaiah 40:13-14, Jeremiah 23:22, Job 15:8-10, John 15:15, Psalms 25:14

[3] Jeremiah 23:19 - 3 Enoch 33:5, Amos 1:14, b.Chagigah 13b, Isaiah 5:25-28 21:1 16:24 66:15-16, Jastrow 273a, Jeremiah 4:11 1:32 6:23, Nahum 1:3-6, Proverbs 1:27 10:25, Psalms 58:10, Zechariah 9:14

[4] LXX *earthquake*

[5] LXX *come violently*

[6] Jeremiah 23:20 - 1 Kings 8:47, 2 Kings 23:26, Deuteronomy 31:29-31:30, Genesis 1:1, Hosea 3:4-3:5, Isaiah 14:24 7:11, Jeremiah 6:24, Proverbs 5:11-5:14 21:30, Zechariah 1:6 8:14-8:15

[7] Jeremiah 23:21 - Acts 13:4, Isaiah 6:8, Jeremiah 14:14 23:32 3:15 4:15 5:9 5:31, John 20:21, Romans 10:15, Saadia Opinions 4:4

[8] Jeremiah 23:22 - 1 Thessalonians 1:9-1:10 5:6, Acts 20:27 26:18-26:20, Ezekiel 2:7 3:17 13:22 18:30, Jeremiah 23:18 1:5 11:15 12:3, Zechariah 1:4

[9] Jeremiah 23:23 - 1 Kings 20:23 20:28, Apocryphon of Ezekiel Frag. 5, Exodus.R 27:2, Ezekiel 20:32-35, Jonah 1:3-1:4, Mekhilta de R'Shimon bar Yochai Amalek 46:2, Mekilta de R'Ishmael Amalek 3:156, Midrash Tanchuma Yitro 6, Psalms 17:5 139:1-10

[10] Jeremiah 23:24 - 1 Kings 8:27, 2 Chronicles 2:5 6:18, Amos 9:2-9:3, Daniel 4:32, Ephesians 1:23, Exodus.R 3:6 3:12 8:2 28:6 30:9, Ezekiel 8:12 9:9, Genesis 16:13, Genesis.R 4:4, Guide for the Perplexed 3:52, Iggeret HaRamban, Isaiah 5:15 9:15 18:1, Jeremiah 1:10, Job 22:13-14 24:13-16, Leviticus.R 4:8, Mekilta de R'Ishmael Beshallah 1:210, Mekilta de R'Ishmael Pisha 1:124 16:47, Mekilta de R'Ishmael Shirata 4:68, Mesillat Yesharim 25:To Acquire Yirah Cheit, Midrash Psalms 8:6 19:6 24:5 62:3, Midrash Tanchuma Bereshit 9, Midrash Tanchuma Beshallach 5, Midrash Tanchuma Bo 11, Midrash Tanchuma Naso 4 5 11, Midrash Tanchuma Reeh 15, Midrash Tanchuma Vaera 9, Midrash Tanchuma Vayakhel 7, Midrash Tanchuma Yitro 11, mt.Hilchot Deot 5:6 5:6, Numbers.R 9:9 12:3 14:22, Pesikta de R'Kahana 10.7, Pesikta Rabbati 5:7, Proverbs 15:3, Psalms 10:12 90:8 19:7 139:11-139:16 4:13, Saadia Opinions 2:13, Siman 1:1, Tanya Igeret Hakodesh §07 §20 §25, Tanya Igeret Hateshuvah §05, Tanya Likutei Aramim §41 §48, z.Bo 32b, z.Lech Lecha 84b, z.Noach 68a, z.Vayera 102a

[11] Jeremiah 23:25 - 1 Corinthians 4:5, Genesis 13:5 13:9, Hebrews 4:13, Jeremiah 8:6 13:27 14:14 16:17 23:28 23:32 5:8 5:23, Joel 3:1, Luke 12:3, Matthew 1:20, Numbers 12:6, Psalms 19:2 19:4, Revelation 2:23

[12] Jeremiah 23:26 - 1 Timothy 4:1-4:2, 2 Peter 2:13-2:16, 2 Thessalonians 2:9-2:11, 2 Timothy 4:3, Acts 13:10, Hosea 8:5, Isaiah 6:10, Jeremiah 4:14 13:27 14:14 17:9, Psalms 4:3

הַחֹשְׁבִים לְהַשְׁכִּיחַ אֶת־עַמִּי שְׁמִי בַּחֲלוֹמֹתָם אֲשֶׁר יְסַפְּרוּ אִישׁ לְרֵעֵהוּ כַּאֲשֶׁר שָׁכְחוּ אֲבוֹתָם אֶת־שְׁמִי בַּבָּעַל	27[1]	Who thinks to cause My people to forget My name by their dreams that they tell every man to his neighbor, as their fathers forgot My name for Baal.
הַנָּבִיא אֲשֶׁר־אִתּוֹ חֲלוֹם יְסַפֵּר חֲלוֹם וַאֲשֶׁר דְּבָרִי אִתּוֹ יְדַבֵּר דְּבָרִי אֱמֶת מַה־לַתֶּבֶן אֶת־הַבָּר נְאֻם־יְהוָה	28[2]	The prophet who has a dream, let him tell a dream; and he who has My word; let him speak My word faithfully. What has the straw to do with the wheat? says the LORD.
הֲלוֹא כֹה דְבָרִי כָּאֵשׁ נְאֻם־יְהוָה וּכְפַטִּישׁ יְפֹצֵץ סָלַע	29[3]	Is not My word like a fire, says the LORD; and like a *hammer*[4] breaking the rock in pieces?
לָכֵן הִנְנִי עַל־הַנְּבִאִים נְאֻם־יְהוָה מְגַנְּבֵי דְבָרַי אִישׁ מֵאֵת רֵעֵהוּ	30[5]	Therefore, behold, I am against the prophets, says the LORD, who steal My words everyone from his neighbor.
הִנְנִי עַל־הַנְּבִיאִם נְאֻם־יְהוָה הַלֹּקְחִים לְשׁוֹנָם וַיִּנְאֲמוּ נְאֻם	31[6]	Behold, I am against the prophets, *says the LORD, who use their tongues and say: 'He says[7].'*
הִנְנִי עַל־נִבְּאֵי חֲלֹמוֹת שֶׁקֶר נְאֻם־יְהוָה וַיְסַפְּרוּם וַיַּתְעוּ אֶת־עַמִּי בְּשִׁקְרֵיהֶם וּבְפַחֲזוּתָם וְאָנֹכִי לֹא־שְׁלַחְתִּים וְלֹא צִוִּיתִים וְהוֹעֵיל לֹא־יוֹעִילוּ לָעָם־הַזֶּה נְאֻם־יְהוָה	32[8]	Behold, I am against those who prophesy lying dreams, says the LORD, and tell them, and cause My people to err by their lies, and by their wantonness; yet I do not sent them, nor commanded them; nor can they profit this people at all, says the LORD.
וְכִי־יִשְׁאָלְךָ הָעָם הַזֶּה אוֹ־הַנָּבִיא אוֹ־כֹהֵן לֵאמֹר מַה־מַשָּׂא יְהוָה וְאָמַרְתָּ אֲלֵיהֶם אֶת־מַה־מַשָּׂא וְנָטַשְׁתִּי אֶתְכֶם נְאֻם־יְהוָה	33[9]	And when this people, or the prophet, or a priest, shall ask you, saying: 'What is the burden of the LORD?' Then you shall say to them: 'What burden? I will cast you off, says the LORD.'
וְהַנָּבִיא וְהַכֹּהֵן וְהָעָם אֲשֶׁר יֹאמַר מַשָּׂא יְהוָה וּפָקַדְתִּי עַל־הָאִישׁ הַהוּא וְעַל־בֵּיתוֹ	34[10]	And as for the prophet, and the priest, and the people, who say: 'The burden of the LORD,' I will punish that man and his house.
כֹּה תֹאמְרוּ אִישׁ עַל־רֵעֵהוּ וְאִישׁ אֶל־אָחִיו מֶה־עָנָה יְהוָה וּמַה־דִּבֶּר יְהוָה	35[11]	Thus you shall tell everyone to his neighbor, and everyone to his brother: 'What has the LORD answered?' and: 'What has the LORD spoken?'

[1] Jeremiah 23:27 - 2 Kings 21:3, 2 Timothy 2:17-18 3:6-8, Acts 13:8, Deuteronomy 13:2-6, Jeremiah 5:8, Judges 3:7 8:33-34 10:6, Ruth.R 4:5

[2] Jeremiah 23:28 - 1 Corinthians 3:12-3:13 4:2, 1 Timothy 1:12, 2 Corinthians 2:17, b.Berachot 55a, b.Nedarim [Ran] 8b, Ein Yaakov Berachot:55a, Luke 12:42, Matthew 24:45, Proverbs 14:5

[3] Jeremiah 23:29 - 2 Corinthians 2:16 10:4-5, Acts 2:3 2:37, b.Bava Batra [Rashbam] 79a, b.Berachot 22a, b.Chagigah 16a, b.Kiddushin 30b, b.Sanhedrin 34a, b.Shabbat 88b, b.Succah 52b, b.Taanit 4a 7a, Chibbur Yafeh 27 {118a}, Ein Yaakov Chagigah 27a, Ein Yaakov Kiddushin 30b, Ein Yaakov Sanhedrin 34a, Ein Yaakov Shabbat 88b, Ein Yaakov Sukkah 52b, Ein Yaakov Taanit:4a 6b, Guide for the Perplexed 3:49, Hebrews 4:12, Jastrow 907b 1145b, Jeremiah 5:14 20:9, John 6:63, Luke 24:32, Mekhilta de R'Shimon bar Yochai Bachodesh 51:2, Mekhilta de R'Shimon bar Yochai Shirata 34:2, Mekilta de R'Ishmael Bahodesh 7:62, Mekilta de R'Ishmael Shirata 8:40, Midrash Psalms 16:7 29:2 38:2, mt.Hilchot Berachot 1:9, mt.Hilchot Kriat Shema 4:8, Numbers.R 11:7, Pesikta de R'Kahana S3.2, Revelation 11:5, Sifre Numbers 111:3, Song of Songs.R 2:16, Tanna Devei Eliyahu 5, Tanya Igeret Hakodesh §32, y.Nedarim 3:2, y.Sheviit 3:8, z.Tetzaveh 182b, z.Yitro 83b

[4] LXX *axe*

[5] Jeremiah 23:30 - 1 Peter 3:12, Deuteronomy 18:20 5:19, Ezekiel 13:8 13:20 15:7, Jeremiah 14:14-15 20:11 20:29, Leviticus 20:3 2:17, Psalms 34:17

[6] Jeremiah 23:31 - 2 Chronicles 18:5 18:10-18:12 18:19-18:21, Isaiah 6:10, Jastrow 887b, Jeremiah 23:17, Micah 2:11

[7] LXX *who put forth prophecies of mere words, and slumber their sleep*

[8] Jeremiah 23:32 - 2 Corinthians 1:17, Deuteronomy 13:2-19 18:20, Ezekiel 13:7-18, Isaiah 3:12, Jeremiah 7:8 23:16 23:21-22 23:25 27:14-22 28:15-17 29:21-23 5:31, Lamentations 2:14, Matthew 15:14, Revelation 19:20, Zechariah 13:2-3, Zephaniah 3:4

[9] Jeremiah 23:33 - 2 Chronicles 15:2, Deuteronomy 31:17-18 32:19-20, Habakkuk 1:1, Hosea 9:12, Isaiah 13:1 14:28, Jeremiah 12:7 17:15 20:7-8 23:39-40, Malachi 1:1, Nahum 1:1, Psalms 78:59-60

[10] Jeremiah 23:34 - Lamentations 2:14, Zechariah 13:3

[11] Jeremiah 23:35 - Hebrews 8:11, Jeremiah 7:35 9:3 18:4

וּמַשָּׂא יְהוָה לֹא תִזְכְּרוּ־ע֑וֹד כִּי הַמַּשָּׂא יִהְיֶה לְאִ֖ישׁ דְּבָר֔וֹ וַהֲפַכְתֶּ֗ם אֶת־דִּבְרֵ֛י אֱלֹהִ֥ים חַיִּ֖ים יְהוָ֥ה צְבָא֖וֹת אֱלֹהֵֽינוּ	36[1]	And the burden of the LORD shall you mention no longer; for every man's own word shall be his burden; and *would you pervert the words of the living God, the LORD of hosts our God*[2]?
כֹּ֥ה תֹאמַ֖ר אֶל־הַנָּבִ֑יא מֶה־עָנָ֣ךְ יְהוָ֔ה וּמַה־דִּבֶּ֖ר יְהוָֽה	37	Thus you shall say to the prophet: 'What has the LORD answered you?' and: 'What has the LORD spoken?'
וְאִם־מַשָּׂ֣א יְהוָה֮ תֹּאמֵרוּ֒ לָכֵ֗ן כֹּ֤ה אָמַר֙ יְהוָ֔ה יַ֧עַן אֲמָרְכֶ֛ם אֶת־הַדָּבָ֥ר הַזֶּ֖ה מַשָּׂ֣א יְהוָ֑ה וָאֶשְׁלַ֤ח אֲלֵיכֶם֙ לֵאמֹ֔ר לֹ֥א תֹאמְר֖וּ מַשָּׂ֥א יְהוָֽה	38[3]	But if you say: 'The burden of the LORD;' therefore, thus says the LORD: because you say this word: 'The burden of the LORD,' and I have sent to you, saying: 'You shall not say: The burden of the LORD;'
לָכֵ֣ן הִנְנִ֔י וְנָשִׁ֥יתִי אֶתְכֶ֖ם נָשֹׁ֑א וְנָטַשְׁתִּ֣י אֶתְכֶ֗ם וְאֶת־הָעִיר֙ אֲשֶׁ֨ר נָתַ֧תִּי לָכֶ֛ם וְלַאֲבוֹתֵיכֶ֖ם מֵעַ֥ל פָּנָֽי	39[4]	Therefore, behold, I will utterly tear you out, and I will cast you off, and the city I gave to you and your fathers, away from My presence;
וְנָתַתִּ֥י עֲלֵיכֶ֖ם חֶרְפַּ֣ת עוֹלָ֑ם וּכְלִמּ֣וּת עוֹלָ֔ם אֲשֶׁ֖ר לֹ֥א תִשָּׁכֵֽחַ	40[5]	and I will bring an everlasting reproach on you, and a perpetual shame, which shall not be forgotten.

Jeremiah – Chapter 24

הִרְאַ֣נִי יְהוָה֒ וְהִנֵּ֗ה שְׁנֵי֙ דּוּדָאֵ֣י תְאֵנִ֔ים מוּעָדִ֕ים לִפְנֵ֖י הֵיכַ֣ל יְהוָ֑ה אַחֲרֵ֣י הַגְל֣וֹת נְבוּכַדְרֶאצַּ֣ר מֶֽלֶךְ־בָּבֶ֡ל אֶת־יְכָנְיָ֣הוּ בֶן־יְהוֹיָקִ֣ים מֶֽלֶךְ־יְהוּדָ֣ה וְאֶת־שָׂרֵ֣י יְהוּדָ֗ה וְאֶת־הֶחָרָ֤שׁ וְאֶת־הַמַּסְגֵּר֙ מִירֽוּשָׁלִַ֔ם וַיְבִאֵ֖ם בָּבֶֽל	1[6]	The LORD showed me, and behold two baskets of figs set before the temple of the LORD; after *Nebuchadrezzar*[7] king of Babylon had carried away captive Jeconiah the son of Jehoiakim, king of Judah, and the princes *of Judah, with the craftsmen and smiths*[8], from Jerusalem, and had brought them to Babylon.
הַדּ֣וּד אֶחָ֗ד תְּאֵנִים֙ טֹב֣וֹת מְאֹ֔ד כִּתְאֵנֵ֖י הַבַּכֻּר֑וֹת וְהַדּ֣וּד אֶחָ֗ד תְּאֵנִים֙ רָע֣וֹת מְאֹ֔ד אֲשֶׁ֥ר לֹא־תֵאָכַ֖לְנָה מֵרֹֽעַ	2[9]	One basket had very good figs, like the figs that are first ripe; and the other basket had very bad figs, which could not be eaten, they were bad.
וַיֹּ֨אמֶר יְהוָ֜ה אֵלַ֗י מָֽה־אַתָּ֤ה רֹאֶה֙ יִרְמְיָ֔הוּ וָאֹמַ֖ר תְּאֵנִ֑ים הַתְּאֵנִ֤ים הַטֹּבוֹת֙ טֹב֣וֹת מְאֹ֔ד וְהָרָעוֹת֙ רָע֣וֹת מְאֹ֔ד אֲשֶׁ֥ר לֹא־תֵאָכַ֖לְנָה מֵרֹֽעַ	3[10]	Then said the LORD to me: 'What do you see, Jeremiah?' And I said: 'Figs; the good figs, very good; and the bad, very bad, that cannot be eaten, they are so bad.'
וַיְהִ֥י דְבַר־יְהוָ֖ה אֵלַ֥י לֵאמֹֽר	4	And the word of the LORD came to me, saying:
כֹּֽה־אָמַ֤ר יְהוָה֙ אֱלֹהֵ֣י יִשְׂרָאֵ֔ל כַּתְּאֵנִ֥ים הַטֹּב֖וֹת הָאֵ֑לֶּה כֵּ֣ן אַכִּ֗יר אֶת־גָּל֤וּת יְהוּדָה֙ אֲשֶׁ֤ר שִׁלַּ֨חְתִּי֙ מִן־הַמָּק֣וֹם הַזֶּ֔ה אֶ֥רֶץ כַּשְׂדִּ֖ים לְטוֹבָֽה	5[11]	'Thus says the LORD, the God of Israel: Like these good figs, so will I regard the captives of Judah, whom I have sent from this place into the land of the Chaldeans, for good.

---

[1] Jeremiah 23:36 - 1 Samuel 17:26 17:36, 1 Thessalonians 1:9, 2 Kings 19:4, 2 Peter 2:17-18 3:16, Acts 14:15, Deuteronomy 5:26, Galatians 1:7-1:9 6:5, Guide for the Perplexed 2:29, Isaiah 3:8 28:13-14 4:22, Jeremiah 10:10, Jude 1:15-16, Luke 19:22, Matthew 12:36, Proverbs 17:20, Psalms 12:4 64:9 24:3 5:9

[2] Missing in LXX

[3] Jeremiah 23:38 - 2 Chronicles 11:13-11:14, z.Vaetchanan 269b

[4] Jeremiah 23:39 - 2 Thessalonians 1:9, Deuteronomy 8:39, Ezekiel 5:8 6:3 8:18 9:6 10:11 10:20, Genesis 6:17, Hosea 4:6 5:14 9:12-17, Isaiah 24:15 3:12, Jeremiah 7:15 23:33 32:28-35 11:17 12:31 4:3, Lamentations 5:20, Leviticus 2:28, Matthew 1:41, Proverbs 13:13, Psalms 51:12

[5] Jeremiah 23:40 - Daniel 9:16 12:2, Deuteronomy 4:37, Ezekiel 5:14-5:15, Hosea 4:7, Jeremiah 20:11 24:9 18:18 44:8-44:12

[6] Jeremiah 24:1 - 1 Samuel 13:19-13:20, 2 Chronicles 12:10, 2 Kings 24:12-24:16, Amos 3:7 7:1 7:4 7:7 8:1-8:2, b.Eruvin 21a, Deuteronomy 26:2-26:4, Ein Yaakov Eruvin:21b, Ezekiel 19:9, Jeremiah 22:24-22:28 5:2, Song of Songs.R 7:20, Zechariah 1:20 3:1

[7] LXX *Nabuchodonosor*

[8] LXX *and the artificers, and the prisoners, and the rich men*

[9] Jeremiah 24:2 - b.Eruvin 21a, Ein Yaakov Eruvin, Ezekiel 15:2-15:5, Genesis.R 22:5, Hosea 9:10, Isaiah 5:4 5:7, Jeremiah 24:5-24:10 5:17, Malachi 1:12-1:14, Matthew 5:13, Micah 7:1

[10] Jeremiah 24:3 - Amos 7:8 8:2, Jeremiah 1:11-1:14, Matthew 25:32-25:33, Zechariah 4:2 5:2 5:5-5:11

[11] Jeremiah 24:5 - 1 Corinthians 8:3, 2 Timothy 2:19, Deuteronomy 8:16, Galatians 4:9, Hebrews 12:5-12:10, John 10:27, Matthew 1:12, Midrash Tanchuma Noach 3, Nahum 1:7, Psalms 94:12-94:14 119:67 119:71, Revelation 3:19, Romans 8:28, Seder Olam 25:Nebuchadnezzar, z.Vaetchanan 269b, Zechariah 13:9

וְשַׂמְתִּ֨י עֵינִ֤י עֲלֵיהֶם֙ לְטוֹבָ֔ה וַהֲשִׁבֹתִ֖ים עַל־הָאָ֣רֶץ הַזֹּ֑את וּבְנִיתִים֙ וְלֹ֣א אֶהֱרֹ֔ס וּנְטַעְתִּ֖ים וְלֹ֥א אֶתּֽוֹשׁ׃ 6[1]

And I will set My eyes on them for good, and I will bring them back to this land; and I will build them, and not pull them down; and I will plant them, and not pluck them up.

וְנָתַתִּ֨י לָהֶ֥ם לֵב֙ לָדַ֣עַת אֹתִ֔י כִּ֥י אֲנִ֖י יְהוָ֑ה וְהָיוּ־לִ֣י לְעָ֗ם וְאָ֣נֹכִ֔י אֶהְיֶ֥ה לָהֶ֖ם לֵאלֹהִ֑ים כִּֽי־יָשֻׁ֥בוּ אֵלַ֖י בְּכָל־לִבָּֽם׃ 7[2]

And I will give them a heart to know Me, that I am the LORD; and they shall be My people, and I will be their God; for they shall return to Me with their whole heart.

וְכַתְּאֵנִים֙ הָֽרָע֔וֹת אֲשֶׁ֥ר לֹא־תֵאָכַ֖לְנָה מֵרֹ֑עַ כִּי־כֹ֣ה ׀ אָמַ֣ר יְהוָ֗ה כֵּ֣ן אֶתֵּ֞ן אֶת־צִדְקִיָּ֤הוּ מֶֽלֶךְ־יְהוּדָה֙ וְאֶת־שָׂרָ֔יו וְאֵ֣ת ׀ שְׁאֵרִ֣ית יְרוּשָׁלִַ֗ם הַנִּשְׁאָרִים֙ בָּאָ֣רֶץ הַזֹּ֔את וְהַיֹּשְׁבִ֖ים בְּאֶ֥רֶץ מִצְרָֽיִם׃ 8[3]

And as the bad figs, which cannot be eaten, they are so bad; surely thus says the LORD: So will I make Zedekiah the king of Judah, and his princes, and the remnant of Jerusalem, who remain in this land, and those who live in the land of Egypt;

וּנְתַתִּים֙ 'לִזְוָעָה' 'לְזַעֲוָה' לְרָעָ֔ה לְכֹ֖ל מַמְלְכ֣וֹת הָאָ֑רֶץ לְחֶרְפָּ֤ה וּלְמָשָׁל֙ לִשְׁנִינָ֣ה וְלִקְלָלָ֔ה בְּכָל־הַמְּקֹמ֖וֹת אֲשֶֽׁר־אַדִּיחֵ֥ם שָֽׁם׃ 9[4]

I will *make them a horror among*[5] all the kingdoms of the earth for evil; a reproach and a proverb, a taunt and a curse, in all places where I drive them.

וְשִׁלַּ֣חְתִּי בָ֗ם אֶת־הַחֶ֙רֶב֙ אֶת־הָרָעָ֣ב וְאֶת־הַדָּ֔בֶר עַד־תֻּמָּ֖ם מֵעַ֣ל הָאֲדָמָ֑ה אֲשֶׁר־נָתַ֥תִּי לָהֶ֖ם וְלַאֲבוֹתֵיהֶֽם׃ 10[6]

And I will send the *sword, the famine, and the pestilence*[7], among them, until they are consumed from off the land I gave to them *and to their fathers*[8].'

Jeremiah – Chapter 25

הַדָּבָ֞ר אֲשֶׁר־הָיָ֤ה עַֽל־יִרְמְיָ֙הוּ֙ עַל־כָּל־עַ֣ם יְהוּדָ֔ה בַּשָּׁנָה֙ הָֽרְבִעִ֔ית לִיהוֹיָקִ֖ים בֶּן־יֹאשִׁיָּ֑הוּ מֶ֖לֶךְ יְהוּדָ֑ה הִ֚יא הַשָּׁנָ֣ה הָרִֽאשֹׁנִ֔ית לִנְבֽוּכַדְרֶאצַּ֖ר מֶ֥לֶךְ בָּבֶֽל׃ 1[9]

The word that came to Jeremiah concerning all the people of Judah in the fourth year of Jehoiakim the son of Josiah, king of Judah, *that was the first year of Nebuchadrezzar king of Babylon*[10];

אֲשֶׁ֨ר דִּבֶּ֜ר יִרְמְיָ֤הוּ הַנָּבִיא֙ עַל־כָּל־עַ֣ם יְהוּדָ֔ה וְאֶ֛ל כָּל־יֹשְׁבֵ֥י יְרוּשָׁלִַ֖ם לֵאמֹֽר׃ 2[11]

Jeremiah the prophet spoke to all the people of Judah, and to all the inhabitants of Jerusalem, saying:

מִן־שְׁלֹ֣שׁ עֶשְׂרֵ֣ה שָׁנָ֗ה לְיֹאשִׁיָּ֤הוּ בֶן־אָמוֹן֙ מֶ֣לֶךְ יְהוּדָ֔ה וְעַ֖ד הַיּ֣וֹם הַזֶּ֑ה זֶ֚ה שָׁלֹ֣שׁ וְעֶשְׂרִ֣ים שָׁנָ֔ה הָיָ֥ה דְבַר־יְהוָ֖ה אֵלָ֑י וָאֲדַבֵּ֧ר אֲלֵיכֶ֛ם אַשְׁכֵּ֥ים וְדַבֵּ֖ר וְלֹ֥א שְׁמַעְתֶּֽם׃ 3[12]

From[13] the thirteenth year of Josiah the son of Amon, king of Judah, to this day, these twenty-three years, *the word of the LORD came to me, and I have spoken to you, speaking before and often; but you have not listened*[14].

[1] Jeremiah 24:6 - 1 Peter 3:12, 2 Chronicles 16:9, Deuteronomy 11:12, Ezekiel 11:15-11:17 12:24, Jeremiah 1:10 12:15 18:7-18:9 21:10 23:3 5:10 8:37 8:41 9:7 18:10, Job 33:27-33:28, Mekhilta de R'Shimon bar Yochai Shirata 36:1, Mekilta de R'Ishmael Shirata 10:10, Nehemiah 5:19, Psalms 34:16

[2] Jeremiah 24:7 - 1 Kings 8:46-8:50, 1 Samuel 7:3, 2 Chronicles 6:38, 4 Ezra 1:26, Deuteronomy 4:29-4:31 26:17-26:19 30:2-30:6, Ezekiel 11:19-11:20 36:24-36:28 13:23 13:27, Hebrews 8:10 11:16, Hosea 14:3-14:5, Isaiah 3:16 55:6-55:7, Jeremiah 3:10 29:12-29:14 6:22 31:34-31:35 32:38-32:40, Jubilees 1:12, Romans 6:17, Shepherd Mandate 12:6 6:1 9:1, Zechariah 8:8 13:9

[3] Jeremiah 24:8 - Ezekiel 12:12-16 17:11-21, Jeremiah 21:10 24:2 24:5 29:16-29:18 32:28-29 34:17-22 13:10 13:17 38:18-23 39:2-9 43:1-44:1 44:26-44:30 52:2-11, z.Vaetchanan 269b

[4] Jeremiah 24:9 - 1 Kings 9:7, 2 Chronicles 7:20, Deuteronomy 4:25 4:37 28:65-28:67, Ezekiel 5:1-5:2 5:12-5:13 1:3 2:2 36:2-36:3, Isaiah 17:15, Jeremiah 15:4 19:8 1:18 2:6 5:18 5:22 10:17 18:16 20:12 20:22, Lamentations 2:15-2:17, Psalms 44:14-44:15 109:18-109:19

[5] LXX *cause them to be dispersed into*

[6] Jeremiah 24:10 - Ezekiel 5:12-17 6:12-14 7:15 14:12-21 9:27, Isaiah 3:19, Jeremiah 5:12 9:17 14:15-16 15:2 16:4 19:7 3:8 10:17

[7] LXX *famine, and pestilence, and the sword*

[8] Missing in LXX

[9] Jeremiah 25:1 - 2 Kings 24:1-24:2, b.Arachin [Rashi] 12a, b.Megillah [Rashi] 11b, Daniel 1:1, Jeremiah 12:1 22:2

[10] Missing in LXX

[11] Jeremiah 25:2 - Jeremiah 18:11 19:14-19:15 2:2 11:13 38:1-38:2, Mark 7:14-7:15, Psalms 49:2-49:3, Seder Olam 24:Jehoachaz

[12] Jeremiah 25:3 - 1 Kings 22:3, 2 Chronicles 10:3 10:8, 2 Timothy 4:2, Exodus 8:16, Genesis 22:3, Isaiah 7:2, Jeremiah 1:2 7:13 11:7 1:4 2:5 5:19 11:13 20:4, John 8:2 8:47, Mark 1:35, Psalms 81:14

[13] LXX *In*

[14] LXX *I have both spoken to you, rising early and speaking*

וְשָׁלַ֨ח יְהֹוָ֤ה אֲלֵיכֶם֙ אֶת־כׇּל־עֲבָדָ֣יו הַנְּבִאִ֔ים הַשְׁכֵּ֖ם
וְשָׁלֹ֑חַ וְלֹ֣א שְׁמַעְתֶּ֔ם וְלֹֽא־הִטִּיתֶ֥ם אֶֽת־אׇזְנְכֶ֖ם
לִשְׁמֹֽעַ

4[1] And the LORD has sent to you all His servants the prophets, sending them *before and often*[2], but you have not listened, nor inclined your ear to hear,

לֵאמֹ֣ר שֽׁוּבוּ־נָ֡א אִ֣ישׁ מִדַּרְכּ֨וֹ הָרָעָה֙ וּמֵרֹ֣עַ
מַעַלְלֵיכֶ֔ם וּשְׁבוּ֙ עַל־הָ֣אֲדָמָ֔ה אֲשֶׁ֨ר נָתַ֧ן יְהֹוָ֛ה לָכֶ֖ם
וְלַאֲבֽוֹתֵיכֶ֑ם לְמִן־עוֹלָ֖ם וְעַד־עוֹלָֽם

5[3] saying: 'Return now everyone from his evil way, and from the evil of your deeds, and live in the land the LORD has given to you and to your fathers, forever and ever;

וְאַל־תֵּלְכ֗וּ אַחֲרֵי֙ אֱלֹהִ֣ים אֲחֵרִ֔ים לְעׇבְדָ֖ם
וּלְהִשְׁתַּחֲוֺ֣ת לָהֶ֑ם וְלֹֽא־תַכְעִ֤סוּ אוֹתִי֙ בְּמַעֲשֵׂ֣ה
יְדֵיכֶ֔ם וְלֹ֥א אָרַ֖ע לָכֶֽם

6[4] And do not go after other gods to serve them, and to worship them, and do not provoke Me with the work of your hands, and I will do you no harm.'

וְלֹֽא־שְׁמַעְתֶּ֥ם אֵלַ֖י נְאֻם־יְהֹוָ֑ה לְמַ֧עַן *הַכְעִסוּנִי* ↑הַכְעִיסֵ֛נִי↓ בְּמַעֲשֵׂ֥ה יְדֵיכֶ֖ם לְרַ֥ע לָכֶֽם

7[5] Yet you have not listened to Me, *says the LORD; so you might provoke Me with the work of your hands to your own harm*[6].

לָכֵ֗ן כֹּ֤ה אָמַר֙ יְהֹוָ֣ה צְבָא֔וֹת יַ֛עַן אֲשֶׁ֥ר לֹֽא־שְׁמַעְתֶּ֖ם
אֶת־דְּבָרָֽי

8[7] Therefore, thus says the LORD of hosts: Because you have not *heard*[8] My words,

הִנְנִ֣י שֹׁלֵ֡חַ וְלָקַחְתִּי֩ אֶת־כׇּל־מִשְׁפְּח֨וֹת צָפ֜וֹן נְאֻם־
יְהֹוָ֗ה וְאֶל־נְבֽוּכַדְרֶאצַּ֣ר מֶֽלֶךְ־בָּבֶל֮ עַבְדִּי֒ וַהֲבִ֨אֹתִ֜ים
עַל־הָאָ֤רֶץ הַזֹּאת֙ וְעַל־יֹ֣שְׁבֶ֔יהָ וְעַ֥ל כׇּל־הַגּוֹיִ֖ם
הָאֵ֣לֶּה סָבִ֑יב וְהַ֣חֲרַמְתִּ֔ים וְשַׂמְתִּים֙ לְשַׁמָּ֣ה וְלִשְׁרֵקָ֔ה
וּלְחׇרְב֖וֹת עוֹלָֽם

9[9] behold, I will send and take all the families of the north, *says the LORD, and I will send to Nebuchadrezzar the king of Babylon, My servant*[10], and will bring them against this land, and against its inhabitants, and against all these nations around; and I will utterly destroy them, and make them an astonishment, and a hissing, and perpetual desolations.

וְהַאֲבַדְתִּ֣י מֵהֶ֗ם ק֤וֹל שָׂשׂוֹן֙ וְק֣וֹל שִׂמְחָ֔ה ק֥וֹל חָתָ֖ן
וְק֣וֹל כַּלָּ֑ה ק֥וֹל רֵחַ֖יִם וְא֥וֹר נֵֽר

10[11] Moreover, I will cause the voice of mirth and the voice of gladness, the voice of the bridegroom and the voice of the bride, the sound of the millstones, and the light of the lamp to cease from among them.

וְהָֽיְתָה֙ כׇּל־הָאָ֣רֶץ הַזֹּ֔את לְחׇרְבָּ֖ה לְשַׁמָּ֑ה וְעָבְד֞וּ
הַגּוֹיִ֤ם הָאֵ֙לֶּה֙ אֶת־מֶ֣לֶךְ בָּבֶ֔ל שִׁבְעִ֖ים שָׁנָֽה

11[12] And this whole land shall be desolate, and a waste; and these nations shall serve *the king of Babylon*[13] seventy years.

וְהָיָ֣ה כִמְלֹ֣אות שִׁבְעִ֣ים שָׁנָ֗ה אֶפְקֹ֨ד עַל־מֶֽלֶךְ־בָּבֶ֤ל
וְעַל־הַגּ֤וֹי הַהוּא֙ נְאֻם־יְהֹוָ֔ה אֶת־עֲוֺנָ֖ם וְעַל־אֶ֣רֶץ
כַּשְׂדִּ֑ים וְשַׂמְתִּ֥י אֹת֖וֹ לְשִֽׁמְמ֥וֹת עוֹלָֽם

12[14] And it shall come to pass, when seventy years are accomplished, I will punish *the king of*

---

[1] Jeremiah 25:4 - 2 Chronicles 36:15-36:16, Acts 7:51-7:52, Hebrews 12:25, Jeremiah 7:24-7:26 11:7-11:10 13:10-13:11 16:12 17:23 18:12 19:15 22:21 1:3 1:7 2:5 5:19 8:33 35:14-35:15 12:31 44:4-44:5, Jubilees 1:12, Zechariah 7:11-7:12

[2] LXX *early*

[3] Jeremiah 25:5 - 2 Kings 17:13-17:14, Acts 2:20, Ezekiel 18:30 9:11, Genesis 17:8, Isaiah 55:6-55:7, James 4:8-4:10, Jeremiah 7:7 17:25 18:11 11:15, Jonah 3:8-3:10, Luke 13:3-13:5, Psalms 37:27 105:10-105:11, Seder Olam 24:Jehoachaz, Zechariah 1:4-1:5

[4] Jeremiah 25:6 - 1 Kings 11:4-11:10 14:22, 2 Kings 17:35, b.Sanhedrin [Rashi] 63a, Deuteronomy 6:14 8:19 13:3 4:14, Exodus 20:3 20:20, Jeremiah 7:6 7:9 11:15, Joshua 24:20

[5] Jeremiah 25:7 - 2 Kings 17:17 21:15, Deuteronomy 8:21, Jeremiah 7:18-19 32:30-33, Mas.Soferim 7:4, Nehemiah 9:26, Proverbs 8:36

Jeremiah 25:7-8 - 4QJerc

[6] Missing in LXX

[7] Jeremiah 25:8 - z.Vaetchanan 269b

[8] LXX *believed*

[9] Jeremiah 25:9 - 1 Kings 9:7-8, Deuteronomy 28:45-50, Ezekiel 2:7 29:18-20 30:10-11, Habakkuk 1:6-1:10, Isaiah 5:26-30 10:5 13:3 15:7 44:28-45:1, Jeremiah 1:15 5:15-16 6:1 6:22-26 8:16 18:16 24:9 25:17-26 27:3-8 16:2 19:10, Leviticus 26:25-46, Proverbs 21:1

[10] Missing in LXX

[11] Jeremiah 25:10 - b.Sanhedrin 32b, Ecclesiastes 12:2-4, Esther 3:13 7:4 8:11, Ezekiel 2:13, Hosea 2:11, Isaiah 24:7-12, Jeremiah 7:34 16:9 33:10-11, Pesikta de R'Kahana S6.1, Revelation 18:22-23

[12] Jeremiah 25:11 - 2 Chronicles 36:21-36:22, Daniel 9:2, Demetrius the Chronographer Fragment 6:1, Isaiah 23:15-23:17, Jeremiah 4:27 12:11-12:12 1:12, Josephus Antiquities 11.1.2, Sibylline Oracles 3.280, Zechariah 1:12 7:5

Jeremiah 25:11-12 - Testament of Moses 3:14

[13] LXX *among the gentiles*

[14] Jeremiah 25:12 - 2 Kings 24:1, 4Q243-245 20-23, b.Succah [Rashi] 28a, Daniel 5:1-31 9:2, Deuteronomy 32:35-42, Ezekiel 11:9, Ezra 1:1-2, Habakkuk 2:1-20, Isaiah 13:1-14 13:19 14:23 15:6 20:1-21:17 46:1-47:1, Jeremiah 23:2 1:14 5:10 50:1-46 51:24-26 51:62-64, Revelation 18:1-24

Babylon, and[1] *that nation, says the LORD, for their iniquity, and the land of the Chaldeans*[2]; *and I will make it perpetual desolations.*

וְהֵבֵאתִי׳ "וְהֵבֵאתִי" עַל־הָאָרֶץ הַהִיא אֶת־כָּל־ דְּבָרַי אֲשֶׁר־דִּבַּרְתִּי עָלֶיהָ אֵת כָּל־הַכָּתוּב בַּסֵּפֶר הַזֶּה אֲשֶׁר־נִבָּא יִרְמְיָהוּ עַל־כָּל־הַגּוֹיִם

13[3] And I will bring on that land all My words that I have pronounced against it, all that is written in this book *that Jeremiah has prophesied against all the nations*[4].

כִּי עָבְדוּ־בָם גַּם־הֵמָּה גּוֹיִם רַבִּים וּמְלָכִים גְּדוֹלִים וְשִׁלַּמְתִּי לָהֶם כְּפָעֳלָם וּכְמַעֲשֵׂה יְדֵיהֶם

14[5] *For many nations and great kings shall make bondsmen of them; and I will recompense them according to their deeds, and according to the work of their own hands*[6].

כִּי כֹה אָמַר יְהוָה אֱלֹהֵי יִשְׂרָאֵל אֵלַי קַח אֶת־כּוֹס הַיַּיִן הַחֵמָה הַזֹּאת מִיָּדִי וְהִשְׁקִיתָה אֹתוֹ אֶת־כָּל־ הַגּוֹיִם אֲשֶׁר אָנֹכִי שֹׁלֵחַ אוֹתְךָ אֲלֵיהֶם

15[7] *For thus says the LORD, the God of Israel, to me: Take this cup of the wine of fury at My hand, and cause all the nations, to whom I send you, to drink it*[8].

וְשָׁתוּ וְהִתְגֹּעֲשׁוּ וְהִתְהֹלָלוּ מִפְּנֵי הַחֶרֶב אֲשֶׁר אָנֹכִי שֹׁלֵחַ בֵּינֹתָם

16[9] *And they shall drink, and reel to and fro, and be like madmen, because of the sword I will send among them*[10].

וָאֶקַּח אֶת־הַכּוֹס מִיַּד יְהוָה וָאַשְׁקֶה אֶת־כָּל־הַגּוֹיִם אֲשֶׁר־שְׁלָחַנִי יְהוָה אֲלֵיהֶם

17[11] *Then took I the cup of the LORD's hand, and made all the nations to drink, to whom the LORD had sent me*[12]:

אֶת־יְרוּשָׁלַ͏ִם וְאֶת־עָרֵי יְהוּדָה וְאֶת־מְלָכֶיהָ אֶת־ שָׂרֶיהָ לָתֵת אֹתָם לְחָרְבָּה לְשַׁמָּה לִשְׁרֵקָה וְלִקְלָלָה כַּיּוֹם הַזֶּה

18[13] *Jerusalem, and the cities of Judah, and its kings, and its princes, to make them an appalment, an astonishment, a hissing, and a curse; as it is this day*[14];

אֶת־פַּרְעֹה מֶלֶךְ־מִצְרַיִם וְאֶת־עֲבָדָיו וְאֶת־שָׂרָיו וְאֶת־כָּל־עַמּוֹ

19[15] *Pharaoh king of Egypt, and his servants, and his princes, and all his people*[16];

וְאֵת כָּל־הָעֶרֶב וְאֵת כָּל־מַלְכֵי אֶרֶץ הָעוּץ וְאֵת כָּל־מַלְכֵי אֶרֶץ פְּלִשְׁתִּים וְאֶת־אַשְׁקְלוֹן וְאֶת־עַזָּה וְאֶת־עֶקְרוֹן וְאֵת שְׁאֵרִית אַשְׁדּוֹד

20[17] *and all the mingled people; and all the kings of the land of Uz, and all the kings of the land of the Philistines, and Ashkelon, and Gaza, and Ekron, and the remnant of Ashdod*[18];

---

[1] Missing in LXX

[2] Missing in LXX

[3] Jeremiah 25:13 - Daniel 5:28 6:1, Jeremiah 1:5 1:10, Revelation 10:11

[4] Missing in LXX

[5] Jeremiah 25:14 - Daniel 5:28, Habakkuk 2:8-2:16, Isaiah 14:2 45:1-45:3 18:6, Jeremiah 3:7 2:9 50:29-50:34 2:41 3:6 51:20-51:28 51:35-51:41, Psalms 17:8, Revelation 18:20-18:24

[6] LXX *The prophesies of Jeremias against the nations of Ælam*

[7] Jeremiah 25:15 - Genesis.R 88:4, Isaiah 3:17 3:22, Jeremiah 13:12-14 3:7, Job 21:20, Midrash Psalms 11:5 75:4, Psalms 11:7 75:9, Revelation 14:10 14:19, Sibylline Oracles Fragment 3.39, z.Vaetchanan 269b
Jeremiah 25:15-17 - 4QJerc

[8] LXX *Thus says the LORD, The bow of Ælam is broken, the chief of their power*

[9] Jeremiah 25:16 - Ezekiel 23:32-23:34, Jeremiah 1:27 3:7 3:39, Lamentations 3:15 4:21, Nahum 3:11, Revelation 14:8 14:10 16:9-16:11 18:3, y.Pesachim 10:1

[10] LXX *And I will bring on Ælam the four winds from the four corners of heaven, and I will disperse them toward all these winds; and there shall be no nation to which they shall not come—even the outcasts of Ælam*

[11] Jeremiah 25:17 - Ezekiel 19:3, Jeremiah 1:10 1:28 3:3 46:1-46:28

[12] LXX *And I will put them in fear before their enemies who seek their life; and I will bring evils upon them according to my great anger; and I will send forth my sword after them, until I have utterly destroyed them*

[13] Jeremiah 25:18 - 1 Kings 8:24, 1 Peter 4:17, 2 Kings 22:19, Amos 2:5 3:2, Daniel 9:12, Ezekiel 9:5-9:8, Ezra 9:7, Isaiah 51:17-51:22, Jeremiah 1:10 19:3-19:9 21:6-21:10 24:9 1:9 1:11 20:22, Joshua 6:18, Nehemiah 9:36, Psalms 60:4

[14] LXX *And I will set my throne in Ælam, and will send forth from there king and rulers*

[15] Jeremiah 25:19 - Ezekiel 29:1-29:21, Jeremiah 43:9-43:11 22:2 46:13-46:26, Nahum 3:8-3:10

[16] LXX *But it shall come to pass at the end of days, I will turn the captivity of Ælam, says the LORD*

[17] Jeremiah 25:20 - 1 Chronicles 1:17, 1 Samuel 6:17, 2 Baruch 42:4, Amos 1:6-1:8, Exodus 12:38, Ezekiel 25:15-25:17 6:5, Genesis 10:23 22:21, Isaiah 20:1, Jeremiah 1:24 47:1-47:7 2:37, Job 1:1, Lamentations 4:21, Nehemiah 13:23-13:27, Zechariah 9:5-9:7, Zephaniah 2:4-2:7

[18] Missing in LXX

Hebrew		English
אֶת־אֱדוֹם וְאֶת־מוֹאָב וְאֶת־בְּנֵי עַמּוֹן	21[1]	Edom, and Moab, and the children of Ammon[2];
וְאֵת כָּל־מַלְכֵי־צֹר וְאֵת כָּל־מַלְכֵי צִידוֹן וְאֵת מַלְכֵי הָאִי אֲשֶׁר בְּעֵבֶר הַיָּם	22[3]	and all the kings of Tyre, and all the kings of Zidon, and the kings of the isle beyond the sea[4];
וְאֶת־דְּדָן וְאֶת־תֵּימָא וְאֶת־בּוּז וְאֵת כָּל־קְצוּצֵי פֵאָה	23[5]	Dedan, Tema, and Buz, and all who have the corners of their hair polled[6];
וְאֵת כָּל־מַלְכֵי עֲרָב וְאֵת כָּל־מַלְכֵי הָעֶרֶב הַשֹּׁכְנִים בַּמִּדְבָּר	24[7]	and all the kings of Arabia, and all the kings of the mingled people who live in the wilderness[8];
וְאֵת כָּל־מַלְכֵי זִמְרִי וְאֵת כָּל־מַלְכֵי עֵילָם וְאֵת כָּל־מַלְכֵי מָדָי	25[9]	and all the kings of Zimri, and all the kings of Elam, and all the kings of the Medes[10];
וְאֵת כָּל־מַלְכֵי הַצָּפוֹן הַקְּרֹבִים וְהָרְחֹקִים אִישׁ אֶל־אָחִיו וְאֵת כָּל־הַמַּמְלְכוֹת הָאָרֶץ אֲשֶׁר עַל־פְּנֵי הָאֲדָמָה וּמֶלֶךְ שֵׁשַׁךְ יִשְׁתֶּה אַחֲרֵיהֶם	26[11]	and all the kings of the north, far and near, one with another; and all the kingdoms of the world, which are upon the face of the earth. And the king of Sheshach shall drink after them.[12]
וְאָמַרְתָּ אֲלֵיהֶם ס כֹּה־אָמַר יְהוָה צְבָאוֹת אֱלֹהֵי יִשְׂרָאֵל שְׁתוּ וְשִׁכְרוּ וּקְיוּ וְנִפְלוּ וְלֹא תָקוּמוּ מִפְּנֵי הַחֶרֶב אֲשֶׁר אָנֹכִי שֹׁלֵחַ בֵּינֵיכֶם	27[13]	And you shall say to them: Thus says the LORD of hosts, the God of Israel: Drink, and be drunken, and spew, and fall, and rise no more, because of the sword I will send among you[14].
וְהָיָה כִּי יְמָאֲנוּ לָקַחַת־הַכּוֹס מִיָּדְךָ לִשְׁתּוֹת וְאָמַרְתָּ אֲלֵיהֶם כֹּה אָמַר יְהוָה צְבָאוֹת שָׁתוֹ תִשְׁתּוּ	28[15]	And it shall be, if they refuse to take the cup at your hand to drink, then shall you say to them: Thus says the LORD of hosts: You shall surely drink[16].
כִּי הִנֵּה בָעִיר אֲשֶׁר נִקְרָא־שְׁמִי עָלֶיהָ אָנֹכִי מֵחֵל לְהָרַע וְאַתֶּם הִנָּקֵה תִנָּקוּ לֹא תִנָּקוּ כִּי חֶרֶב אֲנִי קֹרֵא עַל־כָּל־יֹשְׁבֵי הָאָרֶץ נְאֻם יְהוָה צְבָאוֹת	29[17]	For, lo, I begin to bring evil on the city upon which My name is called, and should you be utterly unpunished? You shall not be unpunished; for I will call for a sword on all the inhabitants of the earth, says the LORD of hosts[18].
וְאַתָּה תִּנָּבֵא אֲלֵיהֶם אֵת כָּל־הַדְּבָרִים הָאֵלֶּה וְאָמַרְתָּ אֲלֵיהֶם יְהוָה מִמָּרוֹם יִשְׁאָג וּמִמְּעוֹן קָדְשׁוֹ	30[19]	Therefore, prophesy against them all these words, and say to them: The LORD roars from

---

[1] Jeremiah 25:21 - Amos 1:11-2:3, Ezekiel 25:2-25:14 8:29 35:1-35:15, Isaiah 15:1-15:9 1:10 34:1-34:17 63:1-63:6, Jeremiah 9:27 3:3 48:1-49:22, Lamentations 4:21-4:22, Malachi 1:2-1:4, Obadiah 1:1-1:16 1:18, Psalms 17:7, Zephaniah 2:8-2:10

[2] Missing in LXX

[3] Jeremiah 25:22 - Amos 1:3-1:5 1:9-1:10, Ezekiel 26:1-26:21 28:22-28:23 5:18 8:30, Jeremiah 3:3 7:11 23:4 49:23-49:27, Joel 4:4-4:8, Zechariah 9:1-9:4

[4] Missing in LXX

[5] Jeremiah 25:23 - 1 Chronicles 1:30, Ezekiel 1:13 3:20, Genesis 10:7 22:21 1:15, Isaiah 21:13-21:14, Jeremiah 9:27 1:8 1:32, Job 6:19

[6] Missing in LXX

[7] Jeremiah 25:24 - 1 Kings 10:15, 2 Chronicles 9:14, Ezekiel 3:21 6:5, Genesis 25:2-4 25:12-16 37:25-28, Isaiah 21:13, Jeremiah 1:20 49:28-33 2:37
Jeremiah 25:24-26 - 4QJerc

[8] Missing in LXX

[9] Jeremiah 25:25 - Daniel 5:28 8:2, Ezekiel 8:24, Genesis 10:22 14:1 1:2, Isaiah 11:11 13:17 22:6, Jeremiah 49:34-49:39 3:11 3:28

[10] Missing in LXX

[11] Jeremiah 25:26 - Daniel 5:1-5:31, Ein Yaakov Shabbat:33a, Ezekiel 8:30, Habakkuk 2:16, Isaiah 13:1-13:14 47:1-47:15, Jastrow 131b, Jeremiah 1:9 1:12 50:1-50:46 3:41, Numbers.R 18:21, Revelation 18:1-18:24

[12] Missing in LXX

[13] Jeremiah 25:27 - Deuteronomy 8:42, Ezekiel 21:9-21:10 24:21-24:25, Habakkuk 2:16, Isaiah 3:21 15:6, Jeremiah 12:12 1:16 22:10 22:14 47:6-47:7 2:35, Lamentations 4:21, Sibylline Oracles 3.356, z.Vaetchanan 269b

[14] Missing in LXX

[15] Jeremiah 25:28 - Acts 4:28, Daniel 4:32, Ephesians 1:11, Isaiah 14:24-14:27 46:10-46:11, Jeremiah 4:28 1:12 3:29, Job 10:33, z.Vaetchanan 269b

[16] Missing in LXX

[17] Jeremiah 25:29 - 1 Kings 8:43, 1 Peter 4:17, Daniel 9:18-9:19, Ezekiel 9:6 14:17 14:21 14:21, Isaiah 10:12, Jeremiah 13:13 6:11 22:28 1:12, Luke 23:31, Mas.Kallah Rabbati 8:9, Midrash Psalms 48:1, Obadiah 1:16, Proverbs 11:21 11:31 17:5, Zechariah 13:7

[18] Missing in LXX

[19] Jeremiah 25:30 - 1 Kings 9:3, 2 Chronicles 6:27, Amos 1:2 3:8, b.Berachot 3a 59a, Deuteronomy 2:15, Ein Yaakov Berachot 3a, Exodus.R 29:9, Hosea 5:14 13:7-8, Isaiah 16:9 18:13, Jastrow 884a, Jeremiah 17:12 24:33, Joel 2:11-13 4:16, Mekilta de R'Ishmael Shirata 10:36, Midrash Psalms 18:12 104:25, Perek Shirah [the Camel], Psalms 11:5 58:6 78:65 12:14, Revelation 14:18-20 19:15,

יִתֵּן קוֹלוֹ שָׁאֹג יִשְׁאַג עַל־נָוֵהוּ הֵידָד כְּדֹרְכִים יַעֲנֶה אֶל כָּל־יֹשְׁבֵי הָאָרֶץ

> on high, and utters His voice from His holy habitation; He mightily roars because of His fold; He gives a shout, as they who tread the grapes, according to ancient tradition, a cipher for Babel, against all the inhabitants of the earth[1].

31[2] בָּא שָׁאוֹן עַד־קְצֵה הָאָרֶץ כִּי רִיב לַיהֹוָה בַּגּוֹיִם נִשְׁפָּט הוּא לְכָל־בָּשָׂר הָרְשָׁעִים נְתָנָם לַחֶרֶב נְאֻם־יְהֹוָה

> A noise comes to the end of the earth; for the LORD has a controversy with the nations, He pleads with all flesh; as for the wicked, He has given them to the sword, says the LORD[3].

32[4] כֹּה אָמַר יְהֹוָה צְבָאוֹת הִנֵּה רָעָה יֹצֵאת מִגּוֹי אֶל־גּוֹי וְסַעַר גָּדוֹל יֵעוֹר מִיַּרְכְּתֵי־אָרֶץ

> Thus says the LORD of hosts: Behold, evil shall go forth from nation to nation, and a great storm shall be raised up from the uttermost parts of the earth[5].

33[6] וְהָיוּ חַלְלֵי יְהֹוָה בַּיּוֹם הַהוּא מִקְצֵה הָאָרֶץ וְעַד־קְצֵה הָאָרֶץ לֹא יִסָּפְדוּ וְלֹא יֵאָסְפוּ וְלֹא יִקָּבֵרוּ לְדֹמֶן עַל־פְּנֵי הָאֲדָמָה יִהְיוּ

> And the slain of the LORD shall be on that day from one end of the earth to the other end of the earth; they shall not be lamented, nor gathered, nor buried; they shall be dung upon the face of the ground[7].

34[8] הֵילִילוּ הָרֹעִים וְזַעֲקוּ וְהִתְפַּלְּשׁוּ אַדִּירֵי הַצֹּאן כִּי־מָלְאוּ יְמֵיכֶם לִטְבוֹחַ וּתְפוֹצוֹתִיכֶם וּנְפַלְתֶּם כִּכְלִי חֶמְדָּה

> Wail, you shepherds, and cry; and wallow yourselves in the dust, you leaders of the flock; for the days of your slaughter have fully come, and I will break you in pieces, and you shall fall like a precious vessel[9].

35[10] וְאָבַד מָנוֹס מִן־הָרֹעִים וּפְלֵיטָה מֵאַדִּירֵי הַצֹּאן

> And the shepherds shall have no way to flee, nor the leaders of the flock to escape[11].

36[12] קוֹל צַעֲקַת הָרֹעִים וִילְלַת אַדִּירֵי הַצֹּאן כִּי־שֹׁדֵד יְהֹוָה אֶת־מַרְעִיתָם

> Listen! the cry of the shepherds, and the wailing of the leaders of the flock, for the LORD despoils their pasture[13].

37[14] וְנָדַמּוּ נְאוֹת הַשָּׁלוֹם מִפְּנֵי חֲרוֹן אַף־יְהֹוָה

> And the peaceable folds are brought to silence because of the fierce anger of the LORD[15].

38[16] עָזַב כַּכְּפִיר סֻכּוֹ כִּי־הָיְתָה אַרְצָם לְשַׁמָּה מִפְּנֵי חֲרוֹן הַיּוֹנָה וּמִפְּנֵי חֲרוֹן אַפּוֹ

> He has forsaken His secret, as the lion; for their land has become a waste because of the fierceness of the oppressing sword, and because of His fierce anger[17].

Siman 1:5, Testament of Moses 10:3, y.Berachot 9:2, z.Vayakhel 196a, z.Vayikra 17a, Zechariah 2:13
Jeremiah 25:30-31 - Mekhilta de R'Shimon bar Yochai Shirata 36:1

[1] Missing in LXX

[2] Jeremiah 25:31 - Ezekiel 20:35-20:36 14:22, Hosea 4:1 12:4, Isaiah 10:8 18:16, Jeremiah 21:5, Joel 4:2, Micah 6:2

[3] Missing in LXX

[4] Jeremiah 25:32 - 2 Chronicles 15:6, Isaiah 5:28 6:30 10:2 18:18, Jeremiah 23:19 6:23, Luke 21:10 21:25, Midrash Psalms 8:8, z.Vaetchanan 269b, Zephaniah 3:8

[5] Missing in LXX

[6] Jeremiah 25:33 - 2 Kings 9:37, Ezekiel 39:4-39:20, Isaiah 5:25 34:2-8 18:16, Jeremiah 8:2 9:22-23 13:12-14 16:4-7 25:18-26, Midrash Psalms 8:8 111:1, Psalms 79:3 83:11, Revelation 11:9 14:19-20 19:17-19:21, Zephaniah 2:12

[7] Missing in LXX

[8] Jeremiah 25:34 - 2 Chronicles 12:10, Amos 5:11, Daniel 11:8, Ezekiel 27:30-31 34:16-34:17 10:20, Isaiah 2:16 10:12 6:14 9:1 10:6, James 5:1-2, Jeremiah 3:19 4:8-9 6:26 19:10-12 22:28 1:12 1:23 1:36 3:7 24:26 2:27 51:20-26, Lamentations 4:21, Psalms 2:9

[9] Missing in LXX

[10] Jeremiah 25:35 - Amos 2:14 9:1-3, Daniel 5:30, Ezekiel 17:15 17:18, Isaiah 2:12-22 24:21-23, Jeremiah 8:4 10:3 14:18 14:23 24:44 52:8-11 52:24-27, Job 11:20, Revelation 6:14-17 19:19-21

[11] Missing in LXX

[12] Jeremiah 25:36 - Jeremiah 4:8 1:34

[13] Missing in LXX

[14] Jeremiah 25:37 - Isaiah 27:10-27:11 8:14

[15] Missing in LXX

[16] Jeremiah 25:38 - Amos 8:8, Hosea 5:14 11:10 13:7-8, Jeremiah 4:7 5:6 1:19 2:44, Psalms 76:3, Zechariah 2:3

[17] Missing in LXX

Jeremiah – Chapter 26[1]

בְּרֵאשִׁ֗ית מַמְלְכ֛וּת יְהוֹיָקִ֥ים בֶּן־יֹאשִׁיָּ֖הוּ מֶ֣לֶךְ יְהוּדָ֑ה הָיָה֙ הַדָּבָ֣ר הַזֶּ֔ה מֵאֵ֥ת יְהוָ֖ה לֵאמֹֽר	1[2]	In the beginning of the reign of Jehoiakim the son of Josiah, king of Judah, came this word from the LORD, saying;
כֹּ֣ה אָמַ֣ר יְהוָ֗ה עֲמֹד֮ בַּחֲצַ֣ר בֵּית־יְהוָה֒ וְדִבַּרְתָּ֞ עַל־כָּל־עָרֵ֣י יְהוּדָ֗ה הַבָּאִים֙ לְהִֽשְׁתַּחֲוֺ֣ת בֵּית־יְהוָ֔ה אֵ֚ת כָּל־הַדְּבָרִ֔ים אֲשֶׁ֥ר צִוִּיתִ֖יךָ לְדַבֵּ֣ר אֲלֵיהֶ֑ם אַל־תִּגְרַ֖ע דָּבָֽר	2[3]	'Thus says the LORD: Stand in the court of the LORD's house, and speak to all the cities of Judah, who come to worship in the LORD's house, all the words I command you to speak to them; diminish not a word.
אוּלַ֣י יִשְׁמְע֔וּ וְיָשֻׁ֕בוּ אִ֖ישׁ מִדַּרְכּ֣וֹ הָרָעָ֑ה וְנִחַמְתִּ֣י אֶל־הָרָעָ֗ה אֲשֶׁ֨ר אָנֹכִ֤י חֹשֵׁב֙ לַעֲשׂ֣וֹת לָהֶ֔ם מִפְּנֵ֖י רֹ֥עַ מַֽעַלְלֵיהֶֽם	3[4]	Perhaps they will listen, and turn from his evil way; so I may repent Me of the evil, which I intend to do to them because of the evil of their deeds.
וְאָמַרְתָּ֣ אֲלֵיהֶ֔ם כֹּ֖ה אָמַ֣ר יְהוָ֑ה אִם־לֹ֤א תִשְׁמְעוּ֙ אֵלַ֔י לָלֶ֙כֶת֙ בְּתֽוֹרָתִ֔י אֲשֶׁ֥ר נָתַ֖תִּי לִפְנֵיכֶֽם	4[5]	And you shall say to them: Thus says the LORD: If you will not listen to Me, to walk in My law, which I have set before you,
לִשְׁמֹ֗עַ עַל־דִּבְרֵ֤י עֲבָדַי֙ הַנְּבִאִ֔ים אֲשֶׁ֥ר אָנֹכִ֖י שֹׁלֵ֣חַ אֲלֵיכֶ֑ם וְהַשְׁכֵּ֥ם וְשָׁלֹ֖חַ וְלֹ֥א שְׁמַעְתֶּֽם	5[6]	to listen to the words of My servants the prophets, whom I send to you, sending them before and often, but you have not listened;
וְנָתַתִּ֛י אֶת־הַבַּ֥יִת הַזֶּ֖ה כְּשִׁלֹ֑ה וְאֶת־הָעִ֤יר הַזֹּאת֙ 'הַזֹּאתָה' "הַזֹּאת" אֶתֵּ֣ן לִקְלָלָ֔ה לְכֹ֖ל גּוֹיֵ֥י הָאָֽרֶץ	6[7]	then will I make this house like Shiloh, and will make this city a curse to all the nations of the earth.'
וַיִּשְׁמְע֛וּ הַכֹּהֲנִ֥ים וְהַנְּבִאִ֖ים וְכָל־הָעָ֑ם אֶת־יִרְמְיָ֙הוּ֙ מְדַבֵּ֣ר אֶת־הַדְּבָרִ֣ים הָאֵ֔לֶּה בְּבֵ֖ית יְהוָֽה	7[8]	So the priests and the [9]prophets and all the people heard Jeremiah speaking these words in the house of the LORD.
וַיְהִ֣י כְּכַלּ֣וֹת יִרְמְיָ֗הוּ לְדַבֵּר֮ אֵ֣ת כָּל־אֲשֶׁר־צִוָּ֣ה יְהוָה֒ לְדַבֵּ֖ר אֶל־כָּל־הָעָ֑ם וַיִּתְפְּשׂ֨וּ אֹת֜וֹ הַכֹּהֲנִ֧ים וְהַנְּבִאִ֛ים וְכָל־הָעָ֖ם לֵאמֹ֥ר מ֥וֹת תָּמֽוּת	8[10]	Now it came to pass, when Jeremiah finished speaking all the LORD commanded him to speak to all the people, that the priests and the prophets and all the people laid hold on him, saying: 'You shall surely die.
מַדּ֩וּעַ֩ נִבֵּ֨יתָ בְשֵׁם־יְהוָ֜ה לֵאמֹ֗ר כְּשִׁלוֹ֙ יִֽהְיֶה֙ הַבַּ֣יִת הַזֶּ֔ה וְהָעִ֥יר הַזֹּ֛את תֶּחֱרַ֖ב מֵאֵ֣ין יוֹשֵׁ֑ב וַיִּקָּהֵ֧ל כָּל־הָעָ֛ם אֶל־יִרְמְיָ֖הוּ בְּבֵ֥ית יְהוָֽה	9[11]	Why have you prophesied in the name of the LORD, saying: This house shall be like Shiloh, and this city shall be desolate, without an inhabitant?' And all the people gathered against Jeremiah in the house of the LORD.
וַיִּשְׁמְע֣וּ שָׂרֵ֣י יְהוּדָ֗ה אֵ֚ת הַדְּבָרִ֣ים הָאֵ֔לֶּה וַיַּעֲל֥וּ מִבֵּית־הַמֶּ֖לֶךְ בֵּ֣ית יְהוָ֑ה וַיֵּֽשְׁב֛וּ בְּפֶ֥תַח שַֽׁעַר־יְהוָ֖ה הֶחָדָֽשׁ	10[12]	When the princes of Judah heard these things, they came up from the king's house to the

---

[1] Chapter 33 in LXX

[2] Jeremiah 26:1 - 2 Chronicles 36:4-5, 2 Kings 23:34-36, b.Arachin 14a, b.Sanhedrin 103a, Ein Yaakov Arachin:17a, Ein Yaakov Sanhedrin 103a, Eupolemus 39:3, Jeremiah 1:3 1:1 3:1 11:1 12:1, Seder Olam 24:Jehoachaz

[3] Jeremiah 26:2 - 2 Chronicles 24:20-21, Acts 5:20-21 5:25 5:42 20:20 20:27, Deuteronomy 4:2 13:1, Ezekiel 3:10 3:17-21, Isaiah 58:1-2, Jeremiah 1:17 7:2 19:14 23:28 12:10 18:4, John 8:2 18:20, Luke 19:47-20:1 21:37-38, Matthew 4:20, Revelation 22:19, z.Vaetchanan 269b

[4] Jeremiah 26:3 - 1 Kings 21:27 21:29, Ezekiel 18:27-18:30, Isaiah 1:16-1:19, Jeremiah 18:7-18:10 12:3 12:7, Jonah 3:8-3:10 4:2, This is the middle verse of the book of Jeremiah per the Massorah

[5] Jeremiah 26:4 - 1 Kings 9:6, 2 Chronicles 7:19-20, Deuteronomy 4:8 4:44 11:32 28:15-68 29:17-27 31:16-18 7:20 32:15-25, Hebrews 6:18, Isaiah 1:20 42:23-25, Jeremiah 20:10, Joshua 23:15-16, Leviticus 26:14-46, Nehemiah 9:26-30, z.Vaetchanan 269b

[6] Jeremiah 26:5 - 2 Kings 9:7 17:13 17:23 24:2, Amos 3:7, Daniel 9:6-9:10, Ezekiel 14:17, Ezra 9:11, Jeremiah 7:13 7:25 11:7 25:3-4, Pesikta de R'Kahana 16.3, Pesikta Rabbati 29/30A:3, Revelation 10:7 11:18, Zechariah 1:6

[7] Jeremiah 26:6 - 1 Samuel 4:10-4:12 4:19-4:22, 2 Kings 22:19, Daniel 9:11, Isaiah 19:28 17:15, Jeremiah 7:12-7:14 24:9 1:18 5:22 18:18 44:8-44:12 20:22, Joshua 18:1, Malachi 3:24, Mas.Soferim 7:2, Psalms 78:60-78:64, Seder Olam 24:Jehoachaz

[8] Jeremiah 26:7 - Acts 4:1-4:6 5:17, Ezekiel 22:25-22:26, Jeremiah 5:31 23:11-23:15, Matthew 21:15, Micah 3:11, Zephaniah 3:4

[9] LXX adds *false*

[10] Jeremiah 26:8 - 2 Chronicles 12:16, Acts 5:33 7:52, Jeremiah 2:30 11:19-11:21 12:5-12:6 18:18 20:1-20:2 20:8-20:11, Lamentations 4:13-4:14, Matthew 21:35-21:39 22:6 23:31-23:35 26:3-26:4 26:59-26:66, Revelation 18:24 Jeremiah 26:8-24 - Josephus Antiquities 11.6.2

[11] Jeremiah 26:9 - 2 Chronicles 1:16, Acts 4:17-4:19 5:28 6:14 13:50 16:19-16:22 17:5-17:8 19:24-19:32 21:30 22:22, Amos 5:10 7:10-7:13, Isaiah 5:21 30:9-30:11, Jeremiah 9:12, John 8:20 8:59, Mark 15:11, Matthew 21:23 3:20, Micah 2:6

[12] Jeremiah 26:10 - 2 Kings 15:35, 4QJera, Ezekiel 22:6 22:27, Jeremiah 26:16-17 2:24 10:19 36:12-19 12:25 37:14-16 38:4-6

house of the LORD; and they sat in the entry of the new gate of the LORD's house[1].

11² וַיֹּאמְרוּ הַכֹּהֲנִים וְהַנְּבִיאִים אֶל־הַשָּׂרִים וְאֶל־כָּל־הָעָם לֵאמֹר מִשְׁפַּט־מָוֶת לָאִישׁ הַזֶּה כִּי נִבָּא אֶל־הָעִיר הַזֹּאת כַּאֲשֶׁר שְׁמַעְתֶּם בְּאָזְנֵיכֶם

11² Then the priests and the prophets spoke to the princes and to all the people, saying: 'This man is worthy of death; for he prophesied against this city, as you have heard with your ears.'

12³ וַיֹּאמֶר יִרְמְיָהוּ אֶל־כָּל־הַשָּׂרִים וְאֶל־כָּל־הָעָם לֵאמֹר יְהוָה שְׁלָחַנִי לְהִנָּבֵא אֶל־הַבַּיִת הַזֶּה וְאֶל־הָעִיר הַזֹּאת אֵת כָּל־הַדְּבָרִים אֲשֶׁר שְׁמַעְתֶּם

12³ Then Jeremiah spoke to all the princes and to all the people, saying: 'The LORD sent me to prophesy against this house and against this city all the words you have heard.

13⁴ וְעַתָּה הֵיטִיבוּ דַרְכֵיכֶם וּמַעַלְלֵיכֶם וְשִׁמְעוּ בְּקוֹל יְהוָה אֱלֹהֵיכֶם וְיִנָּחֵם יְהוָה אֶל־הָרָעָה אֲשֶׁר דִּבֶּר עֲלֵיכֶם

13⁴ Therefore, now amend your ways and your deeds, and listen to the voice of the LORD your God; and the LORD will repent of the evil He has pronounced against you.

14⁵ וַאֲנִי הִנְנִי בְיֶדְכֶם עֲשׂוּ־לִי כַּטּוֹב וְכַיָּשָׁר בְּעֵינֵיכֶם

14⁵ *But as for me*[6], behold, I am in your hand; do with me as is *good and right in your eyes*[7].

15⁸ אַךְ יָדֹעַ תֵּדְעוּ כִּי אִם־מְמִתִים אַתֶּם אֹתִי כִּי־דָם נָקִי אַתֶּם נֹתְנִים עֲלֵיכֶם וְאֶל־הָעִיר הַזֹּאת וְאֶל־יֹשְׁבֶיהָ כִּי בֶאֱמֶת שְׁלָחַנִי יְהוָה עֲלֵיכֶם לְדַבֵּר בְּאָזְנֵיכֶם אֵת כָּל־הַדְּבָרִים הָאֵלֶּה

15⁸ Only know for certain that, if you put me to death, you will bring innocent blood upon yourselves, and upon this city, and upon the inhabitants in it; for of a truth the LORD sent me to you to speak these words in your ears.'

16⁹ וַיֹּאמְרוּ הַשָּׂרִים וְכָל־הָעָם אֶל־הַכֹּהֲנִים וְאֶל־הַנְּבִיאִים אֵין־לָאִישׁ הַזֶּה מִשְׁפַּט־מָוֶת כִּי בְּשֵׁם יְהוָה אֱלֹהֵינוּ דִּבֶּר אֵלֵינוּ

16⁹ Then the princes and all the people said to the priests and to the[10] prophets: 'This man is not worthy of death; for he has spoken to us in the name of the LORD our God.'

17¹¹ וַיָּקֻמוּ אֲנָשִׁים מִזִּקְנֵי הָאָרֶץ וַיֹּאמְרוּ אֶל־כָּל־קְהַל הָעָם לֵאמֹר

17¹¹ Then certain elders of the land rose up, and spoke to all the assembly of the people, saying:

18¹² "מִיכָיָה" "מִיכָה" הַמּוֹרַשְׁתִּי הָיָה נִבָּא בִּימֵי חִזְקִיָּהוּ מֶלֶךְ־יְהוּדָה וַיֹּאמֶר אֶל־כָּל־עַם יְהוּדָה לֵאמֹר כֹּה־אָמַר יְהוָה צְבָאוֹת צִיּוֹן שָׂדֶה תֵחָרֵשׁ וִירוּשָׁלִַם עִיִּים תִּהְיֶה וְהַר הַבַּיִת לְבָמוֹת יָעַר

18¹² 'Micah the Morashtite prophesied in the days of Hezekiah king of Judah; and he spoke to all the people of Judah, saying: Thus says the LORD of hosts: Zion shall be plowed as a field, and Jerusalem shall become heaps, and the mountain of the house as the high places of a forest.

19¹³ הֶהָמֵת הֱמִתֻהוּ חִזְקִיָּהוּ מֶלֶךְ־יְהוּדָה וְכָל־יְהוּדָה הֲלֹא יָרֵא אֶת־יְהוָה וַיְחַל אֶת־פְּנֵי יְהוָה וַיִּנָּחֶם

19¹³ Did Hezekiah king of Judah and all Judah put him to death? Did he not fear the LORD, and entreat the favor of the LORD, and the LORD repented of the evil which He had pronounced

---

Jeremiah 26:10-13 - 4QJerc

[1] Missing in LXX

[2] Jeremiah 26:11 - Acts 6:11-6:14 22:22 24:4-24:9 25:2-25:13, Deuteronomy 18:20, Jeremiah 18:23 14:4, John 18:30 19:7, Luke 23:1-23:5, Matthew 26:66

[3] Jeremiah 26:12 - Acts 4:19 5:29, Amos 7:15-7:17, Jeremiah 1:17-1:18 19:1-19:3 2:2 2:15

[4] Jeremiah 26:13 - Deuteronomy 8:36, Exodus 8:14, Ezekiel 9:11, Hebrews 5:9, Hosea 14:3-14:6, Isaiah 1:19 7:7, Jeremiah 7:3-7:7 18:8 2:3 2:19 11:15 12:3 14:20 18:10, Joel 2:14, Jonah 3:9 4:2, Judges 2:18

[5] Jeremiah 26:14 - 2 Samuel 15:26, Daniel 3:16, Jeremiah 14:5, Joshua 9:25, Mas.Kallah Rabbati 4:14

[6] LXX *And*

[7] LXX *expedient, and as it is best for you*

[8] Jeremiah 26:15 - 1 Thessalonians 2:15-2:16, 2 Kings 24:4, Acts 7:60, Deuteronomy 19:10, Genesis 4:10 18:22, Jeremiah 2:30 2:34 7:6 22:3 22:17, Matthew 23:30-23:36 2:4 2:25, Numbers 11:33, Proverbs 6:17, Revelation 16:6

[9] Jeremiah 26:16 - Acts 5:34-5:39 23:9 23:29 1:25 26:31-26:32, Esther 4:14, Jeremiah 2:11 12:19 12:25 38:7-38:13, Luke 23:14-23:15 23:41 23:47, Mas.Kallah Rabbati 4:4, Matthew 27:23-27:24 3:54, Proverbs 16:7

[10] LXX adds *false*

[11] Jeremiah 26:17 - Acts 5:34, Micah 1:1

[12] Jeremiah 26:18 - 2 Kings 19:25, Isaiah 2:2-2:3, Jeremiah 9:12 17:3 3:37, Josephus Wars 7.2.1, Lamentations.R 5:18 5:18, Micah 1:1 3:12-4:1, Midrash Tanchuma Bereshit 9, Midrash Tanchuma Ki Tavo 4, Midrash Tanchuma Noach 3, Nehemiah 4:2, Psalms 79:1, Sifre Devarim {Ekev} 43, t.Sotah 9:5, y.Berachot 4:1, z.Vaetchanan 269b, Zechariah 8:3
Jeremiah 26:18-19 - t.Sotah 9:5

[13] Jeremiah 26:19 - 2 Chronicles 29:6-29:11 8:20 32:25-32:26 10:21, 2 Samuel 24:16, Acts 5:39, Exodus 8:14, Habakkuk 2:10, Isaiah 2:21 13:1 13:4 37:15-37:20, Jeremiah 2:3 2:15 20:7, Lamentations 4:13-4:14, Luke 3:19-3:20, Matthew 23:35 27:24-27:25, Numbers 17:3 35:33-35:34, Revelation 6:9-6:10 16:6 18:20-18:24

יְהֹוָה אֶל־הָרָעָה אֲשֶׁר־דִּבֶּר עֲלֵיהֶם וַאֲנַחְנוּ עֹשִׂים
רָעָה גְדוֹלָה עַל־נַפְשׁוֹתֵינוּ

וְגַם־אִישׁ הָיָה מִתְנַבֵּא בְּשֵׁם יְהֹוָה אוּרִיָּהוּ בֶּן־
שְׁמַעְיָהוּ מִקִּרְיַת הַיְּעָרִים וַיִּנָּבֵא עַל־הָעִיר הַזֹּאת
וְעַל־הָאָרֶץ הַזֹּאת כְּכֹל דִּבְרֵי יִרְמְיָהוּ

וַיִּשְׁמַע הַמֶּלֶךְ־יְהוֹיָקִים וְכָל־גִּבּוֹרָיו וְכָל־הַשָּׂרִים
אֶת־דְּבָרָיו וַיְבַקֵּשׁ הַמֶּלֶךְ הֲמִיתוֹ וַיִּשְׁמַע אוּרִיָּהוּ
וַיִּרָא וַיִּבְרַח וַיָּבֹא מִצְרָיִם

וַיִּשְׁלַח הַמֶּלֶךְ יְהוֹיָקִים אֲנָשִׁים מִצְרָיִם אֵת אֶלְנָתָן
בֶּן־עַכְבּוֹר וַאֲנָשִׁים אִתּוֹ אֶל־מִצְרָיִם

וַיּוֹצִיאוּ אֶת־אוּרִיָּהוּ מִמִּצְרַיִם וַיְבִאֻהוּ אֶל־הַמֶּלֶךְ
יְהוֹיָקִים וַיַּכֵּהוּ בֶּחָרֶב וַיַּשְׁלֵךְ אֶת־נִבְלָתוֹ אֶל־קִבְרֵי
בְּנֵי הָעָם

אַךְ יַד אֲחִיקָם בֶּן־שָׁפָן הָיְתָה אֶת־יִרְמְיָהוּ לְבִלְתִּי
תֵּת־אֹתוֹ בְיַד־הָעָם לַהֲמִיתוֹ

20[1] And there was also a man who prophesied in the name of the LORD, Uriah the son of Shemaiah of *Kiriath-jearim*[2]; and he prophesied against this city and against this land according to all the words of Jeremiah; and when Jehoiakim the king, with all his mighty men, and all the princes, heard his words, the king sought to put him to death; but when Uriah heard it, he was afraid, and fled, and went into Egypt;

21[3]

22[4] and Jehoiakim[5] the king sent men into Egypt, *Elnathan the son of Achbor, and certain men with him, into Egypt*[6];

23[7] and they *fetched Uriah from Egypt*[8], and brought him to Jehoiakim the king; who killed him with the sword, and cast his dead body into the graves of the children of the people.

24[9] Nevertheless the hand of Ahikam the son of Shaphan was with Jeremiah, that they should not give him into the hand of the people to put him to death.

against them? Thus we might procure great evil against our own souls.'

Jeremiah – Chapter 27[10]

בְּרֵאשִׁית מַמְלֶכֶת יְהוֹיָקִם בֶּן־יֹאושִׁיָּהוּ מֶלֶךְ יְהוּדָה
הָיָה הַדָּבָר הַזֶּה אֶל־יִרְמְיָה מֵאֵת יְהֹוָה לֵאמֹר

כֹּה־אָמַר יְהֹוָה אֵלַי עֲשֵׂה לְךָ מוֹסֵרוֹת וּמֹטוֹת
וּנְתַתָּם עַל־צַוָּארֶךָ

וְשִׁלַּחְתָּם אֶל־מֶלֶךְ אֱדוֹם וְאֶל־מֶלֶךְ מוֹאָב וְאֶל־
מֶלֶךְ בְּנֵי עַמּוֹן וְאֶל־מֶלֶךְ צֹר וְאֶל־מֶלֶךְ צִידוֹן בְּיַד
מַלְאָכִים הַבָּאִים יְרוּשָׁלַ͏ִם אֶל־צִדְקִיָּהוּ מֶלֶךְ יְהוּדָה

1[11] *In the beginning of the reign of Jehoiakim the son of Josiah, king of Judah, came this word to Jeremiah from the LORD, saying*[12]:

2[13] 'Thus says the LORD to me: Make bands and bars, and put them on your neck;

3[14] and send them to the king of *Edom*[15], and to the king of Moab, and to the king of the children of Ammon, and to the king of Tyre, and to the king of Zidon, by the hand of the messengers

---

[1] Jeremiah 26:20 - 1 Samuel 6:21 7:2, Ecclesiastes.R 3:19, Joshua 9:17 15:60 18:14, Pesikta de R'Kahana 13.12, Sifre Devarim Ekev 43
Jeremiah 26:20-23 - Leviticus.R 4:1, t.Sotah 9:5

[2] LXX *Cariathiarim*

[3] Jeremiah 26:21 - 1 Kings 19:1-19:3, 2 Chronicles 16:10, Jeremiah 12:26, Mark 6:19, Matthew 10:23 10:28 10:39 14:5 16:25-16:26, Proverbs 5:25, Psalms 119:109

[4] Jeremiah 26:22 - 2 Kings 22:12 22:14, Jeremiah 12:12 12:25, Proverbs 5:12, Psalms 12:9, Seder Olam 24:Jehoachaz, y.Sanhedrin 11:5

[5] Missing in LXX

[6] Missing in LXX

[7] Jeremiah 26:23 - 1 Thessalonians 2:15, 3Q15 11:9-11, Acts 12:1-12:3, Ezekiel 19:6, Jeremiah 2:30 22:19 2:15 12:30, Matthew 14:10 23:34-23:35, Revelation 11:7

[8] lXX *brought in there*

[9] Jeremiah 26:24 - 1 Kings 18:4, 2 Chronicles 10:20, 2 Kings 22:12-22:14 1:22, Acts 23:10 23:20-23:35 25:3-25:4 3:43, Isaiah 37:32-37:33, Jeremiah 1:18-1:19 15:15-15:21 15:14 40:5-40:7, Revelation 12:16, t.Sotah 9:5, variant בן־ of בני is found

[10] Jeremiah 27 - Derech Hashem Part III 4§08; Chapter 34 in LXX

[11] Jeremiah 27:1 - 2 Chronicles 12:11, Jeremiah 2:1 3:3 3:12 27:19-20 4:1, Ralbag Wars 6part02:2
Jeremiah 27:1-3 - 4QJerc
Jeremiah 27:1-8 - Seder Olam 24:Jehoachaz

[12] Missing in LXX

[13] Jeremiah 27:2 - 1 Kings 11:30-11:31, Amos 7:1 7:4, Ezekiel 4:1-4:5 12:1-12:28 24:3-24:12, Isaiah 20:2-20:4, Jeremiah 13:1-13:11 18:2-18:10 19:1-19:11 3:12 28:10-28:14, Midrash Tanchuma Vayera 13, z.Vaetchanan 269b

[14] Jeremiah 27:3 - 2 Chronicles 12:13, Amos 1:9-2:3, Ezekiel 17:15-17:21 25:1-25:17 5:18, Jeremiah 25:19-25:26 47:1-47:7, Lamentations.R 2:14

[15] LXX *Idumea*

who come to Jerusalem to Zedekiah king of Judah;

4[1] and give them a charge to their masters, saying: Thus says the LORD of hosts, the God of Israel: Thus shall you say to your masters:

5[2] I have made the earth, the man and the beast that are on the face of the earth by My great power and by My outstretched arm; and I give it to whom it seems right to Me.

6[3] And now have I given all these lands into the hand of Nebuchadnezzar the king of Babylon, My servant; and the beasts of the field also have I given him to serve him.

7[4] *And all the nations shall serve him, and his son, and his son's son, until the time of his own land comes; and then many nations and great kings shall make him their bondman*[5].

8[6] *And it shall come to pass, that*[7] the nation and the kingdom which will not serve the *same Nebuchadnezzar*[8] king of Babylon, and that will not put their neck under the yoke of the king of Babylon, that nation will I visit, says the LORD, *with the sword, and with the famine, and with the pestilence*[9], until I have consumed them by his hand.

9[10] *But as for you*[11], do not listen to your prophets, nor to your diviners, nor to your dreams, nor to your soothsayers, nor to your sorcerers, who speak to you, saying: You shall not serve the king of Babylon;

10[12] for they prophesy a lie to you, to remove you far from your land; and *that I should drive you out and you should perish*[13].

11[14] But the nation that shall bring their neck under the yoke of the king of Babylon, and serve him, that nation will I let remain in their own land, says the LORD; they shall till it, and live in it.'

וְצִוִּיתָ אֹתָם אֶל־אֲדֹנֵיהֶם לֵאמֹר כֹּה־אָמַר יְהוָה צְבָאוֹת אֱלֹהֵי יִשְׂרָאֵל כֹּה תֹאמְרוּ אֶל־אֲדֹנֵיכֶם

אָנֹכִי עָשִׂיתִי אֶת־הָאָרֶץ אֶת־הָאָדָם וְאֶת־הַבְּהֵמָה אֲשֶׁר עַל־פְּנֵי הָאָרֶץ בְּכֹחִי הַגָּדוֹל וּבִזְרוֹעִי הַנְּטוּיָה וּנְתַתִּיהָ לַאֲשֶׁר יָשַׁר בְּעֵינָי

וְעַתָּה אָנֹכִי נָתַתִּי אֶת־כָּל־הָאֲרָצוֹת הָאֵלֶּה בְּיַד נְבוּכַדְנֶאצַּר מֶלֶךְ־בָּבֶל עַבְדִּי וְגַם אֶת־חַיַּת הַשָּׂדֶה נָתַתִּי לוֹ לְעָבְדוֹ

וְעָבְדוּ אֹתוֹ כָּל־הַגּוֹיִם וְאֶת־בְּנוֹ וְאֶת־בֶּן־בְּנוֹ עַד בֹּא־עֵת אַרְצוֹ גַּם־הוּא וְעָבְדוּ בוֹ גּוֹיִם רַבִּים וּמְלָכִים גְּדֹלִים

וְהָיָה הַגּוֹי וְהַמַּמְלָכָה אֲשֶׁר לֹא־יַעַבְדוּ אֹתוֹ אֶת־נְבוּכַדְנֶאצַּר מֶלֶךְ־בָּבֶל וְאֵת אֲשֶׁר לֹא־יִתֵּן אֶת־צַוָּארוֹ בְּעֹל מֶלֶךְ בָּבֶל בַּחֶרֶב וּבָרָעָב וּבַדֶּבֶר אֶפְקֹד עַל־הַגּוֹי הַהוּא נְאֻם־יְהוָה עַד־תֻּמִּי אֹתָם בְּיָדוֹ

וְאַתֶּם אַל־תִּשְׁמְעוּ אֶל־נְבִיאֵיכֶם וְאֶל־קֹסְמֵיכֶם וְאֶל חֲלֹמֹתֵיכֶם וְאֶל־עֹנְנֵיכֶם וְאֶל־כַּשָּׁפֵיכֶם אֲשֶׁר־הֵם אֹמְרִים אֲלֵיכֶם לֵאמֹר לֹא תַעַבְדוּ אֶת־מֶלֶךְ בָּבֶל

כִּי שֶׁקֶר הֵם נִבְּאִים לָכֶם לְמַעַן הַרְחִיק אֶתְכֶם מֵעַל אַדְמַתְכֶם וְהִדַּחְתִּי אֶתְכֶם וַאֲבַדְתֶּם

וְהַגּוֹי אֲשֶׁר יָבִיא אֶת־צַוָּארוֹ בְּעֹל מֶלֶךְ־בָּבֶל וַעֲבָדוֹ וְהִנַּחְתִּיו עַל־אַדְמָתוֹ נְאֻם־יְהוָה וַעֲבָדָהּ וְיָשַׁב בָּהּ

---

[1] Jeremiah 27:4 - Exodus 5:1, Jeremiah 10:10 10:16 1:27 3:19, z.Vaetchanan 269b

[2] Jeremiah 27:5 - Acts 14:15 17:24, Colossians 1:16, Daniel 4:14, Deuteronomy 2:7 2:9 2:19 2:21 4:17 4:25 4:32 4:35 5:16 9:29 8:8, Exodus 20:11, Ezra 1:2, Genesis 1:29-30 9:2-3 9:6, Hebrews 1:2 1:10-11, Isaiah 40:21-26 18:5 20:24 21:12 24:13 3:13, Jeremiah 10:11-12 8:17 3:15, Job 26:5-14 38:4-41, John 1:1-1:3, Joshua 1:2-3, Psalms 6:26 115:15-16 135:10-12 136:5-9 146:5-6 148:2-5, Revelation 4:11

[3] Jeremiah 27:6 - b.Shabbat 150a, Daniel 2:37-38 5:18-19, Ezekiel 29:18-20, Isaiah 20:28, Jeremiah 21:7 24:1 1:9 4:14 19:10 51:20-23, Midrash Tanchuma Balak 1, Psalms 50:10-12

[4] Jeremiah 27:7 - 2 Chronicles 36:20-21, Daniel 5:25-31, Esther.R 3:5, Habakkuk 2:7, Isaiah 13:1 13:8-13:22 14:4-6 14:22-23 21:9 47:1-5, Jeremiah 25:11-14 50:1-46 4:31, Leviticus.R 21:7, Midrash Psalms 10:6 17:11, Psalms 37:13 137:8-9, Revelation 13:5-10 14:8 14:15-20 16:19 17:16-17 18:2-8, Zechariah 2:8-9

[5] Missing in LXX

[6] Jeremiah 27:8 - b.Megillah 11a, Ein Yaakov Megillah:11a, Ezekiel 14:21 17:19-21, Jeremiah 24:10 25:28-29 38:17-19 16:9 42:10-18 52:3-6, Leviticus.R 33:6, Mekhilta de R'Shimon bar Yochai Beshallach 21:4, Mekilta de R'Ishmael Beshallah 2:134

[7] Missing in LXX

[8] Missing in LXX

[9] Missing in LXX

[10] Jeremiah 27:9 - Acts 8:11, Deuteronomy 18:10-12 18:14, Exodus 7:11, Isaiah 8:19 47:12-14, Jeremiah 14:14 23:16 23:25 23:32 27:14-16 5:8, Joshua 13:22, Malachi 3:5, Micah 3:7, Revelation 9:21 18:23 21:8 22:15, Zechariah 10:2

[11] Missing in LXX

[12] Jeremiah 27:10 - Ein Yaakov Sanhedrin 21b, Ezekiel 14:9-11, Jeremiah 23:25 3:14 4:16 8:31, Lamentations 2:14

[13] Missing in LXX

[14] Jeremiah 27:11 - Jeremiah 21:9 3:2 3:8 3:12 14:2 40:9-12 42:10-11

וְאֶל־צִדְקִיָּה מֶלֶךְ־יְהוּדָה דִּבַּרְתִּי כְּכָל־הַדְּבָרִים הָאֵלֶּה לֵאמֹר הָבִיאוּ אֶת־צַוְּארֵיכֶם בְּעֹל מֶלֶךְ־בָּבֶל וְעִבְדוּ אֹתוֹ וְעַמּוֹ וִחְיוּ

12[1] And I spoke to Zedekiah king of Judah all these words, saying: 'Bring your necks under the yoke of the king of Babylon, and *serve him and his people, and live*[2].

לָמָּה תָמוּתוּ אַתָּה וְעַמֶּךָ בַּחֶרֶב בָּרָעָב וּבַדָּבֶר כַּאֲשֶׁר דִּבֶּר יְהוָה אֶל־הַגּוֹי אֲשֶׁר לֹא־יַעֲבֹד אֶת־מֶלֶךְ בָּבֶל

13[3] *Why will you die, you and your people, by the sword, by the famine, and by the pestilence, as the LORD spoke concerning the nation that will not serve the king of Babylon?*[4]

וְאַל־תִּשְׁמְעוּ אֶל־דִּבְרֵי הַנְּבִאִים הָאֹמְרִים אֲלֵיכֶם לֵאמֹר לֹא תַעַבְדוּ אֶת־מֶלֶךְ בָּבֶל כִּי שֶׁקֶר הֵם נִבְּאִים לָכֶם

14[5] *And do not listen to the words of the prophets who speak to you, saying: You shall not serve the king of Babylon, for they prophesy a lie*[6] *to you.*

כִּי לֹא שְׁלַחְתִּים נְאֻם־יְהוָה וְהֵם נִבְּאִים בִּשְׁמִי לַשָּׁקֶר לְמַעַן הַדִּיחִי אֶתְכֶם וַאֲבַדְתֶּם אַתֶּם וְהַנְּבִאִים הַנִּבְּאִים לָכֶם

15[7] For I have not sent them, says the LORD, and they prophesy falsely in My name; so I might drive you out, and so you might perish, you, and the prophets who prophesy to you.'

וְאֶל־הַכֹּהֲנִים וְאֶל־כָּל־הָעָם הַזֶּה דִּבַּרְתִּי לֵאמֹר כֹּה אָמַר יְהוָה אַל־תִּשְׁמְעוּ אֶל־דִּבְרֵי נְבִיאֵיכֶם הַנִּבְּאִים לָכֶם לֵאמֹר הִנֵּה כְלֵי בֵית־יְהוָה מוּשָׁבִים מִבָּבֶלָה עַתָּה מְהֵרָה כִּי שֶׁקֶר הֵמָּה נִבְּאִים לָכֶם

16[8] I also spoke to the priests and to all the people, saying: 'Thus says the LORD: do not listen to the words of your prophets who prophesy to you, saying: Behold, the vessels of the LORD's house shall now shortly be brought back from Babylon; for they prophesy a lie to you.

אַל־תִּשְׁמְעוּ אֲלֵיהֶם עִבְדוּ אֶת־מֶלֶךְ־בָּבֶל וִחְיוּ לָמָּה תִהְיֶה הָעִיר הַזֹּאת חָרְבָּה

17[9] *Do no listen to them; serve the king of Babylon, and live; why should this city become desolate?*[10]

וְאִם־נְבִאִים הֵם וְאִם־יֵשׁ דְּבַר־יְהוָה אִתָּם יִפְגְּעוּ־נָא בַּיהוָה צְבָאוֹת לְבִלְתִּי־בֹאוּ הַכֵּלִים הַנּוֹתָרִים בְּבֵית־יְהוָה וּבֵית מֶלֶךְ יְהוּדָה וּבִירוּשָׁלַ͏ִם בָּבֶלָה

18[11] But if they are prophets, and if the word of the LORD is with them, *let them now make intercession to the LORD of hosts, so the vessels that remain in the house of the LORD, and in the house of the king of Judah, and at Jerusalem, do not go to Babylon*[12].

כִּי כֹה אָמַר יְהוָה צְבָאוֹת אֶל־הָעַמֻּדִים וְעַל־הַיָּם וְעַל־הַמְּכֹנוֹת וְעַל יֶתֶר הַכֵּלִים הַנּוֹתָרִים בָּעִיר הַזֹּאת

19[13] *For thus says the LORD of hosts concerning the pillars, and concerning the sea, and concerning the bases, and concerning the remnant of the vessels that remain in this city*[14],

---

[1] Jeremiah 27:12 - 2 Chronicles 36:11-13, Ezekiel 17:11-21, Jeremiah 27:2-3 3:8 4:1 14:17, Midrash Tanchuma Vayera 13, Proverbs 1:33

[2] Missing in LXX

[3] Jeremiah 27:13 - Ezekiel 14:21 18:24 18:31 9:11, Jeremiah 24:9 3:8 14:2 14:20, Proverbs 8:36
Jeremiah 27:13-15 - 4QJerc

[4] Missing in LXX

[5] Jeremiah 27:14 - 1 John 4:1, 1 Kings 22:22-23, 2 Corinthians 11:13-15, 2 Peter 2:1-3, Ezekiel 13:6-15 13:22-23, Isaiah 28:10-13, Jeremiah 14:14 23:21 23:25 27:9-10 4:15 29:8-9, Matthew 7:15, Micah 2:11, Philippians 3:2

[6] LXX *For they prophesy unrighteous words*

[7] Jeremiah 27:15 - 2 Chronicles 18:17-22 1:16, 2 Thessalonians 2:9-12, 2 Timothy 2:17-19 4:3-4, Ezekiel 14:3-10, Jeremiah 6:13-15 8:10-12 14:15-16 20:6 23:15 23:21 3:10 28:16-17 5:9 29:22-23 29:31-32, Matthew 15:14 24:24, Micah 3:5-3:7, Revelation 13:7-8 13:12-14 19:20

[8] Jeremiah 27:16 - 2 Chronicles 36:7-36:10, 2 Kings 24:13, Daniel 1:2, Isaiah 9:16, Jeremiah 3:10 3:14 4:3, Midrash Tanchuma Vayera 13, Pesikta Rabbati 26:4, Sifre Devarim Shoftim 178, z.Vaetchanan 269b

[9] Jeremiah 27:17 - Jeremiah 7:34 27:11-13 14:17 14:23

[10] LXX *I sent them not*

[11] Jeremiah 27:18 - 1 Kings 18:24 18:26, 1 Samuel 7:8 12:19 12:23, 2 Chronicles 8:20, Ezekiel 14:14 14:18-20 22:30, Genesis 18:24-33 20:17, James 5:16-5:18, Jastrow 1133a, Jeremiah 7:16 15:1 18:20 18:2, Job 42:8-9, Malachi 1:9, Mekilta de R'Ishmael Beshallah 111:37
Jeremiah 27:18-22 - Testament of Moses 3:2

[12] LXX *let them meet me, for thus has the LORD said*

[13] Jeremiah 27:19 - 1 Kings 7:15-7:22, 2 Chronicles 4:2-4:16, 2 Kings 1:13 1:17, Ein Yaakov Ketubot:111a, Jeremiah 52:17-52:23, z.Vaetchanan 269b

[14] LXX *And as for the remaining vessels*

אֲשֶׁר לֹא־לְקָחָם נְבוּכַדְנֶאצַּר מֶלֶךְ־בָּבֶל בַּגְלוֹתוֹ אֶת־יְכוֹנְיָה" אֶת־יְכָנְיָה בֶּן־יְהוֹיָקִים מֶלֶךְ־יְהוּדָה מִירוּשָׁלַ͏ִם בָּבֶלָה וְאֵת כָּל־חֹרֵי יְהוּדָה וִירוּשָׁלָ͏ִם

20[1] that Nebuchadnezzar king of Babylon did not take, when he carried away captive Jeconiah *the son of Jehoiakim, king of Judah[2], from Jerusalem to Babylon, and all the nobles of Judah and Jerusalem[3];*

כִּי כֹה אָמַר יְהוָה צְבָאוֹת אֱלֹהֵי יִשְׂרָאֵל עַל־הַכֵּלִים הַנּוֹתָרִים בֵּית יְהוָה וּבֵית מֶלֶךְ־יְהוּדָה וִירוּשָׁלָ͏ִם

21[4] *yes, thus says the LORD of hosts, the God of Israel, concerning the vessels that remain in the house of the LORD, and in the house of the king of Judah, and at Jerusalem[5]:*

בָּבֶלָה יוּבָאוּ וְשָׁמָּה יִהְיוּ עַד יוֹם פָּקְדִי אֹתָם נְאֻם־יְהוָה וְהַעֲלִיתִים וַהֲשִׁיבֹתִים אֶל־הַמָּקוֹם הַזֶּה

22[6] They shall be carried to Babylon, and *there shall they be, until the day I remember them, says the LORD, and bring them up, and restore them to this place[7].'*

Jeremiah – Chapter 28[8]

וַיְהִי בַּשָּׁנָה הַהִיא בְּרֵאשִׁית מַמְלֶכֶת צִדְקִיָּה מֶלֶךְ־יְהוּדָה 'בִּשְׁנַת' "בַּשָּׁנָה" הָרְבִעִית בַּחֹדֶשׁ הַחֲמִישִׁי אָמַר אֵלַי חֲנַנְיָה בֶן־עַזּוּר הַנָּבִיא אֲשֶׁר מִגִּבְעוֹן בְּבֵית יְהוָה לְעֵינֵי הַכֹּהֲנִים וְכָל־הָעָם לֵאמֹר

1[9] *And it came to pass the same year, in the beginning of the reign of Zedekiah king of Judah[10],* in the fourth year, in the fifth month, *that Hananiah the son of Azzur the prophet, who was of Gibeon[11],* spoke to me in the house of the LORD, in the presence of the priests and of all the people, saying:

כֹּה־אָמַר יְהוָה צְבָאוֹת אֱלֹהֵי יִשְׂרָאֵל לֵאמֹר שָׁבַרְתִּי אֶת־עֹל מֶלֶךְ בָּבֶל

2[12] 'Thus speaks the LORD of hosts, the God of Israel, saying: I have broken the yoke of the king of Babylon.

בְּעוֹד שְׁנָתַיִם יָמִים אֲנִי מֵשִׁיב אֶל־הַמָּקוֹם הַזֶּה אֶת־כָּל־כְּלֵי בֵּית יְהוָה אֲשֶׁר לָקַח נְבוּכַדְנֶאצַּר מֶלֶךְ־בָּבֶל מִן־הַמָּקוֹם הַזֶּה וַיְבִיאֵם בָּבֶל

3[13] Within two full years will I bring back into this place all the vessels of the LORD's house, *that Nebuchadnezzar king of Babylon took away from this place, and carried them to Babylon[14];*

וְאֶת־יְכָנְיָה בֶן־יְהוֹיָקִים מֶלֶךְ־יְהוּדָה וְאֶת־כָּל־גָּלוּת יְהוּדָה הַבָּאִים בָּבֶלָה אֲנִי מֵשִׁיב אֶל־הַמָּקוֹם הַזֶּה נְאֻם־יְהוָה כִּי אֶשְׁבֹּר אֶת־עֹל מֶלֶךְ בָּבֶל

4[15] and I will bring back to this place Jeconiah the son of Jehoiakim, king of Judah, with all the captives of Judah, *who went to Babylon, says the LORD[16];* for I will break the yoke of the king of Babylon.'

---

[1] Jeremiah 27:20 - 2 Chronicles 12:10 12:18, 2 Kings 24:14-24:16, Ecclesiastes.R 12:7, Jeremiah 22:28 24:1, Lamentations.R Petichata D'Chakimei:23

[2] LXX *prisoner*

[3] Missing in LXX

[4] Jeremiah 27:21 - z.Vaetchanan 269b

[5] Missing in LXX

[6] Jeremiah 27:22 - 2 Chronicles 36:17-36:18 36:21-1:5, 2 Kings 24:13-24:17 1:13, b.Berachot 24b, b.Ketubot 111a, b.Shabbat 41a, Daniel 5:1-5:4 5:23 9:2, Ein Yaakov Berachot:24b, Ein Yaakov Ketubot:111a, Ein Yaakov Shabbat:41a, Ezra 1:7-1:8 1:11 5:13-5:15 7:9 7:19, Jeremiah 25:11-25:12 5:10 8:5 10:5 52:17-52:21, Midrash Proverbs 23, Midrash Psalms 10:7, mt.Hilchot Melachim uMichamoteihem 5:12, Proverbs 21:30, Sifre Devarim Shoftim 178

[7] LXX *says the LORD*

[8] Chapter 35 in LXX

[9] Jeremiah 28:1 - 4Q339 1:8, b.Sanhedrin 103a, Ein Yaakov Sanhedrin 103a, Isaiah 9:16, Guide for the Perplexed 2:40, Jastrow 308a, Jeremiah 23:28 3:1 3:3 3:12 4:11 12:12 13:13, Joshua 9:3, Pesikta Rabbati 26:4, Sifre Devarim Reeh 84 Sifre Devarim Shoftim 177, y.Sanhedrin 11:5, Zechariah 13:2-4
Jeremiah 28:1-3 - Seder Olam 25:Jehoiachin

[10] Missing in LXX

[11] LXX *Ananias the false prophet, the son of Azor from Gabaon*

[12] Jeremiah 28:2 - b.Sanhedrin 89a, Ein Yaakov Sanhedrin:89a, Ezekiel 13:5-16, Jeremiah 27:2-12, Micah 3:11, y.Sanhedrin 11:5

[13] Jeremiah 28:3 - 2 Chronicles 12:10, 2 Kings 24:13, b.Sotah [Rashi] 41b, Daniel 1:2, Genesis 23:9 23:28, Jeremiah 27:16-22, Psalms 90:10, y.Sanhedrin 11:5

[14] Missing in LXX

[15] Jeremiah 28:4 - 2 Kings 25:27-25:30, Genesis 3:40, Isaiah 9:5, Jeremiah 2:20 22:10 22:24 22:26-22:28 24:1 24:5 4:2 4:10 6:8 52:31-52:34, Nahum 1:13

[16] Missing in LXX

וַיֹּאמֶר יִרְמְיָה הַנָּבִיא אֶל־חֲנַנְיָה הַנָּבִיא לְעֵינֵי הַכֹּהֲנִים וּלְעֵינֵי כָל־הָעָם הָעֹמְדִים בְּבֵית יְהוָה	5[1]	Then the prophet Jeremiah said to the prophet Hananiah in the presence of the priests, and *in the presence of all the people*[2] who stood in the house of the LORD,
וַיֹּאמֶר יִרְמְיָה הַנָּבִיא אָמֵן כֵּן יַעֲשֶׂה יְהוָה יָקֵם יְהוָה אֶת־דְּבָרֶיךָ אֲשֶׁר נִבֵּאתָ לְהָשִׁיב כְּלֵי בֵית־יְהוָה וְכָל־הַגּוֹלָה מִבָּבֶל אֶל־הַמָּקוֹם הַזֶּה	6[3]	The prophet Jeremiah said: 'Amen! The LORD do so! The LORD perform your words that you have prophesied, to bring back the vessels of the LORD's house, and all those who are carried away captive, from Babylon to this place!
אַךְ־שְׁמַע־נָא הַדָּבָר הַזֶּה אֲשֶׁר אָנֹכִי דֹּבֵר בְּאָזְנֶיךָ וּבְאָזְנֵי כָּל־הָעָם	7[4]	Nevertheless hear now *this word*[5] that I speak in your ears, and in the ears of all the people:
הַנְּבִיאִים אֲשֶׁר הָיוּ לְפָנַי וּלְפָנֶיךָ מִן־הָעוֹלָם וַיִּנָּבְאוּ אֶל־אֲרָצוֹת רַבּוֹת וְעַל־מַמְלָכוֹת גְּדֹלוֹת לְמִלְחָמָה וּלְרָעָה וּלְדָבֶר	8[6]	The prophets who have been before me and before you of old prophesied against many countries, and against great kingdoms, of war, and *of evil, and of pestilence*[7].
הַנָּבִיא אֲשֶׁר יִנָּבֵא לְשָׁלוֹם בְּבֹא דְּבַר הַנָּבִיא יִוָּדַע הַנָּבִיא אֲשֶׁר־שְׁלָחוֹ יְהוָה בֶּאֱמֶת	9[8]	The prophet who prophesies of peace, when the word *of the prophet*[9] shall come to pass, then shall the prophet be known, the LORD has truly sent him.'
וַיִּקַּח חֲנַנְיָה הַנָּבִיא אֶת־הַמּוֹטָה מֵעַל צַוַּאר יִרְמְיָה הַנָּבִיא וַיִּשְׁבְּרֵהוּ	10[10]	Then Hananiah *the prophet*[11] took the bar from off the prophet Jeremiah's neck, and broke it.
וַיֹּאמֶר חֲנַנְיָה לְעֵינֵי כָל־הָעָם לֵאמֹר כֹּה אָמַר יְהוָה כָּכָה אֶשְׁבֹּר אֶת־עֹל נְבֻכַדְנֶאצַּר מֶלֶךְ־בָּבֶל בְּעוֹד שְׁנָתַיִם יָמִים מֵעַל צַוַּאר כָּל־הַגּוֹיִם וַיֵּלֶךְ יִרְמְיָה הַנָּבִיא לְדַרְכּוֹ	11[12]	And Hananiah spoke in the presence of all the people, saying: 'Thus says the LORD: so will I break the yoke of *Nebuchadnezzar king of Babylon from off the neck of all the nations within two full years*[13].' And the prophet Jeremiah went his way.
וַיְהִי דְבַר־יְהוָה אֶל־יִרְמְיָה אַחֲרֵי שְׁבוֹר חֲנַנְיָה הַנָּבִיא אֶת־הַמּוֹטָה מֵעַל צַוַּאר יִרְמְיָה הַנָּבִיא לֵאמֹר	12[14]	Then the word of the LORD came to Jeremiah, after that Hananiah the prophet had broken the bar from off the neck of the prophet Jeremiah, saying:
הָלוֹךְ וְאָמַרְתָּ אֶל־חֲנַנְיָה לֵאמֹר כֹּה אָמַר יְהוָה מוֹטֹת עֵץ שָׁבָרְתָּ וְעָשִׂיתָ תַחְתֵּיהֶן מֹטוֹת בַּרְזֶל	13[15]	'Go, and tell Hananiah, saying: Thus says the LORD: you have broken the bars of wood; but you shall make in their stead bars of iron.

[1] Jeremiah 28:5 - Jeremiah 7:2 19:14 2:2 4:1

[2] Missing in LXX

[3] Jeremiah 28:6 - 1 Chronicles 16:36, 1 Corinthians 14:16, 1 Kings 1:36, b.Sheviit 36a, b.Sotah 41b, 2 Corinthians 1:20, Deuteronomy 27:15-26, Ein Yaakov Sotah 41b, Jeremiah 11:5 17:16 18:20 4:3, Matthew 6:13 4:20, Numbers 5:22, Psalms 41:14 72:19 89:53 10:48, Revelation 1:18 3:14 5:14 19:4 22:20-21

[4] Jeremiah 28:7 - 1 Kings 22:28, mt.Hilchot Yesodei haTorah 10:4

[5] LXX *the word of the LORD*

[6] Jeremiah 28:8 - 1 Kings 14:7-14:15 17:1 21:18-21:24 22:8, 1 Samuel 2:27-2:32 3:11-3:14, Amos 1:2, Deuteronomy 4:26-4:27 28:15-28:68 29:17-29:27 31:16-31:17 32:15-32:44, Isaiah 5:1-5:8 6:9-6:12 13:18 24:1-24:23, Joel 1:2-1:20 4:1-4:11, Leviticus 26:14-26:46, Micah 3:8-3:12, Nahum 1:1-1:3

[7] Missing in LXX

[8] Jeremiah 28:9 - Deuteronomy 18:22, Ezekiel 13:10-13:16, Jeremiah 4:10 6:14 8:11 14:13, Midrash Tanchuma Vayera 13, mt.Hilchot Yesodei haTorah 10:4, Ralbag Wars 6part02:13

[9] Missing in LXX

[10] Jeremiah 28:10 - 1 Kings 22:11 22:24-22:25, Jeremiah 3:2 4:2 4:4 36:23-36:24, Malachi 3:13, Midrash Tanchuma Vayera 13

[11] Missing in LXX

[12] Jeremiah 28:11 - 1 Kings 13:18 22:6 22:11-22:12, 2 Chronicles 18:10 18:22-18:23, Ezekiel 13:7, Jeremiah 14:14 23:17 27:2-27:12 28:2-28:4 5:9, Midrash Tanchuma Vayera 13, Proverbs 14:7, z.Vaetchanan 269b

[13] LXX *the king of Babylon from the necks of all the nations*

[14] Jeremiah 28:12 - 1 Chronicles 17:3, 2 Kings 20:4, Daniel 9:2, Jeremiah 1:2 5:30

[15] Jeremiah 28:13 - Jeremiah 3:15, Lamentations 2:14, Psalms 5:8, Sifre Devarim {Haazinu Hashamayim} 318, Sifre Devarim Nitzavim 318, z.Vaetchanan 269b

כִּי כֹה־אָמַר יְהוָה צְבָאוֹת אֱלֹהֵי יִשְׂרָאֵל עֹל בַּרְזֶל נָתַתִּי עַל־צַוַּאר כָּל־הַגּוֹיִם הָאֵלֶּה לַעֲבֹד אֶת־נְבֻכַדְנֶאצַּר מֶלֶךְ־בָּבֶל וַעֲבָדֻהוּ וְגַם אֶת־חַיַּת הַשָּׂדֶה נָתַתִּי לוֹ

14[1] For thus says the LORD of hosts, the God of Israel: I have put a yoke of iron upon the neck of all these nations, so they may serve Nebuchadnezzar king of Babylon; and they shall serve him; and I have given him the beasts of the field also.'

וַיֹּאמֶר יִרְמְיָה הַנָּבִיא אֶל־חֲנַנְיָה הַנָּבִיא שְׁמַע־נָא חֲנַנְיָה לֹא־שְׁלָחֲךָ יְהוָה וְאַתָּה הִבְטַחְתָּ אֶת־הָעָם הַזֶּה עַל־שָׁקֶר

15[2] Then said the prophet Jeremiah to Hananiah the prophet: 'Hear now, Hananiah; the LORD has not sent you; but you make this people trust in a lie.

לָכֵן כֹּה אָמַר יְהוָה הִנְנִי מְשַׁלֵּחֲךָ מֵעַל פְּנֵי הָאֲדָמָה הַשָּׁנָה אַתָּה מֵת כִּי־סָרָה דִבַּרְתָּ אֶל־יְהוָה

16[3] 'Therefore, thus says the LORD: Behold, I will send you away from off the face of the earth; this year you shall die, because you have spoken perversion against the LORD.'

וַיָּמָת חֲנַנְיָה הַנָּבִיא בַּשָּׁנָה הַהִיא בַּחֹדֶשׁ הַשְּׁבִיעִי

17[4] So *Hananiah the prophet died the same year*[5] in the seventh month.

Jeremiah – Chapter 29[6]

וְאֵלֶּה דִּבְרֵי הַסֵּפֶר אֲשֶׁר שָׁלַח יִרְמְיָה הַנָּבִיא מִירוּשָׁלָםִ אֶל־יֶתֶר זִקְנֵי הַגּוֹלָה וְאֶל־הַכֹּהֲנִים וְאֶל־הַנְּבִיאִים וְאֶל־כָּל־הָעָם אֲשֶׁר הֶגְלָה נְבוּכַדְנֶאצַּר מִירוּשָׁלַםִ בָּבֶלָה

1[7] Now these are the words of the *letter*[8] that Jeremiah the prophet sent from Jerusalem to the remnant of the elders of the captivity, and to the priests, and to the [9]prophets, and *to all the people, whom Nebuchadnezzar carried away captive from Jerusalem to Babylon*[10],

אַחֲרֵי צֵאת יְכָנְיָה־הַמֶּלֶךְ וְהַגְּבִירָה וְהַסָּרִיסִים שָׂרֵי יְהוּדָה וִירוּשָׁלַםִ וְהֶחָרָשׁ וְהַמַּסְגֵּר מִירוּשָׁלָםִ

2[11] after that Jeconiah the king, and the queen mother, and the officers, and the princes of Judah and Jerusalem, and the craftsmen, and the smiths, departed from Jerusalem;

בְּיַד אֶלְעָשָׂה בֶן־שָׁפָן וּגְמַרְיָה בֶּן־חִלְקִיָּה אֲשֶׁר שָׁלַח צִדְקִיָּה מֶלֶךְ־יְהוּדָה אֶל־נְבוּכַדְנֶאצַּר מֶלֶךְ בָּבֶל בָּבֶלָה לֵאמֹר

3[12] by the hand of Elasah the son of Shaphan, and Gemariah the son of Hilkiah, whom Zedekiah king of Judah sent to Babylon to Nebuchadnezzar king of Babylon, saying:

כֹּה אָמַר יְהוָה צְבָאוֹת אֱלֹהֵי יִשְׂרָאֵל לְכָל־הַגּוֹלָה אֲשֶׁר־הִגְלֵיתִי מִירוּשָׁלַםִ בָּבֶלָה

4[13] Thus says the LORD of hosts, the God of Israel, to all the captivity, whom I have caused to be carried away captive from Jerusalem to Babylon:

[1] Jeremiah 28:14 - Daniel 2:38, Deuteronomy 4:20 4:48, Ecclesiastes.R 3:13, Isaiah 14:4-14:6, Jeremiah 25:9-25:26 3:4 27:6-27:7 16:4, Revelation 17:12-17:13, z.Vaetchanan 269b

[2] Jeremiah 28:15 - 1 Kings 22:23, Ezekiel 13:2-13:3 13:22 22:28, Jeremiah 14:14-14:15 20:6 23:21 3:15 4:11 5:23 29:31-29:32, Lamentations 2:14, Zechariah 13:3
Jeremiah 28:15-17 - Midrash Tanchuma Vayera 13

[3] Jeremiah 28:16 - 1 Kings 13:34, Acts 13:8-11, Amos 9:8, Deuteronomy 6:15 13:6-11, Exodus 8:12, Ezekiel 13:11-12, Genesis 7:4, Jeremiah 20:6 4:3 5:32, mt.Hilchot Yesodei haTorah 10:1, Numbers 14:37 16:28-35 5:32, Sifre Devarim Shoftim 189, y.Sanhedrin 11:5, z.Vaetchanan 269b
Jeremiah 28:16-17 - Pesikta Rabbati 26:4

[4] Jeremiah 28:17 - Isaiah 44:25-44:26, Seder Olam 25:Jehoiachin, y.Sanhedrin 11:5, Zechariah 1:6

[5] LXX *he*

[6] Chapter 36 in LXX

[7] Jeremiah 29:1 - 2 Chronicles 30:1-30:6, 2 Corinthians 7:8, Acts 15:23, Esther 9:20, Galatians 6:11, Hebrews 13:22, Jeremiah 24:1-7 4:4 29:25-29, Revelation 2:1-2:3, y.Nedarim 6:8, y.Sanhedrin 1:2
Jeremiah 29:1-10 - Seder Olam 25:Jeremiah

[8] LXX *book*

[9] LXX adds *false*

[10] LXX *a letter to Babylon for the captivity, and to all the people*

[11] Jeremiah 29:2 - 2 Chronicles 36:9-36:10, 2 Kings 9:32 20:18 24:12-24:16, Daniel 1:3-1:21, Jastrow 592a, Jeremiah 22:24-22:28 24:1 3:20 4:4, Midrash Tanchuma Shemini 9, Numbers.R 23:14

[12] Jeremiah 29:3 - 1 Chronicles 5:39, 2 Chronicles 10:20, 2 Kings 22:8 22:12, Ezekiel 8:11, Jeremiah 2:24 12:25 15:14

[13] Jeremiah 29:4 - Amos 3:6, Isaiah 5:5 10:5-10:6 21:7 59:1-59:2, Jeremiah 24:5, z.Vaetchanan 269b

בְּנוּ בָתִּים וְשֵׁבוּ וְנִטְעוּ גַנּוֹת וְאִכְלוּ אֶת־פִּרְיָן

5[1] Build houses, and live in them, and plant gardens, and eat its fruit;

קְחוּ נָשִׁים וְהוֹלִידוּ בָּנִים וּבָנוֹת וּקְחוּ לִבְנֵיכֶם נָשִׁים וְאֶת־בְּנוֹתֵיכֶם תְּנוּ לַאֲנָשִׁים וְתֵלַדְנָה בָּנִים וּבָנוֹת וּרְבוּ־שָׁם וְאַל־תִּמְעָטוּ

6[2] take wives, and sire sons and daughters; and take wives for your sons, and give your daughters to husbands, so they may bear sons and daughters; and multiply there, and do not become diminished.

וְדִרְשׁוּ אֶת־שְׁלוֹם הָעִיר אֲשֶׁר הִגְלֵיתִי אֶתְכֶם שָׁמָּה וְהִתְפַּלְלוּ בַעֲדָהּ אֶל־יְהוָה כִּי בִשְׁלוֹמָהּ יִהְיֶה לָכֶם שָׁלוֹם

7[3] And seek the peace of the city where I have caused you to be carried away captive, and pray to the LORD for it; for in its peace you shall have peace.

כִּי כֹה אָמַר יְהוָה צְבָאוֹת אֱלֹהֵי יִשְׂרָאֵל אַל־יַשִּׁיאוּ לָכֶם נְבִיאֵיכֶם אֲשֶׁר־בְּקִרְבְּכֶם וְקֹסְמֵיכֶם וְאַל־תִּשְׁמְעוּ אֶל־חֲלֹמֹתֵיכֶם אֲשֶׁר אַתֶּם מַחְלְמִים

8[4] For thus says the LORD of hosts, the God of Israel: Do not let your prophets who are in your midst, and your diviners, beguile you, nor listen you to your dreams which you cause to be dreamed.

כִּי בְשֶׁקֶר הֵם נִבְּאִים לָכֶם בִּשְׁמִי לֹא שְׁלַחְתִּים נְאֻם־יְהוָה

9[5] For they prophesy falsely to you in My name; I have not sent them, says the LORD.

כִּי־כֹה אָמַר יְהוָה כִּי לְפִי מְלֹאת לְבָבֶל שִׁבְעִים שָׁנָה אֶפְקֹד אֶתְכֶם וַהֲקִמֹתִי עֲלֵיכֶם אֶת־דְּבָרִי הַטּוֹב לְהָשִׁיב אֶתְכֶם אֶל־הַמָּקוֹם הַזֶּה

10[6] For thus says the LORD: After seventy years are accomplished for Babylon, I will remember you, and perform My good word toward you, in causing you to return to this place.

כִּי אָנֹכִי יָדַעְתִּי אֶת־הַמַּחֲשָׁבֹת אֲשֶׁר אָנֹכִי חֹשֵׁב עֲלֵיכֶם נְאֻם־יְהוָה מַחְשְׁבוֹת שָׁלוֹם וְלֹא לְרָעָה לָתֵת לָכֶם אַחֲרִית וְתִקְוָה

11[7] For I know the thoughts I think toward you, says the LORD, thoughts of peace, and not of evil, to give you a future and a hope.

וּקְרָאתֶם אֹתִי וַהֲלַכְתֶּם וְהִתְפַּלַּלְתֶּם אֵלָי וְשָׁמַעְתִּי אֲלֵיכֶם

12[8] And you shall call on Me, and go, and pray to Me, and I will listen to you.

וּבִקַּשְׁתֶּם אֹתִי וּמְצָאתֶם כִּי תִדְרְשֻׁנִי בְּכָל־לְבַבְכֶם

13[9] *And you shall seek Me, and find Me, when[10]* you search for Me with all your heart.

וְנִמְצֵאתִי לָכֶם נְאֻם־יְהוָה וְשַׁבְתִּי 'אֶת־שְׁבִיתְכֶם' "אֶת־שְׁבוּתְכֶם" וְקִבַּצְתִּי אֶתְכֶם מִכָּל־הַגּוֹיִם וּמִכָּל־הַמְּקוֹמוֹת אֲשֶׁר הִדַּחְתִּי אֶתְכֶם שָׁם נְאֻם־

14[11] And I will be found in you, *says the LORD, and I will turn your captivity, and gather you from all the nations, and from all the places where I have driven you, says the LORD; and I*

---

[1] Jeremiah 29:5 - b.Bava Batra 29a, Ezekiel 4:26, Jeremiah 5:10 5:28

[2] Jeremiah 29:6 - 1 Corinthians 7:36-38, 1 Timothy 5:14, b.Ketubot 52b, b.Kiddushin [Rashi] 51b 64b, b.Kiddushin 30b, b.Makkot [Rashi] 8b, Ecclesiastes.R 9:8, Genesis 1:27-28 9:7 21:21 24:3-4 24:51 24:60 28:1-4 5:19 10:4, Jeremiah 16:2-4, Judges 1:12-14 12:9 14:2, Midrash Psalms 7:17, mt.Hilchot Ishut 20:1

[3] Jeremiah 29:7 - 1 Peter 2:13-2:17, 1 Timothy 2:1-2:2, Daniel 4:16 4:24 6:5-6:6, Ezra 6:10 7:23, Midrash Tanchuma Vayigash 10, Romans 13:1 13:5, variant הגליתי of הגילת is found

[4] Jeremiah 29:8 - 2 Corinthians 11:13-11:15, 2 John 1:7-1:9, 2 Peter 2:2-2:3, 2 Thessalonians 2:3 2:9-2:11, 2 Timothy 3:13, Ephesians 4:14 5:6, Jeremiah 5:31 14:14 23:21 23:27 3:9 27:14-27:15 4:15, Luke 6:26 21:8, Mark 13:5-13:6 13:22-13:23, Matthew 24:4-24:5 24:24, Micah 2:11, Revelation 13:14 19:20, Romans 16:18, z.Vaetchanan 269b, Zechariah 13:4

[5] Jeremiah 29:9 - Jeremiah 3:15 5:23 5:31

[6] Jeremiah 29:10 - 2 Chronicles 36:21-1:2, b.Megillah [Rashi] 22a, b.Megillah 11b, b.Yoma [Rashi] 9b, Daniel 9:2, Demetrius the Chronographer Fragment 6:1, Jeremiah 24:6-24:7 1:12 3:7 3:22 32:42-32:44, Josephus Antiquities 11.1.2, Midrash Psalms 7:17 10:7, Pirkei de R'Eliezer 49, Saadia Opinions 8:4, Seder Olam 29:Seventy Years, Song of Songs.R 3:6, Testament of Moses 3:14, y.Sanhedrin 11:5, z.Vaetchanan 269b, Zechariah 7:5, Zephaniah 2:7

[7] Jeremiah 29:11 - Amos 9:8-9:15, b.Taanit 29b, Ezekiel 34:11-34:31 36:1-36:37 39:1-39:29, Genesis.R 10:9, Hosea 2:14-2:25 3:5 14:4-14:11, Isaiah 40:1-40:31 46:10-46:11 55:8-55:12, Jeremiah 3:12-3:19 30:18-30:22 31:2-31:34, Job 23:13, Joel 3:1-3:5, Lamentations 3:26, Micah 4:12 5:5-5:8 7:14-7:20, Midrash Psalms 7:17, Psalms 33:11 40:6, Revelation 14:8-14:14, Sifre Devarim Reeh 53, Zechariah 1:6 8:14-8:15 9:9-9:17 12:5-12:10 14:20-14:21, Zephaniah 3:14-3:20

[8] Jeremiah 29:12 - Daniel 9:3-19, Ezekiel 12:37, Isaiah 6:19 17:24, Jeremiah 7:10 9:3, Matthew 7:7-8, Midrash Psalms 61:1, Nehemiah 2:4-20, Psalms 10:18 50:15 102:17-18 1:19, Zechariah 13:9

[9] Jeremiah 29:13 - 1 Kings 2:4 8:47-8:50, 2 Chronicles 6:37-6:39 22:9 7:21, 2 Kings 23:3, Acts 8:36, Amos 5:4-5:6, Deuteronomy 4:29-4:31 30:1-30:20, Hosea 5:15-6:3, Isaiah 55:6-55:7, Jeremiah 3:10 24:7, Joel 2:12, Jubilees 1:15, Leviticus 26:40-26:45, Luke 11:9-11:10, Matthew 7:7, Midrash Psalms 28:2 61:1, Psalms 32:6 91:15 23:2 23:10 119:145 23:58 119:69, Zephaniah 2:1-2:3

[10] Missing in LXX

[11] Jeremiah 29:14 - 1 Chronicles 4:9, 2 Chronicles 15:12-15, Amos 9:14, Deuteronomy 4:7 6:3, Ezekiel 11:16-20 34:1-31 36:1-38, Isaiah 21:19 7:6, Jeremiah 16:14-15 23:3-8 24:5-7 6:3 6:10 31:9-15 32:37-44 33:7-26 46:27-28 50:4-5 50:19-20 50:33-34 3:10, Micah 4:12, Psalms 32:6 46:2 6:1 6:4, Romans 10:20, Zephaniah 3:20

יְהוָה וַהֲשִׁבֹתִי אֶתְכֶם אֶל־הַמָּקוֹם אֲשֶׁר־הִגְלֵיתִי
אֶתְכֶם מִשָּׁם

כִּי אֲמַרְתֶּם הֵקִים לָנוּ יְהוָה נְבִאִים בָּבֶלָה

כִּי־כֹה׀ אָמַר יְהוָה אֶל־הַמֶּלֶךְ הַיּוֹשֵׁב אֶל־כִּסֵּא דָוִד
וְאֶל־כָּל־הָעָם הַיּוֹשֵׁב בָּעִיר הַזֹּאת אֲחֵיכֶם אֲשֶׁר
לֹא־יָצְאוּ אִתְּכֶם בַּגּוֹלָה

כֹּה אָמַר יְהוָה צְבָאוֹת הִנְנִי מְשַׁלֵּחַ בָּם אֶת־הַחֶרֶב
אֶת־הָרָעָב וְאֶת־הַדָּבֶר וְנָתַתִּי אוֹתָם כַּתְּאֵנִים
הַשֹּׁעָרִים אֲשֶׁר לֹא־תֵאָכַלְנָה מֵרֹעַ

וְרָדַפְתִּי אַחֲרֵיהֶם בַּחֶרֶב בָּרָעָב וּבַדָּבֶר וּנְתַתִּים
'לִזְוָעָה' 'לְזַעֲוָה' לְכֹל מַמְלְכוֹת הָאָרֶץ לְאָלָה
וּלְשַׁמָּה וְלִשְׁרֵקָה וּלְחֶרְפָּה בְּכָל־הַגּוֹיִם אֲשֶׁר־
הִדַּחְתִּים שָׁם

תַּחַת אֲשֶׁר־לֹא־שָׁמְעוּ אֶל־דְּבָרַי נְאֻם־יְהוָה אֲשֶׁר
שָׁלַחְתִּי אֲלֵיהֶם אֶת־עֲבָדַי הַנְּבִאִים הַשְׁכֵּם וְשָׁלֹחַ
וְלֹא שְׁמַעְתֶּם נְאֻם־יְהוָה

וְאַתֶּם שִׁמְעוּ דְבַר־יְהוָה כָּל־הַגּוֹלָה אֲשֶׁר־שִׁלַּחְתִּי
מִירוּשָׁלַ͏ִם בָּבֶלָה

כֹּה־אָמַר יְהוָה צְבָאוֹת אֱלֹהֵי יִשְׂרָאֵל אֶל־אַחְאָב
בֶּן־קוֹלָיָה וְאֶל־צִדְקִיָּהוּ בֶן־מַעֲשֵׂיָה הַנִּבְּאִים לָכֶם
בִּשְׁמִי שָׁקֶר הִנְנִי נֹתֵן אֹתָם בְּיַד נְבוּכַדְרֶאצַּר
מֶלֶךְ־בָּבֶל וְהִכָּם לְעֵינֵיכֶם

וְלֻקַּח מֵהֶם קְלָלָה לְכֹל גָּלוּת יְהוּדָה אֲשֶׁר בְּבָבֶל
לֵאמֹר יְשִׂמְךָ יְהוָה כְּצִדְקִיָּהוּ וּכְאֶחָב אֲשֶׁר־קָלָם
מֶלֶךְ־בָּבֶל בָּאֵשׁ

15[2] For you have said: 'The LORD has raised up prophets in Babylon.'

16[3] *For thus says the LORD concerning the king who sits on the throne of David, and concerning all the people who live in this city, your brethren who are not gone forth with you into captivity;* [4]

17[5] *thus says the LORD of hosts: Behold, I will send upon them the sword, the famine, and the pestilence, and will make them like vile figs, that cannot be eaten, they are so bad[6].*

18[7] *And I will pursue after them with the sword, with the famine, and with the pestilence, and will make them a horror to all the kingdoms of the earth, a curse, and an astonishment, and a hissing, and a reproach, among all the nations where I have driven them;*[8]

19[9] *because they have not listened to My words, says the LORD, with which I sent to them My servants the prophets, sending them often and often; but you would not hear, says the LORD[10].*

20[11] *Hear, therefore, the word of the LORD, all you of the captivity, whom I have sent away from Jerusalem to Babylon[12]:*

21[13] Thus says the LORD *of hosts, the God of Israel[14]*, concerning Ahab *the son of Kolaiah[15]*, and concerning Zedekiah *the son of Maaseiah, who prophesy a lie to you in My name[16]*: Behold, I will deliver them into the hand of Nebuchadrezzar king of Babylon; and he shall kill them before your eyes;

22[17] and of those shall be taken up a curse by all the captivity of Judah who are in Babylon, saying: 'The LORD make you like Zedekiah and like

will bring you back to the place where I caused you to be carried away captive[1].

---

[1] Missing in LXX

[2] Jeremiah 29:15 - Ezekiel 1:1 1:3, Jeremiah 28:1-28:17 29:8-9

[3] Jeremiah 29:16 - Ezekiel 6:1-9 17:12-21 21:14-32 22:31 24:1-14, Jeremiah 24:2 5:3 38:2-3 38:17-23, z.Vaetchanan 269b

[4] Missing in LXX

[5] Jeremiah 29:17 - b.Chullin [Rashi] 7b, b.Sotah [Rashi] 38b, Ezekiel 5:12-17 14:12-21, Jeremiah 15:2-15:3 24:1-24:3 24:8-10 3:8 5:18 34:17-22 19:11 4:6, Luke 21:11 21:23, z.Vaetchanan 269b

[6] Missing in LXX

[7] Jeremiah 29:18 - 1 Kings 9:7-9:8, 2 Chronicles 7:19-7:22 5:8, Amos 9:9, Deuteronomy 4:25 28:64 29:20-29:27, Ezekiel 6:8 12:15 22:15 12:19, Isaiah 17:15, Jeremiah 15:4 19:8 24:9 1:9 2:6 5:22 10:17 18:18, Jubilees 20:6, Lamentations 2:15-16, Leviticus 2:33, Luke 21:24, Psalms 44:12, Zechariah 7:14

[8] Missing in LXX

[9] Jeremiah 29:19 - Hebrews 12:25, Jeremiah 6:19 7:13 7:24-26 25:3-7 2:5 8:33 10:17 35:14-16 44:4-5, Zechariah 1:4-1:6 7:11-13

[10] Missing in LXX

[11] Jeremiah 29:20 - Ezekiel 3:11 3:15, Jeremiah 24:5, Micah 4:10

[12] Missing in LXX

[13] Jeremiah 29:21 - 4Q339 1:5-6, b.Sanhedrin 93ab, Ein Yaakov Sanhedrin:93a, Jeremiah 14:14-15 29:8-9, Lamentations 2:14, z.Vaetchanan 269b

[14] Missing in LXX

[15] Missing in LXX

[16] Missing in LXX

[17] Jeremiah 29:22 - 1 Corinthians 16:22, b.Sanhedrin 93ab, Daniel 3:6 3:21, Ein Yaakov Sanhedrin:93a, Genesis 24:20, Guide for the Perplexed 2:40, Isaiah 17:15, Jastrow 1373a, Midrash Tanchuma Vayikra 6, Numbers.R 9:18 11:1, Pesikta de R'Kahana 13.13 24.15,

Ahab, whom the king of Babylon roasted in the fire;'

יַ֜עַן אֲשֶׁ֧ר עָשׂ֣וּ נְבָלָ֣ה בְּיִשְׂרָאֵ֗ל וַֽיְנַאֲפוּ֙ אֶת־נְשֵׁ֣י רֵֽעֵיהֶ֔ם וַיְדַבְּר֨וּ דָבָ֤ר בִּשְׁמִי֙ שֶׁ֔קֶר אֲשֶׁ֖ר ל֣וֹא צִוִּיתִ֑ם וְאָנֹכִ֧י 'הוֹדֵעַ' "הַיּוֹדֵעַ" וָעֵ֖ד נְאֻם־יְהֹוָֽה	23[1]

because they worked vile deeds in Israel, and committed adultery with their neighbors' wives, and spoke words in My name falsely, which I did not command; but I am he who knows, and am witness, says the LORD.

וְאֶל־שְׁמַעְיָ֥הוּ הַנֶּחֱלָמִ֖י תֹּאמַ֥ר לֵאמֹֽר	24[2]

And concerning Shemaiah the Nehelamite you shall speak, saying:

כֹּֽה־אָמַ֞ר יְהֹוָ֧ה צְבָא֛וֹת אֱלֹהֵ֥י יִשְׂרָאֵ֖ל לֵאמֹ֑ר יַ֡עַן אֲשֶׁ֣ר אַתָּה֩ שָׁלַ֨חְתָּ בְשִׁמְכָ֜ה סְפָרִ֗ים אֶל־כׇּל־הָעָם֙ אֲשֶׁ֣ר בִּירֽוּשָׁלַ֔͏ִם וְאֶל־צְפַנְיָ֤ה בֶן־מַֽעֲשֵׂיָה֙ הַכֹּהֵ֔ן וְאֶ֥ל כׇּל־הַכֹּהֲנִ֖ים לֵאמֹֽר	25[3]

Thus says the LORD of hosts, the God of Israel, saying: Because you sent letters in your own name to all the people who are at Jerusalem[4], and to Zephaniah the son of Maaseiah the priest, and to all the priests, saying:

יְהֹוָ֞ה נְתָנְךָ֣ כֹהֵ֗ן תַּ֚חַת יְהוֹיָדָ֣ע הַכֹּהֵ֔ן לִֽהְי֤וֹת פְּקִדִים֙ בֵּ֣ית יְהֹוָ֔ה לְכׇל־אִ֥ישׁ מְשֻׁגָּ֖ע וּמִתְנַבֵּ֑א וְנָתַתָּ֥ה אֹת֛וֹ אֶל־הַמַּהְפֶּ֖כֶת וְאֶל־הַצִּינֹֽק	26[5]

'The LORD has made you priest in place of Jehoiada the priest, so there should be officers in the house of the LORD for every man who is mad, and makes himself a prophet, [6]so you should put him in *the stocks and in the collar[7].*

וְעַתָּ֗ה לָ֚מָּה לֹ֣א גָעַ֔רְתָּ בְּיִרְמְיָ֖הוּ הָעֲנְּתֹתִ֑י הַמִּתְנַבֵּ֖א לָכֶֽם	27[8]

Now, therefore, why have you not rebuked Jeremiah of Anathoth, who makes himself a prophet to you,

כִּ֣י עַל־כֵּ֞ן שָׁלַ֥ח אֵלֵ֛ינוּ בָּבֶ֖ל לֵאמֹ֑ר אֲרֻכָּ֣ה הִ֑יא בְּנ֤וּ בָתִּים֙ וְשֵׁ֔בוּ וְנִטְע֣וּ גַנּ֔וֹת וְאִכְל֖וּ אֶת־פְּרִיהֶֽן	28[9]

because he has sent to us in Babylon, saying: The captivity is long; build houses, and live in them; and plant gardens, and eat their fruit?'

וַיִּקְרָ֛א צְפַנְיָ֥ה הַכֹּהֵ֖ן אֶת־הַסֵּ֣פֶר הַזֶּ֑ה בְּאׇזְנֵ֖י יִרְמְיָ֥הוּ הַנָּבִֽיא	29[10]

And Zephaniah the priest read this letter in the ears of Jeremiah the prophet.

וַֽיְהִי֙ דְּבַר־יְהֹוָ֔ה אֶל־יִרְמְיָ֖הוּ לֵאמֹֽר	30

Then came the word of the LORD to Jeremiah, saying:

שְׁלַ֞ח עַל־כׇּל־הַגּוֹלָ֣ה לֵאמֹ֗ר כֹּ֣ה אָמַ֤ר יְהֹוָה֙ אֶל־שְׁמַעְיָ֣ה הַנֶּחֱלָמִ֔י יַ֛עַן אֲשֶׁ֧ר נִבָּ֣א לָכֶ֗ם שְׁמַעְיָ֛ה וַאֲנִ֖י לֹ֣א שְׁלַחְתִּ֑יו וַיַּבְטַ֥ח אֶתְכֶ֖ם עַל־שָֽׁקֶר	31[11]

Send to all those of the captivity, saying: Thus says the LORD concerning Shemaiah the Nehelamite: Because that Shemaiah has prophesied to you, and I did not send him, and he has caused you to trust in a lie;

לָכֵ֞ן כֹּֽה־אָמַ֣ר יְהֹוָ֗ה הִנְנִ֨י פֹקֵ֜ד עַל־שְׁמַעְיָ֣ה הַנֶּחֱלָמִי֮ וְעַל־זַרְעוֹ֒ לֹא־יִהְיֶ֨ה ל֜וֹ אִ֣ישׁ ׀ יוֹשֵׁ֣ב ׀ בְּתֽוֹךְ־הָעָ֣ם הַזֶּ֗ה וְלֹֽא־יִרְאֶ֥ה בַטּ֛וֹב אֲשֶׁר־אֲנִ֥י עֹשֶׂ֖ה לְעַמִּ֑י נְאֻם־יְהֹוָ֔ה כִּֽי־סָרָ֥ה דִבֶּ֖ר עַל־יְהֹוָֽה	32[12]

Therefore, thus says the LORD: Behold, I will punish Shemaiah the Nehelamite, and his seed; he shall not have a man live among this people, nor shall he see the good I will do to My

---

Pirkei de R'Eliezer 33, Ruth 4:11, t.Sotah 4:15, The western scrolls read וכאחב *and like Ahab* while eastern scrolls read וכאחאב [found only in the ketiv]

[1] Jeremiah 29:23 - 2 Peter 2:10-2:19, b.Sanhedrin 93ab, Hebrews 4:13, Jeremiah 7:9-7:10 13:27 16:17 23:14 23:21 23:23-23:24 29:8-29:9 5:21, Jude 1:8-1:11, Malachi 2:14 3:5, Midrash Tanchuma Vayikra 7, Pesikta de R'Kahana 24.15, Proverbs 5:21, Psalms 50:16-50:18, Revelation 1:5 3:14, Sifre Devarim {Haazinu Hashamayim} 306, Sifre Devarim Nitzavim 306, Zephaniah 3:4

[2] Jeremiah 29:24 - 4Q339 1:5-6, Jeremiah 29:31-29:32

[3] Jeremiah 29:25 - 1 Kings 21:8-21:13, 2 Chronicles 8:17, 2 Kings 10:1-10:7 19:9 19:14 25:18-25:21, Acts 9:2, Ezra 4:7-4:16, Jeremiah 21:1-21:2 5:29 13:3 4:24, Nehemiah 6:5 6:17 6:19

[4] LXX *I did not send you in my name*

[5] Jeremiah 29:26 - 2 Chronicles 16:10 18:26, 2 Corinthians 5:13-5:15 11:33, 2 Kings 9:11 11:15 11:18, Acts 4:1 5:18 5:24 16:24 2:11 2:24, Deuteronomy 13:2-13:6, Hosea 9:7, Jeremiah 20:1-2 5:27 14:6 14:28, John 8:53 10:20 10:33, Mark 3:21, Matthew 21:23, Revelation 2:10, Zechariah 13:3-6

[6] LXX adds *and to every madman*

[7] LXX *prison, and into the dungeon*

[8] Jeremiah 29:27 - 2 Chronicles 1:16, 2 Timothy 3:8, Acts 4:17-4:21 5:28 5:40, Amos 7:12-7:13, Genesis.R 84:11, Jeremiah 1:1 5:26 43:2-43:3, John 11:47-11:53, Matthew 27:63, Numbers 16:3

[9] Jeremiah 29:28 - Jeremiah 5:1 5:5 5:10

[10] Jeremiah 29:29 - Jeremiah 5:25

[11] Jeremiah 29:31 - 2 Peter 2:1, Ezekiel 13:8-13:16 13:22-13:23, Jeremiah 14:14-14:15 23:21 28:15-28:17 5:9 29:23-29:24, z.Vaetchanan 269b

[12] Jeremiah 29:32 - 1 Samuel 2:30-2:34, 2 Kings 5:27 7:2 7:19-7:20, Amos 7:17, Exodus 20:5, Isaiah 14:20 14:22, Jeremiah 17:6 20:6 22:30 4:16 29:10-29:14 11:19, Joshua 7:24-7:25, Numbers 16:27-16:33, Psalms 109:8-109:15, z.Vaetchanan 269b

people, says the LORD; because he has spoken perversion against the LORD[1].

Jeremiah – Chapter 30[2]

הַדָּבָר אֲשֶׁר הָיָה אֶל־יִרְמְיָהוּ מֵאֵת יְהוָה לֵאמֹר	1[3]	The word that came to Jeremiah from the LORD, saying:
כֹּה־אָמַר יְהוָה אֱלֹהֵי יִשְׂרָאֵל לֵאמֹר כְּתָב־לְךָ אֵת כָּל־הַדְּבָרִים אֲשֶׁר־דִּבַּרְתִּי אֵלֶיךָ אֶל־סֵפֶר	2[4]	'Thus says the LORD, the God of Israel, saying: Write all the words I have spoken to you in a book.
כִּי הִנֵּה יָמִים בָּאִים נְאֻם־יְהוָה וְשַׁבְתִּי אֶת־שְׁבוּת עַמִּי יִשְׂרָאֵל וִיהוּדָה אָמַר יְהוָה וַהֲשִׁבֹתִים אֶל־הָאָרֶץ אֲשֶׁר־נָתַתִּי לַאֲבוֹתָם וִירֵשׁוּהָ	3[5]	For, behold, the days come, says the LORD, that I will turn the captivity of My people Israel and Judah, says the LORD; and I will cause them to return to the land I gave to their fathers, and they shall *possess it*[6].'
וְאֵלֶּה הַדְּבָרִים אֲשֶׁר דִּבֶּר יְהוָה אֶל־יִשְׂרָאֵל וְאֶל־יְהוּדָה	4[7]	And these are the words that the LORD spoke concerning Israel and concerning Judah.
כִּי־כֹה אָמַר יְהוָה קוֹל חֲרָדָה שָׁמָעְנוּ פַּחַד וְאֵין שָׁלוֹם	5[8]	For thus says the LORD: We have heard a voice of trembling, of fear, and not of peace.
שַׁאֲלוּ־נָא וּרְאוּ אִם־יֹלֵד זָכָר מַדּוּעַ רָאִיתִי כָל־גֶּבֶר יָדָיו עַל־חֲלָצָיו כַּיּוֹלֵדָה וְנֶהֶפְכוּ כָל־פָּנִים לְיֵרָקוֹן	6[9]	Ask now, and see whether a man doesn't travail with child; why do I see every man with his hands on his loins, as a woman in travail, and all faces are turned to paleness?
הוֹי כִּי גָדוֹל הַיּוֹם הַהוּא מֵאַיִן כָּמֹהוּ וְעֵת־צָרָה הִיא לְיַעֲקֹב וּמִמֶּנָּה יִוָּשֵׁעַ	7[10]	Alas! For that day is great, so that none is like it; and it is a time of *trouble*[11] to Jacob, but from it he shall be saved.
וְהָיָה בַיּוֹם הַהוּא נְאֻם יְהוָה צְבָאוֹת אֶשְׁבֹּר עֻלּוֹ מֵעַל צַוָּארֶךָ וּמוֹסְרוֹתֶיךָ אֲנַתֵּק וְלֹא־יַעַבְדוּ־בוֹ עוֹד זָרִים	8[12]	And it shall come to pass in that day, says the LORD of hosts, I will break his yoke from off your neck, and will burst your bands; and strangers shall no longer make him their bondman;
וְעָבְדוּ אֵת יְהוָה אֱלֹהֵיהֶם וְאֵת דָּוִד מַלְכָּם אֲשֶׁר אָקִים לָהֶם	9[13]	But they shall serve the LORD their God, and David their king, whom I will raise up to them.

---

[1] Missing in LXX

[2] Chapter 37 in LXX

[3] Jeremiah 30:1 - Jeremiah 1:1-1:2 2:15

[4] Jeremiah 30:2 - 1 Corinthians 10:11, 2 Peter 1:21, b.Bava Batra 8b, Daniel 12:4, Deuteronomy 7:19 31:22-31:27, Exodus 17:14, Habakkuk 2:2-2:3, Isaiah 8:1 6:8, Jeremiah 36:2-36:4 12:32 51:60-51:64, Job 19:23-19:24, Revelation 1:11 1:19, Romans 15:4

[5] Jeremiah 30:3 - Amos 9:14-9:15, Deuteronomy 6:3, Ezekiel 20:42 28:25-28:26 12:24 37:21-37:25 39:25-39:28 23:14, Ezra 3:1 3:8 3:12, Hebrews 8:8, Jeremiah 16:15 23:5 23:7-23:8 3:11 3:22 5:14 6:10 6:18 7:24 7:28 7:32 7:39 8:37 8:44 33:7-33:11 33:14-33:15 9:26, Joel 4:1, Luke 17:22 19:43 21:6, m.Yadayim 4:4, Obadiah 1:19-1:20, Psalms 53:7, Zephaniah 3:20

[6] LXX *be lords of it*

[7] Jeremiah 30:4 - Sifre Devarim Devarim 1

[8] Jeremiah 30:5 - Amos 5:16-5:18 8:10, Isaiah 5:30 11:11, Jeremiah 4:15-4:20 6:23-6:25 8:19 9:20 1:36 31:16-31:17 22:5, Luke 19:41-44 21:25-26 23:29-23:30, Midrash Psalms 20:3, Pesikta Rabbati 27:2, z.Ki Tissa 188b, z.Vaetchanan 269b, Zephaniah 1:10-11 Jeremiah 30:5-7 - Sifre Devarim Devarim 1

[9] Jeremiah 30:6 - 1 Thessalonians 5:3, b.Sanhedrin 98b, Daniel 5:6, Ein Yaakov Sanhedrin 98b, Guide for the Perplexed 1:37, Hosea 13:13, Isaiah 13:6-9 21:3 5:22, Jeremiah 4:31 6:24 13:21 22:23 1:24 2:43, Joel 2:6, John 16:21-22, Mekhilta de R'Shimon bar Yochai Shirata 27:1, Mekhilta de R'Ishmael Shirata 1:79, Micah 4:9-10, Midrash Psalms 20:3 143:1, Nahum 2:11, Pesikta Rabbati 21:21, Psalms 48:7, Sifre Devarim Ekev 37 Sifre Devarim Nitzavim 319, y.Chagigah 2:1, y.Kiddushin 1:8, y.Sheviit 6:1 Jeremiah 30:6-9 - 4QJerc

[10] Jeremiah 30:7 - Acts 2:20, Amos 5:18-5:20, Daniel 9:12 12:1, Deuteronomy.R 2:11, Ezekiel 7:6-7:12, Genesis 8:8 32:25-32:30, Hosea 2:2 12:4-12:6, Isaiah 2:12-2:22 14:1-14:2, Jeremiah 6:10 50:18-50:20 50:33-50:34, Joel 2:11 3:4, Lamentations 1:12 2:13 4:6, Malachi 3:19, Mark 13:19, Matthew 24:21-24:22, Midrash Psalms 20:3 22:5 22:7, Psalms 25:22 34:20, Revelation 6:17, Romans 11:26, y.Taanit 1:1, z.Vayera 119a, Zechariah 14:1-14:2, Zephaniah 1:14-1:18

[11] LXX *straitness*

[12] Jeremiah 30:8 - Ezekiel 10:27, Isaiah 9:5 10:27 14:25, Jeremiah 2:20 1:14 3:2 3:7 4:4 4:10 4:13, Midrash Psalms 81:2, Nahum 1:13

[13] Jeremiah 30:9 - Acts 2:30 13:23 13:34, b.Sanhedrin 98b, Ein Yaakov Sanhedrin:98b, Ezekiel 34:23-34:24 37:23-37:25, Hosea 3:5, Isaiah 55:3-55:5, Jeremiah 23:5, Luke 1:69, z.Noach 72b

Hebrew		English
וְאַתָּ֞ה אַל־תִּירָ֤א עַבְדִּ֣י יַעֲקֹב֙ נְאֻם־יְהֹוָ֔ה וְאַל־ תֵּחַ֖ת יִשְׂרָאֵ֑ל כִּ֣י הִנְנִ֤י מוֹשִֽׁיעֲךָ֙ מֵֽרָח֔וֹק וְאֶֽת־זַרְעֲךָ֖ מֵאֶ֣רֶץ שִׁבְיָ֑ם וְשָׁ֧ב יַעֲקֹ֛ב וְשָׁקַ֥ט וְשַׁאֲנַ֖ן וְאֵ֥ין מַחֲרִֽיד	10[1]	*Therefore, fear you not, O Jacob My servant, says the LORD; nor be dismayed, O Israel; for, lo, I will save you from afar, and your seed from the land of their captivity; and Jacob shall again be quiet and at ease, and no one shall make him afraid*[2].
כִּֽי־אִתְּךָ֥ אֲנִ֛י נְאֻם־יְהֹוָ֖ה לְהוֹשִׁיעֶ֑ךָ כִּי֩ אֶעֱשֶׂ֨ה כָלָ֜ה בְּכָֽל־הַגּוֹיִ֣ם ׀ אֲשֶׁ֧ר הֲפִצוֹתִ֣יךָ שָּׁ֗ם אַ֤ךְ אֹֽתְךָ֙ לֹֽא־ אֶעֱשֶׂ֣ה כָלָ֔ה וְיִסַּרְתִּ֙יךָ֙ לַמִּשְׁפָּ֔ט וְנַקֵּ֖ה לֹ֥א אֲנַקֶּֽךָ	11[3]	*For I am with you, says the LORD, to save you; for I will make a full end of all the nations where I scattered you, but I will not make a full end of you; for I will correct you in measure, and will not utterly destroy you*[4].
כִּ֣י כֹ֥ה אָמַ֛ר יְהֹוָ֖ה אָנ֣וּשׁ לְשִׁבְרֵ֑ךְ נַחְלָ֖ה מַכָּתֵֽךְ	12[5]	For thus says the LORD: *Your hurt is incurable, and your wound is grievous*[6].
אֵֽין־דָּ֥ן דִּינֵ֖ךְ לְמָז֑וֹר רְפֻא֥וֹת תְּעָלָ֖ה אֵ֥ין לָֽךְ	13[7]	*No one deems your wound that it may be bandaged; you have no healing medicines*[8].
כׇּל־מְאַהֲבַ֣יִךְ שְׁכֵח֔וּךְ אוֹתָ֖ךְ לֹ֣א יִדְרֹ֑שׁוּ כִּי֩ מַכַּ֨ת אוֹיֵ֤ב הִכִּיתִ֙יךְ֙ מוּסַ֣ר אַכְזָרִ֔י עַ֚ל רֹ֣ב עֲוֹנֵ֔ךְ עָצְמ֖וּ חַטֹּאתָֽיִךְ	14[9]	All your *lovers*[10] have forgotten you, they do not *seek you*[11]; For I have wounded you with the wound of an enemy, with the chastisement of a cruel one; for the greatness of your iniquity, because your sins were increased.
מַה־תִּזְעַ֣ק עַל־שִׁבְרֵ֔ךְ אָנ֖וּשׁ מַכְאֹבֵ֑ךְ עַ֣ל ׀ רֹ֣ב עֲוֹנֵ֗ךְ עָֽצְמוּ֙ חַטֹּאתַ֔יִךְ עָשִׂ֥יתִי אֵ֖לֶּה לָֽךְ	15[12]	*Why cry for your hurt, so your pain is incurable*[13]? For the greatness of your iniquity, because your sins were increased, I have done these things to you.
לָכֵ֞ן כׇּל־אֹֽכְלַ֙יִךְ֙ יֵֽאָכֵ֔לוּ וְכׇל־צָרַ֥יִךְ כֻּלָּ֖ם בַּשְּׁבִ֣י יֵלֵ֑כוּ וְהָי֤וּ שֹׁאסַ֙יִךְ֙ לִמְשִׁסָּ֔ה וְכׇל־בֹּֽזְזַ֖יִךְ אֶתֵּ֥ן לָבַֽז	16[14]	Therefore, all they who devour you shall be devoured, and all your adversaries, every one of them, shall go into captivity; and they who spoil you shall be spoil, and all who prey on you will I give as prey.
כִּ֣י אַעֲלֶ֥ה אֲרֻכָ֛ה לָ֖ךְ וּמִמַּכּוֹתַ֥יִךְ אֶרְפָּאֵ֖ךְ נְאֻם־ יְהֹוָ֑ה כִּ֤י נִדָּחָה֙ קָ֣רְאוּ לָ֔ךְ צִיּ֣וֹן הִ֔יא דֹּרֵ֖שׁ אֵ֥ין לָֽהּ	17[15]	For I will restore health to you, and I will heal you of your wounds, says the LORD; because

---

[1] Jeremiah 30:10 - b.Taanit 5b, Deuteronomy 31:6-31:8, Ein Yaakov Taanit:5b, Ezekiel 16:52 34:25-34:28 14:11, Genesis 15:1, Hosea 2:18, Isaiah 11:9 41:10-41:15 19:5 20:2 22:11 22:13 1:25 6:4 60:4-60:22, Jeremiah 3:18 23:3 23:6 23:8 5:14 6:3 9:16 46:27-46:28, John 12:15, Leviticus.R 29:2, Micah 4:3-4:4, Midrash Psalms 78:6, Midrash Tanchuma Vayetze 2, Midrash Tanchuma Vayikra 7, Pesikta de R'Kahana 23.2, z.Acharei Mot 57a, z.Balak 199a, z.Terumah 174a, z.Vayetze 165b, z.Vayikra 20b, Zechariah 2:4-2:5 3:10 8:4-8:8, Zephaniah 3:15-3:17

[2] Missing in LXX

[3] Jeremiah 30:11 - 2 Timothy 4:17-4:18 4:22, Acts 18:10, Amos 9:8-9:9, Ezekiel 11:13 11:16-11:17, Isaiah 8:10 27:7-27:8 19:25, Jeremiah 1:8 1:19 4:27 5:10 5:18 10:24 15:20 46:27-46:28, Leviticus.R 29:2, Matthew 1:23 4:20, Midrash Tanchuma Vayetze 2, Pesikta de R'Kahana 23.2, Psalms 6:2, Romans 9:27-9:29 11:5-11:7, Sifre Devarim Nitzavim 325, z.Balak 199a, z.Terumah 174a

[4] Missing in LXX

[5] Jeremiah 30:12 - 2 Chronicles 12:16, Ezekiel 13:11, Isaiah 1:5-1:6, Jeremiah 14:17 15:18 6:15, z.Vaetchanan 269b

[6] LXX *I have brought destruction on you; your stroke is painful*

[7] Jeremiah 30:13 - 1 John 2:1, 1 Peter 2:24, 1 Timothy 2:5-2:6, Deuteronomy 8:39, Exodus 15:26, Ezekiel 22:30, Hosea 6:1 14:6, Isaiah 1:6 11:16, Jeremiah 8:22 14:19 17:14 6:17 9:22 22:11, Job 5:18 10:29, Luke 10:30-10:34, Nahum 3:19, Psalms 10:23 22:5

[8] LXX *There is none to judge your cause: you have been painfully treated for healing, there is no help for you*

[9] Jeremiah 30:14 - Ezekiel 9:8-9:10 23:9 23:22, Hosea 2:5 2:10-2:18 5:14, Jeremiah 2:36 4:30 5:6 6:23 22:20 22:22 6:15 14:22, Job 13:24-13:28 16:9 19:11 6:21, Lamentations 1:2 1:19 2:4-2:5, mt.Hilchot Talmud Torah 2:2, mt.Hilchot Teshuvah 3:2 3:2 3:2, Pesikta de R'Kahana 16.6, Pesikta Rabbati 29/30A:7, Psalms 90:7-90:8, Revelation 17:12-17:18

[10] LXX *friends*

[11] LXX *ask about you at all*

[12] Jeremiah 30:15 - 2 Chronicles 36:14-36:17, Ezekiel 16:1-16:63 20:1-20:49 22:1-22:23, Ezra 9:6-9:7 9:13, Hosea 5:12-5:13, Isaiah 1:4-1:5 1:21-1:24 5:2 30:13-30:14 59:1-59:4 59:12-59:15, Jeremiah 2:19 2:28-2:30 5:6-5:9 5:25-5:31 6:6-6:7 6:13 7:8-7:11 9:2-9:10 11:13 15:18 6:12 6:14 6:17 32:30-32:35 22:11, Job 10:6 10:29, Joshua 9:10-9:11, Lamentations 1:5 3:39 4:13 5:16-5:17, Malachi 3:19-4:20, Micah 1:9 7:9, Nehemiah 9:26-9:36, Zephaniah 3:1-3:5

[13] Missing in LXX

[14] Jeremiah 30:16 - Exodus 23:22, Ezekiel 25:3-7 26:2-21 5:6 11:5, Habakkuk 2:16, Isaiah 14:2 9:1 41:11-12 47:5-6 6:15 6:17, Jeremiah 2:3 10:25 12:14 1:12 25:26-29 50:7-11 50:17-18 2:28 50:33-40 51:34-37, Joel 4:8, Lamentations 1:21 4:21-22, Micah 4:11 7:10, Nahum 1:8, Psalms 9:5 137:8-9, Revelation 13:10, Sifre Devarim Devarim 1, Sifre Devarim Haazinu Hashamayim 319, Zechariah 1:14 2:8 12:2 14:2, Zephaniah 2:8

[15] Jeremiah 30:17 - 1 Peter 2:24, b.Rosh Hashanah 30a, b.Succah 41a, Ein Yaakov Sukkah:41a, Exodus 15:26, Exodus.R 50:3, Ezekiel 10:16 11:12 36:2-3 12:20, Genesis.R 38:14, Hosea 6:1, Isaiah 11:12 6:26, Jeremiah 3:22 8:22 6:13 9:6 9:24, Lamentations 2:15, Lamentations.R 1:52 11:52, Leviticus.R 18:5, Malachi 3:20, Mesillat Yesharim 19:Longing-for-the-Redemption, Midrash Tanchuma

they have called you an outcast: 'She is *Zion*[1], there is no one who cares for her.'

18[2] Thus says the LORD: Behold, I will turn the captivity of Jacob's tents, and have compassion on his dwelling places; and the city shall *be built*[3] on her own mound, and the palace shall be inhabited in its own place.

כֹּה אָמַר יְהוָה הִנְנִי־שָׁב שְׁבוּת אָהֳלֵי יַעֲקוֹב וּמִשְׁכְּנֹתָיו אֲרַחֵם וְנִבְנְתָה עִיר עַל־תִּלָּהּ וְאַרְמוֹן עַל־מִשְׁפָּטוֹ יֵשֵׁב

19[4] And from them shall proceed thanksgiving. And the voice of those who make merry; and I will multiply them, and they shall not be diminished, *I will increase them, and they shall not dwindle away*[5].

וְיָצָא מֵהֶם תּוֹדָה וְקוֹל מְשַׂחֲקִים וְהִרְבִּתִים וְלֹא יִמְעָטוּ וְהִכְבַּדְתִּים וְלֹא יִצְעָרוּ

20[6] Their children also shall be as before, and their assembly shall be established before Me, and I will punish all who oppress them.

וְהָיוּ בָנָיו כְּקֶדֶם וַעֲדָתוֹ לְפָנַי תִּכּוֹן וּפָקַדְתִּי עַל כָּל־לֹחֲצָיו

21[7] And their prince shall be of themselves, and their ruler shall proceed from their midst; and I will cause him to draw near, and he shall approach Me; for who is he who has pledged his heart to approach Me? says the LORD.

וְהָיָה אַדִּירוֹ מִמֶּנּוּ וּמֹשְׁלוֹ מִקִּרְבּוֹ יֵצֵא וְהִקְרַבְתִּיו וְנִגַּשׁ אֵלָי כִּי מִי הוּא־זֶה עָרַב אֶת־לִבּוֹ לָגֶשֶׁת אֵלַי נְאֻם־יְהוָה

22[8] *And you shall be My people, and I will be your God*[9].

וִהְיִיתֶם לִי לְעָם וְאָנֹכִי אֶהְיֶה לָכֶם לֵאלֹהִים

23[10] Behold, a storm of the LORD is gone forth in fury, a sweeping storm; it shall whirl upon the head of the wicked.

הִנֵּה סַעֲרַת יְהוָה חֵמָה יָצְאָה סַעַר מִתְגּוֹרֵר עַל רֹאשׁ רְשָׁעִים יָחוּל

24[11] The fierce anger of the LORD shall not return, until He has executed, and until He has performed the intent of His heart; in the end of days you shall consider it.

לֹא יָשׁוּב חֲרוֹן אַף־יְהוָה עַד־עֲשֹׂתוֹ וְעַד־הֲקִימוֹ מְזִמּוֹת לִבּוֹ בְּאַחֲרִית הַיָּמִים תִּתְבּוֹנְנוּ בָהּ

Ki Tissa 25 26, Midrash Tanchuma Terumah 8, Midrash Tanchuma Vayeshev 9, mt.Hilcnot Shofar Sukkah vLulav 7:15, Nehemiah 4:1-4:4, Pesikta de R'Kahana 18.3, Pesikta Rabbati 29/30B:4 32:2 33:13, Psalms 12:6 23:3 44:14-17 79:9-11 7:3 11:20, Revelation 22:2

Jeremiah 30:17-24 - 4QJerc

[1] LXX *your prey*

[2] Jeremiah 30:18 - 1 Chronicles 5:1 5:19, Ezekiel 7:20-7:22, Ezra 6:3-6:15, Haggai 2:7-2:9, Isaiah 20:26 20:28, Jeremiah 23:3 5:14 6:3 7:5 7:24 7:39 7:41 9:7 9:11 22:27 1:6 1:39, Nehemiah 3:1-3:32 7:4, Pesikta de R'Kahana 20.7, Pesikta Rabbati 39:2 44:7, Psalms 78:69 85:2 6:14, Sifre Devarim Devarim 1, Song of Songs.R 7:11, z.Vaetchanan 269b, Zechariah 1:16 12:6 14:10

[3] MT Feminine; 4QJerc Masculine

[4] Jeremiah 30:19 - 1 Peter 1:7, Ezekiel 36:10-36:15 12:37 13:26, Ezra 3:10-3:13 6:22, Isaiah 12:1 3:6 11:10 3:3 3:11 4:9 12:9 12:19 12:22 62:2-62:3, Jeremiah 7:5 31:13-31:14 7:28 33:9-33:11 9:22, John 17:22, Nehemiah 8:12 8:17 12:43-12:46, Psalms 53:7 126:1-126:2, Zechariah 2:4 8:4-8:5 8:19 9:13-9:17 10:8 12:8, Zephaniah 3:14-3:20

[5] Missing in LXX

[6] Jeremiah 30:20 - Ein Yaakov Bava Batra:8b, Genesis 17:5-17:9, Isaiah 1:26-1:27 1:26 3:22 6:14, Jeremiah 2:3 6:16 8:39 50:33-50:34, Leviticus.R 30:1, mt.Hilchot Matnot Aniyim 7:11, Pesikta de R'Kahana 27.1, Pesikta Rabbati 42:9 51:1, Psalms 90:16-90:17 6:19 6:29

[7] Jeremiah 30:21 - 1 John 2:2, 2 Samuel 7:13, Acts 2:34-2:36 5:31, b.Gittin 56b, b.Kiddushin 70b, b.Sanhedrin 98b, Deuteronomy 18:18 9:5, Ein Yaakov Gittin 56b, Ein Yaakov Kiddushin 70b, Ezekiel 34:23-34:24 13:24, Ezra 2:2 7:25-7:26, Genesis 18:27 18:30 18:32 1:10, Hebrews 1:3 4:14-4:16 7:21-7:26 9:15-9:24, Isaiah 9:7-9:8 15:1, Jeremiah 23:5-23:6 6:9 9:15 1:19 2:44, Job 23:3-23:5 42:3-42:6, John 18:36-18:37 19:19-19:22, Luke 1:32-1:33 24:26, Mark 11:9-10, Matthew 2:2 3:17 21:5-11 3:37, Micah 5:3-5, Midrash Psalms 21:5, Nehemiah 2:9-10 7:2, Numbers 16:5 17:5 17:27-13, Psalms 89:30 110:1-4, Revelation 5:9-10 19:16, Romans 8:34, Tanya Likutei Aramim §33, Zechariah 6:12-13 9:9-10

[8] Jeremiah 30:22 - Deuteronomy 26:17-19, Ezekiel 11:20 12:28 13:27, Hebrews 8:10, Hosea 2:23, Jeremiah 24:7 7:2 7:34 8:38, Matthew 22:32, Revelation 21:3, Song of Songs 2:16, Zechariah 13:9

[9] Missing in LXX

[10] Jeremiah 30:23 - 3 Enoch 35:5, Jastrow 273a 956b, Jeremiah 23:19-23:20 1:32, Proverbs 1:27, Psalms 58:10, Saadia Opinions 9:8, Zechariah 9:14

[11] Jeremiah 30:24 - 1 Samuel 3:12, Daniel 2:28 10:14, Deuteronomy 4:30 7:29, Ezekiel 21:3-20:4 21:10-21:12 14:16, Genesis 1:1, Hosea 3:5, Isaiah 14:24 14:26-14:27 22:11, Jeremiah 4:8 4:28 23:20 24:47 1:39, Job 23:13-23:14, Micah 4:1, Numbers 24:14

בָּעֵת הַהִיא נְאֻם־יְהֹוָה אֶהְיֶה לֵאלֹהִים לְכֹל מִשְׁפְּחוֹת יְ	25[1]	At that time, says the LORD, I will be the God of all the families of Israel, and they shall be My people[2].

Jeremiah – Chapter 31[3]

כֹּה אָמַר יְהֹוָה מָצָא חֵן בַּמִּדְבָּר עַם שְׂרִידֵי חָרֶב הָלוֹךְ לְהַרְגִּיעוֹ יִשְׂרָאֵל	1[4]	Thus says the LORD: The people who remained after the sword found grace in the wilderness, *Israel, when I cause him to rest*[5].
מֵרָחוֹק יְהֹוָה נִרְאָה לִי וְאַהֲבַת עוֹלָם אֲהַבְתִּיךְ עַל־כֵּן מְשַׁכְתִּיךְ חָסֶד	2[6]	'From afar the LORD appeared to me.' 'Yes, I have loved you with an everlasting love; therefore, with *affection*[7] I have drawn you.
עוֹד אֶבְנֵךְ וְנִבְנֵית בְּתוּלַת יִשְׂרָאֵל עוֹד תַּעְדִּי תֻפַּיִךְ וְיָצָאת בִּמְחוֹל מְשַׂחֲקִים	3[8]	I will build you again, and you shall be built, O virgin of Israel; again you shall be adorned with your tambourine, and shall go forth in the dances of those who are merry.
עוֹד תִּטְּעִי כְרָמִים בְּהָרֵי שֹׁמְרוֹן נָטְעוּ נֹטְעִים וְחִלֵּלוּ	4[9]	Again you shall plant vineyards on the mountains of Samaria; The planters shall plant, and *shall have its use*[10].
כִּי יֶשׁ־יוֹם קָרְאוּ נֹצְרִים בְּהַר אֶפְרָיִם קוּמוּ וְנַעֲלֶה צִיּוֹן אֶל־יְהֹוָה אֱלֹהֵינוּ	5[11]	For there shall be a day, that the watchmen shall call on the mount Ephraim: arise and let us go up to Zion, to the LORD our God.'
כִּי־כֹה אָמַר יְהֹוָה רָנּוּ לְיַעֲקֹב שִׂמְחָה וְצַהֲלוּ בְּרֹאשׁ הַגּוֹיִם הַשְׁמִיעוּ הַלְלוּ וְאִמְרוּ הוֹשַׁע יְהֹוָה אֶת־עַמְּךָ אֵת שְׁאֵרִית יִשְׂרָאֵל	6[12]	For thus says the LORD: Sing with gladness for Jacob, and shout at the head of the nations; announce, praise, and say: '*O LORD, save*[13] your people, the remnant of Israel.'

---

[1] Jeremiah 30:25 - b.Kiddushin 70b, Ein Yaakov Kiddushin:70b, Ezekiel 11:20 10:31 12:28 37:16-37:27 15:22, Genesis 17:7-17:8, Hebrews 12:16, Hosea 2:2, Isaiah 11:12-11:13 17:10, Jeremiah 3:18 23:6 6:3 6:10 6:22 6:24 7:34 8:38 9:7 9:14 33:24-33:26 2:4, John 20:17, Leviticus 2:12, Psalms 48:15 24:15, Romans 11:26-11:29, Zechariah 10:6-10:7 13:9

[2] Jeremiah 38:1 in LXX

[3] Chapter 38 in LXX

[4] Jeremiah 31:1 - b.Makkot 24a, Deuteronomy 1:30 1:33 2:7 8:2-8:3 8:16 12:9, Ein Yaakov Makkot:24a, Exodus 1:16 1:22 2:23 5:21 12:37 14:8-14:12 15:9-15:10 17:8-17:13 9:14, Ezekiel 20:14-20:17, Hebrews 4:8-4:9, Isaiah 63:7-63:14, Jeremiah 2:2, Matthew 11:28, Nehemiah 9:12-9:15, Numbers 10:33 14:20, Psalms 78:14-78:16 78:23-78:29 78:52 95:11 105:37-105:43 136:16-136:24
Jeremiah 31:1-9 - 4QJerc
Jeremiah 31:1-19 - Haftarah 2nd day Rosh Hashanah, mt.Hilchot Tefilah 13:10

[5] Missing in 4QJerc

[6] Jeremiah 31:2 - 1 John 4:19, 1 Peter 1:3, 2 Thessalonians 2:13-2:16, 2 Timothy 1:9, b.Berachot 11b, b.Eruvin 54b, b.Sotah 11a, b.Yevamot 62b, Deuteronomy 4:37 7:7-7:9 10:15 9:3 9:26, Ein Yaakov Sotah:11a, Ephesians 1:3-1:5 2:4-2:5, Exodus.R 1:22, Genesis.R 29:3, Hosea 11:1 11:4, Isaiah 21:17 54:8-54:9, James 1:18, John 6:44-6:45, Malachi 1:2, Mekilta de R'Ishmael Shirata 10:69, Psalms 7:17, Ralbag Wars 2:6, Romans 8:30 9:13 11:28-11:29, Song of Songs 1:4, Titus 3:3-3:6, y.Sotah 1:9, z.Mishpatim 125b, z.Shemot 12a, z.Vaetchanan 269b
Jeremiah 31:2-9 - Ahiqar 175

[7] LXX *compassion*

[8] Jeremiah 31:3 - 1 Samuel 18:6-18:7, 2 Kings 19:21, Acts 15:16, Amos 5:2 9:11, Ephesians 2:20-2:22, Exodus 15:20-15:21, Guide for the Perplexed 3:51, Isaiah 13:22, Jeremiah 1:10 14:17 18:13 30:18-30:19 7:14 7:22 9:7, Judges 11:34, Lamentations 1:15 2:13, Lamentations.R Petichata D'Chakimei:24, Luke 15:23, Mekhilta de R'Shimon bar Yochai Shirata 36:3, Midrash Proverbs 14, Psalms 51:19 69:36 5:3 150:3-150:6, Revelation 19:1-19:8 21:10-21:27, z.Bereshit 6a, z.Mikketz 196b, z.Vayera 120a, z.Vayikra 20b

[9] Jeremiah 31:4 - 1 Samuel 21:5, Amos 9:14, Deuteronomy 20:6 4:30, Ezekiel 12:8, Isaiah 62:8-62:9 65:21-65:22, Leviticus 19:23-19:25, Micah 4:4, Obadiah 1:19, Pesikta Rabbati 31:1, Zechariah 3:10

[10] LXX *praise*

[11] Jeremiah 31:5 - 2 Chronicles 13:4 30:5-30:11, Acts 8:5-8:8, Ezekiel 3:17 9:2, Ezra 1:5 8:15-8:20, Hosea 2:2 9:8, Isaiah 2:2-2:4 11:11-11:13 16:9 52:7-52:8 14:6, Jeremiah 6:17 50:4-50:5 2:19, Micah 4:1-4:3, mt.Hilchot Bikkurim 4:16, Sifre Devarim {Ekev} 37, Zechariah 8:20-8:23

[12] Jeremiah 31:6 - Amos 5:15, Deuteronomy 4:13 8:43, Exodus.R 38:4, Ezekiel 6:8, Hosea 1:7, Isaiah 1:9 11:11 12:4-12:6 24:14-24:16 13:4 13:31 42:10-42:12 20:23 13:9, Jeremiah 23:3, Joel 3:5, Lamentations.R 1:52, m.Bikkurim 3:2, Micah 2:12 7:18, Psalms 14:7 28:9 67:2 69:36 96:1-96:3 98:1-98:4 10:47 117:1-117:2 138:4-138:5, Romans 9:27 11:5, Saadia Opinions 7:3, Selichot, t.Menachot 13:23, Tanya Igeret Hakodesh §02, Zephaniah 2:9 3:13-3:20

[13] 4QJerc *The LORD has saved*

הִנְנִי מֵבִיא אוֹתָם מֵאֶרֶץ צָפוֹן וְקִבַּצְתִּים מִיַּרְכְּתֵי־אָרֶץ בָּם עִוֵּר וּפִסֵּחַ הָרָה וְיֹלֶדֶת יַחְדָּו קָהָל גָּדוֹל יָשׁוּבוּ הֵנָּה	7[1] Behold, I will bring them from the north country, and gather them from the uttermost parts of the earth, and with them the blind and the lame, the woman with child and she who travails with child together; they shall return here as a great company.
בִּבְכִי יָבֹאוּ וּבְתַחֲנוּנִים אוֹבִילֵם אוֹלִיכֵם אֶל־נַחֲלֵי מַיִם בְּדֶרֶךְ יָשָׁר לֹא יִכָּשְׁלוּ בָּהּ כִּי־הָיִיתִי לְיִשְׂרָאֵל לְאָב וְאֶפְרַיִם בְּכֹרִי הוּא	8[2] They shall come with weeping, and with supplications I will lead them; I will cause them walk *by*[3] rivers of waters, in a straight way where they shall not stumble; for I became a father to Israel, and Ephraim is My firstborn.
שִׁמְעוּ דְבַר־יְהוָה גּוֹיִם וְהַגִּידוּ בָאִיִּים מִמֶּרְחָק וְאִמְרוּ מְזָרֵה יִשְׂרָאֵל יְקַבְּצֶנּוּ וּשְׁמָרוֹ כְּרֹעֶה עֶדְרוֹ	9[4] Hear the word of the LORD, O you nations, and declare it in the far-off isles, and say: 'He who scattered Israel gathers him, and keeps him, as a shepherd his flock.'
כִּי־פָדָה יְהוָה אֶת־יַעֲקֹב וּגְאָלוֹ מִיַּד חָזָק מִמֶּנּוּ	10[5] For the LORD has ransomed Jacob, and He redeems him from the hand of he who is stronger than he.
וּבָאוּ וְרִנְּנוּ בִמְרוֹם־צִיּוֹן וְנָהֲרוּ אֶל־טוּב יְהוָה עַל־דָּגָן וְעַל־תִּירֹשׁ וְעַל־יִצְהָר וְעַל־בְּנֵי־צֹאן וּבָקָר וְהָיְתָה נַפְשָׁם כְּגַן רָוֶה וְלֹא־יוֹסִיפוּ לְדַאֲבָה עוֹד	11[6] And they shall come and sing in the height of Zion, and shall flow to the goodness of the LORD, to the corn, and to the wine, and to the oil, and to the young of the flock and of the herd; and their soul shall be as a watered garden, and they shall not hunger any longer.
אָז תִּשְׂמַח בְּתוּלָה בְּמָחוֹל וּבַחֻרִים וּזְקֵנִים יַחְדָּו וְהָפַכְתִּי אֶבְלָם לְשָׂשׂוֹן וְנִחַמְתִּים וְשִׂמַּחְתִּים מִיגוֹנָם	12[7] Then the virgin shall rejoice in the dance, and the young men and the old together; for I will turn their mourning into joy, and *will comfort them*[8], and make them rejoice from their sorrow.
וְרִוֵּיתִי נֶפֶשׁ הַכֹּהֲנִים דָּשֶׁן וְעַמִּי אֶת־טוּבִי יִשְׂבָּעוּ נְאֻם־יְהוָה	13[9] And I will satiate the soul of the priests with fatness, and My people shall be satisfied with My goodness, says the LORD.

[1] Jeremiah 31:7 - 1 Corinthians 8:10, 1 Thessalonians 5:14, b.Bava Batra 16a, b.Sanhedrin 91b, b.Shabbat 30b, Deuteronomy 6:4, Ein Yaakov Sanhedrin:91b, Ein Yaakov Shabbat:30b, Ezekiel 20:34 20:41 10:13 10:16, Hebrews 4:15 12:12, Isaiah 16:11 18:16 19:6 21:22 4:10, Jeremiah 3:12 3:18 23:8 5:14, John 21:15, Lamentations.R Petichata D'Chakimei:24, Mas.Kallah Rabbati 2:3, Matthew 12:20, Micah 4:6, Midrash Psalms 33:1 74:3, Psalms 65:6 98:3 11:3, Tanya Igeret Hakodesh §26, z.Vaetchanan 269b, Zechariah 2:6, Zephaniah 3:19

[2] Jeremiah 31:8 - 1 Chronicles 5:10, 2 Corinthians 6:18 7:9-7:11, Daniel 9:17-9:18, Deuteronomy 8:6, Ecclesiastes.R 1:9, Exodus 4:22, Exodus.R 34:3, Ezekiel 34:12-34:14, Hebrews 5:7 12:13 12:23, Hosea 12:6, Isaiah 35:6-35:8 40:3-40:4 41:17-41:19 43:16-43:19 49:9-49:11 9:14 15:13 15:16 16:9, Jeremiah 3:4 3:19 7:21 2:4, Leviticus.R 9:6, Luke 3:4-3:6 6:21, Matthew 3:3 5:4 6:9, Mesillat Yesharim 23:To Acquire Anavah, Midrash Psalms 19:1, Midrash Tanchuma Vayigash 5, Numbers.R 13:2, Pesikta Rabbati 41:5, Psalms 23:2 126:5-126:6, Revelation 7:17, Romans 8:26, Saadia Opinions 2:10, Song of Songs.R 4:32, Zechariah 12:10

[3] 4QJerc *toward*

[4] Jeremiah 31:9 - Acts 20:28-20:29, Deuteronomy 6:4 8:26, Deuteronomy.R 2:24, Ezekiel 5:2 5:10 11:16 20:34 10:12 13:24, Genesis 10:5, Genesis.R 93:12, Isaiah 24:14 3:12 16:11 17:1 18:4 10:6 6:7 12:9 18:19, Jeremiah 1:22 2:17 2:19, John 10:27 11:52, Jubilees 1:24 2:20, Lamentations.R Petichata D'Chakimei:34, Luke 12:32, Micah 2:12 4:6 5:5, Midrash Proverbs 30, Midrash Psalms 18:11 23:1, Pesikta de R'Kahana 24.16, Pesikta Rabbati 21:11 34:2, Psalms 72:10, Song of Songs.R 2:45, z.Mikketz 203a, z.Toledot 146b, z.Vayishlach 175a, Zechariah 9:16, Zephaniah 2:11 3:19

[5] Jeremiah 31:10 - Blessings for Kriat Shema [Maariv], Hebrews 2:14-2:15, Hosea 13:14, Isaiah 20:23 24:20 1:24, Jeremiah 15:21 2:33, Luke 11:21-11:22, Matthew 12:29 20:28 22:29, Pesikta de R'Kahana 13.9, Psalms 22:7, Titus 2:14

[6] Jeremiah 31:11 - Ezekiel 17:23 20:40, Genesis.R 44:22, Hosea 2:20-2:25 3:5, Isaiah 1:30 2:2-2:5 12:1-12:6 11:10 3:11 10:11 12:20 17:19, Jeremiah 7:5 33:9-33:11, Joel 4:18, John 16:22, Micah 4:1-4:2, Midrash Psalms 31:2, Midrash Tanchuma Korach 12, Pesikta de R'Kahana 13.9, Psalms 10:4, Revelation 7:17 21:4, Romans 2:4, Selichot, Sifre Devarim {Ekev} 43, Zechariah 9:15-9:17 Jeremiah 31:11-14 - 4QJerc

[7] Jeremiah 31:12 - b.Berachot 55b, Esther 9:22, Ezra 6:22, Genesis.R 100 [Excl]:12, Isaiah 11:10 3:3 3:11 12:20 13:3 65:18-65:19, Jeremiah 7:5, John 16:22, Mekilta de R'Ishmael Shirata 1:6, Midrash Tanchuma Beshallach 10, Midrash Tanchuma Vayechi 17, Motzoei Shabbat [Viyiten Lecha], Nehemiah 12:27 12:43, Psalms 30:12 5:3, Seder Hatavat Chalom [Order of making good a bad dream] Sifre Devarim Ekev 43, Sifre Devarim {Vezot Habracha} 342, y.Berachot 5:1, z.Vayakhel 220a, Zechariah 8:4-8:5 8:19

[8] Missing in LXX

[9] Jeremiah 31:13 - 1 Peter 2:9, 2 Chronicles 6:41, Deuteronomy 33:8-33:11, Ephesians 1:3 3:19, Genesis.R 97:1, Isaiah 1:6 55:1-55:3 13:6 66:10-66:14, Jeremiah 7:26 9:9, Lamentations.R 1:23 Petichata D'Chakimei:24 Petichata D'Chakimei:34, Matthew 5:6, Nehemiah 10:40, Pesikta de R'Kahana 13.15, Pesikta Rabbati 28:3 37:1, Psalms 17:15 36:9 63:6 65:5 11:9 12:9 12:16, Revelation 5:10 7:16-7:17, Sifre Devarim Vezot Habracha 342, Song of Songs 5:1, Zechariah 9:15-9:17

כֹּה אָמַר יְהֹוָה קוֹל בְּרָמָה נִשְׁמָע נְהִי בְּכִי תַמְרוּרִים רָחֵל מְבַכָּה עַל־בָּנֶיהָ מֵאֲנָה לְהִנָּחֵם עַל־בָּנֶיהָ כִּי אֵינֶנּוּ	14[1] **Thus says the LORD**[2]: A voice is heard in Ramah, lamentation and bitter weeping, Rachel weeping for her children; she refuses to be comforted for her children, because they are not.
כֹּה אָמַר יְהֹוָה מִנְעִי קוֹלֵךְ מִבֶּכִי וְעֵינַיִךְ מִדִּמְעָה כִּי יֵשׁ שָׂכָר לִפְעֻלָּתֵךְ נְאֻם־יְהֹוָה וְשָׁבוּ מֵאֶרֶץ אוֹיֵב	15[3] Thus says the LORD: Refrain your voice from weeping, and your eyes from tears; for your work shall be rewarded, **says the LORD**[4]; and they shall come back from the land of the enemy.
וְיֵשׁ־תִּקְוָה לְאַחֲרִיתֵךְ נְאֻם־יְהֹוָה וְשָׁבוּ בָנִים לִגְבוּלָם	16[5] **And there is hope for your future, says the LORD**[6]; and your children shall return to their own border.
שָׁמוֹעַ שָׁמַעְתִּי אֶפְרַיִם מִתְנוֹדֵד יִסַּרְתַּנִי וָאִוָּסֵר כְּעֵגֶל לֹא לֻמָּד הֲשִׁיבֵנִי וְאָשׁוּבָה כִּי אַתָּה יְהֹוָה אֱלֹהָי	17[7] I have surely heard Ephraim bemoaning himself: 'You have chastised me, and I was chastised, as a calf untrained; turn me, and I shall be turned, for you are the LORD my God.
כִּי־אַחֲרֵי שׁוּבִי נִחַמְתִּי וְאַחֲרֵי הִוָּדְעִי סָפַקְתִּי עַל־יָרֵךְ בֹּשְׁתִּי וְגַם־נִכְלַמְתִּי כִּי נָשָׂאתִי חֶרְפַּת נְעוּרָי	18[8] Surely after that I turned, I repented, and after that I was instructed, I struck my thigh; I was ashamed, yes, confounded, because I bore the reproach of my youth.'
הֲבֵן יַקִּיר לִי אֶפְרַיִם אִם יֶלֶד שַׁעֲשֻׁעִים כִּי־מִדֵּי דַבְּרִי בּוֹ זָכֹר אֶזְכְּרֶנּוּ עוֹד עַל־כֵּן הָמוּ מֵעַי לוֹ רַחֵם אֲרַחֲמֶנּוּ נְאֻם־יְהֹוָה	19[9] Is Ephraim a darling son to Me? Is he a child who is pampered? For as often as I speak of him, I earnestly remember him still; therefore, My heart yearns for him, I will surely have compassion on him, says the LORD.
הַצִּיבִי לָךְ צִיֻּנִים שִׂמִי לָךְ תַּמְרוּרִים שִׁתִי לִבֵּךְ לַמְסִלָּה דֶּרֶךְ הָלָכְתְּ "הָלָכְתִּי" שׁוּבִי בְּתוּלַת יִשְׂרָאֵל שֻׁבִי אֶל־עָרַיִךְ אֵלֶּה	20[10] Set up sign posts, make guide posts; set your heart toward the high way, the way by which

[1] Jeremiah 31:14 - 1 Samuel 7:17, Ezekiel 2:10, Genesis 5:24 11:19 13:35 18:13 18:36, Isaiah 22:4, Jeremiah 10:20 16:1, Job 7:21, Joshua 18:25, Lamentations 5:7, Lamentations.R 1:23 Petichata D'Chakimei:24 Petichata D'Chakimei:34, Matthew 2:16-2:18, Midrash Tanchuma Bo 5, Pesikta de R'Kahana 20.2, Pesikta Rabbati 37:1, Psalms 37:36 77:3, z.Shemot 8a 12b
Jeremiah 31:14-16 - Mekilta de R'Ishmael Pisha 1:60-61

[2] Missing in LXX

[3] Jeremiah 31:15 - 1 Thessalonians 4:14, 2 Chronicles 15:7, b.Taanit 5a, Ecclesiastes 9:7, Ezekiel 11:17-11:18 20:41-20:42, Ezra 1:5-1:11, Genesis 19:31 21:1, Genesis.R 5:4 70:10 71:2 82:10 82:10 97 [Excl], Hebrews 6:10 11:6, Hosea 2:2, Isaiah 1:8 6:19, Jeremiah 23:3 5:14 6:3 6:18 31:5-31:6 9:7 9:11, John 20:13-20:15, Lamentations.R 1:23 Petichata D'Chakimei:24 Petichata D'Chakimei:34, Mark 5:38-5:39, Midrash Psalms 119:67, Midrash Tanchuma Bo 5, Midrash Tanchuma Shemot 3, Pesikta Rabbati 3:4, Psalms 30:6, Ruth 2:12, Ruth.R 7:13, z.Vaera 29b, z.Vaetchanan 269b, z.Vayigash 210a

[4] Missing in LXX

[5] Jeremiah 31:16 - Amos 9:8-9:9, Ezekiel 37:11-37:14 13:25 15:28, Hosea 2:15 3:5, Isaiah 6:13 11:11-11:16, Jeremiah 29:11-29:16 46:27-46:28, Lamentations 3:18 3:21 3:26, Lamentations.R 1:23 Petichata D'Chakimei:24 Petichata D'Chakimei:34, Matthew 24:22, Midrash Psalms 119:67, Pesikta de R'Kahana S5.2, Psalms 102:14-102:15, Romans 11:23-11:26, Selichot, z.Mikketz 203a, z.Vaetchanan 269b, z.Vayetze 158a, z.Vayishlach 175a

[6] Missing in LXX

[7] Jeremiah 31:17 - Acts 3:26, Hebrews 12:5, Hosea 4:16 5:12-5:13 5:15-6:2 10:11 11:8-11:9 14:6-14:10, Isaiah 1:5 9:14 3:20 5:7 57:15-57:18 15:16, James 1:16-1:18, Jeremiah 2:30 3:21-3:22 3:25 5:3 17:14 7:7 7:10 50:4-50:5, Job 5:17 33:27-33:28, Lamentations 3:27-3:30 5:21, Lamentations.R Petichata D'Chakimei:3, Luke 1:17 15:20, Malachi 3:24, Midrash Psalms 119:67, Pesikta Rabbati 3:4, Philippians 2:13, Proverbs 3:11 2:3 5:1, Psalms 32:9 39:9-39:10 80:4 80:8 80:20 85:5 94:12 102:20-102:21 119:75, Revelation 3:19, z.Vayishlach 175a, Zephaniah 3:2
Jeremiah 31:17-18 - Mesillat Yesharim 23:To Acquire Anavah

[8] Jeremiah 31:18 - 2 Corinthians 7:10-7:11, 2 Timothy 2:25, Deuteronomy 6:2 30:6-30:8, Ephesians 2:3-2:5, Ezekiel 6:9 16:61-16:63 20:43-20:44 21:17 23:3 12:26 12:31, Ezra 9:6, Gates of Repentance 1.011 1.018 1.043, Isaiah 6:4, Jastrow 1180a, Jeremiah 3:25 22:21 8:30, Job 13:26 20:11, John 6:44-6:45, Leviticus 26:41-26:42, Leviticus.R 3:7, Luke 15:17-15:19 15:30 18:13, mt.Hilchot Teshuvah 1:1 1:1 2:2 2:2, Psalms 25:7, Romans 6:21, Tanna Devei Eliyahu 6, Titus 3:3-3:7, Zechariah 12:10

[9] Jeremiah 31:19 - 1 Kings 3:26, b.Megillah 31a, Chibbur Yafeh 27 {124b} 27 {126a/Line8}, Deuteronomy 8:36, Gates of Repentance 1.011 1.021 1.022, Genesis 19:30, Hosea 11:8-11:9 14:6, Isaiah 16:11 7:7 57:16-57:18 15:15, Jeremiah 3:19 7:10 24:36, Judges 10:16, Lamentations 3:31-3:32, Luke 15:24 15:32, Mesillat Yesharim 19:Love-of-Hashem Mussaf Rosh Hashanah, Micah 7:18-7:19, Midrash Psalms 70:1 116:5, Midrash Tanchuma Tetzaveh 1, mt.Hilchot Shofar Sukkah vLulav 3:9, Pesikta de R'Kahana 20.2, Philippians 1:8, Proverbs 3:12, Psalms 7:13, Song of Songs 5:4
Jeremiah 31:19-23 - 4QJerc

[10] Jeremiah 31:20 - 1 Chronicles 5:3, 2 Chronicles 11:16 20:3, Deuteronomy 8:46, Deuteronomy.R 2:24 7:11, Ezekiel 16:4, Genesis.R 71:2 82:10, Guide for the Perplexed 1:46, Haggai 1:5, Isaiah 24:20 52:11-12 9:14 14:10, Jastrow 1611b, Jeremiah 3:14 7:5 2:5 3:6

you went; return, O virgin of Israel, return to your cities.

עַד־מָתַי֙ תִּֽתְחַמָּקִ֔ין הַבַּ֖ת הַשּֽׁוֹבֵבָ֑ה כִּֽי־בָרָ֨א יְהוָ֤ה חֲדָשָׁה֙ בָּאָ֔רֶץ נְקֵבָ֖ה תְּס֥וֹבֵֽב גָּֽבֶר

21[1] How long will you turn away coyly, O you backsliding daughter? For the LORD created *a new thing in the earth: a woman shall court a man*[2].

כֹּֽה־אָמַ֞ר יְהוָ֤ה צְבָאוֹת֙ אֱלֹהֵ֣י יִשְׂרָאֵ֔ל ע֣וֹד יֹאמְר֗וּ אֶת־הַדָּבָ֤ר הַזֶּה֙ בְּאֶ֣רֶץ יְהוּדָ֔ה וּבְעָרָ֖יו בְּשׁוּבִ֣י אֶת־שְׁבוּתָ֑ם יְבָרֶכְךָ֧ יְהוָ֛ה נְוֵה־צֶ֖דֶק הַ֥ר הַקֹּֽדֶשׁ

22[3] Thus says the LORD of hosts, *the God of Israel*[4]: Yet again they shall use this speech in the land of Judah and in its cities, when I turn their captivity: 'The LORD bless you, O abode of righteousness, O mountain of holiness.'

וְיָ֥שְׁבוּ בָ֖הּ יְהוּדָ֣ה וְכָל־עָרָ֑יו יַחְדָּ֑ו אִכָּרִ֖ים וְנָסְע֥וּ בַּעֵֽדֶר

23[5] And Judah and all its cities shall live in it together: the husbandmen, and they who go forth with flocks.

כִּ֥י הִרְוֵ֖יתִי נֶ֣פֶשׁ עֲיֵפָ֑ה וְכָל־נֶ֥פֶשׁ דָּאֲבָ֖ה מִלֵּֽאתִי

24[6] For I have satiated the weary soul, and I have replenished every hungry soul.

עַל־זֹ֖את הֱקִיצֹ֣תִי וָאֶרְאֶ֑ה וּשְׁנָתִ֖י עָ֥רְבָה לִּֽי

25[7] Upon this I awoke, and saw, and my sleep was sweet to me.

הִנֵּ֛ה יָמִ֥ים בָּאִ֖ים נְאֻם־יְהוָ֑ה וְזָרַעְתִּ֗י אֶת־בֵּ֤ית יִשְׂרָאֵל֙ וְאֶת־בֵּ֣ית יְהוּדָ֔ה זֶ֥רַע אָדָ֖ם וְזֶ֥רַע בְּהֵמָֽה

26[8] Behold, the days come, says the LORD, that I will sow the house of Israel and the house of Judah with the seed of man, and with the seed of beast.

וְהָיָ֞ה כַּאֲשֶׁ֧ר שָׁקַ֣דְתִּי עֲלֵיהֶ֗ם לִנְת֤וֹשׁ וְלִנְתוֹץ֙ וְלַהֲרֹ֣ס וּלְהַאֲבִ֣יד וּלְהָרֵ֔עַ כֵּ֣ן אֶשְׁקֹ֧ד עֲלֵיהֶ֛ם לִבְנ֥וֹת וְלִנְט֖וֹעַ נְאֻם־יְהוָֽה

27[9] And it shall come to pass, that as I watched over them to pluck up and to break down, and to overthrow and to destroy, and to afflict; so will I watch over them to build and to plant, says the LORD.

בַּיָּמִ֣ים הָהֵ֔ם לֹא־יֹאמְר֣וּ ע֔וֹד אָב֖וֹת אָ֣כְלוּ בֹ֑סֶר וְשִׁנֵּ֥י בָנִ֖ים תִּקְהֶֽינָה

28[10] In those days they shall no longer say: 'The fathers ate sour grapes, and the children's teeth are set on edge.'

כִּ֣י אִם־אִ֥ישׁ בַּעֲוֺנ֖וֹ יָמ֑וּת כָּל־הָֽאָדָ֛ם הָאֹכֵ֥ל הַבֹּ֖סֶר תִּקְהֶ֥ינָה שִׁנָּֽיו

29[11] But everyone shall die for his own iniquity; every man who eats the sour grapes, his teeth shall be set on edge.

הִנֵּ֛ה יָמִ֥ים בָּאִ֖ים נְאֻם־יְהוָ֑ה וְכָרַתִּ֗י אֶת־בֵּ֤ית יִשְׂרָאֵל֙ וְאֶת־בֵּ֣ית יְהוּדָ֔ה בְּרִ֖ית חֲדָשָֽׁה

30[12] Behold, the days come, says the LORD, that I will make a new covenant with the house of Israel, and with the house of Judah;

3:50, Lamentations.R 1:54, Leviticus.R 2:2-3, Midrash Psalms 77:2, Pesikta Rabbati 10:5 37:1, Proverbs 24:32, Psalms 62:11 84:6, Ruth.R 7:13, Saadia Opinions 2:10, Sifre Devarim Ekev 43, Song of Songs.R 5:4, y.Kiddushin 4:1, z.Shemot 12b, Zechariah 2:6-7 10:9

[1] Jeremiah 31:21 - b.Sotah [Rashi] 12a, b.Succah [Rashi] 49a, Ein Yaakov Yevamot:62b, Galatians 4:4, Genesis 3:15, Hosea 4:16 8:5 11:7 14:6, Isaiah 7:14, Jastrow 435a 1275b 1277b, Jeremiah 2:18 2:23 2:36 3:6 3:8 3:11-12 3:14 3:22 4:14 7:24 8:4-6 13:27 14:7 1:4, Luke 1:34-35, Matthew 1:21, Midrash Psalms 73:4, Numbers 16:30, Pesikta Rabbati 33:13, Sifre Devarim Ekev 43, Zechariah 7:11

[2] LXX *safety for a new plantation: men shall go about in safety*

[3] Jeremiah 31:22 - 4 15, Isaiah 1:21 1:26 12:21, Jeremiah 23:5-8 6:18 33:15-26 2:7, Micah 4:1, Midrash Psalms 73:4, Midrash Tanchuma Lech Lecha 15, Obadiah 1:17, Psalms 28:9 48:2-3 87:1-3 122:5-8 8:5 9:8 14:3, Ruth 2:4, Sefer Yetzirah 6:1, Zechariah 8:3

[4] Missing in LXX

[5] Jeremiah 31:23 - Ezekiel 12:10, Genesis.R 82:2, Jeremiah 33:11-13, z.Vaetchanan 269b, Zechariah 2:4 8:4-8

[6] Jeremiah 31:24 - 2 Corinthians 7:6, b.Moed Katan [Tosefot] 2a, Isaiah 8:2 2:4, Jeremiah 7:15, John 4:14, Luke 1:53, Matthew 5:6 11:28, Psalms 11:9

[7] Jeremiah 31:25 - Psalms 7:2, Zechariah 4:1-2
Jeremiah 31:25-26 - 4QJerc

[8] Jeremiah 31:26 - b.Chullin 5b, b.Sotah 22a, Ein Yaakov Sotah:22a, Ezekiel 12:9 12:11, Hosea 2:23, Jeremiah 6:19, Zechariah 10:9

[9] Jeremiah 31:27 - Acts 15:16, Amos 9:11, Daniel 9:14 9:25, Ecclesiastes 3:2-3:3, Ein Yaakov Chullin:5b, Jeremiah 1:10 18:7-18:9 24:6 8:41 20:27 21:4, Psalms 69:36 6:17 3:2

[10] Jeremiah 31:28 - b.Taanit [Rashi] 7b, Ezekiel 18:2-18:3, Jeremiah 7:31, Lamentations 5:7, Ralbag Wars 4:6

[11] Jeremiah 31:29 - b.Eruvin [Rashi] 27b, Deuteronomy 24:16, Ezekiel 3:18-19 3:24 18:4 18:20 9:8 9:13 9:18, Galatians 6:5 6:7-8, Isaiah 3:11, James 1:15, Leviticus.R 15:5, Ralbag Wars 4:6

[12] Jeremiah 31:30 - 1 Corinthians 11:25, 2 Corinthians 3:6, Amos 9:13, Ezekiel 13:26, Galatians 6:16, Hebrews 8:6-13 9:15 10:16-17 12:24 13:20, Jeremiah 23:5 6:3 7:28 31:32-35 8:40 33:14-16 50:4-5, Luke 22:20, Mark 14:24, Mas.Kallah Rabbati 3:25, Matthew 2:28, Philippians 3:3

לֹא כַבְּרִית אֲשֶׁר כָּרַתִּי אֶת־אֲבוֹתָם בְּיוֹם הֶחֱזִיקִי בְיָדָם לְהוֹצִיאָם מֵאֶרֶץ מִצְרָיִם אֲשֶׁר־הֵמָּה הֵפֵרוּ אֶת־בְּרִיתִי וְאָנֹכִי בָּעַלְתִּי בָם נְאֻם־יְהוָה

31 [1] not like the covenant I made with their fathers in the day I took them by the hand to bring them from the land of Egypt; because they broke My covenant, *although I was a lord over them* [2], says the LORD.

כִּי זֹאת הַבְּרִית אֲשֶׁר אֶכְרֹת אֶת־בֵּית יִשְׂרָאֵל אַחֲרֵי הַיָּמִים הָהֵם נְאֻם־יְהוָה נָתַתִּי אֶת־תּוֹרָתִי בְּקִרְבָּם וְעַל־לִבָּם אֶכְתֲּבֶנָּה וְהָיִיתִי לָהֶם לֵאלֹהִים וְהֵמָּה יִהְיוּ־לִי לְעָם

32 [3] But this is the covenant I will make with the house of Israel after those days, says the LORD, I will put My law in their inward parts, and in their heart I will write it; and I will be their God, and they shall be My people;

וְלֹא יְלַמְּדוּ עוֹד אִישׁ אֶת־רֵעֵהוּ וְאִישׁ אֶת־אָחִיו לֵאמֹר דְּעוּ אֶת־יְהוָה כִּי־כוּלָּם יֵדְעוּ אוֹתִי לְמִקְטַנָּם וְעַד־גְּדוֹלָם נְאֻם־יְהוָה כִּי אֶסְלַח לַעֲוֹנָם וּלְחַטָּאתָם לֹא אֶזְכָּר־עוֹד

33 [4] and they shall no longer teach every man his neighbor, and every man his brother, saying: 'Know the LORD;' for they shall all know Me, from the least of them to the great of them, says the LORD; for I will *forgive their iniquity* [5], and I will remember their sin no more.

כֹּה אָמַר יְהוָה נֹתֵן שֶׁמֶשׁ לְאוֹר יוֹמָם חֻקֹּת יָרֵחַ וְכוֹכָבִים לְאוֹר לָיְלָה רֹגַע הַיָּם וַיֶּהֱמוּ גַלָּיו יְהוָה צְבָאוֹת שְׁמוֹ

34 [6] Thus says the LORD, Who gives the sun as a light by day, and the ordinances of the moon and of the stars as a light by night, Who stirs up the sea so its waves roar, The LORD of hosts is His name:

אִם־יָמֻשׁוּ הַחֻקִּים הָאֵלֶּה מִלְּפָנַי נְאֻם־יְהוָה גַּם זֶרַע יִשְׂרָאֵל יִשְׁבְּתוּ מִהְיוֹת גּוֹי לְפָנַי כָּל־הַיָּמִים

35 [7] If these ordinances depart from before Me, says the LORD, then the seed of Israel also shall cease from being a nation before Me forever.

כֹּה אָמַר יְהוָה אִם־יִמַּדּוּ שָׁמַיִם מִלְמַעְלָה וְיֵחָקְרוּ מוֹסְדֵי־אֶרֶץ לְמָטָּה גַּם־אֲנִי אֶמְאַס בְּכָל־זֶרַע יִשְׂרָאֵל עַל־כָּל־אֲשֶׁר עָשׂוּ נְאֻם־יְהוָה

36 [8] *Thus says the LORD: If heaven above can be measured, and the foundations of the earth searched out beneath, then I will cast off all the seed* [9] of Israel for all they have done, says the LORD.

הִנֵּה יָמִים '...' "בָּאִים" נְאֻם־יְהוָה וְנִבְנְתָה הָעִיר לַיהוָה מִמִּגְדַּל חֲנַנְאֵל שַׁעַר הַפִּנָּה

37 [10] Behold, the days come, says the LORD, that the city shall be built to the LORD from the tower of Hananel to the gate of the corner.

---

[1] Jeremiah 31:31 - 1 Kings 8:9, 2 Corinthians 11:2, Apocalypse of Elijah 1:13 2, Deuteronomy 1:31 5:3 28:69 5:20 7:16, Exodus 19:5 24:6-24:8, Ezekiel 16:8 16:59-16:62 20:37 23:4, Hebrews 8:9 9:18-9:22, Hosea 2:2 3:1 11:1 11:3-11:4, Isaiah 24:5 17:13 6:5 63:12-63:14, Jeremiah 2:2 3:14 11:7-11:10 22:9 7:2 10:14, John 3:29, Leviticus 2:15, Mark 8:23, Psalms 73:23, Saadia Opinions 3:8, Song of Songs 8:5, Testament of Benjamin 10:11
[2] LXX *and I disregarded them*
[3] Jeremiah 31:32 - 2 Corinthians 3:3 3:7-3:8, b.Pesachim 50a, Deuteronomy 6:6, Ezekiel 11:19-11:20 36:25-36:27 13:27, Galatians 5:22-5:23, Genesis 17:7-17:8, Hebrews 8:10 10:16, Isaiah 3:7, Jeremiah 24:7 6:22 7:2 8:38 8:40, John 20:17, Midrash Tanchuma Reeh 14, Psalms 37:31 40:9, Revelation 21:3 21:7, Romans 7:22 8:2-8:8, Saadia Opinions 3:8, Zechariah 13:9
[4] Jeremiah 31:33 - 1 Chronicles 4:9, 1 John 2:20 2:27 5:20, 1 Samuel 2:12, 1 Thessalonians 4:9, 2 Corinthians 2:10 4:6, Acts 10:43 13:38-13:39, b.Pesachim 50a, Ecclesiastes.R 2:1, Ephesians 1:7, Habakkuk 2:14, Hebrews 5:12 8:12 10:17-10:18, Isaiah 11:9 6:26 9:24 19:25 20:22 6:13 60:19-60:21, Jeremiah 24:7 9:8 2:20, John 6:45 17:3 17:6, Life of Adam and Eve [Apocalypse] 13:5, Matthew 11:27, Micah 7:18, mt.Hilchot Teshuvah 9:2 9:2, mt.Perek Chelek Intro:11, Pesikta de R'Kahana 10.6 12.21, Romans 11:26-27, Saadia Opinions 3:8, Song of Songs.R 1:15 8:19, Tanya Likutei Aramim §42
[5] LXX *be merciful to their iniquities*
[6] Jeremiah 31:34 - 2 Baruch 77:2, Apocalypse of Elijah 5:4, Deuteronomy 4:19, Exodus 14:21-14:22, Genesis 1:14-1:18, Isaiah 24:2 3:15 6:5 15:12, Jeremiah 5:22 10:16 8:18 22:18 2:34 3:19, Job 2:12 38:10-38:11 14:33, Matthew 5:45 8:25-8:26, Mekilta de R'Ishmael Beshallah 4:28, Midrash Tanchuma Bereshit 1, Midrash Tanchuma Ekev 11, Psalms 19:2-19:7 72:5 72:17 74:13 74:16 78:13 89:3 89:37-89:38 93:3-93:4 10:9 107:25-107:29 114:3-114:5 119:89 136:7-136:9, Saadia Opinions 7:7, z.Vayikra 23a
Jeremiah 31:34-39 - Birchat HaChammah.Vihi Noam, Maamad [Wednesday]
[7] Jeremiah 31:35 - Amos 9:8-9:9, Deuteronomy 8:26, Guide for the Perplexed 2:28, Isaiah 54:9-54:10, Jeremiah 33:20-33:26 22:28, Leviticus.R 35:4, Mekilta de R'Shimon bar Yochai Beshallach 23:1, Mekilta de R'Ishmael Beshallah 4:80, Numbers.R 1:3, Psalms 72:5 72:17 89:37-89:38 6:29 119:89 4:6, Saadia Opinions 3:7, z.Vaetchanan 269b
[8] Jeremiah 31:36 - Esther.R 7:11, Exodus.R 31:10, Isaiah 16:12, Jeremiah 6:11 9:22 33:24-33:26 22:28, Job 11:7-11:9, Lamentations.R 5:20, Midrash Tanchuma Haazinu 1, Midrash Tanchuma Mishpatim 11, Proverbs 6:4, Psalms 89:3, Romans 11:1-11:5 11:26-11:29, Saadia Opinions 3:7
[9] LXX *Though the sky should be raised to a greater height, says the LORD, and though the ground of the earth should be sunk lower beneath, yet I will not cast off the family*
[10] Jeremiah 31:37 - 2 Chronicles 2:9, 2 Kings 14:13, b.Nedarim 37b, Daniel 9:25, Esther.R 7:11, Ezekiel 48:30-48:35, Genesis.R 76:1, Isaiah 20:28, Jeremiah 23:5 6:18 7:28, Mekilta de R'Shimon bar Yochai Beshallach 23:1, Nehemiah 2:17-3:1 12:30-12:40, Pesikta de R'Kahana 19.5, Pesikta Rabbati 33:5, z.Vaetchanan 269b, Zechariah 14:10

וְיָצָא עוֹד 'קָוֵה' "קָו" הַמִּדָּה נֶגְדּוֹ עַל גִּבְעַת גָּרֵב וְנָסַב גֹּעָתָה

38[1] *And the measuring line shall go out straight forward to the hill Gareb, and shall turn about to Goah[2].*

וְכָל־הָעֵמֶק הַפְּגָרִים וְהַדֶּשֶׁן 'וְכָל־הַשְּׁרֵמוֹת' "וְכָל־הַשְּׁדֵמוֹת" עַד־נַחַל קִדְרוֹן עַד־פִּנַּת שַׁעַר הַסּוּסִים מִזְרָחָה קֹדֶשׁ לַיהוָה לֹא־יִנָּתֵשׁ וְלֹא־יֵהָרֵס עוֹד לְעוֹלָם

39[3] And the whole *valley of the dead bodies[4]*, and *of the ashes, and all the fields to the brook[5]* Kidron, to the corner of the horse gate toward the east, shall be holy to the LORD; it shall not be plucked up, nor thrown down again forever.

Jeremiah – Chapter 32[6]

הַדָּבָר אֲשֶׁר־הָיָה אֶל־יִרְמְיָהוּ מֵאֵת יְהוָה 'בִּשְׁנַת' "בַּשָּׁנָה" הָעֲשִׂרִית לְצִדְקִיָּהוּ מֶלֶךְ יְהוּדָה הִיא הַשָּׁנָה שְׁמֹנֶה־עֶשְׂרֵה שָׁנָה לִנְבוּכַדְרֶאצַּר

1[7] The word that came to Jeremiah from the LORD in the tenth year of Zedekiah king of Judah, which was the eighteenth year of Nebuchadrezzar.

וְאָז חֵיל מֶלֶךְ בָּבֶל צָרִים עַל־יְרוּשָׁלָ͏ִם וְיִרְמְיָהוּ הַנָּבִיא הָיָה כָלוּא בַּחֲצַר הַמַּטָּרָה אֲשֶׁר בֵּית־מֶלֶךְ יְהוּדָה

2[8] Now at that time the king of Babylon's army was besieging Jerusalem; and Jeremiah the prophet was shut up in the court of the guard, which was in the king of Judah's house.

אֲשֶׁר כְּלָאוֹ צִדְקִיָּהוּ מֶלֶךְ־יְהוּדָה לֵאמֹר מַדּוּעַ אַתָּה נִבָּא לֵאמֹר כֹּה אָמַר יְהוָה הִנְנִי נֹתֵן אֶת־הָעִיר הַזֹּאת בְּיַד מֶלֶךְ־בָּבֶל וּלְכָדָהּ

3[9] For Zedekiah king of Judah had shut him up, saying: 'Why do you prophesy, and say: Thus says the LORD: behold, I will give this city into the hand of the king of Babylon, and he shall take it;

וְצִדְקִיָּהוּ מֶלֶךְ יְהוּדָה לֹא יִמָּלֵט מִיַּד הַכַּשְׂדִּים כִּי הִנָּתֹן יִנָּתֵן בְּיַד מֶלֶךְ־בָּבֶל וְדִבֶּר־פִּיו עִם־פִּיו וְעֵינָיו 'אֶת־עֵינוֹ' "אֶת־עֵינָיו" תִּרְאֶינָה

4[10] and Zedekiah king of Judah shall not escape from the hand of the Chaldeans, but shall surely be delivered into the hand of the king of Babylon, and shall speak with him mouth to mouth, and his eyes shall see his eyes;

וּבָבֶל יוֹלִךְ אֶת־צִדְקִיָּהוּ וְשָׁם יִהְיֶה עַד־פָּקְדִי אֹתוֹ נְאֻם־יְהוָה כִּי תִלָּחֲמוּ אֶת־הַכַּשְׂדִּים לֹא תַצְלִיחוּ

5[11] *and he shall lead Zedekiah to Babylon, and there he shall he be until I remember him, says the LORD; though you fight with the Chaldeans, you shall not prosper[12]?'*

וַיֹּאמֶר יִרְמְיָהוּ הָיָה דְּבַר־יְהוָה אֵלַי לֵאמֹר

6[13] And Jeremiah said: 'The word of the LORD came to me, saying:

הִנֵּה חֲנַמְאֵל בֶּן־שַׁלֻּם דֹּדְךָ בָּא אֵלֶיךָ לֵאמֹר קְנֵה לְךָ אֶת־שָׂדִי אֲשֶׁר בַּעֲנָתוֹת כִּי לְךָ מִשְׁפַּט הַגְּאֻלָּה לִקְנוֹת

7[14] Behold, Hanamel, the son of Shallum your uncle, shall come to you, saying: Buy my field that is in Anathoth; for the right of redemption it is your to buy.'

---

[1] Jeremiah 31:38 - Ezekiel 16:8, Mas.Soferim 6:8, Zechariah 2:1-2:2

[2] LXX *And the measurement of it shall proceed in front of them as far as the hills of Gareb, and it shall be compassed with a circular wall of choice stones*

[3] Jeremiah 31:39 - 2 Chronicles 23:15, 2 Kings 11:16 23:6 23:12, 2 Samuel 15:23, b.Arachin [Tosefot] 10a, b.Berachot [Rashi] 12b, Ezekiel 13:2 13:25 15:29 45:1-45:6 24:35, Isaiah 3:22, Jastrow 291a, Saadia Opinions 8:7, Jeremiah 7:31-7:32 8:2 18:7 19:11-19:13 8:36, Joel 4:17, John 18:1, Nehemiah 3:28, Zechariah 14:20

[4] LXX *Asaremoth*

[5] LXX *to Nachal*

[6] Chapter 39 in LXX

[7] Jeremiah 32:1 - 2 Chronicles 12:11, 2 Kings 25:1-25:2, b.Bava Batra [Rashi] 28b, Jeremiah 1:1 39:1-39:2 52:4-52:5

[8] Jeremiah 32:2 - b.Bava Batra [Rashi] 28b, Jeremiah 8:3 8:8 9:1 12:5 13:21 14:6 39:13-39:15, Matthew 5:12, Nehemiah 3:25

[9] Jeremiah 32:3 - 2 Chronicles 4:22, 2 Kings 6:31-6:32, Acts 6:12-6:14, Amos 7:13, Exodus 5:4, Jeremiah 2:30 5:3 21:4-21:7 26:8-26:9 3:8 32:28-32:29 34:2-34:3 37:6-37:10 14:4 14:8, Luke 20:2, z.Vaetchanan 269b

[10] Jeremiah 32:4 - 2 Kings 25:4-25:7, Ezekiel 12:12-12:13 17:13-17:21 21:30-21:31, Jeremiah 13:17 14:18 14:23 39:4-39:7 52:8-52:11, Josephus Antiquities 11.7.2

[11] Jeremiah 32:5 - 2 Chronicles 13:12 24:20, Ezekiel 12:13 17:9-17:10 17:15, Jeremiah 2:37 21:4-21:5 3:22 9:5 34:4-34:5 13:10 15:7, Numbers 14:41, Proverbs 21:30

[12] LXX *and Sedekias shall go into Babylon, and live there*

[13] Jeremiah 32:6-27 - Haftarah Behar Sinai [Ashkenaz and Sephard]

[14] Jeremiah 32:7 - 1 Kings 14:5, b.Bava Batra [Rashi] 28b, Jeremiah 1:1 11:21, Joshua 21:18-21:19, Leviticus 1:23 1:25 1:34 1:49, Mark 11:2-11:6 14:13-14:16, Midrash Tanchuma Behar 3, Numbers 11:2, Pesikta de R'Kahana 13.14, Pirkei de R'Eliezer 33, Ruth 4:3-4:9

וַיָּבֹא אֵלַי חֲנַמְאֵל בֶּן־דֹּדִי כִּדְבַר יְהֹוָה אֶל־חֲצַר
הַמַּטָּרָה וַיֹּאמֶר אֵלַי קְנֵה נָא אֶת־שָׂדִי אֲשֶׁר־
בַּעֲנָתוֹת אֲשֶׁר בְּאֶרֶץ בִּנְיָמִין כִּי־לְךָ מִשְׁפַּט
הַיְרֻשָּׁה וּלְךָ הַגְּאֻלָּה קְנֵה־לָךְ וָאֵדַע כִּי דְבַר־יְהֹוָה
הוּא

וָאֶקְנֶה אֶת־הַשָּׂדֶה מֵאֵת חֲנַמְאֵל בֶּן־דֹּדִי אֲשֶׁר
בַּעֲנָתוֹת וָאֶשְׁקֲלָה־לּוֹ אֶת־הַכֶּסֶף שִׁבְעָה שְׁקָלִים
וַעֲשָׂרָה הַכָּסֶף

וָאֶכְתֹּב בַּסֵּפֶר וָאֶחְתֹּם וָאָעֵד עֵדִים וָאֶשְׁקֹל הַכֶּסֶף
בְּמֹאזְנָיִם

וָאֶקַּח אֶת־סֵפֶר הַמִּקְנָה אֶת־הֶחָתוּם הַמִּצְוָה
וְהַחֻקִּים וְאֶת־הַגָּלוּי

וָאֶתֵּן אֶת־הַסֵּפֶר הַמִּקְנָה אֶל־בָּרוּךְ בֶּן־נֵרִיָּה בֶּן־
מַחְסֵיָה לְעֵינֵי חֲנַמְאֵל דֹּדִי וּלְעֵינֵי הָעֵדִים
הַכֹּתְבִים בְּסֵפֶר הַמִּקְנָה לְעֵינֵי כָּל־הַיְּהוּדִים
הַיֹּשְׁבִים בַּחֲצַר הַמַּטָּרָה

וָאֲצַוֶּה אֶת־בָּרוּךְ לְעֵינֵיהֶם לֵאמֹר

כֹּה־אָמַר יְהֹוָה צְבָאוֹת אֱלֹהֵי יִשְׂרָאֵל לָקוֹחַ אֶת־
הַסְּפָרִים הָאֵלֶּה אֵת סֵפֶר הַמִּקְנָה הַזֶּה וְאֵת
הֶחָתוּם וְאֵת סֵפֶר הַגָּלוּי הַזֶּה וּנְתַתָּם בִּכְלִי־חָרֶשׂ
לְמַעַן יַעַמְדוּ יָמִים רַבִּים

כִּי כֹה אָמַר יְהֹוָה צְבָאוֹת אֱלֹהֵי יִשְׂרָאֵל עוֹד יִקָּנוּ
בָתִּים וְשָׂדוֹת וּכְרָמִים בָּאָרֶץ הַזֹּאת

וָאֶתְפַּלֵּל אֶל־יְהֹוָה אַחֲרֵי תִתִּי אֶת־סֵפֶר הַמִּקְנָה
אֶל־בָּרוּךְ בֶּן־נֵרִיָּה לֵאמֹר

אֲהָהּ אֲדֹנָי יְהוִה הִנֵּה אַתָּה עָשִׂיתָ אֶת־הַשָּׁמַיִם
וְאֶת־הָאָרֶץ בְּכֹחֲךָ הַגָּדוֹל וּבִזְרֹעֲךָ הַנְּטוּיָה לֹא־
יִפָּלֵא מִמְּךָ כָּל־דָּבָר

8[1] So *Hanamel my uncle's son*[2] came to me in the court of the guard according to the word of the LORD, and said to me: 'Buy my field, please, that is in Anathoth, which is in the land of Benjamin; for the right of inheritance is yours, and the redemption is yours; buy it for yourself.' Then I knew this was the word of the LORD.

9[3] And I bought the field that was in Anathoth of Hanamel my uncle's son, and weighed him the money, seventeen shekels of silver.

10[4] And I subscribed the deed, and sealed it, and called witnesses, and weighed the money in the balances.

11[5] So I took the deed of purchase, both what was sealed, containing the terms and conditions, and what was open;

12[6] and I delivered the deed of purchase to Baruch the son of Neriah, the son of Mahseiah, in the presence of Hanamel my uncle['s son], and in the presence of the witnesses who subscribed the deed of the purchase, before all the Jews who sat in the court of the guard.

13 And I charged Baruch before them, saying:

14[7] 'Thus says the LORD of hosts, *the God of Israel*[8]: Take these deeds, this deed of purchase, both what is sealed, and this deed which is open, and put them in an earthen vessel; so they may continue many days.

15[9] For thus says the LORD of hosts, the God of Israel: Houses and fields and vineyards shall yet again be bought in this land.'

16[10] Now after I had delivered the deed of the purchase to Baruch the son of Neriah, I prayed to the LORD, saying:

17[11] 'Ah Lord GOD! Behold, you have made the heaven and the earth by Your great power and

---

[1] Jeremiah 32:8 - 1 Chronicles 6:45, 1 Kings 2:26 22:25, 1 Samuel 9:16-17 10:3-7, Acts 10:17-28, b.Megillah [Rashi] 15a, Jeremiah 8:2 8:7 9:1, John 4:53, Midrash Tanchuma Behar 3, Zechariah 11:11

[2] LXX *the son of Salom my father's brother*

[3] Jeremiah 32:9 - 1 Kings 20:39, Esther 3:9, Genesis 23:15-16 13:28, Hosea 3:2, Isaiah 7:2, Midrash Tanchuma Behar 3, Zechariah 11:12-13

[4] Jeremiah 32:10 - 2 Corinthians 1:22, Daniel 8:26, Deuteronomy 8:34, Ephesians 1:13 4:30, Isaiah 8:1-8:2 6:8 20:5, Jeremiah 8:12 8:25 8:44, Job 14:17, John 3:33 6:27, Joshua 18:9, Revelation 7:2 9:4, Ruth 4:9-4:11, Song of Songs 8:6

[5] Jeremiah 32:11 - 1 Corinthians 11:16, Acts 2:3, b.Bava Batra 160b, b.Gittin 20b, b.Kiddushin 9a 26a, Jastrow 1432b, Luke 2:27, variant המצוה ואת of המצוה is found, y.Bava Batra 10:1, y.Gittin 8:10

[6] Jeremiah 32:12 - 2 Corinthians 8:21, Jeremiah 8:16 36:4-36:5 36:16-36:19 12:26 12:32 43:3-43:6 45:1-45:5 3:59 Jeremiah 32:12-16 - 2 Baruch 1:1

[7] Jeremiah 32:14 - b.Bava Batra [Rashbam] 160b, b.Bava Batra 29a, b.Gittin 22b, b.Megillah 26b, b.Menachot [Tosefot] 85a, Guide for the Perplexed 1:13, Sifre Devarim Vaetchanan 31, t.Sheviit 4:2, z.Vaetchanan 269b

[8] Missing in LXX

[9] Jeremiah 32:15 - Amos 9:14-9:15, Jeremiah 6:18 7:6 7:13 7:25 8:37 32:43-32:44 33:12-33:13, Mekhilta de R'Shimon bar Yochai Bachodesh 52:1, z.Vaetchanan 269b, Zechariah 3:10

[10] Jeremiah 32:16 - 2 Samuel 7:18-7:25, Ezekiel 36:35-36:37, Genesis 32:10-32:12, Jeremiah 12:1, Midrash Psalms 90:2, Philippians 4:6-4:7

[11] Jeremiah 32:17 - 2 Baruch 54:2, 2 Kings 19:15, Acts 7:49-7:50 14:15 15:18 17:24, Colossians 1:15-1:16, Daniel 2:22, Ein Yaakov Yoma:69b, Ephesians 3:9-3:11, Exodus 20:11, Ezekiel 9:8 11:13, Genesis 1:1-1:31 18:14, Genesis.R 9:3, Hebrews 1:2-1:3 1:10-1:12, Isaiah 40:26-40:28 18:5 20:24 21:12 46:9-46:10 48:12-48:13, Jeremiah 1:6 4:10 10:11-10:12 14:13 3:5 8:27 3:15 3:19, Job 18:2, John 1:1-1:3, Luke 1:37 18:27, Matthew 19:26, Nehemiah 9:6, Psalms 6:26 136:5-136:9 146:5-146:6, Revelation 4:11, Zechariah 12:1

עֹשֶׂה חֶסֶד לַאֲלָפִים וּמְשַׁלֵּם עֲוֺן אָבוֹת אֶל־חֵיק בְּנֵיהֶם אַחֲרֵיהֶם הָאֵל הַגָּדוֹל הַגִּבּוֹר יְהוָה צְבָאוֹת שְׁמוֹ	18[2]	by Your outstretched arm; *there is nothing too hard for You*[1]; Who shows mercy to thousands, and returns the iniquity of the fathers into the bosom of their children after them; the great, the mighty God, the LORD of hosts is His name;
גְּדֹל הָעֵצָה וְרַב הָעֲלִילִיָּה אֲשֶׁר־עֵינֶיךָ פְקֻחוֹת עַל־כָּל־דַּרְכֵי בְּנֵי אָדָם לָתֵת לְאִישׁ כִּדְרָכָיו וְכִפְרִי מַעֲלָלָיו	19[3]	great in counsel, and mighty in work; whose eyes are open on all the ways of the sons of men, to give everyone according to his ways, and according to the fruit of his deeds;
אֲשֶׁר־שַׂמְתָּ אֹתוֹת וּמֹפְתִים בְּאֶרֶץ־מִצְרַיִם עַד־הַיּוֹם הַזֶּה וּבְיִשְׂרָאֵל וּבָאָדָם וַתַּעֲשֶׂה־לְּךָ שֵׁם כַּיּוֹם הַזֶּה	20[4]	who sets signs and wonders in the land of Egypt, to this day, and in Israel and among other men; and made Yourself a name, as is this day;
וַתֹּצֵא אֶת־עַמְּךָ אֶת־יִשְׂרָאֵל מֵאֶרֶץ מִצְרָיִם בְּאֹתוֹת וּבְמוֹפְתִים וּבְיָד חֲזָקָה וּבְאֶזְרוֹעַ נְטוּיָה וּבְמוֹרָא גָּדוֹל	21[5]	and brought forth Your people Israel from the land of Egypt with signs, and with wonders, and with a strong hand, and with an outstretched arm, and with great *terror*[6];
וַתִּתֵּן לָהֶם אֶת־הָאָרֶץ הַזֹּאת אֲשֶׁר־נִשְׁבַּעְתָּ לַאֲבוֹתָם לָתֵת לָהֶם אֶרֶץ זָבַת חָלָב וּדְבָשׁ	22[7]	and gave them this land, which You swore to their fathers to give them, a land flowing with milk and honey;
וַיָּבֹאוּ וַיִּרְשׁוּ אֹתָהּ וְלֹא־שָׁמְעוּ בְקוֹלֶךָ 'וּבְתרוֹתֶךָ' "וּבְתוֹרָתְךָ" לֹא־הָלָכוּ אֵת כָּל־אֲשֶׁר צִוִּיתָה לָהֶם לַעֲשׂוֹת לֹא עָשׂוּ וַתַּקְרֵא אֹתָם אֵת כָּל־הָרָעָה הַזֹּאת	23[8]	and they came in, and possessed it; but they did not listen to Your voice, nor walked in Your law; they have done nothing of all that you commanded them to do; therefore, you have caused all this evil to befall them;
הִנֵּה הַסֹּלְלוֹת בָּאוּ הָעִיר לְלָכְדָהּ וְהָעִיר נִתְּנָה בְּיַד הַכַּשְׂדִּים הַנִּלְחָמִים עָלֶיהָ מִפְּנֵי הַחֶרֶב וְהָרָעָב וְהַדָּבֶר וַאֲשֶׁר דִּבַּרְתָּ הָיָה וְהִנְּךָ רֹאֶה	24[9]	behold the mounds, they came to the city to take it; and the city is given into the hand of the Chaldeans who fight against it, because of the sword, and of the famine, and of the pestilence; and what you have spoken came to pass; and, behold, you see it.
וְאַתָּה אָמַרְתָּ אֵלַי אֲדֹנָי יְהוִה קְנֵה־לְךָ הַשָּׂדֶה בַּכֶּסֶף וְהָעֵד עֵדִים וְהָעִיר נִתְּנָה בְּיַד הַכַּשְׂדִּים	25[10]	Yet you have said to me, O Lord GOD: Buy the field for money, and call witnesses; while

---

[1] LXX *nothing can be hidden from you*

[2] Jeremiah 32:18 - 1 Kings 14:9-14:10 16:1-16:3 21:21-21:24, 2 Kings 9:26, 2 Samuel 21:1-21:9, b.Berachot 5b, b.Yoma [Rashi] 69a, Deuteronomy 5:9-5:10 7:9-7:10 7:21 10:17, Ein Yaakov Berachot:5b, Exodus 20:5-20:6 10:7, Genesis 1:24, Habakkuk 1:12, Isaiah 9:7 10:21 9:15, Jastrow 593b, Jeremiah 10:16 7:36, Joshua 7:24-7:26, Matthew 23:32-23:36 3:25, Midrash Psalms 19:2, Nehemiah 1:5, Numbers 14:18, Psalms 50:1 145:3-145:6, y.Berachot 7:3, y.Megillah 3:7

[3] Jeremiah 32:19 - 1 Kings 8:32, 2 Chronicles 16:9, 2 Corinthians 5:10, Daniel 4:32, Derech Hashem Part II 3§01, Ecclesiastes 12:14, Ein Yaakov Avodah Zarah:18a, Ephesians 1:11, Exodus 15:11, Guide for the Perplexed 3:17, Hebrews 4:13, Isaiah 9:7 4:29 16:13 46:10-46:11, Jeremiah 16:17 17:10 23:24, Job 10:21, John 5:29, Mas.Semachot 8:11, Matthew 16:27, Mekhilta 8:11, Mekhilta de R'Shimon bar Yochai Beshallach 26:1, Mekhilta de R'Ishmael Beshallah 7:15, mt.Hilchot Temurah 4:13, mt.Shemonah Perakim 4:6, Proverbs 5:21, Psalms 33:13-33:15 34:16 62:13, Ralbag Wars 4:6, Revelation 2:23 22:12, Romans 2:6-2:10 11:33-11:34, Saadia Opinions 5:1, Sifre Devarim {Haazinu Hashamayim} 307, Sifre Devarim Nitzavim 307 Tziduk Hadin, Tanna Devei Eliyahu 7 7

[4] Jeremiah 32:20 - 1 Chronicles 17:21, 2 Samuel 7:23, Acts 7:36, Daniel 9:15, Deuteronomy 4:34 6:22 7:19, Exodus 7:3 9:16 10:2, Isaiah 15:12, Nehemiah 9:10, Psalms 78:43-78:51 105:27-36 15:9

[5] Jeremiah 32:21 - 1 Chronicles 17:21, 1 Kings 8:42, Deuteronomy 4:34 2:8, Exodus 6:1 6:6 13:9 13:14, Psalms 89:9-11 9:37 9:43 106:8-11 136:11-12

[6] LXX *sights*

[7] Jeremiah 32:22 - Deuteronomy 1:8 1:35 6:10 6:18 6:23 7:13 8:1 26:9-26:11, Exodus 3:8 3:17 13:5 33:1-33:3, Ezekiel 20:6 20:15, Genesis 13:15 15:18-15:21 17:7-17:8 24:7 28:13-28:15 35:11-35:12 2:24, Jeremiah 11:5, Joshua 1:6 21:43, Nehemiah 9:15, Numbers 14:16 14:30, Psalms 105:9-105:11

[8] Jeremiah 32:23 - Daniel 9:4-9:6 9:10-9:14, Deuteronomy 28:15-28:68, Ezekiel 20:8 20:18 20:21, Ezra 9:7, Galatians 3:10, James 2:10, Jeremiah 7:23-7:24 11:7-11:8, John 15:14, Joshua 23:16, Judges 2:11-2:13 10:6-10:18, Lamentations 1:8 1:18 5:16-5:17, Leviticus 26:14-26:46, Luke 17:10, Nehemiah 9:15 9:22-9:30, Psalms 44:3-44:4 78:54-78:55 105:44-105:45, Zechariah 1:2-1:4

[9] Jeremiah 32:24 - 2 Samuel 20:15, Deuteronomy 4:26 31:16-31:17 32:24-32:25, Ezekiel 14:21 21:27, Jeremiah 14:12-14:15 15:1-15:3 16:4 21:4-21:7 24:10 8:3 8:25 8:36 9:4 37:6-37:10 4:6, Joshua 23:15-23:16, Lamentations 2:21-2:22 4:3-4:10, Matthew 24:35, Midrash Psalms 90:2, Pesikta de R'Kahana 16.6, Pesikta Rabbati 29/30A:7, Zechariah 1:6
Jeremiah 32:24-25 - 2QJer

[10] Jeremiah 32:25 - b.Bechorot [Tosefot] 13b, Jeremiah 8:24, John 13:7, Psalms 77:20 97:2, Romans 11:33-34

		the city is given into the hand of the Chaldeans.'
וַיְהִי֙ דְּבַר־יְהֹוָ֔ה אֶל־יִרְמְיָ֖הוּ לֵאמֹֽר	26	Then the word of the LORD came to Jeremiah, saying:
הִנֵּה֙ אֲנִ֣י יְהֹוָ֔ה אֱלֹהֵ֖י כׇּל־בָּשָׂ֑ר הֲמִמֶּ֕נִּי יִפָּלֵ֖א כׇּל־דָּבָֽר	27[1]	'Behold, I am the LORD, the God of all flesh; is there anything too hard for Me?
לָכֵ֕ן כֹּ֥ה אָמַ֖ר יְהֹוָ֑ה הִנְנִ֣י נֹתֵן֩ אֶת־הָעִ֨יר הַזֹּ֜את בְּיַ֣ד הַכַּשְׂדִּ֗ים וּבְיַ֛ד נְבֽוּכַדְרֶאצַּ֥ר מֶלֶךְ־בָּבֶ֖ל וּלְכָדָֽהּ	28[2]	Therefore, thus says the LORD: Behold, I will give this city into the *hand of the Chaldeans, and into the*[3] hand of Nebuchadrezzar king of Babylon, and he shall take it;
וּבָ֣אוּ הַכַּשְׂדִּ֗ים הַנִּלְחָמִים֙ עַל־הָעִ֣יר הַזֹּ֔את וְהִצִּ֜יתוּ אֶת־הָעִ֥יר הַזֹּ֛את בָּאֵ֖שׁ וּשְׂרָפ֑וּהָ וְאֵ֣ת הַבָּתִּ֡ים אֲשֶׁר֩ קִטְּר֨וּ עַל־גַּגּֽוֹתֵיהֶ֜ם לַבַּ֗עַל וְהִסִּ֤כוּ נְסָכִים֙ לֵאלֹהִ֣ים אֲחֵרִ֔ים לְמַ֖עַן הַכְעִסֵֽנִי	29[4]	and the Chaldeans, who fight against this city, shall come and set this city on fire, and burn it, with the houses, upon whose roofs they have offered to Baal, and poured out drink offerings to other gods, to provoke Me.
כִּֽי־הָי֣וּ בְנֵֽי־יִשְׂרָאֵ֗ל וּבְנֵ֤י יְהוּדָה֙ אַ֣ךְ עֹשִׂ֥ים הָרַ֛ע בְּעֵינַ֖י מִנְּעֻרֹֽתֵיהֶ֑ם כִּ֣י בְנֵֽי־יִשְׂרָאֵ֗ל אַ֣ךְ מַכְעִסִ֤ים אֹתִי֙ בְּמַעֲשֵׂ֣ה יְדֵיהֶ֔ם נְאֻם־יְהֹוָֽה	30[5]	For the children of Israel and the children of Judah have only done what was evil in My sight from their youth; *for the children of Israel have only provoked Me with the work of their hands, says the LORD*[6].
כִּ֧י עַל־אַפִּ֣י וְעַל־חֲמָתִ֗י הָ֤יְתָה לִּי֙ הָעִ֣יר הַזֹּ֔את לְמִן־הַיּוֹם֙ אֲשֶׁ֣ר בָּנ֣וּ אוֹתָ֔הּ וְעַ֖ד הַיּ֣וֹם הַזֶּ֑ה לַהֲסִירָ֖הּ מֵעַ֥ל פָּנָֽי	31[7]	For this city has been a provocation to Me of My anger and of My fury from the day they built it to this day, so I should remove it from before My face;
עַ֣ל כׇּל־רָעַ֣ת בְּנֵֽי־יִשְׂרָאֵ֡ל וּבְנֵ֣י יְהוּדָה֩ אֲשֶׁ֨ר עָשׂ֜וּ לְהַכְעִסֵ֗נִי הֵ֤מָּה מַלְכֵיהֶם֙ שָׂרֵיהֶ֣ם כֹּהֲנֵיהֶ֔ם וּנְבִֽיאֵיהֶ֑ם וְאִ֣ישׁ יְהוּדָ֔ה וְיֹשְׁבֵ֖י יְרוּשָׁלָֽ͏ִם	32[8]	because of all the evil of the children of Israel and of the children of Judah, which they have done to provoke Me, they, their kings, their princes, their priests, and their prophets, and the men of Judah, and the inhabitants of Jerusalem.
וַיִּפְנ֥וּ אֵלַ֛י עֹ֖רֶף וְלֹ֣א פָנִ֑ים וְלַמֵּ֤ד אֹתָם֙ הַשְׁכֵּ֣ם וְלַמֵּ֔ד וְאֵינָ֥ם שֹׁמְעִ֖ים לָקַ֥חַת מוּסָֽר	33[9]	And they have turned their back to Me, and not their face; and though I taught them, teaching them often and often, yet they have not listened to receive instruction.
וַיָּשִׂ֣ימוּ שִׁקּֽוּצֵיהֶ֗ם בַּבַּ֛יִת אֲשֶׁר־נִקְרָא־שְׁמִ֥י עָלָ֖יו לְטַמְּאֽוֹ	34[10]	But they set their abominations in the house where My name is called, *to defile it*[11].

---

[1] Jeremiah 32:27 - Isaiah 16:9, Jeremiah 8:17, John 17:2, Luke 3:6, Matthew 19:26, Mekhilta de R'Shimon bar Yochai Bachodesh 52:1, Mekhilta de R'Ishmael Kaspa 4:68, Numbers 16:22 3:16, Psalms 65:3, Romans 3:29-30, Sifre Devarim Vaetchanan 31, y.Moed Katan 3:7, y.Sanhedrin 7:8

[2] Jeremiah 32:28 - 2 Chronicles 12:17, Jeremiah 19:7-19:12 20:5 8:3 8:24 8:36, Leviticus.R 12:5, z.Vaetchanan 269b

[3] Missing in LXX

[4] Jeremiah 32:29 - 2 Chronicles 12:19, 2 Kings 1:9, Isaiah 64:11-64:12, Jeremiah 7:18 17:27 19:13 21:10 27:8-27:10 37:7-37:10 15:8 44:17-44:19 20:25 4:13, Lamentations 4:11, Matthew 22:7

[5] Jeremiah 32:30 - 2 Kings 17:9-17:20, Acts 7:51-7:53, Deuteronomy 9:7-9:12 9:22-9:24, Ezekiel 16:15-16:22 20:8 20:28 23:3 23:43-23:44, Genesis 8:21, Isaiah 15:10, Jeremiah 2:7 3:25 7:22-7:26 8:19 22:21 1:7, Nehemiah 9:16-9:37, Psalms 106:6-106:7

[6] Missing in LXX

[7] Jeremiah 32:31 - 1 Kings 11:7-11:8, 2 Baruch 1:1, 2 Kings 21:4-21:7 21:16 22:16-22:17 23:15 23:27 24:3-24:4, b.Niddah 70b, Ezekiel 22:2-22:22, Jeremiah 5:9-5:11 6:6-6:7 23:14-23:15 3:10, Lamentations 1:8, Lamentations.R 2:12, Luke 13:33-13:34, Matthew 23:37, Midrash Proverbs 31, Numbers.R 10:4, Seder Olam 15:Temple, t.Berachot 1:15, z.Beshallach 59a

[8] Jeremiah 32:32 - Daniel 9:6 9:8, Ezekiel 22:6 22:25-22:29, Ezra 9:7, Isaiah 1:4-1:6 1:23 9:15-9:16, Jeremiah 2:26, Micah 3:1-3:5 3:9-3:12, Nehemiah 9:32-9:34, Zephaniah 3:1-3:4

[9] Jeremiah 32:33 - 2 Chronicles 36:15-36:16, b.Sanhedrin [Rashi] 52b, Ezekiel 8:16, Hosea 11:2, Jeremiah 2:27 7:13 7:24 18:17 25:3-25:4 2:5 11:15 20:4, John 8:2, Zechariah 7:11

[10] Jeremiah 32:34 - 2 Chronicles 33:4-33:7 9:15, 2 Kings 21:4-21:7 23:6, Ezekiel 8:5-8:16, Jeremiah 7:30 23:11

[11] LXX *by their uncleannesses*

וַיִּבְנוּ אֶת־בָּמוֹת הַבַּעַל אֲשֶׁר ׀ בְּגֵיא בֶן־הִנֹּם 35[1]
לְהַעֲבִיר אֶת־בְּנֵיהֶם וְאֶת־בְּנוֹתֵיהֶם לַמֹּלֶךְ אֲשֶׁר
לֹא־צִוִּיתִים וְלֹא עָלְתָה עַל־לִבִּי לַעֲשׂוֹת הַתּוֹעֵבָה
הַזֹּאת לְמַעַן ׳הַחֲטִי׳ ״הַחֲטִיא״ אֶת־יְהוּדָה

And they built the high places of Baal in the valley of the son of Hinnom, to *set apart*[2] their sons and their daughters to [3]Molech; which I did not command them, nor did it come into My mind, that they should do this abomination; to cause Judah to sin.

וְעַתָּה לָכֵן כֹּה־אָמַר יְהוָה אֱלֹהֵי יִשְׂרָאֵל אֶל־ 36[4]
הָעִיר הַזֹּאת אֲשֶׁר ׀ אַתֶּם אֹמְרִים נִתְּנָה בְּיַד מֶלֶךְ־
בָּבֶל בַּחֶרֶב וּבָרָעָב וּבַדָּבֶר

And now, therefore, thus says the LORD, the God of Israel, concerning this city, of which you say: It is given into the hand of the king of Babylon by the sword, and by the famine, and by *the pestilence*[5]:

הִנְנִי מְקַבְּצָם מִכָּל־הָאֲרָצוֹת אֲשֶׁר הִדַּחְתִּים שָׁם 37[6]
בְּאַפִּי וּבַחֲמָתִי וּבְקֶצֶף גָּדוֹל וַהֲשִׁבֹתִים אֶל־
הַמָּקוֹם הַזֶּה וְהֹשַׁבְתִּים לָבֶטַח

Behold, I will gather them from all the countries, where I drive them in my anger, and in My fury, and in great wrath; and I will bring them back to this place, and I will cause them to live safely;

וְהָיוּ לִי לְעָם וַאֲנִי אֶהְיֶה לָהֶם לֵאלֹהִים 38[7]

and they shall be My people, and I will be their God;

וְנָתַתִּי לָהֶם לֵב אֶחָד וְדֶרֶךְ אֶחָד לְיִרְאָה אוֹתִי 39[8]
כָּל־הַיָּמִים לְטוֹב לָהֶם וְלִבְנֵיהֶם אַחֲרֵיהֶם

and I will give them one heart and one way, so they may fear Me forever; for their good, and of their children after them;

וְכָרַתִּי לָהֶם בְּרִית עוֹלָם אֲשֶׁר לֹא־אָשׁוּב 40[9]
מֵאַחֲרֵיהֶם לְהֵיטִיבִי אוֹתָם וְאֶת־יִרְאָתִי אֶתֵּן
בִּלְבָבָם לְבִלְתִּי סוּר מֵעָלָי

and I will make an everlasting covenant with them, so I will not turn away from them, to do them good; and I will put My fear in their hearts, so they shall not depart from Me.

וְשַׂשְׂתִּי עֲלֵיהֶם לְהֵטִיב אוֹתָם וּנְטַעְתִּים בָּאָרֶץ 41[10]
הַזֹּאת בֶּאֱמֶת בְּכָל־לִבִּי וּבְכָל־נַפְשִׁי

Yes, I will rejoice over them to do them good, and I will plant them in this land in truth with My whole heart and with My whole soul.

כִּי־כֹה אָמַר יְהוָה כַּאֲשֶׁר הֵבֵאתִי אֶל־הָעָם הַזֶּה 42[11]
אֵת כָּל־הָרָעָה הַגְּדוֹלָה הַזֹּאת כֵּן אָנֹכִי מֵבִיא
עֲלֵיהֶם אֶת־כָּל־הַטּוֹבָה אֲשֶׁר אָנֹכִי דֹּבֵר עֲלֵיהֶם

For thus says the LORD: as I have brought all this great evil on this people, so will I bring on them all the good I have promised them.

וְנִקְנָה הַשָּׂדֶה בָּאָרֶץ הַזֹּאת אֲשֶׁר ׀ אַתֶּם אֹמְרִים 43[12]
שְׁמָמָה הִיא מֵאֵין אָדָם וּבְהֵמָה נִתְּנָה בְּיַד
הַכַּשְׂדִּים

And fields shall be bought in this land, of which you say: it is desolate, without man or beast; it is given into the hand of the Chaldeans.

[1] Jeremiah 32:35 - 1 Kings 11:33 14:16 15:26 15:30 16:19 21:22, 2 Chronicles 28:2-3 9:6 9:9, 2 Kings 3:3 21:11 23:10 23:15, b.Eruvin 19a, Deuteronomy 18:10 24:4, Exodus 8:21, Ezekiel 16:20-21 23:37, Isaiah 9:5, Jeremiah 7:31 19:5-6, Leviticus 18:21 20:2-5, m.Keritot 1:1, Psalms 106:37-138, Sibylline Oracles 2.292, Testament of Solomon 26:1
[2] LXX *offer*
[3] LXX adds *king*
[4] Jeremiah 32:36 - Ephesians 2:3-2:5, Ezekiel 36:31-32, Hosea 2:14, Isaiah 43:24-25 57:17-18, Jeremiah 16:12-15 8:3 8:24 8:28, Romans 5:20, z.Vaetchanan 269b
[5] LXX *banishment*
[6] Jeremiah 32:37 - Amos 9:14-9:15, Deuteronomy 30:3-30:6, Ezekiel 11:17 34:12-34:14 34:25-34:28 12:24 37:21-37:25 39:25-39:29, Hosea 2:2 3:5, Isaiah 11:11-11:16, Jeremiah 23:3 23:6 23:8 5:14 6:18 7:11 9:7 9:16, Joel 4:20, Obadiah 1:17-1:21, Psalms 10:47, Zechariah 2:4-2:5 3:10 14:11, Zephaniah 3:20
[7] Jeremiah 32:38 - Deuteronomy 26:17-26:19, Ezekiel 11:19-11:20 12:28 13:27 15:22 15:28, Genesis 17:7, Hebrews 8:10 11:16, Jeremiah 24:7 6:22 7:2 7:34, Psalms 24:15, Revelation 21:7, Zechariah 13:9
[8] Jeremiah 32:39 - 1 Corinthians 7:14, 2 Chronicles 6:12, 2 Corinthians 13:11, Acts 2:39 3:26 4:32 9:31 13:33, Deuteronomy 5:29 11:18-11:21, Ezekiel 11:19-11:20 12:26 13:22 13:25, Genesis 17:7 18:19 22:12, Hebrews 10:20, Isaiah 11:8 4:8, Jeremiah 6:16 8:40, John 14:6 17:21, Philippians 2:1-2:2, Proverbs 14:26-14:27 23:17, Psalms 16:1 115:13-115:15 8:6, Romans 11:16
[9] Jeremiah 32:40 - 1 Peter 1:5, 2 Samuel 23:4, Ecclesiastes.R 1:36, Ezekiel 12:26 15:29, Galatians 3:14-17, Genesis 17:7-13, Hebrews 4:1 6:13-18 7:24 13:20, Isaiah 24:5 7:3 13:8, James 1:17, Jeremiah 24:7 31:32-34 2:5, John 10:27-30, Luke 1:72-75, Romans 8:28-39 3:7, Song of Songs.R 7:8, Zephaniah 3:17
[10] Jeremiah 32:41 - Amos 9:15, Deuteronomy 6:9, Hosea 2:19-2:22, Isaiah 14:5 17:19, Jeremiah 18:9 24:6 7:29, Jubilees 1:15, Ruth.R 3:7, Song of Songs.R 7:8, Zephaniah 3:17
[11] Jeremiah 32:42 - Jeremiah 7:29 33:10-11, Joshua 23:14-15, Matthew 24:35, z.Vaetchanan 269b, Zechariah 8:14-15
[12] Jeremiah 32:43 - Ezekiel 37:11-14, Jeremiah 8:15 8:36 9:10

שָׂדֹות בַּכֶּסֶף יִקְנוּ וְכָתוֹב בַּסֵּפֶר וְחָתוֹם וְהָעֵד עֵדִים בְּאֶרֶץ בִּנְיָמִן וּבִסְבִיבֵי יְרוּשָׁלַם וּבְעָרֵי יְהוּדָה וּבְעָרֵי הָהָר וּבְעָרֵי הַשְּׁפֵלָה וּבְעָרֵי הַנֶּגֶב כִּי־אָשִׁיב אֶת־שְׁבוּתָם נְאֻם־יְהוָה	44[1]	Men shall buy fields for money, and subscribe the deeds, and seal them, and call witnesses, in the land of Benjamin, and in the places about Jerusalem, and in the cities of Judah, and in the cities of the hill country, and in the cities of the Lowland, and in the cities of the South; for I will cause their captivity to return, *says the LORD*[2].'

Jeremiah – Chapter 33[3]

וַיְהִי דְבַר־יְהוָה אֶל־יִרְמְיָהוּ שֵׁנִית וְהוּא עוֹדֶנּוּ עָצוּר בַּחֲצַר הַמַּטָּרָה לֵאמֹר	1[4]	Moreover, the word of the LORD came to Jeremiah the second time, while he was yet shut up in the court of the guard, saying:
כֹּה־אָמַר יְהוָה עֹשָׂהּ יְהוָה יוֹצֵר אוֹתָהּ לַהֲכִינָהּ יְהוָה שְׁמוֹ	2[5]	Thus says the LORD its Maker, the LORD who formed it to establish it, the LORD is His name:
קְרָא אֵלַי וְאֶעֱנֶךָּ וְאַגִּידָה לְךָ גְּדֹלוֹת וּבְצֻרוֹת לֹא יְדַעְתָּם	3[6]	Call to Me, and I will answer you, and will tell you great and hidden things, which you do not know.
כִּי כֹה אָמַר יְהוָה אֱלֹהֵי יִשְׂרָאֵל עַל־בָּתֵּי הָעִיר הַזֹּאת וְעַל־בָּתֵּי מַלְכֵי יְהוּדָה הַנְּתֻצִים אֶל־הַסֹּלְלוֹת וְאֶל־הֶחָרֶב	4[7]	For thus says the LORD, the God of Israel, concerning the houses of this city, and concerning the houses of the kings of Judah, which are broken down for mounds, and for ramparts;
בָּאִים לְהִלָּחֵם אֶת־הַכַּשְׂדִּים וּלְמַלְאָם אֶת־פִּגְרֵי הָאָדָם אֲשֶׁר־הִכֵּיתִי בְאַפִּי וּבַחֲמָתִי וַאֲשֶׁר הִסְתַּרְתִּי פָנַי מֵהָעִיר הַזֹּאת עַל כָּל־רָעָתָם	5[8]	where they come to fight with the Chaldeans, to fill them with the dead bodies of men, whom I have slain in my anger and in My fury, and for all whose wickedness *I have hid My face from this city*[9]:
הִנְנִי מַעֲלֶה־לָּהּ אֲרֻכָה וּמַרְפֵּא וּרְפָאתִים וְגִלֵּיתִי לָהֶם עֲתֶרֶת שָׁלוֹם וֶאֱמֶת	6[10]	Behold, I will bring it healing and a cure, and I will cure them; and I will reveal to them the abundance of peace and truth.
וַהֲשִׁבֹתִי אֶת־שְׁבוּת יְהוּדָה וְאֵת שְׁבוּת יִשְׂרָאֵל וּבְנִתִים כְּבָרִאשֹׁנָה	7[11]	And I will cause the captivity of Judah and the captivity of Israel to return, and will build them, as before.
וְטִהַרְתִּים מִכָּל־עֲוֹנָם אֲשֶׁר חָטְאוּ־לִי וְסָלַחְתִּי לְכוֹל־לְכָל־עֲוֹנוֹתֵיהֶם אֲשֶׁר חָטְאוּ־לִי וַאֲשֶׁר פָּשְׁעוּ בִי	8[12]	And I will cleanse them from all their iniquity, with which they sinned against Me; and I will pardon all their iniquities, with which they have

---

[1] Jeremiah 32:44 - b.Bava Batra [Rashi] 28b, b.Bava Batra [Tosefot] 162a, b.Bava Batra 28b 160a 160b, b.Eruvin [Tosefot] 81b, b.Gittin 36a, b.Kiddushin [Rashi] 26a, b.Kiddushin 2b 9a 26a, Jastrow 1432b, Jeremiah 17:26 8:10 8:37 9:7 9:11 9:26, Psalms 126:1-126:4, Ruth.R 7:11, y.Kiddushin 1:3 1:5

[2] Missing in LXX

[3] Chapter 40 in LXX

[4] Jeremiah 33:1 - 2 Timothy 2:9, Jeremiah 32:2-32:3 8:8 13:21 14:28, Midrash Psalms 4:3

[5] Jeremiah 33:2 - Amos 5:8 9:6, Exodus 3:14-3:15 6:3 15:3, Hebrews 11:10 11:16, Isaiah 14:32 13:26 19:1 19:21 14:7, Jeremiah 10:16 8:18, Midrash Psalms 4:3, Psalms 87:5 6:17, Revelation 21:2 21:10, z.Vaetchanan 269b

[6] Jeremiah 33:3 - 1 Corinthians 1:2 2:7-2:11, 1 Kings 8:47-8:50, Acts 2:21, Amos 3:7, Deuteronomy 4:7 4:29, Ephesians 3:20, Isaiah 21:3 24:6 55:6-55:7 17:24, Jeremiah 5:12, Joel 3:5, Luke 11:9-11:10, Matthew 13:35, Mekilta de R'Ishmael Pisha 1:161, Micah 7:15, Midrash Psalms 4:3, Psalms 25:14 50:15 91:15 1:18, Revelation 2:17, Romans 10:12-10:13, variant מבצרות of ונצרות is found

[7] Jeremiah 33:4 - Ezekiel 4:2 21:27 2:8, Habakkuk 1:10, Jeremiah 8:24, z.Vaetchanan 269b

[8] Jeremiah 33:5 - Deuteronomy 7:17 8:20, Ezekiel 39:23-39:24 15:29, Isaiah 1:15-1:16 8:17 16:8, Jeremiah 18:17 21:4-21:7 21:10 8:5 37:9-37:10, Micah 3:4, z.Lech Lecha 93b

[9] Mising in LXX

[10] Jeremiah 33:6 - 1 Peter 1:3, Deuteronomy 8:39, Ecclesiastes.R 3:10, Ephesians 6:23, Exodus 10:6, Galatians 5:22-5:23, Hebrews 6:17-6:18, Hosea 6:1 7:1, Isaiah 2:4 11:5-11:9 26:2-26:4 6:26 33:15-33:18 15:8 48:17-48:18 6:13 7:7 10:8 18:12, Jeremiah 17:14 30:12-30:17, John 10:10, Micah 4:3, Psalms 37:11 67:3 72:7 85:11-85:13, Song of Songs.R 4:13, Titus 3:5-3:6

[11] Jeremiah 33:7 - Amos 9:14-15, Hosea 2:15, Isaiah 1:26 11:12-11:16, Jeremiah 23:3 24:6 5:14 6:3 6:18 6:20 7:5 7:29 8:44 9:11 9:26 18:10, Micah 7:14-7:15, Psalms 14:7 85:2 6:1 6:4, Zechariah 1:17, Zephaniah 3:20

[12] Jeremiah 33:8 - 1 John 1:7-1:9, Ezekiel 12:25 12:33, Hebrews 9:11-9:14, Isaiah 4:2 20:22 8:7, Jeremiah 7:35 2:20, Joel 4:21, Micah 7:18-19, Psalms 51:3 65:4 85:3-4, Revelation 1:5, Zechariah 13:1

sinned against Me, and with which they have transgressed against Me.

9[1] And this city shall be to Me a name of joy, for a praise and for a glory, before all the nations of the earth, which shall hear all the good I do to them, and shall fear and tremble for all the good and for all the peace I acquire for it.

10[2] Thus says the LORD: Yet again there shall be heard in this place, of which you say: It is waste, without man and without beast, in the cities of Judah, and in the streets of Jerusalem, that are desolate, without man and without inhabitant and without beast,

11[3] the voice of joy and the voice of gladness, the voice of the bridegroom and the voice of the bride, the voice of those who say: 'Give thanks to the LORD of hosts, for the LORD is good, for His mercy endures forever,' of those who bring offerings of thanksgiving into the house of the LORD. For I will cause the captivity of the land to return as before, says the LORD.

12[4] Thus says the LORD of hosts: yet again shall there be in this place, which is waste, without man and without beast, and in all its cities, a residence of shepherds causing their flocks to lie down.

13[5] In the cities of the hill country, in the cities of the Lowland, and in the cities of the South, and in the land of Benjamin, and in the places about Jerusalem, and in the cities of Judah, shall the flocks again pass under the hands of he who counts them, says the LORD.

14[6] *Behold, the days come, says the LORD, that I will perform that good word which I spoke concerning the house of Israel and concerning the house of Judah[7].*

15[8] *In those days, and at that time, will I cause a shoot of righteousness to grow up to David;*

---

[1] Jeremiah 33:9 - 2 Chronicles 20:29, Avot de R'Natan 34, Esther 8:17, Exodus 15:14-15:16, Hosea 3:5, Isaiah 12:5 62:2-62:3 14:7 14:12, Jeremiah 3:17 13:11 2:6 5:1 7:5 20:8, Micah 7:16-7:17, Nehemiah 6:16, Psalms 40:4 126:2-126:3, Zechariah 8:20-8:23 12:2, Zephaniah 3:17-3:20

[2] Jeremiah 33:10 - Ezekiel 13:11, Jeremiah 8:36 8:43, z.Vaetchanan 269b

[3] Jeremiah 33:11 - 1 Chronicles 16:8 16:34, 2 Chronicles 5:13 7:3 20:21 5:31, b.Berachot 6b, Ein Yaakov Berachot:6b, Ein Yaakov Berachot:6b, Exodus.R 21:1, Ezra 3:11-3:13 6:22, Hebrews 13:15, Isaiah 12:1-12:6 3:3 3:11 4:9, Jeremiah 7:34 16:9 1:10 31:13-31:15 9:7 9:26, John 3:29, Jonah 2:9, Leviticus 7:12-7:13, Leviticus.R 9:7 27:12, Midrash Psalms 100:4, Midrash Tanchuma Devarim 1, Midrash Tanchuma Emor 14, mt.Hilchot Ishut 10:3, Nehemiah 8:12 12:43, Pesikta de R'Kahana 9.12 22.5, Psalms 100:4-100:5 10:1 11:1 11:22 20:17 118:1-118:4 136:1-136:26, Revelation 18:23, Zechariah 8:19 9:17 10:7, Zephaniah 3:14
Jeremiah 33:11-15 - mt.Hilchot Melachim uMichamoteihem 11:2

[4] Jeremiah 33:12 - Ezekiel 34:12-34:15 36:8-36:11, Isaiah 17:10, Jeremiah 17:26 7:25 32:43-32:44 12:29 50:19-50:20 51:62, Obadiah 1:19-1:20, z.Vaetchanan 269b, Zephaniah 2:6-2:7

[5] Jeremiah 33:13 - b.Bechorot 54b, Jeremiah 17:26, John 10:3-10:4, Leviticus 3:32, Luke 15:4, Midrash Tanchuma Ki Tissa 9, Numbers.R 2:11, Pesikta de R'Kahana 2.8, Pesikta Rabbati 10:1

[6] Jeremiah 33:14 - 1 Chronicles 17:13-17:14, 1 Peter 1:10, 2 Corinthians 1:20, Acts 13:32-13:33, Amos 9:11, Daniel 2:44 7:13-7:14 9:25, Ezekiel 34:23-34:25, Genesis 22:18 1:10, Haggai 2:6-2:9, Hebrews 11:40, Isaiah 7:14 9:7-9:8 32:1-32:2, Jeremiah 23:5 5:10 7:28 31:32-31:35 32:38-32:41, Luke 1:69-1:70 2:10-2:11 10:24, Malachi 3:1, Micah 5:3, Revelation 19:10, Zechariah 9:9-9:10, Zephaniah 3:15-3:17

[7] Missing in LXX

[8] Jeremiah 33:15 - 2 Samuel 23:2-23:3, compare צמח צדקה "the branch of righteousness" here with צמח צדיק "a righteous branch" at Jeremiah 33:15, Ezekiel 17:22-17:23, Hebrews 1:8-1:9 7:1-7:2, Isaiah 4:2 9:8 11:1-11:5 32:1-32:2 18:21 5:2, Jeremiah 23:5-23:6, John 5:22-5:29, Psalms 45:5 45:8 72:1-72:5, Revelation 19:11, Testament of Judah 24:4, Zechariah 3:8 6:12-6:13

and he shall execute justice and righteousness in the land[1].

בַּיָּמִים הָהֵם תִּוָּשַׁע יְהוּדָה וִירוּשָׁלַ͏ִם תִּשְׁכּוֹן לָבֶטַח וְזֶה אֲשֶׁר־יִקְרָא־לָהּ יְהוָה ׀ צִדְקֵנוּ

16[2]   *In those days Judah shall be saved, and Jerusalem shall live safely; and this is the name by which she shall be called, The LORD is our righteousness*[3].

כִּי־כֹה אָמַר יְהוָה לֹא־יִכָּרֵת לְדָוִד אִישׁ יֹשֵׁב עַל־כִּסֵּא בֵית־יִשְׂרָאֵל

17[4]   *For thus says the LORD: There shall not be cut off to David a man to sit on the throne of the house of Israel*[5];

וְלַכֹּהֲנִים הַלְוִיִּם לֹא־יִכָּרֵת אִישׁ מִלְּפָנָי מַעֲלֶה עוֹלָה וּמַקְטִיר מִנְחָה וְעֹשֶׂה־זֶּבַח כָּל־הַיָּמִים

18[6]   *Nor shall there be cut off to the priests the Levites a man before Me to offer burnt offerings, and to burn meal offerings, and to do sacrifice continually*[7].

וַיְהִי דְּבַר־יְהוָה אֶל־יִרְמְיָהוּ לֵאמוֹר

19   *And the word of the LORD came to Jeremiah, saying*[8]:

כֹּה אָמַר יְהוָה אִם־תָּפֵרוּ אֶת־בְּרִיתִי הַיּוֹם וְאֶת־בְּרִיתִי הַלָּיְלָה וּלְבִלְתִּי הֱיוֹת יוֹמָם־וָלַיְלָה בְּעִתָּם

20[9]   *Thus says the LORD: If you can break My covenant with the day, and My covenant with the night, So there should not be day and night in their season*[10];

גַּם־בְּרִיתִי תֻפַר אֶת־דָּוִד עַבְדִּי מִהְיוֹת־לוֹ בֵן מֹלֵךְ עַל־כִּסְאוֹ וְאֶת־הַלְוִיִּם הַכֹּהֲנִים מְשָׁרְתָי

21[11]   *Then may also My covenant be broken with David My servant, that he should not have a son to reign on his throne; and with the Levites the priests, My ministers*[12].

אֲשֶׁר לֹא־יִסָּפֵר צְבָא הַשָּׁמַיִם וְלֹא יִמַּד חוֹל הַיָּם כֵּן אַרְבֶּה אֶת־זֶרַע דָּוִד עַבְדִּי וְאֶת־הַלְוִיִּם מְשָׁרְתֵי אֹתִי

22[13]   *As the host of heaven cannot be numbered, the sand of the sea cannot be measured; So will I multiply the seed of David My servant, and the Levites who minister to Me*[14].

וַיְהִי דְּבַר־יְהוָה אֶל־יִרְמְיָהוּ לֵאמֹר

23   *And the word of the LORD came to Jeremiah, saying*[15]:

הֲלוֹא רָאִיתָ מָה־הָעָם הַזֶּה דִּבְּרוּ לֵאמֹר שְׁתֵּי הַמִּשְׁפָּחוֹת אֲשֶׁר בָּחַר יְהוָה בָּהֶם וַיִּמְאָסֵם וְאֶת־עַמִּי יִנְאָצוּן מִהְיוֹת עוֹד גּוֹי לִפְנֵיהֶם

24[16]   *'Do you not consider what this people have said, saying: The two families which the LORD chose, He has cast them off? And they scorn My people, so they should no longer be a nation before them*[17].

---

[1] Missing in LXX

[2] Jeremiah 33:16 - 1 Corinthians 1:30, 2 Corinthians 5:21, 2 Peter 1:1, Deuteronomy 9:12 9:28, Ezekiel 4:26 34:25-34:28 14:8, Isaiah 21:17 21:22 45:24-45:25, Jeremiah 23:6 8:37, Philippians 3:9, Romans 11:26, Tanya Igeret Hakodesh §23
Jeremiah 33:16-20 - 4QJerc

[3] Missing in LXX

[4] Jeremiah 33:17 - 1 Chronicles 17:11-17:14 17:27, 1 Kings 2:4 8:25, 2 Samuel 3:29 7:14-7:16, Isaiah 9:8, Jeremiah 11:19, Luke 1:32-1:33, Psalms 89:30-89:38, z.Vaetchanan 269b

[5] Missing in LXX

[6] Jeremiah 33:18 - 1 Peter 2:5 2:9, Deuteronomy 18:1, Ezekiel 43:19-43:27 44:9-44:11 21:5, Hebrews 13:15-13:16, Isaiah 8:7 13:6, Revelation 1:6 5:10, Romans 1:21 15:16, z.Mishpatim 105b
Jeremiah 33:18 [LXX] - Lives of the Prophets 6:1

[7] Missing in LXX

[8] Missing in LXX

[9] Jeremiah 33:20 - Genesis 8:22, Isaiah 54:9-54:10, Jeremiah 31:36-31:38 33:25-33:26, Psalms 89:38 104:19-104:23, z.Beshallach 46a, z.Vaetchanan 269b
Jeremiah 33:20-21 - Midrash Tanchuma Lech Lecha 20, Midrash Tanchuma Noach 3

[10] Missing in LXX

[11] Jeremiah 33:21 - 2 Chronicles 7:18 21:7, 2 Samuel 23:5, Daniel 7:14, Isaiah 9:7-9:8 7:3, Jeremiah 9:18, Luke 1:32-1:33 1:69-1:70, Matthew 24:35, Psalms 89:35 132:11-132:12 12:17, Revelation 5:10

[12] Missing in LXX

[13] Jeremiah 33:22 - Ezekiel 37:24-37:27 20:15, Genesis 13:16 15:5 22:17 4:14, Greek Apocalypse of Ezra 2:32, Hebrews 11:12, Hosea 2:1, Isaiah 53:10-53:12 18:21, Jeremiah 7:38, Psalms 22:31 89:4-89:5 89:30, Revelation 7:9-7:10, Zechariah 12:8

[14] Missing in LXX

[15] Missing in LXX

[16] Jeremiah 33:24 - Esther 3:6-8, Ezekiel 1:3 2:2 35:10-15 12:2 13:22, Jeremiah 6:17 33:21-22, Lamentations 2:15-16 4:15, Midrash Psalms 109:4, Midrash Tanchuma Lech Lecha 20, Nehemiah 4:2-4, Psalms 44:14-15 71:11 83:5 94:14 123:3-4, Romans 11:1-6

[17] Missing in LXX

כֹּה אָמַר יְהֹוָה אִם־לֹא בְרִיתִי יוֹמָם וָלָיְלָה חֻקּוֹת שָׁמַיִם וָאָרֶץ לֹא־שָׂמְתִּי

25[1] *Thus says the LORD: If My covenant is not with day and night, if I have not appointed the ordinances of heaven and earth[2];*

גַּם־זֶרַע יַעֲקוֹב וְדָוִד עַבְדִּי אֶמְאַס מִקַּחַת מִזַּרְעוֹ מֹשְׁלִים אֶל־זֶרַע אַבְרָהָם יִשְׂחָק וְיַעֲקֹב כִּי־אָשׁוּב "כִּי־אָשִׁיב" אֶת־שְׁבוּתָם וְרִחַמְתִּים

26[3] *then will I cast away the seed of Jacob, and of David My servant, so I will not take of his seed to be rulers over the seed of Abraham, Isaac, and Jacob; for I will cause their captivity to return, and will have compassion on them[4].'*

Jeremiah – Chapter 34

הַדָּבָר אֲשֶׁר־הָיָה אֶל־יִרְמְיָהוּ מֵאֵת יְהֹוָה וּנְבוּכַדְרֶאצַּר מֶלֶךְ־בָּבֶל וְכָל־חֵילוֹ וְכָל־מַמְלְכוֹת אֶרֶץ מֶמְשֶׁלֶת יָדוֹ וְכָל־הָעַמִּים נִלְחָמִים עַל־יְרוּשָׁלַ͏ִם וְעַל־כָּל־עָרֶיהָ לֵאמֹר

1[5] The word which came to Jeremiah from the LORD, when Nebuchadrezzar king of Babylon, and all his army, and all the kingdoms of the land of his dominion, and all the peoples, fought against Jerusalem, and against all its cities, saying:

כֹּה־אָמַר יְהֹוָה אֱלֹהֵי יִשְׂרָאֵל הָלֹךְ וְאָמַרְתָּ אֶל־צִדְקִיָּהוּ מֶלֶךְ יְהוּדָה וְאָמַרְתָּ אֵלָיו כֹּה אָמַר יְהֹוָה הִנְנִי נֹתֵן אֶת־הָעִיר הַזֹּאת בְּיַד מֶלֶךְ־בָּבֶל וּשְׂרָפָהּ בָּאֵשׁ

2[6] Thus says the LORD, the God of Israel: Go, and speak to Zedekiah king of Judah, and tell him: Thus says the LORD: behold, I will give this city into the hand of the king of Babylon, and he shall burn it with fire;

וְאַתָּה לֹא תִמָּלֵט מִיָּדוֹ כִּי תָּפֹשׂ תִּתָּפֵשׂ וּבְיָדוֹ תִּנָּתֵן וְעֵינֶיךָ אֶת־עֵינֵי מֶלֶךְ־בָּבֶל תִּרְאֶינָה וּפִיהוּ אֶת־פִּיךָ יְדַבֵּר וּבָבֶל תָּבוֹא

3[7] and you shall not escape from his hand, but shall surely be taken, and delivered into his hand; and your eyes shall see the eyes of the king of Babylon, and *he shall speak with you mouth to mouth[8]*, and you shall go to Babylon.

אַךְ שְׁמַע דְּבַר־יְהֹוָה צִדְקִיָּהוּ מֶלֶךְ יְהוּדָה כֹּה־אָמַר יְהֹוָה עָלֶיךָ לֹא תָמוּת בֶּחָרֶב

4[9] Yet hear the word of the LORD, O Zedekiah king of Judah: Thus says the LORD *concerning you: you shall not die by the sword[10];*

בְּשָׁלוֹם תָּמוּת וּכְמִשְׂרְפוֹת אֲבוֹתֶיךָ הַמְּלָכִים הָרִאשֹׁנִים אֲשֶׁר־הָיוּ לְפָנֶיךָ כֵּן יִשְׂרְפוּ־לָךְ וְהוֹי אָדוֹן יִסְפְּדוּ־לָךְ כִּי־דָבָר אֲנִי־דִבַּרְתִּי נְאֻם־יְהֹוָה

5[11] you shall die in peace; and *with the burnings of your fathers, the former kings who were before you, so shall they make a burning for you; and they shall lament you[12]*: 'Ah lord!' for I have spoken the word, says the LORD.

---

[1] Jeremiah 33:25 - b.Avodah Zara 3a 10b, b.Megillah 31a, b.Nedarim 31b 32a, b.Pesachim 68b, b.Sanhedrin 99b, b.Shabbat [Rashi] 33a, b.Shabbat 33a 137b, b.Taanit [Rashi] 3b, Ein Yaakov Avodah Zarah 3a, Ein Yaakov Nedarim 31b 32a, Ein Yaakov Pesachim 68b, Ein Yaakov Sanhedrin 99b, Esther.R 7:11 7:13, Exodus.R 47:4, Genesis 8:22 9:9-17, Guide for the Perplexed 3:13, HaMadrikh 35:2, Jeremiah 31:36-37 9:20, Leviticus.R 35:4, m.Nedarim 3:11, Mekhilta de R'Shimon bar Yochai Beshallach 23:1, Mekilta de R'Ishmael Beshallah 4:32, Midrash Psalms 6:1 20:3, Midrash Tanchuma Haazinu 3, Midrash Tanchuma Lech Lecha 20, Midrash Tanchuma Bereshit 1, Midrash Tanchuma Noach 3, Midrash Tanchuma Toledot 2, mt.Hilchot Milah 3:4, Numbers.R 10:1, Pesikta Rabbati 21:21, Pirkei de R'Eliezer 16, Psalms 74:16-17 8:19, t.Nedarim 2:7, y.Nedarim 3:9, z.Bereshit 24b 32a 56a, z.Lech Lecha 89a 96b, z.Noach 59b 66b, z.Vaetchanan 269b, z.Vayeshev 185a 189b, z.Vayikra 14a, z.Yitro 94a
Jeremiah 33:25-26 - Haftarah Mishpatim [continued from 34:8-22 Ashkenaz and Sephard]
[2] Missing in LXX
[3] Jeremiah 33:26 - Ezekiel 15:25, Ezra 2:1 2:70, Genesis 1:10, Hosea 1:7 2:23, Isaiah 14:1 6:8, Jeremiah 7:21 7:38 33:7-33:11, Midrash Psalms 6:1, Romans 11:32, Zechariah 10:6
[4] Missing in LXX
[5] Jeremiah 34:1 - 2 Chronicles 36:12-36:17, 2 Kings 25:1-25:9, Daniel 2:37-2:38 3:31 4:19 5:19, Jeremiah 1:15 27:5-27:7 8:2 10:7 39:1-39:3 52:4-52:11
[6] Jeremiah 34:2 - 2 Baruch 8:2, 2 Chronicles 36:11-36:12, Jeremiah 21:4 21:10 22:1-22:2 8:3 32:28-32:29 10:22 37:1-37:4 37:8-37:10 14:23 15:8, z.Vaetchanan 269b
[7] Jeremiah 34:3 - 2 Kings 25:4-25:7, Ezekiel 12:13 17:18-17:20 21:30, Jeremiah 21:7 8:4 10:21 13:17 14:18 39:4-39:7 52:7-52:11, Josephus Antiquities 11.7.2
[8] Missing in LXX
[9] Jeremiah 34:4 - z.Vaetchanan 269b
[10] Missing in LXX
[11] Jeremiah 34:5 - 2 Chronicles 16:14 21:19-20 10:28, 2 Kings 22:20, b.Avodah Zara 11b, b.Moed Katan 28b, b.Sanhedrin 46b 52b, Daniel 2:46, Ein Yaakov Moed Katan 28b, Ein Yaakov Sanhedrin 46b, Ezekiel 17:16, Jeremiah 22:18, Lamentations 4:20, Mas.Semachot 8:6, mt.Hilchot Evel 14:26, mt.Hilchot Melachim uMichamoteihem 2:1, Numbers.R 11:7, Saadia Opinions 6:5, Seder Olam 28:Daniel, t.Sanhedrin 4:2, t.Shabbat 7:18, y.Avodah Zarah 1:2, y.Sanhedrin 2:6
[12] LXX *and as they wept for your fathers who reigned before you, they shall weep also for you, saying*

וַיְדַבֵּר יִרְמְיָהוּ הַנָּבִיא אֶל־צִדְקִיָּהוּ מֶלֶךְ יְהוּדָה אֵת כָּל־הַדְּבָרִים הָאֵלֶּה בִּירוּשָׁלָם	6[1]	Then Jeremiah the prophet spoke all these words to Zedekiah king of Judah in Jerusalem,
וְחֵיל מֶלֶךְ־בָּבֶל נִלְחָמִים עַל־יְרוּשָׁלַם וְעַל כָּל־עָרֵי יְהוּדָה הַנּוֹתָרוֹת אֶל־לָכִישׁ וְאֶל־עֲזֵקָה כִּי הֵנָּה נִשְׁאֲרוּ בְּעָרֵי יְהוּדָה עָרֵי מִבְצָר	7	when the king of Babylon's army fought against Jerusalem, and against all the cities of Judah that were left, against Lachish and against Azekah; for these alone remained of the cities of Judah as fortified cities.
הַדָּבָר אֲשֶׁר־הָיָה אֶל־יִרְמְיָהוּ מֵאֵת יְהֹוָה אַחֲרֵי כְּרֹת הַמֶּלֶךְ צִדְקִיָּהוּ בְּרִית אֶת־כָּל־הָעָם אֲשֶׁר בִּירוּשָׁלָם לִקְרֹא לָהֶם דְּרוֹר	8[2]	The word that came to Jeremiah from the LORD, after the king Zedekiah had made a covenant with all the people who were at Jerusalem, to proclaim liberty to them;
לְשַׁלַּח אִישׁ אֶת־עַבְדּוֹ וְאִישׁ אֶת־שִׁפְחָתוֹ הָעִבְרִי וְהָעִבְרִיָּה חָפְשִׁים לְבִלְתִּי עֲבָד־בָּם בִּיהוּדִי אָחִיהוּ אִישׁ	9[3]	that every man should let his manservant, and every man his maidservant, being a Hebrew man or a Hebrew woman, go free; that no one should make bondmen of them, of a Jew his brother;
וַיִּשְׁמְעוּ כָל־הַשָּׂרִים וְכָל־הָעָם אֲשֶׁר־בָּאוּ בַבְּרִית לְשַׁלַּח אִישׁ אֶת־עַבְדּוֹ וְאִישׁ אֶת־שִׁפְחָתוֹ חָפְשִׁים לְבִלְתִּי עֲבָד־בָּם עוֹד וַיִּשְׁמְעוּ וַיְשַׁלֵּחוּ	10[4]	and all the princes and all the people listened, who had entered into the covenant to let his man servant, and his maid servant, go free, and not to make bondmen of them any longer; they listened, and let them go;
וַיָּשׁוּבוּ אַחֲרֵי־כֵן וַיָּשִׁבוּ אֶת־הָעֲבָדִים וְאֶת־הַשְּׁפָחוֹת אֲשֶׁר שִׁלְּחוּ חָפְשִׁים 'וַיִּכְבִּישׁוּם' "וַיִּכְבְּשׁוּם" לַעֲבָדִים וְלִשְׁפָחוֹת	11[5]	*but afterwards they turned, and caused the servants and the handmaids, whom they had let go free, return, and brought them into subjection for servants and for handmaids[6];*
וַיְהִי דְבַר־יְהֹוָה אֶל־יִרְמְיָהוּ מֵאֵת יְהֹוָה לֵאמֹר	12[7]	Therefore, the word of the LORD came to Jeremiah *from the LORD[8]*, saying:
כֹּה־אָמַר יְהֹוָה אֱלֹהֵי יִשְׂרָאֵל אָנֹכִי כָּרַתִּי בְרִית אֶת־אֲבוֹתֵיכֶם בְּיוֹם הוֹצִאִי אוֹתָם מֵאֶרֶץ מִצְרַיִם מִבֵּית עֲבָדִים לֵאמֹר	13[9]	Thus says the LORD, the God of Israel: I made a covenant with your fathers in the day that I brought them forth from the land of Egypt, from the house of bondage, saying:
מִקֵּץ שֶׁבַע שָׁנִים תְּשַׁלְּחוּ אִישׁ אֶת־אָחִיו הָעִבְרִי אֲשֶׁר־יִמָּכֵר לְךָ וַעֲבָדְךָ שֵׁשׁ שָׁנִים וְשִׁלַּחְתּוֹ חָפְשִׁי מֵעִמָּךְ וְלֹא־שָׁמְעוּ אֲבוֹתֵיכֶם אֵלַי וְלֹא הִטּוּ אֶת־אָזְנָם	14[10]	*'At the end of seven years[11]* every man shall let go his brother who is a Hebrew, that has been sold to you, and has served you six years, you shall let him go free from you;' but your fathers did not listen to Me, nor inclined their ear.

---

[1] Jeremiah 34:6 - 1 Kings 21:19 22:14, 1 Samuel 3:18 15:16-24, 2 Samuel 12:7-12, Acts 20:27, Ezekiel 2:7, Matthew 14:4

[2] Jeremiah 34:8 - 2 Chronicles 15:12-15:15 23:16 5:10 34:30-34:33, 2 Kings 11:17 23:2-23:3, Deuteronomy 15:12, Exodus 21:2-21:4 23:10-23:11, Isaiah 13:1, Jeremiah 34:14-34:15 10:17, Leviticus 1:10 25:39-25:46, Nehemiah 5:1-5:13 10:1-10:28

Jeremiah 34:8-11 - Seder Olam 26:Zedekiah

Jeremiah 34:8-22 - Haftarah Mishpatim Part One [continues at 33:25-26 Ashkenaz and Sephard]

Jeremiah 34:8-35:19 - Haftarah Mishpatim [Teimon]

[3] Jeremiah 34:9 - 1 Corinthians 6:8, 1 Samuel 4:6 4:9 14:11, 2 Corinthians 11:22, Deuteronomy 15:12, Exodus 2:6 3:18, Genesis 14:13 16:15, Jeremiah 1:14 3:7 6:8 10:10, Leviticus 25:39-25:46, Philippians 3:5

[4] Jeremiah 34:10 - b.Arachin [Tosefot] 33a, b.Arachin 33a, Isaiah 5:13, Jeremiah 3:10-11 2:10 2:16 12:12 36:24-25 14:4, Mark 6:20

[5] Jeremiah 34:11 - 1 Samuel 19:6-11 24:19 2:21, 2 Peter 2:20-22, Ecclesiastes 8:11, Exodus 8:4 8:11 9:28 9:34-35 10:17-20 14:3-9, Hosea 6:4 7:16, Jeremiah 10:21 13:5, Matthew 12:43-45, Proverbs 2:11, Psalms 36:4 78:34-36 5:5, Romans 2:4-5, Zephaniah 1:6

[6] LXX *and gave them over to be man-servants and maid-servants*

[7] Jeremiah 34:12 - Guide for the Perplexed 1:44

[8] Missing in LXX

[9] Jeremiah 34:13 - Deuteronomy 5:2-5:3 5:6 5:27 6:12 7:8 8:14 13:11 15:15 16:12 24:18 28:69, Exodus 13:3 13:14 20:2 24:3 24:7-24:8, Hebrews 8:10-8:11, Jeremiah 7:22 11:4 11:7 7:33, Joshua 24:17, Judges 6:8, Mas.Kallah Rabbati 3:25, z.Vaetchanan 269b

[10] Jeremiah 34:14 - 1 Kings 9:22 21:25, 1 Samuel 8:7-8:8, 2 Chronicles 4:10 12:16, 2 Kings 17:13-17:14, Amos 2:6 8:6, b.Arachin [Rashi] 33a, b.Arachin 33a, Deuteronomy 15:12, Exodus 21:1-21:4 23:10-23:11, Ezekiel 20:4 20:8, Isaiah 2:1 10:6, Jeremiah 7:25-7:26 11:8-11:10 8:30 34:8-34:9, Lamentations.R 1:29, Mas.Kallah Rabbati 3:25, Nehemiah 9:30, Romans 7:14-7:17 7:24, y.Rosh Hashanah 3:5, Zechariah 7:11-7:12

[11] LXX *When six years are accomplished*

וַתָּשֻׁבוּ אַתֶּם הַיּוֹם וַתַּעֲשׂוּ אֶת־הַיָּשָׁר בְּעֵינַי לִקְרֹא דְרוֹר אִישׁ לְרֵעֵהוּ וַתִּכְרְתוּ בְרִית לְפָנַי בַּבַּיִת אֲשֶׁר־נִקְרָא שְׁמִי עָלָיו

15[1] And you were now turned, and did what is right in my eyes, in proclaiming liberty to his neighbor; and you had made a covenant before Me in the house where My name is called;

וַתָּשֻׁבוּ וַתְּחַלְּלוּ אֶת־שְׁמִי וַתָּשִׁבוּ אִישׁ אֶת־עַבְדּוֹ וְאִישׁ אֶת־שִׁפְחָתוֹ אֲשֶׁר־שִׁלַּחְתֶּם חָפְשִׁים לְנַפְשָׁם וַתִּכְבְּשׁוּ אֹתָם לִהְיוֹת לָכֶם לַעֲבָדִים וְלִשְׁפָחוֹת

16[2] but you turned and profaned My name, and caused everyone's servant, and everyone's handmaid, whom you freed at their pleasure, to return; and you brought them into subjection, to be servants and handmaids.

לָכֵן כֹּה־אָמַר יְהֹוָה אַתֶּם לֹא־שְׁמַעְתֶּם אֵלַי לִקְרֹא דְרוֹר אִישׁ לְאָחִיו וְאִישׁ לְרֵעֵהוּ הִנְנִי קֹרֵא לָכֶם דְּרוֹר נְאֻם־יְהֹוָה אֶל־הַחֶרֶב אֶל־הַדֶּבֶר וְאֶל־הָרָעָב וְנָתַתִּי אֶתְכֶם 'לִזְוָעָה' "לְזַעֲוָה" לְכֹל מַמְלְכוֹת הָאָרֶץ

17[3] Therefore, thus says the LORD: You have not listened to Me, to proclaim liberty, every man to his brother, and every man to his neighbor; behold, I proclaim for you a liberty, says the LORD, to the sword, to the pestilence, and to the famine; and I will make you a horror to all the kingdoms of the earth.

וְנָתַתִּי אֶת־הָאֲנָשִׁים הָעֹבְרִים אֶת־בְּרִתִי אֲשֶׁר לֹא־הֵקִימוּ אֶת־דִּבְרֵי הַבְּרִית אֲשֶׁר כָּרְתוּ לְפָנָי הָעֵגֶל אֲשֶׁר כָּרְתוּ לִשְׁנַיִם וַיַּעַבְרוּ בֵּין בְּתָרָיו

18[4] And I will give the men who transgressed My covenant, who have not performed the words of the covenant which they made before Me, when they cut the calf in two and passed between its parts;

שָׂרֵי יְהוּדָה וְשָׂרֵי יְרוּשָׁלַםִ הַסָּרִסִים וְהַכֹּהֲנִים וְכֹל עַם הָאָרֶץ הָעֹבְרִים בֵּין בִּתְרֵי הָעֵגֶל

19[5] the princes of Judah, and the princes of Jerusalem, the officers, and the priests, and all the people *of the land, who passed between the parts of the calf*[6];

וְנָתַתִּי אוֹתָם בְּיַד אֹיְבֵיהֶם וּבְיַד מְבַקְשֵׁי נַפְשָׁם וְהָיְתָה נִבְלָתָם לְמַאֲכָל לְעוֹף הַשָּׁמַיִם וּלְבֶהֱמַת הָאָרֶץ

20[7] I will give them into the hand of their enemies, and *into the hand of those who seek their life*[8]; and their dead bodies shall be food to the fowls of the heaven, and to the beasts of the earth.

וְאֶת־צִדְקִיָּהוּ מֶלֶךְ־יְהוּדָה וְאֶת־שָׂרָיו אֶתֵּן בְּיַד אֹיְבֵיהֶם וּבְיַד מְבַקְשֵׁי נַפְשָׁם וּבְיַד חֵיל מֶלֶךְ בָּבֶל הָעֹלִים מֵעֲלֵיכֶם

21[9] And Zedekiah king of Judah and his princes I will give into the hand of their enemies, and *into the hand of those who seek their life*[10], and into the hand of the king of Babylon's army, who are gone up from you.

הִנְנִי מְצַוֶּה נְאֻם־יְהֹוָה וַהֲשִׁבֹתִים אֶל־הָעִיר הַזֹּאת וְנִלְחֲמוּ עָלֶיהָ וּלְכָדוּהָ וּשְׂרָפֻהָ בָאֵשׁ וְאֶת־עָרֵי יְהוּדָה אֶתֵּן שְׁמָמָה מֵאֵין יֹשֵׁב

22[11] Behold, I will command, says the LORD, and cause them to return to this city; and they shall fight against it, and take it, and burn it with fire; and I will make the cities of Judah desolate, without inhabitant.

---

[1] Jeremiah 34:15 - 1 Kings 21:27-21:29, 2 Kings 10:30-10:31 12:3 14:3 23:3, Isaiah 10:2, Jeremiah 7:10-7:11 8:34 10:8 34:10-34:11, Matthew 15:8, Nehemiah 10:30, Psalms 76:12 119:106

[2] Jeremiah 34:16 - 1 Samuel 15:11, Exodus 20:7, Ezekiel 3:20 17:16-17:19 18:24 20:39 33:12-33:13 15:7, Jeremiah 10:11, Leviticus 19:12, Luke 8:13-8:15, Malachi 1:7 1:12, Matthew 18:28-18:34

[3] Jeremiah 34:17 - Daniel 6:25, Deuteronomy 19:19 4:25 28:64, Esther 7:10, Ezekiel 14:17-14:21, Galatians 6:7, James 2:13, Jeremiah 15:2 15:4 21:7 24:9-24:10 5:18 8:24 8:36 47:6-47:7, Judges 1:6-1:7, Lamentations 1:8, Leviticus 26:34-26:35, Luke 6:37-6:38, Matthew 7:2, Revelation 16:6, z.Vaetchanan 269b

[4] Jeremiah 34:18 - Deuteronomy 17:2, Genesis 15:10 15:17-15:18, Hosea 6:7 8:1, Joshua 7:11 23:16, Psalms 50:1, Seder Olam 26:Zedekiah, Sifre Devarim Shoftim 171

[5] Jeremiah 34:19 - 2 Kings 24:12 24:15, Daniel 9:6-8 9:12, Ezekiel 22:27-31, Jeremiah 5:2 10:10 14:7, Micah 7:1-5, Zephaniah 3:3-4

[6] Missing in LXX

[7] Jeremiah 34:20 - 1 Kings 14:11 16:4 21:23-21:24, 1 Samuel 17:44 17:46, 2 Kings 9:34-9:37, Deuteronomy 4:26, Ezekiel 5:5 8:4 39:17-39:20, Jeremiah 4:30 7:33 11:21 16:4 19:7 21:7 22:25 44:16 20:30 1:37, Revelation 19:17-19:21

[8] Missing in LXX

[9] Jeremiah 34:21 - 2 Kings 25:18-25:21, Ezekiel 17:16, Jeremiah 8:4 34:3-34:5 37:5-37:11 15:6 4:10 52:24-52:27, Lamentations 4:20

[10] Missing in LXX

[11] Jeremiah 34:22 - 2 Chronicles 12:17, 2 Kings 24:2-24:3, 2 Samuel 16:11, Amos 3:6, Ezekiel 33:27-33:28, Isaiah 6:11 10:5-10:7 13:3 24:12 13:26 45:1-45:3 16:11, Jeremiah 4:7 9:12 21:4-21:10 8:29 9:10 37:8-37:10 14:23 39:1-39:2 15:8 44:2-44:6 20:22 4:7 4:13, Lamentations 1:1, Matthew 22:7, Micah 7:13, Zechariah 1:12 7:14

Jeremiah – Chapter 35[1]

הַדָּבָר אֲשֶׁר־הָיָה אֶל־יִרְמְיָהוּ מֵאֵת יְהֹוָה בִּימֵי יְהוֹיָקִים בֶּן־יֹאשִׁיָּהוּ מֶלֶךְ יְהוּדָה לֵאמֹר	1[2]	The word which came to Jeremiah from the LORD in the days of Jehoiakim the son of Josiah, king of Judah, saying:
הָלוֹךְ אֶל־בֵּית הָרֵכָבִים וְדִבַּרְתָּ אוֹתָם וַהֲבִאוֹתָם בֵּית יְהֹוָה אֶל־אַחַת הַלְּשָׁכוֹת וְהִשְׁקִיתָ אוֹתָם יָיִן	2[3]	'Go to the house of the Rechabites, and speak to them, and bring them into the house of the LORD, into one of the chambers, and give them wine to drink.'
וָאֶקַּח אֶת־יַאֲזַנְיָה בֶן־יִרְמְיָהוּ בֶּן־חֲבַצִּנְיָה וְאֶת־אֶחָיו וְאֶת־כָּל־בָּנָיו וְאֵת כָּל־בֵּית הָרֵכָבִים	3	Then I took Jaazaniah the son of Jeremiah, the son of Habazziniah, and his brethren, and all his sons, and the whole house of the Rechabites;
וָאָבִא אֹתָם בֵּית יְהֹוָה אֶל־לִשְׁכַּת בְּנֵי חָנָן בֶּן־יִגְדַּלְיָהוּ אִישׁ הָאֱלֹהִים אֲשֶׁר־אֵצֶל לִשְׁכַּת הַשָּׂרִים אֲשֶׁר מִמַּעַל לְלִשְׁכַּת מַעֲשֵׂיָהוּ בֶן־שַׁלֻּם שֹׁמֵר הַסַּף	4[4]	and I brought them into the house of the LORD, into the chamber of the sons of *Hanan the son of Igdaliah*[5], the man of God, which was by the chamber of the princes, which was above the chamber of Maaseiah the son of Shallum, the keeper of the door;
וָאֶתֵּן לִפְנֵי בְּנֵי בֵית־הָרֵכָבִים גְּבִעִים מְלֵאִים יַיִן וְכֹסוֹת וָאֹמַר אֲלֵיהֶם שְׁתוּ־יָיִן	5[6]	and I set before the sons of the house of the Rechabites goblets full of wine, and cups, and I said to them: 'Drink wine.'
וַיֹּאמְרוּ לֹא נִשְׁתֶּה־יָּיִן כִּי יוֹנָדָב בֶּן־רֵכָב אָבִינוּ צִוָּה עָלֵינוּ לֵאמֹר לֹא תִשְׁתּוּ־יַיִן אַתֶּם וּבְנֵיכֶם עַד־עוֹלָם	6[7]	But they said: 'We will drink no wine; for Jonadab the son of Rechab our father commanded us, saying: You shall drink no wine, ye, nor your sons, forever;
וּבַיִת לֹא־תִבְנוּ וְזֶרַע לֹא־תִזְרָעוּ וְכֶרֶם לֹא־תִטָּעוּ וְלֹא יִהְיֶה לָכֶם כִּי בָּאֳהָלִים תֵּשְׁבוּ כָּל־יְמֵיכֶם לְמַעַן תִּחְיוּ יָמִים רַבִּים עַל־פְּנֵי הָאֲדָמָה אֲשֶׁר אַתֶּם גָּרִים שָׁם	7[8]	Nor shall you build house, nor sow seed, nor plant vineyard, nor have any; but all your days you shall live in tents, so you may live many days in the land in which you sojourn.
וַנִּשְׁמַע בְּקוֹל יְהוֹנָדָב בֶּן־רֵכָב אָבִינוּ לְכֹל אֲשֶׁר צִוָּנוּ לְבִלְתִּי שְׁתוֹת־יַיִן כָּל־יָמֵינוּ אֲנַחְנוּ נָשֵׁינוּ בָּנֵינוּ וּבְנֹתֵינוּ	8[9]	And we have listened to the voice of Jonadab the son of Rechab our father in all he charged us, to drink no wine all our days, we, our wives, our sons, nor our daughters;
וּלְבִלְתִּי בְּנוֹת בָּתִּים לְשִׁבְתֵּנוּ וְכֶרֶם וְשָׂדֶה וָזֶרַע לֹא יִהְיֶה־לָּנוּ	9[10]	nor to build houses for us to live in, nor to have vineyard, or field, or seed;

---

[1] Chapter 42 in LXX

[2] Jeremiah 35:1 - 2 Chronicles 36:5-8, 2 Kings 23:35 24:1-6, Daniel 1:1, History of the Rechabites 8:1a, Jeremiah 1:3 22:13-19 1:1 2:1 12:1 12:9 12:29 22:2

[3] Jeremiah 35:2 - 1 Chronicles 2:55 9:26 9:33 23:28, 1 Kings 6:5-6 6:10, 2 Chronicles 3:9 7:11, 2 Kings 10:15-16, Ezekiel 40:7-13 16:16 41:5-11 42:4-13, Ezra 8:29, Jeremiah 11:4 11:8, Mekhilta de R'Shimon bar Yochai Amalek 47:2, Nehemiah 13:5 13:8-9

[4] Jeremiah 35:4 - 1 Chronicles 9:18-9:19 9:27, 1 Kings 12:22 13:1 13:26 17:18 17:24 20:28, 1 Samuel 2:27 9:6-9:8, 1 Timothy 6:11, 2 Chronicles 8:14 25:7-25:9, 2 Kings 1:9 1:11-1:13 5:14 5:20 6:10 7:2 7:17 8:2-8:8 12:10 23:16-23:17 1:18, 2 Timothy 3:17, Deuteronomy 9:1, Ezekiel 19:8, Jeremiah 2:10 36:10-36:12 4:24, Joshua 14:6, Psalms 84:11

[5] LXX *Joanan, the son of Ananias, the son of Godolias*

[6] Jeremiah 35:5 - 2 Corinthians 2:9, Amos 2:12, Ecclesiastes 9:7, Jeremiah 11:2, Mekhilta de R'Shimon bar Yochai Amalek 47:2

[7] Jeremiah 35:6 - 1 Chronicles 2:55 16:19, 1 Corinthians 7:26-7:31, 1 Peter 2:11, 2 Kings 10:15 10:23, b.Bava Batra [Rashbam] 91b, Ephesians 6:2-6:3, Exodus 20:12, Genesis 1:27 12:7, Genesis.R 98 [Excl]:8, Hebrews 11:9-11:13, History of the Rechabites 9:8, Jehonadab is altered to read, Jeremiah 11:10, Jonadab, Judges 13:7 13:14, Leviticus 10:9 23:42-23:43, Luke 1:15, Midrash Tanchuma Shemini 5, Nehemiah 8:14-8:16, Numbers 6:2-6:5, Psalms 9:12

Jeremiah 35:6-7 - Mekhilta de R'Shimon bar Yochai Amalek 47:2, Midrash Tanchuma Shemini 5

Jeremiah 35:6-11 - History of the Rechabites 8:3

[8] Jeremiah 35:7 - 1 Peter 2:11, Ephesians 5:18 6:2-6:3, Exodus 20:12, Genesis 1:27, Hebrews 11:9-11:13, Jeremiah 11:10, Leviticus 23:42-23:43, Nehemiah 8:14-8:16, Saadia Opinions 10:11

[9] Jeremiah 35:8 - Colossians 3:20, Proverbs 1:8-1:9 4:1-4:2 4:10 6:20 13:1

[10] Jeremiah 35:9 - 1 Timothy 6:6, 2 Kings 5:26, Jeremiah 11:7, Numbers 16:14, Psalms 37:16

וַנֵּ֣שֶׁב בָּאֳהָלִ֔ים וַנִּשְׁמַ֖ע וַנַּ֣עַשׂ כְּכֹ֥ל אֲשֶׁר־צִוָּ֖נוּ יוֹנָדָ֥ב אָבִֽינוּ	10[1]	but we have lived in tents, and have listened, and done according to all Jonadab our father commanded us.
וַיְהִ֗י בַּעֲל֨וֹת נְבוּכַדְרֶאצַּ֥ר מֶֽלֶךְ־בָּבֶל֮ אֶל־הָאָרֶץ֒ וַנֹּ֗אמֶר בֹּ֚אוּ וְנָב֣וֹא יְרוּשָׁלִַ֔ם מִפְּנֵי֙ חֵ֣יל הַכַּשְׂדִּ֔ים וּמִפְּנֵ֖י חֵ֣יל אֲרָ֑ם וַנֵּ֖שֶׁב בִּירוּשָׁלִָֽם	11[2]	But it came to pass, when Nebuchadrezzar king of Babylon came up against the land, we said: Come, and let us go to Jerusalem for fear of the army of the Chaldeans, and for fear of the army of the Arameans; so we live at Jerusalem.'
וַֽיְהִי֙ דְּבַר־יְהֹוָ֔ה אֶֽל־יִרְמְיָ֖הוּ לֵאמֹֽר	12[3]	Then came the word of the LORD to Jeremiah, saying:
כֹּה־אָמַ֞ר יְהֹוָ֤ה צְבָאוֹת֙ אֱלֹהֵ֣י יִשְׂרָאֵ֔ל הָלֹ֤ךְ וְאָֽמַרְתָּ֙ לְאִ֣ישׁ יְהוּדָ֔ה וּלְיֽוֹשְׁבֵ֖י יְרֽוּשָׁלָ֑םִ הֲל֨וֹא תִקְח֥וּ מוּסָ֛ר לִשְׁמֹ֥עַ אֶל־דְּבָרַ֖י נְאֻם־יְהֹוָֽה	13[4]	'Thus says the LORD of hosts, the God of Israel: Go, and say to the men of Judah and the inhabitants of Jerusalem: will you not receive instruction to listen to My words? says the LORD.
הוּקַ֡ם אֶת־דִּבְרֵ֣י יְהוֹנָדָ֣ב בֶּן־רֵ֠כָב אֲשֶׁר־צִוָּ֨ה אֶת־בָּנָ֜יו לְבִלְתִּ֣י שְׁתֽוֹת־יַ֗יִן וְלֹ֤א שָׁתוּ֙ עַד־הַיּ֣וֹם הַזֶּ֔ה כִּ֣י שָֽׁמְע֔וּ אֵ֖ת מִצְוַ֣ת אֲבִיהֶ֑ם וְאָ֨נֹכִ֜י דִּבַּ֤רְתִּי אֲלֵיכֶם֙ הַשְׁכֵּ֣ם וְדַבֵּ֔ר וְלֹ֥א שְׁמַעְתֶּ֖ם אֵלָֽי	14[5]	The words of Jonadab the son of Rechab, that he commanded his sons, not to drink wine, are performed, and to this day they drink none, for they listen to their father's commandment; but I have spoken to you, speaking early and often, and you have not listened to Me.
וָאֶשְׁלַ֣ח אֲלֵיכֶ֣ם אֶת־כׇּל־עֲבָדַ֣י הַנְּבִאִ֣ים ׀ הַשְׁכֵּ֣ים וְשָׁלֹ֣חַ ׀ לֵאמֹ֗ר שֻֽׁבוּ־נָ֞א אִ֣ישׁ מִדַּרְכּ֤וֹ הָֽרָעָה֙ וְהֵיטִ֣יבוּ מַֽעַלְלֵיכֶ֔ם וְאַל־תֵּ֨לְכ֜וּ אַֽחֲרֵ֨י אֱלֹהִ֤ים אֲחֵרִים֙ לְעׇבְדָ֔ם וּשְׁבוּ֙ אֶל־הָ֣אֲדָמָ֔ה אֲשֶׁר־נָתַ֥תִּי לָכֶ֖ם וְלַֽאֲבֹֽתֵיכֶ֑ם וְלֹ֤א הִטִּיתֶם֙ אֶֽת־אׇזְנְכֶ֔ם וְלֹ֥א שְׁמַעְתֶּ֖ם אֵלָֽי	15[6]	I have sent also to you all My servants the prophets, sending them often and often, saying: Return now, everyone, from his evil way, and amend your deeds, and go not after other gods to serve them, and you shall live in the land I have given to you and to your fathers; but you have not inclined your ear, nor listened to Me.
כִּ֣י הֵקִ֗ימוּ בְּנֵי֙ יְהוֹנָדָ֣ב בֶּן־רֵכָ֔ב אֶת־מִצְוַ֥ת אֲבִיהֶ֖ם אֲשֶׁ֣ר צִוָּ֑ם וְהָעָ֣ם הַזֶּ֔ה לֹ֥א שָֽׁמְע֖וּ אֵלָֽי	16[7]	Because the sons of Jonadab the son of Rechab have performed the commandment of their father which he commanded them, but this people has not listened to Me;
לָ֠כֵ֠ן כֹּֽה־אָמַ֨ר יְהֹוָ֜ה אֱלֹהֵ֤י צְבָאוֹת֙ אֱלֹהֵ֣י יִשְׂרָאֵ֔ל הִנְנִ֧י מֵבִ֣יא אֶל־יְהוּדָ֗ה וְאֶ֤ל כׇּל־יֽוֹשְׁבֵי֙ יְר֣וּשָׁלַ֔םִ אֵ֚ת כׇּל־הָ֣רָעָ֔ה אֲשֶׁ֥ר דִּבַּ֖רְתִּי עֲלֵיהֶ֑ם יַ֣עַן דִּבַּ֤רְתִּי אֲלֵיהֶם֙ וְלֹ֣א שָׁמֵ֔עוּ וָאֶקְרָ֥א לָהֶ֖ם וְלֹ֥א עָנֽוּ	17[8]	Therefore, thus says the LORD, *the God of hosts, the God of Israel*[9]: Behold, I will bring upon Judah and upon all the inhabitants of Jerusalem all the evil I have pronounced against them; *because I have spoken to them, but they have not heard, and I have called to them, but they have not answered*[10].'
וּלְבֵ֣ית הָרֵֽכָבִ֗ים אָמַר֙ יִרְמְיָ֔הוּ כֹּֽה־אָמַ֞ר יְהֹוָ֤ה צְבָאוֹת֙ אֱלֹהֵ֣י יִשְׂרָאֵ֔ל יַ֚עַן אֲשֶׁ֣ר שְׁמַעְתֶּ֔ם עַל־	18[11]	And to the house of the Rechabites, Jeremiah said: Thus says the LORD of hosts, the God of

[1] Jeremiah 35:10 - b.Sotah [Rashi] 11a, Jehonadab is altered to read, Jonadab, Mekilta de R'Ishmael Amalek 4:120, Pesikta Rabbati 26:7

[2] Jeremiah 35:11 - 2 Kings 24:1-24:2, Daniel 1:1-1:2, Jeremiah 4:5-4:7 8:14, Luke 21:20-21:21, Mark 13:14, variant אֶל־הָאָרֶץ of עַל־הָאָרֶץ is found

[3] Jeremiah 35:12-19 - History of the Rechabites 10:2

[4] Jeremiah 35:13 - Hebrews 12:25, Isaiah 28:9-28:12 18:23, Jeremiah 5:3 6:8-6:10 9:13 8:33, Proverbs 8:10 19:20, Psalms 32:8-32:9, z.Vaetchanan 269b

[5] Jeremiah 35:14 - 2 Chronicles 36:15-36:16, Isaiah 6:9 2:2, Jeremiah 7:13 7:24-7:26 11:7 25:3-25:4 2:5 5:19 8:33, Midrash Tanchuma Shemini 5, Nehemiah 9:26 9:30, Proverbs 1:20-1:33

[6] Jeremiah 35:15 - 1 Thessalonians 4:8, Acts 2:20, Deuteronomy 6:20, Ezekiel 18:30-18:32, Hosea 14:3-14:6, Isaiah 1:16-1:19, Jeremiah 3:14 4:1 4:14 7:3-7:7 7:25-7:26 17:20-17:25 18:11 22:4 25:5-25:6 2:13 10:14 44:4-44:5, Luke 10:16 13:34-13:35, Zechariah 1:3-1:4

[7] Jeremiah 35:16 - Isaiah 1:3, Jeremiah 11:14, Luke 15:11-15:13 15:28-15:30, m.Taanit 4:5, Malachi 1:6, Matthew 11:28-11:30

[8] Jeremiah 35:17 - Deuteronomy 28:15-28:68 29:18-29:27 31:20-31:21 32:16-32:42, Genesis 6:17, Isaiah 2:2 17:12 18:4, Jeremiah 7:13 7:26-7:27 11:8 15:3-15:4 19:7-19:13 21:4-21:10 2:5 8:33, Joshua 23:15-23:16, Leviticus 26:14-26:46, Luke 13:34-13:35, Micah 3:12, Proverbs 1:24-1:31 13:13 16:2, Romans 10:21, z.Vaetchanan 269b

[9] Missing in LXX

[10] Missing in LXX

[11] Jeremiah 35:18 - b.Sanhedrin [Rashi] 41a, Deuteronomy 5:16, Ephesians 6:1-6:3, Exodus 20:12, z.Vaetchanan 269b

מִצְוַת יְהוֹנָדָב אֲבִיכֶם וַתִּשְׁמְרוּ אֶת־כָּל־מִצְוֹתָיו וַתַּעֲשׂוּ כְּכֹל אֲשֶׁר־צִוָּה אֶתְכֶם

Israel: Because you listened to the commandment of Jonadab your father, and kept all his precepts, and done according to all he commanded you;

19[1]

לָכֵן כֹּה אָמַר יְהוָה צְבָאוֹת אֱלֹהֵי יִשְׂרָאֵל לֹא־יִכָּרֵת אִישׁ לְיוֹנָדָב בֶּן־רֵכָב עֹמֵד לְפָנַי כָּל־הַיָּמִים

Therefore, thus says the LORD of hosts, the God of Israel: Jonadab the son of Rechab shall not be cut off stand before Me forever.'

Jeremiah – Chapter 36[2]

וַיְהִי בַּשָּׁנָה הָרְבִיעִת לִיהוֹיָקִים בֶּן־יֹאשִׁיָּהוּ מֶלֶךְ יְהוּדָה הָיָה הַדָּבָר הַזֶּה אֶל־יִרְמְיָהוּ מֵאֵת יְהוָה לֵאמֹר

1[3]

And it came to pass in the fourth year of Jehoiakim the son of Josiah, king of Judah, that this word came to Jeremiah from the LORD, saying:

קַח־לְךָ מְגִלַּת־סֵפֶר וְכָתַבְתָּ אֵלֶיהָ אֵת כָּל־הַדְּבָרִים אֲשֶׁר־דִּבַּרְתִּי אֵלֶיךָ עַל־יִשְׂרָאֵל וְעַל־יְהוּדָה וְעַל־כָּל־הַגּוֹיִם מִיּוֹם דִּבַּרְתִּי אֵלֶיךָ מִימֵי יֹאשִׁיָּהוּ וְעַד הַיּוֹם הַזֶּה

2[4]

'Take a roll of a book, and write in it all the words I have spoken to you against Israel, and against Judah, and against all the nations, from the day I spoke to you, from the days of Josiah, to this day.

אוּלַי יִשְׁמְעוּ בֵּית יְהוּדָה אֵת כָּל־הָרָעָה אֲשֶׁר אָנֹכִי חֹשֵׁב לַעֲשׂוֹת לָהֶם לְמַעַן יָשׁוּבוּ אִישׁ מִדַּרְכּוֹ הָרָעָה וְסָלַחְתִּי לַעֲוֹנָם וּלְחַטָּאתָם

3[5]

It may be that the house of Judah will hear all the evil I committed to do to them; that they may return from his evil way, and I may forgive their iniquity and their sin.'

וַיִּקְרָא יִרְמְיָהוּ אֶת־בָּרוּךְ בֶּן־נֵרִיָּה וַיִּכְתֹּב בָּרוּךְ מִפִּי יִרְמְיָהוּ אֵת כָּל־דִּבְרֵי יְהוָה אֲשֶׁר־דִּבֶּר אֵלָיו עַל־מְגִלַּת־סֵפֶר

4[6]

Then Jeremiah called Baruch the son of Neriah; and Baruch wrote from the mouth of Jeremiah all the words of the LORD, which He spoke to him, on a roll of a book.

וַיְצַוֶּה יִרְמְיָהוּ אֶת־בָּרוּךְ לֵאמֹר אֲנִי עָצוּר לֹא אוּכַל לָבוֹא בֵּית יְהוָה

5[7]

And Jeremiah commanded Baruch, saying: 'I am detained, I cannot go into the house of the LORD;

וּבָאתָ אַתָּה וְקָרָאתָ בַמְּגִלָּה אֲשֶׁר־כָּתַבְתָּ מִפִּי אֶת־דִּבְרֵי יְהוָה בְּאָזְנֵי הָעָם בֵּית יְהוָה בְּיוֹם צוֹם וְגַם בְּאָזְנֵי כָל־יְהוּדָה הַבָּאִים מֵעָרֵיהֶם תִּקְרָאֵם

6[8]

Therefore, go, and read in the scroll, which you have written from my mouth, the words of the LORD in the ears of the people in the LORD's house on a fast day; and also you also shall read them in the ears of all Judah who come from their cities.

אוּלַי תִּפֹּל תְּחִנָּתָם לִפְנֵי יְהוָה וְיָשֻׁבוּ אִישׁ מִדַּרְכּוֹ הָרָעָה כִּי־גָדוֹל הָאַף וְהַחֵמָה אֲשֶׁר־דִּבֶּר יְהוָה אֶל־הָעָם הַזֶּה

7[9]

Perhaps they will present their supplication before the LORD, and will turn from his evil way; for great is the anger and the fury that the LORD has pronounced against this people.'

---

[1] Jeremiah 35:19 - 1 Chronicles 2:55, Jehonadab is altered to read, Jeremiah 15:19 33:17-33:18, Jonadab, Jude 1:24, Luke 21:36, Mekhilta de R'Shimon bar Yochai Amalek 47:2, Mekilta de R'Ishmael Amalek 4:131, Midrash Tanchuma Bamidbar 26, Midrash Tanchuma Shemini 5, Numbers.R 5:9, Pesikta de R'Kahana S5.2 S5.4, Psalms 5:6, z.Vaetchanan 269b

[2] Jeremiah 36 - mt.Hilchot Teshuvah 5:2; Chapter 43 in LXX

[3] Jeremiah 36:1 - 2 Chronicles 12:5, 2 Kings 24:1-24:2, Eupolemus 39:3, Jeremiah 1:1 11:1 21:1

[4] Jeremiah 36:2 - 2 Kings 17:18-17:20, Deuteronomy 7:24, Exodus 17:14, Ezekiel 2:9 3:1-3:3, Ezra 6:2, Habakkuk 2:2-2:3, Hosea 8:12, Isaiah 8:1 30:8-30:9, Jeremiah 1:2-1:3 1:5 1:10 2:4 3:3-3:10 23:13-23:14 1:3 25:9-25:29 6:2 32:30-32:35 12:6 12:23 12:29 21:1 47:1-47:7 51:60, Job 7:35, Psalms 40:8, Revelation 5:1-5:9, Zechariah 5:1-5:4

[5] Jeremiah 36:3 - 1 Kings 8:48-8:50, 1 Samuel 7:3, 2 Chronicles 6:38-6:39, 2 Peter 3:9, 2 Timothy 2:25-2:26, Acts 3:19 2:18 2:20 4:27, Deuteronomy 5:29 6:2 6:8, Ezekiel 12:3 18:23 18:27-18:28 33:7-33:9 33:14-33:16, Isaiah 6:10 55:6-55:7, Jeremiah 18:8 18:11 23:14 24:7 2:3 11:15 12:7, Jonah 3:8-3:10, Jubilees 5:17, Luke 3:7-9 20:13, Mark 4:12, Matthew 3:7-9 13:15, Nehemiah 1:9, Zephaniah 2:3

[6] Jeremiah 36:4 - 2 Baruch 1:1, Ezekiel 2:9, Isaiah 8:1, Jeremiah 8:12 36:17-36:18 12:21 12:23 12:26 12:28 12:32 19:3 45:1-45:2, Romans 16:22, Zechariah 5:1

[7] Jeremiah 36:5 - 2 Corinthians 11:23, 2 Timothy 2:9, Ephesians 3:1 6:20, Hebrews 11:36, Jastrow 1102b, Jeremiah 20:2 8:2 9:1 13:15 14:6 14:28 16:4

[8] Jeremiah 36:6 - Acts 3:9, Ezekiel 2:3-2:7, Jeremiah 7:2 18:11 19:14 22:2 2:2 36:8-36:9, Leviticus 16:29-16:31 23:27-23:32

[9] Jeremiah 36:7 - 1 Kings 8:33-8:36, 2 Chronicles 33:12-33:13 10:21, 2 Kings 22:13 22:17, Daniel 9:13, Deuteronomy 28:15-28:68 29:17-29:27 7:17, Ezekiel 5:13 8:18 13:13 20:33 22:20 24:8-24:13, Hosea 5:15-6:1 14:3-14:5, Jeremiah 1:3 4:4 16:10 19:15 21:5 1:5 2:3 12:3, Jonah 3:8, Lamentations 4:11, Zechariah 1:4

וַיַּעַשׂ בָּרוּךְ בֶּן־נֵרִיָּה כְּכֹל אֲשֶׁר־צִוָּהוּ יִרְמְיָהוּ הַנָּבִיא לִקְרֹא בַסֵּפֶר דִּבְרֵי יְהוָה בֵּית יְהוָה 8[1]

And Baruch the son of Neriah did according to all Jeremiah the prophet commanded him, reading in the book the words of the LORD in the LORD's house.

וַיְהִי בַשָּׁנָה הַחֲמִשִׁית לִיהוֹיָקִים בֶּן־יֹאשִׁיָּהוּ מֶלֶךְ־יְהוּדָה בַּחֹדֶשׁ הַתְּשִׁעִי קָרְאוּ צוֹם לִפְנֵי יְהוָה כָּל־הָעָם בִּירוּשָׁלִָם וְכָל־הָעָם הַבָּאִים מֵעָרֵי יְהוּדָה בִּירוּשָׁלִָם 9[2]

Now it came to pass in the fifth year of Jehoiakim the son of Josiah, king of Judah, in the ninth month, they proclaimed a fast before the LORD, all the people in Jerusalem, and all the people who came from the cities of Judah to Jerusalem.

וַיִּקְרָא בָרוּךְ בַּסֵּפֶר אֶת־דִּבְרֵי יִרְמְיָהוּ בֵּית יְהוָה בְּלִשְׁכַּת גְּמַרְיָהוּ בֶן־שָׁפָן הַסֹּפֵר בֶּחָצֵר הָעֶלְיוֹן פֶּתַח שַׁעַר בֵּית־יְהוָה הֶחָדָשׁ בְּאָזְנֵי כָּל־הָעָם 10[3]

Then Baruch read in the book the words of Jeremiah in the house of the LORD, in the chamber of Gemariah the son of Shaphan the scribe, in the upper court, at the entry of the new gate of the LORD's house, in the ears of all the people.

וַיִּשְׁמַע מִכָיְהוּ בֶן־גְּמַרְיָהוּ בֶן־שָׁפָן אֶת־כָּל־דִּבְרֵי יְהוָה מֵעַל הַסֵּפֶר 11[4]

And when Micaiah the son of Gemariah, the son of Shaphan, heard from the book all the words of the LORD,

וַיֵּרֶד בֵּית־הַמֶּלֶךְ עַל־לִשְׁכַּת הַסֹּפֵר וְהִנֵּה־שָׁם כָּל־הַשָּׂרִים יוֹשְׁבִים אֱלִישָׁמָע הַסֹּפֵר וּדְלָיָהוּ בֶן־שְׁמַעְיָהוּ וְאֶלְנָתָן בֶּן־עַכְבּוֹר וּגְמַרְיָהוּ בֶן־שָׁפָן וְצִדְקִיָּהוּ בֶן־חֲנַנְיָהוּ וְכָל־הַשָּׂרִים 12[5]

he went down into the king's house, into the scribe's chamber; and, lo, all the princes sat there, Elishama the scribe, and Delaiah the son of Shemaiah, and *Elnathan*[6] the son of Achbor, and Gemariah the son of Shaphan, and Zedekiah the son of Hananiah, and all the princes.

וַיַּגֵּד לָהֶם מִכָיְהוּ אֵת כָּל־הַדְּבָרִים אֲשֶׁר שָׁמֵעַ בִּקְרֹא בָרוּךְ בַּסֵּפֶר בְּאָזְנֵי הָעָם 13[7]

Then Micaiah declared to them all the words he heard, when Baruch read the book in the ears of the people.

וַיִּשְׁלְחוּ כָל־הַשָּׂרִים אֶל־בָּרוּךְ אֶת־יְהוּדִי בֶּן־נְתַנְיָהוּ בֶּן־שֶׁלֶמְיָהוּ בֶן־כּוּשִׁי לֵאמֹר הַמְּגִלָּה אֲשֶׁר קָרָאתָ בָּהּ בְּאָזְנֵי הָעָם קָחֶנָּה בְיָדְךָ וָלֵךְ וַיִּקַּח בָּרוּךְ בֶּן־נֵרִיָּהוּ אֶת־הַמְּגִלָּה בְּיָדוֹ וַיָּבֹא אֲלֵיהֶם 14[8]

Therefore, all the princes sent Jehudi the son of Nethaniah, the son of Shelemiah, the son of Cushi, to Baruch, saying: 'Take in your hand the scroll you have read in the ears of the people, and come.' So Baruch the son of Neriah took the scroll in his hand, and came to them.

וַיֹּאמְרוּ אֵלָיו שֵׁב נָא וּקְרָאֶנָּה בְּאָזְנֵינוּ וַיִּקְרָא בָרוּךְ בְּאָזְנֵיהֶם 15

And they said to him: 'Sit down now, and read it in our ears.' So Baruch read it in their ears.

וַיְהִי כְּשָׁמְעָם אֶת־כָּל־הַדְּבָרִים פָּחֲדוּ אִישׁ אֶל־רֵעֵהוּ וַיֹּאמְרוּ אֶל־בָּרוּךְ הַגֵּיד נַגִּיד לַמֶּלֶךְ אֵת כָּל־הַדְּבָרִים הָאֵלֶּה 16[9]

Now it came to pass, when they heard all the words, they turned in fear one toward another, and said to Baruch: 'We will surely tell the king of all these words.'

וְאֶת־בָּרוּךְ שָׁאֲלוּ לֵאמֹר הַגֶּד־נָא לָנוּ אֵיךְ כָּתַבְתָּ אֶת־כָּל־הַדְּבָרִים הָאֵלֶּה מִפִּיו 17[10]

And they asked Baruch, saying: 'Tell us now: How did you write all these words at his mouth?'

---

[1] Jeremiah 36:8 - 1 Corinthians 16:10, Jeremiah 1:17 12:4, Luke 4:16-4:30, Matthew 16:24, Nehemiah 8:3, Philippians 2:19-2:22
[2] Jeremiah 36:9 - 2 Chronicles 20:3, Esther 4:16, Isaiah 58:1-58:3, Jeremiah 12:1 12:22, Joel 1:13 2:12-2:17, Jonah 3:5, Leviticus 23:27, Nehemiah 9:1, Zechariah 7:5-7:6 8:19
[3] Jeremiah 36:10 - 2 Kings 15:35 18:37, 2 Samuel 8:17 20:25, Jeremiah 2:10 2:24 5:3 11:4 12:6 12:8 12:11 12:25 4:25
[4] Jeremiah 36:11 - 2 Chronicles 10:20, 2 Kings 22:12-22:14 1:22, Jeremiah 12:10
[5] Jeremiah 36:12 - 2 Kings 22:3 22:12 22:14 24:8, Jeremiah 2:22 28:1-28:17 36:10-36:11 36:20-36:21 12:25 17:1
[6] LXX *Jonathan*
[7] Jeremiah 36:13 - 2 Chronicles 34:16-34:18 10:24, 2 Kings 22:10 22:19, Jonah 3:6
[8] Jeremiah 36:14 - 2 Kings 1:23, Ezekiel 2:6-7, Jeremiah 12:2 12:21 16:8 41:1-2 17:16 17:18, Matthew 10:16 10:28, Zephaniah 1:1
[9] Jeremiah 36:16 - Acts 24:25-24:26, Amos 7:10-7:11, Jeremiah 13:18 12:24 38:1-38:4
[10] Jeremiah 36:17 - John 9:10-9:11 9:15 9:26-9:27

וַיֹּאמֶר לָהֶם בָּרוּךְ מִפִּיו יִקְרָא אֵלַי אֵת כָּל־הַדְּבָרִים הָאֵלֶּה וַאֲנִי כֹּתֵב עַל־הַסֵּפֶר בַּדְּיוֹ

18[1] Then Baruch answered them: 'He pronounced all these words to me with his mouth, and I wrote them with ink in the book.'

וַיֹּאמְרוּ הַשָּׂרִים אֶל־בָּרוּךְ לֵךְ הִסָּתֵר אַתָּה וְיִרְמְיָהוּ וְאִישׁ אַל־יֵדַע אֵיפֹה אַתֶּם

19[2] Then said the princes to Baruch: 'Go, hide, you and Jeremiah, and let no one know where you are.'

וַיָּבֹאוּ אֶל־הַמֶּלֶךְ חָצֵרָה וְאֶת־הַמְּגִלָּה הִפְקִדוּ בְּלִשְׁכַּת אֱלִישָׁמָע הַסֹּפֵר וַיַּגִּידוּ בְּאָזְנֵי הַמֶּלֶךְ אֵת כָּל־הַדְּבָרִים

20[3] And they went in to the king into the court; but they had deposited the scroll in the chamber of Elishama the scribe; and they told all the words in the ears of the king.

וַיִּשְׁלַח הַמֶּלֶךְ אֶת־יְהוּדִי לָקַחַת אֶת־הַמְּגִלָּה וַיִּקָּחֶהָ מִלִּשְׁכַּת אֱלִישָׁמָע הַסֹּפֵר וַיִּקְרָאֶהָ יְהוּדִי בְּאָזְנֵי הַמֶּלֶךְ וּבְאָזְנֵי כָּל־הַשָּׂרִים הָעֹמְדִים מֵעַל הַמֶּלֶךְ

21[4] So the king sent Jehudi to fetch the scroll; and he took it from the chamber of Elishama the scribe. And Jehudi read it in the ears of the king, and in the ears of all the princes who stood beside the king.

וְהַמֶּלֶךְ יוֹשֵׁב בֵּית הַחֹרֶף בַּחֹדֶשׁ הַתְּשִׁיעִי וְאֶת־הָאָח לְפָנָיו מְבֹעָרֶת

22[5] Now the king was sitting in the winter house in the ninth month; and the brazier was burning before him.

וַיְהִי כִּקְרוֹא יְהוּדִי שָׁלֹשׁ דְּלָתוֹת וְאַרְבָּעָה יִקְרָעֶהָ בְּתַעַר הַסֹּפֵר וְהַשְׁלֵךְ אֶל־הָאֵשׁ אֲשֶׁר אֶל־הָאָח עַד־תֹּם כָּל־הַמְּגִלָּה עַל־הָאֵשׁ אֲשֶׁר עַל־הָאָח

23[6] And it came to pass, when Jehudi read three or four columns, he cut it with the penknife, and cast it into the fire that was in the brazier, until all the scroll was consumed in the fire in the brazier.

וְלֹא פָחֲדוּ וְלֹא קָרְעוּ אֶת־בִּגְדֵיהֶם הַמֶּלֶךְ וְכָל־עֲבָדָיו הַשֹּׁמְעִים אֵת כָּל־הַדְּבָרִים הָאֵלֶּה

24[7] Yet they were not afraid, nor rent their garments, neither the king, nor any of his servants who heard all these words.

וְגַם אֶלְנָתָן וּדְלָיָהוּ וּגְמַרְיָהוּ הִפְגִּעוּ בַמֶּלֶךְ לְבִלְתִּי שְׂרֹף אֶת־הַמְּגִלָּה וְלֹא שָׁמַע אֲלֵיהֶם

25[8] *Moreover, Elnathan and Delaiah and Gemariah entreated the king not to burn the scroll; but he would not hear them*[9].

וַיְצַוֶּה הַמֶּלֶךְ אֶת־יְרַחְמְאֵל בֶּן־הַמֶּלֶךְ וְאֶת־שְׂרָיָהוּ בֶן־עַזְרִיאֵל וְאֶת־שֶׁלֶמְיָהוּ בֶּן־עַבְדְּאֵל לָקַחַת אֶת־בָּרוּךְ הַסֹּפֵר וְאֵת יִרְמְיָהוּ הַנָּבִיא וַיַּסְתִּרֵם יְהוָה

26[10] And the king commanded Jerahmeel the king's son, and Seraiah the son of Azriel, and Shelemiah the son of Abdeel, to take Baruch the scribe and Jeremiah the prophet; but the LORD hid them.

וַיְהִי דְבַר־יְהוָה אֶל־יִרְמְיָהוּ אַחֲרֵי שְׂרֹף הַמֶּלֶךְ אֶת־הַמְּגִלָּה וְאֶת־הַדְּבָרִים אֲשֶׁר כָּתַב בָּרוּךְ מִפִּי יִרְמְיָהוּ לֵאמֹר

27[11] Then the word of the LORD came to Jeremiah, after the king had burned the scroll, and the words which Baruch wrote at the mouth of Jeremiah, saying:

---

[1] Jeremiah 36:18 - b.Bava Batra 15a, b.Eruvin [Rashi] 15b, b.Gittin [Tosefot] 6b, b.Megillah [Rashi] 15a, b.Megillah 19a, b.Menachot [Rashi] 34a, b.Menachot 30a 34a, Ecclesiastes.R 12:7, Ein Yaakov Bava Batra:14b, Jeremiah 12:2 12:4 43:2-43:3, Lamentations.R Petichata D'Chakimei:23, Mas.Sefer Torah 1:1, Mas.Soferim 1:2, Proverbs 26:4-26:5, Sifre Devarim Vaetchanan 36 Sifre Devarim Vezot Habracha 357, y.Megillah 4:1

[2] Jeremiah 36:19 - 1 Kings 17:3 18:4 18:10, 2 Chronicles 1:15, Acts 5:40 23:16-23:22, Amos 7:12, Jeremiah 26:20-26:24 12:26, Luke 13:31, Proverbs 4:12

[3] Jeremiah 36:20 - Jeremiah 12:12 12:21

[4] Jeremiah 36:21 - 2 Chronicles 10:18, 2 Kings 22:10, Ezekiel 2:4-2:5, Jeremiah 23:28 2:2 12:15

[5] Jeremiah 36:22 - Amos 3:15, Jastrow 39a, Jeremiah 3:20 22:14-22:16 12:9, Midrash Psalms 53:2

[6] Jeremiah 36:23 - 1 Kings 22:8 22:27, b.Moed Katan 26a, Deuteronomy 29:18-29:20, Ein Yaakov Moed Katan:26a, Esther.R Petichata:11, Genesis.R 42:3, Isaiah 5:18-5:19 28:14-28:15 28:17-28:22, Jastrow 39a 1193b, Jeremiah 36:29-36:31, Leviticus.R 11:7, Midrash Psalms 60:2, Midrash Tanchuma Shemini 9, mt.Hilchot Evel 9:9, Proverbs 1:30 5:12 13:13 19:21 21:30 5:1, Psalms 50:17, Revelation 22:19, Ruth.R Petichata:7, y.Moed Katan 3:7

[7] Jeremiah 36:24 - 1 Kings 21:27, 2 Chronicles 34:19-34:31, 2 Kings 19:1-19:2 22:11-22:19, b.Moed Katan 26a, Ein Yaakov Moed Katan:26a, Exodus.R 25:8, Gates of Repentance 2.013, Genesis 13:29, Isaiah 2:11 36:22-37:1, Jeremiah 5:3 12:16, Job 15:4, Jonah 3:6, Matthew 12:41, mt.Hilchot Evel 9:9, Psalms 36:2 64:6, Romans 3:18, y.Moed Katan 3:7

[8] Jeremiah 36:25 - Acts 5:34-5:39, Genesis 13:22 37:26-37:28, Jeremiah 13:15-13:17 2:22 12:12, Matthew 3:4 27:24-27:25, Proverbs 21:29

[9] LXX *But Elnathan and Godolias suggested to the king that he should burn the roll*

[10] Jeremiah 36:26 - 1 Kings 17:3 17:9 18:4 18:10-18:12 19:1-19:3 19:10 19:14, 2 Kings 6:18-6:20, Acts 12:11, Isaiah 2:20, Jeremiah 1:19 2:30 15:20-15:21 26:21-26:23 12:5 12:19, John 7:32 8:20 8:59 11:57, Matthew 23:34-23:37 26:47-26:50, Psalms 27:5 32:7 57:2 64:3 91:1 1:8

[11] Jeremiah 36:27 - b.Eruvin [Rashi] 15b, b.Moed Katan 26a, Jastrow 221a, Jeremiah 12:4, mt.Hilchot Evel 9:9, y.Moed Katan 3:7

שׁוּב קַח־לְךָ מְגִלָּה אַחֶרֶת וּכְתֹב עָלֶיהָ אֵת כָּל־הַדְּבָרִים הָרִאשֹׁנִים אֲשֶׁר הָיוּ עַל־הַמְּגִלָּה הָרִאשֹׁנָה אֲשֶׁר שָׂרַף יְהוֹיָקִים מֶלֶךְ־יְהוּדָה	28[1]	'Take another roll, and write in it all the former words that were in the first scroll, which Jehoiakim the king of Judah has burned.
וְעַל־יְהוֹיָקִים מֶלֶךְ־יְהוּדָה תֹאמַר כֹּה אָמַר יְהוָה אַתָּה שָׂרַפְתָּ אֶת־הַמְּגִלָּה הַזֹּאת לֵאמֹר מַדּוּעַ כָּתַבְתָּ עָלֶיהָ לֵאמֹר בֹּא־יָבוֹא מֶלֶךְ־בָּבֶל וְהִשְׁחִית אֶת־הָאָרֶץ הַזֹּאת וְהִשְׁבִּית מִמֶּנָּה אָדָם וּבְהֵמָה	29[2]	And concerning Jehoiakim king of Judah you shall say: Thus says the LORD: you burned this scroll, saying: Why have you written in it, saying: The king of Babylon shall certainly come and destroy this land, and shall cause to cease from there man and beast?
לָכֵן כֹּה־אָמַר יְהוָה עַל־יְהוֹיָקִים מֶלֶךְ יְהוּדָה לֹא־יִהְיֶה־לּוֹ יוֹשֵׁב עַל־כִּסֵּא דָוִד וְנִבְלָתוֹ תִּהְיֶה מֻשְׁלֶכֶת לַחֹרֶב בַּיּוֹם וְלַקֶּרַח בַּלָּיְלָה	30[3]	Therefore, thus says the LORD concerning Jehoiakim king of Judah: He shall have no one to sit on the throne of David; and his dead body shall be cast out in the day to the heat, and in the night to the frost.
וּפָקַדְתִּי עָלָיו וְעַל־זַרְעוֹ וְעַל־עֲבָדָיו אֶת־עֲוֹנָם וְהֵבֵאתִי עֲלֵיהֶם וְעַל־יֹשְׁבֵי יְרוּשָׁלַ͏ִם וְאֶל־אִישׁ יְהוּדָה אֵת כָּל־הָרָעָה אֲשֶׁר־דִּבַּרְתִּי אֲלֵיהֶם וְלֹא שָׁמֵעוּ	31[4]	And I will visit upon him and his seed and his servants their iniquity; and I will bring upon them, and on the inhabitants of Jerusalem, and on the men of Judah, all the evil I pronounced against them, but they listened not.'
וְיִרְמְיָהוּ לָקַח מְגִלָּה אַחֶרֶת וַיִּתְּנָהּ אֶל־בָּרוּךְ בֶּן־נֵרִיָּהוּ הַסֹּפֵר וַיִּכְתֹּב עָלֶיהָ מִפִּי יִרְמְיָהוּ אֵת כָּל־דִּבְרֵי הַסֵּפֶר אֲשֶׁר שָׂרַף יְהוֹיָקִים מֶלֶךְ־יְהוּדָה בָּאֵשׁ וְעוֹד נוֹסַף עֲלֵיהֶם דְּבָרִים רַבִּים כָּהֵמָּה	32[5]	*Then Jeremiah took another roll, and gave it to Baruch the scribe, the son of Neriah; who wrote in it from the mouth of Jeremiah all the words of the book which Jehoiakim king of Judah burned in the fire; and many like words were added besides them*[6].

Jeremiah – Chapter 37[7]

וַיִּמְלָךְ־מֶלֶךְ צִדְקִיָּהוּ בֶּן־יֹאשִׁיָּהוּ תַּחַת כָּנְיָהוּ בֶּן־יְהוֹיָקִים אֲשֶׁר הִמְלִיךְ נְבוּכַדְרֶאצַּר מֶלֶךְ־בָּבֶל בְּאֶרֶץ יְהוּדָה	1[8]	And Zedekiah the son of Josiah reigned as king, instead of *Coniah the son of Jehoiakim, whom Nebuchadrezzar king of Babylon made king in the land of*[9] Judah.
וְלֹא שָׁמַע הוּא וַעֲבָדָיו וְעַם הָאָרֶץ אֶל־דִּבְרֵי יְהוָה אֲשֶׁר דִּבֶּר בְּיַד יִרְמְיָהוּ הַנָּבִיא	2[10]	But neither he, nor his servants, nor the people of the land, listened to the words of the LORD, which He spoke by the prophet Jeremiah.
וַיִּשְׁלַח הַמֶּלֶךְ צִדְקִיָּהוּ אֶת־יְהוּכַל בֶּן־שֶׁלֶמְיָה וְאֶת־צְפַנְיָהוּ בֶן־מַעֲשֵׂיָה הַכֹּהֵן אֶל־יִרְמְיָהוּ הַנָּבִיא לֵאמֹר הִתְפַּלֶּל־נָא בַעֲדֵנוּ אֶל־יְהוָה אֱלֹהֵינוּ	3[11]	And Zedekiah the king sent Jehucal the son of Shelemiah, and Zephaniah the son of Maaseiah the priest, to the prophet Jeremiah, saying: 'Pray to the LORD our God for us.'

[1] Jeremiah 36:28 - 2 Timothy 2:13, Jeremiah 28:13-28:14 20:28, Job 23:13, Matthew 24:35, Zechariah 1:5-1:6

[2] Jeremiah 36:29 - 1 Corinthians 10:22, Acts 5:28 5:39, Deuteronomy 5:18, Isaiah 5:21 6:10 21:9, Jeremiah 21:4-21:7 21:10 2:9 4:8 8:3 32:28-32:30 34:21-34:22, Job 15:24 16:8, z.Vaetchanan 269b

[3] Jeremiah 36:30 - 2 Kings 24:12-15, Genesis 7:40, Jeremiah 22:18-22:19 22:30, z.Vaetchanan 269b

[4] Jeremiah 36:31 - Deuteronomy 28:15-28:68, Jeremiah 11:8 17:18 19:15 23:34 29:17-29:19 11:17 44:4-44:14, Leviticus 2:14, Matthew 23:37, Proverbs 5:1

[5] Jeremiah 36:32 - Daniel 3:19, Exodus 4:15-4:16 10:1, Jeremiah 12:4 12:18 12:23, Lamentations.R 3:א Petichata D'Chakimei:28, Leviticus 2:18 2:21 2:24 2:28, Mekilta de R'Ishmael Pisha 1:94, Revelation 22:18, Romans 16:22

[6] LXX *And Baruch took another roll, and wrote upon it from the mouth of Jeremias all the words of the book that Joakim burned: and there were yet more words added to it like the former*

[7] Jeremiah 37 - Shabbat preceding Tisha bAv [Pesikta Rabbati 27/28]; Chapter 44 in LXX

[8] Jeremiah 37:1 - 1 Chronicles 3:15-3:16, 2 Chronicles 36:9-36:10, 2 Kings 24:12 24:17, Esther.R Petichata:6, Ezekiel 17:12-17:21, Jeremiah 22:24 22:28 24:1 4:31, Pesikta Rabbati 27/28:1-2

[9] LXX *Joakim, whom Nabuchodonosor appointed to reign over*

[10] Jeremiah 37:2 - 1 Kings 14:18 16:7, 1 Thessalonians 4:8, 2 Chronicles 36:12-36:16, 2 Kings 24:19-24:20, 2 Samuel 10:2 12:25, Exodus 4:13, Ezekiel 21:30, Hosea 12:12, Leviticus 8:36, Pesikta Rabbati 26:3 27/28:1-2, Proverbs 2:6 5:12

[11] Jeremiah 37:3 - 1 Kings 13:6, 1 Samuel 12:19, Acts 8:24, Exodus 8:4 9:28 10:17, Jeremiah 2:27 21:1-21:2 5:21 5:25 14:1 42:2-42:4 18:20 4:24, Numbers 21:7

וְיִרְמְיָהוּ בָּא וְיֹצֵא בְּתוֹךְ הָעָם וְלֹא־נָתְנוּ אֹתוֹ בֵּית ״הַכְּלִיא״ ״הַכְּלוּא״	4[1]	Now Jeremiah came in and went out among the people; for they had not put him into prison.
וְחֵיל פַּרְעֹה יָצָא מִמִּצְרָיִם וַיִּשְׁמְעוּ הַכַּשְׂדִּים הַצָּרִים עַל־יְרוּשָׁלַ͏ִם אֶת־שִׁמְעָם וַיֵּעָלוּ מֵעַל יְרוּשָׁלָ͏ִם	5[2]	And Pharaoh's army came forth from Egypt; and when the Chaldeans *who besieged Jerusalem*[3] heard tidings of them, they *broke*[4] up from Jerusalem.
וַיְהִי דְּבַר־יְהֹוָה אֶל־יִרְמְיָהוּ הַנָּבִיא לֵאמֹר	6	Then came the word of the LORD to the prophet Jeremiah, saying:
כֹּה־אָמַר יְהֹוָה אֱלֹהֵי יִשְׂרָאֵל כֹּה תֹאמְרוּ אֶל־מֶלֶךְ יְהוּדָה הַשֹּׁלֵחַ אֶתְכֶם אֵלַי לְדָרְשֵׁנִי הִנֵּה חֵיל פַּרְעֹה הַיֹּצֵא לָכֶם לְעֶזְרָה שָׁב לְאַרְצוֹ מִצְרָיִם	7[5]	'Thus says the LORD, the God of Israel: Thus shall you say to the king of Judah, who sent you to Me to inquire of Me: Behold, Pharaoh's army, which came forth to help you, shall return to Egypt into their own land.
וְשָׁבוּ הַכַּשְׂדִּים וְנִלְחֲמוּ עַל־הָעִיר הַזֹּאת וּלְכָדֻהָ וּשְׂרָפֻהָ בָאֵשׁ	8[6]	And the Chaldeans shall return, and fight against this city; and they shall take it, and burn it with fire.
כֹּה אָמַר יְהֹוָה אַל־תַּשִּׁאוּ נַפְשֹׁתֵיכֶם לֵאמֹר הָלֹךְ יֵלְכוּ מֵעָלֵינוּ הַכַּשְׂדִּים כִּי־לֹא יֵלֵכוּ	9[7]	Thus says the LORD: Do not deceive yourselves saying: The Chaldeans shall surely depart from us; for they shall not depart.
כִּי אִם־הִכִּיתֶם כָּל־חֵיל כַּשְׂדִּים הַנִּלְחָמִים אִתְּכֶם וְנִשְׁאֲרוּ בָם אֲנָשִׁים מְדֻקָּרִים אִישׁ בְּאָהֳלוֹ יָקוּמוּ וְשָׂרְפוּ אֶת־הָעִיר הַזֹּאת בָּאֵשׁ	10[8]	For though you struck the whole army of the Chaldeans who fight against you, and there remained but wounded men among them, they would yet rise up every man in his tent, and burn this city with fire.'
וְהָיָה בְּהֵעָלוֹת חֵיל הַכַּשְׂדִּים מֵעַל יְרוּשָׁלָ͏ִם מִפְּנֵי חֵיל פַּרְעֹה	11[9]	And it came to pass, when the army of the Chaldeans was broken up from Jerusalem for fear of Pharaoh's army,
וַיֵּצֵא יִרְמְיָהוּ מִירוּשָׁלַ͏ִם לָלֶכֶת אֶרֶץ בִּנְיָמִן לַחֲלִק מִשָּׁם בְּתוֹךְ הָעָם	12[10]	Jeremiah went forth from Jerusalem to go to the land of Benjamin, *to receive his portion there*[11], in the midst of the people.
וַיְהִי־הוּא בְּשַׁעַר בִּנְיָמִן וְשָׁם בַּעַל פְּקִדֻת וּשְׁמוֹ יִרְאִיָּיה בֶּן־שֶׁלֶמְיָה בֶּן־חֲנַנְיָה וַיִּתְפֹּשׂ אֶת־יִרְמְיָהוּ הַנָּבִיא לֵאמֹר אֶל־הַכַּשְׂדִּים אַתָּה נֹפֵל	13[12]	And when he was in the gate of Benjamin, a captain of the ward was there, whose name was *Irijah*[13], the son of Shelemiah, the son of Hananiah; and he laid hold of Jeremiah the prophet, saying: 'You *fall*[14] to the Chaldeans.'

---

[1] Jeremiah 37:4 - Jeremiah 32:2-32:3 13:15

[2] Jeremiah 37:5 - 2 Kings 24:7, Ezekiel 17:15, Jeremiah 10:21 13:7 13:11, Seder Olam 26:Zedekiah

[3] Missing in LXX

[4] LXX *went*

[5] Jeremiah 37:7 - 2 Kings 22:18, Ezekiel 17:17 29:6-29:7 5:16, Isaiah 30:1-30:6 31:1-31:3, Jeremiah 2:36 17:5-17:6 21:2 13:3, Lamentations 4:17, Lamentations.R 4:20, Pesikta Rabbati 26:3, Proverbs 21:30, z.Vaetchanan 269b
Jeremiah 37:7-13 - Pesikta Rabbati 26:4

[6] Jeremiah 37:8 - Jeremiah 8:29 34:21-34:22 14:23 39:2-39:8

[7] Jeremiah 37:9 - 2 Thessalonians 2:3, Ephesians 5:6, Galatians 6:3 6:7, James 1:22, Jeremiah 5:8, Matthew 24:4-24:5, Obadiah 1:3, z.Vaetchanan 269b

[8] Jeremiah 37:10 - Isaiah 10:4 13:15 14:19 6:17, Jeremiah 21:4-21:7 13:8 1:20 2:45 3:4, Joel 2:11, Leviticus 26:36-26:38

[9] Jeremiah 37:11 - Jeremiah 13:5
Jeremiah 37:11-16 - 2 Baruch 2:1
Jeremiah 37:11-21 - Josephus Antiquities 10.7.3

[10] Jeremiah 37:12 - 1 Chronicles 6:45, 1 Kings 19:3 19:9, 1 Thessalonians 5:22, Jeremiah 1:1 32:8-32:9, Joshua 21:17-21:18, Matthew 10:23, Nehemiah 6:11, Pesikta de R'Kahana 13.4

[11] LXX *buy there a property*

[12] Jeremiah 37:13 - 2 Corinthians 6:8, Acts 6:11 24:5-24:9 24:13, Amos 7:10, b.Sotah [Rashi] 41b, b.Sotah 42a, Ein Yaakov Sotah:42a, Jeremiah 18:18 20:10 21:9 3:6 27:12-27:13 4:14 12:12 14:1 14:4 14:7 38:10-38:17, Luke 23:2, Zechariah 14:10

[13] LXX *Saruia*

[14] LXX *are fleeing*

וַיֹּאמֶר יִרְמְיָהוּ שֶׁקֶר אֵינֶנִּי נֹפֵל עַל־הַכַּשְׂדִּים וְלֹא שָׁמַע אֵלָיו וַיִּתְפֹּשׂ יִרְאִיָּיה בְּיִרְמְיָהוּ וַיְבִאֵהוּ אֶל־הַשָּׂרִים	14[1] Then said Jeremiah: 'It is false; I do not fall to the Chaldeans;' but he did not listen to him; so Irijah laid hold on Jeremiah, and brought him to the princes.
וַיִּקְצְפוּ הַשָּׂרִים עַל־יִרְמְיָהוּ וְהִכּוּ אֹתוֹ וְנָתְנוּ אוֹתוֹ בֵּית הָאֵסוּר בֵּית יְהוֹנָתָן הַסֹּפֵר כִּי־אֹתוֹ עָשׂוּ לְבֵית הַכֶּלֶא	15[2] And the princes were angry with Jeremiah, and struck him, and put him in prison in the house of Jonathan the scribe; for they made that the prison.
כִּי בָא יִרְמְיָהוּ אֶל־בֵּית הַבּוֹר וְאֶל־הַחֲנֻיוֹת וַיֵּשֶׁב־שָׁם יִרְמְיָהוּ יָמִים רַבִּים	16[3] When Jeremiah came into the dungeon house, and into the cells, Jeremiah had remained there many days;
וַיִּשְׁלַח הַמֶּלֶךְ צִדְקִיָּהוּ וַיִּקָּחֵהוּ וַיִּשְׁאָלֵהוּ הַמֶּלֶךְ בְּבֵיתוֹ בַּסֵּתֶר וַיֹּאמֶר הֲיֵשׁ דָּבָר מֵאֵת יְהוָה וַיֹּאמֶר יִרְמְיָהוּ יֵשׁ וַיֹּאמֶר בְּיַד מֶלֶךְ־בָּבֶל תִּנָּתֵן	17[4] then Zedekiah the king sent, and fetched him; and the king asked him secretly in his house, and said: 'Is there any word from the LORD?' And Jeremiah said: 'There is.' He said also: 'You shall be delivered into the hand of the king of Babylon.'
וַיֹּאמֶר יִרְמְיָהוּ אֶל־הַמֶּלֶךְ צִדְקִיָּהוּ מֶה חָטָאתִי לְךָ וְלַעֲבָדֶיךָ וְלָעָם הַזֶּה כִּי־נְתַתֶּם אוֹתִי אֶל־בֵּית הַכֶּלֶא	18[5] Moreover, Jeremiah said to king Zedekiah: 'When have I sinned against you, or against your servants, or against this people, that you have put me in prison?
וְאַיּוֹ "וְאַיֵּה" נְבִיאֵיכֶם אֲשֶׁר־נִבְּאוּ לָכֶם לֵאמֹר לֹא־יָבֹא מֶלֶךְ־בָּבֶל עֲלֵיכֶם וְעַל הָאָרֶץ הַזֹּאת	19[6] Where now are your prophets who prophesied to you, saying: The king of Babylon shall not come against you, nor against this land?
וְעַתָּה שְׁמַע־נָא אֲדֹנִי הַמֶּלֶךְ תִּפָּל־נָא תְחִנָּתִי לְפָנֶיךָ וְאַל־תְּשִׁבֵנִי בֵּית יְהוֹנָתָן הַסֹּפֵר וְלֹא אָמוּת שָׁם	20[7] And now hear, please, O my lord the king: let my petition, please, be presented before you; that you do not cause me to return to the house of Jonathan the scribe, lest I die there.'
וַיְצַוֶּה הַמֶּלֶךְ צִדְקִיָּהוּ וַיַּפְקִדוּ אֶת־יִרְמְיָהוּ בַּחֲצַר הַמַּטָּרָה וְנָתֹן לוֹ כִכַּר־לֶחֶם לַיּוֹם מִחוּץ הָאֹפִים עַד־תֹּם כָּל־הַלֶּחֶם מִן־הָעִיר וַיֵּשֶׁב יִרְמְיָהוּ בַּחֲצַר הַמַּטָּרָה	21[8] Then Zedekiah the king commanded, and they committed Jeremiah into the court of the guard, and they gave him daily a loaf of bread from the bakers' street, until all the bread in the city was spent. Thus Jeremiah remained in the court of the guard.

Jeremiah – Chapter 38[9]

וַיִּשְׁמַע שְׁפַטְיָה בֶן־מַתָּן וּגְדַלְיָהוּ בֶּן־פַּשְׁחוּר וְיוּכַל בֶּן־שֶׁלֶמְיָהוּ וּפַשְׁחוּר בֶּן־מַלְכִּיָּה אֶת־הַדְּבָרִים אֲשֶׁר יִרְמְיָהוּ מְדַבֵּר אֶל־כָּל־הָעָם לֵאמֹר	1[10] *And Shephatiah the son of Mattan, and Gedaliah the son of Pashhur, and Jucal the son of Shelemiah, and Pashhur the son of*

---

[1] Jeremiah 37:14 - 1 Peter 3:16 4:14-4:16, b.Sotah 42a, Ein Yaakov Sotah:42a, Jeremiah 40:4-40:6, Luke 6:22-6:23 6:26, Matthew 5:11-5:12, Nehemiah 6:8, Psalms 27:12 35:11 52:2-52:3

[2] Jeremiah 37:15 - 2 Chronicles 16:10 18:26, 2 Corinthians 11:23-27, Acts 5:18 5:28 5:40 12:4-6 16:22-24 23:2-3, Genesis 15:20, Hebrews 11:36-38, Jeremiah 20:1-3 2:16 13:20 14:6 14:26, John 18:22, Luke 20:10-11 22:64, Matthew 21:35 23:34 26:67-68, Revelation 2:10

[3] Jeremiah 37:16 - Genesis 16:15, Jeremiah 14:6 38:10-38:13, Lamentations 3:53 3:55

[4] Jeremiah 37:17 - 1 Kings 14:1-14:4 22:16, 2 Kings 3:11-3:13, Ezekiel 12:12-12:13 17:19-17:21 21:30-21:32, Jeremiah 15:11 21:1-21:2 21:7 24:8 29:16-29:18 32:3-32:5 34:21-34:22 13:3 14:5 38:14-38:16 38:24-38:27 39:6-39:7, Mark 6:20, Pesikta Rabbati 26:4

[5] Jeremiah 37:18 - 1 Samuel 24:9-15 26:18-21, Acts 23:1 24:16 1:11 1:25 2:31, Daniel 6:23, Galatians 4:16, Genesis 7:36, Jeremiah 2:19, John 10:32, Proverbs 17:13 17:26, Sifre.z Numbers Behaalotcha 11:28

[6] Jeremiah 37:19 - 2 Kings 3:13, Deuteronomy 32:36-37, Ezekiel 13:10-16, Jeremiah 2:28 6:14 8:11 14:13-15 23:17 27:14-18 28:1-5 28:10-17 5:31, Lamentations 2:14

[7] Jeremiah 37:20 - Acts 23:16-23:22 25:10-25:11 28:18-28:19, Jeremiah 2:15 12:7 38:6-38:9 14:26, Pesikta Rabbati 26:4

[8] Jeremiah 37:21 - 1 Kings 17:4-6, 2 Kings 1:3, 2 Timothy 1:8 2:9, Acts 12:5 24:27 4:16 4:30, Deuteronomy 28:52-57, Ephesians 4:1 6:20, Isaiah 9:16, Jastrow 1354b, Jeremiah 8:2 8:8 14:9 14:13 14:28 39:14-15 4:6, Job 5:20, Lamentations 2:11-12 2:19-20 4:4-5 4:9-10 5:10, Matthew 6:33, Proverbs 16:7 21:1, Psalms 33:18-19 34:10-11 37:3 37:19, Song of Songs.R 1:41

[9] Jeremiah 38 - Josephus Antiquities 10.7.4-6; Chapter 45 in LXX

[10] Jeremiah 38:1 - 1 Chronicles 9:12, 2 Baruch 5:7, Acts 4:1-4:2 4:6-4:10 5:28, Ezra 2:3, Jeremiah 21:1-21:10 37:3-37:4, Nehemiah 7:9 11:12, Pesikta Rabbati 26:5

Malchiah[1], heard the words Jeremiah spoke to all the people, saying:

כֹּה אָמַר יְהֹוָה הַיֹּשֵׁב בָּעִיר הַזֹּאת יָמוּת בַּחֶרֶב בָּרָעָב וּבַדָּבֶר וְהַיֹּצֵא אֶל־הַכַּשְׂדִּים 'יִחְיֶה' "וְחָיָה" וְהָיְתָה־לּוֹ נַפְשׁוֹ לְשָׁלָל וָחָי

2[2] 'Thus says the LORD: he who remains in this city shall die by the sword, by famine, and *by the pestilence*[3]; but he who goes forth to the Chaldeans shall live, and his life shall be to him as prey, and he shall live.

כֹּה אָמַר יְהֹוָה הִנָּתֹן תִּנָּתֵן הָעִיר הַזֹּאת בְּיַד חֵיל מֶלֶךְ־בָּבֶל וּלְכָדָהּ

3[4] Thus says the LORD: This city shall surely be given into the hand of the army of the king of Babylon, and he shall take it.'

וַיֹּאמְרוּ הַשָּׂרִים אֶל־הַמֶּלֶךְ יוּמַת נָא אֶת־הָאִישׁ הַזֶּה כִּי־עַל־כֵּן הוּא־מְרַפֵּא אֶת־יְדֵי אַנְשֵׁי הַמִּלְחָמָה הַנִּשְׁאָרִים בָּעִיר הַזֹּאת וְאֵת יְדֵי כָל־הָעָם לְדַבֵּר אֲלֵיהֶם כַּדְּבָרִים הָאֵלֶּה כִּי הָאִישׁ הַזֶּה אֵינֶנּוּ דֹרֵשׁ לְשָׁלוֹם לָעָם הַזֶּה כִּי אִם־לְרָעָה

4[5] Then the princes said to the king: 'Let this man, please, be put to death; for he weakens the hands of the men of war who remain in this city, and the hands of all the people, in speaking such words to them; for this man does not seek the welfare of this people, but the hurt.'

וַיֹּאמֶר הַמֶּלֶךְ צִדְקִיָּהוּ הִנֵּה־הוּא בְּיֶדְכֶם כִּי־אֵין הַמֶּלֶךְ יוּכַל אֶתְכֶם דָּבָר

5[6] Then Zedekiah the king said: 'Behold, he is in your hand; *for the king is not he who can do anything against you*[7].'

וַיִּקְחוּ אֶת־יִרְמְיָהוּ וַיַּשְׁלִכוּ אֹתוֹ אֶל־הַבּוֹר מַלְכִּיָּהוּ בֶן־הַמֶּלֶךְ אֲשֶׁר בַּחֲצַר הַמַּטָּרָה וַיְשַׁלְּחוּ אֶת־יִרְמְיָהוּ בַּחֲבָלִים וּבַבּוֹר אֵין־מַיִם כִּי אִם־טִיט וַיִּטְבַּע יִרְמְיָהוּ בַּטִּיט

6[8] Then took they Jeremiah, and cast him into the pit of Malchiah the king's son, who was in the court of the guard; and they let down Jeremiah with cords. And in the pit there was no water, but mire; and Jeremiah sank in the mire.

וַיִּשְׁמַע עֶבֶד־מֶלֶךְ הַכּוּשִׁי אִישׁ סָרִיס וְהוּא בְּבֵית הַמֶּלֶךְ כִּי־נָתְנוּ אֶת־יִרְמְיָהוּ אֶל־הַבּוֹר וְהַמֶּלֶךְ יוֹשֵׁב בְּשַׁעַר בִּנְיָמִן

7[9] Now when *Ebed-melech*[10] the Ethiopian, an officer, who was in the king's house, heard they put Jeremiah in the pit; the king then sat in the gate of Benjamin;

וַיֵּצֵא עֶבֶד־מֶלֶךְ מִבֵּית הַמֶּלֶךְ וַיְדַבֵּר אֶל־הַמֶּלֶךְ לֵאמֹר

8[11] Ebed-melech went forth from the king's house, and spoke to the king, saying:

אֲדֹנִי הַמֶּלֶךְ הֵרֵעוּ הָאֲנָשִׁים הָאֵלֶּה אֵת כָּל־אֲשֶׁר עָשׂוּ לְיִרְמְיָהוּ הַנָּבִיא אֵת אֲשֶׁר־הִשְׁלִיכוּ אֶל־הַבּוֹר וַיָּמָת תַּחְתָּיו מִפְּנֵי הָרָעָב כִּי אֵין הַלֶּחֶם עוֹד בָּעִיר

9[12] 'My lord the king, these men have done evil in all they have done to Jeremiah the prophet, whom they cast into the pit; and he is likely to die in the place where he is because of the famine; for there is no more bread in the city.'

[1] LXX *Saphanias the son of Nathan, and Godolias the son of Paschor, and Joachal the son of Semelias*

[2] Jeremiah 38:2 - Ezekiel 5:12-5:17 6:11 7:15 14:21, Jeremiah 21:8-21:9 24:8 3:13 5:18 10:17 38:17-38:23 15:18 18:17 18:22 20:13 21:5, Matthew 24:7-24:8, Pesikta Rabbati 26:5, Revelation 6:4-6:8, z.Vaetchanan 269b

[3] Missing in LXX

[4] Jeremiah 38:3 - Jeremiah 21:10 32:3-32:5, z.Vaetchanan 269b

[5] Jeremiah 38:4 - 1 Kings 18:17-18:18 21:20, 2 Chronicles 24:21, Acts 16:20 17:6 24:5 4:22, Amos 7:10, Exodus 5:4, Ezekiel 22:27, Ezra 4:12, Jeremiah 2:11 26:21-26:23 5:7 36:12-36:16, John 11:46-11:50, Luke 23:2, Micah 3:1-3:3, Nehemiah 6:9, Zephaniah 3:1-3:3

Jeremiah 38:4-13 - 4 Baruch 3:13

[6] Jeremiah 38:5 - 1 Samuel 15:24 5:9, 2 Samuel 3:39 19:22, John 19:12-19:16, Proverbs 5:25

[7] LXX *for the king could not resist them*

[8] Jeremiah 38:6 - 2 Corinthians 4:8-4:9, Acts 16:24, Genesis 13:24, Genesis.R 40:5, Hebrews 10:36, Jeremiah 12:26 13:16 13:21 38:11-38:12 14:22, Lamentations 3:52-3:55, Lamentations.R 3:17, Luke 3:19-3:20, Mekhilta de R'Shimon bar Yochai Shirata 30:1, Mekhilta de R'Ishmael Shirata 4:99, Midrash Tanchuma Vayigash 10, Pesikta Rabbati 26:5, Psalms 40:3 69:3 69:15-69:16 13:5, Zechariah 9:11

[9] Jeremiah 38:7 - 2 Kings 24:15, Acts 8:27-8:39, Amos 5:10, b.Moed Katan 16b, Deuteronomy 21:19, Ein Yaakov Moed Katan:9b, Jeremiah 13:23 5:2 10:19 13:13 39:16-39:18, Job 29:7-29:17, Luke 10:30-10:36 13:29-13:30, Matthew 8:11-8:12 20:16, Midrash Psalms 7:18, Pesikta Rabbati 26:5, Psalms 68:32, Sifre.z Numbers Behaalotcha 12:1

Jeremiah 38:7-13 - 3 Baruch 2 [Greek]

[10] LXX *Abdemelech*

[11] Jeremiah 38:8 - Midrash Psalms 7:18

[12] Jeremiah 38:9 - Esther 7:4-7:6, Jeremiah 37:21-6 4:6, Job 7:34, Proverbs 24:11-24:12 31:8-31:9

וַיְצַוֶּה הַמֶּלֶךְ אֵת עֶבֶד־מֶלֶךְ הַכּוּשִׁי לֵאמֹר קַח בְּיָדְךָ מִזֶּה שְׁלֹשִׁים אֲנָשִׁים וְהַעֲלִיתָ אֶת־יִרְמְיָהוּ הַנָּבִיא מִן־הַבּוֹר בְּטֶרֶם יָמוּת	10¹	Then the king commanded Ebed-melech the Ethiopian, saying: 'Take from here thirty men with you, and take up Jeremiah the prophet from the pit, before he dies.'
וַיִּקַּח עֶבֶד־מֶלֶךְ אֶת־הָאֲנָשִׁים בְּיָדוֹ וַיָּבֹא בֵית־הַמֶּלֶךְ אֶל־תַּחַת הָאוֹצָר וַיִּקַּח מִשָּׁם בְּלוֹיֵ 'הַסְּחָבוֹת' "סְחָבוֹת" וּבְלוֹיֵ מְלָחִים וַיְשַׁלְּחֵם אֶל־יִרְמְיָהוּ אֶל־הַבּוֹר בַּחֲבָלִים	11²	So Ebed-melech took the men with him, and went into the house of the king under the treasury, and took worn clouts and worn rags, and let them down by cords into the pit to Jeremiah.
וַיֹּאמֶר עֶבֶד־מֶלֶךְ הַכּוּשִׁי אֶל־יִרְמְיָהוּ שִׂים נָא בְּלוֹאֵי הַסְּחָבוֹת וְהַמְּלָחִים תַּחַת אַצִּלוֹת יָדֶיךָ מִתַּחַת לַחֲבָלִים וַיַּעַשׂ יִרְמְיָהוּ כֵּן	12³	And Ebed-melech the Ethiopian said to Jeremiah: '*Put now these worn clouts and rags under your armpits under the cords*[4].' And Jeremiah did so.
וַיִּמְשְׁכוּ אֶת־יִרְמְיָהוּ בַּחֲבָלִים וַיַּעֲלוּ אֹתוֹ מִן־הַבּוֹר וַיֵּשֶׁב יִרְמְיָהוּ בַּחֲצַר הַמַּטָּרָה	13⁵	So they drew up Jeremiah with the cords, and took him up from the pit; and Jeremiah remained in the court of the guard.
וַיִּשְׁלַח הַמֶּלֶךְ צִדְקִיָּהוּ וַיִּקַּח אֶת־יִרְמְיָהוּ הַנָּבִיא אֵלָיו אֶל־מָבוֹא הַשְּׁלִישִׁי אֲשֶׁר בְּבֵית יְהוָה וַיֹּאמֶר הַמֶּלֶךְ אֶל־יִרְמְיָהוּ שֹׁאֵל אֲנִי אֹתְךָ דָּבָר אַל־תְּכַחֵד מִמֶּנִּי דָּבָר	14⁶	*Then Zedekiah the king sent, and brought Jeremiah the prophet to him into the third entry that was in the house of the LORD; and the king said to Jeremiah*[7]: 'I will ask you something; hide nothing from me.'
וַיֹּאמֶר יִרְמְיָהוּ אֶל־צִדְקִיָּהוּ כִּי אַגִּיד לְךָ הֲלוֹא הָמֵת תְּמִיתֵנִי וְכִי אִיעָצְךָ לֹא תִשְׁמַע אֵלָי	15⁸	Then Jeremiah said to Zedekiah: 'If I declare it to you, will you not surely put me to death? and if I give you counsel, you will not listen to me.'
וַיִּשָּׁבַע הַמֶּלֶךְ צִדְקִיָּהוּ אֶל־יִרְמְיָהוּ בַּסֵּתֶר לֵאמֹר חַי־יְהוָה 'אֵת' "..." אֲשֶׁר עָשָׂה־לָנוּ אֶת־הַנֶּפֶשׁ הַזֹּאת אִם־אֲמִיתֶךָ וְאִם־אֶתֶּנְךָ בְּיַד הָאֲנָשִׁים הָאֵלֶּה אֲשֶׁר מְבַקְשִׁים אֶת־נַפְשֶׁךָ	16⁹	So Zedekiah the king swore secretly to Jeremiah, saying: 'As the LORD lives, who made us this soul, I will not put you to death, nor will I give you into the hand of the men who seek your life.'
וַיֹּאמֶר יִרְמְיָהוּ אֶל־צִדְקִיָּהוּ כֹּה־אָמַר יְהוָה אֱלֹהֵי צְבָאוֹת אֱלֹהֵי יִשְׂרָאֵל אִם־יָצֹא תֵצֵא אֶל־שָׂרֵי מֶלֶךְ־בָּבֶל וְחָיְתָה נַפְשֶׁךָ וְהָעִיר הַזֹּאת לֹא תִשָּׂרֵף בָּאֵשׁ וְחָיִתָה אַתָּה וּבֵיתֶךָ	17¹⁰	Then said Jeremiah to Zedekiah: 'Thus says the LORD, the God of hosts, the God of Israel: If you will go forth to the king of Babylon's princes, then your soul shall live, and this city shall not be burned with fire; and you shall live, you, and your house;
וְאִם לֹא־תֵצֵא אֶל־שָׂרֵי מֶלֶךְ בָּבֶל וְנִתְּנָה הָעִיר הַזֹּאת בְּיַד הַכַּשְׂדִּים וּשְׂרָפוּהָ בָּאֵשׁ וְאַתָּה לֹא־תִמָּלֵט מִיָּדָם	18¹¹	but if you will not go forth to the king of Babylon's princes, then this city shall be given into the hand of the Chaldeans, and they shall burn it with fire, and you shall not escape from their hand.'

---

[1] Jeremiah 38:10 - Ein Yaakov Moed Katan:28b, Esther 5:2 8:7, Proverbs 21:1, Psalms 75:11, Saadia Opinions 5:2

[2] Jeremiah 38:11 - Mas.Kallah Rabbati 3:26, Pesikta Rabbati 26:5

[3] Jeremiah 38:12 - b.Menachot [Tosefot] 37a, Ephesians 4:32, Mas.Kallah Rabbati 3:26, Pirkei de R'Eliezer 53, Romans 12:10 12:15

[4] LXX *Put these under the ropes*

[5] Jeremiah 38:13 - 1 Kings 22:27, Acts 23:35 24:23-24:26 4:16 4:30, Jastrow 1081b, Jeremiah 13:21 14:6 14:28 39:14-39:18, Midrash Tanchuma Vayigash 10

[6] Jeremiah 38:14 - 1 Kings 10:5 22:16, 1 Samuel 3:17-18, 2 Chronicles 18:15, 2 Kings 16:18, Jeremiah 21:1-2 13:17 42:2-5 18:20

[7] LXX *the king sent, and called him to himself into the house of Aselisel, which was in the house of the Lord: and the king said to him*

[8] Jeremiah 38:15 - Luke 22:67-22:68

[9] Jeremiah 38:16 - Ecclesiastes 12:7, Guide for the Perplexed 1:41, Hebrews 12:9, Isaiah 18:5 9:16, Jeremiah 10:20 13:17 38:1-38:6, John 3:2, Mas.Soferim 6:9, mt.Shemonah Perakim 8:6, Numbers 16:22 3:16, Saadia Opinions 2:8 6:3, Shemonah Perachim VIII, Zechariah 12:1

[10] Jeremiah 38:17 - 1 Chronicles 17:24, 2 Kings 24:12, Amos 5:27, Ezra 9:4, Jeremiah 7:6-7:7 21:8-21:10 3:12 3:17 14:2 15:3, Job 23:13, Psalms 80:8 80:15, Ralbag Wars 3:4, z.Vaetchanan 269b

[11] Jeremiah 38:18 - 2 Kings 24:12 25:4-25:10 25:27-25:30, Ezekiel 12:13 17:20-17:21 21:30-21:32, Jeremiah 24:8-24:10 32:3-32:5 34:2-34:3 34:19-34:22 13:8 14:3 14:23 15:3 39:5-39:7 52:7-52:11, Ralbag Wars 3:4

וַיֹּאמֶר הַמֶּלֶךְ צִדְקִיָּהוּ אֶל־יִרְמְיָהוּ אֲנִי דֹאֵג אֶת־הַיְּהוּדִים אֲשֶׁר נָפְלוּ אֶל־הַכַּשְׂדִּים פֶּן־יִתְּנוּ אֹתִי בְּיָדָם וְהִתְעַלְּלוּ־בִי	19[1]	And Zedekiah the king said to Jeremiah: 'I am afraid of the Jews who have fallen to the Chaldeans, lest they deliver me into their hand, and they mock me.'
וַיֹּאמֶר יִרְמְיָהוּ לֹא יִתֵּנוּ שְׁמַע־נָא בְּקוֹל יְהֹוָה לַאֲשֶׁר אֲנִי דֹּבֵר אֵלֶיךָ וְיִיטַב לְךָ וּתְחִי נַפְשֶׁךָ	20[2]	But Jeremiah said: 'They shall not deliver you. listen, please, to the voice of the LORD, in what I speak to you; so it shall be well with you, and your soul shall live.
וְאִם־מָאֵן אַתָּה לָצֵאת זֶה הַדָּבָר אֲשֶׁר הִרְאַנִי יְהֹוָה	21[3]	But if you refuse to go forth, this is the word that the LORD has shown me:
וְהִנֵּה כָל־הַנָּשִׁים אֲשֶׁר נִשְׁאֲרוּ בְּבֵית מֶלֶךְ־יְהוּדָה מוּצָאוֹת אֶל־שָׂרֵי מֶלֶךְ בָּבֶל וְהֵנָּה אֹמְרוֹת הִסִּיתוּךָ וְיָכְלוּ לְךָ אַנְשֵׁי שְׁלֹמֶךָ הָטְבְּעוּ בַבֹּץ רַגְלֶךָ נָסֹגוּ אָחוֹר	22[4]	Behold, all the women who are left in the king of Judah's house shall be brought forth to the king of Babylon's princes, and those women shall say: Your familiar friends have set you on, and have prevailed over you; Your feet are sunk in the mire, and they have turned back.
וְאֶת־כָּל־נָשֶׁיךָ וְאֶת־בָּנֶיךָ מוֹצִאִים אֶל־הַכַּשְׂדִּים וְאַתָּה לֹא־תִמָּלֵט מִיָּדָם כִּי בְיַד מֶלֶךְ־בָּבֶל תִּתָּפֵשׂ וְאֶת־הָעִיר הַזֹּאת תִּשְׂרֹף בָּאֵשׁ	23[5]	And they shall bring out all your wives and your children to the Chaldeans; and you shall not escape from their hand, but shall be taken by the hand of the king of Babylon; and you shall cause this city to be burned with fire.'
וַיֹּאמֶר צִדְקִיָּהוּ אֶל־יִרְמְיָהוּ אִישׁ אַל־יֵדַע בַּדְּבָרִים־הָאֵלֶּה וְלֹא תָמוּת	24	Then said Zedekiah to Jeremiah: 'Let no man know of these words, and you shall not die.
וְכִי־יִשְׁמְעוּ הַשָּׂרִים כִּי־דִבַּרְתִּי אִתָּךְ וּבָאוּ אֵלֶיךָ וְאָמְרוּ אֵלֶיךָ הַגִּידָה־נָּא לָנוּ מַה־דִּבַּרְתָּ אֶל־הַמֶּלֶךְ אַל־תְּכַחֵד מִמֶּנּוּ וְלֹא נְמִיתֶךָ וּמַה־דִּבֶּר אֵלֶיךָ הַמֶּלֶךְ	25[6]	But if the princes hear I have talked with you, and they come to you, and say to you: Declare to us now what you have said to the king; hide it not from us, and we will not put you to death; also what the king said to you;
וְאָמַרְתָּ אֲלֵיהֶם מַפִּיל־אֲנִי תְחִנָּתִי לִפְנֵי הַמֶּלֶךְ לְבִלְתִּי הֲשִׁיבֵנִי בֵּית יְהוֹנָתָן לָמוּת שָׁם	26[7]	then you shall say to them: I presented my plea before the king, so he would not cause me to return to Jonathan's house, to die there.'
וַיָּבֹאוּ כָל־הַשָּׂרִים אֶל־יִרְמְיָהוּ וַיִּשְׁאֲלוּ אֹתוֹ וַיַּגֵּד לָהֶם כְּכָל־הַדְּבָרִים הָאֵלֶּה אֲשֶׁר צִוָּה הַמֶּלֶךְ וַיַּחֲרִשׁוּ מִמֶּנּוּ כִּי לֹא־נִשְׁמַע הַדָּבָר	27[8]	Then all the princes came to Jeremiah, and asked him; and he told them according to all the words the king commanded. *So they left after speaking with him; for the matter was not reported*[9].
וַיֵּשֶׁב יִרְמְיָהוּ בַּחֲצַר הַמַּטָּרָה עַד־יוֹם אֲשֶׁר־נִלְכְּדָה יְרוּשָׁלָ͏ִם ס וְהָיָה כַּאֲשֶׁר נִלְכְּדָה יְרוּשָׁלָ͏ִם	28[10]	So Jeremiah lived in the court of the guard until the day Jerusalem was taken. *And it came to pass, when Jerusalem was taken*[11]

---

[1] Jeremiah 38:19 - 1 Samuel 15:24 7:4, Isaiah 45:9-45:10 51:12-51:13 9:11, Jeremiah 14:5 14:22 15:9, Job 7:34, John 12:42 19:12-19:13, Judges 9:54 16:25, Proverbs 5:25

[2] Jeremiah 38:20 - 2 Chronicles 20:20, 2 Corinthians 5:11 5:20 6:1, Acts 2:29, Daniel 4:24, Isaiah 7:3, James 1:22, Jeremiah 11:4 2:13, Philemon 1:8-1:10

[3] Jeremiah 38:21 - Acts 18:6 20:26-20:27, Exodus 10:3-10:4 16:28, Ezekiel 2:4-2:5 2:7 3:17-3:19, Hebrews 12:25, Isaiah 1:19-1:20, Jeremiah 5:3 15:19-15:21 2:15, Job 23:13 10:33, Numbers 23:19-23:20 24:13, Proverbs 1:24-1:31

[4] Jeremiah 38:22 - Isaiah 18:17, Jeremiah 6:12 10:10 38:4-38:6 14:19 17:10 19:6 22:5 22:21, Lamentations 1:2 1:13 5:11, Micah 7:5, Psalms 41:10 69:3 69:15, Tanya Igeret Hakodesh §01

[5] Jeremiah 38:23 - 2 Baruch 2:1, 2 Chronicles 36:20-36:21, 2 Kings 1:7, Ezekiel 14:9 19:3, Jeremiah 27:12-27:13 14:18 15:6 17:10 52:8-52:13

[6] Jeremiah 38:25 - Jeremiah 38:4-38:6 14:27

[7] Jeremiah 38:26 - Esther 4:8, Jeremiah 13:15 13:20 18:2

[8] Jeremiah 38:27 - 1 Samuel 10:15-10:16 16:2-16:5, 2 Kings 6:19, Acts 23:6

[9] LXX *And they were silent, because the word of the LORD was not heard*

[10] Jeremiah 38:28 - 2 Timothy 3:11 4:17-4:18, Esther.R Petichata:11 Petichata:11, Genesis.R 42:3, Jeremiah 15:20-15:21 13:21 14:13 15:14, Leviticus.R 11:7, Midrash Tanchuma Shemini 9, Midrash Tanchuma Shemot 13, Numbers.R 13:5, Pesikta Rabbati 5:8 26:6, Psalms 23:4, Ruth.R Petichata:7

[11] Missing in LXX

Jeremiah – Chapter 39[1]

בַּשָּׁנָה הַתְּשִׁעִית לְצִדְקִיָּהוּ מֶלֶךְ־יְהוּדָה בַּחֹדֶשׁ הָעֲשִׂרִי בָּא נְבוּכַדְרֶאצַּר מֶלֶךְ־בָּבֶל וְכָל־חֵילוֹ אֶל־יְרוּשָׁלַ͏ִם וַיָּצֻרוּ עָלֶיהָ	1[2] in the ninth year of Zedekiah king of Judah, in the tenth[3] month, Nebuchadrezzar king of Babylon and all his army came against Jerusalem, and besieged it;
בְּעַשְׁתֵּי־עֶשְׂרֵה שָׁנָה לְצִדְקִיָּהוּ בַּחֹדֶשׁ הָרְבִיעִי בְּתִשְׁעָה לַחֹדֶשׁ הָבְקְעָה הָעִיר	2[4] in the eleventh year of Zedekiah, in the fourth month, the ninth day of the month, a breach was made in the city
וַיָּבֹאוּ כֹּל שָׂרֵי מֶלֶךְ־בָּבֶל וַיֵּשְׁבוּ בְּשַׁעַר הַתָּוֶךְ נֵרְגַל שַׂר־אֶצֶר סַמְגַּר־נְבוּ שַׂר־סְכִים רַב־סָרִיס נֵרְגַל שַׂר־אֶצֶר רַב־מָג וְכָל־שְׁאֵרִית שָׂרֵי מֶלֶךְ בָּבֶל	3[5] So all the princes of the king of Babylon came in, and sat in the middle gate, *Nergal-sarezer, Samgar-nebo, Sarsechim Rab-saris, Nergal sarezer Rab-mag, with all the remnant of the princes of the king of Babylon*[6].
וַיְהִי כַּאֲשֶׁר רָאָם צִדְקִיָּהוּ מֶלֶךְ־יְהוּדָה וְכֹל אַנְשֵׁי הַמִּלְחָמָה וַיִּבְרְחוּ וַיֵּצְאוּ לַיְלָה מִן־הָעִיר דֶּרֶךְ גַּן הַמֶּלֶךְ בְּשַׁעַר בֵּין הַחֹמֹתָיִם וַיֵּצֵא דֶּרֶךְ הָעֲרָבָה	4[7] *And it came to pass, when Zedekiah the king of Judah and all the men of war saw them, they fled, and went forth from the city by night, by the way of the king's garden, by the gate between the two walls; and he went out the way of the Arabah*[8].
וַיִּרְדְּפוּ חֵיל־כַּשְׂדִּים אַחֲרֵיהֶם וַיַּשִּׂגוּ אֶת־צִדְקִיָּהוּ בְּעַרְבוֹת יְרֵחוֹ וַיִּקְחוּ אֹתוֹ וַיַּעֲלֻהוּ אֶל־נְבוּכַדְרֶאצַּר מֶלֶךְ־בָּבֶל רִבְלָתָה בְּאֶרֶץ חֲמָת וַיְדַבֵּר אִתּוֹ מִשְׁפָּטִים	5[9] *But the army of the Chaldeans pursued after them, and overtook Zedekiah in the plains of Jericho; and when they took him, they brought him up to Nebuchadrezzar king of Babylon to Riblah in the land of Hamath, and he gave judgment upon him*[10].
וַיִּשְׁחַט מֶלֶךְ בָּבֶל אֶת־בְּנֵי צִדְקִיָּהוּ בְּרִבְלָה לְעֵינָיו וְאֵת כָּל־חֹרֵי יְהוּדָה שָׁחַט מֶלֶךְ בָּבֶל	6[11] *Then the king of Babylon killed the sons of Zedekiah in Riblah before his eyes; the king of Babylon also killed all the nobles of Judah*[12].
וְאֶת־עֵינֵי צִדְקִיָּהוּ עִוֵּר וַיַּאַסְרֵהוּ בַּנְחֻשְׁתַּיִם לָבִיא אֹתוֹ בָּבֶלָה	7[13] *Moreover, he put out Zedekiah's eyes, and bound him in fetters, to carry him to Babylon*[14].
וְאֶת־בֵּית הַמֶּלֶךְ וְאֶת־בֵּית הָעָם שָׂרְפוּ הַכַּשְׂדִּים בָּאֵשׁ וְאֶת־חֹמוֹת יְרוּשָׁלַ͏ִם נָתָצוּ	8[15] *And the Chaldeans burned the king's house, and the house of the people, with fire, and broke down the walls of Jerusalem*[16].

---

[1] Chapter 46 in LXX

[2] Jeremiah 39:1 - 2 Kings 25:1-25:12, Ezekiel 24:1-24:2, Jeremiah 52:4-52:7, Josephus Antiquities 10.7.4-6, Zechariah 8:19 Jeremiah 39:1-10 - Josephus Antiquities 10.8.1

[3] LXX *ninth*

[4] Jeremiah 39:2 - 2 Kings 25:3-25:4, b.Bava Batra 28b, Ezekiel 9:21, Jeremiah 5:10 52:6-52:7, Micah 2:12-2:13, mt.Hilchot Taaniot 5:2, y.Taanit 4:5, Zephaniah 1:10

[5] Jeremiah 39:3 - 2 Kings 17:30, b.Sanhedrin 103a, Ecclesiastes.R 3:19 10:7, Ein Yaakov Sanhedrin:103a, Jastrow 513a, Jeremiah 1:15 21:4 14:17 15:13, Leviticus.R 4:1, Midrash Tanchuma Vayikra 6

[6] LXX *Marganasar, and Samagoth, and Nabusachar, and Nabusaris, Nagargas, Naserrabamath, and the rest of the leaders of the king of Babylon*

[7] Jeremiah 39:4 - 2 Chronicles 8:5, 2 Kings 25:4-25:7, Amos 2:14, Deuteronomy 4:25 32:24-32:30, Ezekiel 12:12, Isaiah 30:15-30:16, Jeremiah 38:18-38:20 52:7-52:11, Leviticus 2:17 2:36

[8] Missing in LXX

[9] Jeremiah 39:5 - 2 Baruch 8:5, 2 Chronicles 9:11, 2 Kings 17:24 23:33 1:6, 2 Samuel 8:9, Ezekiel 17:15-17:21, Jeremiah 4:12 32:4-32:5 14:18 14:23 52:8-52:9 52:26-52:27, Joshua 4:13 5:10 13:5, Judges 3:3, Lamentations 1:3 4:20, Numbers 13:21

[10] Missing in LXX

[11] Jeremiah 39:6 - 2 Chronicles 10:28, 2 Kings 22:20 1:7, Deuteronomy 4:34, Esther 8:6, Genesis 21:16 20:34, Isaiah 13:16, Jeremiah 21:7 24:8-10 34:19-21 4:10

[12] Missing in LXX

[13] Jeremiah 39:7 - 2 Kings 1:7, Ein Yaakov Moed Katan:28b, Exodus.R 15:26, Ezekiel 12:13, Jeremiah 32:4-5 4:11, Judges 16:21, Psalms 107:10-11 23:8

[14] Missing in LXX

[15] Jeremiah 39:8 - 2 Chronicles 12:19, 2 Kings 25:9-10, Amos 2:5, Isaiah 5:9, Jeremiah 7:20 9:11-13 17:27 21:10 10:2 10:22 13:10 14:18 52:13-14, Lamentations 1:10 2:2 2:7, Micah 3:12, Nehemiah 1:3

[16] Missing in LXX

וְאֵת יֶ֫תֶר הָעָ֣ם הַנִּשְׁאָרִ֣ים בָּעִ֗יר וְאֶת־הַנֹּפְלִים֙ אֲשֶׁ֣ר נָפְל֣וּ עָלָ֔יו וְאֵת֙ יֶ֣תֶר הָעָ֣ם הַנִּשְׁאָרִ֔ים הֶגְלָ֛ה נְבֽוּזַר־אֲדָ֥ן רַב־טַבָּחִ֖ים בָּבֶֽל	9[1]	*Then Nebuzaradan the captain of the guard carried away captive into Babylon the remnant of the people who remained in the city, the deserters also, who fell away to him, with the rest of the people who remained*[2].
וּמִן־הָעָ֣ם הַדַּלִּ֗ים אֲשֶׁ֤ר אֵֽין־לָהֶם֙ מְא֔וּמָה הִשְׁאִ֛יר נְבֽוּזַר־אֲדָ֥ן רַב־טַבָּחִ֖ים בְּאֶ֣רֶץ יְהוּדָ֑ה וַיִּתֵּ֥ן לָהֶ֛ם כְּרָמִ֥ים וִֽיגֵבִ֖ים בַּיּ֥וֹם הַהֽוּא	10[3]	*But Nebuzaradan the captain of the guard left the poor of the people who had nothing, in the land of Judah, and gave them vineyards and fields on that day*[4].
וַיְצַ֛ו נְבוּכַדְרֶאצַּ֥ר מֶֽלֶךְ־בָּבֶ֖ל עַֽל־יִרְמְיָ֑הוּ בְּיַ֛ד נְבֽוּזַרְאֲדָ֥ן רַב־טַבָּחִ֖ים לֵאמֹֽר	11[5]	*Now Nebuchadrezzar king of Babylon gave charge concerning Jeremiah to Nebuzaradan the captain of the guard, saying*[6]:
קָחֶ֗נּוּ וְעֵינֶ֨יךָ֙ שִׂ֣ים עָלָ֔יו וְאַל־תַּ֥עַשׂ ל֖וֹ מְא֣וּמָה רָ֑ע כִּ֗י "אִם"... "." כַּֽאֲשֶׁ֤ר יְדַבֵּר֙ אֵלֶ֔יךָ כֵּ֖ן עֲשֵׂ֥ה עִמּֽוֹ	12[7]	*'Take him, and look well to him, and do him no harm; but do as he shall say to you*[8].'
וַיִּשְׁלַ֞ח נְבֽוּזַרְאֲדָ֣ן רַב־טַבָּחִ֗ים וּנְבֽוּשַׁזְבָּן֙ רַב־סָרִ֔יס וְנֵֽרְגַ֣ל שַׂר־אֶ֔צֶר רַב־מָ֑ג וְכֹ֖ל רַבֵּ֥י מֶֽלֶךְ־בָּבֶֽל	13[9]	*So Nebuzaradan the captain of the guard sent, and Nebushazban Rab-saris, and Nergal sarezer Rab-mag, and all the chief officers of the king of Babylon*[10]
וַיִּשְׁלְח֣וּ וַיִּקְח֣וּ אֶֽת־יִרְמְיָ֗הוּ מֵֽחֲצַר֙ הַמַּטָּרָ֔ה וַיִּתְּנ֣וּ אֹת֗וֹ אֶל־גְּדַלְיָ֙הוּ֙ בֶּן־אֲחִיקָ֣ם בֶּן־שָׁפָ֔ן לְהוֹצִאֵ֖הוּ אֶל־הַבָּ֑יִת וַיֵּ֖שֶׁב בְּת֥וֹךְ הָעָֽם	14[11]	they sent, and took Jeremiah from the court of the guard, and committed him to Gedaliah the son of Ahikam, the son of Shaphan, so he should carry him home; so he lived among the people.
וְאֶֽל־יִרְמְיָ֖הוּ הָיָ֣ה דְבַר־יְהוָ֑ה בִּֽהְיֹת֣וֹ עָצ֔וּר בַּֽחֲצַ֥ר הַמַּטָּרָ֖ה לֵאמֹֽר	15[12]	Now the word of the LORD came to Jeremiah, while he was shut up in the court of the guard, saying:
הָל֣וֹךְ וְאָֽמַרְתָּ֡ לְעֶֽבֶד־מֶ֨לֶךְ הַכּוּשִׁ֜י לֵאמֹ֗ר כֹּֽה־אָמַ֞ר יְהוָ֤ה צְבָאוֹת֙ אֱלֹהֵ֣י יִשְׂרָאֵ֔ל הִנְנִ֧י "מֵבִי" "מֵבִ֣יא" אֶת־דְּבָרַ֗י אֶל־הָעִ֛יר הַזֹּ֖את לְרָעָ֣ה וְלֹ֣א לְטוֹבָ֑ה וְהָי֥וּ לְפָנֶ֖יךָ בַּיּ֥וֹם הַהֽוּא	16[13]	'Go, and speak to Ebed-melech the Ethiopian, saying: Thus says the LORD of hosts, the God of Israel: Behold, I will bring My words upon this city for evil, and not for good; and *they shall be accomplished before you in that day*[14].
וְהִצַּלְתִּ֥יךָ בַיּוֹם־הַה֖וּא נְאֻם־יְהוָ֑ה וְלֹ֤א תִנָּתֵן֙ בְּיַ֣ד הָֽאֲנָשִׁ֔ים אֲשֶׁר־אַתָּ֥ה יָג֖וֹר מִפְּנֵיהֶֽם	17[15]	But I will deliver you in that day, says the LORD[16]; and you shall not be given into the hand of the men of whom you are afraid.
כִּ֤י מַלֵּט֙ אֲמַלֶּטְךָ֔ וּבַחֶ֖רֶב לֹ֣א תִפֹּ֑ל וְהָֽיְתָ֨ה לְךָ֤ נַפְשְׁךָ֙ לְשָׁלָ֔ל כִּֽי־בָטַ֥חְתָּ בִּ֖י נְאֻם־יְהוָֽה	18[17]	For I will surely deliver you, and you shall not fall by the sword, *but your life shall be a prey*

---

[1] Jeremiah 39:9 - 2 Kings 20:18 1:11 1:20, Deuteronomy 4:27, Genesis 13:36, Isaiah 5:13, Jeremiah 10:18 16:13 20:4-6 39:10-14 16:1 52:12-16 4:26 52:28-30, Leviticus 2:33

[2] Missing in LXX

[3] Jeremiah 39:10 - 2 Kings 1:12, Ezekiel 9:24, Jeremiah 16:7 4:16

[4] Missing in LXX

[5] Jeremiah 39:11 - Acts 24:23, Jeremiah 15:11 15:21 13:2, Job 5:19

[6] Missing in LXX

[7] Jeremiah 39:12 - 1 Peter 3:12-3:13, Acts 7:10, Amos 9:4, Jeremiah 24:6 16:4, Lamentations.R Petichata D'Chakimei:34, Mas.Soferim 6:9, Midrash Tanchuma Tzav 10, Pesikta de R'Kahana 13.9, Pesikta Rabbati 29:3, Proverbs 16:7 21:1 23:5, Psalms 105:14-105:15, Unexpected Dagesh in the letter ר of רַע

[8] Missing in LXX

[9] Jeremiah 39:13 - b.Yoma [Rashi] 54a, Jeremiah 15:3 15:9, Josephus Antiquities 10.8.2, Traditional Small ן in וּנְבֽוּשַׁזְבָּן

[10] Missing in LXX

[11] Jeremiah 39:14 - 2 Baruch 9:2, 2 Kings 22:12 25:22-25, Jeremiah 2:24 13:21 14:13 14:28 15:15 40:1-3, Psalms 9:19

[12] Jeremiah 39:15 - 2 Timothy 2:9, Jeremiah 32:1-2 36:1-5 13:21 15:14 Jeremiah 39:15-18 - 3 Baruch Introduction:2 [Gk]

[13] Jeremiah 39:16 - 2 Chronicles 12:21, Daniel 9:12, Jeremiah 5:14 19:11-12 21:7-10 24:8-10 2:15 2:18 2:20 32:28-29 34:2-3 10:22 11:17 12:31 38:7-13 44:28-29, Joshua 23:14-15, Matthew 24:35, Psalms 91:8-9 92:12, z.Vaetchanan 269b, Zechariah 1:6

[14] Missing in LXX

[15] Jeremiah 39:17 - 2 Samuel 24:14, 2 Timothy 1:16-1:18, Daniel 6:17, Genesis 15:1, Jeremiah 1:19 14:1 14:9, Job 5:19-5:21, Matthew 10:40-10:42 1:40, Psalms 41:2-41:3 50:15 91:14-91:15

[16] LXX *God of Israel*

[17] Jeremiah 39:18 - 1 Chronicles 5:20, 1 Peter 1:21, Ephesians 1:12, Isaiah 2:3, Jeremiah 17:7-17:8 21:9 14:2 45:4-45:5, Psalms 2:12 33:18 34:23 37:3 37:39-37:40 84:13 146:3-6 3:11, Romans 2:12

to you[1]; because you have put your trust in Me, says the LORD.'

Jeremiah – Chapter 40[2]

הַדָּבָ֞ר אֲשֶׁר־הָיָ֤ה אֶֽל־יִרְמְיָ֨הוּ֙ מֵאֵ֣ת יְהֹוָ֔ה אַחַ֣ר ׀ שַׁלַּ֣ח אֹת֗וֹ נְבֽוּזַרְאֲדָ֤ן רַב־טַבָּחִים֙ מִן־הָ֣רָמָ֔ה בְּקַחְתּ֣וֹ אֹת֔וֹ וְהֽוּא־אָס֥וּר בָּאזִקִּ֖ים בְּת֣וֹךְ כׇּל־גָּל֣וּת יְרוּשָׁלַ֤͏ִם וִֽיהוּדָ֔ה הַמֻּגְלִ֖ים בָּבֶֽלָה

1[3] The word that came to Jeremiah from the LORD, after that Nebuzaradan the captain of the guard let him go from Ramah, when he took him being bound in chains among all the captives of Jerusalem and Judah, who were carried away captive to Babylon.

וַיִּקַּ֥ח רַב־טַבָּחִ֖ים לְיִרְמְיָ֑הוּ וַיֹּ֣אמֶר אֵלָ֔יו יְהֹוָ֣ה אֱלֹהֶ֗יךָ דִּבֶּר֙ אֶת־הָרָעָ֣ה הַזֹּ֔את אֶל־הַמָּק֖וֹם הַזֶּֽה

2[4] And the captain of the guard took Jeremiah, and said to him: 'The LORD your God pronounced this evil upon this place;

וַיָּבֵ֥א וַיַּ֖עַשׂ יְהֹוָ֑ה כַּאֲשֶׁ֣ר דִּבֵּ֔ר כִּֽי־חֲטָאתֶ֤ם לַֽיהֹוָה֙ וְלֹֽא־שְׁמַעְתֶּ֣ם בְּקוֹל֔וֹ וְהָיָ֥ה לָכֶ֖ם "הַדָּבָ֥ר" הַזֶּֽה

3[5] and the LORD has brought it, and done according as He spoke; because you have sinned against the LORD, and have not listened to His voice, *Therefore, this thing came upon you[6]*.

וְעַתָּ֞ה הִנֵּ֧ה פִתַּחְתִּ֣יךָ הַיּ֗וֹם מִֽן־הָאזִקִּים֮ אֲשֶׁ֣ר עַל־יָדֶ֒ךָ֒ אִם־ט֨וֹב בְּעֵינֶ֤יךָ לָב֤וֹא אִתִּ֤י בָבֶ֙ל֙ בֹּ֔א וְאָשִׂ֥ים אֶת־עֵינִ֖י עָלֶ֑יךָ וְאִם־רַ֧ע בְּעֵינֶ֛יךָ לָבֽוֹא־אִתִּ֥י בָבֶ֖ל חֲדָ֑ל רְאֵה֙ כׇּל־הָאָ֣רֶץ לְפָנֶ֔יךָ אֶל־ט֨וֹב וְאֶל־הַיָּשָׁ֧ר בְּעֵינֶ֛יךָ לָלֶ֥כֶת שָׁ֖מָּה לֵֽךְ

4[7] And now, behold, I free you this day from the chains on your hand. If it seems good to you to come with me into Babylon, come, and I will look well to you; *but if it seems ill to you to come with me to Babylon, refrain; behold, all the land is before you; where it seems good and right to you to go, go there[8]*.

וְעוֹדֶ֣נּוּ לֹֽא־יָשׁ֗וּב וְשֻׁ֡בָה אֶל־גְּדַלְיָ֣ה בֶן־אֲחִיקָ֣ם בֶּן־שָׁפָ֡ן אֲשֶׁר֩ הִפְקִ֨יד מֶֽלֶךְ־בָּבֶ֜ל בְּעָרֵ֣י יְהוּדָ֗ה וְשֵׁ֤ב אִתּוֹ֙ בְּת֣וֹךְ הָעָ֔ם א֠וֹ אֶל־כׇּל־הַיָּשָׁ֧ר בְּעֵינֶ֛יךָ לָלֶ֖כֶת לֵ֑ךְ וַיִּתֶּן־ל֧וֹ רַב־טַבָּחִ֛ים אֲרֻחָ֥ה וּמַשְׂאֵ֖ת וַֽיְשַׁלְּחֵֽהוּ

5[9] *Yet he would not go back. Go back then to[10]* Gedaliah the son of Ahikam, the son of Shaphan, whom the king of Babylon made governor over the cities of Judah, and live with him among the people; or go wherever it seems right to you to go.' So the captain of the guard gave him an allowance and a present, and let him go.

וַיָּבֹ֧א יִרְמְיָ֛הוּ אֶל־גְּדַלְיָ֥ה בֶן־אֲחִיקָ֖ם הַמִּצְפָּ֑תָה וַיֵּ֤שֶׁב אִתּוֹ֙ בְּת֣וֹךְ הָעָ֔ם הַנִּשְׁאָרִ֖ים בָּאָֽרֶץ

6[11] Then Jeremiah went to Gedaliah the son of Ahikam to Mizpah, and lived with him among the people who remained in the land.

וַיִּשְׁמְעוּ֩ כׇל־שָׂרֵ֨י הַחֲיָלִ֜ים אֲשֶׁ֣ר בַּשָּׂדֶ֗ה הֵ֚מָּה וְאַנְשֵׁיהֶ֔ם כִּֽי־הִפְקִ֥יד מֶֽלֶךְ־בָּבֶ֖ל אֶת־גְּדַלְיָ֣הוּ בֶן־אֲחִיקָ֑ם וְכִ֣י ׀ הִפְקִ֣יד אִתּ֗וֹ אֲנָשִׁ֤ים וְנָשִׁים֙ וָטָ֔ף וּמִדַּלַּ֣ת הָאָ֔רֶץ מֵאֲשֶׁ֖ר לֹא־הׇגְל֥וּ בָּבֶֽלָה

7[12] Now when all the captains of the forces who were in the fields, they and their men, heard the king of Babylon made Gedaliah the son of Ahikam governor in the land, and committed to him men, and women, and *children, and of*

---

[1] LXX *and you shall find your life*

[2] Jeremiah 40 - mt.Hilchot Taaniot 5:2, Mesillat Yesharim 20:Weighing Implementation of Chassidus; Chapter 47 in LXX

[3] Jeremiah 40:1 - 1 Samuel 7:17, Acts 12:6-12:7 21:13 4:20, b.Rosh Hashanah 23b, b.Taanit 5a, Ephesians 6:20, Jeremiah 7:16 39:11-39:14, Joshua 18:25, Lamentations.R Petichata D'Chakimei:34, Pesikta de R'Kahana 13.9, Psalms 68:7 11:16, y.Nedarim 9:1
Jeremiah 40:1-7 - 4 Baruch 4:6, Josephus Wars 4.10.7
Jeremiah 40:1-16 - Josephus Antiquities 10.9.1 10.9.5

[4] Jeremiah 40:2 - 1 Kings 9:8-9:9, 2 Chronicles 7:20-7:22, Deuteronomy 29:23-29:27, Jeremiah 22:8-22:9, Lamentations 2:15-2:17

[5] Jeremiah 40:3 - b.Bava Batra 10b, Daniel 9:11-9:12, Deuteronomy 5:24, Jeremiah 2:7, Nehemiah 9:28 9:33, Pesikta de R'Kahana 2.5, Romans 2:5 3:19

[6] Missing in LXX

[7] Jeremiah 40:4 - Genesis 13:9 20:15, Jeremiah 39:11-39:12, Midrash Psalms 137:2, Pesikta de R'Kahana 13.9, Pesikta Rabbati 26:6

[8] Missing in LXX

[9] Jeremiah 40:5 - 2 Chronicles 10:20, 2 Kings 8:7-8:9 22:12 22:14 25:22-25:24, Acts 3:3 3:43 4:10, Ezra 7:6 7:27, Hebrews 13:6, Jeremiah 15:11 2:24 15:14 16:4 17:2 52:31-52:34, Job 22:29, Nehemiah 1:11 2:4-2:8, Pesikta de R'Kahana 13.9, Proverbs 16:7 21:1

[10] Missing in LXX

[11] Jeremiah 40:6 - 1 Samuel 7:5-7:6, 2 Baruch 9:2, Jeremiah 15:14, Joshua 15:38, Judges 20:1 21:1

[12] Jeremiah 40:7 - 2 Kings 1:4 25:22-25:26, Ezekiel 33:24-33:29 21:16, Jeremiah 15:4 15:10

the poorest of the land, of those who were not carried away captive[1] to Babylon;

8²   then they came to *Gedaliah at Mizpah, Ishmael the son of Nethaniah, and Jochanan and Jonathan the sons of Kareah, and Seraiah the son of Tanhumeth, and the sons of Ephai the Netophathite, and Jezaniah the son of the Maacathite*[3], they and their men.

וַיָּבֹאוּ אֶל־גְּדַלְיָה הַמִּצְפָּתָה וְיִשְׁמָעֵאל בֶּן־נְתַנְיָהוּ וְיוֹחָנָן וְיוֹנָתָן בְּנֵי־קָרֵחַ וּשְׂרָיָה בֶן־תַּנְחֻמֶת וּבְנֵי 'עוֹפָי' "עֵיפַי" הַנְּטֹפָתִי וִיזַנְיָהוּ בֶּן־הַמַּעֲכָתִי הֵמָּה וְאַנְשֵׁיהֶם

9⁴   And Gedaliah the son of Ahikam the son of Shaphan swore to them and to their men, saying: 'Do not fear to serve the Chaldeans; live in the land, and serve the king of Babylon, and it shall be well with you.

וַיִּשָּׁבַע לָהֶם גְּדַלְיָהוּ בֶן־אֲחִיקָם בֶּן־שָׁפָן וּלְאַנְשֵׁיהֶם לֵאמֹר אַל־תִּירְאוּ מֵעֲבוֹד הַכַּשְׂדִּים שְׁבוּ בָאָרֶץ וְעִבְדוּ אֶת־מֶלֶךְ בָּבֶל וְיִיטַב לָכֶם

10⁵   As for me, behold, I will live at Mizpah, to stand before the Chaldeans who may come to us; but you, gather wine and summer fruits and oil, and put them in your vessels, and live in your cities that you have taken.'

וַאֲנִי הִנְנִי יֹשֵׁב בַּמִּצְפָּה לַעֲמֹד לִפְנֵי הַכַּשְׂדִּים אֲשֶׁר יָבֹאוּ אֵלֵינוּ וְאַתֶּם אִסְפוּ יַיִן וָקַיִץ וְשֶׁמֶן וְשִׂמוּ בִּכְלֵיכֶם וּשְׁבוּ בְּעָרֵיכֶם אֲשֶׁר־תְּפַשְׂתֶּם

11⁶   Likewise when all the Jews who were in Moab, and among the children of Ammon, and in *Edom*[7], and who were in all the countries, heard the king of Babylon had left a remnant of Judah, and that he set over them Gedaliah the son of Ahikam, the son of Shaphan;

וְגַם כָּל־הַיְּהוּדִים אֲשֶׁר־בְּמוֹאָב וּבִבְנֵי־עַמּוֹן וּבֶאֱדוֹם וַאֲשֶׁר בְּכָל־הָאֲרָצוֹת שָׁמְעוּ כִּי־נָתַן מֶלֶךְ־בָּבֶל שְׁאֵרִית לִיהוּדָה וְכִי הִפְקִיד עֲלֵיהֶם אֶת־גְּדַלְיָהוּ בֶּן־אֲחִיקָם בֶּן־שָׁפָן

12⁸   then *all the Jews returned from all places where they were driven, and came*[9] to the land of Judah, to Gedaliah, to Mizpah, and gathered wine and summer fruits in great abundance.

וַיָּשֻׁבוּ כָל־הַיְּהוּדִים מִכָּל־הַמְּקֹמוֹת אֲשֶׁר נִדְּחוּ־שָׁם וַיָּבֹאוּ אֶרֶץ־יְהוּדָה אֶל־גְּדַלְיָהוּ הַמִּצְפָּתָה וַיַּאַסְפוּ יַיִן וָקַיִץ הַרְבֵּה מְאֹד

13¹⁰   Moreover, Jochanan the son of Kareah, and all the captains of the forces who were in the fields, came to Gedaliah in Mizpah,

וְיוֹחָנָן בֶּן־קָרֵחַ וְכָל־שָׂרֵי הַחֲיָלִים אֲשֶׁר בַּשָּׂדֶה בָּאוּ אֶל־גְּדַלְיָהוּ הַמִּצְפָּתָה

14¹¹   and said to him: 'Do you know Baalis the king of the children of Ammon sent Ishmael the son of Nethaniah to take your life?' But Gedaliah the son of Ahikam did not believe them.

וַיֹּאמְרוּ אֵלָיו הֲיָדֹעַ תֵּדַע כִּי בַּעֲלִיס מֶלֶךְ בְּנֵי־עַמּוֹן שָׁלַח אֶת־יִשְׁמָעֵאל בֶּן־נְתַנְיָה לְהַכֹּתְךָ נָפֶשׁ וְלֹא־הֶאֱמִין לָהֶם גְּדַלְיָהוּ בֶּן־אֲחִיקָם

15¹²   Then Jochanan the son of Kareah spoke to Gedaliah in Mizpah secretly, saying: 'Let me go, please, and I will kill Ishmael the son of

וְיוֹחָנָן בֶּן־קָרֵחַ אָמַר אֶל־גְּדַלְיָהוּ בַסֵּתֶר בַּמִּצְפָּה לֵאמֹר אֵלְכָה נָּא וְאַכֶּה אֶת־יִשְׁמָעֵאל בֶּן־נְתַנְיָה

---

[1] LXX *whom Nabuchodonosor had not removed*

[2] Jeremiah 40:8 - 1 Chronicles 2:48 2:54 11:30, 2 Kings 1:23 1:25, 2 Samuel 10:6 10:8 23:28-29 23:34, Deuteronomy 3:14, Ezra 2:2 2:22, *Jehochanan* is altered to read *Jochanan*, Jeremiah 13:15 13:20 14:26 16:6 40:11-16 18:1 18:8 19:2 19:5, Joshua 12:5, Mas.Soferim 7:4, Nehemiah 7:26

[3] LXX *Godolias to Massepha Ismael the son of Nathanias, and Joanan son of Caree, and Saraeas the son of Thanaemeth, and the sons of Jophe the Netophathite, and Ezonias son of the Mochathite*

[4] Jeremiah 40:9 - 1 Samuel 20:16-20:17, 2 Kings 1:24, compare מעבוד "to serve" here with מעבדי "because of the servants of" at 2 Kings 25:24, Genesis 1:15, Jeremiah 3:11 38:17-20, Psalms 37:3 8:2

[5] Jeremiah 40:10 - 2 Samuel 16:1, b.Bava Batra [Rashbam] 53b, b.Bava Batra [Rashbam] 67a, b.Kiddushin 26a, Deuteronomy 1:38, Isaiah 16:9, Jeremiah 11:19 15:10 16:6 16:12 24:32, Luke 21:36, Micah 7:1, Proverbs 22:29

[6] Jeremiah 40:11 - 1 Samuel 11:1 12:12, Ezekiel 5:3 5:12 1:2 1:6 1:8 1:12 11:5 11:15, Genesis 12:8, Isaiah 16:4, Jeremiah 24:9, Numbers 22:1 1:1, Obadiah 1:11-14

[7] LXX *Idumea*

[8] Jeremiah 40:12 - Jeremiah 19:5

[9] LXX *they came to*

[10] Jeremiah 40:13 - Jehochanan is altered to read Jochanan, Jeremiah 16:8 18:1

[11] Jeremiah 40:14 - 1 Corinthians 13:5-13:7, 1 Samuel 11:1-11:3, 2 Baruch 5:7, 2 Samuel 10:1-10:6, Amos 1:13-1:15, Ezekiel 25:2-25:6, Isaiah 2:10, Jeremiah 1:21 16:8 17:2 17:10 49:1-49:6, Micah 7:5, Proverbs 26:23-26:26

[12] Jeremiah 40:15 - 1 Samuel 24:4 2:8, 2 Samuel 18:3 21:17, Ezekiel 33:24-33:29, Jehochanan is altered to read Jochanan, Jeremiah 12:3-12:4 18:2, Job 7:31, John 11:50

וְאִישׁ לֹא יֵדַע לָמָּה יַכֶּכָּה נֶפֶשׁ וְנָפֹצוּ כָּל־יְהוּדָה הַנִּקְבָּצִים אֵלֶיךָ וְאָבְדָה שְׁאֵרִית יְהוּדָה

Nethaniah, and no man shall know it; Why should he take your life, so all the Jews who are gathered to you should be scattered, and the remnant of Judah perish?'

וַיֹּאמֶר גְּדַלְיָהוּ בֶן־אֲחִיקָם אֶל־יוֹחָנָן בֶּן־קָרֵחַ אַל־תַּעַשׂ אֶת־הַדָּבָר הַזֶּה כִּי־שֶׁקֶר אַתָּה דֹבֵר אֶל־יִשְׁמָעֵאל

16[1] But Gedaliah the son of Ahikam said to Jochanan the son of Kareah: 'You shall not do this thing; for you speak falsely of Ishmael.'

Jeremiah – Chapter 41[2]

וַיְהִי בַּחֹדֶשׁ הַשְּׁבִיעִי בָּא יִשְׁמָעֵאל בֶּן־נְתַנְיָה בֶן־אֱלִישָׁמָע מִזֶּרַע הַמְּלוּכָה וְרַבֵּי הַמֶּלֶךְ וַעֲשָׂרָה אֲנָשִׁים אִתּוֹ אֶל־גְּדַלְיָהוּ בֶן־אֲחִיקָם הַמִּצְפָּתָה וַיֹּאכְלוּ שָׁם לֶחֶם יַחְדָּו בַּמִּצְפָּה

1[3] Now it came to pass in the seventh month, that Ishmael the son of Nethaniah, the son of Elishama, of the seed royal, and one of the chief officers of the king, and ten men with him, came to Gedaliah the son of Ahikam in Mizpah; and there they ate bread together in Mizpah.

וַיָּקָם יִשְׁמָעֵאל בֶּן־נְתַנְיָה וַעֲשֶׂרֶת הָאֲנָשִׁים אֲשֶׁר־הָיוּ אִתּוֹ וַיַּכּוּ אֶת־גְּדַלְיָהוּ בֶן־אֲחִיקָם בֶּן־שָׁפָן בַּחֶרֶב וַיָּמֶת אֹתוֹ אֲשֶׁר־הִפְקִיד מֶלֶךְ־בָּבֶל בָּאָרֶץ

2[4] Then Ishmael the son of Nethaniah arose, and the ten men who were with him, and struck Gedaliah the son of Ahikam the son of Shaphan with the sword, and killed him, whom the king of Babylon had made governor over the land.

וְאֵת כָּל־הַיְּהוּדִים אֲשֶׁר־הָיוּ אִתּוֹ אֶת־גְּדַלְיָהוּ בַּמִּצְפָּה וְאֶת־הַכַּשְׂדִּים אֲשֶׁר נִמְצְאוּ־שָׁם אֵת אַנְשֵׁי הַמִּלְחָמָה הִכָּה יִשְׁמָעֵאל

3[5] Ishmael also killed all the Jews who were with him, with Gedaliah, at Mizpah, and the Chaldeans who were there, the men of war.

וַיְהִי בַּיּוֹם הַשֵּׁנִי לְהָמִית אֶת־גְּדַלְיָהוּ וְאִישׁ לֹא יָדָע

4[6] And it came to pass the second day after he killed Gedaliah, and no man knew it,

וַיָּבֹאוּ אֲנָשִׁים מִשְּׁכֶם מִשִּׁלוֹ וּמִשֹּׁמְרוֹן שְׁמֹנִים אִישׁ מְגֻלְּחֵי זָקָן וּקְרֻעֵי בְגָדִים וּמִתְגֹּדְדִים וּמִנְחָה וּלְבוֹנָה בְּיָדָם לְהָבִיא בֵּית יְהוָה

5[7] That certain men came from Shechem, from Shiloh, and from Samaria, eighty men, with their beards shaven and their clothes rent, and having cut themselves, with meal offerings and frankincense in their hand to bring to the house of the LORD.

וַיֵּצֵא יִשְׁמָעֵאל בֶּן־נְתַנְיָה לִקְרָאתָם מִן־הַמִּצְפָּה הֹלֵךְ הָלֹךְ וּבֹכֶה וַיְהִי כִּפְגֹשׁ אֹתָם וַיֹּאמֶר אֲלֵיהֶם בֹּאוּ אֶל־גְּדַלְיָהוּ בֶּן־אֲחִיקָם

6[8] And Ishmael the son of Nethaniah went forth from Mizpah to meet them, weeping all along as he went; and it came to pass, as he met them, he said to them: 'Come to Gedaliah the son of Ahikam.'

וַיְהִי כְּבוֹאָם אֶל־תּוֹךְ הָעִיר וַיִּשְׁחָטֵם יִשְׁמָעֵאל בֶּן־נְתַנְיָה אֶל־תּוֹךְ הַבּוֹר הוּא וְהָאֲנָשִׁים אֲשֶׁר־אִתּוֹ

7[9] And it was so, when they came into the midst of the city, that Ishmael the son of Nethaniah killed them, and cast them into the midst of the pit, he, and the men who were with him.

---

[1] Jeremiah 40:16 - Jehochanan is altered to read Jochanan, Jeremiah 17:2, Mas.Soferim 7:2, Matthew 10:16-10:17, Mesillat Yesharim 20:Weighing Implementation of Chassidus, Romans 3:8
[2] Jeremiah 41 - Josephus Antiquities 10.9.1 10.9.5, Mesillat Yesharim 20:Weighing Implementation of Chassidus, Siman 121:2, Jastrow 1310a; Chapter 48 in LXX
[3] Jeremiah 41:1 - 2 Chronicles 22:10, 2 Kings 11:1 1:25, 2 Samuel 3:27 20:9-20:10, b.Megillah 15a, b.Sheviit 20b, Daniel 11:26-11:27, Ezekiel 17:13, James 4:1-4:3, Jeremiah 12:12 12:20 16:6 16:8 40:14-40:16, John 13:18, Luke 22:47-22:48, mt.Hilchot Taaniot 5:2, Proverbs 13:10 26:23-26:26 3:4, Psalms 41:10 13:5
[4] Jeremiah 41:2 - 2 Kings 1:25, 2 Samuel 3:27 20:9-20:10, Jeremiah 16:5 16:7, Pesikta Rabbati 22:5, Psalms 41:10 13:5
[5] Jeremiah 41:3 - 2 Kings 1:25, Ecclesiastes 9:18, Jeremiah 41:11-41:12, Lamentations 1:2
[6] Jeremiah 41:4 - 1 Samuel 3:11, Psalms 52:2-52:3
[7] Jeremiah 41:5 - 1 Kings 12:1 12:25 16:24 16:29, 1 Samuel 1:7, 2 Kings 10:13-10:14 1:9, 2 Samuel 10:4, b.Moed Katan 26a, Deuteronomy 14:1, Genesis 9:18 10:2, Isaiah 15:2, Jeremiah 7:12 7:14, Joshua 18:1 24:32, Judges 9:1, Leviticus 19:27-19:28, mt.Hilchot Evel 9:10, mt.Hilchot Taaniot 5:16, Psalms 6:15, y.Moed Katan 3:7
[8] Jeremiah 41:6 - 2 Samuel 1:2-1:16 3:16, Jeremiah 2:4, Proverbs 26:23-26:26
[9] Jeremiah 41:7 - 1 Kings 15:28-15:29 16:10-16:12, 2 Kings 11:1-11:2 15:25, Ezekiel 22:27 33:24-33:26, Isaiah 11:7, Proverbs 1:16, Psalms 55:24, Romans 3:15

וַעֲשָׂרָה אֲנָשִׁים נִמְצְאוּ־בָם וַיֹּאמְרוּ אֶל־יִשְׁמָעֵאל אַל־תְּמִתֵנוּ כִּי־יֶשׁ־לָנוּ מַטְמֹנִים בַּשָּׂדֶה חִטִּים וּשְׂעֹרִים וְשֶׁמֶן וּדְבָשׁ וַיֶּחְדַּל וְלֹא הֱמִיתָם בְּתוֹךְ אֲחֵיהֶם	8[1]	But ten men were found among those who said to Ishmael: 'Do not kill us; for we have stores hidden in the field, of wheat, and of barley, and of oil, and of honey.' So he stayed his hand, and did not kill them among their brethren.
וְהַבּוֹר אֲשֶׁר הִשְׁלִיךְ שָׁם יִשְׁמָעֵאל אֵת כָּל־פִּגְרֵי הָאֲנָשִׁים אֲשֶׁר הִכָּה בְּיַד־גְּדַלְיָהוּ הוּא אֲשֶׁר עָשָׂה הַמֶּלֶךְ אָסָא מִפְּנֵי בַּעְשָׁא מֶלֶךְ־יִשְׂרָאֵל אֹתוֹ מִלֵּא יִשְׁמָעֵאל בֶּן־נְתַנְיָהוּ חֲלָלִים	9[2]	Now the pit where Ishmael cast all the dead bodies of the men whom he killed by the side of Gedaliah was what Asa the king had made for fear of Baasa king of Israel; the same Ishmael the son of Nethaniah filled with those who were killed.
וַיִּשְׁבְּ יִשְׁמָעֵאל אֶת־כָּל־שְׁאֵרִית הָעָם אֲשֶׁר בַּמִּצְפָּה אֶת־בְּנוֹת הַמֶּלֶךְ וְאֶת־כָּל־הָעָם הַנִּשְׁאָרִים בַּמִּצְפָּה אֲשֶׁר הִפְקִיד נְבוּזַרְאֲדָן רַב־טַבָּחִים אֶת־גְּדַלְיָהוּ בֶּן־אֲחִיקָם וַיִּשְׁבֵּם יִשְׁמָעֵאל בֶּן־נְתַנְיָה וַיֵּלֶךְ לַעֲבֹר אֶל־בְּנֵי עַמּוֹן	10[3]	Then Ishmael carried away captive all the remnant of the people who were in Mizpah, the king's daughters, and all the people who remained in Mizpah, whom Nebuzaradan the captain of the guard committed to Gedaliah the son of Ahikam; Ishmael the son of Nethaniah carried them away captive, and left to go over to the children of Ammon.
וַיִּשְׁמַע יוֹחָנָן בֶּן־קָרֵחַ וְכָל־שָׂרֵי הַחֲיָלִים אֲשֶׁר אִתּוֹ אֵת כָּל־הָרָעָה אֲשֶׁר עָשָׂה יִשְׁמָעֵאל בֶּן־נְתַנְיָה	11[4]	But when Jochanan the son of Kareah, and all the captains of the forces who were with him, heard of all the evil that Ishmael the son of Nethaniah had done,
וַיִּקְחוּ אֶת־כָּל־הָאֲנָשִׁים וַיֵּלְכוּ לְהִלָּחֵם עִם־יִשְׁמָעֵאל בֶּן־נְתַנְיָה וַיִּמְצְאוּ אֹתוֹ אֶל־מַיִם רַבִּים אֲשֶׁר בְּגִבְעוֹן	12[5]	then they took all the men, and went to fight with Ishmael the son of Nethaniah, and found him by the great waters that are in Gibeon.
וַיְהִי כִּרְאוֹת כָּל־הָעָם אֲשֶׁר אֶת־יִשְׁמָעֵאל אֶת־יוֹחָנָן בֶּן־קָרֵחַ וְאֵת כָּל־שָׂרֵי הַחֲיָלִים אֲשֶׁר אִתּוֹ וַיִּשְׂמָחוּ	13[6]	Now it came to pass, that when all the people who were with Ishmael saw Jochanan the son of Kareah, and all the captains of the forces who were with him, *then they were glad*[7].
וַיָּסֹבּוּ כָּל־הָעָם אֲשֶׁר־שָׁבָה יִשְׁמָעֵאל מִן־הַמִּצְפָּה וַיָּשֻׁבוּ וַיֵּלְכוּ אֶל־יוֹחָנָן בֶּן־קָרֵחַ	14[8]	*So all the people that Ishmael had carried away captive from Mizpah cast about and returned, and went to Jochanan the son of Kareah*[9].
וְיִשְׁמָעֵאל בֶּן־נְתַנְיָה נִמְלַט בִּשְׁמֹנָה אֲנָשִׁים מִפְּנֵי יוֹחָנָן וַיֵּלֶךְ אֶל־בְּנֵי עַמּוֹן	15[10]	But Ishmael the son of Nethaniah escaped from Jochanan with eight men, and went to the children of Ammon.
וַיִּקַּח יוֹחָנָן בֶּן־קָרֵחַ וְכָל־שָׂרֵי הַחֲיָלִים אֲשֶׁר־אִתּוֹ אֵת כָּל־שְׁאֵרִית הָעָם אֲשֶׁר הֵשִׁיב מֵאֵת יִשְׁמָעֵאל בֶּן־נְתַנְיָה מִן־הַמִּצְפָּה אַחַר הִכָּה אֶת־גְּדַלְיָה בֶּן־אֲחִיקָם גְּבָרִים אַנְשֵׁי הַמִּלְחָמָה וְנָשִׁים וְטַף וְסָרִסִים אֲשֶׁר הֵשִׁיב מִגִּבְעוֹן	16[11]	Then Jochanan took the son of Kareah, and all the captains of the forces who were with him, all the remnant of the people whom he saved from Ishmael the son of Nethaniah, from Mizpah, after he killed Gedaliah the son of Ahikam, the men, the men of war, and the

---

[1] Jeremiah 41:8 - Isaiah 21:3, Job 2:4, Lamentations.R 1:39, Mark 8:36-8:37, Matthew 6:25 16:26, Pesikta Rabbati 27:1, Philippians 3:7-3:9, Proverbs 13:8, Psalms 49:7-49:9

[2] Jeremiah 41:9 - 1 Kings 15:17-15:22, 1 Samuel 13:6 14:11 14:22 24:3, 2 Chronicles 16:1-16:10, 2 Samuel 17:9, b.Niddah 61a, Hebrews 11:38, Joshua 10:16-10:18, Judges 6:2, Mesillat Yesharim 20:Weighing Implementation of Chassidus

[3] Jeremiah 41:10 - Jeremiah 22:30 15:6 16:7 40:11-40:12 16:14 43:5-43:7 44:12-44:14, Nehemiah 2:10 2:19 4:7-4:8 6:17-6:18 13:4-13:8

[4] Jeremiah 41:11 - Jehochanan is altered to read Jochanan, Jeremiah 40:7-40:8 40:13-40:16 41:2-41:3 17:7 18:1 18:3 43:2-43:5

[5] Jeremiah 41:12 - 1 Samuel 30:1-30:8 30:18-30:20, 2 Samuel 2:13, Genesis 14:14-14:16

[6] Jeremiah 41:13 - Jehochanan is altered to read Jochanan

[7] Missing in LXX

[8] Jeremiah 41:14 - Jehochanan is altered to read Jochanan

[9] LXX *that they returned to Joanan*

[10] Jeremiah 41:15 - 1 Kings 20:20, 1 Samuel 6:17, 2 Kings 1:25, Acts 4:4, Ecclesiastes 8:11-8:12, Jehochanan is altered to read Jochanan, Jeremiah 17:2, Job 21:30, Proverbs 4:17

[11] Jeremiah 41:16 - Jehochanan is altered to read Jochanan, Jeremiah 17:10 18:8 43:4-43:7

women, and *the children*[1], and the officers, whom he brought back from Gibeon;

17[2] וַיֵּלְכוּ וַיֵּשְׁבוּ בְּגֵרוּת "כִּמְהָם' "כְּמוֹהָם' "כְּמָהָם" אֲשֶׁר־אֵצֶל בֵּית לֶחֶם לָלֶכֶת לָבוֹא מִצְרָיִם

and they left, and lived in Geruth Chimham, which is by Bethlehem, to go to enter into Egypt,

18[3] מִפְּנֵי הַכַּשְׂדִּים כִּי יָרְאוּ מִפְּנֵיהֶם כִּי־הִכָּה יִשְׁמָעֵאל בֶּן־נְתַנְיָה אֵת גְּדַלְיָהוּ בֶּן־אֲחִיקָם אֲשֶׁר־הִפְקִיד מֶלֶךְ־בָּבֶל בָּאָרֶץ:

because of the Chaldeans; for they were afraid of them, because Ishmael the son of Nethaniah killed Gedaliah the son of Ahikam, whom the king of Babylon made governor over the land.

Jeremiah – Chapter 42[4]

1[5] וַיִּגְּשׁוּ כָּל־שָׂרֵי הַחֲיָלִים וְיוֹחָנָן בֶּן־קָרֵחַ וִיזַנְיָה בֶּן־הוֹשַׁעְיָה וְכָל־הָעָם מִקָּטֹן וְעַד־גָּדוֹל

Then all the captains of the forces, and *Jochanan the son of Kareah, and Jezaniah the son of Hoshaiah*[6], and all the people from the least to the great, came near,

2[7] וַיֹּאמְרוּ אֶל־יִרְמְיָהוּ הַנָּבִיא תִּפָּל־נָא תְחִנָּתֵנוּ לְפָנֶיךָ וְהִתְפַּלֵּל בַּעֲדֵנוּ אֶל־יְהוָה אֱלֹהֶיךָ בְּעַד כָּל־הַשְּׁאֵרִית הַזֹּאת כִּי־נִשְׁאַרְנוּ מְעַט מֵהַרְבֵּה כַּאֲשֶׁר עֵינֶיךָ רֹאוֹת אֹתָנוּ

and said to Jeremiah the prophet: 'Please let our supplication be accepted before you, and pray for us to the LORD your God, for all this remnant; for but a few of many of us remain, as your eyes see us;

3[8] וְיַגֶּד־לָנוּ יְהוָה אֱלֹהֶיךָ אֶת־הַדֶּרֶךְ אֲשֶׁר נֵלֶךְ־בָּהּ וְאֶת־הַדָּבָר אֲשֶׁר נַעֲשֶׂה

So the LORD your God may tell us the way in which we should walk, and the thing we should do.'

4[9] וַיֹּאמֶר אֲלֵיהֶם יִרְמְיָהוּ הַנָּבִיא שָׁמַעְתִּי הִנְנִי מִתְפַּלֵּל אֶל־יְהוָה אֱלֹהֵיכֶם כְּדִבְרֵיכֶם וְהָיָה כָּל־הַדָּבָר אֲשֶׁר־יַעֲנֶה יְהוָה אֶתְכֶם אַגִּיד לָכֶם לֹא־אֶמְנַע מִכֶּם דָּבָר

Then Jeremiah the prophet said to them: 'I have heard you; behold, I will pray to the LORD your God according to your words; and it shall be, that whatever thing the LORD shall answer, I will declare it to you;

5[10] וְהֵמָּה אָמְרוּ אֶל־יִרְמְיָהוּ יְהִי יְהוָה בָּנוּ לְעֵד אֱמֶת וְנֶאֱמָן אִם־לֹא כְּכָל־הַדָּבָר אֲשֶׁר יִשְׁלָחֲךָ יְהוָה אֱלֹהֶיךָ אֵלֵינוּ כֵּן נַעֲשֶׂה

Then they said to Jeremiah: 'The LORD is a true and faithful witness against us, if we do not according to all the word the LORD your God shall send you to us.

6[11] אִם־טוֹב וְאִם־רָע בְּקוֹל יְהוָה אֱלֹהֵינוּ אֲשֶׁר "אֲנוּ' "אֲנַחְנוּ" שֹׁלְחִים אֹתְךָ אֵלָיו נִשְׁמָע לְמַעַן אֲשֶׁר יִיטַב־לָנוּ כִּי נִשְׁמַע בְּקוֹל יְהוָה אֱלֹהֵינוּ

Whether it is good, or whether it is evil, we will listen to the voice of the LORD our God, to whom we send you; so it may be well with us, when we listen to the voice of the LORD our God.'

7[12] וַיְהִי מִקֵּץ עֲשֶׂרֶת יָמִים וַיְהִי דְבַר־יְהוָה אֶל־יִרְמְיָהוּ

And it came to pass after ten days, the word of the LORD came to Jeremiah.

---

[1] LXX *and the other property*
Jeremiah 41:17 - 2 Samuel 19:37-19:38, Isaiah 30:2-30:3, Jeremiah 18:14 18:19 19:7[2]
[3] Jeremiah 41:18 - 2 Kings 1:25, Isaiah 30:16-30:17 51:12-51:13 9:11, Jeremiah 16:5 18:11 18:16 43:2-43:3, Luke 12:4-12:5
[4] Jeremiah 42 - Josephus Antiquities 10.9.5, Siman 121:2; Chapter 49 in LXX
[5] Jeremiah 42:1 - 2 Kings 1:23, Acts 8:10, Ezekiel 8:11 11:1 14:3-14:4 20:1-20:3 9:31, Isaiah 5:13 24:1 58:1-58:2, Jehochanan is altered to read Jochanan, Jeremiah 5:4-5:5 6:13 8:10 16:8 16:13 17:11 17:16 18:8 18:20 43:4-43:5 20:12, Matthew 15:8
[6] LXX *Joanan, and Azarias the son of Maasaeas*
[7] Jeremiah 42:2 - 1 Kings 13:6, 1 Samuel 7:8 12:19 12:23, Acts 8:24, Deuteronomy 4:27 28:62, Exodus 8:24 9:28, Ezekiel 5:3-4 12:16, Isaiah 1:9 1:15 13:4, James 5:16, Jeremiah 17:15-16 21:2 12:7 13:3 13:20 18:20, Lamentations 1:1, Leviticus 2:22, Matthew 24:22, Zechariah 13:8-9
[8] Jeremiah 42:3 - 1 Kings 8:36, Deuteronomy 5:26 5:29, Ezra 8:21, Isaiah 2:3, Jeremiah 6:16, Mark 12:13-12:14, Micah 4:2, Proverbs 3:6, Psalms 25:4-25:5 27:11 86:11 143:8-143:10
[9] Jeremiah 42:4 - 1 Kings 22:14-22:16, 1 Samuel 3:17-3:18 12:23, 2 Chronicles 18:13-18:15, Acts 20:20 20:27, Exodus 8:25, Ezekiel 2:7, Jeremiah 23:28, Psalms 40:11, Romans 10:1
[10] Jeremiah 42:5 - 1 Samuel 12:5 20:42, Deuteronomy 5:27-5:29, Exodus 20:7 20:16, Genesis 7:50, Jeremiah 5:2, Judges 11:10, Malachi 2:14 3:5, Micah 1:2, Revelation 1:5 3:14, Romans 1:9
[11] Jeremiah 42:6 - Deuteronomy 5:29 5:33 6:2-3, Exodus 24:7, Isaiah 3:10, Jeremiah 7:23, Joshua 24:24, Psalms 81:14-17 8:2, Romans 7:7 7:13 8:7
[12] Jeremiah 42:7 - Habakkuk 2:3, Isaiah 4:16, Mekilta de R'Ishmael Pisha 1:147, Psalms 27:14
Jeremiah 42:7-11 - 2QJer

וַיִּקְרָא אֶל־יוֹחָנָן בֶּן־קָרֵחַ וְאֶל כָּל־שָׂרֵי הַחֲיָלִים אֲשֶׁר אִתּוֹ וּלְכָל־הָעָם לְמִקָּטֹן וְעַד־גָּדוֹל

8[1] Then he called Jochanan the son of Kareah, and all the captains of the forces who were with him, and all the people from the least to the great,

וַיֹּאמֶר אֲלֵיהֶם כֹּה־אָמַר יְהֹוָה אֱלֹהֵי יִשְׂרָאֵל אֲשֶׁר שְׁלַחְתֶּם אֹתִי אֵלָיו לְהַפִּיל תְּחִנַּתְכֶם לְפָנָיו

9[2] *And he said to them*[3]: 'Thus says the LORD, the God of Israel, to whom you sent me to present your petition before Him:

אִם־שׁוֹב תֵּשְׁבוּ בָּאָרֶץ הַזֹּאת וּבָנִיתִי אֶתְכֶם וְלֹא אֶהֱרֹס וְנָטַעְתִּי אֶתְכֶם וְלֹא אֶתּוֹשׁ כִּי נִחַמְתִּי אֶל־הָרָעָה אֲשֶׁר עָשִׂיתִי לָכֶם

10[4] If you will still live in this land, then will I build you, and not pull you down, and I will plant you, and not pluck you up; for I repent of the evil I have done to you.

אַל־תִּירְאוּ מִפְּנֵי מֶלֶךְ בָּבֶל אֲשֶׁר־אַתֶּם יְרֵאִים מִפָּנָיו אַל־תִּירְאוּ מִמֶּנּוּ נְאֻם־יְהֹוָה כִּי־אִתְּכֶם אָנִי לְהוֹשִׁיעַ אֶתְכֶם וּלְהַצִּיל אֶתְכֶם מִיָּדוֹ

11[5] Do not be afraid of the king of Babylon, of whom you are afraid; do not be afraid of him, says the LORD; for I am with you to save you, and to deliver you from his hand.

וְאֶתֵּן לָכֶם רַחֲמִים וְרִחַם אֶתְכֶם וְהֵשִׁיב אֶתְכֶם אֶל־אַדְמַתְכֶם

12[6] And I will grant you compassion, so he may have compassion on you, and cause you to return to your own land.

וְאִם־אֹמְרִים אַתֶּם לֹא נֵשֵׁב בָּאָרֶץ הַזֹּאת לְבִלְתִּי שְׁמֹעַ בְּקוֹל יְהֹוָה אֱלֹהֵיכֶם

13[7] But if you say: We will not live in this land; and you will not listen to the voice of the LORD your God;

לֵאמֹר לֹא כִּי אֶרֶץ מִצְרַיִם נָבוֹא אֲשֶׁר לֹא־נִרְאֶה מִלְחָמָה וְקוֹל שׁוֹפָר לֹא נִשְׁמָע וְלַלֶּחֶם לֹא־נִרְעָב וְשָׁם נֵשֵׁב

14[8] saying: No; but we will go into the land of Egypt, where we shall see no war, nor hear the sound of the horn, nor have hunger of bread; and there will we live;

וְעַתָּה לָכֵן שִׁמְעוּ דְבַר־יְהֹוָה שְׁאֵרִית יְהוּדָה כֹּה־אָמַר יְהֹוָה צְבָאוֹת אֱלֹהֵי יִשְׂרָאֵל אִם־אַתֶּם שׂוֹם תְּשִׂמוּן פְּנֵיכֶם לָבֹא מִצְרַיִם וּבָאתֶם לָגוּר שָׁם

15[9] *Now, therefore, hear the word of the LORD, O remnant of Judah: Thus says the LORD of hosts, the God of Israel*[10]: If you wholly set your faces to enter into Egypt, and go to sojourn there;

וְהָיְתָה הַחֶרֶב אֲשֶׁר אַתֶּם יְרֵאִים מִמֶּנָּה שָׁם תַּשִּׂיג אֶתְכֶם בְּאֶרֶץ מִצְרָיִם וְהָרָעָב אֲשֶׁר־אַתֶּם דֹּאֲגִים מִמֶּנּוּ שָׁם יִדְבַּק אַחֲרֵיכֶם מִצְרַיִם וְשָׁם תָּמֻתוּ

16[11] then it shall come to pass, that the sword, which you fear, shall overtake you there in the land of Egypt, and famine, of which you are afraid, shall follow hard after you there in Egypt; and there you shall die.

וְיִהְיוּ כָל־הָאֲנָשִׁים אֲשֶׁר־שָׂמוּ אֶת־פְּנֵיהֶם לָבֹא מִצְרַיִם לָגוּר שָׁם יָמוּתוּ בַּחֶרֶב בָּרָעָב וּבַדָּבֶר וְלֹא־יִהְיֶה לָהֶם שָׂרִיד וּפָלִיט מִפְּנֵי הָרָעָה אֲשֶׁר אֲנִי מֵבִיא עֲלֵיהֶם

17[12] So it shall be with all the men who set their faces to go into Egypt to sojourn there; they shall die by the sword, by famine, and by pestilence; and none of them shall remain or escape from the evil I will bring upon them.

---

[1] Jeremiah 42:8 - Jehochanan is altered to read Jochanan, Jeremiah 16:8 16:13 41:11-16 18:1 43:2-5

[2] Jeremiah 42:9 - 2 Kings 19:4 19:6 19:20-19:37 22:15-22:20, Jeremiah 18:2, z.Vaetchanan 269b

[3] 2QJer *And their god said* [an error?]

[4] Jeremiah 42:10 - 2 Samuel 24:16, Acts 15:16, Amos 7:3 7:6, Deuteronomy 8:36, Exodus 8:14, Ezekiel 12:36, Genesis 26:2-26:3, Hosea 11:8, Jeremiah 18:7-18:10 24:6 2:19 7:29 9:7, Joel 2:13, Jonah 3:10 4:2, Judges 2:18, Psalms 37:3 69:36 6:17 10:45

[5] Jeremiah 42:11 - 2 Chronicles 32:7-32:8, 2 Kings 1:26, 2 Timothy 4:17, Acts 18:10, Deuteronomy 20:4, Isaiah 8:8-8:10 17:10 19:2 19:5, Jeremiah 1:8 1:19 15:20 3:12 3:17 17:18, Joshua 1:5 1:9, Matthew 10:28 4:20, Numbers 14:9, Psalms 46:8 46:12, Romans 8:31

[6] Jeremiah 42:12 - Nehemiah 1:11, Proverbs 16:7, Psalms 106:45-106:46

[7] Jeremiah 42:13 - Exodus 5:2, Jeremiah 18:10 20:16

[8] Jeremiah 42:14 - 2QJer, Deuteronomy 5:18, Exodus 16:3 17:3, Isaiah 6:16 7:1, Jeremiah 4:19-21 17:17 19:7, Numbers 11:4-5 16:13 Jeremiah 42:14-16 - Mekhilta de R'Shimon bar Yochai Beshallach 22:2

[9] Jeremiah 42:15 - Daniel 11:17, Deuteronomy 17:16, Jeremiah 18:17 44:12-44:14, Luke 9:51, z.Vaetchanan 269b

[10] LXX *then hear the word of the LORD; thus saith the LORD*

[11] Jeremiah 42:16 - Amos 9:1-9:4, Deuteronomy 4:15 4:22 4:45, Esther.R Petichata:3, Ezekiel 11:8, Jeremiah 18:13 44:11-44:13 20:27, John 11:48, Mekhilta de R'Ishmael Beshallah 3:126, Proverbs 13:21, y.Sukkah 5:1, Zechariah 1:6, Esther.R Petichata:3

[12] Jeremiah 42:17 - Jeremiah 24:10 18:22 44:13-44:14 20:28

כִּי כֹה אָמַר יְהוָה צְבָאוֹת אֱלֹהֵי יִשְׂרָאֵל כַּאֲשֶׁר נִתַּךְ אַפִּי וַחֲמָתִי עַל־יֹשְׁבֵי יְרוּשָׁלִַם כֵּן תִּתַּךְ חֲמָתִי עֲלֵיכֶם בְּבֹאֲכֶם מִצְרָיִם וִהְיִיתֶם לְאָלָה וּלְשַׁמָּה וְלִקְלָלָה וּלְחֶרְפָּה וְלֹא־תִרְאוּ עוֹד אֶת־הַמָּקוֹם הַזֶּה

18[1]   For thus says the LORD of hosts, the God of Israel: As my anger and My fury has been poured forth on the inhabitants of Jerusalem, so shall My fury be poured forth on you, when you enter Egypt; and you shall be a blight, and an amazement, and a curse, and a reproof; and you shall never see this place.

דִּבֶּר יְהוָה עֲלֵיכֶם שְׁאֵרִית יְהוּדָה אַל־תָּבֹאוּ מִצְרָיִם יָדֹעַ תֵּדְעוּ כִּי־הַעִידֹתִי בָכֶם הַיּוֹם

19[2]   The LORD has spoken concerning you, O remnant of Judah: Do not go into Egypt; know certainly I have forewarned you this day.

כִּי 'הִתְעֵתֶים' "הִתְעֵיתֶם" בְּנַפְשׁוֹתֵיכֶם כִּי־אַתֶּם שְׁלַחְתֶּם אֹתִי אֶל־יְהוָה אֱלֹהֵיכֶם לֵאמֹר הִתְפַּלֵּל בַּעֲדֵנוּ אֶל־יְהוָה אֱלֹהֵינוּ וּכְכֹל אֲשֶׁר יֹאמַר יְהוָה אֱלֹהֵינוּ כֵּן הַגֶּד־לָנוּ וְעָשִׂינוּ

20[3]   For you have dealt deceitfully against your own souls; for you sent me to the LORD your God, saying: Pray for us to the LORD our God; and according to all the LORD our God shall say, so declare to us, and we will do it;

וָאַגִּד לָכֶם הַיּוֹם וְלֹא שְׁמַעְתֶּם בְּקוֹל יְהוָה אֱלֹהֵיכֶם וּלְכֹל אֲשֶׁר־שְׁלָחַנִי אֲלֵיכֶם

21[4]   and I declared it to you this day; but you have not listened to the voice of the LORD your God in anything which He sent me to you.

וְעַתָּה יָדֹעַ תֵּדְעוּ כִּי בַּחֶרֶב בָּרָעָב וּבַדֶּבֶר תָּמוּתוּ בַּמָּקוֹם אֲשֶׁר חֲפַצְתֶּם לָבוֹא לָגוּר שָׁם

22[5]   Now, therefore, know certainly you shall die by the sword, by famine, and by pestilence, in the place where you desire to go to sojourn.'

Jeremiah – Chapter 43[6]

וַיְהִי כְּכַלּוֹת יִרְמְיָהוּ לְדַבֵּר אֶל־כָּל־הָעָם אֶת־כָּל־דִּבְרֵי יְהוָה אֱלֹהֵיהֶם אֲשֶׁר שְׁלָחוֹ יְהוָה אֱלֹהֵיהֶם אֲלֵיהֶם אֵת כָּל־הַדְּבָרִים הָאֵלֶּה

1[7]   And it came to pass, when Jeremiah finished speaking to all the people the words of the LORD their God, where the LORD their God had sent him to them, all these words,

וַיֹּאמֶר עֲזַרְיָה בֶן־הוֹשַׁעְיָה וְיוֹחָנָן בֶּן־קָרֵחַ וְכָל־הָאֲנָשִׁים הַזֵּדִים אֹמְרִים אֶל־יִרְמְיָהוּ שֶׁקֶר אַתָּה מְדַבֵּר לֹא שְׁלָחֲךָ יְהוָה אֱלֹהֵינוּ לֵאמֹר לֹא־תָבֹאוּ מִצְרַיִם לָגוּר שָׁם

2[8]   then Azariah the son of Hoshaiah spoke, and Jochanan the son of Kareah, and all the proud men, saying to Jeremiah: 'You speak falsely; the LORD our God has not sent you to say: You shall not go into Egypt to sojourn;

כִּי בָּרוּךְ בֶּן־נֵרִיָּה מַסִּית אֹתְךָ בָּנוּ לְמַעַן תֵּת אֹתָנוּ בְיַד־הַכַּשְׂדִּים לְהָמִית אֹתָנוּ וּלְהַגְלוֹת אֹתָנוּ בָּבֶל

3[9]   But Baruch *the son of Neriah*[10] sets you against us, to deliver us into the hand of the Chaldeans, so they may put us to death, and carry us away captives to Babylon.'

[1] Jeremiah 42:18 - 1 Kings 9:7-9:9, 2 Chronicles 10:25 36:16-36:19, 2 Kings 25:4-25:7, b.Moed Katan 16b, Daniel 9:11 9:27, Deuteronomy 29:20-29:21, Ezekiel 22:22, Isaiah 17:15, Jeremiah 6:11 7:20 18:16 22:10-22:12 22:27 24:9 1:9 2:6 5:18 5:22 39:1-39:9 20:12 52:4-52:11, Lamentations 2:4 4:11, Nahum 1:6, Revelation 14:10 16:2-16:21, z.Vaetchanan 269b, Zechariah 8:13
[2] Jeremiah 42:19 - 1 Thessalonians 4:6, 2 Chronicles 24:19, Acts 2:40 20:26-20:27, Deuteronomy 17:16 7:21, Ephesians 4:17, Ezekiel 2:5 3:21 17:15, Isaiah 30:1-30:7 31:1-31:3, Jeremiah 14:21, Nehemiah 9:26 9:29-9:30
[3] Jeremiah 42:20 - Ezekiel 14:3-14:4 9:31, Galatians 6:7, James 1:22, Jeremiah 3:10 17:10 18:2, Matthew 22:15-22:18 22:35, Numbers 17:3, Psalms 18:45 65:4
[4] Jeremiah 42:21 - Acts 20:20 20:26-20:27, Deuteronomy 11:26-11:27 5:18, Ezekiel 2:7 3:17, Jeremiah 7:24-7:27, Zechariah 7:11-7:12
[5] Jeremiah 42:22 - Ezekiel 5:3-5:4 6:11, Hosea 9:6, Jeremiah 18:17 19:11
[6] Chapter 50 in LXX
[7] Jeremiah 43:1 - 1 Samuel 8:10, Acts 5:20 20:27, Exodus 24:3, Jeremiah 1:7 1:17 2:2 2:8 42:3-5 18:22 51:63, Mas.Kallah Rabbati 4:4, Matthew 4:20
Jeremiah 43:1-7 - Josephus Antiquities 10.9.6
[8] Jeremiah 43:2 - 1 Peter 5:5, 2 Chronicles 12:13, Exodus 5:2 9:17, Habakkuk 2:4-2:5, Isaiah 7:9 9:10-9:11, James 4:6, *Jehochanan* is altered to read *Jochanan*, Jeremiah 5:12-13 13:15 16:8 40:13-16 17:16 18:1 19:1, Proverbs 6:17 8:13 16:5 16:18-19 6:9, Psalms 10:5-10:6 12:4 23:21 3:4
Jeremiah 43:2-10 - 4QJerd
[9] Jeremiah 43:3 - Jeremiah 12:4 12:10 12:26 14:4 19:6 45:1-45:3, Luke 6:22-6:23 6:26, Matthew 5:11-5:12, Psalms 13:4
Jeremiah 43:3-6 - 2 Baruch 1:1
[10] Missing in 4QJerd

וְלֹא־שָׁמַע יוֹחָנָן בֶּן־קָרֵחַ וְכָל־שָׂרֵי הַחֲיָלִים וְכָל־הָעָם בְּקוֹל יְהוָה לָשֶׁבֶת בְּאֶרֶץ יְהוּדָה

4[1] So Jochanan *the son of Kareah*[2], and all the captains of the forces, and all the people, did not listen to the voice of the LORD, to live in the land of Judah.

וַיִּקַּח יוֹחָנָן בֶּן־קָרֵחַ וְכָל־שָׂרֵי הַחֲיָלִים אֵת כָּל־שְׁאֵרִית יְהוּדָה אֲשֶׁר־שָׁבוּ מִכָּל־הַגּוֹיִם אֲשֶׁר נִדְּחוּ־שָׁם לָגוּר בְּאֶרֶץ יְהוּדָה

5[3] But Jochanan *the son of Kareah*[4], and all the captains of the forces, took the remnant of Judah, who returned from all the nations *where they were driven*[5] to sojourn in the land of Judah[6]:

אֶת־הַגְּבָרִים וְאֶת־הַנָּשִׁים וְאֶת־הַטַּף וְאֶת־בְּנוֹת הַמֶּלֶךְ וְאֵת כָּל־הַנֶּפֶשׁ אֲשֶׁר הִנִּיחַ נְבוּזַרְאֲדָן רַב־טַבָּחִים אֶת־גְּדַלְיָהוּ בֶּן־אֲחִיקָם בֶּן־שָׁפָן וְאֵת יִרְמְיָהוּ הַנָּבִיא וְאֶת־בָּרוּךְ בֶּן־נֵרִיָּהוּ

6[7] the men, and the women, and the children, and the king's daughters, and every person who Nebuzaradan *the captain of the guard*[8] left with Gedaliah *the son of Ahikam, the son of Shaphan*[9], and Jeremiah the prophet, and Baruch the son of Neriah;

וַיָּבֹאוּ אֶרֶץ מִצְרַיִם כִּי לֹא שָׁמְעוּ בְּקוֹל יְהוָה וַיָּבֹאוּ עַד־תַּחְפַּנְחֵס

7[10] and they went into the land of Egypt; for they did not listen to the voice of the LORD; and they came to Tahpanhes.

וַיְהִי דְבַר־יְהוָה אֶל־יִרְמְיָהוּ בְּתַחְפַּנְחֵס לֵאמֹר

8[11] Then the word of the LORD came to Jeremiah in Tahpanhes, saying:

קַח בְּיָדְךָ אֲבָנִים גְּדֹלוֹת וּטְמַנְתָּם בַּמֶּלֶט בַּמַּלְבֵּן אֲשֶׁר בְּפֶתַח בֵּית־פַּרְעֹה בְּתַחְפַּנְחֵס לְעֵינֵי אֲנָשִׁים יְהוּדִים

9[12] 'Take great stones in your hand, and hide them *in the mortar in the framework, which is at the entry of Pharaoh's house in Tahpanhes*[13], in the sight of the men of Judah;

וְאָמַרְתָּ אֲלֵיהֶם כֹּה־אָמַר יְהוָה צְבָאוֹת אֱלֹהֵי יִשְׂרָאֵל הִנְנִי שֹׁלֵחַ וְלָקַחְתִּי אֶת־נְבוּכַדְרֶאצַּר מֶלֶךְ־בָּבֶל עַבְדִּי וְשַׂמְתִּי כִסְאוֹ מִמַּעַל לָאֲבָנִים הָאֵלֶּה אֲשֶׁר טָמָנְתִּי וְנָטָה אֶת־"שַׁפְרוּרוֹ" "אֶת־שַׁפְרִירוֹ" עֲלֵיהֶם

10[14] and say to them: Thus says the LORD of hosts, the God of Israel: Behold, I will send and take *Nebuchadrezzar*[15] the king of Babylon, My servant, and will set his throne on these stones I have hidden; and he shall spread his royal pavilion over them.

"וּבָאָה" "וּבָא" וְהִכָּה אֶת־אֶרֶץ מִצְרָיִם אֲשֶׁר לַמָּוֶת לַמָּוֶת וַאֲשֶׁר לַשְּׁבִי לַשֶּׁבִי וַאֲשֶׁר לַחֶרֶב לֶחָרֶב

11[16] And he shall come, and shall strike the land of Egypt; such as are for death to death, and such as are for captivity to captivity, and such as are for the sword to the sword.

---

[1] Jeremiah 43:4 - 2 Chronicles 1:16, Ecclesiastes 9:16, Jehochanan is altered to read Jochanan, Jeremiah 42:5-6 42:10-13 20:5, Psalms 37:3

[2] Missing in 4QJerd LXX

[3] Jeremiah 43:5 - 1 Samuel 2:19, Jehochanan reads Jochanan here, Jeremiah 40:11-12 41:15-16

[4] Missing in 4QJerd LXX

[5] Missng in LXX

[6] 4QJerd *away*; Missing in LXX

[7] Jeremiah 43:6 - 4 Baruch 3:15 4:12 4:6, Ecclesiastes 9:1-9:2, Jeremiah 15:10 16:7 17:10 4:10, John 21:18, Lamentations 3:1 Jeremiah 43:6-7 - 2 Baruch 10:2

[8] Missing in 4QJerd LXX

[9] Missing in 4QJerd LXX

[10] Jeremiah 43:7 - 2 Chronicles 1:16, Ezekiel 6:18, Isaiah 6:4, Jeremiah 2:16 20:1 22:14, Lives of the Prophets 2:1

[11] Jeremiah 43:8 - 2 Timothy 2:9, Jeremiah 2:16, Lives of the Prophets 2:2, Psalms 19:7
Jeremiah 43:8-11 - 2QJer
Jeremiah 43:8-13 - Josephus Antiquities 10.9.7

[12] Jeremiah 43:9 - 1 Kings 11:29-11:31, 2 Samuel 12:31, Acts 21:11, Exodus 1:14, Ezekiel 4:1-5:17 12:3-12:16, Hosea 12:12, Isaiah 20:1-20:4, Jeremiah 13:1-13:11 18:2-18:12 19:1-19:15 51:63-51:64, Nahum 3:14, Revelation 18:21

[13] 4QJerd *in the clay in the brick pavement of Pharaoh's palace that is at the entrance of Tahpanhes*; LXX *In the doorway at the entrance of Pharaoh's house of Tahpanhes*

[14] Jeremiah 43:10 - 1 Kings 20:12 20:16, b.Sanhedrin 105a, Daniel 2:21 5:18-5:19, Ezekiel 29:18-29:20, Isaiah 44:28-45:1, Jeremiah 1:15 25:6-25:26 27:6-27:8 46:27-46:28, Matthew 22:7, Midrash Psalms 79:1, Pesikta Rabbati 29/30:1, Psalms 18:12 27:5 31:21, z.Vaetchanan 269b

[15] 2QJer *Nebuchadnezzar*

[16] Jeremiah 43:11 - Ezekiel 5:12 29:19-29:20 30:1-30:26, Isaiah 19:1-19:25, Jeremiah 15:2 1:19 20:13 46:1-46:26, Job 20:29, Mas.Soferim 7:2, Numbers.R 9:49, Pesikta de R'Kahana 13.7 13.8, Zechariah 11:9

וְהִצַּ֤תִּי אֵשׁ֙ בְּבָתֵּי֙ אֱלֹהֵ֣י מִצְרַ֔יִם וּשְׂרָפָ֖ם וְשָׁבָ֑ם וְעָטָה֩ אֶת־אֶ֨רֶץ מִצְרַ֜יִם כַּאֲשֶׁר־יַעְטֶ֤ה הָֽרֹעֶה֙ אֶת־ בִּגְד֔וֹ וְיָצָ֥א מִשָּׁ֖ם בְּשָׁלֽוֹם

12[1] And I will kindle a fire in the houses of the gods of Egypt; and he shall burn them, and carry them away captives; and *he shall fold up the land of Egypt*[2], as a shepherd folds up his garment; and he shall go forth from there in peace.

וְשִׁבַּ֗ר אֶת־מַצְּבוֹת֙ בֵּ֣ית שֶׁ֔מֶשׁ אֲשֶׁ֖ר בְּאֶ֣רֶץ מִצְרָ֑יִם וְאֶת־בָּתֵּ֥י אֱלֹהֵֽי־מִצְרַ֖יִם יִשְׂרֹ֥ף בָּאֵֽשׁ

13[3] He shall also break the pillars of *Beth shemesh, that is in the land of Egypt; and he shall burn the houses of the gods of Egypt*[4] with fire.'

Jeremiah – Chapter 44[5]

הַדָּבָר֙ אֲשֶׁ֣ר הָיָ֣ה אֶֽל־יִרְמְיָ֔הוּ אֶ֥ל כָּל־הַ֨יְּהוּדִ֔ים הַיֹּשְׁבִ֖ים בְּאֶ֣רֶץ מִצְרָ֑יִם הַיֹּשְׁבִ֤ים בְּמִגְדֹּל֙ וּבְתַחְפַּנְחֵ֣ס וּבְנֹ֔ף וּבְאֶ֥רֶץ פַּתְר֖וֹס לֵאמֹֽר

1[6] The word that came to Jeremiah concerning all the Jews who lived in the land of Egypt, who dwelt at Migdol, and at Tahpanhes, and at Noph[7], and in the country of Pathros, saying:

כֹּה־אָמַ֞ר יְהוָ֤ה צְבָאוֹת֙ אֱלֹהֵ֣י יִשְׂרָאֵ֔ל אַתֶּ֣ם רְאִיתֶ֗ם אֵ֤ת כָּל־הָֽרָעָה֙ אֲשֶׁ֤ר הֵבֵ֨אתִי֙ עַל־יְר֣וּשָׁלִַ֔ם וְעַ֖ל כָּל־ עָרֵ֣י יְהוּדָ֑ה וְהִנָּ֤ם חָרְבָּה֙ הַיּ֣וֹם הַזֶּ֔ה וְאֵ֥ין בָּהֶ֖ם יוֹשֵֽׁב

2[8] 'Thus says the LORD of hosts, the God of Israel: You have seen all the evil I brought upon Jerusalem, and upon all the cities of Judah; and, behold, this day they are desolate, and *no one dwells in it*[9];

מִפְּנֵ֣י רָעָתָ֗ם אֲשֶׁ֤ר עָשׂוּ֙ לְהַכְעִסֵ֔נִי לָלֶ֨כֶת֙ לְקַטֵּ֔ר לַעֲבֹ֖ד לֵאלֹהִ֣ים אֲחֵרִ֑ים אֲשֶׁר֙ לֹ֣א יְדָע֔וּם הֵ֖מָּה אַתֶּ֥ם וַאֲבֹתֵיכֶֽם

3[10] Because of their wickedness they committed to provoke Me, in that they went to offer, and to serve other gods, whom they never knew, *neither they, nor you, nor your fathers*[11].

וָאֶשְׁלַ֤ח אֲלֵיכֶם֙ אֶת־כָּל־עֲבָדַ֣י הַנְּבִיאִ֔ים הַשְׁכֵּ֥ים וְשָׁלֹ֖חַ לֵאמֹ֑ר אַל־נָ֣א תַעֲשׂ֗וּ אֵ֛ת דְּבַר־הַתֹּעֵבָ֥ה הַזֹּ֖את אֲשֶׁ֥ר שָׂנֵֽאתִי

4[12] Yet I sent to you all My servants the prophets, sending them often and often, saying: Oh, do not do this abominable thing that I hate.

וְלֹ֤א שָׁמְעוּ֙ וְלֹֽא־הִטּ֣וּ אֶת־אָזְנָ֔ם לָשׁ֖וּב מֵרָֽעָתָ֑ם לְבִלְתִּ֥י קַטֵּ֖ר לֵאלֹהִ֥ים אֲחֵרִֽים

5[13] But they did not listed, nor inclined their ear to turn from their wickedness, to abstain from offering to other gods.

וַתִּתַּ֤ךְ חֲמָתִי֙ וְאַפִּ֔י וַתִּבְעַר֙ בְּעָרֵ֣י יְהוּדָ֔ה וּבְחֻצ֖וֹת יְרֽוּשָׁלִָ֑ם וַתִּהְיֶ֛ינָה לְחָרְבָּ֥ה לִשְׁמָמָ֖ה כַּיּ֥וֹם הַזֶּֽה

6[14] So My fury and My anger was poured forth, and was kindled in the cities of Judah and in the streets of Jerusalem; and they are wasted and desolate, as this day.

---

[1] Jeremiah 43:12 - 2 Samuel 5:21, Colossians 3:12 3:14, Ephesians 4:24 6:11, Esther 6:9, Exodus 12:12, Ezekiel 6:13, Isaiah 19:1 21:9 22:1 1:18 4:1 11:17 13:5 13:10, Jeremiah 22:25 24:7 2:2 3:44, Job 16:10, Psalms 8:2 109:18-19 12:16 12:18, Romans 13:12, Song of Songs.R 1:43, Zephaniah 2:11

[2] LXX *and shall search the land of Egypt*

[3] Jeremiah 43:13 - Isaiah 19:18, Joseph and Aseneth 1:2

[4] LXX *Heliopolis that are in On, and shall burn their houses*

[5] Chapter 51 in LXX

[6] Jeremiah 44:1 - Exodus 14:2, Ezekiel 5:10 5:14 6:14 6:16 6:18, Genesis 10:14, Isaiah 11:11 19:13, Jeremiah 2:16 42:15-18 43:5-8 22:14 22:19
Jeremiah 44:1-3 - 2QJer

[7] Missing in LXX

[8] Jeremiah 44:2 - 2 Kings 21:13, Deuteronomy 5:1, Exodus 19:4, Isaiah 6:11 24:12 64:11-12, Jeremiah 4:7 7:34 9:12 1:11 10:22 39:1-8 20:22, Joshua 23:3, Lamentations 1:1 1:16 5:18, Leviticus 26:32-33 2:43, Micah 3:12, z.Vaetchanan 269b, Zechariah 1:6

[9] Missing in 2QJer

[10] Jeremiah 44:3 - Daniel 9:5, Deuteronomy 13:7 5:25 8:17, Ezekiel 8:17-18 9:9 22:25-31, Ezra 9:6-11, Jeremiah 2:17-19 4:17-18 5:19 5:29 7:19 9:13-15 11:17 16:11-12 19:3-4 22:9 20:8, Lamentations 1:8 4:13, Nehemiah 9:33, Zechariah 7:12-13

[11] LXX Missing in LXX

[12] Jeremiah 44:4 - 1 Peter 4:3, 2 Chronicles 12:15, Ezekiel 8:10 16:36 16:47, Jeremiah 7:13 7:25 16:18 25:3-25:4 2:5 5:19 8:33 11:17, Revelation 17:4-17:5, Zechariah 7:7

[13] Jeremiah 44:5 - 2 Chronicles 12:16, Isaiah 24:4 24:18, Jeremiah 7:24 11:8 11:10 19:13 44:17-44:21, Psalms 81:12-81:14, Revelation 2:21-2:22, Zechariah 7:11-7:12

[14] Jeremiah 44:6 - Daniel 9:12, Ezekiel 5:13 6:12 8:18 20:33 24:8 24:13, Isaiah 6:11 3:17 3:20, Jeremiah 4:4 7:20 7:34 21:5 21:12 12:7 18:18 44:2-44:3, Leviticus 2:28, Nahum 1:2

וְעַתָּ֞ה כֹּֽה־אָמַ֣ר יְהֹוָה֩ אֱלֹהֵ֨י צְבָא֜וֹת אֱלֹהֵ֣י יִשְׂרָאֵ֗ל לָמָה֩ אַתֶּ֨ם עֹשִׂ֜ים רָעָ֤ה גְדוֹלָה֙ אֶל־נַפְשֹׁ֣תֲכֶ֔ם לְהַכְרִ֨ית לָכֶ֧ם אִישׁ־וְאִשָּׁ֛ה עוֹלֵ֥ל וְיוֹנֵ֖ק מִתּ֣וֹךְ יְהוּדָ֑ה לְבִלְתִּ֥י הוֹתִ֛יר לָכֶ֖ם שְׁאֵרִֽית	7[1]	Therefore, now thus says the LORD, the God of hosts, the God of Israel: Why do you commit this great evil against your own souls, to cut off man and woman, infant and suckling, from the midst of Judah, to leave no one remaining;
לְהַכְעִסֵ֙נִי֙ בְּמַעֲשֵׂ֣י יְדֵיכֶ֔ם לְקַטֵּ֛ר לֵאלֹהִ֥ים אֲחֵרִ֖ים בְּאֶ֣רֶץ מִצְרַ֔יִם אֲשֶׁר־אַתֶּ֥ם בָּאִ֖ים לָג֣וּר שָׁ֑ם לְמַ֙עַן֙ הַכְרִ֣ית לָכֶ֔ם וּלְמַ֤עַן הֱיֽוֹתְכֶם֙ לִקְלָלָ֣ה וּלְחֶרְפָּ֔ה בְּכֹ֖ל גּוֹיֵ֥י הָאָֽרֶץ	8[2]	in that you provoke Me with the works of your hands, offering to other gods in the land of Egypt, where you went to sojourn; so you may be cut off, and that you may be a curse and a reproach among all the nations of the earth?
הַֽשְׁכַחְתֶּם֩ אֶת־רָע֨וֹת אֲבֽוֹתֵיכֶ֜ם וְאֶת־רָע֣וֹת ׀ מַלְכֵ֣י יְהוּדָ֗ה וְאֵת֙ רָע֣וֹת נָשָׁ֔יו וְאֵת֙ רָעֹ֣תֵכֶ֔ם וְאֵ֖ת רָעֹ֣ת נְשֵׁיכֶ֑ם אֲשֶׁ֤ר עָשׂוּ֙ בְּאֶ֣רֶץ יְהוּדָ֔ה וּבְחֻצ֖וֹת יְרֽוּשָׁלָֽםִ	9[3]	Have you forgotten the wicked deeds of your fathers, and the wicked deeds of the kings of Judah, and *the wicked deeds of their wives*[4], and your own wicked deeds, and the wicked deeds of your wives, which they committed in the land of Judah, and in the streets of Jerusalem?
לֹ֣א דֻכְּא֔וּ עַ֖ד הַיּ֣וֹם הַזֶּ֑ה וְלֹ֤א יָֽרְאוּ֙ וְלֹא־הָלְכ֣וּ בְתֽוֹרָתִ֗י וּבְחֻקֹּתַי֙ אֲשֶׁר־נָתַ֣תִּי לִפְנֵיכֶ֔ם וְלִפְנֵ֖י אֲבֽוֹתֵיכֶֽם	10[5]	*To this day they are not humbled, nor have they feared, nor walked in My law, nor in My statutes*[6], as I set before you and before your fathers.
לָכֵ֗ן כֹּֽה־אָמַ֞ר יְהֹוָ֤ה צְבָאוֹת֙ אֱלֹהֵ֣י יִשְׂרָאֵ֔ל הִנְנִ֨י שָׂ֥ם פָּנַ֛י בָּכֶ֖ם לְרָעָ֑ה וּלְהַכְרִ֖ית אֶת־כׇּל־יְהוּדָֽה	11[7]	Therefore, thus says the LORD of hosts, the God of Israel: Behold, I will set My face against you *for evil, to cut off all Judah*[8].
וְלָקַחְתִּ֞י אֶת־שְׁאֵרִ֣ית יְהוּדָ֗ה אֲשֶׁר־שָׂ֨מוּ פְנֵיהֶ֜ם לָב֣וֹא אֶֽרֶץ־מִצְרַיִם֮ לָג֣וּר שָׁם֒ וְתַ֙מּוּ֙ כֹ֣ל בְּאֶ֣רֶץ מִצְרַ֔יִם יִפֹּ֕לוּ בַּחֶ֥רֶב בָּרָעָ֖ב יִתַּ֑מּוּ מִקָּטֹן֙ וְעַד־גָּד֔וֹל בַּחֶ֥רֶב וּבָרָעָ֖ב יָמֻ֑תוּ וְהָיוּ֙ לְאָלָ֣ה לְשַׁמָּ֔ה וְלִקְלָלָ֖ה וּלְחֶרְפָּֽה	12[9]	*And I will take the remnant of Judah, who set their faces to go into the land of Egypt to sojourn there, and they shall all be consumed; in the land of Egypt shall they fall*[10]; they shall be consumed by the sword and by famine; they shall die, from the least to the great, *by the sword and by famine; and they shall be an execration, and an astonishment, and a curse, and a reproach*[11].
וּפָקַדְתִּ֗י עַ֤ל הַיּֽוֹשְׁבִים֙ בְּאֶ֣רֶץ מִצְרַ֔יִם כַּֽאֲשֶׁ֥ר פָּקַ֖דְתִּי עַל־יְרוּשָׁלָ֑͏ִם בַּחֶ֥רֶב בָּרָעָ֖ב וּבַדָּֽבֶר	13[12]	For I will punish those who live in the land of Egypt, as I punished Jerusalem, by the sword, by famine, and *by pestilence*[13];

---

[1] Jeremiah 44:7 - 1 Samuel 15:3 22:19, Deuteronomy 8:25, Ezekiel 9:11, Habakkuk 2:10, Jeremiah 7:19 9:22 1:7 2:19 18:20 20:8 44:11-44:12 20:14 44:27-44:28 3:22, Josephus Wars 6.9.1, Joshua 6:21, Judges 21:11, Lamentations 2:11, Numbers 17:3, Proverbs 1:18 5:22 8:36 15:32, z.Vaetchanan 269b

[2] Jeremiah 44:8 - 1 Corinthians 10:21-10:22, 1 Kings 9:7-9:8, 2 Chronicles 7:20, 2 Kings 17:15-17:17, Deuteronomy 32:16-32:17, Ezekiel 18:31-18:32, Hebrews 3:16, Isaiah 3:8 17:15, Jeremiah 18:16 24:9 25:6-25:7 2:6 5:18 18:18 20:3 20:7 20:12, Lamentations 2:15-2:16

[3] Jeremiah 44:9 - Daniel 9:5-8, Ezra 9:7-15, Jeremiah 7:17-18 44:15-19 20:21, Joshua 22:17-20

[4] Missing in LXX

[5] Jeremiah 44:10 - 1 Kings 21:29, 1 Peter 5:6, 2 Chronicles 12:6-12:12 8:26 9:12 9:19 10:27, 2 Kings 22:19, Daniel 5:20-5:22, Ecclesiastes 8:12-8:13, Exodus 9:17 9:30 10:3, Ezekiel 9:4, Isaiah 9:15 18:2, James 4:6-4:10, Jeremiah 8:12 10:7 12:24, Luke 23:40, Malachi 3:20, Matthew 3:54, Proverbs 8:13 14:16 16:6 4:14, Psalms 34:19 51:18, Revelation 15:4, Romans 11:20

[6] LXX *And have not ceased to this day, and they have not kept to my ordinances*

[7] Jeremiah 44:11 - Amos 9:4, Ezekiel 14:7-8 15:7, Jeremiah 21:10, Leviticus 17:10 20:5-6 2:17, Psalms 34:17, z.Vaetchanan 269b

[8] Missing in LXX

[9] Jeremiah 44:12 - Hosea 4:6, Isaiah 1:28 17:15, Jeremiah 18:16 5:18 5:22 42:15-18 18:22 44:7-8 Jeremiah 44:12-14 - 2QJer

[10] LXX *to destroy all the remnant who are in Egypt*

[11] LXX *and they shall be for reproach, and for destruction, and for a curse*

[12] Jeremiah 44:13 - Jeremiah 11:22 21:9 24:10 18:18 19:11 44:27-44:28

[13] Missing in LXX

וְלֹא יִהְיֶה פָּלִיט וְשָׂרִיד לִשְׁאֵרִית יְהוּדָה הַבָּאִים
לָגוּר־שָׁם בְּאֶרֶץ מִצְרַיִם וְלָשׁוּב אֶרֶץ יְהוּדָה
אֲשֶׁר־הֵמָּה מְנַשְּׂאִים אֶת־נַפְשָׁם לָשׁוּב לָשֶׁבֶת שָׁם
כִּי לֹא־יָשׁוּבוּ כִּי אִם־פְּלֵטִים

14 [1] so no one of the remnant of Judah, who went into the land of Egypt to sojourn, shall escape or remain, that they should return into the land of Judah, to which they have a desire to return to live there; for no one shall return save those who escape.'

וַיַּעֲנוּ אֶת־יִרְמְיָהוּ כָּל־הָאֲנָשִׁים הַיֹּדְעִים כִּי־
מְקַטְּרוֹת נְשֵׁיהֶם לֵאלֹהִים אֲחֵרִים וְכָל־הַנָּשִׁים
הָעֹמְדוֹת קָהָל גָּדוֹל וְכָל־הָעָם הַיֹּשְׁבִים בְּאֶרֶץ־
מִצְרַיִם בְּפַתְרוֹס לֵאמֹר

15 [2] Then all the men who knew that their wives offered to other gods, and all the women who stood by, a great assembly, all the people who lived in Pathros in the land of Egypt answered Jeremiah, saying:

הַדָּבָר אֲשֶׁר־דִּבַּרְתָּ אֵלֵינוּ בְּשֵׁם יְהוָה אֵינֶנּוּ
שֹׁמְעִים אֵלֶיךָ

16 [3] 'As for the word you have spoken to us in the name of the LORD, we will not listen to you.

כִּי עָשֹׂה נַעֲשֶׂה אֶת־כָּל־הַדָּבָר אֲשֶׁר־יָצָא מִפִּינוּ
לְקַטֵּר לִמְלֶכֶת הַשָּׁמַיִם וְהַסֵּיךְ־לָהּ נְסָכִים כַּאֲשֶׁר
עָשִׂינוּ אֲנַחְנוּ וַאֲבֹתֵינוּ מְלָכֵינוּ וְשָׂרֵינוּ בְּעָרֵי
יְהוּדָה וּבְחֻצוֹת יְרוּשָׁלַם וַנִּשְׂבַּע־לֶחֶם וַנִּהְיֶה
טוֹבִים וְרָעָה לֹא רָאִינוּ

17 [4] But we will certainly perform every word that comes forth from our mouth, to offer[5] to the queen of heaven, and to pour drink offerings to her, as we have done, we and our fathers, our kings and our princes, in the cities of Judah, and in the streets of Jerusalem; for then had we plenty of food, and were well, and saw no evil.

וּמִן־אָז חָדַלְנוּ לְקַטֵּר לִמְלֶכֶת הַשָּׁמַיִם וְהַסֵּךְ־לָהּ
נְסָכִים חָסַרְנוּ כֹל וּבַחֶרֶב וּבָרָעָב תָּמְנוּ

18 [6] But since we stopped offering to the queen of heaven, and to pour out drink offerings to her, we have wanted all things, and have been consumed by the sword and by famine.

וְכִי־אֲנַחְנוּ מְקַטְּרִים לִמְלֶכֶת הַשָּׁמַיִם וּלְהַסֵּךְ לָהּ
נְסָכִים הֲמִבַּלְעֲדֵי אֲנָשֵׁינוּ עָשִׂינוּ לָהּ כַּוָּנִים
לְהַעֲצִבָה וְהַסֵּךְ לָהּ נְסָכִים

19 [7] And is it we who offer to the queen of heaven, and pour out drink offerings to her? Did we make cakes in her image, and pour out drink offerings to her, without our husbands?'

וַיֹּאמֶר יִרְמְיָהוּ אֶל־כָּל־הָעָם עַל־הַגְּבָרִים וְעַל־
הַנָּשִׁים וְעַל־כָּל־הָעָם הָעֹנִים אֹתוֹ דָּבָר לֵאמֹר

20 [8] Then Jeremiah said to all the people, to the men, and to the women, to all the people who gave an answer, saying:

הֲלוֹא אֶת־הַקִּטֵּר אֲשֶׁר קִטַּרְתֶּם בְּעָרֵי יְהוּדָה
וּבְחֻצוֹת יְרוּשָׁלַם אַתֶּם וַאֲבוֹתֵיכֶם מַלְכֵיכֶם
וְשָׂרֵיכֶם וְעַם הָאָרֶץ אֹתָם זָכַר יְהוָה וַתַּעֲלֶה עַל־
לִבּוֹ

21 [9] 'The offering you offered in the cities of Judah, and in the streets of Jerusalem, you and your fathers, your kings and your princes, and the people of the land, did not the LORD remember them, and did it not come into His mind?

וְלֹא־יוּכַל יְהוָה עוֹד לָשֵׂאת מִפְּנֵי רֹעַ מַעַלְלֵיכֶם
מִפְּנֵי הַתּוֹעֵבֹת אֲשֶׁר עֲשִׂיתֶם וַתְּהִי אַרְצְכֶם
לְחָרְבָּה וּלְשַׁמָּה וְלִקְלָלָה מֵאֵין יוֹשֵׁב כְּהַיּוֹם הַזֶּה

22 [10] So the LORD could no longer bear, because of the evil of your deeds, and because of the abominations you committed; therefore, your land has become desolate, and an

---

[1] Jeremiah 44:14 - Hebrews 2:3, Isaiah 4:2 10:20 30:1-3, Jeremiah 22:26-27 18:17 18:22 44:27-28, Matthew 23:33, Romans 2:3 9:27 11:5-6

[2] Jeremiah 44:15 - 2 Peter 2:1-2:2, Genesis 19:4, Isaiah 1:5, Jeremiah 5:1-5:5, Matthew 7:13, Nehemiah 13:26, Proverbs 11:21

[3] Jeremiah 44:16 - Daniel 3:15, Exodus 5:2, Isaiah 3:9, Jeremiah 8:6 8:12 11:8 11:10 16:15-16:17 18:18 14:4, Job 15:25-15:27 21:14-21:15, Luke 19:14 19:27, Psalms 2:3 73:8-73:9

[4] Jeremiah 44:17 - 1 Peter 1:18, 2 Kings 17:16 22:17, b.Shabbat 152a, Daniel 9:5-9:8, Deuteronomy 23:25, Ein Yaakov Shabbat:152b, Exodus 16:3, Ezekiel 20:8, Hosea 2:5-2:11, Isaiah 24:5, Jeremiah 7:18 19:13 32:29-32:32 20:9 20:21 20:25, Judges 11:36, Mark 6:26, Nehemiah 9:34, Numbers 6:4 6:14, Philippians 3:19, Psalms 12:5 10:6

[5] LXX adds *incense*

[6] Jeremiah 44:18 - Jeremiah 16:12, Job 21:14-21:15, Malachi 3:13-3:15, Numbers 11:5-11:6, Psalms 73:9-73:15

[7] Jeremiah 44:19 - 1 Kings 21:25, 2 Chronicles 21:6, Deuteronomy 7:3-7:4, Genesis 3:6 3:11-3:12 3:16-3:17, Jeremiah 7:18 20:15, Mark 6:19-6:27, Numbers 30:8-30:7, Proverbs 11:21

[8] Jeremiah 44:20 - Jastrow 910a

[9] Jeremiah 44:21 - 1 Kings 17:18, 1 Samuel 15:3, Amos 8:7, Ezekiel 8:10-8:11 16:24 21:28-21:29, Hosea 7:2, Isaiah 16:10, Jeremiah 11:13 14:10 20:9 20:17, Psalms 79:8, Revelation 16:19 18:5

[10] Jeremiah 44:22 - 1 Kings 9:7-9:8, 2 Peter 3:7-3:9, Amos 2:13, Daniel 9:12, Ezekiel 5:13, Genesis 6:3 6:5-6:7 19:13, Isaiah 1:24 7:13 19:24, Jeremiah 15:6 18:16 24:9 1:11 1:18 1:38 2:6 5:19 20:2 20:6 20:12, Lamentations 2:15-2:16, Malachi 2:17, Psalms 95:10-95:11 107:33-34, Romans 2:4-5 9:22

astonishment, and a curse, without an inhabitant, as is this day.

מִפְּנֵי אֲשֶׁר קִטַּרְתֶּם וַאֲשֶׁר חֲטָאתֶם לַיהֹוָה וְלֹא שְׁמַעְתֶּם בְּקוֹל יְהֹוָה וּבְתֹרָתוֹ וּבְחֻקֹּתָיו וּבְעֵדְוֹתָיו לֹא הֲלַכְתֶּם עַל־כֵּן קָרָאת אֶתְכֶם הָרָעָה הַזֹּאת כַּיּוֹם הַזֶּה

23[1] Because you offered, and because you sinned against the LORD, and have not listened to the voice of the LORD, nor walked in His law, nor in His statutes, nor in His testimonies; therefore, this evil has happened to you, *as is this day*[2].'

וַיֹּאמֶר יִרְמְיָהוּ אֶל־כָּל־הָעָם וְאֶל כָּל־הַנָּשִׁים שִׁמְעוּ דְּבַר־יְהֹוָה כָּל־יְהוּדָה אֲשֶׁר בְּאֶרֶץ מִצְרָיִם

24[3] Moreover, Jeremiah said to all the people, and to all the women: 'Hear the word of the LORD, *all Judah who are in the land of Egypt*[4]:

כֹּה־אָמַר יְהֹוָה־צְבָאוֹת אֱלֹהֵי יִשְׂרָאֵל לֵאמֹר אַתֶּם וּנְשֵׁיכֶם וַתְּדַבֵּרְנָה בְּפִיכֶם וּבִידֵיכֶם מִלֵּאתֶם לֵאמֹר עָשֹׂה נַעֲשֶׂה אֶת־נְדָרֵינוּ אֲשֶׁר נָדַרְנוּ לְקַטֵּר לִמְלֶכֶת הַשָּׁמַיִם וּלְהַסֵּךְ לָהּ נְסָכִים הָקֵים תָּקִימְנָה אֶת־נִדְרֵיכֶם וְעָשֹׂה תַעֲשֶׂינָה אֶת־נִדְרֵיכֶם

25[5] Thus says the LORD of hosts, the God of Israel, saying: *You and your wives*[6] have both spoken with your mouths, and with your hands have fulfilled it, saying: We will surely perform the vows that we have vowed, to offer to the queen of heaven, and to pour out drink offerings to her; you shall surely establish your vows, and surely perform your vows.

לָכֵן שִׁמְעוּ דְבַר־יְהֹוָה כָּל־יְהוּדָה הַיֹּשְׁבִים בְּאֶרֶץ מִצְרָיִם הִנְנִי נִשְׁבַּעְתִּי בִּשְׁמִי הַגָּדוֹל אָמַר יְהֹוָה אִם־יִהְיֶה עוֹד שְׁמִי נִקְרָא בְּפִי כָּל־אִישׁ יְהוּדָה אֹמֵר חַי־אֲדֹנָי יְהֹוִה בְּכָל־אֶרֶץ מִצְרָיִם

26[7] Therefore, hear the word of the LORD, all Judah who live in the land of Egypt: Behold, I swear by My great name, says the LORD, that My name shall no longer be named in the mouth of anyone of Judah in all the land of Egypt saying: As the Lord GOD lives.

הִנְנִי שֹׁקֵד עֲלֵיהֶם לְרָעָה וְלֹא לְטוֹבָה וְתַמּוּ כָל־אִישׁ יְהוּדָה אֲשֶׁר בְּאֶרֶץ־מִצְרַיִם בַּחֶרֶב וּבָרָעָב עַד־כְּלוֹתָם

27[8] Behold, I watch over them for evil, and not for good; and all the men of Judah who are in the land of Egypt shall be consumed by the sword and by famine, until there be an end of them.

וּפְלִיטֵי חֶרֶב יְשֻׁבוּן מִן־אֶרֶץ מִצְרַיִם אֶרֶץ יְהוּדָה מְתֵי מִסְפָּר וְיָדְעוּ כָּל־שְׁאֵרִית יְהוּדָה הַבָּאִים לְאֶרֶץ־מִצְרַיִם לָגוּר שָׁם דְּבַר־מִי יָקוּם מִמֶּנִּי וּמֵהֶם

28[9] And they who escape the sword shall return from the land of Egypt into the land of Judah, few in number; and all the remnant of Judah, who went into the land of Egypt to sojourn, shall know whose word shall stand, mine, *or theirs*[10].

וְזֹאת־לָכֶם הָאוֹת נְאֻם־יְהֹוָה כִּי־פֹקֵד אֲנִי עֲלֵיכֶם בַּמָּקוֹם הַזֶּה לְמַעַן תֵּדְעוּ כִּי קוֹם יָקוּמוּ דְבָרַי עֲלֵיכֶם לְרָעָה

29[11] And this shall be the sign to you, *says the LORD, I will punish you in this place, so you may know that My words shall surely stand against you for evil*[12];

[1] Jeremiah 44:23 - 1 Corinthians 10:20, 1 Kings 9:9, 2 Chronicles 12:16, 2 Corinthians 6:16, Daniel 9:11-9:12, Jeremiah 7:13-7:15 32:31-32:33 16:3 20:8 20:18 20:21, Lamentations 1:8, Nehemiah 13:18, Psalms 78:56 119:150 119:155
[2] Missing in LXX
[3] Jeremiah 44:24 - 1 Kings 22:19, Amos 7:16, Ezekiel 2:7 20:32-20:33, Isaiah 1:10 4:14, Jeremiah 18:15 19:7 44:15-44:16 20:26, Matthew 11:15
[4] Missing in LXX
[5] Jeremiah 44:25 - Acts 23:12-23:15, Ezekiel 20:39, Isaiah 4:15, James 1:14-1:15, Jeremiah 44:15-44:19, Job 10:22, Jude 1:13, Matthew 14:9, z.Vaetchanan 269b
[6] LXX *you women*
[7] Jeremiah 44:26 - Amos 6:8 6:10 8:7, Deuteronomy 32:40-32:42, Ezekiel 20:39, Genesis 22:16, Hebrews 3:18 6:13 6:18, Isaiah 48:1-48:2 14:8, Jeremiah 4:2 5:2 7:9 22:5 22:18, Numbers 14:21-14:23 14:28, Psalms 50:16 89:35, Zephaniah 1:4-1:5
[8] Jeremiah 44:27 - 2 Kings 21:14, Ezekiel 7:6, Jeremiah 1:10 21:10 7:29 20:12 20:18
[9] Jeremiah 44:28 - Isaiah 10:19 10:22 14:24-14:27 27:12-27:13 28:16-28:18 46:10-46:11, Jeremiah 20:14 44:16-44:17 44:25-44:26 20:29, Lamentations 3:37-3:38, Matthew 24:35, Numbers 14:28-14:29 14:41, Psalms 33:11, Zechariah 1:6
[10] Missing in LXX
[11] Jeremiah 44:29 - 1 Samuel 2:34, Isaiah 16:8, Jeremiah 20:30, Luke 21:20-21:21 21:29-21:33, Mark 13:14-13:16, Matthew 24:15-24:16 24:32-24:34, Proverbs 19:21
[12] LXX *that I will visit you for evil*

כֹּה אָמַר יְהֹוָה הִנְנִי נֹתֵן אֶת־פַּרְעֹה חָפְרַע מֶלֶךְ־
מִצְרַיִם בְּיַד אֹיְבָיו וּבְיַד מְבַקְשֵׁי נַפְשׁוֹ כַּאֲשֶׁר
נָתַתִּי אֶת־צִדְקִיָּהוּ מֶלֶךְ־יְהוּדָה בְּיַד נְבוּכַדְרֶאצַּר
מֶלֶךְ־בָּבֶל אֹיְבוֹ וּמְבַקֵּשׁ נַפְשׁוֹ

30[1]

Thus says the LORD: Behold, I will give *Pharaoh Hophra*[2] king of Egypt into the hand of his enemies, and into the hand of those who seek his life; as I gave Zedekiah king of Judah into the hand of Nebuchadrezzar king of Babylon, his enemy, and who sought his life.'

Jeremiah – Chapter 45[3]

הַדָּבָר אֲשֶׁר דִּבֶּר יִרְמְיָהוּ הַנָּבִיא אֶל־בָּרוּךְ בֶּן־
נֵרִיָּה בְּכָתְבוֹ אֶת־הַדְּבָרִים הָאֵלֶּה עַל־סֵפֶר מִפִּי
יִרְמְיָהוּ בַּשָּׁנָה הָרְבִעִית לִיהוֹיָקִים בֶּן־יֹאשִׁיָּהוּ
מֶלֶךְ יְהוּדָה לֵאמֹר

1[4]

The word that Jeremiah the prophet spoke to Baruch the son of Neriah, when he wrote these words in a book at the mouth of Jeremiah, in the fourth year of Jehoiakim the son of Josiah, king of Judah, saying:

כֹּה־אָמַר יְהֹוָה אֱלֹהֵי יִשְׂרָאֵל עָלֶיךָ בָּרוּךְ

2[5]

'Thus says the LORD, the God of Israel, concerning you, O Baruch: you did say:

אָמַרְתָּ אוֹי־נָא לִי כִּי־יָסַף יְהֹוָה יָגוֹן עַל־מַכְאֹבִי
יָגַעְתִּי בְּאַנְחָתִי וּמְנוּחָה לֹא מָצָאתִי

3[6]

Woe is me now! For the LORD has added sorrow to my pain; I am weary with my groaning, and I find no rest.

כֹּה תֹּאמַר אֵלָיו כֹּה אָמַר יְהֹוָה הִנֵּה אֲשֶׁר־בָּנִיתִי
אֲנִי הֹרֵס וְאֵת אֲשֶׁר־נָטַעְתִּי אֲנִי נֹתֵשׁ וְאֶת־כָּל־
הָאָרֶץ הִיא

4[7]

Thus shall you say to him: Thus says the LORD: Behold, what I have built will I break down, and what I have planted I will pluck up; and *this in the whole land*[8].

וְאַתָּה תְּבַקֶּשׁ־לְךָ גְדֹלוֹת אַל־תְּבַקֵּשׁ כִּי הִנְנִי מֵבִיא
רָעָה עַל־כָּל־בָּשָׂר נְאֻם־יְהֹוָה וְנָתַתִּי לְךָ אֶת־נַפְשְׁךָ
לְשָׁלָל עַל כָּל־הַמְּקֹמוֹת אֲשֶׁר תֵּלֶךְ־שָׁם

5[9]

And you seek great things for yourself? Do not seek them; for, behold, I will bring evil on all flesh, says the LORD; but your life I will give to you as prey in all places you go.'

Jeremiah – Chapter 46[10]

אֲשֶׁר הָיָה דְבַר־יְהֹוָה אֶל־יִרְמְיָהוּ הַנָּבִיא עַל־
הַגּוֹיִם

1[11]

The word of the LORD came to Jeremiah the prophet concerning the nations[12].

לְמִצְרַיִם עַל־חֵיל פַּרְעֹה נְכוֹ מֶלֶךְ מִצְרַיִם אֲשֶׁר־
הָיָה עַל־נְהַר־פְּרָת בְּכַרְכְּמִשׁ אֲשֶׁר הִכָּה
נְבוּכַדְרֶאצַּר מֶלֶךְ בָּבֶל בִּשְׁנַת הָרְבִעִית לִיהוֹיָקִים
בֶּן־יֹאשִׁיָּהוּ מֶלֶךְ יְהוּדָה

2[13]

Of Egypt: concerning the army of Pharaoh-neco king of Egypt, which was by the river Euphrates in Carchemish, that the king of Babylon, Nebuchadrezzar, struck in the fourth

---

[1] Jeremiah 44:30 - 2 Kings 25:4-7, Exodus.R 8:2, Ezekiel 29:1-21 6:21 31:18-32, Jeremiah 10:21 39:5-7 43:9-13 46:13-26 52:8-11, Midrash Tanchuma Vaera 9, z.Vaetchanan 269b
Jeremiah 44:30-51:30 [LXX] - Eupolemus 30:4
[2] LXX *Uaphres*
[3] Chapter 52:1-5 in LXX
[4] Jeremiah 45:1 - 2 Baruch 1:1, 2 Chronicles 12:5, Jeremiah 1:1 2:1 8:12 8:16 12:1 12:4 36:8-36:9 36:14-36:18 12:26 12:32 43:3-43:6
[5] Jeremiah 45:2 - 2 Corinthians 1:4 7:6, Hebrews 2:18 4:15, Isaiah 15:9, Mark 16:7, z.Vaetchanan 269b
Jeremiah 45:2-5 - 4 Baruch 7:25
[6] Jeremiah 45:3 - 2 Corinthians 4:1 4:16, 2 Thessalonians 3:13, Galatians 6:9, Genesis 37:34-37:35 42:36-42:38, Hebrews 12:3-12:5, Jeremiah 8:18 9:2 15:10-15:21 20:7-20:18, Job 16:11-16:13 23:2, Joshua 7:7-7:9, Lamentations 1:13 1:22 3:1-3:19 3:32, Mekilta de R'Ishmael Pisha 1:149, Mekilta de R'Ishmael Pisha 1:153, Midrash Tanchuma Vayechi 11, Numbers 11:11-11:15, Numbers.R 9:31, Proverbs 24:10, Psalms 6:7 27:13 42:8 69:4 77:4-77:5 24:5, y.Ketubot 2:9, y.Sotah 1:3
[7] Jeremiah 45:4 - Genesis 6:6-6:7, Guide for the Perplexed 2:32, Isaiah 5:2-5:7, Jeremiah 1:10 11:17 18:7-18:10 7:29, Psalms 80:9-80:17, z.Vaetchanan 269b
Jeremiah 45:4-5 - Mekilta de R'Ishmael Pisha 1:157-159
[8] Missing in LXX
[9] Jeremiah 45:5 - 1 Corinthians 7:26-7:32, 1 Timothy 6:6-6:9, 2 Kings 5:26, Genesis 6:12, Guide for the Perplexed 2:32, Hebrews 13:5, Isaiah 18:16, Jeremiah 21:9 1:26 14:2 15:18, Matthew 6:25-6:32, Mekilta de R'Ishmael Pisha 1:163, Romans 12:16, Zephaniah 3:8
[10] Chapter 26 in LXX
[11] Jeremiah 46:1 - Genesis 10:5, Jeremiah 1:10 4:7 25:15-38, Numbers 23:9, Romans 3:29, Zechariah 2:8
Jeremiah 46:1-2 - Seder Olam 24:Jehoachaz
[12] LXX *In the beginning of the reign of king Sedekias, there came this word concerning Ælam*
[13] Jeremiah 46:2 - 2 Chronicles 35:20-35:21, 2 Kings 23:29, b.Chullin [Rashi] 92a, b.Yoma 32b, Ezekiel 29:1-29:21, Isaiah 10:9, Jeremiah 1:1 1:9 1:19 12:1 21:1 22:14

עִרְכוּ מָגֵן וְצִנָּה וּגְשׁוּ לַמִּלְחָמָה

אִסְרוּ הַסּוּסִים וַעֲלוּ הַפָּרָשִׁים וְהִתְיַצְּבוּ בְּכוֹבָעִים מִרְקוּ הָרְמָחִים לִבְשׁוּ הַסִּרְיֹנֹת

מַדּוּעַ רָאִיתִי הֵמָּה חַתִּים נְסֹגִים אָחוֹר וְגִבּוֹרֵיהֶם יֻכַּתּוּ וּמָנוֹס נָסוּ וְלֹא הִפְנוּ מָגוֹר מִסָּבִיב נְאֻם־יְהוָה

אַל־יָנוּס הַקַּל וְאַל־יִמָּלֵט הַגִּבּוֹר צָפוֹנָה עַל־יַד נְהַר־פְּרָת כָּשְׁלוּ וְנָפָלוּ

מִי־זֶה כַּיְאֹר יַעֲלֶה כַּנְּהָרוֹת יִתְגָּעֲשׁוּ מֵימָיו

מִצְרַיִם כַּיְאֹר יַעֲלֶה וְכַנְּהָרוֹת יִתְגֹּעֲשׁוּ מָיִם וַיֹּאמֶר אַעֲלֶה אֲכַסֶּה־אֶרֶץ אֹבִידָה עִיר וְיֹשְׁבֵי בָהּ

עֲלוּ הַסּוּסִים וְהִתְהֹלְלוּ הָרֶכֶב וְיֵצְאוּ הַגִּבּוֹרִים כּוּשׁ וּפוּט תֹּפְשֵׂי מָגֵן וְלוּדִים תֹּפְשֵׂי דֹּרְכֵי קָשֶׁת

וְהַיּוֹם הַהוּא לַאדֹנָי יְהוִה צְבָאוֹת יוֹם נְקָמָה לְהִנָּקֵם מִצָּרָיו וְאָכְלָה חֶרֶב וְשָׂבְעָה וְרָוְתָה מִדָּמָם כִּי זֶבַח לַאדֹנָי יְהוִה צְבָאוֹת בְּאֶרֶץ צָפוֹן אֶל־נְהַר־פְּרָת

עֲלִי גִלְעָד וּקְחִי צֳרִי בְּתוּלַת בַּת־מִצְרָיִם לַשָּׁוְא 'הִרְבֵּיתִי' "הִרְבֵּית" רְפֻאוֹת תְּעָלָה אֵין לָךְ

שָׁמְעוּ גוֹיִם קְלוֹנֵךְ וְצִוְחָתֵךְ מָלְאָה הָאָרֶץ כִּי־גִבּוֹר בְּגִבּוֹר כָּשָׁלוּ יַחְדָּיו נָפְלוּ שְׁנֵיהֶם

year of Jehoiakim the son of Josiah, *king of Judah*[1].

3[2] *Make ready buckler and shield*[3], and draw near to battle.

4[4] Harness the horses, and mount, you horsemen, and stand forth with your helmets; Furbish the spears, put on the coats of mail.

5[5] Why do I see them dismayed and turned back? And their mighty ones are beaten down, and *they flee quickly, and do not look back; Terror is on every side*[6], says the LORD.

6[7] The swift cannot flee, nor the mighty man escape; in the north by the river Euphrates they stumbled and fall.

7[8] Who is this *like the Nile who rises up, like the rivers whose waters toss themselves*[9]?

8[10] *Egypt is like the Nile that rises up, and like the rivers whose waters toss themselves*[11]; and he says: 'I will rise up, I will cover the earth, I will destroy the city and its inhabitants.'

9[12] *Prance, you horses, and rush madly, you chariots; and let the mighty men go forth: Cush and Put, who handle the shield, and the Ludim, who handle and* [13]bend the bow.

10[14] For the Lord GOD of hosts shall have on that day, a day of vengeance, so He may avenge His adversaries; and the sword shall devour and be satiated, and shall be made drunk with their blood; for the Lord GOD of hosts has a sacrifice in the north country by the river Euphrates.

11[15] Go into Gilead, and use balm, O virgin daughter of Egypt; in vain you use many medicines; there is no cure for you.

12[16] The nations have heard of your shame, and the earth is full of your cry; for the mighty man stumbled against the mighty, They both fall together.

---

[1] Missing in LXX

[2] Jeremiah 46:3 - Isaiah 8:9-10 21:5, Jeremiah 51:11-12, Joel 4:9, Nahum 2:2 3:14

[3] LXX *Take up arms and spears*

[4] Jeremiah 46:4 - 1 Samuel 17:5 17:38, 2 Chronicles 2:14, Ezekiel 21:14-16 21:33, Jeremiah 3:3, Nehemiah 4:16

[5] Jeremiah 46:5 - 2 Kings 7:6-7:7, Ezekiel 8:10, Genesis 19:17, Isaiah 19:16, Jeremiah 6:25 20:3-20:4 20:10 22:15 22:21 1:29, Nahum 2:9, Revelation 6:15-6:17

[6] LXX *they have utterly fled, and being hemmed in they have not rallied*

[7] Jeremiah 46:6 - Amos 2:14-2:15 9:1-9:3, Daniel 11:19 11:22, Ecclesiastes 9:11, Isaiah 8:15 30:16-30:17, Jeremiah 1:14 4:6 6:1 20:11 1:9 22:10 22:12 22:16 2:32, Judges 4:15-4:21, Psalms 27:2 33:16-33:17 147:10-147:11

[8] Jeremiah 46:7 - Amos 8:8, Daniel 9:26 11:22, Isaiah 8:7-8:8 15:1, Jeremiah 23:2, Revelation 12:15, Song of Songs 3:6 8:5

[9] LXX *that shall come up as a river, and as rivers roll their waves*

[10] Jeremiah 46:8 - Exodus 15:9-15:10, Ezekiel 5:3 8:2, Isaiah 10:13-10:16 37:24-37:26

[11] LXX *The waters of Egypt shall come up like a river*

[12] Jeremiah 46:9 - 1 Chronicles 1:11, 1 Corinthians 1:8, Acts 2:10, Ezekiel 3:10, Genesis 10:6 10:13, Isaiah 18:19, Jeremiah 6:5 23:3, Nahum 2:4-5 3:9

[13] LXX *Mount the horses, prepare the chariots; go forth, you warriors of the Ethiopians, and Libyans armed with shields; and mount, you Lydians*

[14] Jeremiah 46:10 - 2 Kings 24:7, Deuteronomy 8:42, Ezekiel 39:17-21, Isaiah 13:6 34:5-8 13:2 15:4, Jeremiah 22:2 22:6 2:15 3:6, Joel 1:15 2:1, Luke 21:22, Revelation 19:17-21, Zephaniah 1:7-8 1:14-15

[15] Jeremiah 46:11 - Ezekiel 3:17 30:21-25, Genesis 13:25 19:11, Isaiah 23:1, Jeremiah 8:22 14:17 30:12-15 3:8, Luke 8:43-44, Matthew 5:26, Micah 1:9, Nahum 3:19

[16] Jeremiah 46:12 - 1 Samuel 5:12, Ezekiel 32:9-12, Isaiah 10:4 15:5-8 19:2, Jeremiah 14:2 22:6 24:34 1:21 3:54, Nahum 3:8-10, Zephaniah 1:10

הַדָּבָר אֲשֶׁר דִּבֶּר יְהוָה אֶל־יִרְמְיָהוּ הַנָּבִיא לָבוֹא נְבוּכַדְרֶאצַּר מֶלֶךְ בָּבֶל לְהַכּוֹת אֶת־אֶרֶץ מִצְרָיִם	13[1]	The word the LORD spoke to Jeremiah the prophet, how Nebuchadrezzar king of Babylon should come and strike the land of Egypt.
הַגִּידוּ בְמִצְרַיִם וְהַשְׁמִיעוּ בְמִגְדּוֹל וְהַשְׁמִיעוּ בְנֹף וּבְתַחְפַּנְחֵס אִמְרוּ הִתְיַצֵּב וְהָכֵן לָךְ כִּי־אָכְלָה חֶרֶב סְבִיבֶיךָ	14[2]	*Declare in Egypt, and announce in Migdol, and announce in Noph and in Tahpanhes; Say: 'Stand forth, and prepare, for the sword has devoured around you[3].'*
מַדּוּעַ נִסְחַף אַבִּירֶיךָ לֹא עָמַד כִּי יְהוָה הֲדָפוֹ	15[4]	*Why is your strong one overthrown? He did not stand, because the LORD thrust him down[5].*
הִרְבָּה כּוֹשֵׁל גַּם־נָפַל אִישׁ אֶל־רֵעֵהוּ וַיֹּאמְרוּ קוּמָה וְנָשֻׁבָה אֶל־עַמֵּנוּ וְאֶל־אֶרֶץ מוֹלַדְתֵּנוּ מִפְּנֵי חֶרֶב הַיּוֹנָה	16[6]	He made many to stumble; yes, they fell one upon another, and said: 'Arise, and let us return to our people, and to the land of our birth, from the *oppressing[7]* sword.'
קָרְאוּ שָׁם פַּרְעֹה מֶלֶךְ־מִצְרַיִם שָׁאוֹן הֶעֱבִיר הַמּוֹעֵד	17[8]	They cried there: 'Pharaoh [9]king of Egypt *is but a noise; he let the appointed time pass by[10].'*
חַי־אָנִי נְאֻם־הַמֶּלֶךְ יְהוָה צְבָאוֹת שְׁמוֹ כִּי כְּתָבוֹר בֶּהָרִים וּכְכַרְמֶל בַּיָּם יָבוֹא	18[11]	As I live, says *the King, Whose name is the LORD of hosts[12]*, surely like *Tabor[13]* among the mountains, and like Carmel by the sea, so shall he come.
כְּלֵי גוֹלָה עֲשִׂי לָךְ יוֹשֶׁבֶת בַּת־מִצְרָיִם כִּי־נֹף לְשַׁמָּה תִהְיֶה וְנִצְּתָה מֵאֵין יוֹשֵׁב	19[14]	O you daughter who dwells in Egypt, furnish yourself to go into captivity; for *Noph shall become desolate, and shall be laid waste[15]*, without inhabitant.
עֶגְלָה יְפֵה־פִיָּה מִצְרָיִם קֶרֶץ מִצָּפוֹן בָּא בָא	20[16]	Egypt is a very fair heifer; but the *gadfly[17]* from the north came, it came.
גַּם־שְׂכִרֶיהָ בְקִרְבָּהּ כְּעֶגְלֵי מַרְבֵּק כִּי־גַם־הֵמָּה הִפְנוּ נָסוּ יַחְדָּיו לֹא עָמָדוּ כִּי יוֹם אֵידָם בָּא עֲלֵיהֶם עֵת פְּקֻדָּתָם	21[18]	Also her mercenaries in her midst are like calves of the stall, for they turned back, they fled away together, they did not stand; for the day of their calamity came upon them, the time of their visitation.

---

[1] Jeremiah 46:13 - Isaiah 19:1-19:25 29:1-24, Jeremiah 43:10-13 20:30
Jeremiah 46:13-28 - Haftarah Bo [Ashkenaz and Sephard]
[2] Jeremiah 46:14 - 2 Samuel 2:26, Exodus 14:2, Ezekiel 30:16-18, Isaiah 1:20 7:8 10:6, Jeremiah 2:30 6:1-5 12:12 43:8-9 20:1 46:3-4 22:10, Joel 4:9-12, Nahum 2:14
[3] LXX *Proclaim it at Magdol, and declare it at Memphis: say, Stand up, and prepare; for the sword has devoured your yew-tree*
[4] Jeremiah 46:15 - Deuteronomy 11:23, Exodus 6:1, Isaiah 66:15-16, Jastrow 971b, Jeremiah 22:5 22:21, Judges 5:20-21, Lives of the Prophets 2:8, Midrash Tanchuma Tazria 11, Psalms 18:15 18:40 44:3 68:3 114:2-7
[5] LXX *Wherefore has Apis fled from you? Your choice calf has not remained; for the LORD has utterly weakened him*
[6] Jeremiah 46:16 - Jeremiah 22:6 22:21 2:16 3:9, Leviticus 26:36-37
[7] LXX *Grecian*
[8] Jeremiah 46:17 - 1 Kings 20:10 20:18, b.Moed Katan 16a, Exodus 15:9, Ezekiel 5:3 7:18, Isaiah 19:11-19:16 7:3 37:27-37:29, Sifre Devarim {Vezot Habracha} 356
[9] LXX adds *Nechao*
[10] LXX *Saon esbeie moed*
[11] Jeremiah 46:18 - 1 Kings 18:42-18:43, 1 Timothy 1:17, b.Megillah 29a, Genesis.R 99 [Excl]:1, Isaiah 23:4 24:2, Jastrow 671b, Jeremiah 10:10 20:26 24:15 3:17, Joshua 19:22, Judges 4:6, Malachi 1:14, Matthew 5:35, Mekilta de R'Ishmael Bahodesh 5:43, Midrash Psalms 68:9, Psalms 89:13
[12] LXX *the LORD God*
[13] LXX *Itabyrion*
[14] Jeremiah 46:19 - Ezekiel 12:3-12:12 6:13, Isaiah 20:4, Jastrow 139b, Jeremiah 2:9 10:22 20:1 24:18 51:29-51:30, z.Shemot 6b, Zephaniah 2:5
[15] LXX *Memphis shall be utterly desolate, and shall be called Woe*
[16] Jeremiah 46:20 - Genesis.R 20:5, Hosea 10:11, Jastrow 729a 1278b 1425a, Jeremiah 1:14 1:9 22:6 22:10 22:24 23:2 2:11, Pesikta de R'Kahana 4.9, Pesikta Rabbati 14:2, y.Yoma 3:4, z.Vayigash 210b
[17] LXX *destruction*
[18] Jeremiah 46:21 - 2 Kings 7:6, 2 Samuel 10:6, Amos 6:4, Deuteronomy 8:15, Ezekiel 27:10-27:11 30:4-30:6 11:5, Hosea 9:7, Isaiah 10:3 10:7, Jeremiah 18:17 22:5 22:9 46:15-46:16 2:11 2:27, Micah 7:4, Obadiah 1:13, Proverbs 15:17, Psalms 37:13
Jeremiah 46:21-28 - Philo Quaestiones et Solutiones in Genesin I 100

קוֹלָהּ כַּנָּחָשׁ יֵלֵךְ כִּי־בְחַיִל יֵלֵכוּ וּבְקַרְדֻּמּוֹת בָּאוּ לָהּ כְּחֹטְבֵי עֵצִים

22[1] Its sound shall go like the serpent's; for they march with an army, and come against her with axes, as hewers of wood.

כָּרְתוּ יַעְרָהּ נְאֻם־יְהֹוָה כִּי לֹא יֵחָקֵר כִּי רַבּוּ מֵאַרְבֶּה וְאֵין לָהֶם מִסְפָּר

23[2] They cut down her forest, says the LORD, though it cannot be searched; because they are more than the locusts, and are innumerable.

הֹבִישָׁה בַּת־מִצְרָיִם נִתְּנָה בְּיַד עַם־צָפוֹן

24[3] The daughter of Egypt is put to shame; she is delivered into the hand of the people of the north.

אָמַר יְהֹוָה צְבָאוֹת אֱלֹהֵי יִשְׂרָאֵל הִנְנִי פוֹקֵד אֶל־אָמוֹן מִנֹּא וְעַל־פַּרְעֹה וְעַל־מִצְרַיִם וְעַל־אֱלֹהֶיהָ וְעַל־מְלָכֶיהָ וְעַל־פַּרְעֹה וְעַל הַבֹּטְחִים בּוֹ

25[4] *The LORD of hosts, the God of Israel, says: Behold, I will punish Amon of No, and Pharaoh, and Egypt, with her gods, and her kings; Pharaoh[5], and those who trust in him;*

וּנְתַתִּים בְּיַד מְבַקְשֵׁי נַפְשָׁם וּבְיַד נְבוּכַדְרֶאצַּר מֶלֶךְ־בָּבֶל וּבְיַד־עֲבָדָיו וְאַחֲרֵי־כֵן תִּשְׁכֹּן כִּימֵי־קֶדֶם נְאֻם־יְהֹוָה

26[6] *and I will deliver them into the hand of those who seek their lives, and into the hand of Nebuchadrezzar king of Babylon, and into the hand of his servants; and afterward it shall be inhabited, as in the days of old, says the LORD[7].*

וְאַתָּה אַל־תִּירָא עַבְדִּי יַעֲקֹב וְאַל־תֵּחַת יִשְׂרָאֵל כִּי הִנְנִי מוֹשִׁעֲךָ מֵרָחוֹק וְאֶת־זַרְעֲךָ מֵאֶרֶץ שִׁבְיָם וְשָׁב יַעֲקוֹב וְשָׁקַט וְשַׁאֲנַן וְאֵין מַחֲרִיד

27[8] But fear not, O Jacob My servant, neither be dismayed, O Israel; For, lo, I will save you from afar, and your seed from the land of their captivity; and Jacob shall again be quiet and at ease, and no one shall make him afraid.

אַתָּה אַל־תִּירָא עַבְדִּי יַעֲקֹב נְאֻם־יְהֹוָה כִּי אִתְּךָ אָנִי כִּי אֶעֱשֶׂה כָלָה בְּכָל־הַגּוֹיִם אֲשֶׁר הִדַּחְתִּיךָ שָּׁמָּה וְאֹתְךָ לֹא־אֶעֱשֶׂה כָלָה וְיִסַּרְתִּיךָ לַמִּשְׁפָּט וְנַקֵּה לֹא אֲנַקֶּךָּ

28[9] Fear not, O Jacob My servant, says the LORD, for I am with you; for I will make a full end of all the nations where I have driven you, but I will not make a full end of you; and *I will correct you in measure, but will not utterly destroy you[10].*

Jeremiah – Chapter 47[11]

אֲשֶׁר הָיָה דְבַר־יְהֹוָה אֶל־יִרְמְיָהוּ הַנָּבִיא אֶל־פְּלִשְׁתִּים בְּטֶרֶם יַכֶּה פַרְעֹה אֶת־עַזָּה

1[12] *The word of the LORD that came to Jeremiah the prophet concerning the Philistines, before that Pharaoh smote Gaza[13].*

---

[1] Jeremiah 46:22 - Ecclesiastes.R 10:12, Esther.R Petichata:5, Exodus.R 9:3, Genesis.R 20:5, Guide for the Perplexed 1:24, Isaiah 10:15 10:33-10:34 14:8 5:4 13:24, Jeremiah 51:20-51:23, Micah 1:8 7:16, Midrash Psalms 18:11 120:4, Midrash Tanchuma Vaera 4, z.Bamidbar 119b, Zechariah 11:2

[2] Jeremiah 46:23 - Ezekiel 21:2, Isaiah 10:18, Joel 2:25, Judges 6:5 7:12, Revelation 9:2-9:10

[3] Jeremiah 46:24 - Ezekiel 29:1-29:21, Jeremiah 1:15 22:11 46:19-46:20, Psalms 17:8

[4] Jeremiah 46:25 - Exodus 12:12, Ezekiel 30:13-30:16 32:9-32:12 39:6-39:7, Isaiah 19:1 20:5-20:6 30:2-30:3 31:1-31:3, Jeremiah 17:5-17:6 42:14-42:16 43:12-43:13, Nahum 3:8-3:9, z.Beshallach 49a, Zephaniah 2:11

[5] LXX *Behold, I will avenge Ammon her son upon Pharao*

[6] Jeremiah 46:26 - Ezekiel 29:8-29:14 8:11, Jeremiah 20:30 24:47 1:39

[7] Missing in LXX

[8] Jeremiah 46:27 - Amos 9:14, Ezekiel 34:10-34:14 34:25-34:26 12:24 37:21-37:22 15:25, Isaiah 11:11-11:16 41:13-41:14 19:1 19:5 20:2, Jeremiah 23:3-23:4 23:6 5:14 30:10-30:11 31:9-31:12 8:37 9:16 2:19, Micah 7:11-7:16, z.Toledot 145b Jeremiah 46:27-28 - 2QJer, z.Toledot 145b

[9] Jeremiah 46:28 - 1 Corinthians 11:32, 2 Timothy 4:17, Acts 18:10, Amos 9:8-9:9, Daniel 2:35, Habakkuk 3:2, Hebrews 12:5-12:10, Isaiah 8:9-8:10 3:7 3:9 17:10 19:2 21:23, Jeremiah 1:19 4:27 5:10 5:18 10:24 15:20 1:9 6:11 32:42-32:44 33:24-33:26, Joshua 1:5 1:9, Matthew 1:23 4:20, Numbers.R 10:2, Psalms 46:8 46:12, Revelation 3:19, Romans 11:15-11:17, z.Vayechi 249a

[10] LXX *yet will I chastise you in the way of judgment, and will not hold you entirely guiltless*

[11] Chapter 29:1-7 in LXX

[12] Jeremiah 47:1 - 1 Kings 4:24, Amos 1:6-1:8, Exodus 25:15-25:17, Genesis 10:19, Jeremiah 1:20, Saadia Opinions 7Variant:5, Zechariah 9:5-9:7, Zephaniah 2:4-2:7 Jeremiah 47:1-7 - 2QJer

[13] LXX *Thus says the LORD against the Philistines*

כֹּה ׀ אָמַר יְהֹוָה הִנֵּה־מַיִם עֹלִים מִצָּפוֹן וְהָיוּ לְנַחַל שׁוֹטֵף וְיִשְׁטְפוּ אֶרֶץ וּמְלוֹאָהּ עִיר וְיֹשְׁבֵי בָהּ וְזָעֲקוּ הָאָדָם וְהֵילִל כֹּל יוֹשֵׁב הָאָרֶץ

2 1 *Thus says the LORD*[2]: Behold, waters rise up from the north, and shall become an overflowing stream, and they shall overflow the land and all that is in it, the city and those who live in it; and the men shall cry, and all the inhabitants of the land shall wail.

מִקּוֹל שַׁעֲטַת פַּרְסוֹת אַבִּירָיו מֵרַעַשׁ לְרִכְבּוֹ הֲמוֹן גַּלְגִּלָּיו לֹא־הִפְנוּ אָבוֹת אֶל־בָּנִים מֵרִפְיוֹן יָדָיִם

3 3 At the noise of the stamping of the hoofs of his strong ones, at the rushing of his chariots, at the rumbling of his wheels, the fathers do not look back to their children for feebleness of hands;

עַל־הַיּוֹם הַבָּא לִשְׁדוֹד אֶת־כָּל־פְּלִשְׁתִּים לְהַכְרִית לְצֹר וּלְצִידוֹן כֹּל שָׂרִיד עֹזֵר כִּי־שֹׁדֵד יְהֹוָה אֶת־פְּלִשְׁתִּים שְׁאֵרִית אִי כַפְתּוֹר

4 4 Because of the day that comes, to spoil all the Philistines, *to cut off*[5] from Tyre and Zidon every helper who remains; for the LORD will spoil the Philistines, the remnant of the *isle of Caphtor*[6].

בָּאָה קָרְחָה אֶל־עַזָּה נִדְמְתָה אַשְׁקְלוֹן שְׁאֵרִית עִמְקָם עַד־מָתַי תִּתְגּוֹדָדִי

5 7 Baldness came on Gaza, Ashkelon is brought to nothing, the remnant of their valley; *how long will you cut yourself*[8]?

הוֹי חֶרֶב לַיהֹוָה עַד־אָנָה לֹא תִשְׁקֹטִי הֵאָסְפִי אֶל־תַּעְרֵךְ הֵרָגְעִי וָדֹמִּי

6 9 [10]O you sword of the LORD, how long will it be before you are quiet? Put up yourself into your scabbard. Rest, and be still.

אֵיךְ תִּשְׁקֹטִי וַיהֹוָה צִוָּה־לָהּ אֶל־אַשְׁקְלוֹן וְאֶל־חוֹף הַיָּם שָׁם יְעָדָהּ

7 11 How can you be quiet? For the LORD has given it a charge; against Ashkelon, against the seashore, there He has appointed it.

Jeremiah – Chapter 48

לְמוֹאָב כֹּה־אָמַר יְהֹוָה צְבָאוֹת אֱלֹהֵי יִשְׂרָאֵל הוֹי אֶל־נְבוֹ כִּי שֻׁדָּדָה הֹבִישָׁה נִלְכְּדָה קִרְיָתָיִם הֹבִישָׁה הַמִּשְׂגָּב וָחָתָּה

1 12 Of Moab. Thus says the LORD of hosts, the God of Israel: Woe to Nebo! for it is spoiled; Kiriathaim is put to shame, it is taken; *Misgab is put to shame and dismayed*[13].

אֵין עוֹד תְּהִלַּת מוֹאָב בְּחֶשְׁבּוֹן חָשְׁבוּ עָלֶיהָ רָעָה לְכוּ וְנַכְרִיתֶנָּה מִגּוֹי גַּם־מַדְמֵן תִּדֹּמִּי אַחֲרַיִךְ תֵּלֶךְ חָרֶב

2 14 The praise of Moab has ended; in Heshbon they devised evil against her: 'Come, and let us cut her off from being a nation.' *You also, O Madmen*[15], shall be brought to silence; the sword shall pursue you.

---

[1] Jeremiah 47:2 - 1 Corinthians 10:26 10:28, Amos 9:5-9:6, Daniel 11:22, Isaiah 8:7-8:8 14:31 15:2-15:5 15:8 22:1 22:4-22:5 4:17 11:19, James 5:1, Jeremiah 1:14 8:16 46:6-46:8 22:13 22:20 48:3-48:5 24:39, Nahum 1:8, Psalms 24:1 50:12 96:11 98:7, Revelation 12:15-12:16 17:1 17:15, Saadia Opinions 7:4 7Variant:5, z.Vaetchanan 269b, Zephaniah 1:10-1:11

[2] Missing in LXX

[3] Jeremiah 47:3 - b.Bechorot 5b, b.Sanhedrin 16a, Deuteronomy 28:54-28:55, Ezekiel 26:10-26:11, Jeremiah 8:16 22:9, Job 39:19-39:25, Judges 5:22, Lamentations 4:3-4:4, Nahum 2:5 3:2-3:3

[4] Jeremiah 47:4 - 1 Chronicles 1:12, Amos 1:8-1:10 9:7, Deuteronomy 2:23, Ezekiel 7:5-7:7 7:12 21:30 21:34 1:16 26:1-26:21 6:8, Genesis 10:13-10:14, Hosea 9:7, Isaiah 10:3 20:6 23:1-23:18 7:8, Jeremiah 25:20-25:22 22:10, Job 9:13, Joel 4:4-4:8, Joshua 22:30, Jubilees 8:21, Luke 21:22, Psalms 37:13, Zechariah 9:2-9:5

[5] 2QJer LXX *and I will cut off*

[6] LXX *islands*

[7] Jeremiah 47:5 - 1 Kings 18:28, Amos 1:6-1:8, Deuteronomy 14:1, Ezekiel 7:18 1:16, Isaiah 15:2, Jeremiah 16:1 1:20 17:5 23:1 23:4 24:37, Judges 1:18, Leviticus 19:28 21:5, Mark 5:5, Micah 1:16, Zechariah 9:5-9:7, Zephaniah 2:4-2:7

[8] 2QJer *How long will you scratch yourself*; Missing in LXX

[9] Jeremiah 47:6 - 1 Chronicles 21:27, 2 Samuel 2:26, Deuteronomy 32:41-42, Ezekiel 14:17 21:8-10 21:35, Isaiah 10:5 10:15, Jeremiah 4:21 12:4 12:12 15:3 1:27 51:20-23, John 18:11, Psalms 17:13

[10] LXX adds *How long will you smite*

[11] Jeremiah 47:7 - 1 Samuel 15:3, Amos 3:6, Ezekiel 14:17 1:16, Isaiah 10:6 13:3 13:26 45:1-3 46:10-11, Micah 6:9, Zephaniah 2:6-7

[12] Jeremiah 48:1 - 2 Chronicles 20:10, Amos 2:1-2:2, Ezekiel 25:8-25:11, Genesis 19:37, Isaiah 15:1-15:9 1:10 3:3, Jeremiah 9:27 1:21 3:3 48:22-48:23, Numbers 24:17 8:3 32:37-32:38 9:47, z.Vaetchanan 269b, Zephaniah 2:8-2:11

[13] LXX *Amath and Agath are put to shame*

[14] Jeremiah 48:2 - Esther 3:8-3:14, Isaiah 15:1 15:5 16:8-16:9 16:14 1:10, Jeremiah 1:15 1:17 7:37 9:24 22:28 24:17 48:34-48:35 24:42 24:45 1:3, Numbers 21:25-21:30 8:37, Psalms 83:5-83:9
Jeremiah 48:2-4 - 2QJer

[15] LXX *she*

קוֹל צְעָקָה מֵחֹרוֹנָיִם שֹׁד וָשֶׁבֶר גָּדוֹל	3[1]	Listen! a cry from Horonaim, spoiling and great destruction!
נִשְׁבְּרָה מוֹאָב הִשְׁמִיעוּ זְּעָקָה 'צְעוֹרֶיהָ' "צְעִירֶיהָ"	4[2]	Moab is destroyed; *her little ones have caused a cry to be heard*[3].
כִּי מַעֲלֵה 'הַלֻּחוֹת' "הַלּוּחִית" בִּבְכִי יַעֲלֶה־בֶּכִי כִּי בְּמוֹרַד חוֹרֹנַיִם צָרֵי צַעֲקַת־שֶׁבֶר שָׁמֵעוּ	5[4]	For by the ascent of Luhith[5] with continual weeping shall they go up; for in the going down of Horonaim, they heard the distressing cry of destruction.
נֻסוּ מַלְּטוּ נַפְשְׁכֶם וְתִהְיֶינָה כַּעֲרוֹעֵר בַּמִּדְבָּר	6[6]	Flee, save your lives, and be like a *tamarisk*[7] in the wilderness.
כִּי יַעַן בִּטְחֵךְ בְּמַעֲשַׂיִךְ וּבְאוֹצְרוֹתַיִךְ גַּם־אַתְּ תִּלָּכֵדִי וְיָצָא 'כְמִישׁ' "כְּמוֹשׁ" בַּגּוֹלָה כֹּהֲנָיו וְשָׂרָיו 'יַחַד' "יַחְדָּיו"	7[8]	For, because you have trusted in your *works and in your treasures*[9], you also shall be taken; and Chemosh shall go forth into captivity, his priests and his princes together.
וְיָבֹא שֹׁדֵד אֶל־כָּל־עִיר וְעִיר לֹא תִמָּלֵט וְאָבַד הָעֵמֶק וְנִשְׁמַד הַמִּישֹׁר אֲשֶׁר אָמַר יְהוָה	8[10]	And the spoiler shall come upon every city, and no city shall escape; the valley also shall perish, and the plain shall be destroyed; as the LORD has spoken.
תְּנוּ־צִיץ לְמוֹאָב כִּי נָצֹא תֵּצֵא וְעָרֶיהָ לְשַׁמָּה תִהְיֶינָה מֵאֵין יוֹשֵׁב בָּהֵן	9[11]	*Give wings to Moab, for she must fly and get away*[12]; and her cities shall become desolate, without anyone to live in it.
אָרוּר עֹשֶׂה מְלֶאכֶת יְהוָה רְמִיָּה וְאָרוּר מֹנֵעַ חַרְבּוֹ מִדָּם	10[13]	Cursed is he who does the work of the LORD with a slack hand, and cursed is he who keeps back his sword from blood.
שַׁאֲנַן מוֹאָב מִנְּעוּרָיו וְשֹׁקֵט הוּא אֶל־שְׁמָרָיו וְלֹא־הוּרַק מִכְּלִי אֶל־כֶּלִי וּבַגּוֹלָה לֹא הָלָךְ עַל־כֵּן עָמַד טַעְמוֹ בּוֹ וְרֵיחוֹ לֹא נָמָר	11[14]	Moab has been at ease from his youth, and he has settled on his lees, and has not been emptied from vessel to vessel, nor has he gone into captivity; therefore, his taste remains in him, and his scent has not changed.
לָכֵן הִנֵּה־יָמִים בָּאִים נְאֻם־יְהוָה וְשִׁלַּחְתִּי־לוֹ צֹעִים וְצֵעֻהוּ וְכֵלָיו יָרִיקוּ וְנִבְלֵיהֶם יְנַפֵּצוּ	12[15]	Therefore, behold, the days come, says the LORD, *That I will send to him those who tilt up, and they shall tilt him up; and they shall empty his vessels, and break their bottles in pieces*[16].

---

[1] Jeremiah 48:3 - Isaiah 15:2 15:5 15:8 16:7-16:11 22:4, Jeremiah 4:20-4:21 23:2 24:5 24:34

[2] Jeremiah 48:4 - Esther 8:11, Mas.Soferim 7:4, Numbers 21:27-21:30, Psalms 17:9

[3] LXX *proclaim it to Zogora*

[4] Jeremiah 48:5 - Isaiah 15:5, Mas.Soferim 7:4

[5] LXX *Aloth*

[6] Jeremiah 48:6 - Genesis 19:17, Hebrews 6:18, Jeremiah 17:6 3:6, Job 30:3-30:7, Luke 3:7 17:31-17:33, Matthew 24:16-24:18, Proverbs 6:4-6:5, Psalms 11:2

[7] LXX *wild ass*

[8] Jeremiah 48:7 - 1 Kings 11:7 11:33, 1 Timothy 6:17, 2QJer, Ezekiel 28:2-5, Hosea 10:13, Isaiah 46:1-2 59:4-6, Jeremiah 9:24 13:25 19:12 24:13 24:46 1:3, Judges 11:24, Mas.Soferim 7:1, Numbers 21:29, Psalms 40:5 49:7-8 52:8 62:9-11, Revelation 18:7

[9] LXX *stronghold*

[10] Jeremiah 48:8 - Ezekiel 1:9, Jeremiah 6:26 15:8 1:9 24:18 48:20-48:25 3:56, Joshua 13:9 13:17 13:21

[11] Jeremiah 48:9 - Isaiah 16:2, Jeremiah 22:19 24:28, Psalms 11:2 55:7, Revelation 12:14, Zephaniah 2:9

[12] LXX *Set marks upon Moab, for she shall be touched with a plague spot*

[13] Jeremiah 48:10 - 1 Kings 20:42, 1 Samuel 15:3 15:9 15:13-15:35, 2 Kings 13:19, b.Bava Batra 21b, Ecclesiastes.R 4:1, Ein Yaakov Bava Batra:21b, Jeremiah 23:6 2:25, Judges 5:23, mt.Hilchot Melachim uMichamoteihem 7:15, mt.Hilchot Talmud Torah 2:3, mt.Hilchot Talmud Torah 2:3, Numbers 31:14-31:18, Siman 165:12

[14] Jeremiah 48:11 - b.Beitzah [Rashi] 14a, b.Megillah 12b, b.Sanhedrin [Rashi] 109a, b.Shabbat [Rashi] 40b, b.Shabbat 145b, b.Yoma [Rashi] 31b, Ein Yaakov Megillah:12b, Ein Yaakov Shabbat:145b, Esther.R 4:1, Ezekiel 16:49-16:50, Guide for the Perplexed 1:13, Isaiah 16:6 24:3 1:6, Jastrow 289b, Jeremiah 24:29 3:34, Nahum 2:3 2:11, Pesikta de R'Kahana 12.22, Proverbs 1:32, Psalms 55:20 73:4-73:8 3:4, Tanya Igeret Hakodesh §12, Zechariah 1:15, Zephaniah 1:12

[15] Jeremiah 48:12 - b.Berachot [Rashi] 57b, Ezekiel 25:9-25:10, Isaiah 16:2 6:14, Jeremiah 14:3 19:10 1:9 1:34 24:8 24:11 24:15 24:38, Nahum 2:3, Psalms 2:9

[16] LXX *when I shall send upon him bad leaders, and they shall lead him astray, and they shall utterly break in pieces his possessions, and shall cut his horns asunder*

וּבֹשׁ מוֹאָב מִכְּמוֹשׁ כַּאֲשֶׁר־בֹּשׁוּ בֵּית יִשְׂרָאֵל מִבֵּית אֵל מִבְטֶחָם	13[1]	And Moab shall be ashamed of Chemosh, as the house of Israel was ashamed of Bethel, their confidence.
אֵיךְ תֹּאמְרוּ גִּבּוֹרִים אֲנָחְנוּ וְאַנְשֵׁי־חַיִל לַמִּלְחָמָה	14[2]	How can you say: 'We are mighty men, and valiant men for the war?'
שֻׁדַּד מוֹאָב וְעָרֶיהָ עָלָה וּמִבְחַר בַּחוּרָיו יָרְדוּ לַטָּבַח נְאֻם־הַמֶּלֶךְ יְהוָה צְבָאוֹת שְׁמוֹ	15[3]	Moab is spoiled, and they go up into her cities, and his chosen young men have gone down to the slaughter, *says the King, whose name is the LORD of hosts*[4].
קָרוֹב אֵיד־מוֹאָב לָבוֹא וְרָעָתוֹ מִהֲרָה מְאֹד	16[5]	The calamity of Moab is coming near, and his affliction hastens quickly.
נֻדוּ לוֹ כָּל־סְבִיבָיו וְכֹל יֹדְעֵי שְׁמוֹ אִמְרוּ אֵיכָה נִשְׁבַּר מַטֵּה־עֹז מַקֵּל תִּפְאָרָה	17[6]	Lament him, all who are around him, and all who know his name; Say: 'How is the strong staff broken, that beautiful rod!'
רְדִי מִכָּבוֹד "יֹשְׁבִי" "וּשְׁבִי" בַצָּמָא יֹשֶׁבֶת בַּת־דִּיבוֹן כִּי־שֹׁדֵד מוֹאָב עָלָה בָךְ שִׁחֵת מִבְצָרָיִךְ	18[7]	*O daughter who dwells in Dibon, come down from your glory, and sit in thirst; for the spoiler of Moab came up against you, he has destroyed your strongholds*[8].
אֶל־דֶּרֶךְ עִמְדִי וְצַפִּי יוֹשֶׁבֶת עֲרוֹעֵר שַׁאֲלִי־נָס וְנִמְלָטָה אִמְרִי מַה־נִּהְיָתָה	19[9]	O inhabitant of Aroer, stand by the way, and watch; ask he who flees, and she who escapes; say: 'What has been done?'
הֹבִישׁ מוֹאָב כִּי־חַתָּה "הֵילִילִי" "הֵילִילוּ" "וּזְעָקִי" "וּזְעָקוּ" הַגִּידוּ בְאַרְנוֹן כִּי שֻׁדַּד מוֹאָב	20[10]	Moab is put to shame, for it is dismayed; wail and cry; tell you it in Arnon, Moab is spoiled.
וּמִשְׁפָּט בָּא אֶל־אֶרֶץ הַמִּישֹׁר אֶל־חֹלוֹן וְאֶל־יַהְצָה "וְעַל־מוֹפָעַת" "וְעַל־מֵיפָעַת"	21[11]	And judgment came upon *the country of the Plain*; on Holon, and on Jahzah, and on Mephaath[12];
וְעַל־דִּיבוֹן וְעַל־נְבוֹ וְעַל־בֵּית דִּבְלָתָיִם	22[13]	and on Dibon, and on Nebo, and on Beth-diblathaim;
וְעַל קִרְיָתַיִם וְעַל־בֵּית גָּמוּל וְעַל־בֵּית מְעוֹן	23[14]	and on Kiriathaim, and on Beth-gamul, and on Beth-meon;
וְעַל־קְרִיּוֹת וְעַל־בָּצְרָה וְעַל כָּל־עָרֵי אֶרֶץ מוֹאָב הָרְחֹקוֹת וְהַקְּרֹבוֹת	24[15]	and on Kerioth, and on Bozrah, and on all the cities of the land of Moab, far or near.
נִגְדְּעָה קֶרֶן מוֹאָב וּזְרֹעוֹ נִשְׁבָּרָה נְאֻם יְהוָה	25[16]	The horn of Moab is cut off, and his arm is broken, says the LORD.

---

[1] Jeremiah 48:13 - 1 Kings 11:7 12:28-29 18:26-29 18:40, 1 Samuel 5:3-7, Amos 5:5-6, Hosea 8:5-6 10:5-6 10:14-15, Isaiah 2:20 16:12 21:16 21:20 46:1-2, Jeremiah 24:7 24:39 24:46, Judges 11:24

[2] Jeremiah 48:14 - Ecclesiastes 9:11, Ezekiel 6:6, Isaiah 10:13 10:16 16:6 36:4-36:5, Jeremiah 8:8 9:24 1:16, Psalms 11:2 33:16, Zephaniah 2:10

[3] Jeremiah 48:15 - Daniel 4:34, Isaiah 34:2-34:8 40:30-40:31, James 5:4, Jeremiah 22:18 24:4 48:8-48:25 2:27 3:40 3:57, Malachi 1:14, Psalms 24:8-24:10 47:3, Revelation 19:16, Zechariah 14:9

[4] Missing in LXX

[5] Jeremiah 48:16 - 2 Peter 2:3, Deuteronomy 8:35, Ezekiel 12:23 12:28, Isaiah 13:22 16:13-16:14, Jeremiah 1:12

[6] Jeremiah 48:17 - Ezekiel 19:11-14, Isaiah 9:5 10:5 14:4-5 16:8, Jeremiah 9:18-21 48:31-33 24:39, Revelation 18:14-20, Zechariah 11:10-14

[7] Jeremiah 48:18 - Exodus 17:3, Ezekiel 19:13, Genesis 21:16, Isaiah 5:13 15:2 23:1, Jeremiah 46:18-46:19 24:22, Joshua 13:9 13:17, Judges 15:18, Numbers 21:30 8:3

[8] LXX *Come down from your glory, and sit down in a damp place: Daebon shall be broken, because Moab is destroyed: there has gone up against you one to ravage your stronghold*

[9] Jeremiah 48:19 - 1 Chronicles 5:8, 1 Samuel 4:13-4:14 4:16, 2 Samuel 1:3-1:4 18:24-18:32 24:5, Deuteronomy 2:36, Lamentations.R Petichata D'Chakimei:10, Numbers 8:34

[10] Jeremiah 48:20 - Deuteronomy 2:36, Isaiah 15:1-15:5 15:8 16:2 16:7-16:11, Jeremiah 48:1-48:5, Joshua 13:9, Judges 11:18, Numbers 21:13-21:14 21:26-21:28

[11] Jeremiah 48:21 - Ezekiel 1:9, Isaiah 15:4, Jeremiah 24:8, Joshua 13:18 21:36-37, Mas.Soferim 7:4, Numbers 21:23, Zephaniah 2:9

[12] LXX *the land of Misor, upon Chelon, and Rephas, and Mophas*

[13] Jeremiah 48:22 - Ezekiel 6:14, Jeremiah 24:1 24:18, Numbers 8:34 9:46

[14] Jeremiah 48:23 - Genesis 14:5, Jeremiah 24:1, Joshua 13:17 13:19, Lives of the Prophets 8:1, Numbers 8:38

[15] Jeremiah 48:24 - Amos 2:2, Deuteronomy 4:43, Jeremiah 24:41, Joshua 21:36, Zephaniah 2:8-2:10

[16] Jeremiah 48:25 - Daniel 7:8 8:7-8:9 8:21, Ezekiel 30:21-30:25, Job 22:9, Lamentations 2:3, Numbers 8:37, Psalms 10:16 37:17 75:11, Zechariah 1:19-1:21

Jeremiah 48:25-39 - 2QJer

הַשְׁכִּירֻהוּ כִּי עַל־יְהוָה הִגְדִּיל וְסָפַק מוֹאָב בְּקִיאוֹ וְהָיָה לִשְׂחֹק גַּם־הוּא	26[1] Make *him drunk*[2], *for he magnified himself*[3] against the LORD; and Moab shall wallow in his vomit, and he shall be in derision.
וְאִם לוֹא הַשְּׂחֹק הָיָה לְךָ יִשְׂרָאֵל אִם־בְּגַנָּבִים "נִמְצָאָה" "נִמְצָא" כִּי־מִדֵּי דְבָרֶיךָ בּוֹ תִּתְנוֹדָד	27[4] For was not Israel a derision to you? Was he found among thieves? *For as often as you speak of him, you wag the head*[5].
עִזְבוּ עָרִים וְשִׁכְנוּ בַּסֶּלַע יֹשְׁבֵי מוֹאָב וִהְיוּ כְיוֹנָה תְּקַנֵּן בְּעֶבְרֵי פִי־פָחַת	28[6] O you who live in Moab, leave the cities, and live in the rock; and be like the dove that makes her nest in the sides of the pit's mouth.
שָׁמַעְנוּ גְאוֹן־מוֹאָב גֵּאֶה מְאֹד גָּבְהוֹ וּגְאוֹנוֹ וְגַאֲוָתוֹ וְרֻם לִבּוֹ	29[7] *We have heard of*[8] the pride of Moab; he is very proud; his *loftiness, and his pride*[9], and his haughtiness, and the assumption of his heart.
אֲנִי יָדַעְתִּי נְאֻם־יְהוָה עֶבְרָתוֹ וְלֹא־כֵן בַּדָּיו לֹא־כֵן עָשׂוּ	30[10] *I know his arrogance, says the LORD, and it is ill founded; His boastings have worked nothing well founded*[11].
עַל־כֵּן עַל־מוֹאָב אֲיֵלִיל וּלְמוֹאָב כֻּלֹּה אֶזְעָק אֶל־אַנְשֵׁי קִיר־חֶרֶשׂ יֶהְגֶּה	31[12] Therefore, will I wail for Moab; yes, I will cry out for all Moab; my heart shall moan for the [13]men of *Kir-heres*[14].
מִבְּכִי יַעְזֵר אֶבְכֶּה־לָּךְ הַגֶּפֶן שִׂבְמָה נְטִישֹׁתַיִךְ עָבְרוּ יָם עַד יַם יַעְזֵר נָגָעוּ עַל־קֵיצֵךְ וְעַל־בְּצִירֵךְ שֹׁדֵד נָפָל	32[15] I will weep with more than the weeping of Jazer, O vine of Sibmah; your branches passed over the sea, they reached to the sea of Jazer; upon your summer fruits and upon your vintage the spoiler is fallen.
וְנֶאֶסְפָה שִׂמְחָה וָגִיל מִכַּרְמֶל וּמֵאֶרֶץ מוֹאָב וְיַיִן מִיקָבִים הִשְׁבַּתִּי לֹא־יִדְרֹךְ הֵידָד הֵידָד לֹא הֵידָד	33[16] And gladness and joy is taken away from the fruitful field, and from the land of Moab; and I have caused wine to cease from the winepresses; no one shall tread with shouting; the shouting shall be no shouting.
מִזַּעֲקַת חֶשְׁבּוֹן עַד־אֶלְעָלֵה עַד־יַהַץ נָתְנוּ קוֹלָם מִצֹּעַר עַד־חֹרֹנַיִם עֶגְלַת שְׁלִשִׁיָּה כִּי גַּם־מֵי נִמְרִים לִמְשַׁמּוֹת יִהְיוּ	34[17] From the cry of Heshbon to *Elealeh, to Jahaz they uttered their voice, from Zoar to Horonaim, a heifer of three years old; for the Waters of Nimrim also shall be desolate*[18].
וְהִשְׁבַּתִּי לְמוֹאָב נְאֻם־יְהוָה מַעֲלֶה בָמָה וּמַקְטִיר לֵאלֹהָיו	35[19] Moreover, I will cause to cease in Moab, says the LORD, he who offers in the high place, and he who offers to his gods.

[1] Jeremiah 48:26 - 2 Thessalonians 2:4, Daniel 5:23 8:11-12 11:36, Exodus 5:2 9:17, Ezekiel 23:31-34 35:12-13, Habakkuk 2:16, Isaiah 10:15 19:14 5:9 3:17 15:6, Jeremiah 13:13-14 25:15-17 25:27-29 24:39 24:42 3:7 3:39 3:57, Job 9:4, Lamentations 1:21 3:15 4:21, Nahum 3:11, Psalms 2:4 59:9 60:4 75:9, Revelation 16:19, Sibylline Oracles 3.356, Zephaniah 2:8-10

[2] 2QJer *Make her drunk*

[3] 2QJer *for she has become arrogant*

[4] Jeremiah 48:27 - Ezekiel 1:8 26:2-3 11:15 12:2 12:4, Jeremiah 2:26 18:16, Job 16:4, Lamentations 2:15-17, Mas.Soferim 7:2, Matthew 7:2 2:55 3:38, Micah 7:8-7:10, Obadiah 1:12-13, Proverbs 24:17-18, Psalms 44:14 79:4, Zephaniah 2:8 2:10

[5] LXX *because you fought against him*

[6] Jeremiah 48:28 - 1 Samuel 13:6, Isaiah 2:19, Jeremiah 24:9 1:16, Judges 6:2, Obadiah 1:3-4, Psalms 55:7-8, Song of Songs 2:14

[7] Jeremiah 48:29 - Daniel 4:34, Isaiah 2:11-12 16:6, James 4:6, Job 40:10-12, Luke 14:11, Proverbs 8:13 18:12 6:13, Psalms 18:6, Zephaniah 2:8-15

[8] 2QJer *Now listen to*

[9] 2QJer *his rpice, his vanity*

[10] Jeremiah 48:30 - Genesis.R 51:10, Isaiah 16:6 37:28-29, Jastrow 1066a, Jeremiah 2:36, Job 9:12-13, Proverbs 21:30, Psalms 33:10, Ruth.R 5:14

[11] LXX *But I know his works: is it not enough for him? Has he not done thus?*

[12] Jeremiah 48:31 - 2 Kings 3:25, Isaiah 15:5 16:7-11, Jeremiah 24:36

[13] LXX adds *shorn*

[14] 2QJer *Kir-hareseth*; LXX *a gloomy place*

[15] Jeremiah 48:32 - 4Q248 1 9, Isaiah 16:8-9, Jeremiah 16:10 24:8 24:15 24:18, Joshua 13:19 21:39, Numbers 21:32 8:1 8:35 8:38

[16] Jeremiah 48:33 - Haggai 2:16, Isaiah 5:10 7:23 9:4 16:9-10 24:7-12 32:9-14, Jeremiah 25:9-10, Joel 1:5 1:12-13 1:16, Revelation 18:22-18:23

[17] Jeremiah 48:34 - Deuteronomy 10:3, Genesis 13:10, Isaiah 15:4-6, Jeremiah 48:2-3 24:5, Numbers 8:3 32:36-37

[18] LXX *Ætam their cities uttered their voice, from Zogor to Oronaim, and their tidings as a heifer of three years old, for the water also of Nebrin shall be dried up*

[19] Jeremiah 48:35 - Isaiah 15:2 16:12, Jeremiah 11:13 24:7, Numbers 22:40-41 4:14 28:28-30

עַל־כֵּן לִבִּי לְמוֹאָב כַּחֲלִלִים יֶהֱמֶה וְלִבִּי אֶל־אַנְשֵׁי קִיר־חֶרֶשׂ כַּחֲלִילִים יֶהֱמֶה עַל־כֵּן יִתְרַת עָשָׂה אָבָדוּ

36[1]

Therefore, my heart moans for Moab like pipes, and my heart moans like pipes for the men of Kir-heres; therefore, the abundance he received perishes.

כִּי כָל־רֹאשׁ קָרְחָה וְכָל־זָקָן גְּרֻעָה עַל כָּל־יָדַיִם גְּדֻדֹת וְעַל־מָתְנַיִם שָׂק

37[2]

for every head is bald, and every beard clipped; *upon all the hands are cuttings*[3], and on the loins sackcloth.

עַל כָּל־גַּגּוֹת מוֹאָב וּבִרְחֹבֹתֶיהָ כֻּלֹּה מִסְפֵּד כִּי־שָׁבַרְתִּי אֶת־מוֹאָב כִּכְלִי אֵין־חֵפֶץ בּוֹ נְאֻם־יְהוָה

38[4]

On all the housetops of Moab and in its broad places there is lamentation everywhere; for I have broken Moab like a vessel in which is no pleasure, says the LORD.

אֵיךְ חַתָּה הֵילִילוּ אֵיךְ הִפְנָה־עֹרֶף מוֹאָב בּוֹשׁ וְהָיָה מוֹאָב לִשְׂחֹק וְלִמְחִתָּה לְכָל־סְבִיבָיו

39[5]

'How it is broken down!' Wail! 'How has Moab turned the back with shame!' Shall Moab become a derision and a dismay to all who are around him.

כִּי־כֹה אָמַר יְהוָה הִנֵּה כַנֶּשֶׁר יִדְאֶה וּפָרַשׂ כְּנָפָיו אֶל־מוֹאָב

40[6]

For thus says the LORD: Behold, he shall swoop as a vulture, and shall spread out his wings against Moab.

נִלְכְּדָה הַקְּרִיּוֹת וְהַמְּצָדוֹת נִתְפָּשָׂה וְהָיָה לֵב גִּבּוֹרֵי מוֹאָב בַּיּוֹם הַהוּא כְּלֵב אִשָּׁה מְצֵרָה

41[7]

The cities are taken, and the strongholds are seized, and the heart of the mighty men of Moab at that day shall be like the heart of a woman in her pangs[8].

וְנִשְׁמַד מוֹאָב מֵעָם כִּי עַל־יְהוָה הִגְדִּיל

42[9]

And Moab shall be destroyed from being a people, because he magnified himself against the LORD.

פַּחַד וָפַחַת וָפָח עָלֶיךָ יוֹשֵׁב מוֹאָב נְאֻם־יְהוָה

43[10]

Terror, and the pit, and the trap, are upon you, O inhabitant of Moab, says the LORD.

"הַנִּיס" "הַנָּס" מִפְּנֵי הַפַּחַד יִפֹּל אֶל־הַפַּחַת וְהָעֹלֶה מִן־הַפַּחַת יִלָּכֵד בַּפָּח כִּי־אָבִיא אֵלֶיהָ אֶל־מוֹאָב שְׁנַת פְּקֻדָּתָם נְאֻם־יְהוָה

44[11]

He who flees from the terror shall fall into the pit; and he who gets up from the pit shall be taken in the trap; for I will bring upon her, upon Moab, the year of their visitation, *says the LORD*[12].

בְּצֵל חֶשְׁבּוֹן עָמְדוּ מִכֹּחַ נָסִים כִּי־אֵשׁ יָצָא מֵחֶשְׁבּוֹן וְלֶהָבָה מִבֵּין סִיחוֹן וַתֹּאכַל פְּאַת מוֹאָב וְקָדְקֹד בְּנֵי שָׁאוֹן

45[13]

In the shadow of Heshbon the fugitives stand without strength; for fire goes forth from Heshbon, and a flame from the *midst*[14] of Sihon, and it devours the corner of Moab, and

---

[1] Jeremiah 48:36 - Ecclesiastes 5:14-15, Isaiah 15:5 15:7 16:11 15:15, James 5:2-3, Jeremiah 4:19 17:11, Luke 12:20-21, Numbers.R 20:1, Proverbs 11:4 13:22 18:11

[2] Jeremiah 48:37 - 1 Kings 18:28 21:27, 2 Kings 6:30, Amos 8:10, Ezekiel 7:18 3:31, Genesis 13:29 13:34, Isaiah 3:24 15:2-3 20:2 13:1, Jastrow 271b, Jeremiah 16:6 17:5 23:5, Leviticus 19:28, Mark 5:5, Micah 1:16, Revelation 11:3

[3] LXX *and all hands shall beat the breasts*

[4] Jeremiah 48:38 - 2 Timothy 2:20-21, Hosea 8:8, Isaiah 15:3 22:1 6:14, Jeremiah 22:28 1:34, Psalms 2:9, Revelation 2:27, Romans 9:21-22

[5] Jeremiah 48:39 - Ezekiel 26:16-18, Isaiah 20:4-6, Jeremiah 24:17 48:26-27, Lamentations 1:1 2:1 4:1, Revelation 18:9-10 18:15-16

[6] Jeremiah 48:40 - Daniel 7:4, Deuteronomy 4:49, Ezekiel 17:3, Habakkuk 1:8, Hosea 8:1, Isaiah 8:8, Jeremiah 4:13 1:22, Lamentations 4:19, z.Vaetchanan 269b

[7] Jeremiah 48:41 - 1 Thessalonians 5:3, Isaiah 13:8 21:3 26:17-18, Jeremiah 4:31 6:24 6:6 1:22 1:24 2:43 3:30, Micah 4:9-10, variant נתפשו of נתפשה is found
Jeremiah 48:41-42 - 2QJer

[8] LXX *Carioth is taken, and the strongholds have been taken together*

[9] Jeremiah 48:42 - 2 Thessalonians 2:4, Daniel 11:36, Esther 3:8-3:13, Isaiah 7:8 13:23, Jeremiah 6:11 24:2 48:26-48:30, Matthew 7:2, Proverbs 16:18, Psalms 83:5-83:9, Revelation 13:6

[10] Jeremiah 48:43 - Deuteronomy 32:23-32:25, Isaiah 24:17-18, Lamentations 3:47, Psalms 11:7
Jeremiah 48:43-45 - 2QJer

[11] Jeremiah 48:44 - 1 Kings 19:17 20:30, Amos 2:14-2:15 5:19 9:1-9:4, Hosea 9:7, Isaiah 10:3 24:18 37:36-37:38, Jeremiah 8:12 10:15 11:23 16:16 23:12 22:21 3:18, Micah 7:4

[12] Missing in LXX

[13] Jeremiah 48:45 - According to the Massorah, Amos 2:2, Matthew 21:42, Numbers 21:21 21:26 21:28 24:17, Zechariah 10:4, יצאה was altered to become יצא

[14] 2QJer *town*

the crown of the head of the tumultuous ones[1].

אֽוֹי־לְךָ֤ מוֹאָב֙ אָבַ֣ד עַם־כְּמ֔וֹשׁ כִּֽי־לֻקְּח֤וּ בָנֶ֙יךָ֙ בַּשֶּׁ֔בִי וּבְנֹתֶ֖יךָ בַּשִּׁבְיָֽה	46[2] *Woe to you, O Moab. The people of Chemosh are undone; for your sons are taken captive, and your daughters into captivity*[3].
וְשַׁבְתִּ֧י שְׁבוּת־מוֹאָ֛ב בְּאַחֲרִ֥ית הַיָּמִ֖ים נְאֻם־יְהוָ֑ה עַד־הֵ֖נָּה מִשְׁפַּ֥ט מוֹאָֽב	47[4] *Yet I will turn the captivity of Moab in the end of days, says the LORD. Thus far is the judgment of Moab*[5].

Jeremiah – Chapter 49[6]

לִבְנֵ֣י עַמּ֗וֹן כֹּ֚ה אָמַ֣ר יְהוָ֔ה הֲבָנִ֥ים אֵין֙ לְיִשְׂרָאֵ֔ל אִם־יוֹרֵ֖שׁ אֵ֣ין ל֑וֹ מַדּ֗וּעַ יָרַ֤שׁ מַלְכָּם֙ אֶת־גָּ֔ד וְעַמּ֖וֹ בְּעָרָ֥יו יָשָֽׁב	1[7] Of the children of Ammon. Thus says the LORD: has Israel no sons? Has he no heir? Why then does Malcam take possession of *Gad*[8], and his people live in its cities?
לָכֵ֡ן הִנֵּה֩ יָמִ֨ים בָּאִ֜ים נְאֻם־יְהוָ֗ה וְהִשְׁמַעְתִּ֤י אֶל־רַבַּ֤ת בְּנֵֽי־עַמּוֹן֙ תְּרוּעַ֣ת מִלְחָמָ֔ה וְהָֽיְתָה֙ לְתֵ֣ל שְׁמָמָ֔ה וּבְנֹתֶ֖יהָ בָּאֵ֣שׁ תִּצַּ֑תְנָה וְיָרַ֧שׁ יִשְׂרָאֵ֛ל אֶת־יֹרְשָׁ֖יו אָמַ֥ר יְהוָֽה	2[9] Therefore, behold, the days come, says the LORD, That I will cause an alarm of war to be heard Against Rabbah *of the children of Ammon*[10]; and it shall become a desolate mound, and her *daughters*[11] shall be burned with fire; Then Israel shall *dispossess those who dispossessed him, says the LORD*[12].
הֵילִ֨ילִי חֶשְׁבּ֜וֹן כִּ֣י שֻׁדְּדָה־עַ֗י צְעַקְנָה֮ בְּנ֣וֹת רַבָּה֒ חֲגֹ֣רְנָה שַׂקִּ֔ים סְפֹ֕דְנָה וְהִתְשׁוֹטַ֖טְנָה בַּגְּדֵר֑וֹת כִּ֤י מַלְכָּם֙ בַּגּוֹלָ֣ה יֵלֵ֔ךְ כֹּהֲנָ֥יו וְשָׂרָ֖יו יַחְדָּֽיו	3[13] Wail, O Heshbon, for Ai is ruined; cry, you daughters of Rabbah, gird with sackcloth; lament, and *run to and fro among the folds*[14]; For Malcam shall go into captivity, his priests and his princes together.
מַה־תִּתְהַֽלְלִי֙ בָּעֲמָקִ֔ים זָ֣ב עִמְקֵ֔ךְ הַבַּ֖ת הַשּֽׁוֹבֵבָ֑ה הַבֹּֽטְחָה֙ בְּאֹ֣צְרֹתֶ֔יהָ מִ֖י יָב֥וֹא אֵלָֽי	4[15] Why glory in the *valleys, your flowing valley, O backsliding daughter*[16]? She trusted in her treasures: 'who shall come to me?'
הִנְנִ֩י מֵבִ֨יא עָלַ֜יִךְ פַּ֗חַד נְאֻם־אֲדֹנָ֧י יְהוִ֛ה צְבָא֖וֹת מִכָּל־סְבִיבָ֑יִךְ וְנִדַּחְתֶּם֙ אִ֣ישׁ לְפָנָ֔יו וְאֵ֥ין מְקַבֵּ֖ץ לַנֹּדֵֽד	5[17] *Behold, I will bring terror on you, says the Lord GOD of hosts, from all who are around you; and every man shall be driven out before it, and there shall be no one to gather the wanderers*[18].

---

[1] Missing in LXX

[2] Jeremiah 48:46 - 1 Kings 11:7, 2 Kings 23:13, Jeremiah 24:7 24:13, Judges 11:24, Numbers 21:29

[3] Missing in LXX

[4] Jeremiah 48:47 - Daniel 2:28 10:14, Deuteronomy 4:30 7:29, Ezekiel 16:53-55 14:8, Hosea 3:5, Isaiah 18:7 19:18-19:23 23:18, Jeremiah 12:15 23:20 6:24 22:26 1:6 1:39, Job 19:25, Numbers 24:14, z.Vaetchanan 269b

[5] Missing in LXX

[6] Chapter 30:1-5, 28-33, and 23-27 in LXX

[7] Jeremiah 49:1 - 1 Samuel 11:1-3, 2 Chronicles 20:1 20:23, 2 Kings 10:33 24:2, Amos 1:13-15, b.Yevamot [Tosefot] 76b, Deuteronomy 2:19 23:5, Ezekiel 21:33-37 25:2-25:10, Genesis 19:38, Jeremiah 1:9 1:21 3:3 24:1 1:7 1:23 1:28, Judges 10:7-8 11:13-11:15, Nehemiah 2:19 4:7 13:1-2, Psalms 9:7 83:8, Testament of Solomon 26:1, z.Vaetchanan 269b, Zephaniah 2:8-11

[8] LXX *Galaad*

[9] Jeremiah 49:2 - 2 Samuel 11:1 12:27-29, Amos 1:14, b.Yoma 10a, Deuteronomy 3:11, Ezekiel 16:46-55 21:25 25:4-6, Genesis.R 41:3, Isaiah 14:1-3, Jeremiah 4:19 1:1, Joshua 13:24-25, Lamentations.R 1:38, Numbers 21:25, Obadiah 1:19, Psalms 48:12 97:8

[10] Missing in LXX

[11] LXX *altars*

[12] LXX *succeed to his dominion*

[13] Jeremiah 49:3 - 1 Kings 11:5 11:33, 2 Kings 23:13, Amos 1:15, Isaiah 13:6 14:31 15:2 16:7 23:1 23:6 32:11-32:12, James 5:1, Jeremiah 4:8 6:26 22:25 24:2 24:7 24:20 24:37 1:1 3:8, Job 30:3-30:7, Joshua 8:28, Zephaniah 1:5

[14] Missing in LXX

[15] Jeremiah 49:4 - 1 Timothy 6:17, Ezekiel 28:4-28:7, Hosea 4:16, Isaiah 28:1-28:4 47:7-47:8, Jeremiah 3:14 7:24 9:24 21:13 24:7 1:16, Obadiah 1:4-1:5, Proverbs 10:15, Psalms 49:7 52:8 62:11, Revelation 18:7

[16] LXX *plains of the Enakim, you haughty daughter*

[17] Jeremiah 49:5 - 2 Samuel 7:6-7 19:7, Amos 4:3, Isaiah 16:3, Jeremiah 15:8 20:4 22:5 48:41-44 1:29, Job 15:21, Joshua 2:9, Obadiah 1:12-14, Proverbs 4:1

[18] Missing in LXX

Hebrew	Verse	English
וְאַחֲרֵי־כֵן אָשִׁיב אֶת־שְׁבוּת בְּנֵי־עַמּוֹן נְאֻם־יְהוָה	6[1]	But afterward I will bring back the captivity of the children of Ammon, says the LORD[2].
לֶאֱדוֹם כֹּה אָמַר יְהוָה צְבָאוֹת הַאֵין עוֹד חָכְמָה בְּתֵימָן אָבְדָה עֵצָה מִבָּנִים נִסְרְחָה חָכְמָתָם	7[3]	Of Edom. Thus says the LORD of hosts: Is there no wisdom in Teman? Has counsel perished from the prudent? Has their wisdom vanished[4]?
נֻסוּ הָפְנוּ הֶעְמִיקוּ לָשֶׁבֶת יֹשְׁבֵי דְּדָן כִּי אֵיד עֵשָׂו הֵבֵאתִי עָלָיו עֵת פְּקַדְתִּיו	8[5]	Flee, turn back, live deep, O inhabitants of Dedan; for I bring the calamity of Esau upon him; the time that I shall punish him[6].
אִם־בֹּצְרִים בָּאוּ לָךְ לֹא יַשְׁאִרוּ עוֹלֵלוֹת אִם־גַּנָּבִים בַּלַּיְלָה הִשְׁחִיתוּ דַיָּם	9[7]	If grape gatherers came to you, would they not leave some gleaning grapes? If thieves by night, would they not destroy until they had enough[8]?
כִּי־אֲנִי חָשַׂפְתִּי אֶת־עֵשָׂו גִּלֵּיתִי אֶת־מִסְתָּרָיו וְנֶחְבָּה לֹא יוּכָל שֻׁדַּד זַרְעוֹ וְאֶחָיו וּשְׁכֵנָיו וְאֵינֶנּוּ	10[9]	But I have made Esau bare, I have uncovered his secret places, and he shall not be able to hide himself. His seed is spoiled, and his brethren, and his neighbors, yes he has vanished[10].
עָזְבָה יְתֹמֶיךָ אֲנִי אֲחַיֶּה וְאַלְמְנֹתֶיךָ עָלַי תִּבְטָחוּ	11[11]	Leave your fatherless children, I will rear them, and let your widows trust in Me[12].
כִּי־כֹה אָמַר יְהוָה הִנֵּה אֲשֶׁר־אֵין מִשְׁפָּטָם לִשְׁתּוֹת הַכּוֹס שָׁתוֹ יִשְׁתּוּ וְאַתָּה הוּא נָקֹה תִּנָּקֶה לֹא תִנָּקֶה כִּי שָׁתֹה תִּשְׁתֶּה	12[13]	For thus says the LORD: Behold, those whose judgment was not to drink the cup shall assuredly drink; and are you to remain unpunished? You shall not go unpunished, but you shall surely drink[14].
כִּי בִי נִשְׁבַּעְתִּי נְאֻם־יְהוָה כִּי־לְשַׁמָּה לְחֶרְפָּה לְחֹרֶב וְלִקְלָלָה תִּהְיֶה בָצְרָה וְכָל־עָרֶיהָ תִהְיֶינָה לְחָרְבוֹת עוֹלָם	13[15]	For I have sworn by Myself, says the LORD, that Bozrah shall become an astonishment, a reproach, a waste, and a curse; and all its cities shall be perpetual wastes[16].
שְׁמוּעָה שָׁמַעְתִּי מֵאֵת יְהוָה וְצִיר בַּגּוֹיִם שָׁלוּחַ הִתְקַבְּצוּ וּבֹאוּ עָלֶיהָ וְקוּמוּ לַמִּלְחָמָה	14[17]	I have heard a message from the LORD, and an ambassador is sent among the nations: 'Gather yourselves together, and come against her, and rise up to the battle[18].'

---

[1] Jeremiah 49:6 - b.Berachot 28a, Ein Yaakov Berachot:28a, Ezekiel 16:53, Isaiah 19:18-23 23:18, Jeremiah 22:26 24:47 1:39, m.Yadayim 4:4, t.Yadayim 2:17

[2] Missing in LXX

[3] Jeremiah 49:7 - 1 Chronicles 1:53, Amos 1:11-12, b.Chagigah 5, Daniel 11:41, Deuteronomy 23:9, Ein Yaakov Chagigah:5b, Ezekiel 25:12-14 35:1-15, Genesis 1:30 3:41 12:8 12:11 12:15 12:34, Habakkuk 3:3, Isaiah 19:11-13 5:14 34:1-17 63:1-6, Jastrow 1025a, Jeremiah 18:18 1:9 1:21 1:20, Job 2:11 4:1 5:12-14, Joel 4:19, Lamentations.R 2:11, Malachi 1:3-4, Numbers 20:14-21 24:17-18, Numbers.R 11:1, Obadiah 1:1-21, Psalms 83:5-11 17:7, Romans 1:22-23, Testament of Job 29:3, z.Vaetchanan 269b

[4] Missing in LXX

[5] Jeremiah 49:8 - 1 Samuel 13:6, Amos 9:1-3, Isaiah 2:21 21:13, Jeremiah 6:1 1:23 22:21 24:6 24:28 24:44 1:30 1:32 2:27, Judges 6:2, Lamentations 4:21-22, Matthew 24:15-18, Obadiah 1:3-4, Revelation 6:15

[6] Missing in LXX

[7] Jeremiah 49:9 - Isaiah 17:6, Midrash Psalms 8:1, Obadiah 1:5-6

[8] Missing in LXX

[9] Jeremiah 49:10 - 2QJer, Amos 9:3, Genesis.R 82:12, Isaiah 14:20-14:22 17:14 21:3, Jastrow 812b 1381a, Jeremiah 23:24, Malachi 1:3-1:4, Midrash Psalms 8:1 14:2 28:3 121:3, Obadiah 1:9, Psalms 37:28 37:35-37:36, Romans 9:13

[10] Missing in LXX

[11] Jeremiah 49:11 - 1 Timothy 5:5, b.Bava Metzia 84a, Deuteronomy 10:18, Ein Yaakov Bava Metzia:84a, Hosea 14:5, James 1:27, Jonah 4:11, Malachi 3:5, Proverbs 23:10-23:11, Psalms 10:15-10:19 68:6 82:3 2:9

[12] Missing in LXX

[13] Jeremiah 49:12 - 1 Peter 4:17-4:18, Jeremiah 1:15 25:28-25:29 6:11 22:27, Lamentations 4:21-4:22, Obadiah 1:16, Proverbs 17:5, z.Vaetchanan 269b

[14] Missing in LXX

[15] Jeremiah 49:13 - Amos 1:12 6:8, Ezekiel 25:13-25:14 35:2-35:15, Genesis 22:16 12:33, Isaiah 10:6 34:9-34:15 21:23 15:1, Jeremiah 20:26 49:17-49:18 1:22, Joel 4:19, Malachi 1:3-4, Obadiah 1:18

[16] Missing in LXX

[17] Jeremiah 49:14 - Ezekiel 7:25-26, Isaiah 13:2-3 18:2-3 6:4 13:7, Jeremiah 50:9-16 3:11 51:27-28 3:46, Matthew 24:6, Obadiah 1-4

[18] Missing in LXX

15[1] For, behold, I make you small among the nations, and despised among men[2].

כִּי־הִנֵּה קָטֹן נְתַתִּיךָ בַּגּוֹיִם בָּזוּי בָּאָדָם

16[3] Your terribleness has deceived you, the pride of your heart, O you who lives in the clefts of the rock, that holds the height of the hill; though you should make your nest as high as the eagle, I will bring you down from there, says the LORD[4].

תִּפְלַצְתְּךָ הִשִּׁיא אֹתָךְ זְדוֹן לִבֶּךָ שֹׁכְנִי בְּחַגְוֵי הַסֶּלַע תֹּפְשִׂי מְרוֹם גִּבְעָה כִּי־תַגְבִּיהַ כַּנֶּשֶׁר קִנֶּךָ מִשָּׁם אוֹרִידְךָ נְאֻם־יְהוָה

17[5] And Edom shall become an astonishment; everyone who passes by it shall be astonished and shall hiss at all its plagues[6].

וְהָיְתָה אֱדוֹם לְשַׁמָּה כֹּל עֹבֵר עָלֶיהָ יִשֹּׁם וְיִשְׁרֹק עַל־כָּל־מַכּוֹתֶהָ

18[7] As in the overthrow of Sodom and Gomorrah and its neighbor cities, says the LORD, no man shall live there, nor shall any son of man live in it[8].

כְּמַהְפֵּכַת סְדֹם וַעֲמֹרָה וּשְׁכֵנֶיהָ אָמַר יְהוָה לֹא־יֵשֵׁב שָׁם אִישׁ וְלֹא־יָגוּר בָּהּ בֶּן־אָדָם

19[9] Behold, he shall come up like a lion from the thickets of the Jordan against the strong habitation; for I will suddenly make him run away from it, and whomever is chosen, I will appoint him over it; for who is like Me? And who will appoint Me a time? And who is the shepherd who will stand before Me[10]?

הִנֵּה כְּאַרְיֵה יַעֲלֶה מִגְּאוֹן הַיַּרְדֵּן אֶל־נְוֵה אֵיתָן כִּי־אַרְגִּיעָה אֲרִיצֶנּוּ מֵעָלֶיהָ וּמִי בָחוּר אֵלֶיהָ אֶפְקֹד כִּי מִי כָמוֹנִי וּמִי יֹעִידֶנִּי וּמִי־זֶה רֹעֶה אֲשֶׁר יַעֲמֹד לְפָנָי

20[11] Therefore, hear the counsel of the LORD He has taken against Edom; and the intention He has purposed against the inhabitants of Teman: surely the least of the flock shall drag them away, surely their habitation shall be dismayed at them[12].

לָכֵן שִׁמְעוּ עֲצַת־יְהוָה אֲשֶׁר יָעַץ אֶל־אֱדוֹם וּמַחְשְׁבוֹתָיו אֲשֶׁר חָשַׁב אֶל־יֹשְׁבֵי תֵימָן אִם־לֹא יִסְחָבוּם צְעִירֵי הַצֹּאן אִם־לֹא יַשִּׁים עֲלֵיהֶם נְוֵהֶם

21[13] The earth quakes at the noise of their fall; there is a cry, the noise that can be heard in the Red Sea[14].

מִקּוֹל נִפְלָם רָעֲשָׁה הָאָרֶץ צְעָקָה בְּיַם־סוּף נִשְׁמַע קוֹלָהּ

22[15] Behold, he shall come up and swoop down as the vulture, and spread out his wings against Bozrah; and the heart of the mighty men of Edom at that day shall be as the heart of a woman in her pangs[16].

הִנֵּה כַנֶּשֶׁר יַעֲלֶה וְיִדְאֶה וְיִפְרֹשׂ כְּנָפָיו עַל־בָּצְרָה וְהָיָה לֵב גִּבּוֹרֵי אֱדוֹם בַּיּוֹם הַהוּא כְּלֵב אִשָּׁה מְצֵרָה

[1] Jeremiah 49:15 - 1 Samuel 2:7-2:8 2:30, Luke 1:51, Micah 7:10, Obadiah 1:2, Psalms 53:6

[2] Missing in LXX

[3] Jeremiah 49:16 - Amos 9:2, b.Sanhedrin 89a, Ein Yaakov Sanhedrin:89a, Ezekiel 28:11-28:19, Isaiah 2:21 14:13-14:15 25:4-25:5 1:25, Jeremiah 48:28-48:29, Job 15:27, Midrash Psalms 14:3, Obadiah 1:3-1:4, Pirkei de R'Eliezer 35, Proverbs 16:18 18:21 5:23, Song of Songs 2:14, Tanya Igeret Hateshuvah §07

[4] Missing in LXX

[5] Jeremiah 49:17 - 1 Kings 9:8, 2 Chronicles 7:20-7:21, Ezekiel 1:13 11:7 11:15, Isaiah 34:9-34:15, Jeremiah 18:16 1:13 2:13 3:37, Lamentations 2:15-2:16, Micah 6:16, Zephaniah 2:15

[6] Missing in LXX

[7] Jeremiah 49:18 - 2 Peter 2:6, Amos 4:11, Deuteronomy 5:22, Genesis 19:24-19:25, Isaiah 13:19-13:22 10:10, Jeremiah 1:33 2:40, Job 18:15-18:18, Jude 1:7, Psalms 11:7, Revelation 18:21-18:23, Zephaniah 2:9

[8] Missing in LXX

[9] Jeremiah 49:19 - 1 Chronicles 12:14, Exodus 15:11, Isaiah 16:25, Jeremiah 4:7 12:5 6:21 50:44-50:46, Job 9:19 9:21 23:3-23:7 40:2-40:8 17:2 42:3-42:5, Joshua 3:15, Nahum 1:6, Psalms 76:8 89:7 89:9 113:5-113:6 23:2, Revelation 6:17, Zechariah 11:3

[10] Missing in LXX

[11] Jeremiah 49:20 - 1 Corinthians 1:27-1:29, Acts 4:28, Ein Yaakov Yoma:10a, Ephesians 1:11, Genesis.R 44:17 73:7 75:5 99 [Excl]:2, Guide for the Perplexed 1:47, Isaiah 14:24-14:27 46:10-46:11, Jeremiah 13:10 1:7 1:13 49:17-49:18 2:45, Job 6:19-6:20, Malachi 1:3-1:4, Midrash Tanchuma Ki Tetze 10, Midrash Tanchuma Vayechi 14, Pesikta de R'Kahana 3.13, Proverbs 19:21, Psalms 33:11, Saadia Opinions 8:5, Zechariah 4:6

[12] Missing in LXX

[13] Jeremiah 49:21 - Exodus.R 51:7, Ezekiel 21:21 26:15-26:18 8:10, Genesis.R 44:17, Isaiah 14:4-14:15, Jeremiah 2:46, Lamentations.R 2:1 2:11, Revelation 18:10, Leviticus.R 13:5

[14] Missing in LXX

[15] Jeremiah 49:22 - 1 Thessalonians 5:3, Daniel 7:4, Deuteronomy 4:49, Genesis.R 63:10, Hosea 8:1, Isaiah 13:8 21:3 2:17, Jeremiah 4:13 4:31 6:24 13:21 22:23 6:6 48:40-48:41 1:24, Leviticus.R 13:5, Psalms 18:6

[16] Missing in LXX

לְדַמֶּשֶׂק בּוֹשָׁה חֲמָת וְאַרְפָּד כִּי־שְׁמֻעָה רָעָה שָׁמְעוּ נָמֹגוּ בַּיָּם דְּאָגָה הַשְׁקֵט לֹא יוּכָל

23[1] Of Damascus. Hamath is ashamed, and Arpad; for they have heard evil tidings, they are melted away; there is trouble in the sea; it cannot be quiet.

רָפְתָה דַמֶּשֶׂק הִפְנְתָה לָנוּס וְרֶטֶט הֶחֱזִיקָה צָרָה וַחֲבָלִים אֲחָזַתָּה כַּיּוֹלֵדָה

24[2] Damascus grows feeble, she turns to flee, and trembling seizes on her; anguish and pangs take hold of her, as a woman in childbirth.

אֵיךְ לֹא־עֻזְּבָה עִיר 'תְּהִלָּה' 'תְּהִלָּת' קִרְיַת מְשׂוֹשִׂי

25[3] 'How is the city of praise left unrepaired, the city of my joy?'

לָכֵן יִפְּלוּ בַחוּרֶיהָ בִּרְחֹבֹתֶיהָ וְכָל־אַנְשֵׁי הַמִּלְחָמָה יִדַּמּוּ בַּיּוֹם הַהוּא נְאֻם יְהוָה צְבָאוֹת

26[4] Therefore, her young men shall fall in her broad places, and all the men of war shall be brought to silence in that day, says the LORD of hosts.

וְהִצַּתִּי אֵשׁ בְּחוֹמַת דַּמָּשֶׂק וְאָכְלָה אַרְמְנוֹת בֶּן־הֲדָד

27[5] And I will kindle a fire in the wall of Damascus, and it shall devour the *palaces of Benhadad*[6].

לְקֵדָר וּלְמַמְלְכוֹת חָצוֹר אֲשֶׁר הִכָּה 'נְבוּכַדְרֶאצּוֹר' 'נְבוּכַדְרֶאצַּר' מֶלֶךְ־בָּבֶל כֹּה אָמַר יְהוָה קוּמוּ עֲלוּ אֶל־קֵדָר וְשָׁדְדוּ אֶת־בְּנֵי־קֶדֶם

28[7] Of Kedar, and *of the kingdoms of Hazor*[8], which Nebuchadrezzar king of Babylon struck. Thus says the LORD: Arise, go against Kedar, and *spoil the children of the east*[9].

אָהֳלֵיהֶם וְצֹאנָם יִקָּחוּ יְרִיעוֹתֵיהֶם וְכָל־כְּלֵיהֶם וּגְמַלֵּיהֶם יִשְׂאוּ לָהֶם וְקָרְאוּ עֲלֵיהֶם מָגוֹר מִסָּבִיב

29[10] They shall take their tents and their flocks, they shall carry away for themselves their *curtains*[11], and all their vessels, and their camels; and they shall proclaim against them a terror on every side.

נֻסוּ נֻּדוּ מְאֹד הֶעְמִיקוּ לָשֶׁבֶת יֹשְׁבֵי חָצוֹר נְאֻם־יְהוָה כִּי־יָעַץ עֲלֵיכֶם נְבוּכַדְרֶאצַּר מֶלֶךְ־בָּבֶל עֵצָה וְחָשַׁב 'עֲלֵיהֶם' 'עֲלֵיכֶם' מַחֲשָׁבָה

30[12] Flee, *flit far off, live deep*[13], O you inhabitants of Hazor, says the LORD; Nebuchadrezzar king of Babylon has taken counsel against you, and has conceived a purpose against you.

קוּמוּ עֲלוּ אֶל־גּוֹי שְׁלֵיו יוֹשֵׁב לָבֶטַח נְאֻם־יְהוָה לֹא־דְלָתַיִם וְלֹא־בְרִיחַ לוֹ בָּדָד יִשְׁכֹּנוּ

31[14] Arise, get up against a nation that is at ease, who dwells without care, says the LORD; who has neither gates nor bars, who live alone.

וְהָיוּ גְמַלֵּיהֶם לָבַז וַהֲמוֹן מִקְנֵיהֶם לְשָׁלָל וְזֵרִתִים לְכָל־רוּחַ קְצוּצֵי פֵאָה וּמִכָּל־עֲבָרָיו אָבִיא אֶת־אֵידָם נְאֻם־יְהוָה

32[15] And their camels shall be a spoil, and the multitude of their cattle a spoil; and I will scatter to all winds those who polled their corners; and I will bring their calamity from every side, says the LORD.

[1] Jeremiah 49:23 - 1 Kings 11:24, 2 Chronicles 16:2, 2 Corinthians 11:32, 2 Kings 17:24 18:34 19:13, 2 Samuel 8:9 17:10, Acts 9:2 3:20, Amos 1:3-1:5 6:2, Deuteronomy 20:8, Genesis 14:15 15:2, Isaiah 10:9 11:11 13:7 17:1-17:3 13:13 9:20, Joshua 2:11 14:8, Luke 8:23-8:24 21:25-21:26, Nahum 2:11, Numbers 13:21, Psalms 107:26-107:27, Zechariah 9:1-9:2
[2] Jeremiah 49:24 - Song of Songs.R 1:48
[3] Jeremiah 49:25 - Daniel 4:27, Isaiah 1:26 14:4-14:6, Jeremiah 9:9 24:2 24:39 3:41, Psalms 37:35-36, Revelation 18:10 18:16-19
[4] Jeremiah 49:26 - Amos 4:10, Ezekiel 3:27, Jeremiah 9:22 11:22 2:30 51:3-4, Lamentations 2:21
[5] Jeremiah 49:27 - 1 Kings 15:18-15:20 20:1-22, 2 Kings 13:3 13:5, Amos 1:3-1:5, Jeremiah 19:12
[6] LXX *streets of the son of Ader*
[7] Jeremiah 49:28 - 1 Chronicles 1:29, Ezekiel 3:21, Genesis 1:6 1:13, Genesis.R 45:9, Isaiah 11:14 13:2-13:5 21:13 21:16-21:17 18:11, Jeremiah 2:10 1:14 49:30-49:31 1:33 50:14-50:16, Job 1:3, Judges 6:3, Pirkei de R'Eliezer 30, Song of Songs 1:5, z.Vaetchanan 269b
[8] LXX adds *the Queen of the Palace*
[9] Missing in LXX
[10] Jeremiah 49:29 - 1 Chronicles 5:20-5:21, 2 Corinthians 4:8 7:5, Genesis 13:25, Habakkuk 3:7, Isaiah 13:20 12:7, Jeremiah 4:20 6:25 10:20 20:3-20:4 22:5 1:24, Job 1:3, Judges 6:5 7:12 8:21 8:26, Psalms 31:14 24:5
[11] LXX *garments*
[12] Jeremiah 49:30 - Isaiah 10:7, Jeremiah 1:9 25:24-25:25 3:6
[13] LXX *dig very deep for a dwelling place*
[14] Jeremiah 49:31 - Deuteronomy 9:28, Ezekiel 6:9 14:11 15:6, Isaiah 8:9 8:11 23:8, Jeremiah 24:11, Judges 18:7-18:10 18:27-18:28, Micah 7:14, Nahum 1:12, Numbers 23:9, Psalms 3:4, Zephaniah 2:15
[15] Jeremiah 49:32 - Deuteronomy 28:64, Ezekiel 5:10 5:12 12:14-12:15, Jeremiah 9:27 1:23 1:36

וְהָיְתָה חָצוֹר לִמְעוֹן תַּנִּים שְׁמָמָה עַד־עוֹלָם לֹא־יֵשֵׁב שָׁם אִישׁ וְלֹא־יָגוּר בָּהּ בֶּן־אָדָם

33[1] And Hazor shall be a dwelling place for *jackals*[2], desolate forever; no man shall abide there, nor shall any son of man live there.

אֲשֶׁר הָיָה דְבַר־יְהוָה אֶל־יִרְמְיָהוּ הַנָּבִיא אֶל־עֵילָם בְּרֵאשִׁית מַלְכוּת צִדְקִיָּה מֶלֶךְ־יְהוּדָה לֵאמֹר

34[3] *The word of the LORD that came to Jeremiah the prophet concerning Elam in the beginning of the reign of Zedekiah king of Judah, saying*[4]:

כֹּה אָמַר יְהוָה צְבָאוֹת הִנְנִי שֹׁבֵר אֶת־קֶשֶׁת עֵילָם רֵאשִׁית גְּבוּרָתָם

35[5] *Thus says the LORD of hosts: Behold, I will break the bow of Elam the chief of their might*[6].

וְהֵבֵאתִי אֶל־עֵילָם אַרְבַּע רוּחוֹת מֵאַרְבַּע קְצוֹת הַשָּׁמַיִם וְזֵרִתִים לְכֹל הָרֻחוֹת הָאֵלֶּה וְלֹא־יִהְיֶה הַגּוֹי אֲשֶׁר לֹא־יָבוֹא שָׁם נִדְּחֵי 'עוֹלָם' "עֵילָם"

36[7] *And I will bring against Elam the four winds from the four quarters of heaven, and will scatter them toward all those winds; and there is no nation where the dispersed of Elam shall not go*[8].

וְהַחְתַּתִּי אֶת־עֵילָם לִפְנֵי אֹיְבֵיהֶם וְלִפְנֵי מְבַקְשֵׁי נַפְשָׁם וְהֵבֵאתִי עֲלֵיהֶם רָעָה אֶת־חֲרוֹן אַפִּי נְאֻם־יְהוָה וְשִׁלַּחְתִּי אַחֲרֵיהֶם אֶת־הַחֶרֶב עַד כַּלּוֹתִי אוֹתָם

37[9] *And I will cause Elam to be dismayed before their enemies, and before those who seek their life; and I will bring evil on them, My fierce anger, says the LORD; and I will send the sword after them, until I consume them*[10];

וְשַׂמְתִּי כִסְאִי בְּעֵילָם וְהַאֲבַדְתִּי מִשָּׁם מֶלֶךְ וְשָׂרִים נְאֻם־יְהוָה

38[11] *And I will set My throne in Elam, and will destroy from there king and princes, says the LORD*[12];

וְהָיָה בְּאַחֲרִית הַיָּמִים 'אָשׁוּב' "אָשִׁיב" אֶת־שְׁבִית' "אֶת־שְׁבוּת" עֵילָם נְאֻם־יְהוָה

39[13] *But it shall come to pass in the end of days, that I will bring back the captivity of Elam, says the LORD*[14].

Jeremiah – Chapter 50[15]

הַדָּבָר אֲשֶׁר דִּבֶּר יְהוָה אֶל־בָּבֶל אֶל־אֶרֶץ כַּשְׂדִּים בְּיַד יִרְמְיָהוּ הַנָּבִיא

1[16] The word that the LORD spoke concerning Babylon, concerning the land of the Chaldeans, by Jeremiah the prophet.

הַגִּידוּ בַגּוֹיִם וְהַשְׁמִיעוּ וּשְׂאוּ־נֵס הַשְׁמִיעוּ אַל־תְּכַחֵדוּ אִמְרוּ נִלְכְּדָה בָבֶל הֹבִישׁ בֵּל חַת מְרֹדָךְ הֹבִישׁוּ עֲצַבֶּיהָ חַתּוּ גִּלּוּלֶיהָ

2[17] Declare among the nations and announce, and set up a standard; announce, and do not conceal; Say: 'Babylon is taken, Bel is put to

---

[1] Jeremiah 49:33 - Isaiah 13:20-13:22 14:23 34:9-34:17, Jeremiah 9:12 10:22 49:17-49:18 50:39-50:40 3:37, Malachi 1:3, Revelation 18:2 18:21-18:22, Zephaniah 2:9 2:13-2:15

[2] LXX *ostriches*

[3] Jeremiah 49:34 - 2 Kings 24:17-18, Acts 2:9, Daniel 8:2, Ezekiel 32:24-25, Ezra 4:9, Genesis 10:22 14:1, Isaiah 11:11 21:2, Jeremiah 1:25

[4] Missing in LXX

[5] Jeremiah 49:35 - b.Sanhedrin 89a, Ein Yaakov Sanhedrin:89a, Isaiah 22:6, Jeremiah 2:14 2:29 3:56, Psalms 46:10, Seder Olam 25:Jehoiachin, z.Vaetchanan 269b

[6] Missing in LXX

[7] Jeremiah 49:36 - Amos 9:9, Daniel 7:2-7:3 8:8 8:22 11:4, Deuteronomy 4:25 28:64, Ezekiel 5:10 5:12, Isaiah 11:12 16:3-16:4 3:13 8:8, Jeremiah 6:17 1:32, Psalms 3:2, Revelation 7:1

[8] Missing in LXX

[9] Jeremiah 49:37 - Ezekiel 5:2 5:12 12:14 8:23, Jeremiah 9:17 6:24 34:20-34:21 24:2 24:39 1:5 1:22 1:24 1:29 2:36, Leviticus 2:33, Psalms 48:5-48:7

[10] Missing in LXX

[11] Jeremiah 49:38 - b.Megillah 10b, Daniel 7:9-7:14, Ein Yaakov Megillah:9b, Esther.R Petichata:12, Exodus.R 15:16, Jeremiah 19:10, Lamentations.R 1:54, Mekilta de R'Ishmael Pisha 14:104, Numbers.R 7:10, Pesikta Rabbati 30:2, y.Taanit 1:1

[12] Missing in LXX

[13] Jeremiah 49:39 - Amos 9:14, Daniel 2:28 10:14, Ezekiel 16:53-55 5:14 14:16 15:25, Hosea 3:5, Isaiah 2:2, Jeremiah 24:47 1:6, Job 18:10, Micah 4:1

[14] Missing in LXX

[15] Chapter 27 in LXX

[16] Jeremiah 50:1 - 2 Peter 1:21, 2 Samuel 23:2, Acts 7:4, Genesis 10:10 11:31, Habakkuk 2:5-20, Isaiah 13:1-3 14:4 21:1-21:10 23:13 47:1-47:15, Jeremiah 25:26-25:27 3:7 51:1-51:14, Job 1:17, Psalms 137:8-137:9, Revelation 18:1-18:24, Sibylline Oracles 3.302

[17] Jeremiah 50:2 - According to the Massorah בל "Bel" was not altered to become באל "Baal", Isaiah 12:4 13:2 21:9 13:19 15:1 22:1 24:6 66:18-66:19, Jeremiah 4:16 6:18 7:11 43:12-43:13 22:14 2:46 3:8 3:31 3:44 3:47 3:52 4:31, Mekhilta de R'Shimon bar Yochai Pisha 9:3, Psalms 64:10 96:3, Revelation 14:6-14:8 18:2, Zephaniah 2:11

כִּי עָלָה עָלֶיהָ גּוֹי מִצָּפוֹן הוּא־יָשִׁית אֶת־אַרְצָהּ
לְשַׁמָּה וְלֹא־יִהְיֶה יוֹשֵׁב בָּהּ מֵאָדָם וְעַד־בְּהֵמָה נָדוּ
הָלָכוּ
3[2]

בַּיָּמִים הָהֵמָּה וּבָעֵת הַהִיא נְאֻם־יְהוָה יָבֹאוּ בְנֵי־
יִשְׂרָאֵל הֵמָּה וּבְנֵי־יְהוּדָה יַחְדָּו הָלוֹךְ וּבָכוֹ יֵלֵכוּ
וְאֶת־יְהוָה אֱלֹהֵיהֶם יְבַקֵּשׁוּ
4[3]

צִיּוֹן יִשְׁאָלוּ דֶּרֶךְ הֵנָּה פְנֵיהֶם בֹּאוּ וְנִלְווּ אֶל־יְהוָה
בְּרִית עוֹלָם לֹא תִשָּׁכֵחַ
5[4]

צֹאן אֹבְדוֹת 'הָיָה' 'הָיוּ' עַמִּי רֹעֵיהֶם הִתְעוּם
הָרִים 'שׁוֹבְבִים' "שׁוֹבְבוּם" מֵהַר אֶל־גִּבְעָה הָלָכוּ
שָׁכְחוּ רִבְצָם
6[6]

כָּל־מוֹצְאֵיהֶם אֲכָלוּם וְצָרֵיהֶם אָמְרוּ לֹא נֶאְשָׁם
תַּחַת אֲשֶׁר חָטְאוּ לַיהוָה נְוֵה־צֶדֶק וּמִקְוֵה
אֲבוֹתֵיהֶם יְהוָה
7[7]

נֻדוּ מִתּוֹךְ בָּבֶל וּמֵאֶרֶץ כַּשְׂדִּים 'יָצְאוּ' "צֵאוּ" וִהְיוּ
כְּעַתּוּדִים לִפְנֵי־צֹאן
8[9]

כִּי הִנֵּה אָנֹכִי מֵעִיר וּמַעֲלֶה עַל־בָּבֶל קְהַל־גּוֹיִם
גְּדֹלִים מֵאֶרֶץ צָפוֹן וְעָרְכוּ לָהּ מִשָּׁם תִּלָּכֵד חִצָּיו
כְּגִבּוֹר מַשְׁכִּיל לֹא יָשׁוּב רֵיקָם
9[11]

וְהָיְתָה כַשְׂדִּים לְשָׁלָל כָּל־שֹׁלְלֶיהָ יִשְׂבָּעוּ נְאֻם־
יְהוָה
10[12]

shame, Merdach is dismayed; *her images are put to shame, her idols are dismayed*[1].'

3[2] For from the north a nation comes against her, which shall make her land desolate, and no one shall live in it; they flee, they are gone, both man and beast.

4[3] In those days, and in that time, says the LORD, the children of Israel shall come, they and the children of Judah together; they shall go on their way weeping, and shall seek the LORD their God.

5[4] They shall inquire concerning Zion with their faces toward here: '*Come, and join yourselves to the LORD*[5] In an everlasting covenant shall not be forgotten.'

6[6] My people are lost sheep; the shepherds caused them to go astray, they turned them away on the mountains; they went from mountain to hill, they forgot their resting place.

7[7] All who found them devoured them; and their adversaries said: 'We are not guilty;' because they sinned against the LORD, the habitation of justice, *the LORD, the hope of their fathers*[8].

8[9] Flee from the midst of Babylon, and go forth from the land of the Chaldeans, and be like *the he goats before the flocks*[10].

9[11] For, behold, I will stir and cause an assembly of great nations from the north country to come up against Babylon; and they shall set themselves in array against her, from there she shall be taken; their arrows shall be as of a mighty man who makes childless; no one shall return in vain.

10[12] And Chaldea shall be a spoil; all who spoil her shall be satisfied, says the LORD.

---

[1] Missing in LXX

[2] Jeremiah 50:3 - Exodus 12:12, Genesis 6:7, Isaiah 13:5-13:10 13:17-13:22 14:22-14:24, Jeremiah 7:20 21:6 2:9 50:12-50:13 50:35-50:41 51:8-51:9 3:11 51:25-51:27 51:37-51:44 3:48 51:62, Revelation 18:21-18:23, Zephaniah 1:3

[3] Jeremiah 50:4 - Ezekiel 37:16-37:22 15:25, Ezra 3:12-3:13, Hosea 2:2 3:5, Isaiah 11:12-11:13 14:1 21:19 7:6 15:4, James 4:9, Jeremiah 3:16-3:18 29:12-29:14 30:10-30:11 31:7-31:8 31:10-31:11 7:32 33:6-33:8 9:15 50:19-50:20 50:33-50:34 51:47-51:48, Joel 2:12, Midrash Tanchuma Nitzavim 1, Psalms 9:4 126:4-126:6, Zechariah 8:21-8:23 12:10
Jeremiah 50:4-6 - 4QJere

[4] Jeremiah 50:5 - 1 Kings 19:10 19:14, 2 Corinthians 8:5, 2 Samuel 23:5, Acts 11:23, Genesis 17:7, Hebrews 8:6-8:10, Isaiah 2:3-2:5 11:8 7:3 56:6-56:7, Jeremiah 6:16 31:32-31:37 48:40, John 7:17, Joseph and Aseneth 15:7, Micah 4:1-4:2, Psalms 25:8-25:9 84:8, Verse for names ק-צ [Pisukim Lesheimot Anoshim]

[5] LXX *and they shall come and flee for refuge to the LORD their God*

[6] Jeremiah 50:6 - 1 Peter 2:25, Ezekiel 34:4-34:12 10:14 34:25-34:28, Gates of Repentance 3.159, Isaiah 6:15 8:2 5:6 56:10-56:12, Jeremiah 2:20 2:32 3:6 3:23 10:21 23:11-23:15 2:17 2:19, Luke 15:4-15:7, Matthew 9:36 10:6 15:24 18:10-18:13, Midrash Tanchuma Acharei Mot 8, Psalms 23:2 32:7 90:1 91:1 20:7 119:176, Song of Songs 1:7-1:8, Zechariah 11:4-11:9

[7] Jeremiah 50:7 - 1 Timothy 1:1, Daniel 9:6 9:16, Isaiah 9:13 47:6 56:9, Jeremiah 2:3 12:7-11 14:8 31:24 40:2-3 50:17 50:33, Midrash Psalms 79:5, Psalms 22:5-6 79:7 90:1 91:1, Zechariah 1:15 11:5

[8] Missing in LXX

[9] Jeremiah 50:8 - 2 Corinthians 6:17, Isaiah 48:20 52:1, Jeremiah 51:6 51:45, Numbers 16:26, Proverbs 30:31, Revelation 18:4, Zechariah 2:6-2:7

[10] LXX *serpents before sleep*

[11] Jeremiah 50:9 - 2 Samuel 1:22, Ezra 1:1-1:2, Isaiah 13:2-13:5 13:17-13:18 21:2 41:25 45:1-45:4, Jeremiah 15:14 50:3 50:14 50:21 50:26 50:29 50:41-50:42 51:1-51:4 51:11 51:27-51:28

[12] Jeremiah 50:10 - Isaiah 33:4 33:23 45:3, Jeremiah 25:12 27:7, Revelation 17:16

כִּי 'תִשְׂמְחִי' 'תִשְׂמְחוּ' כִּי 'תַעֲלֹזִי' 'תַעֲלֹזוּ' שֹׁסֵי נַחֲלָתִי כִּי 'תָפוּשִׁי' 'תָפוֹשׁוּ' כְּעֶגְלָה דָשָׁה 'וְתִצְהֲלִי' 'וְתִצְהֲלוּ' כָּאַבִּרִים	11[1]	Because you are glad, because you rejoice, O you who plunders My heritage, because you prance as a heifer at grass, and *neigh as strong horses*[2];
בּוֹשָׁה אִמְּכֶם מְאֹד חָפְרָה יוֹלַדְתְּכֶם הִנֵּה אַחֲרִית גּוֹיִם מִדְבָּר צִיָּה וַעֲרָבָה	12[3]	Your mother shall be grievously ashamed, she who bore you shall be confounded; behold, the last of the nations shall be a wilderness, a dry land, and a desert.
מִקֶּצֶף יְהֹוָה לֹא תֵשֵׁב וְהָיְתָה שְׁמָמָה כֻּלָּהּ כֹּל עֹבֵר עַל־בָּבֶל יִשֹּׁם וְיִשְׁרֹק עַל־כָּל־מַכּוֹתֶיהָ	13[4]	Because of the wrath of the LORD it shall not be inhabited, but it shall be wholly desolate; Everyone who goes by Babylon shall be appalled and hiss at all her plagues.
עִרְכוּ עַל־בָּבֶל סָבִיב כָּל־דֹּרְכֵי קֶשֶׁת יְדוּ אֵלֶיהָ אַל־תַּחְמְלוּ אֶל־חֵץ כִּי לַיהֹוָה חָטָאָה	14[5]	Set yourselves in array around Babylon, all you who bend the bow, shoot at her, spare no arrows; for she sinned against the LORD.
הָרִיעוּ עָלֶיהָ סָבִיב נָתְנָה יָדָהּ נָפְלוּ 'אֲשׁוּיֹתֶיהָ' "אָשְׁיוֹתֶיהָ" נֶהֶרְסוּ חוֹמוֹתֶיהָ כִּי נִקְמַת יְהֹוָה הִיא הִנָּקְמוּ בָהּ כַּאֲשֶׁר עָשְׂתָה עֲשׂוּ־לָהּ	15[6]	Shout against her, she has submitted herself; her supports have fallen, her walls are thrown down; for it is the vengeance of the LORD, take vengeance on her; as she did, do to her.
כִּרְתוּ זוֹרֵעַ מִבָּבֶל וְתֹפֵשׂ מַגָּל בְּעֵת קָצִיר מִפְּנֵי חֶרֶב הַיּוֹנָה אִישׁ אֶל־עַמּוֹ יִפְנוּ וְאִישׁ לְאַרְצוֹ יָנֻסוּ	16[7]	*Cut off the sower from Babylon*[8], and he who handles the sickle in the time of harvest; for fear of the *oppressing*[9] sword everyone shall turn to his people, and everyone shall flee to his own land.
שֶׂה פְזוּרָה יִשְׂרָאֵל אֲרָיוֹת הִדִּיחוּ הָרִאשׁוֹן אֲכָלוֹ מֶלֶךְ אַשּׁוּר וְזֶה הָאַחֲרוֹן עִצְּמוֹ נְבוּכַדְרֶאצַּר מֶלֶךְ בָּבֶל	17[10]	Israel is a scattered sheep, the lions drove him away; first the king of Assyria devoured him, and last this Nebuchadrezzar king of Babylon *broke*[11] his bones.
לָכֵן כֹּה־אָמַר יְהֹוָה צְבָאוֹת אֱלֹהֵי יִשְׂרָאֵל הִנְנִי פֹקֵד אֶל־מֶלֶךְ בָּבֶל וְאֶל־אַרְצוֹ כַּאֲשֶׁר פָּקַדְתִּי אֶל־מֶלֶךְ אַשּׁוּר	18[12]	Therefore, thus says the LORD of hosts, the God of Israel: Behold, I will punish the king of Babylon and his land, as I have punished the king of Assyria.

[1] Jeremiah 50:11 - Amos 4:1, Deuteronomy 32:15, Ezekiel 25:3-25:8 25:15-25:17 26:2-26:3, Hosea 10:11, Isaiah 10:6-10:7 47:6, Jeremiah 5:8 5:28 46:21 50:17 50:27 51:34-51:35, Lamentations 1:21 2:15-2:16 4:21-4:22, Obadiah 1:12, Proverbs 17:5, Psalms 22:13 74:2-74:8 79:1-79:4 83:2-83:6, Zechariah 2:8-2:9 14:1-14:3 14:12

[2] LXX *pushed with the horn as bulls*

[3] Jeremiah 50:12 - 2 Baruch 3:2, Apocalypse of Elijah 2:52, b.Berachot 58ab, Ein Yaakov Berachot:58a, Exodus.R 2:4, Galatians 4:26, Isaiah 13:20-13:22 14:22 23:13, Jeremiah 25:12 25:26 49:2 50:35-50:40 51:25-51:26 51:43 51:62-51:64, mt.Hilchot Berachot 10:11 10:19, Revelation 17:5 18:21-18:23, Siman 60:11, Tanna Devei Eliyahu 1, Upon seeing a gathering of 600,000 non-Jews, Upon seeing pagan graves, y.Berachot 9:2

[4] Jeremiah 50:13 - Habakkuk 2:6-2:18, Isaiah 14:4-14:17, Jeremiah 18:16 19:8 25:12 49:17 51:37, Job 27:23, Lamentations 2:15-2:16, Zechariah 1:15, Zephaniah 2:15

[5] Jeremiah 50:14 - 1 Samuel 17:20, 2 Samuel 10:9, Habakkuk 2:8 2:17, Isaiah 5:28 13:4 13:17-13:18, Jeremiah 46:9 49:35 50:7 50:9 50:11 50:29 50:42 51:2 51:11-51:12 51:27, Psalms 51:5, Revelation 17:5

[6] Jeremiah 50:15 - 1 Chronicles 29:24, 1 Samuel 15:33, 2 Chronicles 30:8, 2 Thessalonians 1:8, Deuteronomy 32:35 32:41 32:43, Ezekiel 17:18 21:27, Isaiah 59:17 61:2 63:4, James 2:13, Jeremiah 46:10 50:14 50:28-50:29 51:6 51:11 51:14 51:25 51:36 51:44 51:58 51:64, Joshua 6:5 6:20, Judges 1:6-1:7, Lamentations 5:6, Luke 21:22, Matthew 7:2, Nahum 1:2, Psalms 94:1 137:8-137:9 149:7, Revelation 16:6 18:6 19:2, Romans 3:5 12:19

[7] Jeremiah 50:16 - Amos 5:16, Isaiah 13:14, Jeremiah 25:38 46:16 51:9 51:23, Joel 1:11

[8] LXX *Utterly destroy seed from Babylon*

[9] LXX *Grecian*

[10] Jeremiah 50:17 - 1 Peter 2:25, 2 Chronicles 28:20 32:1-23 33:11 36:1-23, 2 Kings 15:29 17:6-23 18:9-13 24:1-7, Daniel 6:25, Ezekiel 34:5-6 34:12, Genesis.R 95:1 96:5, Isaiah 7:17-20 8:7-8 10:5-7 36:1-22 47:6, Jeremiah 2:15 4:7 5:6 23:1-2 39:1-8 49:19 50:6 51:34-35 51:38 52:1, Joel 4:2, John 10:10-12, Leviticus.R 4:6, Luke 15:4-6, Matthew 9:36-38, Mekhilta de R'Shimon bar Yochai Bachodesh 49:4, Mekilta de R'Ishmael Bahodesh 2:69, Midrash Tanchuma Acharei Mot 8, Midrash Tanchuma Bamidbar 20, Midrash Tanchuma Vayechi 3, Midrash Tanchuma Vayigash 8, Numbers.R 4:5 9:47, Pesikta Rabbati 53:2, z.Bo 43a

[11] LXX *gnawed*

[12] Jeremiah 50:18 - Ezekiel 31:3-31:17, Isaiah 10:12 37:36-38, Nahum 1:1-3, z.Vaetchanan 269b, Zephaniah 2:13-2:15

וְשֹׁבַבְתִּי אֶת־יִשְׂרָאֵל אֶל־נָוֵהוּ וְרָעָה הַכַּרְמֶל וְהַבָּשָׁן וּבְהַר אֶפְרַיִם וְהַגִּלְעָד תִּשְׂבַּע נַפְשׁוֹ	19[1] And I will bring Israel back to his pasture, and he shall feed on Carmel *and Bashan*[2], and his soul shall be satisfied on the hills of Ephraim and in Gilead.
בַּיָּמִים הָהֵם וּבָעֵת הַהִיא נְאֻם־יְהוָה יְבֻקַּשׁ אֶת־עֲוֺן יִשְׂרָאֵל וְאֵינֶנּוּ וְאֶת־חַטֹּאת יְהוּדָה וְלֹא תִמָּצֶאינָה כִּי אֶסְלַח לַאֲשֶׁר אַשְׁאִיר	20[3] In those days, and in that time, says the LORD, the iniquity of Israel shall be sought, and there shall be none, and the sins of Judah, and they shall not be found; for I will pardon those whom I leave as a remnant[4].
עַל־הָאָרֶץ מְרָתַיִם עֲלֵה עָלֶיהָ וְאֶל־יוֹשְׁבֵי פְּקוֹד חֲרֹב וְהַחֲרֵם אַחֲרֵיהֶם נְאֻם־יְהוָה וַעֲשֵׂה כְּכֹל אֲשֶׁר צִוִּיתִיךָ	21[5] Go against the land of Merathaim, against it, and against the inhabitants of Pekod; waste and utterly destroy them, says the LORD, and do all that I have commanded you.
קוֹל מִלְחָמָה בָּאָרֶץ וְשֶׁבֶר גָּדוֹל	22[6] Listen! Battle is in the land, and great destruction[7].
אֵיךְ נִגְדַּע וַיִּשָּׁבֵר פַּטִּישׁ כָּל־הָאָרֶץ אֵיךְ הָיְתָה לְשַׁמָּה בָּבֶל בַּגּוֹיִם	23[8] How the hammer of the whole earth is cut asunder and broken. How Babylon has become desolate among the nations.
יָקֹשְׁתִּי לָךְ וְגַם־נִלְכַּדְתְּ בָּבֶל וְאַתְּ לֹא יָדָעַתְּ נִמְצֵאת וְגַם־נִתְפַּשְׂתְּ כִּי בַיהוָה הִתְגָּרִית	24[9] I laid a snare for you, and you are taken, O Babylon, and you were not aware; you are found, and also caught, because you fought against the LORD.
פָּתַח יְהוָה אֶת־אוֹצָרוֹ וַיּוֹצֵא אֶת־כְּלֵי זַעְמוֹ כִּי־מְלָאכָה הִיא לַאדֹנָי יְהוִה צְבָאוֹת בְּאֶרֶץ כַּשְׂדִּים	25[10] The LORD has opened His *armory*[11], and has brought forth the weapons of His indignation; for it is a work that the Lord GOD of hosts has to do in the land of the Chaldeans.
בֹּאוּ־לָהּ מִקֵּץ פִּתְחוּ מַאֲבֻסֶיהָ סָלּוּהָ כְמוֹ־עֲרֵמִים וְהַחֲרִימוּהָ אַל־תְּהִי־לָהּ שְׁאֵרִית	26[12] Come against her from every quarter, open her granaries, cast her up as heaps, and destroy her utterly; let nothing of her remain.
חִרְבוּ כָּל־פָּרֶיהָ יֵרְדוּ לַטָּבַח הוֹי עֲלֵיהֶם כִּי־בָא יוֹמָם עֵת פְּקֻדָּתָם	27[13] *Kill all her steers*[14], let them go down to the slaughter; Woe to them, for their day came, the time of their visitation.
קוֹל נָסִים וּפְלֵטִים מֵאֶרֶץ בָּבֶל לְהַגִּיד בְּצִיּוֹן אֶת־נִקְמַת יְהוָה אֱלֹהֵינוּ נִקְמַת הֵיכָלוֹ	28[15] Listen! They flee and escape from the land of Babylon, to declare in Zion the vengeance of

---

[1] Jeremiah 50:19 - Amos 9:14-9:15, Ezekiel 11:17 34:13-34:14 36:24 36:33 37:21-37:22 38:8 39:25-39:29, Isaiah 33:9 35:2 65:9-65:10, Jeremiah 3:18 23:3 24:6-24:7 30:10 30:18 31:7 31:9-31:11 31:15 31:26 32:37 33:7-33:12 50:4-50:5, Joshua 17:15, Micah 7:14 7:18, Numbers 32:1, Obadiah 1:17-1:21, Song of Songs 6:5

[2] Missing in LXX

[3] Jeremiah 50:20 - 2 Peter 3:15, Acts 3:19 3:26, Derech Hashem Part II 8§01, Hebrews 8:10-8:12 10:17-10:18, Isaiah 1:9 11:1-11:2 19:25 20:22, Jeremiah 7:35 9:15 20:14 2:4, Micah 7:19, Midrash Tanchuma Noach 13, Numbers 23:21, Pesikta Rabbati 44:1, Psalms 7:12, Romans 5:16 6:13 8:33-8:34 11:6 11:26-11:27, Selichot

[4] LXX adds *on the land, says the LORD*

[5] Jeremiah 50:21 - 1 Samuel 15:3 15:11-15:24, 2 Chronicles 12:23, 2 Kings 18:25, 2 Samuel 16:11, Ezekiel 23:23, Isaiah 10:6 20:28 24:14, Jeremiah 10:22 24:10 2:3 2:9 2:15, Numbers 31:14-31:18

[6] Jeremiah 50:22 - Isaiah 21:2-21:4, Jeremiah 4:19-4:21 51:54-51:56

[7] LXX *in the land of the Chaldeans*

[8] Jeremiah 50:23 - Isaiah 14:4-14:6 14:12-14:17, Jeremiah 51:20-51:24, Revelation 18:16

[9] Jeremiah 50:24 - 2 Thessalonians 2:4, Daniel 5:30-5:31, Ecclesiastes 9:12, Exodus 10:3, Isaiah 13:11 21:3-21:5 21:9, Jeremiah 3:8 51:31-51:39 3:57, Job 9:4 16:2 16:9, Revelation 18:7-18:8

[10] Jeremiah 50:25 - Amos 3:6, b.Taanit [Tosefot] 2a, Genesis.R 11:10, Isaiah 13:2-13:5 13:17-13:18 14:22-14:24 21:7-21:9 46:10-46:11 48:14-48:15, Jeremiah 2:15 50:35-50:38 51:11-51:12 3:20 3:25 3:55, Midrash Psalms 86:7, Midrash Tanchuma Ki Tissa 33, Pesikta de R'Kahana 24.11, Pesikta Rabbati 23:8, Psalms 45:4 45:6, Revelation 18:8, y.Taanit 2:1

[11] LXX *treasury*

[12] Jeremiah 50:26 - Isaiah 5:26 10:6 14:23 1:10 21:3 63:3-63:4, Jeremiah 2:10 2:13 2:15 2:23 2:41 51:25-51:28 3:44 51:64, Micah 7:10, Revelation 14:19 18:21-18:24 19:15

[13] Jeremiah 50:27 - Ezekiel 7:5-7 39:17-20, Isaiah 10:7, Jeremiah 3:7 22:21 24:44 2:11 2:31, Lamentations 1:21, Psalms 22:13 37:13, Revelation 16:17-19 18:10 19:17

[14] LXX *Dry up all her fruits*

[15] Jeremiah 50:28 - Daniel 5:3-5:5 5:23, Isaiah 24:20, Jeremiah 2:15 51:10-51:11 51:50-51:51, Lamentations 1:10 2:6-2:7, Psalms 149:6-149:9, Zechariah 12:2-12:3

the LORD our God, *the vengeance of His temple*[1].

29[2] Call together the archers against Babylon, all those who bend the bow; encamp around her, let no one in it escape; Return to her according to her work, according to all she has done, do to her: for she has been arrogant against the LORD, against the Holy One of Israel.

הַשְׁמִיעוּ אֶל־בָּבֶל וּ רַבִּים כָּל־דֹּרְכֵי קֶשֶׁת חֲנוּ עָלֶיהָ סָבִיב אַל־יְהִי... "אַל־יְהִי־לָהּ" פְּלֵטָה שַׁלְּמוּ־לָהּ כְּפָעֳלָהּ כְּכֹל אֲשֶׁר עָשְׂתָה עֲשׂוּ־לָהּ כִּי אֶל־יְהוָה זָדָה אֶל־קְדוֹשׁ יִשְׂרָאֵל

30[3] Therefore, her young men shall fall in her broad places, and all her men of war shall be brought to silence in that day, says the LORD.

לָכֵן יִפְּלוּ בַחוּרֶיהָ בִּרְחֹבֹתֶיהָ וְכָל־אַנְשֵׁי מִלְחַמְתָּהּ יִדַּמּוּ בַּיּוֹם הַהוּא נְאֻם־יְהוָה

31[4] Behold, I am against you, O most arrogant, says the Lord GOD of hosts; for your day comes, the time that I will punish you.

הִנְנִי אֵלֶיךָ זָדוֹן נְאֻם־אֲדֹנָי יְהוִה צְבָאוֹת כִּי בָּא יוֹמְךָ עֵת פְּקַדְתִּיךָ

32[5] And the most arrogant shall stumble and fall, and no one shall raise him up; and I will kindle a fire in his cities, and it shall devour all who are around him.

וְכָשַׁל זָדוֹן וְנָפַל וְאֵין לוֹ מֵקִים וְהִצַּתִּי אֵשׁ בְּעָרָיו וְאָכְלָה כָּל־סְבִיבֹתָיו

33[6] Thus says the LORD of hosts: The children of Israel and the children of Judah are oppressed together; and all who took them captive hold them fast; they refuse to let them go.

כֹּה אָמַר יְהוָה צְבָאוֹת עֲשׁוּקִים בְּנֵי־יִשְׂרָאֵל וּבְנֵי־יְהוּדָה יַחְדָּו וְכָל־שֹׁבֵיהֶם הֶחֱזִיקוּ בָם מֵאֲנוּ שַׁלְּחָם

34[7] Their Redeemer is strong, the LORD of hosts is His name; He will thoroughly plead their cause, so He may give rest to the land, and alarm the inhabitants of Babylon.

גֹּאֲלָם חָזָק יְהוָה צְבָאוֹת שְׁמוֹ רִיב יָרִיב אֶת־רִיבָם לְמַעַן הִרְגִּיעַ אֶת־הָאָרֶץ וְהִרְגִּיז לְיֹשְׁבֵי בָבֶל

35[8] A sword is on the Chaldeans, says the LORD, and on the inhabitants of Babylon, and on her princes, and on her wise men.

חֶרֶב עַל־כַּשְׂדִּים נְאֻם־יְהוָה וְאֶל־יֹשְׁבֵי בָבֶל וְאֶל־שָׂרֶיהָ וְאֶל־חֲכָמֶיהָ

36[9] *A sword is on the braggarts, and they shall become fools; a sword is on her mighty men, and they shall be dismayed*[10].

חֶרֶב אֶל־הַבַּדִּים וְנֹאָלוּ חֶרֶב אֶל־גִּבּוֹרֶיהָ וָחָתּוּ

37[11] *A sword is on their horses, and on their chariots, and on all the mingled people in her midst, and they shall become as women; a*

חֶרֶב אֶל־סוּסָיו וְאֶל־רִכְבּוֹ וְאֶל־כָּל־הָעֶרֶב אֲשֶׁר בְּתוֹכָהּ וְהָיוּ לְנָשִׁים חֶרֶב אֶל־אוֹצְרֹתֶיהָ וּבֻזָּזוּ

---

[1] Missing in LXX

[2] Jeremiah 50:29 - 2 Thessalonians 2:4, b.Nedarim 37b, Daniel 4:34 5:23 11:36, Esther.R 5:3, Exodus 10:3, Isaiah 14:13-14 13:23 23:10, Jeremiah 2:9 50:14-15 2:24 2:26 2:32 3:56, Mas.Soferim 6:8, Mekilta de R'Ishmael Beshallah 7:18, Psalms 137:8-9, Revelation 13:5-6 16:6 18:6

[3] Jeremiah 50:30 - Isaiah 13:15-13:18, Jeremiah 9:22 18:21 24:15 1:26 2:36 51:3-51:4 51:56-51:57, Revelation 6:15 19:18

[4] Jeremiah 50:31 - 1 Peter 5:5, Daniel 4:27-4:28, Ezekiel 5:8 5:3 29:9-29:10 14:3 15:1, Habakkuk 2:4-2:5, James 4:6, Jeremiah 21:13 24:29 1:16 2:29 2:32 3:25, Job 40:11-40:12, Nahum 2:14 3:5

[5] Jeremiah 50:32 - Amos 1:4 1:7 1:10 1:12 1:14 2:2 2:5, Daniel 5:20 5:23-5:30, Deuteronomy 8:22, Ezekiel 28:2-28:9, Isaiah 10:12-10:15 14:13-14:15, Jeremiah 21:14 1:27 3:26 51:64, Proverbs 16:18 18:12, Revelation 18:8

[6] Jeremiah 50:33 - Exodus 5:2 7:27 9:2-9:3 9:17-9:18, Isaiah 14:17 23:6 49:24-49:26 3:23 52:4-52:6 10:6, Jeremiah 34:15-34:18 2:7 50:17-50:18 51:34-51:36, Leviticus.R 22:10, Pesikta de R'Kahana 11.5, z.Vaetchanan 269b, Zechariah 1:15-1:16
Jeremiah 50:33-34 - Exodus.R 15:11 20:2, Midrash Tanchuma Behar 3, Midrash Tanchuma Ki Tetze 2, Midrash Tanchuma Vayetze 9

[7] Jeremiah 50:34 - 2 Thessalonians 1:6-1:7, Ecclesiastes.R 4:1, Exodus 6:6, Isaiah 14:3-14:7 17:14 19:14 20:6 44:23-44:24 23:4 3:22 6:5, Jeremiah 15:21 3:19 3:36, Micah 4:10 7:9, Midrash Tanchuma Behar 4, Pesikta de R'Kahana 11.5, Proverbs 22:23 23:11, Psalms 35:1 43:1, Revelation 18:8 19:1-3

[8] Jeremiah 50:35 - Daniel 5:1-5:2 5:7-8 5:30, Ezekiel 14:2, Hosea 11:6, Isaiah 19:11-13 5:14 17:25 20:25 47:13-14 18:16, Jeremiah 8:9 10:7 23:6 2:27 2:30 3:39 3:57, Leviticus 2:25, Zechariah 11:17

[9] Jeremiah 50:36 - 1 Timothy 4:2 6:4, 2 Chronicles 1:16, 2 Samuel 15:31 17:14, 2 Thessalonians 2:9-2:11, b.Berachot 63b, b.Makkot 10a, b.Taanit 7a, Ein Yaakov Berachot:63b, Ein Yaakov Midrash Shmuel 1:6, Ein Yaakov Taanit:6b, Isaiah 19:14 20:25 47:10-47:15, Jeremiah 24:30 1:22 2:30 3:23 3:30 3:32, Mesillat Yesharim 14:Elements of Pe - R'Ishus, Nahum 2:9 3:7 3:13 3:17-3:18, Revelation 19:20 21:8 22:15

[10] LXX *a sword upon her warriors, and they shall be weakened: a sword upon their horses, and upon their chariots*

[11] Jeremiah 50:37 - Ezekiel 6:5 15:20, Haggai 2:22, Isaiah 19:16 21:3, Jeremiah 1:20 1:24 24:41 2:26 3:21 3:30, Nahum 2:3-2:5 2:14 3:13, Psalms 20:8-20:9 46:10 76:7

38² חֹ֤רֶב אֶל־מֵימֶ֙יהָ֙ וְיָבֵ֔שׁוּ כִּ֣י אֶ֤רֶץ פְּסִלִים֙ הִ֔יא וּבָאֵימִ֖ים יִתְהֹלָֽלוּ

sword is on her treasures, and they shall be robbed[1].

A drought is on her waters, and they shall be dried up; for it is a land of graven images, and they are proud of their idols[3].

39⁴ לָכֵ֗ן יֵשְׁב֤וּ צִיִּים֙ אֶת־אִיִּ֔ים וְיָ֥שְׁבוּ בָ֖הּ בְּנ֣וֹת יַֽעֲנָ֑ה וְלֹֽא־תֵשֵׁ֥ב עוֹד֙ לָנֶ֔צַח וְלֹ֥א תִשְׁכּ֖וֹן עַד־דּ֥וֹר וָדֽוֹר

Therefore, the wild cats with the jackals shall live there, and the ostriches shall live in it; and it shall no longer be inhabited forever, nor shall it be lived in from generation to generation[5].

40⁶ כְּמַהְפֵּכַ֨ת אֱלֹהִ֜ים אֶת־סְדֹ֧ם וְאֶת־עֲמֹרָ֛ה וְאֶת־שְׁכֵנֶ֖יהָ נְאֻם־יְהוָ֑ה לֹֽא־יֵשֵׁ֥ב שָׁם֙ אִ֔ישׁ וְלֹֽא־יָג֥וּר בָּ֖הּ בֶּן־אָדָֽם

As when God overthrew Sodom and Gomorrah and its neighbor cities, says the LORD; so shall no man live there, nor shall any son of man live in it.

41⁷ הִנֵּ֛ה עַ֥ם בָּ֖א מִצָּפ֑וֹן וְג֤וֹי גָּדוֹל֙ וּמְלָכִ֣ים רַבִּ֔ים יֵעֹ֖רוּ מִיַּרְכְּתֵי־אָֽרֶץ

Behold, a people come from the north, and a great nation, and many kings shall be stirred from the uttermost parts of the earth.

42⁸ קֶ֣שֶׁת וְכִידֹ֞ן יַחֲזִ֗יקוּ אַכְזָרִ֥י הֵ֙מָּה֙ וְלֹ֣א יְרַחֵ֔מוּ קוֹלָ֖ם כַּיָּ֣ם יֶהֱמֶ֑ה וְעַל־סוּסִ֣ים יִרְכָּ֔בוּ עָר֗וּךְ כְּאִישׁ֙ לַמִּלְחָמָ֔ה עָלַ֖יִךְ בַּת־בָּבֶֽל

They lay hold on bow and spear, they are cruel, and without compassion; their voice is like the roaring sea, and they ride on horses; Set in array, as a man for war against you, O daughter of Babylon[9].

43¹⁰ שָׁמַ֧ע מֶֽלֶךְ־בָּבֶ֛ל אֶת־שִׁמְעָ֖ם וְרָפ֣וּ יָדָ֑יו צָרָה֙ הֶחֱזִיקַ֔תְהוּ חִ֖יל כַּיּוֹלֵדָֽה

The king of Babylon has heard their fame, and his hands grow feeble; anguish has taken hold of him, and pain, as a woman in travail.

44¹¹ הִ֠נֵּה כְּאַרְיֵ֞ה יַעֲלֶ֨ה מִגְּא֣וֹן הַיַּרְדֵּן֮ אֶל־נְוֵ֣ה אֵיתָן֒ כִּֽי־אַרְגִּ֤עָה אֲרוּצֵם֙ מֵֽעָלֶ֔יהָ וּמִ֥י בָח֖וּר אֵלֶ֣יהָ אֶפְקֹ֑ד כִּ֣י מִ֤י כָמ֙וֹנִי֙ וּמִ֣י יֹעִדֶ֔נִּי וּמִֽי־זֶ֣ה רֹעֶ֔ה אֲשֶׁ֥ר יַעֲמֹ֖ד לְפָנָֽי

Behold, he shall come up like a lion from *the thickets of the Jordan against the strong habitation[12]*; for I will suddenly make them run away from it, and whomever is chosen, he will I appoint over it; for who is like Me? and who will appoint Me a time? And who is the shepherd who will stand before Me?

45¹³ לָכֵ֞ן שִׁמְע֣וּ עֲצַת־יְהוָ֗ה אֲשֶׁ֤ר יָעַץ֙ אֶל־בָּבֶ֔ל וּמַ֣חְשְׁבוֹתָ֔יו אֲשֶׁ֥ר חָשַׁ֖ב אֶל־אֶ֣רֶץ כַּשְׂדִּ֑ים אִם־לֹ֤א יִסְחָבוּם֙ צְעִירֵ֣י הַצֹּ֔אן אִם־לֹ֥א יַשִּׁ֛ים עֲלֵיהֶ֖ם נָוֶֽה

Therefore, hear the counsel of the LORD He has taken against Babylon, and His intent that He committed against the land of the Chaldeans: surely the least of the flock shall drag them away, surely their habitation shall be dismayed at them.

---

[1] LXX *a sword upon their warriors and upon the mixed people in the midst of her; and they shall be as women: a sword upon the treasures, and they shall be scattered upon her water*

[2] Jeremiah 50:38 - Acts 17:16, Daniel 3:1-3:30 5:4, Habakkuk 2:18-2:19, Isaiah 20:25 20:27 46:1-46:7, Jeremiah 2:2 2:12 3:7 51:32-51:36 3:44 3:47 3:52, Revelation 16:12 17:5 17:15-17:16

[3] LXX *and they shall be ashamed: for it is a land of graven images; and in the islands, where they boasted*

[4] Jeremiah 50:39 - Isaiah 13:20-13:22 14:23 34:11-34:17, Jeremiah 1:12 50:12-50:13 3:26 51:37-51:38 3:43 51:62-51:64, Revelation 18:2 18:21-18:24

[5] LXX *Therefore, shall idols live in the islands, and the young of monsters shall live in it: it shall not be inhabited anymore forever*

[6] Jeremiah 50:40 - 2 Peter 2:6, Amos 4:11, Deuteronomy 5:22, Genesis 19:24-19:25, Hosea 11:8-11:9, Isaiah 1:9 13:19-13:20, Jeremiah 1:18 3:26, Jude 1:7, Luke 17:28-17:30, Revelation 11:8 18:8-18:9, Zephaniah 2:9

[7] Jeremiah 50:41 - Isaiah 13:2-13:5 13:17-13:18, Jeremiah 6:22-6:23 1:14 50:2-50:3 2:9 51:1-51:2 3:11 51:27-51:28, Revelation 17:16

[8] Jeremiah 50:42 - Habakkuk 1:6-1:8, Isaiah 5:28 5:30 13:17-13:18 14:6 23:6, James 2:13, Jeremiah 6:22-6:23 8:16 23:3 2:14, Psalms 46:3-4 46:7 74:20 137:8-9, Revelation 16:6 19:14-19:18

[9] LXX *the people is fierce, and will have no mercy: their voices shall sound as the sea, they shall ride upon horses, prepared for war, like fire, against you, O daughter of Babylon*

[10] Jeremiah 50:43 - Daniel 5:5-5:6, Isaiah 13:6-13:8 21:3-21:4, Jeremiah 1:22 1:24 3:31

[11] Jeremiah 50:44 - Exodus 15:11, Isaiah 16:18 16:25 17:25 19:10 22:9 22:11, Jeremiah 1:38 49:19-49:21, Job 41:2-41:3, Mas.Soferim 7:4, Numbers 16:5, Psalms 89:7 89:9

[12] LXX *Jordan to Gaethan*

[13] Jeremiah 50:45 - Acts 4:28, Ephesians 1:11, Isaiah 14:24-27 46:10-11, Jeremiah 13:10 1:20 51:10-11, Psalms 33:10-11, Revelation 17:16-17

מִקּוֹל נִתְפְּשָׂה בָבֶל נִרְעֲשָׁה הָאָרֶץ וּזְעָקָה בַּגּוֹיִם נִשְׁמָע	46[1]	At the noise of the taking of Babylon the earthquakes, and the cry is heard among the nations.

Jeremiah – Chapter 51

כֹּה אָמַר יְהֹוָה הִנְנִי מֵעִיר עַל־בָּבֶל וְאֶל־יֹשְׁבֵי לֵב קָמָי רוּחַ מַשְׁחִית	1[2]	Thus says the LORD: Behold, I will raise against Babylon, and against those who live in Leb-kamai[3], a destroying wind.
וְשִׁלַּחְתִּי לְבָבֶל זָרִים וְזֵרוּהָ וִיבֹקְקוּ אֶת־אַרְצָהּ כִּי־הָיוּ עָלֶיהָ מִסָּבִיב בְּיוֹם רָעָה	2[4]	And I will send to Babylon strangers who shall scatter her, and they shall empty her land; for in the day of trouble they shall be against her.
אֶל־יִדְרֹךְ יִדְרֹךְ "..." הַדֹּרֵךְ קַשְׁתּוֹ וְאֶל־יִתְעַל בְּסִרְיֹנוֹ וְאַל־תַּחְמְלוּ אֶל־בַּחֻרֶיהָ הַחֲרִימוּ כָּל־צְבָאָהּ	3[5]	Let the archer bend his bow against her, and let him lift himself up against her in his coat of mail; and do not spare her young men, destroy utterly all her host.
וְנָפְלוּ חֲלָלִים בְּאֶרֶץ כַּשְׂדִּים וּמְדֻקָּרִים בְּחוּצוֹתֶיהָ	4[6]	And they shall fall down slain in the land of the Chaldeans, and thrust through in her streets.
כִּי לֹא־אַלְמָן יִשְׂרָאֵל וִיהוּדָה מֵאֱלֹהָיו מֵיְהֹוָה צְבָאוֹת כִּי אַרְצָם מָלְאָה אָשָׁם מִקְּדוֹשׁ יִשְׂרָאֵל	5[7]	For Israel is not widowed, nor Judah, of his God, of the LORD of hosts; for their land is full of guilt against the Holy One of Israel.
נֻסוּ מִתּוֹךְ בָּבֶל וּמַלְּטוּ אִישׁ נַפְשׁוֹ אַל־תִּדַּמּוּ בַּעֲוֹנָהּ כִּי עֵת נְקָמָה הִיא לַיהֹוָה גְּמוּל הוּא מְשַׁלֵּם לָהּ	6[8]	Flee from the midst of Babylon, and every man save his life, do not be cut off in her iniquity; for it is the time of the LORD's vengeance; He will render to her a recompense.
כּוֹס־זָהָב בָּבֶל בְּיַד־יְהֹוָה מְשַׁכֶּרֶת כָּל־הָאָרֶץ מִיֵּינָהּ שָׁתוּ גוֹיִם עַל־כֵּן יִתְהֹלְלוּ גוֹיִם	7[9]	Babylon has been a golden cup in LORD's hand, who made all the earth drunk; the nations have drunk her wine; therefore, the nations are insane.
פִּתְאֹם נָפְלָה בָבֶל וַתִּשָּׁבֵר הֵילִילוּ עָלֶיהָ קְחוּ צֳרִי לְמַכְאוֹבָהּ אוּלַי תֵּרָפֵא	8[10]	Babylon is suddenly fallen and destroyed, wail for her; take balm for her pain, if so she may be healed.
רִפִּאנוּ "רִפִּינוּ" אֶת־בָּבֶל וְלֹא נִרְפָּתָה עִזְבוּהָ וְנֵלֵךְ אִישׁ לְאַרְצוֹ כִּי־נָגַע אֶל־הַשָּׁמַיִם מִשְׁפָּטָהּ וְנִשָּׂא עַד־שְׁחָקִים	9[11]	We would have healed Babylon, but she is not healed; forsake her, and let everyone go to his own country; For her judgment reaches to the heavens, and is lifted up to the skies.

[1] Jeremiah 50:46 - Ezekiel 2:18 7:16 8:10, Isaiah 14:9-14:10, Jeremiah 1:21, Lamentations.R 2:11, Revelation 18:9-18:19

[2] Jeremiah 51:1 - 2 Kings 19:7, Acts 9:4, Amos 3:6, b.Succah [Rashi] 28a, Ezekiel 19:12, Hosea 13:15, Isaiah 13:3-13:5, Jeremiah 4:11-4:12 1:36 2:9 50:14-50:16 2:21 2:24 2:29 2:33, Sibylline Oracles 5.434, z.Vaetchanan 269b, Zechariah 2:8

[3] i.e., *The heart of those who rises up against Me*. According to ancient tradition, this is a cipher for Chasdim or Chaldea.

[4] Jeremiah 51:2 - Ezekiel 5:12, Guide for the Perplexed 2:47, Isaiah 17:16, Jeremiah 15:7 50:14-50:15 2:29 2:32 51:27-51:28, Matthew 3:12

[5] Jeremiah 51:3 - b.Nedarim 38a, Deuteronomy 8:25, Isaiah 13:10-13:18, James 2:13, Jeremiah 9:22 22:4 2:14 2:21 2:27 50:29-50:30 50:41-50:42, Mas.Soferim 6:9, Psalms 17:9

[6] Jeremiah 51:4 - Isaiah 13:15 14:19, Jeremiah 1:26 2:30 2:37

[7] Jeremiah 51:5 - 1 Kings 6:13, 1 Samuel 12:22, 2 Kings 21:16, Amos 9:8-9:9, Ezekiel 8:17 9:9 22:24-22:31, Ezra 9:9, Hosea 2:1 4:1, Isaiah 20:21 49:14-49:15 54:3-54:11 14:12, Jeremiah 16:18 19:4 23:15 7:38 33:24-33:26 22:28 50:4-50:5 2:20, Lamentations.R 1:3, Micah 7:18 7:20, Midrash Psalms 68:3, Psalms 94:14, Romans 11:1-11:2, Zechariah 2:12 12:6 12:8, Zephaniah 3:1-3:4

[8] Jeremiah 51:6 - 1 Timothy 5:22, Deuteronomy 8:25 8:41 8:43, Genesis 19:15-19:17, Isaiah 24:20, Jeremiah 1:14 1:16 3:7 22:10 2:8 2:15 2:28 2:31 3:9 3:11 3:45 3:50, Numbers 16:26, Proverbs 13:20, Revelation 16:19 18:4-18:6, Zechariah 2:6-2:7

[9] Jeremiah 51:7 - Daniel 2:32 2:38 3:1-3:7, Habakkuk 2:15-2:16, Isaiah 14:4, Jeremiah 1:9 25:14-25:27 2:38, Midrash Psalms 11:5 75:4, mt.Hilchot Deot 1:1, Revelation 14:8 17:2 17:4 18:3 18:23 19:2, Sifre Devarim {Haazinu Hashamayim} 324, Sifre Devarim Nitzavim 324, y.Pesachim 10:1

[10] Jeremiah 51:8 - Daniel 5:24 6:1, Ezekiel 27:30-27:32 6:2, Isaiah 13:6-13:7 21:9 23:9, Jeremiah 8:22 30:12-15 22:11 24:20 24:31 2:2 3:41, Nahum 3:19, Revelation 14:8 18:2 18:8-11 18:17-18:19

[11] Jeremiah 51:9 - 2 Chronicles 4:9, b.Sanhedrin 96b, Daniel 4:17-4:19, Ezra 9:6, Genesis.R 38:5 39:5, Guide for the Perplexed 1:18, Isaiah 13:14 23:15, Jeremiah 8:20 22:16 22:21 2:16, Matthew 25:10-25:13, Revelation 18:5

הוֹצִיא יְהוָה אֶת־צִדְקֹתֵינוּ בֹּאוּ וּנְסַפְּרָה בְצִיּוֹן אֶת־מַעֲשֵׂה יְהוָה אֱלֹהֵינוּ

10[1] The LORD has brought forth our victory; come, and let us declare in Zion the work of the LORD our God.

הָבֵרוּ הַחִצִּים מִלְאוּ הַשְּׁלָטִים הֵעִיר יְהוָה אֶת־רוּחַ מַלְכֵי מָדַי כִּי־עַל־בָּבֶל מְזִמָּתוֹ לְהַשְׁחִיתָהּ כִּי־נִקְמַת יְהוָה הִיא נִקְמַת הֵיכָלוֹ

11[2] Make bright the arrows, fill the quivers, the LORD has roused the spirit of the kings of the Medes; because His device is against Babylon, to destroy it; for it is the vengeance of the LORD, The vengeance of His temple.

אֶל־חוֹמֹת בָּבֶל שְׂאוּ־נֵס הַחֲזִיקוּ הַמִּשְׁמָר הָקִימוּ שֹׁמְרִים הָכִינוּ הָאֹרְבִים כִּי גַם־זָמַם יְהוָה גַּם־עָשָׂה אֵת אֲשֶׁר־דִּבֶּר אֶל־יֹשְׁבֵי בָבֶל

12[3] Set up a standard against the walls of Babylon, make the watch strong, set the watchmen, prepare the ambushes; for the LORD has both devised and done what He spoke concerning the inhabitants of Babylon.

"שֹׁכַנְתִּי" "שֹׁכַנְתְּ" עַל־מַיִם רַבִּים רַבַּת אוֹצָרֹת בָּא קִצֵּךְ אַמַּת בִּצְעֵךְ

13[4] O you who dwells on many waters, abundant in treasures, your end came, the measure of your covetousness.

נִשְׁבַּע יְהוָה צְבָאוֹת בְּנַפְשׁוֹ כִּי אִם־מִלֵּאתִיךְ אָדָם כַּיֶּלֶק וְעָנוּ עָלַיִךְ הֵידָד

14[5] The LORD of hosts has sworn by Himself: surely I will fill you with men, as with *the canker worm*[6], and they shall lift up a shout against you.

עֹשֵׂה אֶרֶץ בְּכֹחוֹ מֵכִין תֵּבֵל בְּחָכְמָתוֹ וּבִתְבוּנָתוֹ נָטָה שָׁמָיִם

15[7] *He who has*[8] made the earth by His power, who has established the world by His wisdom, and has stretched out the heavens by His discernment;

לְקוֹל תִּתּוֹ הֲמוֹן מַיִם בַּשָּׁמַיִם וַיַּעַל נְשִׂאִים מִקְצֵה־אֶרֶץ בְּרָקִים לַמָּטָר עָשָׂה וַיּוֹצֵא רוּחַ מֵאֹצְרֹתָיו

16[9] At the sound of His giving a multitude of waters in the heavens, He causes the vapors to ascend from the ends of the earth; He makes lightnings at the time of the rain, and brings forth the wind from His treasuries;

נִבְעַר כָּל־אָדָם מִדַּעַת הֹבִישׁ כָּל־צֹרֵף מִפָּסֶל כִּי שֶׁקֶר נִסְכּוֹ וְלֹא־רוּחַ בָּם

17[10] Everyone is proven to be brutish, for the knowledge; every goldsmith is put to shame by the graven image, that his molten image is falsehood, and there is no breath in them.

הֶבֶל הֵמָּה מַעֲשֵׂה תַּעְתֻּעִים בְּעֵת פְּקֻדָּתָם יֹאבֵדוּ

18[11] They are vanity, a work of delusion; in the time of their visitation they shall perish,

---

[1] Jeremiah 51:10 - Exodus.R 25:6, Isaiah 16:2 3:11 52:9-52:10, Jeremiah 31:7-31:10 2:28, Micah 7:9-7:10, Pesikta Rabbati 30:4, Psalms 9:15 37:6 102:20-102:22 116:18-116:19 126:1-126:3, Revelation 14:1-14:3 19:1-19:6

[2] Jeremiah 51:11 - 1 Chronicles 5:26, 1 Kings 11:14 11:23, 2 Chronicles 12:22, Ezra 1:1, Habakkuk 2:17-2:20, Isaiah 10:26 13:17-13:18 21:2 21:5 17:25 21:1 21:5 22:11, Jeremiah 22:4 22:9 2:9 50:14-50:15 2:25 50:28-50:29 2:45 3:12 3:24 51:27-51:29 3:35, Midrash Psalms 93:1, Psalms 74:3-74:11 83:4-83:10, Revelation 17:16-17:17, Zechariah 12:2-12:3 14:2 14:12

[3] Jeremiah 51:12 - Isaiah 8:9-8:10 13:2, Jeremiah 46:3-46:5 2:2 3:11 3:27 3:29, Joel 4:2 4:9-4:14, Joshua 8:14, Lamentations 2:17, Nahum 2:2 3:14-3:15, Proverbs 21:30

[4] Jeremiah 51:13 - 1 Peter 4:7, 2 Peter 2:3 2:14-2:15, Amos 8:2, b.Taanit 10a, Daniel 5:26, Ezekiel 7:2-7:12, Genesis 6:13, Habakkuk 2:5-2:11, Isaiah 21:3, Jeremiah 17:11 2:27 2:31 2:37 3:36, Jude 1:11-1:13, Lamentations 4:18, Luke 12:19-12:21, Revelation 17:1 17:15 18:11-18:17 18:19

[5] Jeremiah 51:14 - Amos 6:8, Hebrews 6:13, Jeremiah 22:23 1:13 2:15 3:27, Joel 1:4-1:7 2:3-2:4 2:25, Judges 6:5, Nahum 3:15-3:17

[6] LXX *locusts*

[7] Jeremiah 51:15 - 2 Baruch 21:4, Acts 14:15 17:24, Colossians 1:16-1:17, Genesis 1:1-1:6, Hebrews 1:2-1:3, Isaiah 16:22 16:26 18:5 20:24 21:12 24:13 3:13, Jeremiah 10:12-10:16 8:17 51:15-51:19, Job 9:8, Perek Shirah [the Wind], Proverbs 3:19, Psalms 8:2 8:24 11:25 16:5 146:5-146:6 148:1-5, Revelation 4:11, Romans 1:20 11:33

[8] LXX *the LORD*

[9] Jeremiah 51:16 - Amos 9:7, Exodus 10:13 10:19 14:21, Ezekiel 10:5, Genesis 8:1, Jeremiah 10:12-10:13, Job 36:26-36:33 37:2-37:11 13:13 14:22 38:34-38:38 16:9, Jonah 1:4 4:8, Matthew 8:26-8:27, Perek Shirah [the Waters], Psalms 18:14 29:3-29:10 46:7 68:34 78:26 8:7 15:7 3:18

[10] Jeremiah 51:17 - 1 Corinthians 1:19-1:21, Habakkuk 2:18-2:19, Isaiah 44:18-44:20, Jeremiah 10:14 2:2, Psalms 14:2 53:2-53:3 92:6-92:7 19:5 19:8 135:17-135:18, Romans 1:20-1:23

[11] Jeremiah 51:18 - Acts 14:15, b.Sanhedrin 102a, Exodus 12:12, Isaiah 19:1 22:1, Jeremiah 10:8 10:15 18:15 43:12-43:13 22:25 24:7 2:2, Jonah 2:8, Mas.Kallah 1:18, Zephaniah 2:11

לֹא־כְאֵלֶּה חֵלֶק יַעֲקוֹב כִּי־יוֹצֵר הַכֹּל הוּא וְשֵׁבֶט נַחֲלָתוֹ יְהוָה צְבָאוֹת שְׁמוֹ	19[1]	The portion of Jacob is not like these; for He is the former of all things, and [Israel] is the tribe of His inheritance; the LORD of hosts is His name.
מַפֵּץ־אַתָּה לִי כְּלֵי מִלְחָמָה וְנִפַּצְתִּי בְךָ גוֹיִם וְהִשְׁחַתִּי בְךָ מַמְלָכוֹת	20[2]	You *are My maul and*[3] weapons of war, and with you I will shatter the nations, and with you I will destroy kingdoms;
וְנִפַּצְתִּי בְךָ סוּס וְרֹכְבוֹ וְנִפַּצְתִּי בְךָ רֶכֶב וְרֹכְבוֹ	21[4]	And with you I will shatter the horse and his rider, and with you I will shatter the chariot and he who rides;
וְנִפַּצְתִּי בְךָ אִישׁ וְאִשָּׁה וְנִפַּצְתִּי בְךָ זָקֵן וָנָעַר וְנִפַּצְתִּי בְךָ בָּחוּר וּבְתוּלָה	22[5]	And with you I will *shatter man and woman, and with you I will shatter the old man and the youth, and with you I will shatter the young man and the maid*[6];
וְנִפַּצְתִּי בְךָ רֹעֶה וְעֶדְרוֹ וְנִפַּצְתִּי בְךָ אִכָּר וְצִמְדּוֹ וְנִפַּצְתִּי בְךָ פַּחוֹת וּסְגָנִים	23[7]	And with you I will shatter the shepherd and his flock, and with you I will shatter the farmer and his yoke of oxen, and with you I will shatter governors and deputies.
וְשִׁלַּמְתִּי לְבָבֶל וּלְכֹל יוֹשְׁבֵי כַשְׂדִּים אֵת כָּל־רָעָתָם אֲשֶׁר־עָשׂוּ בְצִיּוֹן לְעֵינֵיכֶם נְאֻם יְהוָה	24[8]	And I will repay to Babylon and to all the inhabitants of Chaldea all the evil they have done in Zion, in your sight; says the LORD.
הִנְנִי אֵלֶיךָ הַר הַמַּשְׁחִית נְאֻם־יְהוָה הַמַּשְׁחִית אֶת־כָּל־הָאָרֶץ וְנָטִיתִי אֶת־יָדִי עָלֶיךָ וְגִלְגַּלְתִּיךָ מִן־הַסְּלָעִים וּנְתַתִּיךָ לְהַר שְׂרֵפָה	25[9]	Behold, I am against you, O destroying mountain, says the LORD, who destroys all the earth; and I will stretch out My hand upon you, and roll you down from the rocks, and will make you a burnt mountain.
וְלֹא־יִקְחוּ מִמְּךָ אֶבֶן לְפִנָּה וְאֶבֶן לְמוֹסָדוֹת כִּי־שִׁמְמוֹת עוֹלָם תִּהְיֶה נְאֻם־יְהוָה	26[10]	And they shall not take from you a stone for a corner, nor a stone for foundations; but you shall be desolate forever, says the LORD.
שְׂאוּ־נֵס בָּאָרֶץ תִּקְעוּ שׁוֹפָר בַּגּוֹיִם קַדְּשׁוּ עָלֶיהָ גוֹיִם הַשְׁמִיעוּ עָלֶיהָ מַמְלְכוֹת אֲרָרַט מִנִּי וְאַשְׁכְּנָז פִּקְדוּ עָלֶיהָ טִפְסָר הַעֲלוּ־סוּס כְּיֶלֶק סָמָר	27[11]	Set up a standard in the land, blow the horn among the nations, prepare the nations against her, *call together against her the kingdoms of Ararat, Minni, and Ashkenaz; appoint a marshal against her; cause the horses to come up like the rough canker worm*[12].
קַדְּשׁוּ עָלֶיהָ גוֹיִם אֶת־מַלְכֵי מָדַי אֶת־פַּחוֹתֶיהָ וְאֶת־כָּל־סְגָנֶיהָ וְאֵת כָּל־אֶרֶץ מֶמְשַׁלְתּוֹ	28[13]	Prepare the nations against her, the kings of the Medes, its governors, and all the deputies, and *all the land of his dominion*[14].

---

[1] Jeremiah 51:19 - 1 Peter 2:9, Deuteronomy 8:9, Exodus 19:5-19:6, Isaiah 23:4, Jeremiah 10:16 12:7-12:10 2:11, Lamentations 3:24, Psalms 16:5 33:12 73:26 74:2 19:3 15:4, Siman 3:2

[2] Jeremiah 51:20 - Isaiah 10:5 10:15 13:5 14:5-14:6 13:26 41:15-41:16, Jeremiah 1:9 1:11 27:5-27:7 2:23, Lamentations.R 2:3, Matthew 22:7, Micah 4:13, Midrash Proverbs 25, Zechariah 9:13-9:14

[3] LXX *scatter for me*

[4] Jeremiah 51:21 - Exodus 15:1 15:21, Ezekiel 15:20, Haggai 2:22, Jeremiah 2:37, Micah 5:11, Nahum 2:14, Psalms 46:10 76:7, Revelation 19:18, Zechariah 10:5 12:4

[5] Jeremiah 51:22 - 1 Samuel 15:3, 2 Chronicles 12:17, Deuteronomy 8:25, Ezekiel 9:6, Isaiah 13:16 13:18 20:4, Jeremiah 6:11, Lamentations 2:11

[6] LXX *scatter youth and maid; and by you I will scatter man and woman*

[7] Jeremiah 51:23 - Jeremiah 3:57

[8] Jeremiah 51:24 - 1 Thessalonians 2:15-16, Isaiah 47:6-9 51:22-51:23 13:2 63:1-4 18:6, Jeremiah 2:15 50:17-18 50:28-29 50:33-34 3:11 3:35 3:49, Midrash Psalms 119:31 121:3, Psalms 137:8-137:9, Revelation 6:10 18:20 18:24 19:2-19:4, Saadia Opinions 4:5

[9] Jeremiah 51:25 - 2 Peter 3:10, Daniel 4:27, Genesis 11:4, Isaiah 13:2, Jeremiah 1:9 25:18-25:27 2:31 3:7 51:20-51:23 3:53 3:58, Revelation 8:8 17:1-17:6 18:9-10, Zechariah 4:7

[10] Jeremiah 51:26 - Isaiah 13:19-22 14:23 34:8-17, Jeremiah 50:12-13 50:40-41 3:29 3:37 3:43, Revelation 18:20-24

[11] Jeremiah 51:27 - 1 Chronicles 1:6, 2 Kings 19:37, Amos 3:6, Genesis 8:4 10:3, Genesis.R 90:3, Isaiah 13:2-5 18:3, Jastrow 548b, Jeremiah 6:1 1:14 22:23 2:2 50:41-42 3:12 3:14, Joel 2:2-3, Judges 6:5, Midrash Psalms 45:6, Nahum 3:15-17, Revelation 9:7-11, Zechariah 14:2

[12] LXX *and that for the people of Achanaz; set against her engines of war; bring up against her horses as a multitude of locusts*

[13] Jeremiah 51:28 - 1 Chronicles 1:5, Daniel 5:28-30 6:9 8:3-4 8:20 9:1, Esther 1:3 10:2, Genesis 10:2, Isaiah 13:17 21:2, Jeremiah 1:25 3:11 3:27

[14] Missing in LXX

וַתִּרְעַשׁ הָאָרֶץ וַתָּחֹל כִּי קָמָה עַל־בָּבֶל מַחְשְׁבוֹת יְהֹוָה לָשׂוּם אֶת־אֶרֶץ בָּבֶל לְשַׁמָּה מֵאֵין יוֹשֵׁב	29[1]	And the land quakes and is in pain; for the machinations of the LORD are performed against Babylon, to make the land of Babylon desolate, without inhabitant.
חָדְלוּ גִבּוֹרֵי בָבֶל לְהִלָּחֵם יָשְׁבוּ בַּמְּצָדוֹת נָשְׁתָה גְבוּרָתָם הָיוּ לְנָשִׁים הִצִּיתוּ מִשְׁכְּנֹתֶיהָ נִשְׁבְּרוּ בְרִיחֶיהָ	30[2]	The mighty men of Babylon failed to fight, they remain in their strongholds; their might has failed, they became as women; her lodgings are set on fire; her bars are broken.
רָץ לִקְרַאת־רָץ יָרוּץ וּמַגִּיד לִקְרַאת מַגִּיד לְהַגִּיד לְמֶלֶךְ בָּבֶל כִּי־נִלְכְּדָה עִירוֹ מִקָּצֶה	31[3]	One post runs to meet another, and one messenger to meet another, to tell the king of Babylon that his city is taken on every quarter;
וְהַמַּעְבָּרוֹת נִתְפָּשׂוּ וְאֶת־הָאֲגַמִּים שָׂרְפוּ בָאֵשׁ וְאַנְשֵׁי הַמִּלְחָמָה נִבְהָלוּ	32[4]	And the fjords are seized, and they burned the *castles*[5] with fire, and the men of war are frightened.
כִּי כֹה אָמַר יְהֹוָה צְבָאוֹת אֱלֹהֵי יִשְׂרָאֵל בַּת־בָּבֶל כְּגֹרֶן עֵת הַדְרִיכָהּ עוֹד מְעַט וּבָאָה עֵת־הַקָּצִיר לָהּ	33[6]	For thus says the LORD of hosts, the God of Israel: the daughter of Babylon is like a threshing floor at the time when it is tread; yet a little while, and the time of harvest shall come for her.
'אֲכָלַנוּ' 'אֲכָלָנִי' 'הֲמָמַנוּ' 'הֲמָמָנִי' נְבוּכַדְרֶאצַּר מֶלֶךְ בָּבֶל 'הִצִּיגַנוּ' 'הִצִּיגַנִי' כְּלִי רִיק 'בְּלָעַנוּ' 'בְּלָעָנִי' כַּתַּנִּין מִלָּא כְרֵשׂוֹ מֵעֲדָנָי 'הֱדִיחַנוּ' 'הֱדִיחָנִי'	34[7]	*Nebuchadrezzar the king of Babylon*[8] consumed me, he crushed me, he set me down as an empty vessel, he swallowed me like a dragon, he filled his mouth with my delicacies; he washed me clean.
חֲמָסִי וּשְׁאֵרִי עַל־בָּבֶל תֹּאמַר יֹשֶׁבֶת צִיּוֹן וְדָמִי אֶל־יֹשְׁבֵי כַשְׂדִּים תֹּאמַר יְרוּשָׁלִָם	35[9]	'The violence done to me and to my flesh is upon Babylon,' shall the inhabitant of Zion say, 'My blood is upon the inhabitants of Chaldea,' shall Jerusalem say.
לָכֵן כֹּה אָמַר יְהֹוָה הִנְנִי־רָב אֶת־רִיבֵךְ וְנִקַּמְתִּי אֶת־נִקְמָתֵךְ וְהַחֲרַבְתִּי אֶת־יַמָּהּ וְהֹבַשְׁתִּי אֶת־מְקוֹרָהּ	36[10]	Therefore, thus says the LORD: behold, I will plead your cause, and take vengeance for you; and I will dry up her sea, and make her fountain dry.
וְהָיְתָה בָבֶל לְגַלִּים מְעוֹן־תַּנִּים שַׁמָּה וּשְׁרֵקָה מֵאֵין יוֹשֵׁב	37[11]	And Babylon shall become ruins, a dwelling place for jackals, an astonishment, and a hissing, without inhabitant.
יַחְדָּו כַּכְּפִרִים יִשְׁאָגוּ נָעֲרוּ כְּגוֹרֵי אֲרָיוֹת	38[12]	They shall roar together like young lions; they shall growl like lions' whelps.

---

[1] Jeremiah 51:29 - Amos 8:8, Isaiah 13:13-14 13:19-20 14:16 14:23-24 46:10-11 47:1-15, Jeremiah 8:16 10:10 2:13 2:36 50:39-40 2:43 2:45 51:11-12 3:43 51:62-64, Joel 2:10, Midrash Psalms 18:1 104:25, Revelation 18:2 18:21-24, y.Berachot 9:2

[2] Jeremiah 51:30 - Amos 1:5, b.Chullin 91a, Isaiah 13:7-13:8 19:16 45:1-45:2, Jeremiah 24:41 50:36-50:37 3:32 3:57, Lamentations 2:9, Nahum 3:13, Psalms 76:6 11:16 3:13, Revelation 18:10

[3] Jeremiah 51:31 - 1 Samuel 4:12-4:18, 2 Chronicles 6:6, 2 Samuel 18:19-18:31, Daniel 5:2-5:5 5:30, Esther 3:13-3:15 8:10 8:14, Isaiah 21:3-21:9 47:11-47:13, Jeremiah 4:20 2:24 2:43, Job 9:25

[4] Jeremiah 51:32 - Isaiah 20:27, Jeremiah 50:37-50:38 3:30

[5] LXX *cisterns*

[6] Jeremiah 51:33 - Amos 1:3, Habakkuk 3:12, Hosea 6:11, Isaiah 17:5-17:11 18:5 21:10 41:15-41:16, Joel 4:13, Matthew 13:30 13:39, Micah 4:13, Midrash Psalms 8:1, Revelation 14:15-14:20, z.Vaetchanan 269b

[7] Jeremiah 51:34 - Amos 8:4, Ezekiel 12:3, Isaiah 24:1-24:3 10:11, Jeremiah 39:1-39:8 48:11-48:12 2:7 2:17 3:44 3:49, Job 20:15, Lamentations 1:1 1:14-1:15 2:16, Matthew 23:13, Nahum 2:3 2:10-2:11, Pesikta de R'Kahana S2.2, Proverbs 1:12, Psalms of Solomon 2:25

[8] LXX *He*

[9] Jeremiah 51:35 - Genesis.R 31:6, Isaiah 26:20-26:21, James 2:13, Jeremiah 2:29, Judges 9:20 9:24 9:56-9:57, Matthew 7:2, Psalms 9:13 12:6 137:8-9, Revelation 6:10 16:6 18:6 18:20, Zechariah 1:15

[10] Jeremiah 51:36 - Deuteronomy 8:35 8:43, Habakkuk 2:8-2:17, Hebrews 10:30-10:31, Isaiah 19:14 20:27 47:6-47:9 49:25-49:26, Jeremiah 50:33-50:34 2:38 3:6, Micah 7:8-7:10, Proverbs 22:23 23:11, Psalms 94:1-94:3 11:33 20:13, Revelation 16:12 19:1-19:3, Romans 12:19, z.Vaetchanan 269b

[11] Jeremiah 51:37 - 2 Chronicles 5:8, Isaiah 13:19-13:22 14:23 34:8-34:17, Jeremiah 18:16 19:8 1:9 1:12 1:18 5:18 50:12-50:13 50:23-50:26 50:38-50:40 51:25-51:26 3:29, Lamentations 2:15-2:16, Micah 6:16, Revelation 18:2 18:21-18:23, Zephaniah 2:15

[12] Jeremiah 51:38 - Isaiah 11:9, Jeremiah 2:15, Job 4:10-4:11, Judges 16:20, Nahum 2:12-2:14, Psalms 34:11 58:7, Zechariah 11:3

Hebrew		English
בְּחֻמָּם אָשִׁית אֶת־מִשְׁתֵּיהֶם וְהִשְׁכַּרְתִּים לְמַעַן יַעֲלֹזוּ וְיָשְׁנוּ שְׁנַת־עוֹלָם וְלֹא יָקִיצוּ נְאֻם יְהוָה	39[1]	*With their poison I will prepare their feast*[2], and I will make them drunk, so they may convulse, and sleep a perpetual sleep, and never waken, says the LORD.
אוֹרִידֵם כְּכָרִים לִטְבוֹחַ כְּאֵילִים עִם־עַתּוּדִים	40[3]	I will bring them down like lambs to the slaughter, like rams with he goats.
אֵיךְ נִלְכְּדָה שֵׁשַׁךְ וַתִּתָּפֵשׂ תְּהִלַּת כָּל־הָאָרֶץ אֵיךְ הָיְתָה לְשַׁמָּה בָּבֶל בַּגּוֹיִם	41[4]	*How Sheshach is*[5] taken, and the praise of the whole earth seized. How Babylon has become an astonishment among the nations.
עָלָה עַל־בָּבֶל הַיָּם בַּהֲמוֹן גַּלָּיו נִכְסָתָה	42[6]	The sea came upon Babylon; She is covered with the multitude of its waves.
הָיוּ עָרֶיהָ לְשַׁמָּה אֶרֶץ צִיָּה וַעֲרָבָה אֶרֶץ לֹא־יֵשֵׁב בָּהֵן כָּל־אִישׁ וְלֹא־יַעֲבֹר בָּהֵן בֶּן־אָדָם	43[7]	Her cities became desolate, a dry land, and a desert, a land in which no man dwells, nor does any son of man pass by.
וּפָקַדְתִּי עַל־בֵּל בְּבָבֶל וְהֹצֵאתִי אֶת־בִּלְעוֹ מִפִּיו וְלֹא־יִנְהֲרוּ אֵלָיו עוֹד גּוֹיִם גַּם־חוֹמַת בָּבֶל נָפָלָה	44[8]	And I will *punish Bel in*[9] Babylon, and I will bring forth from his mouth what he has swallowed, and the nations shall not flow to him any longer; Yes, the wall of Babylon shall fall.
צְאוּ מִתּוֹכָהּ עַמִּי וּמַלְּטוּ אִישׁ אֶת־נַפְשׁוֹ מֵחֲרוֹן אַף־יְהוָה	45[10]	*My people, go from her midst, and save yourselves from the fierce anger of the LORD*[11].
וּפֶן־יֵרַךְ לְבַבְכֶם וְתִירְאוּ בַּשְּׁמוּעָה הַנִּשְׁמַעַת בָּאָרֶץ וּבָא בַשָּׁנָה הַשְּׁמוּעָה וְאַחֲרָיו בַּשָּׁנָה הַשְּׁמוּעָה וְחָמָס בָּאָרֶץ וּמֹשֵׁל עַל־מֹשֵׁל	46[12]	*And do not let your heart faint, nor fear, for the rumor that shall be heard in the land; for a rumor shall come one year, and after that in another year a rumor, and violence in the land, ruler against ruler*[13].
לָכֵן הִנֵּה יָמִים בָּאִים וּפָקַדְתִּי עַל־פְּסִילֵי בָבֶל וְכָל־אַרְצָהּ תֵּבוֹשׁ וְכָל־חֲלָלֶיהָ יִפְּלוּ בְתוֹכָהּ	47[14]	*Therefore, behold, the days come, that I will judge the graven images of Babylon, and her whole land shall be ashamed; and all her slain shall fall in her midst*[15].
וְרִנְּנוּ עַל־בָּבֶל שָׁמַיִם וָאָרֶץ וְכֹל אֲשֶׁר בָּהֶם כִּי מִצָּפוֹן יָבוֹא־לָהּ הַשּׁוֹדְדִים נְאֻם־יְהוָה	48[16]	*Then the heaven and the earth, and all that is in it, shall sing for joy over Babylon; for the spoilers shall come to her from the north, says the LORD*[17].

---

[1] Jeremiah 51:39 - b.Megillah [Rashi] 15a, b.Megillah 15b, Daniel 5:1-5:4 5:30, Ecclesiastes.R 9:2, Ein Yaakov Megillah:15b, Esther.R 3:3, Isaiah 21:4-21:5 22:12-22:14, Jastrow 273a, Jeremiah 1:27 24:26 3:57, Nahum 1:10 3:11, Psalms 13:4 76:6-76:7, Ruth.R 3:2

[2] LXX *In their heat I will give them a draught*

[3] Jeremiah 51:40 - Ezekiel 15:18, Isaiah 10:6, Jeremiah 2:27, Psalms 37:20 44:23

[4] Jeremiah 51:41 - 2 Chronicles 7:21, Daniel 2:38 4:19 4:27 5:1-5:5, Deuteronomy 4:37, Ezekiel 3:35, Isaiah 13:19 14:4, Jeremiah 1:26 1:25 2:23 2:46 3:37, Revelation 18:10-18:19

[5] LXX *How has the boast of all the earth been*

[6] Jeremiah 51:42 - Daniel 9:26, Ezekiel 27:26-27:34, Isaiah 8:7-8:8, Jeremiah 3:55, Luke 21:25, Psalms 18:5 18:17 42:8 65:8 93:3, Revelation 17:15-17:16

[7] Jeremiah 51:43 - Ezekiel 29:10-29:11, Isaiah 13:20, Jeremiah 2:6 2:12 50:39-50:40 3:29 3:37

[8] Jeremiah 51:44 - 2 Chronicles 12:7, According to the Massorah, Daniel 1:2 3:2-3:3 3:29 3:31 4:19 5:2-5:4 5:19 5:26 6:1, Ezra 1:7-1:8, Genesis.R 68:13, Isaiah 2:2 46:1-46:2 12:5, Jeremiah 2:2 2:15 3:18 3:34 3:47 3:53 3:58, Leviticus.R 33:6, Pesikta Rabbati 42:9, Revelation 18:9-18:19, z.Terumah 174b, בל "Bel" was not altered to become באל "Baal"

[9] LXX *vengeance on*

[10] Jeremiah 51:45 - 2 Corinthians 6:17, Acts 2:40, Genesis 19:12-19:16, Isaiah 24:20, Jeremiah 2:8 3:6 3:9 3:50, Numbers 16:26, Revelation 14:8-14:11 18:4, Zechariah 2:7

[11] Missing in LXX

[12] Jeremiah 51:46 - 1 Samuel 14:16-20, 2 Chronicles 20:23, 2 Kings 19:7, Isaiah 13:3-5 19:2 21:2-3, Jeremiah 22:27, Judges 7:22, Luke 21:9-19 21:28, Mark 13:7-8, Matthew 24:6-8, Seder Olam 28:Darius

[13] Missing in LXX

[14] Jeremiah 51:47 - Isaiah 21:9 46:1-46:2, Jeremiah 11:22 13:21 23:34 1:12 2:2 50:12-50:16 50:35-50:40 3:18 3:24 3:43 3:52

[15] Missing in LXX

[16] Jeremiah 51:48 - Isaiah 20:23 24:20 1:13, Jeremiah 2:3 2:9 2:41 51:10-51:11, Proverbs 11:10, Psalms 58:11-58:12, Revelation 15:1-15:4 16:4-16:7 18:20 19:1-19:7

[17] Missing in LXX

גַּם־בָּבֶל לִנְפֹּל חַלְלֵי יִשְׂרָאֵל גַּם־לְבָבֶל נָפְלוּ חַלְלֵי כָל־הָאָרֶץ	49[1]	*As Babylon has caused the slain of Israel to fall, so in Babylon shall the slain of all the land fall[2].*
פְּלֵטִים מֵחֶרֶב הִלְכוּ אַל־תַּעֲמֹדוּ זִכְרוּ מֵרָחוֹק אֶת־יְהוָה וִירוּשָׁלִַם תַּעֲלֶה עַל־לְבַבְכֶם	50[3]	you who have escaped the sword, go, do not stand still; remember the LORD from afar, and let Jerusalem come into your mind.
בֹּשְׁנוּ כִּי־שָׁמַעְנוּ חֶרְפָּה כִּסְּתָה כְלִמָּה פָּנֵינוּ כִּי בָּאוּ זָרִים עַל־מִקְדְּשֵׁי בֵּית יְהוָה	51[4]	'We are ashamed, because we heard reproach, confusion has covered our faces; for strangers come into the sanctuaries of the LORD's house.'
לָכֵן הִנֵּה־יָמִים בָּאִים נְאֻם־יְהוָה וּפָקַדְתִּי עַל־פְּסִילֶיהָ וּבְכָל־אַרְצָהּ יֶאֱנֹק חָלָל	52[5]	So, behold, the days come, says the LORD, that I will judge her graven images; and through all her land the wounded shall groan.
כִּי־תַעֲלֶה בָבֶל הַשָּׁמַיִם וְכִי תְבַצֵּר מְרוֹם עֻזָּהּ מֵאִתִּי יָבֹאוּ שֹׁדְדִים לָהּ נְאֻם־יְהוָה	53[6]	Though Babylon should mount up to heaven, and though she should fortify the height of her strength, yet from Me spoilers shall come to her, says the LORD.
קוֹל זְעָקָה מִבָּבֶל וְשֶׁבֶר גָּדוֹל מֵאֶרֶץ כַּשְׂדִּים	54[7]	Listen. A cry from Babylon, and great destruction from the land of the Chaldeans.
כִּי־שֹׁדֵד יְהוָה אֶת־בָּבֶל וְאִבַּד מִמֶּנָּה קוֹל גָּדוֹל וְהָמוּ גַלֵּיהֶם כְּמַיִם רַבִּים נִתַּן שְׁאוֹן קוֹלָם	55[8]	For the LORD spoils Babylon, and destroys from her the great voice; and their waves roar like many waters, the noise of their voice is uttered;
כִּי בָא עָלֶיהָ עַל־בָּבֶל שׁוֹדֵד וְנִלְכְּדוּ גִּבּוֹרֶיהָ חִתְּתָה קַשְּׁתוֹתָם כִּי אֵל גְּמֻלוֹת יְהוָה שַׁלֵּם יְשַׁלֵּם	56[9]	For the spoiler came upon her, upon Babylon, and took her mighty men, their bows are crushed; for the LORD is a God of restitution, He will surely requite.
וְהִשְׁכַּרְתִּי שָׂרֶיהָ וַחֲכָמֶיהָ פַּחוֹתֶיהָ וּסְגָנֶיהָ וְגִבּוֹרֶיהָ וְיָשְׁנוּ שְׁנַת־עוֹלָם וְלֹא יָקִיצוּ נְאֻם־הַמֶּלֶךְ יְהוָה צְבָאוֹת שְׁמוֹ	57[10]	*And I will make her princes and her wise men drunk, her governors and her deputies, and her mighty men; and they shall sleep a perpetual sleep, and not awaken[11],* says the King, whose name is the LORD of hosts.
כֹּה־אָמַר יְהוָה צְבָאוֹת חֹמוֹת בָּבֶל הָרְחָבָה עַרְעֵר תִּתְעַרְעָר וּשְׁעָרֶיהָ הַגְּבֹהִים בָּאֵשׁ יִצַּתּוּ וְיִגְעוּ עַמִּים בְּדֵי־רִיק וּלְאֻמִּים בְּדֵי־אֵשׁ וְיָעֵפוּ	58[12]	Thus says the LORD of hosts: the broad walls of Babylon shall be utterly overthrown, and her high gates shall be burned with fire; and the peoples shall labor for vanity, and the nations for the fire; and they shall be weary.

[1] Jeremiah 51:49 - Ecclesiastes.R 12:7, James 2:13, Jeremiah 2:11 50:17-50:18 2:29 50:33-50:34 51:10-51:11 3:24 3:35, Judges 1:7, Lamentations.R Petichata D'Chakimei:23, Matthew 7:2, Psalms 137:8-137:9, Revelation 18:5-18:6, y.Berachot 4:1
[2] LXX *and in Babylon the slain men of all the earth shall fall*
[3] Jeremiah 51:50 - Daniel 9:2-3 9:16-19, Deuteronomy 4:29-31 30:1-4, Ezra 1:3-5, Isaiah 24:20 3:11 4:2 52:11-12, Jeremiah 29:12-29:14 7:22 20:28 2:8 3:6 3:45, Midrash Psalms 70:1, Midrash Tanchuma Vayigash 10, Nehemiah 1:2-4 2:3-5, Psalms 102:14-15 2:6 137:5-6, Revelation 18:4, Zechariah 2:7-9
[4] Jeremiah 51:51 - Daniel 8:11-8:14 9:26-9:27 11:31, Ezekiel 7:18 7:21-7:22 9:7 24:21 12:30, Jeremiah 3:22-3:25 14:3 7:20 4:13, Lamentations 1:10 2:15-2:17 2:20 5:1, Lamentations.R Petichata D'Chakimei:9, Micah 7:10, Psalms 44:14-44:17 69:8-69:14 71:13 74:3-74:7 74:18-74:21 79:1 79:4 79:12 13:29 123:3-123:4 137:1-137:3, Revelation 11:1-11:2
[5] Jeremiah 51:52 - Daniel 5:30-5:31, Ezekiel 6:24, Isaiah 13:15-13:16, Jeremiah 2:38 3:47
[6] Jeremiah 51:53 - Amos 9:4, Daniel 4:27, Ezekiel 31:9-11, Genesis 11:4, Isaiah 10:6-7 13:2-5 13:17 14:12-15 17:25 45:1-5 23:5 23:7, Jeremiah 1:16 50:9-10 2:21 2:25 50:31-34 2:45 51:1-4 3:11 3:25 3:48 3:58, Obadiah 1:3-1:4, Psalms 139:8-10
[7] Jeremiah 51:54 - Isaiah 13:6-13:9 15:5, Jeremiah 48:3-48:5 2:22 2:27 2:43 2:46, Revelation 18:17-18:19, Zephaniah 1:10
[8] Jeremiah 51:55 - Ezekiel 2:3, Isaiah 15:1 17:13 24:8-24:11 23:5, Jeremiah 1:10 50:10-50:15 51:38-51:39 3:42, Luke 21:25, Psalms 18:5 65:8 93:3-93:4, Revelation 17:15 18:22-18:23
[9] Jeremiah 51:56 - 1 Samuel 2:4, 2 Thessalonians 1:6, Deuteronomy 8:35, Ezekiel 15:3 15:9, Genesis 1:24, Habakkuk 2:8, Isaiah 21:2 10:8 11:4 11:18, Jeremiah 1:35 2:10 50:28-29 2:36 3:6 3:24 3:30 3:48, Midrash Tanchuma Naso 30, Psalms 37:15 46:10 76:4 94:1-2 17:8, Revelation 17:16 18:5-6 18:20 19:2
[10] Jeremiah 51:57 - Daniel 5:1-5:4 5:30-5:31, Habakkuk 2:15-2:17, Isaiah 21:4-21:5 13:36, Jeremiah 1:27 22:18 24:15 3:39, Malachi 1:14, Nahum 1:10, Psalms 76:6-76:7, Revelation 18:6-18:7 18:9, y.Berachot 9:1, y.Sheviit 4:8
[11] LXX *The LORD recompenses, and will make her leaders and her wise men and her captains completely drunk*
[12] Jeremiah 51:58 - Habakkuk 2:13, Isaiah 45:1-45:2 17:23, Jeremiah 2:15 3:9 3:30 3:44 51:64, Lamentations.R 5:1, Midrash Psalms 137:8, Midrash Tanchuma Ki Tetze 9, Pesikta de R'Kahana 3.7 18.2 20.2, Pesikta Rabbati 32:2, Psalms 7:1, z.Vaetchanan 269b

הַדָּבָ֞ר אֲשֶׁר־צִוָּ֣ה יִרְמְיָ֣הוּ הַנָּבִ֗יא אֶת־שְׂרָיָ֣ה בֶן־נֵרִיָּה֮ בֶּן־מַחְסֵיָה֒ בְּלֶכְתּ֞וֹ אֶת־צִדְקִיָּ֤הוּ מֶֽלֶךְ־יְהוּדָה֙ בָּבֶ֔ל בִּשְׁנַ֥ת הָרְבִעִ֖ית לְמָלְכ֑וֹ וּשְׂרָיָ֖ה שַׂ֥ר מְנוּחָֽה	59[1]	The word Jeremiah the prophet commanded Seraiah the son of Neriah, the son of Mahseiah, when he went with Zedekiah the king of Judah to Babylon in the fourth year of his reign. Now Seraiah was quartermaster.
וַיִּכְתֹּ֣ב יִרְמְיָ֗הוּ אֵ֧ת כָּל־הָרָעָ֛ה אֲשֶׁר־תָּב֥וֹא אֶל־בָּבֶ֖ל אֶל־סֵ֣פֶר אֶחָ֑ד אֵ֚ת כָּל־הַדְּבָרִ֣ים הָאֵ֔לֶּה הַכְּתֻבִ֖ים אֶל־בָּבֶֽל	60[2]	And Jeremiah wrote in one book all the evil that should come upon Babylon, all these words that are written concerning Babylon.
וַיֹּ֥אמֶר יִרְמְיָ֖הוּ אֶל־שְׂרָיָ֑ה כְּבֹאֲךָ֣ בָבֶ֔ל וְֽרָאִ֔יתָ וְֽקָרָ֔אתָ אֵ֥ת כָּל־הַדְּבָרִ֖ים הָאֵֽלֶּה	61[3]	And Jeremiah said to Seraiah: 'When you come to Babylon, then see that you read all these words,
וְאָמַרְתָּ֗ יְהֹוָה֙ אַתָּ֣ה דִבַּ֗רְתָּ אֶל־הַמָּק֤וֹם הַזֶּה֙ לְהַכְרִית֔וֹ לְבִלְתִּ֤י הֱיֽוֹת־בּוֹ֙ יוֹשֵׁ֔ב לְמֵאָדָ֖ם וְעַד־בְּהֵמָ֑ה כִּֽי־שִׁמְמ֥וֹת עוֹלָ֖ם תִּֽהְיֶֽה	62[4]	and say: O LORD, you have spoken concerning this place, to cut it off, that no one shall live in it, neither man nor beast, but that it shall be desolate forever.
וְהָיָה֙ כְּכַלֹּ֣תְךָ֔ לִקְרֹ֖א אֶת־הַסֵּ֣פֶר הַזֶּ֑ה תִּקְשֹׁ֤ר עָלָיו֙ אֶ֔בֶן וְהִשְׁלַכְתּ֖וֹ אֶל־תּ֥וֹךְ פְּרָֽת	63[5]	And it shall be, when you have made an end of reading this book, you shall bind a stone to it, and cast it into the midst of the Euphrates;
וְאָמַרְתָּ֗ כָּ֠כָה תִּשְׁקַ֤ע בָּבֶל֙ וְלֹֽא־תָק֔וּם מִפְּנֵ֥י הָרָעָ֖ה אֲשֶׁ֣ר אָנֹכִ֣י מֵבִ֣יא עָלֶ֑יהָ וְיָעֵ֑פוּ עַד־הֵ֖נָּה דִּבְרֵ֥י יִרְמְיָֽהוּ	64[6]	and you shall say: Thus shall Babylon sink, and shall not rise again because of the evil that I will bring upon her; and they shall be weary.' Thus far are the words of Jeremiah.

Jeremiah – Chapter 52[7]

בֶּן־עֶשְׂרִ֨ים וְאַחַ֤ת שָׁנָה֙ צִדְקִיָּ֣הוּ בְמָלְכ֔וֹ וְאַחַ֤ת עֶשְׂרֵה֙ שָׁנָ֔ה מָלַ֖ךְ בִּירֽוּשָׁלָ֑͏ִם וְשֵׁ֤ם אִמּוֹ֙ 'חֲמִיטַ֔ל' "חֲמוּטַ֔ל" בַּת־יִרְמְיָ֖הוּ מִלִּבְנָֽה	1[8]	Zedekiah was twenty-one years old when he began to reign; and he reigned eleven years in Jerusalem; and his mother's name was Hamutal the daughter of Jeremiah of Libnah.
וַיַּ֥עַשׂ הָרַ֖ע בְּעֵינֵ֣י יְהֹוָ֑ה כְּכֹ֥ל אֲשֶׁר־עָשָׂ֖ה יְהוֹיָקִֽים	2[9]	*And he did what was evil in the sight of the LORD, according to all Jehoiakim had done[10].*
כִּ֣י ׀ עַל־אַ֣ף יְהֹוָ֗ה הָֽיְתָה֙ בִּירֽוּשָׁלַ֣͏ִם וִֽיהוּדָ֔ה עַד־הִשְׁלִיכ֥וֹ אוֹתָ֖ם מֵעַ֣ל פָּנָ֑יו וַיִּמְרֹ֥ד צִדְקִיָּ֖הוּ בְּמֶ֥לֶךְ בָּבֶֽל	3[11]	*For through the anger of the LORD it came to pass in Jerusalem and Judah, until He cast them from His presence. and Zedekiah rebelled against the king of Babylon[12].*
וַיְהִי֩ בַשָּׁנָ֨ה הַתְּשִׁעִ֜ית לְמָלְכ֗וֹ בַּחֹ֨דֶשׁ הָעֲשִׂירִ֜י בֶּעָשׂ֣וֹר לַחֹ֗דֶשׁ בָּ֠א נְבֽוּכַדְרֶאצַּ֨ר מֶֽלֶךְ־בָּבֶ֥ל ה֛וּא	4[13]	And it came to pass in the ninth year of his reign, in the tenth month, in the tenth day of the month, that Nebuchadrezzar king of Babylon came, he and all his army, against

---

[1] Jeremiah 51:59 - 2 Baruch 1:1 5:5, Jastrow 798b, Jeremiah 4:1 8:12 12:4 21:1 4:1, Lamentations.R 2:10, Numbers.R 8:9 10:5, Testament of Solomon 8:6

[2] Jeremiah 51:60 - Daniel 12:4, Habakkuk 2:2-2:3, Isaiah 8:1-8:4 6:8, Jeremiah 30:2-30:3 36:2-36:4 12:32, Revelation 1:11 1:19

[3] Jeremiah 51:61 - 1 Thessalonians 4:18 5:27, 2 Baruch 5:5, Colossians 4:16, Jeremiah 29:1-29:2, Mark 13:1, Matthew 24:1, Revelation 1:3

[4] Jeremiah 51:62 - Ezekiel 11:9, Isaiah 13:19-13:22 14:22-14:23, Jeremiah 1:9 1:12 2:3 2:13 50:39-50:40 51:25-51:26 3:29 3:37, Revelation 18:20-18:23

[5] Jeremiah 51:63 - Jeremiah 19:10-19:11, Revelation 18:21

[6] Jeremiah 51:64 - Habakkuk 2:13, Jeremiah 1:27 3:42 3:58, Job 7:40, Nahum 1:8-1:9, Pesikta de R'Kahana 13.14, Psalms 72:20 76:13, Revelation 14:8 18:2 18:21, Sifre Devarim Devarim 1 Sifre Devarim Vezot Habracha 342, y.Berachot 5:1

[7] Chapter 52:5b-34

[8] Jeremiah 52:1 - 2 Chronicles 12:11, 2 Kings 8:22 24:18, Joshua 10:29 15:42
Jeremiah 52:1-30 - Josephus Antiquities 10.8.2-7

[9] Jeremiah 52:2 - 1 Kings 14:22, 2 Chronicles 36:12-13, 2 Kings 24:19-20, Ezekiel 17:16-20 21:30, Jeremiah 26:21-23 36:21-23 36:29-31

[10] Missing in LXX

[11] Jeremiah 52:3 - 1 Kings 10:9, 2 Chronicles 12:13, 2 Samuel 24:1, Ecclesiastes 10:16, Ezekiel 17:12-17:21, Isaiah 3:1 3:4-3:5 19:4, Proverbs 4:2

[12] Missing in LXX

[13] Jeremiah 52:4 - 2 Kings 25:1-25:27, Deuteronomy 28:52-28:57, Ezekiel 4:1-4:7 21:27 24:1-24:2, Isaiah 5:3 42:24-25, Jeremiah 6:3-6 8:24 15:1 4:7, Leviticus 2:25, Luke 19:43 21:20, Zechariah 8:19
Jeremiah 52:4-12 - Seder Olam 27:Siege

וְכָל־חֵילוֹ עַל־יְרוּשָׁלִַם וַיַּחֲנוּ עָלֶיהָ וַיִּבְנוּ עָלֶיהָ דָּיֵק סָבִיב

Jerusalem, and encamped against it; and they built forts against it.

5[1] וַתָּבֹא הָעִיר בַּמָּצוֹר עַד עַשְׁתֵּי עֶשְׂרֵה שָׁנָה לַמֶּלֶךְ צִדְקִיָּהוּ

5[1] So the city was besieged to the eleventh year of king Zedekiah.

6[2] בַּחֹדֶשׁ הָרְבִיעִי בְּתִשְׁעָה לַחֹדֶשׁ וַיֶּחֱזַק הָרָעָב בָּעִיר וְלֹא־הָיָה לֶחֶם לְעַם הָאָרֶץ

6[2] In the fourth month, in the ninth day of the month, the famine was bitter in the city, so there was no bread for the people of the land.

7[3] וַתִּבָּקַע הָעִיר וְכָל־אַנְשֵׁי הַמִּלְחָמָה יִבְרְחוּ וַיֵּצְאוּ מֵהָעִיר לַיְלָה דֶּרֶךְ שַׁעַר בֵּין־הַחֹמֹתַיִם אֲשֶׁר עַל־גַּן הַמֶּלֶךְ וְכַשְׂדִּים עַל־הָעִיר סָבִיב וַיֵּלְכוּ דֶּרֶךְ הָעֲרָבָה

7[3] Then a breach was made in the city, and all the men of war fled, and went forth from the city by night by the way of the gate between the two walls, which was by the king's garden, now the Chaldeans were against the city, and they went by the way of the Arabah.

8[4] וַיִּרְדְּפוּ חֵיל־כַּשְׂדִּים אַחֲרֵי הַמֶּלֶךְ וַיַּשִּׂיגוּ אֶת־צִדְקִיָּהוּ בְּעַרְבֹת יְרֵחוֹ וְכָל־חֵילוֹ נָפֹצוּ מֵעָלָיו

8[4] But the army of the Chaldeans pursued after the king, and overtook Zedekiah in the plains of Jericho; and his army scattered from him.

9[5] וַיִּתְפְּשׂוּ אֶת־הַמֶּלֶךְ וַיַּעֲלוּ אֹתוֹ אֶל־מֶלֶךְ בָּבֶל רִבְלָתָה בְּאֶרֶץ חֲמָת וַיְדַבֵּר אִתּוֹ מִשְׁפָּטִים

9[5] Then they took the king, and carried him up to the king of Babylon to Riblah in the land of Hamath; and he gave judgment upon him.

10[6] וַיִּשְׁחַט מֶלֶךְ־בָּבֶל אֶת־בְּנֵי צִדְקִיָּהוּ לְעֵינָיו וְגַם אֶת־כָּל־שָׂרֵי יְהוּדָה שָׁחַט בְּרִבְלָתָה

10[6] And the king of Babylon killed the sons of Zedekiah before his eyes; he also killed all the princes of Judah in *Riblah*[7].

11[8] וְאֶת־עֵינֵי צִדְקִיָּהוּ עִוֵּר וַיַּאַסְרֵהוּ בַנְחֻשְׁתַּיִם וַיְבִאֵהוּ מֶלֶךְ־בָּבֶל בָּבֶלָה וַיִּתְּנֵהוּ 'בְבֵית־הַפְּקֻדֹּת' עַד־יוֹם מוֹתוֹ

11[8] And he put out the eyes of Zedekiah; and the king of Babylon bound him in fetters, and carried him to Babylon, and put him in *prison*[9] until the day of his death.

12[10] וּבַחֹדֶשׁ הַחֲמִישִׁי בֶּעָשׂוֹר לַחֹדֶשׁ הִיא שְׁנַת תְּשַׁע־עֶשְׂרֵה שָׁנָה לַמֶּלֶךְ נְבוּכַדְרֶאצַּר מֶלֶךְ־בָּבֶל בָּא נְבוּזַרְאֲדָן רַב־טַבָּחִים עָמַד לִפְנֵי מֶלֶךְ־בָּבֶל בִּירוּשָׁלִָם

12[10] Now in the fifth month, in the tenth day of the month, *which was the nineteenth year of king Nebuchadrezzar, king of Babylon*[11], the captain of the guard, Nebuzaradan, who stood before the king of Babylon, came into Jerusalem;

13[12] וַיִּשְׂרֹף אֶת־בֵּית־יְהוָה וְאֶת־בֵּית הַמֶּלֶךְ וְאֵת כָּל־בָּתֵּי יְרוּשָׁלִַם וְאֶת־כָּל־בֵּית הַגָּדוֹל שָׂרַף בָּאֵשׁ

13[12] and he burned the house of the LORD, and the king's house; and all the houses of Jerusalem, every great man's house, he burned with fire.

---

[1] Jeremiah 52:5 - b.Megillah [Rashi] 11b

[2] Jeremiah 52:6 - 2 Kings 1:3, b.Rosh Hashanah 18b, b.Taanit 28b, Deuteronomy 28:52-28:53 8:24, Ezekiel 4:9-4:17 5:10-5:12 7:15 14:21, Isaiah 3:1, Jeremiah 15:2 19:9 21:9 1:10 14:9 15:2, Lamentations 4:4-4:6 5:10, Lamentations.R 1:39, Leviticus 2:26, Pesikta Rabbati 26:6, Zechariah 8:19
Jeremiah 52:6-7 - Siman 121:4

[3] Jeremiah 52:7 - 2 Kings 1:4, b.Rosh Hashanah 18b, b.Taanit 28b, Deuteronomy 4:25 8:30, Ein Yaakov Rosh Hashanah:18b, Jeremiah 34:2-3 39:4-7 1:26 3:32, Joshua 7:8-12, Leviticus 2:17 2:36

[4] Jeremiah 52:8 - Amos 2:14-15 9:1-4, Ezekiel 12:12-12:14 17:20-21, Isaiah 30:16-17, Jeremiah 21:7 8:4 10:21 13:18 14:23 15:5, Lamentations 4:19-20

[5] Jeremiah 52:9 - 1 Kings 14:22, 2 Chronicles 8:3 9:11, 2 Kings 23:33 1:6, Ezekiel 21:30-32, Jeremiah 32:4-5 15:5, Joshua 13:5, Numbers 13:21 10:11

[6] Jeremiah 52:10 - 2 Kings 1:7 25:18-21, Deuteronomy 4:34, Ezekiel 9:6 11:7-11, Genesis 21:16 20:34, Jeremiah 22:30 39:6-7 52:24-27

[7] LXX *Deblatha*

[8] Jeremiah 52:11 - Ezekiel 12:13, Jeremiah 34:3-5, Sifre.z Numbers Behaalotcha 11:15, z.Yitro 85a

[9] LXX *grinding house*

[10] Jeremiah 52:12 - 2 Kings 24:12 1:8, b.Megillah [Rashi] 11b, b.Sanhedrin 96a, b.Taanit 29a, Ein Yaakov Sanhedrin:96a, Genesis 13:36, Jeremiah 15:9 4:14 4:29, t.Taniyot 3:10, Zechariah 7:3-7:5 8:19
Jeremiah 52:12-13 - mt.Hilchot Taaniot 5:3

[11] Missing in LXX

[12] Jeremiah 52:13 - 2 Chronicles 12:19, 2 Kings 1:9, Acts 6:13-14, Amos 2:5 3:10-11 6:11, b.Sanhedrin 96a, Ein Yaakov Sanhedrin:96a, Ezekiel 7:20-22 24:1-14 24:21, Isaiah 64:11-12, Jeremiah 7:14 22:14 10:22 37:8-10 14:23 39:8-9, Lamentations 2:7, Matthew 24:2, Micah 3:12, Pesikta de R'Kahana 4.1, Pesikta Rabbati 14:2, Psalms 74:6-8 79:1, Zechariah 11:1

וְאֶת־כָּל־חֹמ֣וֹת יְרוּשָׁלַ֛͏ִם סָבִ֖יב נָתְצ֑וּ כָּל־חֵ֣יל
כַּשְׂדִּ֔ים אֲשֶׁ֖ר אֶת־רַב־טַבָּחִֽים

14[1] And all the army of the Chaldeans, who were with the captain of the guard, broke down all the walls of Jerusalem.

וּמִדַּלּ֨וֹת הָעָ֜ם וְֽאֶת־יֶ֥תֶר הָעָ֣ם׀ הַנִּשְׁאָרִ֣ים בָּעִ֗יר
וְאֶת־הַנֹּֽפְלִים֙ אֲשֶׁ֤ר נָֽפְלוּ֙ אֶל־מֶ֣לֶךְ בָּבֶ֔ל וְאֵ֖ת יֶ֣תֶר
הָֽאָמ֑וֹן הֶגְלָ֕ה נְבוּזַרְאֲדָ֖ן רַב־טַבָּחִֽים

15[2] *Then Nebuzaradan the captain of the guard carried away captive of the poorest sort of the people, and the remnant of the people who remained in the city, and those who fell away, who fell to the king of Babylon, and the remnant of the multitude[3].*

וּמִדַּלּ֣וֹת הָאָ֔רֶץ הִשְׁאִ֕יר נְבוּזַרְאֲדָ֖ן רַב־טַבָּחִ֑ים
לְכֹרְמִ֖ים וּלְיֹגְבִֽים

16[4] But Nebuzaradan the captain of the guard left the poorest of the land to be vinedressers and husbandmen.

וְאֶת־עַמּוּדֵ֨י הַנְּחֹ֜שֶׁת אֲשֶׁ֣ר לְבֵית־יְהֹוָ֗ה וְֽאֶת־
הַמְּכֹנ֞וֹת וְאֶת־יָ֧ם הַנְּחֹ֛שֶׁת אֲשֶׁ֥ר בְּבֵית־יְהֹוָ֖ה שִׁבְּר֣וּ
כַשְׂדִּ֑ים וַיִּשְׂא֥וּ אֶת־כָּל־נְחֻשְׁתָּ֖ם בָּבֶֽלָה

17[5] And the pillars of brass that were in the house of the LORD, and the bases and the brazen sea that were in the house of the LORD, the Chaldeans broke in pieces, and carried all the brass to Babylon.

וְאֶת־הַ֠סִּר֠וֹת וְאֶת־הַיָּעִ֨ים וְאֶת־הַֽמְזַמְּר֜וֹת וְאֶת־
הַמִּזְרָקֹ֣ת וְאֶת־הַכַּפּ֗וֹת וְאֵ֨ת כָּל־כְּלֵ֧י הַנְּחֹ֛שֶׁת אֲשֶׁר־
יְשָׁרְת֥וּ בָהֶ֖ם לָקָֽחוּ

18[6] *The pots also, and the shovels, and the snuffers, and the basins, and the pans, and all the vessels of brass with which they ministered, they took away[7].*

וְאֶת־הַ֠סִּפִּ֠ים וְאֶת־הַמַּחְתּ֨וֹת וְאֶת־הַמִּזְרָק֜וֹת וְאֶת־
הַסִּיר֣וֹת וְאֶת־הַמְּנֹר֗וֹת וְאֶת־הַכַּפּוֹת֙ וְאֶת־הַמְּנַקִיּ֔וֹת
אֲשֶׁ֤ר זָהָב֙ זָהָ֔ב וַאֲשֶׁר־כֶּ֖סֶף כָּ֑סֶף לָקַ֖ח רַב־טַבָּחִֽים

19[8] *And the cups, and the fire pans, and the basins, and the pots, and the candlesticks, and the pans, and the bowls, which were of gold, in gold, and which were of silver, in silver, the captain of the guard took away[9].*

הָעַמּוּדִ֣ים׀ שְׁנַ֗יִם הַיָּ֤ם אֶחָד֙ וְהַבָּקָ֞ר שְׁנֵים־עָשָׂ֤ר
נְחֹ֙שֶׁת֙ אֲשֶׁר־תַּ֣חַת הַמְּכֹנ֔וֹת אֲשֶׁ֥ר עָשָׂ֖ה הַמֶּ֣לֶךְ
שְׁלֹמֹ֑ה לְבֵ֣ית יְהֹוָ֔ה לֹא־הָיָ֣ה מִשְׁקָ֔ל לִנְחֻשְׁתָּ֖ם כָּל־
הַכֵּלִ֥ים הָאֵֽלֶּה

20[10] The two pillars, the one sea, and the twelve brazen bulls that were under the *bases[11]*, which king Solomon made for the house of the LORD, the brass of all these vessels was without weight.

וְהָעַמּוּדִ֗ים שְׁמֹנֶ֨ה עֶשְׂרֵ֤ה אַמָּה֙ ׳קֹומָה׳ ״קֹומַת״
הָעַמֻּ֣ד הָאֶחָ֔ד וְח֛וּט שְׁתֵּים־עֶשְׂרֵ֥ה אַמָּ֖ה יְסֻבֶּ֑נּוּ
וְעׇבְי֛וֹ אַרְבַּ֥ע אַצְבָּע֖וֹת נָבֽוּב

21[12] And as for the pillars, the height of the one pillar was *eighteen[13]* cubits; and a line of twelve cubits around it; and its thickness was four fingers; *it was hollow[14].*

וְכֹתֶ֨רֶת עָלָ֜יו נְחֹ֗שֶׁת וְקוֹמַ֨ת הַכֹּתֶ֥רֶת הָאַחַ֛ת חָמֵ֥שׁ
אַמּ֖וֹת וּשְׂבָכָ֣ה וְרִמּוֹנִ֧ים עַֽל־הַכּוֹתֶ֛רֶת סָבִ֖יב הַכֹּ֣ל
נְחֹ֑שֶׁת וְכָאֵ֛לֶּה לַעַמּ֥וּד הַשֵּׁנִ֖י וְרִמּוֹנִֽים

22[15] And a *capital[16]* of brass was on it; and the *height[17]* of the one capital was five cubits, with network and pomegranates around the

---

[1] Jeremiah 52:14 - 2 Kings 1:10, Nehemiah 1:3

[2] Jeremiah 52:15 - Jeremiah 15:1-2, Zechariah 14:2

[3] Missing in LXX

[4] Jeremiah 52:16 - 2 Kings 1:12, b.Shabbat 26a, Ezekiel 9:24, Jastrow 466a, Jeremiah 39:9-10 40:5-7

[5] Jeremiah 52:17 - 1 Kings 7:15-7:37 7:50, 2 Chronicles 4:12-4:15 12:18, 2 Kings 25:13-25:17, Daniel 1:2, Jeremiah 27:19-27:22 52:21-52:23, Lamentations 1:10, Testament of Solomon 21:4 Jeremiah 52:17-19 - 4 Baruch 3:18

[6] Jeremiah 52:18 - 1 Chronicles 4:17, 1 Kings 7:40 7:45 7:50, 2 Chronicles 4:8 4:11 4:16 4:22, 2 Kings 25:14-16, Exodus 1:29 3:3 13:16 13:23 14:3, Ezekiel 46:20-24, Ezra 1:10, Numbers 4:7 4:14 7:13-14 7:19-20 7:26 7:32 7:38 7:44 7:50 7:56, t.Shekalim 2:6

[7] LXX *Also the rim, and the bowls, and the flesh-hooks, and all the brazen vessels, with which they ministered*

[8] Jeremiah 52:19 - 1 Kings 7:49-7:50, 2 Chronicles 4:6-4:22, 2 Kings 1:15, Apocalypse of Elijah 2:43, Exodus 25:31-25:39, Leviticus 2:12, Numbers 17:11, Revelation 8:3-8:5

[9] LXX *and the basons, and the snuffers, and the oil-funnels, and the candlesticks, and the censers, and the cups, the golden, of gold, and the silver, of silver, the captain of the guard took away*

[10] Jeremiah 52:20 - 1 Chronicles 22:14, 1 Kings 7:47, 2 Chronicles 4:18, 2 Kings 1:16

[11] LxX *sea*

[12] Jeremiah 52:21 - 1 Kings 7:15-7:21, 2 Chronicles 3:15-3:17, 2 Kings 1:17

[13] LXX *thirty-five*

[14] Missing in LXX

[15] Jeremiah 52:22 - 1 Kings 7:16-17, 2 Chronicles 3:15 4:12-13, 2 Kings 1:17, Exodus 28:14-22 4:25 39:15-18

[16] LXX *chapter*

[17] LXX *length*

capital, all of brass; and *the second pillar also was similar, and pomegranates*[1].

23[2] וַיִּהְיוּ הָרִמֹּנִים תִּשְׁעִים וְשִׁשָּׁה רוּחָה כָּל־הָרִמּוֹנִים מֵאָה עַל־הַשְּׂבָכָה סָבִיב

And there were ninety-six pomegranates on the outside; all the pomegranates were a hundred on the network around it.

24[3] וַיִּקַּח רַב־טַבָּחִים אֶת־שְׂרָיָה כֹּהֵן הָרֹאשׁ וְאֶת־צְפַנְיָה כֹּהֵן הַמִּשְׁנֶה וְאֶת־שְׁלֹשֶׁת שֹׁמְרֵי הַסַּף

And the captain of the guard *took Seraiah the chief priest, and Zephaniah the second priest, and the three keepers of the door*[4];

25[5] וּמִן־הָעִיר לָקַח סָרִיס אֶחָד אֲשֶׁר־הָיָה פָקִיד עַל־אַנְשֵׁי הַמִּלְחָמָה וְשִׁבְעָה אֲנָשִׁים מֵרֹאֵי פְנֵי־הַמֶּלֶךְ אֲשֶׁר נִמְצְאוּ בָעִיר וְאֵת סֹפֵר שַׂר הַצָּבָא הַמַּצְבִּא אֶת־עַם הָאָרֶץ וְשִׁשִּׁים אִישׁ מֵעַם הָאָרֶץ הַנִּמְצָאִים בְּתוֹךְ הָעִיר

and from the city he took an officer who was set over the men of war; and seven men of those who saw the king's face, who were found in the city; and the scribe of the captain of the host, who mustered the people of the land; and sixty men of the people of the land, who were found in the midst of the city.

26 וַיִּקַּח אוֹתָם נְבוּזַרְאֲדָן רַב־טַבָּחִים וַיֹּלֶךְ אוֹתָם אֶל־מֶלֶךְ בָּבֶל רִבְלָתָה

And Nebuzaradan the captain of the guard took them, and brought them to the king of Babylon to Riblah.

27[6] וַיַּכֶּה אוֹתָם מֶלֶךְ בָּבֶל וַיְמִתֵם בְּרִבְלָה בְּאֶרֶץ חֲמָת וַיִּגֶל יְהוּדָה מֵעַל אַדְמָתוֹ

And the king of Babylon struck them, and put them to death at Riblah in the land of Hamath. *So Judah was carried away captive from his land*[7].

28[8] זֶה הָעָם אֲשֶׁר הֶגְלָה נְבוּכַדְרֶאצַּר בִּשְׁנַת־שֶׁבַע יְהוּדִים שְׁלֹשֶׁת אֲלָפִים וְעֶשְׂרִים וּשְׁלֹשָׁה

This is the people whom Nebuchadrezzar carried away captive: in the seventh year 3,023 Jews[9];

29[10] בִּשְׁנַת שְׁמוֹנֶה עֶשְׂרֵה לִנְבוּכַדְרֶאצַּר מִירוּשָׁלַ͏ִם נֶפֶשׁ שְׁמֹנֶה מֵאוֹת שְׁלֹשִׁים וּשְׁנָיִם

In the eighteenth year of Nebuchadrezzar, from Jerusalem, 832 persons[11];

30[12] בִּשְׁנַת שָׁלֹשׁ וְעֶשְׂרִים לִנְבוּכַדְרֶאצַּר הֶגְלָה נְבוּזַרְאֲדָן רַב־טַבָּחִים יְהוּדִים נֶפֶשׁ שְׁבַע מֵאוֹת אַרְבָּעִים וַחֲמִשָּׁה כָּל־נֶפֶשׁ אַרְבַּעַת אֲלָפִים וְשֵׁשׁ מֵאוֹת

In the twenty-third year of Nebuchadrezzar Nebuzaradan the captain of the guard carried away captive of the Jews 745 persons; all the persons were 4,600[13].

31[14] וַיְהִי בִשְׁלֹשִׁים וָשֶׁבַע שָׁנָה לְגָלוּת יְהוֹיָכִן מֶלֶךְ יְהוּדָה בִּשְׁנֵים עָשָׂר חֹדֶשׁ בְּעֶשְׂרִים וַחֲמִשָּׁה לַחֹדֶשׁ נָשָׂא אֱוִיל מְרֹדַךְ מֶלֶךְ בָּבֶל בִּשְׁנַת מַלְכֻתוֹ אֶת־רֹאשׁ יְהוֹיָכִין מֶלֶךְ־יְהוּדָה וַיֹּצֵא אוֹתוֹ מִבֵּית "הַכְּלִיא' "הַכְּלוּא"

And it came to pass in the thirty-seventh year of the captivity of Jehoiachin king of Judah, in the twelfth month, in the twenty-fifth day of the month, that *Evil-merodach*[15] king of Babylon, in the first year of his reign, *lifted*

---

[1] LXX *and correspondingly the second pillar had eight pomegranates to a cubit for the twelve cubits*

[2] Jeremiah 52:23 - 1 Kings 7:20, t.Oholot 13:9

[3] Jeremiah 52:24 - 1 Chronicles 5:40 9:19-9:26, 2 Kings 1:18, Ezra 7:1, Jeremiah 21:1 5:25 5:29 11:4 13:3 4:12 4:15, Lamentations.R 2:10, m.Sheviit 1:7, mt.Hilchot Sanhedrin vHainshin Hameurim Lahem 2:4, Psalms 84:11, y.Sanhedrin 1:2

[4] LXX *took the chief priest, and the second priest, and those who kept the way*

[5] Jeremiah 52:25 - 2 Kings 1:19, b.Megillah [Tosefot] 23a, b.Sanhedrin [Tosefot] 10b, Esther 1:14, Matthew 18:10, Numbers.R 11:3, y.Sanhedrin 1:2

[6] Jeremiah 52:27 - 2 Kings 17:20 17:23 23:27 25:20-21, 2 Samuel 8:9, Deuteronomy 4:26 4:36 28:64, Ezekiel 8:11-18 11:1-11 9:28, Isaiah 6:11-12 24:3 3:10 32:13-14, Jeremiah 6:13-15 20:4 24:9-10 25:9-11 15:10 4:9, Lamentations.R 1:28, Leviticus 26:33-35, Micah 4:10, Numbers 34:8-11, Seder Olam 27:Siege
Jeremiah 52:27-30 - 4 Baruch 4:6

[7] Missing in LXX

[8] Jeremiah 52:28 - 2 Chronicles 12:20, 2 Kings 24:2-24:3 24:12-24:16, b.Arachin 12a, b.Megillah [Rashi] 11b, Daniel 1:1-1:3, Seder Olam 25:Nebuchadnezzar 25:Nebuchadnezzar 27:Siege

[9] Missing in LXX

[10] Jeremiah 52:29 - 2 Chronicles 12:20, 2 Kings 1:11, b.Megillah [Rashi] 11b, Exodus 1:5, Genesis 12:5, Jeremiah 15:9 4:12, Seder Olam 26:Zedekiah 27:Siege

[11] Missing in LXX

[12] Jeremiah 52:30 - Jeremiah 6:9 4:15

[13] Missing in LXX

[14] Jeremiah 52:31 - 2 Kings 25:27-30, b.Megillah 11b, Genesis 16:13 16:20, Genesis.R 85:2, Job 22:29, Proverbs 21:1, Psalms 3:4 27:6, Seder Olam 28:Daniel

[15] LXX *Ulaemadachar*

the head of Jehoiachin king of Judah, and
brought him forth from prison[1].

וַיְדַבֵּר אִתּוֹ טֹבֹות וַיִּתֵּן אֶת־כִּסְאוֹ מִמַּעַל לְכִסֵּא   32[2]
'מְלָכִים' "הַמְּלָכִים" אֲשֶׁר אִתּוֹ בְּבָבֶל

32[2] And he spoke kindly to him, and set his throne
above the throne of the kings who were with
him in Babylon.

וְשִׁנָּה אֵת בִּגְדֵי כִלְאוֹ וְאָכַל לֶחֶם לְפָנָיו תָּמִיד כָּל־   33[3]
יְמֵי חַיָּו

33[3] And he changed his prison garments, and ate
bread before him continually all the days of
his life.

וַאֲרֻחָתוֹ אֲרֻחַת תָּמִיד נִתְּנָה־לֹּו מֵאֵת מֶלֶךְ־בָּבֶל   34[4]
דְּבַר־יוֹם בְּיוֹמוֹ עַד־יוֹם מֹותוֹ כָּל יְמֵי חַיָּו

34[4] And for his allowance, there was a continual
allowance given him of the king of Babylon,
every day a portion until the day of his death,
all the days of his life.

---

[1] LXX *raised the head of Joakim king of Juda, and shaved him, and brought him from the house where he was kept*
[2] Jeremiah 52:32 - Daniel 2:37 5:18-19, Jeremiah 27:6-11, Proverbs 12:25
[3] Jeremiah 52:33 - 1 Kings 2:7, 2 Samuel 9:7 9:13, Genesis 17:14 17:42, Isaiah 61:1-3, Psalms 30:12, Sifre Devarim Ekev 43,
Zechariah 3:4
[4] Jeremiah 52:34 - 2 Samuel 9:10, Luke 11:3, Matthew 6:11, Midrash Psalms 4:12, Midrash Tanchuma Massei 12

Yechezkiel b'Buzi

Ezekiel[1] – Chapter 01[2]

וַיְהִי בִּשְׁלֹשִׁים שָׁנָה בָּרְבִיעִי בַּחֲמִשָּׁה לַחֹדֶשׁ וַאֲנִי בְתוֹךְ־הַגּוֹלָה עַל־נְהַר־כְּבָר נִפְתְּחוּ הַשָּׁמַיִם וָאֶרְאֶה מַרְאוֹת אֱלֹהִים	1[3]	Now it came to pass in the thirtieth year, in the fourth month, in the fifth day of the month, as I was among the captives by the river Chebar, when the heavens were opened, and I saw visions of God.
בַּחֲמִשָּׁה לַחֹדֶשׁ הִיא הַשָּׁנָה הַחֲמִישִׁית לְגָלוּת הַמֶּלֶךְ יוֹיָכִין	2[4]	In the fifth day of the month, which was the fifth year of king Jehoiachin's captivity,
הָיֹה הָיָה דְבַר־יְהֹוָה אֶל־יְחֶזְקֵאל בֶּן־בּוּזִי הַכֹּהֵן בְּאֶרֶץ כַּשְׂדִּים עַל־נְהַר־כְּבָר וַתְּהִי עָלָיו שָׁם יַד־יְהוָה	3[5]	the word of the LORD came expressly to Ezekiel the priest, the son of Buzi, in the land of the Chaldeans by the river Chebar; and the hand of the LORD was on him there.
וָאֵרֶא וְהִנֵּה רוּחַ סְעָרָה בָּאָה מִן־הַצָּפוֹן עָנָן גָּדוֹל וְאֵשׁ מִתְלַקַּחַת וְנֹגַהּ לוֹ סָבִיב וּמִתּוֹכָהּ כְּעֵין הַחַשְׁמַל מִתּוֹךְ הָאֵשׁ	4[6]	And I looked, and, behold, a stormy wind came out of the north, a great cloud, with a fire flashing up, so that a brightness was around it; and out of its midst as the color of *bright bronze*[7], out of the midst of the fire[8].
וּמִתּוֹכָהּ דְּמוּת אַרְבַּע חַיּוֹת וְזֶה מַרְאֵיהֶן דְּמוּת אָדָם לָהֵנָּה	5[9]	And out of its midst came the likeness of four living creatures. And this was their appearance: they had the likeness of a man.
וְאַרְבָּעָה פָנִים לְאֶחָת וְאַרְבַּע כְּנָפַיִם לְאַחַת לָהֶם	6[10]	And each had four faces, and each of them had four wings.

---

[1] Ezekiel - Ein Yaakov Berachot:57b

[2] Ezekiel 1 - Ein Yaakov Chagigah:12b, Ein Yaakov Pesachim:119a, Haftarah Shavuot [continues at Ezekiel 3:12 Ashkenaz and Sephard], Mekhilta de R'Shimon bar Yochai Nezikin 58:2, mt.Hilchot Tefilah 13:9, Pesikta Rabbati 36:1, Shavuot Day One Part One Haftarah, Siman 79:9, Tanya Igeret Hakodesh §28, Tanya Kuntress Acharon §04

[3] Ezekiel 1:1 - 2 Baruch 22:1, 2 Corinthians 12:1, 2 Enoch 1a:4 20:1, 3 Enoch 1:1, Acts 7:56 9:10-9:12 10:3 10:11, b.Megillah 31a, Daniel 8:1-8:2, Ecclesiastes 9:1-9:2, Exodus 24:10, Ezekiel 1:3 3:15 3:23 8:3 10:15 10:20 10:22 11:24 16:2 19:3, Ezekiel has 29 Sedarim, Genesis 15:1 22:2, Genesis.R 16:3, Greek Apocalypse of Ezra 2:26, Guide for the Perplexed 3:7, Hosea 12:12, Isaiah 1:1, Jeremiah 24:5-24:7, Joel 3:1, John 1:51, Lamentations.R Petichata D'Chakimei:33, Leviticus.R 2:8, Life of Adam and Eve [Vita] 25:2, Lives of the Prophets 3:5, Luke 3:21 3:23, m.Chagigah 2:1, m.Megillah 4:10, Mark 1:10, Mas.Soferim 9:10, Matthew 3:16 17:9, Mekhilta de R'Shimon bar Yochai Bachodesh 53:3, Mekhilta de R'Shimon bar Yochai Shirata 29:1, Mekilta de R'Ishmael Shirata 3:31, Midrash Tanchuma Bo 5, Numbers 4:3 12:6, Pesikta Rabbati 33:11, Revelation 4:1 19:11, Tanna Devei Eliyahu 6, Testament of Levi 2:5, Yalchut Jeremiah:327, z.Bereshit 6b, z.Terumah 166a, z.Yitro 82a

Ezekiel 1:1-3 - 2 Baruch 1:1, Seder Olam 26:Law was Found

Ezekiel 1:1-2:2 - Haftarah Shavuot [continues at Ezekiel 3:12 Teimon]

[4] Ezekiel 1:2 - 2 Kings 24:12-15, Ezekiel 8:1 20:1 5:1 5:17 7:1 16:1, *Jehoiachin* altered to *Joiachin*, Sifre Devarim Vaetchanan 31

[5] Ezekiel 1:3 - 1 Kings 18:46, 1 Timothy 4:1, 2 Kings 3:15, b.Moed Katan 25a, Ein Yaakov Moed Katan:25a, Exodus.R 23:5, Ezekiel 1:1 3:14 3:22 8:1 9:22 13:1 16:1, Guide for the Perplexed 2:41 3:7, Hosea 1:1, Jeremiah 1:2 1:4, Joel 1:1, Leviticus.R 2:8, Lives of the Prophets 3:1, Mekhilta de R'Shimon bar Yochai Pisha 3:1, Mekilta de R'Ishmael Pisha 1:66, Pesikta de R'Kahana 13.2 13.12, Seder Olam 20:Zephaniah, z.Shemot 2a 5a, z.Yitro 82a 82a 82b

Ezekiel 1:3-5 - z.Terumah 131a

[6] Ezekiel 1:4 - 2 Chronicles 5:13-6:1 7:1-7:3, b.Chagigah 13a 13b, Bahir 34, Deuteronomy 4:11-4:12, Exodus 19:16-19:18 24:16-24:17, Ezekiel 1:27 8:2 10:2-10:4 10:8-10:9, Guide for the Perplexed 2:29 3:5 3:7, Habakkuk 1:8-1:9 3:3-3:5, Hebrews 12:29, Isaiah 19:1 21:1, Jeremiah 1:13-1:14 4:6 6:1 23:19 1:9 1:32, Leviticus.R 2:8, Midrash Proverbs 10, Nahum 1:3-1:6, Psalms 18:12-18:14 50:3 97:2-97:3 104:3-104:4, Revelation 1:15, Saadia Opinions 6:7, Sefer Yetzirah 5:2 6:1, Tanna Devei Eliyahu 6, Tanya Likutei Aramim §06, z.Vayakhel 203a, z.Yitro 69a 78a 81b

Ezekiel 1:4-28 - Kuzari 4.3

[7] LXX *amber*

[8] LXX adds *and brightness in it*

[9] Ezekiel 1:5 - 3 Enoch 21:1, Deuteronomy.R 2:20 8:2, Ezekiel 1:26, Guide for the Perplexed 3:2 3:7, Jastrow 528b, Midrash Proverbs 10, Numbers.R 14:22, Pesikta Rabbati 33:11, Revelation 4:6-4:8 6:6, z.Shemot 4b, z.Yitro 82a, z.Yitro 82b

Ezekiel 1:5-10 - Siman 168:1

Ezekiel 1:5-11 - 2 Enoch 12:1

[10] Ezekiel 1:6 - 1 Kings 6:24-6:27, b.Chagigah 13b, Exodus 1:20, Ezekiel 1:8-1:11 1:15 10:10 10:14 10:21-10:22, Isaiah 6:2, Midrash Tanchuma Emor 16, Pesikta Rabbati 33:11, Pirkei de R'Eliezer 4, Revelation 4:7-4:8

וְרַגְלֵיהֶם רֶגֶל יְשָׁרֶה וְכַף רַגְלֵיהֶם כְּכַף רֶגֶל עֵגֶל וְנֹצְצִים כְּעֵין נְחֹשֶׁת קָלָל

7[1]　And their feet were straight feet; and the soles of their feet were like the soles of calves' feet; and they sparkled like the color of burnished brass.

וְיָדוֹ "וִידֵי" אָדָם מִתַּחַת כַּנְפֵיהֶם עַל אַרְבַּעַת רִבְעֵיהֶם וּפְנֵיהֶם וְכַנְפֵיהֶם לְאַרְבַּעְתָּם

8[2]　And they had the hands of a man under their wings on their four sides; and as for their faces and wings: four,

חֹבְרֹת אִשָּׁה אֶל־אֲחוֹתָהּ כַּנְפֵיהֶם לֹא־יִסַּבּוּ בְלֶכְתָּן אִישׁ אֶל־עֵבֶר פָּנָיו יֵלֵכוּ

9[3]　their wings were joined one to another; they did not turn when they went; they, together went straight forward.

וּדְמוּת פְּנֵיהֶם פְּנֵי אָדָם וּפְנֵי אַרְיֵה אֶל־הַיָּמִין לְאַרְבַּעְתָּם וּפְנֵי־שׁוֹר מֵהַשְּׂמֹאול לְאַרְבַּעְתָּן וּפְנֵי־נֶשֶׁר לְאַרְבַּעְתָּן

10[4]　As for the likeness of their faces, they had the face of a man; and they four had the face of a lion on the right side; and *they four*[5] had the face of an ox on the left side; they four had also the face of an eagle.

וּפְנֵיהֶם וְכַנְפֵיהֶם פְּרֻדוֹת מִלְמָעְלָה לְאִישׁ שְׁתַּיִם חֹבְרֹות אִישׁ וּשְׁתַּיִם מְכַסּוֹת אֵת גְּוִיֹתֵיהֶנָה

11[6]　Thus were their faces; and their wings were stretched upward; two wings of every one were joined one to another, and two covered their bodies.

וְאִישׁ אֶל־עֵבֶר פָּנָיו יֵלֵכוּ אֶל אֲשֶׁר יִהְיֶה־שָּׁמָּה הָרוּחַ לָלֶכֶת יֵלֵכוּ לֹא יִסַּבּוּ בְּלֶכְתָּן

12[7]　And they went every one straight forward; whither the spirit was to go, they went; they turned not when they went.

וּדְמוּת הַחַיּוֹת מַרְאֵיהֶם כְּגַחֲלֵי־אֵשׁ בֹּעֲרוֹת כְּמַרְאֵה הַלַּפִּדִים הִיא מִתְהַלֶּכֶת בֵּין הַחַיּוֹת וְנֹגַהּ לָאֵשׁ וּמִן־הָאֵשׁ יוֹצֵא בָרָק

13[8]　As for the likeness of the living creatures, their appearance was like coals of fire, burning like the appearance of torches; it flashed up and down among the living creatures; and there was brightness to the fire, and out of the fire went forth lightning.

וְהַחַיּוֹת רָצוֹא וָשׁוֹב כְּמַרְאֵה הַבָּזָק

14[9]　*And the living creatures ran and returned as the appearance of a flash of lightning*[10].

Ezekiel 1:6-12 - Apocalypse of Abraham 18:3

[1] Ezekiel 1:7 - 8 16, b.Berachot 10b, b.Chagigah 13b, b.Kiddushin [Rashi] 66a, b.Yoma 19b, Daniel 10:6, Ein Yaakov Berachot:10b, Ein Yaakov Yoma:19b, Ezekiel 1:13, Guide for the Perplexed 2:10 3:2, Jastrow 1401b, Leviticus 11:3 11:47, Leviticus.R 27:3, Midrash Psalms 1:2 15:22, Midrash Tanchuma Emor 16, mt.Hilchot Tefilah 5:4, Pesikta de R'Kahana 9.3, Psalms 8:4, Revelation 1:15, Siman 20:4, y.Berachot 1:1, z.Vaera 24b

[2] Ezekiel 1:8 - b.Pesachim 119a, Ezekiel 1:17 8:3 10:2 10:7-10:8 10:11 10:18 10:21, Guide for the Perplexed 3:2, Isaiah 6:6, Jastrow 1703a, z.Yitro 75b

[3] Ezekiel 1:9 - 1 Corinthians 1:10, 1 Enoch 14:18, 2 Chronicles 3:11-3:12, Ezekiel 1:11-1:12 10:11 10:22, Guide for the Perplexed 3:2, Luke 9:51 9:62, Proverbs 4:25-4:27

[4] Ezekiel 1:10 - 1 Chronicles 12:7, 1 Corinthians 9:9-9:10 14:20, 3 Enoch 15B:2 2:1 26:3, b.Chagigah 13b, b.Menachot [Tosefot] 109b, Daniel 7:4, Deuteronomy 4:49, Exodus.R 15:26 23:13 42:5 43:8, Ezekiel 10:14, Guide for the Perplexed 1:49, Isaiah 16:31 22:8, Jastrow 664b, Job 15:27, Judges 14:18, Luke 15:10, Midrash Proverbs 20, Midrash Psalms 103:16, Midrash Tanchuma Emor 16, Midrash Tanchuma Ki Tissa 21, Numbers 2:3 2:10 2:18 2:25, Pesikta Rabbati 47:3, Proverbs 14:4, Revelation 4:7 5:5, Song of Songs.R 1:48, Tanya Igeret Hakodesh §20, Tanya Likutei Aramim §39, Testament of Naphtali 5:6, z.Bamidbar 118b, z.Bereshit 18b 19a, z.Noach 71b, z.Pekudei 237a, z.Vaera 27a, z.Vayakhel 211b, z.Vayikra 14a, z.Yitro 80b

Ezekiel 1:10-13 - 4QEzekb

[5] 4QEzekb *all four of them*

[6] Ezekiel 1:11 - Ezekiel 1:23 10:16 10:19, Guide for the Perplexed 3:2, Isaiah 6:2, Sefer Yetzirah 3:6

[7] Ezekiel 1:12 - Ezekiel 1:9 1:17 1:20-21 10:22, Hebrews 1:14, Mesillat Yesharim 16:Trait of Taharah

[8] Ezekiel 1:13 - Daniel 10:5-10:6, Ezekiel 1:7, Genesis 15:17, Guide for the Perplexed 1:1 3:2 3:3, Lamentations.R 3:8, Matthew 4:3, Midrash Tanchuma Behaalotcha 5, Midrash Tanchuma Terumah 11, Midrash Tanchuma Tetzaveh 6, Numbers.R 12:8 15:7, Psalms 8:4, Revelation 4:5 10:1 18:1, Saadia Opinions 6:7, Song of Songs.R 3:24, z.Tzav 30a, z.Vayakhel 216a

[9] Ezekiel 1:14 - 3 Enoch 22C:5 24:15, b.Chagigah 13b, b.Eruvin [Rashi] 104a, Daniel 9:21, Genesis.R 42:3, Guide for the Perplexed 3:2, Jastrow 154a 396a 504b, Luke 17:24, Mark 13:27, Matthew 24:27 24:31, Mesillat Yesharim 6:Trait of Zerizus, Midrash Proverbs 10, mt.Hilchot Yesodei haTorah 2:7, Numbers.R 12:8, Psalms 3:15, Sefer Yetzirah 1:6 Sefer Yetzirah [Short] 1:8, Song of Songs.R 3:24, Tanya Igeret Hakodesh §01 §31, Tanya Likutei Aramim §50, z.Bereshit 21a, Zechariah 2:3-2:4 4:10

Ezekiel 1:14 [Targum] - Guide for the Perplexed 3:2

[10] Missing in LX

וָאֵרֶא הַחַיּוֹת וְהִנֵּה אוֹפַן אֶחָד בָּאָרֶץ אֵצֶל הַחַיּוֹת לְאַרְבַּעַת פָּנָיו

15[1] Now as I looked at the living creatures, behold one wheel at the *base*[2] by the living creatures, at their four faces.

מַרְאֵה הָאוֹפַנִּים וּמַעֲשֵׂיהֶם כְּעֵין תַּרְשִׁישׁ וּדְמוּת אֶחָד לְאַרְבַּעְתָּן וּמַרְאֵיהֶם וּמַעֲשֵׂיהֶם כַּאֲשֶׁר יִהְיֶה הָאוֹפַן בְּתוֹךְ הָאוֹפָן

16[3] The appearance of the wheels and their work was like the color of a topaz; and the four had one likeness; and their appearance and their work was as a wheel within a wheel.

עַל־אַרְבַּעַת רִבְעֵיהֶן בְּלֶכְתָּם יֵלֵכוּ לֹא יִסַּבּוּ בְּלֶכְתָּן

17[4] When they went, they went toward their four sides; they did not turn when they went.

וְגַבֵּיהֶן וְגֹבַהּ לָהֶם וְיִרְאָה לָהֶם וְגַבֹּתָם מְלֵאֹת עֵינַיִם סָבִיב לְאַרְבַּעְתָּן

18[5] As for their rings, they were high and they were dreadful; and the four had their rings full of eyes around it.

וּבְלֶכֶת הַחַיּוֹת יֵלְכוּ הָאוֹפַנִּים אֶצְלָם וּבְהִנָּשֵׂא הַחַיּוֹת מֵעַל הָאָרֶץ יִנָּשְׂאוּ הָאוֹפַנִּים

19[6] And when the living creatures went, the wheels went hard by them; and when the living creatures were lifted from the bottom, the wheels were lifted.

עַל אֲשֶׁר יִהְיֶה־שָּׁם הָרוּחַ לָלֶכֶת יֵלֵכוּ שָׁמָּה הָרוּחַ לָלֶכֶת וְהָאוֹפַנִּים יִנָּשְׂאוּ לְעֻמָּתָם כִּי רוּחַ הַחַיָּה בָּאוֹפַנִּים

20[7] Wherever[8] the spirit went, as the spirit was to go there, so they went; and the wheels were lifted beside them; for the spirit of the living creature was in the wheels.

בְּלֶכְתָּם יֵלֵכוּ וּבְעָמְדָם יַעֲמֹדוּ וּבְהִנָּשְׂאָם מֵעַל הָאָרֶץ יִנָּשְׂאוּ הָאוֹפַנִּים לְעֻמָּתָם כִּי רוּחַ הַחַיָּה בָּאוֹפַנִּים

21[9] When those went, these went, and when those stood, these stood; and when those lifted up from the earth, the wheels lifted up beside them; for the spirit of the living creature was in the wheels.

וּדְמוּת עַל־רָאשֵׁי הַחַיָּה רָקִיעַ כְּעֵין הַקֶּרַח הַנּוֹרָא נָטוּי עַל־רָאשֵׁיהֶם מִלְמָעְלָה

22[10] And over the heads of the living creatures there was the likeness of a firmament, like the color of an awesome crystal, stretched forth above their heads.

וְתַחַת הָרָקִיעַ כַּנְפֵיהֶם יְשָׁרוֹת אִשָּׁה אֶל־אֲחוֹתָהּ לְאִישׁ שְׁתַּיִם מְכַסּוֹת לָהֵנָּה וּלְאִישׁ שְׁתַּיִם מְכַסּוֹת לָהֵנָּה אֵת גְּוִיֹתֵיהֶם

23[11] And under the firmament were their wings stretched from one to the other; this one had two which covered, and that one had two which covered their bodies.

---

[1] Ezekiel 1:15 - 3 Enoch 25:5, b.Chagigah 13b, Daniel 7:9, Exodus.R 33:4, Ezekiel 1:6 1:19-1:21 10:9 10:13-10:17, Guide for the Perplexed 3:2 3:4, Jastrow 31b, Mas.Derek Eretz Rabbah 2:31, Revelation 4:7, Sefer Yetzirah 1:12, z.Beshallach 48b Ezekiel 1:15-25 - Apocalypse of Abraham 18:12

[2] LXX *ground*

[3] Ezekiel 1:16 - 3 Enoch 2:2 21:3, b.Chullin [Rashi] 91b, Daniel 10:6, Ephesians 3:10, Exodus 15:13, Ezekiel 10:9-10:11, Guide for the Perplexed 3:2, Job 9:10, Mekhilta de R'Shimon bar Yochai Kaspa 82:2, Midrash Proverbs 10, mt.Hilchot Yesodei haTorah 2:7, Psalms 36:7 40:6, Romans 11:33 Ezekiel 1:16-17 - 4QEzekb

[4] Ezekiel 1:17 - 3 Enoch 9:5, Ezekiel 1:9 1:12 10:1-10:11, Guide for the Perplexed 3:2, Isaiah 7:11, Siman 18:5

[5] Ezekiel 1:18 - 3 Enoch 18:25 22:9 25:6 26:5, Bahir 145, Ezekiel 10:12, Isaiah 7:9, Job 37:22-37:24, Mekhilta de R'Shimon bar Yochai Kaspa 82:2, Midrash Tanchuma Toledot 14, Proverbs 15:3, Psalms 77:17-77:20 97:2-97:5, Revelation 4:6 4:8, Song of Songs.R 6:25, Zechariah 4:10

[6] Ezekiel 1:19 - b.Chullin [Tosefot] 92a, Ezekiel 10:16 10:19, Guide for the Perplexed 3:2, Psalms 7:20, y.Sukkah 4:6, y.Yoma 1:5 5:2, z.Pekudei 241b Ezekiel 1:19-24 - 4QEzekb

[7] Ezekiel 1:20 - 1 Corinthians 14:32, b.Chullin [Tosefot] 92a, Exodus.R 33:4, Ezekiel 1:12 10:17, Guide for the Perplexed 3:2 3:3, z.Terumah 136b, Zechariah 6:1-6:8

[8] LXX adds *the cloud happened to be, there was*

[9] Ezekiel 1:21 - Ezekiel 1:19-1:20 10:17, Guide for the Perplexed 3:2, Romans 8:2, z.Pekudei 241b

[10] Ezekiel 1:22 - 3 Enoch 44:7, b.Chagigah 13a, b.Megillah 25a, Ein Yaakov Chagigah:12b, Exodus 24:10, Ezekiel 1:26 10:1, Guide for the Perplexed 3:7, Job 13:22, Midrash Psalms 90:12, Midrash Tanchuma Terumah 11, Numbers.R 12:8, Pirkei de R'Eliezer 4, Revelation 4:3 4:6 21:11, Sefer Yetzirah 4:1, Song of Songs.R 3:24, z.Bereshit 16a 21a, z.Beshallach 56b, z.Vayakhel 211a, z.Vayigash 211a

[11] Ezekiel 1:23 - Apocalypse of Abraham 18:3, Ezekiel 1:11-12 1:24, Job 4:18, Luke 17:10, Midrash Psalms 93:7, Psalms 89:8, z.Vayigash 211a

וָאֶשְׁמַ֣ע אֶת־ק֣וֹל כַּנְפֵיהֶ֡ם כְּקוֹל֩ מַ֨יִם רַבִּ֤ים כְּקוֹל־ 24[1]
שַׁדַּי֙ בְּלֶכְתָּ֔ם ק֥וֹל הֲמֻלָּ֖ה כְּק֣וֹל מַחֲנֶ֑ה בְּעָמְדָ֖ם
תְּרַפֶּ֥ינָה כַנְפֵיהֶֽן

And when they went, I heard the noise of their wings like the noise of great waters, like the voice of the Almighty, a noise of furor like the noise of an army; when they stood, they let down their wings.

וַֽיְהִי־ק֕וֹל מֵעַ֕ל לָרָקִ֖יעַ אֲשֶׁ֣ר עַל־רֹאשָׁ֑ם בְּעָמְדָ֖ם 25[2]
תְּרַפֶּ֥ינָה כַנְפֵיהֶֽן

For, when there was a voice above the firmament that was over their heads, as they stood, they let down their wings.

וּמִמַּ֗עַל לָרָקִ֙יעַ֙ אֲשֶׁ֣ר עַל־רֹאשָׁ֔ם כְּמַרְאֵ֥ה אֶֽבֶן־ 26[3]
סַפִּ֛יר דְּמ֥וּת כִּסֵּ֖א וְעַל֙ דְּמ֣וּת הַכִּסֵּ֔א דְּמ֞וּת כְּמַרְאֵ֥ה
אָדָ֛ם עָלָ֖יו מִלְמָֽעְלָה

And above the firmament that was over their heads was the likeness of a throne, as the appearance of a sapphire; and on the likeness of the throne was the appearance of a man upon it above.

וָאֵ֣רֶא ׀ כְּעֵ֣ין חַשְׁמַ֗ל כְּמַרְאֵה־אֵ֤שׁ בֵּֽית־לָהּ֙ סָבִ֔יב 27[4]
מִמַּרְאֵ֥ה מָתְנָ֖יו וּלְמָ֑עְלָה וּמִמַּרְאֵ֤ה מָתְנָיו֙ וּלְמַ֔טָּה
רָאִ֙יתִי֙ כְּמַרְאֵה־אֵ֔שׁ וְנֹ֥גַֽהּ ל֖וֹ סָבִֽיב

And I saw as the color of polished bronze, as the appearance of fire within and around it, from the appearance of his loins and upward; and from the appearance of his loins and downward I saw the appearance of fire, and there was brightness around him.

כְּמַרְאֵ֣ה הַקֶּ֡שֶׁת אֲשֶׁר֩ יִֽהְיֶ֨ה בֶעָנָ֜ן בְּי֣וֹם הַגֶּ֗שֶׁם כֵּ֣ן 28[5]
מַרְאֵ֤ה הַנֹּ֙גַהּ֙ סָבִ֔יב ה֕וּא מַרְאֵ֖ה דְּמ֣וּת כְּבוֹד־יְהוָ֑ה
וָֽאֶרְאֶה֙ וָאֶפֹּ֣ל עַל־פָּנַ֔י וָֽאֶשְׁמַ֖ע ק֥וֹל מְדַבֵּֽר

As the appearance of the rainbow in the cloud in the day of rain, so was the appearance of the brightness around it. [6]This was the appearance of the glory of the LORD. And when I saw it, I fell on my face, and I heard a voice of one who spoke.

Ezekiel – Chapter 02[7]

וַיֹּ֖אמֶר אֵלָ֑י בֶּן־אָדָם֙ עֲמֹ֣ד עַל־רַגְלֶ֔יךָ וַאֲדַבֵּ֖ר אֹתָֽךְ 1[8]

And He said to me: 'Son of man, stand upon your feet, and I will speak with you.'

וַתָּ֧בֹא בִ֣י ר֗וּחַ כַּֽאֲשֶׁר֙ דִּבֶּ֣ר אֵלַ֔י וַתַּֽעֲמִדֵ֖נִי עַל־רַגְלָ֑י 2[9]
וָֽאֶשְׁמַ֖ע אֵ֥ת מִדַּבֵּ֖ר אֵלָֽי

And spirit entered me when He spoke to me, and set me on my feet; and I heard he who spoke to me.

---

[1] Ezekiel 1:24 - 2 Kings 7:6, Daniel 10:6, Exodus.R 43:4, Ezekiel 10:5 19:2, Genesis.R 65:21, Job 13:2 37:4-5, Midrash Psalms 93:7, Psalms 18:14 29:3-9 68:34, Ralbag Wars 6part02:6, Revelation 1:15 19:6, Sefer Yetzirah 1:8, Testament of Adam 1:5, z.Noach 71b
[2] Ezekiel 1:25 - 3 Enoch 22C:5, Ezekiel 1:22, Midrash Tanchuma Kedoshim 6
[3] Ezekiel 1:26 - 1 Enoch 14:18 18:8, 1 Peter 3:22, b.Chullin 89a, b.Menachot 43b, b.Sotah 14a, Bahir 96, Daniel 7:9-7:10 7:14 10:18, Ecclesiastes.R 2:26 8:1, Ein Yaakov Chullin:89a, Ein Yaakov Sotah:17a, Ephesians 1:21-1:22, Exodus 24:10, Ezekiel 1:22 10:1, Genesis 32:25-32:30, Genesis.R 27:1, Guide for the Perplexed 1:1 1:46, Hebrews 1:8 8:1 12:2, Isaiah 6:1 9:7-9:8 6:11, Jastrow 1271b, Jeremiah 23:5-23:6, Joshua 5:13-6:2, Matthew 1:13 4:18, Mekhilta de R'Shimon bar Yochai Vayassa 43:1, Mekilta de R'Ishmael Vayassa 7:57, Midrash Tanchuma Chukkat 6, mt.Hilchot Yesodei haTorah 2:7, Numbers.R 4:13 19:4, Pesikta de R'Kahana 4.4, Pesikta Rabbati 14:1, Philippians 2:9-2:10, Psalms 45:7, Revelation 1:13 3:21 4:2-4:3 5:13 14:14 20:11, Saadia Opinions 2:10, Sefer Yetzirah 1:6 3:6, Tanya Igeret Hakodesh §07 §28, Tanya Kuntress Acharon §01, y.Sukkah 4:3, z.Mishpatim 122a, z.Noach 71b, z.Pekudei 238a, z.Tazria 48a, z.Vayakhel 217a, z.Vayigash 211a, z.Yitro 80b 90a, Zechariah 6:13
Ezekiel 1:26-27 - z.Terumah 139a
Ezekiel 1:26-28 - Apocalypse of Abraham 18:14
[4] Ezekiel 1:27 - 2 Thessalonians 1:8, b.Chagigah 13a, Deuteronomy 4:24, Ein Yaakov Chagigah:12b, Ezekiel 1:4 8:2, Guide for the Perplexed 3:5, Hebrews 12:29, Jastrow 162b 511b, Life of Adam and Eve [Vita] 25:3, Midrash Proverbs 10, mt.Hilchot Yesodei haTorah 2:7, Psalms 50:3 97:2, Revelation 1:14-1:16, Saadia Opinions 6:7
[5] Ezekiel 1:28 - 1 Corinthians 13:12, 1 Kings 8:10-11, 3 Enoch 21:4, Acts 9:4, b.Chagigah 16a, b.Sheviit [Rashi] 5b, Daniel 8:17 10:7-9 10:16-17, Ein Yaakov Chagigah:12b, Ein Yaakov Chagigah:16a, Exodus 16:7 16:10 24:16 33:18-23, Ezekiel 3:23 8:4 10:19-20 11:22-23 43:3-5 20:4, Genesis 9:13-16 17:3, Genesis.R 35:3, Guide for the Perplexed 2:44 3:7, Isaiah 54:8-10, Leviticus 9:24, Matthew 17:5-6, Midrash Psalms 24:12 90:18 103:5, Numbers 12:6-8, Numbers.R 14:3, Psalms of Solomon 2:5, Revelation 1:17-18 4:3 10:1, z.Bereshit 18a 39b, z.Noach 71b, z.Vayishlach 170b, b.Berachot 28a
[6] This begins Chapter 2 in LXX
[7] Ezekiel 2 - mt.Hilchot Yesodei haTorah 7:3
[8] Ezekiel 2:1 - 2 Baruch 13:2, Acts 9:6 2:16, b.Chagigah 13a, Daniel 8:17 10:11 10:19, Ein Yaakov Chagigah:12b, Ezekiel 1:28 2:3 2:6 2:8 3:1 3:4 3:10 3:17 4:1 5:1 7:2 12:3 14:3 14:13 15:2 16:2 17:2 20:3 13:3, John 3:13 3:16, Joseph and Aseneth 14:8, Leviticus.R 2:8, Matthew 16:13-16:16 17:7, Mekhilta de R'Shimon bar Yochai Shirata 33:1, Mekilta de R'Ishmael Shirata 7:7, Midrash Tanchuma Tzav 13, Psalms 8:5, Saadia Opinions 2:10, z.Terumah 166b
[9] Ezekiel 2:2 - 1 Samuel 16:13, Daniel 8:18, Ezekiel 3:12 3:14 3:24 12:27, Joel 3:1-3:2, Judges 13:25, Nehemiah 9:30, Numbers 11:25-11:26, Revelation 11:11

Hebrew	Verse	English

וַיֹּאמֶר אֵלַי בֶּן־אָדָם שׁוֹלֵחַ אֲנִי אוֹתְךָ אֶל־בְּנֵי
יִשְׂרָאֵל אֶל־גּוֹיִם הַמּוֹרְדִים אֲשֶׁר מָרְדוּ־בִי הֵמָּה
וַאֲבוֹתָם פָּשְׁעוּ בִי עַד־עֶצֶם הַיּוֹם הַזֶּה

3[1] And He said to me: 'Son of man, I send you to the children of Israel, to rebellious converts, who rebelled against Me; they and their fathers transgressed against Me, to this very day;

וְהַבָּנִים קְשֵׁי פָנִים וְחִזְקֵי־לֵב אֲנִי שׁוֹלֵחַ אוֹתְךָ
אֲלֵיהֶם וְאָמַרְתָּ אֲלֵיהֶם כֹּה אָמַר אֲדֹנָי יְהוִֹה

4[2] *And the children are brazen faced and stiff hearted, I send you to them*[3]; and you shall say to them: Thus says the Lord GOD.

וְהֵמָּה אִם־יִשְׁמְעוּ וְאִם־יֶחְדָּלוּ כִּי בֵּית מְרִי הֵמָּה
וְיָדְעוּ כִּי נָבִיא הָיָה בְתוֹכָם

5[4] And they, whether they will hear, or whether they will fear, for they are a rebellious house, yet shall know there has been a prophet among them.

וְאַתָּה בֶן־אָדָם אַל־תִּירָא מֵהֶם וּמִדִּבְרֵיהֶם אַל־
תִּירָא כִּי סָרָבִים וְסַלּוֹנִים אוֹתָךְ וְאֶל־עַקְרַבִּים
אַתָּה יוֹשֵׁב מִדִּבְרֵיהֶם אַל־תִּירָא וּמִפְּנֵיהֶם אַל־
תֵּחָת כִּי בֵּית מְרִי הֵמָּה

6[5] And you, son of man, Do not be afraid of them, nor be *afraid of their words*[6], though defiers and despisers be with you, and you live among scorpions; do not be afraid of their words, nor be dismayed at their glances, for they are a rebellious house.

וְדִבַּרְתָּ אֶת־דְּבָרַי אֲלֵיהֶם אִם־יִשְׁמְעוּ וְאִם־יֶחְדָּלוּ
כִּי מְרִי הֵמָּה

7[7] And you shall speak My words to them, whether they will hear, or whether they will fear; for they are most rebellious.

וְאַתָּה בֶן־אָדָם שְׁמַע אֵת אֲשֶׁר־אֲנִי מְדַבֵּר אֵלֶיךָ
אַל־תְּהִי־מֶרִי כְּבֵית הַמֶּרִי פְּצֵה פִיךָ וֶאֱכֹל אֵת
אֲשֶׁר־אֲנִי נֹתֵן אֵלֶיךָ

8[8] And you, son of man, hear what I say to you: do not be rebellious like that rebellious house; open your mouth, and eat what I give you.'

וָאֶרְאֶה וְהִנֵּה־יָד שְׁלוּחָה אֵלָי וְהִנֵּה־בוֹ מְגִלַּת־סֵפֶר

9[9] And when I looked, behold, a hand was put forth to me; and, lo, a roll of a book was in it;

וַיִּפְרֹשׂ אוֹתָהּ לְפָנַי וְהִיא כְתוּבָה פָּנִים וְאָחוֹר
וְכָתוּב אֵלֶיהָ קִנִים וָהֶגֶה וָהִי

10[10] and He spread it before me, and it was written within and without; and there was written in it lamentations, moaning, and woe.

Ezekiel – Chapter 03[11]

וַיֹּאמֶר אֵלַי בֶּן־אָדָם אֵת אֲשֶׁר־תִּמְצָא אֱכוֹל אֱכוֹל
אֶת־הַמְּגִלָּה הַזֹּאת וְלֵךְ דַּבֵּר אֶל־בֵּית יִשְׂרָאֵל

1[12] And He said to me: 'Son of man, *eat what you find*[13]; eat this roll, and go, speak to the house of Israel.'

---

[1] Ezekiel 2:3 - 1 Samuel 8:7-8:8, 2 Chronicles 36:15-36:16, 2 Kings 17:17-17:20, Acts 7:51, Daniel 9:5-9:13, Deuteronomy 9:24 9:27, Ezekiel 3:4-3:8 16:1-16:63 20:1-20:49 23:1-23:49, Ezra 9:7, Isaiah 6:8-6:10, Jeremiah 1:7 3:25 7:2 16:11-16:12 25:3-25:7 26:2-26:6 12:2 20:21, John 20:21-20:22, Luke 24:47-24:48, Mark 12:2-12:5, Nehemiah 9:16-9:18 9:26 9:33-9:35, Numbers 20:10 32:13-32:14, Psalms 106:16-106:21 10:28 106:32-106:40, Romans 10:15, y.Sanhedrin 10:5

[2] Ezekiel 2:4 - 1 Kings 22:14, 2 Chronicles 6:8 12:13, Acts 20:26-27, Deuteronomy 10:16 7:27, Ezekiel 3:7, Isaiah 24:4, Jeremiah 3:3 5:3 6:15 8:12 26:2-3, Matthew 10:16, Proverbs 21:29, Psalms 95:8, z.Vaetchanan 269b

[3] Missing in LXX

[4] Ezekiel 2:5 - 2 Corinthians 2:15-17, Acts 13:46, Ezekiel 2:7 3:10-11 3:19 3:27 9:9 9:33, John 15:22, Luke 10:10-12, Matthew 10:12-10:15, mt.Hilchot Yesodei haTorah 10:5, Romans 3:3

[5] Ezekiel 2:6 - 1 Peter 3:14, 2 Kings 1:15, 2 Samuel 23:6-7, 2 Timothy 1:7, Acts 4:13 4:19 4:29, Amos 7:10-7:17, Ephesians 6:19, Esther.R 7:11, Ezekiel 3:8-9 3:26-27 4:24, Guide for the Perplexed 2:38, Hebrews 11:27, Isaiah 9:19 3:7 3:12, Jeremiah 1:8 1:17 6:28 18:18, Luke 10:19 12:4, Matthew 10:28, Micah 3:8 7:4, Philippians 1:28, Proverbs 30:13-14, Revelation 9:3-9:6, Saadia Opinions Intro:6

[6] LXX *dismayed at their face*

[7] Ezekiel 2:7 - Ezekiel 2:5 3:10 3:17, Jeremiah 1:7 1:17 23:28 2:2, Jonah 3:2, Matthew 4:20

[8] Ezekiel 2:8 - 1 Kings 13:21-13:22, 1 Peter 5:3, 1 Timothy 4:14-4:16, Ezekiel 3:1-3:3 3:10, Isaiah 2:5, Jeremiah 15:16, Leviticus 10:3, Numbers 20:10-20:13 20:24, Revelation 10:9

[9] Ezekiel 2:9 - b.Kiddushin 2b, Daniel 5:5 10:10 10:16-10:18, Ezekiel 3:1 8:3, Guide for the Perplexed 2:43, Hebrews 10:7, Jeremiah 1:9 12:2, Revelation 5:1-5:5 10:8-10:11

[10] Ezekiel 2:10 - Avot de R'Natan 25, Avot de R'Natan 25, b.Arachin 21a, Habakkuk 2:2, Isaiah 3:11 30:8-30:11, Jeremiah 36:29-36:32, Revelation 8:13 9:12 11:14, Tanya Kuntress Acharon §06

[11] Ezekiel 3 - mt.Hilchot Yesodei haTorah 7:3

[12] Ezekiel 3:1 - 1 Timothy 4:15, Ezekiel 2:3 2:8-2:9 3:10-3:11 3:15 3:17-3:21, Jeremiah 24:1-24:7, Revelation 10:9-10:10 Ezekiel 3:1-3 - Exodus.R 47:7

[13] Missing in LXX

וָאֶפְתַּח אֶת־פִּי וַיַּאֲכִלֵנִי אֵת הַמְּגִלָּה הַזֹּאת	2[1] So I opened my mouth, and He caused me to eat the roll.
וַיֹּאמֶר אֵלַי בֶּן־אָדָם בִּטְנְךָ תַאֲכֵל וּמֵעֶיךָ תְמַלֵּא אֵת הַמְּגִלָּה הַזֹּאת אֲשֶׁר אֲנִי נֹתֵן אֵלֶיךָ וָאֹכְלָה וַתְּהִי בְּפִי כִּדְבַשׁ לְמָתוֹק	3[2] And He said to me: 'Son of man, cause your belly to eat, and fill your body with this roll I give you.' Then I ate it; and it was sweet as honey in my mouth.
וַיֹּאמֶר אֵלַי בֶּן־אָדָם לֶךְ־בֹּא אֶל־בֵּית יִשְׂרָאֵל וְדִבַּרְתָּ בִדְבָרַי אֲלֵיהֶם	4[3] And He said to me: 'Son of man, go, get to the house of Israel, and speak with My words to them.
כִּי לֹא אֶל־עַם עִמְקֵי שָׂפָה וְכִבְדֵי לָשׁוֹן אַתָּה שָׁלוּחַ אֶל־בֵּית יִשְׂרָאֵל	5[4] For you are not sent to a people of *an unintelligible speech and of a slow tongue*[5], but to the house of Israel;
לֹא אֶל־עַמִּים רַבִּים עִמְקֵי שָׂפָה וְכִבְדֵי לָשׁוֹן אֲשֶׁר לֹא־תִשְׁמַע דִּבְרֵיהֶם אִם־לֹא אֲלֵיהֶם שְׁלַחְתִּיךָ הֵמָּה יִשְׁמְעוּ אֵלֶיךָ	6[6] Not to many peoples of an unintelligible speech and of a slow tongue, whose words you cannot understand. Surely, if I sent you to them, they would listen to you.
וּבֵית יִשְׂרָאֵל לֹא יֹאבוּ לִשְׁמֹעַ אֵלֶיךָ כִּי־אֵינָם אֹבִים לִשְׁמֹעַ אֵלָי כִּי כָּל־בֵּית יִשְׂרָאֵל חִזְקֵי־מֵצַח וּקְשֵׁי־לֵב הֵמָּה	7[7] But the house of Israel will not willingly listen to you; for they will not willingly listen to Me; for all the house of Israel have a hard forehead and a stiff heart.
הִנֵּה נָתַתִּי אֶת־פָּנֶיךָ חֲזָקִים לְעֻמַּת פְּנֵיהֶם וְאֶת־מִצְחֲךָ חָזָק לְעֻמַּת מִצְחָם	8[8] Behold, I have made your face hard against their faces, and your forehead hard against their foreheads.
כְּשָׁמִיר חָזָק מִצֹּר נָתַתִּי מִצְחֶךָ לֹא־תִירָא אוֹתָם וְלֹא־תֵחַת מִפְּנֵיהֶם כִּי בֵּית־מְרִי הֵמָּה	9[9] *I have made your forehead adamant, harder than flint*[10]; do not fear them, nor be dismayed at their glances, they are a rebellious house.'
וַיֹּאמֶר אֵלַי בֶּן־אָדָם אֶת־כָּל־דְּבָרַי אֲשֶׁר אֲדַבֵּר אֵלֶיךָ קַח בִּלְבָבְךָ וּבְאָזְנֶיךָ שְׁמָע	10[11] Moreover, He said to me: 'Son of man, all My words that I shall speak to you receive in your heart, and hear with your ears.
וְלֵךְ בֹּא אֶל־הַגּוֹלָה אֶל־בְּנֵי עַמֶּךָ וְדִבַּרְתָּ אֲלֵיהֶם וְאָמַרְתָּ אֲלֵיהֶם כֹּה אָמַר אֲדֹנָי יְהוִה אִם־יִשְׁמְעוּ וְאִם־יֶחְדָּלוּ	11[12] And go, get to those of the captivity, to the children of your people, and speak to them, and tell them: Thus says the Lord GOD; whether they will hear, or whether they will forebear.'
וַתִּשָּׂאֵנִי רוּחַ וָאֶשְׁמַע אַחֲרַי קוֹל רַעַשׁ גָּדוֹל בָּרוּךְ כְּבוֹד־יְהוָה מִמְּקוֹמוֹ	12[13] Then a spirit lifted me up, and I heard behind me the voice of a great *rushing*[14]: 'Blessed be the glory of the LORD from His place;'

---

[1] Ezekiel 3:2 - Acts 2:19, b.Yoma 86b, Guide for the Perplexed 2:46, Jeremiah 1:17

[2] Ezekiel 3:3 - Colossians 3:16, Ezekiel 2:10, Guide for the Perplexed 2:46, Jeremiah 6:11 15:16 20:9, Job 23:12 32:18-32:19, John 6:53-6:63 7:38, Proverbs 2:10-2:11, Psalms 19:11 119:103 23:11 119:97, Revelation 10:9-10:10

[3] Ezekiel 3:4 - Acts 1:8, Ezekiel 2:3 2:7 3:11, Matthew 10:5-10:6 15:24

[4] Ezekiel 3:5 - Acts 26:17-26:18, Ezekiel 3:6, Isaiah 4:11 9:19, Jonah 1:2 3:2-3:4, Psalms 81:6

[5] LXX *hard speech*

[6] Ezekiel 3:6 - Acts 3:28, Jastrow 48b, Jonah 3:5-10, Luke 11:30-32, Matthew 11:20-24 12:41-42, Romans 9:30-33

[7] Ezekiel 3:7 - 1 Samuel 8:7, Ezekiel 2:4 24:7, Isaiah 3:9, Jeremiah 3:3 5:3 25:3-4 44:4-5 20:16, John 5:40-47 15:20-24, Luke 10:16 13:34 19:14, Pesikta Rabbati 33:13

[8] Ezekiel 3:8 - 1 Kings 21:20, Acts 7:51-56, Exodus 4:15-16 11:4-8, Hebrews 11:27 11:32-37, Isaiah 2:7, Jeremiah 1:18 15:20, Micah 3:8

[9] Ezekiel 3:9 - 1 Timothy 2:3, 2 Timothy 2:6, Ezekiel 2:6, Isaiah 17:10 17:14 2:7, Jeremiah 1:8 1:17 17:18, Micah 3:8, Zechariah 7:12

[10] LXX *And it shall be continually stronger than a rock*

[11] Ezekiel 3:10 - 1 Thessalonians 2:13 4:1, Ezekiel 2:8 3:1-3:3, Job 22:22, Luke 8:15, Proverbs 8:10 19:20, Psalms 23:11

[12] Ezekiel 3:11 - Acts 20:26-20:27, Daniel 6:14 12:1, Deuteronomy 9:12, Exodus 8:7, Ezekiel 2:5 2:7 3:15 3:27 11:24-11:25 9:2 9:12 9:17 9:30 13:18, z.Vaetchanan 269b

[13] Ezekiel 3:12 - 1 Kings 18:12, 1 Samuel 4:21-4:22, 2 Kings 2:16, 3 Enoch 1:12 48B:2, Acts 2:2 8:39, b.Chagigah 13b, b.Chullin [Tosefot] 92a, b.Chullin 91b, Bahir 90 130, Blessings for Kriat Shema [Shacharit, Derech Hashem Part IV 6§14, Deuteronomy.R 11:10, Ein Yaakov Chullin:91b, Exodus 40:34-40:35, Exodus.R 23:14, Ezekiel 2:2 3:14 8:3 9:3 10:4 10:18-10:19 11:1 11:22-11:24 40:1-40:2, Genesis.R 65:21, Guide for the Perplexed 1:8, Haftarah Shavuot [continued from Ezekiel 1:1-28], Hammeir Laharetz], Isaiah 6:3, Kedusha [all Services], Leviticus.R 2:8, Maariv Motzoei Shabbat], Midrash Psalms 103:5, Midrash Tanchuma Kedoshim 6, mt.Hilchot Tefilah 7:17 8:4 9:5, Pesikta Rabbati 20:4, Pirkei de R'Eliezer 4, Psalms 72:18-19 103:20-21 4:2, Revelation 1:10 1:15 5:11-14 19:6, Saadia Opinions 2:13, Sefer Yetzirah [Long] 4:2, Shabbat and Yom Tov Minchah, Shavuot Day One Part Two Haftarah, Siman 17:9 79:9, t.Berachot 1:9, Tanna Devei Eliyahu 6, Tanya Likutei Aramim §49, Uvah Letzion [Shacharit, z.Beshallach 58a, z.Tzav 30a, z.Vayakhel 207a, z.Vayera 103a

[14] LXX *earthquake*

וְקוֹל ׀ כַּנְפֵי הַחַיּוֹת מַשִּׁיקוֹת אִשָּׁה אֶל־אֲחוֹתָהּ וְקוֹל הָאוֹפַנִּים לְעֻמָּתָם וְקוֹל רַעַשׁ גָּדוֹל	13[1]	also the noise of the wings of the living creatures as they touched one another, and the noise of the wheels beside them, the noise of a great *rushing*[2].
וְרוּחַ נְשָׂאַתְנִי וַתִּקָּחֵנִי וָאֵלֵךְ מַר בַּחֲמַת רוּחִי וְיַד־יְהוָה עָלַי חָזָקָה	14[3]	So a spirit lifted me up, and took me away; and I went in *bitterness, in the heat*[4] of my spirit, and the hand of the LORD was strong on me.
וָאָבוֹא אֶל־הַגּוֹלָה תֵּל אָבִיב הַיֹּשְׁבִים אֶל־נְהַר־כְּבָר "וָאֵשֵׁב" הֵמָּה יוֹשְׁבִים שָׁם וָאֵשֵׁב שָׁם שִׁבְעַת יָמִים מַשְׁמִים בְּתוֹכָם	15[5]	Then I came to those of the captivity *at Tel Aviv*[6], who lived by the river Chebar, and I sat where they sat; and I remained there, appalled among them, seven days.
וַיְהִי מִקְצֵה שִׁבְעַת יָמִים פ וַיְהִי דְבַר־יְהוָה אֵלַי לֵאמֹר	16[7]	And it came to pass at the end of seven days, that the word of the LORD came to me, saying:
בֶּן־אָדָם צֹפֶה נְתַתִּיךָ לְבֵית יִשְׂרָאֵל וְשָׁמַעְתָּ מִפִּי דָּבָר וְהִזְהַרְתָּ אוֹתָם מִמֶּנִּי	17[8]	'Son of man, I have appointed you a watchman to the house of Israel; and when you hear a word at My mouth, you shall give them My warning.
בְּאָמְרִי לָרָשָׁע מוֹת תָּמוּת וְלֹא הִזְהַרְתּוֹ וְלֹא דִבַּרְתָּ לְהַזְהִיר רָשָׁע מִדַּרְכּוֹ הָרְשָׁעָה לְחַיֹּתוֹ הוּא רָשָׁע בַּעֲוֹנוֹ יָמוּת וְדָמוֹ מִיָּדְךָ אֲבַקֵּשׁ	18[9]	When I say to the wicked: you shall surely die; and you do not warn him, nor speak to warn the wicked from his wicked way, to save his life; the wicked man shall die in his iniquity, but I will require his blood at your hand.
וְאַתָּה כִּי־הִזְהַרְתָּ רָשָׁע וְלֹא־שָׁב מֵרִשְׁעוֹ וּמִדַּרְכּוֹ הָרְשָׁעָה הוּא בַּעֲוֹנוֹ יָמוּת וְאַתָּה אֶת־נַפְשְׁךָ הִצַּלְתָּ	19[10]	Yet, if you warn the wicked, and he does not turn from his wickedness, nor from his wicked way, he shall die in his iniquity; but you have delivered your soul.
וּבְשׁוּב צַדִּיק מִצִּדְקוֹ וְעָשָׂה עָוֶל וְנָתַתִּי מִכְשׁוֹל לְפָנָיו הוּא יָמוּת כִּי לֹא הִזְהַרְתּוֹ בְּחַטָּאתוֹ יָמוּת וְלֹא תִזָּכַרְןָ צִדְקֹתָו אֲשֶׁר עָשָׂה וְדָמוֹ מִיָּדְךָ אֲבַקֵּשׁ	20[11]	Again, when a righteous man turns from his righteousness, and commits iniquity, I will lay a stumbling block before him, and he shall die; because you have not given him warning, he shall die in his sin, and righteous deeds he has done will not be remembered; but I will require his blood at your hand.

---

[1] Ezekiel 3:13 - 2 Samuel 5:24, b.Chullin 92a, Ezekiel 1:15 1:24 10:5 10:16-17, Jastrow 941b, Pesikta de R'Kahana 16.1, Song of Songs.R 1:16

[2] LXX *earthquake*

[3] Ezekiel 3:14 - 1 Kings 18:46, 2 Kings 2:16 3:15, Ezekiel 1:3 3:12 8:1 8:3 13:1, Jeremiah 6:11 20:7-9 20:14-18, John 4:1 4:3 4:9, Numbers 11:11-19

[4] LXX *the impulse*

[5] Ezekiel 3:15 - Ezekiel 1:1 3:23 10:15 19:3, Genesis 2:10, Habakkuk 3:16, Jeremiah 23:9, Job 2:13, Psalms 17:1, Seder Olam 26:Law was Found
Ezekiel 3:15-16 - Mekilta de R'Ishmael Pisha 1:145-146

[6] Missing in LXX

[7] Ezekiel 3:16 - 4Q385b frag 1 l.1, Jeremiah 18:7
Ezekiel 3:16-21 - Apocryphon of Ezekiel Fragment 2

[8] Ezekiel 3:17 - 1 Corinthians 4:14 12:28, 1 Thessalonians 5:14, 2 Chronicles 19:10, 2 Corinthians 5:11 5:20, Acts 20:28-20:31, Avot de R'Natan 34, Colossians 1:28, Ezekiel 33:2-33:9, Habakkuk 2:1, Hebrews 13:17, Isaiah 21:6 21:8 21:11-21:12 4:8 8:10 10:1 14:6, Jeremiah 6:10 6:17 7:7, Matthew 3:7, mt.Hilchot Sanhedrin vHainshin Hameurim Lahem 4:6, Numbers.R 20:1, Song of Songs 3:3 5:7
Ezekiel 3:17-19 - Tanna Devei Eliyahu 11

[9] Ezekiel 3:18 - 1 Timothy 4:16 5:22, 2 Kings 1:4, 2 Samuel 4:11, Acts 2:40 3:19 20:26-20:27, Ephesians 5:5-5:6, Ezekiel 3:20 18:4 18:13 18:20 18:30-18:32 9:6 33:8-33:10 10:10, Genesis 2:17 3:3-3:4 9:5-9:6 18:22, Isaiah 3:11, James 5:19-5:20, John 8:21 8:24, Liber Antiquitatum Biblicarum 37:2, Luke 11:50-11:51 13:3 13:5, Numbers 26:65, Proverbs 14:32

[10] Ezekiel 3:19 - 1 Thessalonians 4:6, 1 Timothy 4:16, 2 Chronicles 36:15-16, 2 Corinthians 2:15-17, 2 Kings 17:13-23, 2 Thessalonians 1:8-9, Acts 13:45-46 18:5-6 20:26, Ezekiel 3:18 3:21 14:14 14:20 9:5 9:9, Hebrews 2:1-2:3 10:26-27 12:25, Isaiah 49:4-5, Jeremiah 42:19-22 44:4-5, Luke 10:10-11, Proverbs 5:1, z.Noach 68a

[11] Ezekiel 3:20 - 1 Corinthians 1:23, 1 John 2:19, 1 Peter 2:8, 2 Chronicles 19:2-4 24:2 24:17-22 1:15, 2 Peter 2:18-22, 2 Samuel 12:7-13, 2 Thessalonians 2:9-12, Daniel 9:18, Deuteronomy 13:4, Ein Yaakov Yoma:86b, Ezekiel 3:18 7:19 14:3 14:7-9 18:24 18:26 9:6 33:12-13 9:18, Hebrews 10:38 13:17, Isaiah 8:14 16:7, Jeremiah 6:21, Leviticus 19:17, Luke 2:34 8:15, Matthew 12:43-45 13:20-21 18:15, Midrash Psalms 34:2, Proverbs 1:12, Psalms 36:4 119:165 5:5, Romans 2:7-2:8 9:32-33 11:9, t.Kippurim 4:12, y.Peah 1:1, Zephaniah 1:6

וְאַתָּ֞ה כִּֽי־הִזְהַרְתּ֣וֹ צַדִּ֗יק לְבִלְתִּ֤י חֲטֹא֙ צַדִּ֔יק וְה֖וּא לֹא־חָטָ֑א חָיֹ֤ו יִֽחְיֶה֙ כִּ֣י נִזְהָ֔ר וְאַתָּ֖ה אֶֽת־נַפְשְׁךָ֥ הִצַּֽלְתָּ׃	21[1]	Nevertheless, if you warn the righteous man, so the righteous does not sin, and he does not sin, he shall surely live, because he took warning; and you have delivered your soul.'
וַתְּהִ֥י עָלַ֛י שָׁ֖ם יַד־יְהוָ֑ה וַיֹּ֣אמֶר אֵלַ֗י ק֥וּם צֵ֤א אֶל־הַבִּקְעָ֔ה וְשָׁ֖ם אֲדַבֵּ֥ר אוֹתָֽךְ	22[2]	And there the hand of the LORD came on me; and He said to me: 'Arise, go forth into the plain, and I will speak with you there.'
וָאָק֜וּם וָאֵצֵ֣א אֶל־הַבִּקְעָ֗ה וְהִנֵּה־שָׁ֤ם כְּבוֹד־יְהוָה֙ עֹמֵ֔ד כַּכָּב֕וֹד אֲשֶׁ֥ר רָאִ֖יתִי עַל־נְהַר־כְּבָ֑ר וָאֶפֹּ֖ל עַל־פָּנָֽי׃	23[3]	Then I arose, and went forth into the plain; and, behold, the glory of the LORD stood there, as the glory I saw by the river Chebar; and I fell on my face.
וַתָּבֹא־בִ֣י ר֗וּחַ וַתַּֽעֲמִדֵ֙נִי֙ עַל־רַגְלָ֔י וַיְדַבֵּ֥ר אֹתִ֖י וַיֹּ֣אמֶר אֵלַ֑י בֹּ֥א הִסָּגֵ֖ר בְּת֥וֹךְ בֵּיתֶֽךָ	24[4]	Then spirit entered into me, and set me on my feet; and He spoke with me, and said to me: 'Go, shut yourself within your house.
וְאַתָּ֣ה בֶן־אָדָ֗ם הִנֵּ֨ה נָתְנ֤וּ עָלֶ֙יךָ֙ עֲבוֹתִ֔ים וַאֲסָר֖וּךָ בָּהֶ֑ם וְלֹ֥א תֵצֵ֖א בְּתוֹכָֽם	25[5]	But you, son of man, behold, bands shall be put on you, and you shall be bound with them, and you shall not go out among them;
וּלְשֽׁוֹנְךָ֙ אַדְבִּ֣יק אֶל־חִכֶּ֔ךָ וְנֶֽאֱלַ֔מְתָּ וְלֹא־תִֽהְיֶ֥ה לָהֶ֖ם לְאִ֣ישׁ מוֹכִ֑יחַ כִּ֛י בֵּ֥ית מְרִ֖י הֵֽמָּה	26[6]	and I will make your tongue cleave to the roof of your mouth, so you shall be dumb, and shall not be a reprove to them; for they are a rebellious house.
וּֽבְדַבְּרִ֤י אֽוֹתְךָ֙ אֶפְתַּ֣ח אֶת־פִּ֔יךָ וְאָמַרְתָּ֣ אֲלֵיהֶ֔ם כֹּ֥ה אָמַ֖ר אֲדֹנָ֣י יְהֹוִ֑ה הַשֹּׁמֵ֤עַ ׀ יִשְׁמָע֙ וְהֶחָדֵ֣ל ׀ יֶחְדָּ֔ל כִּ֛י בֵּ֥ית מְרִ֖י הֵֽמָּה	27[7]	But when I speak with you, I will open your mouth, and you shall say to them: Thus says the Lord GOD; he who hears, let him hear, and he who fears, let him fear; for they are a rebellious house.

Ezekiel – Chapter 04[8]

וְאַתָּ֤ה בֶן־אָדָם֙ קַח־לְךָ֣ לְבֵנָ֔ה וְנָתַתָּ֥ה אוֹתָ֖הּ לְפָנֶ֑יךָ וְחַקּוֹתָ֥ עָלֶ֛יהָ עִ֖יר אֶת־יְרוּשָׁלָֽ͏ִם	1[9]	You also, son of man, take a tile, and lay it before you, and trace on it a city, Jerusalem;
וְנָתַתָּ֨ה עָלֶ֜יהָ מָצ֗וֹר וּבָנִ֤יתָ עָלֶ֙יהָ֙ דָּיֵ֔ק וְשָׁפַכְתָּ֥ עָלֶ֖יהָ סֹלְלָ֑ה וְנָתַתָּ֨ה עָלֶ֧יהָ מַחֲנ֛וֹת וְשִׂים־עָלֶ֥יהָ כָּרִ֖ים סָבִֽיב	2[10]	And lay siege against it, and build forts against it, and cast up a mound against it; set camps against it, and set *battering rams* [11]against and around it.
וְאַתָּ֣ה קַח־לְךָ֗ מַחֲבַ֣ת בַּרְזֶ֔ל וְנָתַתָּ֥ה אוֹתָ֛הּ קִ֥יר בַּרְזֶ֖ל בֵּֽינְךָ֣ וּבֵ֣ין הָעִ֑יר וַהֲכִינֹתָה֩ אֶת־פָּנֶ֨יךָ אֵלֶ֜יהָ וְהָיְתָ֤ה בַמָּצוֹר֙ וְצַרְתָּ֣ עָלֶ֔יהָ א֥וֹת הִ֖יא לְבֵ֥ית יִשְׂרָאֵֽל	3[12]	And take an iron griddle, and set it as a wall of iron between you and the city; and set your face toward it, and it shall be besieged, and you

---

[1] Ezekiel 3:21 - 1 Corinthians 4:14 10:12, 1 John 3:6-9, 1 Thessalonians 4:6-8 5:14, 1 Timothy 4:16, Acts 20:31, Colossians 1:28 3:5-8, Ephesians 4:17-21 5:5-6, Ezekiel 3:19-20, Galatians 1:6-1:10 2:11-13 5:2-7, James 5:20, Matthew 24:24-25, Proverbs 9:9 17:10, Psalms 19:12, Revelation 19:12, Saadia Opinions 4:5, Titus 2:15

[2] Ezekiel 3:22 - Acts 9:6, b.Nedarim 8a, Ein Yaakov Nedarim:8a, Ezekiel 1:3 3:14 8:4 13:1, Genesis.R 39:9 55:7, Mekilta de R'Ishmael Pisha 1:71, Midrash Psalms 18:29, Midrash Tanchuma Bo 5
Ezekiel 3:22-23 - Midrash Tanchuma Ki Tissa 15

[3] Ezekiel 3:23 - Acts 7:55, b.Nedarim 8a, Daniel 8:17 10:8-9, Ezekiel 1:1-4 1:28 9:3 10:18, Midrash Psalms 18:29, Numbers 16:19 17:7, Revelation 1:17 4:10 5:8 5:14

[4] Ezekiel 3:24 - Daniel 10:8-10 10:19, Ezekiel 2:2 4:1-4 13:10

[5] Ezekiel 3:25 - Acts 9:16 20:23 21:11-13, Ezekiel 4:8, John 21:18, Mark 3:21

[6] Ezekiel 3:26 - Amos 5:10 8:11-12, Ezekiel 2:3-8 24:27, Hosea 4:17, Isaiah 1:2, Jeremiah 1:17, Lamentations 2:9, Luke 1:20-22, Micah 3:6-3:7, Psalms 36:12-13 51:16 17:6

[7] Ezekiel 3:27 - Ephesians 6:19, Exodus 4:11-4:12, Ezekiel 2:5 3:9 3:11 3:26 11:25 12:2-3 24:27 5:21 9:22 9:32, Luke 21:15, Matthew 11:15 13:9, Revelation 22:10-11, z.Vaetchanan 269b

[8] Ezekiel 4 - Derech Hashem Part III 4§8

[9] Ezekiel 4:1 - 1 Kings 11:30-31, 1 Samuel 15:27-28, Amos 3:2, Ezekiel 5:1-17 12:3-16, Guide for the Perplexed 2:46, Hosea 1:2-9 3:1-5 12:12, Isaiah 20:2-4, Jeremiah 6:6 13:1-14 18:2-12 19:1-15 25:15-38 27:2-22 8:31

[10] Ezekiel 4:2 - Ezekiel 21:27, Jeremiah 6:6 39:1-2 4:4, Luke 19:42-44

[11] LXX *[siege] machines*

[12] Ezekiel 4:3 - b.Berachot 32b, Ein Yaakov Berachot:32b, Ezekiel 12:6 12:11 24:24-27, Hebrews 2:4, Isaiah 8:18 20:3, Jeremiah 15:1, Leviticus 2:5, Luke 2:34
Ezekiel 4:3-6 - 11QEzek

shall lay siege against it. This shall be a sign to the house of Israel.

4[1] Moreover, you shall lie on your left side, and lay the iniquity of the house of Israel on it; according to the number of the [2]days that you shall lie on it, you shall bear their iniquity.

וְאַתָּה שְׁכַב עַל־צִדְּךָ הַשְּׂמָאלִי וְשַׂמְתָּ אֶת־עֲוֹן בֵּית־יִשְׂרָאֵל עָלָיו מִסְפַּר הַיָּמִים אֲשֶׁר תִּשְׁכַּב עָלָיו תִּשָּׂא אֶת־עֲוֹנָם

5[3] For I have appointed the years of their iniquity to be to you a number of days, *three*[4] hundred and ninety days; so shall you bear the iniquity of the house of Israel.

וַאֲנִי נָתַתִּי לְךָ אֶת־שְׁנֵי עֲוֹנָם לְמִסְפַּר יָמִים שְׁלֹשׁ־מֵאוֹת וְתִשְׁעִים יוֹם וְנָשָׂאתָ עֲוֹן בֵּית־יִשְׂרָאֵל

6[5] And again, when you have accomplished these, you shall lie on your right side, and shall bear the iniquity of the house of Judah; forty days, each day for a year, have I appointed *it to you*[6].

וְכִלִּיתָ אֶת־אֵלֶּה וְשָׁכַבְתָּ עַל־צִדְּךָ 'הַיְמוֹנִי' "הַיְמָנִי" שֵׁנִית וְנָשָׂאתָ אֶת־עֲוֹן בֵּית־יְהוּדָה אַרְבָּעִים יוֹם יוֹם לַשָּׁנָה יוֹם לַשָּׁנָה נְתַתִּיו לָךְ

7[7] And you shall set your face toward the siege of Jerusalem, with your arm uncovered; and you shall prophesy against it.

וְאֶל־מְצוֹר יְרוּשָׁלַ͏ִם תָּכִין פָּנֶיךָ וּזְרֹעֲךָ חֲשׂוּפָה וְנִבֵּאתָ עָלֶיהָ

8[8] And, behold, I lay bands upon you, and you shall not turn from one side to another, until you have accomplished the days of your siege.

וְהִנֵּה נָתַתִּי עָלֶיךָ עֲבוֹתִים וְלֹא־תֵהָפֵךְ מִצִּדְּךָ אֶל־צִדֶּךָ עַד־כַּלּוֹתְךָ יְמֵי מְצוּרֶךָ

9[9] Also take wheat, and barley, and beans, and lentils, and millet, and spelt, and put them in one vessel, and make bread from them; according to the number of the days you shall lie upon your side, *three*[10] hundred and ninety days, shall you eat of it.

וְאַתָּה קַח־לְךָ חִטִּין וּשְׂעֹרִים וּפוֹל וַעֲדָשִׁים וְדֹחַן וְכֻסְּמִים וְנָתַתָּה אוֹתָם בִּכְלִי אֶחָד וְעָשִׂיתָ אוֹתָם לְךָ לְלָחֶם מִסְפַּר הַיָּמִים אֲשֶׁר־אַתָּה שׁוֹכֵב עַל־צִדְּךָ שְׁלֹשׁ־מֵאוֹת וְתִשְׁעִים יוֹם תֹּאכְלֶנּוּ

10[11] And the food you eat shall be by weight, twenty shekels a day; from time to time you shall eat it.

וּמַאֲכָלְךָ אֲשֶׁר תֹּאכְלֶנּוּ בְּמִשְׁקוֹל עֶשְׂרִים שֶׁקֶל לַיּוֹם מֵעֵת עַד־עֵת תֹּאכְלֶנּוּ

11[12] You shall drink also water by measure, the sixth part of a hin; from time to time you shall drink.

וּמַיִם בִּמְשׂוּרָה תִשְׁתֶּה שִׁשִּׁית הַהִין מֵעֵת עַד־עֵת תִּשְׁתֶּה

12[13] And you shall eat it as barley cakes, and you shall bake it in their sight with human dung.'

וְעֻגַת שְׂעֹרִים תֹּאכְלֶנָּה וְהִיא בְּגֶלְלֵי צֵאת הָאָדָם תְּעֻגֶנָה לְעֵינֵיהֶם

13[14] And the LORD said: 'Thus shall the children of Israel eat their bread unclean, among the nations there I will drive them.'

וַיֹּאמֶר יְהֹוָה כָּכָה יֹאכְלוּ בְנֵי־יִשְׂרָאֵל אֶת־לַחְמָם טָמֵא בַּגּוֹיִם אֲשֶׁר אַדִּיחֵם שָׁם

---

[1] Ezekiel 4:4 - 1 Peter 2:24, 2 Kings 17:21-23, b.Sanhedrin 39a, Ein Yaakov Sanhedrin:39a, Ezekiel 4:5 4:8, Hebrews 9:28, Isaiah 53:11-12, Leviticus 10:17 16:22, Matthew 8:17, Numbers 14:34 18:1
Ezekiel 4:4-6 - Seder Olam 26:Law was Found, Sifre Devarim {Vezot Habracha} 344
[2] LXX adds *hundred and fifty*
[3] Ezekiel 4:5 - Isaiah 5:6, Numbers 14:34, Saadia Opinions 8:3
[4] LXX *one*
[5] Ezekiel 4:6 - b.Sanhedrin 39a, Daniel 9:24-26 12:11-12, Ein Yaakov Sanhedrin:39a, Numbers 14:34, Revelation 9:15 11:2-3 12:14 13:5
[6] LXX *you a day for a year*
[7] Ezekiel 4:7 - Ezekiel 4:3 6:2 21:7, Isaiah 4:10
[8] Ezekiel 4:8 - Ezekiel 3:25, Guide for the Perplexed 2:46
[9] Ezekiel 4:9 - b.Chullin [Rashi] 37b, b.Eruvin 81a, Ezekiel 4:13 4:16, Isaiah 4:25, Leviticus.R 28:6, Pesikta de R'Kahana 8.4, Pesikta Rabbati 18:4/5
[10] LXX *one*
[11] Ezekiel 4:10 - Deuteronomy 28:51-68, Ezekiel 4:16 14:13 21:12, Isaiah 3:1, Leviticus 2:26
[12] Ezekiel 4:11 - b.Bava Batra [Rashbam] 89b, Ezekiel 4:16, Isaiah 5:13, John 3:34, Leviticus.R 21:7, m.Avot 6:4, Mas.Kallah Rabbati 8:4, Midrash Psalms 10:7
[13] Ezekiel 4:12 - b.Eruvin 81a, Genesis 18:6, Isaiah 12:12, Jastrow 1040b, Mekilta de R'Ishmael Pisha 14:27, Pirkei de R'Eliezer 51
[14] Ezekiel 4:13 - 1Q5b 5:26, b.Sotah 4b, Daniel 1:8, Hosea 9:3-9:4, z.Terumah 152b

Hebrew		English
וָאֹמַר אֲהָהּ אֲדֹנָי יְהֹוִה הִנֵּה נַפְשִׁי לֹא מְטֻמָּאָה וּנְבֵלָה וּטְרֵפָה לֹא־אָכַלְתִּי מִנְּעוּרַי וְעַד־עַתָּה וְלֹא־בָא בְּפִי בְּשַׂר פִּגּוּל	14[1]	Then I said: 'Ah Lord GOD! Behold, my soul has not been polluted; for from my youth up until now have I not eaten of what dies of itself, or is torn of beasts; nor has abhorred flesh entered my mouth.'
וַיֹּאמֶר אֵלַי רְאֵה נָתַתִּי לְךָ "אֶת־צְפוּעֵי" "אֶת־צְפִיעֵי" הַבָּקָר תַּחַת גֶּלְלֵי הָאָדָם וְעָשִׂיתָ אֶת־לַחְמְךָ עֲלֵיהֶם	15[2]	Then He said to me: 'See, I have given you cow's dung for man's dung, and you shall prepare your bread on it.'
וַיֹּאמֶר אֵלַי בֶּן־אָדָם הִנְנִי שֹׁבֵר מַטֵּה־לֶחֶם בִּירוּשָׁלַ͏ִם וְאָכְלוּ־לֶחֶם בְּמִשְׁקָל וּבִדְאָגָה וּמַיִם בִּמְשׂוּרָה וּבְשִׁמָּמוֹן יִשְׁתּוּ	16[3]	Moreover He said to me: 'Son of man, behold, I will break the staff of bread in Jerusalem, and they shall eat bread by weight, and with anxiety; and they shall drink water by measure, and in disgust;
לְמַעַן יַחְסְרוּ לֶחֶם וָמָיִם וְנָשַׁמּוּ אִישׁ וְאָחִיו וְנָמַקּוּ בַּעֲוֹנָם	17[4]	so they may want bread and water, and be appalled with each another, and pine away in their iniquity.

Ezekiel – Chapter 05

Hebrew		English
וְאַתָּה בֶן־אָדָם קַח־לְךָ חֶרֶב חַדָּה תַּעַר הַגַּלָּבִים תִּקָּחֶנָּה לָּךְ וְהַעֲבַרְתָּ עַל־רֹאשְׁךָ וְעַל־זְקָנֶךָ וְלָקַחְתָּ לְךָ מֹאזְנֵי מִשְׁקָל וְחִלַּקְתָּם	1[5]	And you, son of man, take a sharp sword as a barber's razor; take it to you, and make it to pass along your head and on your beard; then take weight balances, and divide the hair.
שְׁלִשִׁית בָּאוּר תַּבְעִיר בְּתוֹךְ הָעִיר כִּמְלֹאת יְמֵי הַמָּצוֹר וְלָקַחְתָּ אֶת־הַשְּׁלִשִׁית תַּכֶּה בַחֶרֶב סְבִיבוֹתֶיהָ וְהַשְּׁלִשִׁית תִּזְרֶה לָרוּחַ וְחֶרֶב אָרִיק אַחֲרֵיהֶם	2[6]	A *third*[7] part you shall burn in the fire in the midst of the city, when the days of the siege are fulfilled; [8]and you shall take a *third*[9] part, and strike it with the sword around her; and a *third*[10] part you shall scatter to the wind, and I will draw out a sword after them.
וְלָקַחְתָּ מִשָּׁם מְעַט בְּמִסְפָּר וְצַרְתָּ אוֹתָם בִּכְנָפֶיךָ	3[11]	You shall also take from it a few by number, and bind them in your skirts.
וּמֵהֶם עוֹד תִּקָּח וְהִשְׁלַכְתָּ אוֹתָם אֶל־תּוֹךְ הָאֵשׁ וְשָׂרַפְתָּ אֹתָם בָּאֵשׁ מִמֶּנּוּ תֵצֵא־אֵשׁ אֶל־כָּל־בֵּית יִשְׂרָאֵל	4[12]	And yet of those shall you take some, and cast them into the midst of the fire, and burn them in the fire; from there a fire shall come forth into all the house of Israel.
כֹּה אָמַר אֲדֹנָי יְהֹוִה זֹאת יְרוּשָׁלַ͏ִם בְּתוֹךְ הַגּוֹיִם שַׂמְתִּיהָ וּסְבִיבוֹתֶיהָ אֲרָצוֹת	5[13]	Thus says the Lord GOD: This is Jerusalem! I have set her in the midst of the nations, and countries are around her.

---

[1] Ezekiel 4:14 - Acts 10:14, b.Avodah Zara [Tosefot] 20b, b.Chullin 37b 44b, Deuteronomy 14:3, Ein Yaakov Chullin:37b, Exodus 22:31, Ezekiel 9:8 21:5 20:31, Isaiah 17:4 18:17, Jeremiah 1:6, Leviticus 11:39-40 17:15 19:7, Mesillat Yesharim 14:Elements of Pe - R'Ishun, Psalms of Solomon 8:12, z.Vayeshev 191a

[2] Ezekiel 4:15 - b.Bava Kamma [Rashi] 3a, b.Shabbat [Rashi] 151b, Mas.Soferim 7:4

[3] Ezekiel 4:16 - Ezekiel 4:10-11 5:16 12:18-19 14:13, Isaiah 3:1, Lamentations 1:11 4:9:10 5:9, Leviticus 2:26, Psalms 60:4 9:16 Ezekiel 4:16-17 - 1QEzek

[4] Ezekiel 4:17 - Ezekiel 24:23 9:10, Leviticus 2:39, Midrash Tanchuma Vayera 21

[5] Ezekiel 5:1 - 1QEzek, Daniel 5:27, Ezekiel 20:20, Isaiah 7:20, Leviticus 21:5

[6] Ezekiel 5:2 - Amos 9:2-9:3, Ezekiel 4:1-4:8 5:12 12:14, Jeremiah 9:17 9:22-9:23 15:2 24:10 14:2, Leviticus 2:33

[7] LXX *fourth*

[8] LXX adds *and you shall take a fourth part, and burn it up in the midst of it*

[9] LXX *fourth*

[10] LXX *fourth*

[11] Ezekiel 5:3 - 1 Peter 4:18, 2 Kings 1:12, Jeremiah 15:10 16:6 4:16, Luke 13:23-24, Matthew 7:14

[12] Ezekiel 5:4 - 2 Kings 1:25, Jeremiah 4:4 41:1-41:18 24:45 4:30

[13] Ezekiel 5:5 - 1 Corinthians 10:4, 1 Enoch 26:2, Deuteronomy 4:6, Ezekiel 4:1 16:14, Jeremiah 6:6, Leviticus.R 21:6 23:5, Luke 22:19-20, Matthew 5:14, Micah 5:8, Pesikta Rabbati 10:2, Sifre Devarim Ekev 39, Song of Songs.R 2:8, z.Vaetchanan 269b

וַתֶּמֶר אֶת־מִשְׁפָּטַי לְרִשְׁעָה מִן־הַגּוֹיִם וְאֶת־חֻקּוֹתַי מִן־הָאֲרָצוֹת אֲשֶׁר סְבִיבוֹתֶיהָ כִּי בְמִשְׁפָּטַי מָאָסוּ וְחֻקּוֹתַי לֹא־הָלְכוּ בָהֶם

6[1] *And she has rebelled against My ordinances in doing wickedness more than the nations, and against My statutes more than the countries around her; for they have rejected My ordinances, and as for My statutes, they have not walked in them[2].*

לָכֵן כֹּה־אָמַר אֲדֹנָי יְהוִה יַעַן הֲמָנְכֶם מִן־הַגּוֹיִם אֲשֶׁר סְבִיבוֹתֵיכֶם בְּחֻקּוֹתַי לֹא הֲלַכְתֶּם וְאֶת־מִשְׁפָּטַי לֹא עֲשִׂיתֶם וּכְמִשְׁפְּטֵי הַגּוֹיִם אֲשֶׁר סְבִיבוֹתֵיכֶם לֹא עֲשִׂיתֶם

7[3] Therefore, thus says the Lord GOD: Because you have outdone the nations around you, in that you have not walked in My statutes, nor have kept My ordinances, nor have walked after the ordinances of the nations around you;

לָכֵן כֹּה אָמַר אֲדֹנָי יְהוִה הִנְנִי עָלַיִךְ גַּם־אָנִי וְעָשִׂיתִי בְתוֹכֵךְ מִשְׁפָּטִים לְעֵינֵי הַגּוֹיִם

8[4] Therefore, thus says the Lord GOD: Behold, I, I, am against you, and I will execute judgments in your midst in the sight of the nations.

וְעָשִׂיתִי בָךְ אֵת אֲשֶׁר לֹא־עָשִׂיתִי וְאֵת אֲשֶׁר־לֹא־אֶעֱשֶׂה כָמֹהוּ עוֹד יַעַן כָּל־תּוֹעֲבֹתָיִךְ

9[5] And I will do in you what I have not done, and what I will not do again, because of all your abominations.

לָכֵן אָבוֹת יֹאכְלוּ בָנִים בְּתוֹכֵךְ וּבָנִים יֹאכְלוּ אֲבוֹתָם וְעָשִׂיתִי בָךְ שְׁפָטִים וְזֵרִיתִי אֶת־כָּל־שְׁאֵרִיתֵךְ לְכָל־רוּחַ

10[6] Therefore, the fathers shall eat the sons in your midst, and the sons shall eat their fathers; and I will execute judgments in you, and I will scatter your whole remnant to all the winds.

לָכֵן חַי־אָנִי נְאֻם אֲדֹנָי יְהוִה אִם־לֹא יַעַן אֶת־מִקְדָּשִׁי טִמֵּאת בְּכָל־שִׁקּוּצַיִךְ וּבְכָל־תּוֹעֲבֹתָיִךְ וְגַם־אֲנִי אֶגְרַע וְלֹא־תָחוֹס עֵינִי וְגַם־אֲנִי לֹא אֶחְמוֹל

11[7] Why, as I live, says the Lord GOD, surely, because you defiled My sanctuary with all your detestable things, and with all your abominations; therefore, I will I diminish you; My eye will not spare, nor will I have pity.

שְׁלִשִׁתֵיךְ בַּדֶּבֶר יָמוּתוּ וּבָרָעָב יִכְלוּ בְתוֹכֵךְ וְהַשְּׁלִשִׁית בַּחֶרֶב יִפְּלוּ סְבִיבוֹתָיִךְ וְהַשְּׁלִישִׁית לְכָל־רוּחַ אֱזָרֶה וְחֶרֶב אָרִיק אַחֲרֵיהֶם

12[8] A *third*[9] part of you shall die with the pestilence, and [10]they shall be consumed with famine in your midst; and a *third*[11] part shall fall by the sword around you; and I will scatter a *third*[12] part to all the winds, and will draw out a sword after them.

וְכָלָה אַפִּי וַהֲנִחוֹתִי חֲמָתִי בָּם וְהִנֶּחָמְתִּי וְיָדְעוּ כִּי־אֲנִי יְהוָה דִּבַּרְתִּי בְּקִנְאָתִי בְּכַלּוֹתִי חֲמָתִי בָּם

13[13] Thus My anger shall spend itself, and I will satisfy My fury on them, and I will be eased;

---

[1] Ezekiel 5:6 - 1 Corinthians 5:1, 2 Kings 17:8-17:20, Deuteronomy 32:15-32:21, Ezekiel 16:47-16:48 16:51, Jeremiah 5:3 8:5 9:7 11:10, Jude 1:4, Nehemiah 9:16-9:17, Pesikta Rabbati 27/28:2, Psalms 78:10 10:20, Romans 1:23-1:25, Zechariah 7:11
[2] LXX *And you shall declare my ordinances to the lawless one from out of the nations; and my statutes to the sinful one of the countries around her: because they have rejected my ordinances, and have not walked in my statutes*
[3] Ezekiel 5:7 - 2 Chronicles 9:9, 2 Kings 21:9-21:11, b.Sanhedrin 39b, Ein Yaakov Sanhedrin:39b, Ezekiel 5:11 16:47-16:48 16:54, Jastrow 1382a, Jeremiah 2:10-2:11, z.Vaetchanan 269b
[4] Ezekiel 5:8 - 1 Kings 9:8-9, Deuteronomy 5:19 29:22-27, Ezekiel 11:9 15:7 21:8 25:2-6 26:2-3 4:22 29:6-7 11:3 35:10-15 15:1, Jeremiah 21:5 21:13 22:8-9 24:9 2:7, Lamentations 2:5 2:15-17 3:3, Leviticus 26:17-46, Matthew 22:7, z.Vaetchanan 269b, Zechariah 14:2-3
[5] Ezekiel 5:9 - Amos 3:2, Daniel 9:12, Lamentations 4:6 4:9, Matthew 24:21
[6] Ezekiel 5:10 - 2 Kings 6:29, Amos 9:9, Deuteronomy 4:27 28:53-28:57 28:64 8:26, Ezekiel 5:2 5:12 6:8 12:14 20:23 22:15 12:19, Isaiah 9:21 1:26, Jeremiah 9:17 19:9 20:12 2:17, Lamentations 2:20 4:10, Lamentations.R 1:45, Leviticus 2:29 2:33, Luke 21:24, Nehemiah 1:8, Pesikta Rabbati 29:2, Psalms 44:12, Zechariah 2:6 7:14
[7] Ezekiel 5:11 - 2 Chronicles 9:4 9:7 12:14, 2 Kings 21:4 21:7 23:12, 2 Peter 2:4-5, Amos 8:7, Deuteronomy 7:25-26 5:19, Ezekiel 7:4 7:9 7:20 8:5-6 8:16 8:18 9:5 9:10 11:18 11:21 23:28 24:14 5:15 20:7, Hebrews 6:13, Jastrow 850b, Jeremiah 7:9-11 10:24 16:18 8:34 20:4, Lamentations 2:21, Malachi 3:17, Numbers 14:28-35, Psalms 95:11 11:39, Psalms of Solomon 1:8, Romans 8:32 11:12 11:21, t.Shevuot 1:3, Zechariah 11:6
Ezekiel 5:11-17 - 11QEzek
[8] Ezekiel 5:12 - Amos 9:4, Deuteronomy 28:65, Ezekiel 5:2 5:10 5:17 6:8 6:11-12 12:14, Jeremiah 9:17 15:2 21:9 42:16-17 18:22 43:10-11 20:27, Leviticus 2:33, Sibylline Oracles 3.544, Zechariah 7:14 13:7-9
[9] LXX *fourth*
[10] LXX adds *a fourth part of you shall be consumed in your midst*
[11] LXX *fourth*
[12] LXX *fourth*
[13] Ezekiel 5:13 - b.Berachot 59a, Daniel 9:2 11:36, Deuteronomy 8:36, Ezekiel 6:10 6:12 7:8 13:15 16:42 16:63 20:8 20:21 21:22 23:25 24:13 36:5-36:6 38:18-38:19, Isaiah 1:21 1:24 9:8 11:17, Jeremiah 1:12, Lamentations 4:11 4:22, Midrash Psalms 85:3, Zechariah 6:8

וָאֶתְּנֵךְ לְחָרְבָּה וּלְחֶרְפָּה בַּגּוֹיִם אֲשֶׁר סְבִיבוֹתָיִךְ לְעֵינֵי כָּל־עוֹבֵר

14[1] and they shall know I, the LORD, have spoken in My zeal, when I spent My fury on them. Moreover, I will make you *an amazement and a reproach, among the nations around you*[2], in the sight of all who pass by.

וְהָיְתָה חֶרְפָּה וּגְדוּפָה מוּסָר וּמְשַׁמָּה לַגּוֹיִם אֲשֶׁר סְבִיבוֹתָיִךְ בַּעֲשׂוֹתִי בָךְ שְׁפָטִים בְּאַף וּבְחֵמָה וּבְתֹכְחוֹת חֵמָה אֲנִי יְהוָה דִּבַּרְתִּי

15[3] So it shall be a reproach and a taunt, an instruction and an astonishment, to the nations who are around you, when I shall execute judgments in you in anger and in fury, and in furious rebukes; I, the LORD, have spoken it;

בְּשַׁלְּחִי אֶת־חִצֵּי הָרָעָב הָרָעִים בָּהֶם אֲשֶׁר הָיוּ לְמַשְׁחִית אֲשֶׁר־אֲשַׁלַּח אוֹתָם לְשַׁחֶתְכֶם וְרָעָב אֹסֵף עֲלֵיכֶם וְשָׁבַרְתִּי לָכֶם מַטֵּה־לָחֶם

16[4] when I send on them the evil arrows of famine, that are for destruction, which I will send to destroy you; and I will increase the famine on you, and will break your staff of bread;

וְשִׁלַּחְתִּי עֲלֵיכֶם רָעָב וְחַיָּה רָעָה וְשִׁכְּלֻךְ וְדֶבֶר וָדָם יַעֲבָר־בָּךְ וְחֶרֶב אָבִיא עָלַיִךְ אֲנִי יְהוָה דִּבַּרְתִּי

17[5] and I will send famine and evil beasts, and they shall bereave you; and pestilence and blood shall pass through you; and I will bring the sword on you. I, the LORD, have spoken it.'

Ezekiel – Chapter 06

וַיְהִי דְבַר־יְהוָה אֵלַי לֵאמֹר

1[6] And the word of the LORD came to me, saying:

בֶּן־אָדָם שִׂים פָּנֶיךָ אֶל־הָרֵי יִשְׂרָאֵל וְהִנָּבֵא אֲלֵיהֶם

2[7] 'Son of man, set your face toward the mountains of Israel, and prophesy against them,

וְאָמַרְתָּ הָרֵי יִשְׂרָאֵל שִׁמְעוּ דְּבַר־אֲדֹנָי יְהוִה כֹּה־אָמַר אֲדֹנָי יְהוִה לֶהָרִים וְלַגְּבָעוֹת לָאֲפִיקִים "וְלַגֵּאָיֹת" "וְלַגֵּאָיוֹת" הִנְנִי אֲנִי מֵבִיא עֲלֵיכֶם חֶרֶב וְאִבַּדְתִּי בָּמוֹתֵיכֶם

3[8] and say: You mountains of Israel, hear the word of the Lord GOD: Thus says the Lord GOD concerning the mountains and concerning the hills, concerning the ravines and concerning the valleys: Behold, I, I, will bring a sword upon you, and I will destroy your high places.

וְנָשַׁמּוּ מִזְבְּחוֹתֵיכֶם וְנִשְׁבְּרוּ חַמָּנֵיכֶם וְהִפַּלְתִּי חַלְלֵיכֶם לִפְנֵי גִּלּוּלֵיכֶם

4[9] And your altars shall become desolate, and your sun images shall be broken; and I will cast down your slain men before your idols.

וְנָתַתִּי אֶת־פִּגְרֵי בְּנֵי יִשְׂרָאֵל לִפְנֵי גִּלּוּלֵיהֶם וְזֵרִיתִי אֶת־עַצְמוֹתֵיכֶם סְבִיבוֹת מִזְבְּחוֹתֵיכֶם

5[10] And I will lay the carcasses of the children of Israel before their idols; and I will scatter your bones around your altars.

בְּכֹל מוֹשְׁבוֹתֵיכֶם הֶעָרִים תֶּחֱרַבְנָה וְהַבָּמוֹת תִּישָׁמְנָה לְמַעַן יֶחֶרְבוּ וְיֶאְשְׁמוּ מִזְבְּחוֹתֵיכֶם

6[11] In all your dwelling places the cities shall be laid waste, and the high places shall be desolate; that your altars may be laid waste and made desolate, and your idols may be broken

---

[1] Ezekiel 5:14 - 2 Chronicles 7:20-7:21, Deuteronomy 4:37, Ezekiel 22:4, Isaiah 64:11-64:12, Jeremiah 19:8 24:9-24:10 18:18, Lamentations 1:4 1:8 2:15-2:17 5:18, Leviticus 26:31-26:32, Micah 3:12, Nehemiah 2:17, Psalms 74:3-74:10 79:1-79:4

[2] LXX *desolate, and your daughters around you*

[3] Ezekiel 5:15 - 1 Corinthians 10:11, 1 Kings 9:7, Deuteronomy 29:23-27, Ezekiel 1:17, Isaiah 2:9 66:15-16, Jeremiah 22:8-9, Nahum 1:2, Psalms 79:4

[4] Ezekiel 5:16 - 2 Kings 6:25, Deuteronomy 32:23-32:24, Ezekiel 4:16 14:13, Isaiah 3:1, Lamentations 3:12, Leviticus 2:26, Psalms 7:14 91:5-91:7, Psalms of Solomon 2:24, Sifre Devarim {Haazinu Hashamayim} 321, Sifre Devarim Nitzavim 321

[5] Ezekiel 5:17 - 2 Kings 17:25, Deuteronomy 8:24, Exodus 23:29, Ezekiel 5:12-15 5:16 14:15 14:19 14:21-22 17:21 17:24 21:8 21:37 22:14 23:47 2:14 9:27 34:25-28 13:14, Jeremiah 15:3, Leviticus 2:22, Matthew 24:35, Pesikta de R'Kahana 3.11 16.11

[6] Ezekiel 6:1 - Apocalypse of Elijah 1:1, Guide for the Perplexed 2:29

[7] Ezekiel 6:2 - Avot de R'Natan 34, Ezekiel 4:7 13:17 19:9 21:2 21:7 1:2 9:28 10:14 11:12 12:1 13:22 38:2-3, Joshua 11:21, Micah 6:1-2

[8] Ezekiel 6:3 - Ezekiel 36:1-4 12:8, Isaiah 3:9, Jeremiah 2:20 3:6 3:23 22:29, Leviticus 2:30, Micah 6:2, z.Vaetchanan 269b

[9] Ezekiel 6:4 - 1 Kings 13:2, 2 Chronicles 14:4 34:4-5, 2 Kings 23:14 23:16-20, Ezekiel 6:5-6 6:13, Jeremiah 8:1-2 19:13, Leviticus 2:30

[10] Ezekiel 6:5 - 2 Kings 23:14 23:16, Jeremiah 8:1-8:2, Psalms of Solomon 4:19

[11] Ezekiel 6:6 - Ezekiel 5:14 6:4 16:39 6:13, Habakkuk 2:18, Hosea 10:2 10:8, Isaiah 1:31 2:18 2:20 6:11 24:1-12 3:9 32:13-14 16:11, Jastrow 129a, Jeremiah 2:15 9:12 9:20 10:22 17:3 10:22, Leviticus 2:30, Micah 1:7 3:12 5:14, Psalms 19:8, Zechariah 13:2, Zephaniah 1:2-6 1:18 3:6-7

וְנִשְׁבְּרוּ וְנִשְׁבָּתוּ גִּלּוּלֵיכֶם וְנִגְדְּעוּ חַמָּנֵיכֶם וְנִמְחוּ מַעֲשֵׂיכֶם

and cease, and your sun images may be hewn down, and your works may be blotted out.

7[1] וְנָפַל חָלָל בְּתוֹכְכֶם וִידַעְתֶּם כִּי־אֲנִי יְהֹוָה

And the slain shall fall in your midst, and you shall know I am the LORD.

8[2] וְהוֹתַרְתִּי בִּהְיוֹת לָכֶם פְּלִיטֵי חֶרֶב בַּגּוֹיִם בְּהִזָּרוֹתֵיכֶם בָּאֲרָצוֹת

Yet will I leave a remnant, so you shall have some who escape the sword among the nations, when you are scattered through the countries.

9[3] וְזָכְרוּ פְלִיטֵיכֶם אוֹתִי בַּגּוֹיִם אֲשֶׁר נִשְׁבּוּ־שָׁם אֲשֶׁר נִשְׁבַּרְתִּי אֶת־לִבָּם הַזּוֹנֶה אֲשֶׁר־סָר מֵעָלַי וְאֵת עֵינֵיהֶם הַזֹּנוֹת אַחֲרֵי גִּלּוּלֵיהֶם וְנָקֹטּוּ בִּפְנֵיהֶם אֶל־הָרָעוֹת אֲשֶׁר עָשׂוּ לְכֹל תּוֹעֲבֹתֵיהֶם

And they who escape shall remember Me among the nations where they shall be carried captives, how I have been anguished with their straying heart, which has departed from Me, and with their eyes, which are gone astray after their idols; and they shall loathe themselves in their own sight for the evils they have committed in all their abominations.

10[4] וְיָדְעוּ כִּי־אֲנִי יְהֹוָה לֹא אֶל־חִנָּם דִּבַּרְתִּי לַעֲשׂוֹת לָהֶם הָרָעָה הַזֹּאת

And they shall know *I am the LORD; I have not vainly said that I will do this evil to them*[5].

11[6] כֹּה־אָמַר אֲדֹנָי יְהֹוִה הַכֵּה בְכַפְּךָ וּרְקַע בְּרַגְלְךָ וֶאֱמָר־אָח אֶל כָּל־תּוֹעֲבוֹת רָעוֹת בֵּית יִשְׂרָאֵל אֲשֶׁר בַּחֶרֶב בָּרָעָב וּבַדֶּבֶר יִפֹּלוּ

Thus says the Lord GOD: Strike with your hand, and stamp with your foot, and say: Alas! Because of all the evil abominations of the house of Israel; for they shall fall by the sword, by the famine, and by the pestilence.

12[7] הָרָחוֹק בַּדֶּבֶר יָמוּת וְהַקָּרוֹב בַּחֶרֶב יִפּוֹל וְהַנִּשְׁאָר וְהַנָּצוּר בָּרָעָב יָמוּת וְכִלֵּיתִי חֲמָתִי בָּם

He who is far off shall die of the pestilence; and he who is near shall fall by the sword; and he who remains and is besieged shall die by the famine; thus I will spend My fury on them.

13[8] וִידַעְתֶּם כִּי־אֲנִי יְהֹוָה בִּהְיוֹת חַלְלֵיהֶם בְּתוֹךְ גִּלּוּלֵיהֶם סְבִיבוֹת מִזְבְּחוֹתֵיהֶם אֶל כָּל־גִּבְעָה רָמָה בְּכֹל רָאשֵׁי הֶהָרִים וְתַחַת כָּל־עֵץ רַעֲנָן וְתַחַת כָּל־אֵלָה עֲבֻתָּה מְקוֹם אֲשֶׁר נָתְנוּ־שָׁם רֵיחַ נִיחֹחַ לְכֹל גִּלּוּלֵיהֶם

And you shall know I am the LORD, when their slain men shall be among their idols around their altars, upon every high hill, in all the tops of the mountains, and under every leafy tree, and under every thick terebinth, the place where they offered sweet savor to all their idols.

14[9] וְנָטִיתִי אֶת־יָדִי עֲלֵיהֶם וְנָתַתִּי אֶת־הָאָרֶץ שְׁמָמָה וּמְשַׁמָּה מִמִּדְבַּר דִּבְלָתָה בְּכֹל מוֹשְׁבוֹתֵיהֶם וְיָדְעוּ כִּי־אֲנִי יְהֹוָה

And I will stretch out My hand upon them, and make the land desolate and waste, more than the wilderness of Diblah, throughout all their habitations; they shall know I am the LORD.'

Ezekiel – Chapter 07[10]

1[11] וַיְהִי דְבַר־יְהֹוָה אֵלַי לֵאמֹר

Moreover, the word of the LORD came to me, saying:

---

[1] Ezekiel 6:7 - 2 Kings 19:19, Daniel 4:32-34 6:27-28, Exodus 7:5 14:4 14:18, Ezekiel 6:13 7:4 7:9 9:7 11:10 11:12 12:15 13:9 13:14 13:21 13:23 14:8 15:7 20:38 20:42 20:44 23:49 24:24 24:27 1:17 2:6 4:23 6:26 11:15 14:23, Jeremiah 14:18 18:21 1:33, Lamentations 2:20-21 4:9, Psalms 83:18-19

[2] Ezekiel 6:8 - 4Q298 1 iii, Ezekiel 5:2 5:12 7:16 12:16 14:22, Isaiah 6:13 27:7-8, Jeremiah 6:11 20:14 20:28 22:28, Romans 9:27 11:5-6

[3] Ezekiel 6:9 - 2 Kings 16:10, 2 Peter 2:14, Amos 2:13, Daniel 9:2-9:3, Deuteronomy 4:29-4:31 30:1-30:3, Ezekiel 5:13 7:16 12:16 14:4-14:7 16:43 16:63 20:7 20:24 20:28 20:43 23:14-23:16 36:31-36:32, Isaiah 7:13 19:24 15:10 16:7, Jeremiah 3:6 3:13 30:18-30:19 3:50, Job 18:6, Leviticus 26:39-26:41, Numbers 15:39, Psalms 78:40 17:1, Song of Songs.R 2:1, y.Taanit 4:2, Zechariah 10:9

[4] Ezekiel 6:10 - Daniel 9:12, Ezekiel 6:7 14:22-14:23, Jeremiah 5:12-5:14 20:28, Zechariah 1:6

[5] LXX *I, the LORD, have spoken*

[6] Ezekiel 6:11 - Amos 5:16, Ezekiel 5:12 9:4 14:21 21:19-21:22 1:6, Isaiah 10:1, Jeremiah 9:2 9:11 15:2-15:3 16:4 24:10 6:7, Joel 1:15, Mas.Semachot 3:3, Numbers 24:10, Revelation 18:10 18:16-18:19, z.Vaetchanan 269b

[7] Ezekiel 6:12 - Daniel 9:7, Ezekiel 5:13, Isaiah 16:2, Lamentations 4:11 4:22

[8] Ezekiel 6:13 - 1 Kings 14:23, 2 Kings 16:4, Ezekiel 6:4-6:7 20:28, Hosea 4:13, Isaiah 1:29 13:20 37:36-37:38 57:5-57:7 65:3-65:4 18:17, Jeremiah 2:20 3:6

[9] Ezekiel 6:14 - Ezekiel 14:13 16:27 20:33-20:34, Isaiah 5:25 9:13 9:18 9:22 10:4 2:11, Jeremiah 24:22, Numbers 9:46

[10] MT verses are found in this order in LXX: 01-3a, 7, 3b, 8-9, 6, 4-5, 10-27

[11] Ezekiel 7:1 - Pesikta Rabbati 26:6, z.Vayigash 210b

וְאַתָּה בֶן־אָדָם כֹּה־אָמַר אֲדֹנָי יְהוִה לְאַדְמַת יִשְׂרָאֵל קֵץ בָּא הַקֵּץ עַל־אַרְבַּעַת 'עַל־אַרְבַּע' כַּנְפוֹת הָאָרֶץ	2[1]	'And you, son of man, thus says the Lord GOD concerning the land of Israel: An end! The end has come upon the four corners of the land.
עַתָּה הַקֵּץ עָלַיִךְ וְשִׁלַּחְתִּי אַפִּי בָּךְ וּשְׁפַטְתִּיךְ כִּדְרָכָיִךְ וְנָתַתִּי עָלַיִךְ אֵת כָּל־תּוֹעֲבֹתָיִךְ	3[2]	Now is the end upon you, *and I will send My anger on you, and will judge you according to your ways; and I will bring upon you all your abominations.*
וְלֹא־תָחוֹס עֵינִי עָלַיִךְ וְלֹא אֶחְמוֹל כִּי דְרָכַיִךְ עָלַיִךְ אֶתֵּן וְתוֹעֲבוֹתַיִךְ בְּתוֹכֵךְ תִּהְיֶיןָ וִידַעְתֶּם כִּי־אֲנִי יְהוָה	4[3]	And My eye shall not spare you, nor will I pity; but I will bring your ways upon you, and your abominations shall be in your midst; and you shall know I am the LORD.
כֹּה אָמַר אֲדֹנָי יְהוִה רָעָה אַחַת רָעָה הִנֵּה בָאָה	5[4]	Thus says the Lord GOD: *An evil, a singular evil; behold, it comes[5].*
קֵץ בָּא בָּא הַקֵּץ הֵקִיץ אֵלָיִךְ הִנֵּה בָּאָה	6[6]	*An end has come, the end has come, it awakens against you; behold, it comes.[7]*
בָּאָה הַצְּפִירָה אֵלַיִךְ יוֹשֵׁב הָאָרֶץ בָּא הָעֵת קָרוֹב הַיּוֹם מְהוּמָה וְלֹא־הֵד הָרִים	7[8]	The turn has come to you, O inhabitant of the land; the time has come, the day of tumult is near, and not of joyful shouting on the mountains.
עַתָּה מִקָּרוֹב אֶשְׁפּוֹךְ חֲמָתִי עָלַיִךְ וְכִלֵּיתִי אַפִּי בָּךְ וּשְׁפַטְתִּיךְ כִּדְרָכָיִךְ וְנָתַתִּי עָלַיִךְ אֵת כָּל־תּוֹעֲבוֹתָיִךְ	8[9]	Now I will shortly pour out My fury on you, and spend My anger on you, and will judge you according to your ways; and I will bring upon you all your abominations.
וְלֹא־תָחוֹס עֵינִי וְלֹא אֶחְמוֹל כִּדְרָכַיִךְ עָלַיִךְ אֶתֵּן וְתוֹעֲבוֹתַיִךְ בְּתוֹכֵךְ תִּהְיֶיןָ וִידַעְתֶּם כִּי אֲנִי יְהוָה מַכֶּה	9[10]	And My eye shall not spare, nor will I have pity; I will bring on you according to your ways, and your abominations shall be in your midst; and you shall know I, the LORD, strikes.
הִנֵּה הַיּוֹם הִנֵּה בָאָה יָצְאָה הַצְּפִרָה צָץ הַמַּטֶּה פָּרַח הַזָּדוֹן	10[11]	Behold the day; behold, it comes; the turn has come forth; the rod has blossomed, arrogance has budded.
הֶחָמָס קָם לְמַטֵּה־רֶשַׁע לֹא־מֵהֶם וְלֹא מֵהֲמוֹנָם וְלֹא מֶהֱמֵהֶם וְלֹא־נֹהַּ בָּהֶם	11[12]	Violence is risen up into a rod of wickedness; nothing comes from them, nor from their tumult, nor from their turmoil, nor is there eminency among them.

---

[1] Ezekiel 7:2 - 1 Peter 4:7, 2 Chronicles 10:7, Amos 8:2 8:10, Cairo Damascus 16:15, Deuteronomy 8:20, Ezekiel 7:3 7:5-7:6 11:13 12:22 21:7 16:2, Genesis 6:13, Jeremiah 5:31 3:13, Lamentations 1:9 4:18, Matthew 24:6 24:13-24:14, z.Vaetchanan 269b

[2] Ezekiel 7:3 - Ezekiel 5:13 6:3-7 6:12-13 7:8-9 7:27 11:10-11 16:38 18:30 9:20 34:20-22 12:19, Revelation 20:12-20:13

[3] Ezekiel 7:4 - Ezekiel 5:11 6:7 6:14 7:9 7:27 8:18 9:10 11:21 12:20 16:43 22:31 23:31 23:49 24:14, Hebrews 10:30, Hosea 9:7 12:4, Jeremiah 13:14 16:18 1:14, Zechariah 11:6

[4] Ezekiel 7:5 - 2 Kings 21:12-13, Amos 3:2, Daniel 9:12, Ezekiel 5:9, Matthew 24:21, Nahum 1:9, z.Vaetchanan 269b, z.Vayigash 210b

[5] LXX *Behold, the end has come*

[6] Ezekiel 7:6 - 2 Peter 2:5, Ezekiel 7:3 7:10 21:30 15:8, Jeremiah 20:27, Midrash Psalms 105:2, Zechariah 13:7

[7] LXX *Now the end has come to you, and I will send judgment upon you: and I will take vengeance on your ways, and will recompense all your abominations upon you*

[8] Ezekiel 7:7 - 1 Peter 4:17, Amos 4:13, Ezekiel 7:12 12:23-25 12:28, Genesis 19:15 19:24, Isaiah 13:22 17:14 22:5, Jeremiah 20:7, Zephaniah 1:14-16

[9] Ezekiel 7:8 - 2 Chronicles 10:21, Daniel 9:11 9:27, Ezekiel 6:12 7:3-7:4 9:8 14:19 20:8 20:13 20:21 20:33 22:31 6:15 36:18-36:19, Hosea 5:10, Isaiah 18:25, Jeremiah 7:20, Lamentations 2:4 4:11, Nahum 1:6, Psalms 79:6, Revelation 14:10 16:2-16:21

[10] Ezekiel 7:9 - 11QEzek, Galatians 6:7, Isaiah 9:14, Micah 6:9, Revelation 20:13

[11] Ezekiel 7:10 - 1 Thessalonians 5:3, Daniel 4:34, Ezekiel 7:6 19:14 21:15 21:18, Isaiah 10:5 4:1, James 4:6, Numbers 17:23, Proverbs 14:3 16:18, Psalms 89:33, t.Taniyot 3:5

[12] Ezekiel 7:11 - 3 Enoch 31:2, Amos 3:10 6:3, b.Sanhedrin 18a, Ein Yaakov Sanhedrin:108a, Ezekiel 5:4 5:11 6:11 7:2 7:16 7:23 24:16-24:24, Genesis.R 31:1, Isaiah 5:7 9:5 14:29 59:6-59:8, James 2:13, Jastrow 1675b, Jeremiah 6:7 16:5-16:6 22:18 1:33, Micah 2:2 3:3 6:12, Midrash Tanchuma Noach 4, Psalms 78:64, Zephaniah 1:18
Ezekiel 7:11-12 - 11QEzek

בָּא הָעֵת הִגִּיעַ הַיּוֹם הַקּוֹנֶה אַל־יִשְׂמָח וְהַמּוֹכֵר אַל־יִתְאַבָּל כִּי חָרוֹן אֶל־כָּל־הֲמוֹנָהּ

12[1] The time has come, the day draws near; let not the buyer rejoice, nor the seller mourn; for wrath is upon all the multitude.

כִּי הַמּוֹכֵר אֶל־הַמִּמְכָּר לֹא יָשׁוּב וְעוֹד בַּחַיִּים חַיָּתָם כִּי־חָזוֹן אֶל־כָּל־הֲמוֹנָהּ לֹא יָשׁוּב וְאִישׁ בַּעֲוֹנוֹ חַיָּתוֹ לֹא יִתְחַזָּקוּ

13[2] For the seller shall not return to what is sold, although they be yet alive; for the vision is touching the whole multitude, which shall not return; nor shall any stand possessed of the iniquity of his life.

תָּקְעוּ בַתָּקוֹעַ וְהָכִין הַכֹּל וְאֵין הֹלֵךְ לַמִּלְחָמָה כִּי חֲרוֹנִי אֶל־כָּל־הֲמוֹנָהּ

14[3] They have blown the horn, and have made all ready, but no one goes to the battle; for My wrath is upon all the multitude.

הַחֶרֶב בַּחוּץ וְהַדֶּבֶר וְהָרָעָב מִבָּיִת אֲשֶׁר בַּשָּׂדֶה בַּחֶרֶב יָמוּת וַאֲשֶׁר בָּעִיר רָעָב וָדֶבֶר יֹאכְלֶנּוּ

15[4] The sword is outside, and the pestilence and the famine within; he who is in the field shall die with the sword, and, famine and pestilence shall devour he who is in the city.

וּפָלְטוּ פְּלִיטֵיהֶם וְהָיוּ אֶל־הֶהָרִים כְּיוֹנֵי הַגֵּאָיוֹת כֻּלָּם הֹמוֹת אִישׁ בַּעֲוֹנוֹ

16[5] But they who shall at all escape, shall be on the mountains like doves of the valleys, all of them moaning, everyone in his iniquity.

כָּל־הַיָּדַיִם תִּרְפֶּינָה וְכָל־בִּרְכַּיִם תֵּלַכְנָה מָּיִם

17[6] All hands shall be slack, and all knees shall drip with water.

וְחָגְרוּ שַׂקִּים וְכִסְּתָה אוֹתָם פַּלָּצוּת וְאֶל כָּל־פָּנִים בּוּשָׁה וּבְכָל־רָאשֵׁיהֶם קָרְחָה

18[7] They shall also gird themselves with sackcloth, and horror shall cover them; and shame shall be on all faces, and baldness on all their heads.

כַּסְפָּם בַּחוּצוֹת יַשְׁלִיכוּ וּזְהָבָם לְנִדָּה יִהְיֶה כַּסְפָּם וּזְהָבָם לֹא־יוּכַל לְהַצִּילָם בְּיוֹם עֶבְרַת יְהוָה נַפְשָׁם לֹא יְשַׂבֵּעוּ וּמֵעֵיהֶם לֹא יְמַלֵּאוּ כִּי־מִכְשׁוֹל עֲוֹנָם הָיָה

19[8] They shall cast their silver in the streets, and their gold shall be as an unclean thing; their silver and their gold shall not be able to deliver them in the day of the wrath of the LORD; they shall not satisfy their souls, nor fill their bellies; because it has been the stumbling block of their iniquity.

וּצְבִי עֶדְיוֹ לְגָאוֹן שָׂמָהוּ וְצַלְמֵי תוֹעֲבֹתָם שִׁקּוּצֵיהֶם עָשׂוּ בוֹ עַל־כֵּן נְתַתִּיו לָהֶם לְנִדָּה

20[9] And as for the beauty of their ornament, which was set for pride, they made the images of their abominations and their detestable things; therefore, I made it to them as an unclean thing.

וּנְתַתִּיו בְּיַד־הַזָּרִים לָבַז וּלְרִשְׁעֵי הָאָרֶץ לְשָׁלָל "וְחִלְּלָהָ" "וְחִלְּלוּהוּ"

21[10] And I will give it into the hands of the strangers as prey, and to the wicked of the earth as spoil; and they shall profane it.

[1] Ezekiel 7:12 - 1 Corinthians 7:29-7:31, b.Bava Batra [Rashbam] 168a, Ezekiel 6:11-6:12 7:5-7:7 7:10 7:13-7:14, Isaiah 5:13-5:14 24:1-24:2, James 5:8-5:9, Jeremiah 32:7-32:8 32:24-32:25

[2] Ezekiel 7:13 - b.Arachin 33a, b.Megillah 14b, Ecclesiastes 8:8, Ein Yaakov Megillah:14b, Ezekiel 13:22 33:26-27, Job 15:25, Leviticus 25:24-25:28 1:31, Psalms 52:8

[3] Ezekiel 7:14 - Ezekiel 7:11-12, Isaiah 24:1-24:7, Jeremiah 4:5 6:1 6:11 7:20 12:12 3:27

[4] Ezekiel 7:15 - Deuteronomy 32:23-25, Ezekiel 5:12 6:12, Jeremiah 14:18 15:2-3, Lamentations 1:20, Sifre Devarim Haazinu Hashamayim 321, Sifre Devarim Nitzavim 321

[5] Ezekiel 7:16 - Ecclesiastes.R 7:15, Ezekiel 6:8-9 12:31, Ezra 9:15, Isaiah 1:9 13:31 14:14 11:11, Jeremiah 7:10 31:19-20 20:14 20:28 50:4-5, Mekhilta de R'Shimon bar Yochai Beshallach 25:2, Mekilta de R'Ishmael Beshallah 6:110, Midrash Tanchuma Beshallach 23, Proverbs 5:11-14, y.Taanit 4:2, Zechariah 12:10-14

[6] Ezekiel 7:17 - Ezekiel 21:12 22:14, Hebrews 12:12, Isaiah 13:7-13:8, Jeremiah 6:24

[7] Ezekiel 7:18 - Amos 8:10, Ezekiel 3:31, Genesis 15:12, Isaiah 3:24 15:2-3, Jeremiah 3:25 24:37, Job 21:6, Psalms 35:26 55:5-6, Revelation 6:15-17

[8] Ezekiel 7:19 - 2 Kings 7:7-7:8 7:15, Apocalypse of Elijah 1:19, b.Gittin 56a, Ecclesiastes 5:11, Ecclesiastes.R 12:7, Ein Yaakov Gittin:56a, Exodus.R 31:4, Ezekiel 14:3-14:4 14:7 20:12, Isaiah 2:20 6:22 7:2, Job 20:12-20:23, Lamentations.R Petichata D'Chakimei:23, Luke 12:19-12:20, Matthew 16:26, Midrash Psalms 119:58, Midrash Tanchuma Mishpatim 9, Proverbs 11:4, Psalms 78:30-78:31, Romans 11:9, Zephaniah 1:18

[9] Ezekiel 7:20 - 1 Chronicles 29:1-2, 2 Chronicles 2:8 3:1-17 33:4-7 12:14, 2 Kings 21:4 21:7 23:11-12, Ezekiel 5:11 7:22 8:7-10 8:15-16 9:7 24:21, Ezra 3:12, Haggai 2:3, Isaiah 16:12, Jeremiah 7:14 7:30, Lamentations 1:10 2:1 2:7, Psalms 48:3 50:2 87:2-3

[10] Ezekiel 7:21 - 2 Chronicles 36:18-19, 2 Kings 24:13 1:9 25:13-16, Jeremiah 52:13-23, Mas.Soferim 7:1, Psalms 74:2-8 79:1

וַהֲסִבּוֹתִי פָנַי מֵהֶם וְחִלְּלוּ אֶת־צְפוּנִי וּבָאוּ־בָהּ פָּרִיצִים וְחִלְּלוּהָ

22[1] I will also turn My face from them, and they shall profane My secret place; and robbers shall enter into it, and profane it.

עֲשֵׂה הָרַתּוֹק כִּי הָאָרֶץ מָלְאָה מִשְׁפַּט דָּמִים וְהָעִיר מָלְאָה חָמָס

23[2] *Make the chain; for the land is full of bloody crimes, and the city is full of violence*[3].

וְהֵבֵאתִי רָעֵי גוֹיִם וְיָרְשׁוּ אֶת־בָּתֵּיהֶם וְהִשְׁבַּתִּי גְּאוֹן עַזִּים וְנִחֲלוּ מְקַדְשֵׁיהֶם

24[4] *Why, I will bring the worst of the nations, and they shall possess their houses*[5]; I will also make the pride of the strong cease; and their holy places shall be profaned.

קְפָדָה־בָא וּבִקְשׁוּ שָׁלוֹם וָאָיִן

25[6] *Horror comes*[7]; and they shall seek peace, and there shall be none.

הֹוָה עַל־הֹוָה תָּבוֹא וּשְׁמֻעָה אֶל־שְׁמוּעָה תִּהְיֶה וּבִקְשׁוּ חָזוֹן מִנָּבִיא וְתוֹרָה תֹּאבַד מִכֹּהֵן וְעֵצָה מִזְּקֵנִים

26[8] Calamity shall come upon calamity, and rumor shall be on rumor; and they shall seek a vision of the prophet, and instruction shall perish from the priest, and counsel from the elders.

הַמֶּלֶךְ יִתְאַבָּל וְנָשִׂיא יִלְבַּשׁ שְׁמָמָה וִידֵי עַם־הָאָרֶץ תִּבָּהַלְנָה מִדַּרְכָּם אֶעֱשֶׂה אוֹתָם וּבְמִשְׁפְּטֵיהֶם אֶשְׁפְּטֵם וְיָדְעוּ כִּי־אֲנִי יְהוָה

27[9] *The king shall mourn*[10], and the prince shall be clothed with appalment, and the hands of the people of the land shall be enfeebled; I will do to them after their way, and I will judge them according to their deserts; and they shall know I am the LORD.'

Ezekiel – Chapter 08

וַיְהִי בַּשָּׁנָה הַשִּׁשִּׁית בַּשִּׁשִּׁי בַּחֲמִשָּׁה לַחֹדֶשׁ אֲנִי יוֹשֵׁב בְּבֵיתִי וְזִקְנֵי יְהוּדָה יוֹשְׁבִים לְפָנָי וַתִּפֹּל עָלַי שָׁם יַד אֲדֹנָי יְהוִה

1[11] And it came to pass in the sixth year, in the sixth month, in the fifth day of the month, as I sat in my house, and the elders of Judah sat before me, that the hand of the Lord GOD fell on me there.

וָאֶרְאֶה וְהִנֵּה דְמוּת כְּמַרְאֵה־אֵשׁ מִמַּרְאֵה מָתְנָיו וּלְמַטָּה אֵשׁ וּמִמָּתְנָיו וּלְמַעְלָה כְּמַרְאֵה־זֹהַר כְּעֵין הַחַשְׁמַלָה

2[12] Then I beheld, and behold a likeness as the appearance of fire: from the appearance of his loins and downward, fire; and from his loins and upward, as the appearance of brightness, as the color of polished metal.

וַיִּשְׁלַח תַּבְנִית יָד וַיִּקָּחֵנִי בְּצִיצִת רֹאשִׁי וַתִּשָּׂא אֹתִי רוּחַ בֵּין־הָאָרֶץ וּבֵין הַשָּׁמַיִם וַתָּבֵא אֹתִי

3[13] And the form of a hand was put forth, and I was taken by a lock of my head; and a spirit

---

[1] Ezekiel 7:22 - b.Avodah Zara 52b, b.Bechorot 50a, b.Nedarim 62a, Ein Yaakov Nedarim:62a, Ezekiel 39:23-39:24, Jeremiah 18:17, Psalms 10:12 35:22 74:10-74:11 74:18-74:23

[2] Ezekiel 7:23 - 2 Kings 21:16 24:4, Ecclesiastes.R 8:2, Ezekiel 8:17 9:9 11:6 19:3-19:6 22:3-22:6 22:9 22:13 22:27, Hosea 4:2, Isaiah 1:15 11:3 11:7, Jeremiah 2:34 7:6 22:17 3:2 16:1, Lamentations 3:7, Micah 2:2 7:2, Nahum 3:10, Zephaniah 3:3-3:4

[3] LXX *And they shall work uncleanness: because the land is full of strange nations, and the city is full of iniquity*

[4] Ezekiel 7:24 - 2 Chronicles 7:19-7:20, Ezekiel 21:7 21:36 24:21 4:7 9:28, Genesis.R 43:4, Habakkuk 1:6-1:10, Isaiah 5:14, Jeremiah 4:7 6:12 12:12, Lamentations 5:2, Psalms 83:13 10:41, the original עזם was voweled as either עֻזָּם "the strong" or עֻזָּם "their strength"

[5] Missing in LXX

[6] Ezekiel 7:25 - Ezekiel 13:10 13:16, Isaiah 9:21 59:8-59:12, Jeremiah 8:15-8:16, Lamentations 4:17-4:18, Micah 1:12

[7] LXX *And though propitiation shall come*

[8] Ezekiel 7:26 - Amos 8:11-12, Avot de R'Natan 25, b.Arachin 21a, b.Eruvin [Tosefot] 13a, Deuteronomy 8:23, Ezekiel 8:1 14:1 20:1-3 9:31, Isaiah 23:11, Jeremiah 4:20 18:18 21:2 13:17 38:14-28, Lamentations 2:9, Leviticus 2:18 2:21 2:24 2:28, Micah 3:6, Midrash Psalms 119:15, Psalms 74:9

[9] Ezekiel 7:27 - 1 Kings 20:28, Ezekiel 7:4-7:8 12:10-12:22 17:15-17:21 18:30 21:30 2:16, Isaiah 3:11, James 2:13, Jeremiah 52:8-52:11, Joel 4:17, Matthew 7:2, Psalms 9:17, Romans 2:5-2:10

[10] Missing in LXX

[11] Ezekiel 8:1 - Acts 20:33, Ezekiel 1:2-1:3 3:12 3:14 3:22 14:1 14:4 20:1 24:1 2:1 5:1 5:17 7:1 8:17 9:31 13:1 16:1, Guide for the Perplexed 2:46, Liber Antiquitatum Biblicarum 28:6, Malachi 2:7, Seder Olam 26:Law was Found

[12] Ezekiel 8:2 - Daniel 7:9-7:10, Ezekiel 1:4 1:26-1:27, Revelation 1:14-1:15

[13] Ezekiel 8:3 - 1 Corinthians 10:21-22, 1 Kings 18:12, 2 Corinthians 12:2-4, 2 Kings 2:16 16:14 21:7, Acts 8:39, b.Menachot 42a, b.Yevamot 13b, b.Yoma 76b, Daniel 5:5 10:10 10:18, Deuteronomy 4:24 5:9 6:15 8:16 8:21, Exodus 20:5 10:14, Exodus.R 3:6, Ezekiel 2:9 3:12 3:14 5:11 7:20 8:5 11:1 11:24 16:2, Genesis.R 23:3, Guide for the Perplexed 1:3 2:46, Jeremiah 7:30 8:34, Joshua 24:19, Lives of the Prophets 3:14, Midrash Tanchuma Bereshit 5, mt.Hilchot Pesulei haMikdashim 1:12, mt.Hilchot Tzitzit 1:1, mt.Perek Chelek Intro:11, Psalms 78:58, Revelation 1:10-1:20 4:2-11, western wrote ירושלמה and Eastern wrote ירולם [j.Megillah 1:9]

יְרוּשָׁלַ֔͏ְמָה בְּמַרְאֹ֣ות אֱלֹהִ֑ים אֶל־פֶּ֜תַח שַׁ֤עַר
הַפְּנִימִית֙ הַפֹּונֶ֣ה צָפֹ֔ונָה אֲשֶׁר־שָׁ֖ם מֹושַׁ֥ב סֵ֛מֶל
הַקִּנְאָ֖ה הַמַּקְנֶֽה

lifted me up between the earth and the heaven, and brought me in the visions of God to Jerusalem, to the door of the gate of the inner court that looks toward the north; where was the seat of the image of jealousy, which provokes to jealousy.

וְהִנֵּה־שָׁ֔ם כְּבֹ֖וד אֱלֹהֵ֣י יִשְׂרָאֵ֑ל כַּמַּרְאֶ֖ה אֲשֶׁ֥ר
רָאִ֖יתִי בַּבִּקְעָֽה

4[1] And, behold, the glory of the God of Israel was there, similar to the vision I saw in the plain.

וַיֹּ֣אמֶר אֵלַ֗י בֶּן־אָדָם֙ שָׂא־נָ֤א עֵינֶ֨יךָ֙ דֶּ֣רֶךְ צָפֹ֔ונָה
וָאֶשָּׂ֤א עֵינַי֙ דֶּ֣רֶךְ צָפֹ֔ונָה וְהִנֵּ֤ה מִצָּפֹון֙ לְשַׁ֣עַר
הַמִּזְבֵּ֔חַ סֵ֛מֶל הַקִּנְאָ֥ה הַזֶּ֖ה בַּבִּאָֽה

5[2] Then said He to me: 'Son of man, lift up your eyes now the way toward the north.' So I lifted up my eyes the way toward the north, *and behold northward of the gate of the altar this image of jealousy in the entry*[3]

וַיֹּ֣אמֶר אֵלַ֔י בֶּן־אָדָ֕ם הֲרֹאֶ֥ה אַתָּ֖ה 'מהם' "מָ֣ה"
"הֵם" עֹשִׂ֑ים תֹּועֵבֹ֨ות גְּדֹלֹ֜ות אֲשֶׁ֥ר בֵּֽית־יִשְׂרָאֵ֣ל ׀
עֹשִׂ֣ים פֹּ֗ה לְרָֽחֳקָה֙ מֵעַ֣ל מִקְדָּשִׁ֔י וְעֹוד֙ תָּשׁ֣וּב תִּרְאֶ֔ה
תֹּועֵבֹ֖ות גְּדֹלֹֽות

6[4] And He said to me: 'Son of man, see you what they do? The great abominations that the house of Israel commit here, that I should go far off from My sanctuary? But you shall again see yet greater abominations.'

וַיָּבֵ֥א אֹתִ֖י אֶל־פֶּ֣תַח הֶֽחָצֵ֑ר וָאֶרְאֶ֕ה וְהִנֵּ֥ה חֹר־אֶחָ֖ד
בַּקִּֽיר׃

7[5] And He brought me to the door of the court; *and when I looked, behold a hole in the wall*[6].

וַיֹּ֣אמֶר אֵלַ֔י בֶּן־אָדָ֖ם חֲתָר־נָ֣א בַקִּ֑יר וָאֶחְתֹּ֣ר בַּקִּ֔יר
וְהִנֵּ֖ה פֶּ֥תַח אֶחָֽד

8[7] Then said He to me: 'Son of man, *dig now in the wall;' and when I had dug in the wall*[8], behold a door.

וַיֹּ֖אמֶר אֵלָ֑י בֹּ֤א וּרְאֵה֙ אֶת־הַתֹּועֵבֹ֣ות הָרָעֹ֔ות אֲשֶׁ֛ר
הֵ֥ם עֹשִׂ֖ים פֹּֽה

9[9] And He said to me: 'Go in, and see the wicked abominations they do here.'

וָאָבֹוא֮ וָֽאֶרְאֶה֒ וְהִנֵּ֨ה כָל־תַּבְנִ֜ית רֶ֤מֶשׂ וּבְהֵמָה֙
שֶׁ֔קֶץ וְכָל־גִּלּוּלֵ֖י בֵּ֣ית יִשְׂרָאֵ֑ל מְחֻקֶּ֥ה עַל־הַקִּ֖יר
סָבִ֥יב ׀ סָבִֽיב

10[10] So I went in and saw; and behold every detestable form of creeping things and beasts, and all the idols of the house of Israel, portrayed on the wall around it.

וְשִׁבְעִ֣ים אִ֣ישׁ מִזִּקְנֵ֣י בֵֽית־יִ֠שְׂרָאֵל וְיַאֲזַנְיָ֨הוּ בֶן־
שָׁפָ֜ן עֹמֵ֤ד בְּתֹוכָם֙ עֹמְדִ֣ים לִפְנֵיהֶ֔ם וְאִ֕ישׁ מִקְטַרְתֹּ֖ו
בְּיָדֹ֑ו וַעֲתַ֥ר עֲנַֽן־הַקְּטֹ֖רֶת עֹלֶֽה

11[11] And there stood before them seventy men of the elders of the house of Israel, and in their midst stood *Jaazaniah*[12] the son of Shaphan, every man with his censer in his hand; and a thick cloud of incense went up.

וַיֹּ֣אמֶר אֵלַי֮ הֲרָאִ֣יתָ בֶן־אָדָם֒ אֲשֶׁ֨ר זִקְנֵ֤י בֵֽית־
יִשְׂרָאֵל֙ עֹשִׂ֣ים בַּחֹ֔שֶׁךְ אִ֖ישׁ בְּחַדְרֵ֣י מַשְׂכִּיתֹ֑ו כִּ֣י
אֹמְרִ֗ים אֵ֤ין יְהוָה֙ רֹאֶ֣ה אֹתָ֔נוּ עֹזֵ֥ב יְהוָ֖ה אֶת־הָאָֽרֶץ

12[13] Then said He to me: 'Son of man, have you seen what the elders of the house of Israel do in the dark, every man in his chambers of

---

[1] Ezekiel 8:4 - 2 Corinthians 3:18 4:4-6, Exodus 1:22 40:34-35, Ezekiel 1:26-1:28 3:22-23 9:3 10:1-4 11:22-11:23 43:2-43:4, Hebrews 1:3, Mekilta de R'Ishmael Shirata 4:69

[2] Ezekiel 8:5 - Deuteronomy.R 2:20, Ezekiel 8:3, Jastrow 160b, Jeremiah 3:2 8:34, Lamentations.R Petichata D'Chakimei:22, Leviticus.R 17:7, Numbers.R 9:49, Psalms 48:3 78:58, Zechariah 5:5-5:11

[3] LXX *I looked from the north toward the eastern gate*

[4] Ezekiel 8:6 - 2 Chronicles 36:14-17, 2 Kings 23:4-6, Deuteronomy 31:16-18, Ezekiel 5:11 7:20-22 8:9 8:11-12 8:14 8:16-17 10:19 11:22 23:38-39, Jeremiah 3:6 7:17 7:30 23:11 2:6 8:34, Lamentations 2:6-7, Mas.Soferim 7:3, Proverbs 5:14, Psalms 78:60

[5] Ezekiel 8:7 - 1 Kings 7:12, 2 Kings 21:5, Guide for the Perplexed 2:46

[6] Mising in LXX

[7] Ezekiel 8:8 - Amos 9:2-9:3, Isaiah 5:15, Jeremiah 2:34 23:24, Job 10:22
Ezekiel 8:8-16 - Testament of Moses 2:9

[8] LXX *dig, so I dug*

[9] Ezekiel 8:9 - Ezekiel 20:8

[10] Ezekiel 8:10 - b.Sanhedrin 92b, Deuteronomy 4:18 14:3 14:7-14:8, Ein Yaakov Sanhedrin:92b, Exodus 20:4, Isaiah 57:6-57:10, Jeremiah 2:26-2:27 3:9 16:18, Leviticus 11:10-11:12 11:29-11:31 11:42-11:44, Ralbag SOS Pesichta, Romans 1:23, Sibylline Oracles 3.589, Sifre Devarim {Haazinu Hashamayim} 306, Sifre Devarim Nitzavim 306, Tanna Devei Eliyahu 5

[11] Ezekiel 8:11 - 2 Chronicles 2:16 2:19 10:20, 2 Kings 22:3 22:8 22:12 22:14 1:22, b.Yoma 76b, Daniel 9:8, Exodus 24:1 24:9, Jeremiah 5:5 7:9 19:1 2:24 5:3 12:10, Numbers 11:16 11:25 16:17 16:35, Pesikta Rabbati 29/30:1 33:13

[12] LXX *Jechonias*

[13] Ezekiel 8:12 - Ephesians 5:12, Ezekiel 8:6-8 8:11 8:15 8:17 9:9 14:1 20:1, Guide for the Perplexed 3:19 3:54, Isaiah 5:15, Job 22:12-13 24:13-17, John 3:19-3:20, Lamentations.R Petichata D'Chakimei:22, Midrash Tanchuma Noach 4, mt.Perek Chelek Intro:11, Pesikta Rabbati 31:2, Psalms 10:12 73:11 94:7-10, 321, Sifre Devarim Nitzavim 321

וַיֹּאמֶר אֵלַי עוֹד תָּשׁוּב תִּרְאֶה תוֹעֵבוֹת גְּדֹלוֹת
אֲשֶׁר־הֵמָּה עֹשִׂים

וַיָּבֵא אֹתִי אֶל־פֶּתַח שַׁעַר בֵּית־יְהוָה אֲשֶׁר אֶל־
הַצָּפוֹנָה וְהִנֵּה־שָׁם הַנָּשִׁים יֹשְׁבוֹת מְבַכּוֹת אֶת־
הַתַּמּוּז

וַיֹּאמֶר אֵלַי הֲרָאִיתָ בֶן־אָדָם עוֹד תָּשׁוּב תִּרְאֶה
תּוֹעֵבוֹת גְּדֹלוֹת מֵאֵלֶּה

וַיָּבֵא אֹתִי אֶל־חֲצַר בֵּית־יְהוָה הַפְּנִימִית וְהִנֵּה־
פֶתַח הֵיכַל יְהוָה בֵּין הָאוּלָם וּבֵין הַמִּזְבֵּחַ כְּעֶשְׂרִים
וַחֲמִשָּׁה אִישׁ אֲחֹרֵיהֶם אֶל־הֵיכַל יְהוָה וּפְנֵיהֶם
קֵדְמָה וְהֵמָּה מִשְׁתַּחֲוִיתֶם קֵדְמָה לַשָּׁמֶשׁ

וַיֹּאמֶר אֵלַי הֲרָאִיתָ בֶן־אָדָם הֲנָקֵל לְבֵית יְהוּדָה
מֵעֲשׂוֹת אֶת־הַתּוֹעֵבוֹת אֲשֶׁר עָשׂוּ־פֹה כִּי־מָלְאוּ
אֶת־הָאָרֶץ חָמָס וַיָּשֻׁבוּ לְהַכְעִיסֵנִי וְהִנָּם שֹׁלְחִים
אֶת־הַזְּמוֹרָה אֶל־אַפָּם

וְגַם־אֲנִי אֶעֱשֶׂה בְחֵמָה לֹא־תָחוֹס עֵינִי וְלֹא אֶחְמֹל
וְקָרְאוּ בְאָזְנַי קוֹל גָּדוֹל וְלֹא אֶשְׁמַע אוֹתָם

imagery? For they say: The LORD does not see us, the LORD has forsaken the land.'

13[1] He said also to me: 'You shall again see yet greater abominations which they do.'

14[2] Then He brought me to the door of the gate of the LORD's house toward the north; and, behold, women sat there weeping for Tammuz.

15[3] Then said He to me: 'You seen this, O son of man? You shall again see yet greater abominations than these.'

16[4] And He brought me into the inner court of the LORD's house, and, behold, at the door of the temple of the LORD, between the porch and the altar, were about *twenty-five*[5] men, with their backs toward the temple of the LORD, and their faces toward the east; and they worshipped the sun toward the east.

17[6] Then He said to me: ' you seen this, O son of man? Is it a light thing to the house of Judah that they commit the abominations, which they commit here, in that they fill the land with violence, *and provoke Me still more, and, lo, they put the branch to their nose?*[7]

18[8] Therefore, I will I deal in fury; My eye will not spare, nor will I pity; *though they cry in My ears with a loud voice, I will not hear them*[9].'

Ezekiel – Chapter 09

וַיִּקְרָא בְאָזְנַי קוֹל גָּדוֹל לֵאמֹר קָרְבוּ פְּקֻדּוֹת הָעִיר
וְאִישׁ כְּלִי מַשְׁחֵתוֹ בְּיָדוֹ

וְהִנֵּה שִׁשָּׁה אֲנָשִׁים בָּאִים מִדֶּרֶךְ־שַׁעַר הָעֶלְיוֹן
אֲשֶׁר מָפְנֶה צָפוֹנָה וְאִישׁ כְּלִי מַפָּצוֹ בְּיָדוֹ וְאִישׁ־

1[10] Then he called in my ears with a loud voice, saying: 'Cause them who have charge over the city to draw near, every man with his destroying weapon in his hand.'

2[11] And, behold, six men came from the upper gate, which lies toward the north, every man

---

[1] Ezekiel 8:13 - 2 Timothy 3:13, Ezekiel 8:6 8:15, Jeremiah 9:4

[2] Ezekiel 8:14 - Ezekiel 20:4 22:9, Jastrow 169b

[3] Ezekiel 8:15 - 2 Timothy 3:13, Ezekiel 8:6 8:9 8:12-13

[4] Ezekiel 8:16 - 1 Kings 8:29, 2 Chronicles 7:7 5:6, 2 Kings 16:14 23:5 23:11, Acts 7:42-7:43, b.Kiddushin 72b, b.Succah 53b, b.Yoma 77a, Deuteronomy 4:19 17:3, Ein Yaakov Kiddushin:72b, Ezekiel 10:3 11:1 23:35 16:28 19:5 21:19, Guide for the Perplexed 3:45, Jastrow 345b 1235a 1552b, Jeremiah 2:27 8:33 20:17, Job 31:26-31:28, Joel 2:17, Josephus Wars 5.214, m.Chagigah 2:1, m.Sukkah 5:4, Mekhilta de R'Shimon bar Yochai Pisha 16:1, Sifre Devarim {Haazinu Hashamayim} 318, Sifre Devarim Nitzavim 318 321, Song of Songs.R 1:39, y.Berachot 4:4, y.Sukkah 5:5

[5] LXX *twenty*

[6] Ezekiel 8:17 - 2 Kings 21:16 24:4, Amos 3:10 6:3, Ezekiel 7:11 7:23 9:9 11:6 16:26, Genesis 6:13, Genesis.R 31:5, Jastrow 240b, Jeremiah 6:7 7:18-7:19 19:4 20:8, Lamentations.R 1:57, Mekilta de R'Ishmael Shirata 6:25, Micah 2:2 6:12, Midrash Tanchuma Beshallach 16, Midrash Tanchuma Ki Tetze 10 , Zephaniah 1:9 , Numbers.R 13:3, Pesikta Rabbati 33:13, Sifre.z Numbers Behaalotcha 12:12 , The tenth of the Eighteen Emendations of the Sopherim should read, according to some authorities *They put the branch to My nose* by substituting אפי [appai My nose] to אפם [appam their nose]. "Branch" refers to the Asherah which was a phallus-shaped object of worship and the evil is spoken of as placing the Asherah to the very nose of Hashem.

[7] LXX *and, behold, these are as scorners*

[8] Ezekiel 8:18 - Ezekiel 5:11-5:13 7:4-7:9 9:5 9:10 16:42 24:13, Isaiah 1:15 11:2, Jeremiah 11:11 14:12, Judges 10:13-10:14, Luke 13:25, Micah 3:4, Nahum 1:2, Proverbs 1:28, Zechariah 7:13

[9] Missing in LXX

[10] Ezekiel 9:1 - 1 Chronicles 21:15, 2 Kings 10:24, Amos 3:7-3:8, b.Sanhedrin 102a, Ein Yaakov Sanhedrin:102a, Exodus 12:23, Ezekiel 43:6-43:7, Isaiah 6:8 10:6-10:7, Lamentations.R 2:3, Numbers.R 9:49, Revelation 1:10-1:11 14:7

[11] Ezekiel 9:2 - 2 Chronicles 4:1 3:3, 2 Kings 15:35, b.Zevachim [Tosefot] 60a, Ein Yaakov Shabbat:55a, Exodus 27:1-27:7 16:29, Ezekiel 10:2 10:6-10:7, Genesis.R 21:5, Jeremiah 1:15 5:15-5:17 8:16-8:17 1:9 2:10, Lamentations.R 2:3, Leviticus 16:4, Midrash Tanchuma Tazria 9, Revelation 15:6, Testament of Levi 8:2
Ezekiel 9:2-7 - Mekilta de R'Ishmael Pisha 1:128-132

אֶחָד בְּתוֹכָם לָבֻשׁ בַּדִּים וְקֶסֶת הַסֹּפֵר בְּמָתְנָיו
וַיָּבֹאוּ וַיַּעַמְדוּ אֵצֶל מִזְבַּח הַנְּחֹשֶׁת

with his *weapon of destruction*[1] in his hand; and one man in the midst of them clothed in linen, with a writer's inkhorn on his side. And they went in, and stood beside the brazen altar.

3[2]

וּכְבוֹד אֱלֹהֵי יִשְׂרָאֵל נַעֲלָה מֵעַל הַכְּרוּב אֲשֶׁר הָיָה עָלָיו אֶל מִפְתַּן הַבָּיִת וַיִּקְרָא אֶל־הָאִישׁ הַלָּבֻשׁ הַבַּדִּים אֲשֶׁר קֶסֶת הַסֹּפֵר בְּמָתְנָיו

And the glory of the God of Israel lifted from the cherub, upon which it was, to the threshold of the house; and He called to the man clothed in linen, with the writer's inkhorn on his side.

4[3]

וַיֹּאמֶר יְהֹוָה אֵלָו "אֵלָיו" עֲבֹר בְּתוֹךְ הָעִיר בְּתוֹךְ יְרוּשָׁלָ͏ִם וְהִתְוִיתָ תָּו עַל־מִצְחוֹת הָאֲנָשִׁים הַנֶּאֱנָחִים וְהַנֶּאֱנָקִים עַל כָּל־הַתּוֹעֵבוֹת הַנַּעֲשׂוֹת בְּתוֹכָהּ

And the LORD said to him: 'Go through the midst of the city, through the midst of Jerusalem, and set a mark on the foreheads of the men who sigh and who cry for all the abominations done in its midst.'

5[4]

וּלְאֵלֶּה אָמַר בְּאָזְנַי עִבְרוּ בָעִיר אַחֲרָיו וְהַכּוּ "עַל"־אַל־תָּחֹס "עֵינֵיכֶם" "עֵינְכֶם" וְאַל־תַּחְמֹלוּ

And to the others He said in my hearing: 'Go you through the city after him, and strike; let not your eye spare, nor have pity;

6[5]

זָקֵן בָּחוּר וּבְתוּלָה וְטַף וְנָשִׁים תַּהַרְגוּ לְמַשְׁחִית וְעַל־כָּל־אִישׁ אֲשֶׁר־עָלָיו הַתָּו אַל־תִּגַּשׁוּ וּמִמִּקְדָּשִׁי תָּחֵלּוּ וַיָּחֵלּוּ בָּאֲנָשִׁים הַזְּקֵנִים אֲשֶׁר לִפְנֵי הַבָּיִת

slay utterly the old man, the young man, and the maiden, and little children, and women; but do not come near any man upon whom is the mark; and begin at My sanctuary.' Then they began at the elders who were before the house.

7[6]

וַיֹּאמֶר אֲלֵיהֶם טַמְּאוּ אֶת־הַבַּיִת וּמַלְאוּ אֶת־הַחֲצֵרוֹת חֲלָלִים צֵאוּ וְיָצָאוּ וְהִכּוּ בָעִיר

And He said to them: 'Defile the house, and fill the courts with the slain; *go forth.' And they went forth, and struck the city*[7].

8[8]

וַיְהִי כְּהַכּוֹתָם וְנֵאשַׁאר אָנִי וָאֶפְּלָה עַל־פָּנַי וָאֶזְעַק וָאֹמַר אֲהָהּ אֲדֹנָי יְהֹוִה הֲמַשְׁחִית אַתָּה אֵת כָּל־שְׁאֵרִית יִשְׂרָאֵל בְּשָׁפְכְּךָ אֶת־חֲמָתְךָ עַל־יְרוּשָׁלָ͏ִם

And it came to pass, while they were striking, and I was left, that I fell on my face, and cried, and said: 'Ah Lord GOD! will you destroy all the residue of Israel in the pouring out of Your fury on Jerusalem?'

9[9]

וַיֹּאמֶר אֵלַי עֲוֺן בֵּית־יִשְׂרָאֵל וִיהוּדָה גָּדוֹל בִּמְאֹד מְאֹד וַתִּמָּלֵא הָאָרֶץ דָּמִים וְהָעִיר מָלְאָה מֻטֶּה כִּי אָמְרוּ עָזַב יְהֹוָה אֶת־הָאָרֶץ וְאֵין יְהֹוָה רֹאֶה

Then said He to me: 'The iniquity of the house of Israel and Judah is very great, and the land is full of blood, and the city full of wresting of judgment; for they say: The LORD has forsaken the land, and the LORD does not see.

10[10]

וְגַם־אֲנִי לֹא־תָחוֹס עֵינִי וְלֹא אֶחְמֹל דַּרְכָּם בְּרֹאשָׁם נָתָתִּי

And as for Me, My eye shall not spare, nor will I pity, but I will bring their way on their head.'

---

[1] LXX *axe*

[2] Ezekiel 9:3 - b.Rosh Hashanah 31a, Ein Yaakov Rosh Hashanah 31a, Ezekiel 3:23 8:4 10:4 11:22-23 43:2-4, Ladder of Jacob 5:7, Lamentations.R Petichata D'Chakimei:25, Pesikta de R'Kahana 13.11

[3] Ezekiel 9:4 - 2 Corinthians 1:22 12:21, 2 Kings 22:13 22:19-22:20, 2 Peter 2:8-2:9, 2 Timothy 2:19, b.Avodah Zara [Rashi] 4a, b.Shabbat 55a, Cairo Damascus 19:11-12, Cairo Damascus 19:12, Cairo Damascus 19.12, Ein Yaakov Shabbat:55a, Ephesians 4:30, Esther.R 1:9, Exodus 12:7 12:13, Ezekiel 6:11 21:11, Gates of Repentance 3.196, Isaiah 9:15, Jastrow 460b 1500b 1663b, Jeremiah 13:17, Lamentations.R 2:3, Malachi 3:16, Midrash Psalms 12:2 78:9, Midrash Tanchuma Mishpatim 7, Midrash Tanchuma Tazria 9, Psalms 119:136 23:53, Revelation 7:2-7:3 9:4 13:6-13:7 14:1 20:4, Ruth.R 1:5, z.Bereshit 2b, z.Noach 72b, z.Vayera 101b

[4] Ezekiel 9:5 - 1 Kings 18:40, 1 Samuel 9:15, Deuteronomy 32:39-42, Exodus 8:27, Ezekiel 5:11 7:4 7:9 8:18 9:10 24:14, Isaiah 5:9 22:14, Lamentations.R 2:3, Midrash Psalms 12:2, Numbers 25:7-8

[5] Ezekiel 9:6 - 1 Peter 4:17-4:18, 1 Samuel 15:3, 2 Chronicles 12:17, 2 Timothy 2:19, Amos 3:2, b.Avodah Zara 4a, b.Ketubot [Rashi] 8b, b.Shabbat 55a, Deuteronomy 2:34 3:6, Ein Yaakov Shabbat:55a, Exodus 12:23, Ezekiel 8:5-8:16 11:1, Gates of Repentance 3.196, Jastrow 1319b, Jeremiah 1:29, Joshua 2:18-2:19 6:17-6:25, Jubilees 23:23, Lamentations.R 2:3, Luke 12:47, Midrash Psalms 12:2, Midrash Tanchuma Mishpatim 7, Midrash Tanchuma Tazria 9, Numbers 31:15-31:17, Revelation 7:3 9:4 14:4, z.Noach 68a

[6] Ezekiel 9:7 - 2 Chronicles 12:17, Ezekiel 7:20-7:22, Lamentations 2:4-2:7, Lamentations.R 2:3, Luke 13:1, Psalms 79:1-79:3

[7] LXX *and smite*

[8] Ezekiel 9:8 - 1 Chronicles 21:16, Amos 7:2-6, Deuteronomy 9:18, Ezekiel 4:14 11:13, Ezra 9:5, Genesis 18:23, Jeremiah 4:10 14:13 14:19, Joshua 7:6, Lamentations.R 2:8 2:8 4:14, Numbers 14:5 16:4 16:21-22 17:10

[9] Ezekiel 9:9 - 2 Chronicles 36:14-36:16, 2 Kings 17:7-17:23 21:16 24:4, b.Bava Kamma 79b, Deuteronomy 7:29 8:5 32:15-32:22, Ein Yaakov Bava Kamma:79a, Ezekiel 7:23 8:12 8:17 22:2-22:12 22:25-22:31, Genesis.R 28:5, Guide for the Perplexed 3:17, Isaiah 1:4 5:15 59:2-59:8 59:12-59:15, Jeremiah 2:34 5:1-5:9 7:8-7:9 22:17, Job 22:13, Lamentations 4:13-4:14, Lamentations.R 4:9, Luke 11:50, Matthew 23:35-23:37, Mekilta de R'Ishmael Nezikin 15:28, Micah 3:1-3:3 3:9-3:12 7:3-7:4, Psalms 10:12 94:7, Song of Songs.R 1:25, Zephaniah 3:1-3:4

[10] Ezekiel 9:10 - 2 Chronicles 6:23, Deuteronomy 8:41, Ezekiel 5:11 7:4 7:8-7:9 8:18 9:5 11:21 21:36-21:37 22:31, Hebrews 10:30, Hosea 9:7, Isaiah 17:6, Joel 4:4

וְהִנֵּה הָאִישׁ לְבֻשׁ הַבַּדִּים אֲשֶׁר הַקֶּסֶת בְּמָתְנָיו מֵשִׁיב דָּבָר לֵאמֹר עָשִׂיתִי "כַּאֲשֶׁר" "כְּכֹל" "אֲשֶׁר" צִוִּיתָנִי

11[1] And, behold, the man clothed in linen with the inkhorn on his side, reported, saying: 'I have done according to all you commanded me.'

Ezekiel – Chapter 10[2]

וָאֶרְאֶה וְהִנֵּה אֶל־הָרָקִיעַ אֲשֶׁר עַל־רֹאשׁ הַכְּרֻבִים כְּאֶבֶן סַפִּיר כְּמַרְאֵה דְּמוּת כִּסֵּא נִרְאָה עֲלֵיהֶם

1[3] Then I looked, and, behold, upon the firmament over the head of the cherubim, there appeared above them as it were a sapphire stone, as the appearance of the likeness of a throne.

וַיֹּאמֶר אֶל־הָאִישׁ לְבֻשׁ הַבַּדִּים וַיֹּאמֶר בֹּא אֶל־בֵּינוֹת לַגַּלְגַּל אֶל־תַּחַת לַכְּרוּב וּמַלֵּא חָפְנֶיךָ גַחֲלֵי־אֵשׁ מִבֵּינוֹת לַכְּרֻבִים וּזְרֹק עַל־הָעִיר וַיָּבֹא לְעֵינָי

2[4] And He spoke to the man clothed in linen, and said: 'Go in between the wheelwork, under the cherub, and fill both your hands with coals of fire from between the cherubim, and dash them against the city.' And he went in, in my sight.

וְהַכְּרֻבִים עֹמְדִים מִימִין לַבַּיִת בְּבֹאוֹ הָאִישׁ וְהֶעָנָן מָלֵא אֶת־הֶחָצֵר הַפְּנִימִית

3[5] Now the cherubim stood on the right side of the house, when the man went in; and the cloud filled the inner court.

וַיָּרָם כְּבוֹד־יְהוָה מֵעַל הַכְּרוּב עַל מִפְתַּן הַבָּיִת וַיִּמָּלֵא הַבַּיִת אֶת־הֶעָנָן וְהֶחָצֵר מָלְאָה אֶת־נֹגַהּ כְּבוֹד יְהוָה

4[6] And the glory of the LORD lifted from the cherub to the threshold of the house; and the house was filled with the cloud, and the court was full of the brightness of the LORD's glory.

וְקוֹל כַּנְפֵי הַכְּרוּבִים נִשְׁמַע עַד־הֶחָצֵר הַחִיצֹנָה כְּקוֹל אֵל־שַׁדַּי בְּדַבְּרוֹ

5[7] And the sound of the wings of the cherubim was heard to the outer court, as the voice of God Almighty when He speaks.

וַיְהִי בְּצַוֺּתוֹ אֶת־הָאִישׁ לְבֻשׁ־הַבַּדִּים לֵאמֹר קַח אֵשׁ מִבֵּינוֹת לַגַּלְגַּל מִבֵּינוֹת לַכְּרוּבִים וַיָּבֹא וַיַּעֲמֹד אֵצֶל הָאוֹפָן

6[8] And it came to pass, when He commanded the man clothed in linen, saying: 'Take fire from between the wheelwork, from between the cherubim,' that he went in, and stood beside a wheel.

וַיִּשְׁלַח הַכְּרוּב אֶת־יָדוֹ מִבֵּינוֹת לַכְּרוּבִים אֶל־הָאֵשׁ אֲשֶׁר בֵּינוֹת הַכְּרֻבִים וַיִּשָּׂא וַיִּתֵּן אֶל־חָפְנֵי לְבֻשׁ הַבַּדִּים וַיִּקַּח וַיֵּצֵא

7[9] And the cherub[10] stretched forth his hand from between the cherubim to the fire between the cherubim, and took of it, and put it into the hands of he who was clothed in linen, who took it and went out.

---

[1] Ezekiel 9:11 - b.Kiddushin [Rashi] 72a, b.Yoma 77a, Exodus.R 33:4, Isaiah 46:10-11, Mekilta de R'Ishmael Pisha 1:117, Mekilta de R'Ishmael Pisha 1:135, Psalms 7:20, Revelation 16:2 16:17, There is a כ with both sjwa and cholem in כְּ אֲשֶׁר, to be read as כְּכֹל אֲשֶׁר., Zechariah 1:10-11 6:7-8

[2] Ezekiel 10 - Midrash Proverbs 10

[3] Ezekiel 10:1 - 1 Peter 3:22, 3 Enoch 22:12 22:16, b.Sotah [Tosefot] 14a, Ephesians 1:20, Exodus 24:10, Ezekiel 1:22-26 10:20 11:22, Genesis 18:2 18:17 18:22 18:31 8:25 8:31, Guide for the Perplexed 3:7, Habakkuk 2:1, Isaiah 21:8-9, Jeremiah 13:6 13:8 13:18-22, John 1:18, Joshua 5:13-15 6:2, Life of Adam and Eve [Vita] 25:2, Psalms 18:11 68:18-19, Revelation 1:13 4:2-3, y.Berachot 1:2

[4] Ezekiel 10:2 - 2 Kings 1:9, 3 Enoch 24:16, b.Yoma 77a, Exodus 9:8-9:10, Ezekiel 1:13 1:15-1:20 9:2-9:3 9:11 10:7-10:13 10:16 21:3-20:4 24:9-24:14, Isaiah 6:6-6:7 6:30, Jastrow 1089a, Jeremiah 24:8-24:10, Lamentations.R 1:41, Leviticus.R 26:8 31:1, Midrash Tanchuma Emor 3, Midrash Tanchuma Tazria 9, Psalms 18:13-18:14 20:11, Revelation 8:5

[5] Ezekiel 10:3 - 3 Enoch 19:1, Ezekiel 8:16 9:3 19:4, Pesikta de R'Kahana 13.11

[6] Ezekiel 10:4 - 1 Kings 8:10-12, 2 Chronicles 5:13-14, Avot de R'Natan 34, b.Rosh Hashanah 31a, Exodus 16:35, Ezekiel 1:28 9:3 10:18 11:22-23 19:5, Haggai 2:9, Ladder of Jacob 5:7, Lamentations.R Petichata D'Chakimei:25, Numbers 16:19, Pesikta de R'Kahana 13.11, Revelation 15:8, Song of Songs.R 3:20

[7] Ezekiel 10:5 - 1 Kings 7:9, 2 Chronicles 4:9, 3 Enoch 22:15, Deuteronomy 4:12-13, Exodus 19:16 19:19 20:15-19, Ezekiel 1:24 22:21, Hebrews 12:18-19, Job 37:2-5 16:9, John 12:28-29, Numbers.R 14:21, Pesikta de R'Kahana 16.1, Pesikta Rabbati 29/30A:1, Psalms 29:3-9 68:34 77:18, Revelation 10:3-4

[8] Ezekiel 10:6 - Ezekiel 10:2, mt.Hilchot Yesodei haTorah 2:7, Psalms 80:2 99:1
Ezekiel 10:6-12 - Apocalypse of Abraham 18:12
Ezekiel 10:6-22 - 4QEzeka

[9] Ezekiel 10:7 - b.Yoma 77a, Ezekiel 1:13 10:6 41:23-26, Jastrow 1248b, Lamentations.R 1:41, Leviticus.R 26:8, Matthew 13:41-42 13:49-50 24:34-35, Midrash Tanchuma Emor 3, Midrash Tanchuma Tazria 9
Ezekiel 10:7-15 - mt.Hilchot Yesodei haTorah 2:7

[10] LXX he

וַיֵּרָא לַכְּרֻבִים תַּבְנִית יַד־אָדָם תַּחַת כַּנְפֵיהֶם	8[1] And there appeared in the cherubim the form of a man's hand under their wings.
וָאֶרְאֶה וְהִנֵּה אַרְבָּעָה אוֹפַנִּים אֵצֶל הַכְּרוּבִים אוֹפַן אֶחָד אֵצֶל הַכְּרוּב אֶחָד וְאוֹפַן אֶחָד אֵצֶל הַכְּרוּב אֶחָד וּמַרְאֵה הָאוֹפַנִּים כְּעֵין אֶבֶן תַּרְשִׁישׁ	9[2] And I looked, and behold four wheels beside the cherubim, one wheel beside one cherub, and another wheel beside another cherub; and the appearance of the wheels was as the color of a *stone of Tarshish*[3].
וּמַרְאֵיהֶם דְּמוּת אֶחָד לְאַרְבַּעְתָּם כַּאֲשֶׁר יִהְיֶה הָאוֹפַן בְּתוֹךְ הָאוֹפָן	10[4] And as for their appearance, the four had one likeness, as if a wheel had been within a wheel.
בְּלֶכְתָּם אֶל־אַרְבַּעַת רִבְעֵיהֶם יֵלֵכוּ לֹא יִסַּבּוּ בְּלֶכְתָּם כִּי הַמָּקוֹם אֲשֶׁר־יִפְנֶה הָרֹאשׁ אַחֲרָיו יֵלֵכוּ לֹא יִסַּבּוּ בְּלֶכְתָּם	11[5] When they went, they went toward their four sides; they did not turn as they went, but to the place where the head looked they followed it; they did not turn as they went.
וְכָל־בְּשָׂרָם וְגַבֵּהֶם וִידֵיהֶם וְכַנְפֵיהֶם וְהָאוֹפַנִּים מְלֵאִים עֵינַיִם סָבִיב לְאַרְבַּעְתָּם אוֹפַנֵּיהֶם	12[6] *And their whole body*[7], and their backs, and their hands, and their wings, and the wheels were full of eyes all around, the wheels that the four possessed.
לָאוֹפַנִּים לָהֶם קוֹרָא הַגַּלְגַּל בְּאָזְנָי	13[8] As for the wheels, they were called in my hearing *The wheelwork*[9].
וְאַרְבָּעָה פָנִים לְאֶחָד פְּנֵי הָאֶחָד פְּנֵי הַכְּרוּב וּפְנֵי הַשֵּׁנִי פְּנֵי אָדָם וְהַשְּׁלִישִׁי פְּנֵי אַרְיֵה וְהָרְבִיעִי פְּנֵי־נָשֶׁר	14[10] *And everyone had four faces: the first face was the face of the cherub, and the second face was the face of a man, and the third the face of a lion, and the fourth the face of an eagle*[11].
וַיֵּרֹמּוּ הַכְּרוּבִים הִיא הַחַיָּה אֲשֶׁר רָאִיתִי בִּנְהַר־כְּבָר	15[12] And the *cherubim lifted up—this is the*[13] living creature I saw by the river Chebar.
וּבְלֶכֶת הַכְּרוּבִים יֵלְכוּ הָאוֹפַנִּים אֶצְלָם וּבִשְׂאֵת הַכְּרוּבִים אֶת־כַּנְפֵיהֶם לָרוּם מֵעַל הָאָרֶץ לֹא־יִסַּבּוּ הָאוֹפַנִּים גַּם־הֵם מֵאֶצְלָם	16[14] And when the cherubim went, the wheels went beside them; and when the cherubim lifted up their wings to rise up from the earth, the same wheels also did not turn from beside them.
בְּעָמְדָם יַעֲמֹדוּ וּבְרוֹמָם יֵרוֹמּוּ אוֹתָם כִּי רוּחַ הַחַיָּה בָּהֶם	17[15] When they stood, these stood, and when they raised, these raised with them; for the spirit of the living creature was in them.
וַיֵּצֵא כְּבוֹד יְהוָה מֵעַל מִפְתַּן הַבָּיִת וַיַּעֲמֹד עַל־הַכְּרוּבִים	18[16] And the glory of the LORD went from the threshold of the house, and stood over the cherubim.

---

[1] Ezekiel 10:8 - Ezekiel 1:8 10:21, Guide for the Perplexed 3:7, Isaiah 6:6, Lamentations.R 1:41, Leviticus.R 26:8, Midrash Tanchuma Emor 3

[2] Ezekiel 10:9 - Daniel 10:6, Ezekiel 1:15-1:17, Revelation 21:20

[3] LXX *carbuncle*

[4] Ezekiel 10:10 - Ezekiel 1:16, Psalms 36:7 97:2 8:24, Romans 11:33
Ezekiel 10:10-22 - Mas.Soferim 9:10

[5] Ezekiel 10:11 - 11QEzek, Ezekiel 1:17 1:20 10:22, Guide for the Perplexed 3:3, Matthew 8:8-10

[6] Ezekiel 10:12 - 2 Enoch 1a:4, 3 Enoch 24:18 25:5, Ezekiel 1:18, Guide for the Perplexed 3:3, Revelation 4:6 4:8, Saadia Opinions 6:7

[7] Missing in LXX

[8] Ezekiel 10:13 - Guide for the Perplexed 3:3, Midrash Proverbs 10
Ezekiel 10:13 [Targum] - Guide for the Perplexed 3:3

[9] LXX *Gelgel*

[10] Ezekiel 10:14 - 1 Kings 7:29 7:36, 3 Enoch 2:1, b.Chagigah 13b, b.Kiddushin [Rashi] 70a, b.Succah 5b, Ezekiel 1:6-1:10 10:21, Guide for the Perplexed 3:1, Lamentations.R Petichata D'Chakimei:25, Midrash Psalms 20:3, Midrash Tanchuma Emor 16, Revelation 4:7

[11] Missing in LXX

[12] Ezekiel 10:15 - Ezekiel 1:3 1:5 1:13-14 8:6 10:18-20 11:22 19:3, Guide for the Perplexed 3:2-3, Hosea 9:12

[13] LXX And the cherubs were the same

[14] Ezekiel 10:16 - Ezekiel 1:19-1:21, Guide for the Perplexed 3:3

[15] Ezekiel 10:17 - Ezekiel 1:12 1:20-1:21, Genesis 2:7, Revelation 11:11, Romans 8:2

[16] Ezekiel 10:18 - 2 Kings 2:11, Avot de R'Natan 34, Avot de R'Natan 34.09.01, Ezekiel 7:20-22 10:3-4, Genesis 3:24, Hosea 9:12, Jeremiah 6:8 7:12-7:14, Ladder of Jacob 5:7, Lamentations.R Petichata D'Chakimei:25, Matthew 23:37-39, Pesikta de R'Kahana 13.11, Psalms 18:11 68:18-19 78:60-61, Psalms of Solomon 1:8

וַיִּשְׂא֣וּ הַכְּרוּבִ֗ים אֶת־כַּנְפֵיהֶם֙ וַיֵּרֹ֙ומּוּ֙ מִן־הָאָ֔רֶץ
לְעֵינַ֖י בְּצֵאתָ֑ם וְהָאֹ֣ופַנִּ֔ים לְעֻמָּתָ֖ם וַֽיַּעֲמֹד֮ פֶּ֣תַח
שַׁ֣עַר בֵּית־יְהוָה֮ הַקַּדְמֹונִי֒ וּכְבֹ֧וד אֱלֹהֵֽי־יִשְׂרָאֵ֛ל
עֲלֵיהֶ֖ם מִלְמָֽעְלָה

19[1] And the cherubim lifted up their wings, and mounted up from the earth in my sight when they went forth, and the wheels beside them; and they stood at the door of the east gate of the LORD's house; and the glory of the God of Israel was over them above.

הִ֣יא הַֽחַיָּ֗ה אֲשֶׁ֥ר רָאִ֛יתִי תַּ֥חַת אֱלֹהֵֽי־יִשְׂרָאֵ֖ל
בִּֽנְהַר־כְּבָ֑ר וָאֵדַ֕ע כִּ֥י כְרוּבִ֖ים הֵֽמָּה

20[2] This is the living creature I saw under the God of Israel by the river Chebar; and I knew they were cherubim.

אַרְבָּעָ֨ה אַרְבָּעָ֤ה פָנִים֙ לְאֶחָ֔ד וְאַרְבַּ֥ע כְּנָפַ֖יִם לְאֶחָ֑ד
וּדְמוּת֙ יְדֵ֣י אָדָ֔ם תַּ֖חַת כַּנְפֵיהֶֽם

21[3] Everyone had four faces apiece, and everyone *four*[4] wings; and the likeness of the hands of a man was under their wings.

וּדְמ֣וּת פְּנֵיהֶ֔ם הֵ֣מָּה הַפָּנִ֗ים אֲשֶׁ֤ר רָאִ֙יתִי֙ עַל־נְהַר־
כְּבָ֔ר מַרְאֵיהֶ֖ם וְאֹותָ֑ם אִ֛ישׁ אֶל־עֵ֥בֶר פָּנָ֖יו יֵלֵֽכוּ

22[5] And as for the likeness of their faces, they were the faces I saw by the river Chebar, their appearances and themselves; everyone went straight forward.

Ezekiel – Chapter 11

וַתִּשָּׂ֨א אֹתִ֜י ר֗וּחַ וַתָּבֵ֣א אֹתִ֣י אֶל־שַׁ֩עַר֩ בֵּית־יְהוָ֨ה
הַקַּדְמֹונִ֜י הַפֹּונֶ֣ה קָדִ֗ימָה וְהִנֵּה֙ בְּפֶ֣תַח הַשַּׁ֔עַר
עֶשְׂרִ֥ים וַחֲמִשָּׁ֖ה אִ֑ישׁ וָאֶרְאֶ֨ה בְתֹוכָ֜ם אֶת־יַאֲזַנְיָ֧ה
בֶן־עַזֻּ֛ר וְאֶת־פְּלַטְיָ֥הוּ בֶן־בְּנָיָ֖הוּ שָׂרֵ֥י הָעָֽם

1[6] Then a spirit raised me up, and brought me to the east gate of the LORD's house, which looks eastward; and behold at the door of the gate twenty-five men; and I saw in their midst Jaazaniah the son of Azzur, and Pelatiah the son of Benaiah, princes of the people.

וַיֹּ֖אמֶר אֵלָ֑י בֶּן־אָדָ֕ם אֵ֣לֶּה הָאֲנָשִׁ֗ים הַחֹשְׁבִ֥ים אָ֖וֶן
וְהַיֹּעֲצִ֥ים עֲצַת־רָ֖ע בָּעִ֥יר הַזֹּֽאת

2[7] And He said to me: 'Son of man, these are the men who devise iniquity, and who give wicked counsel in this city;

הָאֹ֣מְרִ֔ים לֹ֥א בְקָרֹ֖וב בְּנֹ֣ות בָּתִּ֑ים הִ֣יא הַסִּ֔יר
וַאֲנַ֖חְנוּ הַבָּשָֽׂר

3[8] Who say: The time is not near to build houses! This city is the caldron, and we are the flesh.

לָכֵ֖ן הִנָּבֵ֣א עֲלֵיהֶ֑ם הִנָּבֵ֖א בֶּן־אָדָֽם

4[9] Therefore, prophesy against them. Prophesy, O son of man.'

וַתִּפֹּ֤ל עָלַי֙ ר֣וּחַ יְהוָ֔ה וַיֹּ֣אמֶר אֵלַ֗י אֱמֹר֙ כֹּה־אָמַ֣ר
יְהוָ֔ה כֵּ֥ן אֲמַרְתֶּ֖ם בֵּ֣ית יִשְׂרָאֵ֑ל וּמַעֲלֹ֣ות רֽוּחֲכֶ֔ם אֲנִ֖י
יְדַעְתִּֽיהָ

5[10] And the spirit of the LORD fell on me, and He said to me: 'Speak: Thus says the LORD: Thus have you said, O house of Israel; for I know the things that come to your mind.

הִרְבֵּיתֶ֖ם חַלְלֵיכֶ֑ם בָּעִ֣יר הַזֹּ֔את וּמִלֵּאתֶ֥ם חוּצֹתֶ֖יהָ
חָלָֽל

6[11] You have multiplied the slain in this city, and you have filled its streets with the dead.

---

[1] Ezekiel 10:19 - Ezekiel 1:17-1:21 1:26-1:28 8:16 10:1 11:1 11:22-23 19:4, Lamentations.R Petichata D'Chakimei:25, Pesikta de R'Kahana 13.11, Seder Olam 26:Law was Found

[2] Ezekiel 10:20 - 1 Kings 6:29-6:35 7:36, Ezekiel 1:1 1:5 1:22-28 3:23 10:15, Genesis.R 21:9, Guide for the Perplexed 3:3, z.Mishpatim 126a, z.Pekudei 242a

[3] Ezekiel 10:21 - b.Chullin 92a, Ezekiel 1:6 1:8-10 10:14 41:18-19, Revelation 4:7

[4] LXX *eight*

[5] Ezekiel 10:22 - Ezekiel 1:10 1:12 10:11, Hosea 14:11

[6] Ezekiel 11:1 - 1 Kings 18:12, 2 Corinthians 12:1-4, 2 Kings 2:16 1:23, Acts 8:39, Apocalypse of Zephaniah A, b.Kiddushin 73b, Ein Yaakov Kiddushin:72b, Ezekiel 3:12 3:14 8:3 8:16 10:19 11:13 11:24 22:27 13:1 40:1-2 17:1 43:4-5, Hosea 5:10, Isaiah 1:10 1:23, Revelation 1:10, Testament of Naphtali 5:3
Ezekiel 11:1-11 - 4QEzeka

[7] Ezekiel 11:2 - Esther 8:3, Isaiah 6:1 11:4, Jeremiah 5:5 18:18, Micah 2:1-2, Psalms 2:1-2 36:5 52:3

[8] Ezekiel 11:3 - 2 Peter 3:4, Amos 6:5, Ezekiel 7:7 11:7-11:11 12:22 12:27 24:3-24:14, Isaiah 5:19, Jeremiah 1:11-1:13

[9] Ezekiel 11:4 - Ezekiel 3:2-3:15 3:17-3:21 21:2-20:3 21:7 1:2, Hosea 6:5 8:1, Isaiah 10:1

[10] Ezekiel 11:5 - 1 Chronicles 4:9, 1 Samuel 10:6 10:10, Acts 10:44 11:15, Ezekiel 2:2 2:4-2:5 2:7 3:11 3:24 3:27 8:1 4:2 5:3 38:10-38:11, Hebrews 4:13, Isaiah 4:15 10:1, James 3:6, Jeremiah 16:17 17:10, John 2:24-2:25 21:17, Malachi 3:13-3:14, Mark 2:8 3:22-3:30, Numbers 11:25-11:26, Psalms 7:10 50:21 139:2-139:3, Revelation 2:23, z.Vaetchanan 269b

[11] Ezekiel 11:6 - 2 Kings 21:16, Ezekiel 7:23 9:9 22:2-22:6 22:9 22:12 22:27 24:6-24:9, Hosea 4:2-4:3, Isaiah 1:15, Jeremiah 2:30 2:34 7:6 7:9, Lamentations 4:13, Matthew 23:35, Micah 3:2-3:3 3:10 7:2, Zephaniah 3:3

7[1] Therefore, thus says the Lord GOD: Your slain whom you have laid in its midst, they are the flesh, and this city is the caldron; but you shall be brought forth from its midst.

לָכֵ֗ן כֹּֽה־אָמַר֮ אֲדֹנָ֣י יְהֹוִה֒ חַלְלֵיכֶם֙ אֲשֶׁ֣ר שַׂמְתֶּ֣ם בְּתוֹכָ֔הּ הֵ֥מָּה הַבָּשָׂ֖ר וְהִ֣יא הַסִּ֑יר וְאֶתְכֶ֖ם הוֹצִ֥יא מִתּוֹכָֽהּ

8[2] You have feared the sword; and I will bring the sword on you, says the Lord GOD.

חֶ֖רֶב יְרֵאתֶ֑ם וְחֶ֙רֶב֙ אָבִ֣יא עֲלֵיכֶ֔ם נְאֻ֖ם אֲדֹנָ֥י יְהֹוִֽה

9[3] And I will bring you forth from its midst, and deliver you into the hands of strangers, and will execute judgments among you.

וְהוֹצֵאתִ֤י אֶתְכֶם֙ מִתּוֹכָ֔הּ וְנָתַתִּ֥י אֶתְכֶ֖ם בְּיַד־זָרִ֑ים וְעָשִׂ֥יתִי בָכֶ֖ם שְׁפָטִֽים

10[4] You shall fall by the sword: I will judge you on the border of Israel; and you shall know I am the LORD.

בַּחֶ֣רֶב תִּפֹּ֔לוּ עַל־גְּב֥וּל יִשְׂרָאֵ֖ל אֶשְׁפּ֣וֹט אֶתְכֶ֑ם וִידַעְתֶּ֖ם כִּֽי־אֲנִ֥י יְהֹוָֽה

11[5] *Though this city shall not be your caldron, you shall be the flesh in its midst; I will judge you on the border of Israel[6];*

הִ֗יא לֹֽא־תִהְיֶ֤ה לָכֶם֙ לְסִ֔יר וְאַתֶּ֛ם תִּהְי֥וּ בְתוֹכָ֖הּ לְבָשָׂ֑ר אֶל־גְּב֥וּל יִשְׂרָאֵ֖ל אֶשְׁפֹּ֥ט אֶתְכֶֽם

12[7] *and you shall know I am the LORD; for you have not walked in My statutes, nor have you executed My ordinances, but have gone after the ordinances of the nations around you[8].'*

וִידַעְתֶּ֞ם כִּֽי־אֲנִ֣י יְהֹוָ֗ה אֲשֶׁ֤ר בְּחֻקַּי֙ לֹ֣א הֲלַכְתֶּ֔ם וּמִשְׁפָּטַ֖י לֹ֣א עֲשִׂיתֶ֑ם וּֽכְמִשְׁפְּטֵ֧י הַגּוֹיִ֛ם אֲשֶׁ֥ר סְבִיבוֹתֵיכֶ֖ם עֲשִׂיתֶֽם

13[9] And it came to pass, when I prophesied, that Pelatiah the son of Benaiah died. Then I fell down on my face, and cried with a loud voice, and said: 'Ah Lord GOD! will you make a full end of the remnant of Israel?'

וַֽיְהִי֙ כְּהִנָּ֣בְאִ֔י וּפְלַטְיָ֥הוּ בֶן־בְּנָיָ֖ה מֵ֑ת וָאֶפֹּ֨ל עַל־פָּנַ֜י וָאֶזְעַ֣ק קֽוֹל־גָּד֗וֹל וָאֹמַר֙ אֲהָהּ֙ אֲדֹנָ֣י יְהֹוִ֔ה כָּלָ֙ה אַתָּ֣ה עֹשֶׂ֔ה אֵ֖ת שְׁאֵרִ֥ית יִשְׂרָאֵֽל

14 And the word of the LORD came to me, saying:

וַיְהִ֥י דְבַר־יְהֹוָ֖ה אֵלַ֥י לֵאמֹֽר

15[10] 'Son of man, as for your brothers, your brethren, the men of your kindred, and all the house of Israel, all of them, concerning whom the inhabitants of Jerusalem have said: Get far from the LORD! This land was given to us as a possession;

בֶּן־אָדָ֗ם אַחֶ֤יךָ אַחֶ֙יךָ֙ אַנְשֵׁ֣י גְאֻלָּתֶ֔ךָ וְכׇל־בֵּ֥ית יִשְׂרָאֵ֖ל כֻּלֹּ֑ה אֲשֶׁר֩ אָמְר֨וּ לָהֶ֜ם יֹשְׁבֵ֣י יְרוּשָׁלַ֗͏ִם רַֽחֲקוּ֙ מֵעַ֣ל יְהֹוָ֔ה לָ֥נוּ הִ֛יא נִתְּנָ֥ה הָאָ֖רֶץ לְמוֹרָשָֽׁה

16[11] therefore say: Thus says the Lord GOD: Although I have removed them far off among the nations, and although I have scattered them among the countries, yet I have been as a little sanctuary in the countries where they reside;

לָכֵ֣ן אֱמֹ֗ר כֹּֽה־אָמַר֮ אֲדֹנָ֣י יְהֹוִה֒ כִּ֤י הִרְחַקְתִּים֙ בַּגּוֹיִ֔ם וְכִ֥י הֲפִֽיצוֹתִ֖ים בָּאֲרָצ֑וֹת וָאֱהִ֤י לָהֶם֙ לְמִקְדָּ֣שׁ מְעַ֔ט בָּאֲרָצ֖וֹת אֲשֶׁר־בָּ֥אוּ שָֽׁם

---

[1] Ezekiel 11:7 - 2 Kings 25:18-25:22, Ezekiel 3:9-3:11 24:3-24:13, Jeremiah 52:24-52:27, Micah 3:2-3:3, z.Vaetchanan 269b

[2] Ezekiel 11:8 - 1 Thessalonians 2:15-2:16, Amos 9:1-9:4, Isaiah 24:17-24:18 30:16-30:17 18:4, Jeremiah 38:19-38:23 42:14-42:16 44:12-44:13, Job 3:26 20:24, John 11:48, Proverbs 10:24

[3] Ezekiel 11:9 - 2 Kings 24:4, Deuteronomy 4:36 28:49-28:50, Ecclesiastes 8:11, Ezekiel 5:8 5:10 5:15 16:38 16:41 21:36 6:19, Jeremiah 5:15-5:17 15:6, John 5:27, Jude 1:15, Nehemiah 9:36-9:37, Psalms 10:30 10:41, Romans 13:4

[4] Ezekiel 11:10 - 1 Kings 8:65 2 Kings 14:25 25:19-25:21, Ezekiel 6:7 13:9 13:14 13:21 13:23, Jeremiah 9:25 15:6 52:9-52:10 52:24-52:27, Joshua 13:5, Numbers 34:8-34:9, Psalms 9:17

[5] Ezekiel 11:11 - Ezekiel 11:3 11:7-10

[6] Missing in LXX

[7] Ezekiel 11:12 - 1 Kings 11:33, 2 Chronicles 13:9 4:3 33:2-9 12:14, 2 Kings 16:3 16:10-11 17:11-23 18:12 21:2 21:22, b.Sanhedrin 39b, Daniel 9:10, Deuteronomy 12:30-31, Ezekiel 8:10 8:14 8:16 11:21 16:44-47 18:9 20:16 20:21 20:24, Ezra 9:7, Jeremiah 6:16 10:2, Leviticus 18:3 18:2428 2:40, Nehemiah 9:34, Psalms 78:10 106:35-39

[8] Missing in LXX

[9] Ezekiel 11:13 - 1 Chronicles 21:16-21:17, 1 Kings 13:4, Acts 5:5 5:10 13:11, Amos 7:2 7:5, b.Kiddushin 73b, Deuteronomy 7:4 9:18-19, Ein Yaakov Kiddushin:72b, Ezekiel 9:8 11:1 13:7, Hosea 6:5, Jeremiah 28:15-17, Joshua 7:6-9, Numbers 14:35-37, Proverbs 6:15, Psalms 10:23 119:120

[10] Ezekiel 11:15 - Ezekiel 9:24, Isaiah 17:5 18:5, Jeremiah 24:1-5, John 16:2, Saadia Opinions Intro:7

[11] Ezekiel 11:16 - 2 Kings 24:12-16, Deuteronomy 30:3-4, Ein Yaakov Megillah:29a, Isaiah 4:5 8:14, Jeremiah 24:5-6 2:7 2:11 6:11 7:11 18:11, Leviticus 2:44, mt.Hilchot Tefilah 11:5, Proverbs 18:10, Psalms 31:21 44:12 90:1 91:1 91:9-16, Siman 13:1, z.Vaetchanan 269b

לָכֵן אֱמֹר כֹּה־אָמַר אֲדֹנָי יְהוִה וְקִבַּצְתִּי אֶתְכֶם מִן־הָעַמִּים וְאָסַפְתִּי אֶתְכֶם מִן־הָאֲרָצוֹת אֲשֶׁר נְפֹצוֹתֶם בָּהֶם וְנָתַתִּי לָכֶם אֶת־אַדְמַת יִשְׂרָאֵל

17[1] therefore say: Thus says the Lord GOD: I will gather you from the peoples, and assemble you out of the countries where you have been scattered, and I will give you the land of Israel.

וּבָאוּ־שָׁמָּה וְהֵסִירוּ אֶת־כָּל־שִׁקּוּצֶיהָ וְאֶת־כָּל־תּוֹעֲבוֹתֶיהָ מִמֶּנָּה

18[2] And they shall come there, and they shall take away all its detestable things and all its abominations from there.

וְנָתַתִּי לָהֶם לֵב אֶחָד וְרוּחַ חֲדָשָׁה אֶתֵּן בְּקִרְבְּכֶם וַהֲסִרֹתִי לֵב הָאֶבֶן מִבְּשָׂרָם וְנָתַתִּי לָהֶם לֵב בָּשָׂר

19[3] And I will give them *one*[4] heart, and I will put a new spirit within you; and I will remove the stony heart from their flesh, and will give them a heart of flesh;

לְמַעַן בְּחֻקֹּתַי יֵלֵכוּ וְאֶת־מִשְׁפָּטַי יִשְׁמְרוּ וְעָשׂוּ אֹתָם וְהָיוּ־לִי לְעָם וַאֲנִי אֶהְיֶה לָהֶם לֵאלֹהִים

20[5] So they may walk in My statutes, and keep My ordinances, and do them; and they shall be My people, and I will be their God.

וְאֶל־לֵב שִׁקּוּצֵיהֶם וְתוֹעֲבוֹתֵיהֶם לִבָּם הֹלֵךְ דַּרְכָּם בְּרֹאשָׁם נָתַתִּי נְאֻם אֲדֹנָי יְהוִה

21[6] But as for those whose heart walks after the heart of their detestable things and their abominations, I will bring their way on their own heads, says the Lord GOD.'

וַיִּשְׂאוּ הַכְּרוּבִים אֶת־כַּנְפֵיהֶם וְהָאוֹפַנִּים לְעֻמָּתָם וּכְבוֹד אֱלֹהֵי־יִשְׂרָאֵל עֲלֵיהֶם מִלְמָעְלָה

22[7] Then the cherubim lifted up their wings, and the wheels were beside them; and the glory of the God of Israel was above them.

וַיַּעַל כְּבוֹד יְהוָה מֵעַל תּוֹךְ הָעִיר וַיַּעֲמֹד עַל־הָהָר אֲשֶׁר מִקֶּדֶם לָעִיר

23[8] And the glory of the LORD went up from the midst of the city, and stood upon the mountain on the east side of the city.

וְרוּחַ נְשָׂאַתְנִי וַתְּבִיאֵנִי כַשְׂדִּימָה אֶל־הַגּוֹלָה בַּמַּרְאֶה בְּרוּחַ אֱלֹהִים וַיַּעַל מֵעָלַי הַמַּרְאֶה אֲשֶׁר רָאִיתִי

24[9] And a spirit lifted me up, and brought me in the vision by the spirit of God into Chaldea, to those of the captivity. So the vision that I had seen went up from Me.

וָאֲדַבֵּר אֶל־הַגּוֹלָה אֵת כָּל־דִּבְרֵי יְהוָה אֲשֶׁר הֶרְאָנִי

25[10] Then I spoke to those of the captivity all the things that the LORD had shown me.

---

[1] Ezekiel 11:17 - Amos 9:14-15, Ezekiel 20:41 4:25 10:13 12:24 37:21-28 39:27-29, Hosea 2:1-2, Isaiah 11:11-16, Jeremiah 3:12 3:18 24:5 30:10-11 6:18 31:9-11 32:37-41, z.Vaetchanan 269b

[2] Ezekiel 11:18 - Colossians 3:5-8, Ezekiel 5:11 7:20 11:21 13:23 42:7-8, Hosea 14:10, Isaiah 1:25-27 6:22, Jeremiah 16:18, Micah 5:11-15, Saadia Opinions 10:8, Titus 2:12

[3] Ezekiel 11:19 - 1 Corinthians 1:10, 2 Chronicles 6:12, 2 Corinthians 3:3 5:17, 2 Kings 22:19, Acts 4:32, Deuteronomy 6:6, Ephesians 4:3-4:6 4:23, Ezekiel 18:31 36:26-36:27, Galatians 6:15, Isaiah 24:4, Jeremiah 24:7 7:34 32:39-32:40, John 14:26 17:21-17:23, Luke 11:13, Philippians 2:1-2:5, Psalms 51:11, Romans 2:4-2:5 11:2, Zechariah 7:12, Zephaniah 3:9

[4] LXX *another*

[5] Ezekiel 11:20 - 1 Corinthians 11:2, Ezekiel 11:12 14:11 36:27-36:28 13:27, Hebrews 8:10 11:16, Hosea 2:23, Jeremiah 11:4 24:7 6:22 7:34 8:38, Luke 1:6 1:74-1:75, Psalms 9:45 119:4-119:5 23:32, Romans 16:26, Titus 2:11-2:12, Zechariah 13:9

[6] Ezekiel 11:21 - Ecclesiastes 11:9, Ezekiel 9:10 11:18 16:43 20:31 20:38 22:31, Hebrews 3:12-3:13 10:38, James 1:14-1:15, Jeremiah 1:16 2:20 17:9 29:16-29:19, Jude 1:19, Mark 7:21-7:23

[7] Ezekiel 11:22 - Ein Yaakov Sanhedrin:39b, Ezekiel 1:19-1:20 10:19, Ladder of Jacob 5:7

[8] Ezekiel 11:23 - Avot de R'Natan 34, Avot de R'Natan 34.09.01, b.Rosh Hashanah 31a, Ein Yaakov Rosh Hashanah:31a, Ezekiel 8:4 9:3 10:4 10:18 19:2 19:4, Lamentations.R Petichata D'Chakimei:25, Matthew 23:37-24:2, Pesikta de R'Kahana 13.11, Seder Olam 26:Law was Found, Testament of Naphtali 5:2, Zechariah 14:4

[9] Ezekiel 11:24 - 2 Corinthians 12:2-12:4, 2 Kings 2:16, Acts 10:16, Ezekiel 1:3 3:12 3:15 8:3 11:1, Genesis 17:22 11:13, Psalms 17:1

[10] Ezekiel 11:25 - Ezekiel 2:7 3:4 3:17 3:27

Ezekiel – Chapter 12

וַיְהִ֥י דְבַר־יְהוָ֖ה אֵלַ֥י לֵאמֹֽר	1[1]	The word of the LORD came to me, saying:
בֶּן־אָדָ֗ם בְּת֤וֹךְ בֵּית־הַמֶּ֙רִי֙ אַתָּ֣ה יֹשֵׁ֔ב אֲשֶׁ֨ר עֵינַ֜יִם לָהֶ֤ם לִרְאוֹת֙ וְלֹ֣א רָא֔וּ אָזְנַ֨יִם לָהֶ֤ם לִשְׁמֹ֙עַ֙ וְלֹ֣א שָׁמֵ֔עוּ כִּ֛י בֵּ֥ית מְרִ֖י הֵֽם	2[2]	'Son of man, you dwell in the midst of the *rebellious house*[3], who have eyes to see, yet not see, who have ears to hear, yet not hear; for they are a rebellious house.
וְאַתָּ֣ה בֶן־אָדָ֗ם עֲשֵׂ֤ה לְךָ֙ כְּלֵ֣י גוֹלָ֔ה וּגְלֵ֥ה יוֹמָ֖ם לְעֵֽינֵיהֶ֑ם וְגָלִ֜יתָ מִמְּקֽוֹמְךָ֙ אֶל־מָק֣וֹם אַחֵ֔ר לְעֵ֣ינֵיהֶ֔ם אוּלַ֣י יִרְא֔וּ כִּ֛י בֵּ֥ית מְרִ֖י הֵֽמָּה	3[4]	Therefore, son of man, prepare your belongings for exile, and leave as though for exile by day in their sight; and you shall leave your place to another place in their sight; perhaps they will perceive, for they are a rebellious house.
וְהוֹצֵאתָ֨ כֵלֶ֜יךָ כִּכְלֵ֥י גוֹלָ֛ה יוֹמָ֖ם לְעֵֽינֵיהֶ֑ם וְאַתָּ֗ה תֵּצֵ֤א בָעֶ֙רֶב֙ לְעֵ֣ינֵיהֶ֔ם כְּמוֹצָאֵ֖י גוֹלָֽה	4[5]	And you shall bring forth your belongings by day in their sight, as belongings for exile; and you shall go forth at evening in their sight, as when men go forth into exile.
לְעֵ֣ינֵיהֶ֔ם חֲתָר־לְךָ֖ בַקִּ֑יר וְהוֹצֵאתָ֖ בּֽוֹ	5[6]	Dig through the wall in their sight, and carry out through here.
לְעֵ֨ינֵיהֶ֜ם עַל־כָּתֵ֤ף תִּשָּׂא֙ בָּעֲלָטָ֣ה תוֹצִ֔יא פָּנֶ֣יךָ תְכַסֶּ֔ה וְלֹ֥א תִרְאֶ֖ה אֶת־הָאָ֑רֶץ כִּֽי־מוֹפֵ֥ת נְתַתִּ֖יךָ לְבֵ֥ית יִשְׂרָאֵֽל	6[7]	In their sight shall you bear it on your shoulder, and carry it forth in the darkness; you shall cover your face, so you do not see the ground; for I set you for a sign to the house of Israel.'
וָאַ֣עַשׂ כֵּן֮ כַּאֲשֶׁ֣ר צֻוֵּיתִי֒ כֵּלַ֞י הוֹצֵ֤אתִי כִּכְלֵ֤י גוֹלָה֙ יוֹמָ֔ם וּבָעֶ֗רֶב חָתַ֧רְתִּי־לִ֛י בַקִּ֖יר בְּיָ֑ד בָּעֲלָטָ֥ה הוֹצֵ֛אתִי עַל־כָּתֵ֥ף נָשָׂ֖אתִי לְעֵינֵיהֶֽם	7[8]	And I as I was commanded: I brought forth my belongings by day, as belongings for exile, and in the evening I dug through the wall with my hand; I carried out in the darkness, and bore it on my shoulder in their sight.
וַיְהִ֧י דְבַר־יְהוָ֛ה אֵלַ֖י בַּבֹּ֥קֶר לֵאמֹֽר	8	And in the morning the word of the LORD came to me, saying:
בֶּן־אָדָ֗ם הֲלֹ֨א אָמְר֤וּ אֵלֶ֙יךָ֙ בֵּ֣ית יִשְׂרָאֵ֔ל בֵּ֖ית הַמֶּ֑רִי מָ֖ה אַתָּ֥ה עֹשֶֽׂה	9[9]	'Son of man, has not the house of Israel, the rebellious house, said to you: What do you do?
אֱמֹ֣ר אֲלֵיהֶ֗ם כֹּ֤ה אָמַר֙ אֲדֹנָ֣י יְהֹוִ֔ה הַנָּשִׂ֥יא הַמַּשָּׂ֖א הַזֶּ֣ה בִּירוּשָׁלִָ֑ם וְכָל־בֵּ֥ית יִשְׂרָאֵ֖ל אֲשֶׁר־הֵ֥מָּה בְתוֹכָֽם	10[10]	Say to them: Thus says the Lord GOD: Concerning the prince, this burden, in Jerusalem, and all the house of Israel among whom they are,
אֱמֹ֖ר אֲנִ֣י מֽוֹפֶתְכֶ֑ם כַּאֲשֶׁ֤ר עָשִׂ֙יתִי֙ כֵּ֚ן יֵעָשֶׂ֣ה לָהֶ֔ם בַּגּוֹלָ֥ה בַשְּׁבִ֖י יֵלֵֽכוּ	11[11]	say: I am your sign: like as I have done, so shall it be done to them. They shall go into exile, into captivity.
וְהַנָּשִׂ֨יא אֲשֶׁר־בְּתוֹכָ֜ם אֶל־כָּתֵ֤ף יִשָּׂא֙ בָּעֲלָטָ֣ה וְיֵצֵ֔א בַּקִּ֥יר יַחְתְּר֖וּ לְה֣וֹצִיא ב֑וֹ פָּנָ֣יו יְכַסֶּ֔ה יַ֗עַן אֲשֶׁ֨ר לֹא־יִרְאֶ֧ה לַעַ֛יִן ה֖וּא אֶת־הָאָֽרֶץ	12[12]	And the prince who is among them shall bear on his shoulder, and go forth in the darkness; they shall dig through the wall to carry out

---

[1] Ezekiel 12:1 - Apocalypse of Elijah 1:1

[2] Ezekiel 12:2 - 2 Corinthians 3:14 4:3-4, 2 Thessalonians 2:10-11, Acts 7:51-52 28:26-227, Daniel 9:5-9, Deuteronomy 9:7 9:24 5:3 7:27, Ephesians 4:18, Ezekiel 2:3 2:5-8 3:9 3:26-27 17:12 24:3 20:6, Guide for the Perplexed 1:2, Isaiah 1:23 6:9-10 29:9-12 6:1 6:9 42:19-20 17:2, Jeremiah 4:17 5:21 5:23 9:2-7, John 9:39-41 12:40, Luke 8:10, Mark 4:12 8:17-18, Matthew 13:13-14, Psalms 78:40, Romans 11:7-8

[3] LXX *iniquities of those*

[4] Ezekiel 12:3 - 2 Timothy 2:25, b.Nedarim 40b, Deuteronomy 5:29 8:29, Ein Yaakov Nedarim:40b, Ezekiel 4:1-17 12:10-12 9:11, Jastrow 1554a, Jeremiah 13:1-11 18:2-12 19:1-15 25:4-7 2:3 3:2 12:3 12:7, Lamentations.R 1:22, Luke 13:8-9 13:34 20:13, Psalms 81:14

[5] Ezekiel 12:4 - 2 Kings 1:4, Ezekiel 12:12, Jeremiah 15:4 4:7

[6] Ezekiel 12:5 - 2 Kings 1:4, Jeremiah 39:2-39:4

[7] Ezekiel 12:6 - 1 Samuel 4:8, 2 Samuel 15:30, Ezekiel 4:3 12:11-12:12 24:24, Isaiah 8:18 20:2-20:4, Job 24:17

[8] Ezekiel 12:7 - Acts 2:19, Ezekiel 2:8 12:3 24:18 13:7 13:10, Jeremiah 32:8-12, John 2:5-2:8 15:14, Mark 14:16, Matthew 21:6-7

[9] Ezekiel 12:9 - Ezekiel 2:5-2:8 12:1-12:3 17:12 21:5 24:19

[10] Ezekiel 12:10 - 2 Kings 9:25, Ezekiel 7:27 17:13-21 21:30-32, Isaiah 13:1 14:28, Jeremiah 21:7 24:8 14:18, Malachi 1:1, z.Vaetchanan 269b

[11] Ezekiel 12:11 - Ezekiel 12:6, Jeremiah 15:2 4:15 52:28-52:30

[12] Ezekiel 12:12 - 2 Kings 1:4, Ezekiel 12:6, Jeremiah 15:4 18:7 4:7

there; he shall cover his face, so he cannot see the ground with his eyes.

וּפָרַשְׂתִּי אֶת־רִשְׁתִּי עָלָיו וְנִתְפַּשׂ בִּמְצוּדָתִי וְהֵבֵאתִי אֹתוֹ בָבֶלָה אֶרֶץ כַּשְׂדִּים וְאוֹתָהּ לֹא־יִרְאֶה וְשָׁם יָמוּת

13[1] I will spread My net on him, and he shall be taken in My snare; and I will bring him to Babylon to the land of the Chaldeans; yet he shall not see it, though he shall die there.

וְכֹל אֲשֶׁר סְבִיבֹתָיו 'עֶזְרֹה' "עֶזְרוֹ" וְכָל־אֲגַפָּיו אֱזָרֶה לְכָל־רוּחַ וְחֶרֶב אָרִיק אַחֲרֵיהֶם

14[2] And I will disperse toward every wind all who are around to help him, and all his troops; and I will draw out the sword after them.

וְיָדְעוּ כִּי־אֲנִי יְהוָה בַּהֲפִיצִי אוֹתָם בַּגּוֹיִם וְזֵרִיתִי אוֹתָם בָּאֲרָצוֹת

15[3] And they shall know that I am the LORD, when I scatter them among the nations, and disperse them in the countries.

וְהוֹתַרְתִּי מֵהֶם אַנְשֵׁי מִסְפָּר מֵחֶרֶב מֵרָעָב וּמִדָּבֶר לְמַעַן יְסַפְּרוּ אֶת־כָּל־תּוֹעֲבוֹתֵיהֶם בַּגּוֹיִם אֲשֶׁר־בָּאוּ שָׁם וְיָדְעוּ כִּי־אֲנִי יְהוָה

16[4] But I will leave a few men from the sword, from the famine, and from the pestilence; so they may declare all their abominations among the nations where they go; and they shall know that I am the LORD.'

וַיְהִי דְבַר־יְהוָה אֵלַי לֵאמֹר

17[5] Moreover, the word of the LORD came to me, saying:

בֶּן־אָדָם לַחְמְךָ בְּרַעַשׁ תֹּאכֵל וּמֵימֶיךָ בְּרָגְזָה וּבִדְאָגָה תִּשְׁתֶּה

18[6] 'Son of man, eat your bread with quaking, and drink your water with trembling and anxiety;

וְאָמַרְתָּ אֶל־עַם הָאָרֶץ כֹּה־אָמַר אֲדֹנָי יְהוִה לְיוֹשְׁבֵי יְרוּשָׁלִַם אֶל־אַדְמַת יִשְׂרָאֵל לַחְמָם בִּדְאָגָה יֹאכֵלוּ וּמֵימֵיהֶם בְּשִׁמָּמוֹן יִשְׁתּוּ לְמַעַן תֵּשַׁם אַרְצָהּ מִמְּלֹאָהּ מֵחֲמַס כָּל־הַיֹּשְׁבִים בָּהּ

19[7] and say to the people of the land: Thus says the Lord GOD concerning the inhabitants of Jerusalem in the land of Israel. They shall eat their bread with anxiety, and drink their water with fear, so her land may be desolate from all that is in it, because of the violence of all those who dwell in it.

וְהֶעָרִים הַנּוֹשָׁבוֹת תֶּחֱרַבְנָה וְהָאָרֶץ שְׁמָמָה תִהְיֶה וִידַעְתֶּם כִּי־אֲנִי יְהוָה

20[8] And the inhabited cities shall be laid waste, and the land shall be desolate; and you shall know that I am the LORD.'

וַיְהִי דְבַר־יְהוָה אֵלַי לֵאמֹר

21 And the word of the LORD came to me, saying:

בֶּן־אָדָם מָה־הַמָּשָׁל הַזֶּה לָכֶם עַל־אַדְמַת יִשְׂרָאֵל לֵאמֹר יַאַרְכוּ הַיָּמִים וְאָבַד כָּל־חָזוֹן

22[9] 'Son of man, what is that proverb you have in the land of Israel, saying: The days are prolonged, and every vision fails?

לָכֵן אֱמֹר אֲלֵיהֶם כֹּה־אָמַר אֲדֹנָי יְהוִה הִשְׁבַּתִּי אֶת־הַמָּשָׁל הַזֶּה וְלֹא־יִמְשְׁלוּ אֹתוֹ עוֹד בְּיִשְׂרָאֵל כִּי אִם־דַּבֵּר אֲלֵיהֶם קָרְבוּ הַיָּמִים וּדְבַר כָּל־חָזוֹן

23[10] Tell them therefore: Thus says the Lord GOD: I will make this proverb end, and they no longer will use it as a proverb in Israel; but say to them: The days are at hand, and the word of every vision.

---

[1] Ezekiel 12:13 - 2 Kings 25:5-25:7, Ezekiel 17:16 17:20 19:8-19:9 8:3, Hosea 7:12, Isaiah 24:17-18, Jeremiah 10:3 15:7 2:24 52:8-52:11, Job 19:6, Josephus Antiquities 10.7.2, Lamentations 1:13 3:47 4:19-4:20, Luke 21:35, Psalms 11:7

[2] Ezekiel 12:14 - 2 Kings 25:4-25:5, Ezekiel 5:2 5:10-5:12 14:17 14:21 17:21, Jeremiah 18:16 18:22, Leviticus 2:33

[3] Ezekiel 12:15 - Ezekiel 5:13 6:7 6:14 7:4 11:10 12:16 12:20 14:18 24:27 1:11 2:6 4:26 9:33 15:28, Psalms 9:17, Testament of Levi 10:4

[4] Ezekiel 12:16 - 1 Kings 9:6-9, Amos 9:8-9, Daniel 9:5-12, Deuteronomy 29:23-27, Ezekiel 6:8-10 14:22-23 12:31, Genesis 13:16, Isaiah 1:9 6:13 10:19 10:22 24:13, Jeremiah 3:24-25 4:27 22:8-9 6:11, Leviticus 26:40-41, Matthew 7:14 24:22, Romans 9:27 11:4-5

[5] Ezekiel 12:17 - Jastrow 1222b

[6] Ezekiel 12:18 - Deuteronomy 4:48 28:65, Ezekiel 4:16-17 23:33, Job 3:25, Lamentations 5:9, Leviticus 2:26 2:36, Psalms 60:3-4 80:6 102:5-10

[7] Ezekiel 12:19 - 1 Corinthians 10:26 10:28, 1 Kings 17:10-12, Ezekiel 4:16 6:6-7 6:14 7:23 12:3, Genesis 6:11-13, Isaiah 6:11, Jeremiah 4:27 6:7 9:11-12 10:22 18:16 8:28 9:10 9:12, Micah 3:10-12 7:13, Psalms 24:1 11:34, z.Vaetchanan 269b, Zechariah 7:14

[8] Ezekiel 12:20 - Daniel 9:17, Ezekiel 15:6 15:8, Isaiah 3:26 7:23-7:24 24:3 24:12 64:11-64:12, Jeremiah 4:7 4:23-4:29 12:10-12:12 16:9 19:11 24:8-24:10 1:9 10:22, Lamentations 5:18

[9] Ezekiel 12:22 - 2 Peter 3:3-3:4, Amos 6:3, Ezekiel 11:3 12:27 16:44 18:2-18:3, Genesis.R 64:5, Isaiah 5:19, Jeremiah 5:12-5:13 23:33-23:40, Midrash Psalms 74:3

[10] Ezekiel 12:23 - Ezekiel 7:2 7:5-7:7 7:10-7:12 12:25 18:3, Isaiah 4:22, James 5:8-5:9, Joel 2:1, Malachi 3:19, Matthew 24:34, Psalms 37:13, z.Vaetchanan 269b, Zephaniah 1:14

כִּי לֹא יִהְיֶה עוֹד כָּל־חֲזוֹן שָׁוְא וּמִקְסַם חָלָק בְּתוֹךְ בֵּית יִשְׂרָאֵל

24[1] No longer shall there be any vain vision or smooth divination within the house of Israel.

כִּי אֲנִי יְהוָה אֲדַבֵּר אֵת אֲשֶׁר אֲדַבֵּר דָּבָר וְיֵעָשֶׂה לֹא תִמָּשֵׁךְ עוֹד כִּי בִימֵיכֶם בֵּית הַמֶּרִי אֲדַבֵּר דָּבָר וַעֲשִׂיתִיו נְאֻם אֲדֹנָי יְהוָה

25[2] For I am the LORD; I will speak, whatever word I shall speak, and it shall be performed; it shall no longer be delayed; for in your days, O rebellious house, will I speak the word, and will perform it, says the Lord GOD.'

וַיְהִי דְבַר־יְהוָה אֵלַי לֵאמֹר

26[3] Again the word of the LORD came to me, saying:

בֶּן־אָדָם הִנֵּה בֵית־יִשְׂרָאֵל אֹמְרִים הֶחָזוֹן אֲשֶׁר הוּא חֹזֶה לְיָמִים רַבִּים וּלְעִתִּים רְחוֹקוֹת הוּא נִבָּא

27[4] 'Son of man, behold, they of the house of Israel say: The vision he sees is for many days to come, and he prophesies of times far off.

לָכֵן אֱמֹר אֲלֵיהֶם כֹּה אָמַר אֲדֹנָי יְהוָה לֹא־תִמָּשֵׁךְ עוֹד כָּל־דְּבָרָי אֲשֶׁר אֲדַבֵּר דָּבָר וְיֵעָשֶׂה נְאֻם אֲדֹנָי יְהוָה

28[5] Therefore, say to them: Thus says the Lord GOD: None of My words shall be delayed any longer, but the word I shall speak shall be performed, says the Lord GOD.'

Ezekiel – Chapter 13

וַיְהִי דְבַר־יְהוָה אֵלַי לֵאמֹר

1[6] And the word of the LORD came to me, saying:

בֶּן־אָדָם הִנָּבֵא אֶל־נְבִיאֵי יִשְׂרָאֵל הַנִּבָּאִים וְאָמַרְתָּ לִנְבִיאֵי מִלִּבָּם שִׁמְעוּ דְּבַר־יְהוָה

2[7] 'Son of man, prophesy against the prophets of Israel who prophesy, and say you to those who prophesy out of their own heart: Hear the word of the LORD

כֹּה אָמַר אֲדֹנָי יְהוָה הוֹי עַל־הַנְּבִיאִים הַנְּבָלִים אֲשֶׁר הֹלְכִים אַחַר רוּחָם וּלְבִלְתִּי רָאוּ

3[8] Thus says the Lord GOD: Woe to the vile prophets, who follow their own spirit, and things that they have not seen!

כְּשֻׁעָלִים בָּחֳרָבוֹת נְבִיאֶיךָ יִשְׂרָאֵל הָיוּ

4[9] O Israel, your prophets are like foxes in ruins.

לֹא עֲלִיתֶם בַּפְּרָצוֹת וַתִּגְדְּרוּ גָדֵר עַל־בֵּית יִשְׂרָאֵל לַעֲמֹד בַּמִּלְחָמָה בְּיוֹם יְהוָה

5[10] *You have not gone up to the breaches, nor made up the hedge for*[11] the house of Israel, to stand in the battle in the day of the LORD.

חָזוּ שָׁוְא וְקֶסֶם כָּזָב הָאֹמְרִים נְאֻם־יְהוָה וַיהוָה לֹא שְׁלָחָם וְיִחֲלוּ לְקַיֵּם דָּבָר

6[12] They have seen vanity and lying divination, who say: The LORD says; and the LORD has

---

[1] Ezekiel 12:24 - 1 Kings 22:11-22:13 22:17, 1 Thessalonians 2:5, 2 Peter 2:2-2:3, Ezekiel 13:6 13:23, Jeremiah 14:13-14:16 23:14-23:29, Lamentations 2:14, Proverbs 2:28, Romans 16:18, Zechariah 13:2-13:4

[2] Ezekiel 12:25 - Daniel 9:12, Ecclesiastes.R 8:11, Ezekiel 6:10 12:1-2 12:28, Habakkuk 1:5, Isaiah 14:24 7:11, Jeremiah 16:9, Lamentations 2:17, Lamentations.R Petichata D'Chakimei:12, Luke 21:13 21:33, Mark 13:30-31, Matthew 24:35, Numbers 14:28-34, Zechariah 1:6

[3] Ezekiel 12:26 - y.Nazir 5:3, y.Nedarim 9:2

[4] Ezekiel 12:27 - 2 Peter 3:4, Daniel 10:14, Ecclesiastes.R 8:11, Ezekiel 12:22, Isaiah 28:14-15, Lamentations.R Petichata D'Chakimei:12

[5] Ezekiel 12:28 - 1 Thessalonians 5:2-5:3, Ezekiel 12:23-12:25, Jeremiah 4:7 20:28, Luke 21:34-21:36, Mark 13:32-13:37, Matthew 24:48-24:51, Revelation 3:3, z.Vaetchanan 269b

[6] Ezekiel 13:1 - Apocalypse of Elijah 1:1

[7] Ezekiel 13:2 - 1 Kings 22:19, 2 Chronicles 18:18-18:24, 2 Peter 2:1-2:3, Amos 7:16-7:17, Ezekiel 13:3 13:17 14:9-14:10 22:25 22:28 10:7 10:9, Isaiah 9:16 4:14 56:9-56:12, Jeremiah 5:31 6:13-6:14 8:10 14:13-14:15 23:2 23:11-23:22 23:25-23:26 3:14 3:18 28:12-28:17 29:8-29:9 29:20-29:24 29:31-29:32 13:19, Lamentations 4:13, Micah 3:6 3:11, variant אל of על is found, Zephaniah 3:4

[8] Ezekiel 13:3 - 1 Corinthians 9:16, 1 Timothy 6:4, 2 Timothy 3:9, Ezekiel 13:6-13:7 13:18 10:2, Hosea 9:7, Jeremiah 23:1 23:28-23:32, Lamentations 2:14, Luke 11:40 11:42-11:47 11:52, Matthew 23:13-23:29, Proverbs 15:2 15:14, Saadia Opinions 5:8, z.Vaetchanan 269b, Zechariah 11:15

[9] Ezekiel 13:4 - 1 Timothy 4:1-4:2, 2 Corinthians 11:13-11:15, 2 Thessalonians 2:9-2:10, Ephesians 4:14, Galatians 2:4, Jastrow 1296b, Matthew 7:15, Micah 2:11 3:5, Revelation 13:11-13:14 19:20, Romans 16:18, Ruth.R Petichata:5, Song of Songs 2:15, Song of Songs.R 1:23, Titus 1:10-1:12

[10] Ezekiel 13:5 - 1 Samuel 12:23, 1 Thessalonians 5:2, 2 Peter 3:10, Amos 5:18-5:20, Ephesians 6:13-6:14, Exodus 17:9-17:13 32:11-32:12, Ezekiel 7:19 22:30 6:3, Isaiah 2:12 13:6 13:9 3:4 10:8 10:12, Jeremiah 15:1 23:22 3:18, Job 16:9, Joel 1:15 2:1 3:4 4:14, Lamentations 2:13-2:14, Malachi 1:9 3:23, Numbers 16:21-16:22 17:12-16:48, Psalms 76:8 10:23, Revelation 6:17 16:14 20:8-20:9, Ruth.R 2:2, Zephaniah 1:14-1:18 2:2-2:3

[11] LXX *They have not continued steadfast, and they have gathered flocks against*

[12] Ezekiel 13:6 - 1 Kings 22:6 22:27 22:37, 2 Peter 2:18, 2 Thessalonians 2:11, Ezekiel 12:23-24 13:7 13:22-23 21:28 21:34 22:28, Jeremiah 14:14 23:31-32 4:2 4:15 5:8 5:31 13:19, Lamentations 2:14, Mark 13:6 13:22-23, Proverbs 14:15, Zechariah 10:2

not sent them, yet they hope that the word will be confirmed!

הֲלֹוא מַחֲזֵה־שָׁוְא חֲזִיתֶם וּמִקְסַם כָּזָב אֲמַרְתֶּם וְאֹמְרִים נְאֻם־יְהֹוָה וַאֲנִי לֹא דִבַּרְתִּי

7[1] Have you not seen a vain vision, and have you not spoken a lying divination, because you say: The LORD says; although I have not spoken?

לָכֵן כֹּה אָמַר אֲדֹנָי יְהֹוִה יַעַן דַּבֶּרְכֶם שָׁוְא וַחֲזִיתֶם כָּזָב לָכֵן הִנְנִי אֲלֵיכֶם נְאֻם אֲדֹנָי יְהֹוִה

8[2] Therefore, thus says the Lord GOD: Because you have spoken vanity, and seen lies, behold, I am against you, says the Lord GOD.

וְהָיְתָה יָדִי אֶל־הַנְּבִיאִים הַחֹזִים שָׁוְא וְהַקֹּסְמִים כָּזָב בְּסוֹד עַמִּי לֹא־יִהְיוּ וּבִכְתָב בֵּית־יִשְׂרָאֵל לֹא יִכָּתֵבוּ וְאֶל־אַדְמַת יִשְׂרָאֵל לֹא יָבֹאוּ וִידַעְתֶּם כִּי אֲנִי אֲדֹנָי יְהֹוִה

9[3] And My hand shall be against the prophets who see vanity, and who divine lies; they shall not be in the council of My people, nor shall they be written in the register of the house of Israel, nor shall they enter into the land of Israel; and you shall know that I am the Lord GOD.

יַעַן וּבְיַעַן הִטְעוּ אֶת־עַמִּי לֵאמֹר שָׁלוֹם וְאֵין שָׁלוֹם וְהוּא בֹּנֶה חַיִץ וְהִנָּם טָחִים אֹתוֹ תָּפֵל

10[4] Because, because they have led My people astray, saying: Peace, and there is no peace; and when it builds up a slight wall, behold, they daub it with whited plaster[5];

אֱמֹר אֶל־טָחֵי תָפֵל וְיִפֹּל הָיָה גֶּשֶׁם שׁוֹטֵף וְאַתֵּנָה אַבְנֵי אֶלְגָּבִישׁ תִּפֹּלְנָה וְרוּחַ סְעָרוֹת תְּבַקֵּעַ

11[6] say to those who daub it with whited plaster, so it shall fall; there shall be an overflowing shower, and you, O great hailstones, shall fall, and a stormy wind shall break forth,

וְהִנֵּה נָפַל הַקִּיר הֲלוֹא יֵאָמֵר אֲלֵיכֶם אַיֵּה הַטִּיחַ אֲשֶׁר טַחְתֶּם

12[7] and, lo, when the wall falls, shall it not be said to you: Where is the daubing that you have done?

לָכֵן כֹּה אָמַר אֲדֹנָי יְהֹוִה וּבִקַּעְתִּי רוּחַ־סְעָרוֹת בַּחֲמָתִי וְגֶשֶׁם שֹׁטֵף בְּאַפִּי יִהְיֶה וְאַבְנֵי אֶלְגָּבִישׁ בְּחֵמָה לְכָלָה

13[8] Therefore, thus says the Lord GOD: I will cause a stormy wind to break forth in My fury; and there shall be an overflowing shower in My anger, and great hailstones in fury to consume it.

וְהָרַסְתִּי אֶת־הַקִּיר אֲשֶׁר־טַחְתֶּם תָּפֵל וְהִגַּעְתִּיהוּ אֶל־הָאָרֶץ וְנִגְלָה יְסֹדוֹ וְנָפְלָה וּכְלִיתֶם בְּתוֹכָהּ וִידַעְתֶּם כִּי־אֲנִי יְהֹוָה

14[9] So will I break down the wall you have daubed with whited plaster, and bring it down to the ground, so that its foundation shall be uncovered; and it shall fall, and you shall be consumed in its midst; and you shall know that I am the LORD.

וְכִלֵּיתִי אֶת־חֲמָתִי בַּקִּיר וּבַטָּחִים אֹתוֹ תָּפֵל וְאֹמַר לָכֶם אֵין הַקִּיר וְאֵין הַטָּחִים אֹתוֹ

15[10] Thus I will spend My fury on the wall, and on those who have daubed it with whited plaster; and I will say to you: The wall is no more, nor they who daubed it;

---

[1] Ezekiel 13:7 - Ezekiel 13:2-13:3 13:6, Matthew 24:23-24:24

[2] Ezekiel 13:8 - 1 Peter 3:12, 1 Timothy 4:1 4:8, Ezekiel 5:8 21:8 2:3 4:22 29:3-29:4 5:10 11:3 38:3-38:4 15:1, Jeremiah 50:31-50:32 3:25, Nahum 2:14 3:5-3:6, z.Vaetchanan 269b

[3] Ezekiel 13:9 - 1 Kings 22:24-22:25, b.Ketubot 112a, Daniel 12:1, Ein Yaakov Ketubot:112a, Exodus 32:32-32:33, Ezekiel 11:10 11:12-11:13 12:20 14:9-14:10 20:38, Ezra 2:59 2:62-2:63, Hebrews 12:23, Hosea 9:3, Isaiah 4:3, Jastrow 779b 961b, Jeremiah 17:13 20:3-20:6 23:20 28:15-28:17 29:21-29:22 29:31-29:32, Luke 10:20, mt.Hilchot Melachim uMichamoteihem 5:12, Nehemiah 7:62 7:64, Philippians 4:3, Psalms 69:6 69:29 87:6 5:7, Revelation 13:8 19:20 20:12 20:15, y.Rosh Hashanah 2:5, y.Sanhedrin 1:2

[4] Ezekiel 13:10 - 1 John 2:26, 1 Timothy 4:1, 2 Baruch 48:32, 2 Chronicles 18:12, 2 Kings 21:9, 2 Timothy 3:13, Ezekiel 7:25 13:16 22:28, Isaiah 6:10 9:21, Jastrow 455a, Jeremiah 4:10 5:31 8:11 8:15 14:13 23:13-23:15 23:17 4:9 2:6, Malachi 3:15, Micah 2:11, Proverbs 12:26, Revelation 2:20, Tanna Devei Eliyahu 4, y.Sheviit 3:6

[5] LXX adds *it shall fall*

[6] Ezekiel 13:11 - 3 Enoch 34:1, Ahiqar 169, Ezekiel 14:22, Isaiah 1:4 4:2 28:15-28:18 5:6 8:19, Job 3:21, Luke 6:48-6:49, Matthew 7:25 7:27, Nahum 1:3 1:7-1:8, Psalms 11:7 18:14-18:15 32:6

[7] Ezekiel 13:12 - 2 Kings 3:13, Deuteronomy 8:37, Jeremiah 2:28 29:31-29:32 13:19, Judges 9:38 10:14, Lamentations 2:14-2:15

[8] Ezekiel 13:13 - 3 Enoch 34:1, Exodus 9:18-29, Haggai 2:17, Isaiah 6:30, Jeremiah 23:19, Jonah 1:4, Leviticus 2:28, Psalms 18:13-14 9:32 11:25 4:8, Revelation 8:7 11:19 16:21, z.Vaetchanan 269b

[9] Ezekiel 13:14 - 1 Corinthians 3:11-15, Ezekiel 13:9 13:21 13:23 14:8, Habakkuk 3:13, Jeremiah 6:15 8:12 14:15 23:15, Luke 6:49, Matthew 7:26-27, Micah 1:6, Psalms 11:4

[10] Ezekiel 13:15 - Isaiah 6:13, Nehemiah 4:3, Psalms 62:4

נְבִיאֵי יִשְׂרָאֵל הַנִּבְּאִים אֶל־יְרוּשָׁלַ͏ִם וְהַחֹזִים לָהּ חֲזוֹן שָׁלֹם וְאֵין שָׁלֹם נְאֻם אֲדֹנָי יְהוִה

16[1] namely, the prophets of Israel who prophesy concerning Jerusalem, and who see visions of peace for her, but there is no peace, says the Lord GOD.

וְאַתָּה בֶן־אָדָם שִׂים פָּנֶיךָ אֶל־בְּנוֹת עַמְּךָ הַמִּתְנַבְּאוֹת מִלִּבְּהֶן וְהִנָּבֵא עֲלֵיהֶן

17[2] And you, son of man, set your face against the daughters of your people, who prophesy out of their own heart; and prophesy against them,

וְאָמַרְתָּ כֹּה־אָמַר אֲדֹנָי יְהוִה הוֹי לִמְתַפְּרוֹת כְּסָתוֹת עַל כָּל־אַצִּילֵי יָדַי וְעֹשׂוֹת הַמִּסְפָּחוֹת עַל־רֹאשׁ כָּל־קוֹמָה לְצוֹדֵד נְפָשׁוֹת הַנְּפָשׁוֹת תְּצוֹדֵדְנָה לְעַמִּי וּנְפָשׁוֹת לָכֶנָה תְחַיֶּינָה

18[3] and say: Thus says the Lord GOD: Woe to the women who sew cushions on every elbow, and make pads for the head of persons of every stature to hunt souls. Will you hunt the souls of My people, and save souls for yourselves?

וַתְּחַלֶּלְנָה אֹתִי אֶל־עַמִּי בְּשַׁעֲלֵי שְׂעֹרִים וּבִפְתוֹתֵי לֶחֶם לְהָמִית נְפָשׁוֹת אֲשֶׁר לֹא־תְמוּתֶנָה וּלְחַיּוֹת נְפָשׁוֹת אֲשֶׁר לֹא־תִחְיֶינָה בְּכַזֶּבְכֶם לְעַמִּי שֹׁמְעֵי כָזָב

19[4] And you have profaned Me among My people for handfuls of barley and for crumbs of bread, to kill the souls who should not die, and to save the souls who should not live, by your lying to My people who listen to lies.

לָכֵן כֹּה־אָמַר אֲדֹנָי יְהוִה הִנְנִי אֶל־כִּסְּתוֹתֵיכֶנָה אֲשֶׁר אַתֵּנָה מְצֹדְדוֹת שָׁם אֶת־הַנְּפָשׁוֹת לְפֹרְחוֹת וְקָרַעְתִּי אֹתָם מֵעַל זְרוֹעֹתֵיכֶם וְשִׁלַּחְתִּי אֶת־הַנְּפָשׁוֹת אֲשֶׁר אַתֶּם מְצֹדְדוֹת אֶת־נְפָשִׁים לְפֹרְחֹת

20[5] Thus says the Lord GOD: Behold, I am against your cushions, *with which you hunt the souls as birds, and I will tear them from your arms; and I will let the souls go, the souls you hunt as birds*[6].

וְקָרַעְתִּי אֶת־מִסְפְּחֹתֵיכֶם וְהִצַּלְתִּי אֶת־עַמִּי מִיֶּדְכֶן וְלֹא־יִהְיוּ עוֹד בְּיֶדְכֶן לִמְצוּדָה וִידַעְתֶּן כִּי־אֲנִי יְהוִה

21[7] Your pads also will I tear, and deliver My people out of your hand, and they shall no longer be in your hand to be hunted; and you shall know that I am the LORD.

יַעַן הַכְאוֹת לֵב־צַדִּיק שֶׁקֶר וַאֲנִי לֹא הִכְאַבְתִּיו וּלְחַזֵּק יְדֵי רָשָׁע לְבִלְתִּי־שׁוּב מִדַּרְכּוֹ הָרָע לְהַחֲיֹתוֹ

22[8] Because with lies you have cowed the heart of the righteous, when I have not grieved him; and strengthened the hands of the wicked, so he should not turn from his wicked way to save his life;

לָכֵן שָׁוְא לֹא תֶחֱזֶינָה וְקֶסֶם לֹא־תִקְסַמְנָה עוֹד וְהִצַּלְתִּי אֶת־עַמִּי מִיֶּדְכֶן וִידַעְתֶּן כִּי־אֲנִי יְהוִה

23[9] Therefore, you shall no longer see vanity, nor divine divinations; and I will deliver My people from your hand; and you shall know I am the LORD.'

Ezekiel – Chapter 14

וַיָּבוֹא אֵלַי אֲנָשִׁים מִזִּקְנֵי יִשְׂרָאֵל וַיֵּשְׁבוּ לְפָנָי

1[10] Then certain elders of Israel came to me, and sat before me.

וַיְהִי דְבַר־יְהוָה אֵלַי לֵאמֹר

2[11] And the word of the LORD came to me, saying:

---

[1] Ezekiel 13:16 - Ezekiel 13:10, Isaiah 24:22 57:20-21, Jeremiah 5:31 6:14 8:11 4:1 28:9-17 5:31

[2] Ezekiel 13:17 - 11QEzek, 2 Kings 22:14, 2 Peter 2:1, Ezekiel 4:3 13:2 21:2 21:7, Isaiah 3:16-3:26 4:4, Judges 4:4, Luke 2:36, Revelation 2:20, variant אל־ of על־ is found

[3] Ezekiel 13:18 - 2 Peter 2:14, 2 Timothy 4:3, b.Avodah Zara [Tosefot] 65a, b.Menachot [Tosefot] 37a, b.Moed Katan [Tosefot] 28a, b.Shabbat [Tosefot] 92a, Ephesians 4:14, Ezekiel 13:10 13:16 13:20 22:25, Jeremiah 4:10 6:14, Mas.Kallah Rabbati 6:1, z.Vaetchanan 269b

[4] Ezekiel 13:19 - 1 Corinthians 8:11, 1 Peter 5:2, 1 Samuel 2:16-2:17, 2 Peter 2:2-2:3, b.Arachin 64b, Ezekiel 13:22 20:39 22:26, Jeremiah 23:14 23:17, Malachi 1:10, Micah 3:5 3:11, Numbers.R 10:5, Proverbs 19:27 4:21, Romans 14:15 16:18

[5] Ezekiel 13:20 - 2 Timothy 3:8-3:9, b.Pesachim [Rashbam] 11a, Ezekiel 13:8-13:9 13:15-16 13:18, z.Vaetchanan 269b

[6] LXX *whereby you confound souls, and I will tear them away from your arms, and will set at liberty their souls which you pervert to scatter them*

[7] Ezekiel 13:21 - Psalms 91:3

[8] Ezekiel 13:22 - 2 Peter 2:18-2:19, Ezekiel 9:4 13:16 18:21 33:14-33:16, Genesis 3:4-3:5, Jeremiah 4:10 6:14 8:11 14:13-14:17 23:9 23:14 23:17 27:14-27:17 4:16 5:32, Lamentations 2:11-2:14

[9] Ezekiel 13:23 - 1 Corinthians 11:19, 2 Timothy 3:9, Deuteronomy 18:20, Ezekiel 12:24 13:6-13:16 13:21 14:8 15:7 10:10, Jude 1:24, Mark 13:22, Matthew 24:24, Micah 3:6, Revelation 12:9 12:11 13:5 13:8 15:2, Zechariah 13:3

[10] Ezekiel 14:1 - 2 Kings 6:32, Acts 4:5 4:8 22:3, Ezekiel 8:1 20:1 9:31, Isaiah 5:13, Luke 10:39

[11] Ezekiel 14:2 - 1 Kings 14:4, Amos 3:7, Apocalypse of Elijah 1:1

בֶּן־אָדָם הָאֲנָשִׁים הָאֵלֶּה הֶעֱלוּ גִלּוּלֵיהֶם עַל־לִבָּם וּמִכְשׁוֹל עֲוֺנָם נָתְנוּ נֹכַח פְּנֵיהֶם הַאִדָּרֹשׁ אִדָּרֵשׁ לָהֶם	**3**[1] 'Son of man, these men *set up their idols in their mind*[2], and put the *stumbling block*[3] of their iniquity before their face; should I be inquired by them?
לָכֵן דַּבֵּר־אוֹתָם וְאָמַרְתָּ אֲלֵיהֶם כֹּה־אָמַר אֲדֹנָי יְהֹוָה אִישׁ אִישׁ מִבֵּית יִשְׂרָאֵל אֲשֶׁר יַעֲלֶה אֶת־גִּלּוּלָיו אֶל־לִבּוֹ וּמִכְשׁוֹל עֲוֺנוֹ יָשִׂים נֹכַח פָּנָיו וּבָא אֶל־הַנָּבִיא אֲנִי יְהֹוָה נַעֲנֵיתִי לוֹ "בָה" "בָא" בְּרֹב גִּלּוּלָיו	**4**[4] Therefore, speak to them, and say to them: Thus says the Lord GOD: Every man of the house of Israel who sets up his idols in his mind, and puts the stumbling block of his iniquity before his face, and comes to the prophet, I, the LORD, will answer *he who comes according to the multitude of his idols*[5];
לְמַעַן תְּפֹשׂ אֶת־בֵּית־יִשְׂרָאֵל בְּלִבָּם אֲשֶׁר נָזֹרוּ מֵעָלַי בְּגִלּוּלֵיהֶם כֻּלָּם	**5**[6] So I may take the house of Israel in their own heart, because they all turned away from Me through their idols.
לָכֵן אֱמֹר אֶל־בֵּית יִשְׂרָאֵל כֹּה אָמַר אֲדֹנָי יְהֹוָה שׁוּבוּ וְהָשִׁיבוּ מֵעַל גִּלּוּלֵיכֶם וּמֵעַל כָּל־תּוֹעֲבֹתֵיכֶם הָשִׁיבוּ פְּנֵיכֶם	**6**[7] Therefore, say to the house of Israel: Thus says the Lord GOD: Return, and turn yourselves from your idols; and turn away your faces from all your abominations.
כִּי אִישׁ אִישׁ מִבֵּית יִשְׂרָאֵל וּמֵהַגֵּר אֲשֶׁר־יָגוּר בְּיִשְׂרָאֵל וְיִנָּזֵר מֵאַחֲרַי וְיַעַל גִּלּוּלָיו אֶל־לִבּוֹ וּמִכְשׁוֹל עֲוֺנוֹ יָשִׂים נֹכַח פָּנָיו וּבָא אֶל־הַנָּבִיא לִדְרָשׁ־לוֹ בִי אֲנִי יְהֹוָה נַעֲנֶה־לּוֹ בִּי	**7**[8] for every one of the house of Israel, or of the strangers who sojourn in Israel, who separates himself from Me, and takes his idols into his heart, and puts the stumbling block of his iniquity before his face, and comes to the prophet, to inquire for him of Me, I, the LORD, will answer him *by Myself*[9],
וְנָתַתִּי פָנַי בָּאִישׁ הַהוּא וַהֲשִׂמֹתִיהוּ לְאוֹת וְלִמְשָׁלִים וְהִכְרַתִּיו מִתּוֹךְ עַמִּי וִידַעְתֶּם כִּי־אֲנִי יְהֹוָה	**8**[10] and I will set My face against that man, and will make him a *sign and a proverb*[11], and I will cut him off from the midst of My people; and you shall know that I am the LORD.
וְהַנָּבִיא כִי־יְפֻתֶּה וְדִבֶּר דָּבָר אֲנִי יְהֹוָה פִּתֵּיתִי אֵת הַנָּבִיא הַהוּא וְנָטִיתִי אֶת־יָדִי עָלָיו וְהִשְׁמַדְתִּיו מִתּוֹךְ עַמִּי יִשְׂרָאֵל	**9**[12] And when the prophet is enticed and speaks a word, I, the LORD, have enticed that prophet, and I will stretch out My hand on him, and will destroy him from the midst of My people Israel.
וְנָשְׂאוּ עֲוֺנָם כַּעֲוֺן הַדֹּרֵשׁ כַּעֲוֺן הַנָּבִיא יִהְיֶה	**10**[13] And they shall bear their iniquity; the iniquity of the prophet shall be as the iniquity of he who inquires;

---

[1] Ezekiel 14:3 - 1 Peter 2:8, 1 Samuel 4:6, 2 Kings 3:13, Ephesians 5:5, Ezekiel 3:20 6:9 7:19 11:21 14:4 14:7 20:3 20:16 20:31 12:25 20:12, Isaiah 1:15 9:15, Jeremiah 7:8-7:11 11:11 17:1-17:2 17:9 42:20-42:21 44:16-44:18, Luke 20:8, Proverbs 15:8 15:29 21:27 4:9, Psalms 66:18 5:3, Revelation 2:14, Zechariah 7:13, Zephaniah 1:3
[2] LXX *conceived their devices in their hearts*
[3] LXX *punishment*
[4] Ezekiel 14:4 - 1 Kings 21:20-21:25, 2 Kings 1:16, Ezekiel 2:7 3:4 3:17-3:21 14:7, Isaiah 3:11 18:4, z.Vaetchanan 269b
[5] LXX *him according to the things in which his mind is entangled*
[6] Ezekiel 14:5 - 2 Thessalonians 2:9-11, b.Chullin 142a, b.Kiddushin 39b 40a, Colossians 1:21, Deuteronomy 32:15-16, Ein Yaakov Chullin:142a, Ein Yaakov Kiddushin:39b 40a, Ephesians 4:18, Ezekiel 14:9-10, Galatians 6:7, Hebrews 3:12, Hosea 10:2, Isaiah 1:4, Jeremiah 2:5 2:11-13 2:31-32, mt.Hilchot Ishut 8:5, Romans 1:21-23 1:28 1:30 8:7, Saadia Opinions 5:8, Zechariah 7:11-14 11:8
[7] Ezekiel 14:6 - 1 Kings 8:47-49, 1 Samuel 7:3, 2 Chronicles 5:6, Acts 3:19 17:30 2:20, Ezekiel 8:16 14:4 16:63 18:30 36:31-36:32, Hosea 14:3-14:5 14:10, Isaiah 2:20 6:22 55:6-7, James 4:8-10, Jeremiah 8:5-6 13:27 31:19-21 50:4-5, Jonah 3:7-9, Lamentations 3:39-3:41, Matthew 3:8-3:10, Nehemiah 1:8-1:9, Romans 6:21, z.Vaetchanan 269b, Zephaniah 3:11
[8] Ezekiel 14:7 - 2 Kings 8:8-8:15, Exodus 12:48 20:10, Ezekiel 14:3-14:4 14:7-14:8 33:30-33:32, Hosea 4:14 9:10, Isaiah 58:1-58:2, Jeremiah 21:1-21:2 37:1-37:3 37:9-37:10 13:17 38:14-38:23, Jude 1:19, Leviticus 16:29 20:2 24:22, Numbers 15:15 15:29
[9] LXX *according to the things in which he is entangled*
[10] Ezekiel 14:8 - 1 Corinthians 10:11, Deuteronomy 4:37, Ezekiel 5:15 6:7 13:23 15:7, Isaiah 17:15, Jeremiah 21:10 24:9 5:22 20:11, Leviticus 17:10 20:3-20:6 22:3 2:17, Numbers 19:20 2:10, Psalms 34:17 37:22 44:14-44:15, Romans 11:22
[11] LXX *desolate and ruined*
[12] Ezekiel 14:9 - 1 Kings 22:20-22:23, 2 Samuel 12:11-12:12, 2 Thessalonians 2:9-2:12, Ezekiel 16:27 20:25, Isaiah 5:25 9:13 9:18 9:22 10:4 15:16 18:4, Jeremiah 4:10 14:15, Job 12:16, Psalms 81:12-81:13, Saadia Opinions 4:6
[13] Ezekiel 14:10 - Deuteronomy 13:2-13:11 17:2-17:7, Ezekiel 14:4 14:7-14:8 17:18-17:20 23:49, Galatians 6:5, Genesis 4:13, Jeremiah 6:14-6:15 8:11-8:12 14:15, Micah 7:9, Numbers 5:31, Revelation 19:19-19:21

לְמַעַן לֹא־יִתְעוּ עֹוד בֵּית־יִשְׂרָאֵל מֵאַחֲרַי וְלֹא־ יִטַּמְּאוּ עֹוד בְּכָל־פִּשְׁעֵיהֶם וְהָיוּ לִי לְעָם וַאֲנִי אֶהְיֶה לָהֶם לֵאלֹהִים נְאֻם אֲדֹנָי יְהוִה	11[1]	So the house of Israel may no longer go astray from Me, nor defile themselves any longer with all their transgressions; but that they may be My people, and I may be their God, says the Lord GOD.'
וַיְהִי דְבַר־יְהוָה אֵלַי לֵאמֹר	12	And the word of the LORD came to me, saying:
בֶּן־אָדָם אֶרֶץ כִּי תֶחֱטָא־לִי לִמְעָל־מַעַל וְנָטִיתִי יָדִי עָלֶיהָ וְשָׁבַרְתִּי לָהּ מַטֵּה־לָחֶם וְהִשְׁלַחְתִּי־בָהּ רָעָב וְהִכְרַתִּי מִמֶּנָּה אָדָם וּבְהֵמָה	13[2]	'Son of man, when a land sins against Me by trespassing grievously, and I stretch out My hand upon it, and break the staff of its bread, and send famine upon it, and cut off from it man and beast;
וְהָיוּ שְׁלֹשֶׁת הָאֲנָשִׁים הָאֵלֶּה בְּתוֹכָהּ נֹחַ 'דָּנִאֵל' "דָּנִיֵאל" וְאִיּוֹב הֵמָּה בְצִדְקָתָם יְנַצְּלוּ נַפְשָׁם נְאֻם אֲדֹנָי יְהוִה	14[3]	though these three men, Noah, Daniel, and Job, were in it, they should deliver their own souls by their righteousness, says the Lord GOD.
לוּ־חַיָּה רָעָה אַעֲבִיר בָּאָרֶץ וְשִׁכְּלָתָּה וְהָיְתָה שְׁמָמָה מִבְּלִי עוֹבֵר מִפְּנֵי הַחַיָּה	15[4]	If I cause evil beasts to pass through the land, and they bereave it, and it becomes desolate, so no man may pass through because of the beasts;
שְׁלֹשֶׁת הָאֲנָשִׁים הָאֵלֶּה בְּתוֹכָהּ חַי־אָנִי נְאֻם אֲדֹנָי יְהוִה אִם־בָּנִים וְאִם־בָּנוֹת יַצִּילוּ הֵמָּה לְבַדָּם יִנָּצֵלוּ וְהָאָרֶץ תִּהְיֶה שְׁמָמָה	16[5]	though these three men were in it, as I live, says the Lord GOD, they shall deliver neither sons nor daughters; they only shall be delivered, but the land shall be desolate.
אוֹ חֶרֶב אָבִיא עַל־הָאָרֶץ הַהִיא וְאָמַרְתִּי חֶרֶב תַּעֲבֹר בָּאָרֶץ וְהִכְרַתִּי מִמֶּנָּה אָדָם וּבְהֵמָה	17[6]	Or if I bring a sword upon that land, and say: Let the sword go through the land, so that I cut off from it man and beast;
וּשְׁלֹשֶׁת הָאֲנָשִׁים הָאֵלֶּה בְּתוֹכָהּ חַי־אָנִי נְאֻם אֲדֹנָי יְהוִה לֹא יַצִּילוּ בָּנִים וּבָנוֹת כִּי הֵם לְבַדָּם יִנָּצֵלוּ	18	though these three men were in it, as I live, says the Lord GOD, they shall deliver neither sons nor daughters, but they only shall deliver themselves.
אוֹ דֶּבֶר אֲשַׁלַּח אֶל־הָאָרֶץ הַהִיא וְשָׁפַכְתִּי חֲמָתִי עָלֶיהָ בְּדָם לְהַכְרִית מִמֶּנָּה אָדָם וּבְהֵמָה	19[7]	Or if I send a pestilence into that land, and pour out My fury upon it in blood, to cut off from it man and beast;
וְנֹחַ 'דָּנִאֵל' "דָּנִיֵאל" וְאִיּוֹב בְּתוֹכָהּ חַי־אָנִי נְאֻם אֲדֹנָי יְהוִה אִם־בֵּן אִם־בַּת יַצִּילוּ הֵמָּה בְצִדְקָתָם יַצִּילוּ נַפְשָׁם	20[8]	though Noah, Daniel, and Job, were in it, as I live, says the Lord GOD, they shall deliver neither son nor daughter; they shall but deliver their own souls by their righteousness.

---

[1] Ezekiel 14:11 - 2 Peter 2:15, Deuteronomy 13:12 19:20, Ezekiel 11:18-11:20 34:10-34:31 36:25-36:29 13:23 13:27 15:22 20:10 20:15 24:11, Genesis 17:7, Hebrews 8:10 11:16, Isaiah 9:17, Jeremiah 11:4 23:15 7:34 8:38 2:6, Psalms 119:67, Revelation 21:7, Zechariah 13:9

[2] Ezekiel 14:13 - Daniel 9:5 9:10-9:12, Ezekiel 4:16 5:16 9:9 14:17 14:19 14:21 15:8 20:27 1:13, Ezra 9:6, Genesis 6:7, Isaiah 3:1 24:20, Jeremiah 7:20 15:2-15:3 8:43 12:29, Lamentations 1:8 1:20 4:9-4:10, Leviticus 2:26
Ezekiel 14:13-23 - Psalms of Solomon 13:3

[3] Ezekiel 14:14 - 2 Peter 2:9, Daniel 1:6 9:21 10:11, Ezekiel 14:16 14:18 14:20 18:20 4:3, Genesis 6:8 7:1 8:20-8:21, Hebrews 11:7, Jeremiah 7:16 11:14 14:11-14:12 15:1, Job 1:1 1:5 42:8-42:9, Proverbs 11:4, Song of Songs.R 2:45

[4] Ezekiel 14:15 - 1 Kings 20:36, 2 Kings 17:25, Ezekiel 5:17, Jeremiah 15:3, Leviticus 2:22

[5] Ezekiel 14:16 - Acts 3:24, Ezekiel 14:14 14:18 14:20 18:20 9:11, Genesis 18:23-18:33 19:29, Hebrews 11:7, James 5:16, Job 22:20, Matthew 18:19-18:20, Numbers 14:28-14:29

[6] Ezekiel 14:17 - Ezekiel 5:12 5:17 14:13 21:8-9 21:14-21:20 1:13 5:8 38:21-22, Hosea 4:3, Jeremiah 1:9 9:12 23:6, Leviticus 2:25, Zephaniah 1:3

[7] Ezekiel 14:19 - 1 Kings 8:37, 2 Chronicles 6:28 7:13 20:9, 2 Samuel 24:13 24:15, Amos 4:10, Deuteronomy 28:21-28:22 28:59-28:61, Ezekiel 5:12 7:8 12:18 14:22, Isaiah 13:36, Jeremiah 14:12 21:6 21:9 24:10, Matthew 24:7, Numbers 14:12 17:11-16:50, Psalms 91:3 91:6, Revelation 16:3-16:6

[8] Ezekiel 14:20 - 1 John 2:29 3:7 3:10, Acts 10:35, Ezekiel 14:14 14:16 18:20 18:22, Hosea 10:12, Isaiah 3:10, Job 5:19-5:24, Psalms 33:18-33:19, Zephaniah 2:3

כִּי כֹה אָמַר אֲדֹנָי יְהֹוִה אַף כִּי־אַרְבַּעַת שְׁפָטַי
הָרָעִים חֶרֶב וְרָעָב וְחַיָּה רָעָה וָדֶבֶר שִׁלַּחְתִּי אֶל־
יְרוּשָׁלָ͏ִם לְהַכְרִית מִמֶּנָּה אָדָם וּבְהֵמָה

21[1] For thus says the Lord GOD: How much more when I send My four grievous judgments against Jerusalem, the sword, and the famine, and the evil beasts, and the pestilence, to cut off from it man and beast.

וְהִנֵּה נוֹתְרָה־בָּהּ פְּלֵטָה הַמּוּצָאִים בָּנִים וּבָנוֹת
הִנָּם יוֹצְאִים אֲלֵיכֶם וּרְאִיתֶם אֶת־דַּרְכָּם וְאֶת־
עֲלִילוֹתָם וְנִחַמְתֶּם עַל־הָרָעָה אֲשֶׁר הֵבֵאתִי עַל־
יְרוּשָׁלַ͏ִם אֵת כָּל־אֲשֶׁר הֵבֵאתִי עָלֶיהָ

22[2] And, behold, a remnant remains in it who shall be brought forth, both sons and daughters; behold, when they come forth to you, and you see their way and their deeds, then you shall be comforted concerning the evil that I have brought upon Jerusalem, concerning all that I have brought upon it;

וְנִחֲמוּ אֶתְכֶם כִּי־תִרְאוּ אֶת־דַּרְכָּם וְאֶת־עֲלִילוֹתָם
וִידַעְתֶּם כִּי לֹא חִנָּם עָשִׂיתִי אֵת כָּל־אֲשֶׁר־עָשִׂיתִי
בָהּ נְאֻם אֲדֹנָי יְהֹוִה

23[3] and they shall comfort you, when you see their way and their deeds, and you shall know that I have not done without cause all that I have done in it, says the Lord GOD.'

Ezekiel – Chapter 15

וַיְהִי דְבַר־יְהֹוָה אֵלַי לֵאמֹר

1[4] And the word of the LORD came to me, saying:

בֶּן־אָדָם מַה־יִּהְיֶה עֵץ־הַגֶּפֶן מִכָּל־עֵץ הַזְּמוֹרָה
אֲשֶׁר הָיָה בַּעֲצֵי הַיָּעַר

2[5] 'Son of man, *what is the vine tree more than any tree, the vine branch which grew up among the trees of the forest*[6]?

הֲיֻקַּח מִמֶּנּוּ עֵץ לַעֲשׂוֹת לִמְלָאכָה אִם־יִקְחוּ מִמֶּנּוּ
יָתֵד לִתְלוֹת עָלָיו כָּל־כֶּלִי

3[7] Shall wood be taken from there to make any work? or will men take a pin of it to hang any vessel on it?

הִנֵּה לָאֵשׁ נִתַּן לְאָכְלָה אֵת שְׁנֵי קְצוֹתָיו אָכְלָה
הָאֵשׁ וְתוֹכוֹ נָחָר הֲיִצְלַח לִמְלָאכָה

4[8] Behold, it is cast into the fire for fuel; the fire has devoured both its ends, and its midst is singed; is it profitable for any work?

הִנֵּה בִּהְיוֹתוֹ תָמִים לֹא יֵעָשֶׂה לִמְלָאכָה אַף כִּי־אֵשׁ
אֲכָלַתְהוּ וַיֵּחָר וְנַעֲשָׂה עוֹד לִמְלָאכָה

5[9] Behold, when it was whole, it was not useful for work; how much less, when the fire has devoured it, and it is singed, shall it yet be useful for any work?

לָכֵן כֹּה אָמַר אֲדֹנָי יְהֹוִה כַּאֲשֶׁר עֵץ־הַגֶּפֶן בְּעֵץ
הַיַּעַר אֲשֶׁר־נְתַתִּיו לָאֵשׁ לְאָכְלָה כֵּן נָתַתִּי אֶת־
יֹשְׁבֵי יְרוּשָׁלָ͏ִם

6[10] Therefore, thus says the Lord GOD: As the vine tree among the trees of the forest, which I have given to the fire for fuel, so I give the inhabitants of Jerusalem.

וְנָתַתִּי אֶת־פָּנַי בָּהֶם מֵהָאֵשׁ יָצָאוּ וְהָאֵשׁ תֹּאכְלֵם
וִידַעְתֶּם כִּי־אֲנִי יְהֹוָה בְּשׂוּמִי אֶת־פָּנַי בָּהֶם

7[11] And I will set My face against them; they come forth out of the fire, and the fire shall devour

---

[1] Ezekiel 14:21 - Amos 4:6-4:12, Ezekiel 5:12 5:17 6:11-6:12 14:13 14:15 14:17 14:19 9:27, Jeremiah 15:2-15:3, Midrash Tanchuma Vayera 9, Revelation 6:4-6:8, z.Vaetchanan 269b

[2] Ezekiel 14:22 - 2 Chronicles 12:20, Deuteronomy 4:31, Ezekiel 6:8-6:10 12:16 16:54 36:31 20:43 12:31, Genesis.R 28:5, Hebrews 12:6-12:11, Isaiah 6:13 10:20-10:22 17:4-17:6 24:13 40:1-40:2 65:8-65:9, Jeremiah 3:21-3:25 4:27 5:19 6:11 31:18-31:22 52:27-52:30, Mark 13:20, Micah 5:8, Song of Songs.R 1:25

[3] Ezekiel 14:23 - Daniel 9:7 9:14, Deuteronomy 8:2, Ezekiel 8:6-8:18 9:8-9:9, Genesis 18:22-18:33, Jeremiah 7:17-7:28 22:8-22:9, Lamentations.R Petichata D'Chakimei:5, Nehemiah 9:33, Proverbs 2:2, Revelation 15:4 16:6, Romans 2:5

[4] Ezekiel 15:1 - 3 Baruch 1:2

[5] Ezekiel 15:2 - Deuteronomy 32:32-33, Hosea 10:1, Isaiah 5:1-7 20:23, Jeremiah 2:21, John 15:1-6, Luke 20:9-16, Mark 12:1-9, Matthew 21:33-41, Micah 3:12, Psalms 80:9-17, Song of Songs 2:13 2:15 6:11 7:13 8:11-12, Zechariah 11:2

[6] LXX *of all the wood, of the branches that are among the trees of the forest, what shall be made of the wood of the vine*

[7] Ezekiel 15:3 - Jeremiah 24:8, Luke 14:34-14:35, Mark 9:50, Matthew 5:13

[8] Ezekiel 15:4 - Amos 4:11, b.Shabbat 20a, Ezekiel 19:14, Hebrews 6:8 12:29, Isaiah 1:31 27:11, John 15:6, Malachi 3:19, Matthew 3:12, Psalms 80:17

[9] Ezekiel 15:5 - Genesis.R 92:7, Jeremiah 3:16

[10] Ezekiel 15:6 - Ezekiel 15:2 17:3-17:10 21:3-20:4, Isaiah 5:1-5:6 5:24-5:25, Jeremiah 4:7 7:20 21:7 24:8-24:10 25:9-25:11 25:18 44:21-44:27, z.Vaetchanan 269b, Zechariah 1:6

[11] Ezekiel 15:7 - 1 Kings 19:17, Amos 5:19 9:1-4, b.Bava Batra 79a, Ezekiel 6:7 7:4 11:10 14:8 20:38 20:42 20:44, Ein Yaakov Bava Batra 79a, Isaiah 24:18, Jeremiah 21:10 48:43-44, Psalms 9:17 34:17, Song of Songs.R 2:42, Leviticus 17:10 20:3-6 26:17, Mekhilta de R'Shimon bar Yochai Bachodesh 51:1

them; and you shall know that I am the LORD, when I set My face against them.

וְנָתַתִּי אֶת־הָאָרֶץ שְׁמָמָה יַעַן מָעֲלוּ מַעַל נְאֻם אֲדֹנָי יְהוִה

8[1] And I will make the land desolate, because they have acted treacherously, says the Lord GOD.'

Ezekiel – Chapter 16[2]

וַיְהִי דְבַר־יְהֹוָה אֵלַי לֵאמֹר

1[3] Again the word of the LORD came to me, saying:

בֶּן־אָדָם הוֹדַע אֶת־יְרוּשָׁלַם אֶת־תּוֹעֲבֹתֶיהָ

2[4] 'Son of man, cause Jerusalem to know her abominations,

וְאָמַרְתָּ כֹּה־אָמַר אֲדֹנָי יְהוִה לִירוּשָׁלַם מְכֹרֹתַיִךְ וּמֹלְדֹתַיִךְ מֵאֶרֶץ הַכְּנַעֲנִי אָבִיךְ הָאֱמֹרִי וְאִמֵּךְ חִתִּית

3[5] and say: Thus says the Lord GOD to Jerusalem: your origin and your nativity is of the land of the Canaanite; the Amorite was your father, and your mother was a Hittite.

וּמוֹלְדוֹתַיִךְ בְּיוֹם הוּלֶּדֶת אֹתָךְ לֹא־כָרַּת שָׁרֵּךְ וּבְמַיִם לֹא־רֻחַצְתְּ לְמִשְׁעִי וְהָמְלֵחַ לֹא הֻמְלַחַתְּ וְהָחְתֵּל לֹא חֻתָּלְתְּ

4[6] And as for your nativity, in the day you were born your navel was not cut, nor were you washed in water for cleansing; you were not salted at all, nor swaddled at all.

לֹא־חָסָה עָלַיִךְ עַיִן לַעֲשׂוֹת לָךְ אַחַת מֵאֵלֶּה לְחֻמְלָה עָלָיִךְ וַתֻּשְׁלְכִי אֶל־פְּנֵי הַשָּׂדֶה בְּגֹעַל נַפְשֵׁךְ בְּיוֹם הֻלֶּדֶת אֹתָךְ

5[7] No eye pitied you, to do any of these to you, to have compassion on you; but you were cast out in the open field in the loathsomeness of your person, in the day you were born.

וָאֶעֱבֹר עָלַיִךְ וָאֶרְאֵךְ מִתְבּוֹסֶסֶת בְּדָמָיִךְ וָאֹמַר לָךְ בְּדָמַיִךְ חֲיִי וָאֹמַר לָךְ בְּדָמַיִךְ חֲיִי

6[8] And when I passed by you, and saw you wallowing in your blood, I said to you: *In your blood, live; yes, I said to you: In your blood, live*[9];

רְבָבָה כְּצֶמַח הַשָּׂדֶה נְתַתִּיךְ וַתִּרְבִּי וַתִּגְדְּלִי וַתָּבֹאִי בַּעֲדִי עֲדָיִים שָׁדַיִם נָכֹנוּ וּשְׂעָרֵךְ צִמֵּחַ וְאַתְּ עֵרֹם וְעֶרְיָה

7[10] I cause you to increase, as the growth of the field. And you increased and grew up, and you came to excellent beauty: your breasts were fashioned, and your hair was grown; yet you were naked and bare.

---

[1] Ezekiel 15:8 - 2 Chronicles 36:14-16, Ezekiel 6:14 14:13-21 17:20 33:29, Isaiah 6:11 24:3-12, Jeremiah 25:10-11, Zephaniah 1:18

[2] Ezekiel 16 - Ein Yaakov Shabbat:129b, Mas.Soferim 9:10, Pesikta Rabbati 21:6 states this chapter allegorically describes the events leading to our redemption from Egypt

[3] Ezekiel 16:1-14 - Haftarah Shemot [Teimon]

[4] Ezekiel 16:2 - b.Megillah 25ab, Ezekiel 8:9-8:17 20:4 22:2 23:36 33:7-33:9, Hosea 8:1, Isaiah 58:1, t.Megillah 3:34, y.Megillah 4:12

[5] Ezekiel 16:3 - 1 John 3:10, 1 Kings 21:26, 2 Kings 21:11, b.Sanhedrin 44b, Deuteronomy 7:1 20:17, Ecclesiastes.R 3:10, Ein Yaakov Sanhedrin:44b, Ephesians 2:3, Ezekiel 16:45 21:35, Ezra 9:1, Genesis 11:25 11:29 15:16, Genesis.R 45:1 99 [Excl]:7, Isaiah 1:10 51:1-51:2, Jastrow 784b 1066a, John 8:44, Joshua 24:14, Luke 3:7, Matthew 3:7 11:24, Midrash Tanchuma Vayechi 9, Nehemiah 9:7, z.Vaetchanan 269b

[6] Ezekiel 16:4 - Acts 7:6-7:7, b.Berachot 24a, b.Shabbat 129b, b.Sotah 11b, Deuteronomy 5:6 15:15, Ein Yaakov Shabbat:129b, Ein Yaakov Sotah:11b, Exodus 1:11-1:14 2:23-2:24 5:16-5:21, Ezekiel 20:8 20:13, Genesis 15:13, Hosea 2:3, Joshua 24:2, Lamentations 2:20 2:22, Luke 2:7 2:12, Nehemiah 9:7-9:9, Unexpected Dagesh in the letter ר of לֹא־כָרַּת שָׁרֵּךְ and . Exodus 16:4-5 - Exodus 1:12 23:8

[7] Ezekiel 16:5 - Deuteronomy 32:10, Exodus 1:22, Ezekiel 2:6, Genesis 21:10, Isaiah 49:15, Jeremiah 9:22-9:23 22:19, Lamentations 2:11 2:19 4:3 4:10, Numbers 19:16

[8] Ezekiel 16:6 - Acts 7:34, b.Kereitot 9a, b.Succah [Rashi] 14a, Deuteronomy 9:4, Ephesians 2:4-5, Exodus 2:24-25 3:7-8 19:4-6, Exodus.R 17:3 19:5, Ezekiel 20:5-10, Guide for the Perplexed 3:46, Hebrews 10:29, Isaiah 14:19 51:23, John 5:25, Matthew 5:13, Mekilta de R'Ishmael Pisha 5:10 16:170, Micah 7:10, Midrash Psalms 114:5, Midrash Tanchuma Vayera 4, Numbers.R 14:12, Pesach Haggadah, Pesikta de R'Kahana 7.4, Pesikta Rabbati 17:3, Pirkei de R'Eliezer 29, Psalms 105:10-15 105:26-37, Revelation 14:20, Romans 9:15, Ruth.R 6:1, Seder Brit Milah Kriat Hashem [naming the baby], Song of Songs.R 1:34 5:3, Titus 3:3-7, z.Bo 35b

[9] LXX *Let there be life out of your blood*

[10] Ezekiel 16:7 - Acts 7:17, b.Kiddushin 81b, b.Niddah [Rashi] 49a, b.Niddah 48a, b.Sotah 11b, Deuteronomy 1:10 4:8 32:10-32:14 33:26-33:29, Ein Yaakov Sotah:11b, Exodus 1:7 3:22 12:37, Exodus.R 1:12 1:35 23:8, Ezekiel 16:10-16:13 16:16 16:22, Genesis 22:17, Genesis.R 60:13, Hosea 2:3 2:9-2:12, Isaiah 61:10 62:3, Jastrow 1046a, Job 1:21, Mekilta de R'Shimon bar Yochai Beshallach 20:2, Mekilta de R'Shimon bar Yochai Pisha 15:8, Mekilta de R'Ishmael Beshallah 1:78, Mekilta de R'Ishmael Pisha 5:7 12:83 13:144, Midrash Tanchuma Bo 8, Midrash Tanchuma Shemot 12, mt.Hilchot Chametz uMatzah Haggadah, mt.Hilchot Issurei Biah 21:7, mt.Hilchot Kriat Shema 3:19, Nehemiah 9:18-9:25, Numbers.R 13:20, Pesach Haggadah, Psalms 135:4 147:20 148:14 149:2-149:4, Revelation 3:17-3:18, Song of Songs 4:5, Song of Songs.R 1:55 2:43

וָאֶעֱבֹר עָלַיִךְ וָאֶרְאֵךְ וְהִנֵּה עִתֵּךְ עֵת דֹּדִים וָאֶפְרֹשׂ כְּנָפִי עָלַיִךְ וָאֲכַסֶּה עֶרְוָתֵךְ וָאֶשָּׁבַע לָךְ וָאָבוֹא בִבְרִית אֹתָךְ נְאֻם אֲדֹנָי יְהוִה וַתִּהְיִי לִי	8[1]	Now when I passed by you, and looked on you, and, behold, your time was the time of *love*[2], I spread my *skirt*[3] over you, and covered your nakedness; yes, I swore to you, and entered into a covenant with you, says the Lord GOD, and you became Mine.
וָאֶרְחָצֵךְ בַּמַּיִם וָאֶשְׁטֹף דָּמַיִךְ מֵעָלָיִךְ וָאֲסֻכֵךְ בַּשָּׁמֶן	9[4]	Then I washed you with water; Yes, I cleansed away your blood, and I anointed you with oil.
וָאַלְבִּישֵׁךְ רִקְמָה וָאֶנְעֲלֵךְ תָּחַשׁ וָאֶחְבְּשֵׁךְ בַּשֵּׁשׁ וָאֲכַסֵּךְ מֶשִׁי	10[5]	I clothed you also with richly woven work, and shod you with *sealskin*[6], and I wound fine linen about your head, and covered you with silk.
וָאֶעְדֵּךְ עֶדִי וָאֶתְּנָה צְמִידִים עַל־יָדַיִךְ וְרָבִיד עַל־גְּרוֹנֵךְ	11[7]	I decked you also with ornaments, and I put bracelets on your hands, and a chain on your neck.
וָאֶתֵּן נֶזֶם עַל־אַפֵּךְ וַעֲגִילִים עַל־אָזְנָיִךְ וַעֲטֶרֶת תִּפְאֶרֶת בְּרֹאשֵׁךְ	12[8]	And I put a ring on your nose, and earrings in your ears, and a beautiful crown on your head.
וַתַּעְדִּי זָהָב וָכֶסֶף וּמַלְבּוּשֵׁךְ "שֵׁשׁי" שֵׁשִׁי וָמֶשִׁי וְרִקְמָה סֹלֶת וּדְבַשׁ וָשֶׁמֶן "אָכָלְתִּי" אָכָלְתְּ וַתִּיפִי בִּמְאֹד מְאֹד וַתִּצְלְחִי לִמְלוּכָה	13[9]	Thus were you decked with gold and silver; and your raiment was of fine linen, and silk, and richly woven work; you ate fine flour, and honey, and oil; and you became very beautiful, *and you were useful for royal estate*[10].
וַיֵּצֵא לָךְ שֵׁם בַּגּוֹיִם בְּיָפְיֵךְ כִּי כָּלִיל הוּא בַּהֲדָרִי אֲשֶׁר־שַׂמְתִּי עָלַיִךְ נְאֻם אֲדֹנָי יְהוִה	14[11]	And your renown went forth among the nations for your beauty; for it was perfect, through My splendor that I had put on you, says the Lord GOD.
וַתִּבְטְחִי בְיָפְיֵךְ וַתִּזְנִי עַל־שְׁמֵךְ וַתִּשְׁפְּכִי אֶת־תַּזְנוּתַיִךְ עַל־כָּל־עוֹבֵר לוֹ־יֶהִי	15[12]	But you trusted in your beauty and played the harlot because of your renown, and poured out your harlotries on everyone who passed by; *his it was*[13].

---

[1] Ezekiel 16:8 - 1 Samuel 12:22, Deuteronomy 4:31 7:6-7:8, Exodus 19:4-19:8 24:1-24:8 8:13, Exodus.R 23:8 25:8, Ezekiel 16:6 20:5-20:6, Hosea 2:18-2:22 11:1, Isaiah 41:8-41:9 19:4 63:7-63:9, Jeremiah 2:2-2:3 7:4 7:33, Leviticus.R 6:5, Malachi 1:2, Mekilta de R'Ishmael Pisha 5:4, Romans 5:8 9:10-9:13, Ruth 3:9, Song of Songs.R 4:26

[2] LXX *resting*

[3] LXX *wings*

[4] Ezekiel 16:9 - 1 Corinthians 6:11 10:2, 1 John 2:20 2:27 5:8, 2 Corinthians 1:21, Ecclesiastes.R 11:1, Ezekiel 16:4 12:25, Genesis.R 48:10, Hebrews 9:10-9:14, Isaiah 4:4, John 13:8-13:10, Midrash Tanchuma Tetzaveh 1, Numbers.R 14:2 17:1, Pesikta de R'Kahana 11.8, Pesikta Rabbati 33:10 47:2, Psalms 23:5 51:8, Revelation 1:5-1:6, Ruth 3:3
Ezekiel 16:9-10 - Exodus.R 5:9 20:11 23:8 25:5 25:6, Midrash Tanchuma Shelach 14

[5] Ezekiel 16:10 - 11, 1 Peter 3:3-3:4, b.Yevamot [Rashi] 101a, b.Yevamot 102b, Exodus 1:5 2:14 2:36 4:5 39:27-39:28, Ezekiel 16:7 16:13 16:18 2:16 3:7 3:16, Genesis 17:42, Isaiah 13:3 13:10, Jastrow 104b 1148a 1636a, Lamentations.R 1:1, Luke 15:22, Midrash Psalms 23:4 103:8, Midrash Tanchuma Tetzaveh 1, Pesikta de R'Kahana 11.8 12.11, Pesikta Rabbati 33:10 47:2, Proverbs 7:22, Psalms 45:14-45:15, Revelation 7:9-7:14 18:12 19:8 21:2, Song of Songs.R 4:24
Ezekiel 16:10-12 - Song of Songs.R 4:26
Ezekiel 16:10-13 - Midrash Tanchuma Terumah 5

[6] Lxx *purple*

[7] Ezekiel 16:11 - Daniel 5:7 5:16 5:29, Esther 2:17, Exodus 8:2 11:22, Ezekiel 23:40 23:42, Genesis 24:22 24:47 24:53 11:4 17:42, Genesis.R 48:17, Hosea 2:13, Isaiah 3:19 3:21 4:5, Jastrow 1045a, Job 18:11, Judges 8:24, Lamentations 5:16, Leviticus 8:9, Midrash Tanchuma Tetzaveh 1, Numbers 7:50, Pesikta Rabbati 10:6 33:10, Proverbs 1:9 4:9 1:12, Revelation 2:10 4:4 4:10, Song of Songs 1:10 4:9
Ezekiel 16:11-12 - Exodus.R 45:2

[8] Ezekiel 16:12 - Exodus.R 21:4, Isaiah 3:21 4:5, Jeremiah 13:18, Mas.Kallah Rabbati 8:9, Midrash Tanchuma Ki Tissa 35, Midrash Tanchuma Tetzaveh 1, Pesikta Rabbati 33:1, y.Shabbat 6:4

[9] Ezekiel 16:13 - 1 Kings 4:21, 1 Samuel 10:1 12:12, 2 Samuel 8:15, Deuteronomy 8:8 32:13-32:14, Ezekiel 16:14-16:15 16:19, Ezra 4:20 5:11, Genesis 17:6, Hosea 2:5, Isaiah 16:12, Jeremiah 13:20, Lamentations 2:15, Mekhilta de R'Shimon bar Yochai Bachodesh 49:2, Psalms 45:14-45:15 48:3 50:2 81:17 3:14, Song of Songs.R 4:26

[10] Missing in LXX

[11] Ezekiel 16:14 - 1 Corinthians 4:7, 1 Kings 10:1-10:13 10:24, 2 Chronicles 2:10-2:11 9:23, b.Sanhedrin 21a, Deuteronomy 4:6-4:8 4:32-4:38, Exodus.R 44:1, Joshua 2:9-2:11 9:6-9:9, Lamentations 2:15, Midrash Tanchuma Shoftim 1, Pesikta de R'Kahana 4.4, Pesikta Rabbati 10:6 21:6 28:1, Song of Songs.R 4:26

[12] Ezekiel 16:15 - 1 Kings 15:12 12:28, 2 Kings 17:7 21:3, Deuteronomy 8:15, Exodus 32:6-32:35, Ezekiel 16:25 16:36-16:37 20:8 23:3 23:8 23:11-23:21 3:3 9:13, Hosea 1:2 4:10, Isaiah 1:21 24:1 9:8, Jeremiah 2:20 3:1 7:4, Judges 2:12 3:6 10:6, Matthew 3:9, Micah 3:11, Numbers 25:1-25:2, Psalms 10:35, Revelation 17:5, Zephaniah 3:11

[13] Missing in LXX

וָאֶקַּ֣ח מִבְּגָדַ֗יִךְ וַתַּעֲשִׂי־לָךְ֙ בָּמ֣וֹת טְלֻא֔וֹת וַתִּזְנִ֖י עֲלֵיהֶ֑ם לֹ֥א בָא֖וֹת וְלֹ֥א יִהְיֶֽה׃	16[1]	And you took of your garments, and made high places decked with diverse colors, and played the harlot on them; the like things shall not come, nor shall it be so.
וַתִּקְחִ֞י כְּלֵ֣י תִפְאַרְתֵּ֗ךְ מִזְּהָבִ֤י וּמִכַּסְפִּי֙ אֲשֶׁ֣ר נָתַ֣תִּי לָ֔ךְ וַתַּעֲשִׂי־לָ֖ךְ צַלְמֵ֣י זָכָ֑ר וַתִּזְנִי־בָֽם׃	17[2]	You took your fair jewels of My gold and of My silver, which I gave you, and made images of men, and played the harlot with them;
וַתִּקְחִ֛י אֶת־בִּגְדֵ֥י רִקְמָתֵ֖ךְ וַתְּכַסִּ֑ים וְשַׁמְנִי֙ וּקְטָרְתִּ֔י ״נָתַתְּ״ לִפְנֵיהֶֽם׃	18	and you took your richly woven garments and covered them, and set My oil and My incense before them.
וְלַחְמִי֩ אֲשֶׁר־נָתַ֨תִּי לָ֜ךְ סֹ֣לֶת וָשֶׁ֤מֶן וּדְבַשׁ֙ הֶאֱכַלְתִּ֔יךְ וּנְתַתִּ֧יהוּ לִפְנֵיהֶ֛ם לְרֵ֥יחַ נִיחֹ֖חַ וַיֶּ֑הִי נְאֻ֖ם אֲדֹנָ֥י יְהֹוִֽה׃	19[3]	My bread also that I gave you, fine flour, and oil, and honey, with which I fed you, you set it before them for a sweet savor, and thus it was; says the Lord GOD.
וַתִּקְחִ֞י אֶת־בָּנַ֤יִךְ וְאֶת־בְּנוֹתַ֙יִךְ֙ אֲשֶׁ֣ר יָלַ֣דְתְּ לִ֔י וַתִּזְבָּחִ֥ים לָהֶ֖ם לֶאֱכ֑וֹל הַמְעַ֖ט ״מִתַּזְנֻתֵךְ״ ״מִתַּזְנוּתָֽיִךְ״׃	20[4]	Moreover, you took your sons and your daughters, whom you bore to Me, and these you sacrificed to them to be devoured. Were your harlotries a small matter,
וַֽתִּשְׁחֲטִ֖י אֶת־בָּנָ֑י וַֽתִּתְּנִ֔ים בְּהַעֲבִ֥יר אוֹתָ֖ם לָהֶֽם׃	21[5]	that you have killed My children, and delivered them up, in setting them apart to them?
וְאֵ֤ת כׇּל־תּוֹעֲבֹתַ֙יִךְ֙ וְתַזְנֻתַ֔יִךְ לֹ֥א ״זָכַרְתִּי״ ״זָכַרְתְּ״ אֶת־יְמֵ֣י נְעוּרָ֑יִךְ בִּֽהְיוֹתֵךְ֙ עֵרֹ֣ם וְעֶרְיָ֔ה מִתְבּוֹסֶ֥סֶת בְּדָמֵ֖ךְ הָיִֽית׃	22[6]	And in all your abominations and your harlotries you have not remembered the days of your youth, when you were naked and bare, and were wallowing in your blood.
וַיְהִ֕י אַחֲרֵ֖י כׇּל־רָעָתֵ֑ךְ א֣וֹי א֣וֹי לָ֔ךְ נְאֻ֖ם אֲדֹנָ֥י יְהֹוִֽה׃	23[7]	And it came to pass after all your wickedness, *woe, woe to you*[8]! says the Lord GOD
וַתִּבְנִי־לָ֖ךְ גָּ֑ב וַתַּעֲשִׂי־לָ֥ךְ רָמָ֖ה בְּכׇל־רְחֽוֹב׃	24[9]	that you have built an eminent place, and have made a lofty place in every street.
אֶל־כׇּל־רֹ֣אשׁ דֶּ֗רֶךְ בָּנִית֙ רָֽמָתֵ֔ךְ וַתְּתַֽעֲבִי֙ אֶת־יׇפְיֵ֔ךְ וַתְּפַשְּׂקִ֥י אֶת־רַגְלַ֖יִךְ לְכׇל־עוֹבֵ֑ר וַתַּרְבִּ֖י ״אֶת־תַּזְנֻתֵךְ״ ״אֶת־תַּזְנוּתָֽיִךְ״׃	25[10]	You built your lofty place at every intersection, and made your beauty an abomination, and have opened your feet to everyone who passed by, and multiplied your harlotries.
וַתִּזְנִ֧י אֶל־בְּנֵֽי־מִצְרַ֛יִם שְׁכֵנַ֖יִךְ גִּדְלֵ֣י בָשָׂ֑ר וַתַּרְבִּ֥י אֶת־תַּזְנֻתֵ֖ךְ לְהַכְעִיסֵֽנִי׃	26[11]	You also played the harlot with the Egyptians, your neighbors, great of flesh; and multiplied your harlotry, to provoke Me.
וְהִנֵּ֨ה נָטִ֤יתִי יָדִי֙ עָלַ֔יִךְ וָאֶגְרַ֖ע חֻקֵּ֑ךְ וָאֶתְּנֵ֞ךְ בְּנֶ֤פֶשׁ שֹׂנְאוֹתַ֙יִךְ֙ בְּנ֣וֹת פְּלִשְׁתִּ֔ים הַנִּכְלָמ֖וֹת מִדַּרְכֵּ֥ךְ זִמָּֽה׃	27[12]	Behold, therefore I have stretched out My hand over you, and have *diminished your allowance*[13], and delivered you to the will of

---

[1] Ezekiel 16:16 - 2 Chronicles 4:24, 2 Kings 23:7, Ezekiel 7:20, Hosea 2:8

[2] Ezekiel 16:17 - Exodus 32:1-4, Ezekiel 7:19-20 16:11 23:14-21, Hosea 2:13 10:1, Isaiah 44:19-20 57:7-8, Jeremiah 2:27-28 3:9

[3] Ezekiel 16:19 - Deuteronomy 32:14-32:17, Exodus.R 5:9 25:3 41:1, Ezekiel 16:13, Genesis 8:21, Hosea 2:8-2:15, Midrash Psalms 3:3, Midrash Tanchuma Ki Tissa 14, Midrash Tanchuma Reeh 16, Midrash Tanchuma Shelach 14, Midrash Tanchuma Shemot 25, Numbers.R 17:1, Pesikta de R'Kahana 10.8 12.25, z.Vaetchanan 269b

[4] Ezekiel 16:20 - 2 Chronicles 9:6, 2 Kings 16:3, Deuteronomy 29:10-11, Exodus 13:2 13:12, Ezekiel 8:17 16:21 20:26 20:31 23:4 23:37 23:39, Genesis 17:7, Isaiah 9:5, Jeremiah 2:34-35 7:31 8:35, Lamentations.R 1:36, Micah 6:7, Pesikta Rabbati 29/30:1, Psalms 106:37-38, Testament of Moses 2:8

[5] Ezekiel 16:21 - 2 Kings 17:17 21:6 23:10, Deuteronomy 18:10, Jeremiah 19:5, Leviticus 18:21 20:1-20:5, Psalms 10:37

[6] Ezekiel 16:22 - b.Arachin [Rashi] 19a, Ezekiel 16:3-16:7 16:43 16:60-16:63, Hosea 2:3 11:1, Jastrow 1643b, Jeremiah 2:2

[7] Ezekiel 16:23 - Ezekiel 2:10 13:3 13:18 24:6, Jeremiah 13:27, Matthew 11:21 23:13-23:29, Revelation 8:13 12:12, Zephaniah 3:1

[8] Missing in LXX

[9] Ezekiel 16:24 - 2 Chronicles 33:3-33:7, 2 Kings 21:3-21:7 23:5-23:7 23:11-23:12, Ezekiel 16:31 16:39 20:28-20:29, Isaiah 9:5 9:7, Jeremiah 2:20 3:2 17:3, Lamentations.R Petichata D'Chakimei:22, Leviticus 2:30, Psalms 78:58

[10] Ezekiel 16:25 - b.Ketubot 39b, Ezekiel 16:15 16:31 23:9-23:10 23:32, Genesis 14:14 14:21, Isaiah 3:9, Jastrow 1167a 1201b, Jeremiah 2:23-2:24 3:2 6:15, Lamentations.R Petichata D'Chakimei:22, Leviticus.R 33:6, Proverbs 9:14-9:15, Revelation 17:1-17:5 17:12-17:13 17:16, Sifre Devarim {Haazinu Hashamayim} 306, Sifre Devarim Nitzavim 306

[11] Ezekiel 16:26 - Deuteronomy 29:15-29:16, Exodus 8:4, Ezekiel 8:10 8:14 8:17 20:7-20:8 23:3 23:8 23:19-23:21, Isaiah 6:21, Jeremiah 7:18-7:19, Joshua 24:14, Leviticus.R 25:7

[12] Ezekiel 16:27 - 2 Chronicles 28:18-28:19, 2 Kings 24:2, Deuteronomy 28:48-28:57, Ezekiel 5:6-5:7 14:9 16:37 16:47 16:57 23:22 23:25 23:28-23:29 23:46-23:47, Hosea 2:9-2:14, Isaiah 3:1 5:25 9:13 9:18, Jeremiah 10:21, Psalms 10:41, Revelation 17:16

[13] LXX *abolish your statutes*

those who hate you, the daughters of the Philistines, who are ashamed of your lewd way.

28[1] וַתִּזְנִי֙ אֶל־בְּנֵ֣י אַשּׁ֔וּר מִבִּלְתִּ֖י שָׂבְעָתֵ֑ךְ וַתִּזְנִ֕ים וְגַ֖ם לֹ֥א שָׂבָֽעַתְּ

You have played the harlot also with the Assyrians, without having enough; yes, you have played the harlot with them, and yet you were not satisfied.

29[2] וַתַּרְבִּ֧י אֶת־תַּזְנוּתֵ֛ךְ אֶל־אֶ֥רֶץ כְּנַ֖עַן כַּשְׂדִּ֑ימָה וְגַם־בְּזֹ֖את לֹ֥א שָׂבָֽעַתְּ

You have moreover multiplied your *harlotry with the land of traffic, with Chaldea[3]*; and yet you did not have enough.

30[4] מָ֤ה אֲמֻלָה֙ לִבָּתֵ֔ךְ נְאֻ֖ם אֲדֹנָ֣י יְהוִ֑ה בַּעֲשׂוֹתֵךְ֙ אֶת־כָּל־אֵ֔לֶּה מַעֲשֵׂ֥ה אִשָּֽׁה־זוֹנָ֖ה שַׁלָּֽטֶת

How weak is your heart, says the Lord GOD, seeing you do all these things, the work of a wanton harlot[5];

31[6] בִּבְנוֹתַ֤יִךְ גַּבֵּךְ֙ בְּרֹ֣אשׁ כָּל־דֶּ֔רֶךְ וְרָמָתֵ֥ךְ 'עָשִׂיתִי' "עָשִׂית" בְּכָל־רְח֑וֹב 'וְלֹא־הָיִיתִי' "וְלֹא־הָיִית" כַּזּוֹנָ֖ה לְקַלֵּ֥ס אֶתְנָֽן

in that you build your eminent place in the head of every way, and make your lofty place in every street; and have not been as a harlot who enhances her hire.

32[7] הָאִשָּׁ֖ה הַמְּנָאָ֑פֶת תַּ֣חַת אִישָׁ֔הּ תִּקַּ֖ח אֶת־זָרִֽים

You, the wife who commits adultery, who take strangers instead of your husband[8]

33[9] לְכָל־זֹנ֖וֹת יִתְּנוּ־נֵ֑דֶה וְאַ֨תְּ נָתַ֤תְּ אֶת־נְדָנַ֙יִךְ֙ לְכָל־מְאַהֲבַ֔יִךְ וַתִּשְׁחֳדִ֣י אוֹתָ֗ם לָב֥וֹא אֵלַ֛יִךְ מִסָּבִ֖יב בְּתַזְנוּתָֽיִךְ

to all harlots gifts are given; but you have given your gifts to all your lovers, and have bribed them to come to you from every side in your harlotries.

34[10] וַיְהִי־בָ֨ךְ הֵ֤פֶךְ מִן־הַנָּשִׁים֙ בְּתַזְנוּתַ֔יִךְ וְאַחֲרַ֖יִךְ לֹ֣א זוּנָּ֑ה וּבְתִתֵּ֣ךְ אֶתְנָ֗ן וְאֶתְנַ֛ן לֹ֥א נִתַּן־לָ֖ךְ וַתְּהִ֥י לְהֶֽפֶךְ

And the contrary is in you from other women, in that you solicited harlotry, and were not solicited; and in that you gave hire, and no hire is given to you, thus you are contrary.

35[11] לָכֵ֣ן זוֹנָ֔ה שִׁמְעִ֖י דְּבַר־יְהוָֽה

Why, O harlot, hear the word of the LORD!

36[12] כֹּה־אָמַ֣ר אֲדֹנָ֣י יְהֹוִ֗ה יַ֣עַן הִשָּׁפֵ֤ךְ נְחֻשְׁתֵּךְ֙ וַתִּגָּלֶ֣ה עֶרְוָתֵ֔ךְ בְּתַזְנוּתַ֖יִךְ עַל־מְאַהֲבָ֑יִךְ וְעַל֙ כָּל־גִּלּוּלֵ֣י תוֹעֲבוֹתַ֔יִךְ וְכִדְמֵ֣י בָנַ֔יִךְ אֲשֶׁ֥ר נָתַ֖תְּ לָהֶֽם

Thus says the Lord GOD: Because your filthiness was poured out, and your nakedness uncovered through your harlotries with your lovers; and because of all the idols of your abominations, and for the blood of your children, that you gave to them;

37[13] לָ֠כֵן הִנְנִ֨י מְקַבֵּ֜ץ אֶת־כָּל־מְאַהֲבַ֗יִךְ אֲשֶׁ֣ר עָרַ֣בְתְּ עֲלֵיהֶ֔ם וְאֵת֙ כָּל־אֲשֶׁ֣ר אָהַ֔בְתְּ עַ֖ל כָּל־אֲשֶׁ֣ר שָׂנֵ֑את וְקִבַּצְתִּ֨י אֹתָ֤ם עָלַ֙יִךְ֙ מִסָּבִ֔יב וְגִלֵּיתִ֥י עֶרְוָתֵ֖ךְ אֲלֵהֶ֑ם וְרָא֖וּ אֶת־כָּל־עֶרְוָתֵֽךְ

therefore behold, I will gather all your lovers, to whom you have been pleasant, and all those who you have loved, with all those whom you have hated; I will gather them against you from every side, and will uncover your nakedness to them, so they may see all your nakedness.

---

[1] Ezekiel 16:28 - 2 Chronicles 4:16 28:20-28:21 4:23, 2 Kings 16:7 16:10-16:18 21:11, Ezekiel 23:5-23:9 23:12-23:21, Hosea 10:6, Jeremiah 2:18 2:36, Judges 10:6

[2] Ezekiel 16:29 - 2 Kings 21:9, Ezekiel 13:14-13:23 23:14-23:21, Judges 2:12-2:19

[3] LXX *covenants with the land of the Chaldeans*

[4] Ezekiel 16:30 - Isaiah 1:3 3:9, Jeremiah 2:12-2:13 3:3 4:22, Judges 16:15-16:16, Proverbs 7:11-7:13 7:21 9:13, Revelation 17:1-17:6

[5] LXX *Why should I make a covenant with your daughter, says the LORD, while you do all these things, the works of a harlot? and you have gone a-whoring in a threefold degree with your daughters*

[6] Ezekiel 16:31 - Ezekiel 16:24-25 16:33-34 16:39, Hosea 12:13, Isaiah 4:3, Pesikta de R'Kahana 13.4 Ezekiel 16:31 33 - 3QEzek

[7] Ezekiel 16:32 - 2 Corinthians 11:2-3, Ezekiel 16:8 23:37 23:45, Hosea 2:2 3:1, Jeremiah 2:25 2:28 3:1 3:8-9 3:20, Mekilta de R'Ishmael Bahodesh 8:81, Midrash Tanchuma Naso 7, Numbers.R 9:34 9:49

[8] LXX *An adulteress resembles you, taking rewards of her husband*

[9] Ezekiel 16:33 - Deuteronomy 23:19-23:19, Ezekiel 16:41, Genesis 38:16-38:18, Hosea 2:12 8:9-8:10, Isaiah 6:3 30:6-30:7 9:9, Joel 4:3, Luke 15:30, Micah 1:7, t.Temurah 4:5

[10] Ezekiel 16:34 - b.Avodah Zara 14a, b.Temurah 29b, t.Temurah 4:8

[11] Ezekiel 16:35 - 1 Kings 22:19, Amos 7:16, Exodus.R 50:3, Ezekiel 13:2 21:3 10:7, Hosea 2:5 4:1, Isaiah 1:10 1:21 23:15-16 4:14, Jeremiah 3:1 3:6-3:8, John 4:10 4:18, Nahum 3:4, Revelation 17:5

[12] Ezekiel 16:36 - b.Niddah 41b, b.Shabbat [Rashi] 41a, Ezekiel 16:15-16:22 22:15 23:8 23:10 23:18 23:29 24:13 12:25, Genesis 3:7 3:10-11, Jeremiah 2:34 13:22-26 19:5, Lamentations 1:9, Psalms 139:11-12, Revelation 3:18, z.Vaetchanan 269b, Zephaniah 3:1

[13] Ezekiel 16:37 - Ezekiel 23:9-23:10 23:22-23:30, Hosea 2:3 2:10 8:10, Jeremiah 4:30 13:22 13:26 22:20, Lamentations 1:8 1:19, Nahum 3:5-3:6, Revelation 17:16

וּשְׁפַטְתִּיךְ מִשְׁפְּטֵי נֹאֲפוֹת וְשֹׁפְכֹת דָּם וּנְתַתִּיךְ דַּם חֵמָה וְקִנְאָה	38[1]	And I will judge you, as women who break wedlock and shed blood are judged; and I will bring on you the blood of fury and jealousy.
וְנָתַתִּי אוֹתָךְ בְּיָדָם וְהָרְסוּ גַבֵּךְ וְנִתְּצוּ רָמֹתַיִךְ וְהִפְשִׁיטוּ אוֹתָךְ בְּגָדַיִךְ וְלָקְחוּ כְּלֵי תִפְאַרְתֵּךְ וְהִנִּיחוּךְ עֵירֹם וְעֶרְיָה	39[2]	I will give you into their hand, and they shall throw down your eminent place, and break down your lofty places; and they shall strip you of your clothes, and take your fair jewels; and they shall leave you naked and bare.
וְהֶעֱלוּ עָלַיִךְ קָהָל וְרָגְמוּ אוֹתָךְ בָּאָבֶן וּבִתְּקוּךְ בְּחַרְבוֹתָם	40[3]	They shall also bring up an assembly against you, and they shall stone you with stones, and thrust you through with their swords.
וְשָׂרְפוּ בָתַּיִךְ בָּאֵשׁ וְעָשׂוּ בָךְ שְׁפָטִים לְעֵינֵי נָשִׁים רַבּוֹת וְהִשְׁבַּתִּיךְ מִזּוֹנָה וְגַם אֶתְנַן לֹא תִתְּנִי עוֹד	41[4]	And they shall burn your houses with fire, and execute judgments on you in the sight of many women; and I will cause you to cease from playing the harlot, and *you shall also give no hire any longer*[5].
וַהֲנִחֹתִי חֲמָתִי בָּךְ וְסָרָה קִנְאָתִי מִמֵּךְ וְשָׁקַטְתִּי וְלֹא אֶכְעַס עוֹד	42[6]	So will I satisfy My fury on you, and My jealousy shall depart from you, and I will be quiet, and will be angry no longer.
יַעַן אֲשֶׁר לֹא זָכַרְתְּי לֹא זָכַרְתְּ אֶת יְמֵי נְעוּרַיִךְ וַתִּרְגְּזִי לִי בְּכָל אֵלֶּה וְגַם אֲנִי הֵא דַרְכֵּךְ בְּרֹאשׁ נָתַתִּי נְאֻם אֲדֹנָי יְהוִה וְלֹא עָשִׂיתִי עָשִׂית אֶת הַזִּמָּה עַל כָּל תּוֹעֲבֹתָיִךְ	43[7]	Because you have not remembered the days of your youth, but have grieved Me in all these things; lo, therefore, I will bring your way on your head, says the Lord GOD; or have you not committed this lewdness above all your abominations?
הִנֵּה כָּל הַמֹּשֵׁל עָלַיִךְ יִמְשֹׁל לֵאמֹר כְּאִמָּה בִּתָּהּ	44[8]	*Behold, everyone who uses proverbs shall use this proverb against you*[9], saying: As the mother, so her daughter.
בַּת אִמֵּךְ אַתְּ גֹּעֶלֶת אִישָׁהּ וּבָנֶיהָ וַאֲחוֹת אֲחוֹתֵךְ אַתְּ אֲשֶׁר גָּעֲלוּ אַנְשֵׁיהֶן וּבְנֵיהֶן אִמְּכֶן חִתִּית וַאֲבִיכֶן אֱמֹרִי	45[10]	You are your mother's daughter, who hates her husband and her children; and you are the sister of your sisters, who hates their husbands and their children; your mother was a Hittite, and your father an Amorite.
וַאֲחוֹתֵךְ הַגְּדוֹלָה שֹׁמְרוֹן הִיא וּבְנוֹתֶיהָ הַיּוֹשֶׁבֶת עַל שְׂמֹאולֵךְ וַאֲחוֹתֵךְ הַקְּטַנָּה מִמֵּךְ הַיּוֹשֶׁבֶת מִימִינֵךְ סְדֹם וּבְנוֹתֶיהָ	46[11]	And your elder sister is Samaria, who dwells at your left hand, she and her daughters; and your younger sister, who dwells at your right hand, is Sodom and her daughters.
וְלֹא בְדַרְכֵיהֶן הָלַכְתְּ וּבְתוֹעֲבוֹתֵיהֶן עָשִׂיתִי עָשִׂית כִּמְעַט קָט וַתַּשְׁחִתִי מֵהֵן בְּכָל דְּרָכָיִךְ	47[12]	Yet you have not walked in their ways, nor ran after their abominations; but in a short time you dealt more corruptly than they in all your ways.

[1] Ezekiel 16:38 - Deuteronomy 22:22-22:24, Exodus 21:12, Ezekiel 16:20-16:21 16:36 16:40 23:25 23:45-23:47, Genesis 9:6 14:11 14:24, Jeremiah 18:21, John 8:3-8:5, Leviticus 20:10, Matthew 1:18-1:19, Nahum 1:2, Numbers 11:31, Psalms 79:3-79:5, Psalms of Solomon 2:24, Revelation 16:6, Zephaniah 1:17

[2] Ezekiel 16:39 - Ezekiel 7:22-7:24 16:10-16:20 16:24-16:25 16:31 23:26 23:29, Hosea 2:3 2:9-2:15, Isaiah 3:16-3:24 3:9

[3] Ezekiel 16:40 - Ezekiel 23:10 23:47 24:21, Habakkuk 1:6-1:10, Jeremiah 1:9, John 8:5-8:7, Jubilees 20:4

[4] Ezekiel 16:41 - 1 Timothy 5:20, 2 Kings 1:9, Deuteronomy 13:12 13:17 22:21 22:24, Ezekiel 5:8 23:10 23:27 23:48 13:23, Hosea 2:6-2:19, Isaiah 1:25-1:26 2:18 3:9, Jeremiah 15:8 4:13, Job 10:26, Micah 3:12 5:11-5:15, Psalms of Solomon 2:24, Zechariah 13:2

[5] LXX *I will no longer give you rewards*

[6] Ezekiel 16:42 - 2 Samuel 21:14, Ezekiel 5:13 21:22 15:29, Isaiah 1:24 40:1-40:2 54:9-54:10, Zechariah 6:8

[7] Ezekiel 16:43 - Acts 7:51, Amos 2:13, Deuteronomy 8:21, Ephesians 4:30, Ezekiel 6:9 7:3-4 7:8-9 9:10 11:21 16:22 22:31, Isaiah 15:10, Jeremiah 2:32, Psalms 78:40 78:42 95:10 10:13, Romans 2:8-9

[8] Ezekiel 16:44 - 1 Kings 21:16, 1 Samuel 24:13, 2 Kings 17:11 17:15 21:9, Ezekiel 12:22 16:3 16:45 18:2-18:3, Ezra 9:1, Genesis.R 80:1, Psalms 106:35-106:38, y.Sanhedrin 2:6

Ezekiel 16:44-45 - Midrash Tanchuma Vayishlach 7

[9] LXX *These are all the things they have spoken against you in a proverb*

[10] Ezekiel 16:45 - Deuteronomy 5:9 12:31, Ezekiel 16:8 16:15 16:20-21 23:2 23:37-39, Isaiah 1:4, Romans 1:30-31, Zechariah 11:8

[11] Ezekiel 16:46 - 2 Peter 2:6, Deuteronomy 5:22 8:32, Ezekiel 16:27 16:48-16:49 16:51 16:53-16:56 16:61 23:4 23:11 23:31-23:33 2:6, Genesis 13:10-13:13 14:8 18:20-18:33 19:24-19:25 19:29, Hosea 11:8, Isaiah 1:9-1:10, Jeremiah 3:8-3:11 23:14, Josephus Antiquities 13.9.1 m.Maaser Sheni 5:2 m.Shekalim 1:5, Jude 1:7, Lamentations 4:6, Luke 17:28-17:30, Micah 5:5, Midrash Tanchuma Vayera 7, Revelation 11:8, Song of Songs.R 8:12

[12] Ezekiel 16:47 - 1 Corinthians 5:1, 1 Kings 16:31, 2 Kings 21:9 21:16, Ezekiel 5:6-5:7 8:17 16:48 16:51, John 15:21-15:22

חַי־אָ֗נִי נְאֻם֮ אֲדֹנָ֣י יְהוִה֒ אִם־עָֽשְׂתָה֙ סְדֹ֣ם אֲחוֹתֵ֔ךְ הִ֖יא וּבְנוֹתֶ֑יהָ כַּאֲשֶׁ֥ר עָשִׂ֖ית אַ֥תְּ וּבְנוֹתָֽיִךְ	48[1] As I live, says the Lord GOD, Sodom your sister has not done, she nor her daughters, as you and your daughters have done.
הִנֵּה־זֶ֣ה הָיָ֔ה עֲוֺ֖ן סְדֹ֣ם אֲחוֹתֵ֑ךְ גָּא֨וֹן שִׂבְעַת־לֶ֜חֶם וְשַׁלְוַ֣ת הַשְׁקֵ֗ט הָ֤יָה לָהּ֙ וְלִבְנוֹתֶ֔יהָ וְיַד־עָנִ֥י וְאֶבְי֖וֹן לֹ֥א הֶחֱזִֽיקָה	49[2] Behold, this was the iniquity of your sister Sodom: pride, fullness of bread, and careless ease was in her and in her daughters; nor did she strengthen the hand of the poor and needy.
וַֽתִּגְבְּהֶ֔ינָה וַתַּעֲשֶׂ֥ינָה תוֹעֵבָ֖ה לְפָנָ֑י וָאָסִ֥יר אֶתְהֶ֖ן כַּאֲשֶׁ֥ר רָאִֽיתִי	50[3] And they were haughty, and committed abominations before Me; therefore I removed them when I saw it.
וְשֹׁ֣מְר֔וֹן כַּחֲצִ֥י חַטֹּאתַ֖יִךְ לֹ֣א חָטָ֑אָה וַתַּרְבִּ֤י אֶת־תּוֹעֲבוֹתַ֙יִךְ֙ מֵהֵ֔נָּה וַתְּצַדְּקִ֖י 'אֶת־אֲחוֹתֵךְ' "אֶת־אֲחוֹתַיִךְ" בְּכָל־תּוֹעֲבוֹתַ֖יִךְ אֲשֶׁ֥ר 'עָשִׂיתי' "עָשִׂית"	51[4] Nor has Samaria committed half of your sins; but you have multiplied your abominations more than they, and have justified your sisters by all the abominations you have done.
גַּם־אַ֣תְּ ׀ שְׂאִ֣י כְלִמָּתֵ֗ךְ אֲשֶׁ֤ר פִּלַּלְתְּ֙ לַֽאֲחוֹתֵ֔ךְ בְּחַטֹּאתַ֛יִךְ אֲשֶׁר־הִתְעַ֥בְתְּ מֵהֵ֖ן תִּצְדַּ֣קְנָה מִמֵּ֑ךְ וְגַם־אַ֣תְּ בּ֔וֹשִׁי וּשְׂאִ֣י כְלִמָּתֵ֔ךְ בְּצַדֶּקְתֵּ֖ךְ אַחְיוֹתֵֽךְ	52[5] You also, bear your own shame, in that you have given judgment for your sisters; through the sins that you have committed are more abominable than they, they are more righteous than you; yes, be confused, and bear your shame, in that you have justified your sisters.
וְשַׁבְתִּי֙ אֶת־שְׁבִ֣יתְהֶ֔ן 'אֶת־שְׁבִית' "אֶת־שְׁבוּת" סְדֹ֖ם וּבְנוֹתֶ֑יהָ 'וְאֶת־שְׁבִית' "וְאֶת־שְׁבוּת" שֹׁמְר֖וֹן וּבְנוֹתֶ֑יהָ 'וּשְׁבִית' "וּשְׁבוּת" שְׁבִיתַ֖יִךְ בְּתוֹכָֽהְנָה	53[6] And I will turn their captivity, the captivity of Sodom and her daughters, and the captivity of Samaria and her daughters, and the captivity of your captives in their midst;
לְמַ֙עַן֙ תִּשְׂאִ֣י כְלִמָּתֵ֔ךְ וְנִכְלַ֕מְתְּ מִכֹּ֖ל אֲשֶׁ֣ר עָשִׂ֑ית בְּנַחֲמֵ֖ךְ אֹתָֽן	54[7] so you may bear your own shame, and may be ashamed because of all you have done, *in that you are a comfort to them*[8].
וַאֲחוֹתַ֗יִךְ סְדֹ֤ם וּבְנוֹתֶ֙יהָ֙ תָּשֹׁ֣בְןָ לְקַדְמָתָ֔ן וְשֹֽׁמְר֥וֹן וּבְנוֹתֶ֖יהָ תָּשֹׁ֣בְןָ לְקַדְמָתָ֑ן וְאַ֣תְּ וּבְנוֹתַ֔יִךְ תְּשֻׁבֶ֖ינָה לְקַדְמַתְכֶֽן	55[9] And your sisters, Sodom and her daughters, shall return to their former estate, and Samaria and her daughters shall return to their former estate, and you and your daughters shall return to your former estate.
וְל֤וֹא הָֽיְתָה֙ סְדֹ֣ם אֲחוֹתֵ֔ךְ לִשְׁמוּעָ֖ה בְּפִ֑יךְ בְּי֖וֹם גְּאוֹנָֽיִךְ	56[10] For your sister Sodom was not mentioned by your mouth in the day of your pride;

[1] Ezekiel 16:48 - Acts 7:52, Luke 10:12, Mark 6:11, Matthew 10:15 11:23-11:24, Mekhilta de R'Shimon bar Yochai Shirata 28:1, Numbers.R 9:24, Sifre Devarim {Haazinu Hashamayim} 318
Ezekiel 16:48-49 - Sifre Devarim Nitzavim 318
Ezekiel 16:48-50 - Sifre Devarim {Ekev} 43, t.Sotah 3:12
[2] Ezekiel 16:49 - 1 Peter 5:5, Amos 5:11-12 6:3-6 8:4-6, b.Sanhedrin 42a, Daniel 4:27 4:34 5:23, Deuteronomy 8:15, Ein Yaakov Sanhedrin 104b, Exodus.R 30:19, Ezekiel 18:7 18:12 18:16 4:2 4:9 4:17 5:3, Gates of Repentance 3.015, Genesis 13:10 18:20 19:9, Isaiah 3:9 3:14-15 16:6 22:13-14, Leviticus.R 4:1, Luke 12:16-20 16:19-21 17:28 21:34, Mekilta de R'Ishmael Shirata 2:45, Micah 3:2-4, Numbers.R 9:24, Obadiah 1:3, Pirkei de R'Eliezer 25, Proverbs 16:5 16:18 18:12 21:4 21:13, Psalms 18:6
Ezekiel 16:49-50 - Midrash Tanchuma Beshallach 12
[3] Ezekiel 16:50 - 2 Kings 23:7, 2 Peter 2:6, Amos 4:11, Deuteronomy 23:19 5:22, Genesis 13:13 18:20 19:5 19:24, Isaiah 13:19, Jeremiah 20:16 1:18 2:40, Job 18:15, Jude 1:7, Lamentations 4:6, Leviticus 18:22, Mekilta de R'Ishmael Shirata 2:43, Proverbs 16:18 18:12, Revelation 18:9, Romans 1:26-27, Zephaniah 2:9
[4] Ezekiel 16:51 - Jeremiah 3:8-3:11, Luke 12:47-12:48, Matthew 12:41-12:42, Romans 3:9-3:20
[5] Ezekiel 16:52 - 1 Kings 2:32, 1 Samuel 24:17, Ezekiel 16:54 16:56 16:63 36:6-36:7 12:15 36:31-36:32 15:26 20:13, Genesis 14:26, Hosea 10:6, Jeremiah 23:40 7:20 3:51, Luke 6:37, Matthew 7:1-7:5, Romans 1:32-2:1 2:10 2:26-2:27 6:21
[6] Ezekiel 16:53 - Ezekiel 16:60-16:61 5:14 15:25, Isaiah 1:9 19:24-19:25, Jeremiah 12:16 20:16 7:24 24:47 1:6 1:39, Job 18:10, Joel 4:1, Psalms 14:7 85:2 6:1, Romans 11:23-31, Saadia Opinions 8:8
[7] Ezekiel 16:54 - Ezekiel 14:22-14:23 16:52 16:53 36:31-36:32, Jeremiah 2:26
[8] LXX *in provoking me to anger*
[9] Ezekiel 16:55 - Exodus.R 15:21, Ezekiel 16:53 12:11, Malachi 3:4, Saadia Opinions 8:8
[10] Ezekiel 16:56 - Isaiah 17:5, Luke 15:28-15:30 18:11, Zephaniah 3:11

בְּטֶ֤רֶם תִּגָּלֶה֙ רָעָתֵ֔ךְ כְּמ֣וֹ עֵ֗ת חֶרְפַּ֛ת בְּנוֹת־אֲרָ֖ם וְכָל־סְבִיבוֹתֶ֛יהָ בְּנ֥וֹת פְּלִשְׁתִּ֖ים הַשָּׁאט֣וֹת אוֹתָ֑ךְ מִסָּבִֽיב	57[1]	before your wickedness was uncovered, as at the time of the taunt of the daughters of *Aram*[2], and of all who are around her, the daughters of the Philistines, who disdain you.
אֶת־זִמָּתֵ֥ךְ וְאֶת־תּוֹעֲבוֹתַ֖יִךְ אַ֣תְּ נְשָׂאתִ֑ים נְאֻ֖ם יְהוָֽה	58[3]	You have borne your lewdness and your abominations, says the LORD.
כִּ֣י כֹ֤ה אָמַר֙ אֲדֹנָ֣י יְהוִ֔ה "וְעָשִׂית֙" "וְעָשִׂ֙יתִי֙" אוֹתָ֔ךְ כַּאֲשֶׁ֖ר עָשִׂ֑ית אֲשֶׁר־בָּזִ֥ית אָלָ֖ה לְהָפֵ֥ר בְּרִֽית	59[4]	For thus says the Lord GOD: I will deal with you as you have done, who have despised the oath in breaking the covenant.
וְזָכַרְתִּ֥י אֲנִ֛י אֶת־בְּרִיתִ֥י אוֹתָ֖ךְ בִּימֵ֣י נְעוּרָ֑יִךְ וַהֲקִמוֹתִ֥י לָ֖ךְ בְּרִ֥ית עוֹלָֽם	60[5]	Nevertheless, I will remember My covenant with you in the days of your youth, and I will establish with you an everlasting covenant.
וְזָכַ֣רְתְּ אֶת־דְּרָכַ֗יִךְ וְנִכְלַמְתְּ֮ בְּקַחְתֵּ֣ךְ אֶת־אֲחוֹתַ֙יִךְ֙ הַגְּדֹל֣וֹת מִמֵּ֔ךְ אֶל־הַקְּטַנּ֖וֹת מִמֵּ֑ךְ וְנָתַתִּ֨י אֶתְהֶ֥ן לָ֛ךְ לְבָנ֖וֹת וְלֹ֥א מִבְּרִיתֵֽךְ	61[6]	Then you shall remember your ways, and be ashamed, when you shall receive your sisters, your elder sisters and your younger; and I will give them to you for daughters, but not because of your covenant.
וַהֲקִימוֹתִ֥י אֲנִ֛י אֶת־בְּרִיתִ֖י אִתָּ֑ךְ וְיָדַ֖עַתְּ כִּֽי־אֲנִ֥י יְהוָֽה	62[7]	And I will establish My covenant with you, and you shall know that I am the LORD;
לְמַ֣עַן תִּזְכְּרִי֮ וָבֹ֒שְׁתְּ֒ וְלֹ֤א יִֽהְיֶה־לָּךְ֙ ע֔וֹד פִּתְח֣וֹן פֶּ֔ה מִפְּנֵ֖י כְּלִמָּתֵ֑ךְ בְּכַפְּרִי־לָ֙ךְ֙ לְכָל־אֲשֶׁ֣ר עָשִׂ֔ית נְאֻ֖ם אֲדֹנָ֥י יְהוִֽה	63[8]	so you may remember, and be confounded, and never open your mouth any longer, because of your shame; when I have forgiven you all that you have done, says the Lord GOD.'

Ezekiel – Chapter 17

וַיְהִ֥י דְבַר־יְהוָ֖ה אֵלַ֥י לֵאמֹֽר	1	And the word of the LORD came to me, saying:
בֶּן־אָדָ֕ם ח֥וּד חִידָ֖ה וּמְשֹׁ֣ל מָשָׁ֑ל אֶל־בֵּ֖ית יִשְׂרָאֵֽל	2[9]	'Son of man, proclaim a riddle, and speak a mashal to the house of Israel,
וְאָמַרְתָּ֞ כֹּה־אָמַ֣ר ׀ אֲדֹנָ֣י יְהוִ֗ה הַנֶּ֤שֶׁר הַגָּדוֹל֙ גְּד֤וֹל הַכְּנָפַ֙יִם֙ אֶ֣רֶךְ הָאֵ֔בֶר מָלֵא֙ הַנּוֹצָ֔ה אֲשֶׁר־ל֖וֹ הָרִקְמָ֑ה בָּ֚א אֶל־הַלְּבָנ֔וֹן וַיִּקַּ֖ח אֶת־צַמֶּ֥רֶת הָאָֽרֶז	3[10]	and say: Thus says the Lord GOD: A great eagle with great wings and long pinions, full of feathers, with varied colors, came to Lebanon, and took the top of the cedar;

[1] Ezekiel 16:57 - 1 Corinthians 4:5, 2 Chronicles 28:5-28:6 28:18-28:23, 2 Kings 16:5-16:7, Ezekiel 16:36-16:37 21:29 23:18-23:19, Genesis 10:22-10:23, Hosea 2:10 7:1, Isaiah 7:1 14:28, Jeremiah 9:24, Lamentations 4:22, Numbers 23:7, Psalms 50:21
[2] LXX *Syria*
[3] Ezekiel 16:58 - Ezekiel 23:49, Genesis 4:13, Lamentations 5:7
[4] Ezekiel 16:59 - 2 Chronicles 34:31-34:32, Deuteronomy 29:9-29:14 5:24, Exodus 24:1-24:8, Ezekiel 7:4 7:8-7:9 14:4 17:13-17:16 17:19, Isaiah 3:11 24:5, Jeremiah 2:19 22:9 7:33, Matthew 7:1-7:2, Romans 2:8-2:9, z.Vaetchanan 269b
[5] Ezekiel 16:60 - 2 Samuel 23:5, Ezekiel 16:8 37:26-37:27, Hebrews 8:10 12:24 13:20, Hosea 2:15 2:19-2:22, Isaiah 7:3, Jeremiah 2:2 31:32-35 32:38-41 33:20-26 2:5, Leviticus 2:42 2:45, Luke 1:72, mt.Hilcnot Shofar Sukkah vLulav 3:9, Mussaf Rosh Hashanah, Nehemiah 1:5-11, Psalms 9:8 10:45
[6] Ezekiel 16:61 - Ephesians 2:12-2:14 3:6, Ezekiel 6:9 16:53-16:55 16:63 20:43 36:31-36:32, Galatians 4:26-4:31, Hebrews 8:13, Hosea 1:9-1:11, Isaiah 2:2-2:5 11:9-11:10 49:18-49:23 54:1-54:2 12:4 66:7-66:12, Jastrow 662b, Jeremiah 31:19-31:21 31:32-31:41 50:4-50:5, Job 42:5-42:6, John 15:16, Psalms 23:59, Romans 11:11 15:8-15:9 15:16, Song of Songs 8:8-8:9, Song of Songs.R 1:36
[7] Ezekiel 16:62 - Daniel 9:27, Ezekiel 6:7 16:60 20:37 20:43-20:44 39:22, Hosea 2:18-2:25, Jeremiah 24:7, Joel 4:17
[8] Ezekiel 16:63 - 1 Corinthians 4:7, Daniel 9:7-8, Ein Yaakov Berachot 12b, Ephesians 2:3-2:5, Ezekiel 16:61 36:31-32, Ezra 9:6, Gates of Repentance 1.22 3.2, Job 40:4-5, Lamentations 3:39, Midrash Psalms 31:3, Midrash Tanchuma Vayakhel 10, Psalms 39:10 65:4 79:9, Romans 2:1 3:19 3:27 5:1-2 9:19-20, Titus 3:3-7
[9] Ezekiel 17:2 - 1 Corinthians 13:12, 2 Samuel 12:1-12:4, Avot de R'Natan 34, Ecclesiastes.R 1:31, Ezekiel 21:5 24:3, Guide for the Perplexed 1:Introduction, Hosea 12:12, Judges 9:8-9:15 14:12-14:19, Mark 4:33-4:34, Matthew 13:13-13:14 13:35, Mekhilta de R'Shimon bar Yochai Shirata 33:1, Mekilta de R'Ishmael Shirata 7:8, Midrash Psalms 78:1, Ralbag SOS Pesichta
[10] Ezekiel 17:3 - 2 Chronicles 36:9-10, 2 Kings 24:10-16, Daniel 2:38 4:19 7:4, Deuteronomy 28:49, Ezekiel 17:7 17:12-21, Hosea 8:1, Jeremiah 4:13 22:23-28 24:1 48:40 49:16, Lamentations 4:19, Matthew 24:28, Sifre Devarim Devarim 6, Testament of Naphtali 5:6, z.Vaetchanan 269b
Ezekiel 17:3-9 - 2 Baruch 36:2

אֵת רֹאשׁ יְנִיקוֹתָיו קָטָף וַיְבִיאֵהוּ אֶל־אֶרֶץ כְּנַעַן בְּעִיר רֹכְלִים שָׂמוֹ	4[1]	He cropped off the *topmost of its young twigs, and carried it into a land of traders; he set it in a city of merchants*[2].
וַיִּקַּח מִזֶּרַע הָאָרֶץ וַיִּתְּנֵהוּ בִּשְׂדֵה־זָרַע קַח עַל־מַיִם רַבִּים צַפְצָפָה שָׂמוֹ	5[3]	He also took of the seed of the land, and planted it in a fruitful soil; he placed it beside many waters, he set it *as a slip*[4].
וַיִּצְמַח וַיְהִי לְגֶפֶן סֹרַחַת שִׁפְלַת קוֹמָה לִפְנוֹת דָּלִיּוֹתָיו אֵלָיו וְשָׁרָשָׁיו תַּחְתָּיו יִהְיוּ וַתְּהִי לְגֶפֶן וַתַּעַשׂ בַּדִּים וַתְּשַׁלַּח פֹּארוֹת	6[5]	And it grew, and became a spreading vine of low stature, whose tendrils might turn toward him, and its roots under him; it became a vine, and produced branches, and shot forth sprigs.
וַיְהִי נֶשֶׁר־אֶחָד גָּדוֹל גְּדוֹל כְּנָפַיִם וְרַב־נוֹצָה וְהִנֵּה הַגֶּפֶן הַזֹּאת כָּפְנָה שָׁרָשֶׁיהָ עָלָיו וְדָלִיּוֹתָיו שִׁלְחָה־לּוֹ לְהַשְׁקוֹת אוֹתָהּ מֵעֲרֻגוֹת מַטָּעָהּ	7[6]	There was also another great eagle with great wings and many *feathers*[7]; and, behold, this vine bent *its roots*[8] toward him, and shot forth its branches toward him, from the beds of its plantation, so he might water it.
אֶל־שָׂדֶה טוֹב אֶל־מַיִם רַבִּים הִיא שְׁתוּלָה לַעֲשׂוֹת עָנָף וְלָשֵׂאת פֶּרִי לִהְיוֹת לְגֶפֶן אַדָּרֶת	8[9]	It was planted in a good soil by many waters, so it might bring forth branches, and that it might bear fruit, so it might be a stately vine.
אֱמֹר כֹּה אָמַר אֲדֹנָי יְהֹוִה תִּצְלָח הֲלוֹא אֶת־שָׁרָשֶׁיהָ יְנַתֵּק וְאֶת־פִּרְיָהּ יְקוֹסֵס וְיָבֵשׁ כָּל־טַרְפֵּי צִמְחָהּ תִּיבָשׁ וְלֹא־בִזְרֹעַ גְּדוֹלָה וּבְעַם־רָב לְמַשְׂאוֹת אוֹתָהּ מִשָּׁרָשֶׁיהָ	9[10]	Say: Thus says the Lord GOD: shall it prosper? shall he not pull up its roots, and cut off its fruit, so it withers, Yes, wither in all its sprouting leaves? Nor shall great power or many people be at hand when it is plucked up by the roots.
וְהִנֵּה שְׁתוּלָה הֲתִצְלָח הֲלוֹא כְגַעַת בָּהּ רוּחַ הַקָּדִים תִּיבַשׁ יָבֵשׁ עַל־עֲרֻגֹת צִמְחָהּ תִּיבָשׁ	10[11]	Yes, behold, being planted, shall it prosper? Shall it not wither when the east wind touches it in the beds where it grew it shall wither[12]?'
וַיְהִי דְבַר־יְהֹוָה אֵלַי לֵאמֹר	11	Moreover, the word of the LORD came to me, saying:
אֱמָר־נָא לְבֵית הַמֶּרִי הֲלֹא יְדַעְתֶּם מָה־אֵלֶּה אֱמֹר הִנֵּה־בָא מֶלֶךְ־בָּבֶל יְרוּשָׁלַ͏ִם וַיִּקַּח אֶת־מַלְכָּהּ וְאֶת־שָׂרֶיהָ וַיָּבֵא אוֹתָם אֵלָיו בָּבֶלָה	12[13]	[14]"Say now to the rebellious house: Do you not know what these things mean? Tell them: Behold, the king of Babylon came to Jerusalem, and took the king, and the princes, and brought them to him in Babylon;
וַיִּקַּח מִזֶּרַע הַמְּלוּכָה וַיִּכְרֹת אִתּוֹ בְּרִית וַיָּבֵא אֹתוֹ בְּאָלָה וְאֶת־אֵילֵי הָאָרֶץ לָקָח	13[15]	And he took of the seed royal, and made a covenant with him, and brought him under an oath, and the mighty of the land he took away;

---

[1] Ezekiel 17:4 - Exodus.R 1:12, Isaiah 43:14 47:15, Jeremiah 51:13, Revelation 18:3 18:11-19

[2] LXX *ends of the tender twigs, and brought them into the land of Chanaan; he laid them up in a walled city*

[3] Ezekiel 17:5 - 2 Kings 24:17, b.Succah 34a, Deuteronomy 8:7-9, Ezekiel 17:13 19:11-12, Isaiah 15:7 44:4, Jastrow 1298a, Jeremiah 37:1

[4] LXX *in a conspicuous place*

[5] Ezekiel 17:6 - b.Bava Batra [Tosefot] 68a, Ezekiel 17:14, Proverbs 16:18-16:19, Ralbag SOS 2

[6] Ezekiel 17:7 - 2 Chronicles 26:13, 2 Kings 24:20, Exodus.R 1:12, Ezekiel 17:15 31:4, Jeremiah 37:5-37:7

[7] LXX *claws*

[8] LXX *itself round toward him, and her roots were turned*

[9] Ezekiel 17:8 - Ezekiel 17:5-17:6

[10] Ezekiel 17:9 - 2 Chronicles 13:12 20:20, 2 Kings 25:4-7, b.Bava Batra [Rashi] 93b, Ezekiel 17:10 17:15-17, Isaiah 8:9-10 30:1-7 31:1-3, Jeremiah 21:4-7 24:8-24:10 29:4-7 32:5 37:10 52:7-11, Numbers 14:41, z.Vaetchanan 269b

[11] Ezekiel 17:10 - Ezekiel 19:12-19:14, Hosea 12:3 13:15, John 15:6, Jude 1:12, Mark 11:20, Matthew 21:19

[12] LXX adds *together with the growth of its shoots*

[13] Ezekiel 17:12 - 2 Chronicles 36:9-10, 2 Kings 24:10-16, Acts 8:30, Deuteronomy 6:20, Exodus 12:26, Ezekiel 1:2 2:3-5 2:8 3:9 12:9-11 17:3 24:19, Isaiah 1:2 39:7, Jeremiah 22:24-28 52:31-34, Joshua 4:6 4:21, Luke 9:45, Mark 4:13, Matthew 13:51 15:16-17 16:11, Sifre Devarim Devarim 6

[14] LXX adds *Son of man*

[15] Ezekiel 17:13 - 2 Chronicles 36:13, 2 Kings 24:15-24:17, b.Bava Batra 88b, b.Kereitot 5b, b.Nedarim 65a, b.Rosh Hashanah [Rashi] 32a, b.Sheviit 36a, b.Yevamot 21a, b.Yoma 67b, Ein Yaakov Nedarim:65a, Ein Yaakov Yevamot:21a, Ezekiel 17:5, Genesis.R 64:4, Jeremiah 5:2 24:1 29:2 37:1, Midrash Psalms 29:1, Midrash Tanchuma Noach 3, mt.Hilchot Shevuot 2:1, Numbers.R 12:1

לִהְיוֹת מַמְלָכָה שְׁפָלָה לְבִלְתִּי הִתְנַשֵּׂא לִשְׁמֹר אֶת־בְּרִיתוֹ לְעָמְדָהּ	14[1]	so his [seed] might be a lowly kingdom, so it would not lift itself up, but that by keeping his covenant it might stand.
וַיִּמְרָד־בּוֹ לִשְׁלֹחַ מַלְאָכָיו מִצְרַיִם לָתֶת־לוֹ סוּסִים וְעַם־רָב הֲיִצְלָח הֲיִמָּלֵט הָעֹשֵׂה אֵלֶּה וְהֵפֵר בְּרִית וְנִמְלָט	15[2]	But he rebelled against him in sending his ambassadors into Egypt, so they might give him horses and many people. Shall he prosper? Shall he who does such things escape? Shall he break the covenant, and yet escape?
חַי־אָנִי נְאֻם אֲדֹנָי יְהוִה אִם־לֹא בִּמְקוֹם הַמֶּלֶךְ הַמַּמְלִיךְ אֹתוֹ אֲשֶׁר בָּזָה אֶת־אָלָתוֹ וַאֲשֶׁר הֵפֵר אֶת־בְּרִיתוֹ אִתּוֹ בְתוֹךְ־בָּבֶל יָמוּת	16[3]	As I live, says the Lord GOD, surely in the place where the king dwells who made him king, whose oath he despised, and whose covenant he broke, with him in the midst of Babylon he shall die.
וְלֹא בְחַיִל גָּדוֹל וּבְקָהָל רָב יַעֲשֶׂה אוֹתוֹ פַרְעֹה בַּמִּלְחָמָה בִּשְׁפֹּךְ סֹלְלָה וּבִבְנוֹת דָּיֵק לְהַכְרִית נְפָשׁוֹת רַבּוֹת	17[4]	Nor shall Pharaoh with his mighty army and great company support him in the war when they cast up mounds and build forts, to cut off many souls;
וּבָזָה אָלָה לְהָפֵר בְּרִית וְהִנֵּה נָתַן יָדוֹ וְכָל־אֵלֶּה עָשָׂה לֹא יִמָּלֵט	18[5]	Seeing he has despised the oath by breaking the covenant, when, lo, he gave his hand, and has done all these things, he shall not escape.
לָכֵן כֹּה־אָמַר אֲדֹנָי יְהוִה חַי־אָנִי אִם־לֹא אָלָתִי אֲשֶׁר בָּזָה וּבְרִיתִי אֲשֶׁר הֵפִיר וּנְתַתִּיו בְּרֹאשׁוֹ	19[6]	Therefore, thus says the Lord GOD: As I live, surely My oath that he despised, and My covenant that he broke, I will bring it upon his own head.
וּפָרַשְׂתִּי עָלָיו רִשְׁתִּי וְנִתְפַּשׂ בִּמְצוּדָתִי וַהֲבִיאוֹתִיהוּ בָבֶלָה וְנִשְׁפַּטְתִּי אִתּוֹ שָׁם מַעֲלוֹ אֲשֶׁר מָעַל־בִּי	20[7]	And I will spread My net on him, and he shall be taken in My snare, *and I will bring him to Babylon, and will plead with him there for his treachery that he has committed against Me*[8].
וְאֵת כָּל־מִבְרָחוֹ "כָּל־מִבְרָחָיו" בְּכָל־אֲגַפָּיו בַּחֶרֶב יִפֹּלוּ וְהַנִּשְׁאָרִים לְכָל־רוּחַ יִפָּרֵשׂוּ וִידַעְתֶּם כִּי אֲנִי יְהוָה דִּבַּרְתִּי	21[9]	*And all his mighty men in all his bands*[10] shall fall by the sword, and those who remain shall be scattered toward every wind; and you shall know that I, the LORD, have spoken it.
כֹּה אָמַר אֲדֹנָי יְהוִה וְלָקַחְתִּי אָנִי מִצַּמֶּרֶת הָאֶרֶז הָרָמָה וְנָתָתִּי מֵרֹאשׁ יֹנְקוֹתָיו רַךְ אֶקְטֹף וְשָׁתַלְתִּי אָנִי עַל הַר־גָּבֹהַּ וְתָלוּל	22[11]	Thus says the Lord GOD: Moreover I will take, I, of the lofty top of the cedar, and will set it; I will crop off from the topmost of its young twigs a tender one, and I will plant it on a high and eminent mountain;

[1] Ezekiel 17:14 - 1 Samuel 2:7 2:30, Deuteronomy 28:43, Ezekiel 17:6 29:14, Jeremiah 27:12-27:17 38:17, Lamentations 5:10, Matthew 22:17-22:21, Nehemiah 9:36-9:37

[2] Ezekiel 17:15 - 2 Chronicles 36:13, 2 Kings 24:20, Deuteronomy 17:16 29:11-14, Ezekiel 17:7 17:9 17:18 21:30, Hebrews 2:3, Isaiah 30:1-4 31:1-3 36:6-9, Jeremiah 22:29-30 32:4 34:3 37:5-7 38:18 38:23 52:3, Matthew 23:33, Proverbs 19:5, Psalms 55:24

[3] Ezekiel 17:16 - 1 Timothy 1:10, 2 Kings 24:17, 2 Samuel 21:2, 2 Timothy 3:3, Exodus 7:27 20:7, Ezekiel 12:13 16:59 17:10 17:13 17:18-17:19, Hosea 10:4, Jeremiah 32:4-32:5 34:3-34:5 39:7 52:11, Joshua 9:20, Malachi 3:5, Numbers 30:4, Psalms 15:4, Romans 1:31, Zechariah 5:3-5:4

[4] Ezekiel 17:17 - Ezekiel 4:2 29:6-7, Isaiah 36:6, Jeremiah 33:5 37:5 37:7 52:4, Lamentations 4:17

[5] Ezekiel 17:18 - 1 Chronicles 29:24, 2 Chronicles 30:8, Lamentations 5:6

[6] Ezekiel 17:19 - Deuteronomy 5:11, Ezekiel 21:28-32, Jeremiah 5:2 5:9 7:9-15, Leviticus.R 6:5, z.Vaetchanan 269b

[7] Ezekiel 17:20 - 2 Chronicles 33:11, 2 Samuel 18:9, Ecclesiastes 9:12, Ezekiel 12:13 20:35-36 32:3 38:22, Hosea 2:2 7:12, Jeremiah 2:9 2:35 39:5-7 50:44, Job 10:16, Josephus Antiquities 10.7.2, Joshua 10:16-18, Lamentations 1:13 4:20, Luke 21:35, Micah 6:2

[8] Missing in LXX

[9] Ezekiel 17:21 - 2 Kings 25:5 25:11, Amos 9:1 9:9-10, Ezekiel 5:10 5:12 6:7 6:10 12:14 13:14 13:23 15:7, Isaiah 26:11, Jeremiah 48:44 52:8

[10] LXX *In every battle of his they*

[11] Ezekiel 17:22 - Daniel 2:35 2:44-45, Ezekiel 20:40 34:29 37:22 40:2, Isaiah 2:2-3 4:2 11:1-5 53:2, Jeremiah 23:5-6 33:15-16, Micah 4:1, Psalms 2:6 72:16 80:16, z.Vaetchanan 269b, Zechariah 3:8 4:12-4:14 6:12-13

Ezekiel 17:22-18:32 - Haftarah Haazinu [Teimon]

בְּהַר מְרוֹם יִשְׂרָאֵל אֶשְׁתֳּלֶנּוּ וְנָשָׂא עָנָף וְעָשָׂה פֶּרִי
וְהָיָה לְאֶרֶז אַדִּיר וְשָׁכְנוּ תַחְתָּיו כֹּל צִפּוֹר כָּל־כָּנָף
בְּצֵל דָּלִיּוֹתָיו תִּשְׁכֹּנָּה

23 [1] in the mountain of the height of Israel I will plant it; and it shall bring forth boughs, and bear fruit, and be a stately cedar; and under it shall dwell all fowl of every wing, in the shadow of its branches they shall dwell.

וְיָדְעוּ כָּל־עֲצֵי הַשָּׂדֶה כִּי אֲנִי יְהוָה הִשְׁפַּלְתִּי עֵץ
גָּבֹהַּ הִגְבַּהְתִּי עֵץ שָׁפָל הוֹבַשְׁתִּי עֵץ לָח וְהִפְרַחְתִּי
עֵץ יָבֵשׁ אֲנִי יְהוָה דִּבַּרְתִּי וְעָשִׂיתִי

24 [2] And all the trees of the field shall know that I, the LORD, brought down the high tree, exalted the low tree, dried up the green tree, and made the dry tree to flourish; I, the LORD, have spoken and did it.'

Ezekiel – Chapter 18

וַיְהִי דְבַר־יְהוָה אֵלַי לֵאמֹר

1 [3] And the word of the LORD came to me, saying:

מַה־לָּכֶם אַתֶּם מֹשְׁלִים אֶת־הַמָּשָׁל הַזֶּה עַל־אַדְמַת
יִשְׂרָאֵל לֵאמֹר אָבוֹת יֹאכְלוּ בֹסֶר וְשִׁנֵּי הַבָּנִים
תִּקְהֶינָה

2 [4] 'What do you mean, that you use this proverb in the land of Israel, saying: The fathers have eaten *sour*[5] grapes, And the children's teeth are set on edge?

חַי־אָנִי נְאֻם אֲדֹנָי יְהוִה אִם־יִהְיֶה לָכֶם עוֹד מְשֹׁל
הַמָּשָׁל הַזֶּה בְּיִשְׂרָאֵל

3 [6] As I live, says the Lord GOD, you shall no longer have occasion to use this proverb in Israel.

הֵן כָּל־הַנְּפָשׁוֹת לִי הֵנָּה כְּנֶפֶשׁ הָאָב וּכְנֶפֶשׁ הַבֵּן
לִי־הֵנָּה הַנֶּפֶשׁ הַחֹטֵאת הִיא תָמוּת

4 [7] Behold, all souls are Mine; as the soul of the father, so also the soul of the son is Mine; the soul who sins, it shall die.

וְאִישׁ כִּי־יִהְיֶה צַדִּיק וְעָשָׂה מִשְׁפָּט וּצְדָקָה

5 [8] But if a man be just, and do what is lawful and right,

אֶל־הֶהָרִים לֹא אָכָל וְעֵינָיו לֹא נָשָׂא אֶל־גִּלּוּלֵי
בֵּית יִשְׂרָאֵל וְאֶת־אֵשֶׁת רֵעֵהוּ לֹא טִמֵּא וְאֶל־אִשָּׁה
נִדָּה לֹא יִקְרָב

6 [9] and has not eaten on the mountains, nor has lifted up his eyes to the idols of the house of Israel, nor has defiled his neighbor's wife, nor has come near to a woman in her impurity;

וְאִישׁ לֹא יוֹנֶה חֲבֹלָתוֹ חוֹב יָשִׁיב גְּזֵלָה לֹא יִגְזֹל
לַחְמוֹ לְרָעֵב יִתֵּן וְעֵירֹם יְכַסֶּה־בָּגֶד

7 [10] and has not wronged any, but has restored his pledge for a debt, has taken nothing by robbery,

[1] Ezekiel 17:23 - Acts 10:11-10:12, b.Shabbat 30b, Colossians 3:11, Daniel 4:7-4:11 4:18-4:20, Ein Yaakov Shabbat:30b, Ezekiel 31:6, Galatians 3:28, Genesis 49:10, Hosea 14:9, Isaiah 2:2 11:6-11:10 27:6 49:18 60:4-60:12, John 12:24 15:5-15:8, Luke 14:21-14:23, Matthew 13:32 13:47-13:48, Mekilta de R'Ishmael Shirata 10:14, Psalms 22:28-22:31 72:8-72:11 92:13-92:14, Revelation 11:15, Saadia Opinions 7Variant:5, y.Sanhedrin 11:3

[2] Ezekiel 17:24 - 1 Corinthians 1:27-28, 1 Samuel 2:7-8, Amos 9:11, Ezekiel 12:25 21:31 22:14 24:14, Genesis.R 53:1, Isaiah 2:13-14 9:7-8 11:1-9 26:5 55:12-13, Job 5:11 40:12, Luke 1:33 1:52-53 21:33, Matthew 24:35, Midrash Tanchuma Vayera 15, Pirkei de R'Eliezer 52, Psalms 75:7-8 89:39 89:46 96:11-12, Ralbag SOS 2, z.Tzav 32a

[3] Ezekiel 18:1 - b.Sanhedrin [Tosefot] 81a, m.Megillah 5:10, z.Chayyei Sarah 121b

[4] Ezekiel 18:2 - b.Sanhedrin 39a, b.Shabbat 55a, Ein Yaakov Sanhedrin:39a, Ezekiel 6:2-3 7:2 17:12 25:3 36:1-6 37:11 37:19 37:25, Isaiah 3:15, Jeremiah 15:4 31:30-31, Lamentations 5:7, Matthew 23:36, Ralbag Wars 4:6, Romans 9:20

[5] LXX *unripe*

[6] Ezekiel 18:3 - 3 Enoch 1:2, Ezekiel 18:19-20 18:30 33:11-20 36:31-32, Romans 3:19

[7] Ezekiel 18:4 - b.Makkot 24a, Ein Yaakov Makkot:24a, Ezekiel 18:20, Hebrews 12:9, Isaiah 42:5, Galatians 3:10-13 3:22, Leviticus.R 34:10 37:1, Mekhilta de R'Shimon bar Yochai Shirata 27:1, Mekhilta de R'Ishmael Shirata 1:116, Midrash Tanchuma Beshallach 11, Numbers 16:22 27:16, Pesikta de R'Kahana 24.7, Pirkei de R'Eliezer 34, Romans 6:23, Saadia Opinions 6:5, y.Makkot 2:6, Zechariah 12:1

[8] Ezekiel 18:5 - 1 John 2:3 2:29 3:7 5:2-5, Ein Yaakov Sanhedrin:81a, Ezekiel 33:14, Genesis 18:19, James 1:22-25 2:14-26, Jeremiah 22:15, Matthew 7:21-27, Midrash Psalms 15:7, Proverbs 21:3, Psalms 15:2-5 24:4-6, Revelation 22:14, Romans 2:7-10, Sifre Devarim Ki Tetze 286

[9] Ezekiel 18:6 - 1 Corinthians 6:9-6:11 10:20, b.Avodah Zara [Tosefot] 14a, b.Sanhedrin [Tosefot] 37a, b.Sanhedrin 81a, b.Shabbat 13a, Deuteronomy 4:19 22:22-30, Exodus 34:15, Ezekiel 6:13 18:11-18:12 18:15 20:7 20:24 20:28 22:9-11 33:25-26, Galatians 5:19-21, Hebrews 13:4, Jeremiah 5:8-5:9, Leviticus 18:19-20 20:10 20:18, Mas.Kallah Rabbati 6:1, Matthew 5:28, Mesillat Yesharim 11:Traits-of-Nekuyut, Midrash Psalms 15:7, mt.Hilchot Deot 5:13, Numbers 25:2, Psalms 121:1 123:1-2

[10] Ezekiel 18:7 - 1 John 3:16-19, 1 Samuel 12:3-4, 2 Corinthians 8:7-9 9:6-14, 2 Enoch 63:1 9:1, Amos 2:6 2:8 3:10 5:11-12 6:3 8:4-6, Deuteronomy 15:7-11 24:12-13 24:17, Exodus 22:21-24 22:26 23:9, Ezekiel 7:23 18:12 18:16 18:18 22:12-13 22:27-29 33:15, Genesis 6:11-12, Isaiah 1:17 5:7 33:15 58:6-11 59:6-7, James 2:13-17 5:1-6, Jeremiah 7:6-7 22:3 22:16-17, Job 22:6 24:3 24:9 31:13-22, Leviticus 19:15 25:14, Luke 3:11, Malachi 3:5, Matthew 25:34-46, Micah 2:1 3:2, Proverbs 3:31 11:24-25 14:31 22:22-23 28:8 28:27, Psalms 41:2 112:4 112:9, Pseudo-Phocylides 12, Tanna Devei Eliyahu 5, Zechariah 7:9-11, Zephaniah 1:9

has given his bread to the hungry, and has covered the naked with a garment;

בַּנֶּשֶׁךְ לֹא־יִתֵּן וְתַרְבִּית לֹא יִקָּח מֵעָוֶל יָשִׁיב יָדוֹ מִשְׁפַּט אֱמֶת יַעֲשֶׂה בֵּין אִישׁ לְאִישׁ **8**[1]

he who has not given forth on interest, nor has taken any increase, who has withdrawn his hand from iniquity, has executed true justice between man and man,

בְּחֻקּוֹתַי יְהַלֵּךְ וּמִשְׁפָּטַי שָׁמַר לַעֲשׂוֹת אֱמֶת צַדִּיק הוּא חָיֹה יִחְיֶה נְאֻם אֲדֹנָי יְהוִה **9**[2]

has walked in My statutes, and has kept My ordinances, to deal truly; he is just, he shall surely live, says the Lord GOD.

וְהוֹלִיד בֵּן־פָּרִיץ שֹׁפֵךְ דָּם וְעָשָׂה אָח מֵאַחַד מֵאֵלֶּה **10**[3]

If he fathers a son who is a robber, a shedder of blood, and *who does to a brother any of these things*[4],

וְהוּא אֶת־כָּל־אֵלֶּה לֹא עָשָׂה כִּי גַם אֶל־הֶהָרִים אָכַל וְאֶת־אֵשֶׁת רֵעֵהוּ טִמֵּא **11**[5]

while he himself had not done any of these things[6], for he has eaten on the mountains, and defiled his neighbor's wife,

עָנִי וְאֶבְיוֹן הוֹנָה גְּזֵלוֹת גָּזָל חֲבֹל לֹא יָשִׁיב וְאֶל־הַגִּלּוּלִים נָשָׂא עֵינָיו תּוֹעֵבָה עָשָׂה **12**[7]

has wronged the poor and needy, has taken by robbery, has not restored the pledge, and has lifted up his eyes to the idols, has committed abomination,

בַּנֶּשֶׁךְ נָתַן וְתַרְבִּית לָקַח וָחָי לֹא יִחְיֶה אֵת כָּל־הַתּוֹעֵבוֹת הָאֵלֶּה עָשָׂה מוֹת יוּמָת דָּמָיו בּוֹ יִהְיֶה **13**[8]

has given forth on interest, and has taken increase; shall he then live? he shall not live; he has done all these abominations; he shall surely be put to death, his blood shall be on him.

וְהִנֵּה הוֹלִיד בֵּן וַיַּרְא אֶת־כָּל־חַטֹּאת אָבִיו אֲשֶׁר עָשָׂה וַיִּרְאֶה וְלֹא יַעֲשֶׂה כָּהֵן **14**[9]

Now, behold, if he fathers a son who sees all his father's sins he has done, and considers, and does not behave in like manner,

עַל־הֶהָרִים לֹא אָכַל וְעֵינָיו לֹא נָשָׂא אֶל־גִּלּוּלֵי בֵּית יִשְׂרָאֵל אֶת־אֵשֶׁת רֵעֵהוּ לֹא טִמֵּא **15**[10]

he has not eaten on the mountains, nor lifted up his eyes to the idols of the house of Israel, has not defiled his neighbor's wife,

וְאִישׁ לֹא הוֹנָה חֲבֹל לֹא חָבָל וּגְזֵלָה לֹא גָזָל לַחְמוֹ לְרָעֵב נָתָן וְעֵרוֹם כִּסָּה־בָגֶד **16**[11]

nor has wronged any, has not taken nothing to pledge, nor has taken by robbery, but has given his bread to the hungry, and has covered the naked with a garment,

---

[1] Ezekiel 18:8 - 2 Enoch 42:7, 2 Samuel 22:24, Deuteronomy 1:16-1:17 16:18-16:20 23:21-23:21, Exodus 22:25, Ezekiel 18:13 18:17 22:12, Isaiah 1:17 33:15, Jeremiah 15:10 22:15-22:16, Job 29:7-29:17, Leviticus 19:15 19:35 25:35-25:37, Nehemiah 5:1-5:11 5:15, Proverbs 28:8 31:8-31:9, Psalms 15:5, Zechariah 7:9-7:10 8:16

[2] Ezekiel 18:9 - 1 John 2:29 3:7, Acts 24:16, Amos 5:4 5:14 5:24, b.Sanhedrin 81a, Deuteronomy 4:1 5:1 6:1-6:2 10:12-10:13 11:1, Ein Yaakov Sanhedrin:81a, Ezekiel 18:17 20:11 20:13 33:15 36:27 37:24, Habakkuk 2:4, James 1:22-1:25 2:18-2:26, John 14:21, Leviticus 18:5, Luke 1:6 10:27-10:29, Nehemiah 9:13-9:14, Psalms 19:8-19:12 24:4-24:6 105:44-105:45 119:1-119:6, Romans 1:17, Sifre Devarim {Ki Tetze} 286, Sifre Devarim Ki Tetze 286

[3] Ezekiel 18:10 - 1 John 3:12, b.Bava Metzia [Tosefot] 61b, b.Bava Metzia 105a, b.Sanhedrin 81a, b.Temurah 6b, Exodus 21:12 22:2, Genesis 9:5-9:6, John 18:40, Leviticus 19:13, Malachi 3:8-3:9, Numbers 35:31

[4] LXX *committing sins*

[5] Ezekiel 18:11 - 1 John 3:22, 1 Kings 13:8 13:22, b.Sanhedrin 81a, Ezekiel 18:6-18:7 18:15, James 2:17, John 13:17 15:14, Luke 11:28, Matthew 7:21-7:27, Philippians 4:9, Revelation 22:14

[6] LXX *who has not walked in the way of his righteous father*

[7] Ezekiel 18:12 - 2 Kings 21:11 23:13, Amos 4:1, b.Sanhedrin 81a, Ezekiel 8:6 8:17 18:6-18:7 18:16, Hosea 12:9, Isaiah 59:6-59:7, James 2:6, Jeremiah 22:17, Leviticus 18:22 18:26-18:30, Zechariah 7:10

[8] Ezekiel 18:13 - Acts 1:18, b.Bava Metzia 61b, b.Sanhedrin 81a, b.Temurah 6b, Exodus 22:25, Exodus.R 31:4 31:6 31:13 31:14 31:15, Ezekiel 3:18 18:8 18:17 18:24 18:28 18:32 33:4-33:5, Gates of Repentance 3.025, Leviticus 20:9 20:11-20:13 20:27, Mesillat Yesharim 11:Traits-of-Nekuyut, Midrash Tanchuma Mishpatim 9 12 15, Siman 65:1

[9] Ezekiel 18:14 - 1 Peter 1:18, 2 Chronicles 29:3-11 34:21, Ezekiel 18:10 18:28 20:18, Haggai 1:5 1:7 2:18, Hosea 7:2, Isaiah 44:19, Jeremiah 8:6 9:15 44:17, Luke 15:17-19, Matthew 23:32, Proverbs 17:21 23:24, Psalms 119:59-60

[10] Ezekiel 18:15 - Ezekiel 18:6-7 18:11-13

[11] Ezekiel 18:16 - Ecclesiastes 11:1-11:2, Ezekiel 18:7, Isaiah 58:7-10, Job 22:7 31:19, Luke 11:41 14:13, mt.Hilchot Deot 5:13, Proverbs 22:9 25:21 31:20, Psalms 41:2

מֵעָנִ֞י הֵשִׁ֣יב יָד֗וֹ נֶ֤שֶׁךְ וְתַרְבִּית֙ לֹ֣א לָקָ֔ח מִשְׁפָּטַ֣י עָשָׂ֔ה בְּחֻקּוֹתַ֖י הָלָ֑ךְ ה֚וּא לֹ֣א יָמ֔וּת בַּעֲוֺ֥ן אָבִ֖יו חָיֹ֥ה יִחְיֶֽה

17[1] *that has withdrawn his hand from the poor[2]*, who has not received interest nor increase, has executed My ordinances, has walked in My statutes; he shall not die for the iniquity of his father, he shall surely live.

אָבִ֞יו כִּֽי־עָ֣שַׁק עֹ֗שֶׁק גָּזַל֙ גֵּ֣זֶל אָ֔ח וַאֲשֶׁ֥ר לֹא־ט֖וֹב עָשָׂ֣ה בְּת֣וֹךְ עַמָּ֑יו וְהִנֵּה־מֵ֖ת בַּעֲוֺנֽוֹ

18[3] As for his father, because he cruelly oppressed, *committed robbery on his brother[4]*, and did what is not good among his people, behold, he dies for his iniquity.

וַאֲמַרְתֶּ֕ם מַדֻּ֛עַ לֹֽא־נָשָׂ֥א הַבֵּ֖ן בַּעֲוֺ֣ן הָאָ֑ב וְהַבֵּ֞ן מִשְׁפָּ֧ט וּצְדָקָ֣ה עָשָׂ֗ה אֵ֣ת כָּל־חֻקּוֹתַ֥י שָׁמַ֛ר וַיַּעֲשֶׂ֥ה אֹתָ֖ם חָיֹ֥ה יִחְיֶֽה

19[5] Yet say: Why does the son not bear the iniquity of the father with him? When the son does what is lawful and right, and keeps all My statutes, and does them, he shall surely live.

הַנֶּ֥פֶשׁ הַחֹטֵ֖את הִ֣יא תָמ֑וּת בֵּ֞ן לֹא־יִשָּׂ֣א ׀ בַּעֲוֺ֣ן הָאָ֗ב וְאָב֙ לֹ֤א יִשָּׂא֙ בַּעֲוֺ֣ן הַבֵּ֔ן צִדְקַ֤ת הַצַּדִּיק֙ עָלָ֣יו תִּֽהְיֶ֔ה וְרִשְׁעַ֥ת "רָשָׁ֖ע" "הָרָשָׁ֖ע" עָלָ֥יו תִּֽהְיֶֽה

20[6] The soul who sins shall die; the son shall not bear the iniquity of the father with him, nor shall the father bear the iniquity of the son with him; the righteousness of the righteous shall be on him, and the wickedness of the wicked shall be on him.

וְהָרָשָׁ֗ע כִּ֤י יָשׁוּב֙ "מִכָּל־חַטֹּאתָו֙" "מִכָּל־חַטֹּאתָיו֙" אֲשֶׁ֣ר עָשָׂ֔ה וְשָׁמַר֙ אֶת־כָּל־חֻקּוֹתַ֔י וְעָשָׂ֥ה מִשְׁפָּ֖ט וּצְדָקָ֑ה חָיֹ֥ה יִחְיֶ֖ה לֹ֥א יָמֽוּת

21[7] But if the wicked turn from all his sins that he has committed, and keep all My statutes, and do what is lawful and right, he shall surely live, he shall not die.

כָּל־פְּשָׁעָיו֙ אֲשֶׁ֣ר עָשָׂ֔ה לֹ֥א יִזָּכְר֖וּ ל֑וֹ בְּצִדְקָת֥וֹ אֲשֶׁר־עָשָׂ֖ה יִֽחְיֶֽה

22[8] None of his transgressions he has committed shall be remembered against him; for the righteousness he has done he shall live.

הֶחָפֹ֤ץ אֶחְפֹּץ֙ מ֣וֹת רָשָׁ֔ע נְאֻ֖ם אֲדֹנָ֣י יְהוִ֑ה הֲל֛וֹא בְּשׁוּב֥וֹ מִדְּרָכָ֖יו וְחָיָֽה

23[9] Do I have any pleasure at all that the wicked should die? says the Lord GOD; and not rather that he should return from his ways, and live?

וּבְשׁ֣וּב צַדִּ֣יק מִצִּדְקָתוֹ֮ וְעָ֣שָׂה עָ֒וֶל֒ וְעָשָׂ֗ה כְּכֹ֣ל הַתּוֹעֵב֜וֹת אֲשֶׁר־עָשָׂ֣ה הָרָשָׁ֘ע יַעֲשֶׂ֗ה וָחָ֑י "כָּל־צִדְקָתוֹ" "כָּל־צִדְקֹתָיו" אֲשֶׁר־עָשָׂה֙ לֹ֣א תִזָּכַ֔רְנָה בְּמַעֲל֧וֹ אֲשֶׁר־מָעַ֛ל וּבְחַטָּאת֥וֹ אֲשֶׁר־חָטָ֖א בָּ֥ם יָמֽוּת

24[10] But when the righteous turns away from his righteousness, and commits iniquity, and does according to all the abominations that the wicked man does, shall he live? None of the righteous deeds that he has done shall be remembered; for his trespass that he trespassed,

---

[1] Ezekiel 18:17 - Daniel 4:24, Ezekiel 3:21 18:8-9 18:13 18:19-21 18:28 20:18 20:30 33:13 33:15-16, Jeremiah 16:11-13 16:19 22:16, Job 29:16, Leviticus 18:4 18:26 18:30, Luke 19:8, Malachi 3:7, Matthew 18:27-35 23:29-33, Proverbs 14:31 29:7 29:14

[2] LXX *and has turned back his hand from unrighteousness*

[3] Ezekiel 18:18 - b.Sheviit 31a, Ein Yaakov Shevuot:31a, Ezekiel 3:18 18:4 18:20 18:24 18:26, Isaiah 3:11, John 8:21 8:24, mt.Hilchot Sheluchin vShutafin 3:5, Siman 181:15

[4] LXX *or plunder*

[5] Ezekiel 18:19 - 2 Kings 23:26 24:3-4, Deuteronomy 5:9, Exodus 20:5, Ezekiel 18:2 18:9 20:18-20 20:24 20:30, Jeremiah 15:4, Lamentations 5:7, Zechariah 1:3-6

[6] Ezekiel 18:20 - 1 Kings 8:32 14:13, 1 Peter 2:24, 2 Chronicles 6:23 6:30 25:4, 2 Kings 14:6 22:18-22:20, Derech Hashem Part II 3§07, Deuteronomy 24:16, Ein Yaakov Shabbat:55a, Exodus.R 31:6, Ezekiel 4:4 18:4 18:13 18:30 33:10, Gates of Repentance 3.214, Hebrews 9:28, Isaiah 3:10-3:11 53:11, Jeremiah 31:30-31:31, Leviticus 5:1 5:17 10:17 16:22 19:8, Leviticus.R 37:1, Mas.Kallah Rabbati 6:1, Matthew 16:27, Mekhilta de R'Shimon bar Yochai Bachodesh 53:3, Midrash Tanchuma Vayikra 6, Numbers 18:1, Revelation 2:23 20:12 22:12-22:15, Romans 2:6-2:9, Saadia Opinions 9:3

[7] Ezekiel 18:21 - 1 Timothy 1:13-1:16, 2 Chronicles 33:12-33:13, Acts 3:19 26:18-26:20, Exodus.R 31:6, Ezekiel 3:21 18:5 18:9 18:17 18:19 18:27-18:28 18:30 33:11-33:16 33:19 36:27, Galatians 5:22-5:24, Genesis 26:5, Isaiah 1:16-1:20 55:6-7, James 2:14 2:26 4:8-4:10, Luke 1:6 24:47, Proverbs 28:13, Psalms 119:1 119:112 119:80, Romans 8:13, Saadia Opinions 5:6, Titus 2:11-2:14

[8] Ezekiel 18:22 - 1 John 3:7, 1 Kings 17:18, 2 Chronicles 6:23, 2 Peter 1:5-1:11, Exodus.R 31:1, Ezekiel 18:24 33:16, Galatians 6:7-6:8, Hebrews 8:12 10:3-10:4, Isaiah 43:25, James 2:21-2:26, Jeremiah 31:35 50:20, Micah 7:19, Psalms 18:21-18:25 19:12 25:7 32:1-32:2 51:2 103:12, Romans 2:6-2:7 8:1, Saadia Opinions 5:2

[9] Ezekiel 18:23 - 1 Timothy 2:4, 2 Peter 3:9, Exodus 34:6-34:7, Ezekiel 18:32 33:11, Hosea 11:8, James 2:13, Jeremiah 31:21, Job 33:27-33:28, Lamentations 3:33, Luke 15:4-15:7 15:10 15:22-15:24 15:32, Micah 7:18, Psalms 147:11, Saadia Opinions 4:4, Tanya Shaar Hayichud §08, Tefilah Zakkah [Neilah Yom Kippur], z.Toledot 140a, z.Vayechi 227a

[10] Ezekiel 18:24 - 1 John 2:19 5:16-5:18, 1 Samuel 15:11, 2 Chronicles 24:2 24:17-24:22, 2 Corinthians 12:20-12:21, 2 John 1:8, 2 Peter 2:18-2:22, 2 Timothy 3:1-3:5, b.Berachot 29a, Ein Yaakov Berachot:29a, Ezekiel 3:20-3:21 18:10-18:13 18:18 18:22 18:26 20:27 33:12-33:13 33:18, Galatians 3:4 5:7, Hebrews 6:4-6:6 10:26-10:31 10:38-10:39, John 6:66-6:70 8:21 8:24, Jude 1:12, Mark 13:13, Matthew 7:22-7:23 12:43-12:45 13:20-13:21, Midrash Psalms 52:3, Proverbs 14:32 21:16, Psalms 36:4-36:5 125:5, Revelation 2:10 3:11, Romans 1:28-1:31, Saadia Opinions 5:2, y.Peah 1:1, Zephaniah 1:6

and for his sin that he has sinned, for those shall he die.

וַאֲמַרְתֶּ֖ם לֹ֣א יִתָּכֵ֣ן דֶּ֑רֶךְ אֲדֹנָ֖י שִׁמְעוּ־נָ֣א בֵּ֣ית יִשְׂרָאֵ֗ל הֲדַרְכִּ֣י לֹ֣א יִתָּכֵ֔ן הֲלֹ֣א דַרְכֵיכֶ֖ם לֹ֥א יִתָּכֵֽנוּ ‏ **25**[1]

Yet you say: The way of the Lord is not *equal*[2]. Hear now, O house of Israel: Is it My way that is not *equal*[3]? *Is it not your ways that are unequal*[4]?

בְּשׁוּב־צַדִּ֤יק מִצִּדְקָתוֹ֙ וְעָ֣שָׂה עָ֔וֶל וּמֵ֖ת עֲלֵיהֶ֑ם בְּעַוְלוֹ֥ אֲשֶׁר־עָשָׂ֖ה יָמֽוּת ‏ **26**[5]

When the righteous man turns away from his righteousness, and commits iniquity, he shall die in it; for the iniquity he has done he shall die.

וּבְשׁ֣וּב רָשָׁ֗ע מֵֽרִשְׁעָתוֹ֙ אֲשֶׁ֣ר עָשָׂ֔ה וַיַּ֥עַשׂ מִשְׁפָּ֖ט וּצְדָקָ֑ה ה֖וּא אֶת־נַפְשׁ֥וֹ יְחַיֶּֽה ‏ **27**[6]

Again, when the wicked man turns away from the wickedness he has committed, and does what is lawful and right, he shall save his soul.

וַיִּרְאֶ֣ה וַיָּשׁוֹב֮ "וַיָּ֣שָׁב" מִכָּל־פְּשָׁעָ֖יו אֲשֶׁ֣ר עָשָׂ֑ה חָי֥וֹ יִחְיֶ֖ה לֹ֥א יָמֽוּת ‏ **28**[7]

Because he considers, and turns away from all his transgressions he has committed, he shall surely live, he shall not die.

וְאָמְרוּ֙ בֵּ֣ית יִשְׂרָאֵ֔ל לֹ֥א יִתָּכֵ֖ן דֶּ֣רֶךְ אֲדֹנָ֑י הַדְּרָכַ֞י לֹ֣א יִתָּכֵ֗נוּ בֵּ֣ית יִשְׂרָאֵ֔ל הֲלֹ֥א דַרְכֵיכֶ֖ם לֹ֥א יִתָּכֵֽן ‏ **29**[8]

Yet, says the house of Israel: The way of the Lord is not *equal*[9]. O house of Israel, is it My way that is not *equal*[10]? Is it not your ways *that are unequal*[11]?

לָכֵן֩ אִ֨ישׁ כִּדְרָכָ֜יו אֶשְׁפֹּ֤ט אֶתְכֶם֙ בֵּ֣ית יִשְׂרָאֵ֔ל נְאֻ֖ם אֲדֹנָ֣י יְהוִ֑ה שׁ֤וּבוּ וְהָשִׁ֙יבוּ֙ מִכָּל־פִּשְׁעֵיכֶ֔ם וְלֹֽא־יִהְיֶ֥ה לָכֶ֛ם לְמִכְשׁ֖וֹל עָוֺֽן ‏ **30**[12]

Therefore, I will judge you, O house of Israel, everyone according to his ways, says the Lord GOD. Return, and turn yourselves from all your transgressions; so they shall not be a stumbling block of iniquity to you.

הַשְׁלִ֣יכוּ מֵעֲלֵיכֶ֗ם אֶת־כָּל־פִּשְׁעֵיכֶם֙ אֲשֶׁ֣ר פְּשַׁעְתֶּ֣ם בָּ֔ם וַעֲשׂ֥וּ לָכֶ֛ם לֵ֥ב חָדָ֖שׁ וְר֣וּחַ חֲדָשָׁ֑ה וְלָ֥מָּה תָמֻ֖תוּ בֵּ֥ית יִשְׂרָאֵֽל ‏ **31**[13]

Cast away all your transgressions, in which you have transgressed; and make for yourself a new heart and a new spirit; for why will you die, O house of Israel?

כִּ֣י לֹ֤א אֶחְפֹּץ֙ בְּמ֣וֹת הַמֵּ֔ת נְאֻ֖ם אֲדֹנָ֣י יְהוִ֑ה וְהָשִׁ֖יבוּ וִחְיֽוּ ‏ **32**[14]

For I have no pleasure in the death of he who dies, says the Lord GOD. *Turn and live*[15].

---

[1] Ezekiel 18:25 - Deuteronomy 32:4, Ezekiel 18:29 33:17 33:20, Genesis 18:25, Jeremiah 2:17-2:23 2:29-2:37 12:1 16:10-16:13, Job 32:2 34:5-34:10 35:2 40:8 42:4-42:6, Malachi 2:17 3:13-3:15, Matthew 20:11-20:15, Per Massorah: Soferim altered "Hashem" to "Adonai", Psalms 50:6 50:21 145:17, Romans 2:5-2:6 3:5 3:20 9:20 10:3, Zephaniah 3:5

[2] LXX *straight*

[3] LXX *straight*

[4] LXX *Is your way straight?*

[5] Ezekiel 18:26 - y.Peah 1:1

[6] Ezekiel 18:27 - 1 Timothy 4:16, Acts 2:40 3:19 20:21 26:20, Ezekiel 18:21 33:5, Isaiah 1:18 55:7, Matthew 9:13 21:28-21:32, Saadia Opinions 5:2, Song of Songs.R 6:1, y.Peah 1:1

[7] Ezekiel 18:28 - 1 Samuel 7:3-4, Colossians 3:5-9, Deuteronomy 32:29, Ezekiel 12:3 18:14 18:21 18:31 33:12, James 2:10-12, Jeremiah 31:19-21, Luke 15:17-18, Psalms 119:1 119:6 119:59, Titus 2:14

[8] Ezekiel 18:29 - Ezekiel 18:2 18:25, Per Massorah: Soferim altered "Hashem" to "Adonai", Proverbs 19:3

[9] LXX *right*

[10] LXX *right*

[11] LXX *wrong*

[12] Ezekiel 18:30 - 1 Peter 1:17, 2 Corinthians 5:10-5:11, Acts 26:20, Apocryphon of Ezekiel Fragment 4, Bahir 67, Daniel 9:13, Ecclesiastes 3:17 12:14, Ezekiel 7:3 7:8-7:9 7:27 14:6 18:21 33:9 33:11 33:20 34:20, Galatians 6:4-6:5, Hosea 12:8, James 1:15, Joel 2:12-2:13, Josephus Antiquities 9.9.1, Luke 13:3 13:5, Malachi 3:18, Matthew 3:2 3:8 16:27 25:32, Revelation 2:5 2:16 2:21-2:23 20:12 22:12, Romans 2:5

[13] Ezekiel 18:31 - 1 Peter 1:14 1:22 2:1 4:2-4:4, Acts 3:19 13:46, Apocryphon of Ezekiel Fragment 2, Colossians 3:5-3:9, Deuteronomy 30:15 30:19, Ephesians 4:22-4:32, Ezekiel 11:19 20:7 33:11 36:26, Isaiah 1:16-1:17 30:22 55:7, James 1:21 4:8, Jeremiah 21:8 27:15 32:39, Life of Adam and Eve [Apocalypse] 13:5, Matthew 12:33 23:26, Proverbs 8:36, Psalms 34:15 51:11, Romans 8:13 12:2

[14] Ezekiel 18:32 - 2 Peter 3:9, b.Niddah 70b, Ecclesiastes.R 9:4, Ezekiel 18:23 33:11, Lamentations 3:33, Midrash Tanchuma Tazria 7, Midrash Tanchuma Vayera 8, Pesikta Rabbati 50:3, Saadia Opinions 4:4, Song of Songs.R 6:1, Tefilah Zakkah [Neilah Yom Kippur], y.Berachot 2:3

[15] Missing in LXX

Ezekiel – Chapter 19

וְאַתָּה שָׂא קִינָה אֶל־נְשִׂיאֵי יִשְׂרָאֵל	**1**[1] Moreover, take up a lamentation for the princes of Israel,
וְאָמַרְתָּ מָה אִמְּךָ לְבִיָּא בֵּין אֲרָיוֹת רָבָצָה בְּתוֹךְ כְּפִרִים רִבְּתָה גוּרֶיהָ	**2**[2] and say: How was your mother a lioness! Among lions she couched, in the midst of the young lions she reared her whelps.
וַתַּעַל אֶחָד מִגֻּרֶיהָ כְּפִיר הָיָה וַיִּלְמַד לִטְרָף־טֶרֶף אָדָם אָכָל	**3**[3] And she brought up one of her whelps, he became a young lion; and he learned to catch the prey, he devoured men.
וַיִּשְׁמְעוּ אֵלָיו גּוֹיִם בְּשַׁחְתָּם נִתְפָּשׂ וַיְבִאֻהוּ בַחַחִים אֶל־אֶרֶץ מִצְרָיִם	**4**[4] Then the nations assembled against him, he was taken in their pit; and they brought him with hooks to the land of Egypt.
וַתֵּרֶא כִּי נוֹחֲלָה אָבְדָה תִּקְוָתָהּ וַתִּקַּח אֶחָד מִגֻּרֶיהָ כְּפִיר שָׂמָתְהוּ	**5**[5] Now when she saw, *she was disappointed*[6], and her hope was lost; then she took another of her whelps, and made him a young lion.
וַיִּתְהַלֵּךְ בְּתוֹךְ־אֲרָיוֹת כְּפִיר הָיָה וַיִּלְמַד לִטְרָף־טֶרֶף אָדָם אָכָל	**6**[7] And he went up and down among the lions, he became a young lion; and he learned to catch the prey, he devoured men.
וַיֵּדַע אַלְמְנוֹתָיו וְעָרֵיהֶם הֶחֱרִיב וַתֵּשַׁם אֶרֶץ וּמְלֹאָהּ מִקּוֹל שַׁאֲגָתוֹ	**7**[8] And he *knew their castles*[9], and laid waste their cities; and the land and its fullness was desolate, because of the noise of his roaring.
וַיִּתְּנוּ עָלָיו גּוֹיִם סָבִיב מִמְּדִינוֹת וַיִּפְרְשׂוּ עָלָיו רִשְׁתָּם בְּשַׁחְתָּם נִתְפָּשׂ	**8**[10] Then the nations cried out against him on every side from the provinces; and they spread their net over him. He was taken in their pit.
וַיִּתְּנֻהוּ בַסּוּגַר בַּחַחִים וַיְבִאֻהוּ אֶל־מֶלֶךְ בָּבֶל יְבִאֻהוּ בַּמְּצֹדוֹת לְמַעַן לֹא־יִשָּׁמַע קוֹלוֹ עוֹד אֶל־הָרֵי יִשְׂרָאֵל	**9**[11] And they put him in a cage with hooks, and brought him to the king of Babylon so they might bring him into strongholds, so his voice should no longer be heard on the mountains of Israel.
אִמְּךָ כַגֶּפֶן בְּדָמְךָ עַל־מַיִם שְׁתוּלָה פֹּרִיָּה וַעֲנֵפָה הָיְתָה מִמַּיִם רַבִּים	**10**[12] Your mother was like a vine, *in your likeness*[13], planted by the waters; she was fruitful and full of branches because of many waters.
וַיִּהְיוּ־לָהּ מַטּוֹת עֹז אֶל־שִׁבְטֵי מֹשְׁלִים וַתִּגְבַּהּ קוֹמָתוֹ עַל־בֵּין עֲבֹתִים וַיֵּרָא בְגָבְהוֹ בְּרֹב דָּלִיֹּתָיו	**11**[14] And she had strong rods to be scepters for those who bore rule; and her stature was exalted among the thick branches, and she was seen in her height with the multitude of her tendrils.

[1] Ezekiel 19:1 - 2 Chronicles 35:25 36:3 36:6 36:10, 2 Kings 23:29-23:30 23:34 24:6 24:12 25:5-25:7, Ezekiel 2:10 19:14 26:17 27:2 27:32 32:16 32:18, Jeremiah 9:2 9:11 9:18-9:19 13:17-13:18 22:10-22:12 22:18-22:19 22:28 22:30 24:1 24:8 52:10-52:11 52:25-52:27, Lamentations 4:20 5:12, z.Vayikra 6a

[2] Ezekiel 19:2 - b.Sotah 11b, Ein Yaakov Sotah:11b, Exodus.R 1:16 29:9, Isaiah 5:29 11:6-9, Job 4:11, Midrash Tanchuma Vayishlach 1, Nahum 2:12-13, Psalms 58:7, Zechariah 11:3, Zephaniah 3:1-4

[3] Ezekiel 19:3 - 2 Chronicles 36:1-36:2, 2 Kings 23:31-23:32, Ezekiel 19:6 22:25, Leviticus.R 22:6

[4] Ezekiel 19:4 - 2 Chronicles 36:4 36:6, 2 Kings 23:31 23:33-23:34, Jeremiah 22:11-22:12 22:18

[5] Ezekiel 19:5 - 2 Kings 23:34-23:37, Ezekiel 19:3

[6] LXX *he was driven away from her*

[7] Ezekiel 19:6 - 2 Chronicles 36:5 36:9, 2 Kings 24:1-24:7 24:9, Jeremiah 22:13-17 26:1-24 36:1-32

[8] Ezekiel 19:7 - Amos 6:8, b.Sotah [Rashi] 5a, Ezekiel 12:19 22:25 30:12, Leviticus.R 19:6, Micah 1:2, mt.Pirkei Avot 4:4, Proverbs 19:12 28:3 28:15-16

[9] LXX *prowled in his boldness*

[10] Ezekiel 19:8 - 2 Kings 24:1-24:6 24:11, Ezekiel 12:13 17:20 19:4, Lamentations 4:20

[11] Ezekiel 19:9 - 2 Chronicles 36:6, 2 Kings 24:15, Ezekiel 6:2 19:7 36:1, Jeremiah 22:18-19 36:30-31, Leviticus.R 19:6
Ezekiel 19:9 [LXX] - Testament of Job 27:1

[12] Ezekiel 19:10 - Deuteronomy 8:7 8:9, Ezekiel 15:2-15:8 17:6 19:2, Hosea 2:2 2:5, Isaiah 5:1-5:4, Matthew 21:33-21:41, Numbers 24:6-24:7, Psalms 80:9-80:12 89:26-89:30

[13] LXX *and as a blossom on a pomegranate tree*

[14] Ezekiel 19:11 - Daniel 4:8 4:17-4:18, Ezekiel 19:12 19:14 21:15 21:18 31:3, Ezra 4:20 5:11, Genesis 49:10, Isaiah 11:1, Numbers 24:7-24:9 24:17, Psalms 2:8-2:9 80:16 80:18 110:2

וַתֻּתַּשׁ בְּחֵמָה לָאָרֶץ הֻשְׁלָכָה וְרוּחַ הַקָּדִים הוֹבִישׁ פִּרְיָהּ הִתְפָּרְקוּ וְיָבֵשׁוּ מַטֵּה עֻזָּהּ אֵשׁ אֲכָלָתְהוּ

12[1] But she was plucked up in fury, she was cast down to the ground, and the east wind dried up her fruit. Her strong rods were broken off and withered. The fire consumed her.

וְעַתָּה שְׁתוּלָה בַמִּדְבָּר בְּאֶרֶץ צִיָּה וְצָמָא

13[2] And now she is planted in the wilderness, in a dry and thirsty ground.

וַתֵּצֵא אֵשׁ מִמַּטֵּה בַדֶּיהָ פִּרְיָהּ אָכָלָה וְלֹא־הָיָה בָהּ מַטֵּה־עֹז שֵׁבֶט לִמְשׁוֹל קִינָה הִיא וַתְּהִי לְקִינָה

14[3] And fire is gone out of the rod of her *branches. It devoured her fruit, so there is in her no strong rod to be a scepter to rule.' This is a lamentation, and it was for a lamentation[4].*

Ezekiel – Chapter 20

וַיְהִי בַּשָּׁנָה הַשְּׁבִיעִית בַּחֲמִשִׁי בֶּעָשׂוֹר לַחֹדֶשׁ בָּאוּ אֲנָשִׁים מִזִּקְנֵי יִשְׂרָאֵל לִדְרֹשׁ אֶת־יְהוָה וַיֵּשְׁבוּ לְפָנָי

1[5] And it came to pass in the seventh year, *in the fifth month, the tenth day of the month[6],* that certain elders of Israel came to inquire of the LORD, and sat before me.

וַיְהִי דְבַר־יְהוָה אֵלַי לֵאמֹר

2[7] And the word of the LORD came to me, saying:

בֶּן־אָדָם דַּבֵּר אֶת־זִקְנֵי יִשְׂרָאֵל וְאָמַרְתָּ אֲלֵהֶם כֹּה אָמַר אֲדֹנָי יְהוִה הֲלִדְרֹשׁ אֹתִי אַתֶּם בָּאִים חַי־אָנִי אִם־אִדָּרֵשׁ לָכֶם נְאֻם אֲדֹנָי יְהוִה

3[8] 'Son of man, speak to the elders of Israel, and say to them: Thus says the Lord GOD: Have you come to inquire of Me? As I live, says the Lord GOD, you will not inquire of me.

הֲתִשְׁפֹּט אֹתָם הֲתִשְׁפּוֹט בֶּן־אָדָם אֶת־תּוֹעֲבֹת אֲבוֹתָם הוֹדִיעֵם

4[9] *Will you judge them, son of man, will you judge them[10]?* Cause them to know the abominations of their fathers;

וְאָמַרְתָּ אֲלֵיהֶם כֹּה־אָמַר אֲדֹנָי יְהוִה בְּיוֹם בָּחֳרִי בְיִשְׂרָאֵל וָאֶשָּׂא יָדִי לְזֶרַע בֵּית יַעֲקֹב וָאִוָּדַע לָהֶם בְּאֶרֶץ מִצְרָיִם וָאֶשָּׂא יָדִי לָהֶם לֵאמֹר אֲנִי יְהוָה אֱלֹהֵיכֶם

5[11] and say to them: Thus says the Lord GOD: In the day when I chose Israel, and lifted up My hand to the seed of the house of Jacob, and made Myself known to them in the land of Egypt, when I lifted up My hand to them, saying: I am the LORD your God.

---

[1] Ezekiel 19:12 - 2 Kings 23:29 23:34 24:6 24:14-16 25:6-7, Deuteronomy 32:22, Ezekiel 15:4 15:6-8 17:10 19:11 21:3-20:4 28:17, Hosea 13:15, Isaiah 5:5-6 27:11, Jeremiah 4:11-12 22:10-11 22:18-19 22:25-27 22:30 31:29, John 15:6, Matthew 3:10, Psalms 52:6 80:13-14 80:17 89:41-46

[2] Ezekiel 19:13 - 2 Kings 24:12-16, Deuteronomy 28:47-48, Ezekiel 19:10 20:35, Hosea 2:3, Jeremiah 52:27-31, Psalms 63:2 68:7

[3] Ezekiel 19:14 - 2 Chronicles 36:13, 2 Kings 24:20, Amos 9:11, Ezekiel 15:4 17:18-20 19:1 19:11 21:3 21:30-21:32, Genesis 49:10, Hosea 3:4 10:3, Isaiah 9:19-9:20, Jeremiah 38:23 52:3, John 19:15, Judges 9:15, Lamentations 4:20, Luke 19:41, Nehemiah 9:37, Psalms 79:7 80:16-17, Romans 9:2-9:4

[4] LXX *choice boughs, and has devoured her; and there was no rod of strength in her. Her race is become a parable of lamentation, and it shall be for a lamentation*

[5] Ezekiel 20:1 - 1 Kings 14:2-6 22:15-28, 2 Kings 3:13, Acts 22:3, Ezekiel 1:2 8:1 14:1-3 24:1 26:1 29:1 29:17 30:20 31:1 32:1 33:30-33 40:1, Isaiah 29:13 58:2, Jeremiah 37:17, Liber Antiquitatum Biblicarum 28:6, Luke 2:46 8:35 10:39, Matthew 22:16, Midrash Tanchuma Nitzavim 3, Song of Songs.R 7:14

Ezekiel 20:1-4 - Seder Olam 26:Zedekiah

Ezekiel 20:1-15 - Haftarah Kedoshim [Teimon]

[6] LXX *on the fifteenth day of the month*

[7] Ezekiel 20:2-20 - Haftarah Kedoshim [Sephard], Italk]

[8] Ezekiel 20:3 - 1 Samuel 28:6, Ezekiel 14:3-14:4 14:7-14:8 20:31, Isaiah 1:12 1:15, John 4:24, Luke 3:7, Matthew 3:7 15:8-15:9, Micah 3:7, Proverbs 15:8 21:27 28:9, Psalms 50:15-50:21, Song of Songs.R 7:14, z.Vaetchanan 269b

[9] Ezekiel 20:4 - 1 Corinthians 6:2, Acts 7:51-7:52, Ezekiel 14:14 14:20 16:2-16:3 22:2 23:36 23:45, Genesis.R 36:6, Isaiah 5:3, Jeremiah 7:16 11:14 14:11-14:14 15:1, Luke 11:47-11:51 13:33-13:35, Matthew 23:29-23:37

[10] LXX *Shall I utterly take vengeance on them, son of man*

[11] Ezekiel 20:5 - Deuteronomy 4:34 4:37 7:6 11:2-7 14:2 32:40, Exodus 3:6 3:8 3:16 4:31 6:2 6:6-7 19:4-6 20:2-3, Exodus.R 3:16, Ezekiel 20:15 20:23 35:11 47:14, Genesis 14:22, Isaiah 41:8-9 43:10 44:1-2, Jeremiah 33:24, Mark 13:20, Midrash Tanchuma Behaalotcha 8, Midrash Tanchuma Shemot 27, Numbers.R 15:12, Psalms 33:12 103:7, Revelation 10:5, z.Vaetchanan 269b

בַּיּוֹם הַהוּא נָשָׂאתִי יָדִי לָהֶם לְהוֹצִיאָם מֵאֶרֶץ מִצְרָיִם אֶל־אֶרֶץ אֲשֶׁר־תַּרְתִּי לָהֶם זָבַת חָלָב וּדְבַשׁ צְבִי הִיא לְכָל־הָאֲרָצוֹת

6[1] In that day I lifted up My hand to them, to bring them forth out of the land of Egypt into a land I had pursued for them, flowing with milk and honey, which is the beauty of all lands.

וָאֹמַר אֲלֵהֶם אִישׁ שִׁקּוּצֵי עֵינָיו הַשְׁלִיכוּ וּבְגִלּוּלֵי מִצְרַיִם אַל־תִּטַּמָּאוּ אֲנִי יְהוָה אֱלֹהֵיכֶם

7[2] And I said to them: Every can, cast away the detestable things of his eyes, and do not defile yourselves with the idols of Egypt; I am the LORD your God.

וַיַּמְרוּ־בִי וְלֹא אָבוּ לִשְׁמֹעַ אֵלַי אִישׁ אֶת־שִׁקּוּצֵי עֵינֵיהֶם לֹא הִשְׁלִיכוּ וְאֶת־גִּלּוּלֵי מִצְרַיִם לֹא עָזָבוּ וָאֹמַר לִשְׁפֹּךְ חֲמָתִי עֲלֵיהֶם לְכַלּוֹת אַפִּי בָּהֶם בְּתוֹךְ אֶרֶץ מִצְרָיִם

8[3] But they rebelled against Me, and would not listen to Me; they did not cast away the detestable things from their eyes, nor did they forsake the idols of Egypt; then I said I would pour out My fury on them, to spend My anger on them in the midst of the land of Egypt.

וָאַעַשׂ לְמַעַן שְׁמִי לְבִלְתִּי הֵחֵל לְעֵינֵי הַגּוֹיִם אֲשֶׁר־הֵמָּה בְתוֹכָם אֲשֶׁר נוֹדַעְתִּי אֲלֵיהֶם לְעֵינֵיהֶם לְהוֹצִיאָם מֵאֶרֶץ מִצְרָיִם

9[4] But I decided, for My name's sake, that it should not be profaned in the sight of the nations, among whom they were, in whose sight I made Myself known to them, so as to bring them forth out of the land of Egypt.

וָאוֹצִיאֵם מֵאֶרֶץ מִצְרָיִם וָאֲבִאֵם אֶל־הַמִּדְבָּר

10[5] *So I caused them to go forth out of the land of Egypt,[6] and brought them into the wilderness.*

וָאֶתֵּן לָהֶם אֶת־חֻקּוֹתַי וְאֶת־מִשְׁפָּטַי הוֹדַעְתִּי אוֹתָם אֲשֶׁר יַעֲשֶׂה אוֹתָם הָאָדָם וָחַי בָּהֶם

11[7] And I gave them My statutes, and taught them My ordinances, which if a man does, he shall live by them.

וְגַם אֶת־שַׁבְּתוֹתַי נָתַתִּי לָהֶם לִהְיוֹת לְאוֹת בֵּינִי וּבֵינֵיהֶם לָדַעַת כִּי אֲנִי יְהוָה מְקַדְּשָׁם

12[8] Moreover, I gave them My sabbaths, to be a sign between Me and them, so they might know that I am the LORD who sanctifies them.

וַיַּמְרוּ־בִי בֵית־יִשְׂרָאֵל בַּמִּדְבָּר בְּחֻקּוֹתַי לֹא־הָלָכוּ וְאֶת־מִשְׁפָּטַי מָאָסוּ אֲשֶׁר יַעֲשֶׂה אֹתָם הָאָדָם וָחַי בָּהֶם וְאֶת־שַׁבְּתֹתַי חִלְּלוּ מְאֹד וָאֹמַר לִשְׁפֹּךְ חֲמָתִי עֲלֵיהֶם בַּמִּדְבָּר לְכַלּוֹתָם

13[9] But the house of Israel rebelled against Me in the wilderness; they did not walk in My statutes, and they rejected My ordinances, which if a man do, he shall live by them, and My sabbaths they greatly profaned; then I said I would pour My fury on them in the wilderness, to consume them.

וָאֶעֱשֶׂה לְמַעַן שְׁמִי לְבִלְתִּי הֵחֵל לְעֵינֵי הַגּוֹיִם אֲשֶׁר הוֹצֵאתִים לְעֵינֵיהֶם

14[10] But I decided, for My name's sake, that it should not be profaned in the sight of the nations, in whose sight I brought them out.

---

[1] Ezekiel 20:6 - Daniel 8:9 11:16 11:41, Deuteronomy 6:3 8:7-9 11:9 11:11-12 26:9 26:15 27:3 31:20 32:8 32:13-14, Exodus 3:8 3:17 13:5 14:1-15 33:3, Ezekiel 20:5 20:15 20:23 20:42, Genesis 15:13-14, Guide for the Perplexed 2:30, Jastrow 1258a, Jeremiah 11:5 32:22, Joshua 5:6, Leviticus 20:24, Midrash Tanchuma Massei 6, Numbers 13:27 14:8, Numbers.R 23:7, Psalms 48:3, Zechariah 7:14

[2] Ezekiel 20:7 - 2 Chronicles 15:8, Deuteronomy 29:15-17, Exodus 16:12 20:2 20:4, Exodus.R 6:5, Ezekiel 6:9 14:6 18:6 18:15 18:31 20:8 20:19 23:3 23:8, Isaiah 2:20-21 31:7, Joshua 24:14, Leviticus 11:44 17:7 18:3 20:7, Leviticus.R 7:1, Midrash Psalms 44:1 Ezekiel 20:7-8 - Mekilta de R'Shimon bar Yochai Sanya 2:2 Ezekiel 20:7-9 - Mekilta de R'Ishmael Pisha 5:61-64, Mekilta de R'Ishmael Pisha 16:178-179

[3] Ezekiel 20:8 - b.Shabbat [Rashi] 139a, Deuteronomy 9:7, Exodus 32:4-32:6, Exodus.R 5:17 16:2, Ezekiel 5:13 7:8 20:7 20:13 20:21, Isaiah 63:10, Leviticus.R 7:1, Midrash Tanchuma Behaalotcha 8, Nehemiah 9:26, Numbers.R 5:6 15:12, Song of Songs.R 1:34 Ezekiel 20:8-9 - Mekhilta de R'Shimon bar Yochai Bachodesh 49:2, Mekhilta de R'Shimon bar Yochai Pisha 13:1

[4] Ezekiel 20:9 - 1 Samuel 4:8 12:22, Deuteronomy 9:28 32:26-32:27, Exodus 32:12, Exodus.R 1:35 1:36, Ezekiel 20:14 20:22 36:21-36:22 39:7, Joshua 2:10 7:9 9:9-9:10, Leviticus.R 2:8 7:1 7:1, Mekhilta de R'Shimon bar Yochai Sanya 2:2, Numbers 14:13-14:25

[5] Ezekiel 20:10 - Exodus 13:17-13:18 14:17-14:22 15:22 20:2

[6] LXX *And I*

[7] Ezekiel 20:11 - 4Q504 frag 6 l.17, Deuteronomy 4:8 20:15-20:16, Ezekiel 20:13 20:21, Galatians 3:12, Leviticus 18:5, Luke 10:28, Nehemiah 9:13-9:14, Psalms 147:19-147:20, Romans 3:2 10:5

[8] Ezekiel 20:12 - 1 Thessalonians 5:23, Colossians 2:16, Deuteronomy 5:12-5:15, Exodus 16:29 19:5-19:6 20:8-20:11 31:13-31:17 35:2, Ezekiel 20:20 37:28, Genesis 2:3, John 17:17-17:19, Jubilees 2:19 2:21, Jude 1:1, Leviticus 20:8 21:8 21:15 21:23 23:3 23:24 23:32 23:39 25:4, Mark 2:27-2:28, Nehemiah 9:14

[9] Ezekiel 20:13 - 1 Samuel 8:8, 1 Thessalonians 4:8, 2 Samuel 12:9, Amos 2:4, Deuteronomy 9:8 9:12-9:24 31:27, Exodus 16:27-16:28 32:8 32:10, Exodus.R 5:17 25:12, Ezekiel 20:16 20:21 20:24, Hebrews 10:28-10:29, Isaiah 56:6 63:10, Leviticus 26:15 26:43, Nehemiah 9:16-9:18, Numbers 14:11-14:12 14:22 14:29 15:31-15:36 16:20-16:21 17:10 26:25, Numbers.R 5:6, Proverbs 1:25 13:13, Psalms 78:40-78:41 95:8-95:11 106:13-106:33

[10] Ezekiel 20:14 - Ephesians 1:6 1:12, Ezekiel 20:9 20:22 36:22-36:23, Leviticus.R 2:8

וְגַם־אֲנִי נָשָׂאתִי יָדִי לָהֶם בַּמִּדְבָּר לְבִלְתִּי הָבִיא אוֹתָם אֶל־הָאָרֶץ אֲשֶׁר־נָתַתִּי זָבַת חָלָב וּדְבַשׁ צְבִי הִיא לְכָל־הָאֲרָצוֹת	15[1]	Yet, I lifted up My hand to them in the wilderness, so I would not bring them into the land which I had given them, flowing with milk and honey, which is the beauty of all lands;
יַעַן בְּמִשְׁפָּטַי מָאָסוּ וְאֶת־חֻקּוֹתַי לֹא־הָלְכוּ בָהֶם וְאֶת־שַׁבְּתוֹתַי חִלֵּלוּ כִּי אַחֲרֵי גִלּוּלֵיהֶם לִבָּם הֹלֵךְ	16[2]	because they rejected My ordinances, and did not walk in My statutes, and profaned My Sabbaths, for their heart went after *their idols*[3].
וַתָּחָס עֵינִי עֲלֵיהֶם מִשַּׁחֲתָם וְלֹא־עָשִׂיתִי אוֹתָם כָּלָה בַּמִּדְבָּר	17[4]	Nevertheless, My eye spared them from destruction, nor did I make a full end of them in the wilderness.
וָאֹמַר אֶל־בְּנֵיהֶם בַּמִּדְבָּר בְּחוּקֵּי אֲבוֹתֵיכֶם אַל־תֵּלֵכוּ וְאֶת־מִשְׁפְּטֵיהֶם אַל־תִּשְׁמֹרוּ וּבְגִלּוּלֵיהֶם אַל־תִּטַּמָּאוּ	18[5]	And I said to their children in the wilderness: Do not walk in the statutes of your fathers, nor observe their ordinances, nor defile yourselves with their idols;
אֲנִי יְהוָה אֱלֹהֵיכֶם בְּחֻקּוֹתַי לֵכוּ וְאֶת־מִשְׁפָּטַי שִׁמְרוּ וַעֲשׂוּ אוֹתָם	19[6]	I am the LORD your God; walk in My statutes, and keep My ordinances, and do them;
וְאֶת־שַׁבְּתוֹתַי קַדֵּשׁוּ וְהָיוּ לְאוֹת בֵּינִי וּבֵינֵיכֶם לָדַעַת כִּי אֲנִי יְהוָה אֱלֹהֵיכֶם	20[7]	and hallow My sabbaths, for they shall be a sign between Me and you, so you may know that I am the LORD your God.
וַיַּמְרוּ־בִי הַבָּנִים בְּחֻקּוֹתַי לֹא־הָלְכוּ וְאֶת־מִשְׁפָּטַי לֹא־שָׁמְרוּ לַעֲשׂוֹת אוֹתָם אֲשֶׁר יַעֲשֶׂה אוֹתָם הָאָדָם וָחַי בָּהֶם אֶת־שַׁבְּתוֹתַי חִלֵּלוּ וָאֹמַר לִשְׁפֹּךְ חֲמָתִי עֲלֵיהֶם לְכַלּוֹת אַפִּי בָּם בַּמִּדְבָּר	21[8]	But the children rebelled against Me; they did not walk in My statutes, nor kept My ordinances to do them, which if a man does, he shall live by them. They profaned My sabbaths; then I said I would pour My fury on them, to spend My anger on them in the wilderness.
וַהֲשִׁבֹתִי אֶת־יָדִי וָאַעַשׂ לְמַעַן שְׁמִי לְבִלְתִּי הֵחֵל לְעֵינֵי הַגּוֹיִם אֲשֶׁר־הוֹצֵאתִי אוֹתָם לְעֵינֵיהֶם	22[9]	*Nevertheless, I withdrew My hand, and*[10] decided for My name's sake, it should not be profaned in the sight of the nations, in whose sight I brought them forth.
גַּם־אֲנִי נָשָׂאתִי אֶת־יָדִי לָהֶם בַּמִּדְבָּר לְהָפִיץ אֹתָם בַּגּוֹיִם וּלְזָרוֹת אוֹתָם בָּאֲרָצוֹת	23[11]	I lifted up My hand to them in the wilderness, so I would scatter them among the nations, and disperse them through the countries;
יַעַן מִשְׁפָּטַי לֹא־עָשׂוּ וְחֻקּוֹתַי מָאָסוּ וְאֶת־שַׁבְּתוֹתַי חִלֵּלוּ וְאַחֲרֵי גִּלּוּלֵי אֲבוֹתָם הָיוּ עֵינֵיהֶם	24[12]	because they had not executed My ordinances, but rejected My statutes, and profaned My sabbaths, and their eyes were after their fathers' idols.
וְגַם־אֲנִי נָתַתִּי לָהֶם חֻקִּים לֹא טוֹבִים וּמִשְׁפָּטִים לֹא יִחְיוּ בָּהֶם	25[13]	For this reason I gave them statutes that were not good, and ordinances which they should not live;

---

[1] Ezekiel 20:15 - Deuteronomy 1:34-35, Ezekiel 20:23, Hebrews 3:11 3:18 4:3, Numbers 14:23-30 26:64-65, Psalms 95:11 106:26

[2] Ezekiel 20:16 - Acts 7:39-7:43, Amos 5:25-5:26, Exodus 32:1-32:8, Ezekiel 14:3-14:4 20:8 20:13-20:14 23:8, Numbers 15:39 25:2

[3] LXX *the imaginations of their hearts*

[4] Ezekiel 20:17 - 1 Samuel 24:10, Ezekiel 7:2 8:18 9:10 11:13, Jeremiah 4:27 5:18, Nahum 1:8-1:9, Nehemiah 9:19, Psalms 78:37-38

[5] Ezekiel 20:18 - 1 Peter 1:18, Acts 7:51, Deuteronomy 4:3-4:6, Ezekiel 20:7, Jeremiah 2:7 3:9, Luke 11:47-11:48, Midrash Psalms 44:1, Numbers 14:32-14:33 32:13-15, Psalms 78:6-8, Zechariah 1:2-1:4

[6] Ezekiel 20:19 - Deuteronomy 4:1 5:1 5:6-5:7 5:32-6:8 7:4-7:6 8:1 10:1-10:12 11:1 12:1, Exodus 20:2-20:3, Ezekiel 11:20 36:27 37:24, Jeremiah 3:22-3:23, Nehemiah 9:13-9:14, Psalms 19:8-19:12 81:10-81:11 105:45, Titus 2:11-2:14

[7] Ezekiel 20:20 - Exodus 20:11 31:13-31:17, Ezekiel 20:12 44:24, Isaiah 58:13, Jeremiah 17:22 17:24 17:27, Nehemiah 13:15-13:22, Numbers.R 10:1, Song of Songs.R 6:4

[8] Ezekiel 20:21 - 2 Chronicles 34:21 34:25, Acts 13:18, Daniel 11:36, Deuteronomy 9:23-9:24 31:27, Ezekiel 7:8 13:15 20:8 20:11 20:13 21:36, Lamentations 4:11, Numbers 21:5 25:1-25:8, Numbers.R 5:6, Pesikta Rabbati 27:4 27/28:2, Psalms 106:29-106:33, Revelation 16:1, Saadia Opinions 9:3, y.Nedarim 3:9

[9] Ezekiel 20:22 - Daniel 9:17 9:19, Ezekiel 20:9 20:14 20:17, Isaiah 48:9-11, Jeremiah 14:7 14:21, Job 13:21, Lamentations 2:8, Psalms 25:11 78:38 79:9-10 115:1

[10] LXX *but I*

[11] Ezekiel 20:23 - Deuteronomy 28:64-28:68 32:26-32:27 32:40, Ezekiel 20:15, Jeremiah 15:4, Leviticus 26:33, mt.Hilcnot Shofar Sukkah vLulav 3:9, Psalms 106:27, Revelation 10:5-10:6

[12] Ezekiel 20:24 - Amos 2:4, Deuteronomy 4:19, Ezekiel 6:9 18:6 18:12 18:15 20:13 20:16, Job 31:26-27

[13] Ezekiel 20:25 - 2 Thessalonians 2:9-2:11, b.Berachot 24b, b.Megillah 32a, Deuteronomy 4:27-4:28 28:36, Ein Yaakov Berachot:24b, Ein Yaakov Megillah:32a, Exodus.R 30:22, Ezekiel 14:9-14:11 20:26 20:39, Isaiah 66:4, Mas.Soferim 3:10, Midrash Tanchuma Mishpatim 3, mt.Hilchot Shabbat 2:3, Pesikta de R'Kahana 144, Psalms 81:13, Romans 1:21-1:28, Song of Songs.R 1:42,

וָאֲטַמֵּא אוֹתָם בְּמַתְּנוֹתָם בְּהַעֲבִיר כָּל־פֶּטֶר רָחַם לְמַעַן אֲשִׁמֵּם לְמַעַן אֲשֶׁר יֵדְעוּ אֲשֶׁר אֲנִי יְהוָה	26[1]	*and I polluted them in their own gifts, in that they set apart all who open the womb, that I might destroy them, to the end that they might know that I am the LORD*[2].
לָכֵן דַּבֵּר אֶל־בֵּית יִשְׂרָאֵל בֶּן־אָדָם וְאָמַרְתָּ אֲלֵיהֶם כֹּה אָמַר אֲדֹנָי יְהוִה עוֹד זֹאת גִּדְּפוּ אוֹתִי אֲבוֹתֵיכֶם בְּמַעֲלָם בִּי מָעַל	27[3]	Therefore, son of man, speak to the house of Israel, and say to them: Thus says the Lord GOD: In this moreover have your fathers blasphemed Me, in that they dealt treacherously with Me.
וָאֲבִיאֵם אֶל־הָאָרֶץ אֲשֶׁר נָשָׂאתִי אֶת־יָדִי לָתֵת אוֹתָהּ לָהֶם וַיִּרְאוּ כָל־גִּבְעָה רָמָה וְכָל־עֵץ עָבֹת וַיִּזְבְּחוּ־שָׁם אֶת־זִבְחֵיהֶם וַיִּתְּנוּ־שָׁם כַּעַס קָרְבָּנָם וַיָּשִׂימוּ שָׁם רֵיחַ נִיחוֹחֵיהֶם וַיַּסִּיכוּ שָׁם אֶת־נִסְכֵּיהֶם	28[4]	For when I brought them into the land, which I lifted up My hand to give to them, then they saw every high hill, and every thick tree, and they offered there their sacrifices, and there they presented the provocation of their offering, there also they made their sweet savor, and there they poured out their drink offerings.
וָאֹמַר אֲלֵהֶם מָה הַבָּמָה אֲשֶׁר־אַתֶּם הַבָּאִים שָׁם וַיִּקָּרֵא שְׁמָהּ בָּמָה עַד הַיּוֹם הַזֶּה	29[5]	Then I said to them: *What is the high place where you go? So its name is called Bamah*[6] to this day.
לָכֵן אֱמֹר אֶל־בֵּית יִשְׂרָאֵל כֹּה אָמַר אֲדֹנָי יְהוִה הַבְּדֶרֶךְ אֲבוֹתֵיכֶם אַתֶּם נִטְמְאִים וְאַחֲרֵי שִׁקּוּצֵיהֶם אַתֶּם זֹנִים	30[7]	For this reason, say to the house of Israel: Thus says the Lord GOD: When you pollute yourselves in the manner of your fathers, and go after their abominations,
וּבִשְׂאֵת מַתְּנֹתֵיכֶם בְּהַעֲבִיר בְּנֵיכֶם בָּאֵשׁ אַתֶּם נִטְמְאִים לְכָל־גִּלּוּלֵיכֶם עַד־הַיּוֹם וַאֲנִי אִדָּרֵשׁ לָכֶם בֵּית יִשְׂרָאֵל חַי־אָנִי נְאֻם אֲדֹנָי יְהוִה אִם־אִדָּרֵשׁ לָכֶם	31[8]	*and when, in offering your gifts, in making your sons pass through the fire, you pollute yourselves with all your idols, to this day; shall you inquire of Me, O house of Israel? As I live, says the Lord GOD, you shall not inquire of me*[9];
וְהָעֹלָה עַל־רוּחֲכֶם הָיוֹ לֹא תִהְיֶה אֲשֶׁר אַתֶּם אֹמְרִים נִהְיֶה כַגּוֹיִם כְּמִשְׁפְּחוֹת הָאֲרָצוֹת לְשָׁרֵת עֵץ וָאָבֶן	32[10]	and what comes into your mind shall not be at all; in that you say: We will be as the nations, as the families of the countries, to serve wood and stone.
חַי־אָנִי נְאֻם אֲדֹנָי יְהוִה אִם־לֹא בְּיָד חֲזָקָה וּבִזְרוֹעַ נְטוּיָה וּבְחֵמָה שְׁפוּכָה אֶמְלוֹךְ עֲלֵיכֶם	33[11]	As I live, says the Lord GOD, surely with a mighty hand, and with an outstretched arm, and with fury poured out, will I be king over you;

---

y.Eruvin 3:9

[1] Ezekiel 20:26 - 2 Chronicles 28:3 33:6, 2 Kings 17:17 21:6, Exodus 13:12, Ezekiel 6:7 16:20-16:21 20:31, Isaiah 63:17, Jeremiah 19:9 32:35, Leviticus 18:21, Luke 2:23, Romans 11:7-11:10, Testament of Moses 2:8

[2] LXX *And I will defile them by their own decrees, when I pass through upon every one who opens the womb, that I may destroy them*

[3] Ezekiel 20:27 - Ezekiel 2:7 3:4 3:11 3:27 18:24, Revelation 13:5, Romans 2:24, z.Vaetchanan 269b

[4] Ezekiel 20:28 - Ezekiel 6:13 16:19 20:6 20:15, Genesis 15:18-15:21 26:3-26:4, Isaiah 57:5-57:7, Jeremiah 2:7 3:6, Joshua 23:3-23:4 23:14, Jubilees 1:10, Nehemiah 9:22-9:26, Psalms 78:55-78:58 105:8-105:11

[5] Ezekiel 20:29 - Ezekiel 16:24-16:25 16:31

[6] LXX *What is Abama, that you go in there? And they called its name Abama*

[7] Ezekiel 20:30 - Acts 7:51, Jeremiah 7:26 9:15 16:12, Judges 2:19, Matthew 23:32, Numbers 32:14, z.Vaetchanan 269b

[8] Ezekiel 20:31 - 1 Samuel 28:5-28:6, 2 Kings 3:13-3:14, Deuteronomy 18:10-18:12, Ezekiel 14:3-14:4 16:20 20:3 20:26, Isaiah 1:15, James 4:1-4:3, Jeremiah 7:31 14:12 19:5, Job 27:8 27:10, Jubilees 1:11, Matthew 25:11-25:12, Midrash Tanchuma Vayera 13, Numbers.R 11:7, Proverbs 1:27-1:28 28:9, Psalms 66:18 106:37-106:39, Zechariah 7:13

[9] LXX *and do you pollute yourselves with the firstfruits of your gifts, in the offerings wherewith you pollute yourselves in all your imaginations, until this day; and shall I answer you, O house of Israel? As I live, says the LORD, I will not answer you, neither shall this thing come upon your spirit*

[10] Ezekiel 20:32 - 1 Samuel 8:5, b.Sanhedrin 105a, Daniel 5:4, Deuteronomy 4:28 28:36 28:64 29:16, Ein Yaakov Sanhedrin:105a, Ezekiel 11:5 38:10, Guide for the Perplexed 3:51, Isaiah 37:19, Jeremiah 44:17 44:29, Lamentations 3:37, Leviticus.R 7:3, Midrash Tanchuma Nitzavim 3, Midrash Tanchuma Tzav 13, Numbers.R 2:16, Proverbs 19:21, Psalms 139:2, Revelation 9:20, Romans 12:2, y.Sheviit 1:5, y.Yoma 8:7

[11] Ezekiel 20:33 - b.Rosh Hashanah 32b, b.Sanhedrin 105a, Daniel 9:11-12, Ein Yaakov Sanhedrin 105a, Exodus.R 3:6, Ezekiel 8:18, Jastrow 1503a, Jeremiah 21:5 42:18 44:6, Lamentations 2:4, m.Rosh Hashanah 4:6, Midrash Tanchuma Nitzavim 3, Numbers.R 2:16, Sifre.z Numbers Shelah 15:40, y.Rosh Hashanah 4:7

וְהוֹצֵאתִי אֶתְכֶם מִן־הָעַמִּים וְקִבַּצְתִּי אֶתְכֶם מִן־הָאֲרָצוֹת אֲשֶׁר נְפוֹצֹתֶם בָּם בְּיָד חֲזָקָה וּבִזְרוֹעַ נְטוּיָה וּבְחֵמָה שְׁפוּכָה	34[1]

and I will bring you out from the peoples, and will gather you out of the countries in which you are scattered, with a mighty hand, and with an outstretched arm, and with fury poured out;

וְהֵבֵאתִי אֶתְכֶם אֶל־מִדְבַּר הָעַמִּים וְנִשְׁפַּטְתִּי אִתְּכֶם שָׁם פָּנִים אֶל־פָּנִים	35[2]

and I will bring you into the wilderness of the peoples, and there will I plead with you face to face.

כַּאֲשֶׁר נִשְׁפַּטְתִּי אֶת־אֲבוֹתֵיכֶם בְּמִדְבַּר אֶרֶץ מִצְרָיִם כֵּן אִשָּׁפֵט אִתְּכֶם נְאֻם אֲדֹנָי יְהוִה	36[3]

Like I pleaded with your fathers in the wilderness of the land of Egypt, so will I plead with you, says the Lord GOD.

וְהַעֲבַרְתִּי אֶתְכֶם תַּחַת הַשָּׁבֶט וְהֵבֵאתִי אֶתְכֶם בְּמָסֹרֶת הַבְּרִית	37[4]

And I will cause you to pass under the rod, and I will bring you *into the bond of the covenant*[5];

וּבָרוֹתִי מִכֶּם הַמֹּרְדִים וְהַפּוֹשְׁעִים בִּי מֵאֶרֶץ מְגוּרֵיהֶם אוֹצִיא אוֹתָם וְאֶל־אַדְמַת יִשְׂרָאֵל לֹא יָבוֹא וִידַעְתֶּם כִּי־אֲנִי יְהוָה	38[6]

and I will purge from among you the rebels, and those who transgress against Me; I will bring them forth out of the land where they sojourn, but they shall not enter the land of Israel; and you shall know I am the LORD[7].

וְאַתֶּם בֵּית־יִשְׂרָאֵל כֹּה־אָמַר אֲדֹנָי יְהוִה אִישׁ גִּלּוּלָיו לְכוּ עֲבֹדוּ וְאַחַר אִם־אֵינְכֶם שֹׁמְעִים אֵלָי וְאֶת־שֵׁם קָדְשִׁי לֹא תְחַלְּלוּ־עוֹד בְּמַתְּנוֹתֵיכֶם וּבְגִלּוּלֵיכֶם	39[8]

As for you, O house of Israel, thus says the Lord GOD: everyone, go serve his idols, because you will not listen to Me; but you shall profane My holy name no longer with your gifts, and with your idols.

כִּי בְהַר־קָדְשִׁי בְּהַר מְרוֹם יִשְׂרָאֵל נְאֻם אֲדֹנָי יְהוִה שָׁם יַעַבְדֻנִי כָּל־בֵּית יִשְׂרָאֵל כֻּלֹּה בָּאָרֶץ שָׁם אֶרְצֵם וְשָׁם אֶדְרוֹשׁ אֶת־תְּרוּמֹתֵיכֶם וְאֶת־רֵאשִׁית מַשְׂאוֹתֵיכֶם בְּכָל־קָדְשֵׁיכֶם	40[9]

For in My holy mountain, in the mountain of the height of Israel, says the Lord GOD, there all the house of Israel, all of them, shall serve Me in the land; there I will accept them, *and there I will require your terumah, and the first of your gifts*[10], with all your holy things.

בְּרֵיחַ נִיחֹחַ אֶרְצֶה אֶתְכֶם בְּהוֹצִיאִי אֶתְכֶם מִן־הָעַמִּים וְקִבַּצְתִּי אֶתְכֶם מִן־הָאֲרָצוֹת אֲשֶׁר נְפֹצֹתֶם בָּם וְנִקְדַּשְׁתִּי בָכֶם לְעֵינֵי הַגּוֹיִם	41[11]

With your sweet savor will I accept you, when I bring you out from the peoples, and gather you out of the countries in which you have been scattered; and I will be sanctified in you in the sight of the nations.

---

[1] Ezekiel 20:34 - Amos 9:9-9:10, Ezekiel 20:38 34:16, Isaiah 27:9-27:13, Jeremiah 44:6, Lamentations 2:4

[2] Ezekiel 20:35 - 4Q161 2.18, 4Q161 5+6 15-17, Ezekiel 17:20 19:13 20:36 38:8 38:22, Hosea 2:14 4:1, Jeremiah 2:9 2:35 25:31, Micah 4:10 6:1-6:2 7:13-7:15, Revelation 12:14, Saadia Opinions 8:5

[3] Ezekiel 20:36 - 1 Corinthians 10:5-10:10, Exodus 32:7-32:35, Ezekiel 20:13 20:21, Numbers 11:1-11:35 14:1-14:45 16:1-16:50 25:1-25:18, Psalms 106:15-106:48, Saadia Opinions 8:5

[4] Ezekiel 20:37 - Amos 3:2, Ezekiel 16:59-16:60 34:17, Jeremiah 33:13, Leviticus 26:25 27:32, Matthew 25:32-25:33, Midrash Psalms 94:2, Psalms 89:31-89:33, Saadia Opinions 8:5

[5] LXX *in by number*

[6] Ezekiel 20:38 - 1 Corinthians 10:5, Amos 9:9-9:10, b.Nedarim 20b, Ezekiel 6:7 11:21 13:9 15:7 23:49 34:17-34:22, Hebrews 4:3 4:6, Jeremiah 44:14, Jude 1:5, Malachi 3:3 3:19-4:21, Matthew 3:9-3:10 3:12 25:32-25:33, Midrash Tanchuma Behaalotcha 8, Numbers 14:28-14:30, Numbers.R 15:12, Psalms 9:17 95:11, Romans 9:27-9:29, Saadia Opinions 8:5, Zechariah 13:8-13:9

[7] LXX adds *even the Lord*

[8] Ezekiel 20:39 - 2 Kings 3:13, 2 Thessalonians 2:11, Amos 4:4-4:5, Apocalypse of Abraham 29:16, b.Kiddushin 40a, Ezekiel 20:25-20:26 23:37-23:39 43:7, Gates of Repentance 3.045, Hosea 4:17, Isaiah 1:13-1:15 66:3, Jeremiah 7:9-7:11 44:25-44:26, Judges 10:14, Leviticus.R 22:6, Matthew 6:24, Midrash Psalms 27:5, Pesikta Rabbati 24:3, Proverbs 21:27, Psalms 81:13, Revelation 3:15-3:16, Romans 1:24-1:28, y.Nedarim 3:9, z.Vaetchanan 269b, Zephaniah 1:4-1:5

[9] Ezekiel 20:40 - 1 Peter 2:5, b.Chullin 135b, Ezekiel 17:23 37:22-37:28 43:27, Hebrews 12:20-12:22 13:15, Isaiah 2:2-2:3 56:7 60:7 66:20 66:23, Jeremiah 31:13, Joel 4:17-4:18, Malachi 1:11 3:4, Mekhilta de R'Shimon bar Yochai Shirata 36:1, Mekhilta de R'Ishmael Shirata 10:13, Micah 4:1-4:2, Obadiah 1:16, Pesikta Rabbati 24:3, Psalms 2:6 68:16-68:17, Revelation 12:1 21:10, Saadia Opinions 5:7, Zechariah 8:20-8:23

[10] LXX *and there I will have respect to your firstfruits, and the firstfruits of your offerings*

[11] Ezekiel 20:41 - 1 Peter 3:15, Amos 9:14, Ephesians 5:2, Ezekiel 6:13 11:17 20:28 28:22 28:25 34:19 36:23-36:24 37:25 38:8 38:23 39:27-39:29, Genesis 8:21, Isaiah 5:16 11:11-11:16 27:12-27:13, Jeremiah 23:3 30:3 30:18 32:37, Leviticus 1:9 1:13 1:17 10:3, Luke 2:14, Micah 7:12-7:16, Obadiah 1:17-1:21, Philippians 4:18

וִידַעְתֶּם֙ כִּֽי־אֲנִ֣י יְהוָ֔ה בַּהֲבִיאִ֥י אֶתְכֶ֖ם אֶל־אַדְמַ֣ת יִשְׂרָאֵ֑ל אֶל־הָאָ֗רֶץ אֲשֶׁ֤ר נָשָׂ֙אתִי֙ אֶת־יָדִ֔י לָתֵ֥ת אוֹתָ֖הּ לַאֲבֽוֹתֵיכֶֽם

42[1] And you shall know that I am the LORD, when I bring you into the land of Israel, into the country that I lifted up My hand to give to your fathers.

וּזְכַרְתֶּם־שָׁ֗ם אֶת־דַּרְכֵיכֶם֙ וְאֵת֙ כָּל־עֲלִיל֣וֹתֵיכֶ֔ם אֲשֶׁ֥ר נִטְמֵאתֶ֖ם בָּ֑ם וּנְקֹֽטֹתֶם֙ בִּפְנֵיכֶ֔ם בְּכָל־רָע֥וֹתֵיכֶ֖ם אֲשֶׁ֥ר עֲשִׂיתֶֽם

43[2] And there you shall remember your ways, and all your deeds, in which you have polluted yourselves; and you shall loathe yourselves in your sight for all the evil you have committed.

וִידַעְתֶּ֞ם כִּֽי־אֲנִ֣י יְהוָ֗ה בַּעֲשׂוֹתִ֤י אִתְּכֶם֙ לְמַ֣עַן שְׁמִ֔י לֹא֩ כְדַרְכֵיכֶ֨ם הָרָעִ֜ים וְכַעֲלִילֽוֹתֵיכֶ֤ם הַנִּשְׁחָתוֹת֙ בֵּ֣ית יִשְׂרָאֵ֔ל נְאֻ֖ם אֲדֹנָ֥י יְהוִֽה

44[3] And you shall know I am the LORD, when I have worked with you for My name's sake, not according to your evil ways, nor according to your corrupt deeds, O you house of Israel, says the Lord GOD.'

Ezekiel – Chapter 21[4]

וַיְהִ֥י דְבַר־יְהוָ֖ה אֵלַ֥י לֵאמֹֽר

1 And the word of the LORD came to me, saying:

בֶּן־אָדָ֗ם שִׂ֤ים פָּנֶ֙יךָ֙ דֶּ֣רֶךְ תֵּימָ֔נָה וְהַטֵּ֖ף אֶל־דָּר֑וֹם וְהִנָּבֵ֛א אֶל־יַ֥עַר הַשָּׂדֶ֖ה נֶֽגֶב

2[5] 'Son of man, set your face toward the *South*[6], and preach toward the *South*[7], and prophesy against the *forest of the field in the South*[8];

וְאָמַרְתָּ֙ לְיַ֣עַר הַנֶּ֔גֶב שְׁמַ֖ע דְּבַר־יְהוָ֑ה כֹּֽה־אָמַ֣ר אֲדֹנָ֣י יְהוִ֡ה הִנְנִ֣י מַצִּֽית־בְּךָ֣ ׀ אֵ֡שׁ וְאָכְלָ֣ה בְךָ֣ כָל־עֵץ־לַח֩ וְכָל־עֵ֨ץ יָבֵ֜שׁ לֹֽא־תִכְבֶּה֙ לַהֶ֣בֶת שַׁלְהֶ֔בֶת וְנִצְרְבוּ־בָ֥הּ כָּל־פָּנִ֖ים מִנֶּ֥גֶב צָפֽוֹנָה

3[9] and say to the forest of the *South*[10]: Hear the word of the LORD: Thus says the Lord GOD: Behold, I will kindle a fire in you, and it shall devour every green tree in you, and every dry tree, it shall not be quenched, a flaming flame; and all faces from the south to the north shall be seared by it.

וְרָאוּ֙ כָּל־בָּשָׂ֔ר כִּ֛י אֲנִ֥י יְהוָ֖ה בִּעַרְתִּ֑יהָ לֹ֖א תִּכְבֶּֽה

4[11] all flesh shall see that I, the LORD, have kindled it; it shall not be quenched.'

וָאֹמַ֕ר אֲהָ֖הּ אֲדֹנָ֣י יְהוִ֑ה הֵ֚מָּה אֹמְרִ֣ים לִ֔י הֲלֹ֛א מְמַשֵּׁ֥ל מְשָׁלִ֖ים הֽוּא

5[12] Then said I: 'Ah Lord GOD! they say of me: Is he not a maker of parables?'

וַיְהִ֥י דְבַר־יְהוָ֖ה אֵלַ֥י לֵאמֹֽר

6 Then the word of the LORD came unto me, saying:

בֶּן־אָדָ֗ם שִׂ֤ים פָּנֶ֙יךָ֙ אֶל־יְר֣וּשָׁלִַ֔ם וְהַטֵּ֖ף אֶל־מִקְדָּשִׁ֑ים וְהִנָּבֵ֖א אֶל־אַדְמַ֥ת יִשְׂרָאֵֽל

7[13] 'Son of man, set your face toward Jerusalem, and preach toward the sanctuaries, and prophesy against the land of Israel;

וְאָמַרְתָּ֙ לְאַדְמַ֣ת יִשְׂרָאֵ֔ל כֹּ֖ה אָמַ֣ר יְהוָ֑ה הִנְנִ֣י אֵלַ֗יִךְ וְהוֹצֵאתִ֤י חַרְבִּי֙ מִתַּעְרָ֔הּ וְהִכְרַתִּ֥י מִמֵּ֖ךְ צַדִּ֥יק וְרָשָֽׁע

8[14] say to the land of Israel: Thus says the LORD: Behold, I am against you, and will draw forth

---

[1] Ezekiel 20:42 - 1 John 5:20, Ezekiel 11:17-11:20 20:38 20:44 24:24 26:13 34:13 36:23-24 37:21 37:25 38:23, Jeremiah 24:7 31:35, John 17:3

[2] Ezekiel 20:43 - 2 Corinthians 7:11, Ezekiel 6:9 16:61-16:63 36:31, Hosea 5:15, Jeremiah 31:19, Job 42:6, Leviticus 26:39-26:41, Luke 18:13, Nehemiah 1:8-1:10, Zechariah 12:10-12:14

[3] Ezekiel 20:44 - 1 Timothy 1:16, Ephesians 1:6, Ezekiel 20:9 20:14 20:22 20:38 24:24 36:21-22, Pesikta Rabbati 33:8, Psalms 79:9 115:1

[4] In LXX, this is 20:45 – 21:32

[5] Ezekiel 21:2 - Amos 7:16, Deuteronomy 32:2, Ezekiel 4:7 6:2 21:7, Isaiah 30:6, Jeremiah 13:19 22:7, Job 29:22, Micah 2:6, Midrash Psalms 73:4, Zechariah 11:1-11:2

[6] LXX *Thaeman*

[7] LXX *Darom*

[8] LXX *chief forest of Nageb*

[9] Ezekiel 21:3 - 3 Enoch 32:1, Deuteronomy 32:22, Ezekiel 15:6-15:7 17:24 19:14 21:8-21:9 22:20-22:21, Isaiah 9:19-9:20 13:8 24:1-24:6 30:33 66:24, Jeremiah 21:14, Luke 23:31, Mark 9:43-9:49, z.Vaetchanan 269b

[10] LXX *Nageb*

[11] Ezekiel 21:4 - 2 Chronicles 7:20-7:22, Deuteronomy 29:23-29:27, Isaiah 26:11, Jeremiah 7:20 40:2-40:3, Lamentations 2:16-2:17

[12] Ezekiel 21:5 - Acts 17:18, Ezekiel 17:2, Guide for the Perplexed 1:Introduction, John 16:25, Matthew 13:13-13:14

[13] Ezekiel 21:7 - Acts 6:13-6:14, Amos 7:16, Deuteronomy 32:2, Ephesians 6:19, Ezekiel 4:3 4:7 6:2 21:2 25:2 28:21 29:2 36:1 38:2, Jeremiah 26:11-26:12, Micah 2:6 2:11

[14] Ezekiel 21:8 - b.Avodah Zara 4a, b.Bava Kamma 60a, Deuteronomy 32:41-32:42, Ecclesiastes 9:2, Ein Yaakov Bava Kamma:60a, Exodus 15:9, Ezekiel 5:8 5:12 9:5-9:6 14:17 14:21 21:14-21:16 21:24 26:3, Isaiah 10:5 34:5, Jeremiah 15:2-15:4 21:13 47:6-47:7

My sword out of its sheath, and will cut off from you the righteous and the wicked.

Seeing then that I will cut off from you the *righteous*[2] and the wicked, therefore shall My sword go forth out of its sheath against all flesh from the south to the north;

יַ֚עַן אֲשֶׁר־הִכְרַ֣תִּי מִמֵּ֔ךְ צַדִּ֖יק וְרָשָׁ֑ע לָכֵ֞ן תֵּצֵ֤א חַרְבִּי֙ מִתַּעְרָ֔הּ אֶל־כָּל־בָּשָׂ֖ר מִנֶּ֥גֶב צָפֽוֹן 9[1]

and all flesh shall know that I, the LORD, have drawn My sword from its sheath; it shall not return any more.

וְיָֽדְעוּ֙ כָּל־בָּשָׂ֔ר כִּ֚י אֲנִ֣י יְהֹוָ֔ה הוֹצֵ֥אתִי חַרְבִּ֖י מִתַּעְרָ֑הּ לֹ֥א תָשׁ֖וּב עֽוֹד 10[3]

Sigh, therefore, son of man; with the breaking of your loins and with bitterness shall you sigh before their eyes.

וְאַתָּ֥ה בֶן־אָדָ֖ם הֵאָנַ֑ח בְּשִׁבְר֤וֹן מָתְנַ֙יִם֙ וּבִמְרִיר֔וּת תֵּֽאָנַ֖ח לְעֵינֵיהֶֽם 11[4]

And it shall be, when they say to you: Why do you sigh? You shall say: Because of the tidings, for it comes; and every heart shall melt, and all hands shall be slack, and every spirit shall be faint, and all knees shall drip with water; behold, it comes, and it shall be done, says the Lord GOD.'

וְהָיָה֙ כִּֽי־יֹאמְר֣וּ אֵלֶ֔יךָ עַל־מָ֖ה אַתָּ֣ה נֶאֱנָ֑ח וְאָמַרְתָּ֗ אֶל־שְׁמוּעָ֤ה כִֽי־בָאָה֙ וְנָמֵ֣ס כָּל־לֵ֗ב וְרָפ֤וּ כָל־יָדַ֙יִם֙ וְכִהֲתָ֣ה כָל־ר֔וּחַ וְכָל־בִּרְכַּ֖יִם תֵּלַ֣כְנָה מָּ֑יִם הִנֵּ֤ה בָאָה֙ וְנִֽהְיָ֔תָה נְאֻ֖ם אֲדֹנָ֥י יְהֹוִֽה 12[5]

And the word of the LORD came to me, saying:

וַיְהִ֥י דְבַר־יְהֹוָ֖ה אֵלַ֥י לֵאמֹֽר 13[6]

'Son of man, prophesy, and say: Thus says the LORD: Say: A sword, a sword, it is sharpened, And also furbished:

בֶּן־אָדָ֞ם הִנָּבֵ֣א וְאָמַרְתָּ֗ כֹּ֚ה אָמַ֣ר אֲדֹנָ֔י אֱמֹ֕ר חֶ֥רֶב חֶ֛רֶב הוּחַ֖דָּה וְגַם־מְרוּטָֽה 14[7]

It is sharpened so it may make a terrible slaughter, It is furbished so it may glitter; Or shall we make mirth? Against the rod of My son, condemning every tree.

לְמַ֨עַן טְבֹ֤חַ טֶ֙בַח֙ הוּחַ֔דָּה לְמַעַן־הֱיֵה־לָ֖הּ בָּרָ֑ק מֹרָ֕טָה א֣וֹ נָשִׂ֔ישׂ שֵׁ֥בֶט בְּנִ֖י מֹאֶ֥סֶת כָּל־עֵֽץ 15[8]

And it is given to be furbished, so it may be handled; The sword, it is sharpened, yes, it is furbished, To give it into the hand of the slayer.

וַיִּתֵּ֥ן אֹתָ֛הּ לְמׇרְטָ֖ה לִתְפֹּ֣שׂ בַּכָּ֑ף הִֽיא־הוּחַ֤דָּה חֶ֙רֶב֙ וְהִ֣יא מֹרָ֔טָה לָתֵ֥ת אוֹתָ֖הּ בְּיַד־הוֹרֵֽג 16[9]

Cry and wail, son of man; for it is on My people, it is on all the princes of Israel; *they are thrust down to the sword with My people; strike, therefore, on your thigh*[11].

זְעַ֤ק וְהֵילֵל֙ בֶּן־אָדָ֔ם כִּי־הִיא֙ הָיְתָ֣ה בְעַמִּ֔י הִ֕יא בְּכָל־נְשִׂיאֵ֖י יִשְׂרָאֵ֑ל מְגוּרֵ֤י אֶל־חֶ֙רֶב֙ הָי֣וּ אֶת־עַמִּ֔י לָכֵ֖ן סְפֹ֥ק אֶל־יָרֵֽךְ 17[10]

For there is a trial; and what if it contemns the rod? It shall be no more, says the Lord GOD.

כִּ֣י בֹ֔חַן וּמָ֕ה אִם־גַּם־שֵׁ֖בֶט מֹאֶ֑סֶת לֹ֣א יִֽהְיֶ֔ה נְאֻ֖ם אֲדֹנָ֥י יְהֹוִֽה 18[12]

50:31 51:20 51:25, Job 9:22, Leviticus 26:25 26:33, Mekilta d e R'Ishmael Pisha 11:63, Midrash Tanchuma Mishpatim 7, Nahum 2:14 3:5, Psalms 17:13, Zechariah 13:7, Zephaniah 2:12

[1] Ezekiel 21:9 - Ezekiel 6:11-6:14 7:2 21:3, z.Vaetchanan 269b

[2] LXX *unrighteous*

[3] Ezekiel 21:10 - 1 Kings 9:7-9:9, 1 Samuel 3:12, Deuteronomy 29:23-29:27, Ezekiel 21:4 21:35, Isaiah 45:23 55:11, Jeremiah 23:20, Nahum 1:9, Numbers 14:21-14:23

[4] Ezekiel 21:11 - b.Berachot 58b, b.Ketubot 62a, Daniel 5:6 8:27, Ein Yaakov Berachot:58b, Ein Yaakov Ketubot:62a, Ezekiel 4:12 6:11 9:4 12:3-5 21:17 37:20, Habakkuk 3:16, Isaiah 16:11 21:3 22:4, Jeremiah 4:19 9:18-22 19:10 30:6, John 11:33-35, Nahum 2:11

[5] Ezekiel 21:12 - 1 Peter 4:7, 2 Kings 21:12, 2 Samuel 17:10, b.Berachot 58b, b.Ketubot 62a, Deuteronomy 20:8, Ein Yaakov Berachot 58b, Exodus 15:15, Ezekiel 7:2-12 7:17 7:26 12:9-11 12:22-28 21:5 24:19, Hebrews 12:12, Isaiah 7:2 13:7 28:19 35:3, Jeremiah 6:22-6:24 8:18 49:23 50:43, Job 4:3-4:4, Joshua 2:9-11 5:1, Lamentations 5:17, Leviticus 26:36, Luke 21:26, Mekilta de R'Ishmael Shirata 9:95, Nahum 2:11, Pesikta Rabbati 27:2

[6] Ezekiel 21:13 - Per Massorah: Soferim altered "Hashem" to "Adonai"

[7] Ezekiel 21:14 - Amos 9:4, Avot de R'Natan 33, Deuteronomy 32:41-42, Ezekiel 21:8 21:20 21:33, Isaiah 27:1 34:5-34:6 66:16, Jeremiah 12:12 15:2, Job 20:25, Psalms 7:12-7:14

[8] Ezekiel 21:15 - 2 Samuel 7:14, Amos 6:3-7, b.Tamid [Pirush] 30a, b.Yoma [Rashi] 28a, Ecclesiastes 3:4, Esther 3:15, Ezekiel 19:11-14 21:3 21:30-32, Habakkuk 3:11, Isaiah 5:12-14 22:12-14 34:5-6, Jeremiah 46:4, Luke 21:34-35, Nahum 1:10 3:3, Psalms 2:7-9 89:27-33 89:39-46 110:5-6, Revelation 2:27

[9] Ezekiel 21:16 - Ezekiel 21:24, Jeremiah 25:9 25:33 51:20-23

[10] Ezekiel 21:17 - b.Yoma 9b, Ein Yaakov Yoma:9a, Exodus.R 1:34, Ezekiel 6:11 9:8 21:11 21:19 30:2, Gates of Repentance 1.018, Jeremiah 25:34 31:13 31:20, Joel 1:13, Micah 1:8, z.Yitro 75b

[11] LXX *they shall be as strangers: judgment with the sword has come upon my people: therefore clap your hands, for sentence has been passed*

[12] Ezekiel 21:18 - 2 Corinthians 8:2, Ezekiel 21:15 21:30, Job 9:23

וְאַתָּה בֶן־אָדָם הִנָּבֵא וְהַךְ כַּף אֶל־כָּף וְתִכָּפֵל חֶרֶב שְׁלִישִׁתָה חֶרֶב חֲלָלִים הִיא חֶרֶב חָלָל הַגָּדוֹל הַחֹדֶרֶת לָהֶם

19[1]   You therefore, son of man, prophesy, and strike your hands together; *and let the sword be doubled the third time, the sword of those to be killed; it is the sword of the great one that is to be killed, which encircles them*[2].

לְמַעַן לָמוּג לֵב וְהַרְבֵּה הַמִּכְשֹׁלִים עַל כָּל־שַׁעֲרֵיהֶם נָתַתִּי אִבְחַת־חָרֶב אָח עֲשׂוּיָה לְבָרָק מְעֻטָּה לְטָבַח

20[3]   *I have set the point of the sword against all their gates, so their heart may melt, and their stumbling shall be multiplied; ah! it is made glittering, it is sharpened for slaughter*[4].

הִתְאַחֲדִי הֵימִנִי הָשִׂימִי הַשְׂמִילִי אָנָה פָּנַיִךְ מֻעָדוֹת

21[5]   Go one way to the right, or direct yourself to the left; wherever your face is set?

וְגַם־אֲנִי אַכֶּה כַפִּי אֶל־כַּפִּי וַהֲנִחֹתִי חֲמָתִי אֲנִי יְהוָה דִּבַּרְתִּי

22[6]   I will also strike My hands together, and I will satisfy My fury; I, the LORD, have spoken it.'

וַיְהִי דְבַר־יְהוָה אֵלַי לֵאמֹר

23[7]   And the word of the LORD came to me, saying:

וְאַתָּה בֶן־אָדָם שִׂים־לְךָ שְׁנַיִם דְּרָכִים לָבוֹא חֶרֶב מֶלֶךְ־בָּבֶל מֵאֶרֶץ אֶחָד יֵצְאוּ שְׁנֵיהֶם וְיָד בָּרֵא בְּרֹאשׁ דֶּרֶךְ־עִיר בָּרֵא

24[8]   'Now, son of man, make two ways, so the sword of the king of Babylon may come; the two shall come forth out of one land; and mark a signpost, mark it clear at the head of the way to the city.

דֶּרֶךְ תָּשִׂים לָבוֹא חֶרֶב אֵת רַבַּת בְּנֵי־עַמּוֹן וְאֶת־יְהוּדָה בִירוּשָׁלַ͏ִם בְּצוּרָה

25[9]   You shall make a way, so the sword may come to Rabbah of the children of Ammon, and to Judah in the fortified Jerusalem.

כִּי־עָמַד מֶלֶךְ־בָּבֶל אֶל־אֵם הַדֶּרֶךְ בְּרֹאשׁ שְׁנֵי הַדְּרָכִים לִקְסָם־קָסֶם קִלְקַל בַּחִצִּים שָׁאַל בַּתְּרָפִים רָאָה בַּכָּבֵד

26[10] For the king of Babylon stands at the parting of the way, at the head of the two ways, to use divination; he shakes the arrows to and fro, he inquires of the *teraphim, he looks in the liver*[11].

בִּימִינוֹ הָיָה הַקֶּסֶם יְרוּשָׁלַ͏ִם לָשׂוּם כָּרִים לִפְתֹּחַ פֶּה בְּרֶצַח לְהָרִים קוֹל בִּתְרוּעָה לָשׂוּם כָּרִים עַל־שְׁעָרִים לִשְׁפֹּךְ סֹלְלָה לִבְנוֹת דָּיֵק

27[12] In his right hand is the lot for Jerusalem, to set battering rams, to open the mouth for the slaughter, to lift up the voice with shouting, to set battering rams against the gates, to cast up mounds, to build forts.

וְהָיָה לָהֶם 'כִּקְסוֹם־כִּקְסָם־שָׁוְא בְּעֵינֵיהֶם שְׁבֻעֵי שְׁבֻעוֹת לָהֶם וְהוּא־מַזְכִּיר עָוֹן לְהִתָּפֵשׂ

28[13] *And it shall be a false divination in their sight, who have weeks on weeks! but it brings iniquity to remembrance, so they may be taken*[14].

---

[1] Ezekiel 21:19 - 1 Kings 20:30 22:25, 2 Kings 24:1 24:10-24:16 25:1-25:7, Amos 9:2, Daniel 3:19, Ezekiel 6:11 8:12 21:22, Leviticus 26:21 26:24, Leviticus.R 13:5, Numbers 24:10

[2] LXX *and take a second sword: the third sword is the sword of the slain, the great sword of the slain: and thou shalt strike them with amazement, lest the heart should faint*

[3] Ezekiel 21:20 - 2 Samuel 17:10, Ezekiel 15:7 21:3 21:12 21:15 21:27 21:33, Jeremiah 17:27, Leviticus.R 13:5, Mekhilta de R'Shimon bar Yochai Shirata 35:4, Mekilta de R'Ishmael Shirata 9:96, Psalms 22:15

[4] LXX *and the weak ones be multiplied at every gate; they are given up to the slaughter of the sword: it is well fitted for slaughter, it is well fitted for glittering*

[5] Ezekiel 21:21 - Ezekiel 14:17 16:46 21:9 21:25, Genesis 13:9, Midrash Psalms 31:6 78:19

[6] Ezekiel 21:22 - b.Berachot 59a, b.Sanhedrin 95b, Deuteronomy 28:63, Ein Yaakov Sanhedrin:95b, Ezekiel 5:13 16:42 21:19 22:13, Isaiah 1:24, Midrash Psalms 137:3, Numbers 24:10, Pesikta Rabbati 27/28:2 28:2, Zechariah 6:8

[7] Ezekiel 21:23-24 - mt.Hilchot Beit HaBechirah 5:7

[8] Ezekiel 21:24 - Ezekiel 4:1-3 5:1-17, Jeremiah 1:10, z.Vaetchanan 269b

[9] Ezekiel 21:25 - 2 Chronicles 26:9 32:5 33:14, 2 Samuel 5:9 12:26, Amos 1:14, Deuteronomy 3:11, Ezekiel 25:5, Isaiah 22:10, Jeremiah 49:2, Lamentations 4:12, Psalms 48:13-14 125:1-2

[10] Ezekiel 21:26 - 1 Samuel 15:23, 2 Kings 23:24, Acts 16:16, Deuteronomy 18:10, Ecclesiastes.R 12:7, Genesis 31:19 31:30, Hosea 3:4 4:12, Jastrow 184a 421b 1651b, Judges 17:5 18:14 18:18 18:20 18:24, Lamentations.R Petichata D'Chakimei:23, Midrash Psalms 74:2 79:2, Numbers 22:7 23:23 23:28, Proverbs 16:10 16:33 21:1, Sefer Yetzirah 1:2, z.Vaetchanan 269b, Zechariah 10:2

[11] LXX *graven images, and to examine the victims.*

[12] Ezekiel 21:27 - 1 Samuel 17:20, Ecclesiastes.R 12:7, Exodus 32:17-32:18, Ezekiel 4:2 26:9, Jastrow 534a 611b 643a 669b 1017a, Jeremiah 32:24 33:4 51:14 52:4, Job 39:25, Joshua 6:10 6:20, Lamentations.R Petichata D'Chakimei:23

[13] Ezekiel 21:28 - 1 Kings 17:18, 2 Chronicles 36:13, 2 Kings 24:20-7, Ecclesiastes.R 12:7, Ezekiel 11:3 12:22 17:13-19 21:29 29:16, Isaiah 28:14-15, Jeremiah 52:3-11, Lamentations.R Petichata D'Chakimei:23, Numbers 5:15, Revelation 16:19, z.Vaetchanan 269b

[14] LXX *And he was to them as one using divination before them, and he himself recounting his iniquities, that they might be borne in mind*

לָכֵ֞ן כֹּֽה־אָמַ֣ר ׀ אֲדֹנָ֣י יְהוִ֗ה יַ֚עַן הַזְכַּֽרְכֶ֣ם עֲוֺנְכֶ֔ם בְּהִגָּל֤וֹת פִּשְׁעֵיכֶם֙ לְהֵרָאוֹת֙ חַטֹּ֣אותֵיכֶ֔ם בְּכֹ֖ל עֲלִילֽוֹתֵיכֶ֑ם יַ֚עַן הִזָּ֣כֶרְכֶ֔ם בַּכַּ֖ף תִּתָּפֵֽשׂוּ

29[1] Therefore thus says the Lord GOD: Because you have made your iniquity to be remembered, in that your transgressions are uncovered, so that your sins appear in all your deeds; because that you are come to remembrance, you shall be taken with the hand.

וְאַתָּה֙ חָלָ֣ל רָשָׁ֔ע נְשִׂ֖יא יִשְׂרָאֵ֑ל אֲשֶׁר־בָּ֣א יוֹמ֔וֹ בְּעֵ֖ת עֲוֺ֥ן קֵֽץ

30[2] And you, O wicked one, who are to be slain, the prince of Israel, whose day is come, in the time of the iniquity of the end;

כֹּ֤ה אָמַר֙ אֲדֹנָ֣י יְהוִ֔ה הָסִיר֙ הַמִּצְנֶ֔פֶת וְהָרִ֖ים הָֽעֲטָרָ֑ה זֹ֣את לֹא־זֹ֔את הַשָּׁפָלָ֣ה הַגְבֵּ֔הַ וְהַגָּבֹ֖הַ הַשְׁפִּֽיל

31[3] thus says the Lord GOD: The mitre shall be removed, and the crown taken off; this shall be no more the same: what is low shall be exalted, and what is high abased.

עַוָּ֥ה עַוָּ֖ה עַוָּ֣ה אֲשִׂימֶ֑נָּה גַּם־זֹאת֙ לֹ֣א הָיָ֔ה עַד־בֹּ֗א אֲשֶׁר־ל֥וֹ הַמִּשְׁפָּ֖ט וּנְתַתִּֽיו

32[4] *A ruin, a ruin, a ruin*[5], will I make it; this also shall be no more, until he come whose right it is, and I will give it him.

וְאַתָּ֣ה בֶן־אָדָ֗ם הִנָּבֵ֤א וְאָֽמַרְתָּ֙ כֹּ֤ה אָמַר֙ אֲדֹנָ֣י יְהוִ֔ה אֶל־בְּנֵ֥י עַמּ֖וֹן וְאֶל־חֶרְפָּתָ֑ם וְאָמַרְתָּ֗ חֶ֣רֶב חֶ֤רֶב פְּתוּחָה֙ לְטֶ֣בַח מְרוּטָ֔ה לְהָכִ֖יל לְמַ֥עַן בָּרָֽק

33[6] And you, son of man, prophesy, and say: Thus says the Lord GOD concerning the children of Ammon, and concerning their taunt; and say: O sword, O sword *keen edged, furbished for the slaughter to the uttermost, because of the glittering*[7];

בַּחֲזֽוֹת לָךְ֙ שָׁ֔וְא בִּקְסׇם־לָ֖ךְ כָּזָ֑ב לָתֵ֣ת אוֹתָ֗ךְ אֶל־צַוְּארֵי֙ חַֽלְלֵ֣י רְשָׁעִ֔ים אֲשֶׁר־בָּ֣א יוֹמָ֔ם בְּעֵ֖ת עֲוֺ֥ן קֵֽץ

34[8] While they see falsehood unto thee, While they divine lies unto you, To lay you upon the necks of the wicked to be slain, Whose day is come, in the time of the iniquity of the end!

הָשַׁ֖ב אֶל־תַּעְרָ֑הּ בִּמְק֧וֹם אֲשֶׁר־נִבְרֵ֛את בְּאֶ֥רֶץ מְכֻרוֹתַ֖יִךְ אֶשְׁפֹּ֥ט אֹתָֽךְ

35[9] Cause it to return into its sheath! In the place where you were created, in the land of your origin, will I judge you.

וְשָׁפַכְתִּ֤י עָלַ֙יִךְ֙ זַעְמִ֔י בְּאֵ֥שׁ עֶבְרָתִ֖י אָפִ֣יחַ עָלָ֑יִךְ וּנְתַתִּ֗יךְ בְּיַד֙ אֲנָשִׁ֣ים בֹּֽעֲרִ֔ים חָרָשֵׁ֖י מַשְׁחִֽית

36[10] And I will pour out My indignation upon you, I will blow upon you with the fire of My wrath; And I will deliver you into the hand of brutish men, skillful to destroy.

לָאֵ֤שׁ תִּֽהְיֶה֙ לְאׇכְלָ֔ה דָּמֵ֥ךְ יִהְיֶ֖ה בְּת֣וֹךְ הָאָ֑רֶץ לֹ֣א תִזָּכֵ֔רִי כִּ֛י אֲנִ֥י יְהֹוָ֖ה דִּבַּֽרְתִּי

37[11] You shall be for fuel to the fire; Your blood shall be in the midst of the land, You shall be no more remembered; For I, the LORD, have spoken it.'

---

[1] Ezekiel 21:29 - Amos 9:1-9:3, Ezekiel 16:16-22 22:3-12 22:24-31 23:5-21 24:7, Hosea 4:2, Isaiah 3:9 22:17-18, Jeremiah 2:34 3:2 5:27-28 6:15 8:12 9:3-8 15:2, Micah 3:10-12

[2] Ezekiel 21:30 - 2 Chronicles 36:13, b.Berachot 18b, Ecclesiastes.R 8:13, Ezekiel 7:6 17:19 21:34 30:3 35:5, Jeremiah 24:8 51:13 52:2, Midrash Tanchuma Vezot Habracha 7, Psalms 7:10 9:6-9:7

[3] Ezekiel 21:31 - 1 Samuel 2:7-2:8, 2 Kings 25:6 25:27, b.Gittin 7a, Ein Yaakov Gittin:6b, Ezekiel 12:12-12:13 16:12 17:24, Jastrow 1460a, Jeremiah 13:18 39:6-39:7 52:9-52:11 52:31-52:34, Lamentations 5:16, Luke 1:52, Mesillat Yesharim 22:Trait of Anavah, mt.Hilchot Taaniot 5:15, Psalms 75:8 113:7-113:8, Ruth.R 3:1, y.Sotah 9:15

[4] Ezekiel 21:32 - 1 Peter 3:22, Amos 9:11-9:12, b.Avodah Zara 3a, Daniel 2:44 9:25, Ephesians 1:20-1:22, Ezekiel 17:22-17:23 21:18 34:23 37:24-37:25, Genesis 49:10, Genesis.R 26:7, Haggai 2:7 2:21-2:22, Hebrews 12:26-12:27, Hosea 3:5, Isaiah 9:7-9:8, Jastrow 1262a, Jeremiah 23:5-23:6 30:21 33:15-33:16 33:21 33:26, John 1:4 1:9, Lamentations.R 3:?, Luke 1:32 1:69 2:11, Malachi 3:1 3:20, Matthew 28:18, Micah 5:3, Numbers 24:19, Philippians 2:9-10, Psalms 2:6 72:7-10, Revelation 19:11-16, Zechariah 6:12-13 9:9

[5] LXX Injustice, injustice, injustice

[6] Ezekiel 21:33 - Amos 1:13-1:15, Ezekiel 21:14-21:15 21:25 25:2-25:7, Jeremiah 12:12 49:1-49:5, Zephaniah 2:8-2:10

[7] LXX *drawn for slaughter, and drawn for destruction, awake, that you may gleam*

[8] Ezekiel 21:34 - b.Sanhedrin [Rashi] 88a, b.Sotah 45b, b.Taanit [Rashi] 5a, Ein Yaakov Sotah:45b, Ezekiel 12:24 13:6 13:10 13:23 21:30 22:28 35:5, Isaiah 44:25 47:13, Jeremiah 27:9, Job 18:20, Lamentations 2:14, Psalms 37:13, y.Sotah 9:3

[9] Ezekiel 21:35 - Ezekiel 16:3-16:4 16:38 21:9-21:10 28:13 28:15, Genesis 15:14, Jeremiah 47:6-47:7

[10] Ezekiel 21:36 - Ezekiel 7:8 14:19 22:20-22:22, Habakkuk 1:6-1:10, Haggai 1:9, Isaiah 14:4-14:6 30:33 37:7 40:7, Jeremiah 4:7 6:22-6:23 51:20-51:23, Nahum 1:6, Psalms 18:16, Sifre Devarim {Haazinu Hashamayim} 308, Song of Songs.R 2:47

Ezekiel 21:36-37 - Sifre Devarim Nitzavim 308

[11] Ezekiel 21:37 - Ezekiel 21:3-4 21:35 25:10, Isaiah 34:3-7, Malachi 3:19, Matthew 3:10 3:12 24:35, Numbers 23:19, Zephaniah 2:9

Ezekiel – Chapter 22[1]

וַיְהִי דְבַר־יְהוָה אֵלַי לֵאמֹר	1[2]	Moreover the word of the LORD came unto me, saying:
וְאַתָּה בֶן־אָדָם הֲתִשְׁפֹּט הֲתִשְׁפֹּט אֶת־עִיר הַדָּמִים וְהוֹדַעְתָּהּ אֵת כָּל־תּוֹעֲבוֹתֶיהָ	2[3]	'Now, you, son of man, will you judge, will you judge the bloody city? then cause her to know all her abominations.
וְאָמַרְתָּ כֹּה אָמַר אֲדֹנָי יְהוִֹה עִיר שֹׁפֶכֶת דָּם בְּתוֹכָהּ לָבוֹא עִתָּהּ וְעָשְׂתָה גִלּוּלִים עָלֶיהָ לְטָמְאָה	3[4]	And you shall say: Thus says the Lord GOD: O city that sheds blood in the midst of you, that your time may come, and that make idols unto yourself to defile you;
בְּדָמֵךְ אֲשֶׁר־שָׁפַכְתְּ אָשַׁמְתְּ וּבְגִלּוּלַיִךְ אֲשֶׁר־עָשִׂית טָמֵאת וַתַּקְרִיבִי יָמַיִךְ וַתָּבוֹא עַד־שְׁנוֹתָיִךְ עַל־כֵּן נְתַתִּיךְ חֶרְפָּה לַגּוֹיִם וְקַלָּסָה לְכָל־הָאֲרָצוֹת	4[5]	you are guilty in the blood you have shed, and are defiled in your idols you have made; and you have caused your days to draw near, and have come to your years; therefore have I made you a reproach to the nations, and a mocking to all the countries!
הַקְּרֹבוֹת וְהָרְחֹקוֹת מִמֵּךְ יִתְקַלְּסוּ־בָךְ טְמֵאַת הַשֵּׁם רַבַּת הַמְּהוּמָה	5[6]	Those who are near, and those who are far from you, shall mock you, you defiled of name and full of tumult.
הִנֵּה נְשִׂיאֵי יִשְׂרָאֵל אִישׁ לִזְרֹעוֹ הָיוּ בָךְ לְמַעַן שְׁפָךְ־דָּם	6[7]	Behold, the princes of Israel, every one according to his might, have been in you to shed blood.
אָב וָאֵם הֵקַלּוּ בָךְ לַגֵּר עָשׂוּ בַעֹשֶׁק בְּתוֹכֵךְ יָתוֹם וְאַלְמָנָה הוֹנוּ בָךְ	7[8]	In you have they made light of father and mother; in the midst of you have they dealt by oppression with the stranger; in you have they wronged the fatherless and the widow.
קָדָשַׁי בָּזִית וְאֶת־שַׁבְּתֹתַי חִלָּלְתְּ	8[9]	You have despised My holy things, and have profaned My sabbaths.
אַנְשֵׁי רָכִיל הָיוּ בָךְ לְמַעַן שְׁפָךְ־דָּם וְאֶל־הֶהָרִים אָכְלוּ בָךְ זִמָּה עָשׂוּ בְתוֹכֵךְ	9[10]	*In you have been talebearers*[11] to shed blood; and in you they have eaten upon the mountains; in your midst they have committed lewdness.
עֶרְוַת־אָב גִּלָּה־בָךְ טְמֵאַת הַנִּדָּה עִנּוּ־בָךְ	10[12]	In you have they uncovered their fathers' nakedness; in you have they humbled her who was unclean in her impurity.

[1] Ezekiel 22 - Ein Yaakov Taanit:5a

[2] Ezekiel 22:1-16 - Haftarah Acharei Mot Sephard
Ezekiel 22:1-19 - Haftarah Acharei Mot

[3] Ezekiel 22:2 - 1 Timothy 5:20, 2 Kings 21:16 24:3-24:4, Acts 7:52, Ezekiel 8:9-8:17 16:1-16:63 20:4 23:1-23:49 24:6 24:9, Hosea 4:2, Isaiah 58:1, Jeremiah 2:30 2:34, Luke 11:50, Matthew 23:35 27:25, Nahum 3:1, Tanna Devei Eliyahu 5

[4] Ezekiel 22:3 - 2 Kings 21:2-21:9, 2 Peter 2:3, Ezekiel 7:2-7:12 12:25 22:4 22:6 22:27 23:37 23:45 24:6-24:9, Jeremiah 2:1-2:3, Romans 2:5, z.Vaetchanan 269b, Zephaniah 3:3

[5] Ezekiel 22:4 - 1 Kings 9:7, 1 Thessalonians 2:16, 2 Chronicles 7:20, 2 Kings 21:16, Daniel 9:16, Deuteronomy 28:37 29:23, Ezekiel 5:14-5:15 16:57 21:33 22:2, Jeremiah 18:16 24:9 44:8, Lamentations 2:15-2:16, Leviticus 26:32, Matthew 23:32-23:33, Numbers 32:14, Numbers.R 9:7, Psalms 44:14-44:15 79:4 89:42-89:43, variant עד of עת is found

[6] Ezekiel 22:5 - Isaiah 22:2, Jeremiah 15:2-15:3, Midrash Tanchuma Shoftim 1

[7] Ezekiel 22:6 - Daniel 9:8, Ezekiel 22:27, Isaiah 1:23, Jeremiah 2:26-2:27 5:5 32:32, Micah 2:1 3:1-3:3 3:9-3:11, Midrash Tanchuma Shoftim 8, Nehemiah 9:34, Zechariah 3:3

[8] Ezekiel 22:7 - Deuteronomy 5:16 27:16 27:19, Exodus 20:12 21:17 22:21-22, Ezekiel 18:12 22:29, Jeremiah 7:6, Leviticus 20:9, Malachi 3:5, Mark 7:10, Matthew 15:4-6, Pesikta de R'Kahana 13.4 13.8, Pesikta Rabbati 27:4, Proverbs 20:20 22:22-23 30:11 30:17, Zechariah 7:10

[9] Ezekiel 22:8 - Amos 8:4-8:6, Ezekiel 20:13 20:21 20:24 22:26 23:38-23:39, Leviticus 19:30, Malachi 1:6-1:8 1:12, Midrash Tanchuma Terumah 1, Pesikta de R'Kahana 13.8

[10] Ezekiel 22:9 - 1 Corinthians 10:18-21, 1 Kings 21:10-13, Acts 6:11-13 24:5 24:13, Apocalypse of Elijah 1:13, Exodus 20:13 23:1, Ezekiel 16:43 18:6 18:11 18:15 24:13, Gates of Repentance 3.222, Hosea 4:2 4:10 4:14 6:9 7:4, Jeremiah 6:28 9:5 37:13-15 38:4-6, Judges 20:6, Leviticus 19:16, Matthew 26:59, Proverbs 10:18 18:8 26:22, Psalms 50:20 101:5 106:28, Revelation 12:9-10

[11] LXX *There are robbers in you*

[12] Ezekiel 22:10 - 1 Chronicles 5:1, 1 Corinthians 5:1, 2 Samuel 16:21-16:22, Amos 2:7, Deuteronomy 27:20 27:23, Ezekiel 18:6, Genesis 35:22 49:4, Leviticus 18:7-18:8 18:19 20:11 20:18

Hebrew		English
וְאִישׁ אֶת־אֵשֶׁת רֵעֵהוּ עָשָׂה תּוֹעֵבָה וְאִישׁ אֶת־ כַּלָּתוֹ טִמֵּא בְזִמָּה וְאִישׁ אֶת־אֲחֹתוֹ בַת־אָבִיו עִנָּה־ בָּךְ	11[1]	And each has committed abomination with his neighbor's wife; and each has lewdly defiled his daughter in law; and each in you has humbled his sister, his father's daughter.
שֹׁחַד לָקְחוּ־בָךְ לְמַעַן שְׁפָךְ־דָּם נֶשֶׁךְ וְתַרְבִּית לָקַחַתְּ וַתְּבַצְּעִי רֵעַיִךְ בַּעֹשֶׁק וְאֹתִי שָׁכַחַתְּ נְאֻם אֲדֹנָי יֱהוִה	12[2]	In you have they taken gifts to shed blood; you have taken interest and increase, and you have greedily gained of your neighbors by oppression, and have forgotten Me, says the Lord GOD.
וְהִנֵּה הִכֵּיתִי כַפִּי אֶל־בִּצְעֵךְ אֲשֶׁר עָשִׂית וְעַל־דָּמֵךְ אֲשֶׁר הָיוּ בְּתוֹכֵךְ	13[3]	Behold, therefore, I have smitten My hand at your dishonest gain that you have made, and at your blood that has been in your midst.
הֲיַעֲמֹד לִבֵּךְ אִם־תֶּחֱזַקְנָה יָדַיִךְ לַיָּמִים אֲשֶׁר אֲנִי עֹשֶׂה אוֹתָךְ אֲנִי יֱהוָה דִּבַּרְתִּי וְעָשִׂיתִי	14[4]	Can your heart endure, or can your hands be strong, in the days that I shall deal with you? I, the LORD, have spoken it, and will do it.
וַהֲפִיצוֹתִי אוֹתָךְ בַּגּוֹיִם וְזֵרִיתִיךְ בָּאֲרָצוֹת וַהֲתִמֹּתִי טֻמְאָתֵךְ מִמֵּךְ	15[5]	And I will scatter you among the nations, and disperse you through the countries; and I will consume your filthiness out of you.
וְנִחַלְתְּ בָּךְ לְעֵינֵי גוֹיִם וְיָדַעַתְּ כִּי־אֲנִי יֱהוָה	16[6]	And you shall be profaned in yourself, in the sight of the nations; and you shall know that I am the LORD.'
וַיְהִי דְבַר־יֱהוָה אֵלַי לֵאמֹר	17	And the word of the LORD came unto me, saying:
בֶּן־אָדָם הָיוּ־לִי בֵית־יִשְׂרָאֵל לְסוּגִ' לְסִיג' כֻּלָּם נְחֹשֶׁת וּבְדִיל וּבַרְזֶל וְעוֹפֶרֶת בְּתוֹךְ כּוּר סִגִים כֶּסֶף הָיוּ	18[7]	'Son of man, the house of Israel has become dross to Me; all of them are brass and tin and iron and lead, *in the midst of the furnace; they are the dross of silver*[8].
לָכֵן כֹּה אָמַר אֲדֹנָי יֱהוִה יַעַן הֱיוֹת כֻּלְּכֶם לְסִגִים לָכֵן הִנְנִי קֹבֵץ אֶתְכֶם אֶל־תּוֹךְ יְרוּשָׁלָ͏ִם	19[9]	Therefore thus says the Lord GOD: Because you are all become dross, therefore, behold, I will gather you into the midst of Jerusalem.
קְבֻצַת כֶּסֶף וּנְחֹשֶׁת וּבַרְזֶל וְעוֹפֶרֶת וּבְדִיל אֶל־תּוֹךְ כּוּר לָפַחַת־עָלָיו אֵשׁ לְהַנְתִּיךְ כֵּן אֶקְבֹּץ בְּאַפִּי וּבַחֲמָתִי וְהִנַּחְתִּי וְהִתַּכְתִּי אֶתְכֶם	20[10]	As they gather silver and brass and iron and lead and tin into the midst of the furnace, to blow the fire upon it, to melt it; so will I gather you in My anger and in My fury, and I will cast you in, and melt you.
וְכִנַּסְתִּי אֶתְכֶם וְנָפַחְתִּי עֲלֵיכֶם בְּאֵשׁ עֶבְרָתִי וְנִתַּכְתֶּם בְּתוֹכָהּ	21[11]	Yes, I will gather you, and blow upon you with the fire of My wrath, and you shall be melted in the midst thereof.

[1] Ezekiel 22:11 - 1 Corinthians 6:9, 2 Samuel 13:1 13:14 13:28-13:29, Deuteronomy 22:22 27:22, Deuteronomy.R 2:21, Ezekiel 18:11, Galatians 5:19, Hebrews 13:4, Jastrow 394b, Jeremiah 5:7-5:8 9:3 29:23, Job 31:9-11, Leviticus 18:9 18:15 18:20 20:10 20:12 20:17, Malachi 3:5, Matthew 5:27-28

[2] Ezekiel 22:12 - 1 Corinthians 5:11 6:10, 1 Timothy 3:3 6:9-6:10, Deuteronomy 16:19 23:21 27:25 32:18, Exodus 22:25-22:26 23:7-23:8, Ezekiel 18:8 18:13 23:35, Isaiah 1:23 56:11, James 5:1-5:4, Jeremiah 2:32 3:21, Jude 1:11, Leviticus 19:13 25:35-25:36, Luke 3:13 18:11 19:8, Micah 7:2-7:3, Nehemiah 5:1 5:7, Proverbs 1:19, Psalms 15:5 106:21, Zephaniah 3:3-3:4

[3] Ezekiel 22:13 - 1 Thessalonians 4:6, Amos 2:6-2:8 3:10 8:4-8:6, Ecclesiastes.R 1:32 3:12, Ezekiel 21:19 21:22 22:27, Isaiah 33:15, Jeremiah 5:26-5:27 7:9-7:11, Leviticus.R 33:3, Micah 2:1-2:3 6:10-6:11, Numbers 24:10, Proverbs 28:8

[4] Ezekiel 22:14 - 1 Corinthians 10:22, 1 Samuel 15:29, Ecclesiastes.R 1:36, Ezekiel 5:13 17:24 21:12 24:14 28:9, Hebrews 10:31, Isaiah 31:3 45:9, Jeremiah 13:21, Job 40:9, Mark 13:31, Pesikta de R'Kahana 16.2, Pesikta Rabbati 29/30A:2

[5] Ezekiel 22:15 - 1 Peter 4:12, Deuteronomy 4:27 28:25 28:64, Ezekiel 5:12 12:14-12:15 20:38 22:18 22:22 23:27 23:47-23:48 24:6-24:14 34:6 36:19, Isaiah 1:25, Jeremiah 15:4, Leviticus 26:33, Malachi 3:3 3:19, Matthew 3:12, Nehemiah 1:8, Zechariah 7:14 13:9

[6] Ezekiel 22:16 - 1 Kings 20:13 20:28, Daniel 4:22 4:29-4:32, Exodus 8:18, Ezekiel 6:7 7:24 25:3 39:6-39:7 39:28, Isaiah 37:20 43:28 47:6, Psalms 9:17 83:19

[7] Ezekiel 22:18 - Ezekiel 22:20, Isaiah 1:22 1:25 31:9 48:4 48:10, Jastrow 975a, Jeremiah 6:28-6:30, Lamentations 4:1-4:2, Mas.Soferim 7:4, Numbers.R 13:8, Pesikta Rabbati 7:7, Proverbs 17:3, Psalms 119:119, Song of Songs.R 4:17

[8] LXX *they are mixed up in the midst of the silver*

[9] Ezekiel 22:19 - Ezekiel 11:7 24:3-24:6, Matthew 13:30 13:40-42, Micah 4:12, z.Vaetchanan 269b

[10] Ezekiel 22:20 - Ezekiel 21:36-21:37 22:21 24:13, Isaiah 54:16, Jeremiah 4:11-4:12 4:20, Song of Songs.R 2:47

[11] Ezekiel 22:21 - 2 Kings 25:9, Cairo Damascus 20:3, Cairo Damascus 20:3, Deuteronomy 4:24 29:19 32:22, Ezekiel 15:6-15:7 21:3-20:4 22:20-22:22, Isaiah 30:33 64:3 64:8, Jeremiah 9:8 21:12, Nahum 1:6, Psalms 21:10 50:3 68:3 112:10, Zephaniah 1:18

Hebrew		English
כְּהִתּוּךְ כֶּסֶף בְּתוֹךְ כּוּר כֵּן תֻּתְּכוּ בְתוֹכָהּ וִידַעְתֶּם כִּי־אֲנִי יְהוָה שָׁפַכְתִּי חֲמָתִי עֲלֵיכֶם	22[1]	As silver is melted in the midst of the furnace, so shall you be melted in the midst thereof; and you shall know that I, the LORD, have poured out My fury upon you.'
וַיְהִי דְבַר־יְהוָה אֵלַי לֵאמֹר	23	And the word of the LORD came unto me, saying:
בֶּן־אָדָם אֱמָר־לָהּ אַתְּ אֶרֶץ לֹא מְטֹהָרָה הִיא לֹא גֻשְׁמָהּ בְּיוֹם זָעַם	24[2]	'Son of man, say unto her: you are a land that is not cleansed, nor rained upon in the day of indignation.
קֶשֶׁר נְבִיאֶיהָ בְּתוֹכָהּ כַּאֲרִי שׁוֹאֵג טֹרֵף טָרֶף נֶפֶשׁ אָכָלוּ חֹסֶן וִיקָר יִקָּחוּ אַלְמְנוֹתֶיהָ הִרְבּוּ בְתוֹכָהּ	25[3]	There is a conspiracy of her prophets in the midst thereof, like a roaring lion ravening the prey; they have devoured souls, they take treasure and precious things, they have made her widows many in the midst thereof.
כֹּהֲנֶיהָ חָמְסוּ תוֹרָתִי וַיְחַלְּלוּ קָדָשַׁי בֵּין־קֹדֶשׁ לְחֹל לֹא הִבְדִּילוּ וּבֵין־הַטָּמֵא לְטָהוֹר לֹא הוֹדִיעוּ וּמִשַּׁבְּתוֹתַי הֶעְלִימוּ עֵינֵיהֶם וָאֵחַל בְּתוֹכָם	26[4]	Her priests have done violence to My law, and have profaned My holy things; they have put no difference between the holy and the common, neither have they taught difference between the unclean and the clean, and have hid their eyes from My sabbaths, and I am profaned among them.
שָׂרֶיהָ בְקִרְבָּהּ כִּזְאֵבִים טֹרְפֵי טָרֶף לִשְׁפָּךְ־דָּם לְאַבֵּד נְפָשׁוֹת לְמַעַן בְּצֹעַ בָּצַע	27[5]	Her princes in the midst thereof are like wolves ravening the prey: to shed blood, and to destroy souls, so as to get dishonest gain.
וּנְבִיאֶיהָ טָחוּ לָהֶם תָּפֵל חֹזִים שָׁוְא וְקֹסְמִים לָהֶם כָּזָב אֹמְרִים כֹּה אָמַר אֲדֹנָי יְהוִה וַיהוָה לֹא דִבֵּר	28[6]	And her prophets have daubed for them with whited plaster, seeing falsehood, and divining lies unto them, saying: Thus says the Lord GOD, when the LORD has not spoken.
עַם הָאָרֶץ עָשְׁקוּ עֹשֶׁק וְגָזְלוּ גָּזֵל וְעָנִי וְאֶבְיוֹן הוֹנוּ וְאֶת־הַגֵּר עָשְׁקוּ בְּלֹא מִשְׁפָּט	29[7]	The people of the land have used oppression, and exercised robbery, and have wronged the poor and needy, and have oppressed the stranger unlawfully.
וָאֲבַקֵּשׁ מֵהֶם אִישׁ גֹּדֵר־גָּדֵר וְעֹמֵד בַּפֶּרֶץ לְפָנַי בְּעַד הָאָרֶץ לְבִלְתִּי שַׁחֲתָהּ וְלֹא מָצָאתִי	30[8]	And I sought for a man among them, that should make up the hedge, and stand in the breach before Me for the land, that I should not destroy it; but I found none.
וָאֶשְׁפֹּךְ עֲלֵיהֶם זַעְמִי בְּאֵשׁ עֶבְרָתִי כִּלִּיתִים דַּרְכָּם בְּרֹאשָׁם נָתַתִּי נְאֻם אֲדֹנָי יְהוִה	31[9]	Therefore have I poured out My indignation upon them; I have consumed them with the fire of My wrath; their own way have I brought upon their heads, says the Lord GOD.'

---

[1] Ezekiel 22:22 - Ezekiel 20:8 20:33 22:16 22:31, Hosea 5:10, Revelation 16:1

[2] Ezekiel 22:24 - 2 Chronicles 28:22 36:14-36:16, b.Zevachim 113a, Deuteronomy.R 3:6, Ecclesiastes.R 8:13, Ezekiel 24:13, Genesis.R 33:6, Isaiah 1:5 9:14, Jastrow 1675b, Jeremiah 2:30 5:3 6:29 44:16-44:19, Leviticus.R 31:11, Pirkei de R'Eliezer 23, Song of Songs.R 1:66 4:2, z.Vayakhel 197a, Zephaniah 3:2

[3] Ezekiel 22:25 - 1 Kings 22:11-22:13 22:23, 2 Peter 2:1-2:3, Ezekiel 13:10-13:16 13:19 22:27-22:29, Hosea 6:9, Isaiah 56:11, Jeremiah 2:30 2:34 5:30-5:31 6:13 11:9 15:8, Lamentations 2:14 4:13, Luke 20:47, Mark 12:40, Matthew 23:13, Micah 3:5-3:7, Revelation 13:11 13:15 17:6 18:13

[4] Ezekiel 22:26 - 1 Samuel 2:12-2:17 2:22 2:29, b.Shabbat 119b, Ein Yaakov Shabbat:119b, Ezekiel 20:12-20:13 22:8 36:20 44:23, Haggai 2:11-2:14, Jeremiah 2:8 2:26-2:27 15:19, Lamentations 4:13, Leviticus 10:1-10:3 10:10 11:47 20:25 22:2-22:33, Malachi 1:6-1:8 2:1-2:3 2:8, Micah 3:11-3:12, Midrash Tanchuma Terumah 1, Romans 2:24, Zephaniah 3:3-3:4

[5] Ezekiel 22:27 - Ezekiel 19:3-19:6 22:6 22:13 22:25 45:9, Hosea 7:1-7:7, Isaiah 1:23, James 2:6-2:7 5:1-5:4, Matthew 21:13, Micah 3:2-3:3 3:9-3:11 7:8, Zephaniah 3:3

[6] Ezekiel 22:28 - Ezekiel 13:6-7 13:10-16 13:22-23 21:34 22:25, Isaiah 30:10, Jeremiah 8:10-8:11 23:21 23:25-23:32 28:2 28:15 29:8-9 37:19, Lamentations 2:14, z.Vaetchanan 269b, Zephaniah 3:4

[7] Ezekiel 22:29 - Amos 3:10, Exodus 22:21 23:9, Ezekiel 18:12 22:7, Isaiah 5:7 10:2 59:3-59:7, James 5:4, Jeremiah 5:26-5:28 5:31 6:13, Leviticus 19:33, Matthew 25:43, Micah 2:2 3:3, Pirkei de R'Eliezer 25, Psalms 94:6

[8] Ezekiel 22:30 - Exodus 32:10-32:14, Ezekiel 13:5, Genesis 18:23-18:32, Isaiah 59:16 63:5, Jeremiah 5:1 15:1, Psalms 106:23, Song of Songs.R 2:44

[9] Ezekiel 22:31 - Ezekiel 7:3 7:8-7:9 9:10 11:21 16:43 22:21-22:22, Romans 2:8-2:9

Ezekiel – Chapter 23

וַיְהִ֥י דְבַר־יְהֹוָ֖ה אֵלַ֥י לֵאמֹֽר

1 And the word of the LORD came unto me, saying:

בֶּן־אָדָ֑ם שְׁתַּ֣יִם נָשִׁ֔ים בְּנ֥וֹת אֵם־אַחַ֖ת הָיֽוּ

2[1] 'Son of man, there were two women, the daughters of one mother;

וַתִּזְנֶ֣ינָה בְמִצְרַ֔יִם בִּנְעוּרֵיהֶ֖ן זָנ֑וּ שָׁ֚מָּה מֹעֲכ֣וּ שְׁדֵיהֶ֔ן וְשָׁ֣ם עִשּׂ֔וּ דַּדֵּ֖י בְּתוּלֵיהֶֽן

3[2] and they committed harlotries in Egypt; they committed harlotries in their youth; *there were their bosoms pressed, and there their virgin breasts were bruised*[3].

וּשְׁמוֹתָ֗ן אׇהֳלָ֤ה הַגְּדוֹלָה֙ וְאׇהֳלִיבָ֣ה אֲחוֹתָ֔הּ וַתִּהְיֶ֣ינָה לִ֔י וַתֵּלַ֖דְנָה בָּנִ֣ים וּבָנ֑וֹת וּשְׁמוֹתָ֗ן שֹׁמְר֤וֹן אׇהֳלָה֙ וִירוּשָׁלַ֖͏ִם אׇהֳלִיבָֽה

4[4] And the names of them were Oholah the elder, and Oholibah her sister; and they became Mine, and they bore sons and daughters. And as for their names, Samaria is Oholah[5], and Jerusalem Oholibah[6].

וַתִּ֥זֶן אׇהֳלָ֖ה תַּחְתָּ֑י וַתַּעְגַּב֙ עַֽל־מְאַֽהֲבֶ֔יהָ אֶל־אַשּׁ֖וּר קְרוֹבִֽים

5[7] And Oholah played the harlot when she was Mine; and she doted on her lovers, on the Assyrians, warriors,

לְבֻשֵׁ֤י תְכֵ֙לֶת֙ פַּח֣וֹת וּסְגָנִ֔ים בַּחוּרֵ֥י חֶ֖מֶד כֻּלָּ֑ם פָּרָשִׁ֕ים רֹכְבֵ֖י סוּסִֽים

6[8] clothed with blue, governors and rulers, handsome young men all of them, horsemen riding upon horses.

וַתִּתֵּ֤ן תַּזְנוּתֶ֙יהָ֙ עֲלֵיהֶ֔ם מִבְחַ֥ר בְּנֵֽי־אַשּׁ֖וּר כֻּלָּ֑ם וּבְכֹ֧ל אֲשֶׁר־עָגְבָ֛ה בְּכׇל־גִּלּוּלֵיהֶ֖ם נִטְמָֽאָה

7[9] And she bestowed her harlotries upon them, the choicest men of Assyria all of them; and on whomsoever she doted, with all their idols she defiled herself.

וְאֶת־תַּזְנוּתֶ֤יהָ מִמִּצְרַ֙יִם֙ לֹ֣א עָזָ֔בָה כִּ֤י אוֹתָהּ֙ שָׁכְב֣וּ בִנְעוּרֶ֔יהָ וְהֵ֥מָּה עִשּׂ֖וּ דַּדֵּ֣י בְתוּלֶ֑יהָ וַיִּשְׁפְּכ֥וּ תַזְנוּתָ֖ם עָלֶֽיהָ

8[10] Neither has she left her harlotries brought from Egypt; for in her youth they lay with her, and they bruised her virgin breasts; and they poured out their lust upon her.

לָכֵ֣ן נְתַתִּ֔יהָ בְּיַד־מְאַ֣הֲבֶ֔יהָ בְּיַ֖ד בְּנֵ֣י אַשּׁ֑וּר אֲשֶׁ֥ר עָגְבָ֖ה עֲלֵיהֶֽם

9[11] Why I delivered her into the hand of her lovers, into the hand of the Assyrians, upon whom she doted.

הֵ֩מָּה֩ גִּלּ֨וּ עֶרְוָתָ֜הּ בָּנֶ֤יהָ וּבְנוֹתֶ֙יהָ֙ לָקָ֔חוּ וְאוֹתָ֖הּ בַּחֶ֣רֶב הָרָ֑גוּ וַתְּהִי־שֵׁם֙ לַנָּשִׁ֔ים וּשְׁפוּטִ֖ים עָ֥שׂוּ בָֽהּ

10[12] These uncovered her nakedness; they took her sons and her daughters, and her they slew with the sword; and she became a byword among women, for judgments were executed upon her.

וַתֵּ֙רֶא֙ אֲחוֹתָ֣הּ אׇהֳלִיבָ֔ה וַתַּשְׁחֵ֥ת עַגְבָתָ֖הּ מִמֶּ֑נָּה וְאֶ֨ת־תַּזְנוּתֶ֔יהָ מִזְּנוּנֵ֖י אֲחוֹתָֽהּ

11[13] And her sister Oholibah saw this, yet was she more corrupt in her doting than she, and in her harlotries more than her sister in her harlotries.

אֶל־בְּנֵי֩ אַשּׁ֨וּר עָגָ֜בָה פַּח֤וֹת וּסְגָנִים֙ קְרֹבִ֔ים לְבֻשֵׁ֖י מִכְל֑וֹל פָּרָשִׁ֕ים רֹכְבֵ֣י סוּסִ֔ים בַּחוּרֵ֥י חֶ֖מֶד כֻּלָּֽם

12[14] She doted upon the Assyrians, governors and rulers, warriors, clothed most gorgeously, horsemen riding upon horses, all of them handsome young men.

---

[1] Ezekiel 23:2 - Ezekiel 16:44-16:46, Jeremiah 3:7-3:10, Tanna Devei Eliyahu 9
[2] Ezekiel 23:3 - Deuteronomy 29:15, Ezekiel 16:22 20:8 23:8 23:19 23:21, Hosea 2:15, Joshua 24:14, Leviticus 17:7
[3] LXX *there their breasts fell, there they lost their virginity*
[4] Ezekiel 23:4 - 1 Kings 8:29 12:20 12:26-12:33, Exodus 19:5-19:6, Ezekiel 16:8 16:20 16:40, Jeremiah 2:2-2:3, John 4:22, Psalms 45:12-45:17 76:3 132:13-132:14, Romans 7:4
[5] i.e., *her tent*
[6] i.e., *my tent is in her*
[7] Ezekiel 23:5 - 1 Kings 14:9 14:16 15:26 15:30 16:31-32 21:26, 2 Kings 15:19 16:7 17:3 17:7-18, Ezekiel 16:28 16:37 23:7 23:9 23:12 23:16 23:20, Hosea 5:13 8:9-10 10:6 12:3, Jeremiah 50:38
[8] Ezekiel 23:6 - Ezekiel 23:23
[9] Ezekiel 23:7 - Ezekiel 16:15 20:7 22:3-22:4 23:30, Genesis 10:22, Hosea 5:3 6:10, Psalms 106:39
[10] Ezekiel 23:8 - 1 Kings 12:28, 2 Kings 10:29 17:16, Exodus 32:4, Ezekiel 23:3 23:19 23:21
[11] Ezekiel 23:9 - 1 Chronicles 5:26, 2 Kings 15:29 17:3-17:6 17:23 18:9-18:12, Hosea 11:5, Revelation 17:12-17:13 17:16
[12] Ezekiel 23:10 - Ezekiel 16:37-16:41 23:29 23:48, Hosea 2:3 2:10, Jeremiah 22:8-22:9, Midrash Tanchuma Vaera 9
[13] Ezekiel 23:11 - Ezekiel 16:47-16:51 23:4, Jeremiah 3:8-3:11
[14] Ezekiel 23:12 - 2 Chronicles 28:16-28:23, 2 Kings 16:7-16:15, Ezekiel 16:28 23:5-23:6 23:23

וָאֵרֶא כִּי נִטְמָאָה דֶּרֶךְ אֶחָד לִשְׁתֵּיהֶן

13[1] And I saw that she was defiled; they both took one way.

וַתּוֹסֶף אֶל־תַּזְנוּתֶיהָ וַתֵּרֶא אַנְשֵׁי מְחֻקֶּה עַל־הַקִּיר צַלְמֵי 'כַשְׂדִּיִּים' "כַשְׂדִּים" חֲקֻקִים בַּשָּׁשַׁר

14[2] And she increased her harlotries; for she saw men portrayed upon the wall, the images of the Chaldeans portrayed with vermilion,

חֲגוֹרֵי אֵזוֹר בְּמָתְנֵיהֶם סְרוּחֵי טְבוּלִים בְּרָאשֵׁיהֶם מַרְאֵה שָׁלִשִׁים כֻּלָּם דְּמוּת בְּנֵי־בָבֶל כַּשְׂדִּים אֶרֶץ מוֹלַדְתָּם

15[3] *girded with*[4] girdles upon their loins, with pendant turbans upon their heads, all of them captains to look upon, the likeness of the sons of Babylon, of Chaldea, the land of their nativity.

'וַתַּעְגַּב' "וַתַּעְגְּבָה" עֲלֵיהֶם לְמַרְאֵה עֵינֶיהָ וַתִּשְׁלַח מַלְאָכִים אֲלֵיהֶם כַּשְׂדִּימָה

16[5] [6]And as soon as she saw them she doted upon them, and sent messengers unto them into Chaldea.

וַיָּבֹאוּ אֵלֶיהָ בְנֵי־בָבֶל לְמִשְׁכַּב דֹּדִים וַיְטַמְּאוּ אוֹתָהּ בְּתַזְנוּתָם וַתִּטְמָא־בָם וַתֵּקַע נַפְשָׁהּ מֵהֶם

17[7] And the Babylonians came to her into the bed of love, and they defiled her with their lust; and she was polluted with them, and her soul was alienated *from them*[8].

וַתְּגַל תַּזְנוּתֶיהָ וַתְּגַל אֶת־עֶרְוָתָהּ וַתֵּקַע נַפְשִׁי מֵעָלֶיהָ כַּאֲשֶׁר נָקְעָה נַפְשִׁי מֵעַל אֲחוֹתָהּ

18[9] So she uncovered her harlotries, and uncovered her nakedness; then My soul was alienated from her, like as My soul was alienated from her sister.

וַתַּרְבֶּה אֶת־תַּזְנוּתֶיהָ לִזְכֹּר אֶת־יְמֵי נְעוּרֶיהָ אֲשֶׁר זָנְתָה בְּאֶרֶץ מִצְרָיִם

19[10] Yet she multiplied her harlotries, remembering the days of her youth, in which she had played the harlot in the land of Egypt.

וַתַּעְגְּבָה עַל פִּלַגְשֵׁיהֶם אֲשֶׁר בְּשַׂר־חֲמוֹרִים בְּשָׂרָם וְזִרְמַת סוּסִים זִרְמָתָם

20[11] And she doted upon *concubinage with them*[12], whose flesh is as the flesh of asses, and whose *issue is like the issue*[13] of horses.

וַתִּפְקְדִי אֵת זִמַּת נְעוּרָיִךְ בַּעְשׂוֹת מִמִּצְרַיִם דַּדַּיִךְ לְמַעַן שְׁדֵי נְעוּרָיִךְ

21[14] Thus you called to remembrance the lewdness of your youth, when they from Egypt bruised your breasts for the bosom of your youth.

לָכֵן אָהֳלִיבָה כֹּה־אָמַר אֲדֹנָי יְהוִה הִנְנִי מֵעִיר אֶת־מְאַהֲבַיִךְ עָלַיִךְ אֵת אֲשֶׁר־נָקְעָה נַפְשֵׁךְ מֵהֶם וַהֲבֵאתִים עָלַיִךְ מִסָּבִיב

22[15] Therefore, O Oholibah, thus says the Lord GOD: Behold, I will raise up your lovers against you, from whom your soul is alienated, and I will bring them against you on every side:

---

[1] Ezekiel 23:13 - 2 Kings 17:18-17:19, Ezekiel 23:31, Hosea 12:3-12:4

[2] Ezekiel 23:14 - Ezekiel 8:10 16:29, Isaiah 46:1, Jastrow 497b, Jeremiah 22:14 50:2, Leviticus.R 33:6, Song of Songs.R 8:16 Ezekiel 23:14-18 - 4QEzeka

[3] Ezekiel 23:15 - 1 Samuel 18:4, 2 Samuel 14:25, Isaiah 22:21, Judges 8:18

[4] LXX *having variegated*

[5] Ezekiel 23:16 - 2 Kings 24:1, 2 Peter 2:14, 2 Samuel 11:2, Ezekiel 16:17 16:29 23:40-23:41, Genesis 3:6 6:2 39:7, Job 31:1, Mas.Soferim 7:2, Matthew 5:28, Proverbs 6:25 23:33, Psalms 119:37

[6] There is not enough spce in 4QEzeka to contain all of the verse. Perhaps the scribe skipped a whole line when copying the text.

[7] Ezekiel 23:17 - 2 Samuel 13:15, Ezekiel 16:37 23:22 23:28, Genesis 10:10 11:9, Song of Songs.R 3:9

[8] LXX *her sister*

[9] Ezekiel 23:18 - Amos 5:21 6:8, Deuteronomy 32:19, Ezekiel 16:36 21:29, Genesis.R 77:3, Hosea 2:2 7:1, Isaiah 3:9, Jeremiah 6:8 8:12 12:8 15:1, Lamentations 2:7, Psalms 78:59 106:40, y.Peah 1:1, Zechariah 11:8

[10] Ezekiel 23:19 - Amos 4:4, Ezekiel 16:22 16:25 16:29 16:51 20:7 23:3 23:8 23:14 23:21, Midrash Tanchuma Lech Lecha 5, y.Peah 1:1

[11] Ezekiel 23:20 - b.Arachin 19a, b.Bava Kamma [Rashi] 88a, b.Bechorot [Rashi] 46a, b.Berachot 25b 58a, b.Ketubot [Rashi] 44b, b.Ketubot 3b, b.Niddah 45a, b.Sanhedrin [Tosefot] 74b, b.Shabbat 150a, b.Yevamot [Rashi] 22a 97b, b.Yevamot 98a, Ein Yaakov Berachot:58a, Exodus.R 15:1 18:10, Ezekiel 16:20 16:26 17:15, Genesis.R 96:5, Jeremiah 5:8, Lamentations.R 1:37, Leviticus.R 23:7, Midrash Psalms 22:17, Midrash Tanchuma Acharei Mot 8, Midrash Tanchuma Bamidbar 20, Midrash Tanchuma Ki Tissa 30, Midrash Tanchuma Vayechi 3, Midrash Tanchuma Vayeshev 5, Numbers.R 4:5 9:14 9:47, t.Arachin 3:2, z.Ki Tissa 192b, z.Vayechi 222b, z.Vayikra 14b, z.Vayishlach 173a

[12] LXX *Chaldeans*

[13] LXX *members as the members*

[14] Ezekiel 23:21 - b.Niddah [Rashi] 49a, b.Niddah 45a, Jastrow 673a, y.Taanit 4:5

[15] Ezekiel 23:22 - Ezekiel 16:37 23:9 23:28, Habakkuk 1:6-1:10, Isaiah 10:5-10:6 39:3-39:4, Jeremiah 6:22-6:23 12:9-12:12, Revelation 17:16, z.Vaetchanan 269b

בְּנֵי בָבֶל וְכָל־כַּשְׂדִּים פְּקוֹד וְשׁוֹעַ וְקוֹעַ כָּל־בְּנֵי
אַשּׁוּר אוֹתָם בַּחוּרֵי חֶמֶד פַּחוֹת וּסְגָנִים כֻּלָּם
שָׁלִשִׁים וּקְרוּאִים רֹכְבֵי סוּסִים כֻּלָּם

23[1] the Babylonians and all the Chaldeans, *Pekod and Shoa and Koa*[2], and all the Assyrians with them, handsome young men, governors and rulers all of them, captains and counselors, all of them riding upon horses.

וּבָאוּ עָלַיִךְ הֹצֶן רֶכֶב וְגַלְגַּל וּבִקְהַל עַמִּים צִנָּה
וּמָגֵן וְקוֹבַע יָשִׂימוּ עָלַיִךְ סָבִיב וְנָתַתִּי לִפְנֵיהֶם
מִשְׁפָּט וּשְׁפָטוּךְ בְּמִשְׁפְּטֵיהֶם

24[3] And they shall come against you[4] with hosts, chariots, and wheels, and with an assembly of peoples; they shall set themselves in array against you with buckler and shield and helmet; and I will commit the judgment unto them, and they shall judge you according to their judgments.

וְנָתַתִּי קִנְאָתִי בָּךְ וְעָשׂוּ אוֹתָךְ בְּחֵמָה אַפֵּךְ וְאָזְנַיִךְ
יָסִירוּ וְאַחֲרִיתֵךְ בַּחֶרֶב תִּפּוֹל הֵמָּה בָּנַיִךְ וּבְנוֹתַיִךְ
יִקָּחוּ וְאַחֲרִיתֵךְ תֵּאָכֵל בָּאֵשׁ

25[5] And I will set My jealousy against you, and they shall deal with you in fury; they shall take away your nose and your ears, and your residue shall fall by the sword; they shall take your sons and your daughters, and your residue shall be devoured by the fire.

וְהִפְשִׁיטוּךְ אֶת־בְּגָדָיִךְ וְלָקְחוּ כְּלֵי תִפְאַרְתֵּךְ

26[6] They shall also strip you of your clothes, and take away your fair jewels.

וְהִשְׁבַּתִּי זִמָּתֵךְ מִמֵּךְ וְאֶת־זְנוּתֵךְ מֵאֶרֶץ מִצְרָיִם
וְלֹא־תִשְׂאִי עֵינַיִךְ אֲלֵיהֶם וּמִצְרַיִם לֹא תִזְכְּרִי־עוֹד

27[7] Thus will I make your lewdness to cease from you, and your harlotry brought from the land of Egypt, so that you shall not lift up your eyes unto them, nor remember Egypt any more.

כִּי כֹה אָמַר אֲדֹנָי יְהוִֹה הִנְנִי נֹתְנָךְ בְּיַד אֲשֶׁר
שָׂנֵאת בְּיַד אֲשֶׁר־נָקְעָה נַפְשֵׁךְ מֵהֶם

28[8] For thus says the Lord GOD: Behold, I will deliver you into the hand of them whom you hate, into the hand of them from whom your soul is alienated;

וְעָשׂוּ אוֹתָךְ בְּשִׂנְאָה וְלָקְחוּ כָּל־יְגִיעֵךְ וַעֲזָבוּךְ
עֵירֹם וְעֶרְיָה וְנִגְלָה עֶרְוַת זְנוּנַיִךְ וְזִמָּתֵךְ וְתַזְנוּתָיִךְ

29[9] and they shall deal with you in hatred, and shall take away all your labor, and shall leave you naked and bare; and the nakedness of your harlotries shall be uncovered, both your lewdness and your harlotries.

עָשֹׂה אֵלֶּה לָךְ בִּזְנוֹתֵךְ אַחֲרֵי גוֹיִם עַל אֲשֶׁר־
נִטְמֵאת בְּגִלּוּלֵיהֶם

30[10] These things shall be done unto you, for that you have gone astray after the nations, and because you are polluted with their idols.

בְּדֶרֶךְ אֲחוֹתֵךְ הָלָכְתְּ וְנָתַתִּי כוֹסָהּ בְּיָדֵךְ

31[11] In the way of your sister have you walked; therefore will I give her cup into your hand.

כֹּה אָמַר אֲדֹנָי יְהוִֹה כּוֹס אֲחוֹתֵךְ תִּשְׁתִּי הָעֲמֻקָּה
וְהָרְחָבָה תִּהְיֶה לִצְחֹק וּלְלַעַג מִרְבָּה לְהָכִיל

32[12] Thus says the Lord GOD: You shall drink of your sister's cup, Which is deep and large; *You*

---

[1] Ezekiel 23:23 - 2 Kings 20:14-20:17 24:2 25:1-25:3, Acts 7:4, Ezekiel 21:24-21:32 23:6 23:12, Ezra 6:22, Genesis 2:14 25:18, Genesis.R 5:9, Isaiah 23:13, Jeremiah 50:21, Job 1:17, Mekilta de R'Ishmael Beshallah 2:201
[2] *LXX Phacuc, and Sue, and Hychue*
[3] Ezekiel 23:24 - 2 Samuel 24:14, Ezekiel 16:38 21:28 23:45 26:10, Jeremiah 39:5-39:6 47:3, Nahum 2:4-2:5 3:2-3:3
[4] LXX adds *from the north*
[5] Ezekiel 23:25 - Deuteronomy 29:19 32:21-32:22, Exodus 34:14, Ezekiel 5:13 8:1-8:18 15:6-15:7 16:38-16:42 21:3-20:4 22:18-22:22 23:47, Hosea 2:4-2:7, Proverbs 6:34, Revelation 18:8, Song of Songs 8:6, Zephaniah 1:18
[6] Ezekiel 23:26 - 1 Peter 3:3-3:4, Exodus.R 46:4, Ezekiel 16:16 16:37 16:39 23:29, Hosea 2:3 2:9-2:12, Isaiah 3:17-24, Jeremiah 13:22, Midrash Tanchuma Vayigash 10, Revelation 17:16 18:14-17
[7] Ezekiel 23:27 - Ezekiel 16:41 22:15 23:3 23:19, Isaiah 3:9, Micah 5:11-5:15, Zechariah 13:2
[8] Ezekiel 23:28 - Ezekiel 16:37 23:17 23:22, Jeremiah 21:7-21:10 24:8 10:20, z.Vaetchanan 269b
[9] Ezekiel 23:29 - 2 Samuel 13:15, Deuteronomy 28:47-28:51, Ezekiel 16:36-16:37 16:39 23:18 23:25-23:26 23:45-23:47
[10] Ezekiel 23:30 - Ezekiel 6:9 23:7 23:12-23:21, Jeremiah 2:18-2:20 16:11-16:12 22:8-22:9, Psalms 106:35-106:38
[11] Ezekiel 23:31 - 2 Kings 21:13, Daniel 9:12, Ezekiel 16:47-51 23:13, Jeremiah 3:8-3:11 7:14-15 1:15, Seder Olam 26:Zedekiah, y.Sanhedrin 10:5
[12] Ezekiel 23:32 - 1 Kings 9:7, Deuteronomy 4:37, Ezekiel 22:4-22:5 1:6 2:2 11:15 12:3, Isaiah 3:17, Jeremiah 1:9 25:15-25:28 24:26, Lamentations 2:15-2:16, Matthew 20:22-20:23, Micah 7:8, Midrash Psalms 75:4, Psalms 60:4 79:3, Revelation 16:19 18:6, y.Bikkurim 2:3, z.Vaetchanan 269b

shall be for a scorn and a derision; It is full to the uttermost[1].

שִׁכָּרוֹן וְיָגוֹן תִּמָּלֵאִי כּוֹס שַׁמָּה וּשְׁמָמָה כּוֹס אֲחוֹתֵךְ שֹׁמְרוֹן   33[2]

You shall be *filled with drunkenness and sorrow*[3], With the cup of astonishment and appalment, With the cup of your sister Samaria.

וְשָׁתִית אוֹתָהּ וּמָצִית וְאֶת־חֲרָשֶׂיהָ תְּגָרֵמִי וְשָׁדַיִךְ תְּנַתֵּקִי כִּי אֲנִי דִבַּרְתִּי נְאֻם אֲדֹנָי יְהוִה   34[4]

You shall drink it and drain it, And you shall craunch the sherds thereof, And shall tear your breasts[5]; For I have spoken it, says the Lord GOD.

לָכֵן כֹּה אָמַר אֲדֹנָי יְהוִה יַעַן שָׁכַחַתְּ אוֹתִי וַתַּשְׁלִיכִי אוֹתִי אַחֲרֵי גַוֵּךְ וְגַם־אַתְּ שְׂאִי זִמָּתֵךְ וְאֶת־תַּזְנוּתָיִךְ   35[6]

Therefore thus says the Lord GOD: Because you have forgotten Me, and cast Me behind your back, therefore bear you also your lewdness and your harlotries.'

וַיֹּאמֶר יְהוָה אֵלַי בֶּן־אָדָם הֲתִשְׁפּוֹט אֶת־אָהֳלָה וְאֶת־אָהֳלִיבָה וְהַגֵּד לָהֶן אֵת תוֹעֲבוֹתֵיהֶן   36[7]

The LORD said moreover unto me: 'Son of man, will you judge Oholah and Oholibah? Then declare unto them their abominations.

כִּי נִאֵפוּ וְדָם בִּידֵיהֶן וְאֶת־גִּלּוּלֵיהֶן נִאֵפוּ וְגַם אֶת־בְּנֵיהֶן אֲשֶׁר יָלְדוּ־לִי הֶעֱבִירוּ לָהֶם לְאָכְלָה   37[8]

For they have committed adultery, and blood is in their hands, and with their idols have they committed adultery; and their sons, whom they bore unto Me, they have also set apart unto them to be *devoured*[9].

עוֹד זֹאת עָשׂוּ לִי טִמְּאוּ אֶת־מִקְדָּשִׁי בַּיּוֹם הַהוּא וְאֶת־שַׁבְּתוֹתַי חִלֵּלוּ   38[10]

Moreover this they have done unto Me: they have defiled My sanctuary in the same day, and have profaned My sabbaths.

וּבְשַׁחֲטָם אֶת־בְּנֵיהֶם לְגִלּוּלֵיהֶם וַיָּבֹאוּ אֶל־מִקְדָּשִׁי בַּיּוֹם הַהוּא לְחַלְּלוֹ וְהִנֵּה־כֹה עָשׂוּ בְּתוֹךְ בֵּיתִי   39[11]

For when they had slain their children to their idols, then they came the same day into My sanctuary to profane it; and, lo, thus have they done in the midst of My house.

וְאַף כִּי תִשְׁלַחְנָה לַאֲנָשִׁים בָּאִים מִמֶּרְחָק אֲשֶׁר מַלְאָךְ שָׁלוּחַ אֲלֵיהֶם וְהִנֵּה־בָאוּ לַאֲשֶׁר רָחַצְתְּ כָּחַלְתְּ עֵינַיִךְ וְעָדִית עֶדִי   40[12]

And furthermore you have sent for men that come from far; unto whom a messenger was sent, and, lo, they came; for whom you washed yourself, painted your eyes, and decked yourself with ornaments;

וְיָשַׁבְתְּ עַל־מִטָּה כְבוּדָּה וְשֻׁלְחָן עָרוּךְ לְפָנֶיהָ וּקְטָרְתִּי וְשַׁמְנִי שַׂמְתְּ עָלֶיהָ   41[13]

and sat upon a stately bed, with a table prepared before it, upon which you set My incense and My oil.

---

[1] LXX *to cause complete drunkenness*

[2] Ezekiel 23:33 - Habakkuk 2:16, Isaiah 3:17 3:22, Jeremiah 25:15-25:16 1:27

[3] LXX *thoroughly weakened*

[4] Ezekiel 23:34 - Ezekiel 23:3 23:8, Isaiah 3:17, Psalms 75:9, Revelation 18:7, Sifre Devarim Nitzavim 324

[5] LXX *drink it, and I will take away her festivals and her new moons*

[6] Ezekiel 23:35 - 1 Kings 14:9, Ezekiel 7:4 22:12 23:45-23:49 20:10, Hosea 8:14 13:6, Isaiah 17:10, Jeremiah 2:32 3:21 13:25 23:27 8:33, Leviticus 24:15, Nehemiah 9:26, Numbers 14:34 18:22, Romans 1:28, z.Vaetchanan 269b

[7] Ezekiel 23:36 - 1 Corinthians 6:2-6:3, Acts 7:51-7:53, Ezekiel 16:2 20:4 22:2, Hosea 2:2, Isaiah 10:1, Jeremiah 1:10 11:14 14:11, Luke 11:39-11:52, Matthew 23:13-23:35, Micah 3:8-3:11

[8] Ezekiel 23:37 - 2 Kings 17:17 21:6 24:4, b.Nedarim 91b, Deuteronomy 12:31, Ezekiel 16:20-21 16:32 16:36 16:38 16:45 20:26 20:31 22:2-4 23:4-5 23:39 23:45 24:6-9, Hosea 1:2 3:1 4:2, Isaiah 1:15, Jeremiah 7:6 7:9 7:31 8:35, Leviticus 18:21 20:2-5, Luke 13:34, Micah 3:10, Psalms 106:37-38, Sifre Devarim Haazinu Hashamayim 324, y.Avodah Zarah 2:3

[9] LXX *passed through the fire*

[10] Ezekiel 23:38 - 2 Kings 21:4 21:7 23:11-12, Exodus.R 49:2, Ezekiel 5:11 7:20 8:5-8:16 20:13 20:24 22:8, Jeremiah 17:27, Nehemiah 13:17-18, Psalms of Solomon 1:8

[11] Ezekiel 23:39 - 2 Chronicles 33:4-7, 2 Kings 21:4, Ezekiel 23:38 20:7, Isaiah 3:9, Jeremiah 7:8-11 11:15 23:11, John 18:28, Micah 3:11

[12] Ezekiel 23:40 - 2 Kings 9:30 20:13-15, Esther 2:12, Ezekiel 16:13-16 23:13, Isaiah 3:18-23 9:9, Jeremiah 4:30, Proverbs 7:10, Ruth 3:3

[13] Ezekiel 23:41 - Amos 2:8 6:4, Esther 1:6, Ezekiel 16:18-16:19 20:16, Hosea 2:8-2:11, Isaiah 9:7 17:11, Jeremiah 20:17, Malachi 1:7, Proverbs 7:16-7:17

וְקוֹל הָמוֹן שָׁלֵו בָהּ וְאֶל־אֲנָשִׁים מֵרֹב אָדָם מוּבָאִים 'סוֹבָאִים' "סָבָאִים" מִמִּדְבָּר וַיִּתְּנוּ צְמִידִים אֶל־יְדֵיהֶן וַעֲטֶרֶת תִּפְאֶרֶת עַל־רָאשֵׁיהֶן

42[1] And the voice of a multitude being at ease was in it; and for the sake of men, they were so many, brought drunken from the wilderness, they put bracelets upon their hands, and beautiful crowns upon their heads.

וָאֹמַר לַבָּלָה נִאוּפִים 'עַתְּ' "עַתָּה" 'יִזְנֶה' "יִזְנוּ" תַזְנוּתֶהָ וָהִיא

43[2] Then said I of her that was worn out by adulteries: Still they commit harlotries with her, her.

וַיָּבוֹא אֵלֶיהָ כְּבוֹא אֶל־אִשָּׁה זוֹנָה כֵּן בָּאוּ אֶל־אָהֳלָה וְאֶל־אָהֳלִיבָה אִשֹּׁת הַזִּמָּה

44[3] for everyone went in unto her, as men go in unto a harlot; so went they in unto Oholah and unto Oholibah, the lewd women.

וַאֲנָשִׁים צַדִּיקִם הֵמָּה יִשְׁפְּטוּ אוֹתְהֶם מִשְׁפַּט נֹאֲפוֹת וּמִשְׁפַּט שֹׁפְכוֹת דָּם כִּי נֹאֲפֹת הֵנָּה וְדָם בִּידֵיהֶן

45[4] But righteous men, they shall judge them as adulteresses are judged, and as women who shed blood are judged; because they are adulteresses, and blood is in their hands.

כִּי כֹּה אָמַר אֲדֹנָי יְהוִה הַעֲלֵה עֲלֵיהֶם קָהָל וְנָתֹן אֶתְהֶן לְזַעֲוָה וְלָבַז

46[5] For thus says the Lord GOD: An assembly shall be brought up against them, and they shall be made a horror and a spoil.

וְרָגְמוּ עֲלֵיהֶן אֶבֶן קָהָל וּבָרֵא אוֹתְהֶן בְּחַרְבוֹתָם בְּנֵיהֶם וּבְנוֹתֵיהֶם יַהֲרֹגוּ וּבָתֵּיהֶן בָּאֵשׁ יִשְׂרֹפוּ

47[6] And the assembly shall stone them with stones, and dispatch them with their swords; they shall slay their sons and their daughters, and burn up their houses with fire.

וְהִשְׁבַּתִּי זִמָּה מִן־הָאָרֶץ וְנִוַּסְּרוּ כָּל־הַנָּשִׁים וְלֹא תַעֲשֶׂינָה כְּזִמַּתְכֶנָה

48[7] Thus will I cause lewdness to cease out of the land, that all women may be taught not to do after your lewdness.

וְנָתְנוּ זִמַּתְכֶנָה עֲלֵיכֶן וַחֲטָאֵי גִלּוּלֵיכֶן תִּשֶּׂאינָה וִידַעְתֶּם כִּי אֲנִי אֲדֹנָי יְהוִה

49[8] And your lewdness shall be recompensed upon you, and you shall bear the sins of your idols; and you shall know that I am the Lord GOD.'

Ezekiel – Chapter 24

וַיְהִי דְבַר־יְהוָה אֵלַי בַּשָּׁנָה הַתְּשִׁיעִית בַּחֹדֶשׁ הָעֲשִׂירִי בֶּעָשׂוֹר לַחֹדֶשׁ לֵאמֹר

1[9] And the word of the LORD came unto me in the ninth year, in the tenth month, in the tenth day of the month, saying:

בֶּן־אָדָם 'כְּתוֹב־כְּתָב־לְךָ' אֶת־שֵׁם הַיּוֹם אֶת־עֶצֶם הַיּוֹם הַזֶּה סָמַךְ מֶלֶךְ־בָּבֶל אֶל־יְרוּשָׁלִַם בְּעֶצֶם הַיּוֹם הַזֶּה

2[10] 'Son of man, write *the name of the day, of this selfsame day*[11]; this selfsame day the king of Babylon has invested Jerusalem.

---

[1] Ezekiel 23:42 - Amos 6:1-6:6, Exodus 8:6 32:18-32:19, Ezekiel 16:11-16:12, Genesis 24:30, Hosea 13:6, Jastrow 294a 13248, Job 1:15, Joel 4:8, Leviticus.R 33:6, Revelation 12:3

[2] Ezekiel 23:43 - b.Yoma 83b, Chibbur Yafeh 23 {97b}, Daniel 9:16, Ein Yaakov Yoma:83b, Ezekiel 23:3, Ezra 9:7, Jastrow 172b, Jeremiah 13:23, Leviticus.R 33:6, Mas.Soferim 7:2, Psalms 10:6

[3] Ezekiel 23:44 - Ezekiel 23:3 23:9-23:13
Ezekiel 23:44-47 - 4QEzeka

[4] Ezekiel 23:45 - Deuteronomy 22:21-22:24, Ezekiel 16:38-16:43 23:36-23:39, Hosea 6:5, Jeremiah 5:14, John 8:3-8:7, Leviticus 20:10 21:9, Leviticus.R 5:7, Saadia Opinions 10:7, y.Sanhedrin 6:4, y.Sotah 1:5 1:6, y.Terumot 8:3, Zechariah 1:6

[5] Ezekiel 23:46 - Ezekiel 16:40 23:22-23:26, Jeremiah 15:4 24:9 1:9 10:17, z.Vaetchanan 269b

[6] Ezekiel 23:47 - 2 Chronicles 36:17-36:19, b.Bava Batra [Rashbam] 118a, b.Chullin [Rashi] 43b, b.Succah [Rashi] 44b, Deuteronomy 13:17, Ezekiel 9:6 16:40-16:41 23:25 23:29 24:21, Jastrow 666b, Jeremiah 33:4-33:5 15:8 4:13

[7] Ezekiel 23:48 - 1 Corinthians 10:6-11, 2 Peter 2:6, b.Sanhedrin 45a, b.Sotah [Rashi] 32b, b.Sotah 7b 8b, Deuteronomy 13:12, Ezekiel 5:15 6:6 16:41 22:15 23:27 12:25, Isaiah 2:9, Jastrow 582b, m.Sotah 1:6, Micah 5:12-15, mt.Hilchot Sotah 3:5, Numbers.R 9:33, Zephaniah 1:3

[8] Ezekiel 23:49 - Ezekiel 6:7 7:4 7:9 9:10 11:21 16:43 20:38 20:42 20:44 22:31 23:35 1:5, Isaiah 11:18, Psalms 9:17

[9] Ezekiel 24:1 - 2 Kings 24:12, b.Rosh Hashanah 18b, Ein Yaakov Rosh Hashanah:18b, Ezekiel 1:2 8:1 20:1 2:1 5:1 5:17 7:1 8:1 8:17 9:21 16:1, y.Taanit 4:5
Ezekiel 24:1-2 - Seder Olam 26:Tenth of Tevet

[10] Ezekiel 24:2 - 2 Kings 1:1, b.Rosh Hashanah 18b, Ein Yaakov Rosh Hashanah:18b, Habakkuk 2:2-3, Isaiah 8:1 30:8-9, Jeremiah 15:1 4:4, Midrash Tanchuma Tazria 9, mt.Hilchot Taaniot 5:2, y.Taanit 4:5
Ezekiel 24:2-3 - 4QEzekc

[11] LXX *daily*

r44

444

וּמְשֹׁל אֶל־בֵּית־הַמֶּרִי מָשָׁל וְאָמַרְתָּ אֲלֵיהֶם כֹּה אָמַר אֲדֹנָי יְהוִה שְׁפֹת הַסִּיר שְׁפֹת וְגַם־יְצֹק בּוֹ מָיִם

3[1] And utter a parable concerning the rebellious house, and say unto them: Thus says the Lord GOD: Set on the pot, *set it on*[2], And also pour water into it;

אֱסֹף נְתָחֶיהָ אֵלֶיהָ כָּל־נֵתַח טוֹב יָרֵךְ וְכָתֵף מִבְחַר עֲצָמִים מַלֵּא

4[3] Gather into it the pieces belonging to it, every good piece, the thigh, and the *shoulder; Fill it with the choice bones*[4].

מִבְחַר הַצֹּאן לָקוֹחַ וְגַם דּוּר הָעֲצָמִים תַּחְתֶּיהָ רַתַּח רְתָחֶיהָ גַּם־בָּשְׁלוּ עֲצָמֶיהָ בְּתוֹכָהּ

5[5] Take the choice of the flock, And pile also the bones under it; Make it boil well, That the bones thereof may also be seethed in the midst of it.

לָכֵן כֹּה־אָמַר אֲדֹנָי יְהוִה אוֹי עִיר הַדָּמִים סִיר אֲשֶׁר חֶלְאָתָה בָהּ וְחֶלְאָתָהּ לֹא יָצְאָה מִמֶּנָּה לִנְתָחֶיהָ לִנְתָחֶיהָ הוֹצִיאָהּ לֹא־נָפַל עָלֶיהָ גּוֹרָל

6[6] Why thus says the Lord GOD: Woe to the bloody city, to the pot whose filth is in it, and whose filth is not gone out of it! bring it out piece by piece; no lot is fallen upon it.

כִּי דָמָהּ בְּתוֹכָהּ הָיָה עַל־צְחִיחַ סֶלַע שָׂמָתְהוּ לֹא שְׁפָכַתְהוּ עַל־הָאָרֶץ לְכַסּוֹת עָלָיו עָפָר

7[7] For her blood is in the midst of her; she set it upon the bare rock; she poured it not upon the ground, to cover it with dust;

לְהַעֲלוֹת חֵמָה לִנְקֹם נָקָם נָתַתִּי אֶת־דָּמָהּ עַל־צְחִיחַ סָלַע לְבִלְתִּי הִכָּסוֹת

8[8] that it might cause fury to come up, that vengeance might be taken, I have set her blood upon the bare rock, that it should not be covered.

לָכֵן כֹּה אָמַר אֲדֹנָי יְהוִה אוֹי עִיר הַדָּמִים גַּם־אֲנִי אַגְדִּיל הַמְּדוּרָה

9[9] Therefore thus says the Lord GOD: *Woe to the bloody city! I also will make the pile great*[10],

הַרְבֵּה הָעֵצִים הַדְלֵק הָאֵשׁ הָתֵם הַבָּשָׂר וְהַרְקַח הַמֶּרְקָחָה וְהָעֲצָמוֹת יֵחָרוּ

10[11] heaping on the wood, kindling the fire, that the flesh may be consumed; *and preparing the mixture, that the bones also may be burned*[12];

וְהַעֲמִידֶהָ עַל־גֶּחָלֶיהָ רֵקָה לְמַעַן תֵּחַם וְחָרָה נְחֻשְׁתָּהּ וְנִתְּכָה בְתוֹכָהּ טֻמְאָתָהּ תִּתֻּם חֶלְאָתָהּ

11[13] then will I set it empty upon the coals thereof, that *it may be hot, and the bottom thereof may burn, and that the impurity of it may be molten in it, that the filth of it may be consumed*[14]

תְּאֻנִים הֶלְאָת וְלֹא־תֵצֵא מִמֶּנָּה רַבַּת חֶלְאָתָהּ בָּאֵשׁ חֶלְאָתָהּ

12[15] *It has wearied itself with toil; yet its great filth goes not forth out of it, Yes, its noisome filth*[16].

---

[1] Ezekiel 24:3 - Acts 7:51, b.Avodah Zara [Rashi] 12a, b.Berachot 56b, Deuteronomy.R 3:2, Ezekiel 2:3 2:6 2:8 3:9 11:3 11:7 11:11 12:2 12:25 17:2 17:12 19:2-19:14 21:5 24:6, Isaiah 1:2 6:1 6:9 15:10, Jeremiah 1:13 50:13-50:14, Luke 8:10, Mark 12:12, Micah 2:4, Pesikta de R'Kahana S2.8, Psalms 78:2, z.Vaetchanan 269b

[2] Missing in LXX

[3] Ezekiel 24:4 - b.Yoma 25b, Ezekiel 22:18-22:22, Matthew 7:2, Micah 3:2-3:3

[4] LXX *shoulder taken off from the bones*

[5] Ezekiel 24:5 - b.Shabbat [Rashbam] 116b, Ezekiel 21:3 24:9-10 34:16-17 10:20, Jeremiah 15:6 4:10 52:24-27, Revelation 19:20

[6] Ezekiel 24:6 - 1 Samuel 14:40-42, 2 Kings 21:16 24:4, 2 Samuel 8:2, Ezekiel 9:5-6 11:6-9 11:11 22:2 22:6-9 22:12 22:27 23:37-45 24:9 24:11-13, Jastrow 493a 768a 1377a 1385a, Jeremiah 6:29, Joel 4:3, Jonah 1:7, Joshua 7:16-18 10:22, Lamentations.R Petichata D'Chakimei:5, Matthew 23:35, Micah 7:2, Nahum 3:1 3:10, Obadiah 1:11, Revelation 11:7-8 17:6 18:24, z.Vaetchanan 269b

[7] Ezekiel 24:7 - 1 Kings 21:19, Deuteronomy 12:16 12:24, Ecclesiastes.R 3:19, Isaiah 3:9 2:21, Jeremiah 2:34 6:15, Job 16:18, Jubilees 7:30, Lamentations.R 2:4 Petichata D'Chakimei:5 Petichata D'Chakimei:23, Leviticus 17:13, Midrash Tanchuma Vayikra 6, Pesikta de R'Kahana 15.7, y.Taanit 4:5

[8] Ezekiel 24:8 - 1 Corinthians 4:5, 2 Chronicles 10:25 36:16-17, 2 Kings 22:17, b.Gittin 57b, Deuteronomy 29:21-27 32:21-22, Ecclesiastes.R 10:5, Ein Yaakov Gittin:57b, Ezekiel 5:13 8:17-18 16:37-38 22:30-31 23:45, Jeremiah 7:18 7:20 15:1-4 22:8-9, Lamentations.R 2:4 Petichata D'Chakimei:5 D'Chakimei:23, Matthew 7:2, Pesikta de R'Kahana 15.7, Revelation 17:1-6 18:5-10 18:16, y.Taanit 4:5

[9] Ezekiel 24:9 - 2 Peter 3:7-3:12, 2 Thessalonians 1:8, Ezekiel 22:19-22:22 22:31 24:6, Habakkuk 2:12, Isaiah 6:33 7:9, Jude 1:7, Lamentations.R Petichata D'Chakimei:5, Luke 13:34-13:35, Nahum 3:1, Revelation 14:20 16:6 16:19 21:8, z.Vaetchanan 269b

[10] LXX *I will also make the firebrand great*

[11] Ezekiel 24:10 - Genesis.R 22:6, Jastrow 847b, Jeremiah 17:3 20:5, Lamentations 1:10 2:16, Lamentations.R Petichata D'Chakimei:5

[12] LXX *and the liquor boiled away*

[13] Ezekiel 24:11 - 1 Corinthians 3:12-13, Ezekiel 20:38 22:15-23 23:26-27 23:47-48 12:25, Isaiah 1:25 4:4 3:9, Jeremiah 21:10 8:29 3:10 14:18 15:8 4:13, Lamentations.R Petichata D'Chakimei:5, Malachi 4:13, Matthew 3:12, Micah 5:12-15, Zechariah 13:1-2 13:8-9

[14] LXX *her brass may be thoroughly heated, and be melted in the midst of her filthiness, and her scum may be consumed*

[15] Ezekiel 24:12 - Daniel 9:13-9:14, Ezekiel 24:6 24:13, Genesis 6:5-6:7 8:21, Habakkuk 2:13 2:18-2:19, Hosea 12:3, Isaiah 1:5 23:13 57:9-57:10, Jeremiah 2:13 5:3 9:6 10:14-10:15 44:16-44:17 3:58

[16] LXX *and her abundant scum may not come forth from her*

Hebrew	Verse	English

בְּטֻמְאָתֵךְ זִמָּה יַעַן טִהַרְתִּיךְ וְלֹא טָהַרְתְּ מִטֻּמְאָתֵךְ לֹא תִטְהֲרִי־עוֹד עַד־הֲנִיחִי אֶת־חֲמָתִי בָּךְ — **13[1]**

Because of your filthy lewdness, because I have purged you and you were not purged, you shall not be purged from your filthiness any more, till I have satisfied My fury upon you[2].

אֲנִי יְהוָה דִּבַּרְתִּי בָּאָה וְעָשִׂיתִי לֹא־אֶפְרַע וְלֹא־אָחוּס וְלֹא אֶנָּחֵם כִּדְרָכַיִךְ וְכַעֲלִילוֹתַיִךְ שְׁפָטוּךְ נְאֻם אֲדֹנָי יְהוִֹה — **14[3]**

I, the LORD, have spoken it; it shall come to pass, and I will do it; I will not go back, neither will I spare, neither will I repent; according to your ways, and according to your deeds, shall they judge you, says the Lord GOD.'

וַיְהִי דְבַר־יְהוָה אֵלַי לֵאמֹר — **15[4]**

Also the word of the LORD came to me, saying:

בֶּן־אָדָם הִנְנִי לֹקֵחַ מִמְּךָ אֶת־מַחְמַד עֵינֶיךָ בְּמַגֵּפָה וְלֹא תִסְפֹּד וְלֹא תִבְכֶּה וְלוֹא תָבוֹא דִּמְעָתֶךָ — **16[5]**

'Son of man, behold, I take away the desire of your eyes from you with a stroke; yet you shall not lament nor weep, nor shall your tears flow.

הֵאָנֵק דֹּם מֵתִים אֵבֶל לֹא־תַעֲשֶׂה פְאֵרְךָ חֲבוֹשׁ עָלֶיךָ וּנְעָלֶיךָ תָּשִׂים בְּרַגְלֶיךָ וְלֹא תַעְטֶה עַל־שָׂפָם וְלֶחֶם אֲנָשִׁים לֹא תֹאכֵל — **17[6]**

Sigh in silence; make no mourning for the dead[7], bind your headdress on you, and put your shoes on your feet, and do not cover your upper lip, and do not eat the bread of men.'

וָאֲדַבֵּר אֶל־הָעָם בַּבֹּקֶר וַתָּמָת אִשְׁתִּי בָּעָרֶב וָאַעַשׂ בַּבֹּקֶר כַּאֲשֶׁר צֻוֵּיתִי — **18[8]**

So I spoke to the people in the morning, *and at evening my wife died[9]*; and I did in the morning as I was commanded.

וַיֹּאמְרוּ אֵלַי הָעָם הֲלֹא־תַגִּיד לָנוּ מָה־אֵלֶּה לָּנוּ כִּי אַתָּה עֹשֶׂה — **19[10]**

And the people said to me: 'will you not tell us what these things that you do are to us?'

וָאֹמַר אֲלֵיהֶם דְּבַר־יְהוָה הָיָה אֵלַי לֵאמֹר — **20**

Then I said to them: 'The word of the LORD came to me, saying:

אֱמֹר לְבֵית יִשְׂרָאֵל כֹּה־אָמַר אֲדֹנָי יְהוִֹה הִנְנִי מְחַלֵּל אֶת־מִקְדָּשִׁי גְּאוֹן עֻזְּכֶם מַחְמַד עֵינֵיכֶם וּמַחְמַל נַפְשְׁכֶם וּבְנֵיכֶם וּבְנוֹתֵיכֶם אֲשֶׁר עֲזַבְתֶּם בַּחֶרֶב יִפֹּלוּ — **21[11]**

Speak to the house of Israel: Thus says the Lord GOD: Behold, I will profane My sanctuary, the pride of your power, the desire of your eyes, and the longing of your soul; and your sons and your daughters whom you have left behind shall fall by the sword.

וַעֲשִׂיתֶם כַּאֲשֶׁר עָשִׂיתִי עַל־שָׂפָם לֹא תַעְטוּ וְלֶחֶם אֲנָשִׁים לֹא תֹאכֵלוּ — **22[12]**

And you shall do as I have done: *you shall not cover your upper lips[13]*, nor eat the bread of men;

---

[1] Ezekiel 24:13 - 2 Chronicles 36:14-36:16, 2 Corinthians 7:1, Amos 4:6-4:12, b.Bava Kamma 92b, Chibbur Yafeh 26 {111b}, Ein Yaakov Bava Kamma:92b, Ezekiel 5:13 8:18 16:42 22:24 23:36-23:48 24:11, Hosea 7:1 7:9-7:16, Isaiah 5:4-5:6 9:14-9:18, Jeremiah 6:28-6:30 25:3-25:7 7:19, Luke 13:7-13:9, Matthew 23:37-23:38, Revelation 22:11, Romans 2:8-2:9, Zephaniah 3:2 3:7

[2] LXX *her scum shall become shameful, because you defiled yourself: and what if you shall be purged no more until I have accomplished my wrath?*

[3] Ezekiel 24:14 - 1 Samuel 15:29, 2 Enoch 29:4, Ezekiel 5:11 7:4 7:9 8:18 9:10 16:43 18:30 22:31 23:24 23:29 12:19, Isaiah 3:11 7:11, Jeremiah 4:18 13:14 23:20, Matthew 16:27 24:35, Numbers 23:19, Psalms 33:9, Romans 2:5-2:6

[4] Ezekiel 24:15-27 - Mas.Semachot 8:9

[5] Ezekiel 24:16 - 1 Thessalonians 4:13, b.Moed Katan 28a, b.Sanhedrin 22a, Ein Yaakov Moed Katan:28a, Exodus.R 3:6, Ezekiel 24:18 24:21-24:25, Genesis.R 25:1, Jeremiah 9:2 9:19 13:17 16:5 22:10 22:18, Job 12:18, Lamentations 2:18, Leviticus 10:2-10:3, Mas.Derek Eretz Zutta 9:8, Midrash Tanchuma Shemot 29, Proverbs 5:19, Song of Songs 7:11 Ezekiel 24:16-18 - Ein Yaakov Sanhedrin:21b

[6] Ezekiel 24:17 - 2 Samuel 15:30, Amos 8:3, b.Bava Batra [Rashbam] 60b, b.Berachot 11a 16b, b.Eruvin [Rashi] 81a, b.Ketubot 6b, b.Moed Katan 15ab 27b, b.Succah 25b, b.Taanit [Rashi] 16a, Ezekiel 24:22-24:23, Habakkuk 2:20, Hosea 9:4, Jastrow 965b 1131b 1266b, Jeremiah 16:4-16:7, Josephus Wars 2.1.1, Leviticus 10:6 13:45 21:10, Mas.Semachot 6:1, Micah 3:7, mt.Hilchot Evel 4:9 5:6 5:15 5:19, mt.Hilchot Taaniot 4:1, Psalms 37:7 39:10 46:11, Ralbag SOS 1, y.Moed Katan 3:5

[7] LXX *you shall groan for blood, and have mourning upon your loins*

[8] Ezekiel 24:18 - 1 Corinthians 7:29-7:30, b.Moed Katan 28a, b.Sanhedrin 22a, Ein Yaakov Moed Katan:28a

[9] LXX *as he commanded me in the evening*

[10] Ezekiel 24:19 - Ezekiel 12:9 17:12 21:5 21:12 13:18, Malachi 3:7-3:8 3:13

[11] Ezekiel 24:21 - Acts 6:13-6:14, b.Bava Batra 4a, b.Sanhedrin 22a, Daniel 11:31, Ein Yaakov Bava Batra:4a, Ein Yaakov Sanhedrin:21b, Ezekiel 7:20-22 9:7 23:25 23:47 24:16, Isaiah 17:11, Jeremiah 6:11 7:14 9:22 16:3-16:4, Lamentations 1:10 2:6-2:7, Leviticus.R 17:7, Psalms 27:4 74:7 79:1 84:2 96:6 9:4 12:8, z.Vaetchanan 269b

[12] Ezekiel 24:22 - Amos 6:9-6:10, Ezekiel 24:16-24:17, Jeremiah 16:4-7 23:3, Job 3:15, Psalms 78:64

[13] LXX *you shall not be comforted at their mouth*

וּפְאֵרֵכֶם עַל־רָאשֵׁיכֶם וְנַעֲלֵיכֶם בְּרַגְלֵיכֶם לֹא תִסְפְּדוּ וְלֹא תִבְכּוּ וּנְמַקֹּתֶם בַּעֲוֺנֹתֵיכֶם וּנְהַמְתֶּם אִישׁ אֶל־אָחִיו	23[1]	and your *headdresses*[2] shall be on your heads, and your shoes on your feet; you shall not lament nor weep; but you shall pine away in your iniquities, and moan one toward another.
וְהָיָה יְחֶזְקֵאל לָכֶם לְמוֹפֵת כְּכֹל אֲשֶׁר־עָשָׂה תַּעֲשׂוּ בְּבֹאָהּ וִידַעְתֶּם כִּי אֲנִי אֲדֹנָי יְהוִה	24[3]	Thus Ezekiel shall be a sign to you; all he has done you shall do; when this occurs, you shall know that I am the Lord GOD.
וְאַתָּה בֶן־אָדָם הֲלוֹא בְּיוֹם קַחְתִּי מֵהֶם אֶת־מָעוּזָּם מְשׂוֹשׂ תִּפְאַרְתָּם אֶת־מַחְמַד עֵינֵיהֶם וְאֶת־מַשָּׂא נַפְשָׁם בְּנֵיהֶם וּבְנוֹתֵיהֶם	25[4]	And, son of man, shall it not be in the day when I take from them their stronghold, the joy of their glory, the desire of their eyes, and the yearning of their soul, their sons and their daughters,
בַּיּוֹם הַהוּא יָבוֹא הַפָּלִיט אֵלֶיךָ לְהַשְׁמָעוּת אָזְנָיִם	26[5]	In that day he who escapes shall come to you, to cause you to hear it with your ears?
בַּיּוֹם הַהוּא יִפָּתַח פִּיךָ אֶת־הַפָּלִיט וּתְדַבֵּר וְלֹא תֵאָלֵם עוֹד וְהָיִיתָ לָהֶם לְמוֹפֵת וְיָדְעוּ כִּי־אֲנִי יְהוִה	27[6]	In that day your mouth shall be opened together with he who is escaped, and you shall speak, and no longer more dumb; so you shall be a sign to them; and they shall know that I am the LORD.'

Ezekiel – Chapter 25

וַיְהִי דְבַר־יְהוָה אֵלַי לֵאמֹר	1	And the word of the LORD came to me, saying:
בֶּן־אָדָם שִׂים פָּנֶיךָ אֶל־בְּנֵי עַמּוֹן וְהִנָּבֵא עֲלֵיהֶם	2[7]	'Son of man, set your face toward the children of Ammon, and prophesy against them;
וְאָמַרְתָּ לִבְנֵי עַמּוֹן שִׁמְעוּ דְּבַר־אֲדֹנָי יְהוִה כֹּה־אָמַר אֲדֹנָי יְהוִה יַעַן אָמְרֵךְ הֶאָח אֶל־מִקְדָּשִׁי כִי־נִחָל וְאֶל־אַדְמַת יִשְׂרָאֵל כִּי נָשַׁמָּה וְאֶל־בֵּית יְהוּדָה כִּי הָלְכוּ בַּגּוֹלָה	3[8]	and say to the children of Ammon: Hear the word of the Lord GOD: Thus says the Lord GOD: Because you said: Aha! against My sanctuary, when it was profaned, and against the land of Israel, when it was made desolate, and against the house of Judah, when they went into captivity;
לָכֵן הִנְנִי נֹתְנָךְ לִבְנֵי־קֶדֶם לְמוֹרָשָׁה וְיִשְּׁבוּ טִירוֹתֵיהֶם בָּךְ וְנָתְנוּ בָךְ מִשְׁכְּנֵיהֶם הֵמָּה יֹאכְלוּ פִרְיֵךְ וְהֵמָּה יִשְׁתּוּ חֲלָבֵךְ	4[9]	Therefore, behold, I will deliver you to the children of the east as property, and they shall set their encampments in you, and make their homes in you; they shall eat your fruit, and they shall drink your milk.
וְנָתַתִּי אֶת־רַבָּה לִנְוֵה גְמַלִּים וְאֶת־בְּנֵי עַמּוֹן לְמִרְבַּץ־צֹאן וִידַעְתֶּם כִּי־אֲנִי יְהוָה	5[10]	And I will make *Rabbah*[11] a pasture for camels, and the children of Ammon a couching place for flocks; and you shall know I am the LORD.

---

[1] Ezekiel 24:23 - Ecclesiastes.R 12:7, Ezekiel 4:17 9:10, Isaiah 11:11, Job 3:15, Lamentations.R Petichata D'Chakimei:23, Leviticus 2:39, Mas.Semachot 6:1, Psalms 78:64, y.Shabbat 6:4

[2] LXX *hair*

[3] Ezekiel 24:24 - 1 Samuel 10:2-7, Ezekiel 4:3 6:7 7:9 7:27 12:6 12:11 17:24 1:5 1:7 1:11 1:14 1:17, Hosea 1:2-1:9 3:1-4, Isaiah 8:18 20:3, Jeremiah 17:15, John 13:19 14:29 16:4, Lamentations.R 1:22, Luke 11:29-30 21:13, Mas.Semachot 8:9

[4] Ezekiel 24:25 - Deuteronomy 4:32, Ezekiel 24:21, Jeremiah 7:4 11:22 4:10, Midrash Tanchuma Bamidbar 1, Psalms 48:3 50:2 122:1-9

[5] Ezekiel 24:26 - 1 Samuel 4:12-4:18, Ezekiel 33:21-33:22, Job 1:15-19

[6] Ezekiel 24:27 - Ephesians 6:19, Exodus 6:11-12, Ezekiel 3:26-27 5:21 9:22, Luke 21:15, Psalms 51:16

[7] Ezekiel 25:2 - Amos 1:13-15, Ezekiel 6:2 21:2 21:7 21:33-37 11:2, Genesis 19:38, Jeremiah 9:26-27 1:21 3:3 49:1-6, Zephaniah 2:8-11

[8] Ezekiel 25:3 - Ezekiel 1:6 1:8 26:2-26:21 35:10-35:15 12:2, Lamentations 2:21-2:22 4:21, Micah 7:8, Proverbs 17:5 24:17-24:18, Psalms 70:3-70:4, z.Vaetchanan 269b

[9] Ezekiel 25:4 - 1 Kings 4:30, 2 Samuel 12:26, Deuteronomy 4:33 4:51, Genesis 5:1, Isaiah 1:7 32:8-32:9 17:2 17:22, Judges 6:3-6:6 6:33 7:12 8:10, Leviticus 2:16, Numbers 23:7

[10] Ezekiel 25:5 - 2 Samuel 12:26, Deuteronomy 3:11, Ezekiel 21:25 24:24 1:8 2:6 6:8 11:9 14:23, Isaiah 17:2 8:14 13:20, Psalms 83:19, Zephaniah 2:14-15

[11] LXX *the city of Ammon*

Hebrew	Verse	English

כִּי כֹה אָמַר֮ אֲדֹנָ֣י יְהֹוָה֒ יַ֚עַן מַחְאֲךָ֣ יָ֔ד וְרַקְעֲךָ֖ בְּרָ֑גֶל וַתִּשְׂמַ֤ח בְּכָל־שָׁאטְךָ֙ בְּנֶ֔פֶשׁ אֶל־אַדְמַ֖ת יִשְׂרָאֵֽל — 6[1]

For thus says the Lord GOD: Because you have clapped your hands, and stamped with the feet, and rejoiced with all the disdain of your soul against the land of Israel;

לָכֵ֡ן הִנְנִי֩ נָטִ֨יתִי אֶת־יָדִ֜י עָלֶ֗יךָ וּנְתַתִּ֣יךָֽ־לְבַג֮ 'וּנְתַתִּ֤יךָֽ־לְבַז֙' לַגּוֹיִ֔ם וְהִכְרַתִּ֖יךָ מִן־הָ֣עַמִּ֑ים וְהַאֲבַדְתִּ֙יךָ֙ מִן־הָ֣אֲרָצ֔וֹת אַשְׁמִידְךָ֖ וְיָדַעְתָּ֥ כִּֽי־אֲנִ֖י יְהֹוָֽה — 7[2]

therefore, behold, I stretch out My hand on you, and will deliver you as spoil to the nations; and I will cut you off from the peoples, and I will cause you to perish from the countries; I will destroy you, and you shall know that I am the LORD.

כֹּ֤ה אָמַר֙ אֲדֹנָ֣י יְהֹוִ֔ה יַ֗עַן אֲמֹ֤ר מוֹאָב֙ וְשֵׂעִ֔יר הִנֵּ֥ה כְּכָל־הַגּוֹיִ֖ם בֵּ֥ית יְהוּדָֽה — 8[3]

Thus says the Lord GOD: Because Moab *and Seir*[4] say: Behold, the house of Judah is like all the nations,

לָכֵן֩ הִנְנִ֨י פֹתֵ֜חַ אֶת־כֶּ֤תֶף מוֹאָב֙ מֵהֶ֣עָרִ֔ים מֵֽעָרָ֖יו מִקָּצֵ֑הוּ צְבִ֣י אֶ֗רֶץ בֵּ֤ית הַיְשִׁימֹת֙ בַּ֣עַל מְע֔וֹן 'וְקִרְיָתָֽמָה' 'וְקִרְיָתָֽיְמָה' — 9[5]

therefore, behold, I will open the *flank of Moab on the side of the cities, on the side of his cities which are on his frontiers, the beauteous country of Beth-jeshimoth, Baal-meon, and Kiriathaim*[6],

לִבְנֵי־קֶ֙דֶם֙ עַל־בְּנֵ֣י עַמּ֔וֹן וּנְתַתִּ֖יהָ לְמֽוֹרָשָׁ֑ה לְמַ֛עַן לֹא־תִזָּכֵ֥ר בְּנֵֽי־עַמּ֖וֹן בַּגּוֹיִֽם — 10[7]

together with the children of Ammon, to the children of the east, and I will give them as property, so the children of Ammon may not be remembered among the nations[8];

וּבְמוֹאָ֖ב אֶעֱשֶׂ֣ה שְׁפָטִ֑ים וְיָדְע֖וּ כִּֽי־אֲנִ֥י יְהֹוָֽה — 11[9]

and I will execute judgments on Moab; and they shall know I am the LORD.

כֹּ֤ה אָמַר֙ אֲדֹנָ֣י יְהֹוִ֔ה יַ֣עַן עֲשׂ֥וֹת אֱד֛וֹם בִּנְקֹ֥ם נָקָ֖ם לְבֵ֣ית יְהוּדָ֑ה וַיֶּאְשְׁמ֥וּ אָשׁ֖וֹם וְנִקְּמ֥וּ בָהֶֽם — 12[10]

Thus says the Lord GOD: Because *Edom*[11] has dealt against the house of Judah by taking vengeance, and has greatly offended, and revenged himself upon them;

לָכֵ֗ן כֹּ֤ה אָמַר֙ אֲדֹנָ֣י יְהֹוִ֔ה וְנָטִ֤תִי יָדִי֙ עַל־אֱד֔וֹם וְהִכְרַתִּ֥י מִמֶּ֖נָּה אָדָ֣ם וּבְהֵמָ֑ה וּנְתַתִּ֤יהָ חׇרְבָּה֙ מִתֵּימָ֔ן וּדְדָ֖נֶה בַּחֶ֥רֶב יִפֹּֽלוּ — 13[12]

Therefore, thus says the Lord GOD: I will stretch out My hand on Edom, and will cut off man and beast from it; and I will make it desolate from Teman to *Dedan*[13]; they shall fall by the sword.

וְנָתַתִּ֨י אֶת־נִקְמָתִ֜י בֶּאֱד֗וֹם בְּיַד֙ עַמִּ֣י יִשְׂרָאֵ֔ל וְעָשׂ֤וּ בֶֽאֱדוֹם֙ כְּאַפִּ֣י וְכַחֲמָתִ֑י וְיָדְע֖וּ אֶת־נִקְמָתִ֑י נְאֻ֖ם אֲדֹנָ֥י יְהֹוָֽה — 14[14]

And I will lay My vengeance upon Edom by the hand of My people Israel; and they shall do in Edom according to My anger and according

---

[1] Ezekiel 25:6 - Ezekiel 6:11 1:15 11:15 12:5, Jeremiah 24:27, Job 3:23 10:37, Lamentations 2:15, Nahum 3:19, Nehemiah 4:3-4:4, Obadiah 1:12, Proverbs 24:17, z.Vaetchanan 269b, Zephaniah 2:8 2:10 2:15

[2] Ezekiel 25:7 - Amos 1:14-1:15, Esther.R 3:12, Ezekiel 6:14 14:9 1:13 1:16 11:3, Jastrow 137a, Jeremiah 1:2, Zephaniah 1:4

[3] Ezekiel 25:8 - 4Q177 10 & 14, 4Q177 2.13-14, Amos 2:1-3 2:11-12, Deuteronomy 2:5, Ezekiel 25:12-14 35:1-15, Isaiah 10:9-11 15:1-9 1:10 34:1-17 36:18-20 63:1-63:6, Jeremiah 1:21 3:3 48:1-48:47 49:7-49:22, Lamentations.R Petichata D'Chakimei:9, Numbers 24:17, Obadiah 1:1-9, Pesikta de R'Kahana 19.1, Psalms 83:5-9, z.Vaetchanan 269b, Zephaniah 2:8-11

[4] Missing in LXX

[5] Ezekiel 25:9 - 1 Chronicles 5:8, Genesis.R 41:3, Jeremiah 24:1 24:23, Joshua 12:3 13:17 13:19-20, Numbers 8:3 32:37-38 9:49

[6] LXX *shoulder of Moab from his frontier cities, even the choice land, the house of Bethasimuth above the fountain of the city, by the seaside*

[7] Ezekiel 25:10 - Ezekiel 21:37 1:4, Isaiah 23:16, Lamentations.R 1:38, Psalms 83:4-7

[8] LXX *I have given him the children of Kedem in addition to the children of Ammon for an inheritance, that there may be no remembrance of the children of Ammon*

[9] Ezekiel 25:11 - Ezekiel 5:8 5:10 5:15 11:9 16:41 1:5 1:17 6:14 6:19 11:15 15:21, Jeremiah 9:26-9:27 1:21 48:1-47, Jude 1:15, Lamentations.R 1:38, Psalms 9:17 5:7

[10] Ezekiel 25:12 - 2 Chronicles 28:17-18, Amos 1:11-12, Ezekiel 1:8 35:1-15, Genesis 27:41-42, Jeremiah 49:7-22, Obadiah 1:10-16, Psalms 17:7, z.Vaetchanan 269b

[11] LXX *Idumeans*

[12] Ezekiel 25:13 - Amos 1:12, Ezekiel 14:8 14:13 14:17 14:19-21 1:7 1:16 5:8, Genesis 6:7 12:11, Habakkuk 3:3, Isaiah 34:1:17 63:1-6, Jeremiah 7:20 1:23 49:7-8 1:20, Lamentations 4:21-22, Malachi 1:3-4, Mekilta de R'Ishmael Shirata 9:19, Obadiah 1:9, Testament of Job 29:3, z.Vaetchanan 269b

[13] LXX *Thaeman*

[14] Ezekiel 25:14 - b.Gittin 56a, Deuteronomy 32:35-32:36, Ezekiel 11:11, Genesis 3:29, Genesis.R 6:5, Hebrews 10:30-10:31, Isaiah 11:14 63:1-63:6, Jeremiah 1:2, Leviticus.R 34:9 35:8, Midrash Psalms 18:28, Nahum 1:2-1:4, Numbers.R 2:13, Pesikta de R'Kahana S2.2, Pesikta Rabbati 11:5, Psalms 58:11-58:12, Revelation 6:16-6:17, Ruth.R 5:9, Saadia Opinions 8:6

to My fury; and they shall know my vengeance, says the Lord GOD.

כֹּה אָמַר אֲדֹנָי יְהֹוִה יַעַן עֲשׂוֹת פְּלִשְׁתִּים בִּנְקָמָה וַיִּנָּקְמוּ נָקָם בִּשְׁאָט בְּנֶפֶשׁ לְמַשְׁחִית אֵיבַת עוֹלָם

15[1] Thus says the Lord GOD: Because the Philistines have dealt with revenge, and have taken vengeance with disdain of soul to destroy, *for the old hatred*[2];

לָכֵן כֹּה אָמַר אֲדֹנָי יְהֹוִה הִנְנִי נוֹטֶה יָדִי עַל־פְּלִשְׁתִּים וְהִכְרַתִּי אֶת־כְּרֵתִים וְהַאֲבַדְתִּי אֶת־שְׁאֵרִית חוֹף הַיָּם

16[3] Therefore, thus says the Lord GOD: Behold, I will stretch out My hand on the Philistines, and I will cut off the *Cherethites*[4], and destroy the remnant of the sea coast.

וְעָשִׂיתִי בָם נְקָמוֹת גְּדֹלוֹת בְּתוֹכְחוֹת חֵמָה וְיָדְעוּ כִּי־אֲנִי יְהֹוָה בְּתִתִּי אֶת־נִקְמָתִי בָּם

17[5] And I will execute great vengeance on them with furious rebukes; and they shall know that I am the LORD, when I shall lay My vengeance upon them.'

Ezekiel – Chapter 26

וַיְהִי בְּעַשְׁתֵּי־עֶשְׂרֵה שָׁנָה בְּאֶחָד לַחֹדֶשׁ הָיָה דְבַר־יְהֹוָה אֵלַי לֵאמֹר

1[6] And it came to pass in the eleventh year, in the first day of the month, that the word of the LORD came to me, saying:

בֶּן־אָדָם יַעַן אֲשֶׁר־אָמְרָה צֹּר עַל־יְרוּשָׁלַם הֶאָח נִשְׁבְּרָה דַּלְתוֹת הָעַמִּים נָסֵבָּה אֵלָי אִמָּלְאָה הָחֳרָבָה

2[7] 'Son of man, because Tyre has said against Jerusalem: Aha, she who was the gate of the peoples is broken; She has turned to me; I shall be filled with her who is laid waste;

לָכֵן כֹּה אָמַר אֲדֹנָי יְהֹוִה הִנְנִי עָלַיִךְ צֹר וְהַעֲלֵיתִי עָלַיִךְ גּוֹיִם רַבִּים כְּהַעֲלוֹת הַיָּם לְגַלָּיו

3[8] Therefore, thus says the Lord GOD: Behold, I am against you, O Tyre, And will cause many nations to come up against you, As the sea causes its waves to come up.

וְשִׁחֲתוּ חֹמוֹת צֹר וְהָרְסוּ מִגְדָּלֶיהָ וְסִחֵיתִי עֲפָרָהּ מִמֶּנָּה וְנָתַתִּי אוֹתָהּ לִצְחִיחַ סָלַע

4[9] And they shall destroy the walls of Tyre, And break down her towers; I will also scrape her dust from her, And make her a bare rock.

מִשְׁטַח חֲרָמִים תִּהְיֶה בְּתוֹךְ הַיָּם כִּי אֲנִי דִבַּרְתִּי נְאֻם אֲדֹנָי יְהֹוִה וְהָיְתָה לְבַז לַגּוֹיִם

5[10] She shall be a place for the spreading of nets In the midst of the sea; For I have spoken it, says the Lord GOD; And she shall become spoil to the nations.

וּבְנוֹתֶיהָ אֲשֶׁר בַּשָּׂדֶה בַּחֶרֶב תֵּהָרַגְנָה וְיָדְעוּ כִּי־אֲנִי יְהֹוָה

6[11] And her daughters who are in the field shall be killed with the sword; and they shall know that I am the LORD.

---

[1] Ezekiel 25:15 - 1 Chronicles 7:21, 1 Samuel 4:1-4:6 13:1-13:14 17:1-17:58 21:1-21:15, 2 Chronicles 4:18, 2 Samuel 8:1-8:18, Amos 1:6-1:8, Ezekiel 1:6 1:12, Isaiah 9:13 14:29-31, Jeremiah 1:20 47:1-47:7, Joel 4:4-4:21, Judges 14:1-14:16, Psalms 83:8, z.Vaetchanan 269b, Zechariah 9:5-9:8, Zephaniah 2:4-2:7

[2] LXX *the Israelites to a man*

[3] Ezekiel 25:16 - 1 Samuel 6:14, 2 Samuel 15:18, Ezekiel 1:7 1:13, Jeremiah 47:1-47:7, Mekhilta de R'Shimon bar Yochai Shirata 35:1, Mekhilta de R'Ishmael Shirata 9:18, z.Vaetchanan 269b, Zephaniah 2:4-2:15

[4] LXX *Cretans*

[5] Ezekiel 25:17 - Ezekiel 5:15 6:7 1:5 1:11 1:14, Psalms 9:17

[6] Ezekiel 26:1 - Ezekiel 1:2 8:1 20:1, Jeremiah 15:2, Numbers.R 1:1, This is the middle verse of the book of Ezekiel per the Massorah, y.Taanit 4:5

[7] Ezekiel 26:2 - 2 Samuel 5:11, Acts 2:5-2:10, Amos 1:9-1:10, b.Ketubot 111a, b.Megillah 6a, b.Pesachim 42b, Ein Yaakov Megillah:6a, Ezekiel 25:2-25:3 1:6 1:10 27:1-27:28 12:2, Isaiah 23:1-23:18, Jastrow 498a 785b, Jeremiah 1:22 3:3 23:4 1:1, Joel 4:4, Joshua 19:29, Lamentations 1:1, Psalms 35:21 40:16 70:4 83:3-83:5 83:8, y.Taanit 4:5, z.Pekudei 235a, Zechariah 9:2-9:4 Ezekiel 26:2-3 - Mekhilta de R'Ishmael Pisha 13:34-37

[8] Ezekiel 26:3 - Ezekiel 5:8 21:8 3:26 27:32-34 4:22 14:3, Isaiah 5:30, Jeremiah 6:23 21:13 2:31 2:42 3:42, Luke 21:25, Mekhilta de R'Ishmael Shirata 2:89, Micah 4:11, Midrash Tanchuma Beshallach 12, Nahum 2:13, Psalms 93:3-4 11:25, z.Vaetchanan 269b, Zechariah 14:2

[9] Ezekiel 26:4 - Amos 1:10, Ezekiel 24:7-24:8 2:9 2:12, Isaiah 23:11, Jeremiah 5:10, Leviticus 14:41-14:45, Zechariah 9:3

[10] Ezekiel 26:5 - Ezekiel 1:7 2:14 2:19 3:32 5:19 23:10

[11] Ezekiel 26:6 - Ezekiel 16:46 16:48 1:5 1:7 1:11 1:14 1:17 2:8, Jeremiah 1:2

כִּי כֹה אָמַר אֲדֹנָי יְהוִֹה הִנְנִי מֵבִיא אֶל־צֹר 7[1]
נְבוּכַדְרֶאצַּר מֶלֶךְ־בָּבֶל מִצָּפוֹן מֶלֶךְ מְלָכִים בְּסוּס
וּבְרֶכֶב וּבְפָרָשִׁים וְקָהָל וְעַם־רָב

For thus says the Lord GOD: Behold, I will bring on Tyre *Nebuchadrezzar king of Babylon, king of kings*[2], from the north, with horses, and with chariots, and with horsemen, and a company, and many people.

בְּנוֹתַיִךְ בַּשָּׂדֶה בַּחֶרֶב יַהֲרֹג וְנָתַן עָלַיִךְ דָּיֵק וְשָׁפַךְ 8[3]
עָלַיִךְ סֹלְלָה וְהֵקִים עָלַיִךְ צִנָּה

He shall kill your daughters in the field with the sword; and he shall make forts against you, *And cast up a mound against you, and set up bucklers against you*[4].

וּמְחִי קָבֳלּוֹ יִתֵּן בְּחֹמוֹתָיִךְ וּמִגְדְּלֹתַיִךְ יִתֹּץ 9[5]
בְּחַרְבוֹתָיו

And he shall set his battering engines against your walls, and with his axes He shall break down your towers.

מִשִּׁפְעַת סוּסָיו יְכַסֵּךְ אֲבָקָם מִקּוֹל פָּרַשׁ וְגַלְגַּל 10[6]
וָרֶכֶב תִּרְעַשְׁנָה חוֹמוֹתַיִךְ בְּבֹאוֹ בִּשְׁעָרַיִךְ כִּמְבוֹאֵי
עִיר מְבֻקָּעָה

Because of his abundance of horses, their dust shall cover you; at the noise of the horsemen, and of the wheels, and of the chariots. Your walls shall shake when he shall enter in your gates, As men enter a city through a breach.

בְּפַרְסוֹת סוּסָיו יִרְמֹס אֶת־כָּל־חוּצוֹתָיִךְ עַמֵּךְ 11[7]
בַּחֶרֶב יַהֲרֹג וּמַצְּבוֹת עֻזֵּךְ לָאָרֶץ תֵּרֵד

With the hoofs of his horses he shall tread down all your streets; he shall kill your people with the sword, and the pillars of your strength shall go down to the ground.

וְשָׁלְלוּ חֵילֵךְ וּבָזְזוּ רְכֻלָּתֵךְ וְהָרְסוּ חוֹמוֹתַיִךְ וּבָתֵּי 12[8]
חֶמְדָּתֵךְ יִתֹּצוּ וַאֲבָנַיִךְ וְעֵצַיִךְ וַעֲפָרֵךְ בְּתוֹךְ מַיִם
יָשִׂימוּ

And they shall make a spoil of your riches, and make a prey of your merchandise; and they shall break down your walls, and destroy the houses of your delight, and your stones and your timber; and they shall lay your dust in the midst of the waters.

וְהִשְׁבַּתִּי הֲמוֹן שִׁירָיִךְ וְקוֹל כִּנּוֹרַיִךְ לֹא יִשָּׁמַע עוֹד 13[9]

And I will cause the noise of your songs to cease, And the sound of your harps shall not be heard again.

וּנְתַתִּיךְ לִצְחִיחַ סֶלַע מִשְׁטַח חֲרָמִים תִּהְיֶה לֹא 14[10]
תִבָּנֶה עוֹד כִּי אֲנִי יְהוָה דִּבַּרְתִּי נְאֻם אֲדֹנָי יְהוִֹה

And I will make you a bare rock; you shall be a place for the spreading of nets, You shall not be built any longer; For I, the LORD, have spoken, says the Lord GOD.

כֹּה אָמַר אֲדֹנָי יְהוִֹה לְצוֹר הֲלֹא מִקּוֹל מַפַּלְתֵּךְ 15[11]
בֶּאֱנֹק חָלָל בֵּהָרֵג הֶרֶג בְּתוֹכֵךְ יִרְעֲשׁוּ הָאִיִּים

Thus says the Lord GOD to Tyre: Shall the isles not shake at the sound of your fall, when the wounded groan, when the slaughter is made in your midst?

וְיָרְדוּ מֵעַל כִּסְאוֹתָם כֹּל נְשִׂיאֵי הַיָּם וְהֵסִירוּ אֶת־ 16[12]
מְעִילֵיהֶם וְאֶת־בִּגְדֵי רִקְמָתָם יִפְשֹׁטוּ חֲרָדוֹת
יִלְבָּשׁוּ עַל־הָאָרֶץ יֵשֵׁבוּ וְחָרְדוּ לִרְגָעִים וְשָׁמְמוּ
עָלָיִךְ

Then all the princes of the sea shall come down from their thrones, and lay away their robes, and strip off their richly woven garments; they shall clothe themselves with trembling; they

---

[1] Ezekiel 26:7 - Daniel 2:37 2:47, Ezekiel 17:14 23:24 2:3 26:10-26:11 4:7 29:18-29:20 30:10-30:11 32:11-32:12, Ezra 7:12, Hosea 8:10, Isaiah 10:8, Jeremiah 4:13 6:23 1:9 1:22 27:3-6 4:32, Nahum 2:4-5 3:2-3, Testament of Moses 8:1, z.Vaetchanan 269b
[2] LXX *Nabuchodonosor king of Babylon*
[3] Ezekiel 26:8 - 2 Samuel 20:15, Ezekiel 21:27, Jeremiah 6:6 8:24 4:4
[4] LXX *and carry a rampart round against you, and set up warlike works, and array his spears against you*
[5] Ezekiel 26:9 - 2 Chronicles 2:15
[6] Ezekiel 26:10 - Ezekiel 2:7 2:15 3:28, Jeremiah 4:13 23:3, Joshua 6:5 6:20, Nahum 2:4-2:5
[7] Ezekiel 26:11 - Habakkuk 1:8, Isaiah 5:28 2:5, Jeremiah 19:13 3:27
[8] Ezekiel 26:12 - 2 Chronicles 8:27 12:10, Amos 5:11, Daniel 11:8, Ezekiel 2:5 27:3-36 4:8, Hosea 13:15, Isaiah 23:8 23:11 23:17-18 8:12, Jeremiah 1:34, Matthew 6:19-20, Nahum 2:10, Revelation 18:11-13, Zechariah 7:14 9:3-4
[9] Ezekiel 26:13 - Amos 6:4-7, Ezekiel 4:13, Hosea 2:11, Isaiah 5:12 14:11 22:2 23:7 23:16 24:8-9, James 5:1-5, Jeremiah 7:34 16:9 1:10, Revelation 18:22-23
[10] Ezekiel 26:14 - Deuteronomy 13:17, Ezekiel 5:13 5:15 5:17 17:21-24 21:37 22:14 26:4-5 2:12 6:12, Isaiah 14:27, Job 12:14 16:8, Malachi 1:4, Matthew 24:35, Numbers 23:19
[11] Ezekiel 26:15 - Ezekiel 2:18 3:28 3:35 7:16 8:10, Hebrews 12:26-12:27, Isaiah 2:19, Jeremiah 1:21, z.Vaetchanan 269b
[12] Ezekiel 26:16 - 1 Peter 5:5, Daniel 5:6, Exodus 15:15 33:4-5, Ezekiel 7:8 27:29-36 8:10 32:21-32, Hosea 11:10, Isaiah 3:26 14:9-13 23:1-8 23:11 4:2, Job 2:12-13 8:22, Jonah 3:6, Lamentations 2:10, Psalms 35:26 13:18 13:29 12:18, Revelation 18:11-19

shall sit on the ground, and shall tremble every moment, and be disgusted at you.

וְנָשְׂא֨וּ עָלַ֤יִךְ קִינָה֙ וְאָ֣מְרוּ לָ֔ךְ אֵ֚יךְ אָבַ֣דְתְּ נוֹשֶׁ֣בֶת מִיַּמִּ֔ים הָעִ֖יר הַהֻלָּלָ֑ה אֲשֶׁר֩ הָיְתָ֨ה חֲזָקָ֤ה בַיָּם֙ הִ֣יא וְיֹשְׁבֶ֔יהָ אֲשֶׁר־נָתְנ֥וּ חִתִּיתָ֖ם לְכָל־יוֹשְׁבֶֽיהָ

17[1]   And they shall take up a lamentation for you, and say to you: How you are destroyed, as were peopled from the seas. The renowned city, that was strong in the sea, You and your inhabitants, who caused your terror to be on all who inhabit the earth.

עַתָּה֙ יֶחְרְד֣וּ הָֽאִיִּ֔ן יֹ֖ום מַפַּלְתֵּ֑ךְ וְנִבְהֲל֧וּ הָאִיִּ֛ים אֲשֶׁר־בַּיָּ֖ם מִצֵּאתֵֽךְ

18[2]   Now the isles shall tremble In the day of your fall; *Yes, the isles in the sea shall be terrified at your destruction*[3].

כִּ֣י כֹ֤ה אָמַר֙ אֲדֹנָ֣י יְהֹוִ֔ה בְּתִתִּ֤י אֹתָךְ֙ עִ֣יר נֶחֱרֶ֔בֶת כֶּעָרִ֖ים אֲשֶׁ֣ר לֹא־נוֹשָׁ֑בוּ בְּהַעֲל֤וֹת עָלַ֙יִךְ֙ אֶת־תְּה֔וֹם וְכִסּ֖וּךְ הַמַּ֥יִם הָרַבִּֽים

19[4]   For thus says the Lord GOD: When I make you a desolate city, like the cities that are not inhabited; when I shall bring up the deep upon you, and the great waters shall cover you;

וְהוֹרַדְתִּ֜יךְ אֶת־י֣וֹרְדֵי ב֗וֹר אֶל־עַ֣ם עוֹלָ֔ם וְ֠הוֹשַׁבְתִּיךְ בְּאֶ֨רֶץ תַּחְתִּיּ֜וֹת כׇּחֳרָב֤וֹת מֵֽעוֹלָם֙ אֶת־יֹ֣ורְדֵי ב֔וֹר לְמַ֖עַן לֹ֣א תֵשֵׁ֑בִי וְנָתַתִּ֥י צְבִ֖י בְּאֶ֥רֶץ חַיִּֽים

20[5]   then will I bring you down with those who descend into the pit, to the people of old time, and will make you dwell in the nether parts of the earth, like the places that are desolate of old, with those who down to the pit, so you will not be inhabited; and I will set glory in the land of the living;

בַּלָּה֣וֹת אֶתְּנֵ֔ךְ וְאֵינֵ֑ךְ וּתְבֻקְשִׁ֗י וְלֹֽא־תִמָּצְאִ֥י עוֹד֙ לְעוֹלָ֔ם נְאֻ֖ם אֲדֹנָ֥י יְהֹוִֽה

21[6]   I will make you a terror, and you shall cease to exist; though you be sought, yet shall you never be found again, says the Lord GOD.'

Ezekiel – Chapter 27

וַיְהִ֥י דְבַר־יְהֹוָ֖ה אֵלַ֥י לֵאמֹֽר

1[7]   Moreover the word of the LORD came to me, saying:

וְאַתָּ֣ה בֶן־אָדָ֔ם שָׂ֥א עַל־צֹ֖ר קִינָֽה

2[8]   'And you, son of man, take up a lamentation for Tyre,

וְאָמַרְתָּ֣ לְצ֗וֹר הַיֹּשֶׁ֙בֶתִּ֙י הַיֹּשֶׁ֔בֶת עַל־מְבוֹאֹ֣ת יָ֔ם רֹכֶ֙לֶת֙ הָֽעַמִּ֔ים אֶל־אִיִּ֖ים רַבִּ֑ים כֹּ֤ה אָמַר֙ אֲדֹנָ֣י יְהֹוִ֔ה צ֕וֹר אַ֣תְּ אָמַ֔רְתְּ אֲנִ֖י כְּלִ֥ילַת יֹֽפִי

3[9]   and say to Tyre, that dwells at the entry of the sea, that is the merchant of the peoples to many isles: Thus says the Lord GOD: You, O Tyre, have said: I am perfectly beautiful.

בְּלֵ֥ב יַמִּ֖ים גְּבוּלָ֑יִךְ בֹּנַ֕יִךְ כָּלְל֖וּ יׇפְיֵֽךְ

4[10]   Your borders are in the heart of the seas, your builders have perfected your beauty.

[1] Ezekiel 26:17 - 2 Samuel 1:19 1:25-27, Ezekiel 19:1 19:14 27:2-36 28:2-10 28:12-19 8:2 8:16, Isaiah 14:12 23:4 23:8, Jeremiah 6:26 7:29 9:21, Joel 1:18, Joshua 19:29, Lamentations 1:1, Micah 2:4, Midrash Tanchuma Bereshit 7, Obadiah 1:5, Revelation 18:9-10 18:16-19, Zephaniah 2:15

[2] Ezekiel 26:18 - Ezekiel 2:15 27:28-30 3:35, Isaiah 23:5-7 23:10-12 17:5

[3] Missing in LXX

[4] Ezekiel 26:19 - Daniel 9:26 11:40, Ezekiel 2:3, Isaiah 8:7-8, Midrash Tanchuma Bereshit 7, Revelation 17:15, z.Vaetchanan 269b

[5] Ezekiel 26:20 - Amos 9:2, Avot de R'Natan 34, Ein Yaakov Ketubot:111a, Ezekiel 28:25-26 32:18-32 34:1-31 15:7 39:25-29, Isaiah 4:5 14:11-19 11:10, Jastrow 1258b, Job 30:3-6, Jonah 2:2 2:6, Lamentations 3:6, Luke 10:15, Midrash Tanchuma Bereshit 7, Numbers 16:30 16:33, Psalms 27:13 28:1 88:4-7, Tanya Igeret Hakodesh §8, Zechariah 2:8

[6] Ezekiel 26:21 - Ezekiel 26:14-16 3:36 4:19, Jeremiah 51:64, Lamentations.R 2:1, Midrash Tanchuma Noach 12, Psalms 37:36, Revelation 18:21

[7] Ezekiel 27:1-2 - t.Sotah 6:10

[8] Ezekiel 27:2 - Amos 5:1 5:16, Ezekiel 19:1 2:17 3:32 4:12 8:2, Jeremiah 7:20 9:11 9:18-21, Midrash Tanchuma Balak 1, Numbers.R 20:1

[9] Ezekiel 27:3 - Exodus.R 36:1, Ezekiel 2:17 3:4 27:10-27:36 28:2-28:3 28:12-28:17, Isaiah 23:2-23:3 23:8-23:9 23:11, Lamentations.R 2:19, Mekhilta de R'Shimon bar Yochai Beshallach 24:4, Mekhilta de R'Ishmael Shirata 2:88, Midrash Psalms 48:2, Pesikta Rabbati 41:2, Psalms 50:2, Revelation 18:3 18:11-15, z.Vaetchanan 269b
Ezekiel 27:3-4 - Midrash Tanchuma Beshallach 12

[10] Ezekiel 27:4 - Ezekiel 2:5, Jastrow 703b

בְּרוֹשִׁים מִשְּׂנִיר בָּנוּ לָךְ אֵת כָּל־לֻחֹתָיִם אֶרֶז מִלְּבָנוֹן לָקָחוּ לַעֲשׂוֹת תֹּרֶן עָלָיִךְ	5[1]	They have they fashioned all your planks of cypress trees from Senir. They have taken cedars from Lebanon to make your masts.
אַלּוֹנִים מִבָּשָׁן עָשׂוּ מִשּׁוֹטָיִךְ קַרְשֵׁךְ עָשׂוּ־בַת־שֵׁן אֲשֻׁרִים מֵאִיֵּי 'כִּתִּיִם' "כִּתִּיִּים"	6[2]	They have made your oars from the oaks of Bashan. They made your deck of ivory from the coasts of Chittim, the daughter of Assyria.
שֵׁשׁ־בְּרִקְמָה מִמִּצְרַיִם הָיָה מִפְרָשֵׂךְ לִהְיוֹת לָךְ לְנֵס תְּכֵלֶת וְאַרְגָּמָן מֵאִיֵּי אֱלִישָׁה הָיָה מְכַסֵּךְ	7[3]	Your sail was of fine linen with richly woven work from Egypt, so it might be an ensign for you; your awning was blue and purple from the isles of Elishah.
יֹשְׁבֵי צִידוֹן וְאַרְוַד הָיוּ שָׁטִים לָךְ חֲכָמַיִךְ צוֹר הָיוּ בָךְ הֵמָּה חֹבְלָיִךְ	8[4]	The inhabitants of Sidon and Arvad were your rowers; your wise men, O Tyre, were yours, they were your pilots.
זִקְנֵי גְבַל וַחֲכָמֶיהָ הָיוּ בָךְ מַחֲזִיקֵי בִּדְקֵךְ כָּל־אֳנִיּוֹת הַיָּם וּמַלָּחֵיהֶם הָיוּ בָךְ לַעֲרֹב מַעֲרָבֵךְ	9[5]	The elders of *Gebal*[6] and their wise men were your caulkers; all the ships of the sea with their mariners were yours in exchange for your merchandise.
פָּרַס וְלוּד וּפוּט הָיוּ בְחֵילֵךְ אַנְשֵׁי מִלְחַמְתֵּךְ מָגֵן וְכוֹבַע תִּלּוּ־בָךְ הֵמָּה נָתְנוּ הֲדָרֵךְ	10[7]	Persia and Lud and *Put*[8] were in your army, your men of war hung your shield and helmet, they set forth your splendor.
בְּנֵי אַרְוַד וְחֵילֵךְ עַל־חוֹמוֹתַיִךְ סָבִיב וְגַמָּדִים בְּמִגְדְּלוֹתַיִךְ הָיוּ שִׁלְטֵיהֶם תִּלּוּ עַל־חוֹמוֹתַיִךְ סָבִיב הֵמָּה כָּלְלוּ יָפְיֵךְ	11[9]	The men of Arvad and *Helech*[10] were on your walls, and the *Gammadim*[11] were in your towers; they hung their shields around your walls; they perfected your beauty.
תַּרְשִׁישׁ סֹחַרְתֵּךְ מֵרֹב כָּל־הוֹן בְּכֶסֶף בַּרְזֶל בְּדִיל וְעוֹפֶרֶת נָתְנוּ עִזְבוֹנָיִךְ	12[12]	*Tarshish was*[13] your merchants because of the multitude of all kinds of riches; with silver[14], iron, tin, and lead, they traded for your wares.
יָוָן תֻּבַל וָמֶשֶׁךְ הֵמָּה רֹכְלָיִךְ בְּנֶפֶשׁ אָדָם וּכְלֵי נְחֹשֶׁת נָתְנוּ מַעֲרָבֵךְ	13[15]	*Javan, Tubal, and Meshech*[16], they were your traders; they traded slaves and vessels of brass for your merchandise.
מִבֵּית תּוֹגַרְמָה סוּסִים וּפָרָשִׁים וּפְרָדִים נָתְנוּ עִזְבוֹנָיִךְ	14[17]	Those of the house of Togarmah traded for your wares with horses and horsemen *and mules*[18].

---

[1] Ezekiel 27:5 - 1 Kings 5:1 5:6, b.Bava Batra 73a, Deuteronomy 3:9, Isaiah 14:8, Jastrow 1658a, Psalms 29:5 92:13 8:16, Song of Songs 4:8

[2] Ezekiel 27:6 - b.Bava Batra 73a, Genesis 10:4, Genesis.R 83:1, Isaiah 2:13 23:12, Jeremiah 2:10 22:20, Numbers 21:33 24:24, Zechariah 11:2

[3] Ezekiel 27:7 - 1 Chronicles 1:7, 1 Kings 10:28, b.Bava Batra 73a, b.Megillah [Rashi] 6b, Exodus 1:4, Genesis 10:4, Isaiah 19:9, Jeremiah 10:9, Proverbs 7:16

[4] Ezekiel 27:8 - 1 Kings 5:6 9:27, 2 Chronicles 2:12-13, Ezekiel 3:11 3:28, Genesis 10:15 10:18 1:13, Isaiah 10:9, Jeremiah 1:23, Joshua 11:8

[5] Ezekiel 27:9 - 1 Kings 5:18, Joshua 13:5, Psalms 83:8

[6] LXX *the Biblians*

[7] Ezekiel 27:10 - 1 Chronicles 1:8 1:11 1:17, Daniel 5:28, Ezekiel 3:11 6:5 14:5, Genesis 10:6 10:13 10:22, Isaiah 18:19, Jeremiah 22:9, Nahum 3:9, Song of Songs 4:4

[8] LXX *Libyans*

[9] Ezekiel 27:11 - Ezekiel 27:3-27:4, Jastrow 703b

[10] LXX *your army*

[11] LXX *guards*

[12] Ezekiel 27:12 - 1 Kings 10:22 22:48, 2 Chronicles 20:36-20:37, Ezekiel 3:16 3:18 14:13, Genesis 10:4, Isaiah 2:16 23:6 23:10 23:14 12:9, Jeremiah 10:9, Jonah 1:3, Psalms 72:10

[13] LXX *The Carthaginians were*

[14] LXX adds *and gold*

[15] Ezekiel 27:13 - 1 Chronicles 1:5 1:7, Daniel 8:21 10:20 11:2, Ezekiel 3:19 8:26 38:2-38:3 15:1, Genesis 10:2 10:4, Isaiah 18:19, Joel 4:3, Jubilees 9:10, Revelation 18:13

[16] LXX *Greece, both the whole world, and the adjacent coasts*

[17] Ezekiel 27:14 - 1 Chronicles 1:6, Ezekiel 14:6, Genesis 10:3

[18] Missing in LXX

בְּנֵי דְדָן רֹכְלַיִךְ אִיִּים רַבִּים סְחֹרַת יָדֵךְ קַרְנוֹת שֵׁן "וְהוֹבְנִים" "וְהָבְנִים" הֵשִׁיבוּ אֶשְׁכָּרֵךְ

15¹ The *men of Dedan were your traders; many isles traded under your rule;* they brought you tribute of horns of ivory and ebony².

אֲרָם סֹחַרְתֵּךְ מֵרֹב מַעֲשָׂיִךְ בְּנֹפֶךְ אַרְגָּמָן וְרִקְמָה וּבוּץ וְרָאמֹת וְכַדְכֹּד נָתְנוּ בְּעִזְבוֹנָיִךְ

16³ *Aram was your merchant because of the multitude of your wealth;* they traded for your wares with carbuncles, purple, and richly woven work, and fine linen, and coral, and rubies⁴.

יְהוּדָה וְאֶרֶץ יִשְׂרָאֵל הֵמָּה רֹכְלָיִךְ בְּחִטֵּי מִנִּית וּפַנַּג וּדְבַשׁ וָשֶׁמֶן וָצֹרִי נָתְנוּ מַעֲרָבֵךְ

17⁵ Judah, and the land of Israel, they were your traders; they traded for your merchandise *wheat of Minnith, and balsam, and honey, and oil, and balm*⁶.

דַּמֶּשֶׂק סֹחַרְתֵּךְ בְּרֹב מַעֲשַׂיִךְ מֵרֹב כָּל־הוֹן בְּיֵין חֶלְבּוֹן וְצֶמֶר צָחַר

18⁷ Damascus was your merchant for the *multitude of your wealth, because the multitude of all riches, with the wine of Helbon, and white wool*⁸.

וְדָן וְיָוָן מְאוּזָּל בְּעִזְבוֹנָיִךְ נָתָנּוּ בַּרְזֶל עָשׁוֹת קִדָּה וְקָנֶה בְּמַעֲרָבֵךְ הָיָה

19⁹ *Vedan and Javan traded with yarn for your wares;* massive iron, cassia, and calamus, were among your merchandise¹⁰.

דְּדָן רֹכַלְתֵּךְ בְבִגְדֵי־חֹפֶשׁ לְרִכְבָּה

20¹¹ Dedan was your trader *in precious riding cloths*¹².

עֲרַב וְכָל־נְשִׂיאֵי קֵדָר הֵמָּה סֹחֲרֵי יָדֵךְ בְּכָרִים וְאֵילִם וְעַתּוּדִים בָּם סֹחֲרָיִךְ

21¹³ Arabia, and all the princes of Kedar, they were the merchants of your hand; in lambs, and rams, and goats, in these they were your merchants.

רֹכְלֵי שְׁבָא וְרַעְמָה הֵמָּה רֹכְלָיִךְ בְּרֹאשׁ כָּל־בֹּשֶׂם וּבְכָל־אֶבֶן יְקָרָה וְזָהָב נָתְנוּ עִזְבוֹנָיִךְ

22¹⁴ The traders of Sheba and Raamah, they were your traders; they traded for your wares with chief of all spices, and with all precious stones, and gold.

חָרָן וְכַנֵּה וָעֶדֶן רֹכְלֵי שְׁבָא אַשּׁוּר כִּלְמַד רֹכַלְתֵּךְ

23¹⁵ *Haran and Canneh and Eden, the traders of Sheba, Asshur was your apprentice in trading*¹⁶.

הֵמָּה רֹכְלַיִךְ בְּמַכְלֻלִים בִּגְלוֹמֵי תְּכֵלֶת וְרִקְמָה וּבְגִנְזֵי בְּרֹמִים בַּחֲבָלִים חֲבֻשִׁים וַאֲרֻזִים בְּמַרְכֻלְתֵּךְ

24¹⁷ *These were your traders in gorgeous fabrics,* in wrappings of blue and richly woven work, and in chests of rich apparel, bound with cords and cedar lined, among your merchandise¹⁸.

---

¹ Ezekiel 27:15 - 1 Chronicles 1:9 1:32, 1 Kings 10:22, Ezekiel 1:13 3:20, Genesis 10:7 1:3, Jeremiah 1:23 1:8, Pesikta Rabbati 33:10, Revelation 18:12
² LXX *sons of the Rhodians were your merchants; from the islands they multiplied your merchandise, even elephants' teeth: and to those who came in you returned your prices*
³ Ezekiel 27:16 - 2 Samuel 8:5 10:6 15:8, Ezekiel 4:13, Genesis 10:22 4:5, Isaiah 7:1-8, Judges 10:6
⁴ LXX *even men as your merchandise, from the multitude of your trading population, myrrh, and embroidered works from Tharsis: Ramoth also and Chorchor furnished your market*
⁵ Ezekiel 27:17 - 1 Kings 5:9, 2 Chronicles 2:9, Acts 12:20, Deuteronomy 8:8 8:14, Ecclesiastes.R 1:23, Ezra 3:7, Genesis 19:11, Jastrow 801b, Jeremiah 8:22, Judges 11:33, Lamentations.R 3:6
⁶ LXX *corn and ointments and cassia: and they gave the best honey, and oil, and resin, to your trading population*
⁷ Ezekiel 27:18 - 1 Kings 11:24-11:25, Acts 9:2, Ezekiel 47:16-47:18, Genesis 14:15 15:2, Genesis.R 98 [Excl]:9, Isaiah 7:8
⁸ LXX *abundance of all your power; wine out of Chelbon, and wool from Miletus; and they brought wine into your market*
⁹ Ezekiel 27:19 - Exodus 30:23-24, Jastrow 38a, Judges 18:29, Psalms 45:9, Song of Songs 4:13-14
¹⁰ LXX *Out of Asel came wrought iron, and there is the sound of wheels among your trading population.*
¹¹ Ezekiel 27:20 - Ezekiel 27:15, Genesis 25:3
¹² LXX *with choice cattle for chariots*
¹³ Ezekiel 27:21 - 1 Chronicles 1:29, 1 Kings 10:15, 2 Chronicles 17:11, Acts 2:11, Galatians 4:25, Genesis 25:13, Isaiah 21:16 60:7, Jeremiah 25:24, Song of Songs 1:5
¹⁴ Ezekiel 27:22 - 1 Chronicles 1:9, 1 Kings 10:1-13, 2 Chronicles 9:1-12, Ezekiel 14:13, Genesis 10:7 19:11, Isaiah 12:6, Psalms 72:10 72:15
¹⁵ Ezekiel 27:23 - 2 Kings 19:12, Acts 7:4, Amos 1:5 6:2, Genesis 2:8 10:10 10:22 11:31-32 12:4 1:3 8:23, Isaiah 7:18 7:20 10:9 13:12, Job 1:15, Numbers 24:22, Psalms 83:9
¹⁶ LXX *Charra, and Chanaa, these were your merchants: Assur, and Charman, were your merchants*
¹⁷ Ezekiel 27:24 - 2 Kings 2:8, b.Berachot [Rashi] 26a, b.Megillah [Rashi] 26b
¹⁸ LXX *bringing for merchandise blue, and choice stores bound with cords, and cypress wood*

אֳנִיּוֹת תַּרְשִׁישׁ שָׁרוֹתַיִךְ מַעֲרָבֵךְ וַתִּמָּלְאִי וַתִּכְבְּדִי מְאֹד בְּלֵב יַמִּים 25¹

The ships of Tarshish brought you tribute for your merchandise[2]; So you were replenished, and made very heavy in the heart of the seas.

בְּמַיִם רַבִּים הֱבִיאוּךְ הַשָּׁטִים אֹתָךְ רוּחַ הַקָּדִים שְׁבָרֵךְ בְּלֵב יַמִּים 26³

Your rowers brought you into great waters; the *east*[4] wind has broken you in the heart of the seas.

הוֹנֵךְ וְעִזְבוֹנַיִךְ מַעֲרָבֵךְ מַלָּחַיִךְ וְחֹבְלַיִךְ מַחֲזִיקֵי בִדְקֵךְ וְעֹרְבֵי מַעֲרָבֵךְ וְכָל־אַנְשֵׁי מִלְחַמְתֵּךְ אֲשֶׁר־בָּךְ וּבְכָל־קְהָלֵךְ אֲשֶׁר בְּתוֹכֵךְ יִפְּלוּ בְּלֵב יַמִּים בְּיוֹם מַפַּלְתֵּךְ 27⁵

Your riches, and your wares, your product, your mariners, your pilots, your *caulkers*[6], and the exchangers of your merchandise, and all your men of war, who are in you, with all your company which is in your midst, shall fall into the heart of the seas in the day of your ruin.

לְקוֹל זַעֲקַת חֹבְלָיִךְ יִרְעֲשׁוּ מִגְרֹשׁוֹת 28⁷

At the sound of the cry of your pilots the waves shall shake.

וְיָרְדוּ מֵאֳנִיּוֹתֵיהֶם כֹּל תֹּפְשֵׂי מָשׁוֹט מַלָּחִים כֹּל חֹבְלֵי הַיָּם אֶל־הָאָרֶץ יַעֲמֹדוּ 29⁸

And all who handle the oar, the mariners, and all the pilots of the sea, shall come down from their ships, they shall stand upon the land,

וְהִשְׁמִיעוּ עָלַיִךְ בְּקוֹלָם וְיִזְעֲקוּ מָרָה וְיַעֲלוּ עָפָר עַל־רָאשֵׁיהֶם בָּאֵפֶר יִתְפַּלָּשׁוּ 30⁹

And shall cause their voice to be heard over you, and shall cry bitterly, and shall cast dust upon their heads. They shall roll themselves in the ashes;

וְהִקְרִיחוּ אֵלַיִךְ קָרְחָה וְחָגְרוּ שַׂקִּים וּבָכוּ אֵלַיִךְ בְּמַר־נֶפֶשׁ מִסְפֵּד מָר 31¹⁰

And they shall make themselves utterly bald for you, and clothe themselves with sackcloth, and they shall weep for you in bitterness of soul with bitter lamentation[11].

וְנָשְׂאוּ אֵלַיִךְ בְּנִיהֶם קִינָה וְקוֹנְנוּ עָלָיִךְ מִי כְצוֹר כְּדֻמָּה בְּתוֹךְ הַיָּם 32¹²

And *in their wailing they*[13] shall take up a lamentation for you, *and lament over you: who was like Tyre, fortified in the midst of the sea*[14]?

בְּצֵאת עִזְבוֹנַיִךְ מִיַּמִּים הִשְׂבַּעַתְּ עַמִּים רַבִּים בְּרֹב הוֹנַיִךְ וּמַעֲרָבַיִךְ הֶעֱשַׁרְתְּ מַלְכֵי־אָרֶץ 33¹⁵

When your wares came forth out of the seas, you filled many peoples with the multitude of your riches and of your merchandise you enriched the kings of the earth.

עֵת נִשְׁבֶּרֶת מִיַּמִּים בְּמַעֲמַקֵּי־מָיִם מַעֲרָבֵךְ וְכָל־קְהָלֵךְ בְּתוֹכֵךְ נָפָלוּ 34¹⁶

Now that you are broken by the seas, in the depths of the waters, and your merchandise and all your company *are fallen in your midst*[17],

---

[1] Ezekiel 27:25 - 1 Kings 10:22, Isaiah 2:16 23:14 12:9, Psalms 48:8

[2] LXX *Ships were your merchants*

[3] Ezekiel 27:26 - Acts 3:14 3:41, Ezekiel 2:19 3:34, Isaiah 9:23, Jeremiah 18:17, Mekhilta de R'Shimon bar Yochai Beshallach 24:4, Mekilta de R'Ishmael Beshallah 5:97, Psalms 48:8 93:3-93:4, Revelation 17:15

[4] LXX *south*

[5] Ezekiel 27:27 - Ezekiel 2:12 2:14 2:21 27:7-27:9 3:12 27:18-27:19 3:22 3:24 3:34, Mas.Derek Eretz Rabbah 2:11, Pesikta de R'Kahana 4.9 5.19, Pesikta Rabbati 14:15 15:25, Proverbs 11:4, Revelation 18:11-18:24

[6] LXX *counselors*

[7] Ezekiel 27:28 - Exodus 15:14, Ezekiel 2:10 26:15-26:18 3:35 7:16, Nahum 2:4

[8] Ezekiel 27:29 - b.Bava Batra 73a, b.Yevamot 63a, Ecclesiastes.R 5:6, Ein Yaakov Yevamot:63a, Ezekiel 2:16 8:10, Leviticus.R 22:1, Revelation 18:17-24

[9] Ezekiel 27:30 - 1 Samuel 4:12, 2 Samuel 1:2, Esther 4:1-4:4, Ezekiel 2:17 27:31-27:32, Isaiah 23:1-23:6, Jeremiah 6:26 1:34, Job 2:8 2:12 18:6, Jonah 3:6, Lamentations 2:10, Micah 1:10, Revelation 18:9-18:19

[10] Ezekiel 27:31 - Amos 8:10, Deuteronomy 14:1, Ezekiel 7:18, Isaiah 15:2 16:9 22:4 22:12, Jeremiah 16:6 23:5 24:37, Leviticus 21:5, Micah 1:8 1:16

[11] Missing in LXX

[12] Ezekiel 27:32 - Ezekiel 26:4-26:5 2:17 3:2 3:26, Lamentations 1:12 2:13, Revelation 18:18
Ezekiel 27:32-36 - Testament of Job 25:1

[13] LXX *their sons*

[14] LXX *even a lamentation for Sor*

[15] Ezekiel 27:33 - Ezekiel 3:3 27:12-36 28:4-5 4:16, Isaiah 23:3-8, Revelation 18:3 18:12-15 18:19

[16] Ezekiel 27:34 - Ezekiel 26:12-15 26:19-21 27:26-27, Zechariah 9:3-4

[17] LXX *all your rowers have fallen*

כָּל־יֹשְׁבֵי הָאִיִּים שָׁמְמוּ עָלֶיךָ וּמַלְכֵיהֶם שָׂעֲרוּ שַׂעַר רָעֲמוּ פָּנִים	35[1]	All the inhabitants of the isles are appalled at you, and their kings are horribly afraid, they tremble in their countenance;
סֹחֲרִים בָּעַמִּים שָׁרְקוּ עָלֶיךָ בַּלָּהוֹת הָיִיתָ וְאֵינְךָ עַד־עוֹלָם	36[2]	The merchants among the peoples hiss at you; you have become a terror, and never shall be again.'

Ezekiel – Chapter 28[3]

וַיְהִי דְבַר־יְהֹוָה אֵלַי לֵאמֹר	1[4]	And the word of the LORD came to me, saying:
בֶּן־אָדָם אֱמֹר לִנְגִיד צֹר כֹּה־אָמַר אֲדֹנָי יֱהֹוִה יַעַן גָּבַהּ לִבְּךָ וַתֹּאמֶר אֵל אָנִי מוֹשַׁב אֱלֹהִים יָשַׁבְתִּי בְּלֵב יַמִּים וְאַתָּה אָדָם וְלֹא־אֵל וַתִּתֵּן לִבְּךָ כְּלֵב אֱלֹהִים	2[5]	'Son of man, say to the prince of Tyre: Thus says the Lord GOD: Because your heart is haughty, and you have said: I am a god, I sit in the seat of God, In the heart of the seas; yet you are man, and not God, though you set your heart as the heart of God
הִנֵּה חָכָם אַתָּה 'מִדָּנִאֵל' "מִדָּנִיֵּאל" כָּל־סָתוּם לֹא עֲמָמוּךָ	3[6]	*Behold, you are*[7] wiser than Daniel! There is no secret they can hide from you!
בְּחָכְמָתְךָ וּבִתְבוּנָתְךָ עָשִׂיתָ לְּךָ חָיִל וַתַּעַשׂ זָהָב וָכֶסֶף בְּאוֹצְרוֹתֶיךָ	4[8]	By your wisdom and by your discernment You got riches, and received gold and silver into your treasures;
בְּרֹב חָכְמָתְךָ בִּרְכֻלָּתְךָ הִרְבִּיתָ חֵילֶךָ וַיִּגְבַּהּ לְבָבְךָ בְּחֵילֶךָ	5[9]	In your great wisdom, by your trading, you increased your riches, and your heart is haughty because of your riches
לָכֵן כֹּה אָמַר אֲדֹנָי יֱהֹוִה יַעַן תִּתְּךָ אֶת־לְבָבְךָ כְּלֵב אֱלֹהִים	6[10]	Therefore, thus says the Lord GOD: Because you have set your heart as the heart of God;
לָכֵן הִנְנִי מֵבִיא עָלֶיךָ זָרִים עָרִיצֵי גּוֹיִם וְהֵרִיקוּ חַרְבוֹתָם עַל־יְפִי חָכְמָתֶךָ וְחִלְּלוּ יִפְעָתֶךָ	7[11]	Therefore, behold, I will bring *strangers upon you, the terrible of the nations*[12]; and they shall draw their swords against the beauty of your wisdom, *and they shall defile your brightness*[13]. *They shall bring you down to the pit*[15]; and you shall die the deaths of those slain in the heart of the seas.
לַשַּׁחַת יוֹרִדוּךָ וָמַתָּה מְמוֹתֵי חָלָל בְּלֵב יַמִּים	8[14]	

---

[1] Ezekiel 27:35 - Ezekiel 26:15-26:18 28:17-19 8:10, Isaiah 23:6, Revelation 18:9-10

[2] Ezekiel 27:36 - 1 Kings 9:8, Ezekiel 2:2 2:14 2:21, Jeremiah 18:16 19:8 1:17 2:13, Lamentations 2:15, Psalms 37:10 37:36, Zephaniah 2:15

[3] Ezekiel 28 - Mas.Kallah Rabbati 6:1

[4] Ezekiel 28:1 - 2 Enoch 29:3, Leviticus.R 18:2, Mekhilta de R'Shimon bar Yochai Shirata 33:1

[5] Ezekiel 28:2 - 1 Peter 5:5, 1 Timothy 3:6, 2 Chronicles 2:16, 2 Thessalonians 2:4, Acts 12:22-12:23, b.Bava Kamma [Tosefot] 38a, b.Chullin 89a, b.Yevamot [Tosefot] 61a, Daniel 4:27-28 5:22-23, Deuteronomy 8:14, Ein Yaakov Chullin 89a, Exodus.R 8:2, Ezekiel 27:3-4 27:26-27 28:5-6 4:9 28:12-14 4:17 7:10, Genesis 3:5, Genesis.R 85:3 96:5, Habakkuk 2:4, Isaiah 2:12 14:13-14 7:3, Mekhilta de R'Shimon bar Yochai Shirata 28:1 34:1, Mekhilta de R'Ishmael Shirata 2:91, Mekhilta de R'Ishmael Shirata 8:32, Midrash Tanchuma Bereshit 7, Midrash Tanchuma Beshallach 12, Midrash Tanchuma Vaera 9, Midrash Tanchuma Vayechi 3, Proverbs 16:18 18:12, Psalms 9:21 72:6-7 82:6-7, Revelation 17:3, Sibylline Oracles 5.173, z.Acharei Mot 61a, z.Vaetchanan 269b

[6] Ezekiel 28:3 - 1 Kings 4:29-4:32 10:3, Daniel 1:20 2:22 2:27-2:28 2:47-2:48 5:11-5:12, Genesis.R 96:5, Job 15:8, Lamentations.R 4:1, Midrash Tanchuma Vayechi 3, Psalms 25:14, Zechariah 9:2-9:3

[7] LXX *are you*

[8] Ezekiel 28:4 - Deuteronomy 8:17-8:18, Ecclesiastes 9:11, Ezekiel 5:3, Habakkuk 1:16, Proverbs 18:11 23:4-23:5, Zechariah 9:2-9:4

[9] Ezekiel 28:5 - 1 Timothy 6:17, 2 Chronicles 1:19 32:23-25, Ahiqar 137, Daniel 4:27 4:34, Deuteronomy 6:11-12 8:13-14, Ezekiel 16:49 27:12-36 4:2, Hosea 12:9-10 13:6, Isaiah 5:21 10:8-14 23:3 23:8, James 4:13-14, Job 31:24-25, Luke 12:16-21, Proverbs 11:28 2:12 6:9, Psalms 52:8 62:11, Romans 12:16, Zechariah 9:3

[10] Ezekiel 28:6 - 1 Corinthians 10:22, 2 Thessalonians 2:4, Exodus 9:17, Ezekiel 4:2, James 1:11, Job 9:4 40:9-12, z.Vaetchanan 269b

[11] Ezekiel 28:7 - Amos 3:6, Daniel 7:7, Deuteronomy 28:49-28:50, Ezekiel 26:7-26:14 6:11 7:12 8:12, Habakkuk 1:6-1:8, Isaiah 23:8-23:9 25:3-25:4, Mekhilta de R'Shimon bar Yochai Shirata 33:1, Mekhilta de R'Ishmael Shirata 7:42

[12] LXX *on you strange plagues from the nations*

[13] Missing in LXX

[14] Ezekiel 28:8 - Ezekiel 27:26-27 3:34 32:18-30, Isaiah 14:17, Job 17:16 9:18 9:28, Proverbs 1:12 4:17, Psalms 28:1 30:10 55:16 88:5-88:6

[15] LXX *and they shall bring down your beauty to destruction. And they shall bring you down*

הֶאָמֹר תֹּאמַר אֱלֹהִים אָנִי לִפְנֵי הֹרְגֶךָ וְאַתָּה אָדָם וְלֹא־אֵל בְּיַד מְחַלְלֶיךָ	9[1]	Will you say before he who slays you: I am God? But you are man, and not God in the hand of those who defile you.
מוֹתֵי עֲרֵלִים תָּמוּת בְּיַד־זָרִים כִּי אֲנִי דִבַּרְתִּי נְאֻם אֲדֹנָי יְהוִה	10[2]	You will die the deaths of the uncircumcised by the hand of strangers; for I have spoken, says the Lord GOD.'
וַיְהִי דְבַר־יְהוָה אֵלַי לֵאמֹר	11	Moreover, the word of the LORD came to me, saying:
בֶּן־אָדָם שָׂא קִינָה עַל־מֶלֶךְ צוֹר וְאָמַרְתָּ לּוֹ כֹּה אָמַר אֲדֹנָי יְהוִה אַתָּה חוֹתֵם תָּכְנִית מָלֵא חָכְמָה וּכְלִיל יֹפִי	12[3]	'Son of man, take up a lamentation for the king of Tyre, and say to him: Thus says the Lord GOD: you were the *seal most accurate, full of wisdom, and perfect in beauty*[4],
בְּעֵדֶן גַּן־אֱלֹהִים הָיִיתָ כָּל־אֶבֶן יְקָרָה מְסֻכָתֶךָ אֹדֶם פִּטְדָה וְיָהֲלֹם תַּרְשִׁישׁ שֹׁהַם וְיָשְׁפֵה סַפִּיר נֹפֶךְ וּבָרְקַת וְזָהָב מְלֶאכֶת תֻּפֶּיךָ וּנְקָבֶיךָ בָּךְ בְּיוֹם הִבָּרַאֲךָ כּוֹנָנוּ	13[5]	you were in *Eden the garden of God*[6]; every precious stone was your covering, the *carnelian, the topaz, and the emerald, the beryl, the onyx, and the jasper, the sapphire, the carbuncle, and the emerald, and gold; the workmanship of your settings and of your sockets was in you, in the day you were created they were prepared*[7].
אַתְּ־כְּרוּב מִמְשַׁח הַסּוֹכֵךְ וּנְתַתִּיךָ בְּהַר קֹדֶשׁ אֱלֹהִים הָיִיתָ בְּתוֹךְ אַבְנֵי־אֵשׁ הִתְהַלָּכְתָּ	14[8]	You were the far covering cherub; and I set you, so you were on the holy mountain of God; you walked up and down in the midst of stones of fire.
תָּמִים אַתָּה בִּדְרָכֶיךָ מִיּוֹם הִבָּרְאָךְ עַד־נִמְצָא עַוְלָתָה בָּךְ	15[9]	You were perfect in your ways from the day you were created, until unrighteousness was found in you.
בְּרֹב רְכֻלָּתְךָ מָלוּ תוֹכְךָ חָמָס וַתֶּחֱטָא וָאֶחַלֶּלְךָ מֵהַר אֱלֹהִים וָאַבֶּדְךָ כְּרוּב הַסֹּכֵךְ מִתּוֹךְ אַבְנֵי־אֵשׁ	16[10]	By the multitude of your trading they filled you with violence, and you have sinned; therefore, have I cast you as profane out of the mountain of God; and I have destroyed you, O covering cherub, from the midst of the stones of fire.
גָּבַהּ לִבְּךָ בְּיָפְיֶךָ שִׁחַתָּ חָכְמָתְךָ עַל־יִפְעָתֶךָ עַל־אֶרֶץ הִשְׁלַכְתִּיךָ לִפְנֵי מְלָכִים נְתַתִּיךָ לְרַאֲוָה בָךְ	17[11]	Your heart was haughty because of your beauty, you corrupted your wisdom because of your brightness; I have cast you to the ground, I

---

[1] Ezekiel 28:9 - Acts 12:22-12:23, b.Avodah Zara [Tosefot] 3a, Daniel 4:28-4:29 5:23-5:30, Ezekiel 4:2, Isaiah 7:3, Psalms 82:7

[2] Ezekiel 28:10 - 1 Samuel 17:26 17:36, Acts 7:51, Ezekiel 11:9 4:7 7:18 8:19 8:21 32:24-32:30 20:7 20:9, Jeremiah 6:10 9:26-9:27 1:9, John 8:24, Leviticus 2:41, Mekhilta de R'Shimon bar Yochai Shirata 28:1 34:1, Mekhilta de R'Ishmael Shirata 2:92, Midrash Tanchuma Beshallach 12, Philippians 3:3

[3] Ezekiel 28:12 - 1 Corinthians 1:19-1:20 3:19, 2 Chronicles 11:25, 2 Corinthians 1:22, Acts 6:3, b.Taanit [Rashi] 29a, Colossians 1:9 2:3, Ecclesiastes.R 7:28 8:2, Ezekiel 19:1 19:14 2:17 27:2-27:4 3:32 28:2-28:5 8:2 8:16, Isaiah 10:13 14:4, James 3:13-3:18, Jeremiah 9:18-9:21 9:24, Luke 2:40, Pesikta de R'Kahana 4.4, Pesikta Rabbati 14:1, Proverbs 21:30, Romans 15:28, z.Vaetchanan 269b Ezekiel 28:12 [LXX] - Greek Apocalypse of Ezra 6:17

[4] LXX *are a seal of resemblance, and crown of beauty*

[5] Ezekiel 28:13 - 2 Enoch 8:3, b.Bava Batra [Rashbam] 73b, b.Bava Batra 75a, Ein Yaakov Bava Batra:75a, Exodus 28:17-28:20 39:10-39:21, Ezekiel 21:35 2:13 3:16 3:22 4:15 31:8-31:9 12:35, Genesis 2:8 2:11-2:12 3:23-3:24 13:10, Genesis.R 9:3 15:2 18:1, Isaiah 14:11 23:16 6:32 3:3 54:11-54:12, Joel 2:3, Leviticus.R 20:2, Mas.Kallah Rabbati 6:1, Midrash Tanchuma Acharei Mot 2, Pesikta de R'Kahana 4.4, Pesikta Rabbati 14:1, Pirkei de R'Eliezer 12, Revelation 2:7 17:4 21:19-21:20

[6] LXX *the delight of the paradise of God*

[7] LXX *sardius, and topaz, and emerald, and carbuncle, and sapphire, and jasper, and silver, and gold, and ligure, and agate, and amethyst, and chrysolite, and beryl, and onyx: and you have filled your treasures and your stores with gold*

[8] Ezekiel 28:14 - 2 Thessalonians 2:4, Daniel 2:37-38 4:32 5:18-23, Exodus 9:16 25:17-20 6:26 16:9, Ezekiel 20:40 4:2 4:13 28:16-17, Genesis.R 9:3, Isaiah 10:6 10:15 14:12-15 37:26-27, John 11:51, Midrash Tanchuma Bereshit 7, Psalms 75:6-8, Revelation 9:17 18:16

[9] Ezekiel 28:15 - 2 Peter 2:4, Ecclesiastes 7:29, Ezekiel 27:3-27:4 28:3-28:6 4:12 28:17-28:18, Genesis 1:26-1:27 1:31 6:5-6:6, Isaiah 14:12, Lamentations 5:16, Midrash Tanchuma Bereshit 7, Proverbs 14:34, Romans 7:9

[10] Ezekiel 28:16 - 1 Timothy 6:9-10, 2 Enoch 29:3, 2 Peter 2:4-6, Amos 3:9, Ezekiel 8:17 27:12-36 4:14, Genesis 3:24 6:11, Habakkuk 2:8 2:17, Hosea 12:9, Isaiah 22:19 23:9 23:17-18, John 2:16, Leviticus 18:24-28, Luke 19:45-46, Micah 2:2 2:10 6:12, Revelation 12:9, Zephaniah 1:9

[11] Ezekiel 28:17 - 1 Corinthians 1:19-21, Exodus.R 8:2, Ezekiel 16:14-15 16:41 23:48 4:2 4:5 4:7 7:10 8:10, Genesis.R 96:5, Isaiah 14:9-11 19:11-13, James 4:6, Jeremiah 8:9, Job 40:11-12, Luke 14:11, Midrash Tanchuma Vaera 9, Midrash Tanchuma Vayechi 3, Proverbs 11:2 16:18, Psalms 73:18 3:6, Romans 1:22-25

have laid you before kings, so they may gaze on you.

18[1] By the multitude of your iniquities, in the unrighteousness of your trading, you have profaned your sanctuaries; therefore have I brought forth a fire from your midst, it has devoured you, and I have turned you to ashes on the earth in the sight of all who see you.

מֵרֹב עֲוֺנֶיךָ בְּעֶוֶל רְכֻלָּתְךָ חִלַּלְתָּ מִקְדָּשֶׁיךָ וָאוֹצִא־אֵשׁ מִתּוֹכְךָ הִיא אֲכָלָתְךָ וָאֶתֶּנְךָ לְאֵפֶר עַל־הָאָרֶץ לְעֵינֵי כָּל־רֹאֶיךָ

19[2] All those who know you among the peoples shall be appalled at you; you have become a terror, and you shall never be again.'

כָּל־יוֹדְעֶיךָ בָּעַמִּים שָׁמְמוּ עָלֶיךָ בַּלָּהוֹת הָיִיתָ וְאֵינְךָ עַד־עוֹלָם

20 And the word of the LORD came to me, saying:

וַיְהִי דְבַר־יְהוָה אֵלַי לֵאמֹר

21[3] 'Son of man, set your face toward Zidon, and prophesy against it,

בֶּן־אָדָם שִׂים פָּנֶיךָ אֶל־צִידוֹן וְהִנָּבֵא עָלֶיהָ

22[4] and say: Thus says the Lord GOD: Behold, I am against you, O Zidon, And I will be glorified in your midst; And they shall know I am the LORD, when I shall have executed judgments in her, and shall be sanctified in her.

וְאָמַרְתָּ כֹּה אָמַר אֲדֹנָי יְהוִה הִנְנִי עָלַיִךְ צִידוֹן וְנִכְבַּדְתִּי בְּתוֹכֵךְ וְיָדְעוּ כִּי־אֲנִי יְהוָה בַּעֲשׂוֹתִי בָהּ שְׁפָטִים וְנִקְדַּשְׁתִּי בָהּ

23[5] For I will send pestilence into her and blood in her streets; And the wounded shall fall in her midst by the sword upon her on every side; and they shall know I am the LORD.

וְשִׁלַּחְתִּי־בָהּ דֶּבֶר וָדָם בְּחוּצוֹתֶיהָ וְנִפְלַל חָלָל בְּתוֹכָהּ בְּחֶרֶב עָלֶיהָ מִסָּבִיב וְיָדְעוּ כִּי־אֲנִי יְהוָה

24[6] And there shall no longer be a pricking brier to the house of Israel, nor a piercing thorn of any who are around them who held them in disdain; and they shall know I am the Lord GOD.

וְלֹא־יִהְיֶה עוֹד לְבֵית יִשְׂרָאֵל סִלּוֹן מַמְאִיר וְקוֹץ מַכְאִב מִכֹּל סְבִיבֹתָם הַשָּׁאטִים אוֹתָם וְיָדְעוּ כִּי אֲנִי אֲדֹנָי יְהוִה

25[7] Thus says the Lord GOD: When I gathered the house of Israel from the peoples among whom they are scattered, and I am sanctified in them in the sight of the nations, then they shall dwell in their own land, which I gave to My servant Jacob.

כֹּה־אָמַר אֲדֹנָי יְהוִה בְּקַבְּצִי אֶת־בֵּית יִשְׂרָאֵל מִן־הָעַמִּים אֲשֶׁר נָפֹצוּ בָם וְנִקְדַּשְׁתִּי בָם לְעֵינֵי הַגּוֹיִם וְיָשְׁבוּ עַל־אַדְמָתָם אֲשֶׁר נָתַתִּי לְעַבְדִּי לְיַעֲקֹב

26[8] And they shall live safely in it, and shall build houses, and plant vineyards; yes, they shall live safely; when I have executed judgments on all those around them who have them in disdain; and they shall know that I am the LORD their God[9].'

וְיָשְׁבוּ עָלֶיהָ לָבֶטַח וּבָנוּ בָתִּים וְנָטְעוּ כְרָמִים וְיָשְׁבוּ לָבֶטַח בַּעֲשׂוֹתִי שְׁפָטִים בְּכֹל הַשָּׁאטִים אֹתָם מִסְּבִיבוֹתָם וְיָדְעוּ כִּי אֲנִי יְהוָה אֱלֹהֵיהֶם

---

[1] Ezekiel 28:18 - 2 Peter 2:6, Amos 1:9-1:10 1:14 2:2 2:5, Exodus.R 1:26, Ezekiel 5:4 4:2 28:13-28:14 4:16, Judges 9:15 9:20, Leviticus.R 18:2, Malachi 3:21, Mark 8:36, Midrash Psalms 11:5, Midrash Tanchuma Shemot 8, Revelation 18:8

[2] Ezekiel 28:19 - Ezekiel 2:14 2:21 27:35-36, Isaiah 14:16-19, Jeremiah 51:63-64, Psalms 76:13, Revelation 18:9-10 18:15-18:19 18:21

[3] Ezekiel 28:21 - Ezekiel 6:2 1:2 3:8 5:2 8:30, Genesis 10:15, Isaiah 23:2-4 23:12, Jeremiah 1:22 3:3 23:4, Joel 4:4-4:8, Zechariah 9:2

[4] Ezekiel 28:22 - 1 Samuel 17:45-17:47, Exodus 9:16 14:4 14:17 15:21, Ezekiel 5:8 20:41 21:8 2:3 28:25-28:26 5:3 5:10 6:19 12:23 14:3 38:23-39:3 15:13, Isaiah 5:15-5:16 13:20, Jeremiah 21:13 2:31, Leviticus 10:3, Nahum 1:6 2:14 3:5, Psalms 9:17 21:13-21:14 83:18, Revelation 19:1-19:2, z.Vaetchanan 269b

[5] Ezekiel 28:23 - Ezekiel 5:12 1:7 1:11 1:17 2:6 14:22, Jeremiah 15:2, z.Beshallach 56a

[6] Ezekiel 28:24 - 2 Corinthians 12:7, Esther.R 9:2, Ezekiel 2:6 4:23 4:26 36:36-36:38 15:28, Isaiah 11:9 7:13, Jeremiah 12:14, Joshua 23:13, Judges 2:3, Micah 7:4, Numbers 9:55, Revelation 21:4
Ezekiel 28:24-29:21 - Haftarah Voayroh [Teimon]

[7] Ezekiel 28:25 - Amos 9:14-15, Deuteronomy 30:3-30:4, Ezekiel 11:17 20:41 4:22 10:13 10:27 36:23-24 12:28 13:21 13:25 14:23 15:27, Genesis 28:13-14, Hosea 2:2, Isaiah 5:16 11:12-11:13 27:12-13, Jeremiah 23:8 3:11 6:18 31:9-11 8:37, Joel 4:7, Leviticus 26:44-26:45, Micah 7:11-14, Obadiah 1:17-1:21, Psalms 10:47, z.Vaetchanan 269b, Zephaniah 3:19-3:20
Ezekiel 28:25-29:21 - Haftarah Vayera [Ashkenaz and Sephard]

[8] Ezekiel 28:26 - 1 Kings 4:25, Amos 9:13-9:14, Deuteronomy 12:10, Exodus 5:46, Ezekiel 25:1-25:17 4:22 4:24 34:25-34:28 34:31-35:15 36:22-36:23 14:8 14:11 15:10, Habakkuk 2:8, Hosea 2:18, Isaiah 13:1-13:21 17:14 9:1 65:21-65:22, Jeremiah 23:6-23:8 29:5-29:6 5:28 6:16 31:5-31:6 8:15 9:16 46:1-46:28, Lamentations 1:8, Leviticus 25:18-25:19, Midrash Tanchuma Terumah 7, Proverbs 14:26, Zechariah 1:15 2:4-2:5, Zephaniah 2:8-2:9

[9] LXX adds *and the God of their fathers*

Ezekiel – Chapter 29

בַּשָּׁנָה הָעֲשִׂירִית בָּעֲשִׂרִי בִּשְׁנֵים עָשָׂר לַחֹדֶשׁ הָיָה דְבַר־יְהֹוָה אֵלַי לֵאמֹר

1¹ In the *tenth year, in the tenth month, in the twelfth²* day of the month, the word of the LORD came to me, saying:

בֶּן־אָדָם שִׂים פָּנֶיךָ עַל־פַּרְעֹה מֶלֶךְ מִצְרָיִם וְהִנָּבֵא עָלָיו וְעַל־מִצְרַיִם כֻּלָּהּ

2³ 'Son of man, set your face against Pharaoh king of Egypt, and prophesy against him, and against all Egypt;

דַּבֵּר וְאָמַרְתָּ כֹּה־אָמַר ׀ אֲדֹנָי יְהֹוִה הִנְנִי עָלֶיךָ פַּרְעֹה מֶלֶךְ־מִצְרַיִם הַתַּנִּים הַגָּדוֹל הָרֹבֵץ בְּתוֹךְ יְאֹרָיו אֲשֶׁר אָמַר לִי יְאֹרִי וַאֲנִי עֲשִׂיתִנִי

3⁴ speak, and say: Thus says the Lord GOD: Behold, I am against you, Pharaoh King of Egypt, the great dragon that lies In the midst of his rivers, that has said: My river is mine, and I have made it for myself.

וְנָתַתִּי 'חַחִיִּים' "חַחִים" בִּלְחָיֶיךָ וְהִדְבַּקְתִּי דְגַת־יְאֹרֶיךָ בְּקַשְׂקְשֹׂתֶיךָ וְהַעֲלִיתִיךָ מִתּוֹךְ יְאֹרֶיךָ וְאֵת כָּל־דְּגַת יְאֹרֶיךָ בְּקַשְׂקְשֹׂתֶיךָ תִּדְבָּק

4⁵ And I will put hooks in your jaws, and I will cause the fish of your rivers to stick to your scales; and I will bring you up out of the midst of your rivers, *and all the fish of your rivers shall stick to your scales⁶*.

וּנְטַשְׁתִּיךָ הַמִּדְבָּרָה אוֹתְךָ וְאֵת כָּל־דְּגַת יְאֹרֶיךָ עַל־פְּנֵי הַשָּׂדֶה תִּפּוֹל לֹא תֵאָסֵף וְלֹא תִקָּבֵץ לְחַיַּת הָאָרֶץ וּלְעוֹף הַשָּׁמַיִם נְתַתִּיךָ לְאָכְלָה

5⁷ And I will cast you into the wilderness, you and all the fish of your rivers; you shall fall on the open field; you shall not be brought together, nor gathered. I give you as food to the beasts of the earth and to the fowls of the heaven.

וְיָדְעוּ כָּל־יֹשְׁבֵי מִצְרַיִם כִּי אֲנִי יְהֹוָה יַעַן הֱיוֹתָם מִשְׁעֶנֶת קָנֶה לְבֵית יִשְׂרָאֵל

6⁸ And all the inhabitants of Egypt shall know that I am the LORD, Because they have been a staff of reed to the house of Israel.

בְּתָפְשָׂם בְּךָ 'בַכַּפְּךָ' "בַכַּף" תֵּרוֹץ וּבָקַעְתָּ לָהֶם כָּל־כָּתֵף וּבְהִשָּׁעֲנָם עָלֶיךָ תִּשָּׁבֵר וְהַעֲמַדְתָּ לָהֶם כָּל־מָתְנָיִם

7⁹ When they take hold of you with the hand, you break, And rend all their shoulders; and when they lean on you, you break, and make all their loins to be still.

לָכֵן כֹּה אָמַר אֲדֹנָי יְהֹוִה הִנְנִי מֵבִיא עָלַיִךְ חָרֶב וְהִכְרַתִּי מִמֵּךְ אָדָם וּבְהֵמָה

8¹⁰ Therefore, thus says the Lord GOD: Behold, I will bring a sword on you, and will cut from you man and beast.

וְהָיְתָה אֶרֶץ־מִצְרַיִם לִשְׁמָמָה וְחָרְבָּה וְיָדְעוּ כִּי־אֲנִי יְהֹוָה יַעַן אָמַר יְאֹר לִי וַאֲנִי עָשִׂיתִי

9¹¹ And the land of Egypt shall be desolate and waste, and they shall know I am the LORD; because he said: The river is mine, and I have made it.

---

¹ Ezekiel 29:1 - Ezekiel 1:2 8:1 20:1 2:1 5:17 16:1
Ezekiel 29:1-2 - Seder Olam 26:Tenth of Tevet
² LXX *twelfth year, in the tenth month, on the first*
³ Ezekiel 29:2 - Ezekiel 6:2 21:2 21:7 1:2 28:21-22 30:1-32, Isaiah 18:1-19:17 20:1-20:6, Jeremiah 9:26-9:27 25:18-25:19 43:8-43:13 20:30 46:2-46:16, Joel 4:19, Zechariah 14:18-19
Ezekiel 29:2-3 - Exodus.R 3:12 5:14 8:1 8:2 9:4 10:2 20:6
⁴ Ezekiel 29:3 - 9, Daniel 4:27-28, Deuteronomy 8:17, Ezekiel 4:2 4:22 29:9-10 8:2, Genesis.R 100 [Excl]:1, Isaiah 10:13-14 3:1 3:9, Jeremiah 20:30, Mekhilta de R'Shimon bar Yochai Amalek 46:3, Mekhilta de R'Shimon bar Yochai Shirata 34:1, Mekilta de R'Ishmael Amalek 3:198, Mekilta de R'Ishmael Shirata 8:28, Midrash Tanchuma Bereshit 7, Midrash Tanchuma Beshallach 10, Midrash Tanchuma Tzav 2, Midrash Tanchuma Vaera 5 9, Nahum 1:6, Pesikta Rabbati 21:2, Psalms 74:13-74:14 76:8, Psalms of Solomon 2:25, Revelation 12:3-12:4 12:16-17 13:2 13:4 13:11 16:13 20:2, Saadia Opinions 1:2, Tanya Likutei Aramim §22, z.Bo 34a, z.Lech Lecha 93b, z.Vaera 28a 29a, z.Vaetchanan 269b
⁵ Ezekiel 29:4 - 2 Kings 19:28, Amos 4:2, Ezekiel 14:4, Habakkuk 1:14-15, Isaiah 13:29, Job 40:25-26, Leviticus.R 19:6, z.Vaera 27b 28a
⁶ Missing in LXX
⁷ Ezekiel 29:5 - 1 Samuel 17:44, Ezekiel 7:18 32:4-32:6 39:4-39:6 39:11-39:20, Jeremiah 7:33 8:2 16:4 1:33 10:20, Psalms 74:14 110:5-110:6, Psalms of Solomon 4:19, Revelation 19:17-19:18
⁸ Ezekiel 29:6 - 2 Kings 18:21, Exodus 9:14 14:18, Ezekiel 28:22-28:24 4:26, Isaiah 20:5-20:6 30:2-30:7 31:1-31:3 12:6, Jeremiah 2:36, Lamentations 4:17
⁹ Ezekiel 29:7 - Ezekiel 17:15-17, Isaiah 12:6, Jeremiah 17:5-6 37:5-11, Proverbs 1:19, Psalms 118:8-9 146:3-4
¹⁰ Ezekiel 29:8 - Exodus 12:12, Ezekiel 14:17 1:13 29:19-20 6:4 6:10 32:10-13, Genesis 6:7, Jeremiah 7:20 8:43 46:13-26, z.Vaetchanan 269b
¹¹ Ezekiel 29:9 - Ezekiel 5:3 29:10-12 30:7-8 30:13-19, Jeremiah 43:10-13, Proverbs 16:18 18:12 5:23, Tanya Likutei Aramim §22, z.Shemot 6b

לָכֵן הִנְנִי אֵלֶיךָ וְאֶל־יְאֹרֶיךָ וְנָתַתִּי אֶת־אֶרֶץ מִצְרַיִם לְחָרְבוֹת חֹרֶב שְׁמָמָה מִמִּגְדֹּל סְוֵנֵה וְעַד־גְּבוּל כּוּשׁ	10[1]	Therefore, behold, I am against you, and against your rivers, and I will make the land of Egypt utterly waste and desolate, from Migdol to Syene to the border of Ethiopia.
לֹא תַעֲבָר־בָּהּ רֶגֶל אָדָם וְרֶגֶל בְּהֵמָה לֹא תַעֲבָר־בָּהּ וְלֹא תֵשֵׁב אַרְבָּעִים שָׁנָה	11[2]	No foot of man shall pass through it, nor foot of beast shall pass through it, nor shall it be inhabited forty years.
וְנָתַתִּי אֶת־אֶרֶץ מִצְרַיִם שְׁמָמָה בְּתוֹךְ אֲרָצוֹת נְשַׁמּוֹת וְעָרֶיהָ בְּתוֹךְ עָרִים מַחֳרָבוֹת תִּהְיֶיןָ שְׁמָמָה אַרְבָּעִים שָׁנָה וַהֲפִצֹתִי אֶת־מִצְרַיִם בַּגּוֹיִם וְזֵרִיתִים בָּאֲרָצוֹת	12[3]	And I will make the land of Egypt desolate in the midst of the countries that are desolate, and her cities among the cities that are laid waste shall be desolate forty years; and I will scatter the Egyptians among the nations, and will disperse them through the countries.
כִּי כֹּה אָמַר אֲדֹנָי יְהֹוִה מִקֵּץ אַרְבָּעִים שָׁנָה אֲקַבֵּץ אֶת־מִצְרַיִם מִן־הָעַמִּים אֲשֶׁר־נָפֹצוּ שָׁמָּה	13[4]	For thus says the Lord GOD: At the end of forty years will I gather the Egyptians from the peoples where they were scattered;
וְשַׁבְתִּי אֶת־שְׁבוּת מִצְרַיִם וַהֲשִׁבֹתִי אֹתָם אֶרֶץ פַּתְרוֹס עַל־אֶרֶץ מְכוּרָתָם וְהָיוּ שָׁם מַמְלָכָה שְׁפָלָה	14[5]	and I will turn the captivity of Egypt, and will cause them to return to the land of *Pathros*[6], into the land of their origin; *and there they shall be a lowly kingdom*[7].
מִן־הַמַּמְלָכוֹת תִּהְיֶה שְׁפָלָה וְלֹא־תִתְנַשֵּׂא עוֹד עַל־הַגּוֹיִם וְהִמְעַטְתִּים לְבִלְתִּי רְדוֹת בַּגּוֹיִם	15[8]	It shall be the lowliest of the kingdoms, nor shall it lift itself up above the nations; and I will diminish them, so they shall not rule over the nations.
וְלֹא יִהְיֶה־עוֹד לְבֵית יִשְׂרָאֵל לְמִבְטָח מַזְכִּיר עָוֹן בִּפְנוֹתָם אַחֲרֵיהֶם וְיָדְעוּ כִּי אֲנִי אֲדֹנָי יְהֹוִה	16[9]	And it shall not be the confidence of the house of Israel, bringing iniquity to remembrance, when they turn after them; and they shall know that I am the Lord GOD.'
וַיְהִי בְּעֶשְׂרִים וָשֶׁבַע שָׁנָה בָּרִאשׁוֹן בְּאֶחָד לַחֹדֶשׁ הָיָה דְבַר־יְהֹוָה אֵלַי לֵאמֹר	17[10]	And it came to pass in the twenty-seventh year, *in the first month, in*[11] the first day of the month, the word of the LORD came to me, saying:
בֶּן־אָדָם נְבוּכַדְרֶאצַּר מֶלֶךְ־בָּבֶל הֶעֱבִיד אֶת־חֵילוֹ עֲבֹדָה גְדֹלָה אֶל־צֹר כָּל־רֹאשׁ מֻקְרָח וְכָל־כָּתֵף מְרוּטָה וְשָׂכָר לֹא־הָיָה לוֹ וּלְחֵילוֹ מִצֹּר עַל־הָעֲבֹדָה אֲשֶׁר־עָבַד עָלֶיהָ	18[12]	'Son of man, Nebuchadrezzar king of Babylon caused his army to serve a great service against Tyre; every head was made bald, and every shoulder was peeled; yet he had no wages, nor his army, from Tyre, for the service that he had served against it;
לָכֵן כֹּה אָמַר אֲדֹנָי יְהֹוִה הִנְנִי נֹתֵן לִנְבוּכַדְרֶאצַּר מֶלֶךְ־בָּבֶל אֶת־אֶרֶץ מִצְרָיִם וְנָשָׂא הֲמֹנָהּ וְשָׁלַל שְׁלָלָהּ וּבָזַז בִּזָּהּ וְהָיְתָה שָׂכָר לְחֵילוֹ	19[13]	Therefore thus says the Lord GOD: Behold, I will give the land of Egypt to Nebuchadrezzar king of Babylon; and he shall carry off her

---

[1] Ezekiel 29:10 - Exodus 14:2, Ezekiel 5:11 30:6-30:9 6:12, Habakkuk 3:8, Jeremiah 20:1 22:14, Mekhilta de R'Shimon bar Yochai Shirata 34:1, mt.Hilchot Melachim uMichamoteihem 5:7

[2] Ezekiel 29:11 - 2 Chronicles 12:21, Daniel 9:2, Ezekiel 30:10-13 7:12 8:13 9:28 12:28, Isaiah 23:15 23:17, Jeremiah 25:11-12 5:10 43:11-12

[3] Ezekiel 29:12 - Ezekiel 6:7 6:23 6:26, Genesis.R 89:9, Jeremiah 25:15-19 27:6-11 22:19

[4] Ezekiel 29:13 - b.Yevamot 76b, Isaiah 19:22, Jeremiah 22:26, Saadia Opinions 8:3, z.Vaetchanan 269b

[5] Ezekiel 29:14 - 1 Chronicles 1:12, Ezekiel 6:14, Genesis 10:14, Isaiah 11:11, Jeremiah 20:1

[6] LXX *Phathore*

[7] Missing in LXX

[8] Ezekiel 29:15 - Daniel 11:42-43, Exodus.R 22:1, Ezekiel 17:6 17:14 6:13 7:2 8:2, Mekilta de R'Ishmael Shirata 6:104, Nahum 3:8-9, Seder Olam 20:Obadiah, Zechariah 10:11

[9] Ezekiel 29:16 - 1 Kings 17:18, Ezekiel 17:15-17 21:28 28:22-24 4:26 29:6-7 5:9 5:21, Hebrews 10:3 10:17, Hosea 5:13 7:11 8:13 9:9 12:3 14:5, Isaiah 20:5 30:1-6 31:1-3 36:4-6 16:10, Jeremiah 2:18-19 2:36-37 14:10 37:5-7, Lamentations 4:17, Leviticus.R 27:3, Midrash Tanchuma Emor 8, Midrash Tanchuma Noach 13, Numbers 5:15, Pesikta de R'Kahana 9.3, Psalms 25:7 79:8, Revelation 16:19

[10] Ezekiel 29:17 - b.Sotah [Rashi] 33a, Ezekiel 1:2 24:1 5:1

[11] Missing in LXX

[12] Ezekiel 29:18 - Ezekiel 26:7-12, Jeremiah 1:9 3:6 24:37

[13] Ezekiel 29:19 - Ezekiel 29:8-10 6:4 30:10-12 30:24-25 8:11, Jeremiah 43:10-13, z.Vaetchanan 269b

abundance, and take her spoil, and take her prey; and it shall be the wages for his army.

פְּעֻלָּתוֹ אֲשֶׁר־עָבַד בָּהּ נָתַתִּי לוֹ אֶת־אֶרֶץ מִצְרַיִם אֲשֶׁר עָשׂוּ לִי נְאֻם אֲדֹנָי יְהוִה

20[1] I have given him the land of Egypt as his hire for which he served, because they work for Me, says the Lord GOD.

בַּיּוֹם הַהוּא אַצְמִיחַ קֶרֶן לְבֵית יִשְׂרָאֵל וּלְךָ אֶתֵּן פִּתְחוֹן־פֶּה בְּתוֹכָם וְיָדְעוּ כִּי־אֲנִי יְהוָה

21[2] In that day will I cause a horn to shoot up unto the house of Israel, and I will give you the opening of the mouth in their midst; and they shall know I am the LORD.'

Ezekiel – Chapter 30

וַיְהִי דְבַר־יְהוָה אֵלַי לֵאמֹר

1[3] And the word of the LORD came to me, saying:

בֶּן־אָדָם הִנָּבֵא וְאָמַרְתָּ כֹּה אָמַר אֲדֹנָי יְהוִה הֵילִילוּ הָהּ לַיּוֹם

2[4] 'Son of man, prophesy, and say: Thus says the Lord GOD: Wail: woe worth the day!

כִּי־קָרוֹב יוֹם וְקָרוֹב יוֹם לַיהוָה יוֹם עָנָן עֵת גּוֹיִם יִהְיֶה

3[5] For the day is near, the day of the LORD is near, a day of clouds, it shall be the time of the nations.

וּבָאָה חֶרֶב בְּמִצְרַיִם וְהָיְתָה חַלְחָלָה בְּכוּשׁ בִּנְפֹל חָלָל בְּמִצְרָיִם וְלָקְחוּ הֲמוֹנָהּ וְנֶהֶרְסוּ יְסוֹדֹתֶיהָ

4[6] And a sword shall come upon Egypt, and convulsion shall be in Ethiopia, when the slain shall fall in Egypt; and they shall take away her abundance, and her foundation shall be broken down.

כּוּשׁ וּפוּט וְלוּד וְכָל־הָעֶרֶב וְכוּב וּבְנֵי אֶרֶץ הַבְּרִית אִתָּם בַּחֶרֶב יִפֹּלוּ

5[7] *Ethiopia, and Put, and Lud, and all the mingled people, and Cub, and the children of the land that is in league, shall fall with them by the sword*[8].

כֹּה אָמַר יְהוָה וְנָפְלוּ סֹמְכֵי מִצְרַיִם וְיָרַד גְּאוֹן עֻזָּהּ מִמִּגְדֹּל סְוֵנֵה בַּחֶרֶב יִפְּלוּ־בָהּ נְאֻם אֲדֹנָי יְהוִה

6[9] *Thus says the LORD*[10]: Those who uphold Egypt shall fall, and the pride of her power shall come down; from Migdol to Syene shall they fall in it by the sword, says the Lord GOD.

וְנָשַׁמּוּ בְּתוֹךְ אֲרָצוֹת נְשַׁמּוֹת וְעָרָיו בְּתוֹךְ־עָרִים נַחֲרָבוֹת תִּהְיֶינָה

7[11] And they shall be desolate in the midst of the countries who are desolate, And her cities shall be in the midst of the cities that are wasted.

וְיָדְעוּ כִּי־אֲנִי יְהוָה בְּתִתִּי־אֵשׁ בְּמִצְרַיִם וְנִשְׁבְּרוּ כָּל־עֹזְרֶיהָ

8[12] And they shall know that I am the LORD, When I have set a fire in Egypt, And all her helpers are destroyed.

---

[1] Ezekiel 29:20 - 2 Kings 10:30, Isaiah 10:6-7 45:1-3, Jeremiah 1:9, Tanya Igeret Hakodesh §27a

[2] Ezekiel 29:21 - 1 Samuel 2:10, Amos 3:7-8, b.Sanhedrin 99a, Colossians 4:3-4, Ein Yaakov Sanhedrin:97b, Ezekiel 3:26 24:27 28:25-26 5:6 5:9 5:16 9:22, Isaiah 3:6, Jeremiah 23:5, Luke 1:69 21:15, Psalms 51:16 92:11 16:9 12:17 4:14

[3] Ezekiel 30:1 - Esther.R 1:10, Guide for the Perplexed 2:41

[4] Ezekiel 30:2 - Ezekiel 21:17, Isaiah 13:6 14:31 15:2 16:7 23:1 23:6 17:14, James 5:1, Jeremiah 4:8 23:2, Joel 1:5 1:11, Revelation 18:10, z.Vaetchanan 269b, Zechariah 11:2, Zephaniah 1:11

[5] Ezekiel 30:3 - Amos 5:16-5:20, Exodus 14:20 14:24, Ezekiel 7:7 7:12 7:19 5:12 6:18 8:7 10:12, Isaiah 19:1 24:21-24:23 34:2-34:17, James 5:9, Jeremiah 25:15-25:29, Joel 1:15 2:1-2:2 4:11-4:14, Matthew 24:33, Obadiah 1:15, Philippians 4:5, Psalms 37:13 14:6 149:7-149:9, Revelation 6:17 19:13-19:21, Zechariah 14:3-14:19, Zephaniah 1:7 1:14 3:6-3:7

[6] Ezekiel 30:4 - Exodus 15:14-15:16, Ezekiel 5:8 5:12 5:19 30:9-30:10, Isaiah 16:7 19:2 19:16-19:17, Jeremiah 2:15 50:35-50:37, Psalms 48:7-48:8, Revelation 18:9-18:10

[7] Ezekiel 30:5 - Ezekiel 3:10, Genesis.R 37:2, Isaiah 18:1 20:4, Jastrow 616a, Jeremiah 1:20 1:24 20:27 22:9 2:37, Nahum 3:8-3:9

[8] LXX *Persians, and Cretans, and Lydians, and Libyans, and all the mixed multitude, and they of the children of my covenant, shall fall by the sword*

[9] Ezekiel 30:6 - Ezekiel 5:10, Isaiah 20:3-20:6 7:3, Job 9:13, Leviticus.R 5:7, Nahum 3:9, z.Vaetchanan 269b

[10] Missing in LXX

[11] Ezekiel 30:7 - Ezekiel 5:12 32:18-32:32, Jeremiah 25:18-25:26 46:1-46:28

[12] Ezekiel 30:8 - Amos 1:4 1:7 1:10 1:12 1:14 2:2 2:5, Deuteronomy 8:22, Ezekiel 22:31 4:24 4:26 5:6 5:9 5:16 6:14 6:16, Isaiah 18:25, Lamentations 4:11, Nahum 1:5-1:6, Psalms 58:12

Hebrew		English
בַּיּ֣וֹם הַה֡וּא יֵצְא֣וּ מַלְאָכִים֩ מִלְּפָנַ֨י בַּצִּ֜ים לְהַחֲרִ֣יד אֶת־כּ֣וּשׁ בֶּ֗טַח וְהָיְתָ֧ה חַלְחָלָ֛ה בָהֶ֖ם בְּי֣וֹם מִצְרַ֑יִם כִּ֥י הִנֵּ֖ה בָּאָֽה	9[1]	In that day messengers shall go forth *from before Me in ships to make the confident Ethiopians afraid*[2]; and convulsion shall come on them in the day of Egypt; For, lo, it comes.
כֹּ֥ה אָמַ֖ר אֲדֹנָ֣י יְהֹוִ֑ה וְהִשְׁבַּתִּי֙ אֶת־הֲמ֣וֹן מִצְרַ֔יִם בְּיַ֖ד נְבוּכַדְרֶאצַּ֥ר מֶֽלֶךְ־בָּבֶֽל	10[3]	Thus says the Lord GOD: I will also make the multitude of Egypt cease, by the hand of Nebuchadrezzar king of Babylon.
ה֣וּא וְעַמּ֤וֹ אִתּוֹ֙ עָרִיצֵ֣י גוֹיִ֔ם מֽוּבָאִ֖ים לְשַׁחֵ֣ת הָאָ֑רֶץ וְהֵרִ֤יקוּ חַרְבוֹתָם֙ עַל־מִצְרַ֔יִם וּמָלְא֥וּ אֶת־הָאָ֖רֶץ חָלָֽל	11[4]	He and his people with him, the terrible of the nations, shall be brought in to destroy the land; and they shall draw their swords against Egypt, And fill the land with the slain.
וְנָתַתִּ֤י יְאֹרִים֙ חָֽרָבָ֔ה וּמָכַרְתִּ֥י אֶת־הָאָ֖רֶץ בְּיַד־רָעִ֑ים וַהֲשִׁמֹּתִ֞י אֶ֤רֶץ וּמְלֹאָהּ֙ בְּיַד־זָרִ֔ים אֲנִ֥י יְהֹוָ֖ה דִּבַּֽרְתִּי	12[5]	And I will make the rivers dry, and will give the land over into the hand of evil men; and I will make the land desolate, and all that is in it, by the hand of strangers; I, the LORD, have spoken it.
כֹּֽה־אָמַ֞ר אֲדֹנָ֣י יְהֹוִ֗ה וְהַאֲבַדְתִּ֤י גִלּוּלִים֙ וְהִשְׁבַּתִּ֤י אֱלִילִים֙ מִנֹּ֔ף וְנָשִׂ֥יא מֵאֶֽרֶץ־מִצְרַ֖יִם לֹ֣א יִֽהְיֶה־ע֑וֹד וְנָתַתִּ֥י יִרְאָ֖ה בְּאֶ֥רֶץ מִצְרָֽיִם	13[6]	Thus says the Lord GOD: I will also destroy the *idols, and I will cause the things of nothing to cease from Noph; and there shall not be a prince from the land of Egypt; And I will put a fear in the land of Egypt*[7].
וַהֲשִׁמֹּתִי֙ אֶת־פַּתְר֔וֹס וְנָתַ֥תִּי אֵ֖שׁ בְּצֹ֑עַן וְעָשִׂ֥יתִי שְׁפָטִ֖ים בְּנֹֽא	14[8]	And I will make Pathros desolate, and will set a fire in *Zoan*[9], and will execute judgments in *No*[10].
וְשָׁפַכְתִּ֣י חֲמָתִ֔י עַל־סִ֖ין מָע֣וֹז מִצְרָ֑יִם וְהִכְרַתִּ֖י אֶת־הֲמ֥וֹן נֹֽא	15[11]	And I will pour My fury upon *Sin*[12], the stronghold of Egypt; And I will cut off the multitude of *No*[13].
וְנָתַ֤תִּי אֵשׁ֙ בְּמִצְרַ֔יִם ח֤וּל 'תָּחִיל' "תָּחוּל'" סִ֔ין וְנֹ֖א תִּֽהְיֶ֣ה לְהִבָּקֵ֑עַ וְנֹ֖ף צָרֵ֥י יוֹמָֽם	16[14]	And I will set a fire in Egypt; *Sin*[15] shall be in great convulsion, *and No shall be rent asunder; and in Noph adversaries will come in the daytime*[16].
בַּח֤וּרֵי אָ֙וֶן֙ וּפִי־בֶ֔סֶת בַּחֶ֣רֶב יִפֹּ֑לוּ וְהֵ֖נָּה בַּשְּׁבִ֥י תֵלַֽכְנָה	17[17]	The young men of *Aven and of Pi-beseth*[18] shall fall by the sword; And *these cities*[19] shall go into captivity.

[1] Ezekiel 30:9 - 1 Thessalonians 5:2, Amos 4:2, Ezekiel 2:16 3:35 30:4-30:6 32:9-32:10 9:33 14:11 15:6, Isaiah 18:1-18:2 19:17 20:3 20:5 23:5 32:9-32:11 23:8, Jeremiah 1:21 1:31, Judges 18:7, Zechariah 11:2-11:3, Zephaniah 2:12 2:15

[2] LXX *hasting to destroy Ethiopia utterly*

[3] Ezekiel 30:10 - Ezekiel 29:4-29:5 5:19 30:24-30:25 32:11-32:16, z.Vaetchanan 269b

[4] Ezekiel 30:11 - Deuteronomy 4:50, Ezekiel 4:7 7:12 8:12 11:8 15:4 39:11-39:20, Habakkuk 1:6-1:9, Isaiah 14:4-14:6 34:3-34:7, Jeremiah 51:20-51:23, Zephaniah 1:17-1:18

[5] Ezekiel 30:12 - 1 Corinthians 10:26, Esther.R 1:13, Ezekiel 4:10 5:3 29:9-29:10 7:12, Isaiah 19:4-19:10 20:27, Jeremiah 2:38 3:36, Judges 2:14, Midrash Psalms 24:2, Nahum 1:4, Revelation 16:12

[6] Ezekiel 30:13 - Exodus 12:12, Ezekiel 29:14-29:15, Hosea 9:6, Isaiah 19:1-19:16, Jeremiah 2:16 43:12-44:1 22:5 22:14 22:25, Mekilta de R'Ishmael Shirata 6:103, Pesikta Rabbati 17:4, z.Vaetchanan 269b, Zechariah 10:11 13:2, Zephaniah 2:11

[7] LXX *nobles from Memphis, and the princes of Memphis out of the land of Egypt; and they shall be no more*

[8] Ezekiel 30:14 - Ezekiel 5:14, Isaiah 11:11 19:11 6:4, Jeremiah 22:25, Nahum 3:8, Numbers 13:22, Pesikta Rabbati 17:4, Psalms 78:12 78:43

[9] LXX *Tanis*

[10] LXX *Diospolis*

[11] Ezekiel 30:15 - Nahum 1:6, Pesikta de R'Kahana 7.5, Psalms 11:7, Revelation 16:1

[12] LXX *Sais*

[13] LXX *Memphis*

[14] Ezekiel 30:16 - Ezekiel 4:18 30:8-9, Mekhilta de R'Shimon bar Yochai Pisha 15:1 16:5, Seder Olam 28:Belshazzar

[15] LXX *Syrene*

[16] LXX *and there shall be a breaking in Diospolis, and waters shall be poured out*

[17] Ezekiel 30:17 - Genesis 17:45

[18] LXX *Heliopolis and Bubastum*

[19] LXX *the women*

וּבִתְחַפְנְחֵס חָשַׂךְ הַיּוֹם בְּשִׁבְרִי־שָׁם אֶת־מֹטוֹת מִצְרַיִם וְנִשְׁבַּת־בָּהּ גְּאוֹן עֻזָּהּ הִיא עָנָן יְכַסֶּנָּה וּבְנוֹתֶיהָ בַּשְּׁבִי תֵלַכְנָה	18[1]	*At Tehaphnehes also the day shall withdraw itself, when I shall break the yokes[2] of Egypt,* and the pride of her power shall cease in her; as for her, a cloud shall cover her, and her daughters shall go into captivity.
וְעָשִׂיתִי שְׁפָטִים בְּמִצְרָיִם וְיָדְעוּ כִּי־אֲנִי יְהוָה	19[3]	Thus I will execute judgments in Egypt; And they shall know that I am the LORD.'
וַיְהִי בְּאַחַת עֶשְׂרֵה שָׁנָה בָּרִאשׁוֹן בְּשִׁבְעָה לַחֹדֶשׁ הָיָה דְבַר־יְהוָה אֵלַי לֵאמֹר	20[4]	And it came to pass in the eleventh year, in the first month, in the seventh day of the month, that the word of the LORD came to me, saying:
בֶּן־אָדָם אֶת־זְרוֹעַ פַּרְעֹה מֶלֶךְ־מִצְרַיִם שָׁבָרְתִּי וְהִנֵּה לֹא־חֻבְּשָׁה לָתֵת רְפֻאוֹת לָשׂוּם חִתּוּל לְחָבְשָׁהּ לְחָזְקָהּ לִתְפֹּשׂ בֶּחָרֶב	21[5]	'Son of man, I have broken the arm of Pharaoh king of Egypt; and, lo, it has not been bound up to be healed, to put a roller, so it is bound up and made strong, so it holds the sword.
לָכֵן כֹּה־אָמַר אֲדֹנָי יְהוִה הִנְנִי אֶל־פַּרְעֹה מֶלֶךְ־מִצְרַיִם וְשָׁבַרְתִּי אֶת־זְרֹעֹתָיו אֶת־הַחֲזָקָה וְאֶת־הַנִּשְׁבָּרֶת וְהִפַּלְתִּי אֶת־הַחֶרֶב מִיָּדוֹ	22[6]	Therefore thus says the Lord GOD: Behold, I am against Pharaoh king of Egypt, and will break his *arms, the strong, and what was broken[7]*; and I will cause the sword to fall out of his hand.
וַהֲפִצוֹתִי אֶת־מִצְרַיִם בַּגּוֹיִם וְזֵרִיתִם בָּאֲרָצוֹת	23[8]	And I will scatter the Egyptians among the nations, and will disperse them through the countries.
וְחִזַּקְתִּי אֶת־זְרֹעוֹת מֶלֶךְ בָּבֶל וְנָתַתִּי אֶת־חַרְבִּי בְּיָדוֹ וְשָׁבַרְתִּי אֶת־זְרֹעוֹת פַּרְעֹה וְנָאַק נַאֲקוֹת חָלָל לְפָנָיו	24[9]	And I will strengthen the arms of the king of Babylon, and put My sword in his hand; *but I will break the arms of Pharaoh, and he shall groan before him with the groaning of a mortally wounded man[10]*.
וְהַחֲזַקְתִּי אֶת־זְרֹעוֹת מֶלֶךְ בָּבֶל וּזְרֹעוֹת פַּרְעֹה תִּפֹּלְנָה וְיָדְעוּ כִּי־אֲנִי יְהוָה בְּתִתִּי חַרְבִּי בְּיַד מֶלֶךְ־בָּבֶל וְנָטָה אוֹתָהּ אֶל־אֶרֶץ מִצְרָיִם	25[11]	And I will hold up the arms of the king of Babylon, and the arms of Pharaoh shall fall down; and they shall know I am the LORD, when I put My sword into the hand of the king of Babylon, and he shall stretch it out upon the land of Egypt.
וַהֲפִצוֹתִי אֶת־מִצְרַיִם בַּגּוֹיִם וְזֵרִיתִי אוֹתָם בָּאֲרָצוֹת וְיָדְעוּ כִּי־אֲנִי יְהוָה	26[12]	And I will scatter the Egyptians among the nations, and disperse them through the countries; and they shall know I am the LORD.'

[1] Ezekiel 30:18 - b.Yoma 38b, Exodus 10:15, Ezekiel 5:15 6:3 7:18 32:18-32, Isaiah 5:30 9:5 9:20 10:27 13:10 14:11 14:25 19:1, Jeremiah 2:16 43:7-9 22:14 46:20-26, Joel 4:15, Leviticus 2:13, Matthew 24:29, Mekhilta de R'Shimon bar Yochai Pisha 15:1 16:5, Mekhilta de R'Shimon bar Yochai Shirata 31:1, Mekilta de R'Ishmael Shirata 5:12, Pesikta Rabbati 17:4, Ralbag Wars 6part02:5, Seder Olam 28:Belshazzar

[2] LXX *And the day shall be darkened in Taphnae, when I have broken the scepters there*

[3] Ezekiel 30:19 - Ezekiel 5:8 5:15 1:11 6:14 15:21, Numbers 9:4, Psalms 9:17 5:7, Revelation 17:1, Romans 2:5

[4] Ezekiel 30:20 - Ezekiel 1:2 2:1 5:1 5:17 7:1
Ezekiel 30:20-21 - Seder Olam 26:Tenth of Tevet

[5] Ezekiel 30:21 - Ezekiel 6:24, Isaiah 1:6, Jeremiah 6:13 22:11 24:25 51:8-51:9, Nahum 3:16, Pesikta Rabbati 19:1 33:11, Psalms 10:16 37:17, Revelation 18:21

[6] Ezekiel 30:22 - 2 Kings 24:7, Ezekiel 5:3 10:16, Jeremiah 13:7 46:1-46:12 46:21-46:25, Psalms 37:17, z.Vaetchanan 269b

[7] LXX *strong and outstretched arms*

[8] Ezekiel 30:23 - Ezekiel 29:12-29:13 30:17-30:18 6:26

[9] Ezekiel 30:24 - Deuteronomy 32:41-42, Exodus.R 1:34, Ezekiel 2:15 6:10 6:25, Isaiah 10:5-6 10:15 21:1 21:5, Jeremiah 27:6-8 3:52, Job 24:12, Lamentations.R Petichata D'Chakimei:32, Nehemiah 6:9, Psalms 17:13 18:33 18:40 24:1, Saadia Opinions 4:5, Zechariah 10:11-12, Zephaniah 2:12

[10] LXX *and he shall bring it upon Egypt, and shall take her plunder and seize her spoils*

[11] Ezekiel 30:25 - Ezekiel 5:16 5:21 6:19 6:26 8:15 14:16 14:23 39:21-22, Psalms 9:17

[12] Ezekiel 30:26 - Daniel 11:42, Ezekiel 6:13 5:12 30:17-18 6:23

Ezekiel – Chapter 31

וַיְהִי בְּאַחַת עֶשְׂרֵה שָׁנָה בַּשְּׁלִישִׁי בְּאֶחָד לַחֹדֶשׁ הָיָה דְבַר־יְהוָה אֵלַי לֵאמֹר	1[1] And it came to pass in the eleventh year, in the third month, in the first day of the month, that the word of the LORD came to me, saying:
בֶּן־אָדָם אֱמֹר אֶל־פַּרְעֹה מֶלֶךְ־מִצְרַיִם וְאֶל־הֲמוֹנוֹ אֶל־מִי דָּמִיתָ בְגָדְלֶךָ	2[2] 'Son of man, say to Pharaoh king of Egypt, and to his multitude: Whom are you like in your greatness?
הִנֵּה אַשּׁוּר אֶרֶז בַּלְּבָנוֹן יְפֵה עָנָף וְחֹרֶשׁ מֵצַל וּגְבַהּ קוֹמָה וּבֵין עֲבֹתִים הָיְתָה צַמַּרְתּוֹ	3[3] Behold, the Assyrian was a *cedar*[4] in Lebanon, with fair branches, and with a shadowing shroud, and of a high stature; and its top *was among the thick boughs*[5].
מַיִם גִּדְּלוּהוּ תְּהוֹם רֹמְמָתְהוּ אֶת־נַהֲרֹתֶיהָ הֹלֵךְ סְבִיבוֹת מַטָּעָהּ וְאֶת־תְּעָלֹתֶיהָ שִׁלְחָה אֶל כָּל־עֲצֵי הַשָּׂדֶה	4[6] The waters nourished it, the deep made it grow; her rivers ran around her plantation, and she sent out her conduits to all the trees of the field.
עַל־כֵּן גָּבְהָא קֹמָתוֹ מִכֹּל עֲצֵי הַשָּׂדֶה וַתִּרְבֶּינָה סַרְעַפֹּתָיו וַתֶּאֱרַכְנָה 'פֹארֹתָו' "פֹארֹתָיו" מִמַּיִם רַבִּים בְּשַׁלְּחוֹ	5[7] Therefore, its stature was exalted above all the trees of the field; and its boughs were multiplied, and its branches became long, because of the multitude of waters, when it shot them forth.
בִּסְעַפֹּתָיו קִנְנוּ כָּל־עוֹף הַשָּׁמַיִם וְתַחַת פֹּארֹתָיו יָלְדוּ כֹּל חַיַּת הַשָּׂדֶה וּבְצִלּוֹ יֵשְׁבוּ כֹּל גּוֹיִם רַבִּים	6[8] All the fowls of heaven made their nests in its boughs, and all the beasts of the field brought forth their young under its branches, and under its shadow lived all great nations.
וַיְּיִף בְּגָדְלוֹ בְּאֹרֶךְ דָּלִיּוֹתָיו כִּי־הָיָה שָׁרְשׁוֹ אֶל־מַיִם רַבִּים	7[9] Thus, it was fair in its greatness, in the length of its branches; for its root was in many waters.
אֲרָזִים לֹא־עֲמָמֻהוּ בְּגַן־אֱלֹהִים בְּרוֹשִׁים לֹא דָמוּ אֶל־סְעַפֹּתָיו וְעַרְמֹנִים לֹא־הָיוּ כְּפֹארֹתָיו כָּל־עֵץ בְּגַן־אֱלֹהִים לֹא־דָמָה אֵלָיו בְּיָפְיוֹ	8[10] The cedars in the garden of God could not hide it; the cypress trees were not like its boughs, and the plain trees were not as its branches; nor was any tree in the garden of God like unto it in its beauty.
יָפֶה עֲשִׂיתִיו בְּרֹב דָּלִיּוֹתָיו וַיְקַנְאֻהוּ כָּל־עֲצֵי־עֵדֶן אֲשֶׁר בְּגַן הָאֱלֹהִים	9[11] I made it fair by the multitude of its branches; so that all the trees of Eden, that were in the garden of God, envied it.
לָכֵן כֹּה אָמַר אֲדֹנָי יְהוִֹה יַעַן אֲשֶׁר גָּבַהְתָּ בְּקוֹמָה וַיִּתֵּן צַמַּרְתּוֹ אֶל־בֵּין עֲבֹתִים וְרָם לְבָבוֹ בְּגָבְהוֹ	10[12] Therefore, thus says the Lord GOD: Because you are exalted in stature, and he has set his top among the thick boughs, and his heart is lifted up in his height;

[1] Ezekiel 31:1 - Ezekiel 1:2 6:20, Jeremiah 52:5-6
Ezekiel 31:1-2 - Seder Olam 26:Tenth of Tevet
[2] Ezekiel 31:2 - Ezekiel 5:19 6:10 7:18, Isaiah 14:13-14:14, Jeremiah 1:5 1:17, Mekhilta de R'Shimon bar Yochai Shirata 32:2, Nahum 3:8-3:10, Pesikta Rabbati 30:1 33:11, Revelation 10:11
[3] Ezekiel 31:3 - b.Bava Batra [Rashbam] 68b, b.Succah [Rashi] 45a, Daniel 4:7 4:9 4:17-20, Exodus.R 23:5, Ezekiel 17:3-4 17:22 7:6 7:16, Isaiah 10:33-34 13:24, Jastrow 1377a, Judges 9:15, Mekilta de R'Ishmael Shirata 6:89, Midrash Tanchuma Beshallach 9, Midrash Tanchuma Vayera 15, Nahum 3:1-19, Pesikta de R'Kahana 16.7, Pesikta Rabbati 30:1 33:11, Song of Songs.R 2:42, Zechariah 11:2, Zephaniah 2:13
Ezekiel 31:3-4 - Midrash Tanchuma Bereshit 7
[4] LXX *cypress*
[5] LXX *reached to the midst of the clouds*
[6] Ezekiel 31:4 - Ezekiel 17:5 17:8, Jeremiah 3:36, Pesikta Rabbati 33:11, Proverbs 14:28, Revelation 17:1 17:15
[7] Ezekiel 31:5 - Daniel 4:8, Ezekiel 17:5, Genesis.R 44:9, Isaiah 10:8-10:14 12:4 36:18-36:19 37:11-37:13, Psalms 1:3 37:35-37:36
[8] Ezekiel 31:6 - Daniel 4:9 4:18, Ezekiel 17:23, Matthew 13:32, Midrash Psalms 119:46
[9] Ezekiel 31:7 - Midrash Tanchuma Bereshit 7
[10] Ezekiel 31:8 - 2 Enoch 8:7, b.Berachot 53b, b.Pesachim 75b, b.Shabbat 77b, Ezekiel 4:13 7:16 7:18, Genesis 2:8-9 13:10, Guide for the Perplexed 1:1, Isaiah 10:7-14 36:4-18 37:11-13 3:3, Jastrow 77b, Joseph and Aseneth 18:9, Mas.Kallah Rabbati 8:9, Psalms 37:35 80:11
[11] Ezekiel 31:9 - 1 Samuel 18:15, Daniel 2:21 2:37-38 4:19-22 5:20-23, Ecclesiastes 4:4, Exodus 9:16, Ezekiel 16:14 17:22 17:24 4:13 7:16 7:18, Genesis 2:8-9 13:10 2:14 13:11, Genesis.R 15:2, Isaiah 3:3 7:12, James 4:5-4:6, Jastrow 256a, Judges 9:8-20, Proverbs 3:4, Psalms 75:7-8 96:12-13, Zechariah 11:2
[12] Ezekiel 31:10 - 2 Chronicles 1:19 8:25, Daniel 4:27 5:20, Ezekiel 4:17 7:14, Isaiah 10:12 14:13-15, James 4:6, Job 11:11-12, Matthew 23:12, Obadiah 1:3, Proverbs 16:18 18:12, z.Vaetchanan 269b

וָאֶתְּנֵהוּ בְּיַד אֵיל גּוֹיִם עָשׂוֹ יַעֲשֶׂה לּוֹ כְּרִשְׁעוֹ גֵּרַשְׁתִּהוּ	11[1]	I deliver him into the hand of the mighty one of the nations; he will surely deal with him; I will drive him out according to his wickedness.
וַיִּכְרְתֻהוּ זָרִים עָרִיצֵי גוֹיִם וַיִּטְּשֻׁהוּ אֶל־הֶהָרִים וּבְכָל־גֵּאָיוֹת נָפְלוּ דָלִיּוֹתָיו וַתִּשָּׁבַרְנָה פֹארֹתָיו בְּכֹל אֲפִיקֵי הָאָרֶץ וַיֵּרְדוּ מִצִּלּוֹ כָּל־עַמֵּי הָאָרֶץ וַיִּטְּשֻׁהוּ	12[2]	And strangers, the terrible of the nations, cut him off, and cast him down; on the mountains and in all the valleys his branches are fallen, and his boughs lie broken in all the channels of the land; and all the peoples of the earth go down from his shadow, and leave him.
עַל־מַפַּלְתּוֹ יִשְׁכְּנוּ כָּל־עוֹף הַשָּׁמָיִם וְאֶל־פֹּארֹתָיו הָיוּ כֹּל חַיַּת הַשָּׂדֶה	13[3]	On his carcass all the fowls of the heaven live, and on his branches are all the beasts of the field;
לְמַעַן אֲשֶׁר לֹא־יִגְבְּהוּ בְקוֹמָתָם כָּל־עֲצֵי־מַיִם וְלֹא־יִתְּנוּ אֶת־צַמַּרְתָּם אֶל־בֵּין עֲבֹתִים וְלֹא־יַעַמְדוּ אֲלֵיהֶם בְּגָבְהָם כָּל־שֹׁתֵי מָיִם כִּי־כֻלָּם נִתְּנוּ לַמָּוֶת אֶל־אֶרֶץ תַּחְתִּית בְּתוֹךְ בְּנֵי אָדָם אֶל־יוֹרְדֵי בוֹר	14[4]	To the end that none of all the trees by the waters exalt themselves in their stature, nor set their top among the thick boughs, nor that their mighty ones stand up in their height, all that drink water; for they are all delivered to death, to the nether parts of the earth, in the midst of the children of men, with them who go down to the pit.
כֹּה־אָמַר אֲדֹנָי יְהוִה בְּיוֹם רִדְתּוֹ שְׁאוֹלָה הֶאֱבַלְתִּי כִּסֵּתִי עָלָיו אֶת־תְּהוֹם וָאֶמְנַע נַהֲרוֹתֶיהָ וַיִּכָּלְאוּ מַיִם רַבִּים וָאַקְדִּר עָלָיו לְבָנוֹן וְכָל־עֲצֵי הַשָּׂדֶה עָלָיו עֻלְּפֶה	15[5]	Thus says the Lord GOD: In the day when he went down to the nether world, I caused the deep to mourn and cover itself for him, and I restrained its rivers, and the great waters stayed; and I caused Lebanon to mourn for him, and all the trees of the field fainted for him.
מִקּוֹל מַפַּלְתּוֹ הִרְעַשְׁתִּי גוֹיִם בְּהוֹרִדִי אֹתוֹ שְׁאוֹלָה אֶת־יוֹרְדֵי בוֹר וַיִּנָּחֲמוּ בְּאֶרֶץ תַּחְתִּית כָּל־עֲצֵי־עֵדֶן מִבְחַר וְטוֹב־לְבָנוֹן כָּל־שֹׁתֵי מָיִם	16[6]	I made the nations shake at the sound of his fall, when I cast him down to the *nether world*[7] with them who descend to the pit; and all the trees of Eden, the choice and best of Lebanon, all that drink water, were comforted in the *nether parts*[8] of the earth.
גַּם־הֵם אִתּוֹ יָרְדוּ שְׁאוֹלָה אֶל־חַלְלֵי־חָרֶב וּזְרֹעוֹ יָשְׁבוּ בְצִלּוֹ בְּתוֹךְ גּוֹיִם	17[9]	They also went down into the *nether world*[10] with him to those who are slain by the sword; yes, they who were in his arm, who lived under his shadow in the midst of the nations.
אֶל־מִי דָמִיתָ כָּכָה בְּכָבוֹד וּבְגֹדֶל בַּעֲצֵי־עֵדֶן וְהוּרַדְתָּ אֶת־עֲצֵי־עֵדֶן אֶל־אֶרֶץ תַּחְתִּית בְּתוֹךְ	18[11]	To whom are you, like in glory and in greatness among the trees of Eden? Yet you shall be brought down with the trees of Eden to the nether parts of the earth; you shall lie in the

[1] Ezekiel 31:11 - 1 Timothy 1:20, Daniel 5:18-5:19, Deuteronomy 18:12, Ezekiel 11:9 21:36 23:28 32:11-32:12, James 2:13, Jeremiah 1:9, Judges 1:7 16:23, Lamentations 1:21, Leviticus 18:24-18:28 20:22-20:23, Matthew 7:1-7:2, Nahum 3:18 Ezekiel 31:11-37:15 [frags only] - MasEzek

[2] Ezekiel 31:12 - Daniel 4:9-11, Ezekiel 4:7 6:11 32:4-5 8:12 11:5 11:8 15:4, Habakkuk 1:6 1:11, Isaiah 34:5-7, Nahum 3:1718, Pesikta Rabbati 30:1, Revelation 17:16

[3] Ezekiel 31:13 - Ezekiel 5:5 8:4, Isaiah 18:6, Revelation 19:17-19:18

[4] Ezekiel 31:14 - 1 Corinthians 10:11, 2 Peter 2:6, b.Eruvin [Tosefot] 19a, Daniel 4:29 5:22-23, Deuteronomy 13:12 21:21, Ezekiel 2:20 7:18 32:18-32, Hebrews 9:27, Nehemiah 13:18, Psalms 63:10-11 82:7

[5] Ezekiel 31:15 - Ecclesiastes.R 3:23, Exodus.R 14:2, Genesis.R 33:1, Jastrow 1085b, Leviticus.R 27:1, Malachi 3:4, Midrash Tanchuma Bereshit 7, Midrash Tanchuma Bo 2, Midrash Tanchuma Emor 5, Nahum 2:9-11, Numbers.R 1:1, Pesikta de R'Kahana 9.1, Revelation 18:9-11 18:18-19, z.Vaetchanan 269b

[6] Ezekiel 31:16 - Ezekiel 14:22 2:10 2:15 3:28 7:9 7:14 7:18 32:18-32, Habakkuk 2:17, Haggai 2:7, Hebrews 12:26-27, Isaiah 14:8 14:15, Nahum 2:4, Revelation 11:13 18:9-24

[7] LXX *hades*

[8] LXX *hell*

[9] Ezekiel 31:17 - Daniel 4:8-9, Ezekiel 30:6-8 30:21-25 7:3 7:6 32:20-31, Isaiah 14:9, Lamentations 4:20, Mark 4:32, Nehemiah 3:17-18, Psalms 9:18

[10] LXX *hell*

[11] Ezekiel 31:18 - 1 Corinthians 10:14, 1 Samuel 17:26 17:36, 2 Chronicles 4:22, 2 Samuel 1:20, Ezekiel 4:10 7:2 7:9 7:16 8:10 8:19 8:21 32:24-32, Jeremiah 9:26-27, Matthew 13:19 26:26-28, Psalms 52:8, z.Vaetchanan 269b

עֲרֵלִים תִּשְׁכַּב֙ אֶת־חַלְלֵי־חָ֔רֶב ה֥וּא פַרְעֹ֖ה וְכָל־הֲמוֹנ֔ה נְאֻ֖ם אֲדֹנָ֥י יְהוִֽה

midst of the uncircumcised, with those who are slain by the sword. This is Pharaoh and all his multitude, says the Lord GOD.'

Ezekiel – Chapter 32

וַיְהִ֗י בִּשְׁתֵּ֤י עֶשְׂרֵה֙ שָׁנָ֔ה בִּשְׁנֵי־עָשָׂ֥ר חֹ֖דֶשׁ בְּאֶחָ֣ד לַחֹ֑דֶשׁ הָיָ֥ה דְבַר־יְהוָ֖ה אֵלַ֥י לֵאמֹֽר

1[1]   And it came to pass in the twelfth year, in the *twelfth*[2] month, in the first day of the month, the word of the LORD came to me, saying:

בֶּן־אָדָ֗ם שָׂ֤א קִינָה֙ עַל־פַּרְעֹ֣ה מֶֽלֶךְ־מִצְרַ֔יִם וְאָמַרְתָּ֣ אֵלָ֔יו כְּפִ֥יר גּוֹיִ֖ם נִדְמֵ֑יתָ וְאַתָּה֙ כַּתַּנִּ֣ים בַּיַּמִּ֔ים וַתָּ֣גַח בְּנַהֲרוֹתֶ֗יךָ וַתִּדְלַח־מַ֙יִם֙ בְּרַגְלֶ֔יךָ וַתִּרְפֹּ֖ס נַהֲרוֹתָֽם

2[3]   'Son of man, take up a lamentation for Pharaoh king of Egypt, and say to him: You liken yourself to a young lion of the nations; whereas you are as a dragon in the seas, and you gushed forth with your rivers, and troubled the waters with your feet and fouled their rivers.

כֹּ֤ה אָמַר֙ אֲדֹנָ֣י יְהוִ֔ה וּפָרַשְׂתִּ֤י עָלֶ֙יךָ֙ אֶת־רִשְׁתִּ֔י בִּקְהַ֖ל עַמִּ֣ים רַבִּ֑ים וְהֶעֱל֖וּךָ בְּחֶרְמִֽי

3[4]   Thus says the Lord GOD: I will, therefore, spread out My net over you with a company of many peoples; and they shall bring you up in My net.

וּנְטַשְׁתִּ֣יךָ בָאָ֗רֶץ עַל־פְּנֵ֤י הַשָּׂדֶה֙ אֲטִילֶ֔ךָ וְהִשְׁכַּנְתִּ֥י עָלֶ֖יךָ כָּל־ע֣וֹף הַשָּׁמַ֑יִם וְהִשְׂבַּעְתִּ֥י מִמְּךָ֖ חַיַּ֥ת כָּל־הָאָֽרֶץ

4[5]   And I will cast you on the land, I will hurl you on the open field, and will cause all the fowls of the heavens to settle on you, and I will fill the beasts of the whole earth with you.

וְנָתַתִּ֥י אֶת־בְּשָׂרְךָ֖ עַל־הֶֽהָרִ֑ים וּמִלֵּאתִ֥י הַגֵּאָי֖וֹת רָמוּתֶֽךָ

5[6]   And I will lay your flesh on the mountains, And fill the valleys with your foulness.

וְהִשְׁקֵיתִ֨י אֶ֧רֶץ צָפָתְךָ֛ מִדָּמְךָ֖ אֶל־הֶהָרִ֑ים וַאֲפִקִ֖ים יִמָּלְא֥וּן מִמֶּֽךָ

6[7]   *I will water the land in which you swim with your blood, to the mountains; and the channels shall be full of you*[8].

וְכִסֵּיתִ֤י בְכַבּֽוֹתְךָ֙ שָׁמַ֔יִם וְהִקְדַּרְתִּ֖י אֶת־כֹּֽכְבֵיהֶ֑ם שֶׁ֚מֶשׁ בֶּעָנָ֣ן אֲכַסֶּ֔נּוּ וְיָרֵ֖חַ לֹא־יָאִ֥יר אוֹרֽוֹ

7[9]   And when I extinguish you, I will cover the heavens, and make the stars black; I will cover the sun with a cloud, and the moon will not give her light.

כָּל־מְא֤וֹרֵי אוֹר֙ בַּשָּׁמַ֔יִם אַקְדִּירֵ֖ם עָלֶ֑יךָ וְנָתַ֤תִּי חֹ֙שֶׁךְ֙ עַֽל־אַרְצְךָ֔ נְאֻ֖ם אֲדֹנָ֥י יְהוִֽה

8[10]   I will make all the bright lights of heaven black over you, and set darkness on your land, says the Lord GOD.

וְהִכְעַסְתִּ֔י לֵ֖ב עַמִּ֣ים רַבִּ֑ים בַּהֲבִיאִ֤י שִׁבְרְךָ֙ בַּגּוֹיִ֔ם עַל־אֲרָצ֖וֹת אֲשֶׁ֥ר לֹֽא־יְדַעְתָּֽם

9[11]   I will also *vex*[12] the hearts of many peoples, when I bring your destruction among the nations, into the countries which you have not known.

---

[1] Ezekiel 32:1 - Ezekiel 1:2 5:1 5:17 6:20 7:1 8:17 9:21

[2] LXX *tenth*

[3] Ezekiel 32:2 - b.Taanit 30b, Ezekiel 19:1-19:6 3:2 3:32 4:12 5:3 8:16 8:18 10:18 14:13, Genesis 1:9, Isaiah 3:1 3:9, Jeremiah 4:7 9:19 22:8, Nahum 2:12-2:14, Numbers 24:9, Proverbs 4:15, Psalms 74:13-74:14, Psalms of Solomon 2:25 2

[4] Ezekiel 32:3 - Ecclesiastes 9:12, Ezekiel 12:13 17:20, Habakkuk 1:14-17, Hosea 7:12, Jeremiah 16:16, Lamentations 1:13, z.Vaetchanan 269b

[5] Ezekiel 32:4 - 1 Samuel 17:44-17:46, Ezekiel 5:5 31:12-31:13 39:4-39:5 39:17-39:20, Isaiah 14:19 18:6 34:2-34:7 18:24, Jeremiah 8:2 1:33, Joel 4:19, Psalms 63:11 74:14 79:2-79:3 83:10-83:11 110:5-110:6, Revelation 19:17-19:18

[6] Ezekiel 32:5 - Ezekiel 7:12

[7] Ezekiel 32:6 - Exodus 7:17, Isaiah 10:3 10:7, Revelation 14:20 16:6

[8] LXX *And the land shall be drenched with your dung, because of your multitude upon the mountains: I will fill the valleys with you*

[9] Ezekiel 32:7 - Amos 8:9, Exodus 10:21-23, Ezekiel 6:3 6:18, Guide for the Perplexed 2:29, Isaiah 13:10 10:4, Jeremiah 13:16, Job 18:5-6, Joel 2:2 3:4 4:15, Mark 13:24, Matthew 24:29, Proverbs 13:9, Revelation 6:12-13 8:12

[10] Ezekiel 32:8 - Genesis 1:14, Mekilta de R'Ishmael Shirata 5:9, Proverbs 20:20

[11] Ezekiel 32:9 - Ezekiel 5:12 6:23 6:26, Jeremiah 25:15-25:25, Revelation 11:18 18:10-18:15
Ezekiel 32:9-10 - Mekhilta de R'Shimon bar Yochai Shirata 31:1

[12] LXX *provoke to anger*

וַהֲשִׁמּוֹתִי עָלֶיךָ עַמִּים רַבִּים וּמַלְכֵיהֶם יִשְׂעֲרוּ עָלֶיךָ שַׂעַר בְּעוֹפְפִי חַרְבִּי עַל־פְּנֵיהֶם וְחָרְדוּ לִרְגָעִים אִישׁ לְנַפְשׁוֹ בְּיוֹם מַפַּלְתֶּךָ	10[1]	Yes, I will make many peoples appalled at you, and their kings shall be horribly afraid for you, when I brandish My sword before them; and they shall tremble at every moment, every man for his own life, in the day of your fall.
כִּי כֹּה אָמַר אֲדֹנָי יְהוִה חֶרֶב מֶלֶךְ־בָּבֶל תְּבוֹאֶךָ	11[2]	For thus says the Lord GOD: The sword of the king of Babylon shall come upon you.
בְּחַרְבוֹת גִּבּוֹרִים אַפִּיל הֲמוֹנֶךָ עָרִיצֵי גוֹיִם כֻּלָּם וְשָׁדְדוּ אֶת־גְּאוֹן מִצְרַיִם וְנִשְׁמַד כָּל־הֲמוֹנָהּ	12[3]	By the swords of the mighty I will cause your multitude to fall; the terrible of the nations are they all; and they shall spoil the pride of Egypt, and all its multitude shall be destroyed.
וְהַאֲבַדְתִּי אֶת־כָּל־בְּהֶמְתָּהּ מֵעַל מַיִם רַבִּים וְלֹא תִדְלָחֵם רֶגֶל־אָדָם עוֹד וּפַרְסוֹת בְּהֵמָה לֹא תִדְלָחֵם	13[4]	I will destroy also all its beasts, from beside many waters; nor shall the foot of man trouble them any longer, nor the hoofs of beasts trouble them.
אָז אַשְׁקִיעַ מֵימֵיהֶם וְנַהֲרוֹתָם כַּשֶּׁמֶן אוֹלִיךְ נְאֻם אֲדֹנָי יְהוִה	14[5]	Then will I make their waters settle, and cause their rivers to run like oil, says the Lord GOD.
בְּתִתִּי אֶת־אֶרֶץ מִצְרַיִם שְׁמָמָה וּנְשַׁמָּה אֶרֶץ מִמְּלֹאָהּ בְּהַכּוֹתִי אֶת־כָּל־יוֹשְׁבֵי בָהּ וְיָדְעוּ כִּי־אֲנִי יְהוִה	15[6]	When I make the land of Egypt desolate and waste, a land destitute of that which was full, when I shall strike all those who dwell in it, Then shall they know that I am the LORD.
קִינָה הִיא וְקוֹנְנוּהָ בְּנוֹת הַגּוֹיִם תְּקוֹנֵנָּה אוֹתָהּ עַל־מִצְרַיִם וְעַל־כָּל־הֲמוֹנָהּ תְּקוֹנֵנָּה אוֹתָהּ נְאֻם אֲדֹנָי יְהוִה	16[7]	This is the lamentation they shall lament; The daughters of the nations shall lament; for Egypt, and for all her multitude, shall they lament, says the Lord GOD.'
וַיְהִי בִּשְׁתֵּי עֶשְׂרֵה שָׁנָה בַּחֲמִשָּׁה עָשָׂר לַחֹדֶשׁ הָיָה דְבַר־יְהוָה אֵלַי לֵאמֹר	17[8]	It came to pass also in the twelfth year, in the fifteenth day of the month, that the word of the LORD came to me, saying:
בֶּן־אָדָם נְהֵה עַל־הֲמוֹן מִצְרַיִם וְהוֹרִדֵהוּ אוֹתָהּ וּבְנוֹת גּוֹיִם אַדִּרִם אֶל־אֶרֶץ תַּחְתִּיּוֹת אֶת־יוֹרְדֵי בוֹר	18[9]	'Son of man, wail for the *multitude*[10] of Egypt, and cast them down, her, with the daughters of the mighty nations, to the nether parts of the earth, with them who go down into the pit.
מִמִּי נָעָמְתָּ רְדָה וְהָשְׁכְּבָה אֶת־עֲרֵלִים	19[11]	*Whom do you pass in beauty? Go down, and be laid with the uncircumcised*[12].
בְּתוֹךְ חַלְלֵי־חֶרֶב יִפֹּלוּ חֶרֶב נִתָּנָה מָשְׁכוּ אוֹתָהּ וְכָל־הֲמוֹנֶיהָ	20[13]	They shall fall in the midst of those who are killed by the sword; *she is delivered to the sword; draw her down and all her multitudes*[14].

[1] Ezekiel 32:10 - 1 Kings 9:8, Deuteronomy 5:23 8:41, Exodus 15:14-16, Ezekiel 2:16 3:35 6:9, Jeremiah 3:9, Revelation 18:10, Zechariah 11:2

[2] Ezekiel 32:11 - Ezekiel 2:7 6:4 30:22-25, Jeremiah 19:10 22:13 46:24-26, z.Vaetchanan 269b

[3] Ezekiel 32:12 - Deuteronomy 28:49-50, Ezekiel 4:7 5:19 6:11 7:11, Habakkuk 1:6-7, Isaiah 25:2-3

[4] Ezekiel 32:13 - Ezekiel 5:8 5:11 6:12 8:2 10:18

[5] Ezekiel 32:14 - b.Sanhedrin 98a, Ein Yaakov Sanhedrin:97b

[6] Ezekiel 32:15 - Exodus 7:5 14:4 14:18, Ezekiel 6:7 5:12 29:19-29:20 6:26, Psalms 9:17 24:1 83:18-83:19 107:33-107:34

[7] Ezekiel 32:16 - 2 Chronicles 11:25, 2 Samuel 1:17 3:33-3:34, Avot de R'Natan 25, b.Eruvin 21a, Ezekiel 2:17 8:2, Jeremiah 9:18

[8] Ezekiel 32:17 - Ezekiel 1:2 7:1 8:1 9:21

Ezekiel 32:17-18 - Seder Olam 26:Tenth of Tevet

[9] Ezekiel 32:18 - Exodus.R 19:4, Ezekiel 21:11-21:12 2:20 7:14 7:16 8:2 8:16 8:21 32:24-32:32 19:3, Hosea 6:5, Isaiah 14:15 16:9, Jeremiah 1:10, Leviticus.R 5:7, Luke 19:41, Mekilta de R'Ishmael Shirata 7:74, Micah 1:8, Midrash Proverbs 9, Midrash Psalms 6:1, Midrash Tanchuma Balak 12, Midrash Tanchuma Metzora 1, Numbers.R 20:19, Psalms 30:10 63:10, Romans 12:15

Ezekiel 32:18-30 - Midrash Tanchuma Lech Lecha 20, Midrash Tanchuma Tazria 5

[10] LXX *strength*

[11] Ezekiel 32:19 - 1 Samuel 17:26 17:36, b.Ketubot 14a, b.Shabbat 149b, Ezekiel 27:3-4 4:10 28:12-17 7:2 7:18 8:21 8:24 32:29-30, Isaiah 14:9-14:15, Jeremiah 9:26-27, Midrash Psalms 6:1 116:7

[12] Missing in LXX

[13] Ezekiel 32:20 - Ezekiel 29:8-29:12 32:23-32:26 32:29-32:30, Jeremiah 22:19, Proverbs 24:11, Psalms 28:3

[14] LXX *and all his strength shall perish: the giants also shall say to you*

יְדַבְּרוּ־לֹ֧ו אֵלֵ֛י גִבֹּורִ֖ים מִתֹּ֣וךְ שְׁאֹ֑ול אֶת־עֹ֣זְרָ֔יו יָֽרְד֛וּ שָׁכְב֥וּ הָעֲרֵלִ֖ים חַלְלֵי־חָֽרֶב	**21[1]** The strong among the mighty shall speak of him out of the midst of the nether world with those who helped him; they are gone down, they lie still, the uncircumcised, slain by the sword.
שָׁ֤ם אַשּׁוּר֙ וְכָל־קְהָלָ֔הּ סְבִֽיבֹותָ֖יו קִבְרֹתָ֑יו כֻּלָּ֣ם חֲלָלִ֔ים הַנֹּפְלִ֖ים בֶּחָֽרֶב	**22[2]** Asshur is there and all her company; their graves are around them; *all of them slain, fallen by the sword[3]*;
אֲשֶׁ֤ר נִתְּנ֣וּ קִבְרֹתֶ֗יהָ בְּיַרְכְּתֵי־בֹ֔ור וַיְהִ֣י קְהָלָ֔הּ סְבִיבֹ֖ות קְבֻרָתָ֑הּ כֻּלָּ֤ם חֲלָלִים֙ נֹפְלִ֣ים בַּחֶ֔רֶב אֲשֶׁר־נָתְנ֥וּ חִתִּ֖ית בְּאֶ֥רֶץ חַיִּֽים	**23[4]** whose graves are set in the uttermost parts of the pit, and her company is around her grave; all of them slain, fallen by the sword, who caused terror in the land of the living.
שָׁ֤ם עֵילָם֙ וְכָל־הֲמֹונָ֔הּ סְבִיבֹ֖ות קְבֻרָתָ֑הּ כֻּלָּ֣ם חֲלָלִים֩ הַנֹּפְלִ֨ים בַּחֶ֜רֶב אֲשֶׁר־יָרְד֥וּ עֲרֵלִ֣ים׀ אֶל־אֶ֣רֶץ תַּחְתִּיֹּ֗ות אֲשֶׁ֨ר נָתְנ֤וּ חִתִּיתָם֙ בְּאֶ֣רֶץ חַיִּ֔ים וַיִּשְׂא֥וּ כְלִמָּתָ֖ם אֶת־יֹ֥ורְדֵי בֹֽור	**24[5]** There is *Elam[6]* and all her multitude around her grave; all of them slain, fallen by the sword, who are gone down uncircumcised into the nether parts of the earth, who caused their terror in the land of the living; yet they have borne their shame with those who go down to the pit.
בְּתֹ֣וךְ חֲלָלִים֩ נָתְנ֨וּ מִשְׁכָּ֜ב לָ֣הּ בְּכָל־הֲמֹונָ֗הּ סְבִֽיבֹותָיו֙ קִבְרֹתֶ֔הָ כֻּלָּ֤ם עֲרֵלִים֙ חַלְלֵי־חֶ֔רֶב כִּֽי־נִתַּ֤ן חִתִּיתָם֙ בְּאֶ֣רֶץ חַיִּ֔ים וַיִּשְׂא֥וּ כְלִמָּתָ֖ם אֶת־יֹ֣ורְדֵי בֹ֑ור בְּתֹ֥וךְ חֲלָלִ֖ים נִתָּֽן	**25[7]** *They have set her a bed in the midst of the slain with all her multitude; her graves are around them; all of them uncircumcised, killed by the sword; because their terror was caused in the land of the living, yet they have borne their shame with those who go down to the pit; they are put[8]* in the midst of those who are killed.
שָׁ֣ם מֶ֤שֶׁךְ תֻּבַל֙ וְכָל־הֲמֹונָ֔הּ סְבִֽיבֹותָ֖יו קִבְרֹותֶ֑יהָ כֻּלָּ֤ם עֲרֵלִים֙ מְחֻ֣לְלֵי חֶ֔רֶב כִּֽי־נָתְנ֥וּ חִתִּיתָ֖ם בְּאֶ֥רֶץ חַיִּֽים	**26[9]** There is Meshech, Tubal, and all her multitude; her graves are around them; all of them uncircumcised, killed by the sword; because they caused their terror in the land of the living.
וְלֹ֤א יִשְׁכְּבוּ֙ אֶת־גִּבֹּורִ֔ים נֹפְלִ֖ים מֵעֲרֵלִ֑ים אֲשֶׁ֣ר יָרְדֽוּ־שְׁאֹ֣ול בִּכְלֵֽי־מִלְחַמְתָּם֮ וַיִּתְּנ֣וּ אֶת־חַרְבֹותָם֮ תַּ֣חַת רָאשֵׁיהֶם֒ וַתְּהִ֤י עֲוֹֽנֹתָם֙ עַל־עַצְמֹותָ֔ם כִּֽי־חִתִּ֥ית גִּבֹּורִ֖ים בְּאֶ֥רֶץ חַיִּֽים	**27[10]** *And those who are inferior to the uncircumcised shall not lie with the mighty[11]* that went down to the nether world with their weapons of war, whose swords are laid under their heads, and whose iniquities are upon their bones; because the terror of the mighty was in the land of the living.
וְאַתָּ֗ה בְּתֹ֧וךְ עֲרֵלִ֛ים תִּשָּׁבַ֥ר וְתִשְׁכַּ֖ב אֶת־חַלְלֵי־חָֽרֶב	**28[12]** But you, in the midst of the uncircumcised shall be broken and lie, with those who are killed by the sword.

[1] Ezekiel 32:21 - Ezekiel 8:19 32:24-25 8:27, Isaiah 1:31 14:9-10, Luke 16:23-24, Numbers 16:30-34, Proverbs 14:32, Psalms 9:18 55:16, Sifre Devarim Nitzavim 311

[2] Ezekiel 32:22 - Ezekiel 31:3-18 8:24 8:26 32:29-30, Isaiah 6:33 37:36-38, Nahum 1:7-12 3:1-19, Numbers 24:24, Psalms 83:9-11, Sifre Devarim {Haazinu Hashamayim} 311

[3] Missing in LXX

[4] Ezekiel 32:23 - Ezekiel 2:17 2:20 32:24-27 8:32, Isaiah 14:15-16 14:11 51:12-13, Jeremiah 11:19, Job 4:13, Psalms 27:13 20:9 22:6 Ezekiel 32:23-27 - Gates of Repentance 3.162

[5] Ezekiel 32:24 - 1 Chronicles 1:17, Daniel 8:2, Ezekiel 16:52 16:54 2:20 7:14 8:18 8:21 8:25 8:30 10:29 36:6-7 12:15 15:26 20:13, Genesis 10:22 14:1, Habakkuk 2:16, Isaiah 11:11, Jastrow 461a, Jeremiah 3:24-25 1:25 49:34-39, Job 4:13

[6] LXX Ælam

[7] Ezekiel 32:25 - 1 Chronicles 10:4, 2 Samuel 1:20, Acts 7:51, Ezekiel 8:19 8:21 20:7 20:9, Luke 12:4-5, Psalms 19:8, Revelation 2:22

[8] Missing in LXX

[9] Ezekiel 32:26 - 1 Chronicles 1:5, Ezekiel 3:13 32:19-20 32:23-24 8:27 8:32 38:2-3 15:1, Gates of Repentance 1.27, Genesis 10:2 10:12

[10] Ezekiel 32:27 - 2 Corinthians 10:4, Ezekiel 18:20 8:21, Gates of Repentance 4.013, Isaiah 14:18-14:19 6:17, Job 3:14-3:16 20:11, John 8:24, mt.Hilchot Taaniot 5:7, Proverbs 14:32, Psalms 49:15 92:8 92:10 13:18, Saadia Opinions 6:5, y.Bava Batra 8:6

[11] LXX And they are laid with the giants who fell of old

[12] Ezekiel 32:28 - Daniel 2:34-2:35

<table>
<tr><td>

שָׁמָּה אֱדוֹם מְלָכֶיהָ וְכָל־נְשִׂיאֶיהָ אֲשֶׁר־נִתְּנוּ בִגְבוּרָתָם אֶת־חַלְלֵי־חָרֶב הֵמָּה אֶת־עֲרֵלִים יִשְׁכָּבוּ וְאֶת־יֹרְדֵי בוֹר

</td><td>29[1]</td><td>

There is Edom, her kings and all her princes, who for all their might are laid with those who are killed by the sword; they shall lie with the uncircumcised, and with those who go down to the pit[2].

</td></tr>
<tr><td>

שָׁמָּה נְסִיכֵי צָפוֹן כֻּלָּם וְכָל־צִדֹנִי אֲשֶׁר־יָרְדוּ אֶת־חֲלָלִים בְּחִתִּיתָם מִגְּבוּרָתָם בּוֹשִׁים וַיִּשְׁכְּבוּ עֲרֵלִים אֶת־חַלְלֵי־חֶרֶב וַיִּשְׂאוּ כְלִמָּתָם אֶת־יוֹרְדֵי בוֹר

</td><td>30[3]</td><td>

There are the princes of the north, all of them, and all the *Zidonians[4],* who went down with the slain, *ashamed for all the terror they caused by their might, and they lie uncircumcised with those who are killed by the sword, and bear their shame[5]* with those who go down to the pit.

</td></tr>
<tr><td>

אוֹתָם יִרְאֶה פַרְעֹה וְנִחַם 'עַל־כָּל־הֲמוֹנֹה' "עַל־כָּל־הֲמוֹנוֹ" חַלְלֵי־חֶרֶב פַּרְעֹה וְכָל־חֵילוֹ נְאֻם אֲדֹנָי יְהוִה

</td><td>31[6]</td><td>

These Pharaoh shall see, and will be comforted over all his multitude; *Pharaoh and all his army, killed by the sword[7],* says the Lord GOD.

</td></tr>
<tr><td>

כִּי־נָתַתִּי אֶת־חִתִּיתוֹ "אֶת־חִתִּיתִי" בְּאֶרֶץ חַיִּים וְהֻשְׁכַּב בְּתוֹךְ עֲרֵלִים אֶת־חַלְלֵי־חֶרֶב פַּרְעֹה וְכָל־הֲמוֹנֹה נְאֻם אֲדֹנָי יְהוִה

</td><td>32[8]</td><td>

For I have put My terror in the land of the living; and he shall be laid in the midst of the uncircumcised, with those who are slain by the sword, Pharaoh and all his multitude, says the Lord GOD.'

</td></tr>
</table>

Ezekiel – Chapter 33

<table>
<tr><td>

וַיְהִי דְבַר־יְהוָה אֵלַי לֵאמֹר

</td><td>1[9]</td><td>

And the word of the LORD came to me, saying:

</td></tr>
<tr><td>

בֶּן־אָדָם דַּבֵּר אֶל־בְּנֵי־עַמְּךָ וְאָמַרְתָּ אֲלֵיהֶם אֶרֶץ כִּי־אָבִיא עָלֶיהָ חָרֶב וְלָקְחוּ עַם־הָאָרֶץ אִישׁ אֶחָד מִקְצֵיהֶם וְנָתְנוּ אֹתוֹ לָהֶם לְצֹפֶה

</td><td>2[10]</td><td>

'Son of man, speak to the children of your people, and say to them: When I bring the sword upon a land, if the people of the land take a man from among them, and set him for their watchman;

</td></tr>
<tr><td>

וְרָאָה אֶת־הַחֶרֶב בָּאָה עַל־הָאָרֶץ וְתָקַע בַּשּׁוֹפָר וְהִזְהִיר אֶת־הָעָם

</td><td>3[11]</td><td>

If, when he sees the sword come upon the land, he blows the horn, and warns the people;

</td></tr>
<tr><td>

וְשָׁמַע הַשֹּׁמֵעַ אֶת־קוֹל הַשּׁוֹפָר וְלֹא נִזְהָר וַתָּבוֹא חֶרֶב וַתִּקָּחֵהוּ דָּמוֹ בְרֹאשׁוֹ יִהְיֶה

</td><td>4[12]</td><td>

then whoever hears the sound of the horn, and does not take warning, if the sword comes, and takes him away, his blood shall be on his own head;

</td></tr>
<tr><td>

אֵת קוֹל הַשּׁוֹפָר שָׁמַע וְלֹא נִזְהָר דָּמוֹ בּוֹ יִהְיֶה וְהוּא נִזְהָר נַפְשׁוֹ מִלֵּט

</td><td>5[13]</td><td>

He heard the sound of the horn, and did not take warning, his blood shall be on him;

</td></tr>
</table>

[1] Ezekiel 32:29 - Amos 1:11-1:12, b.Avodah Zara 10b, Chibbur Yafeh 23 {99a}, Ein Yaakov Avodah Zarah:10b, Ezekiel 25:1-25:17 35:1-35:15, Genesis 1:30 36:1-36:19, Isaiah 34:1-34:17 63:1-63:6, Jeremiah 49:7-22, Malachi 1:3-4, Numbers.R 10:2, Obadiah 1:1-9, Sifre Devarim {Haazinu Hashamayim} 311, Sifre Devarim Nitzavim 311

[2] LXX *There are laid the princes of Assur, who yielded their strength to a wound of the sword: these are laid with the slain, with them who go down to the pit*

[3] Ezekiel 32:30 - Ezekiel 4:21 32:24-25 14:6 14:15 15:2, Jeremiah 1:22 1:26, Midrash Psalms 2:8, Midrash Tanchuma Bo 4, Sifre Devarim {Haazinu Hashamayim} 311, Sifre Devarim Nitzavim 311

[4] LXX *captains of Assur*

[5] LXX *they lie uncircumcised among the slain with the sword together with their terror and their strength, and they have received their punishment with them who go down to the pit*

[6] Ezekiel 32:31 - Exodus.R 30:17, Ezekiel 14:22 7:16, Lamentations 2:13, mt.Hilchot Teshuvah 2:3

[7] Missing in LXX

[8] Ezekiel 32:32 - 2 Corinthians 5:11, Ezekiel 8:27, Genesis 11:5, Hebrews 10:31, Jeremiah 25:15-25:38, Job 7:23, Revelation 6:15-6:17, Zephaniah 3:6-3:8

[9] Ezekiel 33:1 - Apocalypse of Elijah 1:1, Perek Shirah
Ezekiel 33:1-6 - Life of Adam and Eve [Apocalypse] 22:2

[10] Ezekiel 33:2 - 2 Kings 9:17-9:20, 2 Samuel 18:24-18:27, Ezekiel 3:11 3:27 6:3 11:8 14:17 14:21 21:14-21:21 9:7 9:12 9:17 9:30 13:18, Hosea 9:8, Isaiah 21:6-21:9 56:9-56:10 14:6, Jeremiah 12:12 15:2-15:3 1:31 47:6-47:7 3:12, Leviticus 2:25, Zechariah 13:7

[11] Ezekiel 33:3 - Ezekiel 33:8-33:9, Hosea 8:1, Isaiah 10:1, Jeremiah 4:5 6:1 3:27, Joel 2:1, Nehemiah 4:18 4:20

[12] Ezekiel 33:4 - 1 Kings 2:37, 2 Chronicles 1:16, 2 Samuel 1:16, Acts 18:6 20:26, Ezekiel 18:13 9:5 9:9, James 1:22, Jeremiah 6:17 42:20-22, Leviticus 20:9 20:11-20:27, Proverbs 5:1, Zechariah 1:2-4

[13] Ezekiel 33:5 - 2 Kings 6:10, Acts 2:37-2:41, Exodus 9:19-9:21, Hebrews 2:1-2:3 11:7, Isaiah 3:2, John 8:39, Psalms 95:7

whereas if he had taken warning, he would have delivered his soul.

6[1] וְהַצֹּפֶה כִּי־יִרְאֶה אֶת־הַחֶרֶב בָּאָה וְלֹא־תָקַע בַּשּׁוֹפָר וְהָעָם לֹא־נִזְהָר וַתָּבוֹא חֶרֶב וַתִּקַּח מֵהֶם נָפֶשׁ הוּא בַּעֲוֹנוֹ נִלְקָח וְדָמוֹ מִיַּד־הַצֹּפֶה אֶדְרֹשׁ

But if the watchman sees the sword come, and does not blow the horn, and the people are not warned, and the sword comes, and takes any person from among them, he is taken away in his iniquity, but his blood I will require at the watchman's hand.

7[2] וְאַתָּה בֶן־אָדָם צֹפֶה נְתַתִּיךָ לְבֵית יִשְׂרָאֵל וְשָׁמַעְתָּ מִפִּי דָּבָר וְהִזְהַרְתָּ אֹתָם מִמֶּנִּי

So you, son of man, I have set you a watchman to the house of Israel; therefore, when you hear the word at My mouth, warn them from Me.

8[3] בְּאָמְרִי לָרָשָׁע רָשָׁע מוֹת תָּמוּת וְלֹא דִבַּרְתָּ לְהַזְהִיר רָשָׁע מִדַּרְכּוֹ הוּא רָשָׁע בַּעֲוֹנוֹ יָמוּת וְדָמוֹ מִיָּדְךָ אֲבַקֵּשׁ

When I say to the wicked: O wicked man, you shall surely die, and you do not speak to warn the wicked from his way; that wicked man shall die in his iniquity, but his blood I will require at your hand.

9[4] וְאַתָּה כִּי־הִזְהַרְתָּ רָשָׁע מִדַּרְכּוֹ לָשׁוּב מִמֶּנָּה וְלֹא־שָׁב מִדַּרְכּוֹ הוּא בַּעֲוֹנוֹ יָמוּת וְאַתָּה נַפְשְׁךָ הִצַּלְתָּ

Nevertheless, if you warn the wicked of his way, to turn from it, and he does not turn from his way; he shall die in his iniquity, but you have delivered your soul.

10[5] וְאַתָּה בֶן־אָדָם אֱמֹר אֶל־בֵּית יִשְׂרָאֵל כֵּן אֲמַרְתֶּם לֵאמֹר כִּי־פְשָׁעֵינוּ וְחַטֹּאתֵינוּ עָלֵינוּ וּבָם אֲנַחְנוּ נְמַקִּים וְאֵיךְ נִחְיֶה

Therefore, O you son of man, say to the house of Israel: you shall speak, saying: Our transgressions and our sins are on us, and we pine away in them; how then can we live?

11[6] אֱמֹר אֲלֵיהֶם חַי־אָנִי נְאֻם אֲדֹנָי יְהֹוִה אִם־אֶחְפֹּץ בְּמוֹת הָרָשָׁע כִּי אִם־בְּשׁוּב רָשָׁע מִדַּרְכּוֹ וְחָיָה שׁוּבוּ שׁוּבוּ מִדַּרְכֵיכֶם הָרָעִים וְלָמָּה תָמוּתוּ בֵּית יִשְׂרָאֵל

Say to them: As I live, says the Lord GOD, I take no pleasure in the death of the wicked, but that the wicked should turn from his way and live; turn, turn from your evil ways; for why should you die, O house of Israel?

12[7] וְאַתָּה בֶן־אָדָם אֱמֹר אֶל־בְּנֵי־עַמְּךָ צִדְקַת הַצַּדִּיק לֹא תַצִּילֶנּוּ בְּיוֹם פִּשְׁעוֹ וְרִשְׁעַת הָרָשָׁע לֹא־יִכָּשֶׁל בָּהּ בְּיוֹם שׁוּבוֹ מֵרִשְׁעוֹ וְצַדִּיק לֹא יוּכַל לִחְיוֹת בָּהּ בְּיוֹם חֲטֹאתוֹ

And you, son of man[8], say to the children of your people: The righteousness of the righteous shall not deliver him in the day of his transgression; and as for the wickedness of the wicked, he shall not stumble by them in the day he turns from his wickedness; nor shall he who is righteous be able to live by them in the day he sins.

---

[1] Ezekiel 33:6 - 2 Samuel 4:11, Ezekiel 3:18-3:20 18:20 18:24 33:8-33:9 10:10, Genesis 9:5 18:22, Isaiah 56:10-56:11, John 8:21-8:24, Proverbs 14:32

[2] Ezekiel 33:7 - 1 Corinthians 11:23 15:3, 1 Kings 22:14 22:16-28, 1 Thessalonians 4:1-4:2, 2 Chronicles 19:10, Acts 5:20 20:20 20:26-20:27, Colossians 1:28-1:29, Ephesians 4:11, Ezekiel 2:7-2:8 3:17-3:21, Hebrews 13:17, Isaiah 14:6, Jeremiah 1:17 6:27 23:28 2:2 7:7, Micah 7:4, Pesikta de R'Kahana 24.1, Song of Songs 3:3 5:7
Ezekiel 33:7-9 - Sifre Devarim {Devarim} 13

[3] Ezekiel 33:8 - Acts 20:26-20:27, Ecclesiastes 8:13, Ezekiel 13:9-13:10 18:4 18:10-18:13 18:18 18:20 9:6 9:14, Genesis 2:17 3:4, Isaiah 3:11, Jeremiah 8:11-8:13 14:13-14:16, Numbers 3:3, Pesikta de R'Kahana 24.1, Proverbs 11:21

[4] Ezekiel 33:9 - 1 Thessalonians 4:3-8 5:14, 2 Corinthians 2:15-17, Acts 13:40 13:46 18:5-6 20:26 28:23-28, Ephesians 5:3-6, Ezekiel 3:19 3:21, Galatians 5:19-21 6:7-8, Hebrews 2:3 12:25, John 8:24, Luke 12:47, Pesikta de R'Kahana 24.1, Philippians 3:18-19, Proverbs 15:10 5:1

[5] Ezekiel 33:10 - Ezekiel 4:17 24:23 13:11, Isaiah 1:14 3:20, Jeremiah 2:25, Leviticus 2:39, Perek Shirah, Psalms 10:7

[6] Ezekiel 33:11 - 1 Timothy 2:4, 2 Peter 3:9, 2 Samuel 14:14, Acts 3:19 2:20, Daniel 9:13, Ecclesiastes.R 9:4, Exodus.R 9:1, Ezekiel 5:11 14:6 14:16-18 16:48 18:23 18:30-32, Gates of Repentance 1.11, Hellenistic Synagogal Prayers 11:6, Hosea 11:8 14:3, Isaiah 1:18 55:6-7, Jeremiah 3:22 22:24 31:19-21 22:18, Lamentations 3:33, Luke 15:20-32, Midrash Proverbs 1, Midrash Psalms 5:7, Midrash Tanchuma Tazria 9, Midrash Tanchuma Tzav 5, Midrash Tanchuma Vaera 11, Midrash Tanchuma Vayera 8, mt.Hilchot Rotzeach Ushmirat Nefesh 13:14, Neilah Yom Kippur [Tefilah Zakkah], Numbers 14:21 14:28, Numbers.R 10:1 11:7, Pesikta de R'Kahana 24.1, Pesikta Rabbati 40:1 44:1 44:7, Proverbs 1:23 8:36, Romans 14:11, Saadia Opinions 4:4, Siman 189:5, Song of Songs.R 6:1, Zephaniah 2:9

[7] Ezekiel 33:12 - 1 John 2:1, 1 Kings 8:48-50, 2 Chronicles 7:14, b.Kiddushin 40b, Ein Yaakov Kiddushin:40b, Ezekiel 3:20-21 18:21 18:24-32 9:2 33:18-19, Matthew 21:28-31, mt.Hilchot Teshuvah 1:3 3:3, Numbers.R 10:1, Romans 3:25, Song of Songs.R 6:1, t.Kiddushin 1:15-16
Ezekiel 33:12-20 - Apocryphon of Ezekiel Fragment 4
[8] Missing in LXX

בְּאָמְרִי לַצַּדִּיק חָיֹה יִחְיֶה וְהוּא־בָטַח עַל־צִדְקָתוֹ וְעָשָׂה עָוֶל כָּל־'צִדְקָתוֹ' "כָּל־צִדְקָתָיו" לֹא תִזָּכַרְנָה וּבְעַוְלוֹ אֲשֶׁר־עָשָׂה בּוֹ יָמוּת	13[1]	When I say to the righteous, that he shall surely live; if he trusts in his righteousness, and commits iniquity, none of his righteous deeds shall be remembered; but for his iniquity he has committed, for it he shall die.
וּבְאָמְרִי לָרָשָׁע מוֹת תָּמוּת וְשָׁב מֵחַטָּאתוֹ וְעָשָׂה מִשְׁפָּט וּצְדָקָה	14[2]	Again, when I say to the wicked: you shall surely die; if he turn from his sin, and do what is lawful and right;
חֲבֹל יָשִׁיב רָשָׁע גְּזֵלָה יְשַׁלֵּם בְּחֻקּוֹת הַחַיִּים הָלַךְ לְבִלְתִּי עֲשׂוֹת עָוֶל חָיוֹ יִחְיֶה לֹא יָמוּת	15[3]	if the wicked restores the pledge, give back what he had taken by robbery, walks in the statutes of life, committing no iniquity; he shall surely live, he shall not die.
כָּל־חַטֹּאתוֹ' "כָּל־חַטֹּאתָיו" אֲשֶׁר חָטָא לֹא תִזָּכַרְנָה לוֹ מִשְׁפָּט וּצְדָקָה עָשָׂה חָיוֹ יִחְיֶה	16[4]	None of his sins he has committed shall be remembered against him; he has done what is lawful and right; he shall surely live.
וְאָמְרוּ בְּנֵי עַמְּךָ לֹא יִתָּכֵן דֶּרֶךְ אֲדֹנָי וְהֵמָּה דַרְכָּם לֹא־יִתָּכֵן	17[5]	Yet the children of your people say: The way of the Lord is not equal[6]; but as for them, their way is not equal[7].
בְּשׁוּב־צַדִּיק מִצִּדְקָתוֹ וְעָשָׂה עָוֶל וּמֵת בָּהֶם	18[8]	When the righteous turns from his righteousness, and commits iniquity, he shall die by them.
וּבְשׁוּב רָשָׁע מֵרִשְׁעָתוֹ וְעָשָׂה מִשְׁפָּט וּצְדָקָה עֲלֵיהֶם הוּא יִחְיֶה	19[9]	And when the wicked turns from his wickedness, and does what is lawful and right, he shall live by them.
וַאֲמַרְתֶּם לֹא יִתָּכֵן דֶּרֶךְ אֲדֹנָי אִישׁ כִּדְרָכָיו אֶשְׁפּוֹט אֶתְכֶם בֵּית יִשְׂרָאֵל	20[10]	Yet you say: The way of the Lord is not equal[11]. O house of Israel, I will judge everyone after his ways.'
וַיְהִי בִּשְׁתֵּי עֶשְׂרֵה שָׁנָה בָּעֲשִׂרִי בַּחֲמִשָּׁה לַחֹדֶשׁ לְגָלוּתֵנוּ בָּא־אֵלַי הַפָּלִיט מִירוּשָׁלַםִ לֵאמֹר הֻכְּתָה הָעִיר	21[12]	And it came to pass in the twelfth[13] year of our captivity, in the tenth[14] month, in the fifth day of the month, that one who escaped out of Jerusalem came to me, saying: 'The city is struck.'
וְיַד־יְהֹוָה הָיְתָה אֵלַי בָּעֶרֶב לִפְנֵי בּוֹא הַפָּלִיט וַיִּפְתַּח אֶת־פִּי עַד־בּוֹא אֵלַי בַּבֹּקֶר וַיִּפָּתַח פִּי וְלֹא נֶאֱלַמְתִּי עוֹד	22[15]	Now the hand of the LORD had been on me in the evening, before he who escaped arrived; and He opened my mouth regarding his coming to me in the morning; and my mouth opened, and I was no longer dumb.

---

[1] Ezekiel 33:13 - 1 John 2:19, 2 Peter 2:20-22, Ezekiel 3:20 18:4 18:24, Hebrews 10:38, Luke 18:9-14, Philippians 3:9, Romans 10:3

[2] Ezekiel 33:14 - Acts 3:19, Ezekiel 3:18-19 18:21 18:27 9:8, Hosea 14:3, Isaiah 3:11 7:7, Jeremiah 4:1 18:7-8, Luke 13:3-5, Matthew 9:13, Micah 6:8, Proverbs 4:13

[3] Ezekiel 33:15 - Amos 2:8, b.Bava Kamma 60b, Deuteronomy 24:6 24:10-13 24:17, Exodus 22:1-4 22:26-27, Ezekiel 18:7 18:12 18:16 18:27-28 20:11 20:13 20:21, Job 22:6 24:3 24:9, Leviticus 6:2-5 18:5, Luke 1:6 19:8, Midrash Tanchuma Noach 4, mt.Hilchot Teshuvah 2:9 2:9, Numbers 5:6-5:8, Psalms 119:93, Revelation 22:12-14, Saadia Opinions 5:6

[4] Ezekiel 33:16 - 1 John 2:1-3, Ezekiel 18:22, Isaiah 1:18 19:25 20:22, Micah 7:18-19, Romans 5:16 5:21

[5] Ezekiel 33:17 - Ezekiel 18:25 18:29 9:20, Guide for the Perplexed 3:16, Job 11:2 16:8, Luke 19:21-22, Matthew 25:24-26, Per Massorah: Soferim altered "Hashem" to "Adonai"

[6] LXX straight

[7] LXX straight

[8] Ezekiel 33:18 - 2 Peter 2:20-22, Ezekiel 3:20 18:26-18:27 33:12-13, Hebrews 10:38

[9] Ezekiel 33:19 - b.Yoma 86b, Chibbur Yafeh 27 {130a}, Ein Yaakov Yoma:86b, Exodus.R 31:1, Ezekiel 18:27-28 9:14, Numbers.R 10:1

[10] Ezekiel 33:20 - 2 Corinthians 5:10, Ecclesiastes 12:14, Ezekiel 18:25 18:29-30 9:17, John 5:29, Matthew 16:27, Proverbs 19:3, Psalms 62:13, Revelation 20:12-15 22:12

[11] LXX straight

[12] Ezekiel 33:21 - 2 Chronicles 36:17-21, 2 Kings 24:4-7 1:4 1:10, b.Rosh Hashanah 18b, Ein Yaakov Rosh Hashanah:18b, Ezekiel 1:2 24:26-27 8:1 16:1, Jastrow 1593a, Jeremiah 39:1-8 52:4-14, Pirkei de R'Eliezer 27, Seder Olam 26:Tenth of Tevet, Sifre Devarim {Vaetchanan} 31

[13] LXX tenth

[14] LXX twelfth

[15] Ezekiel 33:22 - Ezekiel 1:3 3:22 3:26-27 24:26-27 13:1 16:1, Luke 1:64

וַיְהִי דְבַר־יְהוָה אֵלַי לֵאמֹר	23	Then the word of the LORD came to me, saying:
בֶּן־אָדָם יֹשְׁבֵי הֶחֳרָבוֹת הָאֵלֶּה עַל־אַדְמַת יִשְׂרָאֵל אֹמְרִים לֵאמֹר אֶחָד הָיָה אַבְרָהָם וַיִּירַשׁ אֶת־הָאָרֶץ וַאֲנַחְנוּ רַבִּים לָנוּ נִתְּנָה הָאָרֶץ לְמוֹרָשָׁה	24[1]	'Son of man, they who inhabit those waste places in the land of Israel speak, saying: Abraham was one, and he inherited the land; but we are many; the land is given to us for inheritance.
לָכֵן אֱמֹר אֲלֵהֶם כֹּה־אָמַר אֲדֹנָי יְהוִֹה עַל־הַדָּם תֹּאכֵלוּ וְעֵינֵכֶם תִּשְׂאוּ אֶל־גִּלּוּלֵיכֶם וְדָם תִּשְׁפֹּכוּ וְהָאָרֶץ תִּירָשׁוּ	25[2]	*Why say to them: Thus says the Lord GOD. You eat with the blood, and lift up your eyes to your idols, and shed blood; and you shall possess the land[3]?*
עֲמַדְתֶּם עַל־חַרְבְּכֶם עֲשִׂיתֶן תּוֹעֵבָה וְאִישׁ אֶת־אֵשֶׁת רֵעֵהוּ טִמֵּאתֶם וְהָאָרֶץ תִּירָשׁוּ	26[4]	*You stand on your sword, you work abominations, and everyone defiles his neighbor's wife; and you shall possess the land[5]?*
כֹּה־תֹאמַר אֲלֵהֶם כֹּה־אָמַר אֲדֹנָי יְהוִֹה חַי־אָנִי אִם־לֹא אֲשֶׁר בֶּחֳרָבוֹת בַּחֶרֶב יִפֹּלוּ וַאֲשֶׁר עַל־פְּנֵי הַשָּׂדֶה לַחַיָּה נְתַתִּיו לְאָכְלוֹ וַאֲשֶׁר בַּמְּצָדוֹת וּבַמְּעָרוֹת בַּדֶּבֶר יָמוּתוּ	27[6]	Thus shall you say to them: Thus says the Lord GOD: As I live, surely those who are in the waste places shall fall by the sword, and he who is in the open field I will give to the beasts to be devoured, and those who are in the strongholds and in the caves shall die of the pestilence.
וְנָתַתִּי אֶת־הָאָרֶץ שְׁמָמָה וּמְשַׁמָּה וְנִשְׁבַּת גְּאוֹן עֻזָּהּ וְשָׁמְמוּ הָרֵי יִשְׂרָאֵל מֵאֵין עוֹבֵר	28[7]	And I will make the land more desolate, and the pride of her power shall cease; and the mountains of Israel shall be desolate, so that no one shall pass through.
וְיָדְעוּ כִּי־אֲנִי יְהוָה בְּתִתִּי אֶת־הָאָרֶץ שְׁמָמָה וּמְשַׁמָּה עַל כָּל־תּוֹעֲבֹתָם אֲשֶׁר עָשׂוּ	29[8]	Then they shall know I am the LORD, when I have made the land more desolate, because of all the abominations they have committed.
וְאַתָּה בֶן־אָדָם בְּנֵי עַמְּךָ הַנִּדְבָּרִים בְּךָ אֵצֶל הַקִּירוֹת וּבְפִתְחֵי הַבָּתִּים וְדִבֶּר־חַד אֶת־אַחַד אִישׁ אֶת־אָחִיו לֵאמֹר בֹּאוּ־נָא וְשִׁמְעוּ מָה הַדָּבָר הַיּוֹצֵא מֵאֵת יְהוָה	30[9]	And as for you, son of man, the children of your people who talk of you by the walls and in the doors of the houses, and speak one to another, everyone to his brother, saying: Come, please, and hear what is the word that comes forth from the LORD;

[1] Ezekiel 33:24 - 1 Thessalonians 5:3, Acts 7:5, Ecclesiastes.R 4:7, Esther.R 6:3, Ezekiel 5:3-4 11:15 9:27 10:2 12:4, Genesis.R 30:8 38:6 46:1 90:1 94:1, Isaiah 3:2, Jastrow 38b, Jeremiah 15:10 16:7, John 8:33 8:39, Leviticus.R 29:7, Luke 3:8, Matthew 3:9, Micah 3:11, Midrash Psalms 53:2 117:3, Midrash Tanchuma Lech Lecha 9, Midrash Tanchuma Shemot 17, Numbers.R 2:14 10:5 14:11, Pesikta de R'Kahana 23.7, Pesikta Rabbati 11:4 15: 21:12 40:5, Romans 4:12 9:7, Sifre Devarim Vaetchanan 31, Song of Songs.R 6:20 8:10, t.Sotah 6:9, z.Lech Lecha 85b
[2] Ezekiel 33:25 - 1 Samuel 14:32-14:34, Acts 15:20-15:21 15:29 21:25, Deuteronomy 4:19 12:16, Ezekiel 9:9 18:6 18:12 18:15 22:6 22:9 22:27, Genesis 9:4, Jeremiah 7:9-7:10 44:15-44:19, Leviticus 3:17 7:26-7:27 17:10-17:14 19:26, Psalms 24:4, Sifre Devarim {Vaetchanan} 31, z.Vaetchanan 269b
Ezekiel 33:25-26 - Sifre Devarim Vaetchanan 31, t.Sotah 6:9
[3] Missing in LXX
[4] Ezekiel 33:26 - 1 Kings 11:5-7, 1 Peter 4:3, 1 Samuel 2:30, Deuteronomy 4:25-26 29:17-22, Ezekiel 18:6 18:11-12 18:15 22:9-11, Genesis 3:40, Jeremiah 5:8-9, Joshua 23:15-16, Leviticus 18:25-30 20:13 20:22, Micah 2:1-2, Psalms 50:16-20 94:20-21, Revelation 21:8 21:27, Zephaniah 3:3
[5] Missing in LXX
[6] Ezekiel 33:27 - 1 Samuel 13:6 22:1 23:14 24:3, Ezekiel 5:12-5:17 6:11-6:14 9:24 15:4, Isaiah 2:19, Jeremiah 15:2-15:4 17:9 18:22 20:12, Judges 6:2, z.Vaetchanan 269b
[7] Ezekiel 33:28 - 2 Chronicles 12:21, Ezekiel 6:2-6:6 6:14 7:24 12:20 15:8 24:21 30:6-30:7 12:4 36:34-36:35, Isaiah 6:11, Jeremiah 9:12 16:16 1:11 20:2 20:6 20:22, Micah 7:13, Zechariah 7:13-7:14
[8] Ezekiel 33:29 - 2 Chronicles 36:14-17, 2 Kings 17:9-18, Exodus 14:18, Ezekiel 6:7 6:11 7:27 8:6-15 22:2-15 22:25-31 23:49 1:11 36:17-18, Jeremiah 5:1-9 5:25-31, Micah 6:9-12, Per Massorah: Soferim altered "Hashem" to "Adonai", Psalms 9:17 83:18-19, Zephaniah 3:1-4
[9] Ezekiel 33:30 - Isaiah 5:13 10:2, Jeremiah 11:18-11:19 18:18 23:35 42:1-6 18:20, Matthew 15:8 22:16-17

וְיָבֹ֣ואוּ אֵלֶ֣יךָ כִּמְבֹוא־עָ֗ם וְיֵשְׁב֤וּ לְפָנֶ֨יךָ֙ עַמִּ֔י	31[1]	and come to you as the people come, and sit before you as My people, and hear your words, but do not do them, for with their mouth they show much love, but their heart goes after their covetousness;
וְשָׁמְעוּ֙ אֶת־דְּבָרֶ֔יךָ וְאֹותָ֖ם לֹ֣א יַעֲשֹׂ֑וּ כִּֽי־עֲגָבִ֤ים בְּפִיהֶם֙ הֵ֣מָּה עֹשִׂ֔ים אַחֲרֵ֥י בִצְעָ֖ם לִבָּ֥ם הֹלֵֽךְ		
וְהִנְּךָ֤ לָהֶם֙ כְּשִׁ֣יר עֲגָבִ֔ים יְפֵ֥ה קֹ֖ול וּמֵטִ֣ב נַגֵּ֑ן	32[2]	and, lo, you are to them as a love song of one who has a pleasant voice, and can play well on an instrument; so they hear your words, but they do not do them
וְשָׁמְעוּ֙ אֶת־דְּבָרֶ֔יךָ וְעֹשִׂ֥ים אֵינָ֖ם אֹותָֽם		
וּבְבֹאָ֖הּ הִנֵּ֣ה בָאָ֑ה וְיָ֣דְע֔וּ כִּ֥י נָבִ֖יא הָיָ֥ה בְתֹוכָֽם	33[3]	when this comes to pass [behold, it comes] then they shall know that a prophet has been among them.'

Ezekiel – Chapter 34

וַיְהִ֥י דְבַר־יְהוָ֖ה אֵלַ֥י לֵאמֹֽר	1[4]	And the word of the LORD came to me, saying:
בֶּן־אָדָ֕ם הִנָּבֵ֖א עַל־רֹועֵ֣י יִשְׂרָאֵ֑ל הִנָּבֵ֣א וְאָמַרְתָּ֩ אֲלֵיהֶ֨ם לָרֹעִ֜ים כֹּ֥ה אָמַ֣ר ׀ אֲדֹנָ֣י יְהוִ֗ה הֹ֤וי רֹעֵֽי־יִשְׂרָאֵל֙ אֲשֶׁ֤ר הָיוּ֙ רֹעִ֣ים אֹותָ֔ם הֲלֹ֣וא הַצֹּ֔אן יִרְע֖וּ הָרֹעִֽים	2[5]	'Son of man, prophesy against the shepherds of Israel, prophesy, and say to them, to the shepherds: Thus says the Lord GOD: Woe to the shepherds of Israel who fed themselves! Should not the shepherds feed the sheep?
אֶת־הַחֵ֤לֶב תֹּאכֵ֨לוּ֙ וְאֶת־הַצֶּ֣מֶר תִּלְבָּ֔שׁוּ הַבְּרִיאָ֖ה תִּזְבָּ֑חוּ הַצֹּ֖אן לֹ֥א תִרְעֽוּ	3[6]	You ate the fat, and you clothed yourself with the wool, you killed the fatlings but you did not feed the sheep.
אֶֽת־הַנַּחְלֹות֩ לֹ֨א חִזַּקְתֶּ֜ם וְאֶת־הַחֹולָ֣ה לֹֽא־רִפֵּאתֶ֗ם וְלַנִּשְׁבֶּ֨רֶת֙ לֹ֣א חֲבַשְׁתֶּ֔ם וְאֶת־הַנִּדַּחַת֙ לֹ֣א הֲשֵׁבֹתֶ֔ם וְאֶת־הָאֹבֶ֖דֶת לֹ֣א בִקַּשְׁתֶּ֑ם וּבְחָזְקָ֛ה רְדִיתֶ֥ם אֹתָ֖ם וּבְפָֽרֶךְ	4[7]	You have not strengthened the weak, nor have you healed the sick, nor have you bound up broken, nor have you brought back what was driven away, nor have you sought the lost; but with force you ruled over them and with *rigor*[8].
וַתְּפוּצֶ֖ינָה מִבְּלִ֣י רֹעֶ֑ה וַתִּהְיֶ֧ינָה לְאָכְלָ֛ה לְכָל־חַיַּ֥ת הַשָּׂדֶ֖ה וַתְּפוּצֶֽינָה	5[9]	So they were scattered, because there was no shepherd; and they became food to all the beasts of the field, and were scattered.
יִשְׁגּ֤וּ צֹאנִי֙ בְּכָל־הֶ֣הָרִ֔ים וְעַ֖ל כָּל־גִּבְעָ֣ה רָמָ֑ה וְעַ֣ל כָּל־פְּנֵ֤י הָאָ֨רֶץ֙ נָפֹ֣צוּ צֹאנִ֔י וְאֵ֥ין דֹּורֵ֖שׁ וְאֵ֥ין מְבַקֵּֽשׁ	6[10]	My sheep wandered through all the mountains, and on every high hill; yes, on all the face of the earth My were sheep scattered, and there was no one who searched or looked.
לָכֵ֣ן רֹעִ֔ים שִׁמְע֖וּ אֶת־דְּבַר־יְהוָֽה	7[11]	Therefore, you shepherds, hear the word of the LORD:

[1] Ezekiel 33:31 - 1 John 3:17-3:18, 1 Timothy 6:9-6:10, Acts 10:33, b.Sotah 47b, Deuteronomy 5:28-29, Ein Yaakov Sotah:47b, Ephesians 5:5, Ezekiel 8:1 14:1 20:1-32 22:27, Isaiah 4:13 5:13, James 1:22-24 2:14-16, Jastrow 74b, Jeremiah 6:16-17 23:33-38 43:1-7 20:16, Luke 6:48-49 8:21 10:39 11:28 12:15-21 16:14, Matthew 6:24 7:24-27 13:22 19:22, Numbers.R 13:15-16, Psalms 78:36-37, Sifre Devarim {Haazinu Hashamayim} 308, Sifre Devarim Nitzavim 308, t.Sotah 14:8
[2] Ezekiel 33:32 - b.Succah 47b, John 5:35, Mark 4:16-4:17 6:20, Tanna Devei Eliyahu 5
[3] Ezekiel 33:33 - 1 Samuel 3:19-3:20, 2 Kings 5:8, Ezekiel 2:5 9:29, Jeremiah 4:9, Luke 10:11, Tanna Devei Eliyahu 5
[4] Ezekiel 34:1 - Apocalypse of Elijah 5:31
Ezekiel 34:1-27 - Haftarah Bechukosai [Teimon]
[5] Ezekiel 34:2 - 1 Peter 5:2-4, 2 Peter 2:3, 2 Samuel 5:2, Acts 20:26 20:29, Ezekiel 13:19 9:24 34:8-10, Isaiah 16:11, Jeremiah 2:8 3:15 10:21 12:10 23:1, John 10:1-2 10:11-12 21:15-17, Luke 12:42-46 20:46-47, Matthew 24:48-51, Micah 3:1-3 3:11-12, Midrash Tanchuma Vayishlach 7, Psalms 78:71-72, Romans 16:18, z.Vaetchanan 269b, Zechariah 11:17, Zephaniah 3:3-4
[6] Ezekiel 34:3 - 1 Kings 21:13-16, 2 Kings 21:16, Ezekiel 19:3 19:6 22:25-28 33:25-26, Isaiah 1:10 1:15 56:11-12, Jeremiah 2:30 22:17, Micah 3:1-3:3, Zephaniah 3:3
[7] Ezekiel 34:4 - 1 Peter 5:2-3, 2 Corinthians 1:24, Exodus 1:13-14, Ezekiel 10:16, Hebrews 12:12, Isaiah 8:10, James 5:1-6, Jeremiah 8:22 22:13, Luke 15:4-6, Matthew 9:36 10:6 18:12-13 21:35 24:49, Midrash Tanchuma Vayishlach 7, Revelation 13:14-17 17:5-6, Zechariah 11:15-16
[8] LXX *labor*
[9] Ezekiel 34:5 - 1 Kings 22:17, 2 Chronicles 18:16, Acts 20:29-20:31, Ezekiel 9:21 9:28 10:6 10:8 10:28, Isaiah 8:9, Jeremiah 12:9-12:12 23:2 50:6-50:7 2:17, John 10:2, Matthew 9:36, Numbers 3:17, Zechariah 10:2-10:3 13:7
[10] Ezekiel 34:6 - 1 Peter 2:25, b.Sotah 49a, Ezekiel 7:16, Hebrews 11:37-38, Jeremiah 5:1 13:16 40:11-12, John 10:16, Psalms 22:5
[11] Ezekiel 34:7 - Ezekiel 10:9, Isaiah 1:10, Jeremiah 13:13 13:18 22:2-3, Luke 11:39-54, Malachi 2:1, Matthew 23:13-36, Micah 3:8-9, Psalms 82:1-7

חַי־אָנִי נְאֻם אֲדֹנָי יְהוִה אִם־לֹא יַעַן הֱיוֹת־צֹאנִי
לָבַז וַתִּהְיֶינָה צֹאנִי לְאָכְלָה לְכָל־חַיַּת הַשָּׂדֶה
מֵאֵין רֹעֶה וְלֹא־דָרְשׁוּ רֹעַי אֶת־צֹאנִי וַיִּרְעוּ
הָרֹעִים אוֹתָם וְאֶת־צֹאנִי לֹא רָעוּ

8[1] As I live, says the Lord GOD, surely since My sheep became prey, and My sheep became food for all the beasts of the field, because there was no shepherd, nor did My shepherds search for My sheep, but the shepherds fed themselves, and did not feed My sheep;

לָכֵן הָרֹעִים שִׁמְעוּ דְּבַר־יְהוָה

9 *Therefore, shepherds, hear the word of the LORD[2]:*

כֹּה־אָמַר אֲדֹנָי יְהוִה אֶל־הָרֹעִים וְדָרַשְׁתִּי
אֶת־צֹאנִי מִיָּדָם וְהִשְׁבַּתִּים מֵרְעוֹת צֹאן וְלֹא־יִרְעוּ
עוֹד הָרֹעִים אוֹתָם וְהִצַּלְתִּי צֹאנִי מִפִּיהֶם וְלֹא־
תִהְיֶיןָ לָהֶם לְאָכְלָה

10[3] Thus says the Lord GOD: Behold, I am against the shepherds; and I will require My sheep at their hand, and cause them to cease from feeding the sheep; nor shall the shepherds feed themselves any longer; and I will deliver My sheep from their mouth, so they may not be their food.

כִּי כֹּה אָמַר אֲדֹנָי יְהוִה הִנְנִי־אָנִי וְדָרַשְׁתִּי אֶת־
צֹאנִי וּבִקַּרְתִּים

11[4] For thus says the Lord GOD: Behold, *I am here, and I will search for My sheep, and seek them out[5]*.

כְּבַקָּרַת רֹעֶה עֶדְרוֹ בְּיוֹם־הֱיוֹתוֹ בְתוֹךְ־צֹאנוֹ
נִפְרָשׁוֹת כֵּן אֲבַקֵּר אֶת־צֹאנִי וְהִצַּלְתִּי אֶתְהֶם
מִכָּל־הַמְּקוֹמֹת אֲשֶׁר נָפֹצוּ שָׁם בְּיוֹם עָנָן וַעֲרָפֶל

12[6] As a shepherd seeks out his flock in the day he is among his sheep that are separated, so will I seek out My sheep; and I will deliver them from all places in which they were scattered in the day of clouds and thick darkness.

וְהוֹצֵאתִים מִן־הָעַמִּים וְקִבַּצְתִּים מִן־הָאֲרָצוֹת
וַהֲבִיאֹתִים אֶל־אַדְמָתָם וּרְעִיתִים אֶל־הָרֵי
יִשְׂרָאֵל בָּאֲפִיקִים וּבְכֹל מוֹשְׁבֵי הָאָרֶץ

13[7] And I will bring them out from the nations, and gather them from the countries, and will bring them into their own land; and I will feed them on the mountains of Israel, by the streams, and in all the habitable places of the country.

בְּמִרְעֶה־טּוֹב אֶרְעֶה אֹתָם וּבְהָרֵי מְרוֹם־יִשְׂרָאֵל
יִהְיֶה נְוֵהֶם שָׁם תִּרְבַּצְנָה בְּנָוֶה טּוֹב וּמִרְעֶה שָׁמֵן
תִּרְעֶינָה אֶל־הָרֵי יִשְׂרָאֵל

14[8] I will feed them in a good pasture, and their fold shall be on the high mountains of Israel; there they shall lie down in a good fold, and in a fat pasture they shall they on the mountains of Israel.

אֲנִי אֶרְעֶה צֹאנִי וַאֲנִי אַרְבִּיצֵם נְאֻם אֲדֹנָי יְהוִה

15[9] I will feed My sheep, and I will cause them to *lie down[10]*, says the Lord GOD.

אֶת־הָאֹבֶדֶת אֲבַקֵּשׁ וְאֶת־הַנִּדַּחַת אָשִׁיב
וְלַנִּשְׁבֶּרֶת אֶחֱבֹשׁ וְאֶת־הַחוֹלָה אֲחַזֵּק וְאֶת־
הַשְּׁמֵנָה וְאֶת־הַחֲזָקָה אַשְׁמִיד אֶרְעֶנָּה בְמִשְׁפָּט

16[11] I will seek what was lost, and will bring back what was driven away, and will bind up the broken, and will strengthen the sick; and I will destroy the fat and the strong, I will feed them in justice.

---

[1] Ezekiel 34:8 - 1 Corinthians 9:15, 2 Peter 2:13, Acts 20:33, Ezekiel 34:2-34:3 34:5-34:6 10:10 10:18 10:31, Jude 1:12

[2] LXX *For this cause, O shepherds*

[3] Ezekiel 34:10 - 1 Peter 3:12, 1 Samuel 2:29-36, Exodus.R 31:11, Ezekiel 3:18 3:20 5:8 13:8 21:8 33:6-8 10:2 10:8 10:22 11:3, Hebrews 13:17, Jeremiah 13:18-20 21:13 15:6 2:31 52:9-11 52:24-27, Nahum 2:14, Psalms 23:5 72:12-14 102:20-21, z.Vaetchanan 269b, Zechariah 10:3

[4] Ezekiel 34:11 - Deuteronomy 8:39, Ezekiel 5:8 6:3, Genesis 6:17, Hosea 5:14, Isaiah 40:10-40:11 21:12 24:15 3:12 8:8, Jeremiah 23:3 7:9, John 10:16, Leviticus 2:28, Luke 19:10, Matthew 13:11-13:12, Psalms 23:1-23:3 80:2 119:176, z.Vaetchanan 269b

[5] LXX *I will seek out my sheep, and will visit them*

[6] Ezekiel 34:12 - 1 Samuel 17:34-17:35, Acts 2:19-2:21, Amos 5:18-5:20, Ezekiel 6:3, Isaiah 16:11 2:10, Jeremiah 13:16 7:11, Joel 2:1-2:3, John 10:11-10:12, Luke 15:4-15:6 19:10, Midrash Tanchuma Vayishlach 7, Numbers.R 16:25, Zephaniah 1:15

[7] Ezekiel 34:13 - Amos 9:14, Ezekiel 11:17 20:41 28:25-28:26 34:18-34:25 12:24 37:21-37:22 14:8 15:27, Isaiah 11:11-11:16 65:9-10 66:19-20, Jeremiah 23:3-4 23:8 6:3 6:18 7:9 8:37, Micah 7:14-15, Psalms 10:47, Saadia Opinions 8:8, Zephaniah 3:19-20

[8] Ezekiel 34:14 - Ezekiel 10:27 36:29-30, Isaiah 1:6 30:23-24 16:11, Leviticus.R 27:1, Jeremiah 7:26 31:13-15 33:12-13, Genesis.R 33:1, Midrash Tanchuma Emor 5, John 10:9, Psalms 23:1-2 31:9-11, Midrash Proverbs 27, Midrash Psalms 24:5, Numbers.R 1:1, Pesikta de R'Kahana 9.1, Revelation 7:16

Ezekiel 34:14-16 - Apocryphon of Ezekiel Fragment 5

[9] Ezekiel 34:15 - Ezekiel 10:23, Hosea 2:18, Isaiah 11:6-11:7 3:10 65:9-65:10, Jeremiah 3:15, John 21:15, Midrash Psalms 23:7 24:5, Pesikta Rabbati 34:2, Psalms 23:1-23:2, Song of Songs 1:7-1:8, Zephaniah 3:13

[10] LXX *rest; and they shall know that I am the LORD*

[11] Ezekiel 34:16 - Amos 4:1-4:3, Deuteronomy 32:15, Ezekiel 34:4 34:11 39:18, Isaiah 5:17 10:16 40:11 49:26 61:1-61:3, Jeremiah 9:16 10:24 23:15 50:11, Luke 5:31-5:32 15:4-15:7 19:10, Mark 2:17, Matthew 15:24 18:10-18:14, Micah 4:6-4:7 7:14

Hebrew	Verse	English
וְאַתֵּ֣נָה צֹאנִ֔י כֹּ֤ה אָמַר֙ אֲדֹנָ֣י יְהוִ֔ה הִנְנִ֧י שֹׁפֵ֛ט בֵּין־שֶׂ֥ה לָשֶׂ֖ה לָאֵילִ֥ים וְלָעַתּוּדִֽים	17[1]	And as for you, O My flock, thus says the Lord GOD: Behold, I judge between *cattle and cattle*[2], the rams and the male goats.
הַמְעַ֣ט מִכֶּ֗ם הַמִּרְעֶ֤ה הַטּוֹב֙ תִּרְע֔וּ וְיֶ֨תֶר֙ מִרְעֵיכֶ֔ם תִּרְמְס֖וּ בְּרַגְלֵיכֶ֑ם וּמִשְׁקַע־מַ֣יִם תִּשְׁתּ֔וּ וְאֵת֙ הַנּוֹתָרִ֔ים בְּרַגְלֵיכֶ֖ם תִּרְפֹּשֽׂוּן	18[3]	It seems it is a small thing for you to have fed on the good pasture, but must you tread down the residue of your pasture with your feet? And to have drunk in the still waters, but must you foul the residue with your feet?
וְצֹאנִ֑י מִרְמַ֤ס רַגְלֵיכֶם֙ תִּרְעֶ֔ינָה וּמִרְפַּ֥שׂ רַגְלֵיכֶ֖ם תִּשְׁתֶּֽינָה	19[4]	And as for My sheep, they eat what you have trodden with your feet, and they drink what you have fouled with your feet.
לָכֵ֗ן כֹּ֥ה אָמַ֛ר אֲדֹנָ֥י יְהוִ֖ה אֲלֵיהֶ֑ם הִנְנִי־אָ֕נִי וְשָֽׁפַטְתִּי֙ בֵּֽין־שֶׂ֣ה בִרְיָ֔ה וּבֵ֥ין שֶׂ֖ה רָזָֽה	20[5]	Therefore, thus says the Lord GOD to them: Behold, I, I, will judge between the *fat cattle and the lean cattle*[6].
יַ֗עַן בְּצַ֤ד וּבְכָתֵף֙ תֶּהְדֹּ֔פוּ וּבְקַרְנֵיכֶ֥ם תְּנַגְּח֖וּ כָּל־הַנַּחְל֑וֹת עַ֣ד אֲשֶׁ֧ר הֲפִיצוֹתֶ֛ם אוֹתָ֖נָה אֶל־הַחֽוּצָה	21[7]	Because you thrust with side and with shoulder, and push all the weak with your horns, *until you scattered them abroad*[8];
וְהוֹשַׁעְתִּ֣י לְצֹאנִ֔י וְלֹֽא־תִהְיֶ֥ינָה ע֖וֹד לָבַ֑ז וְשָׁפַטְתִּ֕י בֵּ֥ין שֶׂ֖ה לָשֶֽׂה	22[9]	Therefore, I will save My flock, and they shall no longer be a prey; and I will judge between *cattle and cattle*[10].
וַהֲקִמֹתִ֨י עֲלֵיהֶ֜ם רֹעֶ֣ה אֶחָ֗ד וְרָעָ֤ה אֶתְהֶן֙ אֵ֚ת עַבְדִּ֣י דָוִ֔יד ה֥וּא יִרְעֶ֣ה אֹתָ֔ם וְהֽוּא־יִהְיֶ֥ה לָהֶ֖ן לְרֹעֶֽה	23[11]	And I will set up one shepherd over them, and he shall feed them, My servant David; *he shall feed them*[12], and he shall be their shepherd.
וַאֲנִ֣י יְהוָ֗ה אֶהְיֶ֤ה לָהֶם֙ לֵֽאלֹהִ֔ים וְעַבְדִּ֥י דָוִ֖ד נָשִׂ֣יא בְתוֹכָ֑ם אֲנִ֥י יְהוָ֖ה דִּבַּֽרְתִּי	24[13]	And I, the LORD, will be their God, and My servant David prince among them; I, the LORD, have spoken.
וְכָרַתִּ֨י לָהֶ֜ם בְּרִ֣ית שָׁל֗וֹם וְהִשְׁבַּתִּ֤י חַיָּֽה־רָעָה֙ מִן־הָאָ֔רֶץ וְיָשְׁב֤וּ בַמִּדְבָּר֙ לָבֶ֔טַח וְיָשְׁנ֖וּ בַּיְּעָרִֽים	25[14]	And I will make with them a covenant of peace, and will cause evil beasts to disappear from the land; and they shall dwell safely in the wilderness, and sleep in the woods.
וְנָתַתִּ֥י אוֹתָ֛ם וּסְבִיב֥וֹת גִּבְעָתִ֖י בְּרָכָ֑ה וְהוֹרַדְתִּ֤י הַגֶּ֨שֶׁם֙ בְּעִתּ֔וֹ גִּשְׁמֵ֥י בְרָכָ֖ה יִהְיֽוּ	26[15]	And I will make them and the places around My hill a blessing; and I will cause the shower to come down in its season; there shall be showers of blessing.

[1] Ezekiel 34:17 - Ezekiel 20:37-38 34:20-22, Matthew 25:32-33, Midrash Psalms 78:21, Numbers.R 20:19, z.Vaetchanan 269b, Zechariah 10:3

[2] LXX *sheep and sheep*

[3] Ezekiel 34:18 - 2 Samuel 7:19, Exodus.R 31:1, Ezekiel 16:20 16:47 32:2 34:2-3, Genesis 30:15, Isaiah 7:13, Luke 11:52, Matthew 15:6-9 23:13, Micah 2:2, Numbers 16:9 16:13

[4] Ezekiel 34:19 - Jastrow 846a, Pirkei de R'Eliezer 47

[5] Ezekiel 34:20 - Exodus.R 30:17, Ezekiel 34:10 34:17, Matthew 25:31-46, Psalms 22:13-17, z.Vaetchanan 269b

[6] LXX *strong sheep and the weak sheep*

[7] Ezekiel 34:21 - Daniel 8:3-10, Deuteronomy 33:17, Ezekiel 34:3-5, Luke 13:14-16, z.Terumah 162b, Zechariah 11:5 11:16-17

[8] LXX *and you cruelly treated all the sick*

[9] Ezekiel 34:22- Ezekiel 34:10, Jeremiah 23:2-23:3, Midrash Psalms 29:1 119:55, Psalms 72:12-72:14, Zechariah 11:7-11:9

[10] LXX *ram and ram*

[11] Ezekiel 34:23 - 1 Peter 2:25 5:4, Ecclesiastes 12:11, Ezekiel 37:24-37:25, Hebrews 13:20, Hosea 3:5, Isaiah 11:1 40:11 55:3-55:4, Jeremiah 23:4-23:6 30:9, John 10:11, Micah 5:3-5:6, Midrash Psalms 29:1, Numbers.R 20:19, Revelation 22:16, Zechariah 13:7

[12] Missing in LXX

[13] Ezekiel 34:24 - 1 Corinthians 15:25, Acts 5:31, Ephesians 1:21-22, Exodus 29:45-46, Ezekiel 34:30-31 36:28 37:23 37:27 39:22, Hebrews 2:9-10, Isaiah 9:7-8 42:3-2:3, Jeremiah 23:5-6 30:9 31:2 31:34 32:38 33:15-17, Joshua 5:13-15, Luke 1:31-33, Matthew 28:18, Micah 5:3, Philippians 2:9-11, Psalms 2:6, Revelation 19:13-16 21:3, Zechariah 13:9

[14] Ezekiel 34:25 - Ezekiel 34:28 37:26, Hebrews 13:20, Hosea 2:18-2:25, Isaiah 11:6-11:9 35:9 55:3, Jeremiah 23:6 31:32-31:34 33:16, Job 5:22, Leviticus 26:6, Psalms 4:9, Sifre Devarim Vezot Habracha 352 356, Zechariah 6:13
Ezekiel 34:25-31 - Maamad [Thursday]

[15] Ezekiel 34:26 - Deuteronomy 11:13-15 28:12, Ezekiel 20:40, Genesis 12:2, Isaiah 2:2-4 19:24 32:15 32:20 44:3 56:7, Leviticus 26:4, Leviticus.R 35:12, Malachi 3:10, Micah 4:1-2, Psalms 2:6 68:10 68:17 132:14-16 133:3, Sifre Devarim Ekev 42, Zechariah 8:13 8:23

וְנָתַן עֵץ הַשָּׂדֶה אֶת־פִּרְיוֹ וְהָאָרֶץ תִּתֵּן יְבוּלָהּ וְהָיוּ עַל־אַדְמָתָם לָבֶטַח וְיָדְעוּ כִּי־אֲנִי יְהֹוָה בְּשִׁבְרִי אֶת־מֹטוֹת עֻלָּם וְהִצַּלְתִּים מִיַּד הָעֹבְדִים בָּהֶם

27[1] And the tree of the field shall yield its fruit, and the earth shall yield her produce, and they shall be safe in their land; and they shall know that I am the LORD, when I have broken the bars of their yoke, and have delivered them from the hand of those who made them bondsmen.

וְלֹא־יִהְיוּ עוֹד בַּז לַגּוֹיִם וְחַיַּת הָאָרֶץ לֹא תֹאכְלֵם וְיָשְׁבוּ לָבֶטַח וְאֵין מַחֲרִיד

28[2] And they shall no longer be prey to the nations, nor shall the beast of the earth devour them; but they shall dwell safely, and no one shall make them afraid.

וַהֲקִמֹתִי לָהֶם מַטָּע לְשֵׁם וְלֹא־יִהְיוּ עוֹד אֲסֻפֵי רָעָב בָּאָרֶץ וְלֹא־יִשְׂאוּ עוֹד כְּלִמַּת הַגּוֹיִם

29[3] And I will raise them up a *plantation for renown*[4], and they shall no longer be consumed with hunger in the land, nor bear the shame of the nations any more.

וְיָדְעוּ כִּי אֲנִי יְהֹוָה אֱלֹהֵיהֶם אִתָּם וְהֵמָּה עַמִּי בֵּית יִשְׂרָאֵל נְאֻם אֲדֹנָי יְהֹוִה

30[5] And they shall know that I, the LORD, their God is with them, and that they, the house of Israel, are My people, says the Lord GOD.

וְאַתֵּן צֹאנִי צֹאן מַרְעִיתִי אָדָם אַתֶּם אֲנִי אֱלֹהֵיכֶם נְאֻם אֲדֹנָי יְהֹוִה

31[6] And you My sheep, the sheep of My pasture, are men, and I am your God, says the Lord GOD.'

Ezekiel – Chapter 35

וְאַתֵּן צֹאנִי צֹאן מַרְעִיתִי אָדָם אַתֶּם אֲנִי אֱלֹהֵיכֶם נְאֻם אֲדֹנָי יְהֹוִה

1[7] Moreover the word of the LORD came to me, saying:

בֶּן־אָדָם שִׂים פָּנֶיךָ עַל־הַר שֵׂעִיר וְהִנָּבֵא עָלָיו

2[8] 'Son of man, set your face against mount Seir, and prophesy against it,

וְאָמַרְתָּ לּוֹ כֹּה אָמַר אֲדֹנָי יְהֹוִה הִנְנִי אֵלֶיךָ הַר־שֵׂעִיר וְנָטִיתִי יָדִי עָלֶיךָ וּנְתַתִּיךָ שְׁמָמָה וּמְשַׁמָּה

3[9] and say to it: Thus says the Lord GOD: Behold, I am against you, O mount Seir, and I will stretch out My hand against you, and I will make you most desolate.

עָרֶיךָ חָרְבָּה אָשִׂים וְאַתָּה שְׁמָמָה תִהְיֶה וְיָדַעְתָּ כִּי־אֲנִי יְהֹוָה

4[10] I will lay your cities waste, and you shall be desolate; and you shall know I am the LORD.

יַעַן הֱיוֹת לְךָ אֵיבַת עוֹלָם וַתַּגֵּר אֶת־בְּנֵי־יִשְׂרָאֵל עַל־יְדֵי־חָרֶב בְּעֵת אֵידָם בְּעֵת עֲוֹן קֵץ

5[11] Because you have *had an old hatred*[12], and have hurled the children of Israel unto the power of the sword in the time of their calamity, in the time of the iniquity of the end;

---

[1] Ezekiel 34:27 - Ezekiel 33:29 34:10 39:28 47:12, Isaiah 4:2 9:5 10:27 14:2-3 35:1-2 52:2-3 61:3, Jeremiah 2:20 25:14 27:7 30:8, John 15:5-8, Leviticus 26:4 26:13, Psalms 85:13 92:13-15

[2] Ezekiel 34:28 - Ezekiel 34:8 34:25 34:29 36:4 36:15 39:26, Jeremiah 30:10 46:27

[3] Ezekiel 34:29 - Ezekiel 34:26-27 36:3-6 36:15 36:29, Isaiah 4:2 9:7 11:1-6 49:9-10 53:2 60:21 61:3, Jeremiah 23:5 33:15, Psalms 72:17, Revelation 7:16, Zechariah 3:8 6:12

[4] LXX *plant of peace*

[5] Ezekiel 34:30 - Ezekiel 14:11 16:62 34:24 37:27, Isaiah 8:9-8:10, Matthew 1:23 28:20, Psalms 46:8 46:12, z.Vaetchanan 269b

[6] Ezekiel 34:31 - 1 Peter 5:2-5:3, Acts 20:28, b.Avodah Zara [Tosefot] 3a, b.Bava Batra [Tosefot] 58a, b.Bava Metzia 114b, b.Kereitot 6b, b.Sanhedrin [Rashi] 58b, b.Yevamot 61a, Deuteronomy.R 1:2, Ecclesiastes.R 3:21, Esther.R 7:11, Exodus.R 24:3 34:3 40:1, Ezekiel 36:38, Genesis.R 34:13 53:3 65:14 75:6 78:13, Isaiah 40:11, Jastrow 1417b, Jeremiah 23:1, John 10:11 10:16 10:26-10:30 20:15-20:17, Lamentations.R 1:52, Leviticus.R 5:3 17:1, Luke 12:32, Micah 7:14, Midrash Proverbs 27, Midrash Psalms 23:1 24:5 78:17 145:1, Midrash Tanchuma Ki Tissa 4, Midrash Tanchuma Vayakhel 3, Midrash Tanchuma Vayishlach 1, mt.Hilchot Tumat Meit 1:13, Numbers.R 10:2 12:14, Pesikta de R'Kahana 2.3, Pesikta de R'Kahana 16.9, Pesikta Rabbati 10:6 26:1/2 47:4, Psalms 78:52 80:2 95:7 100:3, Song of Songs.R 2:45, z.Naso 147a, z.Shemot 21a, z.Vaera 25a, z.Yitro 86a

[7] Ezekiel 35:1 - 2 Peter 1:21, Ezekiel 21:6 22:1 34:1

[8] Ezekiel 35:2 - 2 Chronicles 20:10 20:22-23 25:11-14, Amos 1:11-12, Deuteronomy 2:5, Ephesians 6:19, Ezekiel 6:2 21:2 21:7 25:2 25:8 25:12-14 32:29, Genesis 32:4 36:8-9, Isaiah 34:1-17 50:7 63:1-6, Jeremiah 9:26-27 49:7-22, Joshua 24:4, Lamentations 4:21-22, Obadiah 1:1 1:10-14, Psalms 83:4-83:19

[9] Ezekiel 35:3 - Ezekiel 5:8 5:15 6:14 21:8 25:13 29:3 29:10 35:7, Jeremiah 6:12 15:6 21:13 51:25, Nahum 2:14 3:5, z.Vaetchanan 269b

[10] Ezekiel 35:4 - Exodus 9:14 14:4, Ezekiel 6:6-6:7 35:9 35:12, Joel 4:19, Malachi 1:3-1:4

[11] Ezekiel 35:5 - Amos 1:11, Daniel 9:24, Ezekiel 21:30 21:34 25:12 25:15 35:12, Genesis 27:41-27:42, Jeremiah 18:21, Obadiah 1:10-1:16, Psalms 137:7

[12] LXX *been a perpetual enemy*

לָכֵן חַי־אָנִי נְאֻם אֲדֹנָי יֱהֹוִה כִּי־לְדָם אֶעֶשְׂךָ וְדָם יִרְדְּפֶךָ אִם־לֹא דָם שָׂנֵאתָ וְדָם יִרְדְּפֶךָ

6[1] Therefore, as I live, says the Lord GOD, I will prepare you for blood, and blood shall pursue you; surely you have hated your own blood, therefore, blood shall pursue you.

וְנָתַתִּי אֶת־הַר שֵׂעִיר לְשִׁמְמָה וּשְׁמָמָה וְהִכְרַתִּי מִמֶּנּוּ עֹבֵר וָשָׁב

7[2] Thus I will make mount Seir *most desolate, and cut off from it he who passes through and he who returns*[3].

וּמִלֵּאתִי אֶת־הָרָיו חֲלָלָיו גִּבְעוֹתֶיךָ וְגֵאוֹתֶיךָ וְכָל־אֲפִיקֶיךָ חַלְלֵי־חֶרֶב יִפְּלוּ בָהֶם

8[4] And I will fill *his mountains with his slain; in your hills and in your valleys and in all your streams they shall fall who are slain with the sword*[5].

שִׁמְמוֹת עוֹלָם אֶתֶּנְךָ וְעָרֶיךָ לֹא 'תֵישַׁבְנָה' "תָּשֹׁבְנָה" וִידַעְתֶּם כִּי־אֲנִי יְהֹוָה

9[6] I will make you perpetual desolations, and your cities shall not return; and you shall know that I am the LORD.

יַעַן אֲמָרְךָ אֶת־שְׁנֵי הַגּוֹיִם וְאֶת־שְׁתֵּי הָאֲרָצוֹת לִי תִהְיֶינָה וִירֵשְׁנוּהָ וַיהֹוָה שָׁם הָיָה

10[7] Because you have said: These two nations and these two countries shall be mine, and we will possess it; but the LORD was there;

לָכֵן חַי־אָנִי נְאֻם אֲדֹנָי יֱהֹוִה וְעָשִׂיתִי כְּאַפְּךָ וּכְקִנְאָתְךָ אֲשֶׁר עָשִׂיתָה מִשִּׂנְאָתֶיךָ בָּם וְנוֹדַעְתִּי בָם כַּאֲשֶׁר אֶשְׁפְּטֶךָ

11[8] Therefore, as I live, says the Lord GOD, I will do according to your anger and according to your envy, which you have used out of your hatred against them; and I will make Myself known among them, when I shall judge you.

וְיָדַעְתָּ כִּי־אֲנִי יְהֹוָה שָׁמַעְתִּי אֶת־כָּל־נָאָצוֹתֶיךָ אֲשֶׁר אָמַרְתָּ עַל־הָרֵי יִשְׂרָאֵל לֵאמֹר 'שָׁמֵמָה' "שָׁמֵמוּ" לָנוּ נִתְּנוּ לְאָכְלָה

12[9] And you shall know that I, the LORD, have heard all the blasphemies you have spoken *against the mountains of Israel*[10], saying: They are laid desolate, they are ours to devour.

וַתַּגְדִּילוּ עָלַי בְּפִיכֶם וְהַעְתַּרְתֶּם עָלַי דִּבְרֵיכֶם אֲנִי שָׁמָעְתִּי

13[11] And you have *magnified yourselves against Me with your mouth, and have multiplied your words against Me*[12]; I have heard it.

כֹּה אָמַר אֲדֹנָי יֱהֹוִה כִּשְׂמֹחַ כָּל־הָאָרֶץ שְׁמָמָה אֶעֱשֶׂה־לָּךְ

14[13] Thus says the Lord GOD: When the whole earth rejoices, I will make you desolate.

כְּשִׂמְחָתְךָ לְנַחְלַת בֵּית־יִשְׂרָאֵל עַל אֲשֶׁר־שָׁמֵמָה כֵּן אֶעֱשֶׂה־לָּךְ שְׁמָמָה תִהְיֶה הַר־שֵׂעִיר וְכָל־אֱדוֹם כֻּלָּהּ וְיָדְעוּ כִּי־אֲנִי יְהֹוָה

15[14] *As you rejoiced over the inheritance of the house of Israel, because it was desolate, so I will do to you; you shall be desolate, O mount Seir, and all Edom, all of it*[15]; and they shall know that I am the LORD.

---

[1] Ezekiel 35:6 - Genesis.R 63:13, Isaiah 63:2-63:6, Mas.Kallah Rabbati 7:1, Matthew 7:2, Mekhilta de R'Shimon bar Yochai Amalek 44:3, Mekilta de R'Ishmael Amalek 1:176, Midrash Tanchuma Beshallach 28, Numbers.R 4:8, Obadiah 1:15, Psalms 109:16-17, Revelation 16:5-7 18:6 18:24 19:2-3

[2] Ezekiel 35:7 - 2 Chronicles 15:5-15:6, Ezekiel 29:11 33:28 35:3 35:9, Judges 5:6-5:7

[3] LXX *a waste, and desolate, and I will destroy from off it men and cattle*

[4] Ezekiel 35:8 - Ezekiel 31:12 32:4-32:5 39:4-39:5, Isaiah 34:2-34:7

[5] LXX *your hills and your valleys with slain men, and in all your plains there shall fall in you men slain with the sword*

[6] Ezekiel 35:9 - Ezekiel 6:7 7:4 7:9 25:13 35:4 36:11, Jeremiah 49:13 49:17-49:18, Malachi 1:3-1:4, Zephaniah 2:9

[7] Ezekiel 35:10 - Ezekiel 36:2 36:5 48:35, Genesis.R 67:8, Isaiah 12:6 31:9, Jeremiah 49:1, Midrash Psalms 14:2, Obadiah 1:13, Psalms 48:2-48:4 76:2 83:5-83:13 132:13-132:14, Zechariah 2:5, Zephaniah 3:15

[8] Ezekiel 35:11 - Amos 1:11, Ezekiel 25:14, James 2:13, Matthew 7:2, Psalms 9:17 73:17-18 137:7

[9] Ezekiel 35:12 - Ezekiel 6:7 35:9 36:2, Jeremiah 50:7, Psalms 83:13 94:9-94:10

[10] Missing in LXX

[11] Ezekiel 35:13 - 1 Samuel 2:3, 2 Chronicles 32:15 32:19, 2 Kings 19:28, 2 Peter 2:18, b.Taanit 20a, Daniel 11:36, Ecclesiastes 10:14, Exodus 16:12, Ezekiel 35:12, Isaiah 10:13-10:19 36:20 37:10 37:23 37:29, Jeremiah 29:23, Job 34:37 35:16, Jude 1:15, Malachi 3:13, Numbers 14:27, Numbers.R 11:1, Psalms 73:8-73:9, Revelation 13:5-13:6

[12] LXX *spoken swelling words against me with your mouth*

[13] Ezekiel 35:14 - Isaiah 14:7-8 65:13-15, Jeremiah 51:48, Midrash Psalms 95:1, z.Vaetchanan 269b

[14] Ezekiel 35:15 - Ezekiel 35:3-35:4 35:9 36:2-36:5 39:6-39:7, Isaiah 34:5-34:6, Jeremiah 50:11, Lamentations 4:21, Mark 3:8, Obadiah 1:12 1:15, Proverbs 17:5, Psalms 137:7

[15] LXX *You shall be desert, O mount Seir, and all Idumea; and it shall be utterly consumed*

Ezekiel – Chapter 36

וְאַתָּה בֶן־אָדָם הִנָּבֵא אֶל־הָרֵי יִשְׂרָאֵל וְאָמַרְתָּ הָרֵי יִשְׂרָאֵל שִׁמְעוּ דְּבַר־יְהוָה

1[1] And you, son of man, prophesy to the mountains of Israel, and say: You mountains of Israel, hear the word of the LORD.

כֹּה אָמַר אֲדֹנָי יְהוִה יַעַן אָמַר הָאוֹיֵב עֲלֵיכֶם הֶאָח וּבָמוֹת עוֹלָם לְמוֹרָשָׁה הָיְתָה לָּנוּ

2[2] Thus says the Lord GOD: Because the enemy has said against you: Aha! The ancient high places are ours in possession;

לָכֵן הִנָּבֵא וְאָמַרְתָּ כֹּה אָמַר אֲדֹנָי יְהוִה יַעַן בְּיַעַן שַׁמּוֹת וְשָׁאֹף אֶתְכֶם מִסָּבִיב לִהְיוֹתְכֶם מוֹרָשָׁה לִשְׁאֵרִית הַגּוֹיִם וַתֵּעֲלוּ עַל־שְׂפַת לָשׁוֹן וְדִבַּת־עָם

3[3] Therefore prophesy, and say: Thus says the Lord GOD: *Because, because they have made you desolate, and swallowed you on every side*[4], so you might be a possession to the rest of the nations, and you are taken up in the lips of talkers, and the evil report of the people;

לָכֵן הָרֵי יִשְׂרָאֵל שִׁמְעוּ דְּבַר־אֲדֹנָי יְהוִה כֹּה־אָמַר אֲדֹנָי יְהוִה לֶהָרִים וְלַגְּבָעוֹת לָאֲפִיקִים וְלַגֵּאָיוֹת וְלֶחֳרָבוֹת הַשֹּׁמְמוֹת וְלֶעָרִים הַנֶּעֱזָבוֹת אֲשֶׁר הָיוּ לְבַז וּלְלַעַג לִשְׁאֵרִית הַגּוֹיִם אֲשֶׁר מִסָּבִיב

4[5] Therefore, mountains of Israel, hear the word of the Lord GOD: Thus says the Lord GOD to the mountains and to the hills, to the streams and to the valleys, to the desolate wastes and to the forsaken cities that became prey and a scorn to the residue of the surrounding nations;

לָכֵן כֹּה־אָמַר אֲדֹנָי יְהוִה אִם־לֹא בְּאֵשׁ קִנְאָתִי דִבַּרְתִּי עַל־שְׁאֵרִית הַגּוֹיִם וְעַל־אֱדוֹם כֻּלָּא אֲשֶׁר נָתְנוּ־אֶת־אַרְצִי לָהֶם לְמוֹרָשָׁה בְּשִׂמְחַת כָּל־לֵבָב בִּשְׁאָט נֶפֶשׁ לְמַעַן מִגְרָשָׁהּ לָבַז

5[6] Therefore thus says the Lord GOD: Surely in the fire of My jealousy I have spoken against the residue of the nations, and against all Edom, who appointed My land to themselves as a possession with the joy of all their heart, with disdain of soul, to cast it out as prey;

לָכֵן הִנָּבֵא עַל־אַדְמַת יִשְׂרָאֵל וְאָמַרְתָּ לֶהָרִים וְלַגְּבָעוֹת לָאֲפִיקִים וְלַגֵּאָיוֹת כֹּה־אָמַר אֲדֹנָי יְהוִה הִנְנִי בְקִנְאָתִי וּבַחֲמָתִי דִּבַּרְתִּי יַעַן כְּלִמַּת גּוֹיִם נְשָׂאתֶם

6[7] Therefore prophesy concerning the land of Israel, and say to the mountains and to the hills, to the streams and to the valleys: Thus says the Lord GOD: Behold, I have spoken in My jealousy and in My fury, because you have borne the shame of the nations;

לָכֵן כֹּה אָמַר אֲדֹנָי יְהוִה אֲנִי נָשָׂאתִי אֶת־יָדִי אִם־לֹא הַגּוֹיִם אֲשֶׁר לָכֶם מִסָּבִיב הֵמָּה כְּלִמָּתָם יִשָּׂאוּ

7[8] Therefore thus says the Lord GOD: I have lifted My hand: Surely the nations who are around you shall bear their shame.

וְאַתֶּם הָרֵי יִשְׂרָאֵל עַנְפְּכֶם תִּתֵּנוּ וּפֶרְיְכֶם תִּשְׂאוּ לְעַמִּי יִשְׂרָאֵל כִּי קֵרְבוּ לָבוֹא

8[9] *But you, O mountains of Israel, you shall shoot forth your branches, and yield your fruit to My people Israel; for they are at hand to come*[10].

[1] Ezekiel 36:1 - Ezekiel 6:2-6:3 21:3 33:28 34:14 36:4 36:8 37:4 37:22, Jeremiah 22:29

[2] Ezekiel 36:2 - Deuteronomy 32:13, Ezekiel 25:3 26:2 35:10 36:5, Habakkuk 3:19, Isaiah 58:14, Jeremiah 49:1, Lamentations.R 2:8, Mekhilta de R'Shimon bar Yochai Shirata 31:2, Mekilta de R'Ishmael Shirata 5:73, Midrash Tanchuma Beshallach 15, Psalms 78:69, z.Vaetchanan 269b

[3] Ezekiel 36:3 - 1 Corinthians 4:13, 1 Kings 9:7-9:8, Daniel 9:16, Deuteronomy 28:37, Ezekiel 13:10, Jeremiah 18:16 24:9 33:24 39:1-39:18 41:1-41:18 51:34 52:1-1:5, Job 30:1-30:10, Lamentations 2:2 2:5 2:15-2:16, Leviticus 26:43, Matthew 27:39-27:44, Proverbs 1:12, Psalms 35:15-35:16 35:25 44:14-44:15 61:2 69:13 79:10, z.Vaetchanan 269b

[4] LXX Because ye have been dishonoured, and hated by those round about you

[5] Ezekiel 36:4 - 2 Chronicles 36:17-36:21, Deuteronomy 11:11, Ezekiel 6:3 6:14 34:28 36:1 36:6 36:33-36:35, Isaiah 6:11 24:1-24:12 64:11-64:12, Jeremiah 25:9-25:13 29:10, Jastrow 971a, Tanna Devei Eliyahu 1, z.Vaetchanan 269b

[6] Ezekiel 36:5 - Amos 1:11-1:12, Deuteronomy 4:24, Ezekiel 25:8-25:15 35:1-35:15 36:3 38:19, Isaiah 34:1-34:17 63:1-63:6 66:15-66:16, Jeremiah 25:9 25:15-25:29 49:1 49:7-49:22 50:11, Lamentations 4:21, Malachi 1:2-1:4, Micah 7:8, Obadiah 1:1-1:9 1:12, Proverbs 17:5 24:17-24:18, Psalms 83:5-83:13 137:7, z.Vaetchanan 269b, Zechariah 1:15, Zephaniah 2:8-2:10 3:8

[7] Ezekiel 36:6 - Ezekiel 34:29 36:4-5 36:15, Psalms 74:10 74:18 74:23 123:3-4, z.Vaetchanan 269b

[8] Ezekiel 36:7 - Amos 1:1-1:15, Deuteronomy 32:40, Ezekiel 20:5 20:15 25:1-25:17, Jeremiah 25:9 25:15-25:29 47:1-47:7, Revelation 10:5-10:6, Sifre Devarim {Haazinu Hashamayim} 330, Sifre Devarim Nitzavim 330, z.Vaetchanan 267b 269b, Zephaniah 2:1-2:15

[9] Ezekiel 36:8 - Amos 9:13-9:15, b.Megillah 14b, b.Sanhedrin 98a, Ein Yaakov Megillah:17b, Ein Yaakov Sanhedrin:97b, Ezekiel 12:25 17:23 34:26-34:27, Hebrews 10:37, Hosea 2:21-2:25, Isaiah 4:2 27:6 30:23, James 5:8-5:9, Midrash Tanchuma Tetzaveh 13, Pesikta de R'Kahana S6.2, Philippians 4:5, Psalms 67:7 85:13, y.Berachot 2:4

[10] LXX *But your grapes and your fruits, O mountains of Israel, shall my people eat; for they are hoping to come*

כִּי הִנְנִי אֲלֵיכֶם וּפָנִיתִי אֲלֵיכֶם וְנֶעֱבַדְתֶּם וְנִזְרַעְתֶּם	9[1]	For, behold, I am for you, and I will turn to you, and you shall be tilled and sown;
וְהִרְבֵּיתִי עֲלֵיכֶם אָדָם כָּל־בֵּית יִשְׂרָאֵל כֻּלֹּה וְנֹשְׁבוּ הֶעָרִים וְהֶחֳרָבוֹת תִּבָּנֶינָה	10[2]	and I will multiply men on you, all the house of Israel, all of it; and the cities shall be inhabited, and the waste places shall be built;
וְהִרְבֵּיתִי עֲלֵיכֶם אָדָם וּבְהֵמָה וְרָבוּ וּפָרוּ וְהוֹשַׁבְתִּי אֶתְכֶם כְּקַדְמוֹתֵיכֶם וְהֵטִבֹתִי מֵרֵאשֹׁתֵיכֶם וִידַעְתֶּם כִּי־אֲנִי יְהוָה	11[3]	and I will multiply man and beast on you, and they shall increase and be fruitful; and I will cause you to be inhabited like your former estate, and will do better to you than at your beginnings; and you shall know that I am the LORD.
וְהוֹלַכְתִּי עֲלֵיכֶם אָדָם אֶת־עַמִּי יִשְׂרָאֵל וִירֵשׁוּךָ וְהָיִיתָ לָהֶם לְנַחֲלָה וְלֹא־תוֹסִף עוֹד לְשַׁכְּלָם	12[4]	Yes, I will cause men to walk upon you, my people Israel, and they shall possess you, and you shall be their inheritance; and you shall no more henceforth bereave them of children.
כֹּה אָמַר אֲדֹנָי יְהוִה יַעַן אֹמְרִים לָכֶם אֹכֶלֶת אָדָם 'אָתְּי' 'אָתְּ' וּמְשַׁכֶּלֶת 'גּוֹיֵךְ' 'גּוֹיַיִךְ' הָיִית	13[5]	Thus says the Lord GOD: Because they say unto you: you land are a devourer of men, and have been a bereavement of your nations;
לָכֵן אָדָם לֹא־תֹאכְלִי עוֹד 'וְגוֹיֵךְ' 'וְגוֹיַיִךְ' לֹא 'תְכַשְּׁלִי־תְשַׁכְּלִי־עוֹד' נְאֻם אֲדֹנָי יְהוָה	14[6]	therefore you shall devour men no more, neither bereave your nations any more, says the Lord GOD;
וְלֹא־אַשְׁמִיעַ אֵלַיִךְ עוֹד כְּלִמַּת הַגּוֹיִם וְחֶרְפַּת עַמִּים לֹא תִשְׂאִי־עוֹד 'וְגוֹיֵךְ' 'וְגוֹיַיִךְ' לֹא־תַכְשִׁלִי עוֹד נְאֻם אֲדֹנָי יְהוִה	15[7]	neither will I suffer the shame of the nations any more to be heard against you, neither shall you bear the reproach of the peoples any more, neither shall you cause your nations to stumble any more, says the Lord GOD.'
וַיְהִי דְבַר־יְהוָה אֵלַי לֵאמֹר	16[8]	Moreover the word of the LORD came unto me, saying:
בֶּן־אָדָם בֵּית יִשְׂרָאֵל יֹשְׁבִים עַל־אַדְמָתָם וַיְטַמְּאוּ אוֹתָהּ בְּדַרְכָּם וּבַעֲלִילוֹתָם כְּטֻמְאַת הַנִּדָּה הָיְתָה דַרְכָּם לְפָנָי	17[9]	'Son of man, when the house of Israel dwelt in their own land, they defiled it by their way and by their deeds; their way before Me was as the uncleanness of a woman in her impurity.
וָאֶשְׁפֹּךְ חֲמָתִי עֲלֵיהֶם עַל־הַדָּם אֲשֶׁר־שָׁפְכוּ עַל־הָאָרֶץ וּבְגִלּוּלֵיהֶם טִמְּאוּהָ	18[10]	Why I poured out My fury upon them *for the blood which they had shed upon the land, and because they had defiled it with their idols*[11];
וָאָפִיץ אֹתָם בַּגּוֹיִם וַיִּזָּרוּ בָּאֲרָצוֹת כְּדַרְכָּם וְכַעֲלִילוֹתָם שְׁפַטְתִּים	19[12]	and I scattered them among the nations, and they were dispersed through the countries; according to their way and according to their deeds I judged them.

[1] Ezekiel 36:9 - Ezekiel 36:34, Haggai 2:19, Hosea 2:21-25, Joel 4:18, Malachi 3:10-11, Psalms 46:12 99:8, Romans 8:31, Zechariah 8:12

[2] Ezekiel 36:10 - Amos 9:14, Ezekiel 36:33 36:37, Isaiah 27:6 41:17-41:23 49:17-49:23 51:3 52:9 58:12 61:4, Jeremiah 30:19 31:11-31:15 31:28-31:29 33:12, Zechariah 8:3-8:6
Ezekiel 36:10-14 - Tanna Devei Eliyahu 5

[3] Ezekiel 36:11 - 1 John 5:20, Amos 9:15, Ezekiel 16:55 35:9 36:35 37:6 37:13, Haggai 2:6-9, Hebrews 8:8-13 11:40, Hosea 2:20, Isaiah 30:26 52:4-6 54:7-10, Jeremiah 23:5-8 30:18 31:28 31:39-41 33:12, Job 42:12, Joel 4:18-21, Micah 7:14, Obadiah 1:19-21, Zechariah 8:11-15

[4] Ezekiel 36:12 - Ezekiel 36:13 47:14, Jeremiah 15:7 32:15 32:44, Numbers 13:32, Obadiah 1:17-21

[5] Ezekiel 36:13 - Numbers 13:32, z.Vaetchanan 269b

[6] Ezekiel 36:14 - Amos 9:15, Ezekiel 37:25-28, Isaiah 60:21

[7] Ezekiel 36:15 - Ezekiel 34:29 36:6, Isaiah 54:4 60:14, Micah 7:8-10, Psalms 89:51, Zephaniah 2:8 3:19-20

[8] Ezekiel 36:16-36 - Haftarah Parshat Parah [Sephard and Teimon]
Ezekiel 36:16-38 - Haftarah Parshat Parah [Ashkenaz], mt.Hilchot Tefilah 13:20, Siman 140:2

[9] Ezekiel 36:17 - Isaiah 24:5 64:7, Jeremiah 2:7 3:1-3:2 3:9 16:18, Lamentations.R 3:7, Leviticus 15:19-15:33 18:24-18:28, Micah 2:10, Midrash Tanchuma Kedoshim 11, Midrash Tanchuma Metzora 9, Numbers 35:33-35:34, Numbers.R 9:45, Pesikta Rabbati 33:13, Pirkei de R'Eliezer 8, Psalms 106:37-106:38, y.Bikkurim 3:3

[10] Ezekiel 36:18 - 2 Chronicles 34:21 34:26, Ezekiel 7:8 14:19 16:36-16:38 21:36 23:37, Isaiah 42:25, Jeremiah 7:20 44:6, Lamentations 2:4 4:11, Nahum 1:6, Revelation 14:10 16:1-16:21

[11] Missing in LXX

[12] Ezekiel 36:19 - Amos 9:9, Deuteronomy 28:64, Ezekiel 5:12 7:3 7:8 18:30 22:15 22:31 39:24, Leviticus 26:38, Revelation 20:12-15, Romans 2:6

וַיָּבוֹא אֶל־הַגּוֹיִם אֲשֶׁר־בָּאוּ שָׁם וַיְחַלְּלוּ אֶת־שֵׁם
קָדְשִׁי בֶּאֱמֹר לָהֶם עַם־יְהוָה אֵלֶּה וּמֵאַרְצוֹ יָצָאוּ

20[1]

And when they came unto the nations, whither they came, they profaned My holy name; in that men said of them: These are the people of the LORD, and are gone forth out of His land.

וָאֶחְמֹל עַל־שֵׁם קָדְשִׁי אֲשֶׁר חִלְּלוּהוּ בֵּית יִשְׂרָאֵל
בַּגּוֹיִם אֲשֶׁר־בָּאוּ שָׁמָּה

21[2]

But I had pity for My holy name, which the house of Israel had profaned among the nations, whither they came.

לָכֵן אֱמֹר לְבֵית־יִשְׂרָאֵל כֹּה אָמַר אֲדֹנָי יְהוִה לֹא
לְמַעַנְכֶם אֲנִי עֹשֶׂה בֵּית יִשְׂרָאֵל כִּי אִם־לְשֵׁם־
קָדְשִׁי אֲשֶׁר חִלַּלְתֶּם בַּגּוֹיִם אֲשֶׁר־בָּאתֶם שָׁם

22[3]

Therefore say unto the house of Israel: Thus says the Lord GOD: I do not this for your sake, O house of Israel, but for My holy name, which you have profaned among the nations, where you came.

וְקִדַּשְׁתִּי אֶת־שְׁמִי הַגָּדוֹל הַמְחֻלָּל בַּגּוֹיִם אֲשֶׁר
חִלַּלְתֶּם בְּתוֹכָם וְיָדְעוּ הַגּוֹיִם כִּי־אֲנִי יְהוָה נְאֻם
אֲדֹנָי יְהוִה בְּהִקָּדְשִׁי בָכֶם לְעֵינֵיהֶם

23[4]

And I will sanctify My great name, which has been profaned among the nations, which you have profaned in the midst of them; and the nations shall know that I am the LORD, says the Lord GOD, when I shall be sanctified in you before their eyes.

וְלָקַחְתִּי אֶתְכֶם מִן־הַגּוֹיִם וְקִבַּצְתִּי אֶתְכֶם מִכָּל־
הָאֲרָצוֹת וְהֵבֵאתִי אֶתְכֶם אֶל־אַדְמַתְכֶם

24[5]

For I will take you from among the nations, and gather you out of all the countries, and will bring you into your own land.

וְזָרַקְתִּי עֲלֵיכֶם מַיִם טְהוֹרִים וּטְהַרְתֶּם מִכֹּל
טֻמְאוֹתֵיכֶם וּמִכָּל־גִּלּוּלֵיכֶם אֲטַהֵר אֶתְכֶם

25[6]

And I will sprinkle clean water upon you, and you shall be clean; from all your uncleannesses, and from all your idols, will I cleanse you.

וְנָתַתִּי לָכֶם לֵב חָדָשׁ וְרוּחַ חֲדָשָׁה אֶתֵּן בְּקִרְבְּכֶם
וַהֲסִרֹתִי אֶת־לֵב הָאֶבֶן מִבְּשַׂרְכֶם וְנָתַתִּי לָכֶם לֵב
בָּשָׂר

26[7]

A new heart also will I give you, and a new spirit will I put within you; and I will take away the stony heart out of your flesh, and I will give you a heart of flesh.

וְאֶת־רוּחִי אֶתֵּן בְּקִרְבְּכֶם וְעָשִׂיתִי אֵת אֲשֶׁר־
בְּחֻקַּי תֵּלֵכוּ וּמִשְׁפָּטַי תִּשְׁמְרוּ וַעֲשִׂיתֶם

27[8]

And I will put My spirit within you, and cause you to walk in My statutes, and you shall keep My ordinances, and do them.

---

[1] Ezekiel 36:20 - 2 Kings 18:30 18:35 19:10-12, b.Yoma 38a, Daniel 3:15, Ein Yaakov Yoma:86a, Exodus 32:11-13, Ezekiel 12:16, Gates of Repentance 3.113, Isaiah 52:5, Jeremiah 33:24, Joshua 7:9, Kuzari 2.056, Lamentations.R Petichata D'Chakimei:16, Mekhilta de R'Shimon bar Yochai Shirata 27:1, Mekilta de R'Ishmael Shirata 1:46, Numbers 14:15-14:16, Pesikta Rabbati 27/28:2 28:2, Romans 2:24

Ezekiel 36:20-22 - Mekilta de R'Ishmael Shirata 3:91-96

Ezekiel 36:20-23 - Mekhilta de R'Shimon bar Yochai Shirata 29:1

[2] Ezekiel 36:21 - Deuteronomy 32:26-27, Ezekiel 20:9 20:14 20:22, Isaiah 37:35 48:9, Psalms 74:18

[3] Ezekiel 36:22 - Deuteronomy 7:7-7:8 9:5-9:7, Ezekiel 36:32, Psalms 106:8 115:1-115:2, z.Vaetchanan 269b

[4] Ezekiel 36:23 - 1 Peter 2:9 3:15, Daniel 2:47 3:28-3:29 3:32-3:33 4:31-4:34 6:27-6:28, Exodus 15:4-15:16, Ezekiel 20:41 28:22 38:22-38:23 39:7 39:28, Isaiah 5:16, Numbers 20:12-20:13, Numbers.R 5:6, Psalms 46:11 102:14-102:17 126:1-126:3

[5] Ezekiel 36:24 - Amos 9:14-9:15, Deuteronomy 30:3-30:5, Ezekiel 11:17 34:13 37:21 37:25 39:27-39:28, Hosea 2:2, Isaiah 11:11-11:16 27:12-27:13 43:5-43:6, Jeremiah 23:3-23:8 30:3 30:18 31:9 32:37 50:17-50:20, Lamentations.R Petichata D'Chakimei:34, Psalms 107:2-107:3, Romans 11:25-26

[6] Ezekiel 36:25 - 1 Corinthians 6:11, 1 John 1:7 5:6, 2 Corinthians 7:1, Acts 22:16, b.Megillah 30a, b.Niddah [Tosefot] 70b, b.Sotah 72b, b.Yoma 85b, Ein Yaakov Yoma:85b 87a, Ephesians 5:26-27, Ezekiel 36:17 36:29 37:23, Genesis.R 99 [Excl]:8, Hebrews 9:13-14 9:19 10:22, Hosea 14:5 14:10, Isaiah 2:18-20 4:4 17:7-8 52:15, Jastrow 944a, Jeremiah 3:22-23 33:8, John 3:5, Leviticus 14:5-7, Leviticus.R 15:9, m.Yoma 8:9, Midrash Tanchuma Metzora 9, Midrash Tanchuma Tazria 9, mt.Hilchot Mikvaot 11:12, Numbers 8:7 19:13-20, Numbers.R 7:10 9:49, Pesikta de R'Kahana 4.1, Pesikta Rabbati 14:2, Proverbs 30:12, Psalms 51:3 51:8, Revelation 1:5 7:14, Selichot, Song of Songs.R 1:19, t.Kiddushin 5:4, t.Megillah 3:3, Titus 2:14 3:5-6, y.Kiddushin 3:13, y.Yoma 8:7, z.Emor 102b, z.Shemini 42a, z.Vayeshev 184b, Zechariah 13:1-2

[7] Ezekiel 36:26 - 2 Corinthians 3:3 3:18 5:17, b.Berachot 32a, b.Megillah [Rashi] 20a, b.Succah 52ab, Chibbur Yafeh 27 {117b}, Deuteronomy 30:6, Ecclesiastes.R 1:36 9:24, Ein Yaakov Sukkah:52a, Ephesians 2:10, Exodus.R 15:6 41:7, Ezekiel 11:19-20, Galatians 6:15, Genesis.R 34:15, Jastrow 180a 198b, Jeremiah 32:39, John 3:3-5, Leviticus.R 35:5, Life of Adam and Eve [Apocalypse] 13:5, Mark 4:16-17, Matthew 13:5 13:20-21, Midrash Psalms 14:6, Midrash Tanchuma Behaalotcha 10, Midrash Tanchuma Ekev 11, Midrash Tanchuma Ki Tissa 19, Midrash Tanchuma Metzora 9, Midrash Tanchuma Noach 13, Midrash Tanchuma Terumah 7, Midrash Tanchuma Vayikra 6, mt.Hilchot Teshuvah 9:2 9:2, Numbers.R 9:49 14:4 15:16 17:6, Pesikta de R'Kahana 22.5a 24.17, Pirkei de R'Eliezer 29, Psalms 51:11, Revelation 21:5, Saadia Opinions 8:6, Song of Songs.R 1:15 6:26, Tanna Devei Eliyahu 4, y.Yoma 4:1, z.Bereshit 28a, z.Vayechi 231b, z.Vayeshev 192b, Zechariah 7:12

Ezekiel 36:26-27 - Midrash Tanchuma Kedoshim 15, Midrash Tanchuma Shelach 15, Midrash Tanchuma Toledot 13

[8] Ezekiel 36:27 - 1 Corinthians 3:16, 1 John 1:6-1:7 3:24, 1 Peter 1:2 1:22, 2 John 1:6, 2 Thessalonians 2:13, b.Berachot 32a, b.Succah 52b, Colossians 2:6, Ephesians 1:13-1:14, Ezekiel 37:14 37:24 39:29, Galatians 5:5 5:16 5:22-5:23, Hebrews 13:21, Isaiah 44:3-44:4

וִישַׁבְתֶּם בָּאָרֶץ אֲשֶׁר נָתַתִּי לַאֲבֹתֵיכֶם וִהְיִיתֶם לִי לְעָם וְאָנֹכִי אֶהְיֶה לָכֶם לֵאלֹהִים	28[1]	And you shall dwell in the land that I gave to your fathers; and you shall be My people, and I will be your God.
וְהוֹשַׁעְתִּי אֶתְכֶם מִכֹּל טֻמְאוֹתֵיכֶם וְקָרָאתִי אֶל־הַדָּגָן וְהִרְבֵּיתִי אֹתוֹ וְלֹא־אֶתֵּן עֲלֵיכֶם רָעָב	29[2]	And I will save you from all your uncleannesses; and I will call for the corn, and will increase it, and lay no famine upon you.
וְהִרְבֵּיתִי אֶת־פְּרִי הָעֵץ וּתְנוּבַת הַשָּׂדֶה לְמַעַן אֲשֶׁר לֹא תִקְחוּ עוֹד חֶרְפַּת רָעָב בַּגּוֹיִם	30[3]	And I will multiply the fruit of the tree, and the increase of the field, that you may receive no more the reproach of famine among the nations.
וּזְכַרְתֶּם אֶת־דַּרְכֵיכֶם הָרָעִים וּמַעַלְלֵיכֶם אֲשֶׁר לֹא־טוֹבִים וּנְקֹטֹתֶם בִּפְנֵיכֶם עַל עֲוֹנֹתֵיכֶם וְעַל תּוֹעֲבוֹתֵיכֶם	31[4]	Then shall you remember your evil ways, and your deeds that were not good; and you shall loathe yourselves in your own sight for your iniquities and for your abominations.
לֹא לְמַעַנְכֶם אֲנִי־עֹשֶׂה נְאֻם אֲדֹנָי יְהוִה יִוָּדַע לָכֶם בּוֹשׁוּ וְהִכָּלְמוּ מִדַּרְכֵיכֶם בֵּית יִשְׂרָאֵל	32[5]	Not for your sake do I this, says the Lord GOD, be it known unto you; be ashamed and confounded for your ways, O house of Israel.
כֹּה אָמַר אֲדֹנָי יְהוִה בְּיוֹם טַהֲרִי אֶתְכֶם מִכֹּל עֲוֹנוֹתֵיכֶם וְהוֹשַׁבְתִּי אֶת־הֶעָרִים וְנִבְנוּ הֶחֳרָבוֹת	33[6]	Thus says the Lord GOD: In the day that I cleanse you from all your iniquities, I will cause the cities to be inhabited, and the waste places shall be built.
וְהָאָרֶץ הַנְשַׁמָּה תֵּעָבֵד תַּחַת אֲשֶׁר הָיְתָה שְׁמָמָה לְעֵינֵי כָּל־עוֹבֵר	34[7]	And the land that was desolate shall be tilled, whereas it was a desolation in the sight of all who passed by.
וְאָמְרוּ הָאָרֶץ הַלֵּזוּ הַנְשַׁמָּה הָיְתָה כְּגַן־עֵדֶן וְהֶעָרִים הֶחֳרֵבוֹת וְהַנְשַׁמּוֹת וְהַנֶּהֱרָסוֹת בְּצוּרוֹת יָשָׁבוּ	35[8]	And they shall say: This land that was desolate is become like the garden of Eden; and the waste and desolate and ruined cities are fortified and inhabited.
וְיָדְעוּ הַגּוֹיִם אֲשֶׁר יִשָּׁאֲרוּ סְבִיבוֹתֵיכֶם כִּי אֲנִי יְהוָה בָּנִיתִי הַנֶּהֱרָסוֹת נָטַעְתִּי הַנְשַׁמָּה אֲנִי יְהוָה דִּבַּרְתִּי וְעָשִׂיתִי	36[9]	Then the nations that remain around you shall know that I, the LORD, have built the ruined places, and planted what was desolate; I, the LORD, have spoken it, and I will do it.
כֹּה אָמַר אֲדֹנָי יְהוִה עוֹד זֹאת אִדָּרֵשׁ לְבֵית־יִשְׂרָאֵל לַעֲשׂוֹת לָהֶם אַרְבֶּה אֹתָם כַּצֹּאן אָדָם	37[10]	Thus says the Lord GOD: I will yet for this be inquired of by the house of Israel, to do it for them; I will increase them with men like a flock.

59:21, Jeremiah 31:34, Joel 3:1-3:2, Luke 11:13, Midrash Psalms 73:4, Numbers.R 9:49, Philippians 2:12-2:13, Proverbs 1:23, Romans 8:9 8:14-8:16, Saadia Opinions 4:6, Titus 2:11-2:14 3:3-3:6, z.Noach 76a, Zechariah 12:10

[1] Ezekiel 36:28 - 2 Corinthians 6:16-7:1, Ezekiel 11:20 14:11 28:25 36:10 37:23 37:25 37:27 39:28, Hebrews 8:10 11:16, Hosea 2:1, Jeremiah 30:22-30:23 31:34 32:38, Matthew 22:32, Pesikta Rabbati 21:11, Revelation 21:3 21:7, Song of Songs 6:3, Zechariah 13:9

[2] Ezekiel 36:29 - b.Berachot 55a, Ein Yaakov Berachot:55a, Ezekiel 34:27-34:29 36:8-36:9 12:25, Hosea 2:21-2:25 14:4 14:6 14:10, Jeremiah 9:8, Joel 4:21, John 1:7-1:9, Mas.Kallah Rabbati 8:9, Matthew 1:21 6:33, Micah 7:19, Midrash Tanchuma Shemini 3, Numbers.R 9:49, Psalms 9:6, Romans 6:14 11:26, Titus 2:14, Zechariah 13:1

[3] Ezekiel 36:30 - Deuteronomy 29:22-29:27, Ezekiel 10:27, Genesis.R 63:14, Joel 2:17 2:26, Leviticus 2:4

[4] Ezekiel 36:31 - 2 Corinthians 7:10-7:11, Daniel 9:4-9:20, Ezekiel 6:9 16:61-16:63 20:43, Ezra 9:6-9:15, Isaiah 6:5 16:7, Jeremiah 31:19-31:21, Job 18:6, Leviticus 2:39, Luke 18:13, Nehemiah 9:26-9:35, Romans 6:21, Zechariah 12:10-12:11

[5] Ezekiel 36:32 - 1 Peter 4:2-3, 2 Timothy 1:9, Daniel 9:18-19, Deuteronomy 9:5, Ezekiel 16:63 12:22, Ezra 9:6, Gates of Repentance 1.22, Numbers.R 9:49, Romans 6:21, Titus 3:3-6

[6] Ezekiel 36:33 - Amos 9:14-9:15, Ezekiel 12:10, Isaiah 10:12, Jeremiah 8:43 9:10 50:19-50:20, z.Vaetchanan 269b, Zechariah 8:7-8:8

[7] Ezekiel 36:34 - 2 Chronicles 12:21, Deuteronomy 29:22-29:27, Ezekiel 6:14, Jeremiah 25:9-25:11

[8] Ezekiel 36:35 - Ezekiel 13:13, Genesis 2:8-2:9 13:10, Isaiah 3:3, Jeremiah 9:9, Joel 2:3, Psalms 58:12 64:10 6:2

[9] Ezekiel 36:36 - Ezekiel 17:24 22:14 24:14 10:30 13:14 13:28 39:27-29, Hosea 14:6-11, Matthew 24:35, Micah 7:15-17, Midrash Tanchuma Vayera 17, Numbers 23:19, Pesikta Rabbati 42:5

[10] Ezekiel 36:37 - 1 John 5:14, Ezekiel 14:3 20:3 20:31, Hebrews 4:16 10:21-22, Isaiah 55:6-7, James 4:2-3, Jeremiah 29:11-13 50:4-5, Matthew 7:7-8, Midrash Tanchuma Vayera 13, Philippians 4:6, Psalms 10:18 6:18, Song of Songs.R 7:14, z.Vaetchanan 269b, Zechariah 10:6 10:9 13:9

Ezekiel 36:37-37:14 - Pesach Intermediate Shabbat Haftarah Sephard
Ezekiel 36:37-37:17 - Haftarah Shabbat Chol Hamoed Pesach [Teimon]

כְּצֹאן קָדָשִׁים כְּצֹאן יְרוּשָׁלַם בְּמוֹעֲדֶיהָ כֵּן תִּהְיֶינָה הֶעָרִים הֶחֳרֵבוֹת מְלֵאוֹת צֹאן אָדָם וְיָדְעוּ כִּי־אֲנִי יְהוָה	38[1]	As the flock for sacrifice, as the flock of Jerusalem in her appointed seasons, so shall the waste cities be filled with flocks of men; and they shall know that I am the LORD.'

Ezekiel – Chapter 37[2]

הָיְתָה עָלַי יַד־יְהוָה וַיּוֹצִאֵנִי בְרוּחַ יְהוָה וַיְנִיחֵנִי בְּתוֹךְ הַבִּקְעָה וְהִיא מְלֵאָה עֲצָמוֹת	1[3]	The hand of the LORD was upon me, and the LORD carried me out in a spirit, and set me down in the midst of the valley, and it was full of [4]bones;
וְהֶעֱבִירַנִי עֲלֵיהֶם סָבִיב סָבִיב וְהִנֵּה רַבּוֹת מְאֹד עַל־פְּנֵי הַבִּקְעָה וְהִנֵּה יְבֵשׁוֹת מְאֹד	2[5]	and He caused me to pass by them, and, behold, there were very many in the open valley; and, lo, they were very dry.
וַיֹּאמֶר אֵלַי בֶּן־אָדָם הֲתִחְיֶינָה הָעֲצָמוֹת הָאֵלֶּה וָאֹמַר אֲדֹנָי יְהוִה אַתָּה יָדָעְתָּ	3[6]	And He said unto me: 'Son of man, can these bones live?' And I answered: 'O Lord GOD, you know.'
וַיֹּאמֶר אֵלַי הִנָּבֵא עַל־הָעֲצָמוֹת הָאֵלֶּה וְאָמַרְתָּ אֲלֵיהֶם הָעֲצָמוֹת הַיְבֵשׁוֹת שִׁמְעוּ דְּבַר־יְהוָה	4[7]	Then He said unto me: 'Prophesy over these bones, and say unto them: O you dry bones, hear the word of the LORD:
כֹּה אָמַר אֲדֹנָי יְהוִה לָעֲצָמוֹת הָאֵלֶּה הִנֵּה אֲנִי מֵבִיא בָכֶם רוּחַ וִחְיִיתֶם	5[8]	Thus says the Lord GOD unto these bones: Behold, I will *cause breath to enter into you, and you shall live*[9].
וְנָתַתִּי עֲלֵיכֶם גִּדִים וְהַעֲלֵתִי עֲלֵיכֶם בָּשָׂר וְקָרַמְתִּי עֲלֵיכֶם עוֹר וְנָתַתִּי בָכֶם רוּחַ וִחְיִיתֶם וִידַעְתֶּם כִּי־אֲנִי יְהוָה	6[10]	And I will lay sinews upon you, and will bring up flesh upon you, and cover you with skin, and put *breath*[11] in you, and you shall live; and you shall know that I am the LORD.'
וְנִבֵּאתִי כַּאֲשֶׁר צֻוֵּיתִי וַיְהִי־קוֹל כְּהִנָּבְאִי וְהִנֵּה־רַעַשׁ וַתִּקְרְבוּ עֲצָמוֹת עֶצֶם אֶל־עַצְמוֹ	7[12]	So I prophesied as I was commanded; and as I prophesied, there was a noise, and behold a commotion, and *the*[13] bones *came together, bone to its bone*[14].
וְרָאִיתִי וְהִנֵּה־עֲלֵיהֶם גִּדִים וּבָשָׂר עָלָה וַיִּקְרַם עֲלֵיהֶם עוֹר מִלְמָעְלָה וְרוּחַ אֵין בָּהֶם	8[15]	And I beheld, and, lo, there were sinews upon them, and flesh came up, and skin covered them above; but there was no breath in them.

---

[1] Ezekiel 36:38 - 1 Kings 8:63, 2 Chronicles 7:8 30:21-27 35:7-19, Acts 2:5-11, Deuteronomy 16:16, Exodus 23:17 10:23, Exodus.R 24:3, Ezekiel 10:31 36:33-35, Jeremiah 6:19 31:28-29, John 10:16, Pirkei de R'Eliezer 40, Revelation 7:4-9, Song of Songs.R 6:14, z.Shemot 21a, Zechariah 8:19-23

[2] Ezekiel 37 - Jastrow 454a, mt.Hilchot Tefilah 13:16

[3] Ezekiel 37:1 - 1 Kings 18:12, 2 Kings 2:16, 3 Enoch 23:7, Acts 8:39, Deuteronomy.R 7:6, Ecclesiastes.R 3:18, Ezekiel 1:3 3:14 3:22 8:3 11:24 9:22 16:1, Genesis.R 13:6, Guide for the Perplexed 2:41 2:46, Jeremiah 7:32 8:2, Luke 4:1, Midrash Psalms 10:6 78:5, Revelation 1:10, Saadia Opinions 7:7, Tanna Devei Eliyahu 5

Ezekiel 37:1-6 - Odes of Solomon 22:9

Ezekiel 37:1-10 - Sibylline Oracles 2.224 4.181

Ezekiel 37:1-14 - Haftarah Shabbat Chol Hamoed Pesach [Ashkenaz and Sephard], Lives of the Prophets 3:12

[4] LXX adds *human*

[5] Ezekiel 37:2 - b.Sanhedrin 92b, Deuteronomy 11:30, Ein Yaakov Sanhedrin:92b, Ezekiel 13:11, Psalms 21:7

[6] Ezekiel 37:3 - 1 Samuel 2:6, 2 Corinthians 1:9-1:10, 4 Maccabees 18:18, Acts 2:8, Deuteronomy 8:29 8:39, Genesis.R 19:11, Hebrews 11:19, John 5:21 6:5-6:6 11:25-11:26, Kuzari 2.034 3.011, Pirkei de R'Eliezer 33, Romans 4:17, z.Balak 200a

[7] Ezekiel 37:4 - 27:2, 1 Kings 13:2, b.Megillah 31a, b.Sanhedrin 92b, Ecclesiastes.R 4:3, Ein Yaakov Sanhedrin:92b, Ezekiel 12:1 13:11 37:15-37:16, Isaiah 2:19 18:18, Jeremiah 22:29, John 2:5 5:25 5:28-5:29, Matthew 21:21, Micah 6:2, Midrash Tanchuma Yitro 4, Numbers 20:8, Pesikta de R'Kahana 14.4, Pesikta Rabbati 27:2, Pirkei de R'Eliezer 33

[8] Ezekiel 37:5 - Ephesians 2:5, Ezekiel 37:9-10 13:14, Genesis.R 2:7, John 20:22, Psalms 104:29-30, Romans 8:2, z.Vaetchanan 269b

[9] LXX *bring upon you the breath of life*

[10] Ezekiel 37:6 - 1 Kings 20:28, Deuteronomy 5:5, Ezekiel 6:7 6:13 7:4 7:9 11:10 11:12 20:38 28:22-28:26 8:15 10:27 11:9 11:12 11:15 13:14 14:23 15:6 15:22 15:28, Isaiah 1:23, Jastrow 623b, Joel 2:27 4:17, y.Shekalim 3:3

[11] LXX *my Spirit*

[12] Ezekiel 37:7 - 1 Kings 19:11-13, Acts 2:2 2:37 4:19 5:20-29 16:26-29, Jeremiah 13:5-7 2:8, Pirkei de R'Eliezer 33, z.Pinchas 222a

Ezekiel 37:7-8 - Midrash Tanchuma Yitro 4

[13] Missing in MasEzek

[14] LXX *approached each one to his joint*

[15] Ezekiel 37:8 - b.Niddah [Tosefot] 25a, Genesis.R 14:5, Leviticus.R 14:9, Pirkei de R'Eliezer 33, z.Pinchas 222a

Hebrew	Verse	English

וַיֹּאמֶר אֵלַי הִנָּבֵא אֶל־הָרוּחַ הִנָּבֵא בֶן־אָדָם וְאָמַרְתָּ אֶל־הָרוּחַ כֹּה־אָמַר אֲדֹנָי יְהוִה מֵאַרְבַּע רוּחוֹת בֹּאִי הָרוּחַ וּפְחִי בַּהֲרוּגִים הָאֵלֶּה וְיִחְיוּ — 9[1]

Then said He unto me: 'Prophesy unto the *breath*[2], prophesy, son of man, and say to the breath: Thus says the Lord GOD: Come from the four winds, O breath, and breath upon these slain, that they may live.'

וְהִנַּבֵּאתִי כַּאֲשֶׁר צִוָּנִי וַתָּבוֹא בָהֶם הָרוּחַ וַיִּחְיוּ וַיַּעַמְדוּ עַל־רַגְלֵיהֶם חַיִל גָּדוֹל מְאֹד־מְאֹד — 10[3]

So I prophesied as He commanded me, and the breath came into them, and they lived, and stood up upon their feet, a very great host.

וַיֹּאמֶר אֵלַי בֶּן־אָדָם הָעֲצָמוֹת הָאֵלֶּה כָּל־בֵּית יִשְׂרָאֵל הֵמָּה הִנֵּה אֹמְרִים יָבְשׁוּ עַצְמוֹתֵינוּ וְאָבְדָה תִקְוָתֵנוּ נִגְזַרְנוּ לָנוּ — 11[4]

Then He said unto me: 'Son of man, these bones are the whole house of Israel; behold, they say: Our bones are dried up, and our hope is lost; we are clean cut off.

לָכֵן הִנָּבֵא וְאָמַרְתָּ אֲלֵיהֶם כֹּה־אָמַר אֲדֹנָי יְהוִה הִנֵּה אֲנִי פֹתֵחַ אֶת־קִבְרוֹתֵיכֶם וְהַעֲלֵיתִי אֶתְכֶם מִקִּבְרוֹתֵיכֶם עַמִּי וְהֵבֵאתִי אֶתְכֶם אֶל־אַדְמַת יִשְׂרָאֵל — 12[5]

Therefore prophesy, and say unto them: Thus says the Lord GOD: Behold, I will open your graves, and cause you to come up out of your graves, O My people; and I will bring you into the land of Israel.

וִידַעְתֶּם כִּי־אֲנִי יְהוָה בְּפִתְחִי אֶת־קִבְרוֹתֵיכֶם וּבְהַעֲלוֹתִי אֶתְכֶם מִקִּבְרוֹתֵיכֶם עַמִּי — 13[6]

And you shall know that I am the LORD, when I have opened your graves, and caused you to come up out of your graves, *O My people*[7].

וְנָתַתִּי רוּחִי בָכֶם וִחְיִיתֶם וְהִנַּחְתִּי אֶתְכֶם עַל־אַדְמַתְכֶם וִידַעְתֶּם כִּי־אֲנִי יְהוָה דִּבַּרְתִּי וְעָשִׂיתִי נְאֻם־יְהוָה — 14[8]

And I will put My spirit in you, and you shall live, and I will place you in your own land; and you shall know that I, the LORD, have spoken, and performed it, says the LORD.'

וַיְהִי דְבַר־יְהוָה אֵלַי לֵאמֹר — 15[9]

And the word of the LORD came unto me, saying:

וְאַתָּה בֶן־אָדָם קַח־לְךָ עֵץ אֶחָד וּכְתֹב עָלָיו לִיהוּדָה וְלִבְנֵי יִשְׂרָאֵל "חֲבֵרָיו" "חֲבֵרוֹ" וּלְקַח עֵץ אֶחָד וּכְתוֹב עָלָיו לְיוֹסֵף עֵץ אֶפְרַיִם וְכָל־בֵּית יִשְׂרָאֵל "חֲבֵרוֹ" "חֲבֵרָיו" — 16[10]

'And you, son of man, take you one stick, and write upon it: For Judah, and for the children of Israel his companions; then take another stick, and write upon it: For Joseph, the stick of Ephraim, and of all the house of Israel his companions;

וְקָרַב אֹתָם אֶחָד אֶל־אֶחָד לְךָ לְעֵץ אֶחָד וְהָיוּ לַאֲחָדִים בְּיָדֶךָ — 17[11]

and join them for you one to another into one stick, *that they may become one in your hand*[12].

---

[1] Ezekiel 37:9 - Ezekiel 13:5 13:14, John 3:8, Midrash Psalms 78:5, Pirkei de R'Eliezer 33, Pirkei de R'Eliezer 33, Psalms 8:30, Saadia Opinions 6:8, Sifre Devarim {Haazinu Hashamayim} 306, Sifre Devarim Nitzavim 306, Song of Songs 4:16, Song of Songs.R 7:15, Tanna Devei Eliyahu 5, z.Shemot 13a, z.Vaetchanan 269b, z.Vayechi 235a, z.Vayishlach 175b
[2] LXX *wind*
[3] Ezekiel 37:10 - Avot de R'Natan 34, Pirkei de R'Eliezer 33, Psalms 8:30, Revelation 11:11 20:4-20:5, Saadia Opinions 7:7
[4] Ezekiel 37:11 - 2 Corinthians 5:14, b.Sanhedrin 92b, Ein Yaakov Sanhedrin:92b, Ephesians 2:1, Ezekiel 12:10 37:1-37:8 13:16 13:19 15:25, Hosea 2:2, Isaiah 16:27 1:14, Jastrow 855b, Jeremiah 2:25 7:2 33:24-33:26, Kuzari 3.011, Lamentations 3:54, Numbers 17:27-17:13, Pirkei de R'Eliezer 33, Psalms 77:8-77:10 21:7, Romans 11:26, Saadia Opinions 7:3 7Variant:4 7Variant:4 7Variant:4 7Variant:4, Tanna Devei Eliyahu 5, z.Vayechi 233a
[5] Ezekiel 37:12 - 1 Samuel 2:6, 1 Thessalonians 4:16, Amos 9:14-9:15, Deuteronomy 8:39, Ezekiel 4:25 12:24 13:21 13:25, Ezra 1:1-1:2, Genesis.R 13:6 73:4 96:5, Hosea 6:2 13:14, Isaiah 2:19 18:14, Jastrow 1253b, Job 35:14-35:15, Midrash Proverbs 10, Midrash Psalms 85:3, Midrash Tanchuma Vayechi 3, Pesikta Rabbati 1:6 42:7, Pirkei de R'Eliezer 33, Revelation 20:13, Saadia Opinions 7:3 7:8 7Variant:4 7Variant:4 7Variant:4 7Variant:8, y.Ketubot 12:3, y.Kilayim 9:3, z.Noach 69a, z.Shemot 16b, z.Vaetchanan 269b
[6] Ezekiel 37:13 - b.Shabbat [Rashi] 152b, b.Taanit 2b, Deuteronomy.R 7:6, Ein Yaakov Shabbat:152b, Ein Yaakov Taanit:2a, Ezekiel 16:62 37:6, Mekilta de R'Ishmael Bahodesh 7:46, Midrash Psalms 78:5, Pesikta Rabbati 1:6, Psalms 126:2-3, Saadia Opinions 7:3 7Variant:4
[7] Missing in LXX
[8] Ezekiel 37:14 - 1 Corinthians 15:45, Acts 2:16-2:17, b.Shekalim 9b, Exodus.R 48:4, Ezekiel 11:19 17:24 22:14 12:27 12:36 13:9 15:29, Genesis.R 14:8 96:5 96 [Excl]:1, Isaiah 8:15, Joel 3:1-3:2, Midrash Psalms 85:3, Midrash Tanchuma Vayakhel 5, Midrash Tanchuma Vayechi 3, Pesikta Rabbati 1:6, Pirkei de R'Eliezer 33, Romans 8:2 8:11, Saadia Opinions 7:3 7Variant:4, Song of Songs.R 1:9, Titus 3:5-3:6, y.Ketubot 12:3, y.Kilayim 9:3, y.Shabbat 1:3, z.Noach 69a, Zechariah 12:10
[9] Ezekiel 37:15-28 - Haftarah Vayegash
[10] Ezekiel 37:16 - 1 Kings 12:16-20, 2 Chronicles 10:17 10:19 11:11-17 15:9 30:11-18, Genesis.R 98 [Excl]:2, Numbers 17:17-13
[11] Ezekiel 37:17 - Bahir 109, Ecclesiastes.R 3:10, Ezekiel 37:22-37:24, Hosea 2:2, Isaiah 11:13, Jeremiah 2:4, Zephaniah 3:9
[12] LXX *and they shall be in your hand*

וְכַאֲשֶׁר יֹאמְרוּ אֵלֶיךָ בְּנֵי עַמְּךָ לֵאמֹר הֲלוֹא־תַגִּיד לָנוּ מָה־אֵלֶּה לָּךְ	18[1] And when the children of your people shall speak unto you, saying: will you not tell us what you meanest by these?
דַּבֵּר אֲלֵהֶם כֹּה־אָמַר אֲדֹנָי יְהוִה הִנֵּה אֲנִי לֹקֵחַ אֶת־עֵץ יוֹסֵף אֲשֶׁר בְּיַד־אֶפְרַיִם וְשִׁבְטֵי יִשְׂרָאֵל 'חֲבֵרָו' "חֲבֵרָיו" וְנָתַתִּי אוֹתָם עָלָיו אֶת־עֵץ יְהוּדָה וַעֲשִׂיתִם לְעֵץ אֶחָד וְהָיוּ אֶחָד בְּיָדִי	19[2] say into them: Thus says the Lord GOD: Behold, I will take the stick of Joseph, which is in the hand of Ephraim, and the tribes of Israel his companions; and I will put them unto him together with the stick of Judah, and make them one stick, and they shall be *one in My hand*[3].
וְהָיוּ הָעֵצִים אֲשֶׁר־תִּכְתֹּב עֲלֵיהֶם בְּיָדְךָ לְעֵינֵיהֶם	20[4] And the sticks whereon you write shall be in your hand before their eyes.
וְדַבֵּר אֲלֵיהֶם כֹּה־אָמַר אֲדֹנָי יְהוִה הִנֵּה אֲנִי לֹקֵחַ אֶת־בְּנֵי יִשְׂרָאֵל מִבֵּין הַגּוֹיִם אֲשֶׁר הָלְכוּ־שָׁם וְקִבַּצְתִּי אֹתָם מִסָּבִיב וְהֵבֵאתִי אוֹתָם אֶל־אַדְמָתָם	21[5] And say unto them: Thus says the Lord GOD: Behold, I will take the children of Israel from among the nations, where they are gone, and will gather them on every side, and bring them into their own land;
וְעָשִׂיתִי אֹתָם לְגוֹי אֶחָד בָּאָרֶץ בְּהָרֵי יִשְׂרָאֵל וּמֶלֶךְ אֶחָד יִהְיֶה לְכֻלָּם לְמֶלֶךְ וְלֹא יִהְיֶה־יִהְיוּ־עוֹד' לִשְׁנֵי גוֹיִם וְלֹא יֵחָצוּ עוֹד לִשְׁתֵּי מַמְלָכוֹת עוֹד	22[6] and I will make them one nation in the land, upon the mountains of Israel, and one king shall be king to them all; and they shall be no more two nations, neither shall they be divided into two kingdoms any more at all;
וְלֹא יִטַמְּאוּ עוֹד בְּגִלּוּלֵיהֶם וּבְשִׁקּוּצֵיהֶם וּבְכֹל פִּשְׁעֵיהֶם וְהוֹשַׁעְתִּי אֹתָם מִכֹּל מוֹשְׁבֹתֵיהֶם אֲשֶׁר חָטְאוּ בָהֶם וְטִהַרְתִּי אוֹתָם וְהָיוּ־לִי לְעָם וַאֲנִי אֶהְיֶה לָהֶם לֵאלֹהִים	23[7] neither shall they defile themselves any more with their idols, nor with their detestable things, nor with any of their transgressions; but I will save them out of all their dwelling places, in which they have sinned, and will cleanse them; so shall they be My people, and I will be their God.
וְעַבְדִּי דָוִד מֶלֶךְ עֲלֵיהֶם וְרוֹעֶה אֶחָד יִהְיֶה לְכֻלָּם וּבְמִשְׁפָּטַי יֵלֵכוּ וְחֻקֹּתַי יִשְׁמְרוּ וְעָשׂוּ אוֹתָם	24[8] And My servant David shall be king over them, and they all shall have one shepherd; they shall also walk in My ordinances, and observe My statutes, and do them.
וְיָשְׁבוּ עַל־הָאָרֶץ אֲשֶׁר נָתַתִּי לְעַבְדִּי לְיַעֲקֹב אֲשֶׁר יָשְׁבוּ־בָהּ אֲבוֹתֵיכֶם וְיָשְׁבוּ עָלֶיהָ הֵמָּה וּבְנֵיהֶם וּבְנֵי בְנֵיהֶם עַד־עוֹלָם וְדָוִד עַבְדִּי נָשִׂיא לָהֶם לְעוֹלָם	25[9] And they shall dwell in the land that I have given unto Jacob My servant, in which your fathers dwelt; and they shall dwell in it, they, and their children, and their children's children, forever; and David My servant shall be their prince forever.

---

[1] Ezekiel 37:18 - Ezekiel 12:9 17:12 21:5 24:19

[2] Ezekiel 37:19 - 1 Chronicles 9:1-3, Colossians 3:11, Ephesians 2:13-14, Ezekiel 37:16-317, z.Vaetchanan 269b, Zechariah 10:6

[3] LXX *one rod in the hand of Juda*

[4] Ezekiel 37:20 - Ezekiel 12:3, Hosea 12:12, Numbers 17:21-17:9

[5] Ezekiel 37:21 - Amos 9:14-9:15, Deuteronomy 30:3-30:4, Ezekiel 10:13 12:24 15:25 15:27, Isaiah 11:11-11:16 27:12-27:13 43:5-43:6 1:12, Jeremiah 16:15 23:3 23:8 5:14 6:3 6:10 6:18 31:9-31:11 8:37 9:7 9:11 2:19, Micah 7:11-7:12, Midrash Proverbs 18, Obadiah 1:17-21, z.Vaetchanan 269b
Ezekiel 37:21-28 - Numbers.R 9:49

[6] Ezekiel 37:22 - Ephesians 2:19-2:22, Ezekiel 34:23-24 13:24, Genesis 1:10, Genesis.R 98 [Excl]:2, Hosea 2:2 3:4-5, Isaiah 9:7-8 11:12-11:13, Jeremiah 3:18 23:5-6 8:39 33:14-17 9:26 2:4, John 10:16, Luke 1:32-33, mt.Hilchot Melachim uMichamoteihem 11:1, Psalms 2:6 2:12 72:1 72:8, Revelation 11:15, z.Toledot 145b

[7] Ezekiel 37:23 - 1 John 1:7 1:9, 4Q174 3:16-17 4QFlor 1.16-17, Ephesians 5:26-5:27, Ezekiel 20:43 36:24-36:25 36:28-36:29 12:31 13:27 15:22 43:7-43:8, Genesis 17:7-17:8, Hebrews 9:13-9:14, Hosea 2:1 14:10, Isaiah 2:18, Jeremiah 7:2 7:34 32:38-32:39, Leviticus 20:7-20:8, Micah 7:14, Midrash Proverbs 18, Psalms 68:21 68:36, Revelation 21:3-21:4 21:7, Zechariah 13:1-13:2 13:9 14:21

[8] Ezekiel 37:24 - 1 Corinthians 11:2, 1 John 2:6, 1 Peter 5:4, Deuteronomy 6:6, Ecclesiastes 12:11, Ephesians 2:10 4:4-4:6, Ezekiel 34:23-34:24 12:27 13:22 13:25, Hebrews 13:20, Hosea 3:5, Isaiah 16:11 55:3-55:4, Jeremiah 23:5 6:9 7:34 8:39, John 10:11 10:14-16, Luke 1:32, Micah 5:3 5:5, Midrash Psalms 57:3, Philippians 2:12-13, Psalms 78:71-72 80:2, Titus 2:11-13 3:3-8, Zechariah 13:7

[9] Ezekiel 37:25 - Amos 9:15, Avot de R'Natan 41, b.Sanhedrin 98b, Daniel 2:44-2:45, Ein Yaakov Sanhedrin:98b, Ezekiel 4:25 12:28 13:21 13:24 13:26, Genesis.R 97:1, Hebrews 7:2 7:21, Isaiah 9:7-8 11:1 12:21 18:22, Jeremiah 6:3 7:25 8:41, Joel 4:20, John 12:34, Luke 1:32-33, Midrash Tanchuma Korach 12, Midrash Tanchuma Tetzaveh 10, Sifre Devarim Vaetchanan 27, Zechariah 6:12-13 14:11, Zephaniah 3:14-15

וְכָרַתִּ֤י לָהֶם֙ בְּרִ֣ית שָׁל֔וֹם בְּרִ֥ית עוֹלָ֖ם יִהְיֶ֣ה אוֹתָ֑ם וּנְתַתִּים֙ וְהִרְבֵּיתִ֣י אוֹתָ֔ם וְנָתַתִּ֥י אֶת־מִקְדָּשִׁ֛י בְּתוֹכָ֖ם לְעוֹלָֽם	26[1] Moreover I will make a covenant of peace with them—it shall be an everlasting covenant with them; and I will establish them, and multiply them, and will set My sanctuary in the midst of them forever.
וְהָיָ֤ה מִשְׁכָּנִי֙ עֲלֵיהֶ֔ם וְהָיִ֥יתִי לָהֶ֖ם לֵֽאלֹהִ֑ים וְהֵ֖מָּה יִֽהְיוּ־לִ֥י לְעָֽם	27[2] My dwelling place also shall be over them; and I will be their God, and they shall be My people.
וְיָֽדְעוּ֙ הַגּוֹיִ֔ם כִּ֚י אֲנִ֣י יְהֹוָ֔ה מְקַדֵּ֖שׁ אֶת־יִשְׂרָאֵ֑ל בִּהְי֧וֹת מִקְדָּשִׁ֛י בְּתוֹכָ֖ם לְעוֹלָֽם	28[3] And the nations shall know that I am the LORD who sanctifies Israel, when My sanctuary shall be in their midst forever.'

Ezekiel – Chapter 38[4]

וַיְהִ֥י דְבַר־יְהֹוָ֖ה אֵלַ֥י לֵאמֹֽר	1[5] And the word of the LORD came unto me, saying:
בֶּן־אָדָ֗ם שִׂ֤ים פָּנֶ֙יךָ֙ אֶל־גּוֹג֙ אֶ֣רֶץ הַמָּג֔וֹג נְשִׂ֕יא רֹ֖אשׁ מֶ֣שֶׁךְ וְתֻבָ֑ל וְהִנָּבֵ֖א עָלָֽיו	2[6] 'Son of man, set your face toward Gog, of the land of Magog, *the chief*[7] prince of Meshech and Tubal, and prophesy against him,
וְאָ֣מַרְתָּ֔ כֹּ֥ה אָמַ֖ר אֲדֹנָ֣י יְהֹוִ֑ה הִנְנִ֤י אֵלֶ֙יךָ֙ גּ֔וֹג נְשִׂ֕יא רֹ֖אשׁ מֶ֥שֶׁךְ וְתֻבָֽל	3[8] and say: Thus says the Lord GOD: Behold, I am against you, O Gog, *chief*[9] prince of Meshech and Tubal;
וְשׁ֣וֹבַבְתִּ֔יךָ וְנָתַתִּ֥י חַחִ֖ים בִּלְחָיֶ֑יךָ וְהוֹצֵאתִי֩ אוֹתְךָ֨ וְאֶת־כָּל־חֵילֶ֜ךָ סוּסִ֣ים וּפָרָשִׁ֗ים לְבֻשֵׁ֤י מִכְלוֹל֙ כֻּלָּ֔ם קָהָ֥ל רָב֙ צִנָּ֣ה וּמָגֵ֔ן תֹּֽפְשֵׂ֥י חֲרָב֖וֹת כֻּלָּֽם	4[10] *and I will turn you about, and put hooks into your jaws, and I will bring you forth, and all your army, horses and horsemen, all of them clothed most gorgeously, a great company with buckler and shield, all of them handling swords*[11]:
פָּרַ֛ס כּ֥וּשׁ וּפ֖וּט אִתָּ֑ם כֻּלָּ֖ם מָגֵ֥ן וְכוֹבָֽע	5[12] Persia, *Cush, and Put with them*[13], all of them with shield and helmet;
גֹּ֚מֶר וְכָל־אֲגַפֶּ֔יהָ בֵּ֣ית תּֽוֹגַרְמָ֗ה יַרְכְּתֵ֥י צָפ֖וֹן וְאֶת־כָּל־אֲגַפָּ֑יו עַמִּ֥ים רַבִּ֖ים אִתָּֽךְ	6[14] Gomer, and all his bands; the house of Togarmah in the uttermost parts of the north, and all his bands; many peoples with you.
הִכֹּ֣ן וְהָכֵ֣ן לְךָ֗ אַתָּ֛ה וְכָל־קְהָלֶ֖ךָ הַנִּקְהָלִ֣ים עָלֶ֑יךָ וְהָיִ֥יתָ לָהֶ֖ם לְמִשְׁמָֽר	7[15] Be prepared, and prepare for yourself, you, and all your company who are assembled unto you, and be guarded of them.

---

[1] Ezekiel 37:26 - 1 Kings 8:20-21, 2 Corinthians 6:16, 2 Samuel 23:5, Ezekiel 11:16 34:25 43:7 36:10 36:37 16:62 10:25 12:10 12:37 19:7 45:1-6, Genesis 17:7, Hebrews 6:14 13:20-13:21, Hosea 2:18-25, Isaiah 3:6 1:21 7:3 59:20-21, Jeremiah 6:19 7:28 8:40, John 14:27, Leviticus 26:11-12, Psalms 68:19 89:4-5, Zechariah 2:5 8:4-5

[2] Ezekiel 37:27 - 2 Corinthians 6:16, b.Kiddushin 70b, Colossians 2:9-2:10, Ein Yaakov Kiddushin 70b, Ezekiel 11:20 14:11 12:28 13:23, Genesis.R 26:6, Hosea 2:23, John 1:14, Leviticus 26:11-26:12, Revelation 21:3 21:22

[3] Ezekiel 37:28 - 1 Corinthians 1:30, 1 Thessalonians 5:23, Ephesians 5:26, Exodus 7:13, Ezekiel 20:12 12:23 12:36 14:23 15:7 15:23, John 17:17-17:19, Leviticus 20:8 21:8, Psalms 79:10 6:16 6:2, Romans 11:15

[4] Ezekiel 38 - Ein Yaakov Pesachim:118a, Haftarah Shabbat Chol Hamoed Sukkot [Teimon], mt.Hilchot Melachim uMichamoteihem 12:2, Sifre Devarim Ekev 43, Jastrow 726b

[5] Ezekiel 38:1 - Leviticus.R 27:11 30:5, Numbers.R 15:19, Sibylline Oracles 3.319 3.663
Ezekiel 38:1-39:29 - Pesikta Rabbati 23:1 51:7

[6] Ezekiel 38:2 - 1 Chronicles 1:5, 3 Enoch 45:5, Ezekiel 2:1 6:2 21:2 1:2 3:13 8:26 35:2-3 14:3 15:1 15:6 15:11, Genesis 10:2, Isaiah 18:19, Lamentations.R 1:40, m.Eduyot 2:10, Revelation 20:8-9

[7] LXX *Rhos*

[8] Ezekiel 38:3 - b.Berachot 58a, Ein Yaakov Berachot:58a, Ezekiel 13:8 5:3 11:3 39:1-39:10, z.Vaetchanan 269b

[9] LXX *Rhos*

[10] Ezekiel 38:4 - 1 Chronicles 12:7, 2 Chronicles 1:5, 2 Kings 19:28, Daniel 11:40, Ezekiel 23:12 5:4 14:15 15:2, Isaiah 13:29, Jeremiah 22:9

[11] LXX *and I will gather you, and all your host, horses and horsemen, all wearing breastplates, with a great multitude, shields and helmets and swords*

[12] Ezekiel 38:5 - 1 Chronicles 1:8, Ezekiel 3:10 6:5, Genesis 10:6 10:8, Nahum 3:9, Sibylline Oracles 3.323

[13] LXX *Ethiopians, and Libyans*

[14] Ezekiel 38:6 - 1 Chronicles 1:5-1:6, Daniel 11:40, Ezekiel 3:14, Genesis 10:2-10:3

[15] Ezekiel 38:7 - 2 Chronicles 1:8, Amos 4:12, Isaiah 8:9-8:10 13:22, Jeremiah 46:3-46:5 46:14-46:16 3:12, Joel 4:9-4:12, Psalms 2:1-2:4, Zechariah 14:2-14:3

Hebrew	Verse	English
מִיָּמִים רַבִּים֙ תִּפָּקֵ֔ד בְּאַחֲרִ֤ית הַשָּׁנִים֙ תָּב֣וֹא ׀ אֶל־אֶ֗רֶץ מְשׁוֹבֶ֣בֶת מֵחֶ֔רֶב מְקֻבֶּ֙צֶת֙ מֵעַמִּ֣ים רַבִּ֔ים עַ֖ל הָרֵ֣י יִשְׂרָאֵ֑ל אֲשֶׁר־הָי֥וּ לְחָרְבָּ֖ה תָּמִ֑יד וְהִיא֙ מֵעַמִּ֣ים הוּצָ֔אָה וְיָשְׁב֥וּ לָבֶ֖טַח כֻּלָּֽם	8[1]	After many days you shall be mustered for service, in the latter years you shall come against the land that is brought back from the sword, that is gathered out of many peoples, against the mountains of Israel, which have been a continual waste; but it is brought forth out of the peoples, and they dwell safely all of them.
וְעָלִ֙יתָ֙ כַּשֹּׁאָ֣ה תָב֔וֹא כֶּעָנָ֛ן לְכַסּ֥וֹת הָאָ֖רֶץ תִּֽהְיֶ֑ה אַתָּה֙ וְכָל־אֲגַפֶּ֔יךָ וְעַמִּ֥ים רַבִּ֖ים אוֹתָֽךְ	9[2]	And you shall ascend, you shall come like a storm, you shall be like a cloud to cover the land, you, and all your bands, and many peoples with you.
כֹּ֥ה אָמַ֖ר אֲדֹנָ֣י יְהֹוִ֑ה וְהָיָ֣ה ׀ בַּיּ֣וֹם הַה֗וּא יַעֲל֤וּ דְבָרִים֙ עַל־לְבָבֶ֔ךָ וְחָשַׁבְתָּ֖ מַחֲשֶׁ֥בֶת רָעָֽה	10[3]	Thus says the Lord GOD: It shall come to pass in that day, that things shall come into your mind, and you shall devise an evil device;
וְאָמַרְתָּ֗ אֶֽעֱלֶה֙ עַל־אֶ֣רֶץ פְּרָז֔וֹת אָבוֹא֙ הַשֹּׁ֣קְטִ֔ים יֹשְׁבֵ֖י לָבֶ֑טַח כֻּלָּ֗ם יֹֽשְׁבִים֙ בְּאֵ֣ין חוֹמָ֔ה וּבְרִ֥יחַ וּדְלָתַ֖יִם אֵ֥ין לָהֶֽם	11[4]	and you shall say: I will go up against the *land of unwalled villages*[5]; I will come upon them who are quiet, who dwell safely, all of them dwelling without walls, and having neither bars nor gates;
לִשְׁלֹ֤ל שָׁלָל֙ וְלָבֹ֣ז בַּ֔ז לְהָשִׁ֤יב יָֽדְךָ֙ עַל־חֳרָב֣וֹת נוֹשָׁב֔וֹת וְאֶל־עַ֗ם מְאֻסָּף֙ מִגּוֹיִ֔ם עֹשֶׂה֙ מִקְנֶ֣ה וְקִנְיָ֔ן יֹשְׁבֵ֖י עַל־טַבּ֥וּר הָאָֽרֶץ	12[6]	to take the spoil and to take the prey; to turn your hand against the waste places that are now inhabited, and against the people who are gathered out of the nations, that have gotten cattle and goods, that dwell in the middle of the earth.
שְׁבָ֡א וּ֠דְדָ֠ן וְסֹחֲרֵ֨י תַרְשִׁ֤ישׁ וְכָל־כְּפִרֶ֙יהָ֙ יֹאמְר֣וּ לְךָ֔ הֲלִשְׁלֹ֤ל שָׁלָל֙ אַתָּ֣ה בָ֔א הֲלָבֹ֥ז בַּ֖ז הִקְהַ֣לְתָּ קְהָלֶ֑ךָ לָשֵׂ֣את ׀ כֶּ֣סֶף וְזָהָ֗ב לָקַ֙חַת֙ מִקְנֶ֣ה וְקִנְיָ֔ן לִשְׁלֹ֖ל שָׁלָ֥ל גָּדֽוֹל	13[7]	Sheba, and Dedan, and the *merchants of Tarshish*[8], with all the magnates thereof, shall say unto you: Come you to take the spoil? have you assembled your company to take the prey? to carry away silver and gold, to take away cattle and goods, to take great spoil?
לָכֵן֙ הִנָּבֵ֣א בֶן־אָדָ֔ם וְאָמַרְתָּ֣ לְג֔וֹג כֹּ֥ה אָמַ֖ר אֲדֹנָ֣י יְהֹוִ֑ה הֲל֣וֹא ׀ בַּיּ֣וֹם הַה֗וּא בְּשֶׁ֨בֶת עַמִּ֧י יִשְׂרָאֵ֛ל לָבֶ֖טַח תֵּדָֽע	14[9]	Therefore, son of man, prophesy, and say unto Gog: Thus says the Lord GOD: In that day when My people Israel dwells safely, shall you not know it?
וּבָ֤אתָ מִמְּקֽוֹמְךָ֙ מִיַּרְכְּתֵ֣י צָפ֔וֹן אַתָּ֕ה וְעַמִּ֥ים רַבִּ֖ים אִתָּ֑ךְ רֹכְבֵ֤י סוּסִים֙ כֻּלָּ֔ם קָהָ֥ל גָּד֖וֹל וְחַ֥יִל רָֽב	15[10]	And you shall come from your place out of the uttermost parts of the north, you, and many peoples with you, all of them riding upon horses, a great company and a mighty army;

---

[1] Ezekiel 38:8 - 1 Peter 2:9, Amos 9:14-9:15, Deuteronomy 4:30, Exodus 20:5, Ezekiel 4:26 10:13 34:25-34:28 36:1-36:8 36:24-36:38 37:21-37:28 38:11-38:12 14:16 39:27-39:29, Genesis 1:1, Habakkuk 2:3, Hosea 3:3-3:5, Isaiah 11:11-11:16 24:22 5:6, Jeremiah 23:6 6:3 6:18 8:5 8:37 9:16 24:47 1:39, Lamentations 4:22, Numbers 24:14

[2] Ezekiel 38:9 - Daniel 11:40, Ezekiel 13:11 14:16, Isaiah 8:9-8:10 21:1-21:2 1:4 4:2, Jeremiah 4:13, Joel 2:2

[3] Ezekiel 38:10 - 1 Corinthians 4:5, Acts 5:3 5:9 8:22, Isaiah 10:7, John 13:2, Mark 7:21, Micah 2:1, Proverbs 6:14 6:18 12:2 19:21, Psalms 36:5 83:4-83:5 19:2, z.Vaetchanan 269b

[4] Ezekiel 38:11 - Exodus 15:9, Ezekiel 14:8, Isaiah 37:24-25, Jeremiah 49:31-32, Judges 18:7 18:27, Proverbs 1:11-1:16 3:29-30, Psalms 10:10, Romans 3:15, Saadia Opinions 8:6, Zechariah 2:4-5

[5] LXX *rejected land*

[6] Ezekiel 38:12 - 1 Enoch 26:1, Amos 1:8, b.Bava Batra [Rashbam] 74a, Ecclesiastes.R 1:9, Ezekiel 5:19 36:33-36:35 14:8, Isaiah 1:24-1:25 10:6, Jeremiah 6:16 32:43-32:44 33:12-33:13, Jubilees 8:12 8:19, Judges 9:37, Midrash Psalms 19:1, Midrash Tanchuma Kedoshim 10, Prayer of Jacob 1:8, Saadia Opinions 2:10, Zechariah 1:12 1:17 10:8-10:10 13:7

[7] Ezekiel 38:13 - Ezekiel 19:3-19:6 1:13 3:12 3:15 3:20 27:22-27:23 3:25 8:2, Isaiah 10:6, Jeremiah 15:13 2:17 3:38, Mekhilta de R'Shimon bar Yochai Shirata 33:1, Nahum 2:12-2:14, Psalms 57:5, Zechariah 11:3

[8] LXX *Carthaginian merchants*

[9] Ezekiel 38:14 - Ezekiel 13:28 14:8 14:11, Isaiah 4:1-4:2, Jeremiah 23:6, z.Vaetchanan 269b, Zechariah 2:5 2:8

[10] Ezekiel 38:15 - Daniel 11:40, Ezekiel 14:4 14:6 15:2, Joel 4:2, Revelation 16:14 16:16 20:8, Saadia Opinions 8:6, Zechariah 12:2-12:4 14:2-14:3, Zephaniah 3:8

וְעָלִיתָ עַל־עַמִּי יִשְׂרָאֵל כֶּעָנָן לְכַסּוֹת הָאָרֶץ
בְּאַחֲרִית הַיָּמִים תִּהְיֶה וַהֲבִאוֹתִיךָ עַל־אַרְצִי
לְמַעַן דַּעַת הַגּוֹיִם אֹתִי בְּהִקָּדְשִׁי בְךָ לְעֵינֵיהֶם גּוֹג

16[1] and you shall come up against My people Israel, as a cloud to cover the land; it shall be in the end of days, and I will bring you against My land, that the nations may know Me, when I shall be sanctified through you, O Gog, before their eyes.

כֹּה־אָמַר אֲדֹנָי יְהוִה הַאַתָּה־הוּא אֲשֶׁר־דִּבַּרְתִּי
בְּיָמִים קַדְמוֹנִים בְּיַד עֲבָדַי נְבִיאֵי יִשְׂרָאֵל
הַנִּבְּאִים בַּיָּמִים הָהֵם שָׁנִים לְהָבִיא אֹתְךָ עֲלֵיהֶם

17[2] Thus says the Lord GOD: Are you he of whom I spoke in old times by My servants the prophets of Israel, who prophesied in those days for many years, that I would bring you against them?

וְהָיָה בַּיּוֹם הַהוּא בְּיוֹם בּוֹא גוֹג עַל־אַדְמַת
יִשְׂרָאֵל נְאֻם אֲדֹנָי יְהוִה תַּעֲלֶה חֲמָתִי בְּאַפִּי

18[3] And it shall come to pass in that day, when Gog shall come against the land of Israel, says the Lord GOD, that My fury shall arise up in My nostrils.

וּבְקִנְאָתִי בְאֵשׁ־עֶבְרָתִי דִּבַּרְתִּי אִם־לֹא בַּיּוֹם
הַהוּא יִהְיֶה רַעַשׁ גָּדוֹל עַל אַדְמַת יִשְׂרָאֵל

19[4] For in My jealousy and in the fire of My wrath have I spoken: Surely in that day there shall be a great shaking in the land of Israel;

וְרָעֲשׁוּ מִפָּנַי דְּגֵי הַיָּם וְעוֹף הַשָּׁמַיִם וְחַיַּת הַשָּׂדֶה
וְכָל־הָרֶמֶשׂ הָרֹמֵשׂ עַל־הָאֲדָמָה וְכֹל הָאָדָם אֲשֶׁר
עַל־פְּנֵי הָאֲדָמָה וְנֶהֶרְסוּ הֶהָרִים וְנָפְלוּ הַמַּדְרֵגוֹת
וְכָל־חוֹמָה לָאָרֶץ תִּפּוֹל

20[5] so that the fishes of the sea, and the fowls of the heaven, and the beasts of the field and all creeping things that creep upon the ground, and all the men who are upon the face of the earth, shall shake at My presence, and the mountains shall be thrown down, and the steep places shall fall, and every wall shall fall to the ground.

וְקָרָאתִי עָלָיו לְכָל־הָרַי חֶרֶב נְאֻם אֲדֹנָי יְהוִה
חֶרֶב אִישׁ בְּאָחִיו תִּהְיֶה

21[6] And I will call for a sword against him throughout all my mountains, says the Lord GOD; every man's sword shall be against his brother.

וְנִשְׁפַּטְתִּי אִתּוֹ בְּדֶבֶר וּבְדָם וְגֶשֶׁם שׁוֹטֵף וְאַבְנֵי
אֶלְגָּבִישׁ אֵשׁ וְגָפְרִית אַמְטִיר עָלָיו וְעַל־אֲגַפָּיו
וְעַל־עַמִּים רַבִּים אֲשֶׁר אִתּוֹ

22[7] And I will plead against him with pestilence and with blood; and I will cause to rain upon him, and upon his bands, and upon the many peoples who are with him, an overflowing shower, and great hailstones, fire, and brimstone.

וְהִתְגַּדִּלְתִּי וְהִתְקַדִּשְׁתִּי וְנוֹדַעְתִּי לְעֵינֵי גּוֹיִם רַבִּים
וְיָדְעוּ כִּי־אֲנִי יְהוָה

23[8] Thus will I magnify Myself, and sanctify Myself, and I will make Myself known in the

---

[1] Ezekiel 38:16 - 1 Samuel 17:45-47, 1 Timothy 4:1, 2 Kings 19:19, 2 Timothy 3:1, Daniel 2:28 3:24-29 4:29-34 6:16-28 10:14, Deuteronomy 7:29, Exodus 14:4, Ezekiel 12:23 38:8-9 14:23 15:21, Genesis.R 98 [Excl]:2, Hosea 3:5, Isaiah 2:2 5:23, Matthew 6:9-10, Micah 4:1 7:15-17, Psalms 83:18-19

[2] Ezekiel 38:17 - b.Sanhedrin 14a, Daniel 11:40-45, Ein Yaakov Sanhedrin:17a, Ezekiel 38:10-11 14:16, Isaiah 3:1 34:1-6 63:1-6 66:15-16, Joel 4:9-14, Midrash Tanchuma Behaalotcha 12, Psalms 110:5-6, z.Vaetchanan 269b, Zechariah 12:2-8 14:1-21

[3] Ezekiel 38:18 - b.Megillah 31a, b.Shabbat 118a, Deuteronomy 8:22, Ein Yaakov Shabbat:118a, Ezekiel 36:5-6, Hebrews 12:29, Midrash Psalms 8:8, Nahum 1:2, Psalms 18:8-9 89:47
Ezekiel 38:18-20 - Mekhilta de R'Shimon b'Yochai Shirata 33:1, Mekilta de R'Ishmael Shirata 7:67-69
Ezekiel 38:18-39:16 - Haftarah Shabbat Chol Hamoed Sukkot [Ashkenaz and Sephard], mt.Hilchot Tefilah 13:16

[4] Ezekiel 38:19 - Deuteronomy 5:19, Ezekiel 5:13 15:25, Haggai 2:6-2:7 2:21-2:22, Hebrews 12:26, Isaiah 18:13, Joel 2:18 4:16, Psalms 18:8, Psalms of Solomon 2:24, Revelation 11:13 16:18 16:20, z.Vaetchanan 266b, Zechariah 1:14

[5] Ezekiel 38:20 - 2 Corinthians 10:4, Hosea 4:3, Isaiah 6:25, Jeremiah 4:23-4:26, Jubilees 23:19, Nahum 1:4-1:6, Revelation 6:12-6:13, Sibylline Oracles 3.677, Zechariah 14:4-14:5

[6] Ezekiel 38:21 - 1 Samuel 14:20, 2 Chronicles 20:23, Ezekiel 14:17, Haggai 2:22, Judges 7:22, Midrash Psalms 8:8, Psalms 9:16, Saadia Opinions 8:6

[7] Ezekiel 38:22 - 16, Exodus 9:22-9:25, Exodus.R 12:2, Ezekiel 5:17 13:11, Fragments of Pseudo-Greek Poets 6, Genesis 19:24, Isaiah 4:17 5:6 30:30-30:33 18:16, Jeremiah 1:31, Joshua 10:11, Matthew 7:27, Mekhilta de R'Shimon bar Yochai Beshallach 26:2, Mekilta de R'Ishmael Beshallah 7:36, Midrash Tanchuma Beshallach 7, Midrash Tanchuma Bo 4, Midrash Tanchuma Reeh 9, Midrash Tanchuma Vaera 10 16, Pesikta de R'Kahana 7.11, Pesikta Rabbati 17:8, Psalms 11:7 18:13-18:15 77:17-19, Revelation 16:21, Saadia Opinions 8:6, Sibylline Oracles 3.287 3.690, Zechariah 14:12-15
Ezekiel 38:22-23 - Mekilta de R'Ishmael Beshallah 2:83-84

[8] Ezekiel 38:23 - Ezekiel 12:23 13:28 14:16 15:7 15:13 15:27, Leviticus.R 24:1, Midrash Psalms 8:8, Midrash Tanchuma Beshallach 7, Midrash Tanchuma Reeh 9, Psalms 9:17, Revelation 15:3-15:4 19:1-19:6, Sibylline Oracles 3.693, z.Shemot 7b, z.Terumah 174a

eyes of many nations; and they shall know that I am the LORD.

Ezekiel – Chapter 39

וְאַתָּה בֶן־אָדָם הִנָּבֵא עַל־גּוֹג וְאָמַרְתָּ כֹּה אָמַר אֲדֹנָי יְהוִה הִנְנִי אֵלֶיךָ גּוֹג נְשִׂיא רֹאשׁ מֶשֶׁךְ וְתֻבָל

1[1] And you, son of man, prophesy against Gog, and say: Thus says the Lord GOD: Behold, I am against you, O Gog, *chief*[2] prince of Meshech and Tubal;

וְשֹׁבַבְתִּיךָ וְשִׁשֵּׁאתִיךָ וְהַעֲלִיתִיךָ מִיַּרְכְּתֵי צָפוֹן וַהֲבִאוֹתִךָ עַל־הָרֵי יִשְׂרָאֵל

2[3] and I will turn you about and lead you on, and will cause you to come up from the uttermost parts of the north; and I will bring you upon the mountains of Israel;

וְהִכֵּיתִי קַשְׁתְּךָ מִיַּד שְׂמֹאולֶךָ וְחִצֶּיךָ מִיַּד יְמִינְךָ אַפִּיל

3[4] and I will smite your bow out of your left hand, and will cause your arrows to fall out of your right hand.

עַל־הָרֵי יִשְׂרָאֵל תִּפּוֹל אַתָּה וְכָל־אֲגַפֶּיךָ וְעַמִּים אֲשֶׁר אִתָּךְ לְעֵיט צִפּוֹר כָּל־כָּנָף וְחַיַּת הַשָּׂדֶה נְתַתִּיךָ לְאָכְלָה

4[5] You shall fall upon the mountains of Israel, you, and all your bands, and the peoples who are with you; I will give you unto the ravenous birds of every sort and to the beasts of the field, to be devoured.

עַל־פְּנֵי הַשָּׂדֶה תִּפּוֹל כִּי אֲנִי דִבַּרְתִּי נְאֻם אֲדֹנָי יְהוִה

5[6] You shall fall upon the open field; for I have spoken it, says the Lord GOD.

וְשִׁלַּחְתִּי־אֵשׁ בְּמָגוֹג וּבְיֹשְׁבֵי הָאִיִּים לָבֶטַח וְיָדְעוּ כִּי־אֲנִי יְהוָה

6[7] And I will send a fire on Magog, *and on those who dwell safely in the isles*[8]; and they shall know that I am the LORD.

וְאֶת־שֵׁם קָדְשִׁי אוֹדִיעַ בְּתוֹךְ עַמִּי יִשְׂרָאֵל וְלֹא־אַחֵל אֶת־שֵׁם־קָדְשִׁי עוֹד וְיָדְעוּ הַגּוֹיִם כִּי־אֲנִי יְהוָה קָדוֹשׁ בְּיִשְׂרָאֵל

7[9] And My holy name will I make known in the midst of My people Israel; neither will I suffer My holy name to be profaned any longer; and the nations shall know that I am the LORD, the Holy One in Israel.

הִנֵּה בָאָה וְנִהְיָתָה נְאֻם אֲדֹנָי יְהוִה הוּא הַיּוֹם אֲשֶׁר דִּבַּרְתִּי

8[10] Behold, it comes, and it shall be done, says the Lord GOD; This is the day whereof I have spoken.

וְיָצְאוּ יֹשְׁבֵי עָרֵי יִשְׂרָאֵל וּבִעֲרוּ וְהִשִּׂיקוּ בְּנֶשֶׁק וּמָגֵן וְצִנָּה בְּקֶשֶׁת וּבְחִצִּים וּבְמַקֵּל יָד וּבְרֹמַח וּבִעֲרוּ בָהֶם אֵשׁ שֶׁבַע שָׁנִים

9[11] And they who dwell in the cities of Israel shall go forth, and shall make fires of the weapons and use them as fuel, both the shields and the bucklers, the bows and the arrows, and the hand staves, and the spears, and they shall make fires of them seven years;

[1] Ezekiel 39:1 - Ezekiel 11:3 38:2-38:3, Midrash Psalms 150:1, Nahum 2:14 3:5, z.Vaetchanan 269b

[2] LXX *Rhos*

[3] Ezekiel 39:2 - Daniel 11:40, Ezekiel 14:15, Isaiah 13:29, Leviticus.R 9:6, Midrash Psalms 150:1, Numbers.R 13:2, Psalms 40:15 68:3, Song of Songs.R 4:32

[4] Ezekiel 39:3 - Ezekiel 20:21-24, Hosea 1:5, Jeremiah 21:4-21:5, Midrash Psalms 150:1, Psalms 46:10 76:4 Ezekiel 39:3-4 - 4Q285 frag 4 ll.3-4

[5] Ezekiel 39:4 - Ezekiel 5:5 32:4-32:5 9:27 14:21 39:17-39:20, Isaiah 34:2-34:8, Jastrow 1156a, Jeremiah 15:3, Lamentations.R 1:40, Midrash Psalms 150:1, Revelation 19:17-19:21, y.Nazir 1:11

[6] Ezekiel 39:5 - Ezekiel 5:5 8:4, Jeremiah 8:2 22:19, Midrash Psalms 150:1

[7] Ezekiel 39:6 - 3 Enoch 45:5, Amos 1:4 1:7 1:10, Judges 18:7, Ezekiel 6:8 6:16 14:6 14:11 14:13 38:19-22, Isaiah 18:19, Jeremiah 1:22, Midrash Psalms 11:5, Nahum 1:6, Psalms 72:10, Zephaniah 2:11

[8] LXX *and the islands shall be securely inhabited*

[9] Ezekiel 39:7 - Exodus 20:7, Ezekiel 20:9 20:14 20:39 36:20-36:21 12:23 12:36 14:16 14:23 15:22, Isaiah 12:6 19:3 19:14 7:5 12:9 12:14, Leviticus 18:21, Midrash Psalms 150:1

[10] Ezekiel 39:8 - 2 Peter 3:8, Ezekiel 7:2-10 14:17, Isaiah 33:10-12, Mekilta de R'Ishmael Pisha 12:33, Midrash Psalms 150:1, Revelation 16:17 21:6

[11] Ezekiel 39:9 - Ezekiel 15:10, Isaiah 18:24, Jastrow 37a 1219b, Joshua 11:6, Leviticus.R 11:2, Malachi 1:5, Psalms 46:10 111:2-111:3, Saadia Opinions 8:8, Sibylline Oracles 3.649 3.727 5.381, Zechariah 9:10

וְלֹא־יִשְׂאוּ עֵצִים מִן־הַשָּׂדֶה וְלֹא יַחְטְבוּ מִן־
הַיְּעָרִים כִּי בַנֶּשֶׁק יְבַעֲרוּ־אֵשׁ וְשָׁלְלוּ אֶת־
שֹׁלְלֵיהֶם וּבָזְזוּ אֶת־בֹּזְזֵיהֶם נְאֻם אֲדֹנָי יְהוִה

10[1] so that they shall take no wood out of the field, neither cut down any out of the forests, for they shall make fires of the weapons; and they shall *spoil those who spoiled them, and rob those who robbed*[2] them, says the Lord GOD.

וְהָיָה בַיּוֹם הַהוּא אֶתֵּן לְגוֹג מְקוֹם־שָׁם קֶבֶר
בְּיִשְׂרָאֵל גֵּי הָעֹבְרִים קִדְמַת הַיָּם וְחֹסֶמֶת הִיא אֶת־
הָעֹבְרִים וְקָבְרוּ שָׁם אֶת־גּוֹג וְאֶת־כָּל־הֲמוֹנֹה
וְקָרְאוּ גֵּיא הֲמוֹן גּוֹג

11[3] And it shall come to pass in that day, that I will give to Gog a place fit for burial in Israel, the valley of those who pass through on the east of the sea; and it shall stop them that pass through; and there shall they bury Gog and all his multitude; and they shall call it the valley of Hamon-gog.

וּקְבָרוּם בֵּית יִשְׂרָאֵל לְמַעַן טַהֵר אֶת־הָאָרֶץ
שִׁבְעָה חֳדָשִׁים

12[4] And seven months shall the house of Israel be burying them, that they may cleanse the land.

וְקָבְרוּ כָּל־עַם הָאָרֶץ וְהָיָה לָהֶם לְשֵׁם יוֹם הִכָּבְדִי
נְאֻם אֲדֹנָי יְהוִה

13[5] Yes, all the people of the land shall bury them, and it shall be a renown to them; in the day that I shall be glorified, says the Lord GOD.

וְאַנְשֵׁי תָמִיד יַבְדִּילוּ עֹבְרִים בָּאָרֶץ מְקַבְּרִים אֶת־
הָעֹבְרִים אֶת־הַנּוֹתָרִים עַל־פְּנֵי הָאָרֶץ לְטַהֲרָהּ
מִקְצֵה שִׁבְעָה־חֳדָשִׁים יַחְקֹרוּ

14[6] And they shall set apart men of continual employment, who shall pass through the land to bury with those who pass through those who remain on the face of the land, to cleanse it; after the end of seven months shall they search.

וְעָבְרוּ הָעֹבְרִים בָּאָרֶץ וְרָאָה עֶצֶם אָדָם וּבָנָה
אֶצְלוֹ צִיּוּן עַד קָבְרוּ אֹתוֹ הַמְקַבְּרִים אֶל־גֵּיא הֲמוֹן
גּוֹג

15[7] And when those who pass through shall pass through the land, and see a man's bone, then shall he set up a sign by it, till the buriers have buried it in the valley of Hamon-gog.

וְגַם שֶׁם־עִיר הֲמוֹנָה וְטִהֲרוּ הָאָרֶץ

16 And Hamonah shall also be the name of a city. Thus shall they cleanse the land.

וְאַתָּה בֶן־אָדָם כֹּה־אָמַר אֲדֹנָי יְהוִה אֱמֹר לְצִפּוֹר
כָּל־כָּנָף וּלְכֹל חַיַּת הַשָּׂדֶה הִקָּבְצוּ וָבֹאוּ הֵאָסְפוּ
מִסָּבִיב עַל־זִבְחִי אֲשֶׁר אֲנִי זֹבֵחַ לָכֶם זֶבַח גָּדוֹל עַל
הָרֵי יִשְׂרָאֵל וַאֲכַלְתֶּם בָּשָׂר וּשְׁתִיתֶם דָּם

17[8] And you, son of man, thus says the Lord GOD: Speak to the birds of every sort, and to every beast of the field: Assemble yourselves and come; gather yourselves on every side to My festival that I prepare for you, a great festival, on the mountains of Israel, so you may eat flesh and drink blood.

בְּשַׂר גִּבּוֹרִים תֹּאכֵלוּ וְדַם־נְשִׂיאֵי הָאָרֶץ תִּשְׁתּוּ
אֵילִים כָּרִים וְעַתּוּדִים פָּרִים מְרִיאֵי בָשָׁן כֻּלָּם

18[9] You shall eat the flesh of the mighty, and you drink the blood of the princes of the earth shall; rams, lambs, and goats, *bullocks, fatlings of Bashan they are. All of them*[10].

---

[1] Ezekiel 39:10 - Exodus 3:22 12:36, Habakkuk 2:8 3:8, Isaiah 14:2 9:1, Matthew 7:2, Micah 5:9, Revelation 13:10 18:6, Zephaniah 2:9-10

[2] LXX *plunder those who plundered them, and spoil those who spoiled*

[3] Ezekiel 39:11 - Ezekiel 14:2 23:18, Genesis.R 36:6, Jastrow 488a, John 6:1, Luke 5:1, Midrash Tanchuma Noach 15, Numbers 11:34 10:11

[4] Ezekiel 39:12 - Deuteronomy 21:23, Ezekiel 15:14 15:16, Numbers 19:16

[5] Ezekiel 39:13 - 1 Peter 1:7, Deuteronomy 2:19, Ezekiel 4:22 39:21-22, Jeremiah 9:9, Psalms 126:2-3 149:6-9, Zephaniah 3:19-20

[6] Ezekiel 39:14 - Ezekiel 15:12, Numbers 19:11-19

[7] Ezekiel 39:15 - b.Eruvin 54b, b.Moed Katan 5a, b.Niddah 57a, b.Shekalim 3a, Ein Yaakov Eruvin, Ein Yaakov Moed Katan:5a, HaMadrikh 35:9, Jastrow 1275b 1277b, Luke 11:44, y.Maaser Sheni 5:1, y.Moed Katan 1:2, y.Shekalim 1:1, y.Sotah 9:1

[8] Ezekiel 39:17 - 1 Samuel 9:13 16:3 17:46, b.Chullin 139b, Ezekiel 15:4, Genesis 7:54, Genesis.R 32:8, Isaiah 18:6 10:6 8:9, Jeremiah 12:9 22:10, Leviticus.R 11:2, Midrash Psalms 150:1, Midrash Tanchuma Bo 4, Pesikta Rabbati 17:8, Psalms of Solomon 4:19, Revelation 19:17-19:18, Sifre Devarim {Haazinu Hashamayim} 332, Sifre Devarim Nitzavim 332, z.Vaetchanan 269b, Zephaniah 1:7

Ezekiel 39:17-19 - Pesikta de R'Kahana 7.11

Ezekiel 39:17-22 - Tanna Devei Eliyahu 5

[9] Ezekiel 39:18 - Amos 4:1, Deuteronomy 8:14, Ezekiel 5:5 10:8 10:17, Isaiah 10:7, Jeremiah 2:11 2:27 3:40, Leviticus.R 11:2, Midrash Psalms 150:1, Psalms 22:13 68:31, Revelation 19:17-19:18 19:21, Sifre Devarim Nitzavim 332

[10] LXX *and they are all fatted calves*

וַאֲכַלְתֶּם־חֵלֶב לְשָׂבְעָה וּשְׁתִיתֶם דָּם לְשִׁכָּרוֹן מִזִּבְחִי אֲשֶׁר־זָבַחְתִּי לָכֶם	19[1] And you shall eat fat until you are full, and drink blood until you are drunk of My festival I have prepared for you.
וּשְׂבַעְתֶּם עַל־שֻׁלְחָנִי סוּס וָרֶכֶב גִּבּוֹר וְכָל־אִישׁ מִלְחָמָה נְאֻם אֲדֹנָי יְהוִה	20[2] And you shall be filled at My table with horses and horsemen, with mighty men, and with all men of war, says the Lord GOD.
וְנָתַתִּי אֶת־כְּבוֹדִי בַּגּוֹיִם וְרָאוּ כָל־הַגּוֹיִם אֶת־מִשְׁפָּטִי אֲשֶׁר עָשִׂיתִי וְאֶת־יָדִי אֲשֶׁר־שַׂמְתִּי בָהֶם	21[3] And I will set My glory among the nations, and all the nations shall see My judgment that I have executed, and My hand that I have laid on them.
וְיָדְעוּ בֵּית יִשְׂרָאֵל כִּי אֲנִי יְהוָה אֱלֹהֵיהֶם מִן־הַיּוֹם הַהוּא וָהָלְאָה	22[4] So the house of Israel shall know that I am the LORD their God, from that day forward.
וְיָדְעוּ הַגּוֹיִם כִּי בַעֲוֹנָם גָּלוּ בֵית־יִשְׂרָאֵל עַל אֲשֶׁר מָעֲלוּ־בִי וָאַסְתִּר פָּנַי מֵהֶם וָאֶתְּנֵם בְּיַד צָרֵיהֶם וַיִּפְּלוּ בַחֶרֶב כֻּלָּם	23[5] And the nations shall know that the house of Israel went into captivity for their iniquity, because they broke faith with Me, and I hid My face from them; so I gave them into the hand of their adversaries, and all of them fell by the sword.
כְּטֻמְאָתָם וּכְפִשְׁעֵיהֶם עָשִׂיתִי אֹתָם וָאַסְתִּר פָּנַי מֵהֶם	24[6] I did to them according to their uncleanness and according to their transgressions; and I hid My face from them.
לָכֵן כֹּה אָמַר אֲדֹנָי יְהוִה עַתָּה אָשִׁיב אֶת־שְׁבִית 'אֶת־שְׁבוּת' יַעֲקֹב וְרִחַמְתִּי כָּל־בֵּית יִשְׂרָאֵל וְקִנֵּאתִי לְשֵׁם קָדְשִׁי	25[7] Therefore, thus says the Lord GOD: Now I will bring back the captivity of Jacob, and have compassion on the whole house of Israel; and I will be jealous for My holy name.
וְנָשׂוּ אֶת־כְּלִמָּתָם וְאֶת־כָּל־מַעֲלָם אֲשֶׁר מָעֲלוּ־בִי בְּשִׁבְתָּם עַל־אַדְמָתָם לָבֶטַח וְאֵין מַחֲרִיד	26[8] And they shall bear their shame, and all their breach of faith which they have committed against Me, when they dwell safely in their land, and no one shall make them afraid;
בְּשׁוֹבְבִי אוֹתָם מִן־הָעַמִּים וְקִבַּצְתִּי אֹתָם מֵאַרְצוֹת אֹיְבֵיהֶם וְנִקְדַּשְׁתִּי בָם לְעֵינֵי הַגּוֹיִם רַבִּים	27[9] When I have brought them back from the nations, and gathered them out of their enemies' lands, and am sanctified in them in the sight of many nations.
וְיָדְעוּ כִּי אֲנִי יְהוָה אֱלֹהֵיהֶם בְּהַגְלוֹתִי אֹתָם אֶל־הַגּוֹיִם וְכִנַּסְתִּים עַל־אַדְמָתָם וְלֹא־אוֹתִיר עוֹד מֵהֶם שָׁם	28[10] And they shall know that I am the LORD their God, in that I caused them to go into captivity among the nations, and have gathered them to their own land; and I will leave none of them there anymore;

[1] Ezekiel 39:19 - Midrash Psalms 150:1, Sifre Devarim Nitzavim 332

[2] Ezekiel 39:20 - Ezekiel 14:4, Haggai 2:22, Leviticus.R 11:2, Psalms 76:6-7, Revelation 19:18, Sifre Devarim Nitzavim 332, z.Vaetchanan 269b

[3] Ezekiel 39:21 - 1 Samuel 5:7 5:11 6:9, Exodus 7:4 8:15 9:16 14:4, Ezekiel 12:23 14:16 14:23 15:13, Isaiah 2:11 13:20, Malachi 1:11, Psalms 32:4

[4] Ezekiel 39:22 - 1 John 5:20, Apocryphon of Ezekiel Fragment 2, Ezekiel 4:26 10:30 15:7 15:28, Jeremiah 24:7 7:35, John 17:3, Psalms 9:17

[5] Ezekiel 39:23 - 2 Chronicles 7:21-22, Deuteronomy 31:17-18 8:20 8:30, Ezekiel 36:18-23 12:36 15:29, Isaiah 1:15 8:17 18:24 11:2 16:8, Jeremiah 22:8-9 9:5 40:2-3, Judges 2:14 3:8, Lamentations 1:8 2:15-17, Leviticus 2:25, Psalms 10:2 30:8 10:41

[6] Ezekiel 39:24 – 2 Kings 17:7-23, Daniel 9:5-10, Ezekiel 12:19, Isaiah 1:20 3:11 59:17-18, Jeremiah 2:17 2:19 4:18 5:25, Leviticus 2:24

[7] Ezekiel 39:25 - Amos 9:14, Ezekiel 20:40 10:13 36:4-36:6 36:21-36:24 37:21-37:22, Hosea 2:2, Isaiah 27:12-27:13 8:8, Jeremiah 3:18 23:3 6:3 6:10 6:18 7:2 7:4 8:37 9:7, Joel 2:18, Romans 11:26-11:31, z.Vaetchanan 269b, Zechariah 1:14 8:2

[8] Ezekiel 39:26 - 1 Kings 4:25, Daniel 9:16, Deuteronomy 28:47-28:48 32:14-32:15, Ezekiel 16:52 16:57-16:58 16:63 32:25 32:30 8:25 8:30 10:25 34:27-34:28, Isaiah 17:2, Jeremiah 3:24-3:25 6:11, Leviticus 26:5-26:6, Micah 4:4, Psalms 99:8

[9] Ezekiel 39:27 - Ezekiel 28:25-28:26 36:23-36:24 13:21 14:16 14:23 15:13 15:25, Isaiah 5:16, Leviticus 10:3

[10] Ezekiel 39:28 - Amos 9:9, Deuteronomy 30:3-4, Ezekiel 10:30 15:22, Hosea 2:20, Isaiah 3:12, Nehemiah 1:8-10, Romans 9:6-8 11:1-7

וְלֹא־אַסְתִּיר עוֹד פָּנַי מֵהֶם אֲשֶׁר שָׁפַכְתִּי אֶת־רוּחִי עַל־בֵּית יִשְׂרָאֵל נְאֻם אֲדֹנָי יְהֹוִה

29[1] Nor will I hide My face from them any longer; for I have poured out My spirit on the house of Israel, says the Lord GOD.'

Ezekiel – Chapter 40

בְּעֶשְׂרִים וְחָמֵשׁ שָׁנָה לְגָלוּתֵנוּ בְּרֹאשׁ הַשָּׁנָה בֶּעָשׂוֹר לַחֹדֶשׁ בְּאַרְבַּע עֶשְׂרֵה שָׁנָה אַחַר אֲשֶׁר הֻכְּתָה הָעִיר בְּעֶצֶם הַיּוֹם הַזֶּה הָיְתָה עָלַי יַד־יְהֹוָה וַיָּבֵא אֹתִי שָׁמָּה

1[2] In the twenty-fifth year of our captivity, in the beginning of the year, in the tenth day of the month, in the fourteenth year after that the city was struck, in the selfsame day, the hand of the LORD was on me, and He brought me there.

בְּמַרְאוֹת אֱלֹהִים הֱבִיאַנִי אֶל־אֶרֶץ יִשְׂרָאֵל וַיְנִיחֵנִי אֶל־הַר גָּבֹהַּ מְאֹד וְעָלָיו כְּמִבְנֵה־עִיר מִנֶּגֶב

2[3] In the visions of God, He brought me into the land of Israel, and set me down on a very high mountain, upon which was, as it were, the frame of a city *on the south*[4].

וַיָּבֵיא אוֹתִי שָׁמָּה וְהִנֵּה־אִישׁ מַרְאֵהוּ כְּמַרְאֵה נְחֹשֶׁת וּפְתִיל־פִּשְׁתִּים בְּיָדוֹ וּקְנֵה הַמִּדָּה וְהוּא עֹמֵד בַּשָּׁעַר

3[5] And He brought me there, and, behold, there was a man, whose appearance was like the appearance of brass, with a *line of flax*[6] in his hand, and a measuring reed; and he stood in the gate.

וַיְדַבֵּר אֵלַי הָאִישׁ בֶּן־אָדָם רְאֵה בְעֵינֶיךָ וּבְאָזְנֶיךָ שְׁמָע וְשִׂים לִבְּךָ לְכֹל אֲשֶׁר אֲנִי מַרְאֶה אוֹתָךְ כִּי לְמַעַן הַרְאוֹתְכָה הֻבָאתָה הֵנָּה הַגֵּד אֶת־כָּל־אֲשֶׁר־אַתָּה רֹאֶה לְבֵית יִשְׂרָאֵל

4[7] And the man said to me: 'Son of man, see with your eyes, and hear with your ears, and set your heart on all that I shall show you, for you are brought here because I intend to show them to you; declare all that you see to the house of Israel.'

וְהִנֵּה חוֹמָה מִחוּץ לַבַּיִת סָבִיב סָבִיב וּבְיַד הָאִישׁ קְנֵה הַמִּדָּה שֵׁשׁ־אַמּוֹת בָּאַמָּה וָטֹפַח וַיָּמָד אֶת־רֹחַב הַבִּנְיָן קָנֶה אֶחָד וְקוֹמָה קָנֶה אֶחָד

5[8] And behold a wall around the outside of the house, and in the man's hand a measuring reed of six cubits long, of a cubit and a hand breadth each; so he measured the breadth of the building, one reed, and the height, one reed.

וַיָּבוֹא אֶל־שַׁעַר אֲשֶׁר פָּנָיו דֶּרֶךְ הַקָּדִימָה וַיַּעַל 'בְּמַעֲלוֹתוֹ' "בְּמַעֲלוֹתָיו" וַיָּמָד אֶת־סַף הַשַּׁעַר קָנֶה אֶחָד רֹחַב וְאֵת סַף אֶחָד קָנֶה אֶחָד רֹחַב

6[9] Then he came to the gate looking toward the east, and went up the [10]steps; and he measured the *jamb*[11] of the gate, one reed broad, *and the other jamb, one reed broad*[12].

---

[1] Ezekiel 39:29 - 1 John 3:24, Acts 2:17-18 2:33, Ezekiel 36:25-27 37:26-27 39:23-25, Isaiah 8:15 44:3-5 21:17 54:8-10 59:20-21, Joel 3:1, Lamentations.R 2:8 4:14, Zechariah 12:10
[2] Ezekiel 40:1 - 2 Kings 25:1-30, b.Arachin 12a-13a, b.Zevachim 118b, Ein Yaakov Zevachim 118b, Exodus 12:41, Ezekiel 1:2-3 3:14 3:22 8:1 11:24 5:17 8:1 8:17 9:21 13:1, Jeremiah 39:1-18 52:1-34, Mekhilta de R'Shimon bar Yochai Bachodesh 48:1, Mekilta de R'Ishmael Bahodesh 1:13, Revelation 1:10, Saadia Opinions 8:6, Seder Olam 11:Caleb 26:Tenth of Tevet, y.Rosh Hashanah 1:1
Ezekiel 40:1-42:20 - Lives of the Prophets 3:15
Ezekiel 40:1-44:31 - mt.Hilchot Beit Habechirah 1:4
Ezekiel 40:1-48:35 - Greek Apocalypse of Ezra 2:22
[3] Ezekiel 40:2 - 1 Chronicles 4:12 4:19, 2 Corinthians 12:1-7, Acts 2:17 16:9, Daniel 2:34-35 7:1 7:7, Ezekiel 1:1 8:3 17:22-23 48:30-35, Galatians 4:26, Isaiah 2:2-3 14:13 24:2, Micah 4:1, Revelation 21:10-21:23
[4] LXX *before me*
[5] Ezekiel 40:3 - Daniel 10:5-10:6, Ezekiel 1:7 1:27 23:3, Genesis.R 1:8, Guide for the Perplexed 2:44, Isaiah 8:20 4:17, Revelation 1:15 11:1 21:15, y.Eruvin 5:3, z.Pekudei 233a, Zechariah 2:1-2
[6] LXX *builder's line*
[7] Ezekiel 40:4 - 1 Corinthians 11:23, Acts 20:27, Ezekiel 2:1 2:7-8 3:17 19:10 20:5, Isaiah 21:10, Jeremiah 2:2, Matthew 10:27 13:9 13:51-52
[8] Ezekiel 40:5 - b.Eruvin 58a, Deuteronomy 3:11, Ezekiel 18:20, Isaiah 2:1 12:18, Psalms 5:2, Revelation 21:12, Zechariah 2:5
[9] Ezekiel 40:6 - 1 Chronicles 9:18 9:24, 1 Kings 6:8, Ezekiel 8:16 10:18 11:1 16:5 16:7 16:20 16:26 19:1 19:8 20:1 46:1-2 22:12 23:1, Jeremiah 19:2, Nehemiah 3:29, Psalms 84:11
[10] LXX adds *seven*
[11] LXX *porch*
[12] Missing in LXX

וְהַתָּא קָנֶה אֶחָד אֹרֶךְ וְקָנֶה אֶחָד רֹחַב וּבֵין הַתָּאִים חָמֵשׁ אַמּוֹת וְסַף הַשַּׁעַר מֵאֵצֶל אוּלָם הַשַּׁעַר מֵהַבַּיִת קָנֶה אֶחָד	7[1]	*And every cell was one reed long, and one reed broad; and the space between the cells was five cubits; and the jambs of the gate by the porch of the gate within were one reed[2].*
וַיָּמָד אֶת־אֻלָם הַשַּׁעַר מֵהַבַּיִת קָנֶה אֶחָד	8	*He also measured the porch of the gate toward the house, one reed[3].*
וַיָּמָד אֶת־אֻלָם הַשַּׁעַר שְׁמֹנֶה אַמּוֹת 'וְאֵילָו' "וְאֵילָיו" שְׁתַּיִם אַמּוֹת וְאֻלָם הַשַּׁעַר מֵהַבָּיִת	9[4]	Then he measured the porch of the gate[5], eight cubits; and its posts, two cubits; and the porch of the gate was inward.
וְתָאֵי הַשַּׁעַר דֶּרֶךְ הַקָּדִים שְׁלֹשָׁה מִפֹּה וּשְׁלֹשָׁה מִפֹּה מִדָּה אַחַת לִשְׁלָשְׁתָּם וּמִדָּה אַחַת לָאֵילִם מִפֹּה וּמִפֹּו	10	And the cells of the gate eastward were three on this side, and three on that side; they three were of one measure; and the posts had one measure on this side and on that side.
וַיָּמָד אֶת־רֹחַב פֶּתַח־הַשַּׁעַר עֶשֶׂר אַמּוֹת אֹרֶךְ הַשַּׁעַר שְׁלוֹשׁ עֶשְׂרֵה אַמּוֹת	11	And he measured the breadth of the entry of the gate, ten cubits; and the length of the gate, thirteen cubits;
וּגְבוּל לִפְנֵי הַתָּאוֹת אַמָּה אֶחָת וְאַמָּה־אַחַת גְּבוּל מִפֹּה וְהַתָּא שֵׁשׁ־אַמּוֹת מִפֹּו וְשֵׁשׁ אַמּוֹת מִפֹּו	12	*and a border before the cells, one cubit [on this side], and a border[6], one cubit on that side; and the cells, six cubits on this side, and six cubits on that side.*
וַיָּמָד אֶת־הַשַּׁעַר מִגַּג הַתָּא לְגַגּוֹ רֹחַב עֶשְׂרִים וְחָמֵשׁ אַמּוֹת פֶּתַח נֶגֶד פָּתַח	13	And he measured the gate from the roof of the one cell to the roof of the other, a breadth of twenty-five cubits; door to door.
וַיַּעַשׂ אֶת־אֵילִים שִׁשִּׁים אַמָּה וְאֶל־אֵיל הֶחָצֵר הַשַּׁעַר סָבִיב סָבִיב	14[7]	*He also made posts of sixty cubits; to the posts of the court in the gates around it[8].*
וְעַל פְּנֵי הַשַּׁעַר 'הַיֵּאתוֹן' "הָאִיתוֹן" עַל־לִפְנֵי אֻלָם הַשַּׁעַר הַפְּנִימִי חֲמִשִּׁים אַמָּה	15[9]	And from the forefront of the gate of the entrance to the forefront of the inner porch of the gate were fifty cubits.
וְחַלֹּנוֹת אֲטֻמוֹת אֶל־הַתָּאִים וְאֶל אֵלֵיהֵמָה לִפְנִימָה לַשַּׁעַר סָבִיב סָבִיב וְכֵן לָאֵלַמּוֹת וְחַלּוֹנוֹת סָבִיב סָבִיב לִפְנִימָה וְאֶל־אַיִל תִּמֹרִים	16[10]	*And there were narrow windows to the cells and to their posts within the gate, and likewise to the arches; and windows were around inward; and on each post were palm trees[11].*
וַיְבִיאֵנִי אֶל־הֶחָצֵר הַחִיצוֹנָה וְהִנֵּה לְשָׁכוֹת וְרִצְפָה עָשׂוּי לֶחָצֵר סָבִיב סָבִיב שְׁלֹשִׁים לְשָׁכוֹת אֶל־הָרִצְפָה	17[12]	*Then he brought me into the outer court, and, behold, there were chambers and a pavement, made for the court around it; thirty chambers were on the pavement[13].*
וְהָרִצְפָה אֶל־כֶּתֶף הַשְּׁעָרִים לְעֻמַּת אֹרֶךְ הַשְּׁעָרִים הָרִצְפָה הַתַּחְתּוֹנָה	18	And the *pavement was by the side of[14]* the gates, corresponding to the length of the gates, the lower *pavement[15].*

---

[1] Ezekiel 40:7 - 1 Chronicles 9:26 23:28, 1 Kings 6:5-10, 2 Chronicles 3:9 7:11, b.Bava Batra 61a, Ezekiel 16:29 16:33 16:36 18:5, Ezra 8:29, Jeremiah 11:4

[2] LXX *And the chamber was equal in length to the reed, and equal in breadth to the reed; and the porch between the chambers six cubits; and the second chamber equal in breadth to the reed, and equal in length to the reed, and the porch five cubits*

[3] LXX *And the third chamber equal in length to the reed, and equal in breadth to the reed*

[4] Ezekiel 40:9 - Ezekiel 21:19

[5] LXX adds *(near the porch of the gate)*

[6] LXX *And the space before the chambers was narrowed to a cubit in front of the chambers*

[7] Ezekiel 40:14 - 1 Chronicles 4:6, Exodus 3:9 11:17, Ezekiel 8:7 18:1, Isaiah 14:9, Leviticus 6:16, Psalms 4:4

[8] LXX *And the open space of the porch of the gate without, was twenty cubits to the chambers around the gate*

[9] Ezekiel 40:15 - Midrash Tanchuma Vayechi 10

[10] Ezekiel 40:16 - 1 Corinthians 13:12, 1 Kings 6:4 6:29 6:32 6:35, 2 Chronicles 3:5, Ezekiel 16:7 16:12 40:21-22 16:25 16:30 41:15-16 17:18 17:26 18:3, John 5:2, Midrash Tanchuma Behaalotcha 5, Numbers.R 15:7, Psalms 92:13, Revelation 7:9

[11] LXX *And there were secret windows to the chambers, and to the porches within the gate of the court round about, and in the same manner windows to the porches round about within: and on the porch there were palm-trees on this side and on that side*

[12] Ezekiel 40:17 - 1 Chronicles 9:26 23:28, 1 Kings 6:5, 2 Chronicles 7:11, 2 Kings 23:11, Ezekiel 10:5 16:38 17:6 18:1 18:4 21:5 22:21, Jastrow 1495a, Revelation 11:2

[13] LXX *And he brought me into the inner court, and, behold, there were chambers, and peristyles round about the court; thirty chambers within the ranges of columns*

[14] LXX *porticos were behind*

[15] LXX *peristyle*

וַיָּמָד רֹחַב מִלִּפְנֵי֙ הַשַּׁעַר֙ הַתַּחְתּ֔וֹנָה לִפְנֵ֖י הֶחָצֵ֑ר הַפְּנִימִ֣י מִח֔וּץ מֵאָ֣ה אַמָּ֑ה הַקָּדִ֖ים וְהַצָּפֽוֹן׃

19[1] *Then he measured the breadth from the forefront of the lower gate to the forefront of the inner court without, a hundred cubits, eastward as also northward[2].*

וְהַשַּׁעַר אֲשֶׁ֤ר פָּנָיו֙ דֶּ֣רֶךְ הַצָּפ֔וֹן לֶחָצֵ֖ר הַחִֽיצוֹנָ֑ה מָדַ֥ד אָרְכּ֖וֹ וְרָחְבּֽוֹ׃

20[3] *And the gate of the outer court that looked toward the north[4], he measured its length and its breadth.*

וְתָאָ֞ו שְׁלוֹשָׁ֣ה מִפּ֗וֹ וּשְׁלֹשָׁה֙ מִפּ֔וֹ "וְאֵילָו" "וְאֵלַמּוֹ" הָיָ֖ה כְּמִדַּ֣ת הַשַּׁ֣עַר הָרִאשׁ֑וֹן חֲמִשִּׁ֤ים אַמָּה֙ אָרְכּ֔וֹ וְרֹ֕חַב חָמֵ֥שׁ וְעֶשְׂרִ֖ים בָּאַמָּֽה׃

21[5] And its cells were three on this side and three on that side; and its *posts and the arches[6]* thereof were the same measure of the first gate; its length was fifty cubits, and the breadth twenty-five cubits.

"וְחַלּוֹנוֹ" "וְחַלּוֹנָיו" "וְאֵלַמּוֹ" "וְתִמֹרוֹ" "וְתִמֹרָיו" כְּמִדַּ֤ת הַשַּׁ֙עַר֙ אֲשֶׁ֣ר פָּנָ֔יו דֶּ֖רֶךְ הַקָּדִ֑ים וּבְמַעֲל֥וֹת שֶׁ֙בַע֙ יַעֲלוּ־ב֔וֹ "וְאֵֽילַמּוֹ" "וְאֵילַמָּ֖יו" לִפְנֵיהֶֽם׃

22[7] And its windows, and its *arches[8]*, and its palm trees, were the same measure of the gate that looks toward the east; and it was ascended by seven steps; and its arches were before them.

וְשַׁ֙עַר֙ לֶחָצֵ֣ר הַפְּנִימִ֔י נֶ֣גֶד הַשַּׁ֔עַר לַצָּפ֖וֹן וְלַקָּדִ֑ים וַיָּ֧מָד מִשַּׁ֛עַר אֶל־שַׁ֖עַר מֵאָ֥ה אַמָּֽה׃

23[9] And there was a gate to the inner court *over against the other gate, northward as also eastward[10]*; and he measured from gate to gate a hundred cubits.

וַיּוֹלִכֵ֙נִי֙ דֶּ֣רֶךְ הַדָּר֔וֹם וְהִנֵּה־שַׁ֖עַר דֶּ֣רֶךְ הַדָּר֑וֹם וּמָדַ֤ד "אֵילָו" "אֵילָיו" "וְאֵלַמּוֹ" "וְאֵילַמָּ֖יו" כַּמִּדּ֥וֹת הָאֵֽלֶּה׃

24[11] And he led me toward the south, and behold a gate toward the south; and he measured its *posts, and its arches[12]* according to these measures.

וְחַלּוֹנִ֨ים ל֜וֹ "וּלְאֵילַמּוֹ" "וּלְאֵילַמָּ֤יו" סָבִ֣יב ׀ סָבִ֗יב כְּהַחֲלֹּנֹ֖ת הָאֵ֑לֶּה חֲמִשִּׁ֣ים אַמָּ֣ה אֹ֔רֶךְ וְרֹ֕חַב חָמֵ֥שׁ וְעֶשְׂרִ֖ים אַמָּֽה׃

25[13] *And there were windows in it and in its arches around it, like those windows[14]*; the length was fifty cubits, and the breadth twenty-five cubits.

וּמַעֲל֤וֹת שִׁבְעָה֙ "עֹלוֹתָו" "עֹלוֹתָ֔יו" "וְאֵלַמּוֹ" "וְאֵילַמָּ֖יו" לִפְנֵיהֶ֑ם וְתִמֹרִ֣ים ל֗וֹ אֶחָ֤ד מִפּוֹ֙ וְאֶחָ֣ד מִפּ֔וֹ "אֶל־אֵילָו" "אֶל־אֵילָֽיו"׃

26[15] And there were seven steps to go up to it, and its arches were before them; and it had palm trees, one on this side, and another on that side, upon its posts.

וְשַׁ֙עַר֙ לֶחָצֵ֣ר הַפְּנִימִ֔י דֶּ֖רֶךְ הַדָּר֑וֹם וַיָּ֣מָד מִשַּׁ֧עַר אֶל־הַשַּׁ֛עַר דֶּ֥רֶךְ הַדָּר֖וֹם מֵאָ֥ה אַמּֽוֹת׃

27[16] And there was a gate to the inner court toward the south; and he measured from gate to gate toward the south a hundred cubits.

וַיְבִיאֵ֙נִי֙ אֶל־חָצֵ֣ר הַפְּנִימִ֔י בְּשַׁ֖עַר הַדָּר֑וֹם וַיָּ֙מָד֙ אֶת־הַשַּׁ֣עַר הַדָּר֔וֹם כַּמִּדּ֖וֹת הָאֵֽלֶּה׃

28[17] Then he brought me to the inner court by the south gate; and he measured the south gate according to these measures;

---

[1] Ezekiel 40:19 - Ezekiel 16:23 16:27 46:1-2
[2] LXX *And he measured the breadth of the court, from the open space of the outer gate inwards to the open space of the gate looking outwards: a hundred cubits was the distance to the place of the gate looking eastward: and he brought me to the north*
[3] Ezekiel 40:20 - Ezekiel 16:6, Midrash Tanchuma Metzora 9
[4] LXX *and behold a gate looking northwards belonging to the outer court*
[5] Ezekiel 40:21 - Ezekiel 40:7-8 40:10-16 40:25-26 40:29-30 16:34 40:36-37
[6] LXX *porches, and the palm-trees*
[7] Ezekiel 40:22 - 1 Kings 6:29 6:32 6:35 7:36, 2 Chronicles 3:5, Ezekiel 16:6 16:16 16:26 16:31 16:34 16:37 16:49, Hebrews 6:1, Revelation 7:9
[8] LXX *porches*
[9] Ezekiel 40:23 - Exodus 27:9-27:18 38:9-38:12, Ezekiel 16:19 40:27-40:28 16:44
[10] LXX *looking toward the north gate, after the manner of the gate looking toward the east*
[11] Ezekiel 40:24 - Ezekiel 16:6 40:20-40:21 40:28-40:29 16:33 40:35-40:36 22:9
[12] LXX *it, and its chambers, and its posts, and its porches*
[13] Ezekiel 40:25 - 1 Corinthians 13:12, 2 Peter 1:19, Ezekiel 16:16 40:21-22 16:29 16:33, John 12:46, Midrash Tanchuma Behaalotcha 5, Numbers.R 15:7, Pesikta de R'Kahana 21.5
[14] LXX *And its windows and its porches round about were according to the windows of the porch*
[15] Ezekiel 40:26 - 2 Peter 3:18, Ezekiel 16:6 16:16 16:22 16:29, Psalms 92:13-14, Song of Songs 7:8-9
[16] Ezekiel 40:27 - Ezekiel 40:19 40:23 40:32 40:47
[17] Ezekiel 40:28 - Ezekiel 40:32 40:35

יְתָאָו ״וְתָאָיו״ ״וְאֵילָו״ ״וְאֵילָיו״ ״וְאֵלַמּוֹ״ ״וְאֵלַמָּיו״ כַּמִּדּוֹת הָאֵלֶּה וְחַלּוֹנוֹת לוֹ ״וּלְאֵלַמּוֹ״ ״וּלְאֵלַמָּיו״ סָבִיב סָבִיב חֲמִשִּׁים אַמָּה אֹרֶךְ וְרֹחַב עֶשְׂרִים וְחָמֵשׁ אַמּוֹת	29[1]	and its cells, and its posts, *and its arches*[2], according to these measures; and there were windows in it and in its arches around it; it was fifty cubits long, and twenty-five cubits broad.
וְאֵלַמּוֹת סָבִיב סָבִיב אֹרֶךְ חָמֵשׁ וְעֶשְׂרִים אַמָּה וְרֹחַב חָמֵשׁ אַמּוֹת	30[3]	*And there were arches around it, twenty-five cubits long, and five cubits broad*[4].
וְאֵלַמָּו אֶל־חָצֵר הַחִצוֹנָה וְתִמֹרִים ״אֶל־אֵילָו״ ״אֶל־אֵילָיו״ וּמַעֲלוֹת שְׁמוֹנֶה ״מַעֲלוֹ״ ״מַעֲלָיו״	31[5]	And its arches were toward the *outer*[6] court; and palm trees were upon its posts; and the going up to it had eight steps.
וַיְבִיאֵנִי אֶל־הֶחָצֵר הַפְּנִימִי דֶּרֶךְ הַקָּדִים וַיָּמָד אֶת־הַשַּׁעַר כַּמִּדּוֹת הָאֵלֶּה	32[7]	And he brought me into the inner court toward the east; and he measured the gate according to these measures;
יְתָאָו ״וְתָאָיו״ ״וְאֵלָו״ ״וְאֵילָיו״ ״וְאֵלַמּוֹ״ ״וְאֵלַמָּיו״ כַּמִּדּוֹת הָאֵלֶּה וְחַלּוֹנוֹת לוֹ ״וּלְאֵלַמּוֹ״ ״וּלְאֵלַמָּיו״ סָבִיב סָבִיב אֹרֶךְ חֲמִשִּׁים אַמָּה וְרֹחַב חָמֵשׁ וְעֶשְׂרִים אַמָּה	33[8]	and its *cells, and its posts, and its arches, according to these measures; and there were windows in it and in its arches around it*[9]; it was fifty cubits long, and twenty-five cubits broad.
וְאֵלַמּוֹ ״וְאֵלַמָּיו״ לֶחָצֵר הַחִיצוֹנָה וְתִמֹרִים אֶל־אֵלוֹ ״אֶל־אֵלָיו״ מִפּוֹ וּמִפּוֹ וּשְׁמֹנֶה מַעֲלוֹת ״מַעֲלוֹ״ ״מַעֲלָיו״	34[10]	And its arches were toward the outer court; and palm trees were upon its posts, on this side, and on that side; and the going up to it had eight steps.
וַיְבִיאֵנִי אֶל־שַׁעַר הַצָּפוֹן וּמָדַד כַּמִּדּוֹת הָאֵלֶּה	35[11]	And he brought me to the north gate; and he measured it according to these measures;
״תָּאָו״ ״תָּאָיו״ אֵלוֹ ״אֵלָיו״ ״וְאֵלַמּוֹ״ ״וְאֵלַמָּיו״ וְחַלּוֹנוֹת לוֹ סָבִיב סָבִיב אֹרֶךְ חֲמִשִּׁים אַמָּה וְרֹחַב חָמֵשׁ וְעֶשְׂרִים אַמָּה	36[12]	its cells, its posts, and its arches; and there were windows in it around it; the length was fifty cubits, and the breadth twenty-five cubits.
״וְאֵילָו״ ״וְאֵילָיו״ לֶחָצֵר הַחִיצוֹנָה וְתִמֹרִים אֶל־אֵלוֹ ״אֶל־אֵילָיו״ מִפּוֹ וּמִפּוֹ וּשְׁמֹנֶה מַעֲלוֹת ״מַעֲלוֹ״ ״מַעֲלָיו״	37[13]	And its posts were toward the *outer*[14] court; and palm trees were on its posts, on this side, and on that side; and the going up to it had eight steps.
וְלִשְׁכָּה וּפִתְחָהּ בָּאֵילִים הַשְּׁעָרִים שָׁם יָדִיחוּ אֶת־הָעֹלָה	38[15]	*And a chamber with its entry was by the posts at the gates; there was the burnt offering to be washed*[16].
וּבְאֻלָם הַשַּׁעַר שְׁנַיִם שֻׁלְחָנוֹת מִפּוֹ וּשְׁנַיִם שֻׁלְחָנוֹת מִפֹּה לִשְׁחוֹט אֲלֵיהֶם הָעוֹלָה וְהַחַטָּאת וְהָאָשָׁם	39[17]	*And in the porch of the gate were two tables on this side, and two tables on that side, to slay upon them the burnt offering and the sin offering and the guilt offering*[18].

---

[1] Ezekiel 40:29 - 1 Chronicles 28:11-12, 2 Chronicles 31:11, Ezekiel 40:7 40:10 40:12 40:16 40:21-22 40:25, Jeremiah 35:2-4 36:10, Nehemiah 13:5 13:9

[2] Missing in LXX

[3] Ezekiel 40:30 - Ezekiel 40:21 40:25 40:29 40:33 40:36

[4] Missing in LXX

[5] Ezekiel 40:31 - Ezekiel 40:22 40:26 40:34 40:37

[6] LXX *inner*

[7] Ezekiel 40:32 - Ezekiel 40:28-40:31 40:35

[8] Ezekiel 40:33 - Ezekiel 40:21 40:25 40:36

[9] LXX *chambers, and the posts, and the porches according to these measures: and there were windows to it, and porches around it*

[10] Ezekiel 40:34 - Ezekiel 40:6 40:16 40:22 40:26 40:31 40:37 40:49

[11] Ezekiel 40:35 - Ezekiel 40:27 40:32 44:4 47:2

[12] Ezekiel 40:36 - Ezekiel 40:7 40:16 40:21 40:29

[13] Ezekiel 40:37 - Ezekiel 40:31 40:34

[14] LXX *inner*

[15] Ezekiel 40:38 - 1 Kings 6:8, 2 Chronicles 4:6, Ein Yaakov Sanhedrin:97b, Ezekiel 40:12 40:17 41:10-11 42:13, Hebrews 10:22, Leviticus 1:9 8:21

[16] LXX *Its chambers and its door-ways, and its porches at the second gate served as a drain*

[17] Ezekiel 40:39 - 1 Corinthians 10:16-21, 2 Corinthians 5:21, Ezekiel 40:42 41:22 42:13 44:16 46:2, Isaiah 53:5 53:10, Leviticus 1:3-17 4:2-3 4:13-35 5:6-13 6:6 7:1-2, Luke 22:30, Malachi 1:7 1:12

[18] LXX *that they might slay in it the sin-offerings, and the trespass-offerings*

וְאֶל־הַכָּתֵף מִחוּצָה לָעוֹלֶה לְפֶתַח הַשַּׁעַר הַצָּפוֹנָה שְׁנַיִם שֻׁלְחָנוֹת וְאֶל־הַכָּתֵף הָאַחֶרֶת אֲשֶׁר לְאֻלָם הַשַּׁעַר שְׁנַיִם שֻׁלְחָנוֹת	40

And outside on the one side, as one goes up to the entry of the gate toward the north, were two tables; and on the other side of the porch of the gate were two tables[1].

אַרְבָּעָה שֻׁלְחָנוֹת מִפֹּה וְאַרְבָּעָה שֻׁלְחָנוֹת מִפֹּה לְכֶתֶף הַשָּׁעַר שְׁמוֹנָה שֻׁלְחָנוֹת אֲלֵיהֶם יִשְׁחָטוּ	41[2]

Four tables were on this side, and four tables on that side, by the side of the gate; eight tables, upon which to kill the sacrifices.

וְאַרְבָּעָה שֻׁלְחָנוֹת לָעוֹלָה אַבְנֵי גָזִית אֹרֶךְ אַמָּה אַחַת וָחֵצִי וְרֹחַב אַמָּה אַחַת וָחֵצִי וְגֹבַהּ אַמָּה אֶחָת אֲלֵיהֶם וְיַנִּיחוּ אֶת־הַכֵּלִים אֲשֶׁר יִשְׁחֲטוּ אֶת־הָעוֹלָה בָּם וְהַזָּבַח	42[3]

Moreover there were four tables for the burnt offering, of hewn stone, *a cubit and a half long, and a cubit and a half broad[4],* and one cubit high, upon which to lay the instruments with which the burnt offering and the sacrifice are killed.

וְהַשְׁפַתַּיִם טֹפַח אֶחָד מוּכָנִים בַּבַּיִת סָבִיב סָבִיב וְאֶל־הַשֻּׁלְחָנוֹת בְּשַׂר הַקָּרְבָן	43[5]

And the slabs, a handbreadth long, were fastened within around it; and on the tables was to be the flesh of the offering[6].

וּמִחוּצָה לַשַּׁעַר הַפְּנִימִי לִשְׁכוֹת שָׁרִים בֶּחָצֵר הַפְּנִימִי אֲשֶׁר אֶל־כֶּתֶף שַׁעַר הַצָּפוֹן וּפְנֵיהֶם דֶּרֶךְ הַדָּרוֹם אֶחָד אֶל־כֶּתֶף שַׁעַר הַקָּדִים פְּנֵי דֶּרֶךְ הַצָּפֹן	44[7]

And outside the inner gate were chambers for the guard in the inner court, which was at the side of the north gate, and their vista was toward the south; one at the side of the east gate having the vista toward the north.

וַיְדַבֵּר אֵלָי זֶה הַלִּשְׁכָּה אֲשֶׁר פָּנֶיהָ דֶּרֶךְ הַדָּרוֹם לַכֹּהֲנִים שֹׁמְרֵי מִשְׁמֶרֶת הַבָּיִת	45[8]

And he said to me: 'This chamber, whose vista is toward the south, is for the priests, the keepers of the charge of the house.

וְהַלִּשְׁכָּה אֲשֶׁר פָּנֶיהָ דֶּרֶךְ הַצָּפוֹן לַכֹּהֲנִים שֹׁמְרֵי מִשְׁמֶרֶת הַמִּזְבֵּחַ הֵמָּה בְנֵי־צָדוֹק הַקְּרֵבִים מִבְּנֵי־לֵוִי אֶל־יְהוָה לְשָׁרְתוֹ	46[9]

And the chamber whose vista is toward the north is for the priests, the keepers of the charge of the altar; these are the sons of Zadok, who from among the sons of Levi come near to the LORD to minister to Him.'

וַיָּמָד אֶת־הֶחָצֵר אֹרֶךְ מֵאָה אַמָּה וְרֹחַב מֵאָה אַמָּה מְרֻבָּעַת וְהַמִּזְבֵּחַ לִפְנֵי הַבָּיִת	47[10]

And he measured the court, a hundred cubits long, and a hundred cubits broad, foursquare; and the altar was before the house.

וַיְבִאֵנִי אֶל־אֻלָם הַבַּיִת וַיָּמָד אֵל אֻלָם חָמֵשׁ אַמּוֹת מִפֹּה וְחָמֵשׁ אַמּוֹת מִפֹּה וְרֹחַב הַשַּׁעַר שָׁלֹשׁ אַמּוֹת מִפּוֹ וְשָׁלֹשׁ אַמּוֹת מִפּוֹ	48[11]

Then he brought me to the porch of the house, and measured each post of the porch, five cubits on this side, and five cubits on that side; and the breadth of the *gate was three cubits on this side[12],* and three cubits on that side.

אֹרֶךְ הָאֻלָם עֶשְׂרִים אַמָּה וְרֹחַב עַשְׁתֵּי עֶשְׂרֵה אַמָּה וּבַמַּעֲלוֹת אֲשֶׁר יַעֲלוּ אֵלָיו וְעַמֻּדִים אֶל־הָאֵילִים אֶחָד מִפֹּה וְאֶחָד מִפֹּה	49[13]

The length of the porch was twenty cubits, and the breadth *eleven[14]* cubits; and it was by steps that it was ascended; and there were

---

[1] LXX *And behind the drain for the whole-burnt-offerings at the north gate, two tables eastward behind the second gate; and behind the porch of the gate two tables eastward*

[2] Ezekiel 40:41 - Ezekiel 40:39-40:40

[3] Ezekiel 40:42 - Exodus 20:22, Ezekiel 40:39

[4] LXX *their breadth was a cubit and a half, and their length two cubits and a half*

[5] Ezekiel 40:43 - Leviticus 1:6 1:8 8:20

[6] LXX *And they shall have within a border of hewn stone round about of a span broad, and over the tables above screens for covering them from the wet and from the heat*

[7] Ezekiel 40:44 - 1 Chronicles 6:16-17 16:41-43 25:1-31, Colossians 3:16, Ephesians 5:19, Ezekiel 40:7 40:10 40:17 40:23 40:27 40:29 40:38

[8] Ezekiel 40:45 - 1 Chronicles 6:34 9:23, 1 Timothy 6:20, 2 Chronicles 13:11, Ezekiel 8:5, Leviticus 8:35, Malachi 2:4-2:7, Numbers 3:27-3:28 3:32 3:38 18:5, Psalms 134:1, Revelation 1:6

[9] Ezekiel 40:46 - 1 Kings 2:35, Ephesians 2:13, Ezekiel 42:13 43:19 44:15 45:4 48:11, Leviticus 6:12-13 10:3, Numbers 16:5 17:5 18:5

[10] Ezekiel 40:47 - Ezekiel 40:19 40:23 40:27

[11] Ezekiel 40:48 - 1 Kings 6:3, 2 Chronicles 3:4, b.Arachin [Tosefot] 2a

[12] LXX *door was fourteen cubits, and the side-pieces of the door of the porch*

[13] Ezekiel 40:49 - 1 Kings 6:3 7:15-21, 2 Chronicles 3:17, Ezekiel 40:31 40:34 40:37, Jeremiah 52:17-23, Revelation 3:12

[14] LXX *twelve*

pillars by the posts, one on this side, and
another on that side.

Ezekiel – Chapter 41

וַיְבִיאֵנִי אֶל־הַהֵיכָל וַיָּמָד אֶת־הָאֵילִים שֵׁשׁ־אַמּוֹת
רֹחַב־מִפּוֹ וְשֵׁשׁ־אַמּוֹת־רֹחַב מִפּוֹ רֹחַב הָאֹהֶל

1[1] And he brought me to the temple, and
measured the posts, six cubits broad on the
one side, and six cubits *broad on the other
side, which was the breadth of the tent*[2].

וְרֹחַב הַפֶּתַח עֶשֶׂר אַמּוֹת וְכִתְפוֹת הַפֶּתַח חָמֵשׁ
אַמּוֹת מִפּוֹ וְחָמֵשׁ אַמּוֹת מִפּוֹ וַיָּמָד אָרְכּוֹ אַרְבָּעִים
אַמָּה וְרֹחַב עֶשְׂרִים אַמָּה

2[3] And the breadth of the entrance was ten
cubits; and the sides of the entrance were five
cubits on the one side, and five cubits on the
other side; and he measured its length, forty
cubits, and the breadth, twenty cubits.

וּבָא לִפְנִימָה וַיָּמָד אֵיל־הַפֶּתַח שְׁתַּיִם אַמּוֹת
וְהַפֶּתַח שֵׁשׁ אַמּוֹת וְרֹחַב הַפֶּתַח שֶׁבַע אַמּוֹת

3[4] Then went he inward, and measured each post
of the entrance, two cubits; and the entrance,
six cubits; *and the breadth of the entrance,
seven cubits*[5].

וַיָּמָד אֶת־אָרְכּוֹ עֶשְׂרִים אַמָּה וְרֹחַב עֶשְׂרִים אַמָּה
אֶל־פְּנֵי הַהֵיכָל וַיֹּאמֶר אֵלַי זֶה קֹדֶשׁ הַקֳּדָשִׁים

4[6] And he measured its length, *twenty*[7] cubits,
and the breadth, twenty cubits, before the
temple; and he said to me: 'This is the most
holy place.'

וַיָּמָד קִיר־הַבַּיִת שֵׁשׁ אַמּוֹת וְרֹחַב הַצֵּלָע אַרְבַּע
אַמּוֹת סָבִיב סָבִיב לַבַּיִת סָבִיב

5[8] Then he measured the wall of the house, six
cubits; and the breadth of every side chamber,
four cubits, around the house on every side.

וְהַצְּלָעוֹת צֵלָע אֶל־צֵלָע שָׁלוֹשׁ וּשְׁלֹשִׁים פְּעָמִים
וּבָאוֹת בַּקִּיר אֲשֶׁר־לַבַּיִת לַצְּלָעוֹת סָבִיב סָבִיב
לִהְיוֹת אֲחוּזִים וְלֹא־יִהְיוּ אֲחוּזִים בְּקִיר הַבָּיִת

6[9] *And the side chambers were one over another,
thirty-three times; and there were brows in the
wall which belonged to the house for the side
chambers around it, that they might have hold
in it, and not have hold in the wall of the
house*[10].

וְרָחֲבָה וְנָסְבָה לְמַעְלָה לְמַעְלָה לַצְּלָעוֹת כִּי מוּסַב־
הַבַּיִת לְמַעְלָה לְמַעְלָה סָבִיב סָבִיב לַבַּיִת עַל־כֵּן
רֹחַב־לַבַּיִת לְמָעְלָה וְכֵן הַתַּחְתּוֹנָה יַעֲלֶה עַל־
הָעֶלְיוֹנָה לַתִּיכוֹנָה

7[11] *And the side chambers were broader as they
wound around higher and higher; for the
winding of the house went higher and higher
around the house; therefore, the breadth of
the house continued upward; and so one went
up from the lowest row to the highest by the
middle*[12].

וְרָאִיתִי לַבַּיִת גֹּבַהּ סָבִיב סָבִיב 'מְיֻסָּדוֹת'
"מוּסָדוֹת" הַצְּלָעוֹת מְלוֹ הַקָּנֶה שֵׁשׁ אַמּוֹת אַצִּילָה

8[13] I saw also that the house had a raised
basement around it; the foundations of the

---

[1] Ezekiel 41:1 - 1 Kings 6:2, 1 Peter 2:5, Ephesians 2:20-2:22, Ezekiel 40:2-40:3 40:9 40:17 41:3 41:21 41:23, Revelation 3:12 11:1-11:2 21:3 21:15, Saadia Opinions 7Variant:8, Zechariah 6:12-6:13
[2] LXX *the breadth of the porch on the other side*
[3] Ezekiel 41:2 - 1 Kings 6:2 6:17 6:31-6:35, 2 Chronicles 3:3 3:7 29:7, Exodus 26:36 36:37, John 10:7 10:9
[4] Ezekiel 41:3 - Ezekiel 40:16
Ezekiel 41:3-6 - 4QEzeka
[5] LXX *and the side-pieces of the door, seven cubits on one side, and seven cubits on the other side*
[6] Ezekiel 41:4 - 1 Kings 6:5 6:16 6:20, 2 Chronicles 3:8, Exodus 26:33-26:34, Hebrews 9:3-9:8, Revelation 21:16
[7] LXX *forty*
[8] Ezekiel 41:5 - 1 Kings 6:5-6:6, b.Bava Batra [Tosefot] 61a, b.Yoma [Tosefot] 52a, Ezekiel 41:6-41:9 42:3-42:14
[9] Ezekiel 41:6 - 1 Kings 6:5-6:6 6:10, 1 Peter 1:5, b.Bava Batra [Rashbam] 75b, b.Bava Batra 61a 75b, b.Yoma [Tosefot] 52a, Ein Yaakov Bava Batra:75b, Ezekiel 40:17
[10] LXX *And the sides were twice ninety, side against side; and there was a space in the wall of the house at the sides round about, that they should be for them that take hold of them to see, that they should not at all touch the walls of the house*
[11] Ezekiel 41:7 - 1 Kings 6:8, b.Bava Batra [Rashbam] 61a, Hebrews 6:1, Matthew 13:32, Midrash Psalms 61:2, Midrash Tanchuma Tzav 12, Pesikta de R'Kahana 20.7, Pesikta Rabbati 41:2, Sifre Devarim Devarim 1, Song of Songs.R 7:11, z.Pekudei 234a
[12] LXX *And the breadth of the upper side was made according to the projection out of the wall, against the upper one round about the house, that it might be enlarged above, and that men might go up to the upper chambers from those below, and from the ground-sills to the third story*
[13] Ezekiel 41:8 - Ezekiel 40:5, Revelation 21:16

side chambers were a full reed of six cubits to the joining.

רֹחַב הַקִּיר אֲשֶׁר־לַצֵּלָע אֶל־הַחוּץ חָמֵשׁ אַמּוֹת וַאֲשֶׁר מֻנָּח בֵּית צְלָעוֹת אֲשֶׁר לַבָּיִת **9**[1]

The breadth of the outer wall which belonged to the side chambers was five cubits; and so what was left by the structure of the side chambers that belonged to the house.

וּבֵין הַלְּשָׁכוֹת רֹחַב עֶשְׂרִים אַמָּה סָבִיב לַבַּיִת סָבִיב סָבִיב **10**[2]

And between the chambers was a breadth of twenty cubits around the house on every side.

וּפֶתַח הַצֵּלָע לַמֻּנָּח פֶּתַח אֶחָד דֶּרֶךְ הַצָּפוֹן וּפֶתַח אֶחָד לַדָּרוֹם וְרֹחַב מְקוֹם הַמֻּנָּח חָמֵשׁ אַמּוֹת סָבִיב סָבִיב **11**[3]

And the doors of the side chambers were toward the place that was left, one door toward the north, and another door toward the south; and the breadth of the place that was left was five cubits around it.

וְהַבִּנְיָן אֲשֶׁר אֶל־פְּנֵי הַגִּזְרָה פְּאַת דֶּרֶךְ־הַיָּם רֹחַב שִׁבְעִים אַמָּה וְקִיר הַבִּנְיָן חָמֵשׁ־אַמּוֹת רֹחַב סָבִיב סָבִיב וְאָרְכּוֹ תִּשְׁעִים אַמָּה **12**[4]

And the building that was before the separate place at the side toward the west was seventy cubits broad; and the wall of the building was five cubits thick, and its length ninety cubits.

וּמָדַד אֶת־הַבַּיִת אֹרֶךְ מֵאָה אַמָּה וְהַגִּזְרָה וְהַבִּנְיָה וְקִירוֹתֶיהָ אֹרֶךְ מֵאָה אַמָּה **13**[5]

And he measured the house, a hundred cubits long; and the separate place, and the building, with its walls, a hundred cubits long;

וְרֹחַב פְּנֵי הַבַּיִת וְהַגִּזְרָה לַקָּדִים מֵאָה אַמָּה **14**

also the breadth of the face of the house and of the separate place toward the east, a hundred cubits.

וּמָדַד אֹרֶךְ־הַבִּנְיָן אֶל־פְּנֵי הַגִּזְרָה אֲשֶׁר עַל־אַחֲרֶיהָ ׳וְאַתּוּקֵיהָא׳ ״וְאַתִּיקֶיהָא״ מִפּוֹ וּמִפּוֹ מֵאָה אַמָּה וְהַהֵיכָל הַפְּנִימִי וְאֻלַמֵּי הֶחָצֵר **15**[6]

And he measured the length of the building before the separate place that was at its back, and its galleries on the one side and on the other side, a hundred cubits. Now the temple, and the inner place, and the porches of the court,

הַסִּפִּים וְהַחַלּוֹנִים הָאֲטֻמוֹת וְהָאַתִּיקִים סָבִיב לִשְׁלָשְׁתָּם נֶגֶד הַסַּף שְׂחִיף עֵץ סָבִיב סָבִיב וְהָאָרֶץ עַד־הַחַלֹּנוֹת וְהַחַלֹּנוֹת מְכֻסּוֹת **16**[7]

the jambs, and the narrow windows, and the galleries, that they three had around it, over against the jambs there was a veneering of wood around it, and from the ground up to the windows; and the windows were covered[8];

עַל־מֵעַל הַפֶּתַח וְעַד־הַבַּיִת הַפְּנִימִי וְלַחוּץ וְאֶל־כָּל־הַקִּיר סָבִיב סָבִיב בַּפְּנִימִי וּבַחִיצוֹן מִדּוֹת **17**[9]

to the space above the door, to the inner house, and outside, and on all the walls around inside and outside, by measure.

וְעָשׂוּי כְּרוּבִים וְתִמֹרִים וְתִמֹרָה בֵּין־כְּרוּב לִכְרוּב וּשְׁנַיִם פָּנִים לַכְּרוּב **18**[10]

And it was made with cherubim and palm trees; and a palm tree was between cherub and cherub, and every cherub had two faces;

וּפְנֵי אָדָם אֶל־הַתִּמֹרָה מִפּוֹ וּפְנֵי־כְפִיר אֶל־הַתִּמֹרָה מִפּוֹ עָשׂוּי אֶל־כָּל־הַבַּיִת סָבִיב סָבִיב **19**[11]

so that there was the face of a man toward the palm tree on the one side, and the face of a young lion toward the palm tree on the other side; thus was it made through all the house around it.

---

[1] Ezekiel 41:9 - Ezekiel 41:11 42:1 42:4

[2] Ezekiel 41:10 - Ezekiel 40:17

[3] Ezekiel 41:11 - b.Middot [Rashi] 36b, Ezekiel 41:9 42:4

[4] Ezekiel 41:12 - Ezekiel 41:13-41:15 42:1 42:10 42:13, Revelation 21:27 22:14-22:15

[5] Ezekiel 41:13 - b.Pesachim [Rashbam] 116b, Ezekiel 40:47

[6] Ezekiel 41:15 - Ezekiel 41:12 41:17 42:1 42:3 42:5 42:15, Genesis.R 31:10, Mas.Soferim 7:4, Song of Songs 1:17 7:6, Zechariah 3:7

[7] Ezekiel 41:16 - 1 Corinthians 13:12, 1 Kings 6:4 6:15, 2 Chronicles 3:5, Ezekiel 16:16 16:25 41:25-26 18:3, Haggai 1:4, Isaiah 6:4

[8] LXX *And the windows were latticed, giving light round about to the three stories, so as to look through: and the house and the parts adjoining were planked round about, and so was the floor, and from the floor up to the windows, and the window shutters folded back in three parts for one to look through*

[9] Ezekiel 41:17 - Ezekiel 18:15

[10] Ezekiel 41:18 - 1 Kings 6:29-32 6:35 7:36, 2 Chronicles 3:5 3:7, Ezekiel 1:10 10:14 10:21 16:16 16:22 17:20 17:25, Revelation 4:7-9 7:9

[11] Ezekiel 41:19 - Ezekiel 1:10 10:14

מֵהָאָ֫רֶץ עַד־מֵעַ֣ל הַפֶּ֑תַח הַכְּרוּבִ֖ים וְהַתִּמֹרִ֑ים עֲשׂוּיִ֑ם וְקִ֖יר הַהֵיכָֽל	20[1]	From the ground to above the door cherubim and palm trees were *made; and so on the wall of the temple*[2].
הַֽהֵיכָל֙ מְזוּזַ֣ת רְבֻעָ֔ה וּפְנֵ֣י הַקֹּ֔דֶשׁ הַמַּרְאֶ֖ה כַּמַּרְאֶֽה	21[3]	*As for the temple, the jambs were squared; and the face of the sanctuary had an appearance such as is the appearance*[4]
הַמִּזְבֵּ֡חַ עֵ֣ץ שָׁלֹושׁ֩ אַמֹּ֨ות גָּבֹ֜הַּ וְאָרְכֹּ֣ו שְׁתַּֽיִם־אַמֹּ֗ות וּמִקְצֹעֹותָ֥יו לֹ֛ו וְאָרְכֹּ֥ו וְקִֽירֹתָ֖יו עֵ֑ץ וַיְדַבֵּ֣ר אֵלַ֔י זֶ֚ה הַשֻּׁלְחָ֔ן אֲשֶׁ֖ר לִפְנֵ֥י יְהוָֽה	22[5]	The altar, three cubits high, and its length two cubits, was of wood, and so its corners; its length, and its walls, were also of wood; and he said to me: 'This is the table that is before the LORD.'
וּשְׁתַּ֥יִם דְּלָתֹ֖ות לַהֵיכָ֥ל וְלַקֹּֽדֶשׁ	23[6]	And the temple and the sanctuary had two doors.
וּשְׁתַּ֥יִם דְּלָתֹ֖ות לַדְּלָתֹ֑ות שְׁתַּ֚יִם מוּסַבֹּות֙ דְּלָתֹ֔ות שְׁתַּ֙יִם֙ לְדֶ֣לֶת אֶחָ֔ת וּשְׁתֵּ֥י דְלָתֹ֖ות לָאַחֶֽרֶת	24[7]	And the doors had two leaves each, two turning leaves; two leaves for the one door, and two leaves for the other.
וַעֲשׂוּיָ֨ה אֲלֵיהֶ֜ן אֶל־דַּלְתֹ֤ות הַהֵיכָל֙ כְּרוּבִ֣ים וְתִֽמֹרִ֔ים כַּאֲשֶׁ֥ר עֲשׂוּיִ֖ם לַקִּירֹ֑ות וְעָ֥ב עֵ֛ץ אֶל־פְּנֵ֥י הָאוּלָ֖ם מֵהַחֽוּץ	25[8]	And cherubim and palm trees were made on them, on the doors of the temple, as were made on the walls; and there were thick beams of wood on the face of the porch outside.
וְחַלֹּונִ֨ים אֲטֻמֹ֤ות וְתִֽמֹרִים֙ מִפֹּ֣ו וּמִפֹּ֔ו אֶל־כִּתְפֹ֖ות הָאוּלָ֑ם וְצַלְעֹ֥ות הַבַּ֖יִת וְהָעֻבִּֽים	26[9]	*And there were narrow windows and palm trees on the one side and on the other side, on the sides of the porch; there were also the brackets of the house, and the thick beams*[10].

Ezekiel – Chapter 42

וַיֹּוצִאֵ֗נִי אֶל־הֶֽחָצֵר֙ הַחִ֣יצֹונָ֔ה הַדֶּ֖רֶךְ דֶּ֣רֶךְ הַצָּפֹ֑ון וַיְבִאֵ֣נִי אֶל־הַלִּשְׁכָּ֗ה אֲשֶׁ֨ר נֶ֧גֶד הַגִּזְרָ֛ה וַאֲשֶֽׁר־נֶ֥גֶד הַבִּנְיָ֖ן אֶל־הַצָּפֹֽון	1[11]	Then he brought me into the *outer court, the way toward the north*[12]; and he brought me in *the chamber that was over against the separate place, and which was over against the building, toward the north*[13],
אֶל־פְּנֵי־אֹ֨רֶךְ֙ אַמֹּ֣ות הַמֵּאָ֔ה פֶּ֖תַח הַצָּפֹ֑ון וְהָרֹ֖חַב חֲמִשִּׁ֥ים אַמֹּֽות	2[14]	To the front of the length of a hundred cubits, with the door on the north, and the breadth of fifty cubits,
נֶ֣גֶד הָעֶשְׂרִ֗ים אֲשֶׁ֤ר לֶֽחָצֵר֙ הַפְּנִימִ֔י וְנֶ֣גֶד רִֽצְפָ֔ה אֲשֶׁ֖ר לֶחָצֵ֣ר הַחִֽיצֹונָ֑ה אַתִּ֥יק אֶל־פְּנֵֽי־אַתִּ֖יק בַּשְּׁלִשִֽׁים	3[15]	*over against the twenty cubits which belonged to the inner court, and over against the*

---

[1] Ezekiel 41:20 - Extraordinary points of the Soferim: A dittography הֵיכָל exists at the end of this verse and at the beginning of the following verse. When excluded, the passage can be rendered "*As for the wall of the Temple the doorposts were squared; and as for the face of the Temple etc.*", Ezekiel 17:18

[2] LXX *carved*

[3] Ezekiel 41:21 - 1 Kings 6:33, Ezekiel 16:14 17:1

[4] LXX *And the holy place and the temple opened on four sides; in front of the holy places the appearance was as the look of*

[5] Ezekiel 41:22 - 1 Corinthians 10:21, 1 Kings 6:20 6:22 7:48, 2 Chronicles 4:19, b.Berachot 55a, b.Chagigah 16a, b.Menachot 97ab, b.Yoma [Tosefot] 21b, Exodus 1:23 25:28-30 30:1-3 6:8, Ezekiel 23:41 20:16, Jastrow 661b, Leviticus 24:6, Malachi 1:7 1:12, Midrash Shmuel 3:4, mt.Pirkei Avot 3:4 [Shabbat afternoon], Proverbs 9:2, Revelation 3:20 8:3, Song of Songs 1:12, y.Chagigah 3:8, z.Acharei Mot 62a, z.Terumah 153ab 168b

[6] Ezekiel 41:23 - 1 Kings 6:31-6:35, 2 Chronicles 4:22, b.Middot 36b, Ezekiel 17:1, m.Middot 4:1, mt.Hilchot Beit Habechirah 4:7

[7] Ezekiel 41:24 - 1 Kings 6:34, b.Middot 36b, Ezekiel 16:48, m.Middot 4:1, mt.Hilchot Beit Habechirah 4:7

[8] Ezekiel 41:25 - Ezekiel 17:18

[9] Ezekiel 41:26 - b.Bava Kamma 67a, Ezekiel 16:16 17:5 17:16, Jastrow 789b 1046b

[10] LXX *And there were secret windows; and he measured from side to side, to the roofing of the porch; and the sides of the house were closely planked*

[11] Ezekiel 42:1 - Ezekiel 40:2-40:3 16:17 16:20 16:24 17:1 17:9 41:12-41:15 18:4 18:10 18:13, Revelation 11:2

[12] LXX *inner court eastward, opposite the northern gate*

[13] LXX *and behold five chambers near the vacant space, and near the northern partition*

[14] Ezekiel 42:2 - Ezekiel 17:13

[15] Ezekiel 42:3 - 2 Chronicles 7:3, Ezekiel 40:17-18 17:10 41:15-16 18:5, Song of Songs 1:17 7:6

וְלִפְנֵי הַלְּשָׁכוֹת מַהֲלַךְ עֶשֶׂר אַמּוֹת רֹחַב אֶל־הַפְּנִימִית דֶּרֶךְ אַמָּה אֶחָת וּפִתְחֵיהֶם לַצָּפוֹן	4[2]
וְהַלְּשָׁכוֹת הָעֶלְיוֹנֹת קְצֻרוֹת כִּי־יוֹכְלוּ אַתִּיקִים מֵהֵנָה מֵהַתַּחְתֹּנוֹת וּמֵהַתִּכֹנוֹת בַּבִּנְיָן	5[4]
כִּי מְשֻׁלָּשׁוֹת הֵנָּה וְאֵין לָהֶן עַמּוּדִים כְּעַמּוּדֵי הַחֲצֵרוֹת עַל־כֵּן נֶאֱצַל מֵהַתַּחְתּוֹנוֹת וּמֵהַתִּיכֹנוֹת מֵהָאָרֶץ	6[6]
וְגָדֵר אֲשֶׁר־לַחוּץ לְעֻמַּת הַלְּשָׁכוֹת דֶּרֶךְ הֶחָצֵר הַחִצוֹנָה אֶל־פְּנֵי הַלְּשָׁכוֹת אָרְכּוֹ חֲמִשִּׁים אַמָּה	7[7]
כִּי־אֹרֶךְ הַלְּשָׁכוֹת אֲשֶׁר לֶחָצֵר הַחִצוֹנָה חֲמִשִּׁים אַמָּה וְהִנֵּה עַל־פְּנֵי הַהֵיכָל מֵאָה אַמָּה	8[8]
וּמִתַּחְתָּה לְשָׁכוֹת וּמִתַּחַת הַלְּשָׁכוֹת הָאֵלֶּה הַמֵּבוֹא הַמֵּבִיא מֵהַקָּדִים בְּבֹאוֹ לָהֵנָּה מֵהֶחָצֵר הַחִצֹנָה	9[9]
בְּרֹחַב גֶּדֶר הֶחָצֵר דֶּרֶךְ הַקָּדִים אֶל־פְּנֵי הַגִּזְרָה וְאֶל־פְּנֵי הַבִּנְיָן לְשָׁכוֹת	10[10]
וְדֶרֶךְ לִפְנֵיהֶם כְּמַרְאֵה הַלְּשָׁכוֹת אֲשֶׁר דֶּרֶךְ הַצָּפוֹן כְּאָרְכָּן כֵּן רָחְבָּן וְכֹל מוֹצָאֵיהֶן וּכְמִשְׁפְּטֵיהֶן וּכְפִתְחֵיהֶן	11[11]
וּכְפִתְחֵי הַלְּשָׁכוֹת אֲשֶׁר דֶּרֶךְ הַדָּרוֹם פֶּתַח בְּרֹאשׁ דָּרֶךְ דֶּרֶךְ בִּפְנֵי הַגְּדֶרֶת הַגִּינָה דֶּרֶךְ הַקָּדִים בְּבוֹאָן	12
וַיֹּאמֶר אֵלַי לִשְׁכוֹת הַצָּפוֹן לִשְׁכוֹת הַדָּרוֹם אֲשֶׁר אֶל־פְּנֵי הַגִּזְרָה הֵנָּה לִשְׁכוֹת הַקֹּדֶשׁ אֲשֶׁר יֹאכְלוּ־שָׁם הַכֹּהֲנִים אֲשֶׁר־קְרוֹבִים לַיהוָה קָדְשֵׁי הַקֳּדָשִׁים שָׁם יַנִּיחוּ קָדְשֵׁי הַקֳּדָשִׁים וְהַמִּנְחָה וְהַחַטָּאת וְהָאָשָׁם כִּי הַמָּקוֹם קָדֹשׁ	13[12]

pavement which belonged to the outer court; *with gallery against gallery in three stories*[1]. And before the chambers was a walk of ten cubits breadth inward, *a way of one cubit*[3]; and their doors were toward the north.

Now the upper chambers were shorter; for the galleries took away from these, more than from the lower and the middlemost, in the building[5].

For they were in three stories, and they did not have pillars like the pillars of the courts; therefore, room was taken away from the lowest and the middlemost, in comparison with the ground.

And the wall that was outside by the side of the chambers, toward the outer court in front of the chambers, its length was fifty cubits.

For the length of the chambers that were toward the outer court was fifty cubits; and, lo, before the temple were a hundred cubits.

And from under these chambers was the entry on the east side, as one goes into them from the outer court.

In the breadth of the wall of the court toward the east, before the separate place, and before the building, there were chambers,

with a way before them; like the appearance of the chambers which were toward the north, with the same length and breadth, with the same layout, and the same designs and doors,

so also the doors of the chambers that were toward the south, there was a door in the head of the way, the way directly before the wall, toward the way from the east, as one enters into them.

Then said he to me: 'The north chambers and the south chambers, *which are before the separate place, they are the holy chambers, where the priests who are near to the LORD*[13] shall eat the most holy things; there they shall lay the most holy things, and the meal

---

[1] LXX *ornamented accordingly as the gates of the inner court, and arranged accordingly as the peristyles of the outer court, with triple porticos fronting one another*
[2] Ezekiel 42:4 - Ezekiel 22:19, Luke 13:24, Matthew 7:14, mt.Hilchot Beit Habechirah 4:6
[3] LXX *the length reaching to a hundred cubits*
[4] Ezekiel 42:5 - b.Bava Batra [Rashi] 14a, Ezekiel 17:7
[5] LXX *And the upper walks were in like manner: for the peristyle projected from it, even from the range of columns below, and there was a space between; so were there a peristyle and a space between, and so were there two porticos*
[6] Ezekiel 42:6 - 1 Kings 6:8, Ezekiel 17:6
[7] Ezekiel 42:7 - Ezekiel 18:10 18:12
[8] Ezekiel 42:8 - Ezekiel 41:13-41:14
[9] Ezekiel 42:9 - Ezekiel 20:5 22:19, Mas.Soferim 7:4
[10] Ezekiel 42:10 - Ezekiel 16:17 41:12-41:15 18:1 18:7 18:13
[11] Ezekiel 42:11 - Ezekiel 18:4
[12] Ezekiel 42:13 - Deuteronomy 21:5, Exodus 5:31, Ezekiel 16:46 18:10, Leviticus 2:3 2:10 6:14-17 6:25-26 6:29 7:1 7:6 10:3 10:13-14 10:17 14:13 21:22 24:9, Nehemiah 13:5, Numbers 1:9-10 16:5 17:5 18:7 18:9-18:10
[13] LXX *in front of the void spaces, these are the chambers of the sanctuary, in which the priests the sons of Sadduc, who draw night to the LORD*

offering, and the sin offering, and the guilt offering; for the place is holy.

בְּבֹאָם הַכֹּהֲנִים וְלֹא־יֵצְאוּ מֵהַקֹּדֶשׁ אֶל־הֶחָצֵר הַחִיצוֹנָה וְשָׁם יַנִּיחוּ בִגְדֵיהֶם אֲשֶׁר־יְשָׁרְתוּ בָהֶן כִּי־קֹדֶשׁ הֵנָּה "וְלָבְשׁוּ" "וְלָבְשׁוּ" בְּגָדִים אֲחֵרִים וְקָרְבוּ אֶל־אֲשֶׁר לָעָם

14[1] When the priests enter in, then they shall not go out of the holy place into the outer court, but there they shall lay their garments in which they minister, for they are holy; and they shall put on other garments, and shall approach the area open to the people.'

וְכִלָּה אֶת־מִדּוֹת הַבַּיִת הַפְּנִימִי וְהוֹצִיאַנִי דֶּרֶךְ הַשַּׁעַר אֲשֶׁר פָּנָיו דֶּרֶךְ הַקָּדִים וּמְדָדוֹ סָבִיב סָבִיב

15[2] Now when he finished measuring the inner house, he brought me by the way of the gate whose vista is to the east, and measured it.

מָדַד רוּחַ הַקָּדִים בִּקְנֵה הַמִּדָּה 'חֲמֵשׁ־אֵמוֹת' "חֲמֵשׁ־מֵאוֹת" קָנִים בִּקְנֵה הַמִּדָּה סָבִיב

16[3] He measured the east side with the measuring reed, five hundred reeds, with the measuring reed around it.

מָדַד רוּחַ הַצָּפוֹן חֲמֵשׁ־מֵאוֹת קָנִים בִּקְנֵה הַמִּדָּה סָבִיב

17 He measured the north side, five hundred reeds, with the measuring reed around it.

אֵת רוּחַ הַדָּרוֹם מָדַד חֲמֵשׁ־מֵאוֹת קָנִים בִּקְנֵה הַמִּדָּה

18 He measured the *south*[4] side, five hundred reeds, with the measuring reed.

סָבַב אֶל־רוּחַ הַיָּם מָדַד חֲמֵשׁ־מֵאוֹת קָנִים בִּקְנֵה הַמִּדָּה

19 He turned about to the *west*[5] side, and measured five hundred reeds with the measuring reed.

לְאַרְבַּע רוּחוֹת מְדָדוֹ חוֹמָה לוֹ סָבִיב סָבִיב אֹרֶךְ חֲמֵשׁ מֵאוֹת וְרֹחַב חֲמֵשׁ מֵאוֹת לְהַבְדִּיל בֵּין הַקֹּדֶשׁ לְחֹל

20[6] He measured it by the four sides; it had a wall around it, the length five hundred, and the breadth five hundred, to make a *separation between what was holy and what was common*[7].

Ezekiel – Chapter 43

וַיּוֹלִכֵנִי אֶל־הַשָּׁעַר שַׁעַר אֲשֶׁר פֹּנֶה דֶּרֶךְ הַקָּדִים

1[8] Afterward he brought me to the gate, the gate that looks toward the east;

וְהִנֵּה כְּבוֹד אֱלֹהֵי יִשְׂרָאֵל בָּא מִדֶּרֶךְ הַקָּדִים וְקוֹלוֹ כְּקוֹל מַיִם רַבִּים וְהָאָרֶץ הֵאִירָה מִכְּבֹדוֹ

2[9] and, behold, the glory of the God of Israel came from the way of the east; *and His voice was like the sound of many waters*[10]; and the earth shone with His glory.

וּכְמַרְאֵה הַמַּרְאֶה אֲשֶׁר רָאִיתִי כַּמַּרְאֶה אֲשֶׁר־רָאִיתִי בְּבֹאִי לְשַׁחֵת אֶת־הָעִיר וּמַרְאוֹת כַּמַּרְאֶה אֲשֶׁר רָאִיתִי אֶל־נְהַר־כְּבָר וָאֶפֹּל אֶל־פָּנָי

3[11] And the appearance of the vision I saw was like the vision I saw when I came to *destroy*[12] the city; and the visions [13]were like the vision

---

[1] Ezekiel 42:14 - 1 Peter 5:5, Exodus 28:40-43 29:4-9, Ezekiel 20:19, Galatians 3:27, Isaiah 13:10, Leviticus 8:7 8:13 8:33-35, Luke 9:62, Romans 3:22 13:14, Zechariah 3:4-5

[2] Ezekiel 42:15 - Ezekiel 40:6-16 41:2-5 17:15 19:1

[3] Ezekiel 42:16 - Ezekiel 16:3, Revelation 11:1-11:2, Zechariah 2:1

[4] LXX *west*

[5] LXX *south*

[6] Ezekiel 42:20 - 1 Enoch 77:1, 2 Corinthians 6:17, Ezekiel 22:26 16:5 20:23 21:2 24:15 24:20, Isaiah 1:1 2:1 12:18, Leviticus 10:10, Luke 16:26, Micah 7:11, Revelation 21:10-21:27, Song of Songs 2:9, Zechariah 2:5

[7] LXX *division between the sanctuary and the outer wall, that belonged to the design of the house*

[8] Ezekiel 43:1 - Ezekiel 10:19 16:6 18:15 19:4 20:1 22:1, Testament of Naphtali 5:3 Ezekiel 43:1-11 - Leviticus.R 2:8

[9] Ezekiel 43:2 - Avot de R'Natan 2, Exodus.R 36:4, Ezekiel 1:24 1:28 3:23 9:3 10:4 10:18-10:19 11:23, Genesis.R 3:4, Guide for the Perplexed 3:9, Habakkuk 2:14 3:3, Isaiah 6:3 60:1-60:3, Jastrow 1574a, John 12:41, Leviticus.R 31:7, Mekhilta de R'Shimon bar Yochai Bachodesh 51:1, Mekhilta de R'Shimon bar Yochai Shirata 30:1, Mekilta de R'Ishmael Bahodesh 4:13, Mekhilta de R'Ishmael Beshallah 1:213, Mekhilta de R'Ishmael Shirata 4:69, Midrash Proverbs 20, Midrash Psalms 1:4 104:4, Midrash Tanchuma Yitro 13, mt.Hilchot Tefilah 7:1, Pesikta de R'Kahana 21.5, Revelation 1:15 14:2 18:1 19:1 19:6 21:23, Testament of Naphtali 5:2

[10] LXX *and there was a voice of an army, as the sound of many redoubling their shouts*

[11] Ezekiel 43:3 - Ezekiel 1:3-28 3:23 8:4 9:1 9:3 9:5 10:1-22 11:22-23 8:18, Jeremiah 1:10, Leviticus.R 1:14, Revelation 11:3-6, z.Mikketz 196a

[12] LXX *anoint*

[13] LXX adds *and the vision of the chariot that I saw*

	I saw by the river Chebar; and I fell on my face.
וּכְבוֹד יְהֹוָה בָּא אֶל־הַבָּיִת דֶּרֶךְ שַׁעַר אֲשֶׁר פָּנָיו דֶּרֶךְ הַקָּדִים	**4** [1] And the glory of the LORD came in the house through the gate whose vista is to the east.
וַתִּשָּׂאֵנִי רוּחַ וַתְּבִיאֵנִי אֶל־הֶחָצֵר הַפְּנִימִי וְהִנֵּה מָלֵא כְבוֹד־יְהֹוָה הַבָּיִת	**5** [2] And a spirit took me up, and brought me into the inner court; and, behold, the glory of the LORD filled the house.
וָאֶשְׁמַע מִדַּבֵּר אֵלַי מֵהַבָּיִת וְאִישׁ הָיָה עֹמֵד אֶצְלִי	**6** [3] And I heard one speaking to me out of the house; and a man stood by me.
וַיֹּאמֶר אֵלַי בֶּן־אָדָם אֶת־מְקוֹם כִּסְאִי וְאֶת־מְקוֹם כַּפּוֹת רַגְלַי אֲשֶׁר אֶשְׁכָּן־שָׁם בְּתוֹךְ בְּנֵי־יִשְׂרָאֵל לְעוֹלָם וְלֹא יְטַמְּאוּ עוֹד בֵּית־יִשְׂרָאֵל שֵׁם קָדְשִׁי הֵמָּה וּמַלְכֵיהֶם בִּזְנוּתָם וּבְפִגְרֵי מַלְכֵיהֶם בָּמוֹתָם	**7** [4] And He said to me: 'Son of man, this is the place of My throne, and the place of the soles of My feet, where I will dwell in the midst of the children of Israel forever; and the house of Israel shall defile My holy name no longer, nor they, nor their kings, by their harlotry, and by the carcasses of their kings in their high places;
בְּתִתָּם סִפָּם אֶת־סִפִּי וּמְזוּזָתָם אֵצֶל מְזוּזָתִי וְהַקִּיר בֵּינִי וּבֵינֵיהֶם וְטִמְּאוּ אֶת־שֵׁם קָדְשִׁי בְּתוֹעֲבוֹתָם אֲשֶׁר עָשׂוּ וָאֲכַל אֹתָם בְּאַפִּי	**8** [5] When they set their threshold by My threshold, and their doorpost beside My doorpost, and there was but the wall between Me and them; and they defiled My holy name by their abominations which they committed; Why I have consumed them in My anger.
עַתָּה יְרַחֲקוּ אֶת־זְנוּתָם וּפִגְרֵי מַלְכֵיהֶם מִמֶּנִּי וְשָׁכַנְתִּי בְתוֹכָם לְעוֹלָם	**9** [6] Now let them throw away their harlotry and the carcasses of their kings, far from Me, and I will live in their midst forever.
אַתָּה בֶן־אָדָם הַגֵּד אֶת־בֵּית־יִשְׂרָאֵל אֶת־הַבַּיִת וְיִכָּלְמוּ מֵעֲוֹנוֹתֵיהֶם וּמָדְדוּ אֶת־תָּכְנִית	**10** [7] You, son of man, show the house to the house of Israel, so they may be ashamed of their iniquities; and let them measure accurately.
וְאִם־נִכְלְמוּ מִכֹּל אֲשֶׁר־עָשׂוּ צוּרַת הַבַּיִת וּתְכוּנָתוֹ וּמוֹצָאָיו וּמוֹבָאָיו וְכָל־צוּרֹתָו וְאֵת כָּל־חֻקֹּתָיו וְכָל־צוּרֹתָי" וְכָל־צוּרֹתָיו" וְכָל־תּוֹרֹתָו" וְכָל־תּוֹרֹתָיו" הוֹדַע אוֹתָם וּכְתֹב לְעֵינֵיהֶם וְיִשְׁמְרוּ אֶת־כָּל־צוּרָתוֹ וְאֶת־כָּל־חֻקֹּתָיו וְעָשׂוּ אוֹתָם	**11** [8] And if they are ashamed of all they have done, make known to them the form of the house, and the fashion, and the goings out, and the comings in, and all the forms, and all the ordinances, and all the forms, and all the laws, and write it in their sight; so they may keep the whole form, and all the ordinances, and do them.
זֹאת תּוֹרַת הַבָּיִת עַל־רֹאשׁ הָהָר כָּל־גְּבֻלוֹ סָבִיב סָבִיב קֹדֶשׁ קָדָשִׁים הִנֵּה־זֹאת תּוֹרַת הַבָּיִת	**12** [9] This is the law of the house: on the top of the mountain its whole limit around it shall be most holy. *Behold, this is the law of the house*[10].

[1] Ezekiel 43:4 - b.Shekalim 14a, Ezekiel 10:18-19 19:2 20:2

[2] Ezekiel 43:5 - 1 Kings 8:10-8:11 18:12, 2 Chronicles 5:14, 2 Corinthians 12:2-12:4, 2 Kings 2:16, Acts 8:39, Exodus 16:34, Ezekiel 3:12-3:14 8:3 10:4 11:24 13:1 16:2 20:4, Haggai 2:7-2:9, Isaiah 6:3, Song of Songs 1:4

[3] Ezekiel 43:6 - Ezekiel 16:3, Isaiah 18:6, Leviticus 1:1, Revelation 16:1

[4] Ezekiel 43:7 - 1 Chronicles 4:2, 2 Corinthians 6:16, Acts 7:48-49, Exodus 5:45, Ezekiel 1:26 10:1 20:39 23:38-39 37:26-28 15:7 19:9 24:35, Guide for the Perplexed 1:46, Hosea 14:10, Isaiah 6:1 18:1, Jeremiah 3:17 14:21 16:18 17:12, Joel 4:17, John 1:14 14:23, Leviticus 2:30, Leviticus.R 2:8, Matthew 5:34-35 4:20, Mekhilta de R'Shimon bar Yochai Shirata 36:1, Psalms 47:9 68:19 99:1 99:5 12:14, Revelation 21:2-3 22:3, Zechariah 13:2 14:20-21

[5] Ezekiel 43:8 - 2 Chronicles 9:4 9:7, 2 Kings 16:14-16:15 21:4-21:7 23:11-23:12, Ecclesiastes.R 5:4, Ezekiel 5:11 8:3-8:16 23:39 20:7, Mekhilta de R'Shimon bar Yochai Pisha 13:1, Mekilta de R'Ishmael Pisha 6:4, Mekilta de R'Ishmael Pisha 11:37, Midrash Tanchuma Haazinu 4, Pesikta de R'Kahana S7.3, y.Berachot 4:4, y.Pesachim 9:5, y.Sanhedrin 10:2

[6] Ezekiel 43:9 - 2 Corinthians 6:16, Colossians 3:5-3:9, Ezekiel 18:30-18:31 13:23 37:26-37:28 19:7, Hosea 2:2

[7] Ezekiel 43:10 - 1 Chronicles 4:11 4:19, Exodus 1:40, Ezekiel 16:61 40:4 16:63 43:11 23:31-23:32 16:4 19:11, Midrash Tanchuma Tzav 14, Romans 6:21
Ezekiel 43:10-27 - Haftarah Tetzaveh, Haftarah Tetzaveh [Ezekiel 43:10-43:27]

[8] Ezekiel 43:11 - 1 Corinthians 11:2, Ezekiel 11:20 12:3 12:27 40:1-40:42 44:5-44:6, Hebrews 8:5, John 13:17, Leviticus.R 7:3, Matthew 4:20, Midrash Tanchuma Tzav 14, Pesikta de R'Kahana 6.3, Pesikta Rabbati 16:7, Saadia Opinions 8:8

[9] Ezekiel 43:12 - Ezekiel 16:2 18:20, Joel 4:17, Pesikta Rabbati 16:7, Psalms 93:5, Revelation 21:27, Zechariah 14:20-14:21

[10] Missing in LXX

Hebrew		English
וְאֵלֶּה מִדּוֹת הַמִּזְבֵּחַ בָּאַמּוֹת אַמָּה אַמָּה וָטֹפַח וְחֵיק הָאַמָּה וְאַמָּה־רֹחַב וּגְבוּלָהּ אֶל־שְׂפָתָהּ סָבִיב זֶרֶת הָאֶחָד וְזֶה גַּב הַמִּזְבֵּחַ	13[1]	And these are the measurements of the altar by cubits: the cubit is a cubit and a *handbreadth*[2]: the bottom shall be a cubit, and the breadth a cubit, and its border by its edge around a span; and this shall be the base of the altar.
וּמֵחֵיק הָאָרֶץ עַד־הָעֲזָרָה הַתַּחְתּוֹנָה שְׁתַּיִם אַמּוֹת וְרֹחַב אַמָּה אֶחָת וּמֵהָעֲזָרָה הַקְּטַנָּה עַד־הָעֲזָרָה הַגְּדוֹלָה אַרְבַּע אַמּוֹת וְרֹחַב הָאַמָּה	14[3]	And from the bottom *on the ground to the lower settle*[4] shall be two cubits, and the breadth one cubit; and from the lesser settle to the greater settle shall be four cubits, and the breadth a cubit.
וְהַהַרְאֵל אַרְבַּע אַמּוֹת וּמֵהָאֲרִאֵיל וּמֵהָאֲרִאֵל וּלְמַעְלָה הַקְּרָנוֹת אַרְבַּע	15[5]	*And the hearth shall be four cubits; and from the hearth and upward there shall be four horns*[6].
וְהָאֲרִאֵיל וְהָאֲרִאֵל שְׁתֵּים עֶשְׂרֵה אֹרֶךְ בִּשְׁתֵּים עֶשְׂרֵה רֹחַב רָבוּעַ אֶל אַרְבַּעַת רְבָעָיו	16[7]	And the hearth shall be twelve cubits long by twelve broad, square in its four sides.
וְהָעֲזָרָה אַרְבַּע עֶשְׂרֵה אֹרֶךְ בְּאַרְבַּע עֶשְׂרֵה רֹחַב אֶל אַרְבַּעַת רְבָעֶיהָ וְהַגְּבוּל סָבִיב אוֹתָהּ חֲצִי הָאַמָּה וְהַחֵיק־לָהּ אַמָּה סָבִיב וּמַעֲלֹתֵהוּ פְּנוֹת קָדִים	17[8]	And the *seat*[9] shall be fourteen cubits long by fourteen broad in its four sides; and the border about it shall be half a cubit; and its bottom shall be a cubit about; and its steps shall look toward the east.'
וַיֹּאמֶר אֵלַי בֶּן־אָדָם כֹּה אָמַר אֲדֹנָי יְהוִה אֵלֶּה חֻקּוֹת הַמִּזְבֵּחַ בְּיוֹם הֵעָשׂוֹתוֹ לְהַעֲלוֹת עָלָיו עוֹלָה וְלִזְרֹק עָלָיו דָּם	18[10]	And He said to me: 'Son of man, thus says the Lord GOD: These are the ordinances of the altar in the day when they shall make it, to offer burnt offerings on it, and to dash blood against it.
וְנָתַתָּה אֶל־הַכֹּהֲנִים הַלְוִיִּם אֲשֶׁר הֵם מִזֶּרַע צָדוֹק הַקְּרֹבִים אֵלַי נְאֻם אֲדֹנָי יְהוִה לְשָׁרְתֵנִי פַּר בֶּן־בָּקָר לְחַטָּאת	19[11]	You shall give to the priests the Levites who are of the seed of Zadok, who are near to Me, to minister to Me, says the Lord GOD, a young bullock for a sin offering.
וְלָקַחְתָּ מִדָּמוֹ וְנָתַתָּה עַל־אַרְבַּע קַרְנֹתָיו וְאֶל־אַרְבַּע פִּנּוֹת הָעֲזָרָה וְאֶל־הַגְּבוּל סָבִיב וְחִטֵּאתָ אוֹתוֹ וְכִפַּרְתָּהוּ	20[12]	And you shall take of its blood, and put it on its four horns, and on the four corners of the seat, and on the border around it; thus shall you purify it and make atonement for it.
וְלָקַחְתָּ אֵת הַפָּר הַחַטָּאת וּשְׂרָפוֹ בְּמִפְקַד הַבַּיִת מִחוּץ לַמִּקְדָּשׁ	21[13]	You shall also take the bullock of the sin offering, and it shall be burnt in the appointed place of the house, without the sanctuary.

---

[1] Ezekiel 43:13 - 2 Chronicles 4:1, b.Eruvin 4a, b.Menachot 97a 98a, b.Middot [Rambam] 36a, Exodus 27:1-27:8, Ezekiel 16:5 17:8, mt.Hilchot Beit HaBechirah 2:5, t.Kelim Bava Metzia 6:13
Ezekiel 43:13-17 - mt.Hilchot Beit Habechirah 2:3 2:3

[2] LXX *span*

[3] Ezekiel 43:14 - Lamentations.R 3:22 Petichata D'Chakimei:8, Midrash Tanchuma Ki Tetze 9, Pesikta de R'Kahana 3.6, Pesikta Rabbati 12:1

[4] lXX *at the commencement of the hollow part to this great mercy-seat, from beneath*

[5] Ezekiel 43:15 - 1 Kings 2:28, b.Zevachim 53a, Exodus 3:2, Isaiah 29:1-29:2 5:7, Leviticus 9:9, m.Middot 4:7, Psalms 22:27

[6] LXX *And the altar shall be four cubits; and from the altar and above the horns a cubit*

[7] Ezekiel 43:16 - 2 Chronicles 4:1, b.Menachot 97b, b.Middot 35b, b.Zevachim [Rashi] 60a, b.Zevachim [Tosefot] 62a, b.Zevachim 59b, Exodus 3:1 38:1-2, Ezra 3:3, m.Middot 3:1 4:7

[8] Ezekiel 43:17 - 1 Kings 6:8 18:32, b.Succah [Rashi] 48b, b.Zevachim 62b, Exodus 20:23 1:25 6:3, Ezekiel 8:16 16:6, Jastrow 459b 441a 388b 1636a, Nehemiah 9:4

[9] LXX *mercy-seat*

[10] Ezekiel 43:18 - b.Menachot [Tosefot] 45a, Exodus 16:29, Ezekiel 2:1 45:18-19, Hebrews 9:13 9:21-22 10:4-12 12:24, Leviticus 1:5-17 8:18-21 16:19, z.Vaetchanan 269b

[11] Ezekiel 43:19 - 1 Kings 2:27 2:35, 1 Peter 2:5 2:9, 1 Samuel 2:35-36, 2 Corinthians 5:21, Exodus 29:10-11, b.Menachot [Tosefot] 45a, Ezekiel 16:46 20:15 45:18-19 24:11, Hebrews 7:27, Isaiah 13:6 18:22, Jeremiah 33:18-22, Leviticus 4:3-35 8:14-15, m.Arachin 9:8, Numbers 16:5 17:5 18:5

[12] Ezekiel 43:20 - b.Menachot [Tosefot] 45a, Exodus 5:12 5:36, Ezekiel 43:15-17 19:22 19:26, Hebrews 9:21-23, Jastrow 699b, Leviticus 4:25 4:30 4:34 8:15 9:9 16:19

[13] Ezekiel 43:21 - Exodus 5:14, Hebrews 13:11-13:12, Leviticus 4:12 8:17

וּבַיּוֹם֙ הַשֵּׁנִ֔י תַּקְרִ֛יב שְׂעִיר־עִזִּ֥ים תָּמִ֖ים לְחַטָּ֑את וְחִטְּאוּ֙ אֶת־הַמִּזְבֵּ֔חַ כַּאֲשֶׁ֥ר חִטְּא֖וּ בַּפָּֽר

22[1] And on the second day you shall offer a male goat without blemish for a sin offering; and they shall purify the altar, as they purified it with the bullock.

בְּכַלּוֹתְךָ֖ מֵֽחַטֵּ֑א תַּקְרִיב֙ פַּ֣ר בֶּן־בָּקָ֣ר תָּמִ֔ים וְאַ֥יִל מִן־הַצֹּ֖אן תָּמִֽים

23[2] When you finish purifying it, you shall offer a young bullock without blemish, and a ram out of the flock without blemish.

וְהִקְרַבְתָּ֖ם לִפְנֵ֣י יְהֹוָ֑ה וְהִשְׁלִ֨יכוּ הַכֹּהֲנִ֤ים עֲלֵיהֶם֙ מֶ֔לַח וְהֶעֱל֥וּ אוֹתָ֛ם עֹלָ֖ה לַֽיהֹוָֽה

24[3] And you shall present them before the LORD, and the priests shall cast salt on them, and they shall offer them up for a burnt offering to the LORD.

שִׁבְעַ֣ת יָמִ֗ים תַּעֲשֶׂ֛ה שְׂעִיר־חַטָּ֖את לַיּ֑וֹם וּפַ֧ר בֶּן־בָּקָ֛ר וְאַ֥יִל מִן־הַצֹּ֖אן תְּמִימִ֥ם יַעֲשֽׂוּ

25[4] Every day for seven days you shall prepare a goat for a sin offering; they shall also prepare a young bullock, and a ram out of the flock, without blemish.

שִׁבְעַ֣ת יָמִ֗ים יְכַפְּרוּ֙ אֶת־הַמִּזְבֵּ֔חַ וְטִֽהֲר֖וּ אֹת֑וֹ וּמִלְא֖וּ יָדָֽו״

26[5] Seven days they shall make atonement for the altar and cleanse it; so they shall consecrate it.

וִֽיכַלּ֣וּ אֶת־הַיָּמִ֗ים ס וְהָיָה֩ בַיּ֨וֹם הַשְּׁמִינִ֜י וָהָ֗לְאָה יַעֲשׂ֨וּ הַכֹּהֲנִ֤ים עַל־הַמִּזְבֵּ֙חַ֙ אֶת־עוֹלֽוֹתֵיכֶ֔ם וְאֶת־שַׁלְמֵיכֶ֔ם וְרָצִ֖אתִי אֶתְכֶ֑ם נְאֻ֖ם אֲדֹנָ֥י יְהֹוִֽה

27[6] And when they have finished the days, it shall be on the eighth day and forward, the priests shall make your burnt offerings upon the altar, and your peace offerings; and I will accept you, says the Lord GOD.'

Ezekiel – Chapter 44

וַיָּ֣שֶׁב אֹתִ֗י דֶּ֩רֶךְ֩ שַׁ֨עַר הַמִּקְדָּ֜שׁ הַחִ֥יצוֹן הַפֹּנֶ֣ה קָדִ֑ים וְה֖וּא סָגֽוּר

1[7] Then he brought me back the way of the outer gate of the sanctuary, which looks toward the east; and it was shut.

וַיֹּ֨אמֶר אֵלַ֜י יְהֹוָ֗ה הַשַּׁ֤עַר הַזֶּה֙ סָג֣וּר יִהְיֶ֔ה לֹ֣א יִפָּתֵ֔חַ וְאִ֖ישׁ לֹא־יָ֣בֹא ב֑וֹ כִּ֣י יְהֹוָ֧ה אֱלֹהֵֽי־יִשְׂרָאֵ֛ל בָּ֥א ב֖וֹ וְהָיָ֥ה סָגֽוּר

2[8] And the LORD said to me: 'This gate shall be shut, it shall not be opened, nor shall any man enter in it, for the LORD, the God of Israel, has entered in it; therefore, it shall be shut.

אֶת־הַנָּשִׂ֕יא נָשִׂ֣יא ה֗וּא יֵֽשֶׁב־בּ֛וֹ לֶאֱכוֹל־לֶ֖חֶם לִפְנֵ֣י יְהֹוָ֑ה מִדֶּ֩רֶךְ֩ אֻלָ֨ם הַשַּׁ֤עַר יָבוֹא֙ וּמִדַּרְכּ֖וֹ יֵצֵֽא

3[9] As for the prince, being a prince, he shall sit in it to eat bread before the LORD; he shall enter by the way of the porch of the gate, and shall go out by the way of the same.'

וַיְבִיאֵ֣נִי דֶּֽרֶךְ־שַׁ֣עַר הַצָּפוֹן֮ אֶל־פְּנֵ֣י הַבַּיִת֒ וָאֵ֕רֶא וְהִנֵּ֛ה מָלֵ֥א כְבוֹד־יְהֹוָ֖ה אֶת־בֵּ֣ית יְהֹוָ֑ה וָאֶפֹּ֖ל אֶל־פָּנָֽי

4[10] Then he brought me the way of the north gate before the house; and I looked, and, behold, the glory of the LORD filled the house of the LORD; and I fell on my face.

וַיֹּ֣אמֶר אֵלַ֣י יְהֹוָ֗ה בֶּן־אָדָ֞ם שִׂ֤ים לִבְּךָ֙ וּרְאֵ֣ה בְעֵינֶ֔יךָ וּבְאָזְנֶ֖יךָ שְׁמָ֑ע אֵ֣ת כׇּל־אֲשֶׁ֤ר אֲנִי֙ מְדַבֵּ֣ר אֹתָ֔ךְ לְכׇל־

5[11] And the LORD said to me: 'Son of man, mark well, and see with your eyes, and hear with your ears all that I say to you concerning all the ordinances of the house of the LORD, and

---

[1] Ezekiel 43:22 - 1 Peter 1:19, b.Menachot [Tosefot] 45a, Exodus 29:15-18, Ezekiel 19:20 43:25-26, Isaiah 5:6 5:10, Leviticus 8:18-21

[2] Ezekiel 43:23 - b.Menachot [Tosefot] 45a, Exodus 5:1

[3] Ezekiel 43:24 - 2 Chronicles 13:5, b.Menachot 21b, Colossians 4:6, Leviticus 2:13, Mark 9:49-9:50, Matthew 5:13, Numbers 18:19

[4] Ezekiel 43:25 - b.Menachot [Tosefot] 45a, Exodus 29:35-29:37, Leviticus 8:33 8:35

[5] Ezekiel 43:26 - Exodus 5:24 8:29, Leviticus 8:34

[6] Ezekiel 43:27 - 1 Peter 2:5, Colossians 1:20-21, Ephesians 1:6, Ezekiel 20:40-41, Hebrews 13:15, Hosea 8:13, Job 18:8, Leviticus 3:1 9:1 17:5, Philippians 2:17, Romans 12:1 15:16

[7] Ezekiel 44:1 - 2 Chronicles 4:9 20:5 9:5, Acts 21:28-30, Ezekiel 16:6 16:17 18:14 19:1 19:4 22:1

[8] Ezekiel 44:2 - Avot de R'Natan 34.7.1, b.Middot 36b, b.Tamid 30b, Exodus 24:10, Ezekiel 43:2-43:4, Guide for the Perplexed 1:22, Isaiah 6:1-6:5, m.Middot 4:2, m.Tamid 3:7, Midrash Tanchuma Ki Tissa 15, mt.Hilchot Beit HaBechirah 5:6, Pirkei de R'Eliezer 51

[9] Ezekiel 44:3 - 1 Corinthians 10:18-10:33, 2 Chronicles 23:13 10:31, Deuteronomy 12:7 12:17-12:18, Exodus 24:9-24:11, Ezekiel 10:24 13:25 16:9 22:2 46:8-10, Genesis 7:54, Isaiah 23:18 14:9, Revelation 3:20, variant לאכל of לֶאֱכוֹל is found, Zechariah 6:12-13

[10] Ezekiel 44:4 - Ezekiel 1:28 3:23 10:4 10:18-10:19 11:22-11:23 16:20 16:40 43:3-43:5, Genesis 17:3, Haggai 2:7, Isaiah 6:3-6:4, Malachi 3:1, Numbers 17:7-16:45, Psalms 89:8, Revelation 1:17

[11] Ezekiel 44:5 - 1 Chronicles 22:19, 2 Chronicles 11:16, Acts 8:36, Daniel 10:12, Deuteronomy 13:1 8:46, Exodus 9:21, Ezekiel 16:4 43:10-43:11, Matthew 4:20, Proverbs 24:32, Psalms 96:8-96:9 23:4, Sifre Devarim {Haazinu Hashamayim} 335

חֻקּוֹת בֵּית־יְהֹוָה "וּלְכׇל־תּוֹרֹתָו "וּלְכׇל־תּוֹרֹתָיו
וְשָׁמַרְתָּ לְבֹא לְמִבְוֹא הַבַּיִת בְּכֹל מוֹצָאֵי הַמִּקְדָּשׁ:
וְאָמַרְתָּ אֶל־מֶרִי אֶל־בֵּית יִשְׂרָאֵל כֹּה אָמַר אֲדֹנָי
יְהֹוָה רַב־לָכֶם מִכׇּל־תּוֹעֲבוֹתֵיכֶם בֵּית יִשְׂרָאֵל

all its laws; and note well who can enter the house, with every exclusion to the sanctuary.

[6][1] And you shall say to the rebellious, to the house of Israel: Thus says the Lord GOD: O you house of Israel, let it be enough of all your abominations,

בַּהֲבִיאֲכֶם בְּנֵי־נֵכָר עַרְלֵי־לֵב וְעַרְלֵי בָשָׂר לִהְיוֹת
בְּמִקְדָּשִׁי לְחַלְּלוֹ אֶת־בֵּיתִי בְּהַקְרִיבְכֶם אֶת־לַחְמִי
חֵלֶב וָדָם וַיָּפֵרוּ אֶת־בְּרִיתִי אֶל כׇּל־תּוֹעֲבוֹתֵיכֶם

[7][2] For you have brought in aliens, uncircumcised in heart and uncircumcised in flesh, to be in My sanctuary, to profane it, My house, when you offer My bread, the fat and the blood, and they have broken My covenant, to add to all your abominations.

וְלֹא שְׁמַרְתֶּם מִשְׁמֶרֶת קׇדָשָׁי וַתְּשִׂימוּן לְשֹׁמְרֵי
מִשְׁמַרְתִּי בְּמִקְדָּשִׁי לָכֶם

[8][3] And you have not kept the charge of My holy things; but you have set keepers of My charge in My sanctuary to please yourselves.

כֹּה־אָמַר אֲדֹנָי יְהֹוִה כׇּל־בֶּן־נֵכָר עֶרֶל לֵב וְעֶרֶל
בָּשָׂר לֹא יָבוֹא אֶל־מִקְדָּשִׁי לְכׇל־בֶּן־נֵכָר אֲשֶׁר
בְּתוֹךְ בְּנֵי יִשְׂרָאֵל

[9][4] Thus says the Lord GOD: No alien, uncircumcised in heart and uncircumcised in flesh, shall enter in My sanctuary, any alien who is among the children of Israel.

כִּי אִם־הַלְוִיִּם אֲשֶׁר רָחֲקוּ מֵעָלַי בִּתְעוֹת יִשְׂרָאֵל
אֲשֶׁר תָּעוּ מֵעָלַי אַחֲרֵי גִּלּוּלֵיהֶם וְנָשְׂאוּ עֲוֹנָם

[10][5] But the Levites, who went far from Me, when Israel went astray, who went astray from Me after their idols, they shall bear their iniquity;

וְהָיוּ בְמִקְדָּשִׁי מְשָׁרְתִים פְּקֻדּוֹת אֶל־שַׁעֲרֵי הַבַּיִת
וּמְשָׁרְתִים אֶת־הַבָּיִת הֵמָּה יִשְׁחֲטוּ אֶת־הָעֹלָה
וְאֶת־הַזֶּבַח לָעָם וְהֵמָּה יַעַמְדוּ לִפְנֵיהֶם לְשָׁרְתָם

[11][6] and they shall be ministers in My sanctuary, having charge at the gates of the house, and ministering in the house: they shall kill the burnt offering and the sacrifice for the people, and they shall stand before them to minister to them.

יַעַן אֲשֶׁר יְשָׁרְתוּ אוֹתָם לִפְנֵי גִלּוּלֵיהֶם וְהָיוּ לְבֵית־
יִשְׂרָאֵל לְמִכְשׁוֹל עָוֹן עַל־כֵּן נָשָׂאתִי יָדִי עֲלֵיהֶם
נְאֻם אֲדֹנָי יְהֹוִה וְנָשְׂאוּ עֲוֹנָם

[12][7] Because they ministered to them before their idols, and became a stumbling block of iniquity to the house of Israel; therefore I have lifted My hand against them, says the Lord GOD, and they shall bear their iniquity.

וְלֹא־יִגְּשׁוּ אֵלַי לְכַהֵן לִי וְלָגֶשֶׁת עַל־כׇּל־קׇדָשַׁי
אֶל־קׇדְשֵׁי הַקֳּדָשִׁים וְנָשְׂאוּ כְּלִמָּתָם וְתוֹעֲבוֹתָם
אֲשֶׁר עָשׂוּ

[13][8] And they shall not come near to Me, to minister to Me in the priest's office, nor to come near to any of My holy things, to the most holy things; but they shall bear their shame, and the abominations they committed.

---

[1] Ezekiel 44:6 - 1 Peter 4:3, Ezekiel 2:5-2:8 3:9 3:26-3:27 21:9, z.Vaetchanan 269b

[2] Ezekiel 44:7 - Acts 7:51 21:28, b.Zevachim 22b, Colossians 2:11-2:13, Deuteronomy 10:16 6:6 7:16 7:20, Exodus 12:48, Ezekiel 7:20 22:26 43:7-43:8 20:9, Genesis 17:14, Hebrews 8:9, Isaiah 24:5 56:6-56:7, Jeremiah 4:4 9:27 11:10 7:33, John 6:52-6:58, Lamentations.R 1:36, Leviticus 3:13-3:17 17:11 21:6 21:8 21:17 21:21 22:25 2:15 2:41, Malachi 1:7 1:12-1:14, Midrash Tanchuma Lech Lecha 20, mt.Hilchot Teshuvah 2:10, Romans 2:28-2:29

[3] Ezekiel 44:8 - 1 Chronicles 23:32, 1 Timothy 6:13, 2 Timothy 4:1, Acts 7:53, Ezekiel 40:45-40:46 20:14 20:16, Ezra 8:24-8:30, Leviticus 22:2-22:33, Numbers 18:3-18:5 18:7

[4] Ezekiel 44:9 - 4QFlor 1.02-3, b.Bava Batra [Rashbam] 123b, b.Moed Katan 5a, b.Sanhedrin 22b, b.Taanit 14b, b.Yoma 71b, b.Zevachim 18b 22b, Ein Yaakov Moed Katan:5a, Ezekiel 20:7, Joel 4:17, John 3:3-3:5, Mark 16:16, Mekilta de R'Ishmael Pisha 15:20, Midrash Tanchuma Lech Lecha 20, mt.Hilchot Biat haMikdash 6:8, mt.Hilchot Sanhedrin vHainshin Hameurim Lahem 19:4, Psalms 50:16 93:5, Psalms of Solomon 17:28, Titus 1:5-1:9, z.Vaetchanan 269b, Zechariah 14:21

[5] Ezekiel 44:10 - 1 Timothy 5:22, 2 Chronicles 29:4-29:5, 2 Kings 23:8-23:9, Ezekiel 22:26 20:15 24:11, Genesis 4:13, Isaiah 5:11, Jeremiah 23:11, Leviticus 19:8, mt.Hilchot Biat haMikdash 9:13, Nehemiah 9:34, Numbers 5:31 18:23, Psalms 38:5, Zephaniah 3:4 Ezekiel 44:10[?] - 4QFlor 1.16-17

[6] Ezekiel 44:11 - 1 Chronicles 26:1-19, 2 Chronicles 5:34 6:17 35:10-11, 3 Enoch 45:2, Ezekiel 16:45 20:14, Numbers 3:5-37 16:9 18:6

[7] Ezekiel 44:12 - 1 Samuel 2:29-30, 2 Kings 16:10-16, Amos 8:7, b.Avodah Zara [Rashi] 52b, b.Menachot 109a, Deuteronomy 32:40-42, Ezekiel 14:3-4 20:6 20:15 20:23 20:28 20:10 20:13, Hosea 4:6 5:1, Isaiah 9:17, Malachi 2:8-9, Psalms 10:26, Revelation 10:5-6

[8] Ezekiel 44:13 - 2 Kings 23:9, b.Avodah Zara [Rashi] 52b 54a, b.Menachot 109a, Ezekiel 40:5 41:8 8:20 12:7, mt.Hilchot Biat haMikdash 9:13, Numbers 18:3

וְנָתַתִּי אוֹתָם שֹׁמְרֵי מִשְׁמֶרֶת הַבַּיִת לְכֹל עֲבֹדָתוֹ וּלְכֹל אֲשֶׁר יֵעָשֶׂה בּוֹ

14[1] And I will make them keepers of the charge of the house, for all its service, and for all that shall be done in it.

וְהַכֹּהֲנִים הַלְוִיִּם בְּנֵי צָדוֹק אֲשֶׁר שָׁמְרוּ אֶת־מִשְׁמֶרֶת מִקְדָּשִׁי בִּתְעוֹת בְּנֵי־יִשְׂרָאֵל מֵעָלַי הֵמָּה יִקְרְבוּ אֵלַי לְשָׁרְתֵנִי וְעָמְדוּ לְפָנַי לְהַקְרִיב לִי חֵלֶב וָדָם נְאֻם אֲדֹנָי יְהוִה

15[2] But the priests the Levites, the sons of Zadok, who kept the charge of My sanctuary when the children of Israel went astray from Me, they shall come near to Me to minister to Me; and they shall stand before Me to offer to Me the fat and the blood, says the Lord GOD;

הֵמָּה יָבֹאוּ אֶל־מִקְדָּשִׁי וְהֵמָּה יִקְרְבוּ אֶל־שֻׁלְחָנִי לְשָׁרְתֵנִי וְשָׁמְרוּ אֶת־מִשְׁמַרְתִּי

16[3] they shall enter My sanctuary, and they shall come near to My table, to minister to Me, and they shall keep My charge.

וְהָיָה בְּבוֹאָם אֶל־שַׁעֲרֵי הֶחָצֵר הַפְּנִימִית בִּגְדֵי פִשְׁתִּים יִלְבָּשׁוּ וְלֹא־יַעֲלֶה עֲלֵיהֶם צֶמֶר בְּשָׁרְתָם בְּשַׁעֲרֵי הֶחָצֵר הַפְּנִימִית וָבָיְתָה

17[4] And it shall be when they enter the gates of the inner court, they shall be clothed with linen garments; and no wool shall come on them, while they minister in the gates of the inner court, *and within*[5].

פַּאֲרֵי פִשְׁתִּים יִהְיוּ עַל־רֹאשָׁם וּמִכְנְסֵי פִשְׁתִּים יִהְיוּ עַל־מָתְנֵיהֶם לֹא יַחְגְּרוּ בַּיָּזַע

18[6] They shall have linen headdresses on their heads, and shall have linen breeches on their loins; *they shall not clothe themselves with anything that causes sweat*[7].

וּבְצֵאתָם אֶל־הֶחָצֵר הַחִיצוֹנָה אֶל־הֶחָצֵר הַחִיצוֹנָה אֶל־הָעָם יִפְשְׁטוּ אֶת־בִּגְדֵיהֶם אֲשֶׁר־הֵמָּה מְשָׁרְתִם בָּם וְהִנִּיחוּ אוֹתָם בְּלִשְׁכֹת הַקֹּדֶשׁ וְלָבְשׁוּ בְּגָדִים אֲחֵרִים וְלֹא־יְקַדְּשׁוּ אֶת־הָעָם בְּבִגְדֵיהֶם

19[8] And when they go forth into the outer court, into the outer court to the people, they shall take off their garments in which they minister, and lay them in the holy chambers, and they shall put on other garments, so they do not sanctify the people with their garments.

וְרֹאשָׁם לֹא יְגַלֵּחוּ וּפֶרַע לֹא יְשַׁלֵּחוּ כָּסוֹם יִכְסְמוּ אֶת־רָאשֵׁיהֶם

20[9] Nor shall they shave their heads, *nor allow their hair to grow long; they shall only trim their heads*[10].

וְיַיִן לֹא־יִשְׁתּוּ כָּל־כֹּהֵן בְּבוֹאָם אֶל־הֶחָצֵר הַפְּנִימִית

21[11] Nor shall any priest drink wine when they enter into the inner court.

וְאַלְמָנָה וּגְרוּשָׁה לֹא־יִקְחוּ לָהֶם לְנָשִׁים כִּי אִם־בְּתוּלֹת מִזֶּרַע בֵּית יִשְׂרָאֵל וְהָאַלְמָנָה אֲשֶׁר תִּהְיֶה אַלְמָנָה מִכֹּהֵן יִקָּחוּ

22[12] Nor shall they marry a widow, nor a divorcee; but they shall take virgins of the seed of the house of Israel, or a widow who is the widow of a priest.

---

[1] Ezekiel 44:14 - 1 Chronicles 23:28-23:32, Numbers 18:4
[2] Ezekiel 44:15 - 1 Kings 2:35, 1 Samuel 2:35, 1 Timothy 3:3-10, 2 Timothy 2:2, 4Q266 frag 23.19-20, b.Bechorot 4a, b.Chullin 24b, b.Tamid 16a, b.Yevamot 86b, Cairo Damascus 3:20-4:2, Cairo Damascus 3.21-4.2, Deuteronomy 10:8, Ein Yaakov Yevamot:86b, Ezekiel 16:46 19:19 20:7 20:10 24:11, Jeremiah 9:18, Leviticus 3:16-17 17:5-6, m.Arachin 9:8, mt.Hilchot Beit Habechirah 8:4, Numbers.R 12:7, Revelation 2:1 2:8 2:12 2:18 3:1 3:7 3:14 3:22, Tanya Likutei Aramim §50, y.Maaser Sheni 5:3, y.Sotah 7:4, z.Beshallach 62a, z.Shemot 20b, Zechariah 3:1-7
Ezekiel 44:15-31 - Haftarah Emor
[3] Ezekiel 44:16 - Deuteronomy 33:8-33:10, Ezekiel 17:22, Malachi 1:7 1:12, Numbers 18:5 18:7-18:8, Revelation 1:6
[4] Ezekiel 44:17 - Exodus 28:39-40 4:43 39:27-9, Leviticus 16:4, Revelation 4:4 19:8, y.Kilayim 9:1
[5] Missing in LXX
[6] Ezekiel 44:18 - 1 Corinthians 11:4-11:10 14:40, b.Yoma 71b, b.Zevachim [Rashi] 88a, b.Zevachim 18b, Exodus 28:40-28:43 15:28, Isaiah 3:20, Leviticus 16:4, y.Kilayim 9:1, y.Shabbat 2:3
[7] LXX *and they shall not tightly gird themselves*
[8] Ezekiel 44:19 - 1 Corinthians 3:5-6, b.Yoma 35b, Exodus 5:37 6:29, Ezekiel 42:13-14 22:20, Leviticus 6:10-11 6:27, Matthew 23:17-19
[9] Ezekiel 44:20 - 1 Corinthians 11:14, b.Nazir 3a, b.Nedarim 54a, b.Sanhedrin 22b, b.Taanit 14ab, Deuteronomy 14:1, Leviticus 21:5-21:24, mt.Hilchot Beit Habechirah 77:20, mt.Hilchot Biat haMikdash 1:8, mt.Hilchot Klei haMikdash Vihaovdim Bo 5:6, Numbers 6:5, Numbers.R 9:24 10:17, t.Sotah 3:16
[10] LXX *nor shall they pluck off their hair; they shall carefully cover their heads*
[11] Ezekiel 44:21 - 1 Timothy 3:8 5:23, b.Sanhedrin 22b, b.Taanit [Rashi] 14a, Leviticus 10:9, Luke 1:15, mt.Hilchot Beit Habechirah 7:20 7:20, mt.Hilchot Biat haMikdash 1:8, Titus 1:7-1:8
[12] Ezekiel 44:22 - 1 Timothy 3:2 3:4-3:5 3:11-3:12, b.Kiddushin 78ab, Deuteronomy 24:1-24:4, Leviticus 21:7 21:13-21:14, mt.Hilchot Issurei Biah 18:3, Titus 1:6, y.Bikkurim 1:5, y.Kiddushin 4:6

וְאֶת־עַמִּי יוֹרוּ בֵּין קֹדֶשׁ לְחֹל וּבֵין־טָמֵא לְטָהוֹר יוֹדִעֵם

23[1] And they shall teach My people the difference between the holy and the *common*[2], and help them know between the unclean and the clean.

וְעַל־רִיב הֵמָּה יַעַמְדוּ *לִשְׁפֹּט* "לְמִשְׁפָּט" בְּמִשְׁפָּטַי *יִשְׁפְּטֻהוּ* "יִשְׁפְּטוּהוּ" וְאֶת־תּוֹרֹתַי וְאֶת־חֻקֹּתַי בְּכָל־מוֹעֲדַי יִשְׁמֹרוּ וְאֶת־שַׁבְּתוֹתַי יְקַדֵּשׁוּ

24[3] *And in a controversy they shall stand to judge; and they shall judge according to My ordinances*[4]; and they shall keep My laws and My statutes in all My appointed seasons, and they shall hallow My sabbaths.

וְאֶל־מֵת אָדָם לֹא יָבוֹא לְטָמְאָה כִּי אִם־לְאָב וּלְאֵם וּלְבֵן וּלְבַת לְאָח וּלְאָחוֹת אֲשֶׁר־לֹא־הָיְתָה לְאִישׁ יִטַּמָּאוּ

25[5] And they shall not come near a dead person to defile themselves; but for father, or for mother, or for son, or for daughter, for brother, or for sister who has not had a husband, they may defile themselves.

וְאַחֲרֵי טָהֳרָתוֹ שִׁבְעַת יָמִים יִסְפְּרוּ־לוֹ

26[6] And after he is cleansed, they shall count for him seven days.

וּבְיוֹם בֹּאוֹ אֶל־הַקֹּדֶשׁ אֶל־הֶחָצֵר הַפְּנִימִית לְשָׁרֵת בַּקֹּדֶשׁ יַקְרִיב חַטָּאתוֹ נְאֻם אֲדֹנָי יְהוִה

27[7] And in the day he goes into the sanctuary, into the inner court, to minister in the sanctuary, he shall offer his sin offering, says the Lord GOD.

וְהָיְתָה לָהֶם לְנַחֲלָה אֲנִי נַחֲלָתָם וַאֲחֻזָּה לֹא־תִתְּנוּ לָהֶם בְּיִשְׂרָאֵל אֲנִי אֲחֻזָּתָם

28[8] And it shall be to them as an inheritance: I am their inheritance; and you shall give them no possession in Israel: I am their possession.

הַמִּנְחָה וְהַחַטָּאת וְהָאָשָׁם הֵמָּה יֹאכְלוּם וְכָל־חֵרֶם בְּיִשְׂרָאֵל לָהֶם יִהְיֶה

29[9] The meal offering, and the sin offering, and the guilt offering, they, they, shall eat; *and every devoted thing in Israel shall be theirs*[10].

וְרֵאשִׁית כָּל־בִּכּוּרֵי כֹל וְכָל־תְּרוּמַת כֹּל מִכֹּל תְּרוּמוֹתֵיכֶם לַכֹּהֲנִים יִהְיֶה וְרֵאשִׁית עֲרִסוֹתֵיכֶם תִּתְּנוּ לַכֹּהֵן לְהָנִיחַ בְּרָכָה אֶל־בֵּיתֶךָ

30[11] And the first of all the firstfruits of everything, and every heave offering of everything, of all your offerings, shall be for the priests; you shall also give to the priest the first of your dough, to cause a blessing to rest on your house.

כָּל־נְבֵלָה וּטְרֵפָה מִן־הָעוֹף וּמִן־הַבְּהֵמָה לֹא יֹאכְלוּ הַכֹּהֲנִים

31[12] The priests shall not eat anything that dies of itself, or is *torn*[13], whether fowl or beast.

Ezekiel – Chapter 45

וּבְהַפִּילְכֶם אֶת־הָאָרֶץ בְּנַחֲלָה תָּרִימוּ תְרוּמָה לַיהוָה קֹדֶשׁ מִן־הָאָרֶץ אֹרֶךְ חֲמִשָּׁה וְעֶשְׂרִים אֶלֶף

1[14] Moreover, when you divide the land by lot for inheritance, you shall set apart an offering to

---

[1] Ezekiel 44:23 - 2 Timothy 2:24-2:25, Deuteronomy 9:10, Ezekiel 22:26, Haggai 2:11-2:13, Hosea 4:6, Leviticus 10:10-10:11, Malachi 2:6-2:9, Micah 3:9-3:11, Titus 1:9-1:11, Zephaniah 3:4

[2] LXX *profane*

[3] Ezekiel 44:24 - 1 Chronicles 23:4, 1 Timothy 3:15, 2 Chronicles 19:8-19:10, Deuteronomy 17:8-17:13, Ezekiel 22:26, Ezra 2:63, Isaiah 58:13-58:14, Leviticus 23:1-23:44, Nehemiah 8:1-8:18, Numbers 28:1-28:29

[4] LXX *And these shall attend at a judgment of blood to decide it: they shall rightly observe my ordinances, and judge my judgments*

[5] Ezekiel 44:25 - 1 Thessalonians 4:13-4:15, 2 Corinthians 5:16, Leviticus 21:1-21:6 22:4, Luke 9:59-9:60, Matthew 8:21-8:22

[6] Ezekiel 44:26 - b.Moed Katan 7b 15b, Hebrews 9:13-14, Numbers 6:10-21 19:11-14, y.Nazir 3:5

[7] Ezekiel 44:27 - b.Chagigah [Tosefot] 42ab, b.Menachot [Rashi] 18a, b.Menachot [Tosefot] 62b, b.Moed Katan 15b 16a, b.Zevachim [Tosefot] 75a, Ezekiel 20:17, Hebrews 7:26-7:28, Leviticus 4:3-4:35 8:14-8:36, Numbers 6:9-6:11

[8] Ezekiel 44:28 - 1 Peter 5:2-5:4, Deuteronomy 10:9 18:1-18:2, Ezekiel 21:4 48:9-48:11, Joshua 13:14 13:33, Numbers 18:20

[9] Ezekiel 44:29 - 1 Corinthians 9:13-9:14, b.Avodah Zara 13a, Hebrews 13:10, Leviticus 2:3 2:10 6:14-6:18 6:26 6:29 7:6 3:21 3:28, Numbers 18:9-11 18:14

[10] LXX *and every special offering in Israel shall be theirs*

[11] Ezekiel 44:30 - 2 Chronicles 31:4-31:6 7:10, b.Shabbat 32b, b.Yevamot 62b, Bahir 103, Deuteronomy 18:4 26:10-26:15, Ecclesiastes.R 9:8, Ein Yaakov Shabbat:32b, Ein Yaakov Yevamot:62b, Exodus 13:2 13:12 22:29 23:19, Genesis.R 17:2, James 1:18, Malachi 3:10-3:11, Mas.Soferim 19:11, mt.Pirkei Avot 5:7, Nehemiah 10:36-10:38, Numbers 3:13 15:19-15:21 18:12-18:18 18:27-18:30, Proverbs 3:9-3:10, y.Bikkurim 2:3, y.Terumot 4:3

[12] Ezekiel 44:31 - 1 Corinthians 8:13, b.Menachot 45a, b.Shabbat [Rashi] 13b, Deuteronomy 14:21, Ein Yaakov Shabbat:13a, Exodus 22:31, Ezekiel 4:14, Leviticus 17:15 22:8, Romans 14:20

[13] LXX *taken of wild beasts*

[14] Ezekiel 45:1 - 3 Enoch 2:3, Ezekiel 45:2-45:7 47:21-47:22 48:8-48:23 24:29, Joshua 13:6 14:2, Leviticus 1:23, Midrash Tanchuma Massei 4, Numbers 10:13, Numbers.R 23:6, Proverbs 3:9, Psalms 16:5-16:6, Zechariah 14:20-14:21

אֹ֣רֶךְ וְרֹ֗חַב עֲשָׂרָ֥ה אֶ֛לֶף קֹ֥דֶשׁ־ה֖וּא בְּכָל־גְּבוּלָ֥הּ סָבִֽיב		the LORD, a holy portion of the land; the length shall be the length of twenty-five thousand reeds, and the breadth shall be *ten*[1] thousand; it shall be holy in all its border around it.
יִהְיֶ֣ה מִזֶּ֣ה אֶל־הַקֹּ֗דֶשׁ חֲמֵ֧שׁ מֵא֛וֹת בַּחֲמֵ֥שׁ מֵא֖וֹת מְרֻבָּ֣ע סָבִ֑יב וַחֲמִשִּׁ֥ים אַמָּ֛ה מִגְרָ֖שׁ ל֥וֹ סָבִֽיב	2[2]	Of this there shall be for the holy place five hundred in length by five hundred in breadth, square around it; and fifty cubits for the open land around it.
וּמִן־הַמִּדָּ֣ה הַזֹּאת֮ תָּמ֣וֹד אֹרֶךְ֒ "חֲמֵשׁ" "חֲמִשָּׁה" וְעֶשְׂרִים֙ אֶ֔לֶף וְרֹ֖חַב עֲשֶׂ֣רֶת אֲלָפִ֑ים וּבוֹ־יִֽהְיֶ֥ה הַמִּקְדָּ֖שׁ קֹ֥דֶשׁ קָדָשִֽׁים	3[3]	And of this you shall measure twenty-five thousand in length, and a breadth of *ten*[4] thousand; and in it shall be the sanctuary, which is most holy.
קֹ֣דֶשׁ מִן־הָאָ֜רֶץ ה֗וּא לַכֹּ֤הֲנִים֙ מְשָׁרְתֵ֣י הַמִּקְדָּ֔שׁ יִֽהְיֶ֔ה הַקְּרֵבִ֖ים לְשָׁרֵ֣ת אֶת־יְהוָ֑ה וְהָיָ֨ה לָהֶ֤ם מָקוֹם֙ לְבָתִּ֔ים וּמִקְדָּ֖שׁ לַמִּקְדָּֽשׁ	4[5]	It is a holy portion of the land; it shall be for the priests, the ministers of the sanctuary, who come near to minister to the LORD; and it shall be a place for their houses, and a place consecrated for the sanctuary.
וַחֲמִשָּׁ֨ה וְעֶשְׂרִ֥ים אֶ֙לֶף֙ אֹ֔רֶךְ וַעֲשֶׂ֥רֶת אֲלָפִ֖ים רֹ֑חַב יִֽהְיֶ֣ה "וְהָיָֽה" לַלְוִיִּ֗ם מְשָׁרְתֵ֤י הַבַּ֙יִת֙ לָהֶ֣ם לַֽאֲחֻזָּ֔ה עֶשְׂרִ֖ים לְשָׁכֹֽת	5[6]	And twenty-five thousand in length, and *ten*[7] thousand in breadth, which shall be to the Levites, the ministers of the house, as a possession, *for twenty chambers*[8].
וַאֲחֻזַּ֨ת הָעִ֜יר תִּתְּנ֗וּ חֲמֵ֤שֶׁת אֲלָפִים֙ רֹ֔חַב וְאֹ֗רֶךְ חֲמִשָּׁ֤ה וְעֶשְׂרִים֙ אֶ֔לֶף לְעֻמַּ֖ת תְּרוּמַ֣ת הַקֹּ֑דֶשׁ לְכָל־בֵּ֥ית יִשְׂרָאֵ֖ל יִֽהְיֶֽה	6[9]	And you shall appoint the possession of the city five-thousand broad, and twenty-five thousand long, side by side with the offering of the holy portion; it shall be for the whole house of Israel.
וְלַנָּשִׂ֡יא מִזֶּ֣ה וּמִזֶּה֩ לִתְרוּמַ֨ת הַקֹּ֜דֶשׁ וְלַאֲחֻזַּ֣ת הָעִ֗יר אֶל־פְּנֵ֤י תְרֽוּמַת־הַקֹּ֙דֶשׁ֙ וְאֶל־פְּנֵי֙ אֲחֻזַּ֣ת הָעִ֔יר מִפְּאַת־יָ֣ם יָ֔מָּה וּמִפְּאַת־קֵ֖דְמָה קָדִ֑ימָה וְאֹ֗רֶךְ לְעֻמּוֹת֙ אַחַ֣ד הַחֲלָקִ֔ים מִגְּב֥וּל יָ֖ם אֶל־גְּב֥וּל קָדִֽימָה	7[10]	And for the prince, on the one side and on the other side of the holy offering and of the possession of the city, in front of the holy offering and in front of the possession of the city, on the west side westward, and on the east side eastward; and in length answerable to one of the portions, from the west border to the east border
לָאָ֛רֶץ יִֽהְיֶה־לּ֥וֹ לַֽאֲחֻזָּ֖ה בְּיִשְׂרָאֵ֑ל וְלֹא־יוֹנ֨וּ ע֤וֹד נְשִׂיאַי֙ אֶת־עַמִּ֔י וְהָאָ֛רֶץ יִתְּנ֥וּ לְבֵֽית־יִשְׂרָאֵ֖ל לְשִׁבְטֵיהֶֽם	8[11]	of the land; it shall be a possession to him in Israel, and My princes shall not wrong My people; but they shall give the land to the house of Israel according to their tribes.
כֹּֽה־אָמַ֞ר אֲדֹנָ֣י יְהוִ֗ה רַב־לָכֶ֞ם נְשִׂיאֵ֣י יִשְׂרָאֵ֘ל חָמָ֣ס וָשֹׁד֮ הָסִ֒ירוּ֒ וּמִשְׁפָּ֣ט וּצְדָקָ֖ה עֲשׂ֑וּ הָרִ֤ימוּ גְרֻשֹֽׁתֵיכֶם֙ מֵעַ֣ל עַמִּ֔י נְאֻ֖ם אֲדֹנָ֥י יְהוִֽה	9[12]	Thus says the Lord GOD: Let it be enough, O princes of Israel; remove violence and spoil, and execute *justice and righteousness; take away your extortion*[13] from My people, says the Lord GOD.

---

[1] LXX *twenty*
[2] Ezekiel 45:2 - Ezekiel 3:28 42:16-42:20
[3] Ezekiel 45:3 - b.Yoma [Rashi] 67a, Ezekiel 24:10, Mas.Soferim 7:2
[4] LXX *twenty*
[5] Ezekiel 45:4 - Ezekiel 16:45 19:19 44:13-44:14 20:28 21:1 48:10-48:11, Numbers 16:5
[6] Ezekiel 45:5 - 1 Chronicles 9:26-9:33, 1 Corinthians 9:13-9:14, Ezekiel 16:17 24:10 24:13 24:20, Nehemiah 10:39-10:40
[7] LXX *twenty*
[8] Missing in LXX
[9] Ezekiel 45:6 - Ezekiel 48:15-48:18 48:30-48:35
[10] Ezekiel 45:7 - Ezekiel 10:24 13:24 46:16-18 24:21, Isaiah 9:6-7, Luke 1:32-33, Psalms 2:8-9
[11] Ezekiel 45:8 - Ezekiel 19:3 19:7 22:27 22:18, Isaiah 11:3-11:5 32:1-32:2 60:17-60:18, James 2:6 5:1-5:6, Jeremiah 22:17 23:5, Joshua 11:23, Micah 3:1-3:4, Proverbs 4:16, Psalms of Solomon 17:28, Revelation 19:11-19:16, Zephaniah 3:13
[12] Ezekiel 45:9 - 1 Corinthians 6:7-6:8, 1 Peter 4:3, Ezekiel 43:14-43:16 20:6, Isaiah 1:17, Jastrow 243a, Jeremiah 22:3, Job 20:19 22:9 24:2-24:12, Luke 3:14, Micah 2:1-2:2 2:9, Nehemiah 5:1-5:13, Psalms 82:2-82:5, z.Vaetchanan 269b, Zechariah 8:16
[13] LXX *judgment and justice; take away oppression*

מֹאזְנֵי־צֶדֶק וְאֵיפַת־צֶדֶק וּבַת־צֶדֶק יְהִי לָכֶם

10[1] You shall have just balances, and a just *ephah, and a just bath*[2].

הָאֵיפָה וְהַבַּת תֹּכֶן אֶחָד יִהְיֶה לָשֵׂאת מַעְשַׂר הַחֹמֶר הַבָּת וַעֲשִׂירִת הַחֹמֶר הָאֵיפָה אֶל־הַחֹמֶר יִהְיֶה מַתְכֻּנְתּוֹ

11[3] The ephah and the bath shall be of one measure, that the *bath*[4] may contain the tenth part of a homer, and the ephah the tenth part of a homer; its measure shall be the homer[5].

וְהַשֶּׁקֶל עֶשְׂרִים גֵּרָה עֶשְׂרִים שְׁקָלִים חֲמִשָּׁה וְעֶשְׂרִים שְׁקָלִים עֲשָׂרָה וַחֲמִשָּׁה הַשֶּׁקֶל הַמָּנֶה יִהְיֶה לָכֶם

12[6] *And the shekel shall be twenty gerahs; twenty shekels, twenty-five shekels, fifteen shekels shall be your maneh*[7].

זֹאת הַתְּרוּמָה אֲשֶׁר תָּרִימוּ שִׁשִּׁית הָאֵיפָה מֵחֹמֶר הַחִטִּים וְשִׁשִּׁיתֶם הָאֵיפָה מֵחֹמֶר הַשְּׂעֹרִים

13[8] This is the offering you shall set apart: the sixth part of an ephah out of a homer of wheat, and you shall give the sixth part of an ephah from a homer of barley;

וְחֹק הַשֶּׁמֶן הַבַּת הַשֶּׁמֶן מַעְשַׂר הַבַּת מִן־הַכֹּר עֲשֶׂרֶת הַבַּתִּים חֹמֶר כִּי־עֲשֶׂרֶת הַבַּתִּים חֹמֶר

14[9] and the set portion of oil, the bath of oil, shall be the tithe of the bath out of the kor, which is ten baths, a homer; for ten baths are a homer;

וְשֶׂה־אַחַת מִן־הַצֹּאן מִן־הַמָּאתַיִם מִמַּשְׁקֵה יִשְׂרָאֵל לְמִנְחָה וּלְעוֹלָה וְלִשְׁלָמִים לְכַפֵּר עֲלֵיהֶם נְאֻם אֲדֹנָי יְהוִה

15[10] and one lamb of the flock, out of *two hundred*[11], *from the well-watered pastures of Israel; for a meal offering*[12], and for a burnt offering, and for peace offerings, to make atonement for them, says the Lord GOD.

כֹּל הָעָם הָאָרֶץ יִהְיוּ אֶל־הַתְּרוּמָה הַזֹּאת לַנָּשִׂיא בְּיִשְׂרָאֵל

16[13] All the people of the land shall give this offering for the prince in Israel.

וְעַל־הַנָּשִׂיא יִהְיֶה הָעוֹלוֹת וְהַמִּנְחָה וְהַנֶּסֶךְ בַּחַגִּים וּבֶחֳדָשִׁים וּבַשַּׁבָּתוֹת בְּכָל־מוֹעֲדֵי בֵּית יִשְׂרָאֵל הוּא־יַעֲשֶׂה אֶת־הַחַטָּאת וְאֶת־הַמִּנְחָה וְאֶת־הָעוֹלָה וְאֶת־הַשְּׁלָמִים לְכַפֵּר בְּעַד בֵּית־יִשְׂרָאֵל

17[14] And it shall be the prince's part to give the burnt offerings, and the meal offerings, and the drink offerings, in the festivals, and in the new moons, and in the sabbaths, in all the appointed seasons of the house of Israel; he shall prepare the sin offering, and the meal offering, and the burnt offering, and the peace offerings, to make atonement for the house of Israel.

כֹּה־אָמַר אֲדֹנָי יְהוִה בָּרִאשׁוֹן בְּאֶחָד לַחֹדֶשׁ תִּקַּח פַּר־בֶּן־בָּקָר תָּמִים וְחִטֵּאתָ אֶת־הַמִּקְדָּשׁ

18[15] Thus says the Lord GOD: In the first month, in the first day of the month, you shall take a

---

[1] Ezekiel 45:10 - Amos 8:4-8:6, Deuteronomy 1:15, Isaiah 5:10, Leviticus 19:35-19:36, Micah 6:10-6:11, Proverbs 11:1 16:11 20:10 21:3, Pseudo-Phocylides 12, Tanna Devei Eliyahu 6

[2] LXX *measure, and a just choenix for measure*

[3] Ezekiel 45:11 - b.Bava Batra [Rashbam] 102b, b.Eruvin [Rashi] 83b, b.Menachot 77a, Isaiah 5:10, y.Terumot 4:3

[4] LXX *choenix*, et al.

[5] LXX *gomor*, et al.

[6] Ezekiel 45:12 - b.Bava Batra 90a, b.Bechorot 5a, b.Menachot 77a, Exodus 6:13, Leviticus 3:25, Numbers 3:47, y.Sanhedrin 1:4

[7] LXX *And the weights shall be twenty oboli, your pound shall be five shekels, fifteen shekels and fifty shekels*

[8] Ezekiel 45:13 - b.Chullin [Rashi] 137b, b.Kiddushin [Tosefot] 41a, t.Terumot 5:8, y.Terumot 4:3

[9] Ezekiel 45:14 - b.Bava Batra [Rashbam] 102b, b.Eruvin 14b, b.Menachot 77a

[10] Ezekiel 45:15 - 2 Corinthians 5:19-21, b.Avodah Zara [Rashi] 46a, b.Bava Metzia [Tosefot] 58a, b.Chullin [Tosefot] 116a 140a, b.Chullin 90b, b.Menachot [Rashi] 69b, b.Menachot [Tosefot] 66b 68b 84a, b.Menachot 5a 6a, b.Pesachim [Rashi] 47b, b.Pesachim 48a, b.Sanhedrin [Rashi] 55a, b.Temurah [Tosefot] 28a, b.Temurah 29a, b.Zevachim [Rashi] 34a 88a, Colossians 1:21, Daniel 9:24, Ephesians 2:16, Hebrews 2:17 9:22-23, Jastrow 946a, Leviticus 1:4 6:30, Malachi 1:8 1:14, Proverbs 3:9-10, Romans 5:10, y.Orlah 2:1, y.Sukkah 4:7

[11] LXX *ten*

[12] LXX *as an oblation from all the tribes of Israel, for sacrifices*

[13] Ezekiel 45:16 - Exodus 30:14-30:15, Isaiah 16:1
Ezekiel 45:16-18 - Haftarah Parshat Hachodesh [Ashkenaz], Siman 140:2
Ezekiel 45:16-25 - mt.Hilchot Tefilah 13:20

[14] Ezekiel 45:17 - 1 Chronicles 16:2-16:3 29:3-29:9, 1 Corinthians 5:7-5:8, 1 Kings 8:63-8:64, 1 Peter 2:24 3:18, 2 Chronicles 5:6 7:4-7:5 8:12-8:13 6:24 7:3 35:7-35:8, 2 Samuel 6:19, Colossians 3:17, Ephesians 5:2, Ezekiel 19:27 46:4-46:12, Ezra 1:5 6:8-6:9, Hebrews 13:10 13:15, Isaiah 18:23, John 1:16 6:51-6:57, Leviticus 23:1-23:44, Numbers 28:1-28:29, Psalms 22:16-22:27 22:30 68:19, Romans 11:35-11:36

[15] Ezekiel 45:18 - 1 Peter 1:19, Apocalypse of Abraham 11:3, b.Megillah 30a, Exodus 12:2, Ezekiel 19:22 19:26, b.Menachot 45a, Ezekiel the Tragedian 177, Hebrews 7:26 9:14 9:22-25 10:3-4 10:19-22, Leviticus 16:16 16:33 22:20, Matthew 6:33, Numbers 28:11-15, t.Megillah 3:4, z.Vaetchanan 269b

young bullock without blemish; and you shall purify the sanctuary.

וְלָקַח הַכֹּהֵן מִדַּם הַחַטָּאת וְנָתַן אֶל־מְזוּזַת הַבַּיִת וְאֶל־אַרְבַּע פִּנּוֹת הָעֲזָרָה לַמִּזְבֵּחַ וְעַל־מְזוּזַת שַׁעַר הֶחָצֵר הַפְּנִימִית	19[1] And the priest shall take of the blood of the sin offering, and put it on the door posts of the house, and on the four corners of the seat of the altar, and on the posts of the gate of the inner court.
וְכֵן תַּעֲשֶׂה בְּשִׁבְעָה בַחֹדֶשׁ מֵאִישׁ שֹׁגֶה וּמִפֶּתִי וְכִפַּרְתֶּם אֶת־הַבָּיִת	20[2] And so you shall do on the seventh day of the month for everyone who errs, and for he who is simple; so you shall make atonement for the house.
בָּרִאשׁוֹן בְּאַרְבָּעָה עָשָׂר יוֹם לַחֹדֶשׁ יִהְיֶה לָכֶם הַפָּסַח חָג שְׁבֻעוֹת יָמִים מַצּוֹת יֵאָכֵל	21[3] In the first month, in the fourteenth day of the month, you shall have the Passover; a festival of seven days; matzah shall be eaten.
וְעָשָׂה הַנָּשִׂיא בַּיּוֹם הַהוּא בַּעֲדוֹ וּבְעַד כָּל־עַם הָאָרֶץ פַּר חַטָּאת	22[4] And on that day the prince shall prepare for himself and for all the people of the land a bullock for a sin offering.
וְשִׁבְעַת יְמֵי־הֶחָג יַעֲשֶׂה עוֹלָה לַיהוָה שִׁבְעַת פָּרִים וְשִׁבְעַת אֵילִים תְּמִימִם לַיּוֹם שִׁבְעַת הַיָּמִים וְחַטָּאת שְׂעִיר עִזִּים לַיּוֹם	23[5] And the seven days of the festival he shall prepare a burnt offering to the LORD, seven bullocks and seven rams without blemish daily for seven days; and a male goat daily for a sin offering.
וּמִנְחָה אֵיפָה לַפָּר וְאֵיפָה לָאַיִל יַעֲשֶׂה וְשֶׁמֶן הִין לָאֵיפָה	24[6] And he shall prepare a meal offering, an ephah for a bullock, and an ephah for a ram, and a hin of oil to an ephah.
בַּשְּׁבִיעִי בַּחֲמִשָּׁה עָשָׂר יוֹם לַחֹדֶשׁ בֶּחָג יַעֲשֶׂה כָאֵלֶּה שִׁבְעַת הַיָּמִים כַּחַטָּאת כָּעֹלָה וְכַמִּנְחָה וְכַשָּׁמֶן	25[7] In the seventh month, in the fifteenth day of the month, in the festival, shall he do the same the seven days; to the sin offering as well as the burnt offering, and the meal offering as well as the oil.

Ezekiel – Chapter 46

כֹּה־אָמַר אֲדֹנָי יְהוִה שַׁעַר הֶחָצֵר הַפְּנִימִית הַפֹּנֶה קָדִים יִהְיֶה סָגוּר שֵׁשֶׁת יְמֵי הַמַּעֲשֶׂה וּבְיוֹם הַשַּׁבָּת יִפָּתֵחַ וּבְיוֹם הַחֹדֶשׁ יִפָּתֵחַ	1[8] Thus says the Lord GOD: The gate of the inner court looking eastward shall be shut the six working days; but on the sabbath day it shall be opened, and in the day of the new moon it shall be opened.
וּבָא הַנָּשִׂיא דֶּרֶךְ אוּלָם הַשַּׁעַר מִחוּץ וְעָמַד עַל־מְזוּזַת הַשַּׁעַר וְעָשׂוּ הַכֹּהֲנִים אֶת־עוֹלָתוֹ וְאֶת־שְׁלָמָיו וְהִשְׁתַּחֲוָה עַל־מִפְתַּן הַשַּׁעַר וְיָצָא וְהַשַּׁעַר לֹא־יִסָּגֵר עַד־הָעָרֶב	2[9] And the prince shall enter through the porch of the outside gate, and shall stand by the post of the gate, and the priests shall prepare his burnt offering and his peace offerings, and he shall worship at the threshold of the gate; then he shall go forth; but the gate shall not be shut until the evening.

Ezekiel 45:18-46:15 - Haftarah Parshat Hachodesh [Sephard]

[1] Ezekiel 45:19 - b.Menachot [Tosefot] 45a, Ezekiel 19:14 19:17 19:20, Leviticus 16:18-20

[2] Ezekiel 45:20 - b.Menachot 45a, b.Shabbat [Rashi] 13b, Ezekiel 21:15 21:18, Hebrews 5:2, Leviticus 4:27-35 16:20, Psalms 19:13, Romans 16:18-19

[3] Ezekiel 45:21 - 1 Corinthians 5:7-8, Deuteronomy 16:1-8, Exodus 12:1-51, Leviticus 23:5-23:8, Numbers 9:2-9:14 28:16-28:25

[4] Ezekiel 45:22 - 2 Corinthians 5:21, b.Pesachim [Rashi] 59b, Leviticus 4:14, Matthew 20:28 26:26-26:28

[5] Ezekiel 45:23 - b.Menachot [Tosefot] 44b, Hebrews 10:8-12, Job 18:8, Leviticus 23:8, Numbers 23:1-2 28:15-31 5:5 29:11-38

[6] Ezekiel 45:24 - Ezekiel 46:5-46:7, Numbers 28:12-28:15

[7] Ezekiel 45:25 - 2 Chronicles 5:3 7:8-10, Deuteronomy 16:13-15, John 7:2 7:37-39, Leviticus 23:33-43, Nehemiah 8:14-18, Numbers 29:12-38, Zechariah 14:16-19

[8] Ezekiel 46:1 - Exodus 20:9, Ezekiel 8:16 44:1-44:2 45:17-45:19 22:6, Genesis 3:19, Hebrews 4:9-4:10, Isaiah 18:23, Luke 13:14, Mas.Soferim 17:9, Midrash Tanchuma Ki Tissa 15, Pirkei de R'Eliezer 51, z.Noach 75b, z.Vaetchanan 269b

[9] Ezekiel 46:2 - 1 Chronicles 17:16 29:10-29:12, 1 Kings 8:22-8:23, 2 Chronicles 6:13 23:13 5:29 10:31, b.Menachot 96a, Colossians 1:28, Ezekiel 20:3 21:19 22:8 22:12, Hebrews 5:7-5:8, John 10:1-10:3, Matthew 2:39

וְהִשְׁתַּחֲווּ עַם־הָאָרֶץ פֶּתַח הַשַּׁעַר הַהוּא בַּשַּׁבָּתוֹת וּבֶחֳדָשִׁים לִפְנֵי יְהוָה	3[1]	Likewise the people of the land shall worship at the door of that gate before the LORD on the sabbaths and in the new moons.
וְהָעֹלָה אֲשֶׁר־יַקְרִב הַנָּשִׂיא לַיהוָה בְּיוֹם הַשַּׁבָּת שִׁשָּׁה כְבָשִׂים תְּמִימִם וְאַיִל תָּמִים	4[2]	And the burnt offering the prince shall offer to the LORD on the sabbath day shall be six lambs without blemish and a ram without blemish;
וּמִנְחָה אֵיפָה לָאַיִל וְלַכְּבָשִׂים מִנְחָה מַתַּת יָדוֹ וְשֶׁמֶן הִין לָאֵיפָה	5[3]	and the meal offering shall be an ephah for the ram, and the meal offering for the lambs as he is able to give, and a hin of oil to an ephah.
וּבְיוֹם הַחֹדֶשׁ פַּר בֶּן־בָּקָר תְּמִימִם וְשֵׁשֶׁת כְּבָשִׂם וְאַיִל תְּמִימִם יִהְיוּ	6[4]	And in the day of the new moon it shall be a young bullock without blemish; and six lambs, and a ram; they shall be without blemish;
וְאֵיפָה לַפָּר וְאֵיפָה לָאַיִל יַעֲשֶׂה מִנְחָה וְלַכְּבָשִׂים כַּאֲשֶׁר תַּשִּׂיג יָדוֹ וְשֶׁמֶן הִין לָאֵיפָה	7[5]	and he shall prepare a meal offering, an ephah for the bullock, and an ephah for the ram, and for the lambs according as his means suffice, and a hin of oil to an ephah.
וּבְבוֹא הַנָּשִׂיא דֶּרֶךְ אוּלָם הַשַּׁעַר יָבוֹא וּבְדַרְכּוֹ יֵצֵא	8[6]	And when the prince enters, he shall enter through the porch of the gate, and he shall leave by its way.
וּבְבוֹא עַם־הָאָרֶץ לִפְנֵי יְהוָה בַּמּוֹעֲדִים הַבָּא דֶּרֶךְ־שַׁעַר צָפוֹן לְהִשְׁתַּחֲוֹת יֵצֵא דֶּרֶךְ־שַׁעַר נֶגֶב וְהַבָּא דֶּרֶךְ־שַׁעַר נֶגֶב יֵצֵא דֶּרֶךְ־שַׁעַר צָפוֹנָה לֹא יָשׁוּב דֶּרֶךְ הַשַּׁעַר אֲשֶׁר־בָּא בוֹ כִּי נִכְחוֹ "יֵצֵאוּ" "יֵצֵא"	9[7]	But when the people of the land come before the LORD in the appointed seasons, he who enters through the north gate to worship shall leave through the south gate; and he who enters through the south gate shall leave through the north gate; he shall not return through the gate through which he came, but shall leave straight before him.
וְהַנָּשִׂיא בְּתוֹכָם בְּבוֹאָם יָבוֹא וּבְצֵאתָם יֵצֵאוּ	10[8]	And the prince, when they go in, shall go in their midst them; and when they leave, they shall leave together.
וּבַחַגִּים וּבַמּוֹעֲדִים תִּהְיֶה הַמִּנְחָה אֵיפָה לַפָּר וְאֵיפָה לָאַיִל וְלַכְּבָשִׂים מַתַּת יָדוֹ וְשֶׁמֶן הִין לָאֵיפָה	11[9]	And in the festivals and in the appointed seasons the meal offering shall be an ephah for a bullock, and an ephah for a ram, and for the lambs as he is able to give, and a hin of oil to an ephah.
וְכִי־יַעֲשֶׂה הַנָּשִׂיא נְדָבָה עוֹלָה אוֹ־שְׁלָמִים נְדָבָה לַיהוָה וּפָתַח לוֹ אֶת הַשַּׁעַר הַפֹּנֶה קָדִים וְעָשָׂה אֶת־עֹלָתוֹ וְאֶת־שְׁלָמָיו כַּאֲשֶׁר יַעֲשֶׂה בְּיוֹם הַשַּׁבָּת וְיָצָא וְסָגַר אֶת־הַשַּׁעַר אַחֲרֵי צֵאתוֹ	12[10]	And when the prince prepares a freewill offering, a burnt offering or peace offerings as a freewill offering to the LORD, one shall open for him the gate that looks toward the east, and he shall prepare his burnt offering and his peace offerings, as he does on the sabbath day; then he shall leave; and after he leaves one shall shut the gate.

---

[1] Ezekiel 46:3 - Hebrews 10:19-10:22, John 10:9, Luke 1:10, Pirkei de R'Eliezer 51
[2] Ezekiel 46:4 - Ezekiel 21:17, mt.Hilchot Maaseh haKorbanot 2:15, Numbers 28:9-28:10
[3] Ezekiel 46:5 - Deuteronomy 16:17, Ezekiel 21:24 22:7 46:11-46:12, Leviticus 14:21, Numbers 6:21 4:12
[4] Ezekiel 46:6 - b.Menachot 45a, Ezekiel 22:1
[5] Ezekiel 46:7 - b.Menachot 45a, Ezekiel 22:5
[6] Ezekiel 46:8 - Colossians 1:18, Ezekiel 44:1-44:3 22:2
[7] Ezekiel 46:9 - 2 Peter 2:20-2:21, b.Berachot 62b, b.Megillah 29a, Deuteronomy 16:16, Exodus 23:14-23:17 10:23, Ezekiel 1:12 1:17, Hebrews 10:38, Malachi 3:22, Mas.Soferim 7:1, mt.Hilchot Tefilah 11:10, Philippians 3:13-3:14, Psalms 84:8
[8] Ezekiel 46:10 - 1 Chronicles 5:20 5:22, 2 Chronicles 6:2-6:4 7:4-7:5 20:27-20:28 29:28-29:29 34:30-34:31, 2 Samuel 6:14-6:19, Hebrews 3:6 4:14-4:16, Matthew 18:20 4:20, Nehemiah 8:8-8:9, Psalms 42:5 122:1-122:4, Revelation 2:1
[9] Ezekiel 46:11 - Deuteronomy 16:1-22, Ezekiel 22:5 22:7, Leviticus 23:1-44, Numbers 15:1-41 28:1-29, Sifre Devarim Ki Tetze 294
[10] Ezekiel 46:12 - 1 Chronicles 5:21, 1 Kings 3:4, 2 Chronicles 5:6 7:5-7:7 5:31, Ephesians 5:2, Ezekiel 20:3 21:17 46:1-46:2 22:8, Ezra 1:4 3:5 6:17, Leviticus 1:3 7:16 23:38, Numbers 5:39, Romans 12:1

וְכֶבֶשׂ בֶּן־שְׁנָתוֹ תָּמִים תַּעֲשֶׂה עוֹלָה לַיּוֹם לַיהֹוָה בַּבֹּקֶר בַּבֹּקֶר תַּעֲשֶׂה אֹתוֹ	13[1] And you shall prepare a lamb of the first year without blemish for a burnt offering to the LORD daily; morning by morning you shall prepare it.
וּמִנְחָה תַעֲשֶׂה עָלָיו בַּבֹּקֶר בַּבֹּקֶר שִׁשִּׁית הָאֵיפָה וְשֶׁמֶן שְׁלִישִׁית הַהִין לָרֹס אֶת־הַסֹּלֶת מִנְחָה לַיהֹוָה חֻקּוֹת עוֹלָם תָּמִיד	14[2] And you shall prepare a meal offering with it morning by morning, the sixth part of an ephah, and the third part of a hin of oil, to moisten the fine flour: a meal offering to the LORD continually by a perpetual ordinance.
וַעֲשׂוּ יַעֲשׂוּ אֶת־הַכֶּבֶשׂ וְאֶת־הַמִּנְחָה וְאֶת־הַשֶּׁמֶן בַּבֹּקֶר בַּבֹּקֶר עוֹלַת תָּמִיד	15[3] Thus shall they prepare the lamb, and the meal offering, and the oil, morning by morning, for a continual burnt offering.
כֹּה־אָמַר אֲדֹנָי יֱהֹוִה כִּי־יִתֵּן הַנָּשִׂיא מַתָּנָה לְאִישׁ מִבָּנָיו נַחֲלָתוֹ הִיא לְבָנָיו תִּהְיֶה אֲחֻזָּתָם הִיא בְּנַחֲלָה	16[4] Thus says the Lord GOD: If the prince gives a gift to any of his sons, it is his inheritance, it shall belong to his sons; it is their possession by inheritance.
וְכִי־יִתֵּן מַתָּנָה מִנַּחֲלָתוֹ לְאַחַד מֵעֲבָדָיו וְהָיְתָה לּוֹ עַד־שְׁנַת הַדְּרוֹר וְשָׁבַת לַנָּשִׂיא אַךְ נַחֲלָתוֹ בָּנָיו לָהֶם תִּהְיֶה	17[5] But if he gives of his inheritance a gift to one of his servants, it shall be his to the year of liberty; then it shall return to the prince; but as for his inheritance, it shall be for his sons.
וְלֹא־יִקַּח הַנָּשִׂיא מִנַּחֲלַת הָעָם לְהוֹנֹתָם מֵאֲחֻזָּתָם מֵאֲחֻזָּתוֹ יַנְחִל אֶת־בָּנָיו לְמַעַן אֲשֶׁר לֹא־יָפֻצוּ עַמִּי אִישׁ מֵאֲחֻזָּתוֹ	18[6] Moreover, the prince shall not take of the people's inheritance, to thrust them out of their possession wrongfully; he shall give inheritance to his sons out of his own possession; so My people will not scattered from his possession.'
וַיְבִיאֵנִי בַמָּבוֹא אֲשֶׁר עַל־כֶּתֶף הַשַּׁעַר אֶל־הַלִּשְׁכוֹת הַקֹּדֶשׁ אֶל־הַכֹּהֲנִים הַפֹּנוֹת צָפוֹנָה וְהִנֵּה־שָׁם מָקוֹם בַּיַּרְכֹתם בַּיַּרְכָתַיִם יָמָּה	19[7] Then he brought me through the entry, which was at the side of the gate, into the holy chambers for the priests, which looked toward the north; and, there was a *place on the rear part westward*[8].
וַיֹּאמֶר אֵלַי זֶה הַמָּקוֹם אֲשֶׁר יְבַשְּׁלוּ־שָׁם הַכֹּהֲנִים אֶת־הָאָשָׁם וְאֶת־הַחַטָּאת אֲשֶׁר יֹאפוּ אֶת־הַמִּנְחָה לְבִלְתִּי הוֹצִיא אֶל־הֶחָצֵר הַחִיצוֹנָה לְקַדֵּשׁ אֶת־הָעָם	20[9] And he said to me: 'This is the place where the priests shall boil the guilt offering and the sin offering, where they shall bake the meal offering; so they do not bring them forth into the outer court, to sanctify the people.'
וַיּוֹצִיאֵנִי אֶל־הֶחָצֵר הַחִיצֹנָה וַיַּעֲבִירֵנִי אֶל־אַרְבַּעַת מִקְצוֹעֵי הֶחָצֵר וְהִנֵּה חָצֵר בְּמִקְצֹעַ הֶחָצֵר חָצֵר בְּמִקְצֹעַ הֶחָצֵר	21[10] Then he brought me forth into the outer court, and caused me to pass by the four corners of the court; and, behold, in every corner of the court there was a court.

[1] Ezekiel 46:13 - 1 Peter 1:19-1:20, Daniel 8:11-8:13, Exodus 12:5 29:38-42, Isaiah 2:4, John 1:29, Leviticus 12:6, Numbers 28:3-28:8 4:10, Psalms 92:3, Revelation 13:8

[2] Ezekiel 46:14 - Numbers 4:5

[3] Ezekiel 46:15 - Exodus 5:42, Hebrews 7:27 9:26 10:1-10, Numbers 4:6

[4] Ezekiel 46:16 - 2 Chronicles 21:3, Galatians 4:7, Genesis 25:5-6, John 8:35-36, Luke 10:42, Matthew 1:34, Psalms 37:18, Romans 8:15-8:17 8:29-8:32, z.Vaetchanan 269b

[5] Ezekiel 46:17 - Galatians 4:30-4:31, Leviticus 1:10, Luke 19:25-26, Matthew 25:14-29

[6] Ezekiel 46:18 - 1 Kings 21:19, Ephesians 4:8, Ezekiel 22:27 34:3-6 10:21 21:8, Isaiah 11:3-4 32:1-2, Jastrow 29a, Jeremiah 23:5-6, John 10:28, Micah 1:1-2 2:1-2 3:1-3, Psalms 68:19 72:2-4 78:72

[7] Ezekiel 46:19 - Ezekiel 40:44-46 18:9 44:4-5

[8] LXX *place set apart*

[9] Ezekiel 46:20 - 1 Samuel 2:13-15, 2 Chronicles 11:13, Ezekiel 20:19 20:29, Leviticus 2:4-7 7:1-38, mt.Hilchot Maaseh haKorbanot 12:22

[10] Ezekiel 46:21 - b.Middot [Rashi] 34b, b.Middot 35a, mt.Hilchot Beit Habechirah 5:7

בְּאַרְבַּעַת מִקְצֹעוֹת הֶחָצֵר חֲצֵרוֹת קְטֻרוֹת אַרְבָּעִים
אֹרֶךְ וּשְׁלֹשִׁים רֹחַב מִדָּה אַחַת לְאַרְבַּעְתָּם
מְהֻקְצָעוֹת

22[1]　In the four corners of the court there were enclosed courts, forty cubits long and thirty broad; these four in the corners were the same measure.

וְטוּר סָבִיב בָּהֶם סָבִיב לְאַרְבַּעְתָּם וּמְבַשְּׁלוֹת
עָשׂוּי מִתַּחַת הַטִּירוֹת סָבִיב

23　And there was a row of masonry around in them, around the four, and it was made with boiling places under the rows around it.

וַיֹּאמֶר אֵלַי אֵלֶּה בֵּית הַמְבַשְּׁלִים אֲשֶׁר יְבַשְּׁלוּ־שָׁם
מְשָׁרְתֵי הַבַּיִת אֶת־זֶבַח הָעָם

24[2]　Then said he to me: 'These are the boiling places, where the ministers of the house shall boil the sacrifices of the people.'

Ezekiel – Chapter 47

וַיְשִׁבֵנִי אֶל־פֶּתַח הַבַּיִת וְהִנֵּה־מַיִם יֹצְאִים מִתַּחַת
מִפְתַּן הַבַּיִת קָדִימָה כִּי־פְנֵי הַבַּיִת קָדִים וְהַמַּיִם
יֹרְדִים מִתַּחַת מִכֶּתֶף הַבַּיִת הַיְמָנִית מִנֶּגֶב לַמִּזְבֵּחַ

1[3]　And he brought me back to the door of the house; and, behold, waters issued out from under the threshold of the house eastward, for the forefront of the house looked toward the east; and the waters came down from under, from the right side of the house, on the south of the altar.

וַיּוֹצִאֵנִי דֶּרֶךְ־שַׁעַר צָפוֹנָה וַיְסִבֵּנִי דֶּרֶךְ חוּץ אֶל־
שַׁעַר הַחוּץ דֶּרֶךְ הַפּוֹנֶה קָדִים וְהִנֵּה־מַיִם מְפַכִּים
מִן־הַכָּתֵף הַיְמָנִית

2[4]　Then he brought me out by the way of the gate northward, and led me around to the outside to the outer gate, by the way of the gate that looks toward the east; and, behold, waters trickled forth on the right side.

בְּצֵאת־הָאִישׁ קָדִים וְקָו בְּיָדוֹ וַיָּמָד אֶלֶף בָּאַמָּה
וַיַּעֲבִרֵנִי בַמַּיִם מֵי אָפְסָיִם

3[5]　*When the man went forth eastward with the line in his hand, he measured a thousand cubits, and he made me to pass through the waters, waters that were to the ankles[6].*

וַיָּמָד אֶלֶף וַיַּעֲבִרֵנִי בַמַּיִם מַיִם בִּרְכָּיִם וַיָּמָד אֶלֶף
וַיַּעֲבִרֵנִי מֵי מָתְנָיִם

4[7]　Again he measured a thousand, and made me to pass through the waters, waters that were to the knees. Again he measured a thousand, and caused me to pass through waters that were to the loins.

וַיָּמָד אֶלֶף נַחַל אֲשֶׁר לֹא־אוּכַל לַעֲבֹר כִּי־גָאוּ
הַמַּיִם מֵי שָׂחוּ נַחַל אֲשֶׁר לֹא־יֵעָבֵר

5[8]　Afterward he measured a thousand; and it was a river I could not pass through; *for the waters had risen, waters to swim in, a river that could not be passed through[9].*

---

[1] Ezekiel 46:22 - and the Syriac.], b.Middot [Rashi] 34b, b.Middot 35a, Extraordinary points of the Soferim: The hydrid expression, is considered is pointed by the Massorites for excision. The resulting phrase becomes, Jastrow 1353a, mt.Hilchot Beit Habechirah 5:7, these four are of the same measure. [See LXX, Vulgate, מהקצעות [in the corners] at the end of the verse

[2] Ezekiel 46:24 - 1 Peter 5:2, Ezekiel 22:20, John 21:15-21:17, Matthew 24:45

[3] Ezekiel 47:1 - b.Eruvin [Tosefot] 2a, b.Shekalim [Taklin Chadatin] 14a, Ezekiel 17:2 41:23-41:26 23:12, Isaiah 2:3 6:25 7:1, Jeremiah 2:13, Joel 4:18, John 7:37-7:39, m.Middot 2:6, Pirkei de R'Eliezer 51, Psalms 46:5, Revelation 22:1 22:17, Saadia Opinions 8:8, t.Sukkah 3:3[4], Zechariah 13:1 14:8
Ezekiel 47:1-5 - m.Shekalim 6:3
Ezekiel 47:1-12 - Odes of Solomon 6:8
Ezekiel 47:1-35 - mt.Hilchot Melachim uMichamoteihem 12:3

[4] Ezekiel 47:2 - b.Shekalim 14a, Ezekiel 20:2 20:4, Jastrow 1174b, m.Middot 2:6, t.Sukkah 3:3[4], y.Shekalim 6:2

[5] Ezekiel 47:3 - Acts 2:4 2:33 10:45-10:46 11:16-11:18, b.Shekalim 14a, b.Yoma 77b, Ezekiel 16:3, Jastrow 1423b, Luke 24:49, Pirkei de R'Eliezer 51, Revelation 11:1 21:15, t.Sukkah 3:3[4], y.Shekalim 6:2, Zechariah 2:1

[6] LXX *in the direction in which a man went forth opposite; and there was a measuring line in his hand, and he measured a thousand cubits with the measure*

[7] Ezekiel 47:4 - Acts 19:10-20, b.Yoma 71b, Colossians 1:6, Pirkei de R'Eliezer 51, Romans 15:19, t.Sukkah 3:6 3:3[4], y.Shekalim 6:2

[8] Ezekiel 47:5 - b.Shekalim 14a, b.Yoma 71b, Daniel 2:34-2:35, Habakkuk 2:14, Isaiah 11:9, Jastrow 792b 1531a 1558b, Matthew 13:31-32, Philo the Epic Poet Frags 4-6, Pirkei de R'Eliezer 51, Revelation 7:9 11:15 20:2-20:4, Saadia Opinions 8:8, t.Sukkah 3:6, y.Shekalim 6:2

[9] LXX *for the water rose as of a torrent that men cannot pass over*

וַיֹּאמֶר אֵלַי הֲרָאִיתָ בֶן־אָדָם וַיּוֹלִכֵנִי וַיְשִׁבֵנִי שְׂפַת הַנָּחַל	6¹

And he said to me: ' you seen this, O son of man?' Then he led me, and made me return to the bank of the river.

בְּשׁוּבֵנִי וְהִנֵּה אֶל־שְׂפַת הַנַּחַל עֵץ רַב מְאֹד מִזֶּה וּמִזֶּה:	7²

Now when I was brought back, behold, on the bank of the river were many trees on the one side and on the other.

וַיֹּאמֶר אֵלַי הַמַּיִם הָאֵלֶּה יוֹצְאִים אֶל־הַגְּלִילָה הַקַּדְמוֹנָה וְיָרְדוּ עַל־הָעֲרָבָה וּבָאוּ הַיָּמָּה אֶל־הַיָּמָּה הַמּוּצָאִים "וְנִרְפְּאוּ" "וְנִרְפּוּ" הַמָּיִם	8³

Then said he to me: '*These waters issue forth toward the eastern region, and shall go down into the Arabah; and when they enter into the sea, into the sea of the putrid waters*[4], the waters shall be healed.

וְהָיָה כָל־נֶפֶשׁ חַיָּה אֲשֶׁר־יִשְׁרֹץ אֶל כָּל־אֲשֶׁר יָבוֹא שָׁם נַחֲלַיִם יִחְיֶה וְהָיָה הַדָּגָה רַבָּה מְאֹד כִּי בָאוּ שָׁמָּה הַמַּיִם הָאֵלֶּה וְיֵרָפְאוּ וָחָי כֹּל אֲשֶׁר־יָבוֹא שָׁמָּה הַנָּחַל	9⁵

And it shall come to pass, that every living creature within it swarms, wherever the rivers shall flow, shall live; and there shall be a great multitude of fish; for these waters flow there, so all things can be healed and may live wherever the river flows.

וְהָיָה "יַעַמְדוּ" "עָמְדוּ" עָלָיו דַּוָּגִים מֵעֵין גֶּדִי וְעַד־עֵין עֶגְלַיִם מִשְׁטוֹחַ לַחֲרָמִים יִהְיוּ לְמִינָה תִּהְיֶה דְגָתָם כִּדְגַת הַיָּם הַגָּדוֹל רַבָּה מְאֹד	10⁶

And it shall come to pass, that fishermen shall stand by it from *En-gedi to En-eglaim*[7]; there shall be a place to spread the nets; their fish shall be after their kinds, as the fish of the Great Sea, a multitude.

"בִּצֹּאתוֹ" "בִּצֹּאתָיו" וּגְבָאָיו וְלֹא יֵרָפְאוּ לְמֶלַח נִתָּנוּ	11⁸

But its swamp places, and its marshes, shall not be healed[9]; they shall be given for salt.

וְעַל־הַנַּחַל יַעֲלֶה עַל־שְׂפָתוֹ מִזֶּה וּמִזֶּה כָּל־עֵץ מַאֲכָל לֹא־יִבּוֹל עָלֵהוּ וְלֹא־יִתֹּם פִּרְיוֹ לָחֳדָשָׁיו יְבַכֵּר כִּי מֵימָיו מִן־הַמִּקְדָּשׁ הֵמָּה יוֹצְאִים "וְהָיוּ" "וְהָיָה" פִרְיוֹ לְמַאֲכָל וְעָלֵהוּ לִתְרוּפָה	12¹⁰

And by the river on its bank, on this side and on that side, shall grow every tree for food, whose leaf shall not wither, nor shall its fruit fail; it shall bring forth new fruit every month, because its waters issue out of the sanctuary; and its fruit shall be for food, and its leaf for healing.'

כֹּה אָמַר אֲדֹנָי יְהֹוִה גֵּה גְבוּל אֲשֶׁר תִּתְנַחֲלוּ אֶת־הָאָרֶץ לִשְׁנֵי עָשָׂר שִׁבְטֵי יִשְׂרָאֵל יוֹסֵף חֲבָלִים	13¹¹

Thus says the Lord GOD: 'This shall be the border, where you shall divide the land for inheritance according to the twelve tribes of Israel, *Joseph receiving two portions*[12].

¹ Ezekiel 47:6 - Ezekiel 8:6 8:17 16:4 20:5, Jeremiah 1:11-1:13, Matthew 13:51, Zechariah 4:2 5:2

² Ezekiel 47:7 - 1 Kings 9:26, 2 Kings 2:13, Ezekiel 23:12, Genesis 2:9-2:10, Revelation 22:2

³ Ezekiel 47:8 - 2 Kings 2:19-22, b.Shekalim 14a, Deuteronomy 3:17 4:49, Exodus.R 15:22, Isaiah 11:6-9 11:1 11:7 41:17-19 19:20 44:3-5 1:9, Jeremiah 7:10, Joshua 3:16, Malachi 1:11, Matthew 13:15, Midrash Tanchuma Chayyei Sarah 3, Pirkei de R'Eliezer 51, t.Sukkah 3:9, y.Shekalim 6:2
Ezekiel 47:8-11 - 4 Baruch 9:18

⁴ LXX *This is the water that goes forth to Galilee that lies eastward, and it is gone down to Arabia, and has reached as far as to the sea to the outlet of the water*

⁵ Ezekiel 47:9 - 1 Corinthians 15:45, Acts 2:41 2:47 4:4 5:14 6:7 21:20, Ephesians 2:1-2:5, Exodus 15:26, Exodus.R 15:21, Isaiah 12:3 6:26 1:12 7:1 60:3-10, John 3:16 4:14 5:25 6:63 7:37-38 11:25-26 14:6 14:19, Pesikta Rabbati 33:12, Pirkei de R'Eliezer 51, Psalms 78:16 7:3, Romans 8:2, t.Sukkah 3:9, Zechariah 2:11 8:21-23

⁶ Ezekiel 47:10 - 1 Samuel 23:29, 2 Chronicles 20:2, b.Shekalim 14a, Ezekiel 2:5 23:15 24:28, Isaiah 1:12 1:20, John 21:3-11, Joshua 15:62 23:4, Luke 5:4-10, Mark 1:17, Matthew 4:19 13:47-50, Numbers 10:6, Pirkei de R'Eliezer 51, Psalms 8:25, t.Sukkah 3:10, y.Shekalim 6:2

⁷ LXX *Ingadin to Enagallim*

⁸ Ezekiel 47:11 - 2 Peter 2:19-2:22, b.Shekalim 14a, Deuteronomy 5:22, Hebrews 6:4-6:8 10:26-10:31, Jeremiah 17:6, Judges 9:45, Mark 9:48-9:49, mt.Hilchot Parah Adumah 6:13, Psalms 11:34, Revelation 21:8 22:11, y.Shekalim 6:2

⁹ LXX *But at the outlet of the water, and the turn of it, and where it overflows its banks, they shall not heal at all*

¹⁰ Ezekiel 47:12 - 1 Enoch 25:5, b.Menachot 98a, b.Sanhedrin 1a, b.Shekalim 14a, Deuteronomy.R 1:1, Ein Yaakov Sanhedrin:100a, Exodus.R 15:21, Ezekiel 23:7, Genesis 2:9, Isaiah 1:6 12:21 13:3, Jastrow 714a 1138a 1649b 1697a 1701a, Jeremiah 8:22 17:8, Job 8:16, Midrash Psalms 23:7, Midrash Tanchuma Bereshit 6, Midrash Tanchuma Pinchas 14, Numbers.R 21:22, Pesikta Rabbati 33:13, Psalms 1:3 92:13, Revelation 22:2, Saadia Opinions 8:8, Song of Songs.R 4:28, t.Taniyot 1:1, Testament of Levi 9:12, y.Shekalim 6:2, y.Taanit 1:2

¹¹ Ezekiel 47:13 - 1 Chronicles 5:1, Ezekiel 48:4-48:6, Genesis 24:5 1:26, Jeremiah 3:18 7:2, Midrash Tanchuma Massei 4, Numbers 34:2-34:12, Numbers.R 23:6, Psalms of Solomon 17:28, z.Vaetchanan 269b

¹² Missing in LXX

וּנְחַלְתֶּם אוֹתָהּ אִישׁ כְּאָחִיו אֲשֶׁר נָשָׂאתִי אֶת־יָדִי לְתִתָּהּ לַאֲבֹתֵיכֶם וְנָפְלָה הָאָרֶץ הַזֹּאת לָכֶם בְּנַחֲלָה

14[1] And you shall inherit it, one as well as another, concerning which I lifted up My hand to give it to your fathers; and this land shall fall to you for inheritance.

וְזֶה גְּבוּל הָאָרֶץ לִפְאַת צָפוֹנָה מִן־הַיָּם הַגָּדוֹל הַדֶּרֶךְ חֶתְלֹן לְבוֹא צְדָדָה

15[2] And this shall be the border of the land: on the north side, from the Great Sea, *through Hethlon, to the entrance of Zedad*[3];

חֲמָת בֵּרוֹתָה סִבְרַיִם אֲשֶׁר בֵּין־גְּבוּל דַּמֶּשֶׂק וּבֵין גְּבוּל חֲמָת חָצֵר הַתִּיכוֹן אֲשֶׁר אֶל־גְּבוּל חַוְרָן

16[4] *Hamath, Berothah, Sibraim, which is between the border of Damascus and the border of Hamath; Hazer hatticon, which is by the border of Hauran*[5].

וְהָיָה גְבוּל מִן־הַיָּם חֲצַר עֵינוֹן גְּבוּל דַּמֶּשֶׂק וְצָפוֹן צָפוֹנָה וּגְבוּל חֲמָת וְאֵת פְּאַת צָפוֹן

17[6] *And the border from the sea shall be Hazar-enon at the border of Damascus, and on the north northward is the border of Hamath. This is the north side*[7].

וּפְאַת קָדִים מִבֵּין חַוְרָן וּמִבֵּין־דַּמֶּשֶׂק וּמִבֵּין הַגִּלְעָד וּמִבֵּין אֶרֶץ יִשְׂרָאֵל הַיַּרְדֵּן מִגְּבוּל עַל־הַיָּם הַקַּדְמוֹנִי תָּמֹדּוּ וְאֵת פְּאַת קָדִימָה

18[8] *And the east side, between Hauran and Damascus and Gilead, and the land of Israel, by the Jordan, from the border to the east sea you shall measure. This is the east side*[9].

וּפְאַת נֶגֶב תֵּימָנָה מִתָּמָר עַד־מֵי מְרִיבוֹת קָדֵשׁ נַחֲלָה אֶל־הַיָּם הַגָּדוֹל וְאֵת פְּאַת־תֵּימָנָה נֶגְבָּה

19[10] *And the south side southward shall be from Tamar to the waters of Meriboth-kadesh, to the Brook, to the Great Sea. This is the south side southward*[11].

וּפְאַת־יָם הַיָּם הַגָּדוֹל מִגְּבוּל עַד־נֹכַח לְבוֹא חֲמָת זֹאת פְּאַת־יָם

20[12] *And the west side shall be the Great Sea, from the border to the entrance of Hamath. This is the west side*[13].

וְחִלַּקְתֶּם אֶת־הָאָרֶץ הַזֹּאת לָכֶם לְשִׁבְטֵי יִשְׂרָאֵל

21 So shall you divide this land according to the tribes of Israel.

וְהָיָה תַּפִּלוּ אוֹתָהּ בְּנַחֲלָה לָכֶם וּלְהַגֵּרִים הַגָּרִים בְּתוֹכְכֶם אֲשֶׁר־הוֹלִדוּ בָנִים בְּתוֹכְכֶם וְהָיוּ לָכֶם כְּאֶזְרָח בִּבְנֵי יִשְׂרָאֵל אִתְּכֶם יִפְּלוּ בְנַחֲלָה בְּתוֹךְ שִׁבְטֵי יִשְׂרָאֵל

22[14] And it shall come to pass, that you shall divide it by lot for an inheritance and to the strangers who sojourn among you, who shall birth children among you; and they shall be to you as the home-born among the children of Israel; they shall have inheritance with you among the tribes of Israel.

וְהָיָה בַשֵּׁבֶט אֲשֶׁר־גָּר הַגֵּר אִתּוֹ שָׁם תִּתְּנוּ נַחֲלָתוֹ נְאֻם אֲדֹנָי יְהוִה

23[15] And it shall come to pass, that in whatever tribe the stranger sojourns, there you shall give him his inheritance, says the Lord GOD.

---

[1] Ezekiel 47:14 - Deuteronomy 1:8, Ezekiel 20:5-20:6 20:28 20:42 24:29, Genesis 12:7 13:15 15:7 17:8 2:3 4:13, Numbers 14:16 14:30, Proverbs 16:33

[2] Ezekiel 47:15 - Ezekiel 24:1, Numbers 10:8

[3] LXX *that comes down, and divides the entrance of Emaseldam*

[4] Ezekiel 47:16 - 1 Chronicles 18:5, 1 Kings 8:65, 2 Samuel 8:8, Acts 9:2, Amos 6:14, Ezekiel 23:17 24:1, Genesis 14:15, Numbers 13:21 10:8, Zechariah 9:2

[5] LXX *Maabthera, Ebrameliam, between the coasts of Damascus and the coasts of Emathi, the habitation of Saunan, which places are above the coasts of Auranitis*

[6] Ezekiel 47:17 - Ezekiel 24:1, Numbers 10:9

[7] LXX *These are the borders from the sea, from the habitations of Ænan, the coasts of Damascus, and the northern coasts*

[8] Ezekiel 47:18 - b.Rosh Hashanah 22b, Genesis 13:10 7:23 7:47, Job 16:23, Judges 10:8, Numbers 8:1

[9] LXX *And the eastern coasts between Loranitis, and Damascus, and the land of Galaad, and the land of Israel, the Jordan divides to the sea that is east of the city of palm-trees. These are the eastern coasts*

[10] Ezekiel 47:19 - Deuteronomy 8:51 9:8, Ezekiel 24:28, Isaiah 3:12, Joshua 12:3, Numbers 20:13 10:5, Psalms 81:8

[11] LXX *And the southern and south-western coasts are from Thaeman and the city of palm trees, to the water of Marimoth Cadem, reaching forth to the great sea. This part is the south and southwest*

[12] Ezekiel 47:20 - Ezekiel 24:1, Numbers 10:6

[13] LXX *This part of the great sea forms a border, till one comes opposite the entrance of Emath, even as far as the entrance thereof. These are the parts west of Emath*

[14] Ezekiel 47:22 - Acts 2:5-2:10 11:18 15:9, Colossians 3:11, Ephesians 2:12-2:14 2:19-2:22 3:6, Ezekiel 47:13-47:14, Galatians 3:28-3:29, Isaiah 14:1 56:6-56:7, Numbers 26:55-26:56, Revelation 7:9-7:10, Romans 10:12

[15] Ezekiel 47:23 - Ecclesiastes.R 1:18, Saadia Opinions 7:9, Sifre.z Numbers Shelah 15:26

Ezekiel – Chapter 48

וְאֵ֗לֶּה שְׁמ֣וֹת הַשְּׁבָטִ֑ים מִקְצֵ֤ה צָפ֙וֹנָה֙ אֶל־יַ֣ד דֶּֽרֶךְ־ 1[1]
חֶתְלֹ֜ן לְבֽוֹא־חֲמָ֗ת חֲצַ֤ר עֵינָן֙ גְּב֤וּל דַּמֶּ֙שֶׂק֙ צָפ֙וֹנָה֙
אֶל־יַ֣ד חֲמָ֑ת וְהָיוּ־ל֧וֹ פְאַת־קָדִ֛ים הַיָּ֖ם דָּ֥ן אֶחָֽד

Now these are the names of the tribes: from the north end, near the way of Hethlon to the entrance of Hamath, Hazar-enan, at the border of Damascus, northward, beside Hamath; and they shall have their sides east and west: Dan, one portion[2].

וְעַ֣ל ׀ גְּב֣וּל דָּ֗ן מִפְּאַ֤ת קָדִים֙ עַד־פְּאַת־יָ֔מָּה אָשֵׁ֖ר 2[3]
אֶחָֽד

And by the border of Dan, from the east side to the west *side*[4]: Asher, one portion.

וְעַ֣ל ׀ גְּב֣וּל אָשֵׁ֗ר מִפְּאַ֤ת קָדִ֙ימָה֙ וְעַד־פְּאַת־יָ֔מָּה 3[5]
נַפְתָּלִ֖י אֶחָֽד

And by the border of Asher, from the east side to the west *side*[6]: Naphtali, one portion.

וְעַ֣ל ׀ גְּב֣וּל נַפְתָּלִ֗י מִפְּאַ֤ת קָדִ֙מָה֙ עַד־פְּאַת־יָ֔מָּה 4[7]
מְנַשֶּׁ֖ה אֶחָֽד

And by the border of Naphtali, from the east side to the west *side*[8]: Manasseh, one portion.

וְעַ֣ל ׀ גְּב֣וּל מְנַשֶּׁ֗ה מִפְּאַ֤ת קָדִ֙מָה֙ עַד־פְּאַת־יָ֔מָּה 5[9]
אֶפְרַ֖יִם אֶחָֽד

And by the border of Manasseh, from the east side to the west *side*[10]: Ephraim, one portion.

וְעַ֣ל ׀ גְּב֣וּל אֶפְרַ֗יִם מִפְּאַ֤ת קָדִים֙ וְעַד־פְּאַת־יָ֔מָּה 6[11]
רְאוּבֵ֖ן אֶחָֽד

And by the border of Ephraim, from the east side to the west *side*[12]: Reuben, one portion.

וְעַ֣ל ׀ גְּב֣וּל רְאוּבֵ֗ן מִפְּאַ֤ת קָדִים֙ עַד־פְּאַת־יָ֔מָּה 7[13]
יְהוּדָ֖ה אֶחָֽד

And by the border of Reuben, from the east side to the west *side*[14]: Judah, one portion.

וְעַל֙ ׀ גְּב֣וּל יְהוּדָ֗ה מִפְּאַ֤ת קָדִים֙ עַד־פְּאַת־יָ֔מָּה תִּהְיֶ֣ה 8[15]
הַתְּרוּמָ֣ה אֲשֶׁר־תָּרִ֗ימוּ חֲמִשָּׁ֤ה וְעֶשְׂרִים֙ אֶ֣לֶף רֹ֔חַב
וְאֹ֜רֶךְ כְּאַחַ֤ד הַחֲלָקִים֙ מִפְּאַ֤ת קָדִ֙ימָה֙ עַד־פְּאַת־יָ֔מָּה
וְהָיָ֥ה הַמִּקְדָּ֖שׁ בְּתוֹכֽוֹ

And by the border of Judah, from the east *side to the west side*[16], shall be the offering which you shall set aside, twenty-five thousand reeds in breadth, and in length as one of the portions, from the east side to the west side; and the sanctuary shall be in its midst.

הַתְּרוּמָ֗ה אֲשֶׁ֤ר תָּרִ֙ימוּ֙ לַֽיהֹוָ֔ה אֹ֕רֶךְ חֲמִשָּׁ֥ה 9[17]
וְעֶשְׂרִים֙ אֶ֔לֶף וְרֹ֖חַב עֲשֶׂ֥רֶת אֲלָפִֽים

The offering you shall set apart to the LORD shall be twenty-five thousand reeds in length, and *ten*[18] thousand in breadth.

וּ֠לְאֵ֠לֶּה תִּֽהְיֶ֞ה תְּרֽוּמַת־הַקֹּ֣דֶשׁ לַכֹּהֲנִ֗ים צָפ֜וֹנָה 10[19]
חֲמִשָּׁ֤ה וְעֶשְׂרִים֙ אֶ֔לֶף וְיָ֗מָּה רֹ֚חַב עֲשֶׂ֣רֶת אֲלָפִ֔ים
וְקָדִ֗ימָה רֹ֚חַב עֲשֶׂ֣רֶת אֲלָפִ֔ים וְנֶ֕גְבָּה אֹ֖רֶךְ חֲמִשָּׁ֥ה
וְעֶשְׂרִ֖ים אָ֑לֶף וְהָיָ֥ה מִקְדַּשׁ־יְהֹוָ֖ה בְּתוֹכֽוֹ

And for these, for the priests, shall be the holy offering; toward the north twenty-five thousand in length, and toward the west ten thousand in breadth, and toward the east ten thousand in breadth, and toward the south

---

[1] Ezekiel 48:1 - 1 Kings 12:28-29, 2 Samuel 24:2, Exodus 1:1-5, Ezekiel 47:15-17 23:20, Genesis 30:3-6, Genesis.R 12:2, Joshua 19:40-47, Judges 18:26-29, Matthew 20:15-16, Mekhilta de R'Shimon bar Yochai Shirata 36:1, Numbers 1:5-15 13:4-15 34:7-9, Revelation 7:4-8, Saadia Opinions 7:9
Ezekiel 48:1-7 - Sifre Devarim Reeh 75

[2] LXX *And these are the names of the tribes from the northern corner, on the side of the descent that draws a line to the entrance of Emath the palace of Ælam, the border of Damascus northward on the side of Emath the palace; and they shall have the eastern parts as far as the sea, for Dan, one portion*

[3] Ezekiel 48:2 - Genesis 30:12-30:13, Joshua 19:24-19:31, Sifre Devarim {Haazinu Hashamayim} 315, Sifre Devarim Nitzavim 315

[4] LXX *seacoast*

[5] Ezekiel 48:3 - Genesis 30:7-30:8, Joshua 19:32-19:39, t.Maaser Sheni 5:29

[6] LXX *coast*

[7] Ezekiel 48:4 - Genesis 30:22-30:24 17:51 24:5 48:14-48:20, Joshua 13:29-13:31 17:1-17:11

[8] LXX *coast*

[9] Ezekiel 48:5 - Joshua 16:1-16:10 17:8-17:10 17:14-17:18

[10] LXX *coast*

[11] Ezekiel 48:6 - Genesis 5:32 49:3-4, Joshua 13:15-21, Sifre Devarim Haazinu Hashamayim 315, Sifre Devarim Nitzavim 315

[12] LXX *coast*

[13] Ezekiel 48:7 - Genesis 5:35, Joshua 15:1-63 19:9, Mekilta de R'Ishmael Shirata 10:8, Sifre Devarim Haazinu Hashamayim 315, Sifre Devarim Nitzavim 315, Song of Songs.R 1:36

[14] LXX *coast*

[15] Ezekiel 48:8 - 2 Corinthians 6:16, Colossians 2:9, Ephesians 2:20-22, Ezekiel 45:1-6 24:21 24:35, Isaiah 12:6 33:20-22, Revelation 21:3 21:22 22:3, Zechariah 2:11-2:12

[16] LXX *parts shall be the offering of firstfruits*

[17] Ezekiel 48:9-11 - Haftarah Parshat Hachodesh [Teimon]

[18] LXX *twenty-five*

[19] Ezekiel 48:10 - 1 Corinthians 9:13-9:14, Ezekiel 20:28 21:4, Joshua 21:1-21:45, Matthew 10:10, Numbers 35:1-35:9

twenty-five thousand in length; and the sanctuary *of the LORD*[1] shall be in its midst.

11[2] The sanctified portion shall be for the priests of the sons of Zadok, who kept My charge, who did not go astray when the children of Israel went astray, as the Levites went astray.

לַכֹּהֲנִים הַמְקֻדָּשׁ מִבְּנֵי צָדוֹק אֲשֶׁר שָׁמְרוּ מִשְׁמַרְתִּי אֲשֶׁר לֹא־תָעוּ בִּתְעוֹת בְּנֵי יִשְׂרָאֵל כַּאֲשֶׁר תָּעוּ הַלְוִיִּם

12[3] And it shall be to them a portion set apart from the offering of the land, a thing most holy, by the border of the Levites.

וְהָיְתָה לָהֶם תְּרוּמִיָּה מִתְּרוּמַת הָאָרֶץ קֹדֶשׁ קָדָשִׁים אֶל־גְּבוּל הַלְוִיִּם

13[4] And answerable to the border of the priests, the Levites shall have twenty-five thousand in length, and ten thousand in breadth; all the length shall be twenty-five thousand, and the breadth *ten*[5] thousand.

וְהַלְוִיִּם לְעֻמַּת גְּבוּל הַכֹּהֲנִים חֲמִשָּׁה וְעֶשְׂרִים אֶלֶף אֹרֶךְ וְרֹחַב עֲשֶׂרֶת אֲלָפִים כָּל־אֹרֶךְ חֲמִשָּׁה וְעֶשְׂרִים אֶלֶף וְרֹחַב עֲשֶׂרֶת אֲלָפִים

14[6] And they shall not sell it, nor exchange, nor alienate the first portion of the land; for it is holy to the LORD.

וְלֹא־יִמְכְּרוּ מִמֶּנּוּ וְלֹא יָמֵר וְלֹא ׳יַעֲבוּר׳ ״יַעֲבִיר״ רֵאשִׁית הָאָרֶץ כִּי־קֹדֶשׁ לַיהוָה

15[7] And the five thousand left in the breadth, in front of the twenty-five thousand, shall be for common use, for the city, for living and for open land; and the city shall be in its midst.

וַחֲמֵשֶׁת אֲלָפִים הַנּוֹתָר בָּרֹחַב עַל־פְּנֵי חֲמִשָּׁה וְעֶשְׂרִים אֶלֶף חֹל־הוּא לָעִיר לְמוֹשָׁב וּלְמִגְרָשׁ וְהָיְתָה הָעִיר ׳בְּתוֹכֹה׳ ״בְּתוֹכוֹ״

16[8] And these shall be its measures: the north side forty-five hundred, and the south side forty-five hundred, and on the east side forty-five hundred, and the west side forty-five hundred.

וְאֵלֶּה מִדּוֹתֶיהָ פְּאַת צָפוֹן חֲמֵשׁ מֵאוֹת וְאַרְבַּעַת אֲלָפִים וּפְאַת־נֶגֶב חֲמֵשׁ ״חָמֵשׁ״ ״...״ מֵאוֹת וְאַרְבַּעַת אֲלָפִים וּמִפְּאַת קָדִים חֲמֵשׁ מֵאוֹת וְאַרְבַּעַת אֲלָפִים וּפְאַת־יָמָּה חֲמֵשׁ מֵאוֹת וְאַרְבַּעַת אֲלָפִים

17 And the city shall have open land: toward the north two-hundred fifty, and toward the south two-hundred fifty, and toward the east two-hundred fifty, and toward the west two-hundred fifty.

וְהָיָה מִגְרָשׁ לָעִיר צָפוֹנָה חֲמִשִּׁים וּמָאתַיִם וְנֶגְבָּה חֲמִשִּׁים וּמָאתָיִם וְקָדִימָה חֲמִשִּׁים וּמָאתַיִם וְיָמָּה חֲמִשִּׁים וּמָאתָיִם

18[9] And the residue in the length, answerable to the holy offering, is ten thousand eastward, and ten thousand westward; and it shall be answerable to the holy offering; and its increase is food for those serving the city.

וְהַנּוֹתָר בָּאֹרֶךְ לְעֻמַּת תְּרוּמַת הַקֹּדֶשׁ עֲשֶׂרֶת אֲלָפִים קָדִימָה וַעֲשֶׂרֶת אֲלָפִים יָמָּה וְהָיָה לְעֻמַּת תְּרוּמַת הַקֹּדֶשׁ וְהָיְתָה ׳תְבוּאָתֹה׳ ״תְבוּאָתוֹ״ לְלֶחֶם לְעֹבְדֵי הָעִיר

19[10] And they who serve the city, out of all the tribes of Israel, shall till it.

וְהָעֹבֵד הָעִיר יַעַבְדוּהוּ מִכֹּל שִׁבְטֵי יִשְׂרָאֵל

20[11] All the offering shall be twenty-five thousand by twenty-five thousand; *you shall set apart the holy offering foursquare*[12], with the possession of the city.

כָּל־הַתְּרוּמָה חֲמִשָּׁה וְעֶשְׂרִים אֶלֶף בַּחֲמִשָּׁה וְעֶשְׂרִים אֶלֶף רְבִיעִית תָּרִימוּ אֶת־תְּרוּמַת הַקֹּדֶשׁ אֶל־אֲחֻזַּת הָעִיר

---

[1] Missing in LXX

[2] Ezekiel 48:11 - 1 Peter 5:4, 2 Timothy 4:7-4:8, Ezekiel 16:46 19:19 20:10 44:15-44:16, Matthew 24:45-24:46, Revelation 2:10

[3] Ezekiel 48:12 - Ezekiel 21:4, Leviticus 3:21

[4] Ezekiel 48:13 - Deuteronomy 12:19, Ezekiel 21:3 21:5, Luke 10:7

[5] LXX *twenty*

[6] Ezekiel 48:14 - Exodus 22:29, Ezekiel 24:12, Leviticus 23:20 1:34 27:9-10 3:28 27:32-33, Malachi 3:8-10, Mas.Soferim 7:4, Ralbag Wars 6part2:2

[7] Ezekiel 48:15 - 1 Timothy 3:15, Ezekiel 22:26 18:20 20:23 21:6

[8] Ezekiel 48:16 - b.Nedarim 38a, Mas.Soferim 6:9, Revelation 21:16

[9] Ezekiel 48:18 - Ezekiel 21:6, Ezra 2:43-2:58, Joshua 9:27, Nehemiah 7:46-62

[10] Ezekiel 48:19 - 1 Kings 4:7-23, b.Bava Batra 122a, Ein Yaakov Bava Batra:122a, Ezekiel 21:6, Genesis.R 20:5, Jastrow 1462a, Midrash Psalms 1:10 17A:14, Nehemiah 11:1-11:36, Numbers.R 8:4, y.Kiddushin 4:1, y.Sanhedrin 6:7

[11] Ezekiel 48:20 - Hebrews 12:17, Revelation 21:16

[12] LXX *you shall separate again part of it, the firstfruits of the sanctuary*

וְהַנּוֹתָר לַנָּשִׂיא מִזֶּה וּמִזֶּה לִתְרוּמַת־הַקֹּדֶשׁ וְלַאֲחֻזַּת הָעִיר אֶל־פְּנֵי חֲמִשָּׁה וְעֶשְׂרִים אֶלֶף תְּרוּמָה עַד־גְּבוּל קָדִימָה וְיָמָּה עַל־פְּנֵי חֲמִשָּׁה וְעֶשְׂרִים אֶלֶף עַל־גְּבוּל יָמָּה לְעֻמַּת חֲלָקִים לַנָּשִׂיא וְהָיְתָה תְּרוּמַת הַקֹּדֶשׁ וּמִקְדַּשׁ הַבַּיִת 'בְּתוֹכֹה' "בְּתוֹכוֹ"	21[1] And the residue shall be for the prince, on the one side and on the other of the holy offering and of the possession of the city, in front of the twenty-five thousand of the offering toward the east border, and westward in front of the twenty-five thousand toward the west border, answerable to the portions, it shall be for the prince; and the holy offering and the sanctuary of the house shall be in its midst.
וּמֵאֲחֻזַּת הַלֵּוִיִּם וּמֵאֲחֻזַּת הָעִיר בְּתוֹךְ אֲשֶׁר לַנָּשִׂיא יִהְיֶה בֵּין גְּבוּל יְהוּדָה וּבֵין גְּבוּל בִּנְיָמִן לַנָּשִׂיא יִהְיֶה	22[2] Thus the possession of the Levites, and the possession of the city, shall be in the midst of the prince's; between the border of Judah and the border of Benjamin shall be the prince's.
וְיֶתֶר הַשְּׁבָטִים מִפְּאַת קָדִימָה עַד־פְּאַת־יָמָּה בִּנְיָמִן אֶחָד	23[3] And as for the rest of the tribes: from the east side to the west side: Benjamin, one portion.
וְעַל גְּבוּל בִּנְיָמִן מִפְּאַת קָדִימָה עַד־פְּאַת־יָמָּה שִׁמְעוֹן אֶחָד	24[4] And by the border of Benjamin, from the east side to the west side: Simeon, one portion.
וְעַל גְּבוּל שִׁמְעוֹן מִפְּאַת קָדִימָה עַד־פְּאַת־יָמָּה יִשָּׂשכָר אֶחָד	25[5] And by the border of Simeon, from the east side to the west side: Issachar, one portion.
וְעַל גְּבוּל יִשָּׂשכָר מִפְּאַת קָדִימָה עַד־פְּאַת־יָמָּה זְבוּלֻן אֶחָד	26[6] And by the border of Issachar, from the east side to the west side: Zebulun, one portion.
וְעַל גְּבוּל זְבוּלֻן מִפְּאַת קָדִמָה עַד־פְּאַת־יָמָּה גָּד אֶחָד	27[7] And by the border of Zebulun, from the east side to the west side: Gad, one portion.
וְעַל גְּבוּל גָּד אֶל־פְּאַת נֶגֶב תֵּימָנָה וְהָיָה גְבוּל מִתָּמָר מֵי מְרִיבַת קָדֵשׁ נַחֲלָה עַל־הַיָּם הַגָּדוֹל	28[8] And by the border of Gad, *at the south side southward, the border shall be from Tamar unto the waters of Meribath-kadesh, to the Brook, to the Great Sea*[9].
זֹאת הָאָרֶץ אֲשֶׁר־תַּפִּילוּ מִנַּחֲלָה לְשִׁבְטֵי יִשְׂרָאֵל וְאֵלֶּה מַחְלְקוֹתָם נְאֻם אֲדֹנָי יְהוִה	29[10] This is the land you shall divide by lot to the tribes of Israel for inheritance, and these are their portions, says the Lord GOD.
וְאֵלֶּה תּוֹצְאֹת הָעִיר מִפְּאַת צָפוֹן חֲמֵשׁ מֵאוֹת וְאַרְבַּעַת אֲלָפִים מִדָּה	30[11] These are the borders of the city: on the north side forty-five hundred reeds by measure;
וְשַׁעֲרֵי הָעִיר עַל־שְׁמוֹת שִׁבְטֵי יִשְׂרָאֵל שְׁעָרִים שְׁלוֹשָׁה צָפוֹנָה שַׁעַר רְאוּבֵן אֶחָד שַׁעַר יְהוּדָה אֶחָד שַׁעַר לֵוִי אֶחָד	31[12] and the gates of the city shall be named after the tribes of Israel; three gates northward: the gate of Reuben, one; the gate of Judah, one; the gate of Levi, one;
וְאֶל־פְּאַת קָדִימָה חֲמֵשׁ מֵאוֹת וְאַרְבַּעַת אֲלָפִים וּשְׁעָרִים שְׁלֹשָׁה וְשַׁעַר יוֹסֵף אֶחָד שַׁעַר בִּנְיָמִן אֶחָד שַׁעַר דָּן אֶחָד	32[13] and at the east side forty-five hundred reeds; and three gates: the gate of Joseph, one; the gate of Benjamin, one; the gate of Dan, one;

[1] Ezekiel 48:21 - b.Bava Batra 122a, Ein Yaakov Bava Batra:122a, Ezekiel 34:23-24 13:24 45:7-8 24:8 24:10 24:22, Hosea 2:2, m.Middot 2:5, mt.Hilchot Melachim uMichamoteihem 4:8

[2] Ezekiel 48:22 - m.Middot 2:5

[3] Ezekiel 48:23 - Ezekiel 48:1-48:7, Genesis 35:16-35:19, Joshua 18:21-18:28

[4] Ezekiel 48:24 - Genesis 5:33 49:5-7, Joshua 19:1-9

[5] Ezekiel 48:25 - Genesis 30:14-18, Joshua 19:17-23

[6] Ezekiel 48:26 - Genesis 30:19-20, Joshua 19:10-16

[7] Ezekiel 48:27 - Genesis 30:10-11, Joshua 13:24-28

[8] Ezekiel 48:28 - 2 Chronicles 20:2, Ezekiel 23:10 23:15 47:19-20, Genesis 14:7 15:18, Isaiah 3:12, Joshua 13:3, Numbers 20:1 20:13 10:5, Psalms 10:32

[9] LXX *from the eastern parts to the south-western parts; his coasts shall even be from Thaeman, and the water of Barimoth Cades, for an inheritance, unto the great sea*

[10] Ezekiel 48:29 - b.Bava Batra 122a, Ein Yaakov Bava Batra:122a, Ezekiel 47:13-22, Joshua 13:1-21, Numbers 10:2 10:13

[11] Ezekiel 48:30 - Ezekiel 24:16 48:32-35, Revelation 21:16

[12] Ezekiel 48:31 - b.Bava Batra 122a, Ein Yaakov Bava Batra:122a, Isaiah 26:1-2 6:12 12:11, Revelation 21:12-13 21:21 21:25

[13] Ezekiel 48:32 - b.Bava Batra [Rashbam] 122a

וּפְאַת־נֶגְבָּה חֲמֵשׁ מֵאוֹת וְאַרְבַּעַת אֲלָפִים מִדָּה **33**
וּשְׁעָרִים שְׁלֹשָׁה שַׁעַר שִׁמְעוֹן אֶחָד שַׁעַר יִשָּׂשכָר
אֶחָד שַׁעַר זְבוּלֻן אֶחָד

פְּאַת־יָמָּה חֲמֵשׁ מֵאוֹת וְאַרְבַּעַת אֲלָפִים שַׁעֲרֵיהֶם **34**
שְׁלֹשָׁה שַׁעַר גָּד אֶחָד שַׁעַר אָשֵׁר אֶחָד שַׁעַר
נַפְתָּלִי אֶחָד

סָבִיב שְׁמֹנָה עָשָׂר אָלֶף וְשֵׁם־הָעִיר מִיּוֹם יְהוָה| **35**[1]
שָׁמָּה

33 and at the south side forty-five hundred reeds
by measure; and three gates: the gate of
Simeon, one; the gate of Issachar, one; the
gate of Zebulun, one;

34 at the west side forty-five hundred reeds, with
their three gates: the gate of Gad, one; the gate
of Asher, one; the gate of Naphtali, one.

35[1] It shall be eighteen thousand reeds around it.
And the name of the city from *that day shall
be, The LORD is there*[2].'

―――――――――

[1] Ezekiel 48:35 - 3 Enoch 24:17, b.Bava Batra [Rashbam] 75b, b.Bava Batra 75a, b.Sanhedrin 97b, b.Succah 45b, Ein Yaakov Bava Batra:75b, Ein Yaakov Sukkah:45b, Exodus 15:26 17:15, Ezekiel 11:10, Genesis 22:14, Isaiah 12:6 14:32 24:23, Jeremiah 3:17 14:9 23:6 9:16, Joel 4:21, Judges 6:24, Lamentations.R 1:51, Midrash Psalms 21:2, Pesikta de R'Kahana 22.5a, Psalms 46:6 48:4 48:15 68:19 77:14 12:14, Revelation 21:3 22:3, Zechariah 2:10 14:21

[2] LXX *the day that it shall be finished, shall be its name*

Shneim Asar

Hosea b'Beeri – Chapter 1[1]

דְּבַר־יְהֹוָה‎ ׀ אֲשֶׁר הָיָה אֶל־הוֹשֵׁעַ בֶּן־בְּאֵרִי בִּימֵי
עֻזִּיָּה יוֹתָם אָחָז יְחִזְקִיָּה מַלְכֵי יְהוּדָה וּבִימֵי
יָרׇבְעָם בֶּן־יוֹאָשׁ מֶלֶךְ יִשְׂרָאֵל

1[2] The word of the LORD that came to Hosea[3] the son of Beeri, [came] in the days of Uzziah, Jotham, Ahaz, and Hezekiah, kings of Judah, and in the days of Jeroboam the son of Joash, king of Israel.

תְּחִלַּת דִּבֶּר־יְהֹוָה בְּהוֹשֵׁעַ פ וַיֹּאמֶר יְהֹוָה אֶל־
הוֹשֵׁעַ לֵךְ קַח־לְךָ אֵשֶׁת זְנוּנִים וְיַלְדֵי זְנוּנִים כִּי־
זָנֹה תִזְנֶה הָאָרֶץ מֵאַחֲרֵי יְהֹוָה

2[4] When the LORD first spoke with Hosea, the LORD said to Hosea: 'Go, take a harlot as a wife and children of harlotry to yourself; for the land commits great harlotry, departing from the LORD.'

וַיֵּלֶךְ וַיִּקַּח אֶת־גֹּמֶר בַּת־דִּבְלָיִם וַתַּהַר וַתֵּלֶד־לוֹ בֵּן

3[5] So he went and took Gomer the daughter of Diblaim; and she conceived, and bore him a son.

וַיֹּאמֶר יְהֹוָה אֵלָיו קְרָא שְׁמוֹ יִזְרְעֶאל כִּי־עוֹד מְעַט
וּפָקַדְתִּי אֶת־דְּמֵי יִזְרְעֶאל עַל־בֵּית יֵהוּא וְהִשְׁבַּתִּי
מַמְלְכוּת בֵּית יִשְׂרָאֵל

4[6] And the LORD said to him: 'Call his name Jezreel; for yet a little while, and I will visit the blood of Jezreel upon the house of Jehu, and will cause the kingdom of the house of Israel to cease.

וְהָיָה בַּיּוֹם הַהוּא וְשָׁבַרְתִּי אֶת־קֶשֶׁת יִשְׂרָאֵל
בְּעֵמֶק יִזְרְעֶאל

5[7] And it shall come to pass on that day, that I will break the bow of Israel in the valley of Jezreel.'

וַתַּהַר עוֹד וַתֵּלֶד בַּת וַיֹּאמֶר לוֹ קְרָא שְׁמָהּ לֹא
רֻחָמָה כִּי לֹא אוֹסִיף עוֹד אֲרַחֵם אֶת־בֵּית יִשְׂרָאֵל
כִּי־נָשֹׂא אֶשָּׂא לָהֶם

6[8] And she conceived again, and bore a daughter. And He said to him: 'Call her name Lo-ruhamah; for I will have compassion upon the house of Israel no longer, that I should in any way pardon them.

וְאֶת־בֵּית יְהוּדָה אֲרַחֵם וְהוֹשַׁעְתִּים בַּיהֹוָה
אֱלֹהֵיהֶם וְלֹא אוֹשִׁיעֵם בְּקֶשֶׁת וּבְחֶרֶב וּבְמִלְחָמָה
בְּסוּסִים וּבְפָרָשִׁים

7[9] But I will have compassion upon the house of Judah, and will save them by the LORD their God, and will not save them by bow, nor by sword, nor by battle, nor by horses, nor by

---

[1] Hosea 1 - The Minor Prophets, as a collective, has 21 Sedarim
[2] Hosea 1:1 - 2 Baruch 1:1, 2 Chronicles 26:1-26:23, 2 Kings 13:13 14:16-15:2 15:32 16:1-16:20 18:1-18:37, 2 Peter 1:21, Amos 1:1, b.Pesachim [Rashi] 87b, b.Pesachim 87a 87b, b.Shabbat [Rashi] 138b, Ein Yaakov Pesachim 87a 87b, Ezekiel 1:3, Genesis.R 84:19, Isaiah 1:1, Jehoach is altered to read "Joach", Jeremiah 1:2 1:4, Joel 1:1, John 10:35, Jonah 1:1, Leviticus.R 6:6, Micah 1:1, Pesikta de R'Kahana 13.7 24.9, Pesikta Rabbati 33:9, Romans 9:25, Seder Olam 20:Flee, Zechariah 1:1
[3] LXX *Osee*
[4] Hosea 1:2 - 2 Chronicles 21:13, 2 Peter 2:14, b.Bava Batra 14b, b.Pesachim 87a, Deuteronomy 7:16, Ein Yaakov Bava Batra:14b, Ein Yaakov Pesachim:87a, Exodus 34:15-34:16, Ezekiel 4:1-4:5 6:9 16:1-16:63 23:1-23:49, Genesis.R 82:11 84:19, Guide for the Perplexed 2:41, Hosea 2:4-2:7 3:1 5:3, Isaiah 20:2-20:3, Jeremiah 2:13 3:1-3:4 3:9 13:1-13:11, Mark 1:1, Numbers.R 2:15, Pesikta Rabbati 33:9 50:4, Psalms 73:27 10:39, Revelation 17:1-17:2 17:5, Seder Olam 20:Flee, z.Ki Tissa 190a
[5] Hosea 1:3 - b.Pesachim 87a, Ein Yaakov Pesachim:87a, Isaiah 8:1-8:3, Jastrow 255a 276b 277a
Hosea 1:3-6 - Ein Yaakov Pesachim:87b
[6] Hosea 1:4 - 1 Chronicles 5:25-5:26, 2 Kings 9:24-9:25 10:7-10:8 10:10-10:11 10:17 10:29-10:31 15:10-15:12 15:29 17:6-17:23 18:9-18:12, b.Pesachim 87a, Ezekiel 23:10 23:31, Gates of Repentance 3.219, Hosea 1:6 1:9 2:13 2:22 9:17, Isaiah 7:14 9:7, Jeremiah 3:8 23:2, John 1:42, Luke 1:13 1:31 1:63, Matthew 1:21
[7] Hosea 1:5 - 2 Kings 15:29, b.Pesachim 87a, Hosea 2:18, Jeremiah 49:34-49:35 3:56, Joshua 17:16, Judges 6:33, Psalms 37:15 46:10
[8] Hosea 1:6 - 1 Peter 2:10, 2 Kings 17:6 17:23-17:41, b.Pesachim 87ab, Hosea 2:4 2:23 9:15-9:17, Isaiah 3:11, Pesikta Rabbati 44:2
Hosea 1:6-9 - 4QXIId
[9] Hosea 1:7 - 2 Kings 19:35, b.Pesachim 87a, Hosea 12:1, Isaiah 7:14 12:2 36:1-22 1:6, Jeremiah 23:5-6, Matthew 1:21-23, Psalms 33:16 44:4-7, Titus 3:4-3:6, Zechariah 2:6-11 4:6 9:9-10

horsemen.'

8[1]   וַתִּגְמֹל אֶת־לֹא רֻחָמָה וַתַּהַר וַתֵּלֶד בֵּן

Now when she weaned Lo-ruhamah, she conceived, and bore a son.

9[2]   וַיֹּאמֶר קְרָא שְׁמוֹ לֹא עַמִּי כִּי אַתֶּם לֹא עַמִּי וְאָנֹכִי לֹא־אֶהְיֶה לָכֶם

And He said: 'Call his name Lo-ammi; for you are not My people, and I will not be yours.'

Hosea – Chapter 2

1[3]   וְהָיָה מִסְפַּר בְּנֵי־יִשְׂרָאֵל כְּחוֹל הַיָּם אֲשֶׁר לֹא־יִמַּד וְלֹא יִסָּפֵר וְהָיָה בִּמְקוֹם אֲשֶׁר־יֵאָמֵר לָהֶם לֹא־עַמִּי אַתֶּם יֵאָמֵר לָהֶם בְּנֵי אֵל־חָי

Yet, the number of the children of Israel shall be as the sand of the sea, which can neither be measured nor numbered; and it shall be that, instead of what was said to them: 'You are not My people,' *it shall be said*[4] to them: 'You are the children of the living God.'

2[5]   וְנִקְבְּצוּ בְּנֵי־יְהוּדָה וּבְנֵי־יִשְׂרָאֵל יַחְדָּו וְשָׂמוּ לָהֶם רֹאשׁ אֶחָד וְעָלוּ מִן־הָאָרֶץ כִּי גָדוֹל יוֹם יִזְרְעֶאל

And the children of Judah and the children of Israel shall be gathered together, and they shall appoint themselves one head, and shall go up out of the land; for great shall be the day of Jezreel.

3[6]   אִמְרוּ לַאֲחֵיכֶם עַמִּי וְלַאֲחוֹתֵיכֶם רֻחָמָה

Say you to your brethren: 'Ammi;' and to your sisters, 'Ruhamah.'

4[7]   רִיבוּ בְאִמְּכֶם רִיבוּ כִּי־הִיא לֹא אִשְׁתִּי וְאָנֹכִי לֹא אִישָׁהּ וְתָסֵר זְנוּנֶיהָ מִפָּנֶיהָ וְנַאֲפוּפֶיהָ מִבֵּין שָׁדֶיהָ

Plead with your mother, plead; For she is not My wife, nor am I her husband; And let her put away her harlotries from her face, And her adulteries from between breasts;

5[8]   פֶּן־אַפְשִׁיטֶנָּה עֲרֻמָּה וְהִצַּגְתִּיהָ כְּיוֹם הִוָּלְדָהּ וְשַׂמְתִּיהָ כַמִּדְבָּר וְשַׁתִּהָ כְּאֶרֶץ צִיָּה וַהֲמִתִּיהָ בַּצָּמָא

Lest I strip her naked, And set her as in the day she was born, And make her as a wilderness, And set her like a dry land, And kill her with thirst.

6[9]   וְאֶת־בָּנֶיהָ לֹא אֲרַחֵם כִּי־בְנֵי זְנוּנִים הֵמָּה

And I will not have compassion on her children; For they are children of harlotry.

7[10]   כִּי זָנְתָה אִמָּם הֹבִישָׁה הוֹרָתָם כִּי אָמְרָה אֵלְכָה אַחֲרֵי מְאַהֲבַי נֹתְנֵי לַחְמִי וּמֵימַי צַמְרִי וּפִשְׁתִּי שַׁמְנִי וְשִׁקּוּיָי

For their mother has played the harlot, she who conceived them has done shamefully; for she said: 'I will go after my lovers who give me my

---

[1] Hosea 1:8 - b.Pesachim 87a, b.Rosh Hashanah 23a, Ein Yaakov Pesachim:87b, Prayer of Joseph Fragment A

[2] Hosea 1:9 - b.Pesachim 87b, Ein Yaakov Pesachim:87b, Jeremiah 15:1, Midrash Tanchuma Massei 7, mt.Hilchot Teshuvah 7:6 7:6, Numbers.R 2:15, Pesikta de R'Kahana 13.7, Pesikta Rabbati 44:2, Saadia Opinions 7:8, Jubilees 1:24, Pirkei de R'Eliezer 48

[3] Hosea 2:1 - 1 John 3:1-3:2, 1 Peter 2:9-2:10, 2 Corinthians 6:18, b.Kiddushin 36a, b.Pesachim 87b, b.Yoma 22b, Ein Yaakov Yoma:22b, Exodus.R 13:1 48:6, Galatians 4:6-4:7, Genesis 13:16 22:17 8:13, Hebrews 11:12, Hosea 1:9 2:23, Isaiah 19:6 24:19 49:17-49:22 54:1-54:3 60:4-60:22 18:20, Jeremiah 9:22, John 1:12, Joseph and Aseneth 19:8, Leviticus.R 32:4, Midrash Psalms 2:2 17:4 22:7, Midrash Tanchuma Balak 21, Midrash Tanchuma Chukkat 6, Midrash Tanchuma Ki Tissa 9, mt.Hilchot Teshuvah 7:6 7:6, Numbers.R 2:12-13 2:15 2:17 19:3 20:25, Pesikta de R'Kahana 2.8, Pesikta de R'Kahana 10.1, Pesikta Rabbati 11:4 11:6, Romans 8:14-17 9:25-28, Sifre Devarim Ekev 47, Sifre Devarim Re'eh 96, Tanya Igeret Hakodesh §07, z.Ki Tissa 190a, z.Pekudei 225b Hosea 2:1-5 - 4QXIId, 4QXIIg
Hosea 2:1-22 - Haftarah Bamidbar, Haftarah Bamidbar [Hosea 2:1-2:22]

[4] 4QXIIb *he shall say*

[5] Hosea 2:2 - b.Pesachim 87b 88a, Ein Yaakov Pesachim 88a, Ezekiel 16:60-16:63 34:23-34:24 37:16-37:25, Hosea 2:22-2:25 3:5, Isaiah 11:12-11:13, Jeremiah 3:18-3:19 23:5-23:8 6:3 31:2-31:10 7:34 50:4-50:5 2:19, Micah 2:12-2:13, Midrash Psalms 45:3, Psalms 22:28-22:31 14:3, Romans 11:15 11:25-11:26, Zechariah 10:6-10:9

[6] Hosea 2:3 - 1 Peter 2:10, 1 Timothy 1:13, 2 Corinthians 4:1, Exodus 19:5-19:6, Ezekiel 11:20 12:28 13:27, Hosea 1:9-1:11 2:23, Jeremiah 7:34 8:38, Romans 11:30-11:31, Zechariah 13:9

[7] Hosea 2:4 - 2 Corinthians 5:16, Acts 7:51-7:53, Ezekiel 16:20 16:25 20:4 23:43 23:45, Hosea 1:2 2:5, Isaiah 2:1 10:1, Jeremiah 2:2 3:1 3:6-3:9 3:13 19:3, Matthew 23:37-23:39, Numbers.R 2:16, Pesikta Rabbati 44:2

[8] Hosea 2:5 - Amos 8:11-8:13, Exodus 17:3, Exodus.R 46:4, Ezekiel 16:4-16:8 16:22 16:37-16:39 19:13 20:35-20:36 23:26-23:29, Hosea 2:10, Isaiah 32:13-32:14 9:9 23:3 16:11, Jeremiah 2:6 2:31 4:26 12:10 13:22 13:26 17:6 22:6 3:43, Judges 15:18, Mekhilta de R'Shimon bar Yochai Nezikin 75:1, Midrash Tanchuma Devarim 1, Pesikta Rabbati 44:2, Revelation 17:16

[9] Hosea 2:6 - 2 Kings 9:22, Ezekiel 8:18 9:10, Hosea 1:2 1:6, Isaiah 3:11 9:3, James 2:13, Jeremiah 13:14 16:5, John 8:41, Numbers.R 2:16, Romans 9:18 11:22, z.Yitro 89b, Zechariah 1:12

[10] Hosea 2:7 - b.Horayot 10b, b.Ketubot 65a, b.Nazir 23a, Daniel 9:5-9:8, Exodus.R 46:4, Ezekiel 16:15-16:16 16:28-16:34 23:5-23:11 23:16-23:17 23:40-23:44, Ezra 9:6-9:7, Hosea 2:2 2:8 2:12-2:15 3:1 4:5 4:12-4:15 8:9 9:10, Isaiah 1:21 2:1 57:7-57:8, Jastrow 1540b, Jeremiah 2:20 2:25-2:27 3:1-3:9 11:13 44:17-18, Judges 16:23, Revelation 2:20-2:23 17:1-17:5, y.Sanhedrin 2:6

bread and my water, *my wool and my flax, my oil and my drink*[1].'

לָכֵן הִנְנִי־שָׂךְ אֶת־דַּרְכֵּךְ בַּסִּירֵים וְגָדַרְתִּי אֶת־גְּדֵרָהּ וּנְתִיבוֹתֶיהָ לֹא תִמְצָא	8[2]

Therefore, behold, I will hedge up your way with thorns, and I will make a wall against her, so she shall not find her paths.

וְרִדְּפָה אֶת־מְאַהֲבֶיהָ וְלֹא־תַשִּׂיג אֹתָם וּבִקְשָׁתַם וְלֹא תִמְצָא וְאָמְרָה אֵלְכָה וְאָשׁוּבָה אֶל־אִישִׁי הָרִאשׁוֹן כִּי טוֹב לִי אָז מֵעָתָּה	9[3]

And she shall run after her lovers, but she shall not overtake them, And she shall seek them, but shall not find them; Then she shall say: 'I will go and return to my first husband; For then was it better with me than now.'

וְהִיא לֹא יָדְעָה כִּי אָנֹכִי נָתַתִּי לָהּ הַדָּגָן וְהַתִּירוֹשׁ וְהַיִּצְהָר וְכֶסֶף הִרְבֵּיתִי לָהּ וְזָהָב עָשׂוּ לַבָּעַל	10[4]

For she did not know that it was I who gave her the corn, and the wine, and the oil, and multiplied her silver and gold that they used for Baal.

לָכֵן אָשׁוּב וְלָקַחְתִּי דְגָנִי בְּעִתּוֹ וְתִירוֹשִׁי בְּמוֹעֲדוֹ וְהִצַּלְתִּי צַמְרִי וּפִשְׁתִּי לְכַסּוֹת אֶת־עֶרְוָתָהּ	11[5]

Therefore, I will take back My corn in its time, And My wine in its season, And will snatch away My wool and My flax given to cover her nakedness.

וְעַתָּה אֲגַלֶּה אֶת־נַבְלֻתָהּ לְעֵינֵי מְאַהֲבֶיהָ וְאִישׁ לֹא־יַצִּילֶנָּה מִיָּדִי	12[6]

And now I will uncover her shame in the sight of her lovers, And no one shall deliver her from My hand.

וְהִשְׁבַּתִּי כָּל־מְשׂוֹשָׂהּ חַגָּהּ חָדְשָׁהּ וְשַׁבַּתָּהּ וְכֹל מוֹעֲדָהּ	13[7]

I also will cause all her joy to cease, Her festivals, her new moons, and her sabbaths, And all her appointed seasons.

וַהֲשִׁמֹּתִי גַּפְנָהּ וּתְאֵנָתָהּ אֲשֶׁר אָמְרָה אֶתְנָה הֵמָּה לִי אֲשֶׁר נָתְנוּ־לִי מְאַהֲבָי וְשַׂמְתִּים לְיַעַר וַאֲכָלָתַם חַיַּת הַשָּׂדֶה	14[8]

And I will lay her vines and her fig trees to waste, of which she said: 'These are my hire, what my lovers have given me;' And I will make them a forest, And the beasts of the field shall eat them.

וּפָקַדְתִּי עָלֶיהָ אֶת־יְמֵי הַבְּעָלִים אֲשֶׁר תַּקְטִיר לָהֶם וַתַּעַד נִזְמָהּ וְחֶלְיָתָהּ וַתֵּלֶךְ אַחֲרֵי מְאַהֲבֶיהָ וְאֹתִי שָׁכְחָה נְאֻם־יְהוָה	15[9]

And I will visit upon her the days of the Baalim, in which she offered to them, And decked herself with her earrings and her jewels,

---

[1] LXX *and my garments, and my linen clothes, my oil and my necessaries*

[2] Hosea 2:8 - 4Q166 frag 1 1.7-8, b.Rosh Hashanah 23b, Jastrow 1570b, Job 3:24 19:8, Lamentations 3:7-3:9, Lamentations.R 1:52, Luke 15:14-15:16 19:43, Sibylline Oracles 3.243 3.745
Hosea 2:8 [10] - Sibylline Oracles 8.382

[3] Hosea 2:9 - 2 Chronicles 28:20-28:22, 4Q166 frag 1 1.15-16, b.Berachot 7a, Daniel 4:14 4:22 4:29 5:21, Deuteronomy 6:10-6:12 8:17-8:18 32:13-32:15, Ezekiel 16:8 16:18 20:32 23:4 23:22, Hosea 5:13 5:15-6:1 13:6 14:3, Isaiah 30:2-30:3 6:16 31:1-31:3, Jeremiah 2:2 2:28 2:36-3:1 3:22-3:25 14:22 30:12-30:15 7:19 7:33 50:4-50:5, Lamentations 3:40-3:42, Luke 15:17-15:20, Nehemiah 9:25-9:26, Numbers.R 2:16, Psalms 20:7
Hosea 2:9-10 - Testament of Levi 10:3

[4] Hosea 2:10 - 4Q166 frag 1 2.1-2, Acts 17:23-17:25, b.Berachot 32a, Daniel 5:3-5:4 5:23, Ein Yaakov Berachot:32a, Exodus 32:2-32:4, Ezekiel 16:16-16:19, Genesis.R 28:7, Guide for the Perplexed 3:8, Habakkuk 1:16, Hosea 2:5 4:11 8:4 10:1 13:2, Isaiah 1:3 24:7-24:9 22:6, Jeremiah 7:18 44:17-44:18, Judges 9:27 17:1-17:5, Leviticus.R 27:8, Luke 15:13 16:1-16:2, Midrash Tanchuma Emor 11, Pesikta de R'Kahana 9.8, Pesikta Rabbati 14:8, Romans 1:28

[5] Hosea 2:11 - b.Berachot 35b, Daniel 11:13, Ein Yaakov Berachot:35b, Ezekiel 16:27 16:39 23:26, Haggai 1:6-1:11 2:16-2:17, Hosea 2:3 8:7 9:2, Isaiah 3:18-3:26 17:10-17:11, Jastrow 1666b, Joel 2:14, Malachi 1:4 3:18, Midrash Tanchuma Re'eh 18, Pesikta Rabbati 44:4, Zephaniah 1:13
Hosea 2:11-12 - 4Q166 frag 1 2.8-11

[6] Hosea 2:12 - 1 Corinthians 4:5, b.Shabbat 55a, Ein Yaakov Shabbat:55a, Exodus.R 46:4, Ezekiel 16:36-37 23:29, Hosea 2:3 5:13-5:14 13:7-8, Isaiah 3:17, Jeremiah 13:22 13:26, Leviticus.R 36:6, Luke 12:2-3, Micah 5:9, Proverbs 11:21, Psalms 50:22, y.Sanhedrin 10:1

[7] Hosea 2:13 - 1 Kings 12:32, 4Q166 frag 1 2.14-15, Amos 5:21 8:3 8:5 8:9-8:10, b.Shabbat 145b, b.Taanit 29b, Ein Yaakov Shabbat:145b, Ezekiel 2:13, Hosea 3:4 9:1-9:5, Isaiah 1:13-1:14 24:7-24:11, Jastrow 322a, Jeremiah 7:34 16:9 1:10, Nahum 1:10, Revelation 18:22-18:23, y.Taanit 4:6
Hosea 2:13-15 - 4QXIIc

[8] Hosea 2:14 - 4Q166 frag 1 2.17-19, Hosea 2:5 9:1 13:8, Isaiah 5:5 7:23 5:17 32:13-15, Jeremiah 8:13 2:18, Micah 3:12, Psalms 80:13
Hosea 2:14-19 - 4QXIIg

[9] Hosea 2:15 - 1 Kings 16:31-32 18:18-40, 1 Samuel 12:9, 2 Kings 1:2 10:28 21:3, Deuteronomy 6:12 8:11-14 8:18, Exodus 8:34, Ezekiel 16:17 22:12 23:35 23:40-42, Hosea 2:5 2:7 4:6 4:13 8:14 9:7 9:9-10 11:2 13:1 13:6, Isaiah 17:10, Jeremiah 2:23-25 2:32 7:9 11:13 18:15 23:2, Job 8:13, Judges 2:11-13 3:7 10:6, Lamentations.R Petichata D'Chakimei:21, Psalms 78:11 10:13 10:21

And went after her lovers, And forgot Me, says the LORD.

16[1] Therefore, behold, I will allure her, And bring her into the wilderness, And speak tenderly to her.

לָכֵ֗ן הִנֵּ֤ה אָֽנֹכִי֙ מְפַתֶּ֔יהָ וְהֹֽלַכְתִּ֖יהָ הַמִּדְבָּ֑ר וְדִבַּרְתִּ֖י עַל־לִבָּֽהּ

17[2] And I will give her her vineyards from there, And the valley of Achor *for a door of hope; And she shall respond*[3] there, as in the days of her youth, And as in the day when she came up out of the land of Egypt.

וְנָתַ֨תִּי לָ֤הּ אֶת־כְּרָמֶ֨יהָ֙ מִשָּׁ֔ם וְאֶת־עֵ֥מֶק עָכ֖וֹר לְפֶ֣תַח תִּקְוָ֑ה וְעָ֤נְתָה שָּׁ֨מָּה֙ כִּימֵ֣י נְעוּרֶ֔יהָ וּכְי֖וֹם עֲלֹתָ֥הּ מֵאֶֽרֶץ־מִצְרָֽיִם

18[4] And it shall be on that day, says the LORD, you shall call Me Ishi, and shall no longer call Me Baali.

וְהָיָ֤ה בַיּוֹם־הַהוּא֙ נְאֻם־יְהֹוָ֔ה תִּקְרְאִ֖י אִישִׁ֑י וְלֹֽא־תִקְרְאִי־לִ֥י ע֖וֹד בַּעְלִֽי

19[5] For I will take away the names of the Baalim from her mouth, And they shall no more be mentioned by their name.

וַהֲסִרֹתִ֛י אֶת־שְׁמ֥וֹת הַבְּעָלִ֖ים מִפִּ֑יהָ וְלֹֽא־יִזָּכְר֥וּ ע֖וֹד בִּשְׁמָֽם

20[6] And in that day will I make a covenant for them with the beasts of the field, and with the fowls of heaven, and with the creeping things of the ground; and I will break the bow and the sword and the battle from the land, and will make them to lie down safely.

וְכָרַתִּ֨י לָהֶ֤ם בְּרִית֙ בַּיּ֣וֹם הַה֔וּא עִם־חַיַּ֤ת הַשָּׂדֶה֙ וְעִם־ע֣וֹף הַשָּׁמַ֔יִם וְרֶ֖מֶשׂ הָֽאֲדָמָ֑ה וְקֶ֨שֶׁת וְחֶ֤רֶב וּמִלְחָמָה֙ אֶשְׁבּ֣וֹר מִן־הָאָ֔רֶץ וְהִשְׁכַּבְתִּ֖ים לָבֶֽטַח

21[7] And I will betroth you to Me forever; Yes, I will betroth you to Me in righteousness, and in justice, and in lovingkindness, and in compassion.

וְאֵרַשְׂתִּ֥יךְ לִ֖י לְעוֹלָ֑ם וְאֵרַשְׂתִּ֥יךְ לִי֙ בְּצֶ֣דֶק וּבְמִשְׁפָּ֔ט וּבְחֶ֖סֶד וּֽבְרַחֲמִֽים

22[8] And I will betroth you to Me in faithfulness; And you shall know the LORD.

וְאֵרַשְׂתִּ֥יךְ לִ֖י בֶּאֱמוּנָ֑ה וְיָדַ֖עַתְּ אֶת־יְהֹוָֽה

23[9] And it shall come to pass in that day, I will respond, says the LORD, I will respond to the heavens, And they shall respond to the earth;

וְהָיָ֣ה ׀ בַּיּ֣וֹם הַה֗וּא אֶֽעֱנֶה֙ נְאֻם־יְהֹוָ֔ה אֶעֱנֶ֖ה אֶת־הַשָּׁמָ֑יִם וְהֵ֖ם יַעֲנ֥וּ אֶת־הָאָֽרֶץ

24[10] And the earth shall respond to the corn, and the wine, and the oil; And they shall respond to Jezreel.

וְהָאָ֗רֶץ תַּעֲנֶה֙ אֶת־הַדָּגָ֔ן וְאֶת־הַתִּיר֖וֹשׁ וְאֶת־הַיִּצְהָ֑ר וְהֵ֖ם יַעֲנ֥וּ אֶת־יִזְרְעֶֽאל

---

[1] Hosea 2:16 - Amos 9:11-15, Exodus.R 2:4 19:1 50:3, Ezekiel 20:10 20:35-36 34:22-31 36:8-15 37:11-28 39:25-29, Genesis 10:3, Hosea 2:3, Isaiah 6:18 35:3-4 40:1-2 49:13-26 51:3-23, Jeremiah 2:2 3:12-24 16:14 30:18-22 31:2-38 32:36-41 33:6-26, John 6:44 12:32, Judges 19:3, Micah 7:14-20, Midrash Psalms 78:8 147:3, Pesikta de R'Kahana 5.8, Pesikta Rabbati 15:10 33:8 44:2, Revelation 12:6 12:14, Romans 11:26-27, Ruth.R 5:6, Sifre Devarim Ha'azinu Hashamayim 313, Sifre Devarim Nitzavim 313, Song of Songs 1:4, Song of Songs.R 2:25, Zechariah 1:12-17 8:19-23, Zephaniah 3:9-20

[2] Hosea 2:17 - 4Q434 frag 7b l.2, Acts 14:27, Amos 9:14, b.Sanhedrin 111a, Deuteronomy 30:3-5, Ein Yaakov Sanhedrin:111a, Exodus 15:1-21, Ezekiel 16:8 16:22 4:26 37:11-14, Hosea 2:12 11:1 12:11, Isaiah 17:10 17:21, Jeremiah 2:2 8:15, John 10:9, Joshua 7:26, Lamentations 3:21, Leviticus 26:40-45, Midrash Psalms 147:3, Nehemiah 1:8-1:9, Numbers 21:17, Pesikta Rabbati 44:2, Psalms 10:12, Song of Songs.R 2:25, Zechariah 9:12

[3] LXX *to open her understanding: and she shall be afflicted*

[4] Hosea 2:18 - 2 Corinthians 11:2, b.Ketubot 65a, b.Pesachim 87a, Ein Yaakov Ketubot:71b, Ein Yaakov Pesachim:87a, Ephesians 5:25-5:27, Hosea 2:7, Isaiah 6:5, Jeremiah 3:14, John 3:29, Numbers.R 9:45, Pesikta Rabbati 30:1 44:2, Revelation 19:7

[5] Hosea 2:19 - Exodus 23:13, Jeremiah 10:11, Joshua 23:7, Psalms 16:4, Sifre Devarim Ha'azinu Hashamayim 306, Sifre Devarim Nitzavim 306, z.Vayikra 6b, Zechariah 13:2

[6] Hosea 2:20 - 4Q434 frag 7b ll.2-3, Exodus.R 15:21, Ezekiel 10:25 39:9-10, Isaiah 2:4 2:11 2:17 11:6-9 2:1 17:25, Jeremiah 23:6 6:10 9:16, Job 5:23, Leviticus 26:5-6, Micah 4:3-4:4, Psalms 23:2 46:10 91:1-91:13, Zechariah 2:11 3:10 9:10 14:4 14:9

[7] Hosea 2:21 - 2 Corinthians 11:2, Avot de R'Natan 37, Deuteronomy.R 3:7, Ephesians 1:7-8 5:23-27, Exodus.R 15:31, Ezekiel 37:25-28 15:29, Isaiah 1:27 45:23-25 6:5 54:8-10 6:14 62:3-5, Jeremiah 3:14-15 4:2 31:32-37 32:38-41, Joel 4:20, John 3:29, Psalms 85:11, Revelation 19:7-9 21:2 21:9-10, Romans 3:25-26 7:4, z.Yitro 85b
Hosea 2:21-22 - Mekilta de R'Ishmael Beshallah 7:159, Upon putting on the Tefillin

[8] Hosea 2:22 - 1 John 4:6 5:20, 2 Corinthians 4:6, 2 Timothy 1:12, Colossians 1:10, Ezekiel 14:23, Hebrews 8:11, Hosea 2:19 6:6 13:4, Jeremiah 9:25 24:7 31:34-31:35, John 8:55 17:3, Luke 10:22, Matthew 11:27, Mekhilta de R'Shimon bar Yochai Beshallach 26:6, Midrash Tanchuma Beshallach 10, Midrash Tanchuma Tzav 14, Pesikta Rabbati 22:7, Philippians 3:8
Hosea 2:22-25 - 4QXIIg

[9] Hosea 2:23 - 1 Corinthians 3:21-3:23, Isaiah 7:10 17:24, Jastrow 1092a, Matthew 6:33, Romans 8:32, Sifre Devarim Ha'azinu Hashamayim 306, z.Naso 147a, Zechariah 8:12 13:9
Hosea 2:23-25 - Sifre Devarim Nitzavim 306

[10] Hosea 2:24 - b.Bava Metzia [Rashi] 39a, Hosea 1:4 2:2, Jeremiah 7:13, Joel 2:19, Prayer of Joseph Fragment A

וּזְרַעְתִּיהָ לִּי בָּאָרֶץ וְרִחַמְתִּי אֶת־לֹא רֻחָמָה וְאָמַרְתִּי לְלֹא־עַמִּי עַמִּי־אַתָּה וְהוּא יֹאמַר אֱלֹהָי

25[1] And I will sow her to Me in the land; And I will have compassion on her who *has not obtained compassion*[2]; And I will say to those who were not My people: 'You are My people;' And they shall say: 'You are my God.'

Hosea – Chapter 3[3]

וַיֹּאמֶר יְהוָה אֵלַי עוֹד לֵךְ אֱהַב־אִשָּׁה אֲהֻבַת רֵעַ וּמְנָאָפֶת כְּאַהֲבַת יְהוָה אֶת־בְּנֵי יִשְׂרָאֵל וְהֵם פֹּנִים אֶל־אֱלֹהִים אֲחֵרִים וְאֹהֲבֵי אֲשִׁישֵׁי עֲנָבִים

1[4] And the LORD said to me: 'Go yet, love a woman *beloved of her friend*[6] and an adulteress, as the LORD loves the children of Israel, though they turn to other gods, and love cakes of raisins.

וָאֶכְּרֶהָ לִּי בַּחֲמִשָּׁה עָשָׂר כָּסֶף וְחֹמֶר שְׂעֹרִים וְלֵתֶךְ שְׂעֹרִים

2[6] So I bought her to me for fifteen pieces of silver and a homer of barley, and a half-homer of barley;

וָאֹמַר אֵלֶיהָ יָמִים רַבִּים תֵּשְׁבִי לִי לֹא תִזְנִי וְלֹא תִהְיִי לְאִישׁ וְגַם־אֲנִי אֵלָיִךְ

3[7] and I said to her: 'You shall sit solitary for me many days; you shall not play the harlot, and you shall not be any man's wife; *nor will I be yours*[8].'

כִּי יָמִים רַבִּים יֵשְׁבוּ בְּנֵי יִשְׂרָאֵל אֵין מֶלֶךְ וְאֵין שָׂר וְאֵין זֶבַח וְאֵין מַצֵּבָה וְאֵין אֵפוֹד וּתְרָפִים

4[9] For the children of Israel shall sit solitary many days without king, and without prince, and without *sacrifice, and without pillar, and without ephod or teraphim*[10];

אַחַר יָשֻׁבוּ בְּנֵי יִשְׂרָאֵל וּבִקְשׁוּ אֶת־יְהוָה אֱלֹהֵיהֶם וְאֵת דָּוִד מַלְכָּם וּפָחֲדוּ אֶל־יְהוָה וְאֶל־טוּבוֹ בְּאַחֲרִית הַיָּמִים

5[11] afterward the children of Israel shall return, and seek the LORD their God, and David their king; and shall come trembling to the LORD and to His goodness in the end of days.

Hosea – Chapter 4

שִׁמְעוּ דְבַר־יְהוָה בְּנֵי יִשְׂרָאֵל כִּי רִיב לַיהוָה עִם־יוֹשְׁבֵי הָאָרֶץ כִּי אֵין־אֱמֶת וְאֵין־חֶסֶד וְאֵין־דַּעַת אֱלֹהִים בָּאָרֶץ

1[12] Hear the word of the LORD, you children of Israel. For the LORD has a controversy with the inhabitants of the land, because there is

[1] Hosea 2:25 - 1 Peter 1:1-2 2:9-10, 1 Thessalonians 1:9-10, Acts 8:1-4, b.Pesachim 87b, Deuteronomy 26:17-19, Hosea 1:6 1:9-10 8:2, Isaiah 20:5, James 1:1, Jeremiah 16:19 7:28 8:38, Malachi 1:11, Midrash Tanchuma Massei 7, Numbers.R 2:16 9:48, Pesikta Rabbati 44:2, Psalms 22:28 68:32 72:16 22:28, Revelation 21:3-4, Romans 3:29 9:25-26 11:30-32 15:9-11, Saadia Opinions 7:8, Sifre Devarim Ha'azinu Hashamayim 306, Song of Songs 2:16, Song of Songs.R 7:8, Zechariah 2:11 8:22-23 10:9 13:9 14:9 14:16
[2] LXX *was not loved*
[3] Hosea 3 - Tanna Devei Eliyahu 9
[4] Hosea 3:1 - 1 Corinthians 10:7 10:21, 1 Peter 4:3, 2 Kings 13:23, 2 Samuel 6:19, Amos 2:8 6:6, b.Pesachim 36b, Deuteronomy 7:6-7:7, Exodus 8:6, Hosea 1:2-1:3 4:11 7:5 9:1-9:2 11:8, Isaiah 17:7-17:8 21:22, Jeremiah 3:1-3:4 3:12-3:14 3:20 7:21, Judges 9:27 10:16, Luke 1:54-1:55, Matthew 2:50, Mekilta de R'Ishmael Bahodesh 8:82, Micah 7:7 7:18-7:20, Nehemiah 9:18-9:19 9:31, Numbers.R 4:20, Psalms 106:43-106:46 3:2, Zechariah 1:16
Hosea 3:1-5 - 4QxIIg
[5] LXX *who loves evil things*
[6] Hosea 3:2 - 1 Samuel 18:25, b.Chullin 92a, b.Sanhedrin 96b, b.Sotah [Rashi] 13a, Ein Yaakov Sanhedrin:96b, Exodus 22:17, Ezekiel 21:11, Genesis 7:41 10:12, Isaiah 5:10, Leviticus 3:16, Numbers.R 13:20, Pesikta de R'Kahana 5.10 12.4, Pesikta Rabbati 15:2
Hosea 3:2-4 - 4QXIIc
[7] Hosea 3:3 - Deuteronomy 21:13, Pesikta de R'Kahana 12.4
[8] LXX *and I will be for you*
[9] Hosea 3:4 - 1 Samuel 2:18 14:3 21:9 22:18 23:6 23:9 6:7, 2 Chronicles 15:2, 2 Kings 23:24, 2 Samuel 6:14, Acts 6:13-6:14, b.Arachin 16a, b.Zevachim 88b, Cairo Damascus 20:15-17, Daniel 8:11-8:13 9:27 11:31 12:11, Ein Yaakov Zevachim:88b, Exodus 4:4, Ezekiel 20:32 21:26, Genesis 7:19 1:10, Hebrews 10:26, Hosea 2:11 10:1-10:3 13:11, Isaiah 19:19-19:20, Jeremiah 15:4-15:5, John 19:15, Judges 8:27 17:5 18:17-18:24, Leviticus 8:7, Leviticus.R 10:6, Luke 21:24, Matthew 24:1-24:2, Micah 5:12-5:15, Song of Songs.R 4:8, y.Yoma 7:3, z.Noach 72b, Zechariah 13:2
[10] LXX *altar, and without a priesthood, and without manifestations*
[11] Hosea 3:5 - 1 Kings 12:16, Acts 15:16-15:18, Amos 9:11, b.Megillah 18a, Daniel 2:28 10:14, Deuteronomy 4:30, Ein Yaakov Megillah:18a, Ezekiel 16:63 34:23-34:24 37:22-37:25 14:8 14:16, Genesis.R 48:6, Hosea 5:6 5:15, Isaiah 2:2 27:12-27:13 55:3-55:4, Jastrow 1151a, Jeremiah 3:22-3:23 23:5 6:9 6:24 31:7-31:11 9:9 9:17 50:4-50:5, Kiddush Levonoh, Micah 4:1, Midrash Psalms 24:2, Midrash Tanchuma Lech Lecha 15, Numbers 24:14, Psalms 130:3-130:4, Romans 2:4 11:25, y.Berachot 2:4, z.Pekudei 232b
[12] Hosea 4:1 - 1 Corinthians 15:34, 1 Kings 22:19, 4QXIIg, Amos 7:16, Hosea 5:1 12:4, Isaiah 1:10 1:18 3:13-3:14 5:3 4:14 10:1 10:8 59:13-59:15 18:5, Jeremiah 2:4 4:22 4:28 5:4 6:13 7:2-7:6 7:28 9:21 19:3 1:31 10:4, John 8:55, Micah 6:2 7:2-7:5, Numbers.R 10:1,

neither truth, nor mercy, nor knowledge of God in the land.

2[1] אָלֹה וְכַחֵשׁ וְרָצֹחַ וְגָנֹב וְנָאֹף פָּרָצוּ וְדָמִים בְּדָמִים נָגָעוּ

Swearing and lying, and killing, and stealing, and committing adultery! They break all bounds, and blood touches blood.

3[2] עַל־כֵּן תֶּאֱבַל הָאָרֶץ וְאֻמְלַל כָּל־יוֹשֵׁב בָּהּ בְּחַיַּת הַשָּׂדֶה וּבְעוֹף הַשָּׁמָיִם וְגַם־דְּגֵי הַיָּם יֵאָסֵפוּ

Therefore, the land mourns, And everyone who dwells in it languishes, with the beasts of the field, and the fowls of heaven; yes, the fish of the sea also are taken away.

4[3] אַךְ אִישׁ אַל־יָרֵב וְאַל־יוֹכַח אִישׁ וְעַמְּךָ כִּמְרִיבֵי כֹהֵן

Yet let no man strive, nor let any man reprove; For your people are as those who strive with the priest.

5[4] וְכָשַׁלְתָּ הַיּוֹם וְכָשַׁל גַּם־נָבִיא עִמְּךָ לָיְלָה וְדָמִיתִי אִמֶּךָ

Therefore, you shall stumble in the day, and the prophet *also shall stumble with you in the night; And I will destroy your mother[5]*.

6[6] נִדְמוּ עַמִּי מִבְּלִי הַדָּעַת כִּי־אַתָּה הַדַּעַת מָאַסְתָּ וְאֶמְאָסְאךָ מִכַּהֵן לִי וַתִּשְׁכַּח תּוֹרַת אֱלֹהֶיךָ אֶשְׁכַּח בָּנֶיךָ גַּם־אָנִי

My people are destroyed for lack of knowledge[7]; because you have rejected knowledge, I will also reject you, so you shall be no priest to Me; seeing you have forgotten the law of your God, I also will forget your children.

7[8] כְּרֻבָּם כֵּן חָטְאוּ־לִי כְּבוֹדָם בְּקָלוֹן אָמִיר

The more they increased, the more they sinned against Me; I will change their glory to shame.

8[9] חַטַּאת עַמִּי יֹאכֵלוּ וְאֶל־עֲוֹנָם יִשְׂאוּ נַפְשׁוֹ

They feed on the sin of My people, And set their heart on their iniquity.

9[10] וְהָיָה כָעָם כַּכֹּהֵן וּפָקַדְתִּי עָלָיו דְּרָכָיו וּמַעֲלָלָיו אָשִׁיב לוֹ

And it is like people, like priest; And I will punish him for his ways, And will recompense him for his doings.

Revelation 2:11 2:29, Romans 1:28, Sifre Devarim Ekev 41, Sifre Devarim Ekev 41

Hosea 4:1-19 - 4QXIIc

[1] Hosea 4:2 - 1 Thessalonians 2:15, Acts 7:52, b.Gittin 57b, b.Kiddushin 13a, b.Sheviit 39a, Ein Yaakov Gittin:57b, Ein Yaakov Kiddushin:13a, Ein Yaakov Shevuot:39a, Ezekiel 22:2-22:13 22:25-22:30, Hosea 5:2 6:9 7:1 7:3 10:4 12:16, Isaiah 24:5 24:1 59:2-59:8 59:12-59:15, Jeremiah 5:1-5:2 5:7-5:9 5:26-5:27 6:7 7:6-7:10 9:3-9:9 23:10-23:14, Lamentations 4:13, Lamentations.R Petichata D'Chakimei:23, Matthew 23:35, Mekilta de R'Ishmael Bahodesh 8:86, Micah 2:1-2:3 3:2 3:9 6:10 7:2, Midrash Tanchuma Naso 4, mt.Hilchot Shevuot 11:16, Numbers.R 9:1, Pesikta de R'Kahana 15.7, Revelation 17:6, Saadia Opinions 5:5, Zechariah 5:3 7:9, Zephaniah 3:1

Hosea 4:2-3 - Midrash Tanchuma Vayeshev 2, t.Sotah 7:2

Hosea 4:2-5 - Gates of Repentance 2.002

[2] Hosea 4:3 - Amos 1:2 5:16 8:8, b.Kiddushin 13a, b.Sheviit 39a, Ein Yaakov Kiddushin:13a, Ein Yaakov Shevuot:39a, Ezekiel 14:20, Isaiah 24:4-12 9:9, Jeremiah 4:25 4:27-28 12:4, Joel 1:10-13, Jubilees 23:18, mt.Hilchot Shevuot 11:16, Nahum 1:4, Zephaniah 1:3

[3] Hosea 4:4 - Amos 5:13 6:10, b.Kiddushin 13a, b.Shabbat [Tosefot] 116b, b.Shabbat 149b, Deuteronomy 17:12, Ein Yaakov Kiddushin:70b, Ezekiel 3:26, Gates of Repentance 3.228, Hosea 4:17, Jastrow 534b 1061a, Jeremiah 18:18, Matthew 7:3-7:6, mt.Hilchot Shekalim 1:10, y.Kiddushin 4:1, y.Yevamot 8:3

[4] Hosea 4:5 - 2 Baruch 3:2, b.Menachot 99b, b.Moed Katan 14a, Ezekiel 13:9-13:16 14:7-14:10 16:44-16:45, Galatians 4:26, Hosea 2:2 9:7-9:8, Isaiah 9:14-9:18 2:1, Jeremiah 6:4-6:5 6:12-6:15 8:10-8:12 14:15-14:16 15:8 23:9 2:12, Micah 3:5-3:7, mt.Hilchot Talmud Torah 7:1, western wrote ממנו and Eastern wrote ממני [j.Megillah 1:9], Zechariah 11:8 13:2

[5] LXX *with you shall fall: I have compared your mother unto night*

[6] Hosea 4:6 - 1 Samuel 2:12 2:28-2:36 3:12-3:15, 2 Chronicles 15:3, 2 Corinthians 4:3-4:6, 2 Kings 17:16-17:20, b.Sotah 49a, b.Yoma 38b, Ein Yaakov Sotah:49a, Ein Yaakov Yoma:38b, Exodus.R 38:1, Hosea 2:13 4:1 4:12 6:6 8:1 8:12 8:14 13:6, Isaiah 1:3 3:12 5:13 17:10 3:11 4:7 21:20 56:10-56:12, Jeremiah 2:8 4:22 5:3-5:4 5:21 8:7-8:9, Job 12:12, Luke 20:16-20:18, Malachi 2:1-2:3 2:7-2:9, Mark 12:8-12:9, Mas.Kallah 1:21, Mas.Kallah Rabbati 2:10, Matthew 1:6 15:3-15:6 15:8 15:14 21:41-21:45 23:16-23:26, Mekhilta de R'Shimon bar Yochai Bachodesh 50:2, Midrash Proverbs 6, Midrash Psalms 8:4, Midrash Tanchuma Vayigash 2, Proverbs 1:30-1:32 19:2, Psalms 119:139 119:61, Ralbag Wars 4:3 4:6, Sifre Devarim Ekev 41, Zechariah 11:8-11:9 11:15-11:17

[7] LXX *My people are like as if they had no knowledge*

[8] Hosea 4:7 - 1 Samuel 2:30, As #11 of the Eighteen Emendations of the Sopherim the text read "*My glory they have turned into shame.*" The word כבודי [*kevodi* my glory] was changed to כבודם [*kevodam* their glory], Deuteronomy.R 2:19, Ezra 9:7, Habakkuk 2:16, Hosea 4:10 5:1 6:9 10:1 13:6 13:14, Jeremiah 2:26-27, Malachi 2:9, Midrash Tanchuma Beshallach 16, Philippians 3:19

[9] Hosea 4:8 - 1 Samuel 2:29, 2 Peter 2:3, Ezekiel 14:3 14:7, Isaiah 8:11, Leviticus 26:26 7:6-7, Malachi 1:10, Micah 3:11, Psalms 24:4 25:1, Romans 16:18, Saadia Opinions 5:1, Titus 1:11

[10] Hosea 4:9 - Ezekiel 22:26-31, Hosea 1:4 8:13 9:9, Isaiah 3:10 9:15-9:17 24:2, Jeremiah 5:31 8:10-8:12 23:11-23:12, Matthew 15:14, Proverbs 5:22, Psalms 109:17-109:18, Zechariah 1:6

וְאָכְלוּ וְלֹא יִשְׂבָּעוּ הִזְנוּ וְלֹא יִפְרֹצוּ כִּי־אֶת־יְהוָה עָזְבוּ לִשְׁמֹר	10[1]	And they shall eat, and not have enough, They shall commit harlotry, and shall not increase; because they no longer heed the LORD.
זְנוּת וְיַיִן וְתִירוֹשׁ יִקַּח־לֵב	11[2]	*Harlotry, wine, and new wine take away the heart*[3].
עַמִּי בְּעֵצוֹ יִשְׁאָל וּמַקְלוֹ יַגִּיד לוֹ כִּי רוּחַ זְנוּנִים הִתְעָה וַיִּזְנוּ מִתַּחַת אֱלֹהֵיהֶם	12[4]	My people ask counsel at their stock, And their staff declares to them; For the spirit of harlotry has caused them to err, And they have gone astray from under their God.
עַל־רָאשֵׁי הֶהָרִים יְזַבֵּחוּ וְעַל־הַגְּבָעוֹת יְקַטֵּרוּ תַּחַת אַלּוֹן וְלִבְנֶה וְאֵלָה כִּי טוֹב צִלָּהּ עַל־כֵּן תִּזְנֶינָה בְּנוֹתֵיכֶם וְכַלּוֹתֵיכֶם תְּנָאַפְנָה	13[5]	They sacrifice on the tops of the mountains, and offer upon the hills, under oaks and poplars and terebinths, because its shadow is good; Therefore, your daughters commit harlotry, And your daughters-in-law commit adultery.
לֹא־אֶפְקוֹד עַל־בְּנוֹתֵיכֶם כִּי תִזְנֶינָה וְעַל־כַּלּוֹתֵיכֶם כִּי תְנָאַפְנָה כִּי־הֵם עִם־הַזֹּנוֹת יְפָרֵדוּ וְעִם־הַקְּדֵשׁוֹת יְזַבֵּחוּ וְעָם לֹא־יָבִין יִלָּבֵט	14[6]	I will not punish your daughters when they commit harlotry, nor your daughters-in-law when they commit adultery, for they consort with lewd women, And they sacrifice with harlots; And the people who are without understanding is distraught.
אִם־זֹנֶה אַתָּה יִשְׂרָאֵל אַל־יֶאְשַׁם יְהוּדָה וְאַל־תָּבֹאוּ הַגִּלְגָּל וְאַל־תַּעֲלוּ בֵּית אָוֶן וְאַל־תִּשָּׁבְעוּ חַי־יְהוָה	15[7]	You, Israel, *play the harlot, Yet do not let Judah become guilty; And do not come to Gilgal, nor go up to Beth-aven*[8], nor swear: 'As the LORD lives.'
כִּי כְּפָרָה סֹרֵרָה סָרַר יִשְׂרָאֵל עַתָּה יִרְעֵם יְהוָה כְּכֶבֶשׂ בַּמֶּרְחָב	16[9]	For Israel is *stubborn like a stubborn*[10] heifer; Now shall the LORD feed them as a lamb in a large place?
חֲבוּר עֲצַבִּים אֶפְרָיִם הַנַּח־לוֹ	17[11]	Ephraim is joined to idols; *Let him alone*[12].

---

[1] Hosea 4:10 - 2 Chronicles 24:17, 2 Peter 2:20-22, b.Yevamot 61b, Ezekiel 18:24, Haggai 1:6, Hosea 4:14 9:11-17, Isaiah 65:13-65:16, Jeremiah 10:15, Leviticus 2:26, Malachi 2:1-3, Micah 6:14, Proverbs 13:25, Psalms 36:4 5:5, y.Yevamot 6:5, z.Mishpatim 95a, Zephaniah 1:6
Hosea 4:10-11 - 4QXIIg
[2] Hosea 4:11 - b.Gittin 68a, b.Yoma 76b, Ecclesiastes 7:7, Ein Yaakov Gittin:68a, Hosea 4:12, Isaiah 5:12 4:7, Jastrow 1553b, Lamentations.R 1:47, Luke 21:34, Midrash Psalms 78:12, Numbers.R 20:23, Pirkei de R'Eliezer 47, Proverbs 6:32 20:1 23:27-23:35, Romans 13:11-13:14, Saadia Opinions 10:6, y.Ketubot 5:8
[3] LXX *The heart of my people is gladly engaged in fornication, wine, and strong drink*
[4] Hosea 4:12 - 2 Chronicles 21:13, 2 Thessalonians 2:9-2:11, b.Pesachim 52b, b.Succah 52b, Deuteronomy 7:16, Ein Yaakov Sukkah:52b, Ezekiel 16:1-16:63 21:26 23:1-23:49, Habakkuk 2:19, Hosea 5:4 9:1, Isaiah 44:18-44:20, Jastrow 727b 1396b, Jeremiah 2:27 3:1-3:3 10:8, Leviticus 17:7 20:5, Micah 2:11, mt.Hilchot Avodat Kochavim v'Chukkoteihem 11:6 11:6, Numbers 15:39, Psalms 73:27, Sifre Devarim Shoftim 171, t.Shabbat 7:4, western wrote וּמַקְלוֹ and Eastern wrote וּמִקְלוֹ [j.Megillah 1:9]
[5] Hosea 4:13 - 2 Samuel 12:10-12, Amos 7:17, Ezekiel 6:13 16:16 16:25 20:28-29, Hosea 2:13 11:2, Isaiah 1:29 9:5 9:7, Jeremiah 2:20 3:6 3:13, Job 31:9-10, Lamentations.R Petichata D'Chakimei:22, Pesikta de R'Kahana 5.7 13.4 24.16, Pesikta Rabbati 15:7 33:13, Romans 1:23-28, Sifre Devarim Ha'azinu Hashamayim 306, Sifre Devarim Nitzavim 306, Song of Songs.R 2:22
Hosea 4:13-14 - 4QXIIg
[6] Hosea 4:14 - 1 Corinthians 6:16, 1 Kings 14:23-14:24 15:12, 2 Kings 23:7, b.Sotah 47a, b.Sotah 47b, Daniel 12:10, Deuteronomy 23:19, Ephesians 4:18, Hebrews 12:8, Hosea 4:1 4:5-4:6 4:17 14:11, Isaiah 1:5 44:18-44:20 8:11, John 8:43, Lamentations.R 1:37, m.Sotah 9:9, mt.Hilchot Sotah 3:19, Numbers.R 9:44, Proverbs 4:5, Ralbag Wars 4:3 4:6, Romans 3:11, y.Sotah 9:9
[7] Hosea 4:15 - 1 Kings 12:28-29, 2 Kings 17:18-19, Amos 4:4 5:5 6:10 8:14, Ephesians 5:11, Ezekiel 20:39 23:4-8, Hosea 4:12 5:8 9:15 10:5 10:8 12:1 12:13, Isaiah 24:1, Jeremiah 3:6-11 5:2, Luke 12:47-48, Mas.Sefer Torah 5:12, Mas.Soferim 5:10, Zephaniah 1:5-6
[8] LXX *do not be ignorant, and do not go, men of Juda, to Galgala; and do not go up to the house of On*
[9] Hosea 4:16 - 1 Samuel 15:11, 4Q266 frag 2 1.17, Avot de R'Natan 23, Cairo Damascus 1:13-14, Hosea 11:7, Isaiah 5:17 7:21-7:25 22:18, Jeremiah 3:6 3:8 3:11 5:6 7:24 8:5 14:7, Lamentations.R 1:3 2:8, Leviticus 2:33, Pesikta de R'Kahana 4.1, Pesikta Rabbati 14:15 44:2, Tanna Devei Eliyahu 2, z.Balak 197b, z.Pekudei 237a, Zechariah 7:11
[10] LXX *maddened like a mad*
[11] Hosea 4:17 - Genesis.R 38:6, Hosea 4:4 11:2 12:3 13:2, Mas.Derek Eretz Zutta 9:12, Mas.Kallah Rabbati 8:9, Matthew 15:14, Midrash Tanchuma Shoftim 18, Midrash Tanchuma Tzav 7, mt.Hilchot Teshuvah 6:3, mt.Shemonah Perakim 8:6, Numbers.R 11:7, Pesikta Rabbati 50:5, Psalms 81:13, Revelation 22:11, Shemonah Perakim VIII, z.Mikketz 200b
[12] LXX *has laid stumbling blocks in his own way*

סַר סָבְאָם הַזְנֵה הִזְנוּ אָהֲבוּ הֵבוּ קָלוֹן מָגִנֶּיהָ

18[1]   *When their carouse is over, They take to harlotry; Her rulers deeply love dishonor[2].*

צָרַר רוּחַ אוֹתָהּ בִּכְנָפֶיהָ וְיֵבֹשׁוּ מִזִּבְחוֹתָם

19[3]   *The wind has bound her up in her skirts[4]; And they shall be ashamed because of their sacrifices.*

Hosea – Chapter 5

שִׁמְעוּ־זֹאת הַכֹּהֲנִים וְהַקְשִׁיבוּ בֵּית יִשְׂרָאֵל וּבֵית הַמֶּלֶךְ הַאֲזִינוּ כִּי לָכֶם הַמִּשְׁפָּט כִּי־פַח הֱיִיתֶם לְמִצְפָּה וְרֶשֶׁת פְּרוּשָׂה עַל־תָּבוֹר

1[5]   Hear this, you priests, And attend, you house of Israel, and give ear, O house of the king, for to you befalls the judgment; for you have been a snare on *Mizpah*, and a net spread on *Tabor*[6].

וְשַׁחֲטָה שֵׂטִים הֶעְמִיקוּ וַאֲנִי מוּסָר לְכֻלָּם

2[7]   *And tbhose who fall away are gone deep in making slaughter; and I am rejected by them all[8].*

אֲנִי יָדַעְתִּי אֶפְרַיִם וְיִשְׂרָאֵל לֹא־נִכְחַד מִמֶּנִּי כִּי עַתָּה הִזְנֵיתָ אֶפְרַיִם נִטְמָא יִשְׂרָאֵל

3[9]   I, even I, know Ephraim, and Israel is not hid from Me; for now, O Ephraim, you have committed harlotry, Israel is defiled.

לֹא יִתְּנוּ מַעַלְלֵיהֶם לָשׁוּב אֶל־אֱלֹהֵיהֶם כִּי רוּחַ זְנוּנִים בְּקִרְבָּם וְאֶת־יְהוָה לֹא יָדָעוּ

4[10]   Their deeds will not cause them to return to their God; for the spirit of harlotry is within them, and they do not know the LORD.

וְעָנָה גְאוֹן־יִשְׂרָאֵל בְּפָנָיו וְיִשְׂרָאֵל וְאֶפְרַיִם יִכָּשְׁלוּ בַּעֲוֹנָם כָּשַׁל גַּם־יְהוּדָה עִמָּם

5[11]   But the pride of Israel shall testify to his face; and Israel and Ephraim shall stumble in their iniquity, Judah also shall stumble with them.

בְּצֹאנָם וּבִבְקָרָם יֵלְכוּ לְבַקֵּשׁ אֶת־יְהוָה וְלֹא יִמְצָאוּ חָלַץ מֵהֶם

6[12]   With their flocks and with their herds they shall go to seek the LORD, but they shall not find Him; He has withdrawn Himself from them.

בַּיהוָה בָּגָדוּ כִּי־בָנִים זָרִים יָלָדוּ עַתָּה יֹאכְלֵם חֹדֶשׁ אֶת־חֶלְקֵיהֶם

7[13]   They dealt treacherously against the LORD, for they have sired strange children; Now the *new moon*[14] shall devour them with their portions.

---

[1] Hosea 4:18 - 1 Samuel 8:3 12:3-4, 2 Kings 17:7-17, Amos 5:12, Deuteronomy 16:19 32:32-33, Exodus 23:8, Hosea 4:2 4:10, Isaiah 1:21-22, Jeremiah 2:21, Micah 3:11 7:3, Proverbs 30:15-16, Psalms 47:10

[2] LXX *He has chosen the Chananites: they have grievously gone whoring: they have loved dishonor through her insolence*

[3] Hosea 4:19 - Hosea 10:6 12:3 13:15, Isaiah 1:29 18:17, Jeremiah 2:26-27 2:36-37 3:24-25 4:11-12 17:13 3:1, Zechariah 5:9-11

[4] LXX *You are a blast of wind in her wings*

[5] Hosea 5:1 - 1 Kings 14:7-16 21:18-22, 2 Chronicles 21:12-21:15, 4QXIIc, Amos 7:9, Exodus.R 15:23, Genesis.R 80:1, Habakkuk 1:15-1:17, Hosea 4:1 4:6-4:7 6:9 7:3-5 9:8 9:11-9:17 10:15 13:8, Jeremiah 13:18 22:1-22:9 22:18, Judges 4:6, Malachi 1:6 2:1, Micah 3:1 3:9 7:2, Saadia Opinions 10:12, y.Sanhedrin 2:6

[6] LXX *Scopia, and as a net spread on Itabyrium*

[7] Hosea 5:2 - Acts 23:12-15, Amos 4:6-12, b.Sanhedrin 102a, Ein Yaakov Sanhedrin:102a, Hosea 4:2 6:5 6:9 9:15, Isaiah 1:5 5:15, Jeremiah 5:3 6:28 11:18-19 18:18 25:3-7, Luke 22:2-5, Psalms 64:4-7 140:2-6, Revelation 3:19, y.Avodah Zarah 1:1, Zephaniah 3:1-2

[8] LXX *which they who hunt the prey have fixed: but I will correct you*

[9] Hosea 5:3 - 1 Kings 12:26-33 14:14-16, Amos 3:2 5:12, Deuteronomy 9:17, Ezekiel 23:5-21, Genesis 48:19-20, Hebrews 4:13, Hosea 4:17-18 5:9 5:11 5:13 6:4 8:11 12:3 13:1, Isaiah 7:5 7:8-9 7:17, Midrash Psalms 14:7, Revelation 3:15, Seder Olam 22 Jorobeam

[10] Hosea 5:4 - 1 John 2:3-4, 1 Samuel 2:12, 2 Thessalonians 2:11-12, b.Succah 52b, Ein Yaakov Sukkah:52b, Hosea 4:1 4:6 4:12, Jeremiah 9:7 9:25 22:15-16 24:7 2:38, John 3:19-3:20 8:55 16:3, Psalms 9:11 36:2-5 78:8

[11] Hosea 5:5 - 2 Kings 17:19-17:20, Amos 2:4-2:5 5:2, Ezekiel 23:31-23:35, Hosea 4:5 5:14 7:10 8:14 14:3, Isaiah 3:9 9:10-9:11 28:1-28:3 20:9 11:12, Jeremiah 14:7, Luke 19:22, Matthew 23:31, Mekhilta de R'Shimon bar Yochai Amalek 44:1, Mekilta de R'Ishmael Amalek 1:43, Proverbs 11:5 11:21 14:32 24:16 6:13, y.Kiddushin 1:7

[12] Hosea 5:6 - Amos 5:21-23, b.Berachot [Rashi] 34b, b.Yevamot 102b, Exodus 10:9 10:24-26, Ezekiel 8:6 8:18, Isaiah 1:11-1:15 18:3, Jastrow 472b 473a, Jeremiah 7:4 11:11, John 7:34, Lamentations 3:44, Luke 5:16, Micah 3:4 6:6-7, Midrash Psalms 10:8, Midrash Tanchuma Haazinu 4, Pesikta de R'Kahana S7.1, Proverbs 1:28 15:8 21:27, Song of Songs 5:6

[13] Hosea 5:7 - b.Kiddushin 70a, b.Yevamot 14a, Ein Yaakov Kiddushin:70a, Exodus.R 1:8, Ezekiel 12:28, Gates of Repentance 3.132, Hosea 2:4 2:11 6:7, Isaiah 24:8 11:13, Jeremiah 3:20 5:11, Leviticus.R 19:2, Malachi 2:11-2:15, Mas.Derek Eretz Zutta 10:4, Mas.Kallah Rabbati 2:2, Midrash Tanchuma Shemot 5, Nehemiah 13:23-13:24, Psalms 24:7 24:11, Ruth.R Petichata:3, Song of Songs.R 5:11, y.Sanhedrin 10:5, z.Lech Lecha 93a, z.Mikketz 204a, z.Yitro 90a, Zechariah 11:8

[14] LXX *cankerworm*

תִּקְע֨וּ שׁוֹפָ֜ר בַּגִּבְעָ֗ה חֲצֹצְרָה֙ בָּרָמָ֔ה הָרִ֖יעוּ בֵּ֣ית אָ֑וֶן אַחֲרֶ֖יךָ בִּנְיָמִֽין	8[1]	*Blow the horn in Gibeah, and the trumpet in Ramah; Sound an alarm at Bethaven: 'Behind you, O Benjamin!'[2]*
אֶפְרַ֨יִם֙ לְשַׁמָּ֣ה תִֽהְיֶ֔ה בְּי֖וֹם תּֽוֹכֵחָ֑ה בְּשִׁבְטֵי֙ יִשְׂרָאֵ֔ל הוֹדַ֖עְתִּי נֶאֱמָנָֽה	9[3]	Ephraim shall be desolate in the day of rebuke; Among the tribes of Israel I make known what shall surely be.
הָיוּ֙ שָׂרֵ֣י יְהוּדָ֔ה כְּמַסִּיגֵ֖י גְּב֑וּל עֲלֵיהֶ֕ם אֶשְׁפּ֥וֹךְ כַּמַּ֖יִם עֶבְרָתִֽי	10[4]	The princes of Judah are like those who remove the landmark; I will pour out My wrath upon them like water.
עָשׁ֤וּק אֶפְרַ֙יִם֙ רְצ֣וּץ מִשְׁפָּ֔ט כִּ֣י הוֹאִ֔יל הָלַ֖ךְ אַחֲרֵי־צָֽו	11[5]	*Oppressed is Ephraim, crushed in his right; Because he willingly walked after filth[6].*
וַאֲנִ֥י כָעָ֖שׁ לְאֶפְרָ֑יִם וְכָרָקָ֖ב לְבֵ֥ית יְהוּדָֽה	12[7]	Therefore am I to Ephraim as a *moth[8]*, And to the house of Judah as *rottenness[9]*.
וַיַּ֨רְא אֶפְרַ֜יִם אֶת־חׇלְי֗וֹ וִֽיהוּדָה֙ אֶת־מְזֹר֔וֹ וַיֵּ֤לֶךְ אֶפְרַ֙יִם֙ אֶל־אַשּׁ֔וּר וַיִּשְׁלַ֖ח אֶל־מֶ֣לֶךְ יָרֵ֑ב וְה֗וּא לֹ֤א יוּכַל֙ לִרְפֹּ֣א לָכֶ֔ם וְלֹֽא־יִגְהֶ֥ה מִכֶּ֖ם מָזֽוֹר	13[10]	And when Ephraim saw his sickness, And Judah his wound, Ephraim went to Assyria, And sent to King *Contentious[11]*; But he is not able to heal you, nor shall he cure you of your wound.
כִּ֣י אָנֹכִ֤י כַשַּׁ֙חַל֙ לְאֶפְרַ֔יִם וְכַכְּפִ֖יר לְבֵ֣ית יְהוּדָ֑ה אֲנִ֨י אֲנִ֤י אֶטְרֹף֙ וְאֵלֵ֔ךְ אֶשָּׂ֖א וְאֵ֥ין מַצִּֽיל	14[12]	For I will be to Ephraim as a *lion[13]*, and as a young lion to the house of Judah; I, even I, will tear and go away, I will take away, and there shall be no one to deliver.
אֵלֵ֤ךְ אָשׁ֙וּבָה֙ אֶל־מְקוֹמִ֔י עַ֥ד אֲשֶֽׁר־יֶאְשְׁמ֖וּ וּבִקְשׁ֣וּ פָנָ֑י בַּצַּ֥ר לָהֶ֖ם יְשַׁחֲרֻֽנְנִי	15[14]	I will go and return to My place, until they acknowledge their guilt, and seek My face; In their trouble they will seek Me earnestly:

Hosea – Chapter 6

לְכוּ֙ וְנָשׁ֣וּבָה אֶל־יְהֹוָ֔ה כִּ֛י ה֥וּא טָרָ֖ף וְיִרְפָּאֵ֑נוּ יַ֖ךְ וְיַחְבְּשֵֽׁנוּ	1[15]	'Come, and let us return to the LORD; For He has torn, and He will heal us, He has smitten, and He will bind us up.

---

[1] Hosea 5:8 - 1 Kings 12:29, 1 Samuel 7:17 8:4 15:34, 2 Samuel 21:6, 4Q177 3.13, b.Berachot 56b, b.Rosh Hashanah 32b, b.Taanit 5a, Hosea 4:15 8:1 9:9 10:5 10:8-9, Isaiah 10:29, Jeremiah 4:5 6:1, Joel 2:1 2:15, Joshua 7:2, Judges 5:14 19:12-15 20:4-6, m.Rosh Hashanah 4:6, mt.Hilcnot Shofar Sukkah v'Lulav 3:9

[2] LXX *Blow the trumpet on the hills, sound aloud on the heights: proclaim in the house of On, Benjamin is amazed*

[3] Hosea 5:9 - Amos 3:7 3:14-3:15 7:9 7:17, Hosea 5:12 5:14 8:8 9:11-9:17 11:5-11:6 13:1-13:3 13:15-13:16, Isaiah 28:1-28:4 13:3 22:10 24:3 24:5, Job 12:14, John 16:4, Lamentations.R Petichata D'Chakimei:6, Midrash Psalms 76:1, Numbers.R 13:4, Zechariah 1:6

[4] Hosea 5:10 - 2 Chronicles 28:16-22, 2 Kings 16:7-9, 4Q266 frag 3 3.25-4.1, Apocalypse of Elijah 1:4, Cairo Damascus 19:15-16 8:2-3, Cairo Damascus 19.15-16, Cairo Damascus 8.3, Deuteronomy 19:14 3:17, Ezekiel 7:8, Lamentations.R 1:3 2:8, Luke 6:49, Matthew 7:27, Pesikta Rabbati 44:4, Proverbs 17:14 22:28, Psalms 32:6 88:18 93:3-4

[5] Hosea 5:11 - 1 Kings 12:26-33, 2 Kings 15:16-20 15:29, Amos 5:11-12, Genesis.R 16:6 100 [Excl]:2, b.Sanhedrin 56b, Deuteronomy 4:33, Deuteronomy.R 2:25, Guide for the Perplexed 1:38, Micah 6:16, mt.Hilchot Melachim u'Michamoteihem 9:1, Pesikta de R'Kahana 12.1, Song of Songs.R 1:16

[6] LXX *Ephraim altogether prevailed against his adversary, he trod judgment under foot, for he began to go after vanities*

[7] Hosea 5:12 - Isaiah 2:9 3:8, Job 13:28, Jonah 4:7, Mark 9:43-48, Midrash Tanchuma Vayera 5, Proverbs 12:4

[8] LXX *consternation*

[9] LXX *goad*

[10] Hosea 5:13 - 2 Chronicles 28:16-28:18 28:20-28:21, 2 Kings 15:19 15:29 16:7, 4Q167 frag 2 1.1, b.Sanhedrin 92a, Ein Yaakov Sanhedrin:92a, Hosea 7:11 8:9 10:6 12:3 14:5, Jeremiah 6:12 30:14-30:15, Micah 1:9, Saadia Opinions 4:6

[11] LXX *Jarim*

[12] Hosea 5:14 - 4Q167 frag 2 ll.2-3, Amos 2:14 3:4-3:8, Deuteronomy 4:31, Hosea 13:7-13:8, Isaiah 5:29, Job 10:7 10:16, Lamentations 3:10, Micah 5:9, Psalms 7:3 50:22

[13] LXX *panther*

[14] Hosea 5:15 - 1 Kings 8:10-8:13 8:47-8:48, 2 Chronicles 6:36-6:37 7:14 33:12-33:13, 4Q167 frag 2 ll.5-6, Avot de R'Natan 34, b.Rosh Hashanah 31a, Daniel 9:4-9:12, Deuteronomy 4:29-4:31 30:1-30:3, Ein Yaakov Rosh Hashanah:31a, Exodus 25:21-25:22, Ezekiel 6:9 8:6 10:4 11:23 20:43 12:31, Guide for the Perplexed 1:23 1:24, Hosea 3:5 5:6 14:3-14:5, Isaiah 2:9 2:16 2:21 64:6-64:10, Jeremiah 2:27 3:13 29:12-29:14 31:19-31:21, Job 27:8-27:10 9:27, Judges 4:3 6:6-6:7 10:10-10:16, Lamentations.R Petichata D'Chakimei:24-25, Leviticus 26:40-26:42, Luke 13:25, Micah 1:3, Midrash Psalms 10:2, Midrash Tanchuma Bechukkotai 3, Nehemiah 1:8-1:9, Pesikta de R'Kahana 13.11, Proverbs 1:27-1:28 8:17, Psalms 50:15 78:34 83:17 12:14, Song of Songs.R 4:12, y.Berachot 4:5, Zephaniah 2:1-2:3

[15] Hosea 6:1 - 1 Samuel 2:6, Chibbur Yafeh 20 87b, Deuteronomy 8:39, Hosea 5:12-5:15 13:7-13:9 14:3 14:6, Isaiah 2:3 6:22 6:26 7:7, Jeremiah 3:22 6:12 6:17 9:5 2:4, Job 5:18 10:29, Lamentations 3:32-3:33 3:40-3:41, Pesikta Rabbati 33:7 44:8, Psalms 30:8, Tanna Devei Eliyahu 5, Zephaniah 2:1

יְחַיֵּנוּ מִיֹּמָיִם בַּיּוֹם הַשְּׁלִישִׁי יְקִמֵנוּ וְנִחְיֶה לְפָנָיו	2[1]	After two days He will revive us, On the third day He will raise us up, so we may live in His presence.
וְנֵדְעָה נִרְדְּפָה לָדַעַת אֶת־יְהוָה כְּשַׁחַר נָכוֹן מוֹצָאוֹ וְיָבוֹא כַגֶּשֶׁם לָנוּ כְּמַלְקוֹשׁ יוֹרֶה אָרֶץ	3[2]	And let us know, eagerly strive to know the LORD, His going forth is sure as the morning; And He shall come to us as the rain, As the latter rain that waters the earth.'
מָה אֶעֱשֶׂה־לְּךָ אֶפְרַיִם מָה אֶעֱשֶׂה־לְּךָ יְהוּדָה וְחַסְדְּכֶם כַּעֲנַן־בֹּקֶר וְכַטַּל מַשְׁכִּים הֹלֵךְ	4[3]	O Ephraim, what shall I do to you? O Judah, what shall I do to you? For your goodness is like a morning cloud, and as the dew that early passes away.
עַל־כֵּן חָצַבְתִּי בַּנְּבִיאִים הֲרַגְתִּים בְּאִמְרֵי־פִי וּמִשְׁפָּטֶיךָ אוֹר יֵצֵא	5[4]	Therefore, I hewed them by the prophets, I have killed them by the words of My mouth; And your judgment goes forth as the light.
כִּי חֶסֶד חָפַצְתִּי וְלֹא־זָבַח וְדַעַת אֱלֹהִים מֵעֹלוֹת	6[5]	For I desire mercy, *and not*[6] sacrifice, And the knowledge of God rather than burnt offerings.
וְהֵמָּה כְּאָדָם עָבְרוּ בְרִית שָׁם בָּגְדוּ בִי	7[7]	But they like men have transgressed the covenant; *There have they dealt treacherously against Me*[8].
גִּלְעָד קִרְיַת פֹּעֲלֵי אָוֶן עֲקֻבָּה מִדָּם	8[9]	*Gilead is a city of those who work iniquity, It is covered with footprints of blood*[10].
וּכְחַכֵּי אִישׁ גְּדוּדִים חֶבֶר כֹּהֲנִים דֶּרֶךְ יְרַצְּחוּ־שֶׁכְמָה כִּי זִמָּה עָשׂוּ	9[11]	*And as troops of robbers wait for a man, so the company of priests; they murder in the way toward Shechem; Yes, they commit enormity*[12].
בְּבֵית יִשְׂרָאֵל רָאִיתִי "שַׁעֲרִירִיָּה" "שַׁעֲרוּרִיֶּה" שָׁם זְנוּת לְאֶפְרַיִם נִטְמָא יִשְׂרָאֵל	10[13]	*In the house of Israel I have seen a horrible thing; There harlotry is found in Ephraim, Israel is defiled*[14].

---

[1] Hosea 6:2 - 1 Corinthians 15:4, 2 Kings 20:5, 3 Enoch 28:10, b.Rosh Hashanah 31a, b.Sanhedrin 97a, Chibbur Yafeh 20 87b, Deuteronomy.R 7:6, Ein Yaakov Rosh Hashanah:31a, Ein Yaakov Sanhedrin:97a, Esther.R 9:2, Ezekiel 37:11-13, Genesis 17:18, Genesis.R 56:1 91:7, Hosea 13:14, Isaiah 2:19, John 14:19, Midrash Psalms 22:5, Pirkei de R'Eliezer 51, Psalms 30:5-6 61:8, Romans 14:8, Selichot, Sifre Devarim Ha'azinu Hashamayim 329, Sifre Devarim Nitzavim 329, y.Berachot 5:2, y.Sanhedrin 11:6, y.Taanit 1:1

[2] Hosea 6:3 - 2 Peter 1:19, 2 Samuel 23:4, Acts 17:11, b.Berachot 6b, b.Taanit 4a, Deuteronomy 8:2, Deuteronomy.R 7:6, Ein Yaakov Berachot:6b, Ein Yaakov Taanit:4a, Ezekiel 12:25, Hebrews 3:14, Hosea 2:20 10:12 14:7, Isaiah 5:6 8:15 20:3 6:13, Jeremiah 24:7, Job 5:23, Joel 2:23-2:24, John 7:17 17:3, Luke 1:78, Malachi 3:20, Matthew 13:11, Mesillat Yesharim 7:Elements of Zerizus, Micah 4:2 5:3 5:8, mt.Hilchot Tefilah 8:2, Pesikta de R'Kahana 17.8, Philippians 3:13-3:15, Proverbs 2:1-2:5 4:18, Psalms 19:5 65:10 72:6, Revelation 22:16, Siman 12:11, Song of Songs.R 8:6, y.Berachot 5:1 5:2, y.Taanit 1:1, z.Naso 148a, z.Vayikra 21b, Zechariah 10:1
Hosea 6:3-4 - 4QXIIg

[3] Hosea 6:4 - 2 Peter 2:20-22, 4Q167 frags 5-6 1.3, b.Berachot 59a, b.Taanit 6b, Gates of Repentance 2.026, Hosea 7:1 11:8 13:3, Isaiah 5:3-4, Jeremiah 3:10 3:19 5:7 5:9 5:23 9:8 10:15, Judges 2:18-19, Luke 13:7-9 19:41-42, Matthew 13:21, Psalms 78:34-37 106:12-13

[4] Hosea 6:5 - 1 Kings 14:6 17:1 18:17 19:17, 1 Samuel 13:13 15:22, 2 Chronicles 21:12, 2 Kings 1:16, Acts 7:31, b.Taanit 5b, Ein Yaakov Taanit:5b, Ezekiel 3:9 19:3, Genesis 18:25, Hebrews 4:12, Isaiah 11:4 10:1, Jeremiah 1:10 1:18 5:14 13:13 23:29, Job 10:10, Mas.Semachot 8:11, Psalms 37:6 119:120, Revelation 1:16 2:16 9:15 9:21, Romans 2:5, Zephaniah 3:5

[5] Hosea 6:6 - 1 Chronicles 4:9, 1 John 2:3 3:6, 1 Samuel 15:22, Amos 5:21, Avot de R'Natan 4, Daniel 4:24, Ecclesiastes 5:2, Hosea 2:20 4:1, Isaiah 1:11 10:6, Jeremiah 7:22 22:16, Matthew 5:7 9:13 12:7, Micah 6:6, Midrash Psalms 9:2 89:1, Pirkei de R'Eliezer 12, Pirkei de R'Eliezer 16, Proverbs 21:3, Psalms 50:8, Sibylline Oracles 2.82 8.334, Tanna Devei Eliyahu 6

[6] LXX *rather than*

[7] Hosea 6:7 - 2 Kings 17:15, 4Q167 frags 7-8 1.1, b.Sanhedrin 38b, Ezekiel 16:59-16:61, Genesis 3:6 3:11, Genesis.R 19:9, Hebrews 8:9, Hosea 5:7 8:1, Isaiah 24:5 24:16 24:8, Jeremiah 3:7 5:11 9:7 7:33, Job 7:33, Lamentations.R Petichata D'Chakimei:4, Leviticus.R 6:1 6:5, Pesikta de R'Kahana 15.1, z.Bereshit 56a

[8] Missing in LXX

[9] Hosea 6:8 - 1 Kings 2:5, 2 Samuel 3:27 20:8, Acts 23:12-23:15 1:3, b.Makkot 10a, Hosea 4:2 5:1 12:13, Isaiah 11:6, Jastrow 1104a, Jeremiah 11:19, Joshua 21:38, Matthew 26:15-26:16, Micah 7:2, Psalms 10:9 59:3, y.Avodah Zarah 5:10
Hosea 6:8-11 - 4QXIIg

[10] LXX *there the city Galaad despised me, working vanity, troubling water*

[11] Hosea 6:9 - 1 Kings 12:25, 4Q163 frag 23 2.14, Acts 4:24, b.Makkot 10a, Ezekiel 22:9 22:27, Ezra 8:31, Genesis.R 80:2, Hosea 5:1 7:1, Jeremiah 7:9-7:10 11:9, Job 1:15-1:17, John 11:47, Luke 22:2-22:6, Mark 14:1, Micah 3:9, Midrash Tanchuma Vayishlach 7, Proverbs 1:11-1:19, Zephaniah 3:3
Hosea 6:9-10 - 4Q166 frags 10+26 ll.1-2

[12] LXX *And your strength is that of a robber: the priests have hid the way, they have murdered the people of Sicima; for they have wrought iniquity in the house of Israel*

[13] Hosea 6:10 - 1 Kings 12:8 15:30, 2 Kings 17:7, Ein Yaakov Megillah:14b, Ezekiel 23:5, Hosea 4:11 4:17 5:3, Jeremiah 2:12-2:13 3:6 5:30-31 18:13 23:14

[14] LXX *I have seen horrible things there, even the fornication of Ephraim: Israel and Juda are defiled*

גַּם־יְהוּדָ֕ה שָׁ֥ת קָצִ֖יר לָ֑ךְ בְּשׁוּבִ֖י שְׁב֥וּת עַמִּֽי	11[1]	*Also, O Judah, there is a harvest appointed for you!*[2]

Hosea – Chapter 7

כְּרָפְאִ֣י לְיִשְׂרָאֵ֗ל וְנִגְלָ֞ה עֲוֺ֤ן אֶפְרַ֙יִם֙ וְרָע֣וֹת שֹׁמְר֔וֹן כִּ֥י פָעֲל֖וּ שָׁ֑קֶר וְגַנָּ֣ב יָב֔וֹא פָּשַׁ֥ט גְּד֖וּד בַּחֽוּץ	1[3]	*When I turn the captivity of My people, when I heal Israel, then the iniquity of Ephraim is uncovered, and the wickedness of Samaria, for they commit falsehood; and the thief enters, and the robbers' troop makes a raid*[4].
וּבַל־יֹֽאמְרוּ֙ לִלְבָבָ֔ם כָּל־רָעָתָ֖ם זָכָ֑רְתִּי עַתָּה֙ סְבָב֣וּם מַֽעַלְלֵיהֶ֔ם נֶ֥גֶד פָּנַ֖י הָיֽוּ	2[5]	And let them not say to their heart, I remember all their wickedness; now their own doings have tormented them, They are before My face.
בְּרָעָתָ֖ם יְשַׂמְּחוּ־מֶ֑לֶךְ וּבְכַחֲשֵׁיהֶ֖ם שָׂרִֽים	3[6]	They make the king glad with their wickedness, And the princes with their lies.
כֻּלָּם֙ מְנָ֣אֲפִ֔ים כְּמ֣וֹ תַנּ֔וּר בֹּעֵ֖רָה מֵֽאֹפֶ֑ה יִשְׁבּ֣וֹת מֵעִ֔יר מִלּ֥וּשׁ בָּצֵ֖ק עַד־חֻמְצָתֽוֹ	4[7]	They are all adulterers, as an oven heated by the baker, Who ceases to stir From the kneading of the dough until it be leavened.
י֣וֹם מַלְכֵּ֔נוּ הֶחֱל֣וּ שָׂרִ֔ים חֲמַ֖ת מִיָּ֑יִן מָשַׁ֥ךְ יָד֖וֹ אֶת־לֹצְצִֽים	5[8]	On the day of our king The princes make him sick with the heat of wine, He stretches out his hand with scorners.
כִּֽי־קֵרְב֧וּ כַתַּנּ֛וּר לִבָּ֖ם בְּאָרְבָּ֑ם כָּל־הַלַּ֙יְלָה֙ יָשֵׁ֣ן אֹֽפֵהֶ֔ם בֹּ֕קֶר ה֥וּא בֹעֵ֖ר כְּאֵ֥שׁ לֶהָבָֽה	6[9]	For they have made ready their heart like an oven, while they lie in wait; Their baker sleeps all the night, in the morning it burns as a raging fire.
כֻּלָּ֤ם יֵחַ֙מּוּ֙ כַּתַּנּ֔וּר וְאָכְל֖וּ אֶת־שֹֽׁפְטֵיהֶ֑ם כָּל־מַלְכֵיהֶ֣ם נָפָ֔לוּ אֵֽין־קֹרֵ֥א בָהֶ֖ם אֵלָֽי	7[10]	They all are hot as an oven, And devour their judges; All their kings have fallen, There is no one among them who calls to Me.
אֶפְרַ֕יִם בָּעַמִּ֖ים ה֣וּא יִתְבּוֹלָ֑ל אֶפְרַ֕יִם הָיָ֥ה עֻגָ֖ה בְּלִ֥י הֲפוּכָֽה	8[11]	Ephraim, he mixes himself with the peoples; Ephraim has become an unturned cake.
אָכְל֤וּ זָרִים֙ כֹּח֔וֹ וְה֖וּא לֹ֣א יָדָ֑ע גַּם־שֵׂיבָה֙ זָ֣רְקָה בּ֔וֹ וְה֖וּא לֹ֥א יָדָֽע	9[12]	Strangers have devoured his strength, And he does not know it; Yes, gray hairs are here and there on him, And he does not know it.

---

[1] Hosea 6:11 - 4Q167 frags 10a+4+18+24 ll.1-2, b.Arachin 33a, b.Megillah 14b, Jeremiah 3:33, Job 18:10, Joel 4:13, Micah 4:12, Psalms 6:1, Revelation 14:15, Zephaniah 2:7

[2] LXX *begin together grapes for thyself, when I turn the captivity of my people*

[3] Hosea 7:1 - 4Q167 frags 10a+4+18+24 l.6, 4QXIIg, Amos 8:14, b.Megillah 13b, Ein Yaakov Megillah:13b, Ezekiel 16:46 23:4, Hosea 4:2 4:17 5:1 6:4 6:8-10 7:13 8:5 8:9 10:5 12:1-2, Isaiah 4:1 11:12, Jeremiah 9:3-7 3:9, Josephus Antiquities 13.9.1, Lamentations.R 2:3, Luke 13:34 19:42, m.Maaser Sheni 5:2, m.Shekalim 1:5, Matthew 23:37, Micah 6:16 7:3-7, Saadia Opinions 10:8, Song of Songs.R 4:13

[4] LXX *When I have healed Israel, then shall the iniquity of Ephraim be revealed, and the wickedness of Samaria; for they have wrought falsehood: and a thief shall come in to him, even a robber spoiling in his way*

[5] Hosea 7:2 - 1 Corinthians 4:5, Amos 8:7, Deuteronomy 8:29, Hebrews 4:13, Hosea 8:13 9:9, Isaiah 1:3 5:12 2:16 20:19, Jeremiah 2:19 4:18 14:10 16:17 8:19, Job 20:11-20:29 10:21, Luke 12:2, Numbers 8:23, Proverbs 5:21-5:22, Psalms 9:17 25:7 50:22 90:8

[6] Hosea 7:3 - 1 John 4:5, 1 Kings 22:6 22:13, Amos 7:10-7:13, Hosea 4:2 5:11 7:5, Jeremiah 5:31 9:3 28:1-28:4 13:19, Leviticus.R 27:8, Micah 6:16 7:3, Midrash Tanchuma Emor 11, Pesikta de R'Kahana 9.7, Romans 1:32

[7] Hosea 7:4 - Hosea 4:2 4:12 7:6-7:7, James 4:4, Jeremiah 5:7-5:8 9:3, Midrash Tanchuma Bo 8, Saadia Opinions 7:4 10:6 7Variant:5 Hosea 7:4-5 - Mekilta de R'Ishmael Pisha 13:110-112, Mekilta de R'Ishmael Pisha 14:40-41

[8] Hosea 7:5 - 1 Kings 13:4, 1 Peter 4:3-4, b.Avodah Zara 18b, b.Sanhedrin 103a, b.Sotah 42a, Daniel 5:1-4 5:23, Ein Yaakov Avodah Zarah 18b, Ein Yaakov Sanhedrin 103a, Ein Yaakov Sotah 42a, Ephesians 5:18, Gates of Repentance 3.172, Genesis 16:20, Habakkuk 2:15-16, Isaiah 5:11-12 5:22-23 4:1 28:7-8, Mark 6:21, Matthew 14:6, Proverbs 13:20 20:1 23:29-35, Psalms 1:1 69:13, Siman 30:6, y.Avodah Zarah 1:1

[9] Hosea 7:6 - 1 Samuel 19:11-15, 2 Samuel 13:28-29, According to the Massorah בם כער was altered to become כארבם, According to the Massorah שן was altered to become ישן, Hosea 7:4 7:7, Micah 2:1, Proverbs 4:16, Psalms 10:9-10 21:10, Saadia Opinions 10:7, Tanya Likutei Aramim §30, y.Avodah Zarah 1:1

[10] Hosea 7:7 - 1 Kings 15:28 16:9-11 16:18 16:22, 2 Kings 9:24 9:33 10:7 10:14 15:10 15:14 15:25 15:30, Daniel 9:13, Deuteronomy.R 2:19 5:9, Ezekiel 22:30, Hosea 5:15 7:10 7:14 8:4, Isaiah 9:14 19:22 16:8, Job 12:13, Leviticus.R 36:3, y.Avodah Zarah 1:1, y.Sanhedrin 10:1

[11] Hosea 7:8 - 1 Kings 18:21, Ezekiel 23:4-11, Ezra 9:1 9:12, Hosea 5:7 5:13 8:2-4 9:3, Malachi 2:11, Matthew 6:24, Nehemiah 13:23-25, Psalms 10:35, Revelation 3:15-16, Zephaniah 1:5

[12] Hosea 7:9 - 2 Kings 13:3-13:7 13:22 15:19, Gates of Repentance 2.007, Hosea 8:7, Isaiah 1:7 42:22-42:25 9:1, Midrash Tanchuma Behar 3, Proverbs 23:35, Saadia Opinions 5:7

וְעָנָה גְאוֹן־יִשְׂרָאֵל בְּפָנָיו וְלֹא־שָׁבוּ אֶל־יְהֹוָה אֱלֹהֵיהֶם וְלֹא בִקְשֻׁהוּ בְּכָל־זֹאת

10[1] And the pride of Israel testifies to his face; But they have not returned to the LORD their God, Nor sought Him, for all this.

וַיְהִי אֶפְרַיִם כְּיוֹנָה פוֹתָה אֵין לֵב מִצְרַיִם קָרָאוּ אַשּׁוּר הָלָכוּ

11[2] And Ephraim has become like a silly dove, without understanding; they call to Egypt, they go to Assyria.

כַּאֲשֶׁר יֵלֵכוּ אֶפְרוֹשׁ עֲלֵיהֶם רִשְׁתִּי כְּעוֹף הַשָּׁמַיִם אוֹרִידֵם אַיְסִרֵם כְּשֵׁמַע לַעֲדָתָם

12[3] As they go, I will spread My net over them; I will bring them down as the fowls of the heaven; I will chastise them, *as their congregation has been made to hear*[4].

אוֹי לָהֶם כִּי־נָדְדוּ מִמֶּנִּי שֹׁד לָהֶם כִּי־פָשְׁעוּ בִי וְאָנֹכִי אֶפְדֵּם וְהֵמָּה דִּבְּרוּ עָלַי כְּזָבִים

13[5] Woe to them! for they have strayed from Me; *Destruction to them*[6]! for they have transgressed against Me; Shall I then redeem them, Seeing they have spoken lies against Me?

וְלֹא־זָעֲקוּ אֵלַי בְּלִבָּם כִּי יְיֵלִילוּ עַל־מִשְׁכְּבוֹתָם עַל־דָּגָן וְתִירוֹשׁ יִתְגּוֹרָרוּ יָסוּרוּ בִי

14[7] And they have not cried to Me with their heart, You they wail on their beds; *They assemble themselves for corn and wine, they rebel against Me*[8].

וַאֲנִי יִסַּרְתִּי חִזַּקְתִּי זְרוֹעֹתָם וְאֵלַי יְחַשְּׁבוּ־רָע

15[9] I have trained and strengthened their arms, Yet they devise evil against Me.

יָשׁוּבוּ לֹא עָל הָיוּ כְּקֶשֶׁת רְמִיָּה יִפְּלוּ בַחֶרֶב שָׂרֵיהֶם מִזַּעַם לְשׁוֹנָם זוֹ לַעְגָּם בְּאֶרֶץ מִצְרָיִם

16[10] They return, but not upwards; They have become like *a*[11] deceitful bow; Their princes shall fall by the sword for the rage of their tongue; This shall be their derision in the land of Egypt.

Hosea – Chapter 8

אֶל־חִכְּךָ שֹׁפָר כַּנֶּשֶׁר עַל־בֵּית יְהֹוָה יַעַן עָבְרוּ בְרִיתִי וְעַל־תּוֹרָתִי פָּשָׁעוּ

1[12] *Set the horn to your mouth. As a vulture*[13] he comes against the house of the LORD; Because they have transgressed My covenant, And trespassed against My law.

---

[1] Hosea 7:10 - Amos 4:6-4:13, Hosea 5:5 6:1 7:7, Isaiah 9:14, Jeremiah 3:3 8:5-8:6 25:5-25:7 35:15-35:17, Midrash Tanchuma Beshallach 25, Pesikta Rabbati 44:2, Proverbs 3:22, Psalms 10:5 14:2 53:3, Romans 3:11, Zechariah 1:4

[2] Hosea 7:11 - 2 Kings 15:19 17:3-17:4, Exodus.R 21:5, Ezekiel 23:4-23:8, Hosea 4:11 5:13 8:8-8:9 9:3 12:1 12:3 14:5, Isaiah 30:1-30:6 31:1-31:3, Jastrow 1252b, Jeremiah 2:18 2:36, Lamentations.R 1:45, Mekilta de R'Ishmael Beshallah 3:128, Midrash Psalms 84:2, Midrash Tanchuma Shemini 11, Proverbs 6:32 15:32 17:16, Song of Songs.R 2:34

[3] Hosea 7:12 - 2 Kings 17:13-18, Deuteronomy 28:15-68 29:21-27 31:16-29 32:15-43, Ecclesiastes 9:12, Ezekiel 12:13 17:20 8:3, Jeremiah 16:16 20:4, Job 19:6, Leviticus 26:14-46, Mekhilta de R'Shimon bar Yochai Bachodesh 49:2, Revelation 3:19
Hosea 7:12-13 - 4QXIIc

[4] LXX *with the rumor of their coming affliction*

[5] Hosea 7:13 - 1 John 1:10, 1 Peter 1:18-1:19, b.Avodah Zara 4a, Deuteronomy 15:15, Exodus.R 42:3, Ezekiel 16:23 18:2 18:25 10:6, Gates of Repentance 2.004, Hosea 7:1 7:3 9:12 9:17 11:2 12:1, Isaiah 7:1 17:14 19:1 11:13 15:8, Jastrow 1136b, Jeremiah 14:10 18:11-18:12 18:20 44:17-44:18, Job 21:14-21:15 22:17, Jonah 1:3 1:10, Lamentations 5:16, Lamentations.R Petichata D'Chakimei:2, Malachi 3:13-3:15, Matthew 23:13-23:29 23:37, Micah 6:4, Nehemiah 1:10, Pesikta de R'Kahana 15.4, Psalms 10:10 107:2-107:3 139:7-139:9, Revelation 8:13, This is the middle verse of the book of Hosea per the Massorah
Hosea 7:13-16 - 4QXIIg

[6] LXX *they are cowards*

[7] Hosea 7:14 - Amos 2:8 8:3, Exodus 8:6, Hosea 3:1 14:1, Isaiah 5:13 4:5 17:14, James 4:3 5:1, Jeremiah 3:10, Job 35:9-35:10, Judges 9:27, Micah 2:11, Philippians 3:19, Psalms 78:34-78:37, Romans 16:18, Saadia Opinions 5:8, Zechariah 7:5

[8] LXX *they pined for oil and wine*

[9] Hosea 7:15 - 2 Corinthians 10:5, 2 Kings 13:5 13:23 14:25-27, Acts 4:25, b.Avodah Zara 4a, Gates of Repentance 2.004, Hebrews 12:5, Jeremiah 17:9, Job 5:17, Nahum 1:9, Proverbs 3:11, Psalms 2:1 62:4 94:12 106:43-45, Revelation 3:19, Romans 1:21

[10] Hosea 7:16 - 2 Peter 2:8, Ezekiel 23:32 12:20, Hosea 6:4 7:13 8:13-14 9:3 9:6 11:7, Isaiah 3:8, James 3:5, Jeremiah 3:10 18:18, Luke 8:13 11:24-26, Matthew 12:36, Midrash Tanchuma Shelach 5, Numbers.R 16:8, Pesikta Rabbati 44:4, Psalms 12:5 52:3 57:5 73:9 78:37 78:57, Revelation 13:5

[11] 4QXIIg *the*

[12] Hosea 8:1 - 1 Corinthians 15:52, 2 Kings 18:27, 4QXIIg, Amos 3:6 8:3 9:1, Deuteronomy 4:49, Ezekiel 7:14 16:59 33:3-6, Habakkuk 1:8, Hebrews 8:8-13, Hosea 4:6 5:8 6:7 9:15, Isaiah 18:3 24:5 10:1, Jeremiah 4:5 4:13 6:1 7:33 24:40 3:27, Joel 2:1 2:15, Life of Adam and Eve [Apocalypse] 22:2, Matthew 24:28, Saadia Opinions 6:5, Zechariah 9:14 11:1, Zephaniah 1:16

[13] LXX *he shall come into their midst as the land, as an eagle*

לִ֤י יִזְעָ֨קוּ אֱלֹהַ֖י יְֽדַעֲנ֖וּךָ יִשְׂרָאֵֽל	2[1]	*Will they cry to Me: 'My God, we Israel know You[2]?'*
זָנַ֥ח יִשְׂרָאֵ֖ל ט֑וֹב אוֹיֵ֖ב יִרְדְּפֽוֹ	3[3]	Israel has cast off what is good; The enemy shall pursue him.
הֵ֤ם הִמְלִ֨יכוּ֙ וְלֹ֣א מִמֶּ֔נִּי הֵשִׂ֖ירוּ וְלֹ֣א יָדָ֑עְתִּי כַּסְפָּ֣ם וּזְהָבָ֗ם עָשׂ֤וּ לָהֶם֙ עֲצַבִּ֔ים לְמַ֖עַן יִכָּרֵֽת	4[4]	They have set up kings, but not from Me, They have made princes, and I did not know it; they have made idols from their silver and their gold, so they may be cut off.
זָנַח֙ עֶגְלֵ֣ךְ שֹֽׁמְר֔וֹן חָרָ֥ה אַפִּ֖י בָּ֑ם עַד־מָתַ֕י לֹ֥א יֽוּכְל֖וּ נִקָּיֹֽן	5[5]	Your calf, O Samaria, is cast off; My anger burns against them; How long will it be before they gain innocence?
כִּ֤י מִיִּשְׂרָאֵל֙ וְה֔וּא חָרָ֥שׁ עָשָׂ֖הוּ וְלֹ֣א אֱלֹהִ֣ים ה֑וּא כִּֽי־שְׁבָבִ֣ים יִֽהְיֶ֔ה עֵ֖גֶל שֹׁמְרֽוֹן	6[6]	*For from Israel is this: The craftsman made it, and it is no God; Yes, the calf of Samaria shall be broken in pieces[7].*
כִּ֤י ר֨וּחַ יִזְרָ֔עוּ וְסוּפָ֖תָה יִקְצֹ֑רוּ קָמָ֣ה אֵֽין־ל֗וֹ צֶ֚מַח בְּלִ֣י יַֽעֲשֶׂה־קֶּ֔מַח אוּלַ֖י יַֽעֲשֶׂ֑ה זָרִ֖ים יִבְלָעֻֽהוּ	7[8]	*For they sow the wind, and they shall reap the whirlwind; It has no stalk, the bud[9] that shall yield no meal; If, perchance, it yields, strangers will devour it.*
נִבְלַ֖ע יִשְׂרָאֵ֑ל עַתָּה֙ הָי֣וּ בַגּוֹיִ֔ם כִּכְלִ֖י אֵֽין־חֵ֥פֶץ בּֽוֹ	8[10]	Israel is swallowed up; Now they have become like the nations, As a vessel with no value.
כִּֽי־הֵ֨מָּה֙ עָל֣וּ אַשּׁ֔וּר פֶּ֖רֶא בּוֹדֵ֣ד ל֑וֹ אֶפְרַ֖יִם הִתְנ֥וּ אֲהָבִֽים	9[11]	*For they have gone to Assyria, Like a wild ass alone by himself; Ephraim has hired lovers[12].*
גַּ֛ם כִּֽי־יִתְנ֥וּ בַגּוֹיִ֖ם עַתָּ֣ה אֲקַבְּצֵ֑ם וַיָּחֵ֣לּוּ מְּעָ֔ט מִמַּשָּׂ֖א מֶ֥לֶךְ שָׂרִֽים	10[13]	Yes, though they hire among the nations, Now will I gather them up; And their diminishment begins because of the burden of king and princes.
כִּֽי־הִרְבָּ֥ה אֶפְרַ֛יִם מִזְבְּחֹ֖ת לַחֲטֹ֑א הָיוּ־ל֥וֹ מִזְבְּח֖וֹת לַחֲטֹֽא	11[14]	For Ephraim has multiplied altars *to sin*, Yes[15], altars have been for him to sin.

---

[1] Hosea 8:2 - 1 John 2:4, 2 Kings 10:16 10:29, Hosea 5:15 7:13-14, Isaiah 48:1-2, Jeremiah 7:4, Lamentations.R Petichata D'Chakimei:2, Luke 13:25, Matthew 7:21 1:11, Micah 3:11, Psalms 78:34-37, Titus 1:16
[2] LXX *They shall soon cry out to me, saying, O God, we know you*
[3] Hosea 8:3 - 1 Timothy 5:12, Amos 1:11, Deuteronomy 4:25, Lamentations 3:66 4:19, Leviticus 2:36, Midrash Psalms 60:2, Pesikta de R'Kahana 15.5, Pesikta Rabbati 31:3, Psalms 36:4 81:11-81:12, y.Rosh Hashanah 3:8
[4] Hosea 8:4 - 1 Kings 12:16-12:20 12:28 13:34 16:31, 2 Kings 15:10-15:30, Deuteronomy.R 2:19, Ezekiel 18:31, Galatians 4:9, Gates of Repentance 1.045, Genesis.R 28:7, Hosea 2:8 13:2 13:9-13:10, Jeremiah 44:7-44:8, John 10:14, Leviticus.R 33:6, Luke 13:25 13:27, Matthew 1:12, y.Sanhedrin 7:7
[5] Hosea 8:5 - 2 Kings 17:16-18 17:21-23, Acts 7:41, Deuteronomy 8:22, Hosea 8:6 10:5, Isaiah 21:20, Jeremiah 4:14 13:27, Proverbs 1:22
[6] Hosea 8:6 - 2 Chronicles 7:1 34:6-34:7, 2 Kings 23:15 23:19, 4Q167 frags 11-13 l.3, 4Q167 frags 11-13 l.5, Acts 17:29 19:26, b.Sanhedrin [Rashi] 7a, Habakkuk 2:18, Hosea 10:2 10:5-10:6, Isaiah 44:9-44:20, Jeremiah 10:3-10:9 10:14 43:12-13 2:2, Psalms 106:19-20 115:4-8 135:15-18
[7] LXX *Whereas the workman made it, and it is not God; therefore your calf, Samaria, was a deceiver*
[8] Hosea 8:7 - 2 Kings 13:3-13:7 15:19 15:29, Deuteronomy 4:33, Ecclesiastes 5:17, Galatians 6:7, Hosea 2:9 7:9 10:12-10:13, Isaiah 17:11 18:15, Jeremiah 12:13, Job 4:8, Judges 6:3-6:6, Nahum 1:3, Pesikta Rabbati 44:3, Proverbs 22:8
Hosea 8:7-8 - 4Q167 frags 11-13 ll.6-8
[9] LXX *for they sow blighted seed, and their destruction shall await them, a sheaf of corn*
[10] Hosea 8:8 - 2 Kings 17:1-6 18:11, 2 Timothy 2:20-21, Deuteronomy 4:25 28:64, Ezekiel 12:3, Isaiah 6:14, Jeremiah 22:28 24:38 2:17 3:34, Lamentations 2:2 2:5 2:16, Leviticus 2:33, Pesikta Rabbati 31:1, Romans 9:22
Hosea 8:8 [LXX] - Life of Adam and Eve [Apocalypse] 26:1
[11] Hosea 8:9 - 2 Kings 15:19, Ezekiel 16:33-34 23:5-9, Hosea 2:5-9 2:10 5:13 7:11 12:3, Isaiah 6:6, Jeremiah 2:24, Job 39:5-8, Saadia Opinions 5:5
[12] LXX *For they have gone up to the Assyrians: Ephraim has been strengthened against himself; they loved gifts*
[13] Hosea 8:10 - 1 Chronicles 5:26, 2 Kings 14:26 15:19-20 17:3, b.Bava Batra 8a, Daniel 2:37, Ein Yaakov Bava Batra:8a, Ezekiel 16:37 22:20 23:9-10 23:22-26 23:46-47 2:7, Haggai 2:6, Hosea 10:10, Isaiah 10:8 12:13, Jeremiah 18:2, Leviticus.R 7:3, mt.Hilchot Talmud Torah 6:10, Pesikta de R'Kahana 6.3, Pesikta Rabbati 16:7, Tanna Devei Eliyahu 5
[14] Hosea 8:11 - Deuteronomy 4:28, Hosea 10:1-10:2 10:8 12:13, Isaiah 10:10-10:11, Jeremiah 16:13, Saadia Opinions 5:5
[15] LXX *his beloved*

אֶכְתָּוב־אֶכְתָּב־לֹו׳ ׳רבּו׳ ׳רבּי׳ תּוֹרָתֵי כְּמוֹ־זָר נֶחְשָׁבוּ

12[1] *I write for him never so many things of My Law, They are accounted as a stranger's[2].*

זִבְחֵי הַבְהָבַי יִזְבְּחוּ בָשָׂר וַיֹּאכֵלוּ יְהוָה לֹא רָצָם עַתָּה יִזְכֹּר עֲוֹנָם וְיִפְקֹד חַטֹּאותָם הֵמָּה מִצְרַיִם יָשׁוּבוּ

13[3] As for the sacrifices made by fire to Me, Let them sacrifice flesh and eat it, For the LORD will not accept them. Now He will recall their iniquity, and punish their sins; They shall return to Egypt[4].

וַיִּשְׁכַּח יִשְׂרָאֵל אֶת־עֹשֵׂהוּ וַיִּבֶן הֵיכָלֹות וִיהוּדָה הִרְבָּה עָרִים בְּצֻרֹות וְשִׁלַּחְתִּי־אֵשׁ בְּעָרָיו וְאָכְלָה אַרְמְנֹתֶיהָ

14[5] For Israel has forgotten his Maker, And built palaces, And Judah has multiplied fortified cities; But I will send a fire upon his cities, And it shall devour their *castles*[6].

Hosea – Chapter 9

אַל־תִּשְׂמַח יִשְׂרָאֵל אֶל־גִּיל כָּעַמִּים כִּי זָנִיתָ מֵעַל אֱלֹהֶיךָ אָהַבְתָּ אֶתְנַן עַל כָּל־גָּרְנֹות דָּגָן

1[7] Do not rejoice to exultation, O Israel, like the peoples, For you have gone astray from your God, You have loved *a harlot's hire on every corn floor*[8].

גֹּרֶן וָיֶקֶב לֹא יִרְעֵם וְתִירֹושׁ יְכַחֶשׁ בָּהּ

2[9] The threshing floor and the winepress shall not feed them, And the new wine shall fail her.

לֹא יֵשְׁבוּ בְּאֶרֶץ יְהוָה וְשָׁב אֶפְרַיִם מִצְרַיִם וּבְאַשּׁוּר טָמֵא יֹאכֵלוּ

3[10] They shall not live in the LORD's land; But Ephraim *shall return to Egypt*[11], And they shall eat unclean food in Assyria.

לֹא־יִסְּכוּ לַיהוָה יַיִן וְלֹא יֶעֶרְבוּ־לֹו זִבְחֵיהֶם כְּלֶחֶם אֹונִים לָהֶם כָּל־אֹכְלָיו יִטַּמָּאוּ כִּי־לַחְמָם לְנַפְשָׁם לֹא יָבֹוא בֵּית יְהוָה

4[12] They shall not pour out wine offerings to the LORD, *Nor shall they be pleasing to Him; Their sacrifices shall be like the bread of mourners to them*[13], All who eat of it shall be polluted; For their bread shall be for their appetite, It shall not come into the house of the LORD.

מַה־תַּעֲשׂוּ לְיֹום מֹועֵד וּלְיֹום חַג־יְהוָה

5[14] What will you do in the day of the appointed season, And in the day of the festival of the LORD?

---

[1] Hosea 8:12 - 2 Kings 17:15-16, b.Gittin 60b, Deuteronomy 4:6-8, Exodus.R 47:1, Exodus.R 47:1, Ezekiel 20:11, Gates of Repentance 2.13, Hosea 4:6, Isaiah 6:9, Jeremiah 6:16-17, Midrash Tanchuma Ki Tissa 34, Nehemiah 9:13-14 9:26, Numbers.R 14:10, Pesikta Rabbati 5:1-2, Proverbs 22:20, Psalms 50:17 23:18 147:19-20, Romans 3:1 7:12, Saadia Opinions Intro:2, y.Chagigah 1:7, y.Peah 2:4

[2] LXX *I will write down a multitude of commands for him; but his statutes are accounted strange things, even the beloved altars*

[3] Hosea 8:13 - 1 Corinthians 11:20 11:29, 1 Samuel 15:22, Amos 5:22 8:7, Deuteronomy 28:68, Exodus 20:3 8:34, Hosea 4:9 5:6 7:2 7:16 9:3-4 9:6 9:9 11:5 12:13, Isaiah 1:11, Jeremiah 7:21-23 14:10, Josephus Wars 6.9.1, Proverbs 21:27, Revelation 16:19

[4] LXX *and they shall eat unclean things among the Assyrians*

[5] Hosea 8:14 - 1 Kings 12:31 16:31, 2 Chronicles 2:10 3:4, 2 Kings 18:13, 4Q167 frags 15+33 2.1-2, Amos 1:4 1:10 1:12 1:14 2:5, b.Shekalim 15b, Deuteronomy 8:18, Ephesians 2:10, Hosea 2:13 13:6, Isaiah 17:10 22:8-11 5:23 18:13 18:25 19:21, Jastrow 345b, Jeremiah 2:32 3:21 17:27 23:27, Psalms 10:21, y.Shekalim 5:4

[6] LXX *foundations*

[7] Hosea 9:1 - Amos 3:2 6:6-7 6:13 8:10, b.Gittin 7a, b.Menachot [Tosefot] 32b, b.Sanhedrin [Rashi] 51a, Ein Yaakov Gittin:6b, Ezekiel 16:47-16:48 20:32 21:15, Genesis.R 57:4, Hosea 2:12 4:12 5:4 5:7 10:5, Isaiah 17:11 22:12-13, James 4:16 5:1, Jeremiah 20:17, Lamentations 4:21, Ruth.R 5:15, y.Megillah 3:2, y.Sotah 5:6
Hosea 9:1-4 - 4QXIIg

[8] LXX *gifts upon every threshing floor*

[9] Hosea 9:2 - Amos 4:5-11, Haggai 1:9 2:16, Hosea 2:9 2:12, Isaiah 24:7-12, Joel 1:3-7 1:9-13, Micah 6:13-6:16

[10] Hosea 9:3 - 1 Kings 9:7, 2 Kings 17:6, Acts 10:14, Daniel 1:8, Deuteronomy 4:26 28:63 28:68, Ezekiel 4:13, Hosea 7:11 8:13 9:6 11:5 12:1, Isaiah 11:15-11:16, Jeremiah 2:7 16:18, Josephus Wars 6.9.1, Joshua 23:15, Leviticus 18:28 20:22 1:23, Micah 2:10

[11] LXX *dwelt in*

[12] Hosea 9:4 - Amos 4:4-5 5:22 8:11-8:12, Deuteronomy 2:14, Exodus 16:23, Ezekiel 24:17 24:22, Haggai 2:13-14, Hosea 3:4 8:13, Isaiah 1:11-15 9:6 18:3, Jeremiah 6:20, Joel 1:13 2:14, John 6:51, Joseph and Asenath 8:5, Leviticus 17:11 21:6 21:8 21:17 21:21, Malachi 1:9-10 2:13, mt.Hilchot Shevitat Yom Tov 6:18, Nehemiah 8:9-12, Numbers 4:7 19:11 4:2, Siman 103:9

[13] LXX *neither have their sacrifices been sweet to him, but as the bread of mourning to them*

[14] Hosea 9:5 - Hosea 2:11, Isaiah 10:3, Jeremiah 5:31, Joel 1:13

כִּי־הִנֵּה הָלְכוּ מִשֹּׁד מִצְרַיִם תְּקַבְּצֵם מֹף תְּקַבְּרֵם מַחְמַד לְכַסְפָּם קִמּוֹשׂ יִירָשֵׁם חוֹחַ בְּאָהֳלֵיהֶם

6[1] *For, look, they have gone away from destruction, Yet Egypt shall gather them up, Memphis shall bury them; Their precious treasures of silver, nettles shall possess them*[2], Thorns shall be in their tents.

בָּאוּ יְמֵי הַפְּקֻדָּה בָּאוּ יְמֵי הַשִּׁלֻּם יֵדְעוּ יִשְׂרָאֵל אֱוִיל הַנָּבִיא מְשֻׁגָּע אִישׁ הָרוּחַ עַל רֹב עֲוֹנְךָ וְרַבָּה מַשְׂטֵמָה

7[3] The days of visitation has come, The days of recompense has come, *Israel shall know it. The prophet is a fool, the man of the spirit is mad*[4]! For the multitude of your iniquity, the enmity is great.

צֹפֶה אֶפְרַיִם עִם־אֱלֹהָי נָבִיא פַּח יָקוֹשׁ עַל־כָּל־דְּרָכָיו מַשְׂטֵמָה בְּבֵית אֱלֹהָיו

8[5] Ephraim is a watchman with my God; As for the prophet, a fowler's snare is in all his ways, And enmity in the house of his God.

הֶעְמִיקוּ־שִׁחֵתוּ כִּימֵי הַגִּבְעָה יִזְכּוֹר עֲוֹנָם יִפְקוֹד חַטֹּאותָם

9[6] They have corrupted themselves deeply, As in the days of Gibeah; He will remember their iniquity, He will punish their sins.

כַּעֲנָבִים בַּמִּדְבָּר מָצָאתִי יִשְׂרָאֵל כְּבִכּוּרָה בִתְאֵנָה בְּרֵאשִׁיתָהּ רָאִיתִי אֲבוֹתֵיכֶם הֵמָּה בָּאוּ בַעַל־פְּעוֹר וַיִּנָּזְרוּ לַבֹּשֶׁת וַיִּהְיוּ שִׁקּוּצִים כְּאָהֳבָם

10[7] I found Israel like grapes in the wilderness, I saw your fathers as the first ripe in the fig tree at her first season; But so soon as they came to Baal-peor, They separated themselves to the shameful thing, And became detestable like what they loved.

אֶפְרַיִם כָּעוֹף יִתְעוֹפֵף כְּבוֹדָם מִלֵּדָה וּמִבֶּטֶן וּמֵהֵרָיוֹן

11[8] As for Ephraim, their glory shall fly away like a bird; There shall be no birth, and no one with child, and no conception.

כִּי אִם־יְגַדְּלוּ אֶת־בְּנֵיהֶם וְשִׁכַּלְתִּים מֵאָדָם כִּי־גַם־אוֹי לָהֶם בְּשׂוּרִי מֵהֶם

12[9] Yes, though they bring up their children, I will bereave them, so that no man remains; Yes, woe also to them when I depart from them.

אֶפְרַיִם כַּאֲשֶׁר־רָאִיתִי לְצוֹר שְׁתוּלָה בְנָוֶה וְאֶפְרַיִם לְהוֹצִיא אֶל־הֹרֵג בָּנָיו

13[10] Ephraim, *like as I have seen Tyre, is planted in a pleasant place*[11]; But Ephraim shall bring forth his children to the slayer.

תֵּן־לָהֶם יְהוָה מַה־תִּתֵּן תֵּן־לָהֶם רֶחֶם מַשְׁכִּיל וְשָׁדַיִם צֹמְקִים

14[12] Give them, O LORD, whatever You will give; Give them a miscarrying womb and dry breasts.

---

[1] Hosea 9:6 - 1 Samuel 13:6, 2 Kings 13:7, Deuteronomy 28:63-64, Hosea 7:13 7:16 8:13 9:3 10:8 12:1, Isaiah 5:6 7:23 11:11 19:13 3:12 8:13 10:13, Proverbs 24:31, Psalms 11:34, Zechariah 10:10-11

[2] LXX *Therefore, behold, they go forth from the trouble of Egypt, and Memphis shall receive them, and Machmas shall bury them: as for their silver, destruction shall inherit it*

[3] Hosea 9:7 - 2 Corinthians 5:13, 2 Kings 9:11, 2 Thessalonians 2:10-12, Acts 26:24-25, Amos 8:2, Ezekiel 7:2-7 12:22-28 13:3 13:10 14:9-10 1:17 14:23, Hosea 9:8, Isaiah 10:3 2:11 10:8 20:25, Jeremiah 6:14 8:11 10:15 11:23 16:18 23:16-17 5:26 22:21, Lamentations 2:14, Luke 21:22, Mark 3:21, Micah 2:11 7:4, Revelation 16:19, Zechariah 11:15-17, Zephaniah 1:14-18 3:4

[4] LXX *and Israel shall be afflicted as the prophet that is mad, as a man deranged*

[5] Hosea 9:8 - 1 Kings 17:1 18:1 18:19 18:36-18:39 22:6 22:11 22:22 22:28, 2 Kings 2:14 2:21 3:15-3:20 4:1-4:7 4:33-4:37 4:41 4:43 5:14 5:27 6:17-6:18 7:2 7:19 13:21, Ezekiel 3:17 9:7, Hebrews 13:17, Hosea 5:1, Isaiah 14:6, Jeremiah 6:14 6:17 14:13 7:7, John 15:24, Lamentations 2:14 4:13, Mas.Soferim 4:9, Micah 7:4, Romans 3:7, Song of Songs 3:3

[6] Hosea 9:9 - Hosea 8:13 10:9, Isaiah 24:5 7:6, Judges 19:16-20:21
Hosea 9:9-17 - 4QXIIg

[7] Hosea 9:10 - 1 Kings 16:31, Amos 4:5, b.Berachot 56b, b.Sanhedrin 16a, b.Sotah [Rashi] 5a, Deuteronomy 4:3 8:10 8:17, Esther.R 9:2, Exodus 19:4-19:6, Exodus.R 36:1, Ezekiel 20:8, Genesis.R 1:4 29:3 46:1 53:3, Hosea 2:15 4:14 11:1, Isaiah 4:4, Jeremiah 2:2-2:3 5:31 11:13 7:3, Judges 6:32, m.Sanhedrin 7:6, Micah 7:1, Midrash Tanchuma Bamidbar 13, Midrash Tanchuma Naso 11, Numbers 13:23-13:24 15:39 25:1-25:18, Numbers.R 2:6 10:8 16:24, Pesikta Rabbati 33:13 42:5, Psalms 81:13 106:28-106:29, Romans 6:21, Sifre Devarim Ha'azinu Hashamayim 313, Sifre Devarim Nitzavim 313, y.Sanhedrin 10:2

[8] Hosea 9:11 - Amos 1:13, Deuteronomy 4:18 \57 9:17, Ecclesiastes 6:3, Genesis 17:52 48:16-20 1:22, Hosea 4:7 9:14 10:5, Job 18:5 18:18-19, Luke 23:29, Midrash Tanchuma Balak 14, Numbers.R 20:20, Psalms 58:9

[9] Hosea 9:12 - 1 Samuel 16:14 28:15-16, 2 Kings 17:18 17:23, Avot de R'Natan 23, Deuteronomy 4:32 28:41-42 7:17 8:25, Hosea 7:13 9:5-6 9:13 9:16, Jeremiah 15:7 16:3-4, Job 3:14, Judges 4:16, Lamentations 2:20, Numbers 26:65, Pesikta Rabbati 44:3, Saadia Opinions 10:9

[10] Hosea 9:13 - 2 Kings 15:16, Amos 7:17, Exodus.R 20:11, Ezekiel 26:1-26:21 3:3, Hosea 9:16 10:14 13:8 14:1, Jeremiah 9:22

[11] LXX *even as I saw, gave their children for a prey*

[12] Hosea 9:14 - 1 Corinthians 7:26, b.Chullin [Rashi] 55b, b.Shabbat [Rashi] 37b, b.Taanit [Rashi] 19b, Hosea 9:11 9:13 9:16, Job 21:10, Luke 21:23 23:29, Mark 13:17, Matthew 24:19, Pesikta Rabbati 44:3, Sifre Devarim Vezot Habracha 342

כָּל־רָעָתָם בַּגִּלְגָּל כִּי־שָׁם שְׂנֵאתִים עַל רֹעַ
מַעַלְלֵיהֶם מִבֵּיתִי אֲגָרְשֵׁם לֹא אוֹסֵף אַהֲבָתָם כָּל־
שָׂרֵיהֶם סֹרְרִים

15[1] All their wickedness is in Gilgal, For there I hated them; Because of the wickedness of their habits I will drive them out of My house; I will love them no more, All their princes are rebellious.

הֻכָּה אֶפְרַיִם שָׁרְשָׁם יָבֵשׁ פְּרִי 'בְלִי־בָל־יַעֲשׂוּן' גַּם
כִּי יֵלֵדוּן וְהֵמַתִּי מַחֲמַדֵּי בִטְנָם

16[2] Ephraim is smitten, Their root is dried up, They shall bear no fruit; Yes, though they bear, I will kill the beloved fruit of their womb.

יִמְאָסֵם אֱלֹהַי כִּי לֹא שָׁמְעוּ לוֹ וְיִהְיוּ נֹדְדִים בַּגּוֹיִם

17[3] My God will cast them away, Because they did not listen to Him; And they shall be wanderers among the nations.

Hosea – Chapter 10

גֶּפֶן בּוֹקֵק יִשְׂרָאֵל פְּרִי יְשַׁוֶּה־לּוֹ כְּרֹב לְפִרְיוֹ
הִרְבָּה לַמִּזְבְּחוֹת כְּטוֹב לְאַרְצוֹ הֵיטִיבוּ מַצֵּבוֹת

1[4] Israel was a luxuriant vine, Which put forth fruit freely: As his fruit increased, He increased his altars; The more goodly his land, The more goodly were his pillars.

חָלַק לִבָּם עַתָּה יֶאְשָׁמוּ הוּא יַעֲרֹף מִזְבְּחוֹתָם יְשֹׁדֵד
מַצֵּבוֹתָם

2[5] Their heart is divided; Now they shall bear their guilt; He will break down their altars, He will spoil their pillars.

כִּי עַתָּה יֹאמְרוּ אֵין מֶלֶךְ לָנוּ כִּי לֹא יָרֵאנוּ אֶת־
יְהוָה וְהַמֶּלֶךְ מַה־יַּעֲשֶׂה־לָּנוּ

3[6] Surely now they shall say: 'We have no king; For we did not fear the LORD; And the king, what can he do for us?'

דִּבְּרוּ דְבָרִים אָלוֹת שָׁוְא כָּרֹת בְּרִית וּפָרַח כָּרֹאשׁ
מִשְׁפָּט עַל תַּלְמֵי שָׂדָי

4[7] They speak words, They swear falsely, they make covenants; Thus judgment springs up as hemlock In the furrows of the field.

לְעֶגְלוֹת בֵּית אָוֶן יָגוּרוּ שְׁכַן שֹׁמְרוֹן כִּי־אָבַל עָלָיו
עַמּוֹ וּכְמָרָיו עָלָיו יָגִילוּ עַל־כְּבוֹדוֹ כִּי־גָלָה מִמֶּנּוּ

5[8] The inhabitants of Samaria shall be in dread For the calves of *Beth-aven*[9]; its people shall mourn over it, And its priests shall tremble for it, For its glory, because it departed from it.

גַּם־אוֹתוֹ לְאַשּׁוּר יוּבָל מִנְחָה לְמֶלֶךְ יָרֵב בָּשְׁנָה
אֶפְרַיִם יִקָּח וְיֵבוֹשׁ יִשְׂרָאֵל מֵעֲצָתוֹ

6[10] It also shall be carried to Assyria, For a present to King *Contentious*[11]; Ephraim shall receive *shame*[12], And Israel shall be ashamed of his own counsel.

---

[1] Hosea 9:15 - 1 Kings 9:7-9, 1 Samuel 7:16, 2 Kings 17:17-20, Acts 4:5-7 4:27 5:21, Amos 4:4 5:5 5:27, Ezekiel 22:27 23:18, Genesis.R 19:9, Hosea 1:6 1:9 3:4 4:9 4:15 5:1-2 7:2 9:3 9:17 12:13, Isaiah 1:23, Jeremiah 3:8 5:5 11:15 33:24-26, Joshua 4:19-24 5:2-9 10:43, Lamentations.R Petichata D'Chakimei:4, Leviticus 2:30, Micah 3:11 6:5, Pesikta de R'Kahana 15.1, Psalms 78:60, Zechariah 11:8, Zephaniah 3:3

[2] Hosea 9:16 - Exodus.R 3:8, Ezekiel 24:21, Hosea 5:11 8:7 9:11-9:13, Isaiah 5:24 16:24, Job 18:16, Malachi 3:19, Midrash Tanchuma Shemot 29, Pesikta de R'Kahana 16.8 24.10

[3] Hosea 9:17 - 1 Kings 14:15-16, 2 Chronicles 18:13 12:16, 2 Kings 17:14-20, Acts 3:23, Amos 8:2 9:9, Deuteronomy 28:64-65 8:26, Hosea 4:10 7:13, Isaiah 7:13 24:18, James 1:1, Jeremiah 25:3-4 26:4-6 35:15-17, John 7:35 20:17 20:28, Micah 7:7, Midrash Tanchuma Bechukkotai 2, Nehemiah 5:19, Philippians 4:19, Proverbs 5:1, Psalms 31:15 81:12-14, Zechariah 1:4 7:11-14

[4] Hosea 10:1 - 1 Kings 14:23, 2 Corinthians 5:16, Ezekiel 15:1-5, Hosea 2:8 8:4 8:11 12:10 12:13 13:2 13:6, Isaiah 5:1-7, Jeremiah 2:28, John 15:1-6, Joseph and Asenath 2:5, Leviticus 2:1, Mekhilta de R'Shimon bar Yochai Shirata 33:1, Mekilta de R'Ishmael Shirata 7:12, Nahum 2:3, Philippians 2:21, Romans 14:7-8, Zechariah 7:5-6

Hosea 10:1-14 - 4QXIIg

[5] Hosea 10:2 - 1 John 2:15, 1 Kings 18:21, 1 Samuel 5:4, 2 Thessalonians 2:11-2:12, Genesis.R 38:6 38:7, Hosea 7:8 8:5-8:6 10:5-8 14:1, Isaiah 20:18, James 1:8 4:4, Jeremiah 19:13, Luke 16:13, Mas.Derek Eretz Zutta 9:12, Mas.Kallah Rabbati 8:9, Matthew 6:24, Micah 5:14, Midrash Tanchuma Shoftim 18, Numbers.R 11:7, Revelation 3:15-3:16, Zechariah 13:2, Zephaniah 1:5

[6] Hosea 10:3 - Genesis 1:10, Hosea 3:4 10:7 10:15 11:5 13:11, John 19:15, Micah 4:9, Saadia Opinions Intro:7

[7] Hosea 10:4 - 2 Kings 17:3-4, 2 Timothy 3:3, Acts 8:23, Amos 5:7 6:12, b.Sanhedrin 63b, Deuteronomy 5:17, Ezekiel 17:13-19, Gates of Repentance 1.27, Hebrews 12:15, Hosea 4:2 6:7, Isaiah 5:7 59:13-15, Pesikta Rabbati 44:2, Revelation 8:10-11, Romans 1:31

[8] Hosea 10:5 - 1 Kings 12:28-32, 1 Samuel 4:21-22, 2 Chronicles 11:15 13:8, 2 Kings 10:29 17:16 23:5, Acts 19:27, b.Megillah 25b, b.Sanhedrin 63b, Hosea 4:15 5:8 8:5-6 9:11 13:2, Jastrow 607a, Joshua 7:2, Judges 18:24, Mas.Sefer Torah 5:12, Revelation 18:11-19, Zephaniah 1:4

[9] LXX *house of On*

[10] Hosea 10:6 - 2 Kings 17:3, Daniel 11:8, Ezekiel 12:31, Hosea 4:7 4:19 5:13 8:6 11:5-11:6, Isaiah 1:29 6:3 44:9-44:11 21:16 46:1-46:2, Jeremiah 2:26-2:27 2:36-2:37 3:24-3:25 7:24 43:12-43:13 24:13, Job 18:7, Micah 6:16, Seder Olam 22:Hosea

[11] LXX *Jarim*

[12] LXX *a gift*

נִדְמֶה שֹׁמְרוֹן מַלְכָּהּ כְּקֶצֶף עַל־פְּנֵי־מָיִם

7[1] As for Samaria, her king is cut off, As *foam on*[2] the water.

וְנִשְׁמְדוּ בָּמוֹת אָוֶן חַטַּאת יִשְׂרָאֵל קוֹץ וְדַרְדַּר יַעֲלֶה עַל־מִזְבְּחוֹתָם וְאָמְרוּ לֶהָרִים כַּסּוּנוּ וְלַגְּבָעוֹת נִפְלוּ עָלֵינוּ:

8[3] The high places of *Aven*[4] will be destroyed, the sin of Israel. The thorn and the thistle shall come up on their altars; And they shall say to the mountains: 'Cover us,' And to the hills: 'Fall on us.'

מִימֵי הַגִּבְעָה חָטָאתָ יִשְׂרָאֵל שָׁם עָמָדוּ לֹא־תַשִּׂיגֵם בַּגִּבְעָה מִלְחָמָה עַל־בְּנֵי עַלְוָה

9[5] From *the days of Gibeah you have sinned, O Israel*[6]; There they stood; *No battle was to overtake them in Gibeah, Nor the children of arrogancy*[7].

בְּאַוָּתִי וְאֶסֳּרֵם וְאֻסְּפוּ עֲלֵיהֶם עַמִּים בְּאָסְרָם לִשְׁתֵּי 'עֵינֹתָם' "עוֹנֹתָם"

10[8] *When it is My desire, I will chastise them; And the peoples shall be gathered against them, When they are yoked to their two rings*[9].

וְאֶפְרַיִם עֶגְלָה מְלֻמָּדָה אֹהַבְתִּי לָדוּשׁ וַאֲנִי עָבַרְתִּי עַל־טוּב צַוָּארָהּ אַרְכִּיב אֶפְרַיִם יַחֲרוֹשׁ יְהוּדָה יְשַׂדֶּד־לוֹ יַעֲקֹב

11[10] And Ephraim is a *well broken* heifer, *That loves to thresh*, And I have passed over on her fair neck; I will make Ephraim ride, Judah shall plow, Jacob shall break his clods[11].

זִרְעוּ לָכֶם לִצְדָקָה קִצְרוּ לְפִי־חֶסֶד נִירוּ לָכֶם נִיר וְעֵת לִדְרוֹשׁ אֶת־יְהוָה עַד־יָבוֹא וְיֹרֶה צֶדֶק לָכֶם

12[12] Sow according to righteousness, *Reap according to mercy*, Break up your fallow ground; For it is time to seek the LORD, until He comes and causes righteousness to rain on you[13].

חֲרַשְׁתֶּם־רֶשַׁע עַוְלָתָה קְצַרְתֶּם אֲכַלְתֶּם פְּרִי־כָחַשׁ כִּי־בָטַחְתָּ בְדַרְכְּךָ בְּרֹב גִּבּוֹרֶיךָ

13[14] *You have plowed wickedness, you have reaped iniquity, You have eaten the fruit of lies; For you trusted in your way, In the multitude of your mighty men*[15].

וְקָאם שָׁאוֹן בְּעַמֶּךָ וְכָל־מִבְצָרֶיךָ יוּשַּׁד כְּשֹׁד שַׁלְמַן בֵּית אַרְבֵאל בְּיוֹם מִלְחָמָה אֵם עַל־בָּנִים רֻטָּשָׁה

14[16] Therefore, a tumult shall arise among your hosts, And all your fortresses shall be spoiled, As *Shalman spoiled Beth-arbel*[17] in the day of

---

[1] Hosea 10:7 - 1 Kings 21:1, 2 Kings 1:3 15:30 17:4, Hosea 10:3 10:15 13:11, Jude 1:13

[2] LXX *a twig on the surface of*

[3] Hosea 10:8 - 1 Kings 12:28-12:30 13:2 13:34 14:16, 2 Chronicles 7:1 34:5-34:7, 2 Kings 23:15, Amos 8:14, Apocalypse of Elijah 2:33, Deuteronomy 9:21, Hosea 4:13 4:15 5:8 9:6 10:2 10:5, Isaiah 2:19 8:13 10:13, Luke 23:30, Micah 1:5 1:13, Revelation 6:16 9:6

[4] LXX *On*

[5] Hosea 10:9 - Gates of Repentance 3.59, Genesis 6:5 8:21, Hosea 9:9, Judges 19:22-30 20:5 20:13-14 20:17-48, Matthew 23:31-32, Zephaniah 3:6-3:7

[6] LXX *the time the hills existed Israel has sinned*

[7] LXX *war waged against the children of iniquity*

[8] Hosea 10:10 - Deuteronomy 28:63, Ezekiel 5:13 16:37 16:42 23:9 23:46, Hosea 4:9 8:1 8:10, Isaiah 1:24, Jeremiah 15:6 16:16 21:4, Matthew 22:7, Micah 4:10-13, Zechariah 14:2-3

[9] LXX *to chastise them shall not overtake them on the hill, the nations shall be gathered against them, when they are chastened for their two sins*

[10] Hosea 10:11 - 2 Chronicles 28:5-28:8, Avot de R'Natan 23, Deuteronomy 1:4, Genesis.R 48:13 53:3, Guide for the Perplexed 1:70, Hosea 2:5 3:1 4:16 9:1 11:4, Isaiah 4:24, Jeremiah 2:11, Lamentations.R 2:2, Pesikta Rabbati 33:13, Romans 16:18

[11] LXX *taught to love victory, but I will come upon the fairest part of her neck: I will mount Ephraim; I will pass over Juda in silence; Jacob shall prevail against him*

[12] Hosea 10:12 - 1 Corinthians 3:6-7, Acts 2:18, Amos 5:4 5:6 5:8 5:15, b.Avodah Zara 5b, b.Bava Batra [Rashbam] 36a, b.Bava Kamma 14a, b.Bechorot 24a, b.Menachot [Rashi] 85a, b.Succah 49b, Ecclesiastes 11:6, Ein Yaakov Avodah Zarah:5b, Ein Yaakov Sukkah:49a, Ezekiel 10:26, Hosea 6:3 8:7 12:8, Isaiah 5:6 6:23 7:1 8:20 20:3 21:8 7:6, James 3:18, Jeremiah 4:3-4 29:12-14 2:4, Luke 13:24, Mesillat Yesharim 19:Gemillut-Chassidim, Midrash Psalms 30:4 65:4, Pirkei de R'Eliezer 33, Proverbs 11:18 18:21, Psalms 72:6 9:4 126:5-6, Saadia Opinions Intro:3, z.Beshallach 59a, z.Shemot 6a, Zephaniah 2:1-3

[13] LXX *gather in for the fruit of life: light for yourselves the light of knowledge; seek the Lord until the fruits of righteousness come on you*

[14] Hosea 10:13 - 2 Enoch 42:11, Ecclesiastes 9:11, Exodus.R 31:15, Galatians 6:7-6:8, Hosea 7:3 8:7 12:1, Job 4:8, Midrash Tanchuma Mishpatim 12, Proverbs 1:31 12:19 18:20-18:21 19:5 22:8, Psalms 33:16 52:8 62:11

[15] LXX *Why have you passed over ungodliness in silence, and reaped the sins of it? You have eaten false fruit; for thou has trusted in your sins, in the abundance of your power*

[16] Hosea 10:14 - 2 Kings 17:16 18:9-18:10 18:33 19:11-19:13, Amos 3:8 9:5, b.Bava Metzia [Rashi] 39a, b.Bava Metzia 39a, Genesis 8:12, Habakkuk 1:10, Hosea 14:1, Isaiah 13:16-13:18 17:3 22:1-22:4 9:14, Jeremiah 13:14 24:41, Leviticus.R 27:11, Midrash Psalms 22:17 119:32, Midrash Tanchuma Emor 13, Nahum 3:10 3:12, Pesikta de R'Kahana 9.11, Saadia Opinions 7:4 7Variant:5

[17] LXX *a prince Solomon departed out of the house of Jeroboam*

<table>
<tr><td>

בָּכָה עָשָׂה לָכֶם בֵּית־אֵל מִפְּנֵי רָעַת רָעַתְכֶם
בַּשַּׁחַר נִדְמֹה נִדְמָה מֶלֶךְ יִשְׂרָאֵל

</td><td>

15[1]

</td><td>

battle; The mother was dashed in pieces with her children.

So has Bethel done to you Because of your great wickedness; At daybreak the king of Israel is utterly cut off[2].

</td></tr>
</table>

Hosea – Chapter 11

כִּי נַעַר יִשְׂרָאֵל וָאֹהֲבֵהוּ וּמִמִּצְרַיִם קָרָאתִי לִבְנִי	1[3]	[4]When Israel was a child, I loved him, And out of Egypt I called My son.
קָרְאוּ לָהֶם כֵּן הָלְכוּ מִפְּנֵיהֶם לַבְּעָלִים יְזַבֵּחוּ וְלַפְּסִלִים יְקַטֵּרוּן	2[5]	The more they called them, the more they went from them; They sacrificed to the Baalim, And *offered*[6] to graven images.
וְאָנֹכִי תִרְגַּלְתִּי לְאֶפְרַיִם קָחָם עַל־זְרוֹעֹתָיו וְלֹא יָדְעוּ כִּי רְפָאתִים	3[7]	*And I, I taught Ephraim to walk, Taking them by their arms*[8]; But they did not know I healed them.
בְּחַבְלֵי אָדָם אֶמְשְׁכֵם בַּעֲבֹתוֹת אַהֲבָה וָאֶהְיֶה לָהֶם כִּמְרִימֵי עֹל עַל לְחֵיהֶם וְאַט אֵלָיו אוֹכִיל	4[9]	*I drew them with cords of a man*[10], With bands of love; And I was to them as he who removes the yoke from their jaws; *I fed them gently*[11].
לֹא יָשׁוּב אֶל־אֶרֶץ מִצְרַיִם וְאַשּׁוּר הוּא מַלְכּוֹ כִּי מֵאֲנוּ לָשׁוּב	5[12]	He shall not return to the land of Egypt, But the Assyrian shall be his king, Because they refused to return.
וְחָלָה חֶרֶב בְּעָרָיו וְכִלְּתָה בַדָּיו וְאָכָלָה מִמֹּעֲצוֹתֵיהֶם	6[13]	And the sword shall fall upon his cities, *And shall consume his bars, and devour them, Because of their own counsels*[14].
וְעַמִּי תְלוּאִים לִמְשׁוּבָתִי וְאֶל־עַל יִקְרָאֻהוּ יַחַד לֹא יְרוֹמֵם	7[15]	*And My people are in suspense about returning to Me; And though they call them upwards, No one at all will lift himself up*[16].

---

[1] Hosea 10:15 - Amos 7:9-7:17, Hosea 10:3 10:5 10:7, Isaiah 16:14, Mas.Soferim 5:10, Romans 7:13, Song of Songs.R 8:13

[2] LXX *thus will I do to you, O house of Israel, because of the unrighteousness of your sins*

[3] Hosea 11:1 - Deuteronomy 7:7, Deuteronomy.R 5:7, Exodus 4:22, Exodus.R 29:9 43:8, Ezekiel 16:6, Hosea 2:15 12:11 12:15 13:4, Jeremiah 2:2, Malachi 1:2, Matthew 2:15, Numbers.R 12:4, Pesikta de R'Kahana 1.2, Pesikta Rabbati 26:1/2, Sibylline Oracles 3.702, Sifre Devarim Nitzavim 305, Song of Songs.R 3:19, z.Shemot 11b, z.Vayakhel 216a

[4] LXX adds *Early in the morning they were cast off, the king of Israel has been cast off*

[5] Hosea 11:2 - 1 Kings 12:33 16:31-16:32 18:19, 1 Samuel 8:7-8:9, 2 Chronicles 36:15-36:16, 2 Corinthians 2:15-2:16, 2 Kings 17:13-17:16, Acts 7:51, Deuteronomy 29:1-29:3, Hosea 2:13 11:7 13:1-13:2, Isaiah 30:9-30:11 17:7, Jeremiah 18:15 11:13 44:15-44:17, John 3:19, Judges 2:13 3:7 10:6, Luke 13:34, Nehemiah 9:30, Zechariah 1:4 7:11
Hosea 11:2-11 - 4QXIIg

[6] LXX *burnt incense*

[7] Hosea 11:3 - Acts 13:18, Deuteronomy 1:31 8:2 32:10-32:12, Exodus 15:26 19:4 23:25, Gates of Repentance 2.004, Genesis.R 97 [Excl], Hosea 2:8 7:1 7:15 14:6, Isaiah 1:2 6:26 22:3 15:9, Jeremiah 8:22 6:17, Lamentations.R 2:2, Mekhilta de R'Shimon bar Yochai Beshallach 24:2, Mekilta de R'Ishmael Beshallah 5:23, Midrash Tanchuma Beshallach 10, Midrash Tanchuma Vayechi 6, Numbers 11:11-11:12, Pesikta Rabbati 3:4
Hosea 11:3-5 - Josephus Wars 6.9.1

[8] LXX *Yet I bound the feet of Ephraim, I took him on my arm*

[9] Hosea 11:4 - 2 Corinthians 5:14, 2 Samuel 7:14, b.Shabbat 89b, Ein Yaakov Shabbat:89b, Exodus 16:32, Genesis.R 86:1, Hosea 2:8, Isaiah 15:9, Jastrow 63a, Jeremiah 31:3-31:4, John 6:32-6:58 12:32, Leviticus 2:13, mt.Hilchot Issurei Biah 14:2, Pesikta Rabbati 3:4, Psalms 78:23-78:25 9:40, Song of Songs 1:4

[10] LXX *When men were destroyed*

[11] LXX *and I will have respect to him, I will prevail with him*

[12] Hosea 11:5 - 2 Kings 15:19 15:29 17:3-17:6 17:13-17:14 18:11-18:12, Amos 4:6 4:8-4:10 5:27, Hosea 5:13 6:1 7:16 8:13 9:3 9:6 10:6, Isaiah 8:6-8:8, Jeremiah 8:4-8:6, Zechariah 1:4-1:6

[13] Hosea 11:6 - Deuteronomy 4:52 8:25, Ezekiel 15:2-15:7 21:3, Hosea 10:6 10:14 14:1, Isaiah 9:15 18:5 3:10 6:1, Jeremiah 5:17, Leviticus 2:31 2:33, Malachi 3:19, Micah 5:12, Psalms 80:12-80:17 10:39 10:43

[14] LXX *and he ceased to war with his hands: and they shall eat of the fruit of their own devices*

[15] Hosea 11:7 - 2 Chronicles 30:1-30:11, Amos 5:4-5:6 5:14-5:15, Deuteronomy.R 2:19, Hosea 4:16 7:16 11:2 14:6, Jeremiah 3:6-3:8 3:11 8:5 14:7, Proverbs 14:14, Psalms 78:57-78:58 81:12, Ruth.R 1:2 Petichata:7
Hosea 11:7-12:12 - Haftarah Vayetze Sephard [Hosea 11:7-12:12], Haftarah Vayishlach [Hosea 11:7-12:12]
Hosea 11:7-12:14 - Haftarah Vayetze [Teimon]

[16] LXX *and his people shall cleave fondly to their habitation; but God shall be angry with his precious things, and shall not at all exalt him*

אֵיךְ אֶתֶּנְךָ אֶפְרַיִם אֲמַגֶּנְךָ יִשְׂרָאֵל אֵיךְ אֶתֶּנְךָ כְאַדְמָה אֲשִׂימְךָ כִּצְבֹאיִם נֶהְפַּךְ עָלַי לִבִּי יַחַד נִכְמְרוּ נִחוּמָי	8[1]	*How shall I give you up, Ephraim? How shall I surrender you, Israel? How shall I make you as Admah? How shall I set you as Zeboim[2]? My* heart is turned within Me, My compassions are kindled together.
לֹא אֶעֱשֶׂה חֲרוֹן אַפִּי לֹא אָשׁוּב לְשַׁחֵת אֶפְרָיִם כִּי אֵל אָנֹכִי וְלֹא־אִישׁ בְּקִרְבְּךָ קָדוֹשׁ וְלֹא אָבוֹא בְּעִיר	9[3]	I will not execute the fierceness of my anger, I will not return to destroy Ephraim; For I am God, and not man, The Holy One in the midst of you; And I will not *come in fury[4]*.
אַחֲרֵי יְהוָה יֵלְכוּ כְּאַרְיֵה יִשְׁאָג כִּי־הוּא יִשְׁאָג וְיֶחֶרְדוּ בָנִים מִיָּם	10[5]	They shall walk after the LORD, Who shall roar like a lion; For He shall roar, And the *children shall come trembling from the west[6]*.
יֶחֶרְדוּ כְצִפּוֹר מִמִּצְרַיִם וּכְיוֹנָה מֵאֶרֶץ אַשּׁוּר וְהוֹשַׁבְתִּים עַל־בָּתֵּיהֶם נְאֻם־יְהוָה	11[7]	They shall come trembling as a bird out of Egypt, And as a dove out of the land of Assyria; And I will make them dwell in their houses, says the LORD.

Hosea – Chapter 12

סְבָבֻנִי בְכַחַשׁ אֶפְרַיִם וּבְמִרְמָה בֵּית יִשְׂרָאֵל וִיהוּדָה עֹד רָד עִם־אֵל וְעִם־קְדוֹשִׁים נֶאֱמָן	1[8]	*Ephraim encircles Me with lies, And the house of Israel with deceit; And Judah is yet wayward towards God, And towards the Holy One who is faithful[9].*
אֶפְרַיִם רֹעֶה רוּחַ וְרֹדֵף קָדִים כָּל־הַיּוֹם כָּזָב וָשֹׁד יַרְבֶּה וּבְרִית עִם־אַשּׁוּר יִכְרֹתוּ וְשֶׁמֶן לְמִצְרַיִם יוּבָל	2[10]	*Ephraim strives after wind, and follows after the east wind; All the day he multiplies lies and desolation; And they make a covenant with Assyria, And oil is carried into Egypt[11].*
וְרִיב לַיהוָה עִם־יְהוּדָה וְלִפְקֹד עַל־יַעֲקֹב כִּדְרָכָיו כְּמַעֲלָלָיו יָשִׁיב לוֹ	3[12]	The LORD has also a controversy with Judah, And will punish Jacob according to his ways, According to his acts He will recompense him.

---

[1] Hosea 11:8 - 2 Kings 13:23, 2 Peter 2:6, 2 Samuel 24:16, Amos 4:11 7:3 7:6, Deuteronomy 5:22 8:36, Genesis 14:8 19:24-19:25, Hosea 6:4, Isaiah 1:9-1:10 15:15, Jeremiah 3:12 9:8 7:21, Jude 1:7, Judges 10:16, Lamentations 1:20 3:33, Luke 19:41-19:42, Matthew 23:37, Psalms 10:45, Revelation 11:8 18:18, Zephaniah 2:9

[2] LXX *How shall I deal with you, Ephraim? how shall I protect you, Israel? what shall I do with you? I will make you as Adama, and as Seboim*

[3] Hosea 11:9 - 1 Samuel 2:8, 2 Samuel 20:10, b.Taanit 5a 11b, Deuteronomy 13:18 32:26-32:27, Ein Yaakov Taanit:11b 5a, Exodus 32:10-32:14, Ezekiel 20:8-20:9 20:13-20:14 20:21-20:23 37:27-37:28, Hosea 14:6, Isaiah 12:6 27:4-27:8 24:9 55:8-55:9, Jeremiah 6:11 31:2-31:4, Leviticus.R 6:1 6:5, Malachi 3:6, Mekilta de R'Ishmael Shirata 4:72, Micah 7:18-7:20, Midrash Psalms 6:3 122:4, Midrash Tanchuma Pekudei 1, Numbers 23:19, Psalms 78:38, Romans 11:28-11:29, Sifre Devarim Ha'azinu Hashamayim 306, Sifre Devarim Nitzavim 306, Testament of Levi 5:2, z.Naso 147b, z.Pekudei 224b, Zephaniah 3:15-3:17

[4] LXX *enter into the city*

[5] Hosea 11:10 - 2 Peter 2:10, Acts 24:25, Amos 1:2 3:4 3:8, b.Berachot 6b, Ein Yaakov Berachot:6b, Guide for the Perplexed 1:38, Habakkuk 3:16, Hosea 3:5 6:1-6:3, Isaiah 2:5 7:4 18:13 1:10 16:3, Jeremiah 2:2 5:22 7:6 7:9 1:30 7:10 9:9, Job 13:1, Joel 4:16, John 8:12, Mesillat Yesharim 7:Elements of Zerizus, Micah 4:5, Numbers.R 13:4, Psalms 2:11 119:120, Romans 8:1, z.Mishpatim 102b, z.Vayechi 223a, z.Vayetze 160a, Zechariah 8:7 10:12

[6] LXX *children of the waters shall be amazed*

[7] Hosea 11:11 - Amos 9:14-9:15, Exodus.R 20:6, Ezekiel 28:25-28:26 36:33-36:34 13:21 13:25, Hosea 3:5 7:11 9:3-9:6, Isaiah 11:11 12:8, Jeremiah 7:13, Obadiah 1:17, Song of Songs.R 1:64 4:2, Zechariah 10:10, 2 Kings 18:4-18:7, Genesis 8:29, Hosea 4:2 4:15 7:16 12:3 12:9, Isaiah 5:13 20:20 59:3-59:4, Micah 6:12, Psalms 78:36, z.Vayechi 237a

[8] Hosea 12:1 - 1 Corinthians 6:2, 2 Chronicles 29:1-29:32, b.Sotah 37a, Deuteronomy.R 11:10, Ein Yaakov Sotah:37a, Mekhilta de R'Shimon bar Yochai Beshallach 25:1, Mekhilta de R'Ishmael Beshallah 6:30 6:65, Midrash Psalms 76:2, Revelation 1:6 3:21 5:10, Sifre Devarim Ha'azinu Hashamayim 306, Sifre Devarim Nitzavim 306, z.Vayetze 155b, z.Yitro 85a Hosea 12:1-15 - 4QXIIg

[9] LXX *But Ephraim is an evil spirit, he has chased the east wind all the day: he has multiplied empty and vain things, and made a covenant with the Assyrians, and oil has gone in the way of traffic into Egypt*

[10] Hosea 12:2 - 2 Kings 15:19 17:4-17:6, Ezekiel 17:10, Hosea 5:13 8:7 12:1, Isaiah 30:6-30:7, Jastrow 1487a, Jeremiah 22:22, Job 15:2, Lamentations.R 3:? 5:6, z.Haazinu 299a

[11] Missing in LXX

[12] Hosea 12:3 - 2 Kings 17:19-17:20, Ezekiel 23:11-23:21 23:31-23:32, Galatians 6:7, Hosea 2:13 4:1 4:9 8:13 9:9, Isaiah 3:11 8:7-8:8 10:6 10:12 24:21 11:18, Jeremiah 3:8-3:11 1:31, Leviticus.R 27:6, Matthew 16:27, Micah 6:2, Midrash Tanchuma Emor 10, Numbers.R 10:1, Pesikta de R'Kahana 9.5, Prayer of Joseph Fragment A, Romans 2:6, Song of Songs.R 6:2

בְּבֶטֶן עָקַב אֶת־אָחִיו וּבְאוֹנוֹ שָׂרָה אֶת־אֱלֹהִים

4[1]

In the womb he took his brother by the heel, *And by his strength he strove with a godlike being*[2];

וַיָּשַׂר אֶל־מַלְאָךְ וַיֻּכָל בָּכָה וַיִּתְחַנֶּן־לוֹ בֵּית־אֵל יִמְצָאֶנּוּ וְשָׁם יְדַבֵּר עִמָּנוּ

5[3]

So he strove with an angel, and prevailed; He wept, and made a plea to him; At *Bethel*[4] he found him, And there he would speak with us;

וַיהוָה אֱלֹהֵי הַצְּבָאוֹת יְהוָה זִכְרוֹ

6[5]

But the LORD, the God of hosts, The LORD is His name[6].

וְאַתָּה בֵּאלֹהֶיךָ תָשׁוּב חֶסֶד וּמִשְׁפָּט שְׁמֹר וְקַוֵּה אֶל־אֱלֹהֶיךָ תָּמִיד

7[7]

Therefore. turn to your God; Keep mercy and justice, And wait for your God continually.

כְּנַעַן בְּיָדוֹ מֹאזְנֵי מִרְמָה לַעֲשֹׁק אָהֵב

8[8]

As for *the trafficker*[9], the balances of deceit are in his hand. He loves to oppress.

וַיֹּאמֶר אֶפְרַיִם אַךְ עָשַׁרְתִּי מָצָאתִי אוֹן לִי כָּל־יְגִיעַי לֹא יִמְצְאוּ־לִי עָוֹן אֲשֶׁר־חֵטְא

9[10]

And Ephraim said: 'Surely I have become rich, I have found myself wealth; In all my labors they shall find in me No iniquity that were sin.'

וְאָנֹכִי יְהוָה אֱלֹהֶיךָ מֵאֶרֶץ מִצְרָיִם עֹד אוֹשִׁיבְךָ בָאֳהָלִים כִּימֵי מוֹעֵד

10[11]

But I am the LORD your God From the land of Egypt; I will yet again make you to dwell in tents, As in the days *of the appointed season*[12].

וְדִבַּרְתִּי עַל־הַנְּבִיאִים וְאָנֹכִי חָזוֹן הִרְבֵּיתִי וּבְיַד הַנְּבִיאִים אֲדַמֶּה

11[13]

I have also spoken to the prophets, And I have increased visions; And by the ministry of the prophets have I *used similitudes*[14].

אִם־גִּלְעָד אָוֶן אַךְ־שָׁוְא הָיוּ בַּגִּלְגָּל שְׁוָרִים זִבֵּחוּ גַּם מִזְבְּחוֹתָם כְּגַלִּים עַל תַּלְמֵי שָׂדָי

12[15]

If Gilead is given to iniquity Becoming altogether vain, In Gilgal they sacrifice to bullocks[16]; Yea, their altars shall be as heaps In the furrows of the field.

---

[1] Hosea 12:4 - Genesis 1:26 32:25-32:28, James 5:16-5:18, Leviticus.R 27:6, Midrash Tanchuma Emor 10, Romans 9:11, Song of Songs.R 6:2, z.Haazinu 299a, z.Toledot 138a

[2] LXX *and in his labors he had power with God*

[3] Hosea 12:5 - 1 Thessalonians 4:17, Acts 7:30-35, b.Chullin 92a, Exodus 3:2-5, Genesis 28:11-28:19 32:10-12 8:30 35:9-10 11:15 24:15, Genesis.R 78:2 82:2, Hebrews 5:7 6:13-18, Isaiah 15:9, Malachi 3:1, Midrash Psalms 91:6 112:2, Midrash Tanchuma Vayishlach 4, Numbers.R 3:6, Psalms 66:6

[4] LXX *house of On*

[5] Hosea 12:6 - Exodus 3:15, Exodus.R 25:2, Genesis 4:16 8:31, Isaiah 18:8, Psalms 15:13

[6] LXX *But the LORD God Almighty shall be his memorial*

[7] Hosea 12:7 - Acts 2:38 2:20, Amos 5:24, Genesis 1:18, Habakkuk 2:3, Hosea 4:1 6:1-6:3 10:12 14:3, Isaiah 1:16 8:17 6:18 7:6 16:31 55:6-55:7 10:6, James 1:27 2:13, Jeremiah 3:14-3:22 22:15, Joel 2:13, Lamentations 3:25-3:26 3:39-3:41, Mas.Soferim 4:9, Micah 6:8 7:7, Pirkei de R'Eliezer 16, Proverbs 1:23 21:3, Psalms 27:14 37:7 3:2 130:5-130:7, Zechariah 1:3 7:9 8:16, Zephaniah 3:8

[8] Hosea 12:8 - 1 Samuel 12:3, 1 Timothy 6:9-6:10, Amos 2:7 3:9 4:1 5:11 8:5-8:6, b.Bava Batra 75a, b.Pesachim 50a, Ein Yaakov Bava Batra:75a, Ezekiel 16:3 22:29, Genesis.R 59:9, Isaiah 3:5, James 5:4, Jastrow 1623b, John 2:16, Leviticus 19:35-19:36, Malachi 3:5, Micah 2:1 3:1-3:3 6:10-6:11 7:2, Proverbs 11:1 16:11, Pseudo-Phocylides 12, Zechariah 14:21

[9] LXX *Chanaan*

[10] Hosea 12:9 - 1 Timothy 6:5 6:17, Deuteronomy 8:17, Habakkuk 1:16 2:5-6, Isaiah 10:13-14, Jeremiah 2:23 2:35, Job 31:24-25, Luke 10:29 12:19 16:13 16:15, Malachi 2:17 3:13, Proverbs 6:12 6:20, Psalms 49:7 52:8 62:11, Revelation 3:17, Zechariah 11:5

[11] Hosea 12:10 - 2 Samuel 7:2, Exodus 20:2, Ezra 3:4, Genesis 1:27, Guide for the Perplexed 1:Introduction, Hebrews 11:9-11:13, Hosea 13:4, Jeremiah 11:7, John 7:2, Leviticus 19:36 23:40-23:43 2:13, Micah 6:4, Nehemiah 8:15-8:17, Numbers 15:41, Numbers.R 11:2, Pesikta de R'Kahana 5.8, Pesikta Rabbati 15:10, Psalms 81:11, Ruth.R 5:6, Song of Songs.R 2:25, Zechariah 14:16-14:19

[12] 4QXIIg *that I brought you up for the appointed holidays*

[13] Hosea 12:11 - 1 Kings 13:1 14:7-16 17:1 18:21-40 19:10, 2 Corinthians 12:1 12:7, 2 Kings 17:13, Acts 2:17, Amos 7:14, Ezekiel 4:1-5 15:1-8 21:5, Hosea 1:2-5 3:1, Isaiah 5:1-7 20:2-5, Jeremiah 7:25 13:1-14 19:1 19:10 1:4, Joel 3:1, Leviticus.R 1:14, Mekhilta de R'Shimon bar Yochai Shirata 29:1, Mekhilta de R'Ishmael Shirata 3:31, Nehemiah 9:30, Numbers 12:6, Pesikta Rabbati 33:11, z.Bechukkotai 112b, z.Bo 42b

[14] LXX *was represented*

[15] Hosea 12:12 - 1 Kings 17:1, 2 Kings 17:9-11, Amos 4:4 5:5, b.Sanhedrin 102b, Deuteronomy.R 2:19 10:4, Ein Yaakov Sanhedrin 102b, Hosea 4:15 6:8 8:11 9:15 10:1, Jeremiah 2:20 2:28 10:8 10:15, Jonah 2:8, Lamentations.R Petichata D'Chakimei 22, Midrash Psalms 101:4, Numbers.R 12:18, Pesikta de R'Kahana 1.8, Pirkei de R'Eliezer 29 36, Sifre Devarim Ha'azinu Hashamayim 306, Sifre Devarim Nitzavim 306, Song of Songs.R 6:15

[16] LXX *If Galaad did not exist, then the chiefs in Galaad when they sacrificed were false*

וַיִּבְרַ֥ח יַעֲקֹ֖ב שְׂדֵ֣ה אֲרָ֑ם וַיַּעֲבֹ֤ד יִשְׂרָאֵל֙ בְּאִשָּׁ֔ה וּבְאִשָּׁ֖ה שָׁמָֽר	13[1]	And Jacob fled into the field of *Aram, And Israel served for a wife, And for a wife he kept sheep*[2].
וּבְנָבִ֕יא הֶעֱלָ֧ה יְהוָ֛ה אֶת־יִשְׂרָאֵ֖ל מִמִּצְרָ֑יִם וּבְנָבִ֖יא נִשְׁמָֽר	14[3]	And by a prophet the LORD brought Israel up out of Egypt, And by a prophet was he kept.
הִכְעִ֥יס אֶפְרַ֖יִם תַּמְרוּרִ֑ים וְדָמָיו֙ עָלָ֣יו יִטּ֔וֹשׁ וְחֶ֨רְפָּת֔וֹ יָשִׁ֥יב ל֖וֹ אֲדֹנָֽיו	15[4]	Ephraim provokes most bitterly; Therefore, his blood shall be cast upon him; And in his reproach shall his Lord return to him.

Hosea – Chapter 13

כְּדַבֵּ֤ר אֶפְרַ֙יִם֙ רְתֵ֔ת נָשָׂ֥א ה֖וּא בְּיִשְׂרָאֵ֑ל וַיֶּאְשַׁ֥ם בַּבַּ֖עַל וַיָּמֹֽת	1[5]	When Ephraim spoke, *there was trembling, He exalted himself in Israel*[6]; But when he became guilty through Baal, he died.
וְעַתָּ֣ה ׀ יוֹסִ֣פוּ לַחֲטֹ֗א וַיַּעֲשׂ֣וּ לָהֶם֩ מַסֵּכָ֨ה מִכַּסְפָּ֤ם כִּתְבוּנָם֙ עֲצַבִּ֔ים מַעֲשֵׂ֥ה חָרָשִׁ֖ים כֻּלֹּ֑ה לָהֶם֙ הֵ֣ם אֹמְרִ֔ים זֹבְחֵ֣י אָדָ֔ם עֲגָלִ֖ים יִשָּׁקֽוּן	2[7]	And now they sin more and more, And have made molten images of their silver, According to their own understanding, idols, All of them the work of the craftsmen; Of those they say: '*Those who sacrifice men kiss calves*[8].'
לָכֵ֗ן יִֽהְיוּ֙ כַּעֲנַן־בֹּ֔קֶר וְכַטַּ֖ל מַשְׁכִּ֣ים הֹלֵ֑ךְ כְּמֹץ֙ יְסֹעֵ֣ר מִגֹּ֔רֶן וּכְעָשָׁ֖ן מֵאֲרֻבָּֽה	3[9]	Therefore, they shall be as the morning cloud, And as the dew that passes away early, As the chaff that is driven with the wind out of the threshing floor, *And as the smoke out of the window*[10].
וְאָנֹכִ֛י יְהוָ֥ה אֱלֹהֶ֖יךָ מֵאֶ֣רֶץ מִצְרָ֑יִם וֵאלֹהִ֤ים זֽוּלָתִי֙ לֹ֣א תֵדָ֔ע וּמוֹשִׁ֥יעַ אַ֖יִן בִּלְתִּֽי	4[11]	Yet I am the LORD your God[12] from the land of Egypt; And you know no God but Me, And beside Me there is no savior.
אֲנִ֥י יְדַעְתִּ֖יךָ בַּמִּדְבָּ֑ר בְּאֶ֖רֶץ תַּלְאֻבֽוֹת	5[13]	I knew you in the wilderness, in the land of great drought.
כְּמַרְעִיתָם֙ וַיִּשְׂבָּ֔עוּ שָׂבְע֖וּ וַיָּ֣רָם לִבָּ֑ם עַל־כֵּ֖ן שְׁכֵחֽוּנִי	6[14]	When they were fed, they became full, They were filled, and their heart was exalted; Therefore, they have forgotten Me.

---

[1] Hosea 12:13 - Deuteronomy 2:5, Genesis 3:43 28:1-22 29:18-28 7:41 32:28-28, Genesis.R 70:20, Mekilta de R'Ishmael Bahodesh 3:39, Midrash Psalms 3:3, Midrash Tanchuma Massei 1, Midrash Tanchuma Shemini 2, Midrash Tanchuma Vayechi 6, Numbers.R 23:1, Siman 79:6, z.Vayetze 151b
Hosea 12:13-14:10 - Haftarah Vayetze [Ashkenaz], Haftarah Vayetze [Hosea 12:13-14:10]
[2] LXX *Syria, and Israel served for a wife, and waited for a wife*
[3] Hosea 12:14 - 1 Samuel 12:8, Acts 3:22-23 7:35-37, Amos 2:11-12, Exodus 12:50-51 13:3, Hosea 13:4-13:5, Isaiah 63:11-14, Micah 6:4, Pesikta Rabbati 4:2, Psalms 77:21
[4] Hosea 12:15 - 1 Kings 2:33-34, 1 Samuel 2:30, 2 Kings 17:7-18, 2 Samuel 1:16, Daniel 11:18, Deuteronomy 4:37, Ezekiel 18:13 23:2-10 24:7-8 9:5, Hosea 7:16
[5] Hosea 13:1 - 1 Kings 12:25 16:29-33 18:18-18:19, 1 Samuel 15:17, 2 Corinthians 5:14, 2 Kings 17:16-18, 4QXIIg, Genesis 2:17, Hosea 11:2, Isaiah 18:2, Jastrow 129a 1478b, Joshua 3:7, Judges 8:1 12:1, Leviticus.R 12:5, Luke 14:11, Numbers 2:18-21 10:22 13:8 13:16 27:16-23, Pesikta Rabbati 4:2, Proverbs 18:12, Romans 5:12, Yalkut Psalms 214
[6] LXX *he adopted ordinances for himself in Israel*
[7] Hosea 13:2 - 1 Kings 19:18, 1 Samuel 10:1, 2 Chronicles 4:13 9:23, 2 Timothy 3:13, b.Sanhedrin 63b, Gates of Repentance 2.17, Habakkuk 2:18-19, Hosea 2:8 8:4 8:6 10:1 11:6, Isaiah 1:5 6:1 44:17-20 21:20 22:6 22:8, Jeremiah 10:4 10:8, Numbers 8:14, Pesikta de R'Kahana 24.1, Psalms 2:12 115:4-8 135:17-135:18, Romans 1:22-25 2:5 11:4
[8] LXX *Sacrifice men, for the calves have come to an end*
[9] Hosea 13:3 - Daniel 2:35, Hosea 6:4, Isaiah 17:13 41:15-16, Psalms 1:4 68:3 83:13-18
Hosea 13:3-10 - 4QXIIc
[10] LXX *and as a vapor from tears*
[11] Hosea 13:4 - Acts 4:12, Exodus 20:2-20:3, Hosea 12:11, Isaiah 19:3 43:10-13 44:6-8 45:21-22, Psalms 81:10-11, z.Kedoshim 84b
[12] 4QXIIg LXX adds *who fortifies Heaven and creates the Earth, whose hands made the whole host of Heaven, but I will show them to you go afer them, but I brought you up*
[13] Hosea 13:5 - 1 Corinthians 8:3, Deuteronomy 2:7 8:15 8:10, Exodus 2:25, Galatians 4:9, Jeremiah 2:2 2:6, Mesillat Yesharim Afterword, Nahum 1:7, Psalms 1:6 31:8 63:2 22:4
[14] Hosea 13:6 - b.Berachot 32a, b.Succah 52b, Deuteronomy 6:10-12 8:12-14 32:13-15 8:18, Ein Yaakov Berachot:32a, Ein Yaakov Sukkah:52b, Hosea 2:13 8:4 10:1, Isaiah 17:10, Jeremiah 2:31-32, Nehemiah 9:25-26 9:35, Psalms 10:5, Saadia Opinions 10:5
Hosea 13:6-8 - 4QXIIg

וָאֱהִי לָהֶם כְּמוֹ־שָׁחַל כְּנָמֵר עַל־דֶּרֶךְ אָשׁוּר

7[1]

Therefore, I became to them as a *lion; As a leopard I will watch by the way*[2];

אֶפְגְּשֵׁם כְּדֹב שַׁכּוּל וְאֶקְרַע סְגוֹר לִבָּם וְאֹכְלֵם שָׁם כְּלָבִיא חַיַּת הַשָּׂדֶה תְּבַקְּעֵם

8[3]

I will meet them *as a bear that is bereaved of her whelps, And will rend the enclosure of their heart; And there I will devour them like a lioness; The wild beast shall tear them*[4].

שִׁחֶתְךָ יִשְׂרָאֵל כִּי־בִי בְעֶזְרֶךָ

9[5]

It is your destruction, O Israel, that you are against Me, against your help[6].

אֱהִי מַלְכְּךָ אֵפוֹא וְיוֹשִׁיעֲךָ בְּכָל־עָרֶיךָ וְשֹׁפְטֶיךָ אֲשֶׁר אָמַרְתָּ תְּנָה־לִּי מֶלֶךְ וְשָׂרִים

10[7]

Look now, your king[8], So he may save you in all your cities! And your judges, of whom you said: 'Give me a king and princes!'

אֶתֶּן־לְךָ מֶלֶךְ בְּאַפִּי וְאֶקַּח בְּעֶבְרָתִי

11[9]

I gave you a king in My anger, And I take him away in My wrath.

צָרוּר עֲוֺן אֶפְרָיִם צְפוּנָה חַטָּאתוֹ

12[10]

The iniquity of Ephraim is bound up; His sin is *laid up in store*[11].

חֶבְלֵי יוֹלֵדָה יָבֹאוּ לוֹ הוּא־בֵן לֹא חָכָם כִּי־עֵת לֹא־יַעֲמֹד בְּמִשְׁבַּר בָּנִים

13[12]

The throes of a travailing woman shall come upon him; *He is an unwise son; For it is time he should not tarry In the place of the breaking forth of children*[13].

מִיַּד שְׁאוֹל אֶפְדֵּם מִמָּוֶת אֶגְאָלֵם אֱהִי דְבָרֶיךָ מָוֶת אֱהִי קָטָבְךָ שְׁאוֹל נֹחַם יִסָּתֵר מֵעֵינָי

14[14]

Shall I ransom them from the power of the nether-world? Shall I redeem them from death? O your plagues, O death! O your destruction, O netherworld! Repentance is hid from My eyes!

כִּי הוּא בֵּן אַחִים יַפְרִיא יָבוֹא קָדִים רוּחַ יְהוָה מִמִּדְבָּר עֹלֶה וְיֵבוֹשׁ מְקוֹרוֹ וְיֶחֱרַב מַעְיָנוֹ הוּא יִשְׁסֶה אוֹצַר כָּל־כְּלִי חֶמְדָּה

15[15]

For though he is fruitful among the reed plants, An east wind shall come, the wind of the LORD coming up from the wilderness, And his spring shall become dry, and his fountain shall be dried up; He shall spoil the treasure of all precious vessels[16].

---

[1] Hosea 13:7 - Amos 1:2 3:4 3:8, Hosea 5:14, Isaiah 18:13, Jeremiah 5:6, Lamentations 3:10, Pesikta Rabbati 29/30B:2

[2] LXX *panther, and as a leopard*

[3] Hosea 13:8 - 2 Samuel 17:8, Amos 9:1-3, Isaiah 5:29 8:9, Jeremiah 12:9, Midrash Tanchuma Shelach 9, Proverbs 17:12, Psalms 50:22 80:14

[4] LXX *by the way of the Assyrians, as a she-bear excited, and I will rend the caul of their heart, and the lions' whelps of the thicket shall devour them there; the wild beasts of the field shall rend them in pieces*

[5] Hosea 13:9 - 2 Kings 17:7-17, Deuteronomy 9:26 9:29, Ephesians 1:3-5, Hosea 13:4 14:3, Isaiah 3:9 3:11, Jeremiah 2:17 2:19 4:18 5:25, Malachi 1:9, Proverbs 6:32 8:36, Psalms 33:20 46:2 121:1-2 2:5, Titus 3:3-7

[6] LXX *O Israel, who will aid you in your destruction?*

[7] Hosea 13:10 - 1 Kings 12:20, 1 Samuel 8:5-8:6 8:19-8:20 12:11-12:12, 2 Kings 17:4, Deuteronomy 32:37-32:39, Hosea 8:4 10:3 13:4, Isaiah 9:22 19:15, Jeremiah 2:28 8:19, John 1:49, Judges 2:16-2:18, Psalms 10:17 44:5 47:7-47:8 74:12 89:19 5:2, Tanna Devei Eliyahu 6, Zechariah 14:9

[8] LXX *Where is this you king?*

[9] Hosea 13:11 - 1 Kings 12:15-12:16 12:26-12:32 14:7-14:16, 1 Samuel 8:7-8:9 10:19 12:13 15:22-15:23 16:1 31:1-31:7, 2 Kings 17:1-17:4, Hosea 10:3 10:7, Pesikta Rabbati 33:13, Proverbs 4:2 Hosea 13:11-13 - 4QXIIg

[10] Hosea 13:12 - Deuteronomy 32:34-32:35, Job 14:17 21:19, Pesikta de R'Kahana 24.1, Pesikta Rabbati 44:2, Romans 2:5

[11] LXX *hidden*

[12] Hosea 13:13 - 1 Thessalonians 5:3, 2 Corinthians 6:2, 2 Kings 19:3, Acts 16:29-16:34 24:25, b.Shabbat [Rashi] 118a, b.Sotah [Rashi] 11b, Hebrews 3:7-3:8, Isaiah 13:8 21:3 2:17 13:3 18:9, Jeremiah 4:31 13:21 22:23 6:6 1:24, Micah 4:9-4:10, mt.Hilchot Tefilah 7:1, Pesikta de R'Kahana 3.d, Proverbs 22:3, Psalms 48:7

[13] LXX *he is your wise son, because he shall not stay in the destruction of your children*

[14] Hosea 13:14 - 1 Corinthians 15:21-22 15:52-57, 1 Samuel 15:29, 1 Thessalonians 4:14, 2 Corinthians 5:4, b.Pesachim 87b, b.Yevamot [Rashi] 14a, b.Yevamot 14a, Ein Yaakov Pesachim:87b, Ezekiel 37:11-14, Hosea 6:2, Isaiah 1:8 2:19, James 1:17, Jastrow 72a, Jeremiah 15:6, Job 19:25-27 9:24, Malachi 3:6, Midrash Psalms 116:3 140:1, Midrash Tanchuma Tzav 2, Numbers 23:19, Philippians 3:21, Psalms 16:10 30:4 49:16 71:20 86:13, Revelation 20:13 21:4, Romans 11:15 11:29

[15] Hosea 13:15 - 4QXIIc, b.Gittin 31b, b.Shabbat [Rashi] 116b, b.Yevamot [Rashi] 114a, Daniel 11:8, Deuteronomy 9:17, Ein Yaakov Gittin:31b, Ezekiel 17:10 19:12, Genesis 17:52 24:19 1:22, Hosea 4:19 9:11 10:1, Isaiah 14:21 17:13 17:16, Jeremiah 4:11 20:5 3:36, Job 18:16, Mekhilta de R'Shimon bar Yochai Beshallach 24:4, Mekilta de R'Ishmael Beshallah 5:92, Nahum 2:10, Pirkei de R'Eliezer 53, Psalms 1:4 13:13

[16] LXX *For though he will cause a division among his brethren, the LORD shall bring upon him an east wind from the desert, and shall dry up his veins and quite drain his fountains: he shall dry up his land, and spoil all his precious vessels*

Hosea – Chapter 14

תֵּאְשַׁם שֹׁמְרֹון כִּי מָרְתָה בֵּאלֹהֶיהָ בַּחֶרֶב יִפֹּלוּ עֹלְלֵיהֶם יְרֻטָּשׁוּ וְהָרִיֹּותָיו יְבֻקָּעוּ

1[1] Samaria shall *bear her guilt*[2], For she has rebelled against her God; They shall fall by the sword; Their infants shall be dashed in pieces, and their pregnant women shall be ripped open.

שׁוּבָה יִשְׂרָאֵל עַד יְהוָה אֱלֹהֶיךָ כִּי כָשַׁלְתָּ בַּעֲוֹנֶךָ

2[3] Return, O Israel, to the LORD your God; For you have stumbled in your iniquity.

קְחוּ עִמָּכֶם דְּבָרִים וְשׁוּבוּ אֶל־יְהוָה אִמְרוּ אֵלָיו כָּל־תִּשָּׂא עָוֹן וְקַח־טֹוב וּנְשַׁלְּמָה פָרִים שְׂפָתֵינוּ

3[4] Take with you words, And return to the LORD; Say to Him: '*Forgive all iniquity, And accept what is good; So we will render for bullocks the offering of our lips*[5].

אַשּׁוּר לֹא יֹושִׁיעֵנוּ עַל־סוּס לֹא נִרְכָּב וְלֹא־נֹאמַר עֹוד אֱלֹהֵינוּ לְמַעֲשֵׂה יָדֵינוּ אֲשֶׁר־בְּךָ יְרֻחַם יָתֹום

4[6] Asshur shall not save us; We will not ride upon horses; nor longer shall we call as gods the work of our hands; For in You the fatherless finds mercy.'

אֶרְפָּא מְשׁוּבָתָם אֹהֲבֵם נְדָבָה כִּי שָׁב אַפִּי מִמֶּנּוּ

5[7] I will *heal their backsliding*[8], I will love them freely; For My anger is turned away from him.

אֶהְיֶה כַטַּל לְיִשְׂרָאֵל יִפְרַח כַּשֹּׁושַׁנָּה וְיַךְ שָׁרָשָׁיו כַּלְּבָנֹון

6[9] I will be as the dew to Israel; He shall blossom as the lily, And cast forth his roots as Lebanon.

יֵלְכוּ יֹנְקֹותָיו וִיהִי כַזַּיִת הֹודֹו וְרֵיחַ לֹו כַּלְּבָנֹון

7[10] His branches shall spread, his beauty shall be as the olive tree, And his fragrance as Lebanon.

---

[1] Hosea 14:1 - 2 Kings 8:12 15:16 17:6 17:18 19:9-11, Amos 1:13 3:9-4:1 6:1-8 9:1, Hosea 7:14 10:2 10:14-15 11:6, Isaiah 7:8-7:9 8:4 13:16 17:3, Jastrow 1240b, Mas.Soferim 4:9, Micah 1:4 6:16, Nahum 3:10, Pesikta de R'Kahana 24.10-11, Pesikta Rabbati 44:2 50:4, Pirkei de R'Eliezer 43, Psalms 137:8-9, variant עלליהם of עלליה is found
Hosea 14:1-6 - 4QXIIc
Hosea 14:1-10 - Shabbat Shuvah [Pesikta Rabbati 44 50]
[2] LXX *be utterly destroyed*
[3] Hosea 14:2 - 1 Samuel 7:3-4, 2 Chronicles 30:6-9, Acts 26:18-20, b.Yoma 86ab, Chibbur Yafeh 27 128a, Ein Yaakov Yoma:86a 86b, Ezekiel 28:14-16, Genesis.R 84:19, Hosea 5:5 6:1 12:8 13:9, Isaiah 55:6-7, Jastrow 1691a, Jeremiah 2:19 3:12-14 4:1, Joel 2:12-13, Lamentations 5:16, Midrash Proverbs 6, Midrash Tanchuma Tazria 9, mt.Hilchot Teshuvah 7:6, Odes of Solomon 8:2, Pesikta de R'Kahana 24.1-13 24.17, Pesikta Rabbati 44:1-10 50:1-6, Pirkei de R'Eliezer 43, Psalms of Solomon 15:3, Saadia Opinions 5:5, Selichot, Tanya Igeret Hateshuvah §01, Zechariah 1:3-4
Hosea 14:2-10 - Haftarah Minchah [Tisha B'Av; continues at Micah 7:18-20 [Sephard and Teimon]], Haftarah Shabbat Shuva [either Vayilech or Haazinu; continues with Micah 7:18 [Sephard]; continues with Joel 2:15 Ashkenaz], Shabbat Shuvah Part One Haftarah, Tisha B'Av Afternoon Sephard Part Two Haftarah
[4] Hosea 14:3 - 1 John 1:7 3:5, 1 Peter 2:5 2:9, 2 Samuel 12:13 24:10, 2 Timothy 1:9, b.Yoma [Rashi] 36b, b.Yoma 36b 86b, Chibbur Yafeh 27 129b, Ecclesiastes.R 10:9, Ein Yaakov Yoma:86b, Ephesians 1:6-1:7 2:7-2:8, Exodus.R 21:10 38:4, Ezekiel 36:25-36:26, Gates of Repentance 1.041 1.041, Genesis.R 16:5, Hebrews 10:4 13:15, Isaiah 6:7, Jastrow 1655a, Job 7:21 34:31-34:32, Joel 2:17, John 1:29, Luke 11:2-11:4 11:13 15:21-15:24 18:13, Matthew 6:9-6:13 7:11, Micah 7:18-7:19, Midrash Psalms 23:3 37:3 118:3, Midrash Tanchuma Acharei Mot 10, Midrash Tanchuma Korach 1 12, Midrash Tanchuma Tzav 6, Numbers.R 18:2 18:21, Pesikta de R'Kahana 24.18 24.19, Pesikta Rabbati 44:2 44:5 44:7 44:9 50:3, Psalms 51:3-51:11 69:31-69:32, Romans 11:27, Saadia Opinions 5:5 5:5, Sifre Devarim Ha'azinu Hashamayim 306, Sifre Devarim Nitzavim 306, Song of Songs.R 4:12, Titus 2:14, Zechariah 3:4
[5] LXX *that you may not receive the reward of unrighteousness, but that you may receive good things: and we will render in return the fruit of our lips*
[6] Hosea 14:4 - 2 Chronicles 16:7, b.Pesachim 112b, Chibbur Yafeh 27 125b, Deuteronomy 17:16, Exodus 22:22-22:24, Ezekiel 12:25 13:23 43:7-43:9, Hosea 2:17 5:13 7:11 8:6 8:9 12:3 14:10, Isaiah 1:29 2:20 3:9 6:2 6:16 7:1 7:3 12:8, Jeremiah 31:19-31:23, John 14:18, Micah 5:11-5:15, mt.Hilchot Teshuvah 2:2 2:2, Proverbs 23:10-23:11, Psalms 10:15 20:8-20:9 33:17 68:6 2:3 2:9, Saadia Opinions 5:5 5:5, Zechariah 13:2
[7] Hosea 14:5 - 2 Corinthians 5:19-21, 2 Timothy 1:9, 4 Ezra 5:24, b.Pesachim 86a, b.Yoma 86b, Chibbur Yafeh 27 126a, Deuteronomy 7:7-8, Ein Yaakov Yoma:86b, Ephesians 1:6 2:4-9, Exodus 15:26, Exodus.R 48:6, Gates of Repentance 1.23 1.42, Hosea 6:1 11:7, Isaiah 12:1 9:18, Jeremiah 3:22 5:6 8:22 14:7 17:14 9:6, Matthew 9:12-13, Midrash Proverbs 1, Midrash Psalms 85:3, Midrash Tanchuma Bamidbar 17, Midrash Tanchuma Ekev 3, Midrash Tanchuma Pekudei 9, Numbers 1:4 1:11, Numbers.R 10:1, Psalms 78:38, Romans 3:24, Saadia Opinions 5:5, Shemonah Perachim III, Titus 3:4, z.Acharei Mot 74a, Zephaniah 3:17
Hosea 14:5-6 - Sifre Devarim Vezot Habracha 342
Hosea 14:5-7 - Testament of Simeon 6:2
[8] LXX *restore their dwellings*
[9] Hosea 14:6 - 2 Kings 19:30, 2 Samuel 23:4, b.Taanit 4a, Deuteronomy 8:2, Ein Yaakov Taanit:4a, Ephesians 3:17, Ezekiel 17:22-17:24, Isaiah 18:4 2:19 3:6 11:2 20:3, Job 5:19, Leviticus.R 23:6, Luke 12:27, Matthew 6:28, Micah 5:8, Midrash Psalms 45:3, Perek Shirah [the Dew], Pesikta de R'Kahana 16.8 17.8, Pesikta Rabbati 29/30B:2, Proverbs 19:12, Psalms 72:6 72:16, Sifre Devarim Ekev 39, Song of Songs 2:1-2:2 2:16 4:5, Song of Songs.R 1:62 2:9 8:6
[10] Hosea 14:7 - 2 Corinthians 2:14-2:15, b.Berachot 43b, Daniel 4:7-4:12, Ezekiel 17:5-17:8 31:3-31:10, Genesis 3:27, Jastrow 1474a, Jeremiah 11:16, John 15:1, Matthew 13:31, Numbers.R 10:1, Philippians 4:18, Psalms 52:9 80:10-80:12 8:3, Romans 11:16-11:24, Sifre Devarim Ekev 47, Sifre Devarim Devarim 10, Song of Songs 4:11-4:15
Hosea 14:7-8 - Sifre Devarim Vezot Habracha 342

יָשֻׁבוּ יֹשְׁבֵי בְצִלּוֹ יְחַיּוּ דָגָן וְיִפְרְחוּ כַגָּפֶן זִכְרוֹ כְּיֵין לְבָנוֹן	8[1]	*Those who dwell under his shadow shall again make corn to grow*[2], And shall blossom as the vine; *its scent shall be*[3] as the wine of Lebanon.
אֶפְרַיִם מַה־לִּי עוֹד לָעֲצַבִּים אֲנִי עָנִיתִי וַאֲשׁוּרֶנּוּ אֲנִי כִּבְרוֹשׁ רַעֲנָן מִמֶּנִּי פֶּרְיְךָ נִמְצָא	9[4]	*Ephraim [shall say]*[5]: 'What have I to do with idols any longer?' *As for Me, I respond and look on him*[6]; I am like a leafy cypress tree; your fruit is found from Me.
מִי חָכָם וְיָבֵן אֵלֶּה נָבוֹן וְיֵדָעֵם כִּי־יְשָׁרִים דַּרְכֵי יְהוָֹה וְצַדִּקִים יֵלְכוּ בָם וּפֹשְׁעִים יִכָּשְׁלוּ בָם	10[7]	Whoever is wise, let him understand these things, whoever is prudent, let him know them. for the ways of the LORD are right, And the just walk in them; But transgressors stumble in them.

Yoel b'Petuel – Chapter 1

דְּבַר־יְהוָֹה אֲשֶׁר הָיָה אֶל־יוֹאֵל בֶּן־פְּתוּאֵל	1[8]	The word of the LORD that came to Joel the son of Pethuel.
שִׁמְעוּ־זֹאת הַזְּקֵנִים וְהַאֲזִינוּ כֹּל יוֹשְׁבֵי הָאָרֶץ הֶהָיְתָה זֹּאת בִּימֵיכֶם וְאִם בִּימֵי אֲבֹתֵיכֶם	2[9]	Hear this, you old men, And give ear, all you inhabitants of the land. Has this been in your days, Or in the days of your fathers?
עָלֶיהָ לִבְנֵיכֶם סַפֵּרוּ וּבְנֵיכֶם לִבְנֵיהֶם וּבְנֵיהֶם לְדוֹר אַחֵר	3[10]	Tell your children of it, And let your children tell their children, And their children another generation.
יֶתֶר הַגָּזָם אָכַל הָאַרְבֶּה וְיֶתֶר הָאַרְבֶּה אָכַל הַיָּלֶק וְיֶתֶר הַיֶּלֶק אָכַל הֶחָסִיל	4[11]	What the *palmer worm*[12] has left the locust has eaten; And what the locust has left the *canker worm*[13] has eaten; And what the *canker worm*[14] has left the *caterpillar*[15] has eaten.
הָקִיצוּ שִׁכּוֹרִים וּבְכוּ וְהֵילִלוּ כָּל־שֹׁתֵי יָיִן עַל־עָסִיס כִּי נִכְרַת מִפִּיכֶם	5[16]	Awake, you drunkards, and weep, And wail, all you drinkers of wine, Because of the sweet wine, For it is cut off from your mouth.

---

[1] Hosea 14:8 - 1 Corinthians 15:36-38, b.Pesachim [Tosefot] 16a, Ezekiel 17:23, Hosea 2:22 6:2 14:7, Isaiah 32:1-2 61:11, John 11:25 12:24, Leviticus.R 1:2, Midrash Psalms 16:12, Midrash Tanchuma Bereshit 6, Numbers.R 8:1, Psalms 85:7 91:1 138:7, Song of Songs 2:3 6:11, Zechariah 8:12

[2] LXX *They shall return, and dwell under his shadow: they shall live and be satisfied with* corn

[3] LXX *his memorial shall be to Ephraim*

[4] Hosea 14:9 - 1 Peter 1:14-16 4:3-4, 1 Thessalonians 1:9, Acts 19:18-20, Ephesians 5:9, Galatians 5:22-23, Hosea 14:4-5, Isaiah 17:19 7:13 12:13, James 1:17, Jeremiah 31:19-21, Job 9:27 10:32, John 1:16 1:47-1:48 15:1-15:8, Luke 15:20, Philippians 1:11 2:13 4:13, Philo De Mutatione Nominum 139, Philo De Plantatione 138, Song of Songs.R 1:71 7:14, z.Lech Lecha 85b, z.Vayera 115b Hosea 14:9-10 - 4QXIIg

[5] Missing in LXX

[6] LXX *I have afflicted him, and I will strengthen him*

[7] Hosea 14:10 - 1 Peter 2:7-8, 2 Corinthians 2:15-16, 2 Thessalonians 2:9-12, b.Bava Batra 89b, b.Bava Kamma [Tosefot] 11a, b.Horayot 10b, b.Nazir 23a, b.Yevamot [Tosefot] 40a, Daniel 12:10, Deuteronomy 8:4, Ecclesiastes.R 6:1 9:15, Ein Yaakov Bava Batra:89b, Ein Yaakov Nazir:23a, Ezekiel 18:25 33:17-20, Genesis 18:25, Isaiah 1:28 8:13-15 2:7, Jeremiah 9:13, Job 17:9 34:10-12 34:18-19, John 3:19-3:20 8:47 9:39 15:24 18:37, Luke 2:34 4:28-29 7:23, Matthew 11:19 13:11-13:12, Midrash Psalms 1:18, Pesikta de R'Kahana 2.2, Proverbs 1:5-6 4:18 10:29, Psalms 19:8-19:9 84:6 84:8 11:43 111:7-8 119:128 119:75, Romans 7:12 9:32-9:33, Song of Songs.R 1:19, z.Lech Lecha 91b, z.Mikketz 204a, z.Vayishlach 167b 175b, Zephaniah 3:5, Sifre Devarim Shoftim 171

[8] Joel 1:1 - Ecclesiastes.R 1:2, Numbers.R 10:5, Ruth.R 4:3, 2 Peter 1:21, Acts 2:16, Ezekiel 1:3, Hosea 1:1, Jeremiah 1:2, Lives of the Prophets 8:1

[9] Joel 1:2-4 - Sifre Devarim Vezot Habracha 342, Amos 3:1 4:1 5:1, Daniel 12:1, Deuteronomy 4:32-4:35, Hosea 4:1 5:1, Isaiah 7:17 10:1, Jeremiah 5:21 6:7, Job 8:8 12:12 15:10 21:7, Joel 1:14 2:2, Matthew 13:9 24:21, Micah 1:2 3:1 3:9, Psalms 49:2, Revelation 2:7

[10] Joel 1:3 - Exodus.R 13:4, Deuteronomy 6:7, Exodus 10:1-2 13:14, Isaiah 14:19, Joshua 4:6-7 4:21-22, Psalms 44:2 71:18 78:3-8 1:4

[11] Joel 1:4 - b.Shabbat [Rashi] 33a, b.Shabbat 33a, b.Taanit 5a, Ein Yaakov Shabbat 33a, Ein Yaakov Taanit 5a, 1 Kings 8:37, 2 Chronicles 6:28 7:13, Amos 4:9 7:1, Deuteronomy 4:38 4:42, Exodus 10:4 10:12-15, Isaiah 9:4, Jeremiah 3:14 3:27, Joel 2:25, Nahum 3:15-17, Psalms 78:46 9:34, Revelation 9:3-7

[12] LXX *caterpillar*

[13] LXX *palmerworm*

[14] LXX *palmerworm*

[15] LXX *cankerwork*

[16] Joel 1:5 - Pesikta de R'Kahana 16.8, Pesikta Rabbati 29/30B:2, Amos 6:3-6:7, Ezekiel 6:2, Isaiah 24:7-24:11 32:10-12, James 5:1, Jeremiah 4:8, Joel 1:11 1:13 4:3, Luke 16:19 16:23-25 21:34-36, Romans 13:11-14

Hebrew	Verse	English
כִּי־גוֹי עָלָה עַל־אַרְצִי עָצוּם וְאֵין מִסְפָּר שִׁנָּיו שִׁנֵּי אַרְיֵה וּמְתַלְּעוֹת לָבִיא לוֹ	6[1]	For a people have come up on my land, mighty and without number; His teeth are the teeth of a lion, *And he has the fangs of a lioness*[2].
שָׂם גַּפְנִי לְשַׁמָּה וּתְאֵנָתִי לִקְצָפָה חָשֹׂף חֲשָׂפָהּ וְהִשְׁלִיךְ הִלְבִּינוּ שָׂרִיגֶיהָ	7[3]	He has laid my vine to waste, and blasted my fig tree; He has made it clean bare, and cast it down, *its branches are made white*[4].
אֱלִי כִּבְתוּלָה חֲגֻרַת־שַׂק עַל־בַּעַל נְעוּרֶיהָ	8[5]	Lament like a virgin bound with sackcloth for the husband of her youth.
הָכְרַת מִנְחָה וָנֶסֶךְ מִבֵּית יְהוָה אָבְלוּ הַכֹּהֲנִים מְשָׁרְתֵי יְהוָה	9[6]	The meal offering and the drink offering are cut off from the house of the LORD; *The priests mourn, the LORD's ministers*[7].
שֻׁדַּד שָׂדֶה אָבְלָה אֲדָמָה כִּי שֻׁדַּד דָּגָן הוֹבִישׁ תִּירוֹשׁ אֻמְלַל יִצְהָר	10[8]	The field is wasted, the land mourns; For the corn is wasted, the new wine is dried up, and the oil languishes.
הֹבִישׁוּ אִכָּרִים הֵילִילוּ כֹּרְמִים עַל־חִטָּה וְעַל־שְׂעֹרָה כִּי אָבַד קְצִיר שָׂדֶה	11[9]	*Be ashamed, O husbandmen, Wail, O vinedressers, For*[10] the wheat and for the barley; Because the harvest of the field perished.
הַגֶּפֶן הוֹבִישָׁה וְהַתְּאֵנָה אֻמְלָלָה רִמּוֹן גַּם־תָּמָר וְתַפּוּחַ כָּל־עֲצֵי הַשָּׂדֶה יָבֵשׁוּ כִּי־הֹבִישׁ שָׂשׂוֹן מִן־בְּנֵי אָדָם	12[11]	The vine withered, And the fig tree languishes; The pomegranate tree, the palm tree also, the apple tree, all the trees of the field, withered; For joy is withered away from the sons of men.
חִגְרוּ וְסִפְדוּ הַכֹּהֲנִים הֵילִילוּ מְשָׁרְתֵי מִזְבֵּחַ בֹּאוּ לִינוּ בַשַּׂקִּים מְשָׁרְתֵי אֱלֹהָי כִּי נִמְנַע מִבֵּית אֱלֹהֵיכֶם מִנְחָה וָנָסֶךְ	13[12]	Gird yourselves and lament, you priests, Wail, you ministers of the altar; Come, lie all night in sackcloth, you ministers of my God; For the meal offering and the drink offering is withheld from the house of your God.
קַדְּשׁוּ־צוֹם קִרְאוּ עֲצָרָה אִסְפוּ זְקֵנִים כֹּל יֹשְׁבֵי הָאָרֶץ בֵּית יְהוָה אֱלֹהֵיכֶם וְזַעֲקוּ אֶל־יְהוָה	14[13]	Sanctify a fast, Call a solemn assembly, Gather the elders and all the inhabitants of the land to the house of the LORD your God, And cry to the LORD.
אֲהָהּ לַיּוֹם כִּי קָרוֹב יוֹם יְהוָה וּכְשֹׁד מִשַּׁדַּי יָבוֹא	15[14]	*Alas*[15] for the day! For the day of the LORD is at hand, And it shall come as a destruction from the Almighty.
הֲלוֹא נֶגֶד עֵינֵינוּ אֹכֶל נִכְרָת מִבֵּית אֱלֹהֵינוּ שִׂמְחָה וָגִיל	16[16]	Is not the food cut off before our eyes, yes, joy and gladness from the house of our God?

[1] Joel 1:6 - Leviticus.R 5:3, Hosea 9:3, Isaiah 8:8 8:13, Joel 2:2-11 2:25, Proverbs 6:14 30:25-27, Psalms 11:34, Revelation 9:7-10

[2] LXX *and their back teeth those of a lion's whelp*

[3] Joel 1:7 - Amos 4:9, Exodus 10:15, Genesis 30:37-39; Habakkuk 3:17, Hosea 2:12, Isaiah 5:6 24:7, Jeremiah 8:13, Joel 1:12, Psalms 9:33

[4] LXX *he has peeled its branches*

[5] Joel 1:8 - b.Sanhedrin 42a, b.Taanit [Rashi] 29a, Ein Yaakov Sanhedrin 104b, Pesikta Rabbati 33:13, Amos 8:10, Isaiah 22:12 24:7-12 8:11, James 4:8-4:9 5:1, Jeremiah 3:4 9:18-20, Joel 1:13-15 2:12-14, Malachi 2:15, Proverbs 2:17, z.Vayigash 210a
Joel 1:8-20 - 4QXIIc

[6] Joel 1:9 - 2 Chronicles 13:10, Exodus 4:1, Hosea 9:4, Isaiah 13:6, Joel 1:13 1:16 2:14 2:17, Lamentations 1:4 1:16

[7] LXX *mourn, you priests who serve at the altar of the LORD*

[8] Joel 1:10 - Haggai 1:11, Hosea 4:3 9:2, Isaiah 24:3-4 24:11, Jeremiah 12:4 12:11 14:2-6 24:33, Joel 1:5 1:12 1:17-20, Leviticus 2:20

[9] Joel 1:11 - Jastrow 69a, Amos 5:16, Isaiah 17:11, Jeremiah 9:13 14:3-14:4, Romans 5:5

[10] LXX *the husbandmen are consumed: mourn your property on account of*

[11] Joel 1:12 - Habakkuk 3:17-3:18, Haggai 2:19, Hosea 9:1-9:2, Isaiah 9:4 16:10 24:11, Jeremiah 24:3 24:33, Joel 1:10 1:16, Numbers 13:23, Psalms 4:8 92:13, Song of Songs 2:3 4:13 7:8-7:10
Joel 1:12-14 - 4QXIIg

[12] Joel 1:13 - 1 Corinthians 4:1 9:13, 1 Kings 21:27, 2 Corinthians 3:6 6:4 11:23, 2 Samuel 12:16, Ezekiel 7:18, Hebrews 7:13-7:14, Isaiah 61:6, Jeremiah 4:8 9:11, Joel 1:8-1:9 2:17, Jonah 3:5-3:8, Leviticus 2:8-2:10, Numbers 29:6

[13] Joel 1:14 - b.Taanit 12b, Midrash Psalms 22:5, y.Taanit 1:6, 2 Chronicles 20:3-20:4 20:13, Apocalypse of Elijah 1:16 3, Deuteronomy 29:9-29:10, Joel 2:15-2:16, Jonah 3:8, Leviticus 23:36, Nehemiah 8:18 9:2-9:3

[14] Joel 1:15 - Amos 5:16-18, Ezekiel 7:2-12 12:22-28, Isaiah 13:6-9, James 5:9, Jeremiah 30:7, Joel 2:1-2 2:11 3:4, Luke 19:41-44, Psalms 37:13, Revelation 6:17, Zephaniah 1:14-18

[15] LXX *Alas, Alas, Alas*

[16] Joel 1:16 - mt.Hilchot Melachim u'Michamoteihem 7:4, Amos 4:6-7, Deuteronomy 12:6-7 12:11-12 16:10-15, Isaiah 3:7 62:8-9, Joel 1:5-9 1:13, Psalms 43:4 105:3

עָבְשׁוּ פְרֻדוֹת תַּחַת מֶגְרְפֹתֵיהֶם נָשַׁמּוּ אֹצָרוֹת נֶהֶרְסוּ מַמְּגֻרוֹת כִּי הֹבִישׁ דָּגָן

17[1] The *grains shrivel under their hoes*[2]; *The harvests are laid desolate, The barns are broken down*[3]; For the corn has withered.

מַה־נֶּאֶנְחָה בְהֵמָה נָבֹכוּ עֶדְרֵי בָקָר כִּי אֵין מִרְעֶה לָהֶם גַּם־עֶדְרֵי הַצֹּאן נֶאְשָׁמוּ

18[4] *How the beasts groan*[5]! The herds of cattle are perplexed, because they have no pasture; Yes, the flocks of sheep are made desolate.

אֵלֶיךָ יְהוָה אֶקְרָא כִּי אֵשׁ אָכְלָה נְאוֹת מִדְבָּר וְלֶהָבָה לִהֲטָה כָּל־עֲצֵי הַשָּׂדֶה

19[6] I cry to You, O LORD; for the fire devoured the pastures of the wilderness, and the flame has set all the trees of the field ablaze.

גַּם־בַּהֲמוֹת שָׂדֶה תַּעֲרוֹג אֵלֶיךָ כִּי יָבְשׁוּ אֲפִיקֵי מָיִם וְאֵשׁ אָכְלָה נְאוֹת הַמִּדְבָּר

20[7] Yes, the beasts of the field pant to You; for the water brooks are dried up, and the fire has devoured the pastures of the wilderness.

Joel – Chapter 2

תִּקְעוּ שׁוֹפָר בְּצִיּוֹן וְהָרִיעוּ בְּהַר קָדְשִׁי יִרְגְּזוּ כֹּל יֹשְׁבֵי הָאָרֶץ כִּי־בָא יוֹם־יְהוָה כִּי קָרוֹב

1[8] Blow the horn in Zion, and sound an alarm in My holy mountain; let all the inhabitants of the land tremble; for the day of the LORD comes, For it is at hand;

יוֹם חֹשֶׁךְ וַאֲפֵלָה יוֹם עָנָן וַעֲרָפֶל כְּשַׁחַר פָּרֻשׂ עַל־הֶהָרִים עַם רַב וְעָצוּם כָּמֹהוּ לֹא נִהְיָה מִן־הָעוֹלָם וְאַחֲרָיו לֹא יוֹסֵף עַד־שְׁנֵי דּוֹר וָדוֹר

2[9] A day of darkness and gloominess, a day of clouds and thick darkness, *as darkness spreads over the mountains; A great and mighty people*[10], there has not been ever the like, nor shall be any more after them, to the years of many generations.

לְפָנָיו אָכְלָה אֵשׁ וְאַחֲרָיו תְּלַהֵט לֶהָבָה כְּגַן־עֵדֶן הָאָרֶץ לְפָנָיו וְאַחֲרָיו מִדְבַּר שְׁמָמָה וְגַם־פְּלֵיטָה לֹא־הָיְתָה לּוֹ

3[11] A fire devours before them, and behind them a flame blazes; the land is as the Garden of Eden before them, and behind them a desolate wilderness; Yes, nothing escapes them.

כְּמַרְאֵה סוּסִים מַרְאֵהוּ וּכְפָרָשִׁים כֵּן יְרוּצוּן

4[12] Their appearance is as the appearance of horses; and as horsemen, so do they *run*[13].

כְּקוֹל מַרְכָּבוֹת עַל־רָאשֵׁי הֶהָרִים יְרַקֵּדוּן כְּקוֹל לַהַב אֵשׁ אֹכְלָה קָשׁ כְּעַם עָצוּם עֱרוּךְ מִלְחָמָה

5[14] Like the noise of chariots, they leap on the tops of the mountains, like the noise of a flame of fire that devours the stubble, As a mighty people set in battle array.

מִפָּנָיו יָחִילוּ עַמִּים כָּל־פָּנִים קִבְּצוּ פָארוּר

6[15] *At their presence the peoples are in anguish; All faces have gathered blackness*[16].

---

[1] Joel 1:17 - b.Bava Batra [Rashbam] 67b, Jastrow 272a, y.Peah 7:3, Genesis 23:16, Isaiah 17:10-11

[2] 4QXIIc LXX *heifers decay in their stalls*

[3] LXX *the treasures are abolished, the wine presses are broken down*

[4] Joel 1:18 - Mekilta de R'Ishmael Beshallah 2:45, Pesikta de R'Kahana 24.11, y.Taanit 2:1, 1 Kings 18:5, Hosea 4:3, Jeremiah 12:4 14:5-6, Joel 1:20, Romans 8:22

[5] LXX *What shall we store up for ourselves? the herds of cattle have mourned*

[6] Joel 1:19 - Amos 7:4, Habakkuk 3:17-18, Jeremiah 9:11, Joel 2:3, Luke 18:1 18:7, Micah 7:7, Philippians 4:6-7, Psalms 50:15 91:15

[7] Joel 1:20 - 1 Kings 17:7 18:5, Job 38:41, Psalms 104:21 145:15 147:9

[8] Joel 2:1 - 4QXIII, Midrash Psalms 121:3, Pesikta Rabbati 40:7 41:1-5, 1 Chronicles 15:28, 1 Peter 4:7, 1 Thessalonians 5:2, Amos 3:6 8:2, Daniel 6:27 9:16 9:20, Ezekiel 7:5-7:7 7:10 7:12 12:23 33:3 33:6, Ezra 9:3-9:4, Hosea 5:8 8:1, Isaiah 2:12 66:2 66:5, James 5:8, Jeremiah 4:5 5:22 16:7 16:10, Joel 1:15 2:15 4:17, Malachi 3:19, Numbers 10:3 10:5-10:9, Obadiah 1:15, Philippians 2:12, Psalms 87:1 119:120, Zechariah 8:3, Zephaniah 1:14 1:16 3:11

Joel 2:1-27 - Rosh Hashanah [Pesikta Rabbati 41]

[9] Joel 2:2 - Amos 4:13 5:18-20, Daniel 9:12 12:1, Deuteronomy 32:7, Exodus 10:6 10:14 20:18, Hebrews 12:18, Isaiah 5:30 8:22, Jeremiah 13:16, Joel 1:2-3 1:6 2:5 2:10-2:11 2:25 3:4 4:14-15, Jude 1:13, Mark 13:19, Psalms 10:7 97:2, Zephaniah 1:14-15 Joel 2:2-13 - 4QXIIg

[10] LXX *a numerous and strong people shall be spread upon the mountains as the morning*

[11] Joel 2:3 - Saadia Opinions 9:5, Amos 7:4, Exodus 10:5 10:15, Ezekiel 31:8-9, Genesis 2:8 13:10, Isaiah 51:3, Jeremiah 5:17, Joel 1:4-7 1:19-20, Psalms 50:3 105:34-35, Zechariah 7:14

[12] Joel 2:4 - Revelation 9:7

[13] LXX *pursue*

[14] Joel 2:5 - Apocalypse of Elijah 1:5, Isaiah 5:24 30:30, Matthew 3:12, Nahum 2:4-5 3:2-3, Revelation 9:9

[15] Joel 2:6 - Saadia Opinions 9:8, Isaiah 13:8, Jeremiah 8:21 30:6, Lamentations 4:8, Nahum 2:11, Psalms 119:83

[16] LXX *Before them shall the people be crushed: every face shall be as the blackness of a caldron*

Hebrew	Verse	English

כְּגִבּוֹרִים יְרֻצוּן כְּאַנְשֵׁי מִלְחָמָה יַעֲלוּ חוֹמָה וְאִישׁ בִּדְרָכָיו יֵלֵכוּן וְלֹא יְעַבְּטוּן אֹרְחוֹתָם

7[1] They run like mighty men, They climb the wall like men of war; everyone moves in his ways, And they do not entangle their paths.

וְאִישׁ אָחִיו לֹא יִדְחָקוּן גֶּבֶר בִּמְסִלָּתוֹ יֵלֵכוּן וּבְעַד הַשֶּׁלַח יִפֹּלוּ לֹא יִבְצָעוּ

8[2] Nor does one thrust another, everyone marches in his highway; And they break through the weapons, And suffer no harm.

בָּעִיר יָשֹׁקּוּ בַּחוֹמָה יְרֻצוּן בַּבָּתִּים יַעֲלוּ בְּעַד הַחַלּוֹנִים יָבֹאוּ כַּגַּנָּב

9[3] They leap upon the city, They run upon the wall, They climb up into the houses; They enter in at the windows like a thief.

לְפָנָיו רָגְזָה אֶרֶץ רָעֲשׁוּ שָׁמָיִם שֶׁמֶשׁ וְיָרֵחַ קָדָרוּ וְכוֹכָבִים אָסְפוּ נָגְהָם

10[4] Before them the earth quakes, The heavens tremble; The sun and the moon have become black, And the stars dim their shining.

וַיהוָה נָתַן קוֹלוֹ לִפְנֵי חֵילוֹ כִּי רַב מְאֹד מַחֲנֵהוּ כִּי עָצוּם עֹשֵׂה דְבָרוֹ כִּי־גָדוֹל יוֹם־יְהוָה וְנוֹרָא מְאֹד וּמִי יְכִילֶנּוּ

11[5] And the LORD utters His voice before His army; For His camp is very great, For he is mighty who executes His word; For great is the day of the LORD and very terrible; And who can live through it?

וְגַם־עַתָּה נְאֻם־יְהוָה שֻׁבוּ עָדַי בְּכָל־לְבַבְכֶם וּבְצוֹם וּבִבְכִי וּבְמִסְפֵּד

12[6] Yet now, says the LORD, Turn to Me with all your heart, And with fasting, and with weeping, and with lamentation;

וְקִרְעוּ לְבַבְכֶם וְאַל־בִּגְדֵיכֶם וְשׁוּבוּ אֶל־יְהוָה אֱלֹהֵיכֶם כִּי־חַנּוּן וְרַחוּם הוּא אֶרֶךְ אַפַּיִם וְרַב־חֶסֶד וְנִחָם עַל־הָרָעָה

13[7] And rend your heart, and not your garments, and turn to the LORD your God; for He is gracious and compassionate, long-suffering, and abundant in mercy, and repents of the evil.

מִי יוֹדֵעַ יָשׁוּב וְנִחָם וְהִשְׁאִיר אַחֲרָיו בְּרָכָה מִנְחָה וָנֶסֶךְ לַיהוָה אֱלֹהֵיכֶם

14[8] Who knows if He will not turn and repent and leave a blessing behind Him, a meal offering and a drink offering to the LORD your God?

תִּקְעוּ שׁוֹפָר בְּצִיּוֹן קַדְּשׁוּ־צוֹם קִרְאוּ עֲצָרָה

15[9] Blow the horn in Zion, Sanctify a fast, call a solemn assembly;

אִסְפוּ־עָם קַדְּשׁוּ קָהָל קִבְצוּ זְקֵנִים אִסְפוּ עוֹלָלִים וְיֹנְקֵי שָׁדָיִם יֵצֵא חָתָן מֵחֶדְרוֹ וְכַלָּה מֵחֻפָּתָהּ

16[10] Gather the people, Sanctify the congregation, assemble the elders, gather the children, and those who suckle the breasts; let the

---

[1] Joel 2:7 - 2 Samuel 1:23 2:18-19 5:8, Isaiah 5:26-29, Jeremiah 5:10, Joel 2:9, Proverbs 30:27, Psalms 19:6

[2] Joel 2:8 - 2 Chronicles 23:10 8:5, Job 33:18 36:12, Nehemiah 4:17 4:23, Song of Songs 4:13

[3] Joel 2:9 - Pesikta Rabbati 21:20 49:8, Exodus 10:6, Jeremiah 9:22, John 10:1

[4] Joel 2:10 - Lamentations.R 1:23 3:י, Leviticus.R 31:9, Acts 2:20, Amos 5:8, Ezekiel 32:7-32:8, Guide for the Perplexed 2:29, Isaiah 13:10 10:4, Jeremiah 4:23, Joel 2:2 3:4 4:15-16, Life of Adam and Eve [Apocalypse] 36:3, Luke 21:25-26, Mark 13:24-25, Matthew 24:29 3:51, Nahum 1:5, Psalms 18:8 18:7, Revelation 6:12 8:12 20:11, Sibylline Oracles 3.801

[5] Joel 2:11 - Midrash Psalms 103:18, Midrash Tanchuma Pekudei 3, Midrash Tanchuma Vayikra 1, Midrash Tanchuma Vayishlach 2, Pesikta de R'Kahana 24.3, 2 Samuel 22:14-15, Amos 2 5:18 5:20, Ezekiel 22:14, Guide for the Perplexed 2:28 2:47, Isaiah 7:18 13:4 18:13, Jeremiah 1:30 6:7 2:34, Joel 1:15 2:25 3:4 4:16, Malachi 3:2, Nahum 1:6, Numbers 24:23, Psalms 46:7, Revelation 6:17 18:8, z.Vayeshev 192b 193a, z.Vayikra 18b, Zephaniah 1:14-15

[6] Joel 2:12 - 4Q266 frag 11 l.5, 4Q270 frag 7 1.19, 1 Kings 8:47-49, 1 Samuel 7:3 7:6, 2 Chronicles 6:38-39 7:13-14 20:3-4, Acts 2:20, Deuteronomy 4:29-30, Gates of Repentance 1.15 4.12, Hosea 6:1 12:8 14:3, Isaiah 22:12 55:6-7, James 4:8-9, Jeremiah 4:1 29:12-13, Jonah 3:5-8, Judges 20:26, Lamentations 3:40-41, Nehemiah 9:1-2, Shepherd Mandate 12:6 6:1 9:1, Zechariah 1:3-4 7:3 7:5 12:10-14

[7] Joel 2:13 - 4Q266 frag 11 l.5, 4Q270 frag 7 1.19, Avot de R'Natan 17, b.Moed Katan 26b, b.Taanit 15a, Chibbur Yafeh 27 129b, Ecclesiastes.R 1:36, Ein Yaakov Midrash Shmuel 2:15, Ein Yaakov Taanit:15a, Jastrow 1310a, Midrash Proverbs 6, mt.Hilchot Taaniot 4:2, mt.Pirkei Avot 2:16, Pesikta de R'Kahana 24.11, Pirkei Avot 2:18 [Shabbat afternoon], Ralbag Wars 3:6, y.Taanit 2:1, 1 Kings 21:27, 1 Timothy 4:8, 2 Kings 5:7 6:30 22:11 22:19, 2 Samuel 1:11, Amos 7:2-6, Ephesians 2:4, Exodus 34:6-7, Ezekiel 9:4, Genesis 13:29 13:34, Greek Apocalypse of Ezra 1:10, Hellenistic Synagogal Prayers 2:3, Isaiah 9:15 10:5 18:2, James 1:19-20, Jeremiah 18:7-8, Job 1:20, Jonah 4:2, m.Taanit 2:1, Matthew 5:3-4 6:16-18, Micah 7:18, Nahum 1:3, Nehemiah 9:17, Numbers 14:18, Prayer of Manasseh 7, Psalms 34:19 51:18 86:5 86:15 7:8 10:45 145:7-9, Romans 2:4 5:20-21

[8] Joel 2:14 - Saadia Opinions 6:2, 1 Samuel 6:5, 2 Corinthians 9:5-9:11, 2 Kings 19:4, 2 Samuel 12:22, 2 Timothy 2:25, Amos 5:15, Exodus 8:30, Haggai 2:19, Isaiah 17:8, Jeremiah 2:3, Joel 1:9 1:13 1:16, Jonah 1:6 3:9, Joshua 14:12, Zephaniah 2:3

[9] Joel 2:15 - Leviticus.R 24:4, mt.Hilchot Taaniot 3:4, 1 Kings 21:9 21:12, 2 Kings 10:20, Apocalypse of Elijah 1:16, Jeremiah 12:9, Joel 1:14 2:1, Numbers 10:3

Joel 2:15-27 - Haftarah Shabbat Shuva [continued from Hoshea 14:2-10 Ashkenaz]

[10] Joel 2:16 - Mekilta de R'Ishmael Shirata 1:143, Mekilta de R'Ishmael Shirata 1:146, Midrash Tanchuma Beshallach 11, Saadia Opinions 5:7, y.Taanit 2:1, 1 Corinthians 7:5, 1 Samuel 16:5, 2 Chronicles 20:13 5:5 29:23-24 6:17 6:19 11:6, Deuteronomy 29:9-10, Exodus 19:10 19:15 19:22, Job 1:5, Joel 1:14, Jonah 3:7-8, Joshua 7:13, Matthew 9:15, Psalms 19:6, Zechariah 12:11-14

bridegroom leave his chamber, And the bride from her pavilion.

בֵּין הָאוּלָם וְלַמִּזְבֵּחַ יִבְכּוּ הַכֹּהֲנִים מְשָׁרְתֵי יְהוָה וְיֹאמְרוּ חוּסָה יְהוָה עַל־עַמֶּךָ וְאַל־תִּתֵּן נַחֲלָתְךָ לְחֶרְפָּה לִמְשָׁל־בָּם גּוֹיִם לָמָּה יֹאמְרוּ בָעַמִּים אַיֵּה אֱלֹהֵיהֶם

17[1] Let the priests, the ministers of the LORD, weep between the porch and the altar, And let them say: 'Spare your people, O LORD, And do not give Your heritage to reproach, so the nations should make them a byword: Why should they say among the peoples: Where is their God?'

וַיְקַנֵּא יְהוָה לְאַרְצוֹ וַיַּחְמֹל עַל־עַמּוֹ

18[2] Then the LORD was jealous for His land, And had pity on His people.

וַיַּעַן יְהוָה וַיֹּאמֶר לְעַמּוֹ הִנְנִי שֹׁלֵחַ לָכֶם אֶת־הַדָּגָן וְהַתִּירוֹשׁ וְהַיִּצְהָר וּשְׂבַעְתֶּם אֹתוֹ וְלֹא־אֶתֵּן אֶתְכֶם עוֹד חֶרְפָּה בַּגּוֹיִם

19[3] And the LORD answered and said to His people: 'Behold, I will send you corn, and wine, and oil, [4]and you shall be satisfied therewith; And I will make you a reproach among the nations no longer;

וְאֶת־הַצְּפוֹנִי אַרְחִיק מֵעֲלֵיכֶם וְהִדַּחְתִּיו אֶל־אֶרֶץ צִיָּה וּשְׁמָמָה אֶת־פָּנָיו אֶל־הַיָּם הַקַּדְמֹנִי וְסֹפוֹ אֶל־הַיָּם הָאַחֲרוֹן וְעָלָה בָאְשׁוֹ וְתַעַל צַחֲנָתוֹ כִּי הִגְדִּיל לַעֲשׂוֹת

20[5] But I will remove far off from you the northern one, and will drive him into a land barren and desolate, with his face toward the eastern sea, and his hinder part toward the western sea; so his foulness and his ill savor may come up, because he has done great things.'

אַל־תִּירְאִי אֲדָמָה גִּילִי וּשְׂמָחִי כִּי־הִגְדִּיל יְהוָה לַעֲשׂוֹת

21[6] Fear not, O land, be glad and rejoice; For the LORD has done great things.

אַל־תִּירְאוּ בַּהֲמוֹת שָׂדַי כִּי דָשְׁאוּ נְאוֹת מִדְבָּר כִּי־עֵץ נָשָׂא פִרְיוֹ תְּאֵנָה וָגֶפֶן נָתְנוּ חֵילָם

22[7] Be not afraid, you beasts of the field; For the pastures of the wilderness do spring, For the tree bears its fruit, The fig tree and the vine yield their strength.

וּבְנֵי צִיּוֹן גִּילוּ וְשִׂמְחוּ בַּיהוָה אֱלֹהֵיכֶם כִּי־נָתַן לָכֶם אֶת־הַמּוֹרֶה לִצְדָקָה וַיּוֹרֶד לָכֶם גֶּשֶׁם מוֹרֶה וּמַלְקוֹשׁ בָּרִאשׁוֹן

23[8] Be glad then, you children of Zion, and rejoice In the LORD your God; For He gives you the former rain in just measure, And He causes the rain to come down for you, The former rain and the latter rain, just as before.

וּמָלְאוּ הַגֳּרָנוֹת בָּר וְהֵשִׁיקוּ הַיְקָבִים תִּירוֹשׁ וְיִצְהָר

24[9] And the floors shall be full of corn, And the vats shall overflow with wine and oil.

---

[1] Joel 2:17 - Exodus.R 46:4, Tachanun [Monday and Thursday mornings], Taking the Torah from the ark [Ayl Erech Apayim], 1 Kings 6:3 9:7, 2 Chronicles 7:20 8:12, 3 Baruch 1:2 4 Ezra 8:45, Amos 7:2 7:5, Daniel 9:18-19, Deuteronomy 9:16-29 4:37 8:27, Exodus 32:11-13 10:9, Ezekiel 8:16 20:9 36:4-7, Hosea 14:4, Isaiah 13:20 63:17-19 64:10-13, Joel 1:9 1:13, Malachi 1:9, Matthew 23:35 3:43, Micah 7:10, Nehemiah 9:36, Numbers 14:14-16, Psalms 42:4 42:11 44:11-15 74:10 74:18-23 79:4 79:10 89:42 89:52 19:2

[2] Joel 2:18 - b.Sotah 3a, mt.Hilchot Sotah 1:1, Numbers.R 9:12, This is the middle verse of the book of Joel per the Massorah, Deuteronomy 8:16 8:36 8:43, Hosea 11:8-9, Isaiah 18:13 12:10 15:9 15:15, James 5:11, Jeremiah 7:21, Judges 10:16, Lamentations 3:22, Luke 15:20, Psalms 7:13 7:17, Zechariah 1:14 8:2

Joel 2:18-27 – Maamad [Tuesday]

[3] Joel 2:19 - Genesis.R 63:14 75:8, Amos 9:13-9:14, Ezekiel 10:29 12:15 15:29, Haggai 2:16-19, Hosea 2:15, Isaiah 62:8-9 65:21-24, Jeremiah 7:13, Joel 1:10 2:24, Malachi 3:10-12, Matthew 6:33

[4] 4QXIIc adds *and you shall eat*

[5] Joel 2:20 - b.Succah 52a, Chibbur Yafeh 27 117b, Ein Yaakov Sukkah:52a, Jastrow 1297b, MurXII, 2 Kings 8:13, Amos 4:10, Deuteronomy 11:24, Exodus 10:19, Ezekiel 39:12-16 47:7-8 23:18, Isaiah 10:3, Jeremiah 1:14-15, Joel 1:4-6 2:2-11, Zechariah 14:8

[6] Joel 2:21 - Midrash Psalms 138:2, 1 Samuel 12:16 12:24, Deuteronomy 4:32, Genesis 15:1, Hosea 2:21, Isaiah 11:1 17:10 20:23 6:4 7:12, Jeremiah 30:9-10 9:3, Joel 2:20, Psalms 65:13-14 71:19 96:11-12 98:8 126:1-3, Zechariah 8:15, Zephaniah 3:16-17

[7] Joel 2:22 - b.Ketubot 112b, Ein Yaakov Ketubot:112b, Leviticus.R 12:5, Pesikta de R'Kahana S6.2, y.Sheviit 4:8, 1 Corinthians 3:7, Amos 9:14-15, Ezekiel 34:26-27 12:8 12:30 12:35, Genesis 4:12, Haggai 2:16, Hosea 14:7-9, Isaiah 30:23-24 3:3, Joel 1:18-20, Jonah 4:11, Leviticus 26:4-5, Malachi 3:10-12, Psalms 36:7 65:13 67:7 104:11-14 104:27-29 107:35-38 145:15-16 147:8-9, z.Terumah 171a, Zechariah 8:12

[8] Joel 2:23 - b.Shekalim 14a, b.Taanit 5a 6a, Ein Yaakov Taanit:5a, Pesikta de R'Kahana S6.3, Pesikta Rabbati 30:1, Sifre Devarim Ekev 42, t.Taniyot 1:1, y.Shekalim 6:2, y.Taanit 1:2, Amos 4:7, Deuteronomy 11:14 4:12 8:2, Ephesians 4:8-11, Galatians 4:26-27, Habakkuk 3:17-18, Hosea 6:3, Isaiah 12:2-6 6:21 6:23 17:16 13:10, James 5:7-8, Jeremiah 3:3 5:24, Job 9:23, Joel 3:1-2, Lamentations 4:2, Leviticus 2:4, Luke 1:46-47, m.Taanit 1:2, Philippians 3:1 3:3 4:4, Proverbs 16:15, Psalms 28:7 32:11 72:6-7 95:1-3 8:34 5:2, Zechariah 9:9 9:13 10:1 10:7, Zephaniah 3:14-17

[9] Joel 2:24 - b.Bava Batra [Rashbam] 67b, Sifre Devarim Ekev 42, Amos 9:13, Joel 4:13 4:18, Leviticus 2:10, Malachi 3:10, Proverbs 3:9-10

וְשִׁלַּמְתִּי לָכֶם אֶת־הַשָּׁנִים אֲשֶׁר אָכַל הָאַרְבֶּה הַיֶּלֶק וְהֶחָסִיל וְהַגָּזָם חֵילִי הַגָּדוֹל אֲשֶׁר שִׁלַּחְתִּי בָּכֶם

25[1] And I will restore to you the years that the *locust has eaten, The canker worm, and the caterpillar, and the palmer worm*[2]; My great army which I sent among you.

וַאֲכַלְתֶּם אָכוֹל וְשָׂבוֹעַ וְהִלַּלְתֶּם אֶת־שֵׁם יְהוָה אֱלֹהֵיכֶם אֲשֶׁר־עָשָׂה עִמָּכֶם לְהַפְלִיא וְלֹא־יֵבֹשׁוּ עַמִּי לְעוֹלָם

26[3] And you shall eat in plenty and be satisfied, And shall praise the name of the LORD your God, Who has dealt wondrously with you; And My people shall never be ashamed.

וִידַעְתֶּם כִּי בְקֶרֶב יִשְׂרָאֵל אָנִי וַאֲנִי יְהוָה אֱלֹהֵיכֶם וְאֵין עוֹד וְלֹא־יֵבֹשׁוּ עַמִּי לְעוֹלָם

27[4] And you shall know I am in the midst of Israel, And I am the LORD your God, and there is no one else; And My people shall never be ashamed.

Joel – Chapter 3

וְהָיָה אַחֲרֵי־כֵן אֶשְׁפּוֹךְ אֶת־רוּחִי עַל־כָּל־בָּשָׂר וְנִבְּאוּ בְּנֵיכֶם וּבְנוֹתֵיכֶם זִקְנֵיכֶם חֲלֹמוֹת יַחֲלֹמוּן בַּחוּרֵיכֶם חֶזְיֹנוֹת יִרְאוּ

1[5] And it shall come to pass afterward, That I will pour out My spirit upon all flesh; And your sons and your daughters shall prophesy, Your old men shall dream dreams, Your young men shall see visions;

וְגַם עַל־הָעֲבָדִים וְעַל־הַשְּׁפָחוֹת בַּיָּמִים הָהֵמָּה אֶשְׁפּוֹךְ אֶת־רוּחִי

2[6] And in those days will I pour out My spirit also upon the servants and upon the handmaids.

וְנָתַתִּי מוֹפְתִים בַּשָּׁמַיִם וּבָאָרֶץ דָּם וָאֵשׁ וְתִימֲרוֹת עָשָׁן

3[7] And I will show wonders in the heavens and in the earth: blood, and fire, and pillars of smoke.

הַשֶּׁמֶשׁ יֵהָפֵךְ לְחֹשֶׁךְ וְהַיָּרֵחַ לְדָם לִפְנֵי בּוֹא יוֹם יְהוָה הַגָּדוֹל וְהַנּוֹרָא

4[8] The sun shall be turned to darkness, and the moon to blood before the great and terrible day of the LORD come.

וְהָיָה כֹּל אֲשֶׁר־יִקְרָא בְּשֵׁם יְהוָה יִמָּלֵט כִּי בְּהַר־צִיּוֹן וּבִירוּשָׁלַם תִּהְיֶה פְלֵיטָה כַּאֲשֶׁר אָמַר יְהוָה וּבַשְּׂרִידִים אֲשֶׁר יְהוָה קֹרֵא

5[9] And it shall come to pass, that whoever shall call on the name of the LORD shall be delivered; For in mount Zion and in Jerusalem there shall be those who escape, As the LORD has said, And among the remnant those whom the LORD shall call.

---

[1] Joel 2:25 - Sifre Devarim Vezot Habracha 342, Joel 1:4-7 2:2-11, Zechariah 10:6

[2] LXX *locust, and the caterpillar, and the palmerworm, and the cankerworm have eaten*

[3] Joel 2:26 - b.Moed Katan 9b, Ein Yaakov Moed Katan:9b, Midrash Psalms 6:6 18:25 31:3, Tanna Devei Eliyahu 4, 1 John 2:28, 1 Timothy 4:3-5 6:17, Deuteronomy 6:11-6:12 8:10 12:7 12:12 12:18 26:10-11, Genesis 9:11, HaMadrikh 16, Isaiah 1:1 5:22 21:17 1:23 6:4 7:2 62:8-9, Joel 2:20-21, Leviticus 2:5 2:26, Micah 6:14, Nehemiah 9:25, Proverbs 13:25, Psalms 13:7 22:27 25:2-3 37:19 72:18 7:5 20:7 126:2-3, Romans 5:5 9:33 10:11, Song of Songs 5:1, Zechariah 9:15 9:17, Zephaniah 3:11
Joel 2:26-27 - Midrash Tanchuma Bereshit 13, Motzoei Shabbat [Viyiten Lecha]

[4] Joel 2:27 - b.Moed Katan 9b, Deuteronomy.R 1:14, Ein Yaakov Moed Katan:9b, Midrash Psalms 6:6, 1 Peter 2:6, 2 Corinthians 6:16, Deuteronomy 23:16, Ezekiel 37:26-28 15:22 15:28, Isaiah 12:6 21:5 21:18 45:21-22 5:6, Joel 2:26 4:17, Leviticus 26:11-12, Psalms 46:6 68:19, Revelation 21:3, Zephaniah 3:17, Testament of Judah 24:2, Apocalypse of Elijah 1:4 3:7

[5] Joel 3:1 - Avot de R'Natan 34, b.Pesachim 50a, Deuteronomy.R 4:14, Midrash Psalms 14:6 138:2, Midrash Tanchuma Beha'alotcha 16, Midrash Tanchuma Mikketz 2, Numbers.R 15:25, Saadia Opinions 8:6 9:11, Tanna Devei Eliyahu 4, Acts 2:2-4 2:16-21 2:33 2:39 10:44-47 11:15-18 15:7-8 21:9, Ezekiel 15:29, Galatians 3:28, Genesis 37:5-10, Isaiah 8:15 16:5 20:3 1:6 6:13, Jeremiah 23:28, John 7:39, Luke 3:6, Numbers 12:6, Proverbs 1:23, Sibylline Oracles 3.293, Testament of Judah 24:2, z.Bereshit 28a, Zechariah 12:10
Joel 3:1-5 - MurXII, Midrash Psalms 13:4, Life of Adam and Eve [Apocalypse] 36:3

[6] Joel 3:2 - Ecclesiastes.R 2:11, Lamentations.R 4:14 4:14, Saadia Opinions 8:6, 1 Corinthians 12:13, Colossians 3:11, Galatians 3:28

[7] Joel 3:3 - b.Yoma [Rashi] 28b, mt.Hilchot Chametz u'Matzah Haggadah, Pesach Haggadah, Pesikta de R'Kahana 7.11, Pesikta Rabbati 17:8, Saadia Opinions 9:11, Acts 2:19-20, Genesis 19:28, Guide for the Perplexed 2:29, Joshua 8:20, Judges 20:38 20:40, Luke 21:11 21:25-26, Mark 13:24-25, Matthew 24:29, Revelation 6:12-17 18:9 18:18, Song of Songs 3:6
Joel 3:3-4 - Midrash Tanchuma Bo 4

[8] Joel 3:4 - Saadia Opinions 9:11, Isaiah 13:9-10 34:4-5, Joel 2:10 4:1 4:15, Luke 21:25, Malachi 3:19 3:23, Mark 13:24-25, Matthew 24:29 3:45, Revelation 6:12-13, Zephaniah 1:14-16

[9] Joel 3:5 - b.Chullin 133a, b.Sanhedrin 92a, Ein Yaakov Sanhedrin:92a, Jastrow 1631a, Mas.Kallah Rabbati 8:9, Mekilta de R'Ishmael Pisha 12:58, Midrash Psalms 4:3 71:3, Sifre Devarim Ekev 48 49, Tanya Igeret Hakodesh §25, y.Berachot 9:1, 1 Corinthians 1:2, 2 Thessalonians 2:13-14, Acts 2:20-21 2:39 15:17, Guide for the Perplexed 1:34, Hebrews 12:22, Isaiah 4:2 10:22 11:16 11:16 22:13 59:20-21, Jeremiah 7:8 9:3, John 4:22 10:16, Micah 4:6-7 5:4 5:8-9, Obadiah 1:17 1:21, Psalms 50:15, Romans 8:28-30 9:24 9:27 10:11-14 11:5 11:7 11:26, Zechariah 13:9

Joel – Chapter 4

כִּי הִנֵּה בַּיָּמִים הָהֵמָּה וּבָעֵת הַהִיא אֲשֶׁר 'אָשׁוּב' "אָשִׁיב" אֶת־שְׁבוּת יְהוּדָה וִירוּשָׁלָֽם	1[1]	For, behold, in those days, and in that time when I bring back the captivity of Judah and Jerusalem,
וְקִבַּצְתִּי אֶת־כָּל־הַגּוֹיִם וְהוֹרַדְתִּים אֶל־עֵמֶק יְהוֹשָׁפָט וְנִשְׁפַּטְתִּי עִמָּם שָׁם עַל־עַמִּי וְנַחֲלָתִי יִשְׂרָאֵל אֲשֶׁר פִּזְּרוּ בַגּוֹיִם וְאֶת־אַרְצִי חִלֵּֽקוּ	2[2]	I will gather all nations, and will bring them down into the valley of *Jehoshaphat*[3]; and I will enter into judgment with them there, for My people and for My heritage Israel whom they scattered among the nations, and divided My land.
וְאֶל־עַמִּי יַדּוּ גוֹרָל וַיִּתְּנוּ הַיֶּלֶד בַּזּוֹנָה וְהַיַּלְדָּה מָכְרוּ בַיַּיִן וַיִּשְׁתּֽוּ	3[4]	And they have cast lots for My people; And have given a boy for a harlot, And sold a girl for wine, and drank it.
וְגַם מָה־אַתֶּם לִי צֹר וְצִידוֹן וְכֹל גְּלִילוֹת פְּלָשֶׁת הַגְּמוּל אַתֶּם מְשַׁלְּמִים עָלָי וְאִם־גֹּמְלִים אַתֶּם עָלָי קַל מְהֵרָה אָשִׁיב גְּמֻלְכֶם בְּרֹאשְׁכֶֽם	4[5]	And also what are you to Me, O Tyre and Zidon, and all *the regions of Philistia*[6]? Will you render retribution on My behalf? And if you render retribution on My behalf, swiftly, speedily I will return your retribution upon your own head.
אֲשֶׁר־כַּסְפִּי וּזְהָבִי לְקַחְתֶּם וּמַחֲמַדַּי הַטֹּבִים הֲבֵאתֶם לְהֵיכְלֵיכֶֽם	5[7]	Because as you have taken My silver and My gold, and carried into your temples My goodly treasures;
וּבְנֵי יְהוּדָה וּבְנֵי יְרוּשָׁלַם מְכַרְתֶּם לִבְנֵי הַיְּוָנִים לְמַעַן הַרְחִיקָם מֵעַל גְּבוּלָֽם	6[8]	the children also of Judah and the children of Jerusalem you sold to the sons of *Jevanim*[9], so you might remove them far from their border;
הִנְנִי מְעִירָם מִן־הַמָּקוֹם אֲשֶׁר־מְכַרְתֶּם אֹתָם שָׁמָּה וַהֲשִׁבֹתִי גְמֻלְכֶם בְּרֹאשְׁכֶֽם	7[10]	Behold, I will stir them up out of the place where you sold them, and will return your retribution on your own head;
וּמָכַרְתִּי אֶת־בְּנֵיכֶם וְאֶת־בְּנוֹתֵיכֶם בְּיַד בְּנֵי יְהוּדָה וּמְכָרוּם לִשְׁבָאיִם אֶל־גּוֹי רָחוֹק כִּי יְהֹוָה דִּבֵּֽר	8[11]	And I will sell your sons and your daughters into the hand of the children of Judah, and they shall sell them *to the men of Sheba*[12], to a nation far off; for the LORD has spoken.

[1] Joel 4:1 - 2 Chronicles 6:37-38, Amos 9:14, Daniel 12:1, Deuteronomy 6:3, Ezekiel 16:53 37:21-22 38:14-18 15:25 39:28-29, Isaiah 11:11-16, Jeremiah 16:15 23:3-8 5:14 6:3 6:18, Joel 3:2, Psalms 14:7 85:2, Zephaniah 3:19-20
Joel 4:1-16 - MurXII
Joel 4:1-21 - Sifre Devarim Ha'azinu Hashamayim 333
[2] Joel 4:2 - Mekilta de R'Ishmael Beshallah 1:226, Midrash Proverbs 10, Midrash Tanchuma Bamidbar 17, Midrash Tanchuma Beshallach 5, Numbers.R 3:8, Saadia Opinions 8:6, Sifre Devarim Nitzavim 333, 2 Chronicles 20:26, Amos 1:11, Ezekiel 1:8 11:10 12:5 14:22 15:11, Greek Apocalypse of Ezra 3:5, Isaiah 18:16, Jeremiah 12:14 1:31 1:1, Joel 4:12, Obadiah 1:10-16, Revelation 11:18 16:6 16:14 16:16 18:20-21 19:19-21 20:8, Zechariah 12:3-4 14:2-4, Zephaniah 2:8-10 3:8
[3] LXX *Josaphat*
[4] Joel 4:3 - b.Gittin 6b, Esther.R 7:11, Jastrow 281a, Lamentations.R 1:46, Midrash Psalms 8:2, Song of Songs.R 8:15, 2 Chronicles 28:8-28:9, Amos 2:6, Nahum 3:10, Obadiah 1:11, Revelation 18:13
[5] Joel 4:4 - 2 Chronicles 21:16 28:17-18, 2 Thessalonians 1:6, Acts 9:4, Amos 1:6-10 1:12-14, Deuteronomy 8:35, Ezekiel 25:12-17, Isaiah 23:1-2 10:8 11:18, Jeremiah 23:4 3:6, Judges 11:12, Luke 18:7, Matthew 11:21, Zechariah 9:2-8
Joel 4:4-9 - 4QXIIg
[6] LXX *Galilee of the Gentiles*
[7] Joel 4:5 - 1 Samuel 5:2-5, 2 Chronicles 21:16-17, 2 Kings 12:19 16:8 18:15-16 24:13 25:13-17, Daniel 5:2-3 11:38, Jeremiah 2:28 3:11
[8] Joel 4:6 - Midrash Tanchuma Vayigash 10, Deuteronomy 4:32 28:68, Ezekiel 3:13, Joel 4:3 4:8, Psalms of Solomon 2:3
Joel 4:6-21 - 4QXIIc
[9] LXX *the Greeks*
[10] Joel 4:7 - 1 Samuel 15:33, 2 Thessalonians 1:6, Esther 7:10, Ezekiel 34:12-13 12:24 14:8, Isaiah 11:12 43:5-6 1:12, James 2:13, Jeremiah 23:8 6:10 6:16 7:9 8:37, Joel 4:4, Judges 1:7, Matthew 7:2, Psalms of Solomon 2:25, Revelation 13:10 16:6 19:2, Zechariah 10:6-10
[11] Joel 4:8 - Mekilta de R'Ishmael Pisha 12:45, Deuteronomy 8:30, Ezekiel 23:42, Isaiah 14:1-2 12:14, Jeremiah 6:20, Job 1:15, Judges 2:14 4:2 4:9
[12] Missing in LXX

קִרְאוּ־זֹאת בַּגּוֹיִם קַדְּשׁוּ מִלְחָמָה הָעִירוּ הַגִּבּוֹרִים יִגְּשׁוּ יַעֲלוּ כֹּל אַנְשֵׁי הַמִּלְחָמָה	9[1] Proclaim this among the nations, Prepare war; Stir up the mighty men; Let all the men of war draw near, Let them come up.
כֹּתּוּ אִתֵּיכֶם לַחֲרָבוֹת וּמַזְמְרֹתֵיכֶם לִרְמָחִים הַחַלָּשׁ יֹאמַר גִּבּוֹר אָנִי	10[2] Beat your plowshares into swords, And your pruning hooks into spears; Let the weak say: 'I am strong.'
עוּשׁוּ וָבֹאוּ כָל־הַגּוֹיִם מִסָּבִיב וְנִקְבָּצוּ שָׁמָּה הַנְחַת יְהוָה גִּבּוֹרֶיךָ	11[3] Hurry and come, you nations all around, and gather yourselves together; *cause Your mighty ones to come down, O LORD*[4]!
יֵעוֹרוּ וְיַעֲלוּ הַגּוֹיִם אֶל־עֵמֶק יְהוֹשָׁפָט כִּי שָׁם אֵשֵׁב לִשְׁפֹּט אֶת־כָּל־הַגּוֹיִם מִסָּבִיב	12[5] Let the nations be stirred up, and come up to the valley of Jehoshaphat; For there will I sit to judge all the surrounding nations.
שִׁלְחוּ מַגָּל כִּי בָשַׁל קָצִיר בֹּאוּ רְדוּ כִּי־מָלְאָה גַּת הֵשִׁיקוּ הַיְקָבִים כִּי רַבָּה רָעָתָם	13[6] Put in the sickle, for the harvest is ripe; Come, tread, for the winepress is full, the vats overflow; for their wickedness is great.
הֲמוֹנִים הֲמוֹנִים בְּעֵמֶק הֶחָרוּץ כִּי קָרוֹב יוֹם יְהוָה בְּעֵמֶק הֶחָרוּץ	14[7] *Multitudes, multitudes in the valley of decision*[8]! For the day of the LORD is near in the valley of decision.
שֶׁמֶשׁ וְיָרֵחַ קָדָרוּ וְכוֹכָבִים אָסְפוּ נָגְהָם	15[9] The sun and the moon have become black, And the stars withdraw their shining.
וַיהוָה מִצִּיּוֹן יִשְׁאָג וּמִירוּשָׁלִַם יִתֵּן קוֹלוֹ וְרָעֲשׁוּ שָׁמַיִם וָאָרֶץ וַיהוָה מַחֲסֶה לְעַמּוֹ וּמָעוֹז לִבְנֵי יִשְׂרָאֵל	16[10] And the LORD shall roar from Zion, and utter His voice from Jerusalem, and the heavens and the earth shall shake; But the LORD will be a refuge to His people, and a stronghold to the children of Israel.
וִידַעְתֶּם כִּי אֲנִי יְהוָה אֱלֹהֵיכֶם שֹׁכֵן בְּצִיּוֹן הַר־קָדְשִׁי וְהָיְתָה יְרוּשָׁלִַם קֹדֶשׁ וְזָרִים לֹא־יַעַבְרוּ־בָהּ עוֹד	17[11] So, shall you know that I am the LORD your God, Dwelling in Zion My holy mountain; Then Jerusalem shall be holy, and no strangers shall pass through her any longer.
וְהָיָה בַיּוֹם הַהוּא יִטְּפוּ הֶהָרִים עָסִיס וְהַגְּבָעוֹת תֵּלַכְנָה חָלָב וְכָל־אֲפִיקֵי יְהוּדָה יֵלְכוּ מָיִם וּמַעְיָן מִבֵּית יְהוָה יֵצֵא וְהִשְׁקָה אֶת־נַחַל הַשִּׁטִּים	18[12] And it shall come to pass in that day, that the mountains shall drop down sweet wine, And the hills shall flow with milk, And all the brooks of Judah shall flow with waters; And a

---

[1] Joel 4:9 - Midrash Psalms 8:8 118:12, Saadia Opinions 8:6, Ezekiel 21:26-27 14:7, Isaiah 8:9-10 10:1, Jeremiah 7:11 46:3-4 2:2, Micah 3:5, Psalms 96:10

[2] Joel 4:10 - Exodus.R 15:6, Saadia Opinions 8:6, 2 Chronicles 1:8, Isaiah 2:4, Luke 22:36, Micah 4:3, Zechariah 12:8

[3] Joel 4:11 - Midrash Psalms 8:8, Saadia Opinions 8:6, 2 Thessalonians 1:7, Ezekiel 38:9-18, Isaiah 10:34 13:3 13:36, Joel 4:2, Micah 4:12, Psalms 7:20, Revelation 16:14-16 19:14 19:19-20 20:8-9, Zechariah 14:2-3, Zephaniah 3:8
Joel 4:11-14 - 4QXIIg

[4] LXX *let the timid become a warrior*

[5] Joel 4:12 - Genesis.R 82:8, Midrash Psalms 2:14 8:8, Pesikta de R'Kahana S2.2, Saadia Opinions 8:6, 2 Chronicles 20:26, Ezekiel 6:3 15:11, Greek Apocalypse of Ezra 3:5, Isaiah 2:4 3:13, Joel 4:2 4:14, Micah 4:3, Psalms 2:8-2:9 7:7 76:9-10 96:13 98:9 110:5-6, Revelation 19:11, Zechariah 14:4

[6] Joel 4:13 - Midrash Psalms 2:14 8:1 8:8 62:2, Pesikta Rabbati 10:4, Saadia Opinions 8:6, Song of Songs.R 8:19, Deuteronomy 16:9, Genesis 13:13 15:16 18:20, Hosea 6:11, Isaiah 15:3, Jeremiah 3:33, Lamentations 1:15, Mark 4:29, Matthew 13:39, Revelation 14:15-20

[7] Joel 4:14 - Midrash Psalms 2:14 8:8 62:2 111:1, Saadia Opinions 8:6, 2 Peter 3:7, Ezekiel 38:8-38:23 39:8-39:20, Isaiah 34:2-34:8 63:1-63:7, Joel 1:15 2:1 4:2, Philippians 3:2, Psalms 37:13, Revelation 16:14-16:16 19:19-19:21

[8] LXX *Noises have resounded in the valley of judgment*

[9] Joel 4:15 - Lamentations.R 3:10 Petichata D'Chakimei:1, Pesikta de R'Kahana 15.3, Isaiah 13:10, Joel 2:10 3:4, Luke 21:25-26, Matthew 24:29, Revelation 6:12-13

[10] Joel 4:16 - Exodus.R 29:9, Midrash Psalms 62:2, 1 Samuel 15:29, Amos 1:2 3:8, Ezekiel 14:19, Haggai 2:6, Hebrews 12:26, Hosea 11:10, Isaiah 9:16 18:13 51:5-51:6 3:16, Jeremiah 16:19 25:30-25:31, Joel 2:10-2:11, Proverbs 18:10, Psalms 18:3 29:11 46:2-46:12 61:4 91:1-91:2, Revelation 11:13 11:19 16:18, Zechariah 10:6 10:12 12:5-12:8

[11] Joel 4:17 - 4QXIIg, Midrash Psalms 8:8, Saadia Opinions 7:7, Daniel 11:45, Ezekiel 19:12 24:35, Isaiah 4:3 12:6 11:8 4:1, Jeremiah 7:24, Joel 2:27 4:21, Micah 4:7, Nahum 2:1, Obadiah 1:16-17, Psalms 9:12 76:3, Psalms of Solomon 17:28, Revelation 21:27, Zechariah 8:3 14:20-21, Zephaniah 3:14-16

[12] Joel 4:18 - 9, b.Sanhedrin [Rashi] 1a, Ecclesiastes.R 1:1 1:28 3:14, Esther.R Petichata:11, Genesis.R 42:3 51:8 70:6, Jastrow 901a 1560a, Leviticus.R 11:7 12:5, Mekhilta de R'Shimon bar Yochai Pisha 18:4, Mekilta de R'Ishmael Shirata 2:50, Midrash Psalms 73:4 138:2, Midrash Tanchuma Balak 17, Midrash Tanchuma Beshallach 12, Midrash Tanchuma Shemini 5, Midrash Tanchuma Terumah 9, Numbers.R 13:2 13:5 20:22, Pesikta de R'Kahana 16.8, Pesikta Rabbati 29/30B:2 33:13, Ruth.R Petichata:7, Sifre Devarim Ekev 43, Sifre Devarim Ekev 43, Song of Songs.R 1:45, Amos 9:13-9:14, Exodus 3:8, Ezekiel 47:1-47:12, Isaiah 6:25 11:6 41:17-41:18 55:12-55:13, Job 5:6, Micah 6:5, Numbers 1:1, Psalms 46:5, Revelation 22:1-22:2, Zechariah 14:8

fountain shall come forth of the house of the LORD, And shall water the valley of *Shittim*[1].

מִצְרַ֙יִם֙ לִשְׁמָמָ֣ה תִֽהְיֶ֔ה וֶאֱד֖וֹם לְמִדְבַּ֣ר שְׁמָמָ֑ה תִּֽהְיֶ֔ה מֵחֲמַ֖ס בְּנֵ֣י יְהוּדָ֑ה אֲשֶׁר־שָׁפְכ֥וּ דָם־נָקִ֖יא בְּאַרְצָֽם   19[2]

Egypt shall be a desolation, and *Edom*[3] shall be [4]a desolate wilderness, for the violence against the children of Judah, because they shed innocent blood in their land.

וִיהוּדָ֖ה לְעוֹלָ֣ם תֵּשֵׁ֑ב וִירוּשָׁלַ֖͏ִם לְד֥וֹר וָדֽוֹר   20[5]

But Judah shall be inhabited forever, and Jerusalem from generation to generation.

וְנִקֵּ֖יתִי דָּמָ֣ם לֹֽא־נִקֵּ֑יתִי וַֽיהוָ֖ה שֹׁכֵ֥ן בְּצִיּֽוֹן   21[6]

And I will hold as innocent their blood that I have not held as innocent[7]; And the LORD dwells in Zion.

Amos min Tekoa – Chapter 1

דִּבְרֵ֣י עָמ֗וֹס אֲשֶׁר־הָיָ֥ה בַנֹּקְדִ֖ים מִתְּק֑וֹעַ אֲשֶׁר֩ חָזָ֨ה עַל־יִשְׂרָאֵ֜ל בִּימֵ֣י ׀ עֻזִּיָּ֣ה מֶֽלֶךְ־יְהוּדָ֗ה וּבִימֵ֞י יָרָבְעָ֤ם בֶּן־יוֹאָשׁ֙ מֶ֣לֶךְ יִשְׂרָאֵ֔ל שְׁנָתַ֖יִם לִפְנֵ֥י הָרָֽעַשׁ   1[8]

The words of Amos, *who was among the herdmen of Tekoa, which he saw concerning Israel*[9] in the days of Uzziah king of Judah, and in the days of Jeroboam the son of Joash king of Israel, two years before the earthquake.

וַיֹּאמַ֓ר ׀ יְהוָה֙ מִצִּיּ֣וֹן יִשְׁאָ֔ג וּמִירוּשָׁלַ֖͏ִם יִתֵּ֣ן קוֹל֑וֹ וְאָֽבְלוּ֙ נְא֣וֹת הָרֹעִ֔ים וְיָבֵ֖שׁ רֹ֥אשׁ הַכַּרְמֶֽל   2[10]

And he said: The LORD roars from Zion, And utters His voice from Jerusalem; and the pastures of the shepherds shall mourn, and the top of Carmel shall wither.

כֹּ֚ה אָמַ֣ר יְהוָ֔ה עַל־שְׁלֹשָׁה֙ פִּשְׁעֵ֣י דַמֶּ֔שֶׂק וְעַל־אַרְבָּעָ֖ה לֹ֣א אֲשִׁיבֶ֑נּוּ עַל־דּוּשָׁ֛ם בַּחֲרֻצ֥וֹת הַבַּרְזֶ֖ל אֶת־הַגִּלְעָֽד   3[11]

For thus says the LORD: For three transgressions of Damascus; yes, for four I will not reverse it: because they *have threshed Gilead with sledges of iron*[12].

וְשִׁלַּ֥חְתִּי אֵ֖שׁ בְּבֵ֣ית חֲזָאֵ֑ל וְאָכְלָ֖ה אַרְמְנ֥וֹת בֶּן־הֲדָֽד   4[13]

So will I send a fire into the house of Hazael, and it shall devour the *palaces of Ben-hadad*[14];

---

[1] LXX *flags*

[2] Joel 4:19 - b.Bava Kamma [Tosefot] 62a, b.Bava Kamma 119a, b.Bava Metzia [Tosefot] 5b, Ein Yaakov Bava Kamma:119a, Exodus.R 15:17 18:6, Genesis.R 31:6, Midrash Tanchuma Beshallach 5, Numbers.R 10:2 13:4, Pesikta de R'Kahana 3.e, Sifre Devarim Ha'azinu Hashamayim 333, Sifre Devarim Nitzavim 333, 2 Thessalonians 1:6, Amos 1:11-12, Ezekiel 25:1-17 35:1-15, Isaiah 11:15 19:1-15 34:1-17 63:1-6, Jeremiah 1:17 3:35, Lamentations 4:21, Malachi 1:3-1:4, Obadiah 1:1 1:10-16, Psalms 17:7, Zechariah 10:10 14:18-19
Joel 4:19-20 - 4QXIIg
Joel 4:19-21 - Mekilta de R'Ishmael Beshallah 1:229-233

[3] LXX *Idumea*

[4] 4QXIIc adds *a wilderness*

[5] Joel 4:20 - Midrash Tanchuma Beshallach 5, Amos 9:15, Ezekiel 13:25, Isaiah 9:20
Joel 4:20-21 - Sifre Devarim Nitzavim 333

[6] Joel 4:21 - b.Rosh Hashanah 23a, Ein Yaakov Rosh Hashanah:23a, Genesis.R 82:2, Midrash Tanchuma Beshallach 5, Numbers.R 13:4, Pesikta de R'Kahana 2:11 5:6, Shabbat Shacharit [Av Horachamim], Ezekiel 12:25 12:29 24:35, Isaiah 4:4, Joel 4:17, Matthew 3:25, Revelation 21:3

[7] LXX *And I will make inquisition for their blood, and will by no means leave it unavenged*

[8] Amos 1:1 - 1 Corinthians 1:27, 1 Kings 19:19, 2 Chronicles 11:6 20:20 26:1-23, 2 Kings 14:21 14:23-2, 2 Samuel 14:2, Amos 7:9-11 7:14, Exodus 3:1, Hosea 1:1, Isaiah 1:1, Jehoach is altered to read, Jeremiah 1:1 6:1 7:27, Joach, m.Menachot 8:3, m.Parah 1:1, Matthew 1:8-9 4:18, Micah 1:1, Psalms 78:70-72, Seder Olam 20:Flee, Sifre Devarim Devarim 1, Sifre Devarim Devarim 1, Zechariah 14:5

[9] LXX *that came to him in Accarim out of Thecue, which he saw concerning Jerusalem*

[10] Amos 1:2 - 1 Samuel 1:2, Amos 3:7-8 4:7-8 9:3, Hosea 13:8, Isaiah 9:9 11:2 18:13, Jeremiah 12:4 14:2 1:30 2:19, Joel 1:9-13 1:16-18 2:11 4:16, Nahum 1:4, Proverbs 20:2

[11] Amos 1:3 - 1 Kings 19:17, 2 Kings 8:12 10:32-10:33 13:3 13:7, Amos 1:6 1:9 1:11 1:13 2:1 2:4 2:6, Ecclesiastes 11:2, Isaiah 7:8 8:4 17:1-17:3 17:15, Jeremiah 49:23-49:27, Job 5:19 19:3, Pesikta de R'Kahana 19.2, Proverbs 6:16, Sifre Devarim Ha'azinu Hashamayim 322, Sifre Devarim Nitzavim 322, z.Vaetchanan 269b, Zechariah 9:1
Amos 1:3-5 - 5QAmos
Amos 1:3-15 - 4QXIIg

[12] LXX *sawed with iron saws the women with child of the Galaadites*

[13] Amos 1:4 - 1 Kings 19:15 20:1-20:22, 2 Chronicles 16:2, 2 Kings 6:24 8:7-8:15 13:3 13:25, Amos 1:7 1:10 1:12 1:14 2:2 2:5, Ezekiel 6:8 15:6, Hosea 8:14, Jeremiah 17:27 1:27, Judges 9:19-9:20 9:57

[14] LXX *foundations of the son of Ader*

Hebrew	Verse	English

וְשָׁבַרְתִּי בְּרִיחַ דַּמֶּשֶׂק וְהִכְרַתִּי יוֹשֵׁב מִבִּקְעַת־אָוֶן וְתוֹמֵךְ שֵׁבֶט מִבֵּית עֶדֶן וְגָלוּ עַם־אֲרָם קִירָה אָמַר יְהוָה

5[1] — And I will break the bar of Damascus, and cut off the inhabitant *from Bikath-Aven, and he who holds the scepter from Beth-eden; and the people of Aram shall go into captivity to Kir*[2], says the LORD.

כֹּה אָמַר יְהוָה עַל־שְׁלֹשָׁה פִּשְׁעֵי עַזָּה וְעַל־אַרְבָּעָה לֹא אֲשִׁיבֶנּוּ עַל־הַגְלוֹתָם גָּלוּת שְׁלֵמָה לְהַסְגִּיר לֶאֱדוֹם

6[3] — Thus says the LORD: For three transgressions of Gaza; yes, for four I will not reverse it: because they *carried away captive a whole captivity, to deliver them up to Edom*[4].

וְשִׁלַּחְתִּי אֵשׁ בְּחוֹמַת עַזָּה וְאָכְלָה אַרְמְנֹתֶיהָ

7[5] — So will I send a fire on the wall of Gaza, and it shall devour its *palaces*[6];

וְהִכְרַתִּי יוֹשֵׁב מֵאַשְׁדּוֹד וְתוֹמֵךְ שֵׁבֶט מֵאַשְׁקְלוֹן וַהֲשִׁיבוֹתִי יָדִי עַל־עֶקְרוֹן וְאָבְדוּ שְׁאֵרִית פְּלִשְׁתִּים אָמַר אֲדֹנָי יְהוָה

8[7] — And I will cut off the inhabitant from *Ashdod, and he who holds the scepter from Ashkelon; and I will turn My hand against Ekron*[8], and the remnant of the Philistines shall perish, says the Lord GOD.

כֹּה אָמַר יְהוָה עַל־שְׁלֹשָׁה פִּשְׁעֵי־צֹר וְעַל־אַרְבָּעָה לֹא אֲשִׁיבֶנּוּ עַל־הַסְגִּירָם גָּלוּת שְׁלֵמָה לֶאֱדוֹם וְלֹא זָכְרוּ בְּרִית אַחִים

9[9] — Thus says the LORD: For three transgressions of Tyre; yes, for four I will not reverse it: because they *delivered up a whole captivity to Edom*[10], and did not remember the brotherly covenant.

וְשִׁלַּחְתִּי אֵשׁ בְּחוֹמַת צֹר וְאָכְלָה אַרְמְנֹתֶיהָ

10[11] — So will I send a fire on the wall of Tyre, and it shall devour its *palaces*[12].

כֹּה אָמַר יְהוָה עַל־שְׁלֹשָׁה פִּשְׁעֵי אֱדוֹם וְעַל־אַרְבָּעָה לֹא אֲשִׁיבֶנּוּ עַל־רָדְפוֹ בַחֶרֶב אָחִיו וְשִׁחֵת רַחֲמָיו וַיִּטְרֹף לָעַד אַפּוֹ וְעֶבְרָתוֹ שְׁמָרָה נֶצַח

11[13] — Thus says the LORD: For three transgressions of Edom; yes, for four I will not reverse it: because he pursued his brother with the sword, and *cast off all pity*[14], and his anger tore perpetually, and he kept his wrath forever.

וְשִׁלַּחְתִּי אֵשׁ בְּתֵימָן וְאָכְלָה אַרְמְנוֹת בָּצְרָה

12[15] — So will I send a fire upon Teman, and it shall devour the *palaces of Bozrah*[16].

---

[1] Amos 1:5 - 2 Kings 16:9, Amos 9:7, Isaiah 19:14, Jeremiah 2:36 3:30, Lamentations 2:9, Nahum 3:13
Amos 1:5-15 - MurXII
[2] LXX *out of the plain of On, and will cut in pieces a tribe out of the men of Charrhan: and the famous people of Syria shall be led captive*
[3] Amos 1:6 - 1 Samuel 6:17, 2 Chronicles 21:16-21:17 4:18, Acts 8:26, Amos 1:3 1:9 1:11, Ein Yaakov Pesachim:87b, Ezekiel 25:15-25:16 11:5, Isaiah 14:29-14:31, Jeremiah 23:1 47:4-47:5, Joel 4:6, Lamentations.R 1:56, Obadiah 1:11, Pesikta de R'Kahana 19.2, Sifre Devarim Ha'azinu Hashamayim 322, Sifre Devarim Nitzavim 322, z.Vaetchanan 269b, Zechariah 9:5, Zephaniah 2:4-2:7
[4] LXX *took prisoners the captivity of Solomon, to shut them up into Idumea*
[5] Amos 1:7 - 2 Chronicles 2:6, 2 Kings 18:8, Amos 1:4, Deuteronomy 8:35 32:41-32:43, Jeremiah 25:18-25:20 23:1, Psalms 75:8-75:9 94:1-94:5, Romans 12:19, Zechariah 9:5-9:7, Zephaniah 2:4
[6] LXX *foundations*
[7] Amos 1:8 - 2 Chronicles 2:6, Amos 3:9, Ezekiel 1:16, Isaiah 1:25 14:29-31 20:1, Jeremiah 47:4-5, Psalms 81:15, Zechariah 9:6 13:7, Zephaniah 2:4-7
[8] LXX *Azotus, and a tribe shall be cut off from Ascalon, and I will stretch out my hand upon Accaron*
[9] Amos 1:9 - 1 Kings 5:1-5:11 9:11-9:14, 2 Chronicles 2:7-2:15, 2 Samuel 5:11, Amos 1:6 1:11, Avot de R'Natan 9, Avot de R'Natan 9, Ezekiel 26:1-26:21, Isaiah 23:1-23:18, Jeremiah 1:22 23:4, Joel 4:4-4:8, Lamentations.R 1:56, Matthew 11:21, Pesikta de R'Kahana 19.2, Sifre Devarim Ha'azinu Hashamayim 322, Sifre Devarim Nitzavim 322, z.Vaetchanan 269b, Zechariah 9:2-9:4
[10] LXX *shut up the prisoners of Solomon into Idumea*
[11] Amos 1:10 - Amos 1:4 1:7, Ezekiel 2:12, Zechariah 9:4
[12] LXX *foundations*
[13] Amos 1:11 - 2 Chronicles 4:17, b.Sotah 21a, Deuteronomy 2:4-8 23:9, Ecclesiastes 7:9, Ephesians 4:26-27 5:1, Ezekiel 25:12-14 35:1-15, Genesis 27:40-41, Genesis.R 67:10 82:2, Isaiah 21:11-12 34:1-17 9:16 63:1-7, Jastrow 896b, Jeremiah 49:7-22, Joel 4:19, Lamentations 4:21-22, Malachi 1:2 1:4, Micah 7:18, Midrash Psalms 109:3, Midrash Tanchuma Ki Tetze 4 10, Midrash Tanchuma Mikketz 10, Numbers 20:14-21, Obadiah 1:1-14, Pesikta de R'Kahana 3.1, Pesikta Rabbati 12:4-5 12:13 13:3 48:2, Psalms 83:4-9 85:6 17:7, Siman 131:4, z.Vaetchanan 269b
[14] LXX *destroyed the mother upon the earth, and summoned up his anger for a testimony*
[15] Amos 1:12 - Genesis 12:11 12:33, Isaiah 10:6, Jeremiah 1:7 1:13 1:20 1:22, Obadiah 1:9-1:10, Testament of Job 29:3
[16] LXX *foundations of her walls*

כֹּה אָמַר יְהֹוָה עַל־שְׁלֹשָׁה פִּשְׁעֵי בְנֵי־עַמּוֹן וְעַל־אַרְבָּעָה לֹא אֲשִׁיבֶנּוּ עַל־בִּקְעָם הָרוֹת הַגִּלְעָד לְמַעַן הַרְחִיב אֶת־גְּבוּלָם	13[1]	Thus says the LORD: For three transgressions of the children of Ammon; yes, for four I will not reverse it: because they ripped up the women with child in Gilead, so they might enlarge their border.
וְהִצַּתִּי אֵשׁ בְּחוֹמַת רַבָּה וְאָכְלָה אַרְמְנוֹתֶיהָ בִּתְרוּעָה בְּיוֹם מִלְחָמָה בְּסַעַר בְּיוֹם סוּפָה	14[2]	So will I kindle a fire in the wall of Rabbah, and it shall devour its *palaces*[3], with shouting in the day of battle, with a tempest in the day of the whirlwind;
וְהָלַךְ מַלְכָּם בַּגּוֹלָה הוּא וְשָׂרָיו יַחְדָּו אָמַר יְהֹוָה	15[4]	And their king shall go into captivity, he and his princes together, says the LORD.

Amos – Chapter 2

כֹּה אָמַר יְהֹוָה עַל־שְׁלֹשָׁה פִּשְׁעֵי מוֹאָב וְעַל־אַרְבָּעָה לֹא אֲשִׁיבֶנּוּ עַל־שָׂרְפוֹ עַצְמוֹת מֶלֶךְ־אֱדוֹם לַשִּׂיד	1[5]	Thus says the LORD: For three transgressions of Moab; Yes, for four I will not reverse it: Because he burned the bones of the king of Edom into lime.
וְשִׁלַּחְתִּי־אֵשׁ בְּמוֹאָב וְאָכְלָה אַרְמְנוֹת הַקְּרִיּוֹת וּמֵת בְּשָׁאוֹן מוֹאָב בִּתְרוּעָה בְּקוֹל שׁוֹפָר	2[6]	So will I send a fire upon Moab, And it shall devour the *palaces of Kerioth*[7]; And Moab shall die with mayhem, With shouting, and with the sound of the horn;
וְהִכְרַתִּי שׁוֹפֵט מִקִּרְבָּהּ וְכָל־שָׂרֶיהָ אֶהֱרוֹג עִמּוֹ אָמַר יְהֹוָה	3[8]	And I will cut off the judge from its midst, and will kill all its princes with him, Says the LORD.
כֹּה אָמַר יְהֹוָה עַל־שְׁלֹשָׁה פִּשְׁעֵי יְהוּדָה וְעַל־אַרְבָּעָה לֹא אֲשִׁיבֶנּוּ עַל־מָאֳסָם אֶת־תּוֹרַת יְהֹוָה וְחֻקָּיו לֹא שָׁמָרוּ וַיַּתְעוּם כִּזְבֵיהֶם אֲשֶׁר־הָלְכוּ אֲבוֹתָם אַחֲרֵיהֶם	4[9]	Thus says the LORD: For three transgressions of Judah; yes, for four I will not reverse it: Because they rejected the law of the LORD, And have not kept His statutes, *And their lies have caused them to err, in the way in which their fathers walked*[10].
וְשִׁלַּחְתִּי אֵשׁ בִּיהוּדָה וְאָכְלָה אַרְמְנוֹת יְרוּשָׁלָ͏ִם	5[11]	So will I send a fire upon Judah, And it shall devour the *palaces*[12] of Jerusalem.
כֹּה אָמַר יְהֹוָה עַל־שְׁלֹשָׁה פִּשְׁעֵי יִשְׂרָאֵל וְעַל־אַרְבָּעָה לֹא אֲשִׁיבֶנּוּ עַל־מִכְרָם בַּכֶּסֶף צַדִּיק וְאֶבְיוֹן בַּעֲבוּר נַעֲלָיִם	6[13]	Thus says the LORD: For three transgressions of Israel; Yes, for four I will not reverse it:

---

[1] Amos 1:13 - 1 Samuel 11:1-11:2, 2 Chronicles 20:1 20:10, 2 Kings 24:2, 2 Samuel 10:1-10:8, Amos 1:3, Deuteronomy 2:19 23:5-23:5, Ezekiel 21:33 25:2-25:7 11:10, Habakkuk 2:5-2:6, Hosea 14:1, Isaiah 5:8, Jeremiah 49:1-49:6, Judges 10:7-10:9 11:15-11:28, Nehemiah 2:19 4:7-4:23, Psalms 83:8, z.Vaetchanan 269b, Zephaniah 2:8-2:9

[2] Amos 1:14 - 2 Samuel 12:26, Ahiqar 169, Amos 2:2, Daniel 11:40, Deuteronomy 3:11, Ezekiel 1:5, Isaiah 9:6 6:30, Jeremiah 1:2, Job 15:25, Psalms 83:16, Zechariah 7:14

[3] LXX *foundations*

[4] Amos 1:15 - Jeremiah 1:3, Testament of Solomon 26:1

[5] Amos 2:1 - 2 Kings 3:9 3:26-27, 4QXIIg, Amos 1:3 1:6 1:9 1:11 1:13 2:4 2:6, b.Bava Batra 22a, Deuteronomy 23:6, Ein Yaakov Bava Batra 22a, Ezekiel 25:8-25:9, Isaiah 11:14 15:1-9 1:10, Jeremiah 48:1-47, Micah 6:5, MurXII, Numbers 22:1-25, Proverbs 15:3, Psalms 83:5-8, z.Vaetchanan 269b, Zephaniah 2:8-9

[6] Amos 2:2 - Amos 1:14, Isaiah 9:6, Jeremiah 24:24 24:34 24:41

[7] LXX *foundations of its cities*

[8] Amos 2:3 - Isaiah 16:23, Jeremiah 24:7 24:25, Numbers 24:17, Psalms 2:10

[9] Amos 2:4 - 1 Peter 1:18, 1 Thessalonians 4:8, 2 Chronicles 6:7 36:14-17, 2 Kings 17:19 22:11-17, 2 Samuel 12:9-10, Amos 3:2, Daniel 9:5-12, Deuteronomy 31:16-18 32:15-27, Ezekiel 13:6-16 13:22 16:1-63 20:13 20:16 20:18 20:24 20:30 22:8 22:28 23:11-21, Habakkuk 2:18, Hosea 5:12-13 6:11 12:4, Isaiah 5:24-25 9:16-17 4:15 20:20, Jeremiah 6:19 8:2 8:9 9:15 9:26-27 16:12 16:19-20 23:13-15 23:25-32 28:15-16, Judges 2:11-20 10:6, Leviticus 26:14-15, Nehemiah 1:7 9:26 9:29-30, Romans 1:25, Sifre Devarim Ekev 41, Sifre Devarim Ekev 41, z.Vaetchanan 269b

[10] LXX *and their vain idols which they made, which their fathers followed, caused them to err*

[11] Amos 2:5 - Hosea 8:14, Jeremiah 17:27 21:10 37:8-10 15:8 4:13

[12] LXX *foundations*

[13] Amos 2:6 - 2 Kings 17:7-18 18:12, Amos 5:11-12 6:3-7 8:4-6, b.Sanhedrin 7a, b.Yoma 86b, Ein Yaakov Sanhedrin:7a, Ein Yaakov Yoma 86b, Ezekiel 23:5-9, Genesis 37:26-28, Hosea 4:1-2 4:11-14 7:7-10 8:4-6 13:2-3, Isaiah 5:22-23 5:21, Jastrow 1005a, Joel 4:3 4:6, Micah 3:2-3 6:10-16, Midrash Tanchuma Noach 5, mt.Hilchot Teshuvah 3:5, Pirkei de R'Eliezer 38, Saadia Opinions 5:5, t.Kippurim 4:13, z.Vaetchanan 269b

Amos 2:6-3:8 - Haftarah Vayeishev

Because they sell the righteous for silver, and the needy for a pair of shoes[1];

Who pant after the dust of the earth on the head of the poor[3], And turn aside the way of the humble; And a man and his father go into the same maid, to profane My holy name;

הַשֹּׁאֲפִים עַל־עֲפַר־אֶרֶץ בְּרֹאשׁ דַּלִּים וְדֶרֶךְ עֲנָוִים יַטּוּ וְאִישׁ וְאָבִיו יֵלְכוּ אֶל־הַנַּעֲרָה לְמַעַן חַלֵּל אֶת־שֵׁם קָדְשִׁי

7[2]

And they lay themselves down beside every altar, on clothes taken in pledge, and in the house of their God they drink the wine of those who have been condemned[5].

וְעַל־בְּגָדִים חֲבֻלִים יַטּוּ אֵצֶל כָּל־מִזְבֵּחַ וְיֵין עֲנוּשִׁים יִשְׁתּוּ בֵּית אֱלֹהֵיהֶם

8[4]

Yet, I destroyed the Amorite before them, whose height was like the height of the cedars, And he was strong as the oaks; yet I destroyed his fruit above, and his roots beneath.

וְאָנֹכִי הִשְׁמַדְתִּי אֶת־הָאֱמֹרִי מִפְּנֵיהֶם אֲשֶׁר כְּגֹבַהּ אֲרָזִים גָּבְהוֹ וְחָסֹן הוּא כָּאַלּוֹנִים וָאַשְׁמִיד פִּרְיוֹ מִמַּעַל וְשָׁרָשָׁיו מִתָּחַת

9[6]

Also I brought you up out of the land of Egypt, And led you forty years in the wilderness, to possess the land of the Amorites.

וְאָנֹכִי הֶעֱלֵיתִי אֶתְכֶם מֵאֶרֶץ מִצְרָיִם וָאוֹלֵךְ אֶתְכֶם בַּמִּדְבָּר אַרְבָּעִים שָׁנָה לָרֶשֶׁת אֶת־אֶרֶץ הָאֱמֹרִי

10[7]

And I raised up of your sons for prophets, And your young men for Nazirites. Is it not so, O children of Israel? Says the LORD.

וָאָקִים מִבְּנֵיכֶם לִנְבִיאִים וּמִבַּחוּרֵיכֶם לִנְזִרִים הַאַף אֵין־זֹאת בְּנֵי יִשְׂרָאֵל נְאֻם־יְהוָה

11[8]

But you gave the Nazirites wine to drink; And commanded the prophets, saying: 'Do not prophesy.'

וַתַּשְׁקוּ אֶת־הַנְּזִרִים יָיִן וְעַל־הַנְּבִיאִים צִוִּיתֶם לֵאמֹר לֹא תִּנָּבְאוּ

12[9]

[11]Behold, I will make it creak under you, As a cart creaks that is full of sheaves.

הִנֵּה אָנֹכִי מֵעִיק תַּחְתֵּיכֶם כַּאֲשֶׁר תָּעִיק הָעֲגָלָה הַמְלֵאָה לָהּ עָמִיר

13[10]

And flight shall fail the swift, And the strong shall not exert his strength, nor shall the mighty deliver himself;

וְאָבַד מָנוֹס מִקָּל וְחָזָק לֹא־יְאַמֵּץ כֹּחוֹ וְגִבּוֹר לֹא־יְמַלֵּט נַפְשׁוֹ

14[12]

Nor shall he who handles the bow stand; And he who is swift of foot shall not deliver himself; nor shall he who rides the horse deliver himself;

וְתֹפֵשׂ הַקֶּשֶׁת לֹא יַעֲמֹד וְקַל בְּרַגְלָיו לֹא יְמַלֵּט וְרֹכֵב הַסּוּס לֹא יְמַלֵּט נַפְשׁוֹ

15[13]

---

[1] This, midrashically, can point to the sale of Yosef [Genesis 37:28, Midrash Tanchuma Noach 5, Pirkei de R'Eliezer 38]; cf. Deuteronomy 25:8-10, Ruth 4:7

[2] Amos 2:7 - 1 Corinthians 5:1, 1 Kings 21:4, 2 Samuel 12:14, Amos 4:1 5:12 8:4, Deuteronomy.R 2:21, Ezekiel 22:11 12:20, Isaiah 10:2, Leviticus 18:8 18:15 20:3, Micah 2:2 2:9 7:2-7:3, Pesikta Rabbati 15:14/15, Proverbs 4:21, Romans 2:24, Zephaniah 3:3 Amos 2:7-9 - 4QXIIg

[3] LXX *with which to tread on the dust of the earth, and they have smitten upon the heads of the poor*

[4] Amos 2:8 - 1 Corinthians 8:10 10:7 10:21, Amos 4:1 6:4 6:6, Deuteronomy 24:12-24:17, Exodus 22:26-22:27, Ezekiel 18:7 18:12 23:41, Hosea 4:8, Isaiah 9:7, Judges 9:27

[5] LXX *And binding their clothes with cords they have made them curtains near the altar, and they have drunk wine gained by extortion in the house of their God*

[6] Amos 2:9 - 2 Samuel 23:16-22, b.Bechorot 45b, b.Sotah 36a, Deuteronomy 1:28 2:10-11 2:24-33 3:11 9:1-3, Ein Yaakov Sotah 36a, Exodus 3:8 10:11, Ezekiel 17:9, Genesis 15:16, Guide for the Perplexed 1:63 2:47, Isaiah 5:24, Job 18:16, Joshua 3:10 10:12 11:21-22 24:8-12, Judges 11:21-23, Leviticus.R 7:1 10:5, Malachi 3:19, Mekhilta de R'Shimon bar Yochai Shirata 32:2, Mekilta de R'Ishmael Shirata 6:90, Midrash Psalms 29:2 136:11, Midrash Tanchuma Acharei Mot 8, Midrash Tanchuma Chukkat 1, Midrash Tanchuma Devarim 4, Midrash Tanchuma Mishpatim 18, Midrash Tanchuma Re'eh 9, Midrash Tanchuma Tetzaveh 10, Nehemiah 9:22-24, Numbers 13:28-29 13:32-33 21:23-25, Numbers.R 1:2 2:8 18:22, Pesikta Rabbati 47:1, Psalms 135:10-12 136:17-22, Sifre Devarim Ekev 50, Song of Songs.R 2:42, Tanna Devei Eliyahu 2

[7] Amos 2:10 - Acts 7:42 13:18, Amos 3:1 9:7, Deuteronomy 1:20-21 1:39 2:7 8:2-4, Exodus 3:8 12:51 20:2, Ezekiel 20:10, Jeremiah 32:20-21, Micah 6:4, Nehemiah 9:8-12 9:21, Numbers 14:31-35, Psalms 95:10 105:42-43 136:10-11, t.Shabbat 7:24

[8] Amos 2:11 - 1 Kings 17:1 18:4 19:16 20:13 20:35 20:41 22:8, 1 Samuel 3:20 19:20, 1 Thessalonians 2:15-16, 2 Chronicles 12:15, 2 Kings 2:2-5 6:1 17:13, 2 Peter 1:20-21, Acts 4:18 5:28 7:51, Amos 7:12-13, Deuteronomy 18:18, Isaiah 5:3-4 30:10-11, Jeremiah 2:5 2:31 7:25 11:21 2:11, Judges 13:4-7, Lamentations 4:7, Luke 1:3-17, Matthew 21:34-38, Micah 2:6 6:3-4, mt.Nizirut 10:14, Numbers 6:2-3, Saadia Opinions 5:7, Sifre.z Numbers Naso 6:8, z.Vaetchanan 269b Amos 2:11-16 - 4QXIIc

[9] Amos 2:12 - Amos 7:13 7:16, Isaiah 6:10, Jeremiah 11:21, Micah 2:6

[10] Amos 2:13 - Ezekiel 6:9 16:43, Isaiah 1:14 7:13 19:24, Malachi 2:17, Psalms 78:40

[11] LXX adds *Because of this*

[12] Amos 2:14 - Amos 9:1-9:3, Ecclesiastes 9:11, Isaiah 30:16-30:17, Jeremiah 9:24, Job 11:20, Psalms 33:16

[13] Amos 2:15 - 4QXIIg, Ezekiel 15:3, Psalms 33:16-33:17

וְאַמִּיץ לִבּוֹ בַּגִּבּוֹרִים עָרוֹם יָנוּס בַּיּוֹם־הַהוּא נְאֻם־יְהוָה

16[1]   And he who *is courageous*[2] among the mighty shall flee naked in that day, says the LORD.

Amos – Chapter 3

שִׁמְעוּ אֶת־הַדָּבָר הַזֶּה אֲשֶׁר דִּבֶּר יְהוָה עֲלֵיכֶם בְּנֵי יִשְׂרָאֵל עַל כָּל־הַמִּשְׁפָּחָה אֲשֶׁר הֶעֱלֵיתִי מֵאֶרֶץ מִצְרַיִם לֵאמֹר

1[3]   Israel, against the whole family who hear this word the LORD has spoken against you, O you children of whom I brought up out of the land of Egypt, saying:

רַק אֶתְכֶם יָדַעְתִּי מִכֹּל מִשְׁפְּחוֹת הָאֲדָמָה עַל־כֵּן אֶפְקֹד עֲלֵיכֶם אֵת כָּל־עֲוֹנֹתֵיכֶם

2[4]   I have known only You of all the families of the earth; Therefore, I will visit upon you all your iniquities.

הֲיֵלְכוּ שְׁנַיִם יַחְדָּו בִּלְתִּי אִם־נוֹעָדוּ

3[5]   Will two walk together, except they agree?

הֲיִשְׁאַג אַרְיֵה בַּיַּעַר וְטֶרֶף אֵין לוֹ הֲיִתֵּן כְּפִיר קוֹלוֹ מִמְּעֹנָתוֹ בִּלְתִּי אִם־לָכָד

4[6]   Will a lion roar in the forest, when he has no prey? Will a young lion give forth his voice out of his den, if he has taken nothing?

הֲתִפֹּל צִפּוֹר עַל־פַּח הָאָרֶץ וּמוֹקֵשׁ אֵין לָהּ הֲיַעֲלֶה־פַּח מִן־הָאֲדָמָה וְלָכוֹד לֹא יִלְכּוֹד

5[7]   Will a bird fall in a snare upon the earth, where there is no lure for it? will a snare spring up from the ground, and take nothing at all?

אִם־יִתָּקַע שׁוֹפָר בְּעִיר וְעָם לֹא יֶחֱרָדוּ אִם־תִּהְיֶה רָעָה בְּעִיר וַיהוָה לֹא עָשָׂה

6[8]   Shall the horn be blown in a city, and the people not tremble? Shall evil befall a city, and the LORD has not done it?

כִּי לֹא יַעֲשֶׂה אֲדֹנָי יְהוָה דָּבָר כִּי אִם־גָּלָה סוֹדוֹ אֶל־עֲבָדָיו הַנְּבִיאִים

7[9]   For the Lord GOD will do nothing, but He reveals His counsel to His servants the prophets.

אַרְיֵה שָׁאָג מִי לֹא יִירָא אֲדֹנָי יְהוִה דִּבֶּר מִי לֹא יִנָּבֵא

8[10]   The lion has roared, Who will not fear? The Lord GOD has spoken, Who can but prophesy?

הַשְׁמִיעוּ עַל־אַרְמְנוֹת בְּאַשְׁדּוֹד וְעַל־אַרְמְנוֹת בְּאֶרֶץ מִצְרָיִם וְאִמְרוּ הֵאָסְפוּ עַל־הָרֵי שֹׁמְרוֹן וּרְאוּ מְהוּמֹת רַבּוֹת בְּתוֹכָהּ וַעֲשׁוּקִים בְּקִרְבָּהּ

9[11]   Proclaim it *on the palaces at Ashdod, And on the palaces in the land* [12]of Egypt, And say: 'Assemble yourselves upon the mountains of Samaria, And behold the great confusions within, And the oppressions in its midst.'

---

[1] Amos 2:16 - 4QXIIg, 2 Kings 7:8-20, Jeremiah 24:41, Judges 4:17, Mark 14:52, Tanya Igeret Hakodesh §32

[2] 4QXIIc *finds heart*

[3] Amos 3:1 - 4QXIIg, 2 Chronicles 20:15, Amos 2:10, Ezekiel 37:16-17, Hosea 4:1 5:1, Isaiah 22:3 24:12, Jeremiah 8:3 7:2 33:24-26, Micah 3:1, Revelation 2:29
Amos 3:1-15 - 4QXIIc

[4] Amos 3:2 - 1 Peter 4:17, 4QXIIg, Acts 17:26, b.Avodah Zara 4a, Daniel 9:12, Deuteronomy 7:6 10:15 2:18 8:9, Ein Yaakov Avodah Zarah 4a, Exodus 19:5-6, Ezekiel 9:6 20:36-38, Gates of Repentance 4.13, Genesis 10:32, Hosea 2:13 8:13 9:9, Isaiah 15:19, Jeremiah 1:15 9:26 10:25 11:22 13:21 14:10, Kuzari 2.44, Luke 12:47-48, Matthew 11:20-24, Nahum 3:4, Psalms 3:19, Romans 2:9, z.Shemot 17b, Zechariah 14:17-18

[5] Amos 3:3 - 2 Corinthians 6:14-6:16, Genesis 5:22 6:9 17:1

[6] Amos 3:4 - Amos 1:2 3:8, Hosea 5:14 11:10, Psalms 8:21, z.Vayeshev 191a

[7] Amos 3:5 - Daniel 9:14, Deuteronomy.R 5:8, Ecclesiastes 9:12, Jeremiah 7:29, Midrash Psalms 91:3, Numbers.R 12:3

[8] Amos 3:6 - 2 Corinthians 5:11, Acts 2:23 4:28, Derech Hashem Part IV 8§04, Ezekiel 9:3, Genesis 2:20, Hosea 5:8, Isaiah 14:24-27 21:7, Jeremiah 4:5 5:22 6:1 10:7, mt.Hilchot Teshuvah 3:4, Pesikta de R'Kahana 24.1, Pesikta Rabbati 40:5, Zephaniah 1:16

[9] Amos 3:7 - 1 Kings 22:19-23, 2 Kings 3:17-20 6:12 22:13 22:20, b.Sanhedrin 89b, b.Sotah 11a, Daniel 9:22-27 10:21 11:2, Ecclesiastes.R 1:27, Ein Yaakov Sanhedrin:89b, Genesis 6:13 18:17, Genesis.R 49:2 97:1 99 [Excl]:2, Jeremiah 23:22, John 15:15, Mas.Kallah Rabbati 8:1, Mekilta de R'Ishmael Shirata 10:73, Midrash Proverbs 14, Midrash Psalms 25:13 64:1 111:1, Midrash Tanchuma Tazria 9, Midrash Tanchuma Vayechi 14, Midrash Tanchuma Vayera 6, Psalms 25:14, Ralbag Wars 2:3, Revelation 1:1 1:19 4:1 6:1-17, Sifre Devarim Vaetchanan 27, Sifre Devarim Vezot Habracha 357, Song of Songs.R 1:38, t.Yadayim 2:16, y.Sotah 1:9, z.Shemot 6b, z.Vayera 104b, z.Vayeshev 183b, z.Vayikra 15a

[10] Amos 3:8 - 1 Corinthians 9:16, Acts 4:20 5:20 5:29, Amos 1:2 2:12 3:4 7:12-17, Avot de R'Natan 2, b.Chullin [Rashi] 59b, b.Chullin 59b, Ein Yaakov Chullin 59b, Exodus.R 29:9, Guide for the Perplexed 2:37, Jastrow 119a, Jeremiah 20:9, Job 32:18-19, Jonah 1:1-3 3:1-3, Mekhilta de R'Shimon bar Yochai Bachodesh 51:1, Mekhilta de R'Ishmael Bahodesh 4:11, Midrash Proverbs 20, Midrash Psalms 1:4, Midrash Tanchuma Yitro 13, Pesikta de R'Kahana 13.15, Pesikta Rabbati 27/28:1, Revelation 5:5, z.Beha'alotcha 154a, z.Shemot 15a, z.Vaetchanan 270a

[11] Amos 3:9 - 1 Samuel 5:1, 2 Samuel 1:20, Amos 1:8 4:1 6:1 8:6, Deuteronomy 29:23-27, Ezekiel 12:8 13:22, Jeremiah 2:10-11 22:8-9 7:6 31:8-10 22:14 2:2, Josephus Antiquities 13.9.1, m.Maaser Sheni 5:2, m.Shekalim 1:5

[12] LXX *to the regions among the Assyrians, and to the regions*

וְלֹא־יָדְעוּ עֲשׂוֹת־נְכֹחָה נְאֻם־יְהֹוָה הָאוֹצְרִים חָמָס
וָשֹׁד בְּאַרְמְנוֹתֵיהֶם

10[1] For they do not know to do right, says the LORD, who store up violence and robbery in their *palaces*[2].

לָכֵן כֹּה אָמַר אֲדֹנָי יְהֹוִה צַר וּסְבִיב הָאָרֶץ וְהוֹרִד
מִמֵּךְ עֻזֵּךְ וְנָבֹזּוּ אַרְמְנוֹתָיִךְ

11[3] Therefore, the Lord GOD says: An adversary, around the land! And he shall bring down your strength, and your palaces shall be spoiled.

כֹּה אָמַר יְהֹוָה כַּאֲשֶׁר יַצִּיל הָרֹעֶה מִפִּי הָאֲרִי שְׁתֵּי
כְרָעַיִם אוֹ בְדַל־אֹזֶן כֵּן יִנָּצְלוּ בְּנֵי יִשְׂרָאֵל הַיֹּשְׁבִים
בְּשֹׁמְרוֹן בִּפְאַת מִטָּה וּבִדְמֶשֶׁק עָרֶשׂ

12[4] Thus says the LORD: As the shepherd rescues two legs or a piece of an ear out of the mouth of the lion, so shall the children of Israel who dwell in Samaria *escape with the corner of a couch, and the leg of a bed*[5].

שִׁמְעוּ וְהָעִידוּ בְּבֵית יַעֲקֹב נְאֻם־אֲדֹנָי יְהֹוִה אֱלֹהֵי
הַצְּבָאוֹת

13[6] Hear[7], and testify against the house of Jacob, Says the Lord GOD, the God of hosts.

כִּי בְּיוֹם פָּקְדִי פִשְׁעֵי־יִשְׂרָאֵל עָלָיו וּפָקַדְתִּי עַל־
מִזְבְּחוֹת בֵּית־אֵל וְנִגְדְּעוּ קַרְנוֹת הַמִּזְבֵּחַ וְנָפְלוּ
לָאָרֶץ

14[8] For in the day that I shall visit the transgressions of Israel upon him, I will also punish the altars of Bethel, And the horns of the altar shall be cut off, And fall to the ground.

וְהִכֵּיתִי בֵית־הַחֹרֶף עַל־בֵּית הַקָּיִץ וְאָבְדוּ בָּתֵּי
הַשֵּׁן וְסָפוּ בָּתִּים רַבִּים נְאֻם־יְהֹוָה

15[9] And I will strike the *winter*[10] house with the summerhouse; And the houses of ivory shall perish, And the great houses shall have an end, Says the LORD.

Amos – Chapter 4

שִׁמְעוּ הַדָּבָר הַזֶּה פָּרוֹת הַבָּשָׁן אֲשֶׁר בְּהַר שֹׁמְרוֹן
הָעֹשְׁקוֹת דַּלִּים הָרֹצְצוֹת אֶבְיוֹנִים הָאֹמְרֹת
לַאֲדֹנֵיהֶם הָבִיאָה וְנִשְׁתֶּה

1[11] Hear this word, you cattle of Bashan, who are in the mountain of Samaria, who oppress the poor, who crush the needy, who say to their lords: 'Bring, so we may celebrate.'

נִשְׁבַּע אֲדֹנָי יְהֹוִה בְּקָדְשׁוֹ כִּי הִנֵּה יָמִים בָּאִים
עֲלֵיכֶם וְנִשָּׂא אֶתְכֶם בְּצִנּוֹת וְאַחֲרִיתְכֶן בְּסִירוֹת
דּוּגָה

2[12] The Lord GOD has sworn by His holiness: Lo, surely the days shall come on you, that you shall be taken away with *hooks, and your residue with fish-hooks*[13].

---

[1] Amos 3:10 - 2 Peter 3:5, Amos 5:7 6:12, Habakkuk 2:8-11, James 5:3-4, Jeremiah 4:22 5:4, Psalms 14:4, Zechariah 5:3-4, Zephaniah 1:9

[2] LXX *countries*

[3] Amos 3:11 - 2 Chronicles 12:19, 2 Kings 15:19 15:29 17:3-17:6 18:9-11, Amos 2:5 3:10 3:15 6:8 6:14, Hosea 11:5-6, Isaiah 7:17-25 8:7-8 10:5-6 10:9-11, Jastrow 69b, z.Vaetchanan 269b

[4] Amos 3:12 - 1 Kings 20:30 20:34 22:25, 1 Samuel 17:34-37, 2 Kings 16:9, Amos 6:4 9:2-3, b.Bechorot [Tosefot] 37a, Isaiah 8:4 17:1-4 7:4, Mekhilta de R'Shimon bar Yochai Nezikin 73:3, Mekilta de R'Ishmael Nezikin 16:65, Romans 11:4-5, Seder Olam 22:Hosea, z.Vaetchanan 269b

[5] LXX *in the presence of a foreign tribe, and in Damascus*

[6] Amos 3:13 - 1 Thessalonians 4:6, 2 Chronicles 24:19, 2 Kings 17:13 17:15, Acts 2:40 18:5-6 20:21, Amos 5:27, Deuteronomy 8:19 30:18-19, Ephesians 4:17, Ezekiel 2:7, Isaiah 1:24, Joshua 22:22

[7] LXX adds *priests*

[8] Amos 3:14 - 1 Kings 13:2-5, 2 Chronicles 7:1 34:6-7, 2 Kings 23:15, Amos 5:5-6 9:1, Exodus 8:34, Hosea 10:5-8 10:14-15, Micah 1:6-7

[9] Amos 3:15 - 1 Kings 22:39, Amos 3:11 6:11, b.Yoma 10a, Ecclesiastes.R 6:3, Esther.R 1:12, Isaiah 5:9, Jeremiah 12:22, Judges 3:20, Psalms 45:9

[10] LXX *turreted*

[11] Amos 4:1 - 1 Kings 16:24, Amos 2:6-8 3:9-10 5:11 6:1 8:4-6, b.Shabbat 32b, Deuteronomy 15:9-11 4:33 32:14-15, Ecclesiastes 4:1 5:9, Ein Yaakov Shabbat:32b, Exodus 22:21-25, Ezekiel 22:7 22:12 22:27 22:29 15:18, Isaiah 1:17-1:24 5:8 10:6, James 5:1-6, Jeremiah 5:26-29 6:6 7:6 2:11 2:27 3:34, Job 20:19, Joel 4:3, Malachi 3:5, Micah 2:1-3 3:1-3, Proverbs 22:22-23 23:10-11, Psalms 12:6 22:13 20:13, Sifre Devarim Devarim 1, Sifre Devarim Vezot Habracha 342, Zechariah 7:10-11
Amos 4:1-2 - 4QXIIc, 4QXIIg

[12] Amos 4:2 - Amos 6:8, b.Bava Batra 73a, Ezekiel 39:4-5, Habakkuk 1:15-16, Isaiah 13:29, Jeremiah 16:16, Midrash Tanchuma Noach 11, Psalms 89:36

[13] LXX *weapons, and fiery destroyers shall cast those with you into boiling caldrons*

וּפְרָצִים תֵּצֶאנָה אִשָּׁה נֶגְדָּהּ וְהִשְׁלַכְתֶּנָה הַהַרְמוֹנָה נְאֻם־יְהוָה	3[1]	And you shall *go out at the breaches, everyone straight before her; And you shall be cast into Harmon*[2], Says the LORD.
בֹּאוּ בֵית־אֵל וּפִשְׁעוּ הַגִּלְגָּל הַרְבּוּ לִפְשֹׁעַ וְהָבִיאוּ לַבֹּקֶר זִבְחֵיכֶם לִשְׁלֹשֶׁת יָמִים מַעְשְׂרֹתֵיכֶם	4[3]	Come to Bethel and transgress, to Gilgal and multiply transgression; and bring your sacrifices in the morning, and your tithes *after three days*[4];
וְקַטֵּר מֵחָמֵץ תּוֹדָה וְקִרְאוּ נְדָבוֹת הַשְׁמִיעוּ כִּי כֵן אֲהַבְתֶּם בְּנֵי יִשְׂרָאֵל נְאֻם אֲדֹנָי יְהוִה	5[5]	*And offer a leavened sacrifice of thanksgiving, And proclaim freewill offerings and publish them; for you love to do so, O you children of Israel*[6], Says the Lord GOD.
וְגַם־אֲנִי נָתַתִּי לָכֶם נִקְיוֹן שִׁנַּיִם בְּכָל־עָרֵיכֶם וְחֹסֶר לֶחֶם בְּכֹל מְקוֹמֹתֵיכֶם וְלֹא־שַׁבְתֶּם עָדַי נְאֻם־יְהוָה	6[7]	And I have given you *cleanness*[8] of teeth in all your cities, And want of bread in all your places; Yet have you not returned to Me, Says the LORD.
וְגַם אָנֹכִי מָנַעְתִּי מִכֶּם אֶת־הַגֶּשֶׁם בְּעוֹד שְׁלֹשָׁה חֳדָשִׁים לַקָּצִיר וְהִמְטַרְתִּי עַל־עִיר אֶחָת וְעַל־עִיר אַחַת לֹא אַמְטִיר חֶלְקָה אַחַת תִּמָּטֵר וְחֶלְקָה אֲשֶׁר־לֹא־תַמְטִיר עָלֶיהָ תִּיבָשׁ	7[9]	And I have withheld the rain from you, when there were yet three months to the harvest; and I caused it to rain upon one city, and caused it not to rain on another; One plot received rain, and the plot which received no rain withered.
וְנָעוּ שְׁתַּיִם שָׁלֹשׁ עָרִים אֶל־עִיר אַחַת לִשְׁתּוֹת מַיִם וְלֹא יִשְׂבָּעוּ וְלֹא־שַׁבְתֶּם עָדַי נְאֻם־יְהוָה	8[10]	So two or three cities wandered to one city to drink water, and were not satisfied; Yet you have not returned to Me, Says the LORD.
הִכֵּיתִי אֶתְכֶם בַּשִּׁדָּפוֹן וּבַיֵּרָקוֹן הַרְבּוֹת גַּנּוֹתֵיכֶם וְכַרְמֵיכֶם וּתְאֵנֵיכֶם וְזֵיתֵיכֶם יֹאכַל הַגָּזָם וְלֹא־שַׁבְתֶּם עָדַי נְאֻם־יְהוָה	9[11]	I have struck you with blasting and mildew; the multitude of your gardens and your vineyards and your fig trees and your olive trees have been devoured by the palmer-worm, Yet you have not returned to Me, Says the LORD.
שִׁלַּחְתִּי בָכֶם דֶּבֶר בְּדֶרֶךְ מִצְרַיִם הָרַגְתִּי בַחֶרֶב בַּחוּרֵיכֶם עִם שְׁבִי סוּסֵיכֶם וָאַעֲלֶה בְּאֹשׁ מַחֲנֵיכֶם וּבְאַפְּכֶם וְלֹא־שַׁבְתֶּם עָדַי נְאֻם־יְהוָה	10[12]	I have sent among you the pestilence like in Egypt; I have killed your young men with the sword, and have carried away your horses; and I have made the stench of your camp to come up into your nostrils; Yet you have not returned to Me, Says the LORD.

---

[1] Amos 4:3 - 2 Kings 7:7-8 7:15 1:4, Ecclesiastes.R 3:10, Ezekiel 12:5 12:12, Isaiah 2:20 7:7, Matthew 16:26, Ruth.R Petichata:6, Zephaniah 1:18

[2] LXX *be brought forth naked in the presence of each other; and ye shall be cast forth on the mountain Romman*

[3] Amos 4:4 - Amos 3:14 5:5 5:21-22, Deuteronomy 14:28-29 2:12, Ecclesiastes 11:9, Ezekiel 20:39, Hosea 4:15 9:15 12:13, Joel 4:9-12, Mark 5:5 14:41, Matthew 23:32 2:45, Numbers 28:3-4, y.Avodah Zarah 1:1
Amos 4:4-9 - 4QXIIg

[4] LXX *every third day*

[5] Amos 4:5 - 2 Thessalonians 2:10-12, Deuteronomy 12:6-7, Hosea 9:1 9:10, Leviticus 7:12-13 22:18-21 23:17, Matthew 6:2 15:9 15:13-14 23:23, Psalms 81:13, Romans 1:28, y.Avodah Zarah 1:1

[6] LXX *And they read the law without, and called for public professions: proclaim aloud that the children of Israel have loved these things*

[7] Amos 4:6 - 1 Kings 17:1 18:2, 2 Chronicles 4:22, 2 Kings 4:38 6:25-29 8:1, Amos 4:8-9, b.Niddah 65b, Deuteronomy 4:38, Ezekiel 16:27, Haggai 2:17, Hosea 5:15-6:1 7:14-16, Isaiah 3:1 9:14 2:11, Jeremiah 5:3 8:5-7, Joel 2:12-14, Leviticus 2:26, mt.Hilchot Teshuvah 7:6, Revelation 2:21 9:20-21 16:10-11, Zechariah 1:3-6

[8] LXX *dullness*

[9] Amos 4:7 - 1 Corinthians 4:7, 1 Kings 8:35-36, 2 Chronicles 7:13-14, b.Sanhedrin 97a, b.Taanit 6b 18b, Deuteronomy 11:17 28:23-24, Ein Yaakov Sanhedrin:97a, Ein Yaakov Taanit:6b, Exodus 8:18 9:4 9:26 10:23, Haggai 1:10-11, Isaiah 5:6, James 5:17, Jastrow 769b 1648b, Jeremiah 3:3 5:24-25 14:4 14:22, Joel 1:10-18 2:23, John 4:35, Judges 6:37-40, Leviticus 26:18-26:21 26:23-24 26:27-28, m.Taanit 3:3, Mas.Derek Eretz Zutta 10:1, Pesikta de R'Kahana 5.9, Pesikta Rabbati 15:14/15, Revelation 11:6, Song of Songs.R 2:33, y.Taanit 3:3, Zechariah 14:17

[10] Amos 4:8 - 1 Kings 18:5, Amos 4:6 4:9-11, Ezekiel 4:16-17, Haggai 1:6, Hosea 7:10, Isaiah 41:17-18, Jeremiah 3:7 14:3-4 23:14, Micah 6:14

[11] Amos 4:9 - 1 Kings 8:37, 2 Chronicles 6:28, Amos 4:6 4:8 7:1-7:2, b.Shabbat [Rashi] 33a, b.Shabbat 33a, Deuteronomy 4:22 4:42, Ein Yaakov Shabbat:33a, Haggai 2:17, Isaiah 1:5 42:24-42:25, Jeremiah 3:10 5:3, Job 36:8-36:13, Joel 1:4 1:7 2:25

[12] Amos 4:10 - 2 Kings 8:12 10:32 13:3 13:7, Amos 4:6 8:3, Deuteronomy 7:15 4:22 28:26-27 28:60, Exodus 8:15 9:3-6 9:12 9:17 9:34-35 10:3 10:27 12:29-30 14:4 15:26, Isaiah 9:14, Jeremiah 6:11 8:1-2 9:23 11:22 15:3 16:4 18:21 24:15, Joel 2:20, Leviticus 2:16 2:25, Psalms 78:49-50

הֲפַ֣כְתִּי בָכֶ֗ם כְּמַהְפֵּכַ֤ת אֱלֹהִים֙ אֶת־סְדֹ֣ם וְאֶת־
עֲמֹרָ֔ה וַתִּהְי֕וּ כְּא֖וּד מֻצָּ֣ל מִשְּׂרֵפָ֑ה וְלֹֽא־שַׁבְתֶּ֤ם עָדַי֙
נְאֻם־יְהוָֽה

11 [1]

I have overthrown some of you, As God overthrew Sodom and Gomorrah, and you were as a brand plucked out of the coals; Yet you have not returned to Me, Says the LORD.

לָכֵ֕ן כֹּ֥ה אֶֽעֱשֶׂה־לְּךָ֖ יִשְׂרָאֵ֑ל עֵ֚קֶב כִּֽי־זֹ֣את אֶֽעֱשֶׂה־
לָּ֔ךְ הִכּ֥וֹן לִקְרַאת־אֱלֹהֶ֖יךָ יִשְׂרָאֵֽל

12 [2]

Therefore, this will I do to you, O Israel; Because I will do this to you, Prepare to meet your God, O Israel.

כִּ֡י הִנֵּה֩ יוֹצֵ֨ר הָרִ֜ים וּבֹרֵ֣א ר֗וּחַ וּמַגִּ֤יד לְאָדָם֙ מַה־
שֵּׂח֔וֹ עֹשֵׂ֥ה שַׁ֙חַר֙ עֵיפָ֔ה וְדֹרֵ֖ךְ עַל־בָּ֣מֳתֵי אָ֑רֶץ יְהוָ֥ה
אֱלֹהֵֽי־צְבָא֖וֹת שְׁמֽוֹ

13 [3]

For, lo, He who *forms the mountains, and creates the wind, and declares to man his thought*[4], who makes the morning darkness, and treads on the high places of the earth; The LORD, the God of hosts, is His name.

Amos – Chapter 5

שִׁמְע֞וּ אֶת־הַדָּבָ֣ר הַזֶּ֗ה אֲשֶׁ֨ר אָנֹכִ֧י נֹשֵׂ֛א עֲלֵיכֶ֖ם
קִינָ֑ה בֵּ֖ית יִשְׂרָאֵֽל

1 [5]

Hear this word that I take up for a lamentation over you, O house of Israel[6]:

נָ֣פְלָ֔ה לֹֽא־תוֹסִ֥יף ק֖וּם בְּתוּלַ֣ת יִשְׂרָאֵ֑ל נִטְּשָׁ֥ה עַל־
אַדְמָתָ֖הּ אֵ֥ין מְקִימָֽהּ

2 [7]

The virgin of Israel is fallen, *She shall rise no more; She is cast down on her land*[8], There is no one to raise her up.

כִּ֣י כֹ֤ה אָמַר֙ אֲדֹנָ֣י יְהוִ֔ה הָעִ֛יר הַיֹּצֵ֥את אֶ֖לֶף תַּשְׁאִ֣יר
מֵאָ֑ה וְהַיּוֹצֵ֥את מֵאָ֛ה תַּשְׁאִ֥יר עֲשָׂרָ֖ה לְבֵ֥ית יִשְׂרָאֵֽל

3 [9]

For thus says the Lord GOD: The city that went forth a thousand shall have a hundred left, and what went forth a hundred shall have ten left, of the house of Israel.

כִּ֣י כֹ֥ה אָמַ֛ר יְהוָ֖ה לְבֵ֣ית יִשְׂרָאֵ֑ל דִּרְשׁ֖וּנִי וִֽחְיֽוּ

4 [10]

For thus says the LORD to the house of Israel: Seek Me, and live;

וְאַֽל־תִּדְרְשׁוּ֙ בֵּֽית־אֵ֔ל וְהַגִּלְגָּל֙ לֹ֣א תָבֹ֔אוּ וּבְאֵ֥ר
שֶׁ֖בַע לֹ֣א תַעֲבֹ֑רוּ כִּ֤י הַגִּלְגָּל֙ גָּלֹ֣ה יִגְלֶ֔ה וּבֵֽית־אֵ֖ל
יִהְיֶ֥ה לְאָֽוֶן

5 [11]

But do not seek Bethel, Nor enter Gilgal, And do not pass to Beer-sheba; For Gilgal shall surely go into captivity, And Bethel shall come to nothing.

---

[1] Amos 4:11 - 1 Corinthians 3:15, 2 Peter 2:6, Amos 4:6, Ezekiel 22:17-22 24:13, Genesis 19:24-19:25, Hosea 11:8, Isaiah 13:19, Jeremiah 6:28-30 23:14 1:18, Jude 1:7 1:23, Revelation 9:20, Zechariah 3:2

[2] Amos 4:12 - 1 Thessalonians 5:2-4, Amos 2:14 4:2-3 5:4-15 9:1-4, b.Berachot 23a 51b, b.Shabbat 10a, Bahir 13, Deuteronomy.R 3:2, Ecclesiastes.R 4:13, Ein Yaakov Chagigah:12b, Ein Yaakov Shabbat:10a, Ezekiel 13:5 22:30, Hosea 13:8, Isaiah 23:3, James 4:1-10, Jastrow 621b 1139b, Luke 14:31-32 21:3-36, Mark 13:32-37, Matthew 5:25 24:44-25:13, Mesillat Yesharim 19:Honoring-Hashem-Beautify-Mitzvot, mt.Hilchot Tefilah 4:6 4:10 5:5, Revelation 3:3, Siman 12:1, t.Berachot 2:18, Tanya Igeret Hakodesh §27b, y.Berachot 2:3, y.Megillah 1:9, z.Noach 72a

[3] Amos 4:13 - 3 Enoch 23:18, Amos 3:13 5:8 5:27 6:8 8:9 9:6, b.Berachot 52b, b.Chagigah 12b 5b, b.Chullin 87a, b.Niddah 23a, b.Sanhedrin 39a, Daniel 2:28, Deuteronomy 8:13 9:29, Ecclesiastes.R 12:13, Ein Yaakov Chagigah:5b, Ein Yaakov Sanhedrin 39a, Exodus 10:22 14:20, Genesis.R 1:9, Guide for the Perplexed 2:30, Habakkuk 3:19, Isaiah 5:30 16:12 23:4 24:2, Jastrow 977b 1278b 1559a, Jeremiah 10:13 10:16 13:16 3:16 3:19, Job 38:4-11, John 2:25 3:8, Lamentations.R 3:?, Leviticus.R 26:7, Luke 7:39-40, Mas.Kallah Rabbati 3:1, Matthew 9:4, Micah 1:3, Midrash Psalms 104:5 136:5, Midrash Tanchuma Chukkat 1, Midrash Tanchuma Emor 2, mt.Hilchot Deot 5:4, mt.Hilchot Deot 5:4, Numbers.R 18:22, Psalms 65:7 15:7 19:2 3:18, Saadia Opinions 1:3, Siman 150:1, y.Chagigah 2:1, y.Niddah 3:3, z.Vayechi 218b, Zechariah 12:1

[4] LXX *strengthens the thunder, and creates the wind, and proclaims to men his Messiah*

[5] Amos 5:1 - Amos 3:1 4:1 5:16, Ezekiel 19:1 19:14 2:17 3:2 27:27-32 4:12 8:2 8:16, Jeremiah 7:29 9:11 9:18 9:21, Lamentations.R Petichata D'Chakimei:2, Micah 2:4, Pesikta de R'Kahana 15.4, z.Vayikra 6a
Amos 5:1-2 - 4QXIIg

[6] LXX adds *it shall no more rise*

[7] Amos 5:2 - 2 Kings 15:29 17:16, Amos 7:2-7:5 8:14 9:11, b.Berachot 42ab, Ein Yaakov Berachot:4b, Ezekiel 16:36-37, Hosea 6:2 14:3, Isaiah 3:8 14:21 24:20 13:22 19:17 51:17-18, Jeremiah 2:27 4:20 14:17 18:13 30:12-14 7:5 2:32 51:64, Lamentations 1:16-19 2:13, mt.Hilchot Avodat Kochavim v'Chukkoteihem 4:2, Pesikta de R'Kahana 16.8, Pesikta Rabbati 29/30B:2 44:5, z.Bamidbar 119b, z.Shemini 40a, z.Vayikra 6a

[8] Missing in LXX

[9] Amos 5:3 - Amos 6:9, b.Sanhedrin [Rashi] 15b, Deuteronomy 4:27 28:62, Ezekiel 12:16, Isaiah 1:9 6:13 10:22, Romans 9:27, Sifre Devarim Ekev 47, z.Vaetchanan 269b

[10] Amos 5:4 - 1 Chronicles 4:9, 2 Chronicles 15:2 20:3 10:3, Amos 5:6, b.Shabbat 24a, Deuteronomy 30:1-30:8, Ein Yaakov Makkot:24a, Isaiah 7:3 55:6-55:7, Jastrow 1086b, Jeremiah 29:12-29:13, Lamentations 3:25-3:26, Matthew 7:8, Midrash Psalms 17A:24, Midrash Tanchuma Shoftim 9, Numbers.R 10:1, Pesikta de R'Kahana 24.1, Psalms 14:2 22:27 27:8 69:33 105:3-105:4, Song of Songs.R 6:1, z.Vaetchanan 269b, Zephaniah 2:3

[11] Amos 5:5 - 1 Corinthians 1:28 2:6, 1 Samuel 7:16 11:14, Amos 4:4 7:17 8:14, Deuteronomy 4:41, Genesis 21:33, Hosea 4:15 9:15 10:8 10:14-10:15 12:13, Isaiah 8:10 5:20, Job 8:22, Leviticus 26:30-26:32, Psalms 33:10, Revelation 18:17

דִּרְשׁוּ אֶת־יְהוָה וִחְיוּ פֶּן־יִצְלַח כָּאֵשׁ בֵּית יוֹסֵף וְאָכְלָה וְאֵין־מְכַבֶּה לְבֵית־אֵל	6[1]	Seek the LORD, and live, lest He break out like fire in the house of Joseph, and it devour, and there be no one to quench it in Bethel
הַהֹפְכִים לְלַעֲנָה מִשְׁפָּט וּצְדָקָה לָאָרֶץ הִנִּיחוּ	7[2]	You who turn judgment to wormwood, and cast righteousness to the ground;
עֹשֵׂה כִימָה וּכְסִיל וְהֹפֵךְ לַבֹּקֶר צַלְמָוֶת וְיוֹם לַיְלָה הֶחְשִׁיךְ הַקּוֹרֵא לְמֵי־הַיָּם וַיִּשְׁפְּכֵם עַל־פְּנֵי הָאָרֶץ יְהוָה שְׁמוֹ	8[3]	*He who made the Pleiades and Orion*[4], And brings on the shadow of death in the morning, and darkens the day into night; who calls for the waters of the sea, and pours them out upon the face of the earth; the LORD is His name;
הַמַּבְלִיג שֹׁד עַל־עָז וְשֹׁד עַל־מִבְצָר יָבוֹא	9[5]	Who causes destruction to flash upon the strong, so that destruction comes upon the fortress?
שָׂנְאוּ בַשַּׁעַר מוֹכִיחַ וְדֹבֵר תָּמִים יְתָעֵבוּ	10[6]	They hate him who reproves in the gate, And they abhor him who speaks uprightly.
לָכֵן יַעַן בּוֹשַׁסְכֶם עַל־דָּל וּמַשְׂאַת־בַּר תִּקְחוּ מִמֶּנּוּ בָּתֵּי גָזִית בְּנִיתֶם וְלֹא־תֵשְׁבוּ בָם כַּרְמֵי־חֶמֶד נְטַעְתֶּם וְלֹא תִשְׁתּוּ אֶת־יֵינָם	11[7]	Therefore, because you trample on the poor, and take exactions of wheat from him; you have built houses of hewn stone, but you shall not dwell in them, you have planted pleasant vineyards, but you shall not drink its wine.
כִּי יָדַעְתִּי רַבִּים פִּשְׁעֵיכֶם וַעֲצֻמִים חַטֹּאתֵיכֶם צֹרְרֵי צַדִּיק לֹקְחֵי כֹפֶר וְאֶבְיוֹנִים בַּשַּׁעַר הִטּוּ	12[8]	For I know how manifold are your transgressions, and how mighty are your sins; you who afflict the just, that take a ransom, and who turn the needy aside in the gate.
לָכֵן הַמַּשְׂכִּיל בָּעֵת הַהִיא יִדֹּם כִּי עֵת רָעָה הִיא	13[9]	Therefore, the prudent keeps silence in such a time; for it is an evil time.
דִּרְשׁוּ־טוֹב וְאַל־רָע לְמַעַן תִּחְיוּ וִיהִי־כֵן יְהוָה אֱלֹהֵי־צְבָאוֹת אִתְּכֶם כַּאֲשֶׁר אֲמַרְתֶּם	14[10]	Seek good, and not evil, so you may live; and so the LORD, the God of hosts, will be with you, as you say.
שִׂנְאוּ־רָע וְאֶהֱבוּ טוֹב וְהַצִּיגוּ בַשַּׁעַר מִשְׁפָּט אוּלַי יֶחֱנַן יְהוָה אֱלֹהֵי־צְבָאוֹת שְׁאֵרִית יוֹסֵף	15[11]	Hate the evil, and love the good, and establish justice in the gate; it may be that the LORD, the God of hosts, Will be gracious to the remnant of Joseph.

[1] Amos 5:6 - 1 Kings 11:28, 2 Samuel 19:20, Amos 5:4 5:14 6:6, Deuteronomy 4:24, Exodus 22:6, Ezekiel 21:3-20:4 9:11 13:19, Genesis 48:8-48:20, Isaiah 1:31 7:6, Jeremiah 4:4 7:20, Joshua 18:5, Judges 1:22-1:23, Mark 9:43-9:48, Zechariah 10:6

[2] Amos 5:7 - Amos 5:11-5:12 6:12, Deuteronomy 5:17, Ezekiel 3:20 18:24 33:12-33:13 9:18, Habakkuk 1:12-1:14, Hosea 10:4, Isaiah 1:23 5:7 10:1 59:13-59:14, Psalms 36:4 5:5, Zephaniah 1:6

[3] Amos 5:8 - 1 Kings 18:44-45, Amos 4:13 8:9 9:6, b.Berachot 58b, Ecclesiastes.R 3:17, Exodus 10:21-23 14:24-28, Exodus.R 12:3 23:4 28:4, Genesis 7:11-20, Genesis.R 5:6 23:7 25:2, Isaiah 18:16 11:10, Job 9:9 12:22 13:13 38:12-13 38:31-32 14:34, Luke 1:79, Matthew 4:16, Mekilta de R'Ishmael Bahodesh 6:38, Midrash Psalms 88:2, Midrash Tanchuma Noach 18, Midrash Tanchuma Yitro 12 16, Pesikta Rabbati 42:8 48:2, Psalms 104:6-9 8:20 9:28 107:10-14, Sifre Devarim Ekev 43, Testament of Solomon 8:2, z.Terumah 168b 170a

[4] LXX *who makes all things, and changes them*

[5] Amos 5:9 - 2 Kings 13:17 13:25, b.Shabbat 77b, Ein Yaakov Shabbat:77b, Hebrews 11:34, Jeremiah 13:10, Micah 5:12, y.Sotah 9:13
Amos 5:9-18 - 4QXIIg

[6] Amos 5:10 - 1 Kings 18:17 21:20 22:8, 2 Chronicles 24:20-22 1:16 12:16, Amos 7:10-17, Genesis.R 3:8 31:3, Isaiah 5:21, Jeremiah 17:16-17:17 20:7-10, John 3:20 7:7 8:45-47 15:19 15:22-24, Proverbs 9:7-8, Revelation 11:10

[7] Amos 5:11 - Amos 3:15-4:1, Deuteronomy 4:30 28:38-39, Haggai 1:6, Isaiah 5:7-5:8 59:13-14 65:21-22, James 2:6, Leviticus.R 15:9, Micah 2:2 3:1-3:3 6:15, Revelation 11:8-10, Saadia Opinions 10:10, Zephaniah 1:13

[8] Amos 5:12 - 1 Samuel 8:3, 2 Kings 17:7-17, Acts 3:13-14 7:52, Amos 2:6-7 2:16 5:10, Deuteronomy 16:18 7:21, Hebrews 4:12-13, Isaiah 1:23 5:23 10:2 5:21 9:15 23:9 18:18, James 5:4 5:6, Jeremiah 5:23, Job 29:7-25 7:21, Lamentations 3:34, Malachi 3:5, Micah 3:11 7:3, Proverbs 22:22, Psalms 26:9-10, Ruth 4:1, Saadia Opinions 5:7

[9] Amos 5:13 - 2 Timothy 3:1, Amos 6:10, Ecclesiastes 3:7 9:12, Ecclesiastes.R 12:13, Ephesians 5:15-16 6:13, Habakkuk 3:16, Hosea 4:4, Isaiah 12:21 13:3, Matthew 27:12-27:14, Micah 2:3 7:5-7, Zephaniah 2:2-2:3

[10] Amos 5:14 - 1 Chronicles 4:20, 2 Chronicles 15:2, 2 Timothy 4:22, Amos 3:3, Exodus 3:12, Genesis 39:2-3 15:23, Isaiah 1:16-17 8:10 48:1-2 7:2, Jeremiah 7:3-4, Joshua 1:9, Matthew 1:23 6:33 4:20, Micah 3:11 6:8, Numbers 16:3, Philippians 4:8-4:9, Proverbs 11:27, Psalms 34:13-34:17 46:12, Romans 2:7-9

[11] Amos 5:15 - 1 Kings 20:31, 1 Thessalonians 5:21-22, 2 Chronicles 19:6-11, 2 Kings 13:7 14:26-27 15:29 19:4, 2 Samuel 16:12, 3 John 1:11, Amos 5:6 5:10 5:24 6:12, b.Chagigah 42ab, Ein Yaakov Chagigah:4b, Exodus 8:30, Genesis.R 71:2 82:10, Jeremiah 7:5-8, Joel 2:14, Jonah 3:9, Lamentations, Leviticus.R 3:?, Micah 2:12 5:4 5:8-9, Midrash Psalms 3:3 20:3, Midrash Tanchuma Emor 2, mt.Hilchot Sanhedrin v'Hainshin Hameurim Lahem 1:3, Pesikta de R'Kahana 20.2, Psalms 34:15 36:5 37:27 82:2-4 97:10 119:104 139:21-22, Romans 7:15-16 7:22 8:7 12:9, Ruth.R 7:13, This is the middle verse Sefer Amos per the Massorah, y.Chagigah 2:1

לָכֵן כֹּה־אָמַ֣ר יְהוָ֗ה אֱלֹהֵ֤י צְבָאוֹת֙ אֲדֹנָ֔י בְּכָל־רְחֹב֣וֹת מִסְפֵּ֔ד וּבְכָל־חוּצ֖וֹת יֹאמְר֣וּ הוֹ־הֹ֑ו וְקָרְא֤וּ אִכָּר֙ אֶל־אֵ֔בֶל וּמִסְפֵּ֖ד אֶל־י֥וֹדְעֵי נֶֽהִי	16[1]	Therefore, thus says the LORD, the God of hosts, the Lord: lamentation shall be in all the broad places, and they shall say in all the streets: 'Alas! alas!' And they shall call the husbandman to mourning, And proclaim lamentation to those who are skilled at wailing.
וּבְכָל־כְּרָמִ֖ים מִסְפֵּ֑ד כִּֽי־אֶעֱבֹ֥ר בְּקִרְבְּךָ֖ אָמַ֥ר יְהוָֽה	17[2]	*And in all vineyards shall be lamentation*[3]; For I will pass through the midst of you, Says the LORD.
ה֣וֹי הַמִּתְאַוִּ֔ים אֶת־י֖וֹם יְהוָ֑ה לָמָּה־זֶּ֥ה לָכֶ֛ם י֥וֹם יְהוָ֖ה הוּא־חֹ֥שֶׁךְ וְלֹא־אֽוֹר	18[4]	Woe to you who desire the day of the LORD! Why would you want the day of the LORD? It is darkness, and not light.
כַּאֲשֶׁ֨ר יָנ֥וּס אִישׁ֙ מִפְּנֵ֣י הָאֲרִ֔י וּפְגָע֖וֹ הַדֹּ֑ב וּבָ֣א הַבַּ֔יִת וְסָמַ֤ךְ יָדוֹ֙ עַל־הַקִּ֔יר וּנְשָׁכ֖וֹ הַנָּחָֽשׁ	19[5]	As if a man fled from a lion, and a bear met him; and went into the house and leaned his hand on the wall, and a serpent bit him.
הֲלֹא־חֹ֛שֶׁךְ י֥וֹם יְהוָ֖ה וְלֹא־א֑וֹר וְאָפֵ֖ל וְלֹא־נֹ֥גַהּ לֽוֹ	20[6]	Shall not the day of the LORD be darkness, and not light, very dark, and no brightness in it?
שָׂנֵ֥אתִי מָאַ֖סְתִּי חַגֵּיכֶ֑ם וְלֹ֥א אָרִ֖יחַ בְּעַצְּרֹֽתֵיכֶֽם	21[7]	I hate, I despise your festivals, And I will take no delight in your solemn assemblies.
כִּ֣י אִם־תַּעֲלוּ־לִ֥י עֹל֛וֹת וּמִנְחֹתֵיכֶ֖ם לֹ֣א אֶרְצֶ֑ה וְשֶׁ֥לֶם מְרִיאֵיכֶ֖ם לֹ֥א אַבִּֽיט	22[8]	Yes, though you offer me burnt offerings and your meal offerings, I will not accept them; nor will I regard the peace offerings of your *fat beasts*[9].
הָסֵ֥ר מֵעָלַ֖י הֲמ֣וֹן שִׁרֶ֑יךָ וְזִמְרַ֥ת נְבָלֶ֖יךָ לֹ֥א אֶשְׁמָֽע	23[10]	Take away from Me the noise of your songs; And let Me not hear the melody of your psalteries.
וְיִגַּ֥ל כַּמַּ֖יִם מִשְׁפָּ֑ט וּצְדָקָ֖ה כְּנַ֥חַל אֵיתָֽן	24[11]	But let justice well up like waters, And righteousness as a mighty stream.
הַזְּבָחִ֨ים וּמִנְחָ֜ה הִֽגַּשְׁתֶּם־לִ֧י בַמִּדְבָּ֛ר אַרְבָּעִ֥ים שָׁנָ֖ה בֵּ֥ית יִשְׂרָאֵֽל	25[12]	Did you bring to Me sacrifices and offerings in the wilderness forty years, O house of Israel?
וּנְשָׂאתֶ֗ם אֵ֚ת סִכּ֣וּת מַלְכְּכֶ֔ם וְאֵ֖ת כִּיּ֣וּן צַלְמֵיכֶ֑ם כּוֹכַ֖ב אֱלֹֽהֵיכֶ֑ם אֲשֶׁ֥ר עֲשִׂיתֶ֖ם לָכֶֽם	26[13]	*So shall you take up Siccuth your king and Chiun your images, the star of your god*[14], which you made for yourselves.
וְהִגְלֵיתִ֥י אֶתְכֶ֖ם מֵהָ֣לְאָה לְדַמָּ֑שֶׂק אָמַ֛ר יְהוָ֥ה אֱלֹהֵֽי־צְבָא֖וֹת שְׁמֽוֹ	27[15]	Therefore, I will cause you to go into captivity beyond Damascus, says He, whose name is the LORD God of hosts.

---

[1] Amos 5:16 - Amos 3:13 5:27 8:10, Isaiah 15:2-15:5 15:8 22:12, Jeremiah 4:31 9:11 9:18-21, Joel 1:8 1:11 1:14, Micah 1:8 2:4, Per Massorah: Soferim altered "Hashem" to "Adonai", Pesikta Rabbati 21:8, Revelation 18:10 18:15-18:16 18:19, z.Vaetchanan 269b
[2] Amos 5:17 - Exodus 12:12 12:23, Hosea 9:1-2, Isaiah 16:10 32:10-12, Jeremiah 24:33, Joel 4:17, Mekhilta de R'Shimon bar Yochai Pisha 9:3 13:2, Mekilta de R'Ishmael Pisha 11:83, Nahum 1:12 2:1, Zechariah 9:8
[3] LXX *And there shall be lamentation in all the ways*
[4] Amos 5:18 - 2 Peter 3:4 3:10, b.Sanhedrin 98b, Ein Yaakov Sanhedrin:98b, Ezekiel 12:22 12:27, Isaiah 5:19 5:30 9:20 24:11-12 28:15-22, Jeremiah 17:15 6:7, Joel 1:15 2:1-2 2:10 3:4, Malachi 3:1-2 3:19, Midrash Psalms 22:3 121:3, Sibylline Oracles 11.45 3.741, Zephaniah 1:14-15
[5] Amos 5:19 - 1 Kings 20:29-30, Acts 4:4, Amos 9:1-2, b.Sanhedrin 98b, Ein Yaakov Sanhedrin:98b, Esther.R Petichata:5, Isaiah 24:17-18, Jastrow 941b, Jeremiah 15:2-3 48:43-44, Job 20:24-25, Midrash Psalms 15:11, Pirkei de R'Eliezer 37, Pirkei de R'Eliezer 38
[6] Amos 5:20 - Ezekiel 10:12, Isaiah 13:10, Job 3:5-7 10:21-22, Jude 1:13, Matthew 22:13, Nahum 1:8, Revelation 16:10, Zephaniah 1:15
[7] Amos 5:21 - Ephesians 5:2, Genesis 8:21, Hosea 8:13, Isaiah 1:11-16 18:3, Jeremiah 6:20 7:21-23, Leviticus 2:31, Matthew 23:13, Philippians 4:18, Proverbs 15:8 21:27 4:9
[8] Amos 5:22 - Amos 4:4-5, Isaiah 18:3, Leviticus 7:12-15, Micah 6:6-7, Psalms 50:8-14 50:23 107:21-22 20:17
[9] LXX *grand peace offerings*
[10] Amos 5:23 - Amos 6:5 8:3 8:10
[11] Amos 5:24 - Amos 5:7 5:14-15, Hosea 6:6, Jeremiah 22:3, Job 29:12-17, Mark 12:32-34, Micah 6:8, Proverbs 21:3
[12] Amos 5:25 - Acts 7:42-43, b.Chagigah 6b 10b, Deuteronomy 32:17-32:19, Ezekiel 20:8 20:16 20:24, Hosea 9:9-9:10, Isaiah 43:23-43:24, Jastrow 1310a, Joshua 24:14, Leviticus 17:7, Nehemiah 9:18 9:21, Zechariah 7:5
[13] Amos 5:26 - 1 Kings 11:33, 2 Kings 23:12-13, Jubilees 12:5, Leviticus 18:21 20:2-5, Testament of Solomon 26:1 15:5 26:2 Amos 5:26-27 - Cairo Damascus 7:14-15
[14] LXX *Yes, you took up the tabernacle of Moloch, and the star of your god Raephan, the images of those*
[15] Amos 5:27 - 2 Kings 15:29 17:6, Acts 7:43, Amos 4:13

Amos – Chapter 6

הֹוי הַשַּׁאֲנַנִּים בְּצִיּוֹן וְהַבֹּטְחִים בְּהַר שֹׁמְרוֹן נְקֻבֵי רֵאשִׁית הַגּוֹיִם וּבָאוּ לָהֶם בֵּית יִשְׂרָאֵל

1[1] Woe to those who are at ease in Zion, and to those who are secure in the mountain of Samaria, *the notable men of the first of the nations, to whom the house of Israel come*[2]!

עִבְרוּ כַלְנֵה וּרְאוּ וּלְכוּ מִשָּׁם חֲמַת רַבָּה וּרְדוּ גַת־פְּלִשְׁתִּים הֲטוֹבִים מִן־הַמַּמְלָכוֹת הָאֵלֶּה אִם־רַב גְּבוּלָם מִגְּבֻלְכֶם

2[3] *Pass to Calneh, and see, And from there go to Hamath the great*[4]; Then go down to Gath of the Philistines; Are they better than these kingdoms, or is their border greater than yours?

הַמְנַדִּים לְיוֹם רָע וַתַּגִּישׁוּן שֶׁבֶת חָמָס

3[5] *You who put the evil day far away, and cause the seat of violence to come near*[6];

הַשֹּׁכְבִים עַל־מִטּוֹת שֵׁן וּסְרֻחִים עַל־עַרְשׂוֹתָם וְאֹכְלִים כָּרִים מִצֹּאן וַעֲגָלִים מִתּוֹךְ מַרְבֵּק

4[7] Who lie upon beds of ivory, and stretch themselves upon their couches, and eat the lambs from the flock, and the calves from the midst of the stall;

הַפֹּרְטִים עַל־פִּי הַנָּבֶל כְּדָוִיד חָשְׁבוּ לָהֶם כְּלֵי־שִׁיר

5[8] *Who strum on the psaltery, Who devise for themselves instruments of music, like David*[9];

הַשֹּׁתִים בְּמִזְרְקֵי יַיִן וְרֵאשִׁית שְׁמָנִים יִמְשָׁחוּ וְלֹא נֶחְלוּ עַל־שֵׁבֶר יוֹסֵף

6[10] Who drink *wine in bowls*[11], and anoint themselves with the chief ointments; but they are not grieved for the destruction of Joseph.

לָכֵן עַתָּה יִגְלוּ בְּרֹאשׁ גֹּלִים וְסָר מִרְזַח סְרוּחִים

7[12] Therefore, they shall go captive *at the head of those who go captive, and the revelry of those who stretched themselves shall fade away*[13].

נִשְׁבַּע אֲדֹנָי יְהוִה בְּנַפְשׁוֹ נְאֻם־יְהוָה אֱלֹהֵי צְבָאוֹת מְתָאֵב אָנֹכִי אֶת־גְּאוֹן יַעֲקֹב וְאַרְמְנֹתָיו שָׂנֵאתִי וְהִסְגַּרְתִּי עִיר וּמְלֹאָהּ

8[14] The Lord GOD has sworn by Himself, says the LORD, the God of hosts: I abhor the pride of Jacob, and hate his palaces; and I will deliver up the city with all who are within it.

וְהָיָה אִם־יִוָּתְרוּ עֲשָׂרָה אֲנָשִׁים בְּבַיִת אֶחָד וָמֵתוּ

9[15] And it shall come to pass, if ten men remain in one house, they shall die.

---

[1] Amos 6:1 - 1 Kings 16:24, 1 Peter 5:7, Amos 4:1 8:14, Exodus 19:5-19:6, Isaiah 32:9-32:11 9:14, James 1:18 5:5, Jastrow 951a, Jeremiah 7:4 24:11 1:31, Judges 18:7, Lamentations 1:1, Leviticus.R 5:3, Luke 6:24-25 12:17-20, Midrash Tanchuma Shemini 5, MurXII, Numbers.R 10:3, Zephaniah 1:12

Amos 6:1-4 - 4QXIIg

[2] LXX *they have gathered the harvest of the heads of the nations, and they have gone in themselves*

[3] Amos 6:2 - 1 Kings 8:65, 1 Samuel 17:4 17:23, 2 Chronicles 2:6, 2 Kings 17:24 17:30 18:34 19:13, Ezekiel 31:2-31:3, Genesis 10:10, Isaiah 10:9-11 36:18-19 37:12-13, Jastrow 481a 1184a 1601a, Jeremiah 22:10-11, Leviticus.R 5:3, Nahum 3:8, Numbers.R 10:3

[4] LXX *O house of Israel, pass by all of you, and see; and pass by thence to Ematrabba*

[5] Amos 6:3 - 1 Thessalonians 5:3, 2 Peter 3:4, Amos 3:10 5:12 5:18 6:12 9:10, Ecclesiastes 8:11, Ecclesiastes.R 12:7, Ezekiel 12:22 12:27, Isaiah 23:7 8:12, Matthew 24:48, Numbers.R 10:3, Psalms 94:20, Revelation 18:17

[6] LXX *You who are approaching the evil day, who are drawing near and adopting false sabbaths*

[7] Amos 6:4 - 1 Samuel 25:36-25:38, Amos 3:12, b.Kiddushin 71b, b.Pesachim 49a, b.Shabbat 62b, Ein Yaakov Pesachim:49a, Ezekiel 34:2-34:3, Isaiah 5:11-5:12 22:13, James 5:5, Jastrow 1024b 1025a 1358a, Leviticus.R 5:3, Luke 12:19-12:20 16:19, Numbers.R 9:7 10:3, Psalms 73:7, Romans 13:13-13:14, Sifre Devarim Ha'azinu Hashamayim 317 318, Sifre Devarim Nitzavim 317 318

Amos 6:4-7 - Midrash Tanchuma Shemini 5

[8] Amos 6:5 - 1 Chronicles 15:16 23:5, 1 Peter 4:3, Amos 5:23 8:3, Ecclesiastes 2:8, Genesis 7:27, Isaiah 5:12, Jastrow 869b 870b 1224a, Job 21:11-12, Leviticus.R 5:3, Numbers.R 10:3, Revelation 18:22

[9] LXX *who excel in the sound of musical instruments; they have regarded them as abiding, not as fleeting pleasures*

[10] Amos 6:6 - 1 Corinthians 12:26, 1 Timothy 5:23, 2 Kings 15:29 17:3-6, Amos 2:8, b.Shabbat 62b, Esther 3:15, Ezekiel 9:4, Genesis 37:25-28 42:21-22 1:22, Hosea 3:1, Jastrow 411b 1177b, Jeremiah 6:7, John 12:3, Leviticus.R 5:3, Matthew 26:7-9, Numbers.R 10:3 13:15-16 14:9, Romans 12:15, Sifre Devarim Ha'azinu Hashamayim 317 318, Sifre Devarim Nitzavim 317 318, z.Vayakhel 220a

Amos 6:6-14 - 4QXIIg

[11] LXX *strained wine*

[12] Amos 6:7 - 1 Kings 20:16-20:20, Amos 5:5 5:27 7:11 7:17, b.Ketubot 69b, b.Kiddushin 71a, b.Moed Katan 28b, b.Pesachim 49a, b.Shabbat 62b, Daniel 5:4-5:6, Deuteronomy 4:41, Ein Yaakov Ketubot:69b, Ein Yaakov Pesachim:49a, Esther 5:8 5:12-5:14 7:1-7:2 7:8-7:10, Isaiah 21:4, Jastrow 834a 840b 969a 1024b, Leviticus.R 5:3, Luke 21:24, Nahum 1:10, Numbers.R 9:7 10:3, Sifre Devarim Ha'azinu Hashamayim 318, Sifre Devarim Nitzavim 318

[13] LXX *from the dominion of princes, and the neighing of horses shall be cut off from Ephraim*

[14] Amos 6:8 - Amos 3:11 4:2 8:7, Deuteronomy 8:19, Ezekiel 24:21, Genesis 22:16, Hebrews 6:13-6:17, Jeremiah 22:5 3:14, Lamentations 2:5, Leviticus 2:11 2:30, Leviticus.R 5:3, Micah 1:6-1:9, Psalms 47:5 50:12 78:59 10:40, Zechariah 11:8

[15] Amos 6:9 - 1 Samuel 2:33, Amos 5:3, Esther 5:11 9:10, Isaiah 14:21, Job 1:2 1:19 20:28, Psalms 13:13

וְנְשָׂאוֹ דּוֹדוֹ וּמְסָרְפוֹ לְהוֹצִיא עֲצָמִים מִן־הַבַּיִת
וְאָמַר לַאֲשֶׁר בְּיַרְכְּתֵי הַבַּיִת הַעוֹד עִמָּךְ וְאָמַר אָפֶס
וְאָמַר הָס כִּי לֹא לְהַזְכִּיר בְּשֵׁם יְהוָה

10 [1]

[2]And when a man's uncle shall take him up, he who burns him, to bring the bones out of the house, and shall say to him who is in the innermost parts of the house: 'Is there anyone with you?' and he shall say: 'No.' Then he shall say: 'Hold your peace; for we must not make mention of the name of the LORD.'

כִּי־הִנֵּה יְהוָה מְצַוֶּה וְהִכָּה הַבַּיִת הַגָּדוֹל רְסִיסִים
וְהַבַּיִת הַקָּטֹן בְּקִעִים:

11 [3]

For, behold, the LORD commands, And the great house shall be struck into splinters, And the little house into rubble.

הַיְרֻצוּן בַּסֶּלַע סוּסִים אִם־יַחֲרוֹשׁ בַּבְּקָרִים כִּי־
הֲפַכְתֶּם לְרֹאשׁ מִשְׁפָּט וּפְרִי צְדָקָה לְלַעֲנָה

12 [4]

Do horses run on the rocks? *Does one plow there with oxen[5]*? You have turned justice into gall, and the fruit of righteousness into wormwood;

הַשְּׂמֵחִים לְלֹא דָבָר הָאֹמְרִים הֲלוֹא בְחָזְקֵנוּ לָקַחְנוּ
לָנוּ קַרְנָיִם

13 [6]

You who rejoice in a thing of nothing, who say: 'Our power comes by our own strength.'

כִּי הִנְנִי מֵקִים עֲלֵיכֶם בֵּית יִשְׂרָאֵל נְאֻם־יְהוָה
אֱלֹהֵי הַצְּבָאוֹת גּוֹי וְלָחֲצוּ אֶתְכֶם מִלְּבוֹא חֲמָת עַד־
נַחַל הָעֲרָבָה

14 [7]

For, behold, I will raise up against you a nation, O house of Israel, says the LORD, the God of hosts; and they shall afflict *you from the entrance of Hamath to the Brook of the Arabah[8]*.

Amos – Chapter 7

כֹּה הִרְאַנִי אֲדֹנָי יְהוִה וְהִנֵּה יוֹצֵר גֹּבַי בִּתְחִלַּת
עֲלוֹת הַלָּקֶשׁ וְהִנֵּה־לֶקֶשׁ אַחַר גִּזֵּי הַמֶּלֶךְ

1 [9]

Thus, the Lord GOD showed me; and, behold, *He formed locusts in the beginning of the shooting up of the latter growth; and, lo, it was the latter growth after the king's mowings[10]*.

וְהָיָה אִם־כִּלָּה לֶאֱכוֹל אֶת־עֵשֶׂב הָאָרֶץ וָאֹמַר אֲדֹנָי
יְהוִה סְלַח־נָא מִי יָקוּם יַעֲקֹב כִּי קָטֹן הוּא

2 [11]

And if it had come to pass, that when they had made an end of eating the grass of the land, so I said: O Lord GOD, forgive, I beg You; How shall Jacob stand? for he is small.

נִחַם יְהוָה עַל־זֹאת לֹא תִהְיֶה אָמַר יְהוָה

3 [12]

The LORD repented concerning this[13]; 'It shall not be,' says the LORD.

---

[1] Amos 6:10 - 1 Samuel 7:12, 2 Kings 6:33 23:16, Amos 5:13 8:3, b.Sanhedrin 64a, Ezekiel 20:39 24:21, Jeremiah 16:6 20:26, Lamentations.R 1:23, Numbers 17:27, Tanya Igeret Hakodesh §02
[2] LXX adds *But a remnant shall be left behind*
[3] Amos 6:11 - 2 Kings 1:9, Amos 3:6-3:7 3:15 6:8 9:1 9:9, b.Shabbat [Rashi] 80b, Ecclesiastes 10:18, Ecclesiastes.R 10:18, Ezekiel 29:18-29:20, Hosea 14:1, Isaiah 10:5-6 13:3 46:10-11 7:11, Leviticus.R 19:4, Luke 19:44, Nahum 1:14, Psalms 9:16 9:31 9:34, Song of Songs.R 4:30, Zechariah 14:2
[4] Amos 6:12 - 1 Kings 21:7-21:13, Acts 7:51-7:52, Amos 5:7 5:11-5:12, Deuteronomy.R 3:7, Habakkuk 1:3-1:4, Hosea 10:4 10:13, Isaiah 24:4 59:13-59:14, Jeremiah 5:3 6:29-6:30, Micah 7:3, Psalms 94:20-94:21, Zechariah 7:11-7:12
[5] LXX *will they refrain from neighing at mares*
[6] Amos 6:13 - 1 Samuel 4:5, 2 Chronicles 28:6-28:8, 2 Kings 13:25 14:12-14:14 14:25, Daniel 4:27, Ecclesiastes 11:9, Exodus 32:18-32:19, Habakkuk 1:15-1:16, Isaiah 7:1 7:4 8:6 17:3-17:4 28:14-28:15, James 4:16, Jeremiah 9:24 2:11, Job 8:15 7:25 7:29, John 16:20, Jonah 4:6, Judges 9:19-9:20 9:27 16:23-16:25, Luke 12:19-12:20, Revelation 11:10, Sifre Devarim Ha'azinu Hashamayim 322, Sifre Devarim Nitzavim 322, Zephaniah 3:11
Amos 6:13-14 - 4QXIII
[7] Amos 6:14 - 1 Kings 8:65, 2 Kings 14:25 15:29 17:6, Ezekiel 47:15-17, Hosea 10:5, Isaiah 7:20 8:4-8 10:5-6, Jeremiah 5:15-17, Numbers 34:7-8
[8] LXX *so that you shall not enter into Æmath, and as it were from the river of the wilderness*
[9] Amos 7:1 - 4QXIIg, Amos 4:9 7:4 7:7 8:1, b.Taanit [Rashi] 6a, Exodus 10:12-10:16, Ezekiel 11:25, Isaiah 9:4, Jeremiah 1:11-1:16 24:1, Joel 1:4 2:25, Nahum 3:15-3:17, Tanna Devei Eliyahu 6, Zechariah 1:20
Amos 7:1-4 - 4QXIIc
[10] LXX *a swarm of locusts coming from the east; and, behold, one caterpillar, king Gog*
[11] Amos 7:2 - Amos 7:5, b.Chullin [Rashi] 60b, Daniel 9:19, Exodus 10:15 32:11-32:12 10:9, Ezekiel 9:8 11:13, Isaiah 13:4 3:19, James 5:15-5:16, Jeremiah 14:7 14:20-14:21 18:2, Numbers 14:17-14:19, Psalms 12:2 44:25-44:27, Revelation 9:4, Zechariah 4:10
[12] Amos 7:3 - 1 Chronicles 21:15, Amos 7:6, Deuteronomy 8:36, Hosea 11:8, James 5:16, Jeremiah 2:19, Joel 2:14, Jonah 3:10, Psalms 10:45
Amos 7:3-17 - MurXII
[13] LXX *Repent, O Lord, for this*

כֹּה הִרְאַנִי אֲדֹנָי יְהוִה וְהִנֵּה קֹרֵא לָרִב בָּאֵשׁ אֲדֹנָי יְהוִה וַתֹּאכַל אֶת־תְּהוֹם רַבָּה וְאָכְלָה אֶת־הַחֵלֶק

4[1] Thus the Lord GOD showed me; and, behold, the Lord GOD called to contend by fire; and it devoured the great deep, and would have eaten up the land.

וָאֹמַר אֲדֹנָי יְהוִה חֲדַל־נָא מִי יָקוּם יַעֲקֹב כִּי קָטֹן הוּא

5[2] Then said I: O Lord GOD, cease, I beg You; How shall Jacob stand? for he is small.

נִחַם יְהוָה עַל־זֹאת גַּם־הִיא לֹא תִהְיֶה אָמַר אֲדֹנָי יְהוִה

6[3] The LORD repented concerning this; 'This also shall not be,' says the Lord GOD.

כֹּה הִרְאַנִי וְהִנֵּה אֲדֹנָי נִצָּב עַל־חוֹמַת אֲנָךְ וּבְיָדוֹ אֲנָךְ

7[4] Thus He showed me; and, behold, the Lord stood *beside a wall made by a plumbline, with a plumbline in His hand*[5].

וַיֹּאמֶר יְהוָה אֵלַי מָה־אַתָּה רֹאֶה עָמוֹס וָאֹמַר אֲנָךְ וַיֹּאמֶר אֲדֹנָי הִנְנִי שָׂם אֲנָךְ בְּקֶרֶב עַמִּי יִשְׂרָאֵל לֹא־אוֹסִיף עוֹד עֲבוֹר לוֹ

8[6] And the LORD said to me: 'Amos, what do you see?' And I said: '*A plumbline.' Then ther Lord said: Behold, I will set a plumbline in the midst of My people Israel; I will pardon them no longer*[7];

וְנָשַׁמּוּ בָּמוֹת יִשְׂחָק וּמִקְדְּשֵׁי יִשְׂרָאֵל יֶחֱרָבוּ וְקַמְתִּי עַל־בֵּית יָרָבְעָם בֶּחָרֶב

9[8] *And the high places of Isaac shall be desolate, And the sanctuaries of Israel shall be laid waste*[9]; And I will rise against the house of Jeroboam with the sword.

וַיִּשְׁלַח אֲמַצְיָה כֹּהֵן בֵּית־אֵל אֶל־יָרָבְעָם מֶלֶךְ־יִשְׂרָאֵל לֵאמֹר קָשַׁר עָלֶיךָ עָמוֹס בְּקֶרֶב בֵּית יִשְׂרָאֵל לֹא־תוּכַל הָאָרֶץ לְהָכִיל אֶת־כָּל־דְּבָרָיו

10[10] Then Amaziah the priest of Bethel sent to Jeroboam king of Israel, saying: 'Amos has conspired against you in the midst of the house of Israel; the land is not able to bear all his words.

כִּי־כֹה אָמַר עָמוֹס בַּחֶרֶב יָמוּת יָרָבְעָם וְיִשְׂרָאֵל גָּלֹה יִגְלֶה מֵעַל אַדְמָתוֹ

11[11] For thus Amos says: Jeroboam shall die by the sword, And Israel shall surely be led away captive out of his land.'

וַיֹּאמֶר אֲמַצְיָה אֶל־עָמוֹס חֹזֶה לֵךְ בְּרַח־לְךָ אֶל־אֶרֶץ יְהוּדָה וֶאֱכָל־שָׁם לֶחֶם וְשָׁם תִּנָּבֵא

12[12] Also Amaziah said to Amos: 'O you seer, go, flee away into the land of Judah, and eat bread there, and prophesy there;

---

[1] Amos 7:4 - Amos 1:4 1:7 4:11 5:6 7:1 7:7, Deuteronomy 8:22, Exodus 9:23-9:24, Hebrews 1:7, Isaiah 3:4 66:15-66:16, Jeremiah 4:4 21:12, Joel 3:3, Leviticus 10:2, Micah 1:4, Nahum 1:6, Numbers 16:35, Revelation 4:1, Sibylline Oracles 4.173

[2] Amos 7:5 - Amos 7:2-3, b.Chullin 60b, b.Makkot 24a, Ein Yaakov Makkot:24a, Isaiah 1:9 10:25, Jeremiah 6:19, Joel 2:17, Psalms 85:5

[3] Amos 7:6 - Amos 7:3, b.Makkot 24a, Ein Yaakov Makkot:24a, Jeremiah 2:19, Jonah 3:10 4:2, Judges 2:18 10:16, Psalms 90:13 15:14

[4] Amos 7:7 - 2 Kings 21:13, 2 Samuel 8:2, Avot de R'Natan 34.9.1, b.Bava Metzia [Tosefot] 60a, b.Bava Metzia 59a, b.Rosh Hashanah 31a, Ein Yaakov Bava Metzia 59a, Ein Yaakov Rosh Hashanah 31a, Ezekiel 16:3, Guide for the Perplexed 2:43, Isaiah 4:17 10:11, Jastrow 298a 85b, Lamentations 2:8, Lamentations.R Petichata D'Chakimei 25, Leviticus.R 33:2, Midrash Tanchuma Noach 4, Per Massorah: Soferim altered *Hashem* to *Adonai*, Pesikta de R'Kahana 13.11, Revelation 11:1 21:15, Zechariah 2:1-2
Amos 7:7-9 - 4QXIIc
Amos 7:7-12 - 4QXIIg

[5] LXX *upon a wall of adamant, and in his hand was an adamant*

[6] Amos 7:8 - 2 Kings 21:13, Amos 8:2, Ezekiel 7:2-9, Isaiah 4:17, Jeremiah 1:11-13 15:6, Lamentations 2:8, Lamentations.R Petichata D'Chakimei:25, Leviticus.R 33:2, Micah 7:18, Nahum 1:8-9, Per Massorah: Soferim altered "Hashem" to "Adonai", Zechariah 5:2

[7] LXX *An adamant. And the Lord said to me, Behold, I appoint an adamant in the midst of my people Israel: I will not pass by them any more*

[8] Amos 7:9 - 2 Kings 15:8-15:10, Amos 3:14 5:5 8:14, Genesis 26:23-26:25 22:1, Guide for the Perplexed 1:12, Hosea 10:8, Isaiah 15:18, Leviticus 26:30-26:31

[9] LXX And the joyful altars shall be abolished, and the sacrifices of Israel shall be set aside

[10] Amos 7:10 - 1 Kings 12:31-32 13:33 18:17, 2 Chronicles 13:8-9, 2 Kings 14:23-24, Acts 5:28 7:54 24:5, b.Pesachim 87b, Genesis 13:8, Jeremiah 18:18 20:1-3 26:8-11 29:26-27 37:13-15 14:4, Luke 23:2, Matthew 21:23, Song of Songs.R 2:18

[11] Amos 7:11 - 2 Kings 17:6, Acts 6:14, Amos 6:7-6:8 7:9, b.Moed Katan [Tosefot] 7b, Jeremiah 2:9 28:10-28:11, Matthew 26:61, Psalms 56:6, Seder Olam 28:Darius
Amos 7:11-15 - mt.Hilchot Melachim u'Michamoteihem 11:2

[12] Amos 7:12 - 1 Corinthians 2:14, 1 Peter 5:2, 1 Samuel 2:36 9:9, 2 Chronicles 16:10, Acts 16:39, Amos 2:12, Avot de R'Natan 34, Ezekiel 13:19, Isaiah 6:10 8:11, Luke 8:37-38 13:31, Malachi 1:10, Matthew 8:34, Romans 16:18
Amos 7:12-16 - 4QXIIc

וּבֵית־אֵל לֹא־תוֹסִיף עוֹד לְהִנָּבֵא כִּי מִקְדַּשׁ־מֶלֶךְ הוּא וּבֵית מַמְלָכָה הוּא	13[1]	but do not prophesy again at Bethel, for it is the king's sanctuary, and it is a royal house.'
וַיַּעַן עָמוֹס וַיֹּאמֶר אֶל־אֲמַצְיָה לֹא־נָבִיא אָנֹכִי וְלֹא בֶן־נָבִיא אָנֹכִי כִּי־בוֹקֵר אָנֹכִי וּבוֹלֵס שִׁקְמִים	14[2]	Then Amos answered, and said to Amaziah: 'I was no prophet, nor was I a prophet's son; but I was a herdman, and a dresser of sycamore trees;
וַיִּקָּחֵנִי יְהוָה מֵאַחֲרֵי הַצֹּאן וַיֹּאמֶר אֵלַי יְהוָה לֵךְ הִנָּבֵא אֶל־עַמִּי יִשְׂרָאֵל	15[3]	And the LORD took me from following the flock, and the LORD said *to me*[4]: Go, prophesy to My people Israel.
וְעַתָּה שְׁמַע דְּבַר־יְהוָה אַתָּה אֹמֵר לֹא תִנָּבֵא עַל־יִשְׂרָאֵל וְלֹא תַטִּיף עַל־בֵּית יִשְׂחָק	16[5]	Now therefore, hear the word of the LORD: You say: do not prophesy against Israel, and do not preach[6]against the house of Isaac;
לָכֵן כֹּה־אָמַר יְהוָה אִשְׁתְּךָ בָּעִיר תִּזְנֶה וּבָנֶיךָ וּבְנֹתֶיךָ בַּחֶרֶב יִפֹּלוּ וְאַדְמָתְךָ בַּחֶבֶל תְּחֻלָּק וְאַתָּה עַל־אֲדָמָה טְמֵאָה תָּמוּת וְיִשְׂרָאֵל גָּלֹה יִגְלֶה מֵעַל אַדְמָתוֹ	17[7]	Therefore, thus says the LORD: Your wife shall be a harlot in the city, and your sons and your daughters shall fall by the sword, and your land shall be divided by line; and you yourself shall die in an unclean land, and Israel shall surely be led away captive out of his land.[8]'

Amos – Chapter 8

כֹּה הִרְאַנִי אֲדֹנָי יְהוִה וְהִנֵּה כְּלוּב קָיִץ	1[9]	*Thus, the Lord GOD showed me; and behold a basket of summer fruit*[10].
וַיֹּאמֶר מָה־אַתָּה רֹאֶה עָמוֹס וָאֹמַר כְּלוּב קָיִץ וַיֹּאמֶר יְהוָה אֵלַי בָּא הַקֵּץ אֶל־עַמִּי יִשְׂרָאֵל לֹא־אוֹסִיף עוֹד עֲבוֹר לוֹ	2[11]	And He said: 'Amos, what do you see?' And I said: 'A basket of summer fruit.' Then the LORD said to me: The end has come to My people Israel; I will not pardon them any more.
וְהֵילִילוּ שִׁירוֹת הֵיכָל בַּיּוֹם הַהוּא נְאֻם אֲדֹנָי יְהוִה רַב הַפֶּגֶר בְּכָל־מָקוֹם הִשְׁלִיךְ הָס	3[12]	And the *songs*[13] of the palace shall be wailings in that day, Says the Lord GOD; The dead bodies shall be many; In every place silence shall be cast.
שִׁמְעוּ־זֹאת הַשֹּׁאֲפִים אֶבְיוֹן וְלַשְׁבִּית עֲנָיֵי־עַנְוֵי־אָרֶץ	4[14]	Hear this, O you who would swallow the needy, And destroy the poor of the land,

---

[1] Amos 7:13 - 1 Kings 12:29 12:32 13:1, Acts 4:17-4:18 5:28 5:40, Amos 2:12

[2] Amos 7:14 - 1 Corinthians 1:27, 1 Kings 20:35, 2 Chronicles 16:7 19:2 20:34, 2 Kings 2:3 2:5 2:7 4:38 6:1, Amos 1:1, b.Nedarim 38a, Ein Yaakov Nedarim:38a, Leviticus.R 20:6, Pesikta de R'Kahana 26.6/7, Zechariah 13:5
Amos 7:14-17 - 4QXIIg

[3] Amos 7:15 - 2 Samuel 7:8, Acts 1:8 4:20 5:20 5:29-32, Ezekiel 2:3-4, Jeremiah 1:7, Luke 24:46-48, Matthew 4:18-19 9:9, Psalms 78:70-72

[4] Missing in 4QXIIg

[5] Amos 7:16 - 1 Kings 22:19, 1 Samuel 15:16, Amos 7:13, Deuteronomy 8:2, Ezekiel 21:2 21:7, Isaiah 6:10, Jeremiah 28:15-17, Micah 2:6

[6] MurXII adds *any longer*

[7] Amos 7:17 - 2 Kings 17:6, Amos 7:11, b.Ketubot 111a, Ezekiel 4:13, Hosea 4:13-14 9:3, Isaiah 13:16, Jeremiah 20:6 4:12 4:16 5:21 5:25 29:31-32 36:27-32, Lamentations 5:11, Leviticus 26:33-39, mt.Hilchot Melachim u'Michamoteihem 5:11, Pirkei de R'Eliezer 33, Psalms 78:55, Sifre Devarim Ekev 43, Sifre Devarim Ha'azinu Hashamayim 320, Sifre Devarim Nitzavim 320, z.Vaetchanan 269b, Zechariah 14:2

[8] LXX adds *Thus has the LORD God shown me*

[9] Amos 8:1 - Amos 7:1 7:4 7:7
Amos 8:1-5 - 4QXIIg

[10] LXX *And behold a fowler's basket*

[11] Amos 8:2 - 2 Samuel 16:1-2, Amos 7:8, Deuteronomy 26:1-4, Ezekiel 3:7 3:10 7:2-3 7:6 8:6 8:12 8:17 12:23 5:8, Guide for the Perplexed 2:43, Isaiah 4:4, Jeremiah 1:11-14 5:31 24:1-3 16:10, Lamentations 4:18, Micah 7:1, Zechariah 1:18-21 5:2 5:5-6

[12] Amos 8:3 - Amos 4:10 5:16 5:23 6:9-6:10 8:10, Hosea 10:5-10:6, Isaiah 13:36, Jastrow 345b 1512b, Jeremiah 9:22-9:23 22:18, Joel 1:5 1:11 1:13, Leviticus 10:3, Nahum 3:3, Psalms 39:10, Song of Songs.R 1:11, Zechariah 11:1-11:3
Amos 8:3-7 - MurXII

[13] LXX *ceilings*

[14] Amos 8:4 - 1 Kings 22:19, Amos 2:6-7 5:11 7:16, Isaiah 1:10 4:14 32:6-7, James 5:6, Jastrow 129b 1508b, Jeremiah 5:21 4:15, Matthew 23:13, Midrash Psalms 56:2, Midrash Tanchuma Mikketz 2, Proverbs 6:14, Psalms 12:6 14:4 56:2 20:13, Pseudo-Phocylides 19-21
Amos 8:4-6 - Pseudo-Phocylides 12

לֵאמֹר מָתַי יַעֲבֹר הַחֹדֶשׁ וְנַשְׁבִּירָה שֶּׁבֶר וְהַשַּׁבָּת וְנִפְתְּחָה־בָּר לְהַקְטִין אֵיפָה וּלְהַגְדִּיל שֶׁקֶל וּלְעַוֵּת מֹאזְנֵי מִרְמָה	5[1]	Saying: 'When will the new moon be gone, so we may *sell grain*[2]? And the Sabbath, so we may set forth corn? Making the ephah small, and the shekel great, And falsifying the balances of deceit;
לִקְנוֹת בַּכֶּסֶף דַּלִּים וְאֶבְיוֹן בַּעֲבוּר נַעֲלָיִם וּמַפַּל בַּר נַשְׁבִּיר	6[3]	So we may buy the poor for silver, and the needy for a pair of shoes, And sell the refuse of the corn?'
נִשְׁבַּע יְהוָה בִּגְאוֹן יַעֲקֹב אִם־אֶשְׁכַּח לָנֶצַח כָּל־מַעֲשֵׂיהֶם	7[4]	The LORD has sworn by the pride of Jacob: Surely I will never forget any of their works.
הַעַל זֹאת לֹא־תִרְגַּז הָאָרֶץ וְאָבַל כָּל־יוֹשֵׁב בָּהּ וְעָלְתָה כָאֹר כֻּלָּהּ וְנִגְרְשָׁה "וְנִשְׁקָה׳ "וְנִשְׁקְעָה" כִּיאוֹר מִצְרָיִם	8[5]	Shall not the land tremble for this, and everyone mourn who dwells there? Yes, it shall rise up wholly like the River; and it shall be troubled and sink again, like the River of Egypt.
וְהָיָה בַּיּוֹם הַהוּא נְאֻם אֲדֹנָי יְהוִה וְהֵבֵאתִי הַשֶּׁמֶשׁ בַּצָּהֳרָיִם וְהַחֲשַׁכְתִּי לָאָרֶץ בְּיוֹם אוֹר	9[6]	And it shall come to pass in that day, says the Lord GOD, that I will cause the sun to go down at noon, And I will darken the earth in the clear day.
וְהָפַכְתִּי חַגֵּיכֶם לְאֵבֶל וְכָל־שִׁירֵיכֶם לְקִינָה וְהַעֲלֵיתִי עַל־כָּל־מָתְנַיִם שָׂק וְעַל־כָּל־רֹאשׁ קָרְחָה וְשַׂמְתִּיהָ כְּאֵבֶל יָחִיד וְאַחֲרִיתָהּ כְּיוֹם מָר	10[7]	And I will turn your festivals into mourning, and all your songs into lamentation; and I will bring up sackcloth on all loins, and baldness on every head; and I will make it as the mourning *for an only son*[8], And its end as a bitter day.
הִנֵּה יָמִים בָּאִים נְאֻם אֲדֹנָי יְהוִה וְהִשְׁלַחְתִּי רָעָב בָּאָרֶץ לֹא־רָעָב לַלֶּחֶם וְלֹא־צָמָא לַמַּיִם כִּי אִם־לִשְׁמֹעַ אֵת דִּבְרֵי יְהוָה	11[9]	Behold, the days come, says the Lord GOD, that I will send a famine in the land, not a famine of bread, nor a thirst for water, but of hearing the words of the LORD.
וְנָעוּ מִיָּם עַד־יָם וּמִצָּפוֹן וְעַד־מִזְרָח יְשׁוֹטְטוּ לְבַקֵּשׁ אֶת־דְּבַר־יְהוָה וְלֹא יִמְצָאוּ	12[10]	And they shall wander from sea to sea, and from the north to the east; they shall run to and fro to seek the word of the LORD, and shall not find it.

---

[1] Amos 8:5 - 2 Kings 4:23, b.Bava Batra 90b, Colossians 2:16, Deuteronomy 25:13-16, Ein Yaakov Bava Batra:89b, Exodus 20:8-10, Ezekiel 45:10-12, Hosea 12:9, Isaiah 1:13 10:13, Jastrow 1350a, Leviticus 19:36, Malachi 1:13, Mas.Derek Eretz Rabbah 2:5, Micah 6:10-11, Nehemiah 13:15-21, Numbers 10:10 28:11-15, Proverbs 11:1 16:11 20:23, Psalms 81:4-5, Romans 8:6-7

[2] 4QXIIg *be satisfied*

[3] Amos 8:6 - Amos 2:6 8:4, Joel 4:3 4:6, Leviticus 25:39-42, Nehemiah 5:1-5 5:8, Saadia Opinions 10:10

[4] Amos 8:7 - 1 Samuel 15:2-15:3, Amos 6:8, b.Bava Batra 90b, Deuteronomy 33:26-33:29, Ein Yaakov Bava Batra:89b, Exodus 17:16, Hosea 7:2 8:13 9:9, Isaiah 19:25, Jeremiah 17:1 7:35, Luke 2:32, Mas.Derek Eretz Rabbah 2:5, Psalms 10:12 47:5 68:35

[5] Amos 8:8 - According to the Massorah וּנשקעה was altered to become וּנשקה, Amos 8:10 9:5, Daniel 9:26, Habakkuk 3:5-8, Haggai 2:6-7, Hosea 4:3 10:5, Isaiah 5:25 8:7-8 24:19-20, Jeremiah 4:24-26 12:4 22:8, Matthew 24:30, Micah 1:3-5, Nahum 1:5-6, Psalms 18:8 60:3-4 114:3-7

[6] Amos 8:9 - Amos 4:13 5:8, b.Moed Katan 25b, Ein Yaakov Moed Katan:25a, Exodus 10:21-10:23, Guide for the Perplexed 2:29, Isaiah 13:10 29:9-29:10 59:9-59:10, Jastrow 5608a 569a, Jeremiah 15:9, Job 5:14, Luke 23:44, Mark 15:33, Matthew 24:29 3:45, Micah 3:6, Revelation 6:12 8:12

[7] Amos 8:10 - 1 Samuel 25:36-25:38, 2 Samuel 13:28-13:31, Amos 5:23 6:4-6:7 8:3, b.Bava Kamma [Rashi] 11a, b.Berachot [Tosefot] 47b, b.Berachot 16b 48b, b.Chagigah [Tosefot] 18a, b.Moed Katan 15b 20a 21b, b.Nazir [Rashi] 15b, b.Succah 25b, Daniel 5:4-5:6, Deuteronomy 16:14, Deuteronomy.R 9:1, Ezekiel 7:18 27:30-27:31, Genesis.R 100 [Excl]:7, Hosea 2:11, Isaiah 15:2-15:3 21:3-21:4 22:12-22:14, Jeremiah 6:26 24:37, Job 3:6 20:23, Luke 7:12-7:13, Mas.Semachot 5:1, mt.Hilchot Evel 5:7, Nahum 1:10, y.Moed Katan 3:5, Zechariah 12:10

[8] LXX *of a beloved friend*

[9] Amos 8:11 - 1 Samuel 3:1 4:6 4:15, 2 Chronicles 15:3, 4Q387 frag 3 ll.8-9, b.Shabbat 138b, Ezekiel 7:26, Genesis.R 25:3 40:3 64:2, Isaiah 5:6 30:20-30:21, Matthew 9:36, Micah 3:6, Midrash Proverbs 6, Midrash Tanchuma Shemini 8, Numbers.R 3:6, Psalms 74:9, Ruth.R 1:4
Amos 8:11-12 - t.Eduyot 1:1
Amos 8:11-14 - 4QXIIg, MurXII

[10] Amos 8:12 - 2 Timothy 3:6-3:7, b.Shabbat 138b, Daniel 12:4, Ezekiel 20:3 20:31, Guide for the Perplexed 2:36, Matthew 11:25-27 12:30 24:23-26, Midrash Tanchuma Shemini 8, Proverbs 14:6, Romans 9:31-33 11:7-10, Sifre Devarim Ekev 48

בַּיּ֤וֹם הַהוּא֙ תִּ֣תְעַלַּ֔פְנָה הַבְּתוּלֹ֥ת הַיָּפ֖וֹת וְהַבַּחוּרִ֑ים בַּצָּמָֽא

13[1] In that day the fair virgins and the young men shall faint for thirst.

הַנִּשְׁבָּעִים֙ בְּאַשְׁמַ֣ת שֹֽׁמְר֔וֹן וְאָמְר֗וּ חֵ֤י אֱלֹהֶ֙יךָ֙ דָּ֔ן וְחֵ֖י דֶּ֣רֶךְ בְּאֵֽר־שָׁ֑בַע וְנָפְל֖וּ וְלֹא־יָק֥וּמוּ עֽוֹד

14[2] Those who swear by the sin of Samaria, and say, 'As your God, O Dan, lives;' and, 'As the way of Beer-sheba lives;' they shall fall, and never rise up again.

Amos – Chapter 9

רָאִ֨יתִי אֶת־אֲדֹנָ֜י נִצָּ֣ב עַֽל־הַמִּזְבֵּ֗חַ וַיֹּאמֶר֮ הַ֣ךְ הַכַּפְתּוֹר֮ וְיִרְעֲשׁ֣וּ הַסִּפִּים֒ וּבְצַ֣עַם בְּרֹ֣אשׁ כֻּלָּ֔ם וְאַחֲרִיתָ֖ם בַּחֶ֣רֶב אֶהֱרֹ֑ג לֹֽא־יָנ֤וּס לָהֶם֙ נָ֔ס וְלֹֽא־יִמָּלֵ֥ט לָהֶ֖ם פָּלִֽיט׃

1[3] I saw the Lord standing beside the altar; and He said: *Strike the capitals, so the posts will shake; and break them in pieces on the head of all of them*[4]; And I will kill their remnant with the sword; and not one of them shall flee, and not one of them shall escape.

אִם־יַחְתְּר֣וּ בִשְׁא֔וֹל מִשָּׁ֖ם יָדִ֣י תִקָּחֵ֑ם וְאִֽם־יַעֲלוּ֙ הַשָּׁמַ֔יִם מִשָּׁ֖ם אוֹרִידֵֽם

2[5] If they dig into the nether world, there My hand shall take them; and though they climb up to heaven, there will I bring them down.

וְאִם־יֵחָֽבְאוּ֙ בְּרֹ֣אשׁ הַכַּרְמֶ֔ל מִשָּׁ֥ם אֲחַפֵּ֖שׂ וּלְקַחְתִּ֑ים וְאִם־יִסָּ֨תְר֜וּ מִנֶּ֤גֶד עֵינַי֙ בְּקַרְקַ֣ע הַיָּ֔ם מִשָּׁ֛ם אֲצַוֶּ֥ה אֶת־הַנָּחָ֖שׁ וּנְשָׁכָֽם

3[6] And though they hide themselves at the top of Carmel, I will search and take them from there; and though they hide from My sight in the bottom of the sea, there I will command the serpent, and he shall bite them.

וְאִם־יֵלְכ֤וּ בַשְּׁבִי֙ לִפְנֵ֣י אֹֽיְבֵיהֶ֔ם מִשָּׁ֛ם אֲצַוֶּ֥ה אֶת־הַחֶ֖רֶב וַהֲרָגָ֑תַם וְשַׂמְתִּ֨י עֵינִ֧י עֲלֵיהֶ֛ם לְרָעָ֖ה וְלֹ֥א לְטוֹבָֽה

4[7] And though they go into captivity before their enemies, there I will command the sword, and it shall kill them; and I will set My eyes on them For evil, and not for good.

וַאדֹנָ֨י יְהֹוִ֜ה הַצְּבָא֗וֹת הַנּוֹגֵ֤עַ בָּאָ֙רֶץ֙ וַתָּמ֔וֹג וְאָבְל֖וּ כָּל־י֣וֹשְׁבֵי בָ֑הּ וְעָלְתָ֤ה כַיְאֹר֙ כֻּלָּ֔הּ וְשָׁקְעָ֖ה כִּיאֹ֥ר מִצְרָֽיִם

5[8] For the Lord, the GOD of hosts, Is He who touches the land and it melts, and all who dwell in it mourn; and it rises like the River, and sinks again, like the River of Egypt;

הַבּוֹנֶ֤ה בַשָּׁמַ֙יִם֙ *מַעֲלוֹתָו* "מַעֲלוֹתָיו" וַאֲגֻדָּת֖וֹ עַל־אֶ֣רֶץ יְסָדָ֑הּ הַקֹּרֵ֣א לְמֵֽי־הַיָּ֗ם וַֽיִּשְׁפְּכֵ֛ם עַל־פְּנֵ֥י הָאָ֖רֶץ יְהֹוָ֥ה שְׁמֽוֹ

6[9] It is He who builds His upper chambers in the heaven, and *has founded His vault upon the earth*[10]; He who calls for the waters of the sea,

---

[1] Amos 8:13 - Deuteronomy 8:25, Hosea 2:3, Isaiah 16:30 41:17-20, Jeremiah 24:18, Lamentations 1:18 2:10 2:21, Psalms 63:2 144:12-15, Zechariah 9:17

[2] Amos 8:14 - 1 Kings 12:28-29 12:32 13:22-34 14:16 16:24, 2 Chronicles 12:16, 2 Kings 10:29, Acts 9:2 18:25 19:9 19:23 24:14, Amos 5:2 5:5, b.Shabbat 67b, Deuteronomy 9:21 9:11, Genesis.R 70:4, Hosea 4:15 8:5-6 10:5 13:2 14:1, Isaiah 19:17, Jeremiah 1:27 51:64, Proverbs 5:1, Psalms 36:13 20:11, Shemonah Perachim VIII, t.Shabbat 7:3, Tanna Devei Eliyahu 3, y.Shabbat 6:9, Zephaniah 1:5

[3] Amos 9:1 - 2 Chronicles 18:18, 3 Enoch 24:5, 4QXIIg, Acts 2:13, Amos 2:14-15 3:14, Avot de R'Natan 34, b.Rosh Hashanah 31a, Ecclesiastes.R 1:32 3:12, Ein Yaakov Rosh Hashanah 31a, Ezekiel 1:28 9:2 10:4, Genesis.R 68:12, Habakkuk 3:13, Isaiah 6:1 6:3-4 24:17-18 6:16, Jeremiah 24:44, John 1:18 1:32, Lamentations.R Petichata D'Chakimei 25, Leviticus.R 33:3, Mas.Semachot 8:10, Mekhilta de R'Shimon bar Yochai Beshallach 22:2, Mekhilta de R'Shimon bar Yochai Shirata 36:3, Mekilta de R'Ishmael Beshallah 3:84, Mekilta de R'Ishmael Shirata 10:66, Midrash Proverbs 14, Midrash Psalms 78:6, Per Massorah: Soferim altered "Hashem" to "Adonai", Pesikta de R'Kahana 13.11, Psalms 68:22, Revelation 1:17, y.Sotah 1:9, Zechariah 11:1-2, Zephaniah 2:14
Amos 9:1-15 - MurXII

[4] LXX *Smite the mercy-seat, and the porch shall be shaken: and cut through into the heads of all*

[5] Amos 9:2 - Ezekiel 28:13-16, Isaiah 2:19 14:13-16, Jeremiah 1:16 3:53, Job 20:6 2:6, Luke 10:18, Obadiah 1:4, Psalms 139:7-10
Amos 9:2-3 - Exodus.R 15:15
Amos 9:2-4 - Jubilees 24:31, Mekilta de R'Ishmael Pisha 1:77-79

[6] Amos 9:3 - Amos 1:2, Isaiah 3:1, Jeremiah 16:16 23:23-23:24, Job 10:22, Psalms 139:9-139:11

[7] Amos 9:4 - 2 Chronicles 16:9, Deuteronomy 28:63-28:65, Ezekiel 5:2 5:12, Jeremiah 21:10 24:6 15:16 20:11, Leviticus 17:10 2:33 26:36-26:39, Psalms 34:16-34:17, Zechariah 13:8-13:9

[8] Amos 9:5 - Amos 8:8, Habakkuk 3:10, Hosea 4:3, Isaiah 8:7-8:8 16:2, Jeremiah 12:4, Matthew 7:27, Micah 1:3-1:4, Nahum 1:6, Psalms 32:6 46:7 93:3-93:4 24:5, Revelation 20:11

[9] Amos 9:6 - 4QXIIg, Amos 4:13 5:8, Avot de R'Natan 8, b.Chagigah 12a, b.Kereitot 6a, b.Menachot 16a, Ecclesiastes.R 3:17, Ein Yaakov Chagigah:12a, Exodus 3:14-15, Genesis 2:1 7:11-19, Genesis.R 5:6 23:7 25:2, Jeremiah 5:22, Leviticus.R 30:12, m.Avot 3:6, Midrash Tanchuma Beha'alotcha 11, Midrash Tanchuma Emor 17, mt.Pirkei Avot 3:7, Numbers.R 15:17, Pesikta Rabbati 48:2, Pirkei Avot 3:7 [Shabbat afternoon], Psalms 8:3 104:5-6 8:13, Sifre Devarim Re'eh 96, Sifre Devarim Vezot Habracha 346, z.Tzav 35a

[10] LXX *establishes his promise on the earth*

and pours them out upon the face of the earth; the LORD is His name.

הֲל֣וֹא כִבְנֵי֩ כֻשִׁיִּ֨ים אַתֶּ֥ם לִ֛י בְּנֵ֥י יִשְׂרָאֵ֖ל נְאֻם־יְהֹוָ֑ה הֲל֣וֹא אֶת־יִשְׂרָאֵ֗ל הֶעֱלֵ֙יתִי֙ מֵאֶ֣רֶץ מִצְרַ֔יִם וּפְלִשְׁתִּיִּ֥ים מִכַּפְתּ֖וֹר וַאֲרָ֥ם מִקִּֽיר

7[1] Are you not as the children of the Ethiopians to Me, O children of Israel? says the LORD. Did I not bring up Israel out of the land of Egypt, and the Philistines from *Caphtor, and Aram from Kir*[2]?

הִנֵּ֞ה עֵינֵ֣י ׀ אֲדֹנָ֣י יֱהֹוִ֗ה בַּמַּמְלָכָה֙ הַֽחַטָּאָ֔ה וְהִשְׁמַדְתִּ֣י אֹתָ֔הּ מֵעַ֖ל פְּנֵ֣י הָאֲדָמָ֑ה אֶ֗פֶס כִּ֠י לֹ֣א הַשְׁמֵ֥יד אַשְׁמִ֛יד אֶת־בֵּ֥ית יַעֲקֹ֖ב נְאֻם־יְהֹוָֽה

8[3] Behold, the eyes of the Lord GOD are upon the sinful kingdom, and I will destroy it off the face of the earth; saving that I will not utterly destroy the house of Jacob, Says the LORD.

כִּֽי־הִנֵּ֤ה אָנֹכִי֙ מְצַוֶּ֔ה וַהֲנִע֥וֹתִי בְכׇל־הַגּוֹיִ֖ם אֶת־בֵּ֣ית יִשְׂרָאֵ֑ל כַּאֲשֶׁ֤ר יִנּ֙וֹעַ֙ בַּכְּבָרָ֔ה וְלֹֽא־יִפּ֥וֹל צְר֖וֹר אָֽרֶץ

9[4] For, lo, I will command, and I will sift the house of Israel among all the nations, like corn is sifted in a sieve, yet shall not the least grain fall upon the earth.

בַּחֶ֣רֶב יָמ֔וּתוּ כֹּ֖ל חַטָּאֵ֣י עַמִּ֑י הָאֹמְרִ֗ים לֹא־תַגִּ֧ישׁ וְתַקְדִּ֛ים בַּעֲדֵ֖ינוּ הָרָעָֽה

10[5] All the sinners of My people shall die by the sword who say: 'the evil shall neither overtake nor confront us.'

בַּיּ֣וֹם הַה֔וּא אָקִ֛ים אֶת־סֻכַּ֥ת דָּוִ֖יד הַנֹּפֶ֑לֶת וְגָדַרְתִּ֣י אֶת־פִּרְצֵיהֶ֗ן וַהֲרִֽסֹתָיו֙ אָקִ֔ים וּבְנִיתִ֖יהָ כִּימֵ֥י עוֹלָֽם

11[6] In that day will I raise up the tabernacle of David that is fallen, and close its breaches, and I will raise up his ruins, And I will build it as in the days of old;

לְמַ֨עַן יִֽירְשׁ֜וּ אֶת־שְׁאֵרִ֤ית אֱדוֹם֙ וְכׇל־הַגּוֹיִ֔ם אֲשֶׁר־נִקְרָ֥א שְׁמִ֖י עֲלֵיהֶ֑ם נְאֻם־יְהֹוָ֖ה עֹ֥שֶׂה זֹּֽאת

12[7] So they may possess the remnant of Edom, and all the nations, upon whom My name is called, Says the LORD who does this.

הִנֵּ֨ה יָמִ֤ים בָּאִים֙ נְאֻם־יְהֹוָ֔ה וְנִגַּ֤שׁ חוֹרֵשׁ֙ בַּקֹּצֵ֔ר וְדֹרֵ֥ךְ עֲנָבִ֖ים בְּמֹשֵׁ֣ךְ הַזָּ֑רַע וְהִטִּ֤יפוּ הֶֽהָרִים֙ עָסִ֔יס וְכׇל־הַגְּבָע֖וֹת תִּתְמוֹגַֽגְנָה

13[8] Behold, the days come, says the LORD, *that the plowman shall overtake the reaper, And the treader of grapes he who sows seed*[9]; and the mountains shall drop sweet wine, and all the hills shall *melt*[10].

וְשַׁבְתִּי֙ אֶת־שְׁב֣וּת עַמִּ֣י יִשְׂרָאֵ֔ל וּבָנ֞וּ עָרִ֤ים נְשַׁמּוֹת֙ וְיָשָׁ֔בוּ וְנָטְע֣וּ כְרָמִ֔ים וְשָׁת֖וּ אֶת־יֵינָ֑ם וְעָשׂ֥וּ גַנּ֖וֹת וְאָכְל֥וּ אֶת־פְּרִיהֶֽם

14[11] And I will turn away the captivity of My people Israel, and they shall build the waste cities, and inhabit them; and they shall plant

---

[1] Amos 9:7 - 2 Kings 16:9, Amos 1:5 2:10, b.Moed Katan 16b, Deuteronomy 2:23, Ein Yaakov Moed Katan:9b, Exodus 12:51, Hosea 12:15, Isaiah 20:4 22:6 19:3, Jeremiah 9:26-27 13:23 23:4, Jubilees 24:30 8:21, Midrash Psalms 1:14 7:18, Pesikta Rabbati 26:5, Pirkei de R'Eliezer 53, Sifre Devarim Vezot Habracha 346, Sifre.z Numbers Beha'alotcha 12:1, Siman 79:6, Song of Songs.R 1:34, z.Terumah 130a

Amos 9:7-15 - Haftarah Kedoshim [Amos 9:7-9:15], Haftarah Kedoshim [Ashkenaz]

[2] LXX *Cappadocia, and the Syrians out of the deep*

[3] Amos 9:8 - 1 Kings 13:34, Amos 9:4, Deuteronomy 4:31 6:15, Genesis 6:7 7:4, Hosea 1:6 9:11-9:17 13:15-13:16, Isaiah 27:7-27:8, Jeremiah 5:10 6:11 31:36-31:37 33:24-33:26 20:27, Joel 3:5, Obadiah 1:16-1:17, Proverbs 5:21 15:3, Psalms 11:5-11:7, Romans 11:1-11:7 11:28-11:29

[4] Amos 9:9 - Deuteronomy 28:64, Isaiah 6:28, Jastrow 881a, Leviticus 2:33, Luke 22:31, Tanna Devei Eliyahu 5

[5] Amos 9:10 - Amos 6:1 6:3, Ecclesiastes 8:11, Ezekiel 20:38 34:16-34:17, Isaiah 5:19 28:14-28:15 9:14 8:12, Jeremiah 18:18, Malachi 3:2-3:5 3:15 3:19, Mas.Semachot 8:14, Matthew 3:10-3:12 13:41-13:42 13:49-13:50, Midrash Tanchuma Behar 3, Psalms 10:12, Tanna Devei Eliyahu 6, Zechariah 13:8-13:9, Zephaniah 3:11-3:13

[6] Amos 9:11 - 4Q174 3.12, 4QFlor 1-3 ii 11-13, Acts 2:30-36 15:15-17, b.Sanhedrin 96b, Cairo Damascus 7.15-16, Cairo Damascus 7.16, Ecclesiastes.R 3:10, Ein Yaakov Sanhedrin:97a, Ein Yaakov Shabbat:138b, Ezekiel 17:24 21:30-32 34:23-24 12:11 37:24-25, Genesis.R 88:8, Hosea 3:5, Isaiah 5:5 9:7-8 11:1-10 16:5 15:11, Jastrow 907a, Jeremiah 23:5-6 6:9 33:14-16 33:20-26 22:26, Job 1:10, Lamentations 5:21, Luke 1:31-33 1:69-70, Micah 5:3 7:14, Midrash Psalms 76:3, Pesikta de R'Kahana 16.8, Pesikta Rabbati 29/30B:2, Psalms 80:13 89:41 23:5, Tanya Igeret Hakodesh §9 §30, z.Noach 72b, z.Pekudei 239b, z.Shemot 11a 9a, z.Vayikra 6b

[7] Amos 9:12 - Acts 15:17, Daniel 9:18-19, Ein Yaakov Shabbat:138b, Genesis 3:29 3:37, Isaiah 11:14 14:1-2 19:7 15:19 17:1, Jeremiah 14:9 15:16, Joel 4:8, Malachi 1:4, Numbers 24:17-24:18, Obadiah 1:18-21, Psalms 60:9

[8] Amos 9:13 - Amos 9:5, Ezekiel 12:35, Genesis.R 93:5, Hosea 2:21-25, Isaiah 35:1-2 7:13, Joel 4:18 4:20, John 4:35, Judges 5:5, Leviticus 2:5, Leviticus.R 17:4, Pesikta de R'Kahana 710, Pesikta Rabbati 17:6, Psalms 97:5, Ruth.R 2:10, Sifre Devarim Vezot Habracha 342

[9] LXX *when the harvest shall overtake the vintage, and the grapes shall ripen at seedtime*

[10] LXX *be planted*

[11] Amos 9:14 - Amos 5:11, b.Berachot 28a, Ein Yaakov Berachot:28a, Ezekiel 16:53 4:26 36:33-36 37:25-28 15:25, Isaiah 13:4 62:8-9 17:21, Jeremiah 6:3 6:18 7:24 7:29 31:39-41, Joel 4:1-2, m.Yadayim 4:4, Psalms 53:7, t.Yadayim 2:17, Zephaniah 1:13
Amos 9:14-15 - 4QXIIg

vineyards, and drink its wine; they shall also make gardens, and eat the fruit of them.

15[1] And I will plant them upon their land, and they shall no more be plucked up out of their land I have given them, Says the LORD your God.

וּנְטַעְתִּים עַל־אַדְמָתָם וְלֹא יִנָּתְשׁוּ עוֹד מֵעַל אַדְמָתָם אֲשֶׁר נָתַתִּי לָהֶם אָמַר יְהוָה אֱלֹהֶיךָ

Ovadyah haGerim – Chapter 1[2]

חֲזוֹן עֹבַדְיָה כֹּה־אָמַר אֲדֹנָי יְהוִה לֶאֱדוֹם שְׁמוּעָה שָׁמַעְנוּ מֵאֵת יְהוָה וְצִיר בַּגּוֹיִם שֻׁלָּח קוּמוּ וְנָקוּמָה עָלֶיהָ לַמִּלְחָמָה

1[3] [4]The vision of Obadiah. Thus says the Lord GOD concerning Edom: We have heard a message from the LORD, And an ambassador is sent among the nations: 'Arise, and let us rise up against her in battle.'

הִנֵּה קָטֹן נְתַתִּיךָ בַּגּוֹיִם בָּזוּי אַתָּה מְאֹד

2[5] Behold, I make you small among the nations; You are greatly *despised*[6].

זְדוֹן לִבְּךָ הִשִּׁיאֶךָ שֹׁכְנִי בְחַגְוֵי־סֶלַע מְרוֹם שִׁבְתּוֹ אֹמֵר בְּלִבּוֹ מִי יוֹרִדֵנִי אָרֶץ

3[7] The pride of your heart has tricked you, OI you who dwells in the clefts of the rock, your habitation on high; who say in your heart: 'Who shall bring me down to the ground?'

אִם־תַּגְבִּיהַּ כַּנֶּשֶׁר וְאִם־בֵּין כּוֹכָבִים שִׂים קִנֶּךָ מִשָּׁם אוֹרִידְךָ נְאֻם־יְהוָה

4[8] *You you make your nest as high as the eagle*[9], And though you *set it*[10] among the stars, I will bring you down from there, says the LORD.

אִם־גַּנָּבִים בָּאוּ־לְךָ אִם־שׁוֹדְדֵי לַיְלָה אֵיךְ נִדְמֵיתָה הֲלוֹא יִגְנְבוּ דַּיָּם אִם־בֹּצְרִים בָּאוּ לָךְ הֲלוֹא יַשְׁאִירוּ עֹלֵלוֹת

5[11] If thieves came to you, if robbers by night, how you are cut off! Would they not steal until they had enough? If grape gatherers came to you, would they not leave some gleaning grapes?

אֵיךְ נֶחְפְּשׂוּ עֵשָׂו נִבְעוּ מַצְפֻּנָיו

6[12] How Esau is searched out! How his hidden places are sought out!

עַד־הַגְּבוּל שִׁלְּחוּךָ כֹּל אַנְשֵׁי בְרִיתֶךָ הִשִּׁיאוּךָ יָכְלוּ לְךָ אַנְשֵׁי שְׁלֹמֶךָ לַחְמְךָ יָשִׂימוּ מָזוֹר תַּחְתֶּיךָ אֵין תְּבוּנָה בּוֹ

7[13] *All the men of your confederacy have conducted you to the border; the men who were at peace with you have fooled you, and prevailed against you*[14]; they who eat your

---

[1] Amos 9:15 - Deuteronomy.R 3:11, Ecclesiastes.R 3:10, Ezekiel 10:28 13:25, Isaiah 12:21, Jeremiah 24:6 8:41, Joel 4:20, Jubilees 7:34, Mekhilta de R'Shimon bar Yochai Shirata 36:1, Mekilta de R'Ishmael Shirata 10:11, Micah 4:4, Midrash Tanchuma Bechukkotai 2, Midrash Tanchuma Kedoshim 11, Pirkei de R'Eliezer 42

[2] Obadiah - Haftarah Vayishlach [Obadiah 1:1-1:21], MurXII, Siman 79:6

[3] Obadiah 1:1 - Amos 1:11-12, Avot de R'Natan 34, b.Sanhedrin 39b, Ein Yaakov Sanhedrin:39b, Ezekiel 25:12-14 35:3-15, Genesis.R 65:11, Isaiah 18:2-3 21:11 6:4 34:1-17 63:1-6, Jeremiah 6:4-5 9:26-27 1:17 1:21 49:7-22 50:9-15 51:27-28 3:46, Joel 4:19, Lamentations 4:21-22, Lamentations.R 4:25, Malachi 1:3-4, Mark 13:7, Matthew 24:6, Micah 2:13, Midrash Tanchuma Ki Tetze 4, Midrash Tanchuma Tazria 8, Midrash Tanchuma Vayetze 2, Psalms 17:7, Saadia Opinions 3:8, Seder Olam 20:Obadiah, z.Vaetchanan 269b, z.Vayishlach 171a
Obadiah 1:1-5 - 4QXIIg

[4] 4QXIIg adds *In*

[5] Obadiah 1:2 - 1 Samuel 2:7-2:8, b.Avodah Zara 10a, b.Yevamot [Rashi] 91b, Ezekiel 5:15, Genesis.R 65:11, Isaiah 23:9, Job 34:25-34:29, Luke 1:51-1:52, Micah 7:10, Midrash Tanchuma Ki Tetze 10, Numbers 24:18, Pesikta de R'Kahana 3.13 5.18, Pesikta Rabbati 12:5 12:13 15:25, Psalms 107:39-140, Song of Songs.R 2:44, z.Shemot 6a, z.Vayishlach 177a

[6] LXX *dishonored*

[7] Obadiah 1:3 - 2 Chronicles 1:12, 2 Kings 14:7, b.Sanhedrin 89a, Ecclesiastes.R 1:36, Ein Yaakov Sanhedrin:89a, Isaiah 10:14-16 14:13-15 16:6 47:7-8, Jeremiah 48:29-30 1:4 1:16, Malachi 1:4, Mesillat Yesharim Afterword, Proverbs 16:18 18:12 5:23, Revelation 18:7-8

[8] Obadiah 1:4 - Amos 9:2, Habakkuk 2:9, Isaiah 14:12-15, Jeremiah 1:16 3:53, Job 20:6-7 39:27-28, Leviticus.R 29:2, Life of Adam and Eve [Vita] 15:3, Midrash Tanchuma Beha'alotcha 11, Midrash Tanchuma Tzav 2, Midrash Tanchuma Vayetze 2, Numbers.R 15:17, Perek Shirah [the Cat], Pesikta de R'Kahana 23.2, Tanya Igeret Hateshuvah §7, Tanya Likutei Aramim §27 §29, y.Nedarim 3:8

[9] 4QXIIg *Though you mount on high as the eagle, and though you set your nest*

[10] LXX *should make your nest*

[11] Obadiah 1:5 - 2 Samuel 1:19, Deuteronomy 24:21, Genesis.R 63:12, Isaiah 14:12 17:6 24:13, Jeremiah 1:9 2:23, Lamentations 1:1, Micah 7:1, Midrash Psalms 121:3, Midrash Tanchuma Ki Tetze 4, Pesikta de R'Kahana 3 1, Revelation 18:10, Zephaniah 2:15

[12] Obadiah 1:6 - b.Bava Kamma 3b, Daniel 2:22, Isaiah 10:13-10:14 21:3, Jastrow 181a 184b, Jeremiah 1:10 2:37, Matthew 6:19-6:20, Midrash Psalms 14:2 121:3, Psalms 19:1, y.Peah 4:3

[13] Obadiah 1:7 - b.Sanhedrin 92a, Ein Yaakov Sanhedrin:92a, Ezekiel 23:22-25, Hosea 13:13, Isaiah 19:11-14 3:11, Jeremiah 4:30 20:10 6:14 14:22 1:7, John 13:18, Lamentations 1:19, Psalms 41:10 55:13-14, Revelation 17:12-17, Tanya Igeret Hakodesh §1

[14] LXX *They sent you to your coasts: all the men of your covenant have withstood you; your allies have prevailed against you*

bread lay a snare under you and you have no discernment.

8¹ הֲלוֹא בַּיּוֹם הַהוּא נְאֻם יְהוָה וְהַאֲבַדְתִּי חֲכָמִים מֵאֱדוֹם וּתְבוּנָה מֵהַר עֵשָׂו

8¹ Shall I not in that day, says the LORD, destroy the wise men from Edom, and discernment from the mount of Esau?

9² וְחַתּוּ גִבּוֹרֶיךָ תֵּימָן לְמַעַן יִכָּרֶת־אִישׁ מֵהַר עֵשָׂו מִקָּטֶל

9² And your mighty men, O Teman, shall be dismayed, to the end so everyone may be cut off from the mount of Esau by slaughter.

10³ מֵחֲמַס אָחִיךָ יַעֲקֹב תְּכַסְּךָ בוּשָׁה וְנִכְרַתָּ לְעוֹלָם

10³ For the violence done to your brother Jacob, shame shall cover you, And you shall be cut off forever.

11⁴ בְּיוֹם עֲמָדְךָ מִנֶּגֶד בְּיוֹם שְׁבוֹת זָרִים חֵילוֹ וְנָכְרִים בָּאוּ "שְׁעָרָיו" "שְׁעָרוֹ" וְעַל־יְרוּשָׁלִַם יַדּוּ גוֹרָל גַּם־אַתָּה כְּאַחַד מֵהֶם

11⁴ In the day you stood aloof, in the day strangers carried away his substance, and foreigners entered into his gates, and cast lots upon Jerusalem, you were as one of them.

12⁵ וְאַל־תֵּרֶא בְיוֹם־אָחִיךָ בְּיוֹם נָכְרוֹ וְאַל־תִּשְׂמַח לִבְנֵי־יְהוּדָה בְּיוֹם אָבְדָם וְאַל־תַּגְדֵּל פִּיךָ בְּיוֹם צָרָה

12⁵ But you should not have gazed on the day of your brother in the day of his disaster, nor should you have rejoiced over the children of Judah in the day of their destruction; nor should you have spoken proudly in the day of distress.

13⁶ אַל־תָּבוֹא בְשַׁעַר־עַמִּי בְּיוֹם אֵידָם אַל־תֵּרֶא גַם־אַתָּה בְּרָעָתוֹ בְּיוֹם אֵידוֹ וְאַל־תִּשְׁלַחְנָה בְחֵילוֹ בְּיוֹם אֵידוֹ

13⁶ You should not have entered into the gate of My people in the day of their calamity; yes, you should not have gazed on their affliction in the day of their calamity, nor laid hands on their property in the day of their calamity.

14⁷ וְאַל־תַּעֲמֹד עַל־הַפֶּרֶק לְהַכְרִית אֶת־פְּלִיטָיו וְאַל־תַּסְגֵּר שְׂרִידָיו בְּיוֹם צָרָה

14⁷ Nor should you have stood in the crossway, to cut off those of His who escape; nor should you have delivered those of His who remained in the day of distress.

15⁸ כִּי־קָרוֹב יוֹם־יְהוָה עַל־כָּל־הַגּוֹיִם כַּאֲשֶׁר עָשִׂיתָ יֵעָשֶׂה לָּךְ גְּמֻלְךָ יָשׁוּב בְּרֹאשֶׁךָ

15⁸ For the day of the LORD is near upon all the nations; as you have done, it shall be done to you; your deeds shall return upon your head.

16⁹ כִּי כַּאֲשֶׁר שְׁתִיתֶם עַל־הַר קָדְשִׁי יִשְׁתּוּ כָל־הַגּוֹיִם תָּמִיד וְשָׁתוּ וְלָעוּ וְהָיוּ כְּלוֹא הָיוּ

16⁹ For as you have drunk on My holy mountain, so shall all the nations drink continually; yes, they shall drink, and swallow down, and shall be as though they had not been.

---

¹ Obadiah 1:8 - 1 Corinthians 3:19-20, Genesis.R 75:13 89:6, Isaiah 19:3 19:13-14 5:14, Job 5:12-14, Lamentations.R 2:13, Leviticus.R 5:7, Midrash Psalms 9:16, Numbers.R 11:1, Psalms 33:10
Obadiah 1:8-9 - Testament of Job 29:3
Obadiah 1:8-12 - 4QXIIg
² Obadiah 1:9 - 1 Chronicles 1:45, Amos 1:12 2:16, b.Avodah Zara [Tosefot] 2b, Deuteronomy 2:5, Ezekiel 1:13, Genesis 12:11, Isaiah 19:16-19:17 34:5-34:8 63:1-63:3, Jeremiah 1:7 1:20 1:22 50:36-50:37, Job 2:11, Midrash Psalms 9:7, Nahum 3:13, Numbers.R 14:10, Obadiah 1:21, Psalms 76:6-76:7, y.Peah 1:1
³ Obadiah 1:10 - Amos 1:11, Ezekiel 7:18 25:12-14 35:5-7 11:9 35:12-15, Genesis 3:11 3:41, Genesis.R 99 [Excl]:7, Jeremiah 1:13 49:17-20 3:51, Joel 4:19, Lamentations 4:21, Leviticus.R 5:3, Malachi 1:3-4, Micah 7:10, Midrash Psalms 140:1, Midrash Tanchuma Vayechi 9, Numbers 20:14-21, Numbers.R 10:3 11:1, Psalms 69:8 83:6-10 89:46 13:29 12:18 17:7, y.Peah 1:1
⁴ Obadiah 1:11 - 2 Kings 24:10-24:16 1:11, Jeremiah 52:28-30, Joel 4:3, Nahum 3:10, Psalms 50:18 17:7, This is the middle verse of the book of Obadiah per the Massorah.
⁵ Obadiah 1:12 - 1 Samuel 2:3, 2 Peter 2:18, Ezekiel 25:6-7 11:15, Isaiah 13:24, James 3:5, Job 7:29, Jude 1:16, Lamentations 4:21, Luke 19:41, Matthew 27:40-43, Micah 4:11 7:8-10, Proverbs 17:5 24:17-18, Psalms 22:18 31:19 37:13 54:8 59:11 92:12, Revelation 13:5
⁶ Obadiah 1:13 - 2 Samuel 16:12, Ezekiel 11:5 11:10, Psalms 22:18, Zechariah 1:15
⁷ Obadiah 1:14 - Amos 1:6 1:9, Genesis 11:3, Isaiah 13:3, Jeremiah 6:7, Midrash Psalms 121:1, Obadiah 1:12, Psalms 31:9
Obadiah 1:14-15 - 4QXIIg
⁸ Obadiah 1:15 - Ezekiel 6:3 11:15, Habakkuk 2:8, James 2:13, Jeremiah 9:26-27 25:15-29 1:12 2:29, Joel 1:15 4:7-8 4:11-14, Judges 1:7, Lamentations 4:21-22, Matthew 7:2, Micah 5:16, Midrash Psalms 135:1, Numbers.R 11:1, Psalms 110:5-6 17:8, Zechariah 14:14-18
⁹ Obadiah 1:16 - 1 Peter 4:17, b.Chullin [Tosefot] 22b, Habakkuk 1:9, Isaiah 8:9-10 29:7-8 18:14 49:25-26 51:22-23, Jeremiah 25:15-16 25:27-29 1:12, Joel 4:17, Psalms 75:9-10

וּבְהַר צִיּוֹן תִּהְיֶה פְלֵיטָה וְהָיָה קֹדֶשׁ וְיָרְשׁוּ בֵּית יַעֲקֹב אֵת מוֹרָשֵׁיהֶם	17[1]	But in mount Zion there shall be those who escape, and it shall be holy; and the house of Jacob shall possess *their possessions*[2].
וְהָיָה בֵית־יַעֲקֹב אֵשׁ וּבֵית יוֹסֵף לֶהָבָה וּבֵית עֵשָׂו לְקַשׁ וְדָלְקוּ בָהֶם וַאֲכָלוּם וְלֹא־יִהְיֶה שָׂרִיד לְבֵית עֵשָׂו כִּי יְהוָה דִּבֵּר	18[3]	And the house of Jacob shall be a fire, and the house of Joseph a flame, and the house of Esau as stubble, and they shall kindle in them, and devour them; and there shall be none who remain of the house of Esau; for the LORD has spoken.
וְיָרְשׁוּ הַנֶּגֶב אֶת־הַר עֵשָׂו וְהַשְּׁפֵלָה אֶת־פְּלִשְׁתִּים וְיָרְשׁוּ אֶת־שְׂדֵה אֶפְרַיִם וְאֵת שְׂדֵה שֹׁמְרוֹן וּבִנְיָמִן אֶת־הַגִּלְעָד:	19[4]	And they of the South shall possess the mount of Esau; and they of the Lowland, the Philistines; and they shall possess the field of Ephraim, and the field of Samaria; and Benjamin shall possess Gilead.
וְגָלֻת הַחֵל־הַזֶּה לִבְנֵי יִשְׂרָאֵל אֲשֶׁר־כְּנַעֲנִים עַד־צָרְפַת וְגָלֻת יְרוּשָׁלַ͏ִם אֲשֶׁר בִּסְפָרַד יִרְשׁוּ אֵת עָרֵי הַנֶּגֶב	20[5]	And the captivity of this host of the children of Israel, who are among the Canaanites, to Zarephath, and the captivity of Jerusalem, who is in Sepharad, shall possess the cities of the South.
וְעָלוּ מוֹשִׁעִים בְּהַר צִיּוֹן לִשְׁפֹּט אֶת־הַר עֵשָׂו וְהָיְתָה לַיהוָה הַמְּלוּכָה	21[6]	And *saviors*[7] who come up on mount Zion to judge the mount of Esau; and the kingdom shall be the LORD's.

[1] Obadiah 1:17 - Amos 9:8 9:11-9:15, Ezekiel 7:16, Isaiah 1:27 4:3-4:4 14:1-14:2 22:13 12:21, Jeremiah 20:14 20:28 22:28, Joel 3:5 4:17 4:19-4:21, Revelation 21:27, Zechariah 8:3 14:20-14:21
[2] MurXII *those who possess them*
[3] Obadiah 1:18 - 12:6, 1 Corinthians 3:12, 2 Samuel 19:20, Amos 5:15 6:6, b.Avodah Zara 10b, b.Bava Batra 123b, Chibbur Yafeh 23 99a, Deuteronomy.R 1:20, Ein Yaakov Avodah Zarah:10b, Ein Yaakov Bava Batra:123b, Exodus.R 15:6, Ezekiel 13:16 13:19, Genesis.R 77:2 84:5, Isaiah 5:24 10:17 7:9 23:14, Joel 2:5, Lamentations.R Petichata D'Chakimei:2, Leviticus.R 18:2, Mekhilta de R'Shimon bar Yochai Shirata 32:2, Mekilta de R'Ishmael Pisha 12:38, Mekilta de R'Ishmael Shirata 6:74, Micah 5:9, Midrash Psalms 121:3 140:2, Midrash Tanchuma Bamidbar 4, Midrash Tanchuma Ki Tetze 10, Midrash Tanchuma Tzav 2, Midrash Tanchuma Vayeshev 1, Midrash Tanchuma Vayishlach 1, Nahum 1:10, Numbers.R 1:4 11:1, Obadiah 1:9-1:10 1:16, Pesikta de R'Kahana 3.b 15.5, Pesikta Rabbati 10:4, Pirkei de R'Eliezer 37, Pirkei de R'Eliezer 40, Psalms 83:7-83:16, Song of Songs.R 3:9, z.Toledot 143b, z.Vayishlach 173a, Zechariah 12:6
[4] Obadiah 1:19 - 1 Chronicles 5:26, 2 Kings 17:24, Amos 1:8 1:13 9:12, Ezekiel 1:16 36:6-36:12 12:28 37:21-37:25 47:13-47:21 48:1-48:9, Ezra 4:2 4:7-4:10 4:17, Isaiah 11:13-11:14, Jeremiah 31:5-31:7 8:44 1:1, Josephus Antiquities 13.9.1, Joshua 13:2-13:3 13:25 13:31 15:21 15:33 15:45-15:46 18:21-18:28, Judges 1:18-1:19, m.Maaser Sheni 5:2, m.Shekalim 1:5, Malachi 1:4-1:5, Micah 7:14, Numbers 24:18-24:19, Psalms 69:36, Zechariah 9:5-9:7, Zephaniah 2:4-2:7
Obadiah 1:19-21 - Midrash Tanchuma Devarim 4
[5] Obadiah 1:20 - 1 Kings 17:9-10, Amos 9:14-15, Ezekiel 34:12-13, Hosea 2:1-2, Jeremiah 3:18 13:19 8:44 9:13 9:26, Luke 4:26, Zechariah 10:6-10
[6] Obadiah 1:21 - 1 Corinthians 6:2-3, 1 Timothy 4:16, 2 Kings 13:5, Daniel 2:35 2:44 7:14 7:27 12:3, Deuteronomy.R 1:20, Esther.R 1:13, Exodus.R 18:5, Genesis.R 78:14 83:1, Isaiah 9:7-8 19:20, James 5:20, Joel 3:5, Judges 2:16 3:9, Leviticus.R 13:5, Luke 1:32-33 22:30, Matthew 6:10 6:13, Mekhilta de R'Shimon bar Yochai Amalek 45:1, Mekhilta de R'Shimon bar Yochai Beshallach 21:3, Micah 5:5-10, Midrash Psalms 47:2 121:3, Midrash Tanchuma Noach 3, Midrash Tanchuma Terumah 9, Midrash Tanchuma Tetzaveh 10, Midrash Tanchuma Toledot 8, Midrash Tanchuma Tzav 2, mt.Hilcnot Melachim u'Michamoteihem 11:1, mt.Hilcnot Shofar Sukkah v'Lulav 3:9, Mussaf Rosh Hashanah, Psalms 2:6-9 22:29 149:5-9, Revelation 11:15 19:6 19:11-13 20:4, Saadia Opinions 8:5, Shiras Hayam Pesukei D'zimrah [Shacharit], Song of Songs.R 2:32, y.Avodah Zarah 2:1, z.Acharei Mot 77b, z.Toledot 143b 146b, z.Vayishlach 172a, Zechariah 9:11-17 10:5-12 14:9
Zechariah 1:1 - Ezra 4:24-5:1 6:14-6:15, Haggai 1:1 1:15-2:1 2:10 2:20, Josephus Wars 4.6.4, Lives of the Prophets 15:6, Luke 11:51, Matthew 23:35, Nehemiah 12:4 12:16, y.Rosh Hashanah 1:1, Zechariah 1:7 7:1
[7] LXX *they who escape*

Yonah b'Amittai – Chapter 1[1]

וַיְהִי דְּבַר־יְהֹוָה אֶל־יוֹנָה בֶן־אֲמִתַּי לֵאמֹר

1[2] Now the word of the LORD came to Jonah the son of Amittai, saying:

קוּם לֵךְ אֶל־נִינְוֵה הָעִיר הַגְּדוֹלָה וּקְרָא עָלֶיהָ כִּי־עָלְתָה רָעָתָם לְפָנָי

2[3] 'Arise, go to Nineveh, that great city, and proclaim against it; for their wickedness has come up before Me.'

וַיָּקָם יוֹנָה לִבְרֹחַ תַּרְשִׁישָׁה מִלִּפְנֵי יְהֹוָה וַיֵּרֶד יָפוֹ וַיִּמְצָא אָנִיָּה ׀ בָּאָה תַרְשִׁישׁ וַיִּתֵּן שְׂכָרָהּ וַיֵּרֶד בָּהּ לָבוֹא עִמָּהֶם תַּרְשִׁישָׁה מִלִּפְנֵי יְהֹוָה

3[4] But Jonah rose up to flee to Tarshish, from the presence of the LORD; and he went down to Joppa, and found a ship going to Tarshish; so, he paid the fare, and went down into it, to go with them to Tarshish, from the presence of the LORD.

וַיהֹוָה הֵטִיל רוּחַ־גְּדוֹלָה אֶל־הַיָּם וַיְהִי סַעַר־גָּדוֹל בַּיָּם וְהָאֳנִיָּה חִשְּׁבָה לְהִשָּׁבֵר

4[5] But the LORD hurled a great wind into the sea, and there was a mighty tempest in the sea, so that the ship was likely to be broken.

וַיִּירְאוּ הַמַּלָּחִים וַיִּזְעֲקוּ אִישׁ אֶל־אֱלֹהָיו וַיָּטִלוּ אֶת־הַכֵּלִים אֲשֶׁר בָּאֳנִיָּה אֶל־הַיָּם לְהָקֵל מֵעֲלֵיהֶם וְיוֹנָה יָרַד אֶל־יַרְכְּתֵי הַסְּפִינָה וַיִּשְׁכַּב וַיֵּרָדַם

5[6] And the mariners were afraid, and every man cried to his god; and they jettisoned the wares from the ship into the sea, to lighten it for them. But Jonah had gone down into the innermost parts of the ship; and he lay, and was fast asleep[7].

וַיִּקְרַב אֵלָיו רַב הַחֹבֵל וַיֹּאמֶר לוֹ מַה־לְּךָ נִרְדָּם קוּם קְרָא אֶל־אֱלֹהֶיךָ אוּלַי יִתְעַשֵּׁת הָאֱלֹהִים לָנוּ וְלֹא נֹאבֵד

6[8] So the shipmaster came to him, and said to him: 'How is it that you *sleep*[9]? Arise, call on your God, perhaps that God will think on us, so we will not perish.'

וַיֹּאמְרוּ אִישׁ אֶל־רֵעֵהוּ לְכוּ וְנַפִּילָה גוֹרָלוֹת וְנֵדְעָה בְּשֶׁלְּמִי הָרָעָה הַזֹּאת לָנוּ וַיַּפִּלוּ גּוֹרָלוֹת וַיִּפֹּל הַגּוֹרָל עַל־יוֹנָה

7[10] And everyone said to his fellow: 'Come, and let us cast lots, so we may know for whose cause this evil is on us.' So they cast lots, and the lot fell on Jonah.

---

[1] Jonah - Haftarah Minchah Yom Kippur [continues at Micah 7:18-20], Yom Kippur Afternoon Haftarah, Josephus Antiquities 9.10.2
Jonah 1 - mt.Hilchot Sanhedrin v'Hainshin Hameurim Lahem 19:3
[2] Jonah 1:1 - 2 Kings 14:25, Luke 11:29-30 11:32, Matthew 12:39-41 16:4
Jonah 1:1-5 - 4QXIIa
Jonah 1:1-9 - 4QXIIg
Jonah 1:1-16 - MurXII
[3] Jonah 1:2 - 2 Kings 19:36, Exodus.R 45:1, Ezekiel 2:7 3:5-9, Ezra 9:6, Genesis 10:11 18:20-21, Isaiah 10:1, James 5:4, Jeremiah 1:7-10, Jonah 3:2 4:11, Matthew 10:18, Micah 3:8, Midrash Tanchuma Toledot 12, Nahum 1:1 2:2-4, Revelation 18:5, Sifre Devarim Shoftim 177, y.Sanhedrin 11:5, Zephaniah 2:13-15
[4] Jonah 1:3 - 1 Corinthians 9:16, 1 Kings 19:3 19:9, 2 Chronicles 2:15, 2 Thessalonians 1:9, Acts 9:36 9:43 15:38 2:19, b.Chullin [Rashi] 91b, b.Nedarim 38a, Ein Yaakov Nedarim 38a, Exodus 4:13-14, Exodus.R 4:3, Ezekiel 3:14 3:12, Genesis 3:8 4:16, Genesis.R 21:5 98 [Excl]:12, Isaiah 2:16 23:1 23:6 23:10 12:9, Jastrow 1272a, Jeremiah 20:7-9, Job 1:12 2:7, Jonah 4:2, Joshua 19:46, Kuzari 2.14, Lives of the Prophets 10:6, Luke 9:62, m.Sanhedrin 11:5, Mekilta de R'Ishmael Pisha 1:101 1:73, Midrash Tanchuma Shemot 18, Midrash Tanchuma Vayikra 8, Pirkei de R'Eliezer 10, Psalms 139:7-12, y.Sanhedrin 11:5, y.Sukkah 5:1, z.Lech Lecha 84b
[5] Jonah 1:4 - Acts 27:13-20, Amos 4:13, b.Nazir [Tosefot] 12a, Ecclesiastes.R 1:12, Exodus 10:13 10:19 14:21 15:10, Genesis.R 24:4, Matthew 8:24-27, Mekilta de R'Ishmael Pisha 1:88, Midrash Psalms 87:1, Midrash Tanchuma Vayikra 8, Numbers 11:31, Pirkei de R'Eliezer 10, Psalms 107:23-107:31 15:7, y.Berachot 9:2, z.Vayakhel 199a
Jonah 1:4-15 - Midrash Tanchuma Toledot 12
[6] Jonah 1:5 - 1 Kings 18:26, 1 Samuel 24:3, Acts 27:18-19 3:38, b.Bava Kamma [Rashi] 114b, b.Ketubot [Rashi] 85a, Hosea 7:14, Isaiah 44:17-20 21:20, Jeremiah 2:28, Job 2:4, Jonah 1:6 1:14 1:16, Judges 16:19, Luke 22:45-46, Matthew 1:5 26:40-41 2:43 2:45, Philippians 3:7-8, t.Niddah 5:17
[7] LXX adds *and snored*
[8] Jonah 1:6 - 2 Samuel 12:22, Acts 21:13, Amos 5:15, Ephesians 5:14, Esther 4:16, Ezekiel 18:2, Isaiah 3:15, Jastrow 1313b 1660a, Jeremiah 2:27-28, Joel 2:11, Jonah 3:9, Mark 4:37-41, Mas.Kallah Rabbati 6:1, Midrash Tanchuma Vayikra 8, Pesikta Rabbati 47:4, Psalms 78:34 11:6 107:12-13 107:18-20 107:28-29, Romans 13:11
Jonah 1:6-8 - 4QXIIf
[9] LXX *snore*
[10] Jonah 1:7 - 1 Corinthians 4:5, 1 Samuel 10:20-21 14:38-39 14:41-42, Acts 1:23-26 13:19, Esther 3:7, Gates of Repentance 3.72, Isaiah 41:6-7, Job 10:2, Joshua 7:10 7:13-18 22:16-20, Judges 7:13-14 20:9-10, Matthew 3:35, Midrash Tanchuma Vayikra 8, Numbers 8:23, Proverbs 16:33, Psalms 22:19
Jonah 1:7-10 - 4QXIIa

וַיֹּאמְרוּ אֵלָיו הַגִּידָה־נָּא לָנוּ בַּאֲשֶׁר לְמִי־הָרָעָה הַזֹּאת לָנוּ מַה־מְּלַאכְתְּךָ וּמֵאַיִן תָּבוֹא מָה אַרְצֶךָ וְאֵי־מִזֶּה עַם אָתָּה	8[1] Then said they to him: 'Tell us, please, for whose cause this evil is on us? What is your occupation? From where do you come? What is your country? And of what people are you?'
וַיֹּאמֶר אֲלֵיהֶם עִבְרִי אָנֹכִי וְאֶת־יְהוָה אֱלֹהֵי הַשָּׁמַיִם אֲנִי יָרֵא אֲשֶׁר־עָשָׂה אֶת־הַיָּם וְאֶת־הַיַּבָּשָׁה	9[2] And he said to them: 'I am a Hebrew; *and I fear the LORD, the God of heaven*[3], who made the sea and the dry land.[4]'
וַיִּירְאוּ הָאֲנָשִׁים יִרְאָה גְדוֹלָה וַיֹּאמְרוּ אֵלָיו מַה־זֹּאת עָשִׂיתָ כִּי־יָדְעוּ הָאֲנָשִׁים כִּי־מִלִּפְנֵי יְהוָה הוּא בֹרֵחַ כִּי הִגִּיד לָהֶם	10[5] Then the men were exceedingly afraid, and said to him: 'What is this you have done?' For the men knew he fled from the presence of the LORD, because he had told them.
וַיֹּאמְרוּ אֵלָיו מַה־נַּעֲשֶׂה לָּךְ וְיִשְׁתֹּק הַיָּם מֵעָלֵינוּ כִּי הַיָּם הוֹלֵךְ וְסֹעֵר	11[6] Then said they to him: 'What shall we do to you, so the sea may be calm for us?' for the sea grew more and more tempestuous.
וַיֹּאמֶר אֲלֵיהֶם שָׂאוּנִי וַהֲטִילֻנִי אֶל־הַיָּם וְיִשְׁתֹּק הַיָּם מֵעֲלֵיכֶם כִּי יוֹדֵעַ אָנִי כִּי בְשֶׁלִּי הַסַּעַר הַגָּדוֹל הַזֶּה עֲלֵיכֶם	12[7] And he said to them: 'Pick me up, and hurl me forth to the sea; so the sea shall be calm for you; for I know that for my sake this great tempest is on you.'
וַיַּחְתְּרוּ הָאֲנָשִׁים לְהָשִׁיב אֶל־הַיַּבָּשָׁה וְלֹא יָכֹלוּ כִּי הַיָּם הוֹלֵךְ וְסֹעֵר עֲלֵיהֶם	13[8] Nevertheless, the men rowed hard to bring it to the land; but they could not; for the sea grew more and more tempestuous against them.
וַיִּקְרְאוּ אֶל־יְהוָה וַיֹּאמְרוּ אָנָּה יְהוָה אַל־נָא נֹאבְדָה בְּנֶפֶשׁ הָאִישׁ הַזֶּה וְאַל־תִּתֵּן עָלֵינוּ דָּם נָקִיא כִּי־אַתָּה יְהוָה כַּאֲשֶׁר חָפַצְתָּ עָשִׂיתָ	14[9] Therefore, they cried unto the LORD, and said: 'We beg You, O LORD, we bewg You, let us not perish for this man's life, and do not lay on us innocent blood; for You, O LORD, have done as it pleased You.'
וַיִּשְׂאוּ אֶת־יוֹנָה וַיְטִלֻהוּ אֶל־הַיָּם וַיַּעֲמֹד הַיָּם מִזַּעְפּוֹ	15[10] So they took up Jonah, and hurled him into the sea; and the sea ceased its raging.
וַיִּירְאוּ הָאֲנָשִׁים יִרְאָה גְדוֹלָה אֶת־יְהוָה וַיִּזְבְּחוּ־זֶבַח לַיהוָה וַיִּדְּרוּ נְדָרִים	16[11] Then the men feared the LORD exceedingly; and they offered a sacrifice to the LORD, and made vows.

---

[1] Jonah 1:8 - 1 Samuel 14:43 6:13, Genesis 23:3, James 5:16, Joshua 7:19
Jonah 1:8-16 - z.Pekudei 230b

[2] Jonah 1:9 - 2 Kings 17:25 17:28 17:32-35, Acts 14:15 17:23-25 3:23, Daniel 2:18-19 2:44, Ezra 1:2 5:11 7:12-13, Genesis 14:13 15:14, Hosea 3:5, Job 1:9, Midrash Tanchuma Vayikra 8, Nehemiah 1:4 2:4 9:6, Philippians 3:5, Pirkei de R'Eliezer 10, Psalms 95:5-6 16:26 146:5-6, Revelation 11:13 15:4 16:11

[3] 4QXIIa *The LORD, the God of Heaven, and I fear He who*

[4] LXX *And he said to them, I am a servant of the LORD; and I worship the LORD God of Heaven, who made the sea, and the dry land*

[5] Jonah 1:10 - 2 Samuel 24:3, Daniel 5:6-9, Job 3:22, John 19:8, Jonah 1:3, Joshua 7:25, z.Lech Lecha 85a
Jonah 1:10-16 - 4QXIIf

[6] Jonah 1:11 - 1 Samuel 6:2-6:3, 2 Samuel 21:1-6 24:11-13, Micah 6:6-7

[7] Jonah 1:12 - 1 Chronicles 21:17, 2 Samuel 24:17, Acts 3:24, Ecclesiastes 9:18, John 11:50, Joshua 7:12 7:20-21, Mekilta de R'Ishmael Pisha I:105, Midrash Tanchuma Vayikra 8, Pirkei de R'Eliezer 10

[8] Jonah 1:13 - Jastrow 749a, Job 10:29, Midrash Tanchuma Vayikra 8, Pirkei de R'Eliezer 10, Proverbs 21:30

[9] Jonah 1:14 - Acts 4:4, Daniel 4:31-4:32, Deuteronomy 21:8, Ephesians 1:9 1:11, Genesis 9:6, Isaiah 2:16, Jonah 1:5 1:16, Matthew 11:26, Midrash Tanchuma Vayikra 8, Psalms 11:28 19:3 15:6
Jonah 1:14-16 - 8HevXIIgr [Interestingly, this DSS, while in Greek, is written with *Hashem* in Paleohebrew letters]

[10] Jonah 1:15 - 2 Samuel 21:8-21:9, 3 Enoch 14:3, 4QXIIa, Joshua 7:24-7:26, Luke 8:24, Matthew 8:26, Midrash Tanchuma Vayeshev 3, Midrash Tanchuma Vayikra 8, Pirkei de R'Eliezer 10, Psalms 65:8 89:10 93:3-93:4 11:29, z.Chayyei Sarah 121a

[11] Jonah 1:16 - 2 Kings 5:17, 4QXIIa, Acts 5:11, Daniel 4:31-34 6:27, Ecclesiastes 5:5, Genesis 8:20 4:20, Isaiah 2:9 60:5-7, Jonah 1:10, Judges 13:16, Mark 4:31, Midrash Tanchuma Tzav 14, Midrash Tanchuma Vayikra 8, Pirkei de R'Eliezer 10, Psalms 50:14 66:13-16 11:22 20:14
Jonah 1:16 [LXX] - Testament of Zebulun 4:4
Jonah 1:16-2:9 - 3 Maccabees 6:8

Jonah – Chapter 2[1]

וַיְמַן יְהוָה דָּג גָּדוֹל לִבְלֹעַ אֶת־יוֹנָה וַיְהִי יוֹנָה בִּמְעֵי הַדָּג שְׁלֹשָׁה יָמִים וּשְׁלֹשָׁה לֵילוֹת	1[2]	And the LORD prepared a great *fish*[3] to swallow up Jonah; and Jonah was in the belly of the fish three days and three nights.
וַיִּתְפַּלֵּל יוֹנָה אֶל־יְהוָה אֱלֹהָיו מִמְּעֵי הַדָּגָה	2[4]	Then Jonah prayed to the LORD his God out of the fish's belly.
וַיֹּאמֶר קָרָאתִי מִצָּרָה לִי אֶל־יְהוָה וַיַּעֲנֵנִי מִבֶּטֶן שְׁאוֹל שִׁוַּעְתִּי שָׁמַעְתָּ קוֹלִי	3[5]	And he said: I called out *of*[6] my affliction to the LORD, and He answered me; Out of the belly of the netherworld I cried, and you heard my voice.
וַתַּשְׁלִיכֵנִי מְצוּלָה בִּלְבַב יַמִּים וְנָהָר יְסֹבְבֵנִי כָּל־מִשְׁבָּרֶיךָ וְגַלֶּיךָ עָלַי עָבָרוּ	4[7]	For you cast me into the depth, in the heart of the seas, and the flood was around me; all Your waves and Your swells passed over me.
וַאֲנִי אָמַרְתִּי נִגְרַשְׁתִּי מִנֶּגֶד עֵינֶיךָ אַךְ אוֹסִיף לְהַבִּיט אֶל־הֵיכַל קָדְשֶׁךָ	5[8]	And I said: 'I am cast out from before your eyes;' *yet I will*[9] look again toward Your holy temple.
אֲפָפוּנִי מַיִם עַד־נֶפֶשׁ תְּהוֹם יְסֹבְבֵנִי סוּף חָבוּשׁ לְרֹאשִׁי	6[10]	The waters encompassed me, to the soul; the deep was around me; the weeds were wrapped about my head.
לְקִצְבֵי הָרִים יָרַדְתִּי הָאָרֶץ בְּרִחֶיהָ בַעֲדִי לְעוֹלָם וַתַּעַל מִשַּׁחַת חַיַּי יְהוָה אֱלֹהָי	7[11]	I went down to the bottoms of the mountains; the earth with her bars closed upon me forever; yet have you brought up *my life*[12] from the pit, O LORD my God.
בְּהִתְעַטֵּף עָלַי נַפְשִׁי אֶת־יְהוָה זָכָרְתִּי וַתָּבוֹא אֵלֶיךָ תְּפִלָּתִי אֶל־הֵיכַל קָדְשֶׁךָ	8[13]	When my soul fainted within me, I remembered the LORD; and my prayer came to You, into Your holy temple.
מְשַׁמְּרִים הַבְלֵי־שָׁוְא חַסְדָּם יַעֲזֹבוּ	9[14]	Those who listen to lying vanities forsake their own mercy.
וַאֲנִי בְּקוֹל תּוֹדָה אֶזְבְּחָה־לָּךְ אֲשֶׁר נָדַרְתִּי אֲשַׁלֵּמָה יְשׁוּעָתָה לַיהוָה	10[15]	But I will sacrifice to You with the voice of thanksgiving; what I have vowed I will pay. Salvation is of the LORD.

---

[1] Jonah 2 - mt.Hilchot Taaniot 4:12

[2] Jonah 2:1 - 4QXIIa, b.Nedarim 51b, Deuteronomy.R 2:17, Esther.R 9:2, Genesis 1:21, Genesis.R 56:1, Habakkuk 3:2, HellenisticSynagoguePrayers 4:24 6:11, Jonah 4:6, Luke 11:30, Matthew 12:40 16:4, Midrash Psalms 8:7, Midrash Tanchuma Vayikra 8, Psalms 104:25-26, Song of Songs.R 5:20
Jonah 2:1-7 - 8HevXIIgr
Jonah 2:1-11 - MurXII

[3] LXX *whale*, et al

[4] Jonah 2:2 - 2 Chronicles 33:11-13, Acts 16:24-25, b.Nedarim 51b, Deuteronomy.R 2:17, Hosea 5:15-6:3, Isaiah 2:16, James 5:13, Job 13:15, Lamentations 3:53-56, Leviticus.R 15:1, Midrash Psalms 22:5, Pirkei de R'Eliezer 10, Psalms 50:15 91:15 130:1-2, z.Beshallach 48a

[5] Jonah 2:3 - 1 Samuel 1:16 6:6, Acts 2:27, b.Eruvin 19a, b.Taanit [Rashi] 15a, Ein Yaakov Eruvin, Genesis 32:8-12 32:25-28, Hebrews 5:7, Isaiah 14:9, Luke 22:44, Matthew 12:40, Midrash Tanchuma Vayikra 8, Pirkei de R'Eliezer 10, Psalms 4:2 16:10 18:5-7 22:25 34:7 61:3 65:3 86:13 88:2-8 20:3 24:1 142:2-4, Saadia Opinions 2:10, y.Taanit 2:9, z.Naso 122b
Jonah 2:3-11 - 4QXIIg

[6] 8HevXII *in*

[7] Jonah 2:4 - Jastrow 824a, Jonah 1:12-16, Lamentations 3:54, Mekhilta de R'Shimon bar Yochai Shirata 31:1, Mekilta de R'Ishmael Shirata 5:17, Midrash Tanchuma Bereshit 7, Midrash Tanchuma Vayikra 8, Psalms 42:8 69:2-3 69:15-16 88:6-9, Sibylline Oracles 2.240

[8] Jonah 2:5 - 1 Kings 8:38-39 8:42 8:48 9:7, 2 Chronicles 6:38, Daniel 6:11, Ezekiel 13:11, Isaiah 38:10-14 14:17 1:14, Jeremiah 7:15 15:1, Pirkei de R'Eliezer 10, Psalms 5:8 31:23 77:2-8

[9] LXX *shall I indeed*

[10] Jonah 2:6 - Lamentations 3:54, Mekhilta de R'Shimon bar Yochai Shirata 31:1, Mekilta de R'Ishmael Shirata 5:15, Midrash Tanchuma Vayikra 8, Pirkei de R'Eliezer 10, Psalms 40:3 69:2-3

[11] Jonah 2:7 - 4QXIIa, Acts 13:33-13:37, Deuteronomy 8:22, Habakkuk 3:6 3:10, Isaiah 14:17 16:12, Job 9:24 9:28 38:4-38:11, Midrash Psalms 77:1, Midrash Tanchuma Vayikra 8, Proverbs 8:25-8:29, Psalms 16:10 30:4 30:10 55:24 65:7 8:6 8:8 23:7

[12] 4QXIIg *the life of my soul*

[13] Jonah 2:8 - 1 Samuel 6:6, 2 Chronicles 6:27, 2 Corinthians 1:9-10, Ecclesiastes.R 1:12, Genesis.R 24:4, Habakkuk 2:20, Hebrews 12:3, Isaiah 2:10, Jonah 2:4, Lamentations 3:21-26, Micah 1:2, Pirkei de R'Eliezer 10, Psalms 11:5 18:7 20:8 22:15 27:13 42:6 42:12 43:5 65:5 77:11-12 119:81-83 23:5, Selichot, This is the middle verse of the book of Jonah per the Massorah

[14] Jonah 2:9 - 1 Samuel 12:21, 2 Kings 17:15, Habakkuk 2:18-20, Jeremiah 2:13 10:8 10:14-15 16:19, Midrash Tanchuma Vayikra 8, Pirkei de R'Eliezer 10, Psalms 31:7, z.Pekudei 231a

[15] Jonah 2:10 - 2 Samuel 15:7, Acts 4:12, b.Chullin [Tosefot] 2b, Deuteronomy 23:20, Ecclesiastes 5:5-5:6, Genesis 11:3, Hebrews

וַיֹּ֥אמֶר יְהוָ֖ה לַדָּ֑ג וַיָּקֵ֥א אֶת־יוֹנָ֖ה אֶל־הַיַּבָּשָֽׁה	11[1]	*And the LORD spoke to the fish, and it vomited out[2] Jonah upon the dry land.*

Jonah – Chapter 3[3]

וַיְהִ֧י דְבַר־יְהוָ֛ה אֶל־יוֹנָ֖ה שֵׁנִ֥ית לֵאמֹֽר	1[4]	And the word of the LORD came to Jonah the second time, saying:
ק֛וּם לֵ֥ךְ אֶל־נִֽינְוֵ֖ה הָעִ֣יר הַגְּדוֹלָ֑ה וּקְרָ֤א אֵלֶ֨יהָ֙ אֶת־הַקְּרִיאָ֔ה אֲשֶׁ֥ר אָנֹכִ֖י דֹּבֵ֥ר אֵלֶֽיךָ	2[5]	Arise, go to Nineveh, that great city, and make to it the proclamation that I instruct you.'
וַיָּ֣קָם יוֹנָ֗ה וַיֵּ֛לֶךְ אֶל־נִֽינְוֵ֖ה כִּדְבַ֣ר יְהוָ֑ה וְנִֽינְוֵ֗ה הָיְתָ֤ה עִיר־גְּדוֹלָה֙ לֵֽאלֹהִ֔ים מַהֲלַ֖ךְ שְׁלֹ֥שֶׁת יָמִֽים	3[6]	So Jonah arose, and went to Nineveh, according to the word of the LORD. Now Nineveh was an exceeding great city, of three days' journey.
וַיָּ֤חֶל יוֹנָה֙ לָב֣וֹא בָעִ֔יר מַהֲלַ֖ךְ י֣וֹם אֶחָ֑ד וַיִּקְרָא֙ וַיֹּאמַ֔ר ע֚וֹד אַרְבָּעִ֣ים י֔וֹם וְנִֽינְוֵ֖ה נֶהְפָּֽכֶת	4[7]	And Jonah began to enter into the city a day's journey, and he proclaimed, and said: 'Forty days remain, and Nineveh shall be overthrown.'
וַֽיַּאֲמִ֛ינוּ אַנְשֵׁ֥י נִֽינְוֵ֖ה בֵּֽאלֹהִ֑ים וַיִּקְרְאוּ־צוֹם֙ וַיִּלְבְּשׁ֣וּ שַׂקִּ֔ים מִגְּדוֹלָ֖ם וְעַד־קְטַנָּֽם	5[8]	And the people of Nineveh believed God; and proclaimed a fast, and put on sackcloth, from the greatest of them, to the least of them.
וַיִּגַּ֤ע הַדָּבָר֙ אֶל־מֶ֣לֶךְ נִֽינְוֵ֔ה וַיָּ֨קָם֙ מִכִּסְא֔וֹ וַיַּעֲבֵ֥ר אַדַּרְתּ֖וֹ מֵעָלָ֑יו וַיְכַ֣ס שַׂ֔ק וַיֵּ֖שֶׁב עַל־הָאֵֽפֶר	6[9]	And the tidings reached the king of Nineveh, and he arose from his throne, and laid his robe from him, and covered him with sackcloth, and sat in ashes.
וַיַּזְעֵ֗ק וַיֹּ֨אמֶר֙ בְּנִֽינְוֵ֔ה מִטַּ֧עַם הַמֶּ֛לֶךְ וּגְדֹלָ֖יו לֵאמֹ֑ר הָאָדָ֨ם וְהַבְּהֵמָ֜ה הַבָּקָ֣ר וְהַצֹּ֗אן אַֽל־יִטְעֲמוּ֙ מְא֔וּמָה אַ֨ל־יִרְע֔וּ וּמַ֖יִם אַל־יִשְׁתּֽוּ	7[10]	And he caused it to be proclaimed and published through Nineveh by the decree of the king and his nobles, saying: 'Let neither man nor beast, herd nor flock, taste anything; let them not feed, nor drink water;

13:15, Hosea 14:4, Isaiah 21:17, Jeremiah 9:11, Job 22:27, John 4:22, Midrash Psalms 95:1, Midrash Tanchuma Vayikra 8, Pirkei de R'Eliezer 10, Psalms 3:9 37:39-40 50:14 50:23 66:13-15 68:21 11:22 116:17-18, Revelation 7:10, Romans 12:1

[1] Jonah 2:11 - b.Bechorot [Rashi] 8a, Deuteronomy.R 2:29, Ecclesiastes.R 7:1, Genesis 1:3 1:7 1:9 1:11 1:14, Genesis.R 20:3, Guide for the Perplexed 2:47, Isaiah 2:2, Jonah 1:17, Matthew 8:8-9 8:26-27, Midrash Psalms 4:3 22:5 26:7, Midrash Tanchuma Vayakhel 1, Midrash Tanchuma Vayeshev 3, Midrash Tanchuma Vayikra 8, Psalms 33:9 9:31 9:34, y.Berachot 9:1, z.Vayakhel 198b
Jonah 2:11 [10] - Lives of the Prophets 10:2

[2] LXX *And the whale was commanded by the LORD, and it cast up*

[3] Jonah 3 - mt.Hilchot Yesodei haTorah 10:4

[4] Jonah 3:1 - b.Yevamot 98a, Ein Yaakov Yevamot:98a, Hellenistic Synagogal Prayers 11:7, John 21:15-21:17, Jonah 1:1, Mekilta de R'Ishmael Pisha 1:102, z.Beshallach 47b
Jonah 3:1-3 - 4QXIIg
Jonah 3:1-5 - Lives of the Prophets 10:2
Jonah 3:1-10 - MurXII

[5] Jonah 3:2 - 4QXIP, b.Taanit 7b 16a, Ezekiel 2:7 3:17, Genesis.R 51:8, Jeremiah 1:17 15:19-15:21, John 5:14, Jonah 1:2 3:3, Matthew 3:8, Midrash Psalms 111:1, Zephaniah 2:13-2:15
Jonah 3:2-5 - HevXIIgr

[6] Jonah 3:3 - 2 Timothy 4:11, b.Yoma 10a, Exodus.R 4:3, Genesis 22:3 6:8, Genesis.R 37:4 39:9, Matthew 21:28-21:29, Midrash Tanchuma Shemot 18, mt.Hilchot Chametz u'Matzah 27:2, Psalms 36:7 80:11

[7] Jonah 3:4 - 2 Kings 20:1 20:6, Derech Hashem Part III 4§07, Deuteronomy 18:22, Jeremiah 18:7-18:10, Jonah 3:10, Lives of the Prophets 10:3, Pesikta de R'Kahana 24.11, Saadia Opinions 5:6
Jonah 3:4-7 - Exodus.R 45:1

[8] Jonah 3:5 - 2 Chronicles 20:3, Acts 8:10 3:25, Daniel 9:3, Exodus 9:18-9:21, Ezra 8:21, Hebrews 11:1 11:7, Jeremiah 7:35 12:9 18:1 18:8, Joel 1:14 2:12-17, Luke 11:32, Matthew 12:41, Siman 121:1

[9] Jonah 3:6 - Daniel 9:3, Esther 4:1-4:4, Ezekiel 27:30-27:31, James 1:9-1:10 4:6-4:10, Jeremiah 6:26 13:18, Job 2:8 18:6, Lamentations 3:29, Luke 10:13, Matthew 11:21, Micah 1:10, Pesikta Rabbati 33:11, Psalms 2:10-2:12

[10] Jonah 3:7 - 2 Chronicles 20:3, Ezra 8:21, Joel 1:18 2:15-2:16, Jonah 3:5, Midrash Tanchuma Shemini 9, Pesikta Rabbati 33:11, Romans 8:20-22, z.Vayechi 234b
Jonah 3:7-8 - Pesikta de R'Kahana 24.11
Jonah 3:7-10 - HevXIIgr

וְיִתְכַּסּ֣וּ שַׂקִּ֗ים הָֽאָדָם֙ וְהַבְּהֵמָ֔ה וְיִקְרְא֥וּ אֶל־אֱלֹהִ֖ים בְּחׇזְקָ֑ה וְיָשֻׁ֗בוּ אִ֚ישׁ מִדַּרְכּ֣וֹ הָֽרָעָ֔ה וּמִן־הֶחָמָ֖ס אֲשֶׁ֥ר בְּכַפֵּיהֶֽם	8[1]	but let them be covered with sackcloth, both man and beast, and let them cry mightily to God; yea, let everyone turn from his evil way, and from the violence that is in their hands.
מִֽי־יוֹדֵ֣עַ יָשׁ֔וּב וְנִחַ֖ם הָאֱלֹהִ֑ים וְשָׁ֛ב מֵחֲר֥וֹן אַפּ֖וֹ וְלֹ֥א נֹאבֵֽד	9[2]	Who knows whether God will not turn and repent, and turn away from His fierce anger, so we do not perish?'
וַיַּ֤רְא הָֽאֱלֹהִים֙ אֶֽת־מַ֣עֲשֵׂיהֶ֔ם כִּי־שָׁ֖בוּ מִדַּרְכָּ֣ם הָרָעָ֑ה וַיִּנָּ֣חֶם הָאֱלֹהִ֗ים עַל־הָרָעָ֛ה אֲשֶׁר־דִּבֶּ֥ר לַעֲשׂוֹת־לָהֶ֖ם וְלֹ֥א עָשָֽׂה	10[3]	And God saw their work; they turned from their evil way and God repented of the evil He said He would do to them; and He did not do it.

Jonah – Chapter 4

וַיֵּ֥רַע אֶל־יוֹנָ֖ה רָעָ֣ה גְדוֹלָ֑ה וַיִּ֖חַר לֽוֹ	1[4]	But it greatly displeased Jonah, and he was angry.
וַיִּתְפַּלֵּ֣ל אֶל־יְהֹוָה֮ וַיֹּאמַר֒ אָנָּ֤ה יְהֹוָה֙ הֲלוֹא־זֶ֣ה דְבָרִ֗י עַד־הֱיוֹתִי֙ עַל־אַדְמָתִ֔י עַל־כֵּ֥ן קִדַּ֖מְתִּי לִבְרֹ֣חַ תַּרְשִׁ֑ישָׁה כִּ֣י יָדַ֗עְתִּי כִּ֤י אַתָּה֙ אֵֽל־חַנּ֣וּן וְרַח֔וּם אֶ֤רֶךְ אַפַּ֙יִם֙ וְרַב־חֶ֔סֶד וְנִחָ֖ם עַל־הָרָעָֽה	2[5]	And he prayed to the LORD, and said: 'Please, O LORD, was not this my saying, when I was yet in my own country? Therefore, I fled beforehand to Tarshish; for I knew you are a gracious God, compassionate, long-suffering, and abundant in mercy, and repent of the evil.
וְעַתָּ֣ה יְהֹוָ֔ה קַח־נָ֥א אֶת־נַפְשִׁ֖י מִמֶּ֑נִּי כִּ֛י ט֥וֹב מוֹתִ֖י מֵחַיָּֽי	3[6]	Therefore, O LORD, take, please, my life from me; for it is better for me to die than to live.'
וַיֹּ֣אמֶר יְהֹוָ֔ה הַהֵיטֵ֖ב חָ֥רָה לָֽךְ	4[7]	And the LORD said: 'Are you good and angry?'
וַיֵּצֵ֤א יוֹנָה֙ מִן־הָעִ֔יר וַיֵּ֖שֶׁב מִקֶּ֣דֶם לָעִ֑יר וַיַּ֩עַשׂ֩ ל֨וֹ שָׁ֜ם סֻכָּ֗ה וַיֵּ֤שֶׁב תַּחְתֶּ֙יהָ֙ בַּצֵּ֔ל עַ֚ד אֲשֶׁ֣ר יִרְאֶ֔ה מַה־יִּהְיֶ֖ה בָּעִֽיר	5[8]	Then Jonah went out of the city, and sat on the east side of the city, and there made himself a booth, and sat under it in the shadow, so he might see what would become of the city.
וַיְמַ֣ן יְהֹוָֽה־אֱ֠לֹהִ֠ים קִיקָי֞וֹן וַיַּ֣עַל ׀ מֵעַ֣ל לְיוֹנָ֗ה לִהְי֥וֹת צֵל֙ עַל־רֹאשׁ֔וֹ לְהַצִּ֥יל ל֖וֹ מֵרָֽעָת֑וֹ וַיִּשְׂמַ֥ח יוֹנָ֛ה עַל־הַקִּ֖יקָי֑וֹן שִׂמְחָ֥ה גְדוֹלָֽה	6[9]	And the LORD God prepared a gourd, and made it come up over Jonah, so it might be a shadow over his head, to deliver him from his evil. So Jonah was exceeding glad because of the gourd.
וַיְמַ֣ן הָֽאֱלֹהִים֙ תּוֹלַ֔עַת בַּעֲל֥וֹת הַשַּׁ֖חַר לַֽמׇּחֳרָ֑ת וַתַּ֥ךְ אֶת־הַקִּֽיקָי֖וֹן וַיִּיבָֽשׁ	7[10]	But God prepared a worm when the morning rose the next day, and it struck the gourd and it withered.

---

[1] Jonah 3:8 - Acts 3:19 2:20, Daniel 4:24, Ein Yaakov Taanit:16a 18a 7b, Ezekiel 18:21-24 18:27-28 18:30-32 9:11, Gates of Repentance 1.44, Isaiah 1:16-19 55:6-7 10:6 11:6, Jastrow 1558a, Jeremiah 18:11, Jonah 1:6 1:14, Matthew 3:8, Pesikta de R'Kahana 24.11, Psalms 130:1-2, y.Taanit 2:1

[2] Jonah 3:9 - 2 Samuel 12:22, Amos 5:15, Joel 2:13-14, Jonah 1:6, Kuzari 4:5, Luke 15:18-20, Midrash Tanchuma Vayikra 8, Psalms 10:45

[3] Jonah 3:10 - 1 Kings 21:27-29, Amos 7:3 7:6, b.Rosh Hashanah 16b, b.Taanit 15a 16a, Ecclesiastes.R 5:4, Ein Yaakov Rosh Hashanah:16b, Ein Yaakov Taanit:15a 16a, Exodus 8:14, Gates of Repentance 1.44, Genesis.R 21:5 44:12, Jeremiah 18:8 31:19-21, Job 33:27-28, Joel 2:13, Jonah 4:2, Luke 11:32 15:20, m.Tannit 2:1, mt.Hilchot Taaniot 4:2, Pesikta de R'Kahana 28.3, Pesikta Rabbati 52:3, Pirkei de R'Eliezer 43, Siman 121:1, y.Taanit 2:1, z.Noach 61a, Derech Hashem Part III 4§7

[4] Jonah 4:1 - Acts 13:46, James 4:5-6, Jonah 4:4 4:9, Luke 7:39 15:28, Matthew 20:15

Jonah 4:1-2 - HevXIIgr

Jonah 4:1-11 - MurXII

[5] Jonah 4:2 - 1 Kings 19:4, Amos 7:3 7:6, Avot de R'Natan 17, Exodus 8:14 34:6-7, Hosea 11:8-11:9, Jastrow 99b, Jeremiah 18:8 20:7, Joel 2:13-2:14, Jonah 1:3 3:10, Luke 10:29, Micah 7:18, mt.Hilchot Yesodei haTorah 10:4, Numbers 14:18-19, Psalms 78:38 86:5 86:15 90:13 1:8, Saadia Opinions 3:5

[6] Jonah 4:3 - 1 Corinthians 9:15, 1 Kings 19:4, Derech Hashem Part II 3§10, Ecclesiastes 7:1, Jeremiah 20:14-18, Job 3:21-22 6:8-9 7:15-16, Jonah 4:8, Midrash Proverbs 14, Midrash Tanchuma Bereshit 7, Numbers 11:15 20:3, Philippians 1:21-25

[7] Jonah 4:4 - James 1:19-1:20, Jonah 4:9, Matthew 20:15, Micah 6:3, Numbers 20:11-20:12 20:24, Psalms 106:32-33

[8] Jonah 4:5 - 1 Kings 19:9 19:13, Genesis 19:27-19:28, Isaiah 9:17, Jeremiah 17:15-17:16 20:9, Jonah 1:5, Luke 19:41-19:44

Jonah 4:5-8 – HevXIIgr

Jonah 4:5-11 - 4QXIIg

[9] Jonah 4:6 - 1 Corinthians 7:30, Amos 6:13, Esther 5:9, Isaiah 15:2, Jonah 1:17, Luke 10:20, Proverbs 23:5, Psalms 103:10-14

[10] Jonah 4:7 - Isaiah 40:6-8, Job 1:21, Joel 1:12, Psalms 30:7-8 90:5-6 6:11

Hebrew		English
וַיְהִ֣י ׀ כִּזְרֹ֣חַ הַשֶּׁ֗מֶשׁ וַיְמַ֨ן אֱלֹהִ֜ים ר֤וּחַ קָדִים֙ חֲרִישִׁ֔ית וַתַּ֥ךְ הַשֶּׁ֛מֶשׁ עַל־רֹ֥אשׁ יוֹנָ֖ה וַיִּתְעַלָּ֑ף וַיִּשְׁאַ֤ל אֶת־נַפְשׁוֹ֙ לָמ֔וּת וַיֹּ֕אמֶר ט֥וֹב מוֹתִ֖י מֵחַיָּֽי	8[1]	And it came to pass, when the sun arose, that God prepared an intense east wind; and the sun beat on the head of Jonah, so he fainted, and requested that he might die, and said: 'It is better for me to die than to live.'
וַיֹּ֤אמֶר אֱלֹהִים֙ אֶל־יוֹנָ֔ה הַהֵיטֵ֥ב חָרָֽה־לְךָ֖ עַל־הַקִּֽיקָי֑וֹן וַיֹּ֕אמֶר הֵיטֵ֥ב חָֽרָה־לִ֖י עַד־מָֽוֶת	9[2]	And God said to Jonah: 'Are you good and angry for the gourd?' And he said: 'I am greatly angry, to death.'
וַיֹּ֣אמֶר יְהֹוָ֔ה אַתָּ֥ה חַ֨סְתָּ֙ עַל־הַקִּ֣יקָי֔וֹן אֲשֶׁ֛ר לֹא־עָמַ֥לְתָּ בּ֖וֹ וְלֹ֣א גִדַּלְתּ֑וֹ שֶׁבִּן־לַ֥יְלָה הָיָ֖ה וּבִן־לַ֥יְלָה אָבָֽד	10[3]	And the LORD said: 'You had pity on the gourd, for which you have not labored, nor made it grow, which came up in a night, and perished in a night;
וַֽאֲנִי֙ לֹ֣א אָח֔וּס עַל־נִֽינְוֵ֖ה הָעִ֣יר הַגְּדוֹלָ֑ה אֲשֶׁ֣ר יֶשׁ־בָּ֡הּ הַרְבֵּה֩ מִֽשְׁתֵּים־עֶשְׂרֵ֨ה רִבּ֜וֹ אָדָ֗ם אֲשֶׁ֤ר לֹֽא־יָדַע֙ בֵּין־יְמִינ֣וֹ לִשְׂמֹאל֔וֹ וּבְהֵמָ֖ה רַבָּֽה	11[4]	and should I not have pity on Nineveh, that great city, in which live more than 120,000 people who cannot discern between their right hand and their left hand, and also much cattle?'

Mikhah haMorashti– Chapter 1

Hebrew		English
דְּבַר־יְהֹוָ֣ה ׀ אֲשֶׁ֣ר הָיָ֗ה אֶל־מִיכָה֙ הַמֹּ֣רַשְׁתִּ֔י בִּימֵ֥י יוֹתָ֛ם אָחָ֥ז יְחִזְקִיָּ֖ה מַלְכֵ֣י יְהוּדָ֑ה אֲשֶׁר־חָזָ֥ה עַל־שֹׁמְר֖וֹן וִירֽוּשָׁלָֽ͏ִם	1[5]	The word of the LORD came to Micah the Morashtite in the days of Jotham, Ahaz, and Hezekiah, kings of Judah, which he saw concerning Samaria and Jerusalem.
שִׁמְע֣וּ עַמִּ֣ים כֻּלָּ֔ם הַקְשִׁ֥יבִי אֶ֖רֶץ וּמְלֹאָ֑הּ וִיהִ֣י אֲדֹנָ֤י יְהֹוִה֙ בָּכֶ֣ם לְעֵ֔ד אֲדֹנָ֖י מֵהֵיכַ֥ל קׇדְשֽׁוֹ	2[6]	Hear, you people, all of you; Listen, O earth, and all that are within it; And let the Lord GOD be witness against you, the Lord from His holy temple.
כִּֽי־הִנֵּ֥ה יְהֹוָ֖ה יֹצֵ֣א מִמְּקוֹמ֑וֹ וְיָרַ֥ד וְדָרַ֖ךְ עַל־בָּ֥מֳתֵי "עַל־בָּ֥מֳתֵי" אָֽרֶץ	3[7]	For, behold, the LORD comes forth from His place, and will come down, and tread upon the high places of the earth.
וְנָמַ֤סּוּ הֶֽהָרִים֙ תַּחְתָּ֔יו וְהָעֲמָקִ֖ים יִתְבַּקָּ֑עוּ כַּדּוֹנַג֙ מִפְּנֵ֣י הָאֵ֔שׁ כְּמַ֖יִם מֻגָּרִ֥ים בְּמוֹרָֽד	4[8]	And the mountains shall melt under Him, and the valleys shall be divided, as wax before the fire, as waters are poured down a cliff.

[1] Jonah 4:8 - 1 Samuel 3:18, 2 Samuel 15:25-26, b.Bava Batra [Rashi] 25a, b.Gittin 30a, Ein Yaakov Gittin:31b, Ezekiel 19:12, Isaiah 1:10, Job 2:10, Jonah 1:4 1:17 4:3 4:6-7, Leviticus 10:3, Psalms 39:10 1:6, Revelation 3:19 7:16, Song of Songs 1:6

[2] Jonah 4:9 - 2 Corinthians 7:10, b.Yevamot [Tosefot] 99b, Genesis 4:5-14, Job 5:2 18:4 40:4-5, Judges 16:16, Matthew 2:38, Revelation 9:6

[3] Jonah 4:10 - 1 Samuel 20:31, Genesis 17:12

[4] Jonah 4:11 - b.Bava Batra [Rashbam] 173a, b.Bechorot [Rashi] 42ab, b.Bechorot 42ab, b.Kereitot 6b, b.Kiddushin [Rashi] 18a, b.Sotah [Rashi] 45b, b.Temurah 9a, b.Yevamot 61a, Deuteronomy 1:39, Ecclesiastes.R 3:21, Isaiah 1:18, Jonah 1:2 3:2-3 3:10-4:1, Luke 15:28-32, Matthew 18:33, Midrash Tanchuma Vezot Habracha 6, mt.Hilchot Chametz u'Matzah 27:2, Pirkei de R'Eliezer 43, Psalms 36:7 8:14 104:27-28 145:8-9 145:15-16, t.Temurah 1:7

[5] Micah 1:1 - 2 Chronicles 27:1-9, Amos 1:1 2:4-2:8 3:1-2 6:1, Ecclesiastes.R 1:2, Habakkuk 1:1, Hosea 1:1 4:15 5:5-14 6:10-11 8:14 12:3-4, Isaiah 1:1 7:9, Jeremiah 2:18, Josephus Antiquities 13.9.1, Lives of the Prophets 6:1, m.Maaser Sheni 5:2, m.Shekalim 1:5, Micah 1:5 1:14-15, Seder Olam 20:Flee 20:Flee
Micah 1:1-8 - 8HevXIIgr
Micah 1:1-16 - MurXII

[6] Micah 1:2 - Deuteronomy 8:1, Habakkuk 2:20, Isaiah 1:2, Jeremiah 6:19 22:29 5:23, Jonah 2:7, Malachi 2:14 3:5, Mark 7:14-15, Micah 6:1-2, Per Massorah: Soferim altered "Hashem" to "Adonai", Psalms 11:5 24:1 28:2 49:2-3 50:1 50:7 50:12, Revelation 2:7 2:11 2:17 2:29 3:6 3:13 3:22, Sifre Devarim Ha'azinu Hashamayim 306, Sifre Devarim Nitzavim 306
Micah 1:2-5 - 1Q14 frags 1-5 ll.1-5

[7] Micah 1:3 - 1 Enoch 1:4, Amos 4:13, Deuteronomy 8:13 9:29, Ezekiel 3:12, Genesis.R 68:11, Guide for the Perplexed 2:29, Habakkuk 3:19, Hosea 5:14-5:15, Isaiah 2:10-19 1:10 2:21 63:3-4 64:2-3, Job 16:12, Midrash Psalms 91:6, Psalms 19:3, Testament of Moses 10:3
Micah 1:3-4 - Sibylline Oracles 8.433

[8] Micah 1:4 - 2 Peter 3:10-12, 4 Ezra 13:4 8:23, Amos 9:5, Ein Yaakov Sanhedrin:102a, Guide for the Perplexed 2:29, Habakkuk 3:6 3:10, Isaiah 64:2-64:4, Joseph and Asenath 28:10, Judges 5:4, Midrash Psalms 91:6, Nahum 1:5, Psalms 68:3 97:5, Revelation 20:11, Sibylline Oracles 3.680, Zechariah 14:4

בְּפֶשַׁע יַעֲקֹב כָּל־זֹאת וּבְחַטֹּאות בֵּית יִשְׂרָאֵל מִי־פֶשַׁע יַעֲקֹב הֲלוֹא שֹׁמְרוֹן וּמִי בָּמוֹת יְהוּדָה הֲלוֹא יְרוּשָׁלָ͏ִם	5[1]	All this is for the transgression of Jacob, and for the sins of the house of Israel. What is the transgression of Jacob? Is it not Samaria? And what are the high places of Judah? Are they not Jerusalem?
וְשַׂמְתִּי שֹׁמְרוֹן לְעִי הַשָּׂדֶה לְמַטָּעֵי כָרֶם וְהִגַּרְתִּי לַגַּי אֲבָנֶיהָ וִיסֹדֶיהָ אֲגַלֶּה	6[2]	Therefore, I will make Samaria *a heap in the field*[3], a place for planting vineyards; and I will pour down its stones into the valley, and I will uncover her foundations.
וְכָל־פְּסִילֶיהָ יֻכַּתּוּ וְכָל־אֶתְנַנֶּיהָ יִשָּׂרְפוּ בָאֵשׁ וְכָל־עֲצַבֶּיהָ אָשִׂים שְׁמָמָה כִּי מֵאֶתְנַן זוֹנָה קִבָּצָה וְעַד־אֶתְנַן זוֹנָה יָשׁוּבוּ	7[4]	And all her graven images shall be beaten to pieces, and all her hires shall be burned with fire, and all her idols will I lay desolate; *for the price of a harlot she gathered them, and to the hire of a harlot they shall return*[5].
עַל־זֹאת אֶסְפְּדָה וְאֵילִילָה אֵילְכָה 'שֵׁילָל' "שׁוֹלָל" וְעָרוֹם אֶעֱשֶׂה מִסְפֵּד כַּתַּנִּים וְאֵבֶל כִּבְנוֹת יַעֲנָה	8[6]	For this I[7] will wail and howl, I[8] will go stripped and naked; I[9] will make a wailing like the jackals, and a mourning like the ostriches.
כִּי אֲנוּשָׁה מַכּוֹתֶיהָ כִּי־בָאָה עַד־יְהוּדָה נָגַע עַד־שַׁעַר עַמִּי עַד־יְרוּשָׁלָ͏ִם	9[10]	For her wound is incurable; and it has come to Judah; it reaches to the gate of my people, to Jerusalem.
בְּגַת אַל־תַּגִּידוּ בָּכוֹ אַל־תִּבְכּוּ בְּבֵית לְעַפְרָה עָפָר 'הִתְפַּלָּשְׁתִּי' "הִתְפַּלָּשִׁי"	10[11]	Do not tell it in Gath, do not weep at all; *at Beth-le-aphrah roll yourself in the dust*[12].
עִבְרִי לָכֶם יוֹשֶׁבֶת שָׁפִיר עֶרְיָה־בֹשֶׁת לֹא יָצְאָה יוֹשֶׁבֶת צַאֲנָן מִסְפַּד בֵּית הָאֵצֶל יִקַּח מִכֶּם עֶמְדָּתוֹ	11[13]	*Pass along, O inhabitant of Saphir, in nakedness and shame; the inhabitant of Zaanan will not come forth; the wailing of Beth-ezel shall take its standing-place from you*[14].
כִּי־חָלָה לְטוֹב יוֹשֶׁבֶת מָרוֹת כִּי־יָרַד רָע מֵאֵת יְהֹוָה לְשַׁעַר יְרוּשָׁלָ͏ִם	12[15]	*For the inhabitant of Maroth wait anxiously for good*[16]; because evil has come down from the LORD to the gate of Jerusalem.
רְתֹם הַמֶּרְכָּבָה לָרֶכֶשׁ יוֹשֶׁבֶת לָכִישׁ רֵאשִׁית חַטָּאת הִיא לְבַת־צִיּוֹן כִּי־בָךְ נִמְצְאוּ פִּשְׁעֵי יִשְׂרָאֵל	13[17]	Bind the chariots to the swift steeds, O inhabitant of Lachish; she was the beginning of sin to the daughter of Zion; For the transgressions of Israel are found in you.

---

[1] Micah 1:5 - 1 Kings 13:32, 1 Thessalonians 2:15-2:16, 1Q14 frags 8-10 ll.1-3, 2 Chronicles 28:2-4 28:23-25 36:14-16, 2 Kings 16:3-4 16:10-12 17:7-23, Amos 6:1 8:14, Genesis.R 82:10, Hosea 7:1 8:5-8:6, Isaiah 50:1-2 59:1-15, Jeremiah 2:17 2:19 4:18 5:25 6:19, Lamentations 5:16, Midrash Psalms 76:4, Pesikta de R'Kahana 16.8

[2] Micah 1:6 - 1Q14 frags 8-10 ll.10-11 11.5-6, 2 Kings 19:25, Amos 5:11, b.Berachot 58a, b.Eruvin 18b, Ein Yaakov Eruvin:19a, Ezekiel 13:14, Habakkuk 3:13, Hosea 14:1, Isaiah 1:2 1:12, Jeremiah 9:12 3:25 3:37, Lamentations 4:1, Matthew 24:2, Micah 3:12

[3] LXX *as a storehouse of the fruits of the field*

[4] Micah 1:7 - 2 Chronicles 7:1 34:6-7, 2 Kings 23:14-15, 4QXIIg, b.Avodah Zara 14a, Deuteronomy 9:21 23:20, Ecclesiastes.R 1:24, Ein Yaakov Avodah Zarah:17a, Hosea 2:5 2:12 8:6 10:5-6, Isaiah 3:9, Jeremiah 44:17-18, Joel 4:3, Leviticus 2:30, Revelation 18:3 18:9 18:12-13

[5] LXX *because she has gathered of the hires of fornication, and of the hires of fornication has she amassed wealth*

[6] Micah 1:8 - 1Q14 frags 11 l.2, b.Bava Batra 152a, b.Chullin 64b, Isaiah 13:21 16:9 20:2-20:4 21:3 22:4, Jeremiah 4:19 9:2 9:11 9:20 48:36-48:39, Job 6:29, Psalms 6:7
Micah 1:8 [LXX] - 2 Baruch 10:8

[7] LXX *she*

[8] LXX *she*

[9] LXX *she*

[10] Micah 1:9 - 1Q14 frags 11 l.3, 2 Chronicles 32:1-32:23, 2 Kings 18:9-18:13, Isaiah 1:5-1:6 3:26 8:7-8:8 10:28-10:32 37:22-37:36, Jeremiah 15:18 30:11-30:15, Micah 1:12

[11] Micah 1:10 - 2 Samuel 1:20, Amos 5:13 6:10, Jeremiah 6:26, Job 2:8, Joshua 18:23, Lamentations 3:29

[12] LXX *and you Enakim, do not rebuild from the ruins of the house in derision: sprinkle dust in the place of your laughter*

[13] Micah 1:11 - Ezekiel 16:37 23:29, Isaiah 16:2 20:4 47:2-47:3, Jeremiah 13:22 24:6 24:9, Micah 1:8, Nahum 3:5

[14] LXX *The inhabitant of Sennaar, fairly inhabiting her cities, came not forth to mourn for the house next to her: she shall receive of you the stroke of grief*

[15] Micah 1:12 - 1 Samuel 4:13, Amos 3:6, Isaiah 21:7 59:9-11, Jeremiah 8:15 14:19, Job 6:26, Micah 1:9, Ruth 1:20
Micah 1:12-15 - 4QXIIg

[16] LXX *Who has begun to act for good to her that dwells in sorrow?*

[17] Micah 1:13 - 1 Kings 13:33-13:34 14:16 16:31, 2 Chronicles 11:9 8:9, 2 Kings 8:18 16:3-16:4 18:13-18:14 18:17, Exodus 8:21, Ezekiel 23:11, Genesis 19:17, Isaiah 10:31 13:8, Jeremiah 3:8 4:29, Joshua 10:3 15:39, Micah 1:5, Revelation 2:14 2:20 18:1-18:5

לָכֵן תִּתְּנִי שִׁלּוּחִים עַל מוֹרֶשֶׁת גַּת בָּתֵּי אַכְזִיב
לְאַכְזָב לְמַלְכֵי יִשְׂרָאֵל

14[1]

Therefore, you shall give a parting gift to Moresheth-gath; the houses of Achzib shall be a deceitful thing[2] to the kings of Israel.

עֹד הַיֹּרֵשׁ אָבִי לָךְ יוֹשֶׁבֶת מָרֵשָׁה עַד־עֲדֻלָּם יָבוֹא
כְּבוֹד יִשְׂרָאֵל

15[3]

I will yet bring to you, O inhabitant of Mareshah, he who shall possess you; the glory of Israel shall come to Adullam[4].

קָרְחִי וָגֹזִּי עַל־בְּנֵי תַּעֲנוּגָיִךְ הַרְחִבִי קָרְחָתֵךְ כַּנֶּשֶׁר
כִּי גָלוּ מִמֵּךְ

16[5]

Make yourself bald, and poll yourself for the children of your delight; *Enlarge your baldness as the vulture[6]*; For they have gone from you into captivity.

Micah – Chapter 2

הוֹי חֹשְׁבֵי־אָוֶן וּפֹעֲלֵי רָע עַל־מִשְׁכְּבוֹתָם בְּאוֹר
הַבֹּקֶר יַעֲשׂוּהָ כִּי יֶשׁ־לְאֵל יָדָם

1[7]

Woe to they who devise iniquity and work evil upon their beds! When the morning is light, they execute it, because it is in the power of their hand.[8]

וְחָמְדוּ שָׂדוֹת וְגָזָלוּ וּבָתִּים וְנָשָׂאוּ וְעָשְׁקוּ גֶּבֶר
וּבֵיתוֹ וְאִישׁ וְנַחֲלָתוֹ

2[9]

And they covet fields *and seize them; and houses and take them away[10]*; thus they oppress a man and his house, a man and his heritage.

לָכֵן כֹּה אָמַר יְהוָה הִנְנִי חֹשֵׁב עַל־הַמִּשְׁפָּחָה הַזֹּאת
רָעָה אֲשֶׁר לֹא־תָמִישׁוּ מִשָּׁם צַוְּארֹתֵיכֶם וְלֹא
תֵלְכוּ רוֹמָה כִּי עֵת רָעָה הִיא

3[11]

Therefore, thus says the LORD: Behold, against this family I devise an evil, From which you shall not remove your necks, nor shall you walk upright; for it shall be an evil time.

בַּיּוֹם הַהוּא יִשָּׂא עֲלֵיכֶם מָשָׁל וְנָהָה נְהִי נִהְיָה
אָמַר שָׁדוֹד נְשַׁדֻּנוּ חֵלֶק עַמִּי יָמִיר אֵיךְ יָמִישׁ לִי
לְשׁוֹבֵב שָׂדֵינוּ יְחַלֵּק

4[12]

In that day they shall take up a parable against you, and lament with a woeful lamentation, and say: 'We are utterly ruined; He changes the portion of my people; and how he removed it from me! Instead of restoring our fields, he divides them.'

לָכֵן לֹא־יִהְיֶה לְךָ מַשְׁלִיךְ חֶבֶל בְּגוֹרָל בִּקְהַל יְהוָה

5[13]

Therefore, you shall have no one who shall cast the line by lot *in the congregation of the LORD[14].*

---

[1] Micah 1:14 - 2 Chronicles 16:1-3, 2 Kings 16:8 18:14-16, 2 Samuel 8:2, b.Bava Batra [Rashbam] 37ab, b.Sanhedrin [Rashbam] 102a, Ein Yaakov Sanhedrin:102a, Isaiah 6:6, Jastrow 1563a, Jeremiah 15:18, Joshua 15:44, Psalms 62:10 118:8-9 146:3-4
[2] LXX *Therefore shall he cause men to be sent forth as far as the inheritance of Geth, even vain houses; they have become vanity*
[3] Micah 1:15 - 1 Samuel 22:1, 2 Chronicles 11:7, Genesis.R 85:1, Isaiah 7:17-25 10:3 10:5-6, Jeremiah 1:1, Joshua 12:15 15:35 15:44, Ruth.R 2:1
[4] LXX *until they bring the heirs, O inhabitant of Lachis: the inheritance shall reach to Odollam, even the glory of the daughter of Israel*
[5] Micah 1:16 - 2 Kings 17:6, Amos 8:10, Deuteronomy 4:41 28:56-57, Isaiah 3:16-26 15:2 22:12 39:6-7, Jeremiah 6:26 7:29 16:6, Job 1:20, Lamentations 4:5-8, Midrash Psalms 29:2 30:4 32:2 85:2 86:2
[6] LXX *increase your widowhood as an eagle*
[7] Micah 2:1 - Acts 23:12 23:15, Deuteronomy 4:32, Esther 3:8 5:14 9:25, Ezekiel 11:2, Genesis 7:29, Genesis.R 28:5, Hosea 7:6-7, Isaiah 8:7 11:3, Jeremiah 18:18, John 19:11, Luke 20:19 22:2-6, Mark 15:1, Matthew 27:1-27:2, Midrash Psalms 30:4, Nahum 1:11, Proverbs 3:27 4:16 6:12-19 12:2, Psalms 7:15-7:17 36:5 140:2-9, Romans 1:30, Saadia Opinions 4:3, Song of Songs.R 1:25
Micah 2:1-13 - MurXII
[8] LXX *They meditated troubles, and wrought wickedness on their beds, and they put it in execution with the daylight; for they have not lifted up their hands to God*
[9] Micah 2:2 - 1 Kings 21:2-19, 1 Samuel 12:3-4, 1 Timothy 6:10, 2 Kings 9:26, Amos 8:4, b.Gittin 58a, Ein Yaakov Gittin:58a, Exodus 20:14 22:21-24, Ezekiel 18:12 22:12, Habakkuk 2:5-9, Isaiah 5:8, Jeremiah 22:17, Job 24:2-12 7:38, Malachi 3:5, Matthew 23:13, Mekhilta de R'Shimon bar Yochai Bachodesh 55:3, Micah 3:9, mt.Hilchot Gezelah Vaavedah 1:11, Nehemiah 5:1-5, Pesikta de R'Kahana 13.8, Pesikta Rabbati 24:3 27:4
[10] LXX *and plundered orphans, and oppressed families*
[11] Micah 2:3 - Amos 2:14-3:2 5:13 9:1-4, Daniel 4:34 5:20-23, Ephesians 5:16, Isaiah 2:11-12 3:16 5:19 28:14-18, James 2:13, Jeremiah 8:3 13:15-13:17 18:11 3:12 10:17 12:23 19:2, Lamentations 1:14 2:17 5:5, Micah 2:1, Romans 16:4, z.Vaetchanan 269b, Zephaniah 1:17-18
Micah 2:3-4 - 4QXIIg
[12] Micah 2:4 - 2 Chronicles 11:25 36:20-21, 2 Kings 17:23-24, 2 Samuel 1:17, Amos 5:1 5:17, Avot de R'Natan 34, Deuteronomy 4:29, Esther.R 1:10, Ezekiel 2:10 16:44, Habakkuk 2:6, Isaiah 6:11 14:4 24:3 63:17-18, Jeremiah 4:13 9:11 9:18-22 14:18 25:9-11, Job 3:1, Joel 1:8 1:13, Lamentations 1:1-5, Mark 12:12, Micah 1:15 2:10, Numbers 23:7 23:18 24:3 24:15, Zephaniah 1:2
[13] Micah 2:5 - b.Kiddushin 39a, Deuteronomy 23:4 23:10 8:8, Hosea 9:3, Joshua 18:4 18:10, Nehemiah 7:61, Psalms 16:6
[14] Missing in LXX

אַל־תַּטִּפוּ יַטִּיפוּן לֹא־יַטִּפוּ לָאֵלֶּה לֹא יִסַּג כְּלִמּוֹת	6[1]	'Do not preach,' they preach; 'They shall not preach[2] of these things, so they shall not take shame.'
הֶאָמוּר בֵּית־יַעֲקֹב הֲקָצַר רוּחַ יְהֹוָה אִם־אֵלֶּה מַעֲלָלָיו הֲלוֹא דְבָרַי יֵיטִיבוּ עִם הַיָּשָׁר הוֹלֵךְ	7[3]	Do I change, O house of Jacob? Is the spirit of the LORD impoverished? Are these His doings? Do not My words do good to him who walks uprightly[4]?
וְאֶתְמוּל עַמִּי לְאוֹיֵב יְקוֹמֵם מִמּוּל שַׂלְמָה אֶדֶר תַּפְשִׁטוּן מֵעֹבְרִים בֶּטַח שׁוּבֵי מִלְחָמָה	8[5]	But of late, My people has risen up as an enemy; with the garment you strip also the mantle from them who pass by securely, so that they are as men returning from war.
נְשֵׁי עַמִּי תְּגָרְשׁוּן מִבֵּית תַּעֲנֻגֶיהָ מֵעַל עֹלָלֶיהָ תִּקְחוּ הֲדָרִי לְעוֹלָם	9[6]	The women of My people you cast out from their pleasant houses; from their young children you take away My glory forever[7].
קוּמוּ וּלְכוּ כִּי לֹא־זֹאת הַמְּנוּחָה בַּעֲבוּר טָמְאָה תְּחַבֵּל וְחֶבֶל נִמְרָץ	10[8]	Arise, and depart; for this is not your resting place; Because of its uncleanness, it shall destroy you with a sore destruction.
לוּ־אִישׁ הֹלֵךְ רוּחַ וְשֶׁקֶר כִּזֵּב אַטִּף לְךָ לַיַּיִן וְלַשֵּׁכָר וְהָיָה מַטִּיף הָעָם הַזֶּה	11[9]	If a man walking in wind and falsehood lies, 'I will preach to you of wine and of strong drink;' He shall be the preacher of this people[10].
אָסֹף אֶאֱסֹף יַעֲקֹב כֻּלָּךְ קַבֵּץ אֲקַבֵּץ שְׁאֵרִית יִשְׂרָאֵל יַחַד אֲשִׂימֶנּוּ כְּצֹאן בָּצְרָה כְּעֵדֶר בְּתוֹךְ הַדָּבְרוֹ תְּהִימֶנָה מֵאָדָם	12[11]	I will surely assemble, O Jacob, all of you; I will surely gather the remnant of Israel; I will render them all as sheep in a fold; As a flock in the midst of their pasture; They shall make a great noise by reason of the multitude of men[12].
עָלָה הַפֹּרֵץ לִפְנֵיהֶם פָּרְצוּ וַיַּעֲבֹרוּ שַׁעַר וַיֵּצְאוּ בוֹ וַיַּעֲבֹר מַלְכָּם לִפְנֵיהֶם וַיהֹוָה בְּרֹאשָׁם	13[13]	The breaker has gone up before them; They have broken forth and passed on, by the gate, and have gone out from there; And their king

---

[1] Micah 2:6 - 1 Thessalonians 2:15-2:16, 4Q269 frag 3 l.2, 6Q15 frag 1 l.2, Acts 4:17 5:28 5:40 7:51, Amos 2:12 7:13 8:11-8:13, Cairo Damascus 4:19-5:2, Cairo Damascus 4.20, Ezekiel 3:26 21:2 21:7, Isaiah 6:10, Jeremiah 6:14-6:15 8:11-8:12 26:8-26:9 26:20-26:23, Micah 6:16, Psalms 74:9, Song of Songs.R 1:18, y.Avodah Zarah 2:7, y.Berachot 1:4, y.Sanhedrin 11:4
[2] LXX *Weep not with tears in the assembly of the LORD, neither let any weep*
[3] Micah 2:7 - 2 Corinthians 6:12, 2 Timothy 3:5, Hosea 14:11, Isaiah 48:1-2 2:2 10:1 59:1-2, Jeremiah 2:4 15:16, John 8:39, Matthew 3:8, Micah 3:9, Midrash Psalms 42/43:5, Numbers 11:23, Proverbs 2:7 10:9 10:29 14:2 4:18, Psalms 15:2 19:8-12 84:12 119:65 119:70-71 119:92-93 119:99-103, Romans 2:28-29 7:13 9:6-13, Zechariah 4:6
Micah 2:7-8 - 8HevXIIgr
[4] LXX *who says, The house of Jacob has provoked the Spirit of the LORD; are not these his practices? Are not the LORD's words right with him? and have they not proceeded correctly*
[5] Micah 2:8 - 2 Chronicles 28:5-8, 2 Samuel 20:19, Exodus.R 42:7, Isaiah 9:22, Psalms 55:21 120:6-7
[6] Micah 2:9 - 1 Samuel 2:19, 2 Corinthians 3:18 4:6, b.Eruvin 63b, Ezekiel 15:21, Habakkuk 2:14, Jastrow 1093b, Jeremiah 10:20, Joel 4:6, Luke 20:47, Mark 12:40, Matthew 23:13, Micah 2:2, Numbers.R 9:7, Pesikta Rabbati 43:4, Psalms 72:19, Siman 152:17, Zechariah 2:5
Micah 2:10 - 1 Kings 9:7, 2 Chronicles 7:20 36:20-21, 2 Kings 15:29 17:6, Deuteronomy 4:26 12:9 6:18, Ezekiel 36:12-14, Hebrews 4:1-9, Jastrow 846a, Jeremiah 3:2 9:20 10:18, Joshua 23:15-16, Leviticus 18:24-28 20:22-26, Numbers.R 9:7, Psalms 95:11 10:38
[7] LXX *The leaders of my people shall be cast forth from their luxurious houses; they are rejected because of their evil practices; draw near to the everlasting mountains*
[8] Micah 2:10-11 - 4Q177 1.10
[9] Micah 2:11 - 1 John 4:1, 1 Kings 13:18 22:6 22:21-23, 2 Chronicles 18:19-22, 2 Corinthians 11:13-15, 2 Peter 2:1-3 2:13-19, 2 Thessalonians 2:8-11, Ezekiel 13:3-14 13:22, Isaiah 9:16 30:10-11, Jeremiah 5:31 6:13-14 8:10-11 14:14 23:14 23:17 23:25 23:32 27:14-15 28:2-3 4:15 29:21-23, Micah 3:5 3:11, Philippians 3:19, Revelation 16:13-14, Romans 16:18, This is the middle verse of the book of Micah per the Massorah, y.Avodah Zarah 2:7, y.Berachot 1:4, y.Sanhedrin 11:4
[10] LXX *you have fled, no one pursuing you: your spirit has framed falsehood, it has dropped on you for wine and strong drink. But it shall come to pass, that out of the dropping of this people*
[11] Micah 2:12 - Amos 1:12, Ezekiel 10:11 10:22 10:31 12:37 13:21, Genesis 12:33, Hosea 2:2, Isaiah 11:11 3:12 10:6, Jeremiah 3:18 23:3 31:8-11, Micah 4:6-7 5:8 7:14 7:18, Midrash Tanchuma Tazria 9, Zechariah 8:22-23 9:14-15 10:6-8
[12] LXX *they shall rush forth from among men through the breach made before them*
[13] Micah 2:13 - 1 Corinthians 15:21-26, b.Megillah 21b, b.Niddah 63a, b.Pesachim 7b 119b, b.Succah 39a, Bahir 70, Daniel 2:34-35 2:44, Ecclesiastes.R 4:1 9:12, Exodus.R 23:5, Ezekiel 34:23-24, Genesis.R 48:10 69:5 73:11 85:14 96 [Excl]:1, Hebrews 2:9-10 2:14-15 6:20, Hosea 2:2 3:5 13:14, Isaiah 18:7 42:13-16 45:1-2 49:9-10 49:24-25 51:9-10 3:12 4:12 7:4 59:16-19, Jastrow 192a, Jeremiah 23:5-6 51:20-24, John 10:27-30, Lamentations.R 1:57, Leviticus.R 32:8, Midrash Proverbs 6, Numbers.R 2:10 13:14, Pesikta de R'Kahana 16.11, Pesikta Rabbati 8:4 10:11 33:10 33:13 35:4, Revelation 7:17 17:14 19:13-17, Siman 10:19, Song of Songs.R 4:26, Zechariah 9:14-15 10:5-7 10:12 12:3-8

has passed on before them, and the LORD at the head of them.

Micah – Chapter 3

וָאֹמַ֗ר שִׁמְעוּ־נָא֙ רָאשֵׁ֣י יַעֲקֹ֔ב וּקְצִינֵ֖י בֵּ֣ית יִשְׂרָאֵ֑ל הֲל֣וֹא לָכֶ֔ם לָדַ֖עַת אֶת־הַמִּשְׁפָּֽט׃

1[1] And I said: Hear, please, you heads of Jacob, And *rulers*[2] of the house of Israel: is it not for you to know justice?

שֹׂ֥נְאֵי ט֖וֹב וְאֹ֣הֲבֵי ״רָעָ֑ה״ ״רָע״ גֹּזְלֵ֤י עוֹרָם֙ מֵֽעֲלֵיהֶ֔ם וּשְׁאֵרָ֖ם מֵעַ֥ל עַצְמוֹתָֽם׃

2[3] Who hate the good and love the evil, who rob their skin from them and their flesh from their bones;

וַאֲשֶׁ֣ר אָכְלוּ֮ שְׁאֵ֣ר עַמִּי֒ וְעוֹרָם֙ מֵעֲלֵיהֶ֣ם הִפְשִׁ֔יטוּ וְאֶת־עַצְמֹֽתֵיהֶ֖ם פִּצֵּ֑חוּ וּפָרְשׂוּ֙ כַּאֲשֶׁ֣ר בַּסִּ֔יר וּכְבָשָׂ֖ר בְּת֥וֹךְ קַלָּֽחַת׃

3[4] Who also eat the flesh of my people, and flay their skin from them, and break their bones; Yes, they chop them in pieces, as what is in the pot, and as flesh within the caldron.

אָ֚ז יִזְעֲק֣וּ אֶל־יְהֹוָ֔ה וְלֹ֥א יַעֲנֶ֖ה אוֹתָ֑ם וְיַסְתֵּ֨ר פָּנָ֤יו מֵהֶם֙ בָּעֵ֣ת הַהִ֔יא כַּאֲשֶׁ֥ר הֵרֵ֖עוּ מַעַלְלֵיהֶֽם׃

4[5] Then they shall cry to the LORD, but He will not answer them; Yea, He will hide His face from them at that time, because they have produced evil with their deeds.

כֹּ֚ה אָמַ֣ר יְהֹוָ֔ה עַל־הַנְּבִיאִ֖ים הַמַּתְעִ֣ים אֶת־עַמִּ֑י הַנֹּשְׁכִ֤ים בְּשִׁנֵּיהֶם֙ וְקָרְא֣וּ שָׁל֔וֹם וַאֲשֶׁר֙ לֹא־יִתֵּ֣ן עַל־פִּיהֶ֔ם וְקִדְּשׁ֥וּ עָלָ֖יו מִלְחָמָֽה׃

5[6] Thus says the LORD concerning the prophets who make my people error; who cry[7]: 'Peace,' when their teeth have anything to bite; And whomever puts nothing to their mouths, they prepare war against him:

לָכֵ֞ן לַ֤יְלָה לָכֶם֙ מֵֽחָז֔וֹן וְחָשְׁכָ֥ה לָכֶ֖ם מִקְּסֹ֑ם וּבָ֤אָה הַשֶּׁ֙מֶשׁ֙ עַל־הַנְּבִיאִ֔ים וְקָדַ֥ר עֲלֵיהֶ֖ם הַיּֽוֹם׃

6[8] Therefore, it shall be night to you, so you shall have no vision; and it shall be dark for you, so You shall not divine; and the sun shall go down on the prophets, and the day shall be black over them.

וּבֹ֣שׁוּ הַחֹזִ֗ים וְחָֽפְרוּ֙ הַקֹּ֣סְמִ֔ים וְעָט֥וּ עַל־שָׂפָ֖ם כֻּלָּ֑ם כִּ֛י אֵ֥ין מַעֲנֵ֖ה אֱלֹהִֽים׃

7[9] And the seers[10] shall be put to shame, and the diviners confounded; yes, they shall all cover their upper lips; for there shall be no answer from God.

וְאוּלָ֗ם אָנֹכִ֞י מָלֵ֤אתִי כֹ֙חַ֙ אֶת־ר֣וּחַ יְהֹוָ֔ה וּמִשְׁפָּ֖ט וּגְבוּרָ֑ה לְהַגִּ֤יד לְיַֽעֲקֹב֙ פִּשְׁע֔וֹ וּלְיִשְׂרָאֵ֖ל חַטָּאתֽוֹ׃

8[11] But I truly am full of power by the spirit of the LORD, and of justice, and of might, to declare to Jacob his transgression, and to Israel his sin.

---

[1] Micah 3:1 - 1 Corinthians 6:5, 2 Chronicles 19:5-10, Amos 4:1, Deuteronomy 1:13-17 16:18, Hosea 5:1, Isaiah 1:10, Jeremiah 5:4-5 13:15-13:18 22:2-3, Micah 3:9-3:10, Psalms 14:4 82:1-5
Micah 3:1-12 - MurXII
[2] LXX *remnant*
[3] Micah 3:2 - 1 Kings 21:20 22:6-8, 2 Chronicles 19:2, 2 Timothy 3:3, Acts 7:51-52, Amos 5:10-14 8:4-6, Ezekiel 22:27 10:3, Isaiah 3:15, John 7:7 15:18-19 15:23-24 18:40, Luke 19:14, Mas.Soferim 7:2, Proverbs 4:4, Psalms 15:4 53:5 139:21-22, Romans 1:32 12:9, Sifre Devarim Vezot Habracha 342, Zechariah 11:4-5, Zephaniah 3:3
Micah 3:2-3 - Sifre Devarim Vezot Habracha 342
[4] Micah 3:3 - b.Berachot 56b, b.Ketubot 47b, Ezekiel 11:3 11:6-11:7, Jastrow 1509a, Mekhilta de R'Shimon bar Yochai Nezikin 60:4, Mekilta de R'Ishmael Nezikin 3:116, Psalms 14:4, Saadia Opinions 5:6, Sifre Devarim Vezot Habracha 342, Zephaniah 3:3
[5] Micah 3:4 - Deuteronomy 31:17-18 32:19-20, Ezekiel 8:18, Isaiah 1:15 3:11 59:1-15, James 2:13, Jeremiah 2:27-28 5:31 9:5, John 9:31, Luke 13:25, Matthew 7:22, Micah 2:3-4, Proverbs 1:28 4:9, Psalms 18:42, Romans 2:8-9, Saadia Opinions 5:6, Zechariah 7:13
[6] Micah 3:5 - Ezekiel 13:10-16 13:18-19 22:25-29, Isaiah 3:12 9:16-17 56:9-12, Jeremiah 6:14 14:14-15 23:9-17 23:27 23:32 28:15-17 29:21-23, Malachi 2:8, Mas.Kallah Rabbati 4:16, Matthew 7:15 15:14, Micah 2:11 3:11, Pesikta Rabbati 33:13, Romans 16:18, z.Vaetchanan 269b
Micah 3:5-6 - 8HevXIIgr
[7] 8HevXIIgr adds *to him*
[8] Micah 3:6 - Amos 8:9-10, Ezekiel 13:22-23, Isaiah 8:20-22 5:10 11:10, Jeremiah 13:16 15:9, Psalms 74:9, Saadia Opinions 7Variant:5, Zechariah 13:2-4
[9] Micah 3:7 - 1 Samuel 9:9 14:37 4:6 4:15, 2 Timothy 3:8-9, Amos 8:11, Daniel 2:9-11, Exodus 8:14-19 9:11, Ezekiel 24:17 24:22, Isaiah 20:25 47:12-14, Leviticus 13:45, Micah 7:16, Psalms 74:9, Zechariah 13:4
[10] LXX *adds of night visions*
[11] Micah 3:8 - 1 Corinthians 2:4 2:12-13, Acts 4:8-12 4:19-20 7:51-52 7:54-57 13:9-12 18:5-6 18:9-11, compare use of א in the word מלתי with Job 32:18, Ezekiel 3:14 16:2 20:4 22:2 19:10, Isaiah 11:2-3 10:1, Jeremiah 1:18 6:11 15:19-21 20:9, Job 8:18, Mark 3:17, Matthew 3:7-12 7:29

שִׁמְעוּ־נָא זֹאת רָאשֵׁי בֵּית יַעֲקֹב וּקְצִינֵי בֵּית יִשְׂרָאֵל הַמֲתַעֲבִים מִשְׁפָּט וְאֵת כָּל־הַיְשָׁרָה יְעַקֵּשׁוּ	9[1] Hear this, please, you heads of the house of Jacob, and *rulers*[2] of the house of Israel, who abhor justice, and pervert all equity;
בֹּנֶה צִיּוֹן בְּדָמִים וִירוּשָׁלַ͏ִם בְּעַוְלָה	10[3] Who build up Zion with blood, and Jerusalem with iniquity.
רָאשֶׁיהָ בְּשֹׁחַד יִשְׁפֹּטוּ וְכֹהֲנֶיהָ בִּמְחִיר יוֹרוּ וּנְבִיאֶיהָ בְּכֶסֶף יִקְסֹמוּ וְעַל־יְהוָה יִשָּׁעֵנוּ לֵאמֹר הֲלוֹא יְהוָה בְּקִרְבֵּנוּ לֹא־תָבוֹא עָלֵינוּ רָעָה	11[4] Their rulers judge for reward, and their priests teach for hire, And their prophets divine for money; Yet will they lean upon the LORD, and say: 'Is not the LORD in our midst? No evil shall come on us.'
לָכֵן בִּגְלַלְכֶם צִיּוֹן שָׂדֶה תֵחָרֵשׁ וִירוּשָׁלַ͏ִם עִיִּין תִּהְיֶה וְהַר הַבַּיִת לְבָמוֹת יָעַר	12[5] Therefore, for your sake, Zion shall be plowed as a field, and Jerusalem shall become heaps, and the mountain of the house as the high places of a forest.

Micah – Chapter 4

וְהָיָה בְּאַחֲרִית הַיָּמִים יִהְיֶה הַר בֵּית־יְהוָה נָכוֹן בְּרֹאשׁ הֶהָרִים וְנִשָּׂא הוּא מִגְּבָעוֹת וְנָהֲרוּ עָלָיו עַמִּים	1[6] But in the end of days it shall come to pass, the mountain of the LORD's house shall be established as the chief of the mountains, And it shall be exalted above the hills; and peoples shall flow to it.
וְהָלְכוּ גּוֹיִם רַבִּים וְאָמְרוּ לְכוּ וְנַעֲלֶה אֶל־הַר־יְהוָה וְאֶל־בֵּית אֱלֹהֵי יַעֲקֹב וְיוֹרֵנוּ מִדְּרָכָיו וְנֵלְכָה בְּאֹרְחֹתָיו כִּי מִצִּיּוֹן תֵּצֵא תוֹרָה וּדְבַר־יְהוָה מִירוּשָׁלָ͏ִם	2[7] And many nations shall go and say: 'Come and let us go up to the mountain of the LORD, and to the house of the God of Jacob; and He will teach us His ways, and we will walk in His paths;' **For out of Zion shall go forth the law, And the word of the LORD from Jerusalem.**
וְשָׁפַט בֵּין עַמִּים רַבִּים וְהוֹכִיחַ לְגוֹיִם עֲצֻמִים עַד־רָחוֹק וְכִתְּתוּ חַרְבֹתֵיהֶם לְאִתִּים וַחֲנִיתֹתֵיהֶם לְמַזְמֵרוֹת לֹא־יִשְׂאוּ גּוֹי אֶל־גּוֹי חֶרֶב וְלֹא־יִלְמְדוּן עוֹד מִלְחָמָה	3[8] And He shall judge between many peoples, And shall decide concerning mighty nations afar off; and they shall beat their swords into plowshares, and their spears into pruninghooks; nation shall not lift up sword against nation, nor shall they learn war any longer.

---

[1] Micah 3:9 - b.Shabbat 139a, Deuteronomy 3:19, Exodus 3:16, Hosea 5:1, Isaiah 1:23, Jeremiah 5:28, Leviticus 2:15, Micah 3:1, Proverbs 17:15, Psalms 58:2-3
Micah 3:9-11 - Ein Yaakov Shabbat:139a
[2] LXX *remnant*
[3] Micah 3:10 - b.Shabbat 139a, Ezekiel 22:25-28, Habakkuk 2:9-12, Jeremiah 22:13-17, John 11:50, Matthew 3:25, Zephaniah 3:3
[4] Micah 3:11 - 1 Peter 5:2, 1 Samuel 4:3-4:6 8:3 12:3-12:4, 1 Timothy 3:3, 2 Peter 2:1-2:3 2:14-2:15, Acts 8:18-8:20, Amos 9:10, b.Shabbat 139a, b.Yoma 9b, Ein Yaakov Yoma:9a, Ezekiel 22:12 22:27, Hosea 4:18, Isaiah 1:23 24:2 8:11, Jeremiah 6:13 7:4 7:8-7:12 8:10, Jude 1:11, Malachi 1:10, Matthew 3:9, Micah 3:5 7:3, Numbers 16:15, Numbers.R 10:3, Pesikta Rabbati 27/28:2 33:13, Romans 2:17-29, t.Demai 5:20, Testament of Levi 14:6, Titus 1:11, y.Demai 6:2, y.Kiddushin 2:9, y.Nedarim 11:3, Zephaniah 3:3
[5] Micah 3:12 - 4QXIIg, Acts 6:13-6:14, b.Makkot [Rashi] 24b, b.Shabbat 139a, b.Taanit [Rashi] 29a, b.Yoma 9b, Ecclesiastes.R 5:8, Ein Yaakov Makkot:24b, Ein Yaakov Yoma:9a, Genesis.R 22:7 65:23, Isaiah 2:2-2:3, Jastrow 1330b, Jeremiah 2:18, Lamentations.R Petichata D'Chakimei:24, Leviticus.R 22:2, Mas.Semachot 8:14, Matthew 24:2, Micah 1:6 4:1-4:2, Midrash Tanchuma Vayishlach 9, mt.Hilchot Taaniot 5:3, Numbers.R 7:10, Psalms 79:1 11:34, Sifre Devarim Vezot Habracha 352, Siman 121:5, Siman 121:5, t.Demai 5:20, Wars 7.2.1, y.Demai 6:2, y.Kiddushin 2:9, y.Nedarim 11:3, z.Vayakhel 218a
[6] Micah 4:1 - 2 Peter 3:3, Acts 2:17, Daniel 2:28 2:35 2:44 7:14 7:18 7:22 7:27 10:14, Ezekiel 17:22-17:24 14:16 16:2 19:12, Genesis 1:1 1:10, Hebrews 1:2, Hosea 3:5, Isaiah 2:1-2:4 11:9-10 3:13 19:6 1:6 49:19-49:23 6:2 60:3-60:14 66:18-23, Jeremiah 3:17 16:19 24:47, Malachi 1:11, Micah 3:12, Pesikta de R'Kahana 21.4, Psalms 22:28 68:16-17 68:30-33 72:7-11 72:16-19 86:9 14:3, Revelation 11:15 15:4 20:4 21:1-21:8, Romans 11:25-11:26, Zechariah 2:11 8:3 14:16-21, Zephaniah 3:9-10
Micah 4:1-14 - MurXII
[7] Micah 4:2 - Acts 1:8 10:32-33 13:42 13:46-47, b.Chullin 91b, Deuteronomy 6:1, Ein Yaakov Pesachim:88a, Hosea 6:3, Isaiah 2:3 42:1-4 51:4-5 6:13, James 1:19-25, Jeremiah 7:7 50:4-5, John 6:45 7:17, Luke 24:47, Mark 16:15-16 16:20, Matthew 11:25-30 28:19-20, Midrash Psalms 30:1, Psalms 25:8-9 25:12 14:2, Romans 10:12-18 15:19, Sibylline Oracles 3.718 3.772, Tanya Igeret Hakodesh §27, Zechariah 2:11 8:20-8:23 14:8-9 14:16
[8] Micah 4:3 - 1 Samuel 2:10, Acts 17:31, b.Shabbat 63a, Daniel 2:44, Hosea 2:18, Isaiah 2:4 9:8 11:3-9 1:3 3:5 12:12 60:17-18 17:25, Joel 4:2 4:9-16, John 5:22-23 5:27-29 16:8-11, Matthew 25:31-32, Micah 5:16 7:16-17, mt.Perek Chelek Intro:11, Psalms 2:5-12 46:10 68:31-32 72:7 82:8 96:13 98:9 110:1-2 110:5-6, Revelation 19:11 19:17-21 20:8-9, Zechariah 9:10 12:3-6 14:3 14:12-19
Micah 4:3-10 - 8HevXIIgr

וְיָשְׁבוּ אִישׁ תַּחַת גַּפְנוֹ וְתַחַת תְּאֵנָתוֹ וְאֵין מַחֲרִיד
כִּי־פִי יְהוָה צְבָאוֹת דִּבֵּר

4[1]

But every man shall sit under his vine and under his fig tree; and no one shall make them afraid; for the mouth of the LORD of hosts has spoken.

כִּי כָּל־הָעַמִּים יֵלְכוּ אִישׁ בְּשֵׁם אֱלֹהָיו וַאֲנַחְנוּ נֵלֵךְ
בְּשֵׁם־יְהוָה אֱלֹהֵינוּ לְעוֹלָם וָעֶד

5[2]

For all the peoples shall walk in the name of its god, but we will walk in the name of the LORD our God forever and ever.

בַּיּוֹם הַהוּא נְאֻם־יְהוָה אֹסְפָה הַצֹּלֵעָה וְהַנִּדָּחָה
אֲקַבֵּצָה וַאֲשֶׁר הֲרֵעֹתִי

6[3]

In that day, says the LORD, will I assemble her who limps, and I will gather her who is driven away, And her whom I have afflicted;

וְשַׂמְתִּי אֶת־הַצֹּלֵעָה לִשְׁאֵרִית וְהַנַּהֲלָאָה לְגוֹי
עָצוּם וּמָלַךְ יְהוָה עֲלֵיהֶם בְּהַר צִיּוֹן מֵעַתָּה וְעַד־
עוֹלָם

7[4]

And I will make her who limps a remnant, and her who was cast far off a mighty nation; and the LORD shall reign over them in mount Zion from then and forever.

וְאַתָּה מִגְדַּל־עֵדֶר עֹפֶל בַּת־צִיּוֹן עָדֶיךָ תֵּאתֶה
וּבָאָה הַמֶּמְשָׁלָה הָרִאשֹׁנָה מַמְלֶכֶת לְבַת־יְרוּשָׁלָ͏ִם

8[5]

And you, *Migdal-eder, the hill of the*[6] daughter of Zion, to you shall it come; yes, the former dominion shall come, the kingdom of the daughter of Jerusalem.

עַתָּה לָמָּה תָרִיעִי רֵעַ הֲמֶלֶךְ אֵין־בָּךְ אִם־יוֹעֲצֵךְ
אָבָד כִּי־הֶחֱזִיקֵךְ חִיל כַּיּוֹלֵדָה

9[7]

Now, why do you cry out aloud? is there no King in you, has your Counselor died, have the pangs of a woman in labor taken hold of you?

חוּלִי וָגֹחִי בַּת־צִיּוֹן כַּיּוֹלֵדָה כִּי־עַתָּה תֵצְאִי מִקִּרְיָה
וְשָׁכַנְתְּ בַּשָּׂדֶה וּבָאת עַד־בָּבֶל שָׁם תִּנָּצֵלִי שָׁם
יִגְאָלֵךְ יְהוָה מִכַּף אֹיְבָיִךְ

10[8]

Be in pain, and labor to give birth, O daughter of Zion, like a woman in labor; for now you shall go forth out of the city, and shall dwell in the field, And shall come to Babylon; There you shall be rescued; There the LORD shall redeem you from the hand of your enemies.

וְעַתָּה נֶאֶסְפוּ עָלַיִךְ גּוֹיִם רַבִּים הָאֹמְרִים תֶּחֱנָף
וְתַחַז בְּצִיּוֹן עֵינֵינוּ

11[9]

And now many nations have assembled against you, who say: 'Let her be defiled, and let our eyes gaze upon Zion.'

וְהֵמָּה לֹא יָדְעוּ מַחְשְׁבוֹת יְהוָה וְלֹא הֵבִינוּ עֲצָתוֹ
כִּי קִבְּצָם כֶּעָמִיר גֹּרְנָה

12[10]

But they do not know the thoughts of the LORD, nor do they understand His counsel; for He has gathered them as the sheaves to the threshing floor.

קוּמִי וָדוֹשִׁי בַת־צִיּוֹן כִּי־קַרְנֵךְ אָשִׂים בַּרְזֶל
וּפַרְסֹתַיִךְ אָשִׂים נְחוּשָׁה וַהֲדִקּוֹת עַמִּים רַבִּים
וְהַחֲרַמְתִּי לַיהוָה בִּצְעָם וְחֵילָם לַאֲדוֹן כָּל־הָאָרֶץ

13[11]

Arise and thresh, O daughter of Zion; for I will make your horn iron, and I will make your hooves brass; and you shall beat in pieces many

---

[1] Micah 4:4 - 1 Kings 4:25, Ezekiel 10:25 10:28 14:11 15:26, Isaiah 1:20 2:16 16:5 6:14 10:14, Jeremiah 23:5-23:6, Leviticus 2:6, Mekilta de R'Ishmael Pisha 12:36, Zechariah 3:10

[2] Micah 4:5 - 2 Kings 17:29 17:34, Colossians 2:6 3:17, Exodus 3:14-15, Exodus.R 15:15, Genesis 17:1, Isaiah 2:5 2:8, Jeremiah 2:10-11, Joshua 24:15, Midrash Psalms 1:20, Psalms 48:15 71:16 145:1-2, Song of Songs.R 2:3, Tefillat Haderech, Upon leaving the synagogue, z.Shemot 17a, z.Vayishlach 177b, Zechariah 10:12

[3] Micah 4:6 - b.Berachot 32a, b.Succah 52b, Ein Yaakov Berachot:32a, Exodus.R 46:4, Ezekiel 34:12-17 12:24 37:21-22 39:25-29, Hebrews 12:12-13, Isaiah 35:3-6 8:8, Jeremiah 3:18 30:17-18 7:9, John 10:16, Luke 19:10, Micah 2:12, Psalms 38:18 3:2, y.Taanit 3:4, Zephaniah 3:19

[4] Micah 4:7 - Daniel 7:14 7:27, Hosea 2:1, Isaiah 6:13 9:7-8 10:21-22 11:11-16 24:23 49:21-23 12:22 18:8, Joel 4:17, Luke 1:33, Micah 2:12 5:4 5:8-9 7:18, Psalms 2:6, Revelation 11:15, Romans 11:5-6 11:25-27, Zechariah 9:1317 10:5-12

[5] Micah 4:8 - 2 Samuel 5:7, Daniel 2:44 7:18, Ephesians 1:21, Genesis 11:21, Isaiah 1:26 5:2 10:32, Mark 12:1, Matthew 21:33, Numbers 24:19, Obadiah 1:21, Psalms 48:13-14, Revelation 22:5, Zechariah 9:10 9:12

[6] LXX *dark tower of the flock*

[7] Micah 4:9 - Hosea 3:4 10:3 13:10-11, Isaiah 3:1-7 13:8 21:3 2:17, Jeremiah 4:21 8:19 22:23 30:6-7 2:43, Lamentations 4:20

[8] Micah 4:10 - 2 Chronicles 9:11 12:20, 2 Kings 20:18 1:4, Ezra 1:1-2, Hosea 2:1 2:14 13:13, Isaiah 19:14 21:13 24:20 52:9-12 66:7-9, Jeremiah 15:21, John 16:20-22, Micah 7:8-13, Midrash Psalms 5:7 11:3, Midrash Tanchuma Noach 3, Midrash Tanchuma Vayishlach 9, Pesikta de R'Kahana S2.7, Psalms 10:10, Revelation 12:14, y.Sukkah 4:3, Zechariah 2:7-9

[9] Micah 4:11 - Guide for the Perplexed 1:4, Isaiah 5:25-30 8:7-8, Jeremiah 4:4, Joel 4:2-15, Lamentations 2:15-16, Micah 7:10, Midrash Psalms 118:12, Obadiah 1:12

[10] Micah 4:12 - b.Bava Metzia 89b, Genesis.R 42:2, Isaiah 21:10 7:8, Jeremiah 5:11, Joel 4:12-13, Luke 3:17, Revelation 14:14-20, Romans 11:33-34, Saadia Opinions 3:4, Zechariah 14:1-3

[11] Micah 4:13 - 1 Corinthians 16:2, 1QSb 5.26, 2 Samuel 8:10-11, b.Eruvin 101a, Daniel 2:44, Deuteronomy 9:25, Isaiah 5:28 18:7 23:18 41:15-16 60:6-9, Jastrow 426b, Jeremiah 3:33, Joshua 6:19, Micah 5:9-16, Midrash Psalms 62:1, Psalms 68:30 72:10, Revelation 2:26-27 21:24-26, Romans 15:25-15:28, Zechariah 4:14 6:5 9:13-15

peoples; and you shall devote their gain to the
LORD, and their substance to the Lord of the
whole earth.

עַתָּה תִּתְגֹּדְדִי בַת־גְּדוּד מָצוֹר שָׂם עָלֵינוּ בַּשֵּׁבֶט   14[1]   *Now you shall gather yourself in troops, O
יַכּוּ עַל־הַלְּחִי אֵת שֹׁפֵט יִשְׂרָאֵל   daughter of troops*[2]; they laid siege against us;
They strike the judge of Israel with a rod on the
cheek.

Micah – Chapter 5

וְאַתָּה בֵּית־לֶחֶם אֶפְרָתָה צָעִיר לִהְיוֹת בְּאַלְפֵי   1[3]   But you, Bethlehem Ephrathah, who are little
יְהוּדָה מִמְּךָ לִי יֵצֵא לִהְיוֹת מוֹשֵׁל בְּיִשְׂרָאֵל   to be among the thousands of Judah, Out of you
וּמוֹצָאֹתָיו מִקֶּדֶם מִימֵי עוֹלָם   one *shall come forth*[4] to Me who is to be ruler
in Israel; whose goings forth are from of old,
from ancient days.

לָכֵן יִתְּנֵם עַד־עֵת יוֹלֵדָה יָלָדָה וְיֶתֶר אֶחָיו יְשׁוּבוּן   2[5]   Therefore, will He give them up, until the time
עַל־בְּנֵי יִשְׂרָאֵל   when she who labor has given birth; then the
residue of his brethren shall return with the
children of Israel.

וְעָמַד וְרָעָה בְּעֹז יְהוָה בִּגְאוֹן שֵׁם יְהוָה אֱלֹהָיו   3[6]   And he shall stand, and shall feed his flock in
וְיָשָׁבוּ כִּי־עַתָּה יִגְדַּל עַד־אַפְסֵי־אָרֶץ   the strength of the LORD, in the majesty of the
name of the LORD his God; and they shall
abide, for then shall he be great to the ends of
the earth.

וְהָיָה זֶה שָׁלוֹם אַשּׁוּר כִּי־יָבוֹא בְאַרְצֵנוּ וְכִי יִדְרֹךְ   4[7]   And this shall be peace: when the Assyrian
בְּאַרְמְנֹתֵינוּ וַהֲקֵמֹנוּ עָלָיו שִׁבְעָה רֹעִים וּשְׁמֹנָה   come to our land, and when he treads in our
נְסִיכֵי אָדָם   palaces, then we shall raise against him seven
shepherds and eight princes among men.

וְרָעוּ אֶת־אֶרֶץ אַשּׁוּר בַּחֶרֶב וְאֶת־אֶרֶץ נִמְרֹד   5[8]   And they shall waste the land of Assyria with
בִּפְתָחֶיהָ וְהִצִּיל מֵאַשּׁוּר כִּי־יָבוֹא בְאַרְצֵנוּ וְכִי   the sword, and the land of Nimrod with the
יִדְרֹךְ בִּגְבוּלֵנוּ   keen-edged sword; and he shall deliver us from
the Assyrian, when he comes into our land, and
when he treads within our border.

---

[1] Micah 4:14 - 1 Kings 22:24, 1 Samuel 8:5-6, 2 Corinthians 11:20, 2 Kings 24:2 25:1-3, Acts 23:2, Amos 2:3, Deuteronomy 4:49
28:51-57, Ezekiel 21:26-27 24:2, Habakkuk 1:6 3:16, Isaiah 8:9 10:6 9:22, Jeremiah 4:7 1:9, Job 16:10, Joel 4:9, John 18:22 19:3,
Lamentations 3:30, Lamentations.R 1:25, Leviticus.R 10:2, Luke 19:43-44, Matthew 5:39 26:67 3:30, Pesikta de R'Kahana 16.4,
Pesikta Rabbati 29/30A:5
[2] LXX *Now shall the daughter of Sion is completely hedged in*
[3] Micah 5:1 - 1 Chronicles 2:50-2:51 2:54 4:4 5:2, 1 Corinthians 1:27-1:28, 1 John 1:1, 1 Samuel 8:12 10:19 17:12 17:18 23:23, Amos
9:11, Colossians 1:17, Deuteronomy 1:15, Exodus 18:21 18:25, Ezekiel 17:22-17:24 34:23-34:24 37:22-37:25, Genesis 11:19 24:7
1:10, Hebrews 7:14 13:8, Isaiah 9:7-9:8 11:1 5:2, Jeremiah 13:5-13:6 6:21, John 1:1-1:3 7:42 19:14-19:22, Luke 1:31-1:33 2:4-2:7
23:2 23:38, Matthew 2:6 4:18, MurXII, Proverbs 8:22-8:23, Psalms 90:2 102:26-102:28 12:6, Revelation 1:11-1:18 2:8 19:16 21:6,
Ruth 4:11, Sibylline Oracles 8.479, Sifre Devarim Vezot Habracha 352, t.Bava Kamma 9:31, Zechariah 9:9
Micah 5:1-2 - 4QXIIf
Micah 5:1-6 - 8HevXIIgr
[4] 4QXIIf *one who shall not come forth*
[5] Micah 5:2 - 1 Kings 14:16, 2 Chronicles 6:7, b.Sanhedrin 98b, b.Yoma 10a, Ein Yaakov Sanhedrin:98b, Hebrews 1:11-12, Hosea 2:9
2:14 11:8, Isaiah 10:20-21 11:11 66:7-8, Jeremiah 7:2 31:8-10, Matthew 1:21 12:50 1:40, Micah 4:7 4:9-10 6:14 7:13, Midrash Psalms
8:1, Pirkei de R'Eliezer 3, Revelation 12:1-2, Romans 8:29 9:27-28 11:4-6, Song of Songs.R 8:19, t.Sotah 11:13
[6] Micah 5:3 - 1 Chronicles 29:11-12, 1 Peter 1:5, Ephesians 1:3, Exodus 23:21, Ezekiel 34:13-15 34:22-24, Isaiah 40:10-11 1:5 49:9-
10 4:10 4:13, John 5:22-29 10:27-30 10:38 14:9-11 20:17, Jude 1:1, Luke 1:32, Matthew 2:6 16:18 1:31, Micah 7:14, Midrash Psalms
21:2, Psalms 22:28 23:1-2 45:4-7 72:8 72:19 93:1 98:3 1:12, Revelation 1:13-18 11:15, Zechariah 9:10
[7] Micah 5:4 - Amos 1:3 1:6, b.Succah 52b, Colossians 1:20-21, Ecclesiastes 11:2, Ein Yaakov Sukkah 52b, Ephesians 2:14-17,
Esther.R 1:18, Isaiah 7:14 8:7-10 9:7-8 10:24-27 37:31-36 20:28 11:19 17:8, Jeremiah 9:15, Job 5:19, John 14:27 16:33,
Lamentations.R 1:41, Luke 2:14, Mas.Kallah Rabbati 7:1, Midrash Psalms 2:8, Numbers.R 14:1, Proverbs 6:16 6:18 6:29, Psalms
72:7, Revelation 17:14 19:14, Saadia Opinions 7:6 7Variant:7, Song of Songs.R 8:13, Zechariah 1:18-21 9:10 9:13 10:3 12:6
[8] Micah 5:5 - 2 Chronicles 9:11, 2 Kings 15:29 17:3-5 18:9-15 19:32-35, Genesis 10:8-10:11, Isaiah 10:5-12 14:2 14:25 9:1, Luke
1:71 1:74, Nahum 2:12-4, Zephaniah 2:13
Micah 5:5-14 - MurXII

וְהָיָ֣ה ׀ שְׁאֵרִ֣ית יַעֲקֹ֗ב בְּקֶ֙רֶב֙ עַמִּ֣ים רַבִּ֔ים כְּטַל֙ מֵאֵ֣ת יְהֹוָ֔ה כִּרְבִיבִ֖ים עֲלֵי־עֵ֑שֶׂב אֲשֶׁ֤ר לֹֽא־יְקַוֶּה֙ לְאִ֔ישׁ וְלֹ֥א יְיַחֵ֖ל לִבְנֵ֥י אָדָֽם 6[1]

And the remnant of Jacob shall be in the midst of many peoples, as dew from the LORD, as showers on the grass, that no man notices, nor expected for the hands of the sons of men.

וְהָיָה֩ שְׁאֵרִ֨ית יַעֲקֹ֜ב בַּגּוֹיִ֗ם בְּקֶ֙רֶב֙ עַמִּ֣ים רַבִּ֔ים כְּאַרְיֵה֙ בְּבַהֲמ֣וֹת יַ֔עַר כִּכְפִ֖יר בְּעֶדְרֵי־צֹ֑אן אֲשֶׁ֧ר אִם־עָבַ֛ר וְרָמַ֥ס וְטָרַ֖ף וְאֵ֥ין מַצִּֽיל 7[2]

And the remnant of Jacob shall be among the nations, in the midst of many peoples, as a lion among the beasts of the forest, As a young lion among the flocks of sheep, who, if he passes through, chases down and tears in pieces, and there is no one to deliver.

תָּרֹ֥ם יָדְךָ֖ עַל־צָרֶ֑יךָ וְכָל־אֹיְבֶ֖יךָ יִכָּרֵֽתוּ 8[3]

Let Your hand be lifted up above your adversaries, and let your enemies be cut off.

וְהָיָ֤ה בַיּוֹם־הַהוּא֙ נְאֻם־יְהֹוָ֔ה וְהִכְרַתִּ֥י סוּסֶ֖יךָ מִקִּרְבֶּ֑ךָ וְהַאֲבַדְתִּ֖י מַרְכְּבֹתֶֽיךָ 9[4]

And it shall come to pass in that day, says the LORD, that I will cut off your horses from your midst, and will destroy your chariots;

וְהִכְרַתִּ֖י עָרֵ֣י אַרְצֶ֑ךָ וְהָרַסְתִּ֖י כָּל־מִבְצָרֶֽיךָ 10[5]

And I will cut off the cities of your land, and will throw down all your strongholds;

וְהִכְרַתִּ֥י כְשָׁפִ֖ים מִיָּדֶ֑ךָ וּמְעוֹנְנִ֖ים לֹ֥א יִֽהְיוּ־לָֽךְ 11[6]

And I will cut off witchcrafts from your hand; and you shall not have soothsayers any longer;

וְהִכְרַתִּ֧י פְסִילֶ֛יךָ וּמַצֵּבוֹתֶ֖יךָ מִקִּרְבֶּ֑ךָ וְלֹא־תִשְׁתַּחֲוֶ֥ה ע֖וֹד לְמַעֲשֵׂ֥ה יָדֶֽיךָ 12[7]

And I will cut off your graven images and your pillars from your midst; and you shall not worship the work of your hands any longer.

וְנָתַשְׁתִּ֥י אֲשֵׁירֶ֖יךָ מִקִּרְבֶּ֑ךָ וְהִשְׁמַדְתִּ֖י עָרֶֽיךָ 13[8]

And I will pluck up your Asherim from your midst; and I will destroy your *enemies*[9].

וְעָשִׂ֜יתִי בְּאַ֧ף וּבְחֵמָ֛ה נָקָ֖ם אֶת־הַגּוֹיִ֑ם אֲשֶׁ֖ר לֹ֥א שָׁמֵֽעוּ 14[10]

And I will execute vengeance in anger and fury on the nations, because they have not listened.

Micah – Chapter 6

שִׁמְעוּ־נָ֕א אֵ֥ת אֲשֶׁר־יְהֹוָ֖ה אֹמֵ֑ר ק֚וּם רִ֣יב אֶת־הֶֽהָרִ֔ים וְתִשְׁמַ֖עְנָה הַגְּבָע֥וֹת קוֹלֶֽךָ 1[11]

Hear now what the LORD says: Arise, contend before the mountains, And let the hills hear your voice.

שִׁמְע֤וּ הָרִים֙ אֶת־רִ֣יב יְהֹוָ֔ה וְהָאֵתָנִ֖ים מֹ֣סְדֵי אָ֑רֶץ כִּ֣י רִ֤יב לַֽיהֹוָה֙ עִם־עַמּ֔וֹ וְעִם־יִשְׂרָאֵ֖ל יִתְוַכָּֽח 2[12]

Hear, O mountains, the LORD's controversy, and you enduring rocks, the foundations of the

---

[1] Micah 5:6 - 1 Corinthians 3:6, Acts 9:15 11:15 13:46 16:9, Amos 5:15, Deuteronomy 8:2, Esther.R Petichata:11, Exodus.R 25:1, Ezekiel 14:22 23:1, Genesis.R 75:8, Hosea 6:3 14:7, Isaiah 8:15 20:3 7:10 18:19, Jastrow 1509b, Jeremiah 14:22, Joel 3:5, Judges 6:36, Leviticus.R 11:7, Matthew 4:19, Micah 2:12 5:4 5:9, Midrash Tanchuma Shemini 9, Psalms 72:6 14:3, Romans 9:30 10:20 11:5-6 11:12 15:19-20, Sifre Devarim Ekev 39, y.Berachot 5:2, y.Taanit 1:1, z.Mikketz 203b, z.Toledot 146b, Zechariah 14:8, Zephaniah 3:13

Micah 5:6-6:8 - Haftarah Balak, Haftarah Balak [Micah 5:6-6:8]
Micah 5:6-7 - 4QXIIg

[2] Micah 5:7 - 2 Corinthians 2:15-17, Acts 18:6, Esther.R 10:11, Genesis 1:9, Hebrews 2:3 12:25, Hosea 5:14, Isaiah 41:15-16, Matthew 10:14, Micah 4:13, Obadiah 1:18-19, Psalms 2:8-12 50:22 110:5-110:6, Zechariah 9:15 10:5 12:3

[3] Micah 5:8 - 1 Corinthians 15:25, Isaiah 1:25 11:14 14:2-4 2:11 9:10 13:36, Luke 19:27, Psalms 10:13 21:9 10:26, Revelation 19:13-21 20:8-9

[4] Micah 5:9 - Hosea 1:7 14:5, Isaiah 2:7, Jeremiah 3:23, Mas.Kallah Rabbati 8:9, Pirkei de R'Eliezer 48, Psalms 20:8-9 33:16-17, Zechariah 9:10

[5] Micah 5:10 - Amos 5:9, Ezekiel 14:11, Hosea 10:14, Isaiah 2:12-17 6:11, Zechariah 4:6

[6] Micah 5:11 - Deuteronomy 18:10-12, Isaiah 2:6-8 2:18 2:20 8:19-20 3:9, Revelation 19:20 22:15, Zechariah 13:2-4

[7] Micah 5:12 - Ezekiel 6:9 12:25 13:23, Hosea 2:16-19 14:5 14:10, Isaiah 2:8 17:7-8, Zechariah 13:2

[8] Micah 5:13 - Exodus 10:13, m.Avodah Zarah 3:5

[9] LXX *cities*

[10] Micah 5:14 - 2 Thessalonians 1:8, Isaiah 17:12, Micah 5:9, Midrash Psalms 6:3 149:2, Midrash Tanchuma Vezot Habracha 4, Pesikta de R'Kahana S1.15, Psalms 5:7, Sifre Devarim Vezot Habracha 343, Tanna Devei Eliyahu 1

[11] Micah 6:1 - 1 Samuel 15:16, Amos 3:1, Deuteronomy 4:26 8:1, Ezekiel 12:1 12:8 13:4, Genesis.R 84:10, Hebrews 3:7-3:8, Isaiah 1:2 2:12-2:14, Jeremiah 13:15 22:29, Luke 19:40, Micah 1:2 1:4, Psalms 50:1 50:4

Micah 6:1-897 - MurXII

[12] Micah 6:2 - 2 Samuel 22:8 22:16, Apocalypse of Elijah 5:25, b.Rosh Hashanah 11a, b.Sotah 46b, Deuteronomy 8:22, Ein Yaakov Rosh Hashanah:10b, Exodus.R 15:4 15:7 15:26 28:2, Ezekiel 20:35-36, Genesis.R 50:11, Hosea 4:1 12:4, Isaiah 1:18 5:3 19:26, Jastrow 365a, Jeremiah 2:9 2:29-35 1:31 7:38, Leviticus.R 27:6, Midrash Tanchuma Balak 12, Midrash Tanchuma Bechukkotai 5, Midrash Tanchuma Emor 5 10, Midrash Tanchuma Ki Tissa 28, Numbers.R 10:1, Pesikta de R'Kahana 9.5 S5.2, Proverbs 8:29, Psalms 8:5, Sifre Devarim Ha'azinu Hashamayim 306, Sifre Devarim Nitzavim 306, Song of Songs.R 6:2

earth; for the LORD has a controversy with His people, and He will plead with Israel.

3[1] עַמִּי מֶה־עָשִׂיתִי לְךָ וּמָה הֶלְאֵתִיךָ עֲנֵה בִּי

O My people, what have I done to you? *And how have I wearied you? Testify against Me*[2].

4[3] כִּי הֶעֱלִתִיךָ מֵאֶרֶץ מִצְרַיִם וּמִבֵּית עֲבָדִים פְּדִיתִיךָ וָאֶשְׁלַח לְפָנֶיךָ אֶת־מֹשֶׁה אַהֲרֹן וּמִרְיָם

For I brought you up out of the land of Egypt, and redeemed you from the house of bondage, and I sent before you Moses, Aaron, and Miriam.

5[4] עַמִּי זְכָר־נָא מַה־יָּעַץ בָּלָק מֶלֶךְ מוֹאָב וּמֶה־עָנָה אֹתוֹ בִּלְעָם בֶּן־בְּעוֹר מִן־הַשִּׁטִּים עַד־הַגִּלְגָּל לְמַעַן דַּעַת צִדְקוֹת יְהוָה

O My people, remember what Balak king of Moab devised, and what Balaam the son of Beor answered him; from *Shittim*[5] to Gilgal, so you may know the righteous acts of the LORD.

6[6] בַּמָּה אֲקַדֵּם יְהוָה אִכַּף לֵאלֹהֵי מָרוֹם הַאֲקַדְּמֶנּוּ בְעוֹלוֹת בַּעֲגָלִים בְּנֵי שָׁנָה

How shall I come before the LORD, and bow myself before God on high? Shall I come before Him with burnt offerings, with calves in their first year?

7[7] הֲיִרְצֶה יְהוָה בְּאַלְפֵי אֵילִים בְּרִבְבוֹת נַחֲלֵי־שָׁמֶן הַאֶתֵּן בְּכוֹרִי פִּשְׁעִי פְּרִי בִטְנִי חַטַּאת נַפְשִׁי

Will the LORD be pleased with thousands of rams, with ten thousands of rivers of oil? Shall I give my firstborn for my transgression, the fruit of my body for the sin of my soul?'

8[8] הִגִּיד לְךָ אָדָם מַה־טּוֹב וּמָה־יְהוָה דּוֹרֵשׁ מִמְּךָ כִּי אִם־עֲשׂוֹת מִשְׁפָּט וְאַהֲבַת חֶסֶד וְהַצְנֵעַ לֶכֶת עִם־אֱלֹהֶיךָ

It has been told, O man, what is good, And what the LORD requires of you: only to do justly, and to love mercy, and *to walk humbly with*[9] your God.

[1] Micah 6:3 - Guide for the Perplexed 3:47, Isaiah 43:22-23, Jeremiah 2:5 2:31, Leviticus.R 27:6 27:6, Micah 6:5, Midrash Tanchuma Emor 10, Numbers.R 10:1 20:5, Pesikta de R'Kahana 9.5, Pesikta Rabbati 48:3, Psalms 50:7 51:5 81:9 81:14, Romans 3:4-5 3:19, Saadia Opinions 4:3, Sifre.z Numbers Beha'alotcha 11:1, Song of Songs.R 6:2, z.Balak 203b, z.Bechukkotai 112a

[2] LXX *or when have I grieved you? or when have I troubled you? answer me*

[3] Micah 6:4 - 2 Samuel 7:23, Acts 7:36, Amos 2:10, Deuteronomy 4:20 4:34 5:6 7:8 9:26 15:15 24:18, Exodus 4:16 12:51 14:30-31 15:20-15:21 20:2, Exodus.R 15:14, Ezekiel 20:5-9, Isaiah 63:9-12, Jeremiah 8:21, Midrash Tanchuma Bamidbar 2, Midrash Tanchuma Terumah 10, Nehemiah 9:9-11, Numbers 12:1, Numbers.R 1:2 13:20, Psalms 77:21 78:51-53 106:7-10 136:10-11, Sifre Devarim Ki Tetze 275, z.Ki Tissa 190a

[4] Micah 6:5 - 1 John 1:9, 1 Samuel 12:7, 2 Peter 2:15, b.Avodah Zara 42ab, b.Berachot 7a, b.Sanhedrin 105b, Deuteronomy 8:2 8:18 9:7 16:3 23:6, Ein Yaakov Berachot:7a, Ephesians 2:11, Genesis.R 41:3, Joshua 4:19 5:9-10 10:42-43 24:9-10, Jude 1:11, Judges 5:11, Lamentations.R 1:38, Leviticus.R 4:1 24:1, Midrash Tanchuma Emor 10, Numbers 22:1-25 22:41 23:13-14 23:27 1:1 7:8 7:16 9:49, Numbers.R 20:6, Pesikta Rabbati 47:4, Psalms 36:11 71:15-16 71:19 103:1-2 15:4 23:11, Revelation 2:14, Romans 3:25-26, Sifre Devarim Ki Tetze 250, Sifre.z Numbers Beha'alotcha 11:1, western wrote מה "what" and Eastern wrote מי "who" [j.Megillah 1:9], z.Bechukkotai 112a

[5] LXX *the reeds*

[6] Micah 6:6 - 2 Samuel 21:3, Acts 2:37 16:17 16:30, Daniel 3:26 4:6 5:18 5:21, Ephesians 3:14, Exodus 12:5, Gates of Repentance 1.25, Genesis 14:18-22, Genesis.R 55:5, Hebrews 10:4-10, John 6:26, Leviticus 1:3-17, Luke 10:25, Mark 5:7, Matthew 19:16, Midrash Tanchuma Bechukkotai 6, Numbers 23:1-4 23:14-15 23:29-30, Psalms 22:30 40:7-40:9 51:17-18 95:6, Romans 10:2-3
Micah 6:6-7 - Gates of Repentance 1.025
Micah 6:6-8 - 2 Enoch 45:3

[7] Micah 6:7 - 1 Samuel 15:22, 2 Kings 3:27 16:3 21:6 23:10, Amos 5:22, Ezekiel 16:20-16:21 23:37, Gates of Repentance 1.025, Hosea 6:6, Isaiah 1:11-1:15 16:16, Jeremiah 7:21-7:22 7:31 19:5, Job 5:6, Judges 11:31 11:39, Leviticus 18:21, Midrash Tanchuma Bechukkotai 6, Midrash Tanchuma Tzav 1, Pesikta Rabbati 48:1, Philemon 1:12, Psalms 10:9-10:14 50:9 51:17

[8] Micah 6:8 - 1 Corinthians 7:16, 1 Peter 3:8 5:5-6, 1 Samuel 12:23 15:22, 2 Chronicles 6:11 8:26 33:12-13 9:19 9:23 10:27, 2 Peter 1:5-8, 2 Thessalonians 2:16, Amos 5:24, b.Makkot 24b, b.Succah 49b, Colossians 3:12, Daniel 4:34, Deuteronomy 10:12-13, Ecclesiastes 12:13, Ein Yaakov Makkot 24a, Ein Yaakov Sukkah 49a, Ephesians 4:32, Ezekiel 16:63, Gates of Repentance 3.13, Genesis 5:22 18:19, Hosea 6:6 12:8, Isaiah 1:16-19 57:1-2 9:15 58:6-11 18:2, James 2:20 4:6-10, Jeremiah 7:3-6 22:3, Kuzari 2.47-48, Lamentations 3:26, Leviticus 2:41, Luke 6:36 10:42 11:42 18:13-17, Mark 12:30-34, Matthew 3:8-10 5:3 5:7 18:32-35, Mesillat Yesharim 20:Weighing Implementation of Chassidus, Midrash Psalms 17A:22, Midrash Tanchuma Bamidbar 3, Midrash Tanchuma Ki Tissa 31, Midrash Tanchuma Shoftim 9, Nehemiah 9:13, Numbers.R 1:3, Pesikta Rabbati 45:1, Proverbs 21:3, Psalms 37:26 73:28 16:4 16:9, Romans 7:16 9:20 10:1-3, Siman 150:5 3:1, Tanya Igeret Hakodesh §13 §26, Titus 2:11-12, Zephaniah 2:3

[9] LXX *be ready to walk with the LORD*

קוֹל יְהוָה לָעִיר יִקְרָא וְתוּשִׁיָּה יִרְאֶה שְׁמֶךָ שִׁמְעוּ מַטֶּה וּמִי יְעָדָהּ 9[1]

Hear! The LORD cries to the city, And it is wisdom to have regard for Your name. Hear the rod, and who has appointed it[2].

עוֹד הַאִשׁ בֵּית רָשָׁע אֹצְרוֹת רֶשַׁע וְאֵיפַת רָזוֹן זְעוּמָה 10[3]

Are there yet the treasures of wickedness in the house of the wicked, And the scant measure that is abominable[4]?

הַאֶזְכֶּה בְּמֹאזְנֵי רֶשַׁע וּבְכִיס אַבְנֵי מִרְמָה 11[5]

'Shall I be pure with wicked balances, and with a bag of deceitful weights?'

אֲשֶׁר עֲשִׁירֶיהָ מָלְאוּ חָמָס וְיֹשְׁבֶיהָ דִּבְּרוּ־שָׁקֶר וּלְשׁוֹנָם רְמִיָּה בְּפִיהֶם 12[6]

For its rich men are full of violence, and its inhabitants have spoken lies, and their tongues are deceitful in their mouth.

וְגַם־אֲנִי הֶחֱלֵיתִי הַכּוֹתֶךָ הַשְׁמֵם עַל־חַטֹּאתֶךָ 13[7]

Therefore, I will strike you with a grievous wound; I will make you desolate because of your sins[8].

אַתָּה תֹאכַל וְלֹא תִשְׂבָּע וְיֶשְׁחֲךָ בְּקִרְבֶּךָ וְתַסֵּג וְלֹא תַפְלִיט וַאֲשֶׁר תְּפַלֵּט לַחֶרֶב אֶתֵּן 14[9]

You shall eat, but not be satisfied; and your sickness shall be in your inward parts; and you shall conceive, but shall not bring birth; and whomever you birth I will give to the sword.

אַתָּה תִזְרַע וְלֹא תִקְצוֹר אַתָּה תִדְרֹךְ־זַיִת וְלֹא־תָסוּךְ שֶׁמֶן וְתִירוֹשׁ וְלֹא תִשְׁתֶּה־יָּיִן 15[10]

You shall sow, but shall not reap; you shall tread the olives, but shall not anoint yourself with oil; and you will press grapes, but shall not drink wine[11].

וְיִשְׁתַּמֵּר חֻקּוֹת עָמְרִי וְכֹל מַעֲשֵׂה בֵית־אַחְאָב וַתֵּלְכוּ בְּמֹעֲצוֹתָם לְמַעַן תִּתִּי אֹתְךָ לְשַׁמָּה וְיֹשְׁבֶיהָ לִשְׁרֵקָה וְחֶרְפַּת עַמִּי תִּשָּׂאוּ 16[12]

For the statutes of *Omri*[13] are kept, and all the works of the house of Ahab, and you walk in their counsels; so I may make you an astonishment, And its inhabitants a hissing; and you shall bear the reproach of My people.

---

[1] Micah 6:9 - 2 Kings 22:11-20, 2 Samuel 21:1, Amos 2:5 3:8-15 4:6-12 6:1, Avot de R'Natan 34, b.Rosh Hashanah 31a, Ein Yaakov Rosh Hashanah 31a, Exodus 34:5-7, Haggai 1:5-7, Hosea 14:1 14:11, Isaiah 9:14 10:5-6 24:10-12 2:11 3:10 6:27 32:13-14 40:6-8 18:6, Jeremiah 14:18-22 19:11-13 2:6 2:18 37:8-10, Job 5:6-8 5:17 10:2, Joel 2:11-18, Jonah 3:4-10, Lamentations 3:39-42, Lamentations.R Petichata D'Chakimei:25, Micah 3:12, Pesikta de R'Kahana 13.11, Pesikta Rabbati 31:3, Proverbs 22:3, Psalms 9:17 48:11 83:19 11:43, Revelation 3:19, Zephaniah 3:2

[2] LXX *The Lord's voice shall be proclaimed in the city, and he shall save those who fear his name: hear, O tribe; and who shall order the city*

[3] Micah 6:10 - 2 Kings 5:23-24, Amos 3:10 8:5-6, Deuteronomy 25:13-16, Ezekiel 45:9-12, Habakkuk 2:5-11, Hosea 12:9-10, James 5:1-4, Jeremiah 5:26-27, Joshua 7:1, Leviticus 19:35-36, Proverbs 10:2 11:1 20:10 20:23 21:6, Zechariah 5:3-4, Zephaniah 1:9

[4] LXX *Is there not fire, and the house of the wicked heaping up wicked treasures, and that with the pride of unrighteousness*

[5] Micah 6:11 - Hosea 12:9, Leviticus 19:36, Midrash Tanchuma Ki Tetze 8, Pesikta de R'Kahana 3.4, Proverbs 16:11, Pseudo-Phocylides 12, Ruth.R 1:2
Micah 6:11-16 - MurXII

[6] Micah 6:12 - Amos 5:11-12 6:1-3, Ezekiel 22:6-13 22:25-29, Hosea 4:1-2 7:1 7:13, Isaiah 1:23 3:8 5:7 59:3-15, Jeremiah 5:5-6 5:26-29 6:6-7 9:3-7 9:9, Micah 2:1-2 3:1-3 3:9-11 7:2-6, Romans 3:13, Sifre Devarim Ekev 40, Zephaniah 3:3

[7] Micah 6:13 - Acts 12:23, Deuteronomy 28:21-28:22, Hosea 5:9 14:1, Isaiah 1:5-1:7 6:11, Jeremiah 14:18, Job 33:19-33:22, Lamentations 1:13 3:11, Leviticus 2:16, Psalms 107:17-107:18

[8] LXX *Therefore, I will begin to smite you; I will destroy you in your sins*

[9] Micah 6:14 - Amos 2:14-16 9:1-4, Deuteronomy 32:22-25, Ezekiel 4:16-17 5:12, Haggai 1:6 2:16, Hosea 4:10, Isaiah 3:6-8 9:21 24:17-20 6:6 17:13, Jeremiah 24:44, Leviticus 2:26, Sifre Devarim Ekev 40
Micah 6:14-16 - 1Q14 frags 17-19 ll.1-5

[10] Micah 6:15 - Amos 5:11, Deuteronomy 28:38-40, Haggai 1:6, Isaiah 62:8-9 65:21-22, Jeremiah 12:13, Joel 1:10-12, Leviticus 2:20, Zephaniah 1:13

[11] LXX adds *and the ordinances of my people shall be utterly abolished*

[12] Micah 6:16 - 1 Kings 9:8 16:25-33 18:4 21:25-26, 2 Chronicles 29:8-9 10:25, 2 Kings 16:3 21:3, Daniel 9:16, Ezekiel 8:17-18 15:26, Hosea 5:11, Isaiah 9:17 1:8, Jeremiah 7:24 18:15-16 19:8 21:8-9 1:9 3:51, Lamentations 5:1, Psalms 1:1 44:14, Revelation 2:20

[13] LXX *Zambri*

Micah – Chapter 7

אַלְלַי לִי כִּי הָיִיתִי כְּאׇסְפֵּי־קַיִץ כְּעֹלְלֹת בָּצִיר אֵין־אֶשְׁכּוֹל לֶאֱכוֹל בִּכּוּרָה אִוְּתָה נַפְשִׁי

1[1] Woe is me, for I am *the last of the summer fruits*[2], as the grape gleanings of the vintage; there is no cluster to eat; nor first-ripe fig that my soul desires.

אָבַד חָסִיד מִן־הָאָרֶץ וְיָשָׁר בָּאָדָם אָיִן כֻּלָּם לְדָמִים יֶאֱרֹבוּ אִישׁ אֶת־אָחִיהוּ יָצוּדוּ חֵרֶם

2[3] The godly man has perished from the earth, and the upright among men is no more; they all lie in wait for blood; every man hunts his brother with a net.

עַל־הָרַע כַּפַּיִם לְהֵיטִיב הַשַּׂר שֹׁאֵל וְהַשֹּׁפֵט בַּשִּׁלּוּם וְהַגָּדוֹל דֹּבֵר הַוַּת נַפְשׁוֹ הוּא וַיְעַבְּתוּהָ

3[4] *Diligently, their hands are upon what is evil; the prince asks, and the judge is ready for a reward; and the great man, he utters the evil desire of his soul; thus they weave it together*[5].

טוֹבָם כְּחֵדֶק יָשָׁר מִמְּסוּכָה יוֹם מְצַפֶּיךָ פְּקֻדָּתְךָ בָאָה עַתָּה תִהְיֶה מְבוּכָתָם

4[6] *The best of them is as a brier; the most upright is worse than a thorn hedge; the day of your watchmen, your visitation, has come; now is the time of their confuion*[7].

אַל־תַּאֲמִינוּ בְרֵעַ אַל־תִּבְטְחוּ בְּאַלּוּף מִשֹּׁכֶבֶת חֵיקֶךָ שְׁמֹר פִּתְחֵי־פִיךָ

5[8] Do not trust in a friend, *do notyou're your confidence in a familiar friend; Keep the doors of your mouth from her who lies in your bosom*[9].

כִּי־בֵן מְנַבֵּל אָב בַּת קָמָה בְאִמָּהּ כַּלָּה בַּחֲמֹתָהּ אֹיְבֵי אִישׁ אַנְשֵׁי בֵיתוֹ

6[10] For the son dishonors the father, the daughter rises against her mother, the daughter-in-law against her mother-in-law; a man's enemies are the men of his own house.

וַאֲנִי בַּיהוָה אֲצַפֶּה אוֹחִילָה לֵאלֹהֵי יִשְׁעִי יִשְׁמָעֵנִי אֱלֹהָי

7[11] 'But as for me, I will look to the LORD; I will wait for the God of my salvation; my God will hear me.

אַל־תִּשְׂמְחִי אֹיַבְתִּי לִי כִּי נָפַלְתִּי קָמְתִּי כִּי־אֵשֵׁב בַּחֹשֶׁךְ יְהוָה אוֹר לִי

8[12] Do not rejoice against me, O my enemy; though I am fallen, I shall arise; though I sit in darkness, the LORD is a light to me.

---

[1] Micah 7:1 - b.Sotah 47a, Ein Yaakov Sotah:47a, Hosea 9:10, Isaiah 6:5 17:6 24:13 24:16 4:4, Jeremiah 4:31 15:10 21:3, Ladder of Jacob 7:28, m.Sotah 9:9, Psalms 24:5, Sifre Devarim Ha'azinu Hashamayim 323, Sifre Devarim Nitzavim 323, Song of Songs.R 2:44, y.Sotah 9:10
Micah 7:1-20 - MurXII
[2] LXX *as one gathering straw in harvest*
[3] Micah 7:2 - 1 Samuel 24:11 2:20, 4Q271 frag 4 2.14-15, Cairo Damascus 16:14-15, Deuteronomy.R 11:10, Habakkuk 1:15-17, Isaiah 9:1 11:7, Jeremiah 5:16 5:26 16:16, Lamentations 4:18, Micah 3:10, Midrash Psalms 12:1, Proverb 1:11 12:6, Psalms 12:2 14:1-3 57:7, Romans 3:10-18
Micah 7:2-3 - 4QXIIg
[4] Micah 7:3 - 1 Corinthians 4:5, 1 Kings 21:9-14, Amos 5:12, Ezekiel 22:6 22:27, Hosea 4:18, Isaiah 1:23 2:21, Jastrow 1037b 1586a, Jeremiah 3:5 8:10, Luke 12:1-2, Matthew 2:15, Micah 3:11, Proverbs 4:16-17, y.Taanit 2:1
[5] LXX *they prepare their hands for mischief, the prince asks a reward, and the judge speaks flattering words; it is the desire of their soul*
[6] Micah 7:4 - 2 Samuel 23:6-7, Amos 8:2, b.Eruvin 101a, Ein Yaakov Eruvin:101a, Ezekiel 2:6 12:23-24, Hebrews 6:8, Hosea 9:7-8, Isaiah 10:3 22:5 7:13, Jastrow 145a 426a 427a 602a 988b, Jeremiah 8:12 10:15, Luke 21:25, Midrash Psalms 22:27, Nahum 1:10, y.Taanit 2:1
[7] LXX *therefore, I will take away their goods as a devouring moth, and as one who acts by a rigid rule in a day of visitation. Woe, woe, your times of vengeance have come; now shall be their lamentations*
[8] Micah 7:5 - b.Chagigah 16a, b.Taanit 11a, Ein Yaakov Chagigah:16a, Ein Yaakov Taanit:11a, HaMadrikh 35:5, Jastrow 1006b, Jeremiah 9:5, Job 6:14-15, Judges 16:5-20, Matthew 10:16, Psalms 118:8-9, Sifre Devarim Nitzavim 304, z.Lech Lecha 92a, z.Naso 121b
[9] LXX *and confide not in guides: beware of your wife, so as not to commit anything to her.*
[10] Micah 7:6 - 2 Samuel 15:10-12 16:11 16:21-23, 2 Timothy 3:2-3, 3 Baruch 4:17, Ahiqar 139, Ezekiel 22:7, Genesis 9:22-24 1:4, Genesis.R 54:1, Jeremiah 12:6 20:10, John 13:18, Luke 12:53 21:16, Mas.Derek Eretz Zutta 10:1, Matthew 10:21 10:35-36 2:23 26:49-50, Obadiah 1:7, Pesikta de R'Kahana 5.9 11.1, Pesikta Rabbati 15:14/15, Proverbs 6:11 6:17, Psalms 41:10 55:13-15, Sibylline Oracles 8.84, Song of Songs.R 2:33
[11] Micah 7:7 - 1 John 5:14-15, Genesis 1:18, Habakkuk 3:17-19, Isaiah 8:17 12:2 1:9 21:22, Lamentations 3:25-26, Luke 2:25-32 6:11-12, Psalms 4:3-4 5 27:12-14 34:6-7 37:7 38:16 40:2-4 50:15 55:17-55:18 62:2-9 65:3 13:4 10:5 142:5-6
[12] Micah 7:8 - 2 Corinthians 4:6, Acts 2:18, Amos 9:11, Deuteronomy.R 11:10, Esther.R 10:14, Ezekiel 1:6 11:15, Gates of Repentance 2.005, Isaiah 2:5 9:3 1:9 2:10 60:1-60:3 60:19-60:20, Jastrow 1155b, Jeremiah 2:11, Job 7:29, John 8:12 16:20,

זַעַף יְהוָה אֶשָּׂא כִּי חָטָאתִי לוֹ עַד אֲשֶׁר יָרִיב רִיבִי
וְעָשָׂה מִשְׁפָּטִי יוֹצִיאֵנִי לָאוֹר אֶרְאֶה בְּצִדְקָתוֹ

9[1]

I will bear the LORD's indignation, because I have sinned against Him, until He pleads my cause, and execute judgment for me; He will bring me forth to the light, and I shall behold His righteousness.

וְתֵרֶא אֹיַבְתִּי וּתְכַסֶּהָ בוּשָׁה הָאֹמְרָה אֵלַי אַיּוֹ יְהוָה
אֱלֹהָיִךְ עֵינַי תִּרְאֶינָּה בָּהּ עַתָּה תִּהְיֶה לְמִרְמָס
כְּטִיט חוּצוֹת

10[2]

Then my enemy shall see it, and shame shall cover her; who said to me, Where is the LORD your God? My eyes shall gaze on her; Now she shall be trodden as the mud of the streets.'

יוֹם לִבְנוֹת גְּדֵרָיִךְ יוֹם הַהוּא יִרְחַק־חֹק

11[3]

'The day for building your walls, that day, shall be far removed[4].'

יוֹם הוּא וְעָדֶיךָ יָבוֹא לְמִנִּי אַשּׁוּר וְעָרֵי מָצוֹר
וּלְמִנִּי מָצוֹר וְעַד־נָהָר וְיָם מִיָּם וְהַר הָהָר

12[5]

There shall be a day when they shall come to you, from Assyria to the cities of Egypt, and from Egypt to the River[6], And from sea to sea, and from mountain to mountain.

וְהָיְתָה הָאָרֶץ לִשְׁמָמָה עַל־יֹשְׁבֶיהָ מִפְּרִי מַעַלְלֵיהֶם

13[7]

And the land shall be desolate for thoes who live in it, because of the fruit of their deeds.

רְעֵה עַמְּךָ בְשִׁבְטֶךָ צֹאן נַחֲלָתֶךָ שֹׁכְנִי לְבָדָד יַעַר
בְּתוֹךְ כַּרְמֶל יִרְעוּ בָשָׁן וְגִלְעָד כִּימֵי עוֹלָם

14[8]

Tend Your people with Your staff, the flock of Your heritage, who dwell alone, as a forest in the midst of the fruitful field; let them feed in Bashan and Gilead, as in the days of old.

כִּימֵי צֵאתְךָ מֵאֶרֶץ מִצְרָיִם אַרְאֶנּוּ נִפְלָאוֹת

15[9]

'As in the days of your coming forth from the land of Egypt will I show to him marvelous things.'

יִרְאוּ גוֹיִם וְיֵבֹשׁוּ מִכֹּל גְּבוּרָתָם יָשִׂימוּ יָד עַל־פֶּה
אָזְנֵיהֶם תֶּחֱרַשְׁנָה

16[10]

The nations shall see and be put to shame for all their might; they shall lay their hand on their mouth, their ears shall be deaf.

יְלַחֲכוּ עָפָר כַּנָּחָשׁ כְּזֹחֲלֵי אֶרֶץ יִרְגְּזוּ מִמִּסְגְּרֹתֵיהֶם
אֶל־יְהוָה אֱלֹהֵינוּ יִפְחָדוּ וְיִרְאוּ מִמֶּךָּ

17[11]

They shall lick the dust like a serpent; *like crawling things of the earth they shall come trembling out of their bunkers[12]*; They shall come with fear to the LORD our God, and shall be afraid because of You.

Lamentations 4:21-4:22, Luke 1:78-1:79, Malachi 3:20, Matthew 4:16, Micah 7:10, Midrash Psalms 5:1 22:4 22:7 22:13, Midrash Tanchuma Nitzavim 1, Numbers.R 2:10, Obadiah 1:12, Pesikta Rabbati 15: 46:3, Proverbs 24:16-18, Psalms 13:5-7 27:1 35:15-16 35:19 35:24-26 37:21 37:24 38:17 41:11-13 84:12 97:11 107:10-15 16:4, Revelation 11:10-12 21:23 22:5, Song of Songs.R 6:25 6:27, Tanya Igeret Hakodesh §6, y.Berachot 1:1, y.Yoma 3:2, z.Pekudei 241b

[1] Micah 7:9 - 1 Corinthians 4:5, 1 Samuel 3:18 24:15 1:39 2:10, 2 Samuel 16:11-16:12 24:17, 2 Thessalonians 1:5-1:10, 2 Timothy 4:8, Hebrews 12:6-12:7, Isaiah 22:13, Jeremiah 50:17-50:20 50:33-50:34 51:35-51:36, Job 23:10 34:31-34:32, Lamentations 1:18 3:39-3:42, Leviticus 2:41, Luke 15:18-15:19, Malachi 3:18, Midrash Psalms 9:7, Psalms 7:7 37:6 43:1, Revelation 6:10-6:11 18:20

[2] Micah 7:10 - 2 Kings 9:33-37, 2 Samuel 22:43, 3 Baruch 1:2, Daniel 3:15, Ezekiel 7:18, Isaiah 25:10-12 26:5-6 37:10-11 41:15-16 47:5-9 51:22-23 63:2-3, Jeremiah 50:33-34 51:8-10 3:24 3:51, Joel 2:17, Joseph and Aseneth 13:7, Malachi 1:5 3:21, Matthew 3:43, Mekhilta de R'Shimon bar Yochai Beshallach 26:5, Mekhilta de R'Ishmael Beshallach 7:103 7:108, Micah 4:11, Nahum 2:2-4, Obadiah 1:10, Psalms 18:43 35:26 42:4 42:11 58:11 79:10 13:29 19:2 137:8-9, Revelation 17:1-7 18:20, Zechariah 10:5

[3] Micah 7:11 - 4Q266 frag 3 1.6, Amos 9:11-15, Cairo Damascus 4.12, Daniel 9:25, Ezra 4:12-24, Isaiah 6:11, Nehemiah 2:8 2:17 3:1-16 4:3 4:6

[4] LXX *It is the day of making of brick; that day shall be your utter destruction, and that day shall utterly abolish your ordinances*

[5] Micah 7:12 - Ezekiel 5:21 13:21, Hosea 12:1, Isaiah 11:16 19:23-25 27:12-13 19:6 1:12 60:4-9 66:19-20, Jeremiah 3:18 23:3 7:9

[6] LXX *And your cities shall be levelled, and parted among the Assyrians; and your strong cities shall be parted from Tyre to the river*

[7] Micah 7:13 - Daniel 4:23-24, Galatians 6:7-6:8, Isaiah 3:10-11 6:11-13 24:3-8, Jeremiah 17:10 21:14 1:11 8:19, Job 4:8, Leviticus 26:33-39, Luke 21:20-24, Mekhilta de R'Ishmael Amalek 4:137, Micah 3:12 6:13, Midrash Psalms 50:1, Proverbs 1:31 5:22 7:31

[8] Micah 7:14 - Amos 9:11, Deuteronomy 9:28, Ein Yaakov Pesachim:68a, Exodus 9:16, Ezekiel 34:13-14, Gates of Repentance 2.17, Isaiah 11:2 13:24 16:11 1:10 17:10, Jeremiah 50:19-50:20, John 10:27-30 17:16, Lamentations 1:7 5:21, Malachi 3:4, Matthew 2:6, Micah 5:5, Numbers 23:9, Psalms 23:1-4 28:9 77:6-12 95:7 4:3 23:5, Zephaniah 3:13, Sifre Devarim Vezot Habracha 343

[9] Micah 7:15 - Exodus 3:20, Exodus.R 15:11, Isaiah 11:16 3:9 63:11-63:15, Jeremiah 23:7-23:8, Mekhilta de R'Shimon bar Yochai Shirata 34:3, Mekhilta de R'Ishmael Shirata 8:99, Midrash Psalms 149:4, Midrash Tanchuma Ekev 7, Pesikta de R'Kahana 5.8, Pesikta Rabbati 1:7, Psalms 68:23 78:12-78:72, Saadia Opinions 8:1, z.Beshallach 54a, z.Bo 38b, z.Shemot 9a, z.Tazria 52a

[10] Micah 7:16 - Chibbur Yafeh 27 123a, Ezekiel 14:23 39:17-39:21, Genesis.R 99 [Excl]:8, Isaiah 2:11 4:15 18:18, Job 21:5 29:9-29:10 16:4, Micah 5:9, Midrash Tanchuma Shoftim 9, Midrash Tanchuma Vayechi 10, Pesikta de R'Kahana 16.11, Psalms 6:2, Revelation 11:18, Romans 3:19, Zechariah 8:20-8:23 12:9

[11] Micah 7:17 - 1 Samuel 14:11, Exodus 15:14-15:16, Genesis 3:14-3:15, Isaiah 2:19-2:21 1:3 1:23 11:19 12:14 16:3 17:25, Jeremiah 16:16 9:9, Joshua 2:9-2:11 9:24, Lamentations 3:29, Psalms 9:21 18:46 72:9, Revelation 3:9 6:15-6:17 18:9-18:10, Zechariah 14:5

[12] LXX *crawling on the earth, they shall be confounded in their holes*

מִי־אֵל כָּמוֹךָ נֹשֵׂא עָוֹן וְעֹבֵר עַל־פֶּשַׁע לִשְׁאֵרִית
נַחֲלָתוֹ לֹא־הֶחֱזִיק לָעַד אַפּוֹ כִּי־חָפֵץ חֶסֶד הוּא

18[1] Who is a God like You, who pardons the iniquity, and passes by the transgression of the remnant of His heritage? He does not retain His anger forever, because He delights in mercy.

יָשׁוּב יְרַחֲמֵנוּ יִכְבֹּשׁ עֲוֹנֹתֵינוּ וְתַשְׁלִיךְ בִּמְצֻלוֹת יָם
כָּל־חַטֹּאותָם

19[2] He will again have compassion; He will subdue our iniquities; and you will cast all their sins into the depths of the sea.

תִּתֵּן אֱמֶת לְיַעֲקֹב חֶסֶד לְאַבְרָהָם אֲשֶׁר־נִשְׁבַּעְתָּ
לַאֲבֹתֵינוּ מִימֵי קֶדֶם

20[3] You will show faithfulness to Jacob and mercy to Abraham, as you have sworn to our fathers from the days of old.

Nachum haElkoshi – Chapter 1

מַשָּׂא נִינְוֵה סֵפֶר חֲזוֹן נַחוּם הָאֶלְקֹשִׁי

1[4] The burden of Nineveh. The book of the vision of Nahum the Elkoshite.

אֵל קַנּוֹא וְנֹקֵם יְהוָה נֹקֵם יְהוָה וּבַעַל חֵמָה נֹקֵם
יְהוָה לְצָרָיו וְנוֹטֵר הוּא לְאֹיְבָיו

2[5] The LORD is a jealous and avenging God, the LORD avenges and is full of wrath; the LORD takes vengeance on His adversaries, and He *reserves wrath for*[6] His enemies.

יְהוָה אֶרֶךְ אַפַּיִם 'וּגְדוֹל־'וּגְדָל־כֹּחַ' וְנַקֵּה לֹא יְנַקֶּה
יְהוָה בְּסוּפָה וּבִשְׂעָרָה דַּרְכּוֹ וְעָנָן אֲבַק רַגְלָיו

3[7] The LORD is longsuffering, and great in power, and will by no means clear the guilty; the LORD, in the whirlwind and in the storm is His way, and the clouds are the dust of His feet.

[1] Micah 7:18 - 1 Kings 8:23, Acts 13:38-39, Amos 7:8 8:2, b.Arachin 8b, b.Megillah 28a, b.Rosh Hashanah 14a, Bahir 34, Daniel 9:9, Derech Hashem Part II 8§01, Deuteronomy 9:26, Deuteronomy.R 8:1, Ein Yaakov Megillah:27a, Ein Yaakov Rosh Hashanah:17a, Ephesians 2:4-5, Exodus 15:11 33:18-19 34:6-7 10:9, Exodus.R 26:2 32:4, Ezekiel 9:11, Hebrews 8:9-12, Isaiah 1:18 16:18 16:25 19:25 20:22 46:8-9 7:7 9:10 9:16 14:5 17:19, James 2:13, Jastrow 1038b 1039a 1339b 1533b 1561b, Jeremiah 3:5 3:12 7:35 8:41 14:8 2:20, Joel 3:5, Jonah 4:2, Lamentations 3:31-3:32, Lamentations.R 3:9, Luke 15:5-7 15:9-10 15:23-24 15:32 24:47, Mas.Derek Eretz Zutta 8:3, Mas.Soferim 4:9, Mesillat Yesharim 22:Trait of Anavah, Micah 2:12 4:7 5:4 5:8-9 7:14, Midrash Tanchuma Ki Tissa 22, mt.Hilchot Teshuvah 3:5, Nehemiah 9:17, Numbers 14:18-19 23:21, Pesikta de R'Kahana 16.8 25.2, Pesikta Rabbati 1:6 39:2 44:9 4S:1 4S:3, Psalms 35:10 65:4 71:19 77:7-11 85:5-6 86:5 86:15 89:7 89:9 103:2-3 103:8-9 7:13 113:5-6 10:4 130:7-8, Romans 11:4, Tanna Devei Eliyahu 1, Tanya Igeret Hakodesh §05, Tanya Igeret Hateshuvah §11, Tanya Shaar Hayichud §8, y.Kiddushin 1:9, y.Peah 1:1, y.Sanhedrin 10:1, y.Sheviit 1:6, Zephaniah 3:17
Micah 7:18-20 - Haftarah Minchah [Tisha B'Av continued from Hosea 14:1-10 Sephard and Teimon], Haftarah Minchah [Yom Kippur continued from Jonah 1:1-4:11], Haftarah Shabbat Shuva [continued from Hosea 14:2-10 continues with Joel 2:15-27 Sephard], Seder Tashlich Rosh Hashanah, Selichot, Shabbat Shuvah Part Two Haftarah, Sifre Devarim Vezot Habracha 342, Sifre Devarim Vezot Habracha 342, Siman 129:21, Tisha B'Av Afternoon Sephard Part Three Haftarah
[2] Micah 7:19 - 1 John 3:8, b.Arachin 8b, b.Rosh Hashanah 14a, b.Succah [Rashi] 43b, Daniel 9:24, Deuteronomy 6:3 6:6 8:36, Ein Yaakov Rosh Hashanah:17a, Exodus.R 25:6, Ezekiel 11:19-11:20 36:25-27, Ezra 9:8-9, Hosea 14:6, Isaiah 14:17 19:25 63:15-17, James 4:5-6, Jeremiah 7:21 7:35 2:20, Lamentations 3:32, Midrash Psalms 29:2 36:5 38:1, Pesikta de R'Kahana 6.4, Pesikta Rabbati 16:7 39:2 44:10 48:3, Psalms 90:13-14 7:12 10:8, Romans 6:14 6:17-22 7:23-25 8:2-3 8:13, Tanya Igeret Hakodesh §12, Titus 2:14, z.Acharei Mot 63b
[3] Micah 7:20 - 4QXIIg, Acts 3:25-26, Bahir 135 190, Deuteronomy 7:8, Genesis 12:2-3 17:7-8 22:16-18 26:3-4 28:13-14, Genesis.R 40:1 73:2, Hebrews 6:13-18, Jeremiah 33:25-26, Leviticus.R 1:4, Luke 1:54-55 1:72-74, Mas.Kallah Rabbati 10:6, Midrash Psalms 15:6 119:17, Midrash Tanchuma Re'eh 14, Pesikta de R'Kahana 10.6, Psalms 105:8-10, Romans 11:26-31, Seder Hoshanot, Tanya Igeret Hakodesh §6, U'voh Letzion [daily Shacharit Shabbat and Yom Tov Minchah Maariv Motzoei Shabbat], z.Beshallach 57a, z.Lech Lecha 96a, z.Yitro 89b 90a
[4] Nahum 1:1 - Genesis 10:11, Genesis.R 49:8, Isaiah 13:1 14:28 15:1 19:1 21:1 22:1 23:1, Jeremiah 23:33-23:37, Jonah 1:2 3:3-3:4, Lives of the Prophets 11:1, Nahum 2:9, Zechariah 9:1, Zephaniah 2:13
Nahum 1:1-4 - t.Sotah 9:6
Nahum 1:1-14 - MurXII
[5] Nahum 1:2 - 2 Peter 2:9, 4Q270 frag 6 3.19, b.Avodah Zara 4a, Cairo Damascus 9:5, Cairo Damascus 9.5, Deuteronomy 4:24 32:34-32:35 32:41-32:43, Ecclesiastes.R 8:8, Exodus 20:5 10:14, Exodus.R 30:1, Ezekiel 5:13 6:12 8:18 12:6 14:18 15:25, Genesis.R 49:8 55:3, Guide for the Perplexed 1:36 1:54, Hebrews 10:30, Isaiah 18:13 3:17 3:20 59:17-59:18 63:3-63:6 18:15, Jastrow 901b, Jeremiah 3:5 4:4 1:15 12:7, Job 20:23, Joel 2:18, Joshua 24:19, Lamentations 4:11, Leviticus 2:28, Micah 5:16 7:18, Midrash Psalms 94:1 149:6, Psalms 94:1, Romans 2:5-2:6 12:19 13:4, Saadia Opinions 2:12, Tanna Devei Eliyahu 7 7, Zechariah 1:14 8:2
[6] LXX *cuts off*
[7] Nahum 1:3 - 1 Kings 19:11-13, 4Q169 frags 1-2 l.1, b.Chullin 91a, Daniel 7:13, Deuteronomy 5:22-24, Deuteronomy.R 3:17, Ein Yaakov Chullin:91a, Ephesians 1:19-20, Exodus 19:16-19:18 34:6-7, Exodus.R 8:1, Habakkuk 3:5-15, HaMadrikh 35:11, Isaiah 19:1 18:15, James 1:19, Job 9:4 10:14 14:1, Joel 2:13, Jonah 4:2, Lamentations.R 1:1 3:10, Matthew 26:64, Midrash Psalms 21:2 25:11, Midrash Tanchuma Bereshit 7, Midrash Tanchuma Naso 30, Midrash Tanchuma Vaera 8, Midrash Tanchuma Vayishlach 10, Nehemiah 9:17, Numbers 14:18, Numbers.R 14:3, Pesikta de R'Kahana 15.3, Psalms 18:8-16 50:3 62:12 66:3 97:2-5 7:8 8:3 1:8 3:5, Revelation 1:7, Song of Songs.R 3:9, Traditional Small ס in בְּסוּפָה, z.Vayishlach 170a, Zechariah 9:14

גּוֹעֵר בַּיָּם וַיַּבְּשֵׁהוּ וְכָל־הַנְּהָרוֹת הֶחֱרִיב אֻמְלַל בָּשָׁן וְכַרְמֶל וּפֶרַח לְבָנוֹן אֻמְלָל	4[1]	He rebukes the sea, and makes it dry, And dries up all the rivers; Bashan languishes, and Carmel, And the *flower of Lebanon languishes*[2].
הָרִים רָעֲשׁוּ מִמֶּנּוּ וְהַגְּבָעוֹת הִתְמֹגָגוּ וַתִּשָּׂא הָאָרֶץ מִפָּנָיו וְתֵבֵל וְכָל־יֹשְׁבֵי בָהּ	5[3]	The mountains quake at Him, and the hills melt, and the earth is upheaved at His presence; yes, the world, and all who dwell in it.
לִפְנֵי זַעְמוֹ מִי יַעֲמוֹד וּמִי יָקוּם בַּחֲרוֹן אַפּוֹ חֲמָתוֹ נִתְּכָה כָאֵשׁ וְהַצֻּרִים נִתְּצוּ מִמֶּנּוּ	6[4]	Who can stand before His anger? And who can live in the *fierceness of His anger*[5]? His *fury is poured out like fire*[6], and the rocks are broken apart before Him.
טוֹב יְהוָה לְמָעוֹז בְּיוֹם צָרָה וְיֹדֵעַ חֹסֵי בוֹ	7[7]	The LORD is good, *a stronghold in the day of trouble*[8]; and He knows who *takes refuge in Him*[9].
וּבְשֶׁטֶף עֹבֵר כָּלָה יַעֲשֶׂה מְקוֹמָהּ וְאֹיְבָיו יְרַדֶּף־חֹשֶׁךְ	8[10]	But with an overrunning flood He will make a full end of the place, and darkness shall pursue *His enemies*[11].
מַה־תְּחַשְּׁבוּן אֶל־יְהוָה כָּלָה הוּא עֹשֶׂה לֹא־תָקוּם פַּעֲמַיִם צָרָה	9[12]	What do you devise against the LORD? He will make a full end; *trouble shall not rise up the second time*[13].
כִּי עַד־סִירִים סְבֻכִים וּכְסָבְאָם סְבוּאִים אֻכְּלוּ כְּקַשׁ יָבֵשׁ מָלֵא	10[14]	*For though they are like tangled thorns, and are drunken from their drink, They shall be devoured*[15] as stubble fully dry.
מִמֵּךְ יָצָא חֹשֵׁב עַל־יְהוָה רָעָה יֹעֵץ בְּלִיָּעַל	11[16]	Out of you he came forth, who devises evil against the LORD, who counsels wickedness.
כֹּה אָמַר יְהוָה אִם־שְׁלֵמִים וְכֵן רַבִּים וְכֵן נָגֹזּוּ וְעָבָר וְעִנִּתִךְ לֹא אֲעַנֵּךְ עוֹד	12[17]	Thus says the LORD: *they are in full strength, and likewise many, so they shall be cut down, and he shall pass away; and though I have afflicted you, I will afflict you no more*[18].

---

[1] Nahum 1:4 - 4Q169 1-9, 4Q169 frags 1-2 l.3-l.5, Amos 1:2 5:8, b.Chagigah 12a, b.Yoma 21b 39b, Ein Yaakov Chagigah:12a, Ein Yaakov Yoma:39b, Ezekiel 6:12, Isaiah 19:5-10 9:9 20:27 50:2-3 3:10, Job 14:11, Joshua 3:13-15, Matthew 8:26, Midrash Tanchuma Terumah 11, Numbers.R 12:4, Psalms 74:15 8:7 10:9 18:3 18:5, Song of Songs.R 3:22, y.Yoma 4:4, z.Terumah 170a

[2] LXX *flourishing trees of Libanus have come to nought*

[3] Nahum 1:5 - 2 Peter 3:7-3:12, 2 Samuel 22:8, 4Q169 1-2 9-11, Exodus 19:18, Habakkuk 3:10, Isaiah 2:12-14 64:2-3, Jeremiah 4:24, Judges 5:5, Matthew 3:51 4:2, Micah 1:4, Prayer of Manasseh 4, Psalms 29:5-6 46:7 68:9 97:4-5 98:7 18:4 18:6, Revelation 20:11
Nahum 1:5-6 - 4Q169 frags 1-2 ll.9-11

[4] Nahum 1:6 - 1 Kings 19:11, b.Avodah Zara 4a, Deuteronomy 32:22-23, Exodus.R 29:9, Ezekiel 6:16, Isaiah 10:16 3:4, Jeremiah 10:10, Lamentations 2:4 4:11, Malachi 3:2, Nahum 1:2, Psalms 2:12 76:8 90:11, Revelation 6:17 16:1 16:8

[5] LXX *anger of his wrath*

[6] LXX *wrath brings to nought kingdoms*

[7] Nahum 1:7 - 1 Chronicles 5:20 16:34, 1 John 4:8-10, 2 Chronicles 16:8-9 8:8 8:11 8:21, 2 Timothy 2:19, Daniel 3:28 6:24, Exodus.R 30:24, Ezra 3:11, Galatians 4:9, Isaiah 1:4 26:1-4 8:2 37:3-4, Jeremiah 17:7-8 9:11, John 10:14 10:27, Lamentations 3:25, Leviticus.R 17:1, Mas.Derek Eretz Rabbah 2:24, Matthew 7:23 3:43, Midrash Psalms 4:5, Midrash Tanchuma Bamidbar 26, Midrash Tanchuma Noach 7, Numbers.R 5:3, Proverbs 18:10, Psalms 1:6 18:2-3 20:2 25:8 27:5 50:15 59:17 62:7-9 71:3 84:12-13 86:7 91:1-2 91:15 4:5 136:1-26 144:1-2 145:6-10, Romans 11:22, z.Vayishlach 174a
Nahum 1:7-9 - 4QXIIg

[8] LXX *to them who wait on him in the day of affliction*

[9] LXX *reverence him*

[10] Nahum 1:8 - 2 Peter 3:6-3:7, Amos 8:8 9:5-9:6, Daniel 9:26 11:10 11:22 11:40, Ezekiel 13:13, Isaiah 8:7-8:8 8:22 4:17, Jeremiah 13:16, Job 6:15, Matthew 7:27 8:12, Nahum 1:2 2:9, Proverbs 4:19, Zephaniah 2:13

[11] LXX *those who rise up against him and his enemies*

[12] Nahum 1:9 - 1 Samuel 3:12 2:8, 2 Corinthians 10:5, 2 Samuel 20:10, Acts 4:25-4:28, b.Berachot 59a, Ezekiel 38:10-38:11, Isaiah 8:9-8:10, Nahum 1:11, Proverbs 21:30, Psalms 2:1-2:4 21:12 33:10

[13] LXX *he will not take vengeance by affliction twice at the same time*

[14] Nahum 1:10 - 1 Samuel 1:36, 1 Thessalonians 5:2-3, 2 Samuel 13:28 23:6-7, Genesis.R 56:5 73:12, Isaiah 5:24 9:19 10:17-19 3:4, Jeremiah 3:39 3:57, Malachi 3:19, Micah 7:4, Nahum 3:11, Psalms 68:3

[15] LXX *For the enemy shall be laid bare even to the foundation, and shall be devoured as twisted yew*

[16] Nahum 1:11 - 1 Samuel 2:12, 2 Chronicles 13:7 32:15-19, 2 Kings 18:13-14 18:30 19:22-25, 2 Samuel 20:1, b.Sanhedrin [Tosefot] 65a, b.Sanhedrin 87a, Isaiah 10:7-10:15, Nahum 1:9, Pesikta de R'Kahana 16.8, Pesikta Rabbati 29/30B:2, Tanna Devei Eliyahu 7

[17] Nahum 1:12 - 2 Kings 19:35 19:37, b.Gittin 7a 7b, Daniel 11:10, Ein Yaakov Gittin:6b, Exodus 12:12, Isaiah 7:20 8:8 10:32-10:34 14:24-14:27 17:14 6:19 30:28-30:33 7:8 13:36 3:22 60:18-60:20, Joel 2:19, Lamentations 3:31-3:32, Midrash Psalms 71:3 143:2, Midrash Tanchuma Mishpatim 5, Nahum 2:1, Revelation 7:16, z.Mikketz 200b 201a, z.Vaetchanan 269b

[18]18 LXX *who rules over many waters, Even thus shall they be sent away, and the report of you shall not be heard any more*

וְעַתָּה אֶשְׁבֹּר מֹטֵהוּ מֵעָלָיִךְ וּמוֹסְרֹתַיִךְ אֲנַתֵּק

13[1] And now will I break his *yoke*[2] from off you, and will burst and divide your bonds.

וְצִוָּה עָלַיִךְ יְהוָה לֹא־יִזָּרַע מִשִּׁמְךָ עוֹד מִבֵּית אֱלֹהֶיךָ אַכְרִית פֶּסֶל וּמַסֵּכָה אָשִׂים קִבְרֶךָ כִּי קַלּוֹתָ

14[3] And the LORD has commanded concerning you, that your name shall never again be *sown*[4]; Out of the house of your god will I cut off the graven image and the molten image; I will make your grave; *for you have become worthless*[5].

Nahum – Chapter 2[6]

הִנֵּה עַל־הֶהָרִים רַגְלֵי מְבַשֵּׂר מַשְׁמִיעַ שָׁלוֹם חָגִּי יְהוּדָה חַגַּיִךְ שַׁלְּמִי נְדָרָיִךְ כִּי לֹא יוֹסִיף עוֹד 'לַעֲבוֹר־לַעֲבָר־בָּךְ' בְּלִיַּעַל כֻּלֹּה נִכְרָת

1[7] Behold, upon the mountains the feet of he who brings good tidings, who announces peace. Keep your festivals, O Judah, perform your vows; *for the wicked one shall never pass through you again; he is utterly cut off*[8].

עָלָה מֵפִיץ עַל־פָּנַיִךְ נָצוֹר מְצֻרָה צַפֵּה־דֶרֶךְ חַזֵּק מָתְנַיִם אַמֵּץ כֹּחַ מְאֹד

2[9] [10]*A maul is come up before your face; guard the defenses, watch the way, make your loins strong, fortify your power mightily!*[11]

כִּי שָׁב יְהוָה אֶת־גְּאוֹן יַעֲקֹב כִּגְאוֹן יִשְׂרָאֵל כִּי בְקָקוּם בֹּקְקִים וּזְמֹרֵיהֶם שִׁחֵתוּ

3[12] For the LORD restores the pride of Jacob, as the pride of Israel; *for the emptiers have emptied them out*[13], and marred their vine-branches.

מָגֵן גִּבֹּרֵיהוּ מְאָדָּם אַנְשֵׁי־חַיִל מְתֻלָּעִים בְּאֵשׁ־פְּלָדוֹת הָרֶכֶב בְּיוֹם הֲכִינוֹ וְהַבְּרֹשִׁים הָרְעָלוּ

4[14] *The shield of his mighty men are made red, the valiant men are in scarlet; the chariots are fire of steel in the day of his preparation, and the cypress spears are made to quiver*[15].

בַּחוּצוֹת יִתְהוֹלְלוּ הָרֶכֶב יִשְׁתַּקְשְׁקוּן בָּרְחֹבוֹת מַרְאֵיהֶן כַּלַּפִּידִם כַּבְּרָקִים יְרוֹצֵצוּ

5[16] The chariots rush madly in the streets, they jostle one against another in the broad places; the appearances of them are like torches, they run to and fro like the lightnings.

יִזְכֹּר אַדִּירָיו יִכָּשְׁלוּ 'בַּהֲלוּכוֹתָם' "בַּהֲלִיכָתָם" יְמַהֲרוּ חוֹמָתָהּ וְהֻכַן הַסֹּכֵךְ

6[17] He considers himself of his worthies; they stumble in their march; they hurry to the wall, and the *mantelet is*[18] prepared.

---

[1] Nahum 1:13 - Isaiah 9:5 10:27 14:25, Jeremiah 2:20 5:5, Micah 5:6-5:7, Psalms 11:14
Nahum 1:13-14 - 8HevXIIgr

[2] LXX *rod*

[3] Nahum 1:14 - 1 Samuel 3:13, 2 Chronicles 8:21, 2 Kings 19:37, Daniel 11:21, Exodus 12:12, Ezekiel 32:22-23, Isaiah 14:20-22 19:1 9:13 46:1-2, Jeremiah 2:2, Leviticus 2:30, Micah 5:14, Nahum 3:4-6, Proverbs 10:7, Psalms 71:3 13:13

[4] LXX *scattered*

[5] LXX *for they are swift*

[6] Nahum 2 - MurXII

[7] Nahum 2:1 - Acts 10:36, Isaiah 29:7-8 37:36-38 40:9-10 4:1 4:7, Joel 4:17, Leviticus 23:2 23:4, Luke 2:10 2:14, Midrash Tanchuma Bamidbar 14, Nahum 1:11-12 1:14, Numbers.R 2:10, Pesikta de R'Kahana 16.8, Pesikta Rabbati 29/30B:2 33:13 35:4, Psalms 11:8 11:15 107:21-22 116:12-14 116:17-18, Romans 10:15

[8] LXX *for they shall no more pass through you to your decay*

[9] Nahum 2:2 - 2 Chronicles 1:8, Isaiah 14:6, Jeremiah 1:9 46:3-10 2:23 51:11-12 51:20-23, Joel 4:9-11, Nahum 3:14-15

[10] LXX begins Chapter 2 here

[11] LXX *It is all over with him, he has been removed, one who has been delivered from affliction has come up panting into your presence, watch the way, strengthen your loins, be very valiant in your strength*

[12] Nahum 2:3 - Ezekiel 13:23, Genesis 49:22-23, Hosea 10:1, Isaiah 10:5-12 12:15, Jeremiah 1:29 1:9, Psalms 80:13-14, Zephaniah 3:11

[13] LXX *for they have utterly rejected them*

[14] Nahum 2:4 - Ezekiel 23:14-15, Genesis.R 63:12 75:4, Isaiah 14:8 63:1-3, Revelation 6:4 12:3, Zechariah 1:8 6:2 11:2

[15] LXX *they have destroyed the arms of their power from among men, their mighty men sporting with fire: the reins of their chariots shall be destroyed in the day of his preparation, and the horsemen shall be thrown into confusion*

[16] Nahum 2:5 - Daniel 11:40, Ezekiel 2:10, Isaiah 13:24 18:15, Jeremiah 4:13, Leviticus.R 19:3 30:2, Midrash Psalms 11:6, Nahum 3:2-3:3, Pesikta de R'Kahana 27.2, Pesikta Rabbati 51:4, Sifre Devarim Devarim 10, Sifre Devarim Ekev 47, Song of Songs.R 5:14
Nahum 2:5-10 - 8HevXIIgr

[17] Nahum 2:6 - Isaiah 5:27 21:5, Jastrow 1135b, Jeremiah 22:12 2:29 51:27-28, Leviticus.R 19:5, Mas.Soferim 7:4, Nahum 3:3 3:18

[18] LXX *defences are*

שַׁעֲרֵי הַנְּהָרוֹת נִפְתָּחוּ וְהַהֵיכָל נָמוֹג | 7[1] | The gates of the *rivers*[2] are opened, and the palace dissolves.

וְהֻצַּב גֻּלְּתָה הֹעֲלָתָה וְאַמְהֹתֶיהָ מְנַהֲגוֹת כְּקוֹל יוֹנִים מְתֹפְפֹת עַל־לִבְבֵהֶן | 8[3] | And the *queen is uncovered, she is carried away, aAnd her handmaids moan as with the voice of doves, beating upon their breasts*[4].

וְנִינְוֵה כִבְרֵכַת־מַיִם מִימֵי הִיא וְהֵמָּה נָסִים עִמְדוּ עֲמֹדוּ וְאֵין מַפְנֶה | 9[5] | But Nineveh has been from of old like a pool of water; yet they flee; 'Stand, stand;' But no one looks back.

בֹּזּוּ כֶסֶף בֹּזּוּ זָהָב וְאֵין קֵצֶה לַתְּכוּנָה כָּבֹד מִכֹּל כְּלִי חֶמְדָּה | 10[6] | Take the spoil of silver, take the spoil of gold; for there is no end of the store, rich with all precious vessels.

בּוּקָה וּמְבוּקָה וּמְבֻלָּקָה וְלֵב נָמֵס וּפִק בִּרְכַּיִם וְחַלְחָלָה בְּכָל־מָתְנַיִם וּפְנֵי כֻלָּם קִבְּצוּ פָארוּר | 11[7] | *She is empty, and void, and waste; and the heart melts, and the knees knock together, and convulsion is in all the loins, and all their faces have gathered blackness*[8].

אַיֵּה מְעוֹן אֲרָיוֹת וּמִרְעֶה הוּא לַכְּפִרִים אֲשֶׁר הָלַךְ אַרְיֵה לָבִיא שָׁם גּוּר אַרְיֵה וְאֵין מַחֲרִיד | 12[9] | Where is the den of the lions, *which was the feeding-place of the young lions, where the lion and the lioness walked, and the lion's whelp*[10], and no one made them afraid?

אַרְיֵה טֹרֵף בְּדֵי גֹרוֹתָיו וּמְחַנֵּק לְלִבְאֹתָיו וַיְמַלֵּא־טֶרֶף חֹרָיו וּמְעֹנֹתָיו טְרֵפָה | 13[11] | *The lion tore in pieces enough for his whelps, and strangled for his lionesses, and filled his caves with prey, and his dens with torn flesh*[12].

הִנְנִי אֵלַיִךְ נְאֻם יְהוָה צְבָאוֹת וְהִבְעַרְתִּי בֶעָשָׁן רִכְבָּהּ וּכְפִירַיִךְ תֹּאכַל חָרֶב וְהִכְרַתִּי מֵאֶרֶץ טַרְפֵּךְ וְלֹא־יִשָּׁמַע עוֹד קוֹל מַלְאָכֵכֵה | 14[13] | Behold, I am against you, says the LORD of hosts, and I will burn *her chariots*[14] in the smoke, and the sword shall devour your young lions; and I will cut off your prey from the earth, and *the voice of your messengers*[15] shall not be heard again.

Nahum – Chapter 3[16]

הוֹי עִיר דָּמִים כֻּלָּהּ כַּחַשׁ פֶּרֶק מְלֵאָה לֹא יָמִישׁ טָרֶף | 1[17] | Woe to the bloody city! It is all full of lies and plunder; The prey does not leave.

---

[1] Nahum 2:7 - 2 Peter 3:10-11, Isaiah 45:1-2

[2] LXX cities

[3] Nahum 2:8 - Isaiah 8:12 14:14 11:11, Luke 23:27 23:48
Nahum 2:8-13 - Josephus Antiquities 9.11.3

[4] LXX *foundation has been exposed; and she has gone up, and her maid-servants were led away as doves moaning in their hearts*

[5] Nahum 2:9 - Genesis 10:11, Isaiah 13:14 23:13 24:20, Jeremiah 22:5 2:16 3:13 3:30, Nahum 3:17, Revelation 17:1 17:15
Nahum 2:9-11 - 4QXIIg

[6] Nahum 2:10 - 2 Chronicles 12:10, Daniel 11:8, Ezekiel 2:12, Isaiah 9:1 9:4, Jeremiah 1:34 3:56, Nahum 2:13-14, This is the middle verse of the book of Nahum per the Massorah

[7] Nahum 2:11 - 4Q169 3-4i1 4Q169 3-4i1-4, 4Q177 3.3, b.Megillah [Rashi] 14b, b.Sanhedrin [Rashi] 98b, Daniel 5:6, Genesis 1:2, Isaiah 13:7-8 13:19-22 14:23 21:3 24:1 34:10-15, Jeremiah 4:23-26 6:6 51:62, Joel 2:6, Joshua 2:11, Nahum 3:7, Psalms 22:15, Revelation 18:21-23, Zephaniah 2:13-15 3:6

[8] LXX *There is thrusting forth, and shaking, and tumult, and heart-breaking, and loosing of knees, and pangs on all loins; and the faces of all are as the blackening of a pot*

[9] Nahum 2:12 - 4Q169 3-4 i 4-5 4Q169 3-4 i 6-8, 4Q169 frags 3-4 1.4, 4Q169 frags 3-4 1.6, Exodus.R 29:9, Ezekiel 19:2-19:8, Genesis 1:9, Isaiah 5:29 7:4, Jeremiah 2:15 4:7 2:17 2:44, Job 4:10-4:11, Nahum 3:1, western wrote הוא and Eastern wrote היא [j.Megillah 1:9], Zephaniah 3:3

[10] LXX *and the pasture that belonged to the whelps? where did the lion go, that the lion's whelp should enter in there*

[11] Nahum 2:13 - 4Q169 3-4 i 8-9 4Q169 3-4 i 10-ii 1, 4Q169 frags 3-4 1.8-9, 4Q169 frags 3-4 1.9-10, b.Bava Kamma 16b, b.Chullin [Tosefot] 61a, Isaiah 10:6-10:14, Jeremiah 3:34, Psalms 17:12, Saadia Opinions 10:8
Nahum 2:13-14 - 8HevXIIgr

[12] LXX *The lion seized enough prey for his whelps, and strangled for his young lions, and filled his lair with prey, and his dwelling-place with spoil*

[13] Nahum 2:14 - 2 Chronicles 32:9-16 8:19, 2 Kings 18:17 18:19 18:27-35 19:9 19:23, Ezekiel 5:8 2:3 4:22 5:3 5:10 11:3 14:3 15:1, Isaiah 31:8-9 33:1-4 37:36-38 49:24-25, Jeremiah 21:13 2:31 3:25, Joshua 11:9, Nahum 3:1 3:5 3:12, Psalms 46:10

[14] LXX *up your multitude*

[15] LXX *your deeds*

[16] Nahum 3 - MurXII

[17] Nahum 3:1 - 4Q169 3-4 ii 1-2, Ezekiel 22:2-3 24:6-9, Habakkuk 2:12, Hosea 4:2, Isaiah 17:14 24:9 18:24, Nahum 2:13, Zephaniah 3:1-3

Hebrew		English
קוֹל שׁוֹט וְקוֹל רַעַשׁ אוֹפָן וְסוּס דֹּהֵר וּמֶרְכָּבָה מְרַקֵּדָה	2[1]	The voice of a whip and the voice of the rattling of a wheel; and a galloping horse, and a bounding chariot;
פָּרָשׁ מַעֲלֶה וְלַהַב חֶרֶב וּבְרַק חֲנִית וְרֹב חָלָל וְכֹבֶד פָּגֶר וְאֵין קֵצֶה לַגְּוִיָּה "יִכְשְׁלוּ" "וְכָשְׁלוּ" בִּגְוִיָּתָם	3[2]	The horseman charging, and the flashing sword, and the lightning spear; and a multitude of slain, and a heap of carcasses; *And there is no end of the bodies, and they stumble upon their corpses*[3];
מֵרֹב זְנוּנֵי זוֹנָה טוֹבַת חֵן בַּעֲלַת כְּשָׁפִים הַמֹּכֶרֶת גּוֹיִם בִּזְנוּנֶיהָ וּמִשְׁפָּחוֹת בִּכְשָׁפֶיהָ	4[4]	Because of the multitude of the harlotries of the well-favored harlot, The mistress of sorceries, who sells nations through her harlotries, and families through her witchcrafts.
הִנְנִי אֵלַיִךְ נְאֻם יְהוָה צְבָאוֹת וְגִלֵּיתִי שׁוּלַיִךְ עַל־פָּנָיִךְ וְהַרְאֵיתִי גוֹיִם מַעְרֵךְ וּמַמְלָכוֹת קְלוֹנֵךְ	5[5]	Behold, I am against you, says the LORD of hosts, and I will uncover your skirts upon your face, and I will show the nations your nakedness, and the kingdoms your shame.
וְהִשְׁלַכְתִּי עָלַיִךְ שִׁקֻּצִים וְנִבַּלְתִּיךְ וְשַׂמְתִּיךְ כְּרֹאִי	6[6]	And I will cast detestable things upon you, *and make you vile, and will make you as dung*[7].
וְהָיָה כָל־רֹאַיִךְ יִדּוֹד מִמֵּךְ וְאָמַר שָׁדְּדָה נִינְוֵה מִי יָנוּד לָהּ מֵאַיִן אֲבַקֵּשׁ מְנַחֲמִים לָךְ	7[8]	And it shall come to pass, that all who look upon you shall flee from you, And say: 'Nineveh is laid waste; who will wail for her? When shall I seek comforters for you?'
הֲתֵיטְבִי מִנֹּא אָמוֹן הַיֹּשְׁבָה בַּיְאֹרִים מַיִם סָבִיב לָהּ אֲשֶׁר־חֵיל יָם מִיָּם חוֹמָתָהּ	8[9]	*Are you better than No-amon*[10] that was situated among the rivers, that had the waters around her; *whose rampart was the sea, and the sea her wall*[11]?
כּוּשׁ עָצְמָה וּמִצְרַיִם וְאֵין קֵצֶה פּוּט וְלוּבִים הָיוּ בְּעֶזְרָתֵךְ	9[12]	Ethiopia and Egypt were your strength, and it was infinite; *Put and*[13] Lubim were your helpers.
גַּם־הִיא לַגֹּלָה הָלְכָה בַשֶּׁבִי גַּם עֹלָלֶיהָ יְרֻטְּשׁוּ בְּרֹאשׁ כָּל־חוּצוֹת וְעַל־נִכְבַּדֶּיהָ יַדּוּ גוֹרָל וְכָל־גְּדוֹלֶיהָ רֻתְּקוּ בַזִּקִּים	10[14]	Yet *was she carried away, she went into captivity*[15]; her young children also were dashed in pieces at the head of all the streets; and they cast lots for her honorable men, and all her great men were bound in chains.

Nahum 3:1-3 - 4Q169 frags 3-4 2.3-4, 4QXIIg

[1] Nahum 3:2 - Isaiah 9:6, Jeremiah 23:3, Job 39:22-39:25, Judges 5:22, Nahum 2:4-2:5

Nahum 3:2-3 - 4Q169 3-4 ii 3-6

[2] Nahum 3:3 - 2 Kings 19:35, 8HevXIIgr, Ezekiel 31:3-13 15:4, Genesis 3:24, Habakkuk 3:11, Isaiah 10:3 13:36, Nahum 2:5

[3] LXX *and of heavy falling: and there was no end to her nations, but they shall be weak in their bodies*

[4] Nahum 3:4 - 4Q169 3-4 ii 7-10, 4Q169 frags 3-4 2.7, Ezekiel 16:25-29, Isaiah 23:15-17 23:9 47:12-13, Leviticus.R 23:7, Pesikta Rabbati 21:17, Revelation 17:1-17:5 18:2-3 18:9 18:23

[5] Nahum 3:5 - 4Q169 3-4 ii 10-iii 1, Ezekiel 16:37 23:25 23:29, Habakkuk 2:16, Isaiah 47:2-3, Jeremiah 13:22 13:26, Micah 1:11, Nahum 2:14

[6] Nahum 3:6 - 1 Corinthians 4:9 4:13, 1 Kings 9:7-9:8, Hebrews 10:33, Isaiah 14:16-19, Jeremiah 3:37, Job 9:31 6:8 6:19, Jude 1:7, Lamentations 3:16, Malachi 2:2 2:9, Nahum 1:14, Psalms 38:6-8, Zephaniah 2:15

Nahum 3:6-7 - 4Q169 3-4 iii 1-5, 4Q169 frags 3-4 3.1-2

Nahum 3:6-17 - 8HevXIIgr

[7] LXX *according to your unclean ways, and will make you a public example*

[8] Nahum 3:7 - 4Q169 3-4 iii 5-8, 4Q169 frags 3-4 3.5-6, Isaiah 3:19, Jeremiah 15:5 3:9 51:41-51:43, Lamentations 2:13, Midrash Psalms 121:3, Nahum 1:1 2:10-2:11, Numbers 16:34, Pesikta Rabbati 30:1, Revelation 18:10 18:16-19

[9] Nahum 3:8 - 4Q169 3-4 iii 8-11, Amos 6:2, Ezekiel 30:14-16 31:2-3, Genesis.R 1:1, Isaiah 19:5-10, Jastrow 1446b, Jeremiah 46:25-26, Pesikta de R'Kahana 16.7, Pesikta Rabbati 29/30A:8 30:1 33:11

[10] LXX *Prepare a portion, tune the chord, prepare a portion for Ammon*

[11] MurXII8 *whose wall was a rampart of the sea*; HevXIIgr *whose strength Is the sea, water her wall*

[12] Nahum 3:9 - 1 Chronicles 1:8, 2 Chronicles 12:3, 4Q169 3-4 iii 11-iv 1, 4Q169 frags 3-4 3.11-12, b.Bechorot [Tosefot] 5b, b.Shabbat [Tosefot] 51b, Ezekiel 3:10 6:5 14:5, Genesis 10:6, Isaiah 20:5, Jeremiah 22:9, Pesikta Rabbati 30:1

[13] Missing in LXX

[14] Nahum 3:10 - 2 Kings 8:12, 4Q169 3-4 iv 1-4, Amos 1:13, Hosea 14:1, Isaiah 13:6 13:16 20:4, Joel 4:3, Lamentations 2:19 4:1, Midrash Psalms 121:3, Obadiah 1:11, Pesikta Rabbati 30:1, Psalms 33:16-17 17:8

[15] LXX *she shall go as a prisoner into captivity*

גַּם־אַתְּ תִּשְׁכְּרִי תְּהִי נַעֲלָמָה גַּם־אַתְּ תְּבַקְשִׁי מָעוֹז מֵאוֹיֵב

11[1] You also shall be *drunken*[2], you shall swoon; you also shall seek a refuge because of the enemy.

כָּל־מִבְצָרַיִךְ תְּאֵנִים עִם־בִּכּוּרִים אִם־יִנּוֹעוּ וְנָפְלוּ עַל־פִּי אוֹכֵל

12[3] All your fortresses shall be like fig trees *with the first-ripe figs*[4]: if they are shaken, they fall into the mouth of the eater.

הִנֵּה עַמֵּךְ נָשִׁים בְּקִרְבֵּךְ לְאֹיְבַיִךְ פָּתוֹחַ נִפְתְּחוּ שַׁעֲרֵי אַרְצֵךְ אָכְלָה אֵשׁ בְּרִיחָיִךְ

13[5] Behold, your people in your midst are women; the gates of your land are set wide open to your enemies; the fire has devoured your bars.

מֵי מָצוֹר שַׁאֲבִי־לָךְ חַזְּקִי מִבְצָרָיִךְ בֹּאִי בַטִּיט וְרִמְסִי בַחֹמֶר הַחֲזִיקִי מַלְבֵּן

14[6] Draw water for the siege, strengthen your fortresses; go into the clay, and *tread the mortar, lay hold of the brickmould*[7].

שָׁם תֹּאכְלֵךְ אֵשׁ תַּכְרִיתֵךְ חֶרֶב תֹּאכְלֵךְ כַּיָּלֶק הִתְכַּבֵּד כַּיֶּלֶק הִתְכַּבְּדִי כָּאַרְבֶּה

15[8] There the fire shall devour you; the sword shall cut you off, it shall devour you like the *cankerworm*[9]; make yourself many like the cankerworm, *make yourself many like the locusts*[10].

הִרְבֵּית רֹכְלַיִךְ מִכּוֹכְבֵי הַשָּׁמָיִם יֶלֶק פָּשַׁט וַיָּעֹף

16[11] You have multiplied your merchants above the stars of heaven; the *cankerworm*[12] spreads itself, and flies away.

מִנְּזָרַיִךְ כָּאַרְבֶּה וְטַפְסְרַיִךְ כְּגוֹב גֹּבָי הַחוֹנִים בַּגְּדֵרוֹת בְּיוֹם קָרָה שֶׁמֶשׁ זָרְחָה וְנוֹדַד וְלֹא־נוֹדַע מְקוֹמוֹ אַיָּם

17[13] *Your crowns are as the locusts, and your marshals as the swarms of grasshoppers, which camp in the walls in the cold day, but when the sun arises they flee away, and their place is not known*[14].

נָמוּ רֹעֶיךָ מֶלֶךְ אַשּׁוּר יִשְׁכְּנוּ אַדִּירֶיךָ נָפֹשׁוּ עַמְּךָ עַל־הֶהָרִים וְאֵין מְקַבֵּץ

18[15] Your shepherds slumber, *O king of Assyria, your nobles are at rest*[16]; your people are scattered upon the mountains, and there is no one to gather them.

אֵין־כֵּהָה לְשִׁבְרֶךָ נַחְלָה מַכָּתֶךָ כֹּל שֹׁמְעֵי שִׁמְעֲךָ תָּקְעוּ כַף עָלֶיךָ כִּי עַל־מִי לֹא־עָבְרָה רָעָתְךָ תָּמִיד

19[17] There is no healing for your hurt, your wound is grievous; all who hear the report of you clap the hands over you; for upon whom has your wickedness not passed continually?

---

[1] Nahum 3:11 - 1 Samuel 13:6 14:11, 4Q169 3-4 iv 4-6 4Q169 3-4 iv 6-8, Amos 9:3, Hosea 10:8, Isaiah 2:10 2:19 5:9 1:26 15:6, Jeremiah 4:5 8:14 25:15-27 3:57, Luke 23:30, Micah 7:17, Nahum 1:10 2:2, Psalms 75:9, Revelation 6:15-17

[2] LXX *overlooked*

[3] Nahum 3:12 - 4Q169 frags 3-4 4.8-9, Habakkuk 1:10, Isaiah 4:4, Revelation 6:13

[4] LXX *having watchers*

[5] Nahum 3:13 - Isaiah 19:16 45:1-45:2, Jeremiah 2:37 3:30, Nahum 2:7, Psalms 11:16 3:13

[6] Nahum 3:14 - 2 Chronicles 32:3-4 8:11, Isaiah 8:9 22:9-11 13:25, Jeremiah 46:3-4 22:9, Joel 4:9-11, Nahum 2:2

[7] LXX *be trodden in the chaff, make the fortifications stronger than brick*

[8] Nahum 3:15 - Exodus 10:13-15, Joel 1:4 2:25, Nahum 2:14 3:13, Zephaniah 2:13

[9] LXX *locust*

[10] LXX *and you shall be pressed down as a palmerworm*

[11] Nahum 3:16 - Genesis 15:5 22:17, Jeremiah 9:22, Nehemiah 9:23

[12] LXX *palmerworm*

[13] Nahum 3:17 - 4QXIIg, Genesis.R 90:3, Jeremiah 3:27, Revelation 9:7

[14] LXX *Your mixed multitude has suddenly departed as the grasshopper, as the locust perched on a hedge in a frosty day; the sun arises, and it flies off, and knows not its place: woe to them*

[15] Nahum 3:18 - 1 Kings 22:17, Exodus 15:16, Ezekiel 31:3-31:18 32:22-32:23, Isaiah 13:14 23:1 56:9-56:10, Jeremiah 2:18 3:39 3:57, Mekhilta de R'Shimon bar Yochai Bachodesh 54:2, Nahum 2:6-2:7, Psalms 76:6-76:7, Revelation 6:15

[16] LXX *the Assyrian king has laid low your mighty men*

[17] Nahum 3:19 - Ezekiel 1:6 30:21-30:22, Isaiah 10:6-10:14 14:8-14:21 13:18, Jeremiah 10:22 30:13-30:15 22:11, Job 3:23, Lamentations 2:15, Micah 1:9, Midrash Psalms 47:1, Nahum 2:12-2:13, Revelation 13:7 17:2 18:2-18:3 18:20, Saadia Opinions 10:13, y.Berachot 4:1, Zephaniah 2:13-2:15

Havakuk haShulami – Chapter 1

הַמַּשָּׂא אֲשֶׁר חָזָה חֲבַקּוּק הַנָּבִיא

1¹ The burden, which Habakkuk the prophet saw.

עַד־אָנָה יְהֹוָה שִׁוַּעְתִּי וְלֹא תִשְׁמָע אֶזְעַק אֵלֶיךָ חָמָס וְלֹא תוֹשִׁיעַ

2² O LORD, how long shall I cry, and you will not hear? I cry to You because of violence, and you will not save.

לָמָּה תַרְאֵנִי אָוֶן וְעָמָל תַּבִּיט וְשֹׁד וְחָמָס לְנֶגְדִּי וַיְהִי רִיב וּמָדוֹן יִשָּׂא

3³ Why do you show me iniquity, and you behold mischief? And why are destruction and violence before me? And there is strife, and contention rises up.

עַל־כֵּן תָּפוּג תּוֹרָה וְלֹא־יֵצֵא לָנֶצַח מִשְׁפָּט כִּי רָשָׁע מַכְתִּיר אֶת־הַצַּדִּיק עַל־כֵּן יֵצֵא מִשְׁפָּט מְעֻקָּל

4⁴ Therefore, the law is helpless, and jusrtice does not go forth; for the wicked entraps the righteous; therefore, right goes forth perverted.

רְאוּ בַגּוֹיִם וְהַבִּיטוּ וְהִתַּמְּהוּ תְּמָהוּ כִּי־פֹעַל פֹּעֵל בִּימֵיכֶם לֹא תַאֲמִינוּ כִּי יְסֻפָּר

5⁵ Look *among the nations*[6], and see, and be amazed. Be amazed[7]; For, look, a work shall be worked in your days, which you will not believe though it is told to you.

כִּי־הִנְנִי מֵקִים אֶת־הַכַּשְׂדִּים הַגּוֹי הַמַּר וְהַנִּמְהָר הַהוֹלֵךְ לְמֶרְחֲבֵי־אֶרֶץ לָרֶשֶׁת מִשְׁכָּנוֹת לֹא־לוֹ

6⁸ [9]For, behold, I raise up the Chaldeans, that bitter and impetuous nation, who march through the length of the earth, to possess dwelling places that are not theirs.

אָיֹם וְנוֹרָא הוּא מִמֶּנּוּ מִשְׁפָּטוֹ וּשְׂאֵתוֹ יֵצֵא

7¹⁰ They are terrible and dreadful; their judgement and their majesty proceed from themselves[11].

וְקַלּוּ מִנְּמֵרִים סוּסָיו וְחַדּוּ מִזְּאֵבֵי עֶרֶב וּפָשׁוּ פָּרָשָׁיו וּפָרָשָׁיו מֵרָחוֹק יָבֹאוּ יָעֻפוּ כְּנֶשֶׁר חָשׁ לֶאֱכוֹל

8¹² Their horses are swifter than leopards, And are more fierce than the wolves of *the evening*[13]; And their horsemen spread themselves; Yes, their horsemen come from far; they fly as a vulture that hurries to devour.

כֻּלֹּה לְחָמָס יָבוֹא מְגַמַּת פְּנֵיהֶם קָדִימָה וַיֶּאֱסֹף כַּחוֹל שֶׁבִי

9¹⁴ *They all come for violence; their faces are set eagerly as the east wind*[15]; And they gather captives as the sand.

---

[1] Habakkuk 1:1 - Isaiah 22:1, Nahum 1:1
Habakkuk 1:1-2 - 1QpHab 1:1-5, 1QpHab 1.1-2
[2] Habakkuk 1:2 - Chibbur Yafeh 7 28b, Jeremiah 14:9, Lamentations 3:8, Midrash Psalms 7:17 77:1, Pesikta de R'Kahana 16.8, Psalms 13:2-13:3 22:2-22:3 74:9-74:10 94:3, Revelation 6:10
[3] Habakkuk 1:3 - 1QpHab 1:5-10, 1QpHab 1.5, 1QpHab 1.7, 2 Peter 2:8, Ecclesiastes 4:1 5:9, Ezekiel 2:6, Jeremiah 9:3-9:7 20:8, Matthew 10:16, Micah 7:1-7:4, Midrash Psalms 7:17, Psalms 12:2-12:3 55:10-55:12 73:3-73:9 120:5-120:6
Habakkuk 1:3-13 - MurXII
[4] Habakkuk 1:4 - 1 Kings 21:13, 1QpHab 1:10-16, Acts 7:52 7:59 23:12-14, Amos 5:7 5:12, Chibbur Yafeh 7 29a, Deuteronomy 16:19, Ein Yaakov Avodah Zarah:3b, Exodus 23:2 23:6, Ezekiel 9:9 22:25-30, Hosea 10:4, Isaiah 1:21-1:23 5:20 59:2-8 59:13-15, James 2:6-7, Jeremiah 5:27-29 12:1 12:6 2:8 26:21-23 37:14-16 38:4-6, Job 21:7, Mark 7:9, Matthew 23:34-36 26:59-66 27:1-2 27:25-26, Micah 2:1-2 3:1-3 7:2-4, Midrash Psalms 22:25 90:7, Psalms 11:4 22:17 58:2-3 59:3 59:5 82:1-5 94:3 94:20-21 119:126, Romans 3:31, z.Pekudei 233b
[5] Habakkuk 1:5 - 1QpHab 1:16-2:10, 1QpHab 1.16-2.1, Acts 6:13-6:14 13:40-13:41, Daniel 9:12, Deuteronomy 4:27, Ezekiel 12:22-12:28, Isaiah 28:21-28:22 5:9 5:14, Jeremiah 5:12-5:13 9:26-9:27 18:18 25:14-25:29, Lamentations 4:12, Zephaniah 1:2
Habakkuk 1:5-11 - 8HevXIIgr
[6] LXX *you despisers*
[7] LXX adds *and vanish*
[8] Habakkuk 1:6 - 1QpHab 2:10-3:2, 1QpHab 2.10-11, 1QpHab 2.15, 1QpHab 3.2, 2 Chronicles 12:6 12:17, 2 Kings 24:2, Deuteronomy 28:49-28:52, Isaiah 23:13 39:6-39:7, Jeremiah 1:15-1:16 4:6 4:8 5:15 6:22-6:23 21:4 1:9
[9] MT uses plural pronouns [i.e. their], LXX uses singular pronouns [i.e., his]
[10] Habakkuk 1:7 - 1QpHab 3:2-6, 1QpHab 3.2-3, Deuteronomy 5:19 5:27, Exodus.R 30:17 51:7, Isaiah 18:7, Jeremiah 39:5-39:9 52:9-52:11 52:25-27, Leviticus.R 18:2, Midrash Tanchuma Tazria 8
[11] LXX adds *and his dignity shall come out of himself*
[12] Habakkuk 1:8 - Deuteronomy 4:49, Ezekiel 17:3 17:12, Genesis.R 16:4, Hosea 8:1, Isaiah 5:26-5:28, Jeremiah 4:13 5:6, Lamentations 4:19, Leviticus.R 13:5, Luke 17:37, Matthew 24:28, Ruth.R 4:1, Sifre Devarim Ha'azinu Hashamayim 325, Sifre Devarim Nitzavim 325, Zephaniah 3:3
Habakkuk 1:8-9 - 1QpHab 3:6-14, 1QpHab 3.6-9
[13] LXX *Arabia*
[14] Habakkuk 1:9 - 1QpHab 3:14-17, 1QpHab 3.14, Deuteronomy 28:51-28:52, Ezekiel 17:10 19:12, Genesis 17:49, Habakkuk 1:6 2:5-2:13, Hosea 2:1 13:15, Isaiah 3:8, Jeremiah 4:7 4:11 5:15-5:17 15:8 1:9 10:22, Job 5:18, Judges 7:12, Psalms 19:18, Romans 9:27
[15] LXX *Destruction shall come upon ungodly men, resisting with their adverse front*

וְהוּא בַּמְּלָכִים יִתְקַלָּס וְרֹזְנִים מִשְׂחָק לוֹ הוּא לְכָל־מִבְצָר יִשְׂחָק וַיִּצְבֹּר עָפָר וַיִּלְכְּדָהּ	10[1]	And they scoff at kings, and princes are a scorn to them; they scorn every stronghold, for they heap up dirt, and take it.
אָז חָלַף רוּחַ וַיַּעֲבֹר וְאָשֵׁם זוּ כֹחוֹ לֵאלֹהוֹ	11[2]	Then he sweeps on, as a wind, transgresses, and becomes guilty: they impute their might to their god.
הֲלוֹא אַתָּה מִקֶּדֶם יְהוָה אֱלֹהַי קְדֹשִׁי לֹא נָמוּת יְהוָה לְמִשְׁפָּט שַׂמְתּוֹ וְצוּר לְהוֹכִיחַ יְסַדְתּוֹ	12[3]	Are you not from everlasting, O LORD my God, my Holy One? We shall not die, O LORD. You have ordained them for judgment, and You, O Rock, have established them for correction.
טְהוֹר עֵינַיִם מֵרְאוֹת רָע וְהַבִּיט אֶל־עָמָל לֹא תוּכָל לָמָּה תַבִּיט בּוֹגְדִים תַּחֲרִישׁ בְּבַלַּע רָשָׁע צַדִּיק מִמֶּנּוּ	13[4]	You who are of eyes too pure to behold evil, and who cannot look on mischief, why do you look when they deal treacherously, and hold Your peace, when the wicked swallow up *the man who is more righteous than he*[5];
וַתַּעֲשֶׂה אָדָם כִּדְגֵי הַיָּם כְּרֶמֶשׂ לֹא־מֹשֵׁל בּוֹ	14[6]	And make men as the fish of the sea, as the creeping things, who have no ruler over them?
כֻּלֹּה בְּחַכָּה הֵעֲלָה יְגֹרֵהוּ בְחֶרְמוֹ וְיַאַסְפֵהוּ בְּמִכְמַרְתּוֹ עַל־כֵּן יִשְׂמַח וְיָגִיל	15[7]	Every one of them take up the hook, they drag them in their net, And gather them in their fishnet; therefore, he rejoices and exults.
עַל־כֵּן יְזַבֵּחַ לְחֶרְמוֹ וִיקַטֵּר לְמִכְמַרְתּוֹ כִּי בָהֵמָּה שָׁמֵן חֶלְקוֹ וּמַאֲכָלוֹ בְּרִאָה	16[8]	Therefore, he sacrifices to his net, burnt incense to his fishnet; b ecause by them his *portion*[9] grows fat, And his food is enriched.
הַעַל כֵּן יָרִיק חֶרְמוֹ וְתָמִיד לַהֲרֹג גּוֹיִם לֹא יַחְמוֹל	17[10]	*Therefore, he shall empty his*[11] *net*[12], and will continually kill

Habakkuk – Chapter 2

עַל־מִשְׁמַרְתִּי אֶעֱמֹדָה וְאֶתְיַצְּבָה עַל־מָצוֹר וַאֲצַפֶּה לִרְאוֹת מַה־יְדַבֶּר־בִּי וּמָה אָשִׁיב עַל־תּוֹכַחְתִּי	1[13]	I will stand upon my watch, and set myself on the tower, and will look out to see what He will

---

[1] Habakkuk 1:10 - 1QpHab 3:17-4:9, 1QpHab 3.17-4.1, 1QpHab 4.3-4, 2 Chronicles 12:6 12:10, 2 Kings 24:12 25:6-25:7, Isaiah 14:16, Jeremiah 8:24 9:4 52:4-52:7, z.Mishpatim 125b

[2] Habakkuk 1:11 - 1QpHab 4:9-16, 1QpHab 4.13, 1QpHab 4.9-10, Daniel 4:27-4:31 5:3-5:4 5:20, Jeremiah 4:11-4:12, Perek Shirah

[3] Habakkuk 1:12 - 1 Samuel 2:2, 1 Timothy 1:17 6:16, 2 Kings 19:25, Acts 3:14, Amos 9:8-9:9, Deuteronomy 8:4 32:30-32:31 9:27, Exodus.R 38:2, Ezekiel 6:25 37:11-37:14, Guide for the Perplexed 3:17, Habakkuk 3:2, Hebrews 1:10-1:12 12:5-12:6 13:8, Isaiah 10:5-10:7 27:6-27:10 13:26 16:28 19:15 1:7 9:15, Jeremiah 4:27 5:18 25:9-25:14 6:11 31:19-31:21 33:24-33:26 22:28, Lamentations 5:19, Malachi 3:6, Mekilta de R'Ishmael Shirata 6:18, Micah 5:3, Midrash Tanchuma Beshallach 16, Psalms 17:13 18:2 90:2 93:2 22:17, Revelation 1:8 1:11, Sifre.z Numbers Beha'alotcha 12:12, This is #12 of the Eighteen Emendations of the Sopherim. This passuk originally read:"*Are you are not from everlasting O LORD my God My Holy One? You shall not die.*" Interestingly this is the only emendation called out in the Revised Version but does so only in the margin by stating: "*According to an ancient Jewish tradition 'You die not.'*"
Habakkuk 1:12-13 - 1QpHab 4:16-5:8, 1QpHab 4.16-5.2

[4] Habakkuk 1:13 - 1 Kings 2:32, 1 Peter 1:15-1:16, 1QpHab 5:8-12, 2 Samuel 4:11, Acts 2:23 3:13-15, b.Bava Metzia 71a, b.Berachot 7b, b.Megillah 6b, Chibbur Yafeh 7 29b, Ein Yaakov Berachot:7b, Esther 4:14, Guide for the Perplexed 1:4 1:48, Habakkuk 1:3-4, Isaiah 21:2 9:1 16:13, Jeremiah 12:1-2, Job 15:15, Leviticus.R 4:8, Pesikta de R'Kahana 4.10 25.1, Pesikta Rabbati 14:1S 21:19, Proverbs 31:8-9, Psalms 5:5-5:6 10:2-3 10:16 11:5-8 34:16-17 35:22 37:12-15 37:32-33 50:3 50:21 56:2-3 73:3 83:2, Ralbag Wars 4:6

[5] LXX *the just*

[6] Habakkuk 1:14 - b.Avodah Zara 3b, Guide for the Perplexed 3:17, Pesikta Rabbati 21:19, Proverbs 6:7, Sifre Devarim Ha'azinu Hashamayim 306, Sifre Devarim Nitzavim 306
Habakkuk 1:14-16 - 1QpHab 5:12-6:8, 1QpHab 5.12-16
Habakkuk 1:14-17 - 8HevXIIgr

[7] Habakkuk 1:15 - Amos 4:2, Ezekiel 1:6 2:2 29:4-29:5 11:15, Isaiah 19:8, Jeremiah 16:16 2:11, John 21:6-21:11, Lamentations 2:15-2:16, Luke 5:5-5:10, Matthew 17:27, MurXII, Psalms 10:10, Revelation 11:10

[8] Habakkuk 1:16 - 1QpHab 6.2-3, 1QpHab 6.5, b.Eruvin [Rashi] 47b, Daniel 4:27 5:23, Deuteronomy 8:17, Ezekiel 4:3 5:3, Habakkuk 1:11, Isaiah 10:13-10:15 13:24, Mekilta de R'Ishmael Bahodesh 10:10, Midrash Tanchuma Yitro 16

[9] 8HevXIIgr *bread*

[10] Habakkuk 1:17 - 1QpHab 6:8-12, Ezekiel 25:1-17, Habakkuk 1:9-10 2:5-8 2:17, Isaiah 14:6 14:16-17 19:8, Jeremiah 25:9-26 46:1-28 52:1-34

[11] LXX *Therefore he will cast his*

[12] 8HevXIIgr *sword*

[13] Habakkuk 2:1 - 2 Corinthians 13:3, 2 Kings 9:17 17:9, 2 Samuel 18:24, b.Taanit 23a, b.Taanit 23a, Ein Yaakov Taanit:23a, Galatians 1:16, Genesis.R 13.7, Habakkuk 1:12-1:17, Isaiah 21:5 21:8 21:11-21:12 14:6, Jeremiah 12:1, Job 23:5-23:7 7:35 7:37,

speak against me, and what I shall answer when I am reproved.

וַיַּעֲנֵנִי יְהוָה וַיֹּאמֶר כְּתוֹב חָזוֹן וּבָאֵר עַל־הַלֻּחוֹת לְמַעַן יָרוּץ קוֹרֵא בוֹ

2[1] And the LORD answered me, and said: 'Write the vision, and make it plain on tables, so a man may read it swiftly.

כִּי עוֹד חָזוֹן לַמּוֹעֵד וְיָפֵחַ לַקֵּץ וְלֹא יְכַזֵּב אִם־יִתְמַהְמָהּ חַכֵּה־לוֹ כִּי־בֹא יָבֹא לֹא יְאַחֵר

3[2] For the vision is yet for the appointed time, and it declares the end, and does not lie; *though it dalays, wait for it; Because it will surely come, it will not delay[3].'*

הִנֵּה עֻפְּלָה לֹא־יָשְׁרָה נַפְשׁוֹ בּוֹ וְצַדִּיק בֶּאֱמוּנָתוֹ יִחְיֶה

4[4] *Behold, his soul is puffed up, it is not upright in him; But **the righteous shall live by his faith**[5].*

וְאַף כִּי־הַיַּיִן בּוֹגֵד גֶּבֶר יָהִיר וְלֹא יִנְוֶה אֲשֶׁר הִרְחִיב כִּשְׁאוֹל נַפְשׁוֹ וְהוּא כַמָּוֶת וְלֹא יִשְׂבָּע וַיֶּאֱסֹף אֵלָיו כָּל־הַגּוֹיִם וַיִּקְבֹּץ אֵלָיו כָּל־הָעַמִּים

5[6] *Yes, moreover, wine is a treacherous dealer; the haughty man is not content[7];* he who enlarges his desire as the nether world, and is as death, and cannot be satisfied, but gathers to himself all nations, and heaps to himself all peoples.

הֲלוֹא־אֵלֶּה כֻלָּם עָלָיו מָשָׁל יִשָּׂאוּ וּמְלִיצָה חִידוֹת לוֹ וְיֹאמַר הוֹי הַמַּרְבֶּה לֹּא־לוֹ עַד־מָתַי וּמַכְבִּיד עָלָיו עַבְטִיט

6[8] Shall not all these take up a parable against him, and a taunting riddle against him, and say: 'Woe to he who increases what is not his! *How long[9]? And who lades himself with many pledges[10]!'*

הֲלוֹא פֶתַע יָקוּמוּ נֹשְׁכֶיךָ וְיִקְצוּ מְזַעְזְעֶיךָ וְהָיִיתָ לִמְשִׁסּוֹת לָמוֹ

7[11] Shall they who shall exact interest not rise up suddenly, and awaken they who shall violently shake you, and you shall be plunder to them?

כִּי אַתָּה שַׁלּוֹתָ גּוֹיִם רַבִּים יְשָׁלּוּךָ כָּל־יֶתֶר עַמִּים מִדְּמֵי אָדָם וַחֲמַס־אֶרֶץ קִרְיָה וְכָל־יֹשְׁבֵי בָהּ

8[12] Because you have spoiled many nations, all the remnant of the peoples shall spoil you; because

---

Josephus Antiquities 14.2.1, m.Taanit 3:8, Midrash Psalms 1:17 77:1, Midrash Tanchuma Ki Tavo 4, Psalms 5:4 73:16-73:17 85:9
Habakkuk 2:1-2 - 1QpHab 6:16-7:5, 1QpHab 6.12-16
Habakkuk 2:1-8 - 8HevXIIgr

[1] Habakkuk 2:2 - 1 Corinthians 14:19, 1QpHab 7.3, 2 Corinthians 3:12, Daniel 12:4, Deuteronomy 3:8 7:19 7:22, Isaiah 8:1 6:8, Jeremiah 36:2-36:4 36:27-36:32, John 11:28-11:29, Midrash Psalms 7:17 77:1 17A:25, Revelation 1:18-1:19 14:13 19:9 21:5-21:8
Habakkuk 2:2-3 - MurXII

[2] Habakkuk 2:3 - 1QpHab 7:5-14, 1QpHab 7.5-6, 1QpHab 7.9-10, 2 Kings 6:33, 2 Peter 2:3, 2 Thessalonians 2:6-2:8, Acts 1:7 17:26, b.Sanhedrin 97b, Daniel 8:17 8:19 9:24-10:1 10:14 11:27 11:35, Ein Yaakov Sanhedrin:97b, Exodus 12:41, Ezekiel 12:25, Galatians 4:2, Hebrews 10:36-10:37, Isaiah 6:18, James 5:7-5:8, Jastrow 461b, Jeremiah 25:12-25:14 3:7, Lamentations 3:25-3:26, Luke 2:25 18:7-8, Micah 7:7, Midrash Psalms 77:1, mt.Perek Chelek Intro:11, Psalms 27:14 6:14 130:5-6

[3] LXX *though he should tarry, wait for him; for he will surely come, and will not tarry*

[4] Habakkuk 2:4 - 1 John 5:10-12, 1 Peter 5:5, 1QpHab 7:14-8:3, 1QpHab 7.14-15, 1QpHab 7.17, 2 Baruch 54:17, 2 Thessalonians 2:4, 4QXIIg, b.Makkot 24a, Daniel 4:27 4:34 5:20-23, Ecclesiastes.R 3:11, Ein Yaakov Makkot 24a, Exodus.R 23:5, Galatians 2:16 3:11-12, Hebrews 10:38, Job 40:11-12, John 3:36, Luke 18:14, Mekhilta de R'Shimon bar Yochai Beshallach 26:6, Mekilta de R'Ishmael Beshallah 7:155, Midrash Psalms 17A:25, Midrash Tanchuma Beshallach 10, Midrash Tanchuma Shoftim 9, Midrash Tanchuma Terumah 4, Miksat Maaseh Torah, Romans 1:17, Tanya Igeret Hakodesh §27ab, Tanya Likutei Aramim §33

[5] LXX *If he should draw back, my soul has no pleasure in him: but the just shall live by my faith*

[6] Habakkuk 2:5 - 1 Thessalonians 4:11, 1QpHab 8:3-13, 2 Baruch 56:6, 2 Kings 14:10, b.Bava Batra [Rashbam] 96b, b.Bava Batra 98a, b.Sotah 47b, Daniel 5:1-4 5:20-23, Ecclesiastes 5:11, Ein Yaakov Bava Batra:98a, Ein Yaakov Sotah:47b, Habakkuk 2:4 2:8-10, Isaiah 2:11-12 2:17 5:8 5:11-12 5:22-23 10:7-13 14:16-17 16:6 21:5, James 4:6, Jastrow 884b, Jeremiah 1:9 25:17-29 2:29 3:39, Midrash Tanchuma Shemini 5, Nahum 1:9-10, Numbers.R 10:2, Proverbs 20:1 23:29-33 3:20 30:13-16 31:4-5, Psalms 18:6, Saadia Opinions 10:5, Song of Songs.R 1:25
Habakkuk 2:5-11 - MurXII

[7] LXX *But the arrogant man and the scorner, the boastful man, shall not finish anything*

[8] Habakkuk 2:6 - 1 Corinthians 7:29-31, 1 Peter 4:7, 1QpHab 8:3-13, Avot de R'Natan 34, Ezekiel 8:21, Habakkuk 1:9-10 1:15 2:13, Isaiah 14:4-19 20:20 7:2, James 5:1-5:4, Jeremiah 5:22 2:13 51:34-35, Job 20:15-29 22:6-10, Luke 12:20, Mas.Derek Eretz Zutta 2:5, Micah 2:4, Numbers 23:7 23:18, Proverbs 22:16, Psalms 94:3

[9] Missing in 8HevXIIgr

[10] 8HevXIIgr *And loads himelf down with thick mud*; LXX *and who heavily loads his yoke*

[11] Habakkuk 2:7 - 1 Thessalonians 5:3, Daniel 5:25-31, Ecclesiastes 10:8, Isaiah 13:1-5 13:16-18 21:2-9 17:25 45:1-3 22:11 23:11 48:14-15, Jeremiah 8:17 50:21-32 3:11 51:27-28 3:57, Nahum 1:9-10, Proverbs 5:1
Habakkuk 2:7-8 - 1QpHab 8:13-9:7, 1QpHab 8.13-15

[12] Habakkuk 2:8 - 1QpHab 9:8-12, 1QpHab 9.3 4 7, Habakkuk 2:10 2:17, Isaiah 9:1 9:4 23:6, Jeremiah 3:7 6:16 50:10-11 50:17-18 2:28 50:33-34 2:37 3:8 3:13 3:24 51:34-35 3:44 3:48 51:55-56, Micah 4:11-13, Psalms 17:8, Revelation 6:10 18:20-24, Zechariah 1:15 2:8-9 12:2-4 14:12

הוֹי בֹּצֵעַ בֶּצַע רָע לְבֵיתוֹ לָשׂוּם בַּמָּרוֹם קִנּוֹ לְהִנָּצֵל מִכַּף־רָע **9**[1]

יָעַצְתָּ בֹּשֶׁת לְבֵיתֶךָ קְצוֹת־עַמִּים רַבִּים וְחוֹטֵא נַפְשֶׁךָ **10**[2]

כִּי־אֶבֶן מִקִּיר תִּזְעָק וְכָפִיס מֵעֵץ יַעֲנֶנָּה **11**[4]

הוֹי בֹּנֶה עִיר בְּדָמִים וְכוֹנֵן קִרְיָה בְּעַוְלָה **12**[6]

הֲלוֹא הִנֵּה מֵאֵת יְהוָה צְבָאוֹת וְיִיגְעוּ עַמִּים בְּדֵי־אֵשׁ וּלְאֻמִּים בְּדֵי־רִיק יִעָפוּ **13**[7]

כִּי תִּמָּלֵא הָאָרֶץ לָדַעַת אֶת־כְּבוֹד יְהוָה כַּמַּיִם יְכַסּוּ עַל־יָם **14**[8]

הוֹי מַשְׁקֵה רֵעֵהוּ מְסַפֵּחַ חֲמָתְךָ וְאַף שַׁכֵּר לְמַעַן הַבִּיט עַל־מְעוֹרֵיהֶם **15**[10]

שָׂבַעְתָּ קָלוֹן מִכָּבוֹד שְׁתֵה גַם־אַתָּה וְהֵעָרֵל תִּסּוֹב עָלֶיךָ כּוֹס יְמִין יְהוָה וְקִיקָלוֹן עַל־כְּבוֹדֶךָ **16**[12]

כִּי חֲמַס לְבָנוֹן יְכַסֶּךָ וְשֹׁד בְּהֵמוֹת יְחִיתַן מִדְּמֵי אָדָם וַחֲמַס־אֶרֶץ קִרְיָה וְכָל־יֹשְׁבֵי בָהּ **17**[14]

מָה־הוֹעִיל פֶּסֶל כִּי פְסָלוֹ יֹצְרוֹ מַסֵּכָה וּמוֹרֶה שָּׁקֶר כִּי בָטַח יֹצֵר יִצְרוֹ עָלָיו לַעֲשׂוֹת אֱלִילִים אִלְּמִים **18**[15]

of men's blood, and for the violence done to the land, to the city and to all who dwell there. Woe to him who gains evil gains for his house, so he may set his nest on high, so he may be delivered from the power of evil!

You have devised shame to your house by cutting off many peoples, *and have forfeited your life*[3].

For the stone shall cry out of the wall, *and the beam out of the timber shall answer it*[5].

Woe to him who builds a town with blood, and establishes a city by iniquity!

Behold, is it not of the LORD of hosts that the peoples labor for the fire, and the nations weary themselves for vanity?

For the earth shall be filled with the knowledge of the glory of the LORD, *as the waters cover the sea*[9].

Woe to him who gives his neighbor *drink, who puts your venom there*[11], and make him drunk, so you may look on his nakedness!

You are filled with shame instead of glory, drink also, and be uncovered[13]; the cup of the LORD's right hand shall be turned to you, and disgrace shall be upon your glory.

For the violence done to Lebanon shall cover you, and the destruction of the beasts, which made them afraid; because of men's blood, and for the violence done to the land, to the city, and to all who dwell there.

What benefit has an image, for its maker carved it; a molten image, and the *teacher of*

[1] Habakkuk 2:9 - 1 Kings 21:2-4 21:19-24, 1QpHab 9:12-5, 2 Kings 5:20-27, Acts 1:17-25, Deuteronomy 7:25-26, Gates of Repentance 3.24, Genesis 13:10-13 19:26-38, Isaiah 4:15 47:7-9, Jeremiah 22:13-19 1:16, Job 20:19-28, Joshua 7:21-26, Jude 1:11, Obadiah 1:4, Proverbs 18:11-12, Psalms 10:4-7 49:12 52:8, Zechariah 5:1-4
[2] Habakkuk 2:10 - 1 Kings 2:23, 1QpHab 9:12-10:5, 2 Kings 9:26 10:7, Gates of Repentance 3.24, Habakkuk 2:16, Isaiah 14:20-22 9:11, Jeremiah 22:30 2:19 12:31, Matthew 3:25, Nahum 1:14, Numbers 17:3, Proverbs 1:18 8:36
[3] LXX *and your soul has sinned*
[4] Habakkuk 2:11 - 1QpHab 9:12-10:5, 4 Ezra 5:5, b.Bava Batra [Tosefot] 2a, b.Chagigah 16a, b.Taanit 11a, Ein Yaakov Chagigah 16a, Ein Yaakov Taanit:11a, Gates of Repentance 3.024, Genesis 4:10, HaMadrikh 35:5, Hebrews 12:24, James 5:3-4, Jastrow 1454b, Job 31:38-40, Joshua 24:27, Lives of the Prophets 10:11, Luke 19:40, Revelation 6:10, z.Vaera 28a
[5] LXX *beetle out of the timber shall speak*
[6] Habakkuk 2:12 - 1 Kings 16:34, Daniel 4:24-28, Ezekiel 24:9, Genesis 4:11-4:17, Jeremiah 22:13-17, John 11:47-50, Joshua 6:26, Micah 3:10, Nahum 3:1, Revelation 17:6, This is the middle verse of the book of Habakkuk per the Massorah
Habakkuk 2:12-13 - 1QpHab 10:5-13, 1QpHab 10.5-8
[7] Habakkuk 2:13 - 2 Samuel 15:31, Genesis 11:6-9, Isaiah 41:5-8 2:11 7:2, Jeremiah 3:58 51:64, Job 5:13-14, Malachi 1:4, Midrash Psalms 2:2, Proverbs 21:30, Psalms 39:7 127:1-2
Habakkuk 2:13-20 - 8HevXIIgr
[8] Habakkuk 2:14 - 1QpHab 10:14-11:2, 1QpHab 10.14-15, Isaiah 6:3 11:9, Mekilta de R'Ishmael Shirata 10:70, Odes of Solomon 6:8, Psalms 22:28 67:2-3 72:19 86:9 98:1-3, Revelation 11:15 15:4, Zechariah 14:8-9
[9] LXX *it shall cover them as water*
[10] Habakkuk 2:15 - 1QpHab 11.2-3, 1QpHab11:2-8, 2 Samuel 11:13 13:26-13:28, Esther.R 3:1, Exodus 8:25, Genesis 9:22 19:32-19:35, Hosea 7:5, Jeremiah 1:15 3:7, Mekhilta de R'Shimon bar Yochai Shirata 32:1, Revelation 17:2 17:6 18:3
Habakkuk 2:15-16 - Mekilta de R'Ishmael Shirata 6:62, Midrash Tanchuma Beshallach 16
[11] LXX *to drink the thick lees of wine*
[12] Habakkuk 2:16 - 1QpHab 11:8-17, 1QpHab 11.8-11, b.Shabbat 149b, Esther.R 3:1, Hosea 4:7 7:5, Isaiah 20:4 28:7-28:8 23:3 1:26 51:21-51:23, Jastrow 1323a, Jeremiah 1:15 25:26-25:29 3:57, Lamentations 4:21, Mekhilta de R'Shimon bar Yochai Shirata 32:1, Nahum 3:5-3:6, Philippians 3:19, Proverbs 3:35, Psalms 75:9, Revelation 18:6
[13] LXX *Drink also your fill of disgrace instead of glory: shake, O heart, and quake*
[14] Habakkuk 2:17 - 1QpHab 11:17-12:10, 1QpHab 11.17-12.1, 1QpHab 12.6-7, Exodus.R 8:2, Habakkuk 2:8, Jeremiah 2:28 50:33-34 3:24 51:34-37, Midrash Tanchuma Vaera 9, Proverbs 4:17, Psalms 55:24 17:8, Revelation 18:20-24, Zechariah 11:1
[15] Habakkuk 2:18 - 1 Corinthians 12:2, 1 Timothy 4:1-2, 1QpHab 12:10-14, 1QpHab 12.10-12, 2 Thessalonians 2:9-11, Isaiah 1:31

lies[1]; does the maker of make dumb idols trust in his work?

הוֹי אֹמֵר לָעֵץ הָקִיצָה עוּרִי לְאֶבֶן דּוּמָם הוּא יוֹרֶה הִנֵּה־הוּא תָּפוּשׂ זָהָב וָכֶסֶף וְכָל־רוּחַ אֵין בְּקִרְבּוֹ	19[2]	Woe to him who says to the wood: *'Awake,'* to the dumb stone: *'Arise!' can these teach? Behold, it is overlaid with*[3] gold and silver, and there is no breath at all in its midst.
וַיהֹוָה בְּהֵיכַל קָדְשׁוֹ הַס מִפָּנָיו כָּל־הָאָרֶץ	20[4]	But the LORD is in His holy temple; let all the earth *keep silence*[5] before Him.

Habakkuk – Chapter 3

תְּפִלָּה לַחֲבַקּוּק הַנָּבִיא עַל שִׁגְיֹנוֹת	1[6]	A prayer of Habakkuk the prophet. *Upon Shigionoth*[7].
יְהֹוָה שָׁמַעְתִּי שִׁמְעֲךָ יָרֵאתִי יְהֹוָה פָּעָלְךָ בְּקֶרֶב שָׁנִים חַיֵּיהוּ בְּקֶרֶב שָׁנִים תּוֹדִיעַ בְּרֹגֶז רַחֵם תִּזְכּוֹר	2[8]	O LORD, I have heard Your report, and am afraid; *O LORD, revive Your work in the midst of the years, in the midst of the years make it known; in wrath remember compassion*[9].
אֱלוֹהַּ מִתֵּימָן יָבוֹא וְקָדוֹשׁ מֵהַר־פָּארָן סֶלָה כִּסָּה שָׁמַיִם הוֹדוֹ וּתְהִלָּתוֹ מָלְאָה הָאָרֶץ	3[10]	God comes from Teman, And the Holy One from *Mount Paran*[11]. *Selah.*[12] His glory covers the heavens, And the earth is full of His praise.
וְנֹגַהּ כָּאוֹר תִּהְיֶה קַרְנַיִם מִיָּדוֹ לוֹ וְשָׁם חֶבְיוֹן עֻזֹּה	4[13]	And a brightness appears as the light; *He has rays at His side, and there is the covering of His power*[14].

13:38 18:17 44:9-10 44:14-20 21:16 21:20 46:1-2 46:6-8, Jeremiah 2:27-28 10:3-5 10:8 10:14-15 2:2, Jonah 2:8, Psalms 115:4-8 135:15-18, Revelation 13:11-15 19:20, Romans 1:23-25 6:21, Zechariah 10:2
Habakkuk 2:18-20 - MurXII
[1] 8HevXIIgr LXX *lying appearance*
[2] Habakkuk 2:19 - 1 Kings 18:26-29, Acts 17:29, b.Sanhedrin 7b, Daniel 3:1 3:7 3:18 3:29 5:23, Ein Yaakov Sanhedrin:7b, Gates of Repentance 3.194, Isaiah 16:19 20:17 22:6, Jastrow 1695b, Jeremiah 10:4 10:9 10:14 3:47, Jonah 1:5, Psalms 97:7 15:17, Revelation 17:4, y.Bikkurim 3:3
Habakkuk 2:19-20 - 1QpHab 12:14-13:4
[3] LXX *Awake, arise; and to the stone, Be exalted! It is but an image, and this is a casting of*
[4] Habakkuk 2:20 - b.Megillah [Rashi] 31a, b.Sanhedrin 7b, Ephesians 2:21-2:22, Exodus.R 2:2, Gates of Repentance 3.194, Isaiah 6:1 18:1 18:6, Jonah 2:4 2:7, Micah 1:2, Midrash Proverbs 16, Midrash Tanchuma Naso 11, Psalms 11:5 46:11 76:9-76:10 19:3 132:13-132:14, y.Bikkurim 3:3, Zechariah 2:13, Zephaniah 1:7
Habakkuk 2:20-3:19 - Haftarah 2nd day Shavuot [Sephard and Teimon]
[5] LXX *fear*
[6] Habakkuk 3:1 - b.Megillah [Rashi] 31a, b.Megillah 31a, Bahir 68, Chibbur Yafeh 7 29a, Midrash Psalms 7:17 90:2 90:7, Psalms 7:2-18 86:1-17 90:1-17, z.Beshallach 44a
Habakkuk 3:1-19 - Haftarah 2nd day Shavuot [Ashkenaz], mt.Hilchot Tefilah 13:9, MurXII
[7] i.e., *ones who err*, LXX *with a song*
[8] Habakkuk 3:2 - 2 Chronicles 34:27-28, 2 Samuel 24:10-17, b.Moed Katan 14a, b.Sotah 49a, Bahir 68 72 76 77 79, Daniel 8:17 9:2, Ein Yaakov Sotah:49a, Exodus 9:20-21 32:10-12, Ezra 9:8, Habakkuk 1:5-10 3:16, Hebrews 11:7 12:21, Hosea 6:2-3, Isaiah 51:9-11 5:1 6:8 63:15-64:4 18:2, Jastrow 1368b 1456a, Jeremiah 10:24 25:11-25:12 5:10 36:21-24 52:31-34, Job 4:12-21, John 10:10, Lamentations 3:32, Midrash Psalms 22:7 90:2, Midrash Tanchuma Korach 12, Numbers 14:10-23 17:11-47, Philippians 1:6, Psalms 6:2-3 38:2 44:2 78:38 85:7 90:13-17 119:120 138:7-8, Revelation 15:4, Romans 10:16, Saadia Opinions 5:7, Seder Hatavat Chalom [Order of making good a bad dream], Song of Songs.R 1:22, Tachanun, z.Bereshit 7b, z.Beshallach 45a, Zechariah 1:12
[9] LXX *you shall be known between the two living creatures, you shall be acknowledged when the years draw near; you shall be manifested when the time is come; when my soul is troubled, you will in wrath remember mercy*
[10] Habakkuk 3:3 - 1 Samuel 1:1, 2 Corinthians 3:7-11, 3 Enoch 18:18, Amos 1:12, b.Avodah Zara [Tosefot] 2b, b.Avodah Zara 2b, b.Beitzah [Rashi] 16a, Deuteronomy 5:24 9:2, Ein Yaakov Avodah Zarah:2b, Exodus 19:16-20 20:15 24:15-17, Exodus.R 5:9, Genesis 21:21 12:11, Guide for the Perplexed 1:64, Isaiah 6:3 16:4, Jeremiah 1:7, Judges 5:4-5, Mekhilta de R'Shimon bar Yochai Bachodesh 49:2, Midrash Psalms 8:2, Midrash Tanchuma Shemot 25, Midrash Tanchuma Terumah 9, Numbers 10:12, Numbers.R 12:7, Obadiah 1:9, Pesikta Rabbati 5:9, Psalms 3:3 3:5 4:5 9:17 9:21 48:11 68:8-9 68:18 114:3-7, Revelation 5:13-14, Saadia Opinions 3:8, Sifre Devarim Ha'azinu Hashamayim 314, Sifre Devarim Nitzavim 314, Sifre Devarim Vezot Habracha 343, Song of Songs.R 8:15
Habakkuk 3:3-6 - Mekilta de R'Ishmael Bahodesh 1:105-107
[11] LXX *the dark shady*
[12] LXX *pause*
[13] Habakkuk 3:4 - 1 Timothy 6:16, b.Pesachim 8a, Bahir 147 148 187, Exodus 13:21 14:20, Isaiah 60:19-60:20, Job 2:14, Lamentations.R 2:6, Matthew 17:2, Midrash Psalms 19:7 75:5, Midrash Tanchuma Ki Tissa 37, Midrash Tanchuma Terumah 10, Nehemiah 9:12, Pesikta Rabbati 10:6, Proverbs 18:10, Psalms 8:2, Revelation 21:23 22:5, Tanya Likutei Aramim §26
[14] LXX *there were horns in his hands, and he caused a mighty love of his strength*

לְפָנָיו יֵלֶךְ דָּבֶר וְיֵצֵא רֶשֶׁף לְרַגְלָיו 5[1]

Before him proceeds *the pestilence, And fiery bolts go forth at His feet*[2].

עָמַד וַיְמֹדֶד אֶרֶץ רָאָה וַיַּתֵּר גּוֹיִם וַיִּתְפֹּצְצוּ הַרְרֵי־עַד שַׁחוּ גִּבְעוֹת עוֹלָם הֲלִיכוֹת עוֹלָם לוֹ 6[3]

He stands and shakes the earth; He sees and makes the nations tremble; And the everlasting mountains are dashed to pieces, The ancient hills bow; His ways are as of old[4].

תַּחַת אָוֶן רָאִיתִי אָהֳלֵי כוּשָׁן יִרְגְּזוּן יְרִיעוֹת אֶרֶץ מִדְיָן 7[5]

I see the tents of Cushan in affliction; The curtains[6] of the land of Midian tremble.

הֲבִנְהָרִים חָרָה יְהוָה אִם בַּנְּהָרִים אַפֶּךָ אִם־בַּיָּם עֶבְרָתֶךָ כִּי תִרְכַּב עַל־סוּסֶיךָ מַרְכְּבֹתֶיךָ יְשׁוּעָה 8[7]

Did the rivers burn against the LORD? Or was Your anger against the rivers? Or Your fury against the sea? *For you ride upon Your horses, upon Your chariots of salvation?*[8]

עֶרְיָה תֵעוֹר קַשְׁתֶּךָ שְׁבֻעוֹת מַטּוֹת אֹמֶר סֶלָה נְהָרוֹת תְּבַקַּע־אָרֶץ 9[9]

Your bow is made quite bare[10]; sworn are the rods of the word. Selah. You carve the earth with rivers[11].

רָאוּךָ יָחִילוּ הָרִים זֶרֶם מַיִם עָבָר נָתַן תְּהוֹם קוֹלוֹ רוֹם יָדֵיהוּ נָשָׂא 10[12]

The mountains have seen You, and they whirled; *the tempest of waters flows over*[13]; the deep utters its voice, And lifts up its hands on high.

שֶׁמֶשׁ יָרֵחַ עָמַד זְבֻלָה לְאוֹר חִצֶּיךָ יְהַלֵּכוּ לְנֹגַהּ בְּרַק חֲנִיתֶךָ 11[14]

The sun and moon stand still in their dwelling at the light of your arrows; they march at the lightning of Your spear.

---

[1] Habakkuk 3:5 - Bahir 178, Deuteronomy 8:24, Exodus 12:29-30, Midrash Psalms 5:7, Nahum 1:2-3, Numbers 14:12 17:11, Numbers.R 12:3, Psalms 18:8-14 78:50-51

[2] LXX *a report, and it shall go forth into the plains*

[3] Habakkuk 3:6 - Acts 17:26, b.Avodah Zara 2b, b.Bava Kamma 38a, b.Megillah 28b, b.Niddah 73a, b.Sotah 22a, Deuteronomy 8:8 9:15, Ein Yaakov Avodah Zarah:2b, Ein Yaakov Niddah:73a, Ein Yaakov Sotah:22a, Exodus 15:17 21:31, Exodus.R 23:1, Genesis 1:26, Habakkuk 3:10, Hebrews 13:8, Isaiah 3:6 3:8 64:2-4, Jastrow 946a, Joshua 10:42 11:18-23, Judges 5:5, Leviticus.R 13:2, Luke 1:50, Matthew 24:35, Mekilta de R'Ishmael Bahodesh 5:80, Micah 5:9, Midrash Tanchuma Shemini 6, Midrash Tanchuma Vezot Habracha 4, Midrash Tanchuma Yitro 14, mt.Hilchot Megillah v'Chanukah 2:18, Nahum 1:5, Nehemiah 9:22-24, Numbers 34:1-29, Pesikta Rabbati 50:2, Psalms 68:17 90:2 7:17 114:4-7 135:8-12, Sibylline Oracles 3.675 8.433, Sifre Devarim Ha'azinu Hashamayim 311, Sifre Devarim Nitzavim 311, y.Bava Kamma 4:3, y.Megillah 1:5, Zechariah 14:4-5

[4] LXX *the earth stood at his feet and trembled: he beheld, and the nations melted away: the mountains were violently burst through, the everlasting hills melted at his everlasting going forth*

[5] Habakkuk 3:7 - Exodus 15:14-16, Genesis 10:6-7 25:1-4, Joshua 2:10 9:24, Judges 7:24-25, Numbers 22:3-4 31:2-12, Psalms 83:6-83:11

[6] LXX *Because of troubles I looked upon the tents of the Ethiopians: the tabernacles*

[7] Habakkuk 3:8 - Deuteronomy 33:26-27, Exodus 7:20 14:21-22, Genesis.R 68:9, Guide for the Perplexed 1:70, Habakkuk 3:15, Isaiah 19:1 2:2, Jastrow 967a, Joshua 3:16-3:17, Mark 4:39, Midrash Psalms 18:14, Nahum 1:4, Pesikta Rabbati 21:1, Psalms 18:11 45:5 68:5 68:18 8:3 18:3 18:5, Revelation 6:2 16:12 19:11 19:14

[8] LXX *for you will mount on your horses, and your chariots are salvation*

[9] Habakkuk 3:9 - 1 Corinthians 10:4, Avot de R'Natan 33, b.Sanhedrin 92a, Deuteronomy 8:23, Deuteronomy.R 6:5, Exodus 17:6, Exodus.R 44:9, Genesis 15:18-15:21 17:7-17:8 22:16-22:18 26:3-26:4 28:13-28:14, Genesis.R 47:5, Hebrews 6:13-18, Isaiah 51:9-10 4:10, Lamentations 2:4, Luke 1:72-75, Mas.Kallah Rabbati 3:19, Mekhilta de R'Shimon bar Yochai Shirata 30:1, Mekhilta de R'Ishmael Shirata 4:9, Midrash Psalms 80:3, Numbers 20:11, Numbers.R 11:3 13:20, Psalms 7:13-14 35:1-3 78:15-16 105:8-11 9:41 23:6, Sifre Devarim Devarim 8, Sifre.z Numbers Korach 18:2, Song of Songs.R 1:49 3:14, t.Maaser Sheni 5:29 Habakkuk 3:9-15 - 8HevXIIgr

[10] 8HevXIIgr *You indeed awakened your bow*

[11] In LXX this verse reads, "*Surely you bend, they bow at scepters, says the LORD. Pause. The land of rivers shall be torn asunder.*"

[12] Habakkuk 3:10 - 2 Enoch 29:4, Bahir 139, Exodus 14:22-14:28 19:16-19:18, Habakkuk 3:6, Hebrews 11:29, Isaiah 11:15-11:16 19:20 7:12 63:11-63:13 64:2-64:3, Jeremiah 4:24, Joshua 3:15-3:16 4:18 4:23-4:24, Judges 5:4-5:5, Matthew 3:51, Mekhilta de R'Shimon bar Yochai Beshallach 24:4, Mekhilta de R'Ishmael Beshallah 5:17, Micah 1:4, Midrash Psalms 19:8, Midrash Tanchuma Beshallach 28, Midrash Tanchuma Tetzaveh 9, Nahum 1:5, Psalms 18:16 65:14 66:6 68:8-68:9 74:13-74:15 77:17-77:20 93:3 96:11-96:13 97:4-97:5 98:7-98:8 114:3-114:8 136:13-136:15, Revelation 6:14 16:12 20:11, y.Rosh Hashanah 3:8

[13] MurXII *the clouds poured out water*

[14] Habakkuk 3:11 - Avot de R'Natan 33, b.Nedarim [Ran] 39b, b.Nedarim 39b, b.Sanhedrin 11a, Ein Yaakov Nedarim:39b, Ein Yaakov Sanhedrin 110a, Exodus.R 31:15, Gates of Repentance 1.27, Isaiah 4:21 14:8, Joshua 10:11-13, Leviticus.R 31:9, Mekhilta de R'Shimon bar Yochai Shirata 30:1, Mekhilta de R'Ishmael Shirata 4:7, Midrash Psalms 19:8 19:11, Midrash Tanchuma Beha'alotcha 6, Midrash Tanchuma Beshallach 28, Midrash Tanchuma Korach 11, Midrash Tanchuma Mishpatim 12, Midrash Tanchuma Shoftim 14, Numbers.R 15:9 18:20, Perek Shirah [the Sun], Psalms 18:13-115 19:5 77:18-19 144:5-6, Song of Songs.R 1:49, y.Rosh Hashanah 3:8, z.Vayetze 165a

Hebrew	Verse	English

בְּזַעַם תִּצְעַד־אָרֶץ בְּאַף תָּדוּשׁ גּוֹיִם — 12[1] — *In fury, you march in to the land; in anger, You thresh the nations[2].*

יָצָאתָ לְיֵשַׁע עַמֶּךָ לְיֵשַׁע אֶת־מְשִׁיחֶךָ מָחַצְתָּ רֹּאשׁ מִבֵּית רָשָׁע עָרוֹת יְסוֹד עַד־צַוָּאר סֶלָה — 13[3] — You came forth for the deliverance of Your people, For the deliverance of your anointed; You struck the head of the house of the wicked, to make bare the foundation to the neck. Selah

נָקַבְתָּ בְמַטָּיו רֹאשׁ 'פְּרָזוֹ' "פְּרָזָיו" יִסְעֲרוּ לַהֲפִיצֵנִי עֲלִיצֻתָם כְּמוֹ־לֶאֱכֹל עָנִי בַּמִּסְתָּר — 14[4] — *You pierced through with his own rods the head of his rulers who come as a whirlwind to scatter me; they rejoice when they secretly devour the poor[5].*

דָּרַכְתָּ בַיָּם סוּסֶיךָ חֹמֶר מַיִם רַבִּים — 15[6] — You have trodden the sea with your horses, the foaming of mighty waters.

שָׁמַעְתִּי וַתִּרְגַּז בִּטְנִי לְקוֹל צָלֲלוּ שְׂפָתַי יָבוֹא רָקָב בַּעֲצָמַי וְתַחְתַּי אֶרְגָּז אֲשֶׁר אָנוּחַ לְיוֹם צָרָה לַעֲלוֹת לְעַם יְגוּדֶנּוּ — 16[7] — *I heard[8] and my belly trembled, My lips quivered at the voice; Rottenness enters my bones, And I trembles within myself; that I should rest for the day of trouble, When he comes up against the people he invades[9].*

כִּי־תְאֵנָה לֹא־תִפְרָח וְאֵין יְבוּל בַּגְּפָנִים כִּחֵשׁ מַעֲשֵׂה־זַיִת וּשְׁדֵמוֹת לֹא־עָשָׂה אֹכֶל גָּזַר מִמִּכְלָה צֹאן וְאֵין בָּקָר בָּרְפָתִים — 17[10] — Though the fig tree shall not blossom, nor shall fruit be on the vines; the labor of the olive shall fail, and the fields shall yield no food; *the flock shall be cut off from the fold[11]*, and no herds shall be in the stalls;

וַאֲנִי בַּיהוָה אֶעְלוֹזָה אָגִילָה בֵּאלֹהֵי יִשְׁעִי — 18[12] — Yet I will rejoice in the LORD, I will exult in the God of my salvation.

יְהוִה אֲדֹנָי חֵילִי וַיָּשֶׂם רַגְלַי כָּאַיָּלוֹת וְעַל בָּמוֹתַי יַדְרִכֵנִי לַמְנַצֵּחַ בִּנְגִינוֹתָי — 19[13] — GOD, the Lord, is my strength, *And He makes my feet like hinds' feet, And He makes me walk upon my high places. For the Leader, on my string instruments[14].*

---

[1] Habakkuk 3:12 - Acts 13:19, Amos 1:3, Isaiah 17:15, Jeremiah 3:33, Joshua 6:1-6:12, Mekhilta de R'Shimon bar Yochai Shirata 31:2, Mekhilta de R'Ishmael Shirata 5:70, Micah 4:12-4:13, Midrash Tanchuma Beshallach 15, Nehemiah 9:22-9:24, Numbers 21:23-21:35, Pesikta Rabbati 49:6, Psalms 44:2-44:4 78:55, Saadia Opinions 2:3, Song of Songs.R 1:49

[2] LXX *You will bring low the land with threatening, and in wrath you will break down the nations*

[3] Habakkuk 3:13 - b.Nedarim [Ran] 39b, Exodus 12:29-12:30 14:13-14:14 15:1-15:2, Isaiah 15:11, Joshua 10:11 10:24 10:42 11:8 11:12, Midrash Psalms 68:12, Midrash Tanchuma Korach 11, Pesikta de R'Kahana 16.8, Psalms 18:38-18:46 20:7 28:8 68:8 68:20-68:24 74:13-74:14 77:21 89:20-89:22 99:6 9:15 9:26 14:6, Unexpected Dagesh in the letter ר of רֹאשׁ

[4] Habakkuk 3:14 - Acts 4:27-4:28, Avot de R'Natan 33, Daniel 11:40, Exodus 1:10-1:16 1:22 11:4-11:7 12:12-12:13 12:29-12:30 14:5-14:9 14:17-14:18 15:9-15:10, Judges 7:22, Mekhilta de R'Shimon bar Yochai Beshallach 23:1 24:1, Mekilta de R'Ishmael Beshallah 4:56 5:3, Midrash Psalms 114:7 136:7, Midrash Tanchuma Beshallach 10, mt.Pirkei Avot 5:3, Psalms 10:9 64:3-64:8 78:50-78:51 83:3 83:9-83:12 118:10-118:12, Zechariah 9:14

[5] LXX *You cut asunder the heads of princes with amazement, they shall tremble in it; they shall burst their bridles, they shall be as a poor man devouring in secret*

[6] Habakkuk 3:15 - Avot de R'Natan 27, b.Sanhedrin 94b, Ein Yaakov Sanhedrin:94b, Exodus 15:8, Exodus.R 24:1, Habakkuk 3:8, Mekhilta de R'Shimon bar Yochai Beshallach 24:1, Mekilta de R'Ishmael Beshallah 5:5 7:60, Midrash Psalms 18:14 93:7 106:4 114:7 136:7, Midrash Tanchuma Beshallach 13, mt.Pirkei Avot 5:3, Psalms 77:20, Sibylline Oracles 1.315 5.157, Song of Songs.R 1:49

[7] Habakkuk 3:16 - 2 Kings 24:1-24:2, 2 Thessalonians 1:6-1:9, b.Yoma 75b, Daniel 8:27 10:8, Deuteronomy 28:49-28:52, Ezekiel 3:14 9:4-9:6, Gates of Repentance 1.004, Guide for the Perplexed 1:67, Habakkuk 1:5-1:11 3:2, Isaiah 26:20-26:21, Jeremiah 15:10-15:11 23:9 25:9-25:11 45:3-45:5, Psalms 91:15 94:12-94:13 119:120

[8] LXX *watched*

[9] LXX *at the sound of the prayer of my lips, and trembling entered into my bones, and my frame was troubled within me; I will rest in the day of affliction, from going up to the people of my sojourning*

[10] Habakkuk 3:17 - Amos 4:6-10, Deuteronomy 28:15-18 28:30-41, Genesis.R 53:3, Haggai 2:16-17, Jastrow 629a, Jeremiah 5:17 14:2-8, Joel 1:10-13 1:16-18, Midrash Proverbs 23, Midrash Tanchuma Tetzaveh 13, Pesikta de R'Kahana S6.2, Pesikta Rabbati 42:5

[11] LXX *the sheep have failed from the pasture*

[12] Habakkuk 3:18 - 1 Peter 1:8 4:12-4:13, 1 Samuel 2:1, Deuteronomy 12:18, Exodus 15:2, Genesis.R 53:3, Isaiah 12:2 17:16 13:10, James 1:2 1:9-1:10, Job 13:15, Luke 1:46-1:47 2:30, Micah 7:7, Numbers.R 3:3, Pesikta Rabbati 42:5, Philippians 4:4, Psalms 25:5 27:1 33:1 46:2-46:6 85:7 97:12 8:34 118:14-118:15 5:2, Romans 5:2-5:3, Zechariah 10:7

[13] Habakkuk 3:19 - 2 Corinthians 12:9-10, 2 Samuel 22:34, Colossians 1:11, Deuteronomy 8:13 9:29, Ephesians 3:16, Isaiah 12:2 21:24 10:14, Midrash Proverbs 23, Midrash Psalms 22:1, Philippians 4:13, Psalms 4:2-9 6:2-11 18:2 18:34 27:1 46:2 54:2-24 67:2-8 76:2-13, Zechariah 10:12

[14] LXX *and he will perfectly strengthen my feet; he mounts me upon high places, that I may conquer by his song*

Tzefanyah b'Cushi – Chapter 1

דְּבַר־יְהוָה אֲשֶׁר הָיָה אֶל־צְפַנְיָה בֶּן־כּוּשִׁי בֶּן־גְּדַלְיָה בֶּן־אֲמַרְיָה בֶּן־חִזְקִיָּה בִּימֵי יֹאשִׁיָּהוּ בֶּן־אָמוֹן מֶלֶךְ יְהוּדָה	1¹ The word of the LORD that came to Zephaniah the son of Cushi, the son of Gedaliah, the son of Amariah, the son of Hezekiah, in the days of Josiah the son of Amon, king of Judah.
אָסֹף אָסֵף כֹּל מֵעַל פְּנֵי הָאֲדָמָה נְאֻם־יְהוָה	2² *I will utterly consume all things*³ from off the face of the earth, Says the LORD.
אָסֵף אָדָם וּבְהֵמָה אָסֵף עוֹף־הַשָּׁמַיִם וּדְגֵי הַיָּם וְהַמַּכְשֵׁלוֹת אֶת־הָרְשָׁעִים וְהִכְרַתִּי אֶת־הָאָדָם מֵעַל פְּנֵי הָאֲדָמָה נְאֻם־יְהוָה	3⁴ *I will consume man and beast, I will consume the fowls of the heaven, and the fishes of the sea, and the stumbling blocks with the wicked; and I will cut off man*⁵ from off the face of the earth, says the LORD.
וְנָטִיתִי יָדִי עַל־יְהוּדָה וְעַל כָּל־יוֹשְׁבֵי יְרוּשָׁלָ͏ִם וְהִכְרַתִּי מִן־הַמָּקוֹם הַזֶּה אֶת־שְׁאָר הַבַּעַל אֶת־שֵׁם הַכְּמָרִים עִם־הַכֹּהֲנִים	4⁶ And I will stretch out My hand upon Judah, And upon all the inhabitants of Jerusalem; and I will cut off the remnant of Baal from this place, and the name of the *idolatrous priests with the*⁷ priests;
וְאֶת־הַמִּשְׁתַּחֲוִים עַל־הַגַּגּוֹת לִצְבָא הַשָּׁמָיִם וְאֶת־הַמִּשְׁתַּחֲוִים הַנִּשְׁבָּעִים לַיהוָה וְהַנִּשְׁבָּעִים בְּמַלְכָּם	5⁸ And those who worship the host of heaven on the housetops; and those who worship, who swear to the LORD and swear by *Malcam*⁹;
וְאֶת־הַנְּסוֹגִים מֵאַחֲרֵי יְהוָה וַאֲשֶׁר לֹא־בִקְשׁוּ אֶת־יְהוָה וְלֹא דְרָשֻׁהוּ	6¹⁰ They also who are turned back from following the LORD; and those who have not sought the LORD, nor inquired after Him.
הַס מִפְּנֵי אֲדֹנָי יְהוִה כִּי קָרוֹב יוֹם יְהוָה כִּי־הֵכִין יְהוָה זֶבַח הִקְדִּישׁ קְרֻאָיו	7¹¹ Hold your peace at the presence of the Lord GOD; for the day of the LORD is at hand, for the LORD has prepared a sacrifice; He has consecrated His guests.
וְהָיָה בְּיוֹם זֶבַח יְהוָה וּפָקַדְתִּי עַל־הַשָּׂרִים וְעַל־בְּנֵי הַמֶּלֶךְ וְעַל כָּל־הַלֹּבְשִׁים מַלְבּוּשׁ נָכְרִי	8¹² And it shall come to pass in the day of the LORD's sacrifice, that I will punish the princes, and the king's sons, and all such as are clothed with foreign apparel.
וּפָקַדְתִּי עַל כָּל־הַדּוֹלֵג עַל־הַמִּפְתָּן בַּיּוֹם הַהוּא הַמְמַלְאִים בֵּית אֲדֹנֵיהֶם חָמָס וּמִרְמָה	9¹³ In the same day will I punish all those who leap over the threshold, who fill *their master's house with violence*¹⁴ and deceit.

¹ Zephaniah 1:1-2 - 4QXIIb
Zephaniah 1:1-6 - 8HevXIIgr, Apocalypse of Zephaniah 3:4
Zephaniah 1:1-18 - Hanukkah first Shabbat [Pesikta Rabbati 8]
² Zephaniah 1:2 - 2 Chronicles 12:21, 2 Kings 22:16-22:17, b.Avodah Zara 55a, Ein Yaakov Avodah Zarah:55a, Ezekiel 33:27-33:29, Genesis 6:7, Isaiah 6:11, Jeremiah 6:8-6:9 24:8-24:10 10:22 12:29, Mekilta de R'Ishmael Bahodesh 6:120, Micah 7:13, Midrash Psalms 92:2, Pesikta Rabbati 29/30B:2
³ LXX *Let there be an utter cutting off*
⁴ Zephaniah 1:3 - b.Avodah Zara 55a, Ecclesiastes.R 1:3, Ein Yaakov Avodah Zarah:55a, Ezekiel 7:19 14:3-14:7 14:13-14:21 15:6-15:8 20:12, Genesis.R 28:6, Guide for the Perplexed 2:29, Hosea 4:3 14:5 14:10, Isaiah 3:9, Jeremiah 4:23-4:29 12:4, Jubilees 23:19, Matthew 23:39, Mekilta de R'Ishmael Bahodesh 6:123, Micah 5:12-5:15, Revelation 2:14, Zechariah 13:2
⁵ LXX *Let man and cattle be cut off; let the birds of the air and the fishes of the sea be cut off; and the ungodly shall fail, and I will take away the transgressors*
⁶ Zephaniah 1:4 - 2 Chronicles 10:4, 2 Kings 21:13 23:4-23:5, Exodus 15:12, Hosea 10:5, Isaiah 14:26-14:27, Jeremiah 6:12, Lives of the Prophets 13:1, Mekhilta de R'Shimon bar Yochai Shirata 35:1, Mekilta de R'Ishmael Shirata 9:18, Micah 5:14
⁷ Missing in LXX
⁸ Zephaniah 1:5 - 1 Kings 11:5 11:33 18:21, 2 Kings 17:33 17:41 23:12, Amos 5:26, Deuteronomy 10:20, Hosea 4:15, Isaiah 20:5 21:23 24:1, Jeremiah 4:2 5:7 19:13 8:29, Joshua 23:7, Lamentations.R Petichata D'Chakimei:22, Matthew 6:24, Pesikta de R'Kahana 134 13.8, Romans 14:11
⁹ LXX *their king*
¹⁰ Zephaniah 1:6 - 1 Samuel 15:11, 1QS 5:11, 2 Peter 2:18-2:22, Ezekiel 3:20, Hebrews 2:3 10:38-10:39, Hosea 4:15-4:16 7:7 11:7, Isaiah 1:4 9:14 19:22, Jeremiah 2:13 2:17 3:10 15:6, Psalms 10:5 14:2-14:3 36:4 5:5, Romans 3:11
¹¹ Zephaniah 1:7 - 1 Samuel 2:9-10 16:5 20:26, 2 Peter 3:10-12, Amos 5:18-20 6:10, Colossians 1:12, Ezekiel 7:7 7:10 39:17-20, Habakkuk 2:20, Isaiah 2:12 6:5 13:6 10:6, Jeremiah 22:10, Job 40:4-5, Joel 2:1-2 2:11 3:4, Luke 14:16-17, Malachi 3:19, Matthew 22:4, Philippians 4:5, Proverbs 9:1-6, Psalms 46:11 76:9-10, Revelation 19:17-18, Romans 3:19 9:20, Zechariah 2:13, Zephaniah 1:14
¹² Zephaniah 1:8 - 2 Kings 10:22 23:30-34 24:12-13 25:6-7 25:19-21, Deuteronomy 22:5, Isaiah 3:18-24 10:12 24:21 15:7, Jeremiah 22:11-19 22:24-30 39:6-7, Pesikta Rabbati 42:9
¹³ Zephaniah 1:9 - 1 Samuel 2:15-16 5:5, 2 Kings 5:20-27, Acts 16:19, Amos 3:10, Nehemiah 5:15, Proverbs 5:12, y.Avodah Zarah 3:2
¹⁴ LXX *the house of the LORD their God with ungodliness*

Hebrew		English
וְהָיָה בַיּוֹם הַהוּא נְאֻם־יְהֹוָה קוֹל צְעָקָה מִשַּׁעַר הַדָּגִים וִילָלָה מִן־הַמִּשְׁנֶה וְשֶׁבֶר גָּדוֹל מֵהַגְּבָעוֹת	10[1]	And in that day, says the LORD, Hear! A cry from the fish gate, and a wail from the second quarter, and a great crashing from the hills.
הֵילִילוּ יֹשְׁבֵי הַמַּכְתֵּשׁ כִּי נִדְמָה כָּל־עַם כְּנַעַן נִכְרְתוּ כָּל־נְטִילֵי כָסֶף	11[2]	Wail, you inhabitants of *Maktesh, for all the merchant people are undone*[3]; all they who were laden with silver are cut off.
וְהָיָה בָּעֵת הַהִיא אֲחַפֵּשׂ אֶת־יְרוּשָׁלַ͏ִם בַּנֵּרוֹת וּפָקַדְתִּי עַל־הָאֲנָשִׁים הַקֹּפְאִים עַל־שִׁמְרֵיהֶם הָאֹמְרִים בִּלְבָבָם לֹא־יֵיטִיב יְהֹוָה וְלֹא יָרֵעַ	12[4]	And it shall come to pass at that time, that I will search Jerusalem with *lamps; and I will punish the men who are settled on their lees*[5], Who say in their heart: 'The LORD will not do good, nor will He do evil.'
וְהָיָה חֵילָם לִמְשִׁסָּה וּבָתֵּיהֶם לִשְׁמָמָה וּבָנוּ בָתִּים וְלֹא יֵשֵׁבוּ וְנָטְעוּ כְרָמִים וְלֹא יִשְׁתּוּ אֶת־יֵינָם	13[6]	Therefore, their wealth shall become spoil, and their houses a desolation; yes, they shall build houses, but shall not inhabit them, and they shall plant vineyards, but not drink the wine.
קָרוֹב יוֹם־יְהֹוָה הַגָּדוֹל קָרוֹב וּמַהֵר מְאֹד קוֹל יוֹם יְהֹוָה מַר צֹרֵחַ שָׁם גִּבּוֹר	14[7]	The great day of the LORD is near, it is near and hurries greatly, the voice of the day of the LORD, *in which the mighty man cries bitterly*[8].
יוֹם עֶבְרָה הַיּוֹם הַהוּא יוֹם צָרָה וּמְצוּקָה יוֹם שֹׁאָה וּמְשׁוֹאָה יוֹם חֹשֶׁךְ וַאֲפֵלָה יוֹם עָנָן וַעֲרָפֶל	15[9]	That day is a day of wrath, a day of trouble and distress, a day of destruction and desolation, a day of darkness and gloom, a day of clouds and thick darkness,
יוֹם שׁוֹפָר וּתְרוּעָה עַל הֶעָרִים הַבְּצֻרוֹת וְעַל הַפִּנּוֹת הַגְּבֹהוֹת	16[10]	A day of the horn and alarm against the fortified cities, and against the high towers.
וַהֲצֵרֹתִי לָאָדָם וְהָלְכוּ כַּעִוְרִים כִּי לַיהֹוָה חָטָאוּ וְשֻׁפַּךְ דָּמָם כֶּעָפָר וּלְחֻמָם כַּגְּלָלִים	17[11]	And I will bring distress upon men, so they shall walk like the blind, because they have sinned against the LORD; and their blood shall be poured out as dust, and their flesh as dung.
גַּם־כַּסְפָּם גַּם־זְהָבָם לֹא־יוּכַל לְהַצִּילָם בְּיוֹם עֶבְרַת יְהֹוָה וּבְאֵשׁ קִנְאָתוֹ תֵּאָכֵל כָּל־הָאָרֶץ כִּי־כָלָה אַךְ־נִבְהָלָה יַעֲשֶׂה אֵת כָּל־יֹשְׁבֵי הָאָרֶץ	18[12]	Neither their silver nor their gold shall be able to deliver them in the day of the LORD's wrath; but the whole earth shall be devoured by

---

[1] Zephaniah 1:10 - 2 Chronicles 3:1 8:22 9:14, 2 Kings 22:14, 2 Samuel 5:7 5:9, Amos 8:3, Isaiah 22:4-22:5 11:11, Jeremiah 4:19-21 4:31 15:2, Nehemiah 3:3, Pesikta Rabbati 8:3, Zephaniah 1:7 1:15

Zephaniah 1:10-13 - Apocalypse of Zephaniah 2:1

[2] Zephaniah 1:11 - Ezekiel 21:17, Hosea 9:6 12:9-12:10, James 5:1, Jeremiah 4:8 1:34, Joel 1:5 1:13, John 2:16, Nehemiah 3:31-3:32, Pesikta Rabbati 8:3, Revelation 18:11-18:18, Zechariah 11:2-11:3

Zephaniah 1:11-18 - MurXII

[3] LXX *the city that has been broken down, for all the people have become like Chanaan*

[4] Zephaniah 1:12 - 2 Peter 3:4, Amos 6:1 9:1-9:3, b.Pesachim [Rashi] 7b, b.Pesachim 7b 8a, Ezekiel 8:12 9:9, Guide for the Perplexed 3:19, Isaiah 5:19, Jastrow 493a, Jeremiah 10:5 16:16-16:17 24:11, Job 21:15, Lives of the Prophets 13:1, Malachi 3:14-3:15, Mekhilta de R'Shimon bar Yochai Pisha 11:2, Obadiah 1:6, Pesikta de R'Kahana 16.8, Pesikta Rabbati 2:2 8:1-6, Psalms 10:12-10:14 14:1 94:7, Revelation 2:23, t.Pisha 1:1, y.Pesachim 1:1

[5] LXX *a candle, and will take vengeance on the men who despise the things committed to them*

[6] Zephaniah 1:13 - Amos 5:11, Deuteronomy 4:30 4:39 4:51, Ezekiel 7:19 7:21 22:31, Isaiah 5:8-5:9 6:11 24:1-24:3 65:21-65:22, Jeremiah 4:7 4:20 5:17 9:12 9:20 12:10-12:13 15:13, Micah 3:12 6:15, Zephaniah 1:9

Zephaniah 1:13-18 - 8HevXIIgr

[7] Zephaniah 1:14 - 1 Thessalonians 4:16, 2 Peter 2:3, Acts 2:20, Amos 8:2, Ezekiel 7:6-7:7 7:12 12:23 6:3, Hebrews 12:26, Isaiah 15:4 22:4-22:5 9:7 18:6, James 5:9, Jeremiah 1:36 6:7 24:41, Joel 1:15 2:1 2:11 3:4 4:16, Malachi 3:23, Philippians 4:5, Revelation 6:15-6:17, Saadia Opinions 9:3, Zephaniah 1:7 1:10

[8] LXX *is made bitter and harsh*

[9] Zephaniah 1:15 - 2 Peter 3:7, Amos 5:18-5:20, Apocalypse of Elijah 1:19, Apocalypse of Zephaniah 12:5, b.Avodah Zara 18b, b.Bava Batra [Rashbam] 78b, b.Bava Batra 10a 10b 78b 116a 141a, b.Shabbat 118a, Ein Yaakov Bava Batra:10a 10b 116a 141a, Ein Yaakov Shabbat:118a, Isaiah 22:5, Jeremiah 6:7, Job 3:5-3:9, Joel 2:2 2:11, Luke 21:22-21:23, Mekilta de R'Ishmael Pisha 7:26 11:82, Pesikta de R'Kahana 16.8, Revelation 6:17, Romans 2:5, Saadia Opinions 9:3, Zephaniah 1:18 2:2

[10] Zephaniah 1:16 - Amos 3:6, Habakkuk 1:6-10 3:6, Hosea 5:8 8:1, Isaiah 2:12-15 8:14 11:10, Jeremiah 4:19-20 6:1 8:16, Psalms 48:13-14

[11] Zephaniah 1:17 - 1 John 2:11, 2 Corinthians 4:4, 2 Kings 9:33-37, 2 Peter 1:9, Amos 4:10, Apocalypse of Zephaniah 10:8, Daniel 9:5-19, Deuteronomy 28:28-29, Ezekiel 22:25-31, Isaiah 24:5-6 5:10 2:1 59:9-10 59:12-15, Jeremiah 2:17 2:19 4:18 9:22-23 10:18 15:3 16:4-6 18:21, John 9:40-41, Lamentations 1:8 1:14 1:18 2:21 4:13-15 5:16-17, Matthew 15:14, Micah 3:9-12 7:13, Psalms 79:2-3 83:11, Revelation 3:17, Romans 11:7 11:25, Saadia Opinions 9:3

[12] Zephaniah 1:18 - 1 Corinthians 10:22, 1 Kings 14:22, 1Q15 frag 1 ll.1-2, Apocalypse of Elijah 1:19 1:4, Deuteronomy 29:19-29:27 7:17 32:21-32:25, Ezekiel 7:19 8:3-8:5 16:38 36:5-36:6, Genesis 6:7, Isaiah 1:24 2:20-2:21 24:1-24:12, Jeremiah 4:26-4:29 7:20 7:34

the fire of His jealousy; for He will make an end, yes, a terrible end, of all those who dwell in the earth.

Zephaniah – Chapter 2

הִתְקוֹשְׁשׁוּ וָקוֹשּׁוּ הַגּוֹי לֹא נִכְסָף	1[1]	Gather yourselves together; yes, gather together, O shameless nation;
בְּטֶרֶם לֶדֶת חֹק כְּמֹץ עָבַר יוֹם בְּטֶרֶם לֹא־יָבוֹא עֲלֵיכֶם חֲרוֹן אַף־יְהוָה בְּטֶרֶם לֹא־יָבוֹא עֲלֵיכֶם יוֹם אַף־יְהוָה	2[2]	*Before the decree, bring forth the day when one passes as the chaff*[3], before the fierce anger of the LORD comes upon you, before the day of the LORD's anger comes upon you.
בַּקְּשׁוּ אֶת־יְהוָה כָּל־עַנְוֵי הָאָרֶץ אֲשֶׁר מִשְׁפָּטוֹ פָּעָלוּ בַּקְּשׁוּ־צֶדֶק בַּקְּשׁוּ עֲנָוָה אוּלַי תִּסָּתְרוּ בְּיוֹם אַף־יְהוָה	3[4]	Seek the LORD, all the earth who are humble, *who have executed His ordinance; seek righteousness, seek humility*[5]. Perhaps you shall be hidden in the day of the LORD's anger.
כִּי עַזָּה עֲזוּבָה תִהְיֶה וְאַשְׁקְלוֹן לִשְׁמָמָה אַשְׁדּוֹד בַּצָּהֳרַיִם יְגָרְשׁוּהָ וְעֶקְרוֹן תֵּעָקֵר	4[6]	For Gaza shall be forsaken, and Ashkelon a desolation; they shall drive out *Ashdod*[7] at the noonday, and *Ekron*[8] shall be uprooted.
הוֹי יֹשְׁבֵי חֶבֶל הַיָּם גּוֹי כְּרֵתִים דְּבַר־יְהוָה עֲלֵיכֶם כְּנַעַן אֶרֶץ פְּלִשְׁתִּים וְהַאֲבַדְתִּיךְ מֵאֵין יוֹשֵׁב	5[9]	Woe to the inhabitants of the seacoast, *the nation of the Cherethites*[10]! The word of the LORD is against you, O Canaan, the land of the Philistines; *I will destroy you, so there shall be no inhabitant*[11].
וְהָיְתָה חֶבֶל הַיָּם נְוֹת כְּרֹת רֹעִים וְגִדְרוֹת צֹאן	6[12]	And *the seacoast*[13] shall be pastures, meadows for shepherds, and folds for flocks.
וְהָיָה חֶבֶל לִשְׁאֵרִית בֵּית יְהוּדָה עֲלֵיהֶם יִרְעוּן בְּבָתֵּי אַשְׁקְלוֹן בָּעֶרֶב יִרְבָּצוּן כִּי יִפְקְדֵם יְהוָה אֱלֹהֵיהֶם וְשָׁב "שְׁבוּתָם" "שְׁבִיתָם"	7[14]	And *it*[15] shall be a portion for the remnant of the house of Judah, upon which they shall feed; in the houses of Ashkelon shall they lie down in

9:12 9:24-9:25, Job 21:30, Leviticus 26:33-26:35, Luke 12:19-12:21 16:22-16:23, Matthew 16:26, Midrash Psalms 46:1, Proverbs 11:4 18:11, Psalms 49:7-49:10 52:6-52:8 78:58 79:5, Saadia Opinions 9:3, Zephaniah 1:2-1:3 1:11 1:15 3:8

[1] Zephaniah 2:1 - 2 Chronicles 20:4, b.Bava Batra 60b, b.Bava Metzia 107b, b.Sanhedrin [Tosefot] 18b, b.Sanhedrin 18a 19a, Ein Yaakov Bava Metzia:107b, Ein Yaakov Sanhedrin:19a, Esther 4:16, Isaiah 1:4-1:6 1:10-1:15 26:8-26:9, Jastrow 1370b 1429b 1433a, Jeremiah 3:3 6:15 12:7-12:9, Joel 1:14 2:12-2:18, Lamentations.R 3:14, Matthew 18:20, Nehemiah 8:1 9:1, Saadia Opinions 9:3, y.Taanit 2:1, Zechariah 11:8
Zephaniah 2:1-2 - 1Q15 frag 1 ll.2-4
Zephaniah 2:1-15 - Lives of the Prophets 13:2, MurXII
[2] Zephaniah 2:2 - 2 Chronicles 36:16-36:17, 2 Kings 22:16-22:17 23:26-23:27, 2 Peter 3:4-3:10, Ezekiel 12:25, Hosea 13:3, Isaiah 17:13 41:15-41:16, Jeremiah 23:20, Job 21:18, Lamentations 4:11, Luke 13:24-13:28, Malachi 3:19-4:20, Matthew 24:35, Nahum 1:6, Psalms 1:4 2:12 50:22 95:7-95:8, Saadia Opinions 9:3, Zephaniah 1:18 3:8
[3] LXX *before you become as the flower that passes away*
[4] Zephaniah 2:3 - 1 Peter 1:22 3:4, 1 Thessalonians 4:1 4:10, 2 Chronicles 34:27-28, 2 Peter 3:18, 2 Samuel 12:22, Amos 5:4-6 5:14-15, Apocalypse of Elijah 1:19, b.Chagigah 42ab, Colossians 3:2-4, Ecclesiastes.R 12:13, Ein Yaakov Chagigah:4b, Ein Yaakov Yevamot:78b, Exodus 12:27, Genesis 7:15-16, Hosea 7:10 10:12, Isaiah 11:4 26:20-21 55:6-7 13:1, James 1:21-22, Jastrow 620a, Jeremiah 3:13-14 4:1-2 22:15-16 29:12-13 15:18 21:5, Joel 2:13-14, Jonah 3:9, Lamentations.R 3:10, Leviticus.R 26:7, Mas.Kallah Rabbati 3:1, Matthew 5:5 7:7-8, Midrash Tanchuma Emor 2, Numbers.R 8:4, Philippians 3:13-14, Proverbs 18:10, Psalms 22:27 25:8-9 31:21 32:6-7 57:2 76:10 91:1 9:4 5:4, y.Chagigah 2:1, y.Kiddushin 4:1, y.Sanhedrin 6:7, z.Noach 67b, Zechariah 8:19
[5] LXX *do judgment, and seek justice, and answer accordingly*
[6] Zephaniah 2:4 - Amos 1:6-1:8, b.Megillah 6a, b.Yevamot 78b, Ein Yaakov Megillah:6a, Ezekiel 25:15-25:17, Jastrow 1365b, Jeremiah 6:4 15:8 1:20 47:1-47:7, Psalms 91:6, Zechariah 9:5-9:7
[7] LXX *Azotus*
[8] LXX *Accaron*
[9] Zephaniah 2:5 - Amos 3:1 5:1, Ezekiel 1:16, Genesis.R 28:5, Isaiah 14:30, Jastrow 674a, Jeremiah 23:7, Joshua 13:3, Judges 3:3, Mark 12:12, Zechariah 1:6, Zephaniah 3:6
[10] LXX *neighbors of the Cretans*
[11] LXX *and I will destroy you out of your dwelling place*
[12] Zephaniah 2:6 - Ezekiel 1:5, Isaiah 5:17 17:2, Zephaniah 2:14-2:15
[13] LXX *Crete*
[14] Zephaniah 2:7 - Acts 8:26 8:40, Amos 9:14-9:15, Exodus 4:31, Ezekiel 15:25, Genesis 2:24, Haggai 1:12 2:2, Isaiah 11:11 14:1 14:29-14:32, Jeremiah 3:18 23:3 5:14 6:3 30:18-30:19 7:8 8:44 9:7, Luke 1:68 7:16, Micah 2:12 4:7 4:10 5:4-5:9, Obadiah 1:19, Psalms 85:2 126:1-126:4, Romans 11:5, Zechariah 9:6-9:7, Zephaniah 2:9 3:20
[15] LXX *the seacoast*

the evening[1]; for the LORD their God will remember them and remove their captivity.

8² שָׁמַעְתִּי חֶרְפַּת מוֹאָב וְגִדּוּפֵי בְּנֵי עַמּוֹן אֲשֶׁר חֵרְפוּ אֶת־עַמִּי וַיַּגְדִּילוּ עַל־גְּבוּלָם

I have heard the taunt of Moab, and the reviling of the children of Ammon, with which they have taunted My people, and spoke boastfully concerning their border.

9³ לָכֵן חַי־אָנִי נְאֻם יְהוָה צְבָאוֹת אֱלֹהֵי יִשְׂרָאֵל כִּי־מוֹאָב כִּסְדֹם תִּהְיֶה וּבְנֵי עַמּוֹן כַּעֲמֹרָה מִמְשַׁק חָרוּל וּמִכְרֵה־מֶלַח וּשְׁמָמָה עַד־עוֹלָם שְׁאֵרִית עַמִּי יְבָזּוּם וְיֶתֶר "גּוֹיִי" "גּוֹיִי" יִנְחָלוּם

Therefore, as I live, says the LORD of hosts, the God of Israel: surely Moab shall be as Sodom, and the children of Ammon as Gomorrah, *the breeding-place of nettles, and salt pits, and a desolation, forever*[4]; the residue of My people shall spoil them, and the remnant of My nation shall inherit them.

10⁵ זֹאת לָהֶם תַּחַת גְּאוֹנָם כִּי חֵרְפוּ וַיַּגְדִּלוּ עַל־עַם יְהוָה צְבָאוֹת

They shall have this for their pride, because they taunted and spoke boastfully against the people of the LORD of hosts[6].

11⁷ נוֹרָא יְהוָה עֲלֵיהֶם כִּי רָזָה אֵת כָּל־אֱלֹהֵי הָאָרֶץ וְיִשְׁתַּחֲווּ־לוֹ אִישׁ מִמְּקוֹמוֹ כֹּל אִיֵּי הַגּוֹיִם

The LORD will be terrible to them; for He will famish all the gods of the earth; then all the isles of the nations shall worship Him, every one from its place.

12⁸ גַּם־אַתֶּם כּוּשִׁים חַלְלֵי חַרְבִּי הֵמָּה

You Ethiopians also, you shall be slain by My sword.

13⁹ וְיֵט יָדוֹ עַל־צָפוֹן וִיאַבֵּד אֶת־אַשּׁוּר וְיָשֵׂם אֶת־נִינְוֵה לִשְׁמָמָה צִיָּה כַּמִּדְבָּר

And He will stretch out His hand against the north, and destroy Assyria; and will make Nineveh a desolation, and dry like the wilderness.

14¹⁰ וְרָבְצוּ בְתוֹכָהּ עֲדָרִים כָּל־חַיְתוֹ־גוֹי גַּם־קָאַת גַּם־קִפֹּד בְּכַפְתֹּרֶיהָ יָלִינוּ קוֹל יְשׁוֹרֵר בַּחַלּוֹן חֹרֶב בַּסַּף כִּי אַרְזָה עֵרָה

And all beasts of every kind shall lie down in her midst in herds; both the pelican and the bittern shall lodge in its capitals; voices shall sing in the windows; desolation shall be in the posts; for its cedarwork shall be uncovered[11].

15¹² זֹאת הָעִיר הָעַלִּיזָה הַיּוֹשֶׁבֶת לָבֶטַח הָאֹמְרָה בִּלְבָבָהּ אֲנִי וְאַפְסִי עוֹד אֵיךְ הָיְתָה לְשַׁמָּה מַרְבֵּץ לַחַיָּה כֹּל עוֹבֵר עָלֶיהָ יִשְׁרֹק יָנִיעַ יָדוֹ

[13]This is the *joyous*[14] city that lived without care, that said in her heart: 'I am, and there is no one else beside me;' How did she become a

---

[1] LXX adds *because of the children of Juda*

[2] Zephaniah 2:8 - Amos 1:13, Ezekiel 25:3-25:11 12:2, Jeremiah 48:27-48:29 1:1, Psalms 83:5-83:8 Zephaniah 2:8-9 - Pesikta de R'Kahana 19.1

[3] Zephaniah 2:9 - Amos 1:13-2:3, Deuteronomy 5:22, Ezekiel 25:1-25:17, Genesis 19:24-19:25, Genesis.R 41:3, Isaiah 11:14 13:19-13:20 15:1-15:9 1:10 34:9-34:13 1:18, Jeremiah 22:18 48:1-49:6 1:18 2:40, Joel 4:19-4:20, Lamentations.R 1:38 Petichata D'Chakimei:9, Micah 5:8-5:9, Midrash Tanchuma Ki Tetze 2, Numbers 14:21, Romans 14:11, This is the middle verse of the book of Zephaniah per the Massorah, Zephaniah 2:7 2:14 3:13
Zephaniah 2:9-10 - 8HevXIIgr

[4] LXX *and Damascus shall be left as a heap of the threshing floor, and desolate forever*

[5] Zephaniah 2:10 - 1 Peter 5:5, Daniel 4:34 5:20-5:23, Exodus 9:17 10:3, Ezekiel 38:14-38:18, Isaiah 10:12-10:15 16:6 37:22-37:29, Jeremiah 24:29, Obadiah 1:3, Zephaniah 2:8

[6] LXX *This is their punishment in return for their haughtiness, because they have reproached and magnified themselves against the LORD Almighty*

[7] Zephaniah 2:11 - 1 Timothy 2:8, Deuteronomy 8:38, Genesis 10:5, Hosea 2:17, Isaiah 2:2-4 11:9-10 24:14-16 18:4 18:10 1:1, Joel 2:11, John 4:21-23, Malachi 1:11, Micah 4:1-3, Psalms 2:8-12 22:28-31 72:8-11 72:17 86:9 97:6-8 117:1-2 18:4, Revelation 11:15, Zechariah 2:11 8:20 8:23 13:2 14:9-21, Zephaniah 1:4 3:9

[8] Zephaniah 2:12 - Ezekiel 30:4-9, Isaiah 10:5 13:5 18:1-7 20:4-5 19:3, Jeremiah 46:9-10 47:6-7 51:20-23, Psalms 17:13

[9] Zephaniah 2:13 - Ezekiel 31:3-18, Isaiah 10:12 10:16 11:11, Mekhilta de R'Shimon bar Yochai Shirata 35:1, Mekilta de R'Ishmael Shirata 9:17, Micah 5:7, Nahum 1:1 2:11-12 3:7 3:15 3:18-19, Psalms 83:9-10, Zechariah 10:10-11
Zephaniah 2:13-15 - 4QXIIb

[10] Zephaniah 2:14 - Amos 9:1, b.Sotah 48a, Ein Yaakov Sotah:47b, Isaiah 13:19-22 14:23 34:11-17, Jastrow 950a 1488a, Jeremiah 22:14, Revelation 18:2, Zephaniah 2:6

[11] LXX *And flocks, and all the wild beasts of the land, and chameleons shall feed in its midst: and hedgehogs shall lodge in the ceilings; and wild beasts shall cry in the breaches, and ravens in her porches, where her loftiness was as as cedar*

[12] Zephaniah 2:15 - 1 Kings 9:7-8, 4QXIIC, Ezekiel 3:36 4:2 4:9 5:3, Isaiah 10:12-14 14:4-5 22:2 8:9 47:7-8, Jeremiah 19:8, Job 3:23, Lamentations 1:1 2:1 2:15, Matthew 3:39, Nahum 3:19, Psalms 52:7-8, Revelation 18:7-19, Tanya Likutei Aramim §22 §36

[13] in LXX, chapter 3 begins here

[14] LXX *scornful*

desolation, a place for beasts to lie down? Everyone who passes by her shall hiss, and wag his hand.

Zephaniah – Chapter 3

Hebrew	v.	English
הוֹי מֹרְאָה וְנִגְאָלָה הָעִיר הַיּוֹנָה	1[1]	*Woe to her who is disgraced and polluted, to the oppressing city[2]!*
לֹא שָׁמְעָה בְּקוֹל לֹא לָקְחָה מוּסָר בַּיהוָה לֹא בָטָחָה אֶל־אֱלֹהֶיהָ לֹא קָרֵבָה	2[3]	*She[4]* did not listen to the voice, she did not receive correction; she did not trust in the LORD, She did not draw near to her God.
שָׂרֶיהָ בְקִרְבָּהּ אֲרָיוֹת שֹׁאֲגִים שֹׁפְטֶיהָ זְאֵבֵי עֶרֶב לֹא גָרְמוּ לַבֹּקֶר	3[5]	Her princes in her midst are roaring lions; her judges are wolves of *the desert[6]*, they do not leave a bone for tomorrow.
נְבִיאֶיהָ פֹּחֲזִים אַנְשֵׁי בֹּגְדוֹת כֹּהֲנֶיהָ חִלְּלוּ־קֹדֶשׁ חָמְסוּ תּוֹרָה	4[7]	Her prophets are wanton and treacherous persons; her priests have profaned what is holy, they have done violence to the law.
יְהוָה צַדִּיק בְּקִרְבָּהּ לֹא יַעֲשֶׂה עַוְלָה בַּבֹּקֶר בַּבֹּקֶר מִשְׁפָּטוֹ יִתֵּן לָאוֹר לֹא נֶעְדָּר וְלֹא־יוֹדֵעַ עַוָּל בֹּשֶׁת	5	The LORD, who is righteous, is in her midst, He will not do unrighteousness; every morning He brings His right to light, *it does not fail; but the unrighteous knows no shame[8]*.
הִכְרַתִּי גוֹיִם נָשַׁמּוּ פִּנּוֹתָם הֶחֱרַבְתִּי חוּצוֹתָם מִבְּלִי עוֹבֵר נִצְדּוּ עָרֵיהֶם מִבְּלִי־אִישׁ מֵאֵין יוֹשֵׁב	6[9]	I have *cut off nations[10]*, their corners are desolate; I have made their streets waste, so that no one passes by; their cities are destroyed, so there is no man, so there is no inhabitant.
אָמַרְתִּי אַךְ־תִּירְאִי אוֹתִי תִּקְחִי מוּסָר וְלֹא־יִכָּרֵת מְעוֹנָהּ כֹּל אֲשֶׁר־פָּקַדְתִּי עָלֶיהָ אָכֵן הִשְׁכִּימוּ הִשְׁחִיתוּ כֹּל עֲלִילוֹתָם	7[11]	I said: 'Surely you will fear Me, you will receive correction; so her dwelling shall not be cut off, despite all that I have visited upon her;' But they previously corrupted all their doings.
לָכֵן חַכּוּ־לִי נְאֻם־יְהוָה לְיוֹם קוּמִי לְעַד כִּי מִשְׁפָּטִי לֶאֱסֹף גּוֹיִם לְקָבְצִי מַמְלָכוֹת לִשְׁפֹּךְ	8[12]	Therefore, wait for Me, says the LORD, until the day I rise up to *the prey[13]*; for My purpose is to gather the nations, so I may assemble the

---

[1] Zephaniah 3:1 - Amos 3:9 4:1, compare use of א in the word נגאל [cf. 2 Samuel 1:21], Ezekiel 22:7 22:29 23:30, Isaiah 5:7 6:12 11:13, Jastrow 748b, Jeremiah 6:6 22:17, Lamentations.R Petichata D'Chakimei:31, Leviticus 1:16, Malachi 3:5, Micah 2:2, Zechariah 7:10
Zephaniah 3:1-2 - 4QXIIc
Zephaniah 3:1-6 - MurXII
[2] LXX *Alas, the glorious and ransomed city*
[3] Zephaniah 3:2 - Deuteronomy 28:15-28:68, Ezekiel 24:13, Hebrews 10:22, Isaiah 1:5 5:13 30:1-30:3 7:1 19:22, Jeremiah 2:30 5:3 7:23-7:28 17:5-17:6 22:21 8:33 11:13 11:17, John 3:18-3:19, Lamentations.R Petichata D'Chakimei:31, Life of Adam and Eve [Vita] 12:1, Nehemiah 9:26, Proverbs 1:7 5:12, Psalms 10:5 50:17 73:28 78:22, Zechariah 7:11-7:14
[4] LXX *The dove*
[5] Zephaniah 3:3 - Exodus.R 5:9, Ezekiel 22:6 22:25-22:27, Habakkuk 1:8, Isaiah 1:23, Jeremiah 5:6 22:17, Job 4:8-4:11, Micah 3:1-3:4 3:9-3:11, Midrash Proverbs 10, Pesikta Rabbati 33:13, Proverbs 4:15, Psalms 10:9-10:11
Zephaniah 3:3-5 - 4QXIIg
[6] LXX *Arabia*
[7] Zephaniah 3:4 - 1 John 4:1, 1 Samuel 2:12-2:17 2:22, 2 Corinthians 11:13, 2 Peter 2:1-2:3, Ezekiel 13:3-13:16 22:26 44:7-44:8, Hosea 4:6-4:8 9:7, Isaiah 9:16 56:10-56:12, Jeremiah 5:31 6:13-6:14 8:10 14:13-14:15 23:9-23:17 23:25-23:27 23:32 27:14-27:15, Lamentations 2:14, Malachi 2:8, Matthew 7:15, Micah 2:11 3:5-3:6, Revelation 19:20
[8] LXX *and it is not hidden, and he knows not injustice by extortion, nor injustice in strife*
[9] Zephaniah 3:6 - 1 Corinthians 10:6 10:11, Isaiah 10:1-10:34 15:1-15:9 19:1-19:25 37:11-37:13 37:24-37:26 13:36, Jeremiah 25:9-25:11 25:18-25:26, Leviticus 2:31, Midrash Tanchuma Metzora 4, Nahum 2:2-2:4, Zechariah 7:14, Zephaniah 2:5
Zephaniah 3:6-7 - 8HevXIIgr, Midrash Tanchuma Behar 3
[10] LXX *brought down the proud with destruction*
[11] Zephaniah 3:7 - 2 Chronicles 28:6-28:8 32:1-32:2 9:11 36:3-36:10, 2 Peter 3:9, b.Shekalim 2b, b.Yevamot 63a, Deuteronomy 4:16, Gates of Repentance 2.003, Genesis 6:12, Hosea 9:9, Isaiah 5:4 15:8, Jastrow 369b, Jeremiah 7:7 8:6 17:25-17:27 1:5 12:3 14:17, Luke 19:42-19:44, Micah 2:1-2:2, Midrash Tanchuma Metzora 4, Saadia Opinions 10:11, y.Shekalim 1:1, Zephaniah 3:2
[12] Zephaniah 3:8 - 2 Peter 3:10, Deuteronomy 32:21-32:22, Exodus.R 17:3, Ezekiel 36:5-36:6 38:14-38:23, Habakkuk 2:3, Hosea 12:8, Isaiah 6:18 42:13-42:14 59:16-59:18, James 5:7-5:8, Joel 4:2 4:9-4:16, Matthew 1:32, Micah 4:11-4:13 7:7, Pesikta de R'Kahana S2.2, Pesikta Rabbati 34:2, Proverbs 20:22, Psalms 12:6 27:14 37:7 37:34 62:2 62:6 78:65-78:66 3:2 130:5-130:6, Revelation 16:14 19:17-19:19, Saadia Opinions 7:2, Song of Songs 8:6, Zechariah 14:2-14:3, Zephaniah 1:18
Zephaniah 3:8-20 - MurXII
[13] LXX *witness*

עֲלֵיהֶם זַעְמִי כֹּל חֲרוֹן אַפִּי כִּי בְּאֵשׁ קִנְאָתִי תֵּאָכֵל כָּל־הָאָרֶץ

kingdoms, to pour upon them my indignation, all My fierce anger; for all the earth shall be devoured with the fire of My jealousy.

9[1] כִּי־אָז אֶהְפֹּךְ אֶל־עַמִּים שָׂפָה בְרוּרָה לִקְרֹא כֻלָּם בְּשֵׁם יְהֹוָה לְעָבְדוֹ שְׁכֶם אֶחָד

For then will I turn the peoples to a *pure language*[2], so they may all call on the name of the LORD, to serve Him with one *consent*[3].

10[4] מֵעֵבֶר לְנַהֲרֵי־כוּשׁ עֲתָרַי בַּת־פּוּצַי יוֹבִלוּן מִנְחָתִי

From beyond the rivers of Ethiopia they shal bring My petitioners, the daughter of My dispersed, as my offering[5].

11[6] בַּיּוֹם הַהוּא לֹא תֵבוֹשִׁי מִכֹּל עֲלִילֹתַיִךְ אֲשֶׁר פָּשַׁעַתְּ בִּי כִּי־אָז אָסִיר מִקִּרְבֵּךְ עַלִּיזֵי גַּאֲוָתֵךְ וְלֹא־תוֹסִפִי לְגָבְהָה עוֹד בְּהַר קָדְשִׁי

In that day you shall not be ashamed for all your deeds, where you have transgressed against Me; for I will take away your proud gloating ones from your midst, and you shall not be conceited in My holy mountain.

12[7] וְהִשְׁאַרְתִּי בְקִרְבֵּךְ עַם עָנִי וָדָל וְחָסוּ בְּשֵׁם יְהֹוָה

And I will leave an afflicted and poor people in your midst, and they shall take refuge in the name of the LORD[8].

13[9] שְׁאֵרִית יִשְׂרָאֵל לֹא־יַעֲשׂוּ עַוְלָה וְלֹא־יְדַבְּרוּ כָזָב וְלֹא־יִמָּצֵא בְּפִיהֶם לְשׁוֹן תַּרְמִית כִּי־הֵמָּה יִרְעוּ וְרָבְצוּ וְאֵין מַחֲרִיד

The remnant of Israel[10] shall not do iniquity, nor speak lies, nor shall a deceitful tongue be found in their mouth; for they shall feed and lie down, and no one shall make them afraid.

14[11] רָנִּי בַּת־צִיּוֹן הָרִיעוּ יִשְׂרָאֵל שִׂמְחִי וְעָלְזִי בְּכָל־לֵב בַּת יְרוּשָׁלָ͏ִם

Sing, O daughter of Zion; shout, O *Israel*[12]; be glad and rejoice with all the heart, O daughter of Jerusalem.

15[13] הֵסִיר יְהֹוָה מִשְׁפָּטַיִךְ פִּנָּה אֹיְבֵךְ מֶלֶךְ יִשְׂרָאֵל יְהֹוָה בְּקִרְבֵּךְ לֹא־תִירְאִי רָע עוֹד

The LORD has taken away your *judgments, He has cast out your enemy*[14]; the King of Israel, the LORD, is in your midst; you shall *fear*[15] evil no more.

---

[1] Zephaniah 3:9 - 1 Kings 8:41-8:43, 4Q464 3 i 9, 4Q464 frag 3 1.9, Acts 2:4-2:13, b.Avodah Zara 24a, b.Berachot 57b, Birchat HaChammah.LeShem Yichud, Ephesians 4:29, Genesis 11:1, Genesis.R 88:3, Habakkuk 2:14, Isaiah 19:18, Jeremiah 16:19, Matthew 12:35, Midrash Psalms 66:1, Midrash Tanchuma Noach 19, mt.Hilchot Melachim u'Michamoteihem 11:4, Psalms 22:28 86:9-86:10 17:3, Revelation 11:15, Romans 15:6-15:11, Saadia Opinions 8:6, t.Berachot 6:2, Tanya Igeret Hakodesh §25, y.Avodah Zarah 2:1, z.Noach 76b, z.Vayera 118a, z.Vayishlach 178a, Zechariah 2:11 8:20-8:23 14:9, Zephaniah 2:11

[2] LXX *tongue for her generation*

[3] LXX *yoke*

[4] Zephaniah 3:10 - 1 Peter 1:1, Acts 8:27 24:17, Isaiah 11:11 18:1 18:7 27:12-27:13 49:20-49:23 60:4-60:12 66:18-66:21, Malachi 1:11, Psalms 68:32 72:8-72:11, Ralbag Wars 6part02:10, Romans 11:11-11:12 15:16, Saadia Opinions 8:6

[5] LXX *From the boundaries of the rivers of Ethiopia will I receive my dispersed ones; they shall offer sacrifices to me*

[6] Zephaniah 3:11 - 1 Peter 2:6, Daniel 9:16 9:20, Ezekiel 7:20-7:24 24:21, Isaiah 11:9 21:17 48:1-48:2 6:4 13:7 65:13-65:14, Jeremiah 7:4 7:9-7:12, Joel 2:26-2:27, Matthew 3:9, Micah 3:11, Numbers 16:3, Psalms 49:6 87:1-2, Romans 2:17 9:33, Zephaniah 3:19-20

[7] Zephaniah 3:12 - 1 Corinthians 1:27-28, 1 Peter 1:21, b.Sanhedrin 98a, Ein Yaakov Sanhedrin:97b, Ephesians 1:12-13, Isaiah 14:32 2:10 61:1-3, James 2:5, Matthew 5:3 11:5 12:21, Nahum 1:7, Pesikta Rabbati 9:2 41:5, Psalms 37:40, Romans 15:12, Zechariah 11:11 13:8-9

[8] LXX *And I will leave in you a meek and lowly people*

[9] Zephaniah 3:13 - 1 John 3:9-10 5:18, 1 Peter 3:14, b.Bava Metzia [Rashi] 48b 49a, b.Bava Metzia 16b, b.Kiddushin 45b, b.Pesachim 91a, Colossians 3:9, Ezekiel 34:13-15 34:23-28 36:25-27 15:26, Gates of Repentance 3.183, Isaiah 6:13 10:20-22 11:6-9 17:2 11:8 6:14 12:21 15:8 17:10, Jeremiah 23:4 6:10 7:34, Joel 4:17 4:21, John 1:47, Matthew 13:41, Mesillat Yesharim 11:Nekiyut-from-Falsehood 11:Traits-of-Nekuyut, Micah 4:4 4:7 5:5-6 7:14, Midrash Psalms 92:14, mt.Hilchot Mechirah 7:1, Psalms 23:2-3, Revelation 7:15-17 14:5 21:8 21:27, Romans 11:4-7, Siman 62:16, Zechariah 14:20-21, Zephaniah 2:7

[10] LXX adds *shall fear the name of the LORD, and*

[11] Zephaniah 3:14 - Ezra 3:11-13, Isaiah 12:6 24:14-16 11:2 16:9 42:10-12 3:11 6:1 65:13-14 65:18-19, Jeremiah 6:19 7:14 9:11, Luke 2:10-14, Matthew 21:9, Micah 4:8, Midrash Psalms 95:1 147:2, Nehemiah 12:43, Pesikta Rabbati 29/30B:2, Psalms 14:7 47:6-8 81:2-4 95:1-2 100:1-2 126:2-3, Revelation 19:1-6, Zechariah 2:10-11 9:9-10 9:15-17

[12] LXX *daughter of Jerusalem*

[13] Zephaniah 3:15 - Amos 9:15, b.Sanhedrin 98a, b.Shabbat 139a, Ein Yaakov Sanhedrin:97b, Ein Yaakov Shabbat:139a, Ezekiel 37:24-28 15:29 24:35, Genesis 6:23, Habakkuk 2:8 2:17, Isaiah 13:1-14 1:8 9:22 11:10 40:1-2 3:22 6:14 12:18 17:19, Jeremiah 50:1-46, Joel 4:17 4:20-21, John 1:49 12:15 19:19, Micah 7:10 7:16-20, Midrash Psalms 95:1 138:2 147:2, Psalms 85:4, Revelation 7:15 12:10 19:16 21:3-4, Romans 8:33-34, Zechariah 1:14-16 2:8-9 8:13-15 9:9 10:6-7 12:3 14:11, Zephaniah 3:5 3:17

[14] LXX *iniquities, he has ransomed you from the hand of your enemies*

[15] LXX *see*

בַּיּוֹם הַהוּא יֵאָמֵר לִירוּשָׁלִַם אַל־תִּירָאִי צִיּוֹן אַל־ יִרְפּוּ יָדָיִךְ

16¹ In that day Jerusalem *shall be told*[2]: 'Fear not; O Zion, do not let not your hands slacken.

יְהוָה אֱלֹהַיִךְ בְּקִרְבֵּךְ גִּבּוֹר יוֹשִׁיעַ יָשִׂישׂ עָלַיִךְ בְּשִׂמְחָה יַחֲרִישׁ בְּאַהֲבָתוֹ יָגִיל עָלַיִךְ בְּרִנָּה

17³ The LORD your God is in your midst, a Mighty One who will save; He will *rejoice over you with joy, He will be silent in His love, He will sing with joy over you*[4].'

נוּגֵי מִמּוֹעֵד אָסַפְתִּי מִמֵּךְ הָיוּ מַשְׂאֵת עָלֶיהָ חֶרְפָּה

18⁵ I will gather *those who are far from the appointed season, who are of you, who have borne the burden of reproach.*[6]

הִנְנִי עֹשֶׂה אֶת־כָּל־מְעַנַּיִךְ בָּעֵת הַהִיא וְהוֹשַׁעְתִּי אֶת־הַצֹּלֵעָה וְהַנִּדָּחָה אֲקַבֵּץ וְשַׂמְתִּים לִתְהִלָּה וּלְשֵׁם בְּכָל־הָאָרֶץ בָּשְׁתָּם

19⁷ *Behold, at that time I will deal with all those who afflict you; and I will save her who is lame, and gather her who was driven away; and I will make them a praise and a name, whose shame has been in all the earth*[8].

בָּעֵת הַהִיא אָבִיא אֶתְכֶם וּבָעֵת קַבְּצִי אֶתְכֶם כִּי־ אֶתֵּן אֶתְכֶם לְשֵׁם וְלִתְהִלָּה בְּכֹל עַמֵּי הָאָרֶץ בְּשׁוּבִי אֶת־שְׁבוּתֵיכֶם לְעֵינֵיכֶם אָמַר יְהוָה

20⁹ *At that time will I bring you in, And at that time will I gather you*[10]; For I will make you to be a name and a praise Among all the peoples of the earth, When I turn your captivity before your eyes, Says the LORD.

Haggai HaNavi – Chapter 1

בִּשְׁנַת שְׁתַּיִם לְדָרְיָוֶשׁ הַמֶּלֶךְ בַּחֹדֶשׁ הַשִּׁשִּׁי בְּיוֹם אֶחָד לַחֹדֶשׁ הָיָה דְבַר־יְהוָה בְּיַד־חַגַּי הַנָּבִיא אֶל־ זְרֻבָּבֶל בֶּן־שְׁאַלְתִּיאֵל פַּחַת יְהוּדָה וְאֶל־יְהוֹשֻׁעַ בֶּן־יְהוֹצָדָק הַכֹּהֵן הַגָּדוֹל לֵאמֹר

1¹¹ In the second year of Darius the king, in the sixth month, in the first day of the month, the word of the LORD came by[12] Haggai the prophet to Zerubbabel the son of Shealtiel, *governor*[13] of Judah, and to Joshua the son of Jehozadak, the high priest, saying:

כֹּה אָמַר יְהוָה צְבָאוֹת לֵאמֹר הָעָם הַזֶּה אָמְרוּ לֹא עֶת־בֹּא עֶת־בֵּית יְהוָה לְהִבָּנוֹת

2¹⁴ 'Thus speaks the LORD of hosts, saying: This people say: The time has not come, the time that the LORD's house should be built.'

וַיְהִי דְּבַר־יְהוָה בְּיַד־חַגַּי הַנָּבִיא לֵאמֹר

3¹⁵ Then the word of the LORD came by Haggai the prophet, saying:

---

[1] Zephaniah 3:16 - 2 Corinthians 4:1, Ephesians 3:13, Galatians 6:9, Haggai 2:4-5, Hebrews 12:3-5 12:12, Isaiah 35:3-4 16:9 17:10 41:13-14 43:1-2 20:2 6:4, Jeremiah 46:27-28, Job 4:3, John 12:12, Midrash Psalms 138:2, Revelation 2:3, Zechariah 8:15

[2] LXX *the LORD shall say*

[3] Zephaniah 3:17 - Deuteronomy 6:9, Genesis 1:31 2:2 17:1 18:14, Hebrews 7:25, Isaiah 9:7 12:2 12:6 18:4 62:4-5 15:1 15:12 17:19, Jeremiah 8:41, John 13:1 15:11, Luke 15:5-6 15:23-24 15:32, Numbers 14:8, Psalms 24:8-10 3:11 5:4, Zephaniah 3:5 3:15

[4] LXX *refresh you with his love; and he shall rejoice over you with delight as in a festival day*

[5] Zephaniah 3:18 - b.Berachot 28a, Ezekiel 10:13 12:24, Hosea 2:2 9:5, Jastrow 1295a, Jeremiah 23:3 31:9-31:10, Lamentations 1:4 1:7 2:6-2:7, mt.Hilchot Chagigah 1:5, Psalms 42:3-42:5 43:3 63:2-63:3 84:2-84:3 137:3-137:6, Romans 11:25-11:26, Zephaniah 3:20

[6] LXX *your afflicted ones. Alas! Who has taken up a reproach against her?*

[7] Zephaniah 3:19 - Ezekiel 10:16 39:17-39:22 15:26, Hebrews 12:13, Isaiah 25:9-25:12 2:11 41:11-41:16 43:14-43:17 49:25-49:26 51:22-51:23 12:14 12:18 13:7 14:7 66:14-66:16, Jeremiah 6:16 7:9 9:9 22:28 51:35-51:36, Joel 4:2-4:9, Micah 4:6-4:7 7:10, Nahum 1:11-1:14, Revelation 19:17-19:21 20:9, Zechariah 2:8-2:9 12:3-12:4 14:2-14:3, Zephaniah 3:15
Zephaniah 3:19-20 - 4QXIIb

[8] LXX *Behold, I will work in you for your sake at that time, says the LORD: and I will save her who was oppressed, and receive her who was rejected; and I will make them a praise, and honored in all the earth*

[9] Zephaniah 3:20 - Amos 9:14, Birchat Hashachar Shacharit, Ezekiel 16:53 4:25 10:16 13:12 13:21 15:28, Isaiah 11:11-12 27:12-13 8:5 8:8 12:15 13:9 14:7 14:12 18:22, Jeremiah 5:14, Joel 4:1, Malachi 3:12, Pesikta Rabbati 29/30B:2, Psalms 35:6, Zephaniah 2:7 3:19

[10] LXX *And their enemies shall be ashamed at that time, when I shall deal well with you, and at the time when I shall receive you*

[11] Haggai 1:1 - 1 Chronicles 3:17 3:19 5:40-41, 1 Kings 14:18, 2 Kings 14:25, Avot de R'Nathan 1, Exodus 4:13, Ezra 1:8 2:2 2:63 3:2 3:8 4:2 4:24-5:3 6:14, Haggai 1:12 1:14 2:1-2 2:4 2:10 2:20, Luke 3:27, Matthew 1:12-13, Mekhilta de R'Shimon bar Yochai Bachodesh 48:1, MurXII, Nehemiah 5:14 7:7 8:9 12:1 12:10, Sibylline Oracles 3.290, y.Rosh Hashanah 1:1, Zechariah 4:6-10
Haggai 1:1-2 - 4QXIIb

[12] LXX adds *the hand of*

[13] LXX *of the tribe*

[14] Haggai 1:2 - b.Zevachim [Rashi] 61b, Ecclesiastes 9:10 11:4, Ezra 4:23-5:2, Nehemiah 4:10, Numbers 13:31, Proverbs 22:13 26:13-26:16 5:25, Song of Songs 5:2-5:3

[15] Haggai 1:3 - Ezra 5:1, Zechariah 1:1

הַעֵת לָכֶם אַתֶּם לָשֶׁבֶת בְּבָתֵּיכֶם סְפוּנִים וְהַבַּיִת הַזֶּה חָרֵב	4[1] 'Is it a time for you to dwell in your tiled houses, while this house lies waste?
וְעַתָּה כֹּה אָמַר יְהוָה צְבָאוֹת שִׂימוּ לְבַבְכֶם עַל־דַּרְכֵיכֶם	5[2] Now, therefore, thus says the LORD of hosts: Consider your ways.
זְרַעְתֶּם הַרְבֵּה וְהָבֵא מְעָט אָכוֹל וְאֵין־לְשָׂבְעָה שָׁתוֹ וְאֵין־לְשָׁכְרָה לָבוֹשׁ וְאֵין־לְחֹם לוֹ וְהַמִּשְׂתַּכֵּר מִשְׂתַּכֵּר אֶל־צְרוֹר נָקוּב	6[3] You have sown much, and brought in little; you eat, but you do not have enough; you drink, but you are not *filled*[4] with drink; you clothe yourselves, but no one is warm; And he who earns wages earns wages for a bag with holes.
כֹּה אָמַר יְהוָה צְבָאוֹת שִׂימוּ לְבַבְכֶם עַל־דַּרְכֵיכֶם	7[5] Thus says the LORD of hosts: Consider your ways.
עֲלוּ הָהָר וַהֲבֵאתֶם עֵץ וּבְנוּ הַבָּיִת וְאֶרְצֶה־בּוֹ "וְאֶכָּבֵד" "וְאֶכָּבְדָה" אָמַר יְהוָה	8[6] Go up to the hill country, and bring wood, and build the house; and I will take pleasure in it, and I will be glorified, says the LORD.
פָּנֹה אֶל־הַרְבֵּה וְהִנֵּה לִמְעָט וַהֲבֵאתֶם הַבַּיִת וְנָפַחְתִּי בוֹ יַעַן מֶה נְאֻם יְהוָה צְבָאוֹת יַעַן בֵּיתִי אֲשֶׁר־הוּא חָרֵב וְאַתֶּם רָצִים אִישׁ לְבֵיתוֹ	9[7] You looked for much, and, lo, it came to little; and when you brought it home, I blew upon it. Why? Says the LORD of hosts. Because My house lies fallow, while every man runs for his own house.
עַל־כֵּן עֲלֵיכֶם כָּלְאוּ שָׁמַיִם מִטָּל וְהָאָרֶץ כָּלְאָה יְבוּלָהּ	10[8] Therefore, the heaven has held back over you, so that there is no dew, and the earth has kept back her produce.
וָאֶקְרָא חֹרֶב עַל־הָאָרֶץ וְעַל־הֶהָרִים וְעַל־הַדָּגָן וְעַל־הַתִּירוֹשׁ וְעַל־הַיִּצְהָר וְעַל אֲשֶׁר תּוֹצִיא הָאֲדָמָה וְעַל־הָאָדָם וְעַל־הַבְּהֵמָה וְעַל כָּל־יְגִיעַ כַּפָּיִם	11[9] And I *called for a drought*[10] on the land, and on the mountains, and on the corn, and on the wine, and on the oil, and on what the ground brings forth, and on men, and on cattle, and on all the labor of the hands.'
וַיִּשְׁמַע זְרֻבָּבֶל בֶּן־שַׁלְתִּיאֵל וִיהוֹשֻׁעַ בֶּן־יְהוֹצָדָק הַכֹּהֵן הַגָּדוֹל וְכֹל שְׁאֵרִית הָעָם בְּקוֹל יְהוָה אֱלֹהֵיהֶם וְעַל־דִּבְרֵי חַגַּי הַנָּבִיא כַּאֲשֶׁר שְׁלָחוֹ יְהוָה אֱלֹהֵיהֶם וַיִּירְאוּ הָעָם מִפְּנֵי יְהוָה	12[11] Then Zerubbabel the son of Shealtiel[12], and Joshua the son of Jehozadak, the high priest, with all the remnant of the people, listened to the voice of the LORD their God, and to the words of Haggai the prophet, as the LORD their God had sent him; and the people feared before the LORD.

---

[1] Haggai 1:4 - 2 Samuel 7:2, Daniel 9:17-9:18 9:26-27, Ezekiel 24:21, Haggai 1:9, Jeremiah 26:6 26:18 33:10 33:12 52:13, Lamentations 2:7 4:1, Matthew 6:33 24:1-2, Micah 3:12, Philippians 2:21, Psalms 74:7 102:15 132:3-5

[2] Haggai 1:5 - 2 Corinthians 13:5, Daniel 6:15 10:12, Exodus 7:23 9:21, Ezekiel 18:28 40:4, Galatians 6:4, Haggai 1:7 2:15-18, Lamentations 3:40, Luke 15:17, Psalms 48:14, z.Vaetchanan 269b

[3] Haggai 1:6 - 1 Kings 17:12, 2 Samuel 21:1, Amos 4:6-4:9, Deuteronomy 28:38-28:40, Ezekiel 4:16-4:17, Haggai 1:9 2:16, Hosea 4:10 8:7, Isaiah 5:10, Jeremiah 14:4 44:18, Job 20:22 20:28, Joel 1:10-1:13, Leviticus 26:20 26:26, Malachi 2:2 3:9-3:11, Micah 6:14-6:15, Midrash Proverbs 23, Midrash Tanchuma Tetzaveh 13, Pesikta de R'Kahana 16.8, Psalms 107:34, Zechariah 5:4 8:10

[4] LXX *satisfied*

[5] Haggai 1:7 - Haggai 1:5, Isaiah 28:10, Philippians 3:1, Psalms 119:59-60, z.Vaetchanan 269b

[6] Haggai 1:8 - 1 Kings 9:3, 2 Chronicles 2:7-9 7:16, b.Yoma 21b, Ein Yaakov Yoma:21b, Exodus 29:43, Ezra 3:7 6:4, Haggai 1:2-4 2:7 2:9, Isaiah 60:7 60:13 66:11, John 13:31-32, Jonah 3:1-2, Mas.Soferim 7:2, Matthew 3:8-9, Psalms 87:2-3 132:13-14, Song of Songs.R 8:13, y.Horayot 3:2, y.Makkot 2:6, y.Taanit 2:1, Zechariah 11:1-2

[7] Haggai 1:9 - 1 Corinthians 11:30-32, 2 Kings 19:7, 2 Samuel 21:1 22:16, Avot de R'Natan 4, Haggai 1:4 1:6 2:16-17, Isaiah 17:10-17:11 40:7, Job 10:2, Joshua 7:10-15, Leviticus.R 17:7, Malachi 2:2 3:8-11, Matthew 10:37-38, Pesikta de R'Kahana 16.9, Psalms 77:6-11, Revelation 2:4 3:19, Sifre Devarim Ekev 40

[8] Haggai 1:10 - 1 Kings 8:35 17:1, Deuteronomy 28:23-24, Hosea 2:9, Jeremiah 14:1-6, Joel 1:18-20, Leviticus 26:19, Midrash Tanchuma Bechukkotai 2

[9] Haggai 1:11 - 1 Kings 17:1, 2 Kings 8:1, Amos 5:8 7:4 9:6, Deuteronomy 28:22, Haggai 2:17, Job 34:29, Lamentations 1:21, Pesikta Rabbati 29/30B:2

[10] LXX *will bring a sword*

[11] Haggai 1:12 - 1 Thessalonians 1:5-6 2:13-14, Acts 9:31, Colossians 1:6, Deuteronomy 31:12, Ecclesiastes 12:13, Ezra 5:2, Genesis 22:12, Haggai 1:1 1:14 2:2, Hebrews 12:28, Isaiah 50:10 55:10-11, Proverbs 1:7, Psalms 112:1

Haggai 1:12-15 - MurXII

[12] LXX adds *of the tribe of Juda*

<table>
<tr><td>

וַיֹּאמֶר חַגַּי מַלְאַךְ יְהוָה בְּמַלְאֲכוּת יְהוָה לָעָם לֵאמֹר אֲנִי אִתְּכֶם נְאֻם־יְהוָה

</td><td>13[1]</td><td>

Then Haggai the LORD's messenger spoke the LORD's message to the people, saying: 'I am with you, says the LORD.'

</td></tr>
<tr><td>

וַיָּעַר יְהוָה אֶת־רוּחַ זְרֻבָּבֶל בֶּן־שַׁלְתִּיאֵל פַּחַת יְהוּדָה וְאֶת־רוּחַ יְהוֹשֻׁעַ בֶּן־יְהוֹצָדָק הַכֹּהֵן הַגָּדוֹל וְאֶת־רוּחַ כֹּל שְׁאֵרִית הָעָם וַיָּבֹאוּ וַיַּעֲשׂוּ מְלָאכָה בְּבֵית־יְהוָה צְבָאוֹת אֱלֹהֵיהֶם

</td><td>14[2]</td><td>

And the LORD stirred up the spirit of Zerubbabel the son of Shealtiel, *governor of Judah[3]*, and the spirit of Joshua the son of Jehozadak, the high priest, and the spirit of all the remnant of the people; and they came and worked in the house of the LORD of hosts, their God,

</td></tr>
<tr><td>

בְּיוֹם עֶשְׂרִים וְאַרְבָּעָה לַחֹדֶשׁ בַּשִּׁשִּׁי בִּשְׁנַת שְׁתַּיִם לְדָרְיָוֶשׁ הַמֶּלֶךְ

</td><td>15[4]</td><td>

in the twenty-fourth day of the month, in the sixth month, in the second year of Darius the king.

</td></tr>
</table>

Haggai – Chapter 2

<table>
<tr><td>

בַּשְּׁבִיעִי בְּעֶשְׂרִים וְאֶחָד לַחֹדֶשׁ הָיָה דְּבַר־יְהוָה בְּיַד־חַגַּי הַנָּבִיא לֵאמֹר

</td><td>1[5]</td><td>

In the seventh month, in the twenty-first day of the month, the word of the LORD came by Haggai the prophet, saying:

</td></tr>
<tr><td>

אֱמָר־נָא אֶל־זְרֻבָּבֶל בֶּן־שַׁלְתִּיאֵל פַּחַת יְהוּדָה וְאֶל־יְהוֹשֻׁעַ בֶּן־יְהוֹצָדָק הַכֹּהֵן הַגָּדוֹל וְאֶל־שְׁאֵרִית הָעָם לֵאמֹר

</td><td>2[6]</td><td>

'Speak now to Zerubbabel the son of Shealtiel, governor of Judah, and to Joshua the son of Jehozadak, the high priest, and to the remnant of the people, saying:

</td></tr>
<tr><td>

מִי בָכֶם הַנִּשְׁאָר אֲשֶׁר רָאָה אֶת־הַבַּיִת הַזֶּה בִּכְבוֹדוֹ הָרִאשׁוֹן וּמָה אַתֶּם רֹאִים אֹתוֹ עַתָּה הֲלוֹא כָמֹהוּ כְּאַיִן בְּעֵינֵיכֶם

</td><td>3[7]</td><td>

Who is left among you who saw this house in its former glory? And how do you see it now? Is it not as nothing in your eyes?

</td></tr>
<tr><td>

וְעַתָּה חֲזַק זְרֻבָּבֶל נְאֻם־יְהוָה וַחֲזַק יְהוֹשֻׁעַ בֶּן־יְהוֹצָדָק הַכֹּהֵן הַגָּדוֹל וַחֲזַק כָּל־עַם הָאָרֶץ נְאֻם־יְהוָה וַעֲשׂוּ כִּי־אֲנִי אִתְּכֶם נְאֻם יְהוָה צְבָאוֹת

</td><td>4[8]</td><td>

Yet now be strong, O Zerubbabel, says the LORD; and be strong, O Joshua, son of Jehozadak, the high priest; and be strong, all you people of the land, says the LORD, and work; for I am with you, says the LORD of hosts.

</td></tr>
<tr><td>

אֶת־הַדָּבָר אֲשֶׁר־כָּרַתִּי אִתְּכֶם בְּצֵאתְכֶם מִמִּצְרַיִם וְרוּחִי עֹמֶדֶת בְּתוֹכְכֶם אַל־תִּירָאוּ

</td><td>5[9]</td><td>

The word I covenanted with you when you came out of Egypt I have established[10], and My spirit lives among you; do not fear.

</td></tr>
</table>

---

[1] Haggai 1:13 - 2 Chronicles 15:2 20:17 32:8, 2 Corinthians 5:20, 2 Timothy 4:17 4:22, Acts 18:9-18:10, Ezekiel 3:17, Guide for the Perplexed 2:42, Haggai 2:4, Isaiah 8:8-10 41:10 42:19 43:2 44:26, Jeremiah 15:20 20:11 30:11, Judges 2:1, Leviticus.R 1:1, Lives of the Prophets 14:1, Malachi 2:7 3:1, Mas.Perek Hashalom 1:17, Matthew 1:23 18:20 28:20, Midrash Psalms 103:17, Midrash Tanchuma Shelach 1, Psalms 46:8 46:12, Romans 8:31

[2] Haggai 1:14 - 1 Chronicles 5:26, 1 Corinthians 12:4-11 15:58, 2 Chronicles 36:22, 2 Corinthians 8:16, Ezra 1:1 1:5 5:2 5:8 7:27-28, Haggai 1:1 1:12 2:2 2:21, Hebrews 13:21, Lives of the Prophets 14:2, Nehemiah 4:6, Philippians 2:12-13, Psalms 110:3

[3] LXX *of the tribe of Juda*

[4] Haggai 1:15 - b.Rosh Hashanah 3b, Ein Yaakov Rosh Hashanah:3a, Haggai 1:1 2:1 2:10 2:20, Mekilta de R'Ishmael Bahodesh 1:15

[5] Haggai 2:1 - 2 Peter 1:21, b.Rosh Hashanah 3b, Haggai 1:1 1:15 2:10 2:20
Haggai 2:1-8 - MurXII

[6] Haggai 2:2 - Ezra 1:8 2:63, Genesis.R 97:1, Haggai 1:1 1:14, Nehemiah 8:9
Haggai 2:2-4 - 4QXIIb

[7] Haggai 2:3 - Ezekiel 7:20, Ezra 3:12, Haggai 2:9, Luke 21:5-6, Pesikta Rabbati 35:1, Zechariah 4:9-10

[8] Haggai 2:4 - 1 Chronicles 22:13 28:20, 1 Corinthians 16:13, 1 Samuel 16:18, 2 Samuel 5:10, 2 Timothy 2:1 4:17, Acts 7:9, Deuteronomy 31:23, Ephesians 6:10, Exodus 3:12, Haggai 1:13, Joshua 1:6 1:9, Judges 2:18, Mark 16:20, Zechariah 8:9

[9] Haggai 2:5 - 2 Chronicles 20:17, Acts 27:24, Exodus 29:45-29:46 33:12-14 34:8 34:10, Isaiah 41:10 41:13 63:11-14, John 14:16-17, Joshua 8:1, Matthew 28:5, Nehemiah 9:20 9:30, Numbers 11:25-29, Psalms 51:12-13, Revelation 1:17, Zechariah 4:6 8:13 8:15

[10] Missing in LXX

כִּי כֹה אָמַר יְהֹוָה צְבָאוֹת עוֹד אַחַת מְעַט הִיא וַאֲנִי מַרְעִישׁ אֶת־הַשָּׁמַיִם וְאֶת־הָאָרֶץ וְאֶת־הַיָּם וְאֶת־הֶחָרָבָה	6[1]	For thus says the LORD of hosts: Yet once, *it is a little while*[2], and I will shake the heavens, and the earth, and the sea, and the dry land;
וְהִרְעַשְׁתִּי אֶת־כָּל־הַגּוֹיִם וּבָאוּ חֶמְדַּת כָּל־הַגּוֹיִם וּמִלֵּאתִי אֶת־הַבַּיִת הַזֶּה כָּבוֹד אָמַר יְהֹוָה צְבָאוֹת	7[3]	and I will shake all nations, and the choicest things of all nations shall come, and I will fill this house with glory, says the LORD of hosts.
לִי הַכֶּסֶף וְלִי הַזָּהָב נְאֻם יְהֹוָה צְבָאוֹת	8[4]	The silver is Mine, and the gold is Mine, says the LORD of hosts.
גָּדוֹל יִהְיֶה כְּבוֹד הַבַּיִת הַזֶּה הָאַחֲרוֹן מִן־הָרִאשׁוֹן אָמַר יְהֹוָה צְבָאוֹת וּבַמָּקוֹם הַזֶּה אֶתֵּן שָׁלוֹם נְאֻם יְהֹוָה צְבָאוֹת	9[5]	The glory of this latter house shall be greater than that of the former, says the LORD of hosts; and in this place will I give peace, says the LORD of hosts.'
בְּעֶשְׂרִים וְאַרְבָּעָה לַתְּשִׁיעִי בִּשְׁנַת שְׁתַּיִם לְדָרְיָוֶשׁ הָיָה דְּבַר־יְהֹוָה אֶל־חַגַּי הַנָּבִיא לֵאמֹר	10[6]	In the twenty-fourth day of the ninth month, in the second year of Darius, the word of the LORD came by Haggai the prophet, saying:
כֹּה אָמַר יְהֹוָה צְבָאוֹת שְׁאַל־נָא אֶת־הַכֹּהֲנִים תּוֹרָה לֵאמֹר	11[7]	'Thus says the LORD of hosts: Ask now the priests for instruction, saying:
הֵן יִשָּׂא־אִישׁ בְּשַׂר־קֹדֶשׁ בִּכְנַף בִּגְדוֹ וְנָגַע בִּכְנָפוֹ אֶל־הַלֶּחֶם וְאֶל־הַנָּזִיד וְאֶל־הַיַּיִן וְאֶל־שֶׁמֶן וְאֶל־כָּל־מַאֲכָל הֲיִקְדָּשׁ וַיַּעֲנוּ הַכֹּהֲנִים וַיֹּאמְרוּ לֹא	12[8]	If one carries holy flesh in the wing of his garment, and with this wing touches bread, or boiled food, or wine, or oil, or any food, shall it be holy?' And the priests answered and said: 'No.'
וַיֹּאמֶר חַגַּי אִם־יִגַּע טְמֵא־נֶפֶשׁ בְּכָל־אֵלֶּה הֲיִטְמָא וַיַּעֲנוּ הַכֹּהֲנִים וַיֹּאמְרוּ יִטְמָא	13[9]	Then said Haggai: 'If one who is unclean by a dead body touches any of these, shall it be unclean?' And the priests answered and said: 'It shall be unclean.'
וַיַּעַן חַגַּי וַיֹּאמֶר כֵּן הָעָם־הַזֶּה וְכֵן־הַגּוֹי הַזֶּה לְפָנַי נְאֻם־יְהֹוָה וְכֵן כָּל־מַעֲשֵׂה יְדֵיהֶם וַאֲשֶׁר יַקְרִיבוּ שָׁם טָמֵא הוּא	14[10]	Then answered Haggai, and said: 'So is this people, and so is this nation before me, says the LORD; and so is every work of their hands; and what they offer there is unclean[11].

---

[1] Haggai 2:6 - Acts 2:19, b.Sanhedrin 97b, Deuteronomy.R 1:23, Ein Yaakov Sanhedrin:97b, Exodus.R 18:12, Ezekiel 38:20, Guide for the Perplexed 2:29, Haggai 2:21-22, Hebrews 10:37 12:26-28, Isaiah 10:25 29:17 34:4, Jeremiah 4:23-26 51:33, Joel 3:3-5 4:16, Luke 21:25-27, Mark 13:24-26, Matthew 24:29-30, Midrash Tanchuma Devarim 1, Psalms 37:10, Revelation 6:2-17 8:5-12 11:9, Testament of Levi 3:9, This is the middle verse of the book of Haggai per the Massorah, z.Vaetchanan 269b
Haggai 2:6-7 - Testament of Levi 3:10
[2] Missing in LXX
[3] Haggai 2:7 - 1 Kings 8:11, 2 Chronicles 5:14, Colossians 2:9, Daniel 2:44-45 7:20-25, Exodus 40:34-35, Exodus.R 3:8, Ezekiel 21:32, Galatians 3:8, Genesis 3:15 22:18 49:10, Isaiah 60:7, Joel 4:9-16, John 1:14 2:13-17 7:37-39 10:23-38, Luke 2:10-11 2:27 2:46 19:47 20:1 21:10-11 21:38, Malachi 3:1, Psalms 80:2, Romans 15:9-15, Zechariah 9:9-10
Haggai 2:7-8 - Midrash Tanchuma Shemot 29
[4] Haggai 2:8 - 1 Chronicles 29:14-16, 1 Kings 6:20-35, b.Avodah Zara 2b, b.Kiddushin 82b, b.Niddah 70b, b.Sanhedrin 103b, Bahir 52, Ein Yaakov Avodah Zarah:2b, Exodus.R 31:15 33:4-5, HaMadrikh 35:7, Isaiah 60:13 60:17, m.Avot 6:9, Mas.Derek Eretz Zutta 4:3, Mas.Kallah Rabbati 8:9, Mekhilta de R'Shimon bar Yochai Shirata 27:1, Mekilta de R'Ishmael Shirata 1:116, Midrash Psalms 45:1, Midrash Shmuel 6:10, Midrash Tanchuma Beha'alotcha 11, Midrash Tanchuma Beshallach 11, Midrash Tanchuma Mishpatim 12, Midrash Tanchuma Shoftim 9, mt.Pirkei Avot 6:9, Numbers.R 15:17, Pesikta Rabbati 23:7, Pirkei Avot 6:9 [Shabbat afternoon], Pirkei de R'Eliezer 2, Psalms 24:1 50:10-12, z.Terumah 138b, z.Vayakhel 197b, z.Vayechi 217a, z.Yitro 90b
[5] Haggai 2:9 - 1 Timothy 3:16, 2 Corinthians 3:9-10, Acts 10:36, b.Bava Batra 3a, Colossians 1:19-21, Ein Yaakov Bava Batra:3a, Ein Yaakov Kiddushin:82b, Ephesians 2:14-17, Isaiah 9:7-8 57:18-21, James 2:1, John 1:14 14:27, Luke 2:14, Micah 5:6, Midrash Tanchuma Vayigash 10, mt.Hilchot Beit Habechirah 4:3, Pesikta de R'Kahana 5.9, Pesikta Rabbati 15:1, Psalms 24:7-10 85:9-10, Song of Songs.R 2:32, Testament of Benjamin 9:2, y.Megillah 1:12, z.Mishpatim 103a, z.Pinchas 221a
[6] Haggai 2:10 - Haggai 1:1 1:15-2:1 2:20, MurXII
[7] Haggai 2:11 - Deuteronomy 17:8-11 33:10, Ezekiel 44:23-24, Leviticus 10:10-11, Malachi 2:7, Titus 1:9, z.Vaetchanan 269b
[8] Haggai 2:12 - b.Pesachim 14a 16b, b.Sheviit [Rashi] 18b, Exodus 29:37, Ezekiel 44:19, Leviticus 6:27 6:29 7:6, Matthew 23:19, y.Sotah 5:2
Haggai 2:12-23 - MurXII
[9] Haggai 2:13 - b.Pesachim 14a, Leviticus 22:4-6, Numbers 5:2-3 9:6-10 19:11-22, y.Sotah 5:2
[10] Haggai 2:14 - b.Pesachim 14a, Ezra 3:2-3, Haggai 1:4-11, Isaiah 1:11-15, Jude 1:23, Proverbs 15:8 21:4 21:27 28:9, Titus 1:15, y.Sotah 5:2
[11] LXX adds *because of their early burdens: they shall be pained because of their toils; and you hated he who reproved in the gates*

וְעַתָּה שִׂימוּ־נָא לְבַבְכֶם מִן־הַיּוֹם הַזֶּה וָמָעְלָה מִטֶּרֶם שֽׂוּם־אֶבֶן אֶל־אֶבֶן בְּהֵיכַל יְהוָֽה

15[1] And now, please, consider from this day and forward, before a stone is laid upon a stone in the temple of the LORD[2],

מִהְיוֹתָם בָּא אֶל־עֲרֵמַת עֶשְׂרִים וְהָיְתָה עֲשָׂרָה בָּא אֶל־הַיֶּקֶב לַחְשֹׂף חֲמִשִּׁים פּוּרָה וְהָיְתָה עֶשְׂרִֽים

16[3] through all that time, when one came to a heap of twenty measures, there were but ten; when one came to the winevat to draw out fifty press measures, there were but twenty;

הִכֵּיתִי אֶתְכֶם בַּשִּׁדָּפוֹן וּבַיֵּרָקוֹן וּבַבָּרָד אֵת כָּל־מַעֲשֵׂה יְדֵיכֶם וְאֵין־אֶתְכֶם אֵלַי נְאֻם־יְהוָֽה

17[4] I struck you with blight and with mildew and with hail in all the work of your hands; yet you did not turn to Me, says the LORD

שִׂימוּ־נָא לְבַבְכֶם מִן־הַיּוֹם הַזֶּה וָמָעְלָה מִיּוֹם עֶשְׂרִים וְאַרְבָּעָה לַתְּשִׁיעִי לְמִן־הַיּוֹם אֲשֶׁר־יֻסַּד הֵֽיכַל־יְהוָה שִׂימוּ לְבַבְכֶֽם

18[5] consider, please, from this day and forward, from the twenty-fourth day of the ninth month, from the day the foundation of the LORD's temple was laid, consider it;

הַעוֹד הַזֶּרַע בַּמְּגוּרָה וְעַד־הַגֶּפֶן וְהַתְּאֵנָה וְהָרִמּוֹן וְעֵץ הַזַּיִת לֹא נָשָׂא מִן־הַיּוֹם הַזֶּה אֲבָרֵֽךְ

19[6] is the seed yet in the barn? Yes, the vine, and the fig tree, and the pomegranate, and the olive tree has not brought forth; from this day will I bless you.'

וַיְהִי דְבַר־יְהוָה שֵׁנִית אֶל־חַגַּי בְּעֶשְׂרִים וְאַרְבָּעָה לַחֹדֶשׁ לֵאמֹֽר

20 And the word of the LORD came the second time to Haggai in the twenty-fourth day of the month, saying:

אֱמֹר אֶל־זְרֻבָּבֶל פַּֽחַת־יְהוּדָה לֵאמֹר אֲנִי מַרְעִישׁ אֶת־הַשָּׁמַיִם וְאֶת־הָאָֽרֶץ

21[7] 'Speak to Zerubbabel, governor of Judah, saying: I will shake the heavens and the earth;

וְהָֽפַכְתִּי כִּסֵּא מַמְלָכוֹת וְהִשְׁמַדְתִּי חֹזֶק מַמְלְכוֹת הַגּוֹיִם וְהָפַכְתִּי מֶרְכָּבָה וְרֹכְבֶיהָ וְיָרְדוּ סוּסִים וְרֹכְבֵיהֶם אִישׁ בְּחֶרֶב אָחִֽיו

22[8] and I will overthrow the throne of kingdoms, and I will destroy the strength of the kingdoms of the nations; and I will overthrow the chariots, and those who ride in them; and the horses and their riders shall come down, every one by the sword of his brother.

בַּיּוֹם הַהוּא נְאֻם־יְהוָה צְבָאוֹת אֶקָּחֲךָ זְרֻבָּבֶל בֶּן־שְׁאַלְתִּיאֵל עַבְדִּי נְאֻם־יְהוָה וְשַׂמְתִּיךָ כַּֽחוֹתָם כִּי־בְךָ בָחַרְתִּי נְאֻם יְהוָה צְבָאֽוֹת

23[9] In that day, says the LORD of hosts, will I take you, O Zerubbabel, My servant, the son of Shealtiel, says the LORD, and will make you as a signet; for I have chosen you, says the LORD of hosts.'

Zekharyah b'Berechyah – Chapter 1

בַּחֹדֶשׁ הַשְּׁמִינִי בִּשְׁנַת שְׁתַּיִם לְדָרְיָוֶשׁ הָיָה דְבַר־יְהוָה אֶל־זְכַרְיָה בֶּן־בֶּרֶכְיָה בֶּן־עִדּוֹ הַנָּבִיא לֵאמֹֽר

1[10] In the eighth month, in the second year of Darius, the word of the LORD came to

[1] Haggai 2:15 - 1 Corinthians 11:31, Avot de R'Natan 4, Ezra 3:10 4:24, Haggai 1:5 1:7 2:18, Hosea 14:11, Isaiah 5:12, Malachi 3:8-11, Psalms 107:43, Romans 6:21, y.Rosh Hashanah 1:1
[2] LXX adds *what manner of men you were*
[3] Haggai 2:16 - Avot de R'Natan 4, Haggai 1:6 1:9-11, Malachi 2:2, Proverbs 3:9-10, y.Sotah 9:16, Zechariah 8:10-12
[4] Haggai 2:17 - 1 Kings 8:37, 2 Chronicles 6:28 28:22, Amos 4:6 4:8-4:11, Deuteronomy 28:22, Exodus 9:18-9:29, Genesis 42:6 42:23 42:27, Haggai 1:9 1:11, Hosea 7:9-7:10, Isaiah 9:14 28:2 37:27 42:25 62:8, Jeremiah 3:24 5:3 6:16-6:17 8:4-8:7, Job 36:13, Psalms 78:46, Revelation 2:21 9:20-9:21, Zechariah 1:2-1:4 7:9-7:13
[5] Haggai 2:18 - Avot de R'Natan 4, Deuteronomy 32:29, Ezra 5:1-2, Haggai 1:14-15 2:10 2:15, Luke 15:17-20, Zechariah 8:9 8:12 Haggai 2:18-21 - 4QXIIe
[6] Haggai 2:19 - Avot de R'Natan 4, Deuteronomy 15:10 28:2-15, Genesis 26:12, Habakkuk 3:17-18, Jastrow 227b, Leviticus 26:3-13, Malachi 3:10, Matthew 6:33, Pesikta de R'Kahana 16.8, Pesikta Rabbati 29/30B:2, Proverbs 3:9-3:10, Psalms 84:13 128:1-5 133:3, Sifre Devarim Ekev 40, Zechariah 8:11-15
[7] Haggai 2:21 - 1 Chronicles 3:19, Ezekiel 26:15 38:19-38:20, Ezra 2:2 5:2, Haggai 1:1 1:14 2:6-2:7, Hebrews 12:26-12:27, Joel 4:16, Psalms 46:7, Revelation 16:17-16:19, Testament of Levi 3:10, Zechariah 4:6-4:10
[8] Haggai 2:22 - 1 Samuel 14:16, 2 Chronicles 20:22, Daniel 2:34-35 2:44-45 7:25-27 8:25, Exodus 14:17 14:28 15:4 15:19, Exodus.R 18:12, Ezekiel 21:32 39:20, Isaiah 19:2 60:12, Judges 7:22, Matthew 24:7, Micah 5:9 5:11 5:16, Midrash Psalms 47:2 150:1, Midrash Tanchuma Balak 13, Midrash Tanchuma Kedoshim 1, Numbers.R 20:20, Psalms 46:10 76:7, Revelation 11:15, Testament of Levi 3:10, Zechariah 4:6 9:10 10:11 12:2-5 14:3, Zephaniah 3:8
[9] Haggai 2:23 - 1 Peter 2:4, 2 Timothy 2:19, Avot de R'Natan 2, Genesis.R 97:1, Isaiah 42:1 43:10 49:1-49:3, Jeremiah 22:24, John 6:27, Matthew 12:18, Midrash Tanchuma Balak 13, mt.Hilchot Teshuvah 7:6 7:6, Pesikta de R'Kahana 24.11, Pesikta Rabbati 47:1, Sifre Devarim Vaetchanan 27, Song of Songs 8:6, Song of Songs.R 8:5, Zechariah 4:6-4:14
[10] Zechariah 1:1-4 - 8HevXIIgr, MurXII, Avot de R'Nathan 1

Zechariah the son of Berechiah, the son of *Iddo*[1], the prophet, saying:

2² קָצַף יְהוָה עַל־אֲבוֹתֵיכֶם קָצֶף

'The LORD has been sorely displeased with your fathers.

3³ וְאָמַרְתָּ אֲלֵהֶם כֹּה אָמַר יְהוָה צְבָאוֹת שׁוּבוּ אֵלַי נְאֻם יְהוָה צְבָאוֹת וְאָשׁוּב אֲלֵיכֶם אָמַר יְהוָה צְבָאוֹת

Therefore, say to them, Thus says the LORD of hosts: Return to Me, says the LORD of hosts, and I will return to you, says the LORD of hosts.

4⁴ אַל־תִּהְיוּ כַאֲבֹתֵיכֶם אֲשֶׁר קָרְאוּ־אֲלֵיהֶם הַנְּבִיאִים הָרִאשֹׁנִים לֵאמֹר כֹּה אָמַר יְהוָה צְבָאוֹת שׁוּבוּ נָא מִדַּרְכֵיכֶם הָרָעִים 'וּמַעֲלֲלֵיכֶם' "וּמַעַלְלֵיכֶם" הָרָעִים וְלֹא שָׁמְעוּ וְלֹא־הִקְשִׁיבוּ אֵלַי נְאֻם־יְהוָה

Do not be like your fathers, to whom the former prophets proclaimed, saying: Thus says the LORD of hosts: Return now from your evil ways, and from your evil deeds; but they did not hear, nor heeded Me, says the LORD.

5⁵ אֲבוֹתֵיכֶם אַיֵּה־הֵם וְהַנְּבִאִים הַלְעוֹלָם יִחְיוּ

Your fathers, where are they? And the prophets, do they live forever?

6⁶ אַךְ דְּבָרַי וְחֻקַּי אֲשֶׁר צִוִּיתִי אֶת־עֲבָדַי הַנְּבִיאִים הֲלוֹא הִשִּׂיגוּ אֲבֹתֵיכֶם וַיָּשׁוּבוּ וַיֹּאמְרוּ כַּאֲשֶׁר זָמַם יְהוָה צְבָאוֹת לַעֲשׂוֹת לָנוּ כִּדְרָכֵינוּ וּכְמַעֲלָלֵינוּ כֵּן עָשָׂה אִתָּנוּ

But My words and My statutes, which I commanded My servants the prophets, did they not overtake your fathers? Thus, they turned and said: Just like the LORD of hosts purposed to do to us, according to our ways, and according to our doings, so He dealt with us.'

7⁷ בְּיוֹם עֶשְׂרִים וְאַרְבָּעָה לְעַשְׁתֵּי־עָשָׂר חֹדֶשׁ הוּא־חֹדֶשׁ שְׁבָט בִּשְׁנַת שְׁתַּיִם לְדָרְיָוֶשׁ הָיָה דְבַר־יְהוָה אֶל־זְכַרְיָה בֶּן־בֶּרֶכְיָהוּ בֶּן־עִדּוֹא הַנָּבִיא לֵאמֹר

On the twenty-fourth day of the eleventh month, the month Shevat, in the second year of Darius, the word of the LORD came to Zechariah the son of Berechiah, the son of Iddo, the prophet, saying:

8⁸ רָאִיתִי הַלַּיְלָה וְהִנֵּה־אִישׁ רֹכֵב עַל־סוּס אָדֹם וְהוּא עֹמֵד בֵּין הַהֲדַסִּים אֲשֶׁר בַּמְּצֻלָה וְאַחֲרָיו סוּסִים אֲדֻמִּים שְׂרֻקִּים וּלְבָנִים

I saw in the night, and behold a man riding upon a red horse, and he stood *among the myrtle trees that were in the revine; and behind him were horses: red, light brown, and white*[9].

9¹⁰ וָאֹמַר מָה־אֵלֶּה אֲדֹנִי וַיֹּאמֶר אֵלַי הַמַּלְאָךְ הַדֹּבֵר בִּי אֲנִי אַרְאֶךָּ מָה־הֵמָּה אֵלֶּה

Then I said: 'O my lord, what are these?' And the angel who spoke with me said to me: 'I will show you what these are.'

---

[1] LXX *Addo*

[2] Zechariah 1:2 - 2 Chronicles 36:13-36:20, 2 Kings 22:16-22:17 22:19 23:26, Acts 7:52, Daniel 9:11-9:12, Ezekiel 22:31, Ezra 9:6-7 9:13, Jeremiah 20:6, Lamentations 1:12-1:15 2:3-2:5 3:42-3:45 5:7, Matthew 23:30-23:32, Nehemiah 9:26-27, Pesikta de R'Kahana 16.8, Pesikta Rabbati 29/30B:2, Psalms 60:2 79:5-79:6, Zephaniah 2:1-3

[3] Zechariah 1:3 - 1 Kings 8:47-48, 2 Chronicles 15:4 30:6-9, Deuteronomy 4:30-31 30:2-10, Ezekiel 9:11, Hosea 6:1 14:3 14:6, Isaiah 7:6 55:6-7, James 4:8-4:10, Jeremiah 3:12-14 3:22 4:1 12:15 1:5 29:12-29:14 31:19-21 11:15, Joel 2:12, Lamentations 3:39-3:41, Lamentations.R 5:21, Luke 15:18-22, Malachi 3:7, Micah 7:19-20, Nehemiah 9:28, z.Vaetchanan 269b

[4] Zechariah 1:4 - 1 Peter 1:18, 1 Thessalonians 2:15-16, 2 Chronicles 24:19-22 29:6-10 6:7 10:21 36:15-16, Acts 3:19 7:51-52 2:20, Amos 5:13-15 5:24, Ezekiel 3:7-3:9 18:14-17 18:30-32 9:11, Ezra 9:7, Hosea 14:3, Isaiah 1:16-19 30:9-11 7:6, Jeremiah 3:12 6:16-17 7:3-7 11:6-8 13:9-10 13:16-18 17:19-23 18:11 25:3-7 2:5 11:15 36:2-10 36:23-24 44:4-5 20:16, Matthew 3:8-10, Micah 2:6, Nehemiah 9:16 9:26 9:30, Psalms 78:8 106:6-7, z.Vaetchanan 269b, Zechariah 1:3 7:11-13
Zechariah 1:4-6 - 4QXIIe

[5] Zechariah 1:5 - 2 Peter 3:2-4, Acts 13:36, b.Sanhedrin 105a, Ecclesiastes 1:4 9:1-3 12:5 12:7, Ein Yaakov Sanhedrin:105a, Hebrews 7:23-24 9:27, Job 14:10-12, John 8:52, Pesikta de R'Kahana 13.3-4, Psalms 90:10

[6] Zechariah 1:6 - 1 Thessalonians 5:4, 2 Chronicles 36:17-21, Amos 9:10, b.Sanhedrin 105a, Daniel 9:11-12, Deuteronomy 4:15 4:20 4:45, Ein Yaakov Sanhedrin:105a, Ezekiel 12:25-28 20:43 13:11, Hosea 2:6-13 9:15, Isaiah 3:8-11 20:26 7:1, Jeremiah 4:4 12:16-17 18:8-11 23:20 2:15 20:28, Job 6:29, Lamentations 1:18 2:17 4:11-12, Malachi 3:18, Matthew 24:35, Numbers 23:19 8:23 9:56

[7] Zechariah 1:7 - b.Rosh Hashanah 7a, Jastrow 1310a, Zechariah 1:1
Zechariah 1:7-11 - Testament of Adam 4:7

[8] Zechariah 1:8 - 1 Kings 3:5, 2 Baruch 36:1, 3 Enoch 17:8 18:1, b.Bava Batra [Rashbam] 78b, b.Megillah 13a, b.Sanhedrin 93ab, Daniel 2:19 7:2 7:13, Ein Yaakov Megillah:13a, Ein Yaakov Sanhedrin:93a, Esther.R 9:2, Genesis 20:3, Isaiah 17:19 7:13 9:15 63:1-4, Jastrow 1029b, Job 4:13, Joshua 5:13, Leviticus.R 30:9, Midrash Psalms 22:3, Pesikta de R'Kahana 27.9, Pesikta Rabbati 51:2, Psalms 45:4-45:5, Revelation 2:1 6:4 19:19-19:21, Song of Songs 2:16 6:2, Zechariah 6:2-6:7 13:7

[9] LXX *between the shady mountains; and behind him were red horses, and grey, and piebald, and white*

[10] Zechariah 1:9 - Daniel 7:16 8:15-16 9:22-23 10:11-14, Genesis 7:11, Genesis.R 56:2, Revelation 7:13-14 17:1-7 19:9-10 22:8-16, Zechariah 1:19 2:3 4:4-5 4:11 5:5 6:4-5
Zechariah 1:9-10 - 4QXIIe

וַיַּעַן הָאִישׁ הָעֹמֵד בֵּין־הַהֲדַסִּים וַיֹּאמַר אֵלֶּה אֲשֶׁר שָׁלַח יְהוָה לְהִתְהַלֵּךְ בָּאָרֶץ	10[1]	And the man who stood among the myrtle trees answered and said: 'These are those whom the LORD sent to walk to and fro through the earth.'
וַיַּעֲנוּ אֶת־מַלְאַךְ יְהוָה הָעֹמֵד בֵּין הַהֲדַסִּים וַיֹּאמְרוּ הִתְהַלַּכְנוּ בָאָרֶץ וְהִנֵּה כָל־הָאָרֶץ יֹשֶׁבֶת וְשֹׁקָטֶת	11[2]	And they answered the angel of the LORD who stood *among the myrtle trees*[3], and said: 'We have walked to and fro through the earth, and, behold, all the earth sits still, and is at rest.'
וַיַּעַן מַלְאַךְ־יְהוָה וַיֹּאמַר יְהוָה צְבָאוֹת עַד־מָתַי אַתָּה לֹא־תְרַחֵם אֶת־יְרוּשָׁלַ͏ִם וְאֵת עָרֵי יְהוּדָה אֲשֶׁר זָעַמְתָּה זֶה שִׁבְעִים שָׁנָה	12[4]	Then the angel of the LORD spoke and said: 'O LORD of hosts, how long will you lack compassion on Jerusalem and on the cities of Judah, against which you have had indignation these seventy years?
וַיַּעַן יְהוָה אֶת־הַמַּלְאָךְ הַדֹּבֵר בִּי דְּבָרִים טוֹבִים דְּבָרִים נִחֻמִים	13[5]	And the LORD answered the angel who spoke with me with good words, comforting words:
וַיֹּאמֶר אֵלַי הַמַּלְאָךְ הַדֹּבֵר בִּי קְרָא לֵאמֹר כֹּה אָמַר יְהוָה צְבָאוֹת קִנֵּאתִי לִירוּשָׁלַ͏ִם וּלְצִיּוֹן קִנְאָה גְדוֹלָה	14[6]	so the angel who spoke with me said to me: 'Proclaim, saying: Thus says the LORD of hosts: I am jealous for Jerusalem and for Zion with a great jealousy;
וְקֶצֶף גָּדוֹל אֲנִי קֹצֵף עַל־הַגּוֹיִם הַשַּׁאֲנַנִּים אֲשֶׁר אֲנִי קָצַפְתִּי מְּעָט וְהֵמָּה עָזְרוּ לְרָעָה	15[7]	and I am very displeased with the nations who are at ease; for I was but a little displeased, and they helped for evil.
לָכֵן כֹּה־אָמַר יְהוָה שַׁבְתִּי לִירוּשָׁלַ͏ִם בְּרַחֲמִים בֵּיתִי יִבָּנֶה בָּהּ נְאֻם יְהוָה צְבָאוֹת 'וְקָו' 'יִנָּטֶה' עַל־יְרוּשָׁלָ͏ִם	16[8]	Therefore, thus says the LORD: I return to Jerusalem with compassions: My house shall be built in it, says the LORD of hosts, and a line shall be stretched forth over Jerusalem.
עוֹד קְרָא לֵאמֹר כֹּה אָמַר יְהוָה צְבָאוֹת עוֹד תְּפוּצֶינָה עָרַי מִטּוֹב וְנִחַם יְהוָה עוֹד אֶת־צִיּוֹן וּבָחַר עוֹד בִּירוּשָׁלָ͏ִם	17[9]	Again, proclaim, saying: Thus says the LORD of hosts: My cities shall again overflow with prosperity; and the LORD shall yet comfort Zion, and shall yet choose Jerusalem.'

---

[1] Zechariah 1:10 - Derech Hashem Part II 6§03, Ezekiel 1:5-1:14, Genesis 32:25-31, Hebrews 1:14, Hosea 12:5-7, Job 1:7 2:1-2, Psalms 103:20-21, Zechariah 1:8 1:11 4:10 6:5-8 13:7

[2] Zechariah 1:11 - 1 Thessalonians 5:3, 2 Thessalonians 1:7, Daniel 10:20, Isaiah 14:7, Matthew 13:41 13:49 24:30-31 1:31, Psalms 68:18 103:20-21, Revelation 1:1, Zechariah 1:8 1:10 1:15 6:7

[3] LXX *between the mountains*

[4] Zechariah 1:12 - 2 Chronicles 12:21, Daniel 9:2, Demetrius the Chronographer Fragment 6:1, Exodus 23:20-23:23, Exodus.R 18:5, Hebrews 7:25, Isaiah 15:9 64:10-64:13, Jeremiah 25:11-25:12 5:10, Psalms 69:6 74:10 6:14, Revelation 6:10, Seder Olam 29:Seventy Years, Testament of Moses 4:1, Zechariah 1:8 1:10-1:11 7:5

Zechariah 1:12-14 - 8HevXIIgr

[5] Zechariah 1:13 - 4QXIIe, Amos 9:11-9:15, Isaiah 40:1-40:2, Jeremiah 5:10 30:10-30:22 31:4-31:15, Zechariah 1:9 1:14-1:16 2:4-2:12 4:1 8:2-8 8:19, Zephaniah 3:14-3:20

[6] Zechariah 1:14 - 4QXIIe, Hosea 11:8, Isaiah 9:8 14:22 16:1 16:6 18:13 11:17 15:15, Joel 2:18, Nahum 1:2, Song of Songs.R 8:7, z.Vaetchanan 269b, Zechariah 1:9 1:13 1:17 2:3-4 4:1 8:2-3

[7] Zechariah 1:15 - Amos 1:3-13 6:1, Exodus.R 30:15, Ezekiel 25:3-9 25:12-17 2:2 29:6-7 36:4-5, Hebrews 12:6-7, Isaiah 10:5-7 47:6-9 6:8, Jeremiah 48:11-13 3:24 51:34-35, Lamentations.R 2:12, mt.Hilchot Teshuvah 6:5, Numbers.R 10:2, Obadiah 1:10-16, Pesikta de R'Kahana 16.8, Pesikta Rabbati 29/30B:2, Psalms 69:27 83:3-6 3:4 17:7, Revelation 18:7-8, Tanna Devei Eliyahu 1, Zechariah 1:2 1:11

[8] Zechariah 1:16 - Deuteronomy.R 4:11, Ezekiel 37:24-28 39:25-29 16:3 23:3 24:35, Ezra 6:14-15, Genesis.R 5:1 28:2, Haggai 1:14, Isaiah 12:1 10:11 44:26-28 54:8-10, Jeremiah 31:23-26 31:40-41 33:10-12, Job 14:5, Mas.Soferim 7:2, Midrash Psalms 72:1, z.Vaetchanan 269b, Zechariah 2:1-2:2 2:10-11 4:9 8:3

[9] Zechariah 1:17 - 2 Chronicles 6:6, Amos 9:14, Ephesians 1:4, Exodus.R 42:4, Ezekiel 36:10-11 12:33, Isaiah 14:1 40:1-2 41:8-9 20:26 1:13 3:3 3:12 4:9 6:8 61:4-6 18:13, Jastrow 1041a, Jeremiah 7:14 31:24-25 32:43-44 9:13, Nehemiah 11:3 11:20, Obadiah 1:20, Psalms 69:36 132:13-14, Romans 11:28-29, z.Vaetchanan 269b, Zechariah 2:12 3:2, Zephaniah 3:15-17, 2 Kings 15:29 17:1-6 18:9-12 24:1-20, Daniel 2:37-43 7:3-8 8:3-14 11:28-35, Joshua 5:13, Zechariah 2:1 5:1 5:5 5:9, Amos 6:13, Daniel 12:7, Ezra 4:1 4:4 4:7 5:3, Habakkuk 3:14, Jeremiah 50:17-18, Revelation 7:13-14, Zechariah 1:9 1:21 2:2 4:11-14 8:14, 1 Samuel 12:11, Deuteronomy 9:25, Isaiah 54:15-17, Judges 11:16 11:18, Micah 5:6-7 5:9-10, Nehemiah 9:27, Obadiah 1:21, Zechariah 9:12-16 10:3-5 12:2-6, Daniel 12:7, Lamentations 2:17, Psalms 75:5-6 75:11, Zechariah 1:19

Zechariah – Chapter 2

וָאֶשָּׂא אֶת־עֵינַי וָאֵרֶא וְהִנֵּה אַרְבַּע קְרָנוֹת	1¹	And I lifted up my eyes, and saw, and behold four horns.
וָאֹמַר אֶל־הַמַּלְאָךְ הַדֹּבֵר בִּי מָה־אֵלֶּה וַיֹּאמֶר אֵלַי אֵלֶּה הַקְּרָנוֹת אֲשֶׁר זֵרוּ אֶת־יְהוּדָה אֶת־יִשְׂרָאֵל וִירוּשָׁלָ͏ִם	2²	And I said to the angel who spoke with me: 'What are these?' And he said to me: 'These are the horns which have scattered Judah, Israel, and Jerusalem.'
וַיַּרְאֵנִי יְהוָה אַרְבָּעָה חָרָשִׁים	3³	And the LORD showed me four craftsmen.
וָאֹמַר מָה אֵלֶּה בָאִים לַעֲשׂוֹת וַיֹּאמֶר לֵאמֹר אֵלֶּה הַקְּרָנוֹת אֲשֶׁר־זֵרוּ אֶת־יְהוּדָה כְּפִי־אִישׁ לֹא־נָשָׂא רֹאשׁוֹ וַיָּבֹאוּ אֵלֶּה לְהַחֲרִיד אֹתָם לְיַדּוֹת אֶת־קַרְנוֹת הַגּוֹיִם הַנֹּשְׂאִים קֶרֶן אֶל־אֶרֶץ יְהוּדָה לְזָרוֹתָהּ	4⁴	Then said I: 'What do these come to do?' And he spoke, saying: 'Theseare the horns that scattered Judah, so no man lifted up his head; these, then, come to frighten them, to cast down the horns of the nations, which lifted up their horn against the land of Judah to scatter it.'
וָאֶשָּׂא עֵינַי וָאֵרֶא וְהִנֵּה־אִישׁ וּבְיָדוֹ חֶבֶל מִדָּה	5⁵	⁶And I lifted up my eyes, and saw, and behold a man with a measuring line in his hand.
וָאֹמַר אָנָה אַתָּה הֹלֵךְ וַיֹּאמֶר אֵלַי לָמֹד אֶת־יְרוּשָׁלַ͏ִם לִרְאוֹת כַּמָּה־רָחְבָּהּ וְכַמָּה אָרְכָּהּ	6⁷	Then said I: 'Where are you going?' And he said to me: 'To measure Jerusalem, to see what is its breadth, and what is its length.'
וְהִנֵּה הַמַּלְאָךְ הַדֹּבֵר בִּי יֹצֵא וּמַלְאָךְ אַחֵר יֹצֵא לִקְרָאתוֹ	7⁸	And, behold, the angel who spoke with me went forth, and another angel went out to meet him,
וַיֹּאמֶר אֵלָו רֻץ דַּבֵּר אֶל־הַנַּעַר הַלָּז לֵאמֹר פְּרָזוֹת תֵּשֵׁב יְרוּשָׁלַ͏ִם מֵרֹב אָדָם וּבְהֵמָה בְּתוֹכָהּ	8⁹	and said to him: 'Run, speak to this young man, saying: 'Jerusalem shall be inhabited without walls for the multitude of men and cattle within it.
וַאֲנִי אֶהְיֶה־לָּהּ נְאֻם־יְהוָה חוֹמַת אֵשׁ סָבִיב וּלְכָבוֹד אֶהְיֶה בְתוֹכָהּ	9¹⁰	For I, says the LORD, will be surrounding wall of fire to her, and I will be the glory in her midst.

---

[1] Zechariah 2:1 - Ezekiel 16:3 16:5 23:4, Revelation 11:1 21:15, y.Berachot 4:3, Zechariah 1:16 1:18
Zechariah 2:1-17 - Sixth Shabbat after Tisha b'Av [Pesikta Rabbati 35]
[2] Zechariah 2:2 - b.Succah 52b, Ezekiel 16:3 21:6 48:15-17 48:30-35, Jeremiah 7:40, John 16:5, Revelation 11:1 21:15-17, Zechariah 5:10
Zechariah 2:2-4 - 8HevXIIgr
[3] Zechariah 2:3 - b.Succah 52b, Midrash Tanchuma Tazria 9, Numbers.R 14:1, Pesikta de R'Kahana 5.9, Pesikta Rabbati 15:14/15, Song of Songs.R 2:33, Zechariah 1:8-1:11 1:13-1:14 1:19 4:1 4:5 5:5
[4] Zechariah 2:4 - 1 Timothy 4:12, Daniel 1:17, Ezekiel 36:10-11 14:11, Isaiah 9:20 20:26 1:20, Jeremiah 1:6 30:18-19 7:25 7:28 31:39-41 33:10-13 9:22, Micah 7:11, Zechariah 1:17 8:4:5 12:6 14:10-11
[5] Zechariah 2:5 - b.Eruvin 58a, Haggai 2:7-2:9, Isaiah 4:5 12:6 26:1-26:2 9:21 60:18-19, Luke 2:32, Psalms 3:4 46:8-12 48:4 48:13, Revelation 21:10-11 21:23 22:3-5, Sibylline Oracles 3.706, z.Mishpatim 108b, Zechariah 9:8
Zechariah 2:5-9 - Greek Apocalypse of Ezra 2:22
[6] LXX begins Chapter 2 here
[7] Zechariah 2:6 - 2 Corinthians 6:16-17, Amos 9:9, b.Bava Batra [Rashi] 25a, b.Bava Batra 75b, Deuteronomy 28:64, Ein Yaakov Bava Batra:75b, Ezekiel 5:12 11:16 12:14-15 17:21, Genesis 19:17, Isaiah 24:20 52:11-12 7:1, Jeremiah 1:14 3:18 15:4 7:9 7:11 2:8 3:6 3:45 3:50, Revelation 18:4, Ruth 4:1, z.Shemot 5b, Zechariah 2:7
[8] Zechariah 2:7 - Acts 2:40, b.Bava Batra [Rashi] 25a, b.Bava Batra 25a, Ein Yaakov Bava Batra:25a, Genesis 19:17, Isaiah 24:20 4:2 4:11, Jeremiah 2:8 3:6 3:45, Micah 4:10, Numbers 16:26 16:34, Revelation 18:4
Zechariah 2:7-9 - 8HevXIIgr
[9] Zechariah 2:8 - 1 John 4:9-4:10 4:14, 2 Kings 24:2, 2 Thessalonians 1:6, 4Q562 2 2, Acts 9:4, Amos 1:3-1:5 1:9 1:11 1:13, b.Bava Batra [Rashi] 25a, b.Bava Batra 75b, b.Bava Metzia [Rashi] 69b, b.Chullin [Tosefot] 60a, Deuteronomy 8:10, Ein Yaakov Bava Batra:75b, Ezekiel 25:6-7 1:12 1:15 2:2 11:5, Genesis 20:6, Habakkuk 2:8 2:17, Isaiah 48:15-48:16 60:7-60:14, Jeremiah 50:17-50:18 51:34-51:35, Joel 4:2-8, John 14:23-24 14:26 15:21-23 17:18, Malachi 3:1, Matthew 1:40 1:45, Micah 4:11 5:7 7:10, Midrash Psalms 15:2 114:7, Obadiah 1:10-1:16, Psalms 17:8 105:13-15, z.Vaetchanan 269b, Zechariah 1:15-16 2:4-5 2:9 2:11, Zephaniah 2:8
[10] Zechariah 2:9 - b.Bava Kamma 60b, b.Sanhedrin [Rashi] 70b, Ein Yaakov Bava Kamma:60b, Exodus.R 20:18 40:4, Ezekiel 15:10, Habakkuk 2:8 2:17, Isaiah 10:32 11:15 13:2 14:2 19:16 9:1 9:23, Jeremiah 3:7 4:9, John 13:19 16:4, Lamentations.R 1:57, Leviticus.R 7:6, Midrash Psalms 15:2, Midrash Tanchuma Ki Tissa 13, Midrash Tanchuma Tzav 2, Minchah [alternate conclusion Tisha B'av Nacheim], Pesikta de R'Kahana 16.11 20.7, Pesikta Rabbati 30:3 3S:2, Song of Songs.R 7:11, y.Taanit 2:2, z.Bereshit 28a, Zechariah 2:8 4:9 6:15, Zephaniah 2:9

Hebrew	Verse	English
הוֹי הוֹי וְנֻסוּ מֵאֶרֶץ צָפוֹן נְאֻם־יְהוָה כִּי כְּאַרְבַּע רוּחוֹת הַשָּׁמַיִם פֵּרַשְׂתִּי אֶתְכֶם נְאֻם־יְהוָה	10[1]	Ho! Ho! Flee, then, from the land of the north, says the LORD; for I have spread you abroad as the Heaven's four winds, says the LORD.
הוֹי צִיּוֹן הִמָּלְטִי יוֹשֶׁבֶת בַּת־בָּבֶל	11[2]	Ho! Zion, escape, you who dwell with the daughter of Babylon.'
כִּי כֹה אָמַר יְהוָה צְבָאוֹת אַחַר כָּבוֹד שְׁלָחַנִי אֶל־הַגּוֹיִם הַשֹּׁלְלִים אֶתְכֶם כִּי הַנֹּגֵעַ בָּכֶם נֹגֵעַ בְּבָבַת עֵינוֹ	12[3]	For thus says the LORD of hosts who sent me after glory to the nations that spoiled you: *'Surely, he who touches you touches the hollow of his eye*[4].
כִּי הִנְנִי מֵנִיף אֶת־יָדִי עֲלֵיהֶם וְהָיוּ שָׁלָל לְעַבְדֵיהֶם וִידַעְתֶּם כִּי־יְהוָה צְבָאוֹת שְׁלָחָנִי	13[5]	For, behold, I will shake My hand over them, and they shall be a spoil to those who served them;' and you shall know the LORD of hosts has sent me.
רָנִּי וְשִׂמְחִי בַּת־צִיּוֹן כִּי הִנְנִי־בָא וְשָׁכַנְתִּי בְתוֹכֵךְ נְאֻם־יְהוָה	14[6]	'Sing and rejoice, O daughter of Zion; for, lo, I come, and I will dwell in the midst of you, says the LORD.
וְנִלְווּ גוֹיִם רַבִּים אֶל־יְהוָה בַּיּוֹם הַהוּא וְהָיוּ לִי לְעָם וְשָׁכַנְתִּי בְתוֹכֵךְ וְיָדַעַתְּ כִּי־יְהוָה צְבָאוֹת שְׁלָחַנִי אֵלָיִךְ	15[7]	And many nations shall join themselves to the LORD in that day, and shall be My people, and I will dwell in your midst;' and you shall know that the LORD of hosts has sent me to you.
וְנָחַל יְהוָה אֶת־יְהוּדָה חֶלְקוֹ עַל אַדְמַת הַקֹּדֶשׁ וּבָחַר עוֹד בִּירוּשָׁלָ͏ִם	16[8]	And the LORD shall inherit Judah as His portion in the holy land, and shall choose Jerusalem again.
הַס כָּל־בָּשָׂר מִפְּנֵי יְהוָה כִּי נֵעוֹר מִמְּעוֹן קָדְשׁוֹ	17[9]	Be silent, all flesh, before the LORD; for He is aroused from His holy habitation.

Zechariah – Chapter 3

Hebrew	Verse	English
וַיַּרְאֵנִי אֶת־יְהוֹשֻׁעַ הַכֹּהֵן הַגָּדוֹל עֹמֵד לִפְנֵי מַלְאַךְ יְהוָה וְהַשָּׂטָן עֹמֵד עַל־יְמִינוֹ לְשִׂטְנוֹ	1[10]	And he showed me Joshua the high priest standing before the angel of the LORD, and *Satan*[11] standing at his right hand to accuse him.

---

[1] Zechariah 2:10 - 2 Corinthians 6:15-16, b.Avodah Zara 10b, b.Taanit 3b, Ein Yaakov Avodah Zarah:10b, Ein Yaakov Taanit:3b, Ezekiel 13:27, Isaiah 12:6 11:10 40:9-11 18:10 3:11 52:9-10 6:1 13:10 65:18-19 18:14, Jeremiah 6:19 7:13 9:11, John 1:14 14:23, Leviticus 2:12, Malachi 3:1, Matthew 4:20, Mekhilta de R'Shimon bar Yochai Amalek 45:1, Mekhilta de R'Ishmael Amalek 2:153, Philippians 4:4, Psalms 40:8 47:2-10 68:19 98:1-3, Revelation 2:1 21:3, Sibylline Oracles 3.785, Zechariah 8:3 9:9 14:5, Zephaniah 3:14-15 3:17
Zechariah 2:10-14 - 4QXIIe

[2] Zechariah 2:11 - 1 Peter 2:9-10, Acts 4:28, b.Ketubot 111a, Ein Yaakov Ketubot:111a, Exodus 12:49, Ezekiel 9:33, Isaiah 2:2-5 11:9-10 19:24-25 42:1-4 21:14 49:6-7 49:22-23 4:10 60:3-7 18:19, Jeremiah 16:19, John 17:21 17:23 17:25, Luke 2:32, Malachi 1:11, Midrash Tanchuma Noach 3, Psalms 22:28-31 68:30-32 72:8-11 72:17, Revelation 11:15, Zechariah 2:9-10 3:10 8:20-23
Zechariah 2:11-12 - 8HevXIIgr

[3] Zechariah 2:12 - Birchat HaChammah.Ana Bekoach, Deuteronomy 8:9, Exodus 19:5-19:6, Exodus.R 13:1 30:15, Isaiah 17:9, Jastrow 648b, Jeremiah 10:16 3:19, Liber Antiquitatum Biblicarum 19:10, Mekhilta de R'Shimon bar Yochai Sanya 1:2, Mekhilta de R'Ishmael Shirata 6:10, Midrash Tanchuma Beshallach 16, Numbers.R 20:6, Psalms 33:12 82:8 15:4, Sifre Devarim Ha'azinu Hashamayim 313, Sifre Devarim Nitzavim 313, Sifre.z Numbers Beha'alotcha 12:12, Zechariah 1:17

[4] This is #13 of the Eighteen Emendations of the Sopherim: the text should read *He who touches you touches the apple of My eye.*

[5] Zechariah 2:13 - 2 Chronicles 6:27, Deuteronomy 2:15, Habakkuk 2:20, Isaiah 26:20-26:21 42:13-15 3:9 9:5 9:15 15:15, Jeremiah 1:30, Psalms 11:5 46:11 68:6 78:65, Romans 3:19 9:20, Zephaniah 1:7 3:8

[6] Zechariah 2:14 - b.Megillah [Rashi] 31a, Exodus.R 19:4, Kuzari 2.24, Pesikta Rabbati 35:1-4, Siman 139:24-25, Song of Songs.R 1:29-30
Zechariah 2:14-4:7 - Haftarah 1st Shabbat of Hanukkah [Ashkenaz and Sephard], Haftarah Beha'alotcha [Ashkenaz and Sephard], mt.Hilchot Tefilah 13:17
Zechariah 2:14-4:9 - Haftarah Beha'alotcha [Teimon] 1st Shabbat of Hanukkah [Teimon]

[7] Zechariah 2:15 - Exodus.R 19:4, Midrash Tanchuma Shemot 3, Pesikta Rabbati 35:3
Zechariah 2:15 [LXX] - Joseph and Aseneth 15:7

[8] Zechariah 2:16 - 8HevXIIgr, Testament of Job 33:5

[9] Zechariah 2:17 - 8HevXIIgr, Genesis.R 75:1, Jastrow 921b, Song of Songs.R 4:18

[10] Zechariah 3:1 - 1 Chronicles 21:1, 1 Peter 5:8, 1 Samuel 6:20, 2 Chronicles 5:11, 3 Enoch 14:1 26:12, 8HevXIIgr, Acts 7:30-38, b.Sanhedrin 93ab, Deuteronomy 10:8 18:15, Ein Yaakov Sanhedrin:93a, Exodus 3:2-6 23:20-21, Ezekiel 20:11 20:15, Ezra 5:2, Genesis 3:15 24:16, Guide for the Perplexed 3:22, Haggai 1:1 1:12 2:4, Hosea 12:6-7, Jeremiah 15:19, Job 1:6-12 2:1-8, Luke 21:36 22:31, Malachi 3:1, Pirkei de R'Eliezer 33, Psalms 10:23 13:6, Revelation 12:9-10, Tanna Devei Eliyahu 4, z.Balak 185b, z.Pinchas 214a, z.Shelach Lecha 174a, z.Vayera 113a, Zechariah 1:9 1:13 1:19 2:3 3:8 6:11

[11] LXX *the Devil*

וַיֹּאמֶר יְהוָה אֶל־הַשָּׂטָן יִגְעַר יְהוָה בְּךָ הַשָּׂטָן וְיִגְעַר יְהוָה בְּךָ הַבֹּחֵר בִּירוּשָׁלָ͏ִם הֲלוֹא זֶה אוּד מֻצָּל מֵאֵשׁ	2[1] And the LORD said to Satan: 'The LORD rebuke you, O Satan; Yes, the LORD who chose Jerusalem rebuke you; is not this *man*[2] a brand plucked out of the fire?'
וִיהוֹשֻׁעַ הָיָה לָבֻשׁ בְּגָדִים צוֹאִים וְעֹמֵד לִפְנֵי הַמַּלְאָךְ	3[3] Now Joshua was clothed with filthy garments, and stood before the angel.
וַיַּעַן וַיֹּאמֶר אֶל־הָעֹמְדִים לְפָנָיו לֵאמֹר הָסִירוּ הַבְּגָדִים הַצֹּאִים מֵעָלָיו וַיֹּאמֶר אֵלָיו רְאֵה הֶעֱבַרְתִּי מֵעָלֶיךָ עֲוֹנֶךָ וְהַלְבֵּשׁ אֹתְךָ מַחֲלָצוֹת	4[4] And he answered and spoke to those who stood before him, saying: 'Take the filthy garments from off him.' And to him he said: 'Behold, I cause your iniquity to pass from you, and I will clothe you with robes.'
וָאֹמַר יָשִׂימוּ צָנִיף טָהוֹר עַל־רֹאשׁוֹ וַיָּשִׂימוּ הַצָּנִיף הַטָּהוֹר עַל־רֹאשׁוֹ וַיַּלְבִּשֻׁהוּ בְּגָדִים וּמַלְאַךְ יְהוָה עֹמֵד	5[5] And I said: 'Let them set a fair mitre on his head.' So they set a fair mitre on his head, and clothed him with garments; and the angel of the LORD stood near.
וַיָּעַד מַלְאַךְ יְהוָה בִּיהוֹשֻׁעַ לֵאמֹר	6[6] And the angel of the LORD forewarned Joshua, saying:
כֹּה־אָמַר יְהוָה צְבָאוֹת אִם־בִּדְרָכַי תֵּלֵךְ וְאִם אֶת־מִשְׁמַרְתִּי תִשְׁמֹר וְגַם־אַתָּה תָּדִין אֶת־בֵּיתִי וְגַם תִּשְׁמֹר אֶת־חֲצֵרָי וְנָתַתִּי לְךָ מַהְלְכִים בֵּין הָעֹמְדִים הָאֵלֶּה	7[7] 'Thus says the LORD of hosts: If you will walk in My ways, and if you will keep My charge, and will judge My house, and will maintain My courts, then I will give you free access among these who stand near.
שְׁמַע־נָא יְהוֹשֻׁעַ הַכֹּהֵן הַגָּדוֹל אַתָּה וְרֵעֶיךָ הַיֹּשְׁבִים לְפָנֶיךָ כִּי־אַנְשֵׁי מוֹפֵת הֵמָּה כִּי־הִנְנִי מֵבִיא אֶת־עַבְדִּי צֶמַח	8[8] Hear now, O Joshua the high priest, you and your fellows who sit before you; for they are men who are a sign; for, behold, I will bring forth My servant *the Shoot*[9].
כִּי הִנֵּה הָאֶבֶן אֲשֶׁר נָתַתִּי לִפְנֵי יְהוֹשֻׁעַ עַל־אֶבֶן אַחַת שִׁבְעָה עֵינָיִם הִנְנִי מְפַתֵּחַ פִּתֻּחָהּ נְאֻם יְהוָה צְבָאוֹת וּמַשְׁתִּי אֶת־עֲוֹן הָאָרֶץ־הַהִיא בְּיוֹם אֶחָד	9[10] For behold the stone I have laid before Joshua; on the stone are seven *facets*[11]; behold, *I will*

---

[1] Zechariah 3:2 - 1 John 3:8, 2 Chronicles 6:6, 8HevXIIgr, Amos 4:11, b.Berachot 51a, b.Sanhedrin 93ab, Chibbur Yafeh 12 47a, Daniel 12:1, Jastrow 261b, John 13:18, Jude 1:9 1:23, Kriat Shema Al Hamittah, Luke 4:35 9:42 22:32, Mark 1:25, Midrash Tanchuma Vayikra 6, Pesikta de R'Kahana 24.15, Pirkei de R'Eliezer 33, Psalms 13:31, Revelation 12:9-12:10 17:14, Romans 8:33 11:4-11:5 16:20, y.Taanit 4:5, z.Vayera 113b, Zechariah 1:17 2:12
Zechariah 3:2-10 - 4QXIIe

[2] LXX *as*

[3] Zechariah 3:3 - 2 Chronicles 30:18-30:20, b.Sanhedrin 93ab, Daniel 9:18, Ein Yaakov Sanhedrin:93a, Ezra 9:15, Isaiah 16:7, Jastrow 1265a, Matthew 22:11-22:13, mt.Hilchot Teshuvah 4:1 4:1, Ralbag SOS 1, Revelation 7:13-7:14 19:8, z.Pinchas 214a

[4] Zechariah 3:4 - 1 Corinthians 6:11, 1 Kings 22:19, 2 Corinthians 5:21, 2 Samuel 12:13, Colossians 3:10, Ezekiel 12:25, Galatians 3:27-28, Hebrews 8:12, Isaiah 6:2-3 6:5-7 19:25 4:1 13:3 13:10, John 1:29, Luke 1:19 15:22, Micah 7:18, Philippians 3:7-9, Psalms 32:1-32:2 51:10, Revelation 5:11 7:14 19:7-8, Romans 3:22 6:23, Saadia Opinions 9:8, Tefilah Zakkah, Zechariah 3:1 3:7 3:9
Zechariah 3:4-5 - 2 Enoch 22:8, Apocalypse of Elijah 5:6
Zechariah 3:4-7 - 8HevXIIgr

[5] Zechariah 3:5 - Apocalypse of Abraham 11:3, Exodus 28:2-4 5:6, Hebrews 2:8-9, Job 5:14, Leviticus 8:6-9, Revelation 4:4 4:10 5:8-14, y.Shabbat 6:4, Zechariah 6:11

[6] Zechariah 3:6 - Acts 7:35-38, Exodus 23:20-21, Genesis 22:15-16 28:13-17 48:15-16, Hosea 12:6, Isaiah 15:9, Jeremiah 11:7, Zechariah 3:1

[7] Zechariah 3:7 - 1 Chronicles 23:32, 1 Corinthians 6:2-6:3, 1 Kings 2:3, 1 Samuel 2:28-2:30, 1 Timothy 6:13-6:14, 2 Timothy 4:1-4:2, Deuteronomy 17:8-17:13, Exodus.R 25:2, Exodus.R 41:7, Ezekiel 20:8 44:15-44:16 24:11, Gates of Repentance 2.019, Genesis 2:5, Hebrews 12:22-12:23, Jeremiah 15:19-15:21, John 14:2, Leviticus 8:35 10:3, Luke 20:35-20:36 22:30, Malachi 2:5-2:7, Matthew 19:28, Revelation 3:4-3:5 3:21 5:9-5:14, Saadia Opinions 9:8, Sefer Yetzirah 1:7, Tanya Shaar Hayichud §53, z.Chayyei Sarah 129b, z.Pekudei 241b, z.Terumah 170a, z.Vaetchanan 260a 269b, z.Vayera 100a, Zechariah 1:8-1:11 4:14 6:5

[8] Zechariah 3:8 - 1 Corinthians 4:9-13, b.Horayot 13a, b.Sanhedrin 93ab, Ein Yaakov Horayot:13a, Ein Yaakov Sanhedrin:93a, Exodus.R 9:1, Ezekiel 12:11 17:22-24 24:24 34:23-24 10:23 10:24 13:24, Genesis.R 56:11, Isaiah 4:2 8:18 11:1 20:3 18:1 1:3 1:5 4:13 5:2 5:11, Jastrow 867a, Jeremiah 23:5 9:15, Luke 1:78, Midrash Tanchuma Vaera 3, Numbers.R 6:1, Philippians 2:6-8, Psalms 71:7, t.Horayot 2:9, Testament of Judah 24:4, y.Horayot 3:5, Zechariah 6:12
Zechariah 3:8 [LXX] - Testament of Solomon 9:6

[9] LXX *the Branch*

[10] Zechariah 3:9 - 1 John 2:2, 1 Peter 2:4-8, 1 Timothy 2:5-6, 2 Chronicles 16:9, 2 Corinthians 1:22 3:3, 2 Timothy 2:19, 4Q177 10+ 2, 4Q177 2.2, Acts 4:11, Colossians 1:20-21, Daniel 9:24-27, Derech Hashem Part II 8§1, Ephesians 2:16-17, Exodus 4:11 4:21 4:36, Hebrews 7:27 9:25-26 10:10-18, Isaiah 8:14-15 4:16 53:4-12, Jeremiah 7:35 2:20, John 1:29 6:27, Matthew 21:42-44, Micah 7:18-19, Psalms 22:22, Revelation 5:6, Romans 9:33, Sefer Yetzirah 4:4, z.Vayechi 231a, Zechariah 3:4 4:10 13:1

[11] LXX *eyes*

engrave its graving[1], says the LORD of hosts: And I will *remove*[2] the iniquity of that land in one day.

בַּיּוֹם הַהוּא נְאֻם֙ יְהוָ֣ה צְבָא֔וֹת תִּקְרְא֖וּ אִ֑ישׁ לְרֵעֵ֖הוּ אֶל־תַּ֥חַת גֶּ֖פֶן וְאֶל־תַּ֥חַת תְּאֵנָֽה

10[3] In that day, says the LORD of hosts, you shall call every man his neighbor under the vine and under the fig tree.

Zechariah – Chapter 4

וַיָּ֣שָׁב הַמַּלְאָ֔ךְ הַדֹּבֵ֖ר בִּ֑י וַיְעִירֵ֕נִי כְּאִ֖ישׁ אֲשֶׁר־יֵע֥וֹר מִשְּׁנָתֽוֹ

1[4] And the angel who spoke with me returned, and woke me, as a man who is awakened out of his sleep.

וַיֹּ֣אמֶר אֵלַ֔י מָ֥ה אַתָּ֖ה רֹאֶ֑ה "וַיֹּאמַ֞ר" רָאִ֣יתִי וְהִנֵּ֣ה מְנוֹרַת֩ זָהָ֨ב כֻּלָּ֜הּ וְגֻלָּ֣הּ עַל־רֹאשָׁ֗הּ וְשִׁבְעָ֤ה נֵרֹתֶ֙יהָ֙ עָלֶ֔יהָ שִׁבְעָ֤ה וְשִׁבְעָה֙ מֽוּצָק֔וֹת לַנֵּר֖וֹת אֲשֶׁ֥ר עַל־רֹאשָֽׁהּ

2[5] And he said to me: 'What do you see?' And I said: 'I have seen, and behold menorahs all of gold, with a bowl on the top of it, and its seven lights; *there are seven pipes, yes, seven, to the lights, which are on its top*[6];

וּשְׁנַ֥יִם זֵיתִ֖ים עָלֶ֑יהָ אֶחָד֙ מִימִ֣ין הַגֻּלָּ֔ה וְאֶחָ֖ד עַל־שְׂמֹאלָֽהּ

3[7] and two olive trees by it, one on the right side of the bowl, and the other on the left side.'

וָאַ֙עַן֙ וָאֹמַ֔ר אֶל־הַמַּלְאָ֛ךְ הַדֹּבֵ֥ר בִּ֖י לֵאמֹ֑ר מָה־אֵ֖לֶּה אֲדֹנִֽי

4[8] And I answered and spoke to the angel who spoke with me, saying: 'What are these, my lord?'

וַ֠יַּעַן הַמַּלְאָ֞ךְ הַדֹּבֵ֥ר בִּ֛י וַיֹּ֥אמֶר אֵלַ֖י הֲל֣וֹא יָדַ֑עְתָּ מָה־הֵ֣מָּה אֵ֔לֶּה וָאֹמַ֖ר לֹ֥א אֲדֹנִֽי

5[9] Then the angel who spoke with me answered and said to me: 'You do not know what these are?' And I said: 'No, my lord.'

וַיַּ֜עַן וַיֹּ֤אמֶר אֵלַי֙ לֵאמֹ֔ר זֶ֚ה דְּבַר־יְהוָ֔ה אֶל־זְרֻבָּבֶ֖ל לֵאמֹ֑ר לֹ֤א בְחַ֙יִל֙ וְלֹ֣א בְכֹ֔חַ כִּ֣י אִם־בְּרוּחִ֔י אָמַ֖ר יְהוָ֥ה צְבָאֽוֹת

6[10] Then he answered and spoke to me, saying: 'This is the word of the LORD to Zerubbabel, saying: Not by might, nor by power, but by My spirit, says the LORD of hosts.

מִֽי־אַתָּ֧ה הַֽר־הַגָּד֛וֹל לִפְנֵ֥י זְרֻבָּבֶ֖ל לְמִישֹׁ֑ר וְהוֹצִיא֙ אֶת־הָאֶ֣בֶן הָרֹאשָׁ֔ה תְּשֻׁא֕וֹת חֵ֥ן חֵ֖ן לָֽהּ

7[11] Who are you, O great mountain before Zerubbabel? You shall become a plain; and he shall bring forth the top stone with shoutings of Grace, grace, to it.'

וַיְהִ֥י דְבַר־יְהוָ֖ה אֵלַ֥י לֵאמֹֽר

8 Moreover, the word of the LORD came to me, saying:

יְדֵ֣י זְרֻבָּבֶ֗ל יִסְּד֛וּ הַבַּ֥יִת הַזֶּ֖ה וְיָדָ֣יו תְּבַצַּ֑עְנָה וְיָ֣דַעְתָּ֔ כִּֽי־יְהוָ֥ה צְבָא֖וֹת שְׁלָחַ֥נִי אֲלֵיכֶֽם

9[12] 'The hands of Zerubbabel laid the foundation of this house; his hands shall finish it; and you

---

[1] LXX *I am digging a trench*

[2] 4QXIIe *draw out all*

[3] Zechariah 3:10 - 1 Kings 4:25, Hosea 2:18, Isaiah 12:16, John 1:45-1:48, Micah 4:4, Midrash Psalms 72:3, Zechariah 2:11

[4] Zechariah 4:1 - 1 Kings 19:5-7, 4QXIIe, b.Avodah Zara [Rashi] 73a, Daniel 8:18 10:8-10, Guide for the Perplexed 2:43, Jeremiah 7:27, Luke 9:32 22:45-46, Zechariah 1:9 1:13 1:19 2:3 3:6-7

[5] Zechariah 4:2 - 1 Chronicles 4:15, 1 Kings 7:49-50, 2 Chronicles 4:7 4:20-22 13:11, 4QXIIe, b.Megillah [Rashi] 31a, b.Megillah 31a, Ecclesiastes.R 4:1, Exodus 25:31-38 37:17-24 40:24-25, Jastrow 216b, Jeremiah 1:11-13 4:19, Leviticus.R 30:2 32:8, Matthew 5:14-16, Numbers.R 13:8, Pesikta de R'Kahana 27.2, Pesikta Rabbati 7:7 8:4 51:4, Revelation 1:12 1:20-2:1 4:5, Song of Songs.R 4:17, Zechariah 5:2

[6] LXX *and seven oil funnels to the lamps on it*

[7] Zechariah 4:3 - 4QXIIe, b.Sanhedrin 24a, Ein Yaakov Sanhedrin:24a, Jastrow 852a, Judges 9:9, Midrash Psalms 16:12, Pesikta Rabbati 8:4, Revelation 11:4, Romans 11:17 11:24, Sifre Devarim Devarim 10, Zechariah 4:11-12 4:14

[8] Zechariah 4:4 - 4QXIIe, Daniel 7:16-7:19 12:8, Matthew 13:36, Revelation 7:13-14, Zechariah 1:9 1:19 4:12-14 5:6 6:4

[9] Zechariah 4:5 - 1 Corinthians 2:12-15, Daniel 2:30, Genesis 17:16, Guide for the Perplexed 3:22, Mark 4:13, Psalms 19:6, Zechariah 1:9 4:13

[10] Zechariah 4:6 - 1 Corinthians 2:4-5, 1 Peter 1:12, 2 Chronicles 14:10 32:7-8, 2 Corinthians 10:4-5, Ezekiel 37:11-14, Ezra 5:2, Haggai 2:2-5, Hosea 1:7, Isaiah 11:2-4 6:1 8:15 63:10-14, Numbers 3:16, Psalms 20:7-9 33:16 33:20-21 44:4-8, Zechariah 9:13-15

[11] Zechariah 4:7 - 1 Peter 2:7, Acts 4:11, Daniel 2:34-35, Ephesians 1:6-7 2:4-8 2:20, Ezra 3:11-13 6:15-17, Genesis.R 97:1, Habakkuk 3:6, Haggai 2:6-9 2:21-23, Isaiah 4:16 40:3-4 17:15 64:2-4, Jeremiah 9:11 3:25, Job 38:6-7, Luke 3:5 20:17, Mark 12:10, Matthew 21:21 21:42, Mesillat Yesharim Afterword, Micah 1:4 4:1, Midrash Tanchuma Toledot 14, Nahum 1:5-6, Psalms 18:4 18:6 22:22, Revelation 5:9-13 16:20 19:1-6, Romans 11:6, Zechariah 4:9 14:4-5

[12] Zechariah 4:9 - Ezra 3:8-13 5:16 6:14-15, Genesis.R 97:1, Hebrews 12:2, Isaiah 24:16, John 3:17 5:36-37 8:16-18 17:21, Matthew 16:18, z.Toledot 143b, Zechariah 2:8-9 2:11 6:12-13 6:15

shall know that the LORD of hosts has sent me to you.

כִּי מִי בַז לְיוֹם קְטַנּוֹת וְשָׂמְחוּ וְרָאוּ אֶת־הָאֶבֶן הַבְּדִיל בְּיַד זְרֻבָּבֶל שִׁבְעָה־אֵלֶּה עֵינֵי יְהוָה הֵמָּה מְשׁוֹטְטִים בְּכָל־הָאָרֶץ

10[1] For who has despised the day of small things? They shall see with joy the tin in the hand of Zerubbabel, these seven, which are the eyes of the LORD, that run to and fro through the whole earth.'

וָאַעַן וָאֹמַר אֵלָיו מַה־שְּׁנֵי הַזֵּיתִים הָאֵלֶּה עַל־יְמִין הַמְּנוֹרָה וְעַל־שְׂמֹאולָהּ

11[2] Then I answered and said to him: 'What are these two olive trees on the right side of the menorah and on the left side?'

וָאַעַן שֵׁנִית וָאֹמַר אֵלָיו מַה־שְׁתֵּי שִׁבֲּלֵי הַזֵּיתִים אֲשֶׁר בְּיַד שְׁנֵי צַנְתְּרוֹת הַזָּהָב הַמְרִיקִים מֵעֲלֵיהֶם הַזָּהָב

12[3] And I answered the second time, and said to him: 'What are these two olive branches that are beside the two golden *spouts, that empty the golden oil out of themselves*[4]?'

וַיֹּאמֶר אֵלַי לֵאמֹר הֲלוֹא יָדַעְתָּ מָה־אֵלֶּה וָאֹמַר לֹא אֲדֹנִי

13[5] And he answered me and said, 'You do not know what these are?' And I said: 'No, my lord.'

וַיֹּאמֶר אֵלֶּה שְׁנֵי בְנֵי־הַיִּצְהָר הָעֹמְדִים עַל־אֲדוֹן כָּל־הָאָרֶץ

14[6] Then said he: 'These are the two anointed ones who stand by the Lord of the whole earth.'

Zechariah – Chapter 5

וָאָשׁוּב וָאֶשָּׂא עֵינַי וָאֶרְאֶה וְהִנֵּה מְגִלָּה עָפָה

1[7] Then I lifted up my eyes again, and saw, and behold a flying *roll*[8].

וַיֹּאמֶר אֵלַי מָה אַתָּה רֹאֶה וָאֹמַר אֲנִי רֹאֶה מְגִלָּה עָפָה אָרְכָּהּ עֶשְׂרִים בָּאַמָּה וְרָחְבָּהּ עֶשֶׂר בָּאַמָּה

2[9] And he said to me: 'What do you see?' And I answered, 'I see a flying *roll*[10]; its length is twenty cubits, and its breadth ten cubits.'

וַיֹּאמֶר אֵלַי זֹאת הָאָלָה הַיּוֹצֵאת עַל־פְּנֵי כָל־הָאָרֶץ כִּי כָל־הַגֹּנֵב מִזֶּה כָּמוֹהָ נִקָּה וְכָל־הַנִּשְׁבָּע מִזֶּה כָּמוֹהָ נִקָּה

3[11] Then said he to me: 'This is the curse that goes forth over the face of the whole land; for everyone who steals from now on will be cut off; and every one who swears from now on will be cut off.

---

[1] Zechariah 4:10 - 1 Corinthians 1:28-1:29, 2 Chronicles 16:9, Amos 7:7-7:8, b.Sanhedrin [Rashi] 38a, b.Sanhedrin 38a, b.Sotah 48b, Daniel 2:34-2:35, Derech Hashem Part II 6§03, Ein Yaakov Sanhedrin:38a, Ein Yaakov Sotah:48b, Exodus.R 8:2, Ezra 3:12-3:13, Genesis.R 87:5 97:1, Guide for the Perplexed 1:44 1:46, Haggai 2:3, Hosea 6:3, Isaiah 18:11 18:14, Jastrow 1350b, Job 8:7, Lamentations.R 1:50, Leviticus.R 4:8, Luke 15:5-15:10 15:32, Matthew 13:31-13:33, Mekhilta de R'Shimon bar Yochai Shirata 34:2, Mekilta de R'Ishmael Pisha 1:76, Midrash Tanchuma Beha'alotcha 5, Midrash Tanchuma Naso 5, Midrash Tanchuma Tetzaveh 4, Midrash Tanchuma Toledot 14, Midrash Tanchuma Vaera 9, Nehemiah 4:2-4, Numbers.R 9:8 15:5, Proverbs 4:18 15:3, Revelation 5:6 8:2, Sifre Devarim Ekev 40, Tanna Devei Eliyahu 1, y.Maaser Sheni 5:5, z.Bo 38b, z.Terumah 129a, Zechariah 1:10-11 3:9
[2] Zechariah 4:11 - Revelation 11:4, Zechariah 4:3
[3] Zechariah 4:12 - Haggai 1:1, Jastrow 1293b, Matthew 20:23, Revelation 11:4
[4] LXX *pipes that pour into and communicate with the golden oil funnels*
[5] Zechariah 4:13 - Hebrews 5:11-5:12, Zechariah 4:5
[6] Zechariah 4:14 - 1 Kings 17:1, 1 Samuel 10:1 16:1 16:12-13, 4Q254 frag 4 1.2, Avot de R'Natan 34, b.Sanhedrin 24a, Daniel 9:24-26, Deuteronomy 10:8, Ein Yaakov Sanhedrin:24a, Exodus 5:7 16:15, Exodus.R 15:3, Haggai 1:1-12, Hebrews 1:8-9 7:1-2, Isaiah 5:1 6:5 61:1-3, Jastrow 588a, Jeremiah 1:19, Joshua 3:11 3:13, Lamentations.R 1:51, Leviticus 8:12, Luke 1:19, Micah 4:13, Midrash Tanchuma Korach 12, Numbers.R 14:13 18:16, Psalms 2:6 89:21 14:4, Revelation 11:4, Testament of Gad 8:1, Zechariah 3:1-7 6:5 6:13
[7] Zechariah 5:1 - Ezekiel 2:9-10, Isaiah 8:1, Jeremiah 36:1-6 36:20-24 36:27-32, Leviticus.R 6:3, Odes of Solomon 23:5, Revelation 5:1-14 10:2 10:8-11, Zechariah 5:2
Zechariah 5:1-3 [LXX] - Lives of the Prophets 3:5
[8] LXX *sickle*
[9] Zechariah 5:2 - 2 Peter 2:3, Amos 7:8, b.Eruvin 21a, b.Gittin 60a, Genesis 6:11-6:13, Jeremiah 1:11-1:14, Leviticus.R 6:3, Revelation 18:5, Zechariah 4:2, Zephaniah 1:14
[10] LXX *sickle*
[11] Zechariah 5:3 - 1 Corinthians 6:7-6:9, 1 Timothy 1:9, Daniel 9:11, Deuteronomy 11:28-11:29 27:15-27:26 28:15-28:68 29:18-29:27, Ephesians 4:28, Exodus 20:13, Ezekiel 17:13-17:16, Galatians 3:10-3:13, Hebrews 6:6-6:8, Hosea 4:2, Isaiah 24:6 19:28 24:1, James 5:4 5:12, Jeremiah 5:2 7:9 23:10 2:6, Leviticus 19:12, Leviticus.R 6:3, Luke 21:35, Malachi 3:5 3:8-3:10 3:24, Matthew 5:33-5:37 23:16-23:22 1:41, Proverbs 3:33 5:24 6:9, Psalms 109:17-109:20, Revelation 21:8 22:15, Zechariah 5:4 8:17
Zechariah 5:3-4 - t.Shevuot 6:3

הוֹצֵאתִיהָ נְאֻם יְהוָה צְבָאוֹת וּבָאָה אֶל־בֵּית הַגַּנָּב וְאֶל־בֵּית הַנִּשְׁבָּע בִּשְׁמִי לַשָּׁקֶר וְלָנֶה בְּתוֹךְ בֵּיתוֹ וְכִלַּתּוּ וְאֶת־עֵצָיו וְאֶת־אֲבָנָיו

4[1] I cause it to go forth, says the LORD of hosts, and it shall enter into the house of the thief, and into the house of he who swears falsely by My name; and it shall live in the midst of his house, and shall consume it with its timber and its stones.'

וַיֵּצֵא הַמַּלְאָךְ הַדֹּבֵר בִּי וַיֹּאמֶר אֵלַי שָׂא נָא עֵינֶיךָ וּרְאֵה מָה הַיּוֹצֵאת הַזֹּאת

5[2] Then the angel who spoke with me went forth, and said to me: 'Now, lift up your eyes, and see that which goes forth.'

וָאֹמַר מַה־הִיא וַיֹּאמֶר זֹאת הָאֵיפָה הַיּוֹצֵאת וַיֹּאמֶר זֹאת עֵינָם בְּכָל־הָאָרֶץ

6[3] And I said: 'What is it?' And he said: 'This is the ephah that goes forth.' He said moreover: 'This is their *eye*[4] in all the land.

וְהִנֵּה כִּכַּר עֹפֶרֶת נִשֵּׂאת וְזֹאת אִשָּׁה אַחַת יוֹשֶׁבֶת בְּתוֹךְ הָאֵיפָה

7[5] And, behold, a *round piece*[6] of lead was raised, and this is a woman sitting in the midst of the ephah.'

וַיֹּאמֶר זֹאת הָרִשְׁעָה וַיַּשְׁלֵךְ אֹתָהּ אֶל־תּוֹךְ הָאֵיפָה וַיַּשְׁלֵךְ אֶת־אֶבֶן הָעֹפֶרֶת אֶל־פִּיהָ

8[7] And he said: 'This is Wickedness.' And he cast her down into the midst of the ephah, and he cast the weight of lead upon its mouth.

וָאֶשָּׂא עֵינַי וָאֵרֶא וְהִנֵּה שְׁתַּיִם נָשִׁים יוֹצְאוֹת וְרוּחַ בְּכַנְפֵיהֶם וְלָהֵנָּה כְנָפַיִם כְּכַנְפֵי הַחֲסִידָה וַתִּשֶּׂאנָה אֶת־הָאֵיפָה בֵּין הָאָרֶץ וּבֵין הַשָּׁמָיִם

9[8] Then I lifted up my eyes, and saw, and, behold, two women came forth, and the wind was in their wings; for they had wings like the wings of a stork; and they lifted up the ephah between the earth and the heaven.

וָאֹמַר אֶל־הַמַּלְאָךְ הַדֹּבֵר בִּי אָנָה הֵמָּה מוֹלִכוֹת אֶת־הָאֵיפָה

10[9] Then I said to the angel who spoke with me: 'Why do these bear the ephah?'

וַיֹּאמֶר אֵלַי לִבְנוֹת־לָהּ בַיִת בְּאֶרֶץ שִׁנְעָר וְהוּכַן וְהֻנִּיחָה שָּׁם עַל־מְכֻנָתָהּ

11[10] And he said unto me: 'To build her a house in the land of *Shinar*[11]; and when it is prepared, she shall be set there in her own place.

Zechariah – Chapter 6

וָאָשֻׁב וָאֶשָּׂא עֵינַי וָאֶרְאֶה וְהִנֵּה אַרְבַּע מַרְכָּבוֹת יֹצְאוֹת מִבֵּין שְׁנֵי הֶהָרִים וְהֶהָרִים הָרֵי נְחֹשֶׁת

1[12] And again I lifted up my eyes, and saw, and, behold, there came four chariots out from between the two mountains; and the mountains were mountains of *bronze*[13].

בַּמֶּרְכָּבָה הָרִאשֹׁנָה סוּסִים אֲדֻמִּים וּבַמֶּרְכָּבָה הַשֵּׁנִית סוּסִים שְׁחֹרִים

2[14] In the first chariot were red horses; and in the second chariot black horses;

---

[1] Zechariah 5:4 - b.Nedarim [Ran] 7b, b.Sheviit 39a, Deuteronomy 7:26, Ein Yaakov Shevuot:39a, Gates of Repentance 3.045, Habakkuk 2:9-2:11, James 5:2-3, Job 18:15 20:26, Leviticus 14:34-45, Leviticus.R 6:3, Malachi 3:5, Midrash Tanchuma Metzora 4, mt.Hilchot Shevuot 11:16, Numbers.R 7:5, Pesikta Rabbati 22:6, Pirkei de R'Eliezer 38, Proverbs 3:33, t.Sotah 7:2, y.Sheviit 6:5
[2] Zechariah 5:5 - Zechariah 1:9 1:14 1:19 2:3 4:5
[3] Zechariah 5:6 - Amos 8:5, Ezekiel 44:10-11, mt.Hilchot Yesodei haTorah 7:3
[4] LXX *iniquity*
[5] Zechariah 5:7 - Ezekiel 16:1-63 23:1-49, Hosea 1:1-3, Isaiah 13:1 15:1 22:11, Jeremiah 3:1-2, Revelation 17:1-18, z.Shemot 19b
[6] LXX *talent*
[7] Zechariah 5:8 - 1 Thessalonians 2:16, Amos 9:1-4, b.Sanhedrin 64a, b.Yoma 69b, Ein Yaakov Yoma:69b, Genesis 15:16, Lamentations 1:14, Matthew 23:32, Micah 6:11, Proverbs 5:22, Psalms 38:5, Zechariah 5:7
Zechariah 5:8-11 - 4QXIIe
[8] Zechariah 5:9 - Avot de R'Natan 28, b.Kiddushin 49b, b.Sanhedrin 24a, Daniel 9:26-9:27, Deuteronomy 4:49, Ein Yaakov Kiddushin:49a, Exodus.R 25:2, Guide for the Perplexed 1:49, Hosea 8:1, Leviticus 11:19, Matthew 24:28
[9] Zechariah 5:10 - b.Kiddushin 49b, b.Sanhedrin 24a
[10] Zechariah 5:11 - Avot de R'Natan 28, b.Kiddushin 49b, b.Sanhedrin 24a, Daniel 1:2, Deuteronomy 4:59, Genesis 10:10 11:2 14:1, Guide for the Perplexed 1:67, Hosea 3:4, Isaiah 11:11, Jeremiah 5:28, Luke 21:24, Ruth.R 5:5
[11] LXX *Babylon*
[12] Zechariah 6:1 - 1 Samuel 2:8, Acts 4:28, Daniel 2:38-40 4:12 4:32 7:3-7 8:22, Ephesians 1:11 3:11, Exodus.R 15:4, Guide for the Perplexed 2:10 2:29 2:43, Isaiah 14:26-27 19:13 46:10-11, Job 10:29, Midrash Tanchuma Tazria 9, Proverbs 21:30, Psalms 33:11 36:7, Sifre Devarim Ha'azinu Hashamayim 320, Sifre Devarim Nitzavim 313 320, Zechariah 1:18-19 5:1 6:5
Zechariah 6:1-5 - 4QXIIe
[13] 4QXIIe *brass*; LXX *brazen*
[14] Zechariah 6:2 - Revelation 6:2-6:6 12:3 17:3, Zechariah 1:8 6:6

וּבַמֶּרְכָּבָה הַשְּׁלִשִׁית סוּסִים לְבָנִים וּבַמֶּרְכָּבָה הָרְבִעִית סוּסִים בְּרֻדִּים אֲמֻצִּים

3[1]   and in the third chariot white horses; and in the fourth chariot *strong-spotted*[2] horses.

וָאַעַן וָאֹמַר אֶל־הַמַּלְאָךְ הַדֹּבֵר בִּי מָה־אֵלֶּה אֲדֹנִי

4[3]   Then I answered and said to the angel that spoke with me: 'What are these, my lord?'

וַיַּעַן הַמַּלְאָךְ וַיֹּאמֶר אֵלָי אֵלֶּה אַרְבַּע רֻחוֹת הַשָּׁמַיִם יוֹצְאוֹת מֵהִתְיַצֵּב עַל־אֲדוֹן כָּל־הָאָרֶץ

5[4]   And the angel answered and said to me: 'These chariots go forth to the four winds of heaven, after presenting themselves before the Lord of all the earth.

אֲשֶׁר־בָּהּ הַסּוּסִים הַשְּׁחֹרִים יֹצְאִים אֶל־אֶרֶץ צָפוֹן וְהַלְּבָנִים יָצְאוּ אֶל־אַחֲרֵיהֶם וְהַבְּרֻדִּים יָצְאוּ אֶל־אֶרֶץ הַתֵּימָן

6[5]   The black horses went forth toward the north country; and the white went forth after them; and the *spotted*[6] went forth toward the south country;

וְהָאֲמֻצִּים יָצְאוּ וַיְבַקְשׁוּ לָלֶכֶת לְהִתְהַלֵּךְ בָּאָרֶץ וַיֹּאמֶר לְכוּ הִתְהַלְּכוּ בָאָרֶץ וַתִּתְהַלַּכְנָה בָּאָרֶץ

7[7]   and the *strong*[8] went forth.' And they yearned to go so they might walk to and fro through the earth; and he said: 'Get there, walk to and fro through the earth.' So they walked to and fro through the earth.

וַיַּזְעֵק אֹתִי וַיְדַבֵּר אֵלַי לֵאמֹר רְאֵה הַיּוֹצְאִים אֶל־אֶרֶץ צָפוֹן הֵנִיחוּ אֶת־רוּחִי בְּאֶרֶץ צָפוֹן

8[9]   Then he cried out to me, and spoke to me, saying: 'Behold, they who go toward the north country have *eased My spirit*[10] in the north country.'

וַיְהִי דְבַר־יְהוָה אֵלַי לֵאמֹר

9[11]   And the word of the LORD came to me, saying:

לָקוֹחַ מֵאֵת הַגּוֹלָה מֵחֶלְדַּי וּמֵאֵת טוֹבִיָּה וּמֵאֵת יְדַעְיָה וּבָאתָ אַתָּה בַּיּוֹם הַהוּא וּבָאתָ בֵּית יֹאשִׁיָּה בֶן־צְפַנְיָה אֲשֶׁר־בָּאוּ מִבָּבֶל

10[12]   *'Take of them of the captivity, of Heldai, of Tobijah, and of Jedaiah, who come from Babylon; and come the same day, and go into the house of Josiah the son of Zephaniah*[13];

וְלָקַחְתָּ כֶסֶף־וְזָהָב וְעָשִׂיתָ עֲטָרוֹת וְשַׂמְתָּ בְּרֹאשׁ יְהוֹשֻׁעַ בֶּן־יְהוֹצָדָק הַכֹּהֵן הַגָּדוֹל

11[14]   yea, take silver and gold, and make crowns, and set the one upon the head of Joshua the son of Jehozadak, the high priest;

וְאָמַרְתָּ אֵלָיו לֵאמֹר כֹּה אָמַר יְהוָה צְבָאוֹת לֵאמֹר הִנֵּה־אִישׁ צֶמַח שְׁמוֹ וּמִתַּחְתָּיו יִצְמָח וּבָנָה אֶת־הֵיכַל יְהוָה

12[15]   and speak to him, saying: Thus says the LORD of hosts, saying: Behold, a man whose name is *the Shoot, and who shall shoot up out of his place*[16], and build the temple of the LORD;

---

[1] Zechariah 6:3 - Daniel 2:33 2:40-2:41, Revelation 6:2 6:8 19:11 20:11, Zechariah 1:8 6:6-6:7

[2] LXX *piebald and ash-colored horses*

[3] Zechariah 6:4 - Zechariah 1:9 1:19-1:21 5:5-5:6 5:10

[4] Zechariah 6:5 - 1 Kings 19:11 22:19, 2 Chronicles 18:18-18:19, Daniel 7:2 7:10, Ezekiel 1:5-1:28 10:9-10:19 11:22 13:9, Guide for the Perplexed 2:10 3:22, Hebrews 1:7 1:14, Isaiah 6:5, Job 1:6 2:1-2:2, Luke 1:19, Matthew 18:10 24:31, Psalms 68:18 104:3-104:4 4:8, Revelation 7:1 14:6-14:13, Zechariah 1:10-1:11 4:10 4:14

[5] Zechariah 6:6 - Daniel 7:5-6 11:3-6 11:9 11:40, Ezekiel 1:4, Jeremiah 1:14-15 4:6 6:1 1:9 22:10 3:48

[6] LXX *piebald*

[7] Zechariah 6:7 - 2 Chronicles 16:9, Daniel 7:19 7:24, Genesis 13:17, Job 1:6-7 2:1-2, Zechariah 1:10

[8] LXX *ash-colored*

[9] Zechariah 6:8 - Ecclesiastes 10:4, Ezekiel 5:13 16:42 16:42 16:63, Isaiah 1:24 18:3-18:4 42:13-42:15 24:14 51:22-51:23, Jeremiah 51:48-51:49, Judges 8:3 15:7, Revelation 18:21-18:22, Zechariah 1:15

[10] LXX *quieted my anger*

[11] Zechariah 6:9 - Zechariah 1:1 7:1 8:1

[12] Zechariah 6:10 - Acts 24:17, Ezra 7:14-7:16 8:26-8:30, Isaiah 18:20, Jeremiah 4:6, Romans 15:25-15:26

[13] LXX *Take the things of the captivity from the chief men, and from the useful men of it, and from them who have understood it; and you shall enter in that day into the house of Josias the son of Sophonias who came out of Babylon*

[14] Zechariah 6:11 - Exodus 28:36-38 5:6 15:30, Ezra 3:2, Haggai 1:1 1:14 2:4, Hebrews 2:9, Leviticus 8:9, Psalms 21:4, Revelation 19:12, Song of Songs 3:11, Zechariah 3:1 3:5

[15] Zechariah 6:12 - 1 Corinthians 3:9, 1 Peter 2:4-2:5, Acts 13:38 17:31, Ephesians 2:20-2:22, Ezra 3:8 3:10, Hebrews 3:3-3:4 7:4 7:24 8:3 10:12, Isaiah 4:2 11:1 32:1-2 5:2, Jastrow 1287b, Jeremiah 23:5 9:15, John 1:45 2:19-21 19:5, Lamentations.R 1:51, Luke 1:78, Mark 14:58 15:29 15:39, Matthew 16:18 26:61, Micah 5:6, Midrash Proverbs 19, Midrash Tanchuma Korach 12, Numbers.R 18:21, Philo De Cofusione Linguarum 62, Pirkei de R'Eliezer 48, Psalms 80:16-18, Testament of Judah 24:4, Zechariah 3:8 4:6-9 8:9 13:7 Zechariah 6:12 [LXX] - Testament of Solomon 9:6

[16] LXX *The Branch; and he shall spring up from his stem*

<table>
<tr><td>

וְהוּא יִבְנֶה אֶת־הֵיכַל יְהוָה וְהוּא־יִשָּׂא הוֹד וְיָשַׁב
וּמָשַׁל עַל־כִּסְאוֹ וְהָיָה כֹהֵן עַל־כִּסְאוֹ וַעֲצַת
שָׁלוֹם תִּהְיֶה בֵּין שְׁנֵיהֶם

</td><td>13¹</td><td>

he shall build the temple of the LORD; and he shall bear the glory², and shall sit and rule on his throne; and there shall be a priest before his throne; and the counsel of peace shall be between them both.

</td></tr>
<tr><td>

וְהָעֲטָרֹת תִּהְיֶה לְחֵלֶם וּלְטוֹבִיָּה וְלִידַעְיָה וּלְחֵן
בֶּן־צְפַנְיָה לְזִכָּרוֹן בְּהֵיכַל יְהוָה

</td><td>14³</td><td>

And the crowns shall be to *Helem, and to Tobijah, and to Jedaiah, and to Hen the son of Zephaniah, as a memorial in the temple⁴ of the* LORD.

</td></tr>
<tr><td>

וּרְחוֹקִים ׀ יָבֹאוּ וּבָנוּ בְּהֵיכַל יְהוָה וִידַעְתֶּם כִּי־
יְהוָה צְבָאוֹת שְׁלָחַנִי אֲלֵיכֶם וְהָיָה אִם־שָׁמוֹעַ
תִּשְׁמְעוּן בְּקוֹל יְהוָה אֱלֹהֵיכֶם

</td><td>15⁵</td><td>

And they who are far off shall come and build in the temple of the LORD, and you shall know that the LORD of hosts has sent me to you. And it shall come to pass, if you will diligently listen to the voice of the LORD your God.'

</td></tr>
</table>

Zechariah – Chapter 7

<table>
<tr><td>

וַיְהִי בִּשְׁנַת אַרְבַּע לְדָרְיָוֶשׁ הַמֶּלֶךְ הָיָה דְבַר־
יְהוָה אֶל־זְכַרְיָה בְּאַרְבָּעָה לַחֹדֶשׁ הַתְּשִׁעִי בְּכִסְלֵו

</td><td>1⁶</td><td>

And it came to pass in the fourth year of king Darius, that the word of the LORD came to Zechariah in the fourth day of the ninth month, in *Chislev⁷*;

</td></tr>
<tr><td>

וַיִּשְׁלַח בֵּית־אֵל שַׂר־אֶצֶר וְרֶגֶם מֶלֶךְ וַאֲנָשָׁיו
לְחַלּוֹת אֶת־פְּנֵי יְהוָה

</td><td>2⁸</td><td>

When Bethel-sarezer, and Regem-melech and his men, had sent to entreat the favor of⁹ the LORD,

</td></tr>
<tr><td>

לֵאמֹר אֶל־הַכֹּהֲנִים אֲשֶׁר לְבֵית־יְהוָה צְבָאוֹת
וְאֶל־הַנְּבִיאִים לֵאמֹר הַאֶבְכֶּה בַּחֹדֶשׁ הַחֲמִשִׁי
הִנָּזֵר כַּאֲשֶׁר עָשִׂיתִי זֶה כַּמֶּה שָׁנִים

</td><td>3¹⁰</td><td>

and to speak to the priests of the house of the LORD of hosts, and to the prophets, saying: '*Should I weep in the fifth month, separating myself, as I have done these so many years?¹¹*'

</td></tr>
<tr><td>

וַיְהִי דְּבַר־יְהוָה צְבָאוֹת אֵלַי לֵאמֹר

</td><td>4¹²</td><td>

Then came the word of the LORD of hosts to me, saying:

</td></tr>
<tr><td>

אֱמֹר אֶל־כָּל־עַם הָאָרֶץ וְאֶל־הַכֹּהֲנִים לֵאמֹר כִּי־
צַמְתֶּם וְסָפוֹד בַּחֲמִישִׁי וּבַשְּׁבִיעִי וְזֶה שִׁבְעִים
שָׁנָה הֲצוֹם צַמְתֻּנִי אָנִי

</td><td>5¹³</td><td>

'Speak to all the people of the land, and to the priests, saying: When you fasted and mourned in the fifth and in the seventh month, these seventy years, did you at all fast to Me, *to Me¹⁴*?

</td></tr>
</table>

---

¹ Zechariah 6:13 - 1 Peter 3:22, Acts 10:36-43, Colossians 1:2 1:18-20, Daniel 7:13-14 9:25-27, Ephesians 1:20-23 2:13-18, Genesis 14:18, Hebrews 2:7-9 3:1 4:14-16 6:20-7:3 7:24-28 10:12-13, Isaiah 9:7 11:10 22:24 49:5-6 6:10, Jeremiah 23:6, John 13:31-32 17:1-5, Micah 5:5, Philippians 2:7-11, Psalms 21:6 45:4-5 72:17-19 85:10-12 14:4, Revelation 3:21 5:9-13 19:11-16, Romans 5:1, Zechariah 4:14 6:11

² LXX *And he shall receive power*

³ Zechariah 6:14 - 1 Corinthians 11:23-11:26, 1 Samuel 2:30, Acts 10:4, b.Middot 36a, Exodus 12:14 4:12 4:29, Joshua 4:7, Mark 14:9, Matthew 2:13, Numbers 17:5 7:54, Zechariah 6:10

⁴ LXX *those who wait patiently, and to the useful men of the captivity, and to those who have known it, and for the favor of the son of Sophonias, and for a psalm in the house*

⁵ Zechariah 6:15 - 1 Corinthians 3:10-15, 1 Peter 2:4-5, 2 Peter 1:5-1:10, Acts 2:39, Ephesians 2:13-2:22, Isaiah 3:10 56:6-56:8 9:19 58:10-14 12:10, Jeremiah 7:23, John 17:20-21, Romans 16:26, Zechariah 2:8-2:11 3:7 4:8-9 6:12

⁶ Zechariah 7:1 - b.Rosh Hashanah 7a, Ezra 6:14-15, Haggai 2:10 2:20, Nehemiah 1:1, Zechariah 1:1

⁷ LXX *Chaseleu*

⁸ Zechariah 7:2 - 1 Kings 13:6, 1 Samuel 13:12, Exodus 8:11, Ezra 6:10 7:15-23 8:28-30, Isaiah 12:7, Jeremiah 2:19, Zechariah 6:10 8:21

⁹ LXX *And Sarasar and Arbeseer the king and his men sent to Bethel, to propitiate*

¹⁰ Zechariah 7:3 - 1 Corinthians 7:5, 2 Kings 25:8-25:9, Deuteronomy 17:9-17:11 9:10, Ecclesiastes 3:4, Ezekiel 44:23-44:24, Haggai 2:11, Hosea 4:6, Isaiah 22:12-22:13, James 4:8-4:10, Jeremiah 52:12-52:14, Joel 2:17, Malachi 2:7, Matthew 9:15, mt.Shemonah Perakim 4:6, Nehemiah 8:9-8:11 9:1-9:3, Numbers.R 10:8, Shemonah Perachim IV, Zechariah 7:5 8:19 12:12-12:14

¹¹ LXX *The holy offering has come in here in the fifth month, as it has done already many years*

¹² Zechariah 7:4 - b.Rosh Hashanah [Rashi] 18b, Isaiah 10:16

¹³ Zechariah 7:5 - 1 Corinthians 10:31, 2 Corinthians 5:15, 2 Kings 1:23, Colossians 3:23, Isaiah 1:11-12 58:4-6, Jeremiah 1:11 41:1-4, Matthew 5:16-18 6:2 6:5 6:16 23:5, mt.Hilchot Deot 3:1, mt.Shemonah Perakim 4:6, Romans 14:6-9 14:17-18, Zechariah 1:12 7:3 7:6 8:19

¹⁴ Missing in LXX

וְכִי תֹאכְלוּ וְכִי תִשְׁתּוּ הֲלוֹא אַתֶּם הָאֹכְלִים וְאַתֶּם הַשֹּׁתִים

6[1] And when you ate, and when you drank, *are you not they who ate, and they who drank[2]*?

הֲלוֹא אֶת־הַדְּבָרִים אֲשֶׁר קָרָא יְהוָה בְּיַד הַנְּבִיאִים הָרִאשֹׁנִים בִּהְיוֹת יְרוּשָׁלַם יֹשֶׁבֶת וּשְׁלֵוָה וְעָרֶיהָ סְבִיבֹתֶיהָ וְהַנֶּגֶב וְהַשְּׁפֵלָה יֹשֵׁב

7[3] Should you not listen to the words the LORD proclaimed by the former prophets, when Jerusalem was inhabited and in prosperity, and its cities around her, and the South and the Lowland were inhabited?'

וַיְהִי דְּבַר־יְהוָה אֶל־זְכַרְיָה לֵאמֹר

8 And the word of the LORD came to Zechariah, saying:

כֹּה אָמַר יְהוָה צְבָאוֹת לֵאמֹר מִשְׁפַּט אֱמֶת שְׁפֹטוּ וְחֶסֶד וְרַחֲמִים עֲשׂוּ אִישׁ אֶת־אָחִיו

9[4] 'Thus has the LORD of hosts spoken, saying: Every man execute true judgment, and show mercy and compassion to his brother;

וְאַלְמָנָה וְיָתוֹם גֵּר וְעָנִי אַל־תַּעֲשֹׁקוּ וְרָעַת אִישׁ אָחִיו אַל־תַּחְשְׁבוּ בִּלְבַבְכֶם

10[5] and do not oppress the widow, nor the fatherless, the stranger, nor the poor; and let none of you *devise evil against his brother in your heart[6]*.

וַיְמָאֲנוּ לְהַקְשִׁיב וַיִּתְּנוּ כָתֵף סֹרָרֶת וְאָזְנֵיהֶם הִכְבִּידוּ מִשְּׁמוֹעַ

11[7] But they refused to attend, and turned a stubborn shoulder, and stopped their ears so they would not hear.

וְלִבָּם שָׂמוּ שָׁמִיר מִשְּׁמוֹעַ אֶת־הַתּוֹרָה וְאֶת־הַדְּבָרִים אֲשֶׁר שָׁלַח יְהוָה צְבָאוֹת בְּרוּחוֹ בְּיַד הַנְּבִיאִים הָרִאשֹׁנִים וַיְהִי קֶצֶף גָּדוֹל מֵאֵת יְהוָה צְבָאוֹת

12[8] Yes, they made their hearts *as an adamant stone[9]*, lest they should hear the law, and the words which the LORD of hosts sent by His spirit by the hand of the former prophets; therefore, great wrath came there from the LORD of hosts.

וַיְהִי כַאֲשֶׁר־קָרָא וְלֹא שָׁמֵעוּ כֵּן יִקְרְאוּ וְלֹא אֶשְׁמָע אָמַר יְהוָה צְבָאוֹת

13[10] And it came to pass that, as He called, and they would not hear; so they shall call, and I will not hear, said the LORD of hosts;

וְאֵסָעֲרֵם עַל כָּל־הַגּוֹיִם אֲשֶׁר לֹא־יְדָעוּם וְהָאָרֶץ נָשַׁמָּה אַחֲרֵיהֶם מֵעֹבֵר וּמִשָּׁב וַיָּשִׂימוּ אֶרֶץ־חֶמְדָּה לְשַׁמָּה

14[11] but I will scatter them with a whirlwind among all the nations whom they have not known. Thus, the land was desolate after them, so that no man passed through nor returned; for they laid the pleasant land desolate.'

---

[1] Zechariah 7:6 - 1 Chronicles 5:22, 1 Corinthians 10:31 11:20-11:21 11:26-11:29, 1 Samuel 16:7, Colossians 3:17, Deuteronomy 12:7 14:26, Hosea 8:13 9:4, Jeremiah 17:9-17:10, mt.Shemonah Perakim 4:6, Shemonah Perachim IV

[2] LXX *do you not eat and drink for yourselves*

[3] Zechariah 7:7 - Amos 5:14-15, Daniel 9:6-14, Deuteronomy 10:3, Ezekiel 18:30-32, Hosea 14:3-5, Isaiah 1:16-20 7:3 55:6-7, Jeremiah 7:5 7:23 17:26 22:21 8:44 9:13 36:2-3, Micah 6:6-8, Midrash Proverbs 1, Zechariah 1:3-1:6, Zephaniah 2:1-2:3

[4] Zechariah 7:9 - 2 Enoch 42:7, Amos 5:24, Deuteronomy 10:18-19 15:7-14 16:18-20, Ezekiel 21:9, Hosea 10:12-13, Isaiah 58:6-10, James 2:13-17, Jeremiah 7:5 7:23 21:12, John 7:51, Leviticus 19:15 19:35-37, Luke 11:42, Matthew 23:23, Mekilta de R'Ishmael Nezikin 18:99, Micah 6:8, mt.Shemonah Perakim 4:6, Proverbs 21:3, Psalms 82:2-4, Shemonah Perachim IV, Zechariah 7:7 8:16-17 Zechariah 7:9-10 - Exodus.R 30:15

[5] Zechariah 7:10 - 1 Corinthians 6:10, 1 John 3:15, 2 Enoch 42:9 50:6, Amos 4:1 5:11-12, Deuteronomy 24:14-18 3:19, Exodus 22:21-24 23:9, Ezekiel 22:7 22:12 22:29, Isaiah 1:16-17 1:23, James 1:14-15 5:4, Jeremiah 5:28 11:19-20 18:18 22:15-17, Malachi 3:5, Mark 7:21-23, Matthew 23:13, Micah 2:1-3 3:1-4, Proverbs 3:29 6:18 22:22-23 23:10-11, Psalms 21:12 36:5 72:4 20:3, Zechariah 8:17, Zephaniah 3:1-3

[6] LXX *remember in his heart the injury of his brother*

[7] Zechariah 7:11 - 2 Baruch 51:5, 2 Chronicles 9:10, 2 Kings 17:13-17:15, Acts 7:51 7:57, Daniel 9:5, Exodus 10:3, Ezekiel 3:7, Hebrews 10:38-10:39 12:25, Hosea 4:16, Isaiah 1:19-1:20 6:10, Jeremiah 6:16-6:17 7:24 8:5 11:10 13:10 17:23 26:5-26:6 11:15 12:31 20:16, Lamentations.R 1:57, Midrash Proverbs 1, Nehemiah 9:17 9:26 9:29, Pesikta de R'Kahana 16.11, Pesikta Rabbati 33:13, Proverbs 1:24-1:32, Psalms 58:5-58:6, Zechariah 1:4, Zephaniah 3:2

[8] Zechariah 7:12 - 1 Peter 1:11-12, 1 Thessalonians 2:15-16, 2 Chronicles 12:16, 2 Peter 1:21, 2 Thessalonians 2:10-12, Acts 7:51-52 4:27, Daniel 9:11-12, Ezekiel 2:4 3:7-9 11:19 12:26, Isaiah 6:10 24:4, Jeremiah 5:3 17:1 2:19, Job 9:4, John 3:19-20, Lamentations.R 1:57, Luke 8:12, Mark 4:12, Matthew 13:15, Nehemiah 9:29-30, Pesikta de R'Kahana 16.11, Pesikta Rabbati 33:13, Psalms 50:17, Zechariah 7:7

[9] LXX *disobedient*

[10] Zechariah 7:13 - Ezekiel 14:3 20:3, Isaiah 1:15 2:2, James 4:3, Jeremiah 6:16-6:17 11:11 14:12, Lamentations.R Petichata D'Chakimei:12-13 Petichata D'Chakimei:21, Luke 13:25 13:34-13:35 19:42-19:44, Matthew 25:11-25:12, Micah 3:4, Midrash Psalms 10:2 13:1, Midrash Tanchuma Bechukkotai 2, Proverbs 1:24-1:28 21:13 4:9, Psalms 81:9-81:13, Saadia Opinions 5:6

[11] Zechariah 7:14 - 2 Chronicles 12:21, Amos 1:14, Daniel 9:16-9:18, Deuteronomy 4:27 4:33 4:49 28:64, Habakkuk 3:14, Isaiah 17:13 21:1 18:15, Jastrow 1010b, Jeremiah 4:11-4:12 5:15 23:19 25:32-25:33 6:23 12:19 20:6 4:30, Leviticus 2:22 2:33, Nahum 1:3, Numbers.R 9:45, Psalms 58:10, Testament of Levi 10:4, Zechariah 2:6 9:14, Zephaniah 3:6

Zechariah – Chapter 8

וַיְהִ֛י דְּבַר־יְהֹוָ֥ה צְבָא֖וֹת לֵאמֹֽר

1 And the word of the LORD of hosts came, saying:

כֹּ֤ה אָמַר֙ יְהֹוָ֣ה צְבָא֔וֹת קִנֵּ֥אתִי לְצִיּ֖וֹן קִנְאָ֣ה גְדוֹלָ֑ה וְחֵמָ֥ה גְדוֹלָ֖ה קִנֵּ֥אתִי לָֽהּ

2[1] 'Thus says the LORD of hosts: I am jealous for Zion with great jealousy, and I am jealous for her with great fury.

כֹּ֚ה אָמַ֣ר יְהֹוָ֔ה שַׁ֚בְתִּי אֶל־צִיּ֔וֹן וְשָׁכַנְתִּ֖י בְּת֣וֹךְ יְרוּשָׁלָ֑͏ִם וְנִקְרְאָ֤ה יְרוּשָׁלַ֙͏ִם֙ עִ֣יר־הָֽאֱמֶ֔ת וְהַר־יְהֹוָ֥ה צְבָא֖וֹת הַ֥ר הַקֹּֽדֶשׁ

3[2] Thus says the LORD: I return to Zion, and will live in the midst of Jerusalem; and Jerusalem shall be called the city of truth; and the mountain of the LORD of hosts the holy mountain.

כֹּ֚ה אָמַר֙ יְהֹוָ֣ה צְבָא֔וֹת עֹ֤ד יֵֽשְׁבוּ֙ זְקֵנִ֣ים וּזְקֵנ֔וֹת בִּרְחֹב֖וֹת יְרוּשָׁלָ֑͏ִם וְאִ֧ישׁ מִשְׁעַנְתּ֛וֹ בְּיָד֖וֹ מֵרֹ֥ב יָמִֽים

4[3] Thus says the LORD of hosts: There shall yet old men and old women sit in the broad places of Jerusalem, every man with his staff in his hand from his many days.

וּרְחֹב֤וֹת הָעִיר֙ יִמָּ֣לְא֔וּ יְלָדִ֖ים וִֽילָד֑וֹת מְשַׂחֲקִ֖ים בִּרְחֹֽבֹתֶֽיהָ

5[4] And the broad places of the city shall be full of boys and girls playing in the broad places.

כֹּ֤ה אָמַר֙ יְהֹוָ֣ה צְבָא֔וֹת כִּ֣י יִפָּלֵ֗א בְּעֵינֵי֙ שְׁאֵרִית֙ הָעָ֣ם הַזֶּ֔ה בַּיָּמִ֖ים הָהֵ֑ם גַּם־בְּעֵינַי֙ יִפָּלֵ֔א נְאֻ֖ם יְהֹוָ֥ה צְבָאֽוֹת

6[5] Thus says the LORD of hosts: If it is marvelous in the eyes of the remnant of this people in those days, should it also be marvelous in my eyes? Says the LORD of hosts.

כֹּ֤ה אָמַר֙ יְהֹוָ֣ה צְבָא֔וֹת הִנְנִ֥י מוֹשִׁ֖יעַ אֶת־עַמִּ֑י מֵאֶ֥רֶץ מִזְרָ֖ח וּמֵאֶ֥רֶץ מְב֥וֹא הַשָּֽׁמֶשׁ

7[6] Thus says the LORD of hosts: Behold, I will save My people from the east country, and from the west country;

וְהֵבֵאתִ֣י אֹתָ֔ם וְשָׁכְנ֖וּ בְּת֣וֹךְ יְרוּשָׁלָ֑͏ִם וְהָֽיוּ־לִ֣י לְעָ֗ם וַֽאֲנִי֙ אֶֽהְיֶ֤ה לָהֶם֙ לֵֽאלֹהִ֔ים בֶּֽאֱמֶ֖ת וּבִצְדָקָֽה

8[7] And I will bring them, and they shall dwell in the midst of Jerusalem; and they shall be My people, and I will be their God, in truth and in righteousness.

כֹּֽה־אָמַר֮ יְהֹוָ֣ה צְבָאוֹת֒ תֶּחֱזַ֣קְנָה יְדֵיכֶ֔ם הַשֹּֽׁמְעִים֙ בַּיָּמִ֣ים הָאֵ֔לֶּה אֵ֖ת הַדְּבָרִ֣ים הָאֵ֑לֶּה מִפִּי֙ הַנְּבִיאִ֔ים אֲשֶׁ֗ר בְּי֛וֹם יֻסַּ֥ד בֵּית־יְהֹוָ֥ה צְבָא֖וֹת הַהֵיכָ֥ל לְהִבָּנֽוֹת

9[8] Thus says the LORD of hosts: Let your hands be strong, you who hear in these days these words from the mouth of the prophets who were in the day that the foundation of the house of the LORD of hosts was laid, the temple, so it might be built.

כִּ֗י לִפְנֵי֙ הַיָּמִ֣ים הָהֵ֔ם שְׂכַ֤ר הָֽאָדָם֙ לֹ֣א נִֽהְיָ֔ה וּשְׂכַ֥ר הַבְּהֵמָ֖ה אֵינֶ֑נָּה וְלַיּוֹצֵ֨א וְלַבָּ֤א אֵין־שָׁלוֹם֙ מִן־הַצָּ֔ר וַֽאֲשַׁלַּ֥ח אֶת־כָּל־הָֽאָדָ֖ם אִ֥ישׁ בְּרֵעֵֽהוּ

10[9] For before those days there was no work for man, nor any work for beast; nor was there any peace to he who went out or came in because of

---

[1] Zechariah 8:2 - 4QXIIe, Ezekiel 36:5-6, Isaiah 42:13-14 11:17 63:4-6 15:15, Joel 2:18, Midrash Tanchuma Vayigash 10, Nahum 1:2 1:6, Psalms 78:58-59, z.Vaetchanan 269b, Zechariah 1:14-1:16

[2] Zechariah 8:3 - 2 Corinthians 6:16, 4QXIIe, Colossians 2:9, Ephesians 2:21-22, Exodus.R 30:8, Ezekiel 24:35, Isaiah 1:21 1:26 2:2-3 11:9 12:6 12:14 17:25 18:20, Jeremiah 30:10-30:11 7:24 9:16, Joel 4:17 4:21, John 1:14 14:23, Joseph and Aseneth 15:7, Mesillat Yesharim 11:Nekiyut-from-Falsehood, mt.Hilchot Beit Habechirah 6:10, Revelation 21:3 21:10 21:27, z.Vaetchanan 269b, Zechariah 1:16 2:10-11 14:20-21

[3] Zechariah 8:4 - 1 Samuel 2:31, 4QXIIe, b.Makkot [Rambam] 24b, b.Makkot 24b, b.Pesachim 68a, Ein Yaakov Makkot:24b, Ein Yaakov Pesachim:68a, Hebrews 12:22, Isaiah 65:20-22, Jastrow 1338b, Job 5:26 18:17, Lamentations 2:20-22 5:11-15, Lamentations.R 5:18, Midrash Psalms 145:1, Pesikta Rabbati 33:13, Sifre Devarim Ekev 43, z.Vaetchanan 269b

[4] Zechariah 8:5 - b.Makkot [Rambam] 24b, Ecclesiastes.R 3:10, Jeremiah 30:19-20 7:14 7:28 9:11, Lamentations 2:19, Lamentations.R 5:18, Matthew 11:16-17, Midrash Psalms 145:1, Psalms 128:3-4 144:12-15, Zechariah 2:4

[5] Zechariah 8:6 - 2 Kings 7:2, 4QXIIe, b.Succah 52a, Ein Yaakov Sukkah:52a, Genesis 18:14, Jeremiah 8:17 8:27, Luke 1:20 1:37 18:27, Numbers 11:22-23, Psalms 22:23 126:1-3, Romans 4:20-21 6:19-21, z.Vaetchanan 269b

[6] Zechariah 8:7 - 4QXIIe, Amos 9:14-15, Ezekiel 37:19-25, Hosea 11:10-11, Isaiah 11:11-16 27:12-13 43:5-6 1:12 11:19 66:19-20, Jeremiah 7:9, Malachi 1:11, Psalms 50:1 107:2-13 17:3, Romans 11:25-27, Saadia Opinions 8:1, z.Vaetchanan 269b

[7] Zechariah 8:8 - 2 Corinthians 6:16-18, Amos 9:14-15, Ezekiel 11:20 12:28 13:25 13:27, Hosea 2:19-25, Jastrow 1138a, Jeremiah 3:17-18 4:2 23:8 6:22 7:2 7:34 32:38-39 8:41, Joel 4:20, Leviticus 2:12, Obadiah 1:17-21, Revelation 21:3 21:7, Saadia Opinions 8:1, Zechariah 2:11 10:10 13:9, Zephaniah 3:14-3:20

[8] Zechariah 8:9 - 1 Chronicles 22:13 4:20, 2 Timothy 2:1, Ephesians 6:10, Ezra 5:1-2, Haggai 1:1 1:12 2:4-9 2:21, Isaiah 11:4, Joshua 1:6 1:8, Shemonah Perachim IV, z.Vaetchanan 269b, Zechariah 8:13 8:18

[9] Zechariah 8:10 - 2 Chronicles 15:5-15:7, Amos 3:6 9:4, b.Chagigah 10a, Ein Yaakov Sanhedrin:97b, Haggai 1:6-1:11 2:16-2:18, Isaiah 19:2, Jeremiah 16:16, Judges 5:6-5:7 5:11, Matthew 10:34-10:36

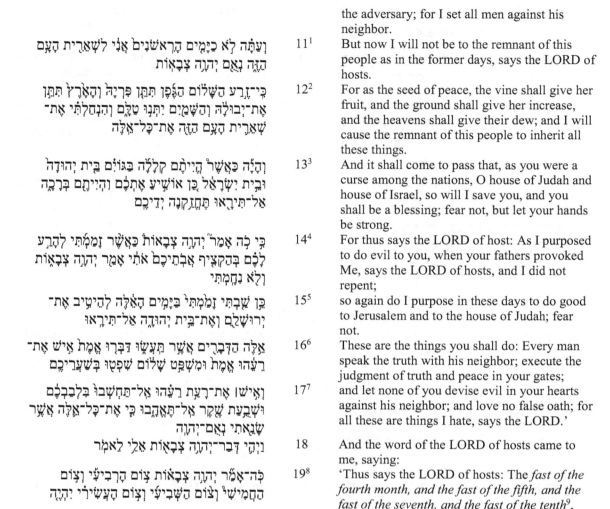

		the adversary; for I set all men against his neighbor.
וְעַתָּ֗ה לֹ֣א כַיָּמִ֤ים הָרִֽאשֹׁנִים֙ אֲנִ֜י לִשְׁאֵרִ֖ית הָעָ֣ם הַזֶּ֑ה נְאֻ֖ם יְהוָ֥ה צְבָאֽוֹת	11[1]	But now I will not be to the remnant of this people as in the former days, says the LORD of hosts.
כִּֽי־זֶ֣רַע הַשָּׁל֗וֹם הַגֶּ֜פֶן תִּתֵּ֤ן פִּרְיָהּ֙ וְהָאָ֙רֶץ֙ תִּתֵּ֣ן אֶת־יְבוּלָ֔הּ וְהַשָּׁמַ֖יִם יִתְּנ֣וּ טַלָּ֑ם וְהִנְחַלְתִּ֗י אֶת־שְׁאֵרִ֛ית הָעָ֥ם הַזֶּ֖ה אֶת־כָּל־אֵֽלֶּה	12[2]	For as the seed of peace, the vine shall give her fruit, and the ground shall give her increase, and the heavens shall give their dew; and I will cause the remnant of this people to inherit all these things.
וְהָיָ֞ה כַּאֲשֶׁ֣ר הֱיִיתֶ֣ם קְלָלָ֗ה בַּגּוֹיִם֙ בֵּ֤ית יְהוּדָה֙ וּבֵ֣ית יִשְׂרָאֵ֔ל כֵּ֖ן אוֹשִׁ֣יעַ אֶתְכֶ֑ם וִהְיִיתֶ֖ם בְּרָכָ֑ה אַל־תִּירָ֖אוּ תֶּחֱזַ֥קְנָה יְדֵיכֶֽם	13[3]	And it shall come to pass that, as you were a curse among the nations, O house of Judah and house of Israel, so will I save you, and you shall be a blessing; fear not, but let your hands be strong.
כִּ֣י כֹ֣ה אָמַר֮ יְהוָ֣ה צְבָאוֹת֒ כַּאֲשֶׁ֣ר זָמַ֗מְתִּי לְהָרַ֣ע לָכֶ֗ם בְּהַקְצִ֤יף אֲבֹֽתֵיכֶם֙ אֹתִ֔י אָמַ֖ר יְהוָ֣ה צְבָא֑וֹת וְלֹ֖א נִחָֽמְתִּי	14[4]	For thus says the LORD of host: As I purposed to do evil to you, when your fathers provoked Me, says the LORD of hosts, and I did not repent;
כֵּ֣ן שַׁ֤בְתִּי זָמַ֙מְתִּי֙ בַּיָּמִ֣ים הָאֵ֔לֶּה לְהֵיטִ֥יב אֶת־יְרוּשָׁלַ֖͏ִם וְאֶת־בֵּ֣ית יְהוּדָ֑ה אַל־תִּירָֽאוּ	15[5]	so again do I purpose in these days to do good to Jerusalem and to the house of Judah; fear not.
אֵ֥לֶּה הַדְּבָרִ֖ים אֲשֶׁ֣ר תַּֽעֲשׂ֑וּ דַּבְּר֤וּ אֱמֶת֙ אִ֣ישׁ אֶת־רֵעֵ֔הוּ אֱמֶת֙ וּמִשְׁפַּ֣ט שָׁל֔וֹם שִׁפְט֖וּ בְּשַׁעֲרֵיכֶֽם	16[6]	These are the things you shall do: Every man speak the truth with his neighbor; execute the judgment of truth and peace in your gates;
וְאִ֣ישׁ׀ אֶת־רָעַ֣ת רֵעֵ֗הוּ אַֽל־תַּחְשְׁבוּ֙ בִּלְבַבְכֶ֔ם וּשְׁבֻ֥עַת שֶׁ֖קֶר אַֽל־תֶּאֱהָ֑בוּ כִּ֧י אֶת־כָּל־אֵ֛לֶּה אֲשֶׁ֥ר שָׂנֵ֖אתִי נְאֻם־יְהוָֽה	17[7]	and let none of you devise evil in your hearts against his neighbor; and love no false oath; for all these are things I hate, says the LORD.'
וַיְהִ֛י דְּבַר־יְהוָ֥ה צְבָא֖וֹת אֵלַ֥י לֵאמֹֽר	18	And the word of the LORD of hosts came to me, saying:
כֹּֽה־אָמַ֞ר יְהוָ֣ה צְבָא֗וֹת צ֣וֹם הָרְבִיעִ֡י וְצ֣וֹם הַחֲמִישִׁ֡י וְצ֣וֹם הַשְּׁבִיעִי֙ וְצ֣וֹם הָעֲשִׂירִ֔י יִהְיֶ֥ה	19[8]	'Thus says the LORD of hosts: The *fast of the fourth month, and the fast of the fifth, and the fast of the seventh, and the fast of the tenth*[9],

---

[1] Zechariah 8:11 - Haggai 2:19, Isaiah 11:13 12:1, Malachi 3:9-3:11, Midrash Tanchuma Kedoshim 7, Psalms 7:9, Zechariah 8:8-8:9 Zechariah 8:11-12 - Midrash Tanchuma Kedoshim 7

[2] Zechariah 8:12 - 1 Corinthians 3:21, 1 Kings 17:1, Amos 9:13-15, Deuteronomy 28:4-12 8:2 9:13 9:28, Ezekiel 34:26-27 12:12 12:30, Genesis 2:12 3:28, Genesis.R 12:6, Haggai 1:10 2:19, Hosea 2:21-25 14:7, Isaiah 6:23 13:7, James 3:18, Joel 2:22, Leviticus 26:4-5, Mas.Perek Hashalom 1:12, Matthew 6:33, Micah 4:6-7, Midrash Tanchuma Kedoshim 7, Numbers.R 13:12, Obadiah 1:17-20, Proverbs 3:9-10 19:12, Psalms 67:7-8 72:3, Zechariah 8:6

[3] Zechariah 8:13 - 1 Corinthians 16:13, 1 Kings 9:7-8, 2 Chronicles 7:20-22, 2 Kings 17:18-20, Daniel 9:11, Deuteronomy 4:37 29:22-27, Ezekiel 5:15 13:11 37:16-19, Galatians 3:14 3:28-29, Genesis 12:2-12:3 2:4, Haggai 2:19, Isaiah 9:21 19:24-25 35:3-4 41:10-16 65:15-16, Jeremiah 24:9 1:18 2:6 5:18 32:30-32 9:24 18:18 20:12 20:22, Jubilees 1:16, Lamentations 2:15-16 4:15, Micah 5:8, Psalms 44:14-15 44:17 72:17 79:4, Ruth 4:11-4:12, Zechariah 1:19 8:9 8:20-23 9:13 10:6-9, Zephaniah 3:20

[4] Zechariah 8:14 - 2 Chronicles 12:16, Ezekiel 24:14, Isaiah 14:24, Jeremiah 4:28 15:1-15:6 20:16 7:29, Psalms 33:11, z.Vaetchanan 269b, Zechariah 1:6

[5] Zechariah 8:15 - Isaiah 43:1-2, Jeremiah 29:11-14 8:42, Luke 12:32, Micah 4:10-13 7:18-20, Zechariah 8:13, Zephaniah 3:16-17

[6] Zechariah 8:16 - 1 Peter 1:13-16, 1 Thessalonians 4:6, 2 Enoch 42:12, Amos 5:15 5:24, b.Sanhedrin [Tosefot] 6a, b.Sanhedrin 6a 6b, Deuteronomy 10:12-13 11:7-8, Ein Yaakov Sanhedrin:6b, Ephesians 4:17 4:25, Hosea 4:1-4:2, Isaiah 9:8 11:3-9, Jeremiah 9:4-6, Leviticus 19:11, Luke 3:8-14, m.Micah 1:18, Mas.Perek Hashalom 1:2, Matthew 5:9, Mekhilta de R'Shimon bar Yochai Amalek 47:1, Mekilta de R'Ishmael Nezikin 18:100, Mesillat Yesharim 11:Nekiyut-from-Falsehood, Micah 6:8 6:12, Midrash Shmuel 1:18, Midrash Tanchuma Mishpatim 6, Midrash Tanchuma Shoftim 15, mt.Hilchot Sanhedrin v'Hainshin Hameurim Lahem 22:4, mt.Pirkei Avot 1:16, Pesikta de R'Kahana 19.6, Pirkei Avot 1:18 [Shabbat afternoon], Proverbs 12:17 12:19, Psalms 15:2, Revelation 21:8, Sifre Devarim Devarim 17, Testament of Dan 5:2, y.Megillah 3:6, y.Sanhedrin 1:1, y.Taanit 4:2, Zechariah 7:9 8:19

[7] Zechariah 8:17 - Habakkuk 1:13, Jeremiah 4:2 4:14 20:4, Malachi 3:5, Matthew 5:28 12:35 15:19, Micah 2:1-2:3, Proverbs 3:29 6:14 6:16-6:19 8:13, Psalms 5:6-5:7 10:4, Saadia Opinions 2:11, Tanya Igeret Hakodesh §22b, Zechariah 5:3-5:4 7:10

[8] Zechariah 8:19 - 2 Kings 25:3-25:4 1:25, b.Rosh Hashanah 18b, b.Sheviit 20a, b.Succah 32b, b.Yevamot 14b, Ein Yaakov Rosh Hashanah:18b, Ein Yaakov Yevamot:14b, Esther 8:17 9:22, Isaiah 12:1 11:10 3:11, Jastrow 1267b, Jeremiah 31:13-31:14 15:2 41:1-41:3 4:4 52:6-52:7 52:12-52:15, Liber Antiquitatum Biblicarum 19:7, Luke 1:74-1:75, mt.Hilchot Taaniot 5:2 5:4 5:19, mt.Shemonah Perakim 4:6, Psalms 30:12, Revelation 22:15, Sifre Devarim Vaetchanan 31, Siman 141:1, t.Sotah 6:10, t.Yevamot 1:109, Titus 2:11-2:12, y.Kiddushin 1:1, y.Taanit 4:5, y.Yevamot 1:6, z.Vaetchanan 269b, Zechariah 7:3 7:5 8:16 Zechariah 8:19-21 - 8HevXIIgr

[9] LXX *fourth fast, and the fifth fast, and the seventh fast, and the tenth fast*

לְבֵית־יְהוּדָה לְשָׂשׂוֹן וּלְשִׂמְחָ֑ה וּלְמֹעֲדִ֖ים טוֹבִ֑ים וְהָאֱמֶ֥ת וְהַשָּׁל֖וֹם אֱהָֽבוּ

shall be to the house of Judah joy and gladness, and cheerful seasons; therefore, love truth and peace.

20[1] כֹּ֤ה אָמַר֙ יְהוָ֣ה צְבָא֔וֹת עֹ֚ד אֲשֶׁ֣ר יָבֹ֣אוּ עַמִּ֔ים וְיֹשְׁבֵ֖י עָרִ֥ים רַבּֽוֹת

Thus says the LORD of hosts: It shall yet come to pass, that people shall come, and the inhabitants of many cities;

21[2] וְֽהָלְכ֡וּ יֹשְׁבֵי֩ אַחַ֨ת אֶל־אַחַ֜ת לֵאמֹ֗ר נֵלְכָ֤ה הָלוֹךְ֙ לְחַלּוֹת֙ אֶת־פְּנֵ֣י יְהוָ֔ה וּלְבַקֵּ֖שׁ אֶת־יְהוָ֣ה צְבָא֑וֹת אֵלְכָ֖ה גַם־אָֽנִי

and the inhabitants of one city shall go to another, saying: Let us go speedily to request the favor of the LORD, and to seek the LORD of hosts; I will go also.

22[3] וּבָ֨אוּ עַמִּ֤ים רַבִּים֙ וְגוֹיִ֣ם עֲצוּמִ֔ים לְבַקֵּ֛שׁ אֶת־יְהוָ֥ה צְבָא֖וֹת בִּירוּשָׁלָ֑͏ִם וּלְחַלּ֖וֹת אֶת־פְּנֵ֥י יְהוָֽה

Yes, many peoples and mighty nations shall come to seek the LORD of hosts in Jerusalem, and to request the favor of the LORD.

23[4] כֹּ֥ה אָמַר֮ יְהוָ֣ה צְבָאוֹת֒ בַּיָּמִ֣ים הָהֵ֔מָּה אֲשֶׁ֤ר יַחֲזִ֨יקוּ֙ עֲשָׂרָ֣ה אֲנָשִׁ֔ים מִכֹּ֖ל לְשֹׁנ֣וֹת הַגּוֹיִ֑ם וְהֶחֱזִ֜יקוּ בִּכְנַ֣ף אִ֣ישׁ יְהוּדִ֗י לֵאמֹר֙ נֵֽלְכָה֙ עִמָּכֶ֔ם כִּ֥י שָׁמַ֖עְנוּ אֱלֹהִ֥ים עִמָּכֶֽם

Thus says the LORD of hosts: In those days it shall come to pass, that ten men out of all the languages of the nations shall take hold, shall take hold of the *corner*[5] of he who is a Jew, saying: We will go with you, for we have heard God is with you.'

Zechariah – Chapter 9

1[6] מַשָּׂ֤א דְבַר־יְהוָה֙ בְּאֶ֣רֶץ חַדְרָ֔ךְ וְדַמֶּ֖שֶׂק מְנֻחָת֑וֹ כִּ֤י לַֽיהוָה֙ עֵ֣ין אָדָ֔ם וְכֹ֖ל שִׁבְטֵ֥י יִשְׂרָאֵֽל

The burden of the word of the LORD against the land of *Hadrach*[7], and in Damascus his resting place; when the eye of every man and all the tribes of Israel shall be toward the LORD.

2[8] וְגַם־חֲמָ֖ת תִּגְבָּל־בָּ֑הּ צֹ֣ר וְצִיד֔וֹן כִּ֥י חָֽכְמָ֖ה מְאֹֽד

And Hamath also borders it; Tyre and Zidon, for she is very wise.

3[9] וַתִּ֥בֶן צֹ֛ר מָצ֖וֹר לָ֑הּ וַתִּצְבָּר־כֶּ֨סֶף֙ כֶּֽעָפָ֔ר וְחָר֖וּץ כְּטִ֥יט חוּצֽוֹת

And Tyre built herself a stronghold, and heaped up silver as the dust, and fine gold as the mire of the streets.

4[10] הִנֵּ֤ה אֲדֹנָי֙ יֽוֹרִשֶׁ֔נָּה וְהִכָּ֥ה בַיָּ֖ם חֵילָ֑הּ וְהִ֖יא בָּאֵ֥שׁ תֵּאָכֵֽל

Behold, the *Lord*[11] will impoverish her, and He will strike her power into the sea; and she shall be devoured with fire.

---

[1] Zechariah 8:20 - 1 Kings 8:41 8:43, 2 Chronicles 6:32-33, Acts 15:14 15:18, Amos 9:12, Hosea 2:1 2:23, Isaiah 2:2-3 11:10 1:6 49:22-23 60:3-12 66:18-20, Jeremiah 16:19, Malachi 1:11, Matthew 8:11, Micah 4:1-2, Psalms 22:28 67:2-5 72:17 89:10 117:1-2 138:4-5, Revelation 11:15, Romans 15:9-12, z.Vaetchanan 269b, Zechariah 2:11 14:16-17

[2] Zechariah 8:21 - Hosea 6:3, Psalms 7:22 122:1-9 146:1-2, Zechariah 7:2

[3] Zechariah 8:22 - Galatians 3:8, Haggai 2:7, Isaiah 1:7 7:5 60:3-22 18:23, Jeremiah 4:2, Micah 4:3, Revelation 15:4 21:24, Zechariah 8:21

[4] Zechariah 8:23 - 1 Chronicles 12:17, 1 Corinthians 14:25, 1 Kings 8:42-8:43, 1 Samuel 15:27-28, 2 Kings 2:6, 2 Samuel 15:19-22, 8HevXIIgr, Acts 13:47-13:48 19:12, b.Shabbat 32b, Deuteronomy 4:6-7, Ecclesiastes 11:2, Ein Yaakov Shabbat:32b, Genesis 7:7 7:41, Isaiah 3:6 4:1 21:14 7:5 12:3 18:18, Job 19:3, Joshua 2:9-13, Luke 8:44, Matthew 18:21-22, Micah 5:6, Midrash Tanchuma Bamidbar 3, Midrash Tanchuma Terumah 9, Numbers 10:29-32 14:14-16 14:22, Numbers.R 1:3, Pesikta Rabbati 36:2, Revelation 7:9-10 14:6-7, Ruth 1:16-17, z.Vaetchanan 269b

[5] LXX *hem*

[6] Zechariah 9:1 - 2 Chronicles 20:12, Amos 1:3-1:5 3:12, Genesis 14:15, Isaiah 9:9-9:22 13:1 17:1-17:3 17:7-17:8 45:20-45:22 4:10, Jeremiah 16:19 23:33-23:38 49:23-49:27, Lamentations.R 1:51, Malachi 1:1, Mekilta de R'Ishmael Bahodesh 4:65, Pesikta de R'Kahana 20.7, Psalms 25:15 1:15, Sifre Devarim Devarim 1, Song of Songs.R 7:11, y.Taanit 3:3 3:4, Zechariah 5:4 8:21-8:23 Zechariah 9:1-17 - Fifth Shabbat after Tisha b'Av [Pesikta Rabbati 34] Zechariah 9:1-5 - 8HevXIIgr

[7] LXX *Sedrach*

[8] Zechariah 9:2 - 1 Kings 17:9, 2 Kings 23:33 1:21, Amos 1:9-1:10 6:14, Ezekiel 26:1-26:21 28:2-28:5 4:12 28:21-28:26, Isaiah 23:1-23:18, Jeremiah 1:23, Joel 4:4-4:8, Numbers 13:21, Obadiah 1:20

[9] Zechariah 9:3 - 1 Kings 10:27, 2 Samuel 24:7, Ezekiel 3:33 28:4-5, Isaiah 23:8, Job 22:24 3:16, Joseph and Aseneth 13:7, Joshua 19:29

[10] Zechariah 9:4 - Amos 1:10, Ezekiel 26:3-5 2:17 27:26-36 4:2 4:8 4:16 4:18, Greek Apocalypse of Ezra 4:36, Isaiah 23:1-7, Joel 4:8, Proverbs 10:2 11:4

[11] 4QXIIe *LORD*, Per Massorah: Soferim altered *Hashem* to *Adonai*

תֵּרֶא אַשְׁקְלוֹן וְתִירָא וְעַזָּה וְתָחִיל מְאֹד וְעֶקְרוֹן כִּי־הֹבִישׁ מֶבָּטָהּ וְאָבַד מֶלֶךְ מֵעַזָּה וְאַשְׁקְלוֹן לֹא תֵשֵׁב	5[1] Ashkelon shall see it, and fear, Gaza also, and shall be sorely pained, and Ekron, for *her expectation shall be ashamed*[2]; and the king shall perish from Gaza, and Ashkelon shall not be inhabited.
וְיָשַׁב מַמְזֵר בְּאַשְׁדּוֹד וְהִכְרַתִּי גְּאוֹן פְּלִשְׁתִּים	6[3] And *a bastard shall dwell in Ashdod*[4], and I will cut off the pride of the Philistines.
וַהֲסִרֹתִי דָמָיו מִפִּיו וְשִׁקֻּצָיו מִבֵּין שִׁנָּיו וְנִשְׁאַר גַּם־הוּא לֵאלֹהֵינוּ וְהָיָה כְּאַלֻּף בִּיהוּדָה וְעֶקְרוֹן כִּיבוּסִי	7[5] And I will take away his blood from his mouth, and his detestable things from between his teeth, and he also shall be a remnant for our God; and he shall be as a chief in Judah, and Ekron as a Jebusite.
וְחָנִיתִי לְבֵיתִי מִצָּבָה מֵעֹבֵר וּמִשָּׁב וְלֹא־יַעֲבֹר עֲלֵיהֶם עוֹד נֹגֵשׂ כִּי עַתָּה רָאִיתִי בְעֵינָי	8[6] And I will encamp around My house against the army, so no one passes through or return; and no oppressor shall pass through them any longer; for now have I seen with my eyes.
גִּילִי מְאֹד בַּת־צִיּוֹן הָרִיעִי בַּת יְרוּשָׁלַ͏ִם הִנֵּה מַלְכֵּךְ יָבוֹא לָךְ צַדִּיק וְנוֹשָׁע הוּא עָנִי וְרֹכֵב עַל־חֲמוֹר וְעַל־עַיִר בֶּן־אֲתֹנוֹת	9[7] Rejoice greatly, O daughter of Zion, Shout, O daughter of Jerusalem; behold, your king comes to you, He is triumphant, and victorious, lowly, and riding on an ass, *upon a colt the foal of an ass*[8].
וְהִכְרַתִּי־רֶכֶב מֵאֶפְרַיִם וְסוּס מִירוּשָׁלַ͏ִם וְנִכְרְתָה קֶשֶׁת מִלְחָמָה וְדִבֶּר שָׁלוֹם לַגּוֹיִם וּמָשְׁלוֹ מִיָּם עַד־יָם וּמִנָּהָר עַד־אַפְסֵי־אָרֶץ	10[9] And I will cut off the chariot from Ephraim, and the horse from Jerusalem, and the battle bow shall be cut off, and he shall speak peace to the nations; and his dominion shall be from sea to sea, and from the River to the ends of the earth.
גַּם־אַתְּ בְּדַם־בְּרִיתֵךְ שִׁלַּחְתִּי אֲסִירַיִךְ מִבּוֹר אֵין מַיִם בּוֹ	11[10] As for you also, because of the blood of your covenant I send forth your prisoners out of the pit, where is no water.

---

[1] Zechariah 9:5 - Acts 8:26, Ezekiel 25:15-17 26:15-21, Isaiah 14:29-31 20:5-6, Jeremiah 23:1 47:4-7 51:8-9, Philippians 1:20, Revelation 18:9-18:17, Romans 5:5, Zephaniah 2:4-7
Zechariah 9:5-11 - Ein Yaakov Sanhedrin:24a
[2] LXX *she is ashamed at her trespass*
[3] Zechariah 9:6 - 1 Peter 5:5, Amos 1:8, Avot de R'Natan 12, b.Kiddushin 72b, Daniel 4:34, Ecclesiastes 2:18-2:21 6:2, Isaiah 2:12-2:17 23:9 4:1, y.Kiddushin 3:13, Zephaniah 2:10
[4] LXX *aliens shall dwell in Azotus*
[5] Zechariah 9:7 - 1 Chronicles 11:4-6 21:15-22:1, 1 Samuel 17:34-36, 2 Samuel 24:16-23, Amos 3:12, b.Megillah 6a, Ein Yaakov Megillah:6a, Ezekiel 16:57-61, Galatians 3:28, Isaiah 11:12-14 19:23-25 49:22-23 60:14-16, Jastrow 248b 1426a, Jeremiah 24:47 1:6 1:39, Psalms 3:8 58:7, Zechariah 8:23
[6] Zechariah 9:8 - 2 Kings 23:29 24:1, 2 Samuel 16:12, Acts 7:34, Amos 9:15, Daniel 11:6-7 11:10-16 11:27-29 11:40-45, Exodus 3:7 3:9, Ezekiel 28:24-25 15:29, Genesis 32:2-3, Isaiah 4:5 2:1 7:5 33:20-22 4:12 6:12 12:18, Jastrow 155a, Jeremiah 7:13 22:2 22:13, Joel 4:16-17, Psalms 34:8 46:2-6 72:4 125:1-2, Revelation 20:1-3 20:9, Zechariah 2:1-13 12:8 14:11
[7] Zechariah 9:9 - b.Berachot 56b, b.Sanhedrin 98a 99a, Deuteronomy.R 4:11, Ecclesiastes.R 1:28, Ein Yaakov Sanhedrin:97b 99a, Epistle to Diognetus 7:4, Exodus.R 30:24, Genesis.R 75:6 98 [Excl]:9 99 [Excl]:8, Isaiah 9:7-8 12:6 32:1-2 16:9 19:3 19:11 21:21 52:9-10 14:11, Jeremiah 23:5-6 6:9, John 1:49 12:13-16 19:15, Luke 19:30-35 19:37-38, Mark 11:7 11:9-10, Matthew 1:21 11:29 21:4-7, Midrash Psalms 60:3, Midrash Tanchuma Acharei Mot 12, Midrash Tanchuma Bereshit 1, Midrash Tanchuma Vayechi 10, Midrash Tanchuma Vayishlach 1, Pesikta de R'Kahana 22.3, Pesikta Rabbati 34:1-2, Pirkei de R'Eliezer 31, Psalms 2:6 45:2 45:7-8 85:10-13 97:6-8 110:1-4, Romans 3:24-26, Sibylline Oracles 8.325, Song of Songs.R 1:29-30, Testament of Dan 6:9, z.Acharei Mot 69a, z.Beshallach 57b, z.Vayechi 238a, z.Vayikra 6b, Zechariah 2:10, Zephaniah 3:14-15
[8] LXX *and a young foal*
[9] Zechariah 9:10 - 1 Kings 4:21, 2 Corinthians 5:18 5:20 10:4-5, Acts 10:36, Colossians 1:20-21, Deuteronomy 11:24, Ephesians 2:13-17, Haggai 2:22, Hosea 1:7 2:18, Isaiah 9:7-8 11:10 1:6 57:18-19 12:12, Micah 4:2-4 5:5 5:11-12, Midrash Tanchuma Shoftim 19, mt.Hilchot Melachim u'Michamoteihem 11:1, Psalms 2:8-12 72:3 72:7-11 72:17 98:1-3, Revelation 11:15, Romans 15:9-13, Zechariah 10:4-5
[10] Zechariah 9:11 - 1 Corinthians 11:25, 2 Chronicles 7:17, 2 Samuel 13:13, Acts 26:17-26:18, b.Shabbat 134a, Colossians 1:13-1:14, Daniel 2:29, Deuteronomy 5:31, Exodus 24:8, Hebrews 9:10-9:26 10:29 13:20, Isaiah 18:7 18:22 1:9 3:14 10:12 13:1, Jeremiah 14:6, Leviticus.R 6:5 19:6, Luke 4:18 16:24 22:20, Mark 14:24, Matthew 2:28, Mekilta de R'Ishmael Pisha 5:11, mt.Hilchot Issurei Biah 14:5, mt.Hilchot Milah 1:7, Psalms 30:4 40:3 69:34 102:20-22 107:10-16, Revelation 20:3

שׁוּבוּ לְבִצָּרוֹן אֲסִירֵי הַתִּקְוָה גַּם־הַיּוֹם מַגִּיד מִשְׁנֶה אָשִׁיב לָךְ	12[1]	Return to the stronghold, you prisoners of hope; today I declare I will render double to you.
כִּי־דָרַכְתִּי לִי יְהוּדָה קֶשֶׁת מִלֵּאתִי אֶפְרַיִם וְעוֹרַרְתִּי בָנַיִךְ צִיּוֹן עַל־בָּנַיִךְ יָוָן וְשַׂמְתִּיךְ כְּחֶרֶב גִּבּוֹר	13[2]	For I bend Judah for Me, I fill the bow with Ephraim; and I will stir up your sons, O Zion, against *your sons, O Javan*[3], and will make you like the sword of a mighty man.
וַיהוָה עֲלֵיהֶם יֵרָאֶה וְיָצָא כַבָּרָק חִצּוֹ וַאדֹנָי יְהוִֹה בַּשּׁוֹפָר יִתְקָע וְהָלַךְ בְּסַעֲרוֹת תֵּימָן	14[4]	And the LORD shall be seen over them, and His arrow shall go forth as the lightning; and the Lord GOD will blow the horn, and will go with whirlwinds of the south.
יְהוָה צְבָאוֹת יָגֵן עֲלֵיהֶם וְאָכְלוּ וְכָבְשׁוּ אַבְנֵי־קֶלַע וְשָׁתוּ הָמוּ כְּמוֹ־יָיִן וּמָלְאוּ כַּמִּזְרָק כְּזָוִיּוֹת מִזְבֵּחַ	15[5]	The LORD of hosts will defend them; and they shall devour, and shall tread down the sling stones; and they shall drink, and make a noise as through wine; and they shall be filled like the basins, like the corners of the altar.
וְהוֹשִׁיעָם יְהוָה אֱלֹהֵיהֶם בַּיּוֹם הַהוּא כְּצֹאן עַמּוֹ כִּי אַבְנֵי־נֵזֶר מִתְנוֹסְסוֹת עַל־אַדְמָתוֹ	16[6]	And the LORD their God shall save them in that day as the flock of His people; for they shall be as the stones of a crown, glittering over His land.
כִּי מַה־טּוּבוֹ וּמַה־יָפְיוֹ דָּגָן בַּחוּרִים וְתִירוֹשׁ יְנוֹבֵב בְּתֻלוֹת	17[7]	For how great is their goodness, and how great is their beauty! Corn shall make the young men flourish, And new wine the *maids*[8].

Zechariah – Chapter 10

שַׁאֲלוּ מֵיְהוָה מָטָר בְּעֵת מַלְקוֹשׁ יְהוָה עֹשֶׂה חֲזִיזִים וּמְטַר־גֶּשֶׁם יִתֵּן לָהֶם לְאִישׁ עֵשֶׂב בַּשָּׂדֶה	1[9]	Ask the LORD for rain in *the time of the latter rain*[10], of the LORD who makes lightnings; and He will give them showers of rain, to every grass in the field.

[1] Zechariah 9:12 - b.Sanhedrin 22a, Ein Yaakov Pesachim:87a, Ein Yaakov Sanhedrin:21b, Ezekiel 13:11, Hebrews 6:18, Hosea 2:15, Isaiah 14:18 16:2 1:9 4:2 13:7, Jeremiah 7:7 7:18 50:4-50:5 2:28 3:10, Job 18:10, Joel 4:16, Lamentations 3:21-3:22, Lives of the Prophets 15:6, Micah 4:8, Midrash Psalms 40:1, Nahum 1:7, t.Sanhedrin 4:7, y.Megillah 1:9

[2] Zechariah 9:13 - 1 Corinthians 1:21-28, 2 Corinthians 10:3-5, 2 Timothy 4:7, Amos 2:11, Daniel 8:21-25 11:32-34, Ein Yaakov Pesachim 87a, Ephesians 6:17, Genesis.R 65:13 93:5, Hebrews 4:12, Isaiah 41:15-16 1:2, Jeremiah 3:20, Joel 4:6-8, Lamentations 4:2, Lamentations.R 1:54, Mark 16:15-20, Micah 4:2-3 5:5-10, Midrash Psalms 8:1, Numbers.R 7:10, Obadiah 1:21, Pesikta Rabbati 2:1, Psalms 18:33-36 45:4 49:3-10 24:1 5:6, Revelation 1:16 2:12 17:14 19:15 19:21, Romans 15:16-20, y.Taanit 1:1, Zechariah 1:21 10:3-7 12:2-8

[3] LXX *the children of the Greeks*

[4] Zechariah 9:14 - 2 Corinthians 10:4-10:5, Acts 4:10-4:11, b.Rosh Hashanah 32b, Exodus 14:24-14:25, Exodus.R 15:16, Genesis.R 56:9 56:9, Habakkuk 3:11, Hebrews 2:4, Isaiah 18:3 21:1 3:13 6:30 7:5 18:15, Joshua 6:4-6:5 10:11-10:14 10:42, Lamentations.R 1:54, Leviticus.R 29:10, Matthew 4:20, Mekilta de R'Ishmael Bahodesh 4:30, mt.Hilcnot Shofar Sukkah v'Lulav 3:9, Pesikta de R'Kahana 23.1, Pesikta Rabbati 39:1, Psalms 18:15 45:4-45:6 77:18-77:19 144:5-144:6, Revelation 6:2, Romans 15:19, Tanya Igeret Hakodesh §23, y.Taanit 2:4, Zechariah 2:5 12:8 14:3
Zechariah 9:14-15 - Mussaf Rosh Hashanah

[5] Zechariah 9:15 - 1 Corinthians 1:18, 1 Samuel 17:45, Acts 2:13-18, b.Pesachim [Rashi] 87a, b.Pesachim 87a, b.Rosh Hashanah 32b, b.Zevachim 54b, Ein Yaakov Pesachim:87a, Ephesians 5:18, Exodus 3:2, Isaiah 13:35 7:1, Leviticus 4:7 4:18 4:25, Micah 5:9, mt.Hilcnot Shofar Sukkah v'Lulav 3:9, Psalms 78:65, Revelation 19:13-21, Song of Songs 1:4 5:1 7:10, Zechariah 9:17 10:5 10:7 12:6 12:8 14:20

[6] Zechariah 9:16 - 1 Peter 5:2-5:4, b.Megillah 12a, Exodus.R 46:2, Ezekiel 34:22-34:26 10:31, Haggai 2:23, Isaiah 11:10-11:12 16:10 12:3 12:14 14:3, Jeremiah 23:3 7:12, John 10:27, Luke 12:32, Mekhilta de R'Shimon bar Yochai Bachodesh 56:1, Micah 5:5 7:14, Pirkei de R'Eliezer 34, Psalms 4:3, Zechariah 8:23, Zephaniah 3:20

[7] Zechariah 9:17 - 1 John 4:8-11, 2 Corinthians 4:4-4:6, Amos 8:11-14 9:13-14, b.Bava Batra 12b, b.Nazir [Rashi] 28a, b.Yoma 76b, Ephesians 1:7-8 2:4-5 3:18-19 5:18-19, Exodus 15:11, Genesis.R 66:3, Hosea 2:21-2:24, Isaiah 9:17 62:8-9 15:7 15:15 65:13-14, Jeremiah 7:13, Joel 2:26 4:18, John 1:14 3:16, Leviticus.R 1:2, Numbers.R 8:1, Psalms 31:20 36:8 45:3 50:2 86:5 86:15 90:17 1:7, Revelation 5:12-14, Romans 5:8 5:20, Song of Songs 5:10 7:10, Titus 3:4-3:7

[8] LXX *virgins*

[9] Zechariah 10:1 - 1 Corinthians 3:6, 1 Kings 17:1 18:41-45, Amos 4:7, b.Taanit 9b, Deuteronomy 11:13-14 4:23, Ezekiel 10:26 12:37, Hosea 6:3 10:12, Isaiah 5:6 6:23 20:3, James 5:7 5:16-18, Jastrow 443b, Jeremiah 10:13 14:22 3:16, Job 5:23 36:27-31 37:1-6, Joel 2:23-24, John 16:23, Leviticus.R 35:12, Matthew 7:7-8, Micah 5:8, Proverbs 16:15, Psalms 65:10 72:6 8:13, Sifre Devarim Ekev 39, Tanna Devei Eliyahu 5

[10] LXX *season, the early and the latter*

2¹ כִּי הַתְּרָפִים דִּבְּרוּ־אָ֫וֶן וְהַקּוֹסְמִים חָזוּ שֶׁקֶר וַחֲלֹמוֹת הַשָּׁוְא יְדַבֵּרוּ הֶבֶל יְנַחֵמוּן עַל־כֵּן נָסְעוּ כְמוֹ־צֹאן יַעֲנוּ כִּי־אֵין רֹעֶה

2¹ For the *teraphim*[2] have spoken vanity, and the diviners have seen a lie, and the dreams speak falsely, they comfort in vain; therefore, they go their way like sheep, they are afflicted, because there is no *shepherd*[3].

3⁴ עַל־הָרֹעִים חָרָה אַפִּי וְעַל־הָעַתּוּדִים אֶפְקוֹד כִּי־פָקַד יְהֹוָה צְבָאוֹת אֶת־עֶדְרוֹ אֶת־בֵּית יְהוּדָה וְשָׂם אוֹתָם כְּסוּס הוֹדוֹ בַּמִּלְחָמָה

3⁴ My anger is kindled against the shepherds, *and I will punish the he-goats; for the LORD of hosts has remembered His flock*[5] the house of Judah, and makes them as His majestic horse in the battle.

4⁶ מִמֶּנּוּ פִנָּה מִמֶּנּוּ יָתֵד מִמֶּנּוּ קֶשֶׁת מִלְחָמָה מִמֶּנּוּ יֵצֵא כָל־נוֹגֵשׂ יַחְדָּו

4⁶ *Out of them shall come forth the cornerstone, out of them the stake, out of them the battle bow, out of them every master, together*[7].

5⁸ וְהָיוּ כְגִבֹּרִים בּוֹסִים בְּטִיט חוּצוֹת בַּמִּלְחָמָה וְנִלְחֲמוּ כִּי יְהֹוָה עִמָּם וְהֹבִישׁוּ רֹכְבֵי סוּסִים

5⁸ And they shall be as mighty men, treading down in the mire of the streets in the battle, and they shall fight, because the LORD is with them; and the riders on horses shall be confused.

6⁹ וְגִבַּרְתִּי אֶת־בֵּית יְהוּדָה וְאֶת־בֵּית יוֹסֵף אוֹשִׁיעַ וְהוֹשְׁבוֹתִים כִּי רִחַמְתִּים וְהָיוּ כַּאֲשֶׁר לֹא־זְנַחְתִּים כִּי אֲנִי יְהֹוָה אֱלֹהֵיהֶם וְאֶעֱנֵם

6⁹ And I will strengthen the house of Judah, and I will save the house of Joseph, and I will bring them back, for I have compassion on them, and they shall be as though I had not cast them off; for I am the LORD their God, and I will hear them.

7¹⁰ וְהָיוּ כְגִבּוֹר אֶפְרַיִם וְשָׂמַח לִבָּם כְּמוֹ־יָיִן וּבְנֵיהֶם יִרְאוּ וְשָׂמֵחוּ יָגֵל לִבָּם בַּיהֹוָה

7¹⁰ And they of Ephraim shall be like a mighty man, and their heart shall rejoice as through wine; yes, their children shall see it, and rejoice, their heart shall be glad in the LORD.

8¹¹ אֶשְׁרְקָה לָהֶם וַאֲקַבְּצֵם כִּי פְדִיתִים וְרָבוּ כְּמוֹ רָבוּ

8¹¹ I will hiss for them, and gather them, for I have redeemed them; and they shall increase as they have increased.

---

[1] Zechariah 10:2 - 1 Kings 22:17, b.Berachot 55b, Ezekiel 13:6-16 13:22-23 21:26 21:34 10:5 10:8, Genesis 7:19, Habakkuk 2:18, Hosea 3:4, Isaiah 20:9 22:5, Jeremiah 6:14 8:11 10:8 13:17-20 14:13 14:22 23:17 23:25-27 3:9 28:4-28:6 4:15 5:8 29:21-22 13:19 2:17 3:23, Job 13:4 21:34, Judges 18:14, Lamentations 2:14, Matthew 9:36, Mesillat Yesharim 11:Nekiyut-in-Character-Traints, Micah 2:12 3:6-11, Midrash Tanchuma Vayetze 12, Numbers 3:17, Pirkei de R'Eliezer 36, Siman 127:18

[2] LXX *speakers*

[3] LXX *healing*

[4] Zechariah 10:3 - 1 Peter 2:12, Exodus 4:31, Ezekiel 10:2 34:7-10 34:16-17 34:20-21, Isaiah 10:12 24:21 56:9-12, Jeremiah 10:21 11:22 23:1-2 1:12 1:34 2:6, Luke 1:68, Matthew 25:32-33, Pesikta Rabbati 42:99, Proverbs 21:31, Ruth 1:6, Song of Songs 1:9, Zechariah 11:5-8 11:17, Zephaniah 1:8 2:7

[5] LXX *and I will visit the lambs; and the LORD God Almighty shall visit his flock*

[6] Zechariah 10:4 - 1 Samuel 14:38, 2 Corinthians 10:4-5, 2 Timothy 2:4, Ein Yaakov Chullin:56b, Ephesians 4:8-11 6:10-17, Exodus.R 37:1, Ezra 9:8, Genesis 1:24, Isaiah 19:13 22:23-25 41:14-16 1:2 6:16, Jeremiah 1:18, Matthew 9:38, Micah 5:6-9, Numbers 24:17, Psalms 22:22, Revelation 17:14 19:13-15, Sifre Devarim Ha'azinu Hashamayim 309, Sifre Devarim Nitzavim 309, Zechariah 1:20-21 9:8 9:10 9:13-16 12:6-8

[7] LXX *And from him he looked, and from him he set the battle in order, and from him came the bow in anger, and from him shall come forth every oppressor together*

[8] Zechariah 10:5 - 1 Samuel 16:18, 2 Corinthians 10:4, 2 Samuel 22:8 22:43, 2 Timothy 4:7 4:17, Acts 7:22 18:24, Amos 2:15, Deuteronomy 20:1, Ezekiel 14:15, Haggai 2:22, Isaiah 8:9 10:6 1:10 17:12, Joel 4:12-17, Joshua 10:14 10:42, Luke 24:19, Matthew 4:3 4:20, Micah 7:10, Psalms 18:43 20:8 33:16 45:4, Revelation 19:13-15 19:17, Romans 8:31-37, Zechariah 9:13 12:4 12:8 14:3 14:13

[9] Zechariah 10:6 - Ezekiel 12:11 12:37 13:16 15:25, Hosea 1:7 2:2 2:23, Isaiah 14:1 17:10 41:17-41:20 49:17-49:21, Jeremiah 3:18 23:6 6:18 7:2 7:21 7:32 33:2-33:3, Micah 4:6 4:13 5:9 7:16 7:18-7:20, Midrash Psalms 119:2, Obadiah 1:18, Psalms 89:22, Romans 11:25-11:26, Zechariah 8:7-8:8 8:11 10:12 13:9, Zephaniah 3:19-3:20

[10] Zechariah 10:7 - 1 Peter 1:8, 1 Samuel 2:1, Acts 2:13-18 2:26 2:39 13:33, Ephesians 5:18-19, Genesis 18:19 19:34, Habakkuk 3:18, Isaiah 14:19 18:14, Jeremiah 8:39, John 16:22, Luke 1:47, Philippians 4:4, Proverbs 31:6-7, Psalms 13:6 28:7 90:16 6:29 8:15, Zechariah 9:15 9:17, Zephaniah 3:14

[11] Zechariah 10:8 - 1 Kings 4:20, 1 Timothy 2:4-2:6, b.Chullin 63a, b.Sanhedrin [Rashi] 11b, Ein Yaakov Chullin:63a, Exodus 1:7, Ezekiel 36:10-11 36:37-38, Genesis.R 44:22, Hosea 2:1, Isaiah 5:26 7:18 11:11-12 27:12-13 20:22 49:19-22 3:11 52:1-3 55:1-3, Jeremiah 30:19-20 31:11-12 9:22, Matthew 11:28, Perek Shirah [the Bee-Eater], Revelation 22:17, Zechariah 9:11

וְאֶזְרָעֵם בָּעַמִּים וּבַמֶּרְחַקִּים יִזְכְּרוּנִי וְחָיוּ אֶת־
בְּנֵיהֶם וָשָׁבוּ

9[1]

And I will sow them among the peoples, and they shall remember Me in far countries; and they shall live with their children, and shall return.

וַהֲשִׁיבוֹתִים מֵאֶרֶץ מִצְרַיִם וּמֵאַשּׁוּר אֲקַבְּצֵם
וְאֶל־אֶרֶץ גִּלְעָד וּלְבָנוֹן אֲבִיאֵם וְלֹא יִמָּצֵא לָהֶם

10[2]

I will bring them back also out of the land of Egypt, and gather them from Assyria; And I will bring them into the land of Gilead and Lebanon; and *place shall not suit them*[3].

וְעָבַר בַּיָּם צָרָה וְהִכָּה בַיָּם גַּלִּים וְהֹבִישׁוּ כֹּל
מְצוּלוֹת יְאֹר וְהוּרַד גְּאוֹן אַשּׁוּר וְשֵׁבֶט מִצְרַיִם
יָסוּר

11[4]

And *over the sea affliction shall pass*[5], and the waves shall be struck in the sea, and all the depths of the Nile shall dry up; and the pride of Assyria shall be brought down, and the scepter of Egypt shall depart.

וְגִבַּרְתִּים בַּיהוָה וּבִשְׁמוֹ יִתְהַלָּכוּ נְאֻם יְהוָה

12[6]

And I will strengthen them in the LORD; And they shall *walk up and down*[7] in His name[8], Says the LORD.

Zechariah – Chapter 11

פְּתַח לְבָנוֹן דְּלָתֶיךָ וְתֹאכַל אֵשׁ בַּאֲרָזֶיךָ

1[9]

Open your doors, O Lebanon, so the fire may devour your cedars.

הֵילֵל בְּרוֹשׁ כִּי־נָפַל אֶרֶז אֲשֶׁר אַדִּרִים שֻׁדָּדוּ
הֵילִילוּ אַלּוֹנֵי בָשָׁן כִּי יָרַד יַעַר 'הַבָּצוּר'
"הַבָּצִיר"

2[10]

Wail, O *cypress*[11] tree, for the cedar is fallen; because the glorious ones are spoiled; wail, O you oaks of Bashan, for the strong forest has been razed.

קוֹל יִלְלַת הָרֹעִים כִּי שֻׁדְּדָה אַדַּרְתָּם קוֹל שַׁאֲגַת
כְּפִירִים כִּי שֻׁדַּד גְּאוֹן הַיַּרְדֵּן

3[12]

Hear! The wailing of the shepherds, for their glory is spoiled; Hear! The roaring of young lions, for the thickets of the Jordan are spoiled.

כֹּה אָמַר יְהוָה אֱלֹהָי רְעֵה אֶת־צֹאן הַהֲרֵגָה

4[13]

Thus said the LORD my God: 'Feed the flock of slaughter;

אֲשֶׁר קֹנֵיהֶן יַהֲרֹגֻן וְלֹא יֶאְשָׁמוּ וּמֹכְרֵיהֶן יֹאמַר
בָּרוּךְ יְהוָה וַאעְשִׁר וְרֹעֵיהֶם לֹא יַחְמוֹל עֲלֵיהֶן

5[14]

whose buyers kill them, and hold themselves not guilty; and they who sell them say: Blessed

---

[1] Zechariah 10:9 - 1 Kings 8:47-48, Acts 2:38-39 3:25-26 8:1 8:4 11:19-21 13:1-38 14:1-21, Amos 9:9, Daniel 3:1-6, Deuteronomy 30:1-4, Ecclesiastes.R 4:1, Esther 8:17, Ezekiel 6:9, Hosea 2:23, Isaiah 17:9 17:23, Jeremiah 7:28 3:50, Micah 5:8, Midrash Psalms 70:1, Nehemiah 1:9, Romans 11:11-17 11:24

[2] Zechariah 10:10 - Ezekiel 47:18-21, Hosea 12:1, Isaiah 11:11-16 19:23-25 27:12-13 49:19-21 54:2-3 12:22, Jeremiah 22:6 2:19, Micah 7:11-12 7:14, Obadiah 1:20, Zechariah 8:7

[3] LXX *and none of them shall be left behind*

[4] Zechariah 10:11 - 2 Kings 2:8 2:14, b.Sanhedrin [Rashi] 103b, b.Sanhedrin 103b, Exodus 14:21-22 14:27-28, Exodus.R 41:1, Ezekiel 29:14-16 6:13, Ezra 6:22, Isaiah 11:15-16 14:25 19:5-7 42:15-16 19:2 3:10, Joshua 3:15-17, Mekilta de R'Ishmael Beshallah 4:74, Mekilta de R'Ishmael Pisha 14:96, Micah 5:6-7, Midrash Psalms 101:2, Midrash Tanchuma Ki Tissa 14, Midrash Tanchuma Re'eh 16, Numbers.R 16:26, Pesikta de R'Kahana 10.8, Psalms 66:10-12 77:17-21 18:3 18:5, Revelation 16:12, Zephaniah 2:13 Zechariah 10:11-12 - 4QXIIg

[5] LXX *they shall pass through a narrow sea*

[6] Zechariah 10:12 - 1 John 1:6-1:7, 1 Thessalonians 2:12 4:1, 2 Timothy 2:1, Colossians 2:6 3:17, Ephesians 6:10, Genesis 5:24 24:40, Isaiah 2:5 17:10 21:24, Micah 4:5, Philippians 4:13, Psalms 68:35-36, Zechariah 10:6 12:5

[7] 4QXIIe *praise*

[8] 4QXIIg *And I will strengthen them in Hashem their God; and they shall boast in his name, says Hashem*

[9] Zechariah 11:1 - 4QXIIg, Avot de R'Natan 4, b.Yoma 39b, Deuteronomy 8:22, Ein Yaakov Yoma:39b, Ezekiel 7:3, Habakkuk 2:8 2:17, Haggai 1:8, Jeremiah 22:6-7 22:23, Luke 19:41-44 21:23-24, Matthew 24:1-2, Mekhilta de R'Shimon bar Yochai Amalek 45:1, Mekilta de R'Ishmael Amalek 2:44, Pesikta Rabbati 33:1, y.Yoma 6:3, Zechariah 10:10 14:1-2

[10] Zechariah 11:2 - 4QXIIg, Amos 6:1, Avot de R'Natan 4, Ezekiel 21:2 31:2-3 7:17, Isaiah 2:12-17 10:33-34 32:15-19, Luke 23:31, Mas.Soferim 7:4, Nahum 3:8-19

[11] LXX *pine*

[12] Zechariah 11:3 - 1 Samuel 4:21-22, Acts 6:11-14 7:52 22:21-22, Amos 8:8, Avot de R'Natan 4, Ezekiel 19:3-19:6 24:21-25, Hosea 1:9-1:10 10:5, Isaiah 17:15, James 5:1-5:6, Jeremiah 2:15 2:30 7:4 7:11-7:14 25:34-36 2:6 1:19 2:44, Joel 1:13, Matthew 3:7-3:10 15:14 21:43-21:45 23:13-38, Psalms 22:22, Romans 11:7-12, Zechariah 11:8 11:15-17, Zephaniah 1:10 3:3 3:11

[13] Zechariah 11:4 - Ephesians 1:3, Ezekiel 34:23-24, Isaiah 40:9-1 49:4-5, John 20:17 21:15-17, Luke 19:41-44, Matthew 15:24 23:37, Micah 5:5, Romans 15:8, z.Vaetchanan 269b, Zechariah 11:7 14:5

[14] Zechariah 11:5 - 1 Timothy 6:5-10, 2 Kings 4:1, 2 Peter 2:3, Deuteronomy 29:18-20, Ezekiel 22:25-27 34:2-4 10:6 10:10 34:18-19 10:21, Genesis 37:26-28, Hosea 12:10, Jeremiah 2:3 23:1-2 2:7, John 10:1 10:12-13 16:2, Matthew 21:12-13 23:13, Micah 3:1-3 3:9-12, Nehemiah 5:8, Revelation 18:13

כִּי לֹא אֶחְמוֹל עוֹד עַל־יֹשְׁבֵי הָאָרֶץ נְאֻם־יְהוָה וְהִנֵּה אָנֹכִי מַמְצִיא אֶת־הָאָדָם אִישׁ בְּיַד־רֵעֵהוּ וּבְיַד מַלְכּוֹ וְכִתְּתוּ אֶת־הָאָרֶץ וְלֹא אַצִּיל מִיָּדָם	6[1]	be the LORD, for I am rich; and their own shepherds do not pity them. For I will no longer pity the inhabitants of the land, says the LORD; but, behold, I will deliver the men into his neighbor's hand, and into the hand of his king; and they shall strike the land, and I will not deliver them out of their hand.'
וָאֶרְעֶה אֶת־צֹאן הַהֲרֵגָה לָכֵן עֲנִיֵּי הַצֹּאן וָאֶקַּח־לִי שְׁנֵי מַקְלוֹת לְאַחַד קָרָאתִי נֹעַם וּלְאַחַד קָרָאתִי חֹבְלִים וָאֶרְעֶה אֶת־הַצֹּאן	7[2]	*So I fed the flock of slaughter, verily the poor of the flock. And I took to me two staves; the one I called Graciousness, and the other I called Binders; and I fed the flock[3].*
וָאַכְחִד אֶת־שְׁלֹשֶׁת הָרֹעִים בְּיֶרַח אֶחָד וַתִּקְצַר נַפְשִׁי בָּהֶם וְגַם־נַפְשָׁם בָּחֲלָה בִי	8[4]	And I cut off the three shepherds in one month; 'for My soul became impatient with them, and their soul also loathed Me.'
וָאֹמַר לֹא אֶרְעֶה אֶתְכֶם הַמֵּתָה תָמוּת וְהַנִּכְחֶדֶת תִּכָּחֵד וְהַנִּשְׁאָרוֹת תֹּאכַלְנָה אִשָּׁה אֶת־בְּשַׂר רְעוּתָהּ	9[5]	Then said I: 'I will not feed you; what dies, let it die; and what is to be cut off, let it be cut off; and let those who remain eat the flesh of another.'
וָאֶקַּח אֶת־מַקְלִי אֶת־נֹעַם וָאֶגְדַּע אֹתוֹ לְהָפִיר אֶת־בְּרִיתִי אֲשֶׁר כָּרַתִּי אֶת־כָּל־הָעַמִּים	10[6]	And I took my *staff, Graciousness[7]*, and cut it apart, 'so I might break My covenant, which I had made with all the people.'
וַתֻּפַר בַּיּוֹם הַהוּא וַיֵּדְעוּ כֵן עֲנִיֵּי הַצֹּאן הַשֹּׁמְרִים אֹתִי כִּי דְבַר־יְהוָה הוּא	11[8]	And it was broken on that day; *and the poor of the flock who listened to me knew of a truth[9]* so it was the word of the LORD.
וָאֹמַר אֲלֵיהֶם אִם־טוֹב בְּעֵינֵיכֶם הָבוּ שְׂכָרִי וְאִם־לֹא חֲדָלוּ וַיִּשְׁקְלוּ אֶת־שְׂכָרִי שְׁלֹשִׁים כָּסֶף	12[10]	And I said to them: 'If you think good, give me my hire; and if not, refuse.' So they weighed for my hire thirty pieces of silver.
וַיֹּאמֶר יְהוָה אֵלַי הַשְׁלִיכֵהוּ אֶל־הַיּוֹצֵר אֶדֶר הַיְקָר אֲשֶׁר יָקַרְתִּי מֵעֲלֵיהֶם וָאֶקְחָה שְׁלֹשִׁים הַכֶּסֶף וָאַשְׁלִיךְ אֹתוֹ בֵּית יְהוָה אֶל־הַיּוֹצֵר	13[11]	And the LORD said to me: '*Cast it into the treasury, the goodly price that I was prized at of them.'* And I took the thirty pieces of silver, *and cast them into the treasury[12]*, in the house of the LORD.

---

[1] Zechariah 11:6 - 1 Thessalonians 2:16, Daniel 9:26-27, Ezekiel 8:18 9:10, Haggai 2:22, Hebrews 2:3 10:26-31, Hosea 1:6 2:10, Isaiah 3:5 9:20-22 3:11, James 2:13, Jeremiah 13:14, John 19:15, Luke 12:52-53 19:43-44 21:16-17 21:22-24, Malachi 3:24, Matthew 10:21 10:34-36 18:33-35 22:7 23:35-38 24:10, Micah 5:9 6:14 7:2-7, Psalms 50:22, Zechariah 8:10 11:5 11:9 11:14 14:13

[2] Zechariah 11:7 - 1 Samuel 17:40 17:43, b.Sanhedrin 24a, Cairo Damascus 19:9, Cairo Damascus 19.9, Ein Yaakov Sanhedrin:24a, Ephesians 2:13-16, Ezekiel 37:16-23, Guide for the Perplexed 2:43 2:46, Isaiah 11:4 13:1, James 2:5, Jastrow 920b, Jeremiah 5:4-5, John 10:16 17:21-23, Leviticus 3:32, Mark 12:37, Matthew 11:5, Psalms 23:4 133:1-3, Zechariah 11:4 11:10-11 11:14 13:8-9, Zephaniah 3:12

[3] LXX *And I will tend the flock of slaughter in the land of Chanaan: and I will take for myself two rods; the one I called Beauty, and the other I called Line; and I will tend the flock*

[4] Zechariah 11:8 - b.Niddah 47a, b.Taanit 9b, Deuteronomy 8:19, Ein Yaakov Taanit:8b, Hebrews 10:38, Hosea 5:7 9:15, Isaiah 1:7, Jeremiah 12:8 14:21, John 7:7 15:18 15:23-25, Leviticus 2:11 2:30 2:44, Luke 12:50 19:14, Matthew 23:34-36 24:50-51, Psalms 5:6 78:9 10:40, Seder Olam 10:Good Providers, Sifre Devarim Nitzavim 305, Song of Songs.R 4:14, t.Sotah 11:8, y.Maasrot 1:2, y.Sheviit 4:6

[5] Zechariah 11:9 - Acts 13:46-47 28:26-28, Deuteronomy 28:53-56, Ezekiel 5:10, Isaiah 9:20-22, Jeremiah 15:2-3 19:9 23:33 23:39 19:11, John 8:21 8:24 12:35, Matthew 13:10-11 15:14 21:19 21:43 23:38-39, Psalms 69:23-29, Revelation 22:11

[6] Zechariah 11:10 - 1 Samuel 2:30, Acts 6:13-14, b.Chullin [Rashi] 92a, Daniel 9:26, Ezekiel 7:20-22 16:59-61 24:21, Galatians 3:16-18, Hebrews 7:17-22 8:8-13, Hosea 1:9, Jeremiah 14:21 31:32-33, Luke 21:5-6 21:32, Numbers 14:34, Psalms 50:2 89:40 90:17, Romans 9:3-5, Zechariah 11:7

[7] LXX *beautiful staff*

[8] Zechariah 11:11 - 4Q163 frag 21 ll.7-8, Acts 1:21-1:22, Deuteronomy 28:49-28:68 7:21 7:29 32:21-32:42, Genesis.R 34:11, Isaiah 8:17 14:32 26:8-26:9 16:31, James 2:5-2:6 5:1-5:6, Jastrow 1300a, Lamentations 3:25-3:26, Leviticus 26:38-26:46, Luke 2:25 2:38 7:22 19:48 23:51 24:49-24:53, Micah 7:7, Midrash Psalms 9:12, Psalms 69:34 72:12-72:14, Romans 11:7-11:12, t.Taniyot 2:13, Zechariah 11:6-11:7, Zephaniah 3:12

[9] LXX *and the Chananites, the sheep that are kept for me, shall know*

[10] Zechariah 11:12 - 1 Kings 21:2, 2 Chronicles 6:4, b.Chullin 92a, Exodus 21:32, Genesis 13:28, Genesis.R 98 [Excl]:9, John 13:2 13:27-13:30, Luke 22:3-22:6, Mark 14:10-14:11, Matthew 2:15, t.Taniyot 2:13, Testament of Gad 2:3, y.Avodah Zarah 2:1

[11] Zechariah 11:13 - Acts 1:18-1:19 4:11, b.Chullin 92a, Isaiah 53:2-53:3 54:7-54:10, Matthew 27:3-27:10 3:12

[12] LXX *Drop them into the furnace, and I will see if it is good metal, as I was proved for their sakes. And I took the thirty pieces of silver, and cast them into the furnace*

14[1] Then I cut asunder my other staff, *Binders*[2], so the brotherhood between Judah and Israel might be broken.

וָאֶגְדַּע אֶת־מַקְלִי הַשֵּׁנִי אֵת הַחֹבְלִים לְהָפֵר אֶת־הָאַחֲוָה בֵּין יְהוּדָה וּבֵין יִשְׂרָאֵל

15[3] And the LORD said to me: 'Take yet the instruments of a *foolish*[4] shepherd.

וַיֹּאמֶר יְהוָה אֵלַי עוֹד קַח־לְךָ כְּלִי רֹעֶה אֱוִלִי

16[5] For, behold, I will raise up a shepherd in the land, who will not think of those who are cut off, nor will seek those who are young, nor heal what is broken; nor will he feed what stands still, but he will eat the flesh of the fat, and *will break their hoofs in pieces*[6].'

כִּי הִנֵּה־אָנֹכִי מֵקִים רֹעֶה בָּאָרֶץ הַנִּכְחָדוֹת לֹא־יִפְקֹד הַנַּעַר לֹא־יְבַקֵּשׁ וְהַנִּשְׁבֶּרֶת לֹא יְרַפֵּא הַנִּצָּבָה לֹא יְכַלְכֵּל וּבְשַׂר הַבְּרִיאָה יֹאכַל וּפַרְסֵיהֶן יְפָרֵק

17[7] Woe to the worthless shepherd who leaves the flock! The sword shall be on his arm, and on his right eye; his arm shall be dried up, and his right eye shall be utterly darkened.

הוֹי רֹעִי הָאֱלִיל עֹזְבִי הַצֹּאן חֶרֶב עַל־זְרוֹעוֹ וְעַל־עֵין יְמִינוֹ זְרֹעוֹ יָבוֹשׁ תִּיבָשׁ וְעֵין יְמִינוֹ כָּהֹה תִכְהֶה

Zechariah – Chapter 12

1[8] The burden of the word of the LORD concerning Israel. The saying of the LORD, who stretched forth the heavens, and laid the foundation of the earth, and formed the spirit of man within him:

מַשָּׂא דְבַר־יְהוָה עַל־יִשְׂרָאֵל נְאֻם־יְהֹוָה נֹטֶה שָׁמַיִם וְיֹסֵד אָרֶץ וְיֹצֵר רוּחַ־אָדָם בְּקִרְבּוֹ

2[9] Behold, I will make Jerusalem *a cup of staggering*[10] to all the peoples around it, and on Judah also shall it fall to be in the siege against Jerusalem.

הִנֵּה אָנֹכִי שָׂם אֶת־יְרוּשָׁלִַם סַף־רַעַל לְכָל־הָעַמִּים סָבִיב וְגַם עַל־יְהוּדָה יִהְיֶה בַמָּצוֹר עַל־יְרוּשָׁלִָם

3[11] And it shall come to pass in that day, that I will make Jerusalem a stone of burden for all the peoples; all who burden themselves with it shall be sorely wounded; and all the nations of the earth shall be gathered together against it.

וְהָיָה בַיּוֹם־הַהוּא אָשִׂים אֶת־יְרוּשָׁלִַם אֶבֶן מַעֲמָסָה לְכָל־הָעַמִּים כָּל־עֹמְסֶיהָ שָׂרוֹט יִשָּׂרֵטוּ וְנֶאֶסְפוּ עָלֶיהָ כֹּל גּוֹיֵי הָאָרֶץ

4[12] In that day, says the LORD, I will smite every horse with bewilderment, and his rider with madness; and I will open my eyes upon the

בַּיּוֹם הַהוּא נְאֻם־יְהֹוָה אַכֶּה כָל־סוּס בַּתִּמָּהוֹן וְרֹכְבוֹ בַּשִּׁגָּעוֹן וְעַל־בֵּית יְהוּדָה אֶפְקַח אֶת־עֵינַי וְכֹל סוּס הָעַמִּים אַכֶּה בַּעִוָּרוֹן

---

[1] Zechariah 11:14 - Acts 23:7-10, Ezekiel 37:16-20, Galatians 5:15, Isaiah 9:22 11:13, James 3:14 3:16 4:1-3, Matthew 24:10, Zechariah 11:7 11:9

[2] LXX *Line*

[3] Zechariah 11:15 - Ezekiel 13:3, Isaiah 6:10-12, Jeremiah 2:26-27, Lamentations 2:14, Luke 11:40, Matthew 15:14 23:17

[4] LXX *unskilled*

[5] Zechariah 11:16 - 1 Samuel 17:34-35, Ezekiel 34:2-6 10:10 10:16 10:21, Genesis 7:38 9:13, Isaiah 16:11, Jeremiah 23:2 23:22, John 10:1 10:12-13, Luke 12:45-46, Matthew 23:2-4 23:13-29

[6] LXX *shall dislocate the joints of their necks*

[7] Zechariah 11:17 - 1 Corinthians 8:4 10:19-10:20, 1 Kings 13:4, 1 Samuel 2:31, Amos 8:9-8:10, Ezekiel 13:3 30:21-30:24 10:2, Hosea 4:5-4:7, Isaiah 6:9-6:10 9:16 5:10 42:19-42:20 20:10, Jeremiah 22:1 23:1 23:32 50:35-50:37, John 9:39 10:12-10:13 12:40, Lamentations.R 2:4, Luke 11:42-11:52, Matthew 23:13 23:16, Micah 3:6-3:7, Romans 11:7, y.Taanit 4:5

[8] Zechariah 12:1 - 2 Enoch 47:4, Ecclesiastes 12:7, Ecclesiastes.R 8:11, Ezekiel 18:4 36:5-36:7, Genesis 2:7, Genesis.R 14:4, Hebrews 1:10-1:12 12:9, Jeremiah 16:22 18:5 20:24 21:12 21:18 24:13 3:13 51:22-51:23 9:16, Jastrow 1270b 1305a, Jeremiah 10:12 6:10 6:16 14:16 2:34 3:15, Job 2:7, Joel 4:19 4:21, Lamentations 2:14, Malachi 1:1, Numbers 16:22, Obadiah 1:16-1:17, Psalms 102:26-102:27 8:2 136:5-136:6, Saadia Opinions 6:1 6:3 6:4, z.Mikketz 197a, Zechariah 9:1
Zechariah 12:1-3 - 4QXIIg

[9] Zechariah 12:2 - Habakkuk 2:16, Isaiah 3:17 51:22-51:23, Jeremiah 8:14 1:15 1:17 1:12 3:7 3:57, Midrash Psalms 119:2, Psalms 75:9, Revelation 14:10 16:19 18:6, Zechariah 14:14

[10] LXX *trembling doorposts*

[11] Zechariah 12:3 - Daniel 2:34-2:35 2:44-2:45, Exodus.R 25:9, Ezekiel 38:1-38:23, Genesis.R 97:1, Habakkuk 2:17, Haggai 2:22, Isaiah 12:12 66:14-66:16, Joel 4:8-4:16, Luke 20:18, Matthew 21:44, Micah 4:11-4:13 5:9 5:16 7:15-7:17, Obadiah 1:18, Revelation 16:14 17:12-17:14 19:19-19:21 20:8-20:9, Tanna Devei Eliyahu 7, Zechariah 2:8-2:9 10:3-10:5 12:4 12:6 12:8-12:9 12:11 13:1 14:2-14:4 14:6 14:8-14:9 14:13, Zephaniah 3:19

[12] Zechariah 12:4 - 1 Kings 8:29, 2 Chronicles 6:20 6:40 7:15, 2 Kings 6:14 6:18, Acts 17:30, Daniel 9:18, Deuteronomy 4:28, Ezekiel 14:4 15:20, Isaiah 24:21 13:17, Jeremiah 24:6, Mekilta de R'Ishmael Shirata 2:134, Nehemiah 1:6, Psalms 76:6-76:8, Zechariah 9:8 10:5 12:3 12:6 12:8-12:9 12:11 14:15

house of Judah, and will stgrike every horse of the nations with blindness.

5[1] And the chiefs of Judah shall say in their heart: 'The inhabitants of Jerusalem are my strength, through the LORD of hosts their God.'

וְאָמְרוּ אַלֻּפֵי יְהוּדָה בְּלִבָּם אַמְצָה לִי יֹשְׁבֵי יְרוּשָׁלַ͏ִם בַּיהוָה צְבָאוֹת אֱלֹהֵיהֶם

6[2] In that day will I make the chiefs of Judah like a pan of fire among the wood, and like a torch of fire among sheaves; and they shall devour all the peoples round about, on the right hand and on the left; and Jerusalem shall be inhabited again in her own place, in Jerusalem.

בַּיּוֹם הַהוּא אָשִׂים אֶת־אַלֻּפֵי יְהוּדָה כְּכִיּוֹר אֵשׁ בְּעֵצִים וּכְלַפִּיד אֵשׁ בְּעָמִיר וְאָכְלוּ עַל־יָמִין וְעַל־שְׂמֹאול אֶת־כָּל־הָעַמִּים סָבִיב וְיָשְׁבָה יְרוּשָׁלַ͏ִם עוֹד תַּחְתֶּיהָ בִּירוּשָׁלָ͏ִם

7[3] The LORD also shall save the tents of Judah first, so the glory of the house of David and the glory of the inhabitants of Jerusalem be not magnified above Judah.

וְהוֹשִׁיעַ יְהוָה אֶת־אָהֳלֵי יְהוּדָה בָּרִאשֹׁנָה לְמַעַן לֹא־תִגְדַּל תִּפְאֶרֶת בֵּית־דָּוִיד וְתִפְאֶרֶת יֹשֵׁב יְרוּשָׁלַ͏ִם עַל־יְהוּדָה

8[4] In that day the LORD shall defend the inhabitants of Jerusalem; and he who stumbles among them at that day shall be as David; and the house of David shall be as a godlike being, as the angel of the LORD before them.

בַּיּוֹם הַהוּא יָגֵן יְהוָה בְּעַד יוֹשֵׁב יְרוּשָׁלַ͏ִם וְהָיָה הַנִּכְשָׁל בָּהֶם בַּיּוֹם הַהוּא כְּדָוִיד וּבֵית דָּוִיד כֵּאלֹהִים כְּמַלְאַךְ יְהוָה לִפְנֵיהֶם

9[5] And it shall come to pass in that day that I will seek to destroy all the nations that come against Jerusalem.

וְהָיָה בַּיּוֹם הַהוּא אֲבַקֵּשׁ לְהַשְׁמִיד אֶת־כָּל־הַגּוֹיִם הַבָּאִים עַל־יְרוּשָׁלָ͏ִם

10[6] And I will pour upon the house of David, and upon the inhabitants of Jerusalem, the spirit of grace and of *supplication*[7]; and they shall look to Me *because they have thrust him through; And they shall mourn for him, as one mourns for his only son, and shall be in bitterness for him, as one that is in bitterness for his firstborn*[8].

וְשָׁפַכְתִּי עַל־בֵּית דָּוִיד וְעַל יוֹשֵׁב יְרוּשָׁלַ͏ִם רוּחַ חֵן וְתַחֲנוּנִים וְהִבִּיטוּ אֵלַי אֵת אֲשֶׁר־דָּקָרוּ וְסָפְדוּ עָלָיו כְּמִסְפֵּד עַל־הַיָּחִיד וְהָמֵר עָלָיו כְּהָמֵר עַל־הַבְּכוֹר

11[9] In that day shall there be a great mourning in Jerusalem, as the mourning of *Hadadrimmon in the valley of Megiddon*[10].

בַּיּוֹם הַהוּא יִגְדַּל הַמִּסְפֵּד בִּירוּשָׁלַ͏ִם כְּמִסְפַּד הֲדַדְ־רִמּוֹן בְּבִקְעַת מְגִדּוֹן

---

[1] Zechariah 12:5 - 2 Corinthians 12:9-12:10, Ezekiel 45:8-9, Isaiah 1:10 1:23 1:26 4:6 5:10 8:1 41:10-16 12:17, Jeremiah 6:21 9:26, Joel 4:16, Judges 5:9, Midrash Psalms 118:13 119:2, Psalms 18:33 18:40 20:7-8 46:2 68:35-36 118:10-14 24:1, Zechariah 10:6 10:12 12:6

[2] Zechariah 12:6 - 2 Corinthians 6:7, Daniel 2:34-35 2:44-45, Ezekiel 48:30-35, Isaiah 9:21 10:16-18 41:15-16 6:3, Jeremiah 6:18 31:39-41, Mekhilta de R'Shimon bar Yochai Shirata 32:2, Mekilta de R'Ishmael Shirata 6:75, Micah 4:13 5:6-9, Midrash Psalms 118:13, Nehemiah 11:1-36, Obadiah 1:18, Psalms 149:6-9, Revelation 19:19-20 20:9, Zechariah 1:16 2:4 2:12 8:3-5 9:15 11:1 14:10-11

[3] Zechariah 12:7 - 1 Corinthians 1:26-31, 2 Corinthians 4:7-12, Amos 9:11, Isaiah 2:11-17 23:9, James 2:5 4:6, Jeremiah 9:24-25 6:18, Job 19:5, John 7:47-49, Luke 1:51-53 10:21, Matthew 11:25-26, Midrash Psalms 107:2, Psalms 35:26 38:17 55:13, Romans 3:27, y.Sukkah 4:3, Zechariah 4:6 11:11 Zechariah 12:7-12 - 4QXIIe

[4] Zechariah 12:8 - 1 Timothy 3:16, 2 Samuel 14:17-20, Acts 7:30-35, Exodus 23:20-21, Ezekiel 34:23-24 37:24-26, Genesis 22:15-17 48:15-16, Hebrews 11:34, Hosea 1:7 3:5 12:5, Isaiah 7:13-14 9:7-8 6:26 1:7 5:3 15:9, Jeremiah 23:5-6 3:10 30:19-22 33:15-16, Joel 4:10 4:16-17, John 17:21-23, Joshua 5:13-14, Leviticus.R 31:4, Malachi 3:1, Matthew 1:23, Mekhilta de R'Shimon bar Yochai Pisha 15:8, Micah 5:3-5 5:9 7:8 7:16, Psalms 2:6-7 45:7-48 82:6 110:1-2, Revelation 22:13 22:16, Romans 1:3-4 9:5, Song of Songs.R 7:12, z.Mishpatim 122a, Zechariah 2:5 3:1-2 9:8 9:15-16

[5] Zechariah 12:9 - b.Avodah Zara 4a, Esther.R 1:6, Haggai 2:22, Isaiah 6:17, Midrash Tanchuma Mishpatim 5, Zechariah 12:2 14:2-3

[6] Zechariah 12:10 - 2 Corinthians 7:9-11, Acts 2:17 2:33 2:37 10:45 11:15, Amos 8:10, b.Succah 52a, Ein Yaakov Sukkah:52a, Ephesians 6:18, Ezekiel 15:29, Genesis.R 29:4, Hebrews 12:2, Isaiah 8:15 44:3-4 59:19-21, Jeremiah 6:26 7:10 2:4, Joel 3:1-2, John 1:29 19:34-37, Lamentations.R 2:8 4:14, Jude 1:20, Matthew 24:30 26:75, Mekhilta de R'Shimon bar Yochai Pisha 15:8, Mekilta de R'Ishmael Pisha 13:137, Midrash Tanchuma Naso 10, Numbers.R 11:6, Proverbs 1:23, Psalms 22:17-18 51:13, Revelation 1:7, Romans 8:15 8:26, Saadia Opinions 8:5, Titus 3:5-6, Two Letters Part II

[7] LXX *compassion*

[8] LXX *because they have mocked me, and they shall make lamentation for him, as for a beloved friend, and they shall grieve intensely, as for a firstborn son*

[9] Zechariah 12:11 - 2 Chronicles 11:24, 2 Kings 23:29, b.Megillah 3a, b.Moed Katan 28b, Ein Yaakov Megillah:3a, Ein Yaakov Moed Katan:28b, Jastrow 695b

[10] LXX *for the omegranate grove cut down in the plain*

וְסָפְדָה הָאָרֶץ מִשְׁפָּחוֹת מִשְׁפָּחוֹת לְבָד מִשְׁפַּחַת בֵּית־דָּוִיד לְבָד וּנְשֵׁיהֶם לְבָד מִשְׁפַּחַת בֵּית־נָתָן לְבָד וּנְשֵׁיהֶם לְבָד	12[1]	And the land shall mourn, every family apart: the family of the house of David apart, and their wives apart; the family of the house of Nathan apart, and their wives apart;
מִשְׁפַּחַת בֵּית־לֵוִי לְבָד וּנְשֵׁיהֶם לְבָד מִשְׁפַּחַת הַשִּׁמְעִי לְבָד וּנְשֵׁיהֶם לְבָד	13[2]	The family of the house of Levi apart, and their wives apart; the family of the Shimeites apart, and their wives apart;
כֹּל הַמִּשְׁפָּחוֹת הַנִּשְׁאָרוֹת מִשְׁפָּחֹת מִשְׁפָּחֹת לְבָד וּנְשֵׁיהֶם לְבָד	14[3]	All the families who remain, every family apart, and their wives apart.

Zechariah – Chapter 13

בַּיּוֹם הַהוּא יִהְיֶה מָקוֹר נִפְתָּח לְבֵית דָּוִיד וּלְיֹשְׁבֵי יְרוּשָׁלָ͏ִם לְחַטַּאת וּלְנִדָּה	1[4]	In that day *there shall be a fountain opened* [5]to the house of David and to the inhabitants of Jerusalem, for *purification and for sprinkling*[6].
וְהָיָה בַיּוֹם הַהוּא נְאֻם יְהוָה צְבָאוֹת אַכְרִית אֶת־שְׁמוֹת הָעֲצַבִּים מִן־הָאָרֶץ וְלֹא יִזָּכְרוּ עוֹד וְגַם אֶת־הַנְּבִיאִים וְאֶת־רוּחַ הַטֻּמְאָה אַעֲבִיר מִן־הָאָרֶץ	2[7]	And it shall come to pass in that day, says the LORD of hosts, that I will cut off the names of the idols from the land, and they shall be remembered no more; and also I will cause the prophets and the unclean spirit to pass from the land.
וְהָיָה כִּי־יִנָּבֵא אִישׁ עוֹד וְאָמְרוּ אֵלָיו אָבִיו וְאִמּוֹ יֹלְדָיו לֹא תִחְיֶה כִּי שֶׁקֶר דִּבַּרְתָּ בְּשֵׁם יְהוָה וּדְקָרֻהוּ אָבִיהוּ וְאִמּוֹ יֹלְדָיו בְּהִנָּבְאוֹ	3[8]	And it shall come to pass that, when any shall yet prophesy, then his father and his mother who begot him shall say to him: 'You shall not live, for you speaks lies in the name of the LORD;' and his father and his mother who begot him shall *thrust him through when*[9] he prophesies.
וְהָיָה בַּיּוֹם הַהוּא יֵבֹשׁוּ הַנְּבִיאִים אִישׁ מֵחֶזְיֹנוֹ בְּהִנָּבְאֹתוֹ וְלֹא יִלְבְּשׁוּ אַדֶּרֶת שֵׂעָר לְמַעַן כַּחֵשׁ	4[10]	And it shall come to pass in that day, that the prophets shall be brought to shame through his vision, when he prophesies; nor shall they wear a hairy mantle to deceive;
וְאָמַר לֹא נָבִיא אָנֹכִי אִישׁ־עֹבֵד אֲדָמָה אָנֹכִי כִּי אָדָם הִקְנַנִי מִנְּעוּרָי	5[11]	but he shall say: 'I am no prophet, I am a tiller of the ground; for I have been made a bondman from my youth.'
וְאָמַר אֵלָיו מָה הַמַּכּוֹת הָאֵלֶּה בֵּין יָדֶיךָ וְאָמַר אֲשֶׁר הֻכֵּיתִי בֵּית מְאַהֲבָי	6[12]	And one shall say to him: 'What are these wounds between your hands?' Then he shall

[1] Zechariah 12:12 - 1 Corinthians 7:5, 2 Samuel 5:14 7:2-7:4 12:1, b.Succah 52a, Ein Yaakov Sukkah:52a, Exodus 12:30, Jeremiah 3:21 4:28 13:18 7:19, Joel 2:16, Jonah 3:5-3:6, Luke 3:31, Matthew 24:30, Revelation 1:7, y.Sukkah 5:2, Zechariah 7:3

[2] Zechariah 12:13 - 1 Chronicles 3:19 4:27 23:7 23:10, 1 Kings 1:8, 2 Chronicles 5:14, 2 Samuel 16:5, Exodus 6:16-6:26, Malachi 2:4-2:9, Numbers 3:1-3:4

[3] Zechariah 12:14 - Proverbs 9:12

[4] Zechariah 13:1 - 1 Corinthians 6:11, 1 John 1:7 5:6, 1 Peter 1:19, b.Niddah [Tosefot] 19b, b.Shekalim 14a, b.Yoma 78b, Ephesians 5:25-5:27, Ezekiel 12:17 12:25 12:29, Hebrews 9:13-9:14, Isaiah 1:16-1:18, Jeremiah 17:13, Job 9:30-9:31, John 1:29 19:34-19:35, Leviticus 15:2-15:33, Numbers 19:9-19:22, Psalms 51:3 51:8, Revelation 1:5-1:6 7:13-7:14, t.Shabbat 8:27, t.Sukkah 3:9, Titus 3:5-3:7, y.Shekalim 6:2, Zechariah 12:3 12:7-12:8 12:10-12:11

[5] LXX *every place shall be opened*

[6] LXX *removal and for separation*

[7] Zechariah 13:2 - 1 John 4:1-2, 1 Kings 22:22, 2 Corinthians 11:13-15, 2 Peter 2:1-3 2:15-19, Deuteronomy 12:3, Exodus 22:13 23:13, Ezekiel 13:12-16 13:23 14:9 6:13 12:25 13:23, Hosea 2:17 14:10, Isaiah 2:18 2:20, Jeremiah 8:10-12 23:14-15 5:23, Joshua 23:7, Luke 11:20, Matthew 7:15 12:43, Micah 2:11 5:13-15, Midrash Tanchuma Chukkat 8, Numbers.R 19:8, Pesikta de R'Kahana 4.7, Pesikta Rabbati 14:1, Psalms 16:4, Revelation 16:13-14 18:2 19:20 20:1-3, Tanya Igeret Hakodesh §12 §26, Tanya Likutei Aramim §7 §33 §37, z.Bereshit 54a 55a, z.Chayyei Sarah 124a 127a 131a, z.Noach 70b 73b, z.Vayera 114a, z.Vayetze 163b, Zephaniah 1:3-4 2:11

[8] Zechariah 13:3 - 2 Corinthians 5:16, Deuteronomy 13:7-13:11 18:20 9:9, Exodus 32:27-32:28, Ezekiel 14:9, Jeremiah 23:34, Luke 14:26, Matthew 10:37, z.Pekudei 269a

[9] LXX *bind him as*

[10] Zechariah 13:4 - 2 Kings 1:8, Isaiah 20:2, Jeremiah 2:26 6:15, Mark 1:6, Martyrdom and Ascension of Isaiah 2:10, Matthew 3:4 11:8-11:9, Micah 3:6-3:7, Revelation 11:3

[11] Zechariah 13:5 - Acts 19:17-19:20, Amos 7:14

[12] Zechariah 13:6 - 1 Kings 18:28, b.Makkot 22b, Jastrow 1214a, John 18:35 19:14-19:16, Leviticus.R 32:1, Mekilta de R'Ishmael

answer: 'Those with which I was wounded in the house of my friends.'

חֶרֶב עוּרִי עַל־רֹעִי וְעַל־גֶּבֶר עֲמִיתִי נְאֻם יְהוָה צְבָאוֹת הַךְ אֶת־הָרֹעֶה וּתְפוּצֶיןָ הַצֹּאן וַהֲשִׁבֹתִי יָדִי עַל־הַצֹּעֲרִים

7[1] Awake, O sword, against My shepherd, and against the man who is near to Me, says the LORD of hosts; smite the shepherd and the sheep shall be scattered; and I will turn My hand upon the little ones.

וְהָיָה בְכָל־הָאָרֶץ נְאֻם־יְהוָה פִּי־שְׁנַיִם בָּהּ יִכָּרְתוּ יִגְוָעוּ וְהַשְּׁלִשִׁית יִוָּתֶר בָּהּ

8[2] And it shall come to pass, that in all the land, says the LORD, two parts of it shall be cut off and die; but the third shall be left in it.

וְהֵבֵאתִי אֶת־הַשְּׁלִשִׁית בָּאֵשׁ וּצְרַפְתִּים כִּצְרֹף אֶת־הַכֶּסֶף וּבְחַנְתִּים כִּבְחֹן אֶת־הַזָּהָב הוּא יִקְרָא בִשְׁמִי וַאֲנִי אֶעֱנֶה אֹתוֹ אָמַרְתִּי עַמִּי הוּא וְהוּא יֹאמַר יְהוָה אֱלֹהָי

9[3] And I will bring the third part through the fire, and will refine them as silver is refined, and will try them as gold is tried; they shall call on My name, And I will answer them; I will say: 'It is My people,' and they shall say: 'The LORD is my God.'

Zechariah – Chapter 14[4]

הִנֵּה יוֹם־בָּא לַיהוָה וְחֻלַּק שְׁלָלֵךְ בְּקִרְבֵּךְ

1[5] Behold, a day of the LORD comes, when your spoil shall be divided in your midst.

וְאָסַפְתִּי אֶת־כָּל־הַגּוֹיִם אֶל־יְרוּשָׁלַ͏ִם לַמִּלְחָמָה וְנִלְכְּדָה הָעִיר וְנָשַׁסּוּ הַבָּתִּים וְהַנָּשִׁים 'תִּשָּׁגַלְנָה' "תִּשָּׁכַבְנָה" וְיָצָא חֲצִי הָעִיר בַּגּוֹלָה וְיֶתֶר הָעָם לֹא יִכָּרֵת מִן־הָעִיר

2[6] For I will gather all nations against Jerusalem to battle; and the city shall be taken, and the houses rifled, and the women ravished; and half of the city shall go forth into captivity, but the residue of the people shall not be cut off from the city.

וְיָצָא יְהוָה וְנִלְחַם בַּגּוֹיִם הָהֵם כְּיוֹם הִלָּחֲמוֹ בְּיוֹם קְרָב

3[7] Then shall the LORD go forth, and fight against those nations, as when He fights in the day of battle.

Bahodesh 6:142, Midrash Psalms 12:5 38:1, mt.Hilchot Talmud Torah 2:1, mt.Hilchot Talmud Torah 2:2, Proverbs 27:5-6, Psalms 22:17, Revelation 13:16-17 14:11

Zechariah 13:6 [LXX] - Ladder of Jacob 7:30

[1] Zechariah 13:7 - 1 John 2:2 4:9-4:10, 1 Peter 1:18-1:20 2:24-2:25 3:18 5:4, 2 Corinthians 5:21, Acts 2:23 4:26-4:28, Avot de R'Natan 38, Cairo Damascus 19:7-9, Cairo Damascus 19:7-9, Cairo Damascus 19:7-9, Colossians 1:15-1:20, Daniel 9:24-9:26, Deuteronomy 32:41-32:42, Ezekiel 21:9-21:10 21:14-21:15 21:33 34:23-34:24 13:24, Galatians 3:13, Hebrews 1:6-1:12 10:5-10:10 13:20, Hosea 12:5-12:7, Isaiah 9:7 3:1 16:11 53:4-53:10, Jeremiah 23:5-23:6 23:6, John 1:1-1:2 1:29 3:14-3:17 5:17-5:18 5:23 8:58 10:10-10:18 10:30 10:38 14:1 14:9-14:11 14:23 16:15 16:32 17:21-17:23 18:8-18:9, Luke 12:32 17:2, Mark 14:27 14:50, Matthew 1:23 10:42 11:27 18:10 18:14 2:31 2:56, Micah 5:3 5:5, Midrash Psalms 80:3, Philippians 2:6, Psalms 2:2, Revelation 1:8 1:11 1:17 2:23 13:8 21:6 22:13-22:16, Romans 3:24-3:26 4:25 5:6-5:10 8:32, z.Pekudei 237a, Zechariah 11:4 11:7 11:11

[2] Zechariah 13:8 - 1 Thessalonians 2:15-2:16, Amos 9:8-9:9, b.Sanhedrin 111a, Daniel 9:27, Deuteronomy 28:49-28:68, Deuteronomy.R 2:33, Ein Yaakov Sanhedrin:111a, Ezekiel 5:2-5:4 5:12, Isaiah 6:13 65:12-65:15 66:4-66:6 18:24, Jastrow 1588b, Jeremiah 6:11, Joel 3:4-3:5, Luke 19:41-19:44 20:16-20:18 21:20-21:24 23:28-23:30, Malachi 3:1-3:2 3:5 3:19-4:21, Mark 13:20, Matthew 3:10-3:12 21:43-21:44 22:7 23:35-23:37 24:21-24:22, Midrash Tanchuma Beha'alotcha 9, Midrash Tanchuma Shoftim 9, Midrash Tanchuma Tzav 2, Numbers.R 15:14, Revelation 8:7-8:12 16:19, Romans 9:27-9:29 11:1-11:5, Sibylline Oracles 3.544 5.103, Zechariah 11:6-11:9 14:1-14:2

[3] Zechariah 13:9 - 1 Corinthians 3:11-3:13, 1 Peter 1:6-1:7 4:12, 4 Ezra 16:73, 4Q176 15 3-5, 4Q176 frag 15 ll.3-5, Acts 2:21, Avot de R'Natan 41, Deuteronomy 26:17-26:19, Ein Yaakov Rosh Hashanah:17a, Ezekiel 11:20 12:28 13:27, Hebrews 8:10, Hosea 2:21-2:25, Isaiah 19:2 44:1-44:6 24:10 10:9 65:23-65:24, James 1:12, Jastrow 1298a, Jeremiah 29:11-29:12 6:22 7:34 8:38, Job 23:10, Joel 3:5, Leviticus 2:12 26:44-26:45, Malachi 3:2-3:3, Matthew 22:29-22:32, mt.Hilchot Teshuvah 3:5 3:5, Proverbs 17:3, Psalms 34:16-34:20 50:15 66:10-66:12 91:15 24:15, Revelation 21:3-21:4 21:7, Romans 10:12-10:14, Saadia Opinions 6:4, Song of Songs.R 1:22, t.Sanhedrin 13:3, Testament of Abraham 12:14, z.Shemot 7b, Zechariah 8:8 10:6 12:10

Zechariah 13:9-14:21 - Haftarah 1st day Sukkot [Teimon]

[4] Zechariah 14 - mt.Hilchot Tefilah 13:12, Sukkot Day One Haftarah

[5] Zechariah 14:1 - Acts 2:20, b.Megillah [Rashi] 31a, b.Megillah 31a, Ecclesiastes.R 5:5, Isaiah 2:12 13:6 13:9, Jastrow 357b, Joel 3:4 4:14, Malachi 3:19 3:23, Midrash Psalms 118:13, Pesikta de R'Kahana S22, Psalms of Solomon 17:21, Revelation 16:14, Saadia Opinions 8:5, Tanna Devei Eliyahu 1, Testament of Naphtali 5:2, z.Metzorah 54a, z.Shemot 19b

Zechariah 14:1-21 - Haftarah 1st day Sukkot [Ashkenaz and Sephard]

[6] Zechariah 14:2 - Amos 7:17, Daniel 2:40-2:43, Deuteronomy 28:9-28:14, Galatians 4:26-4:27, Isaiah 5:26 13:16 65:6-65:9 17:18, Jeremiah 10:1, Joel 4:2, Lamentations 1:10 5:11-5:12, Luke 2:1 19:43-19:44 21:20-21:24, Mark 13:14 13:19, Matthew 22:7 23:37-38 24:15-16 24:19-24:22, Midrash Psalms 2:4 15:5 115:13, Pesikta de R'Kahana S2.2, Pesikta Rabbati 51:7, Romans 9:27-9:29, Ruth.R 5:6, Saadia Opinions 8:5, Song of Songs.R 6:25, To remove indelicate expressions the word ישגלנה [ravish violate outrage] is substituted by ישכבנה [lie with], z.Vayera 119a, Zechariah 13:8-13:9

[7] Zechariah 14:3 - 2 Chronicles 20:15, Daniel 2:34-2:35 2:44-2:45, Esther.R 7:18, Exodus 15:1-15:6, Haggai 2:21-2:22, Isaiah 63:1-

וְעָמְד֣וּ רַגְלָ֣יו בַּיּוֹם־הַ֠הוּא עַל־הַ֨ר הַזֵּתִ֜ים אֲשֶׁ֨ר עַל־פְּנֵ֥י יְרוּשָׁלִַ֘ם֮ מִקֶּ֒דֶם֒ וְנִבְקַע֩ הַ֨ר הַזֵּתִ֜ים מֵחֶצְי֣וֹ מִזְרָ֣חָה וָיָ֗מָּה גֵּ֤יא גְּדוֹלָה֙ מְאֹ֔ד וּמָ֨שׁ חֲצִ֥י הָהָ֛ר צָפ֖וֹנָה וְחֶצְיוֹ־נֶֽגְבָּה

4[1]

And His feet shall stand in that day on the mount of Olives, which is before Jerusalem on the east, and the Mount of Olives shall divide in its midst toward the east and toward the west, so that there shall be a very great valley; and half of the mountain shall move toward the north, and half of it toward the south.

וְנַסְתֶּ֣ם גֵּיא־הָרַ֗י כִּֽי־יַגִּ֣יעַ גֵּי־הָרִים֮ אֶל־אָצַל֒ וְנַסְתֶּ֗ם כַּאֲשֶׁ֤ר נַסְתֶּם֙ מִפְּנֵ֣י הָרַ֔עַשׁ בִּימֵ֖י עֻזִּיָּ֣ה מֶֽלֶךְ־יְהוּדָ֑ה וּבָא֙ יְהוָ֣ה אֱלֹהַ֔י כָּל־קְדֹשִׁ֖ים עִמָּֽךְ

5[2]

And you shall flee to the valley of the mountains; for the valley of the mountains shall reach to Azel; yes, you shall flee, like as you fled from before the earthquake[3] In the days of Uzziah king of Judah; and the LORD my God shall come, and all the holy ones with You.

וְהָיָ֖ה בַּיּ֣וֹם הַה֑וּא לֹֽא־יִהְיֶ֣ה א֔וֹר יְקָר֖וֹת 'יִקְפָּאוֹן' "יְקַפָּאֽוֹן"

6[4]

And it shall come to pass in that day, that there shall not be light, *but heavy clouds and thick[5]*;

וְהָיָ֣ה יוֹם־אֶחָ֗ד ה֛וּא יִוָּדַ֥ע לַֽיהוָ֖ה לֹא־י֣וֹם וְלֹא־לָ֑יְלָה וְהָיָ֥ה לְעֵֽת־עֶ֖רֶב יִֽהְיֶה־אֽוֹר

7[6]

And there shall be one day that shall be known as the LORD's[7], not day, and not night; but it shall come to pass, that at evening time there shall be light.

וְהָיָ֣ה ׀ בַּיּ֣וֹם הַה֗וּא יֵצְא֤וּ מַֽיִם־חַיִּים֙ מִיר֣וּשָׁלִַ֔ם חֶצְיָ֗ם אֶל־הַיָּם֙ הַקַּדְמוֹנִ֔י וְחֶצְיָ֖ם אֶל־הַיָּ֣ם הָאַחֲר֑וֹן בַּקַּ֥יִץ וּבָחֹ֖רֶף יִֽהְיֶֽה

8[8]

And it shall come to pass in that day, that living waters shall go out from Jerusalem: half of them toward the *eastern sea, And half of them toward the western sea[9]*; in summer and in winter it shall be.

וְהָיָ֧ה יְהוָ֛ה לְמֶ֖לֶךְ עַל־כָּל־הָאָ֑רֶץ בַּיּ֣וֹם הַה֗וּא יִהְיֶ֧ה יְהוָ֛ה אֶחָ֖ד וּשְׁמ֥וֹ אֶחָֽד

9[10]

And the LORD shall be King over all the earth; in that day shall the LORD be One, and His name one.

63:6 66:15-66:16, Joel 4:2 4:9-4:17, Joshua 10:42, Leviticus.R 27:11, Mekhilta de R'Shimon bar Yochai Shirata 34:2, Mekilta de R'Ishmael Amalek 2:158, Midrash Psalms 2:4 13:2 17:10 18:5 115:13, Midrash Tanchuma Emor 13, Midrash Tanchuma Lech Lecha 9, Midrash Tanchuma Shoftim 17, Pesikta de R'Kahana 9.11 S2.2, Pesikta Rabbati 9:3, Revelation 6:4-6:17 8:7-8:13, z.Beshallach 47b 56a, z.Vayishlach 174a, Zechariah 2:8-2:9 9:14-9:15 10:4-10:5 12:2-12:6 12:9, Zephaniah 3:19

Zechariah 14:3-4 - Midrash Tanchuma Ekev 3

[1] Zechariah 14:4 - 4 Ezra 5:8, Acts 1:11-1:12, Avot de R'Natan 34, Avot de R'Natan 34.07.01, b.Succah 5a, Ein Yaakov Sukkah:5a, Exodus.R 17:4, Ezekiel 11:23 19:2 47:1-47:12, Guide for the Perplexed 1:13 1 28, Guide for the Perplexed 1:28 [T.Jonathan], Habakkuk 3:6, Isaiah 64:2-64:3, Joel 4:12-4:14, Josephus Antiquities 20.8.6, Lamentations.R 1:50 1:51, m.Maaserot 2:5, m.Middot 1:3, m.Parah 3:9, m.Rosh Hashanah 2:1-2, m.Sukkah 4:5, Mark 11:23, Mekhilta de R'Shimon bar Yochai Shirata 34:2, Micah 1:3-1:4, Nahum 1:5-1:6, Pesikta Rabbati 31:1, Saadia Opinions 8:8, western wrote עמדו ועמדו and Eastern wrote אל־הר הוא ביום רגליו ועמדו עַל־הַר רַגְלָיו וְעָמְדוּ [j.Megillah 1:9], z.Lech Lecha 86a, Zechariah 4:7 14:7 14:10

Zechariah 14:4-7 - Testament of Naphtali 5:1

[2] Zechariah 14:5 - 1 Thessalonians 3:13, 2 Thessalonians 1:7-1:10 2:8, Amos 1:1, Daniel 7:9-7:14 7:21-7:27, Deuteronomy 9:2, Ecclesiastes.R 1:30, Guide for the Perplexed 1:22, Isaiah 5:6 64:2-64:4 66:15-66:16, James 5:8, Joel 4:11, Jude 1:14-1:15, Luke 21:27, Mark 13:26-13:27, Matthew 16:27 24:3 24:27-24:31 1:31, Midrash Psalms 2:4 18:12 18:17, Midrash Tanchuma Tzav 13, Numbers 16:34, Pesikta Rabbati 21:9, Psalms 96:13 97:4-97:6 98:9, Revelation 6:16-6:17 11:13 16:18-16:21 20:4 20:11, Ruth.R Petichata:2, Seder Olam 20:Flee, Song of Songs.R 4:23, Tanna Devei Eliyahu 2, y.Berachot 9:2

[3] LXX *And the valley of my mountains shall be closed up, and the valley of the mountains shall be joined on to Jasod, and shall be blocked up as it was blocked up in the days of the earthquake*

[4] Zechariah 14:6 - 2 Peter 1:19, b.Pesachim 50a, Colossians 1:12, Ein Yaakov Pesachim:50a, Ephesians 5:8-5:14, Genesis.R 82:5, Guide for the Perplexed 2:43, Hosea 6:3, Isaiah 13:10 2:10 60:1-60:3, Jastrow 1295a, Jeremiah 4:23, John 1:5 12:46, Luke 1:78-1:79, Midrash Tanchuma Chukkat 8, Pesikta de R'Kahana 4.7 S2.2, Pesikta Rabbati 8:4 14:13, Proverbs 4:18-4:19, Psalms 97:10-97:11 16:4, Revelation 11:3 11:15, Tanna Devei Eliyahu 2

[5] Missing in LXX

[6] Zechariah 14:7 - 1 Thessalonians 5:2, Acts 1:7 15:18 17:26 17:31, Daniel 12:4, Hosea 3:5, Isaiah 9:8 11:9 6:26 60:19-60:20, Jeremiah 6:7, Mark 13:32, Matthew 24:36, Numbers.R 9:20, Pesikta Rabbati 8:4, Pirkei de R'Eliezer 19 28, Psalms 37:18, Revelation 11:15 14:6 20:2-20:4 21:3 21:23 21:25 22:5, z.Shemot 17a, z.Vaetchanan 266b, z.Vayera 107b

[7] LXX *and there shall be for one day cold and frost, and that day shall be known to the LORD*

[8] Zechariah 14:8 - Avot de R'Natan 35, b.Shekalim 14a, Esther.R Petichata:11, Ezekiel 47:1-47:12, Genesis.R 42:3 48:10 70:6, Isaiah 11:7 41:17-41:18 1:10 10:11, Jastrow 632b, Joel 2:20 4:18, John 4:10 4:14 7:38, Leviticus.R 11:7, Luke 24:47, Midrash Psalms 46:3, Midrash Tanchuma Shemini 9, Numbers.R 13:5, Odes of Solomon 6:8, Pesikta Rabbati 33:12, Pirkei de R'Eliezer 35, Revelation 7:16-7:17 22:1-2 22:17, Ruth.R Petichata:7, t.Sukkah 3:7[8], y.Shekalim 6:2

[9] LXX *latter sea*

[10] Zechariah 14:9 - 1 Samuel 2:10, 3 Enoch 48A:10, Aleinu [Shacharit Minchah Maariv Mussaf Mussaf Rosh Hashanah Kiddush Levonoh Seder Bris Milah] Maariv weekdays [Baruch Hashem L'olam], Amos 9:12, Apocalypse of Elijah 2:11, b.Pesachim 50a, Birchat HaChammah.Alenu, Birchat HaChammah.LeShem Yichud, Daniel 2:44-2:45 7:27, Derech Hashem Part IV 4§01, Deuteronomy 6:4, Deuteronomy.R 5:12, Ein Yaakov Pesachim:50a, Ephesians 3:14-3:15 4:5-4:6, Esther.R 7:18, Genesis 1:10, Guide

Hebrew		English
יִסּ֨וֹב כָּל־הָאָ֜רֶץ כָּעֲרָבָ֗ה מִגֶּ֛בַע לְרִמּ֖וֹן נֶ֣גֶב יְרוּשָׁלִָ֑ם וְֽרָאֲמָ֞ה וְיָ֣שְׁבָ֣ה תַחְתֶּ֗יהָ לְמִשַּׁ֤עַר בִּנְיָמִן֙ עַד־מְק֞וֹם שַׁ֣עַר הָֽרִאשׁ֗וֹן עַד־שַׁ֣עַר הַפִּנִּ֔ים וּמִגְדַּ֣ל חֲנַנְאֵ֔ל עַ֖ד יִקְבֵ֥י הַמֶּֽלֶךְ	10[1]	*All the land shall be turned as the Arabah*[2], from Geba to Rimmon south of Jerusalem; *and she shall be lifted up, and inhabited in her place*[3], from Benjamin's gate to the place of the first gate, to the corner gate, and from the tower of Hananel to the king's winepresses.
וְיָ֣שְׁבוּ בָ֔הּ וְחֵ֖רֶם לֹ֣א יִֽהְיֶה־ע֑וֹד וְיָשְׁבָ֥ה יְרוּשָׁלִַ֖ם לָבֶֽטַח	11[4]	And men shall live there, And there shall be no more *extermination*[5]; but Jerusalem shall dwell safely.
וְזֹ֣את ׀ תִּֽהְיֶ֣ה הַמַּגֵּפָ֗ה אֲשֶׁ֨ר יִגֹּ֤ף יְהוָה֙ אֶת־כָּל־הָ֣עַמִּ֔ים אֲשֶׁ֥ר צָבְא֖וּ עַל־יְרוּשָׁלָ֑͏ִם הָמֵ֣ק ׀ בְּשָׂר֗וֹ וְהוּא֙ עֹמֵ֣ד עַל־רַגְלָ֔יו וְעֵינָיו֙ תִּמַּ֣קְנָה בְחֹֽרֵיהֶ֔ן וּלְשׁוֹנ֖וֹ תִּמַּ֥ק בְּפִיהֶֽם	12[6]	And this shall be the plague that the LORD will strike all the people who have warred against Jerusalem: their flesh shall consume away while they stand on their feet, and their eyes shall consume away in their sockets, and their tongue shall consume away in their mouth.
וְהָיָה֙ בַּיּ֣וֹם הַה֔וּא תִּֽהְיֶ֧ה מְהֽוּמַת־יְהוָ֛ה רַבָּ֖ה בָּהֶ֑ם וְהֶחֱזִ֗יקוּ אִ֚ישׁ יַ֣ד רֵעֵ֔הוּ וְעָלְתָ֥ה יָד֖וֹ עַל־יַ֥ד רֵעֵֽהוּ	13[7]	And it shall come to pass in that day, that a great tumult from the LORD shall be among them; and they shall lay hold everyone on the hand of his neighbor, and his hand shall rise up against the hand of his neighbor.
וְגַ֨ם־יְהוּדָ֔ה תִּלָּחֵ֖ם בִּירֽוּשָׁלִָ֑ם וְאֻסַּף֩ חֵ֨יל כָּל־הַגּוֹיִ֜ם סָבִ֗יב זָהָ֥ב וָכֶ֛סֶף וּבְגָדִ֖ים לָרֹ֥ב מְאֹֽד	14[8]	And Judah also shall fight against Jerusalem; and the wealth of all the nations around them shall be gathered together, gold, and silver, and apparel, in great abundance.
וְכֵ֨ן תִּֽהְיֶ֜ה מַגֵּפַ֣ת הַסּ֗וּס הַפֶּ֙רֶד֙ הַגָּמָ֣ל וְהַחֲמ֔וֹר וְכָ֨ל־הַבְּהֵמָ֔ה אֲשֶׁ֥ר יִהְיֶ֖ה בַּֽמַּחֲנ֣וֹת הָהֵ֑מָּה כַּמַּגֵּפָ֖ה הַזֹּֽאת	15[9]	And so shall be the plague of the horse, of the mule, of the camel, and of the donkey, and of all the beasts that shall be in those camps, as this plague.
וְהָיָ֗ה כָּל־הַנּוֹתָר֙ מִכָּל־הַגּוֹיִ֔ם הַבָּאִ֖ים עַל־יְרֽוּשָׁלָ֑͏ִם וְעָל֞וּ מִדֵּ֧י שָׁנָ֣ה בְשָׁנָ֗ה לְהִֽשְׁתַּחֲוֺת֙ לְמֶ֙לֶךְ֙ יְהוָ֣ה צְבָא֔וֹת וְלָחֹ֖ג אֶת־חַ֥ג הַסֻּכּֽוֹת	16[10]	And it shall come to pass, that everyone who remains of all the nations who came against Jerusalem shall go up from year to year to

for the Perplexed 1:61, Isaiah 2:2-2:4 45:22-45:25 49:6-49:7 6:5 60:12-60:14, Jeremiah 23:6, Lamentations.R 3:23, Leviticus.R 27:11, Matthew 1:23 4:19, Mekhilta de R'Shimon bar Yochai Amalek 45:1, Mekilta de R'Ishmael Amalek 2:159, Micah 4:1-4:3 5:5, Midrash Psalms 2:4 53:3 66:1 96:2 97:1, Midrash Tanchuma Bamidbar 10, Midrash Tanchuma Tetzaveh 10, mt.Hilcnot Shofar Sukkah v'Lulav 3:9, Pesikta de R'Kahana 5.9, Pesikta Rabbati 1:2 15:14/15, Pirkei de R'Eliezer 11, Pirkei de R'Eliezer 31, Psalms 2:6-2:8 22:28-22:32 47:3-47:10 67:5 72:8-72:11 72:17 86:9, Revelation 11:15, Saadia Opinions 2:4 8:8, Seder Hoshanot, Shacharit Pesukei D'zimrah Shiras Hayam [Song at the Sea], Sifre Devarim Vaetchanan 31, Song of Songs.R 2:33, Tanya Igeret Hakodesh §25, z.Acharei Mot 77b, z.Bereshit 18a 27b 29a, z.Noach 76b, z.Pekudei 234a, z.Tazria 52a, z.Terumah 134a, z.Vaera 32a, z.Vaetchanan 260b, z.Vayikra 7b, Zechariah 8:20-8:23 14:16-14:17, Zephaniah 3:9

[1] Zechariah 14:10 - 1 Chronicles 4:32 6:77, 1 Kings 15:22, 2 Chronicles 1:23, Amos 9:11, b.Bava Batra 75b, b.Succah [Rashi] 49a, Birchat HaChammah.Vihi Noam, Ein Yaakov Bava Batra:75b, Guide for the Perplexed 1:11, Isaiah 2:2 10:29 40:3-40:4, Jastrow 591a, Jeremiah 6:18 31:39-31:41 13:13 14:7, Joshua 15:32 21:17, Judges 20:45 20:47 21:13, Luke 3:4-3:6, Nehemiah 3:1 12:39, Pesikta de R'Kahana 20.7, Song of Songs.R 7:11, t.Sotah 11:16, Zechariah 2:4 4:6-4:7 12:6

[2] LXX *compassing all the earth, and the wilderness*

[3] LXX *And Rama shall remain in its place*

[4] Zechariah 14:11 - Amos 9:15, Ezekiel 34:22-34:29 13:26, Isaiah 2:1 12:18 18:22, Jeremiah 23:5-23:6 7:41 33:15-33:16, Joel 4:17 4:20, Numbers 21:3, Revelation 21:4 22:3, Zechariah 2:4 8:4 8:8

[5] LXX *curse*

[6] Zechariah 14:12 - 2 Chronicles 21:15 21:18-21:19, Acts 12:23, b.Ketubot [Rashi] 77a, b.Shabbat [Rashi] 62b, Deuteronomy 4:22 4:59, Ecclesiastes.R 9:14, Ezekiel 38:18-38:22 39:4-39:6 39:17-39:20, Isaiah 34:1-34:17 66:15-66:16, Joel 4:1-4:2, Leviticus 2:16 2:18 2:21 2:24 2:28, Mekhilta de R'Shimon bar Yochai Shirata 28:2, Micah 4:11-4:13 5:9-5:10 7:16-7:17, Midrash Psalms 31:4 118:13, Midrash Tanchuma Tazria 11, Pesikta de R'Kahana 7.11, Pesikta Rabbati 17:8, Psalms 90:11 110:5-16, Revelation 9:5-9:6 16:1-16:21 17:16 18:6-18:8 19:17-21, Saadia Opinions 8:6, z.Beshallach 58b, Zechariah 12:9 14:3
Zechariah 14:12-15 - Mekilta de R'Ishmael Shirata 2:136-137

[7] Zechariah 14:13 - 1 Samuel 14:15-23, 2 Chronicles 20:22-24, Ezekiel 14:21, Judges 7:22, Midrash Psalms 18:18, Revelation 17:12-17, Saadia Opinions 8:6, Zechariah 11:6 12:4

[8] Zechariah 14:14 - 2 Chronicles 14:12-14 20:25-27, 2 Kings 7:6-18, Ezekiel 39:9-10 39:17-20, Isaiah 23:18, Zechariah 10:4-5 12:2 12:5-7

[9] Zechariah 14:15 - Mekhilta de R'Shimon bar Yochai Shirata 28:2, y.Shabbat 5:1, Zechariah 14:12

[10] Zechariah 14:16 - 2 Chronicles 7:8-7:10 8:13, Acts 15:17, Deuteronomy 16:13-16:16 31:10-31:13, Ezra 3:4, Hosea 12:11, Isaiah 6:5 60:6-60:9 66:18-66:21 18:23, Jeremiah 22:18 24:15 3:57, Joel 3:5, John 1:49 7:2 7:37-7:39, Leviticus 23:33-23:36 23:39-23:43, Luke

worship the King, the LORD of hosts, and to keep the festival of tabernacles.

וְהָיָה אֲשֶׁר לֹא־יַעֲלֶה מֵאֵת מִשְׁפְּחוֹת הָאָרֶץ אֶל־יְרוּשָׁלַ͏ִם לְהִשְׁתַּחֲוֹת לְמֶלֶךְ יְהוָה צְבָאוֹת וְלֹא עֲלֵיהֶם יִהְיֶה הַגָּשֶׁם

17[1] And it shall be, that whoever of the families of the earth does not go up to Jerusalem to worship the King, the LORD of hosts, *there shall be no rain upon them*[2].

וְאִם־מִשְׁפַּחַת מִצְרַיִם לֹא־תַעֲלֶה וְלֹא בָאָה וְלֹא עֲלֵיהֶם תִּהְיֶה הַמַּגֵּפָה אֲשֶׁר יִגֹּף יְהוָה אֶת־הַגּוֹיִם אֲשֶׁר לֹא יַעֲלוּ לָחֹג אֶת־חַג הַסֻּכּוֹת

18[3] And if the family of Egypt do not go up, and do not come, they shall have no overflow; there shall be the plague, with which the LORD will strike the nations that go not up to keep the festival of tabernacles.

זֹאת תִּהְיֶה חַטַּאת מִצְרָיִם וְחַטַּאת כָּל־הַגּוֹיִם אֲשֶׁר לֹא יַעֲלוּ לָחֹג אֶת־חַג הַסֻּכּוֹת

19[4] This shall be the *punishment*[5] of Egypt, and the *punishment*[6] of all the nations that go not up to keep the festival of tabernacles.

בַּיּוֹם הַהוּא יִהְיֶה עַל־מְצִלּוֹת הַסּוּס קֹדֶשׁ לַיהוָה וְהָיָה הַסִּירוֹת בְּבֵית יְהוָה כַּמִּזְרָקִים לִפְנֵי הַמִּזְבֵּחַ

20[7] In that day shall there be on the *bells*[8] of the horses: HOLY UNTO THE LORD; and the pots in the LORD's house shall be like the basins before the altar.

וְהָיָה כָּל־סִיר בִּירוּשָׁלַ͏ִם וּבִיהוּדָה קֹדֶשׁ לַיהוָה צְבָאוֹת וּבָאוּ כָּל־הַזֹּבְחִים וְלָקְחוּ מֵהֶם וּבִשְּׁלוּ בָהֶם וְלֹא־יִהְיֶה כְנַעֲנִי עוֹד בְּבֵית־יְהוָה צְבָאוֹת בַּיּוֹם הַהוּא

21[9] Yes, every pot in Jerusalem and in Judah shall be holy to the LORD of hosts; and all those who sacrifice shall come and use them, and boil in them; and in that day a trafficker shall no longer be the house of the LORD of hosts.

Malakhi – Chapter 1

מַשָּׂא דְבַר־יְהוָה אֶל־יִשְׂרָאֵל בְּיַד מַלְאָכִי

1[10] The burden of the word of the LORD to Israel by *Malachi*[11].

אָהַבְתִּי אֶתְכֶם אָמַר יְהוָה וַאֲמַרְתֶּם בַּמָּה אֲהַבְתָּנוּ הֲלוֹא־אָח עֵשָׂו לְיַעֲקֹב נְאֻם־יְהוָה וָאֹהַב אֶת־יַעֲקֹב

2[12] I have loved you, says the LORD. Yet you say: 'How have You loved us?' Was not Esau

---

19:38, Malachi 1:14, Nehemiah 8:14-8:18, Numbers 29:12-29:38, Philippians 2:9-2:11, Psalms 24:7-24:10, Revelation 11:13 11:15-11:17 19:16, Romans 9:23-9:24 11:5 11:16 11:26, Saadia Opinions 8:6, Sibylline Oracles 3.772, Zechariah 8:20-8:23 9:7 14:17-14:19

[1] Zechariah 14:17 - 1 Kings 8:35 17:1, 2 Chronicles 6:26 7:13, Acts 17:26-17:27, Amos 3:2 4:7-4:8, Deuteronomy 11:17 28:23-28:24, Genesis 10:32 12:3 4:14, Isaiah 5:6 21:23 12:12, James 5:17, Jeremiah 10:25 14:4 14:22, Psalms 2:8-2:12 110:5-110:6, Revelation 11:6, Romans 14:10-14:11, Saadia Opinions 8:6, z.Vayera 109a, Zechariah 14:16
Zechariah 14:17-18 - t.Sukkah 3:18

[2] LXX *even these shall be added to the others*

[3] Zechariah 14:18 - 4QXIIa, Deuteronomy 11:10-11, Saadia Opinions 8:6, z.Vaetchanan 268b, z.Vayera 109a, Zechariah 14:12 14:15

[4] Zechariah 14:19 - John 3:19

[5] LXX *sin*

[6] LXX *sin*

[7] Zechariah 14:20 - 1 Corinthians 3:16-3:17, 1 Peter 2:5 2:9 4:11, 1 Samuel 2:14, 2 Chronicles 4:8, Acts 10:15 10:28 11:9 15:9, b.Pesachim 50a, Colossians 3:17 3:22-3:24, Exodus 1:29 28:33-28:36 13:16 15:30, Ezekiel 46:20-24, Isaiah 23:18, Jastrow 826a 1284a, Leviticus 6:28 8:9, Luke 11:41, Malachi 1:11, Numbers 4:7 4:14 7:13 7:19 7:84-7:85, Obadiah 1:17, Proverbs 21:3-21:4, Psalms 14:3, Revelation 1:6 5:10 20:6, Romans 14:17-14:18, Titus 1:15-1:16, y.Pesachim 3:8, Zechariah 9:15, Zephaniah 2:11

[8] LXX *bridle*

[9] Zechariah 14:21 - 1 Corinthians 6:9-11 10:31, 1 Peter 4:17, 1 Timothy 3:15 4:3-5, b.Pesachim 50a, b.Shabbat [Rashi] 63a, Deuteronomy 12:7 12:12, Ephesians 2:19-22, Ezekiel 20:9, Hebrews 3:6, Hosea 12:9, Isaiah 4:3 11:8, Jastrow 1647a, Joel 4:17, John 2:15-16, Mark 11:15-17, Matthew 21:12-13, Nehemiah 8:10, Revelation 18:11-15 21:27 22:15, Romans 14:6-7, Zechariah 7:6 14:20
Zephaniah 1:1 - 2 Chronicles 34:1-34:33, 2 Kings 22:1-22:20, 2 Peter 1:19, 2 Timothy 3:16, b.Megillah 15a, Ezekiel 1:3, Hosea 1:1, Jeremiah 1:2 1:3, MurXII, Pesikta Rabbati 26:1/2, Seder Olam 20:Zephaniah

[10] Malachi 1:1 - Avot de R'Natan 1 34, Exodus.R 28:6, Habakkuk 1:1, Haggai 1:1 2:1, Isaiah 13:1, Midrash Tanchuma Yitro 11, Nahum 1:1, t.Sanhedrin 13:1, Zechariah 9:1 12:1
Malachi 1:1 [LXX] - Lives of the Prophets 16:2
Malachi 1:1-2:7 - Haftarah Toldot [Ashkenaz and Sephard], Haftarah Toledot [Malachi 1:1-2:7]
Malachi 1:1-3:4 - Haftarah Toldot [Teimon]

[11] LXX *His messenger*

[12] Malachi 1:2 - Deuteronomy 4:37 7:6-7:8 10:15 32:8-32:14, Ecclesiastes.R 3:10, Esther.R 7:4, Exodus.R 1:1 49:1, Genesis 1:23 27:27-27:30 3:33 28:3-28:4 28:13-28:14 32:29-32:30 24:4, Genesis.R 80:7 86:1, Isaiah 41:8-41:9 19:4, Jeremiah 2:5 2:31 7:4, Leviticus.R 7:1, Liber Antiquitatum Biblicarum 32:5, Luke 10:29, Malachi 1:6-1:7 2:17 3:7-3:8 3:13-3:14, Mas.Gerim 4:3, Midrash Psalms 22:22, Midrash Tanchuma Mishpatim 17, Midrash Tanchuma Terumah 3 9, Numbers.R 8:2 12:4 17:3, Pesikta Rabbati 48:2, Romans 9:10-9:13 11:28-11:29, Sifre Devarim Devarim 24, Song of Songs.R 2:20 8:7 8:8, z.Bechukkotai 114b

Jacob's brother? Says the LORD; Yet I loved Jacob;

3¹ But Esau I hated, And made his mountains a desolation, And *gave his heritage to the jackals*² of the wilderness.

וְאֶת־עֵשָׂו שָׂנֵאתִי וָאָשִׂים אֶת־הָרָיו שְׁמָמָה וְאֶת־נַחֲלָתוֹ לְתַנּוֹת מִדְבָּר

4³ While Edom says: 'We are beaten down, But we will return and build the ruined places;' Thus says the LORD of hosts: They shall build, but I will throw down; and they shall be called the border of wickedness, and the people whom the LORD denouces forever.

כִּי־תֹאמַר אֱדוֹם רֻשַּׁשְׁנוּ וְנָשׁוּב וְנִבְנֶה חֳרָבוֹת כֹּה אָמַר יְהוָה צְבָאוֹת הֵמָּה יִבְנוּ וַאֲנִי אֶהֱרוֹס וְקָרְאוּ לָהֶם גְּבוּל רִשְׁעָה וְהָעָם אֲשֶׁר־זָעַם יְהוָה עַד־עוֹלָם

5⁴ And your eyes shall see, and you shall say: 'The LORD is great beyond the border of Israel.'

וְעֵינֵיכֶם תִּרְאֶינָה וְאַתֶּם תֹּאמְרוּ יִגְדַּל יְהוָה מֵעַל לִגְבוּל יִשְׂרָאֵל

6⁵ A son honors his father, and a servant his master; if then I am a father, where is My honor? And if I am a master, where is My fear? Says the LORD of hosts to you, O priests, who despise My name. And you say: 'How have we despised Your name?'

בֵּן יְכַבֵּד אָב וְעֶבֶד אֲדֹנָיו וְאִם־אָב אָנִי אַיֵּה כְבוֹדִי וְאִם־אֲדוֹנִים אָנִי אַיֵּה מוֹרָאִי אָמַר יְהוָה צְבָאוֹת לָכֶם הַכֹּהֲנִים בּוֹזֵי שְׁמִי וַאֲמַרְתֶּם בַּמֶּה בָזִינוּ אֶת־שְׁמֶךָ

7⁶ You offer polluted bread on my altar. And you say: 'How have we polluted you?' In this way you say: 'The LORD's table is *contemptible*⁷.'

מַגִּישִׁים עַל־מִזְבְּחִי לֶחֶם מְגֹאָל וַאֲמַרְתֶּם בַּמֶּה גֵאַלְנוּךָ בֶּאֱמָרְכֶם שֻׁלְחַן יְהוָה נִבְזֶה הוּא

8⁸ And when you offer the blind as a sacrifice, is it not evil? And when you offer the lame and sick, is it not evil? Present it now to your governor; will he be pleased with you? Will he lift up your face? Says the LORD of hosts.

וְכִי־תַגִּשׁוּן עִוֵּר לִזְבֹּחַ אֵין רָע וְכִי תַגִּישׁוּ פִּסֵּחַ וְחֹלֶה אֵין רָע הַקְרִיבֵהוּ נָא לְפֶחָתֶךָ הֲיִרְצְךָ אוֹ הֲיִשָּׂא פָנֶיךָ אָמַר יְהוָה צְבָאוֹת

9⁹ And now, please, ask the favor of God so He may be gracious to us! This has been of your doing. Will He lift up your face? Says the LORD of hosts.

וְעַתָּה חַלּוּ־נָא פְנֵי־אֵל וִיחָנֵּנוּ מִיֶּדְכֶם הָיְתָה זֹּאת הֲיִשָּׂא מִכֶּם פָּנִים אָמַר יְהוָה צְבָאוֹת

Malachi 1:2-3 - Midrash Tanchuma Ekev 3, z.Tzav 32a

¹ Malachi 1:3 - Deuteronomy 21:15-16, Ecclesiastes.R 4:3, Ezekiel 25:13-14 35:3-4 35:7-8 36:3-4 12:7 12:9 36:14-15, Genesis 29:30-29:31, Genesis.R 63:7, Isaiah 13:21-22 34:9-14 11:7, Jeremiah 9:12 1:10 49:16-18 3:37, Joel 4:19, Luke 14:26, Midrash Psalms 7:6 9:14 11:4, Midrash Tanchuma Kedoshim 2, Midrash Tanchuma Massei 3, Midrash Tanchuma Terumah 3, Midrash Tanchuma Vayigash 2, Numbers.R 23:4, Obadiah 1:10 1:18-21, Pesikta Rabbati 48:2, Song of Songs.R 1:23, z.Tzav 32a

² LXX *laid waste his borders, and made his heritage as dwellings*

³ Malachi 1:4 - Amos 6:2, b.Avodah Zara [Tosefot] 2b, b.Sheviit [Rashi] 6a, Ezekiel 11:10 1:14 11:9, Genesis.R 63:14, Isaiah 9:10-9:11 10:4 10:15-10:16 11:14 10:5 10:10 63:1-6, James 4:13-16, Jeremiah 7:18, Job 9:4 12:14 10:29, Lamentations 3:37 4:21-4:22, Malachi 1:3, Matthew 12:30, Midrash Psalms 9:7 9:9, Midrash Tanchuma Ki Tetze 9, Numbers.R 11:1 14:1, Pesikta de R'Kahana 3.5, Proverbs 21:30, Psalms 7:1 17:7, z.Vaetchanan 269b

⁴ Malachi 1:5 - 1 Samuel 12:16, 2 Chronicles 5:8, Deuteronomy 4:3 11:7, Ezekiel 14:16 14:23 39:21-22, Joshua 24:7, Luke 10:23-24, Micah 5:5, Numbers.R 11:1, Psalms 35:26-35:27 58:11-12 83:18-19

⁵ Malachi 1:6 - 1 Peter 1:17 2:17-19, 1 Samuel 2:28-30, 1 Timothy 6:1-2, b.Sanhedrin 96a, b.Succah [Rashi] 45b, Deuteronomy 5:16, Ein Yaakov Sanhedrin:96a, Ephesians 6:2, Exodus 4:22-23 20:12, Exodus.R 46:4, Ezekiel 22:26, HaMadrikh 35:10, Hosea 4:6 5:1 12:10, Isaiah 1:2 16:9, Jeremiah 2:21-22 5:30-31 23:11 7:10, John 13:13-17, Leviticus 19:3, Luke 6:36 6:46 10:29 18:20, Malachi 2:8 2:14-17 3:7-8 3:13-14, Mark 7:10 10:19, Matthew 6:9 6:14-15 7:21 15:4 15:6 19:19, Midrash Tanchuma Vayetze 13, Proverbs 6:11 6:17, Testament of Job 29:3, Titus 2:9-2:10, z.Bechukkotai 115b, z.Toledot 146b, z.Vayera 103a

⁶ Malachi 1:7 - 1 Corinthians 10:21 11:21-22 11:27, 1 Samuel 2:15-17, b.Ketubot [Rashi] 24b, Deuteronomy 15:21, Ezekiel 17:22, Leviticus 2:11 21:6, Malachi 1:8 1:12, Midrash Tanchuma Haazinu 7

⁷ LXX *polluted, and that which was set in it you have despised*

⁸ Malachi 1:8 - b.Avodah Zara [Tosefot] 6a, b.Bava Batra [Rashbam] 97ab, b.Bava Batra 97b, b.Chullin [Rashi] 23a, b.Chullin [Tosefot] 3a, b.Menachot [Rashi] 64a, b.Rosh Hashanah [Tosefot] 6b, b.Sotah 14b, b.Succah 50a, b.Zevachim [Rashi] 69a 74b 85b, b.Zevachim 85a, Deuteronomy 15:21, Guide for the Perplexed 3:46, Hosea 8:13, Jeremiah 14:10, Job 18:8, Leviticus 22:19-25, Malachi 1:10 1:13-14, Mesillat Yesharim 19:Honoring-Hashem-Beautify-Mitzvot, Psalms 20:4, Siman 77:5, y.Avodah Zarah 1:5, z.Emor 91a

⁹ Malachi 1:9 - 1 Peter 1:17, 2 Chronicles 6:27, Acts 19:15-16, Ecclesiastes.R 3:11, Exodus 8:11, Exodus.R 43:3, Guide for the Perplexed 3:11, Hebrews 7:26-27, Jeremiah 2:19 3:18, Joel 1:13-14 2:17, John 9:31, Lamentations 2:19, mt.Hilchot Teshuvah 5:4 5:4, Romans 2:11, Saadia Opinions 4:4, Zechariah 3:1-5

מִי גַם־בָּכֶם וְיִסְגֹּר דְּלָתַיִם וְלֹא־תָאִירוּ מִזְבְּחִי
חִנָּם אֵין־לִי חֵפֶץ בָּכֶם אָמַר יְהוָה צְבָאוֹת וּמִנְחָה
לֹא־אֶרְצֶה מִיֶּדְכֶם

10[1]   Oh, that there was one among you who would shut the doors, that you might not kindle fire on my altar in vain! I have no pleasure in you, says the LORD of hosts, nor will I accept an offering from your hand.

כִּי מִמִּזְרַח־שֶׁמֶשׁ וְעַד־מְבוֹאוֹ גָּדוֹל שְׁמִי בַּגּוֹיִם
וּבְכָל־מָקוֹם מֻקְטָר מֻגָּשׁ לִשְׁמִי וּמִנְחָה טְהוֹרָה
כִּי־גָדוֹל שְׁמִי בַּגּוֹיִם אָמַר יְהוָה צְבָאוֹת

11[2]   For from the rising of the sun to the going down of the same, My name is great among the nations; and in every place *offerings are*[3] presented to My name, pure oblations; for My name is great among the nations, says the LORD of hosts.

וְאַתֶּם מְחַלְּלִים אוֹתוֹ בֶּאֱמָרְכֶם שֻׁלְחַן אֲדֹנָי מְגֹאָל
הוּא וְנִיבוֹ נִבְזֶה אָכְלוֹ

12[4]   But you profane it, when you say: 'The table of the LORD is polluted, and the fruit, the food, is contemptible.'

וַאֲמַרְתֶּם הִנֵּה מַתְּלָאָה וְהִפַּחְתֶּם אוֹתוֹ אָמַר יְהוָה
צְבָאוֹת וַהֲבֵאתֶם גָּזוּל וְאֶת־הַפִּסֵּחַ וְאֶת־הַחוֹלֶה
וַהֲבֵאתֶם אֶת־הַמִּנְחָה הַאֶרְצֶה אוֹתָהּ מִיֶּדְכֶם אָמַר
יְהוָה

13[5]   You say also: 'Behold, how wearisome is it[6]!' And you have scoffed at it, says the LORD of hosts; and you have brought *what was taken by violence*[7], and the lame, and the sick; thus you bring the offering; should I accept this from your hand? Says the LORD.

וְאָרוּר נוֹכֵל וְיֵשׁ בְּעֶדְרוֹ זָכָר וְנֹדֵר וְזֹבֵחַ מָשְׁחָת
לַאדֹנָי כִּי מֶלֶךְ גָּדוֹל אָנִי אָמַר יְהוָה צְבָאוֹת וּשְׁמִי
נוֹרָא בַּגּוֹיִם

14[8]   But cursed is he who *deals craftily*[9], where he has in his flock a male, and vows, and sacrifices to the Lord a blemished thing; for I am a great King, says the LORD of hosts, and My name is *feared*[10] among the nations.

Malachi – Chapter 2

וְעַתָּה אֲלֵיכֶם הַמִּצְוָה הַזֹּאת הַכֹּהֲנִים

1[11]   And now, this commandment is for you, O you priests.

אִם־לֹא תִשְׁמְעוּ וְאִם־לֹא תָשִׂימוּ עַל־לֵב לָתֵת
כָּבוֹד לִשְׁמִי אָמַר יְהוָה צְבָאוֹת וְשִׁלַּחְתִּי בָכֶם

2[12]   If you will not listen, and if you will not lay it to heart, to give glory to My name, says the

---

[1] Malachi 1:10 - 1 Corinthians 9:13, 1 Peter 5:2, 4Q266 frag 3 2.19, Amos 5:21-24, b.Bechorot [Rashi] 31a, Cairo Damascus 6:13, Cairo Damascus 6.11-14, Cairo Damascus 6.13, Hebrews 10:38, Hosea 5:6, Isaiah 1:11-15 56:11-12, Jastrow 32b, Jeremiah 6:13 6:20 8:10 14:12, Job 1:9-11, John 10:12, Micah 3:11, Midrash Tanchuma Naso 10, mt.Hilchot Teshuvah 7:7, Numbers.R 11:6, Pesikta de R'Kahana 16.8, Pesikta Rabbati 29/30B:2, Philippians 2:21, t.Demai 2:8

[2] Malachi 1:11 - 1 Timothy 2:8, Acts 10:30-35 15:17-18, Amos 9:12, b.Bava Metzia [Rashi] 114b, b.Menachot [Rashi] 110a, b.Menachot 110a, Guide for the Perplexed 1:36, Hebrews 13:15-16, Hellenistic Synagogal Prayers 2:7, Isaiah 11:9-10 24:14-16 42:10-12 21:6 45:22-23 49:6-7 49:22-23 54:1-3 6:5 11:19 60:1-11 60:16-22 66:19-20, Jastrow 1352b, John 4:21-23, Leviticus.R 7:3 9:1, Luke 1:10, Malachi 1:14, Matthew 6:9-10 4:19, Micah 5:5, Midrash Psalms 19:11 48:1, Midrash Tanchuma Acharei Mot 9, Midrash Tanchuma Ekev 3, Midrash Tanchuma Vayikra 8, Numbers.R 13:4 16:27, Odes of Solomon 10:5, Pesikta de R'Kahana 6.3, Pesikta Rabbati 16:7 48:1, Philippians 4:18, Psalms 22:28-32 50:1 67:3 72:11-17 98:1-3 17:3 21:2, Revelation 5:8 8:3-4 11:15 15:4, Romans 12:1 15:9-11 15:16, Zechariah 8:7 8:20-23, Zephaniah 2:11 3:9

[3] LXX *incense is*

[4] Malachi 1:12 - 2 Samuel 12:14, Amos 2:7, Daniel 5:3-4, Ezekiel 36:21-23, Guide for the Perplexed 3:19, Malachi 1:6-8 1:13 2:8, Midrash Tanchuma Ekev 3, Numbers 11:4-8, Per Massorah: Soferim altered "Hashem" to "Adonai", Romans 2:24

[5] Malachi 1:13 - 1 Samuel 2:29, Amos 5:21-23 8:5, b.Bava Batra [Tosefot] 26b, b.Bava Kamma 67a, b.Succah 30a, Deuteronomy 15:21, Ezekiel 4:14 20:31, Isaiah 1:12 43:22-23 9:6, Jeremiah 7:9-7:11 7:21-24, Leviticus 22:8 22:19-23, Malachi 1:7-8 2:13, Mark 14:4-5 14:37-38, Matthew 6:1-2 6:5 6:16, Mekilta de R'Ishmael Shirata 6:13, Micah 6:3, Midrash Tanchuma Beshallach 16, mt.Shemonah Perakim 8:6, Sifre.z Numbers Beha'alotcha 12:12

[6] This is #14 of the Eighteen Emendations of the Sopherim. The text should read "*You have snuffed at Me*" but אותי [*oti at me*] was changed to אותו [*oto at it*], y.Gittin 5:6, z.Vaetchanan 269b, Zechariah 7:5-6

[7] LXX *in torn victims*

[8] Malachi 1:14 - 1 Timothy 6:15, 2 Corinthians 8:12, 5Q10 frag 1 l.1-3, Acts 5:1-10, Daniel 4:34 9:4, Deuteronomy 4:58, Ecclesiastes 5:5-6, Genesis 3:12, Hebrews 12:29, Isaiah 9:15, Jeremiah 10:10 24:10, Joshua 7:11-12, Leviticus 22:18-21, Luke 12:1-2 12:46, Malachi 1:8 1:11 3:9, Mark 12:41-44 14:8, Matthew 5:35 24:51, Mesillat Yesharim 19:Honoring-Hashem-Beautify-Mitzvot, mt.Hilchot Issurei Mizbeiach 7:1, mt.Hilchot Maaseh haKorbanot 16:4, Per Massorah: Soferim altered "Hashem" to "Adonai", Psalms 47:3 48:3 68:36 76:13 95:3, Revelation 15:4 21:8, Zechariah 14:9

[9] LXX *had the power*

[10] LXX *glorious*

[11] Malachi 2:1 - Hosea 5:1, Jeremiah 13:13, Lamentations 4:13, Malachi 1:6

[12] Malachi 2:2 - 1 Peter 4:11, Abnormal Dagesh in ל on עַל־לֵב, Deuteronomy 28:15-68 30:17-18, Ezekiel 3:7, Exodus.R 51:5, Haggai 1:6 1:9 2:16-17, Hosea 4:7-10 9:11-14, Isaiah 30:8-13 18:25 23:7 9:11, Jeremiah 6:16-20 13:16-17 25:4-9 10:17, Joshua 7:19,

אֶת־הַמְּאֵרָה וְאָרוֹתִי אֶת־בִּרְכוֹתֵיכֶם וְגַם אָרוֹתִיהָ
כִּי אֵינְכֶם שָׂמִים עַל־לֵב

הִנְנִי גֹעֵר לָכֶם אֶת־הַזֶּרַע וְזֵרִיתִי פֶרֶשׁ עַל־פְּנֵיכֶם
פֶּרֶשׁ חַגֵּיכֶם וְנָשָׂא אֶתְכֶם אֵלָיו   3²

וִידַעְתֶּם כִּי שִׁלַּחְתִּי אֲלֵיכֶם אֵת הַמִּצְוָה הַזֹּאת
לִהְיוֹת בְּרִיתִי אֶת־לֵוִי אָמַר יְהוָה צְבָאוֹת   4⁴

בְּרִיתִי הָיְתָה אִתּוֹ הַחַיִּים וְהַשָּׁלוֹם וָאֶתְּנֵם־לוֹ
מוֹרָא וַיִּירָאֵנִי וּמִפְּנֵי שְׁמִי נִחַת הוּא   5⁵

תּוֹרַת אֱמֶת הָיְתָה בְּפִיהוּ וְעַוְלָה לֹא־נִמְצָא
בִשְׂפָתָיו בְּשָׁלוֹם וּבְמִישׁוֹר הָלַךְ אִתִּי וְרַבִּים
הֵשִׁיב מֵעָוֹן   6⁶

כִּי־שִׂפְתֵי כֹהֵן יִשְׁמְרוּ־דַעַת וְתוֹרָה יְבַקְשׁוּ מִפִּיהוּ
כִּי מַלְאַךְ יְהוָה־צְבָאוֹת הוּא   7⁷

וְאַתֶּם סַרְתֶּם מִן־הַדֶּרֶךְ הִכְשַׁלְתֶּם רַבִּים בַּתּוֹרָה
שִׁחַתֶּם בְּרִית הַלֵּוִי אָמַר יְהוָה צְבָאוֹת   8⁸

וְגַם־אֲנִי נָתַתִּי אֶתְכֶם נִבְזִים וּשְׁפָלִים לְכָל־הָעָם
כְּפִי אֲשֶׁר אֵינְכֶם שֹׁמְרִים אֶת־דְּרָכַי וְנֹשְׂאִים
פָּנִים בַּתּוֹרָה   9⁹

LORD of hosts, then will I send the curse upon you, and I will curse your blessings; yes, I curse them[1] because you do not lay it to heart.

Behold, I will rebuke the seed for your hurt, And will spread dung on your faces, the dung of your sacrifices; and you shall be taken away unto it[3].   3²

Know then that I have sent this commandment to you, so My covenant might be with Levi, Says the LORD of hosts.   4⁴

My covenant was with him for life and peace, and I gave them to him, and of fear, and he feared Me, and was afraid of My name.   5⁵

The law of truth was in his mouth, and unrighteousness was not found in his lips; he walked with Me in peace and uprightness, and turned many away from iniquity.   6⁶

For the priest's lips should keep knowledge, and they should seek the law at his mouth; for he is the messenger of the LORD of hosts.   7⁷

But you turned aside from the way; you have caused many to stumble in the law; you have corrupted the covenant of Levi, says the LORD of hosts.   8⁸

Therefore, have I also made you contemptible and base before all the people, because you   9⁹

Leviticus 26:14-46, Luke 17:18 23:28-30, Malachi 3:9, Psalms 69:23 81:12-13 109:7-15, Revelation 14:7 16:9, Zechariah 1:3-1:6 7:11-14

[1] LXX *and I will scatter your blessing, and it shall not exist among you*

[2] Malachi 2:3 - 1 Corinthians 4:13, 1 Kings 14:10, 1 Samuel 2:29-30, 2 Kings 9:36-37, b.Shabbat 151b, Ecclesiastes.R 12:6, Exodus 5:14, Exodus.R 51:5, Gates of Repentance 1.031, Jeremiah 8:2, Job 20:7, Joel 1:17, Leviticus.R 18:1, Life of Adam and Eve [Apocalypse] 6:2, Luke 14:35, Malachi 2:9, mt.Hilchot Deot 5:1, mt.Hilchot Megillah v'Chanukah 2:17, mt.Hilchot Shevitat Yom Tov 6:18, Nahum 3:6, Psalms 83:11, Siman 103:9, y.Moed Katan 3:5, y.Yevamot 16:3, z.Vayakhel 199b, z.Yitro 88b

[3] LXX *Behold, I turn my back upon you, and I will scatter dung upon your faces, the dung of your festivals, and I will carry you away at the same time*

[4] Malachi 2:4 - 1 Kings 22:25, Ezekiel 20:38-41 9:33 14:23 44:9-16, Isaiah 1:24-28 2:11 3:9, Jeremiah 4:9, John 15:2, Luke 10:11, Matthew 3:12, Nehemiah 13:29, Numbers 3:12 3:45

[5] Malachi 2:5 - b.Berachot 12a, Deuteronomy 33:8-33:11, Ein Yaakov Berachot:12a, Ein Yaakov Midrash Shmuel 1:1, Exodus 32:26-32:29, Exodus.R 38:8, Ezekiel 10:25 13:26, Jastrow 897b, Leviticus.R 3:6 21:10, Malachi 2:5-7, Mesillat Yesharim 19:Chassidut-Carrying-Out-Deeds, Midrash Psalms 19:15 25:12, Midrash Tanchuma Bamidbar 24, Midrash Tanchuma Pinchas 1, Numbers 3:45 8:15 16:9-16:10 18:8-18:24 25:12-25:13, Numbers.R 11:7 21:3, Pesikta Rabbati 47:4, Pirkei de R'Eliezer 47, Psalms 106:30-106:31, Sifre.z Numbers Naso 6:26, Song of Songs.R 7:5, Tanna Devei Eliyahu 3, Verse for names א-ב [Pisukim Lesheimot Anoshim], y.Berachot 1:5 2:4 4:1, y.Yoma 7:3, z.Terumah 128b

[6] Malachi 2:6 - 1 Thessalonians 1:9-10, 2 Timothy 2:15-16, Acts 2:18, Avot de R'Natan 12, b.Sanhedrin [Tosefot] 6b, b.Sanhedrin 6b, Bahir 137, Daniel 12:3, Deuteronomy 9:10, Ein Yaakov Sanhedrin:6b, Exodus.R 5:1 5:9 15:14 38:5, Ezekiel 44:23-24, Genesis 5:21-24 6:9 17:1, Genesis.R 99 [Excl]:5, Hosea 4:6, James 5:19-20, Jeremiah 23:22, Leviticus.R 3:6 20:1, Luke 1:6 1:16-17 20:21, Mark 12:14, Mas.Kallah Rabbati 3:4, Matthew 22:16, Midrash Psalms 1:14 2:12 115:7, Midrash Tanchuma Shemini 5, Midrash Tanchuma Shemot 28, mt.Pirkei Avot 1:12, Pesikta de R'Kahana 5.4 26.1, Pesikta Rabbati 33:3, Psalms 37:30, Revelation 14:5, Sifre Devarim Nitzavim 305, t.Sanhedrin 1:2, Tanna Devei Eliyahu 3, Titus 1:7-9, y.Peah 1:1, y.Sanhedrin 1:1, z.Kedoshim 85b, z.Terumah 128b

[7] Malachi 2:7 - 1 Thessalonians 4:8, 2 Chronicles 17:8-17:9 6:22, 2 Corinthians 5:20, 2 Timothy 2:24-25, Acts 16:17, b.Chagigah 15b, b.Moed Katan 14a, b.Sanhedrin [Rashi] 6b, Deuteronomy 17:8-11 21:5 24:8, Ein Yaakov Chagigah:15a, Ein Yaakov Midrash Shmuel 1:3, Ein Yaakov Moed Katan:17a, Exodus.R 33:4 38:3, Ezra 7:10, Galatians 4:14, Haggai 1:13 2:11-13, Isaiah 18:19 20:26, Jeremiah 15:19 18:18, John 13:20 20:21, Leviticus 10:11, Leviticus.R 1:1 3:6 21:12, Malachi 3:1, Mas.Perek Hashalom 1:18, Mesillat Yesharim 26:Trait of Kedushah, Midrash Psalms 52:1 78:6, Midrash Tanchuma Metzora 1, Midrash Tanchuma Shelach 1, Midrash Tanchuma Shemini 5, mt.Hilchot Talmud Torah 4:1, mt.Pirkei Avot 5:13, Nehemiah 8:2-8, Numbers 3:21, Numbers.R 16:1, Pesikta Rabbati 15:4, z.Naso 145b

[8] Malachi 2:8 - 1 Samuel 2:17 2:24 2:30, b.Bechorot 26b, b.Kiddushin [Rashi] 6b, Daniel 9:5-9:6, Ezekiel 20:10, Hebrews 3:12, Isaiah 9:17 6:11 11:13, Jeremiah 17:5 17:13 18:15 23:11-23:15, Leviticus 21:15, Luke 11:45-11:46, Malachi 2:5 2:9-2:10, Matthew 15:2-15:5, mt.Hilchot Terumot 12:18, Nehemiah 13:29, Psalms 22:9 119:102, Romans 2:19-2:24 14:21, t.Demai 5:20

[9] Malachi 2:9 - 1 Kings 22:28, 1 Samuel 2:30, b.Taanit 20a, Daniel 12:2-12:3, Deuteronomy 1:17, Ezekiel 13:12-13:16 13:21, Galatians 2:6, Jeremiah 28:15-28:16 29:20-29:22 29:31-29:32, Luke 10:29 11:42 20:45-20:47, Malachi 2:3 2:8, Mark 7:8-7:14,

have not kept My ways, but respected persons in the law.

10[1] Do we not all have one father? Has not one God created us? Why do we, every man, deal treacherously against his brother, profaning the covenant of our fathers?

הֲלוֹא אָב אֶחָד לְכֻלָּנוּ הֲלוֹא אֵל אֶחָד בְּרָאָנוּ מַדּוּעַ נִבְגַּד אִישׁ בְּאָחִיו לְחַלֵּל בְּרִית אֲבֹתֵינוּ

11[2] Judah has dealt treacherously, and an abomination is committed in Israel and in Jerusalem; for Judah has profaned the holiness of the LORD, which He loves, and has married the *daughter*[3] of a strange god.

בָּגְדָה יְהוּדָה וְתוֹעֵבָה נֶעֶשְׂתָה בְיִשְׂרָאֵל וּבִירוּשָׁלָ͏ִם כִּי חִלֵּל יְהוּדָה קֹדֶשׁ יְהוָֹה אֲשֶׁר אָהֵב וּבָעַל בַּת־אֵל נֵכָר

12[4] May the LORD cut off the man who does this, *He who calls and He who answers*[5] out of the tents of Jacob, and he who offers an offering to the LORD of hosts.

יַכְרֵת יְהוָֹה לָאִישׁ אֲשֶׁר יַעֲשֶׂנָּה עֵר וְעֹנֶה מֵאָהֳלֵי יַעֲקֹב וּמַגִּישׁ מִנְחָה לַיהוָֹה צְבָאוֹת

13[6] And this further you do: you cover the altar of the LORD with tears, with weeping, and with sighing, *so much so, He no longer regards the offering*[7], nor receives it with good will from your hand[8].

וְזֹאת שֵׁנִית תַּעֲשׂוּ כַּסּוֹת דִּמְעָה אֶת־מִזְבַּח יְהוָֹה בְּכִי וַאֲנָקָה מֵאֵין עוֹד פְּנוֹת אֶל־הַמִּנְחָה וְלָקַחַת רָצוֹן מִיֶּדְכֶם

14[9] Yet you say: 'Why?' Because the LORD has been witness between you and the wife of your *youth, against whom you dealt treacherously*[10], she is your companion and the wife of your covenant.

וַאֲמַרְתֶּם עַל־מָה עַל כִּי־יְהוָֹה הֵעִיד בֵּינְךָ וּבֵין אֵשֶׁת נְעוּרֶיךָ אֲשֶׁר אַתָּה בָּגַדְתָּה בָּהּ וְהִיא חֲבֶרְתְּךָ וְאֵשֶׁת בְּרִיתֶךָ

15[11] And not one has done so who has exuberance of spirit! For what seeks the one? A seed given from God. Therefore, listen to your spirit, and let no one deal treacherously against the wife of his youth.

וְלֹא־אֶחָד עָשָׂה וּשְׁאָר רוּחַ לוֹ וּמָה הָאֶחָד מְבַקֵּשׁ זֶרַע אֱלֹהִים וְנִשְׁמַרְתֶּם בְּרוּחֲכֶם וּבְאֵשֶׁת נְעוּרֶיךָ אַל־יִבְגֹּד

Matthew 5:21-5:22 5:27-5:28 5:33-5:37 5:43-5:44 19:17-19:18 23:16-23:24, Micah 3:6-3:7, Midrash Tanchuma Tzav 2, Midrash Tanchuma Vayera 15, Proverbs 10:7, Ralbag SOS 2, Romans 7:7-7:10

[1] Malachi 2:10 - 1 Corinthians 6:6-8 8:6, 1 Thessalonians 4:6, 4Q265 4 1-2, 4Q265 frag 3 ll.1-2, Acts 7:2 7:26 17:25, Ephesians 4:6 4:25, Exodus 19:5 34:10-16, Ezekiel 9:24, Ezra 9:11-9:14 10:2-3, Hebrews 12:9, Isaiah 19:1 19:7 19:15 20:2 3:2 15:16 16:9, Jeremiah 9:5-9:6, Job 7:15, John 8:39 8:41 8:53 8:56, Joshua 23:12-16 24:3, Luke 1:73 3:8, Malachi 1:6 2:8 2:11 2:14-15, Matthew 3:9 10:21 22:16, Micah 7:2-6, Nehemiah 13:29, Psalms 4:3, Romans 4:1 9:10, Tanya Likutei Aramim §44, Testament of Job 29:3 Malachi 2:10-17 - 4QXIIa

[2] Malachi 2:11 - 1 Kings 11:1-8, 2 Corinthians 6:14-18, b.Megillah 15a, b.Sanhedrin 82a, Deuteronomy 7:3-6 14:2 33:26-29, Ein Yaakov Megillah:15a, Exodus 19:5-6, Ezekiel 18:13 22:11, Ezra 9:1-2 9:12 10:2, Genesis 6:1-2, Genesis.R 100 [Excl]:1, Hosea 6:7, Jeremiah 2:3 2:7-8 2:21-22 3:7-9 7:10, Judges 3:6, Leviticus 18:24-30 20:26, Mekilta de R'Ishmael Nezikin 3:91, mt.Hilchot Issurei Biah 12:6, Nehemiah 13:23-29, Psalms 10:28 106:34-39, Revelation 21:8, Sifre Devarim Ha'azinu Hashamayim 306, Sifre Devarim Nitzavim 306

[3] 4QXIIa *house*

[4] Malachi 2:12 - 1 Chronicles 1:8, 1 Samuel 2:31-34 3:14 15:22-23, 2 Timothy 3:13, Amos 5:22, b.Sanhedrin 82a, b.Shabbat 55b, Ein Yaakov Shabbat:55b, Ezekiel 14:10 24:21, Ezra 10:18-19, Gates of Repentance 3.133, Genesis 4:3-5, Hosea 4:4-5, Isaiah 9:15-17 24:1-2 13:8 18:3, Jastrow 1057a, Joshua 23:12-13, Leviticus 18:29 20:3, Malachi 1:10 2:10, Mas.Derek Eretz Rabbah 1:11, Matthew 15:14, mt.Hilchot Issurei Biah 12:6, Nehemiah 13:28-29, Numbers 15:30-31 24:5, Revelation 19:20, y.Shabbat 3:7, Zechariah 12:7

[5] 4QXIIa *one who witnesses or answers*

[6] Malachi 2:13 - 1 Samuel 1:9-10, 2 Samuel 13:19-20, b.Gittin 90b, b.Sanhedrin 22a, Deuteronomy 15:9 2:14, Ecclesiastes 4:1, Ein Yaakov Gittin:90b, Ein Yaakov Sanhedrin:21b, Genesis.R 18:5 54:3, Isaiah 1:11-1:15, Jastrow 1554a, Jeremiah 6:20 14:12, Nehemiah 8:9-8:12, Proverbs 15:8 21:27, Psalms 78:34-78:37

[7] 4QXIIa *because of troubles, does he still regards the offering and accept*

[8] LXX reads *And these things which I hated, you did: you covered with tears the altar of the LORD, and with weeping and groaning because of troubles: is it meet for me to have respect to your sacrifice, or to receive anything from your hands as welcome?*

[9] Malachi 2:14 - 1 Samuel 12:5, b.Gittin 90b, b.Sanhedrin 22a, Ecclesiastes 9:9, Ein Yaakov Gittin:90b, Ein Yaakov Sanhedrin:21b, Ezekiel 16:8, Genesis 2:18 7:50, Isaiah 6:6 10:3, Jeremiah 8:12 18:5, Judges 11:10, Malachi 1:6-1:7 2:15 3:5 3:8, Micah 1:2, Proverbs 2:17 5:18-5:19 6:20, Song of Songs 1:15, This is the middle verse of the book of Malachi per the Massorah

[10] 4QXIIa *youth*

[11] Malachi 2:15 - 1 Corinthians 7:2 7:14, 1 Timothy 3:4-5 3:11-12, 2 Corinthians 6:18, Acts 3:25, Deuteronomy 7:4, Ecclesiastes 12:7, Ephesians 6:4, Ezra 9:4, Genesis 1:27 2:7 2:20-24 6:2 24:3-7 24:44 26:34-35 3:46 28:2-4, Hosea 2:1, James 1:14-15, Jeremiah 2:21, Job 3:3, John 20:22, Malachi 2:14, Mark 10:6-8, Matthew 5:28-29 15:19 19:4-6, Nehemiah 13:24, Proverbs 4:23 6:25 7:25, Titus 1:6

כִּי־שָׂנֵא שַׁלַּח אָמַר יְהֹוָה אֱלֹהֵי יִשְׂרָאֵל וְכִסָּה חָמָס עַל־לְבוּשׁוֹ אָמַר יְהֹוָה צְבָאוֹת וְנִשְׁמַרְתֶּם בְּרוּחֲכֶם וְלֹא תִבְגֹּדוּ

16[1]

For I hate sending away[2], says the LORD, the God of Israel, *And he who covers his garment[3]* with violence, says the LORD of hosts; Therefore, listen to your spirit, so you will not deal treacherously[4].

הוֹגַעְתֶּם יְהֹוָה בְּדִבְרֵיכֶם וַאֲמַרְתֶּם בַּמָּה הוֹגָעְנוּ בֶּאֱמָרְכֶם כָּל־עֹשֵׂה רָע טוֹב בְּעֵינֵי יְהֹוָה וּבָהֶם הוּא חָפֵץ אוֹ אַיֵּה אֱלֹהֵי הַמִּשְׁפָּט

17[5]

You have wearied the *LORD[6]* with your words. Yet you say: 'How have we wearied Him?' In that you say: 'Everyone who does evil is good in the sight of the LORD, and He enjoys them; or where is the God of justice?'

Malachi – Chapter 3[7]

הִנְנִי שֹׁלֵחַ מַלְאָכִי וּפִנָּה־דֶרֶךְ לְפָנָי וּפִתְאֹם יָבוֹא אֶל־הֵיכָלוֹ הָאָדוֹן אֲשֶׁר־אַתֶּם מְבַקְשִׁים וּמַלְאַךְ הַבְּרִית אֲשֶׁר־אַתֶּם חֲפֵצִים הִנֵּה־בָא אָמַר יְהֹוָה צְבָאוֹת

1[8]

[9]Behold, I send My messenger, and he shall clear the way before Me; and the Lord, whom you seek, will suddenly come to His temple, and the *messenger[10]* of the covenant, in whom you delight, behold, he [11]comes, says the LORD of hosts.

וּמִי מְכַלְכֵּל אֶת־יוֹם בּוֹאוֹ וּמִי הָעֹמֵד בְּהֵרָאוֹתוֹ כִּי־הוּא כְּאֵשׁ מְצָרֵף וּכְבֹרִית מְכַבְּסִים

2[12]

But who can *endure the day of his coming[13]*? And who can stand when he appears? For he is like a refiner's fire, and *like fullers' soap[14]*;

וְיָשַׁב מְצָרֵף וּמְטַהֵר כֶּסֶף וְטִהַר אֶת־בְּנֵי־לֵוִי וְזִקַּק אֹתָם כַּזָּהָב וְכַכָּסֶף וְהָיוּ לַיהֹוָה מַגִּישֵׁי מִנְחָה בִּצְדָקָה:

3[15]

And he shall sit *as a refiner and purifier of silver[16]*; and he shall purify the sons of Levi, and purge them as gold and silver; and there shall be those who shall offer to the LORD offerings in righteousness.

---

[1] Malachi 2:16 - 4QXIIa "'But if you should hate your wife and put her away ' says Hashem God of Israel" vs. "'For I hate putting away ' says Hashem the God of Israel", b.Gittin 90b, Deuteronomy 24:1-24:4, Ein Yaakov Gittin:90b, Genesis.R 18:5, Isaiah 4:20 2:1 11:6, Luke 16:18, Mark 10:2-10:12, Matthew 5:31-5:32 19:3-19:9, Micah 7:2-7:3, Proverbs 4:13, y.Kiddushin 1:1

[2] 4QXIIa *For if you hate divorce*

[3] 4QXIIa *they cover my garment*

[4] LXX reads *But if you should hate your wife and put her away, says the LORD God of Israel, then ungodliness shall cover your thoughts, says the LORD Almighty: therefore take heed of your spirit, and do not forsake them*

[5] Malachi 2:17 - 1 Samuel 2:3, 2 Peter 3:3-4, Amos 2:13, Deuteronomy 8:4, Ecclesiastes 8:11, Exodus.R 13:1 30:14, Ezekiel 8:12 9:9 16:43, Gates of Repentance 3.209, Isaiah 1:14 5:18-20 7:13 6:18 19:24, Jastrow 563a, Jeremiah 15:6, Job 34:5-9 10:17 10:36 12:17, Malachi 1:6-7 2:14 3:8 3:13-15, Matthew 11:18-19, Midrash Psalms 39:1, mt.Shemonah Perakim 8:6, Psalms 10:12-14 73:3-15 95:9-10, Shemonah Perakim VIII, z.Naso 146b, Zephaniah 1:12

[6] 4QXIIa *God*

[7] Malachi 3 - 4QXIIa

[8] Malachi 3:1 - Acts 7:38 13:24-13:25 19:4, Deuteronomy.R 4:11, Exodus 23:20, Exodus.R 32:9, Genesis 48:15-48:16, Haggai 2:7-2:9, Hosea 12:5-12:7, Isaiah 7:14 9:7 40:3-40:5 15:9, John 1:6-1:7 1:15-1:23 1:33-1:34 2:14-2:16 3:28-3:30, Luke 1:16-1:17 1:76 2:11 2:21-2:32 2:38 2:46 3:3-3:6 7:19-7:20 7:26-7:28 19:47, Malachi 2:7 3:23, Mark 1:2-1:3, Matthew 3:1-3:3 11:10-11:11 17:10-17:13, Midrash Tanchuma Shelach 7, Numbers.R 16:11, Pirkei de R'Eliezer 29, Psalms 14:1, Saadia Opinions 8:6

[9] 4QXIIa adds *Therefore*

[10] LXX *angel*

[11] 4QXIIa adds *himself*

[12] Malachi 3:2 - 1 Corinthians 3:13-3:15, 1 Peter 2:7-2:8, 4 Maccabees 9:22, Acts 7:52-7:54, Amos 5:18-5:20, Apocalypse of Zephaniah 12:6, Epistle to Diognetus 7:4, Exodus.R 29:9, Ezekiel 22:14, Gates of Repentance 4.012, Hebrews 10:28-10:29 12:25, Isaiah 1:18 4:4, Jeremiah 2:22, John 6:42-6:44 8:41-8:48 8:55 9:39-9:41 15:22-15:24, Luke 2:34 3:9 3:17 7:23 11:37-11:47 11:52-11:54 21:36, Malachi 3:19, Mark 9:3, Matthew 3:7-3:12 21:31-21:44 23:13-23:35 1:10, Midrash Psalms 143:1, Midrash Tanchuma Vayigash 5, Psalms 2:7, Revelation 1:5-1:7 2:23 6:17 7:14 19:8, Romans 9:31-9:33 11:5-11:10, Saadia Opinions 8:6, Sibylline Oracles Fragment 8.4, Testament of Abraham 12:14 13:4, Zechariah 13:9

[13] 4QXIIa *endure them; they come*

[14] LXX *as the herb of fullers*

[15] Malachi 3:3 - 1 Peter 1:7 2:5 2:9 4:12-4:13, 2 Timothy 4:6, b.Kiddushin 71a, Daniel 12:10, Ein Yaakov Kiddushin:71a, Ephesians 5:26-5:27, Ezekiel 22:18-22:22 44:15-44:16, Hebrews 12:10 13:15-13:16, Hosea 14:4, Isaiah 1:25 24:10 13:6 66:19-66:21, Jeremiah 6:28-6:30 33:18-33:22, John 4:23-4:24, Leviticus.R 9:5 9:5 26:3, Luke 3:16, Malachi 1:6-1:11 2:1-2:8, Midrash Psalms 12:4, mt.Hilchot Melachim u'Michamoteihem 12:3, Numbers.R 12:4, Philippians 2:17 4:18, Proverbs 17:3 1:4, Psalms 4:6 50:14 50:23 66:10 69:31-69:32 107:21-107:22 20:17 141:1-141:2, Revelation 1:6 3:18 5:10, Romans 12:1 15:16, Titus 2:14, y.Kiddushin 4:1, y.Yevamot 8:3, Zechariah 13:9

[16] LXX *to melt and purify as it were silver, and as it were gold*

וְעָרְבָה לַיהוָה מִנְחַת יְהוּדָה וִירוּשָׁלָ͏ם כִּימֵי עוֹלָם וּכְשָׁנִים קַדְמֹנִיּוֹת

4[1] Then the offering of Judah and Jerusalem shall be pleasant to the LORD, as in the days of old, and as in ancient years.

וְקָרַבְתִּי אֲלֵיכֶם לַמִּשְׁפָּט וְהָיִיתִי עֵד מְמַהֵר בַּמְכַשְּׁפִים וּבַמְנָאֲפִים וּבַנִּשְׁבָּעִים לַשָּׁקֶר וּבְעֹשְׁקֵי שְׂכַר־שָׂכִיר אַלְמָנָה וְיָתוֹם וּמַטֵּי־גֵר וְלֹא יְרֵאוּנִי אָמַר יְהוָה צְבָאוֹת

5[2] And I will come near you for judgment; and I will be a swift witness against the sorcerers, and against the adulterers, and against false swearers; and against those who oppress the hireling in his wages, the widow, and the orphan, and who turn aside the stranger, and do not fear Me, says the LORD *of hosts*[3].

כִּי אֲנִי יְהוָה לֹא שָׁנִיתִי וְאַתֶּם בְּנֵי־יַעֲקֹב לֹא כְלִיתֶם

6[4] For I the LORD does not change; *and you, O sons of Jacob, are not consumed*[5].

לְמִימֵי אֲבֹתֵיכֶם סַרְתֶּם מֵחֻקַּי וְלֹא שְׁמַרְתֶּם שׁוּבוּ אֵלַי וְאָשׁוּבָה אֲלֵיכֶם אָמַר יְהוָה צְבָאוֹת וַאֲמַרְתֶּם בַּמֶּה נָשׁוּב

7[6] *From the days of your fathers you have turned aside from* [7]my ordinances, and have not kept them. Return unto Me, and I will return to you, Says the LORD of hosts. But you say: 'When shall we return?'

הֲיִקְבַּע אָדָם אֱלֹהִים כִּי אַתֶּם קֹבְעִים אֹתִי וַאֲמַרְתֶּם בַּמֶּה קְבַעֲנוּךָ הַמַּעֲשֵׂר וְהַתְּרוּמָה

8[8] Will a man *rob*[9] God? Yet you *rob*[10] Me. But you say: 'When have we *robbed*[11] You?' In tithes and terumah.

---

[1] Malachi 3:4 - 1 Chronicles 15:26 16:1-16:3 21:26 29:20-29:22, 2 Chronicles 1:6 7:1-7:3 7:10-7:12 8:12-8:14 29:31-29:36 30:21-30:27 31:20-31:21, Deuteronomy.R 4:11, Ezekiel 20:40-20:41 43:26-43:27, Isaiah 1:26-1:27 8:7, Jeremiah 2:2-2:3 30:18-30:20 31:24-31:25, Lamentations.R 5:21, Leviticus.R 7:4 19:3, Maamodot [every day], mt.Hilchot Beit Habechirah 8:12 8:12, mt.Hilchot Teshuvah 7:7 7:7, Numbers.R 17:4, Parshat Haketoress [Shacharit Korbanot] At the end of Amidah, Psalms 51:20, Song of Songs.R 5:14, Zechariah 8:3 14:20-14:21
Malachi 3:4-24 - Haftarah Shabbat Hagodol [Ashkenaz and Sephard], Shabbat Ha-Gadol Haftarah, Siman 115:5
[2] Malachi 3:5 - 1 Corinthians 6:9-6:10, 1 Thessalonians 4:6, b.Chagigah 5a, Deuteronomy 5:11 5:17-5:21 24:14-24:15 24:17 3:19, Ein Yaakov Chagigah:5a, Exodus 1:17 18:21 22:21-22:24, Ezekiel 22:6-22:12 34:20-34:22, Galatians 5:19-5:21, Genesis 20:11 18:18, Hebrews 10:30-10:31 13:4, James 5:4 5:8-5:9 5:12, Jastrow 1623a, Jeremiah 7:9-7:10 22:13-22:17 5:23, Jude 1:14-1:15, Leviticus 19:13 20:6 20:10 20:27, Luke 23:40, Malachi 2:14 2:17, Matthew 23:13-23:35, Mekhilta de R'Shimon bar Yochai Sanya 2:5, Mesillat Yesharim 4:To Acquire Zehirus, Micah 1:2, Midrash Psalms 82:1, Midrash Tanchuma Naso 5 7, Midrash Tanchuma Shoftim 8, Midrash Tanchuma Vayikra 7, mt.Hilchot Teshuvah 2:2, Nehemiah 5:15, Numbers.R 9:9 9:11 9:11 10:2, Pesikta de R'Kahana 24.15, Pesikta Rabbati 44:1, Proverbs 8:13 16:6 22:22-23 23:10-11, Psalms 36:2 50:3-7 81:9 96:13 98:9, Revelation 21:8 22:15, Romans 3:8, Sifre Devarim Ha'azinu Hashamayim 306, Sifre Devarim Nitzavim 306, Testament of Job 12:4, Zechariah 5:3-4
[3] 4QXIIa *God*
[4] Malachi 3:6 - 1 Samuel 15:29, 2 Thessalonians 2:13-14, b.Bava Batra [Rashbam] 115b, b.Sotah 9a, Ein Yaakov Sotah 9a, Exodus 3:14-15, Genesis 15:7 15:18 22:16, Guide for the Perplexed 1:11, Hebrews 6:18 13:8, Hosea 11:9, Isaiah 40:28-31 17:13 42:5-8 43:11-12 20:6 45:5-8, James 1:17, Jastrow 1605a, Jeremiah 8:27, Lamentations 3:22-23, Mas.Perek Hashalom 1:1, Mekhilta de R'Shimon bar Yochai Shirata 30:1, Mekilta de R'Ishmael Shirata 4:40, Midrash Tanchuma Nitzavim 1, Nehemiah 9:7-8, Numbers 23:19, Philippians 1:6, Psalms 78:38 78:57 6:27 7:17 105:7-10, Ralbag Wars 3:6, Revelation 1:8 22:13, Romans 5:10 8:28-32 11:28-29, Saadia Opinions 2:13, Sifre Devarim Ha'azinu Hashamayim 306, Sifre Devarim Nitzavim 306, Tanna Devei Eliyahu 5, Tanya Igeret Hakodesh §6, Tanya Likutei Aramim §20 §29, Tanya Shaar Hayichud §7, Two Letters Part II, z.Beshallach 52a, z.Terumah 176a
Malachi 3:6-7 - 4QXIIc
[5] Missing in LXX
[6] Malachi 3:7 - 1 Kings 8:47-49, Acts 7:51-52, b.Sanhedrin 97b, Bahir 67, Deuteronomy 4:29-31 9:7-21 30:1-4 7:20 31:27-29, Ecclesiastes.R 7:16, Ein Yaakov Sanhedrin:97b, Ezekiel 18:30-32 20:8 20:13 20:21 20:28, Hosea 14:3, Isaiah 55:6-7 17:2, James 4:8, Jeremiah 3:12-14 3:22 7:26, Lamentations.R Petichata D'Chakimei:25, Leviticus 26:40-42, Luke 11:48-51 15:16, Malachi 1:6 3:13, Matthew 23:27, Nehemiah 1:8-9 9:16-17 9:26 9:28-30, Pesikta Rabbati 44:9, Psalms 78:8-10, Romans 7:9 10:3 10:21, Ruth.R 6:2, Zechariah 1:3
[7] LXX *but you, the sons of Jacob, have not refrained from the iniquities of your fathers: you have perverted*
[8] Malachi 3:8 - b.Bava Batra [Rashbam] 60b, b.Rosh Hashanah 26b, Jastrow 1311a, Joshua 7:11, Leviticus 5:15-5:16 27:2-27:34, Luke 20:25, Malachi 1:8 1:13, Mark 12:17, Matthew 22:21, Midrash Psalms 57:2 137:6, Midrash Tanchuma Terumah 9, Nehemiah 13:4-13:14, Numbers 18:21-18:32, Proverbs 3:9-10, Psalms 29:2, Romans 2:22 13:7
[9] LXX *insult*
[10] LXX *insult*
[11] LXX *insulted*

בַּמְּאֵרָה אַתֶּם נֵאָרִים וְאֹתִי אַתֶּם קֹבְעִים הַגּוֹי כֻּלּוֹ

9[1]   *You are cursed with the curse[2], yet you, this whole nation, rob Me[3].*

הָבִיאוּ אֶת־כָּל־הַמַּעֲשֵׂר אֶל־בֵּית הָאוֹצָר וִיהִי טֶרֶף בְּבֵיתִי וּבְחָנוּנִי נָא בָּזֹאת אָמַר יְהוָה צְבָאוֹת אִם־לֹא אֶפְתַּח לָכֶם אֵת אֲרֻבּוֹת הַשָּׁמַיִם וַהֲרִיקֹתִי לָכֶם בְּרָכָה עַד־בְּלִי־דָי

10[4]   *Bring the whole tithe into the storehouse, so there may be food in My house, and try Me now with this[5], Says the LORD of hosts. If I will not open the windows of heaven to you and pour out a blessing, so there shall be more than sufficiency.*

וְגָעַרְתִּי לָכֶם בָּאֹכֵל וְלֹא־יַשְׁחִת לָכֶם אֶת־פְּרִי הָאֲדָמָה וְלֹא־תְשַׁכֵּל לָכֶם הַגֶּפֶן בַּשָּׂדֶה אָמַר יְהוָה צְבָאוֹת

11[6]   *And I will rebuke the devourer for your good, and he shall not destroy the fruits of your land; nor shall your vine cast its fruit before the time in the field[7], says the LORD of hosts.*

וְאִשְּׁרוּ אֶתְכֶם כָּל־הַגּוֹיִם כִּי־תִהְיוּ אַתֶּם אֶרֶץ חֵפֶץ אָמַר יְהוָה צְבָאוֹת

12[8]   *All nations shall call you happy[9]; for you shall be a delightful land, says the LORD of hosts.*

חָזְקוּ עָלַי דִּבְרֵיכֶם אָמַר יְהוָה וַאֲמַרְתֶּם מַה־נִּדְבַּרְנוּ עָלֶיךָ

13[10]   Your words have been all too strong against Me, says the LORD. Yet you say: 'When have we spoken against you?'

אֲמַרְתֶּם שָׁוְא עֲבֹד אֱלֹהִים וּמַה־בֶּצַע כִּי שָׁמַרְנוּ מִשְׁמַרְתּוֹ וְכִי הָלַכְנוּ קְדֹרַנִּית מִפְּנֵי יְהוָה צְבָאוֹת

14[11]   You have said: 'It is vain to serve God; and what profit is there that we have kept His charge, and that we have walked mournfully because of the LORD of hosts?

וְעַתָּה אֲנַחְנוּ מְאַשְּׁרִים זֵדִים גַּם־נִבְנוּ עֹשֵׂי רִשְׁעָה גַּם בָּחֲנוּ אֱלֹהִים וַיִּמָּלֵטוּ

15[12]   And now we call the proud happy; yes, they who work wickedness are built up; yes, they *try*[13] God, and are delivered.'

---

[1] Malachi 3:9 - b.Avodah Zara 36b, b.Bava Batra [Rashbam] 60b, b.Bava Batra 60b, b.Horayot 3b, Deuteronomy 28:15-28:19, Ein Yaakov Bava Batra:60b, Ein Yaakov Horayot:3b, Haggai 1:6-1:11 2:14-2:17, Isaiah 19:28, Joshua 7:12-7:13 22:20, Malachi 2:2, Midrash Psalms 137:6, One of the Eighteen Emendations [actually 27] of the Soferim. The text should say "*You have cursed with with a curse.*" The emendation in this verse involved replacing the מ in the [unemended] word מארים with a נ which renders an active word passive and detaches it from the rest of the sentence.

[2] 4QXIIa *you are looking upon appearances*

[3] LXX reads *and you surely look off from me, and you insult me*

[4] Malachi 3:10 - 1 Chronicles 2:20, 1 Kings 17:13-16, 2 Chronicles 31:4-19, 2 Corinthians 9:6-8, 2 Kings 7:2 7:19, b.Bava Batra [Rashbam] 60b, b.Ketubot [Tosefot] 26b, b.Makkot 23b, b.Shabbat 32b, b.Taanit 9a 22b, Deuteronomy 4:12, Ecclesiastes 11:3, Ein Yaakov Aggadot, Ein Yaakov Midrash Shmuel 1:3, Ein Yaakov Shabbat:32b, Esther.R 10:15, Gates of Repentance 3.30, Genesis 7:11, Haggai 2:19, Jastrow 172b, John 21:6-11, Leviticus 2:10 3:30, Leviticus.R 21:6 35:12, Luke 5:6-7 12:16-17, Matthew 6:33, Midrash Psalms 38:2, Midrash Tanchuma Vayigash 10, Nehemiah 10:34-40 12:44 12:47 13:5 13:10-13, Numbers 18:21, Numbers.R 8:4 12:11, Proverbs 3:9-10, Psalms 37:3, Saadia Opinions 7:2 7Variant:2, y.Berachot 9:5

[5] LXX *The year is completed, and you have brought all the produce into the storehouses; but there shall be the plunder in its house: return now on this behalf*

[6] Malachi 3:11 - Amos 4:9 7:1-3, Deuteronomy 11:14, Deuteronomy.R 3:6, Habakkuk 3:17, Haggai 2:17, Jeremiah 8:13, Joel 1:4 1:7 1:12 2:20 2:22, Zechariah 8:12

[7] LXX *And I will appoint food for you, and I will not destroy the fruit of your land; and your vine in the field shall not fail*

[8] Malachi 3:12 - 2 Chronicles 8:23, Daniel 8:9 11:41, Deuteronomy 4:6-7 8:7-10 11:12, Ecclesiastes.R 1:9 11:3 12:9, Ein Yaakov Shabbat 139a, Exodus.R 1:5, Genesis.R 80:7, Isaiah 13:9 14:4, Jastrow 491a, Jeremiah 9:9, Luke 1:48, Mas.Perek Hashalom 1:1, Mesillat Yesharim 19:Deveikut-Cleaving-to-Hashem, Midrash Psalms 9:2 36:8, Midrash Tanchuma Shemot 3, Numbers.R 14:10, Pesikta de R'Kahana 16.8, Pesikta Rabbati 29/30B:2, Psalms 72:17, Song of Songs.R 6:24, z.Bereshit 13a, Zechariah 8:23, Zephaniah 3:19-20

[9] LXX *blessed*

[10] Malachi 3:13 - 2 Chronicles 32:14-19, 2 Thessalonians 2:4, Esther.R 5:4, Exodus 5:2, Isaiah 5:19 28:14-15 13:23, Jeremiah 8:12, Job 34:7-8 16:8, Malachi 1:6-8 2:14 2:17 3:8, Midrash Psalms 2:1, Midrash Tanchuma Behar 3, Psalms 10:12, Romans 9:20 Malachi 3:13-18 - Guide for the Perplexed 3:19

[11] Malachi 3:14 - Isaiah 10:3, James 4:9, Job 21:14-15 22:17 10:9 11:3, Joel 2:12, mt.Shemonah Perakim 8:6, Numbers.R 11:1, Psalms 73:8-13, Shemonah Perachim VIII, Zechariah 7:3-6, Zephaniah 1:12

[12] Malachi 3:15 - 1 Corinthians 10:9, 1 Peter 5:5, Acts 5:9 12:21, Daniel 4:27 4:34 5:20-28 6:17, Ecclesiastes 9:1-2, Esther 5:10, Habakkuk 1:13-1:17, Hebrews 3:9, Jeremiah 7:10 12:1-2, Job 12:6 21:7-15 21:30 22:23, Malachi 2:17 3:19, Matthew 4:6-7, Midrash Psalms 30:4, Midrash Tanchuma Beshallach 10, mt.Shemonah Perakim 8:6, Numbers 14:22-23, Numbers.R 11:1, Proverbs 12:12, Psalms 10:4 49:19 73:12 78:18 78:41 78:56 95:9 10:14, Shemonah Perachim VIII

[13] LXX *resisted*

אָז נִדְבְּרוּ יִרְאֵי יְהוָה אִישׁ אֶת־רֵעֵהוּ וַיַּקְשֵׁב 16[1]
יְהוָה וַיִּשְׁמָע וַיִּכָּתֵב סֵפֶר זִכָּרוֹן לְפָנָיו לְיִרְאֵי
יְהוָה וּלְחֹשְׁבֵי שְׁמוֹ

Then[2] those who feared the LORD spoke one with another; and the LORD listened, and heard, and a book of remembrance was written before Him, for those who feared the LORD, and who thought upon His name.

וְהָיוּ לִי אָמַר יְהוָה צְבָאוֹת לַ‮יּ‬וֹם אֲשֶׁר אֲנִי עֹשֶׂה 17[3]
סְגֻלָּה וְחָמַלְתִּי עֲלֵיהֶם כַּאֲשֶׁר יַחְמֹל אִישׁ עַל־בְּנוֹ
הָעֹבֵד אֹתוֹ

And they shall be Mine, says the LORD of hosts, in the day that I make my own treasure; and I will spare them, as a man spares His own son who serves him.

וְשַׁבְתֶּם וּרְאִיתֶם בֵּין צַדִּיק לְרָשָׁע בֵּין עֹבֵד 18[4]
אֱלֹהִים לַאֲשֶׁר לֹא עֲבָדוֹ

[5]Then, shall you again discern between the righteous and the wicked, between he who serves God and he who doews not serves Him.

כִּי־הִנֵּה הַיּוֹם בָּא בֹּעֵר כַּתַּנּוּר וְהָיוּ כָל־זֵדִים 19[6]
וְכָל־עֹשֵׂה רִשְׁעָה קַשׁ וְלִהַט אֹתָם הַיּוֹם הַבָּא
אָמַר יְהוָה צְבָאוֹת אֲשֶׁר לֹא־יַעֲזֹב לָהֶם שֹׁרֶשׁ
וְעָנָף

For, behold, the day comes, it burns as a furnace; *and all the proud*[7], and all who work wickedness, shall be stubble; and the day that comes shall set them ablaze, says the LORD of hosts, so it shall leave them neither root nor branch.

וְזָרְחָה לָכֶם יִרְאֵי שְׁמִי שֶׁמֶשׁ צְדָקָה וּמַרְפֵּא 20[8]
בִּכְנָפֶיהָ וִיצָאתֶם וּפִשְׁתֶּם כְּעֶגְלֵי מַרְבֵּק

But to you who fear My name, the sun of righteousness shall arise with healing in *its*[9]

---

[1] Malachi 3:16 - 1 Kings 18:3 18:12, 1 Samuel 23:16-18, 1 Thessalonians 5:11 5:14, 2 Chronicles 6:7, 2 Samuel 7:1, 4 Ezra 6:20, 4Q418 frag 43-45 l.12, Acts 1:13 2:1 4:23-33 9:31 10:2, Apocalypse of Zephaniah 3:8, Avot de R'Natan 8, b.Berachot 6a, b.Kiddushin 40a, b.Makkot 11a, b.Shabbat 63a, Cairo Damascus 20:19-20, Cairo Damascus 20.19-20, Daniel 2:17-18 7:10, Deuteronomy 6:6-8, Ein Yaakov Berachot:6a, Ein Yaakov Kiddushin:40a, Ein Yaakov Shabbat:63a, Ephesians 5:19, Esther 2:23 4:5-17 6:1, Esther.R 6:14, Exodus.R 21:3, Ezekiel 9:4, Gates of Repentance 3.9 3.44, Genesis 22:12, Hebrews 3:13 4:12-13 10:24 12:15, Isaiah 2:3 2:8 2:10 17:6, Jastrow 295a 511a 1272b, Job 19:23-25 4:28, John 1:40-47 12:20-22, Leviticus.R 34:8, Luke 2:38 24:14-31, m.Avot 2:1 3:2 3:6, Malachi 3:5 3:20, Matthew 12:35-37 18:19-20, Mekhilta de R'Shimon bar Yochai Bachodesh 57:1, Mekhilta de R'Shimon bar Yochai Shirata 34:2, Mekilta de R'Ishmael Bahodesh 11:50, Midrash Psalms 30:5, Midrash Tanchuma Emor 16, Midrash Tanchuma Metzora 1, Midrash Tanchuma Vayakhel 7, mt.Hilchot Tumat Tzaraat 16:10, mt.Pirkei Avot 3:3 3:7, Numbers.R 9:20, Pesikta Rabbati 12:1, Pirkei Avot 3:3 3:7 [Shabbat afternoon], Proverbs 13:20, Psalms 10:5 16:3 20:8 33:18 34:16 56:9 66:16 73:15-17 94:19 8:33 111:10-112:1 119:63 19:4 3:11, Revelation 15:4 20:12, Ruth.R 4:5 5:6, Saadia Opinions 5:1 9:3, Song of Songs.R 8:19, Two Letters Part II, z.Mikketz 200b, z.Vaetchanan 265a, z.Vayakhel 200a 217a
Malachi 3:16-18 - 4Q253a frag 1 1.1-5

[2] 4QXIIa *So that*

[3] Malachi 3:17 - 1 Corinthians 3:22-23 6:20 15:23, 1 John 3:1-3, 1 Peter 1:13-16 2:9, 2 Corinthians 6:18, 2 Thessalonians 1:7-10, Deuteronomy 7:6 14:2 26:17-18, Exodus 19:5, Exodus.R 18:7, Ezekiel 16:8 36:27-28, Galatians 5:24, Guide for the Perplexed 1:54, Isaiah 26:20-21 62:3-4, Jeremiah 7:21 7:34 32:38-39, John 10:27-30 17:9-10 17:24, Lamentations.R 1:50 5:21, Malachi 1:6, Matthew 1:34, Mekilta de R'Ishmael Pisha 12:56, Midrash Psalms 31:9, Midrash Tanchuma Noach 12, Nehemiah 13:22, Pesikta de R'Kahana 6.4, Pesikta Rabbati 16:7, Psalms 103:8-13 15:4, Revelation 20:12-20:15, Romans 8:32, Saadia Opinions 9:1 10:15, Song of Songs 2:16, Titus 2:14, y.Megillah 1:5, y.Peah 1:1, Zechariah 13:9, Zephaniah 2:2

[4] Malachi 3:18 - 1 Thessalonians 1:9, 2 Thessalonians 1:5-10, Acts 16:17 3:23, b.Chagigah 9b, Cairo Damascus 20:20-21, Cairo Damascus 20.20-21, Daniel 3:17-26 12:1-3, Ecclesiastes.R 9:7, Ein Yaakov Chagigah:9b, Gates of Repentance 3.9, Genesis 18:25, Isaiah 3:10-3:11, Jeremiah 12:15, Job 6:29 17:10, Joel 2:14, John 12:26, Joshua 24:15, Malachi 1:4 3:14-3:15, Matthew 1:46, Midrash Psalms 31:9, Midrash Tanchuma Shelach 13, mt.Shemonah Perakim 8:6, Numbers.R 11:1 16:23, Psalms 58:11-12, Romans 1:9 2:5-6, Saadia Opinions 5:7 9:1, Shemonah Perachim VIII, Tanya Likutei Aramim §15, Zechariah 1:6

[5] LXX adds *then shall you return*

[6] Malachi 3:19 - 2 Peter 3:7, 2 Thessalonians 1:8, Amos 2:9, Apocalypse of Elijah 1:4, Avot de R'Natan 36, b.Avodah Zara 4a, b.Nedarim 8b, b.Sanhedrin 110b, Ecclesiastes.R 1:11, Ein Yaakov Avodah Zarah:4a, Ein Yaakov Nedarim:8b, Ein Yaakov Sanhedrin:110b, Exodus 15:7, Exodus.R 15:27 18:7, Ezekiel 7:10, Fragments of Pseudo-Greek Poets 6, Gates of Repentance 3.170, Genesis.R 6:6 21:9 26:6 48:8 78:5, Isaiah 2:12-17 5:24 16:24 17:2 23:14, Jastrow 569a, Job 18:16, Joel 2:1 3:4, Luke 19:43 21:20, Malachi 3:2 3:15 3:18 3:23, Mas.Derek Eretz Rabbah 2:9, Matthew 3:12, Midrash Psalms 19:13 21:5 40:4 41:4 52:8 149:6, Midrash Tanchuma Shoftim 9, Midrash Tanchuma Vayera 3, mt.Perek Chelek Intro:11, Nahum 1:5-6 1:10, Numbers.R 14:6, Obadiah 1:18, Pesikta de R'Kahana 52.1, Pesikta Rabbati 41:3, Psalms 21:10-11 119:119, Saadia Opinions 4:2 9:5 9:8, Song of Songs.R 7:8, z.Bereshit 53b, z.Vayechi 218b, Zechariah 14:1, Zephaniah 1:14 1:18

[7] LXX *and all the aliens*

[8] Malachi 3:20 - 1 John 2:8, 2 Peter 1:19 3:18, 2 Samuel 23:4, 2 Thessalonians 1:3, Acts 13:26 13:47 2:18, b.Avodah Zara 4a, b.Gittin [Rashi] 53a, b.Nedarim 8b, b.Taanit 8b, Birchat HaChammah Yiraucha, Ecclesiastes.R 1:11 9:6, Ein Yaakov Avodah Zarah:4a, Ein Yaakov Makkot:23b, Ein Yaakov Nedarim:8b, Ein Yaakov Taanit:8b, Ephesians 5:8-14, Exodus.R 15:21 31:10, Ezekiel 23:12, Genesis.R 68:10 78:5, Hosea 6:1 6:3 14:6-9, Isaiah 9:3 6:26 11:6 1:6 49:9-10 2:10 5:5 55:12-13 57:18-19 60:1-3 60:19-20 66:1-2, Jastrow 593a, Jeremiah 17:14 31:10-15 9:6, John 1:4 1:8 1:14 8:12 9:4 12:35-36 12:40 15:2-5, Joseph and Aseneth 6:2, Luke 1:50 1:78 2:32, Malachi 3:16, Matthew 4:15-16 11:5 23:37, Mekilta de R'Ishmael Bahodesh 8:24, Midrash Psalms 41:4 58:3, Midrash Tanchuma Mishpatim 11, Pesikta de R'Kahana 16.1, Pesikta Rabbati 29/30A:1 33:13 42:4, Proverbs 4:18, Psalms 67:2 84:12 85:10 92:13-15 7:3 3:3, Revelation 2:28 11:18 22:2 22:16, Ruth 2:12, Ruth.R 5:4, Saadia Opinions 9:5 9:8, Sibylline Oracles 3.94, Testament of Judah 24:1, Testament of Zebulun 9:8, z.Beshallach 59a, z.Chayyei Sarah 131a, z.Mikketz 203b

[9] LXX *his*

wings; and you shall go forth, and skip about as calves *of the stall*[1].

וַעֲסוֹתֶם רְשָׁעִים כִּי־יִהְיוּ אֵפֶר תַּחַת כַּפּוֹת רַגְלֵיכֶם בַּיּוֹם אֲשֶׁר אֲנִי עֹשֶׂה אָמַר יְהוָה צְבָאוֹת

21[2]   And you shall *tread down*[3] the wicked; for they shall be ashes under the soles of your feet in the day that I make, says the LORD of hosts.

זִכְרוּ תּוֹרַת מֹשֶׁה עַבְדִּי אֲשֶׁר צִוִּיתִי אוֹתוֹ בְחֹרֵב עַל־כָּל־יִשְׂרָאֵל חֻקִּים וּמִשְׁפָּטִים

22[4]   *Remember the law of Moses My servant, which I commanded to him in Horeb for all Israel, statutes and ordinances*[5].

הִנֵּה אָנֹכִי שֹׁלֵחַ לָכֶם אֵת אֵלִיָּה הַנָּבִיא לִפְנֵי בּוֹא יוֹם יְהוָה הַגָּדוֹל וְהַנּוֹרָא

23[6]   Behold, I will send you Elijah the *prophet*[7] before the coming of the great and terrible day of the LORD.

וְהֵשִׁיב לֵב־אָבוֹת עַל־בָּנִים וְלֵב בָּנִים עַל־אֲבוֹתָם פֶּן־אָבוֹא וְהִכֵּיתִי אֶת־הָאָרֶץ חֵרֶם

24[8]   And he shall turn the heart of the fathers to the children, and the heart of *the children to their fathers*[9]; lest I come and strike the land with utter destruction.

הִנֵּה אָנֹכִי שֹׁלֵחַ לָכֶם אֵת אֵלִיָּה הַנָּבִיא לִפְנֵי בּוֹא יוֹם יְהוָה הַגָּדוֹל וְהַנּוֹרָא

25[10]   Behold, I will send you Elijah the *prophet*[11] before the coming of the great and terrible day of the LORD.

---

[1] LXX *let loose from bonds*

[2] Malachi 3:21 - 2 Samuel 22:43, b.Rosh Hashanah 14a, Daniel 7:18 7:27, Ein Yaakov Rosh Hashanah:17a, Ezekiel 4:18, Gates of Repentance 2.017 3.011, Genesis 3:15, Genesis.R 79:7, Isaiah 1:10 2:6 63:3-6, Jastrow 178a, Job 16:12, Joshua 10:24-25, Malachi 3:17, Micah 5:9 7:10, Midrash Psalms 18:33, Psalms 91:13, Revelation 11:15 14:20, Romans 16:20, Saadia Opinions 9:5, Seder Olam 3:Plagues, t.Sanhedrin 13:4, Tanna Devei Eliyahu 3, z.Bereshit 59a, Zechariah 10:5

[3] 4QXIIa *counsel*

[4] Malachi 3:22 - 3 Enoch 48D:4, b.Shabbat 89a, b.Zevachim [Rashi] 4a, Deuteronomy 4:5-6 4:10, Ecclesiastes.R 9:21, Ein Yaakov Shabbat:89a, Exodus 20:3-21 21:1-23, Exodus.R 1:16 30:4 40:1, Galatians 5:13-14 5:24-25, Isaiah 8:20 18:21, James 2:9-13, John 5:39-47, Leviticus 1:1-7, Luke 10:25-28 16:29-31, m.Tehorot 1:16, Mark 12:28-34, Matthew 5:17-20 19:16-22 22:36-40, Mekhilta de R'Shimon bar Yochai Shirata 27:1, Mechilta Shirata 1, Mekilta de R'Ishmael Shirata 1:37, Midrash Proverbs 14, Midrash Psalms 1:16 19:13 30:4, Midrash Tanchuma Beshallach 10, Midrash Tanchuma Ki Tissa 35, Midrash Tanchuma Shoftim 5, mt.Hilchot Melachim u'Michamoteihem 12:2, mt.Hilchot Yesodei haTorah 9:2, Numbers.R 12:9 14:4, Numbers.R 12:12, Pesikta de R'Kahana 4.5 S1.20, Pesikta Rabbati 5:2 14:11, Psalms 147:19-20, Romans 3:31 13:1-10, Saadia Opinions 3:7, Tanna Devei Eliyahu 6, Traditional Enlarged ז in זִכְרוּ
Malachi 3:22-24 - Sifre Devarim Ekev 41

[5] Missing in LXX

[6] Malachi 3:23 - Acts 2:19-20, Apocalypse of Daniel 14:2, Apocalypse of Elijah 4:7, b.Eruvin 43b, b.Shabbat 118a, b.Shekalim 9b, Deuteronomy.R 3:17 4:11 6:8 11:9, Ein Yaakov Eduyot:10a, Ein Yaakov Shabbat:118a, Exodus.R 3:4, Genesis.R 99 [Excl]:11, Isaiah 16:3, Jastrow 68b, Joel 3:4, John 1:21 1:25, Luke 1:17 7:26-28 9:30, Malachi 3:1 3:19, Mark 9:11-13, Matthew 11:13-14 17:10-13 27:47-49, Midrash Proverbs 19, Midrash Psalms 3:7 42/43:5, Midrash Tanchuma Mishpatim 18, Midrash Tanchuma Vayechi 12, Pesikta Rabbati 4:2 33:8, Pirkei de R'Eliezer 40 43, Revelation 6:17, Saadia Opinions 3:7 8:5 7Variant:7, Sibylline Oracles 2.187, Sifre Devarim Vezot Habracha 342, Song of Songs.R 1:9 4:29, y.Shabbat 1:3

[7] LXX *Tishbite*

[8] Malachi 3:24 - b.Kiddushin [Rashi] 71a, Daniel 9:11 9:26-27, Deuteronomy.R 6:8, Deuteronomy 29:18-28, Ein Yaakov Eduyot:10a, Hebrews 6:8 10:26-31, Isaiah 11:4 24:6 19:28 13:2 17:15, Liber Antiquitatum Biblicarum 23:13, Luke 1:16-17 1:76 19:41-44 21:22-27, m.Eduyot 8:6, Mark 11:21 13:14-26, Matthew 22:7 23:35-38 24:27-24:30, mt.Hilchot Melachim u'Michamoteihem 12:2, Pirkei de R'Eliezer 40 43, Revelation 19:15 22:3 22:20-21, Saadia Opinions 8:5, y.Shabbat 1:3, Zechariah 5:3 11:6 13:8 14:2 14:12
Malachi 3:29 - z.Vayakhel 211b

[9] LXX *a man to his neighbor*

[10] Malachi 3:25 - Acts 2:19-20, Apocalypse of Daniel 14:2, Apocalypse of Elijah 4:7, b.Eruvin 43b, b.Shabbat 118a, b.Shekalim 9b, Deuteronomy.R 3:17 4:11 6:8 11:9, Ein Yaakov Eduyot:10a, Ein Yaakov Shabbat:118a, Exodus.R 3:4, Genesis.R 99 [Excl]:11, Isaiah 16:3, Jastrow 68b, Joel 3:4, John 1:21 1:25, Luke 1:17 7:26-28 9:30, Malachi 3:1 3:19, Mark 9:11-13, Matthew 11:13-14 17:10-13 27:47-49, Midrash Proverbs 19, Midrash Psalms 3:7 42/43:5, Midrash Tanchuma Mishpatim 18, Midrash Tanchuma Vayechi 12, Pesikta Rabbati 4:2 33:8, Pirkei de R'Eliezer 40 43, Revelation 6:17, Saadia Opinions 3:7 8:5 7Variant:7, Sibylline Oracles 2.187, Sifre Devarim Vezot Habracha 342, Song of Songs.R 1:9 4:29, y.Shabbat 1:3

[11] LXX *Tishbite*